2013 IEEE 39th Photovoltaic Specialists Conference (PVSC 2013)
Part 2

Tampa, Florida, USA
16-21 June 2013

IEEE Catalog Number: CFP13PVS-POD
ISBN: 978-1-4799-0511-9

IEEE Catalog Number: CFP13PVS-POD
ISBN 13:   978-1-4799-0511-9

Additional Copies of This Publication Are Available From:

Curran Associates, Inc
57 Morehouse Lane
Red Hook, NY 12571 USA
Phone: (845) 758-0400
Fax: (845) 758-2633
E-mail: curran@proceedings.com
Web: www.proceedings.com

TABLE OF CONTENTS

CHAIRMAN'S MESSAGE

Welcome to the 39th IEEE PV Specialists Conference, the pre-eminent global technical conference in photovoltaics that is sponsored by the world's largest professional association for the advancement of technology, the Institute of Electrical and Electronic Engineers. The 39th PVSC comes at a very exciting time in the evolution of the PV industry. Installations in the Americas grew by more than 76% in 2012 as compared to 2011. The U.S. Solar Market Insight Report: Year In Review, co-authored by GTM Research and the Solar Energy Industries Association, said that 2012 PV solar installations were 3.31 GW, more than 40% more than all previous U.S. solar online capacity. This isn't too surprising considering retail electricity prices have grown by 35% since the start of 2000, and the average price of solar systems dropping by 70% in the same period, according to GTM and SEIA. GTM and SEIA predict another 30% growth of the U.S. market in 2013, with 4.3 GW of new capacity installed. So chances are this will continue to be a very dynamic time for PV.

The one constant is that the PVSC will continue to be the showcase for the technological and manufacturing advances that are the driving force behind this development. Its eleven topical technical focus areas range across fundamentals, characterization, new concepts, all of the major commercial and next generation technologies, space and terrestrial applications, policy and finance developments, and our newest area devoted to the science of PV reliability. The highest quality papers presented at the PVSC will be eligible for inclusion in the IEEE Journal of Photovoltaics, a newly commissioned, peer-reviewed, archival publication reporting original and significant research results that advance the field of photovoltaics. We will also be providing a full slate of tutorials from PV101 to Distributed Generation Integration - Understanding the Current Challenges and Opportunities and a IEA PVPS Task 13 Workshop: Lessons Learned from the Analytical Monitoring and Modeling of PV Systems. Details on the tutorials and workshop can be found within this booklet.

In addition to the technical program, we have a thriving exhibit area where vendors will be showcasing the latest products, technologies and services for the PV research community. There are also a number of booths showcasing some of the leading PV research centers, federal labs, and university research programs. The exhibitor area will also play host to our PV Jobs Fair, our High School PV competition, and of course the Monday evening exhibitors' reception.

This year's conference will be held in the state-of-the-art 600,000-square-foot Tampa Convention and Exhibition Center, whose sparkling waterfront vistas bring the warmth and light of Florida sunshine right into the meeting rooms. Completing this spectacular venue are cafes, restaurants, waterfront gathering areas and spectacular first-class accommodations all within walking distance. We are pleased to offer three organized companion tours through the Bay Area Destination Management Inc. (e.g., Dali Museum Tour, Highlights of Tampa Tour, and the Clearwater Beach Day) and a self-organized day trip.

A highlight of this year's conference is sure to be our Conference Banquet and Cherry Award Reception. The conference banquet will be held at the world famous Busch Gardens. This year's Cherry Reception will be held at Jackson's Bistro, which is walking distance from the convention center and overlooks beautiful Tampa Bay. Space at both of these events will be limited, so if you haven't already registered please do so soon.

In conclusion, I wish to thank all of our sponsors including our corporate sponsor: The U.S. Photovoltaic Manufacturing Consortium (PVMC); our media sponsors: AZoCleantech.com, Latin America Renovable, Photovoltaics International, PVTech, Solar Novus Today, and Photon; and all of our exhibitors (see exhibits directory). I am grateful for your support. I would also like to thank both our program and organizing committees and our supporting organizations for such an outstanding job on all the arrangements. Finally, I would like to recognize all of our authors, presenters, and attendees. Without you, none of this would be possible and it is the work that you do that is making a the world a better place for us all.

Dr. Ryne P. Raffaelle
Vice President, Rochester Institute of Technology
Conference General Chairperson

GENERAL INFORMATION

DATES
The 39th IEEE Photovoltaic Specialists Conference begins Sunday, June 16th, with a day of tutorials. The technical program begins Monday, June 17th, and concludes Friday, June 21st, 2013.

CONFERENCE VENUE
Tampa Convention Center
333 S. Franklin Street
Tampa, FL 33602
Ph: 813.274.8511

REGISTRATION INFORMATION
Name badges and final programs will be distributed at the Registration Desk which is located on the 2nd Floor, East Registration Foyer, Tampa Convention Center. The Registration Desk will be open during the following hours:

Saturday	4:00 PM - 8:00 PM
Sunday	7:00 AM - 8:00 PM
Monday	7:00 AM - 7:00 PM
Tuesday	7:00 AM - 5:00 PM
Wednesday	7:00 AM - 6:00 PM
Thursday	7:00 AM - 5:00 PM
Friday	7:00 AM - 1:00 PM

SPEAKER READY ROOM
The speaker ready room will be available to all oral presenters for required previewing and optional editing of your presentation(s). The speaker ready room in MR 3 will be open during the following hours:

Sunday-Thursday	7:00 AM - 5:00 PM
Friday	7:00 AM - 10:00 AM

INTERNET ACCESS
Free Wifi access is available on the 1st floor in the pre-function area.

NO PHOTOGRAPHY POLICY
Attendees may not take pictures of oral or poster presentations. Only official conference photographers are allowed to take such pictures.

CONFERENCE MESSAGE CENTER
An information and message center will be located in the registration area.

AUTHOR'S BREAKFAST

All poster and oral presenters are required to attend the Author's Breakfast at 7:00 AM the morning of (each of) your presentation(s) for instructions, to meet your session chair, and to be sure all your materials have uploaded correctly. Breakfasts will be in Ballroom A / Rotunda.

COFFEE BREAKS

Coffee and soda breaks will be available each morning and afternoon. Please see below for locations:

8 AM Breaks

Monday - Ballroom A Foyer (1st Floor)
Tuesday - Ballroom A Foyer (1st Floor)
Wednesday - Ballroom A Foyer (1st Floor)
Thursday - Ballroom A Foyer (1st Floor)
Friday - Ballroom A Foyer (1st Floor)

10 AM Breaks

Monday - Ballroom A Foyer (1st Floor)
Tuesday - East Hall (3rd Floor)
Wednesday - East Hall (3rd Floor)
Thursday - East Hall (3rd Floor)
Friday - Ballroom A Foyer (1st Floor)

3 PM Breaks

Monday - Ballroom A Foyer (1st Floor)
Tuesday - East Hall (3rd Floor)
Wednesday - East Hall (3rd Floor)
Thursday - Ballroom A Foyer (1st Floor)

EXHIBITS

The exhibit hall is located on the 3rd floor of the Convention Center in the East Hall and will be open during the following hours:

Monday	5:30 PM - 8:30 PM
Tuesday	10:00 AM - 6:00 PM
Wednesday	10:00 AM - 3:30 PM

IEEE ELECTRON DEVICES SOCIETY

MEMBERSHIP PROMOTIONS FOR 39TH PVSC ATTENDEES

IEEE Members: If you're not currently a member of the Electron Devices Society, don't worry. Your registration fee includes a half-year membership in EDS. Members enjoy free online access to the new IEEE Journal of Photovoltaics!

Non-IEEE Members: Stop by the EDS membership booth in the registration area to learn about special offers to join IEEE and EDS. And, if you are a member of another scientific/technical society, you can receive FREE EDS membership for one-half year by joining IEEE as an Affiliate Member. Enjoy all the benefits of being a part of EDS.

Students: If you registered and paid for the conference at the student, non-member rate, you will receive one half-year of FREE IEEE and EDS.

Learn more! Visit the EDS membership booth located in the PVSC registration area.

EDS Members enjoy a host of benefits to enrich and energize their professional lives:

- Members-only content such as webinars with engineering luminaries like Chenming Hu, leader of the UC Berkeley team that developed the FinFET 3D Transistor

Free Online Access to:
- IEEE Journal of Photovoltaics
- IEEE Transactions on Electron Devices (1954 to current)
- IEEE Electron Device Letters (1980 to current)
- IEEE International Electron Devices Meeting (IEDM)
- Technical Digests (1955 to current)
- IEEE/OSA Journal of Lightwave Technology
- EDS Newsletter
- Discounted Open Access Author Fees in the new Journal of the Electron Devices Society
- Fully Hyperlinked TOC's for Flagship EDS Publications Delivered to your Desktop
- Free Copy-Editing Service of manuscripts submitted to Transactions on Electron Devices or Electron Devices Letters
- Network with EDS's more than 10,000 members

WILLIAM R. CHERRY AWARD

This award is named in honor of William R. Cherry, a founder of the photovoltaic community. In the 1950's, he was instrumental in establishing solar cells as the ideal power source for space satellites and for recognizing, advocating, and nurturing the use of photovoltaic systems for terrestrial applications. The William R. Cherry award was instituted in 1980, shortly after his death. The purpose of the award is to recognize an individual engineer or scientist who devoted a part of his/her professional life to the advancement of the science and technology of photovoltaic energy conversion. The nominee must have made significant contributions to the science and/or technology of PV energy conversion, with dissemination by substantial publications and presentations. Professional society activities, promotional and/or organizational efforts, and achievements are not considerations in the election for the award.

This award is presented at each IEEE Photovoltaic Specialists Conference. The recipient is selected by the William R. Cherry Committee, which is composed of past PVSC conference chairpersons and past recipients of the award. Those nominated for the award do not participate in the process.

To be eligible for the award, the nominee must currently be active in the science and technology of PV conversion. He/she must have been active in the field for an extended period with the expectation of continued activity. Short-term activities in the field, and/or single outstanding contributions are not sufficient to make a person eligible for the award.

WILLIAM R. CHERRY AWARD

To make a nomination, please submit a completed electronic nomination form and accompanying materials at: http://www.ieee-pvsc.org/ePVSC/cherry/form.php. The information required on the electronic form is summarized below:

1. Nominator's name, address, phone, and email
2. Nominee's name, present position, company, address, phone, and email
3. List of Nominee's key activities in the field
4. Nominee's current CV
5. Nominee's photograph
6. Citation: less than 40 words that reflect specific achievements
7. Rationale: less than 150-word summary of nominee's contribution to the advancement of the PV field

The deadline for Cherry Award nominations to be considered for the next IEEE PVSC is January 10 of each year.

Previous Cherry Award Recipients

Dr. Paul Rappaport	1980
Dr. Joseph L. Loferski	1981
Prof. Martin Wolf	1982
Dr. Henry W. Brandhorst	1984
Mr. Eugene L. Ralph	1985
Dr. Charles E. Backus	1987
Dr. David E. Carlson	1988
Dr. Martin A. Green	1990
Mr. Peter A. Iles	1991
Dr. Lawrence L. Kazmerski	1993
Prof. Yoshihiro Hamakawa	1994
Dr. Allen M. Barnett	1996
Dr. Adolf Goetzberger	1997
Dr. Richard J. Schwartz	1998
Dr. Christopher R. Wronski	2000
Dr. Richard M. Swanson	2002
Dr. Ajeet Rohatgi	2003
Dr. Timothy J. Coutts	2005
Dr. Antonio Luque	2006
Dr. Masafumi Yamaguchi	2008
Dr. Stuart Wenham	2009
Dr. Richard King	2010
Dr. Jerry M. Olson	2011
Dr. Sarah Kurtz	2012

THIS YEAR THE WILLIAM R. CHERRY AWARD
WILL BE PRESENTED TO:

KEITH EMERY

Keith Emery is currently a Principal Engineer and Manager of the PV Cell and Module Performance Characterization Group in the National Center for Photovoltaics at the National Renewable Energy Laboratory (NREL). He has collaborated with PV researchers at NREL and around the world in modeling and characterizing one-sun and concentrator terrestrial and space photovoltaics.

Keith received his M.S. in Electrical Engineering at Michigan State University in 1979, with a thesis on "A Theoretical Investigation of Rotational Nonequilibrium Phenomena in the Pulsed Hydrogen Fluoride Laser System." While working on a Ph.D. at Colorado State University, he focused on two different projects—ion-beam-sputtered indium-doped tin oxide on silicon solar cells, and also, laser and electron-beam chemical vapor deposition of silicon nitride, silicon dioxide, and aluminum oxide films.

In 1980, he joined the Solar Energy Research Institute (SERI, now NREL) and established the PV cell performance characterization laboratory. He designed, developed, and implemented the first generation of hardware, software, and procedures to measure current-vs-voltage characteristics as a function of temperature, spectrum, and intensity for single- and multijunction cells and modules. He currently reviews and approves all hardware, software, and procedural changes and is the technical manager of the laboratory. The laboratory is ISO 17025-accredited by A2LA as a calibration laboratory for primary reference cells, secondary reference cells, and secondary modules. In support of the terrestrial PV community, his group averages about 200 cell calibrations and 250 module measurements per month.

Emery provides consulting expertise on PV measurements and solar simulation to hundreds of individuals and groups each year, both internal to NREL as well as within the PV community at large. He has collaborated with several groups in modeling solar spectra, PV sensitivity to solar spectra derived from resource data, and modeling multijunction one-sun and concentrator PV devices for optimal bandgap for maximum energy or efficiency.

Worldwide, Keith Emery is recognized as an expert in efficiency measurements and performance characterization of photovoltaics. He has garnered numerous awards as an individual and as part of a team, including two R&D 100 awards in 2007 and 2011, the 2007 Paul Rapport Award, and the 2012 World Renewable Energy Congress Award.

WILLIAM R. CHERRY AWARD

ORGANIZING COMMITTEE

CONFERENCE CHAIR
Ryne Raffaelle
Rochester Institute of Technology

PAST-CHAIR
BJ Stanbery
HelioVolt Corporation

DEPUTY CONFERENCE CHAIR/SECRETARY
Richard R. King
Spectrolab

TREASURER
Steve Ringel
The Ohio State University

OPERATIONS
Angus Rockett
University of Illinois

DEPUTY OPERATIONS
Martha Symko-Davies
NREL

DEPUTY OPERATIONS
Kelly Trautz
U.S. Naval Research Laboratory

PROGRAM CHAIR
David Wilt
AFRL/RVSV

DEPUTY PROGRAM CHAIR
Angele Reinders
University of Twente

EXHIBITS AND SPONSORSHIP
John Martin
Qioptiq Space Technology

EXHIBITS AND SPONSORSHIP CO-CHAIR
Bill Stueve
Atonometrics

EXHIBITS AND SPONSORSHIP CO-CHAIR
Marc Landry
NREL

REGISTRATION
Martha Symko-Davies
NREL

DEPUTY REGISTRATION
Sylvain Marsillac
Eni S.p.A.

DEPUTY REGISTRATION
Paula Robinson
NREL

PRESENTATIONS AND PUBLICATIONS
Alex Howard
AFRL/RVSV

DEPUTY PRESENTATIONS AND PUBLICATIONS
Seth Hubbard
Rochester Institute of Technology

TUTORIALS
Jennifer Granata
Sandia National Laboratories

POSTERS
Pete Sheldon
NREL

SCHOOL PROGRAM
Keith Emery
NREL

DEPUTY SCHOOL PROGRAM
Chris Ferekides
University of South Florida

SOCIAL PROGRAM
Celeste Raffaelle

AWARDS CHAIR
Cory Cress
US Naval Research Laboratory

DEPUTY AWARDS CHAIR
Annick Anctil
Clemson University

SOLAR DAY CHAIR
Ed Simburger
Aerospace Corporation

DEPUTY SOLAR DAY CHAIR
Jeremiah Mcnatt
NASA

SOLAR DAY LOCAL CO-CHAIR
Tim Anderson
University of Florida

PUBLICITY
Paul Sharps
Emcore Photovoltaics

DEPUTY PUBLICITY
Alex Freundlich
University of Houston

LOCAL ORGANIZING COMMITTEE CHAIR
Chris Ferekides
University of South Florida

PV JOBS CHAIR
Rob Walters
U.S. Naval Research Laboratory

WILLIAM R. CHERRY COMMITTEE

David Wilt, Chair
U.S Air Force Research Laboratory

Richard King, Award Chair
Spectrolab, Inc.

Tim Anderson
University of Florida

Charles Backus
ASU Research Park

Sheila G. Bailey
NASA Glenn Research Center

Allen M. Barnett
University of New South Wales

Paul Basore
Hanwha Solar America

John Benner
Stanford

Henry W. Brandhorst, Jr.
Auburn University

David E. Carlson
BP Solar

Timothy Coutts
National Renewable Energy Laboratory

Dennis J. Flood
North Coast Initiatives Ltd.

Americo F. Forestieri
MOE Consulting

Martin A. Green
University of New South Wales

Lawrence L. Kazmerski
National Renewable Energy Laboratory

Sarah Kurtz
National Renewable Energy Laboratory

Antonio Luque
Instituto De Energia Solar - UPM

John D. Meakin
University of Delaware

Jerry Olson
National Renewable Energy Laboratory

Eugene Ralph
PV consulting

Ajeet Rohatgi
Georgia Institute of Technology

Richard J. Schwartz
Purdue University

BJ Stanbery
Helio Volt Corporation

Richard M. Swanson
SunPower Corporation

Robert J. Walters, Chair
Naval Research Laboratory

Stuart Wenham, Award Chair
University of South Wales

Christopher R. Wronski
Pennsylvania State University

Masafumi Yamaguchi
Toyota Technical Institute

INTERNATIONAL COMMITTEE

Lawrence L. Kazmerski, Chair
National Renewable Energy Lab.

Francesca Ferrazza, Co-chair
Eni S.p.A.

Masafumi Yamaguchi, Co-chair
Toyota Technical Institute

Tim Anderson
University of Florida
USA

Sheila G. Bailey
NASA Glenn Research
Center
USA

A. K. Barua
Indian Assoc. for
Cultivation of Science
INDIA

John Benner
Stanford
USA

Andreas Bett
Fraunhofer ISE
GERMANY

Henry W. Brandhorst
Auburn University
USA

Tim Bruton
NaREC
UNITED KINGDOM

David E. Carlson
BP Solar
USA

Timothy J. Coutts
National Renewable
Energy Laboratory
USA

**Antonia Sonia A.
Cardoso Diniz**
CEMIG
BRAZIL

Dennis J Flood
North Coast Initiatives, Ltd.
USA

Carlo Flores
CESI S.p.A
ITALY

Takashi Fuyuki
Nara Institute of Science
and Technology
JAPAN

Martin A. Green
University of New South
Wales
AUSTRALIA

Huey-Liang Huang
National Tsing Hua
University
TAIWAN, ROC

Donghwan Kim
Korea University
KOREA

Richard J. King
U. S. Department of
Energy
USA

Makoto Konagai
Tokyo Institute of
Technology
JAPAN

Michio Kondo
NIAIST
JAPAN

Kosuke Kurokawa
Tokyo A &T University
JAPAN

JUNE 16-21, 2013 • TAMPA, FLORIDA

IN MEMORIUM

Mature communities-be they nations, professions or groups of people working toward a common objective-identify and honor their heroes, those persons who through their vision, perseverance and commitment helped to launch and enhance the community. The IEEE Photovoltaic Specialists Conference has established this memorial section to recognize those heroes that have passed.

J. David Cohen, Professor of Physics at the University of Oregon died on October 29th 2012 after a long illness. He is survived by his wife and companion of many years, Carol Cohen.

After serving in the U.S. Army, Dave obtained his Ph.D. in physics at Princeton University under Prof. T.R. Carver in 1976, working on microwave properties of ferromagnets. He then took a post-doctoral position at the University of Illinois with Charles Slichter. Dave then joined Bell Labs in 1978 and began the work that defined the remainder of his career – characterization of defects in semiconductors, especially as it relates to the performance of solar cells.

During his time at Bell Labs he published more than 14 papers on the subject of defect states in amorphous Si and their characterization by capacitance, admittance, DLTS and other methods. In 1981 Dave joined the Physics Department at the University of Oregon, where he spent the rest of his career. Dave was a dedicated adviser and mentor to his students who went out of his way to promote their career development.

He continued to keep in touch with them and was actively collaborating with those still working in his area.David Cohen loved the outdoors, folk music and dancing, which contributed to his choice to settle in Eugene Oregon. Those who knew him remember him as a humanitarian with great personal charm who cared deeply about others.

Harold (Harry) Bernhard Lieben, 3/3/24 – 3/12/13. Harry was born in Havana, Cuba of English and German parents. At a young age he moved from Cuba to Germany; then immigrated to the U.S.A. in 1931. He grew up in New Rochelle, NY. He served in the Army during World War II and finished college at NYU after the war and finished his EMBA degree at Baldwin Wallace College in 1993. He served in Army Reserve until 1957. His first job after college was in Cleveland and he's been in Lakewood since 1950.

He was co-owner of West Shore Electric in Lakewood for many years and one of the founding fathers of the Northeast Ohio Electrical Contractors Association (NOECA), now a part of the Independent Electrical Contractors (IEC), a national trade association for merit shop electrical contractors. He was the IEC Executive Director for the NOECA chapter at the time of death.

Harry was a long time foster parent and always very active in the community. He had been a New Rochelle and Bay Village Boy Scout leader, Cleveland Free Clinic volunteer, and the Beck Center. Harry was treasurer of the Lakewood Foundation, a private not for profit organization that supports special community projects, and a Lakewood Foundation Representative on the Lakewood Commission on Aging. Harry loved playing bridge, golf, and traveling. He is survived by his wife, Sheila Brown Bailey, daughter Lisa Lieben and her husband, John Veverka, and step granddaughter Kate Veverka, step son Clark Bailey, step daughter Kathleen Bailey, step daughter Gayle Bailey Ruggiero and her husband Erasmo Ruggiero, step grandchildren Abbygayle, Oliver and Joseph Ruggiero.

Arun Madan, 1946-2013: Arun graduated from Reading University in 1967 and went on to earn his PhD in physics from the University of Dundee in 1973. Arun's professional achievements are immense. While studying for his PhD, Arun helped discover hydrogenated amorphous silicon which paved the way  for the first thin film transistor. He established Glasstech Solar, Inc. in 1984 which later became Solar Cells Inc. and then First Solar. In 1989, Arun started MVSystems, Inc. and served as President and CEO for 23 years.

Over the course of his career, Arun published over 150 scientific papers and co-authored an advanced semiconductor textbook that is used at several universities and has been translated into Russian. Through his work, Arun led teams of scientists/engineers in multi-disciplinary programs involving thin film semiconductors and product development. This includes solar cells, thin film transistors, nuclear particle detectors, tin oxide coatings, Zinc Oxide, photosensor imaging arrays, etc. He is also the holder of 14 basic patents on thin film semiconductor technology as well as advanced vacuum semiconductor deposition systems. The machines developed at MVSystems Inc. have been sold to companies and universities all over the world.

IN MEMORIUM

Manuel Jesus Romero, age 39, was born in Spain near Cadiz. He is survived in Colorado by his loving wife, Nuria Lopez, his beautiful daughter, Virginia del Mar Romero Lopez, and by his parents and family living in Spain.

Dr. Romero, known to many friends and co-workers as "MJ," was a Senior Scientist at the U.S. Department of Energy's National Renewable Energy Laboratory (NREL) in Golden, Colorado, where he has worked since 2001, after receiving his Ph.D. from the Department of Materials Science and Engineering at the University of Cadiz, Spain. He had earlier received his B.S. in Chemistry, and his M.S. in Materials Science and Engineering from the University of Cadiz. At NREL, Dr. Romero worked in the Measurements and Characterization Division focusing on Analytical Microscopy, Renewable Electricity and End Use Systems. He published more than 90 papers in highly prestigious journals, and delivered numerous talks, by invitation, at many international conferences. He was widely recognized for his efforts with multiple awards he received from the U.S. government and professional organizations. He was also working with middle school teachers in Denver and Jefferson Counties to talk with students about science, and to make science attractive to young people, both in English, and in Spanish, which was his first language. Dr. Romero also mentored students from local universities, who would benefit from his knowledge and research in renewable energy.

Personally, Dr. Romero was an excellent competitive tennis player. Further, he enjoyed hiking and was an avid mountain biker. He truly loved the mountains, whether in Colorado, elsewhere in the U.S., or in his native Spain. He had a special ability to make Spanish paella -- seafood, meat and rice – that was the best to be found in Colorado. He was very proud of his Celtic heritage from the Galician area of northwest Spain, and he loved the music of that region. He was a brilliant, witty and charming man, and he will be deeply missed by his family, friends and colleagues.

Jürgen Schmid was one of the pioneers and leading experts in the field of renewable energy. He led Fraunhofer IWES for 14 years before stepping down in the fall of 2012. In 1995 he was appointed to the professorship Efficient Energy Conversion at the  University of Kassel. He became a member of the Board and CEO in 1998 of the former Institute for Solar Energy Supply Technology ISET and since the establishment of the Fraunhofer-Gesellschaft in 2009 Director of the IWES in Kassel in 1996. In addition, he advised 2004-2013 as a member of the Scientific Advisory Council on Global Change (WBGU), the Federal Government and engaged in a nationwide Renewable Energy Research Association (FVEE) and numerous international bodies and initiatives. For his "outstanding contribution in the cultural and scientific life of Hesse", the Hessian Minister of Science and Arts, Jürgen Schmid 2012, the Goethe Plaque awarded the highest award of the Hessian Ministry of Science. The Fraunhofer Board awarded him in 2012 the highest award of the Fraunhofer-Gesellschaft, the Fraunhofer Medal from.

Byron Stafford joined SERI in 1984 with a master's degree in Math and Physics from Northern Illinois University. He was passionate about photovoltaics and especially enjoyed helping people understand and install solar systems all over the world  – from Aurora to Alcatraz to Borneo. Most recently, he was setting up the infrastructure for the solar regional test center in Aurora.

Byron was a leader in the success of the Solar Decathlon. Beginning in 2000, he took on the role of Site Operations Manager and fulfilled this role in every biennial competition. He contributed to the original formulation of the competition rules and was responsible for the safe assembly and disassembly of the 20 student-developed houses, and the entire supporting infrastructure, from water supply to an electrical microgrid. His commitment to the Solar Decathlon project and its safety helped an entire generation of university students understand the interplay of energy efficiency and renewable energy features in buildings.

PV JOBS WEBSITE PORTAL

As a continuous service to our PV community, the PV Jobs Portal can be accessed through our website (www.ieee-pvsc.org). Through this portal, you may post your resume to be viewed by potential employers. If you have a position to fill, you may purchase job postings to be viewed by the entire PV community. Check the PV Jobs Website Portal during the conference to see the latest job and resume postings and to schedule an onsite interview.

PV Jobs at the Conference

The PV Jobs service offers the following during the conference:

- On-site interviews. We have an on-line scheduling system and private rooms available for conducting interviews. Prospective employers and employees may schedule interviews through the PV Jobs Portal (www.ieee-pvsc.org)
- Scrolling job announcements. Active job postings will be scrolled on the oral presentation room screens during breaks
- Job Fair. We will hold a job fair on Tuesday, June 18th from 4:00-6:00 pm in the Exhibit Hall. Organizations with active job postings will be given a table in a sectioned off area to mingle with prospective job applicants.

HIGH SCHOOL PHOTOVOLTAIC DESIGN COMPETITION

The High School Photovoltaic Design Competition sponsored by the IEEE Electron Devices Society has been held in conjunction with the IEEE PVSC for the past 20 years. Schools throughout the metropolitan Tampa area were invited to participate along with outstanding PV related projects at the 58th Florida State Science and Engineering Fair. The students are asked to work on their projects (under the supervision or mentoring of a faculty member, for example) and display their project at the Conference. The design projects must demonstrate the use of photovoltaics in a practical application. The teams will be at their projects during the Exhibitors Opening Reception and their projects will be on display in the Exhibits hall on Tuesday. Awards will be made for the top achievements Monday evening at 8:00 during the Exhibitors opening Reception.

SOCIAL PROGRAM

My name is Celeste Raffaelle and it is my pleasure to be your Social Program Chair for the 39th PVSC to be held in Tampa, Florida. Tampa Bay has all the best of Florida in one place. From wild to mild, there is much to see and do and the one-of-a-kind attractions provide fun for the entire family.

We are pleased to offer three organized companion tours through the Bay Area Destination Management Inc. (e.g., Dali Museum Tour, Highlights of Tampa Tour, and the Clearwater Beach Day). In addition, we have arranged a self-organized day trip. We will board the convenient TECO line Streetcar right in from of the convention center and make stops at Tampa's Channel District where guests may visit The Florida Aquarium, the Tampa Bay History Center, or play and shop at Channelside Bay Plaza; we will then proceed on to the brick-lined streets of Ybor City and the Latin Quarters-"Centro Ybor," where our group will lunch on own at the gem of Spanish Restaurants-Columbia, and get to see their famous Flamenco Dancers!

As has been the practice over the past few conferences, we are asking all the companions to register for the conference. This will make signing up for the various activities quite easy, ensure that you will receive emails regarding any changes and other special events/ opportunities, and will provide you with access to the companions room at the convention center (which includes complimentary continental breakfast each morning). In addition, all PVSC badged individuals will be able to ride the TECO Streetcar at no cost. You only need to present your PVSC badge to the conductor at the time of boarding. Anyone not displaying a PVSC badge will have to pay the normal cost.

Celeste Raffaelle
Social Program Chair

COMPANION ROOM (AVAILABLE DAILY)

Because we are special, we have a dedicated space at the hotel to rendezvous, socialize, and be merry. Start each morning here with a complimentary continental breakfast. Companions are encouraged to make full use of this room. PLEASE NOTE that only companions with badges will be allowed in the companion's room for our continental breakfasts.

Monday - Thursday 7:00 am - 9:00 am
Marriott Tampa Waterside, Meeting Room 1 (Level 3)

SUNDAY, JUNE 16TH

PVSC STUDENT MIXER
6:00 pm - 7:30 pm
MR 18-19

Are you a student or recent graduate attending the PVSC? If so, come to the PVSC Student Mixer sponsored by the Electron Devices Society GOLD (Graduates of the Last Decade) Committee. Join us for an informal reception with a brief presentation about EDS, followed by a mixer with free food. It is a great opportunity to get to know fellow students and recent PV graduates just as the conference kicks off. See you there!

MONDAY, JUNE 17TH

THE SALVADOR DALI MUSEUM
9:00 am - 12:30 pm

St. Petersburg is quickly becoming a Mecca for the arts with the recent opening of the new Dali Museum in the downtown area. This morning your tour will take you through town and along the beautiful waterfront where you will see the new Dali Museum with its Dali-esque facade facing the bay. The Salvador Dali Museum houses the world's most comprehensive collection of works by the late Spanish surrealist Salvador Dali.

Your self guided will provide you with interesting background and insight into the genius of Dali's life and works. Collected by A Reynolds and Eleanor R Morse, Dali's personal friends and scholarly collectors since 1942, this collection includes 94 original oils, over 100 watercolors, and drawings, plus 1,300 graphics, sculptures, holograms, objects of art and photographs.

From the Dali Museum you will continue along Beach Drive and see Snell Isle, the historic Renaissance Vinoy and numerous other sights which make St Petersburg the exciting and thriving area that it's become in the past decade.

Cost per person: $52.00

Inclusions:
- Round trip transportation
- BayArea Destinations Professional tour guide
- Admission to the Dali Museum in St Petersburg
- All taxes and gratuities for included items.

All tours will congregate in the companion's room at the Marriott Tampa Waterside, in Meeting Room 1 (Level 3).

TUESDAY, JUNE 18TH

HIGHLIGHTS OF TAMPA TOUR
9:30 am - 1:00 pm

The city of Tampa comes to life as your guide highlights the area.

Begin with a visit to the old Tampa Bay Hotel at the University of Tampa. This National Historic Landmark features unique Moorish revival architecture and dramatic minarets. Soak in the splendor of days gone by as you see and hear the history of this fabulous hotel and its founder, railroad tycoon, Henry B. Plant. A drive along beautiful Bayshore Boulevard and through the Hyde Park area will show you the diverse architecture that is Tampa.

Your next stop will be in Ybor City, the national historic landmark district located in Tampa. Travel down 7th Avenue and hear the history of the cigar industry, learn of life in this Latin community and the influence these valuable immigrants had on the city of Tampa. Your guide will provide you with a look into this area that was once the Cigar Capital of the World.

Cost per person based on a minimum of 35 passengers: $40.00

Inclusions:

- Round-trip motor coach transportation
- Admission to the Henry Plant Museum
- BayArea Professional Tour Guide
- All taxes & gratuities for items included

All tours will congregate in the companion's room at the Marriott Tampa Waterside, in Meeting Room 1 (Level 3).

WEDNESDAY, JUNE 19TH

SUN RUN
6:15 AM

The IEEE PVSC Sun Run celebrates its silver event anniversary in Tampa! This 25th IEEE PVSC Sun Run (our first run was in 1980!) is scheduled for 6:15 am on Wednesday, June 19, 2013. This will ensure that everyone will be back in time for the presenters' breakfast and the sessions! The course is along the beautiful Bayshore Blvd and waterfront. The starting point is near the Tampa Convention Center. Runners (both competitive and less so!) can register on line or at the meeting. The registration fee covers a special T-shirt, refreshments, recognitions for outstanding performances-and some commemorative materials of great worth. Awards will be made in several age categories for our men and women competitors. Again we will have the Corporate Cup Competition for teams (3 or more runners) for which the times are handicapped by both age and gender using the long-tested (since 1984!) "Modified Arvizu-Kazmerski Adjustment System."

On race morning, we will meet behind (bay side) of the convention center.

Cost:
$25.00

WEDNESDAY, JUNE 19TH

CLEARWATER BEACH DAY
9:00 am - 4:00 pm

Take a day and enjoy the white sands of Florida! Beautiful Clearwater Beach is rated the best beach on the Gulf of Mexico. You can swim, play volleyball, walk or fish on Pier 60. For your convenience there are beach showers, restrooms, concessions, & umbrella rentals. Stroll up & down Beach Drive and shop the souvenir shops for keepsakes & collectables! Shuttles will run throughout the day. The last shuttle back to Tampa will leave at 3:00pm. Important Information:

No alcohol is permitted on Clearwater's public beaches. Swim within the "Safe Bathing Limit" at all times. This area extends 300 feet west of the high water line and is clearly marked by buoys or pilings.

Boaters and jet skiers are not allowed inside the "Safe Bathing Limit" area.

Florida sunshine is intense. Use sunscreen with a high SPF.

Cost per person based on a minimum of 35 passengers: $31.00

Inclusions:
- Roundtrip Shuttle Service to and from Clearwater Beach
- All gratuities for included items.

All tours will congregate in the companion's room at the Marriott Tampa Waterside, in Meeting Room 1 (Level 3).

THURSDAY, JUNE 20TH

CELESTE'S SEMI-INDEPENDENT TOUR
10:00 am - 2:00 pm

Our self-directed tour will be aboard the convenient TECO line Streetcar with stops to Tampa's Channel District where guests may visit The Florida Aquarium, the Tampa Bay History Center, or play and shop at Channelside Bay Plaza; and guests may stroll the brick-lined streets of Ybor City and the Latin Quarters "Centro Ybor" where our group will lunch on own at the gem of Spanish Restaurants-- Columbia.

A 1-day unlimited ride fare card is $5. A family (i.e., 2 adults 3 children or 1 adult 4 children) all day ticket is $12.50. The vending machine for tickets and the departure point is right in front of the convention center. The group will depart from TECO stop at the convention center at 10:00. We will proceed to Ybor City to see the shops and take in the cultural sites. At noon, for those who wish to join us, we will have lunch at the famous Columbia restaurant, Florida's oldest restaurant and the world's largest Spanish Restaurant. You can check out the menu at: http://www. columbiarestaurant.com/ybor.asp

For those who do not wish to eat at Columbia, there are a number of other dining options in a close proximity.
After lunch, the group will once again get on the TECO for the short trip to Channelside http://www. channelsidebayplaza.com/. There is plenty to see and do once there. Whether you want to shop, tour a museum, or even go bowling, there is something for everyone. You can call it a day at any time by just hopping back on the trolley and returning to where it all began. Trolleys leave every 20 minutes.

All tours will congregate in the companion's room at the Marriott Tampa Waterside, in Meeting Room 1 (Level 3).

THURSDAY, JUNE 20TH

PVSC BANQUET - BUSCH GARDENS
6:00 pm - 10:00 pm

This Year's IEEE PVSC Banquet will be held at the world famous Busch Gardens on Thursday evening June 20, 2013. Buses will leave the convention center at 6:00 PM. You will have time to stroll through the park, see the animals, and even ride a few roller coaster (if you wish), as you make your way over to the Desert Grill.

At the Desert Grill you will be treated to a buffet dinner entitled "Taste of Tampa." This will include: Ybor Salad, Fresh Tropical Fruit Salad, Black Beans, Yellow Rice, Plantains, Green Peas and Pimentos, Pork Asado, Mojo Chicken, Shrimp in Caribbean Creole Sauce, Fresh Baked Cuban Bread, Orange Flan, and Treys Leche Cake with Caramel Sauce. There will also be a bar service with Two (2) Beer, Wine, or soft drink tickets per person.

During dinner don't be surprised if a Flamingo, a Sloth (not me), or even a Red Crested Turaco join you at your table. There will also be caricature artists throughout the evening and Jungala themed characters who will perform. However the highlight of the evening will most certainly be the music stylings of the Gasparilla Groove. So, bring your dancing shoes.

The cost for the banquet is $75 per person ($60 for children). Space is limited, so register early.

TAMPA BAY CONVENTION CENTER OUTLET INFORMATION

OUTLET HOURS

Sunday June 16

Bay Bistro (8:30 AM - 3:00 PM)

Monday June 17

Bay Bistro (7:00 AM - 5:00 PM)
Taste of Ybor (11:30 AM - 2:00 PM)
Speed Line (11:30 AM - 2:00 PM)

Tuesday June 18

Bay Bistro (7:00 AM - 5:00 PM)
East Grill (10:00 AM - 4:00 PM
Taste of Ybor (11:30 AM - 2:00 PM)
Speed Line (11:30 AM - 2:00 PM)

Wednesday June 19

Bay Bistro (7:00 AM - 5:00 PM)
East Grill (10:00 AM - 4:00 PM
Taste of Ybor (11:30 AM - 2:00 PM)
Speed Line (11:30 AM - 2:00 PM)

Thursday June 20

Bay Bistro (7:00 AM - 5:00 PM)
East Grill (10:00 AM - 4:00 PM
Taste of Ybor (11:30 AM - 2:00 PM)

Friday June 21

Bay Bistro (7:00 AM - 2:00 PM)

***** Schedule subject to change based on
prior day(s) business levels*****

OUTLET LOCATIONS

Bay Bistro – 1st Floor by Channel Entry/Riverwalk
East Grill – Inside of East Hall
Taste of Ybor – Outside of East Hall
Speed Line – Ballroom BC Foyer

POSTER HALL MAP

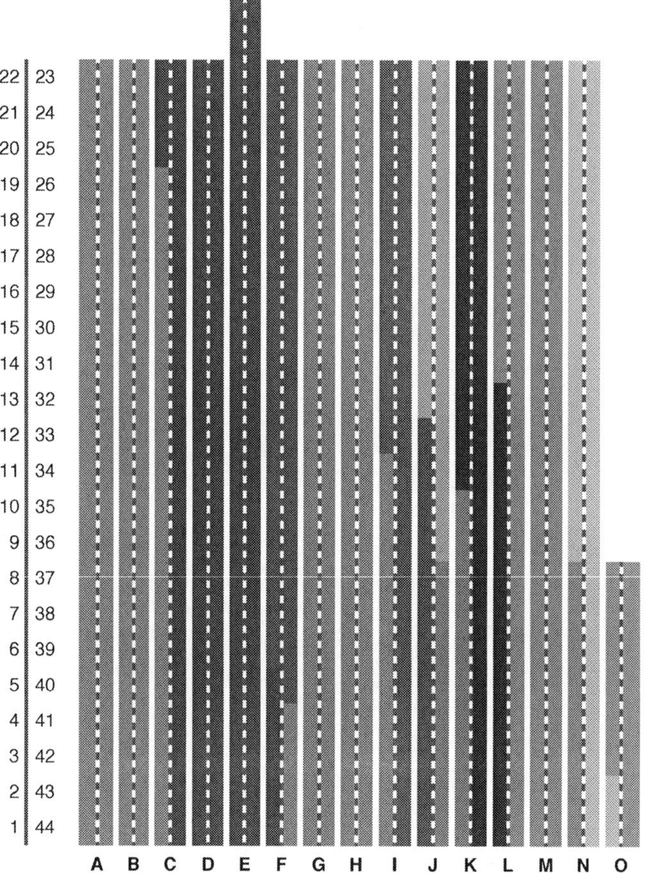

LEGEND

- Area 1: A1 - C19
- Area 2: C20 - F5
- Area 3: F6 - F40
- Area 4: F41 - I11
- Area 5: I12 - J12
- Area 6: J13 - J36
- Area 7: J37 - K10
- Area 8: K11 - L13
- Area 9: L14 - N8
- Area 10: N9 - O2
- Area 11: O3 - O15

VENUE MAP

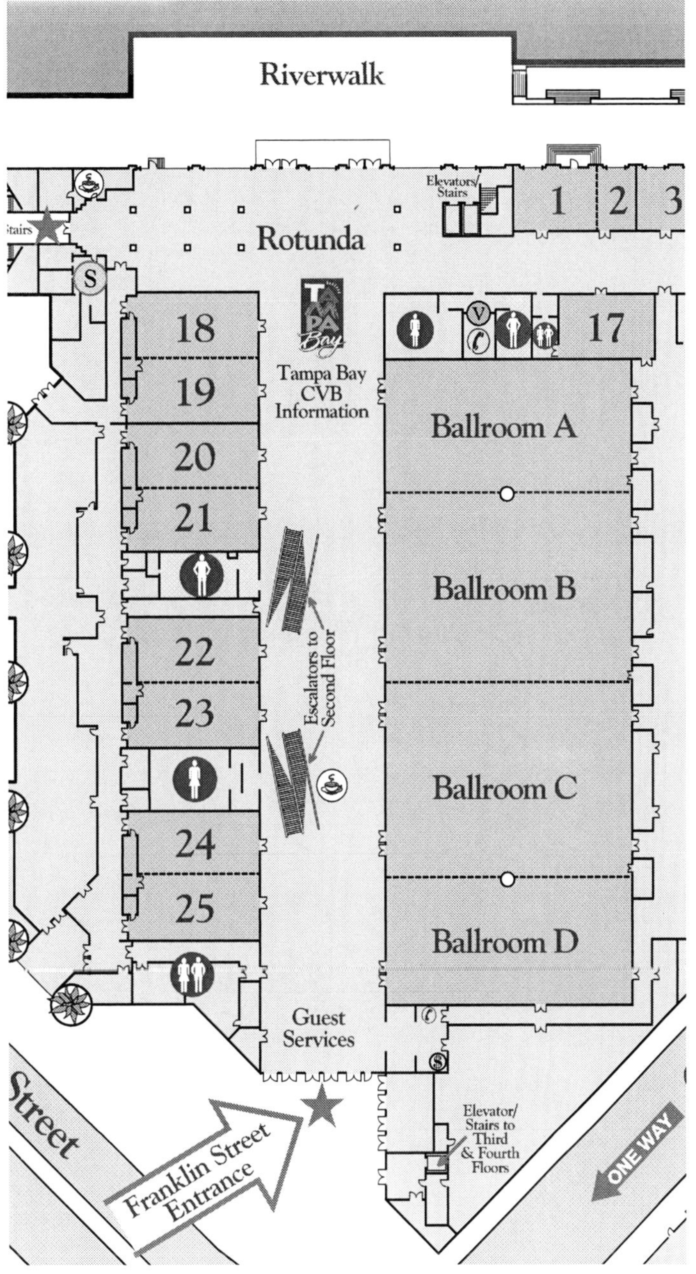

Riverwalk
Elevators/Stairs
1
2
3
Stairs
Rotunda
18
19
20
21
22
23
24
25
17
Tampa Bay
Tampa Bay
CVB
Information
Ballroom A
Ballroom B
Ballroom C
Ballroom D
Escalators to Second Floor
Guest Services
Franklin Street Entrance
Street
Elevator/
Stairs to
Third
& Fourth
Floors
ONE WAY

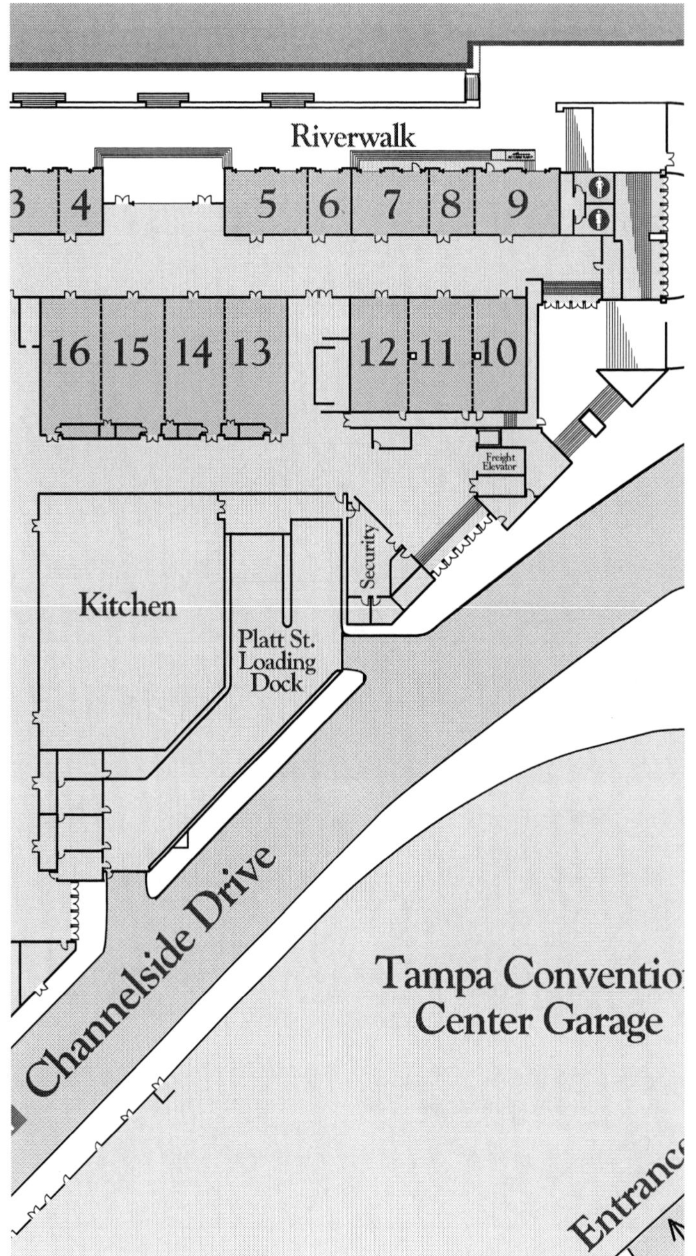

Riverwalk
3
4
5
6
7
8
9
16
15
14
13
12
11
10
Freight Elevator
Security
Kitchen
Platt St. Loading Dock
Channelside Drive
Tampa Convention Center Garage
Entrance

EXHIBIT HALL MAP

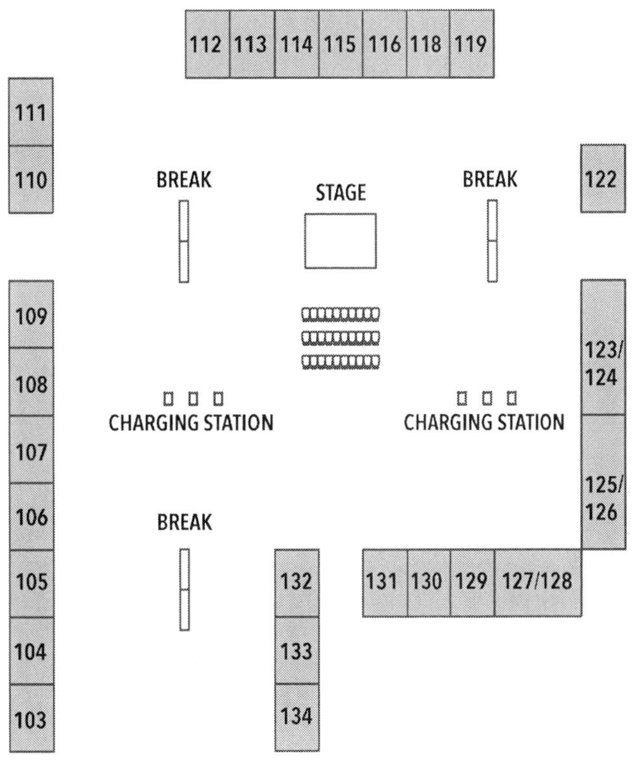

EXHIBITORS

103: Semilab SDI LLC
104: J.A. Woollam Co., Inc.
105: NSERC Photovoltaic Innovation Network
106: Tau Science Corporation
107: Abet Technologies
108: US Photovoltaic Manufacturing Consortium
109: TS Space Systems
110: HORIBA Scientific
111/112: PV Measurements, Inc.
113: SERIIUS/CID
114: Laytec in-line GmbH
115: IEEE Women in Engineering
116: Evans Analytical Group
118: Wiley
119: Qioptiq Space Technology
122: Newport Corp. / Oriel Instruments
123/124: OAI
125/126: NREL
127/128: Sinton Instruments
129: Spire Corporation
130: Semco Engineering, Inc.
131: Atonometrics
132: JASCO
133: Photo Emission Tech
134: ENrG Incorporated

EXHIBIT HALL SCHEDULE & EVENTS

EXHIBIT HOURS
Monday: 5:30 PM - 8:30 PM
Tuesday: 10:00 AM - 6:00 PM
Wednesday: 10:00 AM - 3:00 PM

EXHIBIT GAME
Each attendee bag contains an exhibit bingo. Simply obtain a stamp/sticker from each booth in the exhibit hall and return your bingo card to the registration desk for a chance to win an iPad Mini.

EXHIBITOR'S OPENING RECEPTION
Monday, June 17, 5:30 PM - 8:30 PM
We would like to invite you to the PVSC-39 Exhibitor's Opening Reception in the Exhibition Hall sponsored by the Conference Exhibitors on Monday evening, June 17 from 5:30-8:30 PM. The reception marks the opening of the Exhibits Hall and has become one of the most widely attended social networking events of the conference. This year's opening reception will undoubtedly bring together the biggest-ever gathering of PV experts in the world. Join us as we celebrate the start of another enriching week that only the IEEE Photovoltaic Specialists Conference can provide. Catch up with old friends and meet new colleagues as you enjoy good food and drink. The Welcome Reception is open to all attendees.

JOB FAIR
Tuesday, June 18, 4:00 PM - 6:00 PM
We will hold a job fair on Tuesday, June 18th from 4:00 - 6:00 PM in the Exhibit Hall. Everyone with an active job posting will be given a table in a sectioned off area to mingle with prospective job applicants. Check out the PV Jobs section of the IEEE PVSC website now and return often for updates.

CONFERENCE SPONSORS

Corporate Sponsor

Media Sponsors

Abet Technologies
Booth: 107

Abet Technologies manufactures standard and custom solar cell PV-IV measurement systems. Systems include standards compliant steady state solar simulators, vacuum chuck temperature controlled test stations, comprehensive software, calibrated reference, cells and a range of electronic loads. Systems range in size from 35 mm diameter to 35 x 35 cm. abet-technologies.com

Atonometrics
Booth: 131

Atonometrics, Inc., based in Austin, TX, develops test and measurement technology for the rapidly growing solar energy industry. Products for PV Power Plants include performance, irradiance, soiling, and degradation measurement solutions. Products for manufacturing environments and testing labs include continuous solar simulators, light soakers, I-V systems, and UV exposure chambers. www.atonometrics.com

Center for Inverse Design
Booth: 113

The Center for Inverse Design (CID) is an Energy Frontier Research Center of the U.S. Department of Energy Office of Energy Science. To address a crucial scientific grand challenge, the Center is pursuing a new approach to material science. Rather than using the conventional direct approach ("Given the structure, find the electronic properties"), the CID Is using a "materials by inverse design" approach ("Given the desired property, find the structure"). The CID is led by NREL, with its partners at the University of Colora

Ceramic Technology for Clean Energy

ENrG Incorporated
Booth: 134

ENrG Inc produces ultra flexible 20-40 micron thick ceramic membranes which are finding applications in multiple market segments. For thin film solar, ENrG's Thin E-Strate provides high purity and is chemically inert, a 1200 C process capability, is thermal shock tolerant, and results in faster cycle times. enrg-inc.com

Evans Analytical Group
Booth: 116

Evans Analytical Group (EAG) is the world's leading provider of analytical services for the photovoltaic industry. We analyze all raw materials and processed materials including: c-Si, α-Si/μc-Si, CdTe, CIGS, CZTS and III-V materials. We can determine dopant concentration, dopant profiles, contaminant presence, crystal structure, layer structure, defect location and type, and more. We also look at finished cells for failure analysis and construction analysis. By choosing EAG you gain access to 30+ analytical techniques and to over 200 scientists and engineers with PV materials experience. www.eag.com

HORIBA
Scientific

HORIBA Scientific
Booth: 110

HORIBA Scientific is a world-leading manufacturer of high performance spectroscopic instrumentation. Our products include Raman microscopes, steady-state and lifetime fluorometers, Spectroscopic Ellipsometers, EDXRF, GD-OES for depth-profiling and bulk analysis, as well as optical components and high performance CCDs. Check out HORIBA Products for your Molecular, Elemental and Thin Film analyses. www.horiba.com/scientific

IEEE Women in Engineering
Booth: 115

IEEE Women in Engineering (WIE) is a vessel to support and inform a global community on the best practices and visions in the marketplace for attracting and retaining women in STEM. IEEE WIE facilitates the global recruitment and retention of women in technical disciplines, and envisions a vibrant community of IEEE women and men collectively using their diverse talents to innovate for the benefit of humanity. www.ieee.org/women

J.A. Woollam Co., Inc.
Booth: 104

The J.A. Woollam Company offers a wide range of spectroscopic ellipsometers for nondestructive materials characterization, including thin film thickness (single and multilayer), optical constants, composition, growth/etch rates, and more. Instruments available for research and manufacturing metrology covering spectral ranges from vacuum ultra-violet to far infrared. Offering table-top, in-line, and in-situ models. www.jawoollam.com

JASCO
Booth: 132

JASCO specializes in analytical instruments for spectroscopy and chromatography applications, with over 55 years of experience. Our worldwide presence, superior product quality and outstanding service and support make the company an industry leader. JASCO is recognized for its robust and reliable chromatography instruments including SFC/SFE (analytical, semi-prep, & preparative systems), HPLC and X-LC® (UHPLC). The full line of spectroscopy products includes FT-IR, Portable IR, FT-IR microscopes, UV-Vis/NIR, Fluorescence, Raman, portable Raman, Near-field, Polarimeters, Circular Dichroism and Dissolution testers. www.jascoinc.com

Laytec in-line GmbH
Booth: 114

LayTec is a leading manufacturer of optical, electrical and mechanical in-situ and in-line metrology solutions for the photovoltaic (PV) and semiconductor industry. For c-Si PV wafer and cell production LayTec offers metrology of texture, wafer thickness, layer uniformity and conductivity. The LayTec X Link system controls the lamination process performance of glass/back sheet modules: in-line, reliable and non-destructive. At thin-film PV lines all significant production steps can be monitored.Currently, the Berlin-based company has 100 employees and worldwide more than 1500 metrology systems installed. LayTec offers a worldwide customer support and service network including local representations.   www.laytec.de

National Renewable Energy Laboratory (NREL)
Booths: 125, 126

The NCPV performs research on wide range of PV materials including c-Si, thin-film silicon, CIGS, CdTe, III-V-based devices, and organic PV. The NCPV provides measurements of PV materials, cells and modules, as well as reliability testing. Stop by the booth to meet the PV experts. www.nrel.gov

Newport Corp. / Oriel Instruments
Booth: 122

Oriel® Instruments, a brand of Newport Corporation, is recognition in the optical research field as a highly reliable source for well engineered, durable Light Sources and their dedicated Power Supplies, as well as Light Detection Systems and Spectroscopy Instrumentation. Oriel also manufactures dedicated broadband light sources, monochromatic light sources and detectors for light measurement & characterization in sophisticated dedicated instrumentation. www.newport.com/oriel

NSERC Photovoltaic Innovation Network
Booth: 105

The NSERC Photovoltaic Innovation Network is a partnership between NSERC, university professors, and industry partners across Canada, focused on the development of novel, cost-effective photovoltaic technologies. The network aims to provide a networking ground for the photovoltaic community across the nation. Visit our booth to learn more about our research. www.pvinnovation.ca

OAI
Booths: 123, 124

With over 40 years of experience in the generation, control and mearurement of light, OAI provides solar test systems for R&D or production. OAI's products include Class AAA Trisol Solar Simulators, IV Testers, Test Fixtures, both standard and custom, Calibrated Reference Cells, Solar Power Meters and portable outdoor Solar Array Testers. Trisol Solar Simulators with OAI's advanced beam uniformity optics are available as conintuous/ single long pulse. Other solar simulators for special applications include DSSC, Organic Cells, CPV, 350-1800nm Multijunction cells, and standard cells. OAI offers a full range of IV testers from 1 Amp-20 Amps, and new integrated IV Test System for High Efficiencey Solar Cells. www.oainet.com

Photo Emission Tech
Booth: 133

Manufacturer of Cell Testers & Steady State Solar Simulators Class AAA - Illumination area: 50mm x 50mm to 400mm x 400mm.I-V Measurement Systems - Current Range from 1A to up to 20A, Optional temperature controlSpectral Response & QE Systems- EQE/IPCE; Optional IQE; Flexible configurationSpectro-Radiometers - 300-2,200nm Range. www.photoemission.com

PV Measurements, Inc.
Booths: 111, 112

Manufacturer of the QEX10 Solar Cell Quantum Efficiency Measurement System a series of premier I-V Measurement Systems and reference cell in addition to uniformity mappers and spectroradiometers. www.pvmeasurements.com

Qioptiq Space Technology
Booth: 119

We have served the space industry for more than 40 years and we continue to be world leaders in the design and manufacture of highly specialized optical space components. Our expertise is the manufacture of a series of ultra thin radiation stable glasses for two main applications: Solar Cell Coverglasses and Optical Solar Reflectors, both specifically designed for space applications. Our radiation stable glass has also been used in Terrestrial CPV applications operating in high temperature and high UV conditions. Our approach applies proven technologies and materials in new ways to improve performance tailored to specific mission requirements. www.qioptiq-space.com

Semco Engineering, Inc.
Booth: 130

Semco manufactures high volume and R&D equipment for the c-Si PV industry. Applications include diffusion, oxidation and direct plasma PECVD. Equipment includes: DF series high volume reduced pressure diffusion/oxidation and TWYN series direct plasma PECVD manufacturing systems. For R&D, Semco offers the all-in-one (diffusion, oxidation, PECVD) MiniLab system for process development and lab to fab deployment. Services include a foundry and process development/verification center. www.semcoeng.com

Semilab SDI LLC
Booth: 103

Semilab is a leading metrology provider to the Semiconductor and PV industries, offering a full range of both in-line and off-line mapping tools for Si bricks, wafers, cells and thin film type PV devices. Measurements include lifetime, thickness, resistivity, LBIC, reflectance, ellipsometry, photoluminescence and complete wafer sorting solutions. www.semilab.hu

Sinton Instruments
Booths: 127, 128

Sinton Instruments provides test and measurement instruments for use in Silicon PV manufacturing and R&D that are used at each stage of the solar cell production process. The initial quality of bricks or ingots can be assessed by our unique carrier-lifetime testing instruments. We have lifetime-test instruments for process control and optimization at the as-cut wafer stage and for characterizing the final wafer and surface passivation quality after the high-temperature phosphorus diffusion steps. For the solar cell back-end processes, we provide cell-test and module testing capabilities. Each of these applications involves state-of-the-art analysis including our Suns-Voc testing methodologies.
www.sintoninstruments.com

Solar Energy Research Institute for India and the United States
Booth: 113

The Solar Energy Research Institute for India and the United States (SERIIUS) creates a bi-national network for fostering new ideas and collaborations to expedite a sustainable industry. Supported equally by the Government of India and the U.S. Department of Energy, SERIIUS, through its consortium of 31 national laboratory, university, and industry partners, is developing disruptive technologies through foundational research in photovoltaics (PV) and concentrating solar power (CSP) to address critical barriers for solar energy development I India that intersect with the grand challenges for solar energy in the U.S. www.SERIIUS.org

Spire Corporation
Booth: 129

Spire Corporation is a leading global PV equipment company supplying the industry's best in class simulation systems. We continue our leadership position with the introduction of the 5600SLP Blue simulator, and invest heavily to develop expertise in PV metrology. Our goal is to help the industry be certain about reliably measuring the maximum power performance of today's PV modules. www.spirecorp.com

Tau Science Corporation
Booth: 106

Tau Science builds unique, world class, process control and device characterization equipment for the PV Industry. In addition to custom services and component sales, our signature product lines are: FlashQE, a one second QE measurement; PixEL, a highly configurable PL/EL imaging platform; and IRIS, an inline/ EOL hotspot inspection system.   tauscience.com

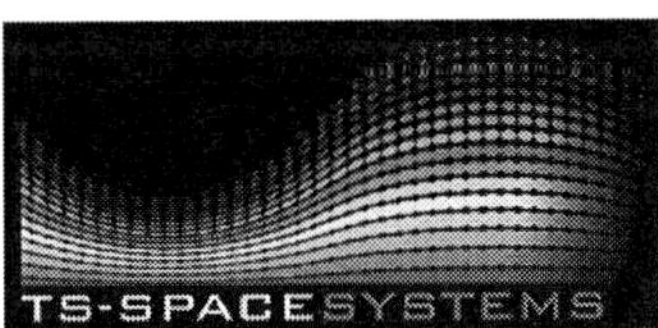

TS Space Systems
Booth: 109

TS-Space Systems™ is an international award winning physics-based group, that has been providing support to the space industry for more than twenty six years. We are continually improving and refining our range of close-match, solar simulators for both the AM0 and AM1.5 solar spectra.At the same time we have continued our work in other space-related fields. We have long-term experience in designing and building high-vacuum thermal cycling chambers and shrouds. Thus, we can supply complete vacuum systems, or use our expertise to customise existing chambers. We also build bespoke rapid thermal cycling equipment. www.ts-space.co.uk

TUTORIAL PROGRAM

AM TUTORIALS
SUNDAY, JUNE 16TH, 8:30 AM – 12:00 PM

AM1. PHOTOVOLTAICS 101/201
(MR 11-12)

Instructor: Dr. Christiana Honsberg, Global Institute of Sustainability, Arizona State University

Synopsis: An introductory tutorial in photovoltaic principles and devices. Basic semiconductor physics will be covered, with an emphasis on semiconductor junctions. The basic current-voltage relationship for a solar cell will be derived. Performance optimization and various loss mechanisms for the general solar cell will be discussed. The course is designed for those with a background in physics, chemistry, and/or engineering, but not yet having a strong background in semiconductor devices.

AM2. TECHNOLOGY STATUS AND CRITICAL ISSUES FOR MANUFACTURING HIGH VOLUME THIN FILM PHOTOVOLTAICS: CDTE, CU(INXGA1-X)SE2 AND A-SI/ NC-SI
(MR 13)

Instructors: Dr. Tim Anderson, Dept. Chemical Engineering, University of Florida, and Dr. Steven Hegedus, Institute of Energy Conversion, University of Delaware

Synopsis: Thin film semiconductors have been investigated as absorber layers for large scale photovoltaic since the 1960's based on the promise of low manufacturing cost for large-area high-throughput PV modules. Three thin film absorber materials emerged in the 1980's as being technically and commercially viable for solar cells: CdTe, CuInSe2-based, and Si-based. The first two are polycrystalline while the Si films are either amorphous or nanocrystalline. Each is configured as a multilayer heterojunction device fabricated on glass, foil, or plastic substrates. Sustained worldwide research and development have significantly increased our understanding of the materials chemistry and physics leading to advanced device structures and high-throughput processing at high yield. Each technology has the benefits common to thin films but each has specific challenges. In this tutorial, we will provide an overview of the basic processing sequence, device structures, manufacturing options, and key challenges for each thin film technology. Based on our 3 decades of direct involvement in thin film PV, we will review the evolution of each thin film technology into today's commercial success and identify critical issues limiting wider commercialization. The course is intended for graduate students, researchers, technologists and managers interested in an overview of the technologies as well as understanding the fundamental materials chemistry, device operation and characterization and process engineering

AM3. POWER ELECTRONICS BALANCE-OF-SYSTEM REQUIREMENTS FOR NON-PLANAR PHOTOVOLTAIC SYSTEMS
(MR 14)

Instructor: Dr. Robert Balog, University of Texas A&M

Synopsis: To present design considerations for photovoltaic systems installed in or on non-planar surfaces and their associated power conditioning architectures. The tutorial begins with a review of traditional planar PV systems, cell electrical models, and thermal models to predict the operating temperature of the module. The tutorial then explores the power electronics needed to interface the PV to the ac utility system. The electrical models previously developed are used to illustrate the phenomenon of maximum power point tracking (MPPT) and to explore the operation of series-connected strings of PV cells and modules under partial shading conditions. The second part of the tutorial introduces emerging applications of non-planar PV.

Detailed analysis is presented for estimating the available electrical power and electrical energy harvest potential for PV systems installed on arbitrarily non-planar curved surface. By way of example, it will be shown that a) conventional "string" PV architectures in which PV modules are connected in series/parallel to a central DC-AC inverter and b) module integrated micro-inverters are not optimal for PV systems installed on curved or irregular surfaces. Several new approaches are then reviewed for extracting maximum power along with possible interconnection of module-integrated converters with PV cells. The concept of a "smart PV pixel" is presented.

AM4. HIGH EFFICIENCY MULTI-JUNCTION CELL TECHNOLOGY
(MR 15)

Instructors: Dr. Ned Edkins-Daukes, Imperial College London and Dr. Robert Walters, Naval Research Laboratory

Synopsis: III-V multi-junction solar cells offer the highest efficiency of any photovoltaic technology, attaining 44% under concentrated sunlight and over 30% commercially for space applications. The operating principles of these solar cells will be reviewed and the present state of the art structures presented together with some possible routes for future development of the technology. Since these devices are used routinely to power spacecraft, their performance in the space environment will be discussed, together with methodologies for determining their degradation and end of life performance.

AM5. PART 1. DISTRIBUTED GENERATION INTEGRATION - UNDERSTANDING THE CURRENT CHALLENGES AND OPPORTUNITIES (MR 16)

Instructors: Michael Coddington, NREL; Blake Lundstrom, NREL; Prof. Ravel Ammerman, Colorado School of Mines/NREL; Robert Broderick, Sandia National Laboratories

Synopsis: Renewable energy resources are widely distributed geographically and are intermittent in nature, so they cannot be directly controlled and dispatched like the more traditional sources of generation. Large electrical power networks have been historically designed using centralized power generating stations supplying customer loads over interconnected transmission and distribution networks. Increasing the penetration level of distributed renewable energy sources requires adjustments to the existing operating procedure and design philosophy of large-scale power systems.

The workshop begins with a high-level overview of energy resources and distributed generation technologies, followed by an in-depth technical discussion of distributed generation interconnection issues. The intent of the workshop is to encourage audience interaction by soliciting input from all participants, using distributed generation interconnection case studies to facilitate discussions. We will cover: Energy System Basics - The Electric Power Grid, Distributed Energy Systems - PV Systems, Applicable Standards and Codes, Interconnection Processes.

PM TUTORIALS
SUNDAY, JUNE 16TH, 1:30 PM – 5:00 PM

PM1. AN END-TO-END (DEVICE-MODULE-SYSTEM) PERSPECTIVE PV RELIABILITY
(MR 11-12)

Instructors: Muhammad (Ashraf) Alam, Purdue University and Mike Fife, Advanced Energy, Inc.

Synopsis: This tutorial will provide attendees with a basic working knowledge of photovoltaic (PV) system reliability. Topics will cover four main sections: physics of PV cell reliability and degradation, cell-to-module efficiency loss, balance-of-system (including inverter) reliability, and system reliability estimation. Topics covered in the PC cell reliability section include the distinction between intrinsic and. extrinsic reliability, theory and practice of active layer degradation and the statistics and universality of shunt formation. The cell-to-module efficiency loss will be discussed in the context of series connectivity, scribing, and shadow degradation. The problem of polymer charging and degradation will also be discussed. A similar overview of balance-of-system reliability will be given with a focus on the inverter, which is known to be responsible for the bulk of PV system downtime. We will then show how to bring individual component reliability estimates into a single plant-wide system reliability model. Some of the metrics discussed will be mean time between failures (MTBF), annualized failure rate, and availability. We will conclude with a discussion on how reliability metrics tie back to plant economics via number of truck rolls, service cost, and lost energy production.

PM2. SILICON SOLAR CELL TECHNOLOGY
(MR 13)

Instructor: Dr. Ron Sinton, Sinton Instruments

Synopsis: This tutorial will look at various aspects of crystalline silicon technologies, from the silicon bricks and ingots through sawing, solar cell production, cell test, and module test. The interactions between the various stages from feedstock to the module testing will be discussed. An emphasis will be placed on device physics as well as test and measurement strategies that are used to optimize the cell and module design and provide real-time feedback for process control at each stage of production.

PM3. DEVELOPING THE MARKET VALUE FOR RESIDENTIAL AND COMMERCIAL PV SYSTEMS - A PRIMER ON METHODS, CHALLENGES AND CURRENT RESEARCH EFFORTS
(MR 14)

Instructors: Geoff Klise, Sandia National Laboratories, Jamie Johnson, Energy Sense Finance, and Sandy Adomatis SRA Adomatis Appraisal Services

Synopsis: This short course will discuss topics surrounding market valuation techniques as applied to photovoltaic (PV) systems during a real estate transaction. More often More often than not, PV systems have been receiving little to no valuation, primarily due to a lack of knowledge by those in the appraisal, real estate, lending and underwriting industry. In response, Energy Sense Finance and Sandia National Laboratories joined forces to develop tools and conduct outreach on standard appraisal techniques and education concepts relevant to solar PV systems. The use of appropriate methodologies when valuing solar PV is key to minimizing risk and conveying the economic benefits of PV to all parties in the real estate transaction.

By the end of this session, you will be able to: Use the PV ValueTM Tool to develop a range of value estimates that can be used by appraisers, real estate agents, and those in leasing and sales. Identify ways the solar industry can provide valuable data through installation and proper commissioning. (Custom derate factors, degradation rates); and Reveal other applications of the PV ValueTM Tool that can be applied to PACE programs.

PM4. NOVEL MATERIALS AND DEVICE CONCEPTS FOR PHOTOVOLTAIC ENERGY CONVERSION
(MR 15)

Instructor: Dr. Nicoleta Sorloaica-Hickman, Associate Professor at Florida Solar Energy Center, University of Central Florida

Synopsis: While the conventional photovoltaic technologies are currently dominating the market and advancing, there are still many exciting research efforts in developing novel materials and device architectures in this area. This tutorial will provide a perspective of the new technologies and materials, as well as novel device concepts which are actively being investigated globally to overcome the current limit of photovoltaic conversion efficiency and further drive down the cost of PV electricity generation.

PM5. PART 2. DISTRIBUTED GENERATION INTEGRATION - UNDERSTANDING THE CURRENT CHALLENGES AND OPPORTUNITIES (MR 16)

Instructors: Michael Coddington, NREL; Blake Lundstrom, NREL; Prof. Ravel Ammerman, Colorado School of Mines/NREL; Robert Broderick, Sandia National Laboratories

Synopsis: Renewable energy resources are widely distributed geographically and are intermittent in nature, so they cannot be directly controlled and dispatched like the more traditional sources of generation. Large electrical power networks have been historically designed using centralized power generating stations supplying customer loads over interconnected transmission and distribution networks. Increasing the penetration level of distributed renewable energy sources requires adjustments to the existing operating procedure and design philosophy of large-scale power systems.

The workshop begins with a high-level overview of energy resources and distributed generation technologies, followed by an in-depth technical discussion of distributed generation interconnection issues. The intent of the workshop is to encourage audience interaction by soliciting input from all participants, using distributed generation interconnection case studies to facilitate discussions. We will cover: Energy System Basics - The Electric Power Grid, Distributed Energy Systems - PV Systems, Applicable Standards and Codes, Interconnection Processes and Procedures, Integrating Distributed Generation - Problems and Mitigation Techniques.

WORKSHOP PROGRAM

SUNDAY, JUNE 16TH, 1:00 PM – 5:00 PM

IEA PVPS TASK 13 WORKSHOP: LESSONS LEARNED FROM THE ANALYTICAL MONITORING AND MODELING OF PV SYSTEMS (MR 7-9, AREA 9)

Optimizing the performance of PV plants is increasingly important as the PV industry becomes more competitive. This workshop will present work being performed as part of the International Energy Agency (IEA) Photovoltaic Power Systems Task 13 on Performance and Reliability of PV Systems. In particular, the workshop will focus on lessons learned from measuring performance from fielded PV systems and methods for analyzing and modeling system performance. Presenters will describe analysis methods and tools for use with PV monitoring data to identify system problems and better understand technology differences in diverse environments.

PROGRAM OUTLINE

1:00 - 1:20 PM
Introduction to IEA PVPS Task 13
Dr. Nils Reich, Fraunhofer Institute for Solar Energy Systems ISE, Germany

1:20 - 1:50 PM
An International Comparison of PV Annual Yield and Performance Ratio
Dr. Wilfried van Sark, Copernicus Institute of Sustainable Development, Utrecht University, Netherlands

1:50 - 2:20 PM
PV Monitoring Data, User Stories, and Interpretation Guidelines
Achim Woyte, PhD, 3E sa, Brussels, Belgium

2:20 - 2:50 PM
The PV Performance Modeling Collaborative
Joshua S Stein Ph.D, Sandia National Laboratories, USA

2:50 - 3:20 PM
Diagnosing System Issues in Real Time
Mike Green, M.G. Lightning Electrical Engineering, Israel

3:20 - 3:50 PM
Networking Break

3:50 - 4:20 PM
An International Comparison of Thin-film Module Performance and the Relevance of Low Irradiance, Spectral and Temperature Effects
Markus Schweiger, TUV Rheinland, Germany

4:20 - 5:00 PM
Q&A, Workshop conclusion

TECHNICAL PROGRAM

PROGRAM CHAIR GREETING

On behalf of the Technical Program Committee, I am honored to welcome you to the 39th IEEE PVSC. The PVSC endeavors to cover all aspects of photovoltaics technology, including the latest in device performance, new module encapsulation technologies, novel characterization techniques, knowledge gained from field experiences, or new PV material science. The chance to share and discuss these important PV developments in a timely and influential forum is what the PVSC is all about.

For PVSC39, we have expanded the number of technical areas to eleven (11), adding a new cross-technology area focused on Reliability of PV, headed up by Dr. Sarah Kurtz of NREL (Area 10). As the PV industry has grown, it has become increasingly critical to have confidence in the long-term performance of the GWs of PV, representing enormous financial investment. This topic cuts across all PV technologies and throughout the supply chain.

Despite the shake-ups and challenges the PV market is experiencing, worldwide research efforts continue to be robust. PVSC39 received more than 1000 submissions, a near record number. From these submissions, as well as invited presentations, an excellent technical program of over 600 posters and 290 oral presentations has been assembled. The technical program consists of up to seven (7) parallel tracks and the Program Committee has strived to minimize conflicts between technical areas with shared audiences. To help alleviate conflict, many joint sessions have been assembled, so please look at the conference schedule carefully.

A significant number of PVSC submissions (approximately 120) were offered the opportunity to publish their PVSC manuscripts in the peer-reviewed IEEE Journal of Photovoltaics (J-PV). This valuable opportunity permits researchers to present their best original research results at the PVSC, while having that work made available to a global audience through a high impact, peer-reviewed journal. If your work wasn't offered this opportunity, you are certainly welcome to add new results to your PVSC paper (30% min) and submit it for consideration by J-PV. And for next year, consider adding all of your high impact data to your review abstract to improve your chances of being offered the opportunity to publish your PVSC paper in J-PV.

As we've done for the past few years, all PVSC papers will be made available to attendees electronically on the Monday following the conference. In addition, we will be uploading the majority of the PVSC papers to IEEE Xplore within a few months of the conference. Once all of the PVSC/J-PV papers complete the peer-review process, the remaining papers will be added to IEEE Xplore and a conference proceedings DVD will be sent to attendees.

In closing, I would like to thank the hundreds of volunteers on the Program Committee for their dedication and hard work. An excellent technical program has been assembled, we have a fantastic venue and a wonderful city in which to meet. I wish you a successful and productive PVSC and I thank you for your participation!

David M. Wilt
Program Chair, 39th PVSC

AREA 1 OVERVIEW

FUNDAMENTALS AND NEW CONCEPTS FOR FUTURE TECHNOLOGIES

Chair
Alex Freundlich, University of Houston, USA

Co-Chairs
Gavin Conibeer, University of New South Wales- Australia
Antonio Marti, Polytechnic University of Madrid, Spain
Masakazu Sugiyama, University of Tokyo, Japan

Sub-Areas & Chairs
1.1: Fundamental Conversion Mechanisms - Seth Hubbard (RIT)
1.2: Quantum-well, Nanowire, and Quantum Dot- Architectured Devices - Jessica Adams (Microlink Devices)
1.3: Hybrid Organic/Inorganic Solar Cells - Nicoleta Hickman (University of Central Florida)
1.4: Advanced Light Management and Spectral Shaping - Peichen Yu (National Chiao Tung University)
1.5: Novel Material Systems - Cory Cress (Naval Research Laboratory)

Papers are sought that describe basic research and breakthroughs in physical, chemical and optical phenomena, new materials and novel device concepts, which are essential to feed the innovation pipeline leading to future-generation PV technologies. General areas of interest include, but are not limited to, recent advances in understanding, simulation, demonstration and optimization of:

1. non-conventional PV conversion processes and devices, intermediate-band solar cells, multiple charge carrier generation, thermophotovoltaics, hot-carrier cells, and other emerging PV device concepts,
2. devices based on quantum wells, nanowires, and quantum dots as well as deciphering the science in photogeneration, recombination, and carrier transport in these devices,
3. cross-cutting hybrid devices that leverage on organic/ inorganic materials and nanostructures,
4. advanced light management concepts and approaches: including new structures and materials for antireflection, light trapping, plasmonic coupling, spectral conversion, and light concentration,
5. novel material systems and associations for increasing performance, functionality, reliability and scalability of PV devices, including new pseudomorphic and metamorphic photovoltaic material systems, alternative inexpensive substrates, novel doping and defect passivation schemes, novel nanostructures, earth abundant thin films and TCO materials. Novel scalable nano/micro fabrication techniques and processes for synthesis of PV materials.

AREA 2 OVERVIEW

CHALCOGENIDE THIN FILM SOLAR CELLS AND RELATED MATERIALS

Chair
Sylvain Marsillac, Old
Dominion University, USA

Co-Chairs
James Sites, Colorado State
University, USA
Takashi Minemoto,
Ritsumeikan University, Japan
Jean-Francois Guillemoles,
IRDEP-CNRS, France

Sub-Areas & Chairs
2.1: Absorber Formation and
Characterization - Harin Ullal (NREL), Ayodhya Tiwari
(EMPA), Shigeru Niki (AIST)
2.2: Substrates, Contacts, Buffer layers and TCO -
IVikash Ranjan (Pilkington), Susanne Siebentritt (U.
Luxembourg), Tokio Nakada (Aoyama University), Marika
Edoff (Uppsala University)
2.3: Robert Collins (University of Toledo), Daniel
Abou Ras (Hemholtz center Berlin), Tetsuya Sakurai
(University of Tsukuba), Mike Scarpulla (University of
Utah)
2.4: Manufacturing Issues: Performance, Metrology,
Process Control, and Reliability - Markus Gloeckler
(First Solar), Paul Mogensen (Avancis), Tadashi Iwakura
(Honda Engineering)

Over the last ten years, chalcogenide thin-film modules
have managed to capture more than 15% of the terrestrial
PV market while the efficiency of the laboratory scale cells
has surpassed the 20% landmark.

Beside the now more traditional CdTe and Cu(In,Ga)
(S,Se)2, new material systems are emerging, such
as Cu2ZnSn(S,Se)4, which brings new technology
challenges but also insight into the other material systems.

There is therefore still a need for understanding and
developing the fundamental science and engineering of
these chalcogenide thin films while pushing the limits of
the industrial applications and solutions for these systems.
Area 2 of the 39th IEEE PVSC invites contributions
addressing recent progress in the fields of Absorber
Formation and Characterization, Substrates, Contacts,
Buffer layers and TCO, Device Properties, Modeling,
Stability, and Defect Characterization, and all aspects
of Manufacturing Issues, which include Performance,
Metrology, Process Control, and Reliability.

AREA 3 OVERVIEW

III-V AND CONCENTRATOR TECHNOLOGIES

Chair
Scott Burroughs, Semprius, Inc., USA

Co-Chairs
Frank Dimroth, Fraunhofer ISE, Germany

Sub-Areas
3.1: Concentrator Solar Cells - Daniel Aiken (Emcore) and Carlos Algora (UPM)
3.2: Concentrator Receivers and Modules - Andreas Gombert (Soitec)
3.3: Concentrator Systems - Damien Buie (EDF Renewable Energy)

This focus area of the IEEE Photovoltaic Specialists Conference covers the latest technical progress in concentrating photovoltaic (CPV) technology. CPV is proving to be a technology that offers very high efficiencies leading to very low LCOE. This area welcomes papers describing advances enabling higher efficiency, lower cost, or more reliable concentrator cells, modules and systems.

AREA 4 OVERVIEW

CRYSTALLINE SILICON PHOTOVOLTAICS

Chair
Nathan Stoddard, SolarWorld, USA

Co-Chairs
Gianluca Coletti, ECN
Zhigang-Rick Li, DuPont

Sub-Areas & Chairs
4.1: Feedstock, Doping and Impurities - Roland Einhaus, Apollon Solar, France
4.2: Crystallization and Wafering - Noritake Usami, Tohoku University
4.3: Passivation and Advanced Devices - Giso Hahn, University of Konstanz, Germany
4.4: Industrial Cell Processing - Ajay Upadhyaya, Georgia Tech
4.5: Fundamentals - Mariana Bertoni, Arizona State University

The downward trend in module prices worldwide continues to drive the need for improved technology in crystalline silicon to maintain competitiveness and meet the demands of a widening market. Refinements in fundamental understanding on topics such as crystallization techniques, defect control and surface passivation drive further improvement in performance. Advances in cell performance demand a difficult balance of performance and manufacturability. We invite papers reporting on all aspects of crystalline silicon technology, encompassing the value chain from feedstock through crystallization, wafer cutting, wafer handling and cell design, as well as the fundamental aspects of defect characterization, gettering, modeling and optics

AREA 5 OVERVIEW

THIN FILM SILICON BASED PV TECHNOLOGIES

Chair
Arno Smets, Delft University of Technology, The Netherlands

Co-Chairs
Ivan Gordon, IMEC, Belgium
Nikolas Podraza, University of Toledo, USA

Sub-Areas & Chairs
5.1: Fundamental Properties of Thin Film Silicon - Erik Johnson, Ecole Polytechnique, France
5.2: Processing Issues for Thin Silicon Films and Devices - Takuya Matsui, AIST, Japan
5.3: Light Management Concepts in Thin Film Silicon Solar Cell Devices - Matthieu Despeisse, EPFL Neuchatel, Switzerland
5.4: Novel Concepts for Thin Film Silicon Solar Cell Devices - Vikram Dalal, Iowa State University, USA
5.5: Polycrystalline and Epitaxial Silicon Technology - David Young, NREL, USA)
5.6: Thin Film Silicon Based Solar Cells, Multijunctions and PV Modules - Bernd Stannowski, Helmholtz Zentrum Berlin, Germany

Thin-film photovoltaics based on amorphous, nano/microcrystalline, polycrystalline and epitaxial silicon on non Si-substrates have matured through three decades of advances in the design and processing of high-quality materials, solar cells and modules. Despite these great advances, many fundamental and technological issues of great importance still remain in order to achieve further progress, like the further increase of the conversion efficiencies and the reduction of cost price of thin silicon film based solar cells. Detailed research studies and visionary papers addressing the entire spectrum of the subject are welcomed. These topics include, but are not limited to: material characterization concerning microstructure, light induced degradation, various silicon based alloy types such as SiGe:H, SiC:H, SiO:H, film oxidation, passivation at heterojunction interfaces; processing issues concerning large throughput, large area, high deposition rates, contamination issues, processing routes for polycrystalline and epitaxial silicon; light trapping using textured interfaces, multi-layers, intermediate reflective layers and new TCO materials or concepts; novel concepts for thin silicon solar cells concerning films with new functionalities, plasmonic approaches, spectral conversion; and all topics related to amorphous/microcrystalline/polycrystalline/epitaxial silicon film solar cells and modules such as multi-junction structures, high performance and long-term reliability.

AREA 6 OVERVIEW

ORGANIC PHOTOVOLTAICS

Chair
Dana Olson, National Renewable
Energy Laboratory (NREL), USA

Co-Chairs
Moritz Riede, IAPP, Technische
Universität Dresden, Germany
Dean DeLongchamp, Nat'l Institute
of Standards and Technology
(NIST), USA

Sub-Areas & Chairs
6.1: Active Layer Materials
6.2: Contacts and Interfaces
6.3: Device Stability and Scale Up
6.4: Tandem, OPV on Inorganic PV, and Light Management
6.5: Hybrid and Dye-Sensitized Solar Cells (DSSCs)

Organic solar cells are rapidly advancing technologies that show potential for low-cost, light-weight, and flexible solar power generation. With efficiencies in organic photovoltaic (OPV) devices approaching or exceeding 11% through both single junction and tandem device architectures, these technologies represent scalable PV technologies that may soon demonstrate initial commercial viability. Despite this remarkable progress, there is a need to increase our understanding of the underlying processes in OPV devices both at the nanoscale and bulk as well as the chemistry, physics, and engineering issues behind OPV systems. Furthermore, commercial viability needs to be enabled to fully realize the advantages of OPV as a technology.

This symposium intends to address recent progress in devices and processing in a wide range of organic related photovoltaic technologies, including polymer solar cells, small molecule solar cells, organic-inorganic hybrid, and dye-sensitized solar cells. Novel interfacial and electrode materials, novel device concepts and architectures, device lifetime, active layer materials and characterization, and large-scale OPV device/module fabrication methods are important topics to be addressed. We especially encourage submissions describing the emerging strategy of using OPV as a low-cost efficiency enhancement layer in tandem with conventional inorganic photovoltaics. The symposium hopes to bring together efforts from a wide range of expertise to further facilitate the development of this technology.

The primary focus will in five main areas that combine many of the themes in the broad set of devices combining inorganic and organic materials to develop low-cost, stable, high-performance solar energy systems.

AREA 7 OVERVIEW

SPACE TECHNOLOGIES

Chair
Philip P. Jenkins, Naval Research Laboratory, USA

Co-Chairs
Mitsuru Imaizumi, JAXA, Japan
Carsten Baur, ESA, The Netherlands

Sub-Areas & Chairs
7.1: Space Devices and Materials - David Scheiman, Naval Research Laboratory
7.2: Space Systems - Brian Spence, Deployable Space Systems
7.3: Flight Performance and Environmental Effects - Justin Likar, Lockheed Martin

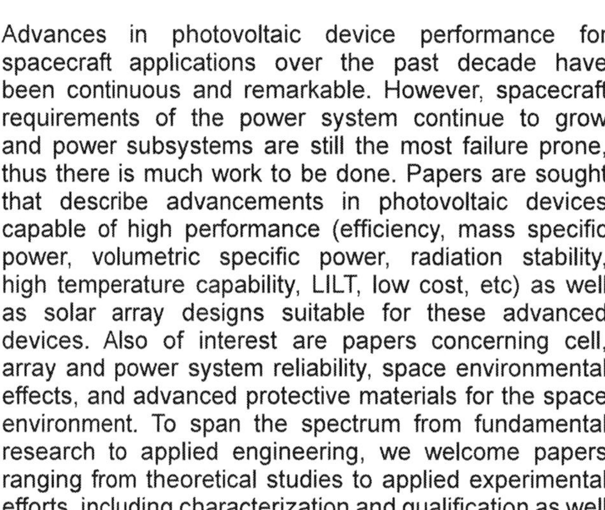

Advances in photovoltaic device performance for spacecraft applications over the past decade have been continuous and remarkable. However, spacecraft requirements of the power system continue to grow and power subsystems are still the most failure prone, thus there is much work to be done. Papers are sought that describe advancements in photovoltaic devices capable of high performance (efficiency, mass specific power, volumetric specific power, radiation stability, high temperature capability, LILT, low cost, etc) as well as solar array designs suitable for these advanced devices. Also of interest are papers concerning cell, array and power system reliability, space environmental effects, and advanced protective materials for the space environment. To span the spectrum from fundamental research to applied engineering, we welcome papers ranging from theoretical studies to applied experimental efforts, including characterization and qualification as well as flight experiments and missions.

TECHNICAL AREA OVERVIEWS

AREA 8 OVERVIEW

CHARACTERIZATION METHODS

Chair
Gerald Siefer, Fraunhofer ISE,
Germany

Co-Chairs
Tonio Buonassisi, M.I.T, USA
Yoshihiro Hishikawa, AIST, Japan
Yanfa Yan, The University of
Toledo, USA

Sub-Areas & Chairs
8.1: Defects in Photovoltaic
Materials and Solar Cells
8.2: Advanced Methods and Instruments for the
Characterization of Solar Cells and Modules
8.3: In-Situ Measurements, Process Control, Defect
Monitoring.
8.4: Challenges in the Characterization of Novel Solar
Cell Devices
8.5: Performance Testing and Standards

It is impossible to understand innovation in science without the support of measurements and characterization. Measurements are needed at all different levels of R&D and production - from the investigation of the operating principles of solar cells to the development of standards for the performance of installed PV systems. Understanding the relations between structure, physical properties, and the resulting PV performance is an exemplary problem in materials science and engineering. Reliable and precise determination of the efficiency and thus power of solar cells and PV modules is crucial for the successful widespread deployment of photovoltaics. Area 8 is intended for the presentation of the latest developments in the characterization of photovoltaics. We encourage members of the PV community to submit their contributions addressing the full range of scientific and technological challenges in the field of characterization.

AREA 9 OVERVIEW

PV MODULES AND TERRESTRIAL SYSTEMS

Chair
Joshua Stein, Sandia National
Laboratories, USA

Co-Chairs
Osamu Onodera, NEDO, Japan

Sub-Areas & Chairs
9.1: Solar Resource Assessment -
Steve Ransome, SRCL, UK
9.2: Optimizing Module-Scale
Performance: Materials, Design, and Construction - Alex
Cronin, Univ. of Arizona
9.3: Inverters, Converters, Embedded Power Electrics,
and BOS - Stephen Pisklak, Dow
9.4: PV Performance Modeling - Nate Blair, NREL
9.5: Interconnecting PV to the Grid - Robert Broderick,
Sandia National Laboratories
9.6: Advanced PV Systems and Smart Grid - Brian
Dougherty, NIST

The amount of innovation in the area of PV modules and
systems has been growing dramatically in recent years.
The PV sector is moving quickly from being a very small
part of the energy generation mix to becoming a major
component of the electrical power system. This rapid
growth is resulting in numerous challenges, including the
need to reduce uncertainty in the available solar resource,
the need to reduce manufacturing costs and increase
performance and reliability by developing new module and
BOS designs and materials, the need to increase system
efficiency at all steps in the power conversion process,
the need to streamline the interconnection process, and
the need to design and operate PV systems to integrate
with the "smart grid" of the future. We have divided this
broad area into six sub-areas, which are described
in more detail below. We welcome papers describing
technical advances in PV modules and systems.

AREA 10 OVERVIEW

RELIABILITY OF PV

Chair
Sarah Kurtz, NREL, USA

Co-Chairs
Tony Sample, JRC, European Commission
Wei Zhou, Trina Solar, China

Sub-Areas & Chairs
10.1: Field Experience -- Jeff Newmiller, BEW Engineering, Yuzuru Ueda, Tokyo Institute of Technology
10.2: Correlation of Accelerated Testing and Field Performance -- John Wohlgemuth, NREL
10.3: Manufacturing Quality Assurance -- Masaaki Yamamichi, AIST
10.4: PV Safety Issues - Joerg Althaus, TÜV Rheinland
10.5: Cell Level Reliability Issues - Allan Ward, First Solar, Kent Whitfield, Solaria
10.6: Reliability Techniques for Application to PV - Carole Graas, Colorado School of Mines, Glenn Alers, University of California, Santa Cruz, Vivek Gade, Jabil

As the PV industry has grown, it has become increasingly critical to have confidence in the long-term performance of the GWs of PV, representing billions of dollars or euros investment. This topic cuts across all technologies and throughout the supply chain. Topics especially critical to the success of the PV industry include: an up-to-date understanding of what is being observed for deployed products, the physics behind observed degradation/ failure modes, and the quantitative correlation between accelerated test results and outcomes seen in the field as a function of climate and installation in order to move toward statistical service life predictions. Submissions are invited for all types of PV technologies.

This area will host joint sessions with other Areas, including Areas 8, 9, and 11. Authors may choose to submit to the area of their choice; abstracts that are relevant to two areas will be reviewed by both areas. If appropriate abstracts are received, a joint session with the Velocity forum will be included: "Demonstrating Reliability to Satisfy the Investor/Customer/Insurance company."

AREA 11 OVERVIEW

PV VELOCITY FORUM

Chair
Elaine Ulrich, U.S. Department of
Energy, USA

Co-Chairs
Kristen Ardani, NREL, USA

Sub-Areas & Chairs
11.1: Deployment: Analysis and
Case Studies
11.2: Technology and Business
Support through Shared
Resources
11.3: Manufacturing

The PV Velocity Forum will address strategies to sustain
or accelerate high growth rates and rapid cost reductions
for PV technologies.

"Deployment: Analysis and Case Studies" will focus
on deployment challenges at the local, national and
international level. This area may include market, finance,
Intellectual Property, business development, outreach,
policy and regulatory studies. This may include workforce
challenges with an emphasis on finding ways to effectively
increase the breadth of expertise engaged in PV R&D,
manufacturing, deployment and technology support.

"Technology and Business support through shared
resources" will focus on the wide variety of R&D centers,
consortia, facilities, road-mapping, and other activities
and resources that can help you to access information
and equipment you need to drive your technology and
business forward in a cost-effective manner. This is an
appropriate forum for showcasing the resources that may
be offered by your organization. This is open (but not
limited to) government programs, non-profits, advocacy
organizations and for-profit facilities and services.

AREA 1 PROGRAM SUMMARY

MONDAY, JUNE 17
Plenary: Area 1
9:30 - 10:00 AM (Ballrooms B-C)

Orals: Fundamentals and New Concepts: Advances in Light Trapping
1:30 - 3:00 PM (MR 20-21)

Orals: Joint Session, Areas 1, 3, & 7: Advances in Science and Engineering of Multijunction Devices
3:30 - 5:00 PM (MR 20-21)

TUESDAY, JUNE 18
Posters: Fundamentals and New Concepts: Quantum Wells, Wires and Dots
10:30 - 12:00 PM (East Hall)

Orals: Fundamentals and New Concepts: Avant-Garde Concepts and Enabling Materials
1:30 - 3:00 PM (MR 20-21)

Posters: Fundamentals and New Concepts: Advanced Concepts and Hybrid Devices
3:30 - 5:00 PM (East Hall)

WEDNESDAY, JUNE 19
Orals: Fundamentals and New Concepts: Progress Toward Intermediate Band Solar Cells
10:30 - 12:00 PM (MR 20-21)

Orals: Fundamentals and New Concepts: Physics and Engineering of Quantum Well and Superlattice Enhanced Solar Cells
1:30 - 3:00 PM (MR 20-21)

Posters: Fundamentals and New Concepts: Light Management Fundamentals
3:30 - 5:00 PM (East Hall)

THURSDAY, JUNE 20
Posters: Fundamentals and New Concepts: Novel Materials
10:30 - 12:00 PM (East Hall)

Orals: Fundamentals and New Concepts: Spectral Management
1:30 - 3:00 PM (MR 20-21)

Orals: Fundamentals and New Concepts: Physics and Engineering of Quantum Dot and Quantum Wire Enhanced Solar Cells
3:30 - 5:00 PM (MR 20-21)

FRIDAY, JUNE 21
Orals: Joint Session, Areas 1 & 6: Emerging Hybrid Approaches to Photovoltaics
8:30 - 10:00 AM (MR 20-21)

Orals: Joint Session, Areas 1 & 7: Advances in III-V Heteroepitaxial Materials and Devices
10:30 - 12:00 PM (MR 20-21)

AREA 2 PROGRAM SUMMARY

MONDAY, JUNE 17
Orals: Progress in CZTS Technology
1:30 - 3:00 PM (Ballroom B)

Orals: Modeling and Defects Characterization
3:30 - 5:00 PM (Ballroom B)

TUESDAY, JUNE 18
Posters: Absorber Formation and Characterization
10:30 - 12:00 PM (East Hall)

Orals: Advances in Buffer Layers Engineering
1:30 - 3:00 PM (Ballroom B)

Posters: Substrates, Contacts, Buffer Layers and TCO
3:30 - 5:00 PM (East Hall)

WEDNESDAY, JUNE 19
Plenary: Area 2
9:30 - 10:00 AM (Ballrooms B-C)

Orals: Progress in CdTe Technology
10:30 - 12:00 PM (Ballroom B)

Orals: Progress in CIGS Technology
1:30 - 3:00 PM (Ballroom B)

Posters: Device Properties and Manufacturing Issues
3:30 - 5:00 PM (East Hall)

THURSDAY, JUNE 20
Posters: Absorber Formation and Characterization 2
10:30 - 12:00 PM (East Hall)

Orals: Metrology
1:30 - 3:00 PM (Ballroom B)

Orals: Worldwide Industry Advances
3:30 - 5:00 PM (Ballroom B)

FRIDAY, JUNE 21
Orals: Back Contacts and Simulations
8:30 - 10:00 AM (Ballroom B)

Orals: New Materials and Ideas
10:30 - 12:00 PM (Ballroom B)

AREA 3 PROGRAM SUMMARY

MONDAY, JUNE 17
Orals: Joint Session, Areas 1, 3, & 7: Advances in
Science and Engineering of Multijunction Devices
3:30 - 5:00 PM (MR 20-21)

TUESDAY, JUNE 18
Posters: CPV Modules, Receivers, and Systems
10:30 - 12:00 PM (East Hall)

Orals: III-V on Si Solar Cells
1:30 - 3:00 PM (MR 25)

WEDNESDAY, JUNE 19
Plenary: Area 3
9:00 - 9:30 AM (Ballrooms B-C)

Orals: Multi-Junction III-V Cells
10:30 - 12:00 PM (MR 25)

Orals: CPV System Design, Modeling, and Field Results
1:30 - 3:00 PM (MR 25)

Posters: CPV Solar Cells
3:30 - 5:00 PM (East Hall)

FRIDAY, JUNE 21
Orals: Single-Junction III-V Cells
8:30 - 10:00 AM (MR 25)

Orals: CPV Module & Receiver Design, Optics &
Modeling
10:30 - 12:00 PM (MR 25)

AREA 4 PROGRAM SUMMARY

MONDAY, JUNE 17
Orals: Silicon Feedstock
1:30 - 3:00 PM (Ballroom C)

Orals: Crystallization and Wafer
3:30 - 5:00 PM (Ballroom C)

TUESDAY, JUNE 18
Posters: Feedstock, Crystallization and Wafering
10:30 - 12:00 PM (East Hall)

Orals: Advanced Devices
1:30 - 3:00 PM (Ballroom C)

Posters: Passivation and Advanced Devices
3:30 - 5:00 PM (East Hall)

WEDNESDAY, JUNE 19
Plenary: Area 4
8:30 - 9:00 AM (Ballrooms B-C)

Orals: Industrial Solar Cells: Texture, Emitter and ARC
10:30 - 12:00 PM (Ballroom C)

Orals: Passivation
1:30 - 3:00 PM (Ballroom C)

Posters: Industrial Solar Cell Processing
3:30 - 5:00 PM (East Hall)

THURSDAY, JUNE 20
Posters: Fundamentals
10:30 - 12:00 PM (East Hall)

Orals: State of the Art Solar Cells
1:30 - 3:00 PM (Ballroom C)

Area 4 Discussion Session
3:30 - 5:00 PM (Ballroom C)

FRIDAY, JUNE 21
Orals: Fundamentals
8:30 - 10:00 AM (Ballroom C)

Orals: Metallization
10:30 - 12:00 PM (Ballroom C)

AREA 5 PROGRAM SUMMARY

MONDAY, JUNE 17
Orals: Film Crystalline Silicon
1:30 - 3:00 PM (MR 22)

Orals: Thin Film Silicon Based Solar Cell Devices and Panels
3:30 - 5:00 PM (MR 22)

TUESDAY, JUNE 18
Plenary: Area 5
8:30 - 9:00 AM (Ballrooms B-C)

Posters: Fundamentals, Processing and Light Management
10:30 - 12:00 PM (East Hall)

Orals: Light Trapping concepts I
1:30 - 3:00 PM (MR 22)

Posters: Thin Film Silicon Solar Cells, Novel Concepts, Polycrystalline and Epitaxial Silicon
3:30 - 5:00 PM (East Hall)

WEDNESDAY, JUNE 19
Orals: Light Trapping Concepts II
10:30 - 12:00 PM (MR 22)

Orals: Metastabiliy, Defect Engineering and Material Processing
1:30 - 3:00 PM (MR 22)

AREA 6 PROGRAM SUMMARY

THURSDAY, JUNE 20
Plenary: Area 6
8:30 - 9:00 AM (Ballrooms B-C)

Posters: Organic PV Posters
10:30 - 12:00 PM (East Hall)

Orals: OPV Active Layers and Scale Up
1:30 - 3:00 PM (MR 22)

Orals: OPV Contacts, Hybrids, and Stability
3:30 - 5:00 PM (MR 22)

FRIDAY, JUNE 21
Orals: Joint Session, Areas 1 & 6: Emerging Hybrid
Approaches to Photovoltaics
8:30 - 10:00 AM (MR 20-21)

AREA 7 PROGRAM SUMMARY

MONDAY, JUNE 17
Orals: Joint Session, Areas 1, 3, & 7: Advances in Science and Engineering of Multijunction Devices
3:30 - 5:00 PM (MR 20-21)

THURSDAY, JUNE 20
Plenary: Area 7
9:00 - 9:30 AM (Ballrooms B-C)

Posters: Space Photovoltaics
10:30 - 12:00 PM (East Hall)

Orals: On-Orbit Performance and Space Environmental Effects
1:30 - 3:00 PM (MR 25)

Orals: Radiation Response of Solar Cells
3:30 - 5:00 PM (MR 25)

FRIDAY, JUNE 21
Orals: Joint Session, Areas 1 & 7: Advances in III-V Heteroepitaxial Materials and Devices
10:30 - 12:00 PM (MR 20-21)

AREA 8 PROGRAM SUMMARY

MONDAY, JUNE 17
Orals: Device Related Characterization
1:30 - 3:00 PM (MR 23)

Orals: Characterization of Silicon Cells and Material (I)
3:30 - 5:00 PM (MR 23)

TUESDAY, JUNE 18
Plenary: Area 8
9:00 - 9:30 AM (Ballrooms B-C)

Posters: Characterization - Device Related
10:30 - 12:00 PM (East Hall)

Orals: Characterization of Silicon Cells and Material (II)
1:30 - 3:00 PM (MR 23)

Posters: Characterization - Cell and Material Related
3:30 - 5:00 PM (East Hall)

WEDNESDAY, JUNE 19
Orals: Characterization of Thin Films (I)
10:30 - 12:00 PM (MR 23)

THURSDAY, JUNE 20
Orals: Characterization of Thin Films (II)
3:30 - 5:00 PM (MR 24)

AREA 9 PROGRAM SUMMARY

MONDAY, JUNE 17
Orals: Advanced PV Module Concepts and Designs
1:30 - 3:00 PM (MR 24)

Orals: System Performance Modeling
3:30 - 5:00 PM (MR 24)

TUESDAY, JUNE 18
Plenary: Area 9
9:30 - 10:00 AM (Ballrooms B-C)

Posters: Performance Modeling
10:30 - 12:00 PM (East Hall)

Orals: Solar Resource Assessment: Measurements and
Analyses
1:30 - 3:00 PM (MR 24)

Posters: Advanced Module Concepts and PV System
Applications
3:30 - 5:00 PM (East Hall)

WEDNESDAY, JUNE 19
Orals: Grid Impacts of PV Systems
10:30 - 12:00 PM (MR 24)

Orals: PV Output Variability
1:30 - 3:00 PM (MR 24)

Posters: Solar Resource and Grid Integration
3:30 - 5:00 PM (East Hall)

THURSDAY, JUNE 20
Posters: Inverters, Converters, Embedded Power
Electrics, and BOS
10:30 - 12:00 PM (East Hall)

Orals: Advanced Grid Interconnection Strategies
1:30 - 3:00 PM (MR 24)

FRIDAY, JUNE 21
Orals: Advanced Power Electronics for Optimized PV
Performance
8:30 - 10:00 AM (MR 24)

AREA 10 PROGRAM SUMMARY

MONDAY, JUNE 17
Plenary: Area 10
8:30 - 9:30 AM (Ballrooms B-C)

Orals: Correlation of Accelerated Testing with Field Performance
1:30 - 3:00 PM (MR 25)

TUESDAY, JUNE 18
Posters: PV Reliability I
3:30 - 5:00 PM (East Hall)

WEDNESDAY, JUNE 19
Orals: Cell Level Reliability and PID
1:30 - 3:00 PM (MR 23)

THURSDAY, JUNE 20
Posters: PV Reliability II
10:30 - 12:00 PM (East Hall)

Orals: Reliability Techniques and PV Safety
1:30 - 3:00 PM (MR 23)

Orals: Field Experience
3:30 - 5:00 PM (MR 23)

AREA 11 PROGRAM SUMMARY

WEDNESDAY, JUNE 19
Posters: PV Velocity Forum
3:30 - 5:00 PM (East Hall)

THURSDAY, JUNE 20
Plenary: Area 11
9:30 - 10:00 AM (Ballrooms B-C)

FRIDAY, JUNE 21
Orals: PV Velocity Forum
8:30 - 10:00 AM (MR 23)

Orals: PV Velocity Forum
10:30 - 12:00 PM (MR 23)

INSTRUCTIONS TO ORAL PRESENTERS

Thank you for participating in the IEEE PVSC as an Oral Presenter! **As an Oral Presenter, the following are your responsibilities:**

- You were required to upload your manuscript, following the guidelines on the PVSC website, by June 10, 2013
- Electronically sign the Copyright form and BRING A COPY WITH YOU
- Upload your presentation at least 24 hours prior to your presentation following the A/V company's guidelines on these pages. Bring your presentation on CD-ROM, compact flash card, memory stick, multi-media card, SD card, and/or a laptop for transfer.
- Even if you upload your presentation prior to the conference, you must check that it uploaded correctly by reviewing it in the Speaker Ready Room at the conference.
- Attend the Author's Breakfast on the morning of (each of) your presentation(s) for instructions, to meet your session chair, and to be sure all your materials have uploaded correctly. Author's Breakfast will be at 7:00 AM in **Ballroom A / Rotunda**
- Please arrive at your session at least 15 minutes before the scheduled start to coordinate with the session chairs, check that the presentation will display properly, and become familiar with the audio-visual equipment in your room.

REMEMBER: No Paper, No Podium

If your manuscript has not been uploaded, you will not be allowed to present. If you (or a co-author) do not give your presentation, the manuscript will not be included in the proceedings.

Be sure to check the online program to confirm your presentation time and length!

Each speaker can bring their presentation to the Speaker Ready Room on CD-ROM, Compact Flash Card, Memory Stick, Multi-media Card, SD Card, or a laptop prior to the scheduled time of their presentation. Also, speakers can submit their presentation via the PRG Upload Center web site http://ieee.presentationupload.com/ prior to the meeting. For technical questions please contact: present@prg.com or call (720) 440-8330 and ask for the IT Department.

Speaker Ready Room: Check in required for all presenters

Production Resource Group requests that all presenters use PowerPoint™ Presentations. All meeting rooms will have presentation computers and will be networked to a central server located in the Speaker Ready Room. Presenters are encouraged and expected to bring their own memory device or CD-ROM to the Speaker Ready Room, where they will have the opportunity to review their presentations or make any last minute changes.

If possible, please check in at the Speaker Ready Room 4 hours BEFORE your presentation.

When reviewing your presentation, you should make sure all fonts appear as expected and all sound/video clips are working properly. You will be able to edit your presentation at this time. When the presentation is to be given, the file will be accessed via the conference menu on the computer in the meeting room. Once the presentation is launched, you (the speaker) will control the program from the podium using a computer mouse.

INSTRUCTIONS TO POSTER PRESENTERS

Congratulations on being chosen to present a poster at the IEEE PVSC! Poster sessions are critical to the success of the conference, contributing to both the breadth and the depth of coverage in photovoltaic technology. Poster papers make it possible for a large number of important developments in the field of photovoltaics to be presented. In addition, the poster sessions allow authors the opportunity to personally interact and network with interested parties, and discuss research results at a level of detail that cannot be approached in formal questions following an oral presentation.

As a Poster Presenter, the following are your responsibilities:

- Manuscripts are required for all poster presentations in Areas 1-11. Be sure to upload your manuscript (Manuscript Instruction), following the guidelines on the PVSC website, **by June 10, 2013.** We value ALL your contributions and expect each to be represented in the Proceedings.
- Electronically sign the Copyright form and BRING A COPY WITH YOU
- Prepare your poster following the guidelines below:
- **Poster Size** - The area available for the poster is limited to a rectangle 40 inches tall by 42 inches wide (101 cm by 106 cm). THE POSTER CHAIR RESERVES THE RIGHT TO TRIM ANY POSTERS LARGER THAN THE ALLOCATED SIZE TO THE ALLOCATED SIZE!!! Tables in front of poster boards are PROHIBITED.
- **Poster Format** - Poster materials must be legible from a distance of two meters. Lettering in text and figures should be at least 5 mm, and the headings should be at least 10 mm. The title of the paper, the authors, and their affiliations should appear near the top of the poster in letters approximately 25 mm high.
- **Poster Mounting** - The surface of the mounting board is pushpin friendly. Posters must be mounted to the boards with pushpins. Push pins will NOT be available at the conference; you must bring your own. We also recommend that you attach an envelope near the bottom of the poster for people to leave business cards for reprints, etc. Please do not leave reprints of the paper on the floor.
- Poster boards will be available when the Posters/

Exhibits Hall opens on Monday, June 17, 2013, for the Exhibitors Reception and must be in place before the first poster session on Tuesday, June 18, 2013 at 10:30 am. The posters will remain on display for most of the week, through the morning poster sessions on Thursday. **Posters must be removed from the poster boards by 3:00 PM on Thursday, June 20, 2013. Any posters not removed on time will be removed and discarded.**

- **Present your poster** in person at the designed time. The posters will all be displayed in the exhibit hall. All posters will be displayed from Monday through Thursday. Poster boards will be arranged with letters designating each aisle and numbered poster position on each aisle. Specific locations for your poster will be available on this website in June.
- **Poster Check-in**: You are required to check-in at the poster registration desk immediately before your poster session time. The poster registration desk will be located in the exhibit hall near the front of the poster area. If you do not check in, your poster will be recorded as not presented and your manuscript will not be published.
- Please be sure to **attend the Author's Breakfast on the morning of (each of) your presentation(s)** for instructions, to meet your session chair, and to be sure all your materials have uploaded correctly. Author's Breakfast will be at 7:00 a.m. in **Ballroom A / Rotunda.**

REMEMBER: No Paper, No Poster

If your manuscript has not been uploaded, you will not be allowed to present your poster. If you (or a co-author) do not check in at the poster registration and present your poster in person, the manuscript will not be included in the proceedings.

BEST POSTER AWARD

As a poster presenter, you are automatically eligible to win the Best Poster Award. The posters will be reviewed in three stages:

1. **Prior to the conference:** Poster session chairs will familiarize themselves with the poster content and review technical content.
2. **After the posters are hung:** Poster session chairs will select the top three to four posters as finalists for best poster; a star will be placed on these posters to indicate their selection.
3. **During the poster session:** The session chairs will listen to the poster presenter's summary.

The poster session chairs will judge the posters based on **Clarity of Presentation, Technical Merit, Impact, and Oral Presentation.** These categories are described in more detail below. One winner will be selected at every poster session and the winner will receive a certificate.

Poster Reviewing Criteria

Clarity of Presentation
- Organized to guide observer through information in a logical order; provides the motivation/objectives and approach of the research, summarizes the key results and highlights the impact of the work.
- Proper use of graphics, figures, text and white space to allow for easy viewing.
- Proper text scaling for comfortable viewing.
- Efficient use of graphics to convey complex information.

Technical Merit
- Research is novel (e.g., discusses novel material development, novel device design, novel conversion mechanism, novel theoretical approach, novel characterization method, etc.).
- Research addresses a critical gap in PV technology.
- Systematic analysis conducted to arrive at results.
- Conclusions are fully supported by data.

Impact
- Results represent a significant advancement over the current status of the field or provide a critical breakthrough that will allow such advancement.

Oral Presentation
- An organized and concise summary of the work is presented, emphasizing the motivation/objectives, approach, key results, and impact of findings.
- Presenter is knowledgeable in all aspects of poster and able to address specific questions about the presented research.
- Presenter understands the broader impact of the work and can suggest potential methods for extending the research.

MONDAY

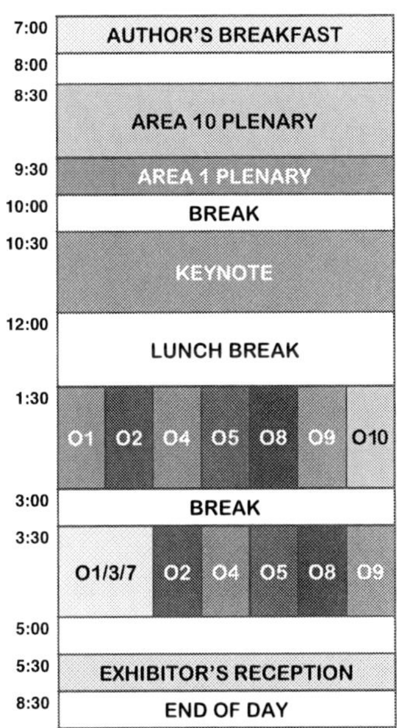

TUESDAY

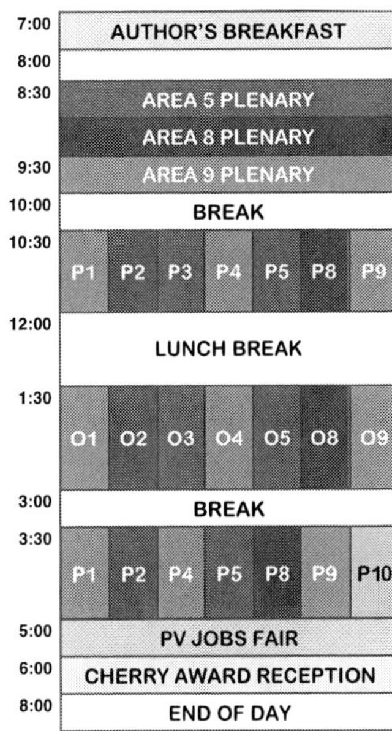

WEDNESDAY

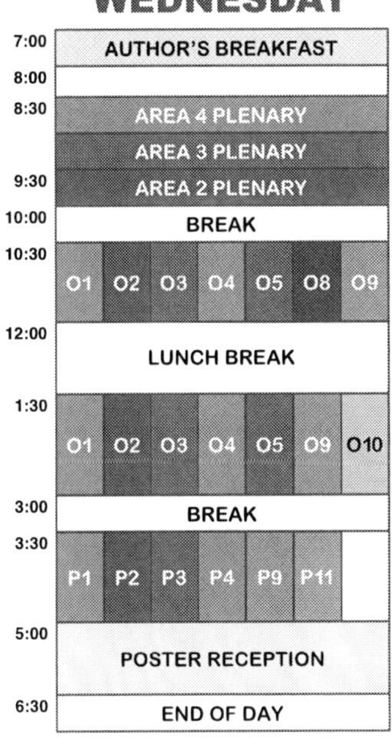

THURSDAY

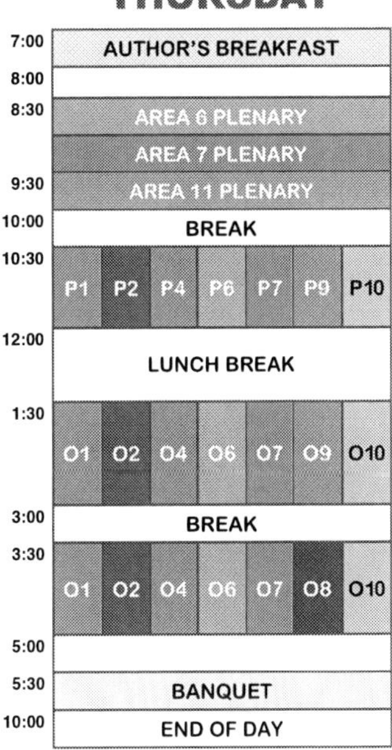

FRIDAY

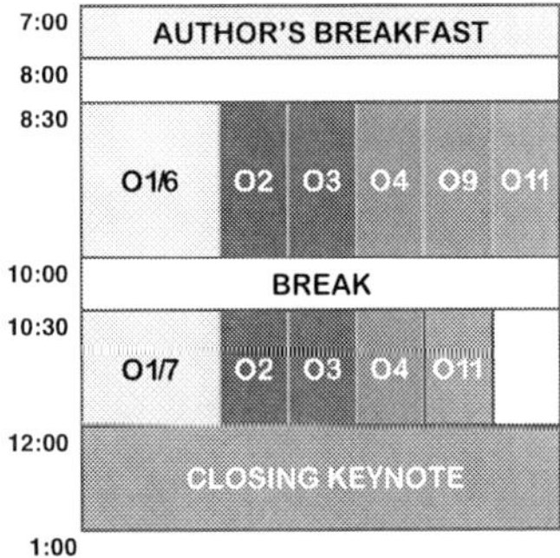

PV Reliability Development Lessons From JPL's Flat Plate Solar Array Project

Ronald G. Ross, Jr.

Abstract—Key reliability and engineering lessons that were learned from the 20-year history of the Jet Propulsion Laboratory's Flat-Plate Solar Array Project and thin-film module reliability research activities are presented and analyzed. Particular emphasis is placed on lessons applicable to evolving new module technologies and the organizations involved with these technologies. The user-specific demand for reliability is a strong function of the application, its location, and its expected duration. Lessons relative to effective means of specifying reliability are described, and commonly used test requirements are assessed from the standpoint of which are the most troublesome to pass, and which correlate best with field experience. Module design lessons are also summarized, including the significance of the most frequently encountered failure mechanisms and the role of encapsulant and cell reliability in determining module reliability. Lessons pertaining to research, design, and test approaches include the historical role and usefulness of qualification tests and field tests.

Index Terms—JPL Flat Plate Solar Array (FSA) project, lessons learned, photovoltaic, reliability.

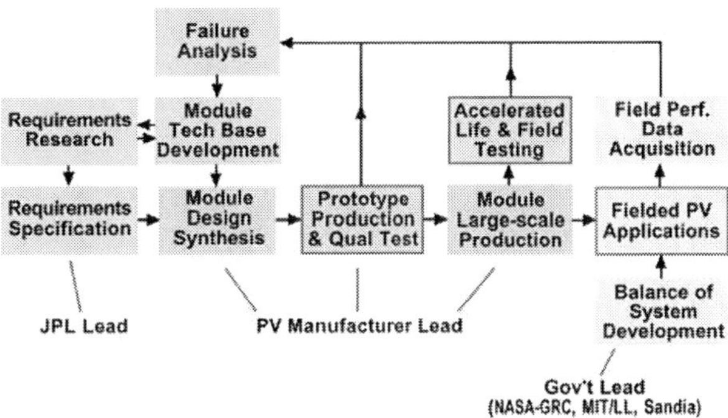

Fig. 1. Flowchart of US DOE PV Program module development activities undertaken in the years 1975 to 1985.

I. INTRODUCTION

DURING the ten years of JPL's flat plate solar array (FSA) Project (from 1975 to 1985) the reliability of crystalline-silicon modules was brought to a high level with lifetimes approaching 20 years, and excellent industry credibility and user satisfaction [1]. At the end of the FSA project, JPL engineering and reliability personnel spent another seven years working with the Solar Energy Research Institute (now NREL) developing reliability technology for thin-film modules. These new thin-film technologies involved new cell materials with more monolithic structures, but were basically responsive to the same reliability drivers and development methods.

At this point, ~20 years later, it is useful to review the lessons learned from JPL's crystalline-Si and thin-film reliability development efforts and apply the technology base, where applicable, to enhance the reliability of today's modules.

To this end, this paper summarizes the key reliability development lessons learned from the JPL module reliability development history with particular emphasis on lessons of use to new technologies and companies. For convenience, the lessons are divided into four topical areas: Reliability Management

Manuscript received July 19, 2013; revised August 30, 2013; accepted September 3, 2013. Date of publication October 1, 2013; date of current version December 16, 2013.

The author is with the Jet Propulsion Laboratory, California Institute of Technology, Pasadena, CA 91109 USA (e-mail: rgrossjr@jpl.nasa.gov).

Color versions of one or more of the figures in this paper are available online at http://ieeexplore.ieee.org.

Digital Object Identifier 10.1109/JPHOTOV.2013.2281102

Lessons, Reliability Requirement Lessons, Reliability Design Lessons, and Reliability Testing Lessons.

II. FLAT PLATE SOLAR ARRAY RELIABILITY MANAGEMENT LESSONS

Critical to successfully managing PV module reliability is understanding the value of increased or decreased module reliability at the PV systems level. Reliability directly influences the economic viability of photovoltaics as an energy source by not only controlling the total number and size of revenue payments received from the future sales of electricity, but it also influences O&M costs, and the cost of money required to build the PV system. After considerations of present-value discounting and escalation of the worth of electricity in future years, a 30-year PV plant, for example, can be worth 25 to 30 percent more than a 20-year-life plant [2]. Based on this economic sensitivity to plant life and the billion dollar cost of a utility-scale PV power plant today, there is a strong incentive to strive for a long life for such systems and a large incentive to allocate substantial funds for improving reliability.

A. Establishing an Overall Reliability Management Approach

During the 1975–1985 time frame, the FSA Project was a key cog in what, in my opinion, was a very well implemented overall U.S. Department of Energy (DOE) National PV Program [1]. Fig. 1 highlights the key module engineering elements of the broad government/industry partnership. These involved all aspects of the problem from requirements definition for future PV applications, to design the synthesis of candidate designs using current technologies, to thoroughly evaluating the designs in both laboratory and field applications, to identifying problem

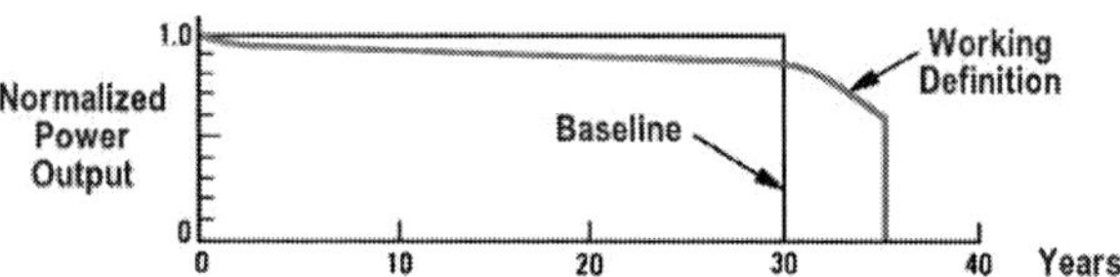

Fig. 2. Allocated degradation versus time for 30-year life photovoltaic system.

TABLE I

LIFE-CYCLE ENERGY COST IMPACT AND ALLOWABLE DEGRADATION LEVELS FOR CRYSTALLINE-SILICON MODULE FAILURE MECHANISMS

Type of Degradation	Failure Mechanism	Units of Degradation	Level for 10% Energy Cost Increase*		Allocation for 30-year Life Module	Economic Penalty
			k = 0	k = 10		
Component failures	Open-circuit cracked cells	%/yr	0.08	0.13	0.005	Energy
	Short circuit cells	%/yr	0.24	0.40	0.050	Energy
	Interconnect open circuits	%/yr^2	0.05	0.25	0.001	Energy
Power Degradation	Cell gradual power loss	%/yr	0.67	1.15	0.20	Energy
	Module optical degradation	%/yr	0.67	1.15	0.20	Energy
	Front surface soiling	%	10	10	3	Energy
Module failures	Module glass breakage	%/yr	0.33	1.18	0.1	O&M
	Module open circuits	%/yr	0.33	1.18	0.1	O&M
	Module hot-spot failures	%/yr	0.33	1.18	0.1	O&M
	Bypass diode failures	%/yr	0.70	2.40	0.05	O&M
	Module shorts to ground	%/yr^2	0.022	0.122	0.01	O&M
	Module delamination	%/yr^2	0.022	0.122	0.01	O&M
Life-limiting wearout	Encapsulant failure due to loss of stabilizers	years of life	27	20	35	End of life

* k=discount rate

areas and root causes, and to developing new improved technologies to resolve identified design weaknesses.

B. Establishment of Mechanism-Specific Reliability Goals

A key step in managing the reliability development process and achieving high reliability was establishing mechanism-specific reliability goals. This forced several disciplines on the design process: first, it required that all failure mechanisms be determined, and that the economic importance at the system level be determined for each failure or degradation occurrence. For some mechanisms, such as encapsulant soiling, the economic impact is directly proportional to the degradation level and is easily calculated. For others, such as open-circuit or short-circuit failures of individual solar cells, elaborate statistical-economic analyses that include the effects of circuit redundancy, maintenance practices, and life-cycle costing were required [2]. Without such analyses, failure levels could not be interpreted with meaning, and cost effective goals could not be established. Thus, the overall FSA reliability process included the generation of the required system's level reliability assessment tools, as well as the extensive tools required for failure mechanism characterization, quantification, and resolution.

As an example, Fig. 2 illustrates a typical power versus time plot for a 30-year life PV system, while Table I lists 13 principal failure mechanisms for flat-plate crystalline-Si photovoltaic modules, together with their economic significance. Similar data were also generated for thin-film modules [2].

The units of degradation listed in the third column of the table provide a convenient means of quantifying the failure levels of the individual mechanisms according to their approximate time dependence. For example, units of %/yr in the context of component or module failures reflect a constant percentage of components failing each year. For components that fail with increasing rapidity, (%/y2) is the unit used. For those mechanisms classified under power degradation, the %/yr units refer to the percentage of power reduction each year.

Using the units described previously, columns 4 and 5 indicate the level of degradation for each mechanism that will result in a 10% increase in the cost of delivered energy from a large PV system. Because the mechanisms will generally occur concurrently, the total cost impact is the sum of the 13 cost contributions. To help manage the reliability development effort, column 6 lists a strawman allocation of allowable degradation among the 13 mechanisms. In this case, the reliability allocations are consistent with a 20% increase in the cost of energy over that from a perfect, failure-free system with a 30-year life. This 20% shortfall is made up by having the eventual wearout and array replacement occur after 35 years.

Although different degradation allocations could have been chosen in Table I, the important point is that these allocations allow the significance of observed failures to be measured, and goals to be developed to guide mechanism-specific research and resolution activities.

Of particular importance is the small size of these allocations relative to there ability to be easily measured: e.g., 1 per 20 000 per year cell failures, 0.2% per year module power degradation, and 1 per 1000 per year module failures. This level of degradation can only be measured using the field experience from a large utility-scale system or from the aggregated results from a large number of smaller-scale systems.

III. FLAT PLATE SOLAR ARRAY RELIABILITY REQUIREMENT LESSONS

Although Table I, defines allowable goals for the acceptable levels of individual failures, the most fundamental requirement that the module reliability design must address is the level of applied stresses in the intended applications. Table II lists the key environments identified as the reliability drivers for crystalline-silicon modules during the FSA tenure (ordered from most significant to least).

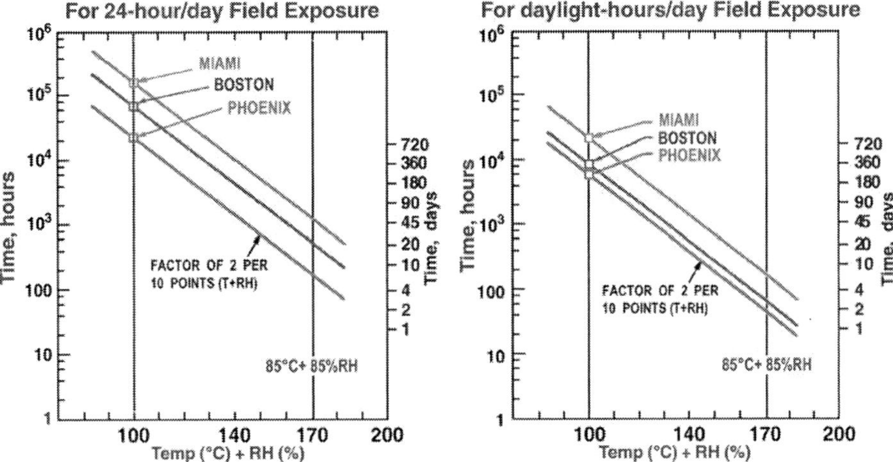

Fig. 3.   T+RH plot describing general Arrhenius relationship between module life expectancy and temperature/humidity conditions.

System voltage heads the list because it impacts a large number of reliability parameters including voltage isolation and grounding requirements, electrochemical corrosion, hot-spot heating, bypass diodes, and the number of series cells in an array source circuit. Since the number of series cells affects the array's tolerance to open-circuit cell failures, system voltage indirectly influences the tolerance of the array to cracked cells and interconnect open circuits [2], [3].

Operating temperature also shares the top of the list by having an accelerating influence on nearly every failure mechanism including voltage isolation, corrosion, hot-spot heating, photothermal degradation of encapsulants, delamination, interconnect fatigue, and cell cracking. All but the last two mechanisms typically have an Arrhenius dependence on temperature (log reaction rate inversely proportioned to reciprocal absolute temperature) with a reaction rate doubling for approximately every 10 °C increase in temperature [4], [5]. This implies that an application that operates 10 °C hotter than another will last only half as long. Interconnect fatigue and cell cracking are sensitive to differential expansion stresses caused by the number of temperature cycles [2], [3] and the high and low temperature extremes.

Humidity, like temperature, has a strong accelerating influence on many degradation mechanisms including corrosion and electrical leakage currents [6]. For such mechanisms, the degradation reaction rate often doubles for approximately every 10% increase in relative humidity [4]. Thus, an application with a 10% higher humidity level may only last half as long. Humidity can also lead to large differential expansion stresses that aggravate delamination and interconnect fatigue.

The remaining environments of soiling, salt-fog, wind, and hail tend to be fairly site specific and have been found to have important, but more limited influences on module reliability [2], [3].

A. Quantifying Application Stress Requirements

Once the important application-dependent and site-dependent stresses are identified, a key difficulty is reducing them to specific stress-time requirements against which the module can be designed and verified. Some environments, such as the system voltage level, are easily identified; others such as hail stone size, temperature and humidity extremes, and maximum wind velocity, require reference to historical weather data and considerations of statistical likelihood over the life of the intended application.

In general, two types of stress-time requirements were found useful: 1) a statement of the actual site-application requirement (such as 30 years of the operating temperatures of a Boston roof-mounted array), and 2) an accelerated qualification test against which the module can be tested.

The site-application requirement is needed for detailed life-prediction simulation analyses, and during the FSA Project, was computed based on SOLMET hourly weather histories for sites in the United States [7]. For example, time-varying module temperature and humidity level can be computed from the hourly weather data using heat transfer and water-sorption models that include the application thermal boundary conditions for an array at a site of interest. This results in a numerical data base description of the application's stress-time environment.

Although the analytical stress-time data base is very useful in life-prediction computer simulations, it fails to provide a requirement that a fabricated module can be quickly and inexpensively tested to; this need is met by a qualification or life test. Ideally the qualification or lifetest stress-time level is selected to correlate to a given application stress-time environment; certainly, this is the desired goal.

Probably the best way to reduce a large hourly data base of environmental parameters to a more easily interpreted test environment is to generate a model for the dependence of the aging mechanism of interest on the hourly environmental parameters.

Fig. 3 illustrates such an approach for generic temperature humidity aging, where the hourly temperature-humidity data for three sites has been aggregated using the model of a degradation rate doubling for each 10 points increase in T+RH level. Each of the curves (Phoenix, Boston and Miami) displays the exposure time to the environment on the lower scale that is equivalent

     3

TABLE III
JPL MODULE QUALIFICATION TEST EVOLUTION

QUAL TEST	I	II	III	IV	V	NOTES
THERMAL CYCLING						
Range (°C)	-40 to+90	-40 to+90	→		→	
Number cycles	100	50	→	→	200	
HUMIDITY CYCLING						
Relative Humidity	90	→	→	→	85	
Temp. Range (°C)	+70*	-23 to+40	→	→	-40 to+85	*No cycling, 70°C
Number cycles	-	5	→	→	10	Constant for 168 h
MECHANICAL CYCLING*						*Excluding shingle
Pressure (kPa)	-	±2.4	→	→	→	modules
Number Cycles	-	100	→	10,000	→	
WIND RESISTANCE (kPa)	-	-	-	1.7*	→	*Shingles only
TWISTED MOUNT (mm/m)	-	20	→	→	→	
HAIL IMPACT						
Diameter (mm)	-	-	-	20	25.4	
Terminal Velocity (m/s)	-	-	-	20.1	23.2	
Num. Impacts	-	-	-	9	10	
HOT-SPOT HEATING (h)	-	-	-	-	100	
ELECTRICAL ISOLATION (volts)	-	1500	→	2000*	3000*	*1500 for resid. modules

to a 20-year operation of a ground-mounted array at that site. Although the curves in this plot are drawn for a rate doubling for each 10 points increase in T+RH, curves of a different slope could easily be drawn for mechanisms with a different rate dependence.

Note that the right-side plot only aggregates T+RH data for daylight hours; this may be more relevant for a mechanism that requires the presence of an array voltage to be active. Details of the theory behind the T+RH relationship and the more broad use of the plot have been described previously [4], [8].

A key advantage of a plot such as Fig. 3 is that equivalent constant-environment test conditions are displayed directly on the lower scale. Thus, a 40 °C/90% RH aging test corresponds to 140 on the lower scale, and an 85 °C/85% RH test corresponds to 170. Thus, for the assumed reaction rate (2× per 10 points T+RH), equivalent test times for these three sites can be read directly off the right-hand time scale. By running tests at parametric stress levels and plotting the corresponding time to failure, one can also use the plot to determine the effective reaction rate for a particular mechanism of interest.

B. Flat Plate Solar Array Qualification Test Experience

During the 10 years of the FSA Project, a number of module qualification tests were developed and refined to the final Block V sequence detailed in Table III [9]–[12]. These test levels were carefully selected and revised with time so as to fail early module designs with a known history of field problems and to pass modules with good field performance. A review of the experience with these tests provides important lessons for designers of future PV modules.

1) Temperature Cycling and Humidity Cycling: Consistent with their importance as key accelerators of degradation mechanisms, the Block V temperature and humidity tests served as the workhorse requirements in the JPL qual test sequence to uncover failures caused by differential expansion and corrosion such as delamination of encapsulants, loss of cell metallization, and open circuiting of cell interconnects. The tests had good correlation to field failures and were generally the most difficult to pass. Typical failure mechanisms included encapsulant delamination, interconnect fatigue, cracked cells, cell metallization corrosion, and warping of plastic parts. The 85 °C and 90 °C upper temperature limits of these tests accurately reflect upper-bound field operating temperatures, and the –40 °C reflects realistic ambient lows.

2) Hot-Spot Testing: The need for hot-spot testing is principally associated with high-voltage applications, which can generate substantial reverse voltages across a temporarily shadowed or cracked cell, and thereby result in damaging hot-spot heating levels. Such heating levels can destroy the module encapsulant system, leading to arcing and electrical safety issues. The complexity of the hot-spot heating phenomenon requires that a number of cell and module parameters be properly accounted for during testing. This resulted in a carefully defined hot-spot test procedure [10]. This hot-spot test was generally easy to meet if generic bypass diode recommendations were followed [14].

3) Mechanical Loading, Twist and Hail Tests: These Block V qual tests were developed to define minimum mechanical-loading requirements for modules intended for generic applications. The tests account for wind, snow, and ice loads, module mounting to nonplanar support structures, and impact by hail stones of 2-cm diameter and less. They are effective design requirements and generally straightforward to meet with 3-mm (1/8-inch) tempered-glass module designs. Annealed glass may pass these tests, but often exhibits excessive numbers of field failures caused by high thermal stresses in the glass resulting from nonuniform solar heating of the module surface. Applications with a significant incidence of large (>2-cm diameter) hail stones may choose to design for a greater resistance to hail impact. The use of 5-mm (3/16-in) tempered glass is generally the maximum needed, and is adequate for 5-cm diameter hail stones [1].

4) Voltage Standoff (Hipot) Testing: This requirement was developed for modules intended for use in applications with system voltages above 50 V. Passing the test requires great care in the design of the module's electrical insulation system and proved troublesome to meet. Typical problems include excessive leakage current through partially conductive gaskets and edge seals, and inadequately insulated electrical leads. It posed special problems for thin-film modules made with tin-oxide coated glass because the edge of the glass is often electrically connected to the cells through the conductive oxide.

C. Postflat Plate Solar Array Reliability Research Thrusts

Although the FSA reliability activities made tremendous progress in understanding and resolving module reliability issues, there were a few remaining reliability areas that were not fully researched and reduced to engineering practice. These included electrochemical corrosion and wet insulation resistance, photothermal aging, overheating of bypass diodes, and soiling.

1) Wet Insulation Resistance and Electrochemical Corrosion: In addition to voltage breakdown issues addressed by the Block V Hipot test, an important additional degradation mechanism is accelerated current leakage between cells and between cells and the module frame that results from high humidity and wet operating conditions. Although no qual test existed during the FSA project for electrical isolation under wet conditions,

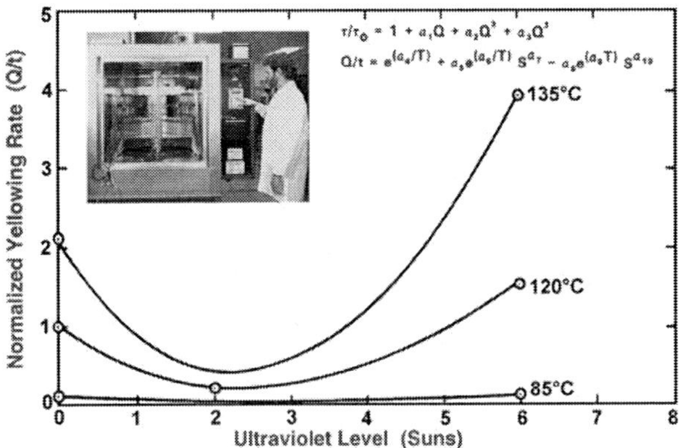

Fig. 4.   Measured dependence of EVA yellowing on aging temperature and UV flux level [5], [24].

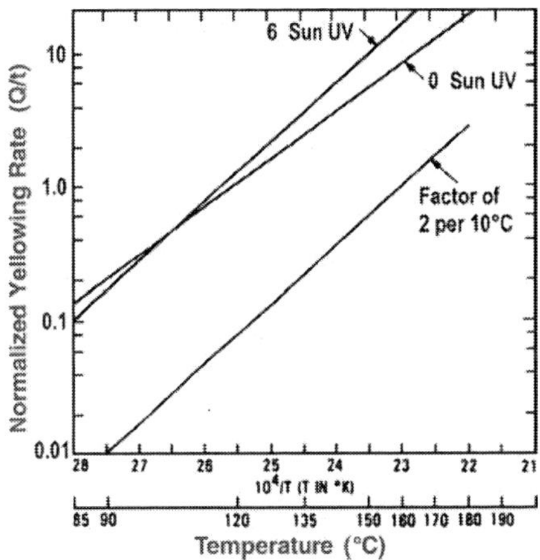

Fig. 5.   Measured dependence of EVA yellowing rate on aging temperature is basically Arrhenius with a reaction rate doubling for approximately every 10 °C increase in temperature [5], [24].

extensive research was carried out at JPL in the post-FSA timeframe that led to extensive improvements in our understanding of the relevant processes [15]–[20].

Key findings included the importance of conductance along encapsulant free surfaces interfaces [15], [16], the strong role of an encapsulant material's ionic cleanliness [17]–[19], and the enormous acceleration (orders of magnitude) associated with humidity level and wet surfaces [15]–[19]. Temperature, as expected, was also determined to be a strong accelerator.

Based on the research results, draft test methods for wet insulation resistance were drafted and published [17], [20], and design guidelines were developed for limiting electrochemical corrosion in both single-crystal and thin-film modules [16]–[20].

2) Photothermal Aging: This requirement addresses the resistance of module encapsulants to ultraviolet photothermal aging. During the FSA and post-FSA years, a large body of research was focused at understanding photothermal aging and deriving accelerated test techniques suitable for characterizing UV/thermal degradation effects and screening new material developments [21], [22]. A key result from this research was the development of PV encapsulant materials, like Ethylene Vinyl Acetate (EVA), with greatly enhanced UV/thermal stability, and a much better understanding of the long-term degradation mechanisms associated with PV encapsulants and their interfacial bonds.

As shown in Fig. 4, a particularly important finding was the very nonlinear dependence of the yellowing of EVA on UV irradiance level. In contrast, as shown in Fig. 5, increased temperature was found to be a highly predictable accelerator, following a classic Arrhenius dependence [5]. This led to the recognition that a useful accelerated test could involve extended exposure at 1-sun UV, together with a carefully controlled elevated temperature such as 85 to 100 °C [23].

As an example of deriving a rough estimate of life expectancy from measured degradation rates and hourly weather data, Table IV utilizes the measured yellowing reaction rates shown in Figs. 4 and 5 to integrate the effects of measured hourly UV and temperature levels derived from SOLMET weather data [5], [24]. The estimated degradation after 20 years is computed as

TABLE IV
20-Year UV Aging Parameters for Phoenix

Cell temperature, °C	Yellowing Rate at each Temperature-UV Level											
	UV level in suns											
	0.05	0.15	0.25	0.35	0.45	0.55	0.65	0.75	0.85	0.95	1.05	1.15
75	65	61	58	55	52	49	48	44	41	39	37	35
65	33	31	29	28	26	25	24	23	21	20	19	18
55	16	15	14	13	13	12	12	11	11	10	10	9
45	7	7	7	6	6	6	6	5	5	5	5	4
35	3	3	3	3	3	3	2	2	2	2	2	2
25	1	1	1	1	1	1	1	1	1	0.9	0.9	0.9
15	0.5	0.5	0.5	0.5	0.4	0.4	0.4	0.4	0.4	0.4	0.4	0.4
5	0.2	0.2	0.2	0.2	0.2	0.2	0.2	0.1	0.1	0.1	0.1	0.1

Cell temperature, °C	Annual Hours at each Temperature-UV Level											
	UV level in suns											
	0.05	0.15	0.25	0.35	0.45	0.55	0.65	0.75	0.85	0.95	1.05	1.15
75	0	0	0	0	0	0	0	0	0	11	4	0
65	0	0	0	0	0	1	17	24	107	294	167	6
55	0	0	0	32	18	56	130	81	201	142	177	17
45	22	74	32	110	62	84	144	73	172	154	55	1
35	134	131	63	124	97	93	113	49	53	17	0	0
25	190	129	92	86	53	21	22	0	0	0	0	0
15	129	94	36	35	8	0	0	0	0	0	0	0
5	66	70	3	0	0	0	0	0	0	0	0	0

20 times the dot product of the two matrices, and leads to an estimate of approximately 3.5% for a ground-mounted array and 8% for a (hotter running) roof-mounted array.

An analysis of the data in Table IV indicates that the primary contributors to this predicted in-field degradation are the periods of high temperature (45–65 °C) and UV flux levels between 0.5 and 1.0 suns. To improve the accuracy of the predictions from the rather sparse dataset in Fig. 4, it would be good to acquire additional data in the 0 to 1-sun range.

A second complicating factor in testing UV stability is the coupled mechanism of the gradual loss of UV screens and antioxidants introduced into encapsulant materials to protect against photothermal degradation. Thus, the working life of these suppression additives was also found to be a key factor in the life of a PV encapsulant system [21].

At the end of JPL's involvement in PV, the complexity of UV degradation mechanisms and the lack of commercially available test facilities precluded the definition of a readily available accelerated qualification test for full-size PV modules. To provide long-term photothermal stability, module designs of the time

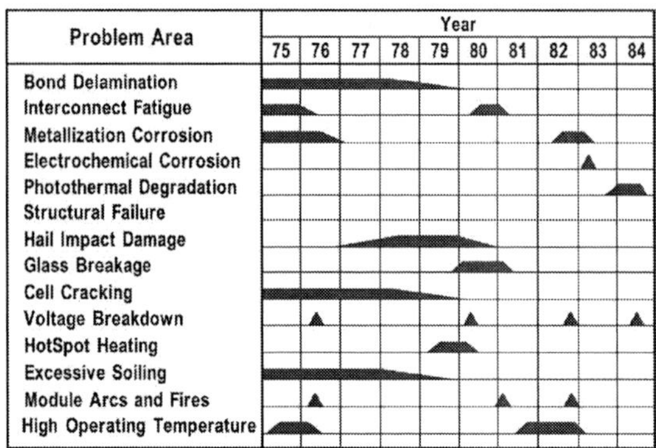

Fig. 6. Flowchart of principal reliability problems as they arose during the FSA's 1975–1985 tenure.

TABLE V
KEY TECHNOLOGY BASE CONTRIBUTION AREAS

- New lamination adhesives, primers, and stabilizers (PVB, EVA, EMA) for lower cost and improved weathering
- Circuit redundancy configurations for controlling cell cracking and broken interconnects
- Interconnect design and test methods
- Cell attachment techniques to minimize losses due to cell cracking
- Glass strength calculation methods
- Bypass diode design and hotspot test methods
- Hail resistance data and test methods
- Cell fracture strength and test methods
- Voltage breakdown data and test methods
- Electrochem corrosion Data and test methods
- UV-thermal durability data and test methods

relied on the use of materials and processes carefully developed to be UV stable in specialized laboratory characterization and life tests.

3) Bypass Diode Overheating: Insufficient heat sinking and excessive current levels were determined to be the primary causes of bypass diode failures. To meet this need, bypass diode design recommendations and a qual test procedure were developed to help achieve acceptable bypass diode thermal design and implementation [13]. The requirement limits the diode junction temperature under hot field conditions (100 mW/cm2, 40 °C ambient) to 50 °C below the diode manufacture's stated maximum allowable junction temperature.

4) Soiling: Front surface soiling by airborne contaminants can lead to the significant degradation of module performance in cases where the illuminated surface is a polymer material. As with photothermal oxidation, no short-term qual tests proved reliable for predicting long-term soling levels, but material selection guidelines and soil-resistant coatings were developed based on long-term field tests [1], [2], [25]. Glass was proven to be an excellent low-soiling surface.

IV. RELIABILITY DESIGN LESSONS

In 1985, after ten years of fielding PV modules in large demonstration systems, an excellent database of design weaknesses had been systematically uncovered as noted in Fig. 6.

As each problem area was identified, technical resolutions were developed including design guidelines, improved materials and fabrication processes, and analysis and test methodologies. These we refer to as the reliability technology base that was developed during the FSA tenure. Key technology base contribution areas are noted in Table V and are heavily documented in nearly 400 reports that are organized by technical topic in top-level summaries [1], [2], [16], [21]–[23], [26].

In lieu of repeating previous reviews of these individual technologies, we examine just one of the more intriguing and recurring issues in module design: The relative role of the module encapsulant system in achieving module reliability.

After many years of testing both bare cells and modules, it became increasingly clear that the encapsulant is the most problem-prone part of the module, and it generally does not enhance the reliability of the solar cells over their performance unencapsulated. For example, in tests at Clemson University, bare crystalline-Si cells routinely demonstrated better reliability than the same cells when encapsulated in any of a variety of typical photovoltaic encapsulant systems [27], [28]. The principal demonstrated function of the encapsulant is to structurally support the cells and isolate them electrically for safety reasons. Secondary functions include providing an easily cleaned external surface and reducing the cell operating temperature by increasing the surface emissivity.

Unfortunately, while attempting to provide these functions, the module encapsulant often aggravates or creates a number of failure mechanisms. These include cracking, yellowing, delamination, accelerated corrosion, and differential expansion stresses. In addition, the encapsulant may fail to perform its intended function, resulting in voltage breakdown, excessive leakage currents, increased soiling, or increased operating temperatures. The conclusion is that cells must be chosen with good inherent reliability, and the encapsulant must be carefully selected to perform its functions while not degrading the reliability and efficiency of the unencapsulated cells.

Aside from failures associated with the encapsulant, the part of a crystalline-Si module that is second most likely to have a failure is the electrical circuit. This includes solar cell electrical interconnects and solder joints, bus wires, and electrical terminal components. Typical failures include mechanical fatigue of conductors, broken solder joints, corrosion of electrical terminals, photothermal degradation of connectors and cabling, and thermal warping of junction boxes.

The most reliable element of a crystalline-Si module is often the cells themselves. Although cell reliability problems were infrequent in the 1980s crystalline-Si modules, historical failure mechanisms included cell cracking, metallization delamination (increased series resistance), and degradation of the antireflective coating. This demonstrated high reliability with 1980s crystalline-Si cells may or may not be achievable with modern advanced-technology or thin-film cells.

Thus, establishing the inherent reliability of unencapsulated cell structures is an important first step in the process of achieving high-reliability long-life PV modules.

V. Reliability Testing Lessons

Because the physics of most failure mechanisms is poorly understood, achieving high reliability requires a strong reliance on empirical characterization and testing. This can take the form of laboratory accelerated tests, outdoor test racks, or complete system application experiments. Each has its lessons.

A. Laboratory Testing

At the root of achieving long-life modules is ensuring that all the important problems are identified early so that they can be systematically addressed. The qualification tests described earlier (see Table I) have been found to be the most cost-effective way to identify obvious reliability problems, and should be applied as early in the design process as possible using prototype hardware manufactured with candidate materials and processes. Even with careful attention to the lessons of the past, *new module designs almost never passed the qual tests on the first try.*

In addition to the qual tests, it is important to conduct long-term life tests at parametric stress levels to achieve a quantitative understanding of the parameter dependences involved with complex failure mechanisms. Photothermal aging and corrosion of cells and modules are obvious examples. Because of the expense and many months required, this type of testing must generally proceed systematically as part of an integrated research effort, as opposed to being a part of a short-term product development cycle. A key advantage of this type of testing is that it provides data to support life predictions.

B. Outdoor Test Racks

A second testing approach requiring extended test durations is outdoor testing on field test racks. Unfortunately, the correlation between this type of testing and observed failures in field applications has historically been poor. Key problems stem from the limited number of samples on test, and the absence of many user-interface stresses such as applied voltages. This type of testing is mostly useful for backing up the qual tests, to catch a not-tested-for mechanism that might become visible after a modest period of field aging. The tests can be enhanced substantially by incorporating as many user-interface stresses as possible and increasing the number of samples on test to a maximum. Important user-interface stresses include module operating point (open circuit, maximum power point, and short circuit), array voltage biasing of the cell string above and below the module-frame ground potential, partial shadows, and increased operating temperatures.

Forcing an elevated, but reasonable operating temperature such as 85 °C or 100 °C can be an effective way to accelerate certain field aging mechanisms in a predictable way. Simultaneous testing at two separate accelerated temperature levels can allow the determination of the degradation-rate temperature dependence and therefore provides improved extrapolation of degradation data to nominal field conditions.

C. Application Experiments

Because of the shortcomings of laboratory and test-rack aging, many problems are not acknowledged as such until they are encountered in a large operating system. The large number of modules involved in such systems is extremely useful in quantifying the significance of the problem, and the user-interface stresses are real. One failure out of 10 in a qualification test, or in a field test rack, is often discounted as a curiosity; 10% failures in a large system is a "problem."

Because of the often-present desire to field a large high-visibility application as soon as possible, there is great pressure to shortcut the laboratory-testing and design-qualification process, and to go directly to the field. This almost always results in tarnished reputations, slipped schedules, minimal learning, cost overruns, and early application retirement. The high cost of failure in the field, together with the need for field testing argues for careful laboratory characterization and life testing, followed by thoughtful selection of a low-risk first field application. This system should be instrumented to obtain quantitative data on failures, and be designed with failure containment features and failure contingency plans.

D. Failure Analysis

Aside from the testing method used to identify a reliability problem, a thorough and careful failure analysis is a critical next step. It is not sufficient to know that a module is open circuited; one must determine where and why in order to effect a corrective action. Did an interconnect fail due to a faulty design, or did someone forget to solder a lead to a solar cell? The correct response is critically dependent on understanding the true root cause of the problem.

VI. Conclusion

Achieving 30-year-life flat-plate PV modules requires a systematic approach to the identification of failure mechanisms, to the establishment of allowable failure levels, to the development of reliability design and test methods, and to the definition of cost-effective solutions. Based on this methodology, the reliability of flat-plate crystalline-Si PV modules was steadily improved from 5-year-life modules of the early 1970s to 10- to 20-year-life modules of the mid 1980s. It is expected that current-day modules have much in common with their 1980s crystalline precursors and will be able to make substantial use of the reliability design and test methods developed during JPL's PV tenure. At the same time, however, new module materials and processes will require a diligent reliability program involving evaluation, testing, and the development of new solution techniques unique to the attributes and peculiarities of today's technologies.

Acknowledgment

This paper summarizes the work conducted at the Jet Propulsion Laboratory, California Institute of Technology, for the U.S. Department of Energy and the National Renewable Energy Laboratory, through an agreement with the National Aeronautics and Space Administration.

REFERENCES

[1] R. G. Ross, Jr., and M. I. Smokler, "The flat-plate solar array project final report Volume VI, Engineering Sciences and Reliability, JPL, Pasadena, CA, USA, JPL Publication 86–31, JPL Document 5101–289, DOE/JPL-1012–125, Oct. 1986.

[2] R. G. Ross, Jr., "Reliability of photovoltaic modules," in *Proc. Photovoltaics for Commercial Solar Power Appl., SPIE Fiber/LASA'86 Symp.*, Cambridge, MA, USA, Sep. 14–20, 1986, vol. 706.

[3] R. G. Ross, Jr., "Technology developments toward 30-year-life of photovoltaic modules," in *Proc. 17th IEEE PV Spec. Conf.*, Orlando, FL, USA, May 1–4, 1984, pp. 464–472.

[4] D. H. Otth and R. G. Ross, Jr., "Assessing photovoltaic module degradation and lifetime from long-term environmental tests," in *Proc. 29th IES Annu. Meeting*, Los Angeles, CA, USA, Apr. 19–21, 1983, pp. 121–126.

[5] C. C. Gonzalez, R. Liang, and R. G. Ross, Jr., "Predicting field performance of photovoltaic modules from accelerated thermal and ultraviolet aging data," in *Proc. Int. Solar Energy Soc.*, Montreal, Canada, Jun. 22–29, 1985.

[6] G. R. Mon, L. C. Wen, J. Meyer, R. G. Ross, Jr., and A. Nelson, "Electrochemical and galvanic corrosion effects in thin-film photovoltaic modules," in *Proc. 20th IEEE PV Spec. Conf.*, Las Vegas, NV, USA, Sep. 26–30, 1988, pp. 108–113.

[7] *SOLMET Volume 1 &2, Hourly Solar Radiation-Surface Meteorological Observations*, TD-9724, National Oceanic and Atmospheric Administration, Asheville, NC, USA, Dec. 1977 and Feb. 1979.

[8] E. F. Cuddihy, The aging correlation (RH+T): Relative humidity (%) + temperature (°C) Jet Propulsion Laboratory, Pasadena, California, USA, JPL Publication 86–7, JPL Document 5101–283, DOE/JPL-1012–121, CA, USA, Jan. 15, 1986.

[9] Block V solar cell module design and test specification for intermediate load applications, Jet Propulsion Laboratory, Pasadena, CA, USA, JPL Internal Document No. 5101–161, Feb. 20, 1981.

[10] A. R. Hoffman, J. S. Griffith, and R. G. Ross, Jr., "Qualification testing of flat plate photovoltaic modules," *IEEE Trans. Rel.*, vol. R-31, no. 3, pp. 252–257, Aug. 1982.

[11] M. I. Smokler and L. D. Runkle, "Experience in design and test of terrestrial solar cell modules," in *Proc. AS/ISES 1982 Annu. Meeting*, Houston, TX, USA, Jun. 1–5, 1982, pp. 1591–1600.

[12] M. I. Smokler, D. H. Otth, and R. G. Ross, Jr., "The block program approach to photovoltaic module development," in *Proc. 18th IEEE Photovoltaic Spec. Conf.*, Las Vegas, NV, USA, Oct. 21–25, 1985, pp. 1150–1158.

[13] D. H. Otth, R. S. Sugimura, and R. G. Ross, Jr., "Development of design criteria and qualification tests for bypass diodes in photovoltaic applications," in *Proc. Inst. Environ. Sci., 31st Annu. Tech. Meeting*, Las Vegas, NV, USA, Apr. 29–May 3, 1985, pp. 242–248.

[14] C. C. Gonzalez, R. W. Weaver, R. G. Ross, Jr., J. C. Arnett, and R. Spenser, "Determination of hot-spot susceptibility of multi-string photovoltaic modules in a central station application," in *Proc. 17th IEEE Photovoltaic Spec. Conf.*, Orlando, FL, USA, May 1–4, 1984, pp. 668–675.

[15] G. R. Mon, L. C. Wen, and R. G. Ross, Jr., "Encapsulant free-surfaces and interfaces: Critical parameters in controlling cell corrosion," in *Proc. 19th IEEE PV Spec. Conf.*, New Orleans, LA, USA, May 4–8, 1987, pp. 1215–1221.

[16] G. R. Mon, L. C. Wen, and R. G. Ross, Jr., "Water-module Interaction Studies," in *Proc. 20th IEEE PV Spec. Conf.*, Las Vegas, NV, USA, Sep. 26–30, 1988, pp. 1098–1102.

[17] G. R. Mon, L. C. Wen, R. S. Sugimura, and R. G. Ross, Jr., "Reliability studies of photovoltaic module insulation systems," in *Proc. 19th Electr./Electron. Insul. Conf.*, Chicago, IL, USA, Set. 25–28, 1989, pp. 324–329.

[18] G. R. Mon, G. Whitla, R. G. Ross, Jr., and M. Neff, "The role of electrical insulation in electrochemical degradation of terrestrial photovoltaic modules," *IEEE Trans. Electr. Insul.*, vol. EI-20, no. 6, pp. 989–996, Dec. 1985.

[19] G. Mon and R. G. Ross, Jr., "Electrochemical degradation of amorphous-silicon photovoltaic modules," in *Proc. 18th IEEE Photovoltaic Spec. Conf.*, Las Vegas, NV, USA, Oct. 21–25, 1985, pp. 1142–1149.

[20] R. S. Sugimura, G. R. Mon, L. C. Wen, and R. G. Ross, Jr., "Electrical isolation design and electrochemical corrosion in thin-film photovoltaic modules," in *Proc. 20th IEEE PV Spec. Conf.*, Las Vegas, NV, USA, Sep. 26–30, 1988, pp. 1103–1109.

[21] E. Cuddihy, C. Coulbert, A. Gupta. and R. Liang, The flat-plate solar array project final report, Volume VII: Module encapsulation, Jet Propulsion Laboratory, Pasadena, CA, USA, JPL Publication 86–31, JPL Document 5101–289, DOE/JPL-1012–125, Oct. 1986.

[22] R. Liang, K. L. Oda, S. Y. Chung, M. V. Smith, and A. Gupta, "Handbook of photothermal test data on encapsulant materials," Jet Propulsion Laboratory, Pasadena, CA, USA, JPL Publication 83–32, JPL Publication No. 5101–230, DOE/JPL-1012–86, May 1, 1983.

[23] G. R. Mon, C. Gonzalez, P. Willis, E. Jetter, R. S. Sugimura, and R. G. Ross, Jr., "Long-term photothermal/humidity testing of photovoltaic module polymer insulations and cover films," in *Proc. 21st IEEE Photovoltaic Spec. Conf.*, Kissimmee, FL, USA, May 21–25, 1990, pp. 1043–1050.

[24] C. C. Gonzalez and R. G. Ross, Jr., "Predicting photothermal field performance," in Proc. 24th FSA Project Integr. Meeting, Jet Propulsion Laboratory, Pasadena, CA, USA, 1985, pp. 121–128. JPL Publication 85-27, JPL Document 5101–259, DOE/JPL-1012–104.

[25] E. F. Cuddihy and P. B. Willis, Antisoiling technology: Theories of surface soiling and performance of antisoiling surface coatings, JPL, Pasadena, CA, USA, JPL Publication 84–72, Nov. 15, 1984.

[26] R. G. Ross, Jr., JPL legacy web site with 480 FSA engineering and reliability documents. [Online]. Available: http://www2.jpl.nasa.gov/adv_tech/photovol/summary.htm

[27] J. L. Prince, J. W. Lathrop, F. W. Morgan, E. L. Royal, and G. W. Witter, "Accelerated stress testing of terrestrial solar cells," in *Proc. 17th IEEE Rel. Phys. Sympo.*, San Francisco, CA, USA, Apr. 24–26, 1979, pp. 77–86.

[28] J. W. Lathrop, "Investigation of reliability attributes and accelerated stress factors on terrestrial solar cells," 1st, 2nd, 3rd and 4th Annual Rep., DOE/JPL-954929–79/4, -80/7, -81/8, and -83/10, Clemson University, Clemson, SC, USA, May 1979, Apr. 1980, Jan. 1981, and Oct. 1983.

Ronald G. Ross, Jr. received the doctoate degree in mechanical engineering from the University of California, Berkeley, USA, in 1968.

He then joined NASA's Jet Propulsion Laboratory (JPL), Pasadena, CA, USA, initially working on large area roll-up solar arrays for spacecraft. When the energy crisis of the mid 1970s occurred, he switched over to terrestrial photovoltaics (PV), where he became the Engineering Sciences and Reliability Manager of the United States Department of Energy (DOE) Flat-Plate Solar Array Project at JPL. Tasked with bringing PV into economic competitiveness for terrestrial power generation as part of DOE's National Photovoltaics Program, he spent the next 15 years leading the development of the engineering and reliability technology base for flat plate PV modules and arrays. Since that time, he has served as a multi-discipline technical manager and project engineer on a wide variety of projects where he specialized in bringing emerging advanced technologies to application readiness. He has authored or coauthored over 190 formal reports and journal articles covering the diverse disciplines of PV, reliability physics, electronic packaging and solder fatigue, cryocooler design and performance, and cryogenic instrument design. He retired from JPL in 2006 but continues to work part time as a JPL consultant.

Light Trapping Textures Designed by Electromagnetic Optimization for Subwavelength Thick Solar Cells

Vidya Ganapati, Owen D. Miller, and Eli Yablonovitch

Abstract—Light trapping in solar cells allows for increased current and voltage, as well as reduced materials cost. It is known that in geometrical optics, a maximum $4n^2$ absorption enhancement factor can be achieved by randomly texturing the surface of the solar cell, where n is the material refractive index. This ray-optics absorption enhancement (AE) limit only holds when the thickness of the solar cell is much greater than the optical wavelength. In subwavelength thin films, the fundamental questions remain unanswered: 1) what is the subwavelength AE limit and 2) what surface texture realizes this optimal AE? We turn to computational electromagnetic optimization in order to design nanoscale textures for light trapping in subwavelength thin films. For high-index thin films, in the weakly absorbing limit, our optimized surface textures yield an angle- and frequency-averaged enhancement factor $\sim$39. They perform roughly 30% better than randomly textured structures, but they fall short of the ray optics enhancement limit of $4n^2$ $\sim$ 50.

Index Terms—Light trapping, optimization, subwavelength.

I. INTRODUCTION

TEXTURING of solar cell surfaces allows for absorption enhancement, owing to the coupling of incident light rays to totally internally reflected modes within the cell, i.e., light trapping. It is known that in the ray-optics regime, where the thickness of the solar cell is much greater than the wavelength of light, the maximum absorption for weakly absorbed rays is given by [1]

$$A = \frac{\alpha d}{\alpha d + \frac{1}{4n^2}} \tag{1}$$

where α is the absorption coefficient, d the thickness of the material, and n the index of refraction. This maximum absorption

Manuscript received July 15, 2013; revised August 27, 2013; accepted August 27, 2013. Date of publication September 17, 2013; date of current version December 16, 2013. This work was supported by the DOE "Light-Material Interactions in Energy Conversion" Energy Frontier Research Center under Grant DE-SC0001293 and the National Energy Research Scientific Computing Center, which is supported by the Office of Science of the U.S. Department of Energy under Contract DE-AC02-05CH11231. The work of V. Ganapati is supported by the Department of Energy Office of Science Graduate Fellowship Program (DOE SCGF), made possible in part by the American Recovery and Reinvestment Act of 2009, administered by ORISE-ORAU under Contract DE-AC05-06OR23100.

The authors are with Material Sciences Division, Lawrence Berkeley National Laboratory, University of California, Berkeley, CA 94704, USA (e-mail: vidyag@berkeley.edu; odmiller@math.mit.edu; eliy@eecs.berkeley.edu).

Color versions of one or more of the figures in this paper are available online at http://ieeexplore.ieee.org.

Digital Object Identifier 10.1109/JPHOTOV.2013.2280340

limit assumes a perfect rear mirror. We can compare this with the single-pass absorption of the weakly absorbed light

$$A = 1 - e^{-\alpha d} \approx \alpha d. \tag{2}$$

The AE is the actual absorption divided by the single-pass absorption. The maximum AE in the ray-optics regime is, thus, given by (1) divided by (2); in the limit of a very weakly absorbing material the AE factor is given by $\text{AE} = 4n^2$.

With light trapping, we can achieve high absorption, even for thin absorber layers. Short-circuit current (J_{sc}) and fill factor improvements occur due to better carrier extraction in thin layers. Additionally, open-circuit voltage (V_{oc}) improvements occur, owing to increased carrier concentration. In high quality materials, such as gallium arsenide, efficiency improvement can be substantial, due to improvement in external fluorescence yield [2], [3]. We also reduce material cost by achieving the same current in a thinner material.

In recent years, light trapping has seen renewed interest in the subwavelength regime, which is applicable to increasingly thin solar cells [4], [5]. In this regime, where the thickness of the solar cell is less than the optical wavelength, traditional ray optics does not hold, and the fundamental unanswered questions are 1) what is the upper bound on absorption enhancement, 2) and what surface texture realizes this limit?

In the subwavelength regime, there are discrete propagating modes (i.e., modes that are totally internally reflected), which can no longer be modeled as a continuum density of states. Stuart and Hall [6] attempted to establish the AE limit in the subwavelength by accounting for these discrete propagating modes, but they make the assumption that the introduced texture does not change the modal structure from that of a flat slab. This assumption does not hold, especially for thin solar cells where the amplitude of the texture is on the order of the thickness. In order to calculate a true limit in the subwavelength, the full modal structure needs to be taken into account, self-consistently. Yu *et al.* [5], [7], [8] also attempt to establish a fundamental limit in the subwavelength regime, but their approach depends on knowledge of the modal structure. In this study, we make no assumptions about the modal structure, instead numerically finding the optimal subwavelength surface texture by using computational inverse electromagnetic design.

Our work differs from prior efforts to find the optimal surface texture for thin absorber layers in the following ways:

1) Our absorber thickness is subwavelength, i.e., the wavelength of the light in the material is greater than the average thickness of the material. Many papers look at texturing

"

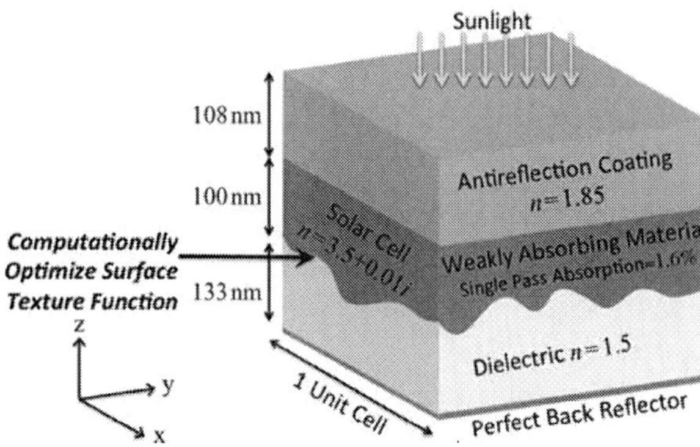

Fig. 1. The bottom surface texture of the absorbing material is computationally optimized. This diagram is a schematic of one unit cell; there are periodic boundary conditions along the y–z and x–z planes.

for absorber thicknesses in the micron range [9]–[20], a regime generally governed by ray optics.

2) To evaluate the light trapping performance of a texture for a flat-plate nonconcentrating, nontracking solar cell, we report the AE averaged over frequency and over all angles in the hemisphere. A valid comparison against the ray optics limit must be angle- and frequency-averaged, instead of over a limited angular range [9]–[11], [20]–[25] or a narrowband of frequencies [26], [27].

3) To derive general principles, we treat a weakly absorbing material with broadband single-pass absorption of 1.6%. This weak single-pass absorption reveals the full benefit of light trapping. Stronger absorbance would saturate the maximum AE possible, as seen in [15], [28]–[36].

4) We utilize a high-index absorber material with $n = 3.5$. Although [4], [5], and [37] exceed the ray optics limit for subwavelength absorber layers, they do so for a low-index absorber ($n < 2$) sandwiched by a higher index cladding.

5) In our optimization, we look for the most general optimal 3-D texture, rather than optimizing a 2-D texture (with no variation along the third dimension) [27], [38] or making constraints on the shape, such as optimizing 1-D or 2-D grating parameters [9], [15], [24], [32] or the arrangement of nanowires [16].

II. Optimization Algorithm

The optimization geometry is shown in Fig. 1, and is meant to be consistent with the practical requirements of a thin-film solar cell. The setup consists of a weakly absorbing semiconductor material of index $n = 3.5$, with average thickness of 100 nm, and a flat top surface that is compatible with a conventional antireflection (AR) coating. The unknown texture on the bottom surface is specified within 2-D periodic boundary conditions. The absorption is evaluated in the important solar frequency range, 350 THz to 400 THz (1.45 to 1.65 eV or 750 to 860 nm free space wavelength), a bandwidth relative to center frequency of 1/8. This is a bandedge photon energy range where even a direct bandgap semiconductor like GaAs needs some absorption assistance. We do not consider the full solar spectral bandwidth

when designing a surface texture, since at most higher frequencies, the direct gap absorption is sufficient. Note that Maxwell's equations are scale invariant, meaning that solutions described here can be scaled to different bandgaps.

The average thickness of 100 nm is less than a half wavelength in the material, placing us in the subwavelength regime. An artificial weakly absorbing material ($n_{\text{real}} = 3.5$ and $\alpha = 1.6 \times 10^3$ cm^{-1}) is chosen in order to arrive at general conclusions related to weak optical absorption. The semiconductor is specified to have a uniform $\alpha d = 0.016$ single-pass absorption throughout the band, small enough to benefit from light trapping, but large enough to allow faster numerical convergence and accuracy. A more highly absorbing material might saturate at 100% absorption, obscuring the benefit of the surface texturing.

An AR coating is applied to the top of the solar cell structure. It is fixed at a quarter wavelength (108 nm) for the center wavelength in the optimization bandwidth, with $n_{\text{AR}} = \sqrt{(n_{\text{air}} \times n_{\text{absorber}})} = 1.85$. A bottom surface texture was chosen for the absorber layer so we can keep the AR coating fixed in our optimization algorithm. Beneath the absorber layer is a nonabsorbing back dielectric layer of $n = 1.5$ (adjusted to 133 nm average thickness) followed by a perfect back reflector.

The periodic surface texture function h is represented by a truncated Fourier series

$$h(x,y) = \sum_{m=-2,-1,0,1,2} \sum_{n=-2,-1,0,1,2} c_{mn} e^{i\frac{m2\pi x}{\Lambda_x}} e^{i\frac{n2\pi y}{\Lambda_y}} \quad (3)$$

where Λ_x and Λ_y are the periodicities in the x- and y-direction, respectively, and c_{mn} are the Fourier coefficients. In our optimization algorithm, we keep the periodicity and the zeroth-order Fourier coefficient (the average absorber layer thickness) fixed, and allow the other Fourier coefficients to evolve. We used a fixed square periodicity of 710 nm; this choice is the result of an optimization further explained in Section III. We truncate the Fourier series to avoid sharp corners and small highly resonant features that would not be robust in manufacturing (it should be noted that the corners in even a square wave fabricated by conventional top down lithography are not perfectly sharp).

Our optimization algorithm scripts are written in MATLAB, following the procedure described in [39]. Our optimization uses an adjoint gradient method to search for a local optimum [40]. To find the absorption of the solar cell, we simulate the solar cell structure of Fig. 1 in "Lumerical FDTD Solutions," a commercial finite-difference time-domain solver for Maxwell's equations, evaluating the absorption at 30 points within the frequency bandwidth. Each iteration takes approximately 15 min on our computational cluster of 128 cores, and the optimization converges after about 25 iterations. Although [38] similarly optimizes a truncated series of Fourier coefficients, they do so for a 2-D surface. The computational burden of optimizing in 3-D is much larger (both due to the increased number of Fourier coefficients and longer simulation time), thus we need to use the method described in [39] to efficiently compute the gradients of the geometric parameters with respect to the figure of merit.

The selection of the figure of merit is critical. We maximize the AE at the frequency with the lowest absorption, a minimax

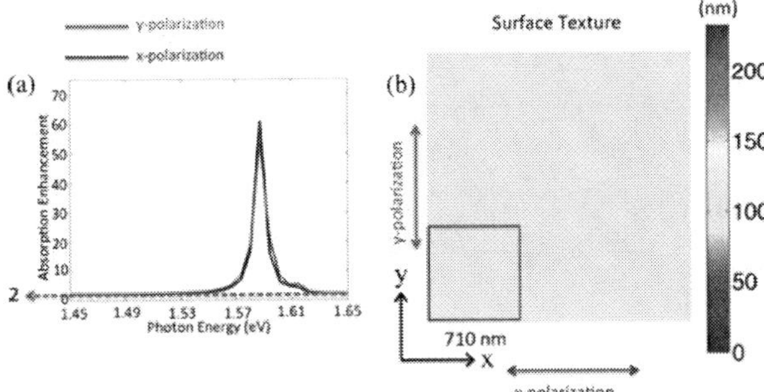

Fig. 2. (a) Initial AE as a function of frequency, at normal incidence and (b) top-down view of the surface texture; the colors show the height of the absorbing material (from the AR coating to the bottom dielectric, as seen in Fig. 1).

figure of merit [41], which allows us to achieve good absorption over the whole frequency band. In one iteration, we evaluate the absorption for each frequency, at each of the two perpendicular polarizations of normally incident light. We then take the lowest AE as the figure of merit (AE_{FOM}). At the end of the optimization, we compute the angle-averaged performance. The Lambertian angle-averaged enhancement (AE_{angle}) as a function of frequency is given by

$$AE_{angle} = \frac{\int_0^{2\pi} \int_0^{\frac{\pi}{2}} AE(\theta, \phi) \times \cos(\theta) \times \sin(\theta) d\theta d\phi}{\int_0^{2\pi} \int_0^{\frac{\pi}{2}} \cos(\theta) \times \sin(\theta) d\theta d\phi} \quad (4)$$

where AE is the absorption enhancement found by dividing the absorption by the average single-pass absorption $\alpha d = 0.016$, and averaging over the two perpendicular polarizations. At the end of the full optimization, we evaluate (4) by simulating 12 angles over the hemisphere, with two orthogonal polarizations for every angle.

III. RESULTS AND DISCUSSION

We started the algorithm from noisy initial conditions with fixed square periodicity of 710 nm ($=3.1\lambda_{n=3.5}$, i.e., approximately three times the wavelength in the absorbing medium). We randomly picked initial Fourier coefficients in the range of 0–8 nm. In this first example, we achieved a minimum absorption enhancement $AE_{FOM} = 32$ for a 100 nm average thickness absorber layer at normal incidence. The progression of the surface texture and AE at normal incidence from the first iteration to the last is shown in Figs. 2 and 3. The reciprocal space representation (the magnitudes and phases of the Fourier coefficients) of the final surface is shown in Fig. 4. The effect of our minimax figure of merit in optimizing for the lowest absorbing frequency and for achieving high absorption over the full band can be seen in this progression. Resonant peaks from the initial case flatten out, and both the minimum and average AE improve. The angle-averaged performance is shown in Fig. 5. Angle- and frequency-averaged, this texture achieves an absorption enhancement of $AE_{angle} = 23$ relative to 1.6% single-pass absorption.

Our optimization algorithm is sensitive to initial conditions; Fig. 6 shows three cases of the final texture and final AE both at

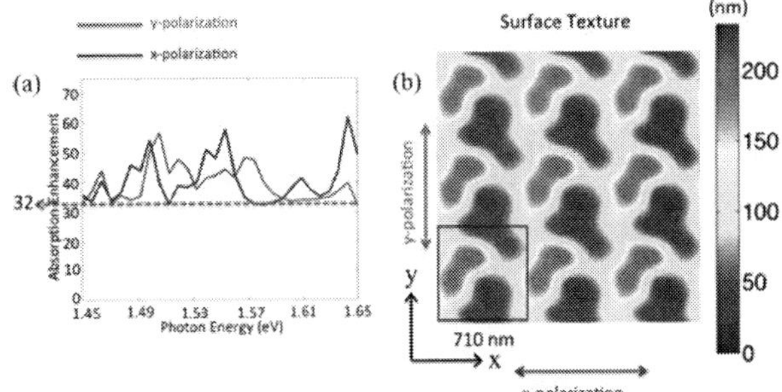

Fig. 3. (a) Final AE as a function of frequency, at normal incidence and (b) top-down view of the surface texture; the colors show the height of the absorbing material (from the AR coating to the bottom dielectric, as seen in Fig. 1).

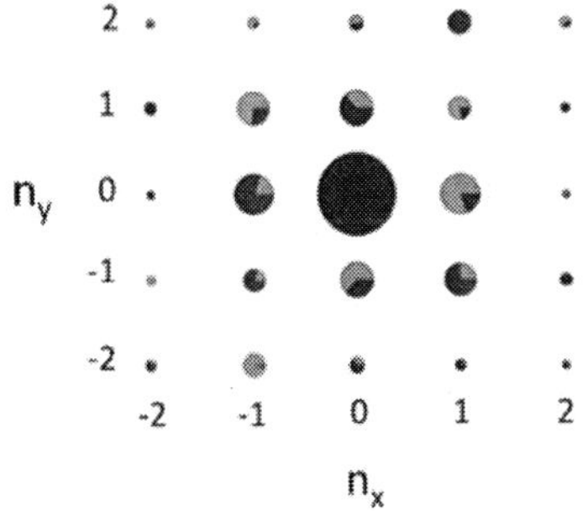

Fig. 4. Reciprocal (k-) space representation for the final texture seen in Fig. 3. The blue pie slices represent the phase of the complex exponential Fourier coefficients.

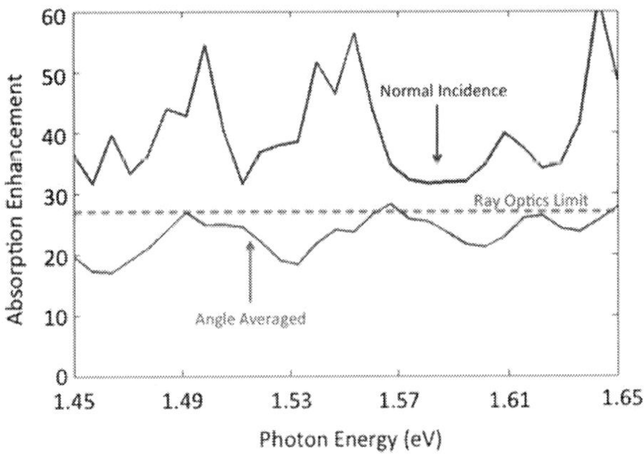

Fig. 5. Absorption enhancement (AE) for the texture in Fig. 3, plotted as a function of frequency at normal incidence, averaged over both polarizations, (blue) and angle averaged (green).

normal incidence and angle averaged for different initial conditions (randomly chosen initial Fourier coefficients in the range of 0–10 nm). Under different initial conditions, we obtain different textures reaching similar angle- and frequency-averaged absorption enhancements of $AE_{angle} = 22$, 24, and 19. The best angle- and frequency-averaged absorption enhancement of $AE_{angle} = 24$ is seen in the texture in Fig. 6(b); the AE for this texture as a function of incident angle is shown in Fig. 7. The

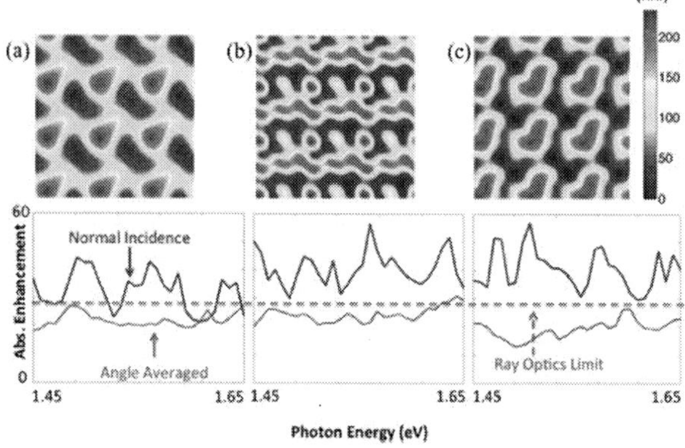

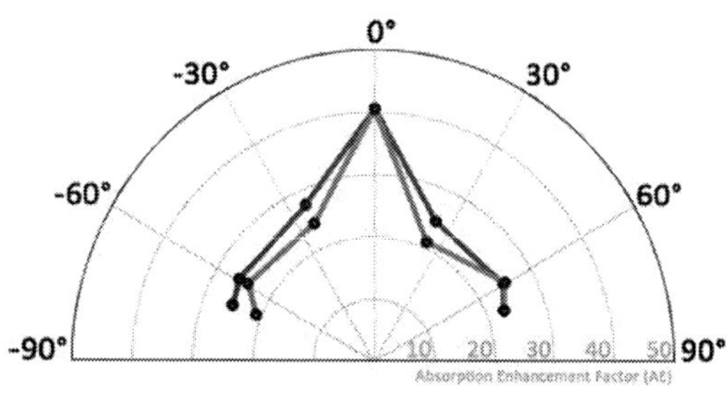

Fig. 6. Surface textures and AE as a function of frequency for different initial conditions, revealing a broad optimum.

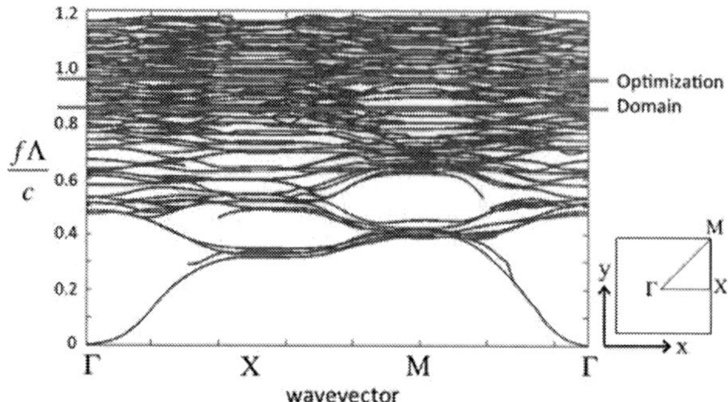

Fig. 8. Photonic bandstructure for the texture in Fig. 6(b).

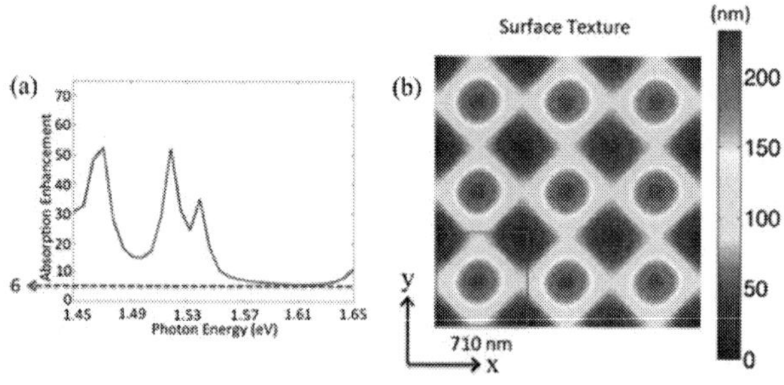

Fig. 7. Absorption enhancement factor (AE) averaged over frequency and polarization, as a function of incident angle θ in the x–z plane (blue) and the y–z plane (red).

Fig. 9. (a) Initial AE as a function of frequency, at normal incidence and (b) top-down view of the surface texture, for a symmetric texture with a slight perturbation along the diagonal.

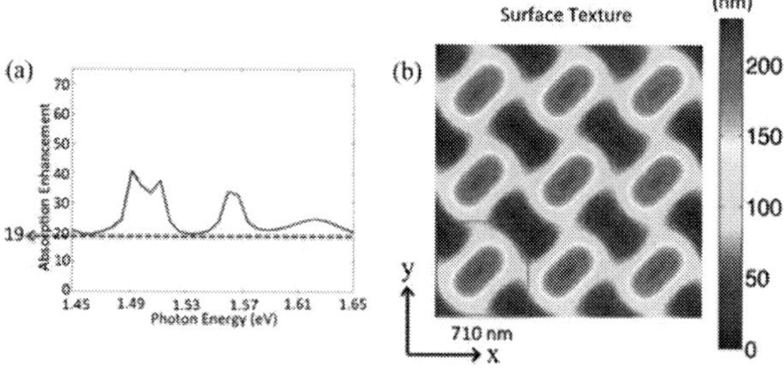

Fig. 10. (a) Final AE as a function of frequency, at normal incidence and (b) top-down view of the surface texture, showing broken mirror symmetry, from almost symmetric initial conditions seen in Fig. 9.

TABLE I

FOURIER COEFFICIENTS (c_{mn}), IN NANOMETERS, APPLIED TO (3) THAT REPRESENT THE TEXTURE IN FIG. 6(b), THE OPTIMIZED TEXTURE WITH THE BEST ANGLE- AND FREQUENCY-AVERAGED AE (AE_{angle})

	$m = -2$	$m = -1$	$m = 0$	$m = 1$	$m = 2$
$n = 2$	1.25 + 2.75i	5.25 + 6i	9 - 17.5i	4.25 - 2.5i	3.25 - 11.75i
$n = 1$	8.5 - 2i	10 - 4.25i	-8.5 + 19i	-6 + 0.25i	-1 - 6.5i
$n = 0$	10 + 6.5i	8 - 1.5i	100	8 + 1.5i	10 - 6.5i
$n = -1$	-1 + 6.5i	-6 - 0.25i	-8.5 - 19i	10 + 4.25i	8.5 + 2i
$n = -2$	3.25 + 11.75i	4.25 + 2.5i	9 + 17.5i	5.25 - 6i	1.25 - 2.75i

Fourier coefficients (c_{mn}) for the texture in Fig. 6(b) are listed in Table I.

A common feature of the final optimized textures is large height amplitude. The full amplitudes for the textures in Figs. 3, 6(a), 6(b), and 6(c) are $\Delta h = 196$, 224, 218, and 217, respectively. The photonic bandstructure of the optimized texture from Fig. 6(b) is shown in Fig. 8. The optimization domain (the bandwidth of frequencies that we simulate) is highlighted in Fig. 8. The bandstructure visually shows the need for a high modal density in the optimization domain; the structure needs modes for the incident light to couple to.

The second common feature we observe is asymmetry within the unit cell. The optimal structures appear to break the inherent mirror symmetries of the problem, with a feature growing along one of the diagonals. To demonstrate that this symmetry breaking is not an artifact of the starting noise, we started another optimization from initial symmetrized conditions, with a slight perturbation along the diagonal, as shown in Fig. 9. The result of the algorithm is shown 15 iterations later in Fig. 10 (reciprocal space diagram in Fig. 11). We see that this perturbation has been amplified along the diagonal, suggesting that symmetry breaking is a fundamental feature of optimal textures. There appears to be no significance to the direction of the asymmetric component: the symmetry will break in the opposite direction (along $x = -y$) if the initial perturbation is in that direction.

In our optimizations, we kept the periodicity fixed at 710 nm. To find the optimal periodicity, we ran a sweep of optimizations with fixed periodicities from 50 to 800 nm in increments of 50 nm. Fig. 12 plots AE_{FOM} (absorption enhancement at the minimum performing frequency at normal incidence) achieved in these optimizations. The smaller periodicities did not optimize well; periodicities less than 350 nm did not achieve

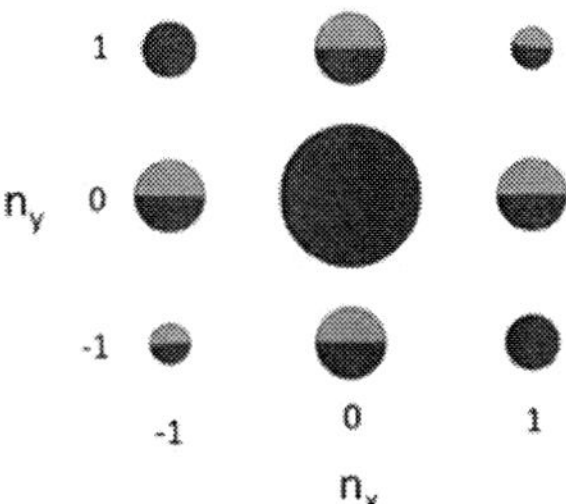

Fig. 11. Reciprocal space representation for the texture with broken mirror symmetry in Fig. 10. The blue pie slices represent the phase of the complex exponential Fourier coefficients.

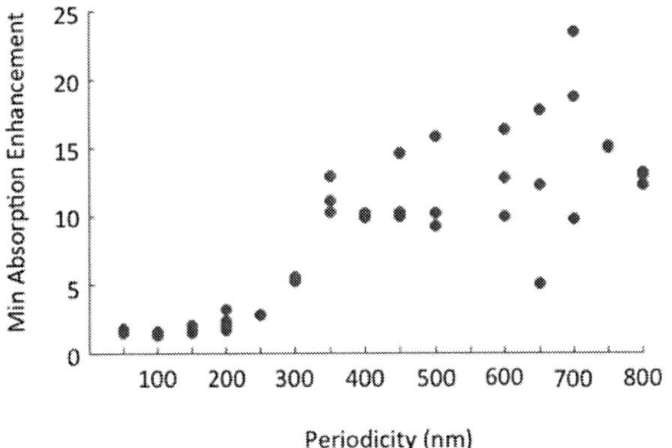

Fig. 12. Optimizations were carried out at periodicities from 50 to 800 nm, in increments of 50 nm. For each periodicity, at least three optimizations were completed for randomly chosen initial starting noise. The AE_{FOM} (absorption enhancement for the worst performing frequency and polarization at normal incidence) is plotted for each optimization.

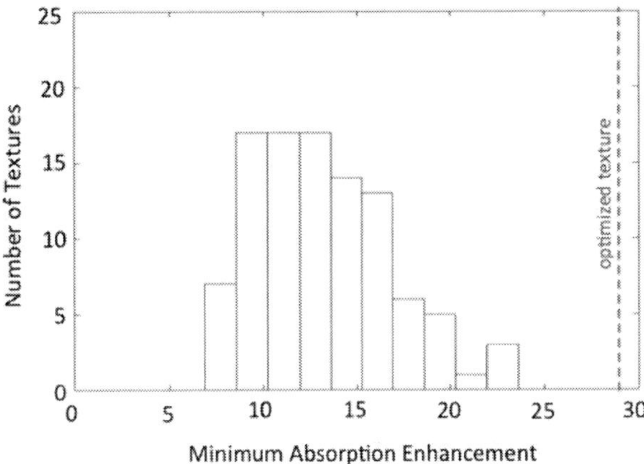

Fig. 13. AE_{FOM} (minimum absorption enhancement at normal incidence) plotted for 100 randomly generated textures of 710-nm periodicity. For comparison, the AE_{FOM} for the optimized texture in Fig. 6(b) is shown by the dotted red line.

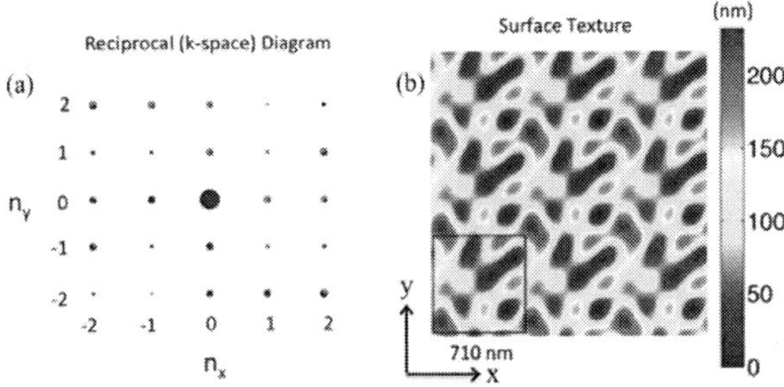

Fig. 14. (a) Reciprocal k-space diagram and (b) real-space top-down view of the median randomly generated texture from Fig. 13.

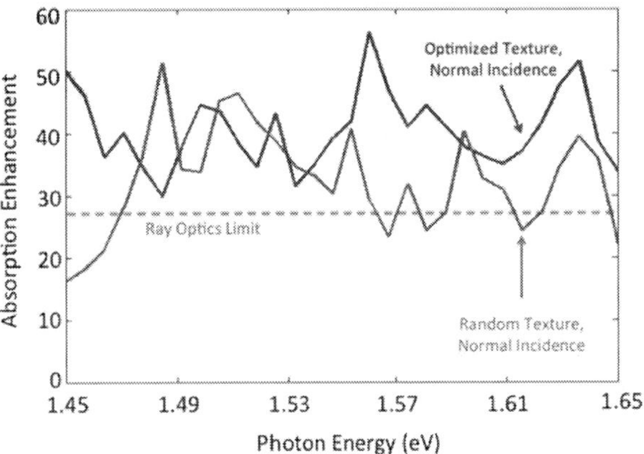

Fig. 15. Absorption enhancement (AE) as a function of frequency at normal incidence for the optimized texture from Fig. 6(b) (blue) compared with the median random texture from Fig. 14 (green). Lines are averaged over the two orthogonal polarizations.

minimum absorption enhancement $AE_{FOM} > 10$. The best optimizations occurred at 700 nm; perhaps because this periodicity brought the optimization frequency band high into the photonic bandstructure where the optical density of states is large and allowed the optimal coupling to the internally propagating modes.

Since the optimum is not unique, it is possible that any randomly generated pattern with large amplitude could achieve a similar figure of merit (AE_{FOM}). To check this, we randomly generated Fourier coefficients for 100 textures with a periodicity of 710 nm, with amplitudes ranging from $\Delta h = 223$ to 233 nm, and simulated the absorption of these structures. The AE_{FOM} (the lowest AE as a function of frequency at normal incidence, for the worst performing polarization) of these random structures are plotted in Fig. 13, and the random texture with the median figure of merit $AE_{FOM} = 13$ is shown in Fig. 14. In Figs. 15 and 16, the random texture with the median AE_{FOM} is compared with the optimized texture shown in Fig. 6(b). The AE_{FOM} for the optimized texture is over two times greater than the median AE_{FOM} in the randomly generated patterns. A comparison of angle-averaged absorption performance (shown in Fig. 16) shows a 33% increase in the optimized texture's AE_{angle} over the AE_{angle} for the median randomly generated pattern.

We also check the performance of a completely random texture (i.e., a texture with infinite periodicity). We randomly generated Fourier coefficients to the fifth order for a periodicity that

          13

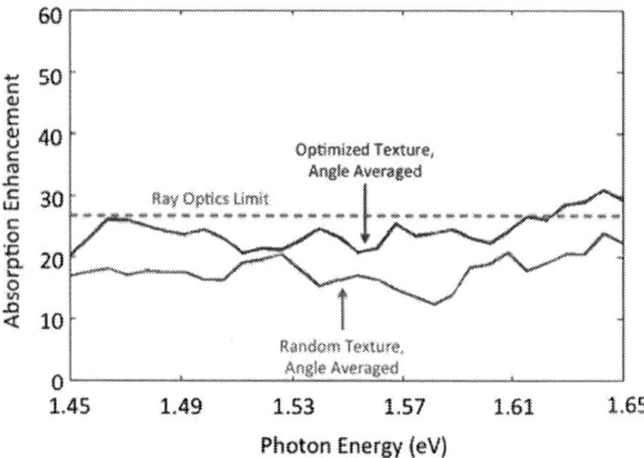

Fig. 16. Absorption enhancement (AE) as a function of frequency, angle averaged, for the optimized texture from Fig. 6(b) (blue) compared with the median random texture from Fig. 14 (green).

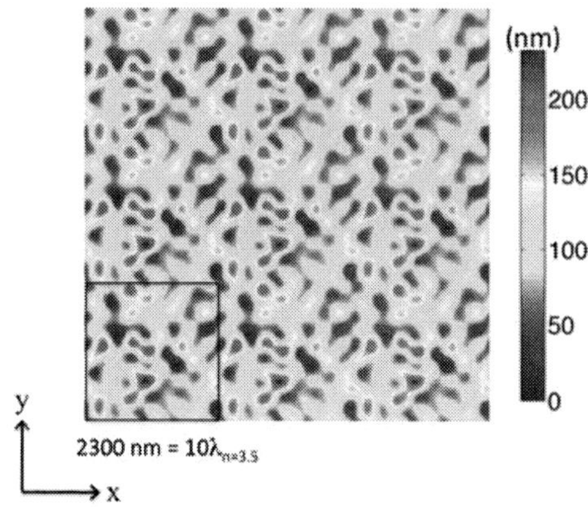

Fig. 18: A top-down view of the surface texture, for the randomly generated texture with periodicity of 2300 nm $= 10\lambda_{n=3.5}$, with median $\mathrm{AE_{FOM}}$ (minimum absorption enhancement at normal incidence).

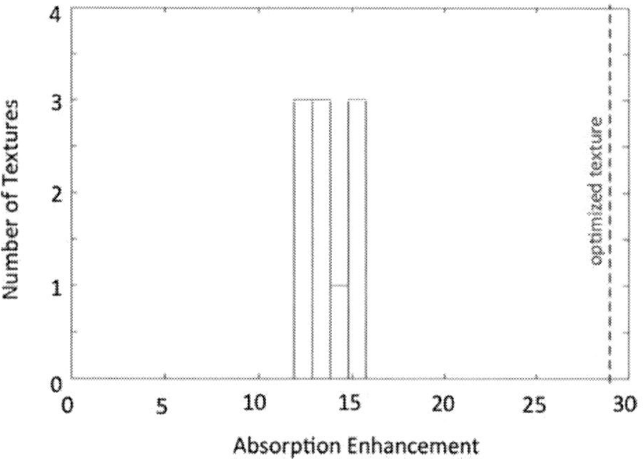

Fig. 17. $\mathrm{AE_{FOM}}$ (minimum absorption enhancement at normal incidence) plotted for 11 randomly generated textures of 2300-nm periodicity. For comparison, the $\mathrm{AE_{FOM}}$ for the optimized texture in Fig. 6(b) is shown by the dotted red line.

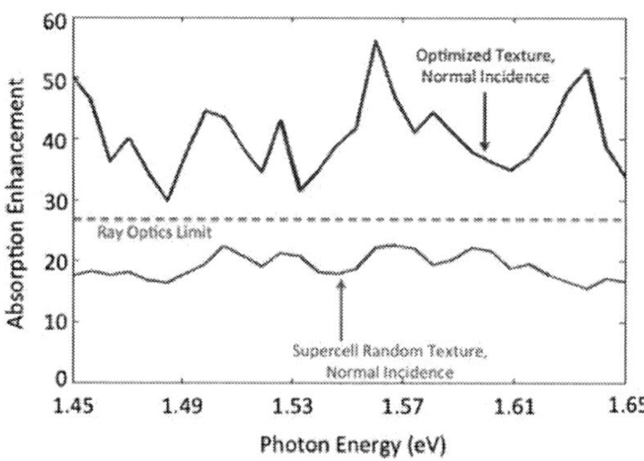

Fig. 19. Absorption enhancement (AE) as a function of frequency at normal incidence for the optimized texture from Fig. 6(b) (blue) compared with the median random texture with 2300-nm periodicity from Fig. 18 (green). Lines are averaged over the two orthogonal polarizations.

is $10\lambda_{n=3.5} = 2300$ nm, with a total texture amplitude between $\Delta h = 223$ nm and 233 nm. Our large periodicity approximates a texture with infinite periodicity (the supercell approach). The resulting $\mathrm{AE_{FOM}}$ for 11 different random supercell textures is shown in Fig. 17. The texture with the median figure of merit of $\mathrm{AE_{FOM}} = 13$ is shown in Fig. 18; this median $\mathrm{AE_{FOM}}$ is the same as for the random textures on a 710-nm periodicity. Fig. 19 compares the median supercell texture with the optimized texture at normal incidence. Additionally, the angle- and frequency-averaged performance (see Fig. 20) of the optimized texture is 26% better than the median random supercell. Our result that a periodic texture can perform better than a random one in the subwavelength regime is in agreement with [42].

In Table II, AE relative to 1.6% single-pass absorption is summarized. To compare these results with the $4n^2$ ray-optics AE limit, we need to account for the finite absorption in our structure. This can be done by using (1), which can be written

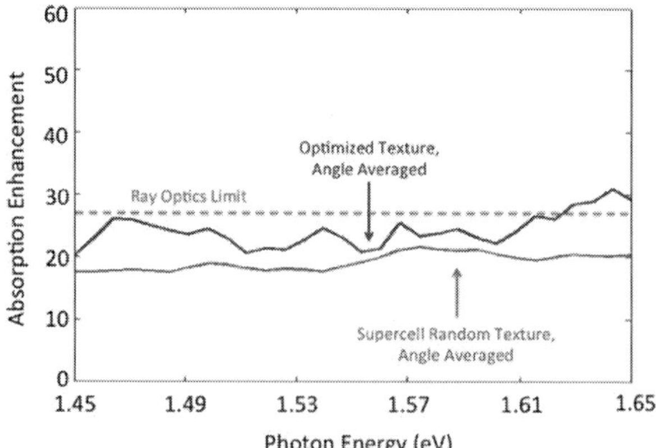

Fig. 20. Absorption enhancement (AE) as a function of frequency, angle averaged, for the optimized texture from Fig. 6(b) (blue) compared with the median random texture with 2300-nm periodicity from Fig. 18 (green).

     14

TABLE II

SUMMARY OF AEs AND WEAK ABSORPTION LIMIT ENHANCEMENTS (E)

	Best Optimized Texture	Median Random Texture (710 nm periodicity)	Median Random Supercell Texture (2300 nm periodicity)	Ray Optics Limit
AE_{FOM} (worst enhancement factor over frequency and polarization at normal incidence)	29	13	13	
AE_{angle} (angle- and frequency-averaged enhancement factor)	24	18	19	27
E (enhancement factor in the weakly absorbing limit)	39	25	27	49

more generally as

$$A = \frac{\alpha d}{\alpha d + \frac{1}{4n^2}} = \frac{\alpha d}{\alpha d + \frac{1}{E}} \tag{5}$$

where E is the limiting enhancement factor when the single-pass absorption is very weak ($\alpha d < 1.6\%$). E represents the highest possible enhancement factor, which should be compared with the ray-optics ideal $E = 4n^2 \sim 50$ case. For our optimized case of $AE_{angle} = 24$ at $\alpha d = 0.016$, $E = 39$. Our AE and weak absorption limit (E) results are summarized in Table II.

IV. CONCLUSION

In the ray optics regime, random structures are optimal to achieve AE [1]. In the subwavelength regime, it appears that computationally optimized surface textures perform better than randomly generated ones. So far, we have discovered a broad optimum, with many textures that achieve similar figures of merit. We have shown that our optimized structures perform about 33% better than randomly generated structures for angle- and frequency-averaged absorption. We report an angle- and frequency-averaged AE factor in the weakly absorbing limit of $E = 39$, for a texture on a high-index material of subwavelength thickness. This enhancement is $\sim 80\%$ of the ray optics limit $E = 4n^2 \sim 50$.

Although we do not prove a fundamental limit, the AE factor that arises from these optimizations is less than the ray-optics limit. It should be noted that for practical purposes, meeting or exceeding the ray-optics limit in the subwavelength might be unnecessary. For example, starting from a 1-μm film thickness, which for some materials makes a good solar cell even without light trapping, an enhancement factor $E = 50$ would permit a reduced film thickness < 100 nm.

In evaluating the performance of a solar cell texture for light trapping, it is important to take into account both the average performance, as well as the worst performance over the frequency. A texture with a few resonant peaks may yield high average performance in theory, but when applied to a real material, the resonant peaks will saturate at 100% absorption, and the total photons absorbed will be low. This electromagnetic optimization procedure obtains both a broadband absorption spectrum and a high average absorption.

Our practical goal in designing a solar cell texture is to achieve complete light absorption in the thinnest possible layer, with a manufacturable texture. This study is meant to be a general discussion of light trapping in the subwavelength thickness regime, and not specific to a certain material. However, this optimization procedure can be used as a tool in designing textures for real materials. Future work also requires the optimization of the AR coating. The one-layer AR coating only works for normal incidence at the center of the chosen frequency band. In reality, the AR coating needs to have good angle-averaged performance, especially for the large energy photons outside the optimized bandwidth. In addition, many authors [43] have attempted to use metal nanostructures to enhance solar cell absorption. Some problems with this approach include parasitic absorption in the metals and shadowing losses. In future work, metal nanostructures can also be included in the optimization of the light trapping structure. Furthermore, we can add manufacturing constraints to the problem. For example, in these calculations, we permitted the minimum film thickness to drop as low as 1 nm, but we could constrain to a more realistic minimum thickness of 50 nm. Finally, in our procedure, we could have fallen into local optima and not found the global optimum. Further work requires us to investigate the question of whether we have really converged.

REFERENCES

[1] E. Yablonovitch, "Statistical ray optics," *J. Opt. Soc. Amer.*, vol. 72, no. 7, pp. 899–907, Jul. 1982.

[2] O. D. Miller, E. Yablonovitch, and S. R. Kurtz, "Strong internal and external luminescence as solar cells approach the Shockley-Queisser limit," *IEEE J. Photovolt.*, vol. 2, no. 3, pp. 303–311, Jul. 2012.

[3] G. Lush and M. Lundstrom, "Thin film approaches for high-efficiency III–V cells," *Sol. Cells*, vol. 30, no. 1–4, pp. 337–344, May 1991.

[4] M. A. Green, "Enhanced evanescent mode light trapping in organic solar cells and other low index optoelectronic devices," *Prog. Photovolt., Res. Appl.*, vol. 19, no. 4, pp. 473–477, Jun. 2011.

[5] Z. Yu, A. Raman, and S. Fan, "Fundamental limit of nanophotonic light trapping in solar cells," *Proc. Nat. Acad. Sci.*, vol. 107, no. 41, pp. 17491–17496, Sep. 2010.

[6] H. R. Stuart and D. G. Hall, "Thermodynamic limit to light trapping in thin planar structures," *J. Opt. Soc. Amer. A*, vol. 14, no. 11, pp. 3001–3008, Nov. 1997.

[7] Z. Yu and S. Fan, "Angular constraint on light-trapping absorption enhancement in solar cells," *Appl. Phys. Lett.*, vol. 98, no. 1, pp. 011106-1–011106-3, 2011.

[8] Z. Yu, A. Raman, and S. Fan, "Thermodynamic upper bound on broadband light coupling with photonic structures," *Phys. Rev. Lett.*, vol. 109, no. 17, pp. 173901-1–173901-5, Oct. 2012.

[9] Z. Yu, A. Raman, and S. Fan, "Fundamental limit of light trapping in grating structures," *Opt. Exp.*, vol. 18, no. S3, pp. A366–A380, Aug. 2010.

[10] L. Zeng, Y. Yi, C. Hong, J. Liu, N. Feng, X. Duan, L. C. Kimerling, and B. A. Alamariu, "Efficiency enhancement in Si solar cells by textured photonic crystal back reflector," *Appl. Phys. Lett.*, vol. 89, no. 11, pp. 111111-1–111111-3, 2006.

[11] E. Garnett and P. Yang, "Light trapping in silicon nanowire solar cells," *Nano Lett.*, vol. 10, no. 3, pp. 1082–1087, Mar. 2010.

[12] D. Shir, J. Yoon, D. Chanda, J.-H. Ryu, and J. A. Rogers, "Performance of ultrathin silicon solar microcells with nanostructures of relief formed by soft imprint lithography for broad band absorption enhancement," *Nano Lett.*, vol. 10, no. 8, pp. 3041–3046, Aug. 2010.

[13] P. Bermel, C. Luo, L. Zeng, L. C. Kimerling, and J. D. Joannopoulos, "Improving thin-film crystalline silicon solar cell efficiencies with photonic crystals," *Opt. Exp.*, vol. 15, no. 25, pp. 16986–17000, 2007.

[14] C. Heine and R. H. Morf, "Submicrometer gratings for solar energy applications," *Appl. Opt.*, vol. 34, no. 14, pp. 2476–2482, May 1995.

[15] N. Senoussaoui, M. Krause, J. Müller, E. Bunte, T. Brammer, and H. Stiebig, "Thin-film solar cells with periodic grating coupler," *Thin Solid Films*, vol. 451/452, pp. 397–401, Mar. 2004.

[16] M. D. Kelzenberg, S. W. Boettcher, J. A. Petykiewicz, D. B. Turner-Evans, M. C. Putnam, E. L. Warren, J. M. Spurgeon, R. M. Briggs, N. S. Lewis, and H. A. Atwater, "Enhanced absorption and carrier collection in Si wire arrays for photovoltaic applications," *Nature Mater.*, vol. 9, pp. 239–244, Feb. 2010.

[17] K. X. Wang, Z. Yu, V. Liu, Y. Cui, and S. Fan, "Absorption enhancement in ultrathin crystalline silicon solar cells with antireflection and light-trapping nanocone gratings," *Nano Lett.*, vol. 12, no. 3, pp. 1616–1619, Mar. 2012.

[18] D. Madzharov, R. Dewan, and D. Knipp, "Influence of front and back grating on light trapping in microcrystalline thin-film silicon solar cells," *Opt. Exp.*, vol. 19, no. S2, pp. A95–A107, Jan. 2011.

[19] P. Kowalczewski, M. Liscidini, and L. C. Andreani, "Engineering Gaussian disorder at rough interfaces for light trapping in thin-film solar cells," *Opt. Lett.*, vol. 37, no. 23, pp. 4868–4870, Nov. 2012.

[20] S. Eyderman, S. John, and A. Deinega, "Solar light trapping in slanted conical-pore photonic crystals: Beyond statistical ray trapping," *J. Appl. Phys.*, vol. 113, no. 15, pp. 154315-1–154315-10, 2013.

[21] I. Tobías, A. Luque, and A. Martí, "Light intensity enhancement by diffracting structures in solar cells," *J. Appl. Phys.*, vol. 104, no. 3, pp. 034502-1–034502-10, 2008.

[22] C. Wang, S. Yu, W. Chen, and C. Sun, "Highly efficient light-trapping structure design inspired by natural evolution," *Sci. Rep.*, vol. 3, Jan. 2013.

[23] E. R. Martins, J. Li, Y. Liu, J. Zhou, and T. F. Krauss, "Engineering gratings for light trapping in photovoltaics: The supercell concept," *Phys. Rev. B*, vol. 86, no. 4, pp. 041404-1–041404-4, Jul. 2012.

[24] A. Abass, K. Q. Le, A. Alù, M. Burgelman, and B. Maes, "Dual-interface gratings for broadband absorption enhancement in thin-film solar cells," *Phys. Rev. B*, vol. 85, no. 11, pp. 115449-1–115449-8, Mar. 2012.

[25] Z. Xia, Y. Wu, R. Liu, Z. Liang, J. Zhou, and P. Tang, "Misaligned conformal gratings enhanced light trapping in thin film silicon solar cells," *Opt. Exp.*, vol. 21, no. S3, pp. A548–A557, May 2013.

[26] P. Sheng, "Wavelength-selective absorption enhancement in thin-film solar cells," *Appl. Phys. Lett.*, vol. 43, no. 6, pp. 579-1–579-3, 1983.

[27] M. B. Dühring and O. Sigmund, "Optimization of extraordinary optical absorption in plasmonic and dielectric structures," *J. Opt. Soc. Amer. B*, vol. 30, no. 5, pp. 1154–1160, Apr. 2013.

[28] J. Zhu, C.-M. Hsu, Z. Yu, S. Fan, and Y. Cui, "Nanodome solar cells with efficient light management and self-cleaning," *Nano Lett.*, vol. 10, no. 6, pp. 1979–1984, Jun. 2010.

[29] P. N. Saeta, V. E. Ferry, D. Pacifici, J. N. Munday, and H. A. Atwater, "How much can guided modes enhance absorption in thin solar cells?" *Opt. Exp.*, vol. 17, no. 23, pp. 20975–20990, Nov. 2009.

[30] D. Zhou and R. Biswas, "Photonic crystal enhanced light-trapping in thin film solar cells," *J. Appl. Phys.*, vol. 103, no. 9, pp. 093102-1–093102-5, 2008.

[31] Y. Park, E. Drouard, O. El Daif, X. Letartre, P. Viktorovitch, A. Fave, A. Kaminski, M. Lemiti, and C. Seassal, "Absorption enhancement using photonic crystals for silicon thin film solar cells," *Opt. Exp.*, vol. 17, no. 16, pp. 14312–14321, Jul. 2009.

[32] C. Eisele, C. E. Nebel, and M. Stutzmann, "Periodic light coupler gratings in amorphous thin film solar cells," *J. Appl. Phys.*, vol. 89, no. 12, pp. 7722-1–7722-5, 2001.

[33] V. E. Ferry, M. A. Verschuuren, H. B. T. Li, E. Verhagen, R. J. Walters, R. E. I. Schropp, H. A. Atwater, and A. Polman, "Light trapping in ultra-thin plasmonic solar cells," *Opt. Exp.*, vol. 18, no. S2, pp. A237–A245, Jun. 2010.

[34] S. Fahr, T. Kirchartz, C. Rockstuhl, and F. Lederer, "Approaching the Lambertian limit in randomly textured thin-film solar cells," *Opt. Exp.*, vol. 19, no. S4, pp. A865–A874, Jun. 2011.

[35] J. Grandidier, D. M. Callahan, J. N. Munday, and H. A. Atwater, "Light absorption enhancement in thin-film solar cells using whispering gallery modes in dielectric nanospheres," *Adv. Mater.*, vol. 23, no. 10, pp. 1272–1276, Mar. 2011.

[36] F. Pratesi, M. Burresi, F. Riboli, K. Vynck, and D. S. Wiersma, "Disordered photonic structures for light harvesting in solar cells," *Opt. Exp.*, vol. 21, no. S3, pp. A460–A468, Apr. 2013.

[37] D. M. Callahan, J. N. Munday, and H. A. Atwater, "Solar cell light trapping beyond the ray optic limit," *Nano Letters*, vol. 12, no. 1, pp. 214–218, Jan. 2012.

[38] X. Sheng, S. G. Johnson, J. Michel, and L. C. Kimerling, "Optimization-based design of surface textures for thin-film Si solar cells," *Opt. Exp.*, vol. 19, no. S4, pp. A841–A850, Jun. 2011.

[39] O. Miller, "Photonic design: From fundamental solar cell physics to computational inverse design," Ph.D. dissertation, EECS Dept., Univ. California, Berkeley, CA, USA, 2012.

[40] M. B. Giles and N. A. Pierce, "An introduction to the adjoint approach to design," *Flow. Turbul. Combust.*, vol. 65, no. 3–4, pp. 393–415, Jan. 2000.

[41] W. Murray and M. L. Overton, "A projected Lagrangian algorithm for nonlinear minimax optimization," *SIAM J. Sci. Stat. Comput.*, vol. 1, no. 3, pp. 345–370, Sep. 1980.

[42] C. Battaglia, C.-M. Hsu, K. Söderström, J. Escarré, F.-J. Haug, M. Charrière, M. Boccard, M. Despeisse, D. T. L. Alexander, M. Cantoni, Y. Cui, and C. Ballif, "Light trapping in solar cells: Can periodic beat random?" *ACS Nano*, vol. 6, no. 3, pp. 2790–2797, Mar. 2012.

[43] V. E. Ferry, J. N. Munday, and H. A. Atwater, "Design considerations for plasmonic photovoltaics," *Adv. Mater.*, vol. 22, no. 43, pp. 4794–4808, Nov. 2010.

Authors' photographs and biographies not available at the time of publication.

High-Efficiency Devices With Pure Solution-Processed Cu$_2$ZnSn(S,Se)$_4$ Absorbers

Teodor Todorov, Hiroki Sugimoto, Oki Gunawan, Tayfun Gokmen, and David B. Mitzi

Abstract—Thin-film kesterite-type Cu$_2$ZnSn(S,Se)$_4$ (CZTSSe) materials comprise readily available and environmentally benign elements. After reaching efficiencies in the 10% range in recent years, they have become some of the most actively studied new contenders for future solar energy production. The quest for efficiencies competitive to CdTe and CIGS has started to address multiple-challenging aspects of CZTSSe device optimization. One of the most evident difficulties is obtaining highly homogeneous material with equally uniform electronic properties—a prerequisite for advanced interface and full device optimization. While hybrid slurry ink deposition approaches have been setting the benchmark for CZTSSe performance, they often suffer from microscale deposition nonuniformities. Pure solution processes offer the potential for superior homogeneity at molecular level during synthesis. This could be advantageous to obtaining higher quality of multinary semiconductors with better uniformity at all levels. Here, we report a pure solution approach for CZTSSe based on zinc salts soluble in selenium-containing hydrazine systems, thus replacing the solid zinc hydrazinate particles used in our previous record-setting works. By this approach, we demonstrate the highest to date efficiency for a pure solution-processed CZTSSe, reaching 10.6%. We observe correlation between PL intensity and device characteristics. Macrospcopic nonuniformities were identified by this technique and addressing these is expected to yield further efficiency improvement.

Index Terms—Copper compounds, photovoltaic cells, semiconductor materials, solar energy, thin-film devices.

I. Introduction

FINDING a cheap, scalable, and efficient solar energy technology unlimited by materials supply is one of the most important goals of the photovoltaic society. Kesterite Cu$_2$ZnSn(S,Se)$_4$ (CZTSSe) materials have fascinated researchers due to their similarities with already commercial direct gap absorbers such as CdTe and CIGS. However, replacing rare indium with earth-abundant Zn and Sn to produce high-efficiency devices has not been trivial due to the complexity of kesterite multinary compounds [1]. Multiple deposition routes have been described, ranging from co-evaporation to nanoparticle processes [2], [3].

Since 2010, we have reported a series of record-setting device results based on hybrid hydrazine slurries containing Cu–Sn–S–Se dissolved species and dispersed Zn–Se hydrazinate nanoparticle species [4]–[6]. While the 11.1% efficiency achieved by this approach remains the highest to date, contrary to pure solution approaches (used for instance for CIGS deposition [7]), the solid phases present in the typical CZTS slurry approach potentially cause microscale non-uniformities during precursor deposition. Enhancing the homogeneity of the absorber layer is therefore expected to lead to more consistent electronic properties that could potentially address key limitations of current devices, such as V_{oc} deficit.

Pure solution processing, in contrast with slurry- and nanoparticle-based approaches, offers precursor homogeneity at a molecular scale and has been used for some of the highest efficiency nonvacuum CIGS absorbers, reaching 15.2% [7]. Successful studies of CZTS deposition from pure solutions have been reported [8], reaching 8.08% [9] by a novel hydrazine–hydrazinocarboxylic acid dissolution of Zn metal. The work employs pure sulfide ink with subsequent selenization.

Here, we report an alternative approach for Zn dissolution based on zinc salts that can be directly dissolved in Cu–Sn–S–Se hydrazine solutions. We demonstrate superior microscale uniformity in comparison with previous slurry-based processes and the highest efficiency achieved with a pure solution kesterite deposition approach—10.6%.

II. Experimental Details

The CZTSSe absorbers for this study were produced by a hydrazine solution-based process that has been described in detail previously [4]–[6]. Key difference from previous works was the use of a zinc salt instead of elemental zinc (see Fig. 2). *Caution: Hydrazine is both highly toxic and reactive and must be handled using appropriate protective equipment to prevent physical contact with either vapor or liquid.*

Multiple layers of the constituent elements in such solutions were spin coated onto Mo-coated soda lime glass and then heat treated at temperatures in excess of 500 °C. Devices were completed using a chemical bath-deposited CdS buffer and RF magnetron sputtered ZnO and indium tin oxide (ITO) window layers. A Ni–Al collection grid and ~110-nm-thick MgF$_2$ antireflection coating were deposited on top of the device by electron-beam evaporation. Each device had a total area of approximately 0.45 cm^2 as defined by mechanical scribing, yielding a standard glass/Mo/CZTSSe/CdS/ZnO/ITO/Ni–Al solar cell [4]–[6].

Manuscript received August 13, 2013; revised September 30, 2013; accepted October 3, 2013. Date of publication November 20, 2013; date of current version December 16, 2013. This work was conducted as part of a joint development project between Tokyo Ohka Kogyo Co., Ltd., DelSolar Co., Ltd., Solar Frontier K. K., and IBM Corporation.

T. Todorov, O. Gunawan, T. Gokmen, and D. B. Mitzi are with the T. J. Watson Research Center, IBM Corporation, Yorktown Heights, NY 10598 USA (e-mail: tktodoro@us.ibm.com; ogunawa@us.ibm.com; tgokmen@us.ibm.com; dmitzi@us.ibm.com).

H. Sugimoto is with Solar Frontier, Atugi, Kanagawa 243-0206, Japan (e-mail: Hiroki.Sugimoto@solar-frontier.com).

Color versions of one or more of the figures in this paper are available online at http://ieeexplore.ieee.org.

Digital Object Identifier 10.1109/JPHOTOV.2013.2287754

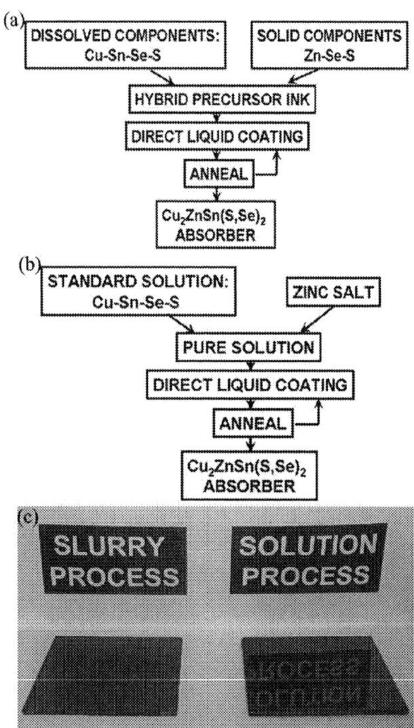

Fig. 1. (a) and (b) Flowcharts for slurry and pure solution-based processes. (c) Image showing better optical reflectivity of solution-processed precursors.

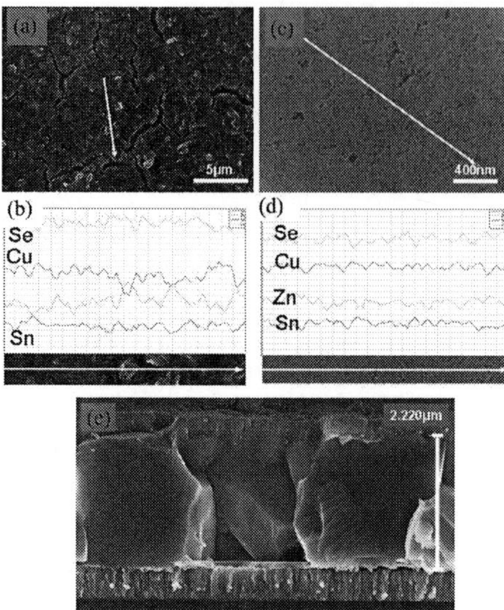

Fig. 2. SEM images of single layers of CZTS precursors on Mo-coated glass with corresponding EDX relative concentration distributions (scan lines indicated with white arrows) by (a), (b) slurry process and (c), (d) pure solution process. (d) SEM image of pure solution CZTSSe device cross section.

Scanning electron microscopy (SEM) was conducted on the CZTSSe films and devices, which were cleaved prior to the SEM analyses and coated with a thin Pd–Au film to prevent charging effects.

III. RESULTS AND DISCUSSION

The superior smoothness of CZTSSe precursor layers in comparison to the slurry-based approaches can be observed by the optical reflection of an image on Fig. 1(c). SEM micrographs confirm this reduced roughness [see Fig. 2(a) and (c)], and EDX line scans demonstrate that while significant fluctuation in slurry precursor layers is present, the smooth solution-processed layers have more uniform elemental distribution at the microscale [see Fig. 2(b) and (d)].

Fig. 3 shows the light J–V and EQE characteristics of the top performing cell. Compared with the 11% generation CZTSSe cells that we recently reported [6], we can make few observations—the bandgap of this cell (extracted from the inflection of the EQE curve) is a little bit higher, $E_g = 1.16$ eV with V_{oc} deficit (i.e., the difference between the bandgap voltage and the V_{oc}), $V_{oc}^{\mathrm{def}} = 0.688$ V quite close to the 11% generation CZTSSe cells at similar bandgap ($E_g \sim 1.13$ eV) [6], where $V_{oc}^{\mathrm{def}} \sim 680$ mV. Although this might not be a fundamental property of the material, it has been empirically observed that lower bandgap CZTS exhibits lower V_{oc} deficit; thus, it will be worthwhile to reduce the bandgap a little bit to optimize this device.

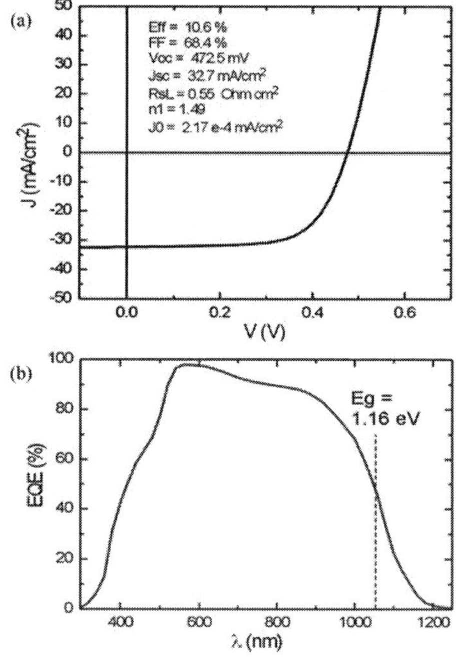

Fig. 3. Light J–V and EQE characteristics of the CZTSSe device.

The fill factor FF $\sim 67\%$ is quite comparable with our 11% generation cells. One dominant factor that limits the FF of our cells is also the low-V_{oc} issue. Low V_{oc} drags down the FF following the empirical relationship between the FF and V_{oc} [11] (ignoring the effect of series resistance):

$$\mathrm{FF} = [V_{\mathrm{OC},N} - \ln(V_{\mathrm{OC},N} + 0.72)]/(V_{\mathrm{OC},N} + 1) \quad (1)$$

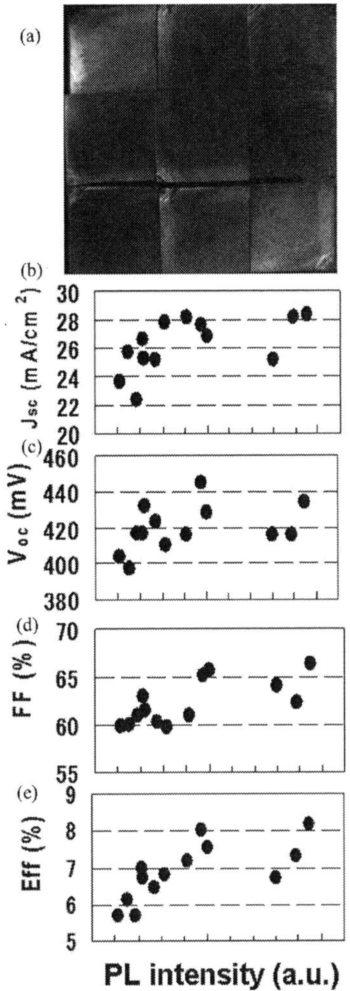

Fig. 4. PL image of solution-processed CZTSSe absorbers and intensity dependence of device parameters: J_{sc}, V_{oc}, FF, Efficiency.

where $V_{OC,N}$ is the normalized V_{OC} given as $V_{OC,N} = e\,V_{OC}/n_1 k_B T$, where n_1 is the diode ideality factor, e is the electron's charge, and k_B is the Boltzmann constant.

The PL imaging technique was employed as a preliminary absorber diagnostic tool, and a trend to better performance is found with increased intensity—including V_{oc}, J_{sc}, and FF (see Fig. 4). Some millimeter-range nonuniformities (darker spots) are observed, possibly limiting device performance as well as broadening the PL reading distribution. Identifying and addressing the causes for these low-performance areas is in progress and is expected to improve device efficiency.

IV. Conclusion

We have reported a 10.6% efficient CZTSSe device—the highest performance achieved with a pure solution-processed kesterite absorber. Superior precursor uniformity at a molecular scale is expected to facilitate more straightforward optimization of CZTSSe absorbers. Currently, macroscopic processing and/or substrate-related nonuniformities identified by PL imaging are being addressed and expected to yield further increases in efficiency.

References

[1] H. Katagiri, K. Jimbo, W. S. Maw, K. Oishi, M. Yamazaki, H. Araki, and A. Takeuchi, "Development of CZTS-based thin film solar cells," *Thin Solid Films*, vol. 517, pp. 2455–2460, 2009.

[2] W. Hsu, I. Repins, C. Beall, C. DeHart, B. To, W. Yang, Y. Yang, and R. Noufi, "Growth mechanisms of co-evaporated kesterite: a comparison of Cu-rich and Zn-rich composition paths," *Progr. Photovoltaic, Res. Appl.*, Early view 2013, DOI: 10.1002/pip.2296.

[3] Q. Guo, G. M. Ford, W.-C. Yang, B. C. Walker, E. A. Stach, H. W. Hillhouse, and R. Agrawal, "Fabrication of 7.2% efficient CZTSSe solar cells using CZTS nanocrystals," *J. Amer. Chem. Soc.*, vol. 132, pp. 17384–17386, 2010.

[4] T. K. Todorov, K. B. Reuter, and D. B. Mitzi, "High-efficiency solar cell with earth-abundant liquid-processed absorber," *Adv. Mater*, vol. 22, pp. E156–E159, 2010.

[5] D. A. R. Barkhouse, O. Gunawan, T. Gokmen, T. K. Todorov, and D. B. Mitzi, "Device characteristics of a 10.1% hydrazine-processed $Cu_2 ZnSn(Se, S)_4$ solar cell," *Progr. Photovolt.*, vol. 20, pp. 6–11, 2012.

[6] T. K. Todorov, J. Tang, S. Bag, O. Gunawan, T. Gokmen, Y. Zhu, and D. B. Mitzi, "Beyond 11% efficiency: Characteristics of state-of-the-art $Cu_2 ZnSn (S, Se)_4$ solar cells," *Adv. Energy Mater.*, vol. 3, pp. 34–38, 2013.

[7] T. K. Todorov, O. Gunawan, T. Gokmen, and D. B. Mitzi, "Solution-processed $Cu(In, Ga)(S, Se)_2$ absorber yielding a 15.2% efficient solar cell," *Progr. Photo-Volt.*, vol. 21, pp. 82–87, 2013.

[8] W. Ki and H. W. Hillhouse, "Earth-abundant element photovoltaics directly from soluble precursors with high yield using a non-toxic solvent," *Adv. Energy Mater.*, vol. 1, pp. 732–735, 2011.

[9] W. Yang, H. S. Duan, B. Bob, H. Zhou, B. Lei, C. H. Chung, S. H. Li, W. W. Hou, and Y. Yang, "Novel solution processing of high-efficiency earth-abundant $Cu_2 ZnSn(S,Se)_4$ solar cells," *Adv. Mater.*, vol. 24, pp. 6323–6329, 2012.

[10] D. B. Mitzi, O. Gunawan, T. K. Todorov, and D. A. R. Barkhouse, "Prospects and performance limitations for Cu–Zn–Sn–S–Se photovoltaic technology," *Phil.Trans. R. Soc. A 13*, vol. 371, no. 1996, p. 20110432, 2013.

[11] M. A. Green, "Solar cell fill factors—General graph and empirical expressions," *Solid State Electron.*, vol. 24, pp. 788–789, 1981.

Authors' photographs and biographies not available at the time of publication.

Impurities through the silicon solar cell value chain

Marisa Di Sabatino[1], Gabriella Tranell[1], Eivind J. Øvrelid[1,2]

[1] Norwegian University of Science and Technology (NTNU), Trondheim, 7491 Norway

[2] SINTEF Materials and Chemistry, Trondheim, 7465 Norway

Abstract — It is accepted that impurities impair the electrical properties of silicon materials used in solar cells. Impurities are incorporated into the material along the entire silicon solar cells value chain. In this paper we review the sources and levels of impurities entering the material during the silicon solar cell process steps from silicon production and refining, crystallization, wafering and cell processing. Solar cell processing technology has made giant steps in the last decade and, as the cell architecture becomes more and more sophisticated, a better understanding of the material quality requirements is essential. This paper will review the different process steps by taking into account the latest progresses in cell manufacturing.

Index Terms — silicon, impurities, solar cell

I. INTRODUCTION

Purity of silicon is one of the main parameters to assess the quality of the material. It is now accepted that the so-called *solar grade silicon* (SoG-Si) has intermediate level of impurities, i.e. its quality lies between the one of metallurgical grade (typically 98-99% purity) and electronic grade silicon (99.9999999% or better). Impurities can be divided in three categories: dopants, which are added to achieve the target resistivity (typically for silicon solar cells, the range is 0.7-1.7 Ωcm); transition elements, which enter the solar cell value chain at different stages; atmospherics, O and C being the most important.

The silicon solar cells value chain starts with the silicon feedstock production. For this process, different qualities of raw materials, i.e. quartz and carbon-bearing compounds, can be used. Silicon made via metallurgical processes undergoes several purification steps in order to achieve typically 6N purity (99.9999%). This feedstock is then used to charge silica crucibles, with or without Si_3N_4 coating layer for multi- or monocrystalline silicon ingots, respectively, where it is heated up to temperatures above 1500°C, melted and solidified. In order to process solar cells, thin wafers (typically 180 µm or thinner) are cut by sawing processes and cleaned/etched before more steps are required for the final solar cell. Most of these processes are aimed at purifying, thus reducing the amount of impurities in the final material. However, they involved the use of different containers, furnaces and atmospheres that can also unintentionally introduce contamination.

It has been reported by several studies that many impurities have a detrimental effect on the electrical properties and final performance of the photovoltaic (PV) device. Typical levels of metallic impurities in the silicon feedstock are approximately hundreds ppbw (10^{15} a/cm^3) and two orders of magnitude lower (10^{13} a/cm^3 or below) in the silicon wafer [1, 2]. Coletti [3] has recently reported on the effect of several impurities (namely Ti, Cr, Fe, Ni and Cu) on minority carried diffusion length and energy conversion efficiency. He indicated that the level of impurity that can be accepted depends on the type of impurity, crystallization process and solar cell architecture.

As PV technology has experienced a fast growth in the last decade and new processes are investigated, new types of impurities and thresholds are proposed. In this paper, we review the types and levels of impurities that enter the silicon material during the different steps of the solar cell value chain. Characterization methods for impurity determination are also briefly reviewed.

II. IMPURITIES IN SILICON FEEDSTOCK

The first step in SoG-Si production is generally the carbothermic production of metallurgical grade silicon (MG-Si) from quartz and carbonaceous materials such as coke, coal, charcoal and wood chips. MG-Si normally has a purity of more than 98% silicon and for special grades, more than 99% Si. A typical chemical composition of MG-Si is listed in Table 1 according to [4]. The purity of the MG-Si product will depend on the purity of raw materials used and on the process operation (e.g. type of electrodes, refractories, fluxes, ladle refining process etc). Typically, transition and alkali elements enter the process mainly through the carbonaceous materials which contain anywhere from less than 1 wt% to more than 10 wt% ash and lattice bound elements. Al, K and Fe based mineral inclusion and lattice impurities are also contained in the quartz. Fe will, in addition, enter the process through the electrodes [5-7]. In terms of the doping elements B and P, quartz and carbon materials are equally responsible for their introduction. In Table 2, average impurity concentrations in raw materials and electrodes are summarized [5, 7, 8]. When the MG-Si is tapped from the electric furnace in which the carbothermic reduction is carried out, the metal is saturated in carbon and will contain SiC particles. This carbon will be reduced in the subsequent ladle refining process, which is standard practice to reduce the Ca- and Al content in the metal. As the production of solar cells with reasonable efficiency requires silicon with 6N purity or higher [3], the MG-Si needs to be purified further.

Table 1. Typical chemical composition of MG-Si [4].

Element:	O	Fe	Al	Ca	C	Mg	Ti	Mn	V	B	P
Low (ppm)	100	300	300	20	50	5	100	10	1	5	5
High (ppm)	5000	250000	5000	2000	1500	200	1000	300	300	70	100

Element:	Cu	Cr	Ni	Zr	Mo
Low (ppm)	5	5	10	5	1
High (ppm)	100	150	100	300	10

Table 2. Average impurity content in quartz, carbon mix and electrode for a Si furnace. Values are in ppmw. After [5, 7, 8].

Element	Quartz	Carbon	Electrode
P	<5-50	<5-300	<5-170
B	<10-45	<10-100	<10
Fe	1000-1500	<100-9000	100-3500
Al	300-3200	<50-10000	<50-4000
Ca	<75-160	<75-4000	200-1500
Ti	20-200	<0.5-4000	<100
Mn	3-600	1-270	50-3500
K	<75-1700	<75-1800	<75-250
Mg	20-140	70-1400	<15-500
Na	50-170	<50-2100	<50-300

Until 1997, the silicon employed for solar cells originated mainly from waste materials from the electronic industry [9]- a Si which typically has a purity of 9-11N. This high-purity, electronic grade silicon (EG-Si) is produced by a chemical refining method, the so-called *Siemens* process [9-11], with MG-Si as starting point. As the market for silicon for solar cells quickly expanded, the concurrent effect of an increase in the demand for solar silicon along with the high energy consumption of the traditional Siemens process, led the photovoltaic industry to focus its efforts on the development of new production processes dedicated to solar silicon (SoG-Si). The development has gone in two different directions:
1) modifications of the chemical process and its evolution into related gas-based chemical processes. Examples of these modified processes include the fluidized bed reactor developed by REC in 2007, the vapor to liquid deposition developed by Tokuyama Corporation [9] or the closed loop process adopted by Wacker Polysilicon [11];
2) metallurgically-based refining and production process developed by, among others, Norwegian Elkem Solar and Fesil Sunergy, American Dow Corning and 6N, Spanish Ferroatlantica, French Photosil consortium, Japanese JFE and Chinese Ningxia, Shanghai Pro-power and Xiamen/Jaco.

While gas-based SoG-Si technologies offer advantages in terms of obtainable high metal purities, metallurgical refining technologies are often more environmentally beneign and energentically beneficial while maintaining 6N or higher purity [12]. Metallurgical methods to remove metallic impurities, include directional solidification or acid leaching processes. Phosphorous levels are possible to reduce with vacuum treatments [13] and/or leaching [14]. Boron levels may be decreased employing oxidative high temperature plasma refining [15], gas treatments [16] or slag refining [17-19].

Reported purity levels of some metallurgical produced SoG-Si materials are reported in Table 3.

Table 3. Reported purities of SoG-Si in ppmw [12].
* Not given
** total Fe, Al, Ti and Cu

Process	B	P	Total Met.
Elkem Solar	0.25±0.02	0.63±0.05	<1-10
Fesil Sunergy	~0.5	~0.4	*
Photosil	~0.3	~1.0	<8.0**
Ningxia	0.3 (min 0.17)	0.4-0.6 (min 0.1)	<1
Shanghai Propower	0.6 (min 0.1)	0.8 (min 0.7)	<1
Xiamen/Jaco	0.8-1.2	2-4	<10

III. IMPURITIES DURING CRYSTALLIZATION

Currently, industrial silicon wafers are either monocrystaline, produced by the Czochralski (CZ) process, or multicrystalline, produced by directional solidification (DS). In both processes, the silicon is melted in a quartz crucible, the furnace is lined with graphite and the furnace shell is water-cooled stainless steel. The electrodes, which connect the graphite heater to the power supply, can either be made from stainless steel or copper. Some details about the impurities in the crucible materials and from the crystallization processes are given below.

A. Crucible

Typical impurity levels in the crucibles used for the CZ and DS process are given in Table 4 [20]. Silica crucibles for the CZ process are typically one or two orders of magnitude purer but also much more expensive.

Table 4. Impurity levels in crucibles in ppmw.

	Al	Ca	Cr	P	Fe	K	B	Mg	Na	Ni	Ti
Conventional	890	89	3·7	2·1	100	2·1	4·5	25	8·9	0·61	110
Clean	15	0·6	0·06		0·5	0·6		0·06	0·9	0·03	1·3

The level of Fe in the conventional crucible used for DS is much higher than in the clean crucible used in the CZ process. Furthermore, the way the impurities enters the silicon from the crucible is different for the two processes; in CZ being mainly due to the dissolution of the crucible material (e.g. several hundred grams of the crucible material dissolves into the melt during a full ingot process).

B. *Directional solidification*

In the DS solidification process, the crucible is coated with silicon nitride. During meltdown of the feedstock and stabilization of the melt, the silicon will be saturated with nitrogen. Some oxygen will enter the silicon due to the vapor pressure of quartz. It is not clear if the metallic impurities in the quartz will enter the melt by dissolution or if the mechanism is solid-state diffusion through the nitride coating. During solidification, the contact area between the molten silicon and the crucible will be reduced, first the bottom, then the side. Therefore, there will always be a reduction in the oxygen level from the bottom to the top of a multicrystalline ingot [21].

For most metals the solubility is lower in the solid than the liquid phase. As the solidification proceeds, impurities will be expelled from the solidification front. Due to the low solidification rate (10-20 mm/hour), it is assumed that there will be total mixing in the melt and low diffusion in the solid. Therefore, for all practical purposes, the Scheil`s equation can be used to estimate the concentration gradient along the ingot, based on the initial concentration of impurities [22].

Table 5 shows the equilibrium segregation coefficient, solid solubility and melt diffusion coefficient for some important transition metal impurities in silicon (from [23]). For the elements with high diffusion coefficient one also have to consider back diffusion, the diffusion of impurities from the crucible wall and into the solid silicon during solidification, and cooldown of the ingot. In Figure 1, the characteristic shape of the contaminated zone by iron is shown as the minority carrier lifetime profile in the cross section of an ingot [24]. The model is based on Shockley Read Hall (SRH) recombination. Olsen et al. [20] showed that by using clean CZ crucibles in the DS process, the minority carrier lifetime could be increased ten times.

Other important impurities are C and N that will form solid particles in the ingot when their level exceeds the solubility limit. C will form SiC particles while N will form Si_3N_4 particles [25]. Figure 2 shows the shape and morphology of these particles. Nitrogen enters the melt from the dissolution of the nitride coating. Carbon has a more complex cicle. Oxygen that enters the melt from the melt will evaporate and react with the graphite parts in the furnace and form CO that goes into the melt. Other sources of C are the feedstock and graphite dust from the interior of the furnace.

Fig. 1. Distribution of lifetime limited by iron based on SRH recombination model [24].

Table 5. Equilibrium segregation coefficient (k^0), solid solubility (S) and melt diffusion coefficient (D_l) for some important transition metal impurities in silicon (from [23]).

Element	k^0	S	D_l
B	0.8	6.0×10^{20}	2.4×10^{-4}
P	0.5	1.3×10^{21}	5.1×10^{-4}
Ti	3.6×10^{-6}	2.1×10^{13}	3.6×10^{-9}
Cr	1.1×10^{-5}	3.1×10^{14}	2.3×10^{-6}
Fe	8.0×10^{-6}	2.9×10^{15}	4.1×10^{-6}
Ni	3.0×10^{-5}	5.0×10^{17}	3.8×10^{-5}
Cu	1.5×10^{-5}	8.0×10^{17}	1.7×10^{-4}

Fig. 2. SiC growth on Si_3N_4 needles [25].

C. *The Czochralski process*

In the Czochralski process, the ingot is pulled from the melt and is therefore newer in contact with the crucible. The crucible and other materials in the furnace usually have lower levels of impurities than in the DS process. The pressure is relatively low, i.e. 20 mbar, compared to 1000-6000 mbar in the DS process, resulting in an efficient flushing of the melt surface and practical no C pick up. The crucible is not coated, resulting in relatively higher levels of oxygen than in the DS process. The crucible is gradually dissolving and thereby adding impurities to the melt. The dissolution rate was measured by Muhe and Muller [26], to be in the range of 10-30 μm/hour. This results in dissolution of approximately 100 g quartz in a 100 kg melt during 1 run, and addition of 0.0015 ppm Ti if we use the values from Table 4. Due to the low distribution coefficient for Ti and other metallic impurities ($\sim 10^{-4}$ or lower), the contamination from the crucible is not significant for a normal run without recharging and pulling of multiple ingots from the same crucible.

IV. IMPURITIES DURING WAFERING AND SOLAR CELL PROCESSING

After the silicon ingot is grown, it proceeds through various steps including wafer sawing, cleaning, etching, diffusion, screen printing and testing. Throughout this process, it is crucial to maintain the purity of the silicon wafer. One of the causes of contamination is the process baths, where wafers are dipped into water and/or chemicals for etching and/or cleaning. The tanks, silicon wafer carriers and handling tools may be made from industrial-grade (IG) materials that desorb impurities, thereby contaminating the baths. Alternatively, the impurities may be extracted from common plastics used in the IG plumbing components or chemical containers [27]. Factors affecting the deposition of impurities on the silicon wafers are: i) the concentration of impurities in the bath, ii) the removal speed of the wafers from the bath, iii) the properties of the liquid including surface tension, density and viscosity. Johnson et al. [27] have pointed out that the first factor has the most significant effect. Graff [28] has reported on different types of contamination during silicon device fabrication. He has reported on liquid-phase contamination of transition metals with higher electronegativity than silicon during wet processing via replating of the metal [28].

There are currently two main sawing technologies: i) the loose abrasive, and ii) fixed abrasive. The former uses SiC particles carried by oil or water slurry. This process gives significant thickness variation and has environmental impact due to the slurries and chemicals used to clean the wafer surfaces after cutting. Furthermore, the technology has the disadvantage of silicon swarf containing SiC particles mixed with silicon powder and other organic coolants, which makes it difficult to filter and separate the particles. Fixed abrasive diamond wire sawing gives thinner wafers and the possibility of recycling the silicon swarf after cutting (no SiC particles are involved with this process). Furthermore, the process uses less

oil based slurries and wafer cleaning chemicals [29]. During fixed abrasive diamond wire sawing coolant mix such as diethylene glycol (DEG) which is toxic, polyethylene glycol (PEG) and water are used. The resulting silicon sludge (or swarf) is highly contaminated with these organic fluids and metallic impurities, such as iron and nickel from the wire core and the electroplated nickel coating used to fasten the diamond particles.

Dhamrin et al. [29] studied impurities in recycled silicon swarf from diamond wire sawing process. They found that CO and N_2 had almost the same evolution all over the temperature range 100-1000°C. The total oxygen content was found to be below 5%. Figure 3 shows the concentration of metallic impurities measured in the swarf before and after the recycling procedures. It was shown that Ni does not significantly affect the electrical properties of the material (e.g. minority carrier diffusion length). Carbon content, on the other hand, was very high before and after the recycling procedures. The diffusion length measurements showed that C had a detrimental role.

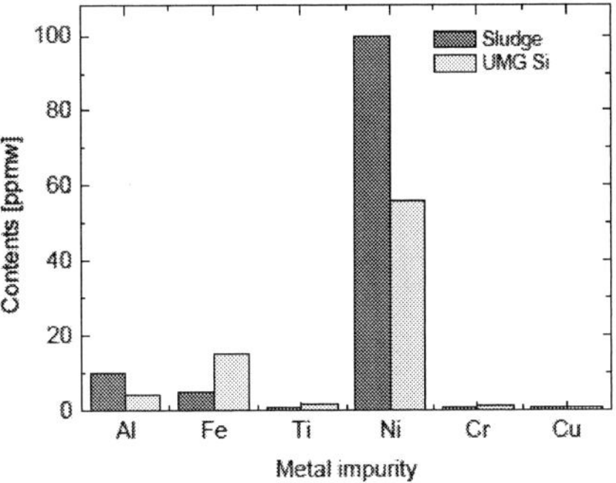

Fig. 3. Concentration of metal impurities measured in the initial silicon swarf (sludge) and after recycling procedures (UMG Si) [29].

During solar cell processing, the wafer undergoes different heat treatments, i.e. emitter diffusion (the most used gases are BBr_3 for n-type base wafer and $POCl_3$ for p-type) which is usually done around 900°C (preferable 1000°C for BBr_3) for 30 min in so-called *tube furnaces*; during antireflection coating (ARC) which is done by, typically, silicon nitride (SiN_x) deposited by plasma-enhanced chemical vapour deposition (PECVD) at around 400°C; and finally metal contacts deposition by means of different pastes and temperatures around 300-400°C. The cleanliness of the furnaces and tools used during these processes plays a crucial role for the impurity contamination, especially the transition metals. Metallic impurities, in fact, can easily diffuse in the silicon bulk and the kinetics of the process is hampered by high temperatures (e.g. above 200°C).

VI. CHARACTERIZATION OF IMPURITIES IN SILICON SOLAR CELLS

Crystalline silicon purity of 99.9999% (6N) or better is required for solar cell fabrication, which means that the total impurity concentration is below 1ppmw. Therefore, accurate measurement of a wide range of impurities in this low level is necessary when studying PV silicon. There are several analytical methods to analyze impurities in silicon. Currently the most used are: neutron activation analysis (NAA), secondary ion mass spectrometry (SIMS), glow discharge mass spectrometry (GDMS), inductively coupled plasma mass spectrometry (ICPMS) and Fourier transform infrared spectrometry (FTIR). Each method has advantages and drawbacks, and the choice of the best method depends on several factors, e.g. the type-, amount- and chemical state of the impurity to be analyzed, the size and shape of the material to be analyzed (e.g. small feedstock chunk or powder, thick quartz crucible materials, thin silicon wafer etc). FTIR is mostly used to measure dissolved oxygen and carbon impurities. NAA, SIMS, GDMS and ICPMS are used when a wide range of elements must be analyzed. They give accurate results both for the doping elements and transition metals. The characteristics of these analytical methods have been recently reviewed by Hockett [30]. NAA can analyze a few grams (typically less than 0.5 cm^3 volume). It is among the tools with the lowest detection limits. However, NAA requires access to neutron activation facility and long analysis time. SIMS has vey good lateral- and depth resolution. It analyzes an area of 10-100 mm^2 but it is less sensitive than NAA and GDMS. ICPMS can analyze an area of the vicinity of few cm. ICPMS have a high detection capability of few ppbw. On the other hand, it requires dissolution of the samples, which involves use of acids (e.g. HF and NO_3). Therefore, attention must be used to not introduce contamination during sample preparation. This is avoided with GDMS measurements. GDMS can analyze in the vicinity of few mm and has detection limits of few ppbw.

Recently, the correction factors for quantitative analysis of silicon matrices have been reported and this enhances the accuracy of the method [31]. Generally the challenges with the analytical tools in PV are many, e.g. representative sampling, impurity level, -type and –distribution may vary from matrix to matrix, sensitivity and stability of the method, etc. One should keep all these factors in mind when choosing the measurement tool.

Finally, as new processes for silicon feedstock production, crystallization methods and solarcell architectures are being developed the analytical tool should follow a similar development.

VI. CONCLUSION

Many types of impurity enter the material during the silicon solar cell process steps from silicon production and refining, crystallization, wafering and cell processing.

The levels and chemical states of these impurities may vary significantly. Some impurities, mainly the transition metals, can be easily removed during crystallization and/or solar cell processing. As the solar cell processes are being developed higher levels of metallic impurities (e.g. Fe and Cu) can be allowed. However, the processes also contaminate the material in different ways.

Since these impurities impair the electrical properties of the final solar cell, it is important to be aware of their sources and levels. Furthermore, it is important to consider their environmental impact.

As new methods (for production, crystallization and manufacturing) are developed, improvements of the analytical methods for impurity detection should also follow.

ACKNOWLEDGEMENT

MDS thanks the "Norwegian Research Centre for Solar Cell Technology" (project nr 193829), a Centre for Environment-friendly Energy Research co-sponsored by the Norwegian Research Council, research- and industry partners in Norway.

REFERENCES

[1] A.A. Istratov, T. Buonassisi, M.D. Pickett, M. Heuer, E.R. Weber, *Materials Science and Engineering B*, vol. 134, pp. 282-286, 2006.

[2] G. Coletti, Impurities in silicon and their impact on solar cell performance, PhD Thesis, Utrecht University, 2012.

[3] G. Coletti, Sensitivity of state-of-the-art and high efficiency crystalline silicon solar cells to metal impurities, *Progress in Photovoltaics: Research and Applications*, DOI: 10.1002/pip.2195, 2012.

[4] A. Schei, J.K. Tuset, H. Tveit, Production of High Silicon Alloys, TapirForlag, 1998.

[5] K. Aasly, Properties and behavior of quartz for the silicon process, PhD Thesis, NTNU, 2008.

[6] V. Myrvågnes, Analyses and characterization of fossil carbonaceous materials for silicon production, PhD Thesis, NTNU, 2008.

[7] E.H. Myrhaug, H. Tveit, Material Balance of Trace Elements in the Ferrosilicon and Silicon Processes, Electric Furnace conference proceedings, vol. 58, 2000.

[8] E. Dal Martello, Study of the impurities behavior from raw materials to poly-silicon, PhD Thesis, NTNU, 2012.

[9] A.F.B. Braga, P.R. Zampieri, J.M. Bacchin, P.R. Mei, New processes for the production of solar-grade polycrystalline silicon: A review, *Solar Energy Materials & Solar Cells*, vol. 92, p.418, 2008.

[10] M.G. Muller, R. Sonnenschein, P. Woditsch, Silicon for photovoltaic applications, *Materials Science and Engineering B*, vol. 134, p. 257, 2006.

[11] E. Schindlbeck, Wacker polysilicon, Alternative Energies Conference proceedings, Paris, 2007.

[12] G. Tranell, M. Di Sabatino, R. Tronstad, *Silicon feedstock for solar cells – availability, quality criteria and future production routes"*, 4th Int workshop on Crystalline Silicon Solar Cells (CSSC4), Taipei (Taiwan), 2010.

[13] J. Safarian, M. Tangstad, Vacuum Refining of Molten Silicon, *Metallurgical and Materials Transactions B*, Vol. 43, pp. 1427-1445, 2012.

[14] Y.V. Meteleva-Fischer, Y. Yang, R. Boom, B. Kraaijveld, H. Kuntzel, Slag treatment followed by acid leaching as a route to solar grade silicon, *Journal of Metals*, vol. 64, pp. 957-967, 2012.

[15] N. Yuge, H. Baba, Y. Sagaguchi, K. Nishikawa, H. Terashima, F. Aratani, Purification of metallurgical silicon up to solar grade, *Solar Energy Materials & Solar Cells*, vol. 34, p. 243, 1994.

[16] E.F. Nordstrand and M. Tangstad, Removal of Boron from Silicon by Moist Hydrogen Gas, *Metallurgical and Materials Transactions B*, Vol. 43, pp. 814-822, 2012.

[17] K. Suzuki, T. Sugiyama, K. Takano, N. Sano, Thermodynamics for removal of boron from metallurgical silicon by flux treatment , *J. Jpn. Inst. Met.*, vol. 54, pp. 168-172, 1990.

[18] E. Krystad, K. Tang, G. Tranell, The kinetics of boron transfer in slag refining of silicon, *Journal of Metals*, vol. 64, pp. 968-972, 2012.

[19] J. Safarian, G. Tranell, M. Tangstad, Thermodynamic and Kinetic Behavior of B and Na Through the Contact of B-Doped Silicon with Na_2O-SiO_2 Slags, *Metallurgical and Materials Transactions B*, Vol. 44, pp. 571-583, 2013.

[20] E. Olsen and E. Øvrelid, Silicon Nitride Coating and Crucible-Effects of Using Upgraded Materials in the Casting of Multicrystalline Silicon Ingots, *Progress in Photovoltaics: Research and Applications*, vol. 16, pp. 93-100, 2008.

[21] M. Syvertsen, K. Tang, C. Modanese, M. Di Sabatino, R. Fagerberg, Model for distribution of dissolved oxygen in directionally solidified silicon, 27th European PVSEC conference proceedings, Hamburg (Germany), pp- 1887-1890, 2011.

[22] E. Øvrelid, B. Geerligs, A. Wærnes, O. Raaness, I. Solheim, R. Jensen, S. Santeen, B. Wiersma, 8th Silicon for the Chemical Industry conference, Trondheim (Norway), pp. 223-234, 2006.

[23] A. Mühlbauer, Technological data, from Landolt-Börnstein database, Springer-Verlag publ., DOI: 10.1007/b53031, 1998.

[24] Y. Boulfrad, G. Stokkan, M. Mhamdi, E. Øvrelid, L. Arnberg, Modeling of lifetime distribution in a multicrystalline silicon ingot, *Solid state Phenomena*, vol. 178, 507-512, 2011.

[25] A.K. Søyland, E.J. Øvrelid, T.A. Engh, O. Lohne, J.K. Tuset, Ø. Gjerstad, SiC and Si3N4 inclusions in multicrystalline silicon ingots, *Materials Science in Semiconductor Processing*, vol. 7, pp. 39-43, 2004.

[26] A. Muhe and G. Muller, Quantitative optical in-situ measurement of the dissolution rate of silica crucible in the silicon Czochralski process, *Materials Science in Semiconductor Processing*, vol. 3, pp. 185-189, 2000.

[27] M.W. Johnson, C.W. Extrand, A. Gildor, S. Tison, Deposition of contaminants on silicon media during wet processing, *Future Photovoltaics*, August 2011.

[28] K. Graff, Metal impurities in silicon-device fabrication, Springer (Berlin), 2000.

[29] M. Dhamrin, T. Saitoh and K. Kamisako, Recycling of silicon powder retrieved from diamond wire slicing kerf, 25th European PVSEC conference proceedings, Valencia (Spain), pp.1600-1603, 2010.

[30] R.S. Hockett, Advanced analytical techniques for solar-grade feedstock, in Advanced Silicon Materials, Ed. by Pizzini, p.215, 2012.

[31] M. Di Sabatino, A.L. Dons, J. Hinrichs, L. Arnberg, Determination of relative sensitivity factors for trace element analysis in PV-silicon by fast-flow glow discharge mass spectrometer, *Spectrochimica Acta Part B*, vol. 66, pp. 144-148, 2011.

Investigation of Lifetime-Limiting Defects After High-Temperature Phosphorus Diffusion in High-Iron-Content Multicrystalline Silicon

David P. Fenning, Annika S. Zuschlag, Jasmin Hofstetter, Alexander Frey, Mariana I. Bertoni, Giso Hahn, and Tonio Buonassisi

Abstract—**Phosphorus diffusion gettering of multicrystalline silicon solar cell materials generally fails to produce material with minority-carrier lifetimes that approach that of gettered monocrystalline wafers, due largely to higher levels of contamination with metal impurities and a higher density of structural defects. Higher gettering temperatures should speed the dissolution of precipitated metals by increasing their diffusivity and solubility in the bulk, potentially allowing for improved gettering. In this paper, we investigate the impact of gettering at higher temperatures on low-purity multicrystalline samples. To analyze the gettering response, we measure the spatially resolved lifetime and interstitial iron concentration by microwave photoconductance decay and photoluminescence imaging, and the structural defect density by Sopori etching and large-area automated quantification. Higher temperature phosphorus diffusion gettering is seen to improve metal-limited multicrystalline materials dramatically, especially in areas of low etch pit density. In areas of high as-grown dislocation density in the multicrystalline materials, it appears that higher temperature phosphorus diffusion gettering reduces the etch pit density, but leaves higher local concentrations of interstitial iron, which degrade lifetime.**

Index Terms—**Dislocation density, iron gettering, minority-carrier lifetime, phosphorus diffusion, silicon solar cells.**

I. Introduction

PHOSPHORUS diffusion gettering (PDG) of metal impurities is a kinetically limited process in multicrystalline

Manuscript received June 16, 2013; revised March 3, 2014; accepted March 11, 2014. Date of current version April 18, 2014. This work, conducted at the Massachusetts Institute of Technology, was supported in part by the National Science Foundation and the Department of Energy under Grant NSF CA EEC-1041895. Samples were made within the SolarFocus project (0327650H), financed by the German Federal Ministry for the Environment, Nature Conservation and Nuclear Safety. The work of D. P. Fenning was supported by a Martin Family Fellowship, the work of A. S. Zuschlag was supported by the Ministry of Science, Research, and the Arts of Baden-Württemberg, Germany, and the work of J. Hofstetter was supported by the Alexander von Humboldt Foundation through a Feodor Lynen Postdoctoral Fellowship.

D. P. Fenning is with the Massachusetts Institute of Technology, Cambridge, MA 02139 USA, and also with the Department of Nanoengineering, University of California San Diego, La Jolla, CA 92093 USA (e-mail: dfenning@alum.mit.edu).

A. S. Zuschlag, A. Frey, and G. Hahn are with the Department of Physics, University of Konstanz, Konstanz 78457, Germany (e-mail: annika.zuschlag@uni-konstanz.de; alexander.frey@uni-konstanz.de; giso.hahn@uni-konstanz.de).

J. Hofstetter and T. Buonassisi are with the Massachusetts Institute of Technology, Cambridge, MA 02139 USA (e-mail: jhofstet@mit.edu; buonassisi@mit.edu).

M. I. Bertoni is with the Department of Electrical, Computer and Energy Engineering, Arizona State University, Tempe, AZ 85287 USA (e-mail: bertoni@asu.edu).

Color versions of one or more of the figures in this paper are available online at http://ieeexplore.ieee.org.

Digital Object Identifier 10.1109/JPHOTOV.2014.2312485

silicon (mc-Si) because the high contamination levels in mc-Si generally exceed the solid solubility at process temperatures [1], [2]. While there are many demands on a phosphorus diffusion profile designed for a high-performance emitter [3], such as achieving a low emitter saturation current, high V_{oc}, and good blue response, iron typically dominates the minority-charge carrier lifetime in the bulk in p-type mc-Si [4]. Current PDG of contaminated mc-Si solar cell materials generally fails to remove significant amounts of precipitated iron [5] and produces material with minority-carrier lifetimes that do not approach that of phosphorus-diffused monocrystalline wafers [6].

Because of the Arrhenius relationship of impurity diffusivity and solubility, higher gettering temperatures should markedly accelerate dissolution of precipitated metals [7]. Recently, confirmation of the improved gettering of precipitated metals at higher temperature has been found by synchrotron-based X-ray fluorescence microscopy [8], [9]. However, in the literature, mixed lifetime results have been seen when performing PDG at higher temperatures. For example, Ballif *et al.* [10] saw lifetime degradation using gettering temperatures above about 875°C in material from the very bottom of a p-type cast multi ingot, suggesting that a high dislocation density and dissolving precipitates could be responsible for the increased recombination activity. An order of magnitude higher interstitial iron concentration was seen after diffusion at 950°C compared with a 830°C diffusion. Alternatively, Möller *et al.* [11]–[13] and Macdonald and Cuevas [14] point to the impact of oxygen precipitates, dislocation decoration with metals, and a rise in dislocation density during annealing to account for lower lifetimes after higher temperature processing. Franke [15] also found a higher dislocation density with higher temperature diffusions in Czochralski (Cz) material. On the other hand, Peters *et al.* [16] showed that millisecond lifetimes could be maintained in float-zone silicon, even with fast ramping rates of roughly 100 K/s using rapid thermal processing, indicating that the existing defects in multicrystalline and Cz materials cause degradation. In this paper, we investigate the impact and limitations of gettering at higher temperatures in high-iron mc-Si, applying detailed microcharacterization to assess potential lifetime-limiting defects, specifically interstitial iron and dislocations.

II. Methods

Seven adjacent wafers along the ingot height (sister wafers) were selected from the top ($\approx$90% ingot height) of a

TABLE I
SQUARE-ROOT-WEIGHTED HARMONIC MEAN LIFETIME AND AREA FRACTION WITH ETCH PIT DENSITY $> 10^6$ CM^{-2}

	As-Grown	820°C	870°C	920°C	920°C N$_2$ + 820°C	920°C + 820°C	920°C + LTA
Sheet Resistance (Ω/sq.)		62.6 ± 1.6	23.2 ± 0.6	10.6 ± 0.2	67.6 ± 1.7	60.3 ± 1.3	11.5 ± 0.1
Post-PDG Avg. Lifetime (μs)		9.6	17.0	14.2	14.7	23.4	22.2
Area Fraction with $> 10^6$ cm^{-2} EPD	0.31	0.24	0.18	0.12	0.26	0.14	0.10
Reduction from As-Grown	–	23%	42%	61%	16%	55%	68%

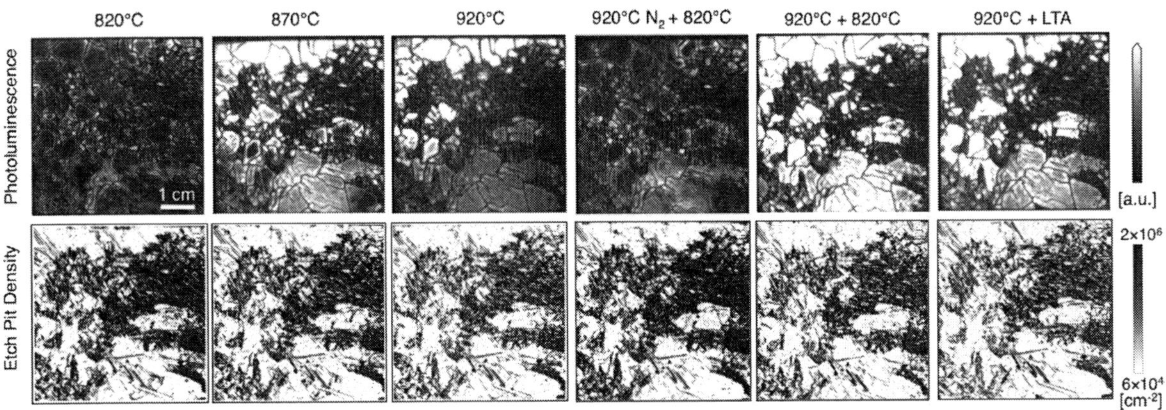

Fig. 1. Photoluminescence images are shown in the first row as a function of sample gettering conditions. Samples are $\approx 5 \times 5$ cm^2. Quantified EPD maps after a 30-s Sopori etch are shown in the second row.

boron-doped mc-Si ingot intentionally contaminated with 20 ppma Fe. Details on the metal concentration in this ingot can be found in [17]. The total Fe concentration in these wafers is about 10^{15} atoms/cm^3. Such high iron concentrations can be found readily in the edge regions of cast multicrystalline ingots [18] that do not use a high-purity crucible and coating [19].

After saw-damage etching and cleaning, the as-grown density of structural defects was measured by performing a 30-s Sopori etch [20] on one of the wafers followed by optical scanning using a flatbed scanner and automated etch pit counting [21].

Single-step phosphorus diffusions were carried out on three sister wafers at different gettering temperatures, namely 820°C, 870°C, and 920°C. Three additional sister samples had two-step gettering processes: one was annealed at 920°C in nitrogen prior to 820°C POCl$_3$ deposition and gettering (designated 920°C N$_2$ + 820°C), the second was gettered at 920°C followed by cooling of several °C/min within the furnace to 600°C and a low-temperature anneal at 600°C for 60 min (920°C + LTA), while the third was P-diffused at 920°C, etched off, and P-diffused again at 820°C (920°C + 820°C). The duration of each P-diffusion step (deposition + drive-in) was about an hour in each case, except the 920°C N$_2$ + 820°C where the P-diffusion was shorter ($\approx$45 min). The resulting emitter sheet resistances are listed in Table I.

After the gettering steps were completed, the emitter was etched off in preparation for photoluminescence imaging (PLI) and microwave photoconductance decay (μ-PCD) lifetime measurements. Finally, defect etching and full-area etch pit density (EPD) quantification was performed on all gettered samples.

III. RESULTS

A. Lifetime Impact of One- and Two-Step High-Temperature Gettering

Photoluminescence images of all gettered samples are shown in the top row of Fig. 1 with all images scaled to the same limits. The sample surfaces were passivated with quinhydrone methanol [22] for the measurement.

One can see immediately from the PLI of the 820°C, 870°C, and 920°C single-step gettering samples shown on the top left that the band-to-band photoluminescence signal, and, by proxy, the bulk lifetime, is strongly influenced by the peak phosphorus diffusion temperature, as reported previously [9]. The 870°C and 920°C processes result in significantly enhanced signal across much of the sample area. This observation is supported by the PLI of the two-step processes as well. The two samples gettered with their phosphorus diffusion conducted at 920°C, on the far right of Fig. 1, show strongly improved lifetime over the 920°C N$_2$ + 820°C sample phosphorus diffused at 820°C.

The local response to higher gettering temperatures within each sample, however, is seen to be strongly dependent on the local structural defect density. Comparing the PLI in Fig. 1 with the EPD maps below reveals that regions of low structural defect density show excellent response to the higher temperature gettering step. However, the heavily dislocated region in the upper right of the samples, for example, degrades somewhat during the single-step 920°C process. The dislocation density is known to play a crucial role in determining the gettering response with improved gettering often seen in areas of low dislocation density [4], [23]–[25].

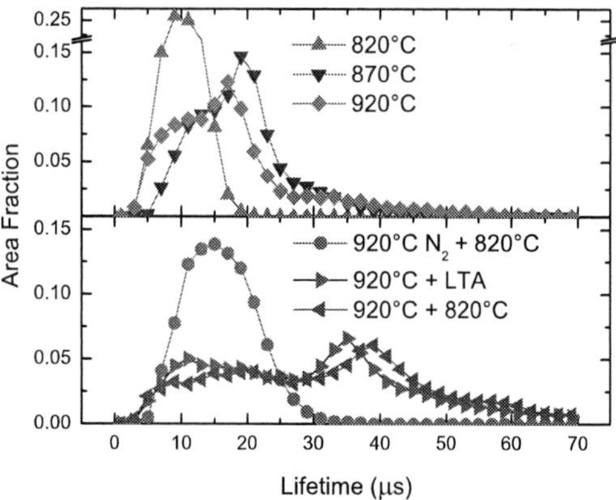

Fig. 2. Lifetime histograms from μ-PCD measurements after gettering. A high-lifetime tail develops in the lifetime distribution by moving to higher phosphorus diffusion temperatures in single-step processes, but by 920°C, this lifetime improvement begins to be offset by degradation in other areas of the sample. The highest lifetimes come from two-step processes where a 920°C P-diffusion step is followed by a lower temperature P-diffusion step or a low-temperature anneal.

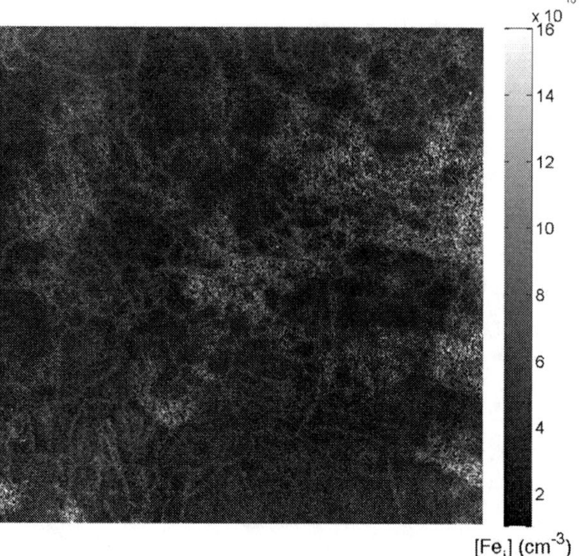

Fig. 3. Iron imaging of the 920°C + 820°C sample by photoconductance-calibrated photoluminescence reveals high local interstitial iron concentration remaining after gettering in the vicinity of structural defects.

Adding a lower temperature step after a 920°C phosphorus diffusion improves lifetime significantly. Comparing the PLI of the single-step 920°C sample with the two rightmost samples phosphorus diffused at 920°C but with lower temperature secondary steps reveals that essentially all areas respond positively to a high-temperature phosphorus diffusion followed by a lower temperature process.

Quantitative spatially resolved lifetime measurements on all samples were obtained before PLI by μ-PCD lifetime measurements with the samples passivated with iodine–ethanol. Spatially resolved lifetimes in the as-grown sample were below 2 μs (not shown). The lifetime histograms from the spatially resolved measurement for the gettered samples are shown in Fig. 2, and the square-root-weighted harmonic mean lifetime for each sample, calculated as $\frac{1}{\sqrt{\tau_{av}}} = \frac{1}{n}\Sigma\frac{1}{\sqrt{\tau_i}}$, which is proportional to the harmonic mean minority-carrier diffusion length and a strong predictor of cell performance [26]–[28], is reported in Table I.

After gettering at the baseline temperature of 820°C, the lifetime is tightly distributed with a calculated average of 9.6 μs, as seen in Fig. 2 (upward triangles) and in Table I. The 920°C N$_2$ + 820°C improves the average lifetime to 14.7 μs, while maintaining a relatively tight distribution (circles). By increasing the phosphorus diffusion temperature to 870°C, the majority of the lifetime distribution shifts to higher values with a high-lifetime tail developing (downward triangles). Compared with the 820°C sample, the average lifetime of the 870°C sample almost doubles to 17.0 μs. From comparison with the PLI in Fig. 1, it is clear that this high-lifetime tail comes from the large-grain areas of low dislocation density. Moving to a 920°C diffusion produces primarily an increase in variation in lifetime across the sample (diamonds). The high-lifetime tail is extended with values reaching 70 μs, but a significant fraction of the wafer degrades with respect to the 870°C lifetime distribution, falling below 15 μs. In comparison with the 870°C PDG, the square-root-weighted harmonic root mean lifetime after 920°C PDG falls to 14.2 μs.

Significant increases in the lifetime distribution are seen by adding a lower temperature step after a 920°C PDG. Both the addition of a low-temperature anneal at 600 °C (22.2 μs average) or an etched off and PDG at 820°C (23.4 μs average) produce superior lifetime response.

B. Interstitial Iron Imaging After Gettering

To better understand the effects of the two-step gettering processes, interstitial iron imaging was performed at low-level injection by the iron–boron pair dissociation method [29] on the highest lifetime sample, the 920°C + 820°C sample. Only in this sample did the injection level under laser illumination easily surpass the onset of trapping at about $\Delta n = 4 \times 10^{14}$ cm^{-3}, allowing for an appropriate calibration of the PLI signal in the injection regime above trapping following the approach taken by Herlufsen *et al.* [30]. The error in the calibration is estimated to be less than 20%. Iron imaging of the other samples were not possible to calibrate but support the results described next qualitatively.

The calibrated interstitial iron concentration measurement, shown in Fig. 3, provides some insight into the defects underlying the observed lifetime distributions after these alternative gettering processes. By comparison with Fig. 1, it appears that the interstitial iron concentration is especially high near most all regions containing structural defects, both grain boundaries and dislocation clusters, contributing to the low local lifetimes. On the other hand, we can see that the intragranular regions of the larger grains show low interstitial iron concentrations (2–3×10^{10} cm^{-3}) and consequently higher PL signal. The

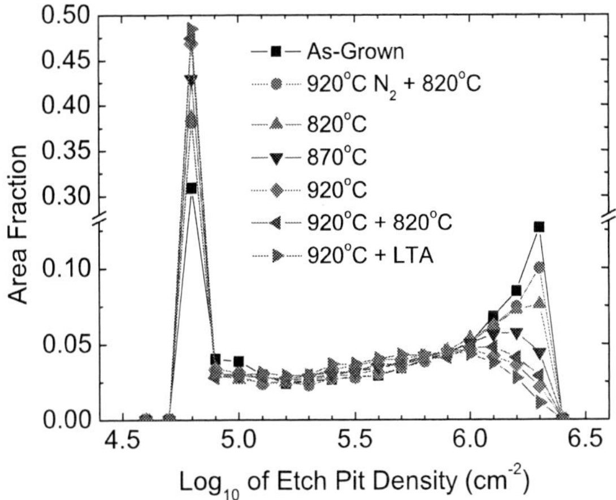

Fig. 4. Histograms of the EPD shown on a log scale. The as-grown distribution is bimodal, with a large number of pixels at the lower limit of the measurement in the large grain, largely dislocation-free areas, but a significant fraction of the wafer contains a high density of etch pits ($> 10^6$ cm^2). Gettering is seen to reduce the frequency of the highest-density areas, while also increasing the fraction of low-density areas. The reduction is monotonic with the phosphorus diffusion temperatures of 820°C, 870°C, and 920°C.

implications of this heterogeneous interstitial iron distribution will be discussed below.

C. Etch Pit Density Reduction During P-Diffusion Gettering

It is interesting to note from the scanner etch pit images of Fig. 1 that the EPD *decreases* as the PDG temperature increases from 820°C to 920°C. The distributions of the EPD in the samples are extracted from the scanner etch pit images of Fig. 1 and plotted in Fig. 4. The upper bound on the observable EPD was limited to $\approx 3 \times 10^6$ cm^2 by the size of the etch pits. The as-grown, 820°C, 870°C, 920°C, and 920°C N$_2$ + 820°C samples were etched at the same time to minimize variation. Scanner images were calibrated to a 2×1 cm^2 optical micrograph of one of the samples. The 920°C + 820°C and 920°C + LTA samples were processed later to add to the dataset and were etched together. A new calibration for these two samples resulted in insignificant differences in the etch pit distribution compared with the calibration used for the other samples, and so the original calibration was used for all samples in Fig. 4. Because all samples were etched prior to diffusion and then again to remove the emitter, the surfaces were effectively chemically polished, reducing false positives in defect detection [21].

The as-grown distribution is largely bimodal, with a significant fraction of the wafer containing $< 10^5$ cm^{-2} and another significant portion containing $> 10^6$ cm^{-2}. Gettering at 820°C increases the frequency below 10^5 cm^{-2} and decreases the frequency of areas containing etch pit densities above $> 10^6$ cm^{-2}. The EPD distribution of the 920°C N$_2$ + 820°C sample is similar to the 820°C standard PDG sample. Higher temperature PDG at 870°C and 920°C monotonically reduces the frequency of the most-heavily pitted areas while increasing the area fraction with few or no pits.

The area fraction in each sample with EPD $> 10^6$ cm^{-2} is reported in Table I, along with a calculation of the percent reduction in area with high EPD with respect to the as-grown sample. The decrease in high-density ($> 10^6$ cm^{-2}) area fraction in the samples with phosphorus diffusion at 920°C sample is dramatic, with 55%, 61%, and 68% reduction with respect to the as-grown sample for the 920°C + 820°C, 920°C, and 920°C + LTA samples, respectively.

To further investigate the wafer-level EPD, 20× optical micrographs were taken in the region from the center right of the wafers that showed areas of both high and low EPD. Fig. 5 shows a portion of the micrographs, with dark areas corresponding to areas of high EPD. The scale bar is 1 mm. Inspection of the images reveals a significant reduction in EPD for all gettered samples with respect to the as-grown sample (which is homogeneously a slightly darker color because of larger surface roughness).

In agreement with the results from the scanner images, the most notable reductions in EPD occur for the higher temperature phosphorus diffusions, including the 870°C sample shown in Fig. 5(c), but especially for the samples with phosphorus diffusions occurring at 920°C, seen in Fig. 5(d), (f), and (g). Comparing the micrographs of the samples that received a 920°C phosphorus diffusion to the as-grown sample reveals a striking decrease in EPD. Importantly, the etch pit distribution in the 920°C N$_2$ + 820°C sample seen in Fig. 5(e) appears much more similar to Fig. 5(b) the 820°C sample than Fig. 5(d) the 920°C.

IV. DISCUSSION

A. Remaining Spatial Nonuniformities in Lifetime Response: Interactions Between Dislocations and Metal Impurities

In a previous study on additional samples from the same ingots and ingot heights, the higher 870°C and 920°C P-diffusion temperatures were found to significantly reduce the size of iron-rich *precipitates* compared with the baseline 820°C phosphorus diffusion temperatures [9]. At higher phosphorus gettering temperatures, more precipitated iron is dissolved and becomes getterable interstitials.

It appears from Fig. 3 that even after 920°C phosphorus diffusion followed by an 820°C diffusion process, there remains a significant amount of iron decorating the structural defects that serves as sources for interstitial injection into the bulk. Some of this iron remains interstitial at the end of the process, having diffused from the structural defects into the surrounding region during processing [31]. The high structural defect density and high interstitial iron concentration lead to low lifetimes after gettering in such regions of the wafer.

While quantitative results were not achieved in iron imaging of the 920°C sample because of trapping effects (not shown), a similarly high local interstitial iron concentration appears to be the cause for degradation in regions rich with structural defects, resulting in the lower average lifetime compared with the 870°C sample despite a much higher lifetime tail.

Adding a lower temperature step after the 920°C phosphorus diffusion appears crucial to ensuring that this mobile, but electronically detrimental, interstitial population is reduced to

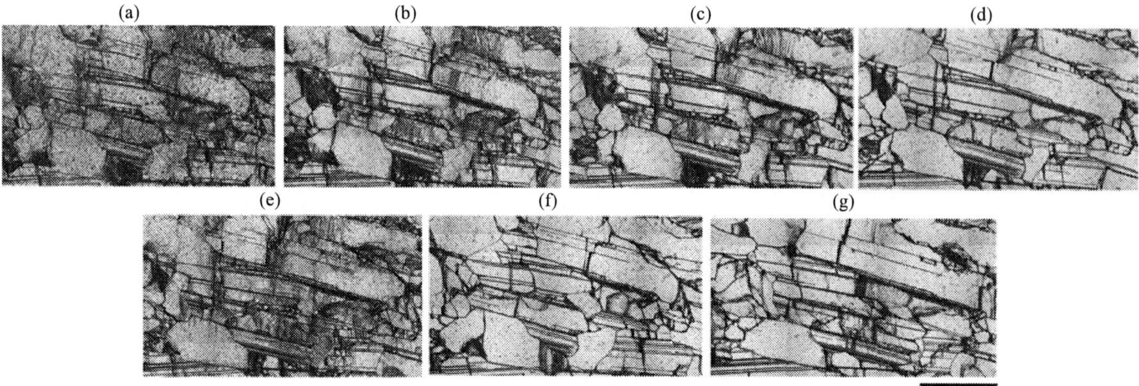

Fig. 5. Optical micrographs of the EPD show a strong correlation with phosphorus diffusion temperature. (a) As-grown. (b) 820°C. (c) 870°C. (d) 920°C. (e) 920°C N_2 + 820°C. (f) 920°C + LTA. (g) 920°C + 820°C. Notably, the 920°C N_2 + 820°C appears more similar to the 820°C sample than the samples phosphorus-diffused at 920°C. Scale bar is 1 mm.

moderate levels before the end of processing, allowing for the highest lifetimes to be achieved in the two-step 920°C PDG processes. Coupling a higher temperature gettering with a lower temperature step is critical, as precipitates remain sources for interstitial injection into the bulk throughout the gettering process and even during firing, the last high-temperature step of the solar cell process.

B. When to Apply Higher Gettering Temperatures

Overall, the mixed performance even within the same material in response to higher temperature processing demands caution. During gettering, the extraction of interstitial iron is effective in intragranular regions with low structural defect density. Thus, in iron-contaminated materials, areas of lower structural defect density that show poor lifetimes in the as-grown material may lead to the highest gettered lifetimes: a reversal is seen in the lifetime contrast across structural defects, save immediately at the defect itself where recombination remains high. This appears to be the case with the heavily Fe-contaminated samples examined here, where one observes that the low as-grown lifetime intragranular regions become the highest gettered lifetime regions after a standard diffusion (cf., lifetime maps in [9] for full comparison). These regions are largely devoid of dislocations or other structural defects that impede gettering [32], demonstrated by dislocation etching and imaging seen in Fig. 1. The lifetime contrast reversal seen here at structural defects in this iron-contaminated mc-Si does not occur, for example, in a study of metal gettering by Bentzen *et al.* in higher quality starting materials [33]. There, the poorest as-grown regions remained the worst areas after gettering.

The presence of higher lifetime denuded zones around structural defects in the as-grown material (see, e.g., [34]) is a potential metric to determine whether higher temperature diffusion will be beneficial. When metals are the principal lifetime-limiting defect in as-grown materials, nucleation and precipitate growth during cooldown from crystallization leads to internal gettering near structural defects, generating higher lifetimes in

areas rich with metal impurities and structural defects [29], [35]. During gettering, these precipitates act as semi-infinite sources for metal point defects, poisoning the local area [31]. In contrast, the worst as-grown areas are dominated by high metal point-defect concentrations, because of a paucity of available nucleation sites. In summary, when lifetime contrast between areas with structural defects and the intragranular bulk reverses after standard gettering, higher temperature phosphorus diffusion may prove useful because the material is likely metal limited.

C. Possible Mechanisms for Change in Etch Pit Density

In the following, it is important to consider whether the EPD corresponds well to the dislocation density. EPD reduction at these relatively low temperatures (below 1000°C) has been observed before by Choi *et al.* [36] during annealing of mc-Si blocks in the presence of a gettering layer, but here we use *standard-thickness wafers*.

The first obvious explanation for a change in EPD is that the effect of the defect etch changes with metal–precipitate decoration, perhaps via a Fermi energy pinning effect. It is also possible that phosphorus pipe-diffusion along dislocations during the annealing influenced defect-etching by altering the local Fermi level. However, these hypotheses are not easy to reconcile with the observation that regions of high EPD remain in all samples. Presumably, if some processing variables were to affect dislocation etching, it would affect all uniformly, which is not our observation. Choi *et al.* [36] also found that the EPD measured for a Secco etch chemistry was the same within experimental error as that found for a Sopori etch chemistry, despite the different etch mechanisms and different energy levels in solution with respect to the Fermi level at the surface.

Furthermore, the sister samples are not perfect controls— the crystal structure changes slightly between each sample— and so care should be taken in interpreting the differences in EPD. The samples order from bottom to top in the ingot was 920°C + LTA, as-grown, 820°C, 870°C, 920°C, 920°C N_2 + 820°C, and 920°C + 820°C. The fact that the EPD reduction in the 920°C N$_2$ + 820°C sample does not continue the trends seen when moving up the ingot, but instead closely resembles the 820°C sample (see Fig. 4), suggests that an overall trend along the ingot height such as metal contamination level cannot explain the differences in EPD distributions after gettering. Likewise, all samples with a phosphorus diffusion at 920°C (the 920°C + LTA, 920°C, and 920°C + 820°C samples) show similar EPD histograms (see Fig. 4) and optical micrographs (see Fig. 5). Apparently, it is the temperature of phosphorus diffusion, rather than the annealing temperature that drives the EPD reduction.

For completeness, we should consider possible mechanisms of long-range dislocation motion that could explain the differences in EPD. Large differences are seen in the etch pit structures between the samples, beyond the simple reduction in number of etch pits (see Fig. 5). Typically, it is considered that homologous temperatures (T/T$_{\text{melting}}$) of 0.8 are required for dislocation climb to occur in silicon, and polygonization and dislocation recovery above these temperatures has been observed in mc-Si [37]. Given that we are operating well below even 1000 $^\circ$C, the significant etch pit redistribution here at phosphorus diffusion temperatures ($0.58 < T/T_m < 0.65$) is surprising. Speculative mechanisms for the significant changes in the etch pit distribution include:

1) Dislocation motion enhanced by the nonequilibrium injection of Si point defects during phosphorus diffusion. As mentioned previously, large EPD reduction was observed in thick slabs (5 mm) of mc-Si during phosphorus diffusion by Choi *et al.* [36], indicating that some other mechanism is active other than, or in addition to, intrinsic point defects to enhance the apparent dislocation motion.

2) A possible reversal of the typical solute-drag effect of dislocations as postulated in [36]. Normally, impurity atoms in solution decorate the dislocation because of the energetically favorable position in the strain field. Dislocation motion is generally slowed by the drag imposed by these solute atoms. However, if during phosphorus diffusion the segregation effect of the gettering layer produces a strong driving force for a net unidirectional flux of impurities to the surface layer, then the impurity atoms collectively may impose a net directional "drag" force act on the dislocation. Such solute-drag reversal has been seen in kinetic Monte Carlo simulations where dislocations moving in a strain field move initially in the direction of nearby impurities [38].

3) The dissolution at high temperature of precipitates decorating the dislocations may unpin the dislocations, allowing the dislocations to move and annihilate. The removal of obstacles pinning dislocations has been previously suggested as a pathway for dislocation recovery based on *in-situ* TEM observations in metals [39].

The possibility of dislocation motion at phosphorus diffusion temperatures warrants further investigation. It is plausible that this effect is simply an artifact of the etching process caused by the change of dislocation metal decoration. Furthermore, confirmation of *dislocation*-density reduction rather than merely EPD reduction is needed, perhaps by photoluminescence measurement of dislocation lines. Unfortunately, the dislocation density in these samples exceeded quantifiable limits when measured by synchrotron-based X-ray topography.

V. Conclusion

Improving lifetime over the entire mc-Si ingot requires an understanding of performance-limiting defects and the development of tailored material-specific defect-engineering approaches. Iron-contaminated materials studied here show strong lifetime improvement with higher gettering temperatures, especially in areas of low dislocation density. Synchrotron-based μ-XRF measurements [9] in samples originating from the same ingot heights as those used here reveal that gettering of precipitated iron improves at these higher temperatures. Coupling higher temperature gettering processes with subsequent lower temperature steps, to avoid degradation because of a high-remaining interstitial impurity concentration, captures the benefit of higher temperature processing that dissolves and getters a higher fraction of the precipitated impurity concentration. As an example, we show here that subsequent low-temperature annealing is effective at further improving lifetime. Alternatively, lower temperature P-diffusion following a high-temperature P-diffusion step produces yet further lifetime benefits, leaving a moderate interstitial iron concentration. Throughput aside, the best performing sample resulted from a sacrificial 920°C P-diffusion targeting impurity-precipitate dissolution, followed by a separate 820°C P-diffusion that lowers final impurity point-defect concentration.

In the most heavily dislocated areas, low lifetimes remain after gettering despite a decrease in the local EPD after P-diffusion at higher temperatures. The reduction in EPD trends monotonically with the P-diffusion temperature, suggesting some interaction with metal gettering, and is most notable in samples with 920°C P-diffusion. Confirmation that this EPD reduction is correlated with dislocation density reduction is still required.

To minimize thermal budgets, higher diffusion temperatures should only be applied when necessary, i.e., to regions of material with high concentrations of iron-rich precipitates, and must be verified on the solar cell level. In multicrystalline materials, a reversal in the lifetime contrast between defect-free and defect-rich areas after gettering may be a good indicator of metal-limited material that can be assumed to respond positively to higher gettering temperatures. A process tradeoff can then be determined between improved average lifetime and lifetime variation across the wafer to optimize the cell efficiency distribution.

Acknowledgment

The authors would like to thank D. Berney Needleman and D. M. Powell for the EPD code support and L. Mahlstaedt for the P-diffusion assistance.

REFERENCES

[1] D. Macdonald, A. Cuevas, A. Kinomura, Y. Nakano, and L. J. Geerligs, "Transition-metal profiles in a multicrystalline silicon ingot," *J. Appl. Phys.*, vol. 97, no. 3, pp. 033523-1–033523-7, 2005.

[2] E. R. Weber, "Transition metals in silicon," *Appl. Phys. A, Mater. Sci. Process.*, vol. 30, no. 1, pp. 1–22, 1983.

[3] A. Dastgheib-Shirazi, M. Steyer, G. Micard, H. Wagner, P. P. Altermatt, and G. Hahn, "Relationships between diffusion parameters and phosphorus precipitation during the POCl$_3$ diffusion process," *Energy Procedia*, vol. 28, pp. 254–262, 2013.

[4] B. Sopori, "Silicon solar-cell processing for minimizing the influence of impurities and defects," *J. Electron. Mater.*, vol. 31, no. 10, pp. 972–980, 2002.

[5] D. P. Fenning, J. Hofstetter, M. I. Bertoni, G. Coletti, B. Lai, C. del Cañizo, and T. Buonassisi, "Precipitated iron: A limit on gettering efficacy in multicrystalline silicon," *J. Appl. Phys.*, vol. 113, no. 4, pp. 044521-1–044521-12, 2013.

[6] G. Coletti, R. Kvande, V. D. Mihailetchi, L. J. Geerligs, L. Arnberg, and E. J. Øvrelid, "Effect of iron in silicon feedstock on p- and n-type multicrystalline silicon solar cells," *J. Appl. Phys.*, vol. 104, no. 10, pp. 104913-1–104913-11, 2008.

[7] P. S. Plekhanov, R. Gafiteanu, U. M. Gösele, and T. Y. Tan, "Modeling of gettering of precipitated impurities from Si for carrier lifetime improvement in solar cell applications," *J. Appl. Phys.*, vol. 86, no. 5, pp. 2453–2458, 1999.

[8] D. Macdonald, S. P. Phang, F. E. Rougieux, S. Y. Lim, D. Paterson, D. L. Howard, M. D. de Jonge, and C. G. Ryan, "Iron-rich particles in heavily contaminated multicrystalline silicon wafers and their response to phosphorus gettering," *Semicond. Sci. Technol.*, vol. 27, pp. 125016-1–125016-5, 2012.

[9] D. P. Fenning, A. S. Zuschlag, M. I. Bertoni, B. Lai, G. Hahn, and T. Buonassisi, "Improved iron gettering of contaminated multicrystalline silicon by high-temperature phosphorus diffusion," *J. Appl. Phys.*, vol. 113, pp. 214504-1–214504-10, 2013.

[10] C. Ballif, S. Peters, D. Borchert, C. Hässler, J. Isenberg, R. Schindler, W. Warta, and G. Willeke, "Lifetime investigations of degradation effects in processed multicrystalline silicon wafers," in *Proc. 17th Eur. Photovoltaic Sol. Energy Conf. Exhib.*, Munich, Germany, 2001, pp. 1818–1821.

[11] H. J. Möller, T. Kaden, S. Scholz, and S. Würzner, "Improving solar grade silicon by controlling extended defect generation and foreign atom defect interactions," *Appl. Phys. A*, vol. 96, no. 1, pp. 207–220, 2009.

[12] H. J. Möller, C. Funke, M. Rinio, and S. Scholz, "Multicrystalline silicon for solar cells," *Thin Solid Films*, vol. 487, no. 1/2, pp. 179–187, 2005.

[13] H. Möller, C. Funke, A. Lawerenz, S. Riedel, and M. Werner, "Oxygen and lattice distortions in multicrystalline silicon," *Sol. Energy Mater. Sol. Cells*, vol. 72, no. 1, pp. 403–416, 2002.

[14] D. Macdonald and A. Cuevas, "The trade-off between phosphorus gettering and thermal degradation in multicrystalline silicon," in *Proc. 16th Eur. Photovoltaic Sol. Energy Conf. Exhib.*, Glasgow, U.K., Jun. 2000, pp. 1707–1710.

[15] D. Franke, "Rise of dislocation density in crystalline silicon wafers during diffusion processing," in *Proc. 3rd World Conf. Photovoltaic Energy Convers.*, Osaka, Japan, May 2003, pp. 1344–1347.

[16] S. Peters, J. Y. Lee, C. Ballif, D. Borchert, S. W. Glunz, W. Warta, and G. Willeke, "Rapid thermal processing: A comprehensive classification of silicon materials," in *Proc. 29th IEEE Photovoltaic Sol. Energy Conf. Exhib.*, New Orleans, LA, USA, May 2002, pp. 214–217.

[17] S. Riepe, I. E. Reis, W. Kwapil, M. A. Falkenberg, J. Schön, H. Behnken, J. Bauer, D. Kreßner-Kiel, W. Seifert, and W. Koch, "Research on efficiency limiting defects and defect engineering in silicon solar cells—Results of the German research cluster SolarFocus," *Phys. Status Solidi (c)*, vol. 8, no. 3, pp. 733–738, 2011.

[18] T. U. Naerland, L. Arnberg, and A. Holt, "Origin of the low carrier lifetime edge zone in multicrystalline PV silicon," *Prog. Photovolt. Res. Appl.*, vol. 17, no. 5, pp. 289–296, 2009.

[19] M. C. Schubert, J. Schön, F. Schindler, W. Kwapil, A. Abdollahinia, B. Michl, S. Riepe, C. Schmid, M. Schumann, S. Meyer, and W. Warta, "Impact of impurities from crucible and coating on mc-silicon quality—The example of iron and cobalt," *IEEE J. Photovoltaics*, vol. 3, no. 4, pp. 1250–1258, Oct. 2013.

[20] B. L. Sopori, "A new defect etch for polycrystalline silicon," *J. Electrochem. Soc.*, vol. 131, no. 3, pp. 667–672, 1984.

[21] D. B. Needleman, H. Choi, D. M. Powell, and T. Buonassisi, "Rapid dislocation-density mapping of as-cut crystalline silicon wafers," *Phys. Status Solidi (RRL)*, vol. 7, no. 12, pp. 1041–1044, 2013.

[22] K. L. Pollock, J. Junge, and G. Hahn, "Detailed investigation of surface passivation methods for lifetime measurements on p-type silicon wafers," *IEEE J. Photovoltaics*, vol. 2, no. 1, pp. 1–6, Jan. 2012.

[23] A. Bentzen, B. G. Svensson, E. S. Marstein, and A. Holt, "The influence of structural defects on phosphorus diffusion in multicrystalline silicon," *Sol. Energy Mater. Sol. Cells*, vol. 90, no. 18/19, pp. 3193–3198, 2006.

[24] O. Schultz, S. W. Glunz, S. Riepe, and G. P. Willeke, "Gettering of multicrystalline silicon for high-efficiency solar cells," in *Proc. 21st Eur. Photovoltaic Sol. Energy Conf. Exhib.*, Dresden, Germany, 2006, pp. 788–791.

[25] M. Kaes, G. Hahn, A. Metz, G. Agostinelli, Y. Ma, J. Junge, A. Zuschlag, and D. Groetschel, "Progress in high efficiency processing of EFG silicon solar cells," in *Proc. 22nd Eur. Photovoltaic Sol. Energy Conf. Exhib.*, Milan, Italy, 2007, pp. 897–902.

[26] J. Isenberg, J. Dicker, and W. Warta, "Averaging of laterally inhomogeneous lifetimes for one-dimensional modeling of solar cells," *J. Appl. Phys.*, vol. 94, no. 6, pp. 4122–4130, 2003.

[27] B. Michl, M. Rüdiger, J. A. Giesecke, M. Hermle, W. Warta, and M. C. Schubert, "Efficiency limiting bulk recombination in multicrystalline silicon solar cells," *Sol. Energy Mater. Sol. Cells*, vol. 98, pp. 441–447, 2012.

[28] H. Wagner, M. Müller, G. Fischer, and P. P. Altermatt, "A simple criterion for predicting multicrystalline Si solar cell performance from lifetime images of wafers prior to cell production," *J. Appl. Phys.*, vol. 114, no. 5, pp. 054501-1–054501-8, 2013.

[29] D. Macdonald, J. Tan, and T. Trupke, "Imaging interstitial iron concentrations in boron-doped crystalline silicon using photoluminescence," *J. Appl. Phys.*, vol. 103, no. 7, pp. 073710-1–073710-7, 2008.

[30] S. Herlufsen, J. Schmidt, D. Hinken, K. Bothe, and R. Brendel, "Photoconductance-calibrated photoluminescence lifetime imaging of crystalline silicon," *Physica Status Solidi RRL*, vol. 2, no. 6, pp. 245–247, 2008.

[31] Y.-C. Fan, J. Tan, S. P. Phang, and D. Macdonald, "Iron imaging in multicrystalline silicon wafers via photoluminescence," in *Proc. 35th IEEE Photovoltaic Sol. Energy Conf. Exhib.*, Honolulu, HI, USA, 2010, pp. 439–442.

[32] A. Bentzen, A. Holt, R. Kopecek, G. Stokkan, J. S. Christensen, and B. G. Svensson, "Gettering of transition metal impurities during phosphorus emitter diffusion in multicrystalline silicon solar cell processing," *J. Appl. Phys.*, vol. 99, no. 9, pp. 093509-1–093509-6, 2006.

[33] A. Bentzen and A. Holt, "Overview of phosphorus diffusion and gettering in multicrystalline silicon," *Mater. Sci. Eng. B*, vol. 159, pp. 228–234, 2009.

[34] J. Haunschild, M. Glatthaar, M. Demant, J. Nievendick, M. Motzko, S. Rein, and E. R. Weber, "Quality control of as-cut multicrystalline silicon wafers using photoluminescence imaging for solar cell production," *Sol. Energy Mater. Sol. Cells*, vol. 94, no. 12, pp. 2007–2012, 2010.

[35] T. Buonassisi, M. D. Pickett, A. A. Istratov, E. Sauer, T. C. Lommasson, E. Marstein, T. Pernau, R. F. Clark, S. Narayanan, S. M. Heald, and E. R. Weber, "Interactions between metals and different grain boundary types and their impact on multicrystalline silicon device performance," in *Proc. 4th World Conf. Photovoltaic Energy Convers.*, Waikoloa, HI, USA, May 2006, pp. 944–947.

[36] H. J. Choi, M. I. Bertoni, J. Hofstetter, D. P. Fenning, D. M. Powell, S. Castellanos, and T. Buonassisi, "Dislocation density reduction during impurity gettering in multicrystalline silicon," *IEEE J. Photovoltaics*, vol. 3, no. 1, pp. 189–198, Jan. 2013.

[37] T. Ervik, M. Kivambe, G. Stokkan, B. Ryningen, and O. Lohne, "High temperature annealing of bent multicrystalline silicon rods," *Acta Materialia*, vol. 60, no. 19, pp. 6762–6769, 2012.

[38] Y. Wang, D. J. Srolovitz, J. M. Rickman, and R. Lesar, "Dislocation motion in the presence of diffusing solutes: A computer simulation study," *Acta Materialia*, vol. 48, no. 9, pp. 2163–2175, 2000.

[39] F. Prinz, A. S. Argon, and W. C. Moffatt, "Recovery of dislocation structures in plastically deformed copper and nickel single crystals," *Acta Metallurgica*, vol. 30, no. 4, pp. 821–830, 1982.

David P. Fenning received the B.S. degree from Stanford University, Stanford, CA, USA, in 2008, and the M.S. and Ph.D. degrees from the Massachusetts Institute of Technology (MIT), Cambridge, MA, USA, in 2010 and 2013, respectively, all in mechanical engineering. His Ph.D. research with the MIT PVLab focused on improving impurity gettering in silicon solar cell materials using defect kinetics simulation and synchrotron-based X-ray characterization.

He is currently a Postdoctoral Researcher with MITs Electrochemical Energy Laboratory, working to develop efficient, low-cost photoelectrochemical devices for water-splitting and CO_2 reduction. He will join the faculty of the Department of Nanoengineering, University of California at San Diego, in 2015, continuing his research in photovoltaics and energy storage technologies.

Mariana I. Bertoni received the B.S. and Diploma degrees in chemical engineering from the Buenos Aires Institute of Technology, Buenos Aires, Argentina, and the Ph.D. degree in materials science and engineering from Northwestern University, Evanston, IL, USA.

She was a Postdoctoral Fellow with Creavis Technologies & Innovation in Germany in 2007 and the Massachusetts Institute of Technology, Cambridge, MA, USA, during 2008–2010. She is currently an Assistant Professor with the School of Electrical Computer and Energy Engineering, Arizona State University, Tempe, AZ, USA. Her research interests include understanding and engineering the defects that govern device performance of photovoltaic materials.

Annika S. Zuschlag was born in Konstanz, Germany, in 1981. She received the Diploma degree in physics from the University of Konstanz, Konstanz, in 2007, where her focus was set on metallic nanostructures and their properties as optical antennas. Since 2007, she has been working toward the Ph.D. degree with the Photovoltaics Division, Department of Physics, University of Konstanz.

She is currently a coordinator of the German research cluster "SolarWinS." Her research interests include defects in crystalline silicon materials, their impact on material quality, and the influence of solar cell processes on defect properties.

Giso Hahn was born in Frankfurt am Main, Germany, in 1969. He received the Diploma degree in physics from the University of Stuttgart, Stuttgart, Germany, in 1995, and the Ph.D. degree in physics from the University of Konstanz, Konstanz, Germany, in 1999.

Since 2009, he has been an Apl. Professor with the Department of Physics, University of Konstanz. His research interests include crystalline silicon materials and solar cell process development, including characterization of promising low-cost materials for photovoltaic applications and the development of adapted solar cell processes for these and other materials.

Dr. Hahn is a member of the scientific committees of various conference series (e.g., IEEE PVSC, EU PVSEC, and SiliconPV) and workshops. Among other scientific and technological achievements, his group is interested in transferring technologies from the laboratory stage to industry.

Jasmin Hofstetter received the degree in physics from Freie Universität Berlin, Berlin, Germany, in 2006 and the Ph.D. degree in photovoltaic solar energy from the Universidad Politcnica de Madrid, Madrid, Spain.

In 2011, she joined the PV Lab, Massachusetts Institute of Technology, Cambridge, MA, USA, as a Postdoctoral Researcher, studying the kinetics of point and structural defects in silicon and in earth-abundant thin-film materials for PV during solar cell processing.

Tonio Buonassisi received the Ph.D. degree in applied science and technology from the University of California at Berkeley, Berkeley, CA, USA, with additional research at the Fraunhofer Institute for Solar Energy Systems and the Max-Planck-Institute for Microstructure Physics.

He is the Head of the Photovoltaic Research Laboratory, Massachusetts Institute of Technology, Cambridge, MA, USA, which combines crystal growth, processing, characterization, defect simulation, and cost-performance modeling to engineer naturally abundant and manufacturable materials into cost-effective, high-performance devices. His research interests include silicon (kerfless absorbers, advanced manufacturing, and defects), Earth-abundant thin films, and high-efficiency concepts.

Alexander Frey received the Diploma degree in physics from the University of Konstanz, Konstanz, Germany, in 2011, where his focus was set on the recombination activity of interstitial iron defects in multicrystalline silicon. Since 2012, he has been working toward the Ph.D. degree with the Department of Photovoltaics, University of Konstanz, where he has been developing high-efficient n-type silicon solar cells with boron emitters from plasma-enhanced chemical vapor deposition layers.

Advanced Bulk Defect Passivation for Silicon Solar Cells

Brett J. Hallam, Phill G. Hamer, Stuart R. Wenham, Malcolm D. Abbott, Adeline Sugianto, Alison M. Wenham, Catherine E. Chan, GuangQi Xu, Jed Kraiem, Julien Degoulange, and Roland Einhaus

Abstract—Through an advanced hydrogenation process that involves controlling and manipulating the hydrogen charge state, substantial increases in the bulk minority carrier lifetime are observed for standard commercial grade boron-doped Czochralski grown silicon wafers from 250–500 μs to 1.3–1.4 ms and from 8 to 550 μs on p-type Czochralski wafers grown from upgraded metallurgical grade silicon. However, the passivation is reversible, whereby the passivated defects can be reactivated during subsequent processes. With appropriate processing that involves controlling the charge state of hydrogen, the passivation can be retained on finished devices yielding independently confirmed voltages on cells fabricated using standard commercial grade boron-doped Czochralski grown silicon over 680 mV. Hence, it appears that the charge state of hydrogen plays an important role in determining the reactivity of the atomic hydrogen and, therefore, ability to passivate defects.

Index Terms—Charge carrier lifetime, hydrogen passivation, photovoltaic cells, silicon.

I. Introduction

THERE is a great need to reduce the cost of photovoltaics, such that solar cells can produce electricity cheaper than conventional fossil fuel technologies. For wafer-based silicon solar cells, there are many approaches which can assist in doing so, such as increasing the efficiency of the solar cells without substantial increases in wafer to cell conversion costs and, therefore, capitalizing on reductions in wafering and encapsulation costs in terms of dollars per Watt. Another approach is to use lower quality silicon wafers which are fabricated at a lower cost, although such wafers typically yield lower efficiency solar cells, which effectively increases the wafer to cell conversion cost and encapsulation costs.

However, there is substantial potential for using silicon wafers of various qualities such as solar grade or upgraded metallurgical grade (UMG) silicon and effectively increasing the quality of such wafers through advanced passivation techniques, therefore allowing higher efficiency devices to be fabricated on what are typically seen as cheaper, lower quality silicon wafers.

In particular, UMG approaches for silicon purification have the potential to be used to fabricate high-efficiency silicon solar cells if processes and technologies can be developed and adapted to the material. UMG silicon typically shows the presence of various contaminants such as transition metals due to the purification methods used such as plasma or aluminum purification [1]–[5]. Due to the high recombination activity of transition metals and their precipitants, such impurities can limit the minority carrier lifetime in UMG silicon, although phosphorus gettering is often used during cell processing to improve the lifetime by removing such contaminants [4]–[8].

In addition, UMG silicon typically contains both n- and p-type dopants, and therefore, both n- and p-type UMG silicon may be subject to the formation of boron–oxygen (B–O) complexes if sufficient quantities of oxygen are present in the silicon [7], [9]–[11]. Furthermore, the presence of contaminants may lead to the formation of crystallographic defects during the crystal growth process leading to additional recombination sites [12], [13]. Subsequently, the passivation of B–O complex defects, metallic impurities, and crystallographic defects is of particular importance for solar cells fabricated using UMG silicon.

However, it is not only UMG silicon which is subject to the presence of transition metals and other impurity-related recombination sites. For example, boron-doped solar grade Czochralski (CZ) and multicrystalline silicon are also subject to the formation of B–O complexes, and the grain boundaries of multicrystalline silicon can be decorated with metallic impurities such as Fe [9], [14]. Therefore, such material can also benefit from improved passivation techniques.

A. Hydrogen in Silicon

The properties and interactions of hydrogen in silicon have been widely studied over multiple decades with beneficial effects shown as early as 1976 [15]. Particularly in the fabrication of multicrystalline silicon solar cells, use of hydrogen containing antireflection coatings, such as plasma-enhanced chemical vapor deposition (PECVD) SiN, is essential for bulk and surface passivation [16]. For monocrystalline silicon, recent studies have shown that hydrogen plays a critical role in the permanent

Manuscript received June 14, 2013; revised August 5, 2013 and September 4, 2013; accepted September 9, 2013. Date of publication September 27, 2013; date of current version December 16, 2013. This work was supported by Roth&Rau, Suntech Power, and the Australian Government through the Australian Renewable Energy Agency.

B. J. Hallam, P. G. Hamer, S. R. Wenham, M. D. Abbott, A. M. Wenham, C. E. Chan, and G. Xu are with the School of Photovoltaic and Renewable Energy Engineering, University of New South Wales, Kensington, N.S.W. 2052, Australia (e-mail: brett.hallam@unsw.edu.au; phillhamer@gmail.com; stuartwenham@gmail.com; mal.abbott@gmail.com; awenham@gmail.com; catherine.chan@unsw.edu.au; guangqi.xu@unsw.edu.au).

A. Sugianto is with the School of Photovoltaic and Renewable Energy Engineering, University of New South Wales, Kensington, N.S.W. 2052, Australia, and also with the Suntech Power Holdings Co., Ltd, Wuxi 214028, China (e-mail: adeline.sugianto@gmail.com).

J. Kraiem, J. Degoulange, and R. Einhaus are with the Apollon Solar, 69002 Lyon, France (e-mail: kraiem@apollonsolar.com; degoulange@apollonsolar.com; einhaus@apollonsolar.com).

Color versions of one or more of the figures in this paper are available online at http://ieeexplore.ieee.org.

Digital Object Identifier 10.1109/JPHOTOV.2013.2281732

deactivation of B–O complexes [17], [18], although the hydrogen content in the dielectric layer alone does not influence the deactivation process, with many factors affecting the passivation [19]–[21].

While the benefits of hydrogen in silicon are widely accepted, the diffusion and passivation mechanisms and dependence on material parameters are reported to be poorly understood with many contradictory theories and large variations in the results and subsequent interpretations reported in the literature [22]–[26]. The complications arise because 1) atomic hydrogen interacts with the lattice and virtually all impurities and defects within the silicon [27]; 2) it is difficult to measure/detect hydrogen in silicon; and 3) hydrogen can be incorporated into films unintentionally during a variety of processing steps [24].

The diffusivity of hydrogen is affected by temperature, electric fields, crystallographic defects, and the type and concentration of almost all impurities and defects within the silicon [23], [25], [28]–[33]. As a result, many experiments and theories yield conflicting results [25] and an uncertainty in the diffusivity of hydrogen with variations of more than five orders of magnitude for a given temperature [22], [25], [26], [32], [34], [35].

Perhaps, one of the least recognized properties of hydrogen in silicon is its ability to assume different charge states, either taking on a positive (H^+), neutral (H°), or negative (H^-) charge state [26], [36], [37]. Due to interactions, large differences are observed for the mobility of the various charge states within crystalline silicon. For example, the neutral charge state of hydrogen is not affected by electric fields and charge effects within the silicon and has a diffusivity of five orders of magnitude higher than that of H^+ [38]. Furthermore, the diffusivity of H^+ is substantially smaller than that of H^- [37].

The ability of hydrogen to assume different charge states in silicon has important implications for the passivation of impurities and defects within silicon. Certain defects can only be passivated by a certain charge state of hydrogen and require the presence of electrons to allow the passivation process to occur. A number of authors have offered interpretations of hydrogen passivation mechanisms in silicon. However, as reported by Van de Walle *et al.*, attempts to explain observed results have led to a number of contradictory assumptions of the charge state of hydrogen and, hence, the passivation reactions which can take place [39]–[43].

By applying an enhanced hydrogenation process, we have achieved an improved passivation of bulk defects. We attribute this improved passivation to the manipulation of the charge state of hydrogen within the silicon. This notion is supported by theoretical calculations based on the literature which indicates that the fraction of neutral and negatively charged hydrogen increases when our enhanced hydrogenation process is applied.

II. Experimental Details

In this paper, 125 mm × 125 mm compensated p-type CZ (CB–CZ) silicon wafers are used from an experimental ingot, using 100% UMG silicon from the PHOTOSIL project, from which ingots and wafers were produced by Apollon Solar [13]. 2-Ω·cm commercial grade boron-doped CZ (B–CZ), 2-Ω·cm commercial grade gallium-doped CZ (Ga–CZ) wafers, and 1 Ω·cm boron-doped FZ (B–FZ) wafers are also used. Each 125 mm × 125 mm wafer is cleaved into nine pieces with pseudocorners to assist with the laboratory processing. Prior to the deposition of the dielectric passivation layer, wafers are saw-damage etched with a resultant thickness of approximately 150 μm and then RCA cleaned.

SiN layers are deposited using standard Roth&Rau remote microwave PECVD systems. Subsequently, the passivation quality is determined by photoluminescence (PL) images [44], [45] obtained using a BTi luminescence imaging system. The quasi-steady-state photoconductance (QSS-PC) and QSS-PL measurement techniques [46]–[48] are used to obtain injection-level-dependent effective minority carrier lifetime curves, 1-sun effective minority carrier lifetime (τ_{eff}), and 1-sun implied open-circuit voltage (iV_{oc}).

Due to the unknown doping densities of both phosphorus and boron in the compensated UMG CZ silicon wafers throughout the ingot, the doping density used for the determination of the electron and hole mobilities and, therefore, the excess minority carrier density and τ_{eff} are the net doping values obtained from dark conductance measurements on the samples. This does not take into account the effect of the reduction in mobility of the minority carriers due to compensation, and therefore, lifetimes presented in this study are underestimated [49]. To eliminate surface effects, the bulk lifetime (τ_{bulk}) is extracted at $\Delta n = 1 \times 10^{16}$ cm^{-3} by removing the Auger and J_{0e} lifetime components associated with the inversion layer formed by the SiN [50].

Two different hydrogenation processes are applied in this study. For process P1, conventional hydrogenation conditions are used whereby there is no attempt to control the hydrogen charge state and, hence, results in a hydrogen charge state which might not be favorable for the passivation of defects such as the B–O complex. Conventional hydrogenation processes such as those implemented via atomic hydrogen being generated through an Alneal process for the world-record PERL cells are performed at approximately 400 °C for typically 5–30 min in the dark [51] and, in this study, consist of 400 °C for 5 min. Industrial processes used for the firing of screen-printed contacts fortuitously implement conditions somewhat better for controlling the charge state of hydrogen, but because the lamps primary function is for heating rather than illumination, conditions are usually far from optimum plus no illumination is provided during cool down. For process P2, the charge state of the hydrogen is controlled to enhance passivation through minority carrier injection. The minority carrier concentration can be controlled through illumination in conduction with the temperature. In this paper, P2 is performed with a peak temperature of approximately 620 °C for 2 s, and improvements in charge state control are achieved through increases in the illumination, while wafers are at peak temperature and during cool down than those achieved using conventional industrial firing processes. For both processes, atomic hydrogen from identical dielectric layers of PECVD SiN is the only source of hydrogen for the passivation

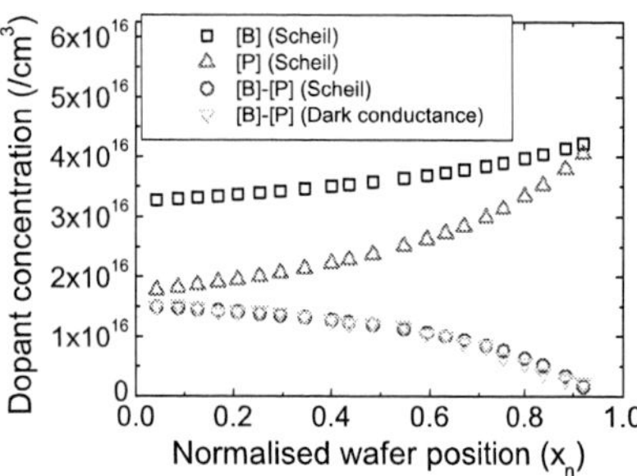

Fig. 1. Doping densities as measured by dark conductance with hypothetical doping profiles from segregation during crystal growth.

process. Subsequently, the wafers are remeasured using the aforementioned techniques.

Solar cells are also fabricated on the B–CZ wafers and processed in an industrial environment using standard commercial production equipment. The wafers are anisotropically textured to expose the (1 1 1) planes, followed by a phosphorus emitter diffusion with a resultant sheet resistance of 100–150 $\Omega/\square$ after the subsequent chemical edge junction isolation process which simultaneously planarizes the rear surface and performs a slight etch back of the front surface to reduce the surface concentration of phosphorus. The front and rear dielectric layers are deposited using an industrial Roth&Rau remote microwave PECVD system.

A commercially available boron spin-on dopant source from Filmtronics is spun onto the rear surface at 2000 r/min for 20 s. Laser doping is performed on the rear surface using a 15-W 532-nm Spectra Physics Millennia Prime laser with a processing speed of 0.5 m/s. The advanced hydrogen process P2 is applied after the laser doping process to passivate laser-induced defects, B–O complexes, and other defects within the device [21]. The p-type metal contact is formed by aluminum sputtering and the n-type contacts are formed using the PLUTO process [52].

III. Results

A. Variation in Effective Doping Density in Upgraded Metallurgical Grade Czochralski Ingots

Raw UMG CB–CZ wafers show a substantial variation in PL response throughout the ingot (not shown). This variation may be due to a change in lifetime of the material and, hence, change in excess minority carrier density, a change in the effective doping of the wafers, or a combination of both [44]. Dark conductance measurements obtained on the wafers after the deposition of the SiN indicate a change in the resistivity of the wafers throughout the ingot, as shown in Fig. 1, where a value of $x_n = 0$ for the normalized wafer position in the ingot corresponds to the top of the ingot and a value of $x_n = 1$ corresponds to the bottom of the ingot. Variations in resistivity throughout CZ ingots are typical, due to the segregation coefficients of the dopants according to the Scheil equation [see (1)] [53]:

$$C(f_S) = C_0 \cdot k_{\text{eff}} \left(1 - f_S\right)^{k_{\text{eff}} - 1} \tag{1}$$

where f_S is the fraction of solidified silicon during ingot growth, $C(f_S)$ is the concentration of the impurity at position f_S, C_0 is the initial concentration of the impurity in the silicon melt, and k_{eff} is the effective segregation coefficient of the impurity in silicon. A value of $f_S = 0$ corresponds to the first silicon to solidify during the CZ growth process at the top of the ingot, and a value of $f_S = 1$ corresponds to the last silicon to solidify at the bottom of the CZ ingot assuming all silicon within the crucible is incorporated into the ingot. However, due to the pot scrap which remains in the crucible after ingot growth and the silicon at the top and bottom of the ingot which are discarded, there are differences in the x_n and f_S values. It is assumed that $f_S = 0.07$ at $x_n = 0$ and $f_S = 0.81$ at $x_n = 1$.

For the case of solar grade Si, typically only one type of dopant is present in the silicon melt, and hence, N_{EFF} increases with increasing f_S in CZ ingots. However, UMG purified silicon may contain many different types of dopant atoms. The CZ ingot used in this study is typical of UMG silicon wafers grown using the 2010/11 version of the PHOTOSIL process; however, this ingot has a P concentration of approximately 1 ppmw in comparison with the PHOTOSIL specifications of 0.5 ppmw. In certain situations, while the concentration of each given dopant increases throughout the CZ ingot, such variations can lead to an inversion of polarity of wafers throughout the ingot [54], [55]. In order to increase the N_{EFF} throughout the ingot, other dopants such as gallium may be added in appropriate addition concentrations which can potentially prevent polarity inversion at the top of the ingot [54], [56]. Dark conductance measurements indicate that no such polarity inversion occurs for the wafers used in this study. A simple segregation model, including only boron and phosphorus, closely matches the measured N_{EFF} (see Fig. 1). Differences in the effective doping density measured by dark conductance and the model using the Scheil equation may be due to the uncertainties in the actual f_S value for a given x_n.

B. Passivation of Slip Lines in Upgraded Metallurgical Grade Czochralski Wafers

In addition to the segregation of dopants which occurs throughout the CZ ingot during crystallization, impurities are incorporated in increasing concentrations throughout the ingot growth process. PL images of the raw wafers and after the deposition of SiN indicate that slip lines are present on wafers near the bottom of the ingot, for $x_n > 0.65$, which appear to be due to increased stresses from higher concentrations of dopants and contaminants in these parts of the ingot [see Fig. 2(a)].

After a typical hydrogenation process (P1), the PL image in Fig. 2(b) indicates the complete passivation of the slip line defects (shown on the same scale). The application of process P2 does not appear to result in any benefit for the passivation of the slip lines over the passivation provided by P1. At this stage, it is unclear whether the passivation of such slip lines can readily occur using a conventional hydrogenation process in noncompensated material or whether the compensation aids in the passivation of the slip lines by increasing the minority hydrogen charge state concentrations. For example, at the maximum process temperature for process P1, a reduction in N_{EFF}

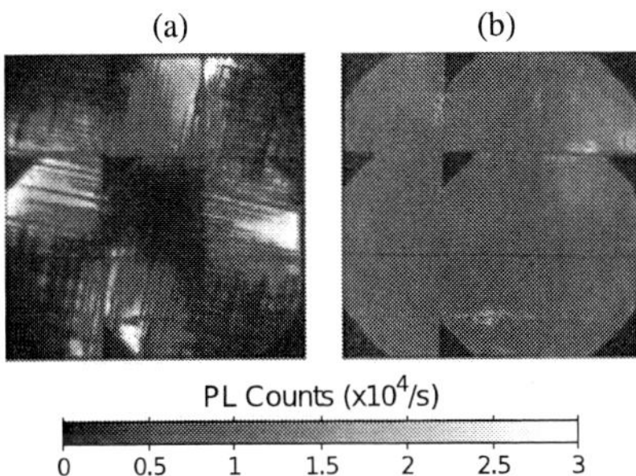

PL Counts (x10^4/s)

Fig. 2. PL images of a wafers with $x_n = 0.72$ (a) before annealing and (b) after process P1.

of one order of magnitude would lead to an enhancement in the concentration of H° and H⁻ by a factor of 2 and 5, respectively. During cool down, this enhancement becomes larger, and at a temperature of 200°C, the H° and H⁻ concentrations would be enhanced by one and two orders of magnitude, respectively (see Fig. 5). If the compensation does assist in the passivation, then impurities such as phosphorus, which are present in increasing concentrations toward the bottom of the ingot and potentially increase the defect concentration, may actually assist with the passivation of such defects. It is also evident that prior to process P1, regions of the wafer without slip lines show substantially higher PL counts and hence higher lifetimes than the corresponding regions after process P1. Hence, it would appear that while a nonoptimal hydrogenation process may be sufficient to passivate certain defects, the same process may in fact be detrimental to other regions of the device. The reduction in τ_{bulk} observed in such areas will be discussed in the following section.

C. Application of Advanced Hydrogenation to Silicon Wafers and Solar Cells

In our previous work, we demonstrated that the effectiveness of hydrogen passivation of B–O complexes on standard commercial grade 2 Ω·cm B–CZ and CB–CZ wafers grown from UMG silicon appears to be heavily dependent on the charge state of the hydrogen and, therefore, the hydrogenation process used [21], [57]. Large changes in the 1-sun effective minority carrier lifetime (τ_{eff}) and 1-sun implied open-circuit voltage (iV_{oc}) of the B–CZ and CB–CZ wafers between processes P1 and P2 were observed, while no significant changes in iV_{oc} are observed for 1-Ω·cm B–FZ wafers or commercial grade 2-Ω·cm Ga–CZ wafers. The hydrogen passivation of B–O defects was also shown to be reversible. Hence, defects passivated using an advanced hydrogenation process (P2) can become reactivated during subsequent processes such as process P1 if the hydrogen is not in the correct state to repassivate any defects which become reactivated during the process, while upon the application of a further P2 process, the defects are once again passivated.

In this paper, we show that such changes are largely due to a change in the bulk lifetime of the wafers. On the UMG CB–CZ wafers, little increase in τ_{bulk} is obtained from performing process P1, while substantial improvements are obtained during

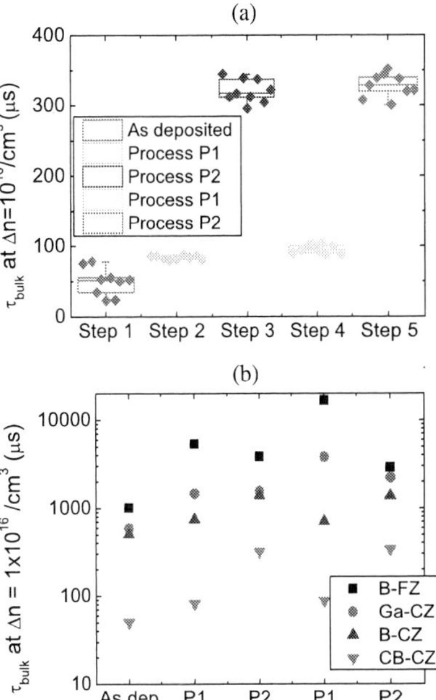

Fig. 3. Reversibility of τ_{bulk} at $\Delta n = 1 \times 10^{16}$ cm^{-3} for different hydrogenation processes on (a) 2-Ω·cm CB–CZ wafers and (b) a variety of wafers including 1-Ω·cm B–FZ, 2-Ω·cm Ga–CZ, 2-Ω·cm B–CZ, and 2-Ω·cm CB–CZ wafers.

process P2 due to the enhanced H° and H⁻ concentrations [see Fig. 3(a)]. The image also highlights the reversibility of the passivation of bulk defects by applying additional hydrogenation treatments P1 and P2 and, therefore, τ_{bulk} toggling in between two values of approximately 100 μs with the application of process P1 and over 300 μs with the application of process P2. It is also observed that there is little spread in the data for the nine samples measured at each stage of processing. Similarly, for B–CZ wafers, after an initial τ_{bulk} of 500 μs, τ_{bulk} toggles between 800 μs with the application of process P1 and 1.4 ms with the application of process P2 [see Fig. 3(b)]. On other B–CZ wafers with a lower initial τ_{bulk} of 250 μs, τ_{bulk} toggles between 700 μs with the application of process P1 and 1.3 ms with the application of process P2, almost reaching the same final value (not shown). However, no such increase in τ_{bulk} is observed for B–FZ or Ga–CZ wafers with the application of process P2. For such wafers, τ_{bulk} typically suffers a slight degradation. It should be noted that PL images do not indicate the presence of thermal donors after P1 or P2.

The PECVD system used in this paper incorporates a thermal process after the deposition of the dielectric layer. This process starts at the deposition temperature of 400 °C and ramps down to a temperature of 250 °C over approximately 20 min before the samples are unloaded. According to the literature, the thermal treatment above 170 °C should result in the lifetime of the B–CZ and CB–CZ wafers being in a nondegraded state [58]. Furthermore, as processes P1 and P2 are performed above 170 °C, the lifetimes after both processes should also be in a nondegraded state.

37

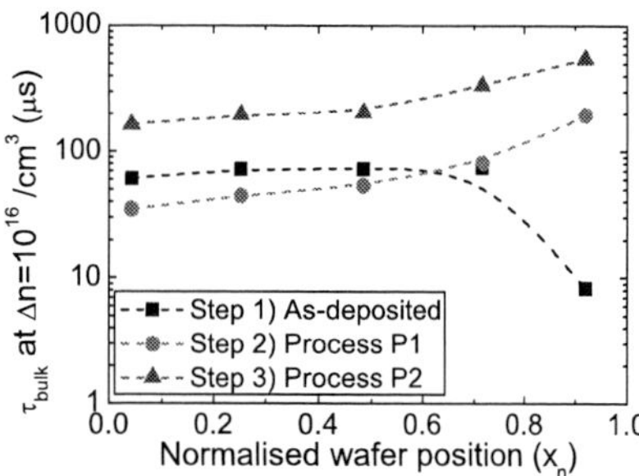

Fig. 4. Bulk lifetimes extracted at $\Delta n = 1 \times 10^{16}$ cm^{-3} from wafers throughout a compensated boron-doped CZ ingot grown from UMG silicon with different hydrogenation processes.

Previous work by Glunz *et al.* reported substantial reductions in the normalized defect density and increased stabilized lifetimes through optimized processing during thermal oxidations. While it was not explicitly reported, the improvements of data presented in the work also resulted in higher lifetimes prior to degradation [59]. Although light soaking will be required to confirm whether or not any increase in stabilized lifetime is achieved, the results by Glunz *et al.* would suggest the possibility of an increase in stabilized lifetime in this paper.

In more recent work on the regeneration process for B–O defects by Wilking *et al.*, minority carrier injection is also used with the authors eluding to the possibility in a change in charge state of hydrogen assisting with the passivation process [20]. At this stage, it remains unclear whether H$^\circ$ or H$^-$ assists in the passivation process. However, one of the recent understandings for the recovery of the slow forming recombination center of the B–O complex is through the capture of an electron [60]. This may suggest the capture of H$^-$ to form a neutral complex.

Furthermore, the response of the UMG wafers to hydrogen passivation processes greatly depends on the position of the wafer within the ingot (see Fig. 4). With the application of process P1, wafers from the top 60% of the ingot ($x_n < 0.6$) show a slight reduction in τ_{bulk}, while wafers from lower regions of the ingot show large improvements. This is despite such wafers only having an initial τ_{bulk} of approximately 8 μs: well below that of wafers from higher regions in the ingot of approximately 60–70 μs. However, it should be noted that due to the reduced mobility of minority carriers in compensated silicon, lifetimes of wafers at the bottom of the ingot may be underestimated by a larger extent than that of wafers at the top of the ingot with lower doping densities of both boron and phosphorus and, therefore, higher mobilities of the charge carriers. The enhanced response to hydrogenation of the wafers at the bottom of the ingot is due to the reduced N_{EFF} from compensation and, hence, higher concentrations of H$^\circ$ and H$^-$, even using a conventional hydrogenation process. This results in such regions of the ingot showing substantially higher τ_{bulk} than wafers from regions of the ingot with higher N_{EFF}. However, by intentionally controlling the charge state of hydrogen through process P2, the τ_{bulk} of all wafers throughout the ingot increase substantially, again with an enhanced response of wafers with lower N_{EFF}. For wafers with $x_n < 0.5$, τ_{bulk} is increased to approximately 200 μs, while for wafers with $x_n = 0.92$, τ_{bulk} is over 550 μs. The corresponding improvement in 1-sun iV_{oc} was on average approximately 160 mV, from 540 mV before hydrogenation to 700 mV after P2 and increase in 1-sun τ_{eff} from 2 to 440 μs, suggesting a great level of passivation of the defects in the material at the bottom of the ingot.

It is common for silicon producers to reject approximately the last 25% of CZ ingots, particularly that grown from UMG silicon due to the differences in wafer resistivity throughout the ingot and high defect densities. For solar cell manufacturers, wafer inspection of raw wafers is often determined by techniques such as PL imaging, whereby material is rejected if the lifetime is deemed too low to make good devices. However, this analysis is carried out before phosphorus gettering and hydrogenation processes take place, which are shown to lead to substantial changes in the τ_{bulk} of the material [61], [62]. If appropriate hydrogenation processes can ensure that adequate passivation is retained on finished devices, it may allow higher efficiency devices to be fabricated on wafers grown from the UMG silicon. Furthermore, higher ingot utilizations may be realized through the use of more effective passivation of material from the bottom of CZ ingots through dopant compensation, even though such regions are typically prone to higher crystallographic defect densities caused by increased impurity concentrations.

The advanced hydrogenation process is applied on cells fabricated from standard commercial grade B–CZ wafers, while ensuring that adequate hydrogen passivation of B–O and other defects is retained on the finished devices. Independently confirmed open-circuit voltages and short-circuit current densities of 681 mV and 40.0 mA/cm^2 are demonstrated, respectively, with pseudo-efficiencies approaching 23%. Further processing details and results of such cells can be found elsewhere [63].

IV. Discussion

A. Enhancing Hydrogen Mobility and Reactivity in Silicon

The charge state of hydrogen is often not considered in the literature on hydrogen passivation of defects in silicon solar cells [64]–[66]. However, considering the literature and theoretical calculations for the concentrations of the various charge states can offer an interpretation of the results obtained in this paper. It appears that the charge state of the hydrogen is of critical importance for several aspects of the passivation process, including

1) the movement of hydrogen into and throughout the solar cell;
2) the activation of the hydrogen once it is inside the silicon to allow the passivation of recombination sites during the hydrogenation process;
3) trapping the hydrogen in the silicon after the hydrogenation process to ensure it does not escape during subsequent processing.

The theoretically calculated fractional charge state concentrations of hydrogen in silicon are greatly dependent on the position of the Fermi level within the bandgap [67]. Subsequently, the temperature, effective doping density (N_{EFF}), and excess minority carrier concentration (Δn) within the silicon play a vital

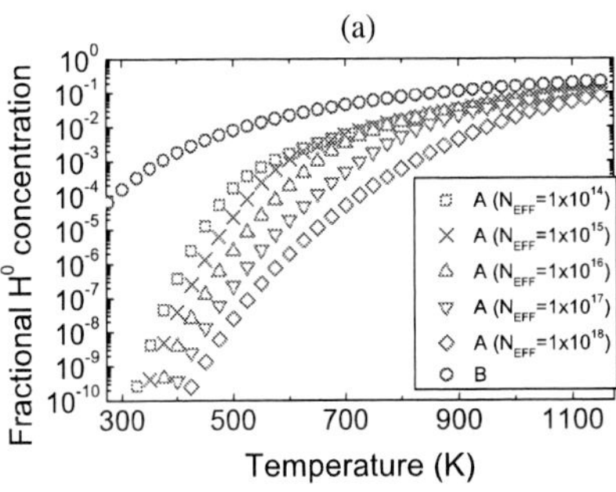

(a)

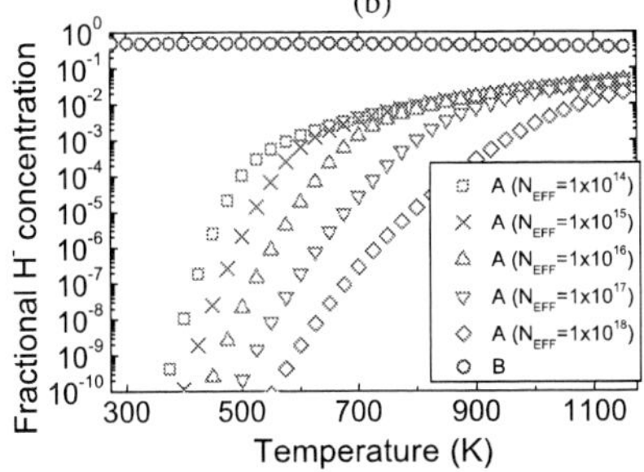

(b)

Fig. 5. Theoretical fractional hydrogen concentrations in p-type silicon of various N_{EFF} (cm^{-3}) for (a) H$^{\circ}$ and (b) H^{-}.

TABLE I
VALUES OF CONSTANTS USED IN (2)–(4)

Constant	Value
m_{de}	0.33 m_0
m_{dh}	0.56 m_0
E_d - E_m at 310 K	0.4 eV
E_m - E_a at 310 K	0.07 eV
v_+	4
v_0	8
v_-	2
Z_+	1
Z_0	1
Z_-	1

role in determining the fractional concentrations of the various hydrogen charge species.

As discussed in Section I, H^{+} and H^{-} have low mobility in silicon. However, by using appropriate minority carrier injection conditions, a significant fraction of hydrogen can be converted into H$^{\circ}$, which is then able to avoid electrostatic effects with a mobility several orders of magnitude higher than that of the positive and negative charge states [37]. Therefore, it would appear advantageous to put the hydrogen into H$^{\circ}$ in order to move the hydrogen throughout the solar cell from the hydrogen source, which is typically a dielectric layer at the wafer surface. Wilking *et al.* recently demonstrated the importance of such a step by the necessity of a firing step for the regeneration process of B–O defects [20].

However, once the hydrogen is dispersed throughout the silicon, it is expected that each given type of recombination site within the silicon requires a specific charge state of hydrogen in order to be passivated, based on the charge and bonding configuration of the recombination site. Given that there are typically multiple impurities and defects within the solar cell requiring passivation throughout the fabrication sequence, it would therefore appear desirable to use conditions which generate sufficient concentrations of the various charge states of hydrogen simultaneously, to allow the passivation of all types of defects within the silicon. As H$^{\circ}$ is always a minority charge species in silicon, it is assumed that conditions should be used to maximize the concentration of H$^{\circ}$.

Furthermore, during subsequent thermal processing, it is essential that the hydrogen is in the appropriate charge state to repassivate any recombination sites which are reactivated during such processes caused by, for example, using temperatures above that which correspond to the reactivation energy of the recombination site. In addition, to trap the hydrogen in the silicon during subsequent processes, it appears desirable to put the unbound hydrogen into a low mobility state to avoid it reaching surfaces or hydrogen sinks within the device such as metal/silicon interfaces or large angle grain boundaries which can lead to the formation of molecular hydrogen or the loss of the hydrogen from the device. Certain structures such as heavily doped p-type silicon regions below the metal/Si interface may assist in trapping the hydrogen in the silicon by converting almost all hydrogen in the heavily doped silicon region into H^{+} and, therefore, reducing mobility.

Fig. 5 shows the fractional concentrations of H$^{\circ}$ and H^{-} in p-type silicon for various N_{EFF} as adapted from [67] taking into account bandgap narrowing, a hydrogen donor level (E_d) of 0.4 eV above mid bandgap, and a hydrogen acceptor level (E_a) 0.07 eV below mid bandgap. The equations are shown below [see (2)–(4)], where f_i is the fractional charge state concentration of charge state i, v_i and Z_i are the number of possible configurations in the unit cell and the vibrational partition function associated with each, respectively, and E_{Fn} is the quasi-electron Fermi level. Due to the importance of electrons as the minority charge carrier in silicon, E_{Fn} is used rather than the Fermi level. Table I shows the values of the constant used in the model, where m_0 is the electron mass (9.11×10^{-31} kg), and m_{de} and m_{dh} are the density of states effective mass for electrons and holes, respectively. It is assumed that the relative positions of E_d and E_a with respect to E_m are independent of temperature. As the temperature dependence of the partition functions is unknown [67], the low-temperature approximation of unity is used in each case. However, this makes it difficult to predict the fractional concentrations precisely. Further details on the theory are given by Herring *et al.* [67]

$$f_0 = \left(1 + \frac{v_+ Z_+}{v_0 Z_0} e^{\left(\frac{E_d - E_{Fn}}{kT} \right)} + \frac{v_- Z_-}{v_0 Z_0} e^{\left(\frac{E_{Fn} - E_a}{kT} \right)} \right)^{-1} \quad (2)$$

$$f_+ = f_0 \frac{v_+ Z_+}{v_0 Z_0} e^{\left(\frac{E_d - E_{Fn}}{kT} \right)} \quad (3)$$

$$f_- = f_0 \frac{v_- Z_-}{v_0 Z_0} e^{\left(\frac{E_{Fn} - E_a}{kT} \right)}. \quad (4)$$

It is observed that with a pure thermal process (A), the fractional concentration of the minority charge species greatly depends on N_{EFF}, particularly at lower temperatures. However, with appropriate minority carrier injection (B), the fractional charge state concentrations of both H$^{\circ}$ and H^{-} are greatly

39

enhanced and become independent of the N_{EFF}. It is also noted that using process B, H$^-$ becomes predominantly independent of temperature. During changes in the temperature throughout the thermal process, based on (2), the optimal E_{Fn} changes slightly, meaning that the excess minority carrier concentration required to maintain optimum H$^\circ$ generation also varies. In Fig. 5, an N_{EFF} of 1×10^{16} cm^{-3} is used for B; however, the values vary by less than 0.05% by changing the doping density over the range indicated in the legend.

V. Conclusion

Using an advanced hydrogenation process which manipulates the charge state of hydrogen, substantial improvements in τ_{bulk} are observed on standard commercial grade B–CZ wafers from 250–500 μs to 1.3–1.4 ms. On UMG CZ silicon wafers, the response to hydrogenation greatly depends on the position of the wafers throughout the ingot, with wafers at the bottom of the ingot showing the most promising increases in bulk lifetime from 8 to over 550 μs. The enhanced response of such wafers is attributed to dopant compensation, which, based on theoretical calculations, results in higher concentrations of the minority hydrogen charge states. However, it is observed that the hydrogen passivation of certain defects is a reversible process, where recombination sites can become reactivated if further thermal processing is performed without controlling the hydrogen charge state. On finished devices fabricated on standard commercial grade B–CZ wafers, independently confirmed V_{OC} over 680 mV have been obtained using the advanced hydrogenation process to control the charge state of hydrogen and to ensure that defects are not reactivated during subsequent processes. The enhanced passivation is attributed to improved control of the hydrogen charge states, which appears to be of critical importance in determining the effectiveness of hydrogen passivation through changes in hydrogen reactivity.

Acknowledgment

The authors would like to acknowledge the support of Suntech Power to allow access to an industrial research production line for this work and Apollon Solar for growth and donation of wafers from an experimental CZ ingot. Responsibility for the views, information, or advice expressed herein is not accepted by the Australian Government.

References

[1] S. De Wolf, J. Szlufcik, Y. Delannoy, I. Perichaud, C. Häßler, and R. Einhaus, "Solar cells from upgraded metallurgical grade (UMG) and plasma-purified UMG multi-crystalline silicon substrates," *Solar Energy Mater. Solar Cells*, vol. 72, no. 1, pp. 49–58, 2002.

[2] A. Braga, S. Moreira, P. Zampieri, J. Bacchin, and P. Mei, "New processes for the production of solar-grade polycrystalline silicon: A review," *Solar Energy Mater. Solar Cells*, vol. 92, no. 4, pp. 418–424, 2008.

[3] N. Yuge, H. Baba, Y. Sakaguchi, K. Nishikawa, H. Terashima, and F. Aratani, "Purification of metallurgical silicon up to solar grade," *Solar Energy Mater. Solar Cells*, vol. 34, no. 1, pp. 243–250, 1994.

[4] I. Périchaud, "Gettering of impurities in solar silicon," *Solar Energy Mater. Solar Cells*, vol. 72, no. 1, pp. 315–326, 2002.

[5] A. Istratov, T. Buonassisi, R. McDonald, A. Smith, R. Schindler, J. Rand, J. Kalejs, and E. Weber, "Metal content of multicrystalline silicon for solar cells and its impact on minority carrier diffusion length," *J. Appl. Phys.*, vol. 94, pp. 6552–6559, 2003.

[6] H. Xu, R. Hong, B. Ai, L. Zhuang, and H. Shen, "Application of phosphorus diffusion gettering process on upgraded metallurgical grade si wafers and solar cells," *Appl. Energy*, vol. 87, no. 11, pp. 3425–3430, 2010.

[7] J. Junge, A. Herguth, G. Hahn, D. Kreßner-Kiel, and R. Zierer, "Investigation of degradation in solar cells from different mc-Si materials," *Energy Procedia*, vol. 8, pp. 52–57, 2011.

[8] T. Taishi, T. Hoshikawa, M. Yamatani, K. Shirasawa, X. Huang, S. Uda, and K. Hoshikawa, "Influence of crystalline defects in czochralski-grown si multicrystal on minority carrier lifetime," *J. Cryst. Growth*, vol. 306, no. 2, pp. 452–457, 2007.

[9] H. Fischer and W. Pschunder, "Investigation of photon and thermal induced changes in silicon solar cells," in *Proc. IEEE 10th Photovoltaic Spec. Conf.*, 1973, p. 404.

[10] J. Reiss, R. King, and K. Mitchell, "Characterization of diffusion length degradation in Czochralski silicon solar cells," *Appl. Phys. Lett.*, vol. 68, no. 23, pp. 3302–3304, 1996.

[11] B. Lim, F. Rougieux, D. Macdonald, K. Bothe, and J. Schmidt, "Generation and annihilation of boron–oxygen-related recombination centers in compensated p-and n-type silicon," *J. Appl. Phys.*, vol. 108, pp. 103722-1–103722-9, 2010.

[12] D. Macdonald and L. Geerligs, "Recombination activity of interstitial iron and other transition metal point defects in p-and n-type crystalline silicon," *Appl. Phys. Lett.*, vol. 85, no. 18, pp. 4061–4063, 2004.

[13] R. Einhaus, J. Kraiem, F. Cocco, Y. Caratini, D. Bernou, D. Sarti, G. Rey, R. Monna, C. Trassy, J. Degoulange, Y. Delannoy, S. Martinuzzi, I. Périchaud, M. Record, and P. Rivat, "Photosil–simplified production of solar silicon from metallurgical silicon," in *Proc. 21st Eur. Solar Energy Conf.*, Dresden, Germany, 2006, pp. 580–584.

[14] T. Buonassisi, A. Istratov, M. Pickett, M. Heuer, J. Kalejs, G. Hahn, M. Marcus, B. Lai, Z. Cai, S. Heald, T. F. Ciszek, R. F. Clark, D. W. Cunningham, A. M. Gabor, R. Jonczyk, S. Narayanan, E. Sauar, and E. R. Weber, "Chemical natures and distributions of metal impurities in multicrystalline silicon materials," *Progr. Photovoltaic: Res. Appl.*, vol. 14, no. 6, pp. 513–531, 2006.

[15] W. Paul, A. Lewis, G. Connell, and T. Moustakas, "Doping, Schottky barrier and p-n junction formation in amorphous germanium and silicon by RF sputtering," *Solid State Commun.*, vol. 20, no. 10, pp. 969–972, 1976.

[16] A. Aberle, "Overview on sin surface passivation of crystalline silicon solar cells," *Solar Energy Mater. Solar Cells*, vol. 65, no. 1, pp. 239–248, 2001.

[17] K. Münzer, "Hydrogenated silicon nitride for regeneration of light induced degradation," in *Proc. 24th Eur. Photovoltaic Solar Energy Conf.*, Hamburg, Germany, 2009, pp. 1558–1561.

[18] G. Krugel, W. Wolke, J. Geilker, S. Rein, and R. Preu, "Impact of hydrogen concentration on the regeneration of light induced degradation," *Energy Procedia*, vol. 8, pp. 47–51, 2011.

[19] B. Lim, K. Bothe, and J. Schmidt, "Impact of oxygen on the permanent deactivation of boron–oxygen-related recombination centers in crystalline silicon," *J. Appl. Phys.*, vol. 107, no. 12, pp. 123707–123707, 2010.

[20] S. Wilking, A. Herguth, and G. Hahn. (2013). Influence of hydrogen on the regeneration of boron-oxygen related defects in crystalline silicon. *J. Appl. Phys.* [Online]. vol. 113, no. 19, p. 194503. Available: http://link.aip.org/link/?JAP/113/194503/1

[21] B. Hallam, S. Wenham, P. Hamer, M. Abbott, A. Sugianto, C. Chan, A. Wenham, M. Eadie, and G. Xu, "Hydrogen passivation of B-O defects in Czochralski silicon," *Energy Procedia*, vol. 38, pp. 561–570, 2013.

[22] B. Sopori, K. Jones, and X. Deng, "Observation of enhanced hydrogen diffusion in solar cell silicon," *Appl. Phys. Lett.*, vol. 61, no. 21, pp. 2560–2562, 1992.

[23] B. Sopori, X. Deng, J. Benner, A. Rohatgi, P. Sana, S. Estreicher, Y. Park, and M. Roberson, "Hydrogen in silicon: A discussion of diffusion and passivation mechanisms," *Solar Energy Mater. Solar Cells*, vol. 41, pp. 159–169, 1996.

[24] C. Seager, R. Anderson, and J. Panitz, "The diffusion of hydrogen in silicon and mechanisms for "unintentional" hydrogenation during ion beam processing," *J. Mater. Res.*, vol. 2, no. 01, pp. 96–106, 1987.

[25] B. Sopori, Y. Zhang, and N. Ravindra, "Silicon device processing in h-ambients: H-diffusion mechanisms and influence on electronic properties," *J. Electron. Mater.*, vol. 30, no. 12, pp. 1616–1627, 2001.

[26] C. Seager and R. Anderson, "Real-time observations of hydrogen drift and diffusion in silicon," *Appl. Phys. Lett.*, vol. 53, no. 13, pp. 1181–1183, 1988.

[27] B. Sopori, "Silicon solar-cell processing for minimizing the influence of impurities and defects," *J. Electron. Mater.*, vol. 31, no. 10, pp. 972–980, 2002.

[28] S. Pearton, J. Corbett, and J. Borenstein, "Hydrogen diffusion in crystalline semiconductors," *Physica B: Condens. Matter*, vol. 170, no. 1, pp. 85–97, 1991.

[29] J. Pankove and N. Johnson, *Hydrogen in Semiconductors: Hydrogen in Silicon.* vol. 34, New York, NY, USA: Academic, 1991.

[30] J. Corbett, J. Lindström, S. Pearton, and A. Tavendale, "Passivation in silicon," *Solar cells*, vol. 24, no. 1, pp. 127–133, 1988.

[31] B. Sopori, "Silicon nitride processing for control of optical and electronic properties of silicon solar cells," *J. Electron. Mater.*, vol. 32, no. 10, pp. 1034–1042, 2003.

[32] N. Johnson and M. Moyer, "Absence of oxygen diffusion during hydrogen passivation of shallow-acceptor impurities in single-crystal silicon," *Appl. Phys. Lett.*, vol. 46, no. 8, pp. 787–789, 1985.

[33] T. Ichimiya and A. Furuichi, "On the solubility and diffusion coefficient of tritium in single crystals of silicon," *Int. J. Appl. Radiat. Isot.*, vol. 19, no. 7, pp. 573–578, 1968.

[34] M. Capizzi and A. Mittiga, "Hydrogen in crystalline silicon: A deep donor?" *Appl. Phys. Lett.*, vol. 50, no. 14, pp. 918–920, 1987.

[35] S. Kleekajai, F. Jiang, M. Stavola, V. Yelundur, K. Nakayashiki, A. Rohatgi, G. Hahn, S. Seren, and J. Kalejs, "Concentration and penetration depth of H introduced into crystalline Si by hydrogenation methods used to fabricate solar cells," *J. Appl. Phys.*, vol. 100, no. 9, pp. 093 517–093 517, 2006.

[36] J. Zhu, N. Johnson, and C. Herring, "Negative-charge state of hydrogen in silicon," *Phys. Rev. B*, vol. 41, no. 17, pp. 12354–12357, 1990.

[37] D. Mathiot, "Modeling of hydrogen diffusion in n-and p-type silicon," *Phys. Rev. B*, vol. 40, no. 8, pp. 5867–5870, 1989.

[38] R. Job, W. Fahrner, N. Kazuchits, and A. Ulyashin, "A two-step low-temperature process for a pn junction formation due to hydrogen enhanced thermal donor formation in p-type Czochralski silicon," *Proc. Mater. Res. Soc.*, vol. 513, no. 1, p. 337, 1998.

[39] C. G. Van de Walle, P. Denteneer, Y. Bar-Yam, and S. Pantelides, "Theory of hydrogen diffusion and reactions in crystalline silicon," *Phys. Rev. B*, vol. 39, no. 15, pp. 10791–10808, 1989.

[40] J. Pankove, R. Wance, and J. Berkeyheiser, "Neutralization of acceptors in silicon by atomic hydrogen," *Appl. Phys. Lett.*, vol. 45, no. 10, pp. 1100–1102, 1984.

[41] J. Pankove, P. Zanzucchi, C. Magee, and G. Lucovsky, "Hydrogen localization near boron in silicon," *Appl. Phys. Lett.*, vol. 46, no. 4, pp. 421–423, 1985.

[42] C. Sah, J. Sun, and J. Tzou, "Deactivation of the boron acceptor in silicon by hydrogen," *Appl. Phys. Lett.*, vol. 43, no. 2, pp. 204–206, 1983.

[43] N. Johnson, C. Herring, and D. Chadi, "Interstitial hydrogen and neutralization of shallow-donor impurities in single-crystal silicon," *Phys. Rev. Lett.*, vol. 56, no. 7, pp. 769–772, 1986.

[44] T. Trupke and R. Bardos, "Photoluminescence: A surprisingly sensitive lifetime technique," in *Proc. IEEE 31st Photovoltaic Spec. Conf.*, 2005, pp. 903–906.

[45] T. Trupke, R. A. Bardos, M. C. Schubert, and W. Warta, "Photoluminescence imaging of silicon wafers," *Appl. Phys. Lett.*, vol. 89, pp. 044107-1–044107-3, 2006.

[46] R. A. Sinton, A. Cuevas, and M. Stuckings, "Quasi-steady-state photoconductance, a new method for solar cell material and device characterization," in *Proc. IEEE 25th Photovoltaic Spec. Conf.*, 1996, pp. 457–460.

[47] R. A. Sinton and A. Cuevas, "Contactless determination of the current-voltage characteristics and minority-carrier lifetimes in semiconductors from quasi-steady-state photoconductance data," *Appl. Phys. Lett.*, vol. 69, no. 17, pp. 2510–2512, 1996.

[48] T. Trupke, R. Bardos, and M. Abbott, "Self-consistent calibration of photoluminescence and photoconductance lifetime measurements," *Appl. Phys. Lett.*, vol. 87, no. 18, pp. 184102-1–184102-3, 2005.

[49] F. Rougieux, D. Macdonald, A. Cuevas, S. Ruffell, J. Schmidt, B. Lim, and A. Knights, "Electron and hole mobility reduction and hall factor in phosphorus-compensated p-type silicon," *J. Appl. Phys.*, vol. 108, pp. 013706-1–013706-5, 2010.

[50] A. Cuevas and D. Macdonald, "Measuring and interpreting the lifetime of silicon wafers," *Solar Energy*, vol. 76, no. 1, pp. 255–262, 2004.

[51] J. Zhao, A. Wang, P. P. Altermatt, S. R. Wenham, and M. A. Green, "24% efficient PERL silicon solar cell: Recent improvements in high efficiency silicon cell research," *Solar Energy Mater. Solar Cells*, vol. 41, pp. 87–99, 1996.

[52] Z. Shi, S. Wenham, and J. Ji, "Mass production of the innovative pluto solar cell technology," in *Proc. IEEE 34th Photovoltaic Spec. Conf.*, 2009, pp. 1922–1926.

[53] E. Scheil, "Remarks on the crystal layer formation," *Z. Metallkd*, vol. 34, p. 70, 1942.

[54] M. Forster, E. Fourmond, R. Einhaus, H. Lauvray, J. Kraiem, and M. Lemiti, "Doping engineering to increase the material yield during crystallization of b and p compensated silicon," in *Proc. 25th Eur. Photovoltaic Sol. Energy Conf.*, 2010, pp. 1250–1253.

[55] T. Trupke, J. Nyhus, and J. Haunschild, "Luminescence imaging for inline characterisation in silicon photovoltaics," *Physica Status Solidi—Rapid Res. Lett.*, vol. 5, no. 4, pp. 131–137, 2011.

[56] M. Forster, E. Fourmond, R. Einhaus, H. Lauvray, J. Kraiem, and M. Lemiti, "Ga co-doping in cz-grown silicon ingots to overcome limitations of b and p compensated silicon feedstock for PV applications," *Physica Status Solidi (c)*, vol. 8, no. 3, pp. 678–681, 2011.

[57] B. Hallam, T. Trupke, Y. Augarten, B. Tjahjono, and S. Wenham, "Photoluminescence imaging for fast determination of the implied open circuit voltage of silicon wafers," in *Proc. 24th Eur. Photovoltaic Solar Energy Conf.*, Hamburg, Germany, 2009, pp. 2015–2018.

[58] J. Schmidt, A. G. Aberle, and R. Hezel, "Investigation of carrier lifetime instabilities in Cz-grown silicon," in *Proc. IEEE 26th Photovoltaic Spec. Conf.*, 1997, pp. 13–18.

[59] S. Glunz, S. Rein, W. Warta, J. Knobloch, and W. Wettling, "Degradation of carrier lifetime in cz silicon solar cells," *Solar Energy Mater. Solar Cells*, vol. 65, no. 1, pp. 219–229, 2001.

[60] V. V. Voronkov and R. Falster, "Latent complexes of interstitial boron and oxygen dimers as a reason for degradation of silicon-based solar cells," *J. Appl. Phys.*, vol. 107, no. 5, pp. 053509–053509, 2010.

[61] J. Haunschild, M. Glatthaar, M. Demant, J. Nievendick, M. Motzko, S. Rein, and E. Weber, "Quality control of as-cut multicrystalline silicon wafers using photoluminescence imaging for solar cell production," *Solar Energy Mater. Solar Cells*, vol. 94, no. 12, pp. 2007–2012, 2010.

[62] M. Rinio, C. Ballif, T. Buonassisi, and D. Borchert, "Defects in the deteriorated border layer of block-cast multicrystalline silicon ingots," in *Proc. 19th Eur. Photovoltaic Solar Energy Conf.*, 2004, vol. 7, pp. 762–765.

[63] A. Sugianto, B. Hallam, X. Bai, P. Han, H. Lu, L. Mai, S. Wenham, and Z. Shi, "Over 20%-efficient laser-doped passivated rear contact solar cells on industrial-sized commercial grade p-type CZ wafers," in *Proc. 27th Eur. Photovoltaic Sol. Energy Conf.*, Frankfurt, Germany, 2012, pp. 700–705.

[64] W. Soppe, H. Rieffe, and A. Weeber, "Bulk and surface passivation of silicon solar cells accomplished by silicon nitride deposited on industrial scale by microwave PECVD," *Progr. Photovoltaic: Res. Appl.*, vol. 13, no. 7, pp. 551–569, 2005.

[65] C. Dube, J. Hanoka, and D. Sandstrom, "Hydrogen diffusion along passivated grain boundaries in silicon ribbon," *Appl. Phys. Lett.*, vol. 44, no. 4, pp. 425–427, 1984.

[66] P. Karzel, J. Junge, and G. Hahn, "Mapping of hydrogen bond energies in EFG silicon samples by analysis of spatially resolved minority charge carrier lifetimes after annealing steps," in *Proc. 24th Eur. Photovoltaic Sol. Energy Conf.*, Hamburg, Germany, 2009, pp. 2023–2027.

[67] C. Herring, N. Johnson, and C. Van de Walle, "Energy levels of isolated interstitial hydrogen in silicon," *Phys. Rev. B*, vol. 64, no. 12, pp. 125209-1–125209-27, 2001.

Authors' photographs and biographies not available at the time of publication.

Improving the Quality of Epitaxial Foils Produced Using a Porous Silicon-based Layer Transfer Process for High-Efficiency Thin-Film Crystalline Silicon Solar Cells

Hariharsudan Sivaramakrishnan Radhakrishnan, *Member, IEEE*, Roberto Martini, Valérie Depauw, Kris Van Nieuwenhuysen, Maarten Debucquoy, Jonathan Govaerts, Ivan Gordon, Robert Mertens, and Jef Poortmans

Abstract—A porous silicon-based layer transfer process to produce thin (30–50 μm) kerfless epitaxial foils (epifoils) is a promising approach toward high-efficiency solar cells. For high efficiencies, the epifoil must have high minority carrier lifetimes. The epifoil quality depends on the properties of the porous layer since it is the template for epitaxy. It is shown that by reducing the thickness of this layer and/or its porosity in the near-surface region, the near-surface void size is reduced to <65 nm and in certain cases achieve a 100 nm-thick void-free zone below the surface. Together with better void alignment, this allows for a smoother growth surface with a roughness of <35 Å and reduced stress in the porous silicon. These improvements translate into significantly diminished epifoil crystal defect densities as low as $\sim$420 defects/cm^2. Although epifoils on very thin porous silicon were not detachable, a significant improvement in the lifetime (diffusion length) of safely detachable n-type epifoils from $\sim$85 ($\sim$300 μm) to $\sim$195 μs ($\sim$470 μm) at the injection level of 10^{15}/cm^3 is achieved by tuning the porous silicon template. Lifetimes exceeding $\sim$350 μs have been achieved in the reference lithography-based epifoils, showing the potential for improvement in porous silicon-based epifoils.

Index Terms—Crystal defects, epitaxy, layer transfer, minority carrier lifetime, porous silicon, stress, surface roughness.

I. Introduction

T HE continuous scaling-down of the silicon solar cell wafer thickness to reduce the consumption of silicon (and hence the cost) has fueled research groups to look into kerf-less production of very thin (<50 μm) silicon and innovative handling

Manuscript received June 16, 2013; revised August 3, 2013; accepted September 3, 2013. Date of publication October 10, 2013; date of current version December 16, 2013. This work was supported in part by the Flemish government in the framework of the project SiLaSol and in part by the European government in the framework of the project R2M.

H. S. Radhakrishnan, R. Martini, R. Mertens, and J. Poortmans are with the IMEC, Leuven B-3001, Belgium and also with the Department of Electrical Engineering, KU Leuven, Heverlee B-3001, Belgium (e-mail: sivarama@imec.be; Roberto.Martini@imec.be; Robert.Mertens@imec.be; Jef.Poortmans@imec.be).

V. Depauw, K. Van Nieuwenhuysen, M. Debucquoy, J. Govaerts, and I. Gordon are with the IMEC, Leuven B-3001, Belgium (e-mail: Valerie.Depauw@imec.be; Kris.VanNieuwenhuysen@imec.be; Maarten.Debucquoy@imec.be; Jonathan.Govaerts@imec.be; Ivan.Gordon@imec.be).

Color versions of one or more of the figures in this paper are available online at http://ieeexplore.ieee.org.

Digital Object Identifier 10.1109/JPHOTOV.2013.2282740

techniques. One such promising route is the electrochemically etched porous silicon-based layer transfer approach that was first proposed by Tayanaka *et al.* [1]. An extensive review of this approach in its various embodiments (sintered porous silicon (SPS) by Sony [1] and the University of Stuttgart [2], [3]; porous silicon process (PSI) by ZAE Bayern [4], [5]); and other associated methods is given by Brendel [6]. Other groups that have also been developing the layer transfer of thin silicon during the early years include Institut National des Sciences Appliquées de Lyon (INSA Lyon) [7] and IMEC [8], [9]. Presently, several institutes and companies are active in this field such as the Institute for Solar Energy Research (ISFH) [10], [11], Solexel [12], Crystal Solar [13], Episun [14], AmberWave [15], and IMEC [16].

In this approach, monocrystalline epitaxial silicon layers of $\sim$30–50 μm thickness, which are grown on sintered porous silicon with a double layer stack of two different porosities, are detached from the silicon parent substrates using a mechanically weak high-porosity porous silicon layer. However, the handling of thin silicon films (epifoils) after detachment from the parent substrate in a free-standing configuration will lead to increased yield loss due to breakages. In order to overcome this issue, the epitaxial film can first be front-side (sunny side) processed while attached to the parent substrate and then bonded to a superstrate glass before further processing into solar cells, such that the thin foils are never handled free-standing, as shown in Fig. 1. Several groups including IMEC follow this route [14], [17]. Alternatively, the epitaxial film can be rear-side (dark side) processed, while it is still attached to the parent substrate and then layer-transferred to a conductive substrate before the front-side is processed while bonded to the foreign substrate. This is the approach followed by AmberWave, where the epitaxial film is transferred to a steel substrate [15].

Although cell processing after the silicon foil is bonded to quartz has its constraints and complications (since compatibility with quartz and silicone is essential), conversion efficiencies of $\sim$18% have been achieved on solar cells processed with FZ silicon bonded to quartz prior to rear-side processing [17]. More impressively, Solexel has announced its world record conversion efficiency of >20% on 156 mm by 156 mm full-square solar cells using a 43 μm-thick epitaxial silicon in a back-contact/back-junction configuration [12]. At IMEC, the

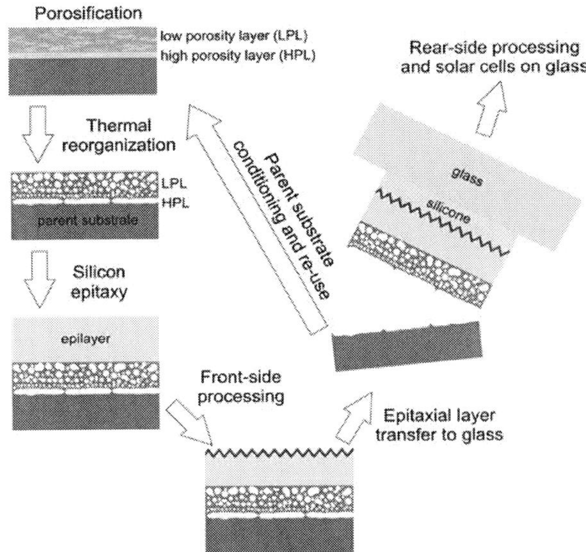

Fig. 1. Process flow for solar cells based on epifoils depicting the main steps of the porous silicon-based layer transfer sequence.

first attempt at processing quartz-bonded epifoils into solar cells have been made recently. Although there were contacting issues, high open-circuit voltages of ~650 mV were already achieved, highlighting the potential of this concept. In both cases, one of the key determinants toward the excellent cell performance characteristics is the high minority carrier lifetime, the improvement of which is the subject of this paper.

II. Porous Silicon as a Template for Epitaxy

Integral to the layer transfer process is the double layer stack of porous silicon (a low porosity layer (LPL) of ~1–2 μm on top of a high porosity layer (HPL) of ~300 nm) that is electrochemically etched on a highly doped silicon substrate. After etching, the porous silicon is sintered at a high temperature and the as-etched, fine columnar pores reorganize such that the HPL becomes a large extended void interrupted by tiny pillars, while the LPL transforms into smaller spheroidal voids embedded in a monocrystalline silicon matrix such that the surface is ideally free of open voids [18], [19], suitable for high-quality epitaxial growth, as depicted in Fig. 1. Thus, the HPL acts as the plane of detachment and the annealed LPL surface acts as the template for epitaxial growth of the epifoil. The efficiency potential of solar cells that is based on epifoils is mainly determined by the minority carrier lifetime achievable in these epifoils, which in turn depends on the quality of the epifoils that are grown on the porous silicon template. Therefore, it is expected that the properties of the porous silicon will strongly influence the crystal quality and hence the minority carrier lifetime of the epifoils.

The porous silicon layer can influence the epifoil quality in several ways. First, prior to epitaxy, since the epitaxial growth starts on the LPL surface, the morphological and topographical nature of the LPL surface will significantly influence the epitaxial growth process. Second, during epitaxy and subsequently,

the evolution of the intrinsically present stress distribution in the porous silicon layer as a whole can cause strain during epitaxial growth or even during the cool down and this is also expected to have an impact on the quality of the epifoil. Finally, in the postepitaxy stage, the morphological nature of the HPL determines the ease of detachment of the epifoil and thereby the amount of mechanical stresses that are induced in the foil during detachment. The easier the detachment, the better will be the epifoil quality.

In this study, the influence of the porous silicon layer on the epitaxial layer quality is studied, particularly focusing on the properties of the LPL, to understand how the epifoil quality can be improved by creating a better porous silicon template.

III. Experimental Method

All the sets of samples that are used in the series of experiments described in this paper were prepared using mirror-polished monocrystalline Czochralski (Cz) silicon wafers with a high boron doping concentration of 10^{19} cm^{-3}. On each of these wafers, a layer of porous silicon, typically with a double-layer structure that consists of an LPL (~30% porosity) on top of an HPL (~60% porosity), was electrochemically etched using an HF/ethanol mixture (22% HF by volume) as the electrolyte. This double layer structure is achieved by applying different current densities for the different layers: 1.4 mA/cm^2 for the LPL and ~73.5 mA/cm^2 for the HPL. The void size and void alignment in the LPL can be varied by altering its thickness and porosity. The thickness of the LPL was varied by varying the etching time between 40 s and 13 min, resulting in LPLs of thicknesses between 160 and 2100 nm. In two of the samples, a third layer of porous silicon of a slightly different porosity was added on top of a typical double-layer structure. This was done by using an applied current density of ~0.36 mA/cm^2 (denoted triple layer A) and ~6.9 mA/cm^2 (denoted triple layer B) for the third layer, respectively. The etching time for the two layers were 150 and 15 s, respectively, such that the thickness of the top layer is ~100 nm.

Following this, the samples were thermally treated at 1130 °C in hydrogen ambient at atmospheric pressure for 10 min. In one set of samples, no epitaxial layer was grown. In the other set, 40-μm-thick, n-type silicon epitaxial layers with an arsenic doping concentration of 10^{16} cm^{-3} were grown using atmospheric pressure chemical vapor deposition (APCVD) with trichlorosilane as the precursor.

Both types of samples were inspected using the Nova NanoSEM scanning electron microscope (SEM) to image the morphology of the different annealed porous silicon layers. From this, the median pore size at the LPL surface can be evaluated.

On the samples without an epilayer, stylus-based high-resolution profilometry measurements were performed on the LPL surface using HRP-200 (distributed by KLA Tencor), in order to analyze the local surface roughness of the growth surface after sintering. A typical scan length of ~20 μm was used and more than 20 profiles were measured in each sample. In addition, some of these samples were also used for noncontact optical profilometry measurements using NT9300 (distributed by Wyko), in order to measure the curvature of the substrate, from which the nature of the stress in porous silicon can be understood.

Some of the samples with an epilayer were defect-etched using the Wright etch solution [20] in order to calculate the crystal defect densities of the epilayers grown on different porous silicon templates. The defect-etched samples were inspected using an optical microscope with a differential interference contrast (DIC) setup in order to visualize and count the defects.

Two of the epilayer samples were also analyzed in cross section using a LabRam micro-Raman spectrometer with a laser of 514.5-nm wavelength to measure the stress distribution in the two porous silicon layers in cross section.

The remaining epilayer samples were passivated on the front side with 20 nm of intrinsic amorphous silicon and 10 nm of n^+ amorphous silicon (i/n^+ a-Si) using plasma-enhanced chemical vapor deposition (PECVD) at 200 °C. The detachment area was then defined by laser grooving using the TruMark Station 7000 distributed by Trumpf. The sample was then bonded to quartz using a 2-component silicone adhesive ("PV6100 Cell encapsulant," provided by Dow Corning), with the adhesive area smaller than the foil to be detached, such that the silicone is shielded during subsequent plasma processes, in order to minimize plasma-silicone interaction that will degrade the surface passivation quality and hence effective minority carrier lifetime [21]. After curing in a vacuum at 200 °C for more than 1 h, the samples were ultrasonicated for a few minutes in order to detach the epifoils from the parent substrates. The detached surface is then etched using an alkaline etchant to remove the residual porous silicon and the rear side is then passivated with PECVD i/n^+ a-Si as before. Minority carrier lifetime measurements are then performed on these passivated samples using the commercially available PL imaging tool (LIS-R1) from BT Imaging in which both quasi-steady-state photoconductance measurements (QSSPC) [22] as well as photoluminescence (PL) measurements can be performed. The samples were illuminated from the side of the quartz.

As a reference for lifetime measurements on porous silicon-based epifoils, lithography-based epifoils were also fabricated whereby the electrochemical etching of mesoporous porous silicon is replaced by dry etching of macropores patterned by deep-ultraviolet (DUV) lithography. This is based on the empty-space-in-silicon technique introduced by Mizushima *et al.* [23] and extended for solar cell applications by Depauw *et al.* [24]. This results in a epitaxial growth template that is close to ideal, as will be explained in Section IV-D. The rest of the process steps are the same as those for the porous silicon-based layer transfer process.

IV. Results and Discussion

The effect of varying the LPL thickness and porosity on the morphology and microstructure of the porous silicon, the stress distribution inside the porous silicon, the crystal defect density of the epilayer, and the lifetime of the epifoils is analyzed and explained in the coming sections.

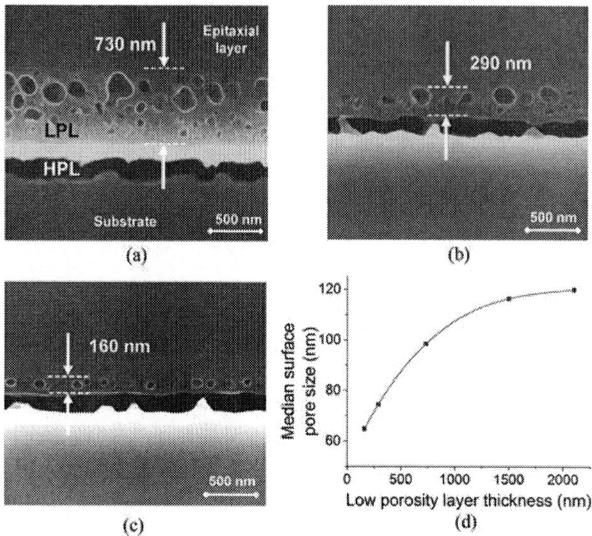

Fig. 2. Cross-sectional SEM images showing an epitaxial layer grown on top of a stack of porous silicon of two different porosities with a (a) 730 nm, (b) 290 nm, and (c) 160 nm thick LPL. (d) A plot depicting the correlation between the LPL thickness and the average surface pore or void size.

A. Annealed Porous Silicon Microstructure

The cross-sectional SEM images of three epifoil samples fabricated as explained previously with three different LPL thicknesses (160, 290 and 730 nm) are shown in Fig. 2(a)–(c). Note that the two samples with thicker LPLs show a distribution of decreasing void sizes in depth, with the voids closer to the HPL being much smaller than those close to the epitaxial layer. This is in contrast with what was observed in [19] (who observed a uniform distribution of void sizes in the separation layer) and in [18] (who observed the opposite trend of increasing void sizes in depth).

This can be explained using the classical sintering theory. Porous silicon reorganization occurs through vacancy diffusion processes driven by a vacancy concentration gradient between the pore (or void) and its surrounding lattice. Voids grow or shrink in size depending on the direction of this vacancy gradient. The vacancy gradient depends on the vacancy concentration at the rim of the pore relative to the lattice vacancy concentration. The vacancy concentration C_v, at the rim of a pore of radius, r, is given by [18]

$$C_v = C_0 \left(\frac{2\alpha}{r} \frac{V_0}{kT} + 1 \right) \tag{1}$$

where C_0 is the equilibrium lattice vacancy concentration in silicon at temperature T (in kelvins), α is the surface tension coefficient, V_0 is the intrinsic vacancy volume in silicon, and k is the Boltzmann constant. From this relation, it is clear that the vacancy concentration surrounding a larger void is smaller. Due to this, there exists a critical void radius r_c beyond which voids grow in size and below which voids shrink and disappear depending on the direction of the vacancy gradient. This critical radius is inversely proportional to the lattice vacancy

44

supersaturation, which is defined as the excess lattice vacancy concentration above the equilibrium value at temperature T [19]. The lower the supersaturation, the higher the critical radius. As a result, as thermal reorganization proceeds and the overall vacancy supersaturation in the porous silicon reduces, the average void size increases throughout the porous silicon.

The surface of the porous silicon layer is a vacancy sink with the vacancy concentration close to the thermodynamic equilibrium (C_0). This results in a steep vacancy gradient that sharply reduces the vacancy supersaturation close to the porous silicon layer surface. This in turn increases the critical void radius near the porous silicon surface, resulting in an overall increase in the sizes of the voids there. As the near-surface vacancy supersaturation reduces, there will be a vacancy gradient from deeper in the porous silicon toward the surface, resulting in a continued growth of voids near the surface, and then subsequently deeper and deeper in the porous silicon. This eventually results in a distribution of smaller and smaller void sizes deeper into the porous silicon layer. A similar vacancy gradient also exists between the LPL and the HPL which drains vacancies from the LPL at the interface region, resulting in the further accentuation of this void size distribution in depth.

This void size enlargement at the porous silicon surface becomes more prominent for the case of the thicker LPLs, since there are greater number of shrinking voids deeper in the LPL contributing to this void growth. A similar consequence for the HPL exists for the samples with very thin LPL, the smaller volume of the LPL contributing to the enhancement of the porosity of the HPL results in a lower porosity in the HPL after annealing compared with a stack with thicker LPL. This results in a greater density of thicker interruptions or pillars, making detachment of epifoil samples on very thin LPL more difficult or impossible. In the case of the thinnest LPL (i.e., 160 nm), the entire LPL interacts with the HPL and the surface, both of which act as vacancy sinks resulting in the shrinking of all LPL voids.

Important morphological differences can be identified among the samples with different LPL thicknesses. First, the median size of the voids closest to the epitaxial growth surface increases with increasing LPL thickness, from ~65 to ~120 nm in the investigated samples. This trend continues to be true up to an LPL thickness of ~2 μm, at which point it appears to saturate, as shown in Fig. 2(d). Second, the LPL voids have only reached their equilibrium shape in the thinnest LPL sample [see Fig. 2(c)], characterized by clearly discernible faceting. In contrast, the majority of the voids in the thicker LPL samples are in constant flux (shrinking or growing), thus having random shapes. Finally, while the voids in the thicker LPL samples are randomly stacked, the voids of the thinnest LPL are well aligned in a single lateral array. These differences are expected to manifest in the quality of the LPL growth surface.

The LPL surface, before epitaxy but after thermal reorganization, was analyzed using high-resolution profilometry. More than 20 profile scans were done and the root-mean-squared (RMS) values of all profiles were calculated, which is indicative of the roughness of the growth surface. Fig. 3 shows the distribution of the RMS values for four different LPL thicknesses. Clearly, the surface roughness of the growth surface

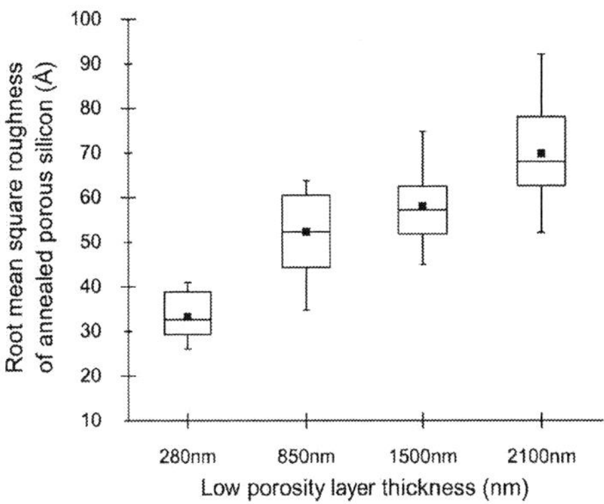

Fig. 3. Distribution of root-mean squared (RMS) values of the surface ordinates of the annealed LPL surface, calculated from more than 20 high resolution profilometry scans for four different LPL thicknesses, namely 280, 850, 1500, and 2100 nm. The three lines of the box plot refer to the 25th, 50th (median), and 75th percentiles and the lines/whiskers above and below the box extend to the 5th and 95th percentiles. The square symbol in the middle of the box plot refers to the mean value.

increases with the thickness of the LPL, because the pores are larger and more misaligned in the thicker LPLs, resulting in a rougher surface. A similar trend in the peak-to-peak roughness values was also observed, with the median peak-to-peak roughness that increases from ~18 nm for the thinnest LPL to ~35 nm for the thickest LPL investigated.

During epitaxy, the reactants are first adsorbed on the wafer surface where they react to form silicon atoms on the surface. This is followed by surface diffusion of the silicon atoms to the lowest energy sites on the surface, typically the edge of a step, leading to step flow growth. One of the factors that determine the quality of the epitaxy is the surface diffusion rate relative the arrival rate of the reactants. For high-quality epitaxy, the surface diffusion rate should be much greater than the arrival rate of the reactants. In a rougher surface, the surface diffusion rate is reduced and this will lead to more defects in the epitaxial layer. Thus, it can be expected that thinner LPL templates should result in a better growth surface for epitaxy.

B. Residual Stress in Porous Silicon

There have been reports on the presence of a residual tensile stress in electrochemically etched porous silicon, shown experimentally using X-ray diffraction [25] and micro-Raman spectroscopy [26] and explained theoretically by considering vacancy relaxation strain at the pore surfaces and thermal strain due to the difference in thermal expansion coefficients of silicon and porous silicon [27]. The residual stress is said to increase with pore size and has been reported to be in the range of a few hundred mega pascasl up to 1–3 GPa [26], [28]. The ultimate tensile strength of silicon is ~7 GPa.

Cross-sectional micro-Raman spectroscopy measurements were performed on the epifoil samples of two different LPL thicknesses, 850 and 1500 nm. In the absence of stress, the Raman peak for unstrained silicon occurs at a wavenumber of $\nu_0 = 520.75$ cm^{-1}. A shift in this wave number is a result of stress or change in crystallinity. Since the porous silicon layer is

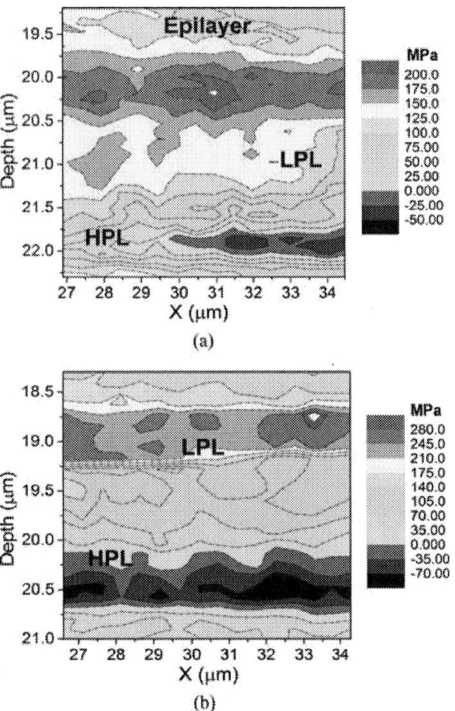

Fig. 4. Stress distribution maps obtained from cross-sectional micro-Raman spectroscopy for an epifoil sample with an LPL thickness of (a) 850 nm and (b) 1500 nm.

a quasi-monocrystal filled with voids, any peak shift is expected to be associated with a residual stress in porous silicon. The shift in the measured wavenumber ν relative to the unstrained silicon peak is then translated into stress values, σ (in Pa) according to [29]

$$\Delta\nu = \nu - \nu_0 = -2 \times 10^{-9}\sigma. \qquad (2)$$

The cross-sectional stress distribution maps of the epifoil samples are shown in Fig. 4. Note that for the sample with an LPL thickness of $\sim$850 nm, the entire porous silicon layer has been mapped [see Fig. 4(a)], while for the sample with an LPL thickness of $\sim$1500 nm, only part of the LPL is shown in Fig. 4(b). Several observations can be made from these maps. First, a band of compressive stress (negative values) corresponding to the region around the HPL be observed. Due to the relatively large spot size of $\sim$1 μm compared with the 200 nm-thick HPL, it is not possible to conclude if this observed compressive stress is from the HPL or from the silicon surrounding this layer.

Second, the region above this band can be expected to correspond to the LPL which is predominantly in tensile stress (positive values) with values in the range of 100–300 MPa. As mentioned previously, this agrees well with investigations reported earlier. In addition, optical profilometry measurements to evaluate the curvature of samples with different LPL thicknesses without epilayer also indicate the presence of a tensile stress in porous silicon.

Third, a band of high tensile stress occurs in the region where the LPL transits into the epilayer. This feature [not shown in Fig. 4(b)] was observed in both samples. It should be noted that while the measured stress distribution gives an averaged value over a relatively large area of porous silicon, the stresses in the porous silicon could be much higher locally and more widely distributed. Although the stress distribution is rather nonuniform, the epifoil sample with a thicker LPL shows a higher average tensile stress compared with that with a thinner LPL.

This has important implications for the quality of the epifoil. First, a higher stress in the porous silicon implies a larger strain (even if we assume negligible difference in the Young's modulus between the two LPLs) and hence a larger lattice mismatch between the porous silicon and the growing epitaxial silicon. Although the silicon epilayer will grow pseudomorphically at the beginning despite the slight lattice mismatch, the strain will eventually be relaxed via dislocations and stacking faults after the film has reached a critical thickness. Second, it has been reported that strain fields are intensified near sharp features [30]. Thus, a rougher porous silicon template with a similar intrinsic stress is likely to have local concentrations of higher stress at the growth surface. Third, a thinner LPL with smaller pore size distribution (and possibly lower porosity [see Fig. 2(c)] is likely to be stiffer than a thicker LPL [31], [32]. A stiffer material with the same intrinsic stress will induce a lower amount of strain in the growing silicon epilayer. All of these support the fact that the intrinsic stress in porous silicon is likely to be more detrimental for epilayers grown on thicker LPL templates.

C. Crystal Defect Density Analysis

To verify the impact of the porous silicon properties on the quality of the epilayers, the defect densities of epifoils grown on different porous silicon templates were evaluated. Three epifoil samples with LPL thicknesses of 250, 1500, and 2100 nm, and two epifoil samples with triple layers (triple layer A and B) of porous silicon as explained in Section III, were defect-etched using Wright etch solution for $\sim$70 s to reveal crystallographic defects present in the epilayer. A DIC optical microscope image of a defect-etched sample is shown in Fig. 5(a). The main defects observed in the epifoils after defect etching are dislocations, stacking faults, multiple stacking faults, and hillocks. Slip lines and orange peel defects were also observed among other defects. The square-shaped features in Fig. 5(a) correspond to etch pits, where stacking faults occur in the epifoil. The oval-shaped etch pits which appear as dots in the image are dislocations.

By sampling more than 50 locations in a defect-etched area of 3 cm $\times$ 3 cm, the areal density of the various crystal defects were calculated and the results are shown in Fig. 5(c). There is a clearly observable reduction in all the crystal defects as the LPL thickness is reduced. The total defect density reduces from $\sim$1230 defects/cm^2 in the sample with a 2100 nm-thick LPL to $\sim$420 defects/cm^2 in the sample with a 250 nm-thick LPL. This confirms our hypothesis that thinner LPL has a smoother surface and lower intrinsic stress, allowing a higher quality epilayer to be grown.

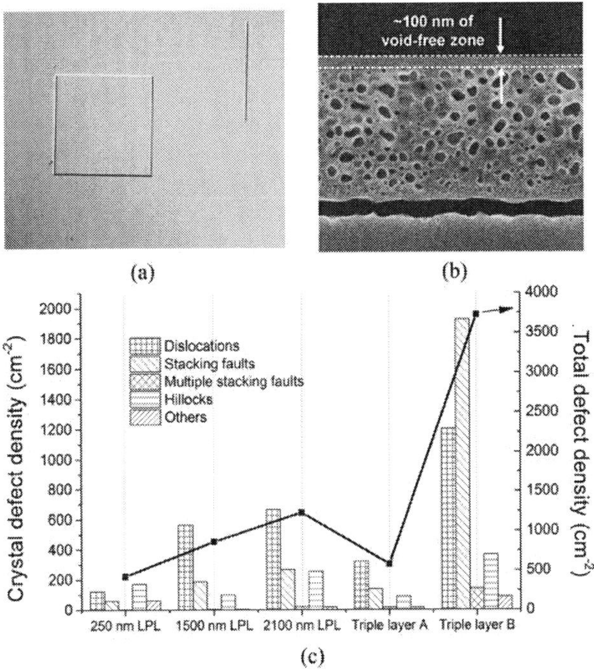

(a) (b)

(c)

Fig. 5. (a) Optical microscope image in differential interference contrast (DIC) mode of an epitaxial layer surface after defect-etching using the Wright etch solution showing stacking faults and dislocations. (b) Cross-sectional SEM image showing the porous silicon template for the trilayer layer A sample with a third layer of lower porosity than that of the LPL, showing ∼100 nm of void-free zone near the surface. (c) Areal density of various crystal defects for epifoil samples with different porous silicon templates. The total defect density is depicted as line and should be read off on the vertical axis on the right side.

For the triple layer sample A, it was observed that the overall defect density is significantly diminished to ∼580 defects/cm^2 compared with a porous silicon template without this 100 nm layer (∼860 defects/cm^2). By inspecting this porous silicon template (without an epilayer) using SEM [see Fig. 5(b)], it was observed that the top 100-nm region was almost void-free and the original lower porosity top layer acted as a sacrificial layer to create a zone free of voids. In contrast, the sample with an additional 100 nm of higher porosity top layer (triple layer B), the defect density is significantly increased to ∼3730 defects/cm^2. This suggests that it is indeed the surface roughness and the stress distribution of the near surface region of the LPL that are critical in determining the crystal quality of the epifoil. In typical double layer stacks, a 10-nm-thick void-free zone near the surface has been reported [19] but besides being much thinner than the triple layer approach, it is not uncommon to find sporadic defects such as open voids breaching this zone.

D. Minority Carrier Lifetime Measurements

The ultimate figure of merit to benchmark the quality of the epifoil is minority carrier lifetime. Lifetime measurements were performed on two sets of glass-bonded n-type arsenic-doped (10^{16}/cm^3) epifoils. The first set was obtained using the porous silicon-based layer transfer approach, while the second

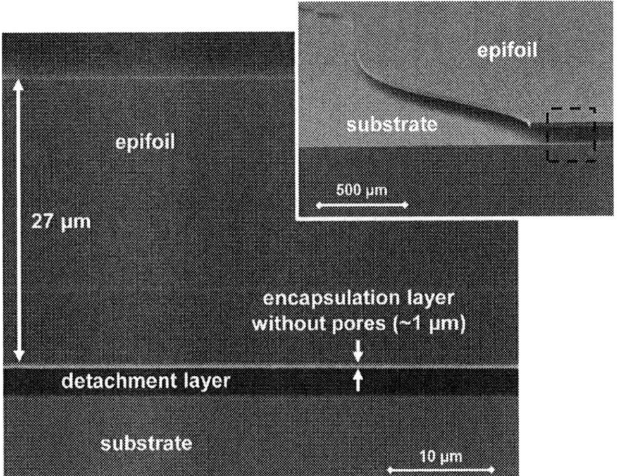

Fig. 6. Cross-sectional SEM image of the DUV lithography-based epifoil, showing pillar-free detachment layer and a pore-less encapsulation layer. (inset) Tilted view of the same sample at lower magnification.

set was fabricated using lithography-based layer transfer process, which creates a pillar-free detachment layer, encapsulated by a pore-free monocrystalline silicon seed layer [24], as depicted in Fig. 6. Since the encapsulating layer is pore free, epifoils produced from this approach can act as a reference for the lifetime measurements on porous silicon-based epifoils. For the porous silicon-based epifoils, three different LPL templates of the following thicknesses were used: 2100, 1400, and 720 nm. These samples were safely detachable with high yield. Much thinner LPL samples ($\leq$250 nm) that were investigated did not detach well, since they had higher densities of thicker pillars in the HPL making detachment impossible. Dedicated optimization is needed to achieve good detachment in samples with very thin LPL.

Lifetime measurements on both sets of epifoils were performed using quasi-steady-state photoconductance (QSSPC), and the best lifetime results are plotted in Fig. 7. Among the porous silicon-based epifoils, a clear trend in the effective lifetime is observed whereby the highest lifetime was measured in the epifoils grown on the thinnest LPL and reaches an excellent lifetime of ∼195 μs at an injection level of 10^{15} cm^{-3}, whereas the epifoil with the thickest LPL only yielded ∼85 μs at the same injection level. A comparison of the reference lithography-based epifoils with the porous silicon-based epifoils show a drastic difference in the best lifetimes obtained thus far, with the lithography-based epifoils exceeding 350 μs at the injection level of 10^{15} cm^{-3}. Since both sets of epifoils are identical except for the template layer for epitaxial growth, it is clear that by reducing the LPL thickness and/or porosity such that the voids in the LPL vanish (at least close to the interface with the epilayer), a drastic improvement in the lifetimes of porous silicon-based epifoils can be achieved. This is why porous silicon stacks like the one of triple layer A have potential in further improving the lifetime of porous silicon-based epifoils.

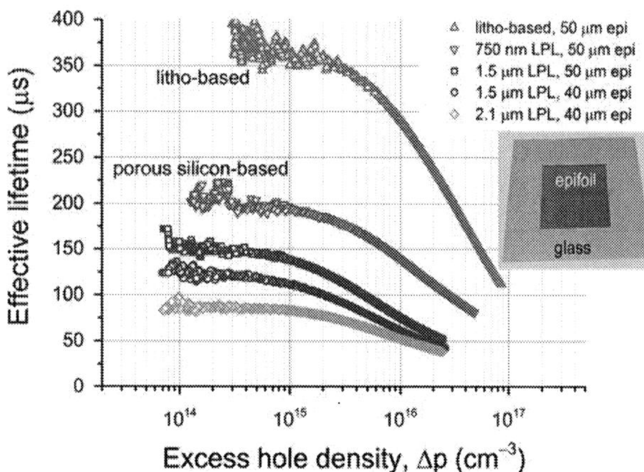

Fig. 7. Effective lifetimes as a function of injection level measured using QSSPC for porous silicon-based epifoils grown on three different porous silicon templates as well as lithography-based epifoils, confirming that higher quality epitaxial growth is obtained on thinner low-porosity layers. (inset) A photograph of a layer-transferred epifoil.

V. Conclusion

The quality of the epifoils produced using a porous silicon-based layer transfer process can be improved by controlling the properties of the LPL, which acts as the template for epitaxy. By reducing the thickness of this layer or the near-surface porosity of the porous silicon, the average near-surface pore size is reduced and better void alignment is achieved. This results in a less-defected and smoother surface with a lower residual stress distribution in porous silicon leading to a lower epilayer defect density of <420 defects/cm^2.

However, epifoils grown on very thin ($\leq$250 nm) LPL templates have detachment issues due to the reduced porosity and increased pillar density and size in the HPL. Thus, for the range of samples investigated, the thinnest LPL that still allows reliable detachment is $\sim$720 nm thick. Therefore, lifetime measurements could only be performed on epifoils grown on templates with an LPL thickness of $\geq$720 nm, which has higher defect densities than the best reported in this paper. Nevertheless, an enhancement in minority carrier lifetime in n-type epifoils of >100 μs has been achieved by reducing the LPL thickness up to $\sim$720 nm, with the effective diffusion length improving from $\sim$300 to $\sim$470 μm. Thus, the best porous silicon stack for achieving high lifetimes while maintaining reliable detachment is the one where the LPL thickness is $\sim$720 nm. This is much less than the standard thickness of $\sim$1–2 μm that is currently used [16], [33]. However, it should be noted that optimization of the porous silicon stack for reliable detachment was not done as part of this study, which leaves scope for improvement of the detachment yield of porous silicon stacks with thinner LPL (which could result in higher lifetimes).

Another alternative that is proposed in this study is to engineer a porous silicon template in such a way that the voids of the LPL are kept as far away from the growth surface as possible after sintering. To this end, a triple layer approach is introduced in this study, whereby a third very low porosity layer is added on top of the LPL to create a 100 nm-thick zone free of voids. This reduces the defect density of the standard detachable stack by more than 1.5 times. However, lifetime measurements on epifoils from such a stack must be performed to prove the actual benefit of this, while still allowing reliable detachment. An ideal reference system is the lithography-based epifoil, which has a seed layer free of enclosed voids. Lifetimes on such epifoils exceeded 350 μs (i.e., 600 μm diffusion length), indicating that it is possible to further improve the lifetime of porous silicon-based epifoils if the presence of voids in the LPL can be completely eliminated. To the best of our knowledge, these lifetime values are the best reported so far in thin silicon.

It must be noted that these results were obtained starting from mirror-polished substrates. It is expected that the nature of the starting surface will also influence the quality of the epitaxial film that is eventually grown on it. One of the corner stones of the layer transfer approach is the reuse of the parent substrate. It can be expected that the starting surface roughness of parent substrates is likely to be higher after the first layer transfer has been performed. Thus, it is worthwhile performing a similar study on reused substrates. Nevertheless, the results reported in this study are expected to largely hold for parent substrates that will be reused after surface conditioning (as indicated in Fig. 1). This is because, first, for an optimized layer transfer process, the surface of the parent substrate after detachment remains highly polished with nanoscale roughness that results from broken pillars during detachment. Second, it is not only the surface roughness that influences the epifoil quality but also the stress in porous silicon as was suggested in this study. Third, the substrate has to be chemically (or electrochemically) polished before reuse to remove the surface layer containing broken pillars which returns the surface close to that of a mirror-polished surface before the next cycle of layer transfer. Polishing removes <5 μm of silicon and this is still an order of magnitude less than the current state-of-the-art kerf loss for wafers [34].

Acknowledgment

The authors would like to thank S. K. P. Veerapandian for the support in processing and M. Moors for the discussions. The authors would also like to the thank the reviewers for the insightful remarks toward the improvement of the paper.

References

[1] H. Tayanaka, K. Yamauchi, and T. Matsushita, "Thin-film crystalline silicon solar cells obtained by separation of a porous silicon sacrificial layer," in *Proc. 2nd World Conf. Exhib. Photovoltaic Solar Energy Convers.*, Vienna, Austria, 1998, pp. 1272–1277.

[2] R. B. Bergmann, T. J. Rinke, R. M. Hausner, M. Grauvogl, M. Vetter, and J. H. Werner, "Thin film solar cells on glass by transfer of monocrystalline Si films," *Int. J. Photoenergy*, vol. 1, no. 2, pp. 89–93, 1999.

[3] R. B. Bergmann, C. Berge, T. J. Rinke, J. Schmidt, and J. H. Werner, "Advances in monocrystalline Si thin film solar cells by layer transfer," *Sol. Energy Mater. Sol. Cells*, vol. 74, no. 1–4, pp. 213–218, 2002.

[4] R. Brendel, "A novel process for ultrathin monocrystalline silicon solar cells on glass," in *Proc. 14th Eur. Photovoltaic Sol. Energy Conf. Exhib.*, Barcelona, Spain, 1997, p. 1354.

[5] R. Brendel, R. Auer, K. Feldrapp, D. Scholten, M. Steinhof, R. Hezel, and M. Schulz, "Crystalline thin-film Si cells from layer transfer using porous Si (PSi-process)," in *Proc. 29th IEEE Photovoltaic Spec. Conf.*, New Orleans, LA, USA, 2002, pp. 86–89.

[6] R. Brendel, "Review of layer transfer processes for crystalline thin-film Si solar cells," *Jpn. J. Appl. Phys.*, vol. 40, no. 7, pp. 4431–4439, 2001.

[7] A. Fave, S. Quoizola, J. Kraiem, A. Kaminski, M. Lemiti, and A. Laugier, "LPE and VPE silicon thin film on porous sacrificial layer," in *Proc. 3rd World Conf. Exhib. Photovoltaic Solar Energy Convers.*, Osaka, Japan, 2003, pp. 1229–1232.

[8] C. S. Solanki, R. R. Bilyalov, G. Beaucarne, and J. Poortmans, "Thin monocrystalline silicon films for solar cells," in *Proc. 3rd World Conf. Photovoltaic Energy Convers.*, Osaka, Japan, 2003, pp. 1320–1323.

[9] H. J. Kim, V. Depauw, F. Duerinckx, G. Beaucarne, and J. Poortmans, "Large-Area thin-film free-standing monocrystalline Si Solar cells by layer transfer," in *Proc. IEEE 4th World Conf. Photovoltaic Energy Convers. Conf. Record*, Waikoloa, HI, USA, 2006, pp. 984–987.

[10] J. H. Petermann, D. Zielke, J. Schmidt, F. Haase, E. Garralaga Rojas, and R. Brendel, "19%-efficient and 43 μm-thick crystalline Si solar cell from layer transfer using porous silicon," *Progress Photovoltaics: Res. Appl.*, vol. 20, pp. 1–5, 2012.

[11] F. Haase, S. Eidelloth, R. Horbelt, K. Bothe, E. Garralaga Rojas, and R. Brendel, "Loss analysis of back-contact back-junction thin-film monocrystalline silicon solar," *J. Appl. Phys.*, vol. 110, no. 12, pp. 124510-1–124510-9, 2011.

[12] M. Moslehi, "World-record 20% + efficiency 156 mm $\times$ 156 mm full square solar cells using low-cost kerfless ultrathin epitaxial silicon and porous silicon lift-off technology for industry-leading high performance smart PV modules," presented at the PV Asia Pacific Conf., Singapore, 2012.

[13] K. V. Ravi, "Poly-less, ingot-less, kerf-less production of very thin (<50 microns) single crystal Si wafers, solar cells and modules," presented at the 21st Workshop Crystalline Silicon Solar Cells Modules: Mater. Processes, Breckenridge, CO, USA, 2011.

[14] A. Bentzen and M. Nese, "A novel integrated approach to module manufacturing using epitaxial silicon layers," presented at the 3rd Int. Conf. Crystalline Silicon Photovoltaics, Hamelin, Germany, 2013.

[15] A. Lochtefeld, L. Wang, M. Carroll, J. Han, D. Stryker, S. Bengtson, Y. Yao, D. Lin, J. Ji, C. Leitz, A. Lennon, R. L. Opila, and A. Barnett, "15%, 20 Micron Thin, Silicon Solar Cells on Steel," presented at the 39th IEEE Photovoltaic Specialists Conf., Tampa, FL, USA, 2013.

[16] K. Van Nieuwenhuysen, V. Depauw, R. Martini, J. Govaerts, M. Debucquoy, H. S. Radhakrishnan, I. Gordon, and J. Poortmans, "High quality epitaxial foils, obtained by a porous silicon based layer transfer process, for integration in back contacted solar cells," in *Proc. 27th Eur. Photovoltaic Solar Energy Conf. Exhib.*, Frankfurt, Germany, 2012, pp. 2471–2474.

[17] F. Dross, K. Van Nieuwenhuysen, T. Bearda, M. Debucquoy, V. Depauw, J. Govaerts, C. Boulord, S. Granata, R. Labie, X. Loozen, R. Martini, B. O'Sullivan, H. S. Radhakrishnan, K. Baert, G. Beaucarne, I. Gordon, and J. Poortmans, "Cell Module integration concept compatible with c-Si epitaxial thin foils and with efficiencies over 18%," in *Proc. 27th Eur. Photovoltaic Solar Energy Conf. Exhib.*, Frankfurt, Germany, 2012, pp. 2207–2211.

[18] V. Labunov, V. Bondarenko, L. Glinenko, A. Dorofeev, and L. Tabulina, "Heat treatment effect on porous silicon," *Thin Solid Films*, vol. 137, pp. 123–134, 1986.

[19] N. Ott, M. Nerding, G. Müller, R. Brendel, and H. P. Strunk, "Evolution of the microstructure during annealing of porous silicon multilayers," *J. Appl. Phys.*, vol. 95, no. 2, pp. 497–503, 2004.

[20] M. W. Jenkins, "A new preferential etch for defects in silicon crystals," *J. Electrochem. Soc.*, vol. 124, pp. 757–759, 1977.

[21] J. Govaerts, S. N. Granata, T. Bearda, F. Dross, C. Boulord, G. Beaucarne, F. Korsos, K. Baert, I. Gordon, and J. Poortmans, "Development of a-Si/c-Si heterojunctions for the i2-module concept: Low-temperature passivation and emitter formation on wafers bonded to glass," *Sol. Energy Mater. Sol. Cells*, vol. 113, pp. 52–60, 2013.

[22] R. A. Sinton and A. Cuevas, "Contactless determination of current-voltage characteristics and minority-carrier lifetimes in semiconductors from quasi-steady-state photoconductance data," *Appl. Phys. Lett.*, vol. 69, pp. 2510–2512, 1996.

[23] I. Mizushima, T. Sato, S. Taniguchi, and Y. Tsunashima, "Empty-space-in-silicon technique for fabricating a silicon-on-nothing structure," *Appl. Phys. Lett.*, vol. 77, no. 20, pp. 3290–3292, 2000.

[24] V. Depauw, I. Gordon, G. Beaucarne, J. Poortmans, R. Mertens, and J.-P. Celis, "Large-area monocrystalline silicon thin-films by annealing of macroporous arrays: Understanding and tackling defects in the material," *J. Appl. Phys.*, vol. 106, pp. 033516-1–033516-10, 2009.

[25] J. M. López-Villegas, M. Navarro, D. Papadimitriou, J. Bassas, and J. Samitier, "Structure and non-uniform strain analysis on p-type porous silicon by X-ray reflectometry and X-ray diffraction," *Thin Film Solids*, vol. 276, pp. 238–240, 1996.

[26] Z.-K. Lei, Y.-L. Kang, M. Hu, Y. Qiu, H. Xu, and H.-P. Niu, "An experimental analysis of residual stress measurements in porous silicon using micro-Raman spectroscopy," *Chinese Phys. Lett.*, vol. 21, no. 2, pp. 403–405, 2004.

[27] M. Y. Ghannam, M. M. Hassan, V. Depauw, G. Beaucarne, J. Poortmans, and R. Mertens, "Study and estimation of the residual stress in porous silicon layer formed on the surface of a crystalline silicon substrate," *Thin Solid Films*, vol. 516, no. 20, pp. 6924–6929, 2008.

[28] Y. H. Ogata, N. Yoshimi, R. Yasuda, T. Tsuboi, and T. Sakka, "Structural change in p-type porous silicon by thermal annealing," *J. Appl. Phys.*, vol. 90, pp. 6487–6492, 2001.

[29] I. de Wolf, *Analytical Application of Raman Spectroscopy*, M. J. Pelletier, Ed. Oxford, U.K: Blackwell, 1999, p. 464.

[30] M. Feron, Z. Zhang, and Z. Suo, "Split singularities and dislocation injection in strained silicon," *J. Appl. Phys.*, vol. 102, pp. 023502-1–023502-6, 2007.

[31] R. Martini, V. Depauw, M. Gonzalez, K. Vanstreels, K. Van Nieuwenhuysen, I. Gordon, and J. Poortmans, "Mechanical properties of sintered meso-porous silicon: A numerical model," *Nanoscale Res. Lett.*, vol. 7, p. 597, 2012.

[32] D. Bellet, P. Lamagnère, A. Vincent, and Y. Bréchet, "Nanoindentation investigation of the Young's modulus of porous silicon," *J. Appl. Phys.*, vol. 80, no. 7, pp. 3772–3776, 1996.

[33] R. Brendel, K. Feldrapp, R. Horbelt, and R. Auer, "15.4%-efficient and 25 μm-thin crystalline Si solar cell from layer transfer using porous silicon," *Physica Status Solidi A*, vol. 197, pp. 497–501, 2003.

[34] International Technology Roadmap for Photovoltaics (ITRPV) Results 2012. (2013, Aug. 1). *SEMI*. [Online]. Available: http://www.itrpv.net

Authors' photographs and biographies not available at the time of publication.

Energy Yield of thin-film PV Modules and the Relevance of low Irradiance, Spectral and Temperature Effects

M. Schweiger, U. Jahn, W. Herrmann, TÜV Rheinland Energie und Umwelt GmbH,
A. Gerber, C. Ulbrich, U. Rau, Forschungszentrum Jülich GmbH

Abstract—The electrical performance and energy yield of 25 PV modules were studied in the laboratory and under moderate climate conditions. The study compares thin-film technologies (a-Si, a-Si/μc-Si, a-Si/a-Si, CIS, CIGS and CdTe) and crystalline silicon technologies (mono- and polycrystalline). Intensive laboratory tests were performed before and after the outdoor exposure with regard to low irradiance behavior as well as sensitivity to spectrum and module temperature. Measurements according to IEC 61853-1 provide information about the non-linear behavior of thin-film modules in respect to irradiance and temperature. The spectral response was determined in the module plane according to IEC 60904-8. Combining the measured spectral response and the measured spectral solar irradiance data, an automated spectral mismatch correction could be implemented to improve monitoring. Additionally, the average photon energy factor was used to determine the dependency of the photo current on spectral shifts for the module technologies under investigation. In a final ranking the energy yield of all tested specimens is compared and the influence of spectrum, temperature and low irradiance behavior on the energy yield is quantified for moderate climate conditions.

Index Terms—APE factor, ECT method, energy yield, low irradiance behavior, module characterization, non-linearity, spectral response, spectrum, thin-film.

Submitted for review in June 10, 2013.

This work was supported by the German Federal Ministry for the Environment, Nature Conservation and Nuclear Safety (BMU) as part of contract no. 0325070A and by the participating PV module suppliers.

M. Schweiger, is with the solar innovation department, TÜV Rheinland Energie und Umwelt GmbH, Cologne, NRW 51105 Germany (e-mail: markus.schweiger@de.tuv.com).

U. Jahn, is with the solar innovation department, TÜV Rheinland Energie und Umwelt GmbH, Cologne, NRW 51105 Germany (e-mail: ulrike.jahn@de.tuv.com).

W. Herrmann, is with the solar innovation department, TÜV Rheinland Energie und Umwelt GmbH, Cologne, NRW 51105 Germany (e-mail: werner.herrmann@de.tuv.com).

A. Gerber, is with the Institute of Energy- and Climate Research, IEK5-Photovoltaics, Forschungszentrum Jülich GmbH, Jülich, NRW 52425 Germany (e-mail: a.gerber@fz-juelich.de).

C. Ulbrich, is with the Institute of Energy- and Climate Research, IEK5-Photovoltaics, Forschungszentrum Jülich GmbH, Jülich, NRW 52425 Germany (e-mail: c.ulbrich@fz-juelich.de).

U. Rau, is director of the Institute of Energy- and Climate Research, IEK5-Photovoltaics, Forschungszentrum Jülich GmbH, Jülich, NRW 52425 Germany (e-mail: u.rau@fz-juelich.de).

I. INTRODUCTION

The predicted specific energy yield (kWh/kW$_{Peak}$) of PV modules is more important for investors than the single maximum power P_{Max} value at standard test conditions (STC). The uncertainties of energy yield predictions are high and errors greater than ±5% occur even with high quality input-data [1]. To calculate the estimated energy yield and guarantee the bankability of PV-systems in particular for thin-film technologies, models must be improved. These models must be validated by comparing calculated performance data with precise measured outdoor performance data [2]. To reach a high accuracy in modeling the crucial input parameters as the temperature coefficients must be determined accurately.

The factors influencing the energy yield are hard to separate. Their influence depends on the outdoor conditions:

- Module efficiency at low irradiance $\eta(G)$
- Temperature coefficient of nominal power γ (TC_{Pmax}) and its dependence on the irradiance G
- Weighted-average module temperature (depends on the module design)
- Adjustment of the external quantum efficiency EQE to the available spectral distribution of solar insolation
- Angular characteristics (textured glass, AR coating)
- Shade, soiling, snow, etc.
- Long-term stability

The aim of the performed high-precision outdoor energy yield measurements is to achieve a low uncertainty in the determination of the parameters needed to model the energy yield. This paper shows how to separate the most important effects influencing the module performance as fluctuations of temperature, solar irradiance and spectral composition. The correction of these effects improves the monitoring of the output power and has enabled us to survey the performance stability outdoors, independent of weather conditions.

II. Experimental techniques

A. Indoor and outdoor characterization

1) Indoor characterization

Prior to the outdoor exposure all modules were first stabilized indoors according to the light-soaking test of IEC 61646 [3] at a temperature of 50°C and an irradiance of 1000 W/m². Afterwards, we characterized the modules by means of a pulsed solar simulator with a classification of AAA according to IEC 60904-9 [4]. *IV*-measurements were carried out both at seven irradiation levels between 100 and 1100 W/m² and four module temperatures between 15 and 75°C as described in the IEC Standard 61853-1 [5]. In addition, we determined the spectral response (SR) of each module in order to investigate the spectral influence on the modules. We used a special *SR* measurement setup for encapsulated modules, developed by AIST [6].

2) Outdoor characterization

The specimens were exposed at the outdoor test-site during two periods, from May, 1st 2010 through April, 30th 2011 and from August, 1st 2011 through July, 31st 2012. The modules were mounted facing south and tilted by 35°. The test-site is located on the rooftop of an office building in Cologne, Germany, at 50°55'22.55" north, 6°59'30.40" east, with a ground elevation of about 60 m MSL. Due to their exposed and careful installation, the modules were not shaded neither by trees or building parts, nor by other solar modules. Each module was equipped with a separate electronic DC load automatically and synchronous performing the P_{MPP}-tracking every 30 s and the IV-curve measurement every 10 min with a measurement duration below 1 s. All sensors have been calibrated and radiation sensors have been cleaned regularly. Temperature and irradiance measurements were taken every 30 s, the solar spectral irradiance was measured every 60 sec.

3) Measurements of the module temperature

The module temperature was measured at the rear side of a module with a Pt-100 sensor. With an infrared camera a representative position for the sensor was chosen. To analyse measurement errors on the back sides of modules, we qualified the temperature measurements using the equivalent cell temperature (ECT-method) for thin-film technologies according to IEC 60904-5 [12]. The equivalent cell temperature *ECT* is determined by the indoor-measured temperature dependency of the open circuit voltage as shown in equation (5) by solving equation (2) for T_2. The *ECT* quantity is an average temperature value of the entire cell (module), whereas the temperature measured by a sensor at the back side of a module is strongly influenced by the thermal properties of the encapsulation material.

$$ECT = 25°C + \frac{1}{\beta_{rel}}\left[\frac{U_{OC2}}{U_{OC,STC}} - 1 - a\,ln\left(\frac{G_2}{1000\ Wm^{-2}} \right) \right] \quad (5)$$

B. Performance monitoring without meteorological influences

The implementation of automated temperature, irradiance and spectral mismatch corrections in the data processing software allows monitoring of the performance stability during outdoor exposure. Typical seasonal sinusoid fluctuations in performance of a-Si modules result for the most part from spectral effects and vanish after the spectral mismatch correction, as shown in Fig. 1. Degradation effects, like the Staebler–Wronski effect, can then be monitored without the disturbance variables of the climatic conditions. Thermal annealing was not detected for the moderate climate of the test-site.

1) Correction of temperature and irradiance effects

Equations (1) and (2) show the correction of irradiance and temperature for each single data point of a recorded *IV* curve to any desired target value according to IEC 60891 [7] procedure 2. The formulas derived for wafer based silicon solar cells are applied to the thin-film technologies being aware of the assumptions made. The norm assumes superposition in the *IV* diode equation. Parameters required for the translation to STC were calculated from indoor data. These parameters are: the relative temperature coefficient of the short circuit current α_{rel}, the relative temperature coefficient of the open circuit voltage β_{rel}, the internal series resistance R'_s, the irradiance correction factor of the open circuit voltage a, and the temperature coefficient of the internal series resistance κ'.

$$I_2 = I_1 \cdot [1 + \alpha_{rel} \cdot (T_2 - T_1)] \cdot G_2 / G_1 \quad (1)$$

$$V_2 = V_1 + V_{OC1} \cdot \beta_{rel} \cdot (T_2 - T_1) + a \cdot \ln G_2 / G_1 \\ - R'_s \cdot (I_2 - I_1) - \kappa' \cdot I_2 \cdot (T_2 - T_1) \quad (2)$$

Where I_1, V_1, V_{OC1} are the coordinates of points on the measured *IV* characteristics and G_1, T_1 are the measured module temperature and irradiance for this *IV* curve. Parameters with the index 2 are the corresponding points on the corrected *IV* curve for the target temperature (25°C) and irradiance (1000 W/m²) values.

2) Correction of spectral effects

Measurements of the spectral response of each specimen $SR_{\mathrm{Spec}}(\lambda)$ according to IEC 60904-8 [8] and the solar spectral irradiance $E_{\mathrm{Mess}}(\lambda)$ at 60 second time intervals allowed for each measured *IV* curve the calculation of the spectral mismatch (*MM*-) factor as shown in (3) according to IEC 60904-7 [9]. This *MM*-factor can be used to perform a spectral mismatch correction to correct deviations from the STC reference spectrum $E_{\mathrm{Ref}}(\lambda)$ according to IEC 60904 3 [10]. If there is a change in the spectrum, the useful fraction for the photo-effect changes, this effect can be balanced out by a change in the irradiance at the module. Therefore, we applied the spectral correction prior to the irradiance correction (see previous paragraph).

$$MM = \frac{\int E_{Ref}(\lambda) \cdot SR_{Ref}(\lambda) d\lambda \cdot \int E_{Mess}(\lambda) \cdot SR_{Spec}(\lambda) d\lambda}{\int E_{Mess}(\lambda) \cdot SR_{Ref}(\lambda) d\lambda \cdot \int E_{Ref}(\lambda) \cdot SR_{Spec}(\lambda) d\lambda} \quad (3)$$

$SR_{Ref}(\lambda)$ is the spectral response of the reference device. In this study a ventilated CMP21 pyranometer from Kipp & Zonen was used. It shows a constant spectral response in the desired wavelength range.

In order to analyze the solar spectral variations in central Europe, we used the so called average photon energy (*APE* factor) [11]. This factor reduces the amount of data by expressing the blue or red shift of a spectrum in one single quantity. The average photon energy is calculated by dividing the integrated energy of a spectrum by the number of photons of a spectrum, as shown in (4). Whereas $E_i(\lambda)$ is the spectral irradiance and $\Phi_i(\lambda)$ is the photon flux density. To get the unit electron-volts the elementary charge q_e is used as a conversion factor.

$$APE = \frac{\int_a^b E_i(\lambda) d\lambda}{q_e' \int_a^b \Phi_i(\lambda) d\lambda} \quad (4)$$

The *APE* strongly depends on the integration limits a and b. The integration interval is defined by the measuring range of the spectrometer. The used spectrometer was equipped with a combined Si/InGaAs-detector operating in a wavelength range between 300 nm and 1600 nm. Therefore, an integral range between $a = 300$ nm and $b = 1600$ nm was chosen for all *APE* calculations. Using the standard AM1.5 spectrum, this leads to an *APE* factor of *APE* = 1.65 eV. Accordingly, the *APE*-factors of spectra which are shifted to the red compared to the AM1.5 spectrum are below 1.65 eV, spectra which show a blue shift, lead to an *APE* factor above 1.65 eV. An integrating sphere combined with a glass dome served as input optic.

III. RESULTS

The following sections give an overview on the reasons leading to differences in the yield of PV modules.

A. Low irradiance behavior

To determine the low irradiance conditions at the test site, we classified the pyranometer measurements. The irradiation in the tilted module-plane and in the horizontal plane was respectively summed up for different irradiance levels in intervals of 100 W/m² and its percentage of the annual insolation calculated. As shown in Fig. 2, a great share of the insolation results from low irradiance. The share is getting even bigger for deviations of the ideal mounting direction 35° tilted, facing south.

For the purposes of illustration five representative modules including the best and worst performing specimens from approx. 60 samples were selected. As shown in Fig. 3 the efficiency reduces to less than 60% at 100W/m² for some modules. Others can increase their efficiency for low irradiance conditions to up to 104%. For all tested specimens a linear behaviour of the short circuit current in the range of 100 W/m² to 1100 W/m² was detected.

For most thin-film modules the low irradiance behaviour is dominated by a small parallel resistance R_P whereas for crystalline silicon the dominating factor was found in a high series resistance R_S in relation to the occurring current at maximum power point. The performance at different irradiance levels depends more on the specific module type than on the given technology. A better low irradiance behaviour of thin-film in comparison to crystalline silicon modules as often claimed could not be confirmed in general.

Given the low irradiance behaviour of each module for constant spectral conditions from the IEC 61853-1 measurements, the frequency distribution of Fig. 2 can be weighted with a low irradiance function of Fig. 3 to calculate the influence on the energy yield. For selected modules, the low irradiance effect on the energy yield without spectral or temperature influences was calculated to result in an annual win/loss of +2% (SP1) and -10% (SP5). The annual win/loss of most of the tested and commercially available modules is found to be in a range of +1 % (SP2) and -5% (SP4). Specimen 3 (SP3) with -3% yield loss represents a typical thin-film module. Other mounting geometries involving a higher low light fraction intensify the effect. For horizontal mounting we have calculated +2%, 0%, - 4%, -7%, -14% for specimens 1 – 5.

B. Temperature effects

Indoor studies of the temperature coefficients and their non-linearity in respect to the irradiance G have been performed. The smallest relative temperature coefficients at STC are achieved by CdTe (-0,16 to -0,25 %/K), followed by a-Si (-0,19 to -0,41 %/K), CI(G)S (-0,30 to -0,46 %/K) and c-Si (-0,41 to -0,51 %/K). Thin-film modules showed a strong dependence on the irradiance for the temperature coefficient γ, as shown in Fig. 4.

From the outdoor data we observed, some modules permanently reach higher module temperatures than others, as shown in Fig. 5. This may be the cause of the device specific mechanical, thermal and optical properties, e.g. the backrails, cooling fins, or mounting bars. For that reason the average module temperature for real operating conditions must be known. To calculate the influence on the energy yield the weighted average module temperature was calculated for each specimen as in (7). Whereas T_{BoM} is the temperature measured at the back of the module.

$$\overline{T}_{BoM,G} = \frac{\sum_{i=1}^{N}(T_{BoM,i} \cdot G_i)}{\sum_{i=1}^{N} G} \qquad (7)$$

The weighted average module temperatures range from 29.7°C to 32.7°C. Given a maximal temperature difference of $\Delta T = 3.5°C$ and a worst-case temperature coefficient of $\gamma = -0.51\%/K$, the difference in the yield of different module designs can be as large as 1.5 %. Relative to STC conditions (25°C) the maximal difference is $\Delta T = 7.7°C$ and the minimal difference is $\Delta T = 4.7°C$ indicating yield losses of up to -1% to -4% depending on the temperature coefficient γ.

The increase of the temperature coefficient due to its non-linearity has a positive effect on the yield of up to +6% compared to calculations for a constant TC value. This is the consequence of the low average module temperature of less than 25°C (STC value) for low irradiance, as shown in Fig. 5.

The error in the temperature measurements on the back of the module was analysed by means of the ECT method. For all tested samples the method works up to the threshold of approximately 200 W/m². The absolute error compared with the Pt100 value was below 2°C. The Pt100 value tends to be too high for low irradiance because of the heat insulation of the sensor. For high irradiance the Pt100 value tends to be too low because of the temperature gradient of the cells on the back of the module. The difference between the two temperature values allows the determination and validation of the irradiance correction factor a of the open circuit voltage. The logarithmic dependency of the open circuit voltage on the irradiance can be adjusted by an accurate correction factor a multiplied with the logarithm. For the ideal correction factor, a linear relationship between ECT and T_{BoM} can be found, as shown in Fig. 6 for $a = 0.045$.

C. Influence of spectrum

Analysis of the spectral data using the APE factor revealed a red shift in the distribution of the solar spectrum for winter and a blue shift for summer. The daily variations are not unitary, but depend mainly on the sky cover, angle of incidence, AirMass and mounting direction. Fig. 7 reveals distinct differences in the daily changes for clear sky days at different months of the year.

The spectral effect on the energy yield depends greatly on the module technology or more precisely on the spectral response of the specimen. The spectral response (see Fig. 8 for exemplary curves), can significantly vary within one module technology.

To illustrate the spectral dependency of the photo current, irradiance and temperature corrected I_{SC} from IV curve measurements were filtered and plotted against the APE values, as shown in Fig. 9. The deployed filter contains all data in the range of 400 W/m² to 1200 W/m² and 0 °C to 60°C. The angle of incidence was restricted to values smaller than 50° to avoid angle effects resulting by the good angle

dependence of the pyranomter and the poor angle characteristics of the modules. The largest spectral influence was detected for a-Si modules. The values of I_{SC} can fluctuate up to ± 20% because of the spectrum alone. For CdTe a slight dependence of ± 5% was calculated. For CI(G)S and c-Si almost no spectral dependence can be ascertained. The a-Si/μc-Si specimens show a combination of a-Si behavior for APE < 1.65 eV (when the current is dominated by the top cell) and μc-Si behaviour for APE > 1.65 eV (when the current is dominated by the bottom cell). Significant yield losses due to current mismatching can be expected because of the large losses of a-Si for red shifts und the small gains of μc-Si for blue shifts.

To evaluate the influence on the energy yield for single-junctions modules, we calculated an average spectrum for the period of September 2011 to August 2012 for irradiance values above 50 W/m². The result was a spectrum with very small deviations to the IEC 60904-3 spectrum. For that reason for single-junction c-Si and CIGS modules with small spectral dependence there is no significant spectral effect on the energy yield. For CdTe small gains of 1% can be calculated. For a-Si single junction and large top layer current-limiting a-Si/a-Si modules maximal gains of 3% of the energy yield are possible over the period in question. For other mounting directions and locations near the equator the average spectrum is suspected to be significantly bluer because of smaller *AirMass* values.

D. Final energy yield ranking

To compare the results of the two years of outdoor exposure, we calculated the performance ratio (*PR*), as shown in (6). The annual absolute energy yield EY$_a$ is the sum of all P_{MPP} values recorded synchronous for all specimens starting at 50W/m². The nominal power $P_{Max,STC}$ is the stabilized outdoor value. The numerator is thus a specific energy yield independent of the module power class. The denominator is the annual insolation H$_{a,Pyr}$ divided by the irradiance at STC G_{STC} (= 1000 W/m²).

$$PR = \frac{EY_a / P_{Max,STC}}{H_{a,Pyr} / G_{STC}} \qquad (6)$$

Differences between the tested modules in their energy yield of up to 11.8% were detected, as shown in the ranking of Fig. 10. The total error bars for the specific energy yield assessment measurements, were estimated at ±5% in 2010-11 and ±4% in 2011-12. The uncertainty is basically resulting from irradiance sensor calibration along with uncertainties in the determination of nominal power and the PMPP-tracking.

IV. SUMMARY

The performance characteristics of different PV module technologies were analysed under indoor and outdoor conditions. From comprehensive indoor characterizations we studied the module performance under various irradiations (100 – 1100 W/m²) and temperatures between 15°C and 75°C. In addition, we used a special SR setup to determine the relative EQE of the modules. With that data we were able to correct the outdoor data, even for a spectral mismatch.

From the outdoor data we conclude, that the energy yield in a moderate climate varied for the tested modules by up to 11.8%. Yield losses due to poor low irradiance performance can increase to up to -10% for ideal mounting, depending mainly on the module manufacturer. Temperature losses of up to -1.5% due to module design and -4% because of the temperature coefficient γ have been calculated. Yield gains of up to +3% due to spectral effects are possible for a-Si and gains of up to +1% for CdTe modules.

Within the research project PVKLIMA the previous investigations will be expanded to different climatic conditions and calculation models will be developed.

REFERENCES

[1] M. Herz, A. Sepanski, D. Nörenberg, M. Schweiger, U. Jahn, "Simulierte Energieerträge von Dünnschicht-Modulen," in 27th PVSOL, Bad Staffelstein, Germany, 2012, pp. 552 - 557.

[2] S. Dittmann, G. Friesen, S. Williams, T. Betts, R. Gottschalg, H.G. Beyer, A. Guérin de Montgareuil, N. van der Borg, A.R. Burgers, T. Huld, B. Müller, C. Reise, J. Kurnik, M. Topic, T. Zdanowicz, F. Fabero (2010, Sep.). Results of the 3rd Modelling Round Robin within the European Project „PERFORMANCE"– Comparison of Module Energy Rating Methods. Presented at 25th EU PVSEC, Valencia, Spain. [Online]. Available: http://www.eupvsec-proceedings.com/proceedings?fulltext=dittmann&paper=7742.

[3] Thin-film terrestrial photovoltaic (PV) modules - Design qualification and type approval, IEC 61646, 2009.

[4] Solar simulator performance requirements, IEC 60904-9, 2008.

[5] Photovoltaic (PV) module performance testing and energy rating: Irradiance and temperature performance measurements and power rating, IEC 61853-1, 2011.

[6] Y. Tsuno, Y. Hishikawa, K. Kurokawa (2008, Sep.). A Method for Spectral Response Measurements of Various PV Modules. Presented at 23rd EU PVSEC, Valencia, Spain. [Online]. Available: http://www.eupvsec-proceedings.com/proceedings?fulltext=tsuno&paper=3611.

[7] Procedures for temperature and irradiance corrections to measured I-V characteristics, IEC 60891, 2010.

[8] Measurement of spectral response of a photovoltaic (PV) device, IEC 60904-8 (CDV), 2012.

[9] Computation of the spectral mismatch correction for measurements of photovoltaic devices, IEC 60904-7, 2009.

[10] Measurement principles for terrestrial photovoltaic (PV) solar devices with reference spectral irradiance data, IEC 61853-3, 2009.

[11] T. Betts, "Investigation of Photovoltaic Device Operation under Varying Spectral Conditions," Ph.D. dissertation, Loughborough University, 2004.

[12] Determination of the equivalent cell temperature (ECT) of photovoltaic (PV) devices by the open-circuit voltage method, IEC 60904-5, 2012.

AUTHOR

M. Schweiger was born in Landshut, Germany, in 1984. He received the B.S. and M.S. degrees in electrical engineering from the Technical University Munich, Germany, in 2009. He is currently pursuing the Ph.D. degree in electrical engineering at the RWTH Aachen University, Germany.

Since 2009, he is working as Project Engineer and Research Assistant with the Solar Innovation Department of TÜV Rheinland Energie und Umwelt GmbH, Cologne, Germany. His research interest includes high-precision PV module characterization, performance behavior of thin-film PV modules and energy yields of different PV module technologies.

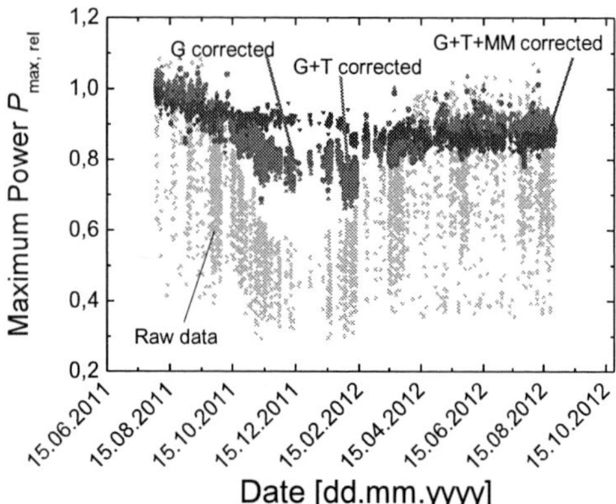

Fig. 1. Raw and corrected outdoor data of a top-limited silicon thin-film a-Si/µc-Si tandem module. Irradiance corrected (G), additionally temperature corrected (G+T) and finally spectral mismatch corrected (G+T+MM) data. The effect of the temperature correction is very little (red and blue data points).

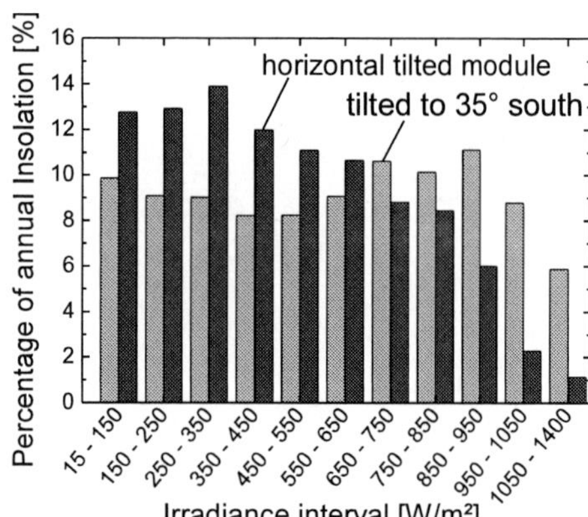

Fig. 2. Distribution of insulation for different irradiance levels, measured with a pyranometer tilted 35° and facing south and horizontal, 01.08.2011 – 31.07.2012, Cologne

56

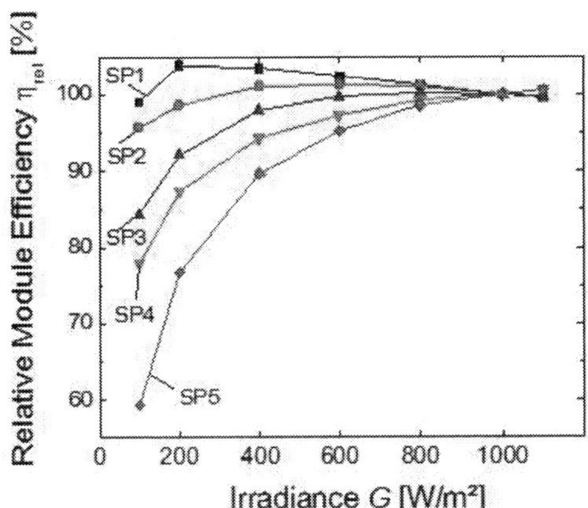

Fig. 3. Low irradiance behavior of 5 representative thin-film modules

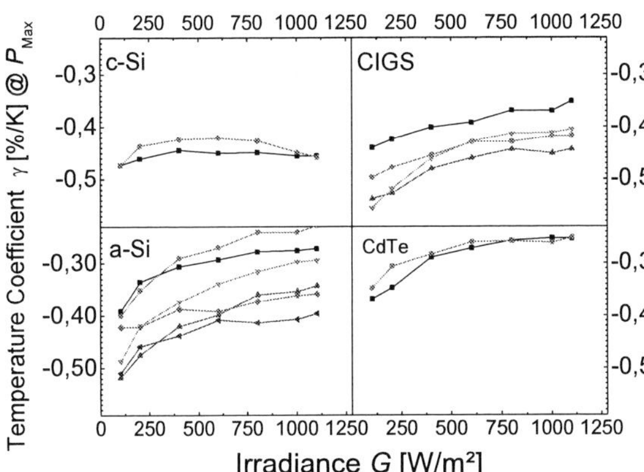

Fig. 4. Temperature coefficient γ of different wafer based silicon and thin-film modules in dependence on the irradiance G measured with a pulsed solar simulator (no spectral shift).

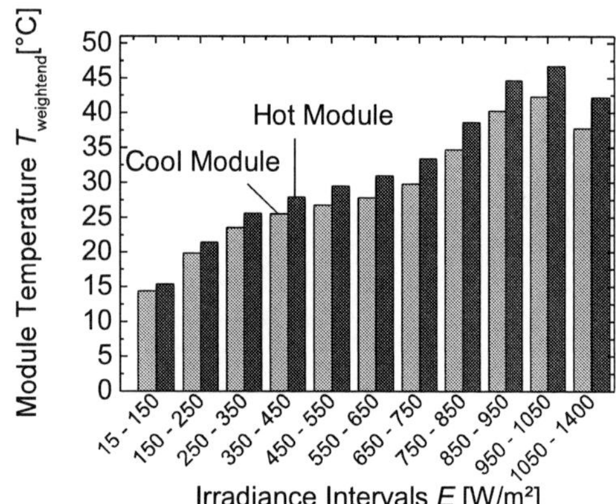

Fig. 5. Average module temperature weighted with irradiance in dependence on the irradiance level.

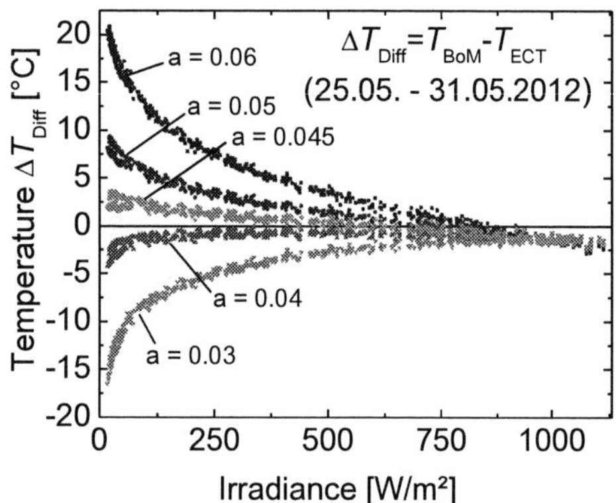

Fig. 6. Difference between temperature measured at the back of the module and calculated by the ECT method for different correction factors a.

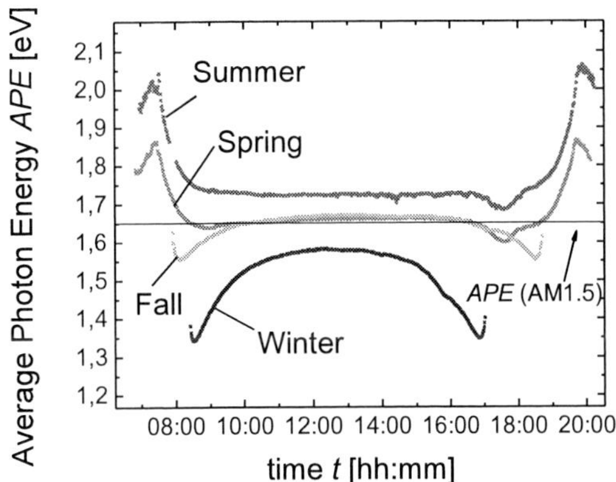

Fig. 7. Average photon energy (APE) for clear-sky days in winter, spring, summer and fall. The horizontal line indicates the APE value of the reference spectrum (AM1.5). During winter the spectrum is significantly shifted towards red wavelength.

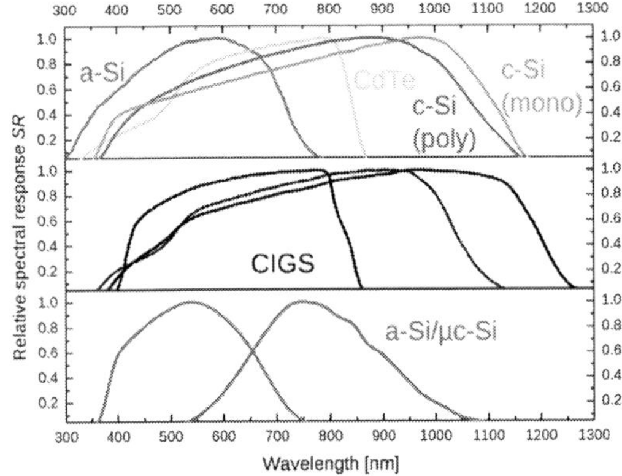

Fig. 8. Relative spectral response (SR) of different PV module technologies. The SR data were used to correct for the spectral mismatch.

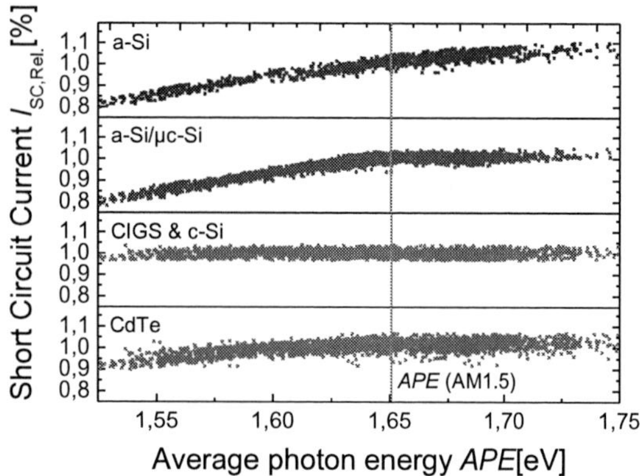

Fig. 9. Dependence of measured ISC on spectral changes (T, G corrected, normalized to ISC, STC at 1.65 eV). Silicon thin-film modules are most sensitive to spectral changes due to the narrow quantum efficiency. In the case of tandem cells, the series connection (matching) restricts the overall current.

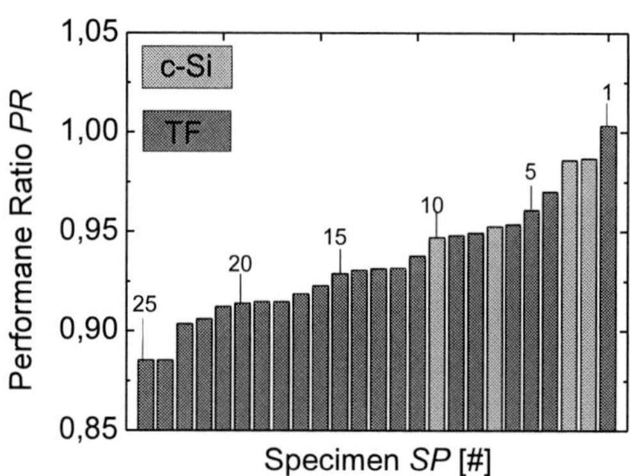

Fig. 10. Final ranking of the performance ratio (PR) for modules exposed in 2010/11 and 2011/12. Significant differences are found between the worst performing module rank 25 and the best performing module rank 1 of 11.8%.

A Comparison of Key PV Backsheet and Module Performance from Fielded Module Exposures and Accelerated Tests

W. Gambogi, Y. Heta, K. Hashimoto, J. Kopchick, T. Felder, S. MacMaster, A. Bradley, B. Hamzavytehrany, L. Garreau-Iles, T. Aoki, K. Stika, T. J. Trout, and T. Sample

Abstract—The performance of photovoltaic (PV) modules and their component materials under the stresses in the outdoor environment is the most important indicator of reliability, durability, and safety of PV modules throughout their service life. Tedlar polyvinyl fluoride films have been a key component in backsheet component structures and used in PV modules that have been in the service environment for over 25 years. The performance of fielded modules and components can be compared with the performance in durability tests using other backsheet materials including polyethylene terephthalate. Accelerated testing protocols are described including UV exposure based on solar irradiance in different climates and relevant albedo levels for exposure of the back of PV modules. The change in critical performance properties in durability tests including damp heat and UV is compared with backsheets that are extracted from fielded modules. Analysis of mechanical and chemical properties of the inner and outer layers of backsheets that are removed from fielded modules is examined. Area-specific coring techniques that are followed by layer composition analysis were also used to understand fielded module failure mechanisms/defects. The impact of extended damp heat and UV on backsheet properties and module performance that is observed in the field is further quantified through measurement of mechanical, optical, electrical, and permeability properties of the backsheet and power, electrical insulation, and physical properties of the modules. Correlations between field performance and accelerated testing are demonstrated. The first results for sequential and combined stress testing are described and compared with the field performance. A comparison of two large and diverse sets of modules from two different locations (EU and Japan) is discussed, and the power loss with field exposure period and the impact of backsheet is described.

Index Terms—Durability, materials, reliability, testing.

I. INTRODUCTION

MATERIALS selection is an important factor in the durability of photovoltaic (PV) modules in the field. Materials are typically tested under durability conditions that are applied to modules in the IEC 61215 qualification standard [1]. While this approach may be appropriate to predict infant mortality, it is generally understood to not be predictive of the long-term module performance.

A more recent approach has been to investigate multistress durability conditions that are based on the expected outdoor environment and compare the performance of these stresses with the performance that is observed in the field. By comparing accelerated durability conditions with the outdoor performance, a better understanding of failure mechanisms and the impact of materials durability can be obtained. This approach is central to the work that is described in this paper.

II. ACCELERATED TESTING PROTOCOLS

A. UV Exposure Accelerated Testing Protocols

The ratio of direct radiation to the reflected light for a given location is referred to as albedo and is represented as a percent ratio. The albedo depends on the reflectance of the ground cover, the time of day, and the wavelength. Albedo in the UVA range is typically higher than in the UVB region. For the work presented, 12% UVA albedo was used, which is based on the average of multiple external literature sources [2], [3].

Using an annual UV exposure average based on various regions [4], [6] and 12% albedo, UVA dosage levels for the junction box side of the PV module over a 25 year period were calculated to be from 171 kWh/m^2 for temperate regions to 275 kWh/m^2 for desert regions. These levels are 11 to 18 times the exposure levels in IEC 61215 [5].

Annual UV exposure levels for exposure of the front of the PV module can also be calculated based on the same literature sources; however, the spectral power distribution of light reaching the inner layer of the backsheet is reduced in the wavelength range from 300 to 360 nm by the absorbance of glass and encapsulant layers. Furthermore, the use of UVA lamps are less effective in exposures through a glass/EVA filter since much of the UVA lamp spectra is within this range. For this reason, we

Manuscript received August 9, 2013; revised November 27, 2013; accepted December 3, 2013.

W. Gambogi, J. Kopchick, T. Felder, S. MacMaster, A. Bradley, B. Hamzavytehrany, K. Stika, and T. J. Trout are with DuPont, Wilmington, DE 19803 USA (e-mail: william.j.gambogi@dupont.com; james.g.kopchick@usa.dupont.com; Thomas.Felder@usa.dupont.com; steven.w.macmaster@usa.dupont.com; alexander.z.bradley@usa.dupont.com; babak.hamzavytehrany@usa.dupont.com; Katherine.M.Stika@usa.dupont.com; t-john.trout@usa.dupont.com).

Y. Heta, K. Hashimoto, and T. Aoki are with DuPont K.K., Utsunomiya 321-3231, Japan (e-mail: Yushi.Heta@jpn.dupont.com; Kana.Hashimoto@jpn.dupont.com; Tomoko.Aoki@jpn.dupont.com).

L. Garreau-Iles is with Du Pont de Nemours International S A , Geneva 1218, Switzerland (e-mail: Lucie.Garreau-Iles@che.dupont.com).

T. Sample is with the European Commission Joint Research Centre, Ispra 21020, Italy (e-mail: tony.sample@jvc.ec.europa.eu).

Color versions of one or more of the figures in this paper are available online at http://ieeexplore.ieee.org.

Digital Object Identifier 10.1109/JPHOTOV.2014.2305472

61

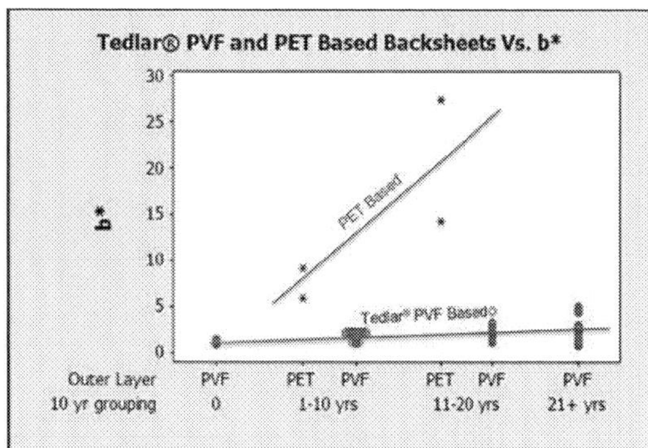

Fig. 1. Yellowing data (b∗) versus age of modules with Tedlar® PVF- or PET-based backsheets.

have selected a metal–halide lamp and exposed the backsheet at higher intensity through a glass/EVA filter to test the UV sensitivity of inner backsheet layers.

B. Testing Protocol

Damp heat (DH) testing was conducted at 85 °C, 85% relative humidity for 1000, 2000, and 3000 h. The 1000-h DH exposure was chosen for durability testing that is based on measurement and correlation of properties in fielded modules. Extended exposure was used for assessment as part of a test-to-failure protocol. Both thermal cycling (TC) and TC with humidity freeze (HF) was done to 3 x the IEC 61215 requirement to better assess the long-term performance.

III. Main Experimental Results

A. Comparison of Accelerated UV and Fielded Modules

Multiple fielded modules containing either Tedlar [poly(vinyl fluoride) (PVF)-] or poly(ethylene terephthalate) (PET)-based backsheets were analyzed for color change, specifically yellowing. Yellowing can represent an important visual indicator of polymer degradation, and we often see cracking of the backsheet associated with yellowing. Fig. 1 shows b∗ data for modules of various ages from the field, and these 227 Tedlar PVF- and four PET-based backsheet containing modules were from a variety of locations. The color coordinates (L∗, a∗, b∗) of the backsheets were measured using an XRite SP64 spectrophotometer. As shown in Fig. 1, a small color change is observed in the DuPont Tedlar® PVF-based backsheets over time, while the PET modules demonstrate a much larger change.

When this yellowing is compared with the accelerated testing of the various backsheets, DH shows very little increase in yellowing out to 3000 h (see Fig. 2). UVA-accelerated testing results in a much more prominent increase in yellowing for the PET-backed modules (see Fig. 3), but not to the same level of yellowing that was observed in the fielded modules (see Fig. 1). Based on these observations, it appears that DH is not a large contributor to yellowing, and is not correlating with field module aging. On the other hand, UV exposure is showing a better agreement with the fielded module data (see

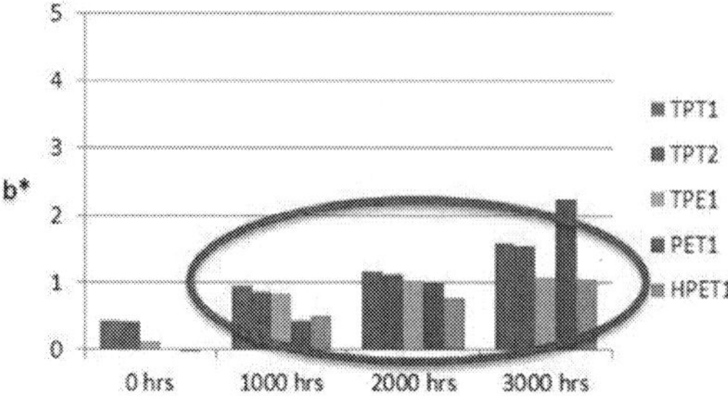

Fig. 2. DH exposure of modules. Yellowing data (b∗) versus exposure time of modules containing Tedlar® PVF- or PET-based backsheets. Two TPT, one TPE, and two PET (PET1 and HPET1) backsheets are compared.

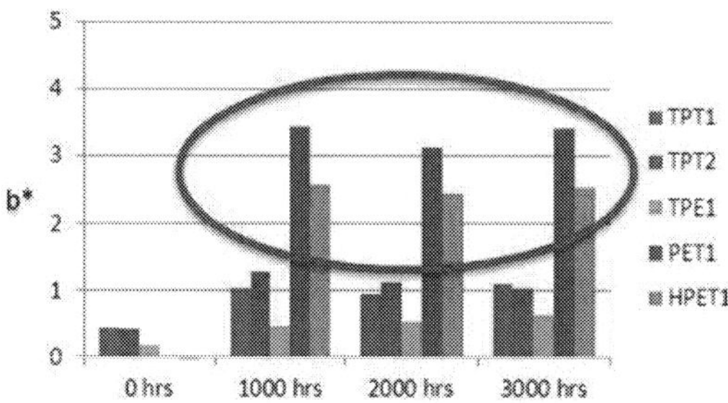

Fig. 3. UVA exposure of modules. Yellowing data (b∗) versus exposure time of modules containing Tedlar PVF- or PET-based backsheets. Two TPT, one TPE, and two PET (PET1 and HPET1) backsheets are compared.

Fig. 1) for Tedlar® PVF-based backsheets (see Fig. 3). Tedlar® PVF containing backsheets include TPT (PVF/PET/PVF) and TPE (PVF/PET/EVA). The fact that the accelerated UV testing is still lower in yellowness level compared with fielded modules will be discussed further in Section III-C.

Yellowing is tracked and compared between outdoor exposure and accelerated test exposure since, in addition to being visually objectionable, it can be an indicator of material degradation. Mechanical properties are also carefully tracked in outdoor and accelerated exposure as they can impact the function of the outer layer to serve as a mechanically stable protection due to the forces associated with thermal expansion/contraction and physical forces associated with weathering.

One of the fielded modules with a yellowing PET-based backsheet was further analyzed due to cracking that is observed in the outer layer of the PET backsheet (see Fig. 4). The backsheet had a cracked 12-μm-thick PET outer layer (thought to originally be clear) and a 50-μm-thick white PET inner layer. Molecular weight (Mw) analyses were conducted of the two layers, and showed that the cracking outer layer of PET had a lower Mw and a broader Mw distribution. This trend is expected for a PET that has undergone hydrolysis, thermal, and/or UV degradation [7]. The loss of mechanical properties (tensile and elongation) of the outer PET layer resulted in cracking and direct exposure of the inner PET layer to the outdoor environment.

We suspect that the reason that UV exposure is a better predictor of change in the outdoor environment when compared with DH exposure is that the degradation mechanism in the outdoor environment is related to photodegradation of the materials and

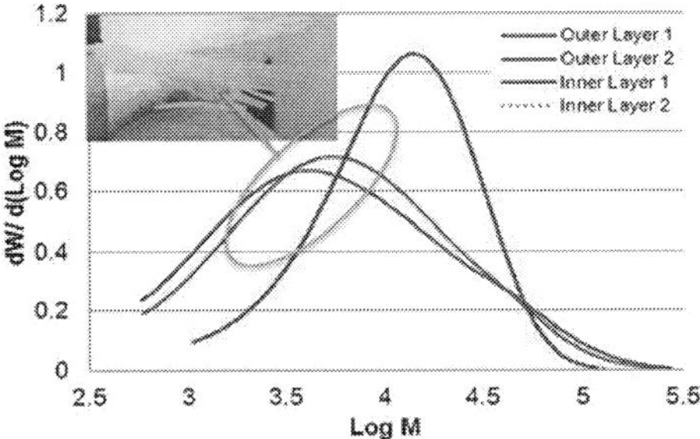

Fig. 4. PET-based backsheet Mw analyses. Cracking of the outer PET layer shown.

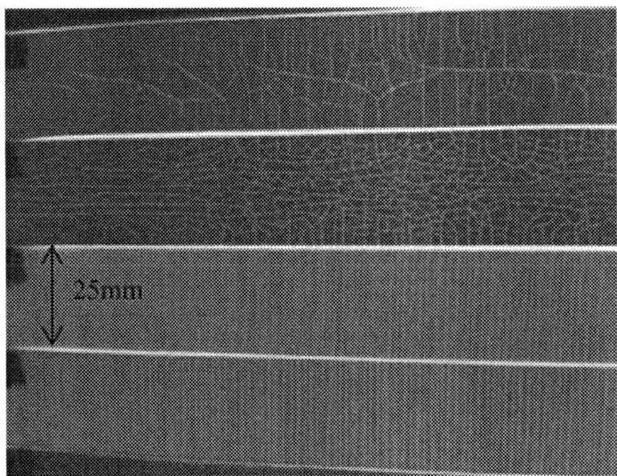

Fig. 5. Four PET-based backsheets with severe inner layer damage after 540 kWh/m^2 TUV from filtered the MH lamp.

not due to hydrolysis damage. In the aforementioned example, the outer layer PET and inner layer PET are exposed to similar relative humidity and temperature but only the outer layer has embrittled suggesting the degradation of the outer layer is primarily due to UV exposure.

To test the UV stability of the inner layer of the backsheet to extended UV exposure, a set of double- and single-sided backsheets (including TPT and TPE) was exposed to high intensity metal halide (MH) lamp exposure using a glass/2 EVA filter that is described in Section II-A. The glass/2 EVA filter uses commercial solar glass and two layers of EVA and absorbs shorter wavelength light (<360 nm) that would not reach the inner layer of the backsheet in a typical PV module. The UV exposure source was a 1500-W/m^2 Iwasaki SUV W151 system and the sample temperature was determined to be about 60 °C during exposure. Both two-sided and single-sided backsheet products were tested and the samples were inspected to crack after a 360-h exposure. Six of the ten single-sided backsheets showed some level of cracking after this period with four PET-based (PET/PET/X) backsheets showing the severe damage, as shown in Fig. 5.

B. Comparison of Accelerated Damp Heat and Fielded Modules

In this section, we look for a correlation of DH durability and fielded module performance. During extended DH testing of both PET and Tedlar® PVF-based backsheets, a large drop-off

in mechanical properties after 1000 h of testing is observed, as shown in Fig. 6. This drop-off in properties is chiefly because of the degradation of the PET core layer in the backsheets, which is responsible for the majority of the mechanical strength of the backsheet. However, this large drop-off in mechanical properties is not observed in field modules that were collected from various regions with a range of time in service (see Fig. 6). It is also interesting to note that no mechanical loss was observed in the backsheet sample removed from the PV module exposed at Miyako Island, Japan, which is considered a humid environment. The disparity between accelerated DH testing and field module analyses suggests that DH testing over 1000 h is not predictive of the field performance.

C. Weathering and Combined Stress Testing

During their service life, photovoltaic modules are exposed to a wide range of stress conditions including: UV, temperature, moisture (water, humidity, and condensation), thermal cycling, and internal voltage. These stresses can operate on the module simultaneously or sequentially causing synergistic effects to be observed.

Using field module observations and analysis, new accelerated testing methods are being developed to better predict the expected performance of materials in the field for 25 years. New testing underway includes test combinations of the following:

1) weathering (light, temperature, and water);
2) sequential stress (UV, DH, TC, and HF);
3) simultaneous stress (UV, DH, TC, and HF);
4) simulated field conditions (weathering, electrical load, and mechanical load).

Initial results of weathering testing (Xenon and water spraying) of backsheets produced cracking of the inner tie layer of the PET backsheet sample after only 1500 h compared with 5000 h needed in the Xenon only accelerated testing. As an example, Fig. 7 shows cracking of the inner tie layer of a PET/PET/tie layer backsheet when the outer (junction box) side of the backsheet is exposed to 1500 h of a xenon weathering condition (ASTM G155 cyc9 (modified), 65 °C BPT, 120 W/m^2 (300–400 nm), 102-min radiation, 18-min radiation + water spray).

When a sequential stress of UVA and TC is applied to Tedlar® PVF- and PET-based backsheets, yellowing becomes much more apparent as compared with the single stress of UVA alone, as shown in Fig. 8. The color coordinate b∗ (yellowing) increased in this case to 8–10 for the PET backsheets, which now correlates with the levels that are observed in the field-analyzed modules (see Fig. 1).

We have also tested four cell mini-modules with sequential stress conditions. In this case, we applied two different sequential stress conditions and found two different failure mechanisms in the backsheet that were not observed in single stress exposures.

The two sequential stress protocols are:

1) Sequence #1 (DH 1000 UVA 1000 TC 200), 1000 h of DH (85 °C, 85%RH) followed by 1000 h of UVA (70 °C BPT, 65 W/m^2 from 300–400 nm) followed by 200 thermal cycles (–40 °C, 85 °C);

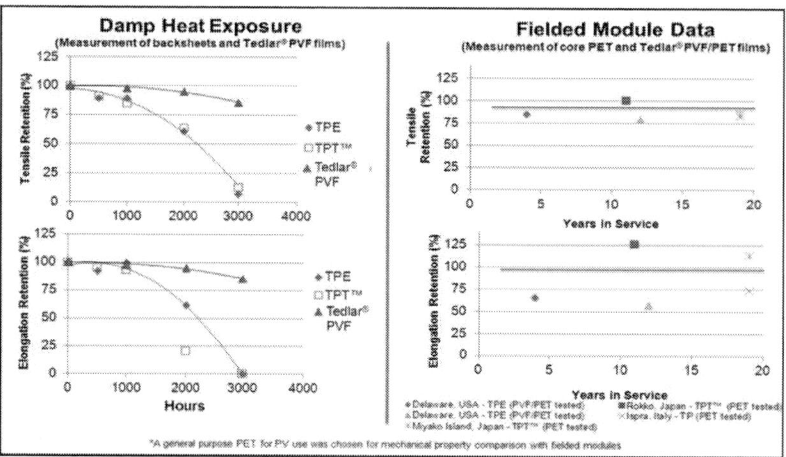

Fig. 6.   Mechanical properties of DH exposure versus fielded module data.

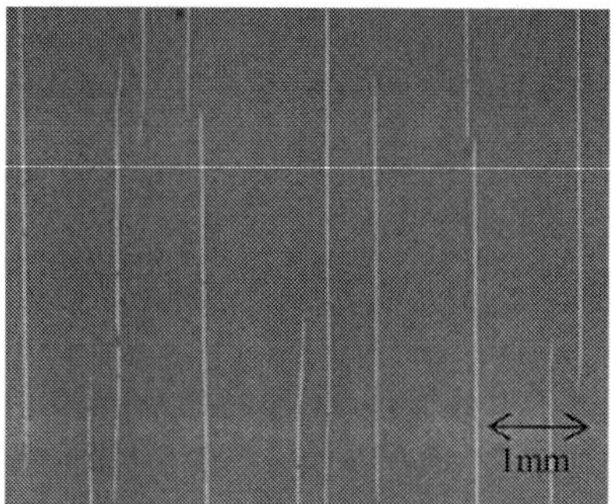

Fig. 7.   Cracking of the inner tie layer of a PET/PET/tie layer backsheet.

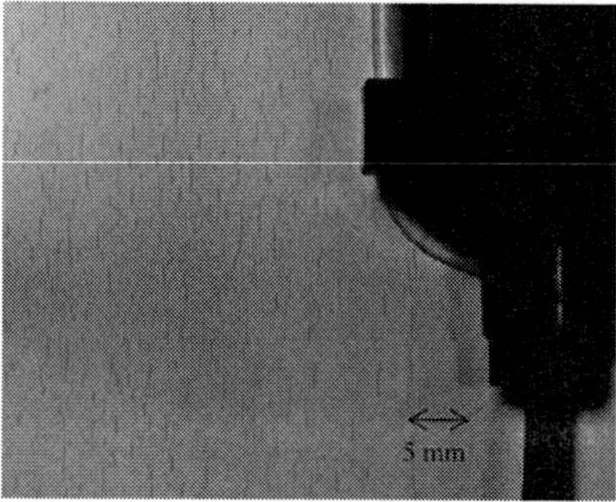

Fig. 9.   Cracking of a single-sided PVDF backsheet after sequential exposure to DH, UV, and TC (contrast altered to highlight cracking).

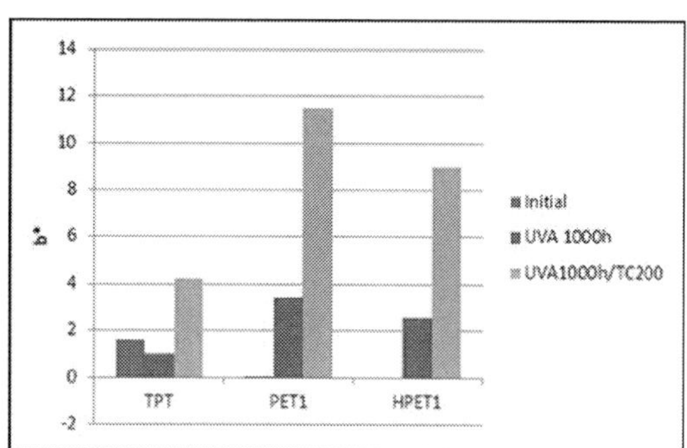

Fig. 8.   PET backsheets show much greater color change after UVA/TC indicating polymer degradation and damage.

2) Sequence #2 (1000 DH 200 TC). 1000 h of DH followed by 200 thermal cycles.

Each sequence was applied to a separate set of mini-modules, and the performance and appearance were assessed after each step in the sequence. These stresses are used individually in the IEC61215 standard to identify infant mortality. By applying them in the sequence, the impact of each stress can be investigated in terms of its effect under another simulated stress condition from the field. In sequence #1, the damage occurring after DH/UV/TC exposure was not observed after DH alone. Similarly, in sequence #2, the result of damage occurring in DH was not observed without TC where the mechanical stress of thermal expansion and contraction is applied.

As shown in Fig. 9, the mini-modules that are stressed using sequence #1 showed fine cracking of the backsheet for a single-sided PVDF backsheet across the entire surface of the back of the modules with the cracks having a specific directionality possibly due to a loss in the mechanical properties in a particular direction for this backsheet. Only one cycle of this test sequence was needed to produce the damage shown.

In the case of sequence #2, two cycles of this stress sequence showed damage in mini-modules made using the same single-sided PVDF backsheet but the damage observed was different than that observed in sequence #1. In sequence #2, large cracking was observed near the junction box and near the frame of the module suggesting a different failure mechanism as shown in Fig. 10. In both cases, a Tedlar® PVF/polyester/EVA (TPE) backsheet was also tested and did not show any signs of the backsheet failures observed in the single-sided PVDF backsheet.

The use of sequential stress testing outlined previously has resulted in observation of cracking and yellowing in some backsheet types. Backsheet cracking and yellowing are two failure

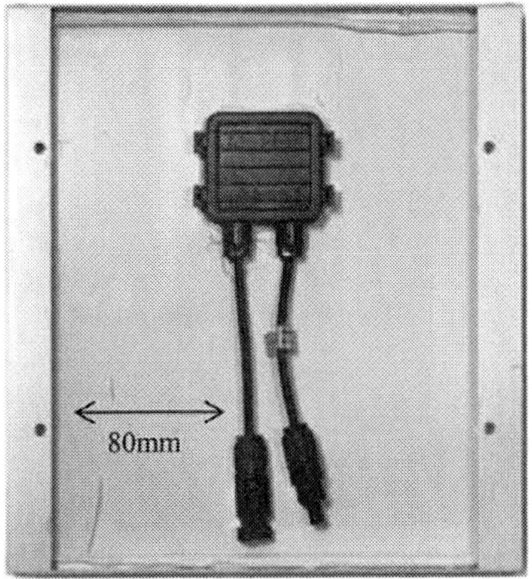

Fig. 10.   Cracking of a single-sided PVDF backsheet after sequential exposure to DH and thermal cycling.

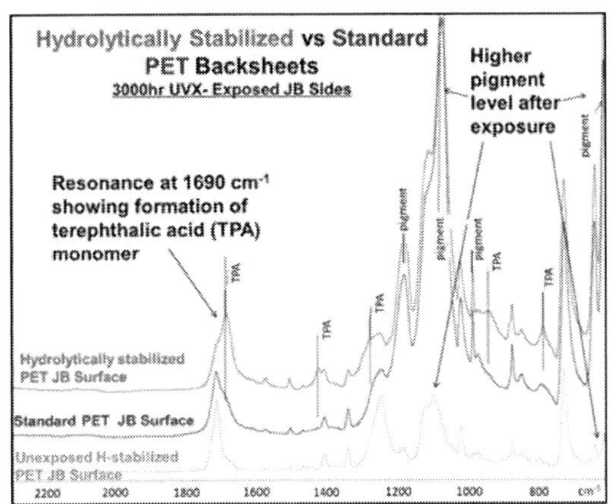

Fig. 11.   FTIR analysis of polyester-based backsheets that underwent accelerated testing in an Atlas Weatherometer.

mechanisms that are observed in the field, which may not be observed in single stress durability test conditions. The use of sequential stress exposures have been shown to more effectively investigate the susceptibility of backsheet to this degradation observed in the field. We also expect that the TC stress might be greater in full-size modules.

D. Infrared Analysis of Backsheet Degradation

Infrared (IR) spectroscopy has been used as an effective method for understanding polymer degradation in accelerated and outdoor exposure. FTIR analysis was carried out on polyester-based backsheets that underwent accelerated testing in an Atlas Ci5000 Weatherometer running a G155 cycle 9 protocol (Xenon lamp, Rightlight/Cira on quartz filters, 120 W/m^2 (300–400 nm), 65 °C BPT, 102 min UV then 18 min water spray with UV) for a total 360 kW hr/m^2 exposure (UV 25 + year desert condition). The FTIR analysis of the exposed outer surface showed that the outer layer of the polymer was degrading to monomers and shedding pigment (see Fig. 11), while the inner

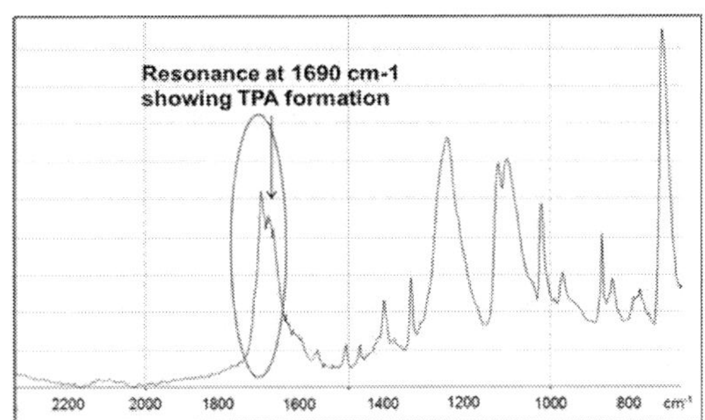

Fig. 12.   FTIR analysis of the polyester backsheet failure in the field.

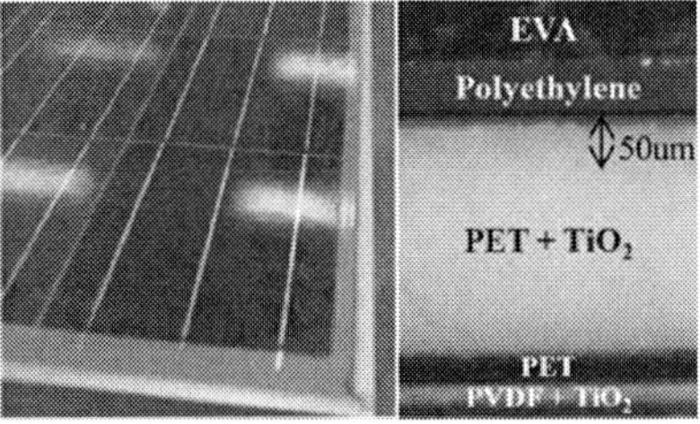

Fig. 13.   Optical images of module with the discolored backsheet.

tie layer was cracked and had degraded to acids, ketones, and lactones from UV transmitted through the backsheet. An FTIR spectrum was taken from a fielded module with a polyester-based backsheet with six years in service in Arizona, USA, this backsheet showed a band forming at 1690 cm^{-1}, evidence of degradation to TPA monomer (see Fig. 12).

IV. Recent Examples of Module Degradation From the Field

Backsheet degradation and durability issues in the field can arise from the combination of multiple stresses in the outdoor environment. In this section, we describe two examples where poor material choices resulted in failure of a majority of the modules in the field and discuss the accelerated testing procedures that might prevent such failures.

Using a modification of the coring procedure described by King *et al.* [8], we examine the core samples for thickness, chemical composition of the individual layers, and any organic degradation signatures using IR spectroscopy in combination with SEM/Energy Dispersive X-Ray. Discoloration and corrosion are assessed using optical and electron micrographs.

In the first case, the module shown in Fig. 13 was part of a commercial MW size system and removed after only two years of service due to severe yellowing and loss of 4% power as a result of a 4% loss in I_{sc} relative to the nameplate rating. Destructive analysis determined the discolored material was not the EVA encapsulant but rather the polyethylene (PE) tie layer and associated adhesive layers in the PVDF/PET/PET/PE backsheet structure. It was further determined that the UV absorbance of the EVA in this case was lower than expected, which would accelerate this degradation mechanism. Testing of the stability of the inner layer to UV exposure, as described in an earlier section,

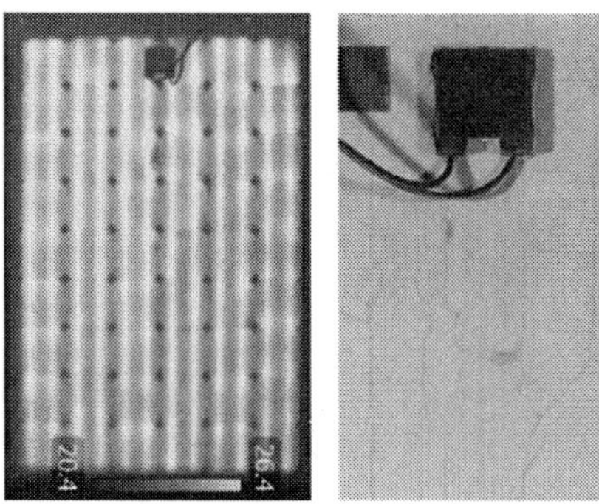

Fig. 14. Thermal (left) and optical (right) image of fielded module with cracking of the outer polyester surface.

TABLE I
SUMMARY OF OBSERVATIONS UNDER FIELD AND ACCELERATED
EXPOSURE CONDITIONS

Location	Junction Box Side of Backsheet	Encapsulant Side of Backsheet
Fielded Modules	Yellowing, Delamination of Outer Layers, Cracking of Outer Layers, No Hydrolysis Damage	Yellowing
UV exposure of JB-side of Backsheet	Yellowing	Cracking
UV exposure of E-side of Backsheet	Yellowing	Yellowing Cracking
1000h Damp Heat Exposure of Backsheet	Yellowing	Yellowing
>1000h Damp Heat of Backsheet	Hydrolysis damage to PET layers, Embrittlement	Yellowing of Some Tie Layers, Embrittlement
UV/Thermal Cycling of Modules	Yellowing, Cracking	No Appreciable Change
DH/UV/Thermal Cycling of Modules	Yellowing, Cracking	No Appreciable Change
UV exposure of E-side of Modules	Yellowing	Yellowing Cracking
>1000h Damp Heat of Modules	Cracking	Yellowing

A thermal image (see Fig. 14) was obtained in the lab under forward bias at I_{sc} conditions. While the overall temperature is not very high, the image identifies a contrast along the tabbing ribbons, indicative of localized thermal stress because of an increase in the series resistance along the back tabbing ribbons. The region behind a tabbing wire and interconnect is also an area of inherent localized mechanical stress because of the flow of polymeric materials during the lamination process. Because of the severity of the polyester degradation, the dielectric withstand performance was less than 40 $M\Omega{\cdot}m^2$, indicating insufficient electrical insulation of the module raising safety concerns.

The damage observed from these fielded modules calls into question the functional performance of the backsheet as an electrical insulator and barrier to weathering stresses (UV, moisture, atmospheric gases). While the measurement of physical properties of the backsheet layers of fielded modules presents challenges in the removal of the backsheet from the package with no damage, analysis of backsheets that are exposed to accelerated test and comparison with the fielded performance provides an opportunity for deeper understanding of the possible materials degradation mechanisms and their effect on the module performance.

A summary of the results of outdoor and accelerated exposure is shown in Table I below.

V. CONCLUSION

The test protocols that are described in Section II were designed to more closely simulate the real environment based on 25 years of UV dosage in different climates. Using these protocols, we have found that degradation in fielded modules is better predicted by combinations of UV, temperature, and moisture than by DH, as shown in Table I. Yellowing of Tedlar® PVF- and PET-based backsheets in fielded modules correlate with accelerated UV and better with UV combined with other stresses. It appears that yellowing is a good visual indication of degradation or possibly more serious problems.

Additional studies are planned to better understand the connection of yellowing to functional properties for specific classes of materials. This needs to be assessed on specific classes of materials because of different compositions and degradation mechanisms for each class of materials.

Based on mechanical properties of both fielded modules and accelerated testing of backsheets in DH, 1000 h of DH exposure is sufficient to mimic hydrolysis damage to the backsheet in the field and exposures over 1000 h does produce a failure mechanism not observed in the field. Weathering and multistress test protocols, compared with single stress tests, are producing effects more consistent with the field-observed performance. Combined UV, DH, and TC are showing weaknesses due to synergistic effects. And testing of stability of backsheets to inner layer exposure using a high-intensity UV source may be used to assess susceptibility to this stress seen in fielded modules. Developing new test methods, which better simulate the combined stresses in the field, may be more predictive of the long-term performance and durability of PV modules.

would identify such instabilities and avoid damage to the modules because of this degradation mechanism as previously described.

In the second example, modules were removed from a commercial MW plant after five years of service for material and I–V analysis. This module demonstrated uniform cracking and delamination of the outer layer of the backsheet along the rear tabbing ribbons as well as in the transverse direction (see Fig. 14). The FTIR spectrum of the outer backsheet surface is consistent with polyester. The I–V measurement indicated a 9% loss in power as a result of an 8% loss in I_{sc} relative to the nameplate rating.

ACKNOWLEDGMENT

The authors would like to thank the European Commission Joint Research Centre and the National Institute of Advanced Industrial Science and Technology for providing some of the field modules studied in this study.

REFERENCES

[1] *Crystalline Silicon Terrestrial Photovoltaic (PV) Modules—Design Qualification and Type Approval*, Int. Electrotech. Comm. 61215 Ed. 2, 2005.

[2] R. Chadysiene and A. Girgzdys, "Ultraviolet radiation on albedo of natural surfaces," *J. Environ. Eng. Landscape Manage.*, vol. 16, no. 2, pp. 83–88, 2008.

[3] "Carcinogens Background Documents for Broad-spectrum ultraviolet (UV) radiation and UVA, and UVB, and UVC," U.S. Department of Health and Human Services, Washington, DC, USA, 2000, Contract # N01-ES-85421.

[4] M. Koehl, "Indoor and outdoor weathering of PV modules," *Proc. SPIE*, vol. 7048, pp. 704806–704904, 2008.

[5] M. Kempe, "Ultraviolet light test and evaluation methods for encapsulants of photovoltaic modules," *Sol. Energy Mater. Sol. Cells*, vol. 94, pp. 246–253, 2010.

[6] G. Wypych, *Weathering of Plastics: Testing to Mirror Real Life Performance*. Amsterdam, The Netherlands: Plastics Design Library, 1999, p. 17.

[7] B. Singh and N. Sharma, "Mechanistic implications of plastic degradation," *Polymer Degradation Stability*, vol. 93, pp. 561–584, 2008.

[8] D. L. King, M. A. Quintana, J. A. Kratochvil, D. E. Ellibee, and B. R. Hansen, "Photovoltaic module performance and durability following long-term field exposure," *Prog. Photovoltaics Res. Appl.*, vol. 8, pp. 241–256, 2000.

Authors' photographs and biographies not available at the time of publication.

Flexible Thin-Film Tandem Solar Cells With >30% Efficiency

Brendan M. Kayes, *Senior Member, IEEE*, Ling Zhang, Rose Twist, I-Kang Ding,
and Gregg S. Higashi, *Fellow, IEEE*

Abstract—Alta Devices, Inc. has previously reported on single-junction thin-film GaAs photovoltaic devices on flexible substrates with efficiencies up to 28.8% under AM1.5G solar illumination at 1-sun intensity. Here, we show that the same technology platform can be extended to tandem devices that are capable of even higher efficiencies: so far up to 30.8%. Specifically, here, we report on a lattice-matched, series-connected, two-junction device with In-GaP as the light-absorbing material of the top cell and GaAs as the absorber in the bottom cell. The material is grown by metal-lorganic chemical vapor deposition, and then, the device is lifted off by the epitaxial liftoff (ELO) process, as previously reported. This demonstrates that ELO is not only capable of record-setting single-junction performance but capable of achieving world-class efficiency with a multijunction architecture as well.

Index Terms—Epitaxial layers, gallium arsenide, indium compounds, photovoltaic cells, solar energy, thin films, thin-film devices, III–V semiconductor materials.

I. INTRODUCTION

THERE are increasing numbers of applications for photovoltaic devices that demand flexible, lightweight solar cells that can be embedded into another material. Unfortunately, almost all of the solutions that are available today convert sunlight into electricity at low efficiency: typically lower than 15% and, in many cases, much lower [1]. Alta Devices has demonstrated [2], [3] the potential for GaAs thin films as a compelling solution that does not compromise conversion efficiency, with 28.8% efficiency demonstrated at the cell level and 24.1% at the module level to date [4].

For some applications, even these efficiencies are not high enough, and to go beyond these numbers, one can consider adding additional pn-junctions to better match the solar spectrum. Prior to the work reported here, the world record 1-sun efficiencies for two- and three-junction solar cells were 30.3% and 37.7%, respectively [5], [4]. Exceeding these efficiencies with a solar cell that is also lightweight and flexible could improve the value of high-efficiency solar cells in areas where specific power (power-to-weight ratio) is at a premium, such as for unmanned aerial vehicles, as well as in other aerial and

Manuscript received June 9, 2013; revised October 19, 2013 and November 24, 2013; accepted December 29, 2013. Date of publication January 30, 2014; date of current version February 17, 2014.

The authors are with Alta Devices, Sunnyvale, CA 94085 USA (e-mail: brendankayes@gmail.com; lingz@altadevices.com; roset@altadevices.com; ikding@gmail.com; greggh@altadevices.com).

Color versions of one or more of the figures in this paper are available online at http://ieeexplore.ieee.org.

Digital Object Identifier 10.1109/JPHOTOV.2014.2299395

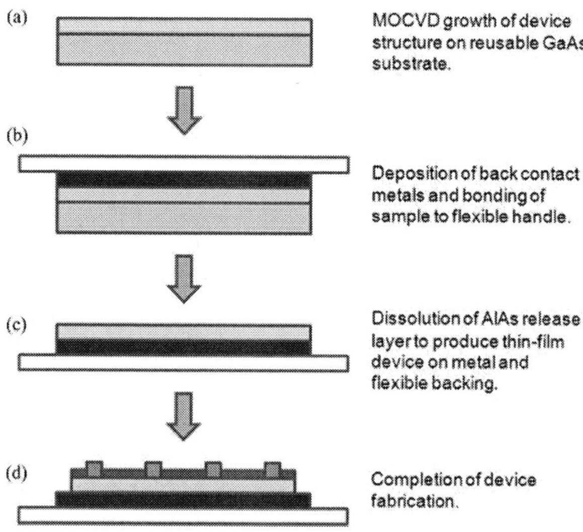

Fig. 1. Schematic illustration of device fabrication process.

extraterrestrial applications. The epitaxial lift-off (ELO) [6] process enables just such a scenario.

II. DEVICE FABRICATION

Our device fabrication process has been described previously [2] and is illustrated schematically in Fig. 1. First, a reusable GaAs growth substrate was introduced into a metal-organic chemical vapor deposition (MOCVD) chamber. A buffer layer of GaAs material was grown, followed by a thin AlAs release layer, on top of which the photovoltaic device structure was grown. What later became the sun-facing side of the device was grown first, and the backside of the device was grown last [see Fig. 1(a)]. This means that the InGaP absorber was grown before the GaAs absorber in a so-called inverted geometry.

The epi surface was then cleaned, and the back contact metal was deposited. This metal-on-semiconductor stack was then attached to a flexible handle using an adhesive [see Fig. 1(b)].

The handle–metal–semiconductor stack was then introduced into a heated bath of aqueous hydrofluoric acid. The acid etches the AlAs release layer but leaves the other layers in the device stack, as well as the metal contact and flexible handle, intact (the ELO process [6]). The etch completes leaving a semiconductor thin film supported by the back metal composite. After being flipped over, rinsed, and dried, the resulting thin-film structure was ready for device processing [see Fig. 1(c)].

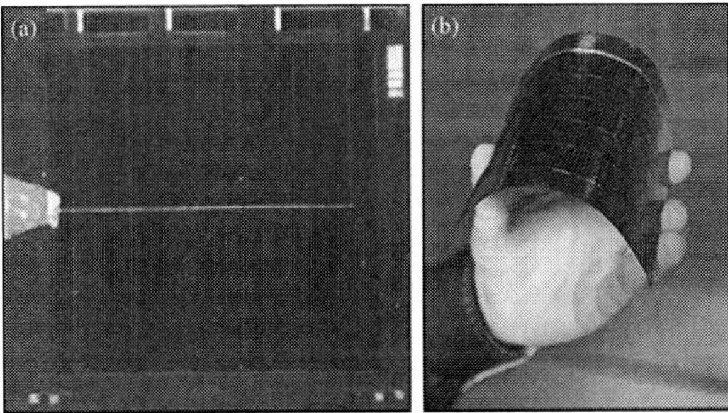

Fig. 2. (a) Finished cell and (b) interconnected 15-cell matrix, demonstrating the flexibility of the cells.

TABLE I

PERFORMANCE CHARACTERISTICS OF 1-cm^2 DEVICE, AS MEASURED AT NREL UNDER AM1.5G ILLUMINATION AT 1-SUN INTENSITY

Area	$0.999\ \text{cm}^2$
Short-circuit current density (J_{sc})	$14.3\ \text{mA/cm}^2$
Open-circuit voltage (V_{oc})	2.547 V
Fill Factor	84.7%
Efficiency	30.8%
Current density at maximum power (J_{max})	$13.7\ \text{mA/cm}^2$
Voltage at maximum power (V_{max})	2.248 V
Temperature coefficient (power)	-0.10 relative % / °C
Temperature coefficient (V_{oc})	-0.0035 V / °C
Temperature coefficient (J_{sc})	$0.013\ \text{mA/cm}^2$ / °C

Front metallization was deposited using an evaporation and lift-off process. This was followed by an etch to define devices of 1-cm^2 area. Finally, an antireflective coating was applied [see Fig. 1(d)].

Fig. 2 shows both the completed 1-cm^2 cell described in this paper [see Fig. 2(a)] and an example of 15 10-cm^2 cells interconnected to a flexible matrix [see Fig. 2(b)].

III. DEVICE CHARACTERIZATION

The devices fabricated as above were then tested both internally at Alta and at NREL [7]. The results of the testing at NREL are displayed in Table I and Figs. 3–6.

The results of current–voltage (*I*–*V*) testing under AM1.5G simulated solar illumination [8] at 1-sun intensity (i.e., without concentration) are shown in Table I and Fig. 3. Device open-circuit voltage (V_{oc}) in particular was significantly higher than previously published values for an InGaP/GaAs solar cell [9].

Fig. 4 shows the (a) cell efficiency, (b) V_{oc}, and (c) short-circuit current density (J_{sc}) of a nominally-identical companion cell as a function of temperature, as measured at NREL. From these data, a temperature coefficient of –0.010 relative power change/°C was derived:

$$\text{Temp. Coefficient} = \frac{\Delta\text{Power}}{\Delta\text{Temp.}}\frac{1}{\text{Power}_{25\,°C}}$$

$$= \frac{\Delta\text{Eff}}{\Delta\text{Temp.}}\frac{1}{\text{Eff}_{25\,°C}}$$

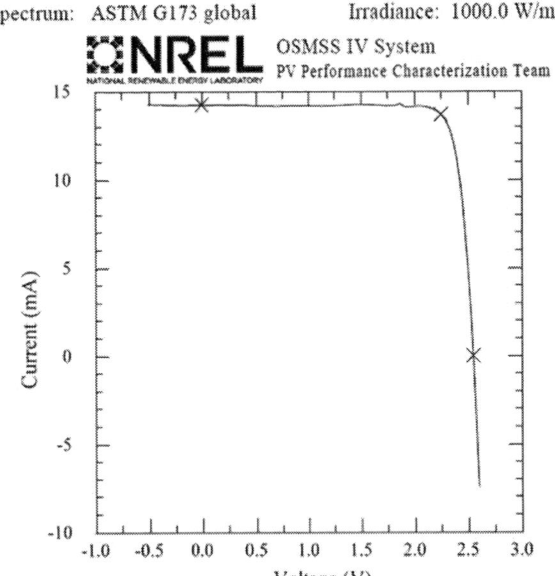

Fig. 3. Current–voltage performance of the device under illumination, as measured at NREL.

$$= \frac{-1.2}{40}\frac{1}{30.8}$$

$$= -0.10\%/°C.$$

Temperature coefficients for V_{oc} and J_{sc} are defined in absolute terms in Table I, i.e., in voltage per degree celsius and milliampere per centimeter square per degree celsius, respectively.

Fig. 5 shows the external quantum efficiency (EQE) of the device as measured at NREL. EQE is a measure of the fraction of incident photons of a given wavelength that are converted into an electrical current in the device. This device was sensitive to light with wavelengths from less than 350 nm to almost 900 nm.

A companion cell with the same layer structure was also tested by NREL for current matching. This was done by testing the cell under calibrated solar illumination and then increasing and decreasing the contribution from wavelengths to which the GaAs cell is sensitive but the InGaP cell is not (i.e., in the range 700–900 nm). Fig. 6 shows J_{sc} and fill factor as a function of relative irradiance of the bottom cell. The graph shows that J_{sc} increased with increasing bottom-cell irradiance until it saturated when bottom-cell irradiance was 1.00 to 1.05 times the top-cell irradiance. In addition, the fill factor was at a minimum in this range of bottom-cell irradiances. This is an indication that the two cells are current-matched to within 5% [10].

Companion samples were weighed at Alta at < 20 mg/cm², implying a power-to-weight ratio of >1.5 W/g. This compares favorably with Alta's single-junction product (1.2 W/g [11]), as well as with other commercially available high-efficiency cells (MicroLink Devices report >0.6 W/g [12], >0.8 W/g [13], and >1 W/g [14] for their one-, two-, and three-junction cells, respectively, while Emcore's [15] and Spectrolab's [16] most

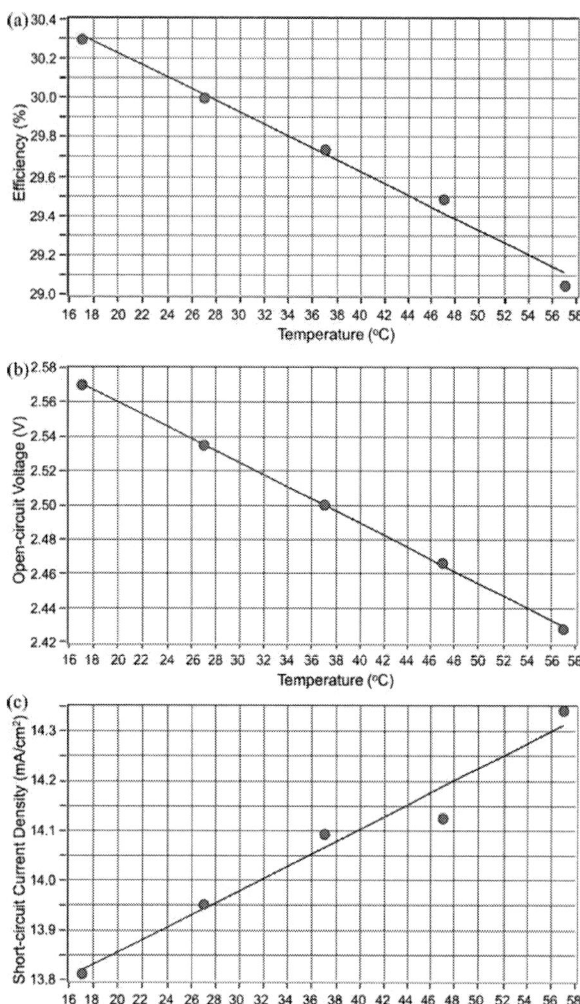

Fig. 4. (a) Efficiency (%), (b) open-circuit voltage (V_{oc}) (V), and (c) short-circuit current density (J_{sc}) (mA/cm^2) versus temperature, as measured at NREL.

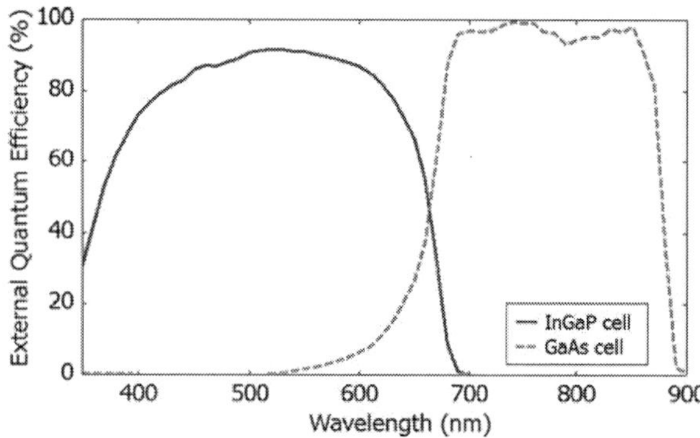

Fig. 5. EQE, as measured at NREL. Data were obtained by applying light bias to enable measurements of the individual subcells.

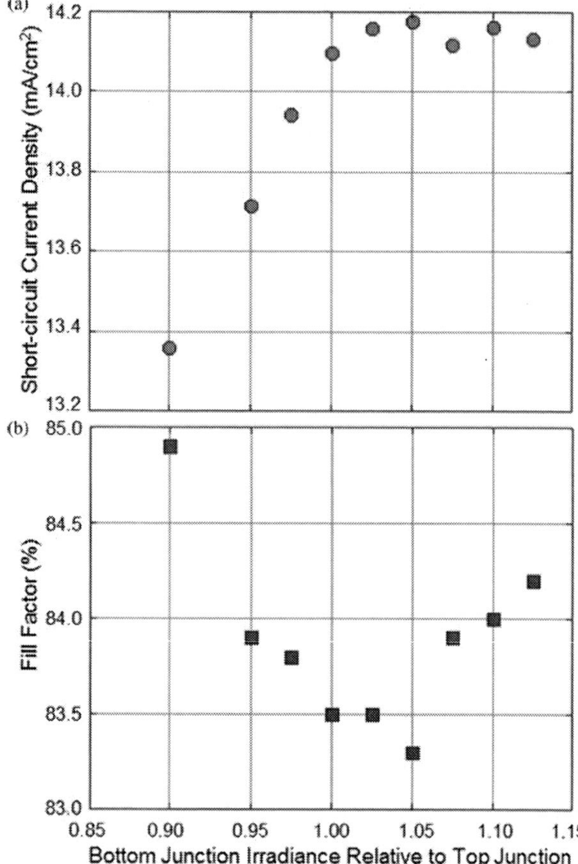

Fig. 6. (a) Short-circuit current density (J_{sc}) and (b) fill factor as a function of relative irradiance of the bottom cell, as measured at NREL.

efficient products promise approximately 0.5 W/g under an AM0 spectrum).

IV. Photon Recycling and Luminescent Coupling

As described previously [2], our use of thin, high-quality absorber materials of well-controlled thickness, combined with a highly optimized back reflector, allows for photons that are emitted internally inside the cell by radiative recombination to be reabsorbed within the absorber material with a high probability for our one-junction cells. This reabsorption provides multiple opportunities for photon escape, as well as for luminescent emission, with corresponding improvements in dark current V_{oc}, external luminescence [17], and overall conversion efficiency [18].

As illustrated in Fig. 7, the situation is more complicated in a two-junction structure, as now, the cell has two different wavelengths at which radiative emission can occur: one at approximately the bandgap energy of InGaP and the other at approximately the bandgap energy of GaAs. Radiative recombination within the GaAs cell [see Fig. 7(a)] is efficiently utilized in the same way as for the one-junction cell as the

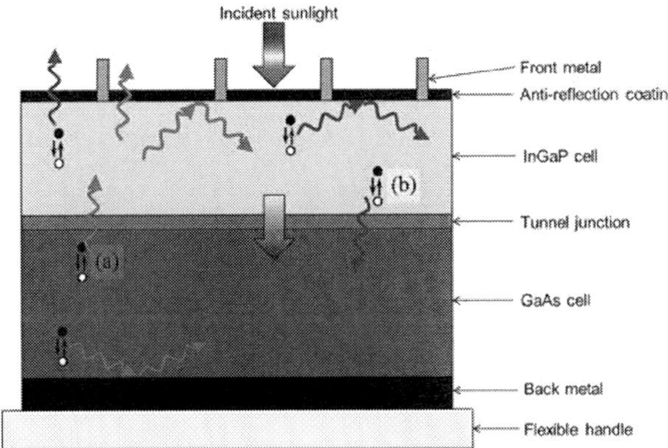

Fig. 7. Photon recycling with a two-junction device. (a) Radiative recombination in the GaAs cell leads to the emission of photons at approximately the bandgap energy of GaAs, shown here in red. These are not absorbed in the InGaP cell, and efficient photon recycling in the GaAs device is possible even in this two-junction architecture. (b) Radiative recombination in the InGaP cell leads to the emission of photons at approximately the bandgap energy of InGaP, shown here in blue. These are strongly absorbed in the GaAs cell, leading to luminescent coupling from the InGaP cell to the GaAs cell, and reducing the potential for photon recycling within the InGaP cell.

InGaP cell is transparent to photons emitted at the GaAs bandgap energy. However, any radiative recombination within the InGaP cell [see Fig. 7(b)] will couple into the GaAs with a high probability as photons emitted at the InGaP bandgap energy are strongly absorbed by GaAs but only weakly absorbed by InGaP. This can be detrimental to peak cell performance in that photons that could in principle be providing voltage to the InGaP cell are instead being absorbed in the GaAs and only contributing a lesser voltage as a result. This reduces the performance advantages of thin-film multijunction devices relative to their on-wafer cousins, compared with single-junction devices where the difference between thin-film and on-wafer devices can be large [2].

However, for real-world applications, efficient optical coupling from the InGaP cell to the GaAs cell creates the potential for the cell to be self-current-balancing to a certain extent. That is, if the GaAs cell is limiting the overall current of the device, the InGaP cell will luminesce and provide more photons to the bottom cell, making the overall device less sensitive to fluctuations in the input spectrum [19].

V. CONCLUSION

A thin-film, flexible, InGaP-GaAs tandem solar cell with NREL-verified efficiency of 30.8% has been described. The fabrication scheme outlined above could be extended to cell structures with three or more junctions.

ACKNOWLEDGMENT

The entire Alta Devices team has contributed in various ways to the development of the technology described in this paper. Specifically, we would like to highlight the technical contributions of S. Amjadi, L. Ang, M. Archer, J. Corbacho, R. Furler, T. Gmitter, R. Hamamjy, G. He, F. Liu, S. Scully, S. Spruytte, T. Suwwan de Felipe, and H. Tam. In addition, this paper benefited from discussions with J. Olson. Finally, we would like to thank K. Emery, T. Moriarty, P. Ciszek, and the Device Performance Characterization team at the National Renewable Energy Laboratory for the cell measurements described herein.

REFERENCES

[1] M. Pagliaro, R. Ciriminna, and G. Palmisano, "Flexible solar cells," *Chem-SusChem*, vol. 1, pp. 880–891, 2008.

[2] B. M. Kayes, H. Nie, R. Twist, S. G. Spruytte, F. Reinhardt, I. C. Kizilyalli, and G. S. Higashi, "27.6% conversion efficiency, a new record for single-junction solar cells under 1 sun illumination," in *Proc. 37th IEEE Photovoltaic Spec. Conf.*, 2011, pp. 4–8.

[3] L. S. Mattos, S. R. Scully, M. Syfu, E. Olson, L. Yang, C. Ling, B. M. Kayes, and G. He, "New module efficiency record: 23.5% under 1-sun illumination using thin-film single-junction GaAs solar cells," in *Proc. 38th IEEE Photovoltaic Spec. Conf.*, 2012, pp. 3187–3190.

[4] M. A. Green, K. Emery, Y. Hishikawa, W. Warta, and E. D. Dunlop, "Solar cell efficiency tables (ver. 41)," *Prog. Photovoltaics: Res. Appl.*, vol. 21, pp. 1–11, 2013.

[5] M. A. Green, K. Emery, Y. Hishikawa, and W. Warta, "Solar cell efficiency tables (ver. 33)," *Progress Photovoltaics: Res. Appl.*, vol. 17, pp. 85–94, 2009.

[6] E. Yablonovitch, T. Gmitter, J. P. Harbison, and R. Bhat, "Extreme selectivity in the lift-off of epitaxial GaAs films," *Appl. Phys. Lett.*, vol. 51, pp. 2222–2224, 1987.

[7] National Renewable Energy Laboratory (NREL), Golden, CO, USA.

[8] ASTM G173 - 03(2012), "Standard Tables for Reference Solar Spectral Irradiances: Direct Normal and Hemispherical on 37° Tilted Surface," ASTM Int., West Conshohocken, PA, 2012, DOI: 10.1520/G0173-03R12, www.astm.org

[9] T. Takamoto, E. Ikeda, H. Kurita, M. Ohmori, M. Yamaguchi, and M. J. Yang, "Two-terminal monolithic $In_{0.5}Ga_{0.5}P$/GaAs tandem solar cells with a high conversion efficiency of over 30%," *Jpn. J. Appl. Phys.*, vol. 36, pp. 6215–6220, 1997.

[10] D. J. Friedman, J. M. Olson, and S. Kurtz, "High-efficiency III–V multijunction Solar Cells," in *Handbook of Photovoltaic Science and Engineering*, A. Luque and S. Hegedus, Eds., 2nd ed. New York, NY, USA: Wiley, 2011, pp. 326–327.

[11] (Jun. 2013). [Online]. Available: http://www.altadevices.com/pdfs/single_cell.pdf

[12] (Jun. 2013). [Online]. Available: http://mldevices.com/images/Datasheets/120213%20uav%20cell%201j.pdf

[13] (Jun. 2013). [Online]. Available: http://mldevices.com/images/Datasheets/120213%20uav%20interconnected%20cell%202j.pdf

[14] (Jun. 2013). [Online]. Available: http://mldevices.com/images/Datasheets/120213%20uav%20interconnected%20cell%203j.pdf

[15] (Jan. 2014). [Online]. Available: http://www.emcore.com/wp-content/uploads/ZTJ-cell.pdf

[16] (Jun. 2013). [Online]. Available: http://www.spectrolab.com/DataSheets/cells/PV%20XTJ%20Cell%205-20-10.pdf

[17] M. A. Green, "Radiative efficiency of state-of-the-art photovoltaic cells," *Prog. Photovoltaics: Res. Appl.*, vol. 20, pp. 472–476, 2012.

[18] O. D. Miller, E. Yablonovitch, and S. R. Kurtz, "Strong internal and external luminescence as solar cells approach the Shockley–Queisser limit," *IEEE J. Photovoltaics*, vol. 2, no. 3, pp. 303–311, Jul. 2012.

[19] M. A. Steiner and J. F. Geisz, "Non-linear luminescent coupling in series-connected multijunction solar cells," *Appl. Phys. Lett.*, vol. 100, pp. 251106-1–251106-5, 2012.

Brendan M. Kayes (SM'13) received the B.A./B.Sc. degrees in philosophy and physics and the B.Sc.(Hons.) degree in applied mathematics from the University of Auckland, Auckland, New Zealand, and the M.S. and Ph.D. degrees in applied physics from the California Institute of Technology, Pasadena, CA, USA. His graduate research involved the design, simulation, fabrication, and characterization of silicon nano- and microstructures for application in low cost photovoltaics.

He joined the device team of Alta Devices, Sunnyvale, CA, USA, in 2008, with a focus on efficiency improvements.

Ling Zhang received the B.S. degree from Zhenjiang University, Hangzhou, China, in 1995 and the Ph.D. degree from the University of Wisconsin–Madison, Madison, WI, USA, in 2002, both in chemical engineering.

Her work has been focused on the crystal growth of III–V compound semiconductors by metal-organic chemical vapor deposition. She has over ten years of industrial experience in R&D and production of epitaxial materials and processes for high-power and high-efficiency optoelectronic devices. Before joining Alta Devices, Sunnyvale, CA, USA, in 2012, she was with several industrial LED companies, including Philips Lumileds Lighting, Bridgelux, and Lattice Power. She served as the Vice President of Epi Manufacturing at Lattice Power, Jiangxi, China, in 2011.

Rose Twist is currently a Senior Technician with Alta Devices, Sunnyvale, CA, USA. Prior to joining Alta Devices in 2009, she was with Hewlett Packard and Agilent Labs., where she worked on the world's first metal-organic chemical vapor deposition (MOCVD)-grown quantum cascade lasers (InP-based, including both ridge and buried heterostructure designs), the world's first all-MOCVD grown RT–CW InGaAsN 1.3-μm vertical cavity surface-emitting laser diode, and HP's first RT–CW GaN blue/UV laser.

I.-Kang Ding received the B.Sc. degree in chemistry from National Taiwan University, Taipei, Taiwan, and the Ph.D. degree in materials sciences and engineering from Stanford University, Stanford, CA, USA. His graduate research involved the design and characterization of light trapping structures in solar cells and the development of advanced characterization techniques to better understand the structure–property relationship of inorganic–organic hybrid devices.

He joined Alta Devices, Sunnyvale, CA, USA, in 2011 as a Senior Device Engineer and focused his R&D efforts on improving the light trapping of III–V solar cells. He is the author or coauthor of more than 15 peer-reviewed papers related to solar cells and LEDs.

Gregg S. Higashi (F'08) received the Bachelor's and Ph.D. degrees in physics from Massachusetts Institute of Technology, Cambridge, MA, USA.

He began his career at Bell Laboratories, Berkeley Heights, NJ, USA, working on understanding chemical vapor decomposition and surface chemistry as it related to silicon-integrated circuit technology. He later helped to develop process technologies spanning 0.5 μm to 90 nm for AT&T Microelectronics, Lucent Technologies, and Agere Systems. At Applied Materials, he was the CTO of the Front End Products Group supporting Si Epi, RTP, gate dielectrics, LPCVD, and ion-implantation technologies before joining Intel to do 65-nm NOR FLASH and phase change nonvolatile memory development. Just prior to joining Alta Devices, Sunnyvale, CA, USA, in 2008, he served as the Managing Director of Applied Materials' SunFab Thin-Film Solar Technology Start-Up Team.

Effect of Luminescent Coupling on the Optimal Design of Multijunction Solar Cells

Daniel J. Friedman, John F. Geisz, and Myles A. Steiner

Abstract—We analyze the implications of luminescent coupling on multijunction cell design and performance, using a recently developed formalism that uses the measured luminescent coupling parameters as inputs to an analytical model of the full current–voltage (*J–V*) characteristic of the cell. This calculation of the full *J–V* curve allows the determination of the cell open-circuit voltage, short-circuit current, fill factor, and efficiency in the presence of luminescent coupling. We show that luminescent coupling affects critical aspects of the cell design that include the optimal junction thicknesses and bandgaps, and affects the dependence of the cell performance on the spectral content of the light illuminating it.

Index Terms—Bandgap optimization, efficiency, luminescent coupling, multijunction solar cells, optical thinning, radiative coupling.

I. Introduction

LUMINESCENT coupling in multijunction solar cells is the generation of the photocurrent in a particular junction by absorption of radiatively emitted light from an overlying higher bandgap junction. For high-quality III–V junctions whose recombination is largely radiative, this effect can have a significant effect on the short-circuit photocurrent densities ($J_{SC}s$) of the junctions. Consequently, there is a significant body of work in the literature on the experimental extraction and modeling of the luminescent coupling parameters from the $J_{SC}s$ [1]–[8]. There have also been theoretical studies of the effect of luminescent coupling on the *efficiencies* of idealized cells [9]–[12], but without a direct link to experimentally measurable luminescent coupling parameters [4] of nonideal cells. We recently extended the analysis of luminescent coupling at short circuit [4] to the full current–voltage curve *V(J)*, with an analytical model allowing the cell efficiency, fill factor, and open-circuit voltage (V_{OC}) to be computed as a function of the luminescent coupling parameters [13].

In this paper, we use the model to analyze several multijunction cell structures of particular interest. We show that strong luminescent coupling can significantly affect the optimal bandgaps and thicknesses of the junctions, and the resulting efficiency of the multijunction cell. Section II briefly reviews the analytical model. Section III then analyzes a simple model two-junction cell, which demonstrates that luminescent coupling affects the optimum junction bandgaps as well as thicknesses; this discussion is extended to the more complex case of a four-junction cell in Section IV. Section V applies the model to the analysis of measured cell parameters, and demonstrates that luminescent coupling can lead to novel features in the functional dependence of the fill factor on junction photocurrents. Finally, Section VI illustrates the calculation of the luminescent coupling currents in a manner that works for any number of junctions.

II. Analytical Model

A. Functional Form for V(J)

We consider a series-connected two-terminal multijunction cell for which each junction can be described by a traditional two-diode model with J_{01} (ideality factor $n = 1$) and J_{02} ($n = 2$) dark current components, and series and shunt resistances can be neglected. We number the junctions in order of decreasing bandgap so that the top highest-bandgap junction is $i = 1$. We treat couplings between nonadjacent junctions as negligible. Elsewhere [4], [13], we show that the voltage $V_i(J)$ of the ith junction at current density J in the presence of luminescent coupling can be written as follows:

$$V_i(J) = \frac{2k_B T}{e} \times$$

$$ln\left[\sqrt{\left(\frac{J_{02,i}}{2J_{01,i}}\right)^2 + 1} + \frac{J_{02,i} + J_i^{\text{Total}}(J) + J}{J_{01,i}} - \frac{J_{02,i}}{2J_{01,i}}\right] \tag{1}$$

with

$$J_i^{\text{Total}}(J) = J_i^{\text{Ext}} + J_{i-1,i}^{LC}(J) \tag{2}$$

and

$$J_{i-1,i}^{LC}(J) = \eta_{i-1,i} J_{01,i-1}\left[\exp\left(\frac{eV_{i-1}(J)}{k_B T}\right) - 1\right]. \tag{3}$$

$J_{i-1,i}^{LC}(J)$ is the coupling photocurrent density that is generated in the ith junction resulting from radiation from the overlying $(i-1)$th junction. The coupling is characterized by the measureable parameters $\eta_{i-1,i}$ and $\varphi_i = J_{02,i}/\left(2\sqrt{J_{01,i}}\right)$, which describe, respectively, the coupling strength and linearity. From the voltages $V_i(J)$ of the m individual junctions, we can then

Manuscript received June 6, 2013; revised December 3, 2013; accepted February 19, 2014. This work was supported by the U.S. Department of Energy under Contract DE-AC36–08GO28308 with the National Renewable Energy Laboratory.

The authors are with the National Renewable Energy Laboratory, Golden, CO 80401 USA (e mail: daniel.friedman@nrel.gov; john.geisz@nrel.gov; myles.steiner@nrel.gov).

Color versions of one or more of the figures in this paper are available online at http://ieeexplore.ieee.org.

Digital Object Identifier 10.1109/JPHOTOV.2014.2308722

calculate the voltage $V(J)$ of the multijunction cell

$$V(J) = \sum_{i=1}^{m} V_i(J) \qquad (4)$$

from which the cell operating parameters, which include V_{OC}, J_{SC}, fill factor, and efficiency, can be computed numerically.

B. Characteristics of $\eta_{i-1,i}$

A convenient model to analyze the luminescent behavior of solar cells, which includes the computation of $\eta_{i-1,i}$, is provided in [14] and [15]. The model allows for the treatment of the detailed optical properties of complex solar cell structures, accounting for optical losses in the interfaces and cladding layers, and for internal luminescent efficiencies η_{int} that can be less than the ideal value of $\eta_{\text{int}} = 1$. To elucidate the trends and fundamental constraints on the value of $\eta_{i-1,i}$, we first consider the idealized case of a cell with no optical losses in the interfaces and cladding layers, an ideal luminescent efficiency $\eta_{\text{int}} = 1$, and zero reflectance at the interface between the $(i-1)$th and ith junctions. The model of [14], [15] then provides simple expressions for $\eta_{i-1,i}$ in the limits of optically thin and optically thick $(i-1)$th junctions

$$\eta_{i-1,i} = \frac{n^2}{1+n^2} \quad \text{[optically thick]} \qquad (5a)$$

and

$$\eta_{i-1,i} = \frac{1}{2}\left(1 + \sqrt{1 - \frac{1}{n^2}}\right) \approx 1 - \frac{1}{4n^2} \quad \text{[optically thin]} \qquad (5b)$$

where n is the index of refraction of the semiconductor material at the bandgap of the $(i-1)$th junction. For the III–V materials out of which high-efficiency multijunction cells are made, a typical value for n would be $n = 3.6$, giving $\eta_{i-1,i} = 0.93$ and 0.98 for the thick and thin limits, respectively. These are upper bounds to η, which thus cannot be precisely 1 even for ideal lossless cells. This is because a small but nonzero fraction of the luminescently emitted light from the junction must escape out the front of the junction rather than being transmitted out the rear to the junction beneath. For nonideal cells with $\eta_{\text{int}} < 1$, the value of $\eta_{i-1,i}$ will be less than these ideal limits, and this decrease from ideality will be greater for thick $(i-1)$th junctions than for thin ones. Optical losses in nonideal absorbing cladding layers will also cause $\eta_{i-1,i}$ to be lower than the ideal limits; however, in this case, the effect on $\eta_{i-1,i}$ will be greatest for thin junctions. Thus, there is no universal trend of $\eta_{i-1,i}$ on the junction thickness. In the following discussions, we treat $\eta_{i-1,i}$ as independent of the junction thickness.

III. Optimal Design of Two-Junction Cells in the Presence of Luminescent Coupling

A. Optical Thinning

The implications of luminescent coupling on the cell design, and specifically on the optical thinning of junctions, are usefully explored by considering a model simulating a GaInP

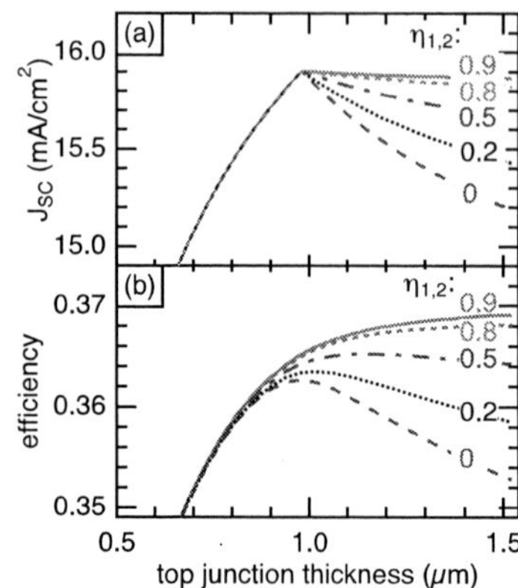

Fig. 1. (a) J_{SC} and (b) efficiency versus top-junction thickness, for several values of the luminescent coupling strength $\eta_{1,2}$, for the GaInP/GaAs model cell described in the text.

(1.85 eV)/GaAs (1.42 eV) two-junction cell under the G173 AM1.5 direct spectrum. The photocurrents resulting from the *external* illumination (i.e., from the AM1.5D spectrum) are computed in the familiar way: the top junction of thickness L and absorption coefficient $\alpha(\lambda)$ is assumed to absorb a fraction $1 - \exp[-\alpha(\lambda)L]$ of the incident light, while the light not absorbed by the top junction is passed to the optically thick bottom junction; all absorbed photons are considered to be converted into the photocurrent. The individual junction $J_{01,i}$ dark currents are computed using the detailed-balance approach assuming zero reflectance at the back of each junction; the dependence of the dark current on the junction thickness is accounted for, as described in [14] and [15]. For simplicity, we take $J_{02,i} = 0$ (i.e., $\varphi_i = 0$). Fig. 1(a) shows the cell's short-circuit current (which includes the luminescent-coupling currents) versus top-junction thickness, which is calculated as a function of the luminescent coupling strength $\eta_{1,2}$ using the model described previously; Fig. 1(b) shows the corresponding cell efficiencies. For $\eta_{1,2} = 0$, we see the familiar result that the optimal design thins the top junction, in order to match the junction photocurrents. However, with increasing $\eta_{1,2}$, the optimal top-junction thickness increases, until at $\eta_{1,2} \geq {\sim}0.8$, the optimal top junction is optically thick. Note that values of η as high as 0.9 have been observed experimentally for a GaAs junction coupling to an InGaAs junction [4].

The efficiencies in Fig. 1(b) are determined not only by the J_{SC} but by the V_{OC} and the fill factor as well, both of which are increased by luminescent coupling [13]. The net result, as seen in Fig. 1, is that luminescent coupling boosts the efficiency even at the current-matched thickness of 0.98 μm, and the boost increases with increasing top-junction thickness. The effects of luminescent coupling on the $V(J)$ curves, fill factor, and V_{OC} are discussed in detail in [13].

B. Optimal Bandgap

Luminescent coupling affects not only the optimal thickness of the top junction, but its optimal bandgap, as well. We explore this by considering the two-junction GaInP/GaAs model cell of Section III-A, now varying the top-junction bandgap.

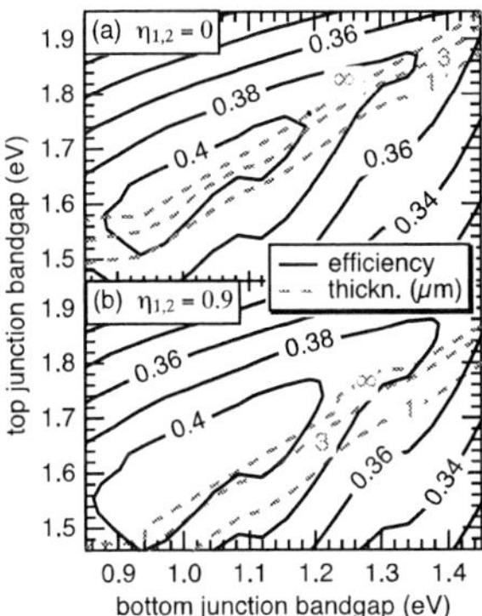

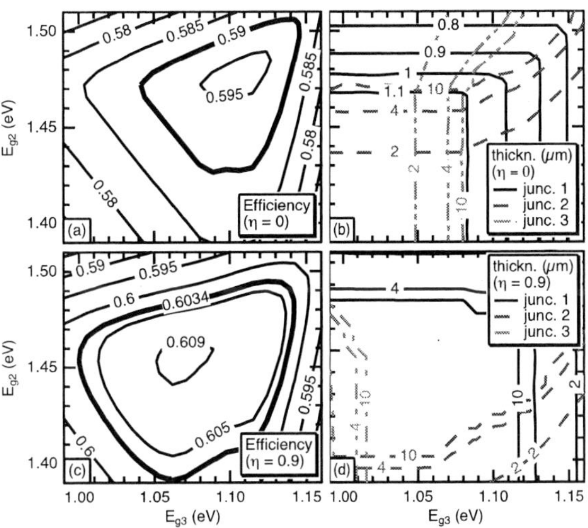

Fig. 2. Efficiency (solid black contours) and corresponding optimal top-junction thickness in micrometers (dashed red contours) as a function of top- and bottom-junction bandgaps for the GaInP/GaAs model cell described in the text, comparing (a) no luminescent coupling ($\eta_{1,2} = 0$) and (b) strong coupling ($\eta_{1,2} = 0.9$). The cell is illuminated at 1 sun; cell temperature is 300 K.

Fig. 2 shows the efficiency and corresponding optimal top-junction thickness as a function of the top- and bottom-junction bandgaps, without (a) and with (b) luminescent coupling. For the case of no luminescent coupling, above the thickness $= \infty$ contour, the external photocurrent of the top junction is less than that of the bottom junction ("top-limited"), even for an optically thick top junction. Below this contour, an optically thick top junction would absorb too much light and cause the cell's current to be limited by the bottom junction ("bottom-limited"); therefore, the optimal cell design thins the top-junction bandgap to match the currents. This is the familiar multijunction picture described, for example, in [16]. In contrast, with strong luminescent coupling, the decrease of the bottom-junction photocurrent with the increasing top-junction thickness is greatly mitigated. Therefore, the optimal top junction thickness is greater than for the case of no luminescent coupling, just as we saw in Fig. 1. As a consequence, the introduction of luminescent coupling slightly lowers the optimal top-junction bandgap and raises the optimal bottom-junction bandgap. Probably of greater practical impact, the luminescent coupling also widens the range of bandgaps for which the efficiency remains near its maximum. Thus, the proper design that accounts for luminescent coupling can affect the optimal bandgaps as well as thicknesses.

IV. Design Optimization of Four-Junction Cells

Luminescent coupling is likely to be important in next-generation four-junction cell structures presently being developed, because of the critical current-matching requirements and the constraints on available bandgap combinations for these cells. One such four-junction bandgap combination of particular interest is the 1.9/1.4/1.0/0.74-eV four-junction structure that can be realized in practice by adding a 0.74-eV InGaAs fourth junction to the well-developed 1.9/1.4/1.0-eV GaInP/GaAs/InGaAs inverted metamorphic multijunction solar cell [17]–[19]. In practice, achieving high-quality junctions with bandgaps higher than 1.9 eV or lower than 0.74 eV in this structure is difficult, but varying the middle two bandgaps is relatively straightforward. This structure is considerably more

Fig. 3. (a) Efficiency and (b) corresponding optimal junction thicknesses versus middle-junction bandgaps E_{g2} and E_{g3}, for the model four-junction cell described in the text, for no luminescent coupling ($\eta_{i-1,i} = 0$). (c) Efficiency and (d) junction thicknesses, as in panels (a) and (b), but for strong luminescent coupling ($\eta_{i-1,i} = 0.9$). The thick contour lines in (a) and (c) indicate the bandgaps for which the efficiency is 99% of its maximum value. In both cases, the fourth junction is fixed at 10 μm (optically thick), and $\varphi_i = 0$. The cell is illuminated at 1000 suns under the G173 AM1.5 direct spectrum; the cell temperature is 300 K.

complex than the two-junction cell analyzed earlier, but its analysis with our model is equally straightforward.

Fig. 3 shows the modeled efficiency and corresponding optimal 1st/2nd/3rd-junction thicknesses of the 1.9/E_{g2}/E_{g3}/0.74-eV structure as a function of the middle two bandgaps E_{g2} and E_{g3}, at 1000 suns concentration and 300-K cell temperature. The 4th junction is fixed at 10 μm (optically thick). The individual junction J_{01} dark currents are computed as described in Section III-A. For each bandgap combination, the optimum junction thicknesses are chosen by numerical search for the maximum efficiency. Fig. 3 compares the case of no luminescent coupling between any of the junctions ($\eta_{i-1,i} = 0$) [see Fig. 3(a) and (b)] with the case of strong luminescent coupling ($\eta_{i-1,i} = 0.9$) [see Fig. (c) and (d)]. For both cases, $\varphi_i = 0$. For each of these two cases, a thick contour line is drawn to indicate the bandgaps for which the efficiency is 99% of its maximum value. With the help of these 99%-of-maximum contours, we can see that with luminescent coupling [see Fig. 3(c)], the efficiency peak becomes broader than without luminescent coupling [see Fig. 3(a)], and centered $\sim$30 meV lower in energy for both E_{g2} and E_{g3}. These trends are comparable with and have the same origin as the simpler case discussed previously of a two-junction cell. The corresponding junction optimal thicknesses are shown for $\eta_{i-1,i} = 0$ and 0.9 in Fig. 3(b) and (d), respectively. For $\eta_{i-1,i} = 0.9$, the junction optimal thicknesses are optically thick ($>$10 μm) over the broad region of the peak efficiency. Thus, the cell that is designed to take advantage of strong luminescent coupling would be less sensitive to unintended deviations from the designed bandgaps and thicknesses than a cell without luminescent coupling.

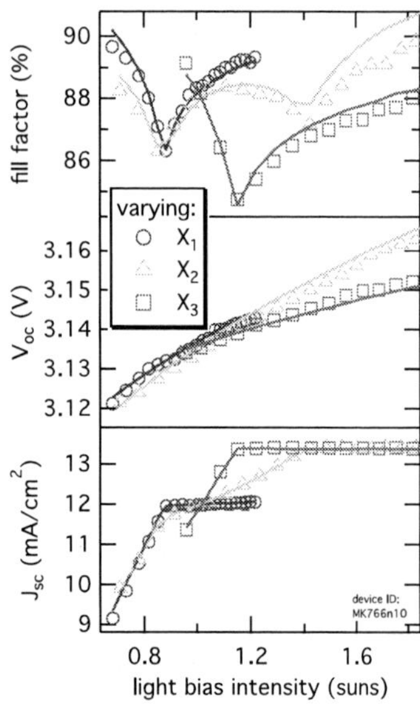

Fig. 4. Measured (open symbols) and modeled (solid lines) J–V parameters of a GaInP/GaAs/GaInAs inverted metamorphic three-junction cell as a function of light bias intensity $X_{1,2,3}$ to each junction, with the light bias to the other junction held constant at 1 sun. Fit parameters are: $J_{01,1} = 1.5 \times 10^{-24}$, $J_{01,2} = 1.1 \times 10^{-17}$, $J_{01,3} = 2.3 \times 10^{-9}$, $J_1^{\mathrm{Ext}} = 13.72$, $J_2^{\mathrm{Ext}} = 13.24$, $J_3^{\mathrm{Ext}} = 11.70$, $\eta_{1,2} = 0.225$, $\eta_{2,3} = 0.844$, $\varphi_1 = 0.500$, $\varphi_2 = 1.998$, $\varphi_3 = 0.930$. Currents are in units of mA/cm^2; φ are in units of (mA/cm^2)$^{1/2}$.

V. MEASUREMENT AND MODELING OF THREE-JUNCTION CELL OPERATING PARAMETERS

The effect of luminescent coupling upon J_{SC}, V_{OC}, and fill factor can be quantified by varying the light bias intensity to each of the junctions in turn, while holding constant the light bias to the other junctions [4], [7], [13]. Fig. 4 compares these measured parameters for a GaInP/GaAs/InGaAs three-junction cell grown and processed in the inverted configuration [20] with a fit to the model that is described here, with excellent agreement. A noteworthy characteristic of the fill factor, which is well reproduced by the model, is the appearance of two separate minima as a function of the light intensity X_2 to the second junction. These minima occur at the values of X_2 for which J_{SC} transitions from middle-junction-limited ($X_2 < 0.85$) to bottom-junction-limited ($0.85 < X_2 < 1.4$) to top-junction-limited ($X_2 > 1.4$), at which two points the slope of J_{SC} discontinuously changes. The appearance of a minimum in the fill factor at the point where the current-limiting junction changes is a long-known feature of multijunction cells; indeed, this phenomenon can be used as a diagnostic of the cell performance [21]. However, the transition through two separate minima as the illumination to one of the junctions is varied is (for junctions without shunts or reverse-bias breakdown) a signature of luminescent coupling.

Further insight into this behavior in a three-junction cell can be gained by examining the dependence of the fill factor on the externally induced photocurrents to the top and middle junctions. Fig. 5(a) shows the calculated fill factor for a three-junction cell using the parameters of Fig. 4, as a function of top- and middle-junction externally induced photocurrents J_1^{Ext} and J_2^{Ext}, with J_3^{Ext} set to 12 mA/cm^2. When $J_1^{\mathrm{Ext}} > J_3^{\mathrm{Ext}}$, the

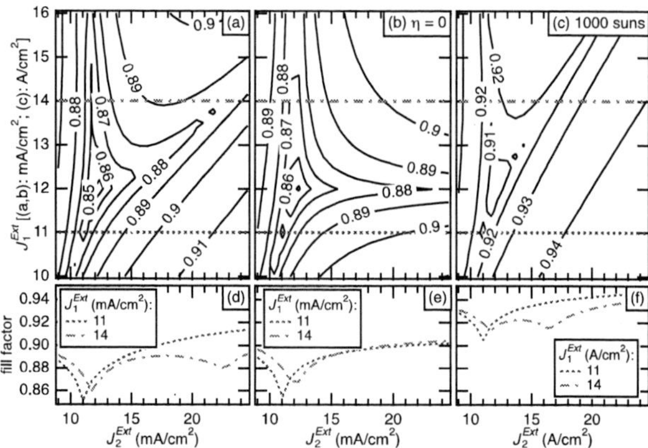

Fig. 5. (a)–(c) Contours of the fill factor for a three-junction cell computed as a function of top and middle junction externally induced photocurrents J_1^{Ext} and J_2^{Ext}. (a) Cell parameters $J_{01,i}$, $J_{02,i}$, $\eta_{i-1,i}$, φ_i set to those of Fig. 4; $J_3^{\mathrm{Ext}} = 12$ mA/cm^2. (b) As in (a) except with $\eta_{1,2} = \eta_{2,3} = 0$. (c) As in (a), except at 1000 suns, i.e., all photocurrents 1000 times that of (a). (d)–(f) Fill factor versus J_2^{Ext} for the two values of J_1^{Ext} indicated in the legends, with the cell parameters the same as in (a)–(c), respectively.

fill factor passes through two minima as J_2^{Ext} is swept. This case is illustrated by the dashed line at $J_1^{\mathrm{Ext}} = 14$ mA/cm^2 [Fig. 5(d) shows the fill factor versus J_2^{Ext} for this $J_1^{\mathrm{Ext}} = 14$ mA/cm^2 case], and approximately corresponds to the case of Fig. 4. When $J_1^{\mathrm{Ext}} \leq J_3^{\mathrm{Ext}}$, as illustrated by the lower dashed line at $J_1^{\mathrm{Ext}} = 11$ mA/cm^2 (also shown in Fig. 5(d)), the fill factor passes through only one minimum as J_2^{Ext} is swept. When the luminescent coupling strength is set to zero as in Fig. 5(b) and (e), the fill factor passes through only one minimum as J_2^{Ext} is swept, regardless of the value of J_1^{Ext}. Finally, Fig. 5(c) and (f) consider the same cell as in Fig. 5(a), except at 1000-sun concentration; i.e., the photocurrents are 1000 times that of Fig. 5(a). In this case, the two minima in the fill factor occur within a significantly smaller range of J_2^{Ext} than in the 1-sun case of Fig. 5(a). This difference occurs because the presence of nonzero J_{02} dark currents results in a nonlinearity of the luminescent coupling current $J_{i-1,i}^{\mathrm{LC}}(J)$ with the current, i.e., with concentration [4], [13].

VI. CALCULATION OF LUMINESCENT COUPLING CURRENTS FOR THREE- AND FOUR-JUNCTION CELLS

Because the model that is described here provides the full multijunction $V(J)$ characteristic including luminescent coupling, it can be used to calculate J_{SC} under any spectrum by searching $V(J)$ for the current J_{SC} for which $V(J_{\mathrm{SC}}) = 0$. Although analytical expressions for J_{SC} are available for two- and three-junction cells (e.g., [4], [8]), the $V(J)$-searching method works for any number of junctions—a vital capability as attention in the multijunction photovoltaics field becomes increasingly focused on cells with more than three junctions. Fig. 6 shows J_{SC} for hypothetical three- and four-junction cells with external illumination going only to the top junction so that the externally induced junction photocurrents are $J_1^{\mathrm{Ext}} = 12$ mA/cm^2, $J_i^{\mathrm{Ext}} = 0$ ($i > 1$). J_{SC} is shown as a function of luminescent coupling strength $\eta_{i-1,i}$; for simplicity, we take

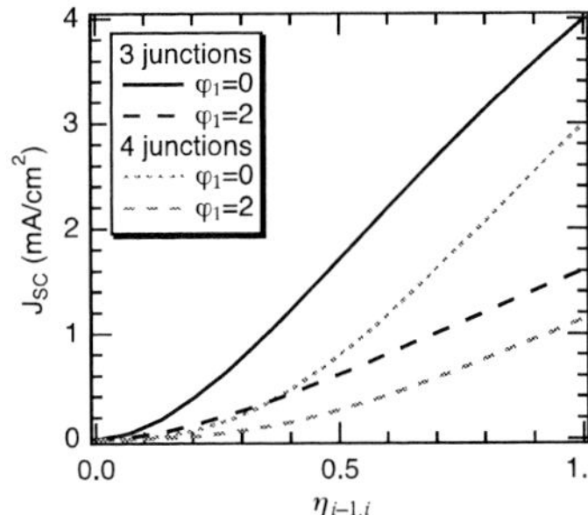

Fig. 6. J_{SC} as a function of the luminescent coupling strength $\eta_{1,2} = \eta_{2,3} = \eta_{3,4}$ for hypothetical three- and four-junction cells with externally induced junction photocurrents $J_1^{Ext} = 12$ mA/cm^2, $J_i^{Ext} = 0$ ($i > 1$). Except where specifically noted in the figure legend, $\varphi_i = 0$.

$\eta_{1,2} = \eta_{2,3} = \eta_{3,4}$. The three-junction J_{SC} is the same (as it must be) as the result computed from the analytical expression of [4, eq. (9)]. The four-junction J_{SC} in this example shows qualitatively similar behavior, with the extra photocurrent in the top junction being distributed through the middle junctions to the bottom junction, to a degree determined by the luminescent coupling strength. This capability to straightforwardly compute J_{SC} (and, as easily, the individual junction coupling currents $J_{i-1,i}^{LC}$) provides the capability to analyze J_{SC} and $J_{i-1,i}^{LC}$ for next-generation cells with four or even more junctions.

VII. SUMMARY

Luminescent coupling between junctions in a multijunction solar cell can significantly alter the optimal design of the cell. Strong luminescent coupling can mitigate or eliminate the need for optical thinning of the junctions, move and broaden the range of optimal bandgaps, and introduce conditions under which new fill factor minima are observed as the relative illumination intensities to the various junctions are varied.

APPENDIX

Here, we clarify the relationship between the quantity η as used here and defined in [4] with the luminescent coupling parameter X_{LC} defined in [8]. When $\varphi = 0$, these two quantities are related by [13]

$$X_{LC} = \eta / (1 + \eta). \tag{A1}$$

For optically thick junctions, we can then apply (5a) to obtain

$$X_{LC} = \frac{n^2}{1 + 2n^2} = 1 - \frac{1 + n^2}{1 + 2n^2}. \tag{A2}$$

This agrees with the value for X_{LC} derived in [8, eq. (21)].

REFERENCES

[1] C. Baur, M. Hermle, F. Dimroth, and A. W. Bett, "Effects of optical coupling in III-V multilayer systems," *Appl. Phys. Lett.*, vol. 90, pp. 192109-1–192109-3, 2007.

[2] K.-H. Lee, K. W. J. Barnham, J. P. Connolly, B. C. Browne, R. Airey, J. S. Roberts, M. Fuhrer, T. N. D. Tibbits, and N. J. EkinsDaukes, "Demonstration of photon coupling in dual multiple-quantum-well solar cells," *IEEE J. Photovoltaics*, vol. 2, no. 1, pp. 68–74, Jan. 2012.

[3] S. H. Lim, J.-J. Li, E. H. Steenbergen, and Y.-H. Zhang, "Luminescence coupling effects on multijunction solar cell external quantum efficiency measurement," *Prog. Photovoltaics*, vol. 21, pp. 344–350, 2011.

[4] M. A. Steiner and J. F. Geisz, "Non-linear luminescent coupling in series-connected multijunction solar cells," *Appl. Phys. Lett.*, vol. 100, pp. 251106-1–251106-5, 2012.

[5] M. A. Steiner, S. R. Kurtz, J. F. Geisz, W. E. McMahon, and J. M. Olson, "Using phase effects to understand measurements of the quantum efficiency and related luminescent coupling in a multijunction solar cell," *IEEE J. Photovoltaics*, vol. 2, no. 4, pp. 424–433, Oct. 2012.

[6] H. Yoon, R. R. King, G. Kinsey, S. Kurtz, and D. D. Krut, "Radiative coupling effects in GaInP/GaAs/Ge multijunction solar cells," in *Proc. 3rd World Conf. Photovoltaics Energy Convers.*, Osaka, Japan, 2003, pp. 745–748.

[7] M. A. Steiner, J. F. Geisz, T. E. Moriarty, R. M. France, W. E. McMahon, J. M. Olson, S. R. Kurtz, and D. J. Friedman, "Measuring IV curves and subcell photocurrents in the presence of luminescent coupling," *IEEE J. Photovoltaics*, vol. 3, no. 2, pp. 879–887, Apr. 2013.

[8] D. Derkacs, D. T. Bilir, and V. A. Sabnis, "Luminescent coupling in GaAs/GaInNAsSb multijunction solar cells," *IEEE J. Photovoltaics*, vol. 3, no. 1, pp. 520–527, Jan. 2013.

[9] A. Marti and G. L. Araujo, "Limiting efficiencies for photovoltaic energy conversion in multigap systems," *Sol. Energy Mater. Sol. Cells*, vol. 43, pp. 203–222, 1996.

[10] A. S. Brown and M. A. Green, "Limiting efficiency for current-constrained two-terminal tandem cell stacks," *Prog. Photovoltaics*, vol. 10, pp. 299–307, 2002.

[11] A. S. Brown and M. A. Green, "Radiative coupling as a means to reduce spectral mismatch in monolithic tandem solar cell stacks-theoretical considerations," in *Proc. IEEE 29th Photovoltaic Spec. Conf.*, New Orleans, LA, USA, 2002, pp. 868–871.

[12] I. Tobias and A. Luque, "Ideal efficiency of monolithic, series-connected multijunction solar cells," *Prog. Photovoltaics*, vol. 10, pp. 323–329, 2002.

[13] D. J. Friedman, J. F. Geisz, and M. A. Steiner, "Analysis of multijunction solar cell current-voltage characteristics in the presence of luminescent coupling," *IEEE J. Photovoltaics*, vol. 3, no. 4, pp. 1429–1436, Oct. 2013.

[14] M. A. Steiner, J. F. Geisz, I. Garcia, D. J. Friedman, A. Duda, and S. R. Kurtz, "Optical enhancement of V_{oc} in high quality GaAs solar cells," *J. Appl. Phys.*, vol. 113, pp. 123109-1–123109-11, 2013.

[15] M. A. Steiner, J. F. Geisz, I. García, D. J. Friedman, A. Duda, W. J. Olavarria, M. Young, and S. R. Kurtz, "Effects of internal luminescence and internal optics on the V_{oc} and J_{sc} of III–V solar cells," *IEEE J. Photovoltaics*, vol. 3, no. 4, pp. 1437–1442, Oct. 2013.

[16] S. R. Kurtz, P. Faine, and J. M. Olson, "Modeling of two-junction, series-connected tandem solar cells using top-cell thickness as an adjustable parameter," *J. Appl. Phys.*, vol. 68, pp. 1890–1895, 1990.

[17] R. M. France, I. Garcia, W. E. McMahon, A. G. Norman, J. Simon, J. F. Geisz, D. J. Friedman, and M. J. Romero, "Lattice-mismatched 0.7 eV GaInAs solar cells using GaInP compositionally graded buffers," *IEEE J. Photovoltaics*, vol. 4, no. 1, pp. 190–195, Jan. 2014.

[18] D. J. Friedman, J. F. Geisz, A. G. Norman, M. W. Wanlass, and S. R. Kurtz, "0.7-eV GaInAs junction for a GaInP/GaAs/GaInAs(1eV)/GaInAs(0.7eV) four-junction solar cell," in *Proc. IEEE 4th World Conf. Photovoltaic Energy Convers.*, 2006, pp. 598–602.

[19] M. Stan, D. Aiken, B. Cho, A. Cornfeld, V. Ley, P. Patel, P. Sharps, and T. Varghese, "High-efficiency quadruple junction solar cells using OMVPE with inverted metamorphic device structures," *J. Cryst. Growth*, vol. 312, pp. 1370–1374, 2010.

[20] J. F. Geisz, S. R. Kurtz, M. W. Wanlass, J. S. Ward, A. Duda, D. J. Friedman, J. M. Olson, W. E. McMahon, T. Moriarty, and J. Kiehl, "High-efficiency GaInP/GaAs/InGaAs triple-junction solar cells grown inverted with a metamorphic bottom junction," *Appl. Phys. Lett.*, vol. 91, pp. 023502-1–023502-3, 2007.

[21] W. E. McMahon, K. Emery, D. J. Friedman, L. Ottoson, M. Young, J. S. Ward, C. Kramer, A. Duda, and S. Kurtz, "Fill factor as a probe of current-matching for GaInP$_2$/GaAs tandem cells in a concentrator system during outdoor operation," *Progress Photovoltaics: Res. Appl.*, vol. 16, pp. 213–224, 2008.

Authors' photographs and biographies not available at the time of publication.

Light Trapping in Thin-Film Cu(InGa)Se₂ Solar Cells

James G. Mutitu, Uwadiae Obahiagbon, Shouyuan Shi, William Shafarman, and Dennis W. Prather

Abstract—A fundamental optical analysis of thin-film $Cu(InGa)Se_2$ solar cell structures is presented, wherein spectroscopic ellipsometry measurements were performed to acquire material optical constants, which were then used as input parameters to perform electromagnetic simulations. The accuracy of the electromagnetic simulation tools, and thus, the validity of the material optical constants, were verified by comparing the values determined from the simulations with experimental measurements obtained using a spectrophotometer. The verified optical modeling tools were then used to analyze thin, <0.7-μm $Cu(InGa)Se_2$ solar cell structures, which do not absorb all incident light within a single optical path length, and hence, the need to incorporate light trapping. To this end, a superstrate device configuration was employed in which the metallic back contact is deposited last, giving rise to an opportunity to incorporate photonic engineering device concepts to the back surface layer of the solar cell. Simulations of superstrate $Cu(InGa)Se_2$ solar cell designs, complete with light trapping structures were then performed and analyzed.

Index Terms—Diffraction, photovoltaic cells, solar energy.

I. Introduction

A GOOD understanding of the interaction between incident light and a solar cell device structure is critical to optimizing device performance. To this end, improving thin-film solar cell performance by increasing the light-trapping capacity has received significant attention in the recent past. Many of these studies have focused on c-Si and a-Si because of the ubiquitous use of these materials throughout the semiconductor industry, in addition to the emergence and growth of the silicon photonics industry [1]–[3]. In contrast, only a handful

Manuscript received July 11, 2013; revised September 20, 2013; accepted October 20, 2013. This work was supported by the Department of Energy under Award DE-EE0005317. This report was prepared as an account of work sponsored by an agency of the United States Government. Neither the United States Government nor any agency thereof, nor any of their employees, makes any warranty, express or implied, or assumes any legal liability or responsibility for the accuracy, completeness, or usefulness of any information, apparatus, product, or process disclosed, or represents that its use would not infringe privately owned rights. Reference herein to any specific commercial product, process, or service by trade name, trademark, manufacturer, or otherwise does not necessarily constitute or imply its endorsement, recommendation, or favoring by the United States Government or any agency thereof. The views and opinions of authors expressed herein do not necessarily state or reflect those of the United States Government or any agency thereof.

J. G. Mutitu and U. Obahiagbon are with the Department of Electrical and Computer Engineering and the Institute of Energy Conversion, University of Delaware, Newark, DE 19716 USA (e-mail: mutitu@udel.edu; uwa@udel.edu).

S. Shi and D. W. Prather are with the Department of Electrical and Computer Engineering, University of Delaware, Newark, DE 19716 USA (e-mail: sshi@mail.eecis.udel.edu; dprather@mail.eecis.udel.edu).

W. Shafarman is with the Institute of Energy Conversion, University of Delaware, Newark, DE 19716 USA (e-mail: wns@udel.edu).

Color versions of one or more of the figures in this paper are available online at http://ieeexplore.ieee.org.

Digital Object Identifier 10.1109/JPHOTOV.2014.2307487

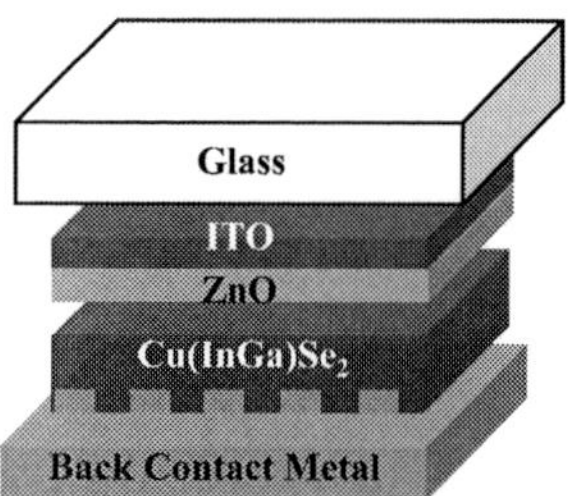

Fig. 1. Structure of the $Cu(InGa)Se_2$ superstrate design complete with diffraction gratings.

of groups have explored light trapping in $Cu(InGa)Se_2$ solar cells, due in part to its high absorption coefficient, which ensures that 95% of the incident illumination is absorbed within a 1-μm thick layer, i.e., within a wavelength band corresponding to the material bandgap. However, when the thickness of the $Cu(InGa)Se_2$ absorber layer is reduced to below 1 μm, a single optical pass of light through the material is insufficient to fully absorb as much light as compared with thicker cells, and thus, the need for incorporating light-trapping schemes arises. The advantages of having thin, <1-μm thick, $Cu(InGa)Se_2$ absorber layers include, reduced material costs and shorter device processing times, which ultimately lead to an increase in manufacturing throughput and lower capital requirements for deposition processes. In practice, however, the efficiency of superstrate devices still lags behind those of conventional substrate devices, which further serves to prove the need for light-trapping studies in thin $Cu(InGa)Se_2$ solar cells.

In the past, studies by Orgassa *et al.* examined the effects of a variety of metallic back contact reflectors on $Cu(InGa)Se_2$ light trapping [4]. Malmström *et al.* investigated the effects of a TiN back contact and reflector, in addition to front and back surface scattering [5]. However, many of these studies have been focused on substrate device configurations, where all the device components are deposited on top of a material substrate, e.g., soda lime glass.

Traditional substrate configurations of $Cu(InGa)Se_2$ solar cells present a major problem when it comes to light-trapping design. The main problem is that a substrate fabrication process requires that the choice of back contact material be inert, in order to withstand the highly corrosive environment that is generated during the $Cu(InGa)Se_2$ deposition step. This limits greatly the choices of available back surface materials. To circumvent this hurdle, a superstrate design configuration is utilized, whereby the constituent solar cell materials are deposited in the order of ITO/ZnO/$Cu(InGa)Se_2$/metal back contact, onto a glass superstrate, as shown in Fig. 1.

The superstrate configuration enables a thinner absorber layer and overcomes the inert metal constraint, which affects

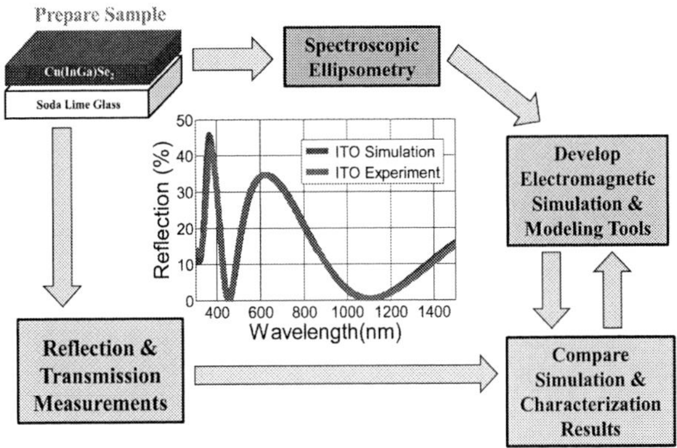

Fig. 2. Integrated Loop approach used to verify optical material characteristics and accuracy of simulation tools. (Inset) Example of the comparison between the simulation and experimental data from ITO.

traditional substrate devices, since the back contact is deposited after the Cu(InGa)Se$_2$ layer has been deposited. Additional advantages of superstrate solar cells include: the elimination of the need for a glass back sheet, which leads to lower cost and lighter weight modules; greater flexibility and simplification in the laser scribing process, which is ultimately necessary for monolithic integration; and finally, the ability to process the TCO layers at elevated temperatures, which leads to improved reliability and performance.

II. Overview

This paper focuses on building a fundamental framework for the study of light-trapping techniques in superstrate configured Cu(InGa)Se$_2$ solar cells. The goal is to develop a reliable electromagnetic simulation tool that can be used to optimize various design parameters in Cu(InGa)Se$_2$ solar cells, such as layer thicknesses, and thus, design better performing devices. To accomplish this, a customized integrated loop approach is employed, whereby samples are prepared and analyzed through two distinct methods, the first being ellipsometry, which gives material optical constants that can then be used to develop the electromagnetic modeling tools. The second method utilizes a spectrophotometer to take alternate measurements that can then be directly compared with the output of the electromagnetic models, thereby verifying the validity of the simulations, as is shown in Fig. 2.

The first step in the integrated loop process is to accurately obtain the optical constants of materials in order to ensure that the subsequent analyses—including the development of simulation tools—are of the highest accuracy. To achieve the desired precision in analysis, there is a strong need to be able to deposit repeatable material compositions and then analyze them using variable angle spectroscopic ellipsometry (VASE) measurements. The second step requires that the deposited samples be prepared, which could entail the need for material etches to smoothen surfaces, in order to obtain reliable instrument readings during the VASE analysis. The VASE analysis, in turn, calls for the modeling of material properties using dispersion equations to obtain the optical constants, which is not a trivial process. In addition, some material systems consist of complex compositional gradients, and hence, exhibit inhomogeneous refractive index profiles. To this end, the optical characterization using VASE may in some cases be used to obtain average, or bulk, material refractive index values. Similarly, it may also be impossible to completely represent the physical structure of a solar cell device using simulation software, especially in situations where a considerable amount of surface roughness is present, and again such situations may call for the use of some approximations. However, to circumvent the accumulation of many erroneous results, further characterization is required. In this case, a spectrophotometer is used; the results obtained from spectrophotometer measurements can be directly compared with simulation results, and hence, provide a reliable means by which to ascertain the veracity of both the VASE characterization and simulation processes. The verified computational tools can thereafter be used to design complex light-trapping structures, such as the one shown in Fig. 1.

III. Experimental Methods

The Cu(InGa)Se$_2$ films were deposited using an elemental coevaporation of Cu, In, Ga, and Se from independent sources in a Belljar evaporator system at a substrate temperature of 550 °C. A single-stage deposition recipe was used, whereby all the fluxes, of all the constituent materials, were held constant throughout the process, producing films with uniform compositions and no Ga gradient [6]–[8]. The resulting films were $\sim$2-μm thick films with a [Cu]/[In+Ga] composition of about 0.9 and a [Ga]/[In+Ga] composition of 0.3, giving rise to a bandgap of 1.2 eV. This coevaporation process produces a film with a high amount of surface roughness, which makes it difficult to acquire accurate optical constants. To circumvent this hurdle, Paulson et al., peeled off the Cu(InGa)Se$_2$ film by exploiting the weakness that occurs at the MoSe$_2$ layer between the Cu(InGa)Se$_2$ and Mo layers [8], [9]. Shafarman et al. also determined the optical constants of Cu(InGa)Se$_2$ by first reducing the roughness and then removing residual Se on the surface using a Br-etch and KCN etch, respectively [7]. In this study, the latter technique was employed using the optimized Br and KCN etch processes. It is worthy to note that, typical values of root-mean-square (rms) roughness measured by atomic force microscopy on Cu(InGa)Se$_2$ films are between 50 and 100 nm making it difficult to make valid ellipsometry measurements. The rms surface roughness is reduced by the Br-Etch process to less than 10–15 nm, which is significantly smaller than the incident ellipsometer beam wavelengths, and hence, does not adversely affect the measurements [10], [11].

Thin films of ZnO and ITO with thicknesses of 162 nm and 92 nm, respectively, were deposited using a sputtering process; the resultant layers had sheet resistances of 5 $\times10^3\,\Omega/\square$ (for ZnO) and 12.1 $\Omega/\square$ (for the ITO). A 200-nm gold layer was deposited using electron beam evaporation, and a similar process was used to produce a 500-nm silver layer. Optical constants of these individual films were obtained using a J. A. Woollam rotating analyzer variable spectroscopic ellipsometer that is equipped with an autoretarder. The VASE instrument works by measuring the change in polarization that light waves experience as they are reflected from surfaces and interfaces through planar multilayered materials [12], [13]. The VASE measurements yield a phase difference (Δ) and an amplitude ratio (ρ), which is the complex reflectance ratio of the parallel (r_p) and perpendicular (r_s) wave polarizations, based on the Fresnel equations for reflection and transmission. The complex reflectance ratio (ρ) used in VASE is measured as function of both angle and wavelength. The relationship between all these terms is shown in

$$\tan(\Psi)e^{i\Delta} = \rho = \frac{r_p}{r_s} \tag{1}$$

where $\tan(\Psi)$ represents the amplitude ratio of the reflected waves (magnitude of reflectance ratio, ρ).

Since VASE measures the complex ratio between two values it can be highly accurate in addition to yielding phase information; the self-referencing nature of the measurement ensures that the effects of fluctuations in lamp intensity, or degradation, do not affect the final results, and hence, the measurements are reproducible.

The reflectance and transmission measurements were acquired using a Perkin–Elmer Lambda 750 spectrophotometer, fitted with an integrating sphere. The spectrophotometer normalizes the results of reflectance and transmission measurements to those achieved using calibrated reflectance standards.

IV. Optical Constant Verification

Throughout the optical characterization process, a number of issues arose. Initially, each material was deposited on a soda-lime glass (SLG) substrate and then analyzed using VASE. It would appear that obtaining the refractive index of a glass substrate, such as SLG should be a straightforward process. However, it turns out that during the Pilkington glass manufacturing process some of the molten tin, on which the glass floats, diffuses into the glass, giving rise to the tin or float side of the SLG [14]. This tin side creates a nonlinear graded refractive index profile, which extends about 900 nm into the 1.6-mm-thick SLG. In addition, the bulk of SLG exhibits birefringence, i.e., the refractive index depends on the polarization and propagation direction of light. The air side also has a different refractive index [14]. This complexity associated with the SLG analysis led to a substitution of c-Si substrates for the ITO and ZnO layers. Crystalline silicon is a well understood material that exhibits a large refractive index contrast between it and ITO or ZnO. Using the c-Si substrate led to the acquisition of lower mean square error values during the VASE analysis, which were 5.4 and 3.8 for the ITO and ZnO films, respectively. The ZnO layer was modeled using a General Oscillator model, which allows for the combination of multiple oscillator models, in this case a P-Semi and Gaussian oscillator were used; the General Oscillator model is one of the dispersion formulae that is released by the J. A. Woollam Company in their CompleteEASE software package, which is used to create the ellipsometer models [15]. The ITO was modeled using a B-Spline dispersion layer, which is a dispersion equation based on the B-Spline recursion relation and is consistent with Kramers–

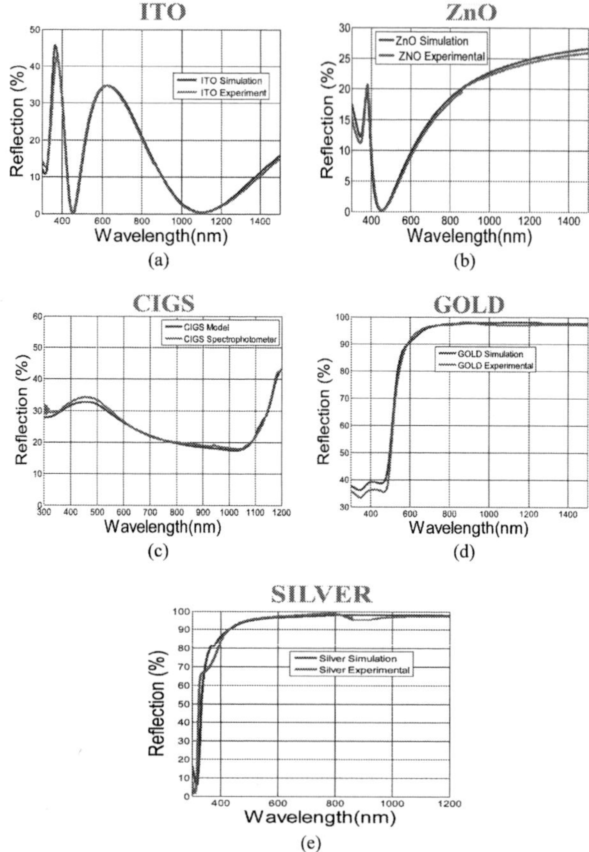

Fig. 3. Comparison between experimental and simulated reflectance for (a) ITO, (b)ZnO, (c) Cu(InGa)Se$_2$, (d) Gold, and (e) Silver.

Kronig relations [16], even though a free carrier Drude model combined with a Lorenz oscillator could also have been used. The gold layer was modeled using a B-Spline layer, which gave an MSE of about 2 [16], whereas with silver, the values were retrieved from the DeltaPsi2 software—from Horiba—based on modified data values obtained from the text *Handbook of optical constants of solids* by E. Palik [17], [18]. The comparison between experimental data, obtained from spectrophotometer measurements, and simulation data is shown in Fig. 3.

Throughout this study with Cu(InGa)Se$_2$, it was found that the material may have a graded index profile, depending on how the deposition process actually occurred. Nevertheless, with multiple measurements, such as spectroscopic transmission intensity measurements—performed on a Cu(InGa)Se$_2$ layer on an SLG substrate—which could be modeled simultaneously with data from more traditional VASE reflectance measurements, it was possible to obtain better complex refractive index values. The Cu(InGa)Se$_2$ was modeled using a B-Spline layer. Additional ellipsometry, simulations and spectrophotometer characterizations were performed on a Cu(InGa)Se$_2$ layer deposited on a crystalline silicon substrate. The resultant simulation data also matched up well with experimental data, as is shown in Fig. 3(c).

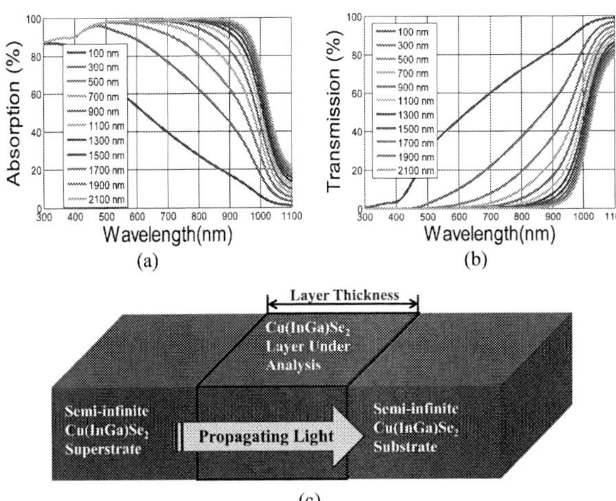

Fig. 4. (a) Absorption and (b) transmission characteristics of Cu(InGa)Se$_2$ layers of various thicknesses. (c) Cu(InGa)Se$_2$ layers that are under analysis, in (a) and (b), are sandwiched between two semiinfinite structures of the same material, and therefore, no front or back surface reflections occur. A light wave propagating through the layer of interest is also shown.

All the other materials properties used in this light-trapping study were obtained from previous studies [3], [8]–[10].

The electromagnetic simulation tool that was used throughout this study is centered on the scattering matrix algorithm, which is a modified version of a transfer matrix-based algorithm that is used to solve Maxwell's equations rigorously for each individual wavelength in the spectrum being considered [20]–[22]. In this algorithm, the structure to be simulated is broken up into many individual layers in the direction of light illumination. The fields in each layer are expanded into Fourier modes, whereby redundant Fourier modes are also incorporated in order to ensure the accuracy of the scattering matrix method; this also includes cases where large index contrast materials are considered. The expansion coefficients for each Fourier mode are then used to form the scattering matrix. The scattering matrices from each of the layers are then cascaded in order to attain an overall system matrix that can be used to provide both reflection and transmission characteristics. The application of periodic boundary conditions makes it possible to significantly reduce the computation time, thus making the S-Matrix method suitable for thin-film solar cell applications.

V. Fundamental Light-Trapping Study

In order to perform a light-trapping study of value, it is necessary to identify the optical characteristics of a material when no optical enhancements or reflections occur. This is calculated by placing the Cu(InGa)Se$_2$ between two semiinfinite structures of the same material, i.e., a superstrate and substrate of Cu(InGa)Se$_2$ in this case, and letting light flow from within the superstrate, through the structure and out into the substrate, as shown in Fig. 4(c). This way, it is possible to determine how much light is absorbed within a certain thickness of the material. This type of analysis was performed on Cu(InGa)Se$_2$ layers with thicknesses ranging from 100 to 2100 nm with a 200-nm

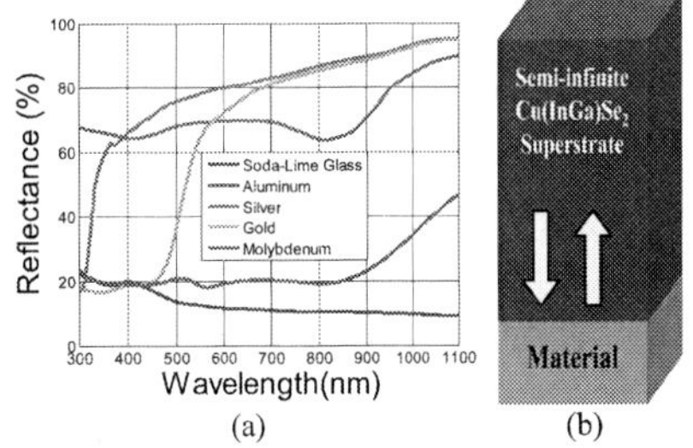

Fig. 5. (a) Reflectance characteristics of different back surface materials into a semiinfinite Cu(InGa)Se$_2$ structure and (b) illustration of the structure under analysis for each material shown in (a).

interval, using the optical constants that had been previously obtained using the integrated loop analysis process, and the results are plotted in Fig. 4(a) and (b).

This exercise enabled the observation of the absorption characteristics of light in a single optical path length. The wavelength range of this analysis was limited to 300–1100 nm, which corresponded to the bandgap of the coevaporated Cu(InGa)Se$_2$, which is about 1.2 eV [6]–[9]. As can be seen in Fig. 4(b), for a structure that is 700-nm thick, only light of wavelengths above 600 nm would hit the back reflector surface, and hence, that is the range where the back reflector design is focused.

The reflectance characteristics were simulated for different back surface materials, including soda-lime glass, aluminum, silver, gold, and molybdenum, with each of these materials placed below a semiinfinite layer of Cu(InGa)Se$_2$. As can be seen in Fig. 5, gold and silver exhibited the best reflectance characteristics especially at longer wavelength regions. Molybdenum, which is the commonly used back contact for Cu(InGa)Se$_2$ solar cells, did not exhibit good reflectance characteristics.

An optimization of the thicknesses of the ITO and ZnO layers was performed using the particle swarm optimization algorithm [3] to reduce the device reflectance. It is pertinent to note that that the soda-lime glass in this case was treated as a semiinfinite superstrate, so as to focus on the ITO and ZnO thicknesses specifically. The optimal design parameters were found to be 150 nm of ITO and 112 nm of ZnO, which gave an average reflectance of 6.5% in the 300–1100 nm range.

Finally, the optimized ITO and ZnO coatings, along with the silver or gold back reflectors, were applied to a superstrate solar cell with 0.7-μm thick Cu(InGa)Se$_2$—in a structure similar to Fig. 1 but without the diffraction gratings—and the light-trapping characteristics were simulated. An additional diffraction grating, with a period of 860 nm and 50% fill factor (similar to Fig. 1)—corresponding to feature sizes that have previously been realized using a deep ultraviolet lithography process [19]—was included to the final design structure and simulated. The resultant absorption characteristics of the different structures are plotted in Fig. 6. It was observed that the absorption characteristics were almost the same, which is what was expected, considering that the reflectance of gold and silver, into Cu(InGa)Se$_2$, is almost identical for wavelengths above 750 nm, as was shown in Fig. 5. Additionally, all wavelengths below 750 nm would be absorbed in the 700-nm Cu(InGa)Se$_2$ layer

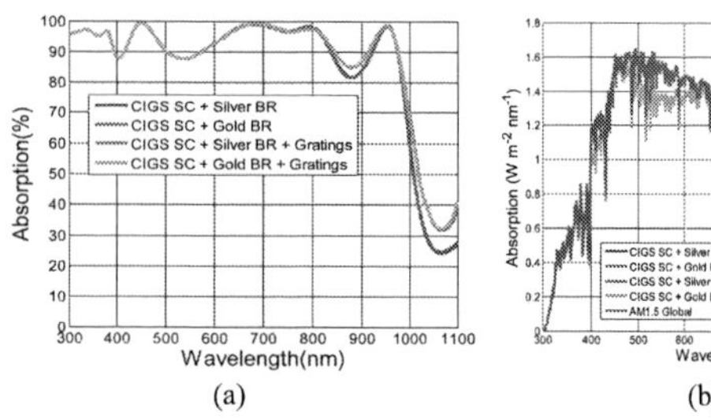

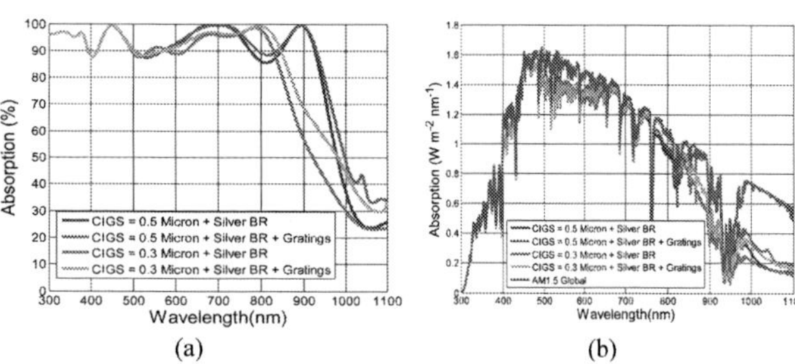

Fig. 6. (a) Percentage and (b) total power absorption characteristics of 700-nm-thick Cu(InGa)Se$_2$ solar cell structures with various optical enhancements; silver and gold back reflectors and silver and gold diffraction gratings.

Fig. 7. (a) Percentage and (b) total power absorption characteristics of 300- and 50-nm Cu(InGa)Se$_2$ solar cell structures with various optical enhancements; silver back reflectors and silver diffraction gratings.

TABLE I

OPTIMAL DESIGN PARAMETERS OF MATERIALS USED IN CU(INGA)SE$_2$ SOLAR CELL STRUCTURE SIMULATIONS

Material	Thickness (nm)
ITO	150
ZnO	112
Cu(InGa)Se$_2$	300/500/700
Grating Thickness	150
Grating Period	860
Back Metal	1000

before ever reaching the back reflector, as can be inferred from Fig. 4.

It was finally decided that silver be used for the rest of the study because of its wider bandwidth of high reflectance, when compared with gold, which would work better for thinner Cu(InGa)Se$_2$ structures; this conclusion was derived from observing the reflectance graphs in Fig. 5(a).

The same optimized design parameters, as used in the structures of Fig. 6, were applied to thinner, i.e., 0.5- and 0.3-μm-thick Cu(InGa)Se$_2$, solar cell structures, but this time only utilizing silver as the back surface and diffraction grating material, and the results are plotted in Fig. 7.

As can be seen in Fig. 7, the structures with the silver diffraction gratings outperformed the other structures, of corresponding thickness, which only had a planar reflector.

The optimal design parameters used for the simulation results of Figs. 6 and 7, are summarized in Table I.

The absorption characteristics, in terms of averaged percentage and total power absorbed, for all the simulation results presented in Figs. 6 and 7 are summarized in Table II.

TABLE II

ABSORPTION CHARACTERISTICS FOR ALL THE SIMULATED CU(INGA)SE$_2$ SOLAR CELL STRUCTURES, ARRANGED IN ORDER OF PERFORMANCE

Structure	Absorption (%)	Absorbed Power (W) (300 – 1100 nm)
300 nm CIGS SC +Silver BR	77	666
300 nm CIGS SC +Silver BR + Grating	81	690
500 nm CIGS SC +Silver BR	83	697
700 nm CIGS SC +Gold BR	85	709
700 nm CIGS SC +Silver BR	85	709
500 nm CIGS SC +Silver BR + Grating	85	711
700 nm CIGS SC +Gold BR + Grating	87	718
700 nm CIGS SC +Silver BR + Grating	87	718
AM1.5 G	100	804.8

VI. CONCLUSION

In this paper, a fundamental optical analysis framework for designing light-trapping schemes for thin-film Cu(InGa)Se$_2$ solar cells was presented. The first part of the study examined the process of obtaining accurate optical material constants using a number of techniques including VASE, electromagnetic simulations, and reflectance measurements obtained using a spectrophotometer. The optical constants that were verified using all the aforementioned methods were then used to accurately develop an electromagnetic simulation tool that was subsequently used to analyze various aspects of light propagation through Cu(InGa)Se$_2$ solar cells. The first aspects to be considered were the absorption and transmission characteristics of Cu(InGa)Se$_2$ layers of varying thickness, thereby giving insights into the wavelengths of interest in light-trapping designs. Subsequently, the simulation tool was used to assess the reflection characteristics of different candidate materials for back surface reflectors in Cu(InGa)Se$_2$ solar cells. Finally, the tool was used to analyze more complex light-trapping schemes, which included diffraction gratings, for thin, 300-, 500-, and 700-nm, Cu(InGa)Se$_2$ solar cells based on superstrate cell configurations. It was found that the structures that incorporated diffraction gratings were the most effective at trapping light.

REFERENCES

[1] J. Zhu, C. Hsu, Z. Yu, S. Fan, and Y. Cui, "Nanodome solar cells with efficient light management and self-cleaning," *Nano Lett.*, vol. 10, pp. 1979–1984, 2010.

[2] J. G Mutitu, S. Shi, A. Barnett, and D. W. Prather, "Hybrid dielectric-metallic back reflector for amorphous silicon solar cells," *Energies*, vol. 3, pp. 1914–1933, 2010.

[3] J. G. Mutitu, S. Shi, C. Chen, T. Creazzo, A. Barnett, C. Honsberg, and D. W. Prather, "Thin film silicon solar cell design based on photonic crystal and diffractive grating structures," *Opt. Exp.*, vol. 16, pp. 15238–15248, 2008.

[4] K. Orgassa, H. W. Schock, and J. H. Werner, "Alternative back contact materials for thin film Cu(In,Ga)Se2 solar cells," *Thin Solid Films*, vol. 431–432, pp. 387–391, May 2003.

[5] J. Malmstrom, O. Lundberg, and L. Stolt, "Potential for light trapping in Cu(In,Ga)Se/sub 2/ solar cells," in *Proc. 3rd World Conf. Photovoltaic Energy Convers.*, May 2003, vol. 1, pp. 344–347.

[6] W. Shafarman and J. Zhu, "Effect of substrate temperature and deposition profile on evaporated Cu(InGa)Se$_2$ films and devices," *Thin Solid Films*, vol. 361–362, pp. 473–477, 2000.

[7] W. N. Shafarman, R. S. Huang, and S. H. Stephens, "Characterization of Cu(InGa)Se2 solar cells using etched absorber layers," in *Proc. Photovoltaic Energy Convers., Conf.*, May 2006, vol. 1, pp. 420–423.

[8] P. D. Paulson, R. W. Birkmire, and W. N. Shafarman, "Optical characterization of CuIn$_1$ − xGa$_x$ Se$_2$ thin films by spectroscopic ellipsometry," *J. Appl. Phys.*, vol. 94, pp. 879–888, 2003.

[9] P. D. Paulson, S. H. Stephens, and W. N. Shafarman, "Analysis of Cu(InGa)Se$_2$ alloy film optical properties and the effect of Cu off-Stoichiometry," *MRS Proc.*, vol. 865, pp. F1.1.1–F1.4.6, 2005.

[10] S. H Stevens, "Modeling Optical Properties of Thin Film Cu(In,Ga)Se$_2$ Solar Cells Using Spectroscopic Ellipsometry," Master's Thesis, Phys. Dept., Univ. Delaware, Newark, DE, USA, 2006.

[11] R. W. Birkmire and B. E. McCandless, "Specular CuInSe$_2$ films for solar cells," *Appl. Phys. Lett.*, vol. 53, pp. 140–141, 1988.

[12] J. Hilfiker, R. Synowicki, and H. G. Tompkins, "Spectroscopic Ellipsometry Methods for Thin Absorbing Coatings," in *Proc. SVC 51st Annu. Tech. Conf.*, 2008, pp. 511–516.

[13] J. A. Woollam, B. Johs, C. Herzinger, J. Hilfiker, R. Synowicki, and C. Bungay, "Overview of variable angle spectroscopic ellipsometry (VASE), Part I: Basic theory and typical applications," in *Proc SPIE*, vol. CR72, pp. 3–28, 1999.

[14] R. A. Synowicki, B. D. Johs, and A. C. Martin, "Optical properties of soda-lime float glass from spectroscopic ellipsometry," *Thin Solid Films*, vol. 519, no. 9, pp. 2907–2913, Feb. 28, 2011.

[15] [Online]. Available: http://www.jawoollam.com

[16] B. Johs and J. S. Hale, "Dielectric function representation by B-Splines," *Phys. Status Solidi, a*, vol. 205, no. 4, pp. 715–719, 2008.

[17] E. D. Palik, *Handbook of Optical Constants of Solids*. New York, NY, USA: Academic, 1985.

[18] Powerful DeltaPsi2 Software Platform drives HORIBA Scientific Ellipsometers–HORIBA. [Online]. Available: www.horiba.com. <http://www.horiba.com/us/en/scientific/products/ellipsometers/software/>

[19] J. G. Mutitu, S. Shi, A. Barnett, and D. W. Prather, "Light trapping in thin silicon solar cells," presented at the 37th IEEE Photovoltaic Spec. Conf., Seattle, WA, USA, Jun. 2011.

[20] A. C. Marsh and J. C. Inkson, "Scattering matrix theory of transport in heterostructures," *Semicond. Sci. Technol.*, vol. 1, pp. 285–290, 1986.

[21] M. Auslender and S. Hava, "S-matrix propagation algorithm in full-vectorial optics of multilayer grating structures," *Opt. Lett.*, vol. 21, pp. 1765–1767, 1996.

[22] D. M. Whittaker and I. S. Culshaw, "Scattering-matrix treatment of patterned multilayer photonic structures," *Phys. Rev. B*, vol. 38, pp. 2610–2618, 1999.

Authors' photograph and biographies not available at the time of publication.

Mono-Like Silicon Growth Using Functional Grain Boundaries to Limit Area of Multicrystalline Grains

Kentaro Kutsukake, Noritaka Usami, Yutaka Ohno, Yuki Tokumoto, and Ichiro Yonenaga

Abstract—We propose a new growth method for mono-like silicon (Si): the suppression of multicrystallization using functional grain boundaries artificially formed by multiseed crystals. In our previous study, we demonstrated such suppression in an ingot 30 mm in diameter. In this paper, we grew mono-like Si ingots of 100 and 400 mm on a side. Functional grain boundaries successfully suppressed the increase in the area of multicrystalline grains nucleated on crucible side walls, which indicates a large volume of quasi-monocrystalline Si up to the top of the ingots. This enables a large increase in the yield of quasi-monocrystalline wafers in an ingot and would lead to a reduction in the cost of the solar cells.

Index Terms—Crystal growth, grain boundary (GB), mono-cast, mono-like Si, multicrystalline Si, quasi-mono, seeded cast.

I. Introduction

THE research and development of a casting-based method for fabricating crystalline silicon (Si) ingots for solar cells using single-crystalline seeds is being actively conducted [1]–[3]. The method is called mono-like, mono-cast, seeded cast, or quasi-mono Si growth. The same facilities of existing standard production lines for multicrystalline Si solar cells can be used for mono-like Si, which is a large advantage of the method. In comparison with solar cells based on multicrystalline Si grown by the conventional casting method, solar cells based on mono-like Si show enhanced conversion efficiency. For example, an increase in the efficiency of 0.6 and 1.4% is reported for solar cells that are processed with isotropic and anisotropic surface texturing processes, respectively [4]. Therefore, mono-like Si growth is promising for the production of crystalline Si for solar cells. The share of mono-like Si within the substrate market of the crystalline Si solar cells was predicted to increase in the international technology roadmap for photovoltaics (ITRPV) reported in March 2012 [5].

However, the predicted share of mono-like Si significantly decreased in the ITRPV reported in March 2013 [6]. This decrease is partially due to problems in the crystalline quality of mono-like Si, i.e., multicrystallization, dislocation generation, and impurity incorporation, as well as problems in additional production costs, i.e., costs of the seed and longer cycling time compared with the conventional casting method for multicrystalline Si. The dislocations are generated from boundaries that are formed at joints between seeds during crystal growth. These dislocations have a negative impact on the solar cell performance [7], [8]. Metallic impurities diffuse from a crucible and Si_3N_4 coating into solid crystals, particularly into seed crystals during a high-temperature process in the crystal growth. These impurities also degenerate solar cell efficiency.

In this paper, we focused on the problem of multicrystallization. During mono-like Si growth, various grains with a different crystallographic orientation from the seeds nucleate at random sites on the inner surface of the crucible side walls. The area of these multicrystalline grains expands with increasing distance from the seeds; finally, the multicrystalline area along the crucible walls surrounds the mono-like area [9]. This multicrystallization results in a significant decrease in conversion efficiency. For example, the gain in conversion efficiency decreases with an increase in the area of multicrystalline grains, and mono-like Si wafers in which the mono-crystalline area is less than 70% of the total area of the wafer surface do not show a gain in conversion efficiency [4].

For the problem mentioned previously, we utilized functional grain boundaries (GBs), arranging them near the crucible side walls [10]. The suppression of multicrystallization is realized by the interaction between functional GBs and grown GBs formed at the side walls of the crucible, as shown in Fig. 1. Functional GBs are expected to control the configuration of grown GBs, resulting in the suppression of the increase in the area of multicrystalline grains. We have demonstrated such a suppression in a columnar crystal 30 mm in diameter and revealed the suppression mechanism by crystal orientation analysis [10]. Here, rectangular ingots of 100×100 mm^2 and 400×400 mm^2 (noted hereafter as 100- and 400-mm ingots, respectively) with artificially arranged multiseed crystals were grown, and the distribution and development of crystal grains were investigated in comparison with results of ingots without the functional GBs.

II. Experiments

To suppress multicrystallization, we selected $\Sigma 5$ GB as a functional GB. We clarified the structure and electrical properties of $\Sigma 5$ GB for the first time [11], [12]. Here, Σ, which is determined by the relative orientation of crystal grains, represents

Manuscript received June 15, 2013; revised August 9, 2013 and September 3, 2013; accepted September 9, 2013. Date of publication September 30, 2013; date of current version December 16, 2013. This work was supported in part by a grant from the Precursory Research for Embryonic Science and Technology and the Japan Science and Technology Agency.

K. Kutsukake is with the Tohoku University, Sendai 980-8577, Japan, and also with the PRESTO, Japan Science and Technology Agency, Tokyo 102-0076, Japan (e-mail: kutukake@imr.tohoku.ac.jp).

N. Usami is with the Graduate School of Engineering, Nagoya University, Nagoya 464-8603, Japan (e-mail: usa@nagoya-u.jp).

Y. Ohno, Y. Tokumoto, and I. Yonenaga are with Tohoku University, Sendai 980-8577, Japan (e-mail: yutakaohno@imr.tohoku.ac.jp; y.tokumoto@imr.tohoku.ac.jp; yonenaga@imr.tohoku.ac.jp).

Color versions of one or more of the figures in this paper are available online at http://ieeexplore.ieee.org.

Digital Object Identifier 10.1109/JPHOTOV.2013.2281730

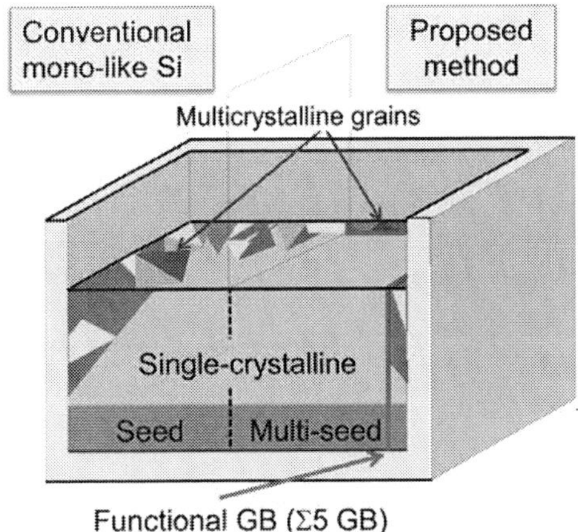

Fig. 1. Schematic illustration of conventional mono-like Si method (left) and proposed method (right). The area of multicrystalline grains nucleated on the crucible side walls is expected to be suppressed by functional GBs artificially formed by multiseed crystals.

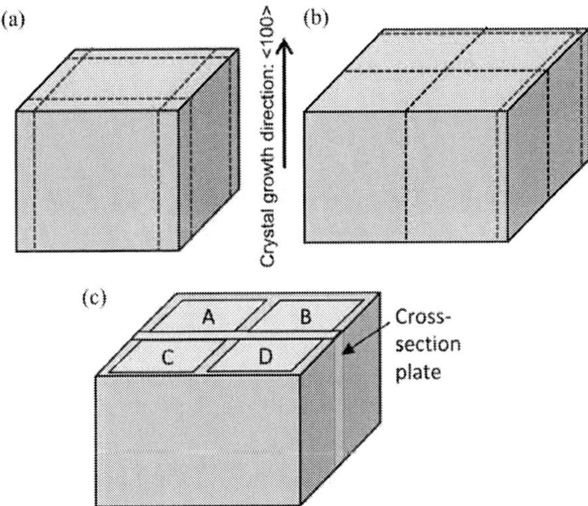

Fig. 2. Schematic illustrations of the multiseed crystals for (a) 100- and (b) 400-mm ingots, and of (c) position of sliced bricks and plate. Broken lines show cutting boundaries between crystal pieces, in which the blue boundaries have a Σ5 configuration, i.e., both multiseeds consist of nine pieces of monocrystalline Si.

the size of the unit cell of the coincident site lattice relative to that of the crystal lattice. Σ5 GB shows a low electrical activity, which is an indispensable condition for solar cell applications, and extends stably in the $\langle 1\,0\,0 \rangle$ growth direction [11]. Thus, in this study, we artificially formed Σ5 GB at certain positions using multiseed crystals.

Fig. 2 shows schematic illustrations of multiseed crystals for the formation of functional GBs. For the growth of the 100-mm ingots, Σ5 GBs were arranged parallel to crucible side walls at a distance of 10 mm. In the case of the 400-mm ingots, Σ5 GBs were arranged parallel to only two crucible side walls at a distance of 15 mm. The crystal orientation in the crystal growth direction was selected to be $\langle 1\,0\,0 \rangle$. The detailed seed preparation for the formation of Σ5 GBs is shown in [11] and [12].

A 100-mm crystal without functional GBs, which was a seed for the conventional mono-like Si method, was also prepared for comparison. Boron-doped p-type Czochralski Si crystals were used as seed crystals. Semiconductor-grade Si feedstock nuggets less than 10 mm in diameter were used for the 100-mm ingots to densely fill a small crucible. In the case of the 400-mm ingot, solar-grade Si nuggets less than 100 mm in diameter were used for the feedstock. The crystals were doped with boron in the range of 0.5–2 $\Omega\cdot$cm. The weights of the 100- and 400-mm ingots including the seeds were approximately 1.7 and 70 kg, respectively. The seed crystals and Si materials were placed in crucibles coated with Si_3N_4 powder. After the upper part of the seeds was melted, crystal growth was carried out in a furnace with a temperature gradient in a flowing Ar gas atmosphere. The crystal growth rate was kept at approximately 0.2 mm/min for the rectangular 100-mm ingots and approximately 0.1 mm/min for the rectangular 400-mm ingots. Note that the 400-mm ingot was grown in a semi-industrial furnace with technical support by Silicon Plus Co., Ltd, Yamagata, Japan. The grown 100-mm ingots were sliced into wafers of 0.3-mm thickness perpendicular to the growth direction. From the 400-mm ingot, four bricks [A to D in Fig. 2(c)] were taken and approximately 450 wafers were sliced from each of them. In addition, a sample plate on the vertical cross section was sliced, as shown in Fig. 2(c). The shape of the crystalline grains was analyzed on the sliced surface by optical microscopy. The photoluminescence (PL) images were taken for the as-sliced wafers using an InGaAs camera and an 800-nm excitation laser. The distribution of electrical resistivity was measured for the cross-sectional plate by the four-point probe method.

III. Results and Discussion

Fig. 3 shows photographs of the wafers cut from the rectangular ingots of 100 mm at just above and 30 mm from the seed. In both wafers just above the seed with and without functional GBs, there are no multicrystalline grains. Only in the wafer with the functional GBs, straight lines along wafer sides can be detected as boundaries between brightness contrasts of the crystal grains. These lines are functional GBs formed and continuing from the boundaries between multiseed crystals. Note that the functional GBs are shown as white broken lines in the figures. In the wafers 30 mm from the seed, multicrystalline grains were observed, which are shown in yellow in the figures. The observations of contiguous wafers in the growth direction revealed that the multicrystalline grains nucleated most frequently around side corners of the ingot. This would be due to a stronger strain or larger under cooling around the side corners than along the side edges, which would be caused by a large heat flux around the side corner. Almost all the GBs formed between the epitaxial grains on the seed and the multicrystalline grains are straight lines along the $\langle 1\,1\,0 \rangle$ direction on the wafer surface. This suggests that these GBs were nucleated on the crucible side walls and were $\{1\,1\,1\}$ Σ3 GBs, as in the cases of multicrystalline Si [13] and the columnar mono-like Si 30 mm [10] and 100 mm [14] in diameter.

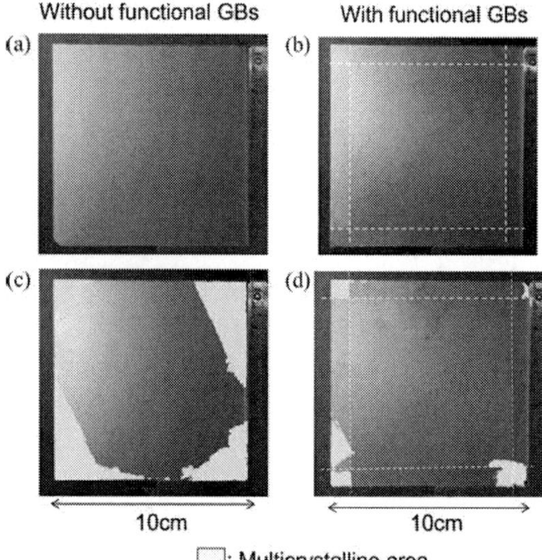

Fig. 3. Wafers cut from the 100 –mm ingots. (a) and (b) Just above the seed and (c) and (d) 30 mm from the seed. In the figures, in the case with functional GBs, positions of the functional GBs are shown as white broken lines. The multicrystalline area is shown in yellow.

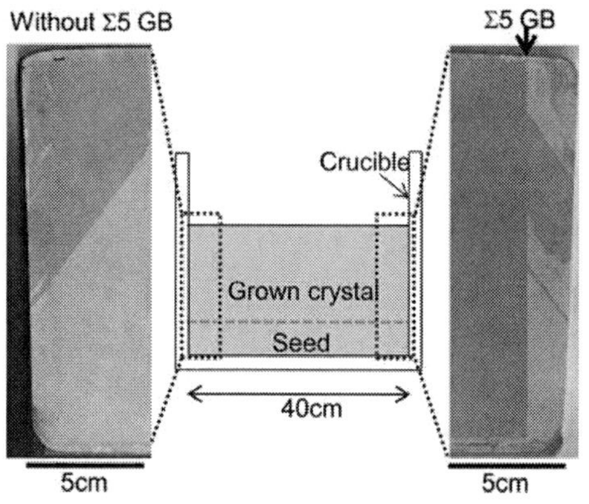

Fig. 4. Vertical cross section of the 400-mm ingot. (Left) Without and (right) with functional GBs.

It is clear that the area of multicrystalline grains nucleated on crucible side walls in the ingot with functional GBs is smaller than that in the case of without functional GBs. The multicrystalline grains extended inward and occupied a large area of the wafer grown without functional GBs. On the other hand, in the ingot with functional GBs, multicrystalline grains that nucleated on the crucible side walls were confined within the spaces between the functional GBs and the crucible side walls except for a small area. Generally, a portion of ingots near the crucible walls cannot be used for solar cell wafers owing to strong impurity contamination from the crucible. Therefore, if multicrystalline grains are confined in the unused area for solar cells by functional GBs, a 100% yield of quasi-single-crystalline wafers in an ingot can be expected.

Fig. 4 shows a photograph of a vertical cross section of the 400-mm ingot. In this ingot, two different types of parts were

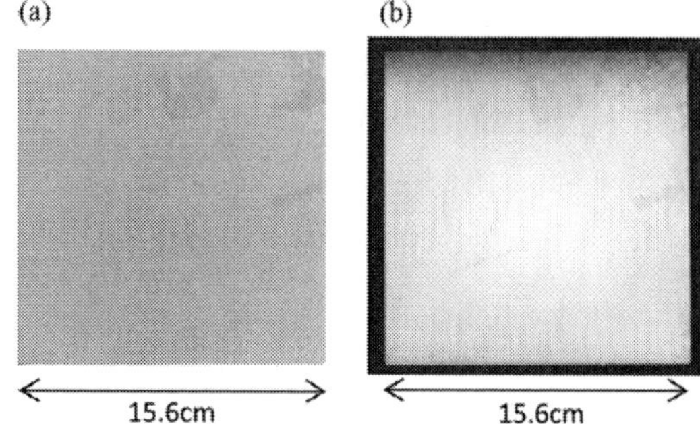

Fig. 5. (a) Photograph and (b) PL image of a wafer sliced from brick B in Fig. 2(c). The wafer position was 20 mm from the top surface of the ingot.

formed: with and without functional GBs near the crucible side wall [see Fig. 2(b)]. As in the case of the ingot 100 mm on a side, straight GBs were generated from the crucible side walls in the ingot 400 mm on a side. They were also analyzed to be {1 1 1} Σ3 GBs. As clearly shown in Fig. 4, although multicrystalline grains, i.e., Σ3 GBs, extended to the inner region of the ingot on a side without functional GBs, the extension of Σ3 GBs from the crucible side walls was intercepted by functional GBs on a side with functional GBs. This result indicates that a large volume of quasi-single crystalline Si is maintained up to the top of the ingot.

The shape of the phase boundary between solid and liquid affects multicrystallization, and some trials to suppress multicrystallization by controlling it are reported [2], [15]. We performed resistivity measurements of the vertical cross section of the 400-mm ingot. The results showed that the phase boundary was slightly convex in the growth direction just above the seed and almost flat in almost the entire ingot. As will be discussed later, the formation of functional GBs and the interaction between GBs do not strongly depend on the growth conditions. Therefore, the functional GB technique applies to not only flat phase boundaries but to convex and concave boundaries as well.

Fig. 5 shows a photograph and a PL image of a wafer sliced from brick B in Fig. 2(c). The wafer was 20 mm from the top surface of the ingot. Σ5 functional GBs were formed along the upper and right outer sides of the wafer. Even at 20 mm from the top surface of the ingot, a large area of mono-like Si was achieved except for a small number of multicrystalline grains. The observation of the morphology of multicrystalline grains in contiguous wafers in the growth direction revealed that many of the grains appeared around the upper-right corner of the wafer. This suggests that the effect of functional GBs of suppressing the inward extension of multicrystalline grains might be small around the cross-point of functional GBs.

In the PL image [see Fig. 5(b)], dark contrasts of dislocations, which differ from those of multicrystalline grains, can be found around the upper-right corner. In general, in mono-like Si, the upper part of a brick is prone to a strong propagation of dislocation and this strongly decreases solar cell efficiency. In our case, we can report good results, as the fraction of dislocations is very small. The analysis of the morphology of multicrystalline grains in continuous wafers in the growth direction shows that many dislocations also appeared around the upper right corner of the wafer. This suggests two mechanisms of dislocation generation. The first is that dislocation generation accompanies multicrystallization through functional GBs. The second is that functional GBs can work as a source of dislocations, especially around the cross-point of functional GBs. Experimentally, this statement is difficult to prove because the functional GBs are located outside of the wafers. In addition to this, concerning the question of whether functional GBs can be used to suppress dislocation generation at the joints of the used seed plates (which is another important problem with mono-like Si), a more sophisticated analysis of dislocations is very necessary. We have reported on dislocation generation from GBs that are artificially formed by multiseed crystals in [16]; however, dislocation generation from functional GBs is still under investigation.

Note that the crystal grown in this study is smaller than that of industry standard ingots. We, however, expect that functional GBs are available for any ingot size because the interaction between GBs, i.e., the suppression mechanism of multicrystallization, is independent of the crystal size.

Moreover, the functional GB technique has another advantage, i.e., the high degree of freedom of the crystal growth conditions. Some trials for suppressing multicrystallization by controlling the growth conditions, such as crystal growth rate, temperature distribution, and the morphology of the crystal growth interface, have been reported. However, the growth conditions also affect the crystal qualities such as the density and distribution of crystal defects, impurities, and residual strain, as well as the productivity and production cost of ingots. On the other hand, the functional GB technique has a wide range of growth conditions because the formation of functional GBs does not seriously depend on the growth conditions. Therefore, the functional GB technique is expected to be compatible with the growth conditions that results in high productivity and high crystal quality.

IV. Conclusion

The suppression of multicrystallization during mono-like Si growth using functional GBs formed by multiseed crystals was investigated on the basis of crystal growth and crystal grain observation of 100- and 400-mm ingots. It was found that multicrystalline grains that nucleated on crucible side walls tended to be confined within the spaces between functional GBs and crucible side walls.

As demonstrated here, multicrystallization in mono-like Si is effectively suppressed by functional GBs. This should increase the yield of the quasi-single crystalline area in a mono-cast ingot.

Acknowledgment

The authors would like to acknowledge K. Nakajima, K. Morishita, and R. Murai of Kyoto University and K. Fujiwara of Tohoku University for their fruitful discussions. They would also like to acknowledge Silicon Plus Co., Ltd., Yamagata, Japan, for their technical support in the crystal growth experiments.

References

[1] N. Stoddard, B. Wu, L. Witting, M. Wagener, Y. Park, G. Rozgonyi, and R. Clark, "Casting single crystal silicon: Novel defect profiles from BP solar's mono2 wafers," *Solid State Phenom.*, vol. 131–133, pp. 1–8, 2008.

[2] A. Jouini, D. Ponthenier, H. Lignier, N. Enjalbert, B. Marie, B. Drevet, E. Pihan, C. Cayron, T. Lafford, and D. Camel, "Improved multicrystalline silicon ingot crystal quality through seed growth for high efficiency solar cells," *Progress Photovoltaics*, vol. 20, pp. 735–746, 2012.

[3] C. W. Lan, W. C. Lan, T. F. Lee, A. Yu, Y. M. Yang, W. C. Hsu, B. Hsu, and A. Yang, "Grain control in directional solidification of photovoltaic silicon," *J. Cryst. Growth*, vol. 360, pp. 68–75, 2012.

[4] M. Mrcaria, "Potential for mono-cast material to achieve high efficiencies in mass production," *Photovoltaics Int.*, vol. 19, pp. 28–36, 2013.

[5] International Technology Roadmap for Photovoltaics (ITRPV) Results 2011 (SEMI PV group, 2012), p. 15, 2012.

[6] International Technology Roadmap for Photovoltaics (ITRPV) Results 2012 (SEMI PV group, 2013), p. 24, 2013.

[7] T. Kaden, K. Petter, R. Bakowskie, Y. Ludwing, R. Lantzsch, D. Raschke, S. Rupp, and T. Spiess, "Analysis of mono-like silicon wafers and solar cells on industrial scale," *Energy Procedia*, vol. 27, pp. 103–108, 2012.

[8] K. Petter, T. Kaden, R. Bakowskie, Y. Ludwing, R. Lantzsch, D. Raschke, S. Rupp, and T. Spiess, "Analysis of mono-cast silicon wafer and solar cells," in *Proc. 27th Eur. Photovoltaic Sol. Energy Conf. Exhib.*, 2012, pp. 984–989.

[9] X. Gu, K. Guo, L. Chen, D. Wang, and D. Yang, "Seed-assisted cast quasi-single crystalline silicon for photovoltaic application: Towards high efficiency and low cost silicon solar cells," *Sol. Energy Mater. Sol. Cells*, vol. 101, pp. 95–101, 2012.

[10] K. Kutsukake, N. Usami, Y. Ohno, Y. Tokumoto, and I. Yonenaga, "Control of grain boundary propagation in mono-like Si: Utilization of functional grain boundaries," *Appl. Phys. Exp.*, vol. 6, pp. 025505-1–025505-3, 2013.

[11] K. Kutsukake, N. Usami, K. Fujiwara, Y. Nose, and K. Nakajima, "Influence of structural imperfection of Sigma 5 grain boundaries in bulk multicrystalline Si on their electrical activities," *J. Appl. Phys.*, vol. 101, pp. 063509-1–063509-5, 2007.

[12] K. Kutsukake, N. Usami, K. Fujiwara, Y. Nose, T. Sugawara, T. Shishido, and K. Nakajima, "Modification of local structure and its influence on electrical activity of near (310) sigma 5 grain boundary in bulk silicon," *Mater. Trans.*, vol. 48, pp. 143–147, 2007.

[13] K. Kutsukake, T. Abe, N. Usami, K. Fujiwara, K. Morishita, and K. Nakajima, "Formation mechanism of twin boundaries during crystal growth of silicon," *Script. Mater.*, vol. 65, pp. 556–559, 2011.

[14] M. Trempa, C. Reimann, J. Friedrich, G. Muller, and D. Oriwol, "Monocrystalline growth in directional solidification of silicon with different orientation and splitting of seed crystals," *J. Cryst. Growth*, vol. 351, pp. 131–140, 2012.

[15] B. Gao, S. Nakano, H. Harada, Y. Miyamura, T. Sekiguchi, and K. Kakimoto, "Reduction of polycrystalline grains region near the crucible wall during seeded growth of monocrystalline silicon in a unidirectional solidification furnace," *J. Cryst. Growth*, vol. 352, pp. 47–52, 2012.

[16] I. Takahashi, N. Usami, K. Kutsukake, G. Stokkan, K. Morishita, and K. Nakajima, "Generation mechanism of dislocations during directional solidification of multicrystalline silicon using artificially designed seed," *J. Cryst. Growth*, vol. 312, pp. 897–901, 2012.

Evaluation of the Silicon Ingot With Addition of SiCl₄ in Atmosphere During Unidirectional Solidification

Evaluation of the Silicon Ingot With Addition
of SiCl$_4$ in Atmosphere During
Unidirectional Solidification

Tomihisa Tachibana, Kuniyuki Sato, Hiroki Kusunoki, Shiro Sakuragi, Yoshio Ohshita, Haruhiko Ono, and Atsushi Ogura

Abstract—Adding SiCl$_4$ to the atmosphere during the growth of a crystal suppressed crystalline defects and impurities from the edge of silicon ingots. Crystalline silicon ingots with seed crystal were grown by using the unidirectional solidification technique. Most of the grain boundaries were inactive $\Sigma 3$ in the ingot with the SiCl$_4$ injection. There were no small-angle grain boundaries at the top and edge of ingots. The carbon concentration with SiCl$_4$ was decreased to less than half of that without the SiCl$_4$ injection. Carbon precipitation did not occur even at the surface of ingots and the surface of grown ingots had a metallic luster.

Index Terms—Grain boundaries, silicon.

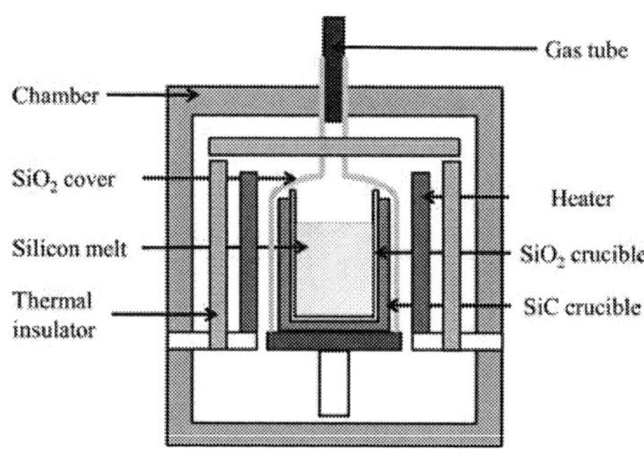

Fig. 1. Schematic diagram of furnace.

I. INTRODUCTION

THE photovoltaic-related industry is developing rapidly worldwide. Crystalline silicon has been the main substrate material to fabricate solar cells because of the low cost and high cell efficiency. However, it is still necessary to increase the conversion efficiency and reduce the production cost for the future market. To provide a high conversion efficiency of the multicrystalline silicon solar cell, the concentration of crystalline defects such as grain boundaries and of impurities in the grown ingot needs to be reduced. Since crystalline defects act as minority carrier recombination centers [1]–[3], the electrical properties deteriorate. To suppress the crystalline defects, some growth techniques are proposed [4]–[6]. One of them is quasi-monocrystalline growth for both multi- and monocrystalline silicon. This technique provides lower production cost than when the Czochralski (Cz) is used, as well as better quality, which results in higher conversion efficiency than that with multicrys-

talline silicon [7], [8]. The quasi-monocrystals are grown by the unidirectional solidification technique with a seed crystal set at the bottom of the crucible. Thus, grain boundary generation from the bottom of ingots is suppressed. However, with this method, grain boundaries are still generated from the edge of the ingot during the growth. In addition, impurities are incorporated due to the contact between the molten silicon and the crucible coated with mold release agent. When the molten silicon reacts with the coating, impurities including nitrogen and carbon are incorporated during the crystal growth. Some of these light element impurities are precipitated and generate secondary defects during the crystal growth [9], [10]. They degrade the crystal quality and decrease the conversion efficiency of a solar cell.

We suppressed the crystalline defect generation and interfusion of impurities from the edge of the ingot by adding SiCl$_4$ in the atmosphere during the unidirectional solidification. To suppress crystalline nucleation and the incorporation of light element impurities from the Si$_3$N$_4$ coating on the crucible, the reaction between the molten silicon and mold release needs to be prevented. Therefore, we used a technique to suppress the wetting properties of molten silicon [11], [12], which is called the "liquinert (inert liquid)" technique. We evaluated the effect of the SiCl$_4$ injection on the crystalline silicon grown by the unidirectional solidification technique.

Manuscript received June 10, 2013; revised September 27, 2013, November 16, 2013, and November 27, 2013; accepted December 9, 2013. This work was supported in part by the New Energy and Industrial Technology Development Organization under the Ministry of Economy, Trade, and Industry.

T. Tachibana and Y. Ohshita are with the Toyota Technological Institute, Nagoya 468-8511, Japan (e-mail: t_tachi@toyota-ti.ac.jp; y_ohshita@toyota-ti.ac.jp).

K. Sato, H. Kusunoki, and A. Ogura are with the Meiji University, Kawasaki, Kanagawa 214-8571, Japan (e-mail: ce31042@meiji.ac.jp; ce11032@meiji.ac.jp; a_ogura@isc.meiji.ac.jp).

S. Sakuragi is with the Union Material Incorporated, Ibaraki 300-1602, Japan (e-mail: u_materials.sakuragi@mbd.nifty.com).

H. Ono is with the Kanagawa Industrial Technology Center, Ebina 243-0435, Japan (e-mail: h_ono@kanagawa-iri.go.jp).

Color versions of one or more of the figures in this paper are available online at http://ieeexplore.ieee.org.

Digital Object Identifier 10.1109/JPHOTOV.2013.2295175

II. EXPERIMENTAL PROCEDURE

Crystalline silicon ingots were grown by using the small furnace shown in Fig. 1. The furnace has heaters around the crucible. We used SiO$_2$ crucible coated with Si$_3$N$_4$ as a mold release agent. The light element impurities are interfused from the

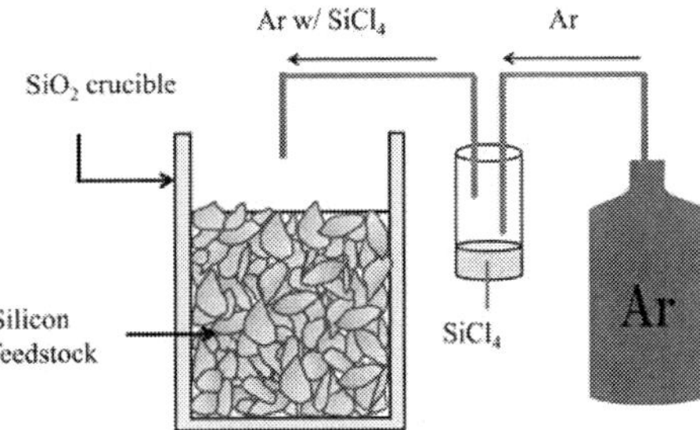

Fig. 2. Schematic diagram of the technique of adding SiCl₄ growth.

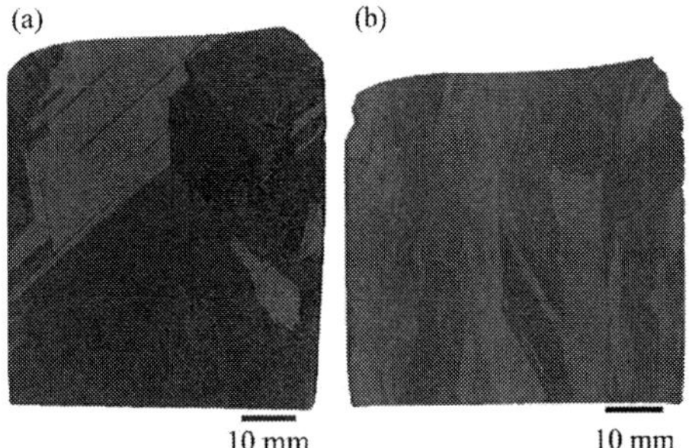

Fig. 3. Cross-sectional view of the (a) crystalline silicon ingot with SiCl₄ injection and (b) reference ingot.

atmosphere during the crystal growth [13], [14]. In particular, carbon impurities come principally from the graphite components such as heaters. Therefore, the furnace was purged with Ar gas, and SiCl₄ was added in the flowing Ar gas to provide liquinert conditions, as shown in Fig. 2. The quartz (SiO_2) cover was set over the crucible to maintain the liquinert atmosphere. The cover also suppresses the carbon incorporation from the atmosphere, in the same way as it is set on the crucible [15]. Crystalline ingots were grown with seed crystal in the atmosphere with SiCl₄ to suppress grain boundaries that were generated from the bottom of the ingot. We used (1 0 0) Cz silicon cylinder with a diameter of ∼60 mm as a seed crystal. Prior to the growth, the seed crystal was etched to remove the surface oxide and damaged layers by a mixture of HF and HNO_3. The crystal was set at the bottom of the SiO_2 crucible. The cylindrical silicon ingot was grown to a diameter of ∼60 mm and a height of ∼70 mm. The feedstock was melted in a SiO_2 crucible. A multicrystalline ingot without SiCl₄ injection was also grown as a reference ingot

The grown ingots were vertically sliced into two half-cylinders and horizontally sliced with a thickness of 2.5 mm for the Fourier transform infrared spectroscopy (FTIR) measurements. The sliced wafers were mirror-polished on both sides to provide a thickness of 2.00 mm. Infrared absorption spectra were obtained by using the Bruker IFS-113v spectrometer. A 2.00-mm-thick floating-zone silicon was used as a reference. The wavenumber resolution was 2.0 cm^{-1} and the scan was repeated 100 times. The absorption spectra were obtained at the center of wafers with 10-mm intervals using an 8-mm-diameter aperture. We evaluated the distribution and concentration of substitutional carbon (C_s), interstitial oxygen (O_i), and nitrogen (NN and/or NNO complexes).

Grain boundary structures and minority carrier recombination properties were evaluated by the electron backscattering diffractometry (EBSD) and electron-beam-induced current (EBIC) measurement. Here, the sliced wafers with a thickness of 0.5 mm were etched with a mixture of HF and HNO_3 to remove the saw damaged layers. The acceleration voltage for the EBSD and EBIC measurements was 20.0 kV and obtained by scanning electron microscopy, using an SU-70 (Hitachi High-Technologies).

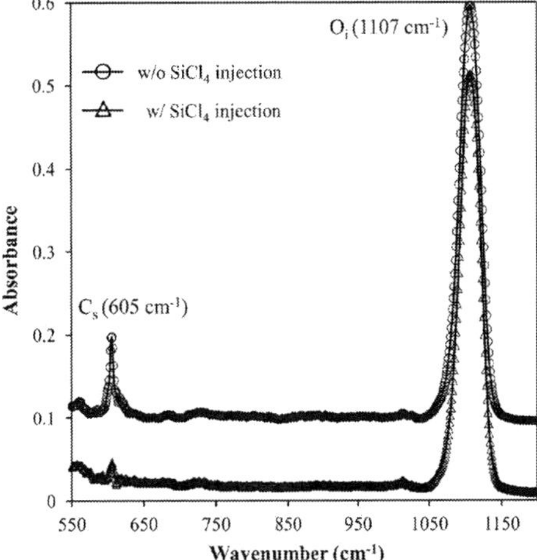

Fig. 4. FTIR spectra of the crystalline silicon wafer with and without SiCl₄ injection.

III. Results and Discussion

The cross-sectional views of a grown ingot with and without SiCl₄ injection are shown in Fig. 3(a) and (b), respectively. The ingot with SiCl₄ injection consisted of relatively large grains without small grains that are generated both at the vicinity of crucible and the top of the ingots. Most of the crystalline defects found at the edge and the top of wafers were inactive Σ3 grain boundaries. There were no small-angle grain boundaries. On the other hand, the reference ingot had small grains. EBSD analysis showed that there were some coincident cite lattice grain boundaries, such as Σ9 and Σ27. By adding SiCl₄, the grain boundary density approximately 31.3 cm/cm² without SiCl₄ injection at the edge of wafer decreased to approximately 8.9 cm/cm². These results suggest that the crystalline nucleation at the interface between the silicon and Si_3N_4 coating may be reduced by SiCl₄ injection.

Infrared absorption spectra from the crystalline silicon with and without SiCl₄ injection are shown in Fig. 4. These spectra were obtained from the bottom of the ingot There are two strong absorption peaks at 605 cm^{-1} that originated from C_s and at 1107 cm^{-1} from O_i. The concentrations of C_s and O_i were evaluated to be of the order of 10^{16} atoms/cm^3 and

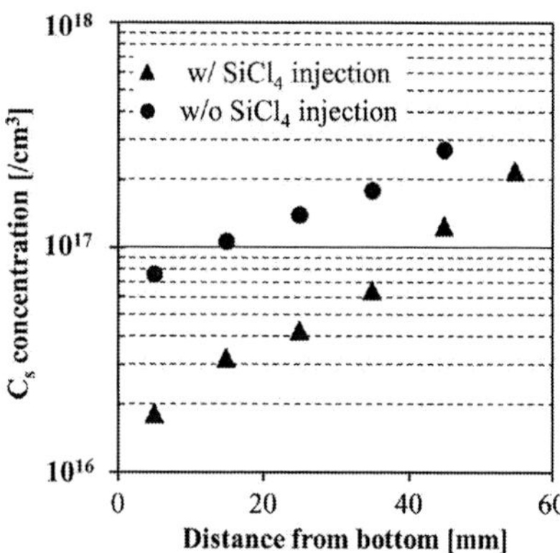

Fig. 5. Relationship between C_s concentrations and distance from the bottom of the crystalline silicon wafer.

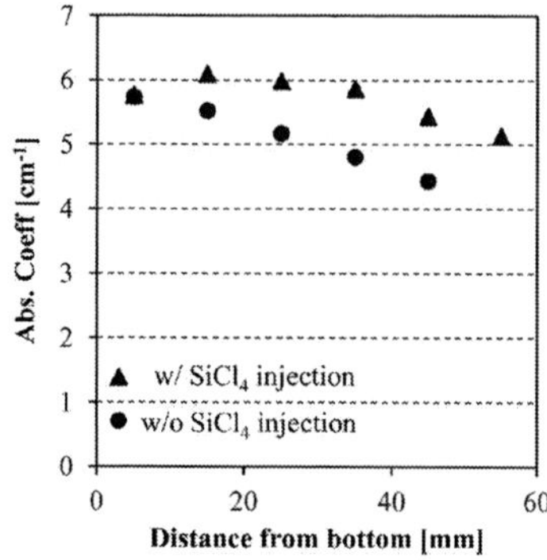

Fig. 6. Relationship between the O_i absorption coefficient and distance from the bottom of the crystalline silicon wafer.

10^{18} atoms/cm^3, respectively. The C_s peak of the ingot with SiCl$_4$ injection is smaller than that without SiCl$_4$ injection. For the detection of NN peaks (766, 963 cm^{-1}) and NNO peaks (801, 996, and 1026 cm^{-1}) [16], [17], a scan was repeated 3000 times and the N concentrations were estimated to be 1×10^{15} atoms/cm^3 or less. The N concentrations were not significantly different between the ingots with and without the SiCl$_4$ injection.

The C_s concentration as a function of the distance from the bottom of the ingot is shown in Fig. 5; C_s concentration with and without SiCl$_4$ injection monotonically increased along the direction of the crystalline growth. In the reference ingot, the C_s concentration is changed from 7.5×10^{16} atoms/cm^3 to 2.7×10^{17} atoms/cm^3. In the ingot with the SiCl$_4$ injection, the concentration is changed from 1.8×10^{16} atoms/cm^3 to 2.2×10^{17} atoms/cm^3. At the bottom of the ingots, the C_s concentration with SiCl$_4$ injection is four times lower than that without SiCl$_4$ injection. The carbon incorporation from Si$_3$N$_4$ coating could be reduced by the SiCl$_4$ injection. The Si$_3$N$_4$ coating material we used contains a small amount of carbon impurities (<0.2%). In the ingot without the injection, molten silicon contacted with the Si$_3$N$_4$ coating during the crystal growth. Thus, carbon impurities in the silicon ingot came from Si$_3$N$_4$ coating. On the other hand, SiCl$_4$ injection might suppress the reaction of molten silicon with Si$_3$N$_4$ coating. The amount of carbon impurity incorporation from the Si$_3$N$_4$ coating decreased in the molten silicon during the crystal growth.

The relationship between the O_i absorption coefficient and the distance from the bottom of the ingot is shown in Fig. 6. The O_i absorption coefficient far from the bottom of the ingot with SiCl$_4$ injection is higher than that of the reference ingot. The concentrations of O_i were of the order of 10^{18} atoms/cm^3. The amount of concentration is of the same order as that of Cz silicon. The difference of the O_i absorption coefficient between the ingot with SiCl$_4$ injection and the reference ingot might be due to the SiO and O$_2$ caused by the chemical reaction between SiCl$_4$ and H$_2$O described as follows:

$$4H_2O + 2SiCl_4 \rightarrow 2SiO + 8HCl + O_2. \tag{1}$$

Large amounts of SiO and O$_2$ in the atmosphere might be incorporated into the molten silicon by the SiCl$_4$ injection during the crystal growth.

IV. CONCLUSION

The multicrystalline nucleation and the incorporation of carbon impurities from the edge of the ingot were reduced by adding SiCl$_4$ in the atmosphere during the unidirectional solidification technique. The SiCl$_4$ injection decreased the contact angle between the molten silicon and Si$_3$N$_4$ coating on the crucible, which indicates the relatively weak interface reaction between them. The grown ingots had relatively large grains with no small-angle grain boundaries. The surface of ingots had a metallic luster with no slugs. The C_s concentration decreased in order of 10^{16} atoms/cm^3 by SiCl$_4$ injection. These results suggest that it is important to suppress the interface reaction between the molten silicon and the crucible to reduce the multi-silicon nucleation at the edge of the ingot and the incorporation amount of the light element impurities from the Si$_3$N$_4$ coating.

REFERENCES

[1] J. Chen, T. Sekiguchi, D. Yang, F. Yin, K. Kido, and S. Tsurekawa, "Electron-beam-induced current study of grain boundaries in multicrystalline silicon," *J. Appl. Phys.*, vol. 96, no. 10, pp. 5490–5495, 2005.

[2] M. Kitamura, N. Usami, T. Tsugawara, K. Kutsukake, K. Fujiwara, Y. Nose, T. Shishido, and K. Nakajima, "Growth of multicrystalline Si with controlled grain boundary configuration by the floating zone technique," *J. Cryst. Growth*, vol. 280, pp. 419–424, 2005.

[3] T. Sameshima, N. Miyazaki, Y. Tsuchiya, H. Hashiguchi, T. Tachibana, T. Kojima, Y. Ohshita, K. Arafune, and A. Ogura, "Interaction between metal impurities and small-angle grain boundaries on recombination properties in multicrystalline silicon for solar cells," *Appl. Phys. Exp.*, vol. 5, no. 4, pp. 042301-1–042301-3, 2012.

[4] K. Arafune, E. Ohishi, H. Sai, Y. Ohshita, and M. Yamaguchi, "Directional solidification of polycrystalline silicon ingots by successive relaxation of supercooling method," *J. Cryst. Growth*, vol. 308, pp. 5–9, 2007.

[5] K. Fujiwara, W. Pan, K. Sawada, M. Tokairin, N. Usami, Y. Nose, A. Nomura, T. Shishido, and K. Nakajima, "Directional growth method to obtain high quality polycrystalline silicon from its melt," *J. Cryst. Growth*, vol. 292, pp. 282–285, 2006.

[6] K. Nakajima, R. Murai, K. Morishita, K. Kutsukake, and N. Usami, "Growth of multicrystalline Si ingots using noncontact crucible method for reduction of stress," *J. Cryst. Growth*, vol. 344, pp. 6–11, 2012.

[7] N. Stoddard, B. Wu, I. Witting, M. Wagener, Y. Park, G. Rozgonyi, and R. Clark, "Casting single crystal silicon: Novel defect profiles from BP

solar's mono^2™ wafers," *Solid State Phenom.*, vol. 131–133, pp. 1–8, 2008.

[8] T. Tachibana, T. Sameshima, T. Kojima, K. Arafune, K. Kakimoto, Y. Miyamura, H. Harada, T. Sekiguchi, Y. Ohshita, and A. Ogura, "Impact of light-element impurities on crystalline defect generation in silicon wafer," *Jpn. J. Appl. Phys.*, vol. 51, pp. 02BP08-1–02BP08-3, 2012.

[9] T. Tachibana, T. Sameshima, T. Kojima, K. Arafune, K. Kakimoto, Y. Miyamura, H. Harada, T. Sekiguchi, Y. Ohshita, and A. Ogura, "Evaluation of defects generation in crystalline silicon ingot grown by cast technique with seed crystal for solar cells," *J. Appl. Phys.*, vol. 111, pp. 074505-1–074505-5, 2012.

[10] T. Tachibana, T. Sameshima, T. Kojima, K. Arafune, K. Kakimoto, Y. Miyamura, H. Harada, T. Sekiguchi, Y. Ohshita, and A. Ogura, "Evaluation of silicon substrates fabricated by seeding cast technique," *Mater. Sci. Forum*, vol. 725, pp. 133–136, 2012.

[11] S. Sakuragi, ""LIQUINERT": A new concept for shaped crystal growth," in *Proc. 19th Eur. Photovoltaic Sol. Energy Conf. Exhib.*, Paris, France, 2004, pp. 1201–1204.

[12] S. Sakuragi, T. Shimasaki, G. Sakuragi, and H. Nanba, "Poly-silicon sheets for solar cells prepared by die-casting," in *Proc. 19th Eur. Photovoltaic Sol. Energy Conf. Exhib.*, 2004, pp. 1197–1200.

[13] B. Gao, S. Nakano, and K. Kakimoto, "Effect of crucible cover material on impurities of multicrystalline silicon in a unidirectional solidification furnace," *J. Cryst. Growth*, vol. 318, p. 255, 2011.

[14] B. Gao, S. Nakano, and K. Kakimoto, "Global simulation of coupled carbon and oxygen transport in a unidirectional solidification furnace for solar cells," *J. Electrochem. Soc.*, vol. 157, pp. H153–H159, 2010.

[15] B. Gao, X. J. Chen, S. Nakano, and K. Kakimoto, "Crystal growth of high-purity multicrystalline silicon using a unidirectional solidification furnace for solar cells," *J. Cryst. Growth*, vol. 312, pp. 1572–1576, 2010.

[16] H. Kusunoki, T. Ishizuka, A. Ogura, and H. Ono, "Complementary Distribution of NN and NNO complexes in cast-grown multicrystalline silicon for photovoltaic cells," *Appl. Phys. Exp.*, vol. 4, pp. 115601-1–115601-3, 2011.

[17] H. Ono, T. Ishizuka, C. Kato, K. Arafune, Y. Ohshita, and A. Ogura, "Microscopic distributions of light elements and their precipitates in multicrystalline silicon for solar cells," *Jpn. J. Appl. Phys.*, vol. 49, pp. 110202-1–110202-3, 2010.

Authors' photographs and biographies not available at the time of publication.

Progress in Laser-Crystallized Thin-Film Polycrystalline Silicon Solar Cells: Intermediate Layers, Light Trapping, and Metallization

Jonathon Dore, Daniel Ong, Sergey Varlamov, Renate Egan, and Martin A. Green

Abstract—Diode laser crystallization of thin silicon films on the glass has been used to form polycrystalline silicon layers for solar cells. Properties of an intermediate layer stack of sputtered $SiO_x/SiN_x/SiO_x$ between the glass and the silicon have been improved by reactively sputtering the SiN_x layer, which result in enhanced optical and electrical performance. Light trapping is further enhanced by texturing the rear surface of the silicon prior to metallization. An initial efficiency of 11.7% with V_{OC} of 585 mV has been achieved using this technique, which are the highest values reported for poly-Si solar cells on glass substrates. Cells suffer a short term, recoverable degradation of V_{OC}, and fill factor. The magnitude of the degradation is reduced via the repeated thermal treatment. A selective p+ metallization scheme has been developed which eliminates the degradation altogether.

Index Terms—Lasers, photovoltaic cells, silicon, thin-film devices.

I. Introduction

LIQUID-PHASE crystallization (LPC) of silicon layers on glass substrates has recently emerged as a promising method of achieving high quality, thin-film, polycrystalline silicon (poly-Si) layers for solar cells. While state of the art cells formed by solid-phase crystallization (SPC) have been limited to the open-circuit voltage (V_{OC}) of around 500 mV [1], much higher values can be achieved using LPC methods. Fraunhofer ISE demonstrated excellent results for proof of concept with their RexWE cells using focused lamp zone-melting recrystallization of seed layers deposited on SiO_2-coated silicon wafers with a best efficiency of 13.5% [2] and best V_{OC} of 614 mV [3]. Similar devices on low-cost Zircon substrates have so far achieved V_{OC} up to 566 mV and efficiency of 8.1% [4]. Likewise, the National Renewable Energy Laboratory, Golden, CO, USA, showed a proof of concept with low-temperature epitaxial thickening of layer-transfer seeds on a display glass reaching V_{OC} of 603 mV and efficiency of 10.6% [5] and with heteroepitaxial cells grown on sapphire reaching V_{OC} of 574 mV and efficiency of 6.8% [6]. Attempts to match these results with layers grown directly on the glass have not yet been as successful.

So far, the most promising devices grown directly on the glass were crystallized by either electron beam, which reaches V_{OC} of 582 mV [7] or diode laser, which reaches over 550 mV [8], [9]. Of these, the highest reported initial efficiency is 8.4% [8], which despite the superior V_{OC}, still lags the SPC record of 10.5%, made by CSG Solar [1], [10], due to lower short-circuit current density (J_{SC}) and fill factor (FF).

The laser-crystallized solar cells described in [8] also suffered from a short term, recoverable degradation of FF and V_{OC}. The cause of this was suggested to be a poor contact between the lightly doped p-type absorber layer and the sputtered aluminum point contacts. This paper describes methods to reduce or prevent this degradation. Further, improvements to the light-trapping scheme and intermediate barrier layer have enabled much higher initial efficiency than previously reported.

II. Methods

A. Silicon Preparation

A borosilicate glass superstrate of 3.3-mm thickness is first coated with a boron-doped, intermediate buffer stack of $SiO_x/SiN_x/SiO_x$ (ONO) by RF magnetron sputtering. A 10-µm thick silicon layer is then deposited by electron-beam evaporation at $\sim$650 °C. The silicon is melted by scanning a line-focused continuous-wave diode laser beam (12-mm top-hat length $\times$ 170-µm FWHM width) across the surface as shown in Fig. 1, causing the boron to diffuse from the intermediate layer into the silicon, creating a p-type absorber. Upon solidification, the silicon recrystallizes with high-quality grains up to several millimeters long, drawn out by the melt front in a self-seeding process [11]. The rear surface of the silicon is chemically etched to achieve a random texture as described by Egan *et al.* [12]. An n-type emitter is created by coating the silicon surface with a spin-on phosphorous source and diffusing in a belt furnace at $\sim$900 °C for < 10 min, with samples supported by a carbon fibre setter to avoid glass distortion. Defects are passivated via a remote-plasma hydrogenation process.

Manuscript received June 6, 2013; revised August 6, 2013; August 19, 2013; accepted August 21, 2013. Date of publication September 10, 2013; date of current version December 16, 2013. This work was supported by the Australian Government through the Australian Renewable Energy Agency (ARENA), supporting Australian research and development in solar photovoltaic and solar thermal technologies to help solar power become cost competitive with other energy sources.

J. Dore is with the University of New South Wales, Sydney 2052, Australia (e-mail: j.dore@unsw.edu.au) and also with the Suntech R&D Australia Pty Ltd, Sydney 2019, Australia.

D. Ong and R. Egan are with the Suntech R&D Australia Pty Ltd., Sydney 2019, Australia (e-mail: daniel.ong@suntech-power.com.au; renate.egan@suntech-power.com.au).

S. Varlamov and M. A. Green are with the University of New South Wales, Sydney NSW 2052, Australia (e-mail: s.varlamov@unsw.edu.au; m.green@unsw.edu.au).

Color versions of one or more of the figures in this paper are available online at http://ieeexplore.ieee.org.

Digital Object Identifier 10.1109/JPHOTOV.2013.2280016

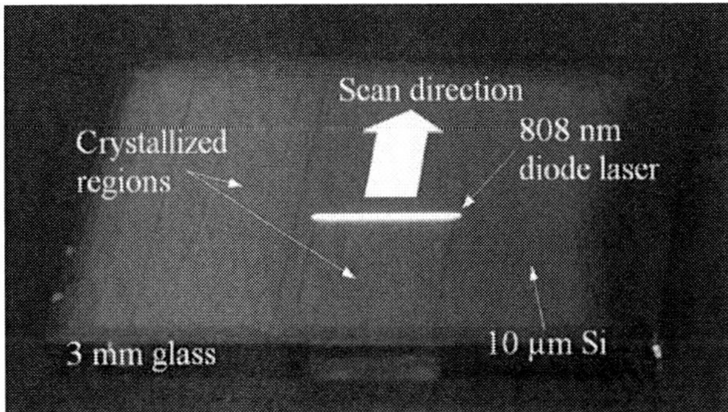

Fig. 1. Diode laser crystallization process.

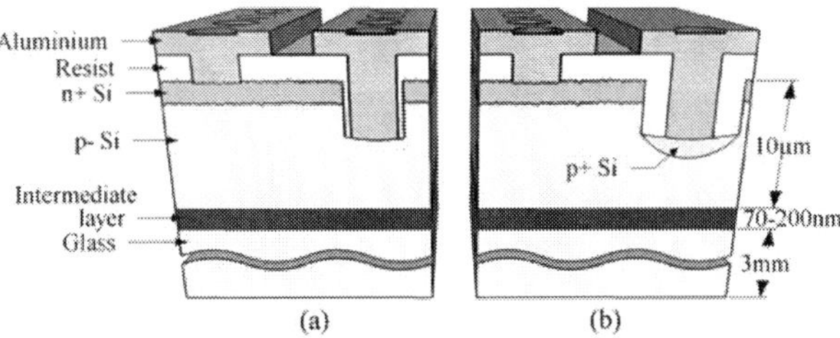

Fig. 2. Device schematics for (a) baseline metallization and (b) selective p+ metallization. Cells are operated in superstrate orientation so that the front side is shown here at the bottom of the image.

B. Metallization

Two different metallization schemes are presented. The simplest is the baseline scheme shown in Fig. 2(a), which is similar to the scheme used by CSG Solar [13]. The 1-cm^2 cell area is defined by laser scribing. The silicon is coated with a TiO_2-impregnated, reflective, isolating resist. Holes are etched through the resist by caustic ink-jet, and then, through the silicon by wet-chemical etching, forming a "crater" to expose the buried absorber layer. The resist is then exposed to solvent to cause it to reflow over the walls of the emitter, but leave the crater floor exposed. A second round of holes is then etched through the resist to expose the emitter layer. The surface is coated with a thin layer of sputtered aluminum, which makes contact with both the absorber and emitter layers, before laser scribing separates the contacts, which are connected to tabs at either side of the cells. Finally, a 1-h contact bake at up to 150 °C completes the process. The cell is designed in superstrate orientation so that the glass is at the front, or sun side, while the aluminum covers the rear side.

The second contact scheme is shown in Fig. 2(b) and uses a selective p+ arrangement to improve the absorber contacts. Via an additional round of etching and masking, a boron spin-on dopant source is applied to the region around the craters and driven in with an additional thermal diffusion process. The p-type contacts are then made directly into this p+ region to create an ohmic contact. Since the junction area etched for each contact is greater than for the baseline scheme, fewer such contacts are used in order to balance the tradeoff between current collection and series resistance.

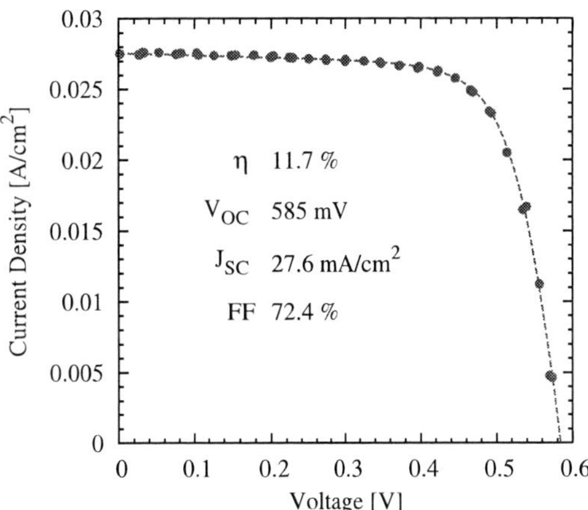

Fig. 3. One-sun current–voltage curve for the best laser-crystallized solar cell. Each point represents an average of three measurements.

C. Characterization

Current–voltage curves were measured at 25 °C with a solar simulator using a xenon lamp. The tool is designed for large modules and as such the voltage steps of around 25 mV are not ideal for single cells but are sufficient at this early stage of the development. The tester is calibrated with a calibration module confirmed by Sandia National Laboratories, Albuquerque, NM, USA, but for the small area used for single cell measurements, local intensity may vary $\pm \sim 2\%$. This error margin should be applied for J_{SC} values stated in the following sections. The data shown are in each case the averages of three measurements.

Quantum efficiency measurements were made using a bias light to ensure realistic operating conditions. The intensity was adjusted so that the J_{SC} calculated by integrating the external quantum efficiency (EQE) over the AM1.5 solar spectrum matched the J_{SC} measured by light I–V.

Further characterization was made with Suns–V_{OC}, spectrophotometry, and dark lock-in thermography (DLIT).

III. RESULTS

A. Light I–V

An initial efficiency of 11.7% and V_{OC} of 585 mV have been measured for a cell using the baseline metallization scheme described earlier. The current–voltage curve is shown in Fig. 3. A degradation of this efficiency occurs over subsequent days and is discussed in Section IV.

B. Dark Lock-In Thermography

Fig. 3 shows a shallow slope at J_{SC}, which suggests a shunt resistance (R_{SH}) of approximately 500 $\Omega.cm^2$, which has a mild impact on FF and efficiency and was the best of its batch. Shunt resistances below 100 $\Omega.cm^2$ have prevented similar cells from achieving higher efficiencies.

One such cell was measured by DLIT and the result is shown in Fig. 4. This cell was processed at the same time, under the same conditions as the best cell, but had R_{SH} of 132 $\Omega.cm^2$

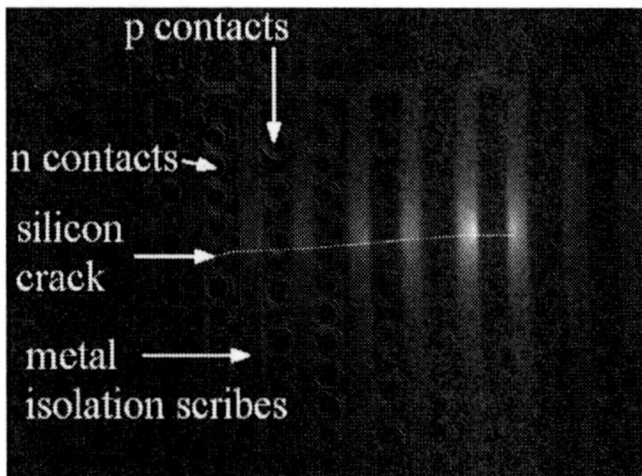

Fig. 4. Dark lock-in thermograph of a cell exhibiting ohmic shunting at a silicon crack. The heat can only be seen in the regions where the aluminum contact has been removed (vertical stripes). Some scattering from the edges of contact features is also visible.

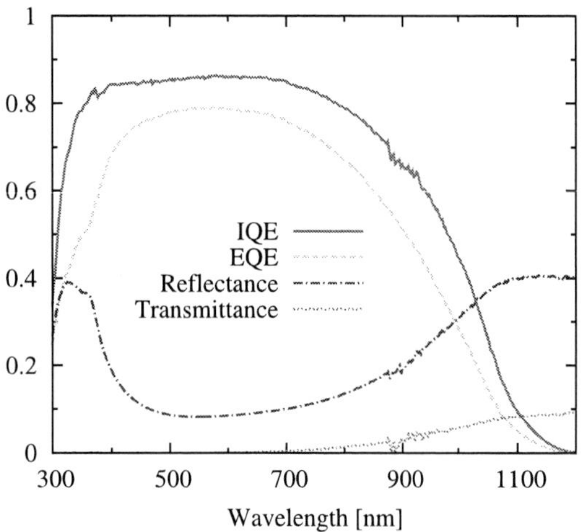

Fig. 5. Spectral response for the best laser-crystallized solar cell.

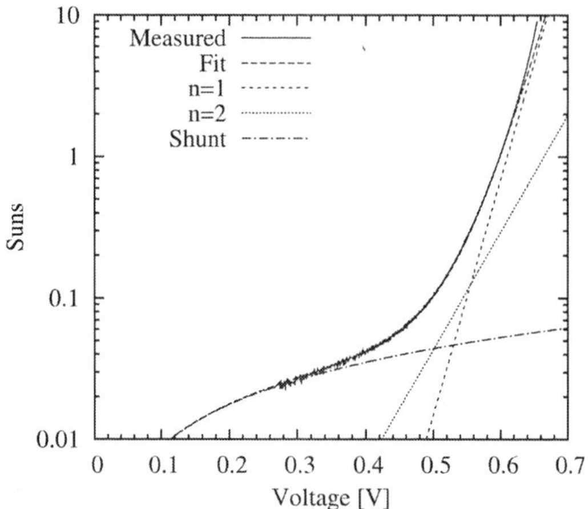

Fig. 6. Suns–V_{OC} curve of the best cell after completion.

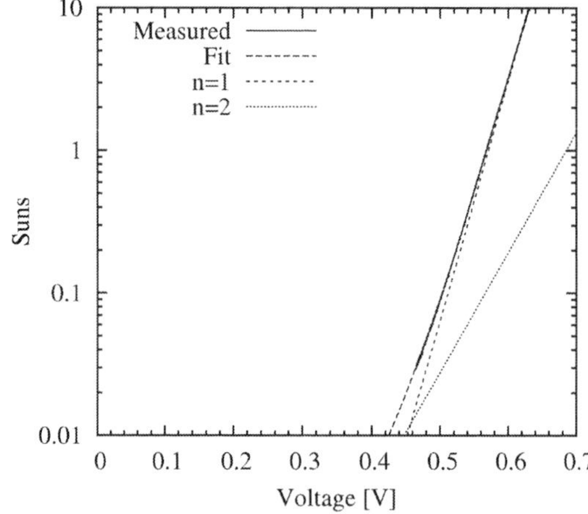

Fig. 7. Suns–V_{OC} curve of a cell measured prior to metallization.

and efficiency of 9.4%. The measurement was taken at forward bias of 0.3 V. A reverse bias measurement was identical, which indicates ohmic shunting coinciding with a crack which runs through the silicon. Such cracks are formed during laser crystallization and can be exacerbated during the P diffusion due to the relaxation of stress around the cracks as the glass begins to soften. The cracks can cause a shunt after cell metallization if they allow the metal of an n-type contact pad to come in contact with the buried absorber layer. Although the cracks are mostly isolated by the resist layer, the DLIT shows that Ohmic shunting still occurs in some instances.

C. Spectral Response

The internal quantum efficiency (IQE) and EQE for the best cell are shown in Fig. 5 along with the reflectance and transmittance. The reflectance shows that the ONO stack is reasonably well optimized as an antireflection coating (ARC). The IQE reduction above 700 nm is likely due to parasitic absorption in the aluminum layer. The plateau region of the IQE is between 0.84 and 0.86 and is stable down to <400 nm. This shows that the diffusion length must be greater than the absorber width. PC1D modeling to fit the IQE suggests that the front surface recombination velocity is not more than about 6500 cm/s in the case that recombination is limited by this surface or that the bulk minority carrier lifetime is at least 90 ns in the bulk-limited case.

D. Suns–opencircuit voltage

Suns–V_{OC} was measured after metallization. The temperature during the measurement was 19.4 °C. The data are not corrected for the low temperature and are, therefore, inflated by around 12 mV compared to standard 25 °C test conditions. Nevertheless, Fig. 6 shows that a reasonable fit is made to a two-diode model, with significant contributions from both $n = 1$ and $n = 2$ type recombination as well as shunt.

Some, but not all cells are measured prior to metallization after completion of hydrogen passivation. Another cell processed similarly to the best cell was measured at this stage (at 26.5 °C) and is shown in Fig. 7. In this case, there is no shunt

TABLE I
ONE-SUN CHARACTERISTICS FOR TWO CELLS MEASURED DIRECTLY AFTER
MOST RECENT BAKE AND FINAL DELAYED MEASUREMENT 7–10 DAYS LATER

Cell	J_{SC}[mA/cm^2]	V_{OC}	FF [%]	η[%]
Cell A (post-bake)	27.6	585	72.4	11.7
Cell A (delayed)	27.7	572	62.9	10.0
Cell B (post-bake)	27.5	573	67.2	10.6
Cell B (delayed)	27.7	569	65.9	10.4

TABLE II
ONE-SUN CHARACTERISTICS FOR CELLS WITHOUT ARCS MEASURED
IMMEDIATELY AFTER CONTACT BAKE AND AGAIN, ONE WEEK LATER

Cell	J_{SC}[mA/cm^2]	V_{OC}	FF [%]	η[%]
Cell X (initial)	24.4	555	56.2	7.6
Cell X (delayed)	24.2	559	56.9	7.7
Cell Y (initial)	23.6	524	62.3	7.7
Cell Y (delayed)	23.9	434	46.4	4.7

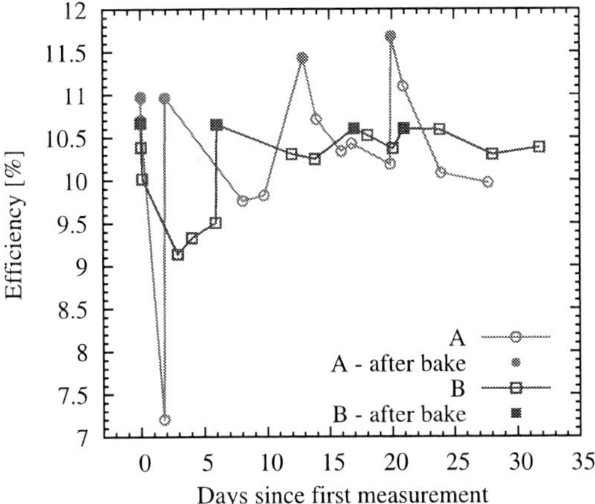

Fig. 8. Efficiency of two cells over time. Solid symbols show measurements made after a contact bake, open symbols show further measurements with no additional bake.

contribution and negligible $n = 2$ recombination. This suggests that the metallization scheme is causing some performance loss and may be optimized to achieve better final efficiency.

IV. STABILIZATION

A. Baseline Metallization

Cells made using the baseline process suffer from degradation in V_{OC} and FF, which begins immediately after the contact bake. The J_{SC} is generally unaffected beyond the margin of error. The peak and final one-sun characteristics are shown in Table I. The degradation is thought to be due to poor contact between the lightly doped p-type absorber layer and the sputtered aluminum point contacts. The performance is fully recoverable if the bake is repeated and in some cases is even improved. Two cells were tracked over a few weeks, with measurements taken at various times, including after repeated baking. The results are shown in Fig. 8.

Two things are obvious from Fig. 8. The first is the difference in the severity of degradation between the two cells. One possible reason for this is the difference in absorber doping. Cell A is doped with ~8e15 cm^{-}3 of boron, while cell B has ~1.5e16 cm^{-}3 (calculated via four-point probe measurements, assuming uniform doping and c-Si mobility). This small difference may have a significant impact on the contact resistance. The second is the reduction in the magnitude of the degradation with repeated baking. This suggests that there is a permanent change occurring at the contacts, which can be accelerated with higher temperature. This is partly supported by the work of Card et al. [14] who showed that the Schottky barrier at lightly doped p-Si/Al contacts reduces to a stable value after around 3 h if held at 150 °C, but takes months to reach the same value at room temperature. However, that would only explain the gradual increase in the stabilized value, while the transient improvement directly after baking is still not understood. By the final measurement, cell A does not appear to have completely stabilized, while cell B has stabilized at around 10.4%.

B. Selective p+ Metallization

In order to address this problem, the alternative metallization scheme described in Section II-B has been developed. The selective p+ metallization eliminates the short-term degradation by reducing and stabilizing the resistance at the absorber–aluminum contact. The best efficiency achieved using this method is 7.7% for a cell with no ARC (only a SiO$_x$ intermediate layer, which is optically indistinguishable from the glass). The one-sun characteristics of this cell are shown in Table II as Cell X. The efficiency matches the previous best initial efficiency achieved for a cell without an ARC, which was made using the baseline metallization scheme and is shown in Table II as Cell Y.

Measurements are shown after the final bake step and after a one week delay. While cell Y exhibits significant degradation in efficiency, FF, and V_{OC}, cell X shows a negligible change between the postbake measurement the delayed measurement.

The selective p+ metallization is a successful proof of concept to show that stable performance can be achieved for rear-contacted, laser-crystallized solar cells, but further development is still required. Although cell X had the advantage of the rear-texture light trapping that is discussed in Section II-A, its J_{SC} is less than 1 mA/cm^2 better than that of cell Y despite the latter having a planar rear surface. Approximately nine times more junction area is etched away for each contact during the selective p+ process compared with the baseline process and this loss of current collection erodes much of the gain made by the light-trapping texture. These contacts are spaced 1 mm apart to minimize the current loss, but this increases resistive losses in lateral transport, which results in a lower FF. Smaller diameter contacts would be necessary to gain the full benefit of this process.

The V_{OC} for cell X is the best measured for a cell with a SiO$_x$ intermediate layer. This may be an additional benefit of the p+ layer but this has not yet been confirmed with a statistically relevant number of samples. Further characterization and

Cell	J_{SC} [mA/cm^2]	V_{OC}	FF [%]	η [%]
Cell A	27.6	585	72.4	11.7
Previous best reported	24.2	557	62.3	8.4

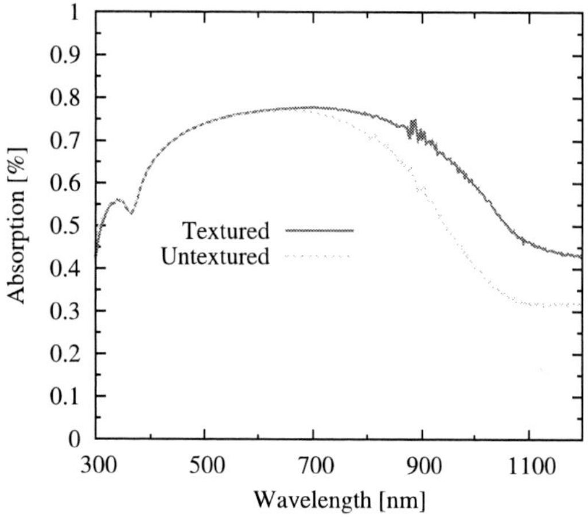

Fig. 9. Absorption improvement due to rear texturing of silicon for cells without an ARC. The absorption at > 1100 nm is likely due to the aluminum layer in each case.

optimization of this process will hopefully lead to stable results with no efficiency penalty.

V. PERFORMANCE IMPROVEMENTS

The peak one-sun characteristics of the best cell made with the baseline metallization are compared in Table III with the previous best reported cell using the laser-crystallization technique, which measured 8.4% efficiency [8]. Differentiating these cells are two significant changes. The first is the addition of the rear texture discussed in Section II-A, which improves near infrared absorption, and thus, J_{SC}. The difference in absorption is shown in Fig. 9 for two cells without an ARC (only glass and SiO$_x$ intermediate layer).

The second is a change to the intermediate layer. While both cells used a sputtered ONO stack between the glass and the silicon, the nitride layer was formed differently. For the 8.4% cell, it was sputtered directly from a SiN$_x$ target in pure argon, producing a silicon-rich nitride, which absorbed significant amounts of a short-medium wavelength light. The SiN$_x$ for the 11.7% cell was sputtered reactively using a silicon target in an nitrogen/argon mix, which reduced parasitic absorption to a negligible level as shown in Fig. 10.

The intermediate layer also has a significant impact on the silicon quality after crystallization. Differences in performance between SiN$_x$, SiO$_x$, and SiC$_x$ layers have been demonstrated in the past [8], [15]. The change in SiN$_x$ formation is most likely the cause of the much improved V_{OC} and FF, although further work must be done to understand the physical mechanism behind this improvement.

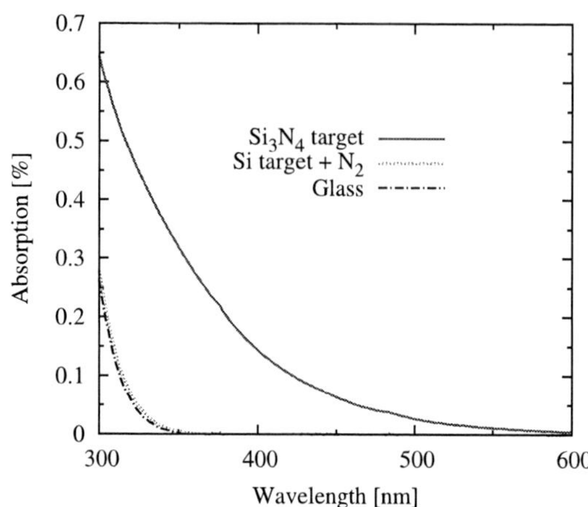

Fig. 10. Parasitic absorption in 75-nm thick silicon nitride layers depending on deposition method. For each layer, the absorption in the glass is included in the data. The absorption in the glass alone is also shown for comparison.

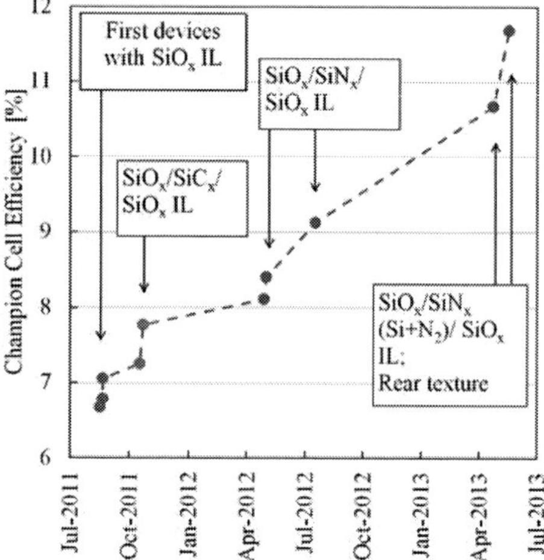

Fig. 11. Efficiency progression for laser-crystallized solar cells showing improvements mostly due to changing intermediate layers (IL).

Over the course of the development of the laser-crystallized solar cells within our group, the changes to the intermediate layer have been responsible for almost all of the performance improvements. Fig. 11 shows the improvements in efficiency over time.

VI. DISCUSSION

While some opportunity for optimization of the intermediate layers may still remain, other areas will need to be addressed in order to continue the rapid trajectory of improvement. For this, it is instructive to look at the results described previously in conjunction with two recent results reported for similar devices, each using either e-beam or diode laser crystallization of 5–10-μm-thick absorber layers deposited on the glass by e-beam evaporation.

The best result achieved for an e-beam crystallized device was reported by the Helmholtz Institute (HZB), Berlin, Germany

[7]. This was created in superstrate configuration with an a-Si:H heterojunction, resulting in a V_{OC} of 582 mV, but a relatively low efficiency of 5.7% due to problems with metallization, lack of light trapping and high recombination rate either in the bulk or at the intermediate layer interface. The Institute for Photonic Technology (IPHT), Jena, Germany, also produced laser crystallized cells reaching 550 mV V_{OC} and 7.8% efficiency [9] with a superstrate configured homojunction device.

Direct comparison of electronic quality such as minority carrier lifetime between such devices is not trivial, primarily due to the effect of carrier emission from shallow traps [16], which is significant in polycrystalline silicon. The only reported lifetimes [17] for the cells discussed here do not account for this. Structurally, the absorber material appears in each case to be similar to that created in our group, with high-quality grains shown to be in the range of tens of microns to several millimeters with a high incidence of twin grain-boundaries [8], [9], [11], [17].

A couple of key differences are worth noting. Both of these cells reported different intermediate layer arrangements to the one discussed in this study—SiO_x/SiC_x for the HZB cell and SiN_x-only for the IPHT cell. Similar arrangements were found in [8] to be inferior to the ONO structure used here. The high voltages achieved despite this suggest that there are either significant differences in those intermediate layer materials or that other advantages balance the result. One possibility regarding the latter is the junction formation. HZB used a heterojunction, which is known to outperform a standard diffused junction when applied to c-Si wafers [18]. In the case of IPHT, the junction was created by depositing a thin layer of highly doped a-Si on the rear surface and epitaxially crystallizing via excimer laser crystallization, thus forming a homojunction with very good control over the doping profile. By combining one of these junction processes with the absorber layers described in this study, it may be possible to reach voltages and efficiencies even higher than those reported here.

Such junctions may have an additional benefit with regard to the metallization scheme. The adaption of the industrially proven superstrate metallization scheme of CSG Solar [19] to laser-crystallized silicon has allowed for rapid efficiency improvement, but shunt losses still need addressing. The shunting related to silicon cracks may be reduced or eliminated by replacing the ~900 °C phosphorous diffusion so that the cracks are not exacerbated by the softening glass. Either of the alternative junction approaches described earlier could achieve this. Another option, which is currently being investigated is a diode laser diffusion process as described in [20]. The other difficulty with the baseline contacting scheme is the degradation. It is worth noting that the two cell results discussed earlier are not reported to exhibit degradation. This may also be related to the different absorber contacting. The HZB cell used COSIMA contacts [21] with evaporated Al, while the IPHT cell was contacted with InGa.

Many other areas are concurrently being investigated to gain further improvements. The rear texture has already helped achieve the latest result by enhancing the optical path length through the absorber, but front texture is ultimately required to gain the additional benefit of reduced reflection. Methods of texturing the glass prior to silicon deposition are, therefore, being tested for their compatibility with laser crystallization. The laser crystallization process itself is also being adapted in order to reduce silicon cracking and to control grain size and orientation. Additionally, improvements to surface and bulk hydrogenation are also under investigation and may increase the effective minority carrier lifetime.

VII. Conclusion

An initial efficiency of 11.7% and Voc of 585 mV have been demonstrated for laser-crystallized thin-film polycrystalline silicon solar cells, which exceeds the best reported results for laser-crystallized cells and for thin-film poly-Si cells grown on the glass. This has been achieved via improvements to the intermediate layer stack and to light trapping via rear silicon texturing. A degradation in FF and Voc occurs in the days following the final bake of the metallization process and is believed to be related to the poor contact between the sputtered aluminum electrode and the lightly doped absorber layer. The best stabilized efficiency is 10.4%. A selective p+ metallization scheme has enabled stable efficiencies to be achieved for such cells with only minor performance penalty. Combining this process with the best intermediate layer stack is expected to enable stable efficiencies over 11% in the near future.

Acknowledgment

The authors would like to thank K. Omaki for e-beam silicon depositions, K. Kim for assistance with processing, and to R. Evans, T. Young, O. Kunz, and S. Partlin for helpful discussions.

References

[1] M. J. Keevers, T. L. Young, U. Schubert, and M. A. Green, "10% efficient CSG minimodules," in *Proc. 22nd Eur. Photovolt. Solar Energy Conf.*, 2007, pp. 1783–1790.

[2] T. Kieliba, J. Pohl, A. Eyer, and C. Schmiga, "Optimization of c-Si films formed by zone-melting recrystallization for thin-film solar cells," in *Proc. 3rd World Conf. Photovolt. Energy Convers.*, 2003, pp. 1170–1173.

[3] S. Lindekugel, T. Rachow, S. Janz, and S. Reber, "Intermediate layer and back surface field optimisations for the recrystallised wafer equivalent," in *Proc. 27th Eur. Photovolt. Solar Energy Conf.*, 2012, pp. 2459–2462.

[4] K. Schillinger, S. Janz, and S. Reber, "Recrystallized silicon thin-film solar cells on zircon ceramics," presented at the IEEE 39th Photovoltaics Specialists Conf., Tampa, FL, USA, 2013.

[5] D. L. Young, C. W. Teplin, S. Grover, B. Lee, J. Oh, V. Lasalvia, D. Amkreutz, S. Gall, M. Chahal, G. J. Couillard, T.-K. Chuang, J. Selj, M. Deceglie, H. Atwater, H. M. Branz, and P. Stradins, "600 mv epitaxial crystal silicon solar cells grown on seeded glass," presented at the IEEE 39th Photovoltaics Specialists Conf., Tampa, FL, USA, 2013.

[6] C. W. Teplin, B. G. Lee, T. R. Fanning, J. Wang, S. Grover, F. Hasoon, R. Bauer, J. Bornstein, P. Schroeter, and H. M. Branz, "Pyramidal light trapping and hydrogen passivation for high-efficiency heteroepitaxial (100) crystal silicon solar cells," *Energy Environ. Sci.*, vol. 5, no. 8, pp. 8193–8198, 2012.

[7] J. Haschke, L. Jogschies, D. Amkreutz, L. Korte, and B. Rech, "Polycrystalline silicon heterojunction thin-film solar cells on glass exhibiting 582 mv open-circuit voltage," *Solar Energy Mater. Solar Cells*, vol. 115, no. 0, pp. 7–10, 2013.

[8] J. Dore, R. Evans, U. Schubert, B. D. Eggleston, D. Ong, K. Kim, J. Huang, O. Kunz, M. Keevers, R. Egan, S. Varlamov, and M. A. Green, "Thin-film polycrystalline silicon solar cells formed by diode laser crystallisation," *Progr. Photovolt.: Res. Appl.*, vol. 21, no. 6, pp. 1377–1383, 2013.

[9] G. Andrä, J. Plentz, A. Gawlik, I. Höger, and F. Falk, "Multicrystalline silicon thin film solar cells based on a two-step liquid phase laser crystallization process," presented at the IEEE 39th Photovoltaics Specialists Conf., Tampa, FL, USA, 2013.

[10] M. A. Green, K. Emery, Y. Hishikawa, and W. Warta, "Solar cell efficiency tables (version 33)," *Progr. Photovolt.: Res. Appl.*, vol. 17, no. 1, pp. 85–94, 2009.

[11] B. D. Eggleston, J. Dore, J. L. Huang, S. Varlamov, and M. A. Green, "Large grained, low defect density multicrystalline silicon on glass substrates by large-area diode laser crystallisation," *MRS Online Proc. Library*, vol. 1426, pp. 251–256, 2012.

[12] R. Egan, M. Keevers, U. Schubert, T. Young, R. Evans, S. Partlin, M. Wolf, J. Schneider, D. Hogg, B. Eggleston, M. Green, F. Falk, A. Gawlik, G. Andrä, M. Werner, C. Hagendorf, P. Dogan, T. Sontheimer, and S. Gall, "CSG minimodules using electron-beam evaporated silicon," in *Proc. 24th Eur. Photovolt. Solar Energy Conf.*, 2009, pp. 2279–2285.

[13] M. A. Green, P. A. Basore, N. Chang, D. Clugston, R. Egan, R. Evans, D. Hogg, S. Jarnason, M. Keevers, P. Lasswell, J. O'Sullivan, U. Schubert, A. Turner, S. R. Wenham, and T. Young, "Crystalline silicon on glass (CSG) thin-film solar cell modules," *Solar Energy*, vol. 77, no. 6, pp. 857–863, 2004.

[14] H. C. Card, "Aluminum-silicon schottky barriers and ohmic contacts in integrated circuits," *IEEE Trans. Electron. Devices*, vol. ED-23, no. 6, pp. 538–544, Jun. 1976.

[15] J. Dore, R. Evans, B. D. Eggleston, S. Varlamov, and M. A. Green, "Intermediate layers for thin-film polycrystalline silicon solar cells on glass formed by diode laser crystallization," *MRS Online Proc. Library*, vol. 1426, pp. 63–68, 2012.

[16] R. K. Ahrenkiel, N. Call, S. W. Johnston, and W. K. Metzger, "Comparison of techniques for measuring carrier lifetime in thin-film and multicrystalline photovoltaic materials," *Solar Energy Mater. Solar Cells*, vol. 94, no. 12, pp. 2197–2204, 2010.

[17] D. Amkreutz, J. Müller, M. Schmidt, T. Hänel, and T. F. Schulze, "Electron-beam crystallized large grained silicon solar cell on glass substrate," *Progr. Photovolt.: Res. Appl.*, vol. 19, no. 8, pp. 937–945, 2011.

[18] M. Taguchi, K. Kawamoto, S. Tsuge, T. Baba, H. Sakata, M. Morizane, K. Uchihashi, N. Nakamura, S. Kiyama, and O. Oota, "Hit cells - high-efficiency crystalline si cells with novel structure," *Progr. Photovolt.: Res. Appl.*, vol. 8, no. 5, pp. 503–513, 2000.

[19] M. A. Green, "Polycrystalline silicon on glass for thin-film solar cells," *Appl. Phys. A: Mater. Sci. Process.*, vol. 96, no. 1, pp. 153–159, 2009.

[20] S. Varlamov, B. Eggleston, J. Dore, R. Evans, D. Ong, O. Kunz, J. Huang, U. Schubert, K. H. Kim, R. Egan, and M. Green, "Diode laser processed crystalline silicon thin-film solar cells," *Proc. SPIE*, vol. 8608, art. no. 86080Q, 2013.

[21] H. Plagwitz, M. Nerding, N. Ott, H. P. Strunk, and R. Brendel, "Low-temperature formation of local al contacts to a-si:h-passivated si wafers," *Progr. Photovolt.: Res. Appl.*, vol. 12, no. 1, pp. 47–54, 2004.

Authors' photographs and biographies not available at the time of publication.

A Complete Fully Thin-Film PV Harvesting and Power-Management System on Plastic With On-Sheet Battery Management and Wireless Power Delivery to Off-sheet Loads

Warren Rieutort-Louis, *Student Member, IEEE*, Liechao Huang, *Student Member, IEEE*, Yingzhe Hu, *Student Member, IEEE*, Josue Sanz-Robinson, Sigurd Wagner, *Fellow, IEEE*, James C. Sturm, *Fellow, IEEE*, and Naveen Verma, *Member, IEEE*

Abstract—Large-area electronics enables the creation of systems with transformational capabilities and form factors. Through the ability to integrate thin-film photovoltaics, batteries, and active transistors, complete power-management subsystems addressing a wide range of applications can also be created. We present, for the first time, a fully flexible system integrating amorphous silicon (a-Si) solar modules with Li-ion thin-film batteries and circuits that are based on a-Si thin-film transistors for battery management and wireless power delivery. A fabricated prototype of the entire system on a plastic sheet is demonstrated. Using a 240 cm^2 solar module under indoor lighting conditions ($\sim$400 μW/cm^2), the system is measured to provide 1) dc power ($\sim$1 mW) to on-sheet loads and 2) ac power ($\sim$10 mW) to off-sheet loads through wireless transmission. Four Li-ion batteries are used for on-sheet energy storage with a battery-management system ensuring discharging at permissible levels, while imposing minimal off-state current ($<$360 nA).

Index Terms—Amorphous semiconductors, battery management systems, energy-harvesting, flexible electronics, photovoltaic systems, thin-film circuits, thin-film transistors.

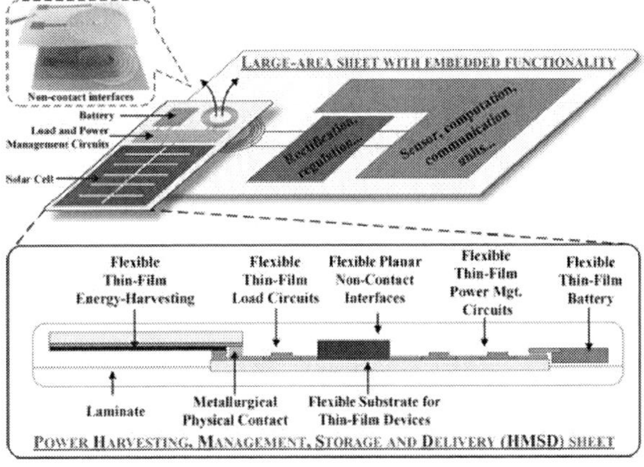

Fig. 1. System concept and physical assembly of power harvesting, management, storage, and delivery (HMSD) sheet system components making use of sheet lamination.

I. INTRODUCTION

THROUGH the deposition of thin-film devices at low temperatures, large-area electronics (LAE) enables the creation of transformational systems with novel form factors on flexible sheets. The simultaneous ability to form amorphous silicon (a-Si) energy-harvesting devices [e.g., photovoltaics (PV)], thin-film transistors (TFTs), thin-film diodes (TFDs), and passives (e.g., inductors, capacitors, resistors) can enable complete self-powered systems for a wide range of embedded applications. Flexible sheets that are based on PV harvesters with in-

tegrated a-Si TFT power electronics for wireless charging of personal devices are such an application, for which two systems have recently been reported. The first system [1] uses two solar modules (dc) from which current is switched in turn by TFTs in order to generate an oscillating output (ac) for transfer over a noncontact capacitive link, while the second system [2] uses a TFT-based *LC* oscillator to transfer power over a noncontact inductive link.

However, to exploit the highly promising sensing and actuation capabilities within LAE [3] in complete systems, integrated thin-film subsystems for continuous power-management are required, by combining energy harvesting with local energy storage (i.e., to account for periods of diminished illumination of, e.g., solar modules). In this study, we present a fully thin-film sheet that accomplishes this.

Fig. 1 illustrates the system concept, showing the proposed power harvesting, management, storage, and delivery (HMSD) sheet for wireless power delivery to large-scale systems (e.g., a large-area sheet with embedded functionality). Interfacing to general large-area sheets is simply achieved by placing the HMSD sheet onto a power-receiving surface without the need for complex metallurgical connections. The aim is a generalized

Manuscript received June 10, 2013; revised August 3, 2013; accepted September 26, 2013. Date of publication October 30, 2013; date of current version December 16, 2013. The work of W. Rieutort-Louis was supported by the IBM Ph.D. Fellowship and the Princeton Andlinger Center Maeder Graduate Fellowship in Energy and the Environment. This work was supported by the National Science Foundation under Grant ECCS-1202168 and Grant CCF-1218206.

The authors are with the Department of Electrical Engineering and the Princeton Institute for the Science and Technology of Materials, Princeton University, Princeton, NJ 08544 USA (e-mail: rieutort@princeton.edu; liechaoh@princeton.edu; yingzheh@princeton.edu; jsanz@princeton.edu; wagner@princeton.edu; sturm@princeton.edu; nverma@princeton.edu).

Color versions of one or more of the figures in this paper are available online at http://ieeexplore.ieee.org.

Digital Object Identifier 10.1109/JPHOTOV.2013.2285959

99

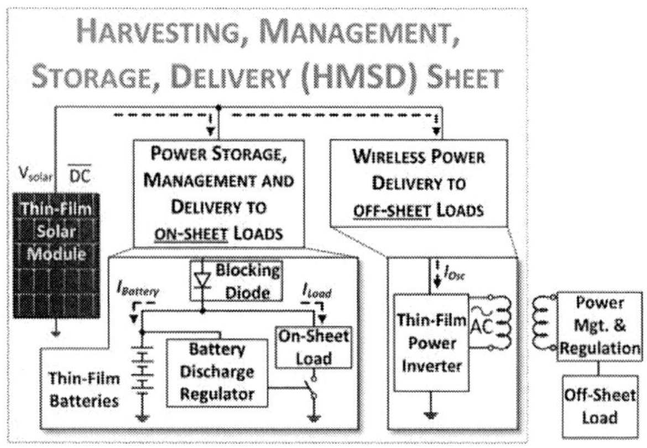

Fig. 2. Schematic representation of the HMSD harvesting, management, storage, and delivery sheet system architecture.

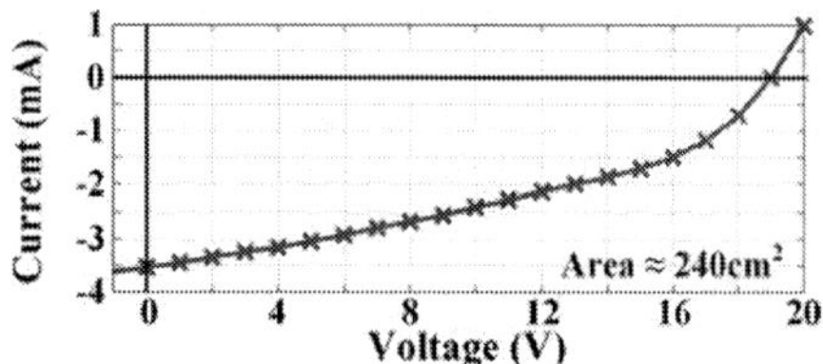

Fig. 3. Solar module *I–V* characteristic under interior illumination.

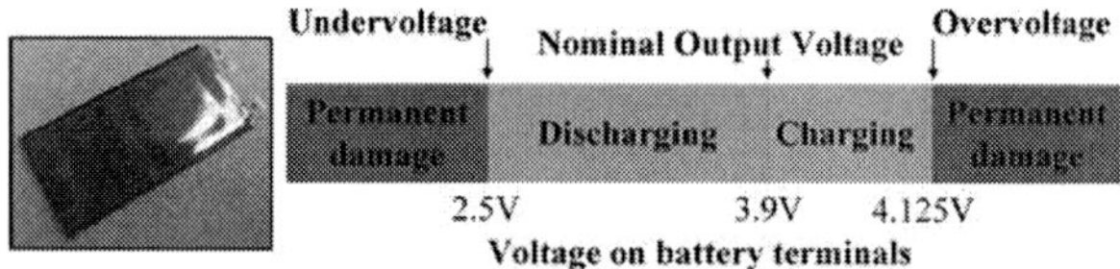

Fig. 4. Permissible operating voltages for charging and discharging of thin-film Li-Ion batteries.

and easy-to-integrate platform for powering various large-area sheets; a flexible HMSD sheet ensures that power delivery is not constrained by the physical form factor of the large-area sheet. In addition to PV harvesters and power inverters for wireless power delivery, the HMSD sheet comprises a TFT-based subsystem for management of commercial, flexible, thin-film lithium-ion batteries, thus also enabling local energy storage and continuous powering of on-sheet loads.

The inset in Fig. 1 shows the physical assembly of the various components of the HMSD sheet. The use of lamination provides a path for low-cost integration of batteries and multiple free-standing substrates onto which on-sheet a-Si thin-film components (e.g., PV, TFTs, TFDs) are patterned. Conductive adhesive [e.g., anisotropic conductive film (ACF)] provides low-resistance, mechanically robust contact between the illustrated planes.

In this paper, we describe all the components of the HMSD sheet, with particular focus on circuits and devices to meet two key requirements of the sheet. First is the need for reliable and safe charging of the thin-film batteries from dc-output solar modules as well as the protection of these batteries from excessive discharge during on-sheet load powering. Second is the need for off-sheet power delivery from solar cells; for this, the dc power output is converted to ac via a thin-film power inverter whose power-transfer efficiency is enhanced by operating beyond the TFT f_t frequency limit [2].

II. System Architecture

Fig. 2 shows a block diagram of the HMSD sheet. The solar module consists of a-Si solar cells in series operating at an output voltage V_{solar}. DC power from the module is distributed on the large-area sheet to

1) an *on-sheet* power-storage, management, and delivery block that comprises batteries, a battery-discharge-regulator subsystem, and on-sheet loads;
2) an *off-sheet* power-delivery block that comprises an inverter for wireless power delivery to off-sheet loads (with their own local energy-storage/regulation circuits).

Under solar illumination, dc current is supplied to both the on-sheet and off-sheet power blocks. In the former, the supplied current is split between charging the batteries (I_{Battery}) and delivering power to the on-sheet load (I_{Load}), while in the latter, current is delivered to the oscillator (I_{Osc}). Without illumination, current is supplied from the batteries to the on-sheet load and the off-sheet block is not operational.

Section III describes the key components and devices that are required for the HSMD sheet. Sections IV and V describe the detailed operation of the on-sheet and off-sheet power-management blocks, respectively.

III. Key Components Required for the Harvesting, Management, Storage, and Delivery Sheet

A. Flexible Thin-Film Solar Modules

Commercial a-Si solar modules fabricated on a 50-μm-thick polymer substrate are used for system demonstration purposes. A typical measured *I–V* characteristic under indoor lighting conditions ($\sim$400 μW/cm^2) is shown in Fig. 3. The thin-film circuitry on the HMSD sheet typically draws modest current levels and, as such, the operating point is close to the open-circuit voltage of the solar module V_{solar} of 19 V.

B. Flexible Thin-Film Batteries

Commercial flexible thin-film lithium-ion (Li-ion) batteries [4] are used for energy storage. These are based on a lithium cobalt oxide cathode, a lithium metal anode, and a lithium phosphorus oxynitride electrolyte. As is typical with Li-ion battery technology, achieving safe and reliable charging/discharging is conditional on drawing charge from (or supplying charge to) the battery within a well-defined window of operating voltages. Failure to do so would result in permanent battery damage. Fig. 4 illustrates the permissible operating voltage range for the thin-film batteries used in the HMSD system, with an open-circuit (nominal output) voltage of 3.9 V.

A method of managing the power drawn from the batteries is thus required to ensure that once the battery reaches the

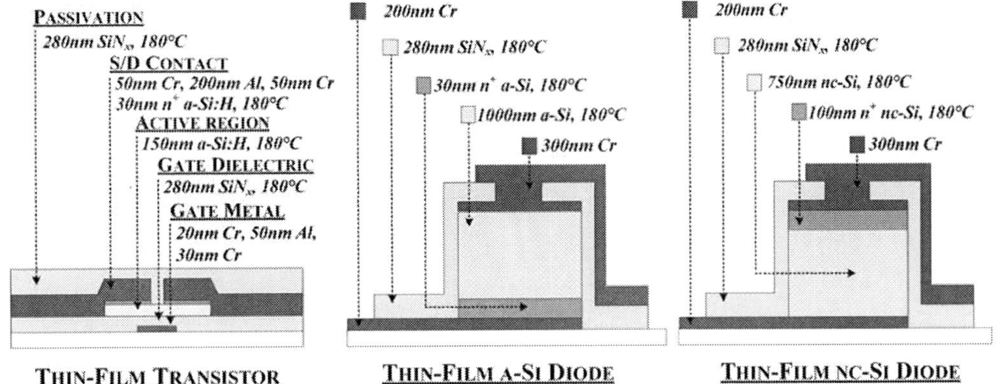

Fig. 5. a-Si TFT and a-Si/nc-Si TFD device structures.

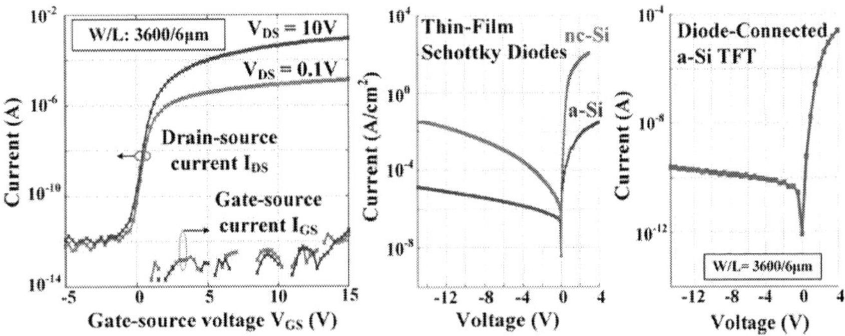

Fig. 6. Thin-film transistor and thin-film diode characteristics.

under-voltage condition, any load is cut off, preventing further battery discharge until the battery has been partly or fully recharged.

C. Flexible, Thin-Film Circuit Technology

A wide variety of materials and processes exist that enable the fabrication of circuits directly patterned on flexible substrates such as polymers or metallic foils. These include, for example, amorphous silicon, organics [5], or metal oxides [6]. For the HMSD sheet, a-Si is used as the primary semiconducting material; its proven commercial viability and established industrial processing on sheets up to 10 m² make it an attractive candidate for a wide range of emerging flexible-system applications.

Our four-chamber PECVD a-Si manufacturing capability allows for the processing of 7.5 cm × 7.5 cm square, 50-µm-thick polyimide substrates onto which the following devices are patterned: thin-film transistors (TFTs), thin-film diodes (TFDs—using amorphous or nano-crystalline Si), thin-film diode-connected transistors, and thin-film resistors (TFRs). Circuits constructed from these components were shielded from light to minimize off-state leakage. Typical device structures and characteristics are shown in Figs. 5 and 6, respectively.

Back-channel etched TFTs are optimized for processing on plastic, with typical channel length of 6 µm; large thin-film resistors (for low static current in the battery-management circuit)

TABLE I
CHALLENGES FOR a-Si TFT POWER CIRCUITS

PROPERTY	CAUSE	IMPLICATION
Low transconductance ($g_m \sim 9 \times 10^{-5}$ A/V for W/L=600, $V_{ds}=V_{gs}=10V$)	Disordered a-Si structure, low electron mobility (~1 cm²/Vs), high threshold voltages ($V_T \sim 2.5V$)	Low-current switches
Only NMOS TFTs	Low field-effect hole mobility (<0.1 cm²/Vs)	CMOS topologies not viable
Large device parasitic capacitances	Large device features and process margins for processing on free-standing substrates	Reduced performance and increased switching losses

are made using n⁺ a-Si with sheet resistance of 30 MΩ/sq [7], [8]. Thin-film a-Si and nc-Si Schottky TFDs [9] are optimized for large on–off ratio as shown; Schottky diodes are used instead of p-i-n diodes due to their simpler fabrication, avoiding the use of p-type thin-film silicon which is not part of a standard a-Si process as used in production of TFT AMLCD technologies. These diodes, where used, are fabricated separately and mounted onto the flexible sheet. From the perspective of power-management circuits, a number of considerations arise due to the performance limitations of the thin-film devices [7]. Table I summarizes the design challenges for circuits.

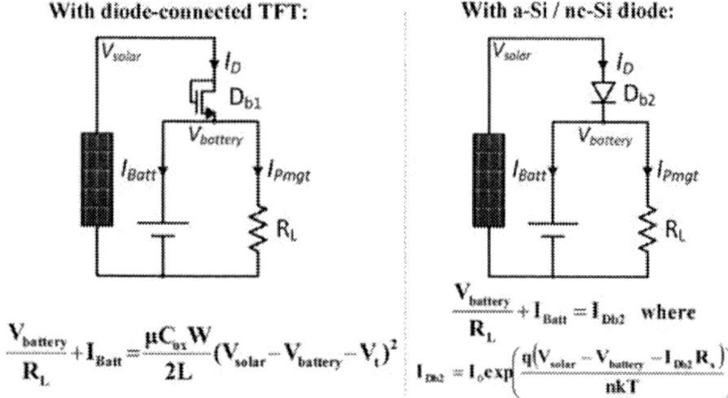

$$\frac{V_{battery}}{R_L} + I_{Batt} = \frac{\mu C_{ox} W}{2L}(V_{solar} - V_{battery} - V_t)^2$$

$$\frac{V_{battery}}{R_L} + I_{Batt} = I_{Db2} \quad \text{where}$$

$$I_{Db2} = I_o \exp\left(\frac{q(V_{solar} - V_{battery} - I_{Db2}R_s)}{nkT}\right)$$

Fig. 7. Options for the blocking diode interfacing the battery management circuitry with the solar module using either diode connected thin-film transistors or thin-film diodes.

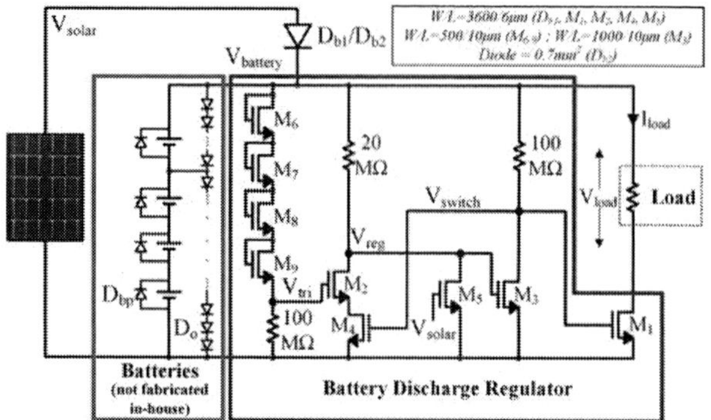

Fig. 8. HMSD sheet subblocks for power storage, management, and delivery to on-sheet loads.

IV. Power Regulation and Delivery to On-Sheet Loads

In this section, the subsystems of the HMSD sheet for power storage, power management, and power delivery to on-sheet-loads will be discussed.

A. Interfacing With the Solar Module: Blocking Diode Design

The blocking diode (D_b) prevents leakage from the batteries under low-illumination conditions (i.e., when V_{solar} drops). It could be implemented using either diode-connected TFTs (attractive from an integration perspective), or either a-Si or nc-Si Schottky diodes, as shown in a generalization of the power-management block circuit in Fig. 5. A first evaluation of the performance of the blocking diode can be made by studying the circuit behavior under a range of different loads R_L. For small resistive loads, $V_{battery}$ droops due to the voltage drop across the blocking diode required to sustain I_{Pmgt}.

A critical condition can be identified where, for a given solar module voltage (V_{solar}), $V_{battery}$ has drooped to the point that the charging current (I_{Batt}) drops to zero (at which point $V_{battery}$ is simply the nominal output voltage of the stack of batteries). This point sets the minimum resistive load that can be powered by the on-sheet block and, thus, serves as a performance metric for the system. When using a diode connected TFT (which is connected to always be in saturation when above V_t), this occurs when:

$$R_L < \frac{V_{battery\,(nominal)}}{\frac{\mu C_{ox} W}{2L}(V_{solar} - V_{battery\,(nominal)} - V_t)^2} \quad (1)$$

whereas for the case of an a-Si or nc-Si diode, this occurs when

$$R_L < \frac{V_{battery\,(nominal)}}{I_{Db2}} \quad (2)$$

where I_{Db2} is defined in Fig. 7, including the diode series resistance component Rs.

A second evaluation of the performance is necessary however, considering the reverse leakage current of the blocking diode under the low-illumination condition. Here, nearly the full nominal voltage of the batteries appears across D_{b1}/D_{b2}; an excessive reverse leakage can result in permanent damage of the batteries due to draining as described previously. An analysis of the three diode options is provided in Section VI.

B. Thin-Film Battery Discharge Regulator

Fig. 8 shows the details of the battery-discharge regulator block. This block is connected to the solar module through the charge-blocking diode, D_{b1}, and it gates the current provided to an on-sheet load through the use of M_1 to ensure safe discharge levels for the batteries. For analysis, a purely resistive load is used to represent on-sheet loads; in practice, these could be embedded functionality circuits (e.g., sensing, power metering...)

Four series-connected 300 μAh thin-film Li-ion batteries as previously described are used for energy storage, providing a nominal output voltage $V_{battery}$ of 15.6 V. This value is chosen to satisfy the voltage-level requirements in typical thin-film circuits. The diode stack D_o ensures proper charging conditions for the batteries, while the TFT circuit ($M1$–$M9$) is used to ensure proper discharging conditions during load powering. During charging, the batteries may not be exposed to a charging voltage greater than $\sim$16.5 V (4 $\times$ 4.125 V); to ensure this, a chain of current-shunting diodes D_o provides regulation if this voltage is exceeded. Bypass diodes D_{bp} are typically included in parallel with each battery to ensure current continuity if one battery fails.

Under low illumination, the batteries take over powering of the load. During discharging, the nominal output voltage of the batteries is maintained until the batteries approach their fully discharged state. At this point, the output voltage begins to drop rapidly; however, following from previous discussion, a drop below $\sim$10 V (4 $\times$ 2.5 V) must be prevented to avoid permanent battery damage.

A low-voltage cut-off circuit is thus implemented, as shown in Fig. 8, to provide rapid turn-off of the load current via a regenerative circuit. V_{tri} follows the battery voltage through the voltage drop across a chain of diode-connected TFTs M_{6-9}. During battery powering, M_2 and M_4 are initially "ON," pulling V_{reg} low; however, the M_{6-9} chain is designed such that when the battery voltage drops below 10 V, V_{reg} rises, thereby pulling V_{switch} low through M_3. This causes M_4 to begin to turn OFF,

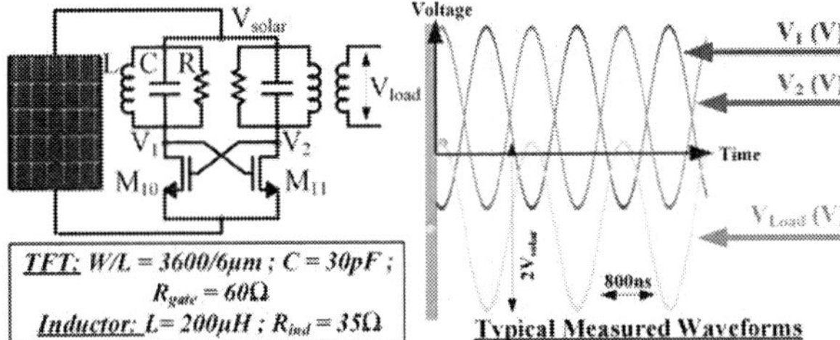

Fig. 9. Circuit diagram, typical device parameters, and measured waveforms of the LC-oscillator inverter for wireless off-sheet power delivery using planar inductors.

triggering regeneration on V_{reg} and V_{switch}. This causes the load current to turn OFF through rapid control of the power TFT M_1.

With full-swing regeneration on V_{switch}, a large on-to-off ratio of 10^5 for the battery current can thus be achieved through M_1 control. Activation of M_1 is subsequently achieved by resetting the circuit through M_5. With M_5 controlled by V_{solar}, battery discharge is prevented until after the battery has been partly/fully recharged, following the return of illumination.

In the "OFF" state, current results primarily from static current through the branches of the regenerative stages and through M_1. M_1's current can be handled as described in the following section, while the current through the regenerative stages can be minimized through sizing of the associated thin-film resistors. After low-voltage cut off occurs, the normal battery operating voltage is redeveloped on V_{battery} and maintained due to the lower current being drawn, with an effective small increase in battery capacity [4]. The width of M_1 is designed so that the level of leakage current is such that low-voltage battery failure would not occur until after *at least* 100 h. For an application, this can be set as desired to be much longer than the expected interval expected between daily illumination periods.

C. Power-Delivery to On-Sheet Load

To design the power-TFT M_1, two optimal conditions can be considered. First, the optimal power point for the load is achieved when M_1 imposes a voltage drop equivalent to the load voltage, i.e., $V_{M1} = V_{\mathrm{load}} = V_{\mathrm{battery}}/2$. Second, the optimal power delivery efficiency is achieved when M_1 exhibits minimal voltage drop. However, this requires either reduction of the load current (and, therefore, load power) or reduction of the effective TFT resistance through increased M_1 width or through an array of parallel-connected TFTs. Though viable, this could increase the off-state leakage and can thus only be pursued to levels permitted by battery discharge limits and expected illumination-cycle periods.

V. WIRELESS POWER DELIVERY TO OFF-SHEET LOADS

Fig. 9 shows the details of the block for wireless power-delivery to off-sheet loads. This block consists of an LC oscillator-based on-sheet inverter [2], enabling inductive coupling for wireless power delivery to an off-sheet load.

The LC oscillator allows operation above the f_t of the TFTs by resonating out the large device parasitic capacitances C. The

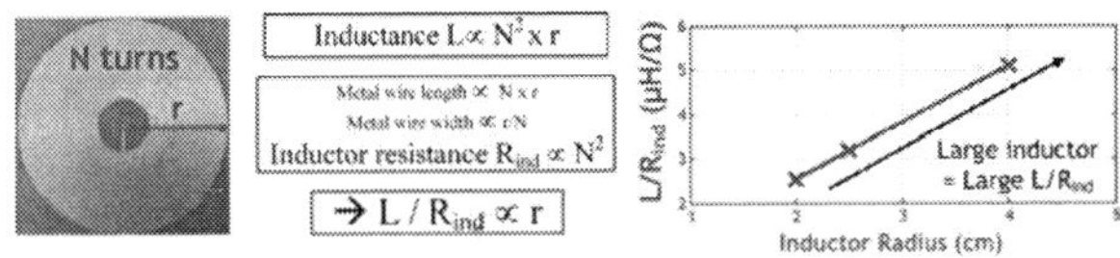

Fig. 10. Design and optimization of the L/R_{ind} ratio of copper planar inductors leveraging large-area inductor sizes to achieve LC oscillator operation and wireless power transfer.

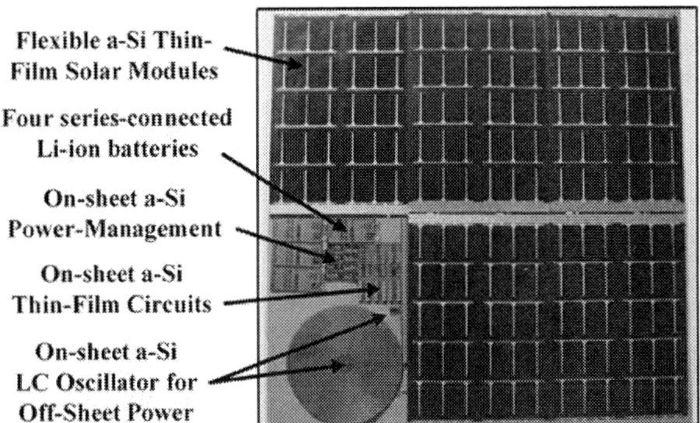

Fig. 11. System prototype on a flexible polyimide sheet (20×15 cm) showing the assembled thin-film components: solar modules, batteries, thin-film circuits, and wireless power transfer inductors.

ability to pattern physically large inductors leads to high-quality factors, thus enabling the resonant tank to be achieved efficiently (i.e., with large effective tank resistance).

In order for oscillations to occur, a positive feedback condition must be satisfied [2].

$$\frac{g_m}{C} \times \frac{L}{R_{\mathrm{ind}} + R_{\mathrm{gate}}} > 1. \tag{3}$$

While this condition depends in part on the modest TFT electrical properties described earlier (low g_m, high gate-source/drain capacitances contributing to C, and large TFT bottom-gate resistance R_{gate}) which can be optimized only to a limited extent [7], the ability to pattern large (cm-scale) inductor coils enables high inductance and small resistance as shown in Fig. 10. This enables robust oscillations, despite the limitations of the TFT devices and their parasitics.

Methods for increasing the output power [2] include increasing solar-module voltage or optimizing TFT-width for the specific loads expected on the large-area sheet that is receiving the power.

VI. EXPERIMENTAL RESULTS

The entire PV-based HMSD sheet is fabricated on 50 μm-thick polyimide, at a maximum temperature of 180 °C. The system prototype is shown in Fig. 11, while the thin-film-circuit micrograph is in Fig. 12, and a system performance summary is in Table II.

Experimental results for all the subsystems are now presented

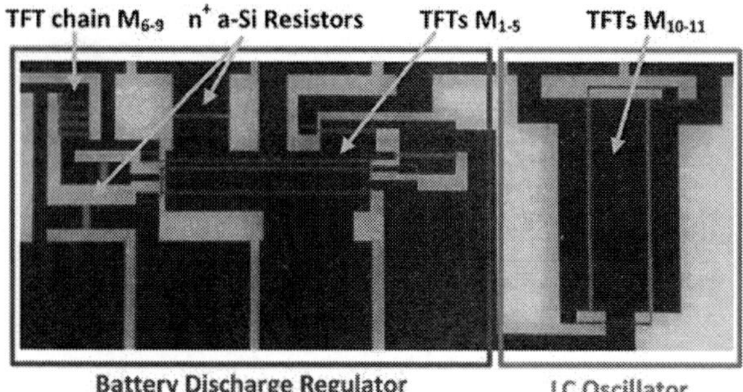

Fig. 12.   Micrographs of HMSD thin-film circuits (10 × 5 mm).

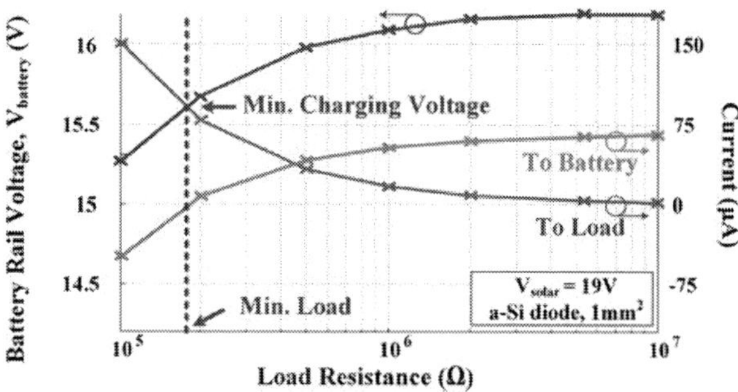

Fig. 13.   Measured effect of blocking diode voltage drop on battery-charging current.

TABLE II
HMSD Sheet System Performance Summary

a-Si Solar Module	V_{oc}=19V, Area=240cm^2, Under indoor illumination=0.4mW/cm^2
Batteries	4 x Li/LiCoO$_2$/LiPON, 300μAh, 3.9V 2.5V<Operating voltage per battery<4.12V
On-Sheet load power	~1.2 mW to 150kΩ
Largest on-sheet load	150kΩ with a 0.7mm^2 a-Si blocking diode
On-sheet standby current	240nA (circuit) + 120nA (blocking diode)
Off-Sheet max. load power	~10mW to 10kΩ at 21% transfer efficiency
Off-Sheet transmission	Frequency ≈ 2MHz, 2cm-radius inductors

TABLE III
Performance Metrics for Blocking Diode Options

BLOCKING DIODE	METRIC 1: ON-CURRENT DELIVERY TO LOAD	METRIC 2: REV. LEAKAGE AT -15.6V
Diode connected TFT (W/L = 3600/6 μm)	For V_{gs}=V_{ds}=3.4V, I_d=10μA → Minimum R$_L$=1.5MΩ	< 500pA
a-Si Schottky Diode (Area = 1 mm^2)	For V_d=3.4V, I_d=200μA → Minimum R$_L$=80kΩ	~ 100nA
nc-Si Schottky Diode (Area = 0.01 mm^2)	For V_d=2V, I_d=5mA → Minimum R$_L$=3kΩ	~3 μA

A. Power Regulation and Delivery to on-Sheet Loads

1) Thin-Film Blocking Diode Optimization: A comparison of the three blocking diode options is performed in Table III using the performance metrics described in Section IV, with $V_{battery}$ = 15.6 V and V_{solar} = 19 V for the TFT-based and a-Si Schottky diodes (leading to a 3.4 V allowable diode-voltage drop). For the nc-Si diodes, a V_{solar} = 17.5 V is used for comparison as voltage drops larger than 3 V are unreliably sustained due to the large current densities achieved.

While the diode-connected TFT provides an attractive on-current to reverse-leakage ratio, for practical TFT dimensions, the on-current is lower than the manufactured a-Si diodes. The a-Si Schottky diode used in this system provides good forward current (~200 μA) when the solar module is charging the battery and powering the load, while giving a reverse leakage (~100 nA at −15.6 V), which is reasonable, in that it is of the same order as the static leakage through the power-management block, as will

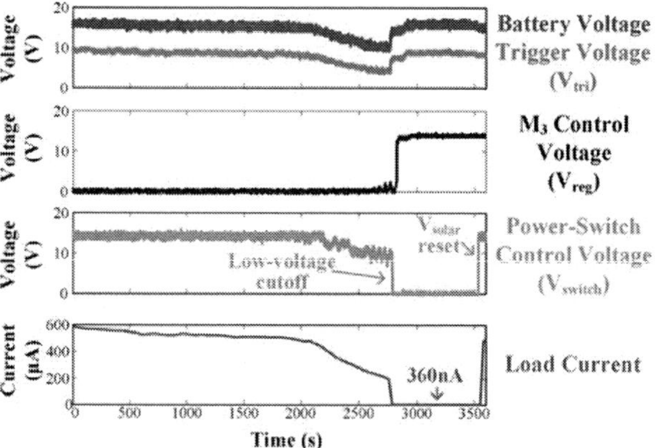

Fig. 14.   Measured waveforms for on-sheet power delivery.

be described later. The diode size could be increased further to support higher load currents at the cost of proportionally higher reverse leakage. The nc-Si diode has a better on–off ratio, potentially allowing for slightly better forward current; however, depending on the required reverse leakage conditions, very small diodes (<0.0005 mm^2) might be required, which are challenging to manufacture.

Fig. 13 shows the drop on the battery-voltage rail that arises due to voltage drops across the blocking diode D_{b1} (a-Si, 1 mm^2 diode) as the load current increases (i.e., due to reduced on-sheet loads).

With a 0.7 mm^2 a-Si TFD, loads less than 150 kΩ are still powered, but the voltage on $V_{battery}$ falls below 15.6 V and is no longer sufficient to provide charging current to the batteries.

2) Thin-Film Battery Discharge Regulator: Fig. 14 shows measured waveforms for the on-sheet battery discharge regulator subsystem. For testing, power at a level of ~5 mW is delivered for 45 min from the batteries to a 10 kΩ load.

As the battery is discharged, the nominal output voltage is initially maintained, but beyond 40 min, it begins to decrease. Once $V_{battery}$ reaches the critical-discharge level (~10 V), the low-voltage cutoff circuit triggers, and the load current is disabled by the power TFT M_1. Subsequently, the current drawn from the batteries drops to below 360 nA, protecting the battery from further discharge.

104

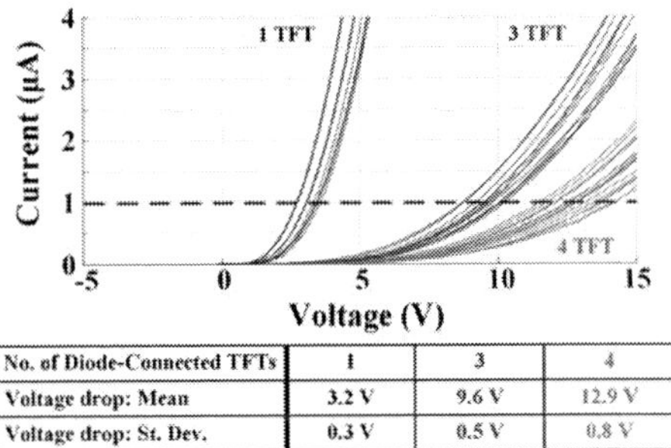

No. of Diode-Connected TFTs	1	3	4
Voltage drop: Mean	3.2 V	9.6 V	12.9 V
Voltage drop: St. Dev.	0.3 V	0.5 V	0.8 V

Fig. 15.   TFT diode chain variability statistics at $I_{\text{diode-chain}} = 1\ \mu A$.

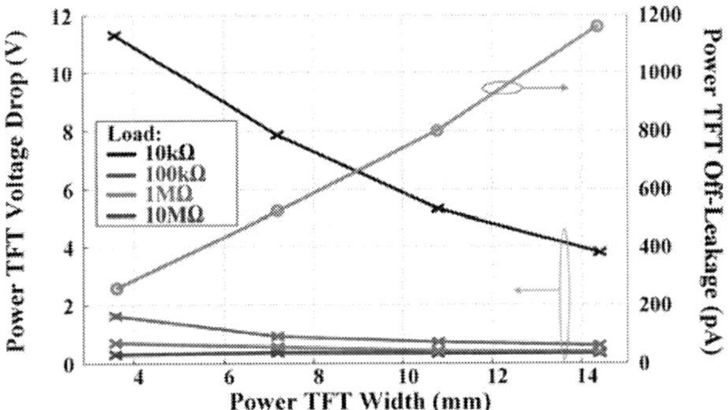

Fig. 16.   Tradeoffs of power-TFT M_1 voltage drop and off-leakage incurred through scaling of the M_1 TFT width.

At this point, the voltage of the batteries returns to a level close to the nominal output voltage due to the greatly reduced current being drawn. A reset through M_5 arising from renewed solar-module illumination is also shown.

The variability of the M_{6-9} voltage drop (i.e., due to TFT threshold-voltage variation) could potentially shift the trigger point; however, measurements across many diode chains found that the range required to ensure correct regeneration can reliably be achieved with modest margining, as set by the standard deviations shown in Fig. 15.

3) Thin-Film Battery Discharge Regulator: Fig. 16 shows how the voltage drop across the power TFT switch scales with the width of the switch (implemented as parallel TFTs for testing performed without charge-blocking diode D_{b1}).

Wider switches result in reduced drops and large V_{load}; however, as shown, this comes at the cost of larger off-state leakage current (shown for $V_{\text{drop}} = 15.6$ V). In the prototyped design, however, this leakage is very small compared with the leakage due to the regenerative branches of the cut-off circuit.

As discussed in Section IV, two optimization approaches may be considered for power delivered to the on-sheet load, optimal power delivery, or power delivery efficiency.

Fig. 17 illustrates this tradeoff whereby with larger resistive loads higher delivery efficiency is achieved at the expense of power delivered to the load.

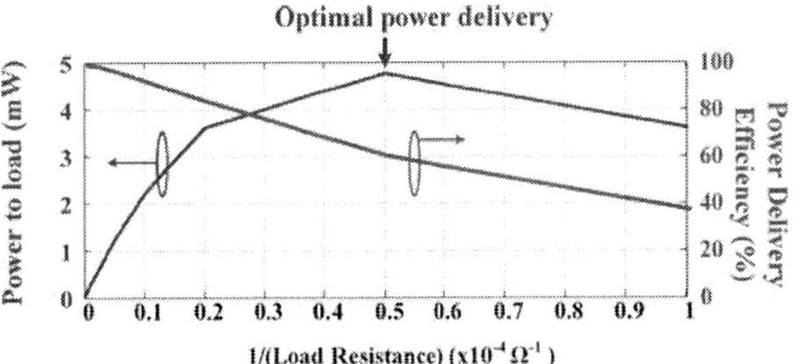

Fig. 17.   Tradeoff of power delivered versus power delivery efficiency to on-sheet loads.

B. Wireless Power Delivery to Off-Sheet Loads

The *LC* oscillator delivers power wirelessly (at 2 MHz) to an off-sheet resistive load via 2 cm-radius patterned 25-μm-thick copper inductors. The inductors could be monolithically fabricated onto the HMSD sheet through an additive process but, for this system demonstration, are fabricated separately and mounted for testing. At a V_{solar} of 19 V and at 1 mm separation distance from the load, the *LC* oscillator delivers 8 mW (under indoor lighting conditions) with 21% power-transfer efficiency, drawing power directly from the solar module.

VII. Conclusion

A fully thin-film power harvesting, management, storage, and delivery (HMSD) sheet is demonstrated based on PV harvesters. It delivers power both locally to an on-sheet battery, battery-management system, and load, as well as wirelessly to off-sheet loads through an *LC*-oscillator-based power inverter. The use of thin-film batteries enables the continuous operation of embedded systems under temporary conditions of reduced illumination. For reliable battery operation, integrated circuitry for controlling the charging and discharging conditions on the batteries is demonstrated, enabling milliwatt-level output power with low off-state leakage.

References

[1] L. Huang, W. Rieutort-Louis, Y. Hu, J. Sanz-Robinson, S. Wagner, J. Sturm, and N. Verma, "Integrated all-silicon thin-film power electronics on flexible sheets for ubiquitous wireless charging stations based on solar-energy harvesting," in *Proc. VLSI Symp. Circuits*, Honolulu, HI, USA, Jun. 13–15, 2012, pp. 198–199.

[2] Y. Hu, W. Rieutort-Louis, L. Huang, J. Sanz-Robinson, S. Wagner, J. Sturm, and N. Verma, "Flexible solar-energy harvesting system on plastic with thin-film LC oscillators operating above ft for inductively-coupled power delivery," in *Proc. Custom Integrated Circuits Conf.*, San Jose, CA, USA, Sep. 2012.

[3] T. Someya, B. Pal, J. Huang, and H. E. Katz, "Organic semiconductor devices with enhanced field and environmental responses for novel applications," *MRS Bulletin*, vol. 33, pp. 690–696, 2008.

[4] *THINERGY MEC220*, Infinite Power Solutions, Littleton, CO, USA, Dec. 7–9, 2009.

[5] T. Someya, T. Sekitani, M. Takamiya, T. Sakurai, U. Zschieschang, and H. Klauk, "Printed organic transistors: Toward ambient electronics," in *Proc. Int. Electron. Device Meeting*, Baltimore, MD, USA, Dec. 7–9, 2009, pp. 1–6.

[6] D. A. Zhao, D. A. Mourey, and T. N. Jackson, "Flexible plastic substrate ZnO thin film transistor circuits," in *Proc. Device Res. Conf.*, Jun. 22–24, 2009, pp. 177–178.

[7] W. Rieutort-Louis, J. Sanz-Robinson, Y. Hu, L. Huang, J. C. Sturm, N. Verma, and S. Wagner, "Device optimization for integration of thin-film power electronics with thin-film energy-harvesting devices to create power-delivery systems on plastic sheets," presented at the Int. Electron Device Meeting, San Francisco, CA, USA, Dec. 2012, Paper 12.3.

[8] B. Hekmatshoar, K. H. Cherenack, A. Z. Kattamis, K. Long, S. Wagner, and J.C. Sturm, "Highly stable amorphous-silicon thin-film transistors on clear plastic," *Appl. Phys. Lett.*, vol. 93, no. 3, Jul. 2008.

[9] J. Sanz-Robinson, W. Rieutort-Louis, N. Verma, S. Wagner, and J. Sturm, "Frequency dependence of amorphous silicon schottky diodes for large-area rectification applications," in *Proc. 70th Device Res. Conf.*, Jun. 18–20, 2012, pp. 117–118.

Warren Rieutort-Louis (S'12) received the B.A. (Hons.) and M.Eng. degrees in electrical and information engineering from Trinity College, Cambridge University, Cambridge, U.K. in 2009 and the M.A. degree in electrical engineering from Princeton University, Princeton, NJ, USA, in 2012, where he is currently working toward the Ph.D. degree.

His research interests include thin-film materials, processes, devices and circuits for large-area electronic systems, as well as the development of hybrid thin-film/complementary metal–oxide semiconductor systems.

Mr. Rieutort-Louis received an IBM Ph.D. Fellowship and the Andlinger Center Maeder Fellowship in Energy and the Environment. He is a Graduate Teaching Fellow with the Princeton McGraw Center for Teaching and Learning.

Liechao Huang (S'12) received the B.S. degree in microelectronics from Fudan University, Shanghai, China, in 2010 and the M.A. degree in electrical engineering from Princeton University, NJ, USA, in 2012, where he is currently working toward the Ph.D. degree.

His research interests include thin-film circuit design for power, radio and sensing interfaces, complementary metal–oxide semiconductor (CMOS) analog and mixed signal design for sensing interfaces and power management and hybrid system design combining thin-film circuits and CMOS integrated circuits.

Mr. Huang received a 2010-2011 Princeton Fellowship.

Yingzhe Hu (S'12) received the B.S. degrees in both physics and microelectronics from Peking University, Beijing, China, in 2009 and the M.A. degree in electrical engineering from Princeton University, Princeton, NJ, USA, in 2011, where he is currently working toward the Ph.D. degree.

His research interests include thin-film circuit and integrated circuit hybrid sensing system design and analog and mixed signal design for sensing interfaces.

Mr. Hu received a 2013 Qualcomm Innovation Fellowship.

Josue Sanz-Robinson received the B.Eng. degree in electrical engineering (Hons.) from McGill University, Montreal, QC, Canada, in 2010 and the M.A. degree in electrical engineering from Princeton University, Princeton, NJ, USA, in 2012, where he is currently working toward the Ph.D. degree in electrical engineering.

His research interests include amorphous/nanocrystalline silicon rectifying diodes and sensors for flexible large-area electronic systems.

Mr. Sanz-Robinson received a 2013 Qualcomm Innovation Fellowship.

Sigurd Wagner (SM'78–F'00) received the Ph.D. degree from the University of Vienna, Vienna, Austria, in 1968.

He was a Postdoctoral Fellow with Ohio State University, Columbus, OH, USA. From 1970 to 1978, he was with the Bell Telephone Laboratories, working on semiconductor memories and heterojunction solar cells, and from 1978 to 1980, he was the Chief of the Photovoltaic Research Branch of the Solar Energy Research Institute (now NREL), Golden, CO, USA. Since 1980, he has been a Professor of electrical engineering, Princeton University, Princeton, NJ, USA, developing materials, processes, and components for flexible large-area electronics, electrotextiles, and electronic skin. He is currently working on backplanes using amorphous and nanocrystalline silicon on plastic and steel foil substrates, elastomeric interconnects and circuit boards, flexible permeation barriers and gate dielectrics, and functional cells for flexible electronics.

Dr. Wagner is a Fellow of the American Physical Society. He received the Nevill Mott Prize "for his groundbreaking research, both fundamental and applied, on amorphous semiconductors as well as chalcopyrites" in 2009.

James C. Sturm (S'81–M'85–SM'95–F'01) received the B.S.E. degree in electrical engineering and engineering physics from Princeton University, Princeton, NJ, USA, and the M.S.E.E and Ph.D. degrees in electrical engineering from Stanford University, Stanford, CA, USA, in 1981 and 1985, respectively.

He was with Intel Corporation as Microprocessor Design Engineer, as well as with Siemens, Munich, Germany. He has been with the Faculty of Princeton University since 1986, where he is currently a Professor of electrical engineering and PRISM Director. During 1994–1995, he was a von Humboldt Fellow with the Institüt Für Halbleitertechnik, University of Stuttgart, Stuttgart, Germany. He has worked in the fields of silicon-based heterojunctions, 3-D integration, silicon-on-insulator, optical interconnects, TFT's, and organic light-emitting diodes. His current research interests include silicon–germanium–carbon and related heterojunctions on silicon, SOI, and 3-D integration, large-area electronics, flat-panel displays, organic semiconductors, and the nanotechnology–biology interface.

Dr. Sturm is a member of the American Physical Society and the Materials Research Society. Formerly, he was a National Science Foundation Presidential Young Investigator. He received ten awards for teaching excellence from both Princeton University and the Keck Foundation and received the President's Distinguished Teaching Award at Princeton in 2004. In 1996 and 1997, he was the Technical Program Chair and General Chair of the IEEE Device Research Conference, for which he is now a charter trustee. He served on the organizing committee of IEDM (1988–1992 and 1997–1999), having chaired both the Solid-State Device and Detectors/Sensors/Displays committees. In 2005, he was named the William and Edna Macaleer Professor of Engineering and Applied Science. He also has been a symposium organizer for the Materials Research Society and on the SOS/SOI, EMC, and several other conference committees. He was the organizing Chair for ISTDM 2006.

Naveen Verma (S'03–M'09) received the B.A.Sc. degree in electrical and computer engineering from the University of British Columbia, Vancouver, BC, Canada, in 2003 and the M.S. and Ph.D. degrees in electrical engineering from the Massachusetts Institute of Technology, Cambridge, MA, USA, in 2005 and 2009, respectively.

Since July 2009, he has been an Assistant Professor of electrical engineering with Princeton University, Princeton, NJ, USA. His research interests include advanced sensing systems, including low-voltage digital logic and SRAMs, low-noise analog instrumentation and data-conversion, large-area sensing arrays based on flexible electronics, and low-energy algorithms for embedded inference, especially for medical applications.

Dr. Verma received/co-received the 2006 DAC/ISSCC Student Design Contest Award, the 2008 ISSCC Jack Kilby Paper Award, the 2012 Princeton Innovation Forum First Prize, the 2012 Alfred Rheinstein Princeton Junior Faculty Award, the 2013 NSF CAREER Award, and the 2013 Intel Early Career Award.

The Comparison of $(Ag,Cu)(In,Ga)Se_2$ and $Cu(In,Ga)Se_2$ Thin Films Deposited by Three-Stage Coevaporation

Lei Chen, JinWoo Lee, and William N. Shafarman

Abstract—$(Ag,Cu)(In,Ga)Se_2$ and $Cu(In,Ga)Se_2$ thin-films with bandgap $\sim$1.35 eV were deposited by a three-stage elemental co-evaporation process. The depositions were conducted at substrate temperatures of 580 °C and 650 °C to understand the effects of Ag alloying and high growth temperature on material properties. Ag/(Ag+Cu) and Ga/(In+Ga) gradients were observed and were reduced with higher growth temperature. Grain size was quantified and found to be enhanced by Ag and high growth temperature, while film texture showed no significant change with different deposition conditions.

Index Terms—$(Ag,Cu)(In,Ga)Se_2$, Ga gradient, grain size, texture, three-stage deposition.

I. INTRODUCTION

Ag incorporation into the $Cu(In,Ga)Se_2$ alloy is expected to reduce the alloy's melting temperature [1] while widening its bandgap simultaneously. Lower melting temperature than its counterpart $Cu(In,Ga)Se_2$ (CIGS) may produce $(Ag,Cu)(In,Ga)Se_2$ (ACIGS) absorbers with lower defect densities [2] and provide a potential pathway to absorber materials for wide-bandgap solar cells with high performance. Three-stage coevaporation [3] has been adopted for wide-bandgap ACIGS deposition and has achieved higher open-circuit voltage (V_{oc}) while maintaining reasonable short-circuit current (J_{sc}) and fill factor (FF) [4], [5]. In addition, higher growth temperature is also of interest for exploration, as thermal energy can directly affect certain film properties.

This work extends the study on ACIGS and focuses on material properties resulting from three-stage growth at different growth temperatures. This study compares ACIGS and CIGS films deposited at two different substrate temperatures, 580 °C and 650 °C. Films were maintained at nominally the same Ga/(In+Ga) and (Ag+Cu)/(In+Ga) ratios and thickness. Film composition, elemental depth profiles, grain sizes, and crystallography will be examined and compared.

II. EXPERIMENTAL PROCEDURES

ACIGS and CIGS thin films were deposited onto Mo-coated, specialty high-temperature glass (HTG) substrates. The HTG has a higher softening temperature than soda-lime glass but similar composition, especially Na and K. The use of HTG allows substrate temperature (T_{ss}) as high as 650 °C for the purpose of this study without any bending of the glass. The films were deposited by elemental coevaporation with a three-stage deposition process. During deposition, In and Ga were deposited in the first stage, followed by Cu and Ag (when used) during the second stage, and then back to In and Ga for the third stage. Se was evaporated at constant flux throughout the process and its overpressure was maintained with a molar flux rate over six times of the total of all metals. The substrate was at $T_{ss} = 350$ °C during the first stage, while T_{ss} of either 580 °C or 650 °C was used for both the second and third stages. The deposition time of the first and second stages was 20 min and 30 min, respectively, while the third stage was terminated after a ratio of (Ag+Cu)/(In+Ga) $\approx$ 0.85 was reached. The termination point of the third stage was determined by the "end point detection" method [6]. This determines the change in film emissivity as its composition changes from having excess Cu or Cu+Ag at the end of the second stage to being Cu or Cu+Ag deficient during the third stage. The deposition was aimed to produce 2 μm thick films with nominal Ag/(Ag+Cu) = 0 or 0.3, Ga/(In+Ga) = 0.5, and (Ag+Cu)/(In+Ga) = 0.85, which corresponds to bandgap (E_g) $\approx$ 1.30 $-$1.35 eV [7].

The elemental composition of the films was determined by energy dispersive X-ray spectroscopy (EDS) stimulated by an electron source with 20-kV acceleration voltage. Composition depth profiles were characterized by secondary ion mass spectroscopy (SIMS). Films prepared for SIMS measurement were capped by 50 nm thick CdS, deposited by chemical bath deposition. Film morphology was examined by scanning electron microscopy (SEM) at $10\,000\times$ magnification, and the film thickness was measured from its cross section. Films were also structurally studied by X-ray diffraction (XRD) using a Cu $K\alpha$ source and Bragg–Brentano focusing geometry. A broad scan in the range of $10° \leq 2\theta \leq 80°$ with a resolution of $\Delta 2\theta = 0.04°$ and 2 s per step was conducted to assess the film texture. A fine scan of $25° \leq 2\theta \leq 30°$ around the chalcopyrite (112) peak with $\Delta 2\theta = 0.01°$ and 5 s per step was conducted to quantify peak shift and broadening. A constant offset correction [8]

Manuscript received June 14, 2013; accepted July 17, 2013. Date of publication September 16, 2013; date of current version December 16, 2013. This work is supported by the National Science Foundation and the Department of Energy (DOE) under NSF CA No. EEC-1041895.

L. Chen and W. N. Shafarman are with the Department of Physics and Astronomy, University of Delaware, Newark, DE 19716 USA and also with the Institute of Energy Conversion, University of Delaware, Newark, DE 19716 USA (e-mail: Lchenud@udel.edu; wns@udel.edu).

J. Lee is with the Institute of Energy Conversion, University of Delaware, Newark, DE 19716 USA (e-mail: jinwoo@udel.edu).

Color versions of one or more of the figures in this paper are available online at http://ieeexplore.ieee.org.

Digital Object Identifier 10.1109/JPHOTOV.2013.2280471

TABLE I

ELEMENTAL COMPOSITION AND THICKNESS OF ACIGS AND CIGS FILMS
DEPOSITED AT $T_{ss} = 580\,°C$ AND $650\,°C$

Film	T_{ss} [°C]	Ag / (Ag+Cu)	Ga / (In+Ga)	(Ag+Cu) / (In+Ga)	Thickness [μm]
ACIGS	580	0.36	0.54	0.85	1.8
ACIGS	650	0.36	0.59	0.87	1.9
CIGS	580	0	0.54	0.78	1.9
CIGS	650	0	0.53	0.83	2.0

was applied to the d-spacing of each diffraction pattern so that the Mo (110) peaks from all samples align with the Mo (110) peak in ICDD card 00-004-0809 [9]. The background signal and diffraction of the Cu $K\alpha_2$ component were subtracted from the broad scans before peak areas were measured. Chalcopyrite (112) peak profiles obtained from the fine scans were fit, excluding background and Cu $K\alpha_2$ contributions, to evaluate peak position and broadening precisely.

Devices were fabricated based on ACIGS and CIGS films, with 50 nm thick chemical bath deposited CdS, followed by RF sputtered 50 nm thick intrinsic ZnO and 150 nm thick ITO, then by electron-beam evaporated Ni–Al grids. Devices showed 14%–17% efficiency without anti-reflection coating. Further device analysis is underway to understand the effects of Ag alloying and growth temperature on device performance, and the results will be reported separately.

III. RESULTS

A. Elemental Composition

The elemental composition ratios of ACIGS and CIGS films are shown in Table I, as well as film thickness. All films present similar Ga/(In+Ga) and (Ag+Cu)/(In+Ga) ratios.

Based on the elemental depth profile obtained from SIMS, the Ga and Ag ratios through each film are plotted and compared in Fig. 1(a). A typical Ga/(In+Ga) notch profile is presented, consistent with what is widely observed for three-stage CIGS deposition [3], [10]. However, an Ag gradient (as shown in Fig. 1(a)) with opposite profile to Ga is also observed even though the Cu profile is relatively flat (not shown here).

Comparing profiles at two different T_{ss} for ACIGS and CIGS, respectively, in Fig. 1(a), it is evident that the higher growth temperature has enhanced diffusion/reaction to reduce or eliminate the Ga/(In+Ga) and Ag/(Ag+Cu) gradients.

Based on the Ag and Ga composition gradients through the films, bandgaps can be calculated as a function of depth [shown in Fig. 1(b)]. The ACIGS bandgap as a function of Ag/(Ag+Cu) and Ga/(In+Ga) ratios has been obtained by Boyle et al. [7] via empirically fitting measured optical bandgaps of a series of samples with known compositions. From Fig. 1(b), one can see that the actual bandgap gradient, while primarily controlled by the Ga gradient, is less steep in ACIGS than in CIGS, because of the opposite effects of gradients in Ag and Ga.

Fig. 2 shows the Na depth profile of each film, also measured by SIMS. The Na concentrations are similar within a factor of $\sim$2 to 3, and there is no clear correlation with the Ag incorporation or change in T_{ss}. For the films deposited at $T_{ss} = 580\,°C$, the Na concentrations in films on HTG were less than in ACIGS

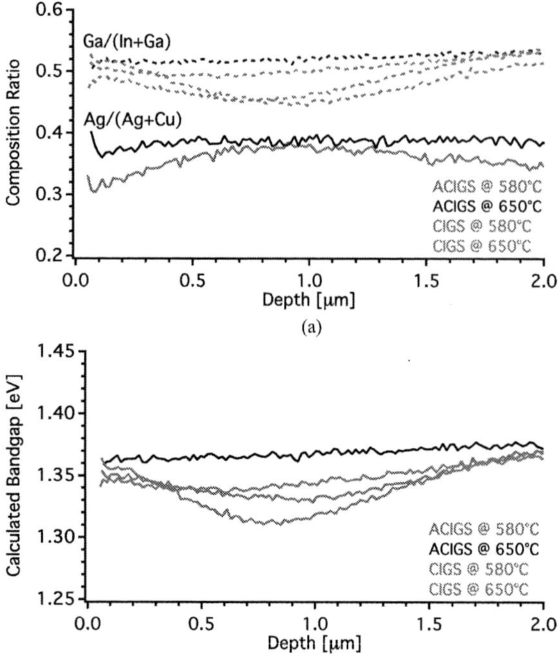

Fig. 1. (a) Composition ratios of Ag/(Ag+Cu) (solid lines) and Ga/(In+Ga) (dashed lines) obtained from SIMS data. (b) Calculated bandgaps based on Ga and Ag gradients.

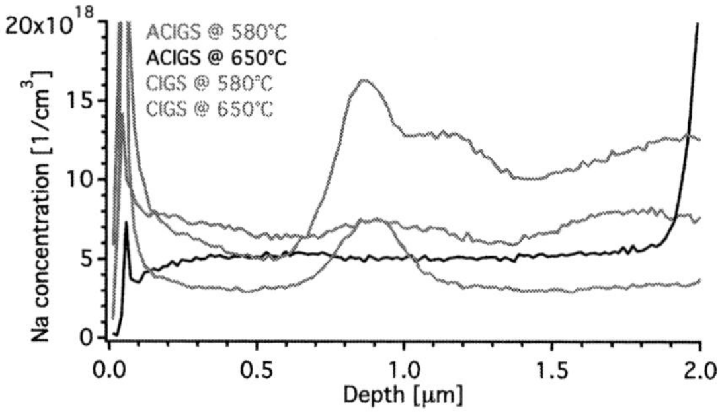

Fig. 2. Na depth profiles in ACIGS and CIGS films deposited at $T_{ss} = 580\,°C$ and $650\,°C$.

or CIGS films deposited, using the same process, on soda-lime glass which typically gives $\sim 2 \times 10^{19}$ cm^{-3}. K concentrations were also measured and were less than Na concentrations by 2 orders of magnitude. Variations in the Na depth profiles, including a peak near the middle of some films, are not understood.

B. Film Morphology and Grain Size

The cross sections of films by SEM show (see Fig. 3) differences in morphology resulting from different growth temperatures and from Ag alloying. Grain sizes were quantified using intercept counting from the cross-sectional images. In this method, the cross sections were examined and 1 or 2 parallel test lines perpendicular to the film growth direction were

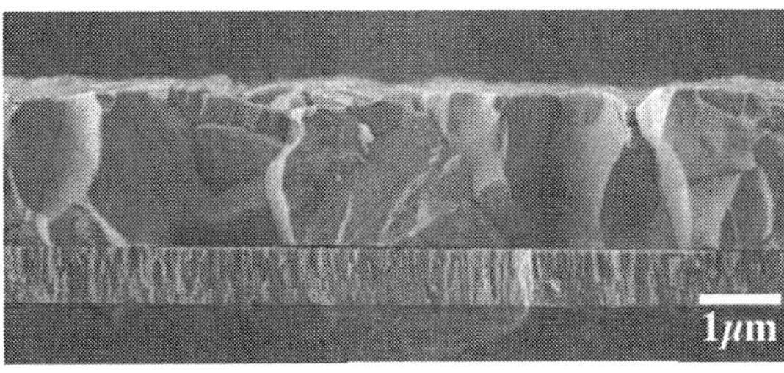

(a)

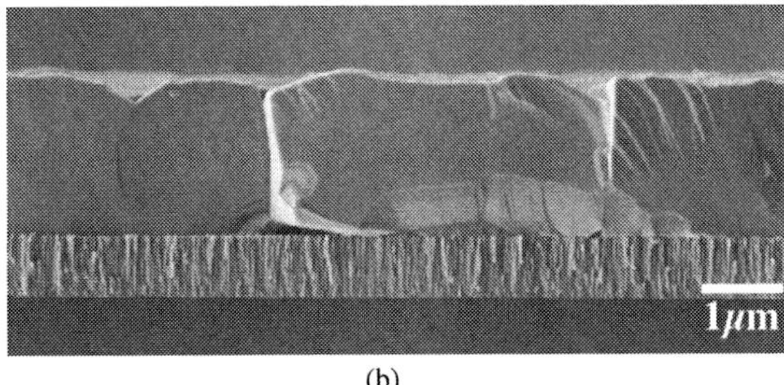

(b)

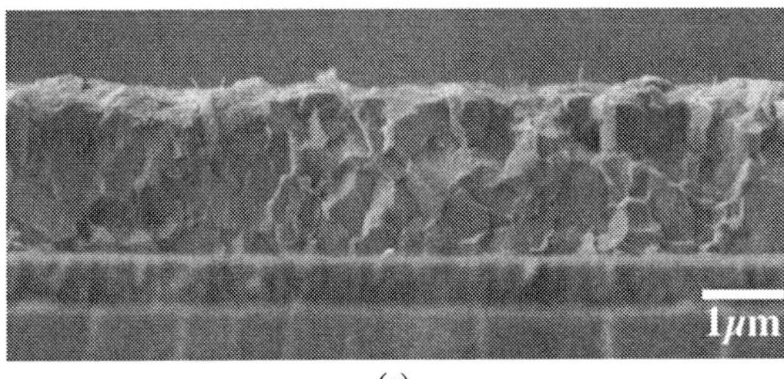

(c)

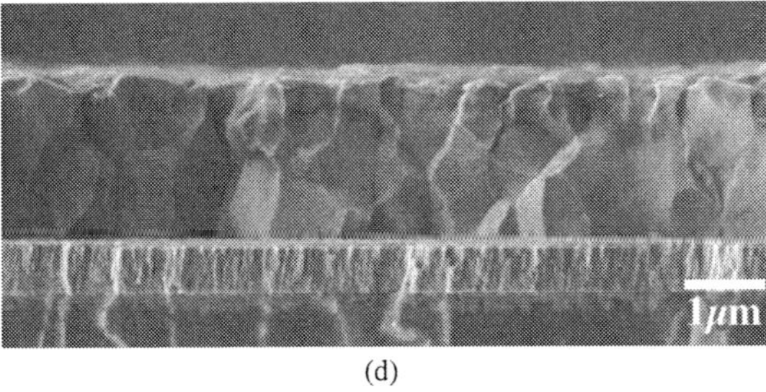

(d)

Fig. 3. Cross-sectional SEM of ACIGS and CIGS films deposited at $T_{ss} =$ 580 °C and 650 °C. The film thickness was measured on these images and shown in Table I. (a) ACIGS at 580 °C. (b) ACIGS at 650 °C. (c) CIGS at 580 °C. (d) CIGS at 650 °C.

drawn through the ACIGS or CIGS layers with lines bisecting or trisecting the layers. Then, the number of intercepts between these lines and grain boundaries was counted. Finally, the average grain size (G) was calculated as $G = L/N$, where L is the total length of test line, and N is the total number of intercepts [11]. To include a statistically significant number of grains, 20 μm long cross-sectional SEM images and ten such images from each film were characterized. In this measurement method, an isotropic grain geometry was assumed.

The results in Table II confirm that higher T_{ss} and Ag alloying both produce larger grain size. Both effects on grain size need to be considered in the context of the three-stage deposition process, especially film growth after the second stage starts, as

TABLE II
CALCULATED AVERAGE GRAIN SIZE (G) OF ACIGS AND CIGS FILMS
DEPOSITED AT $T_{ss} =$ 580 °C AND 650 °C

Sample	G [μm]	ΔG [μm]
ACIGS@580 °C	1.2	0.2
ACIGS@650 °C	2.5	0.4
CIGS@580 °C	0.8	0.1
CIGS@650 °C	1.2	0.2

ΔG is the standard deviation.

Fig. 4. Normalized XRD broad scans of ACIGS and CIGS films deposited at $T_{ss} =$ 580 °C and 650 °C.

neither Ag deposition nor $T_{ss} =$ 580 °C or 650 °C was applied until the beginning of second stage. The grain size that is enhanced by Ag alloying is speculated to be temperature related, as Ag alloying lowers material melting temperature [1].

C. X-ray Diffraction and Film Texture

XRD broad scans, normalized with respect to the chalcopyrite (112) peak in each scan, are shown in Fig. 4. After scans were corrected for d-spacing shift, background and Cu Kα_2 contribution, each peak was assigned according to CuIn$_{0.5}$Ga$_{0.5}$Se$_2$ powder diffraction from ICDD card 00-040-1488 [9]. Both ACIGS and CIGS were peak assigned against the same card since an ACIGS powder diffraction card is currently not available in the ICDD database. Overlapping peaks (220)/(204) and (312)/(116) were not distinguished, while (400)/(008) and (332)/(316) were assigned individually. These overlapping peaks were similarly assigned in the referred power diffraction file. Then diffraction peak areas were measured to calculate the film texture.

The method of Harris [12], [13] was applied to quantify film texture by calculating the orientation parameter, p. Using the chalcopyrite (112) peak as an example here, $p(112)$ is given according to

$$p(112) = N \left[\frac{I(112)}{I_0(112)} \right] \Big/ \sum \left[\frac{I(hkl)}{I_0(hkl)} \right] \qquad (1)$$

where $N = 13$ is the number of peaks observed in the powder diffraction in the 10° to 80° scan range. $I(hkl)$ is the peak area of peak (hkl) generated from the films under study. And $I_0(hkl)$ is the corresponding peak intensity from the CuIn$_{0.5}$Ga$_{0.5}$Se$_2$ powder diffraction file. This assumes proportionality between the peak areas and intensities. Peak area, instead of intensity, was used in the calculation since broadening can originate from

Peaks	Powder	ACIGS@580 °C		ACIGS@650 °C		CIGS@580 °C		CIGS@650 °C	
	I_0	I	p	I	p	I	p	I	p
(112)	100.0	100.0	2.9	100.0	4.7	100.0	1.7	100.0	1.7
(220)(204)	63.0	45.2	2.0	18.6	1.4	99.5	2.7	47.0	1.3
(116)(312)	29.0	4.1	0.4	6.6	1.0	18.7	1.1	13.5	0.8
(400)	5.0	0.0	0.0	1.2	1.1	0.0	0.0	0.0	0.0
(008)	1.0	0.0	0.0	0.0	0.0	1.8	3.0	4.6	7.9
(332)	3.0	8.1	7.7	1.5	2.3	0.0	0.0	0.0	0.0
(316)	7.0	0.0	0.0	3.6	2.4	19.0	4.6	5.0	1.2

I_0 is the intensity of peaks from $CuIn_{0.5}Ga_{0.5}Se_2$ powder diffraction file [9], I is the area of peaks from films under study, and p is the calculated orientation parameter of each peak.

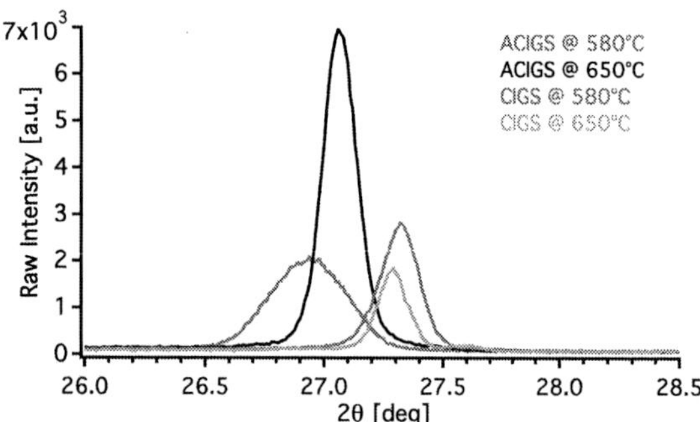

Fig. 5. XRD fine scans of chalcopyrite (112) peaks of ACIGS and CIGS films deposited at T_{ss} = 580 °C and 650 °C.

Sample	Peak Position [°]	d-spacing [Å]	Peak Height [a.u.]	Area	FWHM [°]
ACIGS@580 °C	26.880	3.3142	939	526	0.36
ACIGS@650 °C	26.962	3.3043	4212	874	0.13
CIGS@580 °C	27.262	3.2685	1567	411	0.17
CIGS@650 °C	27.222	3.2733	1158	208	0.12

grain size, stress and composition gradients. The orientation parameter p quantitatively compares grain orientations in the film with that in the powder, such that $p(112) = 1$ means the grains are randomly oriented while $p(112) = 13$ would indicate that only (112) planes are parallel to the film surface.

The peak intensities and orientation parameters are listed in Table III. Overall, there is no significant change of film texture from sample to sample with a small increase in (112) orientation for ACIGS at T_{ss} = 650 °C. In order to further confirm influences on film texture, the texture of the Mo layer underneath ACIGS or CIGS was also determined using the method of Harris. Only slight changes in orientation were determined which could be a result of the position in the Mo sputtering chamber. These changes could not be correlated to the ACIGS or CIGS orientation.

XRD fine scans of the chalcopyrite (112) peaks are shown in Fig. 5 and their peak positions and d-spacings are listed in Table IV. ACIGS crystals have larger lattice constants (i.e., a and/or c in the tetragonal lattice) than CIGS, for similar Ga/(In+Ga) and (Ag+Cu)/(In+Ga) ratios, consistent with what Boyle *et al.* reported [8]. The full-width-at-half-maximum (FWHM) of each peak is slightly larger than the instrumental (112) FWHM of 0.11°. The only exception is the peak of ACIGS at T_{ss} = 580 °C, which shows larger broadening. This can be explained by the fact that 1) the tetragonal lattice constants a and c in CIGS can be considered to linearly increase with *decreased* Ga/(In+Ga) ratio [14], and 2) in ACIGS with Ga/(In+Ga)=0.5, the lattice constant a increases with *increasing* Ag/(Ag+Cu), while the lattice constant c stays nearly constant [8]. Therefore, the opposite Ag/(Ag+Cu) and Ga/(In+Ga) gradients, as shown in the SIMS data (see Fig. 1), could exaggerate the variation in lattice constants and d-spacing. This likely results in the difference in FWHM comparing the ACIGS and CIGS films with T_{ss} = 580 °C. However, it is not possible to rule out other peak broadening mechanisms, such as film stress, until the Ag/(Ag+Cu) gradient effect on d-spacing is quantified.

IV. CONCLUSION

$(Ag,Cu)(In,Ga)Se_2$ and $Cu(In,Ga)Se_2$ films have been grown using a three-stage coevaporation with substrate temperatures of 580 °C and 650 °C. EDS, SIMS, SEM, and XRD techniques were used to characterize material properties. The opposite Ag and Ga gradients were observed resulting from the three-stage process, and high temperature growth has exhibited a force to equilibrate elemental distributions. With the same composition and thickness, both Ag and high temperature growth have shown strong enhancement on grain size, while film texture is nearly unaltered.

ACKNOWLEDGMENT

The authors would like to thank B. McCandless for fruitful discussion, K. Hart and J. Elliott for assistance in sample preparation. Any opinions, findings, and conclusions or recommendations expressed in this material are those of the authors and do not necessarily reflect those of NSF or DOE.

REFERENCES

[1] J. L. Shay and J. H. Wernick, *Ternary Chalcopyrite Semiconductors: Growth, Electronic Properties, and Applications.* New York, NY, USA: Pergamon, 1975.

[2] P. T. Erslev, J. Lee, G. M. Hanket, W. N. Shafarman, and J. D. Cohen, "The electronic structure of $Cu(In_{1-x}Ga_x)Se_2$ alloyed with silver," *Thin Solid Films*, vol. 519, pp. 7296–7299, Aug. 2011.

[3] M. Contreras, J. Tuttle, A. Gabor, A. Tennant, K. Ramanathan, S. Asher, A. Franz, J. Keane, L. Wang, J. Scofield, and R. Noufi, "High efficiency $Cu(In,Ga)Se_2$-based solar cells: Processing of novel absorber structures," in *Proc. IEEE 1st World Conf. Photovolt. Energy Convers.*, Waikoloa, HI, USA, 1994, pp. 68–75.

[4] G. Hanket, J. H. Boyle, and W. N. Shafarman, "Characterization and device performance of $(AgCu)(InGa)Se_2$ absorber layers," in *Proc. 34th IEEE Photovolt. Spec. Conf.*, Philadelphia, PA, USA, 2009, pp. 1240–1245.

[5] G. M. Hanket, J. H. Boyle, W. N. Shafarman, and G. Teeter, "Wide-bandgap $(AgCu)(InGa)Se_2$ absorber layers deposited by three-stage co-evaporation," in *Proc. 35th IEEE Photovolt. Spec. Conf.*, Honolulu, HI, USA, 2010, pp. 3425–3429.

[6] J. Kessler, J. Scholdstrom, and L. Stolt, "Rapid $Cu(In,Ga)Se_2$ growth using "end point detection"," in *Proc. 28th IEEE Photovolt. Spec. Conf.*, Anchorage, AK, USA, 2000, pp. 509–512.

[7] J. Boyle, G. Hanket, and W. Shafarman, "Optical and quantum efficiency analysis of $(Ag,Cu)(In,Ga)Se_2$ absorber layers," in *Proc. 34th IEEE Photovolt. Spec. Conf.*, Philadelphia, PA, USA, 2009, pp. 1349–1354.

[8] J. Boyle, B. McCandless, G. Hanket, and W. Shafarman, "Structural characterization of the $(AgCu)(InGa)Se2$ thin film alloy system for solar cells," *Thin Solid Films*, vol. 519, pp. 7292–7295, Aug. 2011.

[9] *ICDD DDView 4.8.3.4 using PDF-2/Release 2008 RDB 2.0804*, The International Centre for Diffraction Data, Newtown Square, PA, USA, 2008.

[10] A. Gabor, J. Tuttle, M. Bode, A. Franz, A. Tennant, M. Contreras, R. Noufi, D. Jensen, and A. Hermann, "Band-gap engineering in $Cu(In,Ga)Se_2$ thin films grown from $(In,Ga)_2Se_3$ precursors," *Sol. Energ. Mat. Sol. Cells*, vol. 41–42, pp. 247–260, Jun. 1996.

[11] K. J. Kurzydlowski and B. Ralph, *The Quantitative Description of the Microstructure of Materials.* Boca Raton, FL, USA: CRC Press, 1995.

[12] G. Harris, "Quantitative measurement of preferred orientation in rolled uranium bars," *Philos. Mag.*, vol. 43, pp. 113–123, Apr. 1952.

[13] B. E. McCandless, L. V. Moulton, and R. W. Birkmire, "Recrystallization and sulfur diffusion in $CdCl_2$-treated CdTe/CdS thin films," *Prog. Photovolt.: Res. Appl.*, vol. 5, pp. 249–260, Jul. 1997.

[14] D. K. Suri, K. C. Nagpal, and G. K. Chadha, "X-ray study of $CuGa_x In_{1-x}Se_2$ solid solutions," *J. Appl. Crystallogr.*, vol. 22, pp. 578–583, Dec. 1989.

Authors' photographs and biographies not available at the time of publication.

Studying Light-Induced Degradation by Lifetime Decay Analysis: Excellent Fit to Solution of Simple Second-Order Rate Equation

Tine Uberg Nærland, Halvard Haug, Hallvard Angelskår, Rune Søndenå, Erik Stensrud Marstein, and Lars Arnberg

Abstract—Twenty different boron-doped Czochralski silicon materials have been analyzed for light-induced degradation. The carrier lifetime degradation was monitored by an automated quasi-steady-state photoconductance setup with an externally controlled bias lamp for *in-situ* illumination between measurements. Logarithmic plots of the time-resolved lifetime decays clearly displayed the previously reported rapid and slow decays, but a satisfactory fit to a single exponential function could not be achieved. We found, however, that both decay curves, for all the investigated samples, can be fitted very well to the solution of a simple second-order rate equation. This indicates that the defect generation process can be described by second-order reaction kinetics. The new information is used to discuss the role of holes in the defect reaction and the rate-determining steps of the rapid and slow defect reactions.

Index Terms—B–O defects, Czochralski silicon (Cz-Si), light-induced degradation (LID), minority carrier lifetime, rate equations, reaction kinetics.

I. Introduction

BORON-DOPED Czochralski silicon (Cz-Si) is known to be subject to light-induced degradation (LID), decreasing the minority charge carrier lifetime (hereafter lifetime) and thus the solar cell efficiency. It has been shown that a fast initial decay occurs during the first few minutes, while a second slower decay proceeds until lifetime saturation [1], [2]. The two characteristic decays have been reported to be depending on two independent mechanisms, although both mechanisms are related to the si-

multaneous presence of boron and oxygen [1]. According to the Shockley–Read–Hall theory [3], the defect concentration can be directly related to carrier lifetime (τ), provided that the generated defects dominate the recombination behavior.

LID is often described in terms of a normalized defect concentration N_t^* which is related to the measured lifetime by the following equation:

$$N_t^*(t) = \frac{1}{\tau(t)} - \frac{1}{\tau_0} \tag{1}$$

where t is the time, τ_0 is the initial carrier lifetime before LID, and $\tau(t)$ is the carrier lifetime after time t. Upon prolonged illumination at a sufficiently high carrier injection level [4], N_t^* approaches a saturated value $N_{t,\text{sat}}^*$ that has been found to be proportional to the boron concentration and the oxygen concentration squared ($N_{t,\text{sat}}^* \propto [\text{B}]\,[\text{O}]^2$) [5]. A model by Schmidt and Bothe [5], where fast diffusing oxygen dimers capture substitutional boron atoms to form $\text{B}_s\text{–O}_{2i}$ recombination centers, was the first complete model that took this into account and for years this was the prevailing model. In 2009, however, Macdonald *et al.* [6] discovered that in p-type material codoped with boron and phosphorus, where the hole concentration p_0 is smaller than [B], $N_{t,\text{sat}}^*$ was found to be proportional to p_0 and not to [B]. This finding invalidated the model of Schmidt and Bothe, and a new model was later proposed by Voronkov and Falster [7], [8]. In a recent work by Forster *et al.* [9], however, where silicon codoped with boron and gallium was investigated, it was found that the defect concentration was proportional to [B] instead of p_0. Accordingly, how the saturated defect concentration scales with [B] and/or p_0 is still up for debate.

In the model by Voronkov and Falster [7], [8], a latent recombination center is already incorporated in the crystal before carrier injection. According to this model, the centers responsible for the rapid and slow lifetime decays are B_sO_{2i} and B_iO_{2i}, respectively. The reaction model is similar for the two decays, but with some differences. In p-type silicon, the activation of B_sO_{2i} (the defect center responsible for the rapid lifetime decay) is explained through a series of steps where the quadratic proportionality observed between p_0 and lifetime is accounted for by the capture of two holes by a negative latent center (LC_{fast}^-) resulting in the formation of a positive latent center

$$LC_{\text{fast}}^- + 2h^+ \rightarrow LC_{\text{fast}}^+. \tag{2}$$

Manuscript received June 10, 2013; revised August 7, 2013; accepted August 9, 2013. Date of publication August 29, 2013; date of current version September 18, 2013. This work was supported by The Norwegian Research Center for Solar Cell Technology and REC Wafer, REC Solar, Elkem Solar, and the Norwegian Research Council through the KMB project "Defect engineering for crystalline silicon solar cells."

T. U. Nærland is with the Department of Solar Energy, Institute for Energy Technology, Kjeller 2027, Norway, and also with the Department of Material Science and Engineering, Norwegian University of Science and Technology, Trondheim 7491, Norway (e-mail: tine.uberg@gmail.com).

H. Haug, R. Søndenå, and E. S. Marstein are with the Department of Solar Energy, Institute for Energy Technology, Kjeller 2027, Norway (e-mail: Halvard.Haug@ife.no; Rune.Sondeno@ife.no; Erik.Marstein@ife.no).

H. Angelskår is with the Department of Microsystems and Nanotechnology, SINTEF ICT, Oslo 0314, Norway (e-mail: hangelskar@gmail.com).

L. Arnberg is with the Department of Material Science and Engineering, Norwegian University of Science and Technology, Trondheim 7491, Norway (e-mail: lars.arnberg@material.ntnu.no).

Color versions of one or more of the figures in this paper are available online at http://ieeexplore.ieee.org.

Digital Object Identifier 10.1109/JPHOTOV.2013.2278663

The positive latent center is then reconstructed into a transient center (TC_{fast}) by overcoming an energy barrier

$$LC_{\text{fast}}^{+} \xrightarrow{E_{A,1}} TC_{\text{fast}}^{+} \qquad (3)$$

which, due to recharging by injection of electrons, forms a neutral transient center TC_{fast}^{0}

$$TC_{\text{fast}}^{+} + e^{-} \rightarrow TC_{\text{fast}}^{0} \qquad (4)$$

and finally the recombination active center RC_{fast}

$$TC_{\text{fast}}^{0} \xrightarrow{E_{A,2}} RC_{\text{fast}}. \qquad (5)$$

The defect center responsible for the slow lifetime decay also starts from a latent complex, but this time the substitutional boron is replaced by interstitial boron $B_i O_2$. The latent center is now denoted LC_{slow}. In the reaction sequence for the slow decay, the first step is a recharge of the latent center into a neutral state by the assistance of injected minority carriers

$$LC_{\text{slow}}^{+} + e^{-} \rightarrow LC_{\text{slow}}^{0}. \qquad (6)$$

The second step is a temporary recharging to a double positive state by two holes, resulting in a transient center TC_{slow}

$$LC_{\text{slow}}^{0} + 2h^{+} \xrightarrow{E_{A,3}} TC_{\text{slow}}. \qquad (7)$$

The final step is controlled by overcoming a free energy barrier between TC_{slow} and a slow recombination active center RC_{slow} and is thus governed by the attempt frequency and the Boltzmann energy

$$TC_{\text{slow}} \xrightarrow{E_{A,4}} RC_{\text{slow}}. \qquad (8)$$

Voronkov and Falster suggest that in most practical cases, it is the final step that is rate determining for the process [7].

In the work by Schmidt and Bothe [5], [10], the defect generation rate R_{gen}, for both the rapid and the slow decay, has been determined by fitting a single exponential function to the measured lifetime degradation data by the following equation:

$$N_t'(t) = N_0 \left[1 - \exp\left(-kt\right)\right] \qquad (9)$$

where N_t' is the concentration of latent defects, N_0 is the initial latent defect concentration, and k is the rate constant. A rate equation used to describe the defect generation process shows the effect of changing the concentration of the reactant on the rate of the reaction. A fit like this serves as a solution of a first-order rate equation, given by

$$-\frac{dN_t'}{dt} = k\left(N_t'\right). \qquad (10)$$

In [11] and [12], it has, however, been acknowledged that a satisfactory fit between this function and the measured decays is not always obtained. In these works, a double exponential function has been used to fit the lifetime decay data. Such a function can, however, not be directly related to the kinetics of the defect generation reaction and thus gives less physical understanding of the process.

In this study, we show that both the rapid and the slow lifetime decay can be described far better by a second-order rate equation than a first-order rate equation. Information on the defect reaction kinetics extracted from the second-order rate equation fit is used to discuss the rate-determining steps of the rapid and slow defect reactions.

II. Experimental Details

The samples used in this study are boron-doped Cz-Si wafers with a boron concentration ranging from 2×10^{15} to 11×10^{15} cm^{-3}. A boron-doped FZ-Si sample was used as a reference. Prior to the measurements, the wafers were cleaned with RCA [13] and thereafter received a double-side passivation by plasma-enhanced chemical vapor deposited hydrogenated amorphous silicon. The surface recombination velocity is estimated to be below 20 cm/s. In order to ensure that no defect centers are generated before the start of the measurements, the samples were deactivated by an annealing at 200 °C for 15 min on a hotplate in the dark [10] with dummy wafers above and below to avoid contamination.

The normalized B–O defect densities N_t^* were determined by time-resolved lifetime measurements. The lifetime degradation was monitored by an automated quasi-steady-state photoconductance (QSSPC) setup with an externally controlled bias lamp for *in-situ* illumination between measurements. The bias light source was a halogen lamp supplying the sample with an intensity of approximately 50 mW/cm^2. The temperature of the sample was monitored by a resistance temperature detector coupled to the sample stage to ensure that the temperature change of the stage and sample due to illumination by the lamp was too small to significantly influence the measured lifetime. All measurements were performed at $T = 303 \pm 2$ K.

The normalized defect concentration, N_t^*, was calculated from the measured lifetime according to (1). The lifetimes were measured at an injection level corresponding to one-tenth of the doping level for each sample. A doping-independent injection level would be problematic since the doping concentration changes the lifetime dependence on the injection level substantially as seen in Fig. 1.

As an indicator of the mismatch between the measured data and the best fit functions, a calculation of the mean deviation χ^2 was performed (a lower value for χ^2 indicates a better match to the experimental data). χ^2 is defined as

$$\chi^2 = \frac{1}{N} \sum_i \left(\frac{y - y_i}{\sigma_i}\right)^2 \qquad (11)$$

where y is the fitted value for a given point, y_i is the measured data value for the point, and σ_i is the standard deviation of y_i. σ_i is estimated based on algebraic propagation of errors since we do not have multiple repetitions of the measurement for all samples. N is the number of data points minus the number of adjustable coefficients in the fit functions. A Levenberg–Marquardt algorithm is used to search for the minimum value of χ^2 by an iterative process performed by the computer program IGOR [14].

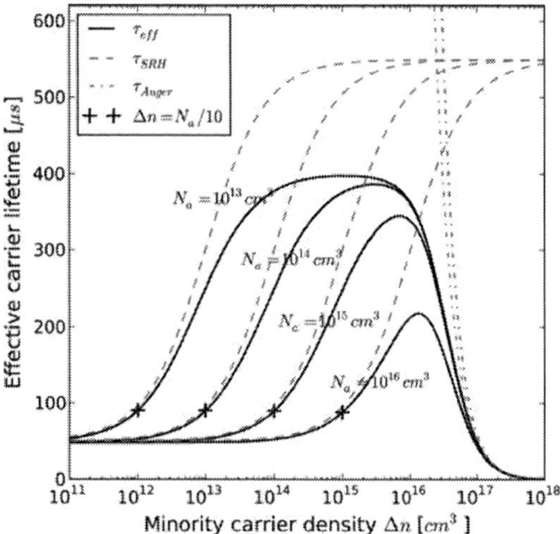

Fig. 1. Simulation showing the impact of the doping concentration on lifetime as a function of carrier injection level. Comparing the lifetime of samples with different doping concentrations measured at a fixed injection level of, e.g., 1×10^{15} may lead to systematic error.

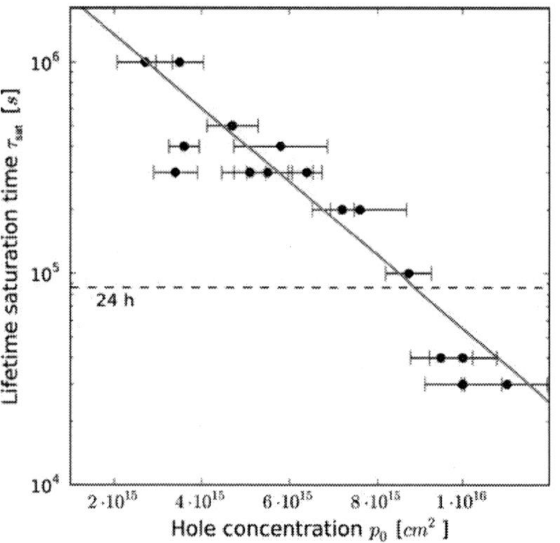

Fig. 2. Time [s] where τ has reached 99% of the total loss as a function of hole concentration. After 24 h, only the samples with a hole concentration above 9×10^{15} cm^{-3} have reached saturation. The red line is a best fit power curve of the data and may serve as an empirical expression predicting the approximate lifetime saturation time t_{sat} in seconds: $t_{\mathrm{sat}} = 9 \times 10^{43} \, [p_0]^{-2.45}$. The oxygen concentration is not measured for all samples but for those that are measured it ranges from 7×10^{17} to 1×10^{18} cm^{-3}. All measurements are performed at $T = 303 \pm 2$ K.

III. RESULTS

Logarithmic plots of the time-resolved lifetime decays clearly display the previously reported rapid and slow decays (see Fig. 3). Other groups have reported that degradation typically occurs during the first hours of illumination [8], [15], [16]. In this study, we experience that only samples with a hole concentration p_0 above 9×10^{15} cm^{-3} saturate within 24 h. This is shown in Fig. 2 where the time where τ has reached 99% of the total lifetime loss is plotted as a function of p_0. Saturation

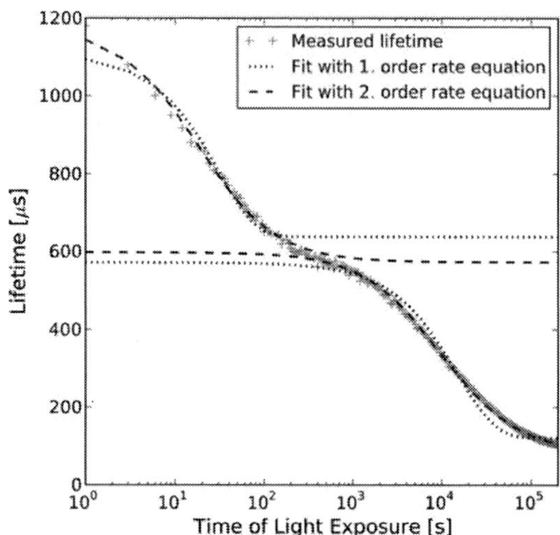

Fig. 3. Plot showing the best fit solutions of two different rate equations for an experimental LID lifetime decay curve.

times were also compared with oxygen concentrations, but no correlation could be seen.

As mentioned in Section I, [11] and [12] commented that the measured decays can be difficult to fit with a single exponential decay, and a double exponential function has, therefore, been used to fit the decay data. In this study, we have found that for both the rapid and the slow decay, for all the investigated samples, a much better fit could be obtained if (10) is replaced by a rate equation of *second* order so that

$$-\frac{dN'_t}{dt} = 2k \left(N'_t\right)^2 . \tag{12}$$

The carrier lifetime as a function of time is then no longer given by an exponential, but as a sigmoidal function on the following form:

$$\tau(t) = \frac{\tau_0 + \tau_\infty \left(\frac{t}{w}\right)}{1 + \left(\frac{t}{w}\right)}. \tag{13}$$

Here, τ_∞ is the defect saturated lifetime and w is the half-life, i.e., the time where the initial lifetime τ_0 is halved

$$w = \frac{1}{2k} \frac{\tau_\infty^2}{\tau_0 - \tau_\infty}. \tag{14}$$

Note that for the slow degradation, τ_0 is in fact the lifetime where the rapid degradation has saturated. A full derivation of (13) from the second-order rate equation is given in the Appendix.

An example showing the best fit curves from the solutions of the first-order (9) and second-order (13) rate equations is given in Fig. 3.

Fig. 4(a) and (b) shows a comparison of the χ^2 values of the fit using the first- and second-order rate equations for the rapid and the slow decays, respectively. The χ^2 values are given as a function of the initial lifetime τ_0 before any light exposure for each sample. χ^2 is increasing with initial lifetime for both the rapid and the slow decay. This is mainly because we need a large dynamic injection range through the entire lifetime decay.

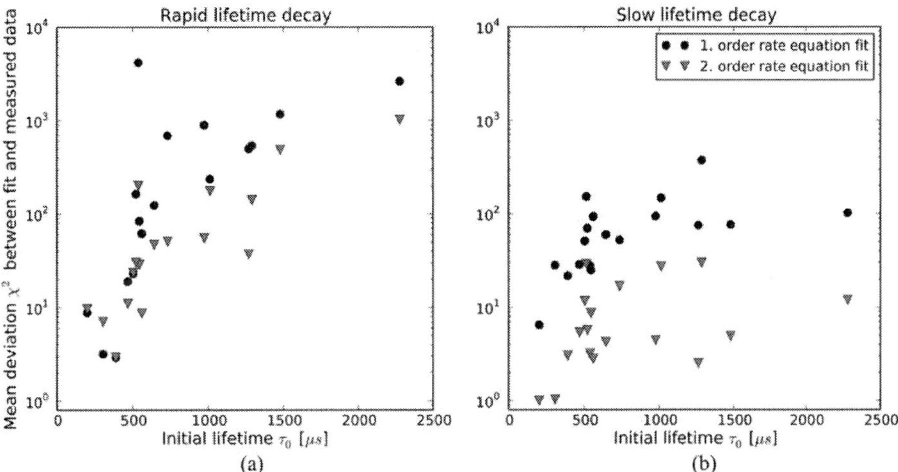

Fig. 4. Mean deviation χ^2 for the two different fit functions is plotted for each sample as a function of initial lifetime before light exposure. (a) Rapid lifetime decay. (b) Slow lifetime decay.

High lifetime samples have a larger lifetime span from start to end, and therefore, the scatter in the lifetime against injection level becomes larger.

For the slow lifetime decay [see Fig. 4(b)], the mean deviation χ^2 is substantially lower for the second-order fit compared with the first-order fit for all investigated samples. This is also true for the rapid lifetime decay [see Fig. 4(a)] except for the samples with the lowest initial lifetimes. This is the region of the plot where the initial lifetime is low and a hypothesis is that the initial lifetime of these samples is limited by some other defect, and that the presence of this defect influences the kinetics of the rapid lifetime decay.

Comparisons of the χ^2 values for the rapid and the slow decay show that χ^2 is in general higher for the rapid decay fits. This is because the number of data points is limited. More measurements during the rapid decay will alter the outcome since the lifetime, at this point, is sensitive to even the short flash from the QSSPC measurement (<1 s).

The half-width w in (14) is the time responsible for 50% of the lifetime degradation. Accordingly, this parameter reveals information on the kinetics of the generation process. In Fig. 5, the half-width of the slow decay is plotted as a function of p_0 for the investigated samples. The plot indicates an approximate quadratic decrease of the half-width with p_0 using the exponent as a free parameter. Lifetime decay analysis has also been performed on a set of compensated p-type boron- and phosphorous-doped Cz-Si samples and the results showed that w for these samples falls far outside the indicated trend lines indicated in Fig. 5 when plotted against $[B_s]$ instead of p_0. Hence, the results from this investigation point toward a correlation between the kinetics of the defect reaction rate and p_0 rather than $[B_s]$. This is in accordance with the work of Macdonald et al. [6].

Oxygen concentration measurements performed by Fourier transform infrared spectroscopy were performed on a selection of the samples. No correlation between the oxygen concentration and the half-width w could be seen, indicating that the oxygen is not playing a role on the kinetics of the defect

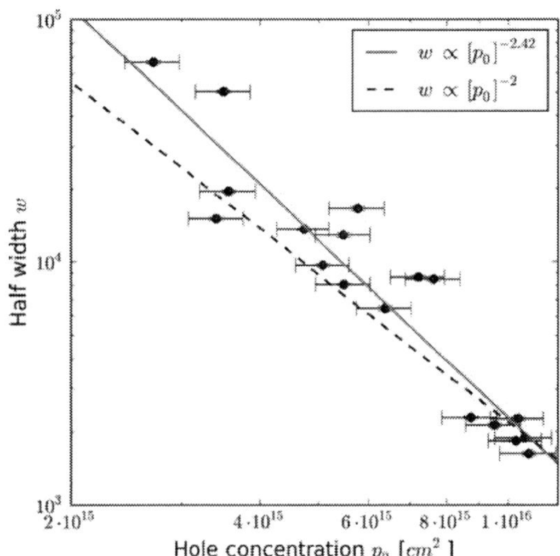

Fig. 5. Half-width w for all measured slow lifetime decays as a function of the hole concentration. For the best fit power curve (solid line), w is proportional to $[p_0]^{-2.42}$. The function corresponding to a decrease proportional to $[p_0]^{-2}$ is indicated by the dashed line.

generation. This is in accordance with the work by Bothe and Schmidt [10].

IV. DISCUSSION

A. Second-Order Reaction Kinetics

The purpose of a kinetic study is to obtain information concerning the reaction mechanism. Agreement between a specific rate equation and the experimental data is then consistent with, but not a proof of, that type of reaction. The second-order rate equation used to describe the lifetime degradation in this study shows that the rate of the reaction is changing with the square of the latent defect concentration $[N_t']^2$. A second-order rate equation often indicates that two species of the same type react

    115

together to form one product species. The rate equation of a reaction with a multistep mechanism cannot, however, in general, be deduced from the stoichiometric coefficients of the overall reaction. The equation may involve fractional exponential coefficients, or it may depend on the concentration of an intermediate species. Nevertheless, the fit to the LID decay by a second-order rate equation might indicate that two defect species of the same kind react in the process of forming the recombination active defect. It is then the concentration of these reactants that acts as N_t' and is depleted during the course of the reaction. The full reaction still involves steps where holes and electrons play a role, and the complete picture of the defect generation process is still missing.

A conclusion we can draw, however, is that a reaction between two individual reactant molecules of different species cannot be the case, as the solution of a second-order rate equation with two different reactants cannot fit the measured data.

B. Role of p_0

From Fig. 5, we saw that for the slow lifetime decay, there is a correlation between the half-life w and the hole concentration p_0. According to (14), w is inversely proportional to k and proportional to $(\tau_\infty^2/\tau_0 - \tau_\infty)$. In our analysis, we do not find any correlation between p_0 and $(\tau_\infty^2/\tau_0 - \tau_\infty)$. We, therefore, conclude that it is mainly k that is influenced by p_0, giving $k \propto p_0^n$, with n being between 2 and 2.5. This opens up the possibility of two potential roles of p_0 in the defect reaction. The first scenario is that p_0 is embedded in the rate constant as an additional reactant, and that k acts as a pseudorate constant for instance as $k = p_0^2 k'$, where k' is the actual rate constant. A requirement for embedding a reactant in a pseudorate constant in this way is that its concentration must not change during the reaction, i.e., it must be in great excess ($p_0 \gg N_t'$). p_0 is commonly occurring in the order of 1×10^{15} to 1×10^{17} cm^{-3} in boron-doped silicon and N_0 is estimated to be less than 1×10^{13} cm^{-3} [17]; hence, the requirement is met. Note that a reactant embedded in the pseudorate constant still influences the rate of the reaction, but it means that the second-order kinetics is describing changes in N_t' exclusively. We can, of course, not rule out that there are other reactants embedded in k, meaning that we cannot exclude other reactants as contributors to the defect. They must, however, also be in great excess.

The other possible explanation for the role of p_0 in the defect reaction is for p_0 to act as a catalyst. This hypothesis can be regarded to support the model of Voronkov *et al.*, presented in Section I, in the sense that they propose that there are two activation barriers for each decay that must be overcome in order to complete the defect. A catalyst will thus work to decrease the activation barrier between one of the intermediate steps in the reaction and thereby decrease the half-width of the degradation decay with increased catalyst concentration. Note that the first explanation model where p_0 is embedded in a pseudorate constant does not contradict Voronkov's model. Several groups have already reported the involvement of two holes/two boron atoms in the reaction kinetics [5]–[9].

C. Rate-Determining Step

The measured overall rate of a reaction is controlled by the rate of the slowest step, the rate-determining step. The rate constant, k, will thus be designated this particular step. According to the data in Fig. 5 and the discussion in Section IV-B, k is strongly correlated with p_0. Relating this to the slow defect reaction model by Voronkov *et al.* [7], [8], summarized in Section I, these results point towards step 2 (7) as the rate-determining step. This, however, contradicts the suggestion by Voronkov *et al.*, which proposes the last step as rate limiting. Step 1 (6) can under any circumstances not be rate-determining since the rate of the defect reaction is independent of Δn [4].

For the fast defect, the reaction steps 1–3, described in (2)–(4), can all be excluded as rate-determining steps because of step 3. In this step, the presence of excess electrons cause a shift of the electron quasi-Fermi level across the energy level of the defect center in its passive state [4], [10]. This cannot be the rate-determining step [4], but it also means that none of the earlier steps can be rate determining since the reaction does not start until the excess carriers are present.

V. Conclusion

A range of boron-doped Cz-Si materials have been analyzed with regard to LID. Curve fitting of the measured data to a single exponential (the solution of a first order rate equation) was attempted, but a much better fit was achieved by a solution of a second-order rate equation indicating that the defect generation process can be described by second-order reaction kinetics. The rate equation describing our system shows that the rate of the reaction is changing with the square of the latent defect concentration $N_t'^2$. The concentration of holes is identified to control the half-life of the degradation process and is either playing the role of reactant in excess or catalyst.

Appendix

Derivation of (7) From the Second-Order Rate Equation

Initial arguments:

$$N_0 = N_t^* + N_t' = \text{constant} \tag{15}$$

$$
\begin{aligned}
t = 0 &: \ N_t^* = 0, N_t' = N_0 \\
t = \infty &: \ N_t^* = N_0, N_t' = 0
\end{aligned}
\tag{16}
$$

where N_0 is the initial latent defect concentration, N_t^* is the concentration of generated defects, and N_t' is the concentration of latent defects. N_0 is equal to saturated defect concentration, which can be calculated in the following way:

$$N_0 = N_{t,\text{sat}}^* = \frac{1}{\tau_\infty} - \frac{1}{\tau_0}. \tag{17}$$

From the initial arguments and (1), we obtain the following relation:

$$N_t'(t) = N_0 - N_t^* = \frac{1}{\tau_\infty} - \frac{1}{\tau(t)}. \tag{18}$$

A second-order rate equation is a simple differential equation

$$-\frac{dN_t'}{dt} = 2k \left(N_t'\right)^2 . \tag{19}$$

Using the boundary conditions in (16), the solution becomes

$$N_t'(t) = \frac{1}{\frac{1}{N_0} + 2kt} . \tag{20}$$

Inserting for $N_t'(t)$ from (15) gives

$$N_t^*(t) = N_0 - \frac{1}{\frac{1}{N_0} + 2kt} \tag{21}$$

and inserting for N_0 (17) and $N_t^*(t)$ (1) in (21) gives the final result

$$\tau(t) = \frac{\tau_0 + \tau_\infty \left(\frac{t}{w}\right)}{1 + \left(\frac{t}{w}\right)} \tag{22}$$

where w is defined as

$$w = 2k \frac{\tau_\infty^2}{\tau_0 - \tau_\infty} . \tag{23}$$

This expression can be successfully fitted to both the rapid and the slow lifetime degradation decay for all investigated samples.

ACKNOWLEDGMENT

The authors would like to acknowledge B. R. Olaisen for making the program that performed the automatic time-resolved LID measurements with the QSSPC setup. They would also like to acknowledge Prof. S. Kjelstrup, with the Norwegian University of Science and Technology, for the valuable discussions on rate equations.

REFERENCES

[1] K. Bothe and J. Schmidt, "Fast-forming boron-oxygen-related recombination center in crystalline silicon," *Appl. Phys. Lett.*, vol. 87, pp. 262108-1–262108-3, 2005.

[2] J. S. H. Nagal, A. G. Aberle, and R. Hezel, "Exceptionally high bulk minority-carrier lifetimes in block-cast multicrystalline silicon," in *Proc. 14th Eur. Photovoltaic Solar Energy Conf.*, 1997, pp. 762–765.

[3] W. Shockley and W. T. Read, "Statistics of the recombination of holes and electrons," *Phys. Rev.*, vol. 87, pp. 835–842, 1952.

[4] T. U. Naerland, H. Angelskar, and E. S. Marstein, "Direct monitoring of minority carrier density during light induced degradation in Czochralski silicon by photoluminescence imaging," *J. Appl. Phys.*, vol. 113, pp. 193707-1–193707-7, 2013.

[5] J. Schmidt and K. Bothe, "Structure and transformation of the metastable boron- and oxygen-related defect center in crystalline silicon," *Phys. Rev. B*, vol. 69, pp. 024107-1–024107-8, 2004.

[6] D. Macdonald, F. Rougieux, A. Cuevas, B. Lim, J. Schmidt, M. Di Sabatino, and L. J. Geerligs, "Light-induced boron-oxygen defect generation in compensated p-type Czochralski silicon," *J. Appl. Phys.*, vol. 105, pp. 093704-1–093704-7, 2009.

[7] V. V. Voronkov and R. Falster, "Latent complexes of interstitial boron and oxygen dimers as a reason for degradation of silicon-based solar cells," *J. Appl. Phys.*, vol. 107, pp. 053509-1–053509-8, 2010.

[8] V. V. Voronkov, R. Falster, K. Bothe, B. Lim, and J. Schmidt, "Lifetime-degrading boron-oxygen centres in p-type and n-type compensated silicon," *J. Appl. Phys.*, vol. 110, pp. 063515-1–063515-7, 2011.

[9] M. Forster, E. Fourmond, F. E. Rougieux, A. Cuevas, R. Gotoh, K. Fujiwara, S. Uda, and M. Lemiti, "Boron-oxygen defect in Czochralski-silicon co-doped with gallium and boron," *Appl. Phys. Lett.*, vol. 100, pp. 042110-1–042110-4, 2012.

[10] K. Bothe and J. Schmidt, "Electronically activated boron-oxygen-related recombination centers in crystalline silicon," *J. Appl. Phys.*, vol. 99, pp. 013701-1–013701-11, 2006.

[11] H. Hashigami, Y. Itakura, and T. Saitoh, "Effect of illumination conditions on Czochralski-grown silicon solar cell degradation," *J. Appl. Phys.*, vol. 93, pp. 4240–4245, 2003.

[12] S. Rein, *Lifetime Spectroscopy: A Method of Defect Characterization in Silicon for Photovoltaic Applications.* Berlin, Germany: Springer-Verlag, 2005, p. 422.

[13] W. Kern, "The evolution of silicon wafer cleaning technology," *J. Electrochem. Soc.*, vol. 137, pp. 1887–1892, Jun. 1, 1990.

[14] *IGOR Pro 6*, WaveMetrics, Inc., Tigard, OR, USA, 2013.

[15] S. W. Glunz, S. Rein, W. Warta, J. Knobloch, and W. Wettling, "On the degradation of Cz-silicon solar cells," presented at the 2nd World Conf. Photovoltaic Energy Convers., Vienna, Austria, 1998.

[16] J. Schmidt, "Light-induced degradation in crystalline silicon solar cells," *Solid State Phenomena*, vol. 95–96, pp. 187–196, 2004.

[17] V. Voronkov, R. Falster, K. Bothe, and B. Lim, "Light-induced lifetime degradation in boron-doped Czochralski silicon: Are oxygen dimers," presented at the Silicon PV, Hamelin, Germany, 2013.

Authors' photographs and biographies not available at the time of publication.

Gettering of Iron in Silicon Solar Cells With Implanted Emitters

Ville Vähänissi, Antti Haarahiltunen, Marko Yli-Koski, and Hele Savin

Abstract—We present here experimental results on the gettering of iron in Czochralski-grown silicon by phosphorus implantation. The gettering efficiency and the gettering mechanisms in a high resistivity implanted emitter are determined as a function of both initial iron level and gettering anneal. The results show that gettering in implanted emitters can be efficient if precipitation at the emitter is activated. This requires low gettering temperatures and/or high initial contamination level. The fastest method to getter iron from the bulk is to rapidly nucleate iron precipitates before the gettering anneal. Here, this was achieved by a fast ramp to the room temperature in between the implantation anneal and the gettering anneal.

Index Terms—Gettering, ion implantation, iron, photovoltaic cells, silicon.

I. Introduction

ION implantation has been widely used in integrated circuit processing. However, it has not raised much interest in the photovoltaic community until recently. The benefits of implantation, such as better process control and fewer processing steps compared with conventional doping techniques [1]–[3], have started to intrigue also the silicon solar cell industry. After all, implantation could provide a great opportunity to reach the ultimate goal: fabrication of low-cost high-efficiency solar cells.

Because of economic reasons, the purity of the silicon feedstock used in photovoltaics is much lower than in integrated circuit industry [4]. Therefore, the high gettering efficiency (GE) [5]–[8] provided by the conventional diffused phosphorus emitter is a great benefit in solar cell processing. There are not many studies on the GE obtained by implanted emitters [9] and even fewer where the GEs of diffused and implanted emitters are directly compared. Implanted emitters have typically lower phosphorus concentration, which is likely to decrease the GE. However, more interesting is the possible role of the electrically inactive phosphorus [10]–[12], which is present after diffusion but not after implantation.

Our goal here is to study the gettering behavior of iron in silicon by phosphorus implantation with well-defined iron concentration levels and varying gettering anneals. In addition to determining the obtainable GE with an implanted emitter, we also study the prevailing mechanisms behind the implantation gettering and compare both the GE and the mechanisms with conventional diffused emitters with higher phosphorus concentration.

II. Experimental Details

In the experiments, p-type silicon wafers with a thickness of 400 μm, a resistivity of 2.7–3.0 $\Omega\cdot$cm, and a low initial oxygen level (7–9 ppma) were intentionally contaminated to two different iron levels: 1) 1×10^{13} cm^{-3} (medium) and 2) 2×10^{14} cm^{-3} (high). The samples are noted as *medium-Fe* and *high-Fe* later on. The contamination was done by a procedure which is described in more detail in [5]. After contamination a 31-nm-thick screen oxide was grown on the wafers at 1000 °C to protect the wafers from low energy debris and to reduce implantation induced damage and channeling [13]. Next, phosphorus with a dose of 1×10^{15} cm^{-2} and energy of 50 keV was implanted on one side of the wafers to form the emitter. Then, the screen oxide was removed in diluted hydrofluoric acid solution and the wafers were cleaned in a sequence of SC-1, SC-2, and HF-dip.

After cleaning, the wafers were annealed at 1000 °C for 30 min to activate the implant and to remove the implantation damage, oxidized at 1000 °C for 10 min to passivate the back surface, and cooled at the rate of 4 K/min down to the gettering anneal temperature. Four different gettering anneals were used. Gettering anneals A through C followed the implantation anneal directly. In gettering anneal D, the wafers were rapidly cooled down to the room temperature, i.e., pulled out from the furnace at 895 °C, after the implantation anneal and then loaded again into the furnace at the gettering temperature 620 °C. Temperatures and times of the gettering anneals are presented in Table I.

After gettering anneals, the back side of the wafers was protected by photoresist. This was followed by the removal of the front side oxide in buffered HF. Then, the sheet resistance of the emitter was measured with four-point probe. The obtained sheet resistance values are presented in Table I.

TABLE I
TEMPERATURES AND TIMES OF THE GETTERING ANNEALS AND THE RESULTING SHEET RESISTANCES

Group	Temperature profile	R_s [$\Omega/\square$]
A	2 h at 800°C	96
B	3.5 h at 750°C	94
C	8 h at 620°C	94
D	pullout at 895°C + 8 h at 620°C	85

Manuscript received June 9, 2013; revised August 2, 2013 and September 15, 2013; accepted October 8, 2013. Date of publication October 30, 2013; date of current version December 16, 2013. This work was supported by the Finnish National Technology Agency, Academy of Finland, Okmetic Oyj, and Semilab Inc. The work of V. Vähänissi was supported by the Walter Ahlström Foundation and the Graduate School in Electronics, Telecommunications, and Automation.

The authors are with the Department of Micro and Nanosciences, Aalto University, 02150 Espoo, Finland (e-mail: ville.vahanissi@aalto.fi; antti.haarahiltunen@aalto.fi; marko.yli-koski@aalto.fi; hele.savin@aalto.fi).

Color versions of one or more of the figures in this paper are available online at http://ieeexplore.ieee.org.

Digital Object Identifier 10.1109/JPHOTOV.2013.2285961

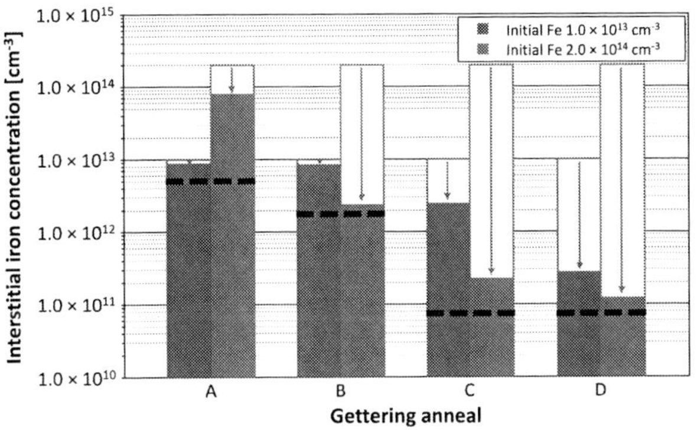

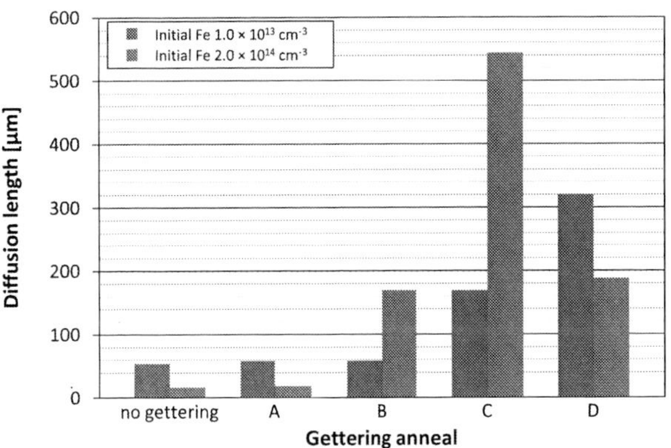

Fig. 1. Measured interstitial iron concentration in the bulk after different gettering anneals. The error estimate of the interstitial iron concentration value is $\pm 2\%$ when iron concentration is below 1×10^{12} cm^{-3} and $\pm 4\%$ when iron concentration is above 1×10^{12} cm^{-3}. The solid solubility of iron at the gettering anneal temperature [14], [15] is marked with a dotted line.

Fig. 2. Measured minority carrier diffusion length prior to dissociating the Fe$_i$B$_s$-pairs in the same samples as in Fig. 1.

Interstitial iron concentration in the wafer bulk was measured using the surface photovoltage (SPV) method, which is well known to measure accurately interstitial iron at low concentrations. The measurement procedure is described in more detail in [5]. In addition, total iron concentration in the phosphorus-doped layer was measured by secondary ion mass spectrometry (SIMS) in selected samples.

Finally, the following supplementary experiments were performed in order to obtain more information about the where-abouts of the gettered iron and the prevailing gettering mechanisms. In the first experiment, some wafers were processed identically to the sample set D but excluding the phosphorus implantation. This means that the samples had no emitter but they experienced the implantation anneal and gettering anneal D. In the second experiment, from some wafers, both the front and back surfaces were removed by etching approximately 23 μm of silicon. The etching was done in a CH$_3$COOH:HF:HNO$_3$ solution. Then, the wafers were annealed at 1000 °C, which is higher than the applied iron in-diffusion temperature, for 20 min, followed by fast cooling. The purpose of the anneal was to dissolve the possible remaining iron in the bulk to the interstitial form. After the dissolution, the interstitial bulk iron concentration was again measured by SPV.

III. RESULTS

A. Gettering Efficiency

Fig. 1 shows a summary of the measured interstitial iron concentration in the bulk after different gettering anneals. At the medium initial iron level (blue columns), the GE is really low with the anneals A and B, but a clear improvement is obtained with the anneal C at lower temperature. Intriguingly, anneal D results in remarkably higher GE than the other anneals.

At the high initial iron level (red columns), the GE is high even with the anneal A and strongly increases with lowering gettering temperature (anneals B and C). Already with the anneal B, the remaining interstitial iron concentration in the high-Fe wafer is below the level of the medium-Fe wafer, and with the anneal C,

the inversion gets even bigger. With the high initial iron level, the difference between anneal C and anneal D is not as high as with the medium initial level. Nonetheless, also with the high initial iron level, anneal D is the most efficient one, and again, there is less interstitial iron left than in the similarly treated medium-Fe wafer.

Fig. 2 presents the minority carrier diffusion length prior to dissociating the Fe$_i$B$_s$-pairs in the corresponding samples. Note that the wafers are not standard lifetime references, but they still have the emitter present when they are measured by SPV. After anneals A through C the diffusion length behavior is in agreement with the measured interstitial iron concentration, i.e., the lower the interstitial iron concentration in the bulk, the longer the diffusion length. However, after anneal D, the diffusion length is in contradiction with the interstitial iron concentration. In the high-Fe wafer, the diffusion length is clearly worse after anneal D, even though the interstitial iron concentration is lower than after anneal C. With the medium iron level the diffusion length after anneal D is significantly better than after anneal C, but it is not as high as one might expect. The measured interstitial iron concentration after anneal D in medium-Fe wafer is equal to high-Fe wafer after anneal C, but the diffusion length is almost a factor of 2 lower.

B. Phosphorus and Iron Profiles

Phosphorus and iron profiles near the wafer surface measured by SIMS from the high-Fe and medium-Fe wafers after gettering anneal C are depicted in Fig. 3. The phosphorus profile is roughly identical in all of our samples since phosphorus diffusion is negligible during the low-temperature gettering anneals, and the ion implantation and the implantation anneal parameters were kept constant. The measured sheet resistance values after the anneals are also in the same range. The peak P concentration is approximately 2×10^{19} cm^{-3}, which is well below the solid solubility value [16] at 1000 °C.

SIMS profiles of the iron show that after gettering anneal C, iron is not collected only right at the emitter surface, but there is a concentration peak that has a maximum approximately at the depth of 60 nm from the wafer surface. A similar iron peak

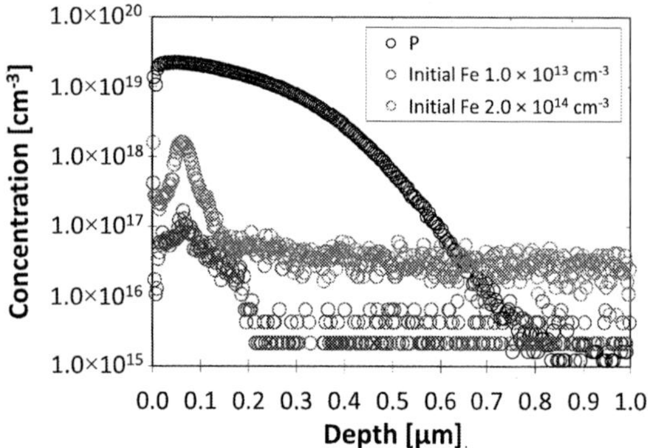

Fig. 3. Phosphorus and iron profiles near the wafer surface measured by SIMS from the high-Fe and medium-Fe wafers after gettering anneal C.

has also been reported by Saga [17] after phosphorus implantation. In that study, the peak was attributed to the gettering by the end of range defects. In our SIMS profiles, there is a clear difference in the measured iron concentrations between the high-Fe and medium-Fe wafer. The peak iron concentration is a decade larger in the high iron level sample. The amount of gettered iron calculated from the profiles is roughly in agreement with the measured decrease in the interstitial iron concentrations presented in Fig. 1. However, there was some lateral variation observed in the SIMS results in the highly contaminated sample.

IV. Discussion

A. Gettering Mechanisms

The obtained low GE in the medium-Fe wafers with the anneals A and B could be explained by segregation to the emitter. With the given temperatures and phosphorus concentration, the segregation coefficient is so low that the GE due to segregation to the emitter is also small. However, with lower temperature (anneal C) a significant improvement is seen, which cannot be explained by pure segregation, indicating the presence of another gettering mechanism. The GE seems to have a steep temperature dependence. Similar steep temperature dependence is seen also in the high-Fe wafers. This, together with the facts that 1) in the high-Fe wafers gettering takes place at higher temperatures, 2) gettering is faster, and 3) "inversion" occurs, supports the conclusion that the enhanced gettering in medium-Fe wafer with anneal C and in high-Fe wafers with anneals A to C takes place due to iron precipitation. It seems that in the medium-Fe wafer, the bulk iron reduction rate in anneal C is limited by the iron precipitation rate. In the case of high-Fe wafers, the iron reduction rate seems to be limited either by the precipitation rate (anneal A) or the diffusion and segregation of iron to the precipitation sites (anneals B and C). To determine the location of the precipitated iron, more information is needed.

The iron precipitation behavior with anneal C seems to be directly linked to the iron supersaturation level at the emitter. Most likely, iron nuclei are already formed at the emitter during the ramp down from the implant anneal to the gettering temperature. Since this is a slow cooling, only a few iron precipitates

form, which then grow further in size when the amount of gettered iron increases. Thus, after the gettering anneal, there are only a few iron precipitates at the emitter, but they are large in size. The nucleation takes place mainly at the emitter due to the implantation induced damage and segregation. This is also supported by the SIMS results: The amount of gettered iron calculated from the profile matches roughly with the measured decrease in the interstitial iron concentration.

Even though the anneal D is almost identical to the anneal C, the results are quite different. The only difference in processing is the fast cooling to the room temperature between the implantation anneal and the gettering anneal in the case of D samples. With the medium-Fe wafers, the GE is significantly higher in case of anneal D, which implies that the prevailing gettering mechanism in anneal D must be precipitation. In anneal D, the rapid cool down to the room temperature allows iron to nucleate fast creating a higher density of iron precipitates [18] than compared with anneal C. Subsequently, the higher density of iron precipitates results in faster precipitation rate during the following anneal at 620 °C. In the best case, the precipitation rate or the gettering of iron can be limited only by diffusion of iron from the bulk. However, it is not clear if the precipitation takes place only at the emitter, and thereby, further experiments are needed.

B. Role of the Electrically Inactive Phosphorus

Previously, we have made corresponding gettering anneals with diffused emitters [6]. In that study, the emitter was formed by in-diffusing phosphorus from a spin-on dopant source for 30 min at 870 °C followed by the gettering anneal. Gettering anneals A and B were identical to this study, but the temperature of the anneal C was 650 °C instead of 620 °C used here. The resulting sheet resistance was $\sim$45 Ω/sq. In those experiments, the prevailing gettering mechanism was found to be segregation in all anneals (A–C). Now, in Fig. 4(a), we compare the GE of the implanted and diffused emitters after gettering anneals A, B, and C and, in Fig. 4(b), the phosphorus profiles of the implanted and diffused emitters measured by SIMS. The GE is naturally lower in implanted emitters due to the lower phosphorus concentration. However, this difference cannot be entirely explained by the lower electrically active phosphorus concentration ($\sim$95 Ω/sq versus $\sim$45 Ω/sq). We can take into account the phosphorus concentration difference using the segregation coefficient from [6] and the measured phosphorus profile presented in Figs. 3 and 4(b). After anneals A and B, the calculated interstitial iron concentration in the bulk is about 7×10^{12} cm^{-3} and 2×10^{12} cm^{-3}, respectively. These values are significantly lower than the concentrations measured here as demonstrated in Fig. 4(a).

One possible reason for the difference in the measured and calculated values is the role of the electrically inactive phosphorus [10]–[12]. In [6], the phosphorus layer was made by diffusion, and the phosphorus concentration near the emitter surface exceeded the solid solubility value, leading to the formation of electrically inactive phosphorus, whereas here at the implanted emitter, there is no electrically inactive phosphorus

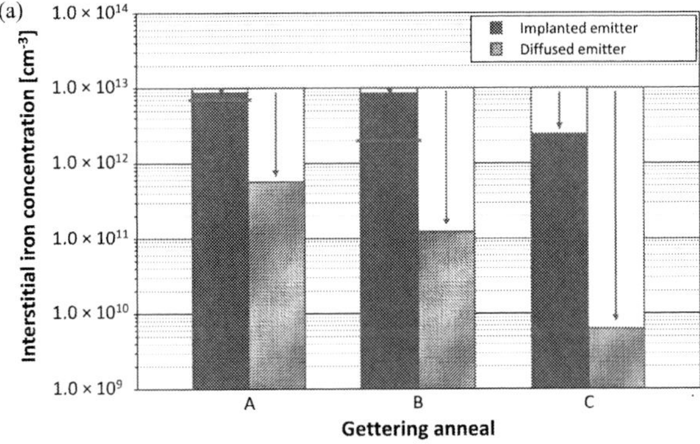

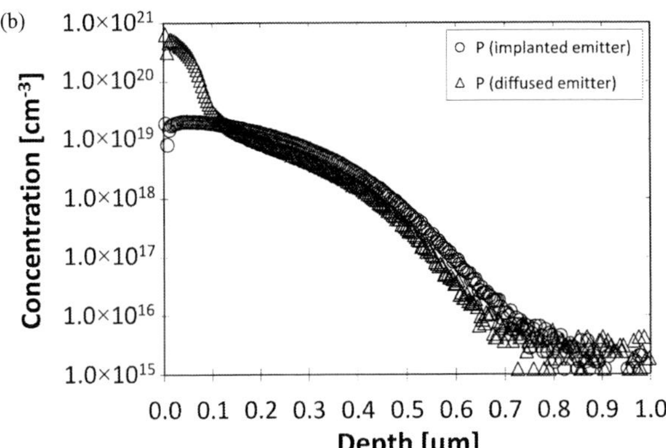

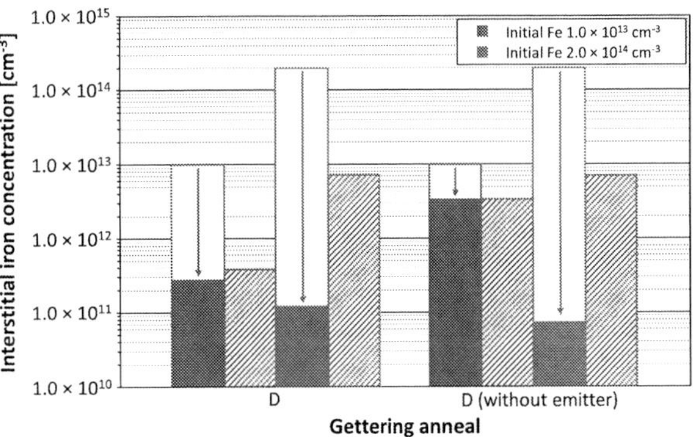

Fig. 5. Interstitial iron concentration in the bulk obtained from the supplementary experiments. Single-colored columns represent the values obtained after gettering anneal D in wafers, which have the implanted emitter (left columns) and in wafers with identical thermal anneals but without implantation (right columns). Striped columns represent the values obtained from the same wafers after they have experienced surface etching and dissolution anneal.

Fig. 4. (a) Comparison of interstitial iron concentration in the bulk after gettering with implanted and diffused emitter. The red lines show the calculated interstitial iron concentration in the bulk obtained using the segregation coefficient from [6] and the measured phosphorus profile. (b) Phosphorus profiles of the implanted and diffused emitters measured by SIMS.

present [see Fig. 4 (b)]. This raises the question if the presence of the dead layer is important at least for the segregation based gettering. Another possibility is that the segregation coefficient scales down much faster with decreasing electrically active phosphorus concentration than assumed in [6].

C. Destination of Gettered Iron

The relatively low minority carrier diffusion length value in high-Fe sample after anneal D was surprising (see Fig. 2). It could indicate that not all of the disappeared interstitial iron was actually gettered to the emitter, but some of the iron was precipitated either in the wafer bulk and/or on the nonimplanted back surface of the wafer due to the aforementioned rapid cooling down to the room temperature. In order to verify the hypothesis, the supplementary experiments mentioned in Section II, i.e., gettering without the presence of an emitter and the combination of surface etching and dissolution anneal, were performed. Fig. 5 presents the interstitial iron concentration in the bulk obtained from these experiments.

We can see from Fig. 5 that the interstitial iron concentration in the medium-Fe sample with the emitter drops approximately a decade lower than without the emitter. This is a clear indication that the iron precipitation rate at the emitter is faster than

at the oxide surface and that segregation and the possible residual damage from the implantation enhance the process. Similar significant difference is also seen in the minority carrier diffusion lengths: 321 μm with the emitter versus 140 μm without the emitter. Thereby, it seems that at the medium contamination level the iron precipitation rate at the emitter is so high that the iron is mostly collected there. Similar strong gettering effect of an implanted layer was observed also in our previous experiments [9], even with a high bulk defect density [19].

In the high-Fe wafers, the results are quite the opposite. The final interstitial iron concentration in the bulk is even a bit smaller without the emitter than with the emitter. This means that high density of iron precipitates, comparable with the density at the emitter, is also formed to the oxide surface in the high-Fe samples. This behavior is clearly different than seen in the medium-Fe samples. The minority carrier diffusion length prior to dissociating the Fe_iB_s-pairs is 188 μm with the emitter and 165 μm without the emitter. The most interesting part is that even though the bulk interstitial iron concentration in the high level wafer with an emitter is smaller than in the medium level wafer, the diffusion length is only approximately a half of the value obtained from the medium level wafer. Thus, the interstitial iron concentration is not limiting the diffusion length in the high-Fe wafer.

The supplementary experiments of surface etching and dissolution provide further information about the location of the gettered iron. In medium-Fe wafers, the interstitial iron concentration remains in the same level after surface etching and dissolution (see the blue-striped columns in Fig. 5) confirming that the gettered iron has not been precipitated in the bulk but has been gettered mainly to the emitter. Again, in the high-Fe wafers, the situation is different. Both with and without an emitter, the bulk interstitial iron concentration increases by approximately two decades as a consequence of the dissolution anneal. In addition, the diffusion length drops down to the vicinity of 70 μm in both cases. This is a clear indication that in the high-Fe wafers, both with and without the emitter, a significant amount of iron

$(7 \times 10^{12}$ cm$^{-3})$ is precipitated in the bulk as well. However, the majority of the gettered iron is still out-diffused and precipitated to the surfaces.

The bulk and surface precipitation in high-Fe samples means that the interstitial iron concentrations or the GE after anneal C and D cannot be directly compared. In addition, in anneal D, it is impossible to make a difference between the precipitation rate to the emitter and to the oxide surface. After both anneal C and anneal D, the iron concentration is close to the solubility value (see Fig. 1), indicating that the precipitation rate is no longer limiting the gettering process. We obtained a similar concentration of iron remaining in the bulk by simulations (iron precipitation in the bulk and ideal out-diffusion to the surfaces [20]) using a precipitate site density of 5×10^6 cm^{-3} with a 50-nm-fixed capture radius or alternatively using a density of 2×10^7 cm^{-3} and growing iron precipitates [21]. These values are in a reasonable range with crystal-originated particles, present in modern high quality Czochralski-grown silicon, which are most likely the nucleation sites for iron in the bulk in this study. Our values for precipitate site densities and capture radiuses are in agreement with [22].

D. Impact on Solar Cell Efficiency

One issue is whether the iron precipitation to the bulk in the high iron level case is desirable, like internal gettering in multicrystalline silicon [23], or mostly just a harmful effect. The minority carrier diffusion length in the high-Fe wafer after anneal C is approximately three times longer than after anneal D (544 μm versus 188 μm), even though the bulk interstitial iron concentrations of the wafers are almost the same after gettering. This can be explained by the differences in the gettered iron, especially in the location of iron precipitates. Our results have shown that in anneal C iron precipitation takes place mainly at the emitter, while in anneal D, some iron precipitates were formed in the bulk as well. Thereby, after anneal C, the minority carrier diffusion length is limited by the interstitial iron concentration, whereas after anneal D, the limit comes from the iron precipitates in the bulk. The calculated capture coefficient for electrons using the iron precipitate densities of 5×10^6 cm^{-3} and 2×10^7 cm^{-3} is in the range of 4–15×10^{-3} cm^{3}s^{-1}. This is roughly ten times higher than the values calculated from the physical surface area and the thermal velocity of the electrons. This apparent discrepancy between physical surface and capture cross section is in agreement with the theoretical results [24].

The GE obtained here for an implanted emitter is much lower than for a diffused emitter [6]. However, if the nucleation of iron precipitates takes place, the gettering is robust, and the iron concentration should always be reduced to the solubility limit. One drawback is that the iron concentration in the material may not be high enough to reach sufficient supersaturation for fast precipitation. Another thing to consider is the size of the precipitates at the emitter. By doing the implant anneal and the gettering anneal as separate steps, very fast emitter precipitation can be maintained. Thereby, the gettering process is limited only by the diffusion of iron from the bulk. This allows the size of the precipitates to be kept small, and thus, the possible problems related to large iron precipitates, e.g., leakage currents at the emitter, could be avoided. However, it should be kept in mind that eventually the increasing amount of precipitated iron at the emitter starts to limit the operation of the solar cell.

V. Conclusion

We have experimentally studied the gettering of iron in Czochralski-grown silicon by phosphorus implantation. The prevailing mechanisms behind the implantation gettering, i.e., gettering with a low phosphorus concentration emitter, were found to differ from those present in typical conventional diffused emitters. In addition, the prevailing gettering mechanisms were found to be case sensitive, i.e., the activated mechanisms depend on the initial contamination level and the gettering anneal parameters. In the case of high initial iron concentration, gettering takes place mainly through precipitation, while in the case of lower iron concentration, precipitation becomes dominating only at relatively low temperatures. Iron precipitation takes place mainly at the emitter if iron level is lower than 1×10^{13} cm^{-3} and the bulk lifetime remains high. If the iron level is high, in the case of a temperature profile that allows iron to form a high density of precipitate nuclei, and thus results in fast gettering, a significant amount of iron can also precipitate in the bulk deteriorating the bulk lifetime, even in high-quality Czochralski-grown silicon. Thus, to reach the best solar cell efficiency, the gettering anneal should be designed to activate the most effective mechanism within the limits of the starting material.

Generally, when the emitter phosphorus concentration is lowered below a certain value (as a result of, e.g., implantation), precipitation begins to dominate. In order to reach the best gettering result in this case, the low-temperature anneal at the end of the process is crucial, annulling the role of a slow cooling. This is the opposite of the diffused emitter, in which segregation dominates, emphasizing the role of the slow cooling to the actual gettering temperature.

Acknowledgment

The authors acknowledge the provision of facilities and technical support by Aalto University at the Micronova Nanofabrication Centre.

References

[1] A. Rohatgi, D. Meier, B. McPherson, Y-W. Ok, A. Upadhyaya, J-H. Lai, and F. Zimbardi, "High-throughput ion-implantation for low-cost high-efficiency silicon solar cells," *Energy Procedia*, vol. 15, pp. 10–19, Apr. 2012.

[2] M. Sheoran, M. Emsley, M. Yuan, D. Ramappa, and P. Sullivan, "Ion-implant doped large-area n-type Czochralski high-efficiency industrial solar cells," in *Proc. 38th IEEE Photovoltaic Spec. Conf. Rec.*, Jun. 2012, pp. 2254–2257.

[3] V. Prajapati, T. Janssens, J. John, J. Poortmans, and R. Mertens, "Diffusion-free high efficiency silicon solar cells," *Prog. Photovoltaics: Res. Appl.*, vol. 21, no. 5, pp. 980–985, Aug. 2013.

[4] A. Müller, M. Ghosh, R. Sonnenschein, and P. Woditsch, "Silicon for photovoltaic applications," *Mater. Sci. Eng. B*, vol. 134, no. 2–3, pp. 257–262, Oct. 2006.

[5] V. Vähänissi, A. Haarahiltunen, H. Talvitie, M. Yli-Koski, and H. Savin, "Impact of phosphorus gettering parameters and initial iron level on silicon

solar cell properties," *Prog. Photovoltaics: Res. Appl.*, vol. 21, no. 5, pp. 1127–1135, Aug. 2013.

[6] H. Talvitie, V. Vähänissi, A. Haarahiltunen, M. Yli-Koski, and H. Savin, "Phosphorus and boron diffusion gettering of iron in monocrystalline silicon," *J. Appl. Phys.*, vol. 109, no. 9, pp. 093505-1–093505-5, May 2011.

[7] S. P. Phang and D. Macdonald, "Direct comparison of boron, phosphorus, and aluminum gettering of iron in crystalline silicon," *J. Appl. Phys.*, vol. 109, no. 7, pp. 073521-1–073521-6, Apr. 2011.

[8] P. Manshanden and L. J. Geerligs, "Improved phosphorous gettering of multi-crystalline silicon," *Sol. Energy Mater. Sol. Cells*, vol. 90, no. 7–8, pp. 998–1012, May 2006.

[9] A. Haarahiltunen, H. Talvitie, H. Savin, O. Anttila, M. Yli-Koski, M. I. Asghar, and J. Sinkkonen, "Gettering of iron in silicon by boron implantation," *J. Mater. Sci.—Mater. Electron.*, vol. 19, no. 1 (suppl.), pp. 41–45, Dec. 2008.

[10] V. Vähänissi, A. Haarahiltunen, H. Talvitie, M. I. Asghar, M. Yli-Koski, and H. Savin, "Effect of oxygen in low temperature boron and phosphorus diffusion gettering of iron in Czochralski-grown silicon," *Solid State Phenomena*, vol. 156–158, pp. 395–400, Oct. 2010.

[11] B. Tryznadlowski, A. Yazdani, R. Chen, and S. T. Dunham, "Coupled modeling of evolution of impurity/defect distribution and cell performance," *Proc. 38th IEEE Photovoltaic Spec. Conf. Rec.*, pp. 217–220, Jun. 2012.

[12] A. Cuevas, D. Macdonald, M. Kerr, C. Samundsett, A. Sloan, S. Shea, A. Leo, M. Mrcarica, and S. Winderbaum, "Evidence of impurity gettering by industrial phosphorus diffusion," *Proc. 28th IEEE Photovoltaic Spec. Conf. Rec.*, pp. 244–247, Sep. 2000.

[13] S. Wolf and R. N. Tauber, "Ion implantation for VLSI," in *Silicon Processing for the VLSI Era—Process Technology*. vol. 1, Sunset Beach, CA, USA: Lattice, 1987, pp. 323–325.

[14] M. Aoki, A. Hara, and A. Ohsawa, "Fundamental properties of intrinsic gettering of iron in a silicon wafer," *J. Appl. Phys.*, vol. 72, no. 3, pp. 895–898, Aug. 1992.

[15] J. D. Murphy and R. J. Falster, "Contamination of silicon by iron at temperatures below 800 °C," *Phys. Status Solidi—Rapid Res. Lett.*, vol. 5, no. 10–11, pp. 370–372, Nov. 2011.

[16] V. E. Borisenko and S. G. Yudin, "Steady-state solubility of substitutional impurities in silicon," *Phys. Status Solidi A*, vol. 101, no. 1, pp. 123–127, May 1987.

[17] K. Saga, "Gettering behavior of transition metals in low energy, high dose ion implanted silicon," *Solid State Phenomena*, vol. 187, pp. 283–286, Apr. 2012.

[18] A. Haarahiltunen, M. Yli-Koski, and H. Savin, "Effect of thermal history on iron precipitation in crystalline silicon," *Energy Procedia*, vol. 8, pp. 355–359, Apr. 2011.

[19] H. Talvitie, M. Yli-Koski, A. Haarahiltunen, V. Vähänissi, M. I. Asghar, and H. Savin, "Experimental study of iron redistribution between bulk defects and boron doped layers in silicon wafers," *Phys. Status Solidi A*, vol. 208, no. 10, pp. 2430–2436, Oct. 2011.

[20] H. Hieslmair, S. Balasubramanian, A. A. Istratov, and E. R. Weber, "Gettering simulator: Physical basis and algorithm," *Semicond. Sci. Technol.*, vol. 16, no. 7, pp. 567–574, Jul. 2001.

[21] H. Hieslmair, A. A. Istratov, T. Heiser, and E. R. Weber, "Evaluation of precipitate densities and capture radii from the analysis of precipitation kinetics," *J. Appl. Phys.*, vol. 84, no. 2, pp. 713–717, Jul. 1998.

[22] J. Murphy and R. Falster, "The relaxation behaviour of supersaturated iron in single-crystal silicon at 500 to 750 °C," *J. Appl. Phys.*, vol. 112, no. 11, pp. 113506-1–113506-7, Dec. 2012.

[23] R. Krain, S. Herlufsen, and J. Schmidt, "Internal gettering of iron in multicrystalline silicon at low temperature," *Appl. Phys. Lett.*, vol. 93, no. 15, pp. 152108-1–152108-3, Oct. 2008.

[24] P. S. Plekhanov and T. Y. Tan, "Schottky effect model of electrical activity of metallic precipitates in silicon," *Appl. Phys. Lett.*, vol. 76, no. 25, pp. 3777–3779, Jun. 2000.

Authors' photographs and biographies not available at the time of publication.

Synthesis of Group IV Clathrates for Photovoltaics

Aaron D. Martinez, Lakshmi Krishna, Lauryn L. Baranowski, Mark T. Lusk, Eric S. Toberer,
and Adele C. Tamboli

Abstract—Although Si dominates the photovoltaics market, only two forms of Si have been thoroughly considered: amorphous Si and Si in the diamond structure (d-Si). Silicon can also form in other allotropes, including clathrate structures. Silicon clathrates are inclusion compounds, which consist of an Si framework surrounding templating guest atoms (e.g., Na). After formation of the type II $Na_{24}Si_{136}$ clathrate, the guest atoms can be removed (Si_{136}), and the material transitions from degenerate to semiconducting behavior with a 1.9 eV direct band gap. This band gap is tunable in the range of 1.9–0.6 eV by alloying the host framework with Ge, enabling a variety of photovoltaic applications that include thin-film single-junction devices, Si_{136} top cells on d-Si for all-Si tandem cells, and multijunction cells with varying Si/Ge ratios. In this study, we present electronic structure calculations that show the evolution of the direct transition as a function of Si/Ge ratio across the alloy range. We demonstrate the synthesis of type II Si/Ge clathrates spanning the whole alloy range. We also demonstrate a technique for forming Si clathrate films on d-Si wafers and sapphire substrates.

Index Terms—Clathrate, density functional theory, photovoltaic cells, Si, Si–Ge.

I. INTRODUCTION

SILICON has been an enabling material for nearly all aspects of microelectronics and currently dominates the photovoltaics market. However, the indirect gap of diamond silicon (d-Si) has been a challenge for optoelectronic applications. The development of a crystalline allotrope of Si with a direct band gap would be transformative. Silicon can form in other allotropes, including semiconducting clathrate structures. In the type II clathrate structure, Si_{136} is a direct wide-band-gap semiconductor and has promise for optoelectronics [1]. This material could be used for a variety of photovoltaic applications that include thin-film single-junction devices, Si_{136} top cells on d-Si for all-Si tandem cells, and multijunction cells with varying Si/Ge ratios.

Manuscript received June 10, 2013; revised July 29, 2013; accepted July 30, 2013. Date of publication August 22, 2013; date of current version September 18, 2013. This work was supported in part by the Center for Revolutionary Solar Photoconversion and the Renewable Energy Materials Research Science and Engineering Center at Colorado School of Mines under the National Science Foundation Grant DMR-0820518. The calculations were done on high performance computing resources provided by the Golden Energy Computing Organization at the Colorado School of Mines (The National Science Foundation Grant CNS-0722415). The work of L. L. Baranowski was supported by the Department of Defense through the National Defense Science and Engineering Graduate Fellowship Program.

The authors are with the Physics Department, Colorado School of Mines, Golden, CO 80401 USA (e-mail: aamartin@mines.edu; lkrishna@mines.edu; lbaranow@mines.edu; mlusk@mines.edu; etoberer@mines.edu; atamboli@mines.edu).

Color versions of one or more of the figures in this paper are available online at http://ieeexplore.ieee.org.

Digital Object Identifier 10.1109/JPHOTOV.2013.2276478

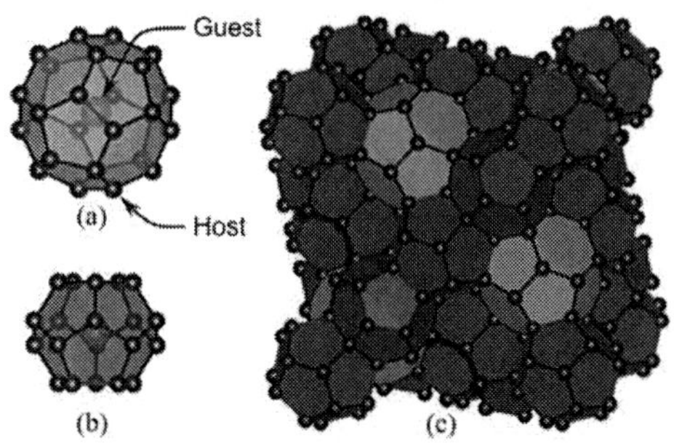

Fig. 1. Type II Si clathrate structure is made up of Si host atoms, covalently bonded to each other, in the form of polyhedral cages with an Na guest atom located within each cage. (a) Si_{28} polyhedral cage. (b) Si_{20} polyhedral cage. (c) Si_{20} and Si_{28} cages are periodically arranged in a face sharing manner, with each Si atom bonded to four other Si atoms, such that there are no voids within the structure.

Generally speaking, clathrates are inclusion compounds, wherein the cage-like host lattice surrounds guest atoms or molecules (see Fig. 1). There are many known clathrate structure types which differ in cage size, bonding, and arrangement [2], [3]. The clathrate crystal structure can be formed by a hydrogen bound framework (e.g., H_2O). These clathrate hydrates were first discovered in 1810 and have been found to exist deep within the oceans, in permafrost regions, and extraterrestrially [2]. More recently, inorganic clathrates have been synthesized using Group IV elements as the host atoms (e.g., Si, Ge, Sn) with Group I or II metals as guests [3]–[5].

Inorganic clathrates are chemically versatile compounds, which can be formed with a variety of different structure types, framework species, and guest species; such a vast phase space results in an incredibly rich and complex material system with applications that include superconductors [6], [7], thermoelectrics [8], [9], and optoelectronics [5]. The substitution of the host framework atoms has been achieved with elements like Ba, Al, Ga, Te, and Zn [3]. Likewise, most alkali and alkali earth metals can be guest atoms in the covalent clathrates. As Zintl compounds, semiconducting behavior can be anticipated through simple valence charge counting. For example, the thermoelectric compound $Ba_8Ga_{16}Ge_{30}$ can be formed as a semiconductor because the framework acceptors (Ga) compensate the guest site donors (Ba) [10].

In this study, we focus on neutral framework type II Si clathrates for photovoltaics. Here, Na guest atoms template cage formation and are removed to achieve semiconducting behavior in Si_{136} [5]. Each Si atom is covalently bound to four other Si atoms in an sp^3 hybridized host network with bond angles ranging from 105.3°–119.9° [11]. In this network, the Si atoms are located at the apices of two different periodically-arranged face-sharing polyhedral cages, as shown in Fig. 1. The conventional cell of the type II clathrate consists of 8 large (Si_{28}) cages [see Fig. 1(a)] and 16 small (Si_{20}) cages [see Fig. 1(b)] for a total unit cell of $Na_{24}Si_{136}$. The conventional cell is face-centered-cubic and has a lattice parameter of 14.64–14.72 Å [12]. The Si framework is electronically neutral; at room temperature every Na guest is ionized and shares an electron with the framework.

After removal of the Na, the guest free Si type II clathrate (Si_{136}) has been shown to be a wide band gap (~ 1.9 eV) semiconductor with complex band edges that have both direct and indirect transitions that differ by less than kT [1], [13], [14]. This band gap should be tunable in the range of 1.9–0.6 eV by alloying the host framework with Ge [15], [16]. The band gaps of pure type II Si and Ge clathrate powders have been experimentally determined through reflectance and transmission measurements. In [14] a band gap of 1.9–2.0 eV for the empty (Na<600ppm) Si clathrate was reported; 1.8 eV was reported for Na_2Si_{136} in [1]. The completely guest-free Ge clathrate, synthesized by Guloy *et al.*, was shown to have a band gap of 0.6 eV [16].

To our knowledge, the synthesis of $Na_{x \leq 24}(Si_{1-y}Ge_y)_{136}$ alloys have not yet been reported. In general, there has been minimal work on framework alloying in type II clathrates, including several reports of Ag and Cu substitution onto Ge clathrate frameworks [17], [18]. In these cases, the level of framework substitution is very low, less than 7 out of a total of 136 framework sites. Silicon–germanium framework alloying has been demonstrated in Type I clathrates ($Ba_8Ga_{16}Si_xGe_{30-x}$) used for thermoelectric applications, where the guest occupancy is fixed (completely filled) [19].

A standard bulk synthesis technique for the type II clathrates consists of the decomposition of a Zintl precursor, e.g., NaSi, under vacuum [5]. During this decomposition, sodium sublimes from the precursor, allowing the framework atoms to crystalize around remaining guest atoms into the cage structures of the clathrate. In the case of Na guests, the majority of them can be removed from the clathrate by additional post-synthesis heating under vacuum. This bulk synthesis technique can lead to impurity phases (e.g., type I clathrate and polycrystalline d-Si) [1]. We employ a slightly modified version of this technique in the synthesis of the type II Si/Ge clathrate alloys.

For PV applications, it is necessary to synthesize Si_{136} as a film rather than a powder; however, there has been little demonstrated success in forming Si_{136} films. Grigorian *et al.* patented a technique that is very similar to the previously discussed bulk synthesis technique [20] where a clathrate film is formed by reacting the surface of a d-Si wafer with elemental Na vapor in a sealed ampule (closed system) at high temperature. This resulted in the formation of a precursor film, which was then decomposed into a clathrate film. In a similar fashion, Narita *et al.* grew an NaSi film through thermal evaporation of Na onto a d-Si substrate (open system); however, they were unable to conclusively demonstrate that the decomposition step produced a clathrate film [21].

In this study, we build on previous density functional theory (DFT) calculations [15] using the more accurate GW approximation; we show the evolution of the direct transition as a function of Si/Ge ratio across the alloy range. We demonstrate the synthesis of type II Si/Ge clathrates spanning the whole alloy range. We also demonstrate the formation of Si clathrate films on d-Si wafers and sapphire substrates.

II. METHOD

A. Theory

Many-body Green function (GW) electronic structure calculations were carried out using the plane-wave ABINIT code [22]. DFT with the Perdew–Burke–Ernzerhof generalized gradient exchange-correlation functional, was used to calculate the electronic band structures of $(Si_{1-y}Ge_y)_{136}$ alloys. Quasi-particle corrections, at the GW_0 level, were then carried out. The DFT plane wave energy cutoffs for wave function representation and dielectric screening were set to 5.0 Hartree (Ha), while the cutoffs for GW wave function representation and the exchange component of the self-energy operator were set to 8.0 Ha. Five hundred bands were used for all calculations and a convergence study of these parameters showed that the band gap at the L-point was converged within 0.05 eV.

B. Experimental Setup

All materials synthesized in this study involved the use of either elemental Na or NaH. All sample handling was done in an Ar filled glovebox ($O_2 < 1$ppm) because Na, NaH, and the Zintl precursors, Na_4Si_4 and Na_4Ge_4, react violently with air and water. The clathrate is stable in air provided that residual metallic Na is washed from the powder. However, it is still prone to oxidation, like d-Si, which can happen quite rapidly in the powder form because of the large surface area. When the clathrate powder oxidizes rapidly, it generates enough heat that the clathrate structure collapses.

To synthesize $Na_{x \leq 24}(Si_{1-y}Ge_y)_{136}$ alloys, crystalline Si and Ge were first mechanically alloyed in a Spex 8000 Mixer/Mill for 8 h. The alloys were further ball-milled with NaH and then reacted under argon for 24–48 h at temperatures between 270 and 395 °C to form the Zintl precursors. The resulting precursors were then decomposed in a custom-built cold wall reactor to yield clathrate powders. The reactor featured local sample heating to 370 °C under rough vacuum (<10 mTorr), with a water cooled plate, adjacent to the sample, on which the Na vapor irreversibly deposited. The resultant powders were washed with ethanol to remove residual Na.

To synthesize $Na_{x < 24}Si_{136}$ films, the surface of a $\langle 100 \rangle$ d-Si wafer was reacted with sodium vapor by placing the wafer over the top of a partially filled Na well, inside a sealed stainless steel vessel [see Fig. 2(a)–(d)]. The vessel was then heated to 550°C for 1–5 h. The Si wafer, with the newly formed precursor film, was subsequently removed from the reactor vessel, sealed in a dynamic high-vacuum vessel ($\sim 10^{-7}$ torr), and then heated in a furnace at 350 °C for 20–24 h to decompose the precursor film into the clathrate structure. To remove the majority of the Na guest atoms from the clathrate structure, further heating of the samples was done in the dynamic high vacuum vessel at 350 °C–390 °C. After the decomposition process, the clathrate films were found to be stable in air. In addition to the use of d-Si

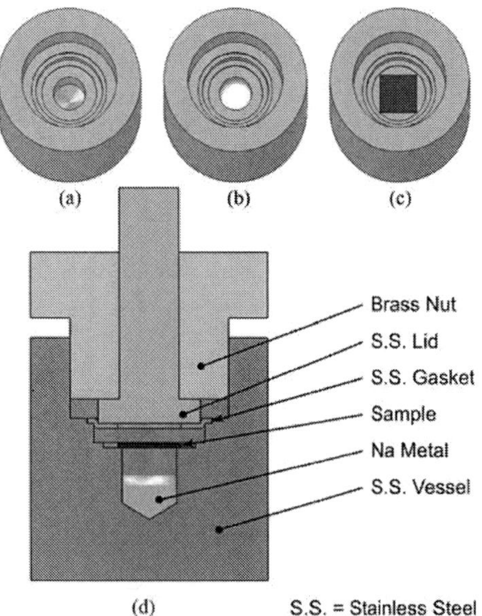

Fig. 2. Na reactor for surface reaction synthesis of clathrate precursor. (a) Empty reactor vessel. (b) Well partially filled with Na metal. (c) Sample placed over the top of the well. (d) Section view of the sealed reactor.

substrates (clathrate-on-Si), this technique was used to convert predeposited 0.6 μm epitaxial Si films on sapphire substrates into clathrate (clathrate-on-sapphire).

The crystallinity of the bulk Si/Ge samples and clathrate-on-Si film samples was analyzed using X-ray diffraction (XRD) data obtained from a PANalytical/Philips X'Pert powder X-ray diffractometer with CuKα radiation (tube current: 40 mA, and voltage: 45 kV). These measurements were coupled with Rietveld refinement, using the General Structure Analysis System (GSAS) code, to determine phase purity and Na content of the clathrate. The instrument file for use with GSAS was generated with a LaB$_6$ NIST standard sample. To eliminate substrate peaks, the clathrate-on-sapphire film samples were analyzed using the glancing angle X-ray diffraction technique (GAXRD), with the incident angle set to 4° (2θ), on a Siemens D500 powder X-ray diffractometer with CuKα radiation. The film morphology was examined with a JEOL JSM7000F FESEM. The JEOL JSM7000F FESEM was equipped with an EDAX energy dispersive X-ray spectroscopy (EDS) system, which was used to approximate the sodium content of the clathrate in the clathrate-on-sapphire samples and the Si/Ge alloying ratios. The absorption measurements of clathrate-on-sapphire samples were obtained by photothermal deflection spectroscopy (PDS) [23]. This instrument was custom-built and consists of a HeNe laser and incandescent light that is passed through a monochrometer. The sample is submerged in carbon tetrachloride (CCl$_4$), which has an index of refraction that changes significantly with temperature. Monochromatic light focused onto the film surface at normal incidence heats the film, which causes the temperature in the CCl$_4$ to increase locally. The resulting temperature gradient in the CCl$_4$ creates a lensing effect that deflects a laser beam, which passes parallel to the film surface. The beam deflection

is a function of the absorbance of the film. PDS is a sensitive technique that is immune to scattering due to the morphology of our samples.

III. RESULTS

A. Ab Initio Calculations

The DFT calculations predict a direct, or nearly direct, band gap over the entire alloy range, which decreases with increasing Ge content (see Fig. 3). For the pure Si clathrate (Si$_{136}$), the band gap calculated by the GW approximation was 1.74 eV; this value dropped to 0.81 eV for the pure Ge clathrate (Ge$_{136}$). These calculations are in agreement with the known experimental end points: E$_g$ (Si$_{136}$) = 1.9 eV (direct) [14] and E$_g$ (Ge$_{136}$) = 0.6 eV (direct) [16]. Selected band structures that were calculated by DFT are shown in Fig. 3(a)–(e). The trend in band gap, as calculated by the GW approximation, is shown in Fig. 3(f). One might expect the trend in band gap as a function of alloying to be roughly linear and possibly exhibit some band-bowing. However, the trend that is observed in previous calculations [15], and confirmed by our own, is more complex. The inspection of the band structures as the Ge fraction is increased [see Fig. 3(a)–(e)] shows the complexity of the transformation. For example, as the Ge fraction is increased from 0 at% to 30 at% [see Fig. 3(a) and (b)], the conduction band changes slightly, while the valance band becomes multiply degenerate; the band gap remains relatively unchanged. This complex trend in band gap over the alloy range is very interesting and warrants a more focused and thorough study, but the ultimate conclusion herein is that the theoretical calculations predict a tunable band gap and that it is the direct transition at the L-point that eventually drops making (Si$_{1-y}$Ge$_y$)$_{136}$ a potentially viable material for photovoltaics.

B. (Si$_{1-y}$Ge$_y$)$_{136}$ Alloys

In addition to pure Si$_{136}$ and Ge$_{136}$, we have synthesized four (Si$_{1-y}$Ge$_y$)$_{136}$ alloys in bulk powder form. We chose to alloy the starting material (Si/Ge) so as to prevent compositional inhomogeneities during decomposition of the clathrate. Alloying was confirmed by XRD at each of the three synthesis steps: the initial mechanically alloyed Si/Ge, the Na$_4$(Si$_{1-y}$Ge$_y$)$_4$ Zintl precursor, and the Na$_{x \leq 24}$(Si$_{1-y}$Ge$_y$)$_{136}$ type II clathrate. For the four (Si$_{1-y}$Ge$_y$)$_{136}$ alloys synthesized, EDS confirmed Si/Ge ratios within a few percent of the starting material.

We extracted the lattice parameter and Na content of our (Si$_{1-y}$Ge$_y$)$_{136}$ samples from Rietveld refinement of the XRD data [see Fig. 4 (a)]. The inset in Fig. 4(a) focuses on the set of peaks around 2θ = 50° and shows the peaks shifting to lower 2θ as the lattice parameter increases due to increased Ge fraction. The lattice parameter is plotted as a function of Ge fraction in Fig. 4(b) along with the previously determined experimental values of the pure Si$_{136}$ and Ge$_{136}$ [1], [16]; the trend appears to obey Vegard's law. It has been shown that the Na$_{x \leq 24}$Si$_{136}$ lattice parameter varies with respect to x between 14.64 and 14.72 Å [12]. We determined the Na content of the samples presented herein to be $1 < x < 5$, which limits the variation in lattice parameter due to Na content to ~0.01 Å. This variation

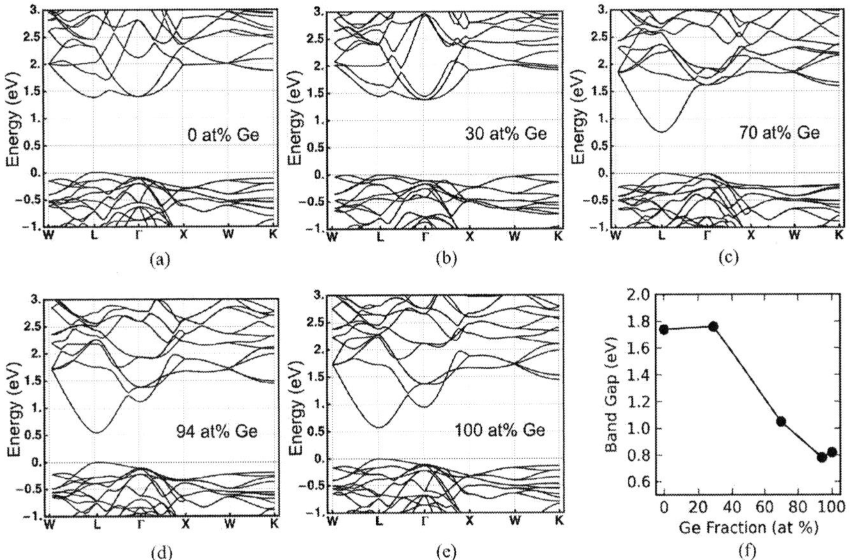

Fig. 3. (a)–(e) Band structures calculated by DFT show direct or nearly direct transitions at the L point over the entire $(Si_{1-y}Ge_y)_{136}$ alloy range. (f) GW calculations show a decreasing trend in band gap with increasing Ge content.

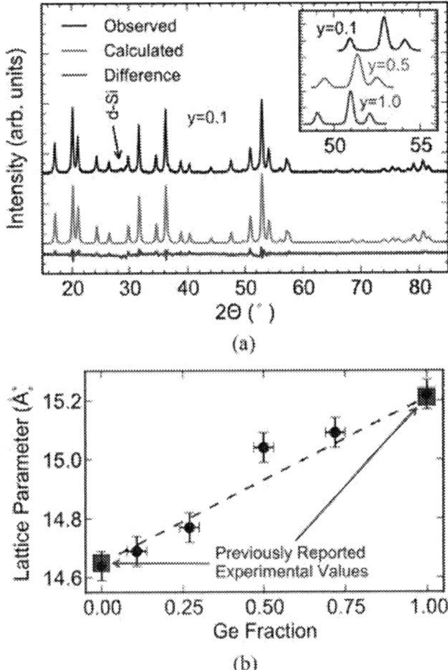

Fig. 4. (a) XRD pattern with Rietveld refinement of $(Si_{1-y}Ge_y)_{136}$ clathrate for y = 0.1; the inset shows the peaks shifting to lower 2θ as y increases. (b) Lattice parameter as a function of Ge fraction (from EDS) as found by Rietveld refinement of XRD data [1], [16].

is small compared with other sources of error. As the peak width did not change across the Si/Ge series and the results are consistent with Vegard's Law, it is inferred that a complete solid solution can be formed across $(Si_{1-y}Ge_y)_{136}$.

Post decomposition heating under vacuum was used to extract the Na guests from within the clathrate. The Na content was found by refining the occupancy of the Na sites in the type II clathrate structure. Assuming $0.6e$ charge sharing [24], the Na level $1 < x < 5$ would yield a carrier concentration of $\sim 1.8 - 9.0 \times 10^{20}$ cm^{-3}. Work to lower the Na content and obtain optical property measurements of these materials is ongoing.

C. Si_{136} Films

In pursuit of materials with a form factor more suitable for optical measurements, we sought a film synthesis technique. Inspired by our bulk synthetic results and previous work [20], [21], a technique was developed to react a d-Si surface with Na vapor, yielding a precursor film. Subsequent decomposition and associated Na removal results in a clathrate film. Two configurations of d-Si were employed: clathrate-on-Si, where the top layer of a d-Si wafer was converted to clathrate, and clathrate-on-sapphire, where a d-Si film on sapphire substrate was converted to clathrate, thus limiting the final clathrate thickness.

Clathrate-on-Si samples were polycrystalline films, which ranged in thickness from 20 to 40 μm. A cross-sectional scanning electron microscope (SEM) image showing the thickness and morphology of a 20-μm-thick film is shown in Fig. 5(a). The phase purity and Na content (Na_5Si_{136}) of these films were verified by Rietveld refinement of XRD data [see Fig. 5(b)]. Although this film synthesis technique closely parallels that of the bulk, it was found to be much less prone to impurity phases (type I clathrate and d-Si). Aside from the presence of forbidden substrate peaks, there appeared to be no polycrystalline d-Si in the XRD pattern and less than 1 at% of type I clathrate [see Fig. 5(b)].

While we were able to synthesize remarkably phase pure films on d-Si substrates, these films were thick and highly fractured due to contraction of the material as it transforms from precursor to clathrate. The adhesion of these films was poor as the clathrate readily washed off the surface by dipping in dilute hydrofluoric

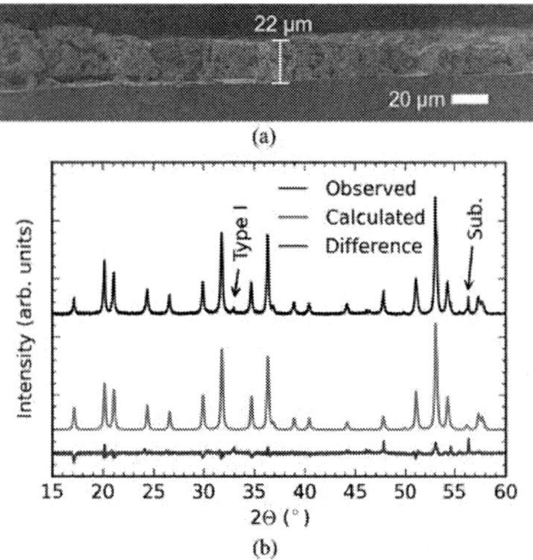

Fig. 5. Na$_5$Si$_{136}$ film on d-Si. (a) Cross-sectional SEM micrograph. (b) Powder XRD pattern.

acid ($<3\%$). The film thickness was not readily controllable, particularly in uniformity. Additionally, Na removal was more challenging than observed in the bulk as it was difficult to get $x < 5$. The difficult Na removal may be due to the dimensionality of diffusion in the films versus powder and larger diffusion length scales: 20–40 μm film thickness versus $\leq \sim 1$ μm particle size. However, these films were well suited for structural characterization of the synthesis technique.

To control film thickness, increase uniformity, and provide a substrate that would not interfere with optical measurements, d-Si on sapphire substrates were also pursued. This route yielded clathrate-on-sapphire films from ~ 0.6 μm thick d-Si films on sapphire. These clathrate films were much more uniform in thickness and displayed minimal porosity, as shown in the SEM images [see Fig. 6(a) and (b)]. The structural integrity of these films is remarkable, given the volume contraction, which occurs during this synthesis technique as these films withstood multiple washes in ethanol, HF, and HCl without delamination.

These clathrate films were polycrystalline as verified by GAXRD [see Fig. 6(c)]. There were minimal impurities phases present in these films: no evidence of the type I clathrate phase and less than 3 at% polycrystalline d-Si phase. The EDS estimates of the Na content of these films was around Na$_4$Si$_{136}$ ($\sim 7 \times 10^{20}$ cm^{-3}).

The preliminary absorption data for a clathrate-on-sapphire film is shown in Fig. 7. The spectrum appears to be dominated by free carriers, which is in agreement with previously reported data taken on bulk material [1], [25]. Equation (1), the free carrier absorption derived from the Drude model, is also plotted in Fig. 7 for reasonable values of the relaxation time τ, carrier concentration n_e, effective mass m^*, and refractive index n. The possible distortion of the conduction band edge by Na guest ions prohibits one from directly referring to the empty Si$_{136}$ band structure [see Fig. 3 (a)] for m^*. While the model demonstrates the free carrier absorption as the low-energy mechanism, more accurate data in the range $E < 1$ eV would enable the

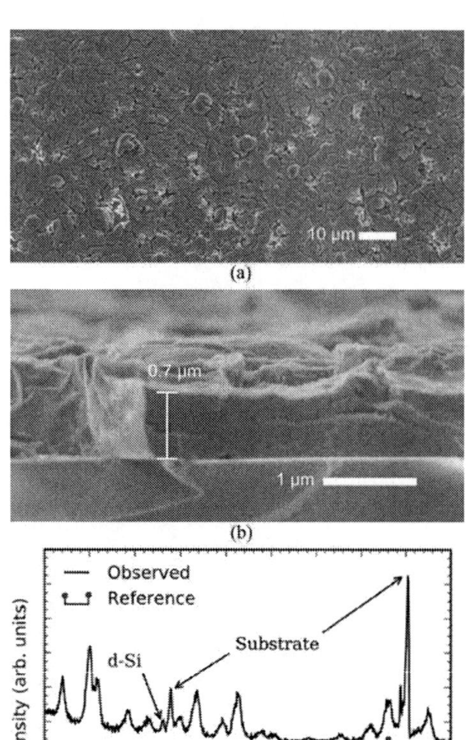

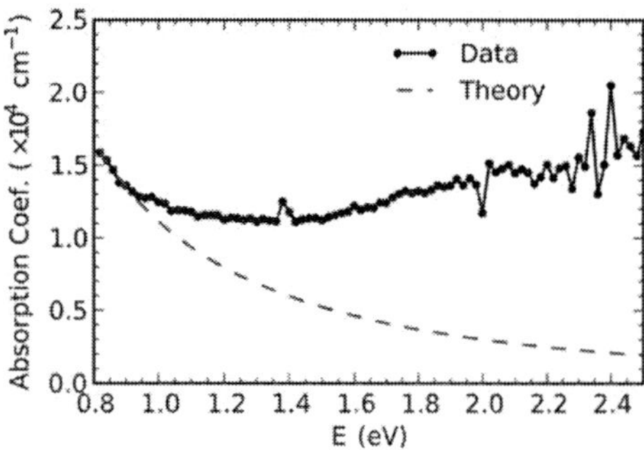

Fig. 6. Na$_3$Si$_{136}$ film on sapphire. (a) SEM micrograph. (b) Cross-sectional SEM micrograph. (c) Glancing Angle XRD pattern with ICDD reference pattern for Na$_{3.8}$Si$_{136}$.

Fig. 7. Absorption spectrum of 700-nm-thick type II Si clathrate film on sapphire from PDS. The free carrier absorption, derived from the Drude model, is plotted for $\tau = 2 \times 10^{-15}$ s, $n_e = 1.35 \times 10^{21}$ cm^{-3}, $m^* = 0.1\,m_e$, and $n = 2$.

extraction of the optical properties. The data does indicate absorption above the band edge of $\sim 1.5 \times 10^4$ cm^{-1} which, from the Beer Lambert law, means a film thickness of 2–3 μm should result in $>95\%$ light absorption.

$$\alpha(E) = \frac{n_e e^2}{4\pi\epsilon_0 c\, n\, m^* \tau \left(\left(\frac{E}{\hbar}\right)^2 + \left(\frac{1}{\tau}\right)^2 \right)} \tag{1}$$

IV. Conclusion

Although it is the leading photovoltaic material, the efficiency and cost of diamond silicon are limited by its indirect band gap. Si clathrates (Si_{136}) have a direct band gap, which is tunable by alloying with Ge, making these materials excellent candidates for photovoltaic applications. We have begun to demonstrate the potential for this material in PV through electronic structure calculations and initial success in the synthesis of $(Si_{1-y}Ge_y)_{136}$ alloys and Si_{136} films. GW calculations show the structure of the trend in band gap over the Si/Ge alloy range, which decreases with increasing Ge fraction. We have experimentally demonstrated the stability of the type II Si/Ge alloyed clathrate spanning the entire alloy range. This understanding of the underlying synthetic pathway enabled the synthesis of type II Si clathrate films on both d-Si wafers and sapphire substrates, from which we were able to collect preliminary optical data indicating that 2–3 μm film thickness should be sufficient for PV absorbers.

Acknowledgment

The authors would like to thank C. A. Koh, C. P. Taylor, and R. T. Collins for the insightful discussions.

References

[1] R. Himeno, F. Ohashi, T. Kume, E. Asai, T. Ban, T. Suzuki, T. Iida, H. Habuchi, Y. Tsutsumi, H. Natsuhara *et al.*, "Optical band gap of semiconductive type II Si clathrate purified by centrifugation," *J. Non-Crystall. Solids*, vol. 358, pp. 2138–2140, 2012.

[2] E. D. Sloan and C. A. Koh, *Clathrate Hydrates of Natural Gases*. Boca Raton, FL, USA: CRC Press, 2008.

[3] A. Shevelkov and K. Kovnir, *Zintl Clathrates*, vol. 990, ser. 0081-5993, T. F. Fassler, Ed. New York, NY, USA: Springer-Verlag, 2011.

[4] J. S. Kasper, P. Hagenmuller, M. Pouchard, and C. Cros, "Clathrate structure of silicon $Na_8 Si_{46}$ and $Na_x Si_{136}$ (x<11)," *Science*, vol. 150, no. 3704, pp. 1713–1714, 1965.

[5] M. Beekman and G. Nolas, "Inorganic clathrate-II materials of group 14: Synthetic routes and physical properties," *J. Mater. Chem.*, vol. 18, no. 8, pp. 842–851, 2008.

[6] K. Tanigaki, T. Shimizu, K. Itoh, J. Teraoka, Y. Moritomo, and S. Yamanaka, "Mechanism of superconductivity in the polyhedral-network compound Ba8Si46," *Nature Mater.*, vol. 2, no. 10, pp. 653–655, 2003.

[7] H. Kawaji, H.-o. Horie, S. Yamanaka, and M. Ishikawa, "Superconductivity in the silicon clathrate compound $(Na, Ba)_x Si_{46}$," *Phys. Rev. Lett.*, vol. 74, no. 8, pp. 1427–1429, 1995.

[8] G. S. Nolas, J. Sharp, and J. Goldsmid, *Thermoelectrics: Basic Principles and New Materials Developments*. vol. 45, New York, NY, USA: Springer-Verlag, 2001.

[9] N. P. Blake, L. Møllnitz, G. Kresse, and H. Metiu, "Why clathrates are good thermoelectrics: A theoretical study of SrGaGe," *J. Chem. Phys.*, vol. 111, no. 7, pp. 3133–3144, 1999.

[10] E. S. Toberer, A. F. May, and G. J. Snyder, "Zintl chemistry for designing high efficiency thermoelectric materials," *Chem. Mater.*, vol. 22, no. 3, pp. 624–634, 2009.

[11] S. Stefanoski, C. D. Malliakas, M. G. Kanatzidis, and G. S. Nolas, "Synthesis and structural characterization of $Na_x Si_{136}$ ($0 < x \leq 24$) single crystals and low-temperature transport of polycrystalline specimens," *Inorgan. Chem.*, vol. 51, no. 16, pp. 8686–8692, 2012.

[12] M. Beekman, E. N. Nenghabi, K. Biswas, C. W. Myles, M. Baitinger, Y. Grin, and G. S. Nolas, "Framework contraction in Na-stuffed Si (cF 136)," *Inorgan. Chem.*, vol. 49, no. 12, pp. 5338–5340, 2010.

[13] X. Blase, "Quasiparticle band structure and screening in silicon and carbon clathrates," *Phys. Rev. B*, vol. 67, no. 3, pp. 035211-1–035211-7, 2003.

[14] J. Gryko, P. McMillan, R. Marzke, G. Ramachandran, D. Patton, S. Deb, and O. Sankey, "Low-density framework form of crystalline silicon with a wide optical band gap," *Phys. Rev. B*, vol. 62, no. 12, pp. R7707–R7710, 2000.

[15] K. Moriguchi, S. Munetoh, and A. Shintani, "First-principles study of $Si_{34-x}Ge_x$ clathrates: Direct wide-gap semiconductors in Si–Ge alloys," *Phys. Rev. B*, vol. 62, no. 11, pp. 7138–7143, 2000.

[16] A. Guloy, R. Ramlau, Z. Tang, W. Schnelle, M. Baitinger, and Y. Grin, "A guest-free germanium clathrate," *Nature*, vol. 443, no. 7109, pp. 320–323, 2006.

[17] A. N. Mansour, M. Beekman, W. Wong-Ng, and G. S. Nolas, "Local structure of Cu in $Cs_8 Na_{16}Cu_5 Ge_{131}$ type II clathrate," *J. Solid State Chem.*, vol. 182, no. 1, pp. 107–114, 2009.

[18] M. Beekman, W. Wong-Ng, J. A. Kaduk, A. Shapiro, and G. S. Nolas, "Synthesis and single crystal x-ray diffraction studies of new framework substituted type II clathrates, $Cs_8 Na_{16} Ag_x Ge_{136-x}$ (x<7)," *J. Solid State Chem.*, vol. 180, no. 1, pp. 1076–1082, 2007.

[19] J. Martin, S. Erickson, G. Nolas, P. Alboni, and T. Tritt, "Thermoelectric properties of Ba-filled Si–Ge alloy type I semiconducting clathrates," in *Proc. 24th IEEE Int. Conf. Thermoelectr.*, 2005, pp. 238–241.

[20] L. Grigorian, P. Eklund, and S. Fang, "Clathrate structure for electronic and electro-optic applications," U.S. Patent 6 103 403, Aug. 15, 2000.

[21] T. Narita, H. Ueno, T. Baba, T. Kume, T. Ban, T. Iida, H. Habuchi, H. Natsuhara, and S. Nonomura, "Preparation of NaSi thin films for the guest free Si clathrate thin films by heat resistance apparatus using NaSi target materials," *Physica Status Solidi (c)*, vol. 7, no. 3–4, pp. 1200–1202, 2010.

[22] M. Torrent, F. Jollet, F. Bottin, G. Zérah, and X. Gonze, "Implementation of the projector augmented-wave method in the ABINIT code: Application to the study of iron under pressure," *Comput. Mater. Sci.*, vol. 42, no. 2, pp. 337–351, 2008.

[23] N. M. Amer and W. B. Jackson, *Semiconductors and Semimetals*, vol. 21, J. I. Pankove, Ed. New York, NY, USA: Academic, 1984, Part B.

[24] J. Conesa, C. Tablero, and P. Wahnon, "First principles calculations of electronic structures and metal mobility of $Na_x Si_{46}$ and $Na_x Si_{34}$ clathrates," *J. Chem. Phys.*, vol. 120, no. 13, pp. 6142–6151, 2004.

[25] R. Himeno, T. Kume, F. Ohashi, T. Ban, and S. Nonomura, "Optical absorption properties of $Na_x Si_{136}$ clathrate studied by diffuse reflection spectroscopy," *J. Alloys Compounds*, vol. 574, pp. 398–401, 2013.

Authors' photographs and biographies not available at the time of publication.

Zn(O, S) Buffer Layers and Thickness Variations of CdS Buffer for Cu$_2$ZnSnS$_4$ Solar Cells

Tove Ericson, Jonathan J. Scragg, Adam Hultqvist, Jörn Timo Wätjen, Piotr Szaniawski, Tobias Törndahl, and Charlotte Platzer-Björkman

Abstract—To improve the conduction band alignment and explore the influence of the buffer–absorber interface, we here investigate an alternative buffer for Cu$_2$ZnSnS$_4$ (CZTS) solar cells. The Zn(O, S) system was chosen since the optimum conduction band alignment with CZTS is predicted to be achievable, by varying oxygen to sulfur ratio. Several sulfur to oxygen ratios were evaluated to find an appropriate conduction band offset. There is a clear trend in open-circuit voltage (V_{oc}), with the highest values for the most sulfur rich buffer, before going to the blocking ZnS, whereas the fill factor peaks at a lower S content. The best alternative buffer cell in this series had an efficiency of 4.6% and the best CdS reference gave 7.3%. Extrapolating V_{oc} values to 0 K gave activation energies well below the expected bandgap of 1.5 eV for CZTS, which indicate that recombination at the interface is dominating. However, it is clear that the values are affected by the change of buffer composition and that increasing sulfur content of the Zn(O, S) increases the activation energy for recombination. A series with varying CdS buffer thickness showed the expected behavior for short wavelengths in quantum efficiency measurements but the final variation in efficiency was small.

Index Terms—Current–voltage characteristics, Cu$_2$ZnSnS$_4$ (CZTS), kesterite, photovoltaic cells, Zn(O, S) buffer.

I. Introduction

THE solar cell material Cu$_2$ZnSn(S,Se)$_4$ (CZTSSe) is a possible alternative to the commercially available Cu(In,Ga)Se$_2$ (CIGS). CZTSSe does not contain indium or gallium, and could therefore be a cheaper and more sustainable solar cell material for the future. Promising efficiencies of up to 11.1% have been achieved [1], but more research is needed to understand what is preventing the devices from being as efficient as CIGS, which has record efficiencies just over 20%.

Several causes for the lower performance have been proposed, such as a MoSe$_2$/MoS$_2$ layer at the back contact [2], secondary phases in the bulk [3], lack of shallow acceptors [4], and a

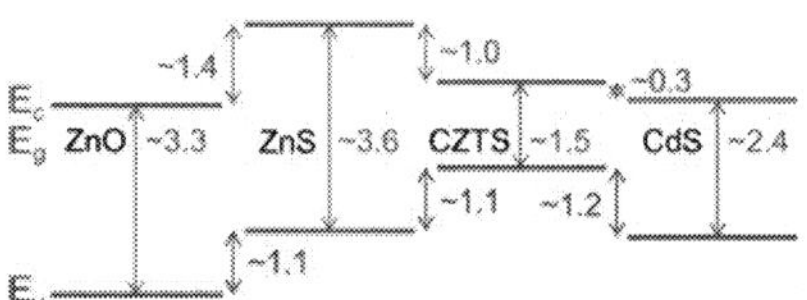

Fig. 1. Approximate conduction band offsets, valence band offsets, and bandgaps, derived from [5], [6], and [8] (values are in eV). The type of the CZTS-CdS conduction band offset is still disputed in the literature, it is shown here as a cliff, following [5]. ZnS forms a barrier toward CZTS and ZnO has a negative conduction band offset with CZTS. The conduction band position of Zn(O, S) has been shown to vary with the oxygen to sulfur ratio [6], so at an intermediate composition, it is likely that the conduction band offset with CZTS is optimal.

nonfavorable alignment of the conduction band at the absorber–CdS buffer interface [5].

To try to improve the conduction band alignment and to explore the influence of the buffer–absorber interface, we here investigate an alternative buffer for Cu$_2$ZnSnS$_4$ (CZTS) solar cells. The Zn(O, S) system was chosen since it has been shown that the conduction band in this material can be changed by varying the ratio of oxygen to sulfur [6], and that the optimum conduction band alignment for CZTS should lie in between the ZnO and the ZnS values (see Fig. 1). Pure ZnO is expected to give a negative conduction band offset with CZTS and has also been shown to give working devices on both CZTS and CZTSSe [7], [8]. ZnS should, according to the theory in [9], cause current blocking due to a high barrier, which has also been observed in experiments [8].

In addition to studying the Zn(O, S) buffer, we performed a small optimization of the CdS buffer thickness on our absorbers. This could also give additional input into understanding the heterojunction formation on CZTS.

II. Experimental Setup

The Mo back contact was sputtered onto soda-lime glass substrates. The absorber was then reactively sputtered in H$_2$S using Zn and Cu:Sn (65:35) alloy targets as described in detail in [10]. The sputtering time was 50 min, giving thicknesses around 2 μm. The precursors had Cu/Sn ratios of 1.91–1.94 and were slightly Zn rich with Zn/(Cu+Sn) equal to 0.39–0.40, as determined by X-ray fluorescence calibrated with Rutherford back scattering (RBS) measurements. The sulfur content was approximately 50% according to energy-dispersive spectroscopy (EDS).

Manuscript received June 5, 2013; revised August 30, 2013; accepted September 15, 2013. Date of publication October 9, 2013; date of current version December 16, 2013. This work was supported by the Swedish Energy Agency and by the Göran Gustafsson Foundation. The work of T. Ericson was supported by a travel scholarship from the C. F. Liljewalchs Fund.

T. Ericson, J. J. Scragg, J. T. Wätjen, P. Szaniawski, T. Törndahl, and C. Platzer-Björkman are with the Solid State Electronics, Ångström Laboratory, Ångström Solar Center, Uppsala SE-751 21, Sweden (e-mail: toer@angstrom.uu.se; josc@angstrom.uu.se; joti@angstrom.uu.se; pisz@angstrom.uu.se; toto@angstrom.uu.se; chpl@angstrom.uu.se).

A. Hultqvist was with the Ångström Solar Center, Uppsala SE-751 21, Sweden. He is now with the Department of Chemical Engineering, Stanford University, Stanford, CA 94305, USA (e-mail: adamhq@stanford.edu).

Color versions of one or more of the figures in this paper are available online at http://ieeexplore.ieee.org.

Digital Object Identifier 10.1109/JPHOTOV.2013.2283058

The precursors were annealed together with 20 mg sulfur in a small graphite box inside a tube furnace under a static argon atmosphere (35 kPa) at 560–565 °C for 10 min. Because of limitations of sample size, the composition after annealing could not be measured for every piece, however, EDS measurement of a dedicated sample showed that the Cu/Sn ratio becomes 2.0, in agreement with our earlier results [11], and that the Zn/(Cu+Sn) ratio is not changed.

The samples were etched in 5 wt% KCN solution for 120 s, rinsed in deionized water, and then, quickly transferred to either chemical bath deposition (CBD) of CdS or to the atomic layer deposition (ALD) system for deposition of Zn(O, S). The ALD was performed at 120 °C in our home-built system called MP3 described in [12], using diethyl zinc (DEZ) as the Zn precursor, H_2O as the O precursor, and H_2S as the S precursor. The buffer composition was varied by changing the number of cycles of DEZ/N_2/H_2O/N_2 versus DEZ/N_2/H_2S/N_2 in the ALD process. This is also how the buffer samples are named: for example, the buffer Zn(O, S)4:1 completes four DEZ/N_2/H_2O/N_2 cycles for every DEZ/N_2/H_2S/N_2 cycle (note that this naming convention differs from some of our previous articles about Zn(O, S) buffer layers for CIGS). A total of 70 cycles was completed for each of the different buffers. For the buffer composition Zn(O, S)6:1, a sample with twice the number of cycles was also prepared.

Samples were prepared on 25 mm × 25 mm substrates. To ensure that the differences observed indeed come from the change of buffer layer, a part of each sample was cut off and processed with the normal CBD CdS buffer. The CBD solution was comprised of 1.1 M ammonia, 0.100 M thiourea, and 0.003 M cadmium acetate. The samples were kept in the solution for 8 min and 15 s at 60 °C, yielding a CdS film thickness of about 50 nm. In the CdS-thickness series, a sample with thinner CdS was produced by shortening the time to 6 min, which is predicted to give roughly half the thickness. For the samples with thick CdS, the CBD procedure was repeated a second time directly after the first, which is expected to give roughly double the thickness of the normal process.

The transparent front contact was deposited with RF-sputtering and consists of a thin intrinsic ZnO and a thicker Al-doped ZnO layer. For one of the samples with double CdS buffer thickness, the intrinsic ZnO was omitted.

The samples were characterized using an I–V–T setup with LED illumination and temperatures from 100 to 330 K. Biased and unbiased quantum efficiency (QE) measurements were made in a setup calibrated by externally measured Hamamatsu Si and InGaAs solar cells. For certain samples, the electron-beam-induced current (EBIC) and transmission electron microscopy (TEM) were performed according to the methods that are described in [13].

Zn(O, S) layers on glass substrates, deposited in the same run as the buffer layers for the solar cells, were further investigated with X-ray reflectivity (XRR) and grazing incidence X-ray diffraction (XRD) in a Philips X'pert MRD diffractometer. The composition of the buffers on the glass substrates was measured with RBS with a 2 MeV He$^+$-beam and a backscattering angle of 170°.

TABLE I

PROPERTIES OF THE ZN(O, S) BUFFERS

Sample name	Buffer	Thickness (XRR) [nm]	Density (XRR) [g/cm^3]	S/Zn (RBS)
B	Zn(O,S) 9:1	16	5.3	0.2
C	Zn(O,S) 6:1 T	33	4.8	0.3
C1	Zn(O,S) 6:1	16	4.5	0.3
D	Zn(O,S) 4:1	16	4.6	0.5

III. RESULTS AND DISCUSSION

A. Zn(O, S) Buffer Composition Variation

For the alternative buffer system, several sulfur to oxygen ratios were evaluated to find an appropriate conduction band offset. The resulting S/Zn-ratios, measured by RBS on glass substrates, are presented in Table I. The oxygen content cannot be determined with this measurement, and therefore, the ratio can only be given with the precision presented in the table. The peak positions from XRD reflect the sample composition, as described in [6], and agree relatively well with our previous measurements on this buffer layer [14]. Measurements with XRR show that the thicknesses of the buffers on the glass are the same for the different compositions and the densities are in the expected range (bulk densities being 5.6 g/cm^3 for ZnO and 4.1 g/cm^3 for ZnS). Doubling the number of ALD cycles roughly doubles the thickness, as seen when comparing sample C and C1. Sample C was also investigated by TEM, and thickness measurements with this technique gave 30 ± 3 nm, which agrees well with the value from XRR.

Varying the composition of the Zn(O, S) buffer layer indeed has a large influence on the electrical properties of the cells, as seen in Table II and Fig. 2. Pure ZnS, as expected, blocks the current, and pure ZnO gives low open-circuit voltage (V_{oc}) values, probably due to a too large negative conduction band offset. The intermediate compositions have a clear trend in V_{oc}, with the highest values for the most sulfur-rich buffer. The currents also show the same, although weaker, trend. The parameter that limits the efficiency for the sulfur rich buffer Zn(O, S)4:1 is the fill factor (FF) which is only 42% compared with 56% for the best alternative buffer, Zn(O, S)6:1.

Shunting seems to increase with higher oxygen content in the buffer. For the Zn(O, S)6:1 buffer, an increased layer thickness was tested in an attempt to decrease the shunt. This seemed to improve FF and V_{oc} slightly (see Table II). However, the shunt conductance, extracted from the dark J–V curve by the method described in [15], was only improved from 2.5 to 1.9 mS/cm^2 for the best cells. Nevertheless, the thicker Zn(O, S)6:1 buffer, denoted as T, yielded 4.6% in efficiency, which was the highest value for the alternative buffers investigated, and is therefore, the sample included in the more detailed measurements and results given here. The CdS reference samples for the complete series gave efficiencies between 4.5–7.3%.

Looking at J–V curves at different temperatures, we notice that the Zn(O, S)4:1 sample is strongly affected by temperature variations already around room temperature. As seen in Fig. 2(b), the other samples have a constant short-circuit current

TABLE II
SOLAR CELL PERFORMANCE FOR SAMPLES WITH VARYING ZN(O, S)-BUFFER LAYER COMPOSITION

Sample name	Buffer	V_{oc}[V]		J_{sc} [mA/cm^2]		FF [%]		Eff. [%]	
		Best	Avg.	Best	Avg.	Best	Avg.	Best	Avg.
A	ZnO	0.152	0.14	14.8	14.0	38.3	36.7	0.9	0.7
B	Zn(O,S) 9:1	0.348	0.26	16.4	15.2	42.6	34.2	2.4	1.5
C	Zn(O,S) 6:1 T	0.482	0.47	17.2	17.0	55.5	50.7	4.6	4.1
C1	Zn(O,S) 6:1	0.461	0.46	17.2	17.1	51.0	50.8	4.1	4.0
D	Zn(O,S) 4:1	0.598	0.55	17.8	17.7	42.4	41.8	4.5	4.0
E	ZnS	0.065	0.05	1.1	1.3	27.0	26.9	0.0	0.0
Ref	CdS	0.652	0.62	17.5	16.4	63.8	57.8	7.3	6.1

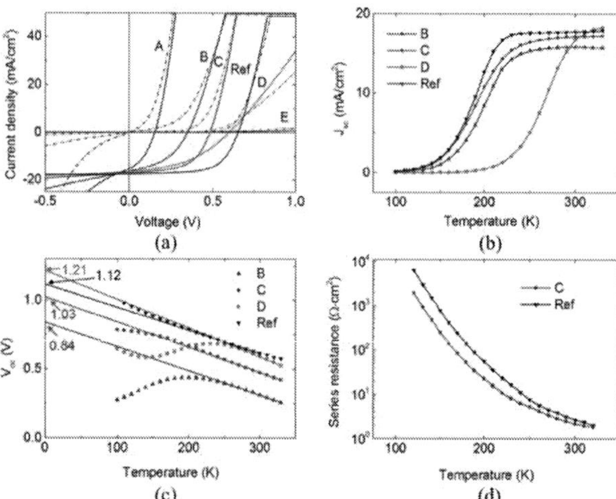

Fig. 2. (a) J–V measurements on samples with different buffer layers. (b) Short-circuit current versus T. (c) Open-circuit voltage versus T and linear extrapolations to 0 K. (d) Series resistance from fitting of J–V curves to a one-diode model. Sample names according to Table II.

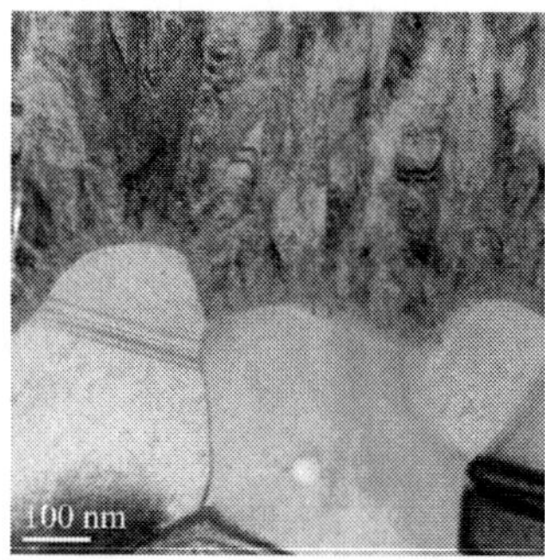

Fig. 3. Bright-field TEM image of a cross section of sample C. The CZTS grains are seen in the lower part of the image. On top are first the buffer layer and then the ZnO window layer.

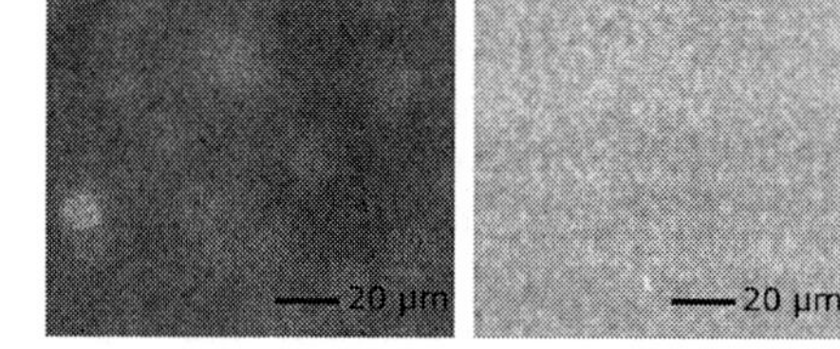

Fig. 4. EBIC on (left) sample C and (right) CdS reference.

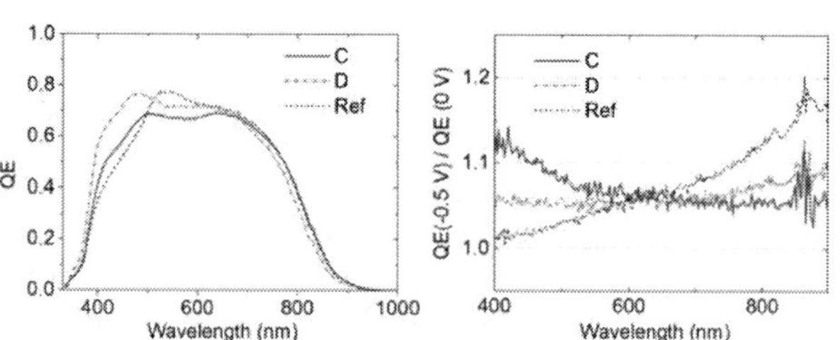

Fig. 5. (Left) QE-measurements on samples with different buffer layers. (Right) Ratio between negative biased (–0.5 V) QE and unbiased QE. Sample names according to Table II.

density (J_{sc}) from 330 K to around 240 K, which then starts decreasing. The Zn(O, S)4:1 sample loses current already between 330 and 320 K. The low *FF* for this buffer together with the sensitivity to decreased temperature suggests that there is a barrier at the interface. Additionally, it has earlier been suggested that these buffer layers are slightly inhomogeneous both in depth and over the area [14]. The area inhomogeneity together with the sensitivity in the band alignment could mean that an optimum alignment is found in some areas, whereas other areas have a too high barrier and block the current unless the temperature is high.

Plotting the V_{oc} against the temperature should yield the activation energy of the dominant recombination path when extrapolated to 0 K. This is described in, for example, [15], and can be seen in (1), where E_A is the activation energy, q is the elemental charge, A is the diode ideality factor, k is the Boltzmann constant, T is the temperature, J_{00} is the saturation current prefactor, and J_L is the photocurrent density

$$V_{OC} = \frac{E_A}{q} - \frac{AkT}{q} \ln\left(\frac{J_{00}}{J_L}\right). \tag{1}$$

As seen in Fig. 2(c), the extrapolations show an increase in activation energy with increasing sulfur content of the Zn(O, S) buffer, but the E_A values are still well below the expected bandgap value of 1.5 eV. This indicates that the band alignment for this buffer can be changed by the oxygen to sulfur ratio, also on the CZTS absorber, but that interface recombination is still dominant, possibly both due to defects and a still nonideal band alignment.

Investigating the interface of the Zn(O, S)6:1 T sample with TEM (bright field in Fig. 3, and high resolution imaging), no

TABLE III
SOLAR CELL PERFORMANCE FOR SAMPLES WITH VARYING CdS-BUFFER LAYER THICKNESS (PROPERTIES OF THE BEST CELL GIVEN)

Sample name	CdS thickness	V_{oc} [V]	J_{sc} [mA/cm^2]	FF [%]	Eff. [%]
X	Thin	0.619	16.2	62.9	6.3
Xref	Normal	0.652	15.1	59.3	5.8
Y	Double	0.657	14.2	58.7	5.5
Yref	Normal	0.646	15.5	58.9	5.9
Z	Double (no i-ZnO)	0.638	14.8	66.3	6.2
Zref	Normal	0.657	16.0	62.3	6.5

obvious causes for bad electrical performance can be seen. The buffer conformally covers the CZTS grains and the crystallinity at the interface seems high. In addition, TEM–EDS across the interface shows a sharp interface without neither clear gradients across the buffer layer nor diffusion of elements between the buffer and absorber.

EBIC was performed on the Zn(O, S)6:1 T sample and the respective CdS reference. Both samples have an intensity variation on the level of the CZTS grain size. Additionally, there is an inhomogeneity on a larger scale for both samples, but, as can be seen in Fig. 4, it is different in shape and size. A TEM comparison between the dark and bright areas seen in the EBIC image, on the Zn(O, S)6:1 T sample, showed no clear differences in thickness, composition, or morphology between the regions.

Trying to fit the J–V curves according to a one-diode model is dubious due to the nonideal behavior, especially at lower temperatures. However, the CdS reference and the best alternative buffer, the double-thickness Zn(O, S)6:1, give fairly reasonable fits. Interestingly, we see that the increase in series resistance for low temperatures, also seen by others [2], is similar for these two buffer layers [see Fig. 2(d)], which indicate that either the two different buffers cause a similar problem, or that the origin of the high series resistance at low temperatures is not the buffer.

Negatively biased QE measurements for the CdS buffer samples gave an increased collection for the long wavelength photons; this is further discussed in the next section. The sample with Zn(O, S)4:1 buffer instead shows an increased QE for all wavelengths at -0.5 V, with only slightly more increase for long wavelengths (see Fig. 5). An explanation for this could be a photocurrent barrier at the buffer–absorber interface, in agreement with the low FF discussed earlier. For the Zn(O, S)6:1 T and Zn(O, S)6:1 samples, there is instead an additional increase of collection toward the short wavelength side. This could originate from the negative bias decreasing interface recombination of holes generated in the top part of the absorber and in the buffer [16].

B. CdS Buffer Thickness Variation

The results from the CdS buffer thickness series are presented in Table III and Fig. 6, together with their respective references, which were taken from the same precursor and annealing run but processed with the standard CdS and window layers. As seen in Fig. 6, the QE signal behaves as expected for the different thicknesses, with higher response at the low wavelength side for the sample with a thin buffer, and a decreased level for the samples with thick CdS buffer. The long wavelength part of the QE curve looks similar for the different samples, but the solar

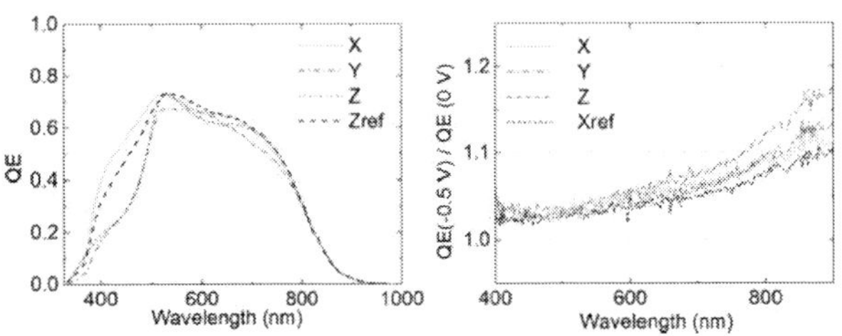

Fig. 6. (Left) QE-measurements on samples with different thickness of the CdS buffer layer. (Right) Ratio between negatively biased (-0.5 V) QE and unbiased QE. Sample names according to Table III.

cell with thickest total window layer (double CdS and including i-ZnO) has a generally lower QE.

When comparing the QE measured without bias with the QE measured at -0.5 V, all samples show an increase in collection for the long wavelengths with negative bias. Such behavior was reported earlier for this material combination, for example in [2], and is usually explained by poor collection toward the back of the absorber [16], possibly due to short diffusion lengths in combination with a narrow space charge region. The behavior is very similar between the different thicknesses of buffer layer, which could indicate that the Fermi level at the interface is pinned by interface states.

The V_{oc} is slightly reduced for the thinnest CdS thickness. Comparing the thick CdS sample (Y) with its own reference also shows this trend, but when comparing with the reference samples in general there is no difference between the normal and the double thickness. A general increase of V_{oc} with increasing CdS thickness was seen in [17] for thicknesses from roughly 30 to 300 nm on monograins of CZTS, whereas the opposite trend was seen in [18], but no thickness range was given in the latter case.

We note that the FF for the sample without i-ZnO is one of the highest reported for the CZTS material in the literature.

The efficiency difference is at most 1% for this series, and the variation between the references is 0.7%, indicating that the performance of the solar cell is rather robust to change of CdS buffer thickness in this range.

IV. CONCLUSION

In summary, we have shown that Zn(O, S) is a viable buffer system for CZTS, in which it is possible to vary the conduction band offset between the absorber and the buffer. The best cell with this alternative buffer had an efficiency of 4.6% and was obtained for the Zn(O, S)6:1 buffer, the same optimum composition as for CIGS [12]. However, judging from the V_{oc} extrapolation to 0 K, a buffer with higher sulfur content gives a higher activation energy for recombination, which indicates that the interface can be further improved. The large increase in series resistance at low temperatures is similar for the CdS and Zn(O, S)6:1 buffer samples.

We have also shown that increasing the CdS buffer thickness causes the expected decrease of short wavelength QE response but did not affect the efficiency values to a large extent, especially if the i-ZnO is omitted for the thickest CdS buffer layer sample.

ACKNOWLEDGMENT

The authors would like to thank D. Primetzhofer for assistance with the RBS measurements, which were made at Uppsala Tandem Laboratory (Ion Technology Center).

REFERENCES

[1] T. K. Todorov, J. Tang, S. Bag, O. Gunawan, T. Gokmen, Y. Zhu, and D. B. Mitzi, "Beyond 11% efficiency: Characteristics of state-of-the-art Cu2ZnSn(S,Se)4 solar cells," *Adv. Energy Mater.*, vol. 3, pp. 34–38, Jan. 2013.

[2] O. Gunawan, T. Todorov, and D. Mitzi, "Loss mechanisms in hydrazine-processed Cu2ZnSn(Se,S)4 solar cells," *Appl. Phys. Lett.*, vol. 97, pp. 233506-1–233506-3, Dec. 2010.

[3] A. Redinger, M. Mousel, M. H. Wolter, N. Valle, and S. Siebentritt, "Influence of S/Se ratio on series resistance and on dominant recombination pathway in Cu2ZnSn(SSe)4 thin film solar cells," *Thin Solid Films*, vol. 535, pp. 291–295, May 2013.

[4] O. Gunawan, T. Gokmen, C. W. Warren, J. D. Cohen, T. K. Todorov, D. A. R. Barkhouse, S. Bag, J. Tang, B. Shin, and D. B. Mitzi, "Electronic properties of the $Cu_2ZnSn(Se,S)_4$ absorber layer in solar cells as revealed by admittance spectroscopy and related methods," *Appl. Phys. Lett.*, vol. 100, pp. 253905-4, Jun. 2012.

[5] M. Bär, B. A. Schubert, B. Marsen, R. G. Wilks, S. Pookpanratana, M. Blum, S. Krause, T. Unold, W. Yang, L. Weinhardt, C. Heske, and H. W. Schock, "Cliff-like conduction band offset and KCN-induced recombination barrier enhancement at the CdS/Cu_2ZnSnS_4 thin-film solar cell heterojunction," *Appl. Phys. Lett.*, vol. 99, pp. 222105-1–222105-3, Nov. 2011.

[6] C. Platzer-Björkman, T. Törndahl, D. Abou-Ras, J. Malmström, J. Kessler, and L. Stolt, "Zn(O, S) buffer layers by atomic layer deposition in $Cu(In,Ga)Se_2$ based thin film solar cells: Band alignment and sulfur gradient," *J. Appl. Phys.*, vol. 100, pp. 044506-1–044506-8, Aug. 2006.

[7] H. Katagiri, K. Jimbo, M. Tahara, H. Araki, and K. Oishi, "The Influence of the Composition Ratio on CZTS-Based Thin Film Solar Cells," in *Proc. Mater. Res. Soc. Symp.*, May 2009, vol. 1165, 12 pp.

[8] D. A. R. Barkhouse, R. Haight, N. Sakai, H. Hiroi, H. Sugimoto, and D. B. Mitzi, "Cd-free buffer layer materials on $Cu_2ZnSn(S_x Se_1 - x_4$: Band alignments with ZnO, ZnS, and In_2S_3," *Appl. Phys. Lett.*, vol. 100, pp. 193904-1–193904-5, May 2012.

[9] A. Nagoya, R. Asahi, and G. Kresse, "First-principles study of Cu2ZnSnS4 and the related band offsets for photovoltaic applications," *J. Phys. Condens. Matter*, vol. 23, pp. 404203-1–404203-6, Oct. 2011.

[10] T. Ericson, T. Kubart, J. J. Scragg, and C. Platzer-Björkman, "Reactive sputtering of precursors for Cu_2ZnSnS_4 thin film solar cells," *Thin Solid Films*, vol. 520, pp. 7093–7099, Oct. 2012.

[11] J. J. Scragg, T. Kubart, J. T. Wätjen, T. Ericson, M. K. Linnarsson, and C. Platzer-Björkman, "Effects of back contact instability on Cu2ZnSnS4 devices and processes," *Chem. Mater.*, vol. 25, pp. 3162–3171, Aug. 2013.

[12] U. Zimmermann, M. Ruth, and M. Edoff, "Cadmium-free CIGS minimodules with ALD-grown Zn(O, S)-based buffer layers," presented at the 21st Eur. Photovoltaic Solar Energy Conf., Dresden, Germany, 2006.

[13] J. T. Wätjen, J. Engman, M. Edoff, and C. Platzer-Björkman, "Direct evidence of current blocking by ZnSe in $Cu_2ZnSnSe_4$ solar cells," *Appl. Phys. Lett.*, vol. 100, pp. 173510-1–173510-3, Apr. 2012.

[14] A. Hultqvist, C. Platzer-Björkman, E. Coronel, and M. Edoff, "Experimental investigation of $Cu(In_{1-x},Ga_x)Se_2/Zn(O_{1-z},S_z)$ solar cell performance," *Sol. Energy Mater. Sol. Cells*, vol. 95, pp. 497–503, Feb. 2011.

[15] S. S. Hegedus and W. N. Shafarman, "Thin-film solar cells: Device measurements and analysis," *Prog. Photovolt.*, vol. 12, pp. 155–176, Mar.–May 2004.

[16] R. Scheer and H. W. Schock, *Chalcogenide Photovoltaics.* Weinheim, Germany: Wiley–VCH Verlag, 2011.

[17] K. Ernits, R. Hall, K. Muska, and T. Holopainen, "Multiple CdS deposition on Cu2ZnSn(S,Se)4 monograins," presented at the 2nd Kesterite Workshop, Barcelona, Spain, 2011.

[18] H. Sugimoto, H. Hiroi, N. Sakai, S. Muraoka, and T. Katou, "Over 8% Efficiency Cu2ZnSnS4 Submodules with Ultra-Thin Absorber," in *Proc. IEEE 38th Photovolt. Spec. Conf.*, Jun. 2012, pp. 2997–3000.

     134

Comparison of Direct Growth and Wafer Bonding for the Fabrication of GaInP/GaAs Dual-Junction Solar Cells on Silicon

Frank Dimroth, Tobias Roesener, Stephanie Essig, Christoph Weuffen, Alexander Wekkeli, Eduard Oliva,
Gerald Siefer, Kerstin Volz, Thomas Hannappel, Dietrich Häussler, Wolfgang Jäger, and Andreas W. Bett

Abstract—Two different process technologies were investigated for the fabrication of high-efficiency GaInP/GaAs dual-junction solar cells on silicon: direct epitaxial growth and layer transfer combined with semiconductor wafer bonding. The intention of this research is to combine the advantages of high efficiencies in III–V tandem solar cells with the low cost of silicon. Direct epitaxial growth of a GaInP/GaAs dual-junction solar cell on a $GaAs_yP_{1-y}$ buffer on silicon yielded a 1-sun efficiency of 16.4% (AM1.5g). Threading dislocations that result from the 4% lattice grading are still the main limitation to the device performance. In contrast, similar devices fabricated by semiconductor wafer bonding on n-type inactive Si reached efficiencies of 26.0% (AM1.5g) for a 4-cm^2 solar cell device.

Index Terms—Heterojunctions, silicon, wafer bonding, III–V multijunction solar cells.

I. INTRODUCTION

THE combination of III–V multijunction solar cells and silicon offers many advantages. The high mechanical strength, excellent heat conductivity, nontoxicity, availability in large diameters, and comparably low cost are just some of the most important properties which favor silicon as a semiconductor material. Therefore, the research and development of monolithic III–V solar cells on Si has a long history, but

Manuscript received June 13, 2013; revised October 7, 2013; accepted December 10, 2013. Date of current version February 17, 2014. This work was supported in part by the German Ministry for education and research BMBF under the Contract III–V-Si Solar 03SF0329A and in part by the European Union by the project NGCPV under Contract 283798. The Ph.D. work of S. Essig and T. Roesener was supported by the German Federal Environmental Foundation (DBU) and Reiner–Lemoine Foundation.

F. Dimroth, S. Essig, C. Weuffen, A. Wekkeli, E. Oliva, G. Siefer, and A.W. Bett are with the Fraunhofer Institute for Solar Energy Systems ISE, D-79110 Freiburg, Germany (e-mail: frank.dimroth@ise.fraunhofer.de; stephanie.essig@ise.fraunhofer.de; christoph.weuffen@ise.fraunhofer.de; alexander.wekkeli@ise.fraunhofer.de; eduard.oliva@ise.fraunhofer.de; gerald.siefer@ise.fraunhofer.de; bett@ise.fraunhofer.de).

T. Roesener was with the Fraunhofer ISE, D-79110 Freiburg, Germany. He is now with the AZUR Space Solar Power GmbH, D-74072 Heilbronn, Germany (e-mail: tobias.roesener@azurspace.com).

K. Volz is with the Philipps University Marburg, D-35032 Marburg, Germany (e-mail: kerstin.volz@physik.uni-marburg.de).

T. Hannappel is with the Technische Universität Ilmenau, D-98693 Ilmenau, Germany (e-mail: Thomas.Hannappel@tu-ilmenau.de).

D. Häussler and W. Jäger are with the Institute of Materials Science, Christian-Albrechts-University, D-24118 Kiel, Germany (e-mail: dih@tf.uni-kiel.de; wj@tf.uni-kiel.de).

Digital Object Identifier 10.1109/JPHOTOV.2014.2299406

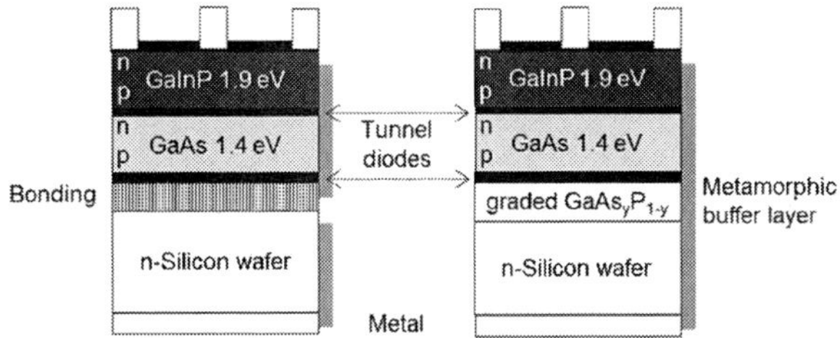

Fig. 1. Schematic of two investigated concepts for the integration of high-efficiency III–V solar cells on silicon. $Ga_{0.5}In_{0.5}P$/GaAs tandem solar cell structure transferred to Si by wafer bonding (left) and direct growth of $Ga_{0.5}In_{0.5}P$/GaAs structure on a GaAsP metamorphic buffer layer on Si (right). Both solar cell structures have an n-on-p polarity and are grown on n-Si. Tunnel diodes are used to connect the top and bottom subcells, as well as the bottom subcell and the n-Si wafer.

challenges in the fabrication processes, cracking or bowing of films because of high thermal mismatch, and high dislocation densities have so far prohibited the commercial success of this technology [2]. This situation is currently changing for optoelectronic devices like GaN-based LEDs, for which the first commercial products are entering the market. The reasons being that the transition between nonpolar Si and polar III–V crystals is better understood and high-quality nucleation layers of III–V on Si are more widely available today [3]–[7]. Furthermore, the understanding of lattice-mismatched growth has significantly improved over the years [8]–[12]. This also opens new opportunities for III–V multijunction solar cells to be manufactured on Si, especially if high efficiencies can be demonstrated. In this paper, we are investigating two pathways to achieve high-efficiency III–V multijunction solar cells on Si: direct epitaxial growth and thin layer transfer combined with wafer bonding (see Fig. 1). Both of these approaches are viable for industrial applications of III–V on Si solar cells.

Direct epitaxial growth of III–V on Si for solar cells was successfully developed in the 1990s, for example, by Umeno *et al.* [13] and Yang *et al.* [14]. They proved efficiencies up to 20% for AlGaAs/Si devices under AM0. Ringel *et al.* were following a different approach by combining SiGe templates grown by chemical vapor deposition with MBE growth of a GaAs or GaInP/GaAs solar cell structure [15]–[18]. The best devices showed a total area efficiency of 16.8% under AM1.5g conditions. More recently, GaP nucleation layers on Si with high crystalline quality and low density of antiphase domains (APDs) became available [3], [4], [7], and publications are concentrating on $GaAs_yP_{1-y}$ transition layers to form III–V on silicon solar cell devices [19], [20].

An alternative approach was used to first create GaAs or Ge on Si templates by wafer bonding and lift-off before starting the epitaxial growth. This was followed by Schöne *et al.* in [21] as well as Zahler and Archer *et al.* [22], [23]. They demonstrated the metal-organic-vapor-phase-epitaxy (MOVPE) growth of GaInP/GaAs tandem solar cell devices on such templates reaching 16% efficiency. Difficulties were connected with the different thermal expansion of silicon and GaAs, which may lead to cracking of the thin solar cell layers when heated to the high growth temperatures of 600–700 °C. Postgrowth wafer bonding avoids such high temperatures and was recently demonstrated in a publication by Derendorf *et al.* [24]. In this case, a GaInP/GaAs tandem solar cell was first grown on a GaAs substrate and then combined with a Si bottom pn-junction to form a triple-junction device. Efficiencies of 23.6% were reported under concentrated illumination showing the high potential of this approach.

This paper presents GaInP/GaAs dual-junction solar cells on inactive n-type silicon. Both wafer bonding and direct growth have been investigated, and the results are discussed, together with challenges of each method.

II. Experimental Details

GaInP/GaAs tandem solar cells with n-on-p polarity were entirely grown by MOVPE. The bandgap energies of the top and bottom subcells were 1.88 and 1.43 eV, respectively. n^+ GaAs/p^+ AlGaAs tunnel diodes were used for the series connection between the top and bottom cells, as well as the bottom subcell and the n-Si substrate. In the wafer bonding approach (see Fig. 1 left), a GaInP/GaAs solar cell structure was first grown inverted on GaAs wafers (100) 6° off toward $\langle 1 -1 \, 1 \rangle$, including an etch-stop layer. The film was polished and then bonded to silicon using fast atom beam activated direct wafer bonding [25] in an Ayumi SAB-100 system at 120 °C and removed from the GaAs substrate by wet chemical etching.

Then, the bonded solar cell structure was annealed for 1 min at 400 °C and finally processed to solar cell devices with a total area of 4 cm². All cells were covered with a TaO_x/MgF_2 antireflective coating on the front side. Standard ohmic metal contacts were applied to the GaAs cap layer on the front side of the cell and the Si rear side, respectively.

In the case of direct growth (see Fig. 1 right), the epitaxy process started with a 300-nm homoepitaxial silicon layer on n-Si, followed by the growth of a 60-nm thick n-GaP nucleation layer and a $GaAs_yP_{1-y}$ graded buffer with seven steps to overcome the 4% difference in lattice constant between Si and GaAs. Typical growth temperatures of 640 °C and growth rates of 0.94 nm/s were used. Afterward, the samples were transferred to a second MOVPE system where the GaInP/GaAs layer structure with n-on-p polarity was deposited. A CRIUS closed-coupled showerhead reactor served for the direct III–V growth on Si, whereas an AIX 2800-G4 system was used for the GaInP/GaAs solar cell structures. In future, both processes shall be combined in

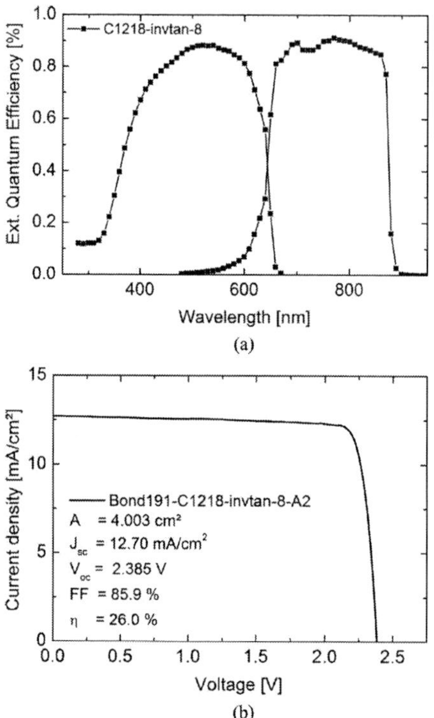

Fig. 2. (a) EQE (b) and *I–V*-characteristic under AM1.5g spectral conditions of a GaInP/GaAs tandem solar cell transferred and bonded to silicon.

the same chamber. Device processing was the same as described previously for wafer bonded solar cells.

Measurements of the external quantum efficiency (EQE) and current–voltage characteristics were carried out in the Fraunhofer ISE Callab. The incident spectral conditions were matched to the AM1.5g spectrum. More details of the procedures can be found in [26] and [27].

III. Results and Discussion

A. Wafer Bonded GaInP/GaAs Solar Cells on Si

Fig. 2(a) shows the EQE of a GaInP/GaAs tandem solar cell (1.0-μm thick $Ga_{0.5}In_{0.5}P$ and 1.8-μm GaAs absorber) which has been first grown inverted on a GaAs substrate and then transferred to n-Si by wafer bonding. The overall thickness of the epitaxy structure including buffer layers and tunnel diodes was 4.6 μm. It is important to note, that such thin crystalline layers are not stable enough to handle and must always be supported by a carrier. This was achieved by bonding the solar cell layers to silicon before removal of the GaAs substrate. The dual-junction solar cell shows an excellent characteristic with both junctions reaching EQE values above 88%.

I–V characteristics of solar cells with 4-cm² total area were measured under AM1.5g standard test conditions [see Fig. 2(b)]. The best devices reach an efficiency of 26.0% with an open-circuit voltage of 2.39 V, a short-circuit current density of 12.7 mA/cm², and a fillfactor of 85.9% (C1218-invtan-8-T504-M43-A2). The high performance is due to the good crystal

136

I–V-Characteristics of GaInP/GaAs Tandem Solar Cells Under AM1.5g Conditions, Cell Area 4 cm^2

Solar Cell Type	J_{sc} [mA/cm2]	V_{oc} [V]	FF [%]	η [%]
GaInP/GaAs tandem cell from Ref. [1]	14.22	2.49	85.6	30.3
Wafer bonded cell on silicon	12.7	2.39	85.9	**26.0**
Upright reference on GaAs substrate	13.15	2.45	84.2	27.1
Upright direct growth on silicon	11.20	1.94	75.3	16.4

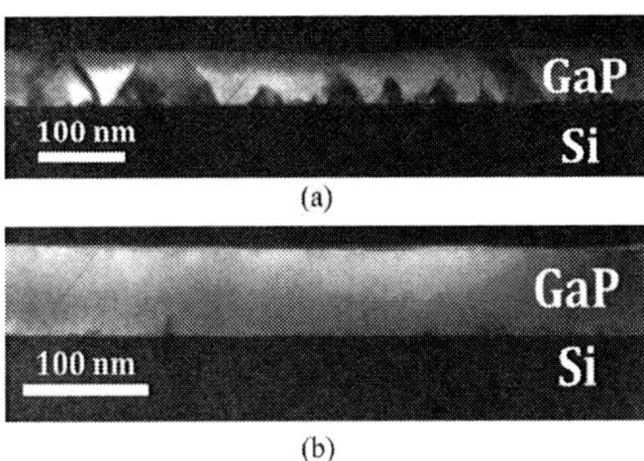

Fig. 3. Dark-field transmission electron microscopy images, (0 0 –2) reflex of GaP nucleation layers on Si with (a) high and (b) low density of APDs.

quality and low dislocation density which are obtained for lattice-matched growth on GaAs. This is also supported by the high open-circuit voltage of 2.39 V, which is only 100 mV below the best GaInP/GaAs tandem solar cell from [1] (see also Table I). Although these solar cell structures are not directly comparable due to the upright versus inverted growth and probable differences in the layer structure, the voltage is a sensitive measure of the crystal quality, and the value of 2.39 V for the GaInP/GaAs tandem solar cells on silicon proves the high material quality which has been achieved.

Further optimization of the GaInP and GaAs solar cell structure is needed especially to increase the short-circuit current density. This requires a reduction of parasitic absorption losses in the window, antireflection, and tunnel diode layers, as well as better current matching of the subcells. The AM1.5g current generation of the GaInP top cell is calculated from the EQE to be 12.9 mA/cm^2 compared with 14.4 mA/cm^2 for the GaAs bottom cell. Improvements of the response in the short-wavelength range are possible and subject of current developments. This should allow us to reach efficiencies above 30% with this approach.

For an economic success of the wafer-bonded cell, multiple reuse of the GaAs substrate is mandatory. The solar cells in this paper were processed after wet-chemical etching of the GaAs substrate which leads to a loss of the GaAs material. In addition, the preparation steps of bonding the 4.6-μm thick inverted III–V layer structure to silicon and removing the GaAs substrate must be carried out with high yield and in high throughput equipment. The wafer bonding process itself can be fast if performed at room temperature, as in the present experiments.

B. Directly Grown GaInP/GaAs Solar Cells on Si

The direct growth of III–V solar cell structures on Si is more challenging but has the advantage of using only one substrate and one epitaxial process. This allows for lower manufacturing costs. In the present experiments, the growth of an n-GaP nucleation layer on Si has been separated from the growth of the GaAs$_{1-y}$P$_y$ metamorphic buffer and the GaInP/GaAs tandem solar cell structure to avoid any source of potential cross contamination. It has to be carefully analyzed in the future how these processes can be combined, avoiding nucleation-related defects on Si induced by previously grown III–V material, as well as high background doping levels of the III–V elements in silicon and *vice versa*.

The n-GaP nucleation layer in our experiments was directly grown on Si to form the transition between the singular group IV and the polar III–V crystal lattice. Modulated flows of TEGa and TBP were used for the monolayer growth of GaP following the procedure described in [3] for singular (1 0 0) Si substrates. In this paper, the process was adapted to the large CRIUS MOVPE reactor and silicon wafers with 6° offcut angle toward $\langle 1 -1\ 1\rangle$.

Fig. 3 shows two dark-field transmission electron microscopy (TEM) images of a 60-nm thick GaP nucleation layer with high (top) and low (bottom) density of APDs. Phases with different polarity appear light or dark under these imaging conditions. It turned out that the formation of APDs is very sensitive to the flow of TEGa during the pulsed nucleation as excess Ga can accumulate on the surface. If the TEGa flow is chosen carefully, the density of remaining APDs was found to be very low [see Fig. 3(b)], and most APDs at the interface annihilate within the first 10–30 nm of GaP growth. The surface of the 60-nm thick GaP nucleation layer was virtually free of APDs which was also confirmed by reflection anisotropy spectroscopy (RAS). A distinct RAS spectrum for single-domain GaP was found for these layers, similar to [28]. Still, in some cases, planar defects like twins or stacking faults are found in the TEM micrographs. These defects originate at the GaP/Si interface and propagate throughout the crystal layers. It is important to avoid such threading dislocations as they can have a severe impact on the minority carrier diffusion length in the active solar cell layers. Further work is required to understand the origin and avoid the formation of these planar defects.

GaAs$_y$P$_{1-y}$ was used for grading the lattice constant between GaP and GaAs. Fig. 4 shows a TEM image of a typical buffer structure that comprises of seven step-graded GaAs$_y$P$_{1-y}$ layers with increasing As content followed by the GaAs target layer. The thickness of each GaAs$_y$P$_{1-y}$ layer was 100 nm in this structure. An additional Ga$_{0.97}$In$_{0.03}$As over-shooting layer (GaInAs-ÜSS) was added on top of the GaAs target layer to fully relax the in-plane lattice constant and ensure that further growth of the GaInP/GaAs tandem cell continues unstrained.

Unfortunately, a rather high density of threading dislocations resulted from the lattice grading in the metamorphic buffer. Counting threading dislocations in the TEM image (see Fig. 4)

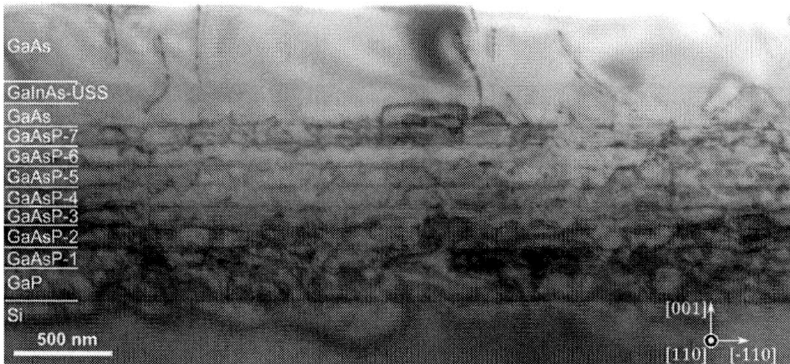

Fig. 4. TEM image of a $GaAs_yP_{1-y}$ metamorphic buffer layer on Si. The structure consists of a GaP nucleation layer on Si, seven $GaAs_yP_{1-y}$ layers, a GaAs target layer, and a GaInAs over shooting layer (ÜSS) to relax the in-plane lattice constant and finally 400 nm of GaAs.

suggest that the density is exceeding 10^8 cm^{-2} after the buffer growth. Atomic force microscopy images of the surface showed small pits with a density of 2×10^8 cm^{-2} in the upper GaAs layer, which correlates well with the TEM results and suggests that the threading dislocations influence the local growth mode. Single-junction GaAs solar cells with p-on-n polarity were investigated on the same $GaAs_{1-y}P_y$ buffer layers on silicon and the devices showed open-circuit voltages of 795 mV (compared with 1038 mV for a reference cell on GaAs). This loss in voltage is expected for a threading dislocation density of 2×10^8 cm^{-2}, following the model of Yamaguchi *et al.* [29]. The different analysis methods lead to the same conclusion that the threading dislocation density in the GaAs target layer on silicon is still high and of the order of 10^8 cm^{-2}. The growth conditions and composition of the buffer layers need to be further optimized in the future. An important parameter to reduce dislocations is for example the grading rate (i.e., lattice mismatch per micrometer of growth) [30].

GaInP/GaAs tandem solar cell structures (790-nm-thick $Ga_{0.5}In_{0.5}P$ and 1.9-μm GaAs absorber) were grown on the GaAsP/Si templates. The thickness of the $GaAs_yP_{1-y}$ layers in the metamorphic buffer was increased to 180 nm. Otherwise, all parameters were identical to the structure in Fig. 4. A reference tandem cell was grown on the GaAs substrate in the same epitaxy process together with the GaAsP/Si template. Fig. 5 shows results for the quantum efficiencies of both devices. While the GaInP top cell shows similar performance on GaAs and Si substrates, the GaAs bottom cell suffers significantly from the low diffusion length of minority carriers. There are two possible explanations for this result: either the additional growth of the GaAs cell and tunnel diodes on the GaAsP buffer layer leads to a reduction of the threading dislocation density, or the GaInP top cell material is less sensitive to dislocations. This can be expected as the thickness of the GaInP base layer (660 nm) is much lower compared with the GaAs base layer (1750 nm). Therefore, minority carriers need higher diffusion length in GaAs to reach the pn-junction and contribute to the photocurrent. Due to the low quantum efficiency of the GaAs bottom cell on Si, this subcell limits the overall current of the tandem cell under AM1.5g.

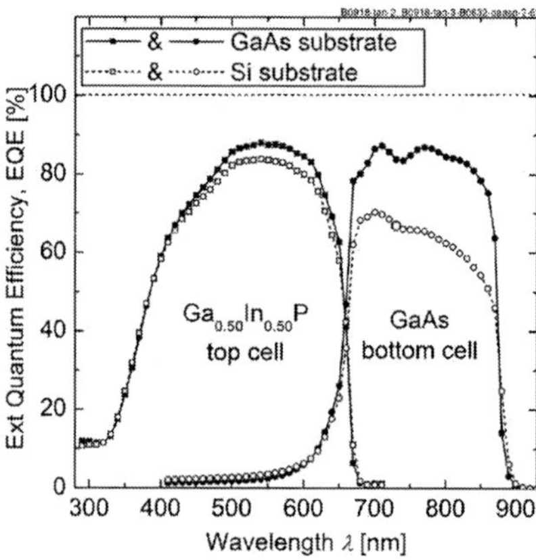

Fig. 5. EQE of a GaInP/GaAs tandem solar cell grown on Si compared with an identical reference structure on GaAs.

An efficiency of 16.4% (AM1.5g) was measured for the best directly grown GaInP/GaAs tandem solar cell on Si in comparison with 27.1% for the reference structure on GaAs (see Table I). It is obvious that the high dislocation density for the growth on silicon leads to losses in short-circuit current density J_{sc}, fillfactor FF, and open-circuit voltage V_{oc}. The V_{oc} of the tandem cell on Si drops by 510 mV compared with the reference structure. This is approximately twice the voltage drop measured for a GaAs single-junction cell on Si. This result is expected as both junctions in the dual-junction device contribute approximately the same voltage loss to the series-connected dual-junction cell. Higher open-circuit voltages of 2.2 V were reported by Lueck *et al.* [16] for GaInP/GaAs tandem cells on SiGe/Si buffer layers with a low dislocation density of 2×10^6 cm^{-2}. This shows that further optimization of the $GaAs_yP_{1-y}$ buffer layer is necessary to improve the threading dislocation density and the overall performance of our tandem solar cells on silicon. It should be mentioned that none of the devices on Si showed any indication of cracking due to differences in the thermal expansion coefficient of Si and GaAs. Direct MOVPE growth of III–V solar cells on Si, therefore, is also a viable process to realize high-efficiency devices.

IV. Conclusion

This paper discusses two approaches how III–V tandem solar cells can be realized on silicon as a substrate material. This is an important step toward reducing the cost of III–V solar cells and making the technology attractive for terrestrial applications. III–V materials in multijunction solar cells offer the opportunity to overcome the Shockley–Queisser limit of single-junction devices [31]. In this paper, we have investigated dual-junction solar cells with an active $Ga_{0.5}In_{0.5}P$ top cell and a GaAs middle cell. The solar cells were realized on inactive silicon as a mechanical support and electrical conductor. One approach was based on the epitaxy of an inverted GaInP/GaAs solar cell on GaAs followed by bonding to Si and GaAs substrate removal. For the first time, such tandem solar cells achieved 26.0% AM1.5g efficiency on Si. A second approach was to grow the III–V materials directly on Si, and an efficiency of 16.4% AM1.5g was obtained. The solar cell structures had different layer thicknesses, but it was evident that a high threading dislocation density was leading to significant losses for the GaInP/GaAs solar cells grown directly on Si. Further optimization of the graded $GaAs_yP_{1-y}$ buffer will be necessary to reduce such dislocations and improve the device performance.

The concept of the III–V solar cell on Si can be further extended to include an active Si junction as a third bottom subcell in the future. With this approach, one-sun efficiencies above 30% are realistic and offer one of the most promising roadmaps for the realization of high-efficiency photovoltaic modules.

Acknowledgment

The authors would like to thank E. Schäffer, E. Fehrenbacher, M. Scheer, K. Wagner, I. Semke, K. Mayer, and R. Koch for solar cell fabrication and characterization at Fraunhofer ISE.

References

[1] M. A. Green, K. Emery, Y. Hishikawa, and W. Warta, "Solar cell efficiency tables (ver. 35)," *Prog. Photovoltaics: Res. Appl.*, vol. 18, pp. 144–150, 2010.

[2] S. F. Fang, K. Adomi, S. Iyer, H. Morkoç, H. Zabel, C. Choi, and N. Otsuka, "Gallium arsenide and other compound semiconductors on silicon," *J. Appl. Phys.*, vol. 68, pp. R31–R58, 1990.

[3] K. Volz, A. Beyer, W. Witte, J. Ohlmann, I. Németh, B. Kunert, and W. Stolz, "GaP-nucleation on exact Si (001) substrates for III/V device integration," *J. Crystal Growth*, vol. 315, pp. 37–47, 2011.

[4] H. Döscher, B. Borkenhagen, G. Lilienkamp, W. Daum, and T. Hannappel, "III–V on silicon: Observation of gallium phosphide anti-phase disorder by low-energy electron microscopy," *Surface Sci.*, vol. 605, pp. L38–L41, 2011.

[5] A. Dadgar, P. Veit, F. Schulze, J. Blasing, A. Krtschil, H. Witte, A. Diez, T. Hempel, J. Christen, R. Clos, and A. Krost, "MOVPE growth of GaN on Si–substrates and strain," *Thin Solid Films*, vol. 515, pp. 4356–4361, 2007.

[6] B. Kunert, I. Németh, S. Reinhard, K. Volz, and W. Stolz, "Si (001) surface preparation for the antiphase domain free heteroepitaxial growth of GaP on Si substrate," *Thin Solid Films*, vol. 517, pp. 140–143, 2008.

[7] T. J. Grassman, J. A. Carlin, B. Galiana, L.-M. Yang, F. Yang, M. J. Mils, and S. A. Ringel, "Nucleation-related defect-free GaP/Si(100) heteroepitaxy via metal-organic chemical vapor deposition," *Appl. Phys. Lett.*, vol. 102, pp. 142102-1–142102-4, 2013.

[8] V. I. Vdovin, "Misfit dislocations in epitaxial heterostructures: Mechanisms of generation and multiplication," *Phys. Status Solidi A*, vol. 171, pp. 239–250, 1999.

[9] W. Guter, J. Schöne, S. P. Philipps, M. Steiner, G. Siefer, A. Wekkeli, E. Welser, E. Oliva, A. W. Bett, and F. Dimroth, "Current-matched triple-junction solar cell reaching 41.1% conversion efficiency under concentrated sunlight," *Appl. Phys. Lett.*, vol. 94, pp. 223504–223506, 2009.

[10] A. W. Bett, C. Baur, F. Dimroth, and J. Schöne, "Metamorphic GaInP–GaInAs layers for photovoltaic applications," in *Proc. Mater. Res. Soc. Symp.*, 2005, vol. 836, pp. 223–234.

[11] T. J. Grassman, M. R. Brenner, M. Gonzalez, A. M. Carlin, R. R. Unocic, R. R. Dehoff, M. J. Mills, and S. A. Ringel, "Characterization of metamorphic GaAsP/Si materials and devices for photovoltaic applications," *IEEE Trans. Electron Devices*, vol. 57, no. 12, pp. 3361–3369, Dec. 2010.

[12] M. W. Wanlass, S. P. Ahrenkiel, R. K. Ahrenkiel, D. S. Albin, J. J. Carapella, A. Duda, J. F. Geisz, S. Kurtz, T. Moriarty, R. J. Wehrer, and B. Wernsman, "Lattice-mismatched approaches for high-performance, III–V photovoltaic energy converters," in *Proc. 31st IEEE Photovolt. Spec. Conf.*, Orlando, FL, USA, 2005, pp. 530–535.

[13] M. Umeno, H. Shimizu, T. Egawa, T. Soga, and T. Jimbo, "First results of AlGaAs/Si monolithic two-terminal tandem solar cell grown by MOCVD," in *Proc. 22nd IEEE Photovolt. Spec. Conf.*, Las Vegas, NV, USA, 1991, pp. 361–364.

[14] M. J. Yang, T. Soga, T. Jimbo, and M. Umeno, "High efficiency monolithic GaAs/Si tandem solar cells grown by MOCVD," in *Proc. 1st World Conf. Photovoltaic Energy Convers.*, Waikoloa, HI, USA, 1994, pp. 1847–1850.

[15] J. A. Carlin, S. A. Ringel, E. A. Fitzgerald, and M. Bulsara, "High quality GaAs growth by MBE on Si using GeSi buffers and prospects for space photovoltaics," *Progress Photovoltaic: Res. Appl.*, vol. 8, pp. 323–332, 2000.

[16] M. R. Lueck, C. L. Andre, A. J. Pitera, M. L. Lee, E. A. Fitzgerald, and S. A. Ringel, "Dual junction GaInP/GaAs solar cells grown on metamorphic SiGe/Si substrates with high open circuit voltage," *IEEE Electron Device Lett.*, vol. 27, no. 3, pp. 142–144, Mar. 2006.

[17] J. A. Carlin, S. A. Ringel, E. A. Fitzgerald, M. Bulsara, and B. M. Keyes, "Impact of GaAs buffer thickness on electronic quality of GaAs grown on graded Ge/GeSi/Si substrates," *Appl. Phys. Lett.*, vol. 76, pp. 1884–1886, 2000.

[18] S. A. Ringel, C. L. Andre, E. A. Fitzgerald, A. J. Pitera, and D. M. Wilt, "Multijunction III–V photovoltaics on lattice-engineered Si substrates," in *Proc. 31st IEEE Photovoltaic Spec. Conf.*, Orlando, FL, USA, 2005, pp. 567–570.

[19] T. Roesener, H. Döscher, A. Beyer, S. Brückner, V. Klinger, A. Wekkeli, P. Kleinschmidt, C. Jurecka, J. Ohlmann, K. Volz, W. Stolz, T. Hannappel, A. W. Bett, and F. Dimroth, "MOVPE growth of III–V solar cells on silicon in 300 mm closed coupled showerhead reactor," in *Proc. 25th Eur. Photovoltaic Sol. Energy Conf. Exhib.*, Valencia, Spain, 2010, pp. 964–968.

[20] S. A. Ringel, J. A. Carlin, T. J. Grassman, B. Galiana, A. M. Carlin, C. Ratcliff, D. Chmielewski, L. Yang, M. J. Mills, A. Mansouri, S. P. Bremner, A. Ho-Baillie, X. Hao, H. Mehrvarz, G. Conibeer, and M. A. Green, "Ideal GaP/Si heterostructures grown by MOCVD: III–V/active-Si subcells, multijunctions, and MBE-to-MOCVD III–V/Si interface science," in *Proc. 39th IEEE Photovoltaic Spec. Conf.*, Tampa, FL, USA, 2013.

[21] J. Schöne, F. Dimroth, A. W. Bett, A. Tauzin, C. Jaussaud, and J. C. Roussin, "III-V solar cell growth on wafer-bonded GaAs/Si-substrates," in *Proc. 4th World Conf. Photovoltaic Energy Convers.*, Waikoloa, HI, USA, 2006, pp. 776–779.

[22] J. M. Zahler, C.-G. Ahn, S. Zaghi, H. A. Atwater, C. Chu, and P. Iles, "Ge layer transfer to Si for photovoltaic applications," *Thin Solid Films*, vol. 403–404, pp. 558–562, 2002.

[23] M. J. Archer, D. C. Law, S. Mesropian, M. Haddad, C. M. Fetzer, A. C. Ackerman, C. Ladous, R. King, and H. A. Atwater, "GaInP/GaAs dual junction solar cells on Ge/Si epitaxial templates," *Appl. Phys. Lett.*, vol. 95, pp. 103503-1–103503-3, 2008.

[24] K. Derendorf, S. Essig, E. Oliva, V. Klinger, T. Roesener, S. P. Philipps, J. Benick, M. Hermle, M. Schachtner, G. Siefer, W. Jäger, and F. Dimroth, "Fabrication of GaInP/GaAs//Si solar cells by surface activated direct wafer bonding," *IEEE J. Photovoltaics*, vol. 3, no. 4, pp. 1–6, Oct. 2013.

[25] T. R. Chung, L. Yang, N. Hosoda, and T. Suga, "Room temperature GaAs-Si and InP-Si wafer direct bonding by the surface activated bonding method," *Nuclear Instrum Methods Phys Res B*, vol. 121, pp. 203–206, 1997.

[26] M. Meusel, R. Adelhelm, F. Dimroth, A. W. Bett, and W. Warta, "Spectral mismatch correction and spectrometric characterization of monolithic III–V multi-junction solar cells," *Prog. Photovoltaics: Res. Appl.*, vol. 10, pp. 243–255, 2002.

[27] M. Meusel, C. Baur, G. Létay, A. W. Bett, W. Warta, and E. Fernandez, "Spectral response measurements of monolithic GaInP/Ga(In)As/Ge triple-junction solar cells: Measurement artifacts and their explanation," *Prog. Photovoltaics: Res. Appl.*, vol. 11, pp. 499–514, 2003.

[28] H. Döscher and T. Hannappel, "In situ reflection anisotropy spectroscopy analysis of heteroepitaxial GaP films grown on Si(100)," *J. Appl. Phys.*, vol. 107, pp. 123523-1–123523-12, 2010.

[29] M. Yamaguchi and C. Amano, "Efficiency calculations of thin-film GaAs solar cells on Si substrates," *J. Appl. Phys.*, vol. 58, pp. 3601–3606, 1985.

[30] A. Y. Kim, W. S. McCullough, and E. Fitzgerald, "Evolution of microstructure and dislocation dynamics in $In_x Ga_{1-x} P$ graded buffers grown on GaP by metalorganic vapor phase epitaxy: Engineering device-quality substrate materials," *J. Vac. Sci. Technol. B (Microelectron. Nanometer Struct.)*, vol. 17, pp. 1485–1501, 1999.

[31] W. Shockley and H. J. Queisser, "Detailed balance limit of efficiency of p-n junction solar cells," *J. Appl. Phys.*, vol. 32, pp. 510–519, 1961.

Authors' photographs and biographies not available at the time of publication.

Record Infrared Internal Quantum Efficiency in Silicon Heterojunction Solar Cells With Dielectric/Metal Rear Reflectors

Zachary C. Holman, *Member, IEEE*, Antoine Descoeudres, Stefaan De Wolf, and Christophe Ballif

Abstract—Inserting a dielectric between the absorber and rear metal electrode of a solar cell increases rear internal reflectance by both limiting the transmission cone and suppressing the plasmonic absorption of light arriving outside of the cone. We fabricate rear reflectors with low-refractive-index magnesium fluoride (MgF_2) as the dielectric, and with local electrical contacts through the MgF_2 layer. These MgF_2/metal reflectors are introduced into amorphous silicon/crystalline silicon heterojunction solar cells in place of the usual transparent conductive oxide/metal reflector. An MgF_2/Ag reflector yields an average rear internal reflectance of greater than 99.5% and an infrared internal quantum efficiency that exceeds that of the world-record UNSW PERL cell. An MgF_2/Al reflector performs nearly as well, enabling an efficiency of 21.3% and a short-circuit current density of nearly 38 mA/cm^2 in a silicon heterojunction solar cell without silver or indium tin oxide at the rear.

Index Terms—Heterojunction, light trapping, magnesium fluoride, parasitic absorption, reflector, silicon, solar cell.

I. Introduction

PANASONIC recently demonstrated an amorphous silicon/crystalline silicon heterojunction solar cell with a near-record certified efficiency of 24.7% [1]. This device had an open-circuit voltage (V_{oc}) of 750 mV—the highest ever reported for a single-junction crystalline silicon device and 44 mV higher than that of the record 25.0%-efficient UNSW PERL cell [2], [3]—thanks to the displacement of the metal contacts from the wafer surface enabled by amorphous silicon (a-Si:H) passivation [4], [5]. The 83.2% fill factor (*FF*) of the Panasonic cell was also slightly higher than that of the UNSW PERL cell, easing fears that silicon heterojunction solar cells could not reach high *FF*s [6]–[9]. However, the short-circuit current density (J_{sc}) was an enormous 3.2 mA/cm^2 lower than that of the UNSW PERL cell; had the Panasonic device duplicated

Manuscript received June 10, 2013; revised July 26, 2013; accepted July 30, 2013. Date of publication August 28, 2013; date of current version September 18, 2013. This work was supported in part by the European Commission (FP7 project 20 plμs, Grant No. 256695), in part by Axpo Naturstrom Fonds, and in part by the Swiss Commission for Technology and Innovation.

Z. C. Holman is with Arizona State University, School of Electrical, Computer, and Energy Engineering, Tempe, AZ, USA (e-mail: zachary.holman@asu.edu).

A. Descoeudres, S. De Wolf, and C. Ballif are with the Ecole Polytechnique Fédérale de Lausanne, Institute of Microengineering, Photovoltaics and Thin-Film Electronics Laboratory, Neuchâtel 2000, Switzerland (e-mail: antoine.descoeudres@epfl.ch; stefaan.dewolf@epfl.ch; christophe.ballif@epfl.ch).

Color versions of one or more of the figures in this paper are available online at http://ieeexplore.ieee.org.

Digital Object Identifier 10.1109/JPHOTOV.2013.2276484

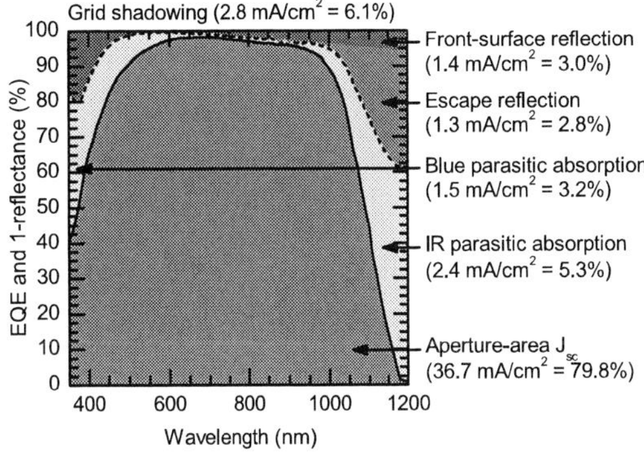

Fig. 1. External quantum efficiency (solid line) and total absorbance (dashed line) of a 20.8%-efficient silicon heterojunction solar cell on a 96-μm-thick wafer. The total reflectance was split into front-surface and escape components by extending a linear fit of the total reflectance between 600–900 nm to longer wavelengths. Shadowing was determined from the ratio of the active-area and aperture-area J_{sc}. The aperture-area J_{sc} and equivalent current associated with each loss mechanism were calculated by integrating over the AM 1.5G photon flux density, reduced by the shadowing loss, and are indicated at right.

the J_{sc} of the record cell, it would have had an efficiency of 26.7%. Much of the difference can be attributed to shadowing (the UNSW PERL cell was measured with a designated illumination area instead of an aperture area [3]) and wafer thickness (98 versus 400 μm [2]). Nevertheless, J_{sc} losses due to parasitic absorption in the front a-Si:H, transparent conductive oxide (TCO), and rear metal electrode layers are a persistent problem in silicon heterojunction solar cells that become increasingly important as the wafer thickness is reduced [4], [10]–[13].

Fig. 1 shows the measured external quantum efficiency (*EQE*) and total absorbance (1-reflectance) of a 96-μm-thick 20.8%-efficient silicon heterojunction solar cell fabricated in our laboratory. The figure has been divided into several regions according to loss mechanism to illustrate the relative importance of each mechanism and to motivate this study. Shadowing from the front screen-printed silver grid accounts for the largest loss, but parasitic absorption at wavelengths greater than 900 nm is nearly as significant. Interestingly, escape reflection due to imperfect light trapping is the least important loss, even in this 96-μm-thick cell, because the random-pyramid texture is excellent at confining light to the wafer. Were infrared (IR) parasitic absorption eliminated, J_{sc} would increase by 1.2 mA/cm^2 in this device; from a recent Panasonic *EQE* spectrum, we estimate that J_{sc} in their devices would increase by 0.8 mA/cm^2, breaking the silicon efficiency record [14]. (Note that reducing IR parasitic absorption increases escape reflectance as well as

EQE; hence the discrepancy between the loss in the figure and the potential gain above.)

We reported that IR parasitic absorption in silicon heterojunction solar cells arises from free-carrier absorption in both the front and rear TCO layers, as well as plasmonic absorption in the rear metal electrode [11]. The plasmonic loss occurs only for *p*-polarized light that is incident on the rear TCO above the critical angle, and only if the metal electrode is within the penetration depth of the resulting evanescent wave [15]. Consequently, one method to mitigate the loss in the metal electrode is to require the rear TCO layer to play an optical as well as electrical role by making it thick and very transparent [11]. An alternative approach is to make the rear TCO very thin so that it serves only an electrical contact function (or dispose of it altogether if a suitable doped a-Si:H/metal junction can be formed [16]), and to add another layer specifically to suppress plasmon excitation in the metal electrode.

It is well known that dielectrics serve as efficient optical buffer layers when inserted between the absorber layer and metal electrode, increasing rear internal reflectance. In PERL-like cells, the silicon nitride (SiN_x), silicon dioxide, or aluminum oxide rear passivation layer (or passivation stack) simultaneously enhances reflectance [17]–[23], and a zinc oxide buffer layer that also acts as a metal diffusion barrier is common in thin-film silicon solar cells [24]–[30]. The reflectance enhancement in PERL-like cells is frequently perceived to occur because the dielectric limits the cone of light that is transmitted to the lossy metal electrode. However, this explanation is incomplete: If sufficiently thick, the dielectric also works by inhibiting plasmonic absorption of light arriving *outside* of the critical angle [15], [23]. In fact, we calculated that lowering the refractive index of the dielectric improves reflectance primarily by reducing the penetration depth and field strength of evanescent waves in the dielectric (generated by super-critical-angle light), not by narrowing the transmission cone [31], [32]. From a purely optical perspective, the best rear dielectric layer for solar cells with micrometer-sized or larger rear textures has the lowest possible refractive index and a thickness greater than ∼200 nm [31].

In 1993, Campbell *et al.* hypothesized excellent internal reflectance if a layer of magnesium fluoride (MgF_2), which has a refractive index of 1.37 at IR wavelengths, were inserted between the rear passivation layer and aluminum rear electrode in PERL-like cells [33]. Although MgF_2 has since been used extensively in double-layer antireflection coatings [2], [34], [35], we are not aware of its implementation in a rear reflector. In this paper, we fabricate and characterize silicon heterojunction solar cells with MgF_2/metal reflectors. These high-performance reflectors are particularly beneficial in silicon heterojunction cells that are being made on ever-thinner wafers to increase V_{oc}. Nonetheless, the design can also be transferred to diffused-junction cells—as Campbell *et al.* originally suggested—by depositing the MgF_2 layer on the rear passivation layer, or even to thin-film silicon cells with some modification.

II. Experimental

High-efficiency silicon heterojunction solar cells were fabricated on 250-μm-thick *n*-type float-zone wafers with a re-sistivity of 3 Ω·cm. The wafers were textured in a potassium hydroxide solution to remove saw damage and reveal random pyramids with (111) faces on both surfaces, and were chemically cleaned [5]. Prior to a-Si:H deposition, the wafers were dipped in diluted hydrofluoric acid to remove the native oxide. Intrinsic and *p*-type a-Si:H layers 5–10 nm thick were deposited on the front (sunward) side of each wafer; intrinsic and *n*-type a-Si:H layers of the same thickness were deposited on the rear. All a-Si:H depositions were performed in an industrial parallel-plate plasma-enhanced chemical vapor deposition (PECVD) reactor powered at very high frequency (40.68 MHz). In several experiments, a-Si:H layers were codeposited on multiple wafers in the large-area reactor to form identical solar cell precursors. Additional details regarding our PECVD a-Si:H layers can be found in [36] and [37].

Hydrogen-doped indium oxide/indium tin oxide (IO:H/ITO) bilayers approximately 75 nm thick were subsequently sputtered on the front of the solar cells using RF (for IO:H) and DC (for ITO) power. As with PECVD, these layers were codeposited on cells that were to be compared. The IO:H sublayer has an electron mobility $\mu_e > 100$ cm^2/V·s and thus provides low-resistance lateral transport with minimal free-carrier absorption [38]–[41]; the ultrathin ITO super-layer forms a low-resistance contact to the silver front electrode grid. Additional details regarding these bilayers can be found in [41]. In one experiment, in which only reflectance was measured, an IR-transparent SiN_x layer was deposited in place of IO:H/ITO using PECVD, and the gas ratios were tuned to yield a layer with similar refractive index to IO:H/ITO.

To form MgF_2/metal rear reflectors, an ITO or aluminum-doped zinc oxide (ZnO) layer 10–20 nm thick was first sputtered over the entire rear surface. The oxygen partial pressure during sputtering was adjusted until the Hall free-electron density (n_e) of the ITO or ZnO film was below 1×10^{20} cm^{-3} [11], [42] so that the film was very transparent. Next, an MgF_2 layer 300–400 nm thick was thermally evaporated onto the rear surface through a fine stainless-steel mesh that acted as a shadow mask. The mesh and wafer were in intimate contact during evaporation and the wafer was not rotated. Finally, a silver or aluminum layer 100–200 nm thick was deposited over the entire rear surface using DC sputtering. As a reference, the same reflectors were fabricated without the MgF_2 layer. Our previous best reflector served as yet another reference; this reflector is comprised of an ITO/Ag stack in which the ITO layer is highly transparent (low free-electron density) and approximately 150 nm thick [11]. Film thicknesses were measured with profilometry on glass substrates that witnessed each deposition. The measured thicknesses were divided by the ratio of the textured to planar surface areas (1.7) to obtain thicknesses on the textured wafers.

Silicon heterojunction solar cells were completed by screen printing a silver grid electrode on the front IO:H/ITO layer. Each wafer had four 4-cm^2 cells and a nonmetallized area for *EQE* and reflectance measurements. The total reflectance of solar cells and solar-cell-like structures was measured with a dual-beam spectrophotometer using an integrating sphere. The total reflectance at a wavelength of 1200 nm was taken as the sub-bandgap reflectance (R_{sub}). *EQE* measurements were performed without voltage bias using a commercial instrument

                142

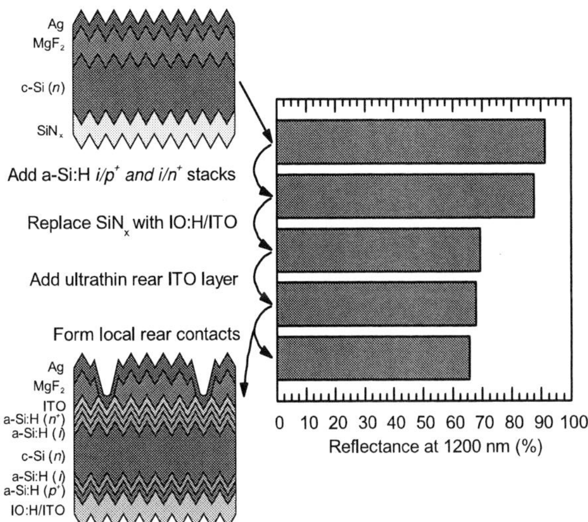

Fig. 2. Sub-bandgap reflectance of structures that increasingly resemble a completed silicon heterojunction solar cell. The starting and finished structures (corresponding to the top and bottom bars, respectively) are shown schematically, and the alterations made to transform the former into the latter are listed. Note that light is incident on these structures from below.

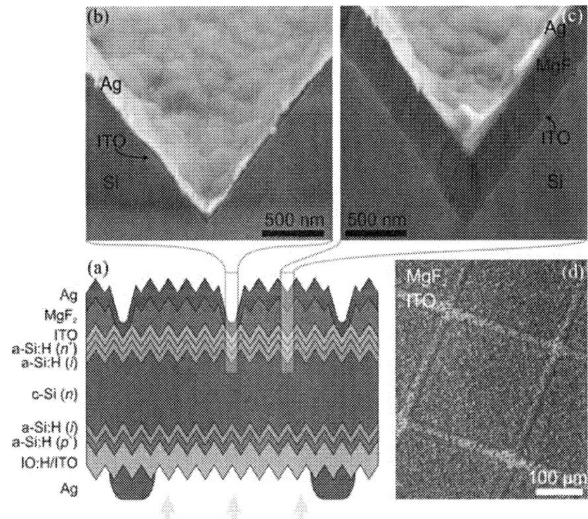

Fig. 3. (a) Schematic of a silicon heterojunction solar cell with the MgF_2/Ag rear reflector and local rear contact design investigated here. SEM images of the cross section of a completed cell (b) in a contact area and (c) not in a contact area. (d) Top-down optical microscope image of the rear side of a solar cell after MgF_2 evaporation and before silver deposition.

that utilizes a lock-in technique, and active-area J_{sc} was calculated by integrating EQE over the AM 1.5G photon flux density. Aperture-area current–voltage characteristics were recorded under AM 1.5G illumination, and the output characteristics of the four cells on each wafer were averaged. Select solar cells were cleaved and their cross sections were imaged with scanning electron microscopy (SEM).

III. RESULTS AND DISCUSSION

A. MgF₂/Metal Reflector Design

We previously measured and simulated a sub-bandgap reflectance of $R_{sub} > 90\%$ for the SiN_x/c-Si/MgF_2/Ag structure depicted in Fig. 2 when the MgF_2 thickness was greater than 200 nm [31]. This structure, which represents the optical equivalent of a silicon solar cell with the least IR parasitic absorption that we can fabricate (average rear internal reflectance greater than 99.5% [15]), provides the basis for the MgF_2/metal reflector developed here. Fig. 2 shows the evolution of the sub-bandgap reflectance—a metric of parasitic absorption—as layers are added consecutively to the aforementioned structure until a completed silicon heterojunction solar cell is constructed. Introducing doped a-Si:H layers and an ultrathin rear ITO layer, as well as structuring the MgF_2 layer, is surprisingly benign. Only replacing the front SiN_x layer with IO:H/ITO causes an appreciable drop in sub-bandgap reflectance because, despite its high mobility and low free-electron density ($n_e \approx 1 \times 10^{20}$ cm^{-3}), the TCO layer absorbs some IR light. This underscores an important point. A high-performance rear reflector will not benefit a cell that has significant parallel IR parasitic absorption processes (e.g., emitter free-carrier absorption) [11]. Despite absorption in the front TCO, $R_{sub} = 65\%$ in the completed device in Fig. 2. Based on the correlation between R_{sub} and J_{sc} [31],

this 250-μm-thick cell should generate 99.5% of the current it would produce if there were no IR parasitic absorption ($R_{sub} = 100\%$).

As shown in Figs. 2 and 3(a), local contacts through the insulating MgF_2 layer are necessary to collect electrons at the rear of the cell. The contact design requirements are relaxed compared with those for PERL-like solar cells because these local contacts are through an optical—not passivation—layer. In particular, a relatively large contact fraction can be tolerated since only internal reflectance will suffer in the contacted areas, and thus current crowding and the associated increase in series resistance are not a concern [43], [44]. Additionally, the pitch between contacts can be up to 500 μm before incurring a 5% increase in the lumped series resistance of the cell caused by lateral transport in the wafer. (The wafer sheet resistance is approximately 100 Ω/sq.) There are several methods available to structure the MgF_2 layer in accordance with the above lenient requirements; we masked cells with a wire mesh during MgF_2 evaporation. The mesh was chosen such that 88% of the cell surface is covered with square MgF_2 patches approximately 200 μm on a side, and the contact openings are 25 μm wide [see Fig. 3(d)]. The SEM images in Fig. 3(b) and (c) confirm that a nearly conformal and visibly porous MgF_2 layer 300 nm thick is deposited everywhere except in the local contacts [45], [46], where the silver electrode makes direct contact to the ultrathin ITO layer. The ITO layer is included to form a low-resistance contact between the n-type a-Si:H layer and silver electrode [11]. For convenience, the ultrathin ITO layer will be left out of the reflector name for the remainder of this paper (e.g., the cell in Fig. 3 will be said to have an MgF_2/Ag reflector), although an ITO layer (or, later, a ZnO layer in its place) is always present when an MgF_2 layer is present.

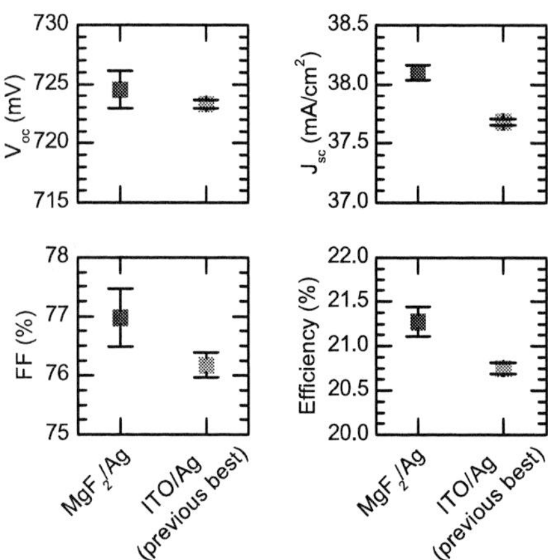

Fig. 4. Output characteristics of codeposited silicon heterojunction solar cells with our newly developed and previous best rear reflectors. Each data point represents the average value of four cells and error bars express standard deviations.

B. Performance of Cells With MgF₂/Ag Reflectors

The average output characteristics of silicon heterojunction solar cells with MgF$_2$/Ag reflectors are shown in Fig. 4. For comparison, codeposited cells were fabricated with our previous best rear reflector, which consists of a full-coverage ITO/Ag stack in which the ITO layer is approximately 150 nm thick and has $n_e < 5 \times 10^{19}$ cm^{-3} [11]. This previous best rear reflector was employed in a certified 22.1%-efficient cell with $J_{sc} = 38.9$ mA/cm^2 [47]. V_{oc} is insensitive to the design of the rear reflector, and J_{sc} is 0.4 mA/cm^2 higher with the MgF$_2$/Ag reflector—as was the aim. FF is also slightly elevated, confirming that the additional lateral transport in the wafer makes a negligible contribution to series resistance. The increase in FF is not statistically significant (although we have observed a similar improvement in other codeposited comparisons); if it is real, however, a possible explanation is the evolution of the properties of ITO with thickness. Although we reported no significant variation in FF for cells with varying rear ITO thickness and nearly constant mobility and free-electron density, we also noted that the deposition recipe had to be adjusted with thickness in order to achieve this constant mobility and density [11]. Here, the same recipe was used for the ultrathin rear ITO contact layer in the MgF$_2$/Ag cell and the thick ITO layer in the previous best cell, and we thus expect that the layers *do not* have the same mobility and carrier density. As a result of both higher J_{sc} and FF, the cells with MgF$_2$ reflectors outperform our previous best device design and achieve an average efficiency of 21.3%. The best cell falls short of our 22.1%-efficient internal record only because of slightly poorer blue response, attributed to thicker front a-Si:H layers, and 2% lower pseudo-FF resulting from inferior surface passivation at low injection (minority-carrier lifetime at maximum power point of 4.4 ms compared with 6.3 ms for our record cell).

The EQE and total absorbance of the solar cells in Fig. 4 are shown in Fig. 5. The cells have identical response and reflectance at UV and visible wavelengths because the layers at their front sides were codeposited. As anticipated, the source of

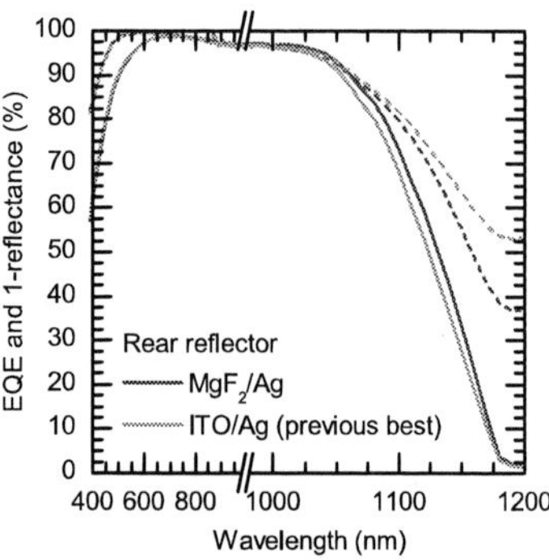

Fig. 5. External quantum efficiency (solid lines) and total absorbance (dashed lines) of silicon heterojunction solar cells with our newly developed and previous best rear reflectors. These spectra were measured on the cells in Fig. 4.

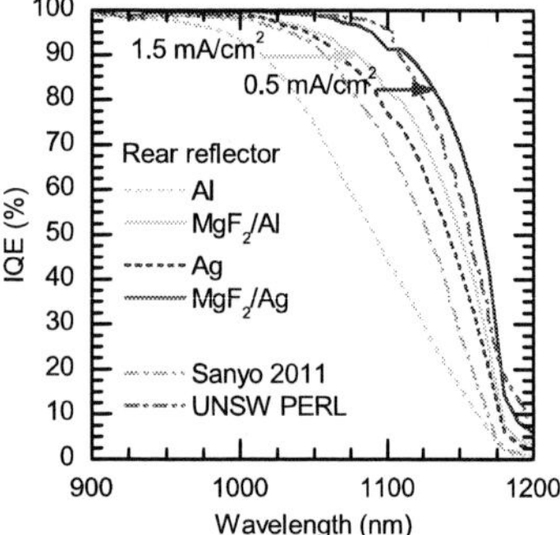

Fig. 6. Internal quantum efficiency of codeposited silicon heterojunction solar cells with and without MgF$_2$ layers, and with aluminum or silver rear electrodes. The active-area J_{sc} gain from the addition of an MgF$_2$ layer is given for each electrode material. Also plotted are the most recently published IQE of the Panasonic (formerly Sanyo) heterojunction cell [48] and the IQE of the UNSW record PERL cell [2].

the J_{sc} enhancement in Fig. 4 is the superior internal reflectance of the MgF$_2$/Ag reflector, which simultaneously increases EQE and escape reflectance. Further attempts to improve this reflector will be futile unless the wafer is extremely thin. For this 250-μm-thick cell, only 0.2 mA/cm^2 remains to be gained by eliminating IR parasitic absorption altogether (consistent with our calculation from the sub-bandgap reflectance in Fig. 2).

C. Practical MgF₂/Al Reflectors for Commercial Solar Cells

Silicon heterojunction solar cells with MgF$_2$/Ag reflectors have higher IR internal quantum efficiency (IQE) than the 25%-efficient UNSW PERL cell (see Fig. 6), despite a thinner wafer and an IR-absorbing front TCO. The reflector therefore seems a likely candidate for inclusion in the next record-efficiency silicon cell, but it is perhaps otherwise not of great practical value. The expense of the additional processing step cannot be justified in a commercial setting, especially because the previous best ITO/Ag reflector was already excellent and, as mentioned earlier, the benefit is realized only if there are no other overpowering sources of IR parasitic absorption in the cell. In silicon heterojunction solar cells, this means that the front TCO must have $\mu_e > 50$ cm^2/V·s; an ITO layer with $\mu_e = 30$ cm^2/V·s that

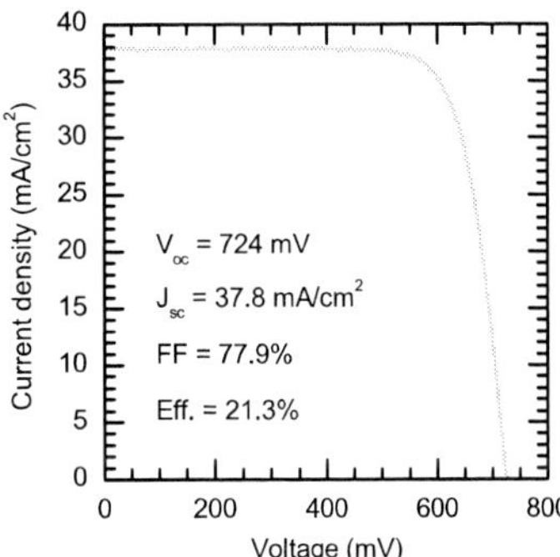

Fig. 7. Current–voltage characteristic of the best 4-cm² screen-printed silicon heterojunction solar cell with an MgF₂/Al reflector.

is optimized according to the $J_{\rm sc}$–FF tradeoff ($n_e \approx 3 \times 10^{20}$ cm²/V·s [10]) will be too absorbing to see much benefit from an improved rear reflector [11]. If, however, an MgF₂ layer could eliminate the $J_{\rm sc}$ loss incurred when switching from a silver to an aluminum rear electrode [21], [31], then its cost may be more than offset by the savings from the cheaper metal (US$ 0.02/W at today's prices for a 200-nm-thick metal layer).

Fig. 6 shows the *IQE* spectra of codeposited silicon heterojunction solar cells with Al, MgF₂/Al, Ag, and MgF₂/Ag reflectors. As before, an ultrathin ITO contact layer was used in cells with silver; in cells with aluminum, ITO was replaced with ZnO to form a good contact, as is typical in thin-film silicon solar cells [27]. Additionally, this replacement adds to the cost benefit of switching from silver to aluminum. (Note that, because they are thin and have very low free-electron densities, both employed ZnO and ITO layers have negligible IR absorption (see Fig. 2) and can be considered optically equivalent). Without an MgF₂ layer, the aluminum electrode is a very poor reflector: $R_{\rm sub} = 19\%$, indicating that 81% of light is absorbed parasitically at 1200 nm, most of it in the aluminum. By adding an MgF₂ layer, however, active-area $J_{\rm sc}$ increases by 1.5 mA/cm² or 4% as the IR *IQE* surpasses the most recently published *IQE* from Panasonic and approaches that of the UNSW PERL cell [2], [48]. Active-area $J_{\rm sc}$ with the MgF₂/Al reflector is also just 0.3 mA/cm² lower than that with the MgF₂/Ag reflector, reaffirming that MgF₂ is a great equalizer: The optical screening it provides reduces the sensitivity of the cell to the reflectance of the metal electrode, and thus the electrode material can be selected based on, e.g., cost or solderability.

Fig. 7 displays the current–voltage characteristic of the best 4-cm² screen-printed silicon heterojunction solar cell we fabricated with an MgF₂/Al reflector and ultrathin ZnO contact layer. It produces nearly 38 mA/cm² at short circuit and has a power conversion efficiency of 21.3%.

IV. Conclusion

We have demonstrated an MgF₂/Ag reflector that gives exceptional rear internal reflectance and, when implemented in a silicon heterojunction solar cell with a high-mobility front TCO, excellent IR *IQE*. An MgF₂/Al reflector performs nearly

as well, and in this case the boost in performance provided by the MgF₂ layer may warrant the additional processing step in a manufacturing line. The reflector concept introduced here, in which local contacts through a low-refractive-index insulating layer are made for an optical rather than passivation gain, may be transferred to other cell structures. For example, an MgF₂/metal reflector is expected to be particularly advantageous in thin-film silicon solar cells grown on metal foils, though the contact pitch will need to be reduced to compensate for the high lateral resistivity of the absorber. This could be accomplished by, e.g., spraying onto the metal foil polymer microspheres that act as a mask during MgF₂ evaporation, and subsequently dissolving them.

ACKNOWLEDGMENT

The authors would like to thank Roth & Rau Research for wafer preparation and N. Badel for screen printing.

REFERENCES

[1] M. Taguchi, A. Yano, S. Tohoda, K. Matsuyama, Y. Nakamura, T. Nishiwaki, K. Fujita, and E. Maruyama, "24.7% record efficiency HIT solar cell on thin wafer," in *Proc. IEEE 39th Photovoltaic Spec. Conf.*, Jun. 2013, pp. 827–837.

[2] J. H. Zhao, A. H. Wang, P. P. Altermatt, S. R. Wenham, and M. A. Green, "24% efficient PERL silicon solar cell: Recent improvements in high efficiency silicon cell research," *Sol. Energy Mater. Sol. Cells*, vol. 41–42, pp. 87–99, Jun. 1996.

[3] M. A. Green, K. Emery, Y. Hishikawa, W. Warta, and E. D. Dunlop, "Solar cell efficiency tables (version 41)," *Prog. Photovoltaics: Res. Appl.*, vol. 21, pp. 1–11, Jan. 2013.

[4] M. Tanaka, M. Taguchi, T. Matsuyama, T. Sawada, S. Tsuda, S. Nakano, H. Hanafusa, and Y. Kuwano, "Development of new a-Si/c-Si heterojunction solar cells: ACJ-HIT (artificially constructed junction-heterojunction with intrinsic thin-layer)," *Jpn. J. Appl. Phys.*, vol. 31, pp. 3518–3522, Nov. 1992.

[5] S. De Wolf, A. Descoeudres, Z. C. Holman, and C. Ballif, "High-efficiency silicon heterojunction solar cells: A review," *Green*, vol. 2, pp. 7–24, Mar. 2012.

[6] A. Kanevce and W. K. Metzger, "The role of amorphous silicon and tunneling in heterojunction with intrinsic thin layer (HIT) solar cells," *J. Appl. Phys.*, vol. 105, pp. 094507-1–094507-7, May 2009.

[7] M. R. Page, E. Iwaniczko, Y. Q. Xu, L. Roybal, F. Hasoon, Q. Wang, and R. S. Crandall, "Amorphous/crystalline silicon heterojunction solar cells with varying i-layer thickness," *Thin Solid Films*, vol. 519, pp. 4527–4530, May 2011.

[8] M. Rahmouni, A. Datta, P. Chatterjee, J. Damon-Lacoste, C. Ballif, and P. R. I. Cabarrocas, "Carrier transport and sensitivity issues in heterojunction with intrinsic thin layer solar cells on N-type crystalline silicon: A computer simulation study," *J. Appl. Phys.*, vol. 107, pp. 054521-1–054521-14, Mar. 2010.

[9] T. F. Schulze, L. Korte, E. Conrad, M. Schmidt, and B. Rech, "High-forward-bias transport mechanism in a-Si:H/c-Si heterojunction solar cells," *Phys. Status Solidi A*, vol. 207, pp. 657–660, Mar. 2010.

[10] Z. C. Holman, A. Descoeudres, L. Barraud, F. Zicarelli, J. P. Seif, S. De Wolf, and C. Ballif, "Current losses at the front of silicon heterojunction solar cells," *IEEE J. Photovoltaics*, vol. 2, no. 1, pp. 7–15, Jan. 2012.

[11] Z. C. Holman, M. Filipic, A. Descoeudres, S. De Wolf, F. Smole, M. Topic, and C. Ballif, "Infrared light management in high-efficiency silicon heterojunction and rear-passivated solar cells," *J. Appl. Phys.*, vol. 113, pp. 013107-1–013107-13, Jan. 2013.

[12] H. Fujiwara and M. Kondo, "Effects of a-Si:H layer thicknesses on the performance of a-Si:H/c-Si heterojunction solar cells," *J. Appl. Phys.*, vol. 101, pp. 054516-1–054516-9, Mar. 1, 2007.

[13] N. Jensen, R. A. Hausner, R. B. Bergmann, J. H. Werner, and U. Rau, "Optimization and characterization of amorphous/crystalline silicon heterojunction solar cells," *Prog. Photovoltaics: Res. Appl.*, vol. 10, pp. 1–13, Jan. 2002.

    145

[14] M. A. Green, K. Emery, Y. Hishikawa, W. Warta, and E. D. Dunlop, "Solar cell efficiency tables (version 40)," *Prog. Photovoltaics: Res. Appl.*, vol. 20, pp. 606–614, Aug. 2012.

[15] Z. C. Holman, S. De Wolf, and C. Ballif, "Improving metal reflectors by suppressing surface plasmon polaritons: A priori calculation of the internal reflectance of a solar cell," *Light: Sci. Appl.*, in press.

[16] M. Bivour, C. Reichel, M. Hermle, and S. W. Glunz, "Improving the a-Si:H(p) rear emitter contact of n-type silicon solar cells," *Sol. Energy Mat. Sol. Cells*, vol. 106, pp. 11–16, Nov. 2012.

[17] A. W. Blakers, A. Wang, A. M. Milne, J. H. Zhao, and M. A. Green, "22.8% efficient silicon solar cell," *Appl. Phys. Lett.*, vol. 55, pp. 1363–1365, Sep. 1989.

[18] A. Wang, J. Zhao, and M. A. Green, "24% efficient silicon solar cells," *Appl. Phys. Lett.*, vol. 57, pp. 602–604, Aug. 1990.

[19] J. Schmidt, A. Merkle, R. Brendel, B. Hoex, M. C. M. van de Sanden, and W. M. M. Kessels, "Surface passivation of high-efficiency silicon solar cells by atomic-layer-deposited Al_2O_3," *Prog. Photovoltaics: Res. Appl.*, vol. 16, pp. 461–466, Sep. 2008.

[20] P. Saint-Cast, J. Benick, D. Kania, L. Weiss, M. Hofmann, J. Rentsch, R. Preu, and S. W. Glunz, "High-efficiency c-Si solar cells passivated with ALD and PECVD aluminum oxide," *IEEE Electron Device Lett.*, vol. 31, no. 7, pp. 695–697, Jul. 2010.

[21] D. Kray, M. Hermle, and S. W. Glunz, "Theory and experiments on the back side reflectance of silicon wafer solar cells," *Prog. Photovoltaics: Res. Appl.*, vol. 16, pp. 1–15, Jan. 2008.

[22] N. Woehrle, J. Greulich, C. Schwab, M. Glatthaar, and S. Rein, "A predictive optical simulation model for the rear-surface roughness of passivated silicon solar cells," *IEEE J. Photovoltaics*, vol. 3, no. 1, pp. 175–182, Jan. 2013.

[23] K. O. Davis, J. Kaiyun, C. Demberger, H. Zunft, H. Haverkamp, D. Habermann, and W. V. Schoenfeld, "Investigation of the internal back reflectance of rear-side dielectric stacks for c-Si solar cells," *IEEE J. Photovoltaics*, vol. 3, no. 2, pp. 641–648, Apr. 2013.

[24] C. Kothandaraman, T. Tonon, C. Huang, and A. E. Delahoy, "Improvement of a-Si:H p-i-n devices using zinc oxide based back-reflectors," in *Proc. Mat. Res. Soc. Symp.*, 1991, vol. 219, pp. 475–480.

[25] W. W. Wenas, A. De, A. Yamada, M. Konagai, and K. Takahashi, "Optimization of ZnO for front and rear contacts in a-Si solar cells," *Sol. Energy Mater. Sol. Cells*, vol. 34, pp. 313–319, Sep. 1994.

[26] J. D. Saunderson, R. Swanepoel, and M. J. van Staden, "The role of the ZnO buffer layer in Al/Si interdiffusion in alpha-Si : H solar cells on flexible substrates," *Sol. Energy Mater. Sol. Cells*, vol. 51, pp. 425–432, Feb. 1998.

[27] J. Muller, B. Rech, J. Springer, and M. Vanecek, "TCO and light trapping in silicon thin film solar cells," *Sol. Energy*, vol. 77, pp. 917–930, Dec. 2004.

[28] T. Soderstrom, F. J. Haug, X. Niquille, and C. Ballif, "TCOs for nip thin film silicon solar cells," *Prog. Photovoltaics: Res. Appl.*, vol. 17, pp. 165–176, May 2009.

[29] F. J. Haug, T. Soderstrom, O. Cubero, V. Terrazzoni-Daudrix, and C. Ballif, "Plasmonic absorption in textured silver back reflectors of thin film solar cells," *J. Appl. Phys.*, vol. 104, pp. 064509-1–064509-7, Sep. 2008.

[30] F. J. Haug, T. Soderstrom, O. Cubero, V. Terrazzoni-Daudrix, and C. Ballif, "Influence of the ZnO buffer on the guided mode structure in Si/ZnO/Ag multilayers," *J. Appl. Phys.*, vol. 106, pp. 044502-1–044502-7, Aug. 2009.

[31] Z. C. Holman, M. Filipic, B. Lipovsek, S. De Wolf, F. Smole, M. Topic, and C. Ballif. (2013). Parasitic absorption in the rear reflector of a silicon solar cell: Simulation and measurement of the sub-bandgap reflectance for common dielectric/metal reflectors. *Solar Energy Mater. Sol. Cells*. [Online]. Available: http://dx.doi.org/10.1016/j.solmat.2013.06.024

[32] N. J. Harrick and F. K. Dupre, "Effective thickness of bulk materials and of thin films for internal reflection spectroscopy," *Appl. Opt.*, vol. 5, pp. 1739–1743, Nov. 1966.

[33] P. Campbell, S. R. Wenham, and M. A. Green, "Light trapping and reflection control in solar cells using tilted crystallographic surface textures," *Sol. Energy Mater. Sol. Cells*, vol. 31, pp. 133–153, Nov. 1993.

[34] D. Bouhafs, A. Moussi, A. Chikouche, and J. M. Ruiz, "Design and simulation of antireflection coating systems for optoelectronic devices: Application to silicon solar cells," *Sol. Energy Mater. Sol. Cells*, vol. 52, pp. 79–93, Mar. 1998.

[35] S. E. Lee, S. W. Choi, and J. Yi, "Double-layer anti-reflection coating using MgF_2 and CeO_2 films on a crystalline silicon substrate," *Thin Solid Films*, vol. 376, pp. 208–213, Nov. 1993.

[36] A. Descoeudres, L. Barraud, R. Bartlome, G. Choong, S. De Wolf, F. Zicarelli, and C. Ballif, "The silane depletion fraction as an indica-tor for the amorphous/crystalline silicon interface passivation quality," *Appl. Phys. Lett.*, vol. 97, pp. 183505-1–183505-3, Nov. 2010.

[37] A. Descoeudres, L. Barraud, S. De Wolf, B. Strahm, D. Lachenal, C. Guerin, Z. C. Holman, F. Zicarelli, B. Demaurex, J. Seif, J. Holovsky, and C. Ballif, "Improved amorphous/crystalline silicon interface passivation by hydrogen plasma treatment," *Appl. Phys. Lett.*, vol. 99, pp. 123506-1–123506-3, Sep. 2011.

[38] T. Koida, H. Fujiwara, and M. Kondo, "Hydrogen-doped In_2O_3 as high-mobility transparent conductive oxide," *Jpn. J. Appl. Phys.*, vol. 46, pp. L685–L687, Jul. 2007.

[39] T. Koida, H. Fujiwara, and M. Kondo, "Reduction of optical loss in hydrogenated amorphous silicon/crystalline silicon heterojunction solar cells by high-mobility hydrogen-doped In_2O_3 transparent conductive oxide," *Appl. Phys. Exp.*, vol. 1, pp. 041501-1–041501-3, Apr. 2008.

[40] T. Koida, H. Fujiwara, and M. Kondo, "High-mobility hydrogen-doped In_2O_3 transparent conductive oxide for a-Si:H/c-Si heterojunction solar cells," *Sol. Energ Mat. Sol. Cells*, vol. 93, pp. 851–854, Jun. 2009.

[41] L. Barraud, Z. C. Holman, N. Badel, P. Reiss, A. Descoeudres, C. Battaglia, S. De Wolf, and C. Ballif, "Hydrogen-doped indium oxide/indium tin oxide bilayers for high-efficiency silicon heterojunction solar cells," *Sol. Energ Mat. Sol. Cells*, vol. 115, pp. 151–156, Aug. 2013.

[42] M. Buchanan, J. B. Webb, and D. F. Williams, "Preparation of conducting and transparent thin films of tin-doped indium oxide by magnetron sputtering," *Appl. Phys. Lett.*, vol. 37, pp. 213–215, Jul. 1980.

[43] A. Cuevas, "Geometrical analysis of solar cells with partial rear contacts," *IEEE J. Photovoltaics*, vol. 2, no. 4, pp. 485–493, Oct. 2012.

[44] R. M. Swanson, "Point-contact solar cells: Modeling and experiment," *Sol. Cells*, vol. 17, pp. 85–118, Mar. 1986.

[45] U. Kaiser, N. Kaiser, P. Weissbrodt, U. Mademann, E. Hacker, and H. Muller, "Structure of thin fluoride films deposited on amorphous sub-strates," *Thin Solid Films*, vol. 217, pp. 7–16, Sep. 1992.

[46] L. Dumas, E. Quesnel, J. Y. Robic, and Y. Pauleau, "Characterization of magnesium fluoride thin films deposited by direct electron beam evaporation," *J. Vac. Sci. Technol. A*, vol. 18, pp. 465–469, Mar. 2000.

[47] A. Descoeudres, Z. C. Holman, L. Barraud, S. Morel, S. De Wolf, and C. Ballif, ">21% efficient silicon heterojunction solar cells on n- and p-type wafers compared," *IEEE J. Photovoltaics*, vol. 3, no. 1, pp. 83–89, Jan. 2013.

[48] T. Mishima, M. Taguchi, H. Sakata, and E. Maruyama, "Development status of high-efficiency HIT solar cells," *Sol. Energ Mat. Sol. Cells*, vol. 95, pp. 18–21, Jan. 2011.

Zachary C. Holman (M'13) received the B.A. degree in physics from Reed College, Portland, OR, USA, and the Ph.D. degree in mechanical engineering from the University of Minnesota, Minneapolis, MN, USA, in 2005 and 2010, respectively.

In 2010, he joined the Photovoltaics and Thin-Film Electronics Laboratory, Ecole Polytechnique Fédérale de Lausanne, Neuchâtel, Switzerland, as a Postdoctoral Researcher. In 2013, he joined the faculty at Arizona State University, Tempe, AZ, USA, as an Assistant Professor within the Quantum Energy and Sustainable Solar Technology center. His research interests include light management in solar cells, high-efficiency silicon solar cells, and novel photovoltaic devices incorporating nanoparticles.

Antoine Descoeudres received the M.Sc. and Ph.D. degrees in physics from Ecole Polytechnique Fédérale de Lausanne, Lausanne, Switzerland, in 2001 and 2006, respectively.

From 2007 to 2009, he was a Postdoctoral Researcher at CERN, Geneva, Swizterland, studying vacuum breakdowns for the development of high-gradient accelerating cavities. Since 2009, he has been a Postdoctoral Researcher at the Photovoltaics and Thin-Film Electronics Laboratory, Ecole Polytechnique Fédérale de Lausanne, Neuchâtel, Switzerland. His current research interests include thin-film deposition with plasma-enhanced chemical vapor deposition and plasma diagnostics for the development of silicon heterojunction solar cells.

Stefaan De Wolf received the Ph.D. degree from the Catholic University of Leuven, Leuven, Belgium, while he was with IMEC, Leuven, focusing on crystalline silicon solar cells.

From 2005 until 2008, he was with the National Institute of Advanced Industrial Science and Technology, Tsukuba, Japan, focusing on silicon heterojunction devices. In 2008, he joined the Photovoltaics and Thin-Film Electronics Laboratory, Ecole Polytechnique Fédérale de Lausanne, Neuchâtel, Switzerland, as Team Leader for its activities on such solar cells.

Christophe Ballif received the M.Sc. and Ph.D. degrees in physics from Ecole Polytechnique Fédérale de Lausanne, Lausanne, Switzerland, in 1994 and 1998, respectively, focusing on novel photovoltaic materials.

He was a Postdoctoral Researcher with the National Renewable Energy Laboratory, Golden, CO, USA, where he was involved in compound semiconductor solar cells (CIGS and CdTe). He then was with the Fraunhofer Institute for Solar Energy Systems, Freiburg, Germany, where he focused on crystalline silicon photovoltaics (monocrystalline and multicrystalline) until 2003. He then joined the Swiss Federal Laboratories for Materials Testing and Research, Thun, Switzerland, before becoming a Full Professor and Chair with the Institute of Microengineering, University of Neuchâtel, Neuchâtel, Switzerland. In 2009, the Institute of Microengineering was transferred to Ecole Polytechnique Fédérale de Lausanne. He is the Director of the Photovoltaics and Thin-Film Electronics Laboratory within the Institute, and since 2013, he has also been the Director of the PV-Center within the Swiss Center for Electronics and Microtechnology, Neuchâtel. His research interests include thin-film silicon, high-efficiency heterojunction crystalline cells, module technology, contributing to technology transfer, and industrialization of novel devices.

Silicon Nanowire Solar Cells With Radial p-n Heterojunction on Crystalline Silicon Thin Films: Light Trapping Properties

Guobin Jia, Annett Gawlik, Joachim Bergmann, Björn Eisenhawer, Sven Schönherr, Gudrun Andrä, and Fritz Falk

Abstract—We present a concept for a core-shell silicon nanowire thin-film solar cell showing strong light trapping. Nanowires are wet chemically etched into a several micrometer-thick laser-crystallized silicon thin film on glass. The nanowires are equipped with an a-Si heteroemitter deposited as a shell around the nanowires by plasma-enhanced chemical vapor deposition to achieve a radial p-n heterojunction. The space between the nanowires is filled with ZnO:Al, acting as a transparent contact. Our core-shell nanowire solar cells reached an efficiency of 8.8%. The main emphasis of this study is on the optical properties of the nanowire solar cell system.

Index Terms—Heterojunction, nanowires, photovoltaic cells, silicon, thin film.

I. Introduction

CRYSTALLINE silicon thin-film solar cells suffer from low absorption, which has to be increased by some light-trapping arrangement. One possibility for this purpose is to use nanowires. Therefore, silicon nanowire (SiNW) solar cells have received growing interest over the past few years [1]–[9]. However, nanowire solar cells usually are based on monocrystalline silicon wafers [1]–[3], [8], [9], for which light trapping is not as strongly needed as in thin-film solar cells. Solar cells that are based on microwires prepared on silicon wafers reached an efficiency of 12.2% [1], which is much lower than that of conventional wafer cells. In our opinion, nanowires are of real interest mostly for solar cells prepared on low-cost substrates such as polycrystalline silicon thin films [4], low-cost metallurgical grade silicon [5], or on metal foils [7].

In this paper, we present a concept for a nanowire solar cell based on n-doped laser crystallized multicrystalline silicon (mc-Si) thin films prepared on glass (see Fig. 1), leading to a

Manuscript received June 15, 2013; revised August 14, 2013; accepted October 30, 2013. Date of publication November 21, 2013; date of current version December 16, 2013. This work was suported by the European Commission under FP7 Program within the projects SiNAPS under Grant 257856 and NanoPV under Grant NMP3-SL-2009–246331.

G. Jia, A. Gawlik, J. Bergmann, B. Eisenhawer, G. Andrä, and F. Falk are with the Institute of Photonic Technology, Jena 07745, Germany (e-mail: guobin.jia@ipht-jena.de; annette.gawlik@ipht-jena.de; joachim.bergmann@ipht-jena.de; bjoern.eisenhawer@ipht-jena.de; gudrun.andrae@ipht-jena.de; fritz.falk@ipht-jena.de).

S. Schönherr is with the Institute of Solid State Physics, Friedrich-Schiller-University, Jena 07743, Germany (e-mail: sven.schoenherr@uni-jena.de).

Color versions of one or more of the figures in this paper are available online at http://ieeexplore.ieee.org.

Digital Object Identifier 10.1109/JPHOTOV.2013.2289873

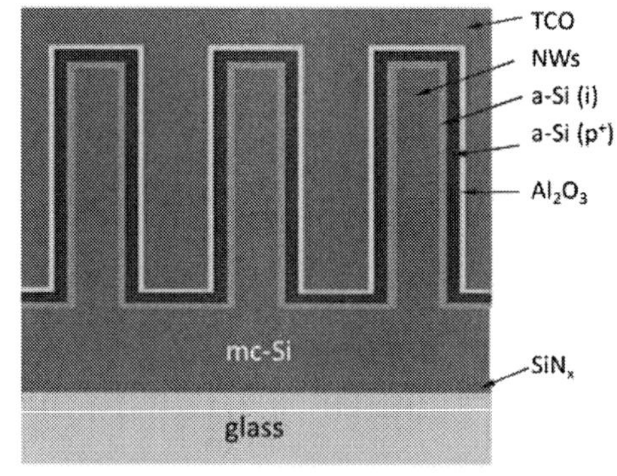

Fig. 1. Concept of a SiNW thin film solar cell.

significant performance gain. The nanowires are produced by wet chemical etching. A radial p-n heterojunction is prepared by depositing a p-doped shell of amorphous silicon around the n-doped nanowires by plasma-enhanced chemical vapor deposition (PECVD). In fact, we use the heterojunction with intrinsic thin layer (HIT) concept [10], i.e., first, a very thin intrinsic a-Si layer is deposited followed by p-type a-Si. Then, this layer system is passivated by an ultrathin layer of Al_2O_3, deposited by atomic layer deposition (ALD). This technique has the advantage to work also in the narrow grooves between the nanowires. The space between the nanowires is filled by ZnO:Al (AZO) acting as a transparent conductive oxide contact for the solar cell. To get information on the optical properties of the nanowire solar cell, measurements were performed not only on the final solar-cell configuration but after intermediate preparation steps as well.

II. Experimental Setup

On a glass substrate (Schott boro33) sputter coated with a thin SiN_x film (80 nm), several micrometer n-doped (about $6 \cdot 10^{16}$ cm^{-3} P) a-Si was deposited by electron beam evaporation. This layer was crystallized by scanning the beam of a high-power line focus diode laser (808-nm wavelength, $10\dots15$ kW/cm^2 power density) at a rate of 1– 3 cm/s. Crystallization occurs via the melt and results in grains 100 μm to 1 mm in size [11], as shown by electron backscatter diffraction (EBSD) (see Fig. 2).

In this layer, SiNW arrays were prepared by metal catalyzed wet chemical etching following the method described by Peng

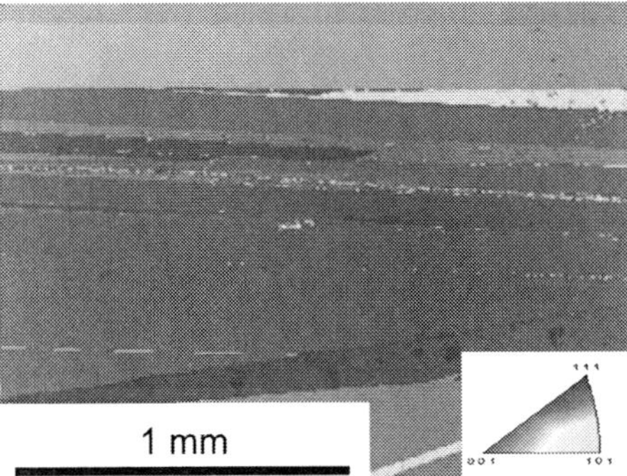

Fig. 2.　EBSD map of a laser crystallized silicon thin film on glass.

Fig. 3.　SEM image of a nanowire array prepared on a mc-Si thin film.

et al. [12]. We used 1:1 a mixture of $AgNO_3$ (0.04 M) and HF (5 M). The etching rate is in the 50–60 nm/min range and the length of the nanowires can simply be controlled by the etching time. Fig. 3 shows as an example a scanning electron microscopy (SEM) image of a SiNW array etched for 10 min into an mc-Si thin film on glass. The resulting SiNWs are densely packed, irregularly shaped, and have a length of 500–600 nm. Silver remnants were carefully removed by HNO_3, applying a procedure developed by our group [5], [9]. A formed silicon dioxide layer was removed by dipping into HF (2%)/2-propanol, where the propanol serves as a surfactant to reduce the surface tension so that the etchant can penetrate into the nanowire array to completely remove the oxide around the NWs. Subsequently, the samples were rinsed by ultrapure deionized water and blown dry with N_2.

a-Si:H deposition was done by PECVD at 225 °C. A thin (about 2 nm) intrinsic *a*-Si:H layer was deposited prior to a highly doped, about 5-nm-thick p-type *a*-Si:H. In this way, a HIT-type core shell p-n heterojunction was formed. The nanowires were then covered by 1.2-nm Al_2O_3 [9] and subsequently by 200 nm of AZO [13], both deposited by ALD.

There arises the suspicion that, when depositing the *a*-Si heteroemitter, deposition might not take place in the deep grooves between the nanowires. This would lead to solar cells with the p-n heterojunction present only at the upper part of the nanowires so that not only a radial junction configuration would result but just an intermediate case between axial and radial junction. In-

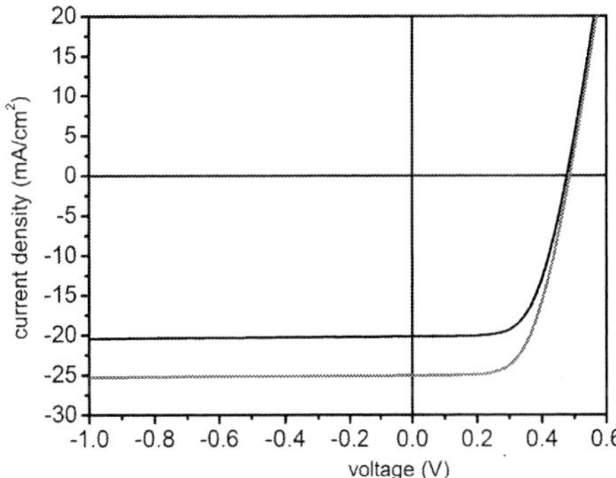

Fig. 4.　*I–V* curves of a nanowire solar cell on a 8-μm-thick mc-Si thin film on glass in substrate (black) and superstrate (red) illumination.

deed, TEM cross-section images demonstrated *a*-Si deposition down to the bottom of the groves [9], [14] with just some variation in thickness.

To define the solar cell, mesa etching was performed down to the mc-Si thin film. In this way, the area of the solar cell (5.4 mm²) was well defined. For contacting, one metal tip was located at the TCO layer and another one on the etched down mc-layer next to the cell. Light being absorbed in the remaining thin mc-layer surrounding of the cell is not expected to contribute to the measured current.

The optical properties of the system after different preparation steps were determined by UV-VIS spectroscopy. Reflectance R and transmission T were measured in an integrating sphere, and absorption A was calculated according to $A = 1 - T - R$. *I–V* curves were measured in a sun simulator under AM1.5 illumination. The spectral response was determined by external quantum efficiency (EQE) measurements.

III. SOLAR CELL RESULTS

Fig. 4 shows the *I–V* curve of a nanowire solar cell prepared on a 8-μm-thick mc-Si film, both in substrate (black line) and in a superstrate (red line) configuration, i.e., with illumination from the front or the glass side, respectively.

In the superstrate configuration, the solar cell shows an open-circuit voltage of 486 mV, a short-circuit current density of 25.1 mA/cm², and a power conversion efficiency of 7.5%, whereas in the substrate configuration, the short-circuit current is 20.2 mA/cm², which is a bit lower. Our best superstrate cell with a 200-nm-thick Ag reflection layer on the TCO reached 8.8% efficiency and an open circuit-voltage of 530 mV. To get this result, an additional hydrogen passivation step of the virgin mc-Si layer was added before nanowire etching.

Reference cells on planar crystalline silicon layers reached, if prepared exactly by the same procedure just omitting the nanowire etching step, only low-current densities of about 10 mA/cm² and open-circuit voltages up to 361 mV.

Fig. 5 shows the EQE measured for both illumination conditions. In the case of superstrate illumination, the EQE curve shows a much stronger response below 800-nm wavelength, which explains the difference of the short-circuit current.

　　　149

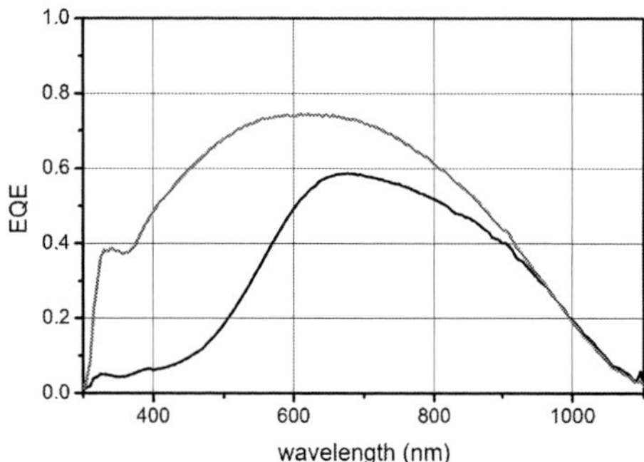

Fig. 5. EQE of the cell of Fig. 4 in case of substrate (black) and superstrate (red) illumination.

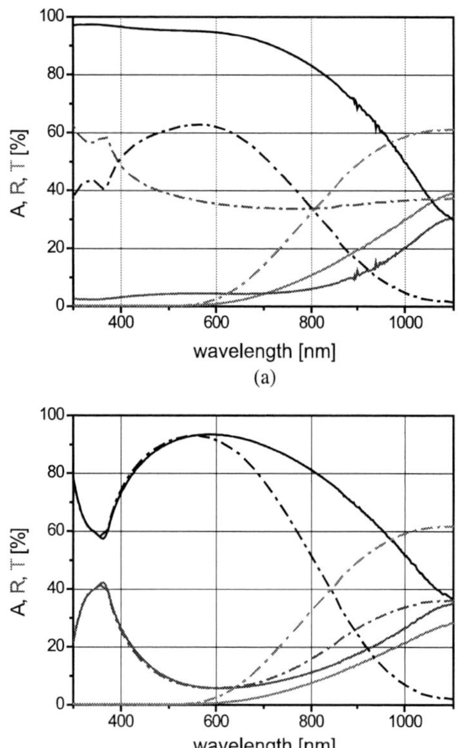

Fig. 6. Absorption (black), reflection (blue), and transmission (red) of a 8-μm thick mc-Si layer on 80-nm SiN on glass with (solid lines) and without (dash–dotted lines) nanowires. (a) Substrate illumination and (b) superstrate illumination.

IV. Optical Results and Discussion

To better understand the properties of SiNW solar cells, optical measurements were performed. Fig. 6 shows the optical properties of an 8-μm-thick flat mc-Si layer on 80-nm SiN on glass, compared with those of a nanowire sample etched into this film. The most important optical result is the strong increase of the absorption in the nanowire sample, as compared with the flat sample. For substrate illumination, the flat sample shows high

reflection (see Fig. 6(a), blue dash–dotted line) and, therefore, low absorption (black dash–dotted line) in the whole spectral range, with the typical Si reflection peak around 360 nm. The nanowire sample has very low reflectivity (blue solid line) and the absorption (black solid line) is very high (>90%) up to 700-nm wavelength. Even for larger wavelengths, the absorption is higher by 40% absolute, as compared with the flat sample, which shows only low absorption in the long wavelength range ($\lambda >$ 800 nm), according to the low-absorption constant of c-Si.

In case of superstrate illumination [see Fig. 6(b)], the flat sample (dash–dotted black line) shows higher absorption in any wavelength range as compared with substrate illumination. This is because of the antireflection properties of the SiN layer between glass and silicon. Nevertheless, the nanowires increase absorption also in the superstrate configuration, particularly in the long wavelength region ($\lambda >$ 600 nm). These observations perfectly demonstrate the light trapping capability of the nanowire array, which is responsible for the relatively high efficiency of our SiNW solar cells on glass substrates.

When comparing the absorption of the nanowire solar cell in both configurations, one finds rather similar behavior in the long wavelength range, whereas at short wavelengths, the substrate configuration shows higher absorption. As a consequence, one would expect higher EQE there under substrate illumination, which is not the case (see Fig. 5). To understand this contradiction, optical measurements were performed after intermediate preparation steps. To better demonstrate the influence of the nanowires and the a-Si and AZO layers, we did these experiments on mc-Si films that are only 1.5 μm thick. Fig. 7 shows the absorption of a flat system (a) and a system with nanowires (b) after the individual deposition steps.

On the flat system without nanowires, we observe, in the substrate configuration, that a thin added a-Si layer does not appreciably change the optical properties, except in the short wavelength range $\lambda <$ 400 nm [compare red and blue solid curve in Fig. 7(a)]. Adding the AZO layer increases the absorption in the wavelength range below 600 nm. This is because AZO acts as an antireflection layer. Moreover, one observes strong interference effects below 500-nm wavelength.

In the superstrate configuration of the flat system, the bare silicon layer without nanowires shows stronger absorption than in the substrate configuration [compare dash dotted and solid red lines in Fig. 7(a)]. This is because the glass/SiN/Si stack acts as an antireflection layer system. Adding a-Si and AZO does not change absorption any more [compare the red, blue, and black dash dotted curves in Fig. 7(a)].

Let us now look at the nanowire system in the substrate configuration [solid lines in Fig. 7(b)]. As compared with the flat system, the absorption is much higher. Adding a-Si increases the absorption by about 10% [compare red and blue solid lines in Fig. 7(b)]. Adding AZO (black solid line) further increases the absorption in the long wavelength range above 800 nm. Both these effects are in contrast with the flat system. This observation is interpreted as resulting from scattering of the incoming light by the nanowires so that the effective thickness of the a-Si and AZO layer traversed by the light is strongly increased. AZO appreciably absorbs only in the IR because of free

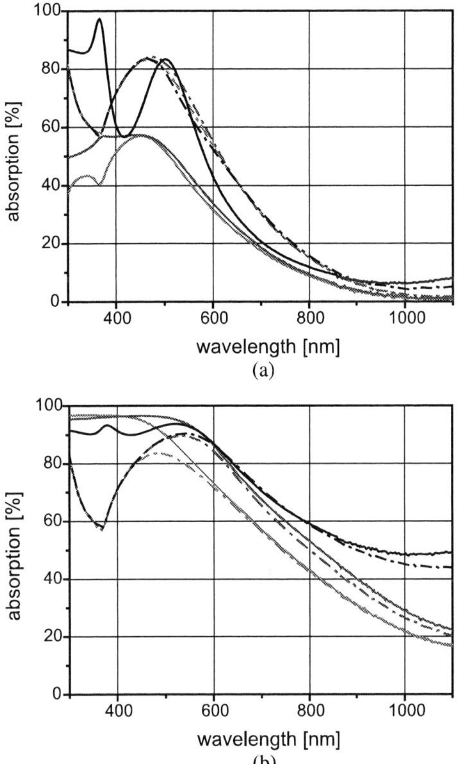

Fig. 7. Absorption of a 1.5-μm-thick flat system without nanowires (a) and of a system with nanowires (b). Just mc-Si (red), mc-Si with a-Si (blue), and additionally with AZO (black), in substrate (solid lines) and in superstrate illumination (dash-dotted lines). 80-nm SiN between glass and mc-Si.

carriers. Absorption in both a-Si and AZO is parasitic and does not contribute too much to the photocurrent of the solar cell.

If we now look at the nanowire system in superstrate configuration, we find that again a-Si increases absorption [compare red and blue dash–dotted lines in Fig. 7(b)], but to a somewhat lower degree. The same applies if AZO is added. (black dash–dotted line). Superstrate and substrate configurations show rather similar properties, except in the short wavelength region (below 500 nm), where the absorption in superstrate configuration is lower. The absorption curves there are similar to the flat system. The effect is because of the increasing reflection of the glass/SiN/Si stack in this wavelength range.

Let us summarize the optical results and compare with the EQE curves. From EQE, we learn that the superstrate configuration gives higher response than the substrate configuration. Part of this effect is because of the parasitic absorption in a-Si and AZO. In substrate configuration, the incoming light absorbed in a-Si and in AZO does not reach the nanowires anymore and does not contribute to the photocurrent much. In the superstrate configuration, only a part of the light in the long wavelength range, which is not absorbed in the silicon film and in the nanowires, reaches the a-Si layer to get partly absorbed there. This effect is beneficial for the superstrate configuration and explains at least partly the difference in the EQE curves of both configurations.

The lower absorption of the nanowire system in superstrate as compared with the substrate configuration at short wavelength should have an adverse effect.

Altogether, we feel that the optical properties of both configurations of the system give hints for the differences in photovoltaic properties but do not completely explain them. This is due to the fact that the increase in absorption by adding a-Si and AZO not only results from the additional absorption within these layers but from the changed optical properties of the whole system as well so that it is not perfectly clear in which of the layers the light is in fact absorbed.

Concerning the influence of recombination on the difference in the response for both illumination conditions, one can state that bulk recombination cannot be responsible. We expect that bulk recombination is identical within the nanowires and in the crystalline silicon layer, since the wires are etched into the layer. In substrate illumination, the short wavelength light is absorbed within the nanowires and the generated minority charge carriers have to travel just across the radius of the nanowires to reach the p-n heterojunction. In superstrate illumination, the short wavelength light is absorbed in the silicon layer near the glass interface, and the generated minorities have to travel much farther through all the layer and the lower part of the nanowires. Since, for short wavelength light, the EQE is larger in superstrate than in substrate illumination, bulk recombination is neither the limiting factor, nor is it the recombination at the interface to SiN/glass. Concerning interface recombination at the heterojunction, its effect is not so clear. In substrate illumination, the carriers generated in the nanowires by the short wavelength light experience the large surface of the nanowires. In the superstrate configuration, the carriers generated near the glass interface by the short wavelength light travelling to the heterojunction probably pass only through the base of the nanowires, experiencing only a small part of the heterojunction area. Therefore, they probably suffer less from interface recombination, which could explain the higher EQE.

Altogether, it is not clear up to now if the optical properties of both configurations of the system or if interface recombination at the heterojunction is responsible for the differences in the response of the nanowire solar cell in the superstrate and in the substrate configuration.

V. CONCLUSION

SiNW solar cells with a core shell structure pre-pared on mc-Si thin films on glass reached an efficiency of up to 8.8%. The nanowires act as a strong light-trapping device, increasing the absorption appreciably, as compared with a flat system of the same thickness. The EQE of the cells is, in the visible wavelength region, lower in substrate than in the superstrate configuration. This may be because of interface recombination at the heterojunction and to parasitic absorption in the a-Si shell and the AZO around the nanowires, which is rather important in substrate illumination, in which the incoming light is scattered by the nanowire array and crosses AZO and the nanowires repeatedly. This effect is not so important in superstrate illumination. In this case, the thickness of the AZO layer on top of the nanowire system does not influence the optical properties too much; therefore, it can be optimized with respect to electrical requirements. Moreover, due to the minor influence of the a-Si absorption in superstrate configuration, the a-Si thickness can as well be optimized with respect to electrical requirements. Altogether, in the case of SiNW solar cells on a glass substrate, superstrate illumination is to be preferred against substrate illumination.

REFERENCES

[1] M. Gharghi, E. Fathi, B. Kante, S. Sivoththaman, and X. Zhang, "Heterojunction silicon microwire solar cells," *Nano Lett.*, vol. 12, pp. 6278–6282, 2012.

[2] S. Perraud, S. Poncet, S. Noel, M. Levis, P. Faucher, E. Rouviere, P. Thony, C. Jaussaud, and R. Delsol, "Full process for integrating silicon nanowire arrays into solar cells," *Sol. Energy Mater. Sol. Cells*, vol. 93, pp. 1568–1571, 2009.

[3] B. Tian, X. Zheng, T. J. Kempa, Y. Fang, N. Yu, G. Yu, J. Huang, and C. M. Lieber, "Coaxial silicon nanowires as solar cells and nanoelectronic power sources," *Nature*, vol. 449, pp. 885–890, 2007.

[4] V. Sivakov, G. Andrä, A. Gawlik, A. Berger, J. Plentz, F. Falk, and S. H. Christiansen, "Silicon nanowire-based solar cells on glass, optical properties, and cell parameters," *Nano Lett.*, vol. 9, pp. 1549–1554, 2009.

[5] G. Jia, I. Höger, A. Gawlik, J. Dellith, L. R. Bailey, A. Ulyashin, and F. Falk, "Wet chemically prepared nanowire arrays on low-cost substrates for photovoltaic applications," *Phys. Status Solidi (a)*, vol. 210, pp. 728–731, 2013.

[6] B. M. Kayes, H. A. Atwater, and N. S. Lewis, "Comparison of the device physics principles of planar and radial p-n junction nanorod solar cells," *J. Appl. Phys.*, vol. 97, art. no. 114302, 2005.

[7] L. Tsakalakos, J. Balch, J. Fronheiser, B. A. Korevaar, O. Sulima, and J. Rand, "Silicon nanowire solar cells," *Appl. Phys. Lett.*, vol. 91, art. no. 233117, 2007.

[8] G. Jia, M. Steglich, I. Sill, and F. Falk, "Core-shell heterojunction solar cells on silicon nanowire arrays," *Sol. Energy Mater. Sol. Cells*, vol. 96, pp. 226–230, 2012.

[9] G. Jia, B. Eisenhawer, J. Dellith, F. Falk, A. Thøgersen, and A. Ulyashin, "Multiple core-shell silicon nanowire based heterojunction solar cells," *J. Phys. Chem. C*, vol. 117, pp. 1091–1096, 2013.

[10] Y. Tsunomura, Y. Yoshimine, M. Taguchi, T. Baba, T. Kinoshita, H. Kanno, H. Sakata, E. Maruyama, and M. Tanaka, "Twenty-two percent efficiency HIT solar cell," *Sol. Energy Mater. Sol. Cells*, vol. 93, pp. 670–673, 2009.

[11] G. Schmidl, G. Andrä, J. Bergmann, A. Gawlik, I. Höger, S. Anders, F. Schmidl, V. Tympel, and F. Falk, "CW-diode laser crystallization of sputtered amorphous silicon on glass, SiN_x, and SiO_2 intermediate layers," *J. Mater. Sci.*, vol. 48, pp. 4177–4182, 2013.

[12] K. Peng, Y. Yan, S. Gao, and J. Zhu, "Synthesis of large-area silicon nanowire arrays via self-assembling nanoelectrochemistry," *Adv. Mater.*, vol. 14, pp. 1164–1167, 2002.

[13] M. Steglich, A. Bingel, G. Jia, and F. Falk, "Atomic layer deposited ZnO:Al for nanostructured silicon heterojunction solar cells," *Sol. Energy Mater. Sol. Cells*, vol. 103, pp. 62–68, 2012.

[14] F. Falk, G. Jia, I. Sill, and N. Petkov, "Silicon nanowire solar cells with a-Si hetero-junction showing 7.3% efficiency," *Proc. SPIE*, vol. 8111, art. no. 81110Q, 2011.

Authors' photographs and biographies not available at the time of publication.

Optical and Electrical Simulation of μc-Si:H Solar Cells: Effect of Substrate Morphology and Crystalline Fraction

Do Yun Kim, René A. C. M. M. van Swaaij, and Miro Zeman

Abstract—Hydrogenated microcrystalline silicon (μc-Si:H) is an important material for high-efficiency multijunction solar cells. Due to its complex microstructural properties, it is difficult to describe the electronic behavior clearly. In this study, we measure opto-electronic properties including the mobility gap of μc-Si:H films in solar cells, as well as physical properties such as the crystalline fraction profile. The height distribution function of the ZnO substrates is obtained by AFM scans, which is used for optical simulation. All the parameters that we obtained from measurements were used as input parameters of a model in the ASA simulator. We obtained a good fit between measurements and simulations

Index Terms—Microcrystalline silicon, mobility gap, optical and electrical simulation, solar cells, TCO morphology.

I. INTRODUCTION

HYDROGENATED amorphous silicon (a-Si:H) is an important material for thin-film solar cell technology. For a better understanding, much effort has been devoted to computer modeling of a-Si:H devices. To date, computer modeling has been quite well established and a fairly good match between experiment and simulation results has been demonstrated, thereby enabling good interpretation of the device operation [1]–[4]. Even though hydrogenated microcrystalline silicon (μc-Si:H) is also regarded as a key material for micromorph solar cells, less work has been carried out on computer modeling of μc-Si:H solar cells. In spite of its importance, the electronic properties of μc-Si:H are not completely understood due to its complicated microstructure, as illustrated in Fig. 1(a). In reality, during the very early stages of μc-Si:H film growth, an incubation layer is formed, followed by microcrystallites growing with different sizes, amorphous tissues surrounding the crystals, grain boundaries, cracks, dislocations, etc.

For the modeling of μc-Si:H, two different methods are used. The first model considers amorphous and crystalline regions, and grain boundaries separately. Depending on their fraction, each factor can affect opto-electrical properties significantly

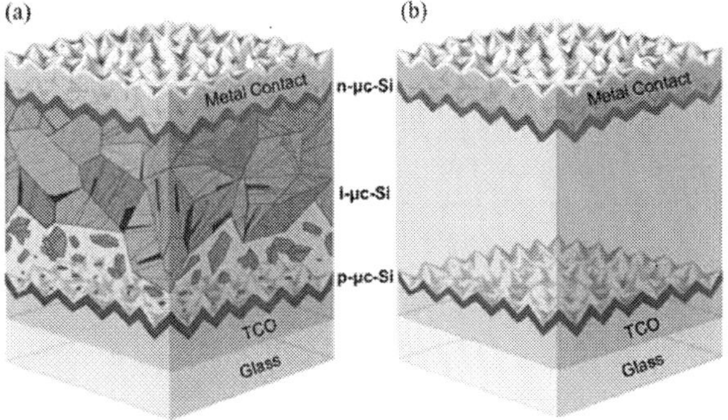

Fig. 1. Schematic representation of (a) μc-Si:H solar cell in reality and (b) μc-Si:H solar cell in the effective medium approximation.

and to a different extent. This approach, however, needs input parameters for each phase, which are difficult to obtain as these material parameters are extracted from general measurements.

The second model uses the effective medium approach (EMA), treating μc-Si:H as if it is a single-phase material instead of considering each respective phase, as illustrated in Fig. 1(b). This approach ignores detailed information of the component materials; however, this is a simple and time-saving method.

To achieve highly efficient μc-Si:H solar cells, securing the material quality is regarded as a key factor. In addition, light management techniques are taken into account for the same objective. Proper light management is generally achieved by tuning the substrate morphology. In the literature, it has been reported that film growth is strongly dependent on the substrate morphology [5]. It has been demonstrated that μc-Si:H grown on highly textured substrates, beneficial for increasing the photocurrent through light trapping, has many cracks in the growth direction, suppressing the efficiency.

In this context, it is necessary to figure out how material parameters of μc-Si:H change under different conditions in order to develop an accurate simulation model that fits the experimental results well, such that solar-cell behavior can be characterized properly and design can be optimized. Therefore, in this contribution, we carry out optical and electrical simulations of μc-Si:H solar cells deposited on different substrates by using the ASA simulator that has been developed at the Delft University of Technology (TU Delft) [6]. For these simulations, the effective medium approximation is adopted to describe the μc-Si:H.

Manuscript received June 16, 2013; revised August 17, 2013; accepted September 10, 2013. Date of publication November 14, 2013; date of current version December 16, 2013. This work was supported by the European Commission under Grant 283501 in the framework of the FP7 project "Fast Track."

The authors are with Photovoltaic Materials and Devices Laboratory, Delft University of Technology, 2628 CD Delft, The Netherlands (e-mail: D.Kim@tudelft.nl; R.A.C.M.M.vanSwaaij@tudelft.nl; M.Zeman@tudelft.nl)

Color versions of one or more of the figures in this paper are available online at http://ieeexplore.ieee.org.

Digital Object Identifier 10.1109/JPHOTOV.2013.2287770

TABLE I
VARIOUS ZnO SUBSTRATES FROM DIFFERENT INSTITUTE

Substrate	Institute	σ_{RMS} (nm)
ZJL	FZJ	105
ZEP1	EPFL	113
ZEP2	EPFL	145
ZEP3	EPFL	158

TABLE II
PHOTOVOLTAIC PARAMETERS OF SOLAR CELLS ON DIFFERENT SUBSTRATES
USED IN THIS STUDY FOR SIMULATIONS

No	Substrates	V_{OC} (V)	J_{SC} (mA/cm²)	FF (-)	η (%)
SJL	ZJL	0.523	24.12	0.64	8.07
SEP1	ZEP1	0.564	22.74	0.71	9.11
SEP2	ZEP2	0.538	24.03	0.67	8.66
SEP3	ZEP3	0.468	23.64	0.63	6.97
SDFT	ZJL	0.556	22.87	0.72	9.16

II. EXPERIMENTAL AND SIMULATION PROCEDURES

In this study, various samples were investigated and characterized, including TCO substrates; p, i and n-type μc-Si:H layers; and solar cells., These layers and devices were fabricated by Forschungszentrum Jülich (FZJ), École polytechnique fédérale de Lausanne (EPFL), and TU Delft. In Table I, various types ZnO substrates used in this study are tabulated. The ZnO:Al from FZJ (crater-like shape), hereafter called ZJL, is fabricated by sputtering, and ZnO:B from EPFL (pyramidal shape), hereafter referred to as ZEP1 to ZEP3 depending on the RMS roughness (σ_{RMS}), is fabricated by low-pressure chemical vapor deposition (LPCVD).

Atomic force microscopy (AFM) scans of 256×256 points over an area of 10 μm $\times$ 10 μm on the ZnO substrates, n-layers, and back ZnOs of p-i-n solar cells were taken to obtain the height distribution functions, $z(x, y)$, which in turn are used for optical simulations that are based on the scalar scattering model as described by Jäger et al. [7]. With this model, the angular intensity distribution (AID) function is calculated. This model is combined with the ASA simulator. Optical film properties, such as the refractive index and extinction coefficient of μc-Si:H layers, are characterized for use as practical and reliable input parameters in our simulations. For the description of μc-Si:H, we have adopted the EMA. μc-Si:H is a heterogeneous material that consists of a-Si:H, silicon crystals, grain boundaries, voids, cracks, etc., and the contribution to the optical properties of each component is difficult to ascertain. Using the EMA, the properties of the μc-Si:H layers that we measured are regarded to represent the entire (or average) properties of the μc-Si:H layers. The electrical properties of films and devices are also measured to be used as input parameters for electrical modeling, where we followed the percolation approach as used by Pieters et al. [8]. In addition, we assumed the infinite surface recombination velocity, because practically no excess minority carriers reach the contacts adjoining the doped layers. Because of the very low carrier lifetimes in the doped layer, the excess minorities recombine before they can reach the contact surface [9]. For comparison of simulation to experimental external solar cell results, quantum efficiency (QE), illuminated current density versus voltage ($J–V$) characteristics, and temperature-dependent dark $J–V$ characteristics of solar cells from FZJ, hereafter called SJL, EPFL, hereafter referred to as SEP1 to 3, and TU Delft, hereafter named SDFT, are measured. The SJL and SEP solar cells have the structure of Front ZnO/p-μc-Si/ i-μc-Si/n-μc-Si/Back ZnO/Back metal contact. The SDFT solar cell also has the same structure, except for the back ZnO, which was omitted. All of the solar cells had the same i-layer thickness of around 1.1 μm. The detailed PV

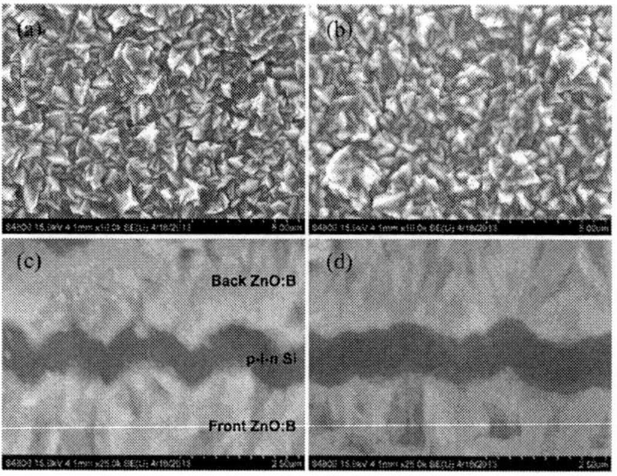

Fig. 2. SEM images of (a) ZEP3, (b) Ag/Cr/Al back contact and cross-section of the (c) SEP3 and (d) SEP1.

parameters of the solar cells used in this simulation are tabulated in Table II. The maximal standard deviation in the measured parameters is 2 mV for the V_{OC}, 0.05 mA/cm² for the J_{SC}, 0.01 for the FF, and 0.07% for η. From the temperature-dependent dark $J–V$, the voltage-dependent dark current activation energy is calculated, from which in turn the mobility gap, E_μ, of the intrinsic layer in a p-i-n device is obtained using a model developed by Pieters et al. [8]. According to this model this activation energy is described by

$$E_a^{\mathrm{p\text{-}i\text{-}n}} = \frac{E_\mu - V}{2} + 3kT. \tag{1}$$

III. RESULTS AND DISCUSSION

In Fig. 2(a) and (b), scanning electron microscope (SEM) images of the front ZnO with σ_{RMS} of 158 nm, Ag/Cr/Al back contact of the p-i-n uc-Si:H solar cell on that ZnO substrate are shown as an example. From this figure, it can be clearly seen that the surface morphology maintains a similar shape even after the deposition of p-i-n- solar cells followed by Ag/Cr/Ar back contact. The difference between the Fig. 2(a) and (b) is obviously small. After the deposition of the p-i-n μc-Si:H solar cells on two different ZnO substrates, as shown in Fig. 2(c) and (d), which are SEP3 and SEP1, respectively, the roughness hardly becomes smaller and the morphology of the front TCO is almost copied. Since there is a big change in refractive index between the front TCO/p-Si, n-Si/back TCO, and the back TCO/Ag/Cr/Al back contact, there must be much reflection at those interfaces. Hence, in order to take into account these phenomena, we also measured the height functions at those surfaces and used them

154

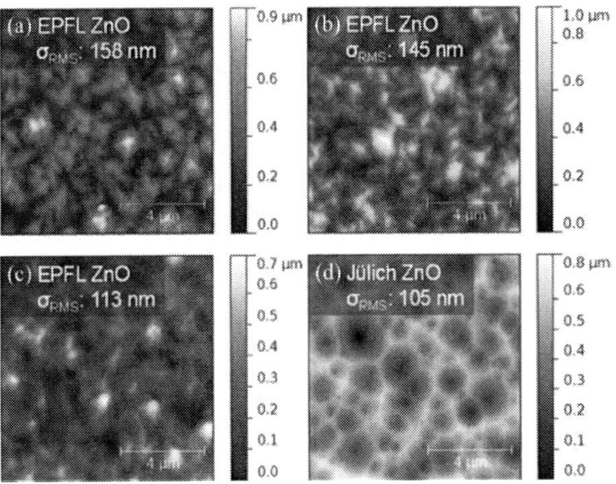

Fig. 3. AFM images of (a) *ZEP3*, (b) *ZEP2*, (c) *ZEP1*, and (d) *ZJL*.

in our simulations. On the other hand, it can be seen from the cross-section images, that a difference in the growing surface of those two solar cells is apparent. In the literature, it has been shown that solar cells on ZnO substrates with rough morphology can have many cracks generated at the sharp and steep valleys of the ZnO [10]–[14]. This can explain the fact that the *SEP3* on the *ZEP3* of σ_{RMS} of 158 nm has J_{sc} induced by better scattering, but lower V_{OC} and FF because of a higher crack density with respect to *SEP1* on the *ZEP1* of σ_{RMS} of 113 nm. We shall discuss this further in this paper.

In Fig. 3(a)–(d), AFM images of ZnO substrates are shown. The *ZEP1* is the as-deposited ZnO:B by LPCVD and has the highest σ_{RMS} among these substrates. The σ_{RMS} is then reduced to a value as low as 113 nm by performing Ar plasma treatment in EPFL. In contrast, the *ZJL* is etched by etchant solution to form textured surfaces in FZJ.

With increasing σ_{RMS} of *ZEP* from 113–158 nm, the haze ratios in transmission (H_T) of all ZnO substrates increase continuously, as shown in Fig. 4(a). In Fig. 4(b), the AID of the ZnO substrates is shown at the wavelength of 600 nm. Here, the specular transmission component is higher for ZnO with lower σ_{RMS} and the diffuse transmission component is higher for ZnO with higher σ_{RMS}. Both results directly indicate better light scattering with σ_{RMS}. The height distribution function of $z(x, y)$ as obtained from AFM scans of these surfaces is used as input in the optical simulation for tracing the propagation of scattered light. The measurements (markers) are remarkably consistent with the simulation results (shown by lines), as depicted in Fig. 4(a) and (b), which validates the application of this optical model to device simulation.

Film growth of μc-Si:H depends to a large extent on the deposition conditions. In addition, the growth is strongly influenced by the surface morphology of the underlying substrate. Several authors have shown [15], [16] that the crystalline fraction increases along the growth direction and that the film growth often starts with an amorphous incubation layer. In this context, we examined the crystalline fraction profile of μc-Si:H solar cells and films, which were fabricated on ZnO substrates having

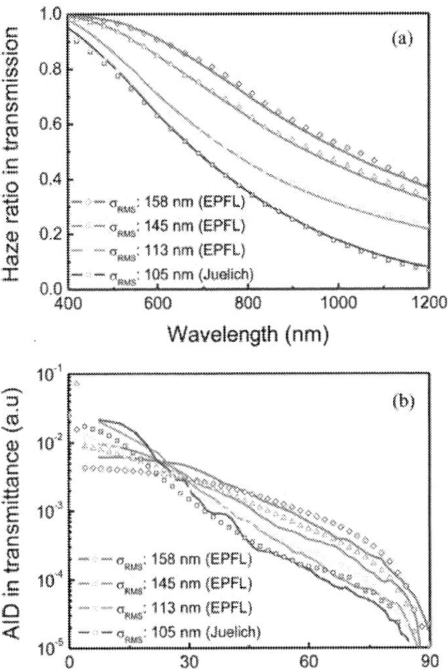

Fig. 4. (a). Haze ratio and (b) AID in transmission of TCO layers. Markers are experimental results and the lines are simulation results.

different σ_{RMS}. We determined the crystalline fraction profile of μc-Si:H p-i-n solar cells and layers by alternating Raman measurements and reactive ion etching. From the Raman measurements, the crystalline fraction (X_C) was determined using the flowing relation:

$$X_C = \frac{I_{510} + I_{518}}{I_{480} + I_{510} + I_{518}} \qquad (2)$$

where I_i denotes an integrated intensity of Raman spectra at i cm^{-1} [17].

Dry etching was carried out using a reactive ion etcher with a gas mixture of CF$_4$, SF$_6$, and N$_2$. The depth profiles of X_C of p-i-n solar cells and intrinsic μc-Si:H layers on different substrates are shown in Fig. 5(a) and 5(b). It is noteworthy that even at a position of ~50 nm from the TCO, X_C of all the solar cells is 40–55 %, whereas X_C of Si films on glass is 15–40%. The X_C of individual films is substantially lower than in the solar cells and continues to increase with thickness. The difference in X_C is induced by the presence of p-μc-Si:H layer, which obviously turns out to promote crystalline growth. The measurements also reveal that the crystalline fraction of solar cells and i-layers are strongly affected by σ_{RMS} of substrates. With high σ_{RMS} substrates the overall X_C of devices stays low. In general, if X_C of i-μc-Si:H increases, the V_{OC} decreases [18]. In contrast, the V_{OC} of *SEP1* is higher than that of *SEP2* and *SEP3* (see Table II), even though their X_C shows an increasing trend as confirmed from Fig. 5. Given that the X_C of the solar cells decreases while the TCO morphology (see Fig. 3) becomes rougher, this feature would be strongly related to the presence

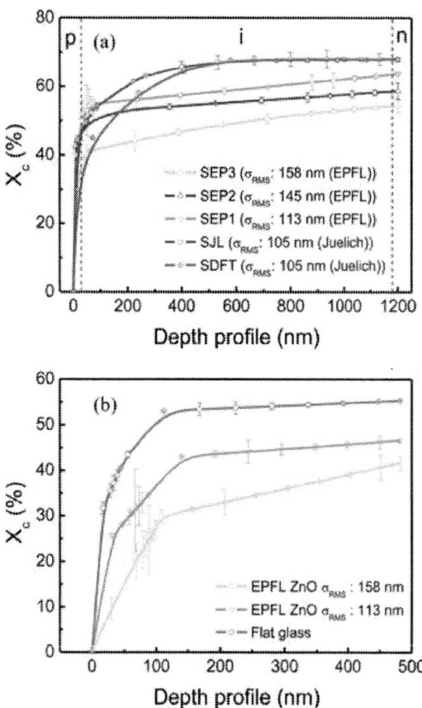

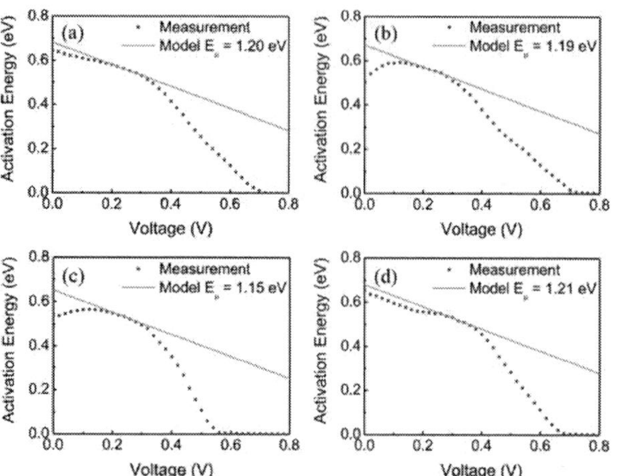

Fig. 6.   Dark current activation energy $E_a^{\mathrm{p\text{-}i\text{-}n}}$ of (a) *SEP1*, (b) *SEP3*, (c) *SJL*, and (d) *SDFT* solar cells.

Fig. 5   (a). Dependence of crystalline fraction profile of p-i-n devices from different institutes. (b) Intrinsic μc-Si:H films from EPFL on different substrates.

of cracks. The decreasing FFs of the solar cells with σ_{RMS} also support this.

We approximated a constant X_C of the i-μc-Si:H layers of those solar cells in the simulations by selecting X_C at the middle of the i-μc-Si:H layers. Similar to the work of Pieters *et al.* [8], the X_C is used to rescale effective density of states (DOS) of i-layer, following the percolation assumption in which electronic transport dominantly takes place through clusters of crystallites (percolation path) [19]–[21]. Thus, a low crystalline fraction indicates low effective DOS in this simulation. This is valid especially when the μc-Si:H has crystallites over the percolation threshold. Several authors have shown theoretically and experimentally that percolation occurs when the crystalline fraction of μcSi:H is around 20–30% [21]–[24]. In particular, Hamma *et al.* showed that the conductivity of μc-Si:H films jumped up more than three orders of magnitudes when X_C reached 30% and the conductivity stayed constant even though X_C increased up to 76% [24].

In order to determine the E_μ of p-i-n devices, we measured dark J–V curves as a function of temperature (from 40 °C to 100 °C at 10 °C intervals). The temperature was set with accuracy of ±0.5 °C. For accurate measurements, we used a Keithley 6517 A electrometer. With this electrometer the current was measured with an accuracy better than 0.01%; the voltage is set with an accuracy of 0.15%. In general, the n-μc-Si:H layer is so conductive that it is not possible to measure precise current in the low-voltage region, which ultimately makes it difficult to obtain E_μ. Therefore, the n-μc-Si:H layer outside of the effective

solar cell is etched after the deposition of the metal back contact. Using this structure, parasitic leakage current is largely reduced in the low-voltage region. The dark current activation energy curves of *SEP1*, *SEP3*, *SJL*, and *SDFT* are shown in Fig. 6. Fitting this result to (1) shows that the E_μ of the intrinsic layers in the p-i-n devices are around 1.20, 1.19, 1.15, and 1.21 eV for *SEP1*, *SEP3*, *SJL*, and *SDFT*, respectively. For *SEP1* and *SEP3*, the difference between the obtained mobility gaps turns out to be negligible, even though their X_C showed quite big difference: ΔX_C at the middle of these cells is approximately 10%.

From the dark J–V measurements, we found that the current density at room temperature of the μc-Si:H solar cells was around $\sim 10^{-5}$ mA/cm^2 at a voltage of 0.02 V, whereas that of typical a-Si:H solar cells is $\sim 10^{-8}$ mA/cm^2 as shown by Kind *et al.* [25]. They also showed that E_μ of a-Si:H solar cells is about 1.69 eV, which is obviously higher than our results. These results are clear indications that the current of our μc-Si:H solar cells flows through percolation paths made up by the crystalline Si phase, thus strongly supporting the validity of the percolation assumption in this study.

Subsequently, optical and electrical simulations were carried out using ASA simulator for the μc-Si:H solar cells, using the parameters obtained by measurements: the wavelength-dependent complex refractive index; the thickness of each layer; the height distribution function of the TCOs, n-layers, and back ZnOs; the activation energy of the p- and n-layers; the dark current activation energy (thereby E_μ); and the X_C of the i-layer in a p-i-n device [thereby re-scaled densities of states at the conduction and valence band edge ($N_{c0/v0}$)]. In addition, other parameters such as electron and hole mobilities ($\mu_{e/h}$), band tail width (E_{tail}) and electron affinity of μc-Si:H are taken from Pieters *et al.* (see [8] and references therein); we assumed a constant band tail width of 31 meV. The defect density (N_{db}) of the intrinsic layer and the cross section for electron (n) or hole (p) capture, of a positively charged (+), neutral (0), or negatively

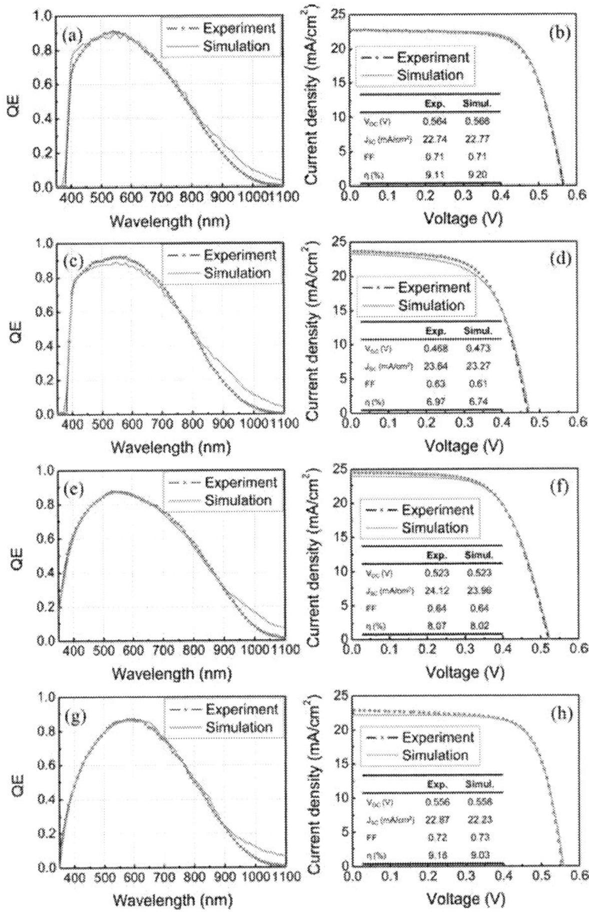

Fig. 7. Simulations and measurements of (a) QEs and (b) illuminated *J–V* curves of *SEP1*, (c) QEs and (d) illuminated *J–V* curves of *SEP3*, (e) QEs and (f) illuminated *J–V* curves of *SJL*, and (g) QEs and (h) illuminated *J–V* curves of *SDFT*.

TABLE III

INPUT PARAMETERS FOR SIMULATIONS

Parameters	Value (for *SJL* / *SEP1* / *SDFT*)
E_μ	$(1.15 / 1.20 / 1.21)$ eV
μ_e	100 cm^{2}V^{-1}s^{-1}
μ_h	30 cm^{2}V^{-1}s^{-1}
N_{v0}	$(1.40 / 1.23 / 1.40) \times 10^{21}$ cm^{-3} eV^{-1}
N_{c0}	$(2.79 / 2.45 / 2.79) \times 10^{21}$ cm^{-3} eV^{-1}
N_{db}	$(5.4 / 5.8 / 1.0) \times 10^{15}$ cm^{-3}
$\sigma^0_{p,db}$	$(1.6 / 4.5 / 2.0) \times 10^{-16}$ cm^2
$\sigma^0_{n,db}$	$(1.6 / 4.5 / 2.0) \times 10^{-16}$ cm^2
$\sigma^-_{p,db}$	$(1.6 / 4.5 / 2.0) \times 10^{-15}$ cm^2
$\sigma^+_{n,db}$	$(1.6 / 4.5 / 2.0) \times 10^{-15}$ cm^2

Furthermore, our simulation results showed that the defect density of *SEP3* was much higher (1.0×10^{16} cm^{-3}) than that of *SEP1* (5.8×10^{15} cm^{-3}). The defect density mainly affects the slope of dark *J–V* curves and FF in the simulation results. Therefore, we changed this value carefully to match the results. This also supports our speculation discussed previously regarding the generation of cracks depending on substrate morphology, which resulted in lower V_{OC} even with lower X_C.

IV. Conclusion

In this study, μc-Si:H films and solar cells were deposited on ZnO substrates having different σ_{RMS} for optical and electrical simulation with percolation assumption. The height function of the ZnO substrates is obtained by AFM scans on the substrates and used for the optical model together with complex refractive index and the thickness of ZnO substrates. The X_C depth profiles of μc-Si:H films and solar cells were measured by Raman spectroscopy and the X_C of the middle of intrinsic layers was chosen to rescale effective DOS. We observed that the X_C of the solar cells is significantly influenced by σ_{RMS}. For the determination of the E_μ of the intrinsic μc-Si:H layer in p-i-n devices, temperature dependent dark *J–V* measurements were carried out. All experimentally obtained parameters were used as input parameters for the optical and electrical models in the ASA simulator. We demonstrated that experimental and simulation results are in good agreement. Although the *ZJL* has lower H_T than the *ZEP*, the J_{SC} of the *SJL* was higher due to its lower E_μ. This result suggests that E_μ determines to a significant extent the J_{SC}. From experiments and simulation results, we found that the V_{OC} is largely affected by σ_{RMS} of substrates, thereby possibly cracks, as well as X_C of the solar cells.

Acknowledgment

The authors would like to thank Dr. M. Meier and Dr. M. Ghosh of the Forschungszentrum Jülich, and S. Hänni, M. Stückelberger, and Dr. M. Despeisse of IMT's PV-lab (EPFL) for preparation of the samples. We would like to thank Dr. A. Čampa from the University of Ljubljana for sharing his ideas on optical measurements.

charged ($-$) gap state ($\sigma^{+/0/-}_{n/p}$) are varied for fitting simulation results to experiment results. As a result, we obtained excellent fits, as shown in Fig. 7. The slight deviation of the QEs at longer wavelengths between experimental and simulation results originate from the extinction coefficients, because μc-Si:H has very low absorption coefficient in the long wavelength region and, therefore, it is hard to measure this accurately.

Important material parameters used in this simulation, such as the E_μ, $\mu_{e/h}$, $N_{c0/v0}$, N_{db}, and $\sigma^{+/0/-}_{n/p}$, are tabulated in Table III. These values are similar to those obtained in the literature [8], [26]. Although the *ZJL* has the lowest σ_{RMS} and thereby lower H_T, the *SJL* on the *ZJL* shows higher J_{SC} than the *SEP* on the *ZEP* due to the lower E_μ of i-layer of the *SJL* of 1.15 eV as obtained by dark current activation energy. This result is in line with the higher X_C of the *SJL* as confirmed by Raman. The lower V_{OC} of the *SJL* in this simulation originates from both the reduced E_μ and increased X_C (thus effective DOS).

REFERENCES

[1] M. Zeman, J. A. Willemen, S. Solntsev, and J. W. Metselaar, "Extraction of amorphous silicon solar cell parameters by inverse modelling," *Sol. Energ. Mat. Sol. C.*, vol. 34, pp. 557–563, 1994.

[2] M. Zeman, J. A. Willemen, L. L. A. Vosteen, G. Tao, and J. W. Metselaar, "Computer modelling of current matching in a-Si:H/a-Si:H tandem solar cells on textured TCO substrates," *Sol. Energ. Mat. Sol. C.*, vol. 46, pp. 81–99, 1997.

[3] A. M. K. Dagamesh, B. Vet, P. Sutta, and M. Zeman, "Modelling and optimization of a-Si:H solar cells with ZnO:Al back reflector," *Sol. Energ. Mat. Sol. C.*, vol. 94, pp. 2119–2123, 2010.

[4] B. Vet and M. Zeman, "Relation between the open-circuit voltage and the band gap of absorber and buffer layers in a-Si:H solar cells," *Thin Solid Films*, vol. 516, pp. 6873–6876, 2008.

[5] M. Python, O. Madani, D. Dominé, F. Meillaud, E. Vallat-Sauvain1, and C. Ballif, "Influence of the substrate geometrical parameters on microcrystalline silicon growth for thin-film solar cells," *Sol. Energ. Mat. Sol. C.*, vol. 93, pp. 1714–1720, 2009.

[6] M. Zeman and J. Krc, "Optical and electrical modeling of thin-film silicon solar cells," *J. Mat. Res.*, vol. 23, pp. 889–898, 2008.

[7] K. Jäger, M. Fischer, R. A. C. M. M. van Swaaij, and M. Zeman, "A scattering model for nano-textured interfaces and its application in opto-electrical simulations of thin-film silicon solar cells," *J. Appl. Phys.*, vol. 111, pp. 083108-1–083108-9, 2012.

[8] B. E. Pieters, H. Stiebig, M. Zeman, and R. A. C. M. M. van Swaaij, "Determination of the mobility gap of intrinsic μc-Si:H in p-i-n solar cells," *J. Appl. Phys.*, vol. 105, pp. 044502-1–044502-10, 2009.

[9] J. A. Willemen, *Modelling of Amorphous Silicon Single- and Multi-Junction Solar Cells*, Ph.D. dissertation. Dept. Elect. Eng., Delft Univ. Tech., Delft, The Netherlands, 1998.

[10] M. Luysberg, P. Hapke, R. Carius, and F. Finger, "Structure and growth of hydrogenated microcrystalline silicon: Investigation by transmission electron microscopy and Raman spectroscopy of films grown at different plasma excitation frequencies," *Philos. Mag. A*, vol. 75, no. 1, pp. 31–47, 1997.

[11] M. Goerlitzer, P. Torres, N. Beck, N. Wyrsch, U. Kroll, H. Keppner, J. Pohl, and A. Shah, "Structural properties and electronic transport in intrinsic microcrystalline silicon deposited by the VHF-GD technique," *J. Non-Cryst. Solids*, vol. 227–230, pp. 996–1000, 1998.

[12] L. Houben, M. Luysberg, P. Hapke, R. Carius, F. Finger, and H. Wagner, "Structural properties of microcrystalline silicon in the transition from highly crystalline to amorphous growth," *Philos. Mag. A*, vol. 77, no. 6, pp. 1447–1460, 1998.

[13] U. Graf, J. Meier, U. Kroll, J. Bailat, C. Droz, E. Vallat-Sauvain, and A. Shah, "High rate growth of microcrystalline silicon by VHF-GD at high pressure," *Thin Solid Films*, vol. 427, pp. 37–40, 2003.

[14] M. Python, D. Dominé, T. Söderström, F. Meillaud, and C. Ballif, "Microcrystalline silicon solar cells: Effect of substrate temperature on cracks and their role in post-oxidation," *Prog. Photovoltaics, Res. Appl.*, vol. 18, pp. 491–499, 2010.

[15] J. Bailat, E. Vallat-sauvain, A. Vallat, and A. Shah, "Simulation of the growth dynamics of amorphous and microcrystalline silicon," *J. Non-Cryst. Solids*, vol. 338–340, pp. 32–36, 2004.

[16] S. N. Agbo, S. Dobrovolskiy, G. Wegh, R. A. C. M. M. van Swaaij, F. D. Tichelaar, P. Sutta, and M. Zeman, "Structural analyses of seeded thin film microcrystalline silicon solar cell," *Prog. Photovoltaics, Res. Appl.*, published online, 2012.

[17] S. Y. Myong, K. Sriprapha, Y. Yashiki, S. Miyajima, A. Yamada, and M. Konagai, "Silicon-based thin-film solar cells fabricated near the phase boundary by VHF PECVD technique," *Sol. Energ. Mat. Sol. C.*, vol. 92, pp. 639–645, 2008.

[18] C. Droz, E. Vallat-Sauvain, J. Bailat, L. Feitknecht, J. Meier, and A. Shah, "Relationship between Raman crystallinity and open-circuit voltage in microcrystalline silicon solar cells," *Sol. Energ. Mat. Sol. C.*, vol. 81, pp. 61–71, 2004.

[19] K. Shimakawa, "Percolation-controlled electronic properties in microcrystalline silicon: Effective medium approach," *J. Non-Cryst. Solids*, vol. 266–269, pp. 223–226, 2000.

[20] P. Hapke, F. Finger, R. Carius, H. Wagner, K. Prasad, and R. Fluckiger, "Annealing studies of the microcrystalline silicon system," *J. Non-Cryst. Solids*, vol. 164–166, pp. 981–984, 1993.

[21] H. Overhof, M. Otte, M. Schmidtke, U. Backhausen, and R. Carius, "Transport mechanism in micro-crystalline silicon," *J. Non-Cryst. Solids*, vol. 227–230, pp. 992–995, 1998.

[22] R. Tsu, J. Gonzalez-Hernandez, S. S. Chao, S. C. Lee, and K. Tanaka, "Critical volume fraction of crystallinity for conductivity percolation in phosphorus-doped Si:F:H alloys," *Appl. Phys. Lett.*, vol. 40, pp. 534–535, 1982.

[23] H. Scher and R. Zallen, "Critical density in percolation processes," *J. Chem. Phys.*, vol. 53, pp. 3759–3761, 1970.

[24] S. Hamma and P. Roca i Cabarrocas, "Low-temperature growth of thick intrinsic and ultrathin phosphorous or boron-doped microcrystalline silicon films: Optimum crystalline fractions for solar cell applications." *Sol. Energ. Mat. Sol. C.*, vol. 69, pp. 217–239, 2001.

[25] R. Kind, R. A. C. M. M. van Swaaij, F. A. Rubinelli, S. Solntsev, and M. Zeman, "Thermal ideality factor of hydrogenated amorphous silicon p-i-n solar cells," *J. Appl. Phys.*, vol. 110, pp. 104512-1–104512-8, 2011.

[26] T. Brammer and H. Stiebig, "Defect density and recombination lifetime in microcrystalline silicon absorbers of highly efficient thin-film solar cells determined by numerical device simulations," *J. Appl. Phys.*, vol. 94, pp. 1035–1042, 2003.

Do Yun Kim was born in Seoul, Korea, in 1982. He received the B.Sc and M.Sc. degrees in materials science and engineering in 2007 and 2009, respectively, both from Yonsei University, Seoul, Korea. He received the Ph.D degree in physical electronics on silicon-based multijunction solar cells, under the supervision of Prof. M. Konagai, in 2012 from the Tokyo Institute of Technology, Tokyo, Japan. His research interests include the characterization and modeling of silicon-based thin-film multijunction solar cells. Since 2012, he has been a Postdoctoral Researcher at the Photovoltaics Materials and Devices Laboratory, the Delft University of Technology, Delft, The Netherlands.

René A. C. M. M van Swaaij was born in Maastricht, the Netherlands, in 1966. He received the M.Sc. and Ph.D. degrees in physics in 1990 and 1995, respectively, both from Utrecht University, Utrecht, The Netherlands.

In 1997, he joined the Delft University of Technology, Delft, The Netherlands, to work on amorphous-silicon-based solar cells. In 2002, he was appointed an Associate Professor within Electronic Components, Technology, and Materials (ECTM). Since January 1, 2009, he has been with the Photovoltaic Materials and Devices Group, Department of Electrical Sustainable Energy Delft University of Technology. His research interests include the fast deposition of amorphous silicon layers and the physics underlying the operation of amorphous silicon solar cells. He has authored and co-authored more than 80 journal and conference papers.

Miro Zeman was born in Slovakia in 1957. He received the B.Sc and Ph.D. degrees in materials science in 1981 and 1989, respectively, both from the Slovak University of Technology, Bratislava, Slovakia.

In 1989, he became a member of the Solar Cell Group, Delft University of Technology, Delft, The Netherlands. In 2009, he was appointed a Full Professor with the Delft University of Technology for the Chair of Photovoltaic Materials and Devices in the Department of Electrical Sustainable Energy. Since 1989, he has been in charge of more than 30 Dutch and six European projects dealing with the development of thin-film solar cells and technology for their fabrication. He has authored and co-authored more than 130 scientific publications and contributed to two scientific books. In 2006, he co-founded the nonprofit organization Slovak Renewable Energy Agency in Slovakia. His research interests include the development of novel concepts for the improvement of thin-film silicon solar cell performance and modeling of devices based on amorphous semiconductors.

158

Progress Toward Realizing an Intermediate Band Solar Cell—Sequential Absorption of Photons in a Quantum Well Solar Cell

Megumi Yoshida, Hemmel Amrania, Daniel J. Farrell, Ben Browne, Edward Yoxall, N. J. Ekins-Daukes, and Chris C. Phillips

Abstract—In order to realize an intermediate band solar cell, which promises high photovoltaic energy conversion efficiency, achieving higher photocurrent while maintaining the cell voltage is essential. We report on a transient photocurrent due to the sequential absorption of photons in a single quantum well by continuously pumping to stimulate interband transitions (from a valence band to an intermediate band) and showing an intersubband transition (from an intermediate band to a conduction band) with a pulsed infrared laser. We demonstrate the extent to which multiple-photon absorption can be achieved in quantum well devices and propose that a quantum well is a suitable candidate for an intermediate band solar cell. From the combination of this and other sequential absorption results, it is clear that enhancing the short lifetime of a carrier in the intermediate band is the next step toward achieving a working intermediate band solar cell. In light of this, we enhance our previous suggestion, the photon ratchet intermediate band solar cell, as a means of increasing the electron lifetime.

Index Terms—Intermediate band (IB) solar cell, intersubband transition, quantum well (QW), sequential photon absorption.

I. Introduction

APPLYING the principle of detailed balance, the efficiency of photovoltaic energy conversion using a single semiconductor bandgap solar cell is fundamentally limited to 31.0% at 1 sun, principally because of the broad spectral distribution of solar radiation [1]. Among other third-generation solar cell concepts [2], the intermediate band solar cell (IBSC) has been proposed to overcome this limit, by introducing a radiatively efficient but electrically isolated band between the conduction band (CB) and valence band (VB) [3], as shown in Fig. 1. The intermediate band (IB) allows additional photocurrent to be generated by the sequential absorption of two subbandgap photons (G_{VI} and G_{IC}), which would otherwise be unabsorbed, thereby

Manuscript received July 12, 2013; revised December 16, 2013; accepted December 27, 2013. Date of current version February 17, 2014. This work was supported by Sharp Laboratories of Europe Ltd.

M. Yoshida, H. Amrania, B. Browne, E. Yoxall, N. J. Ekins-Daukes, and C. C. Phillips are with the Experimental Solid State Physics, Imperial College London, London SW7 2AZ, U.K. (e-mail: megumi.yoshida06@imperial.ac.uk; hemmel.amrania04@imperial.ac.uk; benbrowne@gmail.com; edward.yoxall05@imperial.ac.uk; n.ekins-daukes@imperial.ac.uk; chris.phillips@imperial.ac.uk).

D. J. Farrell is with the Research Center for Advanced Science and Technology, University of Tokyo, Tokyo 153–8904, Japan (e-mail: farrell@mbe.rcast.u-tokyo.ac.jp).

Color versions of one or more of the figures in this paper are available online at http://ieeexplore.ieee.org.

Digital Object Identifier 10.1109/JPHOTOV.2014.2301891

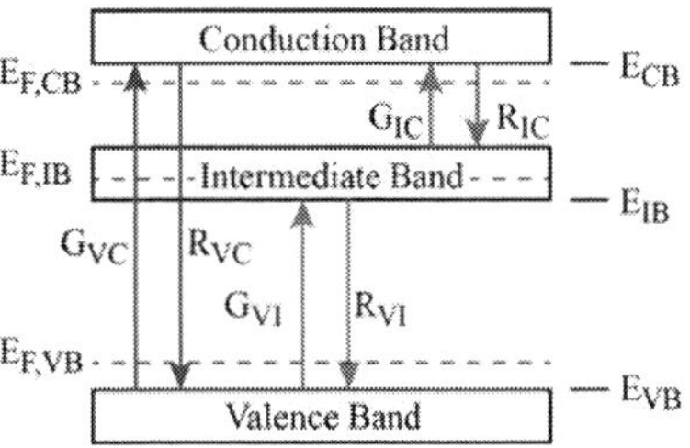

Fig. 1. Energy diagram of an IBSC, in which extra photocurrent is produced due to the sequential absorption of subbandgap photons via the partially filled IB (represented by $E_{F,\mathrm{IB}}$) increasing theoretical limit in the conversion efficiency.

reducing below bandgap and thermalization losses. In principle, by introducing the IB, the current can be enhanced without significantly reducing the voltage (separation of quasi-Fermi levels $E_{F,\mathrm{CB}}$ and $E_{F,\mathrm{VB}}$), hence leading to higher conversion efficiency. Thermodynamical modeling of the IBSC shows that its limiting efficiency can be increased significantly over the Shockley–Queisser limit to 46.8% at 1 sun and 63.2% at full concentration [3].

A number of experimental studies on IBSCs have been reported, including attempts with quantum dots (QDs) [4], [5]. However, even though an increase in a photocurrent has been observed in QD IBSCs, they suffer from significant voltage loss, which results in low conversion efficiency [6]. One of the main causes of the voltage reduction in these IBSCs is the short lifetime of electrons in the excited states, which is often caused by fast nonradiative recombination [7], [8]. Furthermore, since the absorption cross section of QDs is small, the rate of generation (G_{VI} and G_{IC}) is relatively weak in comparison to the rate of recombination/relaxation (R_{VI} and R_{IC}); hence the separation of the quasi-Fermi levels ($E_{F,\mathrm{CB}}$, $E_{F,\mathrm{IB}}$, and $E_{F,\mathrm{VB}}$) is relatively small [9].

In this paper, we show that despite fast nonradiative relaxation, sequential photon absorption can be achieved in a quantum well (QW) heterostructure and that this is common to many other low-dimensional IBSC materials. As a first step toward achieving QW IBSCs, we propose a means by which fast relaxation can be addressed through the introduction of an energy ratchet, designed to promote sequential absorption of photons.

II. Quantum Well as an Intermediate Band Material

One of the possible routes to achieving an IBSC is to use quantum mechanically confined structures such as QWs and

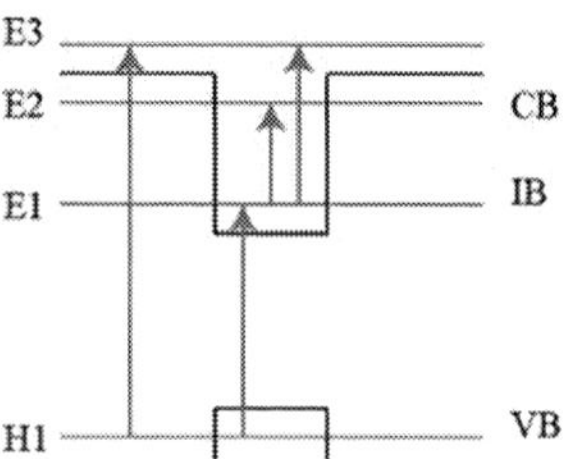

Fig. 2. Schematic energy diagram of a QW IBSC. Ground states which arise as a result of quantum mechanical confinement in QW (E1) act as an IB.

QDs [10]. In these materials, the IB would typically arise from the confined states of the electrons in the CB potential well. An electron can be excited from the VB (H1) to the lowest confined energy states in the CB potential well (E1) by absorbing a photon, followed by optical excitation to higher confined states (E2) or continuum states (E3), where the electron can be extracted to the outer circuit (see Fig. 2).

However, for this two-photon process to be efficient, the long wavelength photon must be absorbed while the electron is still in the confined state (E1), which is acting as the IB. The short lifetime (nanoseconds) of the excited electron in the IB means that it is necessary either to increase the lifetime of the electronic state in the IB, or to increase the photon flux by using a high intensity of long wavelength radiation, in order for the second transition to occur.

It is well known that confined states in both QDs and QWs have much shorter upper-state lifetimes compared with optical interband transitions, because of phonon mediated relaxation. Phonon bottleneck effects have been observed in both QWs and QDs, but under conditions unsuited for solar application [11], [12]. In almost all practical situations, the intersubband relaxation in both QW and QD heterostructures is fast, typically on a picosecond timescale, relative to the nanosecond timescale for radiative processes.

To demonstrate sequential absorption, we choose a single QW p-i-n diode, which has the advantage of a larger optical cross section compared with QDs. Absorption strength can be increased with further QW layers, but the use of a single QW avoids complexity with transport over multiple QWs. The intersubband transition in QWs can only be excited by light polarized normal to the plane of the QWs and thus not by light that is normally incident [13]. By fabricating a grating on the rear of the solar cell, the light can be scattered inside the structure in such a way that it has a component of polarization parallel to the QW [14]. This has successfully been achieved in quantum infrared photodetectors, in which the photocurrent is produced by absorbing scattered infrared light via intersubband excitation. [15].

III. Observation of Two-Photon Absorption Via Intersubband Transition in a Quantum Well

The sample used in this study is a 7-nm $In_{0.2}Ga_{0.8}As$ QW with GaAs barriers in a p-i-n junction. The sample was fabricated using metal-organic chemical vapor deposition. The thickness of the intrinsic region is 319 nm, while the p-type region

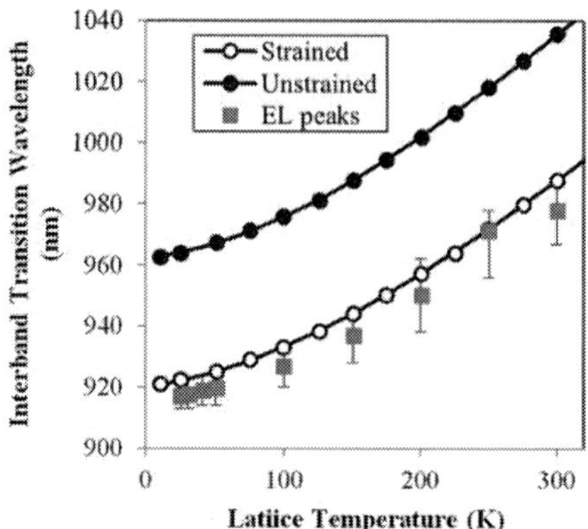

Fig. 3. Wavelength of the interband transition of the sample predicted by the k.p model, with and without considering the lattice strain. The temperature-dependent electroluminescent peaks from the sample (see Fig. 4) are plotted in red.

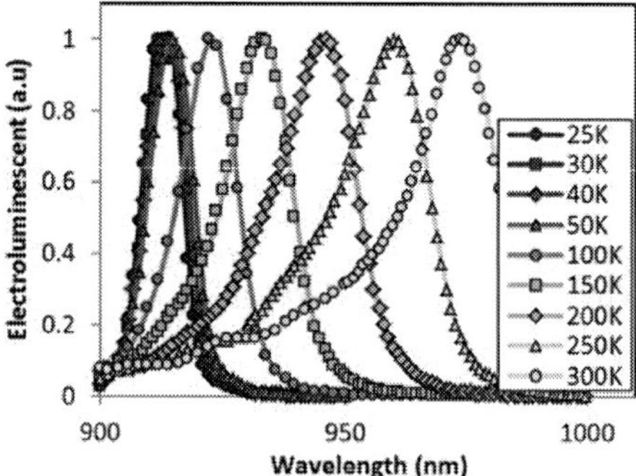

Fig. 4. Normalized temperature-dependent electroluminescence of the sample. Peak PL wavelengths are plotted in the Fig. 3.

is doped with 2.0×10^{18} cm^{-3} carbon and the n-type region is doped with 1.0×10^{18} cm^{-3} silicon. Theoretical modeling, using the k.p theory, gives the predictions for the interband transition wavelength. The model uses an eight-band Pikus–Bir Hamiltonian to accurately treat the VB splitting, which occurs in strained materials; this results in the four energy bands (CB, HH, LH, and SO). The Schrödinger equation is solved by using the finite difference method in real space for each band individually to give the envelope functions and energy levels of the nanostructures. In Fig. 3, the predicted transition wavelength from the VB to the IB is plotted and is shown to vary between 920 and 990 nm depending on its lattice temperature.

These predicted transition wavelengths, when lattice strain is included, match the observed electroluminescence peaks (see Fig. 4). As the temperature of the sample is lowered, the thermal distribution of the carrier is reduced, resulting in sharper peaks.

In order to minimize the background photocurrent, the sample is illuminated at 905 nm, a wavelength below the bandgap of the bulk GaAs material, so that carrier excitation only takes place in the QW, and not in the bulk region. However, since the p-n junction device has a built-in voltage, carriers can escape from the well by tunneling, and this generates a measurable photocurrent even at low temperature, as shown in Fig. 5. The

160

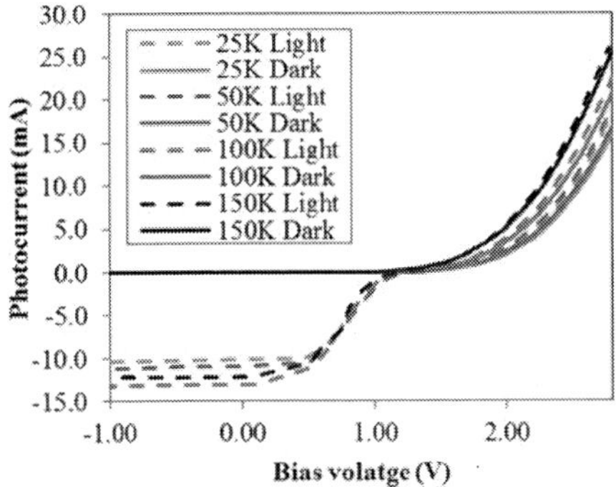

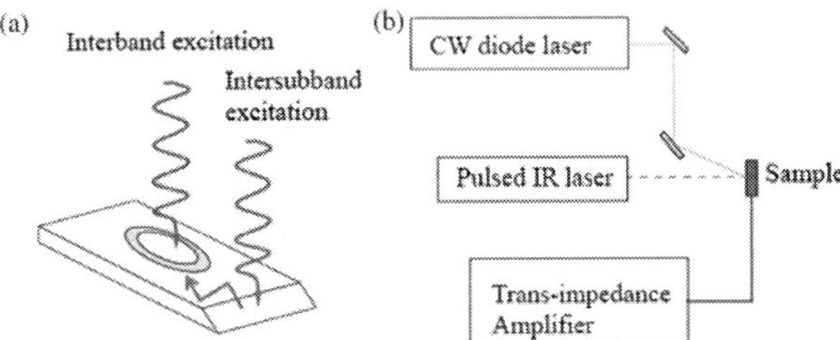

Fig. 5. Light and dark current voltage characteristics of the sample. The light *I–V* is taken with the sample illuminated at 905 nm at a power of 120 mW.

Fig. 6. Sample is processed with a beveled edge from which intersubband excitation can be coupled into the device. The pulsed IR light from the Erbium laser will be deflected at the wedge into total internal reflection mode and reaches active region with component of polarization which can excite intersubband transitions. The sample is illuminated with continuous light populating the ground state of the QW. Intersubband excitation pulsed radiation is coupled from the wedge, while the photocurrent is observed.

temperature variation in the short-circuit current is caused by the difference in effective density of states in the QW, corresponding to the fixed photoexcitation wavelength of 905 nm, as well as variation in the carrier escape rate at different temperatures. [16]–[18]

When a forward bias is applied, the tunneling rate of the carriers reduces and the photocurrent decreases, eventually reaching zero just below the open-circuit voltage [16]. Near this point, the *I–V* curve has a flat region (at an applied bias of between 1.1 and 1.3 V) as shown in Fig. 5. At this bias, carriers cannot escape via tunneling and become trapped in the well [16]. The following experiment is performed at this bias condition so that there is no dc background current and the only photocurrent detected is because of the absorption of infrared photons.

The sample was prepared with a wedge structure in order to increase the optical coupling of IR light into QW intersubband transition, as shown in Fig. 6(a). It was illuminated with continuous 980-nm light, populating the ground state of the QW. While carriers are continuously excited into the well, a 100-ps pulse of light at 2.79 μm from an Erbium laser [19], with energy 2 mJ and 3 Hz repetition rate, was directed at the sample enabling the carriers that are trapped in the QW to be excited into the continuum. Once in this state, the carriers can then be extracted to the external circuit. Fig. 6(b) shows the experimental setup that has been used in this study.

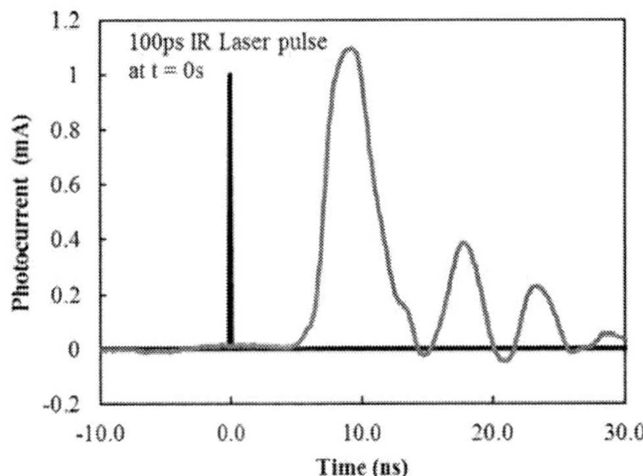

Fig. 7. Photocurrent from the sample after being illuminated with pulsed 100-ps laser of 2.79 μm at $t = 0$ s. The oscillatory behavior and the delay is because of the mismatch in impedance of the electric equipment.

A clear observation of a two-photon photocurrent of 1 mA in a single QW structure has been obtained (see Fig. 7). The oscillatory behavior is an artifact, called ringing, that is caused by incomplete impedance matching in the detection electronics, and the delay of photocurrent enhancement is because of the combination of optical and electrical delays in the detection system. The result demonstrates that multiple-photon absorption can be achieved in QW devices, which is one of the essential conditions needed to be satisfied for IBSCs, [9] and the result indicates that the QW can be in fact a suitable candidate for IBSCs.

IV. Discussion of the Results and Realizing Intermediate Band Solar Cells

Our observation of an increase in photocurrent in QW IBSCs via a transient electrical measurement adds to the growing body of the literature from QD IBSCs in the forms of both quasi-continuous-wave electrical and transient optical measurements. Martí *et al.* reported an increase in the photocurrent in a δ-doped InAs/(Al,Ga)As QD system with continuous infrared light exciting carriers from the IB to the CB [5], which is an essential process in IBSCs. However, the photocurrent increase observed was as small as 10–12% of the initial value. A recent report by Okada *et al.* also shows an increase in quantum efficiency of 0.3% in a δ-doped InAs/GaNAs QD solar cell [4], while Sugiyama *et al.* achieved 0.5% in an InGaAs/GaAsP strain-balanced QW superlattice cell [20]. Kita *et al.* reported proof of sequential absorption of photons via the IB in the form of bleaching and recovery of photoluminescence (PL) in InAs/GaAs QDs in an optical cavity [21]. As an IR radiation pulse excites carriers from the IB to the continuum, Kita *et al.* observed a reduction in the carrier density in the IB, causing a transient suppression of the PL. To achieve sufficient absorption, the quantum dots were located in a photonic cavity and short, high-power pulses were used.

As demonstrated in this paper as well as in the literature, the short excited-state lifetime of the carriers remains a critical problem in realizing efficient IBSCs. In fact, all experimental reports on IBSCs show only a very weak sequential absorption

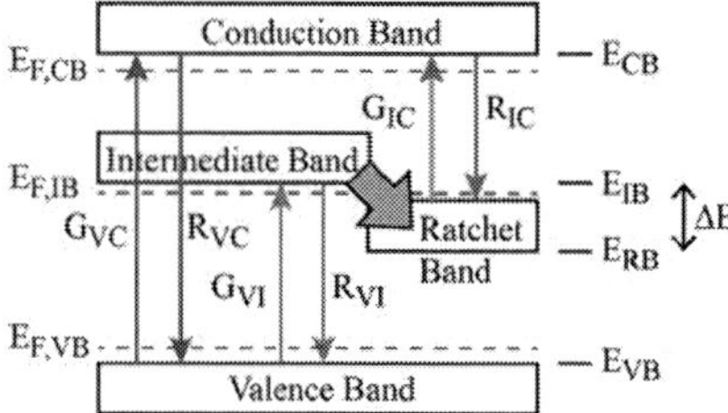

Fig. 8. Energy diagram of a "photon ratchet" IBSC. The photon RB E_{RB} is located at an energy interval ΔE below the IB E_{IB} and the occupation of both IB and RB can be described by a single quasi-Fermi level $E_{F,IB}$. The charge carriers in the IB will quickly scatter to the RB where they may have a long lifetime since the RB is optically isolated from the VB. [23].

of photons, resulting in a negligible gain in energy conversion efficiency. The short lifetime of electrons in the intermediate states is mainly caused by fast nonradiative recombination that proceeds faster than all radiative processes. In most of the solar cells described previously, radiative and nonradiative recombination of carriers of the IB occurs before significant sequential absorption can take place. Thus, as with a conventional two-band solar cell, the product of carrier lifetime and mobility is critical for an efficient operation [22].

One means to extending the IB carrier lifetime is to allow some energy relaxation to take place, forming a so-called "photon ratchet." The photon ratchet IBSC has been proposed to increase the lifetime of the carriers in the IB and CB by introducing an extra energy band called the "ratchet band" (RB), i.e., some energy ΔE below the IB, which is optically decoupled from the VB but thermally coupled to IB [23] (see Fig. 8). In such systems, the photoexcited electrons in the IB rapidly relax into the RB, and when the energy loss ΔE is sufficiently large, their lifetime can become very long. The increase in the carrier lifetime enhances the probability of the second optical excitation process from the RB to the CB (G_{IC}). The enhancement in carrier lifetime is a key to high efficiency PV [24]. To increase the generation rate G_{IC}, the photon ratchet also reduces the population of the IB (as suggested by the quasi-Fermi level $E_{F,IB}$), which, in turn, reduces the recombination rate of the electrons from the IB to the VB (G_{VI}). Both effects increase the photocurrent of the solar cell, leading to higher efficiency. The limiting efficiency of such a system shows an efficiency enhancement from 46.8% to 48.5% when an RB is introduced at ΔE of 270 meV with the globally optimized bandgaps [23].

In practice, introducing the RB to a conventional IBSC adds the very important advantage that it combats the extremely fast nonradiative recombination rates that are typically caused by the introduction of the IB. The RB extends the lifetime of the carriers in the IB and ensures that the two transitions G_{VI} and G_{IC} pump electrons from occupied ground states into vacant excited states. Hence, we propose that the RB is an important component to realizing efficient operation of an IBSC, especially in systems where the ideal situation of achieving degenerate doping, high mobility, and long carrier lifetime in the IB is difficult. The photon ratchet IBSC can be implemented in QW and quantum dot systems by spatially separating the carriers

using type-II structures. In such systems, the photo-generated electrons and holes rapidly separate into positions in the lattice, reducing the strength of both radiative and nonradiative recombination processes; hence, the lifetime of the carriers can be extended [25]–[27]. We note that theoretical calculation of the type-II "ratchet" quantum dots IBSC predicts the enhancement in efficiency [28] and the same would apply to the type-II "ratchet" QW IBSC. The next challenge is to implement a prototype structure and to enhance the conversion efficiencies by extending the carrier lifetime in an IBSC.

V. Conclusion

Clear observation of a photocurrent of $\sim$1 mA arising from the sequential absorption of photons has been obtained by illuminating the sample with a continuum laser to populate the ground state of a QW, followed by a pulsed laser to pump the intersubband transition. The result adds to other published observations that sequential absorption of the photons is possible in both QW and quantum dot systems but the short lifetime of carriers prevents efficiency gains that the IBSC concept promises. Introducing a relaxation step into a nonradiative state, the so-called "ratchet band," can be used to lock carriers into long-lived states thereby promoting sequential absorption. In a low-dimensional material system, the RB could arise from type-II structures.

References

[1] W. Shockley and H. J. Queisser, "Detailed balance limit of efficiency of *p-n* junction solar cells," *J. Appl. Phys.*, vol. 32, pp. 510–519, 1961.

[2] M. A. Green, "Third generation photovoltaics: Ultra-high conversion efficiency at low cost," *Prog. Photovoltaics: Res. Appl.*, vol. 9, pp. 123–135, 2001.

[3] A. Luque and A. Martí, "Increasing the efficiency of ideal solar cells by photon induced transitions at intermediate levels," *Phys. Rev. Lett.*, vol. 78, no. 26, pp. 5014–5017, 1997.

[4] Y. Okada, T. Morioka, K. Yoshida, R. Oshima, Y. Shoji, T. Inoue, and T. Kita, "Increase in photocurrent by optical transitions via intermediate quantum states in direct-doped InAs/GaNAs strain-compensated quantum dot solar cell," *J. Appl. Phys.*, vol. 109, p. 024301, 2011.

[5] A. Martí, E. Antolín, C. R. Stanley, C. D. Farmer, N. López, P. Díaz, E. Cánovas, P. G. Linares, and A. Luque, "Production of photocurrent due to intermediate-to-conduction-band transitions: A demonstration of a key operating principle of the intermediate-band solar cell," *Phys. Rev. Lett.*, vol. 97, p. 247701, 2006.

[6] A. Luque, A. Martí, N. López, E. Antolín, and E. Cánovas, "Operation of the intermediate band solar cell under nonideal space charge region conditions and half filling of the intermediate band," *J. Appl. Phys.*, vol. 99, p. 094503, 2006.

[7] W. Shockley and W. T. Read, Jr., "Statistics of the recombinations of holes and electrons," *Phys. Rev.*, vol. 87, pp. 835–842, 1952.

[8] R. N. Hall, "Electron–hole recombination in germanium," *Phys. Rev.*, vol. 87, p. 387, 1952.

[9] N. J. Ekins-Daukes, C. B. Honsberg, and M. Yamaguchi, "Signature of intermediate band materials from luminescence measurements," in *Proc. 31st IEEE Photovoltaic Spec. Conf.*, 2005, pp. 49–54.

[10] A. Marti, L. Cuadra, and A. Luque, "Quantum dot intermediate band solar cell," in *Proc. Conf. Record 28th IEEE Photovoltaic Spec. Conf.*, 2000, pp. 940–943.

[11] E. A. Zibik, T. Grange, B. A. Carpenter, N. E. Porter, R. Ferreira, G. Bastard, D. Stehr, S. Winnerl, M. Helm, H. Y. Liu, M. S. Skolnick, and L. R. Wilson, "Long lifetimes of quantum-dot intersublevel transitions in the terahertz range," *Nat. Mater.*, vol. 8, pp. 803–809, 2009.

[12] B. Murdin, W. Heiss, C. Langerak, S. Lee, I. Galbraith, G. Strasser, E. Gornik, M. Helm, and C. Pidgeon, "Direct observation of the LO phonon bottleneck in wide GaAs/AlxGa1-xAs quantum wells," *Phys. Rev. B*, vol. 55, pp. 5171–5176, 1997.

[13] D. D. Coon and R. P. G Karunasiri, "New mode of IR detection using quantum wells," *Appl. Phys. Lett.*, vol. 45, no. 6, pp. 649–651, 1984.

[14] M. Helm, "The basic physics of intersubband transitions," *Semiconductors Semimetals*, vol. 62, pp. 1–99, 1999.

[15] B. F. Levine, "Quantum-well infrared photodetectors," *J. Appl. Phys.*, vol. 74, pp. R1–R81, 1993.

[16] J. Nelson, M. Paxman, K. W. J. Barnham, J. S. Roberts, and C. C. Button, "Steady-state carrier escape from single quantum wells," *IEEE J. Quantum. Electron.*, vol. 29, no. 6, pp. 1460–1468, Jun. 1993.

[17] A. Zachariou, J. Barnes, K. W. J. Barnham, J. Nelson, E. S. M. Tsui, J. Epler, and M. Pate, "A carrier escape study from InP/InGaAs single quantum well solar cells," *J. Appl. Phys.*, vol. 83, pp. 877–881, 1998.

[18] M. Paxman, J. Nelson, B. Braun, J. Connolly, K. W. J. Barnham, C. T. Foxon, and J. S. Roberts, "Modeling the spectral response of the quantum-well solar-cell," *J. Appl. Phys.*, vol. 74, pp. 614–621, 1993.

[19] K. L. Vodopyanov and V. G. Voevodin, "Parametric generation of tunable infrared radiation in ZnGeP2 and GaSe pumped at 3 μm," *J. Opt. Soc. Amer. B*, vol. 10, no. 9, pp. 1723–1729, 1995.

[20] M. Sugiyama, Y. Wang, K. Watanabe, T. Morioka, and Y. Okada, "Photocurrent generation by two-step photon absorption with quantum-well superlattice cell," *IEEE J. Photovoltaics*, vol. 2, no. 3, pp. 298–302, Jul. 2012.

[21] T. Kita, T. Maeda, and Y. Harada, "Carrier dynamics of the intermediate state in InAs/GaAs quantum dots coupled in a photonic cavity under two-photon excitation," *Phys. Rev. B*, vol. 86, p. 035301, 2012.

[22] J. J. Krich, B. I. Halperin, and A. Aspuru-Guzik, "Nonradiative lifetimes in intermediate band photovoltaics—Absence of lifetime recovery," *J. Appl. Phys.*, vol. 112, p. 013707, 2012.

[23] M. Yoshida, N. J. Ekins-Daukes, D. J. Farrell, and C. C. Phillips, "Photon ratchet intermediate band solar cells," *Appl. Phys. Lett.*, vol. 100, no. 26, pp. 263902–263902, 2012.

[24] M. J. Y. Tayebjee, A. A. Gray-Weale, and T. W. Schmidt, "Thermodynamic limit of exciton fission solar cell efficiency," *J. Phys. Chem. Lett.*, vol. 3, pp. 2749–2754, 2012.

[25] G. Ru, F.-S. Choa, X. Wei, G. Chen, and J. B. Khurgin, "Measurement of the lifetimes of photo-excited carriers in type-I and type-II quantum well materials," in *Proc. Conf. Lasers Electro-Opt.*, 2006, pp. 1–2.

[26] S. Fukatsu, H. Sunamura, Y. Shiraki, and S. Komiyama, "Phononless radiative recombination of indirect excitons in a Si/Ge type-II quantum dot," *Appl. Phys. Lett.*, vol. 71, pp. 258–260, 1997.

[27] F. Hatami, M. Grundmann, N. N. Ledentsov, F. Heinrichsdorff, R. Heitz, J. Bohrer, D. Bimberg, S. S. Ruvimov, P. Werner, V. M. Ustinof, P. S. Kop'ev, and Z. I. Alferov, "Carrier dynamics in type-II GaSb/GaAs quantum dots," *Phys. Rev. B*, vol. 57, pp. 4635–4641, 1998.

[28] A. M. Kechiantz, L. M. Kocharyan, and H. M. Kechiyants, "Band alignment and conversion efficiency in Si/Ge type-II quantum dot intermediate band solar cells," *Nanotechnology*, vol. 18, p. 405401, 2007.

Authors' photographs and biographies not available at the time of publication.

Nonradiative trapping and localization in intermediate band solar cells

Jacob J. Krich

Department of Physics, University of Ottawa, Ottawa, ON, K1N 6N5, Canada

Abstract—For intermediate band solar cells (IBSC) to achieve high efficiency, the gains in light absorption due to the intermediate band (IB) must exceed the nonradiative losses from mid-gap states. An important proposal holds that in IB's formed from bulk doping, when the energy states of the IB are delocalized (i.e., metallic), they do not significantly reduce the nonradiative lifetime. We show that this proposal is incorrect because the motion of the crystal lattice will always re-localize IB states. We compare this result to band-to-band nonradiative recombination, which is well known to be slow. For IBSC's to realize their potential, research must move away from delocalizing IB states.

Index Terms—charge carrier lifetime, photovoltaic cells, mathematical model.

I. Introduction

The intermediate band solar cell (IBSC) is a potentially transformative concept for high-efficiency photovoltaics [1]. An early version was proposed by Wolf [2], and in-depth theoretical analysis examined and rejected the Si:In system [3]. The IB concept – harnessing subgap light using states inside the semiconductor band gap – was given new life in 1997 by detailed balance calculations showing a maximum conversion efficiency of 63% in fully concentrated sunlight [1], considerably higher than the 41% concentrated Shockley-Queisser limit [4]. Since 1997, there has been much success in developing systems with intermediate bands for intermediate band solar cells (IBSC) [5]. However, intermediate levels deep in the band gap have long been known to be detrimental to carrier lifetime [6], [7]. For this reason, the IBSC has long been dismissed as impossible [8]. A pathbreaking and highly-influential proposal for IBSC's formed from deep-level dopants holds that delocalized (i.e., metallic) states in an intermediate band (IB) do not cause nonradiative recombination [9], [10]. According to this proposal, once such a metallic IB is formed, increasing the dopant concentration *increases* the carrier lifetime. This lifetime recovery proposal has launched a large effort to observe an insulator-to-metal transition in semiconductors doped with high concentrations of deep-level dopants [11]–[16], including experimental claims of lifetime recovery [17], [18].

We show that this proposal will not be effective, and an insulator-to-metal transition (IMT) in an intermediate band will not suppress multiphonon recombination processes. It is possible for carrier lifetimes to increase for other reasons (e.g., chemical changes, energy level shifts), but the delocalization of IB orbitals is necessarily too fragile to prevent nonradiative recombination. Progress in IBSC's requires overcoming the nonradiative recombination problem, but we show that the IMT is not a way forward for the field. The search for IMT's with deep-level dopants has led to great progress in materials

science, and if these materials are sufficiently strongly absorbing of subgap light, they can still produce highly efficient solar cells [19].

The lifetime recovery proposal combines two true statements and arrives at an appealing but erroneous conclusion. A (true): at high impurity concentrations, impurity orbitals can overlap and become delocalized, which is called an insulator-to-metal transition. B (true): the nonradiative capture cross section of a defect generally decreases as the impurity orbital becomes larger. That is, as the impurity state delocalizes, the nonradiative lifetime should increase. C (false): an IMT in an intermediate band delocalizes the impurity orbitals and therefore suppresses nonradiative capture.

II. Argument against lifetime recovery

In this paper, we carefully outline why the conclusion C does not follow from A and B, first described in Ref. [19]. We first go through these three steps in detail. We then compare to the case of band-to-band multiphonon recombination, which is well known to be slow due to the delocalized character of the conduction- and valence-band states. Finally, we describe the conditions under which lifetime recovery may still occur (not due to IMT) and the remaining loopholes in our derivation, none of which we believe would change our conclusions.

A. *High dopant concentration causes delocalization*

Metallic conduction at low temperature relies on delocalized energy eigenstates at the Fermi energy. IMT's have been observed in several shallow-doped semiconductor systems [20], [21]. These results have recently been extended to deep-dopant systems by groups developing IBSC's, including Si:S [12], Si:Se [13] and Si:Ti [15]. It is possible that in the deep-dopant transitions, the impurity band broadens to overlap the conduction band [13], which would make it unsuitable for IBSC.

B. *For isolated defects, delocalization increases nonradiative lifetime*

A defect-mediated recombination event consists of two trapping events: a conduction band (CB) electron is trapped into an empty defect level and a hole is trapped into a filled defect level. The original proposal for lifetime recovery [9] focused on the multiphonon mechanism for nonradiative trapping [22], [23], as opposed to other mechanisms such as cascade capture [24] and Auger recombination [25]. We will focus exclusively on multiphonon trapping and recombination, which we will refer to as simply nonradiative trapping and recombination. For convenience, we will consider only the

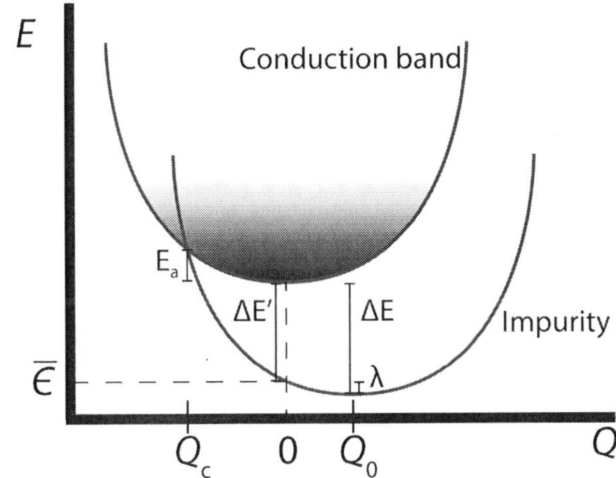

Fig. 1.   Configuration coordinate diagram for trapping of a conduction band (CB) electron by an impurity level. The energy of the CB and impurity level are shwon as a function of a single harmonic vibrational mode with coordinate Q is depicted. Trapping occurs where the levels are degenerate. At high temperatures, trapping is an activated process with barrier E_a at lattice coordinate Q_c. As the impurity wave function becomes larger, Q_0 and λ approach 0, increasing both E_a and Q_c.

CB to IB trapping process, and all results are easily translated into the case of hole trapping from the valence band (VB).

We now present the standard description of the nonradiative trapping process [22], [23]. We model the system in the adiabatic approximation, valid when the electron motion is fast compared to the vibrational motion, allowing the electron problem to be solved separately for each lattice configuration [25]–[27]. The lattice vibrations can be described by normal modes with frequencies ω_i and coordinates Q_i. The physics is clearest when we neglect the lattice momenta and treat the Q_i as classical quantities. Trapping from a CB state into an impurity state occurs when the lattice is in a configuration where these two electronic states are degenerate, marked as Q_c in Fig. 1. We consider the high-temperature, activated limit, in which the trapping rate U is [25]

$$U \propto \exp\left(\frac{-E_a}{k_b T}\right), \tag{1}$$

where T is the temperature, k_b is Boltzmann's constant, and E_a is the activation energy, as shown in Fig. 1. All of the main conclusions hold with low-temperature tunneling-based trapping, too [19]. In Fig. 1, there is only one vibrational mode shown and thus only one intersection; in a real system, there are many vibrational modes, and the lowest-energy degeneracy between the CB and impurity states determines E_a. From the geometry of the parabolae, it is easy to show that

$$E_a = \frac{\Delta E'^2}{4\lambda} = \frac{(\Delta E - \lambda)^2}{4\lambda}, \tag{2}$$

where $\lambda = \Delta E - \Delta E'$ is the reorganization energy, indicated in Fig. 1, and this result is valid with many vibrational modes.

For shallow donors, the wave function is often approximated as a hydrogenic 1s orbital bound to the impurity, screened by the surrounding dielectric. For deeper donors, there is no

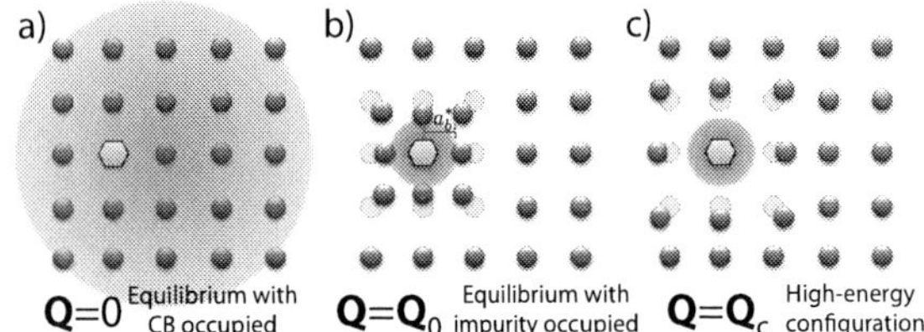

Fig. 2.   Illustration of why localization causes recombination. Each panel is a cartoon of a semiconductor with an isolated impurity atom. a) An electron is in the conduction band, so its charge density is uniformly distributed through the sample. b) When the electron occupies the localized impurity state, the charge density is localized, and the nearby ions are attracted, moving to new equilibrium positions $\vec{Q}_0$. The effective Bohr radius a_b^* is shown. c) Trapping occurs in a lattice configuration $\vec{Q}_c$ where the ions destabilize the impurity state, raising its energy to be degenerate with the conduction band.

systematic accurate approximation for the wave functions. For a hydrogenic 1s orbital in a polar semiconductor,

$$\lambda \propto 1/a_b^*, \tag{3}$$

where a_b^* is the effective Bohr radius, indicated in Fig. 2b [25], [27], [28], so larger orbitals give slower trapping. This result can easily be understood qualitatively by considering the effect of moving an electron from a delocalized conduction band state (Fig. 2a) to the localized impurity state (Fig. 2b). An electron charge that was evenly distributed over large numbers of lattice sites becomes localized. The nearby ions are attracted to it, shifting their equilibrium positions. This shift is precisely the move of equilibrium from $\vec{Q} = 0$ to $\vec{Q}_0$.

Let us examine Fig. 1 more carefully. When the electron-phonon coupling is linear in $\vec{Q}$, the vibrational frequencies are the same in the two electronic states, but the equilibrium position is different: 0 or $\vec{Q}_0$. As a_b^* increases, the electron density in the impurity state becomes less concentrated, so the shift of nearby ions when the impurity becomes occupied (illustrated in Fig. 2b) is reduced, reducing $\vec{Q}_0$. It is clear from Fig. 1 that this reduction increases E_a and thus decreases U. This effect is at the heart of the lifetime recovery proposal [9], and it is in this sense that *localization causes recombination*. But this effect is for isolated defects. We now show that delocalization that originates in superpositions of orbitals is less robust than this "delocalization" of a single orbital, as the electron-phonon interaction localizes the states.

C. IMT delocalization does not *increase nonradiative lifetime*

We now consider the case of trapping into an IB rather than an isolated impurity. We consider the best-case scenario for lifetime recovery: a perfectly periodic superlattice of impurities inside the host semiconductor. Disorder also poses problems for delocalization [16], [29], but disorder is not important for our argument here, though it is not harder to include [19]. We construct a model for the IB system and the electron-phonon coupling, taking care to discuss it in both localized and delocalized bases. We then give a variational argument showing that the delocalization of the IB can only increase the nonradiative lifetime [19].

We begin by considering the lattice in its equilibrium position when the IB is empty, $\vec{Q} = 0$. For convenience, we consider a single electron (initially at the bottom of the conduction band) with the IB states empty. We describe the states inside the IB using a localized basis $|\phi_{\vec{R}}\rangle$ and a delocalized basis $|\psi_{\vec{k}}\rangle$. We begin by taking the isolated impurity states localized at each impurity site $|\phi_{\vec{R}}\rangle$, orthogonalized appropriately, where $\vec{R}$ denotes the impurity locations.[1] As the impurity concentration increases, the electrons can hop between the sites and produce delocalized energy eigenstates $|\psi_{\vec{k}}\rangle$, where $\vec{k}$ denotes the crystal momentum in the superlattice of impurities. In the case of noninteracting electrons, the energy eigenstates are always delocalized, though when interactions are included this delocalization occurs only at a finite concentration [32]. These delocalized energy eigenstates form the second basis for this system; we could equally have arrived at them by invoking Bloch's theorem for a periodic system and noting that our energy eigenstates must be of the form $\psi_{\vec{k}} = e^{i\vec{k}\cdot\vec{r}} u_{\vec{k}}(\vec{r})$, where $u_{\vec{k}}(\vec{r})$ is periodic with the superlattice periodicity.

We can write the Hamiltonian for the IB system as $H = H_e + E_{ph} + H_{e-ph}$, with

$$H_e = \bar{\epsilon} \sum_{\vec{R}} |\phi_{\vec{R}}\rangle \langle \phi_{\vec{R}}| + \sum_{\vec{R} \neq \vec{R}'} t_{\vec{R}\vec{R}'} |\phi_{\vec{R}}\rangle \langle \phi_{\vec{R}'}| \quad (4)$$

$$E_{ph} = \sum_i \omega_i^2 Q_i^2 / 2 \quad (5)$$

$$H_{e-ph} = \sum_{i\vec{R}\vec{R}'} Q_i A^i_{\vec{R}\vec{R}'} |\phi_{\vec{R}}\rangle \langle \phi_{\vec{R}'}|, \quad (6)$$

where $t_{\vec{R}\vec{R}'}$ is the matrix describing the hopping between localized states (i.e., $t_{\vec{R}\vec{R}'}$ describes the delocalizing forces, which become larger with impurity concentration). For each phonon mode i, A^i gives the effect of the lattice vibration on the electronic states, either changing on-site energies (diagonal terms $A^i_{\vec{R}\vec{R}}$) or hopping (off-diagonal terms $A^i_{\vec{R}\vec{R}'}$). There is, in addition, electron-phonon coupling between the IB and the CB, which is responsible for the actual transfer of electrons between these states. This coupling is important only when an IB state described by Eqs. 4-6 is nearly degenerate with the CB. We do not express these terms explicitly, but the nonradiative lifetime depends on their values [25]. If the largest (smallest) eigenvalues of t are $t_{1(2)}$, we define the IB bandwidth $J = (t_1 - t_2)/2$. We must have $J < \Delta E'$, or we do not have an IB.

We can also write

$$H_e = \sum_{\vec{k}} \epsilon(\vec{k}) |\psi_{\vec{k}}\rangle \langle \psi_{\vec{k}}| \quad (7)$$

$$H_{e-ph} = \sum_{i\vec{k}\vec{k}'} Q_i \tilde{A}^i_{\vec{k}\vec{k}'} |\psi_{\vec{k}}\rangle \langle \psi_{\vec{k}'}|, \quad (8)$$

with energies $\epsilon(\vec{k})$ and new matrices $\tilde{A}^i$, related to the A^i by a basis transformation. We further let $H_0 = H_e + H_{e-ph}$.

The bases $\phi_{\vec{R}}$ and $\psi_{\vec{k}}$ allow us to treat different effects easily. When $\vec{Q} = 0$, as in Fig. 2a, the $\psi_{\vec{k}}$ basis is the simplest, as the Hamiltonian is diagonal, and delocalized states

are a natural description. But as thermal fluctuations cause $\vec{Q}$ to vary, we must consider the A^i terms. In the delocalized $\psi_{\vec{k}}$ basis, the matrices $\tilde{A}^i$ are complicated and off-diagonal. The most important physical assumption that we make is that the main effect of the phonons is to change the on-site energies in the local basis, which is generally true in the adiabatic approximation [27], [28]. That is, the matrices A^i are approximately diagonal. This assumption means that as the lattice is distorted, the energy to occupy individual impurity sites changes, but the overlaps between the impurity wave functions, which affect the hopping t, do not change. As the lattice positions $\vec{Q}$ change and the eigenvalues of the matrix $\vec{Q} \cdot \vec{A}$ become larger than the bandwidth J, the phonons localize the energy eigenstates of the system, and the local $\phi_{\vec{R}}$ basis becomes a more useful basis to study the problem.

We now present the variational argument that delocalization does not increase the nonradiative lifetime [19]. We already know, from studying the isolated impurity problem in Section II-B, that there is a $\vec{Q}_c$ such that $|\phi_{\vec{R}_0}\rangle$ gains enough energy $\Delta E'$ to be degenerate with a conduction band state, with reference to Figs. 1 and 2c.[2] That is, when $t = 0$, the largest eigenvalue of $\vec{Q}_c \cdot \vec{A}$ is $\Delta E'$, and the eigenvector $|\rho_0\rangle$ is approximately one of the maximally localized states $|\phi_{R_0}\rangle$ because we know by Eqs. 1-3 that trapping is fastest through the most localized states, as illustrated in Fig. 2.

If the IMT increases the nonradiative lifetime, it must be that E_a increases when the electrons are able to hop to other impurities (encapsulated in $t_{\vec{R}\vec{R}'}$), and having the lattice in configuration $\vec{Q}_c$ must no longer cause an IB state to become degenerate with a CB state. That is, the largest eigenvalue of $H_0(\vec{Q}_c)$ must be less than $(\bar{\epsilon} + \Delta E')$.

We know that $\langle \phi_{\vec{R}_0} | t | \phi_{\vec{R}_0} \rangle = 0$, and we expect in most systems that $\langle \rho_0 | t | \rho_0 \rangle = 0$, too. A finite $\langle \rho_0 | t | \rho_0 \rangle$ shifts the energy of the localized state and can increase or decrease the nonradiative lifetime, depending on its sign, but it is not caused by delocalization or an IMT – see Sec. IV-B1. A perturbative calculation of the effects of such terms is in Ref. [19]. Since we are only interested in studying the effects of delocalization, we therefore assume that $\langle \rho_0 | t | \rho_0 \rangle = 0$.

We then have $\langle \rho_0 | H_0(\vec{Q}_c) | \rho_0 \rangle = (\bar{\epsilon} + \Delta E')$. Therefore, by the variational principle, the largest eigenvalue of $H_0(\vec{Q}_c)$ must be greater than or equal to $(\bar{\epsilon} + \Delta E')$. The effect of delocalization across several impurities is only to possibly *increase* the capture cross section of each impurity, in addition to providing more recombination centers.

This result can be understood to mean that eigenstates initially delocalized across multiple impurity sites are localized by electron-phonon interactions. When $\vec{Q} = 0$, the eigenstates of the IB may be localized or delocalized. As thermal fluctuations bring the lattice into configuration $\vec{Q}_c$, the electron-phonon coupling H_{e-ph} is larger than the effects of t, since $\Delta E' > J$. Therefore, one of the localized states becomes an approximate eigenstate of the system and can become degenerate with the CB minimum, resulting in rapid

---

[1] In non-dopant-based IB systems [30], [31], the localized basis can be constructed from Wannier functions, described in Section III.

[2] In a periodic system with N unit cells, there are N equivalent sites, and we consider one of them here.

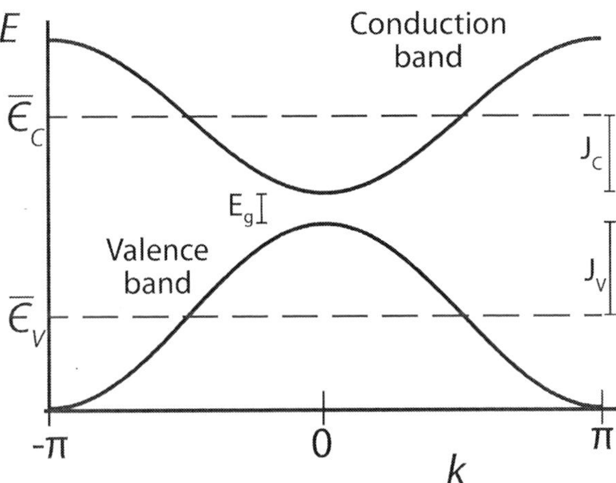

Fig. 3. A simple 1D semiconductor band structure (energy vs. wavevector) illustrating the key energy scales: the band gap E_g, the bandwidths J_α, and the mean energy $\bar{\epsilon}_\alpha$, for $\alpha = C, V$. The nonradiative lifetime is determined by the energy gap $\bar{\epsilon}_C - \bar{\epsilon}_V$, which is generally much larger than E_g. Though this figure shows a direct-gap semiconductor, for our purposes it does not matter whether the semiconductor is direct or indirect.

trapping, just as in the case of independent impurities. Multi-site delocalization, as in an IMT, does not extend nonradiative lifetimes in the same way that increasing the size of a single-impurity state does.

III. COMPARISON TO BAND-BAND MULTIPHONON RECOMBINATION

We have shown that delocalization across many sites in an intermediate band does not increase the nonradiative lifetime compared to the case with independent sites. Yet it is well known that multiphonon recombination is slow (insignificant) for conduction- to valence-band recombination, which is often credited to the delocalization of the conduction and valence band wave functions. We now adapt the model described above to analyze the case of band-to-band recombination and illustrate why the nonradiative lifetime is so long. The essential reason is that the effective energy gap is much larger than $\Delta E'$.

We describe our CB and VB within an effective non-interacting model, as above. By Bloch's theorem, we can diagonalize the Hamiltonian in a basis of states with well-defined crystal-momentum $\vec{k}$. For convenience, we assume that each band has only a single state at each $\vec{k}$. Then we write

$$H_e = \sum_{\vec{k}} \epsilon_C(\vec{k}) \left| \psi_{C,\vec{k}} \right\rangle \left\langle \psi_{C,\vec{k}} \right| + \epsilon_V(\vec{k}) \left| \psi_{V,\vec{k}} \right\rangle \left\langle \psi_{V,\vec{k}} \right|, \quad (9)$$

where $\left| \psi_{C(V),\vec{k}} \right\rangle$ are states in the CB (VB). We define the bandwidth J_C (J_V) of the CB (VB) in Eq. 9 to be half the difference between the maximum and minimum energies in the band, as in Fig. 3. We construct localized states from these Bloch states using Wannier functions [33]. For an appropriate choice of phases on the Bloch states $\psi_{C(V),\vec{k}}$, these can be made maximally localized [34], and we call these localized

states $\left| \phi_{C(V),\vec{R}} \right\rangle$, where $\vec{R}$ are the centers of the unit cells of the crystal. That is, we write

$$\left| \phi_{C,\vec{R}} \right\rangle = \frac{1}{\sqrt{N}} \sum_{\vec{k}} e^{-i\vec{k}\cdot\vec{R}} \left| \psi_{C,\vec{k}} \right\rangle, \quad (10)$$

where N is the number of unit cells in the system and the sum is over the first Brillouin zone; similar results apply for $\left| \phi_{V,\vec{R}} \right\rangle$. These localized states are not eigenstates of H_e, but we can express H_e as in a tight-binding model over these states.

$$H_e = \bar{\epsilon}_C \sum_{\vec{R}} \left| \phi_{C,\vec{R}} \right\rangle \left\langle \phi_{C,\vec{R}} \right| + \sum_{\vec{R} \neq \vec{R}'} t_{C,\vec{R}\vec{R}'} \left| \phi_{C,\vec{R}} \right\rangle \left\langle \phi_{C,\vec{R}'} \right|$$

$$+ \bar{\epsilon}_V \sum_{\vec{R}} \left| \phi_{V,\vec{R}} \right\rangle \left\langle \phi_{V,\vec{R}} \right| + \sum_{\vec{R} \neq \vec{R}'} t_{V,\vec{R}\vec{R}'} \left| \phi_{V,\vec{R}} \right\rangle \left\langle \phi_{V,\vec{R}'} \right|, \quad (11)$$

where $\bar{\epsilon}_\alpha \equiv \sum_{\vec{k}} \epsilon_\alpha(\vec{k})/N$ is the mean energy in the $\alpha = C, V$ band, N is the number of unit cells in the system, and $t_{\alpha,\vec{R}\vec{R}'}$ is the hopping matrix element between sites $\vec{R}$ and $\vec{R}'$, which generally decays rapidly with $\left| \vec{R} - \vec{R}' \right|$. This basis allows us to think of the CB and VB states similarly to the impurity states of Sec. II-C.

We couple in the motion of the lattice, with E_{ph} as in Eq. 5 and H_{e-ph} modified to

$$H_{e-ph} = \sum_{\alpha i \vec{R}\vec{R}'} Q_i A^i_{\alpha,\vec{R}\vec{R}'} \left| \phi_{\alpha,\vec{R}} \right\rangle \left\langle \phi_{\alpha,\vec{R}'} \right|, \quad (12)$$

where the sum goes over all unit cells $\vec{R}$, vibrational modes i, and $\alpha = C, V$. We can equivalently write H_{e-ph} in the delocalized basis,

$$H_{e-ph} = \sum_{\alpha i \vec{k}\vec{k}'} Q_i \tilde{A}^i_{\alpha,\vec{k}\vec{k}'} \left| \psi_{\alpha,\vec{k}} \right\rangle \left\langle \alpha, \psi_{\vec{k}'} \right|. \quad (13)$$

As in the case with the IB, the key physical assumption we make is that A^i_α is an approximately diagonal matrix, which implies that $\tilde{A}^i_\alpha$ has large off-diagonal components. Physically, this assumption means that distortions of the lattice change the energies of localized states but do not cause hopping from localized states to far-away states. In the momentum-basis, distortions of the lattice mainly cause scattering between different $\vec{k}$ states.

We now analyze this problem similarly to Sec. II-C. The nonradiative process has an activation energy $E_a = E_{ph}(\vec{Q})$ with $\vec{Q}$ a lattice configuration where the lowest energy in the CB is degenerate with the highest energy in the VB. If the system has carriers that can recombine, these extremal states are always filled and empty, respectively. We find the $\vec{Q}_c$ satisfying the degeneracy condition and minimizing E_a. For the bands to become degenerate, the electron-phonon coupling must raise a VB state out of the band to approach the CB (or similarly a CB state must approach the VB). Here we consider the case that a VB state is raised to the CB. We assume that the CB states are not strongly modified by this lattice distortion, as this assumption produces the fastest nonradiative process. That is, we seek a degeneracy between a VB state and the delocalized state $|\psi_{C,0}\rangle$ at the CB minimum, where we assume the CB minimum is at $\vec{k} = 0$, as illustrated in Fig. 3.

Let $E_V(\vec{Q})$ be the largest eigenvalue of $t_V + \vec{Q} \cdot \vec{A}_V$, and let the eigenvector be $|\rho_V\rangle$. To satisfy the degeneracy condition, we must find $\vec{Q}$ such $E_V(\vec{Q}) = \epsilon_C(0) - \bar{\epsilon}_V \equiv \Delta E_{\text{eff}}$. Using a standard Lagrange multiplier technique, as in [19], we find the minimal E_a to be

$$E_a = \frac{(\Delta E_{\text{eff}} - \langle \rho_V | t_V | \rho_V \rangle)^2}{4\lambda_{CV}}, \text{ where} \quad (14)$$

$$\lambda_{CV} = \sum_i \frac{\langle \rho_V | A_V^i | \rho_V \rangle^2}{2\omega_i^2}. \quad (15)$$

Since the state $|\rho_V\rangle$ has left the VB, it must be close to being an eigenstate of $\vec{Q}_c \cdot \vec{A}_V$, with t_V as a perturbation. In order to minimize E_a, $|\rho_V\rangle$ must be maximally localized[3] [25], and therefore $\langle \rho_V | t_V | \rho_V \rangle \approx 0$.

We see from Eqs. 2 and 14 that even if the reorganization energies λ, λ_{CV} are similar, the activation energy for band-to-band nonradiative recombination is much larger than for recombination through an impurity in the band gap; ΔE_{eff} is approximately equal to $E_g + J_V$ while the best case for a dopant is $\Delta E' = E_g$. Since semiconductor bandwidths are generally much larger than their band gaps, nonradiative trapping into a mid-gap level can be rapid while band-to-band nonradiative recombination is negligible. We generally expect band-to-band nonradiative recombination to have $\Delta E_{\text{eff}} \approx E_g + \min[J_V, J_C]$, as the band with smaller bandwidth is more easily localized by the electron-phonon coupling.

We note that for band-to-band nonradiative recombination, there are M unit cells per unit volume, which is much greater than the N impurities per unit volume in a doped system. In the band-to-band case, all M of these unit cells contribute to the recombination. But since U is suppressed exponentially by ΔE_{eff}^2, the band-to-band nonradiative process is negligible, despite the large number of independent lattice sites.

IV. LOOPHOLES

We now discuss situations that could cause the above arguments to break down. We do not believe any of these loopholes change our conclusions. We further discuss possibilities for lifetime recovery which are not based in the IMT.

A. Loopholes that could permit IMT-based lifetime recovery

1) Electron-phonon coupling is non-local: As emphasized above, the key physical assumption is that the electronic states most strongly coupled to the lattice vibrations are localized in space. This result is well known for polar semiconductors [25], [28], [35], with the intuition given in Fig. 2, and there are similar results with deformation-potential coupling in nanostructures [36], [37]. But if it were not true, our argument would fail. This assumption is also required, however, for the lifetime recovery proposal, which relies on delocalization to slow recombination, so it is not clear that this loophole would permit IMT-based lifetime recovery.

---

[3]As in footnote 2, for a periodic system with M unit cells there are M such configurations $\vec{Q}_c$, and we choose one here.

2) The matrices $\vec{A}$ vary with t : In this paper, we consider increasing or decreasing the concentration of impurities by turning on or off the hopping matrix t in order to study the system with and without the IMT delocalization. We assume that $\vec{A}$ does not vary with t, as it does not vary in a tight-binding model. Consider, however, an IMT that produces delocalized states that have a different span than the $t = 0$ independent-impurity wave functions. That is, the orthogonalized independent-state wave functions are not superpositions of the delocalized eigenstates. Localized Wannier functions can still be constructed, and $\vec{A}$ should be approximately diagonal in the local basis. In that system, however, $\vec{A}$ of the metallic system is not necessarily related to $\vec{A}$ of the independent-impurity system, and we cannot make further analytical progress. If the delocalized system for some reason has $\vec{A}$ of smaller magnitude, the nonradiative lifetime will increase, giving lifetime recovery. In particular, if the maximally localized Wannier functions are larger than the independent-impurity wave functions, then we would expect $\vec{A}$ to be smaller in magnitude and thus the nonradiative lifetime to increase. We do not see why this loophole should occur, but we cannot rule it out with the methods used here.

3) Adiabatic approximation breaks down: Our discussion has been entirely in the adiabatic approximation. This approximation assumes that the electrons move much more rapidly than the ions, so the ions cannot follow the electron motion and instead feel only an effective averaged potential. We can then write the electron-phonon wave functions as products of electronic and lattice wave functions. The momentum of the lattice is important for describing the actual trapping process, where the electron transfers from one electronic state to another, but in this paper we have only been concerned with finding the lattice configurations where trapping can occur, so we have neglected the lattice momentum. This approximation allows us to write the Hamiltonian H_e and H_{el-ph} in the simple forms above.

The adiabatic approximation is valid when the relevant electronic energies are much larger than the phonon energies [38]. The trapping process itself requires nonadiabatic effects, but only in the near vicinity of degeneracy [22], [23]. As the lattice approaches configuration $\vec{Q}_c$, where the relevant energy levels are degenerate, the corrections to adiabatic coupling cause the transfer from one electronic state to the other. This breakdown of the adiabatic approximation is not a loophole but rather a fundamental part of the trapping process.

If the adiabatic approximation is more generally invalid outside the vicinity of degeneracy, then all of these results are suspect. It is breaks down via polaron formation, then delocalized states are not formed. It is not clear whether a more general breakdown could be associated with lifetime recovery.

4) The linear-coupling approximation is invalid near $\vec{Q}_c$: The linear-coupling approximation of Eq. 6 is not itself well justified but is widely used, because it results in relatively tractable problems. If the electron-phonon coupling is non-linear in $\vec{Q}$, we expect all of the above results to hold qualitatively, but we have not proved that assertion.

5) Interaction effects: While this paper has used models of non-interacting electrons, we cannot rule out that correlated many-body states could have other effects, as in Sec. IV-A2. We expect that the general result – that multi-site delocalized states are localized by electron-phonon interactions when the electron-phonon energy is larger than the bandwidth – remains true in interacting systems.

B. Other possibilities for lifetime recovery, not related to IMT

We now present reasons unrelated to IMT that lifetime recovery could still occur, though all of these effects could make lifetimes increase or decrease.

1) Shifts of $\bar{\epsilon}$: As more states are added to the IB, the intermediate energy levels could shift into or out of the gap, changing $\Delta E'$ and thus E_a as indicated in Eq. 2. In the notation of Sec. II-C, this consists of diagonal terms of the matrix $t_{\vec{R}\vec{R}}$. This effect could be very significant, though it is not related to IMT.

2) Shifts of the CB/VB: The formation of the IB could shift the CB and VB energies, due to chemical bonding or screening effects, which could also affect the nonradiative lifetime.

3) Chemical changes with concentration: As dopants are added to an IB material, they may undergo chemical changes, forming precipitates or occupying different structural states in the semiconductor. These can change the nonradiative lifetime.

V. Summary

Progress in producing highly-efficient IBSC's requires extending nonradiative lifetimes. We show that even for an IB that is metallic when the lattice is in its equilibrium configuration, the delocalized states are fragile; as the lattice vibrates, localized states emerge from the IB to cause nonradiative trapping. The delocalization of the band can only *increase* the trapping rates. Progress in IBSC's will not occur by searching for delocalized intermediate bands.

Acknowledgments

We acknowledge a careful reading by Christie Simmons.

References

[1] A. Luque and A. Martí, "Increasing the efficiency of ideal solar cells by photon induced transitions at intermediate levels," *Phys. Rev. Lett.*, vol. 78, no. 26, pp. 5014–5017, 1997.

[2] M. Wolf, "Limitations and possibilities for improvement of photovoltaic solar energy converters: Part I: Considerations for Earth's surface operation," *Proceedings of the IRE*, vol. 48, no. 7, pp. 1246–1263, 1960.

[3] M. J. Keevers and M. A. Green, "Efficiency improvements of silicon solar cells by the impurity photovoltaic effect," *J. Appl. Phys.*, vol. 75, no. 8, pp. 4022–4031, 1994.

[4] W. Shockley and H. J. Queisser, "Detailed balance limit of efficiency of p-n junction solar cells," *J. Appl. Phys.*, vol. 32, no. 3, pp. 510–519, 1961.

[5] A. Luque, A. Martí, and C. Stanley, "Understanding intermediate-band solar cells," *Nat Photon*, vol. 6, no. 3, pp. 146–152, 2012.

[6] W. Shockley and W. T. Read, "Statistics of the recombinations of holes and electrons," *Phys. Rev.*, vol. 87, no. 5, pp. 835–, 1952.

[7] R. Hall, "Electron-hole recombination in germanium," *Phys. Rev.*, vol. 87, no. 2, pp. 387–387, 1952.

[8] G. Güttler and H. Queisser, "Impurity photovoltaic effect in silicon," *Energy Conversion*, vol. 10, no. 2, pp. 51–55, 1970.

[9] A. Luque, A. Martí, E. Antolín, and C. Tablero, "Intermediate bands versus levels in non-radiative recombination," *Physica B*, vol. 382, no. 1-2, pp. 320–327, 2006.

[10] A. Luque and A. Martí, "A metallic intermediate band high efficiency solar cell," *Prog. Photovolt: Res. Appl.*, vol. 9, no. 2, pp. 73–86, 2001.

[11] J. Olea, G. González-Díaz, D. Pastor, I. Mártil, A. Martí, E. Antolin, and A. Luque, "Two-layer Hall effect model for intermediate band Ti-implanted silicon," *J. Appl. Phys.*, vol. 109, no. 6, pp. 063 718–8, 2011.

[12] M. T. Winkler, D. Recht, M.-J. Sher, A. J. Said, E. Mazur, and M. J. Aziz, "Insulator-to-metal transition in sulfur-doped silicon," *Phys. Rev. Lett.*, vol. 106, no. 17, pp. 178 701–, 2011.

[13] E. Ertekin, M. T. Winkler, D. Recht, A. J. Said, M. J. Aziz, T. Buonassisi, and J. C. Grossman, "Insulator-to-metal transition in selenium-hyperdoped silicon: Observation and origin," *Phys. Rev. Lett.*, vol. 108, no. 2, pp. 026 401–, 2012.

[14] W. M. Reid, T. Driscoll, and M. F. Doty, "Forming delocalized intermediate states with realistic quantum dots," *J. Appl. Phys.*, vol. 111, no. 5, pp. 056 102–3, 2012.

[15] D. Pastor, J. Olea, A. del Prado, E. García-Hemme. R. García-Hernansanz, and G. González-Díaz. "Insulator to metallic transition due to intermediate band formation in Ti-implanted silicon," *Solar Energy Materials and Solar Cells*, vol. 104, pp. 159–164, 2012.

[16] J. J. Krich and A. Aspuru-Guzik, "Scaling and localization lengths of a topologically disordered system," *Phys. Rev. Lett.*, vol. 106, no. 15, pp. 156 405–, 2011.

[17] E. Antolín, A. Martí, J. Olea, D. Pastor, G. González-Díaz, I. Mártil, and A. Luque, "Lifetime recovery in ultrahighly titanium-doped silicon for the implementation of an intermediate band material," *Appl. Phys. Lett.*, vol. 94, no. 4, p. 042115, 2009.

[18] E. Garcia-Hemme, R. Garcia-Hernansanz, J. Olea, D. Pastor, A. del Prado, I. Martil, and G. Gonzalez-Diaz, "Sub-bandgap spectral photo-response analysis of Ti supersaturated Si," *Appl. Phys. Lett.*, vol. 101, no. 19, pp. 192 101–5, 2012.

[19] J. J. Krich, B. I. Halperin, and A. Aspuru-Guzik, "Nonradiative lifetimes in intermediate band photovoltaics—absence of lifetime recovery," *J. Appl. Phys.*, vol. 112, no. 1, pp. 013 707–8, 2012.

[20] P. P. Edwards and M. J. Sienko, "Universality aspects of the metal-nonmetal transition in condensed media," *Phys. Rev. B*, vol. 17, no. 6, pp. 2575–2581, 1978.

[21] M. N. Alexander and D. F. Holcomb, "Semiconductor-to-metal transition in n-type group IV semiconductors," *Rev. Mod. Phys.*, vol. 40, no. 4, pp. 815–, 1968.

[22] D. V. Lang and C. H. Henry, "Nonradiative recombination at deep levels in GaAs and GaP by lattice-relaxation multiphonon emission," *Phys. Rev. Lett.*, vol. 35, no. 22, pp. 1525–, 1975.

[23] C. H. Henry and D. V. Lang, "Nonradiative capture and recombination by multiphonon emission in GaAs and GaP," *Phys. Rev. B*, vol. 15, no. 2, pp. 989–, 1977.

[24] M. Lax, "Cascade capture of electrons in solids," *Phys. Rev.*, vol. 119, no. 5, pp. 1502–, 1960.

[25] P. T. Landsberg, *Recombination in Semiconductors*. Cambridge, 1991.

[26] R. Evrard, E. Kartheuser, and F. Williams, "Polaron formalism applied to donor-acceptor pairs in semiconductors," *Journal of Luminescence*, vol. 14, no. 2, pp. 81–90, 1976.

[27] E. Kartheuser, R. Evrard, and F. Williams, "Radiative recombination of donor-acceptor pairs in polar semiconductors," *Phys. Rev. B*, vol. 21, no. 2, pp. 648–658, 1980.

[28] M. Soltani, M. Certier, R. Evrard, and E. Kartheuser, "Photoluminescence of CdTe doped with arsenic and antimony acceptors," *J. Appl. Phys.*, vol. 78, no. 9, pp. 5626–5632, 1995.

[29] E. Abrahams, P. W. Anderson, D. C. Licciardello, and T. V. Ramakrishnan, "Scaling theory of localization: Absence of quantum diffusion in two dimensions," *Phys. Rev. Lett.*, vol. 42, no. 10, pp. 673–, 1979.

[30] N. López, L. A. Reichertz, K. M. Yu, K. Campman, and W. Walukiewicz, "Engineering the electronic band structure for multiband solar cells," *Phys. Rev. Lett.*, vol. 106, no. 2, pp. 028 701–, 2011.

[31] W. Shan, W. Walukiewicz, J. W. Ager, E. E. Haller, J. F. Geisz, D. J. Friedman, J. M. Olson, and S. R. Kurtz, "Band anticrossing in GaInNAs alloys," *Phys. Rev. Lett.*, vol. 82, no. 6, pp. 1221–, 1999.

[32] N. F. Mott, "Metal-insulator transition," *Rev. Mod. Phys.*, vol. 40, no. 4, pp. 677–, 1968.

[33] G. H. Wannier, "The structure of electronic excitation levels in insulating crystals," *Phys. Rev.*, vol. 52, no. 3, pp. 191–197, 1937.

[34] N. Marzari, A. A. Mostofi, J. R. Yates, I. Souza, and D. Vanderbilt, "Maximally localized Wannier functions: Theory and applications," *Rev. Mod. Phys.*, vol. 84, no. 4, pp. 1419–1475, 2012.

[35] H. L. Malm and R. R. Haering, "Franck-Condon effects in the luminescence of CdS," *Canadian Journal of Physics*, vol. 49, p. 2970, 1971.

[36] T. Takagahara, "Electron-phonon interactions and excitonic dephasing in semiconductor nanocrystals," *Phys. Rev. Lett.*, vol. 71, no. 21, pp. 3577–3580, 1993.

[37] I. V. Bondarev, S. A. Maksimenko, G. Y. Slepyan, I. L. Krestnikov, and A. Hoffmann, "Exciton-phonon interactions and exciton dephasing in semiconductor quantum-well heterostructures," *Phys. Rev. B*, vol. 68, no. 7, pp. 073 310–, 2003.

[38] R. Evrard and F. Williams, *Luminescence of inorganic solids.* Plenum Press, 1978, pp. 419–435.

Photogenerated Current By Two-Step Photon Excitation in ZnTeO Intermediate Band Solar Cells with n-ZnO Window Layer

Tooru Tanaka, *Member, IEEE*, Masaki Miyabara, Yasuhiro Nagao, Katsuhiko Saito, Qixin Guo, Mitsuhiro Nishio, Kin Man Yu, and Wladek Walukiewicz

Abstract—We present the results of systematic experimental studies on ZnTeO intermediate band solar cells (IBSCs) with a n-ZnO window layer. In order to understand photovoltaic (PV) activities of ZnTeO IBSCs, we first describe PV properties of ZnO/ZnTe solar cells without the intermediate band (IB). The improved efficiency of 1.38% is demonstrated by using a n^+-ZnO/i-ZnO/i-ZnTe/p-ZnTe structure. Then, the PV properties of ZnTeO IBSCs fabricated using n-ZnO window layer with and without a blocking barrier for IB are compared. The device with a blocked IB shows higher open-circuit voltage than that without the blocking barrier. High external quantum efficiency (EQE) is observed in the photon energy range in which electron transitions from the valence band to the IB take place in ZnTeO IBSC without the blocking layer, whereas the device with the blocked IB shows a small EQE at the same energy range, implying the electron accumulation in IB. Finally, the production of photogenerated current by two-step photon excitation via IB is demonstrated.

Index Terms—Highly mismatched alloy (HMA), intermediate band solar cell (IBSC), molecular beam epitaxy (MBE), two-step photon excitation (TPE), ZnTeO.

I. Introduction

THE concept of the multiband or intermediate band solar cell (IBSC) has recently attracted renewed attention as a viable approach to achieving high solar power conversion efficiencies [1]–[4]. Several approaches have been employed to demonstrate the concept of IBSC including quantum dots [5],

Manuscript received June 8, 2013; revised August 19, 2013; accepted September 11, 2013. Date of publication October 21, 2013; date of current version December 16, 2013. This work was supported in part by the JST PRESTO program, in part by the JSPS KAKENHI under Grant 24760258, and in part by the Nippon Sheet Glass Foundation for Materials Science and Engineering. The work performed at Lawrence Berkeley National Laboratory was supported by the Director, Office of Science, Office of Basic Energy Sciences, Materials Sciences and Engineering Division, of the U.S. Department of Energy under Contract DE-AC02-05CH11231.

T. Tanaka is with the Department of Electrical and Electronic Engineering, Saga University, Saga 840–8502, Japan, and also with PRESTO, Japan Science and Technology Agency, Kawaguchi, Saitama 332–0012, Japan (e-mail: ttanaka@cc.saga-u.ac.jp).

M. Miyabara, Y. Nagao, K. Saito, Q. Guo, and M. Nishio are with the Department of Electrical and Electronic Engineering, Saga University, Saga 840–8502, Japan (e-mail: miyabara@sc.ec.saga-u.ac. jp; nagao@sc.ec.saga-u.ac.jp; saito@o.m.saga-u.ac.jp; guoq@cc.saga-u.ac.jp; nishiom@cc.saga-u.ac.jp).

K. M. Yu and W. Walukiewicz are with the Materials Sciences Division, Lawrence Berkeley National Laboratory, Berkeley, CA 94720 USA (e-mail: KMYu@lbl.gov; W_Walukiewicz@lbl.gov).

Color versions of one or more of the figures in this paper are available online at http://ieeexplore.ieee.org.

Digital Object Identifier 10.1109/JPHOTOV.2013.2282738

[6] and highly mismatched alloys (HMAs) [1], [3], [7]–[11]. Among them, ZnTe-based HMA of $ZnTe_{1-x}O_x$ (ZnTeO) [2], [10], [11] is a good candidate for the IBSC because the incorporation of a small amount of isoelectronic O in ZnTe leads to the formation of a narrow, O-derived band (E_-) of extended states located well below the conduction band (CB) (E_+) edge of the ZnTe, and the E_- band can be used as an intermediate band (IB) [4], [10].

In a recent report, we demonstrated the growth of ZnTeO layers by the molecular beam epitaxy (MBE) technique and showed that both E_- and E_+ transitions with different O content in the layers are in excellent agreement with the BAC model [11]. For an operational IBSC, however, it is essential to show the evidence of photocurrent induced by two-step photon excitation (TPE) via the IB. Recently, Ahsan *et al.* reported experimental results of the direct observation of photocurrent by TPEs in a GaNAs-based IBSC structure, which is another candidate for HMA-based bulk IBSC [8]. Although a few experimental results on TPE have been reported using laser or light emitting diode as illumination light sources [4], [10], there have been no detailed optical studies on the TPE process in ZnTeO.

In order to understand the nature of the photovoltaic (PV) activity of a ZnTeO IBSC and to achieve good performance, it is necessary to realize high-efficiency ZnTe solar cells. Based on this idea, we previously reported the fabrication of ZnTe homojunction solar cell, in which n-ZnTe layer was prepared by a thermal diffusion of Al into p-ZnTe with a hole concentration of 10^{18} cm^{-3} [12]. By studying the dependence of the n-type layer thickness and the diffusion temperatures on the PV properties, the highest conversion efficiency of 1.42% was achieved in the ZnTe homojunction solar cell [12], [13]. However, the efficiency was relatively small as compared with the value estimated for a single-junction ZnTe solar cell.

In homojunction solar cells based on direct bandgap semiconductors, surface recombination losses are inevitable because most of the incident light is absorbed near the surface region. Thus, a heterojunction structure combined with a highly conductive n-type semiconductor with a wide bandgap is generally used to avoid the surface recombination losses [14]. In ZnTe solar cells, Al-doped n-ZnO can be used as the n-type window layer. So far, the ZnO/ZnTe heterojunction was investigated on GaAs substrate for solar cell applications [15]. However, the reported short-circuit current and open-circuit voltage were relatively small as $J_{sc} \sim 0.8$ mA/cm^2 and $V_{oc} \sim 60$ mV, respectively, because of defects due to the large lattice-mismatch among ZnTe,

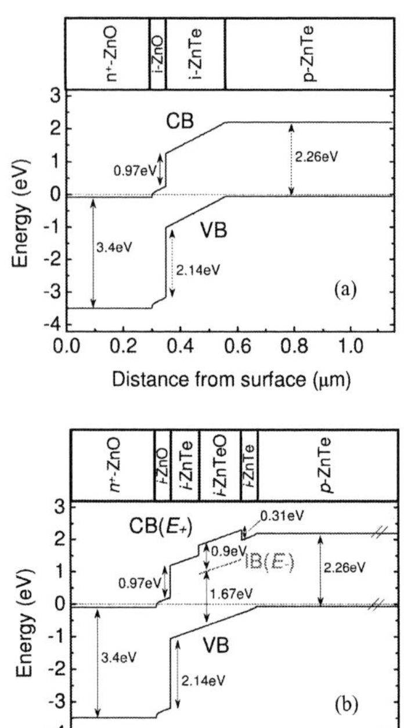

Fig. 1. Device structure and calculated band diagrams of (a) n^+-ZnO/i-ZnO/i-ZnTe/p-ZnTe structure and (b) ZnTeO IBSC with a BIB.

ZnO, and GaAs substrate [15], [16]. The use of ZnTe substrate is expected to improve the efficiency of the heterojunction ZnTe solar cells because of the homoepitaxial growth. In fact, we have achieved the improved efficiency of n^+-ZnO/i-ZnTe/p-ZnTe solar cells on p-ZnTe substrates [13]. Further improvement of the PV performance is expected by optimizing the cell structure and the thickness of absorber layer.

Here, we first present the results of systematic experimental studies on ZnO/ZnTe solar cells and then, based on the results, the cell structure was applied to ZnTeO-based IBSCs. Finally, the production of photocurrent by the TPE process via IB is demonstrated.

II. EXPERIMENTAL

Heterojunction solar cells with n^+-ZnO/i-ZnTe/p-ZnTe and n^+-ZnO/i-ZnO/i-ZnTe/p-ZnTe structures were fabricated on p-ZnTe(100) substrates to clarify the effect of i-ZnO layer on PV properties. The i-ZnTe layer was inserted to increase the width of the depletion region adjacent to the heavily doped p-ZnTe substrate. The thickness of the layer was varied between 150 and 400 nm. The thicknesses of n-ZnO and i-ZnO layers were kept constant at 300 and 50 nm, respectively. Fig. 1(a) shows a band diagram for n^+-ZnO/i-ZnO /i-ZnTe/p-ZnTe structure with i-ZnTe layer thickness of 200 nm drawn using electron affinities for ZnTe and ZnO of 3.53 [17] and 4.5 eV [18], respectively.

For ZnTeO-based IBSCs, two types of IBSC structures, n^+-ZnO/i-ZnO/i-ZnTe/i-ZnTeO/i-ZnTe/p-ZnTe and n^+-ZnO/ i-ZnO/i-ZnTeO/i-ZnTe/p-ZnTe, were prepared in this study. Because the IB should be electrically isolated from any allowed band so that it only acts as a stepping stone for photon

absorption, the former structure was designed to have a blocked intermediate band (BIB) using blocking layers (i-ZnTe) on both the surface and the substrate side, as shown in Fig. 1(b). The latter one has an unblocked intermediate band (UIB), and the IB is connected to the CB of a ZnO window layer. The thickness of n^+-ZnO, i-ZnO, i-ZnTeO, and i-ZnTe (substrate side) layers were 300, 50, 150, and 50 nm, respectively. The thickness of i-ZnTe top blocking layer on the i-ZnTeO layer was changed between 50 and 200 nm to clarify the influence on PV properties. The O content x in ZnTeO layer was set to 1.8%, which was confirmed by X-ray diffraction after the growth. The bandgap energies of ZnTeO estimated using the BAC model [9], [11] were also shown in Fig. 1(b). The UIB device will be our reference sample in this study. Note that the IB is not occupied in this experiment. Therefore, the optical transitions from IB to E_+ band can only occur because of the nonequibrium occupation of the IB through the optical excitations from the valence band (VB) to the IB.

All layers were grown on p-ZnTe(100) substrates with a hole concentration of 10^{18} cm^{-3} by a conventional radio frequency (RF) plasma-assisted MBE system. 7 N Zn, 6 N Te, and 6 N Al were used as source materials. The O atoms were supplied as O radicals using the RF plasma gun. The ZnTe (100) substrates were ultrasonically cleaned in organic solvents and were wet-etched using Br-methanol solution. The substrate temperature was set to 400 °C.

For solar cell characterization, the Al grid contact was fabricated by thermal evaporation of Al, and Pd back contact was deposited by electroless plating. No antireflection coating layers were employed. The current density–voltage (J–V) curves for solar cells were measured under dark and illumination from 1 × sun AM1.5G. External quantum efficiency (EQE) was measured using a 250-W tungsten halogen lamp and a grating monochromator. The light from the tungsten halogen lamp was modulated with a chopper allowing to extract the PV response to the monochromator output by a lock-in amplifier.

III. RESULTS AND DISCUSSION

A. PV Properties of ZnO/ZnTe Solar Cells

Fig. 2(a)–(d) show the dependence of open-circuit voltage (V_{OC}), short-circuit current (J_{SC}), fill factor (F. F.), and power conversion efficiency (η) of the ZnO/ZnTe solar cells on the thickness of i-ZnTe layer, respectively. In the case of n^+-ZnO/i-ZnTe/p-ZnTe solar cells, the maximum efficiency of 1.1% was achieved when the thickness of i-ZnTe layer was 200 nm because the highest V_{OC} and J_{SC} were obtained. However, the observed V_{OC} value of 0.35 V is significantly small as compared with the bandgap of ZnTe of 2.26 eV.

The main reason for the small V_{OC} is because of the small built-in potential of only about 1 eV preventing hole transport from the p-ZnTe layer to the n^+-ZnO/i-ZnTe interface. The recombination of the holes transferred to the interface with the electrons in n$^+$-ZnO enhances dark current and limits the V_{OC} to less than 1 eV.

In order to suppress the interface recombination, the i-ZnO layer was inserted between the n^+-ZnO and i-ZnTe layers. As shown in Fig. 1(a), electrons fed into i-ZnO layer are expected

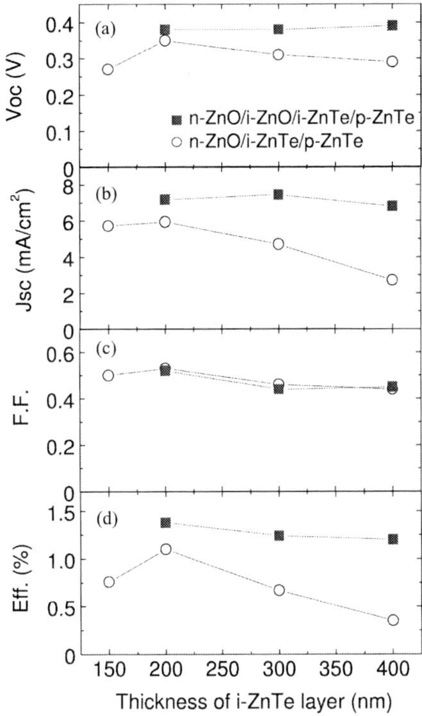

Fig. 2. Dependence of (a) open-circuit voltage (V_{OC}), (b) short-circuit current (J_{SC}), (c) fill factor (F. F.), and (d) power conversion efficiency (η) of ZnO/ZnTe solar cells.

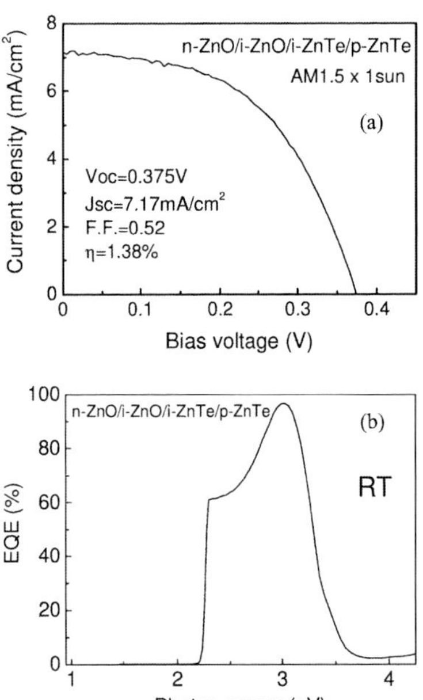

Fig. 3. (a) J–V curve under $1 \times$ sun illumination and (b) EQE curve for the n^+-ZnO/i-ZnO/i-ZnTe/p-ZnTe solar cell with i-ZnTe layer thickness of 200 nm.

to move away from the interface by the electric field in the i-ZnO region, which should reduce the interface recombination. The results of PV properties as a function of the thickness of the i-ZnTe layer are also shown in Fig. 2 (a)–(d) as blue squares. As compared with the case without i-ZnO layer, J_{SC} and V_{OC} are found to be improved significantly. Thus, the interface recombination seems to be reduced by inserting the i-ZnO layer at the n^+-ZnO/i-ZnTe interface.

Fig. 3(a) shows a J–V curve under $1 \times$ sun illumination for the n^+-ZnO/i-ZnO/i-ZnTe/p-ZnTe solar cell with i-ZnTe layer thickness of 200 nm. As a result of the reduced interface recombination, the J_{SC} and V_{OC} are increased to 7.17 mA/cm^2 and 0.375 V, respectively, yielding the power conversion efficiency of 1.38%.

Considering a fraction of the terrestrial solar spectrum ($1 \times$ sun AM1.5G) extending above the ZnTe bandgap of 2.26 eV and assuming 100% quantum efficiency, a functional ZnTe solar cell is expected to generate the theoretical maximum current of 9.6 mA/cm^2. The current density obtained in this ZnO/ZnTe solar cell is approximately 75% of the estimation and is reasonable for the present nonantireflection coating device.

Fig. 3(b) shows an EQE curve for n^+-ZnO/i-ZnO/i-ZnTe/ p-ZnTe solar cell with i-ZnTe layer thickness of 200 nm. High efficiency is obtained between the absorption edge of ZnTe (2.26 eV) and that of ZnO (3.4 eV). The reduction of EQE observed approaching the absorption edge of ZnTe will be because of the interference effect of the incident light and should be reduced by antireflection coating.

Based on these results on ZnO/ZnTe solar cells, we decided to adopt the n^+-ZnO/i-ZnO/i-ZnTe/p-ZnTe structure as a basic solar cell structure for the investigation of ZnTeO-based IBSCs.

B. PV Properties of ZnTeO-Based IBSCs

Fig. 4(a) shows J–V curves of UIB and BIB devices with the top blocking layer thickness of 50, 100, and 200 nm (hereafter, referred to as "BIB-50, 100, and 200-nm-devices", respectively) under AM1.5 $1 \times$ sun illumination. V_{OC} of all BIB devices are comparable to those obtained by the ZnO/ZnTe solar cells, and no degradation of V_{OC} by introducing ZnTeO layer is observed. A slight increase of the V_{OC} is observed in BIB-200-nm-device, although the reason for the improvement is unclear and presently under investigation. On the other hand, V_{OC} of the UIB device is relatively small and less than half of the BIB devices. This is probably because of the smaller bandgap between VB and IB (E_-) of ZnTeO than ZnTe.

J_{SC} of the BIB devices increases with increasing thickness of the i-ZnTe top blocking layer, and the highest J_{SC} of 5.44 mA/cm^2 is obtained in the BIB-200-nm-device. However, the J_{SC} value is still smaller than those obtained in a ZnO/ZnTe solar cell. This is probably because of the higher recombination losses in the ZnTeO layer as compared with a ZnTe layer because the IB of the ZnTeO is not occupied by electrons under equilibrium condition in this experiment. With an absorption coefficient α of the order of 3.3×10^4 cm^{-1} for ZnTe [19], a 200-nm-thick ZnTe absorbs approximately 50% of the photons with energies above the ZnTe bandgap. The rest of the photons are absorbed in the ZnTeO layer and/or the deeper layer. These photons produce electron–hole pairs that partially contribute to the current, although a fraction of them is also lost through

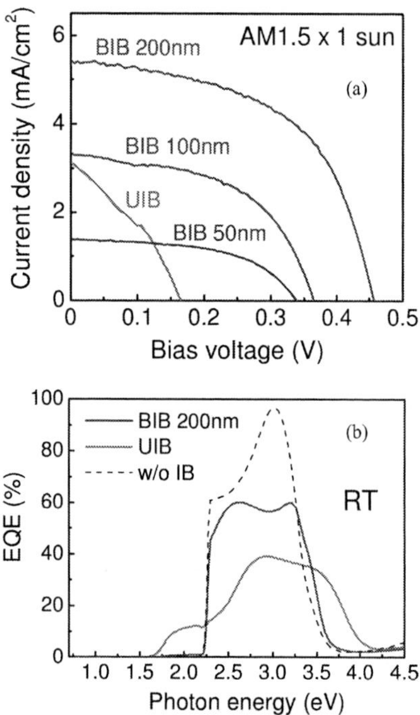

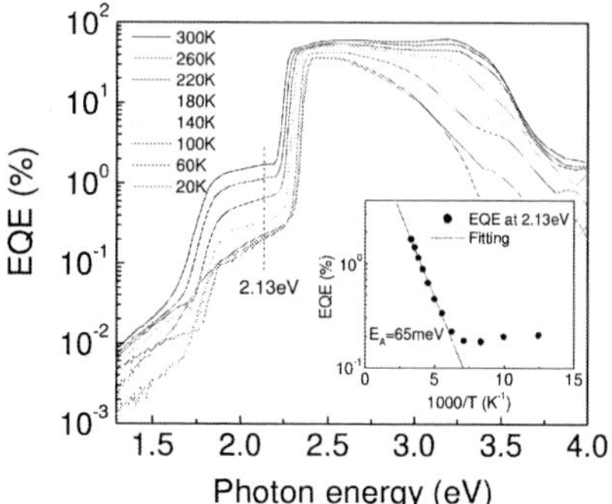

Fig. 5. Temperature dependence of EQE curve on the BIB-200-nm-device. The inset shows Arrhenius plot of EQE at 2.13 eV (580 nm).

Fig. 4. (a) J–V curves of UIB and BIB devices with a blocking layer thickness of 50, 100, and 200 nm. (b) EQE curves for the UIB and the BIB-200-nm-device. EQE spectrum for ZnO/ZnTe solar cell without IB is also shown for comparison.

a recombination in the ZnTeO layer. This recombination loss will be higher when the thickness of i-ZnTe top blocking layer decreases.

Fig. 4(b) shows the EQE curves for UIB and BIB-200-nm-devices. EQE spectrum for the ZnO/ZnTe solar cell without IB is also shown for comparison. The UIB device shows a low-energy photocurrent edge at about 1.65 eV corresponding to the optical transitions from the VB to the IB and the second more diffused edge at about 2.3 eV that can be attributed to the transitions from the VB to E_+ in ZnTeO and from the VB to the CB in ZnTe. For both transitions, the photoexcited electrons can be collected directly at the top contact as there is no barrier confining electrons in IB.

On the other hand, the BIB-200-nm-device shows a well-defined EQE edge at about 2.26 eV corresponding to the transition from the VB to the CB of ZnTe and the E_+ band in ZnTeO absorber. In this case, no current from the lower energy photons is expected because the IB is not occupied under equilibrium conditions and the electrons excited to IB cannot be collected because of the blocking barrier. The very small EQE signal ($<1\%$), which is an order of magnitude smaller than that measured for the UIB device, is detected at the low-energy region between 1.65 and 2.26 eV. This implies that the most of electrons excited from the VB to the IB are accumulated in the IB while some of the electrons in the IB escape directly to the CB. This EQE signal at low-energy region becomes small significantly when the thicker blocking layer above 300 nm is used (not shown). Note that the cutoff at high energy is because of the absorption by the ZnO top layer. Since the electron concentration in the n^+-ZnO

layer in the UIB structure was more than 5×10^{20} cm^{-3}, the absorption edge was shifted to higher energy side because of the band filling effect (Burnstein–Moss shift), while the n^+-ZnO layer for the BIB device has lower electron concentration of 1×10^{20} cm^{-3}, and the absorption coincides with the band gap of ZnO.

The temperature-dependent EQE measurements were carried out from 20 to 300 K on the BIB-200-nm-device in order to identify possible electron escape mechanisms, as shown in Fig. 5. The EQE at low-energy region between 1.65 and 2.26 eV was almost independent of the temperature below 140 K, implying the existence of a temperature-independent escape mechanism because of the tunneling through the blocking barrier. At temperatures above 180 K, the EQE at low-energy region shows a temperature-dependent character. The inset of Fig. 5 shows an Arrhenius plot of the EQE at 2.13 eV (580 nm). By fitting the linear part of the temperature-dependent EQE using $\exp(-E_A/kT)$, where E_A is the activation energy, k the Boltzmann constant, and T the temperature, the activation energy E_A is deduced as 65 meV. The thermal escape of electrons from the IB to the CB at the ZnTe/ZnTeO interface might be considered to be one of the escape mechanisms. However, this is unlikely because the energy difference between the CB of ZnTe and the IB of ZnTeO is much larger than the activation energy. Another possible process is the tunneling facilitated by deep levels in the barrier, which can have thermally activated character dependent on the energy of the deep levels. Further experiments are required to clarify the mechanism.

In order to prove the photocurrent induced by TPE via IB, the EQE of a BIB-50-nm-device was recorded with and without an infrared (IR) light illumination as a bias light at room temperature. A 500-W Xe lamp with a sharp cutoff filter which passes photons with the wavelength longer than 1000 nm or the photon energy below 1.24 eV was used as the IR light source. With the IR illumination, the excess electrons in the IB can be excited to the CB producing an additional photocurrent. The EQE was recorded with and without the IR illumination, and the difference between them, i.e., ΔQE (QE$_{\mathrm{IR-ON}}$ $-$ QE$_{\mathrm{IR-OFF}}$), was calculated.

Fig. 6 shows the ΔQE spectrum measured at the room temperature for the BIB-50-nm-device. The ΔQE increases at photon

174

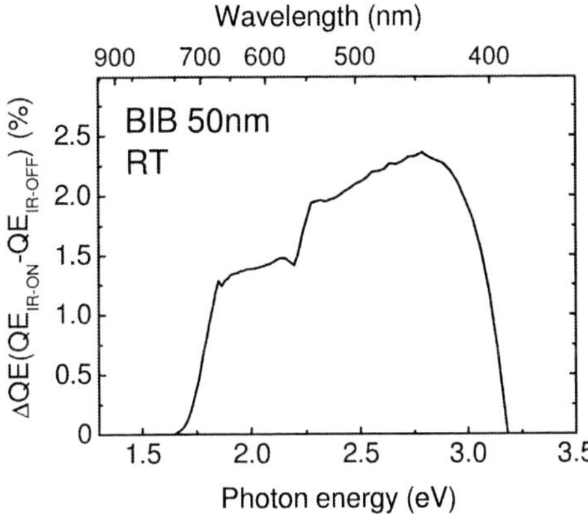

Fig. 6.   ΔQE spectrum measured at room temperature for BIB-50-nm-device.

energies above 1.65 eV. It is considered that the increase of ΔQE at the energy region between 1.65 and 2.25 eV are because of the enhanced IB → CB transitions of electrons excited from the VB to the IB, whereas those at the energy region above 2.25 eV can be explained by the reexcitation of electrons being trapped into the IB after the transition from the VB to the CB by a fast relaxation. Similar results have been reported in the InAs/GaNAs QD-IBSC [6] and the GaNAs-based IBSC [8]. The ratio of ΔQE to the EQE without IR illumination at 2 eV, which implies the ratios of optical transition rate from the IB to the CB with respect to the direct escape rate, were as high as ∼1, which indicates a high optical transition rate from the IB to the CB.

IV. CONCLUSION

The improved efficiency of ZnO/ZnTe heterojunction solar cells was achieved using the n$^+$-ZnO/i-ZnO/i-ZnTe/p-ZnTe structure as a result of reduced interface recombination. Based on the systematic experimental results on ZnO/ZnTe solar cells, ZnTeO IBSCs with n-ZnO window layer were fabricated. As a result, the photogenerated current induced by the TPE process in the ZnTeO IBSC with n-ZnO window layer was demonstrated. The observed high optical transition rate from the IB to the CB clearly indicates the high potential of this HMA for the application of IBSCs.

REFERENCES

[1] A. Luque and A. Martí, "Increasing the efficiency of ideal solar cells by photon induced transitions at intermediate levels," *Phy. Rev. Lett.*, vol. 78, pp. 5014–5017, 1997.

[2] K. M. Yu, W. Walukiewicz, J. Wu, W. Shan, J. W. Beeman, M. A. Scarpulla, O. D. Dubon, and P. Becla, "Diluted II–VI oxide semiconductors with multiple band gaps," *Phys. Rev. Lett.*, vol. 91, pp. 246403-1–246403-4, 2003.

[3] K. M. Yu, W. Walukiewicz, J. Wu, W. Shan, M. A. Scarpulla, O. D. Dubon, J. W. Beeman, and P. Becla, "Diluted ZnMnTe oxide: a multiband semiconductor for high efficiency solar cells," *Phys. Stat. Sol. B*, vol. 241, pp. 660–663, 2004.

[4] W. Wang, A. S. Lin, and J. D. Phillips, "Intermediate-band photovoltaic solar cell based on ZnTeO," *Appl. Phys. Lett.*, vol. 95, pp. 011103-1–011103-2, 2009.

[5] A. Marti, E. Antolin, C. R. Stanley, C. D. Farmer, N. Lopez, P. Diaz, E. Canovas, P. G. Linares, and A. Luque, "Production of photocurrent due to intermediate-to-conduction-band transitions: A demonstration of a key operating principle of the intermediate-band solar cell," *Phys. Rev. Lett.*, vol. 97, pp. 247701-1–247701-4, 2006.

[6] Y. Okada, T. Morioka, K. Yoshida, R. Oshima, Y. Shoji, T. Inoue, and T. Kita, "Increase in photocurrent by optical transitions via intermediate quantum states in direct-doped InAs/GaNAs strain-compensated quantum dot solar cell," *J. Appl. Phys.*, vol. 109, pp. 024301-1–024301-5, 2011.

[7] N. Lopez, L. A. Reichertz, K. M. Yu, K. Campman, and W. Walukiewicz, "Engineering the electronic band structure for multiband solar cells," *Phys. Rev. Lett.*, vol. 106, pp. 028701-1–028701-4, 2011.

[8] N. Ahsan, N. Miyashita, M. M. Islam, K. M. Yu, W. Walukiewicz, and Y. Okada, "Two-photon excitation in an intermediate band solar cell structure," *Appl. Phys. Lett.*, vol. 100, pp. 172111-1–172111-4, 2012.

[9] W. Shan, W. Walukiewicz, J. W. Ager III, E. E. Haller, J. F. Geisz, D. J. Friedman, J. M. Olson, and S. R. Kurtz, "Band anticrossing in GaInNAs alloys," *Phys. Rev. Lett.*, vol. 82, pp. 1221–1224, 1999.

[10] T. Tanaka, K. Yu, A. Levander, O. Dubon, L. Reichertz, N. Lopez, M. Nishio, and W. Walukiewicz, "Demonstration of ZnTe$_{1−x}$O$_x$ intermediate band solar cell," *Jpn. J. Appl. Phys.*, vol. 50, pp. 082304-1–082304-3, 2011.

[11] T. Tanaka, S. Kusaba, T. Mochinaga, K. Saito, Q. Guo, M. Nishio, K. M. Yu, and W. Walukiewicz, "Molecular beam epitaxial growth and optical properties of highly mismatched ZnTe$_{1−x}$O$_x$ alloys," *Appl. Phys. Lett.*, vol. 100, pp. 011905-1–011905-3, 2012.

[12] T. Tanaka, K. M. Yu, P. R. Stone, J. W. Beeman, O. D. Dubon, L. A. Reichertz, V. M. Kao, M. Nishio, and W. Walukiewicz, "Demonstration of homojunction ZnTe solar cells," *J. Appl. Phys.*, vol. 108, pp. 024502-1–024502-3, 2010.

[13] T. Tanaka, M. Miyabara, K. Saito, Q. Guo, M. Nishio, K. M. Yu, and W. Walukiewicz, "Development of ZnTe-based solar cells," *Mater. Sci. Forum*, vol. 750, pp. 80–83, 2013.

[14] R. Menner, B. Dimmler, R. H. Mauch, and H. W. Schock, "II–VI compound thin films for windows in heterojunction solar cells," *J. Cryst. Growth*, vol. 86, pp. 906–911, 1988.

[15] W. Wang, A. Lin, and J. Phillips, "Electrical characteristics and photoresponse of ZnO/ZnTe heterojunction diodes," *J. Electron. Mater.*, vol. 37, pp. 1044–1048, 2008.

[16] W. Wang, J. Phillips, S. Kim, and X. Pan, "ZnO/ZnSe/ZnTe heterojunctions for ZnTe-based solar cells," *J. Electron. Mater.*, vol. 40, pp. 1674–1678, 2011.

[17] H. Dumont, J. Bouree, A. Marbeuf, and O. Gorochov, "Photo-assisted growth of ZnTe by metalorganic chemical vapour deposition," *J. Cryst. Growth*, vol. 130, pp. 600–610, 1993.

[18] K. Jacobi, G. Zwicker, and A. Gutmann, "Work function, electron affinity and band bending of zinc oxide surfaces," *Sur. Sci.*, vol. 141, pp. 109–125, 1984.

[19] M. Lindner, G. Schotz, P. Link, H. Wagner, W. Kuhn, and W. Gebhardt, "Investigation of the hydrostatic pressure dependence of the E_0 gap, the excitonic binding energy and the refractive index of MOCVD-grown ZnTe layers," *J. Phys.: Condens. Matter*, vol. 4, pp. 6401–6416, 1992.

Tooru Tanaka (M'10) received the B.E., M.E., and Ph.D. degrees in electrical and electronic engineering from the Toyohashi University of Technology, Toyohashi, Japan, in 1995, 1997, and 2000, respectively.

From 1998 to 2000, he was a Research Fellow with the Japan Society for the Promotion of Science. In 2000, he joined the Department of Electrical and Electronic Engineering, Saga University, Saga, Japan, as an Assistant Professor, and then became an Assistant Professor with the Synchrotron Light Application Center, Saga University, in 2003. Since 2009, he has been a member of the faculty with the Department of Electrical and Electronic Engineering, Saga University, where he is currently an Associate Professor. From 2009 to 2010, he was a Visiting Scholar with the Materials Sciences Division, Lawrence Berkeley National Laboratory, Berkeley, CA, USA. Since 2010, he has also been a PRESTO-Researcher, Japan Science and Technology Agency, Japan. His current research interests include molecular beam epitaxial growth of II–VI–O dilute oxides and their applications to next-generation ultrahigh-efficiency photovoltaic devices.

Dr. Tanaka is a member of the Japan Society of Applied Physics, the Institute of Electrical Engineers of Japan (IEEJ), and The Japanese Society for Synchrotron Radiation Research. In 1992, he received the Best Paper Award for Young Researchers from the IEEJ.

Masaki Miyabara received the B.E. degree in electrical and electronic engineering from Saga University, Saga, Japan, in 2012, where he is currently working toward the M.E. degree in electrical and electronic engineering.

His research interest includes the growth and characterization of II–VI semiconductor materials for solar cells.

Mr. Miyabara is a member of the Japan Society of Applied Physics and the Institute of Electrical Engineers of Japan (IEEJ). He received the Best Paper Award for Young Researchers from the IEEJ in 2012.

Yasuhiro Nagao received the B.E. degree in electrical and electronic engineering from Saga University, Saga, Japan, in 2012, where he is currently working toward the M.E. degree in electrical and electronic engineering.

His research interest includes the growth and characterization of II–VI semiconductor materials for solar cells.

Mr. Nagao is a member of the Japan Society of Applied Physics and the Institute of Electrical Engineers of Japan.

Katsuhiko Saito received the B.S. and M.S. degrees in physics from Hirosaki University, Hirosaki, Japan, in 1996 and 1998, respectively, and the Ph.D. degree in engineering from Tohoku University, Sendai, Japan, in 2003.

He then spent five and a half years as a Postdoctoral or Special-Appointment Researcher with Saga University, Saga, Japan. In 2009, he became an Assistant Professor with the Synchrotron Light Application Center, Saga University. His present research interests include epitaxial growth of wideband gap semiconductor materials and micro- and nanostructure fabrication for device applications.

Dr. Saito is a member of the Japan Society of Applied Physics and the Japanese Society for Synchrotron Radiation Research.

Qixin Guo received the B.E., M.E., and Ph.D. degrees in electrical and electronic engineering from the Toyohashi University of Technology, Toyohashi, Japan, in 1990, 1992, and 1996, respectively.

In 1992, he joined the Department of Electrical and Electronic Engineering, Saga University, Saga, Japan, as an Assistant Professor and then became an Associate Professor in 1997 and a Full Professor in 2007. Since 2008, he has also been a Member of the Synchrotron Light Application Center, Saga University, where he is currently the Director. His current research interests include epitaxial growth of compound semiconductors and synchrotron light applications in novel material sciences. He has published more than 250 journal papers and book chapters.

Mitsuhiro Nishio received the B.E., M.E, and Ph.D. degrees in electrical engineering from Nagoya University, Nagoya, Japan, in 1974, 1976, and 1986, respectively.

In 1976, he joined the Department of Electrical and Electronic Engineering, Saga University, Saga, Japan, as an Assistant Professor and then became a Lecturer in 1988 and an Associate Professor in 1990. From 1993 to 1995, he was with the Institute for Molecular Science as an Associate Professor, where he studied epitaxial growth using synchrotron radiation as an excitation light source. He returned to the same department at Saga University, again as an Associate Professor in 1995. He then became a Professor in 1999. His current research interests include metalorganic vapor phase epitaxial growth and device applications of ZnTe-based materials such as ZnTe, ZnMgTe, ZnMgSeTe, and so on.

Dr. Nishio is a member of the Japan Society of Applied Physics, the Institute of Electrical Engineers of Japan, and the Japanese Society for Synchrotron Radiation Research.

Kin Man Yu received the B.S. degree in engineering physics and the Ph.D. degree in materials science and mineral engineering from the University of California, Berkeley, in 1982 and 1987, respectively.

Since 1987, he has been a Staff Scientist and a Principal Investigator with the Materials Sciences Division, Lawrence Berkeley National Laboratory, Berkeley, CA, USA, where he conducts fundamental research on defects in semiconductors. His current research interests include structural, optical, and electronic properties of thin-film semiconductors and transparent conductors; design, synthesis, and characterization of group III nitrides, as well as novel highly mismatched III–V and II–V semiconductor alloys for full spectrum photovoltaic applications. He has published more than 400 journal articles with more than 9000 citations. He has also coauthored nine book chapters and invited reviews.

Dr. Yu, together with Dr. W. Walukiewicz, received the 2006 R&D 100 Award (Editor's choice for most promising technology) for their work on multiband semiconductors for high-efficiency solar cells.

Wladek Walukiewicz received the M.S. degree in physics from Warsaw University, Warsaw, Poland, in 1971 and the Ph.D. degree in solid-state physics from the Institute of Physics, Polish Academy of Sciences, Warsaw, in 1974.

From 1974 to 1982, he was with the Institute of Physics. During that time, he was a frequent visitor to the Massachusetts Institute of Technology, Cambridge, MA, USA, where he conducted studies on electrical and optical properties of compound semiconductors. In 1984, he joined the Lawrence Berkeley National Laboratory, Berkeley, CA, USA, as a Staff Scientist. He currently holds a position of Senior Staff Scientist, Principal Investigator in the Materials Sciences Division, and deputy Program Leader of the Electronics Materials Program. His work covers a broad range of topics in the physics of semiconductors. He has developed models of electronic transport in 3-D and 2-D systems. He has made major contributions to understanding the defect properties of semiconductors. Working with a group of collaborators, he has discovered highly mismatched alloys, which is a new class of semiconductor materials. In his most recent work, he has shown that the band gaps of GaInN alloys perfectly match the solar spectrum, offering a potential material system for high efficiency, multijunction solar cells. He has published more than 400 papers, review articles, and book chapters. He is a co-inventor on several patent applications. Recently, he co-edited a special issue of *Semiconductor Science and Technology* on the properties of group III–N–V alloys.

The Nanometer-Resolution Local Electrical Potential and Resistance Mapping of CdTe Thin Films

C.-S. Jiang, H. R. Moutinho, R. G. Dhere, and M. M. Al-Jassim

Abstract—We have investigated the microelectrical properties of CdTe thin films using scanning Kelvin probe force microscopy (SKPFM) and scanning spreading resistance microscopy (SSRM). Two films with the configurations of substrate and superstrate were subjected to the characterization studies. The electrical potential and resistance were properly mapped with the substrate film but not with the superstrate film because the underlying CdS/CdTe junction largely impacted the characterizations. The higher SKPFM potential on grain boundaries (GBs) of the substrate film than on the grain surface indicates positively charged GBs and upward band bending around the GB; therefore, the GBs are either depleted or inverted. The SSRM resistance mapping on this film shows nonuniformities and features that are associated with the grain structure and facets. However, the GBs do not exhibit distinct characteristic resistance. Comparing the low resistance channel along the GBs of high-performance CIGS films, the SSRM mapping of CdTe supports depletion of the GBs. In SSRM measurement, it is critical to adequately indent the probe to the film, and to apply a bias voltage larger than the onset voltage of the probe/film barrier, so that the contact resistance is minimized and that the local spreading resistance of CdTe film beneath the probe is measured.

Index Terms—CdTe, microelectrical property, scanning kelvin probe force microscopy, scanning spreading resistance, thin-film photovoltaic.

I. INTRODUCTION

CdTe thin-film photovoltaic technology has been significantly advanced in recent years and has reached conversion efficiency of $>18\%$ [1]. The improvements are mainly on short-circuit current J_{sc} [1], [2], due to the improvements of the transparent conductive oxide (TCO) window, and CdS buffer layers, etc. [3]. However, open-circuit voltage V_{oc} of the high-performance cell stays relatively low compared with the CdTe bandgap of 1.45 eV [1]–[3]. It is believed that defects in the CdTe thin film are one of the main reasons worsening minority carrier lifetime ($\tau \sim$ ns [4], [5]) and junction quality, both of which are critical factors for V_{oc} and fill factor (FF) of the device [4]. Therefore, defect physics in CdTe have been actively studied [6]; most characterizations are macroscopic investigations that involve a large amount of point and extended defects [7]. The electrical and optical investigations of nanometer resolution, which aim at resolving individual defects and mapping the defect inhomogeneity [8]–[10], have not been reported as much.

We have previously reported on electrical potential and resistance mapping of high-performance Cu(In,Ga)Se$_2$ (CIGS) thin films [11]–[13] using the atomic force microscopy (AFM)-based electrical techniques of scanning Kelvin probe force microscopy (SKPFM) [14] and scanning spreading resistance microscopy (SSRM) [15]. The results are consistent with inverted carrier polarity around grain boundaries (GBs) of the polycrystalline CIGS material. In this paper, we report the electrical properties of CdTe films using similar approaches. Our results support carrier depletions around the GBs, in contrast to the inversion of CIGS film.

II. EXPERIMENTAL SETUP

Two CdTe films were subjected to the measurements. One was deposited in the superstrate scheme, involving a glass superstrate, a SnO$_2$ TCO coating, a CdS buffer layer, and a CdTe film. The other was deposited with a substrate configuration, involving a glass substrate, an Mo layer, a Cu$_x$Te layer, and a CdTe film [16]. The CdTe films in both samples were deposited by close space sublimation and were postannealed with CdCl$_2$. To avoid artifacts from the rough-film surface morphology, the films were polished using 5 kV Ar$^+$ ion beam with a $\sim<5°$ glancing angle. Both SKPFM and SSRM are based on an AFM of Veeco D5000 and Nanoscope V. The AFM is set in an Ar glove box, which is necessary for avoiding oxidation of the film, because a high indentation force and a relatively large bias voltage between the probe and film were applied in the SSRM measurement. In SKPFM, Pt-coated Si probes were used, and surface potential was measured by the second-harmonic mode [17]. In SSRM, highly doped diamond-coated Si probes were used to mitigate wearing off of the tips under the large indentation force.

III. RESULTS AND DISCUSSIONS

The superstrate configuration is commonly used for high-performance CdTe devices [3]. However, there is an underlying CdS/CdTe junction, which makes an essential impact on the electrical measurement. We first show the results from the substrate film and then discuss the superstrate film.

A. Substrate Film

In an SSRM technique, minimizing the probe-sample contact resistance is critical for measuring the local spreading resistance beneath the probe [15], [18]. Strongly indenting the probe against Si made many nonlocalized orbitals of $sp^3 d^1$ and $sp^3 d^2$ in the local area around the probe/Si interface, leading to

Manuscript received June 7, 2013; revised July 16, 2013; accepted July 31, 2013. Date of publication August 29, 2013; date of current version September 18, 2013. This work was supported by the U.S. Department of Energy under Contract DOE-AC36–08GO28308 with the National Renewable Energy Laboratory.

The authors are with the National Renewable Energy Laboratory, Golden, CO 80401, USA (e mail: chun.sheng.jiang@nrel.gov; helio.moutinho@nrel.gov; ramesh.dhere@nrel.gov; mowafak.aljassim@nrel.gov).

Color versions of one or more of the figures in this paper are available online at http://ieeexplore.ieee.org.

Digital Object Identifier 10.1109/JPHOTOV.2013.2276932

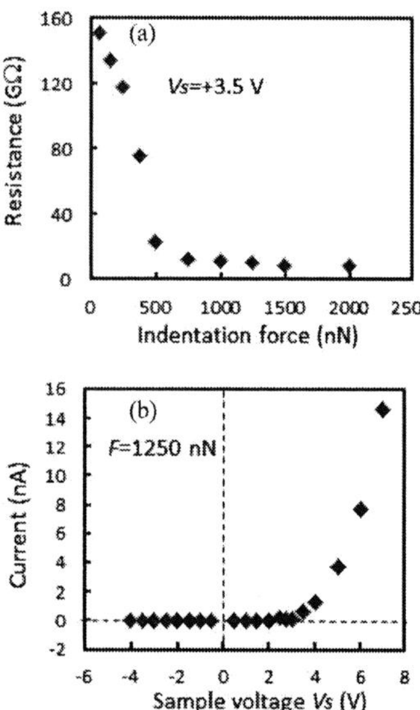

Fig. 1. (a) Change in SSRM resistance with indentation force taken on the substrate film at $Vs = 3.5$ V, (b) I–V characteristic at $F = 1250$ nN.

the minimization of contact resistance [19]. For CdTe, Fig. 1(a) shows a sharp drop in the resistance with increasing indentation force. The resistance value at every data point is an average of 24 lines and 1024 pixels/line. This average gives more reliable data than does positioning the probe at one sample location and sweeping the force [13]. With a force larger than 1000 nN, the contact resistance is minimized. The current–voltage (I–V) curve in Fig. 1(b) shows a significant rectifying characteristic. To minimize the contact resistance, one must apply a sample voltage Vs larger than the onset voltage of $\sim$3.5 V. The back contact resistance of the substrate film is much smaller than the spreading resistance ($\sim$gigaohm). If the probe/film contact resistance is adequately minimized, then the measured overall resistance is dominated by the spreading resistance of the film. The local spreading resistance is dominated by resistivity of the local nanometer-scale volume of the film beneath the probe and an effective contact area of probe/film [15] $R = \rho/4\,r$, with ρ and r being the local resistivity and effective probe radius, respectively.

Fig. 2 shows the images of SKPFM potential, SSRM resistance under a large indentation force of $F = 1250$ nN and a voltage of $V_s = 4$ V, and SSRM under a small $F = 75$ nN and $Vs = 4$ V, taken on the same sample area of the substrate CdTe film. From the potential image of Fig. 2(a), one sees grain structures $\sim$1–5 μm in size. The potential on the GBs is $\sim$100–200 mV larger than on the grain surface, as shown by the potential profile in Fig. 2(e). The AFM surface morphology [see Fig. 2(b)] does not exhibit the grain structure. As discussed previously on CIGS film [11], [12], the higher potential on GBs indicates either a depleted or an inverted GB, and the GB is positively charged. Because surface band bending should make the potential contrast between the GB and grain surface smaller than the contrast in the bulk, it cannot be determined whether the GB is depleted or inverted, solely by the potential measurement [11], [12]. However, if the Fermi level at the GB is

pinned around the middle of bandgap, and the bulk Fermi level is $\sim$0.3 eV above the valance band maximum (estimated from carrier concentration of 10^{14}/cm^3 and effective hole mass of 0.35 m$_0$ [20]), then the surface band bending should be small, in a few hundred millivolt range. Using the measured potential contrast of $\sim$150 mV, and the depletion width of $\sim$0.5 μm, the carrier concentration is estimated: $N_A = 2\varepsilon\varepsilon_0\varphi/qw^2 = 6 \times 10^{14}$/cm^3, where $\varepsilon \sim 10$ [20] is the dielectric constant; $\varepsilon_0 = 8.85 \times 10^{-14}$ F/cm the vacuum dielectric constant; $\varphi \sim 150$ mV the measured potential contrast; $q = 1.6 \times 10^{-19}$ C the elemental charge; and $w \sim 0.5$ μm the measured depletion width.

The SSRM images of Fig. 2(c) and (d) display the resistance in relative logarithm scales, which are brighter with a larger resistance when the $Vs > 0$ and brighter with a smaller resistance when $Vs < 0$. On the scale bars, the middle value [e.g., 4.1×10^9 Ω in Fig. 2(c)] is the average resistance across the image. In order to display the images best, the maximum and minimum values of the scale bars were set much larger than the actual resistance range. From the resistance image taken under a large indentation force [see Fig. 2(c)], the GBs do not exhibit distinct characteristics. Rather than the GBs, the resistance image shows features somehow associated with grains and facets, indicating that the resistance nonuniformity is among the grains and inside a grain. It seems that the most important factor that dominates the resistance map is grain–grain contrast. Therefore, correlating the maps of resistance and grain orientations by using electron backscattering diffraction is expected to get better understanding of the resistance, which is now underway.

The line profile in Fig. 2(f) shows that the nonuniformity is about 1–2 orders of magnitude: $\sim$8 $\times$ 10^8–2 $\times$ 10^{10} Ω. If we use this resistance value, a nominal probe radius of $r = 35$ nm and hole mobility of $\mu = 5$ cm^2/Vs [21] in the polycrystalline thin film, carrier concentration is estimated as $N = 1/e\mu\rho = 1/4e\mu Rr = 1 \times 10^{14}$–$4 \times 10^{12}$/cm^3. This value of carrier concentration can be underestimated by overestimates of effective probe/film contact area (r). On the probe/film contact, not all of the local areas open adequate spreading conductance channels, depending on local strained and dangling bonds under high pressure of the probe. Therefore, the effective r should be smaller than the real probe radius. In addition, the estimate of carrier concentration strongly depends on the mobility value taken, and it is largely scattered in the literature. For these reasons, we believe that the rough resistivity value in orders of magnitude is reliable, but the accurate numbers are not. In fact, the SSRM is a technique for imaging the local resistivity in qualitatively-relative scale with nm spatial resolution, rather than a technique measuring the quantitatively-absolute resistance value.

The resistance map is much different from that of the CIGS films, where a clear low-resistance channel along the GBs was measured (see Fig. 3) [13]. The potential images taken on CdTe and CIGS both show higher GB potential than the grain surface, and the GBs should be either depleted or inverted. The higher conductance on GBs of CIGS is consistent with an inversion region of 30–100 nm around the GBs. However, we have not measured a clear characteristic resistance on the GBs of CdTe. This difference of resistance at the GBs supports the argument that the GBs of CdTe are depleted and that there are charged deep levels at the GBs. Early works that are based on the

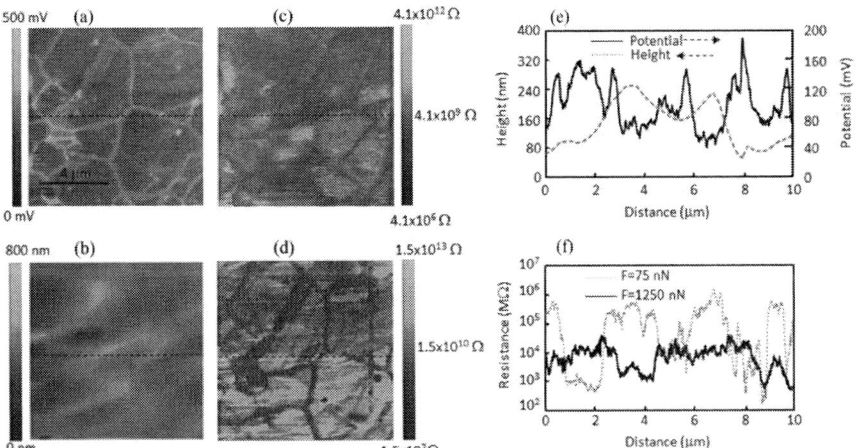

Fig. 2.   Images of (a) SKPFM potential, (b) the corresponding AFM, (c) SSRM resistance under an large $F = 1250$ nN, and (d) SSRM under a small $F = 75$ nN, taken on the same sample area of the substrate CdTe film. (e) and (f) show line profiles along the lines in (a), (b) and (c), (d), respectively.

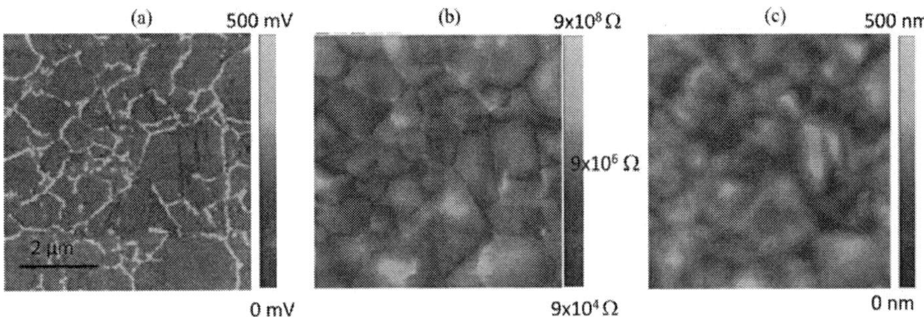

Fig. 3.   (a) SKPFM potential and (b) SSRM resistance images taken on the same sample area of NREL's high-performance CIGS film. (c) Corresponding AFM image.

various characterization tools have proposed different models that carriers around the GBs are either depleted [7], [10] or accumulated [8]. However, our resistance map does not exhibit a larger resistance at the GBs than in the grain interior. A large electrical field should concentrate in a small region beneath the probe with a large positive Vs applied. This field can attract holes and compensate the hole depletion so that no hole depletion was measured. In our substrate film, the carrier concentration could be low and, accordingly, the carrier depletion. If the carrier concentration in the grain bulk increases, the hole attraction beneath the probe may not fully compensate the hole depletion. In this case, we expect to image a higher resistance at the GBs than in the grain interior.

With a small indentation force $F = 75$ nN and $Vs = +4$ V, the measured overall resistance significantly increased [see Fig. 2(d)]. Comparing the resistance and potential images, GBs can be clearly identified in the resistance image, with smaller resistance on the GB than on the grain surface. Because both the overall resistance and the nonuniformity increased significantly under the small indentation force, we believe that the measured resistance is dominated by the probe/film contact resistance but not by the spreading resistance of the film.

When a reverse bias to the probe/film barrier $Vs < 0$ is applied, even under the large $F = 1250$ nN, the overall re-

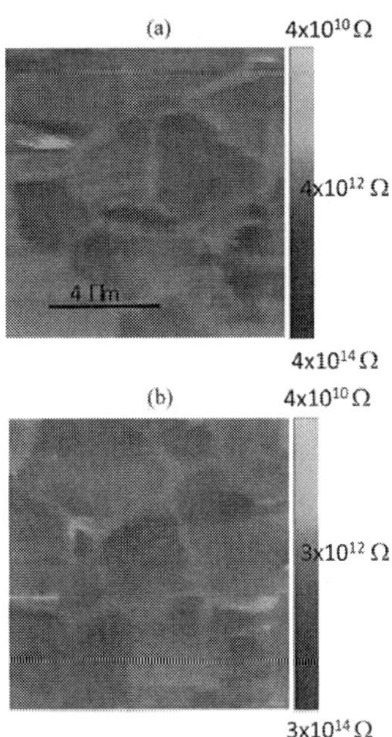

Fig. 4.   (a) and (b) SSRM images taken with negative sample voltages of $Vs = -2$ V and -4 V, respectively.

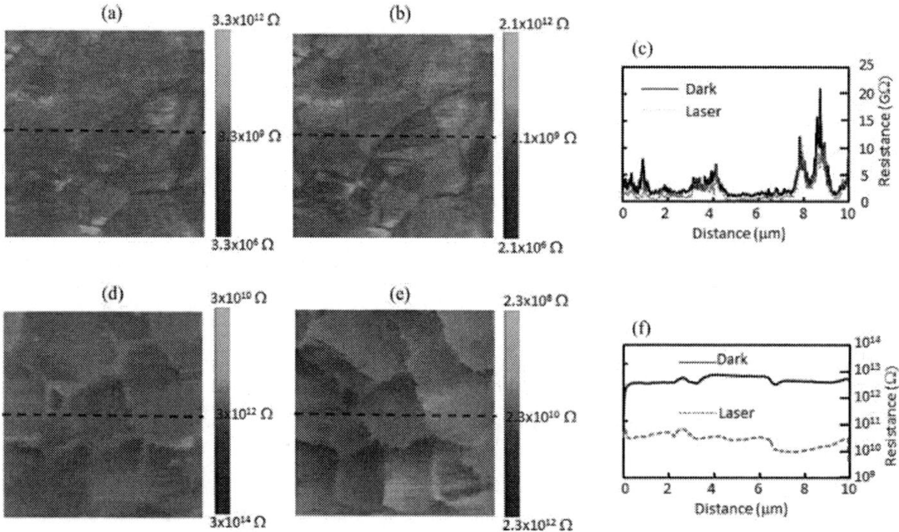

Fig. 5. SSRM images taken with (a), (b) $Vs = 4$ V and (d), (e) $Vs = -4$ V, (a), (d) in the dark and (b), (e) with AFM laser-on, respectively. (c) and (f) show line profiles in (a), (b) and (d), (e), respectively.

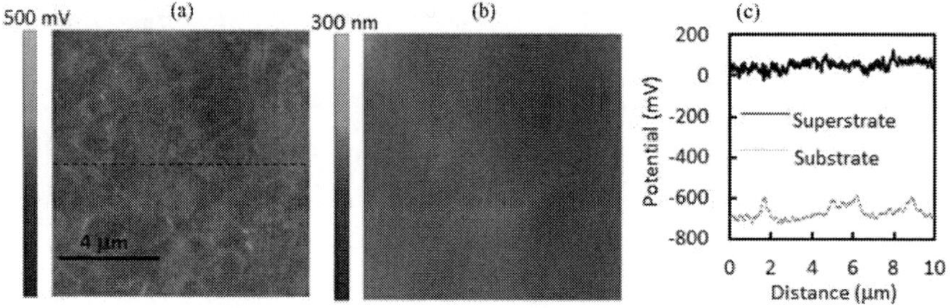

Fig. 6. (a) SKPFM potential and (b) the corresponding AFM images taken on a superstrate CdTe film. (c) Potential profile along the line in (a) and a profile taken on the substrate film using the same probe.

sistance increases by $\sim$3 orders of magnitude (see Fig. 4). Although the absolute resistance value increases, the relative resistance on the GB is smaller than on the grain surface, which is consistent with the case of small F and large forward Vs [Fig. 2(d)]. The resistances under the small F large Vs and large F negative Vs should both be dominated by the probe/film contact. The smaller resistance on the GBs than on the grain surface could originate from a smaller probe/film barrier height at the GBs if the Fermi level at the GB is pinned at a higher energy location in the bandgap than on the grain surface, or in other words, the work function is smaller at the GB than on the grain surface, which is consistent with the higher GB potential in the potential measurement.

In all the data shown above, we turned OFF the AFM laser using "dark lift" mode so that resistance was not affected by the laser. Simultaneously, we got the resistance mapping with laser ON in the same sample area, as shown in Fig. 5. Under a Vs larger than the onset voltage, the resistance with laser on decreased a portion of the resistance; the average value decreased from 3.3×10^9 to 2.1×10^9 Ω. The corresponding conductivity increased by $\Delta C = 1/\rho_l - 1/\rho_d = 1 \times 10^{-5}$ $(\Omega \cdot cm)^{-1}$ with

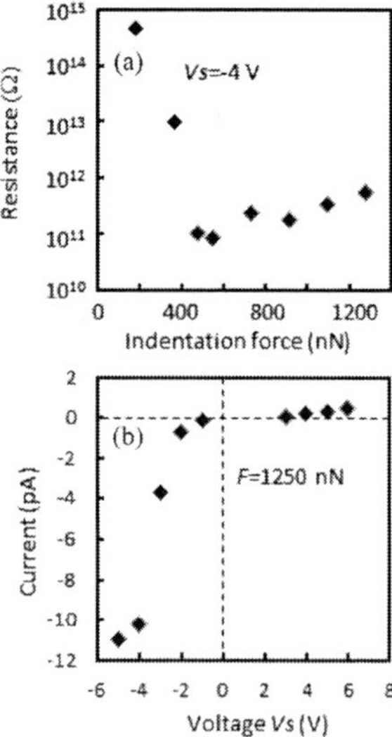

Fig. 7. (a) Change in SSRM resistance with indentation force at $Vs = -4$ V and (b) I–V characteristic at $F = 1250$ nN, taken on the superstrate film.

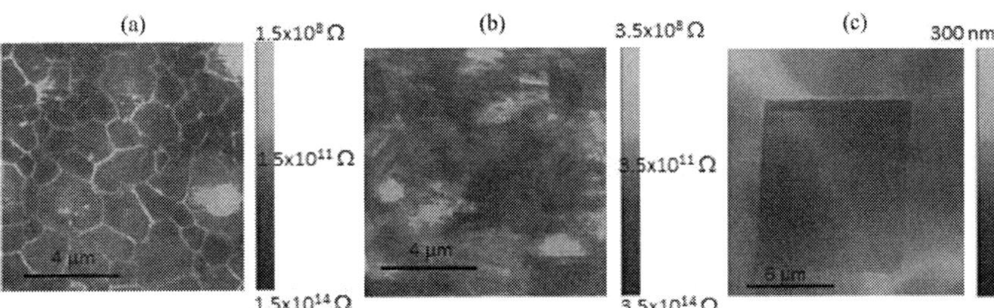

Fig. 8.   (a) and (b) SSRM images taken with $F = 500$ and 1250 nN, respectively; both were with a sample voltage $Vs = -4$ V. (c) AFM image taken in a larger area with a small F $= 50$ nN after Fig. 8(b) was taken.

ρ_l and ρ_d being light and dark resistivity. The conductivity increase or the photoconductivity is about the half of the dark conductivity ($C_d \sim 2 \times 10^{-5}$ 1/Ω·cm). The cantilever of the diamond-coated probe (BrukerNano, DDESP, Width ~ 30 μm) blocked a significant portion of the AFM laser, and the probe apex is shadowed by the cantilever. However, light scattering and carrier diffusion could make the photoconductivity comparable to the dark conductivity of the CdTe material.

With a reverse bias $Vs = -4$ V, the large resistance of 3×10^{12} Ω in the dark decreased largely by two orders of magnitude to 2.3×10^{10} Ω by turning ON the laser. This change of resistance corresponds to a photoconductivity of $\Delta C = 3 \times 10^{-6}$ 1/Ω·cm, which is consistent with the photoconductivity when Vs is $+4$ V ($\Delta C = 1 \times 10^{-5}$ 1/Ω·cm). The reverse Vs is favorable for photo-carrier collection; a considerable portion of the carrier is expected to be collected, dominating the measured resistance under light. The consistency of photoconductivity under opposite bias polarities of $Vs = +4$ and -4 V supports the inference that the measured resistance under an adequate indentation force and a large bias voltage is dominated by the local spreading resistance beneath the probe/film interface.

B. Superstrate Film

In the superstrate configuration, there is an underlying CdS/CdTe junction several micrometer away from the probe/film interface. Both the potential and resistance imaging are largely affected by the existence of the junction. Fig. 6 shows the potential image, exhibiting unclear features like the GBs with much smaller grain sizes than the substrate film. Because SKPFM uses cantilever oscillation for detecting Coulomb force between the probe and sample [14], we cannot turn OFF the AFM laser in the SKPFM measurement. This laser illumination induced a significant photovoltage, as shown in Fig. 6(c), where the potential of the superstrate film is ~ 700 mV higher than the substrate film, which is consistent with V_{oc} of the CdTe device. The different approaches of the same probe to a sample may measure a 100 or 200 mV difference of the surface potential, but should not make a difference as large as 700 mV. This large photovoltage can reduce the potential contrast because the photovoltage on the GBs could be smaller than on grain surface, especially when the GB is active for minority carrier recombination.

The SSRM results (see Fig. 7) are much different from the substrate film. The minimum resistance is two orders of magnitude larger than the substrate film, and the appropriate mea-

surement parameters are a large indentation force and a large negative Vs. In the superstrate configuration, there are two barriers of CdS/CdTe and probe/film in opposite polarities. The direction of rectifying I–V in Fig. 7(b) shows that the dominant barrier is the CdS/CdTe junction, because the quality of the junction should be better than the probe/film barrier. The SSRM image under a negative Vs, which is a forward bias to the CdS/CdTe junction and a reverse bias to the probe/film barrier, shows a clear resistance contrast, with the GB resistance being smaller than on the grain surface [see Fig. 8(a)]. This resistance contrast is consistent with that of the substrate film under similar measurement parameters (see Fig. 4). The image shows smaller grain sizes than the substrate film, which is consistent with electron backscattering diffraction measurement and is induced by oxygen inclusion in the film [22]. However, under a large indentation force the GB resistance contrast was no longer measured [see Fig. 8(b)]. Fig. 8(c) exhibits that the film material was significantly removed by the scan with the large indentation force (the dark square).

IV. SUMMARY

We have investigated the microelectrical properties of CdTe thin films, aiming at understanding the defect physics of the material, using the AFM-based nanometer -resolution electrical techniques of SKPFM and SSRM. The surface potential mapping shows higher potential on the GBs than on the grain surface, demonstrating positively charged GBs; therefore, the GBs are either depleted or inverted. The local spreading resistance mapping shows nonuniformity and features that are associated with grain structure and facets of the polycrystalline material. Comparing the low resistance channel along GBs of CIGS film, the resistance mapping of CdTe indicates that the GB is not inverted, differing from CIGS. To minimize the probe/film contact resistance so that the spreading resistance beneath the probe is measured, the probe should be adequately indented to the film and a forward bias larger than the onset voltage of the probe/film barrier should be applied. This measurement of spreading resistance was verified by examining the resistance data with and without the AFM laser illumination. The surface potential and spreading resistance of the CdTe film were properly mapped in the substrate film. With the superstrate configuration, however, proper characterization of the film electrical property was prohibited by the underlying CdS/CdTe junction.

REFERENCES

[1] M. A. Green, K. Emery, Y. Hishikawa, W. Warta, and E. D. Dunlop,, "Solar cell efficiency tables (version 41)," *Prog. Photovoltaic: Res. Appl.*, vol. 21, no. 1, pp. 1–11, 2013.

[2] M. A. Green, K. Emery, Y. Hishikawa, W. Warta, and E. D. Dunlop,, "Solar cell efficiency tables (version 39)," *Prog. Photovoltaic: Res. Appl.*, vol. 20, no. 12, pp. 12–20, 2012.

[3] X. Wu, J. C. Keane, R. G. Dhere, C. DeHart, A. Duda, T. A. Gessert, S. Asher, D. H. Levi, and P. Sheldon,, "16.5%-efficient CdS/CdTe polycrystalline thin-film solar cell," in *Proc. 17th Eur. Photovoltaic Sol. Energy Conf.*, Munich, Gemanay, Oct. 11–26, 2001, pp. 995–1000.

[4] W. K. Metzger, D. Albin, D. Levi, P. Sheldon, and R. K. Ahrenkiel,, "Time-resolved photoluminescence studies of CdTe solar cells," *J. Appl. Phys.*, vol. 94, pp. 3549–3555, 2003.

[5] D. Kuciauskas, A. Kanevce, J. N. Duenow, P. Dippo, M. Young, J. V. Li, D. H. Levi, and T. A. Gessert,, "Spectrally and time resolved photoluminescence analysis of the CdS/CdTe interface in thin-film photovoltaic solar cells," *Appl. Phys. Lett.*, vol. 102, pp. 173902-1–173902-5, 2013.

[6] For a review, R. Triboulet, and P. Siffert,, *CdTe and related compounds: Physics, Defects, Hetero- and Nanostructures, rystal Growth, Surface and Applications*. Amsterdam, The Netherlands: Elsevier, 2010, ch. V.

[7] L. M. Woods, D. H. Levi, V. Kaydanov, G. Y. Robinson, and R. K. Ahrenkiel,, "Electrical characterization of etched grain-boundary properties from as-processed px-CdTe-based solar cells," in *Proc. Amer. Inst. Phys. Conf.*, 1999, vol. 462, pp. 499–504.

[8] S. A. Galloway, P. R. Edwards, and K. Durose,, "Characterization of thin film CdS/CdTe solar cells using electron and optical beam induced current," *Sol. Energy Mater. Solar Cells*, vol. 57, no. 61, pp. 61–74, 1999.

[9] M. J. Romero, D. S. Albin, M. M. Al-Jassim, X. Wu, H. R. Moutinho, and R. D. Dhere,, "Carrier diffusion and radiative recombination in CdTe thin films," *Appl. Phys. Lett.*, vol. 81, pp. 3161–3163, 2002.

[10] I. Visoly-Fisher, S. R. Cohen, and D. Cahen,, "Direct evidence for grain-boundary depletion in polycrystalline CdTe from nanoscale-resolved measurements," *Appl. Phys. Lett.*, vol. 82, pp. 556–558, 2003.

[11] C.-S. Jiang, R. Noufi, J. A. AbuShama, K. Ramanathan, H. R. Moutinho, J. Pankow, and M. M. Al-Jassim,, "Local built-in potential on grain boundary of Cu(In,Ga)Se2 thin films," *Appl. Phys. Lett.*, vol. 84, pp. 3477–3479, 2004.

[12] C.-S. Jiang, M. A. Contreras, I. Repins, H. R. Moutinho, Y.. Yan, M. J. Romero, L. M. Mansfield, R. Noufi, and M. M. Al-Jassim,, "How grain boundaries in Cu(In,Ga)Se2 thin films are charged: Revisit," *Appl. Phys. Lett.*, vol. 101, pp. 033903-1–033903-4, 2012.

[13] C.-S. Jiang, I. L. Repins, L. M. Mansfield, M. A. Conteras, H. R. Moutinho, K. Ramanathan, R. Noufi, and M. M. Al-Jassim,, "Electrical conduction channel along the grain boundaries of Cu(In,Ga)Se2 thin films," *Appl. Phys. Lett.*, vol. 102, pp. 253905-1–253905-5, 2013.

[14] M. Nonnenmacher, M. P. O'Boyle, and H. K. Wickramasinghe,, "Kelvin probe force microscopy," *Appl. Phys. Lett.*, vol. 58, pp. 2921–2923, 1991.

[15] P. Eyben, S. Denis, T. Clarysse, and W. Vandervorst,, "Progress towards a physical contact model for scanning spreading resistance microscopy," *Mater. Sci. Eng. B*, vol. 102, pp. 132–137, 2003.

[16] R. G. Dhere, J. N. Duenow, C. M. DeHart, J. V. Li, D. Kuciauskas, and T. A. Gessert, "Development of substrate structure CdTe photovoltaic devices with performance exceeding 10%," presented at IEEE 38th Photovoltaic Specialist Conf., Austin, TX, USA, Jun. 3–8, 2012.

[17] A. Kikukawa, S. Hosaka, and R. Imura,, "Silicon pn junction imaging and characterizations using sensitivity enhanced Kelvin probe force microscopy," *Appl. Phys. Lett.*, vol. 66, pp. 3510–3512, 1995.

[18] L. Zhang, K. Ohuchi, K. Adachi, K. Ishimaru, M. Takayanagi, and A. Nishiyama,, "High-resolution characterization of ultrashallow junctions by measuring in vacuum with scanning spreading resistance microscopy," *Appl. Phys. Lett.*, vol. 90, pp. 192103-1–192103-3, 2007.

[19] P. Eyben, F. Clemente, K. Vanstreels, G. Pourtois, T. Clarysse, E. Duriau, T. Hantschel, K. Sankaran, J. Mody, W. Vandervorst, K. Mylvaganam, and L. Zhang,, "Analysis and modeling of the high vacuum scanning spreading resistance microscopy nanocontact on silicon," *J. Vac. Sci. Technol. B*, vol. 28, pp. 401–406, 2010.

[20] B. E. McCandless and J. R. Site, in *Handbook of Photovoltaic Science and Engineering*, A Luque and S Hegedus, Eds., 2nd ed. Chichester, West Sussex, U.K.: Wiley, 2011, ch. 14.

[21] A. S. Gilmore, V. Kaydanov, T. R. Ohno, D. Grecu, and D. Rose,, "Impedance spectroscopy and Hall measurements on CdTe thin film polycrystalline films," in *Proc. Mat. Res. Soc. Symp.*, vol. 668, 2001, pp. H5.10.1–H5.10.6.

[22] D. H. Rose, F. S. Hasoon, R. G. Dhere, D. S. Albin, R. M. Ribelin, X. Li, Y. Mahathongdy, T. A. Gessert, and P. Sheldon,, "Fabrication procedures and progress sensitivities for CdS/CdTe solar cells," *Prog. In Phtovoltaic: Res. Appl.*, vol. 7, pp. 331–340, 1999.

Authors' photographs and biographies not available at the time of publication.

Direct Semiconductor Bonded 5J Cell for Space and Terrestrial Applications

P. T. Chiu, D. C. Law, R. L. Woo, S. B. Singer, D. Bhusari, W. D. Hong, A. Zakaria,
J. Boisvert, S. Mesropian, R. R. King, and N. H. Karam

Abstract—Spectrolab has demonstrated a 2.2/1.7/1.4/1.05/
0.73 eV 5J cell with an efficiency of 37.8% under 1 sun AM1.5G
spectrum and 35.1% efficiency for 1 sun AM0. The top three junctions and bottom two junctions were grown on GaAs and InP
substrates, respectively, by metal organic vapor phase epitaxy. The
GaAs- and InP-based cells were then direct bonded to create a low-
resistance, high-transmissive interface. Both the space and terrestrial cells have high 1 sun V_{oc} between 4.75 and 4.78 V. Initial tests
of the terrestrial cells at concentration are promising with efficiencies increasing up to $10\times$ concentration to a maximum value close
to 41%.

Index Terms—Direct wafer bonding, multijunction cells.

I. Introduction

THE most widely adopted cell for use in space and terrestrial applications is a three junction (3J) design, where
1.9- and 1.4-eV cells are grown lattice-matched to a 0.67-eV
Ge cell. Cell efficiencies for the upright Ge 3J cell have reached
a maximum efficiency of near 30% for space and 41.6% for
terrestrial [1]. While cell designs with 4–6 junctions present
tantalizing opportunities for higher efficiencies, all such designs require near 1-eV bandgap materials. Three monolithic
4–6 junction approaches that incorporate a 1-eV junction include
cells with InGaAsNSb, inverted metamorphic (IMM) cells, and
direct bonded cells. InGaAsN cells have historically suffered
from poor minority carrier lifetimes [2]. Although recent work
suggests that growth using molecular beam epitaxy (MBE) can
improve material quality [3], MBE growth suffers from high
cost and low growth rates. The IMM cells incorporating lattice
mismatched InGaAs have been pursued, but growth of mismatched InGaAs results in degraded cell quality, even with the
use of thick grading layers [4].

An alternative approach is to grow infrared and visible
bandgap cells on InP and GaAs, respectively. The main benefit of this approach is that several high-quality 0.73–1.4-eV
alloys exist that are lattice matched to InP. The InP and GaAs
cells can be bonded directly using a proprietary process at a
relatively low temperature. The resulting bonded cell is termed
a semiconductor bonded technology (SBT) cell that has been

demonstrated previously as a two- or four-junction cell [5], [6].
In this paper, we have implemented a 2.2/1.7/1.4/1.05/0.73 eV 5
junction (5J) SBT cell. The top three junctions (T3J) are grown
on GaAs and the bottom two junctions (B2J) on InP. The resulting SBT cells have achieved a 35.1% efficiency in AM0 and
have been verified by the National Renewable Energy Laboratory, Golden, CO, USA (NREL) for terrestrial $1\times$ AM1.5G
of 37.8%. Initial concentration measurements indicate that the
technology is also promising for concentrator applications.

II. Experimental Setup

All III–V epitaxial layers were grown on a Veeco K475
MOVPE system. The top three subcells with bandgaps of
2.2/1.7/1.4 eV were grown inverted on GaAs substrates. The bottom two subcells with bandgaps of 1.05/0.73 eV were grown upright on InP substrates. The component wafers were chemical-
mechanical polished to a surface roughness of less than 0.5 nm.
The direct bonding was completed in a Karl Suss wafer bon-
der. The bonding parameters such as temperature, pressure, and
bonding time were carefully optimized to achieve high mechanical strength and low electrical resistance across the bonded
interface. Infrared transmission imaging was used to determine
the uniformity and quality of the bonded interface. Following
the direct bond, the GaAs wafer was substrate removed to yield
a 5J stack ready for processing. The bonded pairs were full processed into 4 cm^2 cells for space. For terrestrial, the cells were
processed into 1 cm^2 cells with grid pitches optimized for both
1 sun and 10 suns. The cells were characterized at Spectrolab by
illuminated current–voltage measurements (LIV) and quantum
efficiency spectroscopy. For terrestrial cells, LIV measurements
were confirmed by the NREL using the OSMSS simulator system. Details of the OSMSS simulator system and the associated
testing methodology have been described previously [5].

III. Results and Discussion

A. Bonding Process Improvements

Significant progress has been made in direct bonding process at Spectrolab. Following a thorough optimization of bond
parameters including bonding time, temperature, and applied
pressure, bonding yields have improved dramatically. We have
achieved 50 consecutive 100-mm GaAs epitaxy to 100-mm InP
epitaxy bonds without mechanical breakage, demonstrating the
stability and reliability of the process.

Although optimization of bond time, temperature, and pressure greatly enhances mechanical yield, there *was* a persistent
high density ($\sim$7 per wafer) of large voids (defined as a void

Manuscript received July 2, 2013; revised August 6, 2013; accepted August 7,
2013. Date of publication September 11, 2013; date of current version December
16, 2013. This work was supported by the U.S. government for conducting space
cell work and the Spectrolab internal research and development for conducting
terrestrial work.

The authors are with the Spectrolab Inc., Sylmar, CA, 91342, USA (e-mail:
philip.t.chiu@boeing.com).

Color versions of one or more of the figures in this paper are available online
at http://ieeexplore.ieee.org.

Digital Object Identifier 10.1109/JPHOTOV.2013.2279336

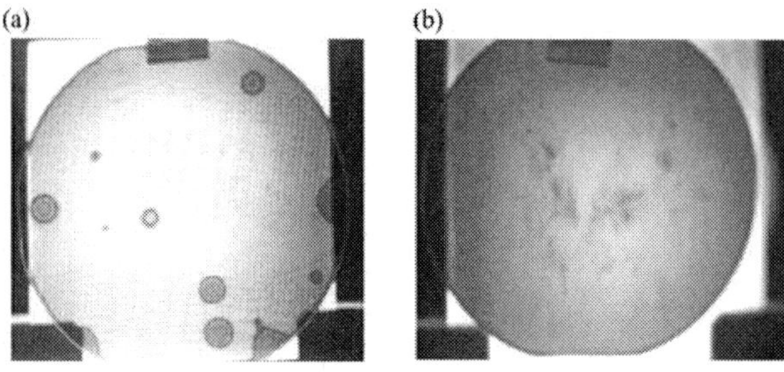

Fig. 1. Infrared bonding images of 100-mm GaAs epitaxy to 100-mm InP epitaxy (a) before and (b) after improvements to reduce particle contamination.

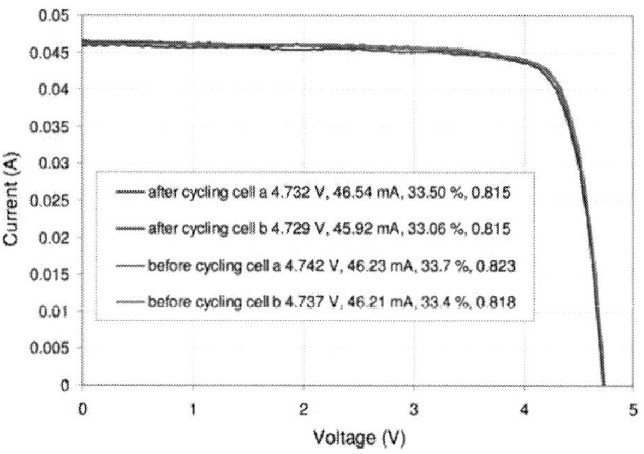

Fig. 2. *LIV* curves of two 4-cm^2 cells before and after five abrupt thermal cycles between 77 and 423 K.

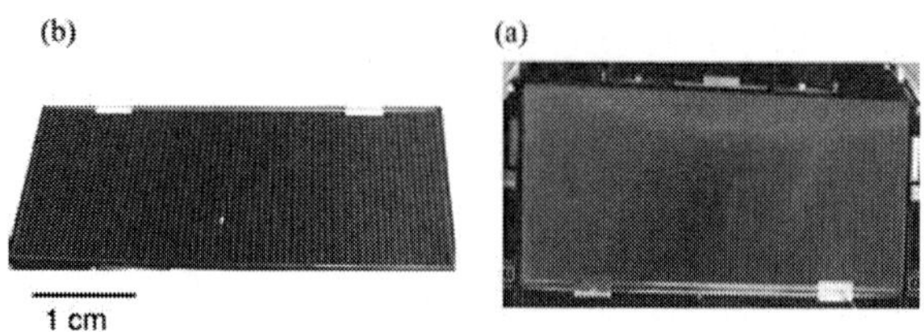

Fig. 3. (a) Picture and (b) unfiltered FBIR image of a bonded SBT 5J wafer optimized for space applications. Wafer contains 20-cm^2 and 1-cm^2 test cells on the perimeter.

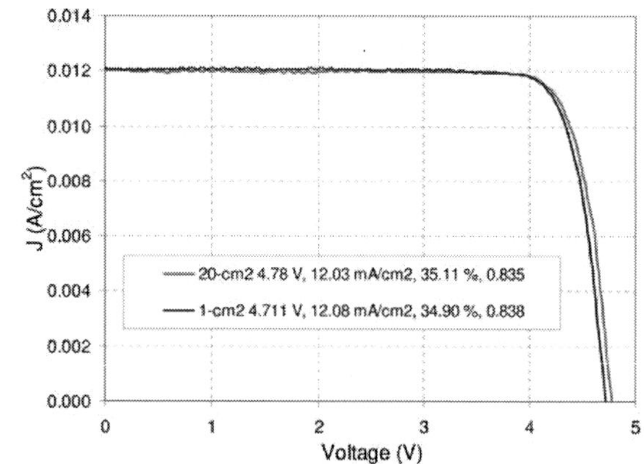

Fig. 4. Illuminated *I–V* curves 1-cm^2 cells and >20-cm^2 cells for the 5J wafer shown in Fig. 3(a). The large area cell measures at 35.1% space at 1 sun AM0 spectrum (1366 W/m^2) and 28 °C. The simulator was calibrated using SBT 5J Learjet standards.

with a diameter greater than 1 mm). Large voids have a pronounced effect on the performance of direct bonded cells. The voids tend to burst during processing, which result in reduced current, and/or shunts through the top three junctions in stack. Based upon previous research of direct bonds, we attribute large void formation to particle contaminants with diameters on the order of a 1 μm [7]. Consequently, we have improved wafer handling and cleaning prior to the bonds to reduce the probability of particle contamination. The result is a decrease in the average large void density from 7 to 2 per 100-mm wafer. Infrared bonding images that demonstrate the improvement of large void density are shown in Fig. 1. We anticipate that further upgrades in the prebonding process will reduce the large void density to 0. This is the large void density achieved in the SOI industry for 300-mm wafer direct bonds [8].

The mechanical strength of the direct bond with the updated and improved bonding process has been verified by thermal cycling tests. Several 4-cm^2 cells were cycled five times in liquid nitrogen (77 K) for 1 min and a 423-K hot plate for 1 min. The cells exhibited no signs of delamination. Moreover, as shown in Fig. 2, the *LIV* of the cells before and after thermal cycling is identical to within measurement error.

1) Space Cell Results: Because of the improvements in the bonding process that increased mechanical yield and reduced large void density, Spectrolab was able to produce multiple 20-cm^2 SBT5J cells with excellent performance under AM0 space irradiance. Large area cells are required for currently used 1 sun space arrays. A picture of one such 5J wafer is shown in Fig. 3(a). The 5J wafer contains two large 20-cm^2 cells in the middle of the wafer and eight 1-cm^2 test cells on the perimeter. The bond exhibits a single large void that reduces the performance of the top large area cell. The rest of the wafer is void free, including the bottom large area cell. The corresponding unfiltered forward bias electroluminescence (FBIR) image of the bottom large area cell is shown in Fig. 3(b). As evident from Fig. 3(b), there is no evidence of debonded areas or other defects in the FBIR image.

The *LIV* results for the cells in Fig. 3(b) are shown in Fig. 4. The *LIV* was measured using SBT 5J Learjet standards to calibrate the simulator. The spectral mismatch factors using the new standards are limited to 1% or less for each of the five junctions. The J_{sc}, V_{oc}, and FF of the best large cell is 12.0 mA/cm^2, 4.78 V, and 83.5%, respectively. This results in an AM0 efficiency of 35.1%. The efficiency of the large area cell is actually 0.2% absolute higher than the 1-cm^2 cells on the same wafer. The difference in efficiency is a direct result of a 70-mV increase in V_{oc} going from 1 to 20-cm^2 cell. We tentatively attribute the increase in V_{oc} to a reduction in perimeter recombination for the larger area cell [9]. In general, the high V_{oc} of both the large and small area 5J cells is a demonstration of the high quality lattice matched components grown on GaAs and InP substrates. Previous data collected on cell fabricated from GaAs T3J and

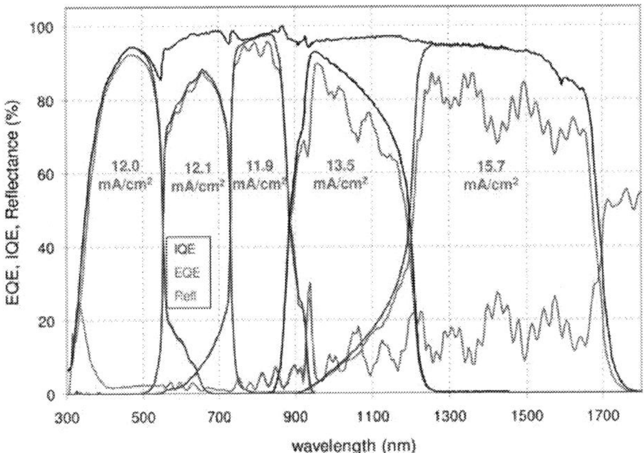

Fig. 5. EQE, IQE, and reflectance curves for space SBT 5J cell. EQE, IQE, and reflectance are given by the red, blue, and green curves, respectively. IQE CUM is given by the black curve. Integrated EQE values after busbar correction are shown in the red numbers.

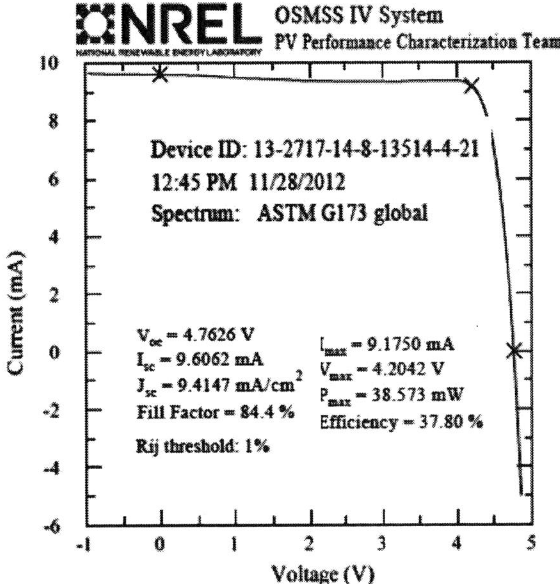

Fig. 6. *LIV* curve for 37.8% terrestrial 5J SBT cell. Cell was measured at 1 sun under AM1.5G spectrum and 25 °C by the NREL.

InP B2J wafers in the same epitaxial runs had V_{oc} of 3.68 and 1.08 V, respectively. In particular, we note that the average voltage bandgap offset of the B2J is 0.335V, attesting to the high quality of the B2J grown on InP. The near ideal agreement 5J cell voltage with that of the GaAs and InP components indicates little to no loss in cell quality due to the direct bonding process.

The quantum efficiency curves for the 5J space cell are shown in Fig. 5. The integrated external quantum efficiency (EQE) currents (after accounting for busbar loss) are also given in red in Fig. 5. The limiting cell from EQE is C3 at 11.9 mA/cm^2. This EQE current agrees within 1% of the measured J_{sc} of 12.0 mA/cm^2. The excellent agreement between the EQE and simulator currents provides further confidence in the accuracy of the 35.1% efficiency value.

B. Terrestrial Cell Results

SBT5J terrestrial cells were based upon the space structure discussed in the previous section because the bulk of the development such cells was for space applications. Small adjustments to the bandgap and thickness were required to improve the current matching in an AM1.5G spectrum. The *LIV* results for the 1.02-cm^2 SBT 5J cells optimized for 1 sun AM1.5G performance are in Fig. 6. The *LIV* measurements were performed by the NREL on the new OSMSS simulator. As evident in Fig. 6, the cell has a V_{oc} of 4.76 V. Similar to the space 5J cells, the V_{oc} of the 5J closely matches the sum of the GaAs and InP components. The J_{sc} of the cell is 9.4 mA/cm^2. The limiting junction from the EQE curves in Fig. 7 is C1 at 9.6 mA/cm^2. Therefore, the J_{sr} (defined as the limiting current density as measured by EQE) and J_{sc} (measured by the NREL) agree reasonably to within 2%. The fill factor of 84.4% is limited by a nonlinearity in between 0.5–3.5 V. The nonlinearity is attributed to current matching between the cells with two lowest integrated EQE: C1 and C2. The difference in current between C1 and C2 is 0.3 mA/cm^2. We note that the current matching between C1 and C2 could only cause a characteristic nonlinearity in the

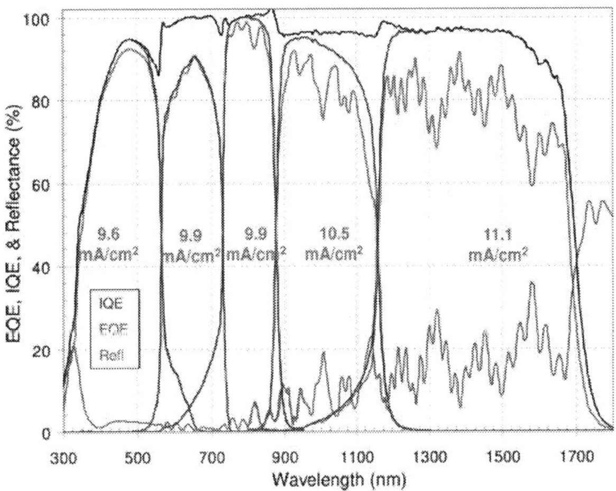

Fig. 7. EQE, IQE, and reflectance curves for terrestrial SBT 5J cell. EQE, IQE, and reflectance are given by the red, blue, and green curves, respectively. IQE CUM is given by the black curve. Integrated EQE values after busbar correction are shown in the red numbers.

I–V curve if limiting junction C1 also had poor reverse bias breakdown.

While the $1\times$ AM1.5G efficiency of 37.8% is encouraging, the SBT 5J cell has opportunities for improvements in cell efficiency that are evident from the QE curves. Fig. 7 plots the internal quantum efficiency (IQE) cumulative (CUM) in black. The CUM is 95% for C1, nearly 100% for C2 and C3, and ~97% for C4 and C5. The 3% loss in CUM in C4 and C5 is not due to an issue with cell quality but rather transmission losses through the bond interface. However, the peak IQE of C1 could be enhanced, which results in a direct increase in J_{sc}

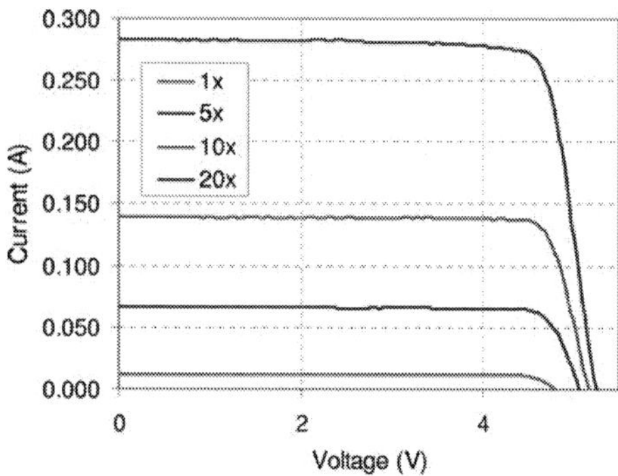

Fig. 8. *LIV* curves measured at concentrations between 1× and 20× for a 1.328-cm² SBT 5J cell optimized for low concentration.

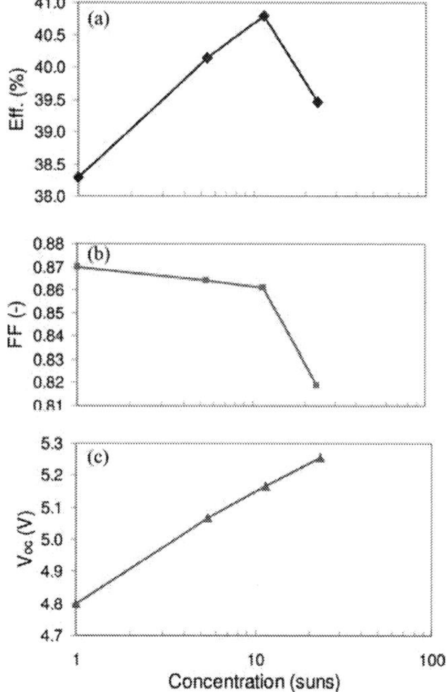

Fig. 9. (a) Efficiency, (b) FF, and (c) V_{oc} as a function of concentration for the terrestrial SBT5J cell.

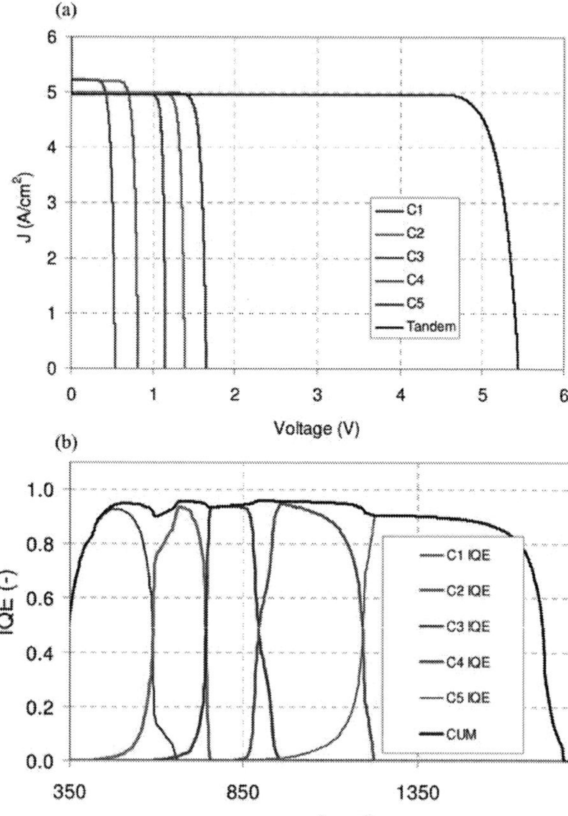

Fig. 10. Modeled (a) *I–V* and (b) IQE curves of an SBT5J cell optimized for 500× AM1.5D.

(as C1 is limiting). Moreover, an increase in C1 current would reduce current imbalance between C1 and C2, which results in an increase in FF.

The *LIV* curves for a 1.328-cm² SBT 5J cell optimized for 10× concentration were measured at Spectrolab. The *LIV* curves at 1×, 5×, 10×, and 20× are shown in Fig. 8. Plots of the efficiency, FF, and V_{oc} as a function of concentration are given in Fig. 9. Although the cell was measured internally at Spectrolab, the internal efficiency of 38.2% agrees reasonably well with that measured by the NREL for a similar cell. As shown in Fig. 9(a), the efficiency increases from 1× to 10× to a maximum of 40.7% at only 10× concentration. The efficiency decreases from 10× to 20× due to a drop in FF [see Fig. 9(b)] or specific resistance. Using the multiple light intensities method [10], the

specific resistance of the cell is 2 $\Omega \cdot cm^2$. Grid, top layer, and contact resistance contributions to the specific resistance should only be of the order of 0.56 $\Omega \cdot cm^2$. The difference in specific resistance is presumably in the tunnel junctions or at the bond interface that were developed and optimized for only 1 sun space applications. In particular, further studies regarding bond resistance with respect to the identity and doping of the bonding layers, chemical pretreatment, and substrate miscut would be required to optimize the bond resistance.

As expected, the V_{oc} is linear with respect to the log concentration as in Fig. 9(c). The slope of this plot is related to the ideality factor of the cell. According to the V_{oc} versus concentration dependence, the ideality factor is 5.6. This is reasonably close to the predicted value for five ideal diodes in series and is a further indication of the high quality of the junctions in the 5J SBT cell.

Next, we model the performance of the SBT 5J cell at 500×, assuming that the specific resistance of the tunnel junctions and bond interface could be reduced to a negligible amount (<5 m$\Omega \cdot cm^2$). The purpose of the modeling is to demonstrate the tantalizing potential of the SBT5J cell in terrestrial concentrator applications. The assumptions used in the model are realistic, which are based largely upon measured SBT5J data.

For example, the cell quality in terms of current collection and voltage bandgap offset of all 5Js is assumed to be equal to that shown in Figs. 5 and 7. We have also utilized tunnel junctions that absorb more than those used in the $1\times$ SBT5J design but have been proven to operate with peak currents significantly higher than the $500\times$ operating currents. In order to improve current matching, only the bandgap and thicknesses of the cells were adjusted for an AM1.5D spectrum. The one major assumption in the model is a total specific resistance of 25 m$\Omega\cdot$cm^2, which is a number that is readily achievable for tunnel junction, and bond interface resistances are suppressed $<$5 m$\Omega\cdot$cm^2. It should be noted that a similar resistance has been previously achieved in direct bonded cells, as evident by high FF in a 4J cell tested at $>$300 suns [11]. The results of the modeling are shown in Fig. 10(a) and (b). The modeled I–V curve has a J_{sc}, V_{oc}, and FF of 4.96 A/cm2, 5.56 V, and 84.7%, respectively. This results in a theoretical $500\times$ efficiency of 46.7%.

IV. Conclusion

Spectrolab has demonstrated high quality 5J cells optimized for space and terrestrial irradiance. The 5J cells were fabricated by direct bonding high-quality, lattice matched, T3J cells grown on GaAs and B2J cells grown on InP. A 20-cm^2 space cell achieved an efficiency of 35.1% for AM0 1 sun. A terrestrial cell reached an efficiency of 37.8%, which was verified independently by the NREL. Both the space and terrestrial efficiencies are among the highest, the highest being measured at 1 sun. Cell measurements at concentration indicate efficiencies approaching 41% at low concentration. Modeling indicates the potential to reach close to 47% at 500 suns. This demonstrates the potential of using direct bonding to couple lattice matched GaAs and InP cells to form a single multijunction stack.

Acknowledgment

The authors would like to thank the hardworking members of the ATP operations team who fabricated and measured the cells discussed in this paper.

References

[1] R. R. King, A. Boca, W. Hong, X.-Q. Liu, D. Bhusari, D. Larrabee, K. M. Edmondson, D. C. Law, C. M. Fetzer, S. Mesropian, and N. H. Karam, "Band-gap engineered architectures for high efficiency multijunction concentrator solar cells," in *Proc. 24th Eur. Photovolatic Sol. Energy Conf.*, 2009, pp. 21–25.

[2] S. R. Kurtz, A. A. Allerman, C. H. Seager, R. M. Sieg, and E. D. Jones, "Minority carrier diffusion, defects and localization in InGaAsN with 2% nitrogen," *Appl. Phys. Lett.*, vol. 77, pp. 400–402, 2000.

[3] D. B. Jackrel, S.R. Bank, H. B. Yuen, M. A. Wistey, J. S. Harris, Jr., A. J. Ptak, S. W. Johnston, D. J. Friedman, and S. R. Kurtz, "Dilute nitride GaInNAs and GaInNAsSb solar cells by molecular beam epitaxy," *J. Appl. Phys.*, vol. 101, pp. 11496-1–11496-8, 2007.

[4] P. M. Patel, D. Aiken, D. Chumney, A. Cornfeld, Y. Lin, C. Mackos, J. McCarty, N. Miller, P. Sharps, and M. Stan, "Initial results of the monolithically grown six junction inverted metamorphic multijunction solar cell," in *Proc. IEEE 38th Photovolatic Spec. Conf.*, 2012, pp. 922–926.

[5] K. Tanabe, A. F. Morral, H. A. Atwater, D. J. Aiken, and M. W. Wanlass, "Direct Bonded GaAs-InGaAs tandem solar cell," *Appl. Phys. Lett.*, vol. 89, pp. 102106-1–102106-3, 2006.

[6] D. Bhusari, D. Law, R. Woo, J. Boisvert, S. Mesropian, D. Larrabee, W. Hong, and N. H. Karam, "Direct semiconductor bonding technology (SBT) for high efficiency multijunction solar cells," in *Proc. IEEE 37th Photovolatic Spec. Conf.*, 2011, pp. 1937–1940.

[7] T. Moriarity and K. Emery, "Algorithm for building a spectrum for NREL's one-sun multi-source simulator," in *Proc. IEEE 38th Photovolatic Spec. Conf.*, 2012, pp. 1291–1295.

[8] Q. Y. Tong and U. Gosele, *Semiconductor Wafer Bonding: Science and Technology.* New York, NY, USA: Wiley Interscience, 1999.

[9] T. B. Stellwag, P. E. Dodd, M. S. Carpenter, M. S. Lundstrom, R. F. Pierret, M. R. Melloch, E. Yablonovitch, and T. J. Gmitter, "Effects of perimeter recombination on GaAs based solar cells," in *Proc. IEEE 20th Photovolatic Spec. Conf.*, 1990, pp. 442–447.

[10] D. K. Schroder, *Semiconductor Material and Device Characterization.* Hoboken, NJ, USA: Wiley Intersicence, 2006.

[11] Fraunhofer ISE. (2013). 43.6% 4 junction solar cell under concentrated sunlight new manufacturing technologies allow for higher efficiencies. [Online]. Available: http://www.ise.fraunhofer.de/en/press-and-media/press-releases/presseinformationen-2013/43.6-four-junction-solar-cell-under-concentrated-sunlight

Authors' photographs and biographies not available at the time of publication.

Effects of Internal Luminescence and Internal Optics on V_{oc} and J_{sc} of III–V Solar Cells

Myles A. Steiner, John F. Geisz, Iván García, Daniel J. Friedman, Anna Duda, Waldo J. Olavarria, Michelle Young, Darius Kuciauskas, and Sarah R. Kurtz

Abstract—**For solar cells dominated by radiative recombination, the performance can be significantly enhanced by improving the internal optics. We demonstrate a detailed model for solar cells that calculates the external luminescent efficiency and discuss the relationship between the external and internal luminescence. The model accounts for wavelength-dependent optical properties in each layer, parasitic optical and electrical losses, multiple reflections within the cell, and assumes isotropic internal emission. For single-junction cells, the calculation leads to V_{oc}, and for multijunction cells, the calculation leads to the V_{oc} of each junction as well as the luminescent coupling constant. In both cases, the effects of the optics are most prominent in cells with high internal radiative efficiency. Exploiting good material quality and high luminescent coupling, we demonstrate a two-junction nonconcentrator cell with a conversion efficiency of $(31.1 \pm 0.9)\%$ under the global spectrum.**

Index Terms—**Luminescence, luminescent coupling, photon recycling, radiative recombination, III–V solar cell.**

I. Introduction

FOR solar cells dominated by radiative recombination, the open-circuit voltage V_{oc}, short-circuit current J_{sc}, and ultimately the efficiency can be significantly enhanced by improving the internal optics and by harnessing the energy of the internal luminescence. Internally radiated photons can be directly emitted from the cell, but if confined by good internal reflectors at the front and back of the cell, they can also be reabsorbed with a significant probability. This so-called photon recycling leads to an increase in the equilibrium minority carrier concentration and, therefore, V_{oc}. In multijunction cells, the internal luminescence from a particular junction can also be coupled into

Manuscript received June 14, 2013; accepted August 8, 2013. Date of publication August 30, 2013; date of current version September 18, 2013. This work was supported by the U.S. Department of Energy under Contract DE-AC36-08GO28308 with the National Renewable Energy Laboratory and in part by the Foundational Program to Advance Cell Efficiency. The work of I. García was supported by an IOF grant from the People Programme (Marie Curie Actions) of the European Union's Seventh Framework Programme (FP7/2007-2013) under REA Grant 299878.

M. A. Steiner, J. F. Geisz, D. J. Friedman, A. Duda, W. J. Olavarria, M. Young, D. Kuciauskas, and S. R. Kurtz are with the National Renewable Energy Laboratory, Golden, CO 80401 USA (e-mail: myles.steiner@nrel.gov; john.geisz@nrel.gov; daniel.friedman@nrel.gov; anna.duda@nrel.gov; waldo.olavarria@nrel.gov; michelle.young@nrel.gov; darius.kuciauskas@nrel.gov; Sarah.Kurtz@nrel.gov).

I. García is with the National Renewable Energy Laboratory, Golden, CO 80401 USA, and also with the Instituto de Energía Solar, Universidad Politécnica de Madrid, Madrid 28040, Spain (e-mail: ivan.garcia@nrel.gov).

Color versions of one or more of the figures in this paper are available online at http://ieeexplore.ieee.org.

Digital Object Identifier 10.1109/JPHOTOV.2013.2278666

a lower bandgap junction where it generates photocurrent in addition to the externally generated photocurrent, which shifts the equilibrium J_{sc} and affects the overall performance of the tandem. Both of these phenomena—photon recycling and luminescent coupling—are enhanced by high radiative efficiency and by the tailored geometrical design of the solar cell. In this paper, we extend the ray-optic model of luminescence that we have developed [1] to multijunction cells and use this model to develop and analyze high-efficiency solar cells that exploit a high internal luminescence and good optical properties.

II. Internal Optics

On thermodynamic grounds, it has been shown [2], [3] that V_{oc} of a solar cell can be expressed as

$$V_{\mathrm{oc}} = V_{\mathrm{db}} + \frac{kT}{q} \ln\left(\eta_{\mathrm{ext}}\right) \tag{1}$$

where V_{db} is the value of V_{oc} in the ideal, detailed-balance limit where there are no nonthermodynamic losses, and η_{ext} is the external luminescent efficiency, or the fraction of electron–hole pairs that recombine radiatively to yield a photon that ultimately escapes the cell. In real devices, however, there are electrical losses due to nonradiative recombination, and we quantify the fraction of electron–hole pairs that recombine radiatively as the internal luminescent efficiency, η_{int}. There are also parasitic optical losses due to imperfect reflectances and transmittances. All of these losses are aggregated into η_{ext}, which represents a loss in voltage and, therefore, conversion efficiency. Consequently, an *increase* in η_{ext} indicates an *improvement* in the internal processes of the cell or, equivalently, a decrease in one or more loss mechanisms.

The effect of the internal optics can be clearly demonstrated in a set of double heterostructures (DHs) by measuring the minority carrier lifetime with time-resolved photoluminescence (TRPL). This simple experiment has the advantage that there is no junction or significant doping profile to complicate the carrier dynamics. We grew a set of 16 DHs of $\mathrm{Ga}_{0.5}\mathrm{In}_{0.5}\mathrm{P}/\mathrm{GaAs}/\mathrm{Ga}_{0.5}\mathrm{In}_{0.5}\mathrm{P}$ on 2°B-miscut (0 0 1) GaAs substrates, with a range of carrier concentrations. We first measured the TRPL decays on the as-grown samples, then removed the GaAs substrates and bonded the epilayers to glass with a transparent low viscosity epoxy and remeasured the TRPL decays. On substrate, the DH is "clad" by air (index of refraction $n = 1$) on one side and GaAs ($n \sim 3.6$) on the other. Bonded to glass, the DH is clad by air on one side and epoxy/glass ($n \sim 1.5$) on the other. Thus, the optical environment has changed. Schematics of the DH samples are shown in Fig. 1(a).

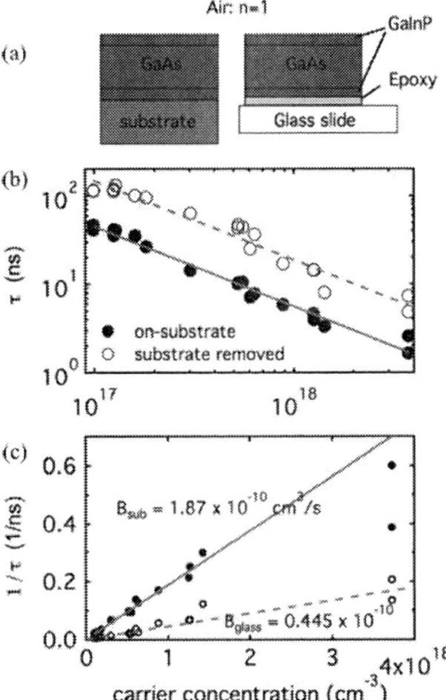

Fig. 1. Minority carrier lifetime of 16 DH samples, as measured by TRPL. (a) Schematics of the samples on-substrate and bonded to glass. (b) Measured lifetime as-grown (solid) and bonded to glass (open). (c) Reciprocal lifetime. The lines show a fit to (2).

Samples were grown by atmospheric pressure metal–organic vapor phase epitaxy. The p-type majority carriers were derived from a triethylzinc source, and the majority carrier concentration was varied from $\sim 1 \times 10^{17}$ to 40×10^{17} cm^{-3} by changing the temperature, growth rate, phosphine overpressure, and dopant flow rate. The carrier concentration in the GaAs layer was measured by standard capacitance–voltage (C–V) methods with a dilute hydrochloric acid electrolyte. Time-correlated single photon counting was used to measure room temperature TRPL decays at 870 nm, with excitation at 630 nm. The average laser power was 0.2 mW, the repetition rate was 1 MHz, and the pulse length was 0.3 ps. The optical-fiber-based TRPL spectrometer is described elsewhere [4]. For all samples, the TRPL was well described by a single exponential decay which enabled a straightforward determination of the lifetime.

Fig. 1(b) shows the measured lifetime as a function of the carrier concentration N_A. For both measurement sets, the measured lifetime varies with N_A as $\tau \sim N_A^{-0.9}$ as shown by the solid and dashed lines. Since we expect the radiative lifetime τ_R to vary with the concentration as $\tau_R = 1/BN_A$, where B is the radiative recombination coefficient, the data indicate that the total recombination is close to the radiative limit. Removing the substrate has the effect of increasing the lifetime by a factor of ~ 4. In Fig. 1(c), the reciprocal of the lifetime is plotted as a function of the carrier concentration and the data are fit to

$$\frac{1}{\tau} = \frac{1}{\tau_{\text{SRH}}} + BN_A \qquad (2)$$

where τ_{SRH} is the nonradiative Shockley–Read–Hall lifetime (Auger recombination can be neglected at these doping levels).

The coefficient B is found to be 1.87×10^{-10} cm^3/s for the on-substrate samples and 0.445×10^{-10} cm^3/s when the substrate was removed. In both cases, $\tau_{\text{SRH}} \sim 2.7 \pm 0.1 \mu$s, and for all data points, $\tau \ll \tau_{\text{SRH}}$. Thus, the samples are indeed dominated by radiative recombination, and by removing the substrate, the effective radiative lifetime has increased solely because of the change in the optical environment surrounding the semiconductor. In Section III, we show that these data can be used to quantify η_{int} and confirm that in this case $\eta_{\text{int}} \approx 1$.

As shown in [5], the functional dependence of the radiative lifetime τ_R can be expressed as

$$\frac{1}{\tau_R} \sim \frac{n_{\text{top}}^2 + n_{\text{bot}}^2}{2n_{\text{sc}}^2} \qquad (3)$$

where n_{top}, n_{bot}, and n_{sc} are the indices of refraction of the top and bottom cladding layers and the semiconductor, respectively. Since the coefficient $B \sim 1/\tau_R$, we calculate the expected ratio of measured coefficients in the radiative limit to be

$$\frac{B_{\text{glass}}}{B_{\text{sub}}} = \frac{(1.5)^2 + 1}{(3.6)^2 + 1} = 0.233 \qquad (4)$$

which is in excellent agreement with the measured ratio of 0.238.

III. Photon Recycling in Single-Junction Solar Cells

The DH experiment illustrates that for optoelectronic devices that are dominated by radiative recombination, the minority carrier lifetime can be significantly enhanced by improving the internal optics of the device. Since the dark current of a solar cell is inversely related to the minority carrier lifetime, we expect the performance of the cell to increase as the lifetime increases.

To understand and predict how the material quality and geometry of the cell affect the performance, we developed a ray-optical model of the external and internal luminescence. The model was described in detail in [1]; here, we summarize the main aspects.

It is useful to think of the solar cell as an optical cavity where photons generated in the absorber layer can reflect multiple times off the two cladding interfaces and possibly interfere with each other. For thick solar cells, it is generally sufficient to treat the cavity with ray optics in which only the intensity of the light varies with location. The optical cavity must have a high absorbance so that most of the incoming light is converted into electron–hole pairs. However, the optical cavity must also manage the internal luminescence: While some of the internally emitted photons will escape out the front of the cell or be reabsorbed parasitically in the cladding layers or in the substrate (if still present), a significant fraction of the photons will be reabsorbed in the absorber layer and reincarnated as new electron–hole pairs.

To escape the cell, an internally emitted photon can escape directly, possibly after bouncing around the cell cavity several times due to the highly reflective cladding surfaces; or it can be reabsorbed, reemitted and then escape; or be reabsorbed again, and so on.

We define $P_{\text{esc}}(\vec{r})$ and $P_{\text{abs}}(\vec{r})$ to be, respectively, the probabilities that a photon emitted at position $\vec{r}$ either escapes directly

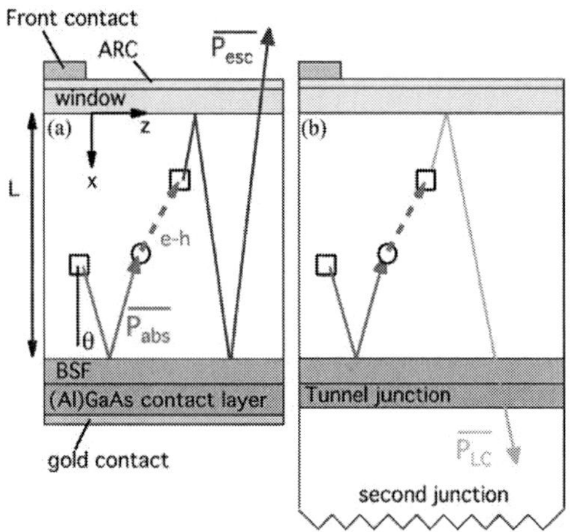

Fig. 2. Schematic of cell geometry and luminescent paths for (a) single-junction and (b) tandem solar cells. The solid lines represent the probabilities $\overline{P_{\mathrm{esc}}}$ (dark blue), $\overline{P_{\mathrm{abs}}}$ (red) and $\overline{P_{LC}}$ (light blue). The green-dashed line represents electron–hole pair diffusion.

or is reabsorbed. Both quantities are already averaged over the spontaneous energy distribution and the uniformly distributed solid angle of internal emission. If η_{int} varies with position, then it can be expressed as $\eta_{\mathrm{int}}(\vec{r})$, and following the derivation in [1], the external luminescent efficiency is

$$\eta_{\mathrm{ext}} = \frac{\int \eta_{\mathrm{int}}(\vec{r}) P_{\mathrm{esc}}(\vec{r}) d\vec{r}}{1 - \int \eta_{\mathrm{int}}(\vec{r}) P_{\mathrm{abs}}(\vec{r}) d\vec{r}}. \tag{5}$$

If we assume, however, that for very high quality cells, η_{int} is uniformly distributed over the cell volume, then (5) simplifies to

$$\eta_{\mathrm{ext}} = \frac{\eta_{\mathrm{int}} \overline{P_{\mathrm{esc}}}}{1 - \eta_{\mathrm{int}} \overline{P_{\mathrm{abs}}}} \tag{6}$$

as derived explicitly in [1], where $\overline{P_{\mathrm{esc}}}$ and $\overline{P_{\mathrm{abs}}}$ now represent energy-, solid-angle-, and volume-averaged probabilities. These quantities are shown schematically in Fig. 2(a). Equation (6) shows that the internal efficiency and the optical-geometrical properties have been effectively separated for high-quality cells. The probabilities can be expressed in (7) and (8), shown at the bottom of the page.

In these expressions, $R_f = R_f(E,\theta), T_f = T_f(E,\theta), R_b = R_b(E,\theta)$, and $T_b = T_b(E,\theta)$ are the effective energy- and angle-dependent Fresnel coefficients for specular reflection and transmission at the front and back interfaces and can be calculated with the transfer matrix method [6] by accounting for the

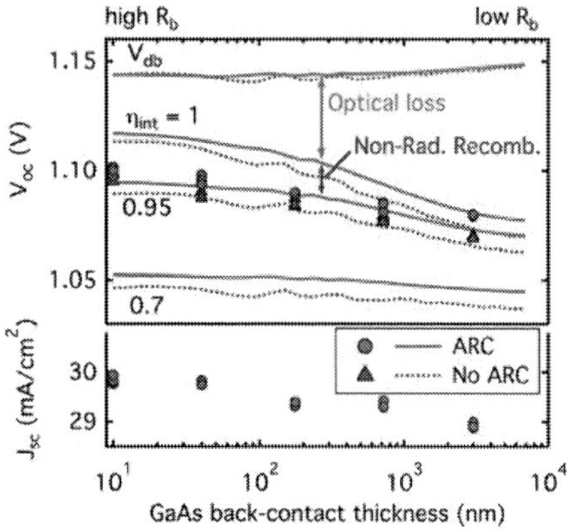

Fig. 3. V_{oc} and J_{sc} for a set of 2-μm GaAs cells, and modeled V_{oc} curves following (1) and (6)–(8). The top curve shows the detailed balance voltage V_{db}. Red points/lines are for AR-coated cells, purple points/lines are for uncoated cells.

thicknesses and optical coefficients of every layer in the cell; $\alpha = \alpha(E)$ is the energy-dependent absorption coefficient of the absorber layer; $\hat{S}(E)$ is the normalized spontaneous emission distribution of the absorber layer; and θ is the polar angle shown in Fig 2(a). Notice that the probabilities, and therefore η_{ext}, do not depend explicitly on the average reflectance at either cladding interface.

To demonstrate the utility of the model, a series of single-junction GaAs cells was grown. The cell geometry is sketched in Fig. 2(a) and consists of an absorber layer of thickness L that is passivated on the front by an AlInP window layer and on the back by a so-called GaInP back-surface field layer (BSF). Behind the BSF layer is an AlGaAs/GaAs contact layer for making Ohmic contact, and behind that is a reflective layer of gold. The front of the cell is covered with an antireflection coating. Details of the fabrication are shown elsewhere [1]. Cells with different absorber layers have the same overall architecture.

Fig. 3 shows the measured V_{oc} for a 2-μm-thick GaAs cell, with and without an antireflection coating, as a function of the thickness of the absorbing GaAs back-contact layer. Although the primary function of the contact layer is to enable ohmic contact between the electroplated gold and the semiconductor, the layer can also serve a secondary purpose of lowering the overall reflectance by absorbing some of the luminescence, to allow a systematic exploration of the optical effects. In Fig. 3, the average back reflectance decreases from left to right. The data show that V_{oc} decreases by $\sim$20 mV as the contact layer is thickened from 10 nm to 3 μm, and that V_{oc} increases by

$$\overline{P_{\mathrm{esc}}} = \int_0^\infty \hat{S}(E) \int_0^{\pi/2} \frac{T_f}{2\alpha L} \frac{\left(1 - e^{-\alpha L/\cos\theta}\right)\left(1 + R_b e^{-\alpha L/\cos\theta}\right)}{1 - R_f R_b e^{-2\alpha L/\cos\theta}} \cos\theta \, \sin\theta \, d\theta \, dE \tag{7}$$

and

$$\overline{P_{\mathrm{abs}}} = 1 - \int_0^\infty \hat{S}(E) \int_0^{\pi/2} \left\{ \frac{\left(1 - e^{-\alpha L/\cos\theta}\right)}{\alpha L} \left(1 - \frac{1}{2}(1 - e^{-\alpha L/\cos\theta})\left(\frac{R_f + R_b + 2R_f R_b e^{-\alpha L/\cos\theta}}{1 - R_f R_b e^{-2\alpha L/\cos\theta}}\right)\right) \right\} \cos\theta \, \sin\theta \, d\theta \, dE \tag{8}$$

$\sim$5 mV when the cell is AR-coated. The cells with the best optics demonstrated conversion efficiencies of $(27.8 \pm 0.8)\%$ under the global spectrum [1].

The solid lines show the modeled $V_{\rm oc}$ as calculated from (1) and (6)–(8) for different values of $\eta_{\rm int}$. We modeled the external quantum efficiency (EQE) of the cell at each value of the back-contact thickness and then calculated the probabilities $\overline{P_{\rm esc}}$ and $\overline{P_{\rm abs}}$ from the modeled structure. The data are reasonably modeled by $\eta_{\rm int} \sim 0.965$ for both coated and uncoated cells, which is not surprising: the antireflection coating affects the optical cavity properties by changing the front reflectance, but it should not have any effect on the relative recombination rates for an electron–hole pair.

The top curves show the value of $V_{\rm db}$ as calculated from the modeled EQE. $V_{\rm db}$ is an important characteristic of a solar cell and must be calculated for the particular geometry. As the optical cavity changes, by changing the absorber thickness or the back reflectance, for example, the value of $V_{\rm db}$ will also change. The data indicate the general trend that $V_{\rm db}$ increases as the cell absorbance decreases. For these 2-μm cells, the GaAs absorber becomes less than optically thick, relative to the incident light, as the back reflectance decreases, and therefore, the absorbance also decreases from left to right as can be seen in the $J_{\rm sc}$ data in the lower panel.

Several important conclusions can be drawn from Fig. 3. $V_{\rm oc}$ is clearly more sensitive to the back reflectance in cells of high material quality (i.e., large $\eta_{\rm int}$), as can be seen from the different slopes of the lines with $\eta_{\rm int} = 1$ and 0.7. Conversely, improved material quality has a more pronounced effect on the performance in cells with good optical properties than with poor optical properties. Finally, in this model of a solar cell, the optical and nonradiative recombination losses are separable, as indicated by the vertical arrows. Even for a cell with perfect material quality, $V_{\rm oc} < V_{\rm db}$ because of the parasitic optical losses during the reflection of light at the front and back surfaces.

Fig. 3 also helps address a concern about the broad applicability of the model. The requirement of uniform internal luminescent efficiency implicitly assumes that the solar cell can be described by a single-diode equation at voltages near $V_{\rm oc}$, for if this is not true and a sizeable depletion region (where $\eta_{\rm int} \approx 0$) causes a second term in the diode equation to be significant at voltages near $V_{\rm oc}$, then $\eta_{\rm int}$ can explicitly no longer be uniform. We write the internal luminescent efficiency as

$$\eta_{\rm int} = \frac{U_{\rm rad}}{U_{\rm rad} + \left(U_{nr}^{\rm bulk} + U_{nr}^{\rm dep} \right)} \qquad (9)$$

where $U_{\rm rad}$ is the radiative recombination rate, and the total nonradiative recombination rate is separated into contributions from the bulk and depletion regions. If recombination in the depletion region is negligible near $V_{\rm oc}$, then $U_{nr}^{\rm dep} \ll U_{nr}^{\rm bulk}$ and $V_{\rm oc}$ depends on $\eta_{\rm int}$, as shown in Fig. 3; as we have already noted, the internal optics are irrelevant for low values of $\eta_{\rm int}$

which could occur if there are many defect sites within the bulk and $U_{nr}^{\rm bulk}$ is high. If recombination in the depletion region is not negligible near $V_{\rm oc}$, however, then $U_{nr}^{\rm dep} \gg U_{nr}^{\rm bulk}$, the denominator of (9) becomes very large and $\eta_{\rm ext} \approx \eta_{\rm int} \overline{P_{\rm esc}} \to 0$, in which case the optics are again irrelevant. Thus, for cells that are dominated by nonradiative recombination, whether in the bulk or in the depletion region, the influence of the internal optics is negligible and the model may not be particularly useful. For cells that are dominated by radiative recombination, however, the model is very useful and can direct the designer to further improvements by means of the internal optics.

The model can also be used to determine the value of $\eta_{\rm int}$ for the samples in the DH experiment of Fig. 1. We expect the radiative recombination coefficient B to be proportional to the probability that an electron–hole pair is not reincarnated, or $B \sim 1 - \eta_{\rm int} \overline{P_{\rm abs}}$. Based on the layer structure, we calculate $\overline{P_{\rm abs}} = 0.711$ for the sample on-substrate, and $\overline{P_{\rm abs}} = 0.951$ when bonded to glass, a $\sim$33% increase in $\overline{P_{\rm abs}}$. Therefore, using the measured ratio $\frac{B_{\rm glass}}{B_{\rm sub}} = 0.238$, we find $\eta_{\rm int} \approx 0.97$ which is consistent with the measurements on the actual GaAs cells. While DHs are usually used to measure the lifetime of a particular sample or to determine the surface recombination velocity at an interface, this experiment shows that they can also be a valuable test structure to determine $\eta_{\rm int}$ and to evaluate whether the internal optics are good enough to result in a high degree of photon recycling.

IV. Luminescent Coupling in Tandem Solar Cells

If the back reflector is replaced by a tunnel junction and a second, lower bandgap junction to form a tandem cell, some fraction of the luminescence can couple into the lower bandgap junction, as shown in Fig. 2(b). The probability that photons directly escape out the back of the top junction can be calculated simply by interchanging $R_b \to R_f$ and $T_f \to T_b'$ in expression (7) for $\overline{P_{\rm esc}}$. Care must be taken to only count those photons in the Fresnel coefficient T_b' that are actually absorbed and collected in the lower junction, and not include any photons that escape out the back of the top junction but are absorbed elsewhere; this consideration is indicated by the prime superscript. For high-quality cells where the diffusion length is comparable with the thickness, the collection efficiency is close to unity, and we assume so in the model.

The new quantity $\overline{P_{LC}}$ can be expressed explicitly in (10), shown at the bottom of the page.

Following the same reasoning as for $\eta_{\rm ext}$, the luminescent coupling constant η_{LC} can then be defined as

$$\eta_{LC} = \frac{\eta_{\rm int} \overline{P_{LC}}}{1 - \eta_{\rm int} \overline{P_{\rm abs}}}. \qquad (11)$$

In a configuration where the tandem cell is current-limited by the bottom junction, the coupling raises the photocurrent of the bottom junction and represents a recovery of photocurrent that

$$\overline{P_{LC}} = \int_0^\infty \hat{S}(E) \int_0^{\pi/2} \frac{T_b'}{2\alpha L} \frac{\left(1 - e^{-\alpha L/\cos\theta}\right)\left(1 + R_f e^{-\alpha L/\cos\theta}\right)}{1 - R_f R_b e^{-2\alpha L/\cos\theta}} \cos\theta \, \sin\theta \, d\theta \, dE. \qquad (10)$$

would otherwise be lost if those photons were simply absorbed parasitically; in all configurations, the coupling raises the overall V_{oc} [7]. In general, high coupling will be driven by high η_{int} in the top junction and by a minimal degree of parasitic absorption between the junctions, for example, in the tunnel junction layers.

We recently showed a technique [8], [9] to measure the coupling constant, defined there as η_{ij} between adjacent junctions i and j, based on the measurement of the tandem J_{sc} as the relative intensities on the two (or more) junctions are systematically varied. Using the modeling shown here, we can compare the measured and modeled coupling constants and, more importantly, use the model to design multijunction cells that take advantage of the coupling [10].

In [11], we demonstrated the ability to artificially control the coupling η_{12} in a two-junction GaInP/GaAs tandem, by thickening an absorbing $Al_{0.2}Ga_{0.8}As$ layer grown between the two junctions. The data there showed η_{12} dropping by a factor of 2, while η_{int} for the top junction remained constant. Here, we demonstrate the value of luminescent coupling by varying the thickness of the top junction, to change the externally induced photocurrents on each junction.

Fig. 4(a) shows the EQE for four GaInP/GaAs tandem cells in which the top junction thickness was varied from 0.6 to 1.2 μm. The bottom junction EQE has been corrected for luminescent coupling [9], [12]. For the three thinnest top junctions, the data show the expected gradual increase in the top junction red response as the junction is thickened, and a corresponding decrease in the bottom junction EQE at those wavelengths. The 1.2-μm top junction has a red response similar to the 1.0-μm junction but a diminished blue response which likely indicates that the emitter thickness has exceeded the minority carrier diffusion length. This last cell, therefore, does not quite satisfy the model's assumption of perfect collection efficiency and should be treated with caution, but is included for completeness.

Fig. 4(b) shows the measured coupling constant η_{12} which remains approximately constant, with some fluctuation, as the top junction gets thicker. Fig. 4(c) shows the measured values of the externally induced top and bottom photocurrents J_1^{ext} and J_2^{ext} [8], as well as the actual J_{sc} values measured at 1 sun under the G173-global spectrum (1000 W/m^2). For thick top junctions, J_1^{ext} exceeds J_2^{ext} by up to 10% and the tandem is clearly bottom-limited. The thickest cell shows a lower value of J_1^{ext} than the 1-μm cell, again because of the reduced collection efficiency. The actual J_{sc} for the three thickest cells exceeds the limiting external photocurrent J_2^{ext} because of the coupling and is much less sensitive to top junction thickness than is J_2^{ext}. As the top junction is thinned to 0.6 μm, however, the cell crosses over to being slightly top-limited. Under the UV-rich AM0 spectrum (1367 W/m^2), the trends are the same but more pronounced.

Without any luminescent coupling, we would expect the decreasing photocurrent to result in a decrease in conversion efficiency, as modeled by the dashed lines in Fig. 4(d). The modeling was adjusted to account for realistic series resistance, but the trends in the model are the most important feature rather than the absolute values. For the global spectrum, the efficiency should peak at a top junction thickness of $\sim$0.7 μm and for

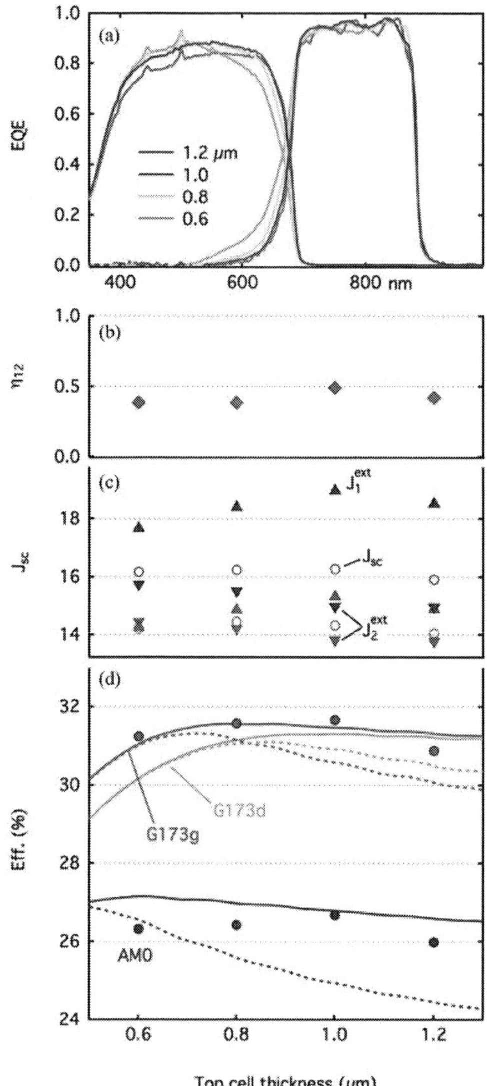

Fig. 4.   GaInP/GaAs tandem cells with varied top junction thickness. (a) EQE after correction for luminescent coupling. The top junction thicknesses are indicated in the legend. (b) Measured value of η_{12}. (c) Measured values of the photocurrents under the G173-global (red) and AM0 (blue) solar spectra. Upward and downward triangles correspond to J_1^{ext} and J_2^{ext}, and circles correspond to J_{sc}. (d) Conversion efficiency under global, direct and AM0 spectra, as indicated. Points show measured values (for global and AM0), solid lines show modeled values, dashed lines show modeled values with $\eta_{LC} = 0$.

the direct spectrum at $\sim$0.8 μm. The sensitivity to thickness is more dramatic for the AM0 spectrum. The data, however, show a significantly reduced sensitivity to top junction thickness, as the luminescent coupling has conspired to recover some of the otherwise-lost photocurrent and boost the J_{sc}, and thereby increase the efficiency. Indeed, the measured efficiencies under both the global and AM0 spectra are nearly flat despite the large variation in externally induced photocurrents, which indicates that, for terrestrial applications, the cells are well positioned to

                    192

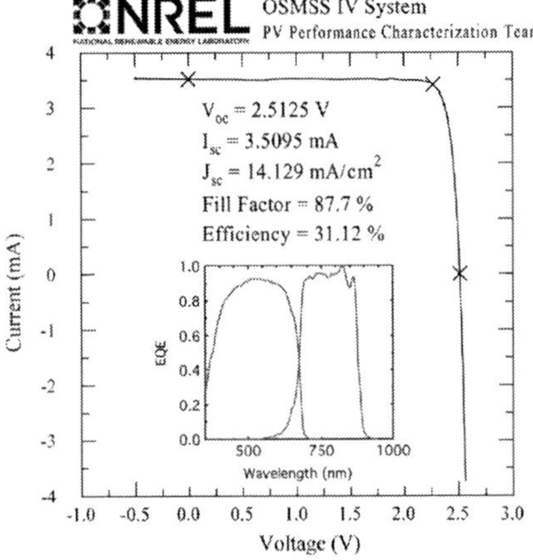

Fig. 5. NREL-certified *I–V* curve for a GaInP/GaAs solar cell, under the AM1.5-G173 global spectrum at 1000 W/m². The EQE is shown in the inset, corrected for luminescent coupling.

mitigate efficiency loss from spectral variation over the course of operation [7], [13].

Fig. 5 shows an NREL-certified *I–V* curve for a tandem that takes advantage of the concepts discussed here. The cell is bottom-limited with a luminescent coupling constant $\eta_{LC} = 0.56$, driven in large part by the high material quality of the GaInP: Using the model, we calculate $\eta_{int} \sim 80\%$ for the top junction [14]. The diffusion barrier on the n-side of the tunnel junction was $Al_{0.3}Ga_{0.7}As$ with a bandgap of ~ 1.66 eV, chosen to minimize the absorption of luminescence. The GaAs bottom junction was thinned to 2 μm and a reflective gold back contact was deposited on an $Al_{0.3}Ga_{0.7}As$ back-contact layer, also designed to minimize the absorption of luminescence. The front metallization grid was designed for 1-sun intensity, with approximately 2% shadowing. The luminescent coupling measurement of this cell shows the externally induced photocurrents to be $J_1^{ext} = 14.95$ and $J_2^{ext} = 13.55$ mA/cm², and the equilibrium photocurrents to be $J_1^{equil} = 14.95$ and $J_2^{equil} = 13.98$ mA/cm²: The bottom photocurrent increases by $\sim 3\%$ because of the coupling. V_{oc} of 2.513 V is higher than baseline examples because of the significant photon recycling in the two junctions. The cell had a conversion efficiency of (31.1 ± 0.9)% under the AM1.5-G173 global spectrum at 1000 W/m², which is the highest demonstrated efficiency for a two-junction 1-sun cell to date.

ACKNOWLEDGMENT

The authors are grateful for conversations with J. Olson, E. Yablonovitch, C.-S. Ho, R. King, W. McMahon and R. France, and to K. Emery and T. Moriarty for the data in Fig. 5.

REFERENCES

[1] M. A. Steiner, J. F. Geisz, I. Garcia, D. J. Friedman, A. Duda, and S. R. Kurtz, "Optical enhancement of the open-circuit voltage in high quality GaAs solar cells," *J. Appl. Phys.*, vol. 113, pp. 123109-1–123109-11, 2013.

[2] U. Rau, "Reciprocity relation between photovoltaic quantum efficiency and electroluminescent emission of solar cells," *Phys. Rev. B*, vol. 76, pp. 085303-1–085303-8, 2007.

[3] O. D. Miller, E. Yablonovitch, and S. R. Kurtz, "Strong internal and external luminescence as solar cells approach the Shockley-Queisser limit," *J. Photovoltaics*, vol. 2, pp. 303–311, 2012.

[4] D. Kuciauskas, J. N. Duenow, J. V. Li, M. R. Young, P. Dippo, and D. H. Levi, "Time resolved photoluminescence spectrometer for thin-film absorber characterization and analysis of TRPL data for CdS/CdTe interface," presented at the 38th IEEE Photovoltaic Spec. Conf., Austin, TX, USA, 2012.

[5] E. Yablonovitch, T. J. Gmitter, and R. Bhat, "Inhibited and enhanced spontaneous emission from optically thin AlGaAs/GaAs double heterostructures," *Phys. Rev. Lett.*, vol. 61, pp. 2546–2549, 1988.

[6] E. Centurioni, "Generalized matrix method for calculation of internal light energy flux in mixed coherent and incoherent multilayers," *Appl. Opt.*, vol. 44, pp. 7532–7539, 2005.

[7] D. J. Friedman, J. F. Geisz, and M. A. Steiner, "Analysis of multijunction solar cell current-voltage characteristics in the presence of luminescent coupling," *J. Photovoltaics*, 2013, to be published.

[8] M. A. Steiner and J. F. Geisz, "Non-linear luminescent coupling in series-connected multijunction solar cells," *Appl. Phys. Lett.*, vol. 100, pp. 251106-1–251106-5, 2012.

[9] M. A. Steiner, J. F. Geisz, T. E. Moriarty, R. M. France, W. E. McMahon, J. M. Olson, S. R. Kurtz, and D. J. Friedman, "Measuring IV curves and subcell photocurrents in the presence of luminescent coupling," *J. Photovoltaics*, vol. 3, pp. 879–887, 2012.

[10] D. J. Friedman, J. F. Geisz, and M. A. Steiner, "Effect of luminescent coupling on the optimal design of multijunction solar cells," *J. Photovoltaics*, 2013, submitted for publication.

[11] M. A. Steiner, J. F. Geisz, I. Garcia, D. J. Friedman, and S. R. Kurtz, "Experimental and modeling analysis of internal luminescence in III-V solar cells," presented at the 9th Int. Conf. Concentrating Photovoltaic Syst., Miyazaki, Japan, 2013.

[12] M. A. Steiner, S. R. Kurtz, J. F. Geisz, W. E. McMahon, and J. M. Olson, "Using phase effects to understand measurements of the quantum efficiency and related luminescent coupling in a multijunction solar cell," *J. Photovoltaics*, vol. 2, pp. 424–433, 2012.

[13] A. S. Brown and M. A. Green, "Radiative coupling as a means to reduce spectral mismatch in monolithic tandem solar cell stacks—Theoretical considerations," in *Proc. 29th IEEE Photovoltaic Spec. Conf.*, New Orleans, LA, USA, 2002, pp. 868–871.

[14] J. F. Geisz, M. A. Steiner, I. García, S. R. Kurtz, and D. J. Friedman, "Enhanced external radiative efficiency for 20.8% efficient single-junction GaInP solar cells," *Appl. Phys. Lett.*, vol. 103, pp. 041118-1–041118-5, 2013.

Authors' photographs and biographies not available at the time of publication.

Fully Ion Implanted and Coactivated Industrial n-Type Cells With 20.5% Efficiency

T. S. Böscke, D. Kania, C. Schöllhorn, D. Stichtenoth, A. Helbig, P. Sadler, M. Braun, M. Dupke, M. Weiß, A. Grohe, J. Lossen, and H.-J. Krokoszinski

Abstract—We present our progress in fully implanted n-type cell for industrial manufacturing. Screen-printed n-type cells with boron emitters are a viable contender to succeed p-type cell in industrial production. A major open topic is the availability of a robust manufacturing flow. The synergistic qualities of ion implantation allow for a very efficient and potentially robust process sequence. We review some of the challenges arising from this approach, such as activation of the implanted boron emitter and the reverse current characteristics. Or current process allows manufacturing of $156 \times 156 \text{ mm}^2$ cells with efficiencies up to 20.5% with a single coactivation anneal.

Index Terms—Ion implant, n-type, screen-printed solar cell.

I. Introduction

THE ongoing consolidation in the solar cell manufacturing industry creates a strong drive toward both cost reduction and technology differentiation. A widely followed evolutionary improvement path for p-type cells is the introduction of a rear side with dielectric passivation and point contacts. However, due to reduced surface recombination and low bulk resistance requirements, this cell type becomes more and more sensitive to light-induced degradation [1], [2]. This can be overcome by the introduction of n-type base material. Further advantages of n-type material are its insensitivity to some common impurities, such as iron, and therefore a high lifetime potential.

We recently presented the development of screen-printed n-type cells type for industrial production [3]. As part of our effort, we screened a number of process flows involving different manufacturing techniques. One of the most interesting options is to employ ion implantation for both the boron emitter and phosphorous back surface field. In this paper, we report our results in the technology screening of the so-called fully implanted n-type cells and review some of the arising challenges.

Manuscript received June 9, 2013; revised August 5, 2013 and August 29, 2013; accepted September 3, 2013. Date of publication November 6, 2013; date of current version December 16, 2013.

The authors are with Bosch Solar Energy, 99310 Arnstadt, Germany (e-mail: t.boescke@ieee.org; daniel.kania@bosch.com; claus.schoellhorn@bosch.com; daniel.stichtenoth@bosch.com; anke.helbig@bosch.com; patrick.sadler@ bosch.com; mathias.braun@bosch.com; martin.dupke@bosch.com; matthias. weiss@bosch.com; andreas.grohe@bosch.com; jan.lossen@bosch.com; hans-joachim.krokoszinksi@bosch.com).

Color versions of one or more of the figures in this paper are available online at http://ieeexplore.ieee.org.

Digital Object Identifier 10.1109/JPHOTOV.2013.2287760

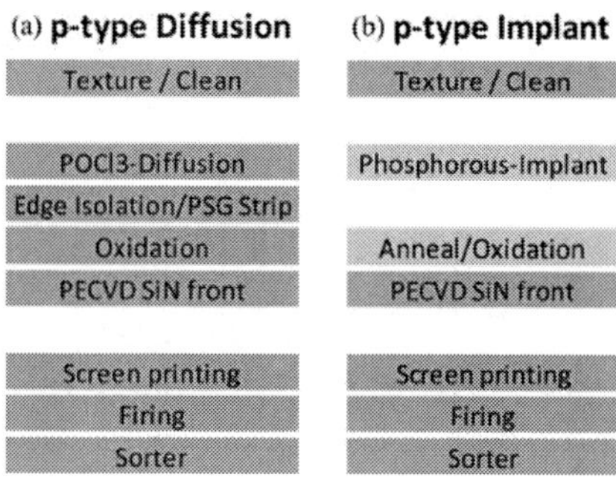

Fig. 1. (a) Process flows for a standard cell with SiO/SiN passivation. (b) Simplified process flow with ion implantation.

II. Synergistic Advantages of Ion Implantation

Ion implantation is a relatively complex vacuum process, which, at the current time, requires a significantly higher tool investment than a conventional diffusion process. In addition, a separate high-temperature activation step is required after the implant. Due to this, it seems counterintuitive to introduce ion implantation into a cost-sensitive manufacturing environment. However, several characteristics of ion implantation may reduce total cost of ownership by omitting other process steps: In contrast with a diffusion process, ion implantation is inherently single sided (no separate edge isolation needed) and does not grow a dopant glass. Furthermore, a high-quality oxide layer can be grown during annealing [4], which can be used to improve emitter passivation. As shown in Fig. 1(b), this allows reducing the process flow complexity compared with diffused cells [see Fig. 1(a)]. Up to 19.5% average production efficiency has been reported with this scheme [5].

Starting from the ion-implant p-type flow [see Fig. 1(b)], an evolutionary upgrade to an n-type process may be possible by adding a boron implant and an additional rear-side passivation step [6]–[8]. Both the boron emitter and the phosphorous back surface field could be passivated by a SiO/SiN stack. Industrial realization of this process flow with acceptable efficiency and total cost of ownership could pose a very attractive upgrade path, especially if only a single coactivation step is used both for boron and phosphorous.

III. Device Structure Used in This Study

To assess the viability of a full-implant flow, we used a different process flow with Al_2O_3/SiN passiviation to decouple the dependence of oxide quality on the anneal process. The back surface field and boron emitter were implanted on a beamline

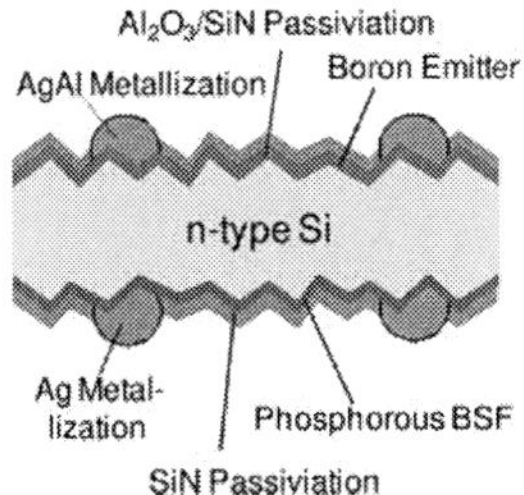

Fig. 2. Schematic cross section of the nPERT-cell used in this study.

TABLE I
IMPACT OF ANNEALING TEMPERATURE ON THE BORON EMITTER PARAMETERS
(DOSE 3e15)

Annealing peak temperature	Voc [mV]	Isc [A]	Rsheet Bor [Ohm]
940°C	600.9	8.77	91.7
970°C	618.9	8.97	71.0
1000°C	630.8	9.24	64.9

implanter and activated in a single coannealing step. H-grid screen-printed silver metallization was used to contact both the front and the rear side. All cells were manufactured on 156×156 mm^2 Czochralski n-type wafers with a starting thickness of 175 μm and a base resistivity between 1 and 6 Ω·cm.

Cell characterization was performed on a production flasher, contacting the front- and rear-side busbars only. The current was calibrated to a reference measured on a gold-coated chuck to emulate the conditions in a module with reflective white back sheet. Averaging of forward and reverse measurement was used to eliminate hysteresis effects [9].

IV. CHALLENGE: BORON IMPLANT ANNEALING

Activation of implanted boron and annealing of the associated damage presents a major challenge compared with phosphorous. Implantation of phosphorous usually leads to an amorphization of the silicon surface and can easily be annealed at temperatures below 850 °C. Boron, in contrast, does not amorphize the surface at room temperature and has a longer range due to its lower mass, leading to a deeper network of structural damage. Furthermore, it tends to form electrically inactive clusters with interstitial silicon atoms. These boron interstitial clusters only dissolve at high temperatures [10].

Effectively, this means that a relatively high thermal budget is required to activate boron and anneal all defects. This becomes apparent in electrical cell data. Table I shows emitter sheet resistance and open-circuit voltage of cells with different annealing temperatures. A significant reduction in sheet resistance is observed with increased temperature. This effect is most likely a combination of improved mobility at higher temperatures, due to the deeper profile, and potentially incomplete electrical activation at lower temperatures. In addition, a drastic improvement in V_{oc} and I_{sc} is observed. From internal quantum-efficiency measurements (see Fig. 3), it is obvious that improved emitter performance is responsible for this observation. Note that hardly any change is observed at longer wavelengths, suggesting that

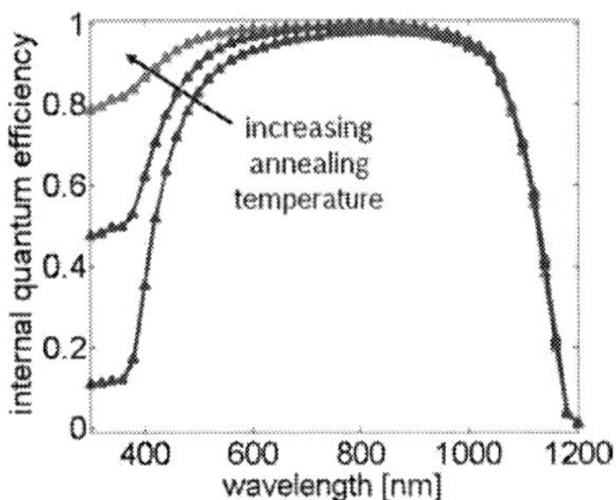

Fig. 3. Internal quantum efficiency for a set of cells annealed at different temperatures (cf., Table II). A drastic improvement of the blue response is apparent with higher temperatures.

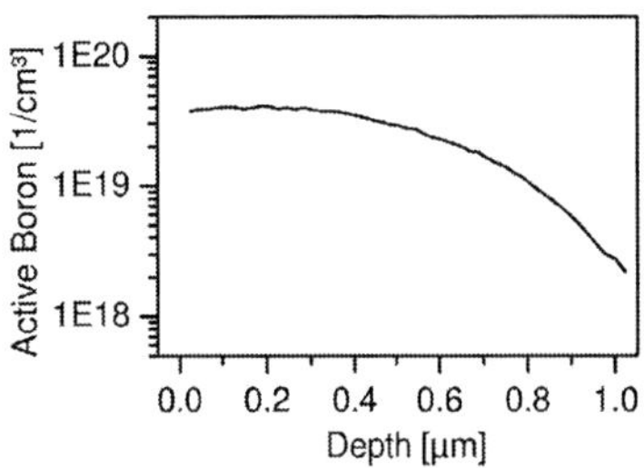

Fig. 4. Electrochemical profiling of the implanted boron emitter after annealing with an optimized process.

TABLE II
CELL PARAMETERS VERSUS BORON IMPLANT ENERGY

Energy	Projected Range	Voc [mV]	Isc [A]	FF [%]	eta [%]
100%	100%	645	9.34	79.1	19.79
75%	80%	646	9.35	79.1	19.86
50%	56%	647	9.37	79.1	19.91

the phosphorous back surface field is completely annealed even at the lowest temperature. The high thermal budget of the annealing process leads to a significant increase in junction depth and reduction of surface concentration of the boron emitter, as shown in Fig. 4.

Although the emitter quality can be optimized, the high thermal budget has several undesirable side effects: While it is still possible to contact boron emitters with a surface concentration below 5e19 1/cm^3, this is not the case for the back surface field where a surface concentration above 2e20 1/cm^3 is necessary to enable a contact to the silver paste. Due to the high thermal budget, this can only be achieved by an increased phosphorous dose, approximately two times as high as for a typical emitter, which leads to increased rear-side recombination and higher free carrier absorption losses. Furthermore, the high temperature may lead to the dissolution of precipitates in n-Cz material and can, therefore, cause a degradation of bulk lifetime. Finally, a high thermal budget leads to an increase cost of ownership of the anneal process.

Apart from the high thermal budget requirements, we also observed a pronounced dependence of emitter quality on implant energy, as shown in Table II. The emitter quality

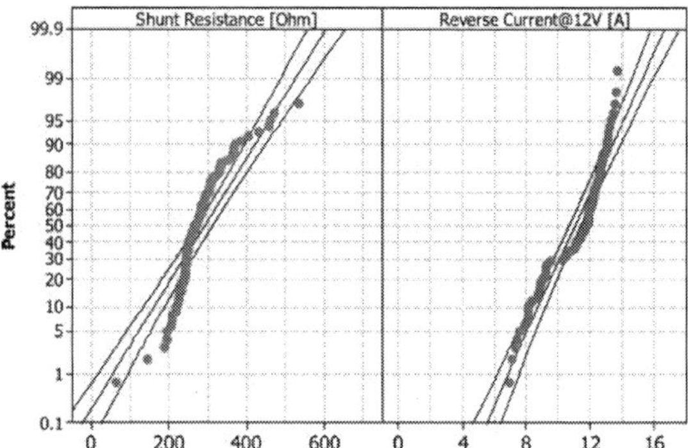

Fig. 5. Probability plots of shunt resistance and reverse current of a batch of implanted n-type cells without additional edge isolation.

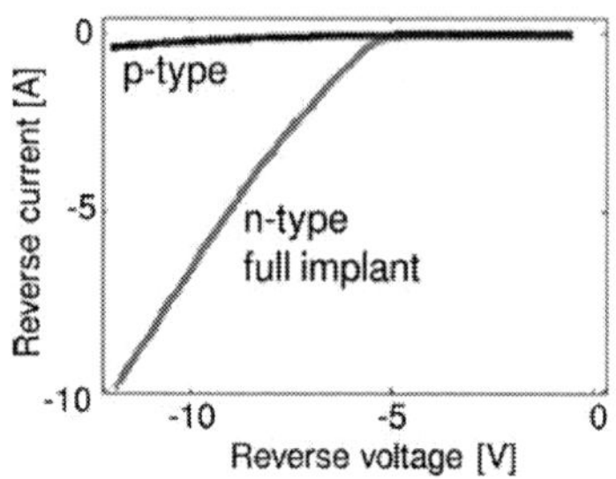

Fig. 6. Comparing the reverse current–voltage characteristics of a standard p-type cell with edge isolation and a fully implanted cell without edge isolation.

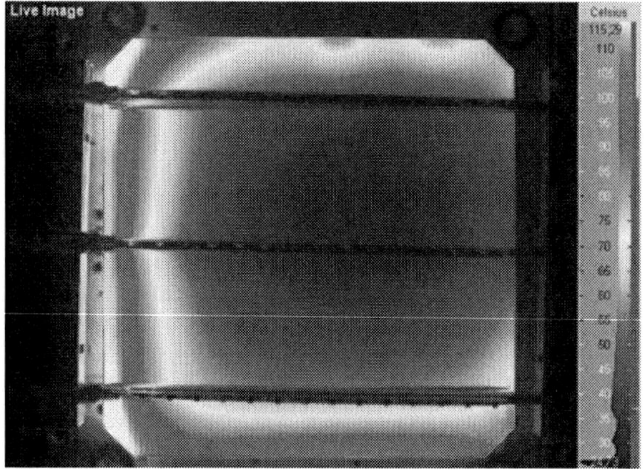

Fig. 7. Static thermography image of a nonedge isolated full-implant cell at a reverse bias of −12 A and 25 °C ambient temperature after 60 s. The cell edge shows heating above 100 °C, which does not meet long-term reliability requirements.

monotonically improved with lower implant energy, suggesting that for high energies not all implant damage could be annealed. This observation may have ramifications for a potential boron implant-production tool: Depending on source configuration, a significant reduction in ion energy may reduce beam current and beam stability, leading to unrealistically low throughputs. Furthermore, it means that the boron implant may be sensitive to the occurrence of high-energy particles that may emerge in nonenergy filtered ion sources in second-generation high-throughput solar implanters.

V. Challenge: Reverse Bias Behavior

A benefit of ion implant for p-type cells is the omission of an additional edge isolation step due to the single-sided nature of implant. In principle, the same would be expected for n-type cells, as the emitter should only be implanted on the front side and the back-surface field only on the back side, leaving a gap between both doped regions at the wafer edge. As shown in Fig. 5, excellent shunt resistances >200 Ω are observed for almost all cells in the test batch, suggesting no impact of shunting on low-light behavior and forward characteristics.

Despite the seemingly good edge isolation, a high reverse current above 10 A (median) is observed when the cells are biased to −12 V. This is a standard test condition to cover an extreme case which may occur during partial shadowing of a 60-cell module. To prevent excessive heating of cells in this operational mode, a reverse current of less than 1 A is required at −12 V, which is exceeded by an order of magnitude. This is also evident from the reverse current–voltage characteristics, as shown in Fig. 6, which show a distinctly nonlinear behavior. Furthermore, static thermography measurements do indeed show local heating of the cell at the edge.

Further investigation showed that all heat generation is limited to the edge of the cell. We attribute this behavior to avalanche breakdown of a p-n junction that is formed at the cell edge by spuriously deposited dopant.

These findings suggest that, unlike implanted p-type cells, n-type cells may require additional measures for edge isolation.

TABLE III
CELL PARAMETERS OF A RECENT RECORD BATCH (68 CELLS, OWN MEASUREMENT)

	Voc [mV]	Jsc [mA/cm²]	FF [%]	eta [%]
Median	654	39.48	78.8	20.34
Best Cell	655	39.52	79.1	20.5

VI. Optimized Cell Results

We processed a cell batch based on optimized annealing and implant parameters and combined it with further optimization of the metallization layout and the passivation. As shown in Table III, excellent median and maximum efficiencies were obtained. To our knowledge, 20.5% is the highest reported efficiency for a fully implanted, large-area, screen-printed n-type cell.

VII. Conclusion

We presented our progress in technology screening of fully implanted nPERT-cells. Excellent cell efficiencies up to 20.5% were obtained, confirming the viability of this approach. We also identified topics for further improvement.

1) Annealing and activation of boron required a high thermal budget which causes undesirable side effects. Further

understanding and fine-tuning of the implant conditions may alleviate this issue.

2) The boron implant may potentially be sensitive to energy contamination.

3) The edge isolation of fully implanted cells proved to be insufficient according to their nonlinear reverse bias characteristics. It is critical to solve this issue without a significant loss in cell efficiency.

Further complexity reduction of the process flow may be possible by utilizing a SiO/SiN stack for boron emitter passivation.

REFERENCES

[1] J. Schmidt and A. Cuevas, "Electronic properties of light-induced recombination centers in boron-doped Czochralski silicon," *J. Appl. Phys.*, vol. 86, pp. 3175–3180, 1999.

[2] K. Ramspeck, S. Zimmermann, H. Nagel, A. Metz, Y. Gassenbauer, B. Birkmann, and A. Seidl, "Light induced degradation of rear passivated mc-Si solar cells," in *Proc. 27th Eur. Photovoltaic Solar Energy Conf.*, Frankfurt, Germany, 2012, pp. 861–865.

[3] T. S. Böscke, D. Kania, A. Helbig, T. Roth, C. Schöllhorn, M. Dupke, P. Sadler, M. Braun, D. Stichtenoth, T. Wütherich, R. Jesswein, D. Fiedler, R. Carl, J. Lossen, and H.-J. Krokoszinski, "Bifacial *n*-type cells with >20% front-side efficiency for low-cost production," presented at the 38th IEEE Photovoltaic Spec. Conf., Austin, TX, USA, Jun, 2012.

[4] A. Gupta, R. J. Low, N. Bateman, D. Ramappa, H.-J. L. Gossman, Q. Zhai, P. Sullivan, W. Skinner, C. Dubé, B. Tsefrekas, and J. Mullin, "High efficiency selective emitter cells using in-situ patterned ion implantation," in *Proc. 25th Eur. Photovoltaic Solar Energy Conf.*, Valencia, Spain, Sep. 6–10, 2010, pp. 1158–1162.

[5] W. Han, W. Shan, Q. Jiang, Y. Li, Z. Qiu, J. Li, and Q. Zhai, "Mass production implementation of soliton ion implantation technology," in *Proc. 27th Eur. Photovoltaic Solar Energy Conf. Exhib.*, Frankfurt, Germany, 2012, pp. 1498–1502.

[6] N. Bateman, "Ion implantation for *n*-type solar cells," presented at the nPV-Workshop 2012, Amsterdam, The Netherlands, May 14–15, 2012.

[7] O. Young-Woo, A. D. Upadhyaya, T. Yugou, F. Zimbardi, S. Ning, and A. Rohatgi, "Ion-implanted and screen-printed large area 19.6% efficient *n*-type bifacial Si solar cell," in *Proc. 38th IEEE Photovoltaic Spec. Conf.*, Jun. 3–8, 2012, pp. 2240–2243.

[8] M. Sheoran, M. Emsley, Y. Min, D. Ramappa, and P. Sullivan, "Ion-implant doped large-area *n*-type Czochralski high-efficiency industrial solar cells," in *Proc. 38th IEEE Photovoltaic Spec. Conf.*, Jun. 3–8, 2012, pp. 2254–2257.

[9] T. Roth, D. Wichmann, K. Meyer, and M. Orlob, "In-depth analysis of transient errors of inline IV measurements," *Energy Procedia*, vol. 8, pp. 82–87, 2011.

[10] S. Mirabella, E. Bruno, F. Priolo, D. De Salvador, E. Napolitani, A. V. Drigo, and A. Carnera, "Dissolution kinetics of boron-interstitial clusters in silicon," *Appl. Phys. Lett.*, vol. 83, pp. 680–682, 2003.

Authors' photographs and biographies not available at the time of publication.

Towards an Optimized Emitter for Screen-Printed Solar Cells

A. Dastgheib-Shirazi[1], G. Micard[1], H. Wagner[2], M. Steyer[1], P.P. Altermatt[2], G. Hahn[1]

[1]Department of Physics, University of Konstanz, 78457 Konstanz
[2]Dept. Solar Energy, Inst. Solid-State Physics, Leibniz University of Hannover, 30167 Hannover, Germany

Abstract — The determination of suitable process parameters for $POCl_3$ diffusion, with the aim of minimizing emitter recombination and obtaining satisfactory contactability of the homogeneous emitter, is the aim of this study. It can be shown that different emitters with low $R_{sheet} < 60$ Ω/sq can result in significantly different emitter saturation current densities. Regarding the screen-printing metallization procedure, we observe that the resistance of a semiconductor-metal contact can vary on different emitters despite of the same sheet resistance.

In this study, the relevant process parameters for emitter optimization using $POCl_3$-diffusion were determined with the help of a design of experiment (DoE). Thus, it is also possible to find optimized diffusion parameters without increasing the sheet resistance of the optimized emitter. To verify the efficiency potential of the emitter, a standard industrial solar cell process is applied, and the outcome is compared with results from simulations using Sentaurus Device. A significant increase in efficiency can be reached, with open circuit voltages >640 mV and average efficiencies well above 19%.

Index Terms — homogeneous emitter, $POCl_3$-diffusion, metallization, simulation

I. INTRODUCTION

The influence of process parameters during $POCl_3$ diffusion on the emitter formation is still the subject of current research [2-7]. The main goal is to fabricate optimized emitters that show low emitter recombination, as well as suitable contactability for screen-printing metallization. A still common but somehow misleading parameter for the evaluation of emitters is the emitter sheet resistance, which reflects only the density of electrically active phosphorus atoms. For a quantitative assessment of emitters in a screen-printing process, more attention should be paid to the profile of the electrically inactive phosphorus [3].

In the first part of this work we discuss the influences of the important diffusion parameters on emitter formation during the pre-deposition phase, using a design of experiment (DoE) approach. Based on previous work [1], we focus on the main parameters of the $POCl_3$-N_2 / O_2 gas flow ratio and diffusion temperature. The evaluation of the DoE allows us to find optimal diffusion parameters for emitter formation. Here, we focus on emitter structures that (in spite of constantly low sheet resistance) have decreased emitter saturation current densities j_{0E} and sufficient metal-semiconductor contactability.

In order to show the extent to which the optimized emitter with $R_{sheet} < 60$ $\Omega/\square$ meets the requirements of a screen-printing process, the optimized emitter has been transferred to an industry-standard screen-printing process.

II. DESIGN OF EXPERIMENT

A DoE approach is used to systematically show the effects of diffusion parameters on emitter formation during the pre-deposition phase. For this purpose, we used the Box-Behnken Design [1], which allows a significant reduction of the diffusion experiments. In this investigation, four process parameters (duration, temperature, $POCl_3$-N_2 gas flow and O_2 gas flow) are systematically varied, but we focus on the parameters temperature and $POCl_3$-N_2 gas flow, which have the strongest influence on emitter formation. For emitter characterization, the following methods are used:

- 4-Point Probe to obtain R_{sheet}
- Quasi-Steady-State Photoconductance (QSSPC) to obtain j_{0E} and $V_{oc,implied}$
- Electrochemical Capacitance Voltage (ECV) to obtain the active dopant profile
- Secondary Ion Mass Spectrometry (SIMS) to obtain the total phosphorus density
- Glow Discharge – Optical Emission Spectroscopy (GD-OES) to obtain the phosphorus density in the PSG layer

The samples used for this part of the study were (100) oriented boron doped FZ wafers ($R_B = 2$ Ωcm & 200 Ωcm) with a thickness of 250 μm. After the cleaning procedure, diffusion processes are carried out in a state of the art $POCl_3$ diffusion furnace from Centrotherm. Only the temperature and the $POCl_3$-N_2 gas flow are varied, while all other parameters are held constant. After the characterization of the phosphorus-silicate glass (PSG) and its removal, the emitter is analyzed using the characterization tools listed above. In order to measure j_{0E} and the implied V_{oc}, the samples are symmetrically passivated by plasma enhanced chemical vapor deposition (PECVD) using a-SiN_x:H. Afterwards, j_{0E} and $V_{oc,implied}$ are measured using the quasi-steady-state photoconductance (QSSPC) tool. The determination of j_{0E} is done using the Kane Swanson method at high injection level ($\Delta n = 1$-3×10^{16} cm^{-3}) [8].

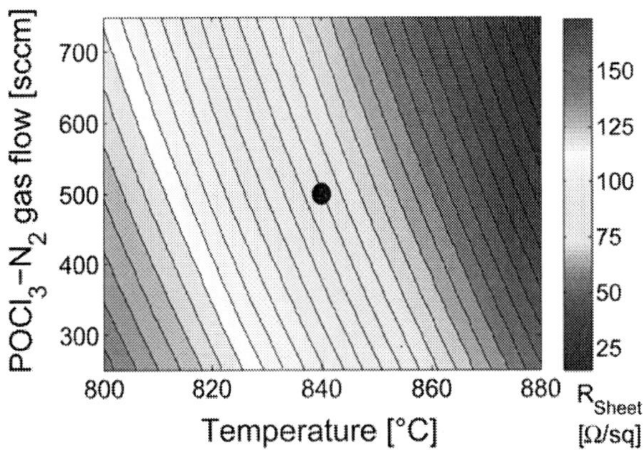

Fig. 1.   Results of the DoE regarding R_{sheet} as a function of $POCl_3$-N_2 gas flow and process temperature.

Fig. 1 shows measured R_{sheet} as a function of $POCl_3$-N_2 gas flow and temperature range during pre-deposition. Here the sheet resistance increases significantly with higher $POCl_3$-N_2 gas flow and temperature.

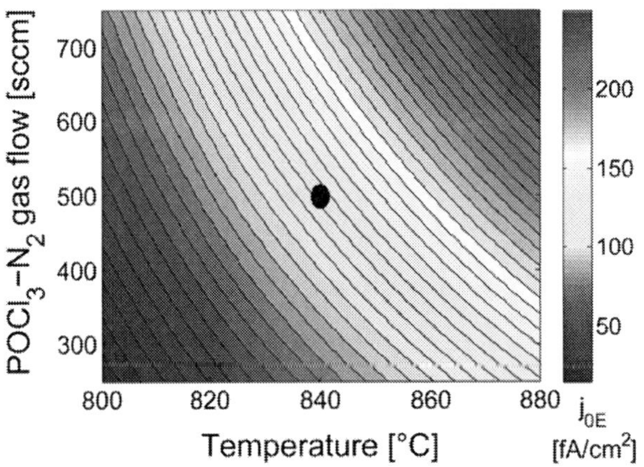

Fig. 2.   Results of the DoE regarding j_{0E} as a function of $POCl_3$-N_2 gas flow and process temperature.

Fig. 2 shows that an increase in temperature as well as $POCl_3$-N_2 gas flow leads to a significant increase in j_{0E}. Through the combination of Fig. 1 and Fig. 2, parameter ranges of constant R_{sheet} and strongly reduced j_{0E} can be determined.

By combining the DoE results with a Sentaurus Device simulation of a standard Si solar cell with Al-BSF, the potential of an optimized homogeneous emitter is visualized in Fig. 3. The isosurfaces in Fig. 3 indicate the diffusion parameter range for constant solar cell efficiency. The reduction of the $POCl_3$-N_2 gas flow and the slight increase of

the diffusion temperature lead to a maximum efficiency region whereby a gain of $0.6\%_{abs}$ can be achieved.

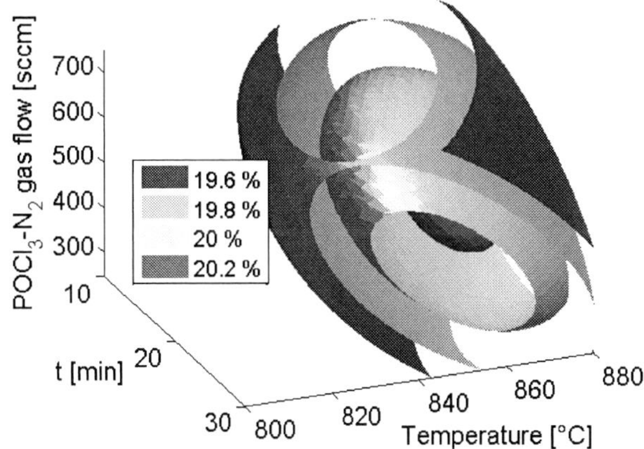

Fig. 3.   3-parameter isosurfaces of solar cell efficiencies as a function of $POCl_3$-N_2/O_2 ratio, temperature and deposition? time, resulting from the combination of the DoE and solar cell simulation by using Sentaurus Device.

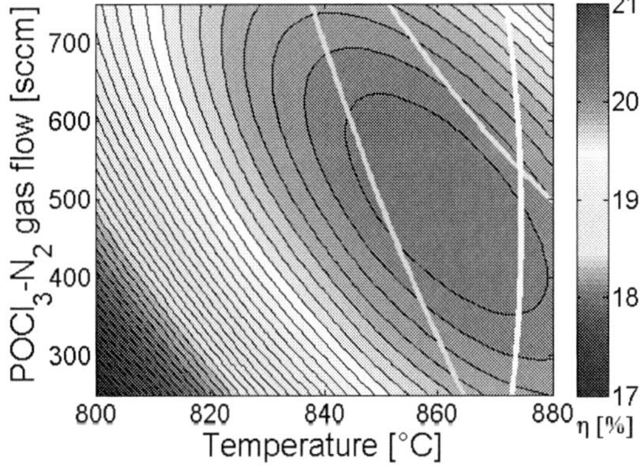

Fig. 4.   2D cross-section of Fig. 3 showing the simulated solar cell efficiencies as a function of $POCl_3$-N_2 gas flow and temperature during pre-deposition.

A 2D cross-section of the soalr cell efficiency as a function of $POCl_3$-N_2 gas flow and temperature during pre-deposition is shown in Fig. 4. An optimized parameter region with maximum solar cell efficiency can be achieved by adjustment of $POCl_3$-N_2 gas flow and temperature. On the left side of the plot the green line indicates the efficiency limitation due to R_{sheet} values higher than 60 Ω/sq. In this region the cell efficiency is limited by lower fill factors (FF). The maximum cell efficiency region is also limited by j_{0E} values above 210 fA/cm^2 as illustrated by the blue line in Fig 4. The j_{sc} limit (yellow line) was calculated using the ECV profiles of the DoE. Here it must be taken into consideration that the contribution of emitter recombination that is caused by the electrically inactive phosphorous was not implemented in the device simulation. Taking into account the electrically inactive phosphorus would significantly reduce solar cell efficiency further in this region.

IV. P-Precipitation

Based on the results from the DoE, we see that the density of P-precipitates at the PSG/Si interface and in the emitter region is strongly affected by adjusting the diffusion parameters of $POCl_3$-N_2 gas flow and temperature.

To show the effect of precipitation at the PSG/Si interface, GD-OES measurements are carried out on PSG structures. Thereby it is possible to measure the course of concentration of P and O in the PSG layer and at the PSG/Si interface.

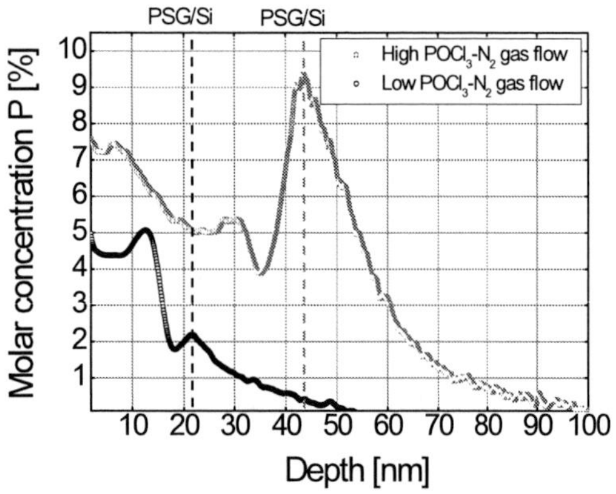

Fig. 5.   Molar concentration profile of P in PSG and at the PSG/Si interface, measured by GD-OES. The PSG/Si interface is indicated by dashed lines for both samples.

Fig. 5 shows the concentration profile of P in the PSG layer as a function of the $POCl_3$-N_2 gas flow. A comparison of the concentration profiles makes it clear that the PSG has to be regarded as a multi-layered dopant source [9]. Furthermore, the reduction of the $POCl_3$-N_2 gas flow leads to several effects in the PSG and at the PSG/Si interface. On the one hand, the P concentration in the PSG layer is significantly lowered by the reduction of the $POCl_3$-N_2 gas flow. On the other hand, Fig. 5 indicates different concentration gradients in the sub-layers of the PSG as a function of the $POCl_3$-N_2 gas flow. The P concentration at the PSG/Si interface is drastically increased in the case of high $POCl_3$-N_2 gas flow condition. Therefore it can be assumed that on the one hand the high $POCl_3$-N_2 gas flow leads to an intensified formation of inactive phosphorous on the Si emitter surface region. On the other hand, this precipitate formation on the Si emitter surface region leads to an accumulation of the P in the PSG close to the PSG/Si interface. To examine the effect of the precipitate formation more closely, the concentration of O in the PSG, at the PSG/Si interface and in silicon is investigated.

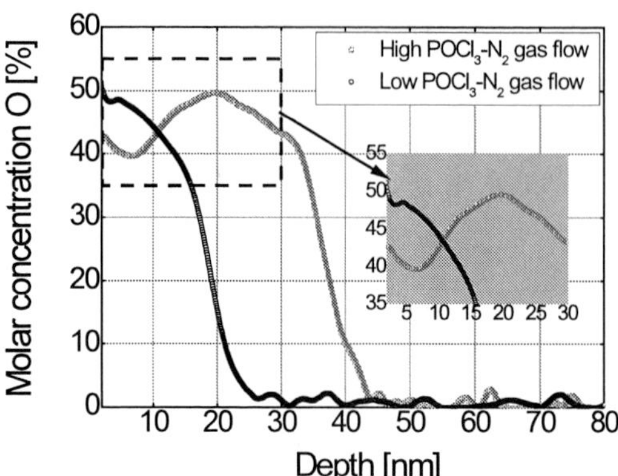

Fig. 6.   Molar concentration profile of oxygen in the PSG and at the PSG/Si interface, measured by GD-OES.

In Fig. 6 the molar concentration profile of O in the PSG and at the PSG/Si interface is shown. It is apparent that for the case of high $POCl_3$-N_2 gas flow, the O concentration drops in the first 5 nm. The comparison with the high P concentration in Fig 5 within the first 5 nm supports the hypothesis of high amount of P_xO_y in this region.

In the depth between 5 nm and 20 nm the O concentration increases in the PSG while the P concentration drops. This leads to a second PSG sublayer consisting of P_xO_y and SiO_2.

In the third sublayer the O concentration sharply decreases and the P concentration increases towards the PSG/Si interface. Fig. 5 and 6 indicate that the composition of the PSG layer and the thickness of the PSG sublayers are significantly correlated with the $POCl_3$-N_2 gas flow. As the O concentration within the first nanometers of the emitter does not seem to drop to zero, but shows molar concentrations of around 3%, we could assume that the mechanisms of precipitate formation on the silicon surface may be influenced not only by P, but also by the relatively high concentration of oxygen in silicon.

To ensure that the developed emitters are optimized to meet the requirements of a screen-printing process, the surface concentrations of the electrically active and inactive P in Si are measured by ECV and SIMS. Previous results show how strongly the $POCl_3$-N_2 gas flow affects the precipitation of P, which leads to a significant increase in the surface concentration of the inactive P [2, 3, 10-15].

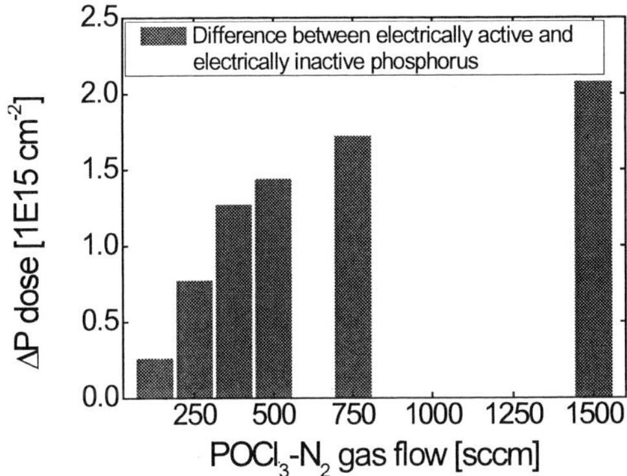

Fig. 7. Difference between the total and electrically active phosphorus surface concentration, ΔP, as a function of the $POCl_3$-N_2 gas flow during pre-deposition, as measured by ECV and SIMS.

By reducing the surface concentration of the inactive P, we can significantly reduce emitter recombination without decreasing the emitter sheet resistance. However, the influence of the reduction of the P-precipitate density on the contact formation has to be investigated, in particular when using the screen-printing metallization procedure. For screen-printing metallization technology, low contact resistivity has to be assured for the metal-semiconductor contact. By the combination of high lateral conductivity and excellent ohmic contacts, a high FF, $\geq$ 80% can be achieved.

The influence of the electrically inactive P on the screen-printing based front-side contact can be illustrated by scanning electron microscopy (SEM) images. Therefore, emitters with different shares of inactive P are contacted via screen-printing. After this, the Ag front grid is wet chemically removed using HF, and the contacts are analyzed by means of SEM.

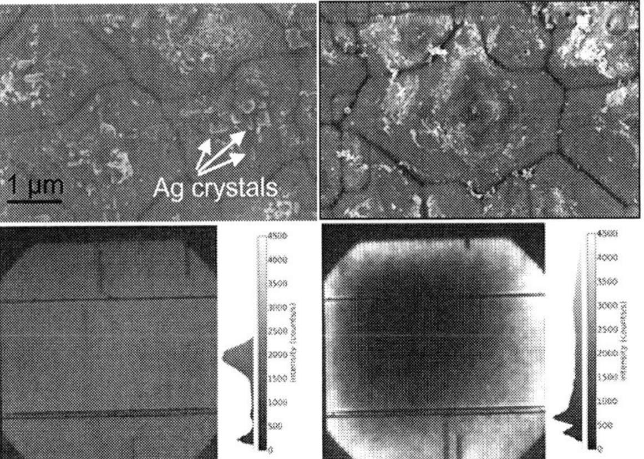

Fig. 8. Top: SEM analysis after removing the Ag finger by a wet chemical HF etching procedure. Bottom: EL images of the same samples.

Fig. 8 shows a comparison of two SEM images of emitters contacted by means of screen-printing. In the image on the left the emitter was processed with an increased $POCl_3$-N_2 gas flow. We see that the formation of Ag crystals is enhanced on the emitter with the higher $POCl_3$-N_2 gas flow. By contrast, in the image on the right, Ag crystals were scarcely formed for the emitter with reduced $POCl_3$-N_2 gas flow. It must thereby be noted that for both emitters the concentration of the active P is at the same level. This finding strengthens the assumption that not only the concentration of the electrically active P, but also the density of the inactive P plays a decisive role in screen-printing metallization of the solar cell front-side. A juxtaposition of these SEM pictures with electroluminescence (EL) images of the same samples underlines this hypothesis. In the left EL image, which represents the emitter with the increased $POCl_3$-N_2 gas flow, the front-side contacting was successful. The measurement of the IV parameters of this sample shows a FF of 80.3% and a series resistance value of 0.29 Ωcm^2. The evaluation of the IV characteristics of the right sample (reduced thickness of the electrically inactive P) shows a FF of only 54% and a series resistance of > 2 Ωcm^2 which can also be illustrated in the inhomogeneous and cloudy EL image.

To investigate the influence of the electrically active and inactive P on the contacting of the presented emitters, the transfer length method (TLM) was used. Results are given in Tab. I.

TABLE I

MEASUREMENTS OF THE CONTACT RESISTIVITY OF TWO EMITTERS IN A SCREEN-PRINTING PROCESS AS A FUNCTION OF $POCL_3$-N_2 GAS FLOW DURING PRE-DEPOSITION

	High POCl₃-N₂ gas flow	Low POCl₃-N₂ gas flow
ρ_c [mΩcm²]	2.0 ± 0.4	117.4 ± 23.4

V. SOLAR CELL RESULTS

To verify the potential of optimized homogeneous emitters from the DoE, screen-printed solar cells with full area Al-BSFs and homogeneous emitters were fabricated on 6" boron doped Cz-Si material with a base resistivity of approximately 2.5 Ωcm. The solar cells have a 3-busbar front grid (single print) and a thickness of approximately 160 µm. A standard PECVD SiN_x deposition (direct plasma, low frequency by centrotherm) is used for emitter passivation. The applied emitters have the same electrically active emitter surface doping of $N_s \sim 2\times10^{20}$ cm^{-3} However, they differ in the surface concentration of the electrically inactive P. For all emitters industrially feasible drive-in times are used.

TABLE II

COMPARISON OF AVERAGE IV PARAMETERS OF SOLAR CELLS WITH STANDARD AND OPTIMIZED HOMOGENEOUS EMITTERS

	j_{sc} [mA/cm²]	V_{oc} [mV]	FF [%]	η [%]
Reference Emitter	36.9	633	79.7	18.6
Optimized Emitter	37.6	643	80.1	19.4

TABLE III

MEASUREMENTS OF THE CONTACT RESISTIVITY OF TWO
EMITTERS IN A SCREEN-PRINTING PROCESS AS A FUNCTION OF
$POCl_3$-N_2 GAS FLOW

	Reference Emitter	Optimized Emitter
ρ_c [mΩcm²]	0.9 ± 0.2	1.2 ± 0.2

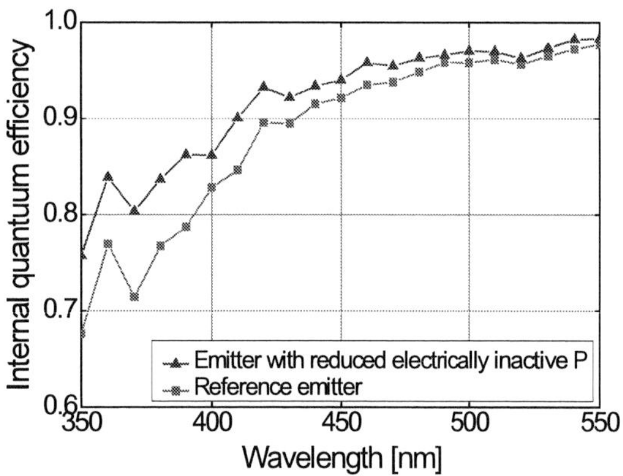

Fig. 9. Comparison between measured internal quantum efficiencies of solar cells with a reference emitter and an optimized emitter with reduced electrically inactive P.

By a slight adjustment of the diffusion parameters during the pre-deposition phase, an increase in j_{sc} of 0.7 mA/cm², and an increase in V_{oc} of up to 10 mV is obtained. Due to the constant level of the FF, a gain in efficiency of 0.6%$_{abs}$ is achieved. The increase in the internal quantum efficiency in the short wavelength region (350-550 nm) of the improved emitter structure shows that the reduction of the electrically inactive P not only reduces emitter recombination, but also increases the emitter's blue response. The analysis of the solar cells studied show that independently of the concentration of the electrically active P, a lower limit of the concentration of the electrically inactive phosphorus must be present for satisfactory contacting. For the emitters examined here, this amounts to ~6×10^{20} cm^{-3}. With the emitter structures studied, the lower limit of the plateau depth of the electrically inactive P is ~60 nm.

These experimental data confirm the simulated data of Fig. 4 and allow an estimation of the maximum achievable efficiency applying an optimized homogeneous emitter. A comparison of the solar cell results with Fig. 4 shows also that by further adjustment of the diffusion parameters even higher solar cell efficiencies may be achieved.

After determination of the optimal parameters in Fig. 4, the optimized emitter can also be transferred to novel multi-busbar solar cell designs [16]. According to the initial results, efficiencies > 19.5% may be achieved.

V. CONCLUSION AND OUTLOOK

In this work, we used a design of experiment (DoE) study for the determination of the influence of diffusion parameters on emitter characteristics. We focused on optimizing the emitter saturation current density without significantly increasing the emitter sheet resistance. The combination of results from the DoE and the Sentaurus Device simulator shows good correlations between the diffusion parameters and the solar cell efficiency. Solar cell results of up to 19.5% have been achieved so far on standard p-type 6'' Cz material.

Further implementation of the electrically inactive P in the device simulation will reduce the gap between simulated and experimental solar cell results. This approach would allow a further gain in the efficiency of screen-printed solar cells via additional adjustment of the diffusion parameters and the front grid metallization structure.

ACKNOWLEDGEMENT

The financial support from the German BMU project FKZ 0325581 is gratefully acknowledged, in particular for the characterization equipment.

REFERENCES

[1] S.L.C. Ferreira, R.E. Bruns, H.S. Ferreira, G.D. Matos, J.M. David, G.C. Brandao, E.G.P. da Silva, L.A. Portugal, P.S. dos Reis, A.S. Souza, W.N.L. dos Santos, "Box-Behnken design: An alternative for the optimization of analytical methods," *Analytica Chimica Acta,* vol. 597, pp. 179-186, 2007.

[2] A. Dastgheib-Shirazi, M. Steyer, G. Micard, H. Wagner, P. Altermatt, G. Hahn, "Effects of process conditions for the n$^+$-emitter formation in crystalline silicon," in *38th IEEE PVSC,* 2012, p. 1584.

[3] A. Dastgheib-Shirazi, M. Steyer, G. Micard, H. Wagner, P. Altermatt, G. Hahn, "Relationships between diffusion parameters and phosphorus precipitation during the POCl$_3$ diffusion process," *Energy Procedia,* in press, 2013.

[4] H. Wagner, A. Dastgheib-Shirazi, R. Chen, S.T. Dunham, M. Kessler, P.P. Altermatt, "Improving the predictive power of modeling the emitter diffusion by fully including the phosphosilicate glass (PSG) layer," in *37th IEEE PVSC,* 2011, p. 2957.

[5] G. Micard, A. Dastgheib-Shirazi, B. Raabe, G. Hahn, "Diffusivity analysis of POCl$_3$ emitter SIMS profiles for semi empirical parameterization in Sentaurus Process," in *26th EU PVSEC,* 2011, p. 1446.

[6] G. Micard, A. Dastgheib-Shirazi, M. Steyer, H. Wagner, P. Altermatt, G. Hahn, "Advances in the understanding of phosphorus silicate glass (PSG) formation for accurate process simulation of phosphorus diffusion," in *27th EU PVSEC,* 2012, p. 1355.

[7] M. Steyer, A. Dastgheib-Shirazi, H. Wagner, G. Micard, P. Altermatt, G. Hahn, "A study of various methods for the analysis of the phosphosilicate glass layer," in *27th EU PVSEC*, 2012, p. 1325.

[8] D.E. Kane and R.M. Swanson, "Measurement of the emitter saturation current by a contactless photoconductivity decay method," in *18th IEEE PVSC*, 1985, p. 578.

[9] R.N. Ghoshtagore , Phosphorus Diffusion Processes in SiO2 Films, Thin Solid Films, 25(2), 1975, p. 501-513

[10] D. Nobili, A. Armigliato, M. Finnetti, S. Solmi, "Precipitation as the phenomenon responsible for the electrically inactive phosphorus in silicon," *Journal of Applied Physics*, vol. 53(3), pp. 1484-1491, 1982.

[11] D.C. Douglass, T.M. Duncan, K.L. Walker, R. Csencsits, "A study of phosphorus in silicate glass with ^{31}P nuclear magnetic resonance spectroscopy," *Journal of Applied Physics*, vol. 58(1), pp. 197-203, 1985.

[12] E. Antoncik, "The influence of the solubility limit on diffusion of phosphorus and arsenic into silicon," *Applied Physics A*, vol. 58, pp. 117-123, 1994.

[13] A. Bentzen, J.S. Christensen, B.G. Svensson, A. Holt, "Understanding phosphorus emitter diffusion in silicon solar cell processing," in *21st EU PVSEC*, 2006, p. 1388

[14] G. Beshkov, V. Krastev, H. Maciel, T.-A. Tang, V. Huang, "X-ray photoelectron spectroscopy study of phosphorus silicate glasses," *Surface and Coatings Technology*, vol, 161, pp. 11-19, 2002.

[15] V. Vais, M. Milica, A.F. Brana, T. Leo, J.M. Fernandez, "Mechanisms involved in the formation of phosphosilicate glass from a phosphoric acid dopant source," *Progress in Photovoltaics: Research and Applications*, vol. 19(3), pp. 280-285, 2010.

[16] S. Braun, R. Nissler, C. Ebert, D. Habermann, G. Hahn, "High efficiency multi-busbar solar cells and modules," in 39th IEEE, PVSC, 2013, in press.

Amir Dastgheib-Shirazi was born in Mashhad, Iran in 1978. He received his Diploma in physics from University of Konstanz, Germany in 2008. He is currently working on his PhD in the Photovoltaic Division at the University of Konstanz. His scientific work is focused on emitter formation and surface morphology effects in crystalline silicon. He is the author/co-author of more than 20 publications in journals and conference proceeding and holds 2 patents.

Gabriel Micard was born in Bordeaux (France), in 1977. He received the B.S. and M.S. degrees in electronics from Bordeaux I university, in 2001 and the Ph.D. degree in Physics from Konstanz University, Konstanz (Germany) in 2011. From 2005 to 2011, he did his PhD degree at the Photovoltaics Departement of the University of Konstanz where he studied nanocrystalline silicon grown by low-energy PECVD for photovoltaics application and developed several analytical theories aiming at extracting electrical parameters of Grain Boundaries in multicrystalline silicon from their light beam induced current (LBIC) contrast profile. Since 2011, he is post-doctoral researcher at the University of Konstanz dealing with crystalline silicon solar cells physical simulation, series resistance numerical and analytical estimation, POCl$_3$ diffusion theoretical studies and porous silicon optical properties numerical estimation. He is the author or coauthor of more than 20 articles, and 1 patent.

Hannes Wagner was born in Hamburg, Germany, in 1982. He received the diploma degree in physics from the University of Göttingen, Germany, in 2010. He is currently pursuing the Ph.D. degree at the Photovoltaics Department of the University of Hannover, Germany. His research focuses on process and device modeling of solar cells. Major tasks have been developing physical models to predict diffusion profiles in silicon, analyzing the influence of lifetime differences in multicrystalline silicon materials, and modeling of solar cell heterostructures.

Michael Steyer received his M.Sc. degree in physics from the University of Konstanz in 2012. He is currently working as Research Assistant in the Photovoltaics Division at the University of Konstanz. His research interests include emitter optimization for screen printed solar cells, PSG characterization and the influence of rear surface morphology on passivation and reflection.

Pietro P. Altermatt received the Ph.D. degree from the University of Konstanz, Germany, in 1996, for his activities at the Centre for Photovoltaics, University of New South Wales, Sydney, Australia. He is currently with the Leibniz University of Hanover, Germany, as Head of the Simulation Group, where Si solar cells are investigated by means of numerical device simulations and by optical modeling. His research interests include the design of test samples for the extraction of device or silicon material parameters, the improvement of simulation models, and the development of solar cell design strategies that are tailored to meet specific demands in terms of materials, geometries, fabrication processes, and applications.

203

Giso Hahn was born in Frankfurt am Main, Germany, in 1969. He received his Diploma in physics from University of Stuttgart, Germany, in 1995 and the Ph.D. degree in physics from University of Konstanz, Germany, in 1999. He received his Venia Legendi (Habilitation) in experimental physics from University of Konstanz in 2005. Since 2009 he is Apl. Professor in the Department of Physics at University of Konstanz.

He is Head of the Photovoltaics Division in the Department of Physics at the University of Konstanz consisting of more than 50 employees. His research interests are focused on crystalline silicon materials and solar cell process development, including characterization of promising low cost materials for photovoltaic applications and development of adapted solar cell processes for these and other materials. He is the author/coauthor of more than 230 publications in journals, books, and conference proceedings and holds several patents.

Prof. Hahn is a member of the scientific committees of various conference series (e.g. IEEE PVSC, EU PVSEC, SiliconPV) and workshops. Among other scientific and technological achievements like e.g. reaching record efficiencies for selected crystalline silicon materials and detailed characterization of efficiency limiting crystal defects, his group is interested in transferring technologies from the laboratory stage to industry.

Leveraging Silicon Epitaxy to Fabricate Excellent Front Surface Regions for Thin Interdigitated Back Contact Solar Cells

Simeon C. Baker-Finch and Paul A. Basore

Abstract—**Epitaxy can be used to fabricate doped front surface regions that enable high interdigitated back contact (IBC) silicon solar cell efficiency. One- and two-dimensional simulations show that an epitaxial layer with a constant phosphorus dopant concentration on the order of 10^{17}–10^{18} cm^{-3} can possess the properties of an excellent front surface region for an n-type IBC cell. With appropriate control of dopant concentration and thickness, the epitaxially grown region passivates a textured surface, and provides the lateral conductivity necessary to enable high fill factor. The combination of these two factors drives a simulated efficiency improvement above 0.3% absolute over an n-type IBC cell with a typical 200-Ω/sq phosphorus diffusion (e.g., from POCl$_3$). Importantly, the epitaxial front surface region can occupy the entire volume of the pyramidal texture. We, therefore, propose an exemplary process sequence for device fabrication that places texture etching after epitaxial growth.**

Index Terms—**Photovoltaic cells, semiconductor device modeling, semiconductor epitaxial layers, silicon, surface texture.**

I. Introduction

THIN Si solar cells may offer the dual advantages of high efficiency and low cost. The costs of crystallization and wafer sawing are eliminated by depositing crystalline Si by epitaxy on an inexpensive or recyclable template. Epitaxial layers with thicknesses in the range of 10–100 μm possess the high efficiency potential and stability of traditional crystalline Si wafers [1]. Additionally, epitaxial Si is compatible with a broad range of well understood proven process technologies [1]. In this study, we describe an opportunity for leveraging epitaxy to simplify the fabrication of a high-efficiency rear-junction all-rear-contact solar cell. We demonstrate that a doped front surface region (a.k.a. "field" [2]) can be "grown-in" during epitaxy and, via detailed modeling, that the region enables high efficiency in an exemplary interdigitated back contact (IBC) architecture.

A. Doped Regions for Solar Cells, Grown by Epitaxy

The utility of epitaxy in forming well-defined doped regions and dopant concentration transitions for solar cells has been investigated extensively (see, e.g., [3]–[6]). Many such studies focus on collector (aka "emitter") formation (usually on the sunward surface) [5], [7]. In this case, the epitaxial layer parameters (viz., doping and depth) must be chosen to meet the competing demands of 1) low Auger recombination, 2) effective field-effect surface passivation, and 3) low resistance contact to front side metal [5], [8]. Texturing the front surface to gain an optical benefit further complicates collector epitaxy. One approach is to texture after epitaxy. In this case, the competing demands outlined earlier can only be met if very little of the doped region is removed during texture formation; plasma texturing has been demonstrated [7]. In a second approach, the substrate can be textured before epitaxy. In this case, epitaxial growth tends not to conform to the texture; it rounds features, thus increasing reflectance [1], [4].

B. Interdigitated Back Contact Cells and their Front Surface Regions

The advantages of IBC cells are well known and numerous. Some key benefits are 1) the elimination of shading by front contacts, 2) the reduction of series resistance by freedom from the tradeoff with finger shading, and 3) potential simplification of module fabrication. High efficiency has been demonstrated on large scale [9]. However, the complexity of the IBC structure can incur high cost.

Typical n-type Si IBC cells feature phosphorus-doped textured front surfaces. Pyramidal texture (as is applied to industrial monocrystalline Si cells) reduces front surface reflectance and enhances light trapping. Doping of the textured front surface to a sheet resistance of 100–200 Ω/sq 1) reduces the sensitivity of the device to the front surface recombination velocity via the field effect [10], 2) increases the fill factor of the device by providing a pathway for lateral conduction of majority carriers [11] and reducing the ideality factor of surface recombination [12], and 3) improves the long-term UV stability of surface passivation [13], [14]. Typical design rules would further require that the front surface region is not too heavily doped so that it neither 1) reduces blue response (collection efficiency near the front surface would be reduced by Auger recombination exacerbated by bandgap narrowing) nor 2) causes parasitic free carrier absorption.

In contrast with the traditional diffusion of dopants, epitaxy facilitates precise selection of dopant concentration. As we show, epitaxy eliminates tradeoffs that typically challenge the practical formation of the optimal front surface region.

Manuscript received June 10, 2013; revised July 29, 2013; accepted August 2, 2013. Date of publication September 16, 2013; date of current version December 16, 2013.

The authors are with the Hanwha Solar America, Santa Clara, CA 95051 USA (e-mail: simeon.bakerfinch@gmail.com; pvspecialist@gmail.com).

Color versions of one or more of the figures in this paper are available online at http://ieeexplore.ieee.org.

Digital Object Identifier 10.1109/JPHOTOV.2013.2278880

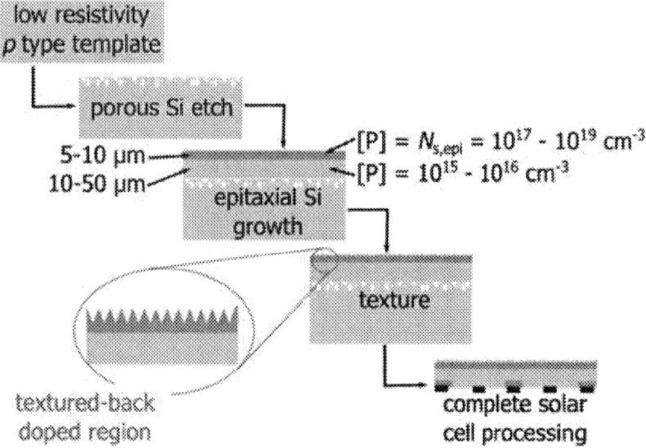

Fig. 1.   Possible process sequence incorporating the epitaxial growth and texturing of a phosphorus doped front surface region.

II. CONCEPT

In this contribution, we describe and assess the epitaxial growth and texturization of a phosphorus-doped region for the front surface of a thin IBC cell. An approximate process sequence is demonstrated in Fig. 1. A template wafer of crystalline Si is etched to form a porous layer that will later allow the exfoliation of the active layer and reuse of the template [15], [16]. The epitaxial growth features a moderately doped n-type base of some 10–50 μm thickness and a top layer of more heavily doped n-type material. Alkaline etching consumes some of this top layer, leaving behind a doped region that is greater than the depth of the pyramidal texture. The remaining cell fabrication processes are performed on the rear side after exfoliation from the template. Note that epitaxy could be further leveraged to form an n- or p-type doped region at the rear. The formation of a p$^+$/n/n$^+$ or n$^+$/n/n$^+$ structure likely offers process simplification and cost reduction.

III. ONE-DIMENSIONAL SIMULATIONS: RECOMBINATION AND COLLECTION EFFICIENCY IN THE DOPED REGION

A. PC1D Model for Pyramidal Texture

The popular 1-D device simulator PC1D [17] mimics the effect of pyramidal texture by accounting for 1) oblique traversal of light and 2) enhanced volume and surface recombination [18]. This second "correction" has important impacts in this study. Key characteristics of the simulations that follow are illustrated in Fig. 2 and include the following.

1) The texture depth $h = 5$ μm is a PC1D input.
2) The texture angle ω is a PC1D input. It is set to 54.7° (assuming $\langle 111 \rangle$-bounded pyramidal texture).
3) PC1D accounts for the increased volume of elements along its solution axis x, with the origin at the center of a texture facet, by assigning each node an area multiplier $A(x) = (A_0 - 1) \exp[-x^2/\sigma^2] + 1$. The front surface area multiplier $A_0 = 1/\cos(\omega)$. The parameter $\sigma = h/6$ so that at $x = h/2$, only 1% of the area enlargement remains.
4) We define the depth d of the epitaxial front surface region along the PC1D solution axis. The doped region with con-

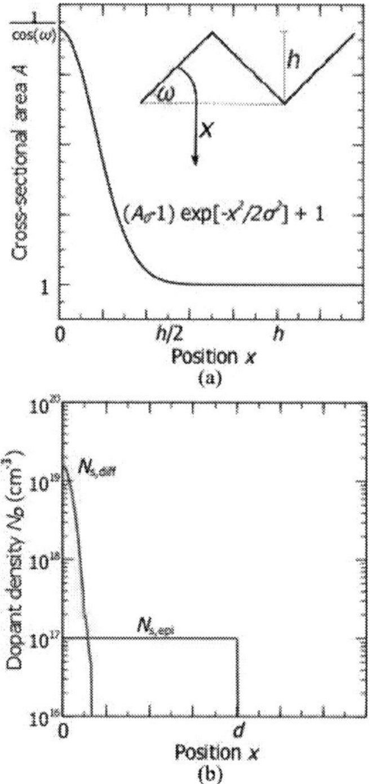

Fig. 2.   (a) Cross-sectional area enhancement. (b) Reference diffused and representative epitaxially grown front surface region dopant densities plotted along the PC1D solution axis. Note that the reference diffusion is shallow with a peak dopant concentration around 2×10^{19} cm^{-3}, while $N_{s,\mathrm{epi}}$ and d are varied in simulations.

centration $N_{s,\mathrm{epi}}$ extends beyond the physical depth of the pyramids when $d \geq h/2$ (i.e., $d \geq 2.5$ μm).
5) We assume that the surface recombination velocity varies with $N_{s,\mathrm{epi}}$ following the parameterization (for SiO$_2$-passivated surfaces) in [19]. Surface charge density Q_s/q is varied. An identical approach is applied when simulating the diffused reference performance.

B. Collection Efficiency at the Doped Front Surface

The impact of the front surface dopant profile on "blue response" (defined here as the quantum efficiency at which carriers generated at $x = 0$ are transported to the high–low front junction) is readily simulated with PC1D. We employ Donolato's reciprocity theorem [20] to arrive at the results illustrated in Fig. 3. To do so, we simulate the application of a forward bias (e.g., 600 mV) in the dark. The normalized pn product at $x = 0$ is equal to the proportion of light generated minority carriers that would be transported from the surface to the high–low junction before recombining.

For lightly doped front surface regions, η_c is high, since both surface and Auger recombination rates are low. Epitaxial front surface regions can outperform a traditional light diffusion ($\sim$200 Ω/sq) for a range of dopant densities below approximately 10^{18} cm^{-3}. Heavy doping reduces η_c by enhancing Auger recombination. Drastic increases in surface recombination and reduction in blue response are caused by a negatively

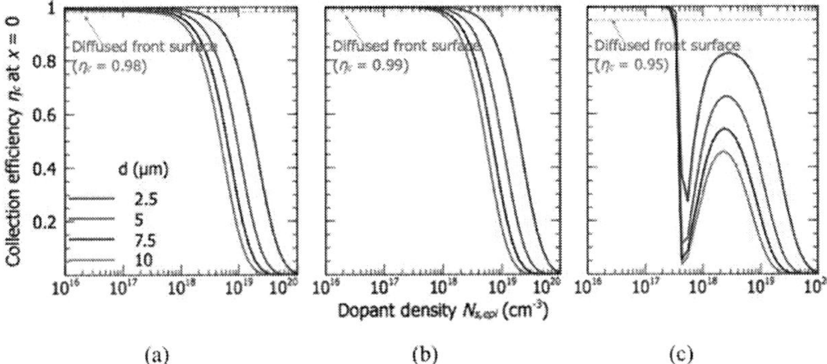

Fig. 3. Simulated "blue response" of epitaxially grown, pyramidally textured front surface regions with various surface charge densities. (a) $Q_s/q = 0$. (b) $Q_s/q = 10^{12}$ cm^{-2}. (c) $Q_s/q = -10^{12}$ cm^{-2}.

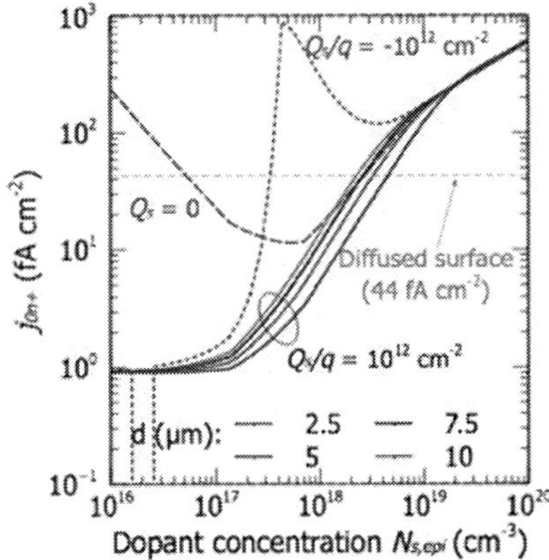

Fig. 4. Simulated recombination current prefactor for passivated, epitaxially grown, and textured front surface regions. Results for neutral and negative surface charges assume $d = 5$ μm. The diffused reference surface is positively charged ($Q_s/q = 10^{12}$ cm^{-2}).

charged passivation layer that depletes surfaces doped to between 5×10^{17} and 10^{18} cm^{-3}.

C. Recombination Current Prefactor

The recombination activity in the front surface region additionally influences the open-circuit voltage of a completed cell. Fig. 4 plots the simulated recombination current density prefactor j_{0n+} for a range of parameters. For a diffused reference dopant profile, assuming surface charge density $Q_s/q = 10^{12}$ cm^{-2}, we calculate $j_{0n+} = 44$ fA cm^{-2} (at 25 °C).

For epitaxial front surface regions, well-known behavior is demonstrated when the surface is charge neutral ($Q_s = 0$; see the dashed line in Fig. 4): highest j_{0n+} is expected at either 1) low dopant concentrations, where poor "screening" of the front surface allows a high rate of surface recombination or 2) high dopant concentrations, which give rise to excessive Auger recombination in the bulk of the front surface region. Negative surface charge ($Q_s/q = -10^{12}$ cm^{-2}; see the dotted line in Fig. 4) leads to depletion of moderately doped surfaces, with maximum surface recombination occurring when electron and

hole concentrations at the surface are approximately equal. An associated increase in j_{0n+} of several orders of magnitude means that negative charge is of little interest, and we do not consider it further. By contrast, a positive surface charge, as is typically present in SiN$_x$, contributes field-effect passivation beyond that already provided by the surface doping. This allows j_{0n+} to be relatively low for all surface dopant concentrations (at least until Auger recombination begins to dominate).

The depth of the doped region determines the dopant concentration at which the onset of Auger recombination begins to increase j_{0n+}. For example, with a positive surface charge and $N_{s,\mathrm{epi}} = 10^{18}$ cm^{-3}, a 2.5-μm deep region exhibits 2.5 fold smaller j_{0n+} than a 10-μm deep equivalent.

IV. PARASITIC FREE CARRIER ABSORPTION

Heavily doped regions reduce the short-circuit current potential of practical devices through parasitic free carrier absorption (FCA) of infrared radiation. By increasing the path length of light in the doped region, front surface texturing can exacerbate FCA. When a front surface region extends beyond the texture, FCA loss can become a significant concern.

To account for the path length enhancement in pyramidal texture, we consider only the first pass of light through the front surface region. Assuming normal incidence, and unity front surface transmission at the first interaction, rays pass into the texture at an angle ψ with respect to the *local* surface normal and into the bulk with angle θ with respect to the macroscopic normal (see [21]). At a wavelength of 1200 nm, assuming encapsulant refractive index of 1.5, and texture angle $\omega = 54.7°$, $\psi = 20.4°$, and $\theta = 34.3°$.

Simplifying the texture to two dimensions, FCA *within* the pyramids is the average of the absorptance of rays evenly distributed across the textured facet. The total FCA A_{FCA} in a doped region extending beyond the pyramid is given by

$$A = \frac{\cos\omega}{h} \int^{h/\cos\omega} 1 - \exp\left[\frac{-\alpha\tan\omega}{\cos(\omega - \varphi)} x\right] dx$$
$$+ \left(1 - \exp\left[-\alpha\frac{(d - h/2)}{\cos\theta}\right]\right)$$

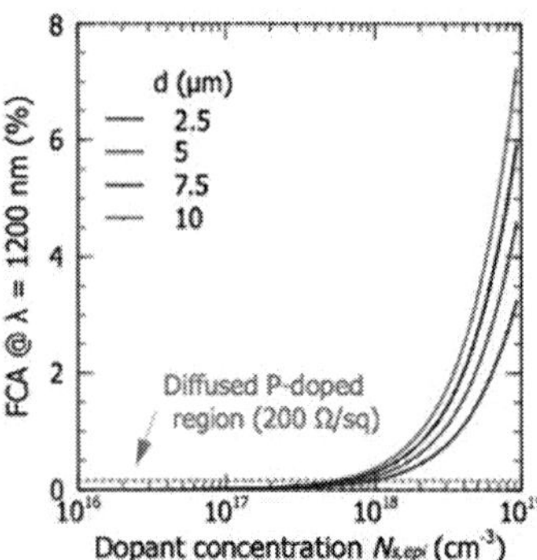

Fig. 5. Simulated FCA loss in the first pass through a textured front surface region with varying depth and dopant density.

where α_{FCA} is the dopant density- and wavelength-dependent FCA coefficient [22]. The first component of the sum is the FCA within the pyramids, while the second is the FCA in the region that extends beyond the pyramids into the cell bulk.

An upper limit on A_{FCA} can be calculated by applying α_{FCA} at 1200 nm (since α_{FCA} increases with wavelength). This upper limit is plotted for epitaxially grown and textured front surface regions in Fig. 5, and is compared with a reference diffused region, which parasitically absorbs just 0.16% of incident radiation in a single pass. Epitaxial regions suffer less FCA loss when $N_{s,\mathrm{epi}} < \sim 5 \times 10^{17}$ cm^{-3}. A precise comparison would require ray tracing of the many passes of light across the substrate and through the front surface region and is beyond the scope of this study. The key conclusion to be drawn here is that, despite their significant volume compared with a diffused reference, epitaxially grown front surface fields do not cause unreasonably large parasitic FCA loss as long as $N_{s,\mathrm{epi}}$ is kept below around 10^{18} cm^{-3}.

V. DEVICE SIMULATIONS

A. Simulation Approach

We employ the 2-D conductive boundary modeling freeware PC2D [23] to approximate the behavior of thin IBC cells with an epitaxially grown and textured front surface region. Simulation parameters are listed in Table I. Device thickness and contact pitch are chosen to be compatible with high-throughput epitaxy and the alignment tolerance possible with industrial metallization approaches.

We incorporate j_{0n+} values calculated previously, and account for "blue response" by reducing the front surface transmittance T in PC2D (since the font surface in PC2D is equivalent to the edge of the high–low junction). We approximate the wavelength dependence of this reduction by an exponential decay from 300 nm with exponential constant 50 nm, such that

$$T(\lambda) = T_0(\lambda) \cdot \left(1 - (1 - \eta_c)\exp\left(\frac{300 - \lambda}{50}\right)\right)$$

where T_0 is the optical transmittance of the front surface (textured and coated with an optimally thick SiN$_x$).

Parameter	Value	Units
Active layer thickness	50	μm
[P] in base	2 or 5×10^{15}	cm^{-3}
Bulk lifetime	300	μs
Pitch	1.2	mm
Rear p^+ (collector) fraction	75	%
Rear p^+ sheet resistance	80	Ω/sq
Rear n^+ sheet resistance	80	Ω/sq
Contact opening width (n+ or p+ contacts)	120	μm
Rear internal reflectance	90	%
Front surface sheet resistance	Fig. 6.	Ω/sq
Front surface j_{0n+}	Fig 4. ($Q_s/q = 10^{12}$ cm^{-2})	fA cm^{-2}
Front surface transmittance	See text and Fig. 3.	%
External series resistance	0.4	Ω cm^2

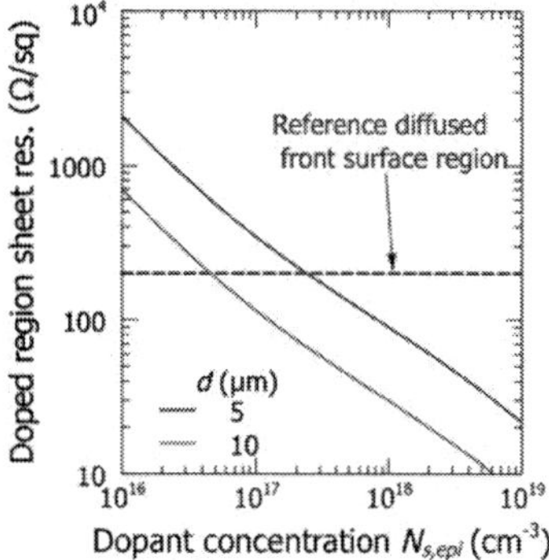

Fig. 6. Sheet resistance of front surfaces used as PC2D inputs.

B. Lateral Transport in an Epitaxially Grown and Textured Region

The front surface region plays a role in the lateral conduction of majority carriers [11]. PC2D simulates this phenomenon by assigning lateral conductivity to boundaries. In the case of a textured epitaxial region, the appropriate choice of conductivity is not obvious. For our purpose, we assume that if $d < h/2$ (i.e., a discontinuous doped region), the region has zero lateral conductivity. Only the region beyond the pyramids contributes boundary conductivity, resulting in the sheet resistivity dependence on d and $N_{s,\mathrm{epi}}$ depth depicted in Fig. 6.

C. Simulation Results

Two-dimensional device simulation results are illustrated in Fig. 7. It is immediately apparent that epitaxially grown and textured front surface regions of well-controlled dopant density have the potential to drive an improvement in the efficiency of thin IBC cells. At optimal $N_{s,\mathrm{epi}} = 2 \times 10^{17}$ cm^{-3} and $d = 10$ μm, such a region outperforms a traditional diffused reference by 0.3–0.4% absolute.

When the base is doped to a density of 5×10^{15} cm^{-3}, there is a plateau in conversion efficiency and j_{sc} for a range of $N_{s,\mathrm{epi}}$ below around 10^{18} cm^{-3} for the range of d. The slight increase

208

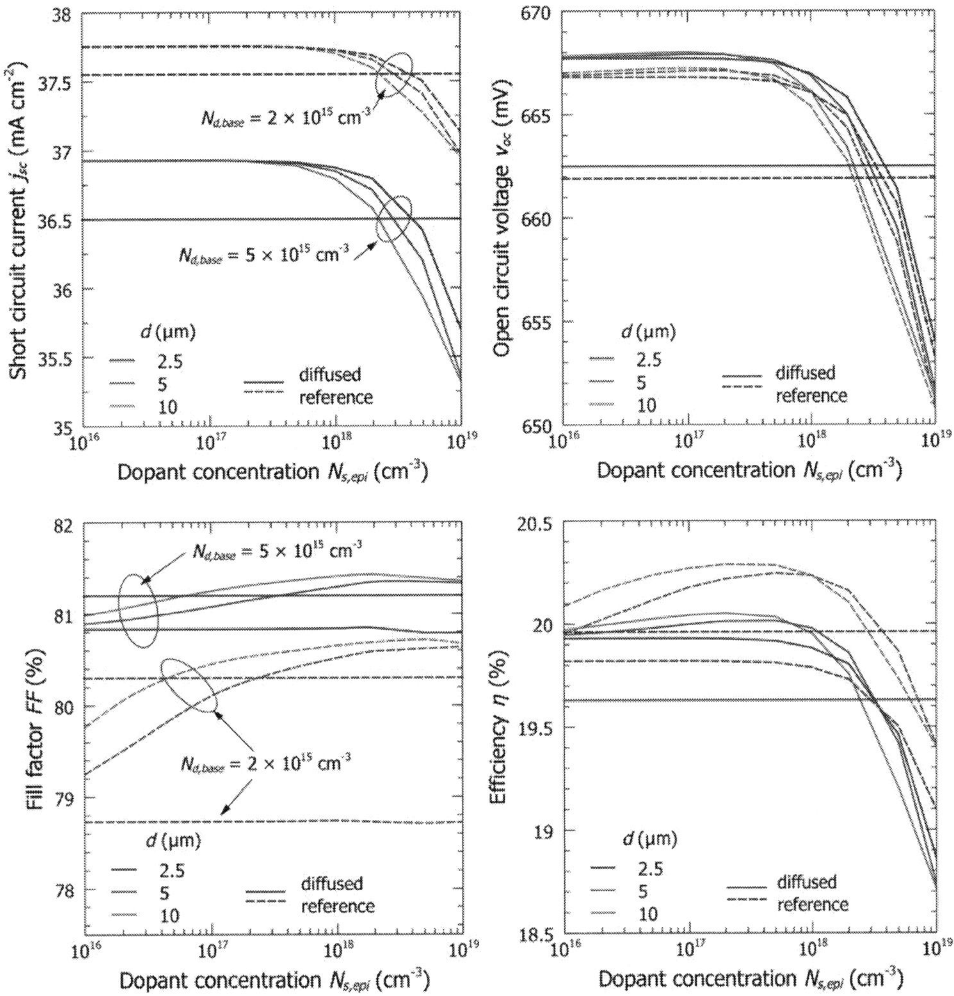

Fig. 7. Two-dimensional simulation results. Thin IBC cell performance parameters and their dependence on front surface region parameters.

in v_{oc} to an optimum between $N_{s,\mathrm{epi}} = 10^{17}$ and 10^{18} cm^{-3} is attributed to a subtle (as yet unidentified) effect of increased front surface region conductivity. Fill factor depends on the front surface region properties, albeit weakly (it varies by 0.4% absolute although the front surface region sheet resistance varies by two orders of magnitude).

On the other hand, with a lesser doped base ($N_d = 2 \times 10^{15}$ cm^{-3}), lateral conduction in the front surface region becomes considerable in comparison with the lateral conductivity provided by the base. Low dopant densities result in series resistance losses, reduced fill factor, and, hence, reduced efficiency.

VI. Scanning Electron Microscope Characterization of an Exemplary Epitaxial Front Surface Region

An epitaxially grown and textured front surface region was prepared as a demonstration of the concept investigated in this study. In particular, two epitaxial layers (a $\sim$60-μm thick lowly doped base and a 20-μm thick highly doped region) were grown

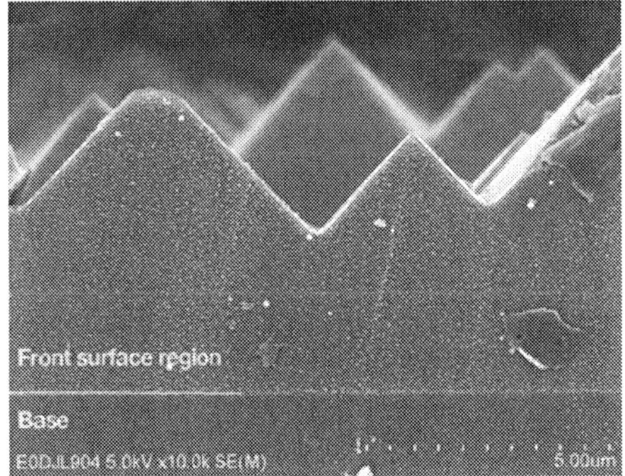

Fig. 8. SEM image illustrating a front surface region that extends beyond the depth of the pyramidal surface texture.

on a low resistivity p-type Cz wafer. The entire stack was etched in an aqueous solution of KOH and texturing additive; a random array of upright pyramids was, hence, formed on the surface of the uppermost epitaxial layer (and removing $\sim$8 μm of that layer). In preparation for inspection under scanning electron microscope (SEM), a cross section was formed by ion milling and junction stain. The wet chemical junction staining process etches more heavily doped regions faster, hence, exposing the interface between the two epitaxial layers. An SEM image is presented in Fig. 8. The junction between front surface region and base is clearly visible and lies below the base of the surface texture pyramids.

VII. CONCLUSION

One- and two-dimensional simulations show that an epitaxially grown, then textured, front surface region possesses the necessary properties to enable high efficiency n-type IBC cell fabrication on thin Si substrates. Optimal process control drives a 0.3% absolute improvement in simulated device efficiency over a cell with a typical 200-Ω/sq phosphorus diffused front surface region.

ACKNOWLEDGMENT

The authors would like to thank Crystal Solar, Santa Clara, CA, USA, for their support of this study (particularly through the provision of epitaxial Si layers); their fellow staff members at Hanwha Solar America for their contributions in the conception and development of this work; V. Noorai for both sage guidance and for preparing the sample depicted in Fig. 8, which they particularly appreciated; and T. Ratcliff and D. Yan of the Australian National University in Canberra, Australia, for providing experimental data for the dopant profile of a reference light POCl$_3$ diffusion.

REFERENCES

[1] G. Beaucarne, F. Duerinckx, I. Kuzma, K. Van Niewenhuysen, H. J. Kim, and J. Poormans, "Epitaxial thin-film Si solar cells," *Thin Solid Films*, vol. 511/512, pp. 533–542, 2006.

[2] A. Cuevas, "Misconceptions and misnomers in solar cells," presented at the 27th Eur. Photovoltaic Solar Energy Conf., Frankfurt, Germany, 2012.

[3] M. J. Keevers, "Fabrication and characterization of parallel multijunction thin film silicon solar cells," *Solar Energy Mater. Solar Cells*, vol. 65, pp. 363–368, 2001.

[4] E. Schmich, "High-temperature CVD processes for crystalline silicon thin-film and wafer solar cells," Ph.D. dissertation, Univ. Konstanz, Fakultat fur Physik (Faculty of Physics), Konstanz, Germany, 2008.

[5] S. Reber, K. Dicker, D. M. Huljic, and S. Bau, "Epitaxy of emitters for crystalline silicon solar cells," in *Proc. 17th Eur. Photovoltaic Solar Energy Conf.*, 2001, pp. 1612–1616.

[6] K. Van Niewenhuysen, D. Van Gestel, I. Kuzma, F. Duerinckx, G. Beaucarne, and J. Poortmans, "Characterization of thin silicon films grown in a batch-type LP-CVD system," in *Proc. 20th Eur. Photovoltaic Solar Energy Conf.*, 2005, pp. 1251–1254.

[7] F. Duerinckx, K. Van Niewenhuysen, H. J. Kim, I. Kuzma-Filipek, G. Beaucarne, and J. Poortmans, "Light trapping for epitaxial thin film crystalline silicon solar cells," in *Proc. 20th Eur. Photovoltaic Solar Energy Conf.*, 2005, pp. 1190–1193.

[8] R. King, R. Sinton, and R. Swanson, "Studies of diffused phosphorus emitters: Saturation current, surface recombination velocity, and quantum efficiency," *IEEE Trans. Electron Devices*, vol. 27, no. 2, pp. 365–371, Feb. 1990.

[9] D. D. Smith, P.J. Cousins, A. Masad, A. Waldhauer, S. Westerberg, M. Johnson, X. Tu, T. Dennis, G. Harley, G. Solomon, S. Rim, M. Shepherd, S. Harrington, M. Defensor, A. Leygo, P. Tomada, J. Wu, T. Pass, L. Ann, L. Smith, N. Bergstrom, C. Nicdao, P. Tipones, and D. Vicente, "Generation III higher efficiency lower cost technology: Transition to full scale manufacturing," in *Proc. 38th IEEE Photovoltaics Spec. Conf.*, 2012, pp. 1594–1597.

[10] P. E. Gruenbaum, R. R. King, and R. Swanson, "Photoinjected hot-electron damage in silicon point-contact solar cells," *J. Appl. Phys.*, vol. 66, pp. 6110-1–6110-5, 1989.

[11] F. Granek, M. Hermle, D. M. Huljic, O. Schultz-Wittmann, and S. W. Glunz, "Enhanced lateral current transport via the front n+ diffused layer of n-type high-efficiency back-junction back-contact silicon solar cells," *Progr. Photovoltaics*, vol. 17, pp. 47–56, 2009.

[12] T. Ohrdes, U. Romer, Y. Larionova, R. Peibst, P. P. Altermatt, and N.-P. Harder, "High fill-factors of back-junction solar cells without front surface field diffusion," in *Proc. 27th Eur. Photovoltaic Solar Energy Conf.*, 2012, pp. 866–869.

[13] F. Granek and C. Reichel, "Back-contact back-junction silicon solar cells under UV illumination," *Solar Energy Mater. Solar Cells*, vol. 94, pp. 1734–1740, 2010.

[14] P. E. Gruenbaum, J. Y. Gan, R. R. King, and R. M. Swanson, "Stable passivations for high-efficiency silicon solar cells," in *Proc. 21st IEEE Photovoltaics Spec. Conf.*, 1990, pp. 317–322.

[15] R. Brendel, "A novel process for ultrathin monocrystalline silicon solar cells on glass," in *Proc. 14th Eur. Photovoltaic Solar Energy Conf.*, 1997, pp. 1354–1357.

[16] H. Tayanaka and T. Matsushita, "Separation of thin epitaxial Si films on porous Si for solar cells," in *Proc. 6th Sony Res. Forum*, 1996, p. 556.

[17] D. A. Clugston and P. A. Basore, "PC1D version 5: 32-bit solar cell modelling on personal computers," in *Proc. IEEE 26th Photovoltaics Spec. Conf.*, 1997, pp. 207–210.

[18] P. A. Basore, "Numerical modelling of textured silicon solar cells," *IEEE Trans. Electron Devices*, vol. 37, no. 2, pp. 337–343, Feb. 1990.

[19] A. Cuevas, G. Giroult-Matlakowski, P. A. Basore, C. Dubois, and R. R. King, "Extraction of the surface recombination velocity of passivated phosphorus-doped silicon emitters," in *Proc. 1st World Conf. Photovoltaic Energy Convers.*, 1994, pp. 1446–1449.

[20] C. Donolato, "A reciprocity theorem for charge collection," *Appl. Phys. Lett.*, vol. 46, no. 3, pp. 270–272, 1985.

[21] P. A. Basore, "Extended spectral analysis of internal quantum efficiency," in *Proc. IEEE 23rd Photovoltaics Spec. Conf.*, 1993, pp. 147–152.

[22] J. Isenberg and W. Warta, "Free carrier absorption in heavily doped silicon layers," *Appl. Phys. Lett.*, vol. 84, no. 13, pp. 2265–2267, 2004.

[23] P. A. Basore and K. Cabanas-Holmen, "PC2D: A circular-reference spreadsheet solar cell device simulator," *IEEE J. Photovoltaics*, vol. 1, no. 1, pp. 72–77, Jul. 2011.

Application of ion Implantation Emitter in PERC Solar Cells

Jian Wu, Yunyu Liu, Xusheng Wang, and Lingjun Zhang

Abstract—Ion-implantation offers numerous advantages (i.e., single-side precise control and reproducibility of the dopant, simultaneous SiO_2 passivation during annealing, no phosphosilicate glass formation) for solar cell manufacturing. Canadian Solar Inc. has developed an average efficiency 19.23% blank emitter solar cell (156 mm Cz) process using a high-throughput Varian (Applied Materials) Solion ion-implant tool. In order to improve solar cell efficiency, focus is placed on the well-known advanced passivated emitter and rear cell solar cell architecture with optimized backside passivation. The approach is to combine the surface passivation provided by a thin atomic layer deposition aluminum oxide layer grown after the post implantation annealing process with a deposited capping silicon nitride layer. Laser ablation and proper aluminum paste is also used to locally remove the dielectric layers and to form local contact. Based on this development, implanted emitter and local Al-BSF with Al_2O_3/SiN_x back passivation are integrated in solar cells, reaching an average efficiency of 19.96% and champion 20.12%.

Index Terms—c-Si, passivated emitter and rear cell (PERC), solar cell.

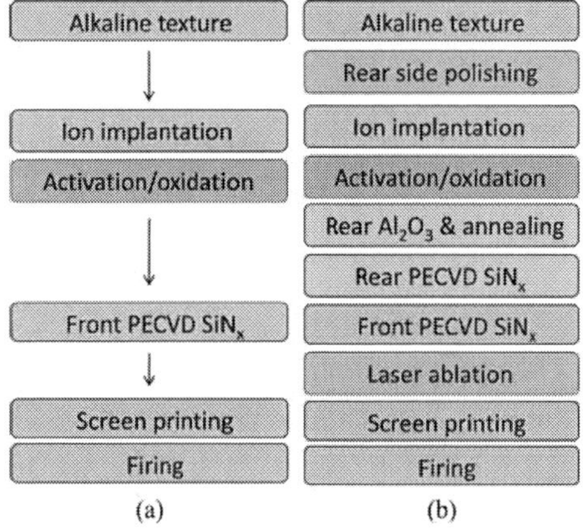

Fig. 1. Process scheme of implanted (a) full Al-BSF and (b) PERC solar cell.

I. INTRODUCTION

ION implantation has been reported as a breakthrough technology in photovoltaic (PV) industry to drive down dollars per Watts cost. This doping approach is unique in that the dopant atoms are directly introduced into the silicon lattice with no external film deposited on the surface that may require removal in subsequent steps. The directional nature of the ion implantation process ensures only the surface exposed to the energetic ions gets doped, enabling single-side doping, which is critical for the advanced cell structures. Emitters that are formed by ion implantation show improved cell efficiency because of the benefit in blue wavelength region. The quality of the emitters that are formed by ion implantation followed by activation has clear advantages, such as no dead layer and better surface passivation with SiO_2/SiN_x stack compared with the single SiN_x layer [1]. Canadian Solar Inc. (CSI) has developed an average efficiency 19.23%, champion efficiency 19.39% solar cell (156 mm) process using a high-throughput Varian (Applied Materials) Solion ion-implant tool based on a beam line design [2], [3], proving that ion implantation technology is mass production ready for PV cell manufacturing.

Manuscript received June 9, 2013; revised August 6, 2013 and August 28, 2013; accepted September 3, 2013. Date of publication October 10, 2013; date of current version December 16, 2013.

The authors are with Canadian Solar Inc., Suzhou 215129, China (e-mail: jian.wu@canadiansolar.com; yunyu.liu@canadiansolar.com; xusheng.wang@canadiansolar.com; lingjun.zhang@canadiansolar.com).

Color versions of one or more of the figures in this paper are available online at http://ieeexplore.ieee.org.

Digital Object Identifier 10.1109/JPHOTOV.2013.2282893

On the other hand, the passivated emitter and rear cell (PERC) solar cell design appears as a great alternative to the standard process employing a full Al-BSF at the backside [4], providing a significantly improved surface passivation and optical reflectivity achieved by dielectric layers [5], [6]. Therefore, the benefit from an implanted emitter using P^+ ions could be combined with integration of a local back surface field (PERC) structure on the backside of the solar cell, enabling cell efficiency up to 20%. There have been reports of PERC cell processes [7], [8] which utilized the thermal oxide layer as a passivation layer for the rear surface, achieving cell efficiency of up to 19.7%.

Up to now, only Dullweber *et al.* have reported Al_2O_3/SiN_y passivated PERC solar cell combined with ion implanted phosphorus emitter [9]. In this paper, we present CSI's approach of combining implantation and PERC passivation by atomic layer deposition (ALD) Al_2O_3 and PECVD SiN_x. The result represents a promising approach for industrial realization of PERC devices.

II. PROCESS DETAILS

A large set of Cz wafers (p-type, $\rho = 3 \pm 0.3$ $\Omega\cdot$cm, pseudo square, 156-mm side, 180-μm starting thickness) were split into two groups. The as-cut wafers in both groups go through conventional saw damage etch and alkaline texture to form random upright pyramids. As a reference, one group proceeded with the standard ion implanted full Al-BSF process, which is shown in Fig. 1(a). P^+ ions are implanted directly into silicon lattice under 10 keV at a certain dose. The wafers, standing back-to-back, are then annealed in a quartz furnace to activate the implanted dopants. The post implantation annealing (PIA) recipe is

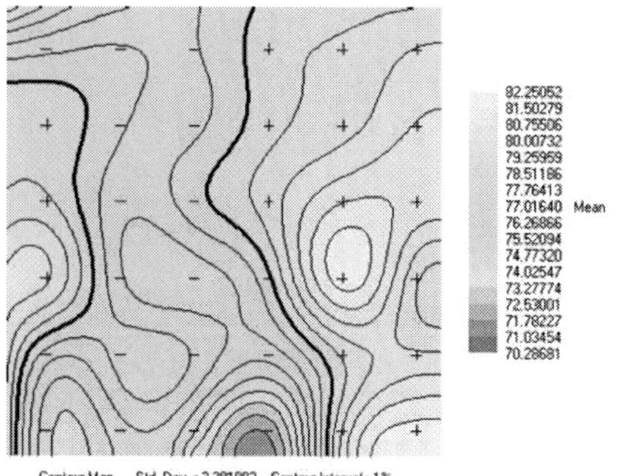

Fig. 2. Sheet resistance mapping (36 point by four-probe method) after thermal activation.

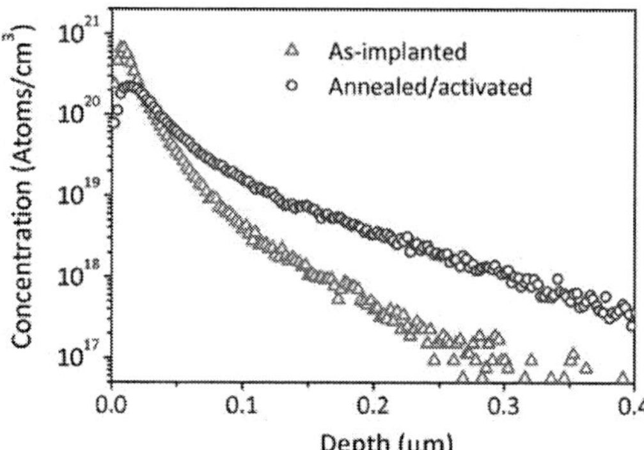

Fig. 3. Comparison of dopant junction profiles for As-implanted and PIA samples.

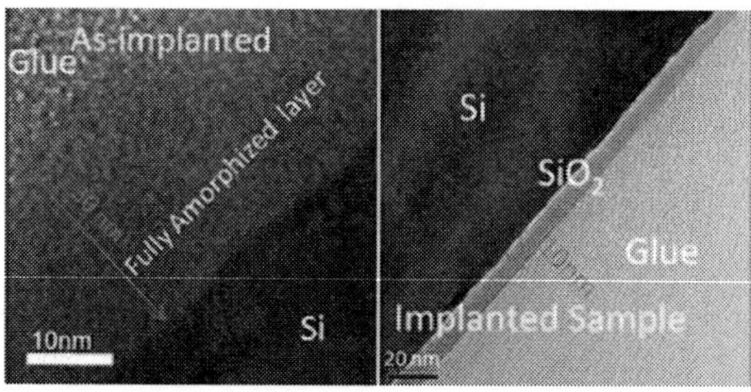

Fig. 4. Cross-sectional images of (left) as implanted and (right) furnace annealed, illustrating no residual defects in the crystal lattice in the implanted emitter.

$\sim$820 °C for 15 min in N_2/O_2 mixture ambience, which is sufficient to activate the implanted dopant. The average emitter sheet resistance after annealing is 77 Ω/sq. A thin thermal silicon dioxide ($\sim$10 nm) is grown on doped texture surface during the anneal process providing excellent passivation of the emitter. At the same time, an ultrathin SiO_x (1$\sim$2 nm) grows on the rear surface.

The other group was processed with an implanted-PERC device following the description illustrated in Fig. 1(b). The ion implantation involved processes (shown in green) are the same as full Al-BSF process. In the PERC process, the polished rear surface was passivated by 10-nm ALD Al_2O_3 capped by 100-nm PECVD SiN_x. A green laser (532 nm) with picosecond pulsewidth and a Gaussian beam profile were used for the local opening on the rear dielectric stack layers. Both groups used the same texture, emitter formation, front side SiN_x, screen printing and firing.

III. Results and Discussions

A. Implanted Emitter and its Passivation

Ion implantation provides a powerful method to precisely control the amount of dopant in the emitter layer. Fig. 2 shows the sheet resistance mapping with 36 points after PIA, setting the target sheet resistance (R_{sq}) $\sim$80 Ω/sq. The R_{sq} standard deviation of implanted wafer is 2.38 Ω/sq. The emitter that is fabricated by ion implantation proves excellent uniformity and, therefore, is acceptable for mass production.

The dopant profile may use an appropriate annealing step to maximize cell performance. Fig. 3 shows the secondary ion mass spectroscopy profile of the emitters before and after annealing. For the dopant activation profiles, the as-implanted sample presents surface concentration of 7×10^{20} cm^{-3}. After high-temperature annealing, phosphorus atoms are activated and driven deeper into Si substrate to form an even lower (2×10^{20} cm^{-3}) concentration dopant emitter.

One concern about the implantation process is whether the implanted regions can be perfectly regrown with no residual damage within the layer. Defects in the regrown lattice may cause increased carrier recombination in the emitter.

Fig. 4 shows transmission electron microscopy pictures comparison of as-implanted annealed sample. Image (left) shows as-implanted sample and reveals a highly uniform and fully amorphized $\sim$30-nm region. After a furnace annealing, the amorphous region completely recrystallized with no defects, as shown at the right side of Fig. 4. The cross-section comparisons illustrate the perfectly regrown Si crystal lattice with no dead regions in the near surface region of the implanted emitter, similar to previous reports [10], [11]. The right side of Fig. 4 also illustrates the presence of a thin layer ($\sim$10 nm) of thermally grown silicon dioxide during PIA.

Emitter passivation properties of thermal oxide capped by SiN_x and firing have been assessed on the same batch of wafers as PERC cell process by measuring the minority carrier lifetime (τ_{eff}) with the Sinton QSSPC method on symmetrically n$^+$-doped and passivated structure. Since ion implantation does not require any parasitic dopant containing layers (such as the phosphor–silicate glass in $POCl_3$ diffusion), it is possible to grow and retain a high-quality thermal oxide for implanted emitters without the removal/ additional process. As shown in Fig. 5, a relatively high effective carrier lifetime (τ_{eff}) is indicative of very low recombination because of the excellent surface passivation after annealing. After SiN_x and firing, the value increases even more, probably due to hydrogen passivation of the Si/SiO_2 interface.

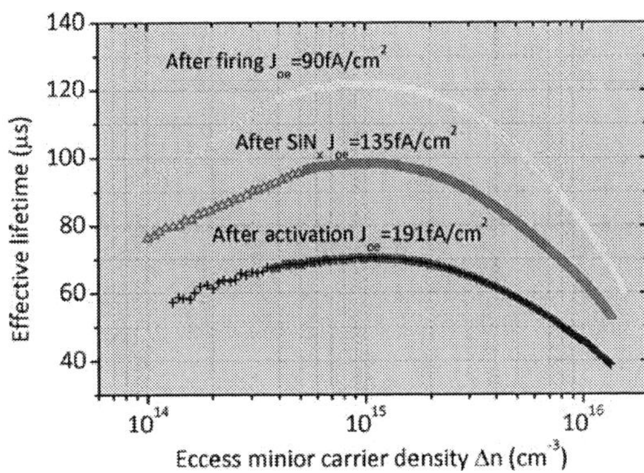

Fig. 5. Measured effective lifetime as a function of the injection density Δn on 3 Ω·cm (substrate doping 4.5 $\times$ 10^{15} cm^{-3}), p-type CZ-Si. The lifetime is tested after three steps: implantation and PIA, further deposition of SiN$_x$ layer on both the surfaces, and firing.

The emitter saturation current density J_{oe} in high injection level was determined from the relation proposed by Kane and Swanson [12] and Glunz *et al.* [13] (radiative recombination neglected)

$$\frac{1}{\tau_{\text{eff}}} - \frac{1}{\tau_{\text{Auger}}} = \frac{1}{\tau_{\text{SHR}}} + \frac{2S_{\text{eff}}}{W} = \frac{1}{\tau_{\text{SHR}}} + \frac{2(J_{oe} + N_A)}{qn_i^2 W}\Delta n \tag{1}$$

where τ_{Auger} is the intrinsic Auger lifetime, τ_{SRH} is the defect-related bulk lifetime, N_A is the base doping level, n_i is the intrinsic carrier concentration of c-Si, q is the elementary charge, Δn is the excess carrier density, and W is the sample thickness.

In high injection, one can neglect the Shockley–Read–Hall recombination when high carrier lifetime material is used. Then, the extraction of J_{oe} can be done by taking into account that the Auger recombination is nonlinearly dependent on the excess carrier density, whereas the emitter recombination increases linearly with the excess carrier density. By plotting the Auger corrected inverse effective carrier lifetime versus the excess carrier density (not shown here), it is possible to extract J_{oe}, which is directly proportional to the slope of the resulting straight line. At the injection level $\Delta n = 1 \times 10^{16}$ cm^{-3}, the extracted J_{oe} values are 191, 135, and 90 fA/cm^2 after annealing, PECVD SiN$_x$, and firing. J_{oe} value, which is as low as 90 fA/cm^2 after firing, indicates an excellent junction quality and very low recombination in the emitters because of the excellent surface passivation by ion implantation.

B. Rear Surface Passivation

More recently, it was shown that thin film of the negatively charged dielectric aluminum oxide (Al$_2$O$_3$) grown by ALD provide an excellent level of surface passivation [14]. As Al$_2$O$_3$ is a negative charge dielectric, no parasitic shunting occurs when applied to the rear of p-type silicon solar cells.

Before the evaluation of ALD-Al$_2$O$_3$ passivation, we studied the interfacial SiO$_x$ layer between ALD-Al$_2$O$_3$ layer and p-Si surface. As mentioned in the process detail section, an ultra-thin SiO$_x$ layer grows on the rear polished surface during PIA. The silicon oxide growth rate in dry O$_2$ depends on temper-

TABLE I
TABLE PRESENTING TOTAL FIXED CHARGE (Q_{fix}) AND INTERFACE DEFECT DENSITY (D_{it}) FOR SINGLE ALUMINUM OXIDE LAYER AND ALUMINUM OXIDE WITH SILICON NITRIDE STACK LAYERS WITH OR WITHOUT PIA

PIA	Layer	Q_{fix} [cm^{-2}]	D_{it} [cm^{-2}eV^{-1}]
No	Al$_2$O$_3$	-3.21×10^{12}	1.43×10^{12}
	Al$_2$O$_3$/SiN$_x$	-4.57×10^{12}	9.44×10^{11}
Yes	SiO$_x$/Al$_2$O$_3$	-3.07×10^{12}	1.59×10^{12}
	SiO$_x$/Al$_2$O$_3$/SiN$_x$	-4.15×10^{12}	9.87×10^{11}

ature, silicon lattice orientation, surface doping concentration, and oxygen partial pressure [15]–[17]. Theoretically, the silicon oxide on front surface ($\langle 1\ 1\ 1\rangle$ orientation, n$^+$ doping $\sim$10^{20} cm^{-3}) should be much thicker than on the rear surface ($\langle 1\ 0\ 0\rangle$ orientation, base doping $\sim$4.5 $\times$ 10^{15} cm^{-3}). As a matter of fact, high-resolution transmission electron microscopy (HRTEM) proves that an ultrathin SiO$_x$ (1$\sim$2 nm) grows on the rear surface (not shown).

It has been reported that a thin (1–2 nm) SiO$_x$ layer is present at the interface between Al$_2$O$_3$ and c-Si during Al$_2$O$_3$ deposition, which is independent of synthesis methods [18]. In this paper, with the presence of ultrathin SiO$_x$ in PIA, SiO$_x$ thickness variation cannot be identified after Al$_2$O$_3$ deposition by means of HRTEM observation (not shown).

The interfacial SiO$_x$ layer is believed to fulfill an important role in the origin of the negative Q_f that is found in Al$_2$O$_3$ films grown on c-Si by inducing a high density of negatively charged Al vacancies close to the interface [19]–[22]. To evaluate the effect of the interfacial SiO$_x$ layer with ALD Al$_2$O$_3$ and capping SiN$_x$ layer, comparison wafers of PERC cell process were double side polished. One half of them proceeded with PIA, and the other half did nothing. Then, both the groups were coated with ALD Al$_2$O$_3$ and capping SiN$_x$ layer symmetrically. A noncontact capacitance–voltage (CV) measurement was performed in order to compare the total fixed charge density (Q_{fix}) and the interface defect density (D_{it}) in Table I. These data demonstrate that for both single Al$_2$O$_3$ and Al$_2$O$_3$/SiN$_x$ stack layers, samples with PIA exhibit relatively higher D_{it} and lower Q_{fix}. However, the differences are not considerably significant. Similar reports from Wolf *et al.* demonstrated the Al$_2$O$_3$/SiN$_x$ stack system with an ultrathin oxide film ($<$4 nm) allows both a low density of interface traps and a high absolute value of negative charges and, thus, efficient field-effect passivation because of strong accumulation [23]. The results presented here are in agreement with Wolf *et al.*, and support the conclusions that the PIA induced SiO$_x$ has little effect on the field-effect passivation.

To examine the Al$_2$O$_3$ passivation with PIA further, effective minor carrier lifetime was characterized using the Sinton QSSPC method. The symmetrical lifetime samples used here were fabricated by the same batch wafers as the PERC cell process, polished on both sides. Al$_2$O$_3$ films were symmetrically deposited on both wafer surfaces by atomic layer deposition and then annealed. The lifetime is tested after SiN$_x$ capping and firing, respectively. As can be seen in Fig. 6, the effective lifetime increases step by step.

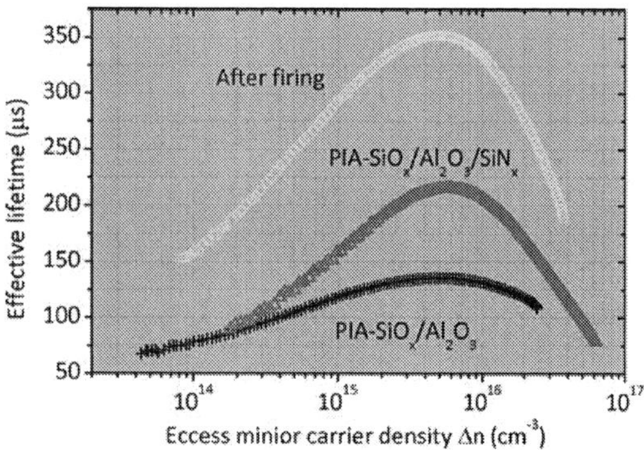

Fig. 6. Measured effective lifetime τ_{eff} versus excess minor carrier density Δn on $3\,\Omega \cdot$cm (substrate doping 4.5×10^{15} cm^{-3}) with PIA. The wafer surfaces are symmetrically passivated by ALD Al$_2$O$_3$ films. Then, the lifetime is tested after SiN$_x$ capping and firing, respectively.

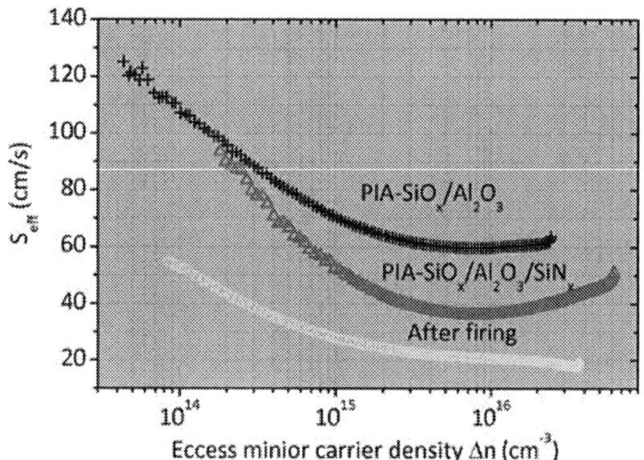

Fig. 7. Maximum effective SRV versus excess minor carrier density calculated from Fig. 6 and (2).

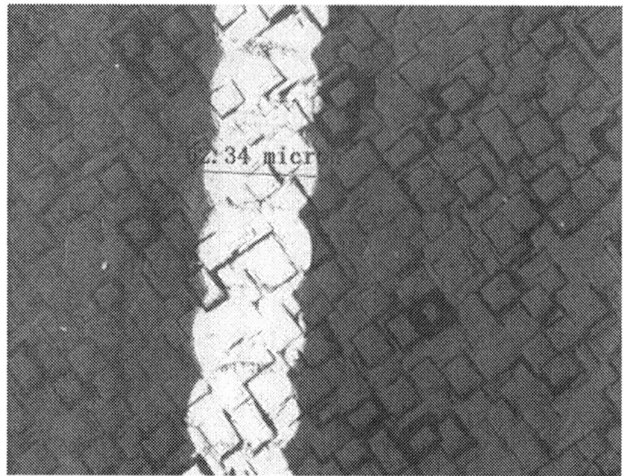

Fig. 8. Optical microscope images of typical line shape opening using nanosecond laser.

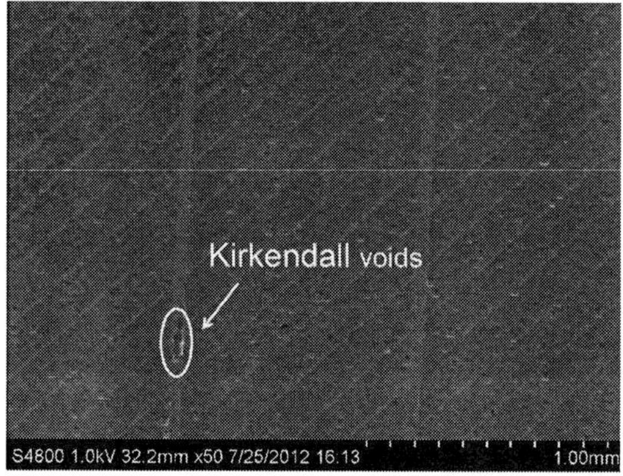

Fig. 9. Al–Si eutectic top view of Al layer removal sample by SEM image.

With the measured lifetime data, the effective surface recombination velocity (SRV) S_{eff} was determined by

$$S_{eff} = \frac{W}{2}\left(\frac{1}{\tau_{\mathrm{eff}}} - \frac{1}{\tau_{\mathrm{bulk,intrinsic}}}\right). \qquad (2)$$

For a sample without an emitter and a very good surface passivation, τ_{eff} would reach the intrinsic bulk carrier lifetime $\tau_{\mathrm{bulk,intrinsic}}$ which is given by the radiative recombination of the Auger recombination and the Shockley–Read–Hall recombination. The radiative recombination can be neglected, since it plays no significant role under low injection conditions. Here, we use the Kerr and Cuevas model [24] to determine the Auger recombination and use the SRH parameters determined from the analysis of the Yablonovitch and Gmitter data [25] as 37 ms. In Fig. 7, the effective SPV S_{eff} as a function of the excess carrier density is calculated by (2) with the polished wafer thickness 170 μm. The calculated S_{eff} of 33 cm/s($@\Delta n = 5 \times 10^{14}$ cm^{-3}), and 23 cm/s($@\Delta n = 3 \times 10^{15}$ cm^{-3}) after Al$_2$O$_3$/SiN$_x$ firing is close to the data of Wolf et al. [23], proving that the PIA induced SiO$_x$ has little effect on the field-effect passivation.

C. Laser Ablation and Rear Local Contact

Fig. 8 depicts the optical image of typical line shape opening using a picosecond laser. There is no evidence of Al$_2$O$_3$/SiN$_x$ stack residue in the ablated area, which indicates that the dielectric layers are completely eliminated there. Line opening width of laser is nearly 63 μm, corresponding to the actual open area ratio $\sim 5.6\%$.

The Kirkendall voids are normally found at the rear of local contact solar cells (see Fig. 8, dark area represents voids, and gray area represents Al–Si eutectic). In the case of large-pitch-contact, silicon beneath the local opening is not sufficient to saturate in the Al paste, which is far away from the opening. The unsaturated Al paste continuously drives Si diffusion away from the contact sites. We optimized the pitch so that over 90% of the local opened area is filled with Al–Si eutectic alloy, and we obtain a maximum remaining passivation area; see Fig. 9.

The quality of the back surface field (BSF) is closely related to the quality of local opening and aluminum paste and, hence, can have a significant effect on the cell performance. In formulating a screen printable aluminum paste for rear local contact application, several factors should be taken into consideration. The paste should have a low contact resistance to silicon and a

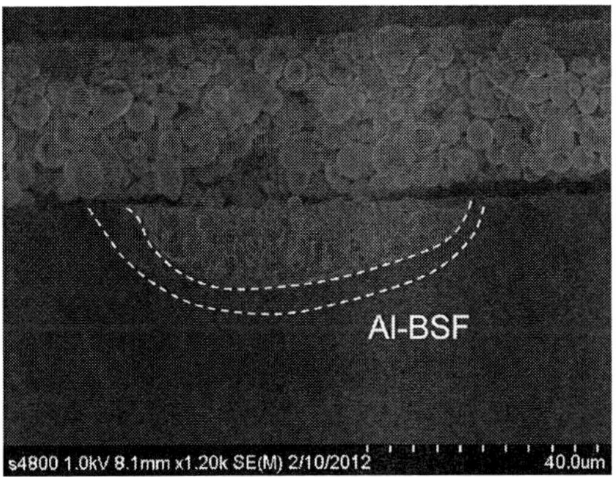

Fig. 10. Cross-sectional view of local contact, Al–Si eutectic, and BSF from an SEM image. BSF is marked between white-dashed lines.

TABLE II
IMPLANTED EMITTER SOLAR CELL PERFORMANCE OF FULL AL-BSF AND PERC STRUCTURE

Type	V_{oc} [V]	J_{sc} [mA/cm^2]	FF [%]	η [%]
Full Al-BSF	0.642	37.50	79.87	19.23
Champion	0.643	37.52	80.36	19.39
PERC	0.657	38.79	78.19	19.93
Champion	0.661	38.88	78.35	20.14

low bulk resistivity to allow for the cell to function in a soldered string with minimum series resistance losses. In addition, the paste must strongly adhere to the passivation dielectric layer so that the integrity of the passivation quality is maintained after contact formation. Furthermore, paste composition should be such that it should be able to enable voids free contact formation in the presence of a sufficiently thick BSF layer over a range of contact sizes with different firing conditions. The quality of BSF was analyzed with cross-section view, using scanning electron microscopy (SEM). Samples cross-section pictures from laser and paste etching were shown in Fig. 10. A continuous Al–Si alloy was found to be thickest in the middle and tapered closer to the edges in both cases with BSF thickness 4–7 μm.

With proper choice of local opening geometry and aluminum paste, more than 90% of the contacts were completely filled with deep enough Al-BSF formation.

D. Emitter-Implanted Passivated Emitter and Rear Cell Cells Performance

Table II summarizes the batch average cell performance parameters of full Al-BSF reference and implanted-PERC group. Rear passivation and local contact structure result in higher V_{oc} (+15 mV) and J_{sc} (+1.29 mA/cm^2), compared with full Al-BSF reference cells. Although they present fill factor loss $\sim$ −1.7%, the average cell efficiency gain due to PERC structure reaches 0.7% abs. The champion cell efficiency of PERC group reaches 20.14%. The efficiency distribution of over 300 pcs cells for each group is shown in Fig. 11.

Fig. 12 illustrates the internal quantum efficiency (IQE) and reflectance of implanted full BSF and PERC solar cell. As fur-

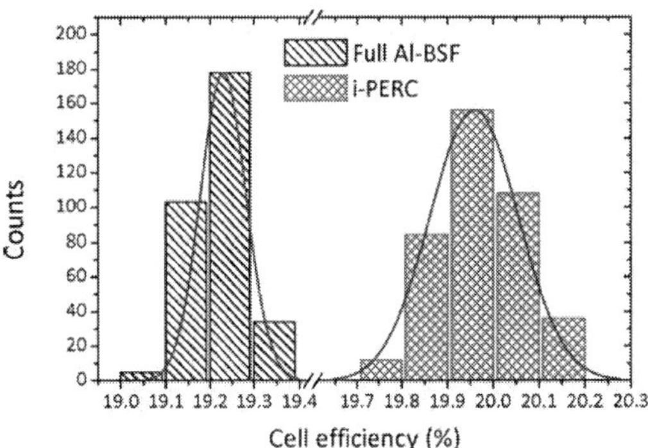

Fig. 11. Histogram of cell efficiency of full Al-BSF and PERC groups.

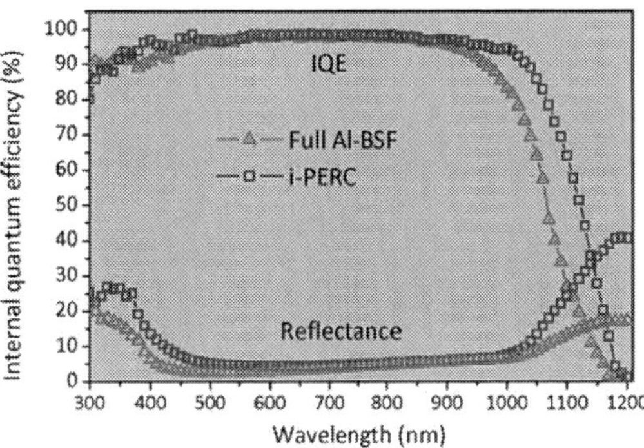

Fig. 12. Comparison of the IQE and reflectance of implanted full BSF and PERC solar cell.

ther evidence of superior emitter quality, the average IQE data of both groups in the short wavelength region (300–450 nm), which is the so-called blue response, exceed 90%. The excellent blue response of the cell is indicative of very low recombination in the emitter and excellent surface passivation, as well as the absence of dead layer of the emitter. The high IQE and reflection in the high wavelength range (950–1200 nm) prove that the rear surface of the solar cells is effectively passivated, and it provides a high internal reflection, which helps to improve the V_{oc} and J_{sc} further.

IV. CONCLUSION

This paper summarizes the technological progress achieved on advanced solar cells integrating a backside engineering and implanted phosphorus emitter. Focus was placed on the emitter doping profile and passivation, rear side passivation evaluation, and local laser ablation and aluminum paste choice. Ion implantation shows an excellent junction quality and very low recombination in the emitters because of the excellent surface passivation. An ultrathin thermal oxide layer (1–2 nm), induced by PIA, located between the Si substrate and ALD Al$_2$O$_3$ layers, does not have significant impact on the interface properties and field-effect passivation. The implanted PERC process described here achieved an average 19.93% and champion 20.14% solar cell efficiency. These results indicate that the combination of ion implantation and PERC technology is a promising approach for an industrial cell process.

ACKNOWLEDGMENT

The authors would like to thank all Varian (Applied Materials) and CSI team members for their efficient cowork.

REFERENCES

[1] M. B. Spitzer and C. J. Keavney, "Low recombination p$^+$ and n$^+$ regions for high performance silicon solar cells," in *Proc. 18th IEEE Photovoltaic Spec. Conf.*, 1985, pp. 43–49.

[2] J. Wu, X. Wang, and L. Zhang, "19.2% efficient c-Si solar cells using ion implantation," presented at the 22th Photovoltaic Sci. Eng. Conf., Hangzhou, China, Nov. 05–09 2012.

[3] X. Wang, Y. Li, and L. Zhang, "Over 19% CE c-Si cells enabled by ion implantation," in *Proc. 27th Eur. Photovoltaic Solar Energy Conf. Exhib.*, 2012, pp. 1558–1562.

[4] M. A. Green, A. W. Blakers, J. Zhao, and A. Wang, "Characterization of 23-percent efficient silicon solar cells," *IEEE Trans. Electron Devices*, vol. 37, no. 2, pp. 331–336, Feb. 1990.

[5] S. Mack, U. Jäger, and G. Kästner, "Towards 19% efficient industrial PERC devices using simultaneous front emitter and rear surface passivation by thermal oxidation," in *Proc. 35th IEEE Photovoltaic Spec. Conf.*, Jun. 20–25, 2010, pp. 34–38.

[6] J. Lai, A. Upadhyaya, S. Ramanathan, A. Das, and A. Rohatgi, "High-efficiency large-area rear passivated silicon solar cells with local Al-BSF and screen-printed contacts," *IEEE J. Photovoltaics*, vol. 1, no. 1, pp. 16–21, Jul. 2011.

[7] L. Bounaas, N. Auriac, B. Grange, M. Pirot, J. Jourdan, S. Mialon, A. Lanterne, R. Cabal, R. Monna, P. J. Ribeyron, S. De Magnienville, and M. Pasquinelli, "Advanced solar cell with back side engineering and implanted phosphorus emitter," in *Proc. 27th Eur. Photovoltaic Solar Energy Conf. Exhib.*, 2012, pp. 1489–1493.

[8] S. Mack, A. Wolf, S. Werner, C. E. Dubé, V. Bhosle, and D. Biro, "Synergistic use of ion implant annealing processes for thermal oxide rear surface passivation," in *Proc. 27th Eur. Photovoltaic Solar Energy Conf. Exhib.*, 2012, pp. 875–878.

[9] T. Dullweber, V. Bhosle, R. Brendel, C. Dube, and R. Hesse, "Ion-implanted PERC solar cells with Al$_2$O$_3$/SiN$_Y$ rear passivation," presented at the 3rd Silicon PV Conf., Hamelin, Germany, 2013.

[10] N. Cagnat, C. Laviron, N. Auriac, J. Liu, S. Mehta, L. Frioulaud, and D. Mathiot, "Defect behavior in BF2 implants for S/D applications as a function of ion beam characteristics," in *Proc. 16th Int. AIP Conf. Ion Implantation Technol.*, 2006, vol. 866, pp. 133–136.

[11] M. Chun, B. Adibi, H. Hieslmair, and L. Mandrell, "Using solid phase expitaxial re-growth ion implantation solar cell fabrications," in *Proc. 26th Eur. Photovoltaic Solar Energy Conf. Exhib.*, 2011, pp. 1293–1296.

[12] D. E. Kane and R. M. Swanson, "Measurement of the emitter saturation current by a contactless photoconductivity decay method," in *Proc. 18th IEEE Photovoltaic Spec. Conf.*, Las Vegas, NV, USA, 1985, pp. 578–583.

[13] C. Reichel, F. Granek, J. Benick, O. Schultz-Wittmann, and S. W. Glunz, "Comparison of emitter saturation current densities determined by quasi-steady-state photoconductance measurements of effective carrier lifetime at high and low injections," in *Proc. 23rd Eur. Photovoltaic Solar Energy Conf. Exhib.*, 2008, pp. 1664–1668.

[14] G. Dingemans, P. Engelhart, R. Seguin, F. Einsele, B. Hoex, M. C. M. van de Sanden, and W. M. M. Kessels, "Stability of Al$_2$O$_3$ and Al$_2$O$_3$/a-SiNx :H stacks for surface passivation of crystalline silicon," *J. Appl. Phys.*, vol. 106, 2009, pp. 114907-1–114907-4.

[15] Y. J. von der Meulen, "Kinetics of thermal growth of ultra-thin layers of SiO$_2$ on silicon," *J. Electrochem. Soc.*, vol. 119, no. 4, pp. 530–534, 1972.

[16] M. A. F. Gomes, E. F. daSilva, Jr, and J. Albino Aguiar, "Growth kinetics of thermal SiO2 thin films," *Semicond. Sci. Technol.*, vol. 10, pp. 1037–1039, 1995.

[17] H. Z. Massoud, J. D. Plummer, and E. A. Irene, "Thermal oxidation of silicon in dry oxygen growth-rate enhancement in the thin regime," *J. Electrochem. Soc.*, vol. 132, no. 11, pp. 2685–2693, 1985.

[18] G. Dingemans and W. M. M. Kessels, "Status and prospects of Al$_2$O$_3$-based surface passivation schemes for silicon solar cells," *J. Vac. Sci. Technol. A*, vol. 30, no. 4, pp. 040802-1–040802-27, 2012.

[19] K. Kimoto, Y. Matsui, T. Nabatame, T. Yasuda, T. Mizoguchi, I. Tanaka, and A. Toriumi, "Coordination and interface analysis of atomic-layer-deposition Al$_2$O$_3$ on Si(001) using energy-loss near-edge structures," *Appl. Phys. Lett.*, vol. 83, pp. 4306–4308, 2003.

[20] R. S. Johnson, G. Lucovsky, and I. Baumvol, "Physical and electrical properties of noncrystalline Al$_2$O$_3$ prepared by remote plasma enhanced chemical vapor deposition," *J. Vac. Sci. Technol. A*, vol. 19, pp. 1353–1360, 2001.

[21] S. Y. No, D. Eom, C. S. Hwang, and H. J. Kim, "Property changes of aluminum oxide thin films deposited by atomic layer deposition under photon radiation," *J. Electrochem. Soc.*, vol. 153, pp. F87–F93, 2006.

[22] B. Hoex, J. J. H. Gielis, M. C. M. van de Sanden, and W. M. M. Kessels, "On the c-Si surface passivation mechanism by the negative-charge-dielectric Al$_2$O$_3$," *J. Appl. Phys.*, vol. 104, pp. 113703-1–113703-7, 2008.

[23] A. Wolf, S. Mack, C. Brosinsky, M. Hofmann, P. Saint-Cast, and D. Biro, "Impact of thin intermediate thermal oxide films on the properties of PECVD passivation layer systems," presented at the IEEE 37th Photovoltaic Spec. Conf., Seattle, WA, USA, 2011.

[24] M. J. Kerr and A. Cuevas, "General parameterization of Auger recombination in crystalline silicon," *J. App. Phys.*, vol. 91, no. 4, pp. 2473–2480, 2002.

[25] E. Yablonovitch and T. Gmitter, "Auger recombination in silicon at low carrier densities," *Appl. Phys. Lett.*, vol. 49, pp. 587–589, 1986.

Jian Wu received the Ph.D. degree in condensed matter physics from Nanjing University, Nanjing, China, in 2006. He was involved in research on fullerene thin-film and nuclear magnetic resonance.

From 2006 to 2009, he was with Gemlight Solar Co., Ltd., as the R&D manager, focusing on the research of CIGS solar cells and modules. After 2009, he joined Canadian Solar, Inc., Ltd. Suzhou, China, as a senior R&D Engineer, where he is currently leading an R&D team which focuses on high-efficient mono crystalline silicon solar cell research and industrial applications.

Yunyu Liu received the Ph.D. degree in condensed matter physics from the Technical Institute of Physics and Chemistry, Chinese Academy of Sciences, Beijing, China, in 2012. He was involved in research on the preparation of 1-D nanometer material and their applications, i.e., fluorescent pH sensor and TiO$_2$ dye-sensitized solar cells.

Since 2012, he has been an R&D Engineer with Canadian Solar, Inc., Suzhou, China, where he focuses on the application of ion implantation on high-efficiency crystalline silicon solar cells.

Xusheng Wang received the Ph.D. degree in mechanical engineering from Hong Kong University of Science and Technology, Hong Kong, China, in 2006. He was involved in research on micro mechanical and electronic devices.

From 2006 to 2008, he was with Lin Yang New energy Co., Ltd., as the main R&D leader, focusing on research into crystalline silicon solar cells. After 2008, he then joined Canadian Solar, Inc., Ltd. Suzhou, China, as a Technical Director, where he is currently leading the R&D group which focuses on new process and efficiency improvement of crystalline silicon solar cells.

Lingjun Zhang received the Bachelor's degree from the Applied Physics Department, Tsinghua University, Beijing, China, in 1986 and the Ph.D. degree from the Shanghai Technical Physics Institute, China Science Academy, Shanghai, China, in 1992, where he was involved in research on semiconductor devices.

From 1993 to 1996, he was with China Hi-tech Group Co., Shanghai, as the Project Manager. From 1997 to 1999, he was with Shanghai Temic Telefunken Semiconductor Co. as the Production Manager. From 1999 to 2003, he was with Shanghai Simconix Electronic Co., Ltd., as the Production Manager and Operation Manager. Since June 2003, he has been with Canadian Solar Inc., Suzhou, China. From 2003 to 2006, he was the Deputy General Manager and Technical Director of CSI Solar Manufacturing Inc. From 2007 to 2012, he was the General Manager of the CSI Cells Ltd. Co. He is currently the VP of Technology of the CSI group.

Implications of TCO Topography on Intermediate Reflector Design for a-Si/μc-Si Tandem Solar Cells—Experiments and Rigorous Optical Simulations

Simon Kirner, Martin Hammerschmidt, Christoph Schwanke, Daniel Lockau, Sonya Calnan, Tim Frijnts, Sebastian Neubert, Andreas Schöpke, Frank Schmidt, Jens-Hendrik Zollondz, Andreas Heidelberg, Bernd Stannowski, Bernd Rech, and Rutger Schlatmann

Abstract—The influence of the transparent conducting oxide (TCO) topography was studied on the performance of a silicon oxide intermediate reflector layer (IRL) in a-Si/μc-Si tandem cells, both experimentally and by 3-D optical simulations. Therefore, cells with varying IRL thickness were deposited on three different types of TCOs. Clear differences were observed regarding the performance of the IRL as well as its ideal thickness, both experimentally and in the simulations. Optical modeling suggests that a small autocorrelation length is essential for a good performance. Design rules for both the TCO topography and the IRL thickness can be derived from this interplay.

Index Terms—3-D rigorous optical modeling, a-Si/μc-Si, intermediate reflector, micromorph, solar cells, transparent conducting oxide (TCO).

I. INTRODUCTION AND BACKGROUND

AS THE demand for affordable clean energy grows, amorphous silicon (a-Si) / microcrystalline silicon (μc-Si) tandem solar cells are an interesting technology, as it combines nontoxic and abundant materials with a low temperature/low cost process. However, the conversion efficiency of these de

vices, which is as high as 12% on lab scale [1], is low compared with other approaches. It is agreed that one of the main limitations of this technology is the limited current provided by the a-Si top cell. Here, a tradeoff regarding the thickness has to be made between 1) high currents and 2) good electronic properties and stability against light-induced degradation. This limits the ideal thickness of the top cell to typically around 200–300 nm. As both subcells are connected in series, this also limits the total current of the tandem device. Prominent strategies to increase the current in the top cell without increasing its thickness, thus circumventing the mentioned tradeoff, are textured transparent conducting oxides (TCOs)—enhancing the optical path through the device—and intermediate reflector layers (IRLs) deposited between the top and the bottom cell [2], [3]. In the superstrate configuration discussed here, the textured TCO acts as a light scatterer, a substrate for the growing film, and as the front electrode. It is known that the different textures obtained—depending on the TCO type and the process conditions—have a significant influence on the amount of light absorbed and on the quality of the absorber layer grown on top of it [4]. Because of differences in the absorption behavior, ideal topographies differ for cells made of a-Si and μc-Si [5].

With respect to the IRL, it was previously found experimentally that the roughness of the TCO also has an influence on the performance of the IRL. As its optical thickness is of the same order of magnitude as the wavelengths that are to be reflected, interference- and near-field effects have to be considered: for a planar system, the variation of the intermediate reflector layer thickness (t_{IRL}) leads to oscillations in the implied photocurrent density of reflectance, which increase in amplitude with increasing light scattering as shown in [6]. The maximum of the first oscillation is the ideal t_{IRL} in case of the top cell limitation. The calculation of the change in ideal t_{IRL} and the maximum gain in the top cell current depending on the TCO topography is one main topic of this publication. It was previously found that the description of the IRL is not sufficiently accurate using 1-D optical models that are based on the tracing of the light [7]. Using a more computationally intensive wave optic theory, it was found that not only the amplitude but also the period (and therewith the ideal t_{IRL}) of the oscillation increases with improved light scattering [8], [9]. This can be explained by the fact that the component of the wave vector going into normal

Manuscript received June 16, 2013; revised August 3, 2013; accepted August 13, 2013. Date of publication September 5, 2013; date of current version December 16, 2013. This work was supported in part by the Federal Ministry of Education and Research, the Federal Ministry of environment, and the state government of Berlin in the framework of the program "Spitzenforschung und Innovation in den Neuen Ländern" under Grant 03IS2151 and the Demo14 project under Grant 0325237.

S. Kirner, C. Schwanke, S. Calnan, S. Neubert, A. Schöpke, B. Stannowski, B. Rech, and R. Schlatmann are with Helmholtz-Zentrum Berlin, Berlin 14109, Germany (e-mail: simon.kirner@helmholtz-berlin.de; cmsa@gmx.de; sonya.calnan@helmholtz-berlin.de; Sebastian.neubert@helmholtz-berlin.de; schoepke@helmholtz-berlin.de; bernd.stannowski@helmholtz-berlin.de; bernd.rech@helmholtz-berlin.de; rutger.schlatmann@helmholtz-berlin.de).

M. Hammerschmidt and F. Schmidt are with Konrad-Zuse-Zentrum für Informationstechnik Berlin, Berlin 10717, Germany (e-mail: hammerschmidt@zib.de; frank.schmidt@zib.de).

D. Lockau is with Helmholtz-Zentrum Berlin, Berlin 14109, Germany, and also with Konrad-Zuse-Zentrum für Informationstechnik Berlin, Berlin 10717, Germany (e-mail: daniel.lockau@helmholtz-berlin.de)

T. Frijnts, J.-H. Zollondz, and A. Heidelberg are with Masdar PV GmbH, Ichtershausen 99334, Germany (e-mail: tfrijnts@masdarpv.com; hzollondz@masdarpv.com; aheidelberg@masdarpv.com).

Color versions of one or more of the figures in this paper are available online at http://ieeexplore.ieee.org.

Digital Object Identifier 10.1109/JPHOTOV.2013.2279204

direction, which sets the resonance condition, is reduced with increasing light scattering.

To investigate this interplay systematically, we analyzed a-Si/μc-Si tandem solar cells with varying t_{IRL} on three different TCOs commonly used in thin-film silicon solar cells (SnO$_2$:F, ZnO:Al, and ZnO:B). The experiments were accompanied by rigorous optical simulations for three wavelengths (600, 650, and 700 nm) and qualitatively good agreement was obtained. As expected, significant differences in the performance of the IRL depending on the topography of the TCO were found.

Through the synthetization of topographies, we were able to analyze the influence of two important characteristics of the topography, independently. By varying the autocorrelation length (ACL) of the synthesized topographies for different root mean square values of the height distribution (RMS), the differences regarding the IRL performance can be explained.

II. Experimental and Simulation Details

The TCOs were in all cases deposited and optimized for large area application in solar cells by external partners. The SnO$_2$:F was deposited by atmospheric pressure chemical vapor deposition, the ZnO:B by low pressure chemical vapor deposition and the ZnO:Al by means of dc sputtering. The texture etching of the ZnO:Al layers was performed before the solar cell deposition using HCl [10]. The solar cells were deposited in an industrial-like AKT-1600 PECVD multichamber system using an excitation frequency of 13.56 MHz on a substrate size of 30 cm × 30 cm with 3-mm glass thickness. Because of reasons described, i.e., in [11], we adjusted the p-layer to the TCO to assure a low ohmic contact resistance. The top- and bottom-cell i-layers have a nominal thickness of 290 and 1800 nm, respectively. The IRL consists of μc-SiO$_x$ and is placed in between two 5–10 nm μc-Si n-layers [12]. The thickness of the IRL (t_{IRL}) was varied between 0 and 150 nm. For the sample where t_{IRL} is zero, the n-layer consisted of 30-nm n-μc-Si. A TCO/Ag stack was used as a back contact and reflector. The cells were structured by means of a laser into a size of 1 cm × 1 cm.

The topography and light scattering properties of the TCOs were characterized using atomic force microscopy (AFM), Haze measurements using a Perkin–Elmer Lambda 1050 UV–Vis-NIR photospectrometer with an integrating sphere, and angular resolved transmission measurements. The solar cells were characterized using a dual source sun simulator (Wacom WXS-155S-L2, class AAA). A differential spectral response setup was used to measure the external quantum efficiency (EQE). To reduce the contribution of the field dependence on the collection efficiency, a high reverse bias voltage of −1.5 V was applied during the EQE measurements. In this way, differences between the devices that originate from the different material qualities obtained on the varying TCOs could be minimized. In addition, the comparison with the simulation, where perfect collection efficiency is assumed, is more reasonable this way. The total reflection measurements were performed using a spectrophotometer.

The finite-element method was used to compute a solution to Maxwell's equations in 3-D in order to determine the EQE of the

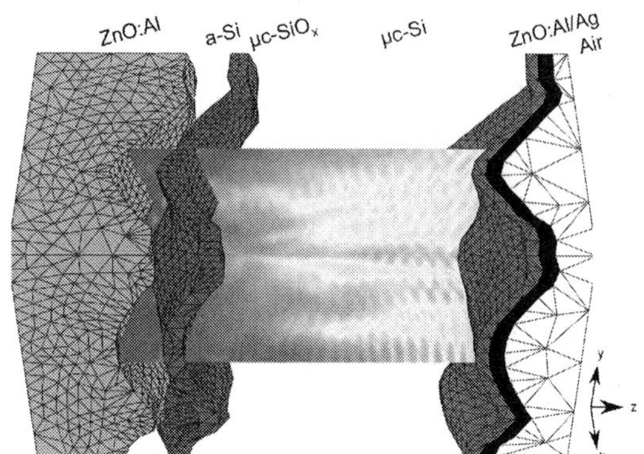

Fig. 1. Example of a 3-D model of an a-Si/μc-Si tandem cell generated based on the measured topography of ZnO:Al TCO. The silicon absorber layers are not shown. The electric field intensity is shown as a false-color plot on a logarithmic scale.

studied solar cell geometries. The employed simulator is based on JCMsuite by JCMwave [13] and an analysis of the numerical accuracy to the simulator can be found in [14]. The different cells were modeled as axis-aligned periodic unit cells based on the AFM scans of the investigated TCOs (cf., Fig. 1). The AFM scans were cut into smaller samples of 1.8 μm × 1.8 μm size and mirrored along x- and y-axes, creating periodic samples, which are manageable in domain size and previously were shown to yield a good agreement with experimental results [15]. Aside from a planar interface between the glass half-space and the TCO, the same measured topography was applied for all material interfaces throughout the cell layer stack. This assumption of conformal growth is a simplification of the actual cell geometry as layer growth is not purely directional with the employed deposition methods. However, for the wavelengths analyzed here (600, 650, 700 nm) the topology of the back reflector is of minor interest, as light of these wavelengths, scattered at the back reflector, will be absorbed in the bottom cell i-layer independently of its scattering direction. The vertical layer stack in illumination direction consists of: glass half-space/TCO/a-Si/IRL/μc-Si/ZnO:Al/Ag/Air half-space with nominally the same thicknesses as in the experiment. The optical constants of the IRL were measured experimentally from a single layer on the glass, by fitting transmission and reflection measurements to the Tauc–Lorentz dispersion model. For the other layers, datasets given in the literature were used [16], [17]. In order to keep computation times reasonable, the doped layers (except for the IRL itself) were not considered in our computational cell model.

In ±z-directions of the finite-element domain, adaptive perfectly matched layers [18] are used as boundary conditions to ensure transparency of the domain in these directions. Because of the mirror symmetric construction of the unit cell only one quarter of it needs to be discretized if appropriate mirror boundary conditions are applied laterally and if the incident field has the same symmetry. As illuminating light source, we used a plane wave in normal incidence with respect to the solar cell stack and with a polarization that matches the applied lateral boundary conditions. The initial reflection of the air/glass interface was calculated analytically using Fresnel's equations.

To synthesize randomly textured topographies with a given circular autocorrelation function (ACF), a method described in [19] and [20] was used. Using the inverse Fourier transform of the amplitude power spectral density (APSD) with randomized phases allows the generation of topographies with specific, parameterized ACFs like the following expression:

$$\mathrm{ACF}(d) = \mathrm{RMS}^2 \cdot \exp\left(\frac{3}{2}\left(\frac{d}{(\mathrm{ACL})}\right)^2\right) \tag{1}$$

where d is the distance from the origin. The APSD can be derived from the Fourier transform of the ACF. It should be mentioned that the synthesized random topologies reproduce the given ACFs well; however, the angular distributions might be different. Each cell simulation was executed using ~5 million degrees of freedom. The simulation results for each cell configuration were averaged over at least six AFM samples or synthesized samples amounting to a large number of overall simulations, hence, the restriction to a small wavelength selection.

III. Results and Discussion

In Fig. 2, the AFM scans of the TCOs are shown together with the two characteristic values RMS and ACL. The ACL gives information about the lateral size distribution of the features and can easily be calculated from the AFM data using the appropriate software. The three types of TCO were also analyzed regarding their electrical properties (carrier density and mobility) as well as their transmittance. The results of these studies are not discussed here, as they do not affect the performance of the IRL directly. The analyzed TCOs have been compared in detail before [21] and it is generally agreed upon that due to the large features obtained by etching, the ZnO:Al films yield high bottom cell (>15 mA/cm^2) and total currents (>29 mA/cm^2) in a-Si/μc-Si tandem solar cells. This is due to a superior light trapping of the long wavelength region, which is in agreement with theoretical predictions [5]. On the other hand, the highest top cell currents (>14 mA/cm^2) reported are usually obtained on ZnO:B [22] or SnO$_2$:F [23], which is generally ascribed to the fact that the features of these TCOs have steeper angles, which scatter the relevant light into wider angles [21]. As can be seen in Fig. 3, our solar cell results are in line with these previously reported observations. It should be mentioned that the use of textured glass substrates, which are not considered here, has led to further improvements in the total photocurrent density in a-Si/μc-Si tandem cells [1], [24] and μc-Si single junction cells [25]–[27], recently.

The TCOs were furthermore characterized using haze–and angular resolved scattering (ARS) measurements. These techniques give direct information about the scattering properties of a given topography against air. In the bottom part of Fig. 2, it can be seen that the ZnO:Al outperforms the other two TCOs in terms of light scattering. However, regarding the application in solar cells, it has previously been found that these characteristics do not necessarily correlate with the implied photocurrent

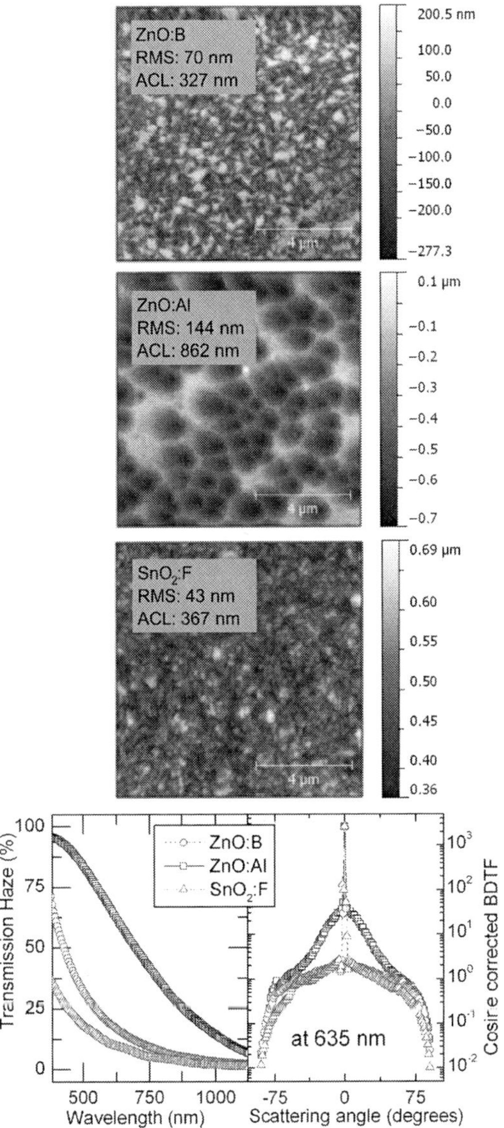

Fig. 2. (Top) AFM scans with the two characteristics, RMS and ACL, and (bottom left) the transmission haze characteristics as a function of wavelength and (bottom right) the cosine corrected bidirectional transmission function (BDTF), as obtained from ARS measurements, of the three analyzed TCOs.

density of the absorbed light in the absorber layers due to the differences in the interface properties. This is in particular the case for the short wavelengths region, and thus, for the top cell [21]. With respect to the intermediate reflector performance studied in this paper and presented in Figs. 3–5, it was found that neither quantitative nor qualitative correlation was found to these optical characteristics. In Fig. 3, three examples of the experimentally obtained quantum efficiencies are depicted of devices deposited on the different TCOs with t_{IRL} of 0, 60, and 120 nm. As can be seen by the magnitude of the current densities, the light in-coupling varies significantly on the different TCOs, i.e., the total current varies between 21.5 and 24.2 mA/cm^2, for

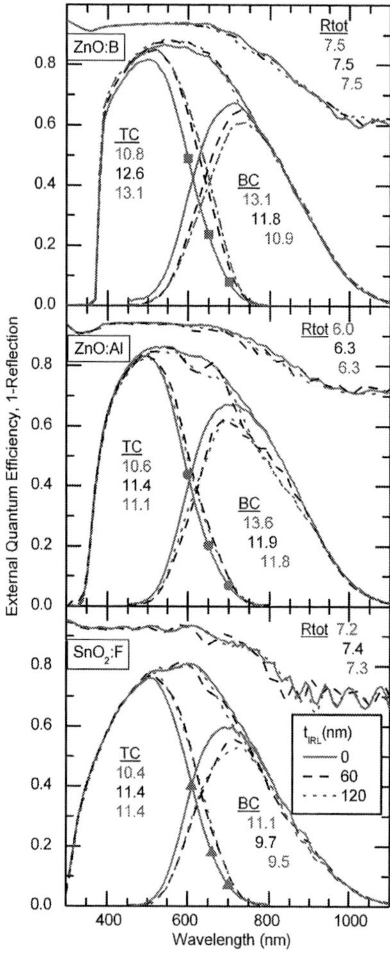

Fig. 3. EQE and total absorptance $(1 - R)$ as a function of wavelength for selected tandem solar cells deposited on the three different TCOs. The numbers indicate the implied photocurrent densities (in mA/cm^2) for the subcells as well as the amount of implied photocurrent of total reflectance (R_{tot}). Some EQE values for the wavelengths, which were also used in the simulation (600, 650, and 700 nm) and are shown in Fig. 5, are marked by symbols.

$t_{\text{IRL}} = 0$ nm, which can be mainly attributed to the differences in light scattering and the differences in the transmittance of the TCO and the top cell p-layer. In addition, the IRL performance, which shall be defined here as the gain in top cell current density compared with the current density obtained without an IRL ($t_{\text{IRL}} = 0$ nm), is significantly different. The highest gain is obtained on the ZnO:B with 2.3 mA/cm^2 at $t_{\text{IRL}} = 120$ nm, which is still below values reported elsewhere [28]. On the other two TCOs, the maximum gain is significantly less and at lower t_{IRL}s. With respect to the total absorptance $(1 - R)$, one can observe that no current is lost with increasing t_{IRL} on the ZnO:B, on the other hand, increasing total reflection can be observed on the SnO$_2$:F and the ZnO:Al, similar to observations reported in [7]. However, the increase in total reflection cannot explain the entire loss in the total absorbed current. It is, thus, believed that parasitic absorption increases significantly, presumably, through

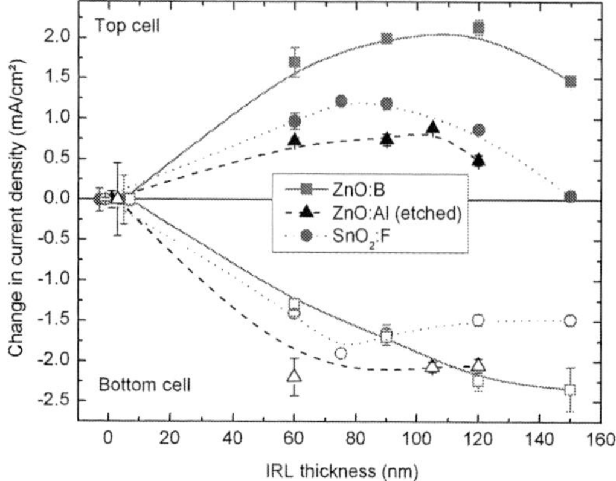

Fig. 4. Experimentally obtained changes in current density in the subcells as obtained by EQE of devices with IRL with indicated thickness compared with devices without IRL. The symbols and error bars indicate the mean and standard deviation of different cells of the same runs. Lines are guides to the eye.

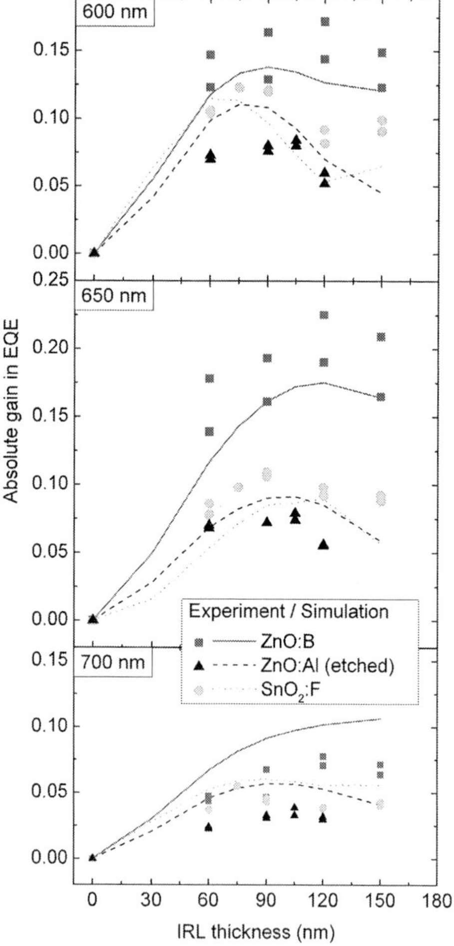

Fig. 5. Experimentally obtained values (symbols) and simulation results (lines) of the gain in top cell EQE at 600, 650, and 700 nm as a function of IRL thickness for the three analyzed TCOs.

reflected light being trapped inside the front TCO [29]. It can be summarized that experimentally, a significant dependence of the IRL performance and ideal t_{IRL} on the type of TCO was observed.

To study the interplay between the IRL performance and the TCO topography in more detail and to gain a better understanding of how the topography affects the performance of the IRL, optical calculations were performed. Therefore, the same variations of t_{IRL} were performed in the simplified layer stacks based on the AFM scans described earlier. Because of the high computation time, the EQE was calculated so far only for three wavelengths (600, 650, and 700 nm), and thus, no integrated current density can be shown. Fig. 5 shows the absolute gain in top cell EQE [i.e., $EQE(t_{IRL}=x)-EQE(t_{IRL} = 0 \text{ nm})$] for the calculated (lines) and the experimentally measured values for two different cells of the same run (as symbols) at the three wavelengths as a function of IRL thickness for the different TCOs. The discrepancy between the two experimentally observed values stems from the spatial inhomogeneity of the top cell i-layer thickness. When looking at the trend of the absolute gain in EQE, one can observe the first maximum of Fabry–Perot oscillations, which occur like on flat interfaces (cf., [6]) despite the roughness of the TCO.

Comparing experiment and simulation, there are rather high discrepancies between the absolute values. Reasons for this can be, for example, differences in the top cell i-layer thickness, which is known to be a function of substrate roughness, imprecisions in the AFM scans and differences in the growth of the IRL and resultant differences in the optical constants, which are all not considered in the simulation. Despite these divergences, one can observe important qualitative parallels between experiment and simulation. First, in both cases, the gain in EQE is the highest on ZnO:B. The other two analyzed TCOs perform fairly similar both experimentally and within the simulation, despite having a significantly different topography. Second, it can be seen that the maximum of the first oscillation shifts to higher t_{IRL} in the case of ZnO:B. The shift in the ideal t_{IRL} toward higher thicknesses can be explained by the fact that the period of the Fabry–Perot oscillations increases due to the reduction in the z-component of the wave vector due to light scattering, as discussed in the beginning and in [8]. Taking the AFM properties of the ZnO:Al and ZnO:B into account and comparing it with the IRL performance, another important conclusion should be drawn. The RMS value is not a solid figure of merit for the performance of the IRL. For example, the highest absolute gain in top cell EQE for ZnO:B (RMS = 70 nm) is >2 mA/cm^2, the highest gain on ZnO:Al (RMS = 144 nm) is <1 mA/cm^2. More important seems to be the lateral dimension (i.e., the ACL).

To emphasize this and to derive implications regarding an ideal topography for the IRL, synthetic topographies were generated using the previously described method with varying ACLs for two different RMS values of 70 and 144 nm. The top cell current gain of a 60 nm IRL compared with no IRL was calculated at a wavelength of 700 nm. As can be seen in Fig. 6, low ACL values are essential for a good performance, rather than high RMS. The calculations indicate, that the high gain in the top cell current obtained on ZnO:B, can be even increased by

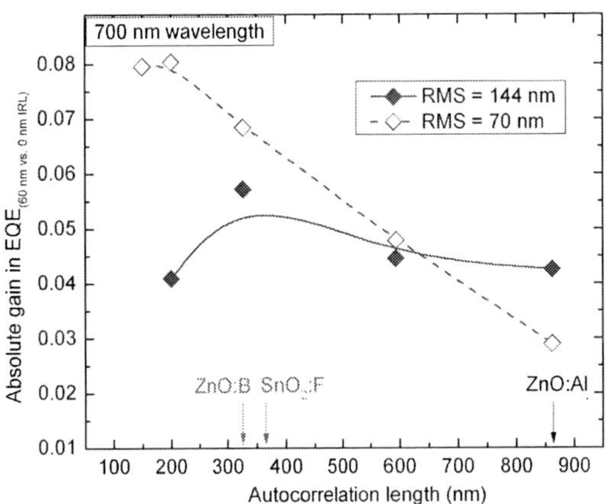

Fig. 6. Simulated gain in top cell current density between 60 and 0 nm IRL at a wavelength of 700 nm as a function of ACL for two different RMS values for synthetically generated topographies. In addition, shown are the experimentally obtained ACL values for the TCOs. Lines are guides to the eye.

a further reduction in the ACL. However, the growth of high quality material becomes presumably more difficult on such topographies as mentioned in the beginning and in [5]. Further wavelengths have to be considered for predictive modeling.

IV. Conclusion

We have analyzed the interplay between TCO topography and IRL performance both experimentally and by rigorous optical calculations. Experimentally, we have obtained significantly different IRL performances on the analyzed TCOs: ZnO:B, ZnO:Al, and SnO$_2$:F. Optical simulations came qualitatively to similar results, which confirm that this is not an experimental artifact. We explain this with the different light scattering properties that lead to significant differences in the ideal IRL design. The difference in the ideal thicknesses can be explained by the reduction of light being reflected in the normal direction and a resulting increase in oscillation period, as predicted by the wave optic theory. The presented approach can be used to calculate improved topographies for high top cell currents.

Acknowledgment

The authors would like to thank M. Zelt and S. Ring for their technical assistance.

References

[1] U. Kroll, J. Meier, L. Fesquet, J. Steinhauser, S. Benagli, J. Orhan, B. Wolf, D. Borrello, L. Castens, Y. Djeridane, X. Multone, G. Choong, D. Domine, J.-F. Boucher, P.-A. Madliger, M. Marmelo, G. Monteduro, B. Dehbozorgi, D. Romang, E. Omnes, M. Chevalley, G. Charitat, A. Pomey, E. Vallat-Sauvain, S. Marjanovic, G. Kohnke, K. Koch, J. Liu, R. Modavis, D. Thelen, S. Vallon, A. Zakharian, and D. Weidman, "Recent developments of high-efficiency micromorph tandem solar cells in Kai-m/plasmabox PECVD reactors," in *Proc. 26th Eur. Photovoltaic Sol. Energy Conf.*, 2011, pp. 2340–2343

[2] A. Lambertz, T. Grundler, and F. Finger, "Hydrogenated amorphous silicon oxide containing a microcrystalline silicon phase and usage as an intermediate reflector in thin-film silicon solar cells," *J. Appl. Phys.*, vol. 109, pp. 113109-1–113109-11, 2011.

[3] P. Buehlmann, J. Bailat, D. Dominé, A. Billet, F. Meillaud, A. Feltrin, and C. Ballif, "In situ silicon oxide based intermediate reflector for thin-film silicon micromorph solar cells," *Appl. Phys. Lett.*, vol. 91, pp. 143505-1–143505-3, 2007.

[4] M. Python, O. Madani, D. Dominé, F. Meillaud, E. Vallat-Sauvain, and C. Ballif, "Influence of the substrate geometrical parameters on microcrystalline silicon growth for thin-film solar cells," *Sol. Energy Mater. Sol. Cells*, vol. 93, pp. 1714–1720, 2009.

[5] B. Lipovsek, M. Cvek, A. Campa, J. Krc, and M. Topic, "Analysis and optimisation of periodic interface textures in thin-film silicon solar cells," in *Proc. 25th Eur. Photovoltaic Sol. Energy Conf.*, 2010, pp. 3120–3123.

[6] N. P. Vaucher, J.-L. Nagel, R. Platz, D. Fischer, and A. Shah, "Light management in tandem cells by an intermediate reflector layer," in *Proc. 2nd World Conf. Photovoltaic Sol. Energy Convers.*, 1998, pp. 729–731.

[7] D. Dominé, J. Bailat, J. Steinhauser, A. Shah, and C. Ballif, "Micromorph solar cell optimization using a ZnO layer as intermediate reflector," *Photovoltaic Energy Convers.*, vol. 2, pp. 1465–1468, 2006.

[8] C. Rockstuhl, F. Lederer, K. Bittkau, T. Beckers, and R. Carius, F. Lederer, K. Bittkau *et al.*, "The impact of intermediate reflectors on light absorption in tandem solar cells with randomly textured surfaces," *Appl. Phys. Lett.*, vol. 94, pp. 211101-1–211101-3, 2009.

[9] S. Fahr, C. Rockstuhl, and F. Lederer, "The interplay of intermediate reflectors and randomly textured surfaces in tandem solar cells," *Appl. Phys. Lett.*, vol. 97, pp. 173510-1–173510-3, 2010.

[10] J. Müller, B. Rech, J. Springer, and M. Vanecek, "TCO and light trapping in silicon thin film solar cells," *Sol. Energy*, vol. 77, pp. 917–930, 2004.

[11] J. Rath and R. Schropp, "Incorporation of p-type microcrystalline silicon films in amorphous silicon based solar cells in a superstrate structure," *Sol. Energy Mater. Sol. Cells*, vol. 53, pp. 189–203, 1998.

[12] S. Kirner, S. Calnan, O. Gabriel, S. Neubert, M. Zelt, B. Stannowski, B. Rech, and R. Schlatmann, "An improved silicon-oxide-based intermediate-reflector for micromorph solar cells," *Phys. Status Solidi C*, vol. 9, pp. 2145–2148, 2012.

[13] J. Pomplun, S. Burger, L. Zschiedrich, and F. Schmidt, "Adaptive finite element method for simulation of optical nano structures," *Phys. Status Solidi B*, vol. 244, pp. 3419–3434, 2007.

[14] M. Hammerschmidt, D. Lockau, S. Burger, F. Schmidt, C. Schwanke, S. Kirner, S. Calnan, B. Stannowski, and B. Rech, "FEM-based optical modeling of silicon thin-film tandem solar cells with randomly textured interfaces in 3D," *Proc. SPIE*, vol. 8620, pp. 86201H-1–86201H-9, 2013.

[15] C. Jandl, K. Hertel, C. Pflaum, and H. Stiebig, "Simulation of thin-film silicon solar cells with integrated AFM scans for oblique incident waves," in *Proc. 26th Eur. Photovoltaic Sol. Energy Conf.*, 2011, pp. 2663–2666.

[16] J. Springer, A. Poruba, and M. Vanecek, "Improved three-dimensional optical model for thin-film silicon solar cells," *J. Appl. Phys.*, vol. 96, pp. 5329–5337, 2004.

[17] M. Zeman, R. A. C. M. M. van Swaaij, J. W. Metselaar, and R. E. I. Schropp, "Optical modeling of a-Si: H solar cells with rough interfaces: Effect of back contact and interface roughness," *J. Appl. Phys.*, vol. 88, pp. 6436–6443, 2000.

[18] L. Zschiedrich, "Transparent boundary conditions for Maxwell's equations," Ph.D. dissertation, Dept. Math. Comput. Sci., Free Univ. Berlin, Berlin, Germany, 2009.

[19] J.-J. Wu, "Simulation of rough surfaces with FFT," *Tribol. Int.*, vol. 33, no. 1, pp. 47–58, 2000.

[20] D. Lockau, L. Zschiedrich, S. Burger, F. Schmidt, F. Ruske, and B. Rech, "Rigorous optical simulation of light management in crystalline silicon thin film solar cells with rough interface textures," *Proc. SPIE*, vol. 7933, pp. 79330M-1–79330M-10, 2011.

[21] C. Rockstuhl, S. Fahr, K. Bittkau, T. Beckers, R. Carius, F.-J. Haug, T. Söderström, C. Ballif, and F. Lederer, "Comparison and optimization of randomly textured surfaces in thin-film solar cells," *Opt. Exp.*, vol. 18, pp. A335–A341, 2010.

[22] P. Cuony, D. T. L. Alexander, I. Perez-Wurfl, M. Despeisse, G. Bugnon, M. Boccard, T. Söderström, A. Hessler-Wyser, C. Hébert, and C. Ballif, "Silicon filaments in silicon oxide for next-generation photovoltaics," *Adv. Mater.*, vol. 24, pp. 1182–1186, 2012.

[23] V. Smirnov, A. Lambertz, B. Grootoonk, R. Carius, and F. Finger, "Microcrystalline silicon oxide alloys: A versatile material for application in thin film silicon single and tandem junction solar cells," *J. Non-Cryst. Solids*, vol. 358, pp. 1954–1957, 2012.

[24] M. Boccard, C. Battaglia, S. Hänni, K. Söderström, J. Escarr, S. Nicolay, F. Meillaud, M. Despeisse, and C. Ballif, "Multiscale transparent electrode architecture for efficient light management and carrier collection in solar cells," *Nano Lett.*, vol. 12, pp. 1344–1348, 2012.

[25] H. Sai, K. Saito, N. Hozuki, and M. Kondo, "Enhanced photocurrent and conversion efficiency in thin-film microcrystalline silicon solar cells using periodically textured back reflectors with hexagonal dimple arrays," *Appl. Phys. Lett.*, vol. 101, pp. 173901-1–173901-5, 2012.

[26] O. Isabella, F. Moll, J. Krc, and M. Zeman, "Modulated surface textures using zinc-oxide films for solar cells applications," *Phys. Status Solidi A*, vol. 207, no. 3, pp. 642–646, 2010.

[27] P. I. Widenborg and A. G. Aberle, "Polycrystalline silicon thin-film solar cells on AIT-textured glass superstrates," *Adv. Opto. Electron.*, vol. 2007, pp. 1–7, 2007.

[28] D. Dominé, P. Buehlmann, J. Bailat, A. Billet, A. Feltrin, and C. Ballif, "Optical management in high-efficiency thin-film silicon micromorph solar cells with a silicon oxide based intermediate reflector," *Phys. Status Solidi, RRL*, vol. 2, no. 4, pp. 163–165, 2008.

[29] F.-J. Haug, K. Söderstrom, A. Naqavi, and C. Ballif, "Resonances and absorption enhancement in thin film silicon solar cells with periodic interface texture," *J. Appl. Phys.*, vol. 109, pp. 084516-1–084516-8, 2011.

Author's photographs and biographies not available at the time of publication.

Fabrication of Light-Scattering Multiscale Textures by Nanoimprinting for the Application to Thin-Film Silicon Solar Cells

M. Meier, U. W. Paetzold, M. Ghosh, W. Zhang, T. Merdzhanova, G. Jost, N. Sommer, S. Michard, and A. Gordijn

Abstract—In this study, nanoimprint processing was used to realize various multiscale textures on glass substrates for application in thin-film photovoltaic devices. The multiscale textures are formed by a combination of large and small features, which proofed to be beneficial for light trapping in silicon thin-film solar cells. Two approaches for the fabrication of multiscale textures are presented in this study. In the first approach, the multiscale texture is realized at the lacquer/transparent conductive oxide (TCO) interface, and in the second approach, the multiscale texture is realized at the TCO/Si interface. Various types of multiscale textures were fabricated and tested in microcrystalline thin-film silicon solar cells in p-i-n configuration to identify the optimal texture for the light management. It was found that the best light-scattering multiscale texture was realized using an imprint-textured glass substrate, which contains large craters, in combination with HF-etched TCO (ZnO:Al), which contains small features, on top of the imprint. With this structure (of the second approach), the short-circuit current density of the solar cell devices was improved by 0.6 mA/cm^{-2} using multiscale textures realized by nanoimprint processing.

Index Terms—Light-trapping, microcrystalline silicon, multiscale textures, nanoimprint, photovoltaics, thin-film.

I. Introduction

LIGHT-TRAPPING textures are essential in thin-film photovoltaic devices. By the application of rough interfaces, the light path in the thin absorber layers is enhanced due to light scattering and light diffraction. Rough interfaces are commonly realized by transparent conductive oxide (TCO) layers used as front contact in thin-film silicon solar cells in p-i-n configuration, which are considered in this study [1]. Novel device concepts use, e.g., textured glass, where the light scattering properties are decoupled from the front contact TCO [2].

Textured glass substrates can be fabricated (among others) by nanoimprint processes, on which this study is focused [3], [4].

Nanoimprint is a high throughput and a highly reproducible process, which is applicable for mass production and thus relevant for the industrial application. Recent studies have shown that nanoimprint processes are suitable in the fabrication chain of thin-film silicon solar cells and modules [5]–[9]. Random and periodic light-trapping textures for photovoltaic devices were fabricated, and solar cells with good performance were demonstrated [10]–[15].

In our recent studies, we focused on the fabrication and integration of random light-trapping textures in thin-film silicon solar cells, which consist of craters in the micrometer range [9], [16]. The crater structures are randomly distributed on the surface, and the dimension distribution of the structures is narrow, thus we call the texture a single-scale texture. It turned out that for this kind of single-scale textures challenging light management issues occur due to decreased light incoupling into the device [16]. Interference effects occur at distinct front TCO layer thicknesses, which are deposited on the imprint-textured glass. These interferences result in an increased cell reflection which (partly) lowers the external quantum efficiency (EQE) and, thus, the short-circuit current density of the solar cells.

To increase the light incoupling and light-scattering properties in thin-film silicon solar cells multiscale textures were used, which has been shown in the past by a double-textured front electrode made of TCO [17], [18]. The multiscale textures consist of various feature sizes, such as small and large craters, which were realized by, e.g., a multiple etching step process.

In this study, we demonstrate a method for the realization of multiscale textures by the application of nanoimprint processes. Two approaches are presented. In the first approach, the glass/TCO interface of the solar cell and in the second approach the TCO/silicon interface of the solar cell contains the multiscale texture. Both approaches aim for improved light management properties that are compared with single-scale-textured substrates. The concepts are tested in microcrystalline silicon (μc-Si:H) solar cells in p-i-n configuration, where light trapping plays an important role.

II. Experimental Details

An UV nanoimprint process was used for the texturing of 5 cm $\times$ 5 cm glass substrates (Corning Eagle) on which μc-Si:H solar cells in p-i-n configuration were fabricated. The whole process flow of the solar cell preparation is schematically shown in Fig. 1.

Manuscript received June 6, 2013; accepted February 25, 2014. Part of this work was carried out in the framework of the FP7 Project "Fast Track," funded by the European Commission, and part was carried out in the framework of the project "Quick μc-Si" (Contract No. 03225260 C) funded by the "Bundesministerium für Umwelt, Naturschutz und Reaktorsicherheit."

The authors are with IEK-5 Photovoltaics, Forschungszentrum Jülich GmbH, Jülich, 52425 Germany (e-mail: m.meier@fz-juelich.de; u.paetzold@fz-juelich.de; m.ghosh@fz-juelich.de; w.zhang@fz-juelich.de; t.merdzhanova@fz-juelich.de; g.jost@fz-juelich.de; n.sommer@fz-juelich.de; s.michard@fz-juelich.de; a.gordijn@fz-juelich.de).

Color versions of one or more of the figures in this paper are available online at http://ieeexplore.ieee.org.

Digital Object Identifier 10.1109/JPHOTOV.2014.2311233

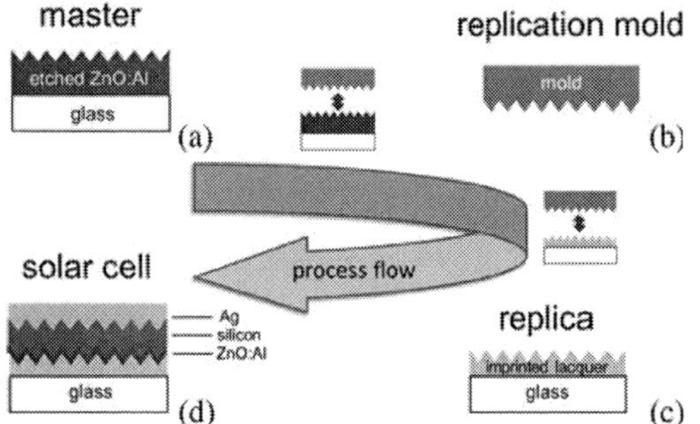

Fig. 1. Process flow of the preparation of thin-film μc-Si:H solar cells on imprint textured glass substrates. (a) Master made of etched ZnO:Al which contains the original texture. (b) Replication mold made of a soft polymeric material and is formed in a hot embossing process using the master as basis. (c) Replica made of transparent lacquer deposited on glass textured in an imprint process using the replication mold. (d) Solar cell in p-i-n configuration fabricated on the imprint textured glass.

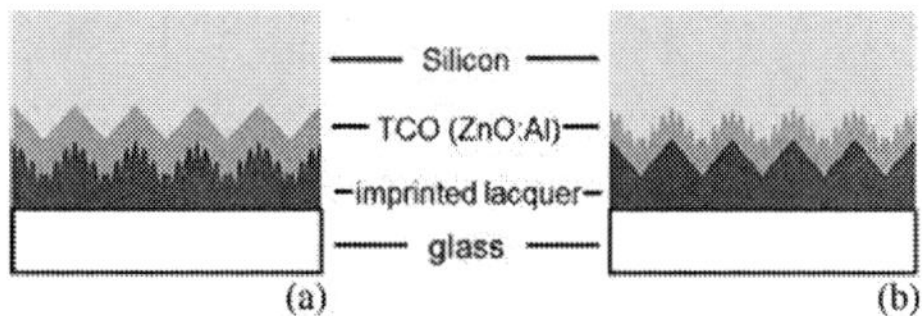

Fig. 2. Two approaches for the realization of multiscale textures containing large and small features in thin-film silicon solar cells. In the first approach, the lacquer/TCO interface contains the multiscale texture (a) whereas, in the second approach, the TCO/silicon interface contains the multiscale textures (b).

First, a master containing the original texture was fabricated [see Fig. 1(a)]. The master is made from aluminum-doped ZnO (ZnO:Al) sputtered on a glass substrate and subsequently textured by liquid acids (HCl and HF). Details of the sputter and the etching processes can be found in [1] and [18].

Second, a replication mold was realized which exhibits the inverse texture of the master [see Fig. 1(b)]. The replication mold is a soft mold made from a polymeric material (polyolefin plastomer). It is fabricated in a hot embossing process in which the polymeric material is pressed against the master [19].

Third, the replica glass substrate used for the solar cells was realized in a UV nanoimprint process [see Fig. 1(c)]. Therefore, a liquid and transparent lacquer is spun onto the glass. Afterward, the replication mold is pressed into the lacquer and UV light is applied to crosslink and to harden the lacquer. The imprint processes were performed using a Nanonex NX 2000 imprint system which works with an air cushion press [20]. Finally, the replication mold and the glass substrate, which contains now the original master texture, are separated. Details of the nanoimprint process parameters can be found in [9].

Fourth, the μc-Si:H solar cell was deposited on the imprint-textured glass substrate [see Fig. 1(d)]. Therefore, a thin ZnO:Al front contact layer of 350 nm thickness is sputtered on top of the textured lacquer. A radiofrequency magnetron sputtering process at a temperature of around 230 °C was used. Subsequently, the silicon layer stack (p-type layer, i-layer, and n-type layer) is deposited on top of the ZnO:Al using parallel plate PECVD processes at 13.56 MHz. The thickness of the i-layer was around 1 μm. The deposition temperature was below 200 °C. Finally, Ag was evaporated through a shadow mask on top of the silicon n-type layer to build the back contact and to define the solar cell active area of 1 cm × 1 cm. Details of the ZnO:Al and the PECVD processes can be found in [1], [18], and [21]. As an alternative TCO material, which is sputtered on top of the imprint lacquer, indium tin oxide (ITO) was investigated.

To investigate the influence of the texture on the light management, EQE measurements were performed at the finalized solar cells. Additionally, the solar cells were characterized using a class A sun simulator.

Two different approaches for the fabrication of multiscale textures for thin-film silicon solar cells were applied. They are schematically shown in Fig. 2. In the first approach, the imprint lacquer was directly patterned with a multiscale texture which consists of small and large features [see Fig. 2(a)]. Therefore, it was necessary to fabricate first the corresponding master with multiscale textures by texturing ZnO:Al on glass [see Fig. 1(a)]. On top of the patterned lacquer, a ZnO:Al layer with a thickness of 350 nm was sputtered. Thus, in this first approach, only the lacquer/TCO interface exhibits multiscale textures. The small features vanish on top of the TCO layer, due to nonperfect conformal growth, and only the large features are available at the TCO/silicon interface.

In the second approach, the nanoimprint process was used to realize the large features of the multiscale texture only [see Fig. 2(b)]. Hence, the lacquer contains a single-scale texture. As in the first approach, ZnO:Al of 350 nm thickness was then sputtered on top of the imprint-textured lacquer. Contrary to the first approach, in the second approach, the ZnO:Al was additionally textured in a short HF wet etch step, leading to small features. In the end, a multiscale texture was built at the TCO/silicon interface.

III. RESULTS

Fig. 3 shows scanning electron microscopy (SEM) images of four master textures, which are used in the first approach of the study [compare Fig. 2(a)]. In Fig. 3(a)–(c), three multiscale textures are shown. The first texture shows a high density of small features with dimensions of about 100 nm, whereas the larger craters are not clearly visible in the SEM image [see Fig. 3(a)]. In Fig. 3(b) and (c), the large craters of the multiscale texture with dimensions in the micrometer range are clearly visible because they are more pronounced. The density of the small features is not as high as at the first texture in Fig. 3(a). The two surfaces of Fig. 3(b) and (c) seem similar in the SEM image, but they are clearly distinguishable from their light scattering behavior measured for example by angle-resolved scattering. The texture of the SEM image shown in Fig. 3(d) is a single-scale texture with only large craters in the micrometer range. This single-scale texture, also called Jülich-like ZnO:Al texture, was used as reference texture because it is usually used (in our Institute) for thin-film silicon solar cell devices fabricated on textured ZnO:Al.

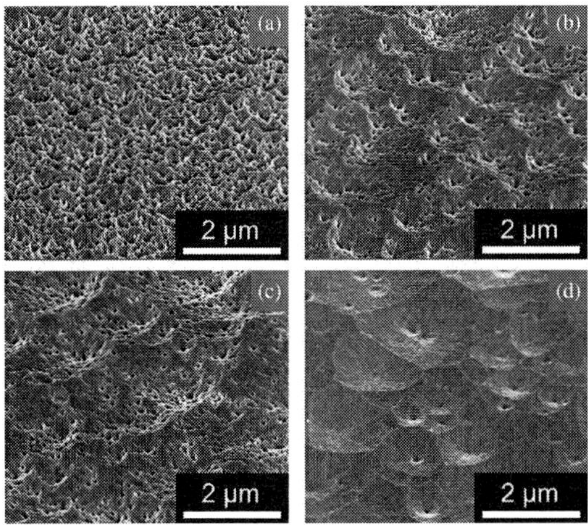

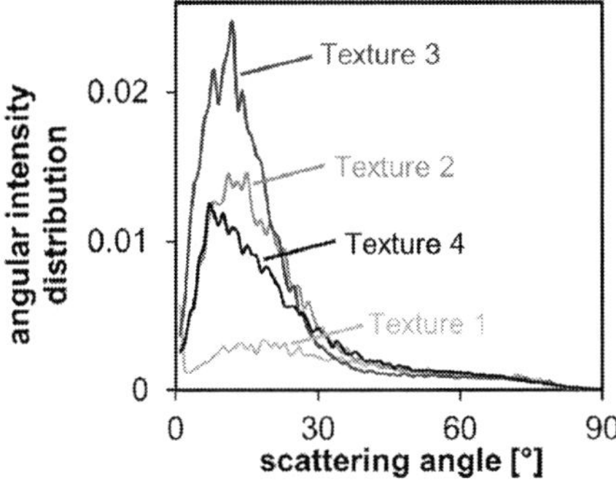

Fig. 3. SEM images of four different multiscale textures used for the first approach of this study [shown in Fig. 2(a)]. Here, the master samples are shown.

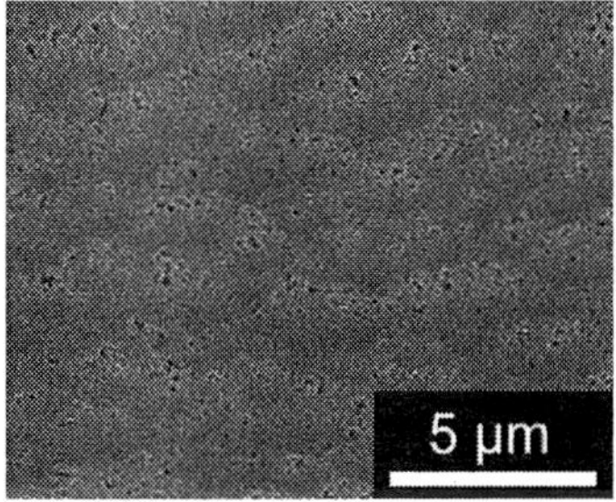

Fig. 5. SEM image of the multiscale texture used in the second approach of this study [shown in Fig. 2(b)].

Fig. 4. Angle resolved scattering spectra of the samples shown in Fig. 3. Measurements were performed in air using a laser wavelength of 550 nm. Texture 1 corresponds to the image of Fig. 3(a), Texture 2 corresponds to the image of Fig. 3(b), Texture 3 corresponds to the image of Fig. 3(c), and Texture 4 corresponds to the image of Fig. 3(d).

TABLE I
SUMMARY OF THE TEXTURES APPLIED AT THE FIRST APPROACH AND THE SECOND APPROACH OF THIS STUDY

Approach 1	Texture 1	Figure 3a)
	Texture 2	Figure 3b)
	Texture 3	Figure 3c)
	Texture 4	Figure 3d)
Approach 2	Texture 5	Figure 5

Fig. 4 shows the angle-resolved scattering spectra of the four different master textures presented in Fig. 3. The scattering behavior of the samples was measured in air using a laser wavelength of 550 nm. This method proofed to be useful for the estimation of the light-scattering properties of the rough surfaces in solar cell devices [22]. Here, the angle-resolved scattering measurements are used to distinguish the different surface textures, which are replicated by nanoimprinting. It can be seen that the four different textures, which are used in the first approach of this study, show a clearly distinguishable scattering behavior, even though they are partly not distinguishable from their SEM images. In the scattering angle range from +0° to 30°, the curve of Texture 1, which corresponds to Fig. 3(a), shows the lowest intensity values, and the curve of Texture 3, which corresponds to Fig. 3(c), shows the highest intensity values, which means, in principle, that Texture 3 shows the best scattering properties in this angular range. The curves of Texture 2 and Texture 4 show medium intensity values which are slightly different but close to each other. Thus, Texture 3 and Texture 4 are clearly dis-

tinguishable due to their scattering behavior, even though they appear similar in Fig. 3.

Fig. 5 shows the SEM image of the multiscale texture which was fabricated with the second approach of this study [compare Fig. 2(b)]. The top side of the ZnO:Al layer, which was deposited on the patterned lacquer, is shown here. The ZnO:Al was etched in an HF solution for 10 s, which causes the small features with dimensions of about 100 nm. The underlying lacquer contains large features in the micrometer range, such that on top of thin-etched ZnO:Al, a multiscale texture occurs.

Table I summarizes the textures of the first approach and the second approach of this study, which is helpful for the following part of description.

Fig. 6 shows the EQE measurements of the solar cells fabricated with the first approach of this study in comparison with the EQE measurement of a reference μc-Si:H solar cell that is fabricated on sputtered and etched ZnO:Al, which exhibits a single-scale texture and is commonly used in our institute. The reference solar cell has no imprinted layer included in its device structure. Fig. 6(a) shows the EQE of the samples with Texture 1 and Texture 2 and Fig. 6(b) shows the EQE of samples with Texture 3 and Texture 4.

It is observed that by applying Texture 1 or Texture 2 to solar cells their EQE curves do not reach the EQE of the reference cell [see Fig. 6(a)]. Especially in the long wavelength range, the EQE of the cell fabricated on Texture 1 is significantly decreased, which indicates a reduced light-trapping effect. For both cells, including imprint textures, a lower EQE at around 500 nm wavelength, in comparison to the reference cell, is also observed. This is an indication of a reduced light incoupling.

By applying Texture 3 and Texture 4, the EQE is increased in the lower wavelength range compared with the reference cell, such that the light incoupling properties are enhanced with these

225

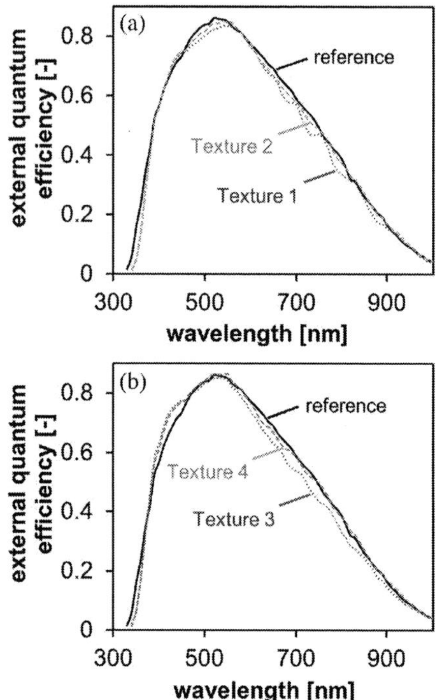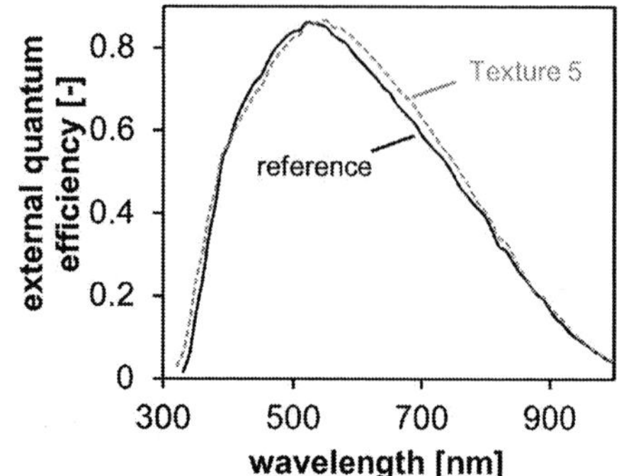

Fig. 6. EQE as a function of wavelength for solar cells deposited on the textures 1–4 of the first approach of this study. For comparison, the external quantum efficiency of a reference cell is shown, which is deposited on sputtered and etched ZnO:Al.

Fig. 7. External quantum efficiency as a function of wavelength for the solar cell deposited on the Textures 5 of the second approach of this study. For comparison, the external quantum efficiency of a reference cell is shown, which is deposited on sputtered and etched ZnO:Al.

TABLE II

PHOTOVOLTAIC PARAMETERS OF SELECTED μc-Si:H SOLAR CELLS

	Ref	Texture 4 ZnO	Texture 4 ITO	Texture 5
η [%]	7.32	6.72	7.1	4.08
V_{OC} [mV]	539	524	539	493
J_{SC} [mA/cm²]	20.09	20.38	20.1	20.70
FF [%]	69.0	65.9	67.5	41.6

two textures [see Fig. 6(b)]. In the long wavelength range, only Texture 4 performs similarly to the reference cell.

The short-circuit current density (J_{SC}) of the solar cells was derived as a spectral-weighted (AM 1.5) integral of the EQE. It is observed that the solar cell with Texture 4 generates a higher J_{SC} of 20.38 mA cm^{-2} than the reference solar cell fabricated on etched ZnO:Al, which generates J_{SC} of 20.09 mA cm^{-2}. For the multiscale textures (Textures 1–3), no improvement of the J_{SC} in comparison with the reference cell was achieved. Thus, only with Texture 4 of the first approach of this study, which is a single-scale texture, an enhancement of J_{SC} is achieved compared with the reference cell.

Fig. 7 shows the EQE measurements of the solar cells fabricated with the second approach of this study (Texture 5) in comparison with the EQE measurement of a reference μc-Si:H solar cell, which is fabricated on sputtered and etched ZnO:Al. Here, a significant enhancement in the EQE of the imprint solar cell compared with the reference cell, especially in the long wavelength range, can be seen. This leads to an increase in J_{SC} of 20.70 mA cm^{-2} for the solar cell fabricated with Texture 5 compared with a J_{SC} of 20.09 mA cm^{-2} of the reference cell. Hence, a significant increase in the optical performance and, thus, a significant increase of J_{SC} was reached using the multiscale texture of the second approach.

The photovoltaic parameters (η: conversion efficiency, V_{OC}: open-circuit voltage, J_{SC}: short-circuit current density, and FF: fill factor) of selected cells are presented in Table II. The refer-

ence cell and the best performing cells, regarding J_{SC}, from the first approach and the second approach are shown. Additionally, the parameters of a solar cell, which was fabricated with ITO (indium tin oxide) as a front contact layer material instead of ZnO:Al, is included.

The values of the conversion efficiency of the reference solar cell were not achieved using either the first or the second approach, even though J_{SC} of the cells is significantly increased. The lower efficiencies are mainly driven by the reduced FF of the solar cells, which are fabricated on imprint-textured glasses compared with the reference cell. This results from the low thickness of the front contact layer which is necessary, on the one hand, to reduce parasitic absorption and, on the other hand, to prevent a smoothening of the texture of glass substrates. By using ITO instead of ZnO:Al, the FF can be increased due to the lower sheet resistance of ITO. This also increases the conversion efficiency, which is shown with the help of the example made with Texture 4 here.

IV. DISCUSSION

With the first approach that is based on an imprint-textured substrate, the J_{SC} of μc-Si:H thin-film solar cells was improved using a single-scale texture (Texture 4) compared with the reference solar cell, which was fabricated on standard texture-etched ZnO:Al. This experiment shows that there is still room for improvement for the multiscale textures, which were designed and optimized for the use as textured ZnO:Al front contact layers in thin-film silicon solar cells. Since an optically different system is applied when imprint-textured substrates are used, compared with the standard solar cell approach wherein textured ZnO:Al is used, the multiscale textures must be optimized for such a different optical layer stack. However, there are several process parameters which can be varied during the fabrication of multiscale-textured master samples. This implies the freedom to realize various textures and, thus, presents the potential to produce optimized multiscale textures for imprint-textured glasses during further experiments [18].

The second approach, wherein multiscale textures are used, results in a significantly higher J_{SC} compared with the reference solar cell. Thus, regarding J_{SC}, it is an excellent alternative process compared with the standard processing of μc-Si:H solar cells, due to the improved light management issues.

Nevertheless, other photovoltaic parameters, like V_{OC} and FF, are also influenced by the solar cell design. We have seen in earlier studies that the FF reduction due to reduced TCO thicknesses has to be compensated [6]. One possible solution is shown here by application of ITO instead of ZnO:Al as a front contact layer, but of course, in the second approach of this study, ITO cannot be an alternative material because ITO cannot be etched like sputtered ZnO:Al for the creation of light-trapping textures. Here, it is important to study and understand the ZnO:Al growth on textured substrates such that, e.g., the following etching step, which is necessary for the fabrication of the multiscale texture, can be adjusted to realize layers which are not only optically optimized but are also optimized with respect to their electrical conductance to improve the FF of the solar cell devices. Studies on the ZnO:Al growth on different textured substrates are therefore currently conducted at our institute [23].

Finally, it is known that the growth of silicon is strongly influenced by the substrate texture, which always must be considered [24]. The different silicon growth and, with it, the different crystalline volume fraction of the μc-Si:H absorber layer mainly has an effect on V_{OC} of the solar cell device, which we already have seen and reported in our recent studies [9], [21]. It can be concluded that the optimization of the solar cell performance is in a more or less early stage because not only optimized textures for the best light management but, in addition, the optimal process parameters like deposition pressure, deposition temperature, plasma frequency, or electrode distance (in a parallel plate PECVD) for the ZnO:Al and Si deposition must be found [1], [18], [21], [23]–[26].

Finally, we demonstrate and use an attractive alternative (nanoimprint) process for the fabrication chain of thin-film silicon solar modules, which implies a high industrial relevance. Hence, not only the highest performance of the device but also the compromise between cost reduction and efficiency gain has to be considered. This kind of tradeoff is conducted by industrial companies (e.g., OM&T Moser Baer Technologies [7]), and it shows that using imprint technologies has the potential to decrease costs for the solar module production, which provides us additional room for the optimization of the device performance.

V. Summary

Two approaches for the fabrication of multiscale textures on glass substrates using nanoimprinting for the integration in thin-film μc-Si:H solar cells were shown. In the first approach, the multiscale texture is realized at the lacquer/TCO interface, and in the second approach, the multiscale texture is realized at the TCO/Si interface. With respect to reference μc-Si:H solar cells fabricated on single-scale-textured ZnO:Al, the short-circuit current density was improved significantly from 20.09 mA cm^{-2} to 20.70 mA cm^{-2} using the second approach of the study. Hence, the implementation of light-trapping multiscale textures shows the potential to significantly improve the light management of the solar cell device. With the imprint technology, an attractive fabrication method is used due to the potential for up-scaling, cheap high through-put processing, and the potential of the reduction of material costs because of the TCO thickness in the solar cell can be significantly reduced.

Acknowledgment

The authors would like to thank A. Schmalen, J. Wolff, D. Weigand, J. Kirchhoff, and W. Appenzeller for technical assistance and M. Prömpers, D. Mayer (both PGI8—Bioelectronics, Forschungszentrum Jülich GmbH), J. Hüpkes, R. Carius, and U. Rau for fruitful discussions.

References

[1] W. Beyer, J. Hüpkes, and H. Stiebig, "Transparent conducting oxide films for thin film silicon photovoltaics," *Thin Solid Films*, vol. 516, pp. 147–154, 2007.

[2] W. Zhang, U. W. Paetzold, M. Meier, A. Gordijn, J. Hüpkes, and T Merdzhanova, "Thin film silicon solar cells on dry etched glass," *Energy Procedia*, vol. 44, pp. 151–159, 2014.

[3] S. Y. Chou, P. R. Krauss, and P. J. Renstrom, "Nanoimprint lithography," *J. Vac. Sci. Technol. B, Microelectron. Process. Phenom.*, vol. 14, pp. 4129–4133, 1996.

[4] L. Jay Guo, "Nanoimprint lithography: Methods and material requirements," *Adv. Mater.*, vol. 19, pp. 495–513, 2007.

[5] C. Battaglia, J. Escarre, K. Söderström, L. Erni, L. Ding, G. Bugnon, A. Billet, M. Boccard, L. Barraud, S. De Wolf, F.-J. Haug, M. Despeisse, and C. Ballif, "Nanoimprint lithography for high-efficiency thin-film silicon solar cells," *Nano Lett.*, vol. 11, pp. 661–665, 2011.

[6] J. Escarré, C. Battaglia, K. Söderström, C. Pahud, R. Biron, O. Cubero, F.-J. Haug, and C. Ballif, "UV imprinting for thin film solar cell application," *J. Opt.*, vol. 14, 024009, 8 pp., 2012.

[7] A. J. M. van Erven, M. Steltenpool, M. Bos, J. Rutten, G. van der Hofstad, J. Muller, H. de Groot, J. de Ruijter, B. Titulaer, and G. Rajeswaran, "Gen5 production tool for light management textures," in *Proc. 38th IEEE Photovoltaic Spec. Conf.*, 2012, pp. 690–693.

[8] M. C. R. Heijna, M. J. A. A. Goris, and W. J. Soppe, "Roll-to-roll nanotexturisation of layers on steel foil substrates for nip silicon solar cells," in *Proc. 25th Eur. Photovoltaic Solar Energy Conf.*, 2010, pp. 3090–3093.

[9] M. Meier, U. W. Paetzold, M. Prömpers, T. Merdzhanova, R. Carius, and A. Gordijn, "UV nanoimprint for the replication of etched ZnO:Al textures applied in thin-film silicon solar cells," *Prog. Photovolt, Res. Appl.*, 2013, doi: 10.1002/pip.2382, to be published.

[10] J. Escarré, K. Söderström, C. Battaglia, F.-J. Haug, and C. Ballif, "High fidelity transfer of nanometric random textures by UV embossing for thin film solar cells applications," *Sol. Energy Mater. Sol. Cells*, vol. 95, pp. 881–886, 2011.

[11] C. Becker, V. Preidel, T. Sontheimer, C. Klimm, E. Rudigier-Voigt, M. Bockmeyer, and B. Rech, "Direct growth of periodic silicon nanostructures on imprinted glass for photovoltaic and photonic applications," *Phys. Status Solidi C*, vol. 9, pp. 2079–2082, 2012.

[12] V. E. Ferry, M. A. Verschuuren, H. B. T. Li, E. Verhagen, R. J. Walters, R. Schropp, H. A. Atwater, and A. Polman, "Light-trapping in ultrathin photovoltaic devices," *Opt. Exp.*, vol. 18, pp. 237–245, 2010.

[13] U. W. Paetzold, E. Moulin, D. Michaelis, W. Böttler, C. Wächter, V. Hagemann, M. Meier, R. Carius, and U. Rau, "Plasmonic reflection grating back contacts for microcrystalline silicon solar cells," *Appl. Phys. Lett.*, vol. 99, p. 181105, 2011.

[14] C. Battaglia, C.-M. Hsu, K. Söderström, J. Escarré, F.-J. Haug, M. Charrière, M. Boccard, M. Despeisse, D. T. L. Alexander, M. Cantoni,

Y. Cui, and C. Ballif, "Light trapping in solar cells: Can periodic beat random?" *ACS Nano*, vol. 6, pp. 2790–2797, 2012.

[15] H. A. Atwater and A. Polman, "Plasmonics for improved photovoltaic devices," *Nat. Mater.*, vol. 9, pp. 205–213, 2010.

[16] U. W. Paetzold, W. Zhang, M. Prömpers, J. Kirchhoff, T. Merdzhanova, S. Michard, R. Carius, A. Gordijn, and M Meier, "Thin-film silicon solar cell development on imprint textured glass substrates," *Mat. Sci. Eng. B*, vol. 178, pp. 617–622, 2013.

[17] M. Boccard, C. Battaglia, S. Hänni, K. Söderström, J. Escarré, S. Nicolay, F. Meillaud, M. Despeisse, and C. Ballif, "Multiscale transparent electrode architecture for efficient light management and carrier collection in solar cells," *Nano Lett.*, vol. 12, pp. 1344–1348, 2012.

[18] J. Hüpkes, J. I. Owen, E. Bunte, H. Zhu, S. E. Pust, J. Worbs, and G. Jost, "New texture etching of zinc oxide: Tunable light trapping FIR Si thin film solar cells," in *Proc. 25th Eur. Photovoltaic Solar Energy Conf.*, 2008.

[19] S. Gilles, M. Meier, M. Prömpers, A. v. d. Hart, C. Kügeler, A. Offenhäusser, and D. Mayer, "UV nanoimprint lithography with rigid polymer molds," *Microelectron. Eng.*, vol. 86, pp. 661–664, 2009.

[20] H. Gao, H. Tan, W. Zhang, K. Morton, and S. Y. Chou, "Air cushion press for excellent uniformity, high yield, and fast nanoimprint across a 100 mm field," *Nano Lett.*, vol. 6, pp. 2438–2441, 2006.

[21] S. Michard, M. Meier, B. Grootoonk, O. Astakhov, A. Gordijn, and F. Finger, "High deposition rate processes for the fabrication of micro-crystalline silicon thin films," *Mat. Sci. Eng. B*, vol. 178, pp. 691–694, 2013.

[22] G. Jost and J. Hüpkes, "Angle resolved scattering measurements as quality analysis of textured ZnO:Al layers," to be published.

[23] N. Sommer, S.Götzendörfer, F. Köhler, M. Ziegner, and J. Hüpkes, "Influence of deposition conditions and substrate morphology on the electrical properties of zinc oxide grown on texture-etched glass substrates," *Thin Solid Films*, to be published.

[24] M. Python, O. Madani, D. Domine, F. Meillaud, E. Vallat-Sauvain, and C. Ballif, "Influence of the substrate geometrical parameters on micro-crystalline silicon growth for thin-film solar cells," *Sol. Energy Mater. Sol. Cells*, vol. 93, pp. 1714–1720, 2009.

[25] G. Bugnon, G. Parascandolo, T. Söderström, P. Cuony, M. Despeisse, S. Hänni, J. Holovský, F. Meillaud, and C. Ballif, "A new view of micro-crystalline silicon: The role of plasma processing in achieving a dense and stable absorber material for photovoltaic applications," *Adv. Functional Mater.*, vol. 22, pp. 3665–3671, 2012.

[26] M. Despeisse, G. Bugnon, A. Feltrin, M. Stueckelberger, P. Cuony, F. Meillaud, A. Billet, and C. Ballif, "Resistive interlayer for improved performance of thin film silicon solar cells on highly textured substrate," *Appl. Phys. Lett.*, vol. 96, p. 073507, 2010.

Authors' photographs and biographies not available at the time of publication.

Light-Trapping and Interface Morphologies of Amorphous Silicon Solar Cells on Multiscale Surface Textured Substrates

Asman Tamang, Aswin Hongsingthong, Porponth Sichanugrist, Vladislav Jovanov, Makoto Konagai, and Dietmar Knipp

Abstract—The short circuit current and quantum efficiency of silicon thin-film solar cells can be increased by using multiscale surface textures consisting of micro- and nanoscale textures. Adding microtextures to the already existing nanosurface textures leads to an increase of the short circuit current from 15.5 mA/cm^2 to almost 17 mA/cm^2 for thin amorphous silicon solar cells. To gain insights into the light-trapping properties, finite difference time domain simulations were carried out using realistic interface morphologies. The simulations reveal that the gain of the short circuit current is caused by an increased effective thickness of the solar cell and the scattering properties of the microtextured back reflector. The thickness of the solar cells is increased by the growth of the silicon p-i-n diode on the microtextured surface. The influence of the nanoscale and multiscale surface textures on the quantum efficiency and short circuit current will be discussed.

Index Terms—Amorphous silicon solar cells, light trapping, transparent conductive oxides (TCOs), 3-D surface growth algorithm.

I. Introduction

LIGHT trapping in thin-film solar cells allows for both a reduction of the reflection losses and an increase in the optical path length of the incident light inside the solar cell. Different light-trapping methods have been proposed for increasing the absorption of light in thin-film solar cells [1]–[10]. It has been shown experimentally and numerically that the highest short circuit current can be achieved if the front and the back contacts of the solar cell are textured [1], [2]. Furthermore, it has been demonstrated that a combination of micro- and nanotextures is a very effective approach to increasing the absorption of light in thin-film solar cells [3]–[6]. Multiscale textures usually consist of a combination of micro- and nanosized textures. The multiscale textures lead to a gain of the quantum efficiency for longer wavelengths. It is commonly believed that the gain in the short circuit current is caused by an improved light trapping of longer wavelengths of light [3]–[6]. The small surface features scatter and diffract shorter wavelengths, while the bigger surface textures scatter and diffract longer wavelengths [3]–[6]. As a consequence, the quantum efficiency for longer wavelengths (red and infrared parts of the optical spectrum) is increased. However, a detailed analysis of the dimensions of the surface textures reveals that this explanation cannot be correct. The dimensions of the microsized surface features are too large to efficiently scatter and diffract red and infrared light [9], [10]. Therefore, the mechanism responsible for the gain in the quantum efficiency and short circuit current remains unclear. The aim of this study is to gain insights into the optics of amorphous silicon thin-film solar cells that are prepared on nano- and multiscale (micro plus nano)-textured substrates. The nanoscale substrates exhibit typical surface feature dimensions (period) of 300 nm, while the multiscale-textured substrates combine surface textures with periods of 2.5–4 μm and 300 nm. Experimental results of solar cells that are prepared on nano- and multiscale-textured solar cells are presented in Section II-A. A model to determine the interface morphology of thin-film solar cells of single- and multiscale textured substrates is presented in Section II-B. The optical simulations of the single- and multiscale-textured solar cells are described in Section II-C. Section II-D presents approaches to optimize light trapping in multiscale solar cells, before summarizing the results in Section III.

II. Results

A. Experimental Results

Cross sections of amorphous silicon thin-film solar cells that are prepared on nano- and multiscale-textured substrates are shown in Fig. 1(a) and (c). Fig. 1(a) exhibits a thin-film solar cell that is prepared on a single (nano)-textured transparent conductive oxide (TCO) layer. The solar cell on the single-textured substrate is used as a reference. The reference solar cell exhibits short circuit currents and conversion efficiencies comparable or even higher than amorphous silicon solar cells on commercial available pyramidal-textured substrates [10]. The front ZnO layer was prepared by metal organic chemical vapor deposition (MOCVD) on a soda lime glass. Before ZnO film deposition, the glass was textured by using a reactive ion etching process.

Manuscript received June 10, 2013; revised August 14, 2013; accepted August 21, 2013. Date of publication September 16, 2013; date of current version December 16, 2013.

A. Tamang, V. Jovanov, and D. Knipp are with the Electronic Devices and Nanophotonics Laboratory, Research Center for Functional Materials and Nanomolecular Science, Jacobs University Bremen, 28759 Bremen, Germany (e-mail: asmantamang2012@gmail.com; v.jovanov@jacobs-university.de; d.knipp@jacobs-university.de).

A. Hongsingthong and P. Sichanugrist are with the Department of Physical Electronics, Tokyo Institute of Technology, Tokyo 1528552, Japan (e-mail: hongsingthong_a_aa@m_titech.ac.jp; sichanugrist.p.aa@m.titech.ac.jp).

M. Konagai is with the Department of Physical Electronics and Photovoltaics Research Center (PVREC), Tokyo Institute of Technology, Tokyo 1528552, Japan (e-mail: konagai.m.aa@m.titech.ac.jp).

Color versions of one or more of the figures in this paper are available online at http://ieeexplore.ieee.org.

Digital Object Identifier 10.1109/JPHOTOV.2013.2280020

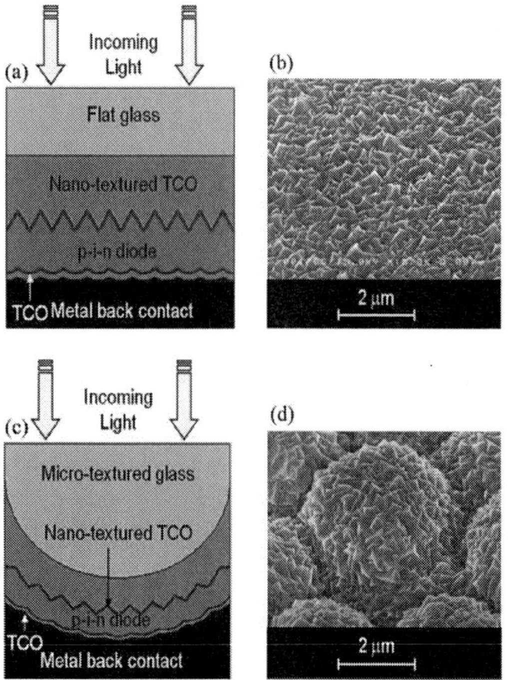

Fig. 1. Schematic cross section of an amorphous silicon thin film solar cell on (a) a single scale (nanotextured) substrate and (b) a multiscale (micro- and nanotextured)-textured substrate. The cross sections of the solar cells are not drawn to scale.

The glass substrate in Fig. 1(b) was etched by using carbon tetrafluoride (CF_4) as etchant gas at a gas pressure of 13 Pa. Further details on the texturing of the glass substrate are given in [5]. Details on the fabrication of the TCO films are given in [5], [11], and [12]. A scanning electron microscope (SEM) image of a ZnO film that is prepared on a glass substrate is shown in Fig. 1(b). The film exhibits a high transmission of >80% and a haze of >20% in the spectral range from 300 to 800 nm. The nanotextured layer exhibits a sheet resistance of <9 $\Omega/\square$ and a root-mean-square (rms) roughness of 63 nm. The cross section of solar cells that are prepared on a multiscale-textured substrate is shown in Fig. 1(c) and its corresponding SEM image is shown in Fig. 1(d). Based on SEM images, an average feature size of 2.5–4 μm was estimated for the microtextured substrate. Besides, the nanotextured TCO was fabricated by MOCVD [5], [11], [12]. The transmission and sheet resistances of the ZnO films prepared on flat (nanotextured cell) and microtextured glass (micro- and nanotextured cell) are equal. However, the haze for the multiscale-textured substrate exceeds 90% for the wavelengths ranging from 300 to 800 nm. Because of the microtexturing of the glass substrate, the rms roughness of the chemically vapor-deposited zinc oxide film is increased to 270 nm. In the next step, the amorphous silicon p-i-n solar cells were prepared on the front ZnO substrates by plasma-enhanced chemical vapor deposition (PECVD). A wide-bandgap silicon oxide ($Si_{1-x} O_x$) film was used as a p-layer to minimize the optical loss in the p-layer [13]. A 20-nm $Si_{1-x} O_x$ thick film was prepared on the textured substrates. The absorber layer of

the amorphous silicon solar cell has a thickness of 300 nm. The n-layer was again alloyed by oxygen to reduce the absorption in the doped layers. A 50-nm zinc oxide layer was prepared on top of the 20-nm thick n-layer to reduce parasitic absorption in the metallic back reflector [10], [14]–[16]. Finally, a silver back reflector was prepared.

The current/voltage characteristics of the nanotextured and multiscale-textured substrate are presented in Fig. 2(a). The nanotextured solar cell exhibits a short circuit current (I_{SC}) of 15.52 mA/cm^2, fill factor (FF) of 65%, and an open circuit voltage (V_{OC}) of 940 mV resulting in energy conversion efficiency (η) of 9.5%. The conversion efficiency is comparable to high efficiency amorphous silicon solar cells on Asahi U-type or Nippon Sheet Glass Tech substrates [10]. The multiscale-textured substrate exhibits a short circuit current of 16.75 mA/cm^2, and therefore, a gain in the short circuit current of 1.23 mA/cm^2 as compared with the nanotextured solar cell is achieved. Furthermore, the solar cell exhibits a FF of 68%, and an open circuit voltage of 940 mV resulting in an energy conversion efficiency of 10.7%. The relatively low FF for both solar cells is caused by the formation of the a-$Si_{1-x}O_x$:H p-layer. Solar cells with a-$Si_{1-x}C_x$:H p-layer that are prepared on the same substrates exhibit FFs in the range of 72–73%. However, the absorption of light by the a-$Si_{1-x}C_x$:H p-layer is higher.

The measured quantum efficiency and total reflection of the amorphous silicon solar cell on the single- and multiscale-textured substrates are shown in Fig. 2(b). The quantum efficiencies were measured under short circuit current conditions. The solar cells on the multiscale-textured glass exhibit a small increase of the quantum efficiency for shorter wavelengths and distinct increase for longer wavelengths and a reduced total reflection in the spectral range from 300 to 700 nm. For longer wavelengths, the total reflection is identical.

B. Determining Interface Morphologies of Nanoscale and Multiscale Thin-Film Solar Cells

The realistic simulation of the optical wave propagation in a silicon thin-film solar cell requires a precise description of the interface morphologies.

Recently, several different models for obtaining realistic interface morphologies have been presented [17]–[21]. In our model, the front-contact morphology of the solar cell is determined by the TCO layer, which is grown on a flat or a textured glass substrate. The morphologies of the subsequent layers are determined by the front-contact morphology, the growth conditions of the amorphous silicon films, and the silicon film thicknesses. Low-temperature amorphous silicon solar cells are commonly deposited by a PECVD process. The preparation of solar cells with good electrical properties is achieved when the films are prepared under CVD-like growth conditions [22], [23]. Under such conditions, the films exhibit low sticking coefficient on the substrate and the surface coverage of amorphous silicon films is excellent. Consequently, amorphous silicon films are uniform and without voids, and exhibit a low density of electronic defects. Taking these considerations into account, it can be assumed that the amorphous silicon film grows in

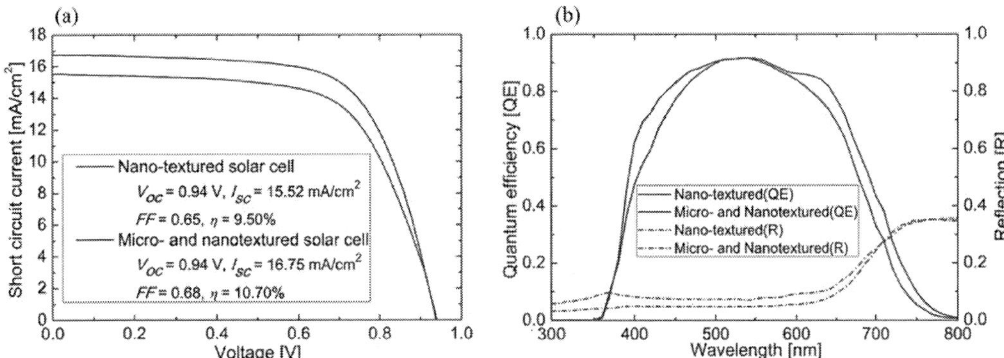

Fig. 2. (a) Current/voltage characteristics and (b) reflection and quantum efficiency of amorphous silicon solar cell prepared on a single- and double-textured substrate.

the direction of local surface normal. To obtain realistic interface morphologies of silicon films and solar cells on arbitrary substrates, a 3-D surface growth algorithm was implemented. The accuracy of the surface coverage algorithm was demonstrated for amorphous silicon films prepared on nanotextured substrates [20], [21]. The calculated surface morphologies were compared with measured morphologies and an excellent agreement was observed [20], [21]. The growth of the silicon film leads to a filling of the valleys between adjacent textures. As a consequence, the effective (average) thickness of the silicon films on the textured substrates is larger than the nominal film thickness. The calculated interface morphologies were used to calculate the effective thicknesses. In the case of a flat substrate, the effective thickness is equal to the nominal thickness. In the case of the nanotextured substrate, the effective thickness of the i-layer is equal to 350 nm assuming a nominal i-layer thickness of 300 nm. In the case of the multiscale-textured substrate, the effective thickness increased up to 380 nm. Sever *et al.* published results in which the surface of amorphous silicon films was described by taking into account a growth component in the direction of the substrate normal [19]. Our experimental results on amorphous silicon films can be described without considering a growth component in the direction of the substrate normal [20], [21]. However, in our study, a growth component in the direction of the substrate normal has to be considered when describing the growth of nano- or microcrystalline silicon. Details on the growth model for nano- or microcrystalline silicon are given in [21]. The concept of the effective thickness refers to the optical thickness of the solar cell. The electrical thickness of the solar cell is roughly equal to the nominal thickness of the solar cell. Only in the valleys between the pyramids, the electrical thickness of the solar cell will be slightly larger than the nominal thickness of the solar cells. The surface textures of the substrates, in particular the multiscale texture, allow for the partial decoupling of the optical and the electrical properties of the solar cell. Similar effects were observed for core/shell nanowire solar cells [24]. Since the electrical thickness is not significantly increased, the light-induced degradation should not significantly increase. This is confirmed by light-induced degradation experiments of core/shell nanowire solar cells [24].

C. Optical Simulation of Amorphous Silicon Solar Cells on Textured Substrates

The calculated interface morphologies of the FTCO (front TCO), p-, i-, n- and back TCO layers were used as input parameters to simulate the optical wave propagation in the textured solar cells. The finite-difference time domain (FDTD) method was used to numerically solve Maxwell's equations in three dimensions [2], [9], [10], [25], [26]. Optical simulations were used to analyze electromagnetic wave propagation in solar cell structures and determine the absorption of the incident light in the individual layers. In the case of the single-textured substrate, the glass substrate is assumed to be flat, while in the case of the multiscale texture, the glass substrate is described by a periodic arrangement of microsized hemispheres. The period and height of the glass-textured hemispheres are assumed to be 3 μm and 1.5 μm, respectively. The period is consistent with the experimental data as shown in Fig. 1(d). The amorphous silicon solar cell consists of a zinc oxide front contact with a thickness of 400 nm. The nanotextures were described by a square-based pyramid with a period and height of 300 nm and 150 nm, respectively. The dimensions of the surface texture were determined by the surface analysis of the nanotextured substrate [26]. In the case of the flat glass substrate, the pyramidal textures are added on top of the 400-nm zinc oxide layer, while in the case of the textured glass substrate, the 3-D surface coverage algorithm is used to describe the interface morphology of the FTCO layer. Afterward, the pyramidal texture is added to the surface morphology. The nominal thicknesses of the individual layers of the amorphous silicon p-i-n diode are 20, 300, and 10 nm. The thickness of the zinc oxide buffer layer was assumed to be 50 nm. The 3-D surface coverage algorithm is used to calculate the interface morphology for each of the layers. The calculated effective thicknesses of the i-layer for the nano- and multiscale-textured solar cell were 364 and 450 nm, respectively. A comparison of the effective thickness for the artificially generated substrates with the effective thickness for the measured substrates shows higher thicknesses for the artificially generated substrate. This is caused by some flat regions between the microtextures on the experimentally realized substrate. Such flat regions do not exist

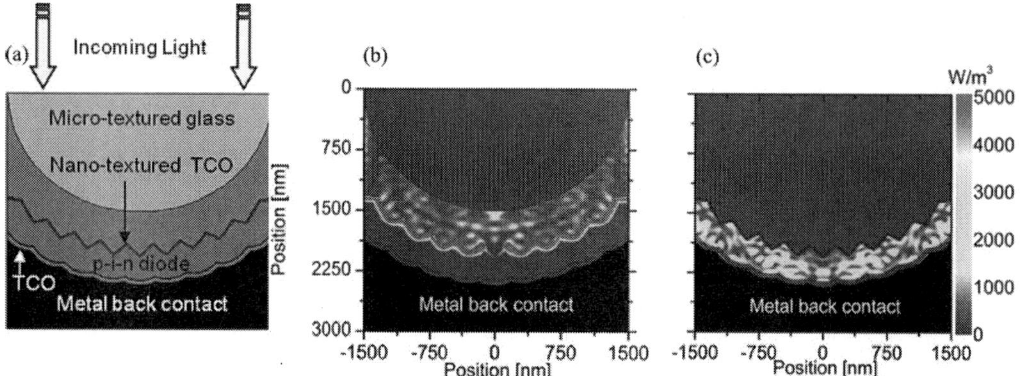

Fig. 3. (a) Schematic cross section of the unit cell of an amorphous silicon thin-film solar cell on a double (micro- and nanotextured)-textured substrate and its simulated power loss profile for a wavelength of (b) 400 nm and (c) 700 nm.

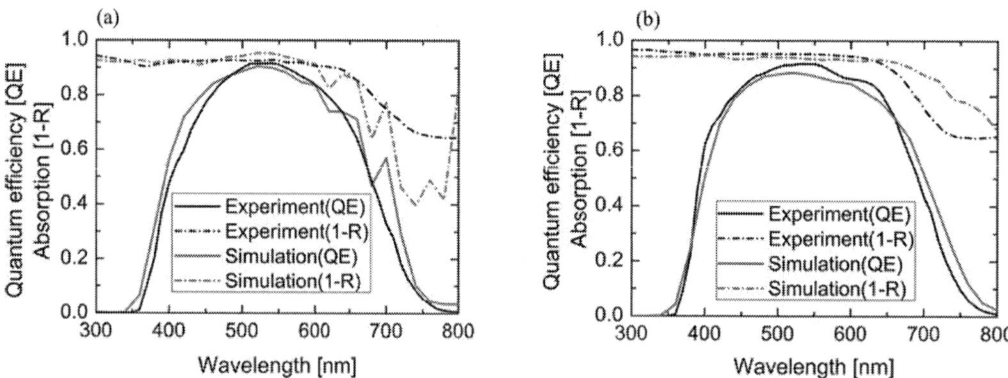

Fig. 4. Comparison of the absorption spectrum and quantum efficiency of (a) simulated and experimentally realized nanotextured solar cell and (b) simulated and experimentally realized multiscale-textured solar cell.

for the artificially generated surfaces. Therefore, the effective thickness for the synthetic is overestimated.

After the realization of solar cell structures, the power loss profiles, the absorption for each layer of the solar cell, the reflection, and the short circuit current were calculated for the different solar cells. Details on the calculations of these parameters are given in [10]. The schematic cross section of the micro- and nanotextured solar cell is shown in Fig. 3(a). The power loss profiles for the solar cell are shown in Fig. 3(b) and (c) for incident wavelength of 400 nm and 700 nm, respectively. For shorter wavelengths, most of the incident light is absorbed by the FTCO. The longer wavelengths [see Fig. 3(c)] reach the metal back contact, where the light is scattered and diffracted. In the next step, the quantum efficiency of the solar cells was determined. It is assumed that all electron/hole pairs that are generated in the i-layer of the p-i-n solar cell are collected. In other words, the internal quantum efficiency of the solar cells is assumed to be unity. The charge carriers that were generated in the p- and n-regions were assumed to recombine due to the low diffusion lengths. The quantum efficiency was calculated as the ratio of the collected charge carriers and the number of input photons of a given energy. The calculated and measured quantum efficiency and total absorptions for nanotextured

and multiscale-textured substrates are shown in Fig. 4(a) and (b). The simulated quantum efficiencies follow the experimentally observed trends. The solar cells on the nanotextured and multiscale-textured substrates exhibit a short circuit current of 16.2 mA/cm^2 and 16.8 mA/cm^2, respectively. The increased short circuit current of 0.6 mA/cm^2 for the multiscale-textured substrate is caused by the gain in the effective thickness of the i-layer and the efficient scattering of the back reflector. The gain in the short circuit current cannot only be explained by an increased effective thickness of the absorber layer. The morphology of the back contact has a distinct influence on the short circuit current. To further characterize the nanotextured solar cells, the absorption in the individual layers of the solar cell was determined. The absorption in the individual region is shown in Fig. 5 for the nano- and the multiscale-textured solar cells. The optical simulations show that the FTCO exhibits excellent optical properties since the absorption of the light by the FTCO is low. Furthermore, the light is efficiently scattered by the front texture. However, the high roughness of the front texture leads to a significant absorption of light by the p-layer even though wide-bandgap silicon oxide material was used as a p-layer. The back contact loss is defined as the absorption in the n-layer of the solar cell, the zinc oxide buffer layer, and the metal back

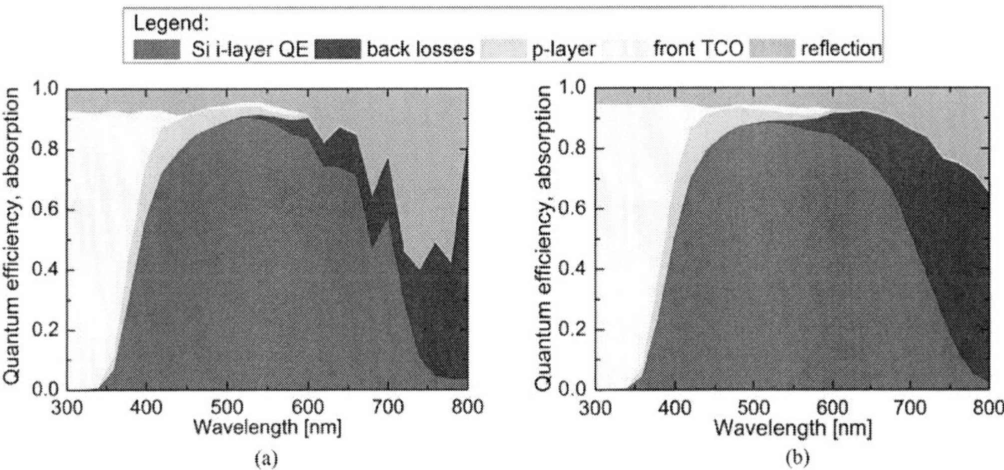

Fig. 5.   Simulated quantum efficiencies and optical losses for (a) nanotextured and (b) multiscale-textured solar cell.

reflector. Good agreement between the measured and simulated quantum efficiencies could only be achieved if aluminum (Al) instead of silver (Ag) was used as a metal reflector. This observation is confirmed by other research groups [27]. A comparison of the measured and simulated total absorption shows that the simulated absorption is underestimated for the nanotextured substrate, while it is overestimated for the multiscale substrate. The deviations are caused by the description of the back-contact morphology. Further investigations are needed to develop a model that exactly resembles the back-contact morphology of solar cells on randomly textured substrates. Often, additional losses of the back contact are caused by nanofeatures that are present at the back contact. Such nanofeatures can be caused by the PECVD deposition of the silicon thin film or the sputtering or polycrystalline zinc oxide films [28], [29]. Optical simulations show that such features can lead to significant absorption losses by the metal back reflectors [29]. However, nanofeatures are not considered in the simulations presented in this paper. In order to consider the additional absorption introduced by the nanofeatures, aluminum was used as metal back contact instead of silver. A certain fraction of the light that reaches the back contact is efficiently scattered, while the remaining fraction is absorbed by the back reflector (see Fig. 5). The absorption in the back contact is determined by the metal/dielectric interface and the morphology of the back reflector. In this case, the zinc oxide buffer layer/metal interface is determined by the front-contact morphology and the film growth on the substrate. Optical simulations and experimental results show that the morphology of the back contact is more important than the dielectric materials involved [28], [29]. Large surface features of the back contact have only a small influence on the absorption of the back contact, while smaller features cause a distinct increase of the absorption by the back contact [29]. Introducing a material with a low dielectric constant between the silicon solar cell and the metal back reflector leads to a drop of the absorption. However, the low refractive index is not sufficient to completely suppress the absorption by the back contact. The optical simulations of the solar cells on the multiscale-textured substrates show that the total absorption of the solar cell is higher than the absorption of the solar cell on the nanotextured substrate. The higher total absorption results in a higher QE and a higher absorption by the back reflector [see Fig. 5(b)].

D. Toward the Optimal Multiscale Surface Texture

Further efforts are needed to increase the quantum efficiency and reduce the parasitic losses. The quantum efficiency of the solar cell on multiscale-textured substrates can be increased by an increased effective thickness of the absorber layer of the solar cell and efficient light trapping. Furthermore, the absorption losses have to be reduced. The absorption losses of the FTCO and the silicon oxide p-layer are already very low. The total absorption losses can be minimized by reducing the absorption of the back reflector [10], [29]–[32]. The back reflector morphology has to be controlled so that the plasmonic losses are reduced. As an alternative, the metal back reflector can be replaced by a ZnO back contact in combination with a white reflector [33]–[35]. However, even in the case of a solar cell with a metal back reflector, the optical losses in the back contact can be distinctly reduced. Calculations of the interface morphology with the surface coverage algorithm show that the roughness of the back reflector can be reduced by increasing the thickness of the ZnO buffer layer. Optical simulations of multiscale-textured solar cells with thicker buffer layers show that a short circuit current of 17–18 mA/cm^2 can be achieved for ZnO buffer layers with a thickness of 200–400 nm.

III. Summary

The short circuit current of silicon thin-film solar cells can be increased by combining micro- and nanoscale surface textures. FDTD simulations were used to gain insights into the light-trapping properties. The interface morphologies of the layers of the amorphous silicon solar cell were determined by a realistic surface growth model. The simulations indicate that the gain of the short circuit current is caused by an increased effective thickness of the solar cells and the morphology of the back reflector.

The morphology of the back reflector allows for an efficient scattering and diffraction of the reflected light. Multiscale texturing of the thin-film solar cells provides a promising route to increasing the short circuit current and conversion efficiency of silicon thin-film solar cells.

REFERENCES

[1] H. Sai, H. Jia, and M. Kondo, "Impact of front and rear texture of thin-film microcrystalline silicon solar cells on their light trapping properties," *J. Appl. Phys.*, vol. 108, pp. 044505-1–044505-9, 2010.

[2] D. Madzharov, R. Dewan, and D. Knipp, "Influence of front and back grating on light trapping in microcrystalline thin-film silicon solar cells," *Opt. Exp.*, vol. 19, pp. A95–A107, 2011.

[3] T. Oyama, M. Kambe, N. Taneda, and K. Masumo, "Requirements for TCO substrate in Si-based thin film solar cells—Toward tandem," in *Proc. Mater. Res. Soc. Symp.*, 2008, vol. 1101, pp. 1101-KK02-01.

[4] J. Bailat, L. Fesquet, J-B. Orhan, Y. Djeridane, B. Wolf, P. Madliger, J. Steinhauser, S. Benagli, D. Borrello, L. Castens, G. Monteduro, M. Marmelo, B. Dehbozorghi, E. Vallat-Sauvain, X. Multone, D. Romang, J.-F. Boucher, J. Meier, U. Kroll, M. Despeisse, G. Bugnon, C. Ballif, S. Marjanovic, G. Kohnke, N. Borrelli, K. Koch, J. Liu, R. Modavis, D. Thelen, S. Vallon, A. Zakharian, and D. Weidman, "Recent developments of high-efficiency micromoph tandem solar cells in KAI-M PECVD reactors," in *Proc. 25th Eur. Photovoltaic Solar Energy Conf. Exhib./5th World Conf. Photovoltaic Energy Convers.*, 2010, pp. 2720–2723.

[5] A. Hongsingthong, T. Krajangsang, A. Limmanee, K. Sriprapha, J. Sritharathikhun, and M. Konagai, "Development of textured ZnO-coated low-cost glass substrate with very high haze ratio for silicon-based thin film solar cells," *Thin Solid Films*, vol. 537, pp. 291–295, 2013.

[6] M. Boccard, C. Battaglia, S. Hänni, K. Söderström, J. Escarré, S. Nicolay, F. Meillaud, M. Despeisse, and C. Ballif, "Multiscale transparent electrode architecture for efficient light management and carrier collection in solar cells," *Nano Lett.*, vol. 12, pp. 1334–1348, 2012.

[7] C. Haase and H. Stiebig, "Optical properties of thin-film silicon solar cells with grating couplers," *Progress Photovoltaics: Res. Appl.*, vol. 14, no. 7, pp. 629–641, 2006.

[8] M. Schulte, K. Bittkau, B. E. Pieters, S. Jorke, H. Stiebig, J. Hüpkes, and U. Rau, "Ray tracing for the optics at nano-textured ZnO-air and ZnO-silicon interfaces," *Progress Photovoltaics: Res. Appl.*, vol. 19, no. 6, pp. 724–732, 2011.

[9] R. Dewan, V. Jovanov, C. Haase, H. Stiebig, and D. Knipp, "Simple and fast method to optimize nanotextured interfaces of thin-film silicon solar cells," *Appl. Phys. Exp.*, vol. 3, no. 9, pp. 092301-1–092301-3, 2010.

[10] U. Palanchoke, V. Jovanov, H. Kurz, P. Obermeyer, H. Stiebig, and D. Knipp, "Plasmonic effects in amorphous silicon thin film solar cells with metal back contacts," *Opt. Exp.*, vol. 20, no. 6, pp. 6340–6347, 2012.

[11] A. Hongsingthong, I. A. Yunaz, S. Miyajima, and M. Konagai, "Preparation of ZnO thin films using MOCVD technique with D_2O/H_2O gas mixture for use as TCO in silicon-based thin film solar cells," *Solar Energy Mater. Solar Cells*, vol. 95, pp. 171–174, 2011.

[12] A. Hongsingthong, T. Krajangsang, I. A. Yunaz, S. Miyajima, and M. Konagai, "ZnO films with very high haze value for use as front transparent conductive oxide films in thin-film silicon solar cells," *Appl. Phys. Exp.*, vol. 3, pp. 051102-1–051102-3, 2010.

[13] S. Inthisang, T. Krajangsang, I. A. Yunaz, A. Yamada, M. Konagai, and C. R. Wronski, "Fabrication of high open-circuit voltage a-$Si_{1-x}O_x$:H solar cells by using p-a-$Si_{1-x}O_x$:H as window layer," *Phys. Status Solidi*, vol. C8, pp. 2990–2993, 2011.

[14] R. Ross, R. Mohr, J. Fournier, and J. Yang, "Status of fluorinated amorphous silicon-germanium alloys and multijunction devices," in *Proc. IEEE PVSC*, New Orleans, LA, USA, 1987, vol. 1, pp. 327–330.

[15] J. Morris, R. R. Arya, J. G. O'Dowd, and S. Wiedeman, "Absorption enhancement in hydrogenated amorphous silicon (a-Si:H) based solar cells," *J. Appl. Phys.*, vol. 67, no. 2, pp. 1079–1087, 1990.

[16] C. Kothandaraman, T. Tonon, C. Huang, and A. E. Delahoy, "Improvement of a-Si: H PIN devices using zinc oxide based back-reflectors," in *Proc. Mater. Res. Soc. Symp.*, 1991, vol. 219, pp. 475–480.

[17] S. Solntsev, O. Isabella, D. Caratelli, and M. Zeman, "Thin-film silicon solar cells on 1-D periodic gratings with nonconformal layers: Optical analysis," *IEEE J. Photovoltaics*, vol. 3, no. 1, pp. 46–52, Jan. 2013.

[18] A. Naqavi, K. Söderström, F. Haug, V. Paeder, T. Scharf, H. Herzig, and C. Ballif, "Understanding of photocurrent enhancement in real thin film solar cells: Towards optimal one-dimensional gratings," *Opt. Exp.*, vol. 19, pp. 128–140, 2011.

[19] M. Sever, B. Lipovšek, J. Krč, A. Čampa, G. S. Plaza, F.-J. Haug, M. Duchamp, W. Soppe, and M. Topič, "Combined model of nonconformal layer growth for accurate optical simulation of thin-film silicon solar cells," *Sol. Energy Mater. Sol. Cells*, (May 30, 2013). [Online]. Available: http://dx.doi.org/10.1016/j.solmat.2013.05.016.

[20] V. Jovanov, X. Xu, S. Shrestha, M. Schulte, J. Hüpkes, M. Zeman, and D. Knipp, "Influence of interface morphologies on amorphous silicon thin film solar cells prepared on randomly textured substrates," *Sol. Energy Mater. Sol. Cells*, vol. 112, pp. 182–189, 2013.

[21] V. Jovanov, X. Xu, S. Shrestha, M. Schulte, J. Hüpkes, and D. Knipp, "Predicting the interface morphologies of silicon films on arbitrary substrates: Application in solar cells," *ACS Appl. Mater. Interfaces*, vol. 5, no. 15, pp. 7109–7116, 2013.

[22] R. A. Street, *Hydrogenated Amorphous Silicon.* Cambridge, U.K.: Cambridge Univ. Press, 1991, ch. 2.

[23] C. C. Tsai, J. C. Knights, G. Chang, and B. Wacker, "Film formation mechanisms in the plasma deposition of hydrogenated amorphous silicon," *J. Appl. Phys.*, vol. 59, pp. 2998–3001, 1986.

[24] M. J. Naughton, K. Kempa, Z. F. Ren, Y. Gao, J. Rybczynski, N. Argenti, W. Gao, Y. Wang, Y. Peng, J. R. Naughton, G. McMahon, T. Paudel, Y. C. Lan, M. J. Burns, A. Shepard, M. Clary, C. Ballif, F.-J. Haug, T. Söderström, O. Cubero, and C. Eminian, "Efficient nanocoax-based solar cells," *Phys. Status Solidi – Rapid Res. Lett.*, vol. 4, pp. 181–183, 2010.

[25] K. Yee, "Numerical solution of initial boundary value problems involving Maxwell's equations in isotropic media," *IEEE Trans. Antennas Propag.*, vol. 14, no. 3, pp. 302–307, May 1966.

[26] R. Dewan, J. I. Owen, D. Madzharov, V. Jovanov, J. Hüpkes, and D. Knipp, "Analyzing nanotextured transparent conductive oxides for efficient light trapping in silicon thin film solar cells," *Appl. Phys. Lett.*, vol. 101, no. 10, pp. 103903-1–103903-4, 2012.

[27] M. Zeman, R. A. C. M. M. van Swaaij, J. W. Metselaar, and R. E. I. Schropp, "Optical modeling of a-Si:H solar cells with rough interfaces: effect of back contact and interface roughness," *J. Appl. Phys.*, vol. 88, pp. 6436–6443, 2000.

[28] U. Palanchoke, V. Jovanov, H. Kurz, R. Dewan, P. Magnus, H. Stiebig, and D. Knipp, "Influence of back contact roughness on light trapping and plasmonic losses of randomly textured amorphous silicon thin film solar cells," *Appl. Phys. Lett.*, vol. 102, no. 8, pp. 083501-1–083501-3, 2013.

[29] V. Jovanov, U. Palanchoke, P. Magnus, H. Stiebig, and D. Knipp, "Influence of back contact morphology on light trapping and plasmonic effects in microcrystalline silicon single junction and micromorph tandem solar cells," *Sol. Energy Mater. Sol. Cells*, vol. 110, pp. 49–57, 2013.

[30] F.-J. Haug, T. Soderstrom, O. Cubero, V. Terrazzoni-Daudrix, and C. Ballif, "Plasmonic absorption in textured silver back reflectors of thin film solar cells," *J. Appl. Phys.*, vol. 104, no. 6, pp. 064509-1–064509-7, 2008.

[31] J. Springer, A. Poruba, L. Müllerova, M. Vanecek, O. Kluth, and B. Rech, "Absorption loss at nanorough silver back reflector of thin-film silicon solar cells," *J. Appl. Phys.*, vol. 95, no. 3, pp. 1427–1429, 2004.

[32] J. Müller, B. Rech, J. Springer, and M. Vanecek, "TCO and light trapping in silicon thin film solar cells," *Sol. Energy*, vol. 77, no. 6, pp. 917–930, 2004.

[33] O. Berger, D. Inns, and A. G. Aberle, "Commercial white paint as back surface reflector for thin-film solar cells," *Sol. Energy Mater. Sol. Cells*, vol. 91, pp. 1215–1221, 2007.

[34] S. Faÿ, J. Steinhauser, N. Oliveira, E. Vallat-Sauvain, and C. Ballif, "Opto-electronic properties of rough LP-CVD ZnO:B for use as TCO in thin-film silicon solar cells," *Thin Solid Films*, vol. 515, pp. 8558–8561, 2007.

[35] B. Lipovsek, J. Krc, O. Isabella, and M. Zeman, "Modeling and optimization of white paint back reflectors for thin-film silicon solar cells," *J. Appl. Phys.*, vol. 108, no. 10, pp. 103115-1–103115-7, 2010.

Authors' photographs and biographies not available at the time of publication.

The Two Approaches of Surface-Texture Optimization in Thin-Film Silicon Solar Cells

Janez Krc, Martin Sever, and Marko Topic

Abstract—Textured interfaces in thin-film silicon solar cells can increase the photocurrent of the devices. However, the challenge is how to design textures (periodic or random) that could outperform the state-of-the-art random ones. Moreover, the textures should enable defect-less semiconductor layer growth, which has often been neglected in the past, resulting in the low open-circuit voltage and fill factor of the devices. In this paper, we present two approaches for the systematic optimization of surface-textures: bottom-up and top-down. Fully 3-D optical simulations, including calibrated nonconformal layer growth model were employed to predict gains in short-circuit current densities in a micromorph solar cell (bottom-up approach) and a single-junction amorphous silicon solar cell (top-down approach). In the bottom-up approach, we start with a simple sinusoidal component and change its shape systematically in the direction of broader valleys, also resulting in better conditions for the layer growth. In the top-down approach, we start from a random texture (morphology fingerprint taken from Asahi U type substrate) and modify it in a spatial frequency domain. We show the role of the presence/absence of different frequency regions as well as the important role of the phase spectrum on the optical characteristics of the device. In both approaches, improved textures have the potential to outperform state-of-the-art random ones, not only from optical point of view but in terms of conversion efficiency as well.

Index Terms—Light trapping, optical modeling, surface textures, thin-film silicon solar cells.

I. INTRODUCTION

INCREASING the conversion efficiency of thin-film solar cells should result in lowering production costs per watt-peak of thin-film PV modules. Besides improving the quality and stability of materials of active and supporting layers, interfaces between the layers play an important role. Both electronic and optical properties of internal interfaces and external surfaces are of importance [1]. Focusing on optical aspects in this paper, interfaces should assist sun light to enter the device and ensure efficient light trapping in absorber layers [2]. In thin-film silicon solar cells, where the absorption coefficient becomes low at photon energies close to the optical gap of the material, it is of key importance to introduce a proper texturization at the

Manuscript received June 10, 2013; revised July 26, 2013; accepted August 7, 2013. Date of publication September 5, 2013; date of current version September 18, 2013. This work was supported in part by the European FP7 project Silicon-Light (GA No. 2412777), in part by the European FP7 project Fast Track (GA No. 283501), and in part by the Slovenian Research Agency (Research Programme P2 0197).

The authors are with the University of Ljubljana, Faculty of Electrical Engineering, University of Ljubljana, Si 1000 Ljubljana, Slovenia (e-mail: janez.krc@fe.uni-lj.si; martin.sever@fe.uni-lj.si; marko.topic@fe.uni-lj.si).

Color versions of one or more of the figures in this paper are available online at http://ieeexplore.ieee.org.

Digital Object Identifier 10.1109/JPHOTOV.2013.2278665

interfaces in order to efficiently scatter incident light. Prolonged optical paths should lead to increased photocurrent and consequently increased conversion efficiency of the cells. Different transparent conductive oxide (TCO) superstrates and substrates with naturally grown or postfabricated (etched) random surface textures have been investigated and developed with respect to improved light scattering and antireflection [3]–[6]. On the other hand, interference and e-beam lithography and thermoplastic and UV embossing techniques have enabled to fabricate various artificial (synthetic) textures on a large scale [7], [8]. Therefore, strategies and systematic approaches are required to design better textures that are either periodic or random, which can outperform current state-of-the-art TCO textures and can be fabricated by the aforementioned techniques [9].

Besides superior optical properties of the textures, one has to pay special attention to layer growth conditions to these textures. It has been demonstrated that sharp valleys on the surface, for example, can lead to the formation of defective regions in semiconductor layers grown on such textures [10], [11]. This results in decreased fill factor and the open-circuit voltage of the device, both reducing the conversion efficiency of the device, despite increased photocurrent. This is an important aspect to be considered in the design and optimization of the textures.

In this paper, two approaches of systematic design of surface textures are presented: *bottom-up* and *top-down*. In the first one, we start with a simple regular periodic texture (sinus) and modify its shape systematically. In the second one, we start from a more complex texture, e.g., natural random texture of a TCO superstrate, and modify it in spatial frequency domain, in this case. The analysis is based on fully 3-D rigorous optical simulations with simulation software COMSOL Multiphysics [12]. The bottom-up approach was applied to a micromorph solar cell (amorphous/microcrystalline silicon, a-Si:H/μc-Si:H cell), in substrate configuration, starting with an ideal 2-D sinusoidal texture. The top-down approach was applied to a single-junction a-Si:H solar cell in substrate configuration, starting with a random texture with morphological properties of Asahi U type SnO_2:F TCO substrate [3]. To consider realistic texture transfer from the substrate to subsequent internal interfaces in the cells and to predict textures that may lead to defective region formation in silicon layers, we used our model of nonconformal layer growth [13], [14].

II. MODELS

A. Optical Model

In the presented 3-D rigorous optical simulations of thin-film silicon solar cells, the COMSOL Multiphysics simulation software was employed [12]. Rigorous solving of Maxwell's

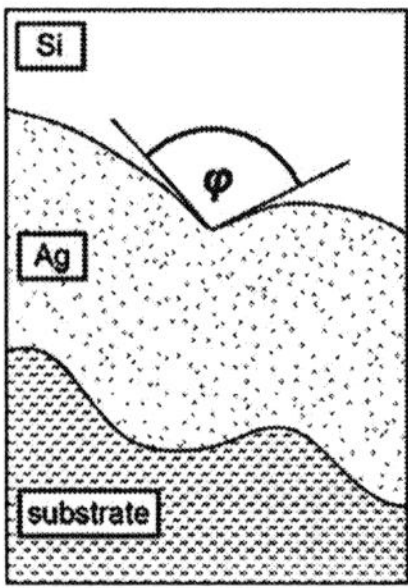

Fig. 1. Opening angle φ of the surface on which semiconductor layers are grown (in this case top Ag surface) as an important parameter for predicting defect formation in semiconductor layers.

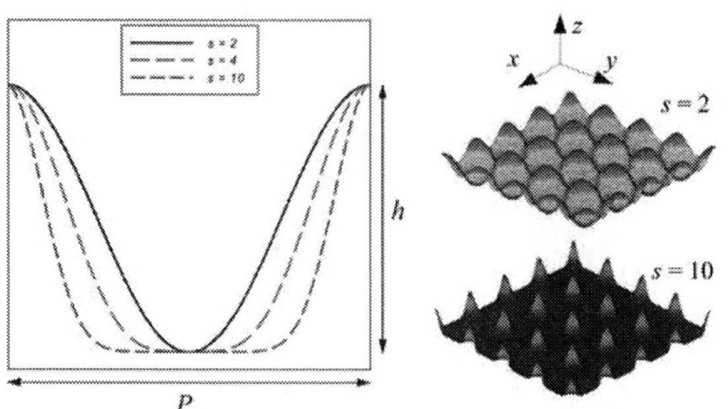

Fig. 2. Variation of substrate surface-texture in the presented bottom-up approach. (Left) Cross section of 2-D sinus-like textures corresponding to different values of the power parameter s and (right) 3-D views on the actual 2-D textures for $s = 2$ and 10.

equations is based on the finite-element method (FEM). Simulated 3-D structures with nanotextured interfaces are imported from the calibrated nonconformal growth model (see the next section). In the case of structures with lateral periodicity and symmetrical properties, integrated symmetry boundary conditions enable simulation over one quarter of a period only, reducing the time of simulation significantly. The simulator also enables dynamic adjustment of the meshing, depending on the wavelength of light.

External quantum efficiency (EQE) of solar cells was calculated from wavelength dependent absorptance of the intrinsic (absorber) layer(s). Assuming ideal charge carrier extraction from the absorber layers and neglecting contributions from p- and n-doped layers, one can directly equal the absorptance to EQE, which is close to realistic case in state-of-the-art devices [15]. J_{SC} was calculated from EQE by applying illumination with AM1.5 g solar spectrum.

B. Model of Nonconformal Layer Growth

In simulations, our nonconformal model of layer growth is used to determine internal interface morphologies [13], [14]. The 3-D model combines 1) conformal and 2) isotropic layer growth mechanisms. The analysis of surface morphologies of the grown thin-film layers on various textured substrates indicated that both growth mechanisms are required to accurately describe the top surfaces of the layers. The conformal growth corresponds to the growth in the vertical direction of the cell, whereas the isotropic growth is the growth in the direction of local surface normal. The key parameter of the model is growth parameter g, which defines the proportion of isotropic and conformal growth (for fully isotropic growth $g = 1$ and for fully conformal growth $g = 0$). The g parameter was calibrated for each layer of the cell using the cross-sectional scanning electron microscopy (SEM) images of device structures [14]. The g is assumed to remain equal for a certain layer if the morphology of a substrate or layer thickness are varied, as in the case of our optimization. Experimental analysis showed that higher probability of defect formation in semiconductor layers are expected if small opening angles (i.e., $\varphi < 130°$; see Fig. 1) are present at the surface on which the semiconduc-

tor layer is grown [14]. Thus, the textures with narrow valleys (small φ) have to be avoided in optimization.

III. Surface Optimization Approaches

A. Bottom-Up Approach

In the *bottom–up approach* of surface texture optimization, we start with a simple regular texture and proceed to more complex textures, aiming to improve the performance of the cell. Here, we selected a 2-D sinusoidal texture as a starting point (see the top right image of Fig. 2). Lateral dimension—period (P), and vertical dimension—height (h), are varied at the first stage of optimization. Sinus-like textures have already been identified as promising textures for efficient light trapping, as well as for defect-free layer growth [11], [14], [16]. Besides optimization of P and h of this texture, in the bottom-up approach, we change its form (shape) systematically. We propose to do the variation of the shape as

$$z(x,y) = h \cdot \left| \sin\left(\frac{2\pi}{P}x\right) \cdot \sin\left(\frac{2\pi}{P}y\right) \right|^{s} \qquad (1)$$

where x and y are lateral axes, and z is the vertical one. Parameter h is the peak-to-peak height of the sinusoidal texture, P is the period (the same in x- and y-direction in our case, $P = P_x = P_y$). Parameter s is introduced as a power factor which is responsible for changing the shape, as presented in Fig. 2. Its initial value is 2. Following trigonometric rules, $s = 2$ (squared sinusoidal function) corresponds to a sinusoidal component with the half of initial period P and an offset plane (discarded when defining thickness). Thus, $s = 2$ still corresponds to the ideal sinusoidal shape (as in case of $s = 1$). By increasing s ($s > 2$), one can observe that the valleys of the starting sinusoidal shape become broader. As indicated by previous experiments and by our growth model, such textures present a better condition for defect-free growth of silicon absorber material. This was our motivation to include such shape modification in the presented bottom-up approach. In Section IV-B, we show the improvements related to J_{SC} of micromorph cell with respect to this optimization.

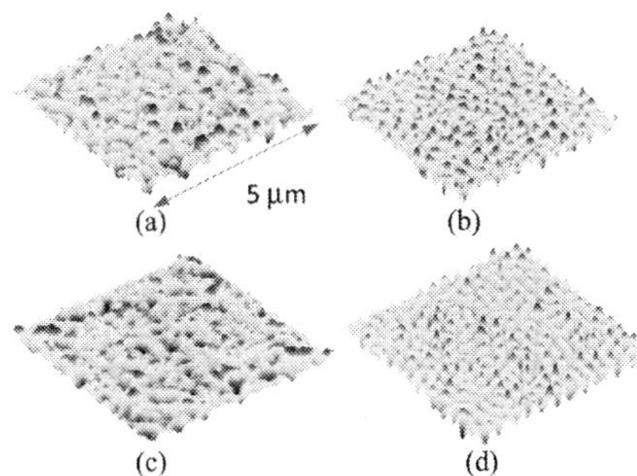

Fig. 3. Selected 2-D textures used in simulation. (a) Initial random texture (as obtained from the AFM scan of Asahi U type TCO), (b) MF filtering of the random texture, (c) random texture with phase spectrum set to zero and (d) a three component texture (with periods $P_1 = 300$ nm, $P_2 = 150$ nm, and $P_3 = 75$ nm).

B. Top-Down Approach

The idea of the *top-down approach* is to start the optimization of the texture from a complex (multicomponent) texture, such as the state-of-the-art random textures. The motivation is that the selected complex texture already exhibits superior optical behavior, but one wants to optimize it further. In this approach, we propose to use spatial frequency space in which we represent the texture with multiple (discrete) sinusoidal components which are described by their peak-to-peak *height spectrum* and the *phase spectrum*. The frequency domain for surface representation has already been used in some of the previous works [13], [17], [18]. Since the surface is represented by discrete points, frequency components are also discrete. In our case, the 2-D discrete fast Fourier transformation present the basis for transformation of the texture to spatial frequency domain. The example of the height spectrum and the phase spectrum for a random texture presented in Fig. 3(a) (Asahi U type TCO) is given in Fig. 4. Since the surface is 2-D as well, the spectra are originally 2-D images. Selected cross sections of the 2-D representations are given on the right hand side of Fig. 4.

The presented texture in Fig. 3(a) corresponds to atomic force microscopy (AFM) measurement of commercially available Asahi U type SnO_2:F TCO with measured vertical root-mean-square roughness $\sigma_{\mathrm{rms}} = 40$ nm. Although the Asahi U type substrate is usually used in solar cells in superstrate configuration (light enters from the substrate side), here, its random texture is applied to the cells in substrate configurations (substrate on the back side). In this case, the Asahi U substrate is used as a master in nanoimprint-lithography (NIL) process to texture the lacquer on the substrate foil, on which the cells in substrate configuration are deposited afterward [7]. Thus, the NIL process can be applied not only to replicate regular (periodic) textures but to random ones on various substrates as well [19].

The AFM scan in Fig. 3(a) is presented for the area of 5 µm × 5 µm and consisting of 256 × 256 discrete points $z(x, y)$. In the height spectrum, we can observe a trend of decreasing of spectral components going toward higher frequencies f ($f = 1/P$, where P represents the period of a certain discrete sinusoidal

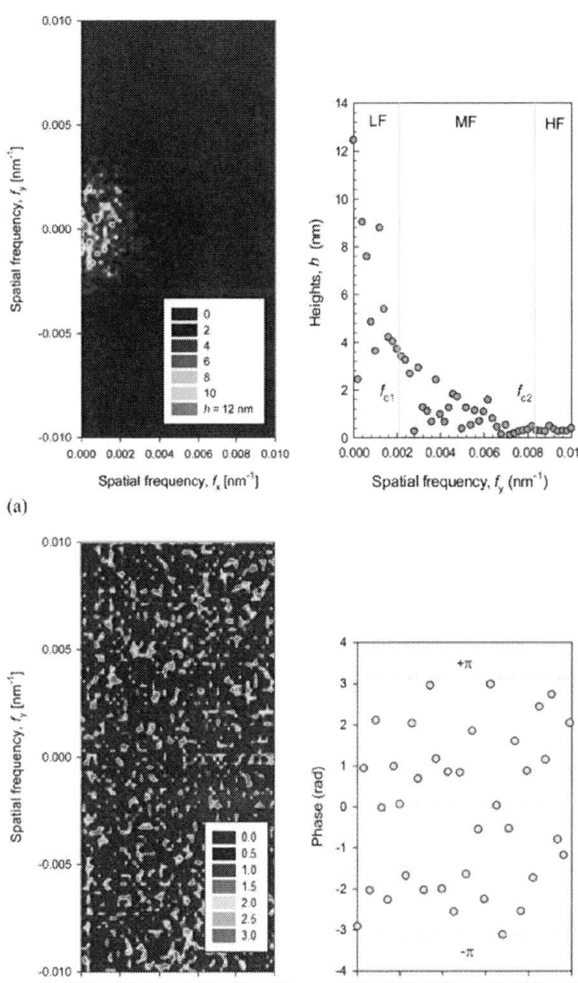

Fig. 4. (a) Height and (b) phase spectrum of the initial random texture [from Fig. 3(a)] (left) represented in contour plots and (right) corresponding scans in the y-direction. Denotations LF, MF, and HF correspond to low-, medium-, and high-frequency regions of the spectrum.

component), whereas in the phase spectrum, fully random character of the surface is manifested.

In the top-down approach, we apply changes in the spatial frequency domain; thus, we change either the height and/or phase spectrum of the surface. In our case, we decided on a strategy to divide the spectra first in three spectral regions: low-frequency LF (including sinusoids with large Ps), middle-frequency MF (medium Ps), and high-frequency region HF (small Ps). The corner frequencies f_{c1} and f_{c2} were set to 2.08×10^{-3} nm^{-1} and 8.33×10^{-3} nm^{-1}, corresponding to the periods $P_{c1} = 480$ nm and $P_{c2} = 120$ nm, respectively. These periods were selected based on the type of the solar cell (a-Si:H) to which the approach is applied. The P_{c2} is related to the appearance of light scattering effect in the silicon layer (lateral dimension of the texturization feature (P) has to be equal or greater to

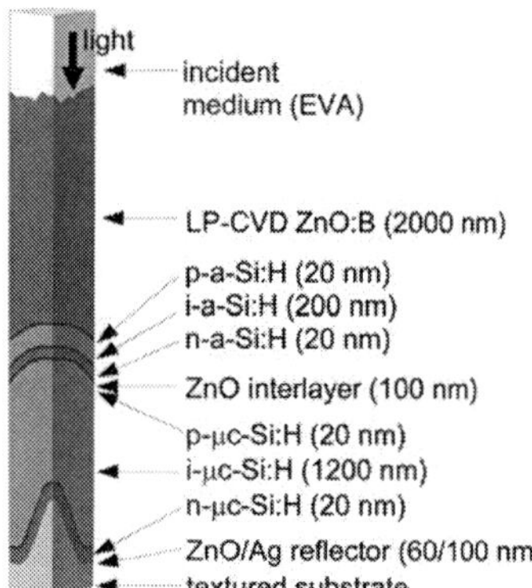

Fig. 5. Structure of the simulated micromorph a-Si:H/μc-Si:H solar cell in substrate configuration.

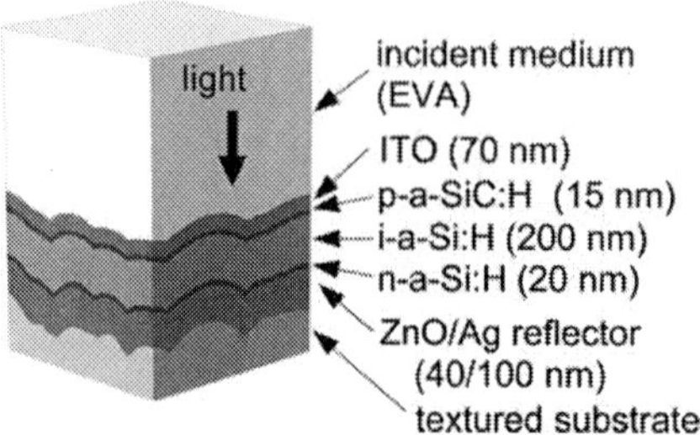

Fig. 6. Structure of the simulated single-junction amorphous solar cell in substrate configuration.

effective wavelength of light in the material). For $\lambda = 550$ nm, the corresponding effective wavelength in a-Si:H material $\lambda_{\text{eff}} \approx 550$ nm $/4.5 \approx 120$ nm, where 4.5 represents the value of the refractive index of a-Si:H. The P_{c1} was selected to be 480 nm, making $P = 300$ nm a central period of the MF region. $P = 300$ was also predicted by simulations to be the optimal single component texture for the analyzed a-Si:H cell for a given $\sigma_{\text{rms}} = 40$ nm of the texture. In the 2-D spectral plots (see the left side of Fig. 4), f_cs would be presented by two circles, with the middle point at $f_x = f_y = 0$ and radius equal to f_c.

Besides testing which region of frequency components is beneficial for high J_{SC} and which one detrimental, it is our aim to decrease the number of components in the spectrum as much as possible, making such artificial texture possible to be fabricated by, e.g., multistep interference or e-beam lithography (one step one 2-D sinus texture or principle of superposition). The role of random phase spectrum will also be addressed in our analysis. Results corresponding to the top-down approach are presented in Section IV-C.

IV. RESULTS

A. Simulated Structures

Two different thin-film solar cells were included in simulations: micromorph (a-Si:H/μc-Si:H) and single-junction amorphous, both in substrate configurations. The bottom-up approach was applied to micromorph, whereas the top-down approach to amorphous cell. Substrate configuration enables the use of light, flexible foils as substrates, and roll-to-roll production integrated with up-scaled nanoimprint lithography can be applied in the fabrication of PV modules [7], [8]. However, the presented approaches are not linked to a specific type or configuration or type of the cell. Nevertheless, different configurations and types of cells require new optimization processes, possibly resulting in different optimal textures, have to be carried out.

The models of the structures that were used in 3-D optical simulations are presented in Figs. 5 and 6, where all layers and their thicknesses are specified. The texture that we address in optimization refers to the texture of the substrate. The textures of subsequent interfaces are defined accordingly by applying the nonconformal growth model. The only exception is the top surface of the front LP-CVD ZnO:B TCO contact in the micromorph solar cell, where its natural random texture was applied directly and was not changed in the optimization process [20].

Defining an appropriate mesh in a 3-D model of solar cells presents a critical point. We tested different grid-meshes in the cells and optimized them, depending on the textures and simulated wavelengths to get reliable simulation results.

In the case of the micromorph cell, where periodic textures were analyzed, symmetrical boundary conditions were applied to the vertical boundaries of the device, enabling only half of the period to be included in simulation. Thus, the simulated area was $P/2 \times P/2$. In the case of random textures in the a-Si:H cell, 1 μm $\times$ 1 μm pitch was used in simulations, and periodic boundary conditions were applied at the sides of the simulation domain. However, the frequency analysis in the top-down approach was done on the texture area 5 μm $\times$ 5 μm. Realistic wavelength-dependent complex refractive indexes of layers were included in simulations [21]. In the EQE and J_{SC} calculations, absorptances in intrinsic (absorber) layers were considered, as explained before. Illumination (AM1.5 g) was applied as a plane wave at the front boundarsy of the model (EVA foil was considered as incident medium in all simulations)

B. Results of the Bottom-Up Approach

Simulated J_{SC} of the top (a-Si:H) and the bottom (μc-Si:H) subcells are presented in Fig. 7. We present the effect of the period (P) and the shape ($s = 2, 4$ and 10) of the texture of the substrate on the J_{SC}s, following the described bottom-up optimization approach. Results are shown for a selected value of $h = 900$ nm, since simulations indicated that such h is required for highest improvements in J_{SC}s. However, the nonconformal model of layer growth indicated that cells with the starting sinusoidal textures ($s = 2$) are expected to have defective regions in semiconductor layers and should be discarded [14]. Therefore, it is important to focus on shapes with $s > 2$.

In both graphs of Fig. 7, a reference line is added, corresponding to a cell where random texture of LP-CVD ZnO with $\sigma_{\text{rms}} = 116$ nm was applied to the substrate surface. The area of 1 μm $\times$ 1 μm of the AFM scan was used in simulation to represent this texture. This random texture is more suitable for thin-film silicon tandem devices, such as micromorph solar cells, than the texture of Asahi U type TCO.

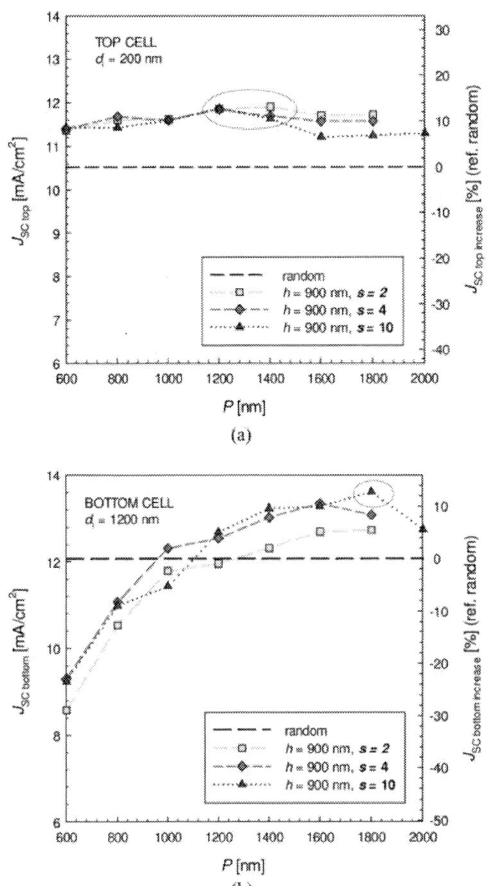

(a)

(b)

Fig. 7. (a) Simulated short-circuit current density of the top amorphous and (b) the bottom microcrystalline cell component in a micromorph solar cell in substrate configuration as a function of the period and texturization shape (bottom up approach).

The cells are not current-matched in our investigation (which can be done by an absorber thickness adjustment later on). We monitor the improvements related to the substrate texture in $J_{SC\,top}$ and $J_{SC\,bottom}$ separately.

When changing P of the substrate texture, no special trend is observed with respect to $J_{SC\,top}$ [see Fig. 7(a)]. The highest influence is obtained for the texture with $s = 10$, where a decrease in $J_{SC\,top}$ is observed for $P > 1400$ nm. Furthermore, one can observe that the shape of the texture affects the $J_{SC\,top}$ much less than the $J_{SC\,bottom}$ [(see Fig. 7(b)]. The highest gain in $J_{SC\,top}$ is simulated for $P = 1400$ nm ($h = 900$ nm) and $s = 2$ (11.91 mA/cm^2 which is +8.4% compared with random ref). However, considering the defect-less material growth, the combination $P = 1200$ nm ($h = 900$ nm) and s $= 10$ with similar increase (11.87 mA/cm^2, presenting +8.0% with respect to random ref) would be preferred. As the gains in the top cell are not really affected by the texture of the substrate (at least not the shape) in the case of micromorph cell in the substrate configuration, we rather focus on optimization with respect to $J_{SC\,bottom}$. By increasing P from 600 nm to 1600 nm, $J_{SC\,bottom}$ increases

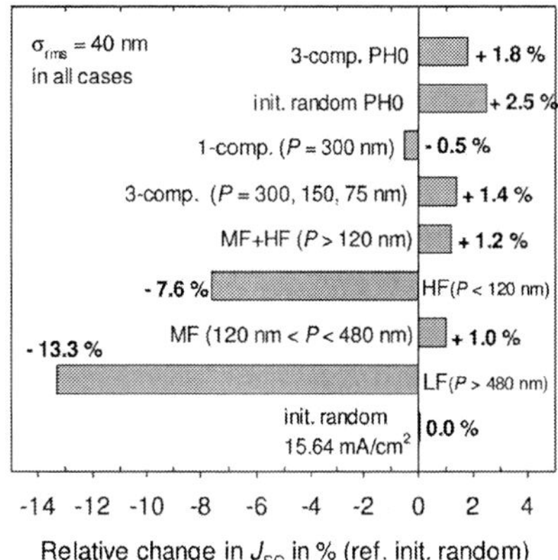

Fig. 8. Simulated relative increases in J_{SC} (%) of the a-Si:H cell in substrate configuration related to the change of the substrate morphology (top-down approach). LF, MF, HF, and MF+HF labels correspond to the random textures with low-, middle-, high- and high+middle-frequency components present in the modified random texture, respectively. Labels 1-comp and 3-comp correspond to the texture with only one and with three frequency components, respectively. The label PH0 indicates that phase spectrum of the texture was set to zero.

for all periodic textures [see Fig. 7(b)]. The highest point was obtained for the texture with $P = 1800$ nm ($h = 900$ nm) and $s = 10$ (13.01 mA/cm^2 presenting 12.8% increase with respect to the random ref). Thus, such smooth textures with broader valleys are not preferred just from the layer-growth point of view but from optical aspects as well, as shown by these simulations.

C. Results of the Top-Down Approach

In the top-down approach, we first analyze the role of the presence/absence of different frequency regions (LP, MF, and HF), defined in Section III-B. At the first stage, we preserve the phase spectrum and filter the height spectrum according to the mentioned three frequency regions. Furthermore, we kept the σ_{rms} of all the textures in the optimization at the same level, i.e., $\sigma_{rms} = 40$ nm (when a certain frequency region is excluded from the texture, consequently, the heights of the remaining components are scaled up accordingly, whereas the ratio between heights of the components remains the same). It is important to keep σ_{rms} fixed and focus on the shape and lateral parameters of the texture separately, since it is known that increasing σ_{rms} of random textures generally leads to improvement in J_{SC} [22]. In our analysis, we want to eliminate this effect. Another issue that has to be mentioned is that the filtering of the texture components (e.g., LF, MF, and HF), as well as the rescaling of the present components (in order to maintain σ_{rms}), affect the distribution of angles of textured surface facettes, For example, keeping only HF components in the texture and scaling up them to $\sigma_{rms} = 40$ nm results in the texture with higher angles of the facettes (angles between facette normal and z-direction). The role of the distribution of angles on scattering characteristics of the surface can be found elsewhere, e.g., in [23].

The results of simulations referring to the top-down approach are presented in Fig. 8. Relative increases in J_{SC} of the a-Si:H cell with respect to initial random texture are presented.

In general, the increases are not so high, since the initial random texture has a fingerprint of the Asahi U type substrate texture, which is already a well-suited texture for a-Si:H cells and since the increases in J_{SC} in cells with a-Si:H absorber related to improved optics are expected to be lower than in the case of μc-Si:H absorbers [24]. Nevertheless, one shall focus on trends of the improvements.

Simulations indicated that among all six combinations between LF, MF, and HF spectral regions (only four selected are represented in Fig. 8), the combination MF+HF is most beneficial ($+1.2\%$ increase in J_{SC}). The MF region alone gives $+1.0\%$ of improvement and is the best choice among single spectral regions [see MF texture appearance in Fig. 2(b)]. Texture with only LF components shows a significant drop in J_{SC}. One of the main reasons for that can be that surface features with large lateral dimensions lead to scattering in smaller angles, which may be inside the escaping zone of light [25]. On the other hand, in MF region the periods, which have a high potential for large-angle scattering, are present, according to analysis done on single sinusoidal components. The benefits of the HF region can be assigned to the antireflecting effect at front interfaces, although one has to be aware that these features are suppressed a lot at the front interfaces of the device in substrate configuration due to non-conformal layer growth. The combination of MF and HF components thus combines scattering in large angles as well as antireflecting properties, which we believe is the main reason for the highest gain in J_{SC} for this combination.

In order to reduce the number of frequency components in the spectrum further, to make such artificial textures possible for fabrication, we selected only three frequency components (3-comp) of the texture in the next step, having periods of $P_1 = 300$ nm, $P_2 = 150$ nm, and $P_3 = 75$ nm [first two from MF and the last from HF, see the appearance of the texture in Fig. 2(d)]. Again, σ_{rms} of the three-component texture was scaled to 40 nm, and the initial random phases were considered first. From the results given in Fig. 8, we can observe even a higher gain than for best spectral region combination (i.e $+1.4\%$ compared with initial random). Thus, the top-down approach indicates that with only a few components, it is possible to achieve and even surpass the J_{SC} obtained with full random spectrum. A question that arises is whether we can get a better result with only one optimized sinusoidal component (1-comp). In the case of the analyzed amorphous cell, the optimal period obtained by simulations was detected to be 300 nm (optimization results not shown here) for a given $h = 113$ nm (corresponding to $\sigma_{\mathrm{rms}} = 40$ nm). In this case, we can see that the optimal single component texture does not beat the random one. The presented results indicate that well designed a-few-component textures can be very promising. However, a proper combination of components has to be selected, since combinations may improve or harm the optical performances of the device (as indicated by HF and combination of MF+HF).

In the last step of investigation, we focus on the phase spectrum of the texture. In all simulations of the top-down approach presented so far, we preserve the phase spectrum of the initial random texture. Here, we set the entire phase spectrum to zero (this change is labeled with PH0), preserving the height spectrum, and repeat the simulations of as-modified initial random texture and the 3-component texture. Simulation results (see the top two horizontal bars in Fig. 8) reveal a further increase in J_{SC} ($+2.5\%$ and $+1.8\%$ compared with the initial random texture). This indicates an important role of the phase spectrum in the optimization of surface textures. This issue could not be included in previous optimizations with the models based on scalar scattering theory for surface optimization and needs to be paid more attention in future investigations of surface textures.

Besides textures with $\sigma_{\mathrm{rms}} = 40$ nm, the top-down approach was also applied to the textures where σ_{rms} was scaled up to 100 nm (not shown here). As expected, higher J_{SC}s were obtained; however, the trends between the presented optimization cases remain similar.

Higher relative improvements in J_{SC}s are expected if the optimization approach is applied to the cells with a μc-Si:H absorber. On the other hand, this approach demonstrates that with a-few-component synthetic texture, we can reach or even overcome the performances of the cells with state-of-the-art random textures. Moreover, the discussed textures are usually also smoother, enabling an increase in σ_{rms}, without deterioration of electrical properties, resulting in a further gain in efficiency.

V. Conclusion

Two approaches of surface-texture optimization were presented: the bottom-up and the top-down. Fully 3-D optical simulations were used to determine the improvements in J_{SC} of the investigated cells, which were related to the substrate texture optimization. A nonconformal layer growth model was used to define the transfer of the substrate texture to all internal interfaces in the cell, which may be substantially different from the starting, substrate one. Another advantage of the growth model is to predict and avoid textures that exhibit a higher probability of formation of defective regions in semiconductor layers.

All these features were considered in the bottom-up approach, which was applied to the optimization of a micromorph cell. Periodic textures with broader valleys exhibit, besides better growth conditions, good optical potential, as well, as shown by simulations. In a particular case, the optimized texture from the bottom-up approach (sinusoidal to the power $s = 10$, $P = 1800$ nm, and $h = 900$ nm) beat the $J_{SC\ \mathrm{bottom}}$ of the state-of-the-art random texture by 12.8%, according to simulations.

In the top-down approach, which was applied to a single-junction a-Si:H solar cell, we started with a random texture, and by systematic modification of the texture in spatial frequency domain, the way toward synthetic textures that are better than state-of-the art random ones was shown. Based on simulations, a-few-component textures have a better potential than optimized single component textures. In addition, simulations indicated the important role of the phase spectrum.

Acknowledgment

The authors would like to thank A. Campa and B. Lipovsek from the University of Ljubljana for useful discussions on optimization of surface textures and O. Isabella and M. Zeman from TU Delft for their help with spatial frequency transformation.

REFERENCES

[1] A. V. Shah, Ed., *Thin-Film Silicon Solar Cells*, 1st ed. Lausanne, Switzerland: EFPL Press, 2010.

[2] J. Krc and M. Topic, *Optical Modeling and Simulation of Thin-Film Photovoltaic Devices*. Boca Raton, FL, USA: CRC, 2013.

[3] K. Sato, Y. Gotoh, Y. Wakayama, Y. Hayashi, K. Adachi, and H. Nishimura, "Reports of the Research Labs," Asahi Glass Co. Ltd., Tokyo, Japan, 1992.

[4] O. Kluth, G. Schope, J. Hupkes, C. Agashe, J. Muller, and B. Rech, "Modified Thornton model for magnetron sputtered zinc oxide: Film structure and etching behaviour," *Thin Solid Films*, vol. 442, no. 1–2, pp. 80–85, Oct. 2003.

[5] S. Fay, J. Steinhauser, N. Oliveira, E. Vallat-Sauvain, and C. Ballif, "Optoelectronic properties of rough LP-CVD ZnO : B for use as TCO in thin-film silicon solar cells," *Thin Solid Films*, vol. 515, no. 24, pp. 8558–8561, Oct. 2007.

[6] T. Oyama, M. Kambe, N. Taneda, and K. Masumo, "Requirements for TCO substrate in Si-based thin film solar cells—Toward tandem," *MRS Proc.*, vol. 1101, 1101-KK02-01, 2008. DOI: 10.1557/PROC-1101-KK02-01.

[7] W. J. Soppe, H. Borg, B. B. Van Aken, C. Devilee, M. Dorenkamper, M. Goris, M. C. R. Heijna, J. Loffler, and P. Peeters, "Roll to roll fabrication of thin film silicon solar cells on nano-textured substrates," *J. Nanosci. Nanotechnol.*, vol. 11, no. 12, pp. 10604–10609, Dec. 2011.

[8] W. J. Soppe, M. Dörenkämper, J. B. Notta, P. P. A. C. Pex, W. Schipper, and R. Wilde, "Nano imprint lithography of textures for light trapping in thin film silicon solar cells," presented at the 27th Eur. Photovoltaic Solar Energy Conf. Exhib., Frankfurt, Germany, 2012, vol. 2012, pp. 2117–2119.

[9] C. Battaglia, C.-M. Hsu, K. Söderström, J. Escarré, F.-J. Haug, M. Charrière, M. Boccard, M. Despeisse, D. T. L. Alexander, M. Cantoni, Y. Cui, and C. Ballif, "Light trapping in solar cells: Can periodic beat random?" *ACS Nano*, vol. 6, no. 3, pp. 2790–2797, Mar. 2012.

[10] M. Python, O. Madani, D. Dominé, F. Meillaud, E. Vallat-Sauvain, and C. Ballif, "Influence of the substrate geometrical parameters on microcrystalline silicon growth for thin-film solar cells," *Solar Energy Mater. Solar Cells*, vol. 93, no. 10, pp. 1714–1720, Oct. 2009.

[11] M. Duchamp, K. Söderström, Q. Jeangros, C. B. Boothroyd, A. Kovács, T. Kasama, F.-J. Haug, C. Ballif, and R. E. Dunin-Borkowski, "Transmission electron microscopy of the textured silver back reflector of a thin-film silicon solar cells from chrystallography to optical absorption," in *Proc. 26th Eur. Photovoltaic Solar Energy Conf. Exhib.*, Hamburg, Germany, 2011, vol. 2011, pp. 2554–2557.

[12] Multiphysics Modelling and Simulation Software, 2012. [Online]. Available: http://www.comsol.com/

[13] M. Sever, B. Lipovšek, J. Krč, and M. Topič, "Optimisation of surface textures in thin-film silicon solar cells with 3-D optical modelling by considering realistic layer growth," presented at the 27th Eur. Photovoltaic Solar Energy Conf. Exhib., Frankfurt, Germany, Sep. 24–28, 2012, vol. 2012, pp. 2129–2131.

[14] M. Sever, B. Lipovsek, J. Krc, A. Campa, G. Sanchez Plaza, F.-J. Haug, M. Duchamp, W. J. Soppe, and M. Topic, "Combined model of non-conformal layer growth for accurate optical simulation of thin-film silicon solar cells," *Solar Energy Mater. Solar cells*, to be published. Available: http://dx.doi.org/10.1016/j.solmat.2013.05.016.

[15] M. Zeman, R. A. C. M. M. van Swaaij, J. W. Metselaar, and R. E. I. Schropp, "Optical modeling of a-Si:H solar cells with rough interfaces: Effect of back contact and interface roughness," *J. Appl. Phys.*, vol. 88, no. 11, pp. 6436–6443, Dec. 2000.

[16] P. Couty, M. Duchamp, K. Söderström, B. A. Kovács, R. E. Dunin-Borkowski, L. Sansonnens, and Y. Ziegler, "Transmission electron microscopy of amorphous tandem thin-film silicon modules produced by a roll-to-roll process on plastic foil," presented at the 26th Eur. Photovoltaic Solar Energy Conf. Exhib., Hamburg, Germany, 2011, vol. 2011, pp. 2395–2398.

[17] O. Isabella, J. Krc, and M. Zeman, "Modulated surface textures for enhanced light trapping in thin-film silicon solar cells," *Appl. Phys. Lett.*, vol. 97, no. 10, pp. 1011061-1–1011061-3, Sep. 2010. DOI: 10.1063/1.3488023.

[18] K. Jäger and M. Zeman, "A scattering model for surface-textured thin films," *Appl. Phys. Lett.*, vol. 95, no. 17, pp. 171108-1–171108-3, Oct. 2009.

[19] C. Battaglia, J. Escarre, K. Soederstroem, M. Charriere, M. Despeisse, F.-J. Haug, and C. Ballif, "Nanomoulding of transparent zinc oxide electrodes for efficient light trapping in solar cells," *Nat. Photonics*, vol. 5, no. 9, pp. 535–538, Sep. 2011.

[20] F. Haug, C. Battaglia, D. Dominé, and C. Ballif, "Light scattering at nano-textured surfaces in thin film silicon solar cells," in *Proc. 35th IEEE Photovoltaic Spec. Conf.*, 2010, pp. 000754–000759.

[21] J. Springer, A. Poruba, and M. Vanecek, "Improved three-dimensional optical model for thin-film silicon solar cells," *J. Appl. Phys.*, vol. 96, no. 9, pp. 5329–5336, 2004.

[22] J. Krc, F. Smole, and M. Topic, "Study of enhanced light scattering in microcrystalline silicon solar cells," *J. Non-Cryst. Solids*, vol. 338, pp. 673–676, Jun. 2004.

[23] W. Böttler, V. Smirnov, J. Hüpkes, and F. Finger, "Texture-etched ZnO as a versatile base for optical back reflectors with well-designed surface morphologies for application in thin film solar cells," *Physica Status Solidi (a)*, vol. 209, no. 6, pp. 1144–1149, 2012.

[24] J. Krc, M. Zeman, E. Smole, and M. Topic, "Optical modelling of thin-film silicon solar cells deposited on textured substrates RID A-5194–2008," *Thin Solid Films*, vol. 451, pp. 298–302, Mar. 2004.

[25] K. Jäger, M. Fischer, R. A. C. M. M. van Swaaij, and M. Zeman, "A scattering model for nano-textured interfaces and its application in optoelectrical simulations of thin-film silicon solar cells," *J. Appl. Phys.*, vol. 111, no. 8, p. 083108, Apr. 2012.

Authors' photographs and biographies not available at the time of publication.

Resonant Absorption Enhancement in Solar Cells With Periodically Textured Interfaces

Franz-Josef Haug, Karin Söderström, and Christophe Ballif

Abstract—We study the interaction of electromagnetic waves in layered media with textured interfaces. Experimental results of a solar cell grown on a sinusoidal back reflector are compared with a theoretical model using an expansion into diffraction modes. We assume the validity of the Rayleigh hypothesis and show that the continuity equations extend the coupling only to neighboring orders for the case of sinusoidal textures. This approach includes all essential aspects of the coupling process and it requires only a moderate amount of mathematical complexity. Our modeling results correctly reproduce the absorption of the periodically textured solar cell for both polarization directions. The absorption phenomena underlying the light-trapping process can thus be studied with a small number of parameters like period, depth, and film thickness.

Index Terms—Amorphous silicon, diffraction efficiency, light trapping.

I. Introduction

INTERFACE textures are used in various electronic components to enhance the coupling between the active layers and external radiation. Prominent examples are emission enhancement in light-emitting diodes and absorption enhancement in detectors and in solar cells. The latter is most widely studied in devices based on weakly absorbing silicon but could also become an interesting option to reduce the film thickness in other solar cell technologies. In thin-film silicon solar cells, the most successful light-scattering designs rely on random textures that were proposed as early as 1983 by Deckman *et al.* [1]. However, in the same year, it was already suggested that cleverly designed periodic interface textures should outperform their random counterparts [2]. In the meantime, processing of devices with periodic textures has advanced significantly [3]–[7], and it was shown that they can perform as well as state-of-the-art random interface textures [8]–[10]. With advancing computing power, rigorous calculations have become accessible to the modeling of solar cells [8], [11]–[14], but the understanding of the actual mechanisms of light trapping is still limited.

In this paper, we study absorption enhancement in solar cells with textured interfaces. In order to clarify the underlying mechanisms, we reduce complexity to the bare minimum, i.e., we use a 1-D interface texture of sinusoidal shape. The 1-D geometry is sufficient to treat the excitation of resonances via grating–coupling, and it has the additional advantage of resolving polarization phenomena. Generally, a 1-D geometry will not enhance the absorption as much as a 2-D geometry since it yields fewer resonance conditions [15], [16]. Likewise, we find that the sinusoidal interface corrugation is the simplest possible coupling mechanism; it is certainly not the most efficient one [17]. Nevertheless, it can serve as a representative of a component in the spatial Fourier expansion of an arbitrary surface texture. Our analytic approach is based on an expansion into diffraction modes and we use the Rayleigh hypothesis. Reducing the complexity in the device design as well as in the mathematical treatment allows us to distinguish the key parameters underneath the light-trapping process, especially the excitation of waveguide modes.

II. Experimental Details

We used nanoimprinting [18] to create several copies of a 1-D sinusoidal grating with 1800 lines/mm (GH series, Thorlabs). The copies have a period P of 550 nm and an amplitude s of 70 nm, i.e., 140-nm peak-to-valley depth. The solar cell was deposited in n-i-p configuration using a stack of ITO/a-Si/ZnO/Ag with respective thicknesses of 65/255/60/120 nm; the deposition is from the same series as the cell on the blazed grating described in [6]. ITO, ZnO, and Ag were deposited by sputtering. The 255-nm-thick silicon film contains n- and p-doped layers with respective thicknesses of 20 and 10 nm, all deposited by plasma-enhanced chemical vapor deposition with an excitation frequency of 70 MHz.

The reflection was measured from 370 to 2000 nm in a spectrophotometer with integrating sphere which yields an angle of incidence of 8° (Lambda 900, Perkin Elmer). The measurement on the small cell surface required reduced spot size and becomes thus somewhat noisy toward the boundaries of the investigated spectral region. A broad-band wire-grid polarizer (ProFlux PPL05C, Moxtek) was used to polarize the incident beam parallel or perpendicular to the grating lines, exciting thus TE or TM modes, respectively.

III. Model

We expand the electromagnetic field of each layer and in the delimiting half-spaces into a series of diffraction modes. An application of this procedure to solar-cell back reflectors can be found elsewhere [19]. For the incident half-space, we assume air as a loss-free medium with relative permittivity $\varepsilon_i = 1$, and we express the incident light by a single plane wave with wave-vector components $k = k_0 \cdot \sin\theta$ and $\gamma_i = (k_0^2 - k^2)^{1/2} = k_0 \cos\theta$. Here, the wavelength λ_0 of the

Manuscript received June 16, 2013; revised March 5, 2014; accepted March 5, 2014. This work was supported by the Swiss National Science Foundation under Grant 200020_137700/1 and by the European Union within the Projects Silicon-Light under Grant 241277 and FastTrack (No. 283501).

The authors are with the Institute of Microengineering, Ecole Polytechnique Fédérale de Lausanne, CH-2000 Neuchâtel, Switzerland (e-mail: franz-josef.haug@epfl.ch; karin.soderstrom@epfl.ch; christophe.ballif@epfl.ch).

Color versions of one or more of the figures in this paper are available online at http://ieeexplore.ieee.org.

Digital Object Identifier 10.1109/JPHOTOV.2014.2310750

242

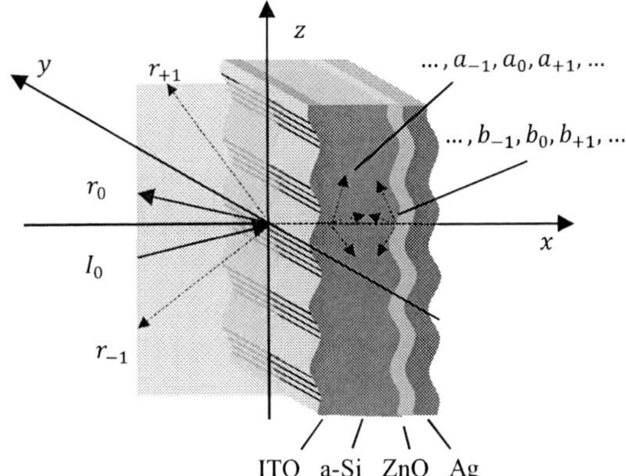

Fig. 1.   Geometry used in this contribution: the incident beam I_0 and the reflected beam r_0 are in the xz-plane. The expansion into forward- and backward-going modes of (2) is illustrated only for the a-Si film.

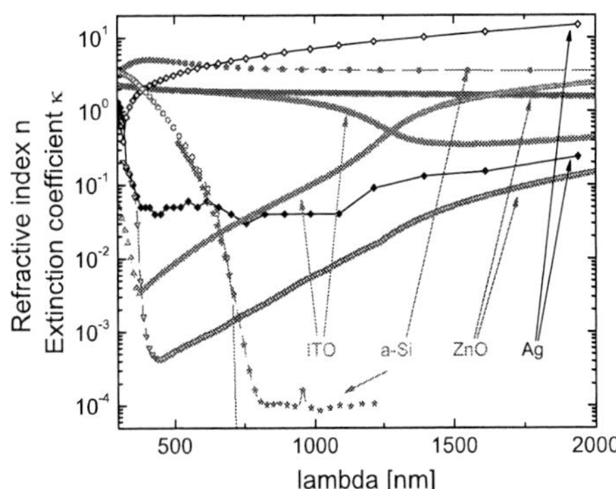

Fig. 2.   Refractive indexes (full symbols) and extinction coefficients (open symbols) of the materials used for modeling. The stars denote data of photothermal deflection spectroscopy which we used in the region close to the bandgap of a-Si.

incident light in air is used to define the wave-vector modulus $k_0 = 2\pi/\lambda_0$, and θ is the incident angle with respect to the surface normal. Reflected light is described by a superposition of diffraction modes. In the in-plane direction, the wave-vector components are $k_p = k + p \cdot G$, where $G = 2\pi/P$ with the grating period P and the mode index p which extends over negative and positive integers including zero. The wave-vector components in the out-of-plane direction are given by $\gamma_{i,p} = (k_0^2 - k_p^2)^{1/2}$. The components $\gamma_{i,p}$ are either purely real or purely imaginary and describe thus propagating and evanescent waves, respectively. Fig. 1 shows the chosen geometry where incident and reflected beams are contained in the xz plane. With grating lines parallel to the y-axis, the diffracted beams are contained in the same plane. The description is simplified by considering transverse fields that have only one component in the y-direction.

We can define two polarization directions where either the electric field $\vec{E}$ or the magnetic field $\vec{H}$ is directed along the y-axis. The former and the latter correspond to TE and TM polarization, respectively, and the field component in the y-direction is expressed by the following expansion with reflection coefficients r_n:

$$F_i = e^{i(\gamma_i x + kz)} + \sum_p r_p e^{i(\gamma_{i,p} x + k_p z)}. \tag{1}$$

In the films that constitute the solar cell, the field is described by superposing forward and backward going diffraction modes. For these modes, the in-plane components k_p are the same as for the incident medium. The out-of-plane components are defined by $\gamma_{f,p} = (\varepsilon_f k_0^2 - k_n^2)^{1/2}$ with the relative permittivities ε_f of each film f. The amplitudes of forward and backward traveling waves are described by the coefficients a_p and b_p:

$$F_f = \sum_p [a_p e^{i(\gamma_{f,p} x + k_p z)} + b_p e^{i(-\gamma_{f,p} x + k_p z)}]. \tag{2}$$

Note that the exponents contain γ_p with both positive and negative signs. The imaginary parts γ_p'' result thus in exponentially decreasing and increasing terms, respectively. Even for

purely real ε_f, the latter can cause numeric instabilities once $k_p > \sqrt{\varepsilon_f} k_0$ (cf., [19, Fig. 2]).

Since the silver back-electrode can be considered opaque for thicknesses like the one used here, we do not take into account its actual thickness, but we assume that it fills the opposing half-space. It contains thus only forward traveling waves with amplitude coefficients t_p that are transmitted from the other layers into the silver film:

$$F_{Ag} = \sum_p t_p e^{i(\gamma_{Ag,p} x + k_p z)}. \tag{3}$$

The dielectric data used in our modeling are shown in Fig. 2. For ITO, a-Si, and ZnO, they were determined from reference layers on glass by combined fitting of ellipsometry data and the total transmission with a Tauc–Lorentz model [20]. Since the model does not contain band tails, we used data from photothermal deflection spectroscopy in the weakly absorbing region of a-Si. For the opaque silver layer, we used tabulated data of Johnson and Christy [21].

We assume conformal coating in this paper; however, the grating depth and its phase can be varied easily at each interface. In order to evaluate the continuity conditions at the interfaces, we make use of the Rayleigh hypothesis [22], i.e., we assume that the expansion into diffraction modes remains valid within the roughness zones and at the interfaces. While not applicable in general [23], [24], the Rayleigh hypothesis was reported to apply reliably for gratings similar to ours [25]. For each interface, the application of the electromagnetic continuity conditions yields two equations that relate the field amplitudes and their normal derivatives.

The equation that relates the derivatives contains the distinction between the polarization directions: in TE polarization, the electric field amplitude is differentiable, whereas in TM polarization, the derivative of the magnetic field amplitude is discontinuous by a factor equal to the inverse of the relative permittivities. At the interface between the films f and $f + 1$, we obtain

$$\left(\frac{1}{\varepsilon_f}\right)^\kappa \left(\frac{\partial F_f}{\partial n}\right) = \left(\frac{1}{\varepsilon_{f+1}}\right)^\kappa \left(\frac{\partial F_{f+1}}{\partial n}\right). \tag{4}$$

The exponent κ is either 0 or 1 to denote TE or TM polarization, respectively (cf., discussion after [26, eq. (3b)]). In addition, the coupling mechanism is also contained in the second continuity condition via the normal derivative:

$$\frac{\partial}{\partial n} = \left(1 + \left(\frac{\partial g(z)}{\partial z}\right)^2\right)^{-\frac{1}{2}} \left(\frac{\partial}{\partial x} - \frac{\partial g(z)}{\partial z}\frac{\partial}{\partial z}\right). \qquad (5)$$

Here, the derivative of the surface profile $g(z) = s \cdot \sin Gz$ appearing in the second term of (5) can be expressed as $Gs \cdot \cos Gz = Gs \cdot [\exp(iGz) + \exp(-iGz)]/2$, i.e., a sum of two exponentials with positive and negative spatial frequency G. Since the z-dependence of the field amplitudes is expanded into multiples of the same frequency G, the sinusoidal corrugation couples only between neighboring orders [27]. It represents, therefore, the simplest possible coupling mechanism.

After evaluating the equalities along the sinusoidal interface, i.e., inserting $x = g(z) = s \cdot \sin Gz$ in all instances of x, the expansion can be sorted by the orders of the diffraction modes $\exp(iGz \cdot p)$ and eventually yields an infinite system of linear equations like [28, eqs. (1)–(8)]. This procedure relies on using the generation function of the Bessel functions (cf., [25, eqs. (4) and (5)]), and the result is mathematically rigorous up to this point.

Finally, the equations are truncated to desired accuracy, e.g., at order n. Each interface yields thus $2 \times (2n + 1)$ linear equations with complex coefficients for the determination of the reflection coefficients r_p, the amplitude coefficients a_p and b_p within each film, and the transmission coefficients t_p. Since the coupling is included before the truncation in a mathematically rigorous manner, the procedure yields fast convergence, typically for three or four orders [19], [25], [28].

A. Absorption

In the absence of transmission, the total absorption A of the whole stack is obtained by $A = 1 - R$, using the total reflection R:

$$R = \sum_p r_p r_p^*. \qquad (6)$$

The absorption within a film can be determined according to Poynting's theorem by integrating the dissipated power density P_{abs}. We choose a volume that is delimited by one grating period P, the sinusoidal interfaces separated by the film thickness d_f, and a distance dy along the y-axis; since the equations are invariant to this coordinate, dy is arbitrary. We obtain for TE polarization

$$P_{\mathrm{abs},f} = \frac{\omega \varepsilon_0 \varepsilon_f''}{2} dy \cdot \int_0^P \int_{s \cdot \sin Gz}^{s \cdot \sin Gz + d_f} \vec{E}_f \vec{E}_f^* \cdot dz dx. \qquad (7)$$

Here, ω is the angular frequency, ε_f'' is the imaginary part of the permittivity of the film, and $\vec{E}_f$ is the electric field vector.

For TE polarization, $\vec{E}_f$ contains only one single component in the y-direction which is given by (2). The relative absorption with respect to the amplitude of the incident wave is then obtained by dividing with the incident flux of energy S_i that impinges on the surface of the probing volume, i.e., the area delimited by P and dy:

$$S_i = \frac{P \cdot dy}{2}\sqrt{\varepsilon_0/\mu_0}. \qquad (8)$$

The integration in (7) can be carried out numerically. More conveniently, we insert the expansion of (2) and obtain four terms like the following:

$$\sum_{p,q}[a_p a_q^* \cdot e^{i(\gamma_{f,p} - \gamma_{f,q}^*)x} e^{i(k_p - k_q)z}]. \qquad (9)$$

Reversing the order of summation and integration, we can carry out the integration along the x-direction. After applying the sinusoidal profiles to the limits of the integration, we obtain terms of the form:

$$(i(\gamma_{f,p} - \gamma_{f,q}^*))^{-1} \cdot \int_0^P e^{i(\gamma_{f,p} - \gamma_{f,q}^*)s \cdot \sin Gz} e^{i(p-q)Gz} dz. \qquad (10)$$

In (10), the integral over a full grating period represents an integral representation of $J_{q-p}((\gamma_{f,p} - \gamma_{f,q}^*)s)$, i.e., the Bessel function of order $q - p$. Dropping the ubiquitous index f, we obtain

$$P_{\mathrm{abs}} = \frac{\omega \varepsilon_0 \varepsilon''}{2} dy \cdot P \cdot \sum_{p,q}$$
$$\left[\frac{a_p a_q^*}{i(\gamma_p - \gamma_q^*)}(e^{i(\gamma_p - \gamma_q^*)d} - 1) \cdot J_{q-p}(\gamma_p - \gamma_q^*)\right.$$
$$+ \frac{a_p b_q^*}{i(\gamma_p + \gamma_q^*)}(e^{i(\gamma_p + \gamma_q^*)d} - 1) \cdot J_{q-p}(\gamma_p + \gamma_q^*)$$
$$+ \frac{a_q^* b_p}{i(-\gamma_p - \gamma_q^*)}(e^{i(-\gamma_p - \gamma_q^*)d} - 1) \cdot J_{q-p}(-\gamma_p - \gamma_q^*)$$
$$\left. + \frac{b_p b_q^*}{i(-\gamma_p + \gamma_q^*)}(e^{i(-\gamma_p + \gamma_q^*)d} - 1) \cdot J_{q-p}(-\gamma_p + \gamma_q^*)\right]. $$
$$(11)$$

The absorption in the film is thus obtained by a summation over analytic terms that involve only the amplitude coefficients a_p and b_p, wave-vector components γ_p and k_p, and Bessel functions thereof. With this procedure, we can avoid issues with the numeric integration at the cost of treating a few more terms. This is particularly helpful for the contribution of the substrate where the integration should be extended to infinity.

B. Absorption in the Films (TM Polarization)

For TM polarization, F_f in (2) describes the y-component of magnetic field vector $\vec{H}_f$; the electric field vector $\vec{E}_f$ must, therefore, be determined via $\vec{E}_f = 1/(i\omega\varepsilon_f) \cdot \nabla \times \vec{H}_f$:

$$P_{\mathrm{abs},f}^{\mathrm{TM}} = \frac{\varepsilon_0 \varepsilon_f'' dy}{2\omega \varepsilon_f \varepsilon_f^*}$$
$$\cdot \int \left[\left(\frac{\partial F_f}{\partial x}\right)\left(\frac{\partial F_f^*}{\partial x}\right) + \left(\frac{\partial F_f}{\partial z}\right)\left(\frac{\partial F_f^*}{\partial z}\right)\right] dz dx. $$
$$(12)$$

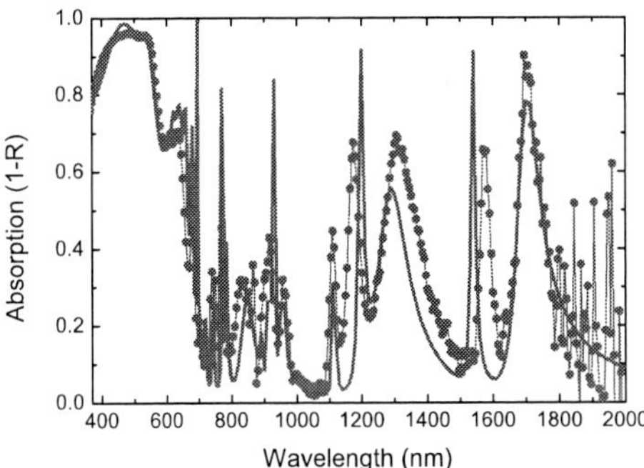

Fig. 3. Symbols show the total reflection of the solar cell over a wide spectral region (TE polarization, angle of incidence equal to 7°). The line illustrates modeling results.

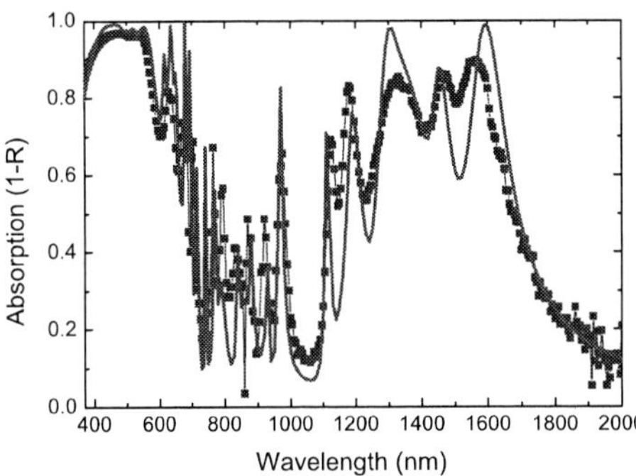

Fig. 4. Symbols show the total reflection of the solar cell over a wide spectral region (TM polarization, angle of incidence equal to 7°). The line illustrates modeling results.

The derivatives with respect to x and z yield additional factors of $i\gamma_{f,p}$ and ik_p or their complex conjugates, respectively, and now the integration extends over two terms. The other considerations of the previous section remain valid and the integrals can be resolved accordingly. Eventually, we obtain again double sums over the amplitude coefficients and Bessel functions.

IV. Results and Discussion

We applied the model to the solar cell on the sinusoidal texture. All modeling results were obtained with truncation after third order. Expansion to fourth order did not yield an improvement and owing to exponentially increasing terms, it even leads to occasional instabilities around resonances.

A. Total Absorption

Figs. 3 and 4 show the total absorption according to (6) in TE and TM polarization, respectively. In both figures, Fabry–Perot interference yields features that are common in both polarization directions. They are easily identified by reducing the grating amplitude to zero. On the resulting flat structure, absorption maxima appear at 1450, 920, 700, and at 575 nm (not shown). The presence of the grating yields blue shifts to 1300, 870, 680, and 555 nm, respectively.

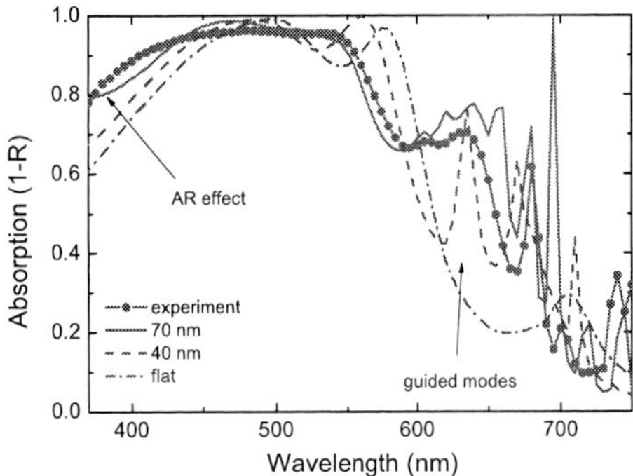

Fig. 5. Detail of the absorption characteristic in TE polarization. The full line denotes the grating amplitude of 70 used in the experiment, the dashed line refer to an intermediate grating amplitudes of 40 nm, and the dashed–dotted line illustrates the properties of a flat structure.

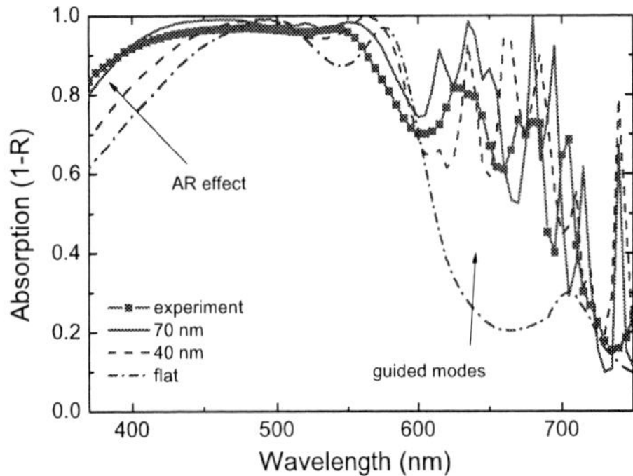

Fig. 6. Detail of the absorption characteristic in TM polarization. The line styles are the same as Fig. 5.

Between the Fabry–Perot interferences, Figs. 3 and 4 show a multitude of guided modes, notably the broad absorption signatures at 1700 nm and around 1500 nm found for TE and TM polarization, respectively. The modeling results denoted by the lines show a good overall correspondence to the measured results; all of the dominant features of the measurement are correctly reproduced.

A closer investigation of Figs. 3 and 4 shows slight misfits of the peak positions, notably around 1200 and 1600 nm. Similarly, the height and width of the peaks show slight deviations. These observations may be related to two shortcomings of our model. First, we assumed perfectly reproduced interfaces, whereas sputtering and CVD processes are known to deviate from fully conformal growth. Second, we used a single film of silicon, whereas the n-i-p stack of the actual solar cell includes the doped layers whose permittivities are likely to differ from the undoped intrinsic layer.

Figs. 5 and 6 zoom in on the range of interest for solar cell operation. For both polarization directions, the low reflection between 400 and 550 nm is related to the ITO front electrode. In combination with the underlying silicon film, its thickness of 65 nm is designed to yield an antireflection condition close to 500 nm (cf., characteristic of the flat structure in Figs. 5 and 6).

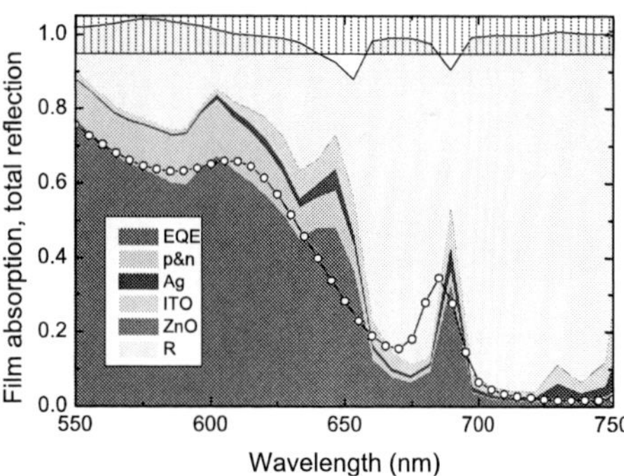

Fig. 7. Stacked plot of reflection and absorption in the individual films. Symbols represent a measurement of the EQE (0° incidence, TE polarization).

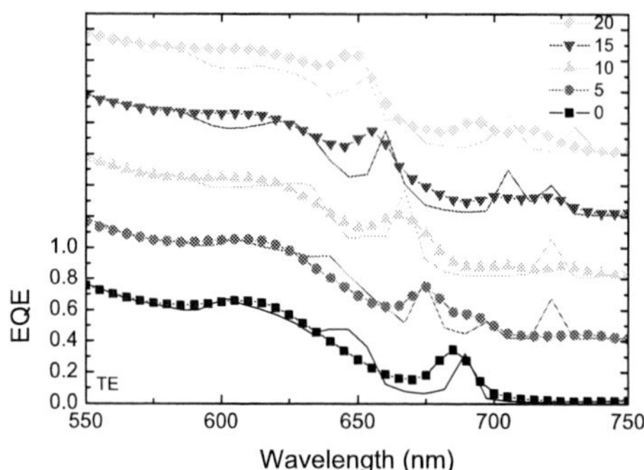

Fig. 8. Angle-resolved EQE (symbols) and modeling results (lines) for TE polarization. The characteristics are shifted with an offset of 0.4.

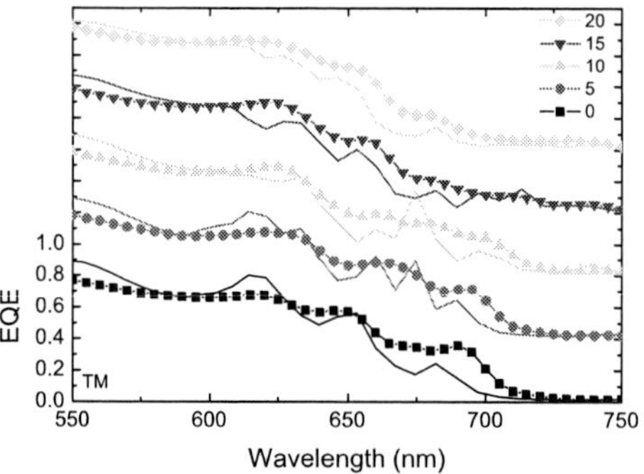

Fig. 9. Angle-resolved EQE for TM polarization; symbols and lines as Fig. 8.

The interface texture enhances the antireflection effect toward shorter wavelengths.

Increasing grating amplitudes yield a blue shift of the dominant Fabry–Perot interference at 570 nm. For TE polarization, a strong drop of absorption appears as the amplitude is stepped down from 70 to 40 nm, for TM polarization this amplitude gives still acceptable absorption enhancement.

In the light-trapping region between 600 and 750 nm, increasing grating amplitude yields more and more efficient coupling to guided modes. The experimental data do not resolve all of the narrow resonances that dominate the modeling results in this region, but absorption enhancement is clearly visible for both polarization directions. Overall, the enhancement appears to be more efficient for TM polarization shown in Fig. 6.

B. Absorption in the Individual Films

We applied the model to calculate the absorption in the individual films of the solar cell. Fig. 7 compares the results to a measurement of the external quantum efficiency (EQE) in the weakly absorbing region between 550 and 750 nm. The EQE is a spectrally resolved ratio between the number of electrons that the solar cell provides to the external circuit with respect to the number of incident photons. A theoretical "EQE" can be estimated by excluding the thickness of the doped layers from the integration boundaries. This estimate assumes that the solar cell collects all electron–hole pairs and transports them to the external circuit without losses. Fig. 7 shows that this theoretical EQE reproduces the measured characteristic rather well, but it predicts a slightly larger wavelength for the resonance at 775 nm and it underestimates the experimental broadening.

Absorption in the individual films and reflection should add up to unity. Except for the resonances at 630 and 680 nm, the dashed band in Fig. 7 shows that the accuracy of the expansion to third order is better than 5%. However, we emphasize that the idea of this study was the demonstration of a simple model that illustrates the ingredients of the light-trapping process.

Fig. 7 shows that there is significant absorption in the regions of the doped layers. In a more recent generation of solar cells than the one studied here, this loss is reduced by using a p-doped layer of nanocrystalline SiO_x which is more transparent [29], [30]. To a lesser extent, parasitic absorption occurs also in the silver back contact and in the ITO front electrode. Absorption in the ZnO buffer layer is negligible.

We also studied the angular properties of the EQE; Figs. 8 and 9 compare experimental and theoretical results for TE and TM polarization, respectively. For TE polarization, the dispersion of the leading resonance is well reproduced as the incident angle is varied from 0° to 20°. The model predicts smaller resonances in the weakly absorbing region beyond 700 nm; however, experimentally these are not well resolved.

For the TM-polarized case shown in Fig. 9, the broadening of the measured data makes it more difficult to distinguish individual resonances. Nevertheless, the agreement between experiment and modeling results is surprisingly good, considering that the expansion is only to third order. A more detailed discussion of the angular properties of this cell including the effect of photonic bandgaps can be found elsewhere [31].

V. CONCLUSION

We presented a numerical treatment for wave propagation in layered media with sinusoidal interface texture. For this kind of texture, we showed that the coupling between incident radiation and eigenmodes of the stack can be expressed in a fast-converging expansion. We applied our model to the case of light trapping in solar cells, using a device with 1-D grating back reflector. We found that the model reproduces most of the experimental findings, but it is still comparatively simple in terms of the underlying mathematics. The model is thus helpful and instructive to understand details of coupling phenomena that arise from interface textures and we are confident that its application is not limited to solar cells.

REFERENCES

[1] H. W. Deckman, C. R. Wronski, H. Witzke, and E. Yablonovitch, "Optically enhanced amorphous silicon solar cells," *Appl. Phys. Lett.*, vol. 42, no. 11, pp. 968–970, 1983.

[2] P. Sheng, A. N. Bloch, and R. S. Stepleman, "Wavelength-selective absorption enhancement in thin-film solar cells," *Appl. Phys. Lett.*, vol. 43, p. 579, 1983.

[3] N. Senoussaoui, M. Krause, J. Müller, E. Bunte, T. Brammer, and H. Stiebig, "Thin-film solar cells with periodic grating coupler," *Thin Solid Films*, vol. 451, pp. 397–401, 2004.

[4] V. E. Ferry, M. A. Verschuuren, H. Li, R. E. I. Schropp, H. A. Atwater, and A. Polman, "Improved red-response in thin film a-Si: H solar cells with soft-imprinted plasmonic back reflectors," *Appl. Phys. Lett.*, vol. 95, pp. 183503-1–183503-3, 2009.

[5] J. Zhu, C. M. Hsu, Z. Yu, S. Fan, and Y. Cui, "Nanodome solar cells with efficient light management and self-cleaning," *Nano Lett.*, vol. 10, no. 6, pp. 1979–1984, 2009.

[6] K. Söderström, F. Haug, J. Escarré, O. Cubero, and C. Ballif, "Photocurrent increase in n-i-p thin film silicon solar cells by guided mode excitation via grating coupler," *Appl. Phys. Lett.*, vol. 96, pp. 213508-1–213508-3, 2010.

[7] U. Paetzold, E. Moulin, D. Michaelis, W. Böttler, C. Wächter, V. Hagemann, M. Meier, R. Carius, and U. Rau, "Plasmonic reflection grating back contacts for microcrystalline silicon solar cells," *Appl. Phys. Lett.*, vol. 99, no. 18, pp. 181105-1–181105-3, 2011.

[8] V. E. Ferry, A. Polman, and H. A. Atwater, "Modeling light trapping in nanostructured solar cells," *ACS Nano*, vol. 5, no. 12, pp. 10055–10064, 2011.

[9] O. Isabella, F. Moll, J. Krč, and M. Zeman, "Modulated surface textures using zinc-oxide films for solar cells applications," *Phys. Status Solidi (a)*, vol. 207, no. 3, pp. 642–646, 2010.

[10] C. Battaglia, C. M. Hsu, K. Söderström, J. Escarré, F. J. Haug, M. Charrière, M. Boccard, M. Despeisse, D. Alexander, M. Cantoni, Y. Cui, and C. Ballif, "Light trapping in solar cells: Can periodic beat random?" *ACS Nano*, vol. 6, no. 3, pp. 2790–2797, 2012.

[11] C. Haase and H. Stiebig, "Thin-film silicon solar cells with efficient periodic light trapping texture," *Appl. Phys. Lett.*, vol. 91, no. 6, pp. 061116-1–061116-3, 2007.

[12] C. Rockstuhl, F. Lederer, K. Bittkau, and R. Carius, "Light localization at randomly textured surfaces for solar-cell applications," *Appl. Phys. Lett.*, vol. 91, pp. 171104-1–171104-3, 2007.

[13] A. Campa, O. Isabella, R. van Erven, P. Peeters, H. Borg, K. J., T. M., and M. Zeman, "Optimal design of periodic surface texture for thin film a-Si:H solar cells," *Progress Photovoltaics, Res. Appl.*, vol. 18, no. 3, pp. 160–167, 2010.

[14] R. Dewan, I. Vasilev, V. Jovanov, and D. Knipp, "Optical enhancement and losses of pyramid textured thin-film silicon solar cells," *J. Appl. Phys.*, vol. 110, no. 1, pp. 013101-1–013101-10, 2011.

[15] Z. Yu, A. Raman, and S. Fan, "Fundamental limit of light trapping in grating structures," *Opt. Exp.*, vol. 18, no. 103, pp. A366–A380, 2010.

[16] Z. Yu, A. Raman, and S. Fan, "Fundamental limit of nanophotonic light trapping in solar cells," *Proc. Nat. Acad. Sci. USA*, vol. 107, no. 41, p. 17491, 2010.

[17] A. Naqavi, K. Söderström, F. J. Haug, V. Paeder, T. Scharf, H. P. Herzig, and C. Ballif, "Understanding of photocurrent enhancement in real thin film solar cells: Towards optimal one-dimensional gratings," *Opt. Exp.*, vol. 19, no. 1, pp. 128–140, 2011.

[18] K. Söderström, J. Escarré, O. Cubero, F.-J. Haug, S. Perregaux, and C. Ballif, "UV nano imprint lithography technique for the replication of back reflectors for n-i-p thin film silicon solar cells," *Progress Photovoltaics, Res. Appl.*, vol. 19, no. 2, pp. 202–210, 2011.

[19] F. J. Haug, A. Naqavi, and C. Ballif, "Diffraction and absorption enhancement from textured back reflectors of thin film solar cells," *J. Appl. Phys.*, vol. 112, pp. 024516-1–024516-7, 2012.

[20] Z. C. Holman, A. Descoeudres, L. Barraud, F. Z. Fernandez, J. P. Seif, S. De Wolf, and C. Ballif, "Current losses at the front of silicon heterojunction solar cells," *IEEE J. Photovoltaics*, vol. 2, no. 1, pp. 7–15, Jan. 2012.

[21] P. B. Johnson and R. W. Christy, "Optical constants of the noble metals," *Phys. Rev. B*, vol. 6, no. 12, p. 4370, 1972.

[22] L. Rayleigh, "On the dynamical theory of gratings," *Proc. Royal Soc. London, A*, vol. 79, no. 532, pp. 399–416, 1907.

[23] R. Petit and M. Cadilhac, "Sur la diffraction d'une onde plane par un reseau infiniment conducteur," *Comptes Rendus le l'Academie des Sci. B*, vol. 262, p. 468, 1966.

[24] P. Van Den Berg and J. Fokkema, "The Rayleigh hypothesis in the theory of reflection by a grating," *J. Opt. Soc. Amer.*, vol. 69, no. 1, pp. 27–31, 1979.

[25] S. H. Zaidi, M. Yousaf, and S. R. J. Brueck, "Grating coupling to surface plasma waves. I—First-order coupling," *J. Opt. Soc. Amer. B*, vol. 8, no. 4, pp. 770–779, 1991.

[26] V. Kiselev, "Diffraction coupling of radiation into a thin-film waveguide," *Soviet J. Quantum Electron.*, vol. 4, p. 872, 1975.

[27] V. Kiselev, "Resonant conversion and reflection of surface waves in a thin-film waveguide with a sinusoidally corrugated surface," *Soviet J. Quantum Electron.*, vol. 4, p. 182, 1974.

[28] S. H. Zaidi, D. Reicher, B. Draper, J. McNeil, and S. Brueck, "Characterization of thin Al films using grating coupling to surface plasma waves," *J. Appl. Phys.*, vol. 71, no. 12, pp. 6039–6048, 1992.

[29] R. Biron, C. Pahud, F.-J. Haug, J. Escarré, K. Söderström, and C. Ballif, "Window layer with p doped silicon oxide for high Voc thin-film silicon nip solar cells," *J. Appl. Phys.*, vol. 110, no. 12, pp. 124511-1–124511-7, 2011.

[30] R. Biron, C. Pahud, F.-J. Haug, and C. Ballif, "Origin of the Voc enhancement with a p-doped nc-SiOx:H window layer in n-i-p solar cells," *J. Non-Crystalline Solids*, vol. 358, no. 17, pp. 1958–1961, 2012.

[31] F. J. Haug, K. Söderström, A. Naqavi, J. Li, and C. Ballif, "Super-Lambertian photocurrent generation in solar cells with periodically textured interfaces," *Appl. Phys. Lett.*, vol. 102, pp. 131108-1–131108-4, 2013.

Authors' photographs and biographies not available at the time of publication.

Critical Points in the Band Structure of Absorber and Buffer Layers of CuIn$_{1-x}$Ga$_x$Se$_2$ Solar Cells by Electroreflectance Spectroscopy

Oliver Kiowski, Wolfram Witte, Michael Hetterich, and Michael Powalla

Abstract—We explore the use of electroreflectance (ER) spectroscopy at room temperature to characterize simultaneously Cu(In,Ga)Se$_2$ (CIGS) absorber and CdS/i-ZnO buffer layers of thin-film solar cells. Absorber layers are coevaporated from elemental sources. The CdS buffer layers are deposited by chemical bath deposition. We apply ER at different incidence angles to distinguish ER signals from interference fringes. Bandgaps, critical point energies, and broadening parameters that describe the band structure of absorber and buffer films are determined by fitting the ER spectra with a third-derivative functional form. Absorbers grown with a vertical gradient in the Ga/(Ga+In) (GGI) ratio are compared with cells without a GGI gradient but the same integral GGI compositions. We also measure samples with no gradient but different integral GGI ratios of 0 (CuInSe$_2$), 0.3, 0.6, and 1 (CuGaSe$_2$). The ER signal of CdS yields three excitonic transitions, consistent with theory.

Index Terms—Bandgap, buffer, CdS, Cu(In,Ga)Se$_2$ (CIGS), critical point, electroreflectance (ER).

I. Introduction

PHOTOVOLTAIC devices that are based on coevaporated Cu(In,Ga)Se$_2$ (CIGS) thin films have reached record efficiencies of 20.3% on glass [1] and 20.4% on polyimide [2] and are now matching those of multicrystalline silicon solar cells [3]. On commercially available 60 cm × 120 cm modules, a conversion efficiency of 14.6% has been demonstrated using coevaporated chalcopyrite absorber layers with selenium [4].

Electroreflectance (ER) spectroscopy is a versatile technique in semiconductor research. Together with photoreflectance (PR), a contactless form of ER, it has been used to investigate the band structure of chalcopyrites (see [5], [6] and references therein, and [7]). Individual layers are usually grown epitaxially on GaAs substrates to examine the effect of polarized light on optical transitions. However, thin-film growth is influenced by the substrate; therefore, separate films of absorber or buffer may differ from those in a solar cell stack. Most publications using ER spectroscopy as a technique for the examination of chalcopyrite absorbers investigated Cu(In,Ga)S$_2$ thin-film solar cells [8], [9] or Cu(In,Ga)Se$_2$ grown by sequential processes [10], [11]. In this contribution, we discuss ER spectra on complete solar cells with inline coevaporated CIGS absorbers and conversion efficiencies of up to 16% in a spectral range that encompasses absorber and buffer layers.

ER spectroscopy in its simplest form measures the change of reflectance ΔR of a sample when an external bias U is applied, divided by (referenced to) the reflectance without an external bias as a function of photon energy E

$$\frac{\Delta R}{R}(U,E) = \frac{R_{(U,E)} - R_{(0,E)}}{R_{(0,E)}}. \tag{1}$$

ER spectra are dominated by points in the Brillouin zone, where the joint density of states for direct transitions shows strong variations as a function of energy (van Hove singularities). These points are called critical points (CPs), and the bandgap is one of them. If the electric field due to the p-n junction and the applied bias is small, i.e., the so-called low-field regime [12], then the ER line shape of a CP is related to the third derivative of the undisturbed dielectric function (TDFF, third derivative functional form) and can be written as

$$\frac{\Delta R}{R}(E) = \mathrm{Re}\left(Ce^{i\theta}\left(E - E_{\mathrm{crit}} + i\Gamma\right)^{-m}\right) \tag{2}$$

where Re() describes the real part of the expression in parentheses, C is an amplitude and θ a phase factor, E_{crit} is the energy, and Γ the broadening parameter of the CP, respectively. The exponent m specifies the dimensionality of the CP with $m = 2.5$ for a 3-D CP and $m = 2$ for an excitonic transition [12]. We use $m = 2.5$ for the chalcopyrite absorber layers and $m = 2$ for the buffer layers CdS and i-ZnO due to their high exciton binding energy of 27–31 meV for CdS [13] and $\sim$60 meV for ZnO [14].

In the low-field regime (already present in the sample plus externally applied), the ER amplitude scales quadratically with the electric field but the line shape is invariant. In the case of higher electric fields, the intermediate-field regime [12], line shapes are no longer independent of the electric field and so-called Franz–Keldysh oscillations (FKOs) appear in the ER spectrum.

Manuscript received June 10, 2013; revised August 26, 2013; accepted September 4, 2013. Date of publication October 4, 2013; date of current version December 16, 2013. This work was supported by the Federal Ministry for the Environment, Nature Conservation and Nuclear Safety under Contract 0329585G.

O. Kiowski and W. Witte are with the Zentrum für Sonnenenergie- und Wasserstoff-Forschung Baden-Württemberg (ZSW), Stuttgart 70565, Germany (e-mail: oliver.kiowski@zsw-bw.de; wolfram.witte@zsw-bw.de).

M. Hetterich is with the Institute of Applied Physics, Karlsruhe Institute of Technology, Karlsruhe 76131, Germany (e-mail: michael.hetterich@kit.edu).

M. Powalla is with the Zentrum für Sonnenenergie und Wasserstoff-Forschung Baden-Württemberg (ZSW), Stuttgart 70565, Germany, and also with the Light Technology Institute, Karlsruhe Institute of Technology, Karlsruhe 76131, Germany (e-mail: michael.powalla@zsw-bw.de).

Color versions of one or more of the figures in this paper are available online at http://ieeexplore.ieee.org.

Digital Object Identifier 10.1109/JPHOTOV.2013.2281741

248

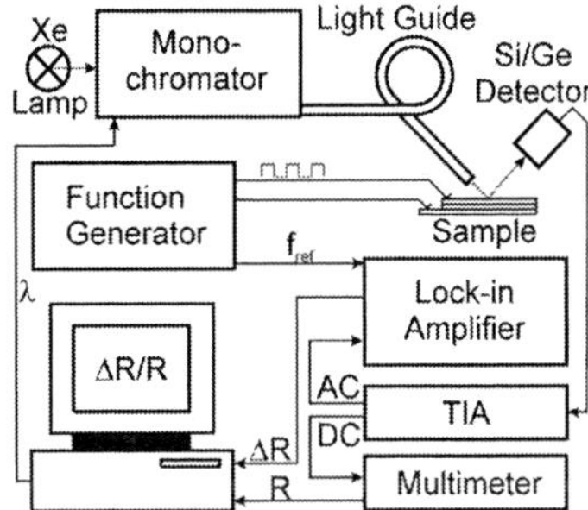

Fig. 1. ER setup. The transimpedance amplifier (TIA) amplifies and separates the ac and the dc components of the signal, which are then measured by a lock-in amplifier and multimeter, respectively.

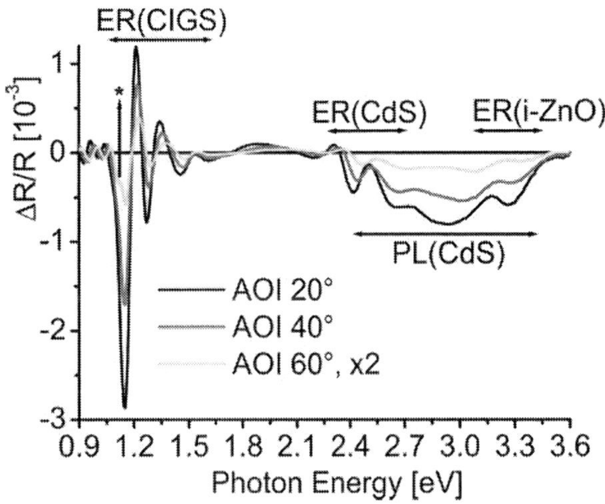

Fig. 2. Typical ER spectra of multistage CIGS/CdS/i-ZnO/ZnO:Al cells for different AOIs. Data for AOI = 60° is magnified by a factor of 2. The asterisk marks a shoulder discussed in the text which is only visible at AOI = 60°.

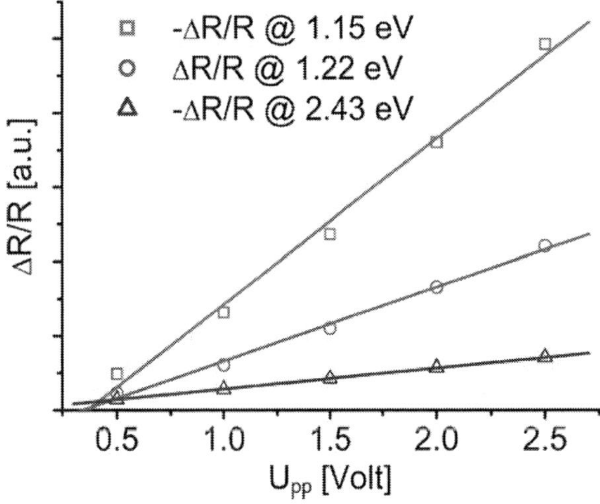

Fig. 3. ER amplitudes at three spectral positions of an ER spectrum versus peak-to-peak square-wave modulation voltage U_{pp}. The linear relation shows that the ER measurements are in the low-field regime and TDFFs can be used to fit the spectra.

II. METHODS

Fig. 1 shows the setup we use to acquire ER spectra. The light of a 100-W Xenon lamp is dispersed by a computer-controlled monochromator and illuminates the sample via a light guide. The light guide randomizes the polarization and allows easy adjustment of the angle of incidence (AOI) for angle-resolved ER. The reflected light is focused onto a Si or Ge photodiode detector. A function generator modulates the electric field of the sample by applying a rectangular reverse ac bias to the sample, typically between 0 and −2 V. All measurements are carried out at room temperature. The optical resolution of the setup is approximately ±3 meV.

CIGS films with a thickness between 2 and 2.5 μm were deposited with an inline multistage co-evaporation process [15] on soda-lime glass covered with 500 nm of sputtered Mo. These cells exhibit a double gradient in the Ga/(Ga+In) ratio (GGI) with an integral GGI as determined by X-ray fluorescence (XRF) of around 0.3 (for the shape of the double gradient see [16, Fig. 5]). The Cu/(Ga+In) ratio (CGI) is around 0.8. Other CIGS films were grown in an inline co-evaporation chamber with approximately the same thickness but without a GGI gradient. These $CuIn_{1-x}Ga_xSe_2$ films have different Ga contents of $x = 0$, 0.3, 0.6, and 1. Absorbers were covered with (thicknesses in nm in parenthesis): CdS(∼50)/i-ZnO(30–60)/ZnO:Al(500). CdS was grown by chemical bath deposition (CBD), the other films were sputtered.

III. RESULTS

Fig. 2 depicts typical ER spectra of a sample with a graded bandgap (efficiency ∼16%) and a CdS/i-ZnO buffer layer at three different AOIs (20°, 40°, and 60° from the surface normal). Each spectrum consists of a measurement with a Ge (0.9–1.4 eV) and Si (1.4–3.6 eV) photodiode detector, merged at 1.4 eV. In order to verify that the obtained ER spectra are within the low-field regime and that the TDFF formalism can be applied, we conducted bias-dependent ER measurements and show the amplitudes at three spectral positions as a function of peak-to-peak voltage U_{pp} in Fig. 3. According to Aspnes et al., the amplitudes of the ER signals scale linearly with an applied voltage U_{pp} and are independent of the dc component U_{DC} and the waveform [12]. In Fig. 3, we vary both U_{DC} and

U_{pp} by applying an AC voltage between 0 and $-U_{pp}$ with $U_{pp} = 0.5 - 2.5$ V. The expected linear relation is obtained. Only the amplitudes of the ER spectrum change, not the line shapes (not shown). In another test, we assumed the maxima and minima of Fig. 2 on the high energy side of the CIGS bandgap (1.16 eV) at AOI = 20° to be FKOs and plotted the number of the extrema versus $(E - E_g)^{3/2}$ (not shown). However, this did not yield a linear relationship as would be expected for FKOs [17]. According to these tests, the presence of FKOs in the ER spectra shown here is unlikely. Interference fringes, e.g., due to light reflected from the Mo back surface emerge at energies below the bandgap energy of CIGS with $E_g = 1.16$ eV as determined by quantum efficiency (QE) measurements. This relation indicates that although ER measurements are self-referencing by plotting

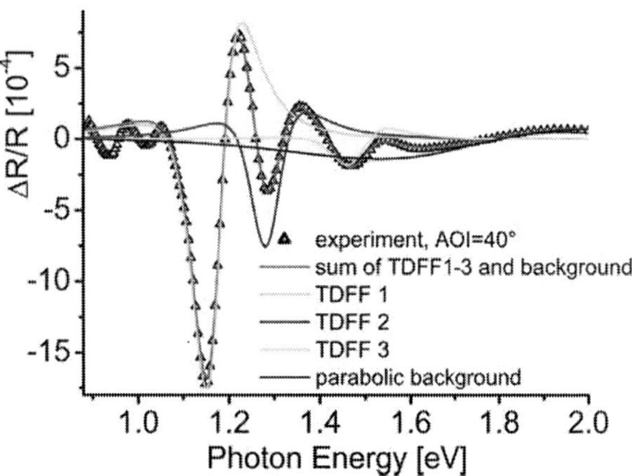

Fig. 4. TDFF fit to the ER signal of CIGS at AOI $= 40°$ from Fig. 2. A quadratic polynomial is used to fit the background. Fitting parameters are listed in Table I.

TABLE I

SUMMARY OF FITTING PARAMETERS E_{crit} (IN eV) AND Γ (IN meV) FOR THE LAYERS CIGS (GRADED), CdS, AND i-ZnO FOR DIFFERENT ANGLES OF INCIDENCE (AOIs)

AOI	CIGS			CdS			i-ZnO
	$E_{\text{crit},1}$	$E_{\text{crit},2}$	$E_{\text{crit},3}$	$E_{\text{crit},1}$	$E_{\text{crit},2}$	$E_{\text{crit},3}$	$E_{\text{crit},1}$
	Γ_1	Γ_2	Γ_3	Γ_1	Γ_2	Γ_3	Γ_1
20°	1.17	1.28	1.46	2.34	2.45	2.62	3.25
	72	74	93	118	122	158	115
40°	1.17	1.29	1.46	2.35	2.44	2.62	3.25
	76	75	80	135	107	167	110
60°	1.15	1.27	1.46	2.35	2.46	2.63	3.25
	79	72	89	123	115	185	119

$\Delta R/R$ and spectral features of the measurement system—e.g., the xenon emission lines—do not show up in the ER spectrum, interference effects do not cancel. By comparison with the reflectance spectrum of a bulk reflectance standard measured with the same setup, we observe that both ΔR and R are affected by interference. We therefore assume that interference is not limited to photon energies below the bandgap but part of the complete ER spectrum. To distinguish ER signals from interference fringes, we measured at different AOIs and fit the spectra with linear or quadratic polynomials (to account for interference fringes with rather long periods). Increasing the AOI increases the R component, which can be understood in terms of the Fresnel equations. The largest fraction of the reflected light intensity results from the air/ZnO:Al interface because of the large difference of refraction index n between air ($n = 1$) and ZnO:Al ($n \approx 2$). The ΔR component decreases for the same reason: increasing the AOI increases the fraction of light that is reflected off the ZnO:Al surface without entering the space charge region. Therefore, the ER signal $\Delta R/R$ strongly diminishes with increasing AOI.

Increasing the AOI shifts all spectral features toward higher energies. However, CP energies E_{crit} and broadening parameters Γ as determined by fitting (2) should remain constant since the material remains the same. The individual fitting functions for the CIGS transitions for AOI $= 40°$ are shown in Fig. 4. The E_{crit} and Γ values for the individual TDFFs of the CIGS, CdS and i-ZnO layers for AOI $= 20°$, $40°$, and $60°$ are listed in Table I.[1] To account for background signals (e.g., interference and photoluminescence, see below), quadratic (see Fig. 4) and linear line shapes were used for CIGS/CdS and i-ZnO CP transitions, respectively. CPs energies agree within ±10 meV and broadening parameters within ±15 meV for CIGS, CdS, and i-ZnO for the different AOI.

<hr>

[1] We assume the TDFF formalism to be applicable to off-normal incidence although the derivation uses normal incidence. We justify this by the good agreement of the CP energies for different AOIs in Table I.

At AOI $= 60°$, a subbandgap shoulder emerges at 1.11 eV (see Fig. 2) which is not taken into account in the fitting process of the CIGS signals. This feature mainly affects the CP energies of $E_{\text{crit},1}$ and $E_{\text{crit},2}$ of CIGS (see Table I), which exhibit lower values compared with the fitting without the shoulder (AOI $= 20°$ and $40°$). The signal could be due to thin-film interference. Interference in this sample is low because of the relatively rough CIGS surface; therefore, the shoulder is only visible at high AOIs and is superimposed by the ER signal at lower AOIs. Another possibility is that this signal is due to electroabsorption (EA). Henninger et $al.$ found two subbandgap transitions for CuInS$_2$ thin-film solar cells deposited by a sequential process about 50 meV below the bandgap [18]. The shoulder in Fig. 2 is also $\sim$50 meV below the bandgap (1.16 eV). They attribute the lower peak to EA of acceptor–donor defects and the higher peak to band-to-band related EA (Franz–Keldysh effect). However, this explanation would indicate that the electric field in the sample is large enough for the Franz–Keldysh effect and therefore for FKOs. This is not in agreement with the results shown in Fig. 3. Therefore, it is more likely that the shoulder is due to thin-film interference. A more detailed investigation and simulation of the electric fields involved are underway.

We ascribe the broad negative background in the spectral range 2.4–3.5 eV (see Fig. 2) to photoluminescence (PL) of the CdS layer. We verify this by putting narrow band-pass filters in front of the detector with their maximum transmission equal to the monochromatic excitation photon energy. For excitation photon energies above the bandgap of CdS ($\sim$2.4 eV), this filter completely blocks the PL which is centered on the bandgap of CdS and transmits only the ER signal which has the same photon energy as the excitation light. We also investigate cells without a CdS layer (Mo/CIGS/i-ZnO/ZnO:Al, not shown) which exhibit no broad background signal. Since the detector is not wavelength sensitive between 2.4–3.5 eV, the PL signal is added to the ER signal and $\Delta R/R$ becomes

$$\frac{\Delta R + \Delta PL}{R + PL}(U, E) \approx \frac{\Delta R + \Delta PL}{R}(U, E). \qquad (3)$$

Where PL is the photoluminescence intensity and ΔPL its change due to the ac bias, respectively. The photoluminescence is modulated by the ac bias we apply to the solar cell and is lower at a bias of -2 V, compared to 0 V. Photogenerated charge

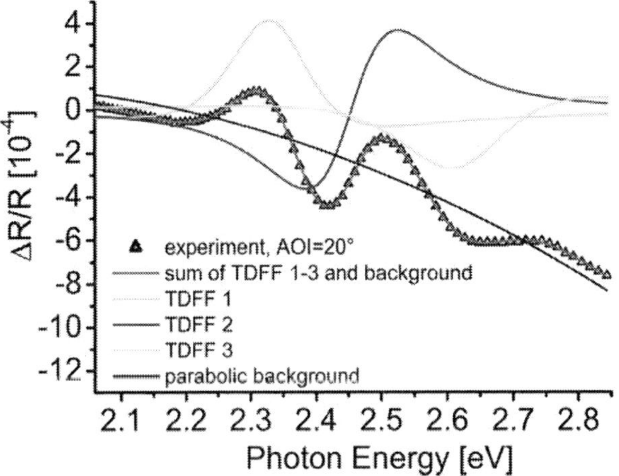

Fig. 5. TDFF fit to the ER signal of CdS at AOI $= 20°$ from Fig. 2. A quadratic polynomial is used to fit the background. Fitting parameters are listed in Table I.

carriers are more effectively separated at negative bias and cannot recombine radiatively. Hence, $\Delta PL = PL(-2\ V,E) - PL(0,E)$ is negative and renders the enumerator of (3), and therefore the ER signal, negative (if $\Delta R < |\Delta PL|$, as is the case). PL can be omitted in the denominator of (3) since R is much larger than the photoluminescence. Placing the monochromator between sample and detector should reduce a background signal due to PL. However, this might require a higher incident light intensity onto the sample in order to get a good signal-to-noise ratio.

Paulson *et al.* determined the three lowest CP transitions by ellipsometry to 1.17–1.18, 1.21–1.23, and 1.45–1.48 eV for CIGS with an integral GGI of 0.31, no GGI gradient, and a CGI of 0.93 [19]. The first and the last value closely match our findings (see Table I). The reason for the deviation of $E_{\mathrm{crit},2}$ is not clear but might be related to the vertical GGI gradient in our samples, differences in the CGI value (0.8 versus 0.93), or the assumption of a simple parabolic background.

Fig. 5 depicts the best fit of three TDFF functions plus a parabolic background used for the ER signal of the CdS buffer layer at AOI $= 20°$. We attribute the three CP energies of $\sim$2.35, 2.45, and 2.62 eV (mean values from Table I) to the $n = 1$ excitonic transitions at the E_0 edge of hexagonal CdS. Imada *et al.* obtained 2.47–2.50, 2.49–2.52, and 2.54–2.57 eV for a hexagonal CdS single crystal at room temperature by PR [13]. (They used three TDFFs with $m = 2$ and three TDFFs with $m = 2.5$.) Cardona *et al.* applied electrolyte electroreflectance (EER) on hexagonal CdS single crystals and epitaxially grown layers of cubic CdS [20]. For the former, the values were slightly lower than the data from Imada *et al.* (2.45, 2.47, and 2.53 eV). For the latter, only one value is presented (2.42 eV), though spin-orbit splitting and therefore two transitions are expected in cubic CdS. Our ER measurements of the CdS buffer layer resemble much more the EER spectrum of hexagonal CdS than of cubic CdS depicted in [20], although our signals are shifted in energy and are broader. Compared to a single crystal, CBD-CdS layers in a working solar cell are much thinner, nanocrystalline,

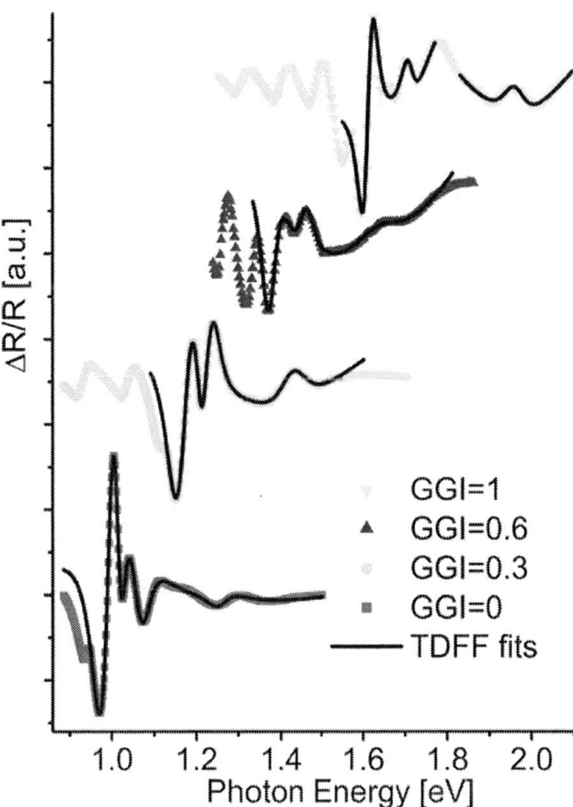

Fig. 6. Experimental ER spectra and TDFF fits for CP transitions in CIGS with different integral GGI at AOI $= 20°$. Spectra are offset on the y-axis for clarity.

"contaminated" by CdO and Cd(OH)$_2$ from the CBD process and doped with Cu and Se which diffuses from the CIGS [21], [22]. These effects could influence the energetic position of CPs and the broadening parameter Γ. Abou-Ras *et al.* investigated the crystal structure of our CBD-CdS layers by electron diffraction in a transmission electron microscope and found the hexagonal modification [21].

We attribute the highest energy feature of the ER spectrum in Fig. 2 to the i-ZnO layer because there is no such signal present in solar cells without this layer (not shown). Sputtered ZnO films are preferably oriented with the crystallographic c-axis perpendicular to the surface. However, since we use unpolarized light, our ER spectrum is a linear combination of the ER spectrum for the electric field vector being parallel and perpendicular to c. Cardona *et al.* measured EER spectra for both orientations [20]. A combination of both spectra would cancel out some spectral features and could explain why we measure only one broad CP for i-ZnO, whereas three excitonic transitions are expected. Cardona *et al.* obtained 2 CP energies (3.306 and 3.340 eV). A more recent study on reactively sputtered epitaxial ZnO layers with a thickness of ca. 300 nm showed a bandgap between 3.10 and 3.26 eV, depending on the oxygen partial pressure [23].

Fig. 6 depicts ER spectra for samples without bandgap grading and with integral GGI values of 0, 0.3, 0.6, and 1. The AOI for all spectra is 20°. The spectra for 40° and 60° were also fitted

251

TABLE II

AVERAGE FITTING PARAMETERS E_{crit} (IN eV) AND Γ (IN meV) FOR NONGRADED CIGS ABSORBERS FOR DIFFERENT GGI RATIOS.

GGI	$E_{\mathrm{crit},1}$ Γ_1	$E_{\mathrm{crit},2}$ Γ_2	$E_{\mathrm{crit},3}$ Γ_3	$E_{\mathrm{crit},4}$ Γ_4	E_g
0	0.99 40	(1.02) (29)	(1.07) (51)	1.26 54	0.98
0.3	1.18 43	1.23 38	1.44 71	- -	1.19
0.6	1.39 37	1.47 40	1.64 112	- -	1.40
1	1.63 30	1.72 42	1.96 60	- -	1.64

The average was taken from 3 measurements at AOIs of 20°, 40°, and 60°. Bandgap energies E_g were determined by QE measurements.

(not shown) and the average values for E_{crit} and Γ are listed in Table II and compared to the bandgap E_g (determined by QE measurements).

The fitting process is ambiguous since all samples exhibit large interference modes and/or EA features (see the aforementioned discussion) which, e.g., for GGI = 0.6, are of the same amplitude as the ER signal. The reason for the former is probably the smoother CIGS surface due to the lower deposition temperature (compared to the graded sample). For GGI = 0 the crystal-field splitting of the valence band is too small to be resolved at room temperature; therefore, only two CPs are expected [19]. Paulson *et al.* found CP energies of 1.02–1.03 eV and 1.25–1.27 eV [19]. Shay *et al.* reported a bandgap of 1.01 eV, determined by ER at 77 K [5]. Qualitatively, their ER spectrum is similar to ours except for a factor of -1 and two additional oscillations centered around 0.94 and 1.06 eV in Fig. 6. Even if we assume these two additional signals to be due to interference effects, fitting only two TDFFs to the remaining line shape is difficult. However, since the literature does not support $E_{\mathrm{crit},2}$ and $E_{\mathrm{crit},3}$ for GGI = 0, they are listed with parenthesis in Table II. For GGI = 1, $E_{\mathrm{crit},i}$ = 1.721/1.806/2.012 eV for i = 1, 2, 3 were reported for a bulk crystal at 77 K by ER [6] and 1.69/1.77/1.98 eV for a CuGaSe$_2$ thin film at room temperature by ellipsometry [19]. Our values are systematically lower. For $E_{\mathrm{crit},4}$, a separate background had to be used for a good fit. The sample with GGI = 0.6 can only be compared to literature values via an empirical bowing curve linking the GGI values with the CP energies. Such a relation yields 1.36/1.45/1.68 eV [19] which is in fair agreement with our values, given that the GGI value of 0.6 is only approximate. A GGI of 0.63 would yield 1.38/1.47/1.70 eV. The CP energies (especially $E_{\mathrm{crit},2}$) obtained for the nongraded CIGS absorber with GGI = 0.3 match the results from Paulson *et al.* better than those of the graded sample. (They also used nongraded CIGS.) It is generally assumed that the bandgap determined by QE represents the smallest bandgap in a graded absorber (in our case: the notch of the double grading profile). Comparing those bandgaps of the graded (1.16 eV) and the nongraded (1.19 eV) CIGS absorber shows that the notch is approximately 30 meV lower. The difference in the ER-determined bandgaps is smaller ($\sim$10 meV), indicating that the origin of the ER signal of the absorber is closer to a point, where the grading profiles intersect, i.e., close to the surface or closer to the bulk of the CIGS absorber. In order to further clarify this aspect simulations are underway.

The broadening parameters Γ for almost all CP energies are lower than those of the graded CIGS absorber. We account this for lattice strain due to the grading [6].

The systematic error introduced by interference modes, EA features, and the chosen background function for the nongraded samples is difficult to quantify. The statistical error for the CP energies and broadening parameters could be estimated from the scatter of the values for the different AOIs. All data are within ±15 meV of the values given in Table II.

IV. CONCLUSION

We measured ER spectra of working CIGS thin-film solar cells and were able to distinguish i-ZnO, CdS, and CIGS layers. If Fabry–Perot interferences and EA features are small and FKOs are absent, CP energies of the layers could be extracted by fitting TDFFs. Angle-resolved ER helped to increase the reliability of the fitting process. We determined CP and broadening energies for i-ZnO, CdS, and for graded (integral GGI = 0.3) CIGS. Three CPs were obtained for CIGS and CdS and one for i-ZnO. We also investigated the CP energies and broadening parameters for nongraded (GGI = 0, 0.3, 0.6, and 1) CIGS absorbers. Interference effects are much stronger for these samples and broadening parameters are lower. The former is possibly due to a lower surface roughness, the latter could be a result of strain induced by the grading. The ER-determined bandgaps of a graded and a nongraded CIGS sample with an integral GGI of 0.3 are similar, whereas the QE-determined bandgaps differ by 30 meV. The ER signal of the CIGS absorber therefore presumably originates from a region closer to the CIGS/buffer heterointerface or the bulk of the absorber where the GGI ratio of both samples is comparable.

ACKNOWLEDGMENT

The authors would like to thank the CIGS team at the ZSW for preparing the samples. O. Kiowski would also like to thank E. Staton and T. Magorian Friedlmeier for proofreading.

REFERENCES

[1] P. Jackson, D. Hariskos, E. Lotter, S. Paetel, R. Würz, R. Menner, W. Wischmann, and M. Powalla, "New world record efficiency for Cu(In,Ga)Se$_2$ thin-film solar cells beyond 20%," *Prog. Photovolt. Res. Appl.*, vol. 19, pp. 894–897, 2011.

[2] EMPA Press Release. Dübendorf, Switzerland. (2013, Jan. 17). [Online]. Available: http://www.empa.ch/plugin/template/empa/*/131441

[3] M. A. Green, K. Emery, Y. Hishikawa, W. Warta, and E. D. Dunlop, "Solar cell efficiency tables (ver. 41)," *Prog. Photovolt: Res. Appl.*, vol. 21, pp. 606–614, 2013.

[4] Manz Press Release. Reutlingen, Germany. (2012, Oct. 3). [Online]. Available: http://www.manz.com/media/news/archive/2012/manz-presents-cigs-world-record-module-with-efficiency-of-146-at-pv-taiwan-425

[5] J. L. Shay and H. L. Kasper, "Direct observation of Cu d levels in I–III–VI$_2$ compounds," *Phys. Rev. Lett.*, vol. 29, pp. 1162–1164, 1972.

[6] S. Shirakata and S. Chichibu, "Photoreflectance of Cu based I–III–VI$_2$ heteroepitaxial layers grown by metalorganic chemical vapor deposition," *J. Appl. Phys.*, vol. 79, pp. 2043–2054, 1996.

[7] D. Fuertes Marrón, E. Cánovas, M. Y. Levy, A. Martí, A. Luque, M. Afshar, J. Albert, S. Lehmann, D. Abou-Ras, S. Sadewasser, and N. Barreau, "Optoelectronic evaluation of the nanostructuring approach to chalcopyrite-based intermediate band materials," *Sol. Energ. Mat. Sol. Cells*, vol. 94, pp. 1912–1918, 2010.

[8] S. Theodoropoulou, D. Papadimitriou, A. G. Mamalis, D. E. Manolakos, R. Klenk, and M.-C. Lux-Steiner, "Band-gap energies and strain effects in $CuIn_{1-x}Ga_xS_2$ based solar cells," *Semicond. Sci. Technol.*, vol. 22, pp. 933–940, 2007.

[9] A. M. Chaparro, A. C. Maffiotte, M. T. Gutierrez, J. Herrero, J. Klaer, K. Siemer, and D. Bräunig, "Characterisation of $CuInS_2$/ZnSe junctions by XPS and electroreflectance," *Thin Solid Films*, vol. 387, pp. 104–107, 2001.

[10] P. J. Dale, A. P. Samantilleke, G. Zoppi, I. Forbes, and L. M. Peter, "Characterization of $CuInSe_2$ material and devices: Comparison of thermal and electrochemically prepared absorber layers," *J. Phys. D, Appl. Phys.*, vol. 41, pp. 085105-1–085105-8, 2008.

[11] D. D. Shivagan, P. J. Dale, A. P. Samantilleke, and L. M. Peter, "Electrodeposition of chalcopyrite films from ionic liquid electrolytes," *Thin Solid Films*, vol. 515, pp. 5899–5903, 2007.

[12] D. E. Aspnes, "Third derivative modulation spectroscopy with low-field electroreflectance," *Surface Sci.*, vol. 37, pp. 418–442, 1973.

[13] A. Imada, S. Ozaki, and S. Adachi, "Photoreflectance spectroscopy of wurtzite CdS," *J. Appl. Phys.*, vol. 92, pp. 1793–1798, 2002.

[14] T. Makino, K. Tamura, C. H. Chia, Y. Segawa, M. Kawasaki, A. Ohtomo, and H. Koinuma, "Temperature quenching of exciton luminescence intensity in ZnO/(Mg,Zn)O multiple quantum wells," *J. Appl. Phys.*, vol. 93, pp. 5929–5933, 2003.

[15] G. Voorwinden, R. Kniese, P. Jackson, and M. Powalla, "In-line Cu(In,Ga)Se$_2$ co-evaporation process on 30 cm x 30 cm substrates with multiple deposition stages," in *Proc. 22nd Eur. Conf. Photovoltaic Energy Convers.*, Milan, Italy, 2007, pp. 2115–2118.

[16] M. Müller, S. Ribbe, T. Hempel, F. Bertram, J. Christen, W. Witte, S. Paetel, and M. Powalla, "Investigation of vertical compositional gradients in Cu(In,Ga)Se$_2$ by highly spatially and spectrally resolved cathodoluminescence microscopy," *Thin Solid Films*, vol. 535, pp. 270–274, 2013.

[17] D. E. Aspnes, "Schottky-barrier electroreflectance of Ge: Nondegenerate and orbitally degenerate critical points," *Phys. Rev. B*, vol. 12, pp. 2297–2310, 1975.

[18] R. Henninger, J. Klaer, K. Siemer, J. Bruns, and D. Bräuig, "Electroreflectance of $CuInS_2$ thin-film solar cells and dependence on process parameters," *J. Appl. Phys.*, vol. 89, pp. 3049–3054, 2001.

[19] P. D. Paulson, R. W. Birkmire, and W. N. Shafarman, "Optical characterization of $CuIn_{1-x}Ga_xSe_2$ alloy thin films by spectroscopic ellipsometry," *J. Appl. Phys.*, vol. 94, pp. 879–888, 2003.

[20] M. Cardona, K. L. Shaklee, and F. H. Pollak, "Electroreflectance at a semiconductor-electrolyte interface," *Phys. Rev.*, vol. 154, pp. 696–720, 1967.

[21] D. Abou-Ras, G. Kostorz, A. Romeo, D. Rudmann, and A. N. Tiwari, "Structural and chemical investigations of CBD- and PVD-CdS buffer layers and interfaces in Cu(In,Ga)Se$_2$-based thin-film solar cells," *Thin Solid Films*, vol. 480–481, pp. 118–123, 2005.

[22] S. Pookpanratana, I. Repins, M. Bär, L. Weinhardt, Y. Zhang, R. Félix, M. Blum, W. Yang, and C. Heske, "CdS/Cu(In,Ga)Se$_2$ interface formation in high-efficiency thin film solar cells," *Appl. Phys. Lett.*, vol. 97, pp. 074101-1–074101-3, 2010.

[23] H. Liu, F. Zeng, Y. Lin, G. Wang, and F. Pan, "Correlation of oxygen vacancy variations to band gap changes in epitaxial ZnO thin films," *Appl. Phys. Lett.*, vol. 102, pp. 181908-1–181908-4, 2013.

Authors' photographs and biographies not available at the time of publication.

High-Speed Imaging/Mapping Spectroscopic Ellipsometry for In-Line Analysis of Roll-to-Roll Thin-Film Photovoltaics

Ambalanath Shan, Miklós Fried, György Juhász, Csaba Major, Olivér Polgár, Ágoston Németh, Péter Petrik, Lila R. Dahal, Jie Chen, Zhiquan Huang, Nikolas J. Podraza, and Robert W. Collins

Abstract—**An expanded-beam spectroscopic ellipsometer has been developed and applied toward *in situ* high-speed imaging/mapping analysis of large area spatial uniformity for multilayer coated substrates in roll-to-roll thin-film photovoltaics (PV). Slower speed instrumentation available in such analyses applies a 1-D detector array for spectroscopic mapping and involves widthwise translation of the ellipsometer optics over the moving coated substrate surface, measuring point-by-point in a time-consuming process. The expanded-beam instrument employs instead a 2-D detector array with no moving optics, exploiting one array index for spectroscopy and the second array index for line imaging across the width of a large area sample. Thus, the instrument enables imaging width-wise and mapping length-wise for uniformity evaluation at the high linear substrate speeds required for real-time, *in situ*, and online analysis in roll-to-roll thin-film PV. In this investigation, we employ the expanded beam technique to characterize the uniformity of the Ag, ZnO, and n-type hydrogenated amorphous silicon (a-Si:H) layers of an a-Si:H n-i-p structure deposited on a flexible polyimide substrate in the roll-to-roll configuration. Spectroscopic ellipsometry data across a line image were collected as the substrate was translated by a roll-to-roll mechanism. Coated areas as large as 12 cm $\times$ 45 cm were analyzed in this study for layer thickness and optical properties by applying the appropriate analytical models for the complex dielectric functions of the Ag, ZnO, and n-type a-Si:H layers.**

Index Terms—**Ellipsometry, photovoltaic cells, thin film.**

Manuscript received July 12, 2013; revised September 9, 2013; accepted September 24, 2013. Date of publication October 22, 2013; date of current version December 16, 2013. The instrumentation development at the University of Toledo was supported by the State of Ohio's Wright Centers of Innovation Program. This work was also supported by the Hungarian National Development Agency under Project KMR_12_1_2012_0225.

A. Shan, J. Chen, Z. Huang, N. J. Podraza, and R. W. Collins are with the Department of Physics and Astronomy, Center for Photovoltaics Innovation and Commercialization, University of Toledo, Toledo, OH 43606 USA (e-mail: ashan@utnet.utoledo.edu; jie.chen3@rockets.utoledo.edu; Zhiquan.Huang@rockets.utoledo.edu; Nikolas.Podraza@utoledo.edu; robert.collins@utoledo.edu).

M. Fried, G. Juhász, C. Major, O. Polgár, A. Németh, and P. Petrik are with the Institute for Technical Physics and Materials Science, Research Centre for Natural Sciences, Budapest H-1525, Hungary (e-mail: fried@mfa.kfki.hu; juhaszgy@mfa.kfki.hu; major@mfa.kfki.hu; polgaro@mfa.kfki.hu; nemeth@mfa.kfki.hu; petrik@mfa.kfki.hu).

L. R. Dahal was with the Department of Physics and Astronomy, Center for Photovoltaics Innovation and Commercialization, University of Toledo, Toledo, OH 43606 USA. He is now with NSG-Pilkington Company, Northwood, OH, USA (e-mail: Lila.Dahal@rockets.utoledo.edu).

Color versions of one or more of the figures in this paper are available online at http://ieeexplore.ieee.org.

Digital Object Identifier 10.1109/JPHOTOV.2013.2284380

I. Introduction

THE highest efficiencies achievable for laboratory-scale thin-film solar cells are often well above those of the best production modules for a given photovoltaics (PV) technology. Thus, in the commercialization of thin-film PV technologies, many key problems are related to manufacturing scale up. The efficiency difference can be caused by multiple nonuniformities of the material's properties over the module area resulting from the processing steps of individual layer components. A limitation of some of the most powerful mapping measurements, such as Kelvin probe scanning for surface potential and laser beam scanning for induced currents, derives from the requirements of first forming the junction, and then making near or full electrical contact to the cell structure. Contactless single-spot optical measurements with analytical power such as spectroscopic ellipsometry (SE) suffer from long mapping times as a result of the need for incident beam polarization state modulation or reflected beam polarization state detection. Thus, in-line 2-D mapping with point-by-point SE at the desired speeds and spatial resolutions is not possible.

In this paper, we demonstrate a high-speed and potentially high-resolution measurement method to monitor thin-film PV fabrication processes in-line over large areas based on novel line imaging SE. As an optical probe, SE determines the angle-of-incidence dependent relative (p-s) amplitude ratios $\tan\psi$, and phase difference (p-s) shifts Δ observed upon specular reflection of polarized light from a planar surface. Thus, conventional ellipsometry applies a collimated light beam with a well-defined angle of incidence at the surface. Here, we describe the design and application of an SE method fundamentally different from conventional techniques [1]–[3].

II. Instrument Design and Calibration

A. Instrument Design

Fig. 1 depicts a schematic of the instrument and its integration into the optical station of a roll-to-roll system for fabrication of thin-film solar cell structures. In the reflection SE method applied here, a diverging beam of polarized light from a bright broad-band point source is focused using a spherical mirror to produce a converging beam that illuminates the roll-to-roll coated substrate inside the chamber. Using a rectangular aperture directly after the source, the expanded beam is defined as a narrow stripe in order to illuminate an area of $\sim$1 cm (along

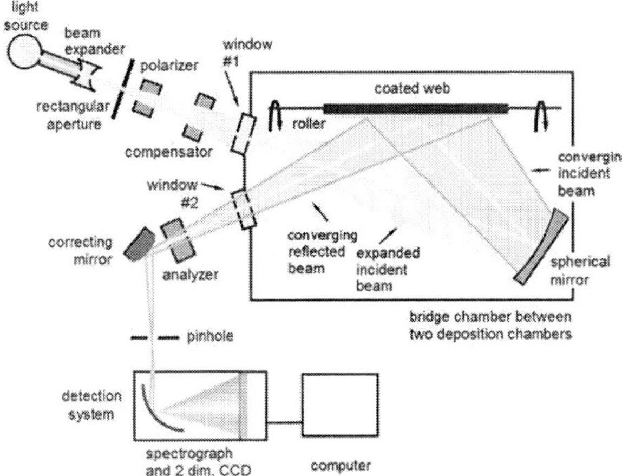

Fig. 1. Expanded beam system for imaging/mapping SE mounted in line at an optical station in a cassette roll-to-roll cluster tool.

the length) $\times$ 12 cm (across the width) of the coated substrate. A nanowire grid polarizer placed after the aperture generates high-purity linearly polarized rays from the incident unpolarized diverging beam. The spherical mirror directs these rays to the sample where they first reflect, with an angle of incidence depending on location across the coated substrate width, and then converge through a second polarizer (or analyzer) with the focal point at a pin hole. Recently, a rotating compensator, consisting of a MgF$_2$ biplate, has been introduced into the beam path for improved accuracy as shown in Fig. 1. This enables the determination of both sin Δ and cos Δ (rather than simply cos Δ as in a rotating polarizer instrument). Angle of incidence selection, or equivalently imaging of the illuminated surface, is performed by the pin hole, acting as a camera whose spatial resolution depends on the pin-hole diameter. By projecting the transmitted image of the substrate surface length-wise along the slit of an imaging spectrograph, the image can be dispersed by a grating onto a charge-coupled device (CCD). Thus, the instrument produces spatial information along one index of the CCD array simultaneously with spectroscopic information along the orthogonal index.

B. Instrument Calibration

In addition to the coated substrate, any mirrors in the system between the two polarizers will change the polarization state upon reflection. This polarization change must be measured in calibration, a procedure in which its dependences on image location and wavelength, i.e., on the vertical and horizontal CCD pixel indices, respectively, are determined. In addition, an angle of incidence calibration is required, which associates an individual CCD pixel row with a specific angle. The two calibrations are performed simultaneously via well-known optimally selected samples that are mounted at the coated substrate position. The calibration samples are three crystalline silicon (c-Si) wafers having different thicknesses of thermal oxide (SiO$_2$). Mirror effects are calculated using the product $\rho_{\mathrm{eff}} = \rho_k \rho_m$, where $\rho_j = r_{pj}/r_{sj} = \tan\psi_j \exp(i\Delta_j)$ $(j = k, m)$ are the com-

plex amplitude reflection ratios (p:s) for the known calibration samples ($k = 1,2,3$) and for the single spherical mirror (m) to be calibrated. In addition, r_{pj} and r_{sj} denote the p and s Fresnel complex amplitude reflection coefficients for light linearly polarized parallel (p) and perpendicular (s) to the plane of incidence, and $\tan\psi_j$ and Δ_j denote the relative amplitude ratios and phase difference shifts upon specular reflection. This approach is based on the assumption that the p and s linear polarization eigenmodes are the same for reflections from the spherical mirror and the sample shown in Fig. 1.

By calibrating with three successive c-Si/SiO$_2$ samples having different thicknesses (d_1, d_2, d_3), six spectra or 6N ($\psi_{\mathrm{eff},i}$, $\Delta_{\mathrm{eff},i}$) values can be obtained for each sample location, where $i = 1, \ldots, N$ is the wavelength index. In the analysis, $2N + 4$ unknown values $\{(\psi_{m,i}, \Delta_{m,i}), i = 1, \ldots, N; \theta, d_1, d_2, d_3\}$ must be determined by fitting in order to achieve the simultaneous mirror and angle of incidence θ calibration at the given sample location. A calibration can be performed for each CCD pixel; however, improved signal-to-noise ratio is obtained by summing the irradiances according to pixel groups, in consideration of the desired spatial and spectral resolution of the instrument. After an initial calibration attempt, the values are smoothed as functions of sample position and wavelength using polynomials in order to reduce statistical errors. Smooth variations are expected for the angle of incidence and for the $\{\psi_m, \Delta_m\}$ calibration values. Window corrections can be performed simultaneously with the polarizer and analyzer azimuthal calibration methods [4].

III. PROCEDURE, RESULTS, AND DISCUSSION

The capability of the instrument is demonstrated first by analyzing a multilayer consisting of Ag/ZnO/(n-type a-Si:H) deposited onto a polyimide polymer substrate roll. This sample structure comprises a standard back-reflector and the initial amorphous layer of a thin-film a-Si:H solar cell in the n-i-p substrate configuration. In this configuration, the p-layer is the last semiconductor layer in the deposition sequence [5], which is used conventionally for Si:H-based solar cells on flexible substrates. The Ag and ZnO films were deposited using radio-frequency (RF) magnetron sputtering at a substrate temperature of 24 °C and an Ar pressure of 5 mTorr. The RF power densities at the target and the deposition times for the Ag and ZnO were varied to obtain the requisite thicknesses, yielding 0.003 and 0.004 W/cm^2, respectively, and $\sim$30 min in each case. At a roll speed of 0.02 cm/s, the final average thickness of Ag was $\sim$0.5 μm and that of ZnO was 0.4 μm. The n-type a-Si:H layer was fabricated by applying an RF plasma-enhanced chemical vapor deposition (PECVD) process with flows of silane (SiH$_4$) and phosphine (PH$_3$) gases set for a ratio of D = [PH$_3$]/[SiH$_4$] = 0.005. An elevated substrate temperature of 200 °C, a total pressure of 350 mTorr, and an RF power density of 0.0095 W/cm^2 (lowest possible for this system) were used. The desired n-layer thickness of $\sim$30 nm was achieved at the higher roll speed of 0.12 cm/s.

A multichambered load-locked system was used for all depositions, ensuring that the entire process was accomplished without exposure to atmosphere. The resulting product was a polyimide/Ag/ZnO/(n-type a-Si:H) roll 12 cm wide with a length of 45 cm. Mapping SE was performed starting from the leading end of the coated substrate roll over the 1.3 to 3.3 eV photon energy range (376 to 954 nm wavelength range) with a spectral resolution of 5.4 nm. This spectral range is of interest for probing many of the component materials of thin-film solar cells, and the optical properties obtained over this range can be used to simulate the quantum efficiency, and the reflectance and absorbance losses [6]. The angle of incidence at the sample surface varied from 67.4° to 72.2° across the 12 cm dimension of the beam (parallel to the plane of incidence) with an angular resolution $\delta\theta$ of 0.16°; the variations along the 1 cm dimension (normal to the plane of incidence) are negligible in comparison to $\delta\theta$. Accurate analysis of the structure and optical properties of thin films using this SE instrument thereby provides sufficient information for simulating the device's performance over the mapped area.

The mapping results that are described in the three succeeding sections are obtained by least-squares regression analysis of the (ψ, Δ) maps obtained from the measured $\rho_{\text{eff}} = \tan\psi_{\text{eff}} \exp(i\Delta_{\text{eff}})$ data via the mirror (m) calibration correction. Thus, the correction was performed according to the expression, $\rho = \tan\psi \exp(i\Delta) = \rho_{\text{eff}}/\rho_m$, where ρ_m is the complex amplitude reflection ratio ($p{:}s$) that describes the mirror reflection, having the same p–s coordinate system as the sample. In least-squares fitting, a set of wavelength independent parameters are deduced including bulk, interface roughness, and surface roughness thicknesses, as well as parameters in analytical expressions for the complex dielectric function.

The maps presented for different component layers have been cropped to ~9 cm × 36 cm, where the mean square errors in the SE fitting are acceptable—excluding the edges of the roll and the leading end of the roll. These regions may be interpretable in the future by incorporation of thickness distributions into the modeling, as well as by an analysis of depolarization [7]. Finally, it should be noted that identically sized maps depict results over the same area of the sample structure.

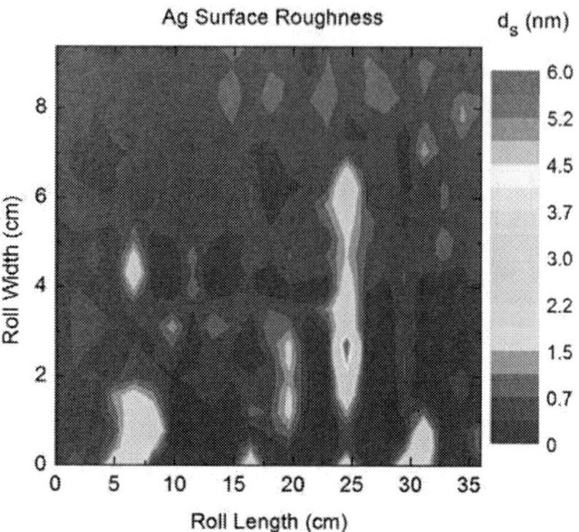

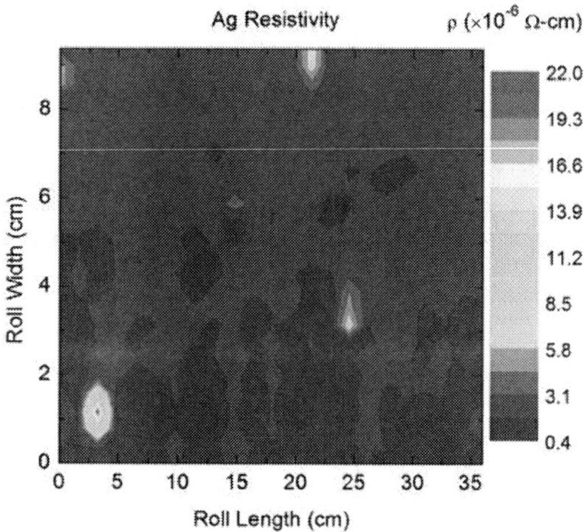

Fig. 2. (Top) Maps of surface roughness layer thickness and (bottom) resistivity for opaque Ag, the first thin film of the multilayer structure. The horizontal axis is the direction of roll advance. The vertical axis is the width of the roll, from which edge-to-edge uniformity of the film is evaluated.

A. Silver Layer

The opaque Ag film is investigated by applying a one-layer bulk/surface-roughness model. The Drude expression was used to simulate the complex dielectric function $\varepsilon = \varepsilon_1 + i\varepsilon_2$ of the bulk Ag with three photon-energy-independent free parameters, including the constant contribution to the real part $\varepsilon_{1\infty}$, the resistivity ρ, and the electron relaxation time τ. The ε spectra of the surface roughness layer of thickness d_s is described by the Bruggeman effective medium approximation (EMA), assuming a 50/50 vol.% mixture of (underlying bulk Ag)/void. Thus, least-squares regression analysis of the experimental (ψ, Δ) spectra provide $\{d_s, \varepsilon_{1\infty}, \rho, \tau\}$. Fig. 2 shows maps of d_s and ρ, and Fig. 3 shows the experimental and best fit (ψ, Δ) spectra at a selected sample location. Bands across the coated substrate width are observed having larger roughness and higher resistivity. These bands, possibly arising from a wrinkling of the polymer, require further study.

B. ZnO Layer

The Ag/ZnO structure is investigated using a two-layer model consisting of ZnO bulk and surface roughness layers of thicknesses, d_b and d_s, respectively. The ε_1 and ε_2 spectra of ZnO are simulated using a complex function that includes both a Sellmeier term in the real part ε_1 and a critical point (CP) oscillator in both real and imaginary parts, ε_1 and ε_2. The CP oscillator, applied to model the ε_2 absorption onset of the ZnO, is based on the assumption of parabolic bands in the electron energy-wavevector $[E(\mathbf{k})]$ band structure, whereas both the CP oscillator and Sellmeier contribute to the dispersion $\varepsilon_1(E)$. The total number of free parameters is nine, including d_s and d_b that describe the structure, three parameters (including $\varepsilon_{1\infty}$) that describe the Sellmeier term, and four parameters that describe the CP term. The two dielectric function terms include amplitudes and resonance energies, indicated by A_j and E_j ($j = 0$: CP; $j = 1$: Sellmeier), and the CP term includes in addition broadening

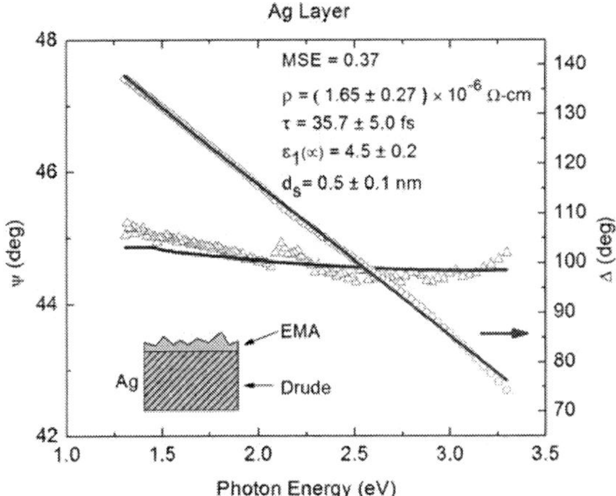

Fig. 3. Example best fit (lines) to experimental (ψ, Δ) spectra (points) via MSE minimization for an opaque Ag film at a single point on the map of Fig. 2; a one-layer model is used with bulk/roughness layer dielectric functions from Drude/EMA expressions, respectively.

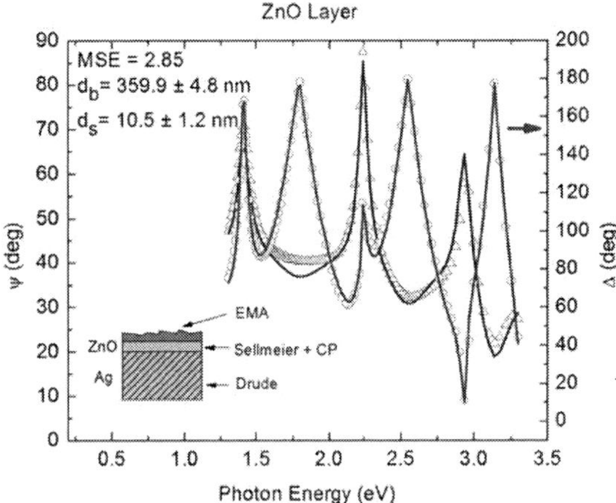

Fig. 5. Example best fit (lines) to experimental (ψ, Δ) spectra (points) via MSE minimization for the Ag/ZnO structure at a single point on the map of Fig. 4; Sellmeier and CP terms are used to describe the ZnO dielectric function.

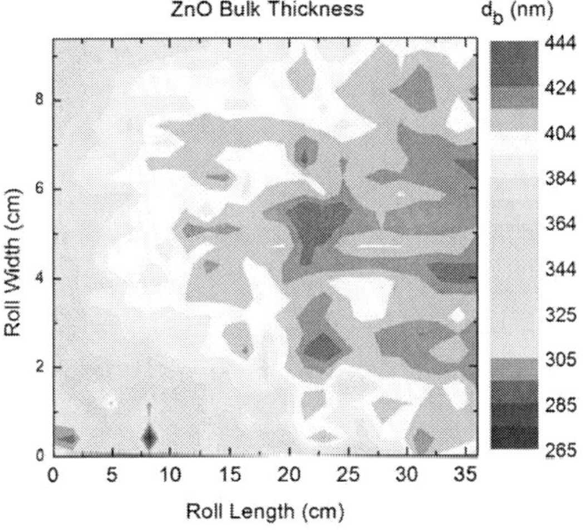

Fig. 4. Map of the bulk layer thickness for ZnO, the second film of the multilayer a-Si:H n-i-p solar cell structure.

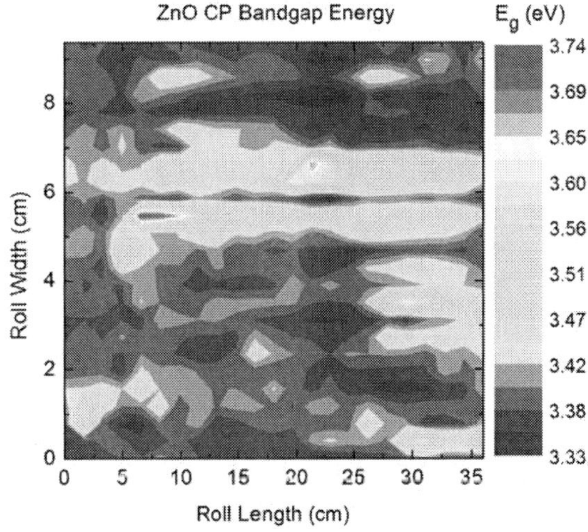

Fig. 6. Map of the band gap CP energy for ZnO, the second film of the multilayer a-Si:H n-i-p solar cell structure.

and phase parameters, indicated by Γ_0 and ϕ_0. (In the fitting, the CP exponent is held constant at 0.5.)

In Fig. 4, a map of the ZnO bulk layer thickness is shown, and in Fig. 5, a representative best fit at a single point is shown. Maps in the parameters of the Sellmeier term are not displayed, however. Since this term incorporates a resonance energy E_1 well above the instrument's spectral range, the parameters do not directly reveal physical information of interest. Fig. 6 depicts the CP energy E_0, describing the band gap of ZnO. A blue shift of E_0 can reveal a shift of the Fermi level as it enters the conduction band upon degenerate doping. A map of the ZnO bulk layer index of refraction n evaluated at 700 nm, $n(700\ \text{nm})$ is shown in Fig. 7, and is of interest due to its relevance in characterizing the operation of the ZnO as a back reflector in the thin-film Si:H solar cell. The ~9 cm × 36 cm $\{d_b, n(700\ \text{nm})\}$ maps in Figs. 4 and 7 exhibit clear features in the lower left

corners. These may be due to a defect in the roll that causes beam distortion and measurement deviations. Further work is underway in the detection of such features and analysis of their origins.

Improvements in the mean square error (MSE) of the best fit in the analysis of the Ag/ZnO structure can be obtained by incorporating an interface layer between the two films, yielding a three-layer model. This interface layer is important as it leads to absorption and dissipation, and thus generates a loss that inhibits optimum operation of the back reflector. A single thickness d_i as a structural free parameter is used to describe the Ag/ZnO interface. The ε spectra of this interface layer can be modeled as a single Lorentz oscillator that represents the dipolar plasmon resonances that are associated with free electron oscillations within the protrusions of the Ag roughness layer. The Lorentz expression incorporates four free parameters,

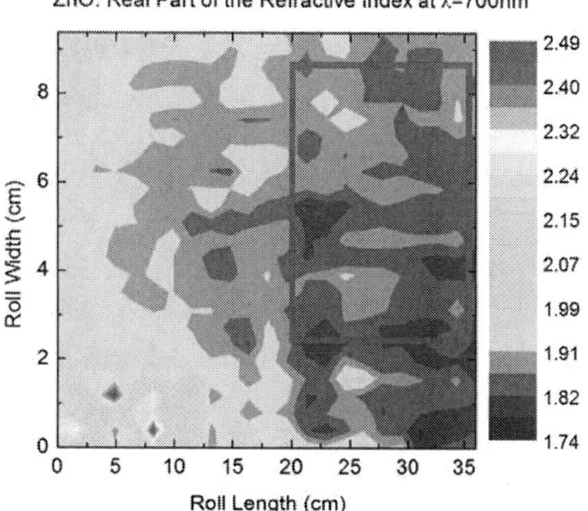

Fig. 7. Map of the real part of the index of refraction for the bulk ZnO layer at a wavelength of 700 nm. The inset box indicates the region shown in the maps of Figs. 8 and 10.

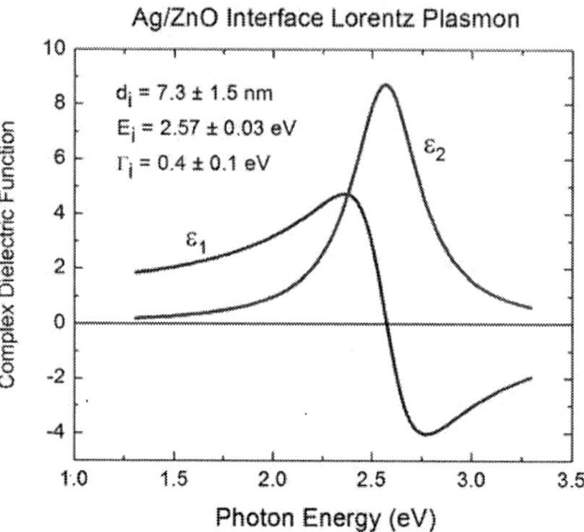

Fig. 9. Real and imaginary parts of the complex dielectric function of the interface layer at a representative point on the map of Fig. 8, based on the assumption that a Lorentz oscillator expression describes plasmon resonances.

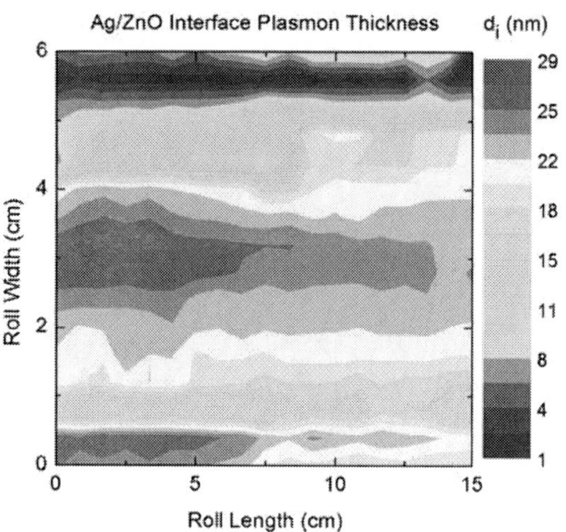

Fig. 8. Map of the thickness of the Ag/ZnO interface layer, whose ε spectra are modeled assuming a Lorentz oscillator.

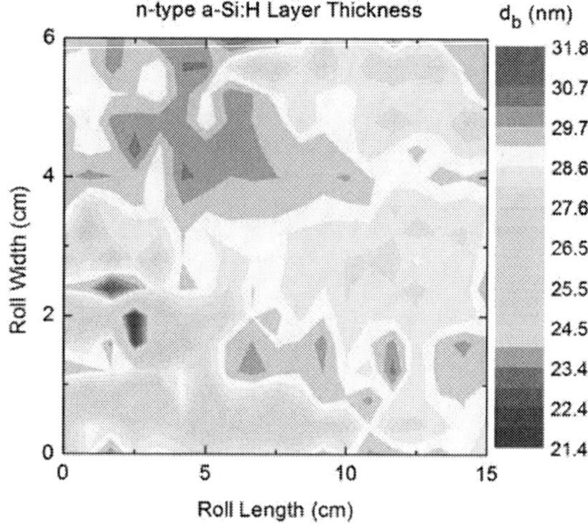

Fig. 10. Map of the bulk layer thickness for the n-type a-Si:H, the third thin film of the multilayer structure of the a-Si:H n-i-p solar cell.

including the constant contribution to the real part of the dielectric function, as well as the amplitude, resonance energy, and broadening parameter. Thus, the interface layer introduces a total of five new parameters designated $\{d_i, \varepsilon_{1\infty i}, A_i, E_i, \Gamma_i\}$. A map of the interface thickness is depicted in Fig. 8, for a reduced section of the coated substrate. For a typical single point on the Ag/ZnO coated substrate, Fig. 9 shows the interface layer dielectric function as a best fit Lorentz oscillator. The resonance energy of the oscillator depends on the index of refraction of the ambient medium, which is ZnO (as in Fig. 7), and on the height and area fraction of the silver protrusions.

C. n-Type a-Si:H Layer

Adding the n-type hydrogenated amorphous silicon (a-Si:H) layer on the Ag/ZnO structure introduces two additional struc-

tural free parameters, the n-layer bulk and surface roughness layer thicknesses, d_b and d_s.

The complex dielectric function of the n-layer is simulated using the Cody–Lorentz dispersion model, which is based on the assumption of square-root densities of valence and conduction band states versus hole and electron energies, respectively, and a constant dipole matrix element for the band-to-band transitions. This dispersion model employs five free parameters, including not only the three parameters of the Lorentz oscillator (A_n, E_n, Γ_n), but also the band gap energy E_g, and a transition energy E_p between the absorption onset behavior just above the band gap and the Lorentz oscillator absorption behavior at higher energies. In this model, it is found that $\varepsilon_{1\infty}$ can be set to unity. In Fig. 10, a map is shown for the n-type a-Si:H bulk layer thickness over a more restricted area than those of Figs. 2, 4, 6, and 7, and in Fig. 11 a representative best fit is shown to the

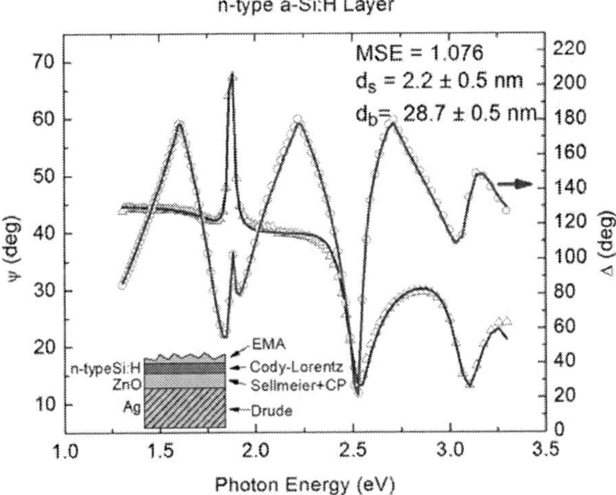

Fig. 11. Example best fit (lines) to experimental (ψ, Δ) spectra (points) via MSE minimization for the Ag/ZnO/(a-Si:H n-layer) structure at a single point on the map of Fig. 10; the Cody–Lorentz dispersion expression is applied for the n-layer complex dielectric function.

experimental (ψ, Δ) spectra at a single point. The thickness over much of the area ranges between 25 and 30 nm, whereby the latter value is the intended thickness. The features in the lower left corner with thicknesses extending above and below this range may arise from a dimpling of the coated substrate which would leave some areas closer to the PECVD electrode, leading to a larger thickness, and some areas further away, leading to a smaller thickness. Alternatively, such a substrate defect may lead to a distortion of the angle of incidence away from the calibrated values, which may then lead to incorrect thicknesses. In either case, the map shows how substrate defects can be detected readily and how the potential exists to characterize their nature and origin.

IV. CONCLUSION

Existing instrumentation for SE using a 1-D detector array requires translation of the ellipsometer optics width-wise in order to map large area roll-to-roll coated flexible substrates. A 12 cm × 12 cm sample area requires ~150 measurements and typically ~12 min to achieve centimeter-scale spatial resolution—meaning a maximum of ~1 cm/min roll-to-roll coated substrate speed. By using a 2-D detector array and imaging across 1-D in parallel via an expanded-beam system, no moving ellipsometer optics are required to map large area roll-to-roll coated substrates. As a result, such a system can measure with similar spatial resolution in <2 min, or with ~10 cm/min maximum substrate speed. Currently a single 40 point line image can be collected in 10 s over a 12 cm width of flexible roll-to-roll photovoltaic material. Prospects exist for reducing this measurement time significantly, achieving meter per minute speeds. Considering the potential of SE for characterizing bulk layer thicknesses, surface roughness thicknesses, and complex dielectric function spectra in analytical form, from which material phase and composition are accessible, in-line expanded-beam SE is expected to achieve considerable analytical power. Future advances are expected in the instrumentation, reference dielectric function databases, and analysis software.

REFERENCES

[1] C. Major, G. Juhász, Z. Horváth, O. Pólgar, and M. Fried, "Wide angle beam ellipsometry for extremely large samples," *Phys. Stat. Sol. (c)*, vol. 5, pp. 1077–1080, 2008.

[2] G. Juhász, Z. Horváth, C. Major, P. Petrik, O. Pólgar, and M. Fried, "Non-collimated beam ellipsometry," *Phys. Stat. Sol. (c)*, vol. 5, pp. 1081–1084, 2008.

[3] C. Major, G. Juhász, P. Petrik, Z. Horváth, O. Pólgar, and M. Fried, "Application of wide angle beam spectroscopic ellipsometry for quality control in solar cell production," *Vacuum*, vol. 84, pp. 119–122, 2009.

[4] R. W. Collins, I. An, and C. Chen, "Rotating polarizer and analyzer ellipsometry," in *Handbook of Ellipsometry*, E. A. Irene and H. G. Tompkins, Eds. Norwich, NY, USA: William Andrew, 2005, ch. 5, pp. 329–432.

[5] L. R. Dahal, D. Sainju, N. J. Podraza, S. Marsillac, and R. W. Collins, "Real time spectroscopic ellipsometry of Ag/ZnO and Al/ZnO interfaces for back-reflectors in thin film Si:H photovoltaics," *Thin Solid Films*, vol. 519, pp. 2682–2687, 2011.

[6] P. Aryal, J. Chen, Z. Huang, L. R. Dahal, M. N. Sestak, D. Attygalle, R. Jacobs, V. Ranjan, S. Marsillac, and R. W. Collins, "Quantum efficiency simulations from on-line compatible mapping of thin-film solar cells," in *Proc. Conf. Rec. 37th IEEE Photovoltaics Spec. Conf.*, Seattle, WA, Jun. 19–24, 2011, pp. 002241–002246.

[7] J. Lee, P. I. Rovira, I. An, and R. W. Collins, "Rotating-compensator multichannel ellipsometry for characterization of the evolution of non-uniformities in diamond thin-film growth," *Appl. Phys. Lett.*, vol. 72, pp. 900–902, 1998.

Ambalanath Shan received the M.S.E.E. degree from the University of Toledo, Toledo, OH, USA, in 1995 and is currently a member of the Department of Physics and Astronomy, University of Toledo.

He is currently a member of the Department of Physics and Astronomy, the University of Toledo, Toledo, OH, USA. His research interest includes mapping ellipsometry instrumentation, hardware and software development, and thin-film optical characterization.

Miklós Fried received the Ph.D. degree from the Hungarian Academy of Sciences, Budapest, Hungary, in 1985.

He is currently the Head of the Department of Photonics, the Research Institute for Technical Physics and Materials Science, Budapest, Hungary. His main research interests include the investigation of surface modification of materials by ellipsometry and ion backscattering spectrometry.

György Juhász is a member of the Department of Photonics, the Research Institute for Technical Physics and Materials Science, Budapest, Hungary. He works on novel imaging ellipsometry techniques, including the computer control and data acquisition and processing problems of the equipment.

Csaba Major received the Ph.D. degree from the Hungarian Academy of Sciences, Budapest, Hungary, in 2009.

He is currently with the Department of Photonics, Research Institute for Technical Physics and Materials Science, Budapest, Hungary. His main research interests include optical system designing, ellipsometer hardware development, evaluation of ellipsometric measurement.

Jie Chen received the Ph.D. degree from the University of Toledo, OH, USA, in 2010.

He is currently a Post-Doctoral Research Scientist at the Center for Photovoltaics Innovation and Commercialization, University of Toledo. His research interests include the development of new metrology and online monitors for CdTe PV technology.

Olivér Polgár received the Ph.D. degree in electrical engineering from the Budapest University of Technology and Economics, Budapest, Hungary.

He is currently with the Department of Photonics, the Research Institute for Technical Physics and Materials Science, Budapest. His research interests include software development, evaluation and parameter search algorithms, and mapping ellipsometry.

Zhiquan Huang is currently working toward the Doctoral degree from the University of Toledo, OH, USA. In his thesis research, he is developing processes for thin-film silicon tandem solar cells and new methods for their characterization by *in situ* and *ex situ* optical methods.

Ágoston Németh received the Ph.D. degree on the topic of ZnO reactive sputtering from the Research Centre for Natural Sciences, Institute for Technical Physics and Materials Science, Budapest, Hungary.

He held a one year Postdoctoral fellowship at the Wright Center for Photovoltaics Innovation and Commercialization, Toledo, OH, USA. He is currently with the Research Institute for Technical Physics and Materials Science, Budapest. His research interest includes thin-film solar cells. He has applied thin-film deposition techniques such as reactive sputtering, evaporation, and VHF PECVD.

Nikolas J. Podraza received the Ph.D. degree in physics from the University of Toledo, OH, USA, in 2008.

He is currently an Assistant Professor at the University of Toledo. His research interests include the physical mechanisms of film growth that control the electromagnetic, optical, and vibrational properties of thin-film materials used in opto-electronic device applications.

Péter Petrik received the M.Sc. and Ph.D. degrees from the Technical University of Budapest, Budapest, Hungary, in engineering and physics, respectively.

He is a Senior Scientist at the Institute for Technical Physics and Materials Science, Hungarian Academy of Sciences, Budapest, heading the Ellipsometry Laboratory. His research interests include the ellipsometric modeling of nonuniform, composite nanostructures including the development of ellipsometric models for the characterization of surface roughness, nanocrystalline semiconductors, photonic and organic structures.

Robert W. Collins received the Ph.D. degree in applied physics from Harvard University, Cambridge, MA, USA, in 1982.

He is a Distinguished University Professor and the Nippon Electric Glass Endowed Chair of Silicate and Materials Science in the Department of Physics and Astronomy, University of Toledo, OH, USA. He co-directs the Center for Photovoltaics Innovation and Commercialization and has been involved in research and development of thin-film PV since 1976.

Lila R. Dahal received the Ph.D. degree in physics from the University of Toledo, OH, USA, in 2013.

He is currently a Research Scientist with NSG-Pilkington Company, Northwood, OH, USA. His research interests include *in situ* real time and *ex situ* mapping analysis of thin film silicon solar cells using spectroscopic ellipsometry.

Improved Bandgap-Voltage Offset in
InGaAs/InAlGaAs Quantum Well Solar Cells

C. G. Bailey[1], M. P. Lumb[1,2], D. V. Forbes[3], M. K. Yakes[1], M. Gonzalez[1,4],
S. M. Hubbard[3], R. Hoheisel[1,2], L. C. Hirst[1], J. G. Tischler[1], I. Vurgaftman[1], J. R. Meyer[1], R. J. Walters[1]

[1]U.S. Naval Research Laboratory, Washington, DC, USA
[2] George Washington University, Washington, DC, USA
[3] NanoPower Research Labs, Rochester Institute of Technology, Rochester, NY, USA
[4]Sotera Defense Solutions, Annapolis Junction, MD, 20701, USA

Abstract — In recent years, the implementation of bandgap engineering techniques for solar energy conversion has been demonstrated with exciting results, using both quantum wells (QWs) and quantum dots. Here, the exploitation of a fully lattice-matched QW / barrier system is introduced as an attractive new possibility for this type of device. Photovoltaic characterization is performed and relevant solar cell parameters are reported. For these devices, sixteen layers of 5 nm InGaAs QWs / 10 nm InAlGaAs barriers were embedded into the *i*-region of a 1.0 eV InAlGaAs solar cell, and the results compared to a 1.0 eV InAlGaAs control solar cell. One-sun J_{sc} is enhanced in the QW cell by 5.3% compared to that of the InAlGaAs control device, while the open circuit voltage is reduced by 153 mV compared to the control. External quantum efficiency measurements reveal a 1.6 mA/cm^2 gain from the QW absorption region.

Index Terms — InAlGaAs, InGaAs, quantum wells, solar, InP

I. INTRODUCTION

There are many potential paths to high solar power conversion efficiency, but the most successful approaches to date have been the multijunction architecture. The recent achievement of a 44% value under concentrated sunlight [1] is close to the fundamental limit for the successful Ge-based lattice-matched (LM) materials [2]. The potential for success using monolithic junctions which are not lattice-matched has been demonstrated using metamorphic growth techniques [3]. However, LM materials, exhibiting superior optical and electrical quality have the most potential for high efficiency photovoltaics [4]. New material systems are being evaluated such as LM InP-based multijunction devices that span the range of bandgaps needed to efficiently collect from the solar spectrum with efficiencies exceeding those of the Ge-based devices [5]. In that work, the optimal bandgaps were calculated to be 1.8/1.18/0.7 eV energies. Since no LM material exists at 0.7 eV, it has been proposed that quantum confinement be used to reduce the bottom junction's bandgap without requiring any lattice-mismatched materials. These structures have had success in the past in both single-junction [6-8] and multijunction cells [9-11].

In the present study, the 1.0 eV InP-lattice-matched InAlGaAs is chosen as a host junction bulk material. LM InGaAs QWs are then investigated in a compositionally identical InAlGaAs barrier matrix. The lattice matching is maintained in order to remove strain as a variable.

Maintaining the lattice-matched condition is important since a wide range of QW/barrier systems can be studied within the $In_xAl_yGa_{1-x-y}As$ system.

In order to experimentally investigate the device architecture of this system, it is necessary to independently evaluate the QWs in a device. Test structures have been grown and studied elsewhere to determine the optical properties of the isolated QWs [12]. Although the bulk solar cell material used here, has been reported as a solar cell material before [13], this is the first report of an InAlGaAs 1.0 eV *n-i-p* solar cell, with embedded QWs in the intrinsic (*i*) region. Figure 1 shows a schematic diagram of the layering and band structure of the 16/17-layer QW/barrier superlattice (SL) device grown on a *p*-InP (100) substrate. The device will be compared to a control device without quantum wells.

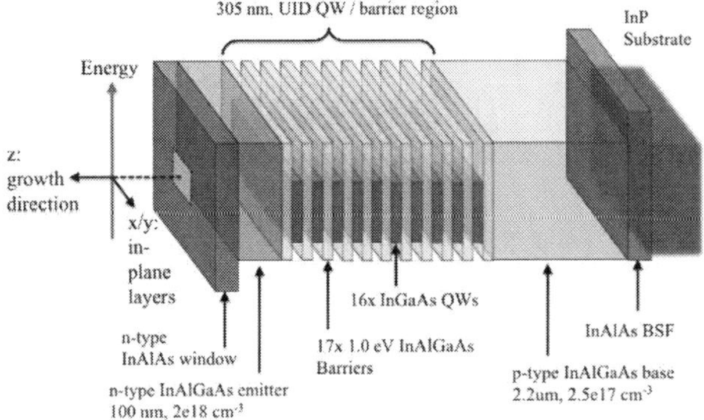

Figure 1. Schematic of InP-lattice matched 16-layer InGaAs / InAlGaAs QW structure. Only 10 layers of QW/barrier material are shown to save space. The vertical direction is the energy axis for the material layers, with the top and bottom surfaces representing conduction and valence bandedges, respectively.

Traditionally, QW/barrier systems studied for photovoltaic purposes have been largely limited to the GaAs-LM systems. The lack of a lattice-matched sub-GaAs bandgap III-V material, results in the need for the strain balancing technique. While well-understood and successful, this technique requires the unavoidable inclusion of strain in the experimental matrix under examination. The material system proposed here, however, represents an exciting extension to the use of quantum wells for photovoltaics, since the InP-based system is relatively immature compared to its GaAs-based counterpart. More importantly, this InP-lattice-matched QW/barrier system is an exciting test-bed for the investigation of physical mechanisms in a QW-based structures without the inclusion of strain. Results can be subsequently ported into feedback for device design. Ultimately, the evaluation of the full devices with these architectures can be used as solar cell parameter test-beds.

II. EXPERIMENTAL

In this study, high resolution x-ray diffraction (HRXRD) is used to evaluate the lattice matching parameters of the devices, with and without QWs. Standard solar cell measurements will then be shown and analyzed, including dark J-V, light J-V, and external quantum efficiency (EQE). Electroluminescence (EL) data are also included as a function of injection current, to further investigate the device ideality parameters.

A multiwafer rotating disk MOVPE reactor was used to grow LM InGaAs QWs embedded in a 1.0 eV InAlGaAs matrix within the i-region of an InAlGaAs n-i-p solar cell. The LM InAlGaAs barrier layers were 10 nm thick, while the LM InGaAs (In = 53%) QW thickness was 5 nm. The solar cell structure depicted in figure 1 consisted of 1.0 eV InAlGaAs material (identical to the barrier material, except in doping concentration) for the base (2.2 μm, Zn-doped, 3.8×10^{17} cm^{-3}), and the emitter (100 nm, Si-doped, 2×10^{18} cm^{-3}). The 305 nm i-region was unintentionally doped. A non-trivial background doping exists in the intrinsic region (n-type, 1×10^{16} cm^{-3}) measured by Hall (not shown). An n-type (p-type) window (BSF) layer was grown using LM InAlAs, of 50 nm thickness and doped with Si (Zn), at 5×10^{18} cm^{-3}. A Si-doped (1.5×10^{18} cm^{-3}) InGaAs contact layer was included for ohmic contacting.

Solar cells were fabricated using standard III-V processing methodology. Metallization of the p-type substrate was completed using a Au/Zn/Au structure and the n-type InGaAs contact layer consisted of Ni/Ge/Au structure. Cells were mesa isolated to 0.5×0.5 cm^2 with grid shadowing of 6%. Antireflective coatings were not used. HRXRD measurements were taken using a *Bede Scientific QC1a Diffractometer* equipped with a GaSb 2-bounce incident monochromator. Dark J-V measurements were obtained using a *Cascade Microtech* 4-point probe station and a *Keithley 4200* parametric analyzer. One-sun AM0-illuminated J-V characteristics were measured by a class A Oriel solar simulator equipped with a Xenon bulb. External quantum efficiency (EQE) measurements were made using a CVI *Instruments Digikrom* monochromator coupled with a *Stanford Research Systems SR830* lock-in amplifier, and were calibrated using an *Oriel* pyroelectric detector.

Electroluminescence measurements were taken using a standard current source and probe station apparatus coupled with an *ASD Inc. Fieldspec* spectroradiometer.

III. RESULTS

HRXRD was performed and the simulated structure was fit to both devices. Figure 2 shows the high resolution x-ray diffraction data from the two devices, along with fits obtained from the simulations. The substrate peak, aligned to the 0 arc-second point of the x-axis, exhibits lower intensity than the major layer peak (609 ppm, compressive) due to diffraction in the thick epitaxial layers. The InAlGaAs layer is slightly lattice mismatched, but within acceptable crystal growth range. slightly indium rich (In = 0.537). The superlattice peaks which appear only in the QW device, as expected, and reveals a periodicity of 20 nm. The rough breakdown to 7 nm QWs, with 12.5 nm barriers, indicates that both growth rates are slightly high and may explain the indium-rich nature of the 0th order SL peak. Fringe peaks arising from the contact layer can be seen clearly in the control device, but are less pronounced in the QW sample.

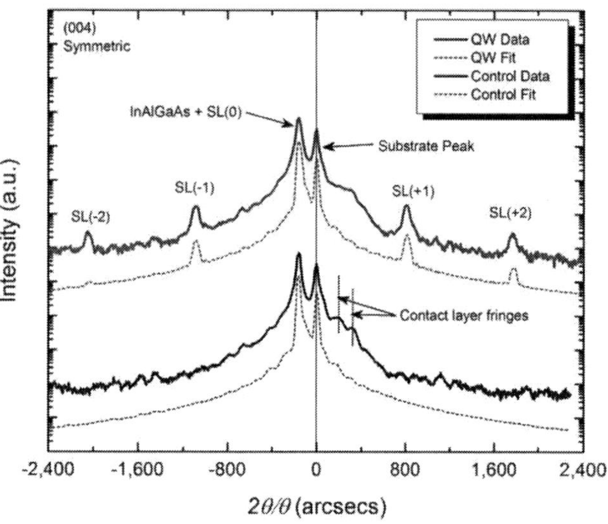

Figure 2. HRXRD of both devices. Offsets are used in the intensity here to separate the measurements, as well as their respective fits.

The fits in figure 2 were performed using the commercially available *RADS* software by *Jordan Valley Semiconductors*. Least squares fitting of the [004] 2-theta-omega scans based on dynamical diffraction theory simulations allowed the thickness and composition of each layer to be determined. This fitting routine has been demonstrated to yield excellent agreement with the structural information obtained from microscopy measurements [14]. For these samples, due to the complexity of the layer structure and the relatively small number of satellite peaks, tetragonal distortion was not taken into account and the uniqueness of the fits could not be verified. The results agree well with the growth parameters.

Figure 3 shows the dark J-V measurements for both solar cell devices. The control cell exhibited characteristics of both diffusion current and generation-recombination (GR) current contributions, and was fit with a standard 2-diode dark J-V model incorporating series and shunt resistance, using the Levenberg-Marquardt fitting algorithm in NRL MultiBands^{TM}. The QW device exhibited higher GR current, indicating a domination of i-region non-radiative recombination mechanisms. This was to be expected, as the effective bandgap is lower. Dark diode parameters extracted from fits were compared. Series resistances for the two samples were $Rs = 0.83\ \Omega$ and $0.87\ \Omega$, for the control and the QW cells respectively. These values are comparatively good for III-V solar cells.

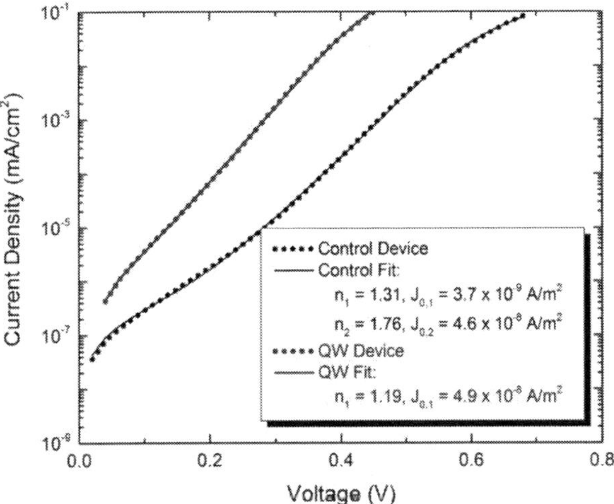

Figure 3. Dark J-V curves of both solar cell samples.

The control sample exhibited ideality factors of $n_1 = 1.31$ and $n_2 = 1.76$. These represent appearance of both quasi-neutral region and i-region recombination mechanisms, since both components are expected to be present. The deviations from 1 and 2 for these idealities result in part from uncertainties associated with the limited voltage fitting range. Additionally, no clear regions are delineated by a transitional kink point in the data, indicating that no specific recombination mechanism dominates. Saturation currents were typical of a 1.0 eV bandgap material, with $J_{0,1} = 3.7 \times 10^{-9}$ A/m^2, indicating good material quality [15]. The QW device was fit with a single diode approximation, due to the complete absence of the characteristic kink, giving $n_1 = 1.19$. This value is quite low for a device expected to be dominated by i-region recombination and is not yet fully understood. Another diode term may be present, indicating an additional

mechanism, such as side-wall recombination. The dark saturation current, $J_{0,2}$ was equivalent to the fitted control cell value (4.9×10^{-8} A/m^2).

Figure 4 shows the illuminated J-V data for the two solar cells under the AM0 spectrum. The open circuit voltage of 521 mV for the control InAlGaAs solar cell is slightly lower than expected for a 1.0 eV bandgap with respect to previous InAlGaAs device and accepted theory [13, 16], and implies an experimental bandgap-voltage offset ($W_{oc} \equiv E_g - V_{oc}$) value of 472 mV [16]. The short-circuit current density is 32.1 mA/cm^2, which indicates a high quantum efficiency of a non-anti-reflection coated device. The QW-embedded sample showed a reduction in open-circuit voltage of about 153 mV from that of the control cell, which is expected due to reduced effective bandgap of the QW device, which agrees with the increased saturation current. The expected confined well depth is more than 200 meV below the barrier/bulk conduction band, indicating that the quasi-fermi-level is largely, but not completely governed by the reduced quasi Fermi level of the effective bandgap. The W_{oc} is in fact lower in value (412 mV) than that of the control sample (472 mV), expected from the fundamental theory of Barnham $et\ al.$ [17].

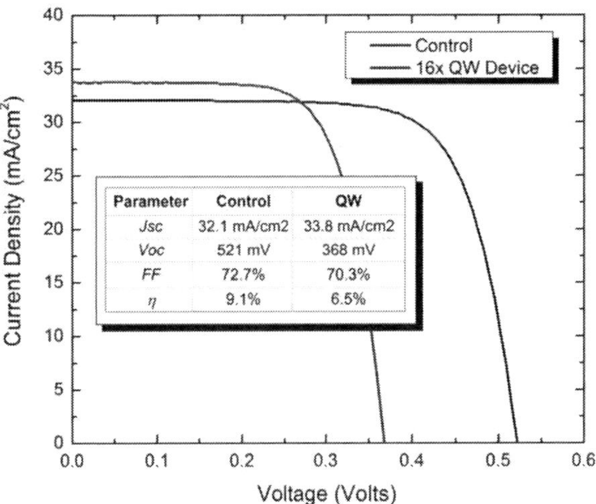

Figure 4. 1-sun AM0 illuminated J-V curves of both solar cell samples. No anti-reflection coatings were used for these devices.

The short circuit current density, shows an increase of 1.7 mA/cm^2 (5.3%), or approximately 0.1 mA/cm^2 per QW. The FF values for these samples are within reasonable values for lower bandgap III-V solar cells, at 72.7 (70.3)% for the control (QW) cells. The solar cell efficiencies were 9.1 (6.5)%. Improvement in FF may be obtained through optimization of grid metallization, and further reduction of W_{oc}. The control device was expected to display a higher efficiency value, since its effective bandgap is much closer to the ideal 1-sun detailed balance bandgap (1.35 eV), than its QW-embedded counterpart [18].

External quantum efficiency measurements were performed on the two devices, shown in figure 5. The peak bulk *EQE* values near 67% are equivalent for both samples. Since measured reflectivities of typical III-V devices are ~30-40%, the peak internal quantum efficiencies are near unity. The QW device's absorption at photon energies below the InAlGaAs bandgap ($\lambda > 1250$ nm) is clearly the primary source of the improved J_{sc} in the light *J-V* measurement. The sub-bandgap peaks at 1320, 1410 and 1570 nm, (equivalent to 939, 879, and 790 eV), arise from the absorption edges of the confined well states.

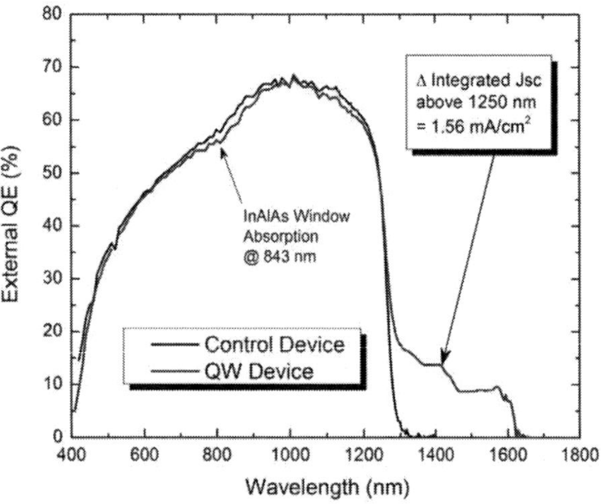

Figure 5. *EQE* plot for both solar cell samples grown for this study.

The product of the spectral responsivity and the AM0 spectrum was numerically integrated. That this calculation deviated only slightly from the illuminated *J-V* measurements, verified the calibration of the solar simulator. In addition, this calculation was performed specifically for the sub-InAlGaAs absorption portion of the spectrum (> 1250 nm). The additional current in the light *J-V* measurement was 1.7 mA/cm^2. The integrated *EQE* spectra returned 30.4 and 31.4 mA/cm^2 for the control and QW samples, respectively. Firstly, the visible difference in the bulk wavelengths between the samples' *EQE* partially offset the influence of the QW device's absorption above 1250 nm on the differences in the J_{sc} values. Secondly, the above-1250 nm integration revealed a gain of 1.6 mA/cm^2 for the QW sample when subtracted from the control. This implies an increase of 0.1 mA/cm^2 per QW layer, and correlates well with the illuminated *J-V*. The small difference in these values may be attributed to the infrared spikes present in the simulator at these wavelengths, which falsely enhance the QW device for the light *J-V* measurement.

Electroluminescence measurements were taken of both devices. Figure 6 shows the spectra emitted from the surface of each structure, overlaid with the sub-band-gap *EQE* of the QW device. The emission from the QW device exhibits strong peaks from radiative recombination between electrons (e) and both heavy [HH] and light [LH] holes. The e1-HH1 (780 meV), e1-LH1 (793 meV), and e1-HH3 (872 meV) transitions

can be seen in the inflection points of the spectra. The overlaid *EQE* data shows good correlation between the emission and absorption from these states. In order to further investigate the recombination mechanisms from these confined and band-to-band states, injection-dependent EL was performed.

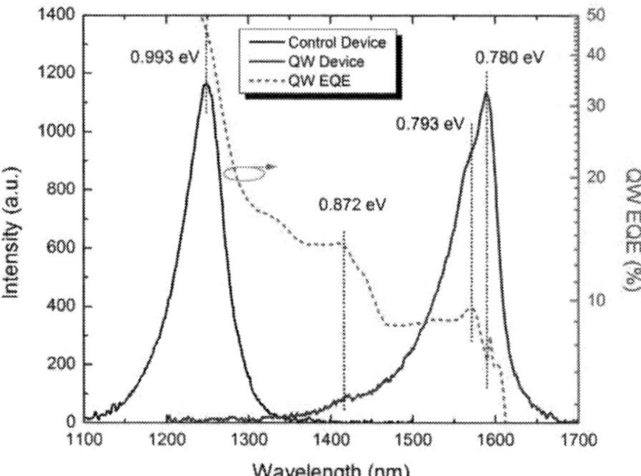

Figure 6. Electroluminescence spectra for both the control and the QW sample overlaid with the QW *EQE* (red, right y-axis). The EL spectra were obtained at a forward injection current of 600 mA/cm^2, equivalent to ~18 suns.

Figure 7 shows the results of integrating the spectra as a function of injection current density. The injection is reported here in number of suns, in order to scale to the injected current, (where # Suns = J_{inj} / J_{sc}). Additionally, the linear diode equation is plotted for a comparison, assuming an ideality of 1. Similar comparisons are made to evaluate the dominant recombination mechanism in the

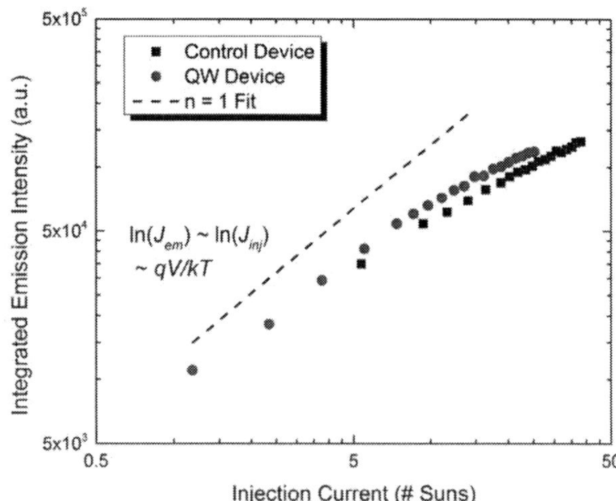

Figure 7. Integrated EL intensity as a function of injection current density (for reference, the x-axis has been converted to suns from the 1-sun short circuit density) for both the control and the QW sample.

          264

electroluminescence data. Here, the data correlates well with the n = 1 regime indicating a lack of Shockley-Read-Hall recombination at the studied injection current densities [19].

IV. CONCLUSION

In conclusion, we report the growth and fabrication of the first InAlGaAs 1.0 eV solar cell to incorporate QWs. For comparison, a lattice matched InAlGaAs control was grown and standard solar cell testing performed. A 5.3% increase in J_{sc} was observed in the QW sample, with a 153 mV drop in V_{oc}, representing the effects of bandgap engineering using QWs. The W_{oc} value of the QW device was 89 mV lower than that of the control, indicating a departure from the theory of Fermi-pinning at the confined energy levels in the intrinsic region. Emission and absorption from the sub-bulk-bandgap states were in good agreement. The demonstration of these devices are important steps toward the ultimate goal of an InP lattice-matched 3-junction solar cell, with projected efficiencies of over 50%. More fundamentally, this unique strain balanced multiple QW system is ideal for studying the optical and electrical characteristics of InP-lattice matched QW devices.

ACKNOWLEDGEMENTS

The authors would like to thank Meng Zhao at the Rochester Institute of Technology for aid in device processing, and David A. Scheiman at the U.S. Naval Research Laboratory for aid in light J-V measurements. This work was supported by the Office of Naval Research. Both C.G.B and L.C.H. acknowledge support from the National Research Council Research Associate Program.

REFERENCES

[1] M. A. Green, K. Emery, Y. Hishikawa, W. Warta, and E. D. Dunlop, *Progress in Photovoltaics,* vol. 21, pp. 1-11, 2013.

[2] P. R. Sharps, D. A. Aiken, A. Boca, B. Cho, D. Chumney, A. Cornfeld, S. S. Je, Y. Lin, J. McCarty, F. Newman, P. Patel, J. Sponn, M. Stan, and J. Steinfeldt, "High Efficiency Multi-junction Solar Cells: Past, Present, and Future," in *Fall Meeting of the Materials Research Society*, Boston, MA, 2012.

[3] W. Guter, J. Schone, S. P. Philipps, M. Stiner, G. Siefer, A. Wekkell, E. Welser, E. Oliva, A. W. Bett, and F. Dimroth, *Appl. Phys. Lett.,* vol. 94, 2009.

[4] N. L. A. Chan, N. J. Ekins-Daukes, J. G. J. Adams, M. P. Lumb, M. Gonzalez, P. P. Jenkins, I. Vurgaftman, J. R. Meyer, and R. J. Walters, "Optimal Bandgap Combinations - Does Material Quality Matter?," *Journal of Photolvoltaics,* vol. 2, 2012.

[5] M. Gonzalez, N. Chan, N. J. Ekins-Daukes, J. G. J. Adams, P. Stavrinou, I. Vurgaftman, J. R. Meyer, J. Abcll, R. J. Walters, C. D. Cress, and P. P. Jenkins, in *Physics and Simulation of Optoelectronic Devices XIX*, San Francisco, CA, 2011.

[6] N. J. Ekins-Daukes, K. W. J. Barnham, J. P. Connolly, J. S. Roberts, J. C. Clark, G. Hill, and M. Mazzer, "Strain-balanced GaAsP/InGaAs quantum well solar cells," *Appl. Phys. Lett.,* vol. 75, 1999.

[7] C. G. Bailey, D. V. Forbes, S. J. Polly, Z. S. Bittner, Y. Dai, C. Mackos, R. P. Raffaelle, and S. M. Hubbard, "Open-circuit voltage improvement of InAs/GaAs quantum-dot solar cells using reduced InAs coverage," *J. Photovoltaics,* vol. 2, 2012.

[8] Y. Wen, Y. Wang, K. Watanabe, M. Sugiyama, and Y. Nakano, "Effect of GaAs Step Layer on InGaAs/GaAsP Quantum Well Solar Cells," *Appl. Phys. Express,* vol. 4, 2011.

[9] M. P. Lumb, A. L. Dobbin, D. B. Bushnell, K. H. Lee, and T. N. D. Tibbits, "Comparing the energy yield of (III-V) multi-junction cells with different numbs of sub-cells," presented at the 6th International Conference on Concentrating Photovoltaic Systems, 2010.

[10] T. N. D. Tibbits, M. P. Lumb, and A. Dobbin, "Quantum wells in multiple junction photovoltaics," presented at the Photonics West, San Francisco, CA, 2011.

[11] C. Kerestes, C. D. Cress, B. C. Richards, D. V. Forbes, Y. Lin, Z. Bittner, S. J. Polly, P. Sharps, and S. M. Hubbard, "Strain effects on radiation tolerance of triple junction solar cells with InAs quantum dots in the GaAs junction," *J. Photovoltaics,* vol. submitted, 2013.

[12] C. G. Bailey, D. V. Forbes, M. P. Lumb, M. K. Yakes, M. Gonzalez, S. M. Hubbard, R. Hoheisel, J. G. Tischler, I. Vurgaftman, J. R. Meyer, and R. J. Walters, "InGaAs quantum wells for InP lattice-matched triple junction solar cells," *Appl. Phys. Lett., in preparation* July, 2013.

[13] H. J. Schimper, Z. Kollonitsch, K. Moller, U. Seidel, U. Bloeck, K. Schwarzburg, F. Willig, and T. Hannappel, "Material studies regarding InP-based high-efficiency solar cells," *J. Cryst. Gro.,* vol. 287, pp. 642-646, 2006.

[14] M. K. Yakes, S. B. Qadri, N. A. Mahadik, C. Yi, D. Lubyshev, J. M. Fastenau, A. W. K. Liu, and E. H. Aifer, "Combined cross sectional scanning tunneling microscopy and high resolution x-ray diffraction study for quantitative structural descriptions of type-II superlattice infrared detectors," *Appl. Phys. Lett.,* vol. 101, 2012.

[15] J. R. Wilcox, A. W. Haas, J. L. Gray, and R. J. Schwartz, "Estimating saturation current based on junction temperature and bandgap," in *7th International Conference on Concentrating Photovoltaic Systems*, 2011, pp. 30-33.

[16] R. R. King, D. Bhusari, A. Boca, D. Larrabee, X.-Q. Liu, W. Hong, C. M. Fetzer, D. C. Law, and N. H. Karam, "Band gap-voltage offset and energy

production in next-generation multijunction solar cells," *Progress in Photovoltaics,* vol. 19, pp. 797-812, 2011.

[17] K. W. J. Barnham and G. Duggan, "A new approach to high efficiency multibandgap solar cells," *J. Appl. Phys.,* vol. 67, 1990.

[18] W. Shockley and H. J. Queisser, "Detailed balance limit of efficiency of p-n junction solar cells," *J. Appl. Phys.,* vol. 32, 1961.

[19] R. Hoheisel, F. Dimroth, A. W. Bett, S. R. Messenger, P. P. Jenkins, and R. J. Walters, "Electroluminescence analysis of irradiated GaInP/GaInAs/Ge space solar cells," *Sol. En. Mat. and Sol. Cells,* vol. 108, pp. 235-240, 2013.

Carrier Escape Time and Temperature-Dependent Carrier Collection Efficiency of Tunneling-Enhanced Multiple Quantum Well Solar Cells

Kasidit Toprasertpong, Hiromasa Fujii, Yunpeng Wang, Kentaroh Watanabe, Masakazu Sugiyama, and Yoshiaki Nakano, *Member, IEEE*

Abstract—Tunneling enhancement of cell performance in In-GaAs/GaAsP multiple quantum well (MQW) solar cells has been studied to investigate the potential in overcoming the carrier collection problem, which hinders the maximum performance of quantum structure solar cells. To accurately investigate the effects of the tunneling effect, the study was carried out in samples with different GaAsP barrier thickness, controlled absorption edge, and constant built-in field. The tunneling effect has been confirmed by evaluating carrier escape times using the time-resolved photoluminescence technique and measuring carrier collection efficiency at various temperatures. The collection efficiencies at low temperature are found to be remarkably improved when barrier thickness was below 3 nm, which can be regarded as the critical thickness for efficiently facilitating tunneling enhancement. It can also be concluded that the carrier transport model based on thermal and tunneling processes is practical enough to describe most of the carrier sweep-out dynamics in MQW solar cells.

Index Terms—Carrier transport, III–V semiconductor materials, photoluminescence, photovoltaic cells, quantum well devices, temperature dependence, tunneling.

I. INTRODUCTION

AMONG the many novel concepts proposed as the next-generation of solar cells, whose conversion efficiency from solar energy can exceed the theoretical limit—the Shockley–Queisser limit—of single bandgap solar cells [1], multijunction solar cells are successful in surpassing the efficiency limit and are currently playing an important role in ultrahigh efficiency solar cell research [2], [3]. Multijunction solar cells consist of materials with different bandgaps, which absorb photons from different solar spectrum ranges. This suppresses both carrier relaxation loss and transmission loss, resulting in higher limiting efficiency than what is possible with single bandgap cells. An InGaP/GaAs/Ge triple junction, with its high crystal quality and comparatively simple fabrication, is known as a standard structure of multijunction solar cells because of their matching lattice constants [4].

However, the comparatively low current density generated from the GaAs middle subcell limits the output current density of the junction cell. One promising way to overcome this problem, and thus increase the current flowing through the entire cell, is to extend the absorption spectrum of the middle subcell to the longer wavelength. Narrow-bandgap InGaAs is one of the suitable candidates for longer wavelength absorber in the middle subcell. However, its larger lattice constant than that of the GaAs/Ge system requires some sophisticated techniques to grow an InGaAs bulk subcell on the GaAs/Ge system with high crystal quality, and these techniques still need improvement [5]. Alternatively, InGaAs/GaAsP multiple quantum well (MQW) structure, with GaAsP layers to compensate for the strain from InGaAs growth, was proposed as a suitable candidate [6], [7].

One challenging issue of MQWs is that the band discontinuity between InGaAs absorbers and GaAsP strain-compensators forms a quantum well structure which traps carriers and obstructs them from escaping [8]. Some carriers excited within active regions cannot be extracted to the external circuit to generate power as expected from ideal solar cells. Hence, understanding carrier escape mechanism and utilizing it are important for designing the structure of high-performance cells. A number of research works have been modeling carrier escape mechanism by using two main processes, a classical process of thermal escape, and a quantum mechanical process of tunneling escape [8]–[13], although a more detailed model is required for precise solar cell simulation.

In this study, the focus was on utilization of the tunneling escape to enhance cell performance. Many research works were carried out by introducing the tunneling effect in quantum well structures for laser or modulator application [14], [15]; however, the application to solar cells could be different since they operate to extract carriers while applying forward bias. A few research works report the performance enhancement of MQW solar cells after decreasing the barrier thickness [11], [12], but analyzing the physical mechanism behind, only by $I-V$ curve or external quantum efficiency (EQE) measurement, is difficult.

Here, the authors systematically show the potential of the tunneling escape by observing shorter carrier sweep-out time and temperature dependence of carrier collection efficiency

Manuscript received June 10, 2013; accepted November 12, 2013. This work was supported in part by Research and Development of Innovative Solar Cell program, New Energy and Industrial Technology Development Organization, Japan.

K. Toprasertpong, H. Fujii, M. Sugiyama, and Y. Nakano are with the Department of Electrical Engineering and Information Systems, School of Engineering, University of Tokyo, Tokyo 113-8654, Japan (e-mail: toprasertpong@hotaka.t.u-tokyo.ac.jp; fujii@hotaka.t.u-tokyo.ac.jp; sugiyama@ee.t.u-tokyo.ac.jp; nakano@ee.t.u-tokyo.ac.jp).

Y. Wang and K. Watanabe are with the Research Center for Advanced Science and Technology, University of Tokyo, Tokyo 153-8904, Japan (e-mail: wangyunpeng@hotaka.t.u-tokyo.ac.jp; kentaroh@hotaka.t.u-tokyo.ac.jp).

Color versions of one or more of the figures in this paper are available online at http://ieeexplore.ieee.org.

Digital Object Identifier 10.1109/JPHOTOV.2013.2293877

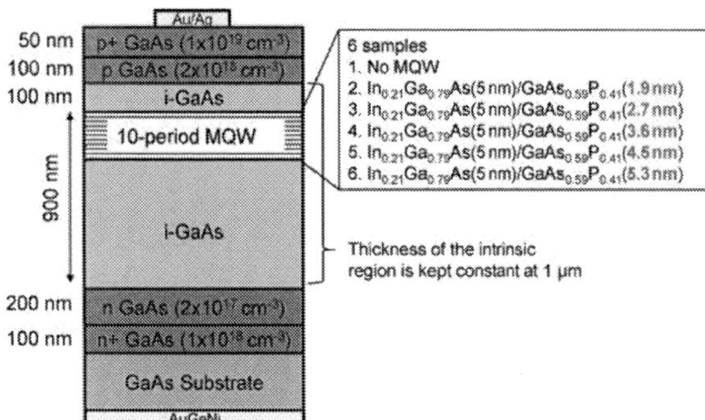

Fig. 1.   Sample structures of solar cells employed in this study. The numbers in parentheses represent doping concentrations or thicknesses.

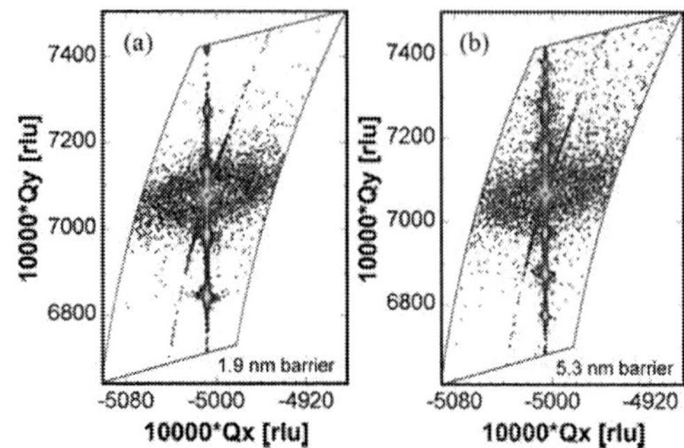

Fig. 2.   Reciprocal space mappings of MQW cells with (a) 1.9-nm and (b) 5.3-nm thick barriers around $(\bar{2}\,\bar{2}\,4)$ GaAs reciprocal lattice point.

(CCE) of a set of MQW solar cells by varying only their barrier thickness. Low temperature suppresses the thermal escape, thus allowing separate study of the tunneling escape. But earlier, the minimum thickness of potential barriers required for effective tunneling enhancement has not been investigated and will be shown here. Advance knowledge of the minimum required thickness would be helpful in cell design since the crystal growth of strain-balanced MQWs is extremely difficult if the barrier is very thin [13].

II. Experimental Details

A. Sample Structures and Fabrication

Fig. 1 shows the structures of the samples employed in this experiment. Five p-i-n GaAs solar cells, with different structures of ten-period InGaAs/GaAsP MQWs in their i-regions, and one typical p-i-n GaAs bulk reference cell were prepared. MQWs consisted of 5.0-nm thick $In_{0.21}Ga_{0.79}As$ wells and $GaAs_{0.59}P_{0.41}$ barriers of varying thickness stacked alternately. The thickness of GaAsP barriers in each cell was designed to be 1.9, 2.7, 3.6, 4.5, and 5.3 nm so that they cover the thicknesses already reported in many research works on the performance improvement [11]–[13], as also the thickness with which the tunneling effect was reported to be weak. Considering the variations in the total thicknesses of MQWs, the thicknesses of i-GaAs spacers were so adjusted that the total thicknesses of i-region were always 1 μm and the built-in fields were kept constant at 14 kV/cm, which was estimated by dividing the built-in potential by the i-region thickness. Other parameters, such as thickness of wells and composition of In and P, were so fixed as to control the effective height of potential barriers in each sample. This resulted in the same thermal escape rate from the wells, thus leaving the tunneling escape as the only variable in each cell. On the other hand, the residual strain could not be controlled when the barrier thickness was varied while all the other structural parameters were kept constant. As strain-balanced cells were reported to have better performance than unbalanced ones [16], the strain balance was tuned for the cells with the thickest barrier based on the expectation that a thinner barrier would be better for carrier transport. With the strain balance tuned for the thickest barrier, the samples with thin-

ner barriers would suffer crystal degradation due to imbalanced strain and consequent degradation of carrier transport. If the thinnest barrier shows the best CCE, it would mean that the enhancement in carrier transport overwhelms the disadvantage of crystal degradation, confirming that thinner barrier is better for carrier transport. Besides, reciprocal space mappings showed no lattice relaxation as can be seen from Fig. 2.

The samples mentioned above were grown by metal-organic vapor phase epitaxy (MOVPE) on (0 0 1) oriented n-GaAs substrates under 100 mbar at 610 °C. The source materials were trimethylgallium, trimethylindium, tertiarybutylarsine, tertiarybutylphosphine, dimethylzinc for p-type doping, and hydrogen sulfide (H_2S) for n-type doping. They were diluted and carried to the reactor by high-purity H_2. All samples were grown starting with a 1×10^{18} cm^{-3} n-GaAs (100 nm), followed by a 2×10^{17} cm^{-3} n-GaAs (200 nm). After growing a 1-μm-thick i-region on the n layer, a 2×10^{18} cm^{-3} p-type emitter (100 nm) and a 1×10^{19} cm^{-3} p-contact (50 nm) were grown. During the growth of the i-region, unintentional background doping by carbon from the organic source materials was compensated with proper amount of sulfur donors. The compensated carrier concentration was confirmed to be below 5×10^{14} cm^{-3} by Hall effect measurements on a separately grown i-GaAs layer. This is low enough to ensure that the 1-μm i-region is intrinsic enough to make the electric field in the i-region almost constant [17].

The parameters shown in Fig. 1 were confirmed by X-ray diffraction measurement. All the samples were confirmed to have had the same well thicknesses and the same atomic contents for both InGaAs and GaAsP. For ohmic contact at n-side, Ni with thickness of 30 nm and AuGe with thickness of 380 nm were prepared by thermal evaporating and annealed at 390 °C for 2 min. Then, 30-nm thick Ag and 750-nm thick Au were thermally evaporated for p-type front contact electrodes.

B. Time-Resolved Photoluminescence Measurement

Time-resolved photoluminescence (TRPL) was measured to assess the transient carrier dynamics inside MQWs, especially the ability of carriers to escape from MQWs after photogeneration. As the absorption length of GaAs at the wavelength of around 400 nm is lower than 20 nm [18], a pulse laser with wavelength of 405 nm was used to excite only those carriers which were nearby to the surfaces of cells. This allow holes to be collected easily at the top contact and only electrons to run across the i-region, avoiding thereby possible complication of cascade dynamics when carriers are generated inside and beyond MQWs. Therefore, electron transport dominates the results of this study. The laser had a pulse width of 50 ps, peak power of 500 mW, and pulse repetition frequency of 312.5 kHz. After each pulse, time-dependent luminescence was measured by using a photomultiplier and a time correlation photon counter. The detected wavelength was adjusted by a monochromter to the wavelength corresponding to the PL peak of MQWs to observe the radiative recombination of carriers inside MQWs.

After carriers were photogenerated, some of them were extracted from cells and the others recombined by radiative or non-radiative process. By observing radiative recombination process after a pulse, the total carrier density left inside MQWs can be directly estimated as a function of time. Therefore, information on carrier escape speed can be experimentally extracted from the decay of TRPL, although theoretical models of these processes are still under development [10], [19], [20].

C. Carrier Collection Efficiency

CCE is defined as the ratio of the number of extracted carriers to the total number of carriers photogenerated in an active region [21]. If all carriers photogenerated in an active region can be extracted out under sufficient reverse bias, as validated in [21], CCE at the excitation wavelength λ under applied bias V can be evaluated by normalizing $\mathrm{EQE}(\lambda, V)$ to the saturated value at reversed-bias $\mathrm{EQE}_{\mathrm{sat}}(\lambda)$

$$\mathrm{CCE}(\lambda, V) = \frac{\mathrm{EQE}(\lambda, V)}{\mathrm{EQE}_{\mathrm{sat}}(\lambda)} . \qquad (1)$$

By convoluting CCE with photon flux density, one can obtain the increment of photocurrent from dark current. CCE is unity in the ideal solar cell, corresponding to the principle of superposition. CCE can provide more useful information about carrier collection mechanism in addition to facilitating evaluation of short-circuit current I_{sc}, open-circuit voltage V_{oc}, or EQE because they include diode characteristics and optical loss. Especially, in temperature-dependent measurement, in which absorbance and band-edge are not constant, CCE is more appropriate to evaluate carrier transport.

Monochromatic light with a power density of 2.5 mW/cm^2 was used in EQE and CCE measurements at room temperature and 405-nm continuous laser with a power of 88 mW and a spot size of 550 μm^2 in temperature-dependent measurement. The reason for using this wavelength is given in Section III-B. In temperature-dependent experiment, CCEs were evaluated at various temperatures ranging from 30 to 298 K.

III. Results and Discussion

A. Validation of Tunneling-Enhancement Discussion

To assume that photogenerated carriers in each MQW cell escape from MQWs with the same thermal escape rate, one needs to control the built-in electric field and the effective potential

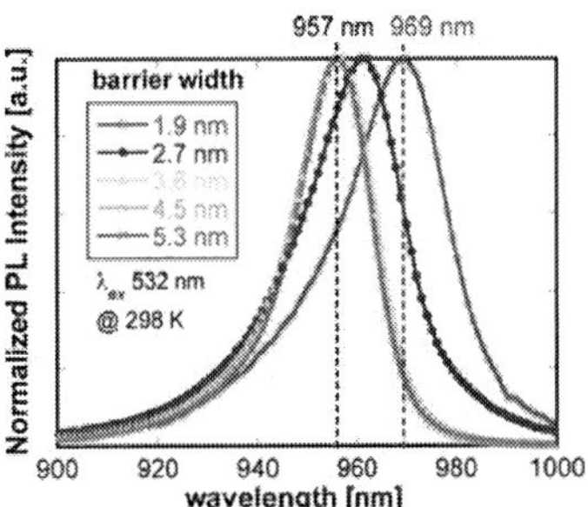

Fig. 3. Normalized CWPL spectra of MQW cells around MQW band-edge under illumination of a 532 nm, 300 μW laser at short-circuit, and room temperature condition.

barrier height in the sample set as discussed in Section II and the same will be experimentally confirmed in this section. The controlled built-in field was assured by maintaining the same doping profile and i-region thickness during the growth. The constant composition of GaAs$_{0.59}$P$_{0.41}$ indicates that the band-edge energy for the barrier is constant, and therefore only the energy levels in the wells have to be discussed to verify the constant effective barrier height. To ascertain that all quantum well structures have the same effective bandgap, continuous-wave photoluminescence (CWPL) were measured by using 532-nm laser with 300-μW power and the result under short-circuit condition is shown in Fig. 3. The PL peaks show that these MQWs have almost the same effective bandgap of 1.295 eV (957 nm) as expected. However, when MQW cells had 2.7-nm- and 1.9-nm-thick barriers, the effective bandgap was 1.290 eV (961 nm) and 1.280 eV (969 nm), respectively, due to energy level splitting after the overlap of wavefunctions from adjacent wells. Fortunately, as will be shown in the next part, this decrease in bandgap, or increase in effective barrier height, can be ignored because enhanced tunneling escape can overcome degraded thermal escape.

Fig. 4 shows the EQE spectra of MQW cells and the reference cell. Peaks beyond the GaAs band-edge were observed as would be expected from MQW solar cells. Similar EQE spectra under sufficient reverse bias confirm that these samples have the same light absorption and are, therefore, appropriate for comparison of carrier transport. On the other hand, under forward bias, the large difference was observed in the EQE spectra because of the difference in carrier transport inside MQW. This is considered critical since solar cells operate under forward bias. This will be discussed further in the next section by introducing CCE.

B. Carrier Transport and Carrier Collection Enhancement

The result of TRPL measurement, under short-circuit and room temperature conditions, is shown in Fig. 5(a), wherein the instrument response function (IRF), measured directly by scattered laser, is also shown. The decay times obtained from the slopes of decay for various applied voltages are shown in Fig. 5(b), together with the time constant of IRF, 0.13 nm. It is known that the decay of TRPL is affected by both escaping and recombination processes, rendering the analysis of escape times

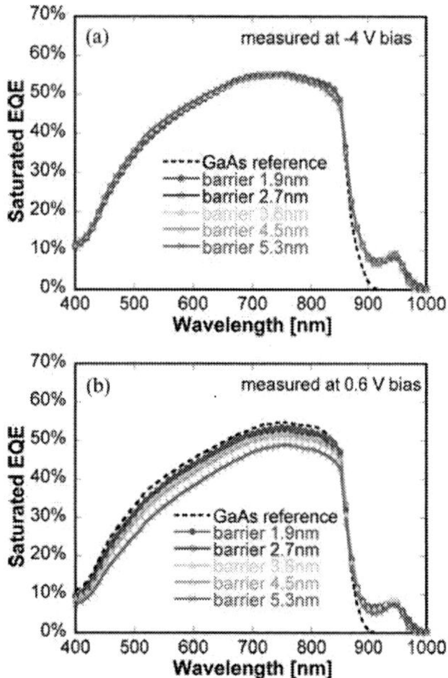

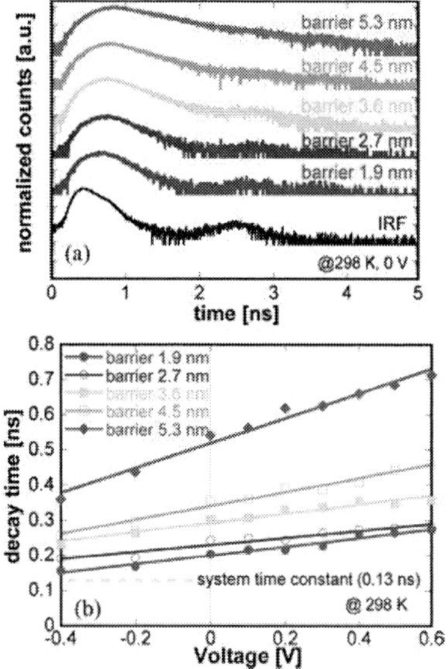

Fig. 4. EQE spectra at room temperature under (a) –4 V and (b) 0.6 V; the intensity of monochromatic light was 2.5 mW/cm^2.

Fig. 5. (a) Normalized TRPL curves of MQW solar cells under the conditions of 405-nm excitation, short-circuit, and room temperature. The IRF measured from incident beam scattering is also shown. At this wavelength, more than 99% of the carriers were excited in the p-region. (b) Fitting decay time constants for different applied voltages. The time constant of IRF is presented as a dashed line.

difficult [22]. However, it can be seen that the decay becomes faster under reverse bias, thus indicating that the escaping process dominates the decay here. The carrier escape from MQWs gets faster when the thickness of GaAsP barriers decreases. This agrees well with the characteristic of tunneling process, implying thereby that, when the barrier thickness is from 5.3

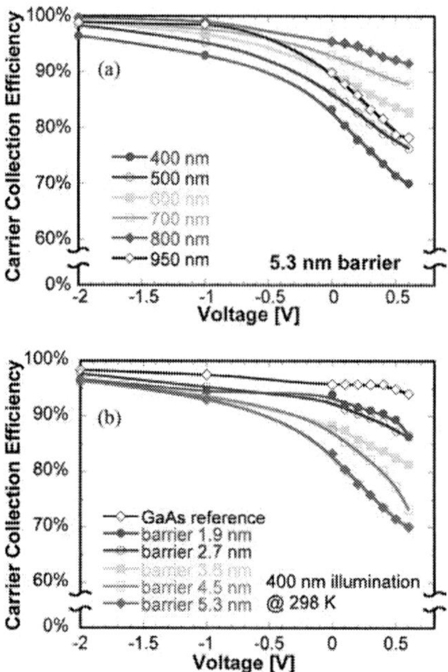

Fig. 6. Carrier collection efficiencies of (a) 5.3-nm-barrier sample excited by various excitation wavelengths and (b) all the samples excited by 400-nm illumination at room temperature.

to 1.9 nm, the tunneling escape improves dramatically. Moreover, MQWs with thicker barriers show stronger dependency on applied bias and hence internal electric field. This indicates that the relation of thermal escape to applied electric field, in the range of electric field applied for this study (8–18 kV/cm), is stronger than that of tunneling escape, although a faster system time constant is necessary for more a detailed study of bias dependency.

The CCE values of MQW cells, measured at room temperature, were found to be comparatively poor at short wavelength excitation [see Fig. 6(a)]. This implies that electron transport is the bottleneck to performance; hence, the focus was on CCE at excitation wavelength of around 400 nm as it allows direct observation of the improvement in electron transport. Fig. 6(b) shows that at 400-nm excitation, CCE declines significantly as the barrier thickness increase from 1.9 to 5.3 nm. Thus, fast tunneling escape rate results in better cell performance of MQW solar cells. When the barrier thickness goes below 2.7 nm, the value of CCE almost converges, thus indicating that this is the critical thickness needed for tunneling enhancement of the cell performance. This result provides cell design criteria needed to improve the cell performance of InGaAs/GaAsP MQW solar cells.

To confirm whether the performance enhancement in MQW solar cells with thin barriers can be attributed to the tunneling escape, low-temperature measurement of CCE was carried out to suppress thermal escape, and thus leaving the tunneling escape alone to drive carrier extraction. The temperature dependence of CCE at short-circuit condition is summarized in Fig. 7. The fact that CCE is almost constant in the GaAs reference cell at

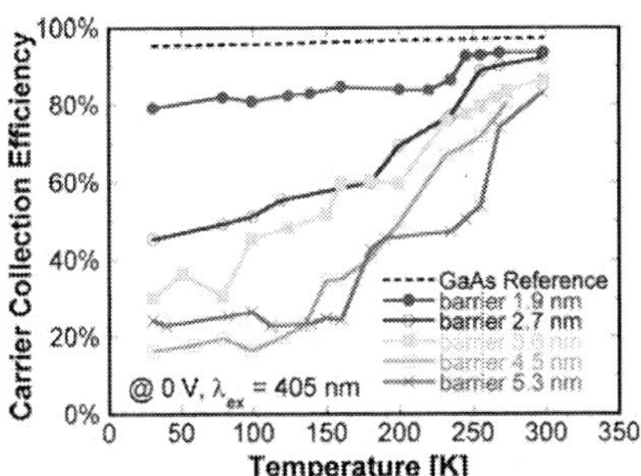

Fig. 7.   Temperature dependence of collection efficiencies of carriers, excited by 405-nm laser under short-circuit condition.

any temperature justifies the validity of introducing CCE for evaluating carrier dynamics attributed to the characteristics of MQWs. The CCE of cells with barrier thickness of more than 3.6 nm dropped by more than 50% at 30 K, as compared with the value at room temperature. In contrast, the CCE of cells with barrier thickness of 2.7 and 1.9 nm dropped by only 45% and 15%, respectively. This can be explained as due to the fact that, in the cells with thin barriers, carriers travel inside MQWs by tunneling process more effectively than by thermal process, thus making CCE less affected after the thermal process is suppressed. Therefore, it confirms that the tunneling process has a remarkable impact on cell performance enhancement.

By cooling and sufficiently increasing barrier thickness, the thermal escape and tunneling escape should be suppressed; hence, the drop in CCE at low temperature and with thick barriers should give values of CCE supported by both processes. However, the value of CCE of the cell with barrier thickness of 5.3 nm at low temperature still remains. This is because the suppression of carrier escape may not be enough, or there might be other dynamics which require consideration. Nevertheless, it can be said that the main carrier collection process can be explained by the thermal-and-tunneling model as suggested by many research workers of carrier escape. This finding enhances the present understanding of carrier transport inside MQWs and consequently confirms the practicality of the cell design using tunneling enhancement. Although this study investigated InGaAs/GaAsP MQW solar cells, the concept is considered applicable to other material systems of MQW solar cells as well.

C. Cell Performance as Middle Subcells in Triple-Junction Solar Cells

The $I-V$ characteristics were measured for discussion on practical cell performance. The AM1.5G spectrum filtered by a 665-nm longpass filter (FGL665 S, Thorlabs) was illuminated to evaluate the cell performance as a midcell since wavelengths longer than 665 nm will be absorbed by an InGaP or AlGaAs topcell. The $I-V$ curves are shown in Fig. 8 and the parameters are summarized in Table I. Under reverse bias, the current density was the same for all the MQW samples at 6.13 mA/cm², as expected from the similar reverse-biased EQE in Fig. 4(a). In contrast, short-circuit current density, open-circuit voltage, and conversion efficiency improved significantly after decreasing

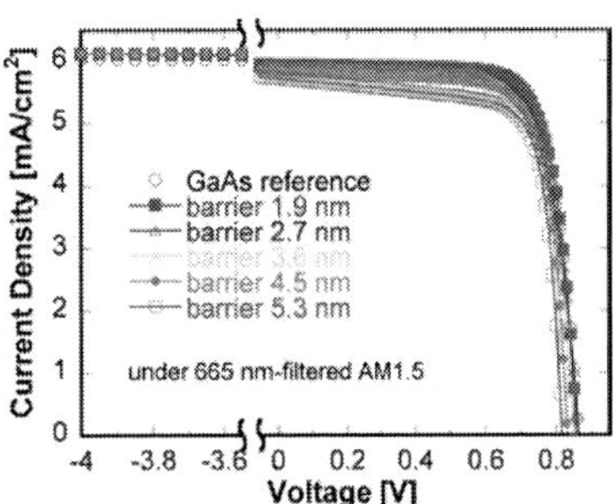

Fig. 8.   Cell performance under illumination of AM1.5G filtered by a 665-nm longpass filter (FGL665 S, Thorlabs) to simulate the performance of middle subcell in triple-junction cell.

TABLE I
CELL PERFORMANCE UNDER 665-NM-FILTERED AM1.5G ILLUMINATION

Barrier Thickness	Short-Circuit Current Density (mA/cm²)	Open-Circuit Voltage (V)	Conversion Efficiency (%)
Reference	5.88	0.862	7.45
1.9 nm	5.95	0.854	7.62
2.7 nm	5.91	0.862	7.34
3.6 nm	5.91	0.848	7.27
4.5 nm	5.84	0.829	7.20
5.3 nm	5.73	0.811	6.87

Prior to illumination, AM1.5G was filtered by a 665 nm longpass filter (FGL665S, Thorlabs) to simulate a light spectrum entering a midcell, whose wavelength of more than 665 nm will be absorbed by a topcell. The filter transmitted less than 5% light when λ < 647 nm and more than 85% when λ > 687 nm. At long wavelengths, the transmittance was around 91%. Illumination intensity after filtering was considered for calculating conversion efficiencies.

the GaAsP barrier thickness. Particularly, the increase in conversion efficiency as midcells was more in the MQW cell with 1.9-nm barrier than in the typical p-i-n GaAs. These may be regarded as improvements in CCE by tunneling enhancement discussed in the last section since the enhanced CCE avoids drop in photocurrent in short-circuit and forward-bias conditions [see (1)]. A small open-circuit voltage drop in a sample with 1.9-nm barriers was caused by decline in bandgap as shown in Fig. 3.

Nonetheless, current density of more than 14 mA/cm² is required for the current matching in the optimized triple-junction solar cells [3]. However, the samples measured here, which were optimized particularly to verify physical phenomena, were obviously insufficient for practical use. Following are some of the issues to be improved in a practical cell: 1) weak absorption in MQW, which can be enhanced by introducing more than 100 periods of MQWs [11] or light management [23]; 2) lack of window layers for the prevention of surface recombination; 3) the lack of AR coating; and 4) larger effective bandgap (1.30 eV) than that of the optimized one (1.20 eV), which can be reached by the development of a crystal growth technique [13]. A promising structure for high-efficiency MQW subcells can be expected after optimizing carrier collection process and satisfying the points mentioned above.

IV. CONCLUSION

Electron escape times of InGaAs/GaAsP MQW solar cells with variable thickness of potential barriers and controlled potential height were studied. The escape time was found to be shorter for the cell with thinner barriers, thus indicating the potential of tunneling escape. Faster tunneling escape, in turn, improves carrier collection efficiency, resulting in the enhancement of solar cell performance as a middle subcell in a triple-junction cell. These results also indicate that a barrier thickness of at least 3 nm is required for the tunneling enhancement of cell performance. This information is useful for the cell design in future works. In addition, the same experiment can be conducted with n-on-p structures to study the hole escape mechanism. Moreover, the practicality of the thermal-and-tunneling model was also investigated. Further quantitative and detailed modeling, on the basis of the present findings, would contribute to the design of better MQW cells for more efficient carrier transport.

REFERENCES

[1] W. Shockley and H. J. Queisser, "Detailed balance limit of efficiency of p–n junction solar cells," *J. Appl. Phys.*, vol. 32, no. 3, pp. 510–519, Mar. 1961.

[2] R. K. Jones, J. H. Ermer, C. M. Fetzer, and R. R. King, "Evolution of multijunction solar cell technology for concentrating photovoltaics," *Jpn. J. Appl. Phys.*, vol. 51, pp. 10ND01-1–10ND01-4, Oct. 2012.

[3] R. R. King, D. Bhusari, D. Larrabee, X.-Q. Liu, E. Rehder, K. Edmondson, H. Cotal, R. K. Jones, J. H. Ermer, C. M. Fetzer, D. C. Law, and N. H. Karam, "Solar cell generations over 40% efficiency," *Prog. Photovolt. Res. Appl.*, vol. 20, no. 6, pp. 801–815, Sep. 2012.

[4] T. Takamoto, M. Kaneiwa, M. Imaizumi, and M. Yamaguchi, "InGaP/GaAs-based multijunction solar cells," *Prog. Photovolt. Res. Appl.*, vol. 13, no. 6, pp. 495–511, Sep. 2005.

[5] W. Guter, J. Schöne, S. P. Philipps, M. Steiner, G. Siefer, A. Wekkeli, E. Welser, E. Oliva, A. W. Bett, and F. Dimroth, "Current-matched triple-junction solar cell reaching 41.1% conversion efficiency under concentrated sunlight," *Appl. Phys. Lett.*, vol. 94, no. 22, pp. 223504-1–223504-3, 2009.

[6] N. J. Ekins-Daukes, J. M. Barnes, K. W. J. Barnham, J. P. Connolly, M. Mazzer, J. C. Clark, R. Grey, G. Hill, M. A. Pate, and J. S. Roberts, "Strained and strain-balanced quantum well devices for high-efficiency tandem solar cells," *Sol. Energy Mater. Sol. Cells*, vol. 68, no. 1, pp. 71–87, Apr. 2001.

[7] B. Browne, J. Lacey, T. Tibbits, G. Bacchin, T. C. Wu, J. Q. Liu, X. Chen, V. Rees, J. Tsai, and J. G. Werthen, "Triple-Junction quantum-well solar cells in commercial production," in *Proc. AIP Conf.*, Miyazaki, Japan, 2013, vol. 1556, no. 3, pp. 3–5.

[8] J. M. Mohaidat, K. Shum, W. B. Wang, and R. R. Alfano, "Barrier potential design criteria in multiple-quantum-well-based solar-cell structures," *J. Appl. Phys.*, vol. 76, no. 9, pp. 5533–5537, Nov. 1994.

[9] A. C. Varonides and R. A. Spalletta, "Tunneling vs. thermionic currents in multi-quantum well photovoltaic structures," *WSEAS Trans. Electron.*, vol. 2, no. 4, pp. 170–174, Oct. 2005.

[10] A. Alemu, J. A. Coaquira, and A. Freundlich, "Dependence of device performance on carrier escape sequence in multi-quantum-well p-i-n solar cells," *J. Appl. Phys.*, vol. 99, no. 8, pp. 084506-1–084506-5, Apr. 2006.

[11] Y. Wang, Y. Wen, H. Sodabunlu, K. Wanatabe, M. Sugiyama, and Y. Nakano, "A superlattice solar cell with enhanced short-circuit current and minimized drop in open-circuit voltage," *IEEE J. Photovolt.*, vol. 2, no. 3, pp. 387–392, Jul. 2012.

[12] G. K. Bradshaw, C. Z. Carlin, J. P. Samberg, N. A. El-Masry, P. C. Colter, and S. M. Bedair, "Carrier transport and improved collection in thin-barrier InGaAs/GaAsP strained quantum well solar cells," *IEEE J. Photovolt.*, vol. 3, no. 1, pp. 278–283, Jan. 2013.

[13] H. Fujii, Y. Wang, K. Wanatabe, M. Sugiyama, and Y. Nakano, "High-aspect ratio structures for efficient light absorption and carrier transport in InGaAs/GaAsP multiple-quantum-well solar cells," *IEEE J. Photovolt.*, vol. 3, no. 2, pp. 859–867, Apr. 2013.

[14] B. A. Vojak, N. Holonyak, R. Chin, E. A. Rezek, R. D. Dupuis, and P. D. Dapkus, "Tunnel injection and phonon-assisted recombination in multiple-quantum-well $Al_x Ga_{1-x}$ As-GaAs p-n heterostructure lasers grown by metalorganic chemical vapor deposition," *J. Appl. Phys.*, vol. 50, no. 9, pp. 5835–5840, Sep. 1979.

[15] I. Mehdi, G. I. Haddad, and R. K. Mains, "Novel use of resonant tunneling structures for optical and IR modulators," *Superlattices Microstructures*, vol. 5, no. 3, pp. 443–449, Jan. 1989.

[16] H. Sodabanlu, S. Ma, K. Watanabe, M. Sugiyama, and Y. Nakano, "Impact of strain accumulation on InGaAs/GaAsP multiple-quantum-well solar cells: Direct correlation between in situ strain measurement and cell performances," *Jpn. J. Appl. Phys.*, vol. 51, pp. 10ND16-1–10ND16-4, Oct. 2012.

[17] H. Fujii, Y. Wang, K. Watanabe, M. Sugiyama, and Y. Nakano, "Enhanced carrier collection efficiency in InGaAs/GaAsP quantum well solar cells by compensation doping," in *Proc. 27th Eur. PV Solar Energy Conf. Exhib.*, Frankfurt, Germany, 2012, pp. 27–31.

[18] E. D. Palik, "Gallium Arsenide (GaAs)," in *Handbook of Optical Constants of Solids*, vol. 1, 1st ed. New York, NY, USA: Academic, 1997, pp. 429–443.

[19] R. Corkish and M. A. Green, "Recombination of carriers in quantum well solar cells," in *Proc. IEEE 23th Photovoltaic Spec. Conf.*, Louisville, KY, USA, 1993, pp. 675–680.

[20] H. Schneider and K. V. Klitzing, "Thermionic emission and Gaussian transport of holes in a $GaAs/Al_x Ga_{1-x}$ As multiple-quantum-well structure," *Phys. Rev. B, Condensed Matter.*, vol. 38, no. 9, pp. 6160–6165, Sep. 1988.

[21] H. Fujii, K. Toprasertpong, K. Watanabe, M. Sugiyama, and Y. Nakano, "Carrier collection efficiency in multiple quantum well solar cells," in *Proc. SPIE*, San Francisco, CA, USA, 2013, p. 86201 F.

[22] K. Watanabe, K. Toprasertpong, H. Fujii, H. Sodabanlu, M. Sugiyama, and Y. Nakano, "Temperature-dependent photoluminescence analysis for InGaAs/GaAsP multiple quantum wells solar cell," presented at the 22th Int. Photovoltaic Sci. Eng. Conf., Hangzhou, China, Nov. 2012.

[23] D. B. Bushnell, N. J. Ekins-Daukes, K. W. J. Barnham, J. P. Connolly, J. S. Roberts, G. Hill, R. Airey, and M. Mazzer, "Short-circuit current enhancement in Bragg stack multi-quantum-well solar cells for multi-junction space cell applications," *Sol. Energy Mater. Sol. Cells*, vol. 75, no. 1–2, pp. 299–305, Jan. 2003.

Kasidit Toprasertpong was born in Bangkok, Thailand, on July 14, 1989. He received the B.E. degree from the Department of Electrical and Electronic Engineering, University of Tokyo, Tokyo, Japan, in 2013, where he is currently working toward the M.S. degree with the Department of Electrical Engineering and Information Systems.

He is currently a Japanese government (Monbukagakusho) Scholarship student. His current research interests include physics of carrier dynamics inside quantum structures and characterization of nanostructure solar cells.

Mr. Toprasertpong is a Member of the Japan Society of Applied Physics.

Hiromasa Fujii received the B.E. degree from the Department of System Innovation and the M.S. degree from the Department of Electrical Engineering, both from the University of Tokyo, Tokyo, Japan, in 2010 and 2012, respectively. He is currently working toward the Ph.D. degree with the Department of Electrical Engineering and Information Systems, University of Tokyo.

He is also a Research Fellow of the Japan Society for the Promotion of Science. His current research interests include metal-organic vapor phase epitaxy of III–V materials for photovoltaic application and device characterization to uncover the underlying physics in the quantum structure devices.

Mr. Fujii is a Member of the Japan Society of Applied Physics.

Yunpeng Wang was born in Dalian, China, on October 23, 1977. He received B.Eng. degree from the Fine Chemistry Department and the M.Eng. degree from the Department of Inorganic Chemistry, Dalian University of Technology (DLUT), Dalian, Liaoning, China, in 2001 and 2004, respectively, and the Ph.D. degree in material engineering from the University of Tokyo, Tokyo, Japan, in 2008. His Ph.D. research focused on the kinetic behavior of III–V compound semiconductor by metal-organic vapor-phase epitaxy (MOVPE).

After graduation, he was a Research Staff member with the Advanced Carbon Material Institute, DLUT, and continued his research on carbon nanomaterial. Since 2008, he has been a Project Researcher with the Research Center for Advanced Science and Technology, University of Tokyo. His research interests include both MOVPE phenomena of compound semiconductor, and nanosize devices implementation, designing, and measurement, especially, multijunction solar cells.

Dr. Wang is a Member of the Japan Society of Applied Physics and the Society of Chemical Engineers, Japan.

Kentaroh Watanabe received the B.S. degree from the Department of Physics, Hokkaido University, Hokkaido, Japan, in 2002, and the M.S. and Ph.D. degrees from the Department of Astronomy, University of Tokyo, Tokyo, Japan, in 2004 and 2007, respectively.

In 2007, he was a Researcher with the Institute of Space and Astrophysical Science, Japan Aerospace Exploration Agency, Kanagawa, Japan. In 2009, he joined the Research Center for Advanced Science and Technology, University of Tokyo, where he is currently a Project Assistant Professor. His current research interests include the ultrahigh-efficiency photovoltaic devices and metal-organic vapor phase epitaxy of III–V compound semiconductors.

Dr. Watanabe is a Member of the Japan Society of Applied Physics, the Astronomical Society of Japan, and the International Society of Optics and Photonics.

Masakazu Sugiyama received the B.E., M.S., and Ph.D. degrees in chemical systems engineering, all from the University of Tokyo, Tokyo, Japan, in 1995, 1997, and 2000, respectively.

He is currently an Associate Professor with the Institute of Engineering Innovation, Graduate School of Engineering, University of Tokyo. He is also with the Department of Electronic Engineering. From 1997 to 2000, he was a Research Fellow of the Japan Society for the Promotion of Science. In 2000, he became a Research Associate with the Department of Chemical System Engineering, University of Tokyo. In 2002, he joined the Department of Electronic Engineering as a Lecturer. He became an Associate Professor in 2005. He authored and coauthored more than 130 refereed journal publications and more than 140 international conference papers. He also holds 15 patents. His research interests include reaction engineering regarding the fabrication processes of nanomicro devices, especially film deposition and plasma etching. His current concern is high-efficiency solar cells with quantum nanostructures and its growth with metalorganic vapor-phase epitaxy, under the Research and Development of Innovative Solar Cell Program NEDO. His other concern is nanomicro fabrication processes, including photon-trapping mechanisms as an efficiency booster for solar cells.

Dr. Sugiyama is a Member of the Japan Society of Applied Physics, the Society of Chemical Engineers, Japan (SCEJ), and the Japanese Association for Crystal Growth. In 2003, he received the Young Investigator Researcher Award from SCEJ.

Yoshiaki Nakano (S'81–M'87) received the B.E., M.S., and Ph.D. degrees in electronic engineering, all from the University of Tokyo, Tokyo, Japan, in 1982, 1984, and 1987, respectively. In 1984, he spent a year with the University of California, Berkeley, CA, USA, as an exchange student.

He is currently the Director and a Professor with the Research Center for Advanced Science and Technology, University of Tokyo. He is also with the Department of Electronic Engineering, School of Engineering, University of Tokyo. In 1987, he joined the Department of Electronic Engineering, University of Tokyo, and became an Associate Professor in 1992, a Professor in 2000, and the Department Head in 2001. He moved to the Research Center for Advanced Science and Technology, University of Tokyo, in 2002, where he is currently a Professor with the Department of Information Systems. In 1992, he was a Visiting Associate Professor with the University of California, Santa Barbara, CA, USA. He has authored and coauthored more than 200 refereed journal publications and more than 400 international conference papers, and he holds 40 patents. His research interests include physics and fabrication technologies of semiconductor distributed feedback lasers, semiconductor optical modulators/switches, and monolithically integrated photonic circuits.

Dr. Nakano was an elected member of the Board of Governors of the IEEE Laser and Electrooptics Society and a Member of the Board of Directors of the Japan Society of Applied Physics (JSAP). He is currently a Member of the Board of Directors of the Japan Institute of Electronics Packaging, the Chairman of the Optoelectronics Technology Trend Research Committee of the Optoelectronics Industry and Technology Development Association (OITDA), and the Chairman of the Optical Interconnect Standardization Committee of Japan Electronics Packaging and Circuits Association. He is also a Fellow of the Institute of Electronics, Information, and Communication Engineers (IEICE), a Member of the IEEE EDS, and the OSA. He served as the Leader of the Japanese National Project on "Research and Development of Innovative Solar Cell program" organized by the Ministry of Economy, Trading, and Industry. He received the 1987 Shinohara Memorial Prize from the IEICE, the 1991 Optics Paper Award from the JSAP, the 1997 Marubun Science Prize, the 2007 Ichimura Prize, the 2007 IEICE Electronics Society Award, and the 2007 Sakurai Medal from the OITDA. He received the Prime Minister Award in Collaborative Research between Academia and Industry in 2007.

Thin-Film InGaAs/GaAsP MQWs Solar Cell With Backside Nanoimprinted Pattern for Light Trapping

Kentaroh Watanabe, Boram Kim, Tomoyuki Inoue, Hassanet Sodabanlu, Masakazu Sugiyama, Masanao Goto, Shinya Hayashi, Kenjiro Miyano, and Yoshiaki Nakano

Abstract—A light-trapping structure of the thin-film GaAs p-i-n single-junction solar cell with InGaAs/GaAsP multiple quantum wells (MQWs) was successfully demonstrated. Using a nanoimprinting method with ultraviolet curing resin, the submicron light-scattering dielectric array was fabricated on the back surface of the cell for enhanced optical absorption in the MQWs. The epitaxially grown photovoltaic active layer approximately 2.5 μm in thickness was successfully transferred to the stainless steel support substrate with backside light-scattering structure from the GaAs growth substrate. The light-trapping pattern-induced sample showed improved absorption in MQWs and resulted in 1.7 times larger quantum efficiency than the cell without the backside pattern.

Index Terms—Light trapping, multiple quantum wells (MQWs), quantum efficiency spectrum, thin-film III–V cell.

I. INTRODUCTION

LIGHT trapping is quite an attractive technology for improving the conversion efficiency of PV cells. The idea of light trapping was proposed for thin-film crystalline silicon and dye sensitized solar cells in order to reduce material consumption and production cost while keeping high-conversion efficiency [1]–[4]. On the other hand, InGaAs/GaAsP strain-balanced multiple quantum wells (MQWs) solar cells essentially have the advantage of variable bandgap energy, lower than the bulk GaAs, and they are more suitable for PV operating under high concentration [5], [6]. One of the important issues of quantum structures for the application of solar cells is insufficient diffusion length of photoexcited carrier. When InGaAs/GaAsP MQWs exist in the i-region of the GaAs p-i-n cell, the carrier

transportation from MQWs is quite important to achieve high PV performance [7]. Until now, such an InGaAs/GaAsP MQWs system has been investigated as a feasible candidate material for a middle subcell of current-matched triple-junction solar cell [8]–[10]. In order to improve the photo-carrier extraction efficiency, smaller stacking numbers of MQW for thinning the i-region thickness is desirable to obtain the large built-in field potential. Furthermore, from the crystallographic point of view, a smaller number of MQWs is also favorable to reduce dislocation density since InGaAs/GaAsP MQWs necessitates elaborate strain balancing [11], [12]. However, such a smaller total number of InGaAs well reduces the photon absorption in the objective wavelength range beyond GaAs band edge. The problem of such a tradeoff relationship between optical-thickness for light absorption and electrical field for carrier transport has not been solved yet.

We have proposed a light-trapping technique for In-GaAs/GaAs MQWs solar cells for realizing the maximum light harvesting in a single-junction cell: the scattering structure on the back surface of the cell induces multiple total reflections of inside the cell, at longer wavelengths than the absorption edge of GaAs. Because the free carrier absorption in a thick conductive GaAs substrate leads to the same order of optical absorption as that of MQWs at the subbandgap wavelength, the thickness of the substrate should be reduced to maximize the light-trapping effect [13], [14]. Recently, the thin-film PV cell with GaAs or III–V epitaxial layers transferred to the other support substrate realized excellent performance and also the feasibility for drastic cost reduction has been suggested for high-efficiency PV production [15]–[18]. Such a methodology of PV thinning by transferring only the epitaxial grown layer should be significantly suitable for the light-trapping effect of eliminating energy loss caused by free carrier absorption in a conductive substrate [19]. In this paper, we report the fabrication of the light-trapping thin-film MQWs solar cell by epitaxial layer transfer on the supporting substrate. Measured external quantum efficiency (EQE) showed clear enhancement by applying the light-trapping backside pattern, which was defined by using nanoimprinted ultraviolet (UV) curing resin array.

II. EXPERIMENTAL DETAILS

A. Concept of the Thin-Film III–V Cell With Light Trapping

Fig. 1 shows the cross-sectional structure of thin-film MQW solar cells with a light-trapping texture. The inverted single-junction GaAs p-i-n structure with ten layers of strain-balanced $In_{0.17}Ga_{0.83}As/GaAs_{0.78}P_{0.22}$ MQW inserted in i-region was

Manuscript received June 10, 2013; revised January 17, 2014; accepted March 6, 2014. This work was supported by the Research and Development of Innovative Solar Cell program, New Energy and Industrial Technology Development Organization, Japan.

K. Watanabe, H. Sodabanlu and K. Miyano are with the Research Center for Advanced Science and Technology, University of Tokyo, Tokyo 153-8904, Japan (e-mail: kentaroh@hotaka.t.u-tokyo.ac.jp; sodabanlu@hotaka.t.u-tokyo.ac.jp; miyano@mbe.rcast.u-tokyo.ac.jp).

B. Kim, T. Inoue, M. Sugiyama, and Y. Nakano are with the Department of Electrical Engineering and Information Systems, School of Engineering, University of Tokyo, Tokyo 113-8654, Japan (e-mail: boram@hotaka.t.utokyo.ac.jp; inoue@hotaka.t.u-tokyo.ac.jp; sugiyama@ee.t.u-tokyo.ac.jp; nakano@ee.t.u-tokyo.ac.jp).

M. Goto and S. Hayashi are with the Central Technical Research Laboratory, JX Nippon Oil and Energy Corporation, Yokohama, Kanagawa 231-0815, Japan (e-mail: masanao.goto@noe.jx-group.co.jp; shinya.hayashi@noe.jx-group.co.jp).

Color versions of one or more of the figures in this paper are available online at http://ieeexplore.ieee.org.

Digital Object Identifier 10.1109/JPHOTOV.2014.2312486

     274

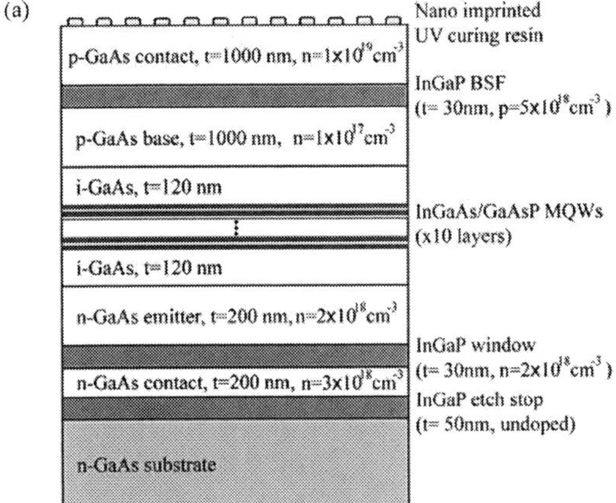

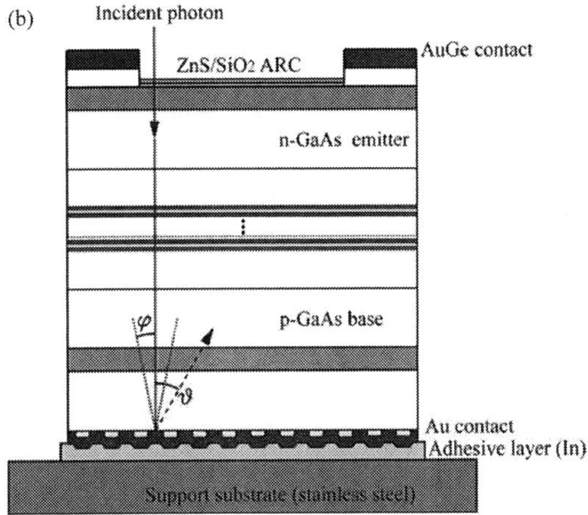

Fig. 1. Schematic figure of a thin-film MQWs solar cell structure with light-scattering pattern. (a) An inverted MOVPE-grown PV active layer and NIR-patterned top surface. (b) A thin-film solar cell with light-trapping pattern transferred on a stainless steel substrate.

grown by metal organic vapor phase epitaxy (MOVPE) on the n-type GaAs (0 0 1) substrate. The thickness (t) and doping concentration (n or p) of GaAs contact, base, emitter, $In_{0.48}Ga_{0.52}P$ window, back surface field (BSF) and etch stop layers are shown in Fig. 1(a). The thicknesses of the InGaAs well and the GaAsP barrier was 8.54 and 15.7 mm, respectively. An accumulated strain was totally compensated by monitoring *in situ* curvature using the multibeam optical strain-sensor system during the MOVPE growth.

Typically, about 15% of free carrier absorption was observed for a 300 μm-thick n-type GaAs substrate (net carrier density $n{\sim}2 \times 10^{18}$ cm^{-3}) at $\lambda = 950$ nm in a single light path [13], [20], [21]. This absorption loss is almost equivalent to the optical absorption in InGaAs/GaAsP MQWs, in which the effective thickness of InGaAs absorber is 300 nm. The light trapping in the cell causes the same enhancement of effective optical path length for both the substrate and the InGaAs absorber when the MQWs PV structure was grown on the n-type GaAs substrate. Therefore, it is necessary to reduce the substrate thickness for minimizing the optical loss due to free-carrier absorption and maximizing the light trapping effect in the PV active layer. In this study, we tried to fabricate a thin-film solar cell by transferring the PV active epitaxial layer on the supporting substrate, as shown in Fig. 1(b), so that the free-carrier absorption loss is reduced drastically.

The backside scattering pattern was fabricated by nanoimprinted UV curing resin on the epitaxial surface of the inverted PV structure for inducing the light-trapping effect in the cell. The scattered photon at the back surface, which has an angle θ from the normal direction, can be confined in cell if θ was larger than the critical angle φ for the total reflection on the front surface, resulting in absorption enhancement in the optically thin medium, where φ is defined by the contrast of refractive index between the PV material and air. In the case of GaAs-based cell, φ is estimated to be approximataly16.6° [14].

B. Nanoimprinted Pattern for Light Scattering

As a light-trapping structure, the submicrometer-scale dielectric array has been attempted by nanoimprinting lithography (NIL) method. Strong light scattering should be caused by a large difference of dielectric constant between the gold electrode, the GaAs layer, and the dielectric material. The nanotextured template of silicon (Si) wafer was fabricated by electron beam lithography (EBL) and inductively-coupled plasma reactive ion etching (ICP-RIE). The obtained Si NIL mold was copied to the heat curable PDMS resin as a UV-transparent mold. Finally, the aligned nanosize box of the UV curing resin was obtained on the surface of an epitaxial wafer as shown in Fig. 1(a), by applying the molding to the resin and subsequently curing with UV irradiation. Fig. 2 shows the picture of the surface with the arrayed bumps of the UV curing resin and a magnified SEM image of the NIL patterns. In order to form the electrode on p-type GaAs contact layer, the residual fim of the UV curing resin was removed by O_2 ashing process using ICP-IRE. The lateral size of each resin bump was 600 nm × 600 nm, and the height was 260 nm, respectively. The period of the lattice was 900 nm. The size and period of NIR pattern were optimized by numerical simulation of the light-trapping effect calculated by the FDTD method to maximize the light-trapping effect. The detail about the numerical FDTD simulation for an optimized structure is described in Section III.

C. Epitaxial Layer Transfer and Cell Fabrication

After NIL patterning of the UV resin, the surface of the epitaxial wafer was coated with a gold contact layer as a backside metal electrode, and then the epitaxial wafer was bonded to a flat stainless steel substrate using a liquid-phase indium paste at 160 C°. After solidification of an adhesive indium metal at room temperature, the n-type GaAs substrate was removed by selective wet etching in the mixture of aqueous ammonia and hydrogen peroxide. After subsequent selective etching only the InGaP etch stop layer by 36% HCl solution, the top contact with a cross finger grid was fabricated by evaporation of the AuGe alloy. Finally, the ZnS/SiO2 dual layer antireflection coating

Fig. 2. Surface picture of nanoimprinted UV curing resin in 1 cm × 1 cm area. (a) A whole surface and (b) SEM image of UV curing resin array.

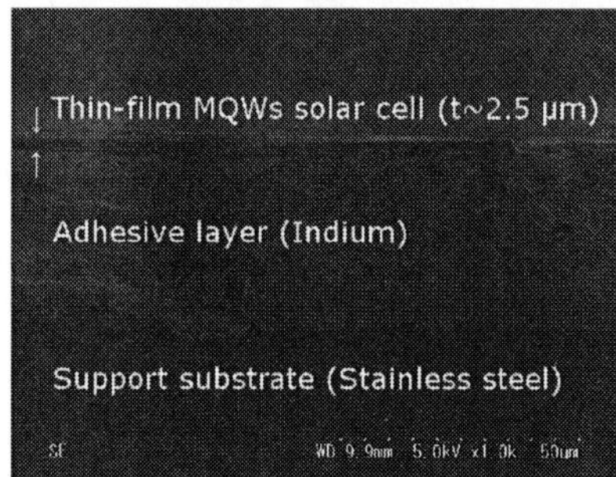

Fig. 3. Cross-sectional SEM image of the thin-film MQWs solar cell.

was applied to the cell surface for minimizing surface reflection loss.

Fig. 3 shows the cross-sectional SEM image of the fabricated thin-film MQWs solar cell. The thickness of the indium adhesive layer was ~50 μm and the thickness of the MQWs solar cell was approximately 2.5 μm, respectively. We also fabricated a thin-film bulk GaAs and MQWs solar cell without any pattern on the epitaxial surface as a reference sample. Because the epitaxially grown surface was sufficiently mirror like, the reference sample with a flat back surface should provide almost double optical path length across the cell for incident photons due to backside reflection.

D. External Quantum Efficiency and Reflectance Measurement

The fabricated cells were evaluated by the EQE and reflectance spectrum. We performed the EQE measurement in the wavelength range of $\lambda = 300–1100$ nm under illumination of white-light simulating AM1.5G spectrum (100 mW/cm^2). The synchronized QE signal with chopped monochromatic irradiation (fixed incident power with 2.5 W/cm^2) was measured by using a lock-in-amplifier. The external bias voltage was set to 0 V during EQE measurement. In an I–V curve, current density was sufficiently flat versus voltage around zero external bias point, indicating that the structure is free from current leakage due to the fabrication process. We also carried out the spectral reflectance measurement using a reflection monitor equipped with a multichannel spectrometer (HAMAMATSU C10178 System). Using a beam splitter and optical fiber systems, the reflectance spectrum at the perpendicular direction to the surface was measured in the samples: the bulk GaAs thin-film cell, MQWs cells with a flat and a NIL-patterned back surface, respectively.

III. RESULT AND DISCUSSION

Fig. 4(a) shows the result of the EQE measurement. Clear enhancement was observed in the wavelength range of 880–1000 nm for the MQWs solar cell with the backside NIL pattern. Comparing observed QE in the wavelength range corresponding to the above GaAs bandgap, there was no difference between the sample with the flat and patterned back surface. This result indicated the optical absorption is sufficiently large in this range even for 2.5 μm-thick device. The averaged EQE enhancement ratio in this wavelength range was 1.7. The NIL patterned cell showed the short-circuit current (J_{SC}) of 23.4 mA/cm^2, as estimated from the integrated EQE under AM1.5G spectrum. Compared with J_{SC} with the flat back surface cell, the improvement in short-circuit current density was $\Delta J_{SC} = 0.65$ mA/cm^2 by applying the light-trapping pattern. From the result of I–V characteristics of each sample, no significant difference was observed in the open-circuit voltage and fill factor affected by applying the backside pattern.

Fig. 4(b) shows the normal reflectance spectrum of the thin-film bulk GaAs cell with a flat back surface, the MQWs cell with a flat back surface, and the MQWs cell with a NIL-patterned back surface. Oscillating fringes appear in the optically thin wavelength range ($\lambda > 880$ nm) for both the bulk GaAs and MQWs cell with flat backside surfaces. This fringe was caused by the Fabry–Perot interference between the top and back surface reflections, and the oscillation period of each spectrum corresponds to the total thickness of thin-film samples. The frequency of the Fabry–Perot oscillation in the reflectance spectrum for the bulk GaAs cell is shorter than the MQW cell with a flat backside due to the thicker base layer applied to the bulk GaAs reference cell. For the samples with a flat back surface, the bulk GaAs cell showed the highest reflection at $\lambda > 880$ nm and the reflectance of the MQWs cell was reduced due to the light absorption by the quantum wells. The MQWs cell with a NIL- patterned backside surface showed significantly reduced normal reflectance compared to the cell with a flat backside surface, which indicates strong light scattering was caused by the backside NIL pattern, as expected.

Fig. 4(c) shows the spectral enhancement of the EQE for the light-trapping cell. The wavelength-dependent enhancement was observed. The maximum enhancement of 2.3 was observed

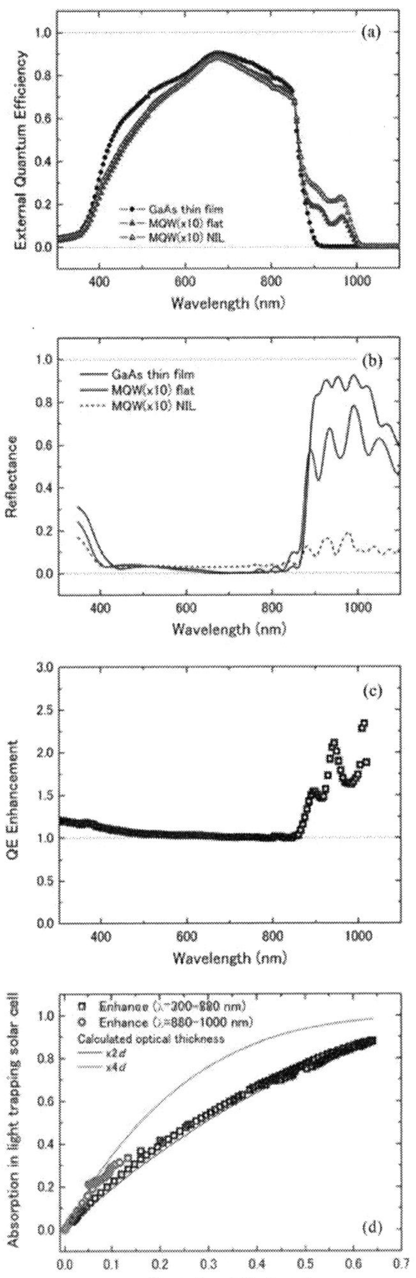

Fig. 4. . (a) EQE spectra of a thin-film bulk GaAs and MQWs solar cells, which have a flat back surface and an NIL-imprinted back surface. (b) Normal surface reflectance on the ARC-applied surface of the cell without the front contact metal. (c) Wavelength-dependent enhancement ratio of EQE for the MQWs cells with a flat back surface and an NIR-imprinted back surface. (d) Estimated effective optical path length in the MQWs cell with a backside NIL pattern, with estimated single-path absorption as the lateral axis.

at 1015 nm. At this wavelength, the absolute value of EQE was sufficiently small and we can assume that the enhancement of optical path length is equivalent to the EQE enhancement.

Further analysis of scattering by NIL pattern would be required to maximize light-trapping effect at the target wavelength of $\lambda = 880$–1000 nm.

Assuming the optical thickness of the MQWs cell with a flat back surface is exactly twice the physical thickness, we can estimate the effective optical path length (*fd*) in the light-trapping MQWs cell, where f means the enhancement factor, and d is the designed physical thickness of the devices. Because the additional backside NIL pattern size is sufficiently small, d can be regarded as common for both the flat sample and the sample with NIL pattern. According to the simple Beer–Lambert law, optical absorption in the solar cells can be expressed as 1-exp(-αfd), where α is the absorption coefficient. Compared to the QE feature in the optically thick wavelength range, there is no significant difference between the flat and patterned sample. Therefore, the observed QE value can be regarded as a light absorption ratio in the cell because the recombination loss rate of photogenerated carrier in the cell is not different between these two samples. Fig. 4(d) shows the light absorption in the light-trapping MQWs cell versus single-path absorption that is estimated from the absorption for the MQWs cell with a flat back surface. The solid lines illustrate the hypothetical absorption calculated under the assumption of $f = 2$ (black, equivalent to the flat sample) and $f = 4$ (red), respectively. By plotting the observed absorption of the light-trapping MQWs cell for the optically thick wavelength range ($\lambda = 300$–880 nm, black squares) and for the optically thin range ($\lambda = 880$–1000 nm, red circles) separately, we can conclude that the absorption enhancement owing to the light-trapping structure is effective only in the optically thin wavelength range. In the optically thick range, the enhancement over the flat cell is not significant. The maximum value of the estimated effective optical pass exceeds four times the single optical path length.

In order to optimize and verify the efficiency of the light-trapping structure of the NIL imprinted pattern, a finite-difference time-domain (FDTD) numerical simulation of an electromagnetic field in a simplified MQWs cell structure was performed [22]. Fig. 5(a) shows the cross-sectional structure of the cell for the simulation. The well-known literature values were used for the optical constants n and k, for all the layers except the MQWs layer [21], [23]. For the MQWs layer, we used effective optical constants measured by the ellipsometer. The sample of 20 periods of MQWs, which have the same structure in the solar cell devices, was prepared by MOVPE growth. As an optimization of the NIL pattern, the variable parameters of D and L were evaluated, where D is the lateral size, and L is the period of the arrayed UV curing resin, respectively. In this simulation, the ratio of D/L and height (h) of resin bump is fixed to 0.65 and 260 nm, respectively. The FDTD simulation result, as shown in Fig. 5(b), indicated approximately three times of a QE enhancement by the light-trapping structure with an NIL-imprinted pattern for $L = 900$ nm. Therefore, the obtained experimental average enhancement, a factor of 1.7 on average, is still to be improved, most likely due to the unexpected absorption at the metal–semiconductor or metal–dielectric interface at the backside of the cell.

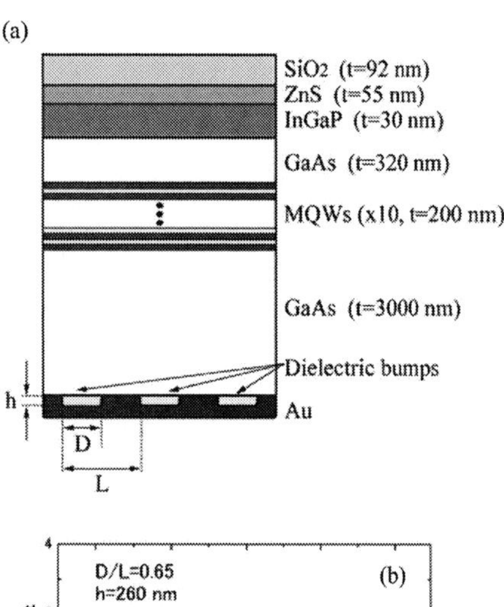

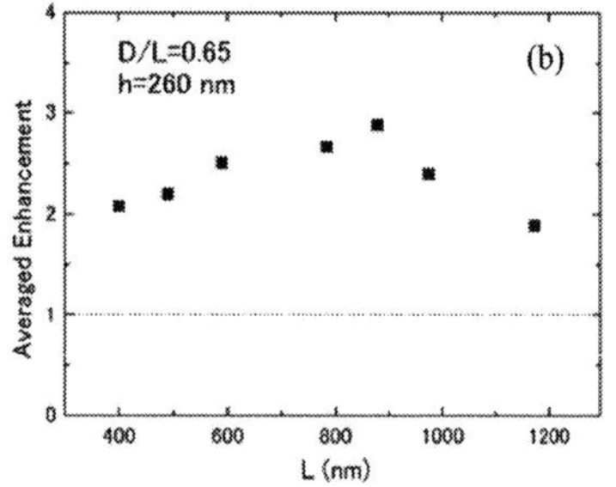

Fig. 5. (a) Simplified structure of thin-film MQWs cell with a backside NIR-imprinted UV curing resin, as modeled for FDTD simulation. (b) Averaged enhancement of MQW absorption averaged in the range of $\lambda = 800–1200$ nm obtained by the FDTD simulation, as a function of the period of NIL pattern.

IV. Conclusion

The thin-film MQWs solar cell with backside light-trapping texture has been successfully fabricated by NIR patterning and transferring the epi-grown layer to the stainless steel support substrate. Compared with the reference cell, which has a flat back surface, 1.7 times larger EQE on average was observed in the wavelength range of 880–1000 nm in the cell with an NIL-patterned UV curing resin on the back surface. Enhancement spectrum of EQE showed strong dependence on wavelength. At the maximum, more than four times longer effective optical path length of the physical thickness of the cell was obtained by the NIL pattern as compared with the single-path of the cell with a planar back surface.

References

[1] E. Yabolonivitch and G. D. Cody, "Intensity enhancement in textured optical sheets for solar cells," *IEEE Trans. Electron. Devices*, vol. ED-29, no. 2, pp. 300–305, Feb. 1982.

[2] M. A. Green, "Lambertian light trapping in textured solar cells and light-emitting diodes: Analytical solutions," *Prog. Photovolt, Res. Appl.*, vol. 10, no. 4, pp. 235–241, Jun. 2002.

[3] S. Mokkapati and K. R. Catchpole, "Nanophotonic light trapping in solar cells," *J. Appl. Phys.*, vol. 112, pp. 101101-1–101101-19, 2012.

[4] S. Foster and S. John, "Light-trapping in dye-sensitized solar cells," *Energy Environ. Sci.*, vol. 6, pp. 2972–2983, 2013.

[5] K. W. J. Barnham, I. Ballard, J. P. Connolly, N. J. Ekins-Daukes, B. G. Kluftinger, J. Nelson, and C. Rohr, "Quantum well solar cells," *Physica. E.*, vol. 14, pp. 27–36, 2002.

[6] W. Shockley and H. J. Queisser, "Detailed balance limit of efficiency of *p-n* junction solar cells," *J. Appl. Phys.*, vol. 32, pp. 510–520, 1961.

[7] H. Fujii, K. Watanabe, M. Sugiyama, and Y. Nakano, "Effect of quantum well on the efficiency of carrier collection in ingaas/gaasp multiple quantum well solar cells," *Jpn. J. Appl. Phys.*, vol. 51, pp. 10ND04-1–10ND04-5, 2012.

[8] N. J. Ekins-Daukes, K. W. J. Barnham, J. P. Connolly, J. S. Roberts, J. C. Clark, G. Hill, and M. Mazzer, "Strain-balanced GaAsP/InGaAs quantum well solar cells," *Appl. Phys. Lett.*, vol. 75, pp. 4195–4197, 1999.

[9] M. Mazzer, K. W. J. Barnham, I. M. Ballard, A. Bessiere, A. Ioannides, D. C. Johnson, M. C. Lynch, T. N. D. Tibbits, J. S. Roberts, G. Hill, and C. Calder, "Progress in quantum well solar cells," *Thin Solid Films*, vol. 511–512, pp. 76–83, 2006.

[10] B. Browne, J. Lacey, T. Tibbits, G. Bacchin, T. Wu, J. Q. Liu, X. Chen, V. Rees, J. Tsai, and J. Werthen, "Triple-junction quantum-well solar cells in commercial production," in *Proc. Int. Conf. Concentrator Photovoltaic Syst.*, Miyazaki, Japan, 2013.

[11] S. Ma, H. Sodabanlu, K. Watanabe, M. Sugiyama, and Y. Nakano, "Strain-conpensation measurement and simulation of InGaAs/GaAsP multiple quantum wells by metal organic vapor phase epitaxy using wafer-curvature," *J. Appl. Phys.*, vol. 110, pp. 113501-1–113501-5, 2011.

[12] H. Fujii, Y. Wang, K. Watanabe, M. Sugiyama, and Y. Nakano, "Suppressed lattice relaxation during InGaAs/GaAsP MQW growth with InGaAs and GaAs ultra-thin interlayers," *J. Cryst. Growth*, vol. 352, pp. 239–244, 2012.

[13] K. Watanabe, B. Kim, H. Sodabanlu, M. Goto, K. Nakayama, S. Hayashi, M. Sugiyama, K. Miyano, and Y. Nakano, "Light trapping with backside scatterer for enhanced photo-absorption by quantum structures," in *Proc. 38th IEEE Photovoltaic Spec. Conf.*, 2012, pp. 000113–000117.

[14] B. Kim, K. Watanabe, M. Sugiyama, and Y. Nakano, "Drastic QE enhancement by light-trapping structure in InGaAs/GaAsP multiple quantum-well solar cells," presented at the 22nd Int. Photovoltaic Science. Eng. Conf., Hangzou, China, 2012.

[15] G. J. Bauhuis, P. Mulder, E. J. Haverkamp, J. C. C. M. Hujiben, and J. J. Schermer, "26.1% thin-film GaAs solar cell using epitaxial lift off," *Sol. Eng. Mater. Sol. Cells*, vol. 93, pp. 1488–1491, 2009.

[16] B. M. Kayes, H. Nie, R. Twist, S. G. Spruytte, F. Reinhardt, I. C. Kizilyalli, and G. S. Higashi, "27.6% Conversion efficiency, a new record for single-junction solar cells under 1 sun illumination," in *Proc. 37th IEEE Photovoltaic Spec. Conf.*, 2011, pp. 000004–000008.

[17] M. A. Steiner, J. F. Geisz, I. García, D. J. Friedman, A. Duda, and S. R. Kurtz, "Optical enhancement of the open-circuit voltage in high quality GaAs solar cells," *J. Appl. Phys.*, vol. 113, pp. 123109-1–123109-11, 2013.

[18] J. Adams, V. Elarde, A. Hains, C. Stender, F. Tuminello, C. Youtsey, A. Wibowo, and M. Osowski, "Demonstration of multiple substrate reuses for inverted metamorphic solar cells," *IEEE J. Photovoltaics*, vol. 3, no. 2, pp. 899–908, Apr. 2013.

[19] E. T. Yu, C. O. McPheeters, X. Li, D. Hu, and D. M. Schaadt, "Light trapping and quantum semiconductor structure for high-efficiency photovoltaics," in *Proc. Opt. Nanostruct. Adv. Mater. Photovoltaics*, 2011.

[20] W. G. Spitzer and J. M. Whelan, "Infrared absorption and electron effective mass in n-type gallium arsenide," *Phys. Rev.*, vol. 114, no. 1, pp. 59–63, 1959.

[21] E. D. Palik, *Handbook of Optical Constants of Solids*. New York, NY, USA: Academic, 1985.

[22] *FDTD solution*. [Online]. Available:http://www.lumerical.com

[23] P. B. Jhonson and R. W. Christy, ed., "Optical constants of the noble metals," *Phys. Rev. B*, vol. 6, pp. 4370–4379, 1972.

Authors' photographs and biographies not available at the time of publication.

A New Mass Production Technology for High-Efficiency Thin-Film CIS-Absorber Formation

Volker Probst, Immo Koetschau, Emmerich Novak, Axel Jasenek, Heinz Eschrich, Frank Hergert, Thomas Hahn, Jochen Feichtinger, Markus Maier, Bernd Walther, and Volker Nadenau

Abstract—A new mass production technology for CIS-absorber formation yielding high-average module efficiencies is introduced. A novel custom-designed oven very successfully exploits the principle of forced convection during heating, CIS formation reaction, and cooling. Cu(In,Ga)(Se,S)$_2$ absorbers are formed by metal precursor deposition on soda lime glass followed by reaction in selenium/sulfur atmosphere. Processing is performed in a multiple-chamber equipment which handles corrosive, flammable, and toxic process gases from atmospheric pressure to vacuum at high durability. The substrates (size: 50 cm × 120 cm) are processed in batches up to 102 substrates, applying forced convection for very homogenous heat transfer and high heating and cooling rates. Multiple-chamber design and batch size yield high throughput at cycle times above 1 h. This approach combines the specific advantages of batch type and inline processing. An excellent average efficiency of 14.3% with a narrow distribution (+/−0.31%) and a peak efficiency of 15.1% is shown with this technology. Module characteristic distributions during pilot production are presented. Detailed layer analytics is discussed. This straightforward reliable mass production technology is a key for highest module performance and for upscaling. Module efficiencies of 17% can be reached, enabling production costs below 0.38 US$/Wp in a projected GWp plant.

Index Terms—Batch, CIGSSe, CIS, costs, high efficiency, inline, mass production, photovoltaic module, thin film.

I. Introduction

COPPER–indium–diselenide-based solar cells have exhibited the maximum cell efficiencies of all thin-film approaches for the past 20 years [1] with the latest world record of 20.4% recently [2]. Nonetheless, the market share of CIS solar cells is still insignificant, since those top efficiencies could not successfully enough be transferred into commercial production so far. Additionally, the efficiency gap to multicrystalline Si solar modules and the ongoing price decline for all types

Manuscript received June 11, 2013; revised September 16, 2013; accepted October 6, 2013.

V. Probst, I. Koetschau, E. Novak, A. Jasenek, H. Eschrich, F. Hergert, T. Hahn, M. Maier, and B. Walther are with the Research and Development, Bosch Solar CISTech GmbH, Brandenburg 14772, Germany (e-mail: volker. probst@bosch.com; Immo.Koetschau@bosch.com; Emmerich.Novak@ bosch.com; Axel.Jasenek@de.bosch.com; heinz.eschrich@bosch.com; frank. hergert@bosch.com; Thomas.Hahn3@bosch.com; Markus.Maier@bosch.com; bernd.walther1@bosch.com).

J. Feichtinger and V. Nadenau are with the Corporate Research, Robert Bosch GmbH, Gerlingen-Schillerhöhe 70893, Germany (e-mail: Jochen.Feichtinger@bosch.com; Volker.Nadenau@bosch.com).

Color versions of one or more of the figures in this paper are available online at http://ieeexplore.ieee.org.

Digital Object Identifier 10.1109/JPHOTOV.2014.2302235

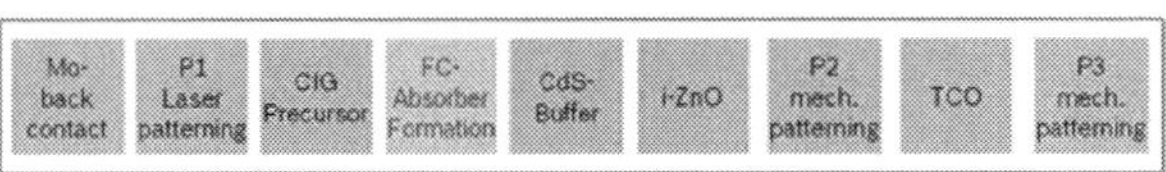

Fig. 1.   Process sequence for CIS module front end processing.

of solar modules remain steadily challenging. Only those thin film technologies that demonstrate 1) the highest efficiency and 2) the largest cost reduction potential will persist under these surrounding conditions. Within a typical CIS process sequence, the strongest impact on those two aspects is found in the CIS-absorber formation. Thus, we have introduced a new CIS formation approach involving forced convection (FC) which quickly yielded the high-average aperture efficiencies in production ambient. This new technology combines batch and inline processing and its benefits in a very effective way and provides an excellent average module efficiency at high throughput and small production floor footprint.

II. Experimental Setup

A. Module Preparation

The process flow for front-end processing is shown in Fig. 1. On standard float glass substrates of 120 cm × 50 cm in size, a molybdenum back contact is formed by dc magnetron sputtering.

Subsequently, laser patterning of the back contact (P1) is performed to define the cell width for the monolithic cell integration. Then, the two-stage absorber formation process is started by dc magnetron sputter deposition of the CuGaIn precursor (CIG) using alternating CuGa and indium targets.

For the subsequent Cu(In,Ga)(Se,S)$_2$ absorber formation (CIGSSe or simply CIS), the new FC technology is applied which is described more in detail next.

After CIS formation, a CdS buffer layer is deposited in a volume-minimized chemical bath that is followed by a sputtered intermediate layer of intrinsic ZnO. Mechanical patterning is performed to prepare for the integrated series connection (P2). The transparent front electrode is dc magnetron sputtered from ZnO:Al targets, and a mechanical insulation cut (P3) finalizes the front-end processing. Details on the typical device structure and module completion done by a chemical-bath-deposited buffer layer, a sputtered window layer, and scribing processes are given in [3].

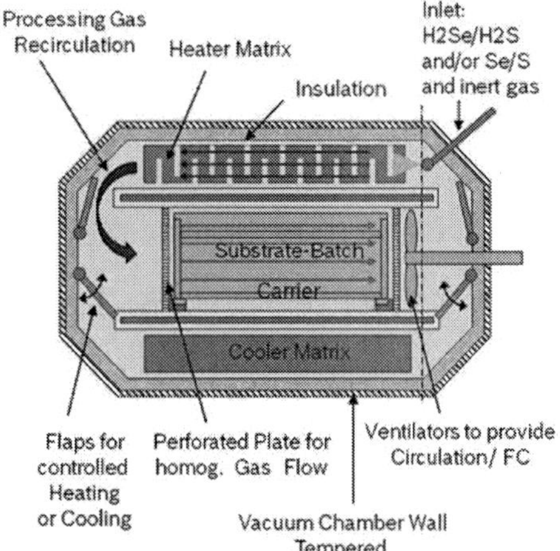

Fig. 2. Schematic cross section of the processing chamber of the new FC oven normal to the production flow.

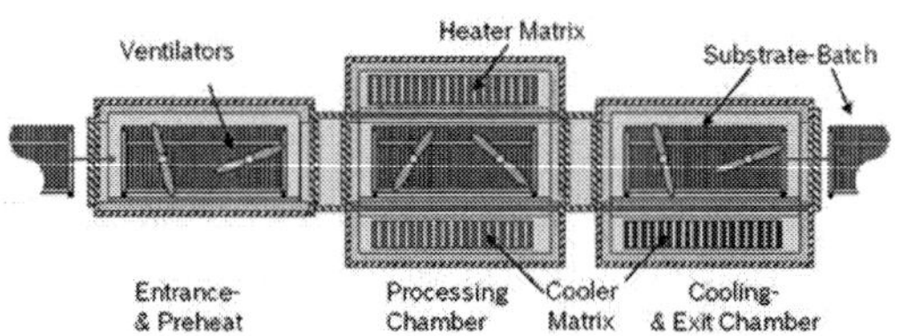

Fig. 3. Schematic section showing the production flow through a three-chamber FC system. The system is extendable to multiple-processing chambers and entrance/exit load locks.

B. Forced Convection Absorber Formation Technology

Fig. 2 schematically displays the processing chamber that is operated at typically from atmospheric pressure and above down to vacuum. It consists of a vacuum chamber with walls kept to an adjustable constant temperature in a range from room temperature to, e.g., 200 °C. Condensation of processing gases can be avoided this way.

At the inner surface of the chamber, a thermal insulation is applied in order to avoid heat loss and protect the chamber walls against processing gas interaction like, e.g., corrosion or condensation. At least one ventilator per chamber provides circulation of the processing gases through the substrate batch and the heater matrix.

One important aspect is the chosen flow regime: for a given number of substrates and distance between the glass plates, the fan speed can be adjusted in such a way that from laminar up to turbulent all flow conditions can occur.

Switching from heating to cooling can be accomplished by changing the position of the flaps accordingly. Intermediate positions can be controlled and are helpful for the adjustment of cooling rates in a wide range.

Fig. 3 displays a schematic cross section in the plane of the production flow of a three-chamber FC system. The absorber formation process step is divided into different sections which are processed in the different chambers specified for the respective task. In the production mode, each chamber contains a full

batch of 72 or optionally 102 substrates. However, the equipment is not limited to this carrier capacity. Tests for even larger substrate load are currently under way.

The full process recipe is applied to each batch by transferring the carriers in an indexing mode from one processing chamber to the next. Heating, metal precursor reaction, and cooling are performed via FC, which allows for very homogenous temperature distribution and CIS formation across the substrates and batch, even at ramp rates significantly above that of conventional batch-type furnaces.

Flexible thermal profiling up to the transition point temperature of soda lime glass is possible and precisely controlled by fast response heating units. During the reaction process, the carrier gas is well controlled in order to exactly adjust the required partial pressure of the respective chalcogens.

The furnace setup enables fast ramp-up and cool-down cycles as well as short-defined temperature plateaus. Process atmosphere and temperature can be changed very easily, and process cycles can be performed significantly faster than those in conventional batch-type diffusion furnaces. A typical total pressure range is from 100 to 1000 mbar. During the reaction process, the carrier gas for FC contains selenium and subsequently sulfur in a well-controlled manner in order to exactly adjust the required partial pressure of the respective chalcogens. The processing gas can also contain H_2Se or H_2S, either on its own or in combination with Se-vapor or S-vapor, respectively. Hydrogen may be present as well.

These benefits result in very low costs of ownership for this new type of CIS formation process and equipment.

III. RESULTS

A. Module Electrical Characteristics and Distribution

In a continuous 24-h/7-d production over a week, an aperture efficiency of $\eta = 14.3\% \pm 0.31\%$ was achieved in average over all modules processed. The furnace showed homogeneous performance nearly independent of carrier position over the whole load of 72 substrates. Correspondent statistics of the module electrical characteristics are shown in Fig. 4.

The excellent reproducibility of absorber formation is not only reflected in a low variation of photovoltaic parameters of the produced modules but in the absence of any significant variation of CIGS material properties as well, as depicted in Fig. 5. Here, a region from X-ray diffraction (XRD) patterns taken in the Bragg–Brentano (BB) geometry covering the two chalcopyrite reflections 112 and 211 is shown together with the CIGSSe composition, as measured by wavelength dispersive X-ray fluorescence (XRF) for series of test modules from consecutive batches. The shape of the 112 reflection is especially determined by the elemental gradients in particular by the Ga-gradient, as will be shown later. Thus, the low variation between the different diffraction patterns concerning shape, intensity, and position of the reflections, as seen in Fig. 5(a), is a direct sign for a high reproducibility of the core CIGS material parameters as is the low-compositional variation from different runs shown in Fig. 5(b). Here, the anion-to-cation ratio shows up slightly above unity because of an additional amount of Se

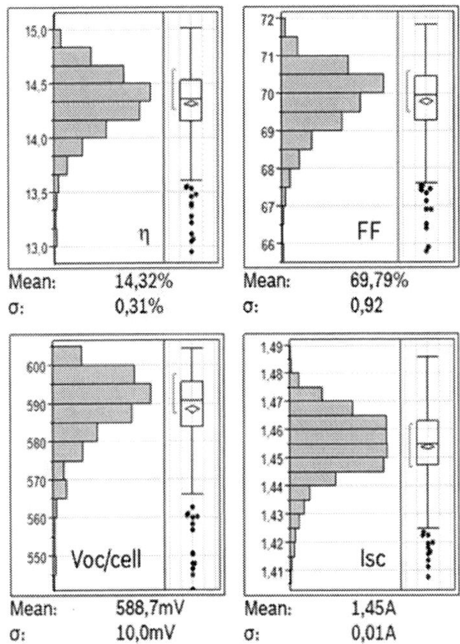

Mean: 14,32% Mean: 69,79%
σ: 0,31%   σ: 0,92

Mean: 588,7mV Mean: 1,45A
σ: 10,0mV   σ: 0,01A

Fig. 4. Result of a 24-h/7-d test run with fixed process parameters. The electrical module data are shown as histograms and box plots (median, quartile, and whiskers of 1.5∗interquartile range, possible outliers). The diamonds symbolize the mean values plus their 95% confidence levels, and the red brackets depict the shortest halves.

that is incorporated during the annealing process in the Mo back contact. Thus, the stable amount of $MoSe_2$ that is formed during annealing is an additional sign for high process stability.

B. Absorber Characterization

In order to investigate the structural properties of the absorber, XRD patterns were recorded in the BB and grazing incidence geometry [grazing-incidence X-ray diffraction (GIXRD)]. Fig. 6 shows the BB-XRD pattern in the range from 16° to 47° (diffraction angle 2θ). All visible peaks can unambiguously be identified with either the chalcopyrite phase, or the features of the back contact, namely, the 110 reflection of metallic molybdenum and a broad peak at 31.7°, which can be attributed to the 100 reflection of the $MoSe_2$ phase because of its increased peak width clearly exceeding those of the neighbored chalcopyrite reflections 112 and 211. The 112 chalcopyrite reflection shows additional diffraction intensity at the peak tail on the right side (see arrow) at 27.5°. This very likely indicates the presence of chalcopyrite absorber material with a smaller lattice constant and may not be attributed to a separate phase. It is well known that the CIGSSe chalcopyrite lattice adopts a smaller lattice constant according to Vegard's law if either Ga is substituted for In and/or sulfur is substituted for selenium [4], [5]. Under the assumption of a lateral homogeneous absorber formation process, as evidenced later on by electroluminescence (EL) and Raman mappings, the diffraction signal at 27.5° can be interpreted in terms of a compositional depth profile of the thin film. A nonde-

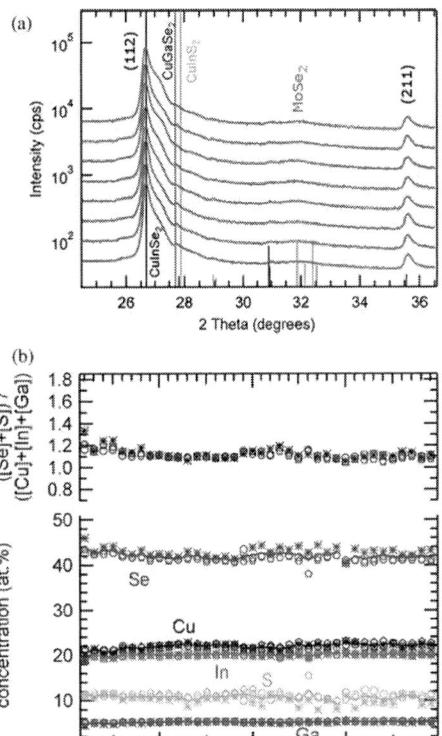

Fig. 5. (a) XRD patterns of CIGS thin films on Mo-coated float glass substrates from eight consecutive runs. The intensities of the diffraction patterns have been shifted for the sake of visibility. (b) Composition of CIGS samples from 40 consecutive runs, derived from WD-XRF measurements. Here, the results from three different module positions are given (□, top left "∘," and bottom right "∗"), together with the average composition (solid line).

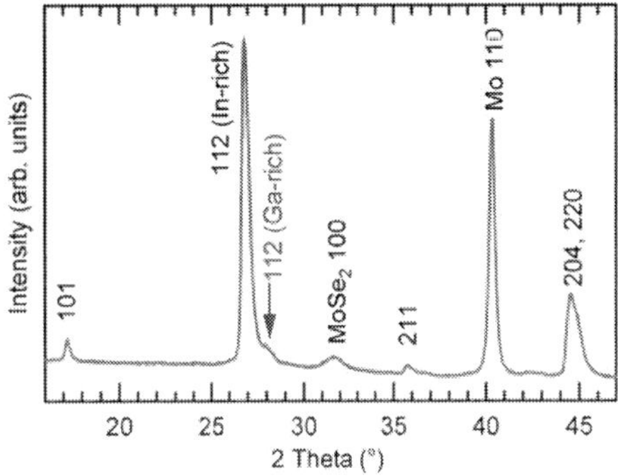

Fig. 6. BB X-ray diffraction pattern of a typical $Cu(In,Ga)(Se,S)_2$ thin film. All peaks can be either assigned to the chalcopyrite phase or to the molybdenum-related phases of $MoSe_2$ (100 reflection) and Mo (110 reflection).

structive method to access this depth profile is GIXRD, which is used to sample the thin film at varying penetration depths [6].

The pattern acquired at the lowest incidence angle generates the most surface-sensitive diffraction pattern, and the measurement at highest incidence angle yields the most bulk-sensitive pattern.

281

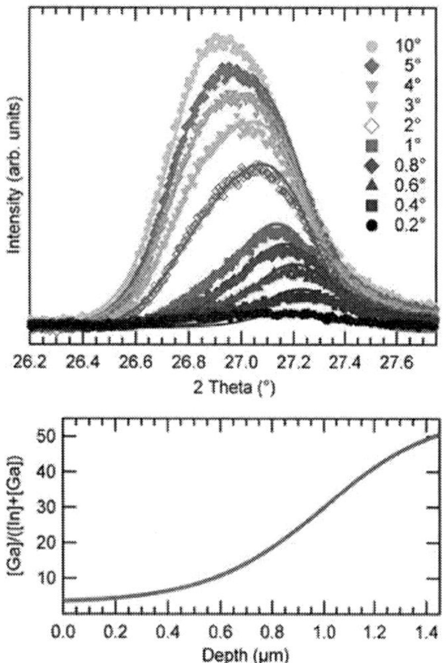

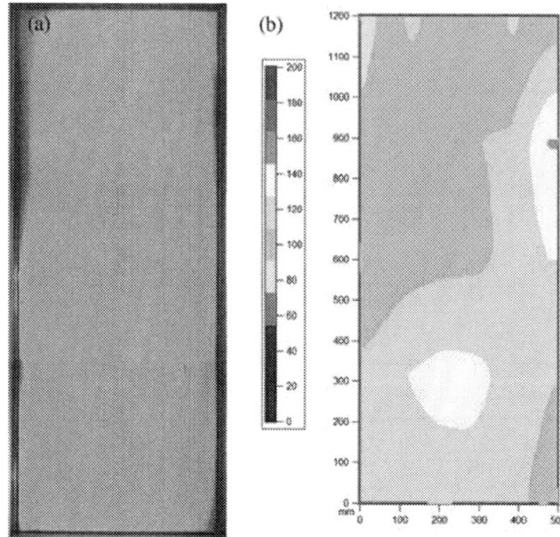

Fig. 7. Determination of the gallium profile by GIXRD. Backside GIXRD patterns of the same Cu(In,Ga)(Se,S)$_2$ thin film for incident angles between 0.2° and 10°. The maximum intensity decreases with smaller incidence angles. The simulations (solid lines) fit the measured data well and result in the Ga/(Ga+In) concentration depth profile of the lower chart.

Fig. 8. (a) EL image of a typical module from a continuous production run. The image is assembled from three single images, each covering one third of the module area, in order to enhance its resolution. (b) Mapping of the S/(Se + S)-ratio at the surface of the same module as recorded by 5 × 6 single Raman spectra covering the whole module area. The mapping is scaled to relative deviations from the target value; the value 100 represents roughly S/(Se + S) = 0.2.

It is also possible to quantitatively refine a set of diffraction patterns taken at various incidence angles simultaneously by a suitable simulation program in order to extract the depth profile of either the Ga/(Ga+In) ratio or the S/(S+Se) ratio [7]. However, some rough information about the depth profiles is essential in order to define a starting point of such quantitative refinements. Cross-sectional energy dispersive X-ray spectroscopy (EDX) measurement gives a first insight here and—as seen in other reactive sequential absorber processes—we also found a strong concentration of Ga near the interface to the back contact [8], [9]. Furthermore, our two-step process is a sulfurization after selenization, and we found that sulfur is enriched at the absorber surface. This finding will further be corroborated by Raman mappings of the sulfur A1-mode. Hence, the absorber is sulfur-rich at the surface and gallium-rich at the back contact. In such a configuration, it is difficult to unambiguously refine GIXRD patterns for a Ga-depth profile at the back contact. The incident X-ray beam penetrates from the absorber surface and the most surface-sensitive measurements are dominated by the sulfur gradient at the surface. In order to circumvent this problem, the GIXRD patterns were recorded from the backside of the film. For this purpose, an amorphous piece of polyethylene (8 mm × 12 mm) was glued to the absorber surface, and the absorber thin film was forcedly separated from the back contact. This sample was then subject to the GIXRD measurements, as shown in Fig. 7. Since the X-rays of the incident beam enter now from the backside of the thin film, the Ga-depth profile, which concentrates at the back contact, is most sensitively ac-

cessed (i.e., low absorption), and at the same time, the influence of sulfur is now strongly attenuated by the bulk material.

In order to obtain a quantitative Ga-depth profile, the parameters of an empirical function describing solid state diffusion were subject to iterative refinements of simulation data [10]. The Ga/(Ga+In)-depth profile in the lower chart of Fig. 7 shows the final result, and the fit between simulated and measured GIXRD data is shown in the upper one. We ensured that the integral Ga content which is given by the simulated Ga/(Ga+In) profile meets the boundary condition of the overall integral Ga content as measured by XRF of the thin film (Ga/(Ga+In) ≈ 0.2). Given that most of the sulfur is in fact found at the surface [see Raman mapping in Fig. 8(b)], the influence of small amounts of sulfur in the bulk of the absorber on the refined Ga profile is rather low and yields only an overall offset of all measured peak positions. In summary, the structural investigation confirms a device structure where most of the Ga is located at the back contact and where only a small amount of Ga ($<$ 2 at.%) is found in the space charge region (0–0.4 μm) of the device.

The homogeneity of our modules is checked regularly with various imaging and mapping methods. A typical example is given in Fig. 8(a), which depicts an EL image and a Raman mapping of a module from a continuous production run. The EL image shown in Fig. 8(a) reveals uniform EL intensity throughout the whole module area, without the appearance of significant shunts or lateral intensity variations. Thus, current density as well as the bandgap at the surface of our modules can be assumed to have a high homogeneity [11]. The latter is confirmed by the S-content in the surface, as measured by a Raman mapping given in Fig. 8(b). Since the Ga content of the CIGS layers is accumulating toward the back contact, any increase of the bandgap at the surface above that of CuInSe$_2$ can be attributed

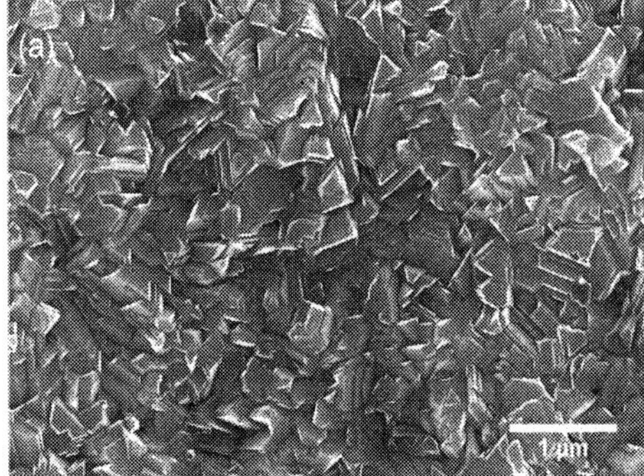

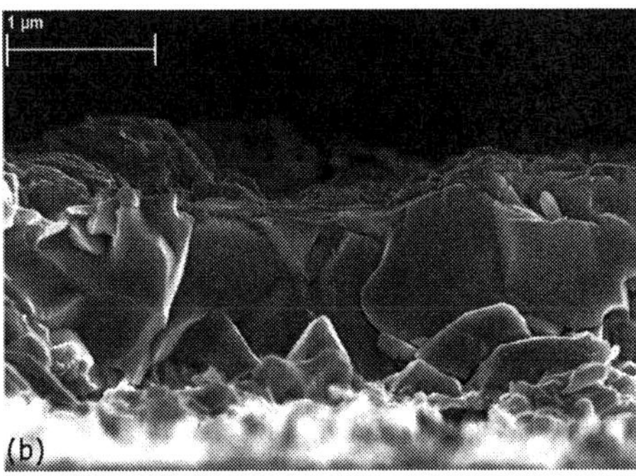

Fig. 9.   SEM pictures from two samples descending from the same annealing process. In (a), the plain view of the CIGSSe surface is shown, and in (b), the cross section of a cleaved CIGSSe layer is shown.

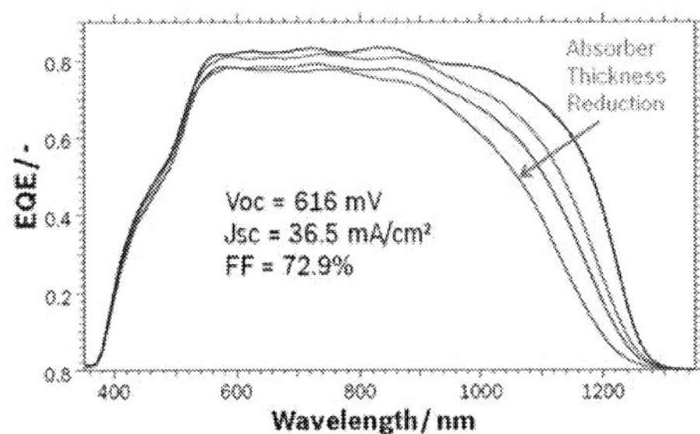

Fig. 10.   EQE spectra reveal decreasing IR response when the absorber thickness is reduced (black: 100%, red: 92%, blue: 85%, green: 77%). The electric data refer to the standard (100%).

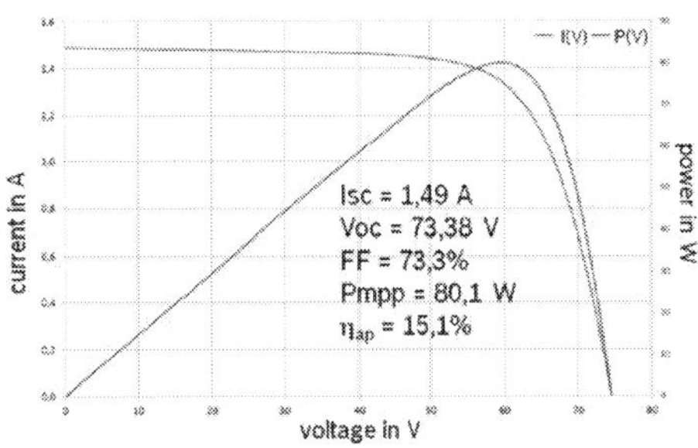

Fig. 11.   I(V) and P(V) curves of the champion module yielding an aperture area efficiency of 15.1%. The module voltage corresponds to an average cell voltage of 611.5 mV.

to the amount of sulfur incorporated there. Raman has been shown to be a sensitive quantitative measurement technique for the Se/S balance in CIGSSe surfaces [12].

In the example given, most of the surface area lies within ±20% deviation from the target value for the sulfur content. Thus, a low lateral variation of the bandgap at the surface resulting from a low lateral variation of the CIGSSe composition can be regarded as a prerequisite for the high EL uniformity shown in Fig. 8(a).

The morphology of CIGSSe layers shows up most prominently in scanning electron microscope (SEM) images (see Fig. 9): The CIGSSe layer is dense and shows a compact surface without significant holes or pronounced grain boundaries; the cross-sectional view confirms the compactness of the absorber material with grain sizes typically in the range of the film thickness.

C. Spectral Response Measurement

In order to understand the electrical properties, we first investigated the spectral response as a function of absorber thickness. Fig. 10 shows four characteristic measurements of the external quantum efficiency (EQE), and as can be readily seen, all devices have an effective bandgap $E_g \approx 1.0$ eV. This finding fits well to the device structure of a Ga-rich back contact. Within the space charge region, only a little Ga is found, and the device works basically like a CuInSe$_2$ cell with an excellent current collection due to the back surface field, which is induced by the

Ga gradient. However, the open-circuit voltage of typical cells is around 590–610 mV and exceeds the expected "rule of thumb value" of $E_g/e - 0.5$ V = 0.5 V), which can be only explained by the sulfur incorporation near the surface. Motivated by material saving, an experiment to reduce the absorber layer thickness showed us clearly that the infrared (IR) response diminishes in thinner absorbers (see Fig. 10). Still, the standard thickness (100%, on which all other investigations of this study are based) yields the best results. This indicates that the crystal quality of the standard thickness is excellent—carrier lifetime and mobility are sufficient to separate and collect the generated charge carriers throughout the absorber thickness. Consequently, a further increase of the IR response, just as efficiency, is expected for thicker absorbers.

D. Champion Module From a 24/7-Run

Fig. 11 displays the current–voltage characteristics of our champion module so far. It yields an aperture area efficiency of 15.1%, a fill factor of 73.3%, and an open-circuit voltage 73.4 V measured and confirmed by TÜV Rheinland.

The processed modules show excellent stability during light soak and climate testing.

IV Production Costs Perspective

We assume a 17% module efficiency (total area) to be achieved, even on a doubled substrate size by using FC technology. For this case, production costs were calculated using a detailed model for the overall process, taking into account

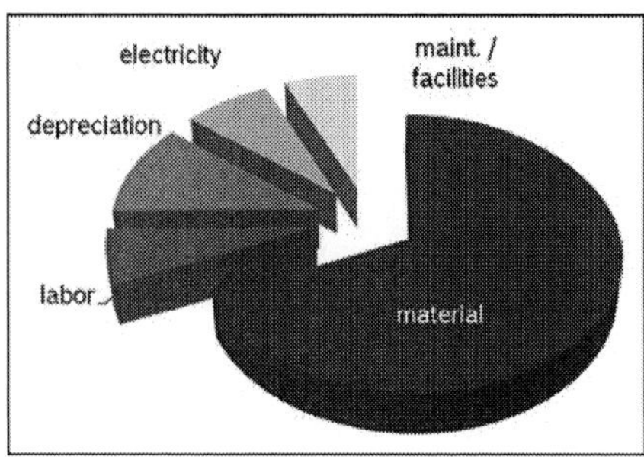

Fig. 12.   Items of expenditures for a 500 MWp CIS factory.

total cost of ownership of each process step. We performed a study for fab sites from 250 MWp to 1 GWp. Scaling up fab and substrate size leads to production costs below 0.38 US\$/Wp in a continuous 1-GWp production. Because of excellent performance of the FC oven (short cycle time and high capacity), low-capital expenditures (CAPEX) and depreciation rates can be reached, and consequently, the total costs will be dominated by material prices (see Fig. 12).

V. Summary and Outlook

A new type of mass production technology for high-efficiency CIS formation has been introduced. It is based on FC during the process steps: heating, CIS reaction, and cooling. The new technology is very beneficial because of
1) high average efficiencies at a narrow distribution reproducibly demonstrated in 24-h/7-d production runs;
2) high throughput at very low production cost, made possible by the combination of batch type and inline processing.

The new FC CIS technology is scalable fourfold: in terms of substrate size, batch size, substrate packing density, and number of equipment chambers. In consequence, highest throughput per production unit is exploitable to lowest photovoltaic module production costs. For a projected 1 GWp, plant production costs below 0.38 US\$/Wp were calculated.

References

[1] National Center for Photovoltaics, NAt. Renewable Energy Lab., Golden, CO, USA. Chart of best research-cell efficiencies. (2013). [Online]. Available: http://www.nrel.gov/ncpv/

[2] Swiss Federal Laboratories for Materials Science and Technology, EMPA, Dübendorf, Switzerland. "New world record 20.4% for flexible CIGS on polyimide foil." Jan. 17, 2013 (Press Release). Available: http://www.empa.ch/plugin/template/empa/1/131438/—/l=2

[3] V. Probst, F. Hergert, B. Walther, R. Thyen, G. Batereau-Neumann, B. Neumann, A. Windeck, T. Letzig, and A. Gerlach, "High performance CIS solar modules: Status of production and development at Johanna solar technology," in *Proc. 24th Eur. Photovoltaic Sol. Energy Conf.*, Hamburg, Germany, 2009, pp. 2455–2459.

[4] D. K. Suri, K. C. Nagpal, and G. K. Chadha, "X-ray study of $CuGa_x In_{1-x} Se_2$ solid solutions," *J. Appl. Cryst.*, vol. 22, pp. 578–583, 1989.

[5] I. M. Kötschau, Strukturelle Eigenschaften von $Cu(In,Ga)(Se,S)_2$ Dünnschichten, Ph.D. dissertation, Univ. Stuttgart, Stuttgart, Germany, 2002.

[6] B. L. Ballard, X. Zhu, P. K. Predecki, D. Albin, A. Gabor, J. Tuttle, and R. Noufi, "Determination of composition and phase depth-profiles in multilayer and gradient solid solution photovoltaic films using grazing incidence," *Adv. X-Ray Anal.*, vol. 38, pp. 269–276, 1995.

[7] I. M. Kötschau and H.-W. Schock, "Compositional depth profiling of polycrystalline thin films by grazing-incidence X-ray diffraction," *J. Appl. Cryst.*, vol. 39, pp. 683–696, 2006.

[8] T. Dalibor, S. Jost, H. Vogt, R. Brenning, A. Heiß, S. Visbeck, T. Happ, J. Palm, A. Avellán, T. Niesen, and F. Karg, "Advanced CIGSSe device for module efficiencies above 15%," in *Proc. 25th Eur. Photovoltaic Sol. Energy Conf.*, Valencia, Spain, 2010, pp. 2854–2857.

[9] G. M. Hanket, W. N. Shafarman, B. E. McCandless, and R. W. Birkmire, "Incongruent reaction of Cu–(InGa) intermetallic precursors in H_2 Se and H_2 S," *J. Appl. Phys.*, vol. 102, pp. 074922-1–074922-10, 2007.

[10] I. M. Kötschau and H.-W. Schock, "Depth profile of the lattice constant of the Cu-poor surface layer in $(Cu2Se)_{1-x}(In2Se3)_x$ evidenced by grazing incidence x-ray diffraction," *J. Phys. Chem. Solids*, vol. 64, pp. 1559–1563, 2003.

[11] T. Ott, P. Mack, F. Trudel, Y. Schulz, T. Walter, D. Hariskos, O. Kiowski, and R. Schäffler, "Accelerated ageing and luminescence of CIGS solar cells," in *Proc. 26th Eur. Photovoltaic Sol. Energy Conf.*, Hamburg, Germany, 2011, pp. 2421–2424.

[12] V. Izquierdo-Roca, A. Pérez-Rodríguez, A. Romano-Rodríguez, J. R. Morante, J. Álvarez-García, L. Calvo-Barrio, V. Bermudez, P. P. Grand, O. Ramdani, L. Parissi, and O. Kerrec, "Raman microprobe characterization of electrodeposited S-rich $CuIn(S,Se)_2$ for photovoltaic applications: Microstructural analysis," *J. Appl. Phys.*, vol. 101, pp. 103517-1–103517-8, 2007.

Authors' photographs and biographies not available at the time of publication.

Semprius Field Results and Progress in System Development

Kanchan Ghosal, Doug Lilly, John Gabriel, Michael Whitehead, Steve Seel,
Brent Fisher, John Wilson, and Scott Burroughs

Abstract—Semprius manufactures HCPV modules with printed microcells that provide cost, performance, and reliability benefits over conventional flat-plate modules. Recent module results exceed 35% efficiency at concentrator standard test condition and current factory built modules average 33%. Semprius has installed several different reference HCPV systems with apertures that range from 54 m^2–140 m^2, suitable for commercial deployment. This paper outlines Semprius' system design approach and presents field results including system efficiency, power production, and tracker error. Results confirm an ac system efficiency of 30%. In addition, Semprius' performance model will be described and results presented.

Index Terms—Concentrated photovoltaics, CPV modules, CPV systems.

I. Introduction

SEMPRIUS is a manufacturer of HCPV modules. A unique feature of Semprius' design is the use of microcells that provide cost, reliability, and performance benefits over existing designs. This module design has been laboratory and field validated over several design cycles and is now factory manufactured. Semprius has also designed several reference systems with large, reliable, and cost effective two-axis trackers that are suitable for commercial deployment. This paper will present the system design approach followed by field results from three such designs along with lessons learned during the installation and operation of such systems.

II. Module Design Approach

Semprius has taken a unique approach to addressing the challenges of designing a reliable high-performance low-cost HCPV system, which is based on a patented microtransfer printing technique [1]. The technique allows microcells to be released from the growth substrate and printed to an engineered substrate in a massively parallel manner. This technique enables the handling of the microcells which are ~600 μm on each side. Semprius' approach has a number of benefits given as follows.

1) The source substrate is not consumed in transfer printing and can be used multiple times reducing the cell cost.
2) A short optical path enables a low-profile module with low enclosure material costs, reduced wind loading and reduced shipping costs.
3) Distributed heat dissipation, due to the use of a large number of microcells per backplane, allows the module to effectively dissipate the heat without the use of heat sinks.
4) It features unique dual stage low-cost high-performance refractive optics.
5) It features improved reliability enabled by low-module current, low cell temperatures, thin-film metallization instead of wire bonds, and glass instead of polymeric materials.
6) It has highly automated, scalable, parallel, and capital efficient manufacturing processes that are based on standard microelectronics and surface mount technology (SMT).

The module backplane has an array of hundreds of printed microcells. The primary optic is a silicone-on-glass lens and the secondary optic is a glass spherical lens. The module is based on a three-junction microtransfer printed cell with a geometric concentration ratio of 1111X. The modules are manufactured in a pilot production line in Henderson, NC, USA.

III. Module Results

Last year, Semprius announced an industry leading module efficiency of 33.9% at CSTC (Concentrator Standard Test Condition: Direct Normal Irradiance of 1000 W/m^2, cell temperature of 25 °C, and spectrum AM 1.5D) [2]. Semprius has continued to make progress in improving module efficiency. Recent flash test results demonstrate an efficiency of >35% at CSTC. The module aperture area is 0.268 m^2. Fig. 1 presents the I–V curve of four such modules, flash tested at CSTC at the Universidad Politecnica de Madrid (IES-UPM). The aperture efficiencies of these modules ranged from 34.8%–35.6%. Recent on-sun module tests at Fraunhofer ISE confirm outdoor module efficiencies ranging from 32–33%. Fig. 2 presents the outdoor I–V curve for one of the modules, tested at Fraunhofer ISE, which had an efficiency of 33.3% at a DNI of 834 W/m^2 and an ambient temperature of 21 °C.

Last year, Semprius commissioned a pilot plant in Henderson, NC, USA, as the next step toward commercializing its technology. All factory built modules are flash tested as an integral part of the manufacturing process. Fig. 3 presents the efficiency distribution of a recent sample of 814 modules, ready for customer shipment. 95% of the modules in this sample have efficiencies between 31.7% and 34.1%, with a mean efficiency of 33%. This

Manuscript received June 10, 2013; revised August 12, 2013; accepted October 8, 2013.

The authors are with Semprius Inc., Durham, NC 27713 USA (e-mail: kanchan.ghosal@semprius.com; Doug.lilly@semprius.com; john.gabriel@semprius.com; Michael.whitehead@semprius.com; Steve.seel@semprius.com; brent.fisher@semprius.com; john.wilson@semprius.com; scott.burroughs@semprius.com).

Color versions of one or more of the figures in this paper are available online at http://ieeexplore.ieee.org.

Digital Object Identifier 10.1109/JPHOTOV.2013.2288026

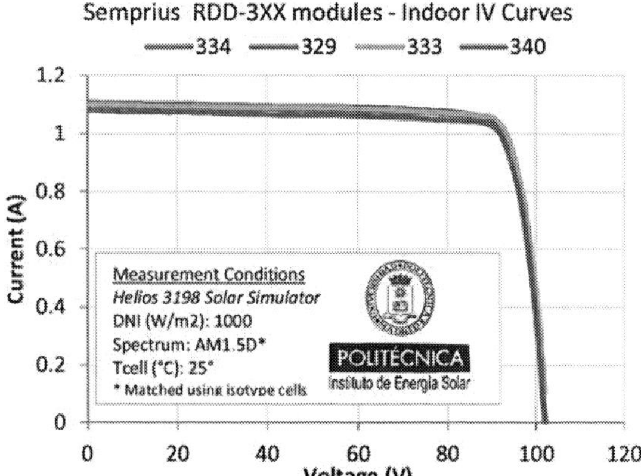

Fig. 1.   Indoor *I–V* curves of recent modules tested at IES-UPM.

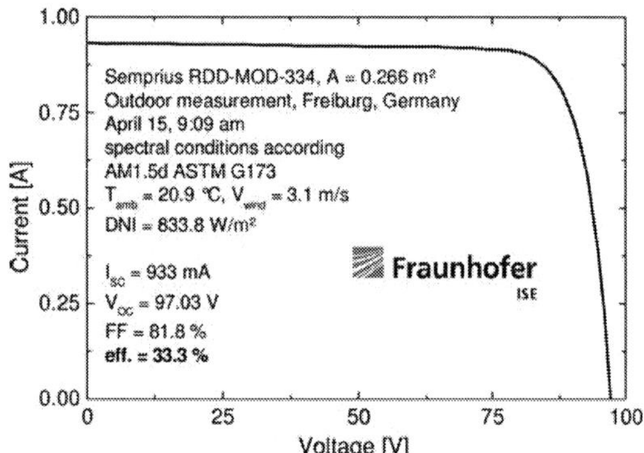

Fig. 2.   On-sun *I–V* curve of a module tested at Fraunhofer ISE.

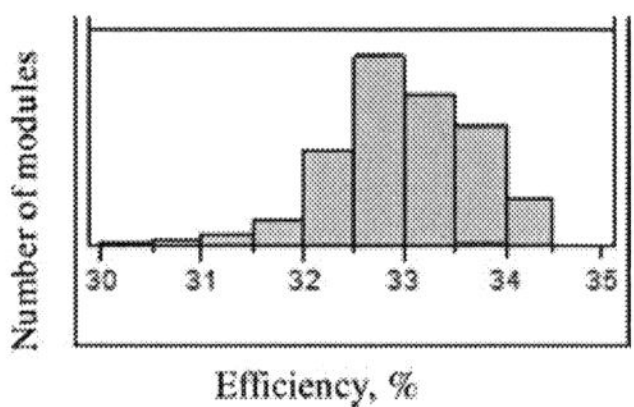

Fig. 3.   Flash test efficiency distribution of a recent shipment.

is one of the highest efficiencies for factory produced modules, using a high-volume process. The factory produced module efficiencies are expected to increase further as new processes are continuously transferred to the production line. The results also demonstrate a relatively tight distribution with a standard deviation of 0.6%. A tight distribution helps reduce module mismatch losses when the modules are field deployed on a tracker array.

Semprius has focused on designs that are compatible with high volume manufacturing and support the expected field lifetime of 20–30 years. From its earliest stages, the design has focused on a continuous cost reduction roadmap. This mindset is necessary to compete in the very cost competitive PV industry. Only those designs that can be implemented in a cost effective

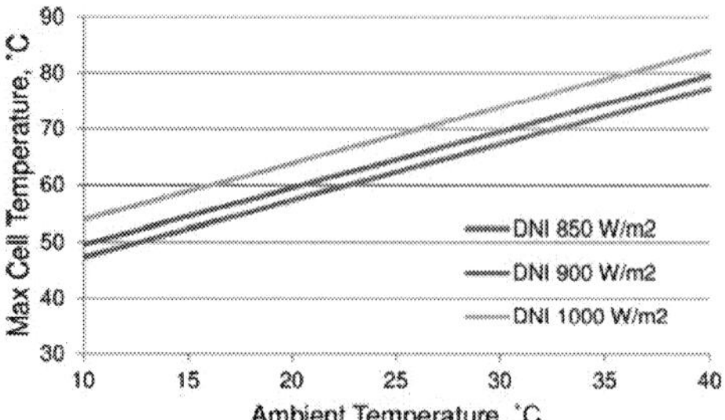

Fig. 4.   Correlation between maximum cell and ambient temperatures and DNI at zero wind condition by thermal simulation.

manner are considered. Design for reliability is another foundational principle in our product development. Materials used in module fabrication were selected for their long-term reliability characteristics and the modules are subjected to a comprehensive battery of severe tests beyond what is required for certification. Semprius is in the process of completing third-party IEC 62108 certification (only outdoor exposure testing remains).

The cell temperature at operating conditions is a critical parameter that influences both the reliability and performance of the module. Increased performance and reliability require low cell temperatures at operating conditions, which is why heat dissipation is an important consideration in CPV module design. One of the benefits of Semprius' approach is that no heat sinks are required in the module even at concentrations above $1000\times$, and the module surface is able to dissipate the heat. In a previous paper [2], indirect cell temperature measurements confirmed that the cell temperature is $<80\,°C$ at ambient temperatures up to $40\,°C$ and a DNI of $850\ W/m^2$. It is difficult to measure the cell temperature directly under operating conditions due to the small size of the cell and because the secondary optic prevents direct access to the cell.

Recently, a novel electroluminescence technique was developed at Semprius [3] that correlated the cell temperature to the wavelength shift of the emitted electroluminescence when the cell is shaded. This technique has been shared with NREL to be developed for the CPV community and was presented separately by NREL at the 39th IEEE PVSC conference [4]. The correlation between ambient temperature, maximum cell temperature, and DNI has been modeled at zero wind conditions by thermal balance and the results are presented in Fig. 4. This model has now been confirmed experimentally by the electroluminescence technique and is consistent with independent measurements made at NREL [4]. It confirms that the cell temperature does not exceed $80\,°C$ for temperature up to $40\,°C$ and DNI up to $900\ W/m^2$.

IV. System Design Approach

Semprius has deployed research, development, and demonstration (RD&D) systems since the fabrication of the initial engineering prototype modules, using field results to validate the modules and initiate further improvements. There are now 10 Semprius systems deployed in the field in three continents. The first 1 kW RD&D system was installed in Tucson, AZ, USA,

Fig. 5. Picture of a 2 × 4 multimodule array.

TABLE I
CPV SYSTEM SUMMARY

System	Area	MMAs	Rating
A	90 m^2	35	24.5 kW
B	64 m^2	25	17.5 kW
C	54 m^2	20	14.0 kW

Fig. 6. Picture of 90 m^2 Semprius CPV system at ISFOC.

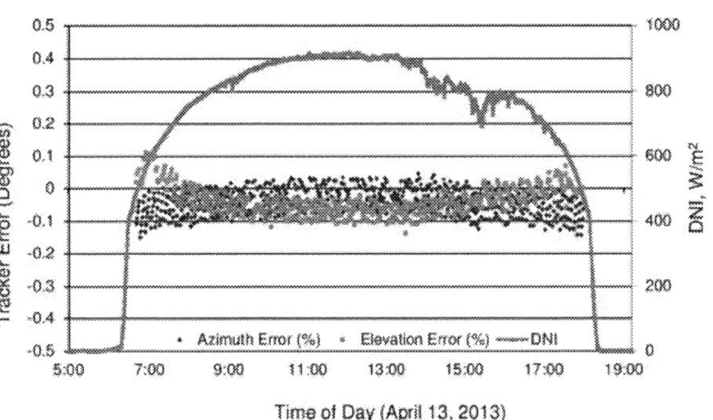

Fig. 7. Tracker error for the 90 m^2 Semprius CPV system.

with Tucson Electric Power in 2010 [5] and provided early field experience on the interplay between each component of the CPV system. This system was later upgraded to a 1.3 kW system with the current design. The Tucson system was followed by 3.5 kW RD&D systems in Huntsville, AL, USA, [2], Puertollano, Spain [6], and other global sites, all using the present design.

Semprius ships 2 × 4 arrays of eight modules each that are preracked, prewired, and prealigned in the factory. The multimodule array (MMA) configuration minimizes the number of operations in the field and reduces assembly time. The MMA design was optimized for shipping, electrical requirements, available tracker configurations, and ease of field assembly. A picture of the MMA is presented in Fig. 5.

HCPV technology requires the use of reliable, cost effective, and accurate two-axis trackers. The availability of such trackers is critical to the success of HCPV commercialization. Tracker selection was, therefore, a key decision point in the system design. Semprius has partnered with several leading tracker suppliers, each with a significant field site design and installation experience and thousands of installed trackers. Each partner brings a unique offering to the table in terms of cost, reliability, performance, geographical diversity, and ability to support the mechanical and civil aspects of the project.

Semprius has developed system designs for several concepts, ranging in aperture size from 54 m^2–140 m^2. Joint design exercises were initiated with each tracker partner to develop mechanical interfaces which mated with the Semprius MMAs. Industry standard string inverters of appropriate sizes were selected for each system design. Cable harnesses were designed for each system for optimum connection of the MMAs to the inverter. Each system was a unique combination of a tracker with the appropriate number of MMAs, dc cables, and inverters, with cost and performance optimization as the major design criteria.

Pilot systems of each design, suitably sized for commercial deployment, have been installed for field validation. Field validation is an essential part of the design process and serves to de-risk commercial projects by demonstrating reliable performance at the expected cost. The pilot units are used to exercise the system design, gather field data, and further validate the performance model. These systems will advance the understanding of the effect of weather events, site conditions, solar insolation, and soiling on energy generation. They also provide platforms for validation and improvement of large-scale tracker and inverter operation, as well as construction concepts for CPV power plants. The results from three such systems, shown in Table I, will be presented.

V. SYSTEM FIELD RESULTS

Fig. 6 presents a picture of the 90 m^2 system at the Instituto de Sistemas Fotovoltaicos de Concentracion (ISFOC) in Puertollano, Spain. This system has a nominal power of 24.5 kW (CSTC) and consists of 35 MMAs arranged in a 7 × 5 configuration. Fig. 7 presents the tracking error of the system, which demonstrates a tracking accuracy of better than ±0.1°, well within the module angle of acceptance of ±0.8°. This test validated the tracker accuracy requirements for a large system such as this one. The preliminary power tests for this system were done with an undersized inverter, which is in the process of being replaced. Fig. 8 presents preliminary AC power and DNI for the system on a relatively sunny day. The inverter limits the power production above a DNI of 850 W/m^2, however, the preliminary results confirm a system AC efficiency exceeding 29%.

The selection of construction methods is an important consideration for large scale CPV deployment. Material, labor, and equipment costs for the foundation (concrete and steel) must

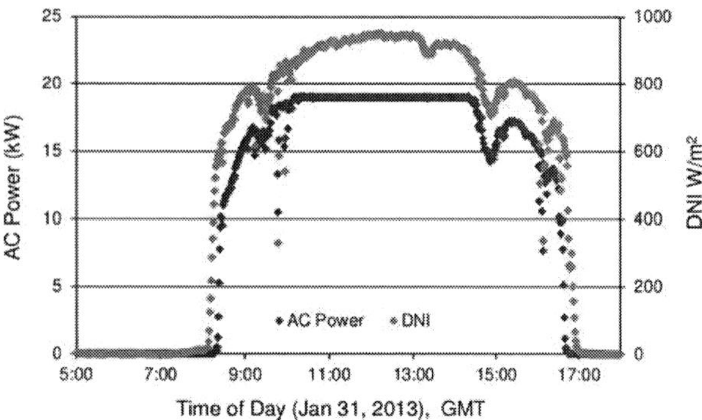

Fig. 8. Power and DNI for the 90 m² system, using an undersized inverter.

Fig. 9. Tracker array being hoisted by a crane during assembly.

Fig. 10. Picture of 64-m² Semprius CPV system.

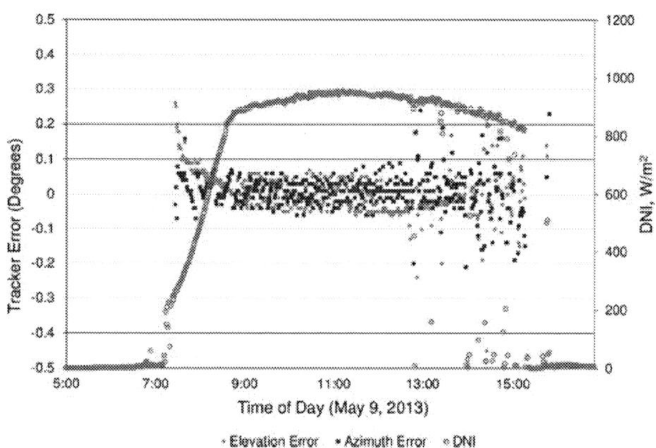

Fig. 11. Tracker error for the 64-m² Semprius CPV system.

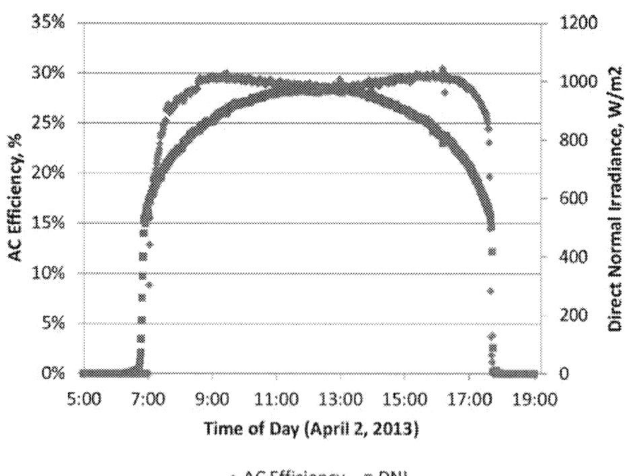

Fig. 12. AC efficiency for the 64 m² system.

be optimized while using methods that are well known to civil engineers and commercial construction firms. Both the system design and the assembly procedure must be optimized for field assembly. Finally, the system must be commissioned and monitored using industry standard control packages. Fig. 9 presents a picture of the 90 m² system during the assembly process. The picture shows the assembled and aligned tracker array being hoisted by a crane to be attached to the mast.

Fig. 10 presents a picture of the 64 m² system at Henderson, NC, USA. This system has a nominal power of 17.5 kW (CSTC) and consists of 25 MMAs, arranged in a 5 × 5 configuration. Fig. 11 presents the tracking error of the system which demonstrates a tracking accuracy of better than ±0.1°. There is minor drift outside this range in the late afternoon due to intermittent clouds that affect the controller sun sensor. This system is equipped with sensors on the four corners to study the structural deformation under load. The results of this study will be presented in a future paper. Fig. 12 presents the ac efficiency for the system on a relatively sunny day. The results demonstrate a peak system ac efficiency of 30%. The inverter efficiency for this system was measured to be 99%, which was more than a percentage point higher than its rating.

288

Fig. 13.   Picture of 54 m^2 Semprius CPV system.

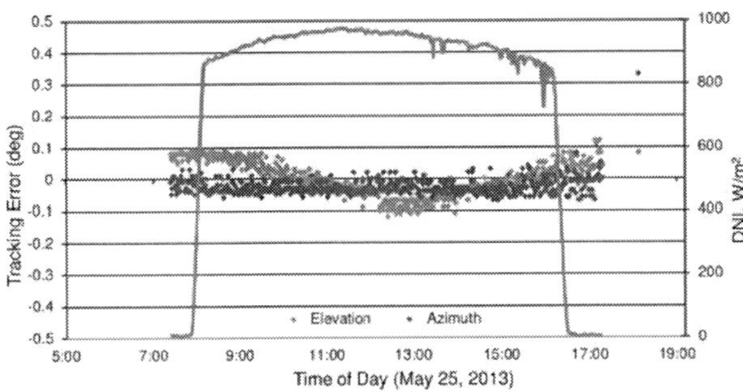

Fig. 14.   Tracker error for the 54 m^2 Semprius CPV system.

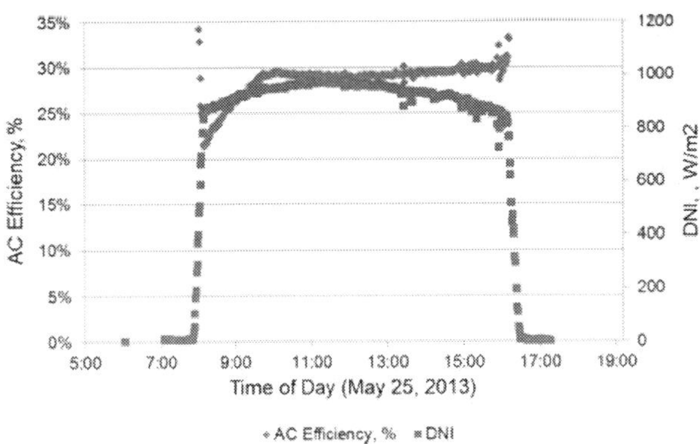

Fig. 15.   AC Efficiency and DNI of the 54-m^2 system.

Fig. 13 presents a picture of the 54 m^2 system at Durham, NC, USA. This system has a nominal power of 14 kW (CSTC) and consists of 20 MMAs, arranged in a 5 × 4 configuration. Fig. 14 presents the tracking error of the system which demonstrates a tracking accuracy of better than ±0.1°. Fig. 15 presents the ac efficiency of the system for one day, which peaks at 30%. This

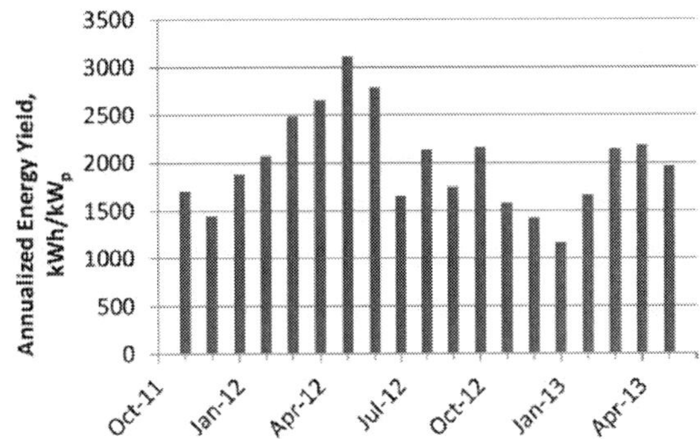

Fig. 16.   Energy yield from the RD&D system in Tucson.

system is installed close to several buildings and receives excessive shading in the morning, which explains its early morning behavior.

Fig. 16 presents the energy yield of the 1.3 kW RD&D system in Tucson, AZ, USA. Since it was upgraded with the current generation module. The energy yield of this system was 2186 kWh/kWp in 2012. This compares favorably with a colocated 1.6 MW 1-axis Si system that yielded 1966 kWh/kWp and a 5 MW fixed tilt system that yielded 1677 kWh/kWp in 2012.

VI. Performance Model

The availability of an accurate performance model is a prerequisite to the commercial deployment of solar power plants. Current commonly used performance tools such as PVSyst, SAM, and PVSol are geared toward conventional thin film and silicon products and are not accurate for HCPV. Semprius used a version of the Sandia Array Performance Model (SAPM) as the basis of its own performance model. SAPM is based on King's classic paper [7] on solar performance modeling, and is a commonly used engine that powers performance tools such as SAM. Semprius collaborated with Sandia National Laboratories to add the required spectral component to the open source MATLAB library that implements SAPM [8]. Semprius then used the modified SAPM and the Sandia led PV Performance Modeling Collaborative's PV-lib package [9] to develop the Semprius Performance Model (SPM). SPM is used for energy production estimation using standard meteorological files. It also has a tracker field layout feature for modeling interrow shading losses for HCPV plants.

SPM has been validated using Semprius' existing field data. Fig. 17 presents the measured and modeled monthly energy yields from the Tucson RD&D system for January to September 2012, using actual weather data but assuming zero soiling. The actual and predicted energy yields for this period are within 1.5% of each other. The underproduction in May and June is presumed to be due to soiling since they were very dry months. There was significant rain in July ($>2''$) that cleaned the system, resulting in better agreement in August and September.

Fig. 18 presents the measured and modeled ac power from the 64 m^2 Semprius CPV System for one day, which are within 0.3% of each other. It is worth noting that there is an inverter

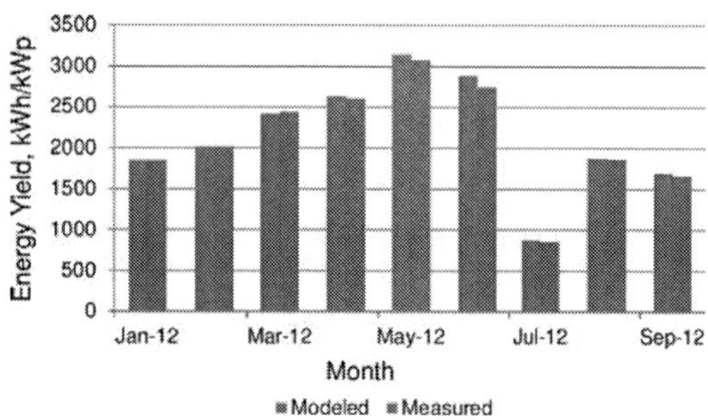

Fig. 17. Measured and modeled energy yield from the Tucson system.

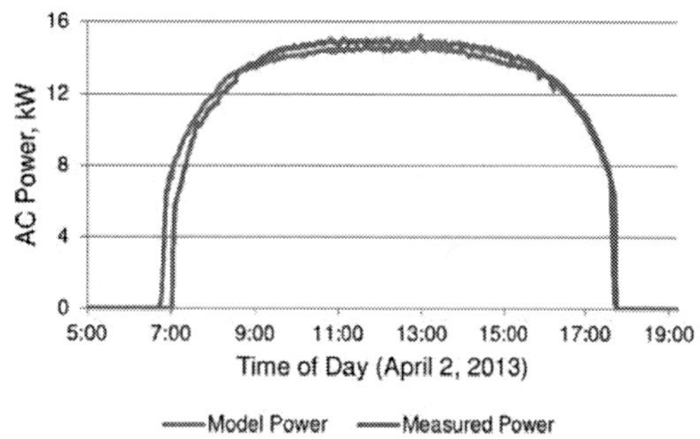

Fig. 18. Measured and modeled ac power from the 64-m^2 system.

start-up delay in the morning, which explains the difference between the two curves in the morning. In addition, the actual inverter performance (99%) is higher than the inverter model from the manufacturer (97.5%), and this exhibits itself as higher measured ac power.

VII. CONCLUSION

Semprius continues to make progress in improving its module efficiency. Flash tested module efficiencies of >35% at CSTC have been demonstrated for recent prototypes, while factory produced modules average 33%. Several reference CPV system designs with apertures of 54 to 140 m^2 have been field deployed. All systems demonstrate tracking accuracy of better than $\pm 0.1°$,

and ac grid efficiencies of around 30%. Semprius' performance model has been completed and validated with existing field data.

ACKNOWLEDGMENT

Semprius would like to acknowledge the productive collaborations from many of the leaders in the field, in particular, S. Askins and Prof. G. Sala from IES-UPM, M. Martinez from ISFOC, G. Siefer from Fraunhofer ISE, K. Emery from NREL, C. Hansen and D. Riley from Sandia National Laboratories, E. Menard from Helioslite and C. Cameron.

REFERENCES

[1] B. Furman, E. Menard, A. Gray, M. Meitl, S. Bonafede, D. Kneeburg, K. Ghosal, R. Bukovnik, W. Wagner, J. Gabriel, S. Seel, and S. Burroughs, "A high concentration photovoltaic module utilizing micro-transfer printing and surface mount technology," in *Proc. 36th IEEE Photovoltaic Spec. Conf.*, 2010, pp. 475–480.

[2] K. Ghosal, D. Lilly, J. Gabriel, S. Seel, E. Menard, S. Burroughs, R. Daniel, S. Lowe, and C. Kudija, "Performance of a microcell based transfer printed HCPV system in the South Eastern US," in *Proc. 8th Int. Conf. Concentrated Photovoltaic Syst.*, Toledo, Spain, 2012.

[3] E. Menard, M Meitl, and S. Burroughs, "Indirect temperature measurement of CPV solar cells using wavelength shift of the sub-cells luminescence emission peaks," in *Proc. 27th Eur. Photovoltaic Solar Energy Conf. Exhib.*, 2012, pp. 189–193.

[4] M. Muller, T. J. Silverman, S. Kurtz, E. Menard, and S. Burroughs, "Optical cell temperature measurements of multiple CPV technologies in outdoor conditions," in *Proc. 39th IEEE Photovoltaic Spec. Conf.*, 2013.

[5] K. Ghosal, J. Gabriel, D. Lilly, B. Furman, E. Menard, M. Meitl, S. Bonafede, D. Kneeburg, B. Kendrick, R. Bukovnik, W. Wagner, S. Seel, S. Burroughs, P. Krause, and M. Fiedler, "On-sun performance of a novel microcell based HCPV system located in the southwest US," in *Proc. 7th Int. Conf. Concentrated Photovoltaic Syst.*, 2011.

[6] K. Ghosal, S. Burroughs, K. Heuser, D. Setz, and E. Rojas, "Performance results from micro-cell based RD&D systems," *Progress Photovoltaics, Res. Appl.*, vol. 21, no. 6, pp. 1370–1376, 2012.

[7] D. L. King, W. E. Boyson, and J. A. Kratochvill, "Photovoltaic array performance model," Sandia National Laboratories, Albuquerque, NM, USA, Report 3535, 2004.

[8] C. Hansen and D. Riley, "Performance model for semprius module," PSEL memorandum, Sep. 5, 2012.

[9] [Onine]. Available http://pvpmc.org/pv-lib

Authors' photographs and biographies not available at the time of publication.

Investigation of Carrier Recombination at the SiO$_2$/c-Si Interface by Photoluminescence Imaging Under Applied Bias

Halvard Haug, Ørnulf Nordseth, Edouard Monakhov, and Erik Stensrud Marstein

Abstract—A new technique to analyze the surface recombination for passivated silicon substrates has been employed to study the SiO$_2$/c-Si interface under various band bending conditions. A photoluminescence imaging setup was used to measure the effective minority carrier lifetime of oxidized Si wafers while applying an external bias over the rear side passivation layer. This method was used to investigate both the effect of substrate doping polarity and postoxidation forming gas anneal (FGA) upon the surface passivation properties. The measured carrier lifetimes as a function of voltage were interpreted in the framework of the extended Shockley–Read–Hall theory. The calculated oxide charge density was found to decrease from $\sim 7 \times 10^{11}$ cm^{-2} to $\sim 4 \times 10^{11}$ cm^{-2} after the FGA treatment for both p-type and n-type substrates, causing a reduction in the field effect passivation. On the contrary, an increased chemical passivation was observed after FGA, shown by a reduction of the effective surface recombination velocity parameters by a factor of 3.8–5.5. In total, a significant increase in the effective carrier lifetime was obtained for both substrate types. Furthermore, the carrier capture efficiency at the surface defects was found to be 2–2.5 times higher for electrons than for holes, regardless of doping polarity and FGA.

Index Terms—Charge carrier lifetime, imaging, photoluminescence, silicon, surfaces.

I. Introduction

IN the development of high efficiency solar cells based on thin silicon wafers, reduction of electronic recombination at the wafer surfaces is a topic of high and increasing importance. The surface recombination velocity (SRV) at a silicon surface is proportional to the interface defect density and is limited by the availability of minority charge carriers near the surface. The recombination losses can therefore be reduced by lowering the interface defect density (chemical passivation) or by reducing the concentration of either electrons or holes in the region near the surface with a built-in electric field (field-effect passivation) [1]. Such band bending towards the surface is normally obtained in solar cells by applying a dielectric passivation layer incorporating fixed charges.

The SRV of a passivated Si surface is normally calculated from measurements of the effective minority charge carrier lifetime τ_{eff} (hereafter: lifetime), which contains contributions from recombination in the bulk of the wafer and at the two surfaces [2]. For characterization purposes, modulation of the surface band bending, and thus the SRV, is possible by applying voltage to a gate electrode placed on top of a dielectric passivation layer [3]–[5] or by deposition of charged ions on the surface in a corona discharge chamber [6], [7]. The latter method has traditionally been preferred in solar cell research, both because of its noninvasive nature and in order to avoid the necessity to make contacts to the sample. Additionally, the presence of metallic electrodes typically interferes with most of the common carrier lifetime measurements.

Recently, we proposed a new technique to analyze the surface recombination for passivated silicon substrates [8]. The technique is based on measurements of the effective lifetime in a photoluminescence (PL) imaging setup [9] while applying a voltage over the rear side passivation layer (PL V). In contrast with corona charging techniques, PL imaging under applied bias requires the presence of metal electrodes on the sample surface. However, the method allows for very fast measurements and simultaneous data collection from multiple areas on the sample. The technique also has the advantage of allowing for repeated voltage sweeps between inversion and accumulation, which can be recorded with little or no influence of the measurement history of the sample.

Thermal oxidation is a well-established technology for surface passivation of Si substrates and can be implemented in both lab-scale and industrial solar cell processes [10]. The passivation properties of the c-Si/SiO$_2$ interface mainly arise from a high degree of chemical passivation, with a reported density of interface states D_{it} as low as 10^9 cm^{-2}eV^{-1} [11]. Thermal SiO$_2$ layers may also give a moderate field-effect passivation, caused by positive fixed charges located at the interface, with a typical density in the range $1–5 \times 10^{11}$ cm^{-3} [12]. In this paper, we have used measurements of effective lifetime as a function of voltage (PL-V) to investigate the surface passivation properties of SiO$_2$ layers formed by high temperature dry oxidation. Furthermore, we present an interpretation of the surface passivation

Manuscript received June 10, 2013; revised September 27, 2013; accepted October 9, 2013. Date of publication October 23, 2013; date of current version December 16, 2013. This work has been supported by the Research Council of Norway through the project "Thin and highly efficient silicon-based solar cells incorporating nanostructures," NFR Project 181884/S1.

H. Haug and E. S. Marstein are with the Department of Solar Energy, Institute for Energy Technology, Kjeller 2027, Norway, and also with the Department of Physics, University of Oslo, Blindern, Oslo 0316, Norway (e-mail: halvard.haug@ife.no; erik.stensrud.marstein@ife.no).

Ø. Nordseth is with the Department of Solar Energy, Institute for Energy Technology, Kjeller 2027, Norway (e-mail: ornulf.nordseth@ife.no).

E. Monakhov is with the Department of Physics, University of Oslo, Blindern, Oslo 0316, Norway (e-mail: edouard.monakhov@fys.uio.no).

Color versions of one or more of the figures in this paper are available online at http://ieeexplore.ieee.org.

Digital Object Identifier 10.1109/JPHOTOV.2013.2285833

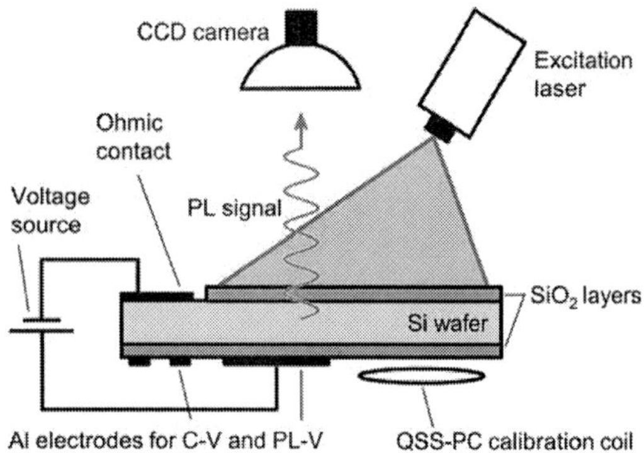

Fig. 1. Schematic overview of the experimental setup for the PL-V method, used to obtain lifetime images while modulating the surface band bending by applying voltage over the rear side passivation layer. Al electrodes for both C–V and PL-V measurements are present on each sample.

properties in terms of the oxide charge density and the effective surface recombination parameters for electrons and holes.

II. EXPERIMENTAL DETAILS

Samples were made from double side polished and thermally oxidized FZ Si (100) wafers. Both n-type (P-doped) and p-type (B-doped) substrates were used, with doping concentrations of 1.7×10^{15} and 5.0×10^{15} cm^{-3}, and thicknesses of 290 and 280 μm, respectively. The wafers had a high bulk lifetime to ensure that the measured effective lifetime was dominated by recombination at the wafer surfaces.

After a standard RCA (1+2) clean and 30-s immersion in a 5% HF solution, the wafers were loaded into a tube furnace and oxidized in dry O$_2$ at 1000 °C for 60 min. The resulting thermal SiO$_2$ layers provide a stable, high quality surface passivation with negligible leakage current, simplifying the interpretation of the results. Subsequently, one wafer of each doping polarity received a postoxidation forming gas anneal (FGA) with 5% H$_2$ in N$_2$ at 400 °C for 30 min. This process is commonly used in the literature to reduce the number of interface states by hydrogen diffusion and passivation of dangling bonds [1]. The oxide thickness was measured by variable-angle spectroscopic ellipsometry and found to be 66–68 nm uniformly across the wafers.

7 mm × 7 mm square electrodes for PL-V measurements and 0.45–2.25 mm diameter circular electrodes for capacitance versus voltage (C–V) measurements were deposited onto the oxide layers by thermal evaporation of Al through a shadow mask. Finally, low resistivity contacts were made to the Si substrate by grinding down the oxide with P200 sand paper and depositing Ag by thermal evaporation in the region opposite the C–V electrodes.

A schematic overview of the experimental setup for the PL-V method is shown in Fig. 1. Steady state carrier lifetime measurements were carried out with a LIS-R1 PL imaging setup from BT imaging with an excitation wavelength of 808 nm and a constant illumination intensity of 33.4 mW/cm^2.

In a PL imaging lifetime measurement, the excess minority carrier concentration (injection level) at each point of the image is calculated from the measured PL intensity. For a p-type sample, Δn is given by

$$\Delta n = \sqrt{\left(\frac{N_A}{2}\right)^2 + \frac{I_{\mathrm{PL}}}{C_{\mathrm{cal}}}} - \frac{N_A}{2} \qquad (1)$$

where N_A is the acceptor doping concentration, I_{PL} is the measured PL intensity, and C_{cal} is an instrument and sample specific calibration constant, which is determined from a quasi-steady state photoconductance (QSSPC) measurement [13]. For the PL-V measurements, a reference region without metal electrodes was used for this purpose. An external voltage source was connected to the sample as shown in Fig. 1 in order to perform the measurements with an applied bias over the rear side passivating oxide layer. The PL intensity in the region over the Al electrodes is enhanced compared with the reference region because of an increased rear side reflectance, causing a larger fraction of the emitted PL light to reach the camera. To account for this, I_{PL} in the region above the metal electrodes was divided by an optical enhancement factor of 1.36. This factor is sample specific and was determined experimentally by measuring the enhancement of the PL intensity after placing the sample over an Al mirror made by thermal evaporation of 100-nm Al on a glass substrate. The steady state effective lifetime image was then calculated from the measured injection level averaged over the electrode area as $\tau_{\mathrm{eff}} = \Delta n / G$, where G is the excess carrier generation rate per volume. An extensive discussion of the optical corrections and other possible errors in the calculation of τ_{eff} is described elsewhere [14]. A typical PL lifetime image measured while applying voltage over the rear side passivation layer is shown in Fig. 2.

The fixed oxide charge density Q_{ox} in the SiO$_2$ layers was extracted from high frequency (1 MHz) C–V curves measured using a Keithley 4200-SCS semiconductor characterization system. The fixed charge density per cm^2 is calculated as

$$Q_{\mathrm{ox}} = C_{\mathrm{ox}} \left(\phi_{\mathrm{ms}} - V_{\mathrm{fb}}\right) / q \qquad (2)$$

where C_{ox} is the measured oxide capacitance per unit area, q is the elementary charge, ϕ_{ms} is the metal–semiconductor work function, and V_{fb} is the flat band voltage. V_{fb} is the voltage that is needed to obtain zero band bending at the Si surface, and can be extracted from the C–V curve following the procedure described in [15]. For a p-type sample, ϕ_{ms} is calculated as

$$\phi_{\mathrm{ms}} = F_m - \chi_{\mathrm{Si}} - \frac{E_g}{2} - \frac{k_B T}{q} \ln\left(\frac{N_A}{n_i}\right) \qquad (3)$$

where F_m is the metal work function, χ_{Si} is the electron affinity of Si, E_g is the band gap, k_B is the Boltzmann constant, T is the temperature, and n_i is the intrinsic carrier concentration. Using an Al work function of 4.1 eV and $\chi_{\mathrm{Si}} = 4.05$ eV, ϕ_{ms} was calculated to be –0.84 eV for the p-type samples and −0.2 eV for the n-type samples. The results from between 10 and 15 measurements using different electrode sizes were averaged in the calculation of Q_{ox}.

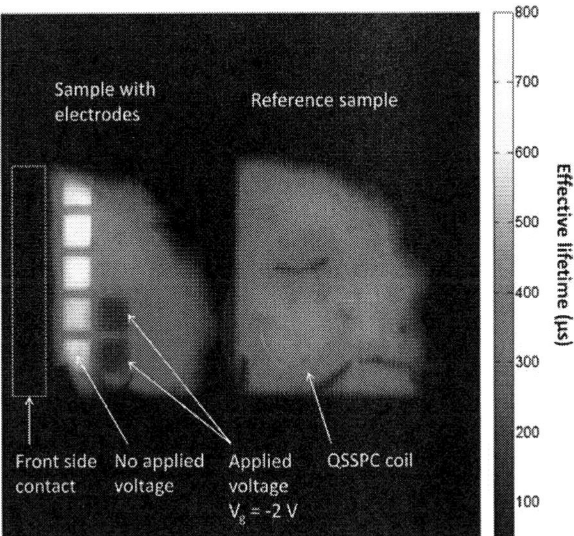

Fig. 2. PL lifetime image measured on the p-type wafer after FGA treatment while applying a voltage of –2 V over two of the rear Al electrodes. In this case, a quarter of the wafer (right) is used for lifetime calibration, whereas Al electrodes are deposited on another quarter (left). Note that the PL signal is larger above the Al electrodes not under bias compared with the surrounding areas, because of the built-in voltage from the Al–Si work function difference and an increased rear reflectance. The C–V electrodes are hidden behind the front side contact covering the left hand side of the left quarter (see Fig. 1).

III. RESULTS

A. Effective Lifetime Versus Voltage

Fig. 3 shows the effective carrier lifetime of the n-type and p-type samples as a function of the applied gate voltage V_g. For both types of substrate doping, the effective lifetime increases after FGA. All the carrier lifetime versus voltage curves show the same general behavior: When a small negative voltage is applied, the effective lifetime decreases as the external bias compensates the effect of the positive oxide charge density. To increase negative voltages, the lifetime drops to a minimum corresponding to depletion conditions at the surface, before it increases as the surface is driven into inversion (n-type samples) or accumulation (p-type samples). The curves are slightly asymmetric, with a lower effective lifetime for large negative voltage as compared with large positive voltage.

The minimum lifetime in the PL-V curve in the as-oxidized state and after FGA is found to be 119 μs and 286 μs for the n-type sample and 27 μs and 190 μs for the p-type sample, respectively. The highest lifetime was observed in the n-type sample under accumulation conditions; with $\tau_{\text{eff}} = 856$ μs. Note that all lifetime images were measured using a constant generation rate so that the injection level Δn changes with the lifetime in the sample according to the relation $\Delta n = \tau_{\text{eff}} G$. For instance, in the n-type sample after FGA, the lifetime variation corresponds to injection levels in the range between 9.4×10^{14} cm^{-3} and 2.8×10^{15} cm^{-3}.

B. Capacitance–Voltage Measurements

Typical C–V curves measured on the p-type sample are shown in Fig. 4. The flat band voltage was observed to decrease after FGA, indicating a lowering of the oxide charge density. Average Q_{ox} values, calculated from 10–15 measurements on each sample, are presented in Table I.

IV. ANALYSIS AND DISCUSSION

A. Calculation of Experimental SRV Values

In order to obtain a more fundamental understanding of the data presented in Fig. 3, front and rear SRVs were calculated from the lifetime measurements in the following manner: The front side SRV S_f was first calculated from the effective lifetime τ_{eff} measured by the QSSPC in the reference region, where the front and rear SRVs are assumed to be identical [2]

$$S_f = \alpha D \tan\left(\frac{\alpha W}{2}\right). \tag{4}$$

Here, D is the minority carrier diffusion coefficient, W is the wafer thickness, and α is given by

$$\alpha = \sqrt{\frac{1}{D}\left(\frac{1}{\tau_{\text{eff}}} - \frac{1}{\tau_{\text{bulk}}}\right)} \tag{5}$$

where τ_{bulk} is the bulk lifetime. It should be noted that the effective lifetime in the reference region does not directly correspond to the lifetime measured at 0 V in the PL-V curves, as the lifetime over the electrodes is also influenced by the change in the rear SRV caused by the built-in potential because of ϕ_{ms}. The rear side SRV S_r was then calculated from S_f and the measured lifetime, over the active electrode at each point of the curves shown in Fig. 3 as [2]

$$S_r = \frac{\tan(\alpha W)\alpha^2 D^2 - \alpha D S_f}{\alpha D + \tan(\alpha W)S_f} \tag{6}$$

with α defined as above. FZ wafers with a high bulk lifetime were used in the experimental investigation to ensure that the contribution from bulk recombination is small. Still, the chosen value for τ_{bulk} has some influence on the result. To ensure that the bulk lifetime did not significantly degrade after oxidation, a quarter of each wafer was dipped in a 5% HF solution for 1 min to strip off the oxide layers, cleaned by a standard RCA 1+2 clean, dipped in 5% HF solution for 30 s and passivated on both sides with a 40-nm thick layer of hydrogenated amorphous Si (a-Si:H) deposited by plasma enhanced chemical vapor deposition. This surface passivation layer ensures a SRV less than 5 cm/s, and thus the measured effective lifetime of these samples give a good indication of the bulk lifetime. Based on these measurements, a constant bulk lifetime of 5 ms was chosen for the calculations, and the error bars on the SRV values were calculated using $\tau_{\text{bulk}} = 2.5$ ms and $\tau_{\text{bulk}} = \infty$ ms as minimum and maximum values. The calculated values for S_f and S_r as a function of V_g for the p-type sample after FGA treatment is shown in Fig. 5.

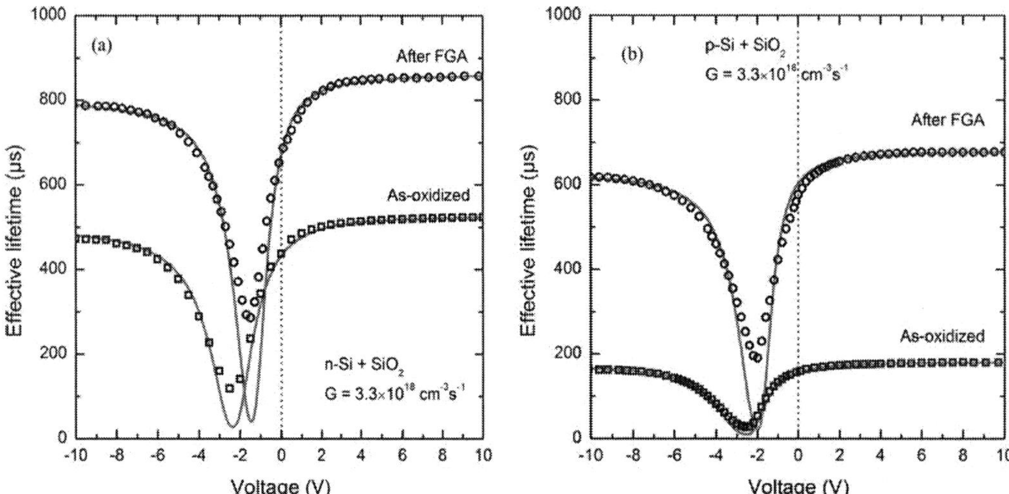

Fig. 3. Effective lifetime of the n-type (a) and the p-type (b) samples as a function of voltage applied to one of the sample surfaces, before and after FGA. The measurements were performed using a constant generation rate of $G = 3.3 \times 10^{18}$ cm^{-3}s^{-1}. The experimental data is shown as open symbols, whereas the simulated curves are shown as solid red lines. The simulation details are given in Section IV-B and the simulation parameters are given in Table I. The line corresponding to zero applied voltage is indicated by a dotted vertical line for clarity.

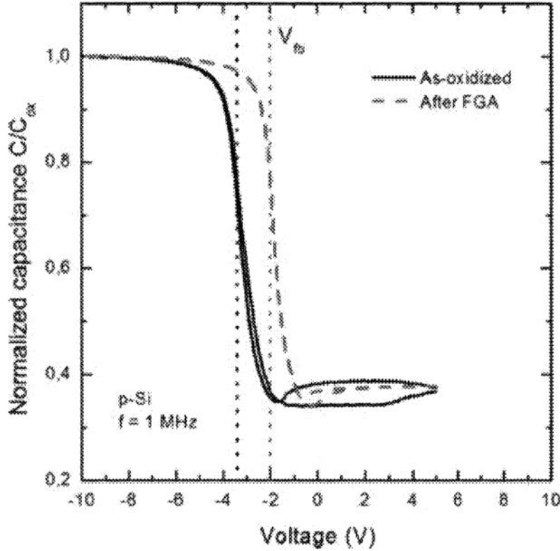

Fig. 4. Normalized C–V curves measured on the p-type sample, before (solid line) and after (dashed line) FGA treatment. The flat band voltage V_{fb} (indicated by dotted lines) is reduced after FGA treatment.

B. Simulation of the Effective SRV

Measurements of effective lifetime (and thus the SRV) with varying surface potential allow for a fundamental understanding of the surface recombination mechanisms, and are particularly useful for separating the contributions from field-effect and chemical passivation. In order to quantitatively extract fundamental properties of the interface traps responsible for carrier recombination, we have fitted the results to an extended Shockley–Read–Hall (SRH) recombination model [16]. No measurements of the (energy dependent) interface state density D_{it} or capture cross sections $\sigma_{n/p}$ have been performed for this study. A simplified model that includes one effective midgap defect level was therefore chosen, and was found to sufficiently describe the observations. The rear effective SRV is then given from standard SRH theory as

$$S_{\mathrm{SRH}} = \frac{1}{\Delta n} \frac{S_{n0} S_{p0} (n_s p_s - n_i^2)}{S_{n0}(n_s + n_i) + S_{p0}(p_s + n_i)} \qquad (7)$$

where n_i is the intrinsic carrier concentration and S_{n0} and S_{p0} are the SRV parameters of electrons and holes, respectively, defined as the product of the electron thermal velocity v_{th}, the concentration of surface states per unit area N_{it} and the corresponding capture cross section σ_n or σ_p. The surface concentrations of electrons and holes n_s and p_s are strongly dependent on the surface potential ψ_s. We use the so-called Girisch formalism [3], [16] to numerically find a self-consistent value for ψ_s (and thus n_s and p_s) for any given values for V_g, Q_{ox}, and ϕ_{ms}. This method is based upon a numerical solution of the charge balance at the interface, under the assumption of constant quasi-Fermi levels throughout the surface space charge region. To simplify the analysis, we have assumed that Q_{ox} is constant with all the charges located at the c-Si/SiO$_2$ interface and that the contribution from the charges in the interface traps Q_{it} can be neglected in the charge balance.

As seen on the experimental SRVs shown in Fig. 5, the SRV could not be enforced arbitrarily low by increasing the voltage, but instead it reaches a minimum value. It was therefore necessary to add a (voltage-independent) contribution to the effective SRV called S_{min} in order to correctly describe the flattening of the lifetime versus voltage curves under large surface band bending

$$S_{\mathrm{eff}} = S_{\mathrm{SRH}} + S_{\mathrm{min}}. \qquad (8)$$

Note that this effect could not be accounted for by recombination at the front surface or in the bulk of the wafers. A similar approach has also previously been used for such simulations [7], [12]. In these works, inclusion of shunt and recombination currents through the space-charge region were used to

     294

TABLE I
SIMULATION PARAMETERS AND Q_{ox} VALUES CALCULATED FROM THE C–V MEASUREMENTS

	Parameter	Description	Unit	n-type sample		p-type sample	
				As-oxidized	FGA	As-oxidized	FGA
Fitting	S_{n0}	SRV parameter for electrons	cm/s	12000	3300	21000	2500
parameters	S_{p0}	SRV parameter for holes	cm/s	5700	1300	8800	990
for simulations	$S_{min,\,n}$	Minimum SRV, $\psi_s < 0$	cm/s	21	9.1	61	14
	$S_{min,\,p}$	Minimum SRV, $\psi_s > 0$	cm/s	17	6.6	53	10
	Q_{ox}	Fixed oxide charge	cm^{-2}	6.8×10^{11}	3.7×10^{11}	6.1×10^{11}	4.0×10^{11}
C-V analysis	Q_{ox}	Fixed oxide charge	cm^{-2}	7.3×10^{11}	2.7×10^{11}	6.9×10^{11}	3.5×10^{11}
		Standard deviation	cm^{-2}	0.3×10^{11}	0.5×10^{11}	0.4×10^{11}	0.2×10^{11}

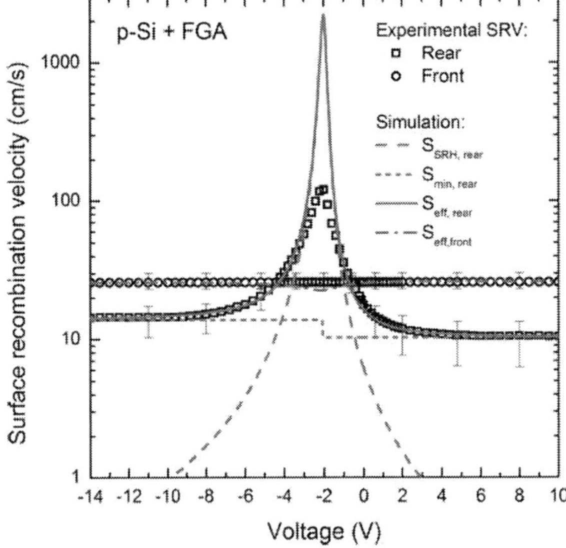

Fig. 5. Front and rear side SRV for the p-type sample after FGA as a function of applied voltage. The experimental values (calculated from the measured carrier lifetime data shown in Fig. 3) are plotted together with the different simulated contributions to the effective SRV. The error bars are calculated from minimum and maximum bulk lifetime values.

theoretically describe measurements of the SRV as function of surface charge and injection level.

The measured minimum SRV was found to be different for large negative voltages compared with large positive voltages. S_{min} was therefore modeled as

$$S_{min} = \begin{cases} S_{min,n} & \text{for } \psi_s < 0 \\ S_{min,p} & \text{for } \psi_s > 0. \end{cases} \tag{9}$$

C. Simulation Results

The model described above was used to numerically calculate the effective SRV for each value of V_g. A least squares optimization algorithm was then used find a best fit between the model and the front and rear experimental SRVs, with $S_{0n}, S_{0p}, Q_{ox}, S_{min,n}$, and $S_{min,p}$ used as free fitting parameters. When simultaneously fitting the model to both S_r and S_f, it is possible to find a relatively unique fit, as each parameter

plays a different role in the determination of the curve: S_{n0} and S_{p0} determine the slope of the left and right hand side of the SRV peak, respectively, Q_{ox} determines the position of the lifetime minimum along the voltage axis, and $S_{min,n}$ and $S_{min,p}$ determine the minimum SRV at large negative and large positive voltages, respectively. The simulated effective lifetime for each measurement is shown in Fig. 3 and the different SRV contributions are shown in Fig. 5 for the p-type sample after FGA. The best fit parameters for each measurement are given in Table I, together with the average Q_{ox} values calculated from the C–V measurements.

From Table I, it can be seen that both S_{n0} and S_{p0} are reduced after FGA for both substrate polarities. The ratio between the capture cross sections for electrons and holes σ_n/σ_p (given by S_{n0}/S_{p0}) are however found to approximately constant, and is found to be between 2 and 2.5 for all measurements, regardless of doping polarity and FGA treatment. The knowledge of this ratio is valuable as it can aid in an identification of the type of defect which is dominating the recombination. It is also interesting from a technological point of view, as the ratio between σ_n and σ_p affects the injection level dependence of the SRV, which again is a contributing factor to the fill factor of high-efficiency Si solar cells with passivated rear surfaces.

The minimum SRV values $S_{min,n}$ and $S_{min,p}$ are also observed to decrease after FGA, with $S_{min,n}$ being larger than $S_{min,p}$ for all the curves. This is consistent with σ_n being larger than σ_p at the interface defects.

Furthermore, Q_{ox} is found to decrease from 6–7×10^{11} to $\sim 4 \times 10^{11}$ cm^{-3} after FGA for both samples, caused by a shift of the lifetime minimum towards lower negative voltages in the PL-V curves. This is in good agreement with the results from the C–V measurements, shown in the lower part of Table I. The observed reduction of both the oxide charge and the effective SRV parameters (and thus D_{it}) is consistent with previous findings in the literature [1, p. 118].

D. Possible Errors and Deviations

Using the best-fit parameters, the model described in Section IV-B gives a good simultaneous agreement with the measured front and rear SRVs under most band bending conditions. The SRH model however overestimates the rear SRV in the region of the curve corresponding to depletion conditions (close to V_{fb}) by more than one order of magnitude. In this region, the applied voltage counteracts the field-effect passivation from the oxide charges, and the rear SRV goes through a maximum where it is limited by chemical passivation only. This discrepancy suggests that the model described in Section IV-B cannot fully describe the surface recombination behavior when the SRV is large. A possible explanation for this may be that the assumption of constant quasi-Fermi levels throughout the surface space region which is used in [3] may not hold for the largest SRVs observed at depletion conditions.

The error bars indicated in Fig. 5 are calculated based on an uncertainty in the bulk lifetime of the samples. This possible error is however the same for all points along the curve, therefore the conclusions based on relative differences, e.g., the difference between $S_{\min,n}$ and $S_{\min,p}$, are still valid. No significant charge build-up was observed during the course of the measurement, meaning that the points along the voltage-lifetime curve could be almost perfectly reproduced when the measurements were repeated without moving the sample. This is consistent with a very small hysteresis in the C–V curves shown in Fig. 3, which implies that Q_{ox} is not changed during the measurement.

V. Concluding Remarks

The PL-V technique has been shown to give reproducible results which are in agreement with both capacitance–voltage measurements and previous findings in the literature. Analysis of the PL-V curves using an extended SRH model gives valuable information about the passivation mechanisms, and can be used to separate the contributions from field-effect and chemical passivation. The method may be used to determine S_{n0}, S_{p0}, and Q_f for a wide range of dielectric passivation layers, and in combination with supplementary measurements of the interface state density D_{it} the method can also be used to determine the absolute values of σ_n and σ_p for the recombination active defects at the interface. The PL-V method allows for very fast measurements to be carried out independently of the measurement history of the sample, and gives the possibility of simultaneous measurements of several areas of the wafer. The PL-V measurements can therefore be used as an attractive alternative method for characterization of the Si surface passivation layers.

Acknowledgment

The authors wish to thank T. U. Nærland for valuable input and discussion of the paper and M. S. Wiig for help with the thermal oxidation process and forming gas annealing of the wafers.

References

[1] A. G. Aberle, "Crystalline silicon solar cells— Advanced surface passivation and analysis," in *Centre for Photovoltaic Engineering*. Kensington, Australia: Univ. of New South Wales, 1999.

[2] A. B. Sproul, "Dimensionless solution of the equation describing the effect of surface recombination on carrier decay in semiconductors," *J. Appl. Phys*, vol. 76, no. 5, pp. 2851–2854, 1994.

[3] R. B. M. Girisch, R. P. Mertens, and R. F. De Keersmaecker, "Determination of Si-SiO2 interface recombination parameters using a gate-controlled point-junction diode under illumination," *IEEE Trans. Electron. Devices*, vol. 35, no. 2, pp. 203–222, Feb. 1988.

[4] E. Yablonovitch, R. M. Swanson, W. D. Eades, and B. R. Weinberger, "Electron-hole recombination at the Si-SiO2 interface," *Appl. Phys. Lett.*, vol. 48, no. 3, pp. 245–247, 1986.

[5] W. E. Jellett and K. J. Weber, "Accurate measurement of extremely low surface recombination velocities on charged, oxidized silicon surfaces using a simple metal-oxide-semiconductor structure," *Appl. Phys. Lett.*, vol. 90, no. 4, pp. 042104–042104-3, 2007.

[6] M. Schofthaler, R. Brendel, G. Langguth, and J. H. Werner, "High-quality surface passivation by corona-charged oxides for semiconductor surface characterization," in *Proc. 1st World Conf. Photovoltaic Energy Convers.*, Waikoloa, HI, USA, 1994, vol. 2, pp. 1509–1512.

[7] S. W. Glunz, D. Biro, S. Rein, and W. Warta, "Field-effect passivation of the SiO2 Si interface," *J. Appl. Phys*, vol. 86, no. 1, pp. 683–691, 1999.

[8] H. Haug, Ø. Nordseth, E. V. Monakhov, and E. S. Marstein, "Photoluminescence imaging under applied bias for characterization of Si surface passivation layers," *Sol. Energy Mater. Sol. Cells*, vol. 106, pp. 60–65, 2012.

[9] T. Trupke, R. A. Bardos, M. C. Schubert, and W. Warta, "Photoluminescence imaging of silicon wafers," *Appl. Phys. Lett.*, vol. 89, no. 4, pp. 44103–44107, 2006.

[10] D. Biro, S. Mack, A. Wolf, A. Lemke, U. Belledin, D. Erath, B. Holzinger, E. A. Wotke, M. Hofmann, L. Gautero, S. Nold, J. Rentsch, and R. Preu, "Thermal oxidation as a key technology for high efficiency screen printed industrial silicon solar cells," in *Proc. 34th IEEE Photovoltaic Spec. Conf..* Philadelphia, PA, USA, 2009, pp. 1594–1599.

[11] A. G. Aberle, S. W. Glunz, A. W. Stephens, and M. A. Green, "High-efficiency silicon solar cells: Si/SiO2 interface parameters and their impact on device performance," *Prog. Photovoltaic Res. Appl.*, vol. 2, no. 4, pp. 265–273, 1994.

[12] S. Mack, A. Wolf, C. Brosinsky, S. Schmeisser, A. Kimmerle, P. Saint-Cast, M. Hofmann, and D. Biro, "Silicon Surface Passivation by Thin Thermal Oxide/PECVD Layer Stack Systems," *IEEE J. Photovoltaics*, vol. 1, no. 2, pp. 135–145, 2011.

[13] R. A. Sinton, A. Cuevas, and M. Stuckings, "Quasi-Steady-State Photo-Conductance, A new method for solar cell material and device characterization," in *Proc. 25th IEEE Photovoltaic Spec. Conf.*, Washington, DC, USA, 1996, pp. 457–460.

[14] H. Haug, S. Olibet, Ø. Nordseth, and E. S. Marstein, "Modulating the field-effect passivation at the SiO2/c-Si interface: Analysis and verification of the photoluminescence imaging under applied bias method," *J. Appl. Phys*, to be published.

[15] D. K. Schroeder, *Semiconductor material and device characterization*, 3rd ed. Hoboken, NJ, USA: Wiley, 2006, p. 334.

[16] A. G. Aberle, S. Glunz, and W. Warta, "Impact of illumination level and oxide parameters on Shockley–Read–Hall recombination at the Si-SiO2 interface," *J. Appl. Phys*, vol. 71, no. 9, pp. 4422–4431, 1992.

Humidity Degradation and Repair of ALD Al$_2$O$_3$ Passivated Silicon

Wensheng. Liang, Klaus J. Weber, Dongchul Suh, Jun Yu and James Bullock

Centre for Sustainable Energy Systems, Australian National University, Canberra, A.C.T. 0200, Australia

Abstract— The effect of humidity on boron diffused and undiffused silicon samples passivated by aluminum oxide (Al$_2$O$_3$) synthesized by plasma-assisted atomic layer deposition (PA-ALD) has been investigated. We found that undiffused samples show a higher degradation rate than diffused samples. Under an ambient of 100% relative humidity and 50°C, the lifetime of an undiffused sample passivated by Al$_2$O$_3$ decreased from 1500 to 400µs after 28 hours of exposure, whereas the saturation current density of the diffused region J_{op+} of a boron diffused sample was nearly unchanged after 7 days of exposure. As expected, for both diffused and undiffused samples, the degradation rate is accelerated by increasing the temperature of the humidity environment. A PECVD SiN$_x$ capping layer acts as an effective protection layer for Al$_2$O$_3$ to resist a damp-heat conditions of 100% relatively humidity at 80°C. The electrical resistance of PA-ALD Al$_2$O$_3$ was observed to degrade in humidity. Fourier Transform Infra-red Spectroscopy (FTIR) measurements indicate that damp heat results in a structural modification of the bulk Al$_2$O$_3$ film and the formation of AlO(OH). This change could be responsible for the fast degradation rate of PA-ALD Al$_2$O$_3$ passivation compared with SiO$_2$. Finally, we experimentally demonstrated that the degraded passivation of an Al$_2$O$_3$ layer can be repaired by light illumination and negative corona charge deposition.

Index Terms—Al$_2$O$_3$, passivation, humidity, FTIR, solar cell.

I. Introduction

In recent years, aluminum oxide (Al$_2$O$_3$) thin films have been used to significantly improve solar cell efficiency by providing effective surface passivation, as they feature both a relatively high fixed negative charge density as well as a low interface defect density[1],[2]. Various deposition techniques have been developed to deposit Al$_2$O$_3$(or AlO$_x$) for surface passivation, including atomic layer deposition (ALD)[1], plasma enhanced chemical vapour deposition (PECVD)[3], sputtering[4], atmospheric pressure chemical vapour deposition (APCVD)[5] and reactive sputter deposition[6].

The stability of the passivation scheme to elevated temperatures, ultraviolet (UV) irradiation and humidity is an important consideration necessary when the material is applied on an illuminated surface in an external environment. Dingemans *et. al.* demonstrated that both PA-ALD Al$_2$O$_3$ single layers and Al$_2$O$_3$/SiN$_x$ stacks exhibit sufficient stability to thermal and UV stress, with the surface passivation of Al$_2$O$_3$ films even improving during UV irradiation[7]. However, to our knowledge, no specific investigations have been carried out into the impact of humidity on the surface passivation of Al$_2$O$_3$, even though it a promising passivation material for further commercialized silicon solar cells[8]. In this paper, the humidity stability of Al$_2$O$_3$ films and Al$_2$O$_3$/SiN$_x$ stacks on different silicon surfaces will therefore be investigated. Fourier transform infrared (FTIR) spectroscopy will also be applied to investigate possible structural modifications to Al$_2$O$_3$ layers following humidity exposure.

Finally, we will demonstrate how the degraded passivation due to humidity exposure can to some extent be healed by light illumination and negative corona charge deposition.

II. Experimental Details

High resistivity >100Ω-cm, n-type, (100), float zone (FZ) silicon wafers were symmetrically diffused to form a p+np+ structure with a sheet resistance R_{sh} ~85Ω/□ and surface concentration of 2×10^{19}cm^3. FZ, p-type, ~0.8Ω-cm, (100) oriented silicon samples were also used as undiffused samples. Before Al$_2$O$_3$ deposition samples received a conventional RCA clean with a final dip in diluted HF (5%). Plasma assisted ALD(PA-ALD) Al$_2$O$_3$ films were deposited using a Beneq TFS-200 ALD system at a temperature of 175°C. All Al$_2$O$_3$ films had a thickness of ~20nm unless stated otherwise. After Al$_2$O$_3$ deposition, on selected samples a capping layer of 70nm SiN$_x$ was deposited on both sides in a PECVD reactor (Oxford Plasmalab 80+) at 400°C. The passivation performance was activated by annealing in forming gas (95% Ar with 5% H$_2$) at 400°C for 30 minutes.

Selected samples were then subjected to a damp-heat atmosphere of 100% relative humidity (RH) at a specific temperature for various durations according to experiment requirements. The influence of damp-heat exposure on passivation performance was evaluated by measuring the effective minority carrier lifetime(τ_{eff}) using a WCT-120 Sinton system[9]. For diffused samples, the saturation current density of the p+ region (J_{op+}) was extracted by applying the model proposed by Kane and Swanson[10].

N-type, >100Ω-cm, silicon wafers were used to test the

resistance of 30nm Al_2O_3 before and after humidity exposure. Following humidity exposure 1μm thick aluminum pads were evaporated 200μm apart through a shadow mask. A current is driven between the two pads and the current-voltage behavior recorded.

The FTIR spectra were measured on double sided polished, FZ, silicon wafers with PA-ALD Al_2O_3 deposited on both sides, using an Bruker Vertex 80V spectrometer with resolution of 6 cm^{-1}. To eliminate the artefact from the non-uniform distribution of O and C in the silicon bulk on the final results, the background spectrum of each sample, which was used for the final analysis, was collected before passivation layer deposition.

Depth resolved XPS (X-ray photoelectron spectroscopy) measurements were performed using an Escalab 220i-XL spectrometer with a monochromatic Al-Kα radiation source (energy 1486.68eV) with a measuring spot of 500μm^2, where the photoelectrons emitted from the samples were collected in the surface normal direction. Depth profiles were obtained alternating narrow-scan measurements and sputtering with 3KeV Ar ion beam (etch area 2.5×2.5mm^2) after every 5s of sputtering.

Corona charging was carried out with a conventional setup by applying a voltage of +/−6 KV to a steel needle ~10cm above the samples.

III.   RESULTS AND DISCUSSION

A. Passivation degradation

In Fig.1, clear degradation due to damp heat is observed for PA-ALD Al_2O_3 passivated p-type samples and boron doped p^+np^+ structures in a temperature range from 50 to 80°C. For the p-type sample, degradation occurs after ~4-hour exposure at a temperature of 50°C, whereas passivation can only survive for ~10 minutes if the exposure temperature increases up to 65°C and 80 °C.

Fig.1(a) suggests that, in terms of exposure time, a threshold indicating the abrupt onset of degradation exists for a given temperature. Passivation is stable before the threshold value while a rapid drop of lifetime occurs after the threshold. In contrast, thermal SiO_2 passivated and alnealed samples exhibit a more gradual degradation in the same ambient[11]. Furthermore, the extent of degradation of the Al_2O_3 surface passivation is much more significant than that of alnealed SiO_2 passivation after a prolonged humidity exposure[11]. Under the same damp heat conditions (RH=100%, 80°C,1×10^4 minutes), τ_{eff} decreased by a factor of 3-5 for thermal SiO_2 passivated samples and by a factor of 1.2–1.4 for those that had received an alneal[11]. In contrast, the effective lifetime of PA-ALD Al_2O_3 passivated samples degrades dramatically from more than 1ms prior to exposure to ~20μs, by a factor>50.

In Fig.1(a), the sample passivated by an Al_2O_3/SiNx stack shows no significant change in effective lifetime. Lifetime stability of such stacks was also observed for boron diffused samples, which are not illustrated in Fig.1. This shows that PECVD SiNx layers can efficiently act as a barrier against the

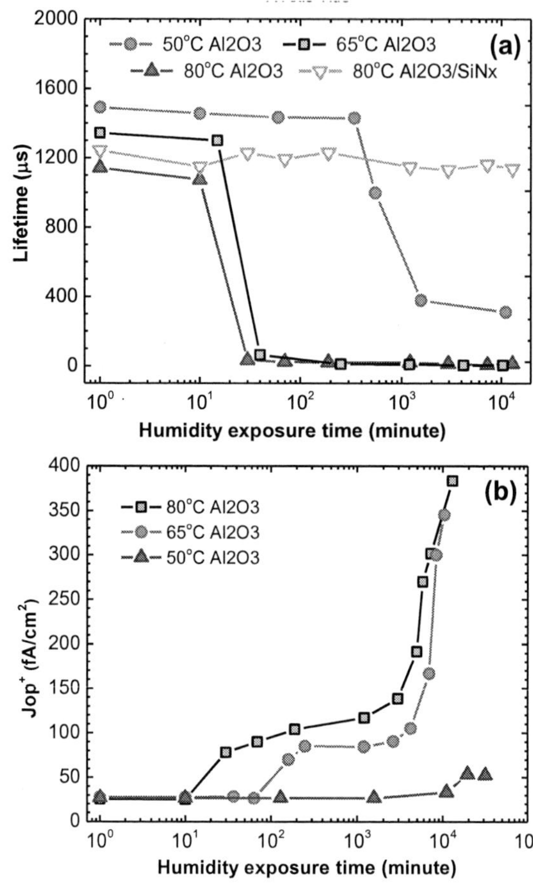

Fig.1. Passivation performance of PA-ALD Al_2O_3 passivated structures as a function of humidity(RH=100%) exposure time at different temperatures of 50, 65 and 80°C respectively. (a) Al2O3 or Al2O3/SiNx passivated p-type substrates; (b) Al2O3 passivated p+np+ structures with a sheet resistance ~85 $\Omega/\square$.

penetration of water vapor for PA-ALD Al_2O_3 films.

Fig.1(b) plots J_{op+} of boron diffused samples as a function of cumulative humidity exposure time. It is evident that higher temperatures accelerate the degradation for Al_2O_3 passivated p^+np^+ samples. Samples subjected to the temperature of 50°C do not significantly degrade until a cumulative exposure time of $1×10^4$ minutes, while the sample exposed at 80°C shows degradation after only 20 minutes. In addition, no clear thresholds, illustrating a rapid J_{op+} increase, are displayed by boron diffused samples; instead the J_{op+} rises gradually with increasing period of exposure time, by a factor of 20 after $1×10^4$ minutes.

It should be stressed that Al_2O_3 single layer can still afford good humidity resistance for boron diffused samples if the environment temperature is lower than 50°C, which is presented by the triangles in Fig.1(b). The J_{op+} is nearly unchanged during the first $1.3×10^4$ minutes, with an increase by a factor of 2 to 50fA/cm^2 during the subsequent period of $2×10^4$ minutes. The shortest humidity exposure duration in Fig.1 is $1.3×10^4$ minutes, which is slightly greater than the 200h required for the humidity-freeze component of standard solar cell module

298

testing[12].

It is noticeable that the onset of degradation appears to be delayed for boron diffused samples compared with undiffused samples. For example, for the 65°C sample, the onset of degradation occurs at 20 minutes for the latter case, while it is 70 minutes for the boron diffused samples. After 1000-minute exposure, J_{op+} of the p+np+ structure increases by a factor of 3, whereas τ_{eff} of the p-type sample has degraded to 20µs. It is possible that, as the recombination of Al_2O_3 passivated p^+np^+ region is dominated by the auger recombination in the diffused region[13], the prominent increase of J_{op+} can only be revealed when the surface recombination due to a humidity exposure exceeds that from the surface doping region. Secondly, as will be shown later, the initial stage of degradation appears to be caused by a decrease of negative charge density, rather than an increase in interface defects. The passivation of the boron diffused surfaces is less sensitive to a reduction in negative charge density than that of undiffused surfaces.

The results above suggest that the power output of silicon solar cells would decrease after prolonged exposure to a damp-heat ambient if the Al_2O_3 passivation layer was not properly protected. However, it is rare to apply a single Al_2O_3 layer to passivate Si surfaces; more commonly Al_2O_3/SiN_x stacks are considered for both superior optical performance and appropriate passivation [14],[15].

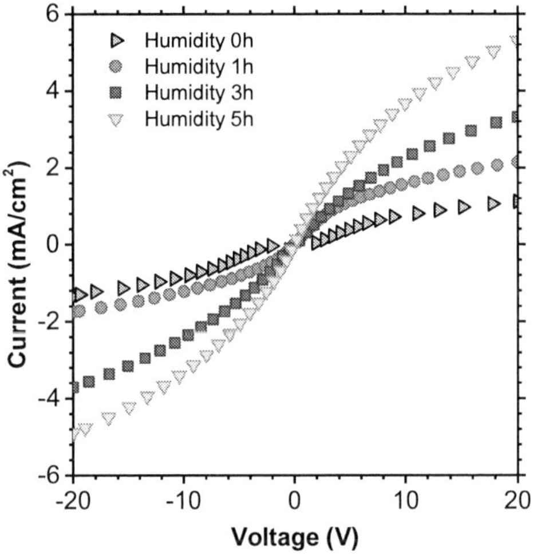

Fig.2. I-V curves obtained from a samples with 30nm Al_2O_3 after different periods of humidity exposure with RH=100%, 80°C.

B. Electric resistance degradation

Further to the passivation requirements of the Al_2O_3 films, electrical insulation properties must also be maintained during the lifetime of the solar cell. This is important as to avoid a low resistance shunting path, for example in the interdigitated back contact solar cell where contacts of opposite polarity are in close vicinity. Fig.2 shows the changing current-voltage behavior as a function of increasing humidity exposure. The sample without humidity exposure exhibits the most resistive behavior, the shape of which is likely due to the opposing junctions faced by current when flowing through the high resistivity silicon between contacts. The current-voltage behavior becomes successively more conductive as a function of humidity exposure indicating the likelihood of an increase Al_2O_3 film conductance.

It is probable that an increase in film conductivity will lead to differences in current flow both through the film and through the silicon making a quantitate inference of the films contribution difficult. An estimation of the increasing contribution of film conductance is made by measuring the resistance in 10 to 20V region. This is seen to decrease by a factor of 4 after just 5 hours of humidity exposure.

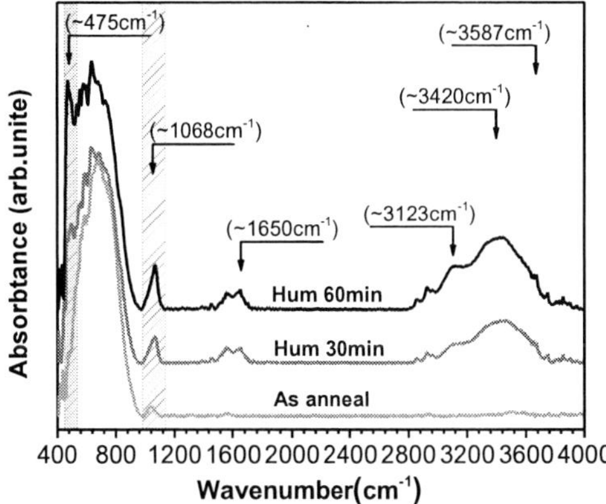

Fig.3. FTIR spectrums of a sample with 30nm Al_2O_3 at as anneal stage, after 30-minute and 60-minute exposure in humidity(RH=100%, 80°C).

C. FTIR spectroscopy analysis

Fig.3 plots the FTIR absorption spectrum for the sample with 30nm Al_2O_3 measured after an initial anneal and after a 60-minute humidity exposure (RH=100%, 80°C). The spectrum of the as annealed sample shows a small absorption peak at 1040cm⁻¹, associated with the asymmetric stretch of the with the asymmetric stretch vibration of Si-O-Si bridging [16], which is attributed to the 1 2nm interfacial SiO_2 layer of Al_2O_3/Si. The band between 400 and 1000cm⁻¹ is assigned to multiple vibrations of Al-O and O-Al-O bonds [17]. Two weak peaks at 1570 and 3500cm⁻¹ are assigned to the bending mode of H-O-H and the stretching mode of O-H, which is often present in ALD-Al_2O_3 due to the use of hydrogen containing reactants $Al(CH_4)_3$[16].

From the spectrum of the same sample after 60-minute exposure to humidity, two broad bands emerge in the range of 2800-3800cm⁻¹ and 1450-1720cm⁻¹ respectively. Both bands are O-H vibration related, indicating the absorption of H_2O on the Al_2O_3 surface or penetration into the Al_2O_3 bulk. A concomitant increase of the two peaks located at 1068 and 480cm⁻¹ is noticeable, and the reasons for this will be discussed in the following section.

Fig.4 displays the expanded region in the vicinity of 1068 and 3420cm⁻¹ bands of FTIR spectrum of Al_2O_3 films of various thicknesses after 60-minute exposure to a damp heat environment. These spectra clearly show that the increase of the intensity of O-H vibrations (2800-3800cm⁻¹) increases with Al_2O_3 thickness. This suggests that the concentration of

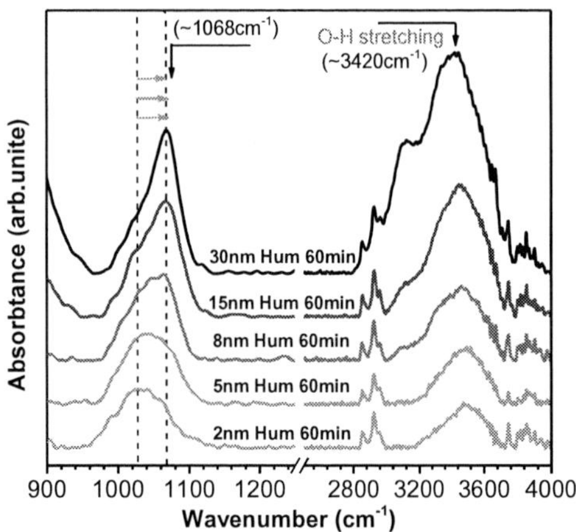

Fig.4. FTIR spectra of Al$_2$O$_3$ with a series of thicknesses from 2nm to 30nm after 60-minute exposure in a damp-heat ambient of RH=100%, 80°C.

moisture in the Al$_2$O$_3$ is not just restricted to the surface, but some diffusion into the bulk of the film has occurred. The penetration of OH species through the Al$_2$O$_3$ film may result in changes to the Si-SiOx interface, resulting in a degradation mechanism similar as that reported for SiO$_2$/Si or SiNx/Si structures [18],[19].

Fig.5 shows the changes in the absorption bands around 1068cm^{-1} and 3420cm^{-1} bands as a function of humidity exposure time. As expected, the intensity of O-H peak at ~3420cm^{-1} increases gradually with cumulative exposure time as more moisture penetrates in the Al$_2$O$_3$ bulk. A concomitant increase is also observed at the peak at 1068cm^{-1}.

On the basis of the degradation mechanism of Si/SiNx[19], it could be suggested that the increase of the peak at ~1068cm^{-1} is due to the further growth of SiO$_2$ at the interface of Al$_2$O$_3$/Si, which is supported by the same increase of the Si-O-Si intensity observed for the SiNx FTIR spectrum after moisture exposure and the fact that there was no other bonds would contribute to this in that study. Moreover, it is interesting that with increasing exposure time, the spectral peak of Si-O species shifts from an as-deposited value of 1040cm^{-1} to 1068cm^{-1} after 1h humidity exposure, which is in agreement with the migration of the same band reported for aged PECVD SiO$_2$ layers[20]. It is explained that the strained Si-O-Si bonds existing in SiO$_2$ react with atmospheric water resulting in near-neighbour Si-OH configurations. The near-neighbour silanol pairs display significant hydrogen bonding interactions. These interaction can slightly alter the characteristic vibration modes of the Si-OH groups, resulting in a peak shift toward higher wavenumber[20].

It must be stressed that the above interpretation for the observed changes from Al$_2$O$_3$ FTIR spectrums is based on the related studies involving the influence of aging on SiO$_2$ and SiNx layers.

Insight into the impact of humidity on the composition and bonding structure of Al$_2$O$_3$/Si is obtained by the depth resolved XPS analysis on the basis of Al$_{2p}$, O$_{1s}$ and Si$_{2p}$ peak intensities.Fig.6 compares the atomic concentrations of a 30nm Al$_2$O$_3$ sample after anneal and 1 hour humidity exposure. No apparent difference can be seen for the Si$_{2p}$ profiles related to

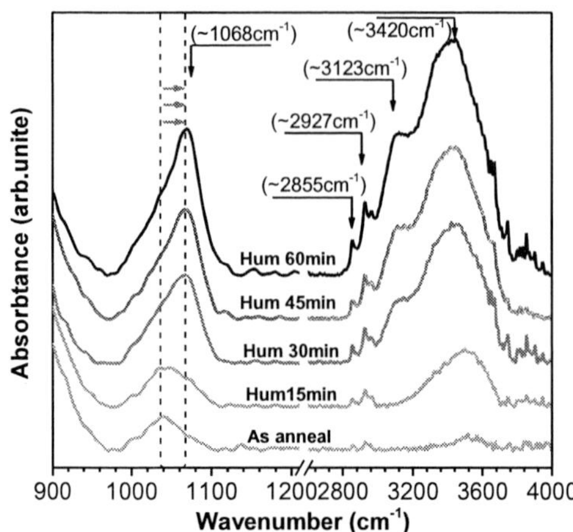

Fig.5. Evolution of the FTIR bands 900-1200cm^{-1}, 2800-4000cm^{-1} with increasing exposure in humidity(RH=100%, 80°C). 30nm PA-ALD Al$_2$O$_3$ was deposited on double sides.

the interfacial SiO$_2$, even though the integrated 1068cm^{-1} peak in Fig.5 after 60-minute humidity exposure is around 4 times of that before humidity exposure.

We conclude that the increase of peak at ~1068cm^{-1} with cumulative humidity exposure time is not induced by a modification of the thin interfacial SiO$_x$ layer, but that other bond vibrations are introduced under the influence of moisture.

Following on the literature data on δ-Al$_2$O$_3$, the band at 1068cm^{-1} could correspond to Al-O stretching bonds localized at the surface of Al$_2$O$_3$ brought about by crystal truncation induced defects[21],[22]. However, any surface process that increases the surface Madelung energy and decreases the surface covalency should lead to the disappearance of the surface mode, such as CO absorption[22] and hydration[23]. According to the data proposed by J. C. Lavalley[23], this surface vibration mode decreases instantaneously after the introduction of water and at the same time the O-H mode appears in the FTIR spectrum, which is contrary to our results shown in Fig. 5. Therefore, this explanation is not well

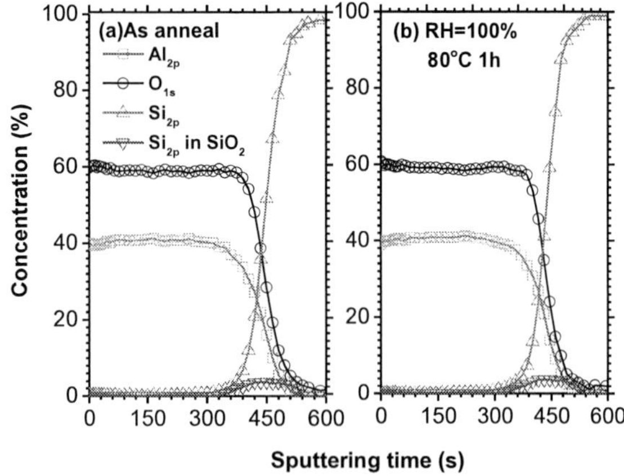

Fig.6 Atomic concentration derived from the XPS Al$_{2p}$, O$_{1s}$ and Si$_{2p}$ peak intensities as a function of sputtering time. (a) 30nm Al$_2$O$_3$, 425°C N$_2$ anneal for 15 minutes; (b) 1h exposure in a humidity ambient (RH=100%, 80°C) after anneal.

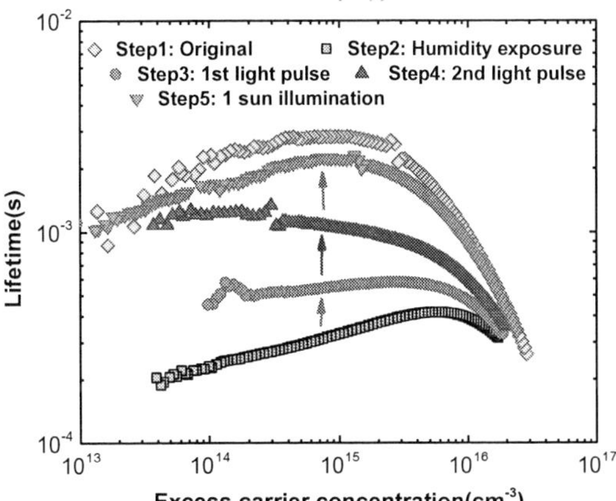

Fig.7 Measured effective lifetime τ_{eff} as a function of the excess carrier concentration for a sample following different consecutive steps. Step 1: As annealed; Step 2: Damp heat exposure in relatively 100% humidity at 80 °C for 20 minutes; Step 3: The first lifetime measurement; Step 4: The second lifetime measurement; Step 5: 1 Sun illumination for 7 hours.

supported by the experimental data either.

A third possibility is that the intensity increase at ~1068 cm^{-1} is due to the generation of some AlO(OH) species from the reaction of amorphous Al_2O_3 and H_2O[24],[25]. The FTIR spectral features of our PA-ALD Al_2O_3 films after 1h humidity exposure are quite similar to those of AlO(OH) crystals, especially the positions of some typical bands, including 475, 1068, 3123, 3420 and 3587 cm^{-1}[25].

The analysis below is on the basis of the vibration definition in Ref [25], where the molecular structure of AlO(OH) is nonlinear with 4 atoms, and 6 fundamental modes of vibrations(v1 to v6) were proposed. The strong and sharp band at 1068cm^{-1} is assigned to the Al=O stretching vibration(v2) of (OH)-Al=O. The fact that a strong band emerges around 475cm^{-1} for the 60-minute sample in Fig.3 also verify the presence of a new chemical phase, which is assigned to the angle deformation (wagging) of Al=O(v6)[25]. These two peaks are always found in the AlO(OH) spectrum[26].

Fig. 5 also shows the evolution of a broad band at 3420cm^{-1}. The spectrum taken after 15-minute exposure shows a distinct asymmetric character which corresponds to the spectrum of H_2O. With an increase in humidity exposure time, the asymmetric feature does not significantly change, but a new feature begins to emerge around 3123cm^{-1}, with the whole band broadening towards the lower wavenumber. The features at 3123 and 3587cm^{-1} are all assigned to the O-H stretching vibration(v1) of AlO(OH). Since the H position and hydrogen bond interaction are critical to the band position and intensity of vibration v1, multiple bands are observed in this range. Moreover, the feature at 3420cm^{-1} is assigned to the stretching modes of O-H of H_2O, and this absorbance is much weaker in the spectrum of AlO(OH), indicating that part of the O-H bonds are present as molecular H_2O in our Al_2O_3. It is worth mentioning that both the appearance of the broad band at 3123cm^{-1} and the extension of the O-H band region to lower wavenumbers imply the production of AlO(OH) during humidity exposure.

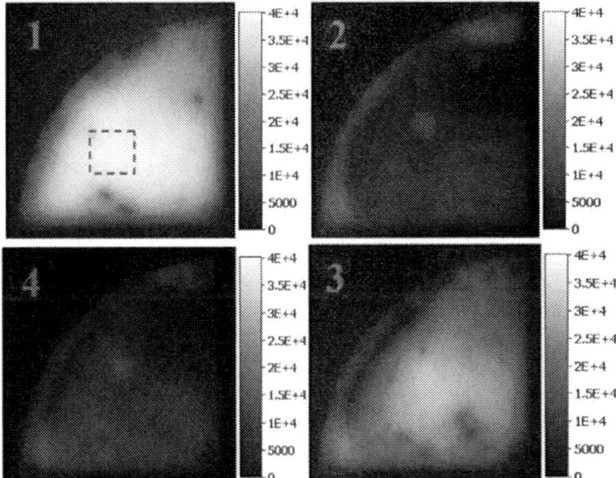

Fig.8 Uncalibrated PL images for a sample after various consecutive steps. 1: Anneal and negative corona charging; 2: Damp heat exposure for 20 minutes (RH=100% 80° C); 3: Negative corona charging until the saturation of lifetime; 4: IPA rinse; PL counts of the selected region indicated by the red square in four images are 38354, 5744, 30695 and 9744 respectively.

Hence, the FTIR results show that humidity exposure results in significant structural changes to the Al_2O_3 film bulk, which are likely to play a key role in the fast degradation rate of PA-ALD Al_2O_3 passivation compared with SiO_2.

D. Impact of surface orientation

Light illumination

We investigated the impact of illumination on the degraded samples following exposure to 100% relative humidity at 80 °C for 20 minutes. One side of the sample used in this experiment was passivated by an Al_2O_3/SiNx stack and the other side is only coated with a single Al_2O_3 layer. As the SiNx is a good barrier against H_2O diffusion, any degradation will be due to the single layer Al_2O_3 film. Following humidity exposure, the sample was illuminated in a Q-Sun Xe-1 chamber which simulates the 1-Sun spectrum at noon.

As shown in Fig.7, the lifetime decreased from 2700μs to 300μs after only 20 minutes exposure, then the degraded lifetime of 300μs after was significantly improved to around 2200μs after a 7-hour illumination (Step 5). Moreover, it is notable that a very short light pulse, decaying from a peak of 20 suns to 0 sun within 10ms, from the Sinton lifetime tester used for lifetime measurement can also improve the degraded passivation apparently(Sept 3 and 4).

Negative corona charge

Fig.8 presents a series of photoluminescence (PL) images for a sample after various consecutive processing steps. Firstly, negative corona charge was deposited on double sides after annealing to get saturated passivation. The sample degraded seriously after being subjected to a damp heat atmosphere. Subsequently, negative corona charge was applied until the effective lifetime saturated. It can be seen that the degradation is uniformly repaired except for the region around the edge. Following a subsequent IPA rinse, the effect from negative corona charge was removed and the image became dark again.

The PL counts of the selected square were measured after each step, with 38354, 5744, 30695 and 9744 respectively, which quantitatively illustrates the repair effect by negative corona charge.

It should be noted that the two repair methods are all low temperature processes, from which we consider the interface was not changed during the repair. In this case, the reason for the repair could be the recovery of negative charge density. This is consistent with the former XPS results and the supposition that the influence of humidity on the PA-ALD Al_2O_3 film implicates bulk effect.

IV. CONCLUSIONS

In conclusion, degradation due to damp heat ambient is observed for PA-ALD Al_2O_3 passivated p-type samples and boron doped p^+np^+ structures at temperature range from 50°C to 80°C. In some cases, a later onset of degradation is observed for boron diffused samples compared with undiffused samples. It is evident that a higher temperature accelerates the degradation, regardless of surface doping. Al_2O_3 single layers can still afford good humidity resistance for boron diffused samples if the environment temperature is lower than 50 °C. A PECVD SiNx capping layer can effectively protect Al_2O_3 from humidity damage, with an environment of RH=100%, temperature from 50°C to 80°C.

The electrical resistance of PA-ALD Al_2O_3 also degrades after the humidity exposure. It was estimated to decrease by a factor of 4 after just 5 hours of humidity exposure.

On the basis on FTIR measurements, two clear bands at ~1068cm^{-1} and ~475cm^{-1} were observed after humidity exposure. It is proposed that these bands are the result of the formation of Al=O(OH). This reaction between amorphous PA-ALD Al_2O_3 and H_2O could be the reason why fast degradation was observed.

We experimentally demonstrated that the degraded passivation of a Al_2O_3 layers can be partly recovered by light illumination and negative corona charge deposition.

ACKNOWLEDGMENTS

The authors would like to thank Dr. Bill Gong at UNSW for helping with XPS measurements and analysis, Dr Sachin Surve for this contribution to fabricating the resistance test samples. We also thank ANFF(Australian National Fabrication Facility) for the PECVD SiNx deposition. The PhD scholarship for Wensheng Liang from the China Scholarship Council and The Australian National University is gratefully acknowledged.

REFERENCES

[1] B. Hoex, J. Schmidt, P. Pohl, M. van de Sanden, and W. Kessels, "Silicon surface passivation by atomic layer deposited Al2O3," *Journal of Applied Physics,* vol. 104, pp. 044903, 2008.

[2] B. Hoex, J. Schmidt, R. Bock, P. Altermatt, M. van de Sanden, and W. Kessels, "Excellent passivation of highly doped p-type Si surfaces by the negative-charge-dielectric Al2O3," *Applied Physics Letters,* vol. 91, pp. 112107, 2007.

[3] P. Saint-Cast, D. Kania, M. Hofmann, J. Benick, J. Rentsch, and R. Preu, "Very low surface recombination velocity on p-type c-Si by high-rate plasma-deposited aluminum oxide," *Applied Physics Letters,* vol. 95, pp. 151502, 2009.

[4] T. T. Li and A. Cuevas, "Effective surface passivation of crystalline silicon by rf sputtered aluminum oxide," *physica status solidi (RRL)-Rapid Research Letters,* vol. 3, pp. 160-162, 2009.

[5] L. E. Black and K. R. McIntosh, "Surface passivation of c-Si by atmospheric pressure chemical vapor deposition of Al2O3," *Applied Physics Letters,* vol. 100, pp. 202107, 2012.

[6] Z. Xinyu, A. Cuevas, and A. Thomson, "Process Control of Reactive Sputter Deposition of AlOx and Improved Surface Passivation of Crystalline Silicon," *Photovoltaics, IEEE Journal of,* vol. 3, pp. 183-188, 2013.

[7] G. Dingemans, P. Engelhart, R. Seguin, F. Einsele, B. Hoex, M. van de Sanden, and W. Kessels, "Stability of Al2O3 and Al2O3/a-SiNx: H stacks for surface passivation of crystalline silicon," *Journal of Applied Physics,* vol. 106, pp. 114907, 2009.

[8] G. Dingemans and W. M. M. Kessels, "Status and prospects of Al2O3-based surface passivation schemes for silicon solar cells," *Journal of Vacuum Science & Technology A: Vacuum, Surfaces, and Films,* vol. 30, pp. 040802, 2012.

[9] R. A. Sinton and A. Cuevas, "Contactless determination of current--voltage characteristics and minority-carrier lifetimes in semiconductors from quasi-steady-state photoconductance data," *Applied Physics Letters,* vol. 69, pp. 2510-2512, 1996.

[10] D. E. Kane and R. M. Swanson, "Measurement of the emitter saturation current by a contactless photoconductivity decay method," in *Proceedings of the 18th IEEE Photovoltaic Specialists Conference,* Las Vegas, 1985, pp. 578.

[11] E. Klampaftis, K. R. McIntosh, and B. S. Richards, "Degradation of an undiffused Si-SiO2 interface due to humidity," in *22nd EU PVSEC* Milan, Italy, 2007, pp. 889-892.

[12] IEC61215, "CrystallineQ3 Silicon Terrestrial Photovoltaic(PV) Modules-Design Qualification and Type Approval," International Electrotechnical Commission: Geneva, Switzerland, April 2005.

[13] W. Liang, K. J. Weber, D. Suh, S. P. Phang, J. Yu, A. K. McAuley, and B. R. Legg, "Surface Passivation of Boron-Diffused p-Type Silicon Surfaces With (1 0 0) and (1 1 1) Orientations by ALD Al2O3 Layers," *IEEE Journal of Photovoltaics,* vol. 3, pp. 678-683, 2013.

[14] J. Schmidt, B. Veith, and R. Brendel, "Effective surface passivation of crystalline silicon using ultrathin Al2O3 films and Al2O3/SiNx stacks," *physica status solidi (RRL)-Rapid Research Letters,* vol. 3, pp. 287-289, 2009.

[15] J. Benick, B. Hoex, M. C. M. van de Sanden, W. M. M. Kessels, O. Schultz, and S. W. Glunz, "High efficiency n-type Si solar cells on Al2O3-passivated boron emitters," *Applied Physics Letters,* vol. 92, pp. 253504, 2008.

[16] V. Verlaan, L. R. J. G. van den Elzen, G. Dingemans, M. van de Sanden, and W. Kessels, "Composition and bonding structure of plasma-assisted ALD Al2O3 films," *physica status solidi (c),* vol. 7, pp. 976-979, 2010.

[17] L. Tsu-Tsung, "Surface Passivation of Crystalline Silicon by Sputtered Aluminium Oxide." vol. PhD Canberra: The Australian National University, 2010, pp. 102-104.

[18] K. R. McIntosh and X. Dai, "Damp-heat degradation and repair of oxide-passivated silicon," *physica status solidi (a),* vol. 208, pp. 1931-1936, 2011.

[19] H. Lin, L. Xu, X. Chen, X. Wang, M. Sheng, F. Stubhan, K.-H. Merkel, and J. Wilde, "Moisture-resistant properties of SiNx films prepared by PECVD," *Thin Solid Films,* vol. 333, pp. 71-76, 1998.

[20] J. A. Theil, D. V. Tsu, M. W. Watkins, S. S. Kim, and G. Lucovsky, "Local bonding environments of Si-OH groups in SiO2 deposited by remote plasmaenhanced chemical vapor deposition and incorporated by postdeposition exposure to water vapor," *Journal of Vacuum Science & Technology A: Vacuum, Surfaces, and Films,* vol. 8, pp. 1374-1381, 1990.

[21] C. Morterra and G. Magnacca, "A case study: surface chemistry and surface structure of catalytic aluminas, as studied by vibrational spectroscopy of adsorbed species," *Catalysis Today,* vol. 27, pp. 497-532, 1996.

[22] L. Marchese, S. Bordiga, S. Coluccia, G. Martra, and A. Zecchina, "Structure of the surface sites of δ-Al2O3 as determined by high-resolution transmission electron microscopy, computer modelling and infrared spectroscopy of adsorbed CO," *J. Chem. Soc., Faraday Trans.,* vol. 89, pp. 3483-3489, 1993.

[23] J.-C. Lavalley and M. Benaissa, "IR spectroscopic evidence for surface vibrational modes formed upon dehydroxylation of alumina," *Journal of the Chemical Society, Chemical Communications,* pp. 908-909, 1984.

[24] S. Rana and S. Ram, "X-Ray Diffraction and IR Spectrum for Activated Surface Hydrolysis of Al Metal into AlO(OH)·αH2O Nanocrystals in a New Monoclinic Crystal Structure," *Journal of Solid State Chemistry,* vol. 157, pp. 40-49, 2001.

[25] S. Ram, "Infrared spectral study of molecular vibrations in amorphous, nanocrystalline and AlO (OH)·αH2O bulk crystals," *Infrared physics & technology,* vol. 42, pp. 547-560, 2001.

[26] S. Shen, W. K. Ng, L. S. O. Chia, Y. Dong, and R. B. H. Tan, "Morphology Controllable Synthesis of Nanostructured Boehmite and γ-Alumina by Facile Dry Gel Conversion," *Crystal Growth & Design,* vol. 12, pp. 4987-4994, 2012.

Assessing the Performance of Surface Passivation Using Low-Intensity Photoluminescence Characterization Techniques

Catherine E. Chan, Malcolm D. Abbott, Mattias K. Juhl, Brett J. Hallam, Bo Xiao, and Stuart R. Wenham

Abstract—**This paper applies quasi-steady-state photoluminescence (QSS-PL) and photoluminescence imaging to characterize the recombination properties of various surface passivation techniques. Particular interest is given to the performance at low excess carrier densities where many types of surface passivation show a strong increase in surface recombination velocity. These techniques are then used to further understand the ability of parasitic effects such as nonuniform illumination, edge recombination and areas of high recombination to affect these measurements. Furthermore, a new technique for edge isolation using laser doping is shown to be effective against the effect of edge recombination. This technique is useful to implement when using QSS-PL to analyze small samples as carriers conducted to the edge regions can dramatically alter the effective lifetime in low injection.**

Index Terms—**Charge carrier lifetime, photoluminescence (PL), silicon, surface passivation.**

I. INTRODUCTION

IT is desirable to be able to characterize various types of surface passivation layers for silicon solar cells using test structures rather than finished devices. When doing so, it is important to cover a wide range of excess carrier densities since some passivation techniques have a strong dependence on injection level. One characterization technique that is capable of covering a wide range of intensities is quasi-steady-state photoluminescence (QSS-PL), which has been shown to measure the effective lifetime as a function of carrier intensity over eight orders of magnitude [1], [2]. When using this technique, it has been widely observed that samples may show a strong decrease in effective lifetime (τ_{eff}) at low excess carrier densities. When performing these measurements, it is of great importance to account for a range of parasitic effects that can affect the measured lifetime such as edge recombination, nonuniform illumination, localized damage or a shunted junction.

For samples with a diffused p-n junction this reduction in τ_{eff} has been shown to be due to edge effects [3]–[5]. However,

p-type undiffused samples with surfaces passivated by SiN_x also show a decrease in τ_{eff} at low injection levels [2], [6]–[9], despite the fact that the lateral path of conduction to the edge is quite resistive. Similar behavior has been observed on n-type silicon passivated by Al_2O_3 [9]–[11]. In both cases, a weak inversion layer is formed at the surface of the silicon due to the fixed positive and negative charges in the SiN_x and Al_2O_3 layers, respectively. This has severe implications for solar cells with undiffused p-type surfaces passivated by SiN_x and n-type surfaces passivated by Al_2O_3, as their performance will deteriorate under low illumination.

Numerous theories have been presented to explain this effect [6]–[8], [11]–[16]. For example, it has been suggested that the degradation in lifetime at low injection levels is due to high asymmetry of the charged and neutral capture cross sections of the defects at the SiN_x/Si interface, causing an increased surface recombination velocity at low injection [6], although no evidence of this has been observed experimentally [7]. It was instead proposed that the fixed charge density in a SiN_x layer is reduced by an order of magnitude when under illumination compared with the value measured by standard dark C–V measurements, causing the observed results, although this was subsequently disproved [8]. Other explanations have involved the introduction of recombination losses in the space charge region [8], [12], [13]. Recently, the effect has been attributed to enhanced SRH recombination in the bulk caused by a surface damage region (SDR) [14], [15], hypothesized to be formed, for the SiN_x case, during PECVD due to an excessive density of hydrogen [15]. The SDR is theorized to have a significantly lower lifetime than elsewhere in the bulk that is particularly detrimental when the surface of the silicon is in weak inversion. In this case, the space charge region lies within the SDR and the electron and hole concentrations are equal at a point of high defect density. When the silicon is passivated by a layer which induces accumulation conditions at the surface, this effect is not seen as there is no point where the electron and hole concentrations are approximately equal. Ma *et al.* simulated two possible causes of the observed injection dependence: 1) the asymmetric electron and hole lifetimes in the bulk, and 2) the SDR of which they identify the latter to be the most likely cause [16]. Throughout all of these works, it is not always clear if parasitic recombination that is present outside of the measured area has been accounted for before analyzing the results. This paper and others show that when measuring the effective lifetime at very low carrier concentrations, it is important to consider the potential for such effects to impact on the experimental data.

Manuscript received June 10, 2013; revised August 6, 2013; accepted September 13, 2013. Date of publication October 7, 2013; date of current version December 16, 2013.

The authors are with the School of Photovoltaic and Renewable Energy Engineering, University of New South Wales, Sydney, NSW 2052, Australia (e-mail: catherine.chan@unsw.edu.au; m.abbott@unsw.edu.au; mattias.juhl@unsw.edu.au; brett.hallam@unsw.edu.au; bo.xiao@unsw.edu.au; s.wenham@unsw.edu.au).

Color versions of one or more of the figures in this paper are available online at http://ieeexplore.ieee.org.

Digital Object Identifier 10.1109/JPHOTOV.2013.2282739

One of the major types of parasitic recombination that has the propensity to impact effective lifetime measurements is edge recombination, particularly when the sample size is small. This has been clearly shown to affect samples with surface diffusions of the opposite polarity to the bulk [3]–[5]. It has also been suggested that Al_2O_3 passivated undiffused n-type wafers show an injection-dependent lifetime that is exclusively due to edge effects [11]. Further, it is suggested that the same is true for SiN_x passivated p-type wafers. In their particular case, Veith *et al.* conclude that the sample size must be greater than 6 cm × 6 cm to eliminate edge effects on the Al_2O_3 passivated wafers [11]. While these studies refer to edge recombination, it is not necessarily the case that the localized regions of enhanced recombination need to be located at the substrate edge.

In this paper, we investigate the ability of various forms of enhanced recombination, which are located outside of the test area, to impact the measurement of effective lifetime. Specifically, we examine samples with SiN_x surface passivation on p-type wafers with and without phosphorus-diffused surfaces as well as on n-type wafers with Al_2O_3 surface passivation. To measure the effective lifetime, we use low-intensity QSS-PL and create spatial maps with photoluminescence (PL) imaging. Two types of enhanced recombination are examined: recombination in dark regions and localized surface damage.

A technique to potentially mitigate these problems is also presented in the form of laser-doped edge isolation. Laser ablation has been used as a technique for edge isolation since the early 1980s, resulting however in damage to the silicon. To minimize the impact of this damage, the laser ablated groove may be damage etched, undergo a thermal groove diffusion that dopes the groove with the opposite polarity to the emitter layer, and subsequently, be passivated [3]. However, the high-temperature groove diffusion will change the characteristics of the original sample which is not ideal. Laser doping, on the other hand, can be used to locally overcompensate and interrupt the conductivity of a diffused layer in a relatively defect-free manner without the need for high-temperature processing [17]. In this paper, the authors propose that this laser-doping technique developed by Hallam *et al*, could be applied to isolate high-recombination areas such as wafer edges or regions that cannot be illuminated (i.e., if the wafer is too large for a given illumination source) from the rest of the device. Importantly, this method of edge isolation could be a useful technique when measuring the effective lifetime of samples with a surface diffusion as it allows the isolation to be performed without the need for high-temperature steps that may alter the results. It is also difficult to achieve edge isolation using laser scribing and cleaving on samples that have diffusions on both sides without shunting the junction on the laser-scribed side. This is particularly important for small samples as a shunted junction has been shown to dramatically affect QSS-PL measurements in low injection [4].

II. Experimental

We examine a variety of symmetric test structures to investigate the potential for parasitic effects to reduce the effective lifetime at very low excess carrier densities (i.e., $\Delta n < 1 \times$ $10^{13}/cm^3$). Samples are prepared with various surface passivation layers that have the potential to introduce a variety of conductive paths away from the measured area and toward sites of recombination that are outside of the measured area.

A. Sample Preparation and Characterization

The experimental samples were divided into three sets; each designed to demonstrate a different aspect of the impact of parasitic effects on the effective lifetime curves.

The first set consisted of relatively large area 156 mm × 156 mm pseudosquare wafers that were used to test the impact of enhanced recombination at greater distances from the test area. These substrates were 180-μm thick, 1–3 Ω·cm boron-doped p-type CZ wafers that were etched in an alkaline solution to produce random upright pyramid texture. Half of the samples were diffused in a standard Centrotherm $POCl_3$ tube furnace to produce an n-type surface diffusion on both sides with a sheet resistance of 100 $\Omega/\square$ and junction depth of 0.3 um. The other half of the set of wafers was not diffused. After cleaning the surfaces with HF, all of the samples were deposited with an industry standard 75-nm SiN_x layer on both front and rear surfaces using a Centrotherm direct PECVD tool. Such films have been shown to contain strong positive charge [8], which induces an inversion layer at the p-type silicon surface. To induce additional damage outside of the test area, the samples were scratched on the surface using a diamond pen. These damaged regions introduce very high recombination in the local area of the scratching. The distance between the scratched area and the measurement area was varied to identify trends in the effective lifetime with progressively more damaged regions.

The second sample set was used to investigate the impact of a different type of surface passivation. The samples were prepared on 265-μm thick 1–3 Ω·cm n-type CZ wafers. These substrates were laser cut into approximately 42 mm × 42 mm pieces (to enable laboratory processing), and were then etched in NaOH to remove surface damage. The samples were RCA cleaned, HF dipped, and both surfaces were coated with a 5-nm layer of Al_2O_3 film. This film was deposited using thermal atomic layer deposition in a Cambridge Nanotech Savannah S200 tool at 200 °C. After deposition, the samples were annealed at 400 °C for 5 min to activate the Al_2O_3 passivation. Such films have been shown to contain strong negative charge [18], [19], which induces a potentially conductive inversion layer at the n-type silicon surface.

The third set of samples used wafers with higher bulk lifetime (potentially even more sensitive to parasitic recombination) to demonstrate the laser-doping technique to mitigate the impact of edge effects on effective lifetime curves. The samples were prepared on p-type 1 Ω·cm FZ wafers. The substrates were laser cut into approximately 42 mm × 42 mm pieces to enable laboratory processing and etched in NaOH to remove any surface damage. The samples were then diffused in a $POCl_3$ furnace to create an n-type-doped layer with a sheet resistance of 100 $\Omega/\square$ on each side. After the diffusion and PSG removal in HF, half of the wafers were spin coated with a commercially available boron spin-on-dopant source followed by laser doping around

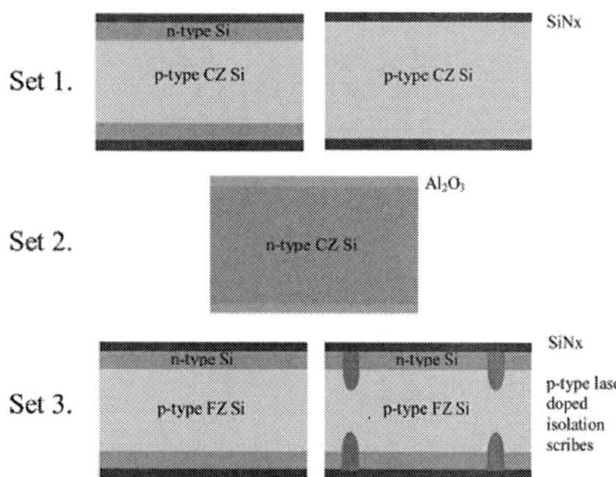

Fig. 1. Schematic cross sections of the samples used in each experimental set.

the edges of the wafer with a high powered 532-nm laser. Further details about the laser-doping process used are described in [17]. The spinning and laser-doping process were repeated on both sides of the wafer. For comparison purposes, the other half of the samples were not processed by the laser and as such did not have any edge isolation. The wafers were then RCA cleaned, HF dipped, and a 75-nm SiN_x layer was deposited on each side using a remote microwave Roth&Rau AK400 PECVD system with a deposition temperature of 400 °C. Samples were then annealed at 400 °C in nitrogen ambient to improve surface passivation. A schematic of the samples from each of the three sets is shown in Fig. 1.

The injection-dependent effective lifetimes of the samples were obtained using a combination of PL and photoconductance (PC) techniques. Details of the theory are covered elsewhere [1], [20], [21]. A Sinton Instruments WCT-120 tool was used, which is modified with the addition of a photodiode inside the PC sensor, which allows simultaneous measurement of PC and PL from the same wafer area. In the case of PL, the measured relative PL signal is converted into an excess carrier density Δn using

$$I_{\mathrm{PL,rel}} = A_i B \Delta n \left(\Delta n + N_{A/D} \right) \qquad (1)$$

where A_i is a scaling factor to account for the fact that the PL measurement is in relative units, B is the coefficient of radiative recombination and $N_{A/D}$ is the bulk dopant density [1]. The injection dependence of the coefficient of radiative recombination B is taken into account using the model presented in [22].

A calibrated 808-nm LED array was used as the light source for the smaller area wafers of Sets 2 and 3, with an illumination area of a circle of diameter 5.5 cm. The QSS-PL signal was calibrated against the QSS-PC signal using the technique that is described in [1]. For the larger area wafers of Set 1, two calibrated light sources were used: a 630-nm LED array and a photographic flash lamp both with an illumination area of a circle of diameter 24 cm. The flash lamp was required to extend the injection level range to obtain PC data that was not affected by DRM or trapping. The QSS-PL signal for this set

was calibrated using the technique that is described in [23], where the scaling factor A_i and the bulk dopant density $N_{A/D}$ were obtained by comparing QSS-PC and QSS-PL signals in high and medium to low injection levels, respectively. A_i was kept constant for both measurements on a sample using the two light sources. As the QSS-PC and QSS-PL signals matched well for both measurements, the change in A_i was deemed to be negligible despite the different spectrums the illumination sources.

All of the samples investigated in this paper were intended to demonstrate the importance of considering parasitic recombination effects that are located outside of the sample area under test. It should be noted, however, that the relative impact of these regions and the ability of the surface layers to transport carriers from the test area into these regions to recombine is specific to the samples under test. This is, particularly, the case for the undiffused samples where the amount of charge contained in the SiN_x and Al_2O_3 films deposited at the University of New South Wales may be different from those used at other institutes. It should also be noted that in the PL images, some of the samples displayed a number of localized regions of increased recombination that were unintentionally introduced during the processing. While the authors assume that the presence of such defects would not change the trends in the results, they cannot be ruled out as a source of recombination that could affect the effective lifetime. It was ensured that the area of the sample within the active measurement area itself was mostly free of these visible defects and laterally homogenous.

B. Impact of Nonilluminated Regions

The impact of a partially illuminated wafer was investigated on the large area samples from Set 1. The QSS-PL measurements were taken with both full area illumination over the entire 156 mm × 156 mm wafer and with only a 4 cm × 4 cm square area in the center of the wafer illuminated (slightly larger than the measurement area, which is a circle of diameter 3.5 cm). The latter was achieved by using a sheet of black paper as an aperture. The resulting effective lifetime versus minority carrier density curves are shown in Fig. 2 with the full area illumination plotted in black (squares) and the reduce area illumination in red (circles). The sample with a more conductive surface layer (diffused n-type emitter) is shown in Fig. 2(a), while the sample with a less conductive surface layer (SiN_x only) is shown in part Fig. 2(b).

The results shown in the figure clearly demonstrate the impact of a dark region close to the area under test and the significance of the surface layer conductivity on its impact. The sample with the highly conductive p-n junction on the front surface showed a significant decrease in effective lifetime at all $\Delta n < 1 \times 10^{13}/cm^3$ measured with the aperture. The difference between effective lifetime for aperture versus full area illumination was greatest at the lowest minority carrier concentration measured. In contrast, the sample with the less conductive surface layer [see Fig. 2(b)] showed very little impact of the dark region, and the differences only occur for much lower illumination intensities with $\Delta n < 1 \times 10^{11}/cm^3$.

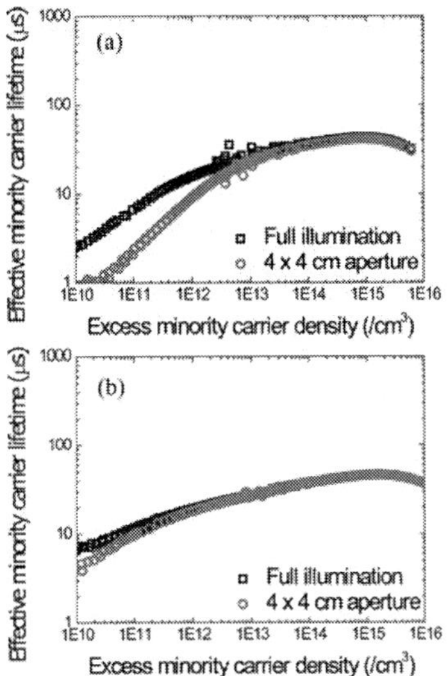

Fig. 2. Effective lifetime versus excess minority carrier density for p-type wafers with (a) 100 $\Omega/\square$ n-type symmetrical diffusion and SiN$_x$ passivation layers (b) no diffusion and SiN$_x$ passivation layers. Measurements were made with QSS-PL using (black) full illumination and (red) partial illumination.

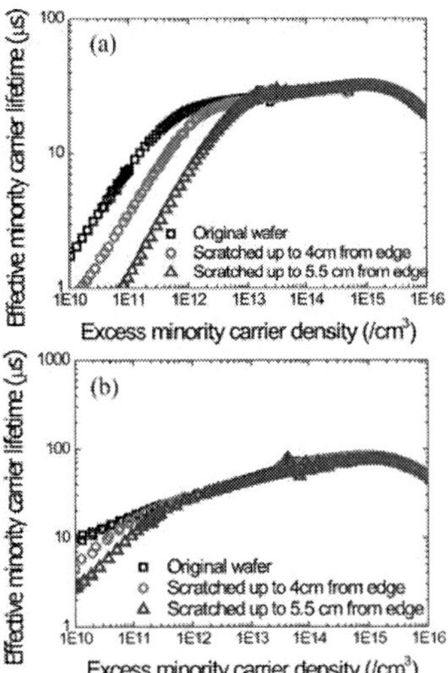

Fig. 3. Effective lifetime versus excess minority carrier density of (a) diffused wafer and (b) undiffused wafer before and after excess damage was applied with a diamond pen.

As there was almost no generation of carriers in the dark, any area of the wafer that was not illuminated acted as a sink for carriers that are in the illuminated area, particularly, at low minority carrier densities. For diffused wafers, this effect was significant due to the low resistance path to the dark regions. These results demonstrate the importance of having light sources that are capable of illuminating the entire area of a wafer, particularly, when measuring low-level injection effects. It is important to be mindful of this effect when taking measurements of samples, both lifetime measurements and I–V testing, when using an aperture or if the entire sample is not uniformly illuminated as this can significantly impact the measurement.

It can also be seen in Fig. 2(b) that the undiffused wafer was only affected at injection levels below 1×10^{11}/cm^3 when using an aperture compared with without. The authors interpret this to be due to the high resistivity of the inversion layer. This seems to suggest that the strong injection dependence of the lifetime on those samples was due to some other recombination mechanism other than the presence of dark regions. As the samples are boron doped, this is likely to be the result of B–O complexes in the bulk as well as a surface effect as described in the literature [8], [12]–[16].

C. Impact of Surface Damage

The ability of localized regions of enhanced recombination, which are located outside of the area under test, to reduce the effective lifetime was demonstrated on the samples from both Sct 1 and Sct 2. In this case, the localized recombination was introduced in the form of surface damage induced by scratching with a diamond tipped pen.

The QSS-PL measurements were taken with full area illumination over the entire 156-mm wafers. Damage was first intro-duced by scratching the edge region of the wafer so that only an 8 cm $\times$ 8 cm area remained relatively damage free in the center. The second stage involved increasing the area of damage so that only a 5 cm $\times$ 5 cm undamaged area remained in the center.

The resulting effective lifetime versus minority carrier density curves are shown in Fig. 3 with the lifetime curve of the original wafer plotted in black (squares), after the first stage of damage in red (circles) and after the second stage of damage in blue (triangles). The sample with a more conductive surface layer (diffused n-type emitter) is shown in Fig. 3(a), while the sample with a less conductive surface layer (SiN$_x$ only) is shown in Fig. 3(b). Fig. 4 shows the PL images of the wafers at 0.1-sun and 1-sun illumination after the second application of damage.

As seen in Fig. 3, τ_{eff} of the diffused wafer deteriorated rapidly at $\Delta n < 1 \times 10^{13}$/cm^3 as the damage approached the measurement area. In contrast, the undiffused wafer τ_{eff} was much less affected by damage outside the measurement area. For that sample, the impact of the enhanced recombination was only observed below carrier densities of 1×10^{12}/cm^3. Again the authors interpret this to be due to the higher resistivity of the induced inversion layer compared with that of the phosphorus-diffused layer resulting in less lateral transport of carriers to the recombination sites. In both cases, the effective lifetime curve only deviated from the reference case at injection levels below those normally measured by PC. The injection dependence was still strong for this wafer even without the introduced damage. It was also evident from the PL images that on the diffused wafers, the damaged regions reduced the apparent τ_{eff} of surrounding high lifetime areas under low injection to a greater extent than the undiffused wafers due to the high lateral conductivity of the diffused layer, consistent with [3]–[5]. This demonstrates that while damaged edge regions are important to consider in samples with diffused p-n junctions, they are less likely to impact the results of p-type wafers passivated by only a SiN$_x$ layer. The

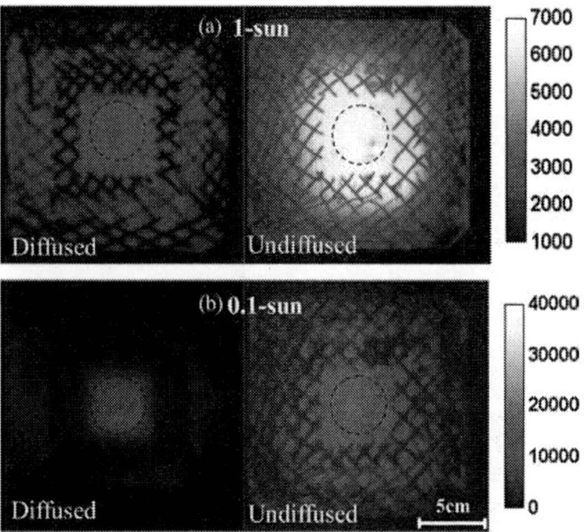

Fig. 4. PL images of (left) diffused and (right) undiffused wafers from Set 1 with excess damage applied with a diamond pen taken at (a) 1-sun and (b) 0.1-sun illumination intensity. The scales shown are in units of counts per exposure time. The exposure time of the 1-sun and 0.1-sun images were 0.1 and 10 s, respectively. The dashed black circles represent the active measurement area used in the QSS-PL test.

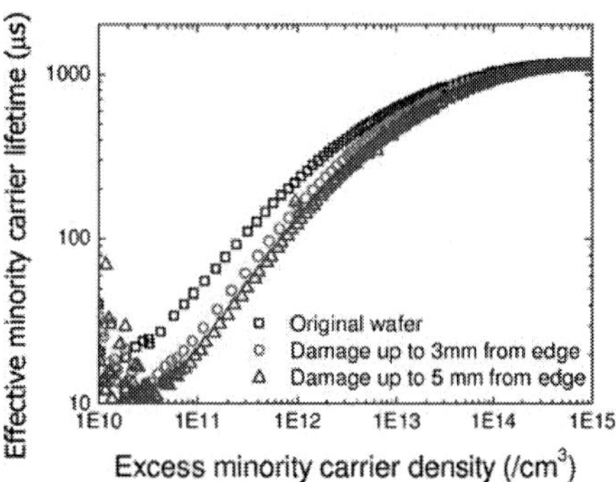

Fig. 5. Effective lifetime versus excess minority carrier density of an n-type wafer passivated with Al_2O_3 with excess damage introduced at increasing distances to the measurement area.

reduction in effective lifetime for low values of excess minority carrier densities was mainly due to another recombination effect either in the bulk, at the surface, or both.

To test the injection-dependent lifetime of n-type wafers passivated by Al_2O_3, measurements were taken in a similar manner on the wafers from Set 2. Effective lifetime curves and PL images are shown in Figs. 5 and 6, respectively. A slight degradation in lifetime at lower injection levels is observed in the case of Al_2O_3 passivation of n-type silicon, when the artificial edge is brought closer to the measurement area indicating that transport to the edge regions plays an important role in the injection-dependent lifetime of the sample, consistent with [13].

The results that are presented in this section demonstrated that regions of high recombination outside of the test area were significant for the cases of the SiN_x coated samples with n-type diffusion on a p-type wafer. For the SiN_x coated, undiffused p-type samples investigated here the presence of large quanti-

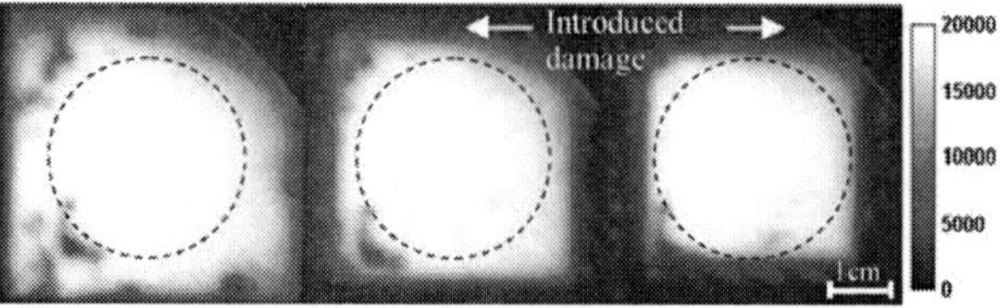

Fig. 6. PL images taken at 1-sun illumination level of an n-type wafer passivated with Al_2O_3 (Set 2) with excess damage introduced at increasing distances to the measurement area (left to right). The scale shown is in units of counts per 0.1 s (exposure time). The black dashed circles indicate the perimeter of the active measurement area.

ties of high surface damage close to the measurement area was found to have smaller impact on the effective lifetime. It is speculated that this was due to the higher lateral resistance of the inversion layer of the SiN_x film as compared with the other surface treatments. It was observed that lateral transport of carriers in the samples with an Al_2O_3 layer on an n-type wafer plays a role in the observed injection-dependent lifetime of such samples. Unfortunately, wafers that are larger than 42 mm × 42 mm were unable to be processed that would enable the authors to determine if edge effects are the main reason for the drop in lifetime at low injection as shown by Veith *et al.* [13] or, like in the p-type Si/SiN_x case earlier, a contributing but not underlying cause.

D. Method of Edge Isolation Using Laser Doping

It has been shown earlier and in the literature [3]–[5] that a diffused layer can provide a low resistance path for carriers to the edge region at low excess minority carrier densities. The wafers from Set 3 were used to determine if laser doping can interrupt this conductive path to regions of high recombination and do so without introducing more damage than already exists at the edge region. QSS-PL measurements were taken before and after extra damage was introduced near the edge of the wafer with a diamond pen. The extra damage was introduced to ensure the edge region was an area of high recombination, as prior to this damage, the edge would have been diffused and passivated with SiN_x, and thus, potentially be a well-passivated edge. For wafers that had the edge isolation scribe, this damage was located between the scribe and the edge of the wafer. The $\tau_{\rm eff}$ curves are shown in Fig. 7 and the PL images taken at 1 and 0.1 sun injection level are shown in Fig. 8.

It was observed that the laser scribe appeared to offer improvement with the $\tau_{\rm eff}$ being significantly higher at injection levels less than 1×10^{13}/cm³ for the edge-isolated case compared with the case with no edge isolation. After excess damage was introduced near the edge region, the $\tau_{\rm eff}$ of wafers with edge isolation was unaffected in contrast with those without edge isolation which deteriorated even further. This confirms that the laser-doped isolation scribe effectively interrupts the conductive path for carriers to the damaged regions and can therefore be used as an edge-isolation technique. This technique could be useful in allowing smaller samples to be used or as a technique to isolate dark regions of a sample if the light source used has a smaller illumination area than the sample.

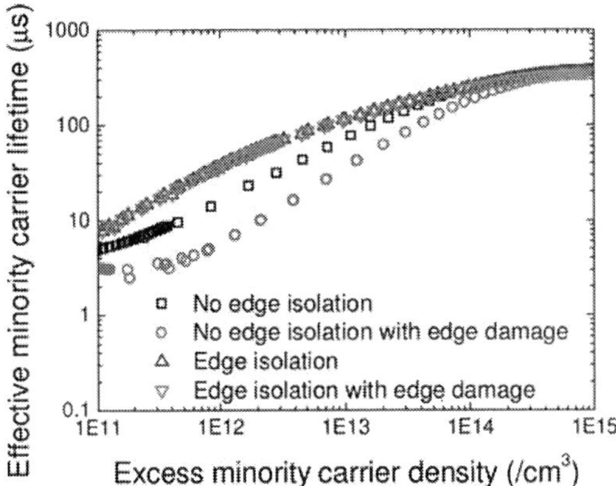

Fig. 7. Effective lifetime versus excess minority carrier density of a wafer with and without laser-doped edge isolation, before and after excess damage is introduced at the edge.

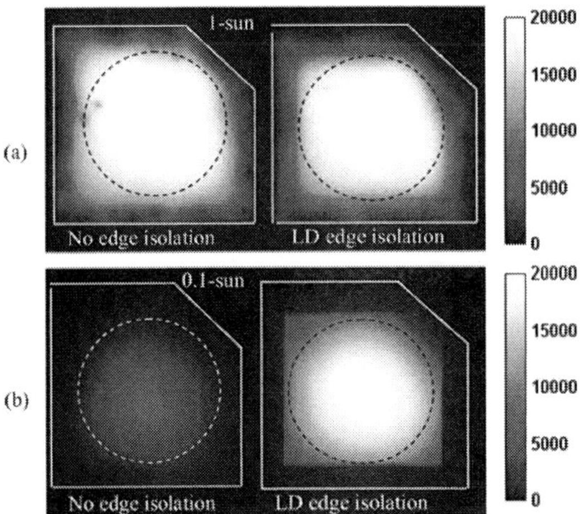

Fig. 8. PL images of wafers from Set 3 without (left) and with (right) laser-doped edge isolation after excess damage was applied at the edge regions with a diamond pen (a) at 1-sun injection level and (b) at 0.1 sun injection level. The scales shown are in units of counts per exposure time. The exposure time of the 1-sun and 0.1-sun images were 1 and 30 s, respectively. The dashed circles represent the active measurement area. The dotted lines show the perimeter of the wafer for clarity.

III. CONCLUSION

In this paper, the ability of various forms of enhanced recombination, which are located outside of the test area, to impact the measurement of effective lifetime was demonstrated. Specifically, the effect of fully versus partially illuminating a wafer during lifetime measurements was shown with the results demonstrating the significance for measurements taken using a light source that has an illumination area less than the size of the wafer under investigation, or for measurements taken using an aperture. It was shown that it is critical to fully illuminate wafers when studying low-illumination lifetime behavior, particularly, with samples containing a highly conductive path that can transport carriers to the edge such as an emitter diffusion.

The ability of edges and local points of high recombination to affect lifetime measurements on SiN_x passivated p-type samples with phosphorus diffusions, and Al_2O_3 passivated n-type samples, was demonstrated and found to be consistent with the results found in the literature. On undiffused p-type wafers, areas of high recombination including edges did not appear to be the underlying cause of the injection-dependent lifetime. It is likely that the cause of the injection dependence exists within the measurement area itself, perhaps in the form of high recombination areas such as pinholes, or a surface damage region as described in the literature. It should be noted that the specific results and conclusions presented in the paper are expected to be highly dependent on the samples used. It is likely that a sample with a SiN_x layer deposited elsewhere may show slightly different behavior. The results do, however, demonstrate that the presence of sources of recombination outside of the area under test can be significant and should be accounted for in any work that seeks to characterize samples at very low values of excess carrier densities.

Finally, a new method of edge isolation using laser doping was shown to be an effective means to interrupting the conductive path from the area under test into the edge or damaged regions that otherwise would result in an enhanced degradation at low illumination intensities. Importantly, it is an edge-isolation process that is able to be performed without the use of high-temperature processes meaning it does not significantly alter the properties of the wafer being measured and could, therefore, be useful to analyze the true properties of diffused wafers. Optimization of the laser-doped edge-isolation process will be performed in future work.

REFERENCES

[1] T. Trupke and R. A. Bardos, "Photoluminescence: A surprisingly sensitive lifetime technique," in *Proc. IEEE 31st Photovolt. Spec. Conf.*, Orlando, FL, USA, 2005, pp. 903–906.

[2] J. A. Giesecke, T. Niewelt, M. Rüdiger, M. Rauer, M. C. Schubert, and W. Warta, "Broad range injection-dependent minority carrier lifetime from photoluminescence," *Sol. Energy Mater. Sol. Cells*, vol. 102, pp. 220–224, 2012.

[3] M. Abbott, J. Cotter, T. Trupke, and R. Bardos, "Investigation of edge recombination effects in silicon solar cell structures using photoluminescence," *Appl. Phys. Lett.*, vol. 88, 114105, 2006.

[4] F. W. Chen, J. E. Cotter, M. D. Abbott, A. Li, and K. C. Fisher, "The influence of parasitic effects on injection-level-dependent lifetime data," *IEEE Trans. Electron. Devices*, vol. 54, no. 11, pp. 2960–2968, Nov. 2007.

[5] M. Kessler, T. Ohrdes, P. P. Altermatt, and R. Brendel, "The effect of sample edge recombination on the averaged injection dependent carrier lifetime in silicon," *J. Appl. Phys*, vol. 111, 054508, 2012.

[6] J. R. Elmiger, R. Schieck, and M. Kunst, "Recombination at the silicon-nitride silicon interface," *J. Vacuum Sci. Technol. A.*, vol. 15, pp. 2418–2425, 1997.

[7] J. Schmidt and A. G. Aberle, "Carrier recombination at silicon-silicon nitride interfaces fabricated by plasma-enhanced chemical vapour deposition," *J. Appl. Phys.*, vol. 85, pp. 3626–3633, 1999.

[8] S. Dauwe, J. Schmidt, A. Metz, and R. Hezel, "Fixed charge density in silicon nitride films on crystalline silicon surfaces under illumination," in *Proc. IEEE 29th Photovolt. Spec. Conf.*, New Orleans, LA, USA, 2002, pp. 162–165.

[9] K. Rühle, M. Rauer, M. Rüdiger, J. Giesecke, T. Niewelt, C. Schmiga, S. W. Glunz, and M. Kasemann, "Passivation layers for indoor solar cells at low irradiation intensities," *Energy Procedia*, vol. 27, pp. 404–411.

[10] B. Hoex, S. B. S. Heil, E. Langereis, M. C. M. van de Sanden, and W. M. M. Kessels, "Ultralow surface recombination of c-Si substrates

passivated by plasma-assisted atomic layer deposited Al_2O_3," *Appl. Phys. Lett.*, vol. 89, 042112, 2006.

[11] B. Veith, T. Ohrdes, F. Werner, R. Brendel, P. P. Altermatt, N.-P. Harder, and J. Schmidt, "Injection dependence of the effective lifetime of n-type Si passivated by Al2O3: An edge effect?," presented at the 3rd Int. Conf. Crystalline Silicon Photovoltaic, Hamelin, Germany, 2013.

[12] S. W. Glunz, D. Biro, S. Rein, and W. Warta, "Field effect passivation of the SiO2Si interface," *J. Appl. Phys.*, vol. 86, pp. 683–691, 1999.

[13] J. Schmidt, J. D. Moschner, J. Henze, S. Dauwe, and R. Hezel, "Recent progress in the surface passivation of silicon solar cells," in *Proc. 19th Eur. Photovolt. Sol. Energy Conf.*, Paris, France, 2004, pp. 391–396.

[14] I. Martin, B. Hoex, M. C. M. Van de Sanden, R. Alcubilla, and W. M. M. Kessels, "The origin of emitter-like recombination for inverted c-Si surfaces," in *Proc. 23rd Eur. Photovolt. Sol. Energy Conf.*, Valencia, Spain, 2008, pp. 1388–1392.

[15] S. Steingrube, P. P. Altermatt, D. S. Steingrube, J. Schmidt, and R. Brendel; "Interpretation of recombination at c-Si/SiN$_x$ interfaces by surface damage," *J. Appl. Phys.*, vol. 108, 014506, 2010.

[16] F. Ma, G. Samudra, M. Peters, A. Aberle, F. Werner, J. Schmidt, and B. Hoex, "Advanced modeling of the effective minority carrier lifetime of passivated crystalline silicon wafers," *J. Appl. Phys.*, vol. 112, 054508, 2012.

[17] B. Hallam, C. Chan, A. Sugianto, and S. Wenham, "Deep junction laser doping for contacting buried layers in silicon solar cells," *Sol. Energy Mater. Sol. Cells*, vol. 113, pp. 124–134, 2013.

[18] R. Hezel and K. Jaeger, "Low temperature surface passivation of silicon for solar cells," *J. Electrochem. Soc.*, vol. 136, no. 2, pp. 518–523, 1989.

[19] G. Agostinelli, P. Vitanov, Z. Alexieva, A. Harizanova, H. F. W. Dekkers, S. De Wolf, and G. Beaucarne, "Surface passivation of silicon by means of negative charge dielectrics," in *Proc. 19th Eur. Photovolt. Sol. Energy Conf.*, Paris, France, 2004, pp. 132–134.

[20] H. Nagel, C. Berge, and A. Aberle, "Generalised analysis of quasi-steady-state and quasi-transient measurements of carrier lifetimes in semiconductors," *J. Appl. Phys.*, vol. 86, pp. 6218–6221, 1999.

[21] T. Trupke, R. Bardos, and M. Abbott, "Self-consistent calibration of photoluminescence and photoconductance lifetime measurements," *Appl. Phys. Lett.*, vol. 87, no. 18, 184102, 2005.

[22] P. P. Altermatt, F. Geelhaar, T. Trupke, X. Dai, A. Neisser, and E. Daub, "Injection dependence of spontaneous radiative recombination in crystalline silicon: Experimental verification and theoretical analysis," *Appl. Phys. Lett.*, vol. 88, 261901, 2006.

[23] Z. Hameiri, T. Trupke, N. Gao, R. Sinton, and J. Weber, "Effective bulk doping concentration of diffused and undiffused silicon wafers obtained from combined photoconductance and photoluminescence measurements," *Progr. Photovolt., Res. Appl.*, vol. 21, no. 5, pp. 942–949, 2013.

Catherine E. Chan received the B.E. (Hons. Class 1) degree in photovoltaic engineering and the B.Sc. degree in physics from the University of New South Wales (UNSW), Sydney, Australia, in 2009, where she is a currently working toward the Ph.D. degree in photovoltaic engineering with an interest in laser doping and passivation for silicon solar cells.

She is working with the Technology Transfer Team, UNSW, which focuses on commercializing UNSW's laser-doped selective emitter technology.

Malcolm D. Abbott received the B.E. degree in electrical engineering and the Ph.D. degree in photovoltaics from the University of New South Wales, Sydney, Australia, in 2001 and 2006, respectively.

He is currently a Senior Research Fellow with the University of New South Wales, working on crystalline silicon solar cell research and development. He is also currently a Senior Research Consultant with PV Lighthouse, where he provides consulting service to the photovoltaic industry, as well as developing online software tools. Prior to this, he was a Senior Device Engineer with Innovalight (later DuPont-Innovalight), where he worked on the development of new solar cell technologies using silicon nanoparticle inks. His current research interests include developing processing technology, characterization techniques, and software models for high-efficiency silicon solar cells.

Mattias K. Juhl received the B.Sc. degree in physics and the B.E. (First-Class Hons.) degree in photovoltaic and solar energy engineering from the University of New South Wales, Sydney, Australia, in 2010, where he is currently working toward the Ph.D. degree in photovoltaic engineering, focusing on the injection dependent photoluminescence analyses of silicon wafers and devices.

Brett J. Hallam received the B.E./B.Sc. degrees in photovoltaics and solar energy/physics and physical oceanography from the University of New South Wales, Sydney, Australia, in 2009, where he is currently working toward the Ph.D. degree in photovoltaic engineering, developing laser doping and hydrogenation processes for high-efficiency silicon solar cells.

He is currently working with the Technology Transfer Team, University of New South Wales, helping to commercialize the laser-doped selective emitter technology. He is also currently undertaking an internship with the Interuniversity Microelectronics Centre (IMEC), Heverlee, Belgium, as part of his Ph.D studies. His research interests include laser, metallization, and passivation processes for high-efficiency silicon solar cells.

Bo Xiao received the B.E. degree in photovoltaic engineering from the University of New South Wales, Sydney, Australia, and the B.E degree in electronic information technology and science from Nankai University, Tianjin, China, in 2008. He is currently working toward the Ph.D. degree in photovoltaic engineering with the University of New South Wales, developing laser doping and advanced passivation processes for high-efficiency silicon solar cells.

His research interests include laser processing and dielectric passivation, particularly aluminum oxide passivation, for high-efficiency silicon solar cells.

Stuart R. Wenham received the Ph.D. degree in electrical engineering and computer science from the University of New South Wales (UNSW), Sydney, Australia, in 1986.

He is currently a Scientia Professor with the University of New South Wales, where he is the Director of the Photovoltaics Centre of Excellence. He is also CTO of Suntech-Power: one of the world's largest solar cell manufacturers. He has been involved in photovoltaics since 1980, when he and B. Godfrey established Australia's first solar cell production line. He has been involved in the successful development and commercialization of several photovoltaic technologies, including the Semiconductor Finger solar cell, BP's Saturn technology, CSG thin silicon on glass modules, and Suntech's Pluto technology. He also headed the team that developed and implemented the world's first Photovoltaic Engineering degree in 2000.

Prof. Wenham has received numerous national and international awards for his work.

Degradation kinetics of amorphous silicon solar cells processed at high pressure and its relation to the nanostructure

Marinus Fischer, Robin J.V. Quax, Miro Zeman, and Arno H.M. Smets

Delft University of Technology, Delft, PO Box 5031, 2600 GA, The Netherlands

Abstract — In this study it is revealed that the light induced defects (LIDs) responsible for the fast degradation of hydrogenated amorphous silicon (a-Si:H) solar cells under light soaking are located at nanosized voids. This important breakthrough in identifying the local environment of LIDs has been achieved by detailed study of the relation between the nanostructure of a-Si:H and metastability of corresponding solar cell devices under light soaking. We propose that a useful tool to define the nanostructure of a-Si:H is to determine the size distribution of the volume deficiencies, which range from small hydrogenated vacancies up to nanosized voids. The processing window used to vary and control the nanostructure in dense a-Si:H is based on a hydrogen rich plasma at unconventional high processing pressures (~10 mbar). The dense absorber layers with different distributions of volume deficiencies are subsequently incorporated in solar cell devices. For the first time a clear relation between nanostructures of the a-Si:H absorber layer and the fast kinetics of the metastable LIDs of the solar cell during light soaking and thermal annealing is observed. The 'fast' degradation (first 10 hours of light soaking) strongly correlates to the density of largest volume deficiencies in the a-Si:H matrix. The "slow" regime (10 tot 1000 hours of light soaking) appears to be independent on the nanostructure of the absorber layer. In addition, the fast metastable defect states are the first ones to be annealed out at relative low annealing temperatures (120-130 C). Although solar cells processed at higher pressure have the same long term degradation kinetics, their FF recovers much faster by thermal annealing when compared to the cells processed at standard low pressure and low hydrogen dilution conditions.

Index Terms — amorphous silicon materials, light induced degradation, metastability, photovoltaic cells, nanostructure, staebler-wronski.

I. Introduction

The micromorph solar cell is a tandem cell based on an amorphous silicon (a-Si:H) p-i-n junction and a nanocrystalline (nc-Si:H) p-i-n junction. An important part of the power (~65%) delivered by a micromorph cell is originating from the a-Si:H top cell. A way to increase the stabilized efficiency is the reduction of the light induced degradation of the a-Si:H based top cell. The degradation of the cell performance originates from a reduction of the photo- and dark conductivity of the a-Si:H absorber layer, due to the so-called Staebler-Wronski effect [SWE]. It is believed that recombination of the by light absorption excited charge carriers can create metastable defects in the bulk. These light induced defects (LIDs) can be annealed out again at moderate temperatures. [1] In spite of extensive studies, the origin and kinetics of the SWE are poorly understood. The main reasons for this poor understanding are *i*) the lack of tools to define

the nanostructure of the various types of a-Si:H networks due to the complex nature of the materials, *ii*) the nature of the dominant native and meta-stable defects and their local environments are not yet identified, *iii*) the lab-to-lab variations in observed meta-stability and its kinetics in solar cells, and *iv*) the overall lack of empirical correlations between the nanostructure, defect entities and performance in solar cells. In this study we report on an important breakthrough in tackling above short-comings, by demonstrating a clear relation between the nanostructure of a-Si:H and the metastability of corresponding solar cell devices.

We propose that a useful tool to define the nanostructure of a-Si:H is to use the size distribution of the volume deficiencies, which ranges from small vacancies up to nanosized voids. From various studies including infrared absorption, Raman spectroscopy and positron annihilation [2] it is known that volume deficiencies ranging from divacancies up to nanosized voids are present in the a-Si:H matrix and determine its nanostructure. The conventional route to increase the stability of a-Si:H is using hydrogen dilution of the silane process gas. The hydrogen dilution ratio R is defined as the ratio between hydrogen flow rate and the silane flow rate, and typically ranges from 0 up to 20 for low pressure conditions (~0.7 mbar). Here we investigate the influence of the hydrogen on the nanostructure by using even higher dilution ratios of R = 50, while maintaining amorphous growth. This is achieved by using elevated processing pressures, which allows to precisely control the dominant vacancy type present in the a-Si:H matrix. Here we present a structural study on the relation between the degradation kinetics of the external parameters of a-Si:H p-i-n solar cells and the size distribution of volume deficiencies in the absorber layer. We demonstrate that the 'fast' LIDs generated in the fist 10 hours of light soaking are related to the largest volume deficiencies, i.e. the nanosized voids.

II. Defining the Nanostructure

In our recent work we have made the case that volume deficiencies in a-Si:H matrix play an important role in determining the various material properties, like the band gap [3] and volume deficiencies are likely to accommodate various defects [4]. Consequently, here the experiment is proposed in which intentionally a variety of size distributions for volume deficiencies in a-Si:H is engineered. Subsequently, the relation between these various nanostructures and the degradation kinetics can be studied. This approach first requires the development of a processing route of dense a-Si:H in which the size distribution of vacancies can be varied. Before we discuss this processing approach the method to determine the distribution of volume deficiencies in the a-Si:H is explained in more detail.

The distribution of volume deficiencies is determined using the analysis of the hydride stretching modes in measured infrared spectra. From FTIR analysis it is known that the silicon hydride stretching modes of amorphous silicon have at least three distinct vibration modes, each represented by a Gaussian distribution at different frequency. [5] The distinct vibration frequencies of the modes are dominated by monohydrides and known as the Low Stretching Mode (LSM ~1985 cm-1), Medium Stretching Mode (MSM ~2034 cm-1) [6] and the High Stretching Mode (HSM: ~2070 – 2099 cm-1) [7]. The shift in frequency for these monohydride modes in reference to the unscreened monohydride (~2100 cm^{-1}) is attributed to both the local density of silicon hydrides and the dielectric screening of the dipole by the local environment [7]. The local environment of the silicon hydride is determined by the size of the volume deficiency as can be defined by the nano-structural parameter K and the structure V_xH_y. V stands here for the missing silicon atom (Vacancy) and H for the hydrogen atoms which can be incorporated in the vacancy. The parameter K is defined as the number of hydrogen atoms bound in the volume deficiency per missing silicon atom of the volume deficiency. Thus in very large volume deficiencies like nanosized voids ($K{\leq}1$), there is moderate shift in frequency, the HSM becomes (~2070-2100) cm-1. The MSM

originates from Si-H in the middle of large vacancies (-VH$_2$-, K=2). The LSM is linked to Si-H situated in hydrogenated di-vacancies (-VH$_3$, K=3). The mono-vacancy (K=4) is presumed to be unstable in a-Si:H at room temperature and thus its mode at ~1950 cm-1 is not observed in a-Si:H. This approach can be used to study the size distribution of volume deficiencies in the material. If a divacancy VH3-VH3 is incorporated in the lattice, the vibrating hydrides only contributes to the LSM in the FTIR spectrum. In case of a trivacancy VH3-VH2-VH3, 6 silicon hydrides contribute to the LSM and 2 silicon hydrides to the MSM. Subsequently, LSM corresponds to outer sides of vacancies (-VH$_3$), the MSM is a signature of the presence of multivacancies V_xH_y (x>2), whereas the HSM reflects large hydrogenated surfaces in nanosized voids. The phase diagram defined by the three axis LSM. MSM and HSM is a helpful tool to show the various distributions of volume deficiencies in the material as illustrated in Figure 1.

III. Experiment

In this study the processing approach to vary the size distribution of volume deficiencies in a-Si:H has been achieved by using the significant higher processing pressures. Typical processing conditions used are a high pressures of ~10 mbar and highly hydrogen diluted (R=50) plasma conditions. These conditions are close to the so-called high-pressure-depletion regime for nc-Si:H,[7] however the RF power is significantly reduced from ~ 1 W/cm^2 to ~ 0,1 W/cm^2 to guarantee a fully amorphous phase. [8] In Figure 2 the deposition regimes for a-Si:H are indicated for various

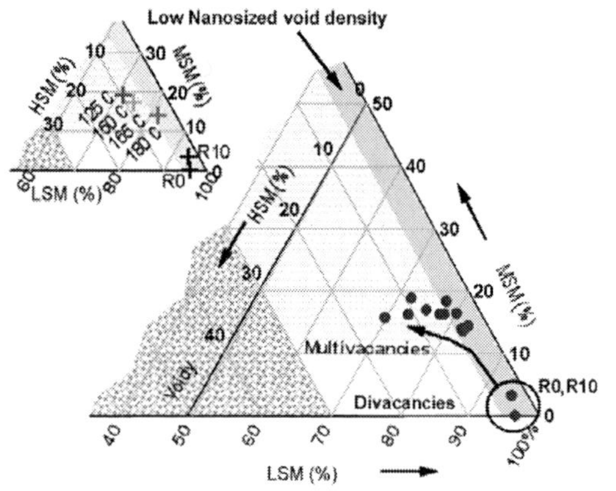

Fig. 1. The nanostructure of the processed a-Si:H conditions given as ratio between the LSM, MSM and HSM contribution in the total FTIR absorption spectrum of the silicon hydride stretching modes.Areas are indicated for device grade a-Si:H with low nanosized void density (low HSM) and increased vacancy size (multi-vacancies).

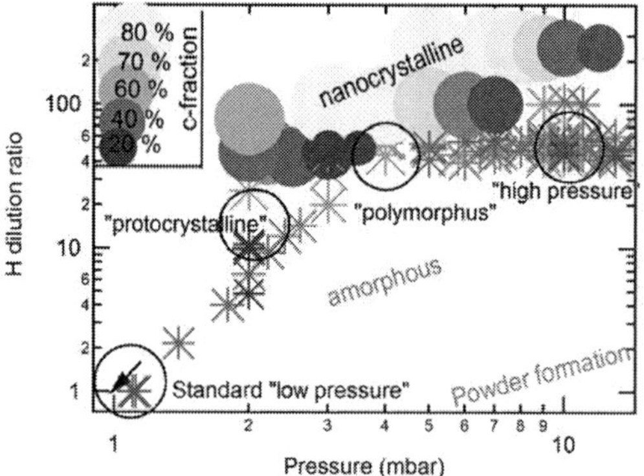

Fig. 2. Processing regimes for optimized a-Si:H in terms of stability against light induced degradation. Depending on the pressure the phase transition to nanocrystalline silicon shifts to larger hydrogen dilution ratio. Processing at the high pressure leads to dense a-Si:H where nanostructure can be varied by Temperature and RF power.

                    312

pressures and hydrogen dilution ratios. In general it is believed to be advantageous to process a-Si:H in solar cells near the transition to nc-Si in terms of stabilized efficiency. Figure 1 demonstrates that increasing the processing pressure, results in a shift of the phase transition to nc-Si to higher hydrogen dilutions. We roughly indicate in Figure 2 four growth regimes, referred to as (or also known as) 'low pressure', 'protocrystalline-',[9] 'polymorphous-'[10] and in our case 'high-pressure' a-Si:H [11]. Deposition of a-Si:H in the high pressure conditions has several advantages. Processing at high pressure has made increasing the average size of the volume deficiencies in the a-Si:H possible, without increasing deposition rate or decreasing hydrogen dilution of the processing gas. The high processing pressure results in a reduced energy of the ions bombarding the growth surface. [12,13] The ion energy at the conventional low pressure conditions contributes to the densification of a-Si:H [14,15]. We believe that under the high pressure plasma conditions, the chemical annealing of the hydrogen during deposition partly takes over the role of the ion bombardment in the densification of the a-Si:H during growth [16]. Using the high hydrogen dilutions is possibly essential in achieving a high passivation degree of hydrogen of the silicon bonds in the volume deficiencies. [17]

The deposition rate is maintained for the strong hydrogen diluted conditions when compared to deposition from pure silane (~15 nm/min) at low pressures. For the "protocrystalline" deposition regime the deposition rate typically quenches to below 5 nm/min. [18] At the high pressure regime even higher growth rates (~30 nm/min) can be achieved while preserving dense a-Si:H without the unwelcome powder formation in the plasma. Powder formation is initiated by the polymerization of radicals and is in general enhanced at high process pressure. [19] However, in the high pressure regime explored powder formation was only observed for low hydrogen dilution. For the a-Si:H films deposited for this study, the processing conditions are only slightly adjusted to vary the average size distribution of the volume deficiencies in the amorphous matrix. For this processing regime a series of different absorber layers with

thickness of 300 nm are deposited and their nanostructure is determined using FTIR. Two reference conditions using pure silane (R=0) and moderate hydrogen dilution of R=10 are deposited at the standard processing regime at ~1 mbar. The 300 nm thick absorber layers are incorporated in p-i-n devices based upon the Asahi-U substrate. The a-Si:H absorber layer is sandwiched between an a-SiC:H p-layer and an a-Si:H n-layer with a silver back contact on top.

The nanostructure of the deposited absorber layers are depicted in the phase diagram (Figure 1), ,where the three axis are obtained by calculating the ratio of the contribution of each hydride stretching modes (LSM, MSM, HSM) to the total absorption of the three stretching modes. The reference a-Si:H absorber layers with $R=0$ and $R=10$ the FTIR absorption signature is dominated by the LSM, as becomes clear in the figure since both films reside close to the MSM = 0 line. This indicates that the hydrogen is predominantly present in the smallest stable volume deficiencies, the divacancies. In addition, the a-Si:H processed at $R=10$ conditions show a slightly reduced HSM contribution. For the films at high pressure the average vacancy size shifts from di- to multivacancy, reflected in the increased contribution of the MSM. For these conditions the contribution of the HSM (nanosized voids in the a-Si:H matrix) is increased by decreasing the processing temperature. Interestingly the absorber layers which have on average multivacancies as the dominant vacancy type, have an increased bandgap resulting in higher Voc when incorporated in a device [11]. It has to be noted that this is essentially different from the conventional observed increased bandgap due to increasing density of the larger nanosized voids.

IV. Results

The metastability of a-Si:H p-i-n junctions with corresponding absorber layers from Fig. 1 has been studied in detail. In figure 3 the FF degradation and annealing kinetics are shown for the two reference cells with a-Si:H processed at low pressures and $R=0$ and $R=10$ and four cells process at high pressure conditions but with varying deposition

TABLE I

	Voc (V)	Voc deg	FF (%)	FF deg	Isc (A/m^2)	Isc deg	Eff (%)	Eff deg
R0 undiluted ref.	0,90	0,85	69,9	53,3	155	144	9,8	6,5
R10 diluted low P	0,91	0,86	71,8	60,0	145	132	9,5	6,8
R50, high P, 180C	0,94	0,89	75,7	59,6	140	133	10,0	7,0
R50, high P, 165C	0,95	0,90	75,0	59,5	138	127	9,8	6,8
R50, high P, 150C	0,95	0,89	75,0	53,8	136	124	9,7	6,4
R50, high P, 125C	0,97	0,90	73,8	50,8	133	118	9,5	5,4

Table 1: Initial and stabilized external parameters of the 2 reference solar cells with conditions (R0, R10) processed at standard pressure, and of 4 solar cells processed at elevated pressure and increased hydrogen dilution (R50). The cells processed at low temperature show higher FF degradation probably related to increased nano-sized void density.

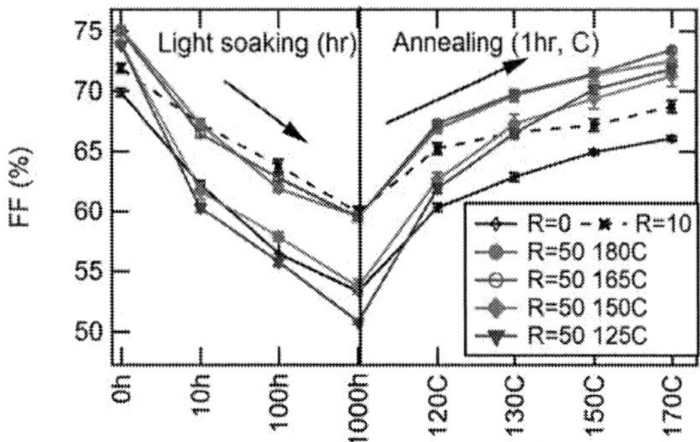

Fig. 3. Kinetics of the FF during light soaking under AM1.5 at 25 C, for 10, 100 and 1000 hours exposure. Followed by the kinetics due to stepwise thermal annealing, each step was for 1 hour. Interestingly the cells processed at high pressure show similar long term degradation kinetics for the 180 C as the R10 low pressure a-Si:H. However when annealed these cells recover much faster.

temperatures. The external parameters of the solar cells for initial and 1000 hours light soaked states are shown in Table 1. The deterioration of the FF in general is an indication for the decreasing photo-conductivity of the absorber layer due to the Staebler-Wronski effect. The recombination of some of light induced charge carriers create metastable LIDs in the a-Si:H bulk. In figure 3 we can identify two degradation regimes. In the first 10 hours of light soaking a large part of the FF degradation occurs. We refer to the defect generated in this regime as the 'fast' LIDs. The defects generated between 10 hours and 1000 hours of light soaking are subsequently referred to as the 'slow' LIDs. [20]For the solar cells in figure 3 it becomes clear that a slight variation in the nanostructure

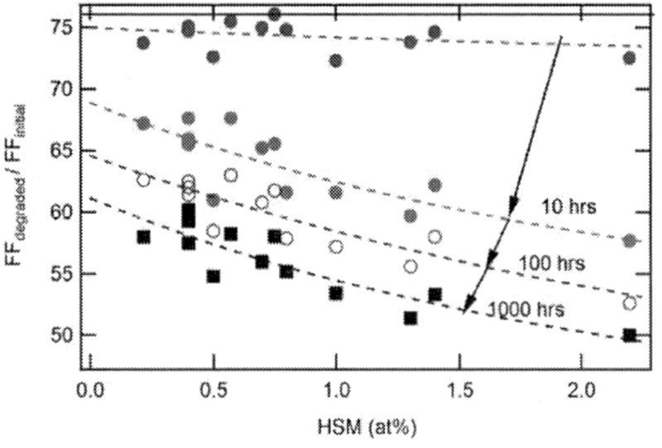

Fig. 4. Kinetics of the FF during light soaking under AM1.5 at 25 C, for 10, 100 and 1000 hours exposure for all solar cells deposited at the high pressure. The HSM contribution in at. % H as determined from FTIR absorption for the silicon hydride stretching modes of the absorber layer is plotted at the x-axis. In the first 10 hours of light soaking the different degree of degradation already is apparent.

of the absorber layer has a major influence on the stability of the material. The degradation kinetics seems similar for the solar cells with a-Si:H processed at high pressure when compared to the reference solar cells with a-Si:H processed at low pressure conditions. The 'high pressure' cells appear to have a larger drop in the FF during the first 10 hours of light soaking ('fast' regime) in reference to the 'low pressure' cells.

The recovery of the FF by thermal annealing for the conditions deposited under high dilution, high pressure is much faster. An additional interesting result of our studies is that for 'high pressure' a-Si:H the role of the nanostructure in the metastability kinetics becomes more obvious. For these p-i-n junctions the FF for solar cells with absorber layers deposited at lower temperature clearly decreases stronger. From the nanostructural characterization it is known that those films had an increased HSM contribution (more nanosized voids)[6]. In Figure 4, the FF results (for initial, 10 hours, 100

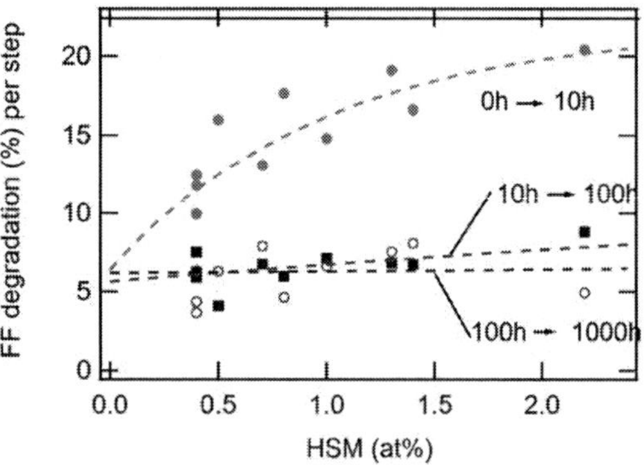

Fig. 5. Relative FF degradation due to light soaking under AM1.5 at 25 C, as calculated between the light soaking steps at 10, 100 and 1000 hours. The HSM contribution in at.% H as determined from FTIR absorption for the silicon hydride stretching modes of the absorber layer is plotted at the x-axis. After 10 hours the FF degradation seems to become independent of the absorber layer properties in terms of nanostructure.

hours and 1000 hours of light soaking) are plotted versus the HSM hydrogen content for all the solar cells processed at the high pressure regime. The decrease in FF within the first 10 hours of light soaking show a clear relation with the HSM, while the decrease in FF after 10 hours appears to be not correlated with the HSM.

This trend is even more evident when the relative FF degradation (initial → 10 hours LS, 10 hours → 100 hours LS and 100 hours → 1000 hours LS) is studied. The relative degradation in FF during the first 10 hours of light soaking is clearly related to the nanostructure, whereas from 10 to 100 hours and 100 hours to 1000 hours of light soaking no correlation is observed. This result is an important breakthrough as it clearly demonstrates the origin of the 'fast' LIDs. The trend demonstrates that the fast part of light induced degradation is mainly a result from metastable defect creation near or at nanosized voids.

, The degradation of the FF clearly becomes independent of the a-Si:H absorber layer used in the solar cell after 10 h of light soaking, as shown in figure 5. Probably the degradation is now dominated by metastable defects that have an isotropic distribution through the silicon matrix, independent on the nanostructure of a-Si:H and independent on a possible contribution of the p-i interface on the FF degradation.

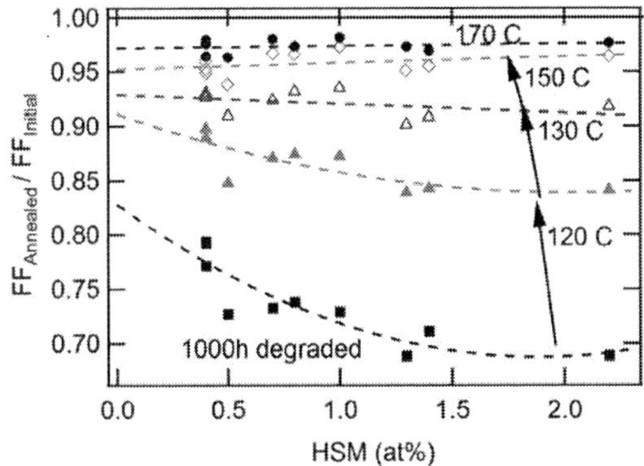

Fig. 6. Annealing behavior of the FF for all 11 solar cells deposited at the high pressure. The relative HSM contribution to the FTIR absorption for the absorber layer is plotted at the x-axis. In the first anneal step most of the FF degradation is already recovered. The lines are a guide for the eye.

Next in figure 6 the recovery of the FF for the same cells after 1000 hrs of light soaking is studied by stepwise annealing. The solar cells are annealed for 1 hr at 120 °C, 130 °C, 150 °C and 170 °C. Again the first step in annealing shows a correlation with the largest volume deficiencies determining the nanostructure of a-Si:H. The FF of the cells with high HSM contribution (more nanosized voids) recover much faster. This suggests that the light induced defects located near the nanosized voids are easy to anneal out. From the annealing steps at temperature above 130 °C, the FF of all of the cells are recovered within 92% of initial FF. In addition the relative recovery of the FF during thermal anneal does not show a relation with the nanostructure, anymore. This suggests that the metastable LIDs generated in the slow light soaking regime (>10 hours), required higher temperatures to be annealed out again. The light soaking and thermal anneal study shows that the LIDs at nanosized voids appear to have the highest level of meta-stability. As the 'fast' LIDs are the largest contributor to the FF-degradation of the a-Si:H p-i-n junctions, the processing of a-Si:H with the lowest possible density of large volume deficiencies appear to be an important design rule for a-Si:H solar cells with improved stabilized efficiencies.

V. Conclusions

The influence of small variations in the nanostructure on light induced degradation of amorphous silicon deposited at high hydrogen dilution (50 times) and high processing pressure (10 mbar) is studied. The degradation kinetics are studied by applying the absorber layers in p-i-n devices and monitoring their FF. It is observed that the kinetics of the fast degradation (first 10 hours) and recovery by annealing (at lowest temperatures) seem to depend on the nanostructure of the absorber layer. Especially the generation of defects near the nanosized voids are the candidate to be the origin of the fast degradation. The long term degradation of the solar cells seems to become independent of the absorber layer properties. These "slow" states might be a result of an isotropic defect state in the silicon matrix. In the thermal annealing experiment temperatures above 130 °C are needed to anneal the cells back to its initial performance.

References

[1] D. L. Staebler and C. R. Wronski, Appl. Phys. Lett. 31, 292 (1977)
[2] J. Melskens, A. Smets, S. Eijt, H. Schut, E. Brck, and M. Zeman, J. Non-Crys. Solids 358, 17 (2012)
[3] A.H.M. Smets, M. Wank , B. Vet , M. Fischer , R.A.C.M.M. van Swaaij , M. Zeman , D.C. Bobela , C.R. Wronski and R.M.C.M. van de Sanden, IEEE Journal of Photovoltaics 2, 94 (2012)
[4] A.H.M. Smets, C.R. Wronski, M. Zeman and M. van de Sanden, MRS Proceedings, 1245, (2010)
[5] D. M. Goldie and S. K. Persheyev, J. Mat. Sci. 41, 5287 (2006).
[6] S. Lebib and P. R. i Cabarrocas, Eur. Phys. J. Appl. Phys. 26, 17 (2004).
[7] A. H. M. Smets and M. C. M. van de Sanden, Phys. Rev. B 76, 073202 (2007).
[8] S. Shimizu, M. Kondo, A. Matsuda, J. Appl. Phys. 97, 033522 (2005)
[7] A.H.M. Smets, T. Matsui, M. Kondo, and M.C.M. van de Sanden, 34th IEEE Photovoltaic Specialists Conference (PVSC), (2009)
[8] G. Lihui and L. Rongming, Thin Solid Films 376, 249 (2000)
[9] J. Müllerová, P. Sutta, G. van Elzakker, M. Zeman and M. Mikula, Appl. Surf. Sci. 254, 3690 (2008)
[10] T. Nguyen-Tran, V. Suendo, P. Roca i Cabarrocas, L. N. Nittala, S. N. Bogle and J. R. Abelson, J. Appl. Phys. 100, 094319 (2006)
[11] M. Fischer, M. Zeman and A.H.M. Smets, Appl. Phys. Lett. Submitted (2013)
[12] M. Kondo, M. Fukawa, L. Guo and A. Matsuda, J. Non-Cryst. Solids 266, 84 (2000)
[13] M. Zeuner, H. Neumann and J. Meichsner, Jpn. J. Appl. Phys. 36, 4711 (1997)
[14] M. H. Francombe ,Thin Films and Nanostructures, Academic Press, San Diego, (2002)
[15] E.A.G. Hamers, W.G.J.H.M. van Sark, J. Bezemer, H. Meiling and W.F. van der Weg, J. Non-Cryst. Solids 226, 205 (1998)
[16] K. Nakamura, K. Yoshino, S. Takeoka, I. Shimizu, Jpn. J. Appl. Phys. 34, 442 (1995)
[17] B.D. Vogt, B. O'Brien, D.R. Allee, D. Loy, B. Akgun and S.K. Satija, J. Non Crys. Sol. 357, 1114 (2011)
[18] M. Isomura, M. Kondo, A. Matsuda, Jpn. J. Appl. Phys. 39, 4721 (2000)
[19] M.H. Brodsky, M. Cardona and J.J. Cuomo, Phys. Rev. B 16, 3556 (1977)
[20] L. Yang and L. Chen Appl. Phys. Lett. 63, 400 (1993)

The Limited Relevance of SWE Dangling Bonds to Degradation in High-Quality a-Si:H Solar Cells

Christopher R. Wronski, *Fellow, IEEE*, and Xinwei Niu, *Member, IEEE*

Abstract—Contributions of different light-induced defect states to degradation of solar cells have been established for high-quality p-i-n solar cells with *i* layers of protocrystalline a-Si:H deposited at very low rates, whose nanostructure is dominated by hydrogen-passivated divacancies. Nature of the different light-induced gap states and their respective roles as electron and hole recombination centers were characterized in the thin films from their photocurrents, and in corresponding solar cells from their Shockley–Reed–Hall carrier recombination currents. The results were directly related to three light-induced states, with "A" and "B" within 0.2 eV and "C" 0.4 eV below midgap, identified from subgap absorption. The A and B states are efficient electron, while the C states are very efficient hole recombination centers. Under 1-sun illumination, the former dominate the electron lifetimes, while the latter are key to solar cell operation as is confirmed by the direct correlation of their creation with the degradation of V_{OC} and 1-sun fill factor (FF). It is also shown that the apparent correlation found earlier between the cell FF and electron lifetimes is due to the same long-term degradation kinetics of the light-induced changes in the B t and C states.

Index Terms—Amorphous silicon, defect states, light-induced degradation, photovoltaic cells, thin films.

I. INTRODUCTION

THE Staebler–Wronski effect (SWE) and its role in the stability of a-Si:H solar cells are still important technological issues as the a-Si:H cells in tandem structures deliver two thirds and in triple junction structures one half of the expected power. Despite the extensive studies of SWE for nearly 40 years on different a-Si:H materials, there is no consensus about either its nature or the role that the light-induced defect states play in the degradation of solar cells. The vast majority of the studies on SWE, based on the view that isolated dangling bonds and their associated midgap states were solely responsible for the light-induced changes in a-Si:H, focused on issues that were related to the physical nature of such isolated dangling bonds as reviewed in detail by Fritzche [1]. In these studies, little attention was given to the nature of the light-induced changes in the gap

states and carrier recombination responsible for the degradation of a-Si:H solar cells. Studies that did address these issues were fewer by far with little, if any, attention being given to their results [2], [3]. These results, however, did offer important insights into light-induced changes in carrier recombination and defect gap states that did not necessarily agree with the widely held "dangling bond" viewpoint, but are highly relevant to a-Si:H solar cell degradation.

Such results included: the extensive evidence for light-induced changes in gap states other than just neutral dangling bond midgap states [4]; two distinct regimes in the kinetics of light-induced changes in carrier recombination degrading under 1-sun illumination [2]; presence of "fast" and "slow" states [5], [6]; and changes in subgap absorption, $\alpha(h\nu)$, inconsistent with a single type of gap states and requiring presence of states away from midgap [7]. It is somewhat surprising that such results are overlooked or ignored in attempts, made even up to now, to explain the contribution of SWE to the degradation of solar cells [8]. In the studies that focused on the nature of light-induced states, and their contribution to the degradation of solar cells, unfortunately, it was not possible to reliably quantify the wide range of results. This was in part due to their being on porous and inhomogeneous a-Si:H, whose microstructural differences could not be adequately characterized. This limitation seriously affected the advances made in improving the stability of a-Si:H cells, because it led to an empirical approach based on just changing their deposition conditions. However, recently, Smets and van Sanden [9] developed a technique based on IR spectroscopy that is able to accurately characterize the nanostructure of a-Si:H. This offers the real possibility of developing a reliable method for relating the changes in SWE, to those in the microstructure, that could lead to a systematic improvement in the stability of a-Si:H solar cells. However, prior to this, it is important to establish the nature of the different light-induced gap states, with their role as both electron and hole recombination centers, so that their respective contributions to the degradation of solar cells can be evaluated.

Here, results are presented and discussed from a study addressing these issues, carried out on dense a-Si:H protocrystalline [10] thin films and corresponding solar cells whose nanostructure is dominated by divacancies [11]. Attention is given to the carrier recombination that is present under 1-sun illumination, which is the normal operating condition for solar cells. It is important to note that under these conditions, carrier recombination occurs not just through the midgap states, but a region of the gap that extends for about 0.9 eV. This study was able to characterize the nature of two states at and one away from midgap, identified with refined dual beam photoconductivity

Manuscript received June 8, 2013; revised February 17, 2014; accepted March 4, 2014. Date of publication April 4, 2014; date of current version April 18, 2014. X. Niu (Corresponding author) was supported in part by research contracts # 2010DFB63080 and 2012AA052401 from Department of Science and Technology, P.R. China.

C. R. Wronski is with the Center for Thin Film Devices, Pennsylvania State University, University Park, PA 16802 USA (e-mail: crwece@engr.psu.edu).

X. Niu is with Chint Solar (Zhejiang) Co., Ltd., Hangzhou 310053, China (e-mail: xinwei.niu@astronergy.com).

Color versions of one or more of the figures in this paper are available online at http://ieeexplore.ieee.org.

Digital Object Identifier 10.1109/JPHOTOV.2014.2311498

(DBP) measurements [12], as electron and hole recombination centers. It was then able to characterize the light-induced changes in them, including those in the fast states [13], and to directly relate them to the degradation of solar cell characteristics under 1-sun illumination.

II. BACKGROUND

The vast majority of studies addressing SWE and light-induced changes were carried out on a-Si:H films consisting of a wide variety of porous undiluted a-Si:H whose microstructure was not well characterized, and no attempts were made to relate the results to solar cell degradation in a quantitative way. It is only recently that SWE studies were undertaken on dense, highly homogeneous, hydrogenated a-Si:H films and solar cells [2], [3]. Such a-Si:H exhibits not only significantly lower light-induced degradation but also under 1-sun illumination at 25 °C attains essentially a degraded steady state (DSS) after around a hundred hours rather than the many hundreds of hours. The studies reported here were carried out on such a-Si:H deposited in the protocrystalline regime [10] with high-quality solar cells as indicated by 1-sun fill factors (FF) of 0.73 in 4000 Å thick cells. It is also important to note that the p/i interfaces in these cells were such as to allow the carrier recombination to be dominated by that in the bulk i layers [14]. The approach taken in establishing the contribution of the different light-induced gap states to the degradation of the solar cells was first to establish their distributions in the gap and then to determine their role as *both* electron and hole recombination centers. To achieve this on the films, it was necessary to refine the DBP measurements and their analysis so as to be able to characterize the different states in detail and measure the electron mobility ($\mu\tau$) products up to 1-sun illumination.

It was also necessary to develop a method to characterize the light-induced gap states in solar cells, which is more direct than that available from the generally used degradation of FF. This was achieved by utilizing the ambipolar (electron and hole) Shockley–Reed–Hall (SRH) recombination in the diffusive currents of the cells under forward bias. This approach was particularly useful in these high-quality cells because of relatively homogeneous low densities of states across the i layers and the low potential barriers confined close to the n and p contacts that lead to essentially a uniform field across the i layer [14], [15].

In detailed studies on carrier transport and carrier recombination mechanisms in cells such as studied here, using an analytically derived model, Deng and Wronski [14] were able to show how the voltage-dependent diode quality factors, $n(V)$, in the forward bias, $J_D - V$, characteristics depend on the densities of states and their conversion into recombination centers with the quasi-Fermi (QF) splitting equal to the applied voltage V. They were was also able to explain the presence of the superposition of the short-circuit current–open-circuit voltage ($J_{sc}-V_{oc}$) and the dark current ($J_D - V$) characteristics over extended regions of current and voltage [15]. This was possible even though the superposition principle, such as exists in the case of c-Si cells, does not apply, since the photocurrents in a-Si:H are not diffusive but field driven and thus voltage de-

pendent. In addition, this model could explain, by separating the contributions of the field-driven transport of photogenerated carriers from the diffusive currents, how the solar cell characteristics in these cells depend on bias and the introduction of light-induced defect states. This methodology was adopted in this study rather than relying on a numerical model where fitting to the experimental data on solar cells involves a large number of unknown and adjustable parameters.

The more direct method of characterizing the light-induced gap states based on SRH recombination allowed the carrier recombination originating from different regions of the gap to be probed by changing the QF splitting equal to the applied voltage. This enabled quantitative correlations to be made between the SRH carrier recombination in cells with the photocurrent recombination in corresponding films and reliable, detailed information to be obtained about the nature of the different light-induced gap states. As a consequence, it was possible to establish the individual contributions of the different defect states directly to the light-induced changes in the thin films and solar cell characteristics, as well as solar cell degradation under 1-sun illumination.

III. EXPERIMENTAL PROCEDURES

The p-i-n superstrate solar cell structures in this study were in the form of glass/specular SnO_2/p a-SiC:H (250 Å)/i a-Si:H (4000 Å)/μc-Si:H (350 Å)/1000 Å Cr fabricated in a multichamber system using RF plasma-enhanced chemical vapor deposition under conditions previously described [16]. The intrinsic layers consisted of protocrystalline a-Si:H obtained with dilution $R = 10$ ($R = [H_2/SiH_4]$ deposited at 0.55 torr, low power, and very low deposition rate of 0.5 Å per second. To control the recombination in the p/i interfaces the i layers were also deposited with a two-step process previously described [17]. The p-SiC:H and n μc-Si:H contacts were of sufficiently high quality as to give under 1-sun illumination an open-circuit voltage of 0.93 V with the i layer bandgap of 1.8 eV. To minimize any external contribution to the $J_D - V$ characteristics at low voltages, small areas (2 mm^2) were defined by the evaporation of the Cr through a shadow mask with subsequent etching off to uncover the n μc-Si:H layer. To eliminate the contributions of external resistance to the cells at higher voltages, a three-probe technique was used, in which two probes on the Cr and ITO contacts of the cells allowed the currents and the voltages to be measured through separate electrical paths. The current–voltage characteristics were obtained with computer-controlled measurements with 25-meV steps with excellent reproducibility in $J_D - V$ characteristics being obtained for different cells on the same substrate.

The procedures in this study also took into account the RT annealing in midgap states [13] and ensured that direct correlations could be made between the results on thin films with those on the corresponding cells. In the characterization of thin films, care was taken to measure the electron $\mu\tau$ products accurately up to 1-sun illumination by having $n^{\pm}$ a-Si:H ohmic contacts in the coplanar structures and careful monitoring of the different carrier generation rates. To take account of the "fast" states in

     317

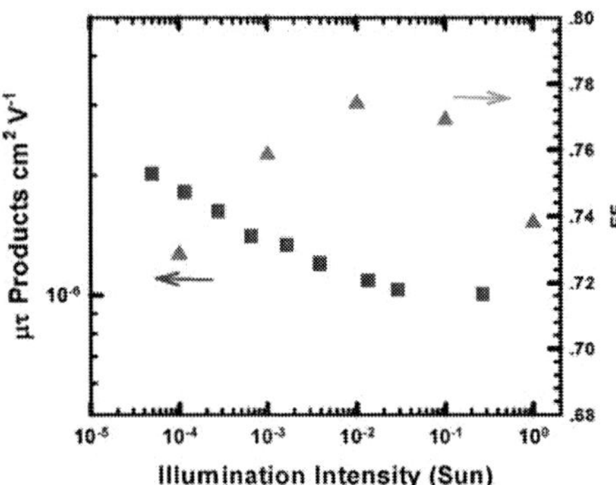

Fig. 1. The film electron $\mu\tau$ products and the corresponding fill factor (FF) in an annealed 4000 Å p-i-n solar cell as a function of illumination intensity up to 1 sun. Observe the inverse behavior of $\mu\tau$ and FF during an increase in Quasi Fermi level splitting.

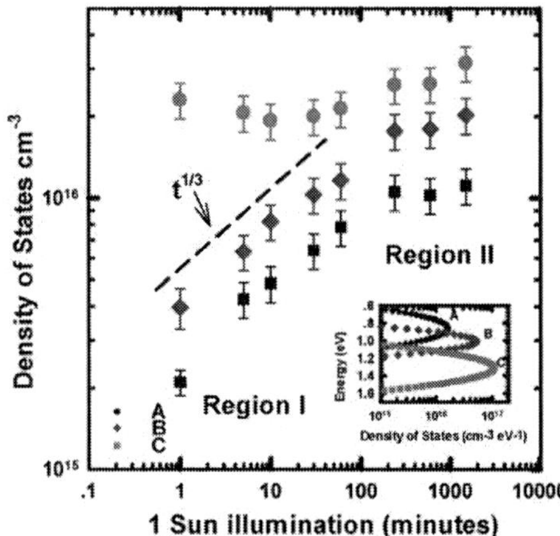

Fig. 2. The light induced changes in the densities of the A, B, and C states, during 1 sun degradation at 25 °C, obtained from subgap absorption measured with DBP. In the inset are the energy distributions of these states shown relative to the conduction band.

the subgap absorption measurements these were not carried out under continuous with 1-sun illumination. Rather a sequence of longer and longer degradations with annealing out of the created light-induced defects prior to subsequent illumination. The reproducible annealed states of the films were obtained after annealing them at 170 °C for 4 h. The derivatives of the DBP measurement results were fitted with three Gaussians, the presence of which was indicated in the self-consistent fitting of previous results on a-Si:H films [4].

In solar cells, the carrier recombination was not characterized with just solar cell characteristics but was also measured directly with SRH recombination. The regions of the gap where the states act as recombination centers were defined by controlling the QF splitting with, intensity of illumination in film photoconductivities, and forward bias in SRH measurements. Such QF splitting enabled the contributions to carrier recombination of different states to be characterized for electron $\mu\tau$ products from photoconductivity and holes from SRH measurements. Because of the large number of the 2-mm^2 cells on any given substrate, it was possible to carry out a new set of experiments on any given cell without having to anneal out any prior degradation.

IV. RESULTS AND DISCUSSION

The contribution of the continuous distribution gap states in a-Si:H to carrier recombination in these films and solar cells was addressed in the annealed state by selectively converting the gap states, at and away from midgap, into recombination centers by increasing the QF splitting with the level of illumination [18]. Fig. 1 shows the results for the electron $\mu\tau$ products obtained from the photocurrents in an a-Si:H film as the illumination is increased up to the level of 1 sun. Also shown are the corresponding results for the FF of a 4000 Å p-i-n solar cell up to 1-sun illumination with a QF splitting of 0.93 eV. There is a striking contrast between the results for electron lifetimes, τ_n, and those of the FF which is determined primarily by the hole lifetimes, τ_p. In the case of the films, there is the generally observed decrease in τ_n with illumination, but in addition there is a clear absence of any further decrease once the QF splitting reaches the value generated by $\sim 10^{-2}$ sun. This shows that the

additional states introduced away from midgap do not act as efficient electron recombination centers as τ_n remains determined by what may be called midgap states.

The results on the FF and, consequently, on τ_p indicate quite an opposite role for the two sets of gap states. While the midgap states act as recombination centers, the FF increases with illumination, as is the case for c-Si cells [19], indicating that introduction of these recombination centers has a small perturbation on hole lifetimes. However, after reaching the $\sim 10^{-2}$ sun illumination, the states away from midgap become hole recombination centers; the FF begins and then continues to decrease. This is a clear indication that those states, which have negligible effect on τ_n, have large hole capture cross sections that limit the FF under 1-sun illumination. The results also clearly show that the midgap states, which for a long time have been recognized as efficient electron recombination centers, have a very much smaller effect on holes than the gap states located away from midgap.

These two sets of gap states and their light-induced changes in the a-Si:H films were identified in a detailed study carried out by Niu [12] who characterized their subgap absorption spectra with DBP and analysis that took into account the presence of multiple defect states. In these studies, where the states that anneal out at room temperature were taken into account, three different Gaussian distributions were identified from the derivatives of $\alpha(h\nu)$. In this a-Si:H with the bandgap of 1.8 eV, there are two states at midgap, A at 0.05 eV above and the B at 0.095 eV below midgap, with the third C states 0.39 eV below midgap. The energy distributions of these three gap states after 30 min of 1-sun illumination at 25 °C are shown relative to the conduction band in the inset of Fig. 2. In this a-Si:H, with a bandgap of 1.8 eV, the peaks of the Gaussians relative to midgap are: A at 0.05 eV above; B at 0.095 eV below; and C at 0.39 eV below. Since the A and B states are located very close to 0.9 eV below the conduction band, they can be termed as the "midgap" states. Even though the C states are close to the valence band tail, it

318

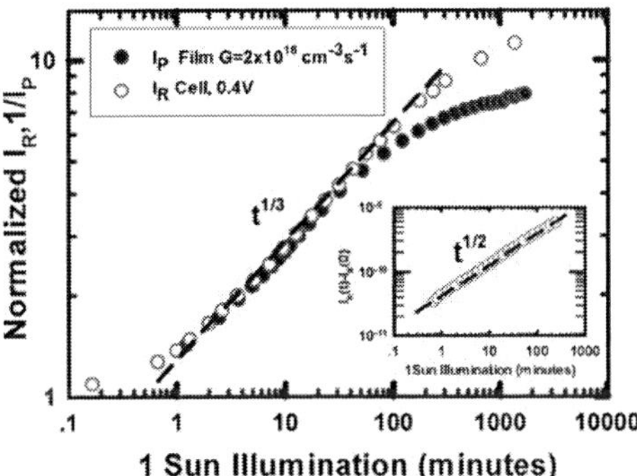

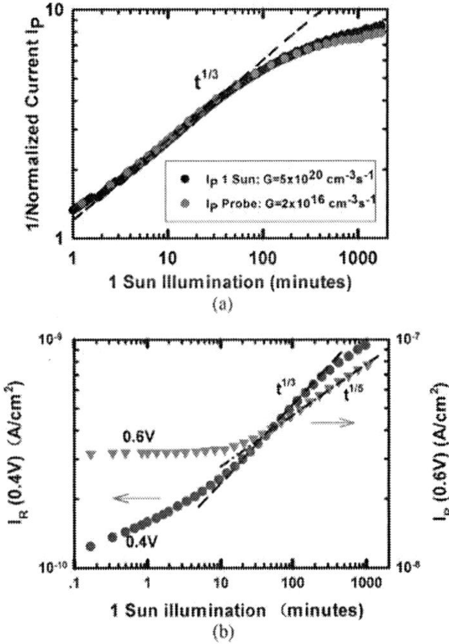

Fig. 3. The SRH recombination current, I_R, and the corresponding inverse of the normalized film photocurrent, I_P, for Quasi Fermi splitting of 0.4 eV during 1sun illumination at 25 °C. The inset illustrates how the $t^{1/3}$ time dependence of the increase in the A and B states reflects a $t^{1/2}$ dependence for their creation rate. R

Fig. 4. (a) The inverse of the normalized 1 sun film photocurrents, I_R, with carrier generation rates of 2×10^{16} and 5×10^{20} cm^{-3} s^{-1} during 1 sun degradation at 25 °C. (b) The Shockley-Reed-Hall (SRH) recombination current, I_R, for QF splitting of 0.4 and 0.6 eV during 1 sun illumination at 25 °C. The former is with just A and B states while the latter is when C states are also present as recombination centers.

was possible to clearly separate them and their evolution from the exponential distribution of the tail states.

During the degradation, the increase in the areas under the Gaussians occurred with very little or no change in their peak energies or half widths. The changes in the respective electron-occupied states, which are obtained from the areas under the Gaussians, are shown in Fig. 2 for a bias illumination of 1 nA. These changes reflect those present in the actual densities of states as the kinetics of the changes are found to be independent of the bias illumination. It can be seen in the figure that in the time frame of the experiments, the changes in the three distributions of states are distinctly different. Nevertheless, all of them exhibit two regimes, I and II, with transitions between the two occurring after about a half hour of illumination. In regime I, there are large increases in both the A and B states, while there is no increase in the C states. Also shown in Fig. 2 is a guide to the eye time dependence of $t^{1/3}$, one that is extensively reported for light-induced changes in a-Si:H photocurrents. On transitioning into regime II, there is no longer any increase in the A states, reflecting their nature as the fast states that anneal out even at 25 °C [13]. On the other hand, the B states now increase at a slower rate which is similar to that for the onset of the increase in the C states.

The role of these states as recombination centers was characterized by selectively converting them into recombination centers by increasing the QF splitting. In the case of the films by changing the carrier generation rates for the photocurrents, I_P, from 5×10^{15} to 5×10^{20} cm^{-3}·s^{-1}, and in the case of cells by changing the forward bias for the SRH recombination currents, I_R, from 0.3 to 0.6 V. These results could be directly related to three gap states in Fig. 2 and applied to characterizing them as electron and hole recombination centers. Fig. 3 shows the results of 1-sun degradation at 25 °C for the cell SRH recombination currents, I_R, at 0.4 V forward bias and the inverse of the film photocurrents, I_P, with a similar QF splitting. The two results correspond to the recombination through the A and B states. Even though I_P depends solely on τ_n and I_R on both τ_n and τ_p, the excellent superposition in the kinetics of their changes

clearly shows that they reflect the same creation of midgap states in the films and solar cells.

The kinetics of these recombination currents clearly exhibit a $t^{1/3}$ time dependence, such as indicated in Fig. 2 for the A and B states, with a transition into the regime II that leads to a DSS after about 100 h. It should be noted here that this $t^{1/3}$ kinetics seen here and in Fig. 2 are for the *increase* in the total densities of the A and B states. As such it does not, as is generally assumed, reflect the actual *creation rate* of the light-induced gap states which can be obtained only after the density of states prior to the degradation is taken into account. This is illustrated in the inset of Fig. 3, where the difference between SRH current at time t, $I_R(t)$, and the initial value, $I_R(0)$, are shown as a function of the 1-sun illumination time. It can now be clearly seen that the time dependence for the actual *creation* rate of the A and B states is $t^{1/2}$ and not $t^{1/3}$. It is important to note that this time dependence holds even when the density of the created states is smaller than that of the intrinsic states, as found in the extensive studies on the creation of metastable defect states in this a-Si:H [20].

There is, however, a striking difference between the kinetics of these two recombination currents when the QF splitting is increased so as to introduce the C states as recombination centers, as illustrated in Fig. 4. In Fig. 4(a), the inverse of the normalized I_P photocurrents are shown for carrier generation rates of $G = 2 \times 10^{16}$ and 5×10^{20} cm^{-3}·s^{-1}. In this case, the intensity dependence of the $\mu\tau$ products during degradation

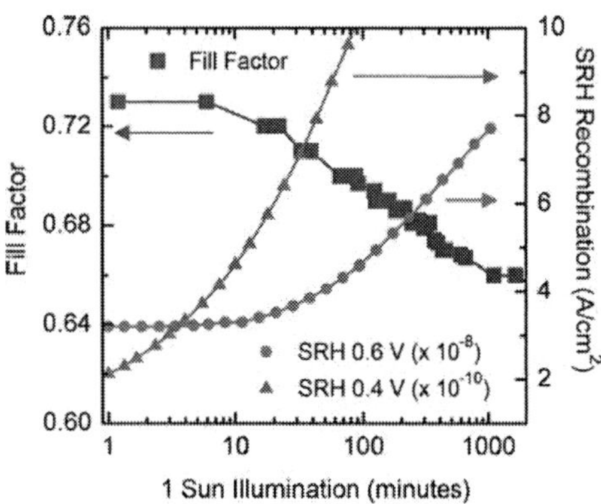

Fig. 5. Changes in the 0.4 V and 0.6 V SRH recombination currents and the 1 sun FF during 1 sun illumination at 25 °C.

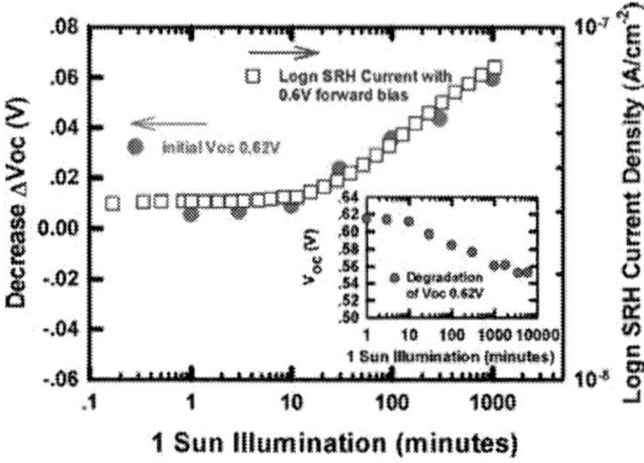

Fig. 6. The inset shows the decrease in the initial V_{OC} of 0.62 V during degradation with 1 sun at 25 °C. The figure illustrates the direct correlation between the decrease in V_{OC}, ΔV_{OC}, and the logarithm of the SRH recombination with 0.6 eV Quasi Fermi splitting.

remained quite similar to that in the annealed state, with intensity-independent values at the high generation rates, when the C states are included as recombination centers. The identical $t^{1/3}$ time dependence in the changes of the photocurrents, when the generation rates change by 10^5, is a clear indication that the electron lifetimes in both cases are dominated by the A and B states. This, just as prior to degradation, shows that the C states are inefficient electron recombination centers so that the light-induced midgap states determine τ_n even at 1-sun illumination. In Fig. 4(b), the SRH recombination currents are shown for the QF splitting of 0.4 and 0.6 V forward bias. In this case, a dramatic change occurs in the kinetics of the SRH recombination currents when the C states are introduced as recombination centers with the QF splitting to 0.6 eV. In this case, the changes in the SRH recombination currents closely follow those of the C states in Fig. 2. There is still the striking absence of any changes during the large $t^{1/3}$ increase of the midgap A and B states in region I, but here the transition into region II can now be clearly identified to have a $t^{1/5}$ time dependence. It is important to remember that even though the C states cannot be detected in electron photocurrent recombination, they can, with SRH ambipolar recombination, be determined by both τ_n and τ_p. Because of their large hole capture cross section of their introduction recombination centers, the SRH currents become dominated by τ_p, rather than τ_n, when carrier recombination occurs through only the A and B states. The differences in the kinetics of the light-induced changes in the A, B, and C states, as well as in their nature as recombination centers, offer fingerprints for their respective contributions to the degradation of solar cells under the 1-sun illumination.

Under this illumination, both the A, B midgap and the C states contribute to the degradation of the solar cells. Results are presented in Fig. 5, where the contribution of A and B states to the degradation of the 1-sun FF can be separated from that of the C states. The figure shows the changes under 1-sun illumination in the SRH currents of just the A and B states, J_R with 0.4 V, as well as when the C states are included as recombination centers, J_R with 0.6 V. Also shown is the corresponding 1-sun FF which exhibits two sets of degradation rates. It can be seen that when initially there is large increase in the A and B states and no change in the C states, there is virtually no change in the FF. On the other hand, as soon as there is an increase in the C states, as expected from their effect on τ_p, there is the onset of degradation in the FF.

A more direct and quantitative correlation can be found between the increase of the C states and the degradation in the cell open-circuit voltage, V_{OC}. In these 4000 Å thick cell structures with the protocrystalline a-Si:H i layer, there was virtually no decrease in the 1-sun short-circuit currents, J_{SC}, even after degradation to a DSS with 1 sun at 25 °C. The J_{SC} was generated with one pass absorption in the i layer, with minimal reflection from the Cr back contact, and no optical enhancement from the specular CTO. As indicated earlier, in the detailed study on the $J_{sc}-V_{oc}$ characteristics over a wide range of illumination, Deng *et al.* [15] found that in these a-Si:H cells, superposition of the $J_{sc}-V_{oc}$ and the dark current J_D-V characteristics was present over extended regions of current and voltage. They then showed that the superposition is present if $J_D = J_{\text{diff}} > J_{RG}$, where J_{diff} is the diffusive forward bias current and J_{RG} is the current corresponding to the recombination of the photogenerated carriers in the bulk i layer. Superposition between $J_{sc}-V_{oc}$ and J_D-V, however, will not be present if at $V = V_{oc}$, J_{RG} is comparable with or larger than J_{diff}, and under these conditions, V_{oc} cannot be related to the SRH recombination currents. Even though superposition is present to high values of voltage, the introduction of light-induced defect states and corresponding increases in J_{RG} can limit such superposition and direct correlation to SRH recombination currents J_D to lower and lower values of V_{oc}.

The inset of Fig. 6 shows the 1-sun degradation in V_{oc} of 0.62 V which also exhibits two regimes similar to those of the FF in Fig. 5. In this case, the QF splitting is close to 0.6 eV; therefore, its light-induced changes should correspond to those in the J_D at 0.6-V forward bias in Fig. 4(b). At this voltage, it is possible to directly relate the light-induced changes in V_{OC} to the those in the bulk C states since $J_D \gg J_{RG}$, as confirmed by the presence of the superposition characteristic even after 10 h of the 1-sun degradation at 25 °C. Fig. 6 then illustrates the decrease, ΔV_{OC}, in this voltage under 1-sun illumination at 25 °C as well as the SRH recombination at 0.6 V such as

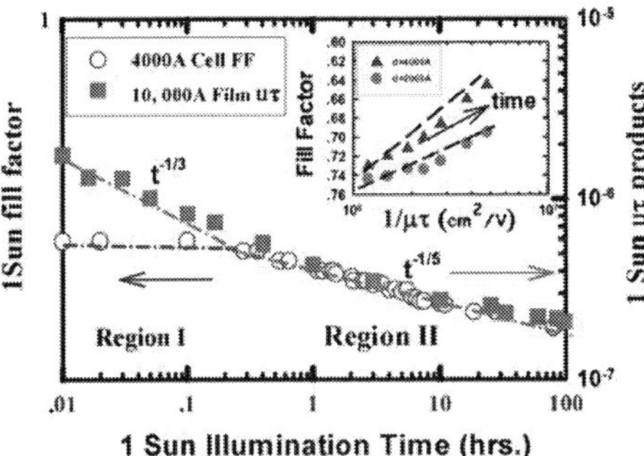

Fig. 7. The inset shows the correlation between the 1 sun FF of p-i-n solar cells with different thickness and the corresponding film $1/\mu\tau$ products, both in region II of 1 sun degradation at 25 °C. The figure shows separately that the 1 sun FF and $\mu\tau$ products where in region II both have the same $t^{-1/5}$ time dependence that leads to the results shown in the inset.

seen in Fig. 5. Excellent superposition can be seen in the figures between ΔV_{OC} and the change in $J_D\,(0.6\ \mathrm{V})$, which is plotted on a logarithmic scale since V_{OC} has a logarithmic dependence on J_D [15]. This quantitative agreement between the change in the C states, as indicated by $J_R\,(0.6\ \mathrm{V})$, and V_{OC} clearly shows the absence of any significant contribution from the light-induced midgap states to cell degradation under close to or at 1-sun illumination.

In analyzing the kinetics in region II of the degradation under 1-sun illumination on protocrystalline films and cells such as those here, Pearce *et al.* found what appears to point to midgap states being responsible for the degradation of the 1-sun FF [3]. This was indicated by the apparent direct correlation between the changes in the midgap states, known to be efficient electron recombination centers that determine the electron $\mu\tau$ products, with those in the 1-sun FF. Such correlations are shown in the inset of Fig. 7, where the 1-sun FF for two cell thicknesses is plotted versus $1/\mu\tau$ during period of about 100 h in region II.

In Fig. 7, the changes in the 1-sun FF and the electron $\mu\tau$ products in films are shown separately with the transitions in their kinetics clearly visible. In region I, there are the previously discussed kinetics of $\mu\tau$ and FF changes that result from the creation of the A, B, and C states. In region II, it can now be seen that the previously seen initial changes in the C states, with a $t^{1/5}$ time dependence, continue as such over the 100 h or so it takes to approach a DSS. This is reflected in the changes of the FF having the time dependence of $t^{-1}/5$. What is new and somewhat surprising in Fig. 7 is the result for the time dependence of changes in the $\mu\tau$ products in region II which is also $t^{-1}/5$. Since in this region the $\mu\tau$ products depend solely on the B states, this points to the changes in the B and C states having the same time dependence. It is such a time dependence, and not the contribution of the midgap B states to hole recombination, that leads to the results in the inset of Fig. 7. It is, therefore, not surprising that without a detailed knowledge about the nature of the different light-induced gap states, a misconception would arise about the importance of midgap states in the degradation of solar cells even operating under 1-sun illumination.

V. Conclusion

The results presented here clearly demonstrate that the degradation in these cells operating under 1-sun illumination is determined by the light-induced changes in C states located 0.4 eV below midgap, with the A and B states within 0.2 eV of midgap having a negligible effect. Under 1-sun illumination at 25 °C, the changes in the gap states exhibit two regimes, with regime I transitioning after about half an hour into regime II which leads to essentially a DSS after around 100 h. In regime I, the A and B states exhibit the same $t^{1/3}$ time dependence for their light-induced changes, while there is no increase in the C states. However, in regime II, while there is no longer any further increase in the A states, the B and C states change with a $t^{1/5}$ time dependence. It is this same time dependence for the changes of the B and C states in regime II, and not the contribution of the midgap states to hole recombination, that leads to a correlation between electron $\mu\tau$ products and FF [3]. A lack of any contribution from the A and B states, and the importance of the C states, to the degradation of the solar cells was clearly identified from their respective effect on the 1-sun FF. On the other hand, the dominant role of the light-induced C states is demonstrated with the quantitative correlation between their increases and the degradation in V_{oc}. Evidence for the two regimes and a $t^{-1}/5$ time dependence in the degradation of Voc were also reported by Liang *et al.* [21]. They attributed such results to carrier recombination through both the tail states and light-induced midgap states. However, it is shown here that the degradation in cell characteristics under 1-sun illumination is determined solely by the light-induced changes in the clearly identified C states.

From the correlation of the results on the electron photocurrents in films and the ambipolar SRH currents in cells, it was possible to obtain insights into the nature of the different states. In this dense protocrystalline a-Si:H, clearly the A states are the fast states [2], [13] for which no evidence was found in 1-sun degradation of the porous a-Si:H films. The very large changes in the $\mu\tau$ products upon their relaxation at RT point to larger electron capture cross sections, S_n, than those for the B states. Despite the large difference in the rates at which the midgap states in the dense and the porous a-Si:H films are created under 1-sun illumination, there are some similarities between the midgap B states and those that have been generally associated with dangling bond D^0 states. This includes their $t^{1/3}$ initial increases and their annealing out at temperatures above 100 °C. In both cases, the states are efficient electron recombination centers and capture cross sections associated with a neutral recombination centers [4]. It is also interesting to note that kinetics of 1-sun light-induced changes similar to those in the B states have been seen in the ESR signal, generally associated with isolated dangling bonds [22].

Evidence pointing to states below midgap, such as the C states clearly identified here, had been found from the self-consistent fitting of different results on thin films using numerical modeling. This could only be obtained using similar three Gaussian distributions and with negatively charged states below midgap [23]. Such C states have very small electron and very large hole capture cross sections that would explain their complete lack of effect on the electron lifetimes and the dominant role in determining the hole lifetimes.

Despite some similarities of the B states to the gap states that are considered to be due to isolated dangling bonds, the states discussed here are associated with divacancies [11], [24], [25]. This is because not only in this dense, a-Si:H is the nanostructure dominated by their presence, but also because of the similarity in the separation in the gap state distributions to those of the defect states in crystalline divacancies [26]. Consequently, in addressing the origin of SWE defects in dense protocrystalline a-Si:H, it is necessary to consider mechanisms related to divacancies [27], [28] rather than just isolated dangling bonds. They must also take into account that the actual creation rate of the defects responsible for midgap states is $t^{1/2}$ and not $t^{1/3}$ as has been generally assumed.

It should be mentioned that in the case of the divacancies in crystalline silicon, there are four sets of gap states; therefore, it may be possible that there is a fourth set of states in the a-Si:H. States, such as those reported to be 0.5–0.6 eV from the conduction band [29], would not have been detected here because of the limitation in the DBP measurements. However, such states would not be "midgap" since they would become recombination centers only at illumination levels similar to those required for the C states.

Acknowledgment

The authors gratefully acknowledge the critical contributions of Dr. J. Deng and Dr. J. Pearce for their results and helpful discussions. They would also like to acknowledge the helpful discussion with Dr. R. Koval and Dr. A. Smets.

References

[1] H. Fritzsche, "Development in understanding and controlling the Staebler-Wronski effect in a-Si:H," *Annu. Rev. Mater. Res.*, vol. 31, pp. 47–79, 2001.

[2] C. R. Wronski, J. M. Pearce, R. J. Koval, X. Niu, A. S. Ferlauto, J. Koh, and R. W. Collins, "Light induced defect creation kinetics in thin film proctocrystalline amorphous silicon materials and their solar cells," *Mater. Res. Soc. Symp. Proc.*, vol. 15, p. 459, 2002.

[3] J. M. Pearce, R. J. Koval, R. W. Collins, C. R. Wronski, M. M. Al-Jassim, and K. M. Jones. "Correlation of light-induced changes in a-Si:H films with characteristics of corresponding solar cells," in *Proc. 29th IEEE Photovoltaic Spec. Conf.*, 2002, p. 1098.

[4] M. Gunes and C. R. Wronski, "Differences in the densities of charged defect states and the kinetics of Staebler-Wrosnki effect in undoped hydrogenated amorphous silicon thin films," *J. Appl. Phys.*, vol. 81, p. 3526, 1997.

[5] L. Yang and L. Chen, ""Fast' and "slow" metastable defects in hydrogenated amorphous silicon," *Appl. Phys. Lett.*, vol. 63, p. 400, 1993.

[6] J. M. Pearce, R. J. Koval, X. Niu, S. J. May, R. W. Collins, and C. R. Wronski, "The 'fast' and 'slow' light induced defects in diluted and undiluted hydrogenated amorphous silicon solar cells and materials," in *Proc. 17th Eur. Photovoltaic Solar Energy Conf.*, 2002, pp. 2842–2845.

[7] Y. Lee, L. Jiao, Z. Lu, R. W. Collins, and C. R. Wronski, "Light induced changes in hydrogen-diluted a-Si:H Materials and Solar Cells: A new perspective on a self-consistent analysis," *Sol. Energy Mater. Solar Cells*, vol. 49, p. 149, 1997.

[8] P. Stradins, "Staebler-Wronski defects: Creation efficiency, stability, and effect on a-Si:H Cell degradation," in *Proc. 35th IEEE Photovoltaic Spec. Conf.*, 2010, pp. 142–146.

[9] A. H. M. Smets and M. C. M. van Sanden, "Relation of the Si-H stretching frequency to the nanostructural Si-H bulk environment," *Phys. Rev. B*, vol. 76, p. 073202, 2007.

[10] Rob Collins, R. W., J. Koh, A. Ferlauto, P. Rovira, Y. Lee, R. Koval, and C. R. Wronski, "Real time analysis of amorphous and microcrystalline silicon film growth by multichannel ellipsometry," *Thin Solid Films*, vol. 364, pp. 129–137, 2000.

[11] A. H. M. Smets, W. M. M. Kessels, and M. C. M. van Sanden, "Vacencies and voids in hydrogenated amorphous silicon," *Appl. Phys. Lett.*, vol. 82, p. 1547, 2003.

[12] X. Niu, "Nature and evolution of light induced defects in hydrogenated amorphous silicon," Ph.D. dissertation, Dept. Elect. Eng., Pennsylvania State University, University Park, PA, USA, 2006.

[13] M. L. Albert, J. Deng, X. Niu, J. M. Pearce, R. W. Collins, and C. R. Wronski, "The creation and annealing kinetics of fast light induced defect states created by 1 sun illumination in a-Si:H," *Mater. Res. Soc. Symp. Proc.*, vol. 862, p. A.13.2.1, 2005.

[14] J. Deng and C. R. Wronski, "Carrier recombination and differential diode quality factors in the dark forward bias current-voltage characteristics of a-Si:H solar cells," *J. Appl. Phys.*, vol. 98, p. 24509, 2005.

[15] J. Deng, J. M. Pierce, V. Vlahos, R. W. Collins, and C. R. Wronski, "Carrier transport and recombination in a-aSi:Hp-i-n solar cells in dark an under illumination," *Mater. Res. Soc. Symp. Proc.*, vol. 762, p. 303, 2003.

[16] R. J. Koval, J. Koh, Z. Lu, L. Jiao, R. W. Collins, and C. R. Wronski, "Performance and stability of Si:Hp-i-n solar cells with i. layers prepared at the thickness-dependentamorphous-to-microcrystalline phase boundary," *Appl. Phys. Lett.*, vol. 75, p. 155, 1991.

[17] J. Koh, Y. Lee, H. Fujiwara, C. R. Wronski, and R. W. Collins, "Optimization of hydrogenated amorphous silicon p-i-n solar cells with two-step i layers guided by real-time spectroscopic ellipsometry," *App. Phys. Lett.*, vol. 73, p. 1526, 1998.

[18] A. Rose, *Concepts in Photoconductivity and Allied Problems.* New York, NY, USA: Interscience, 1962.

[19] H. J. Hovel, *Solar Cells, Semiconductors and Semimetals. Volume 11. Solar Cells.* New York, NY, USA: Academic, 1975.

[20] J. D. Deng, B. Ross, M. Albert, R. W. Collins, and C. R. Wronski, "Characterization of the evolution in metastable defects created by recombination of carriers generated by photo-generation and injection in *p-i-n* a-Si:H solar cells," *Mater. Res. Soc. Symp. Proc.*, vol. 910, p. A.2.2, 2006.

[21] J. J. Liang, E. A. Schiff, S. Guha, B. Yan, and J. Yang, "Light-soaking effects on the open-circuit voltage of a-Si:H solar cells," *Mater. Res. Soc. Symp. Proc.*, vol. 862, p. A13.6.1, 2005.

[22] J. M. Pearce, V. Vlahos, J. Deng, R. W. Collins, C. R. Wronski, J. Whitaker, and P. C. Taylor, "Evolution of D^0 and non-D^0 light induced defect states in a-Si:H materials and their respective contribution to carrier recombination," *Mater. Res. Soc. Symp. Proc.*, vol. 808, p. A2.5, 2004.

[23] L. Jiao, H. Liu, S. Semoushikina, Y. Lee, and C. R. Wronski, "Initial, rapid light-induced changes in hydrogenated amorphous silicon materials and solar cell structures: The effects of charged defects," *Appl. Phys. Lett.*, vol. 69, p. 3713, 1996.

[24] J. Melskens, A. H. M. Smets, S. W. H. Eijt, H. Schut, E. Bruck, and M. Zeman, "Nanostructural analysis of hydrogenated silicon films on positron annihilation studies," *J. Non. Cryst. Solids*, vol. 358, pp. 2015–2018, 2012.

[25] J. Melskens, A. H. M. Smets, M. Schouten, S. W. H. Eijt, H. Schut, and M. Zeman, "New insights in the nanostructure and defect states of hydrogenated amorphous silicon obtained by annealing," *IEEE J. Photovoltaics*, vol. 3, no. 1, pp. 65–71, Jan. 2013.

[26] G. D. Watkins and J. W. Corbett, "Defects in irradiated silicon: Electron paramagnetic resonance of the divacancy," *Phys. Rev.*, vol. 138, p. A543, 1963.

[27] D. E. Carlson and K. Rajan, "Evidence for proton motion in the recovery of light-induced degradation in amorphous silicon solar cells," *J. Appl. Phys.*, vol. 83, p. 1726, 1998.

[28] A. H. M. Smets, C. R. Wronski, M. Zeman, and M. C. M. van Sanden, "The Staebler-Wronski effect: New physical approaches and insight as a route to reveal its origin," *Mater. Res. Soc. Symp. Proc.*, vol. 1245, p. 43, 2010.

[29] F. Zhong and J. D. Cohen, "Measured and calculated distributions of deep defect states in hydrogenated amorphous-silicon verification of deep defect relaxation dynamics," *Phys Rev Lett.*, vol. 71, p. 597, 1993.

Structural Order and Staebler–Wronski Effect in Hydrogenated Amorphous Silicon Films and Solar Cells

Florian Köhler, Thomas Zimmermann, Stefan Muthmann, Aad Gordijn, and Reinhard Carius

Abstract—The structure of hydrogenated amorphous silicon films is investigated by Raman spectroscopy and X-ray diffraction. Raman spectroscopy probes the phonon density of states, whereas X-ray diffraction measures the distribution of the electron density. Yet, both methods can yield information on the microstructure of the material represented by certain parameters like, e.g., the position or the width of the transverse optical phonon or the width of the first scattering peak. Interdependences between these parameters are investigated and evaluated. A correlation was found between the structural disorder and the relative efficiency loss caused by the Staebler–Wronski effect for intrinsic films applied as absorbing layers in solar cells. This correlation could be used to estimate the solar cell degradation without time-consuming light-soaking experiments.

Index Terms—Amorphous semiconductors, degradation, microstructure, photovoltaic cells, Raman scattering, silicon, X-ray diffraction.

I. Introduction

HYDROGENATED amorphous silicon (a-Si:H) is widely used as an absorber material in thin-film solar cells. A common way to deposit a-Si:H layers is plasma-enhanced chemical vapor deposition (PECVD) using silane diluted in hydrogen. However, a-Si:H is prone to the light-induced degradation of optoelectronic properties, commonly known as the Staebler–Wronski effect (SWE). This effect was observed as a reversible change of the conductivity in a-Si:H films and also as a degradation in the solar cell performance after illumination [1], [2]. Despite intensive research on the SWE over the last decades, the microscopic mechanism is not yet fully understood [3]. For prolonged illumination of a-Si:H, an increase of the defect density from 10^{15} up to 10^{17} cm^{-3} is found for device-grade material and the defects are identified as dangling bonds [4]. As proposed by Staebler and Wronski, these defects might originate from a nonradiative recombination process of excess charge carriers [5]. The amount of defects can be reversed by annealing the material at temperatures around 150 °C. In the model

proposed by Stutzmann *et al.* [6], dangling bonds are believed to emerge from broken Si–Si bonds that are not passivated by hydrogen. Hence, reducing the amount of weak bonds should lead to more stable material. Fritzsche reviewed the results of several experiments and proposed, in addition to the creation of defects, light-induced changes of the structural network [7]. Beyond this, a reversible expansion of the material volume was observed during light soaking experiments [8], providing further motivation to investigate the structural order of a-Si:H and its impact on the SWE in more detail.

"Structural order" in amorphous materials is a rather general term that can be specified depending on the length scale it comprises. Short-range order (SRO, 2–5 Å), medium-range order (MRO, 5–20 Å), and long-range structure (LRS, ≥ 20 Å) are distinguished [9]. In silicon, the atoms are covalently bonded, which is why the SRO is characterized in terms of bond length or bond angle deviations from the ideal tetrahedron. The MRO is reflected in the coordination of next-nearest neighbors or the dihedral angle between neighboring tetrahedra. Finally, the LRS deals with clusters of tetrahedra and their coordination. The LRS, however, is rarely addressed in the literature, and experimental results are usually interpreted in terms of SRO and MRO. One has to keep in mind that these definitions are not well defined, and the results of experimental methods addressing one length scale may also be influenced by the order on other length scales.

The SRO and hence the mean bond angle deviation $\Delta\Theta$ from 109.5° of ideally fourfold coordinated Si atoms were derived from the width of the transverse optical (TO) phonon band w_{TO} obtained by Raman spectroscopy [10]. From this experiment, a measure for the MRO can be calculated from the relative intensity of the transverse-acoustical (TA) to the TO phonon I_{MRO} [11]–[13], while we found indications for a correlation between I_{MRO} and the w_{TO} [14]. For this study, a larger range of preparation conditions was investigated, and an excitation wavelength with smaller information depth was used to exclude contributions from the glass substrate that might influence the spectrum in the region of both the TO and the TA phonon band.

Another method to access the MRO is the evaluation of the width of the first scattering peak (FSP) obtained by X-ray diffraction (XRD) measurements. Although the origin of the FSP is not completely understood so far, it was shown that an increase in MRO results in a decreased peak width [15]–[17]. An improved structural order in a-Si:H was found for a film preparation with high hydrogen dilutions close to and above the

Manuscript received June 14, 2013; revised October 14, 2013; accepted October 22, 2013. Date of current version December 16, 2013.

The authors are with the IEK-5 Photovoltaik, Forschungszentrum Jülich GmbH, 52425 Jülich, Germany (e-mail: f.koehler@fz-juelich.de; t.zimmermann@fz-juelich.de; s.muthmann@fz-juelich.de; a.gordijn@fz-juelich.de; r.carius@fz-juelich.de).

Color versions of one or more of the figures in this paper are available online at http://ieeexplore.ieee.org.

Digital Object Identifier 10.1109/JPHOTOV.2013.2287911

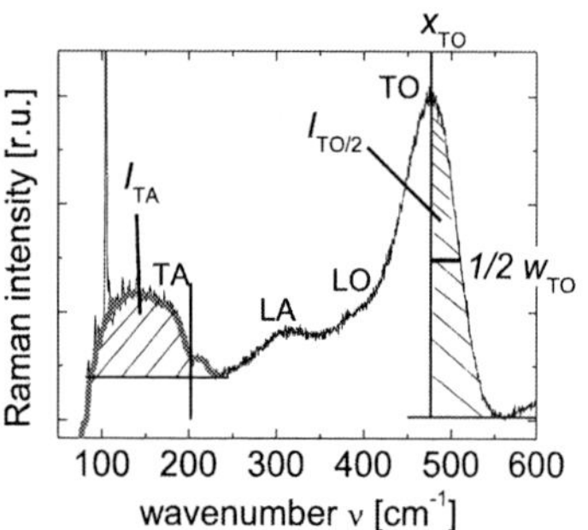

Fig. 1. Typical Raman spectrum of hydrogenated amorphous Silicon excited at 488 nm. Phonon bands are assigned according to [24] as TA, LA, LO, and TO (T = transverse, L = longitudinal, A = acoustical, O = optical). Evaluation of the integrated TO and TA intensity is illustrated (I_{TO} and I_{TA}, respectively). For the latter, the low-wavenumber region was smoothed (grey line) to reduce the effects of the plasma and rotational Raman peaks. Position and width of the TO phonon were fitted with a Gaussian peak between 470 and 560 cm⁻¹.

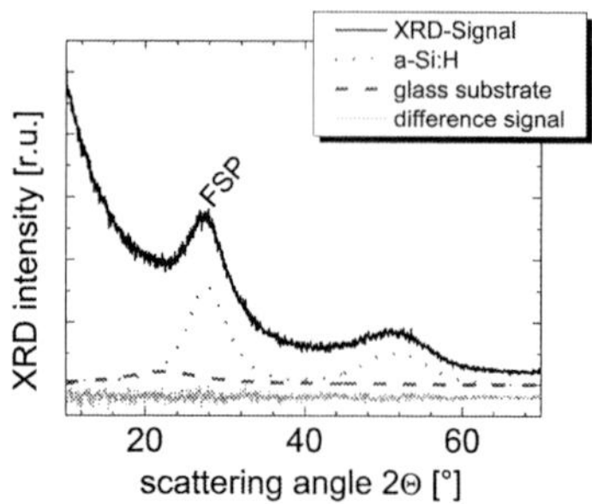

Fig. 2. Typical XRD pattern of the investigated samples (black-solid line) and its numerical deconvolution into contributions of the amorphous silicon (red-dotted line), and the glass substrate (blue dashed line). The gray-solid line shows the difference between measured signal and the deconvolution including the background. It is shifted to lower intensities for a better visibility. The first scattering peak of the pattern is marked as "FSP."

onset of microcrystallinity [18]. Consequently, correlations between the results of XRD and Raman spectroscopy concerning the structural order are expected and investigated in this study.

For deposition conditions toward the microcrystalline growth, thin films and solar cells of a-Si:H show an improved stability against light-soaking [19]–[22]. Ito and Kondo varied the hydrogen dilution periodically during the growth of absorbing layers for solar cells and related the light-induced efficiency loss to a decrease in MRO [23]. However, the initial efficiencies obtained in their study vary between 6% and 9% and correlate strongly with MRO. Thus, it is not obvious that the improved structural order is the cause for an improved stability.

In this study, we provide data on the microstructure of a-Si:H films and absorbing layers of solar cells deposited by PECVD under various conditions in order to obtain data from a broad range of structural order. Raman spectroscopy and XRD were applied to characterize the microstructure and to investigate the connections between SRO and MRO. Solar cell efficiencies were measured before and after degradation in order to find a correlation between the efficiency loss and the structural order. As degradation experiments are very time consuming, it is desirable to have a quick method that can predict the efficiency loss of amorphous silicon solar cells. It will be shown that for the presently studied high-quality samples, an increase of the TO phonon position strongly correlates with the relative efficiency loss. Accordingly, this parameter might serve as a first estimation for the magnitude of the degradation of a-Si:H solar cells.

II. EXPERIMENTAL DETAILS

Hydrogenated amorphous silicon films prepared by PECVD (single layers and absorbing layers applied in solar cells) were investigated using Raman spectroscopy at an excitation wavelength λ_{ex} of 488 nm. Fig. 1 shows a typical Raman spectrum of a-Si:H. The phonon bands are assigned following Brodsky *et al.* [24]. The position of the maximum x_{TO} and the full-width at half-maximum (FWHM) w_{TO} of the TO phonon were obtained from a least-squares fit of a Gaussian peak fitted

between 470 and 560 cm⁻¹. To obtain the intensity ratio of the TO and the TA band, two different baselines were chosen for the corresponding peaks. For the TA band, the minimum around 230 cm⁻¹ served as the baseline intensity. Below 150 cm⁻¹, several narrow lines are present that can be attributed to the laser emission and rotational Raman lines of aerial nitrogen and oxygen. To reduce their impact on the TA intensity, the spectrum was approximated with a percentile filter below 235 cm⁻¹ as illustrated with the gray curve in the low-wavenumber region of the spectrum shown in Fig. 1. The peak at approximately 215 cm⁻¹ was excluded from the evaluation as it is attributed to local Si-H modes and does, therefore, not contribute to the TA band [25]. The residual area between the baseline and the spectrum is then taken as the intensity of the TA band I_{TA}. Concerning the intensity of the TO band, a baseline parallel to the x-axis is defined by the minimum at 560 cm⁻¹. To reduce the influence of the LO band, only the high-wavenumber side of the TO peak was used for the fitting procedure. Consequently, the area defined by x_{TO}, the chosen baseline, and the spectrum was assigned to half of the phonon intensity $I_{TO/2}$. The MRO parameter I_{MRO} is then calculated as

$$I_{MRO} = 2\frac{I_{TO/2}}{I_{TA}}. \tag{1}$$

This definition is inverse to the one usually used, but it has the advantage that an increase of the value of I_{MRO} also means an increase in structural order.

XRD measurements of selected samples were conducted with a parallel beam of the K_{α}-line of Cu and incident angles between 0.1° and 0.3°. Integration times of 48 h per sample were applied to obtain a sufficient signal-to-noise ratio. The diffractograms consist of contributions from the background, the glass substrate, and a-Si:H and were deconvoluted as shown in Fig. 2 using the software TOPAS [26]. In contrast with [18], the whole signal from the a-Si:H was fitted with two pseudo-Voigt functions. Pseudo-Voigt functions are a linear combination of a Lorentzian and a Gaussian with the same position and FWHM. Those functions were folded with the ratios of the K_{α}-lines of Cu that are published in [27]. Assuming a sufficient

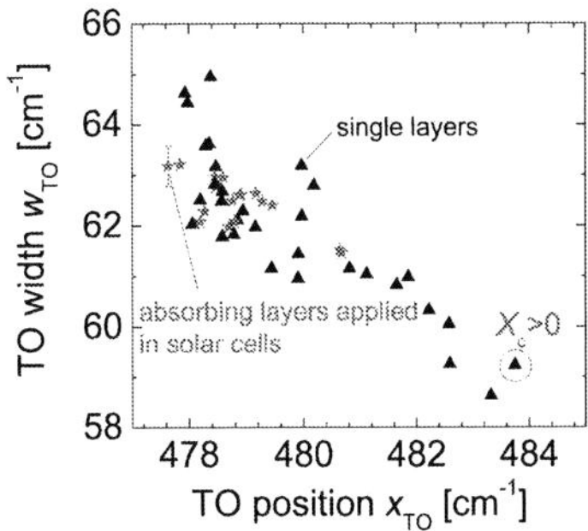

Fig. 3. Plot of the position x_{TO} versus the width w_{TO} of the optical phonon band as evaluated from the Raman spectra. The dominating error was estimated from the homogeneity of the films as derived from different probing positions. As it was similar for all samples, it is exemplarily shown for one data point. The spectrum that exhibits a nonzero crystalline volume fraction is marked with $X_c > 0$.

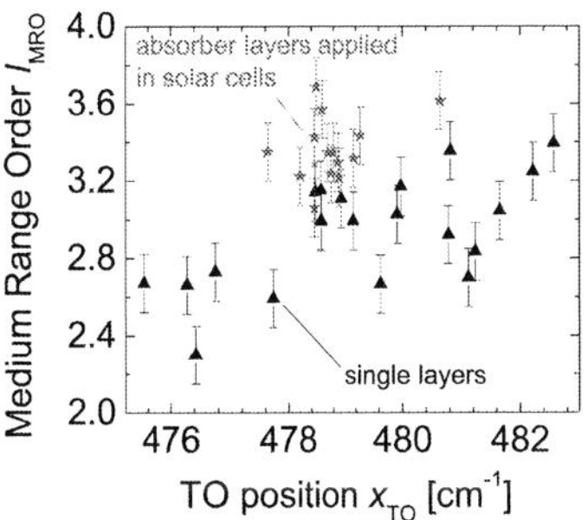

Fig. 4. MRO parameter I_{MRO} as evaluated from Raman spectroscopy plotted versus the TO phonon position x_{TO}.

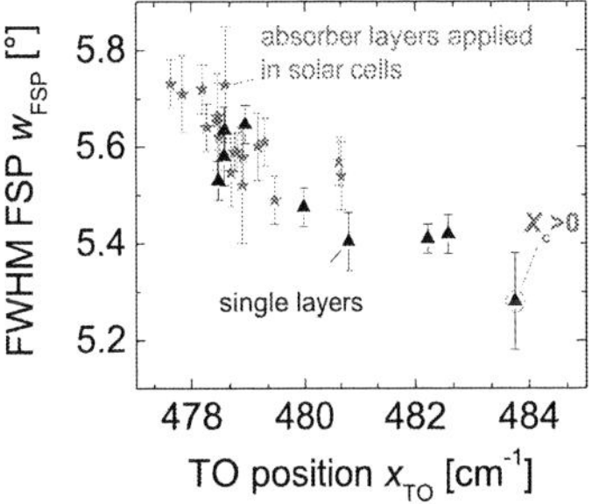

Fig. 5. Width of the FSP w_{FSP} plotted versus the TO phonon position x_{TO}. The error bar is given by the least squares fit of the software TOPAS. The data from the spectrum with a nonzero crystalline volume fraction are marked with $X_c > 0$.

homogeneity of the films, the intensity ratio of the FSP and the second scattering peak was kept constant as well as their ratio of Lorentzian-to-Gaussian contributions. This has the advantage of reducing the amount of free parameters for the fitting procedure. The resulting FWHM of the FSP w_{FSP} was taken as a measure of MRO. A similar approach with a fixed intensity ratio was used to model the glass substrate. Two broad peaks were identified from the pure substrate at 22° and 46°. The latter, however, is not visible in the figure.

Layers that were also used as absorbers in solar cells were deposited by two different methods as published in [28]. The layers were deposited under nominally constant conditions using silane concentrations between 4.6% and 42.8%, power densities of 21 up to 107 mW/cm², and pressures from 0.65 to 4 mbar. Two different excitation frequencies of 13.56 and 60 MHz were used, while the substrate temperature was kept constant at 180 °C for all depositions. The thickness of the absorbing layers in the solar cells was 320–350 nm, whereas the single intrinsic layers had a thickness of around 500 nm. A stack of ZnO/Ag was utilized as the back contact for solar cells. The solar cell efficiencies were measured under standard conditions (AM1.5, 25 °C) before and after prolonged illumination (1000 h, AM1.5, 50 °C, open-circuit conditions).

III. RESULTS

In order to illustrate the parameter range investigated, the correlation between w_{TO} and x_{TO} is shown in Fig. 3 for all samples. Because not all deposition conditions were applied in solar cells, the figure distinguishes between single layers and absorber layers applied in solar cells. The variation of w_{TO} covers a range between 57 and 68 cm⁻¹, which corresponds to mean bond angle deviations $\Delta\theta$ between 7.0° and 8.8° as derived from the equation $w_{\mathrm{TO}} = 15 + 6\,\Delta\theta$ introduced by Beeman et al. [10]. Although the samples were deposited in different systems under various conditions, w_{TO} generally decreases with increasing x_{TO}.

There is one data point marked with $X_c > 0$ that exhibits additional Raman scattering intensities around 520 cm⁻¹. Those intensities are attributed to a crystalline phase of Si.

The corresponding spectrum was fitted with an additional peak around 520 cm⁻¹ to account for a more accurate determination of w_{TO}. The crystalline volume fraction X_c was below 2%. For the evaluation of X_c, an amorphous reference spectrum was fitted to the measured spectrum as sometimes used in the literature [29], [30]. Remarkably, an increase of X_c is accompanied by increased structural order within the amorphous volume, as shown, for example, in [18]. Consequently, a decrease in w_{TO} is expected toward higher crystallinities and the appropriate reference spectrum will change with X_c. This correlation has to be kept in mind for the evaluation of X_c because it bares an additional source for uncertainties.

To demonstrate a correlation between x_{TO} and I_{MRO}, these parameters are plotted in Fig. 4 for selected samples covering the whole range of measured SRO. Despite some scattering, the data from the single layers follow an overall trend of increasing I_{MRO} with increasing x_{TO}. In contrast, the material that was used as an absorber in solar cells exhibits higher values of I_{MRO}, and a general correlation with x_{TO} cannot be confirmed from these data.

To investigate the connection between SRO and MRO derived from Raman spectroscopy and XRD, respectively, the FWHM of the FSP w_{FSP} is plotted versus x_{TO} in Fig. 5. It is important to note that the volume of the samples probed by XRD and Raman spectroscopy differs. From the absorption coefficient α, it can be calculated that for a wavelength of 488 nm approximately 63% (i.e., $1 - 1/e$) of the incident light is absorbed within the

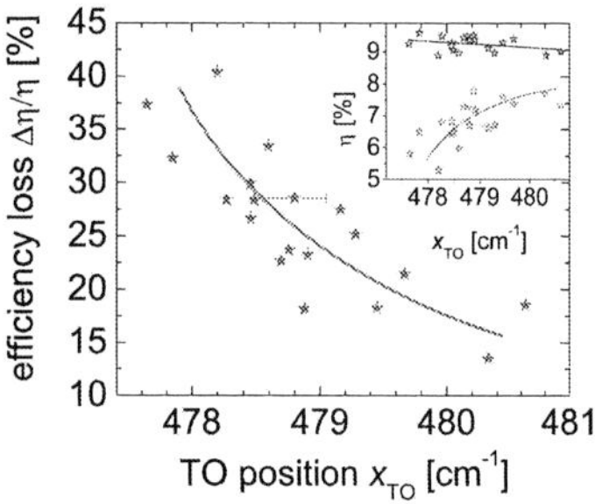

Fig. 6. Relative solar cell efficiency loss (main graph) and solar cell efficiency before and after degradation (inset) plotted versus the position of the TO phonon band x_{TO} obtained by Raman spectroscopy. The dominating error was estimated from the homogeneity of the films as derived from different probing positions. The solid lines are a guide to the eye.

first 60 nm (penetration depth). This means that due to the absorption of the backscattered light, most of the information stems from the topmost 30 nm of the sample (information depth). For X-rays, the penetration depth $\tau_{1/e}$ can be estimated from the incident angle ω and the linear absorption coefficient μ via the relation [31]:

$$\tau_{1/e} = \frac{\sin \omega}{\mu}. \tag{2}$$

With the chosen incident angles between $0.1°$ and $0.3°$ and $\mu = 14.8$ mm^{-1} for Si [31], this gives a penetration depth of 120–470 nm and an according information depth of 60–235 nm. Due to the mounting procedure of the samples for XRD, the exact incident angle could not be determined, which is why these values represent the estimated range of information depths. Despite the fact that the probed volumes for both experiments are not exactly the same, the data correlate over the whole measured range in terms of decreasing w_{FSP} with increasing x_{TO}.

In order to display the influence of structural order on the degradation of a-Si:H devices, the relative efficiency loss of solar cells after light soaking is plotted versus x_{TO} in Fig. 6. After the degradation, the decrease in efficiency is less severe for samples with higher x_{TO}.

The efficiencies before and after degradation are shown in the upper right of the figure. Here, it can be seen that the initial efficiencies scatter between 8.9% and 9.6% with a slight decrease toward higher x_{TO}, whereas the stable efficiencies significantly increase with increasing x_{TO}.

IV. Discussion

To link the structural order to the SWE, it is appropriate to discuss the former parameter first. The width of the optical phonon band w_{TO} can be interpreted as the mean deviation of the bond angle from that of an ideal tetrahedron. This deviation influences the configuration of nearest neighbors, and it accordingly represents a measure of SRO. The data in Fig. 3 show a general correlation of w_{TO} with the position x_{TO} for a reasonably broad range of structural order. This correlation still holds for material with a low crystalline volume fraction which exhibits the highest x_{TO} and almost the narrowest w_{TO}. Assuming the latter being

the most relaxed, i.e., least strained material, the shift of x_{TO} toward lower wavenumbers would indicate tensile stress with respect to the unstrained equilibrium. We also found that as x_{TO} decreases by approximately 1%, the position of the FSP x_{FSP} increases by a similar order of magnitude (not shown). This suggests that variations in bond length affect x_{TO} on a similar scale. In the literature, a volume expansion after light soaking in the order of $\Delta V/V = 10^{-6}$–10^{-5} was observed [8], which results in a relative variation of bond lengths of the same order of magnitude. Such small changes are not detectable with these kinds of experiments. Therefore, it is not surprising that within an experimental error, a change of the values after prolonged illumination was not observed here.

For the single layers that were not included in solar cells, the MRO parameter I_{MRO} increases significantly with higher x_{TO} as can be seen in Fig. 4. However, it is not clear why the samples used as absorbing layers in solar cells tend to show higher values of I_{MRO} and break this trend. An accurate evaluation of I_{MRO} is challenging because the energy shift between the TA phonon band and the exciting laser wavelength is only around 15 meV, while the latter is more intense by a factor of about 10^{11}, which is why these signals are not easy to separate. The absolute values obtained for I_{MRO} are not only influenced by the filter used to cut off the laser intensities, but also by the choice of the baselines as well as the excitation wavelength. These aspects, however, cannot explain the observed deviations because the experimental conditions and the method of evaluation were not altered. There could still be the possibility that a strong correlation of I_{MRO} and x_{TO} or w_{TO} is not generally valid for a-Si:H. It might also be possible that the amount of hydrogen inside the films influences the Raman spectrum in addition to their impact on the structural order of Si atoms.

A comparison of the order parameters derived from XRD and the TO phonon is shown in Fig. 5 to illustrate the correlation between the two different methods that nominally address different length scales. The plot of w_{FSP} versus x_{TO} shows that an increasing x_{TO} correlates with a decreasing w_{FSP}. These findings confirm that variations in the SRO measured by Raman spectroscopy also have a significant impact on the MRO as derived from XRD and vice versa. Consequently, the use of the general term "structural order" is adequate for the question addressed here and it prevents from possible misunderstandings concerning the considered length scales.

The fact that the correlation between x_{TO} and w_{FSP} is much more evident than that between x_{TO} and I_{MRO} begs the question whether I_{MRO} is useful for characterizing the structural order. While XRD basically probes the electron density and hence directly the structural order, the Raman spectrum depends on the bonds between atoms. These bonds are not only influenced by structural order but also by stress or maybe even the presence of hydrogen or charged defects. From this point of view, the interpretation of w_{FSP} as a parameter characterizing the structural order should be favored.

As can be seen from the solar cell efficiencies (see Fig. 6), the SWE is less severe for solar cells in which the absorbing layers show higher values of x_{TO}. Despite the significant variation of the deposition conditions, this trend is clear and we attribute the improved stability of the solar cells to a higher degree of structural order within the absorbing layers. According to the Stutzmann model, weak bonds are attributed to deep tail states. Those bonds can break up under illumination and give rise to defect states within the mobility gap. Thus, a higher degree of structural order is directly linked to a reduction of weak bonds, consequently a lower density of tail states and hence to more stable material.

Fig. 6 also shows that the evaluation of x_{TO} can be a quick method to estimate the relative efficiency loss due to light-induced degradation for the investigated solar cells. The accuracy of this estimation is roughly below $\pm 5\%$ as can be seen from the data. Yet, one has to be careful when applying nonconstant deposition conditions. For this case, detailed depth profiles must be compared with the efficiency loss. Those profiles could be obtained, for example, using different wavelengths or special etching procedures [30], [32], [33].

V. Conclusion

Layers and solar cells of a-Si:H deposited under various conditions were investigated with respect to their structural order and their properties after light-induced degradation. The position and the width of the TO phonon band measured by Raman spectroscopy are often used to characterize the SRO of the material. A correlation of these parameters persists even in material with low crystalline volume fraction indicating an increasing SRO of the amorphous phase also above the onset of microcrystallinity.

The intensity ratio of the TO and the TA phonon band obtained by Raman spectroscopy was evaluated as a measure of the MRO. Only a weak correlation of this parameter with the position of the TO phonon band was observed over a broad range. It was concluded that for our samples, this intensity ratio is hardly useful for estimating the structural order. Contributions from hydrogen or charged dangling bonds might influence the spectra in addition to their impact on the configuration of Si atoms.

As a consequence, the MRO is better reflected in the width of the FSP obtained by XRD measurements. The width of this peak correlates with the position of the phonon band and consequently with the SRO. For the investigated samples, a close interdependence between SRO and MRO can be concluded which is why the general term "structural order" is adequate for the issues addressed here. Even more, a quick fingerprint of the structural order might be obtained simply by evaluating the position of the TO phonon band. A decrease of this parameter was successfully correlated with a relative efficiency loss of amorphous silicon solar cells deposited under nominally constant conditions. This correlation does not only support the Stutzmann model, but it also enables a first quick and easy estimation of the degradation of amorphous silicon solar cells before a time-consuming light soaking procedure.

Acknowledgment

The authors would like to thank W. Appenzeller, C. Grates, W. Fischer, M. Hülsbeck, J. Kirchhoff, D. Weigand, and M. Ziegner for technical support and N. Harder for providing some of the a-Si:H samples. Additionally, U. Rau is gratefully acknowledged for fruitful discussions and his support.

References

[1] D. L. Staebler and C. R. Wronski, "Reversible conductivity changes in discharge-produced amorphous Si," *Appl. Phys. Lett.*, vol. 31, no. 4, pp. 292–294, 1977.

[2] D. E. Carlson, C. Wronski, J. I. Pankove, P. Zanzucchi, and D. Staebler, "Properties of amorphous silicon and a-Si solar cells," *RCA Rev.*, vol. 38, pp. 211–225, 1977.

[3] H. Fritzsche, "Development in understanding and controlling the Staebler-Wronski effect in a-Si:H," *Annu. Rev. Mater. Res.*, vol. 31, pp. 47–79, 2001.

[4] R. A. Street, "Transient photoconductivity studies of the light soaked state of hydrogenated amorphous silicon," *Appl. Phys. Lett.*, vol. 42, no. 6, pp. 507–509, 1983.

[5] D. L. Staebler and C. R. Wronski, "Optically induced conductivity changes in discharge-produced hydrogenated amorphous silicon," *J. Appl. Phys.*, vol. 51, no. 6, pp. 3262–3268, 1980.

[6] M. Stutzmann, W. Jackson, and C. Tsai, "Light-induced metastable defects in hydrogenated amorphous silicon: A systematic study," *Phys. Rev. B*, vol. 32, no. 1, pp. 23–47, Jul. 1985.

[7] H. Fritzsche, "Photo-induced structural changes associated with the Staebler-Wronski effect in hydrogenated amorphous silicon," *Solid State Commun.*, vol. 94, no. 12, pp. 953–955, Jun. 1995.

[8] S. Nonomura, N. Yoshida, T. Gotoh, T. Sakamoto, M. Kondo, A. Matsuda, and S. Nitta, "The light-induced metastable lattice expansion in hydrogenated amorphous silicon," *J. Non-Crystalline Solids*, vol. 266–269, pp. 474–480, May 2000.

[9] S. R. Elliott, "Medium range structural order in covalent amorphous solids," *Nature*, vol. 354, pp. 445–452, 1991.

[10] D. Beeman, R. Tsu, and M. Thorpe, "Structural information from the Raman spectrum of amorphous silicon," *Phys. Rev. B*, vol. 32, no. 2, pp. 874–878, 1985.

[11] R. Tsu, J. Gonzalez-Hernandez, J. Doehler, and S. Ovshinsky, "Order parameters in a-Si systems," *Solid State Commun.*, vol. 46, no. 1, pp. 79–82, 1983.

[12] M. Marinov and N. Zotov, "Model investigation of the Raman spectra of amorphous silicon," *Phys. Rev. B*, vol. 55, no. 5, pp. 2938–2944, 1997.

[13] O. Golikova and V. K. Kudoyarova, "Defects and short-and medium-range order in the structural network of hydrogenated amorphous silicon," *Semiconductors*, vol. 32, no. 7, pp. 779–781, 1998.

[14] S. Muthmann, F. Kohler, R. Carius, and A. Gordijn, "Structural order on different length scales in amorphous silicon investigated by Raman spectroscopy," *Phys. Status Solidi (a)*, vol. 207, no. 3, pp. 544–547, Mar. 2010.

[15] A. Uhlherr and S. Elliott, "Generation of the first sharp diffraction peak by extended-range ordering of atoms and voids in amorphous silicon," *Philosoph. Mag. B*, vol. 71, no. 4, pp. 611–624, 1995.

[16] L. Cervinka, "Several remarks on the medium-range order in glasses," *J. Non-Crystalline Solids*, vol. 232–234, pp. 1–17, Jul. 1998.

[17] K. Tanaka, "Medium-range structure in chalcogenide glasses," *Jpn. J. Appl. Phys.*, vol. 37, pp. 1747–1753, 1998.

[18] D. L. Williamson, "Medium-range order in a-Si:H below and above the onset of microcrystallinity," *Mater. Res. Soc. Symp. Proc.*, vol. 557, pp. 251–261, 1999.

[19] S. Muthmann and A. Gordijn, "Amorphous silicon solar cells deposited with non-constant silane concentration," *Solar Energy Mater. Solar Cells*, vol. 95, no. 2, pp. 573–578, Feb. 2011.

[20] S. Chattopadhyay, S. N. Sharma, R. Banerjee, D. M. Bhusari, S. T. Kshirsagar, Y. Chen, and D. L. Williamson, "Short-range order, microstructure and their correlation with light-induced degradation in hydrogenated amorphous silicon deposited at high growth rates by cathode heating technique," *J. Appl. Phys.*, vol. 76, no. 9, pp. 5208–5213, 1994.

[21] C. Longeaud, J. Kleider, P. Roca i Cabarrocas, S. Hamma, R. Meaudre, and M. Meaudre, "Properties of a new a-Si: H-like material: Hydrogenated polymorphous silicon," *J. Non-Crystalline Solids*, vol. 227, pp. 96–99, 1998.

[22] S. Guha, J. Yang, A. Banerjee, B. Yan, and K. Lord, "High quality amorphous silicon materials and cells grown with hydrogen dilution," *Solar Energy Mater. Solar Cells*, vol. 78, no. 1, pp. 329–347, 2003.

[23] M. Ito and M. Kondo, "Systematic study of photodegradation of tailored nanostructure Si solar cells by controlling their medium range order," *Jpn. J. Appl. Phys., Pt. 2, Lett.*, vol. 45, no. 8, pp. L230–L232, 2006.

[24] M. Brodsky, M. Cardona, and J. Cuomo, "Infrared and Raman spectra of the silicon-hydrogen bonds in amorphous silicon prepared by glow discharge and sputtering," *Phys. Rev. B*, vol. 16, no. 8, pp. 3556–3571, Oct. 1977.

[25] D. Bermejo and M. Cardona, "Raman scattering in pure and hydrogenated amorphous germanium and silicon," *J. Non-Crystalline Solids*, vol. 32, pp. 405–419, Feb. 1979.

[26] TOPAS V4: General profile and structure analysis software for powder diffraction data, Bruker AXS, Billerica, MA, USA, 2008.

[27] H. Berger, "Study of the Kα emission spectrum of copper," *X-Ray Spectrometry*, vol. 15, no. 4, pp. 241–243, Oct. 1986.

[28] T. Zimmermann, A. J. Flikweert, T. Merdzhanova, J. Woerdenweber, A. Gordijn, U. Rau, F. Stahr, K. Dybek, and J. W. Bartha, "Deposition of intrinsic hydrogenated amorphous silicon for thin-film solar cells—A comparative study for layers grown statically by RF-PECVD and dynamically by VHF-PECVD," *Progr. Photovoltaics: Res. Appl.*, Jul. 2012. DOI: 10.1002/pip.2254.

[29] C. Smit, R. van Swaaij, H. Donker, A. Petit, W. Kessels, and M. van de Sanden, "Determining the material structure of microcrystalline silicon from Raman spectra," *J. Appl. Phys.*, vol. 94, no. 5, pp. 3582–3588, 2003.

[30] F. Köhler, S. Schicho, B. Wolfrum, A. Gordijn, S. E. Pust, and R. Carius, "Gradient etching of silicon-based thin films for depth-resolved measurements: The example of Raman crystallinity," *Thin Solid Films*, vol. 520, pp. 2605–2608, Nov. 2012.

[31] M. Birkholz, *Thin Film Analysis by X-Ray Scattering*. Weinheim, Germany: Wiley-VCH Verlag, 2006.

[32] V. Paillard, P. Puech, R. Sirvin, S. Hamma, and P. Roca i Cabarrocas, "Measurement of the in-depth stress profile in hydrogenated microcrystalline silicon thin films using Raman spectrometry," *J. Appl. Phys.*, vol. 90, pp. 3276–3279, 2001.

[33] Y. Mai, S. Klein, R. Carius, J. Wolff, A. Lambertz, F. Finger, and X. Geng, "Microcrystalline silicon solar cells deposited at high rates," *J. Appl. Phys.*, vol. 97, no. 11, p. 114913, 2005.

Authors' photographs and biographies not available at the time of publication.

Potential-Induced Degradation (PID): Introduction of a Novel Test Approach and Explanation of Increased Depletion Region Recombination

Dominik Lausch, Volker Naumann, Otwin Breitenstein, Jan Bauer, Andreas Graff, Jöerg Bagdahn, and Christian Hagendorf

Abstract—In recent years, a detrimental degradation mechanism of solar cells in large photovoltaic fields called potential-induced degradation (PID) has been intensively investigated and discussed. Here, the module efficiency is decreasing down to a fractional part of their original efficiency. In this study, we introduce a PID test at a solar-cell level and for individual module components applicable as a tool for process control in industries and root cause analyses in science departments. Using the proposed method, one example analysis of a solar cell that is degraded by the PID tester is presented. It is shown that PID of the shunting type influences both the parallel resistance (R_p) and the depletion region recombination behavior (J_{02}) of the solar cell. Increased recombination in the depletion region is caused by Na decorated stacking faults crossing the depletion region. This strongly influences recombination behavior in the depletion region, leading to an increased J_{02} and an ideality factor $n_2 > 2$. However, the defects leave the base of the solar cell primarily unaffected, and hence, J_{01} recombination remains rather low. Based on these findings, a model for the shunting and the increased depletion region recombination behavior is discussed.

Index Terms—Crystal defect, potential-induced degradation (PID), recombination.

I. Introduction

ONE of the most important advantages of photovoltaic (PV) technology is its low cost of maintenance and a lifetime of over 30 years. Nevertheless, several degradation mechanisms can decrease solar efficiencies or destroy PV modules. Potential-induced degradation (PID) of crystalline Si solar cells is one of the main degradation mechanisms and has been intensively investigated since the affect was reported more than two years ago [1], [2]. This effect has been most pronounced in large field installations of PV modules that are fabricated using p-type solar cells. In conventional PV systems under working conditions, a voltage difference of a few hundred volts between the framing and the solar cells of a module can occur. If the modules/cells are not resistant to PID, the degradation mechanism can result in yield losses of 20% or more. According to recent publications, the PID shunting effect (PID-s) is the most relevant type of PID [3]–[5]. However, it has also been shown that PID-s can also influence the recombination behavior of the solar cell [3], [6]. In this paper, it is shown that these recombination processes mainly influence the second diode (J_{02}) that is caused by increased recombination in the depletion region because of Na-decorated stacking faults.

To prevent PID in the field, either every solar cell in the module, or module components such as encapsulants or glass must be PID resistant. For PID testing, various methods exist at module and solar-cell level. Generally, PID susceptibility is tested in a climate chamber [7] (damp heat, 85 °C, 85% relative humidity, −1000 V, 48-h test time) or in a water bath on the module level [1]. However, for such tests, a module or minimodule must be prepared, and a climate chamber is necessary.

At the cell level, to prevent PID, the solar cell must be resistant to PID-s. One way to achieve this is to optimize the antireflection coating (ARC). However, in a module every solar cell has to be resistant to PID. To test resistance to PID-s, a quick and direct process control method is required. To test PID susceptibility on a solar-cell level, a high-voltage stress test by corona discharge can be used [4], [8]. Here, a voltage stress of around 20 keV is used. However, single-module components, i.e., encapsulants and glass, cannot be tested using this method. In addition, only single positions to where the cathode is pointing can be tested for PID susceptibility. The high-voltage stress can also lead to a transformation of the SiN, often leading to a visible permanent discoloration on the SiN layer. Repeatability using this method is also difficult since the charging is dependent on climatic factors such as humidity and temperature. Hence, the corona PID test needs well-defined environmental conditions. For an alternative method, a test was proposed in which the solar cell is connected by tab ribbons, with glass-EVA laminates on both sides. Subsequently, the whole sample is then placed in a climate chamber to perform the PID test. However, it was concluded that this method did not work, and laminated minimodules were again produced [7].

Manuscript received June 10, 2013; revised July 26, 2013, November 12, 2013, and December 9, 2013; accepted December 10, 2013.

D. Lausch, V. Naumann J. Bagdahn, and C. Hagendorf are with the Fraunhofer Center for Silicon Photvoltaics CSP, D-06120 Halle (Saale), Germany (e-mail: dominik.lausch@csp.fraunhofer.de; volker.naumann@csp.fraunhofer.de; joerg.bagdahn@csp.fraunhofer.de; christian.hagendorf@csp.fraunhofer.de).

O. Breitenstein and J. Bauer are with the Max Planck Institute of Microstructure Physics, 06120 Halle, Germany (e-mail: breiten@mpi-halle.mpg.de; jbauer@mpi halle.mpg.de).

A. Graff is with the Fraunhofer Institute for Mechanics of Materials IWM, Walter-Hülse Str. 1, 06120 Halle (Saale), Germany (e-mail: a.graff@iwmh.fraunhofer.de).

Color versions of one or more of the figures in this paper are available online at http://ieeexplore.ieee.org.

Digital Object Identifier 10.1109/JPHOTOV.2014.2300238

In this paper, a method to test the resistance against PID on the solar-cell level close to field conditions is introduced in Section III it is capable of testing individual solar cells as well as individual module components. Subsequently, a root cause analysis of a solar cell that is degraded by the PID tester is shown in Section IV, highlighting the influence of PID-s on the shunting and recombination behavior of the solar cell. In order to discuss the increased recombination behavior, a root cause analysis down to the nanometer scale is shown in Section V. Finally, a discussion about a model recently introduced [5] explaining the influence of PID-s on shunting and recombination behavior of the solar cell is presented in Section VI.

II. Experimental Details

The solar cells that are analyzed in this study are full-square monocrystalline silicon (mono-Si) solar cells produced in a commercial environment. The solar cells were degraded by the PID tester as it will be described in Section III. Electroluminescence (EL) images have been acquired with a coolSamBa HR-830 Si camera. The dark lock-in thermography (DLIT) measurements were performed with equipment from Thermosensorik, which offers the opportunity to increase the lateral resolution by different lenses. For more information, see [9]. The scanning electron microscopy (SEM) and electron-beam-induced current (EBIC) were acquired with a SU-70 (Hitachi) tool that is equipped with an EBIC system DISS 5 by point electronic. The electron beam energy for SEM and EBIC was varied between 3 and 30 keV.

Chemical information was measured by time-of-flight secondary ion mass spectroscopy (ToF-SIMS) within a TOF.SIMS 5 by IONTOF with a pulsed Bi primary ion beam scanning over the sample surface. ToF-SIMS depth profiling uses an additional O^{2+} (1 keV) sputter beam for planar erosion of surficial layers. Cross sections have been prepared by focused ion beam (FIB) and imaged by SEM/EBIC. Cross-sectional lamellae have been imaged by scanning transmission electron microscopy (STEM) in FEI TITAN^3 G2 60-300 equipped with spherical aberration correction and a Super-X EDX detector.

III. Introduction of a Novel Test Approach

An experimental setup for PID testing at solar-cell level was developed in order to provide a quick and easy tool for research and process control. With this setup, it is also possible to test partially fabricated solar cells such as wafers with ARC coating. Furthermore, individual module components such as special glasses or alternative foils as encapsulants can be tested as well. This opens the opportunity to test materials and solar cells before an application into the production processes. Here, a few test samples out of the production shall be tested in regular time steps for process control. Additionally, based on a special foil treatment, the solar cell can easily be delaminated without leaving residual contaminations on the solar-cell surface, hence, giving the possibility of performing advanced root cause analysis.

The prototype of the PID tester is shown in Fig. 1. The PID test is performed as follows: The solar cell is placed on a temperature-controlled aluminum chuck to achieve a constant

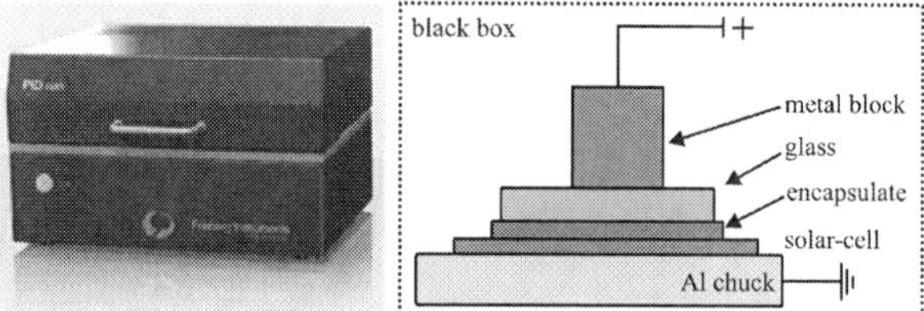

Fig. 1. (Left) PID tester by Freiberg Instruments. (Right) Simplified sketch of the specimen stacking which is similar to the structure of PV modules is visualized.

temperature throughout the testing process. On the front side, a layer of foil and a sheet of glass are placed on top of the solar cell. The specimen stack is shown schematically on the right side of Fig. 1. The stack can be made with all possible materials, but in this paper, only standard materials are used. To measure the solar-cell parameters, electrical contact to the front surface of the solar cell is realized by a contact needle (which is located outside the test region) and electrical contact at the rear is realized by the aluminum chuck. A solid metal block is then placed on top of the front glass to achieve a uniform high voltage across the glass surface within the test area. The test can be performed on samples with or without laminating the foil to the solar cell. Without the lamination process, it is possible to detach the foil after testing and allow for further investigations. A voltage of up to 1000 V is then applied. Under field conditions, the frame and subsequently the glass are grounded, leaving the solar cell at a negative potential. As only the potential difference is important for PID, in our test a positive voltage is applied to the solid metal block, and therefore, the glass surface and ground to the rear contact of the solar cell through the aluminum chuck. During the degradation, the shunt resistance, the I–V curve of the solar cells, and the HV ionic/leakage current can be measured. For our tests, we do not laminate the foil to allow for further investigations. Since the specimen stack approximates the module structure, standard module materials are used. We also use a voltage of 600 V and temperature of 80 °C, similar to that which occur under field operation. Therefore, we assume that test procedure is performed under realistic conditions close to what is experienced in the field, and hence, the results should be trustworthy. However, a conductive layer on top of the solar glass at temperatures of about 80 °C can be doubted since the wet glass surface will dry quickly under real conditions, although the electric field will be still present at the frame. Nevertheless, the method will still be close to standard test conditions. If the standard test conditions for PID are different from those used in this study, then the test procedure can be easily adapted to more appropriate conditions. In addition, all comparisons between our tester and module tests in climate chambers have shown equal results.

In order to test alternative encapsulants and glasses, a PID-prone solar cell has to be used for the PID test. If the solar cell is not PID affected, the encapsulants and glasses, respectively, are preventing PID.

In Fig. 2(a), a dark I–V curve is shown as an example measurement of a solar cell before (black) and after (red) the PID

     330

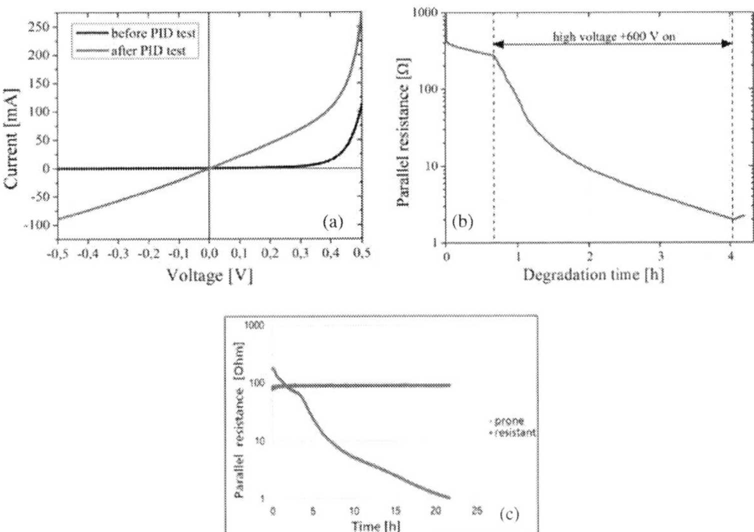

Fig. 2. (a) Dark I–V curve of a solar cell before (black) and after (red) PID test of a 4×4 cm^2 area at 600 V, (b) degradation of the parallel resistance of a tested solar cell, and (c) parallel resistance throughout the test for a solar cell with an encapsulant prone to and resistant to PID.

test of a 4×4 cm^2 area at 600 V. A distinct ohmic behavior of the solar cell is indicated by the linear I–V characteristic around $U = 0$ V. However, the slightly curved shape of the I–V curve for higher voltage indicates the presence of an additional nonlinear current component. The parallel resistance R_p was measured every 30 s during the whole test by applying a voltage $U = -0.1$ V at the solar cell for the duration of each measurement. The time dependence of the degradation is shown in Fig. 2(b). During the test, R_p decreases until the voltage is turned OFF. This indicates PID-s degradation of the solar cell by the PID tester, as has been shown from field experiments by Taubitz et al. [6]. In Fig. 2(c), a PID test of the same solar cell with a PID resistant and a PID-prone encapsulant is shown. The R_p of the solar cell that is tested with the PID resistant encapsulant is nearly constant over the whole test duration, proving that the encapsulant is preventing PID, whereas the R_p decreases when using a PID-prone encapsulant. This result is further supported by tests at the module level.

Since the introduced method uses the same material stack as well as the same materials for the stack as used for modules, and the voltage and temperature is as occurring under field operation (of up to 1000 V and 90 °C), it can be assumed that the introduced procedure is testing on PID susceptibility of solar cells or module components rather than other degradation mechanisms, as could be the case for different test procedures.

IV. Characteristics of Potential-Induced Degradation-s on the Solar-Cell Level

As can be seen in Fig. 2(b) and (c), respectively, R_p is strongly decreased after PID, as shown in [1]. In addition to this, Taubitz et al. [6] and Hacke et al. [3] have shown that the illuminated I–V characteristic cannot be fitted by a decreased R_p alone. It was shown that a second diode must be added in order to

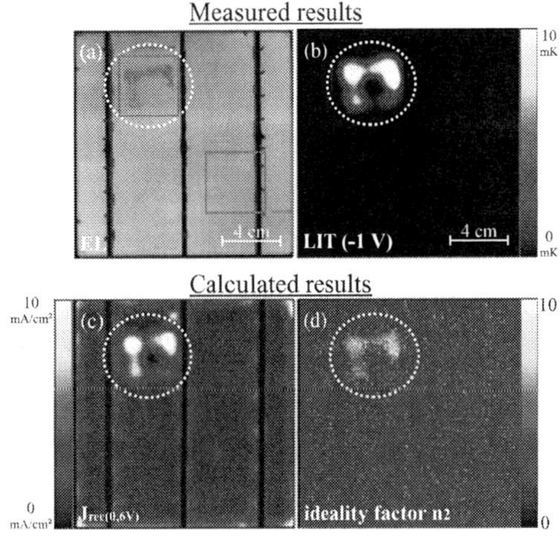

Fig. 3. (a) EL image of a degraded solar cell (measured). The green marked regions have been taken out for dark I–V measurements. (b) DLIT image at -1 V. The shunted region is revealed by the increased DLIT signal (measured). (c) J_{02} distribution calculated from four DLIT measurements at different voltages according to [11] (calculated). (d) Ideality factor n_2 (calculated), scaled from 2 to 10. The PID-s region exhibits a strongly increased J_{02} and an ideality factor n_2 up to 7.

fit the illuminated I–V curve correctly. We assume that this is because of an increased recombination process at PID-s-affected positions. If this is the case, the recombination takes place in the depletion region. This assumption will become clear throughout this paper. This would result in an increased J_{02} and high ideality factor $n_2 > 2$ and will be discussed later.

In Fig. 3(a), an EL image of a PID-s-degraded full-square mono-Si solar cell is shown. The solar cell was PID-s degraded on a 4×4 cm^2 area, which is characterized by a strongly decreased EL signal between the busbars [marked by a white circle in Fig. 3(a)]. In Fig. 3(b), a DLIT image of the same solar cell at -1 V is shown. The DLIT image reveals that strong shunts in the PID-s-affected area are in good agreement with previous results [10]. As already discussed, PID-s degradation results in a strong local decrease of R_p.

Based on a procedure introduced by Breitenstein [11], it is possible to calculate the local I–V curves out of four different DLIT measurements. In addition, the parameters of the two-diode model of each pixel can be imaged, including the ideality factor n_2 of the depletion region recombination current. For this, we have performed DLIT analyses at -1 V, 500, 550, and 600 mV. J_{01} shows a rather even distribution over the whole solar cell (not shown here). Small deviations at the contacts can be observed. These deviations could be caused by a laterally varying serial resistance (R_S). In our calculations, R_S is assumed to be constant. In contrast with this, J_{02} is strongly increased at the degraded area, which can be seen in Fig. 3(c). Based on these results, it is assumed that at PID-s-affected sites, a strong recombination process in the depletion region takes place since J_{02} is influenced by recombination processes within the depletion region. An increased J_{02} can also be observed at the corners of the solar cell. This can be expected if the p-n junction is opened poorly there, having a large number of defects [12]. In Fig. 3(d), the calculated ideality factor n_2 is shown. Fig. 3(d) shows that the ideality factor in severely PID-s-affected areas reaches local values of up to 7.

Strongly increased J_{02} values and ideality factors larger than 2 for PID-s-affected areas can also be observed in multicrystalline Si (multi-Si) solar cells. In contrast with mono-Si, the increased J_{02} in multi-Si solar cells is subjected to recombination-active defect structures, in particular so-called type-A defects [13], which can also result in an increased J_{02}. However, J_{02} for PID-s-affected areas is much higher than that caused by recombination-active defects.

In order to confirm the DLIT results, we have taken two regions out of the degraded solar cell as marked with the green rectangles in Fig. 3(a). In Fig. 4, the dark I–V characteristics of these regions (a PID affected and a reference region) are shown. To discuss the solar-cell parameters, we have fitted the curves with the two-diode model. The parallel resistance of the PID-affected region is about 500 $\Omega \cdot \text{cm}^2$ which is drastically reduced compared with 33 k$\Omega \cdot \text{cm}^2$ of the reference position. The recombination current J_{02} of the PID-affected region is about 5×10^{-16} A/cm^2 and, hence, clearly higher compared with the reference region (1×10^{-19} A/cm^2). The J_{01} currents are quite similar. The calculated ideality factor n_2 of the whole PID-affected region is approximately $n_2 = 3.2$: lower than that determined by the DLIT analysis. However, the n_2 value of the I–V curve is the mean value of the whole region and therefore, includes regions which are not degraded. Hence, the I–V curve analysis confirms the DLIT measurements.

V. Microscopic Investigation of Potential-Induced Degradation

In Fig. 5(a), a DLIT image at -1 V and high magnification can be seen. Two PID-s positions marked with a white-dotted

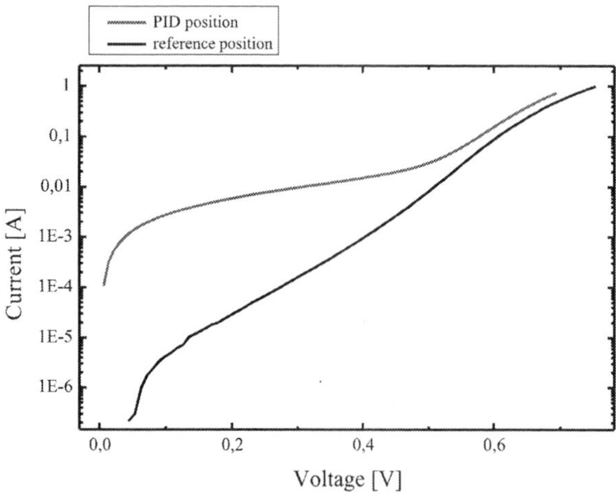

Fig. 4. Dark I–V curve of the two samples which were taken out of the degraded solar cell [marked in Fig. 3(a) with a green rectangle].

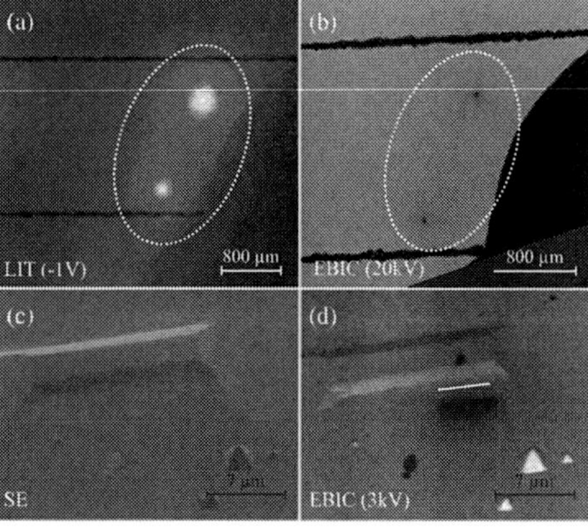

Fig. 5. (a) DLIT image at high magnification of two PID-s positions. (b) EBIC (20 kV) of the same region. The PID-s positions can be seen as reduced EBIC signal. (c) SE image at 3 kV of a PID-s position. No evidence as root cause for PID-s can be seen. (d) EBIC image at 3 kV. Here, PID-s is characterized by a line-shaped reduced EBIC signal.

circle between two contact fingers have been obtained. The EBIC signal at these positions is drastically reduced, as seen in the EBIC image in Fig. 5(b) (20-kV acceleration voltage). In general, the PID-s-affected areas are very localized, as shown in [10]. In Fig. 5(c) and (d), a PID-s-affected area is investigated by SE imaging (c) and EBIC (d) in high magnification and with a lower acceleration voltage 3 kV. Here, two important facts should be emphasized: 1) The SE image in Fig. 5(c) shows no particular feature visible at the surface except small pyramids and the edges of truncated pyramids since the mono-Si solar cell is weakly alkaline textured [14]. 2) The EBIC signal in Fig. 5(d) is reduced and visualized by the white line. The line is approximately 4 μm long and parallel to the pyramidal structures; hence, the long axis of PID-s-affected areas appears to be oriented along a $\langle 1\,1\,0 \rangle$ direction. The fact that the line has one sharp and one smooth edge indicates that the corresponding defect is lying inclined to the (1 0 0) surface [15] because at this

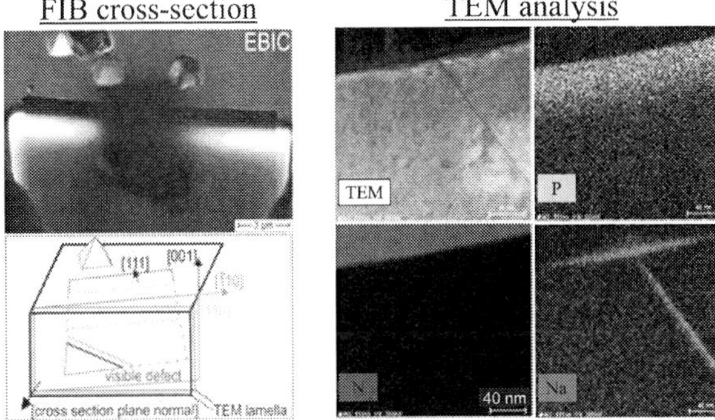

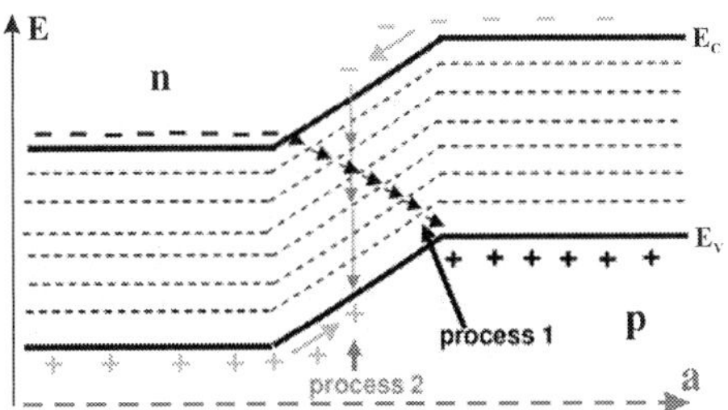

Fig. 6.   (Left) Cross-sectional EBIC view of a shunt position. A disturbed p-n junction and a distinct linear region with low signal both in cross section and on the surface can be seen. The scheme is visualizing the geometrical position of the crystal defect (taken from [15]). (Right) STEM analysis of a FIB-lamella showing a PID-s degraded stacking fault that hits the Si surface. The elemental intensities were measured by EDX in STEM mode (taken from [16]).

Fig. 7.   Band structure along a Na decorated stacking fault [5]. The defect states are illustrated with dotted lines. For sufficiently high concentration levels of Na, hopping conduction of carriers can occur via the introduced defect levels (process 1). For lower concentration levels, electrons and holes can recombine via these defect levels under forward bias in the depletion region, leading to an increased J_{02} and n_2 (process 2). Here, the carriers are generated by illumination.

surface, electrons have a high collection probability, and the interaction volume with the electron beam is small, resulting in a high lateral resolution. Within the silicon material, the signal is blurred because of carrier diffusion and the collection probability of carriers which are generated near the defect. The same behavior has been observed at over 30 different PID-s-affected areas of different samples, even on multi-Si solar cells. It should be noted that in multi-Si solar cells PID-s-affected areas are not located at grain boundaries [1].

For mapping the chemical information at these positions, ToF-SIMS was employed. In [5], an EBIC image of the degraded area was overlaid with a laterally resolved reconstruction of the measured Na intensity near the SiN/Si interface. It was shown that Na accumulates at positions that coincide well with PID-s-affected areas. Additionally, a significant increase of the Na signal was clearly visible at the SiN/Si interface.

In order to localize defects within the Si material and to discuss the increased recombination, cross sections have been prepared toward the shunt position by FIB as shown in detail elsewhere [16]. Here, only the main results shall be summarized to conclude the paper. The EBIC image of the FIB cross section in Fig. 6 reveals a well-defined p-n junction that is weakened substantially over a length of $\sim 10~\mu$m at this PID-s-affected site. Below the location of the weakened p-n junction, a region which is located 0–4 μm below the emitter region shows a drastically reduced EBIC signal. In addition, a darker line indicates a line of defects within the area. These observations can be explained by a plane-like defect, which is lying in the [1 1 1] plane [15]. In Fig. 6, the geometrical situation at the FIB cross section of this defect is visualized. The red line indicates the puncture point of the defect in the cross section. Note that the cross section is not perfectly parallel to the base of the pyramidal structures.

In order to investigate structural properties and elemental composition of individual PID shunts on a nanometer scale, TEM experiments, including elemental analyses (EDX), have been performed in [16]. A FIB-lamella has been prepared at this position for TEM analysis. The TEM imaging at the lamella in

Fig. 6 (right) shows a tilted defect line (a crystal defect) which is lying mainly in the depletion region. The crystal defect is assigned to a stacking fault lying in the [1 1 1] plane, which has been shown previously [9], [11]. Cross sections at nine different PID-s-affected sites have all revealed stacking faults in {1 1 1} planes. In the following, the main results of the EDX measurements in STEM mode will be summarized in order to discuss the observed results. The SiN layer is indicated by a high EDX signal for N (yellow color in Fig. 6). An interlayer that contains O is clearly detected in the SiN/Si interface region (not shown here). The most important result is that the stacking fault is clearly decorated by Na impurities visualized in green in the TEM analysis in Fig. 6. In addition, Na is also detected in the SiO_x interlayer, where the stacking fault touches the interface.

VI. Discussion

Based on our results, the following facts can be claimed as partly done in [5] and [15]: 1) PID-s is influencing the parallel resistance (R_p) and the recombination behavior (J_{02} and n_2) of the solar cell. 2) The PID-s effect is not affecting the whole area but only single microscopic areas. [5], [15]. 3) At PID-s-affected areas, Na atoms have always been detected [5], [15]. 4) PID-s-affected sites always show modified stacking faults decorated with Na atoms which touch the surface [5], [15].

The stacking faults are considered to be present prior to degradation. However, they appear to accumulate Na during PID. In this contribution, the dynamics of Na movement through the SiN layer and at the interfaces or even at the stacking faults will not be discussed. For this discussion, see [11] and [17]. In this contribution, only the shunting and, in particular, the recombination processes will be discussed.

In [16], it is shown that quantitative evaluations of the EDX data for Si and Na reveal an areal density of Na atoms of approximately 6×10^{14} cm^{-2} in the stacking fault plane. Therefore, we assume a density of Na within the stacking fault in an order of magnitude that corresponds to one Si monolayer. In our case, Na atoms should be constrained to the stacking fault plane, probably located on interstitial sites. Since, in metallic Na, the Fermi level is lying in a continuum of states, it can be assumed that the Na atoms lead to a band of gap states at multiple energies within the Si band gap, as sketched in Fig. 7. The blue-dashed arrow in Fig. 7 visualizes a path along the stacking fault, starting from the SiN/Si interface through the emitter across the p-n junction into the base where Na can travel. Here, it depends on the local defect level concentration and how this defect acts electronically.

If the local defect level concentration in the PID-s-affected area is very high, the defect orbitals of neighbored levels overlap, enabling hopping conduction for charge carriers under forward and reverse bias. Then, the monolayer acts like a quasi-metallic Na plane. This process needs no thermal activation and, therefore, leads to an ohmic conductivity across the p-n junction. Therefore, process 1 in Fig. 7 would explain the detrimental decrease of the parallel resistance R_p.

In addition to this, under injection conditions these defect levels will offer recombination paths for interlevel recombination of the electrons and holes in the depletion region (process 2 in Fig. 7). This process can occur already at a relatively low concentration level, where lateral hopping conduction has yet to occur. Process 2 is thermally activated and should lead to an increased J_{02} with an ideality factor n_2 larger than 2, as described by Steingrube et $al.$ [12], because the density of defects is still sufficiently high such that recombination does not occur via isolated defect states, but rather occurs via coupled defect states. Additionally, it was shown in Fig. 6 that the stacking fault which is only about 3 μm in length is crossing the depletion region. Hence, the fact that the decorated stacking fault is mainly influencing the recombination behavior in the depletion region coincides well with our experimental results. In Section IV, an increased J_{02} and an ideality factor larger than 2 was clearly observed by LIT and single dark I–V curve measurements. The charge carriers in Fig. 7 are generated by illumination (light gray in Fig. 7) as minority carriers and recombine via the defect states within the depletion region. However, the measurements in this paper were done under electrical injection. Nevertheless, the physical recombination process is assumed to be identical.

VII. Summary

In this paper, we have introduced a PID test for solar-cell level and module components that is applicable as a tool for process control in industries and for root cause analysis in the laboratory. In addition, an analysis of a solar cell that is degraded by the PID tester is performed. It is shown that PID of the shunting type is influencing both the parallel resistance (R_p) and the depletion region recombination behavior (J_{02}) of the solar cell. The increased recombination in the depletion region is caused by Na-decorated stacking fault crossing the depletion region and, hence, influencing the recombination behavior of the depletion region strongly, reflected by an increased J_{02} and n_2 larger than 2. Since the stacking fault ends only a few micrometers below the surface, the base of the solar cell is primarily unaffected; hence, the J_{01} recombination is not increased. Based on these results, a model explaining the influence of PID-s on the shunting, as well as on the recombination behavior of the solar cell, was discussed. In particular, the increased J_{02} recombination is explained by

an interlevel recombination of the electrons and holes in the depletion region at defect states caused by the Na-decorated stacking fault.

References

[1] S. Pingel, O. Frank, M. Winkler, S. Daryan, T. Geipel, H. Hoehne, and J. Berghold, "Potential induced degradation of solar cells and panels," in *Proc. 35th IEEE Photovoltaic Spec. Conf.*, Honolulu, HI, USA, 2010, pp. 002817–002822.

[2] J. Berghold, O. Frank, H. Hoehne, S. Pingel, B. Richardson, and M. Winkler, "Potential induced degradation of solar cells and panels," in *Proc. 25th Eur. Photovoltaic Sol. Energy Conf. Exhib.*, Valencia, Spain, 2010, pp. 3753–3759.

[3] P. Hacke, K. Terwilliger, R. Smith, S. Glick, J. Pankow, M. Kempe, S. Bennett, and M.o. Kloos, "System voltage potential-induced degradation mechanisms in PV modules and methods for test," in *Proc. 37th IEEE Photovoltaic Spec. Conf.*, Seattle, WA, USA, 2011, pp. 814–820.

[4] H. Nagel, A. Metz, and K. Wangemann, "Crystalline Si solar cells and modules featuring excellent stability against potential-induced degradation," in *Proc. 26th Eur. Photovoltaic Sol. Energy Conf. Exhib.*, Hamburg, Germany, 2011, pp. 3107–3112.

[5] V. Naumann, D. Lausch, A. Hähnel, J. Bauer, O. Breitenstein, A. Graff, M. Werner, S. Swatek, S. Großer, J. Bagdahn, and C. Hagendorf, "Explanation of potential-induced degradation of the shunting type by Na decoration of stacking faults in Si solar cells," *Sol. Energy Mater. Sol. Cells*, vol. 120, pp. 383–389, 2013.

[6] C. Taubitz, M. Schütze, and M. B. Köntopp, "Towards a kinetic model of potential-induced shunting," in *Proc. 27th Eur. Photovoltaic Sol. Energy Conf. Exhib.*, 2012, pp. 3172–3176.

[7] S. Koch, C. Seidel, P. Grunow, S. Krauter, and M. Schoppa, "Polarization effects and tests for crystalline silicon cells," presented at the 26th Eur. Photovoltaic Solar Energy Conf. Exhib., Hamburg, Germany, 2011.

[8] M. Schütze, M. Junghänel, O. Friedrichs, R. Wichtendahl, M. Scherff, J. Müller, and P. Wawer, "Investigations of potential induced degradation of silicon photovoltaic modules," presented at the 26th Eur. Photovoltaic Solar Energy Conf. Exhib., Hamburg, Germany, 2011.

[9] B. Otwin and M. Langenkamp, *Lock-In Thermography: Basics and Use for Functional Diagnostics of Electronic Components.* vol. 10, New York, NY, USA: Springer, 2003.

[10] J. Bauer, V. Naumann, S. Großer, C. Hagendorf, M. Schütze, and O. Breitenstein, "On the mechanism of potential-induced degradation in crystalline silicon solar cells," *Phys. Status Solidi*, vol. 6, no. 8, pp. 331–333, 2012.

[11] O. Breitenstein, "Nondestructive local analysis of current–voltage characteristics of solar cells by lock-in thermography," *Sol. Energy Mater. Sol. Cells*, vol. 95, pp. 2933–2936, 2011.

[12] S. Steingrube, O. Breitenstein, K. Ramspeck, S. Glunz, A. Schenk, and P. Altermatt, "Explanation of commonly observed shunt currents in c-Si solar cells by means of recombination statistics beyond the Shockley–Read–Hall approximation," *J. Appl. Phys.*, vol. 110, pp. 014515-1–014515-10, 2011.

[13] D. Lausch, K. Petter, R. Bakowskie, J. Bauer, O. Breitenstein, and C. Hagendorf. "Classification and investigation of recombination-active defect structures in multicrystalline silicon solar cells," in *Proc. 27th Eur. Photovoltaic Solar Energy Conf. Exhib.*, Frankfurt, Germany, 2012, pp. 723–728.

[14] H. Seidel, L. Csepregi, A. Heuberger, and H. Baumgärtel, "Anisotropic etching of crystalline silicon in alkaline solutions," *J. Electrochem. Soc.*, vol. 137, no. 11, pp. 3612–3626, 1990.

[15] V. Naumann, "Microstructural analysis of crystal defects leading to potential-induced degradation (PID) of Si solar cells," *Energy Procedia*, vol. 33, pp. 76–83, 2013.

[16] V. Naumann, D. Lausch, A. Graff, M. Werner, S. Swatek, J. Bauer, A. Hähnel, O. Breitenstein, S. Großer, J. Bagdahn, and C. Hagendorf, "The role of stacking faults for the formation of shunts during potential-induced degradation of crystalline Si solar cells," *Phys. Status Solidi*, vol. 7, no. 5, pp. 315–318, 2013.

[17] M. Schütze, M. Junghanel, M. B. Koentopp, S. Cwikla, S. Friedrich, J. W. Muller, and P. Wawer, "Laboratory study of potential induced degradation of silicon photovoltaic modules," in *Proc. 37th IEEE Photovoltaic Spec. Conf.*, Seattle, WA, USA, 2011, pp. 821–826.

Dominik Lausch received the diploma degree in physics from the University of Leipzig, Leipzig, Germany, in 2009. During his studies, he was with the company Q-Cells SE on various subjects, including his diploma thesis about the pre-breakdown luminescence of silicon solar cells. In 2012, he received the Ph.D. degree in natural science from the University of Halle, Halle, Germany, in cooperation with the Fraunhofer Center for Silicon Photovoltaics CSP, Halle, and Q-Cells SE, Thalheim, Germany. His dissertation explored the subject of the "*Influence of recombination active defects on the electrical properties of recombination active defects in silicon solar cells,*" which received the PVSEC Student Award in 2012.

He is now a postdoctoral researcher with the Fraunhofer Center for Silicon Photovoltaics CSP, where he is currently dealing with plasma texturing and hydrogen passivation topics.

Andreas Graff received the Diploma in physics from the RWTH Aachen, Aachen, Germany, in 1995 and the Ph.D. degree in physics from the University of Halle, Halle, Germany, in 1999 for the investigations of interface structures during solid-state reactions. The experiments were done at the Max Planck Institute for Microstructure Physics, Halle.

He then spent 3 years with the IFW Dresden, Dresden, Germany, where he worked with analytical transmission electron microscopy (TEM), mostly on carbon-based materials. He joined the Fraunhofer Institute of Mechanics of Materials, Halle, in 2004, where he has been investigating defects in semiconductor devices by analytical TEM with the Center for Applied Microstructure Diagnostics (CAM).

Volker Naumann received the degree in physics from the Martin-Luther-University Halle-Wittenberg, Germany, in Electric properties and microstructure of local contacts on silicon solar cells, in 2009. Currently, he is a young researcher and is pursuing the Ph.D. degree with the Fraunhofer Center for Silicon Photovoltaics CSP (Halle) and Martin-Luther-University Halle-Wittenberg, working on electrical and microstructure characterization of photovoltaic materials and processes.

He is particularly focussed on microstructural diagnostics and elemental analyses of antireflective layers with respect to PID shunting phenomena of crystalline Si-solar cells.

Christian Hagendorf received the Ph.D. degree from the Martin-Luther-University Halle-Wittenberg, Germany, in the field of surface and interface analysis of semiconductor materials.

He is head of the research group "Solar Cell Diagnostics" with the Fraunhofer Center for Silicon Photovoltaics CSP, Germany. He joined Fraunhofer CSP in 2007 and established a research group focussed on defect diagnostics in crystalline and thin-film photovoltaics. His research activities rely on electrical, microstructural, and trace elemental characterization of solar cells and modules.

Otwin Breitenstein received the Ph.D. degree in physics from the University of Leipzig, Leipzig, Germany, in 1980.

Since 1992, he has been with the Max Planck Institute of Microstructure Physics, Halle, Germany, where he investigated defects in semiconductors. Since 1999, he has been using lock-in thermography for detecting internal shunts in silicon solar cells. In 2001, he introduced this technique on a microscopic scale for isolating faults in integrated circuits.

He gives lectures on photovoltaics at Halle University and is author of a book on Lock-in Thermography. He has published more than 200 contributions in scientific journals and international conference proceedings.

Jörg Bagdahn received the diploma and the Ph.D. degrees in material science from the Technical University of Chemnitz and Martin-Luther-University, Halle, Germany, respectively.

From 2000 until 2002, he was a postdoctoral fellow with Johns Hopkins University, Baltimore, MD, USA, working on long term reliability of thin silicon films. In 2003, he joined the Fraunhofer Institute for Mechanics of Materials, where he worked as a group leader and later on as head of the department "Microelectronics and Microsystems." Since 2007, he has been the director of the Fraunhofer Center for Silicon Photovoltaics CSP. Since 2008, he has held a professorship for "Photovoltaic Materials" with the Anhalt University of Applied Sciences.

Jan Bauer received the Diploma in physics from the University of Halle, Halle, Germany, in 2006, for an investigation on shunting precipitates in Si solar cell material, and the Ph.D. degree in solar cell characterization, particularly under reverse bias, from University of Halle in 2009, in cooperation with the Max Planck Institute of Microstructure Physics, Halle.

After being with CaliSolar Inc., Berlin, Germany, he is now a postdoctoral researcher with the Max Planck Institute of Microstructure Physics, Halle. His main research interest is the local loss analysis of solar cells and the microscopic investigation of defects limiting their efficiency.

Evolution of Leakage Current Paths in MC-Si PV Modules From Leading Manufacturers Undergoing High-Voltage Bias Testing

Neelkanth G. Dhere, *Member, IEEE*, Narendra S. Shiradkar, *Member, IEEE*, and Eric Schneller, *Member, IEEE*

Abstract—The evolution of leakage currents in photovoltaic modules undergoing outdoor high-voltage bias testing is studied using data from high-voltage bias testing of multicrystalline silicon modules from leading manufacturers. An analysis of the module leakage currents as a function of environmental conditions including temperature, relative humidity, rain, and wetness is carried out. The behavior of the modules was found to be dependent on the module construction and the materials used. The Arrhenius model was used to fit the experimental data and activation energies were computed for various relative humidity values. The effect of dew and rain (wetness) on the front glass was investigated. Changes in the leakage current during dry conditions were studied using the temperature dependence of resistivity of bulk soda-lime glass. Because of the approximately tenfold increase in leakage currents during the wet conditions, it is suggested that the accelerated tests should not be limited exclusively to noncondensing environments but should also be complemented with tests that include wet conditions.

Index Terms—Degradation, high-voltage bias, leakage current, photovoltaic (PV) cells, photovoltaic systems, potential-induced degradation, reliability, system voltage stress.

I. Introduction

IT is important to accurately estimate the lifetime of photovoltaic (PV) modules in order to provide a quantitative basis for the bankability of the PV projects. Current IEC qualification testing has been successful in eliminating failures that are associated with infant mortality; however, these tests do not guarantee module performance over an extended period of time [1]. Currently, many PV module manufacturers provide a 25-year warranty that the module will maintain a power output of at least 80%. These warranties are provided without an accurate estimation of the useful performance lifetime for the specific PV module type.

Outdoor field testing is the only way to replicate the modes and mechanisms of degradations that would occur within PV modules deployed in real-world conditions [2]. The major disadvantage of this type of testing is the long time *(several years)* it takes to observe various types of degradations in PV modules.

Additionally, the degradation modes and associated degradation time scales will depend on the climate in which the outdoor testing is performed.

Reliability testing in environmental chambers is often used to accelerate the degradation of PV modules [3], [4]. The advantage of this type of testing is the short time *(several months)* it takes for performance degradation to occur. The drawback of this acceleration testing is that it can lead to failure modes that are not observed in field-deployed modules [5].

The reliability of field-deployed PV modules depends on the quality of cells and effectiveness of the complete packaging scheme to offer protection to the PV modules. Some modules in PV systems are subjected to higher voltages, up to 1000 V in US and 1500 V in Europe. The utility companies can step up to even higher system voltages as long as the systems are located within enclosed premises. This has resulted in a unique long-term degradation mode, which is termed potential-induced degradation (PID) or system-voltage-induced degradation (SVID), that is caused when the cell circuit remains at an elevated potential with respect to the grounded frame. It has been shown that the rate of SVID is a function of the leakage current that flows from the internal cell circuit to the grounded frame [6]. Several studies have focused on determining the root cause of PID from accelerated testing in environmental chambers [7], [8]. Several models for the occurrence of PID in varying environmental conditions such as temperature and relative humidity (RH) have been developed [9]. This has led to recommendations for acceleration test plans that could effectively test the susceptibility of PV modules to SVID [10]. Most of these tests are carried out in noncondensing conditions. This excludes the effect of events such as condensation and rain experienced by field-deployed modules that are found to significantly affect the leakage current.

Outdoor high-voltage bias testing has been carried out at the Florida Solar Energy Center, Cocoa, FL, USA, to investigate the robustness of various module types to SVID [11]. In this study, a detailed investigation of the response of the module leakage current as it relates to the various environmental conditions including temperature, RH, rain, and dew is carried out. Several groups have identified the leakage current activation energy as a function of temperature using field-deployed data [12] and environmental chamber testing data [13]. This study provides the leakage currents in a module as it relates to the module packaging materials in real-world environmental conditions. Additionally, this study attempts to deconvolute the effect of module surface wetness and high RH on the leakage current.

Manuscript received June 16, 2013; revised October 9, 2013; accepted November 5, 2013.

The authors are with the Florida Solar Energy Center, University of Central Florida, Cocoa, FL 32922 USA (e-mail: dhere@fsec.ucf.edu; nshiradkar@fsec.ucf.edu; eschneller@fsec.ucf.edu).

Color versions of one or more of the figures in this paper are available online at http://ieeexplore.ieee.org.

Digital Object Identifier 10.1109/JPHOTOV.2013.2294764

II. Experimental Details

Outdoor high-voltage bias testing is being carried out on commercially procured 60-cell multicrystalline silicon (mc-Si) PV modules from leading manufacturers having a standard soda-lime glass/encapsulant/backsheet package. Four different module types are used during this testing with at least three modules of each type for statistical significance. Modules are installed at latitude tilt on an open rack high-voltage platform in which each module is mounted on standoff insulators to electrically isolate the module frame from ground. Modules are connected across a fixed load with both terminals isolated from ground. A negative voltage bias is applied to the negative terminal of the module. The high-voltage test bed is capable of testing modules up to an applied voltage of 3000 V. It is general practice to apply 600 V for a period equivalent to at least one month prior to application of higher voltages to verify integrity of the module insulation. For this study, the initial one month of 600-V data is presented.

The leakage current was continuously monitored along with several meteorological parameters. A Campbell Scientific CR1000 Datalogger was used to store one measurement every 60 s. Meteorological measurements include solar irradiance, UV irradiance, ambient temperature, back of the module temperature, dew point temperature, RH, and rain. A Vaisala DRD11A rain sensor was used to provide a digital on/off output for rain, as well as an analog voltage output corresponding to surface wetness to measure the intensity of rain. In addition, the analog output was found to measure surface wetness due to the occurrence of surface dew formation.

III. Discussion

Fig. 1 shows several meteorological parameters and leakage currents of all four types of modules measured on a typical sunny day. The "module temperature" is an average of temperatures measured at three locations on one representative unbiased control module. The RH remains above 80% from midnight until sunrise. An early morning condensation is identified by a steady increase in the surface wetness. The gradual rise in the module leakage currents during this time is attributed to an increase in surface wetness because of dew formation, as the RH remained almost constant at a value close to 90%. Just after sunrise, the surface wetness drops to zero as the dew evaporates. This event is also marked by a sharp reduction in the module leakage currents.

During the day, when the solar irradiance is close to 1000 W/m^2, the back of the module temperature is found to be approximately 20 °C higher than the ambient temperature. Leakage currents of module type A, C, and D are found to peak at this time. However, the leakage currents for module type B show minimal change with the increase in back of the module temperature. After sunset, the RH again begins to increase, and module types A and B are found to respond immediately by an increase in the leakage currents.

Fig. 2 shows the meteorological parameters and leakage currents of all four types of modules that were measured on a typical rainy day. The events of heavy rain can be identified

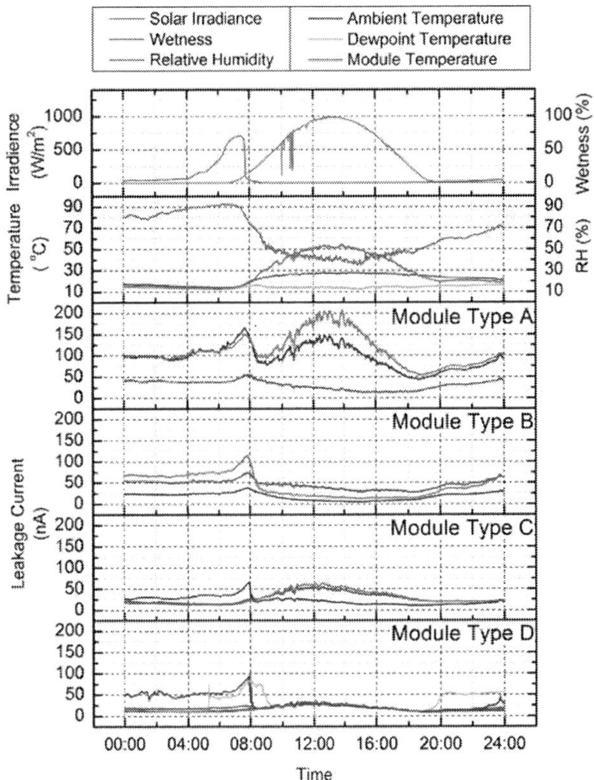

Fig. 1. Meteorological parameters and corresponding leakage currents for one typical sunny day.

by the interval during which values of wetness signal suddenly jump close to 100%, starting from low values. On that day, this happened around 12:00 AM, 2:00 PM, and later around 11:00 PM. The leakage currents of all modules are found to increase significantly coinciding with the rain events. In fact, usually the total charge flown through the module during an event of rain is higher than the total charge flown through the module during rest of the day. The values of leakage currents during the event of rain are also observed to be unstable. This fluctuation in the leakage current is attributed to the surface of the module not remaining in a steady state of complete wetness. As the rain droplets fall and the intensity of the rain changes, the surface area on the module in which there is continuous film will vary. Very high values of wetness are also measured during early morning; however, this is because of dew formation and not rain. This can be concluded from the fact that the values of wetness signal are found to increase gradually during early morning, and no large peaks are observed in the leakage current values during this time.

The behavior of wet modules is considerably different from that of dry modules under similar conditions of ambient temperature and RH. Therefore, leakage current analysis is carried out separately for dry and wet conditions.

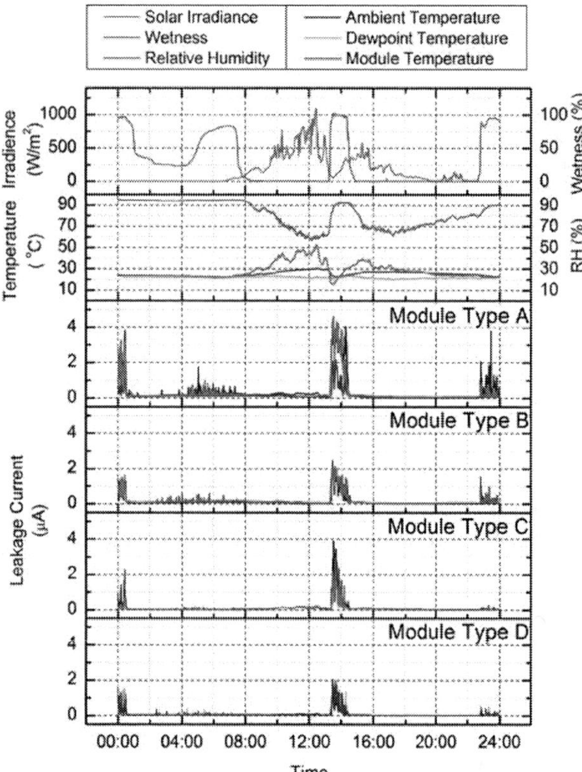

Fig. 2. Meteorological parameters and corresponding leakage currents for one typical rainy day.

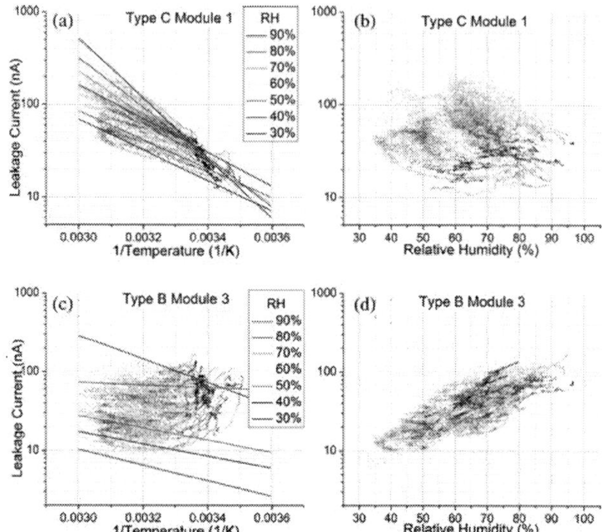

Fig. 3. Leakage current as a function of inverse temperature with best-fit line for various relative humidity ranges for (a) module type C and (c) module type B and the leakage current as a function of relative humidity for (b) module type C and (d) module type B.

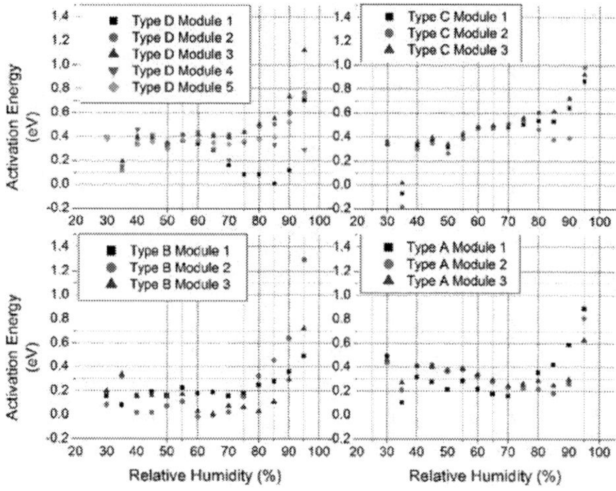

Fig. 4. Activation energy as a function of relative humidity for all module types.

A. Leakage Current Analysis for Dry Conditions

It was necessary to filter the leakage current data to analyze only dry conditions. It was observed that during intervals of high RH, the surface wetness was seen to increase to a small degree. This effect was attributed to the surface adsorbing higher amounts of water vapor and not to the presence of condensed water on the surface. Therefore, data corresponding to wetness values less than 10% were selected for this analysis. The following Arrhenius model was applied to study the experimental data [12]:

$$I = I_0(\mathrm{RH}, V)e^{-E_a(\mathrm{RH})/kT}. \tag{1}$$

The leakage current of the modules was plotted on a logarithmic scale against inverse of back of module temperature. The best-fit lines are found for various RH ranges with a window of ± 2.5% RH values around the selected points. Fig. 3(a) shows this analysis for a type-C module where the experimental data followed the Arrhenius relationship for the leakage current. The model was found adequate for modules of types A, C, and D. This relationship did not correspond to the leakage current data distribution of the type-B modules as shown in Fig. 4(c). The leakage currents show no significant exponential dependence on the temperature, and in fact the leakage current values tend to be temperature independent. The leakage currents that are observed for the type-B modules do show a direct correlation with the RH as shown in Fig. 3(d).

The activation energies were calculated from the slope of the best-fit lines for each RH range from the leakage current versus temperature distributions for all modules. Fig. 4 shows the activation energies of all four types of modules as a function of RH. The activation energies are found to increase at higher RH values.

B. Leakage Current Analysis for Wet Conditions

Analysis was carried out to study the leakage current as a function of surface wetness. As observed during rain events, as

338

Fig. 5. Individual water droplets dispersed across the module surface during a light rain.

shown in Fig. 2, module leakage currents can experience almost a tenfold increase. This is observed only during intense rains and the leakage currents quickly return to lower values after the rain subsides. It is important to note that for this to happen, the modules must be maintained at a minimum tilt that allows for quick draining of rain water. If the modules are maintained in the horizontal position, typically, a puddle of water will remain after a rain event. The resulting leakage current will depend on the surface area of the puddle and whether the film of water is in contact with the frame. If the puddle has good contact with the frame, then the leakage current may remain unnecessarily high for extended periods and result in premature degradation.

It was determined that condensation events, such as dew formation, and light-to-medium rain did not necessarily correspond to a continuous film on the front surface of a module, but instead resulted in individual droplets that were dispersed across the surface of the module. This is shown in Fig 5. There are instances where the leakage current increases and this was attributed to water droplets coalescing and forming a continuous film on a small region of the module surface. If this electrically conductive strip is in contact with the frame for the instant in which the measurement is taken, then an increase in the leakage current will be observed. This instantaneous increase is proportional to the surface area that is electrically conductive and that can vary significantly. This results in a large scatter in the data. As more data are collected for periods of intense rain and high wetness, it may be possible to observe an upper limit to the increase in module leakage currents. This upper limit would correspond to a continuous film on the front surface of the module.

The surface properties of the front glass have a significant effect on the contact angle of water droplets on the surface. This contact angle determines whether condensed moisture is more likely to form isolated islands or a continuous film. It is commonly known that an extremely clean surface has a very low contact angle. On the other hand, if the surface has a large collection of pollutants, as would be the case for a module in the field, the surface will be hydrophobic. This will result in a high contact angle and the formation of isolated droplets dispersed across the module surface.

Since rain events are known to cause the highest levels of leakage currents, any accelerated test for SVID must not exclude this condition of low surface resistivity. The more accurate way to replicate these real-world conditions would be to carry out this testing in a condensing environment. A somewhat easier approach would be to cover the front surface of the module with an aluminum foil sheet intimately in contact with the front surface.

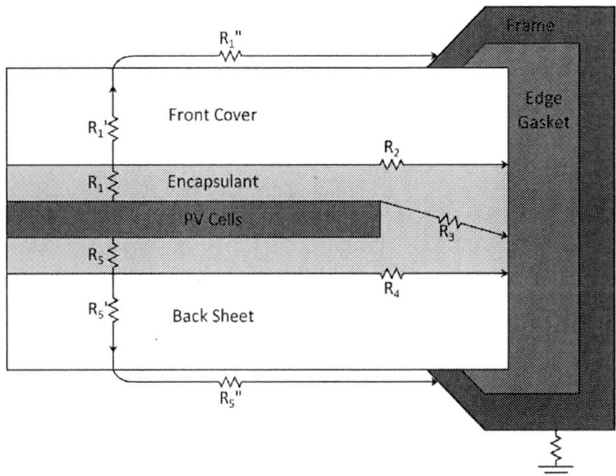

Fig. 6. Cross section of a PV module showing the different module leakage current pathways.

C. Leakage Current Pathways Under Different Environmental Conditions

Fig. 6 shows the cross section of a PV module and various leakage current pathways from the cell circuit to the frame. The top cover that has been used in this study for all modules is soda-lime glass, and the back cover is a polymer backsheet. On the front side, the bulk resistance of encapsulant (R_1), bulk resistance of front glass (R_1'), and surface resistance of the glass (R_1'') are in series. For the back side, since the bulk resistance of the backsheet (R_5') is significantly high, negligible current flows through this path. Therefore, the two major leakage current pathways are through the bulk of the front glass and sideways along the interfaces between glass-encapsulant (R_2) and backsheet-encapsulant (R_4).

The surface resistivity of soda-lime glass is known to be significantly greater than the bulk resistivity. Therefore, if the surface of the module is uniformly wet or covered with a conducting metal foil, then highest leakage currents are observed, as the surface resistance of the glass is reduced to zero. This is evident from significantly increased leakage currents that were measured during intense rains as shown in Fig. 2. If the surface of the module is dry, then the bulk resistivity of the glass plays an important role in determining the total leakage current. It can be seen in Fig. 1 that the daytime leakage current of module type A shows a strong correlation with the temperature. This is because the resistivity of the front glass decreases as the temperature of the module is increased. Fig. 7 is a plot of experimentally measured and calculated values of the leakage current using the literature value for the temperature coefficient of resistivity of soda-lime glass of 0.002/ °C. It can be seen that there is a good correlation.

The leakage currents of other module types, especially module type B, do not show such a strong increase in the leakage current with temperature. This may be due to a much higher resistance in series with the resistance of the bulk glass, and, therefore, the changes in the resistivity of the bulk glass do

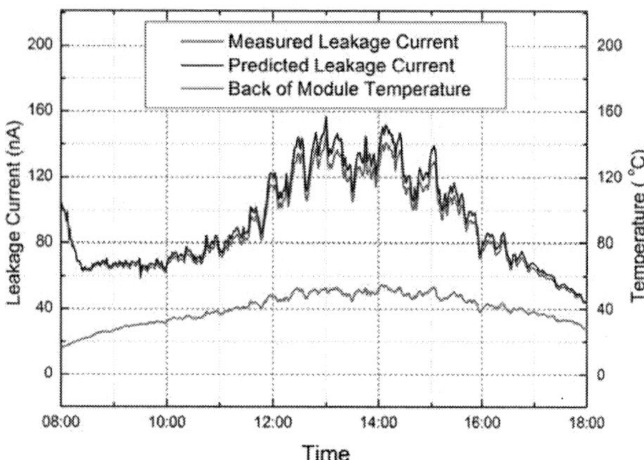

Fig. 7. Comparison of experimental and predicted values of leakage current using the coefficient of resistivity for bulk soda-lime glass.

not significantly affect the amount of leakage current flowing through the module. Additionally, water vapor transport rate of backsheet used will affect the moisture ingress within the module, which will also affect resistivity of the encapsulant [14]. If a glass or another impermeable backsheet is used, then the edge seals used in PV modules will determine the extent of moisture ingress, and in turn affect the magnitude of the leakage current.

IV. Conclusion

Results from the outdoor high-voltage bias testing of mc-Si modules from leading manufacturers are presented. The various trends of the module leakage currents with respect to outdoor environmental conditions were investigated. It was shown that leakage currents are significantly affected by relative humidity, temperature, rain, and dew formation. During dry conditions, for most of the module types, an Arrhenius relationship with respect to temperature for various relative humidity ranges was observed to correlate with the experimental data. There was a large variation in the data during wet conditions because of the dynamic nature of formation of a continuous path on the front surface of the module. Uniform wetting of front glass was determined to be one of the key factors capable of significantly increasing the module leakage currents. For most of the rain events, the charge flown through the module was shown to be greater than the total charge flown through the module during rest of the day. Accelerated testing using exclusively

noncondensing environment must, therefore, be complemented with accelerated tests under condensing conditions.

References

[1] J. H. Wohlgemuth, "Standards for PV modules and components—Recent developments and challenges," in *Proc. 27th Eur. Photovoltaic Sol. Energy Conf.*, 2012, pp. 2976–2980.

[2] J. A. del Cueto and S. R. Rummel, "Degradation of photovoltaic modules under high voltage stress in the field," *Proc. SPIE*, vol. 7773, Reliability of Photovoltaic Cells, Modules, Components, and Systems III, 77730J, 2010.

[3] T. J. McMahon, "Accelerated testing and failure of thin-film PV modules," *Prog. Photovoltaic, Res. Appl.*, vol. 12, pp. 235–248, 2004.

[4] A. Saint-Lary, S. Ed-daoudi, T. Delsol, P. Legrain, and J.-C. Marcel, "Photovoltaic modules reliability on accelerated and natural test: The ELVIRE project," in *Proc. 27th Eur. Photovoltaic Solar Energy Conf.*, 2012, pp. 3523–3525.

[5] J. H. Wohlgemuth, D. W. Cunnigham, P. Monus, J. Miller, and A. Nguyen, "Long term reliability of photovoltaic modules," in *Proc. IEEE 4th World Conf. Photovoltaic Energy Convers.*, 2006, pp. 2199–2201.

[6] G. R. Mon and R. G. Ross, "Electrochemical degradation of amorphous silicon photovoltaic modules," in *Proc. 18th IEEE Photovoltaics Spec. Conf.*, 1985, pp. 1142–1149.

[7] P. Hacke, R. Smith, K. Terwilliger, S. Glick, D. Jordan, S. Johnston, M. Kempe, and S. Kurtz, "Testing and analysis for lifetime prediction of crystalline silicon PV modules undergoing degradation by system voltage stress," *IEEE J. Photovoltaics*, vol. 3, no. 1, pp. 246–253, Jan. 2013.

[8] H. Nagel, R. Pfeiffer, A. Raykov, and K. Wangemann, "Lifetime warranty testing of crystalline silicon modules for potential-induced degradation," in *Proc. 27th Eur. Photovoltaic Solar Energy Conf.*, 2012, pp. 3163–3166.

[9] A. Raykov, H. Nagel, D.-J. Amankwah, and W. Bergholz, "Climate model for potential-induced degradation of crystalline silicon photovoltaic modules," in *Proc. 27th Eur. Photovoltaic Solar Energy Conf.*, 2012, pp. 3399–3404.

[10] J. Hattendorf, R. Loew, W.-M. Gnehr, L. Wulff, M. C. Koekten, D. Koshnicharov, A. Blauaermel, and J. A. Esquivel, "Potential induced degradation in mono-crystalline silicon based modules: An acceleration model," in *Proc. 27th Eur. Photovoltaic Solar Energy Conf.*, 2012, pp. 3404–3410.

[11] N. G. Dhere. 2011. "High voltage bias testing of specially designed c-Si PV modules. in *Proc. Photovoltaic Module Rel. Workshop.* [Online]. Available: www.eere.energy.gov /solar/pv_module_reliability_workshop_2011.html)

[12] J. A. DelCueto and T. J. McMahon, "Analysis of leakage currents in photovoltaic modules under high-voltage bias in the field," *Prog. Photovoltaic, Res. Appl.*, vol. 10, pp. 15–25, 2002.

[13] S. Hoffman and M. Koehl, "Effect of humidity and temperature on potential induced degradation," *Prog. Photovoltaic, Res. Appl.*, 2012. DOI: 10.1002/pip.2238.

[14] M. Kempe, "Modeling of rates of moisture ingress into photovoltaic modules," *Solar Energy Mater. Solar Cells*, vol. 90, pp. 2720–2738, 2006.

Authors' photographs and biographies not available at the time of publication.

Price Development of Photovoltaic Modules, Inverters, and Systems in the Netherlands in 2012

Wilfried G.J.H.M. van Sark[1,2], Peter Muizebelt[3], Jadranka Cace[4], Arthur de Vries[1,5], Peer de Rijk[1,6]

[1]Stichting Monitoring Zonnestroom (SMZ), Utrecht, The Netherlands
[2]Utrecht University, Copernicus Institute, Utrecht, The Netherlands
[3]New-Energy-Works (NEW), Utrecht, the Netherlands
[4]Rencom, Ouderkerk a/d Amstel, the Netherlands
[5]Holland Solar, Utrecht, The Netherlands
[6]Organisatie voor Duurzame Energie (ODE), Utrecht, The Netherlands

Abstract — Since 2010 the Dutch photovoltaic (PV) market has been growing fast, with around doubling of installed capacity in 2011 and 2012. Four quarterly inventories have been made in 2012 for modules, inverters, and systems that are presently available for purchase in the Netherlands. We have found that the average selling price of modules, inverters, and systems decreased with 44.3, 14, and 7.3-10.2 %, respectively: average selling prices are 1.26 €/Wp, 0.41 €/Wp, and 1.46 €/Wp for modules, inverters, and systems on tilted roofs, respectively, at the end of 2012. Average installation costs amount to 0.43 €/Wp. Using an energy yield of 900 kWh/kWp, 25 years system lifetime, 6% discount rate, and 1% operation and maintenance (O&M) cost, a levelized cost of electricity (LCOE) is calculated for a 2.5 kWp system to be 0.194 €/kWh for a system price of 1.98 €/Wp (including installation). Grid parity conditions are apparent, with electricity retail prices of around 0.23 €/kWh.

Index Terms — PV market, price development, grid parity, PV module, inverter, system

I. INTRODUCTION

Deployment of photovoltaic (PV) systems in the Netherlands has been irregular due to changing subsidy schemes, as is illustrated in Fig. 1. After a slow but steady capacity growth up to 2002, a very successful investment subsidy scheme (Energy Premium, EPR) lead to a near doubling of capacity in 2003. However, due to abolishment of this subsidy scheme, capacity growth was near zero for 4 years. A new scheme, based on a feed-in tariff was devised (Stimulation Renewable Energy production, SDE), which lead to a large capacity growth in 2009 and 2010. This was followed by a new scheme (SDE+), which, however, was much less favorable to PV as the 2000-2010 schemes. Nevertheless, market growth in 2011 was 57 MWp, again nearly doubling capacity to 145 MWp. In an earlier study [2], we showed that PV system prices were nearing grid parity at the end of 2011, which at least partly enabled market growth. We therefore extended our market study in the year 2012. The global development of module prices was expected to also influence Dutch module prices, which was corroborated by early 2012 market data [2]. In July 2012 a new investment subsidy became in force for residential PV owners (15% subsidy on material investment costs up to a maximum of 650 € per system). However, right after the announcement in May 2012, market turnover dropped enormously, as consumers waited for final details on the subsidy scheme before making their purchase: this was referred to as 'consumer strike'. The subsidy scheme was questioned by the PV industry as it created yet another market imbalance. Nevertheless, capacity growth in 2012 was expected to at least doubling the cumulative installed capacity. Recently updated figures show that installed capacity has more than doubled to 340 MWp [1] (Fig. 1).

An inventory of the PV market in the Netherlands was made every quarter in 2012, by collecting price data on PV modules, inverters, other system components including installation and consultancy, in order to support private customers in their purchasing decision. VAT was therefore included in the price data. Moreover, for four different typically sized PV systems, performance and cost calculations were performed. This allowed to determine the levelized cost of electricity of PV systems in order to compare with retail electricity prize of typically 0.23 €/kWh, and assessment of consumer grid parity.

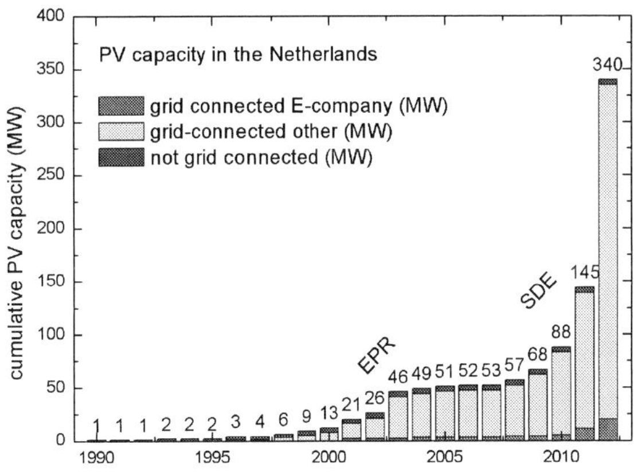

Fig. 1.   Development of the cumulative installed PV capacity in the Netherlands (data source: CBS [1]).

II. METHODOLOGY

The collection of market data was performed using extensive Internet searches that identified the relevant retailers of PV modules, inverters, complete systems, and other BOS components. For most of these retailers price data were available on their web sites. Those for which this information was not available were contacted directly (phone, email) and were asked to provide detailed price information on the products they sell, also including data on installation prices. Note that _all_ prices in this paper are quoted _including_ value-added tax (VAT), which was 19% prior to 1 October 2012 and 21% from that date onwards. The purpose of the study

The Levelized Cost of Electricity (LCOE) was calculated using

$$LCOE = \frac{\alpha I + OM}{E},\qquad(1)$$

where α is the capital recovery factor, I the initial investment, OM the operation and maintenance cost, and E the annual electricity production. The capital recovery factor is defined as

$$\alpha = \frac{r}{1-\left(1+r\right)^{-L}},\qquad(2)$$

with r the discount rate, and L the lifetime of the system.

In the Netherlands a large number of 4-6 module systems were installed, and still are offered: system size then is on average about 600 Wp. Nowadays, a typical household roof system measures about 2.5 kWp. As typical yields range from 800 to 1000 kWh/kWp, depending on correct and optimal installation, such a system would generate 2000-2500 kWh annually. This constitutes 57-71% to the annual electricity demand of an average Dutch household, i.e., 3500 kWh. Present legislation allows for net metering up to 5000 kWh annually, therefore a 5-kWp system is also taken as a size in our study. Larger systems range from 10-50 kWp. We have chosen four typical sizes for the LCOE calculation: 0.6, 2.5, 5, and 50 kWp. A typical, mortgage-related interest rate is 6%, while a lower, soft of green loan rate may be possible at 3%. Commercial rates are 8% or higher. Results will be presented using these ranges of values.

III. RESULTS

A. PV modules

In the quarterly inventories of PV modules the number of unique modules rose from 480 in April to 669 in December 2012, and these were predominantly crystalline silicon modules (49% mono, 49% poly, 2% thin film). The average

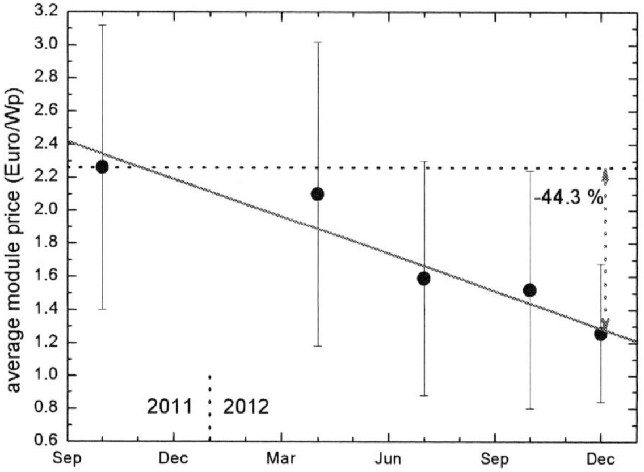

Fig. 2. Development of PV module price (including tax) between October 2011 and December 2012.

selling price decreased from €442 (range €147 - €921) to €287 (range €82 - €840); this translates into values of the price per rated power of 2.10 €/Wp (range 0.95 - 6.69 €/Wp) and 1.26 €/Wp (range 0.64 - 2.63 €/Wp) for April and December 2012, respectively. This development in price is shown in Fig. 2, where the error bars are the standard deviations in the mean values. Data from October 2011 are also shown for comparison. Clearly, a very large price <u>decrease</u> of 44.3 % occurred between October 2011 and December 2012. Similar decreases have been reported globally. The number of modules with lower price than 1.1 €/Wp increased from 10 in April 2012 to 84 (17.5%) in December 2012. Thus, in the Netherlands, PV module price is observed to decrease between October 2011 and December 2012 with 7.5 cent€ every month. Note that the consumer strike of mid 2012 is reflected in the price trend as a relatively low price change in the fall of 2012.

Figure 3 shows the changes in price distribution over the same period. The decrease in price can be cleary observed, as well as the narrowing of the distribution, which may be due to the fact that more expensive modules have been taken off the market. In fact, some 15% of the modules each quarter are new on the market.

B. Inverters

The number of inverters in the inventory rose from 188 in April to 342 in December 2012. The average selling price decreased from €2013 (range €120 - €7921) to €1823 (range €155 - €7399). Note that the range in rated capacity varies from 215 W to 60 kW; this translates into values for the price per rated power of 0.48 €/Wp (range 0.18 - 1.09 €/Wp) and 0.41 €/Wp (range 0.17 - 0.92 €/Wp) for April

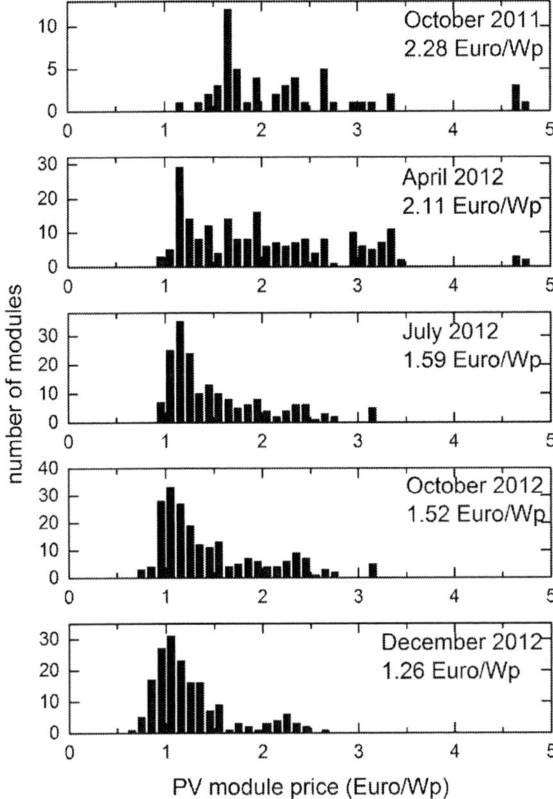

Fig. 3. Development of the distribution of PV module price (including tax) between October 2011 and December 2012.

and December 2012, respectively. The average EU efficiency is 95.2%. Small size inverters are more expensive than large size ones: for size < 1 kW the average price is 0.6 €/Wp; for inverters >10 kW the price is <0.3 €/Wp, as is illustrated in Fig. 4.The development in price is shown in Fig. 5, where the error bars are the standard deviations in the mean values. A modest decrease in price is observed of 14 % occurred between April and December 2012, or 0.8 cent€ in this period.

C. Systems

The number of systems for tilted (flat) roofs in the inventory rose from 1557 (1477) in April to 2352 (2270) in December 2012. The average selling price for tilted systems decreased from 1.63 €/Wp (range 1.28 - 4.44 €/Wp) to 1.46 €/Wp (range 1.05 - 2.73 €/Wp) in April and December 2012, respectively. Similar numbers, albeit slightly higher are found for flat roof systems. The price development is depicted in Fig. 6 for both tilted and flat roof systems. A

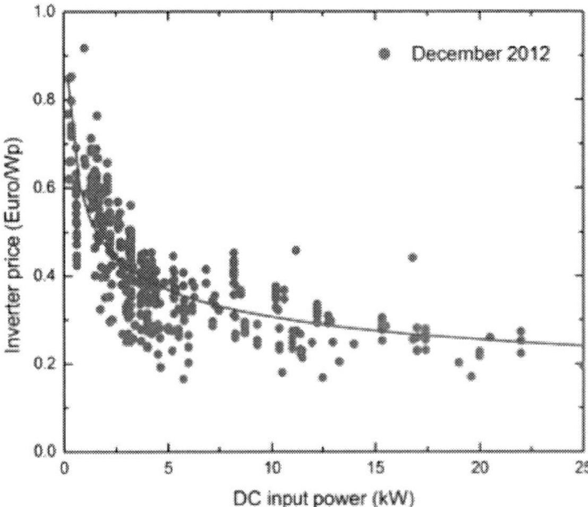

Fig. 4. Inverter price (including tax) as a function of DC input power for December 2012

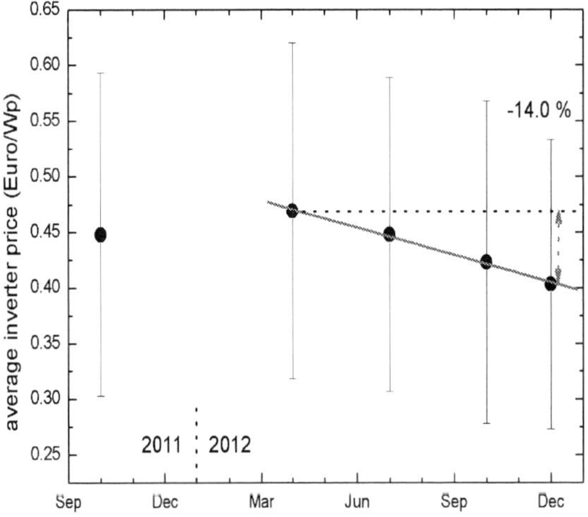

Fig. 5. Development of inverter price (including tax) between October 2011 and December 2012.

decrease in price is observed of 10.2 % for tilted systems (7.3% for flat roof systems) between April and December 2012, or 2 (1.5) cent€ in this period. Note that the average selling price depends on system size: large systems have lower prices than small systems, as illustrated in Fig. 7. The average prices for three system size ranges have been determined, i.e., for 0-1 kWp, 1-5 kWp, and 5-25 kWp, all excluding installation. Figure 8 shows the price development for these ranges. For the smaller systems, the price decrease is clear; the price of the largest systems seems to stabilize.

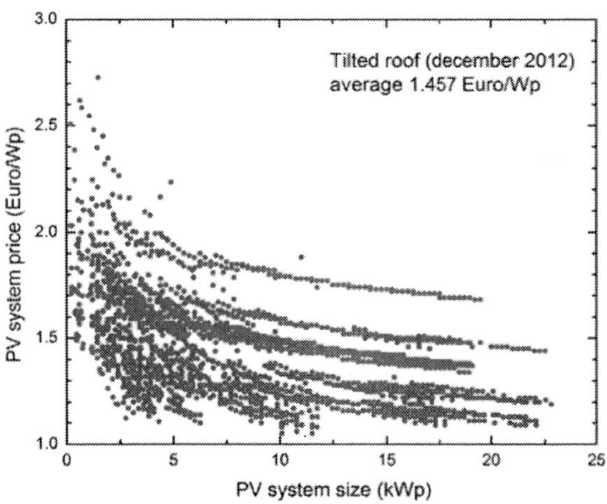

Fig. 6. Development of system price (including tax) for tilted and flat roof systems.

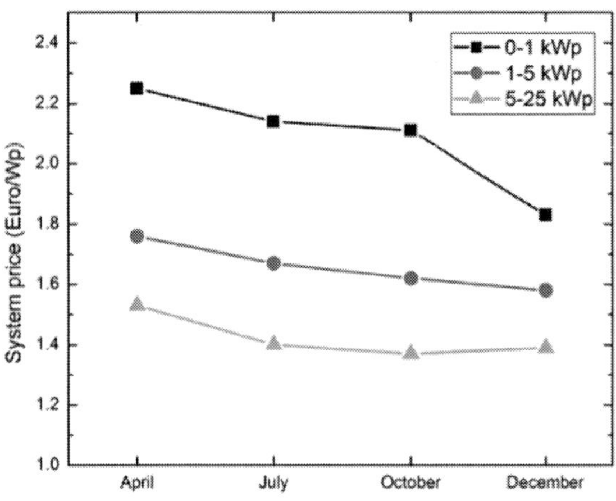

Fig. 7. System price in December 2012 for tilted systems, excluding installation.

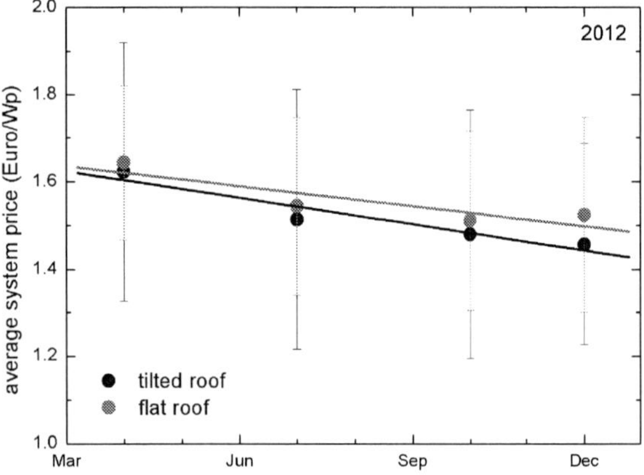

Fig. 8. Development of system price for three different size ranges.

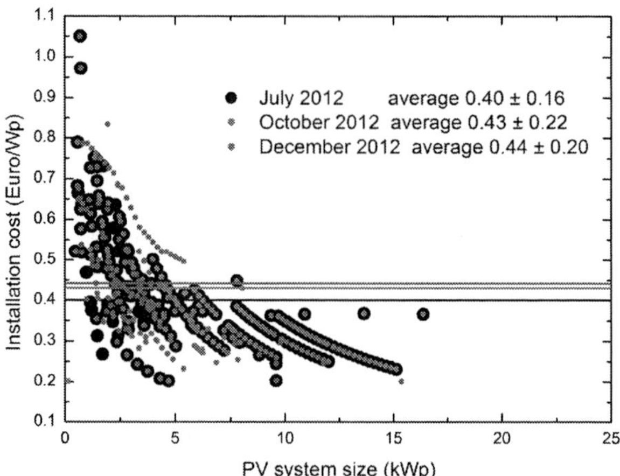

Fig. 9. Development of system installation cost between July 2012 and December 2012.

Average installation costs have been determined to be 0.40 €/Wp in July to 0.44 €/Wp in December, as shown in Fig. 9. This may be caused by lowered system price margins being compensated somewhat by higher installation cost margins. Note that for small systems installation costs are >0.50 €/Wp, while for large systems (>5 kWp) installation costs are <0.30 €/Wp. Based on the December 2012 data, and the size dependent prices from Fig. 7, the system size dependent prices are set as shown in Table I.

TABLE I

PRICES OF FOUR TYPICALLY SIZED PV SYSTEMS

system size	price	installation	total
kWp	€/Wp	€/Wp	€/Wp
0.6	1.83	0.60	2.43
2.5	1.58	0.40	1.98
5	1.39	0.30	1.69
50	1.39	0.20	1.59

D. LCOE for typical systems

For the four system sizes, with associated prices, the LCOE is calculated for three different values of the interest rate. Results are shown in Table II; the yellow marked values are similar or lower than the current (early 2013) price of electricity (0.23 €/kWh) that utilities charge to customers. Clearly, as was found in the previous study as well [2], grid parity has been reached for systems between 2.5 and 5 kWp for high energy rating values. For small systems and low energy ratings only soft and mortgage type loans lead to grid parity. Due to net metering legislation, systems larger than 5.5 kWp (at 900 kWh/kWp) are not considered to be operable below consumer grid parity. Also, consumers/owners installing systems of 50 kWp, most probably pay a much lower fee of about 0.10 €/kWh to

TABLE II

LCOE (€/KWH) FOR VARIOUS COMBINATIONS OF ENERGY
YIELD, SYSTEM SIZE AND PRICE, AND INTEREST RATE.
OTHER ASSUMPTION IS 1% O&M.

energy yield kWh/kWp	size kWp	price €/Wp	3%	6%	8%
800	0.6	2.43	0.205	0.268	0.315
	2.5	1.98	0.167	0.218	0.257
	5	1.69	0.142	0.186	0.219
	50	1.59	0.134	0.175	0.206
850	0.6	2.43	0.193	0.252	0.296
	2.5	1.98	0.157	0.206	0.242
	5	1.69	0.134	0.175	0.206
	50	1.59	0.126	0.165	0.194
900	0.6	2.43	0.182	0.238	0.280
	2.5	1.98	0.148	0.194	0.228
	5	1.69	0.127	0.166	0.195
	50	1.59	0.119	0.156	0.183
950	0.6	2.43	0.162	0.212	0.250
	2.5	1.98	0.132	0.173	0.203
	5	1.69	0.113	0.148	0.174
	50	1.59	0.106	0.139	0.163

utilities, as they are so-called large consumers (and in fact will be owners/tenants of office buildings). In their case, grid parity is not reached, and PV system price should be close to 1 €/Wp. Note, that new legislation in mid 2013 will probably remove the 5000 kWh barrier, which would make larger residential installations more attractive in economical terms.

III. DISCUSSION

The present study in fact is to been as a start of a long-term effort to follow market developments, which would allow identifying price trends much better. Nevertheless, the quarterly price updates have shown rapid decreases in the Netherlands for modules and inverters, but less so for complete systems and installation cost. This is also seen on the global market. Module prices have been about halved globally over 2012 [3].

The average system price cannot be compared directly with summing up average module price, average inverter price and average installation price. Suppose a house owner would like to purchase a 4 kWp system, which comprises of 16 250 Wp modules of 1.26 €/Wp, an inverter of 0.35 €/Wp. and installation of 0.35 €/Wp. Total system price would be 1.96 €/Wp, which is 10-15% larger than the system price used in Table I. Obviously, system installers are able to close better deals on the market than consumers buying individual components.

IV. CONCLUSION

In order to follow price developments in the fast growing and dynamic Dtuch PV market, four 2012 quarterly inventories of PV modules, inverters, and other BOS components, as well as on complete PV systems have been composed. It has been found that prices of modules, inverters, and systems all have decreased by 44.3, 14, and 7.3-10.2 %, respectively. This has lead to a large market growth in 2012, which more than doubled with respect to the installed capacity in 2011. Assessment of grid parity shows that LCOE can be 10-15 cent€ lower than current consumer retail price, for systems of typical household size with high energy yield, i.e., that are properly installed on good locations. Continuation of this market study in 2013 will reveal if a further price reduction can be realized, which will be a challenge in view of the recent EU decision to impose provisional anti-dumping tariffs on Chinese PV panels [4]. Therefore, in our 2013 study we will also distinguish between the countries of origin of the modules [5].

ACKNOWLEDGEMENT

We would like to thank AgentschapNL for financial support.

REFERENCES

[1] CBS Statline, http://statline.cbs.nl/statweb/, last access date 06/04/13.
[2] W.G.J.H.M. van Sark, P. Muizebelt, J. Cace, A. de Vries, P. de Rijk, "Grid parity reached for consumers in the Netherlands," in 38th IEEE Photovoltaic Specialist Conference, 2012, p. 2462-2466.
[3] M. Barker, http://www.displaysearchblog.com/2013/02/pv-c-si-module-asps-continue-steep-decline-in-2012/, last access date 06/08/13.
[4] EU Press release June 4, 2013, EU imposes provisional anti-dumping tariffs on Chinese solar panels, IP/13/501, http://europa.eu/rapid/press-release_IP-13-501_en.htm, last access data 06/08/13.
[5] W.G.J.H.M. van Sark, P. Muizebelt, J. Cace, A. de Vries, P. de Rijk, "Photovoltaic market development in the Netherlands," in 28th EU Photovoltaic Solar Energy Conference, 2013 (in press)

High-Efficiency CdS/CdTe Solar Cells on Commercial SnO_2:F Coated Soda-lime Glass Substrates

Naba R. Paudel and Yanfa Yan

Department of Physics & Astronomy, and Wright Center for Photovoltaics Innovation and Commercialization, The University of Toledo, Toledo, OH 43606, USA

ABSTRACT

High efficiency CdTe-based thin-film solar cells with a superstrate configuration have been fabricated on commercial SnO_2:F/SnO_2-coated soda-lime glass substrates. The CdS window layers were deposited by magnetron sputtering, and the CdTe absorber layers were deposited by close-spaced sublimation. The back-contacts are elemental Cu/Au bilayers. $CdCl_2$ activations were carried out in dry air. Without antireflection coating, the best small-area cell has shown an efficiency of 15.8% with an open-circuit voltage of 845 mV, a short-circuit current of 24.5 mA/cm^2, and a fill-factor of 76.8% measured under an AM1.5 illumination. We find that besides optimizing the growth process of the window and absorber layers and the $CdCl_2$ activation steps, incorporating a small amount of oxygen in the CdS window layers is essential for achieving high efficiency CdTe solar cells.

Key Words- thin-film, solar cell, CdTe, CdS, TEC15, CSS, sputtering.

I.   INTRODUCTION

Cadmium telluride (CdTe) is a promising absorber material for thin-film solar cell applications due to its excellent structural and optical properties such as simple binary structure, high absorption coefficient, direct optical band gap of 1.5 eV which matches the terrestrial soar spectrum for maximum theoretical efficiency, and ease of manufacturing [1]. CdTe technology has now dominated the thin-film solar cell market. So far, laboratory small area CdTe solar cells have achieved a record efficiency of 18.7% [2]. The new record efficiency will stimulate more research on further improving the performance of CdS/CdTe thin-film solar cells. However, the details of the cell structure and substrates used for fabricating these champion cells are not reported. Most record efficiency CdTe solar cells do not use commercially available F-doped SnO_2 (FTO) coated soda-lime glass (SLG) substrates and use carefully engineered antireflection (AR) coating. Therefore these record efficiency cells often exhibit very high short circuit currents (J_{SC}). In order to drive the module cost down below $0.50 per watt, the use of commercial FTO coated SLG as the substrates is highly preferred. Significant research efforts have been paid on fabricating CdTe solar cells using commercial FTO coated SLG substrates. For example, a recent work by Korevaar et al. [3] has reported nearly 15.2% efficiency CdTe solar cells using commercial SnO_2:F coated glass substrates. These cells showed an open circuit voltage (V_{OC}) of 838 mV, a J_{SC} of 23.1 mA/cm^2 and a fill factor (FF) of 78.3% [3]. These devices were finished with a 100 nm MgF_2 layer on the glass side as the AR coating. The details of the type of glass that were used to fabricate these CdTe cells were not reported. In addition, Banai et al. [4] also reported 15.3%

efficiency (V_{OC} = 834 mV, J_{SC} = 24.5 mA/cm^2 and FF = 75.2%) CdTe solar cells using commercial FTO-coated glass substrates.

In this article, we report our progress on the fabrication of high-efficiency CdS/CdTe thin-film solar cells on commercial FTO-coated SLG substrates. Our cells use TEC15 glass substrates with a highly resistive transparent (HRT) buffer layer (i-SnO_2) supplied by NSG, Toledo, OH. The cells have a superstrate configuration - SLG/SnO_2:F/i-SnO_2/CdS/CdTe/Cu/Au [5, 6]. The CdS window layers are deposited by RF magnetron sputtering in a mixed argon and oxygen ambient. The CdTe absorber layers are grown by a home-built close-spaced sublimation (CSS) system. Our fabrication process can be easily scaled up for commercial manufacturing. For comparison we have also synthesized CdS layers using chemical bath deposition (CBD). With careful optimization of the growth process, our best small-area champion cell (0.08 cm^2) has shown an efficiency of 15.8% with a V_{OC} of 845 mV, a J_{SC} of 24.5 mA/cm^2 and a FF of 76.8% under an AM1.5 illumination. The efficiency is anticipated to further improve if an AR coating is applied. We find that besides optimizing the growth process of the window and absorber layers and the $CdCl_2$ activation steps, incorporating a small amount of oxygen in the CdS window layers is essential for achieving high efficiency CdTe solar cells. We also find that the parameters and processes that lead to high efficiency cells are system and substrate dependent. Therefore, the optimal growth conditions and processes reported here may not necessarily be same as that reported in literature.

II.   EXPERIMENTAL DETAILS

The CdS window layers were deposited on TEC15 substrates by either RF magnetron sputtering at a 270 °C substrate temperature or CBD at a 68 °C bath temperature [7, 8]. Oxygen (O) incorporation in sputtered CdS thin layers was realized by allowing 0-5% O_2 (mixed with Ar) flow variation in the sputtering environment. The optical properties of the CdS window   layers with various O concentrations were measured using a UV-VIS-NIR spectrophotometer (Lambda 1050). Unless otherwise specified, our standard CdTe absorber layers have a thickness of about 4 μm. The CdTe layers were deposited by CSS method in mixed oxygen helium ambient. The separation between the source and the substrate was fixed at about 2-3 mm which, consequently, held a temperature difference of 50 °C during the sublimation period. The as-grown CdTe samples received chloride activations at various temperatures in a dry air ambient. After chloride treatment, the samples were cleaned a few times with a methanol rinse and then were transferred to an evaporator for thermal evaporation of Cu (4 nm) and Au (40 nm) contacts. No chemical etching was applied before the deposition of back contacts. The solar cells were finally annealed for 45 minutes at 150 °C in room air ambient for activation of Cu. About 25 dot cells (with cell area

          346

of 0.08 cm^2) were prepared on each quarter of the 3" × 3" sample plates. The finished solar cells were characterized under an AM1.5 illumination for current-voltage (J-V) and external quantum efficiency (EQE) measurements at room temperature.

III.   RESULTS AND DISCUSSIONS

A.   Influence of Sublimation Pressure and Substrate Temperature

Optimizing the CSS deposition of CdTe films is very important for achieving high efficiency CdTe solar cells. Previous studies by Korevaar et al [3], Banai et al. [4] Major et al. [9], Ferekides [10], Wu et al. [11] have reported that the sublimation pressure and substrate temperature can significantly influence the device performance. However, so far, no universal values were found that can be automatically adapted for our device fabrication; even the reported results are very indicative to our research. Therefore, we have also optimized the sublimation pressure and substrate temperature for our growth system. The effects of sublimation pressure and substrate temperature on CdTe growth rate, grain size, surface morphology, crystalinity, and interdiffusion at the CdS/CdTe interface will be published elsewhere [12].   Here, we focus on optimizing the device performance. Figure 1(a) shows the averaged efficiencies over 20 dot cells grown at a 607 °C substrate temperature (with ΔT = 53 °C where ΔT is the temperature difference between source and substrate) with various sublimation pressures ranging from 0.5 − 200 Torr. The deposition time for each pressure is adjusted such that the final CdTe thickness is about 3-4 µm. As seen in Figure 1(a), the cell efficiency increases from 11.8% to 13.5% as the sublimation pressure increases from 0.5 Torr to 20 Torr. Further increase of pressure up to 80 Torr results in a slight decrease in efficiency. At 200 Torr, the average efficiency drops below 12%, suggesting that a sublimation pressure in the range of 5 Torr − 80 Torr is suitable for our system with the selected gas ambient (0.5% O_2 and 99.5% He). The CdTe cells grown in this pressure range usually yielded good V_{OC}, FF and J_{SC}, consistent with the results reported by other groups [3, 4, 9-12], even though the gas ambient was slightly different.

To find the optimal substrate temperature, we have deposited CdTe thin films at various substrate temperatures at a fixed sublimation pressure of 20 Torr. Figure 1(b) presents the averaged cell efficiencies of cells using CdTe films grown at 20 Torr as a function of the substrate temperature. It should be noted that the source temperature was also varied to keep ΔT fixed (50-60 °C). The cell efficiency varies from 12.5% - 14.5% when the substrate temperature varies in the range of 560 °C - 610 °C. This temperature range has also been considered by other groups [3, 9, 11] to fabricate high efficiency CdTe cells.   Outside this temperature range, the efficiency dropped significantly: < 9%. At 500 °C, the growth rate was very slow and grain sizes are very small, leading to poor V_{OC} and FF [12]. At 625 °C, the growth rate was fast during sublimation period but showed unusual growth process. During the post-sublimation cooling period, the CdTe re-sublimates from the substrate resulted in non-preferred surface morphology with a high density of voids and loosely connected CdTe grains [12]. When these samples were finished with Cu/Au back contacts, the voids and opening grain boundaries act as shunting paths and yield cells with very poor performance.

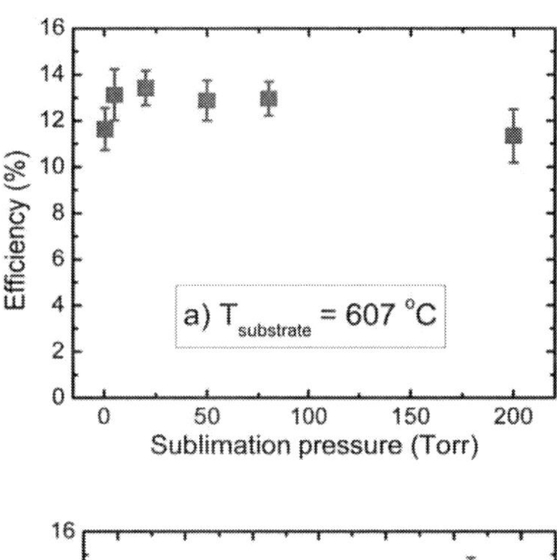

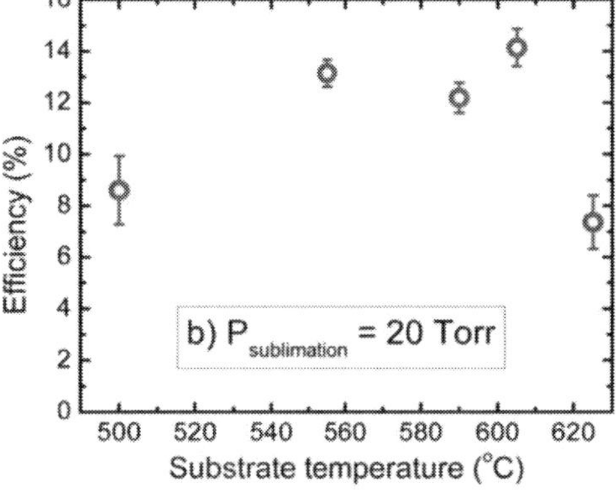

Fig. 1. Averaged efficiencies over 20 dot CdS/CdTe cells as a function of a) sublimation pressure and b) substrate temperature during CSS CdTe absorber layer depositions.

B.   Effect of CdCl$_2$ Activation Temperature

It is well known that polycrystalline CdTe films need to be "activated" in CdCl$_2$ and air ambient at a temperature in the range of 350-450 °C to obtain high efficiency cells [13]. The performance of CdTe cells is sensitive to the heat treatment temperature. CdTe layers deposited at low substrate temperatures prefer heat treatments at temperatures in the range of 370-390 °C [6], whereas CdTe layers deposited at high temperatures prefer heat treatments at temperatures in the range of 390-420 °C [3, 9-11, 14-16].   We have optimized our heat treatment process by varying activation temperature from 370 °C − 430 °C. Figure 2 shows the current-voltage (J-V) characteristics of four CdTe cells which received 10 minutes CdCl$_2$ activation at 370 °C, 390 °C, 410 °C and 430 °C in dry air ambient. We found that the CdTe cells treated below 400 °C outperformed the cells treated at higher temperatures. When activated at temperatures <400 °C, the cells exhibited efficiencies of about 14%; however, efficiencies below 13% were measured when cells were activated at temperatures higher than 400 °C.   For our system, the optimal activation temperature was found to be around 390 °C. The heat treatment significantly improves the V_{OC} and FF. Though the exact mechanism of CdCl$_2$ treatment is still under debate, it is generally accepted that during the treatment Cl atoms diffuse into CdTe to passivate grain boundaries and to form defect complexes that have shallower acceptor levels than Cd vacancies [17]. Furthermore, the treatment facilitates interdiffusion at the CdS/CdTe junction and reduces the non-radiative recombination at the junction [18]. All these effects are expected to improve V_{OC} and FF as was experimentally observed. However, treatment at too high of a temperature may lead to severe interdiffusion and cause complete consumption of CdS layers, leading to shunting. This would lead to low FF and V_{OC}, as experimentally observed.

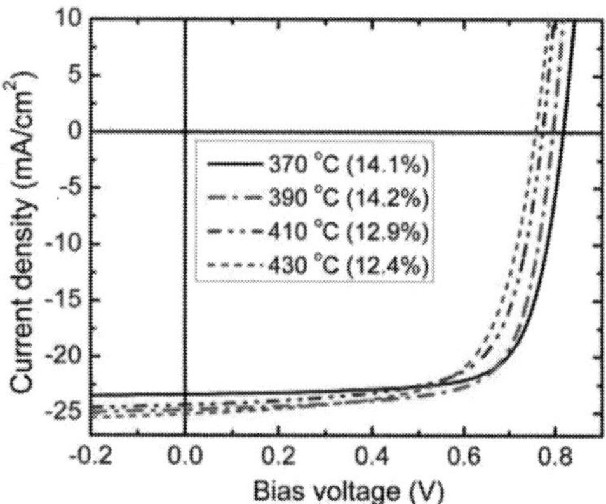

Fig. 2. Light J-V characteristics of CdS/CdTe solar cells received cadmium chloride activation at various temperatures. Each heat treatment was done for 10 minutes in dry air ambient.

C. The Role of Oxygen in CdTe and CdS Layers

It has been shown that incorporating a small amount of O_2 in both CdTe and CdS layers is very beneficial for CdTe solar cell performance. Ferekides et al. [10] reported that the introduction of oxygen during CSS CdTe controls the grain size and will lead to the growth of dense films. It is also suggested that the incorporation of O may enhance the p-type doping of CdTe and improve the cell efficiency. Therefore, most of the high temperature processing options routinely use partial pressure of oxygen during CdTe growth [3, 11, 14]. In our fabrication method, we also have optimized the O_2 concentration in the CSS deposition chamber. We found that 0.5% oxygen mixed helium ambient gives the best cell performance. The cell performances were poor if a significantly higher O_2 concentration was introduced in the deposition chamber.

The presence of O_2 in the CdS window layer can optimize the interdiffusion at the CdS/CdTe interface and lead to improved cell performance. Wu [11] reported that the incorporation of O_2 at room temperature, sputtered CdS films leads to a nanocrystalline CdS:O phase with enhanced optical band gaps: which results in improved J_{SC}. However, in our study, the incorporation of O_2 led to a smaller optical band gap in CdS. Figure 3 shows the transmission spectra of the sputtered CdS layers deposited with various O_2 concentrations. The concentration was measured on the gas flow meter and may not necessarily indicate the same O_2 concentration in the sputtered films. The reference transmission was taken from an HRT coated TEC15 substrate without a CdS layer. It is seen that with the introduction of O_2 in the argon ambient, the CdS absorption edges start to shift toward lower energies; suggesting a decrease in the optical band gap. If the O_2 concentration exceeds 5%, the absorption edge suddenly shifts

back to higher energies. These results are consistent with the data reported by Gupta et al. [19]. Our results are contrary to the results reported Wu [11]. The difference is mainly attributed to the growth temperature. In our case, the CdS layers were deposited at 270 °C, whereas the CdS layers reported by Wu [11] were deposited at room temperature (RT). The nanocrystalline CdS:O phase is not expected to form at 270 °C. We have also deposited CdS:O layers at RT, and we indeed observed increased band gaps. However, our device data revealed that the performance of cells using CdS:O layers deposited at 270 °C is much better than the cells using CdS:O layers deposited at RT. It is important to note that the introduction of oxygen in sputtering ambient significantly slows down the growth rate of the sputtered film. This is mainly due to the bombardment of highly energetic oxygen ions (O^-) onto the substrates. These ions either get incorporated into the film or knock off the already deposited material [20].

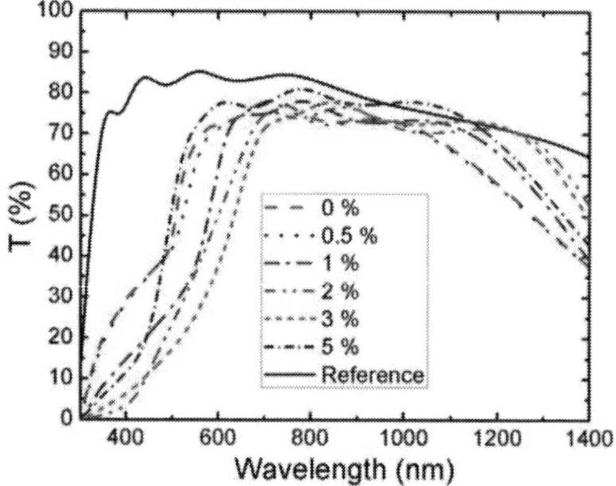

Fig. 3. Transmission spectra of CdS thin films sputtered on TEC15 soda-lime glass substrates with various O_2 concentrations in the deposition ambient.

Figures 4(a) and 4(b) show the device performance averaged over 20 dot cells as a function of oxygen concentration in the sputtering ambient. The results show the incorporation of O_2 in the CdS layer affects V_{OC}, J_{SC}, and FF. The change of J_{SC} correlates well with the change of the optical band gap induced by the incorporation of O_2. The cells with a CdS layer deposited at higher ambient O_2 concentrations resulted in lower J_{SC}, consistent with the transmission data shown in Figure 3. The averaged J_{SC} obtained for cells using CdS layers deposited in 0-1% ambient oxygen concentration are about 24.0 mA/cm². With 2% or higher O_2 concentrations, the J_{SC} drops quickly and reaches the minimum value of 18.7 mA/cm² for 5% O_2 concentration. As suggested in previous studies, the presence of oxygen in CdS layers can effectively suppress the interdiffusion at the CdS/CdTe front junctions [18, 21], which reduces the non-radiative recombination at the junction and leads to improved V_{OC}. It is seen in Figure 4(a) that the V_{OC} first fluctuates within the range of 800-830 mV at low O_2 concentration (0-2%). The V_{OC} starts to decrease as the O_2 concentration increases. The highest V_{OC} obtained is about 845 mV for the 1% O_2 concentration.

Figure 4(b) shows the averaged FFs and efficiencies of CdTe cells as a function of oxygen concentration in the CdS deposition ambient. It is seen that the influence of O_2 concentration on FF is less significant than that on V_{OC} and J_{SC}. The FFs vary in between

　　　348

75% - 70% for 0-3% oxygen ambient but decreases to 65% for 5% ambient oxygen concentration due to shunting effects. With the changes on V_{OC}, J_{SC}, and FF, the averaged cell efficiencies of these devices vary from 8.8% - 14.5%. The optimal O_2 concentration in the sputtering ambient is found to be 1%. It is slightly lower than the O_2 concentration reported in literature (2%) [11]. However, the latter used CdS layers deposited at RT.

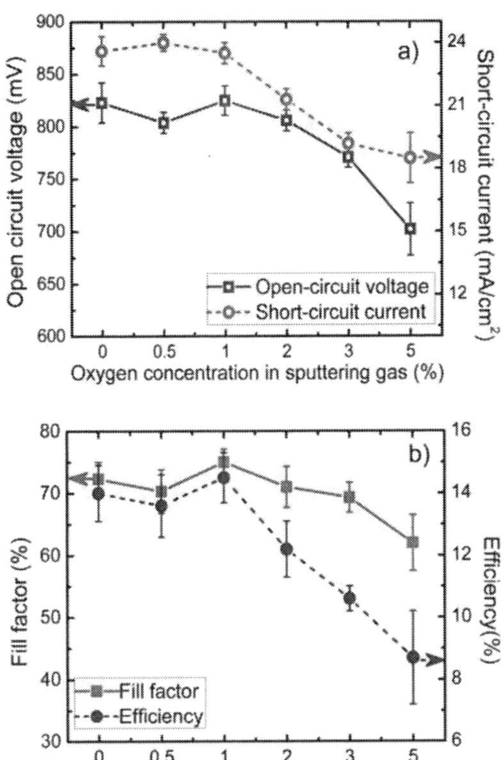

Fig. 4. Averaged solar cell performance parameters over 20 dot CdS/CdTe cells as a function of O_2 concentration in sputtering gas ambient during CdS deposition; a) V_{OC} and J_{SC}; b) efficiencies and FFs.

D. Fabrication of High Efficiency CdTe Cells

After careful optimization of all fabrication parameters discussed above, a series of CdTe solar cells were fabricated with small aperture areas: 0.08 cm^2. For comparison, CBD CdS window layers were also used to finish devices. Table 1 presents the best and the averaged device performance of CdTe cells using CdS window layers grown by RF sputtering and CBD. Previous studies have indicated that CdTe solar cells using CBD CdS window layers outperform CdTe cells using CdS layers deposited by non-CBD methods, such as sputtering [11]. In this study, the cells using sputtered CdS window layers showed slightly better performance than the cells using CBD CdS window layers; specifically the FF and J_{SC}.

Table 1. The best cell performance and 25 cell-averaged performances for solar cells using sputtered CdS and CBD CdS as window layers.

CdS deposition		V_{OC} (mV)	J_{SC} (mA/ cm^2)	FF (%)	Eff (%)	R_S (Ω-cm^2)	R_{SH} (Ω-cm^2)
Sputter	Best	845	24.5	76.8	15.8	2.4	2175
	Ave	827	23.6	75.6	14.6	2.6	1690
CBD	Best	847	23.8	74.3	14.9	2.7	1266
	Ave	829	23.7	73.1	14.2	3.0	1306

The J-V curves and EQE data measured from the two best cells, using sputtered CdS and CBD CdS window layers, are shown in Figure 5(a) and 5(b), respectively. The measured shunt resistances from the light J-V curves reveal that the cell using sputtered CdS as the window layer exhibits a higher resistance than the cell using CBD CdS as the window layer. This explains the observed difference in FF for the two cells. The J-V curves measured from both cells show no cross-over effects, indicating minimum photoconductive behavior of the CdS layers [22]. The EQE data shows noticeable current losses at 400-500 nm, suggesting that the CdS window layers were not consumed completely during CdTe deposition and chloride activation. The thickness of the residual CdS layer is estimated to be 55-60 nm, using the approach suggested by McCandless et al. [14]. The QE response of the cell using CBD CdS as the window layer shows a slightly lower current at the 550-830 nm range than the cell using sputtered CdS as the window layer. The mechanism for this behavior is subjected to further study.

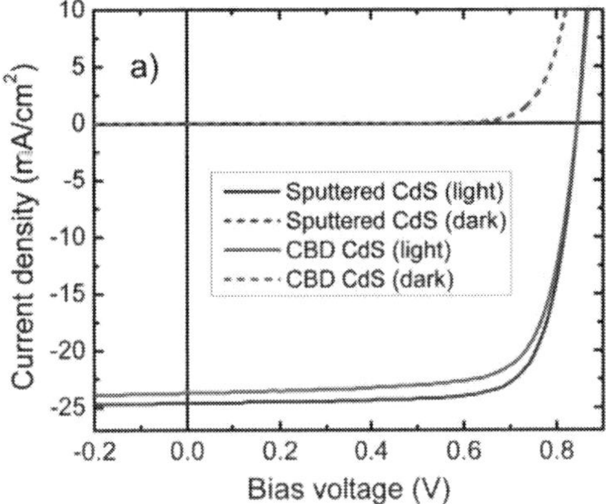

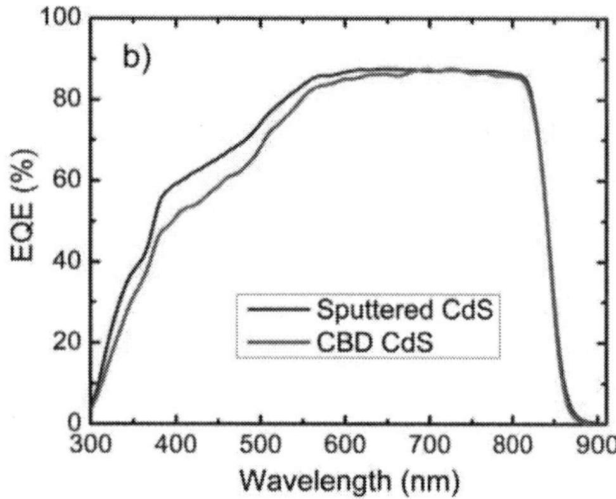

Fig. 5. a) J-V and b) EQE of the best CdS/CdTe cells using sputtered CdS and CBD CdS as the window layers.

IV. CONCLUSIONS

We have fabricated CdS/CdTe thin-film solar cells with a best small-area (0.08 cm^2) cell efficiency of 15.8% on commercial Pilkington TEC15 soda lime glass substrates without an AR coating. We found that, besides optimizing the growth process of the window and absorber layers and the CdCl$_2$ activation steps, incorporating a small amount of oxygen in the CdS window layer is essential for achieving high efficiency CdTe solar cells. We also found that the parameters and processes that lead to high efficiency cells are system and substrate dependent. Our fabrication process is capable of scaling up for commercial manufacturing.

ACKNOWLEDGEMENTS

The Authors would like to thank Professor Alvin D. Compaan for providing access to his lab and for his valuable suggestions. We also would like to thank Dr. David Strickler from NSG (Pilkington NA) Toledo, OH for supplying SnO$_2$:F coated soda-lime glass substrates. This work was partially supported by the U.S. Department of Energy SunShot program under contract No. 0492-1662 and the Ohio Research Scholar Program (ORSP).

REFERENCES

[1] M.D. Wild-Scholten, M. Sturm, M.A. Butturi, M. Noack, K. Heasman, and G. Timo, "Environmental sustainability of concentrator PV systems: preliminary LCA results of the Apollon projects," *in 25th EUPVSEC,* pp. 3908-3911, 2010.

[2] http://investor.firstsolar.com/releases.cfm (press release February 26, 2013).

[3] B.A. Korevaar, A. Halverson, J Cao, J. Choi, C. Collazo-Davila, W. Huber, "High efficiency CdTe cells using manufacturable window layers and CdTe thickness," *Thin Solid Films,* vol. 535, pp. 229-232, 2013.

[4] R. Banai, C. Blissett, C. Buurma, E. Colegrove, P. Bechmann, J. Ellsworth, M. Morley, S. Barnes, C. Lennon, C. Gilmore, R. Dhere, J. Bergeson, M. Scott, and T. Gessert, "Polycrystalline CdTe solar cells on buffered commercial TCO-coated glass with efficiencies above 15%," *in 37th Photovoltaic Specialists Conference,* 2011, pp. 3410.

[5] B.E. McCandless and K.D. Dobson, "Processing options for CdTe thin film solar cells," *Solar Energy,* vol. 77, pp.839-856, 2004.

[6] C.S. Ferekides, U. Balasubramanian, R. Mamazza, V. Viswanathan, H. Zhao, and D.L. Morel, "CdTe thin film solar cells: device and technology issues," *Solar Energy,* vol. 77, pp.823-830, 2004.

[7] N.R. Paudel, K.A. Wieland and A.D. Compaan, "Ultrathin CdS/CdTe solar cells by sputtering," *Solar Energy Materials & Solar Cells,* vol. 105, pp. 109-112, 2012.

[8] T.L. Chu, S.S. Chu, "Recent progress in thin-film cadmium telluride solar cells," *Progress in Photovoltaics: Research and Applications,* vol. 1, pp. 31-42, 1993.

[9] J.D. Major, Y.Y. Proskuryakov, K. Durose, G. Zoppi and I Forbes, "Control of grain size in sublimation-grown CdTe, and the improvement in performance of devices with systematically increased grain size," *Solar Energy Materials & Solar Cells,* vol. 94, pp. 1107-1112, 2010.

[10] C.S. Ferekides, D. Marinskiy, V. Viswanathan, B. Tetali, V. Palekis, P. Selvaraj, D.L. Morel, "High effciency CSS CdTe solar cells," *Thin Solid Films,* vol. 361-362, pp. 520-526, 2000.

[11] X. Wu, "High-efficiency polycrystalline CdTe thin-film solar cells," *Solar Energy,* vol. 77, pp. 803-814, 2004.

[12] N.R. Paudel and Y. Yan, "Fabrication and characterization of high-efficiency CdTe-based thin-film solar cells on commercial SnO$_2$:F coated soda-lime glass substrates," *Surface and Coatings Technology,* (manuscript submitted).

[13] P. V. Meyers, C. H. Liu, and T. J. Frey, "Method of making photovoltaic cell with chloride dip," *U. S. Patent No. 4,873,198,* 1989.

[14] B.E. McCandless and W.A. Buchanan, "High throughput processing of CdTe/CdS solar cells with thin absorber layers," *in 33rd IEEE Photovoltaic Specialists Conference,* 2008, pp. 134-139.

[15] N. Romeo, A. Bosio, V. Canevari, and A. Podesta, "Recent progress on CdTe/CdS thin film solar cells," *Solar Energy,* vol. 77, pp. 795-801, 2004.

[16] R.A. Enzenroth, K. L. Barth, W. S. Sampath, V. Manivannan, A.T. Kirkpatrick and P. Noronha , "Stable Cu-based back contacts for CdTe thin film photovoltaic devices," *Journal of Solar Energy Engineering,* vol. 131 pp. 021012–1, 2009.

[17] J. Krustok, V. Valdna, K. Hjelt and H. Collan, "Does the low-temperature Arrhenius plot of the photoluminescence intensity in CdTe point towards an erroneous activation energy?," *Journal of Applied Physics,* Vol. 80, pp. 1757-1760, 1996.

[18] D. Albin, Y. Yan, and M.M. Al-Jassim, "The effect of oxygen on interface microstructure evolution in the CdS/CdTe solar cells," *Photovoltaics: Research and Applications,* vol. 10, pp.309-322, 2002.

[19] A. Gupta, K. Allada, S.H. Lee, and A.D. Compaan, "Oxygenated CdS window layer for sputtered CdS/CdTe solar cells," *MRS Proceedings*, 763, B8.9, 2003.

[20] K. Ellmer, "Magnetron sputtering of transparent conductive zinc oxide: relation between the sputtering parameters and the electronic properties," *Journal of Physics D: Applied Physics Letters,* vol. 33, pp. R17-R32, 2000.

[21] Y. Yan, D. Albin, and M.M. Al-Jassim, "Do grain boundaries assist S diffusion in polycrystalline CdS/CdTe heterojunctions?," *Appl. Phys. Lett.,* vol. 78, pp.171-173, 2001.

[22] S. Hegedus, D. Ryan, K. Dobson, B. McCandless and D. Desai, "Photoconductive CdS: how does it affect CdTe/CdS solar cell performance," *MRS Proceedings*, vol. 763, B9.5, 2003.

Improved Dislocation Model for Silicon Solar Cells: Calculation of Dark Current

Vinay Budhraja, *Member, IEEE*, B. Sopori, N.M. Ravindra, and D.Misra, *Member, IEEE*

Abstract —We have extended a previous dislocation model to include the effect of front and back surface recombination velocities in a silicon solar cell. This improved dislocation model uses Green's Function approach to solve three dimensional continuity equation in p and n layer of solar cell. Expressions for saturation current components are derived for different dislocation densities and compared with published experimental results. The modeling results also show the variation of cell parameters with dislocation density.

Index Terms — Continuity equation, dislocation, Green's function, modeling, multicrystalline silicon.

I. INTRODUCTION

OUT of various defects, dislocations are the most harmful in multicrystalline silicon. It is important to have a model from which the variation of cell parameters can be observed. The modeling of dislocations has been published by many authors [1-8]. They have been very helpful to develop an understanding of the recombination effects of dislocations. A semi-analytical model was presented by Ghitani, which addresses recombination in the bulk and the depletion regions but did not include surface recombination effects. Recently we developed an improved dislocation model as an extension of dislocation paper introduced by Ghitani et al.[9].

In a previous publication, we have discussed the influence of dislocations on the cell parameters under illumination [10] without a detailed description of dark current. Here we discuss calculation of the dark current components including the effects of surface recombination. The main interest in this work is to develop expression for J_{01} (saturation current density due to diffusion) so that this model can be integrated into network model for calculating cell parameters for large area devices with nonuniformly distributed dislocations [12]. In the forward biased, mainly two components of currents-diffusion current and recombination current in the depletion region are dominant. The diffusion current is determined using the improved dislocation model and described in next section. We use the second (recombination) component of current as calculated by Zolper et. al [7] and Ghitani et. al [11].

II. THEORY

The three dimensional continuity equations were solved for minority carriers in p and n layers of solar cell using Green's function. The assumptions made in the improved dislocation model are:

(i) Dislocations are arranged periodically in a regular array, which extends from top to bottom of the solar cell.

(ii) Dislocations have its effect in vertical as well as in horizontal direction.

(iii) The effect of emitter (which was ignored in previous model) was included.

(iv) The effect of recombination activity at dislocation was also considered.

Fig. 1. shows a schematic of the modeled solar cell.

A. Dark current in n-region

The continuity equation for holes in the n region is given by

$$\nabla^2(p_n - p_{no}) - (p_n - p_{no})/L_p^2 = 0 \tag{1}$$

Boundary conditions used in the n region are:

$$\frac{\partial(p_n - p_{no})}{\partial z} = \frac{S_1}{D_p}(p_n - p_{no}) \quad \text{at } z = 0 \tag{2}$$

$$p_n = p_{no}\exp\left(\frac{qV}{kT}\right) \text{ at } z = Z_j \tag{3}$$

$$\frac{\partial(p_n - p_{no})}{\partial x} = \pm\frac{S_d}{D_p}(p_n - p_{no}) \quad \text{at } x = \pm a \tag{4}$$

$$\frac{\partial(p_n - p_{no})}{\partial y} = \pm\frac{S_d}{D_p}(p_n - p_{no}) \quad \text{at } y = \pm a \tag{5}$$

Green's function method was used to obtain the solution of equation 1. The hole concentration was calculated as

$$(p_n - p_{no})(x_0, y_0, z_0) = \oiint\{(p_n - p_{no})\nabla G - G\nabla(p_n - p_{no})\}.ds \tag{6}$$

The hole current density was determined as

$$J_p = \frac{1}{4a^2}\oiint_{-a}^{a} -qD_p\left|\frac{d(p_n - p_{no})}{dz_0}\right|_{z=Z_j} dx_0 dy_0 \tag{7}$$

$$J_p = J_{p1} + J_{p2} \tag{8}$$

J_{p1} is due to the first term in equation (6) and J_{p2} is due to the second term in equation (6).

$$J_{p1} = f1 \cdot \left(\exp\left(\frac{qV}{kT}\right) - 1\right) \tag{9}$$

Where

$$f1 = qD_p \sum_{m,n} M_a N_a \frac{4\sin^2(ma)\sin^2(na)}{m^2 n^2 a^2} p_{n0}$$

$$\frac{\left(\frac{S_1}{D_p}\right)\cosh\left(\frac{Z_j}{L_2}\right) + \left(\frac{1}{L_2}\right)\sinh\left(\frac{Z_j}{L_2}\right)}{\cosh\left(\frac{Z_j}{L_2}\right) + \left(\frac{S_1 L_2}{D_p}\right)\sinh\left(\frac{Z_j}{L_2}\right)} \tag{10}$$

$$J_{p2} = f2 \cdot \left(\exp\left(\frac{qV}{kT}\right) - 1\right) \tag{11}$$

Where

$$f2 = -\frac{qD_p}{4a^2} \sum_{m,n} M_a N_a \frac{4\sin^2(ma)\sin(ma)}{n} \sum_K \left(\frac{\sin(n+K)a}{(n+K)} + \right.$$

$$\frac{\sin(n-K)a}{(n-K)}\right)\left(\frac{2\sin(Ka)}{Ka+0.5\sin(2Ka)}\right) p_{n0} \left[A_{L2} \int_0^{Z_j} E_1 \sinh\left(\frac{z}{L_2}\right) dz + \right.$$

$$B_{L2} \int_0^{Z_j} E_1 \cosh\left(\frac{z}{L_2}\right) dz - C_{L2} \left. E_1 \sinh\left(\frac{z}{L_2}\right)\right|_{z=Z_j} -$$

$$D_{L2} \left. E_1 \cosh\left(\frac{z}{L_2}\right)\right|_{z=Z_j} \right] \tag{12}$$

Where $B_{L2} = \dfrac{\left(\frac{1}{L_2}\right)\{1/\cosh\left(\frac{Z_j}{L_2}\right)\}}{\{\frac{1}{L_2}+\frac{S_1}{D_p}\tanh\left(\frac{Z_j}{L_2}\right)\}}$, $A_{L2} = \left(\frac{S_1 L_2}{D_p}\right)B_{L2}$,

$$C_{L2} = \frac{\left(\frac{S_1 L_2}{D_p}\right)\sinh\left(\frac{Z_j}{L_2}\right) + \cosh\left(\frac{Z_j}{L_2}\right)}{\{\frac{1}{L_2}+\frac{S_1}{D_p}\tanh\left(\frac{Z_j}{L_2}\right)\}}, \quad D_{L2} = -\tanh\left(\frac{Z_j}{L_2}\right)C_{L2} \text{ and}$$

$$E_1 = \left[\left\{\left(-\frac{S_1 L_1}{D_p}\right) + \left(\frac{S_1 L_1}{D_p \cosh\left(\frac{Z_j}{L_1}\right)}\right)\right\}\sinh\left(\frac{z}{L_1}\right) + \left\{\left(\frac{S_1 L_1}{D_p}\right).\right.\right.$$

$$\tanh\left(\frac{Z_j}{L_1}\right) + \left(\frac{1}{\cosh\left(\frac{Z_j}{L_1}\right)}\right)\right\}\cosh\left(\frac{z}{L_1}\right) - \left\{\left(\frac{S_1 L_1}{D_p}\right)\tanh\left(\frac{Z_j}{L_1}\right) + 1\right\}\right]/$$

$$\left\{1 + \frac{S_1 L_1}{D_p}\tanh\left(\frac{Z_j}{L_1}\right)\right\}$$

B. Dark current in p-region

The continuity equation for electrons in the p region is given by

$$(n_p - n_{p0}) - (n_p - n_{p0})/L_n^2 = 0 \tag{13}$$

Boundary conditions used in the p region are:

$$n_p = n_{p0}\exp\left(\frac{qV}{kT}\right) \quad \text{at } z = Z_j + W \tag{14}$$

$$\frac{\partial(n_p - n_{p0})}{\partial z} = -\frac{S_2}{D_n}(n_p - n_{p0}) \quad \text{at } z = d \tag{15}$$

$$\frac{\partial(n_p - n_{p0})}{\partial x} = \pm\frac{S_d}{D_n}(n_p - n_{p0}) \quad \text{at } x = \mp a \tag{16}$$

$$\frac{\partial(n_p - n_{p0})}{\partial y} = \pm\frac{S_d}{D_n}(n_p - n_{p0}) \quad \text{at } y = \mp a \tag{17}$$

The electron current density was determined as

$$J_n = \frac{1}{4a^2} \oiint_{-a}^{a} qD_n \left.\left|\frac{d(n_p - n_{p0})}{dz_0}\right|\right|_{z=H} dx_0 dy_0 \tag{18}$$

$$J_n = J_{n1} + J_{n2} \tag{19}$$

$$J_{n1} = f3 \cdot \left(\exp\left(\frac{qV}{kT}\right) - 1\right) \tag{20}$$

Where

$$f3 = -q\,D_n \sum_{m,n} M_a N_a \frac{4\sin^2(ma)\sin^2(na)}{m^2 n^2 a^2} n_{p0} \cdot$$

$$\frac{\left(\frac{1}{L_2}\right)\cosh\left(\frac{H}{L_2}\right) - \left(\frac{1}{L_2}\right)\left(\frac{A_{11}}{A_{22}}\right)\sinh\left(\frac{H}{L_2}\right)}{\sinh\left(\frac{H}{L_2}\right) - \left(\frac{A_{11}}{A_{22}}\right)\cosh\left(\frac{H}{L_2}\right)} \tag{21}$$

$$J_{n2} = f4 \cdot \left(\exp\left(\frac{qV}{kT}\right) - 1\right) \tag{22}$$

where

$$f4 = \frac{qD_n}{4a^2} \sum_{m,n} M_a N_a \frac{4\sin^2(ma)\sin(ma)}{n} \sum_K \left(\frac{\sin(n+K)a}{(n+K)} + \right.$$

$$\frac{\sin(n-K)a}{(n-K)}\right)\left(\frac{2\sin(Ka)}{Ka+0.5\sin(2Ka)}\right) n_{p0} \left[A_{L2}\left. E_2 \sinh\left(\frac{z}{L_2}\right)\right|_{z=H} + \right.$$

$$B_{L2}\left. E_2 \cosh\left(\frac{z}{L_2}\right)\right|_{z=H} + C_{L2}\int_H^d E_2 \sinh\left(\frac{z}{L_2}\right) dz - $$

$$D_{L2}\int_H^d E_2 \cosh\left(\frac{z}{L_2}\right) dz\right] \tag{23}$$

Where $H = Z_j + W$,

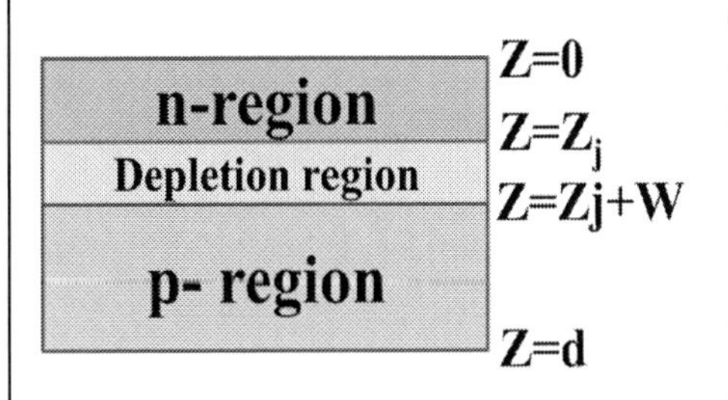

Fig. 1. Side view of the modeled device

$$B_{L2} = \frac{\sinh\left(\frac{H}{L_2}\right) - \left(\frac{A_{11}}{A_{22}}\right)\cosh\left(\frac{H}{L_2}\right)}{\left(\frac{1}{L_2}\right) - \left(\frac{1}{L_2}\right)\left(\frac{A_{11}}{A_{22}}\right)\coth\left(\frac{H}{L_2}\right)}, \quad A_{L2} = -\coth\left(\frac{H}{L_2}\right)B_{L2}$$

$$C_{L2} = \frac{1/\sinh\left(\frac{H}{L_2}\right)}{1 - \left(\frac{A_{11}}{A_{22}}\right)\coth\left(\frac{H}{L_2}\right)}, \quad D_{L2} = -\left(\frac{A_{11}}{A_{22}}\right)C_{L2} \quad \text{and}$$

$$E_2 = \left[\left\{\frac{1}{\sinh\left(\frac{H}{L_1}\right)} - \coth\left(\frac{H}{L_1}\right)\cosh\left(\frac{d}{L_1}\right) + \left(\frac{A_1}{A_2}\right)\coth\left(\frac{H}{L_1}\right).\right.\right.$$

$$\sinh\left(\frac{d}{L_1}\right)\right\}\sinh\left(\frac{z}{L_1}\right) + \left\{-\left(\frac{A_1}{A_2}\right)\frac{1}{\sinh\left(\frac{H}{L_1}\right)} + \cosh\left(\frac{d}{L_1}\right) - \right.$$

$$\left(\frac{A_1}{A_2}\right)\sinh\left(\frac{d}{L_1}\right)\} \cosh\left(\frac{z}{L_1}\right) + \{\left(\frac{A_1}{A_2}\right)\coth\left(\frac{H}{L_1}\right) - 1\}] \Big/$$

$$\{1 - \left(\frac{A_1}{A_2}\right)\coth\left(\frac{H}{L_1}\right)\}$$

$$A_1 = \frac{1}{L_1}\cosh\left(\frac{d}{L_1}\right) + \frac{S_2}{D_n}\sinh\left(\frac{d}{L_1}\right)$$

$$A_2 = \frac{1}{L_1}\sinh\left(\frac{d}{L_1}\right) + \frac{S_2}{D_n}\cosh\left(\frac{d}{L_1}\right)$$

$$A_{11} = \frac{1}{L_2}\cosh\left(\frac{d}{L_2}\right) + \frac{S_2}{D_n}\sinh\left(\frac{d}{L_2}\right)$$

$$A_{22} = \frac{1}{L_2}\sinh\left(\frac{d}{L_2}\right) + \frac{S_2}{D_n}\cosh\left(\frac{d}{L_2}\right)$$

$$M_a = m/(ma + \left(\frac{1}{2}\right)\sin(2ma))$$

$$N_a = n/(na + \left(\frac{1}{2}\right)\sin(2na))$$

$$\frac{1}{L_1{}^2} = \frac{1}{L_n{}^2} + K^2 \; ; \quad \frac{1}{L_2{}^2} = \frac{1}{L_n{}^2} + m^2 + n^2$$

The total diffusion current density in the dark is given by

$$J_{diffusion} = J_p + J_n \tag{24}$$

$J_{diffusion}$ can also be expressed as

$$J_{diffusion} = (f1 + f2 + f3 + f4)\left(\exp\left(\frac{qV}{kT}\right) - 1\right) = J_{01}.$$
$$\left(\exp\left(\frac{qV}{kT}\right) - 1\right) \tag{25}$$

where J_{01} is the saturation current density of the diffusion component. f1, f2, f3 and f4 were calculated in equations (10), (12), (21) and (23) respectively. In the summation of J_n and J_p, the term $(\exp(qV/kT)-1)$ is common; J_{01} is the expression other than $(\exp(qV/kT)-1)$ in this summation. Other details of calculations of diffusion currents are given in reference [13].

To calculate the recombination in the depletion region, we follow the formalism of Fossum et al. [14], which gives

$$J_{recombination} = J_{02}.\exp(\frac{qV}{2kT}) \tag{26}$$

where $J_{02} = (q/2)(S_n S_p)^{1/2} n_i W N_d$

Ghitani [11] introduced one more component of current, which arises due to the shunting provided by dislocations. This shunt component of current is given as

$$J_{shunt} = J_{03}.\left(\exp\left(\frac{qV}{2kT}\right) - 1\right) \tag{27}$$

where $J_{03} = (2kT\, n_i \mu \Pi r^2 N_d)/W$, r is the radius of dislocation pipe.

We also incorporate this component of current and calculated the total current density which is the sum of $J_{diffusion}$, $J_{recombination}$ and J_{shunt}. The total current density in dark is given as

$$J_{total} = J_{diffusion} + J_{recombination} + J_{shunt} \tag{28}$$

III. RESULTS

The values of input parameters taken for dark current calculations are given in the Table I.

TABLE I
VALUES OF PARAMETERS TAKEN IN MODELING

S.No	Parameter	Value
1.	N_D (Donor concentration)	10^{18} cm^{-3}
2.	N_A (Acceptor concentration)	10^{16} cm^{-3}
3.	L_n (Diffusion length for electron)	1000 µm
4.	L_p (Diffusion length for hole)	10 µm
5.	S_d (Recombination activity)	10^4 cm/s
6.	S_1 (Front surface recombination Velocity)	10^3 (cm/s)
7.	S_2 (Back surface recombination Velocity)	10^4 (cm/s)
8.	Z_j (Junction depth)	0.3 µm
9.	Dn (Diffusion coefficient for electron)	50 (cm^2/V.s)
10.	Dp (Diffusion coefficient for hole)	20 (cm^2/V.s)
11.	d (thickness of the cell)	180 µm
12.	r (Radius of dislocation pipe)	0.15 µm

Fig. 2. shows the calculated dark J-V at different dislocation densities. As expected, an increase in dislocation density increases, both q/kT and q/2kT components of the dark saturation current.

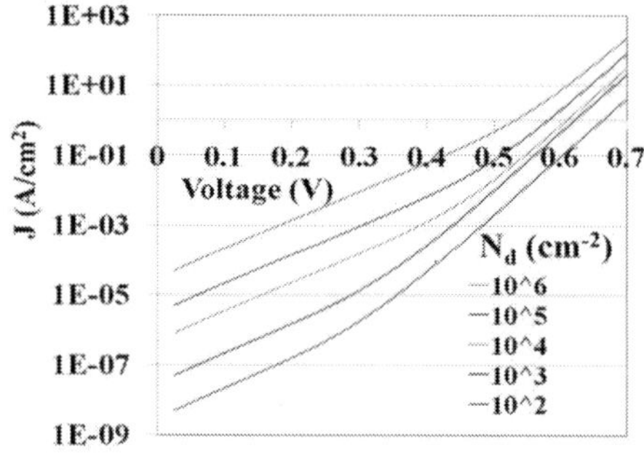

Fig. 2. Calculated dark J-V characteristics at different dislocation densities

Fig. 3. shows the variation of diffusion component of dark current density with dislocation density. The saturation current density due to diffusion increases with increase in dislocation density. Both, the increase in dislocation density and increase in saturation current density has an adverse effect on the performance of solar cell.

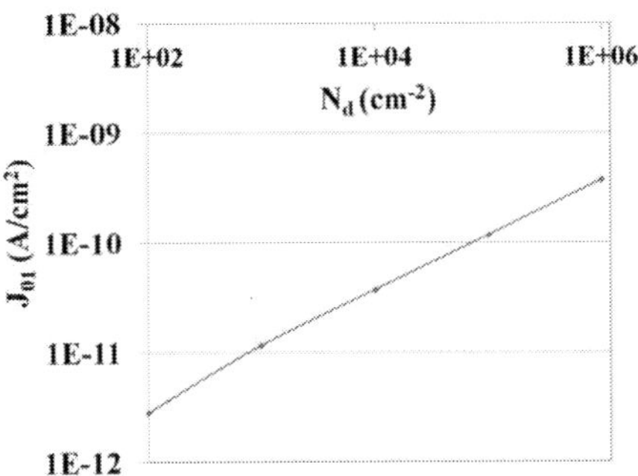

Fig. 3. Calculated diffusion component of dark current density as a function of dislocation density

The variation in dark current at different recombination activity of dislocations was also determined. This variation is shown in figure 4. As seen from this figure, there is not must change in the dark current with S_d, which tells that the dislocation density is the more dominant parameter than S_d in the calculation of dark current. The calculations done under light conditions (published elsewhere [10]) showed significant difference w.r.t S_d. In dark conditions, the diffusion of carriers is mainly effected by dislocation density because there is significant change in dark current with dislocation density.

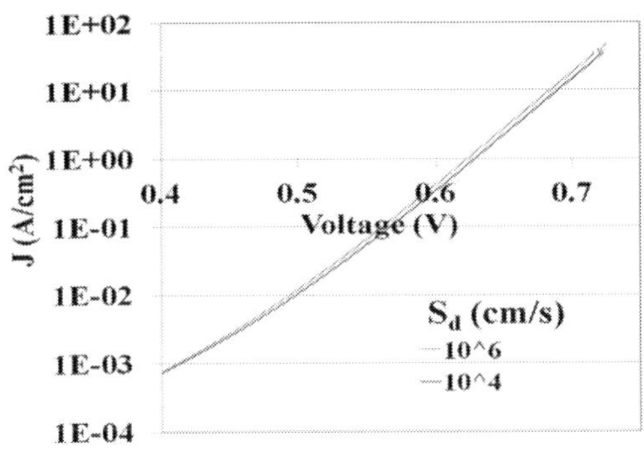

Fig. 4. Calculated dark J-V characteristics at different S_d

We used our model to determine the effect of S_1 and S_2 on the performance of solar cell, whereas this effect was neglected in earlier dislocation models. Fig. 5 a shows the variation of J_{01} with respect to S_1 for different dislocation densities. There is a significant change in J_{01} for lower values of dislocation density. This shows that the surface passivation is more effective in silicon wafers having low dislocation density. Fig. 5 b shows the dark J-V at different values of S_1. There is an increase in dark current with S_1. This shows that the effect of S_1 can no longer be neglected in a dislocation model.

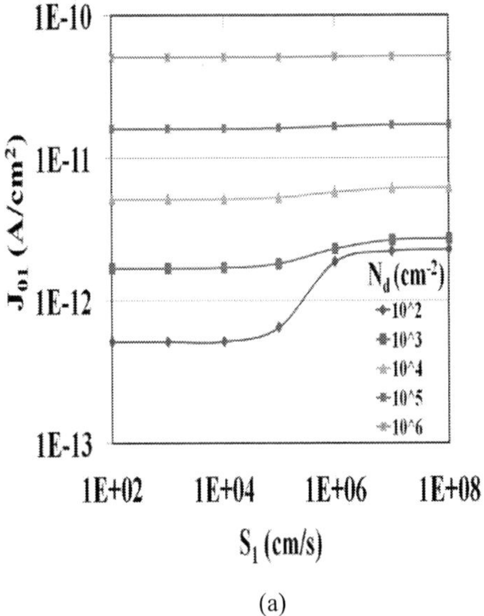

(a)

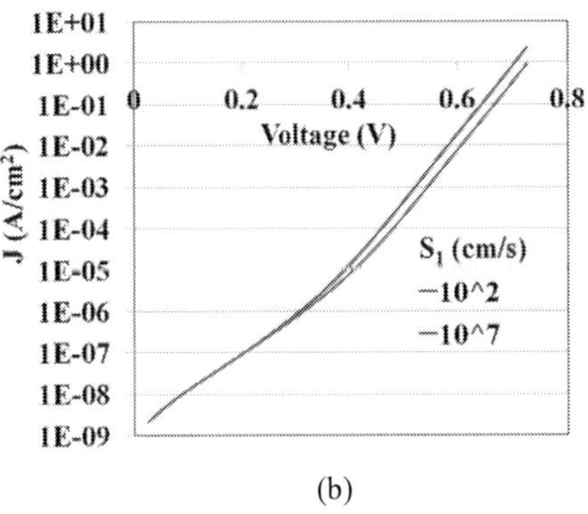

(b)

Fig. 5. (a) Calculated J_{01} vs. S_1 at different dislocation densities, (b) Dark J-V at lower and higher values of S_1

Fig. 6 a shows the variation of J_{01} with respect to S_2. Again, there is a significant change for lower dislocation density. However, this change is less in comparison to the change in J_{01} with respect to S_1 as we seen earlier in fig. 5 a. Fig. 6 b shows the dark J-V at different values of S_2. Again, there is an increase in dark current with S_2 but this increase is less in comparison to increase in dark current with S_1 as we seen earlier in fig. 5 b.

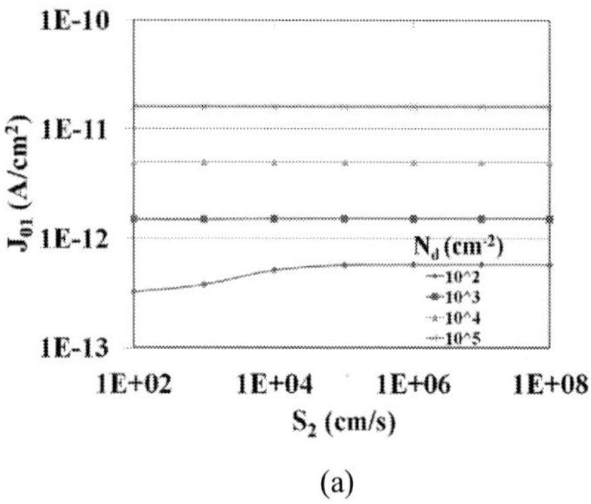

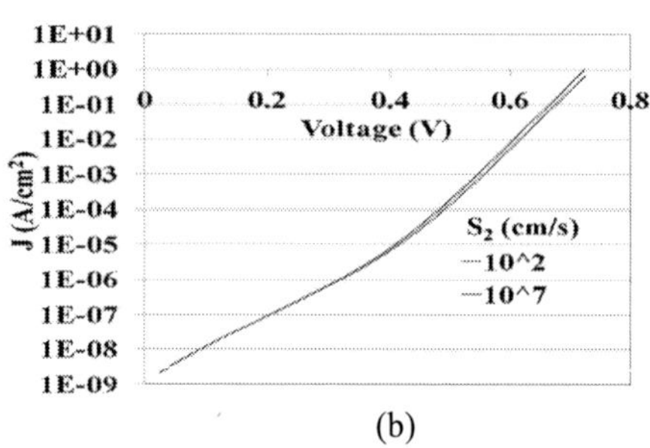

Fig. 6. (a) Calculated J_{01} vs. S_2 at different dislocation densities, (b) Dark J-V at lower and higher values of S_2

Fig.7 a and 7 b show the logarithmic plot of the dark current components w.r.t voltage at low and high dislocation densities respectively. In this figure, the diffusion component is $J_{diffusion}$, the shunt component is J_{shunt} and recombination in space charge region (SCR) is $J_{recombination}$. From this figure we observed that the recombination component of current is always negligible at all voltages. At low voltages i.e. $\leq$ 0.3 V the component of current due to the recombination in space charge region (SCR) is dominant. The diffusion component of current is dominant at higher voltages i.e. $\geq$ 0.4 V and we have already shown that the saturation current is affected by dislocation density.

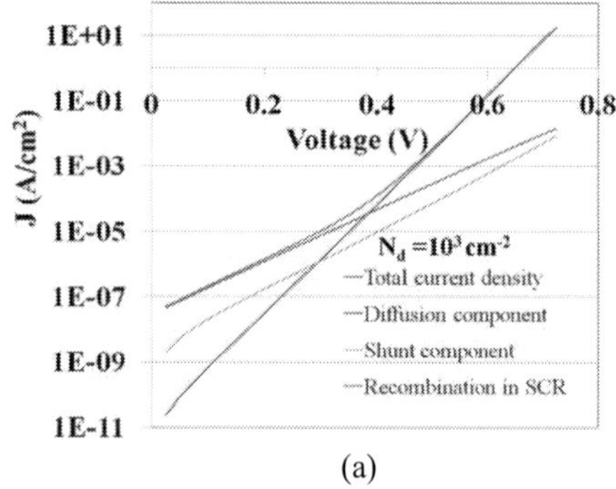

(a)

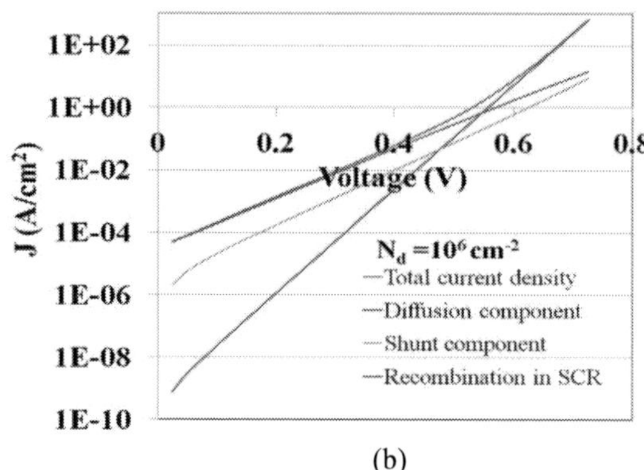

(b)

Fig. 7. Calculated dark current density vs. voltage at (a)$N_d=10^3$ cm^{-2}, and (b)$N_d=10^6$ cm^{-2}

The dark J-V was calculated at low, moderate and high dislocation densities and compared with the previously published experimental results. This comparison is shown in fig 8. In experimental studies [11, 15], measurements were taken on mesa diodes on different defect density regions. The experimental results suggest that there is an enhancement in current as the density of dislocation increases. The experimental results are in qualitative agreement with the modeling results. This agreement is significantly pronounced at higher voltages on which our theoretical model is based.

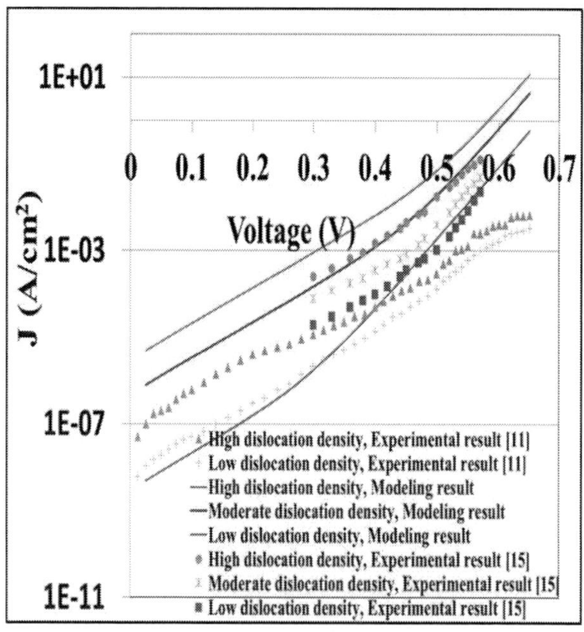

Fig. 8. Comparison of experimental [11, 15] and modeling results of dark J-V at low, moderate and high dislocation density.

IV. CONCLUSION

We have developed a model which calculates the effect of dislocations on the dark current of solar cells that includes the effect of surface recombination. The diffusion component of current was calculated by solving the continuity equation in three dimension using Green's function. The diffusion component of current showed the variation with dislocation density. The recombination component of current proposed by others was also inserted in this work to compare their effects on total current. The diffusion component of current was dominant at higher voltages. We compared the modeling results with the previously published experimental results and achieved qualitative agreement between these two results.

REFERENCES

[1] J.Cousins and J. E. Cotter, "The influence of diffusion-induced dislocations on high efficiency silicon solar cells. *IEEE Trans. Electron Dev.*, vol. 53, pp. 457-464, 2006.

[2] T. Kieliba, S. Riepe and W. Warta, " Effect of dislocations on open circuit voltage in crystalline silicon solar cells", *J. Appl. Phys.*, vol. 100, pp. 093708, 2006.

[3] K. L. Pauls, K. W. Mitchell and W. Chesarek, "The effect of dislocations on the performance of silicon solar cells", in *Proc. 18th IEEE PVSC*, pp. 209-213, 1993.

[4] C. V. Opdorp, A. T. Vink and C. Werkhoven, "Minority carrier recombination at surfaces, dislocations and microdefects: evaluation of parameters from near band edge luminescence," in *Proc. 6th III-V Symposium St. Louis MO*, edited by L.F.Eastman, Inst. Phys. Conf. Ser. 33b, pp. 317, 1977.

[5] M. Lax, "Junction current and luminescence near a dislocation or a surface," *J. Appl. Phys.*, vol. 49, pp. 2796-2810, 1978.

[6] M. Yamaguchi, A. Yamamoto and Y. Itoh, "Effect of dislocation on the efficiency of thin-film GaAs solar cells on Si substrate," *J. Appl. Phys.*, vol. 59, pp. 1751-1753, 1986.

[7] J. C. Zolper and A. M. Barnett, "The effect of dislocations on the open circuit voltage of gallium arsenide solar cell," *IEEE Trans. Electron Dev.*, vol. 37, pp. 478-484, 1990.

[8] C. Donolato, "Modeling the effect of dislocations on the minority carrier diffusion length of a semiconductor," *J. Appl. Phys.*, vol. 84, pp. 2656-2664, 1998.

[9] H. E. Ghitani and S. Martinuzzi, "Influence of dislocations on electrical properties of large grained polycrystalline silicon cells. I. Model," *J. Appl. Phys.*, vol. 66, pp. 1717-1722, 1989.

[10] V. Budhraja, B. Sopori, N. M. Ravindra and D. Misra, "Improved dislocation model of silicon solar cells with the effect of front and back surface recombination velocity," accepted for publication in *Prog. Photovolt: Res. Appl.*

[11] H. E. Ghitani and M. Pasquinelli, "Influence of dislocations on dark current of multicrystalline silicon N^+P junction, *J. Phys. III France*, vol. 3, pp. 1931-1939, 1993.

[12] B. L. Sopori and R. Murphy, "Theoritical analysis of large-area inhomogenous solar cell," in *Proc. 12th European Photovoltaic Solar Energy Conference*, pp. 1797-1799, 1994.

[13] N. C. Halder and T. R. Williams, "Grain boundary effects in polycrystalline silicon solar cells I: solution of the three dimensional diffusion equation by the Green's function method," *Solar Cells*, vol. 8, pp. 201-223, 1983.

[14] J. G. Fossum and F. A. Lindholm, " Theory of grain boundary and intragrain recombination currents in polysilicon p-n junction solar cells," *IEEE Trans. Electron Dev.*, vol. 26, pp. 692-700, 1980.

[15] B. L. Sopori, "Crystal defects in RTR ribbons: their characteristics and influence on the ribbon cell performance," *J. Cryst. Growth*, vol. 82, pp. 228-236, 1987.

Vinay Budhraja has received B. Tech degree in Electronics and Communication Engineering from Institute of Engineering and Technology, Kanpur in 2004 and M. Tech degree in Materials Science Programme from Indian Institute of Technology Kanpur in 2007 and PhD degree in Electrical Engineering from New Jersey Institute of Technology (NJIT) in 2012. During PhD, from July, 2008 - December, 2012 he worked full time at National Renewable Energy Laboratory (NREL) through the joined collaboration of NJIT with NREL. Since spring, 2012 he has been a postdoctoral research fellow at Department of Electrical Engineering of University of Arkansas at Fayetteville. His research interests include semiconductor devices like silicon solar cells, MOS, thin film transistors etc. In 2009, he received best poster award at 34th IEEE PVSC.

Bhushan Sopori is a Principal Engineer at the National Center for Photovoltaics, National Renewable Energy Laboratory (NREL). Prior to joining NREL in June 1987, he worked at Motorola Inc. for ten years and was Manager, Optoelectronic Analysis, at Solavolt International, a joint venture of Motorola Inc. and Shell Oil Co. He has extensive experience in solar cell and module fabrication. Dr Sopori is currently performing research in Defect Engineering for advanced device fabrication, development of instrumentation for material growth and device fabrication, and development of new processing techniques. He works with the photovoltaic industry partners, helping both large and small companies to improve their products and lower their costs. He managed the NREL/DOE Silicon Program for about 12 years and was Task Leader for Device Processing and Modeling. Dr. Sopori has published over 200 papers (in the areas of optics, holography, lasers, integrated optics, semiconductor devices, and crystal growth), written two book chapters, has 22 awarded patents, and developed several instruments and solar cell fabrication methods that have either been licensed or are being negotiated for license to industry for commercial production. He has received numerous awards including three prestigious R&D 100 awards.

Durgamadhab (Durga) Misra has received his M.S. and Ph.D. degrees both in Electrical Engineering from University of Waterloo, Waterloo, Canada in 1985 and 1988 respectively. He has been with the Department of Electrical and Computer Engineering of New Jersey Institute of Technology (NJIT) as a faculty member since the fall of 1988 where he is currently a full professor. His current research focus is deep-submicron CMOS gate stacks and device reliability and solar cell devices. He received several research awards from the National Science Foundation, NASA and various Industries. In 1997 he worked on plasma charging damage to CMOS devices at the VLSI Research Department of Bell Laboratories of Lucent Technologies. He served as the Chair of the IEEE north Jersey Section for two years and subsequently received the IEEE Member Geographical Activities Board's International Leadership Award. He is a Senior Member of IEEE and is currently a Distinguished Lecturer of Electron Device Society. He is also EDS SRC Chair for North America East (Region 1, 2, 3 and 7). He has organized many International Symposiums on Solid-State Science and Technology field during the Technical Meetings of the Electrochemical Society and IEEE. He is a Fellow of the Electrochemical Society (ECS) and received the Thomas D. Collinan Award from the Dielectric Science and Technology Division and the Electronic and Photonic Division Award of ECS.

N.M. Ravindra, Member (1987) is a professor & chair of physics at the New Jersey Institute of Technology. His research interests include semiconductor materials and devices, magnetic field assisted assembly of semiconductors and energy. He is the Director of the Interdisciplinary program in materials science and engineering at NJIT and is the Editor-in-Chief of Emerging Materials Research.

Upconverter Silicon Solar Cell Devices for Efficient Utilization of Sub-Band-Gap Photons Under Concentrated Solar Radiation

Stefan Fischer, Aruna Ivaturi, Benjamin Fröhlich, Marc Rüdiger, Armin Richter, Karl W. Krämer,
Bryce S. Richards, and Jan Christoph Goldschmidt

Abstract—Upconversion (UC) of sub-band-gap photons has the potential to increase the efficiency of solar cells significantly. We realized an upconverter solar cell device, by attaching an upconverter layer of β-NaYF$_4$ doped with 25% Er^{3+} embedded in the polymer perfluorocyclobutyl to the rear side of a bifacial silicon solar cell. We determined the external quantum efficiency of such upconverter solar cell devices under broad-band sub-band-gap excitation. Under consideration of spectral mismatch, we calculated the expected increase of the short-circuit current density due to UC under the air mass 1.5 global illumination. We determined an enhancement of 2.2 mA/cm^2 for a spectral excitation band ranging from 1450 to 1600 nm and a comparatively low solar concentration of 78 suns. Subsequently, a system of concentrator lens and upconverter solar cell device was characterized with a solar simulator. We determined an increase of the short-circuit current density due to UC of sub-band-gap photons of 13.1 mA/cm^2 under a concentration of 210 suns. This corresponds to a potential relative increase of the solar cell efficiency of 0.19%.

Index Terms—Optical frequency conversion, photovoltaic cells, silicon, spectral conversion, upconversion (UC).

I. INTRODUCTION

IN silicon solar cells, more than 45% of all the photons of the solar spectrum cannot be utilized, because the energy of these photons is below the band gap energy of silicon. These photons carry about 20% of the whole energy of the sun's radiation. As a consequence, transforming these sub-band-gap photons into

Manuscript received June 10, 2013; revised August 6, 2013 and August 22, 2013; accepted August 27, 2013. Date of publication October 9, 2013; date of current version December 16, 2013.

S. Fischer, B. Fröhlich, M. Rüdiger, and A. Richter are with the Fraunhofer Institute for Solar Energy Systems, Freiburg 79110, Germany (e-mail: stefan.fischer@ise.fraunhofer.de; benjamin.froehlich@ise.fraunhofer.de; marc.ruediger@ise.fraunhofer.de; armin.richter@ise.fraunhofer.de).

A. Ivaturi is with the Institute of Photonics and Quantum Sciences, Heriot-Watt University, Edinburgh EH14 4AS, Scotland (e-mail: A.Ivaturi@hw.ac.uk).

K. W. Krämer is with the Department of Chemistry and Biochemistry, University of Bern, Bern 3012, Switzerland (e-mail: karl.kraemer@iac.unibe.ch).

B. S. Richards is with the Institute of Photonics and Quantum Sciences, Heriot-Watt University, Edinburgh, EH14 4AS, Scotland, and also with the Nelson Mandela African Institute of Science and Technology, Tengeru, Arusha, Tanzania (e-mail: b.s.richards@hw.ac.uk).

J. C. Goldschmidt is with the Fraunhofer Institute for Solar Energy Systems, Freiburg 79110, Germany, and also with the Imperial College, South Kensington Campus, London SW7 2AZ, U.K. (e-mail: jan.christoph.goldschmidt@ise.fraunhofer.de).

Color versions of one or more of the figures in this paper are available online at http://ieeexplore.ieee.org.

Digital Object Identifier 10.1109/JPHOTOV.2013.2282744

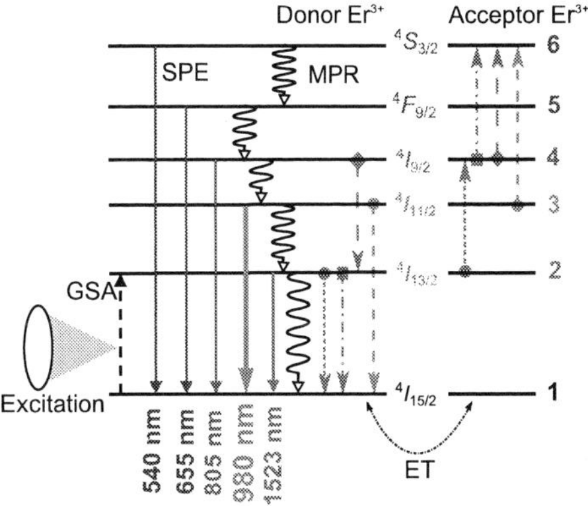

Fig. 1. Most important processes for upconversion in β-NaYF$_4$ doped with Er^{3+} are shown in this energy level scheme.

higher energy photons has the potential to enhance the efficiency of the solar cells considerably. The process of generating high-energy photons from a larger number of lower energy photons is called upconversion (UC).

For silicon solar cells, lanthanide-doped materials like hexagonal sodium yttrium fluoride (β-NaYF$_4$) doped with trivalent erbium (Er^{3+}), make especially suitable upconverter materials [1]. This upconverter materials feature broad ground state absorption (GSA) spectra around 1523 nm and a dominant UC emission around 980 nm, which can be utilized by the silicon solar cells. The energy level structure is sketched in Fig. 1 including the most important UC processes, which are energy transfer (ET), multiphonon relaxation (MPR), and spontaneous emission (SPE) [2].

A first experimental approach to enhance the efficiency of a solar cell by UC was investigated by Gibart *et al.* in 1996 with a GaAs solar cell [3]. Successful proof-of-concept experiments with silicon solar cells have been performed with the upconverter material β-NaYF$_4$ with a Er^{3+} doping concentration of 20% [4], [5]. In these experiments, the upconverter was attached on the rear side of the solar cell and the upconverter solar cell device was illuminated with monochromatic laser excitation.

For solar cells with larger band gaps other upconverter materials are potentially better suited. The β-NaYF$_4$ with 18% Yb^{3+} and 2% Er^{3+} are investigated for a-Si:H solar cells, and an enhanced external quantum efficiency (EQE) of the solar cell due to UC of photons with wavelengths of around 980 nm was found [6]. Organic compounds represent another group of

"

upconverter materials. Due to triplet–triplet annihilation photons with wavelengths up to approximately 750 nm can be up-converted to shorter wavelengths. It has been shown that such organic upconverters improve the performance of a-Si:H [7] and organic solar cells [8]. At this point, we would also like to refer to the overview articles of de Wild *et al.* [9] and Liu *et al.* [10].

To investigate the potential of UC for harvesting solar radiation, however, experiments under broad-band excitation or even concentrated sun light are much more meaningful. Typically, the spectral bandwidth of the laser excitation is much smaller than the absorption line of the Er^{3+} transition. In contrast, the solar spectrum, and also the fraction of the spectrum transmitted by bifacial silicon solar cells, is considerably wider than these absorption lines. Under broad-band excitation, in addition to GSA also other UC processes, like excited state absorption (ESA), may be in resonance with the excitation and affect the UC dynamics. Hence, not only the spectral width but also the spectral intensity distribution of the excitation has to be taken into account.

Up to now, only few experimental investigations of UC under broad-band excitation have been performed [11]–[13] and even fewer such experiments on upconverter solar cell devices [14], [15]. In this study, we will investigate bifacial silicon solar cells with an upconverter attached to the rear side under monochromatic laser and broad-band excitation to determine the EQE of the devices due to UC of sub-band-gap photons. Additionally, we determine the additional short-circuit current due to UC from current–voltage *(I–V)*-curves of the upconverter solar cell device under concentrated light of a solar simulator.

II. Experimental Details

A. Device Fabrication

We produced bifacial silicon solar cells that were adapted for an UC application [16]. The solar cells that are used in this study feature a double-layer front side antireflection coating (ARC) optimized to achieve a low reflection up to ~1800 nm (120 nm MgF_2 on top of 110 nm SiN_x), and a rear side single layer ARC optimized for low reflection of sub-band-gap photons and for low reflection of upconverted photons with wavelengths larger than 950 nm (120 nm SiN_x). Thus overall transmittance of sub-band-gap photons was maximized, and the solar cell's efficiency for photons emitted by the upconverter increased. We fabricated both planar and front side textured solar cells on 1 Ωcm, 200 μm thick, n-type FZ silicon wafers. The size of the solar cells A_{cell} is 2 cm × 2 cm. Both surfaces were passivated with Al_2O_3 prior to the deposition of the ARC.

The bifacial solar cells were soldered to copper frames, which form the rear contact of the solar cells. The copper frames are then applied on polytetrafluoroethylene (PTFE) blocks with a recess for the upconverter. The PTFE is a good diffuse reflector and serves as a rear reflector for the upconverted and the incident excitation light.

In this study, we used the upconverter powder β-NaYF$_4$ doped with 25% Er^{3+}, which showed a larger UC quantum yield than the one with a 20% Er^{3+} doping concentration we used in previous investigations. The β-NaYF$_4$ doped with 25% Er^{3+}

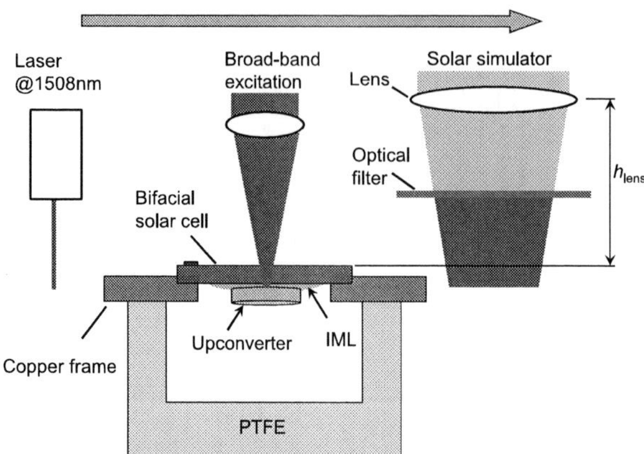

Fig. 2. Upconverter solar cell device, consisting of a bifacial silicon solar cell with an upconverter material embedded in a polymer attached to the rear side of the solar cell, was characterized under monochromatic laser and broad-band excitation. Furthermore, a Fresnel lens was placed in front of the device, and the whole system was characterized with a solar simulator. The additional short-circuit current density due to upconversion $\Delta j_{SC,UC}$ was determined for the different concentration levels that could be achieved by adjusting the height of the lens above the measurement chuck h_{lens}.

was embedded in the polymer perfluorocyclobutyl (PFCB) with a powder to polymer concentration of 75.7 w/w%. We used a sample with the same concentration of un-doped β-NaYF$_4$ in the polymer as a reference. The samples have a cylindrical shape with a diameter of 12.6 mm and a thickness of 1 mm [17]. Hence, the upconverter and the reference sample do not cover the complete active area of the solar cell. This will be important for the later discussed determination of the short-circuit current density. The solidified upconverter and reference sample were attached to the solar cells with the index matching liquid (IML) immersion oil (Type 300, Cargille), as depicted in Fig. 2.

B. Measurement Setups

For the monochromatic measurements, we used an ECL-210 NIR laser from Santec to illuminate the upconverter solar cell devices with a wavelength of 1508 nm and different laser powers. Due to laser stability a wavelength of 1508 nm was used which shows around 87% of the UC luminescence compared with the commonly used 1523 nm excitation wavelength. The laser power and the beam profile were measured to determine the incident irradiance. More details of the setup for monochromatic measurements can be found in [5].

For the broad-band experiments, the spectrum of a halogen lamp was clipped by several longpass and shortpass filters to four different excitation spectra, as shown in Fig. 3(a). The intensity of the broad-band excitation was adjusted by several neutral density filters. The light from the halogen lamp was focused with lenses into an optical fiber. On the other end of the optical fiber lenses were used to focus the light on the sample. The height of the lens system above the upconverter solar cell device was adjusted to obtain the largest short-circuit current due to UC of the photons transmitted through the solar cell. The beam profile was determined with a digital camera and a pixel counting method. The excitation spectra from the halogen lamp

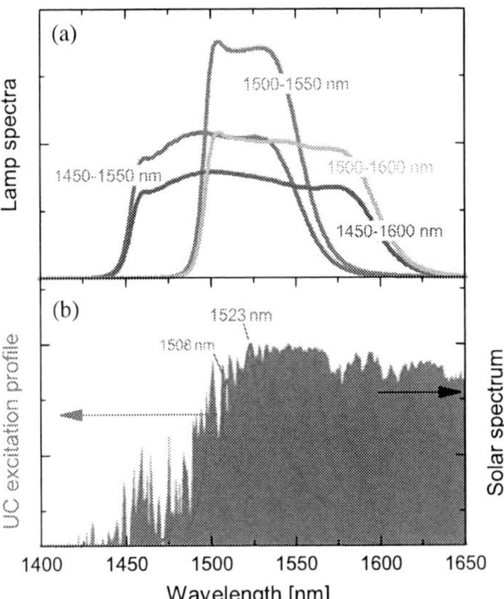

Fig. 3. (a) Normalized excitation spectra as used in the broad-band excitation experiments. (b) Excitation profile of the upconverter for emission of photons at 980 nm (shown in red) overlaps well with the AM1.5G solar spectrum shown in photons per area and time (shown in gray).

were recorded with a Jobin Yvon grating monochromator H25 and an InGaAs detector from OptoElectronic components.

In the third measurement setup, we used a Fresnel lens to focus the light of a standard solar simulator (Wacom, WXS-150 S-10, class A) onto the upconverter solar cell device. The Fresnel lens features a focal length of 169 mm and a dimension A_{lens} of 100 mm $\times$ 100 mm. The height of the lens above the upconverter solar cell device h_{lens} can be adjusted with a translation stage. Hence, the concentration of the white light on the sample is altered. From the geometrical data of our setup, we calculated an illuminated area A_{spot} ranging from 39.3 $\pm$ 8.9 mm^2 at a height h_{lens} of 160 mm to 541.0 $\pm$ 29.9 mm^2 at a height h_{lens} of 135 mm. Herein, we assumed that for h_{lens} equal to the focal length, the focus had a spot size of 1 mm. The errors stem from the uncertainty of the height measurement of h_{lens}.

We applied two filters above the solar cell to clip photons that can be utilized by the silicon solar cell. First, a monocrystalline 750 μm thick silicon wafer blocks the UV, visible (VIS) and near-infrared (NIR) parts of the lamp spectrum. For a large transmittance of sub-band-gap photons, ARCs of 120 nm TiO$_2$ and 120 nm MgF$_2$ were deposited on both sides, resulting in a transmittance above 80% in the absorption range of the upconverter. Second, a longpass filter from Edmund Optics with a cut-on wavelength of 1200 nm serves as an additional NIR filter for photons close to the band gap of silicon, which are transmitted through the silicon filter.

We measured the I–V-curves of the upconverter solar cell devices with attached upconverter as a function of the height h_{lens} between lens and the front side of the silicon solar cell. Subsequently, we repeated the measurement with the reference sample attached on the rear side of the bifacial silicon solar cell.

C. External Quantum Efficiency Due to Upconversion

The same solar cell and the same upconverter sample were used in all measurements. In all three setups, the short-circuit current of the solar cell $I_{\text{SC,UC}}$ was recorded with the upconverter attached to the rear of the solar cell. Additionally, the short-circuit current of the solar cell $I_{\text{SC,ref}}$ was recorded, with the un-doped reference sample attached instead of the upconverter sample. Finally, the short-circuit current of a germanium solar cell at the sample position $I_{\text{SC,Ge}}$ was recorded for calibration purposes. The external quantum efficiency EQE_{Ge} of this solar cell is known from calibrated measurements with an uncertainty of 1% absolute. In all these measurements no bias illumination was applied, and care was taken to avoid contributions from scattered light, that could be directly utilized by the solar cell or that could excite the upconverter.

From this data, the EQE due to UC of sub-band-gap photons EQE_{UC} was determined for the monochromatic laser and the broad-band excitation via

$$\int EQE_{\text{UC}}(\Phi) = \frac{I_{\text{SC,UC}} - I_{\text{SC,Ref}}}{I_{\text{SC,Ge}}} \frac{\int EQE_{\text{Ge}}(\lambda)\Phi_\lambda(\lambda)d\lambda}{\int \Phi_\lambda(\lambda)d\lambda}.$$
(1)

In (1), the EQE_{Ge} is weighted with the spectral photon flux density of the excitation spectrum $\Phi_\lambda(\lambda)$, which is a delta function in case of the monochromatic laser excitation. For the broad-band excitation, we used the spectra shown in Fig. 3(a).

D. Spectral Mismatch Corrections

Fig. 3(b) shows the excitation profile for UC emission around 980 nm of the investigated upconverter β-NaYF$_4$: 25% Er^{3+} in comparison to the solar spectrum. The excitation profile was measured with a photoluminescence setup that features a double monochromator (Jobin Yvon, H25) with a halogen lamp as excitation source and a monochromator (Jobin Yvon, H25) with an attached Si detector (OptoElectronic Components) for detection of the 980 nm emission. The excitation wavelength was changed in 0.5 nm steps from 1400 to 1650 nm. The full width at half maximum of the excitation was approximately 1 nm.

The solar spectrum provides many photons above wavelengths of $\sim$1475 nm, which can be efficiently used by the upconverter, while below $\sim$1450 nm less photons impinge on the earth due to absorption by water molecules in the atmosphere. Since neither the broad-band excitation spectrum nor the spectrum of the solar simulator match precisely the solar spectrum, we applied a spectral mismatch correction on the experimental EQE_{UC} data to determine the EQE_{UC} values that could be expected under illumination with the solar AM1.5G spectrum, if restricted to the same spectral range and the same effective concentration level. [13]

The mismatch correction has two parts: first the irradiance I is transferred for the different excitation spectra to equivalent solar concentration factors of the solar spectrum AM1.5G in suns C. Second, the experimental EQE_{UC} values are transferred to values which can be expected with the spectral distribution of the solar spectrum at this concentration level. The irradiance I is connected to the spectral photon flux density of the excitation

$\Phi_\lambda(\lambda)$ by

$$I = \int \Phi_\lambda(\lambda)\frac{hc}{\lambda}d\lambda \qquad (2)$$

with the Planck constant h and the speed of light c. For the broad-band excitation, the solar concentration factor C

$$C = \frac{\int A(\lambda)T_{\mathrm{cell}}(\lambda)\Phi_\lambda(\lambda)d\lambda}{\int A(\lambda)T_{\mathrm{cell}}(\lambda)\Phi_{\lambda,\mathrm{AM1.5G}}(\lambda)d\lambda} \qquad (3)$$

describes how much the solar radiation has to be concentrated to reach the same integrated photon flux density of absorbed photons as for the considered broad-band excitation spectrum. The limits of the integral are the lower and upper wavelength of the respective broad-band excitation spectrum. T_{cell} is the transmittance of the bifacial silicon solar cell.

In principal, the same methodology can be applied to the monochromatic laser measurements. Here, the spectral bandwidth is very narrow, which results in very high equivalent solar concentration factors.

In the case of the solar simulator, the solar concentration factor C was accessible by geometrical considerations. We used the area of the lens A_{lens} and the calculated area of the light spot A_{spot} for the different settings of h_{lens}, as already mentioned previously, to calculate the solar concentration C. The transmittances of the filters and the lens have to be considered as well. We used a transmittance of the lens T_{lens} of 0.92, which is basically determined by the reflectance of the glass surfaces, and 0.80 for the transmittance of the filters T_{filter}, which is an average value over the range from 1400 to 1700 nm. The solar concentration factor is consequently

$$C = \frac{T_{\mathrm{lens}}T_{\mathrm{filter}}}{c_{\mathrm{mismatch,sun}}}\frac{A_{\mathrm{lens}}}{A_{\mathrm{spot}}}. \qquad (4)$$

The spectral mismatch correction factor $c_{\mathrm{mismatch,sun}}$ describes how the geometrical concentration of the solar simulator translates to a concentration of solar radiation. Therefore, the spectral photon flux density of the standard solar spectrum AM1.5G $\Phi_{\lambda,\mathrm{AM1.5G}}(\lambda)$, the absorption spectrum of the upconverter $A(\lambda)$, and the spectral photon flux density of the solar simulator $\Phi_{\lambda,\mathrm{sun}}(\lambda)$ have to be considered. Due to an uncertainty of the area of the light spot A_{spot}, we determined an error of around 28% on the largest concentration value C.

To calculate the EQE_{UC} under illumination with the solar spectrum AM1.5G $\Phi_{\lambda,\mathrm{AM1.5G}}(\lambda)$, a spectral mismatch correction was applied on the EQE_{UC} data. We determined the mismatch correction factors c_{mismatch} by

$$\begin{aligned} c_{\mathrm{mismatch}} &= \frac{\int A(\lambda)T_{\mathrm{cell}}(\lambda)\Phi_{\lambda,\mathrm{AM1.5G}}(\lambda)d\lambda}{\int A(\lambda)T_{\mathrm{cell}}(\lambda)\Phi_\lambda(\lambda)d\lambda} \\ &\quad \times \frac{\int T_{\mathrm{cell}}(\lambda)\Phi_\lambda(\lambda)d\lambda}{\int T_{\mathrm{cell}}(\lambda)\Phi_{\lambda,\mathrm{AM1.5G}}(\lambda)d\lambda}. \end{aligned} \qquad (5)$$

The c_{mismatch} describes how the EQE_{UC} is altered when illuminated with the solar spectrum instead of the respective broad-band excitation spectrum

$$EQE_{\mathrm{UC,solar}}(C) = c_{\mathrm{mismatch}}EQE_{\mathrm{UC}}(C). \qquad (6)$$

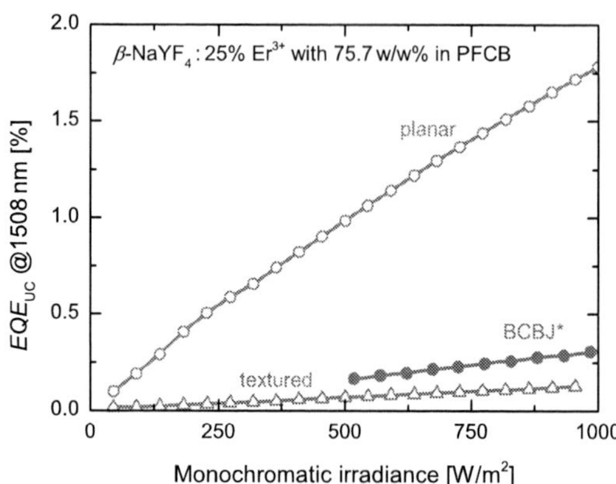

Fig. 4. EQE_{UC} of a planar bifacial solar cell could be increased by a factor of around 6, compared with [5], by optimizing the transmittance of the solar cell and due to a more efficient upconverter. In [5], a bifacial back-contact back-junction (BCBJ) silicon solar was used. For the front side textured solar cells the effect of the upconverter is fairly low, because of the poor transmittance of sub-band-gap photons through the solar cell.

E. Calculation of Expected Short-Circuit Current Density

Using the spectral mismatch correction for the EQE_{UC}, an expected additional short-circuit current density $\Delta j_{\mathrm{SC,UC}}$ due to UC of sub-band-gap photons under the illumination with the AM1.5G solar spectrum can be calculated by

$$\begin{aligned} &\Delta j_{\mathrm{SC,UC}}(C) \\ &= ec_{\mathrm{mismatch}}EQE_{\mathrm{UC}}(C)C\int_{\lambda_{\mathrm{low}}}^{\lambda_{\mathrm{up}}}\Phi_{\lambda,\mathrm{AM1.5G}}(\lambda)d\lambda \end{aligned} \qquad (7)$$

for broad-band excitation and the laser illumination.

In the case of the solar simulator, we calculated the short-circuit current density due to UC by

$$\Delta j_{\mathrm{SC,UC}} = \frac{(I_{\mathrm{SC,UC}} - I_{\mathrm{SC,ref}})}{A_{\mathrm{spot}}}c_{\mathrm{mismatch,sun}} \qquad (8)$$

with the short-circuit currents determined with attached upconverter $I_{\mathrm{SC,UC}}$, reference sample $I_{\mathrm{SC,ref}}$ and the mismatch correction factor $c_{\mathrm{mismatch,sun}}$, as described previously. For a spot area A_{spot} larger than the actual solar cell area A_{cell} of 400 mm^2 we used A_{cell} instead of A_{spot}.

III. RESULTS

A. Monochromatic Laser Excitation

The results of the monochromatic measurements are shown in Fig. 4. We measured an EQE_{UC} of 1.79% for an irradiance of 1000 Wm^{-2} and an incident wavelength of 1508 nm. This translates to a normalized efficiency of 0.179 cm^2/W. For comparison, the best values for upconverter silicon solar cell devices presented in the literature so far are 0.014 cm^2/W in [4] and 0.030 cm^2/W in [5]. In comparison to [5], the EQE_{UC} could be enhanced by nearly a factor of 6. However, for the same material as investigated in this study, an external UC quantum yield of 0.550 cm^2/W is reported, which was determined directly by photoluminescence measurements [17].

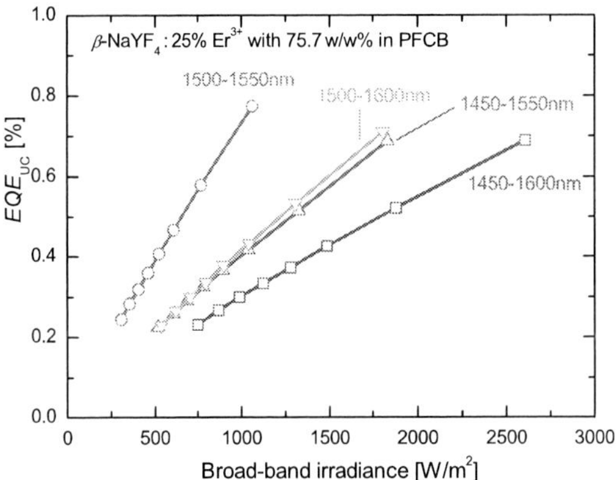

Fig. 5. External quantum efficiency of the planar solar cell due to upconversion of sub-band-gap photons increases for narrower excitation bands, as a larger ratio of the excitation photons have a wavelength corresponding to the most efficient spectral region of the upconverter.

We found that solar cells textured on the front side with planar rear are not suitable for UC applications. In such cells, the transmittance of sub-band-gap photons through the solar cell is fairly poor ($\sim$20%) due to a large portion of internal total reflection at the rear side interface. For planar cells, the transmittance of sub-band-gap photons was above approximately 80%. Consequently, in the following we will focus on the planar bifacial silicon solar cell.

B. Broad-Band Excitation

The results of the experiments under broad-band excitation are presented in Fig. 5. We determined an EQE_{UC} of 0.77% for an irradiance of 1063 W/m^2 with a corresponding normalized efficiency of 0.072 cm^2/W for the narrowest considered excitation spectrum, ranging from 1500 to 1550 nm. The broader the excitation spectrum the more photons impinge on the upconverter. However, a smaller ratio of these incident photons is absorbed compared with the case of a narrower excitation spectrum around the peak at 1523 nm. In consequence, the EQE_{UC} drops with broader excitation spectra and larger irradiance values are necessary to achieve as large EQE_{UC} values as found for narrower excitation spectra. However, one has to keep in mind that the solar spectrum provides much more photons when broader spectral bands are considered.

C. Concentrated Light From a Solar Simulator

The results of the measurement with the solar simulator are shown in Fig. 6. The measured short-circuit current I_{SC} of the upconverter solar cell device increases with the height of the lens above the solar cell. Since the used heights are below the focal length of the lens of 169 mm, a larger h_{lens} translates into a larger concentration of the light from the solar simulator. The I_{SC} with attached reference sample is considerably lower and decreases with the height h_{lens}, possibly due to a smaller fraction of ambient scattered light.

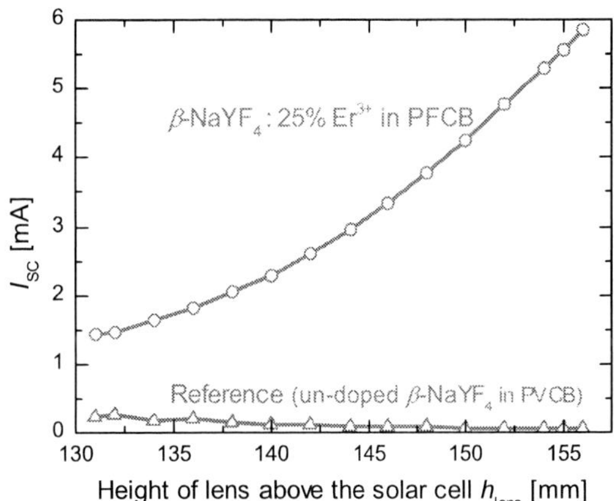

Fig. 6. Short-circuit current I_{SC} as measured with a solar simulator and a Fresnel lens with a height h_{lens} above the planar solar cell. With attached upconverter, I_{SC} increases with increasing height h_{lens}, which translates in a larger concentration. On the other hand, with attached reference sample, the I_{SC} decreases with h_{lens}.

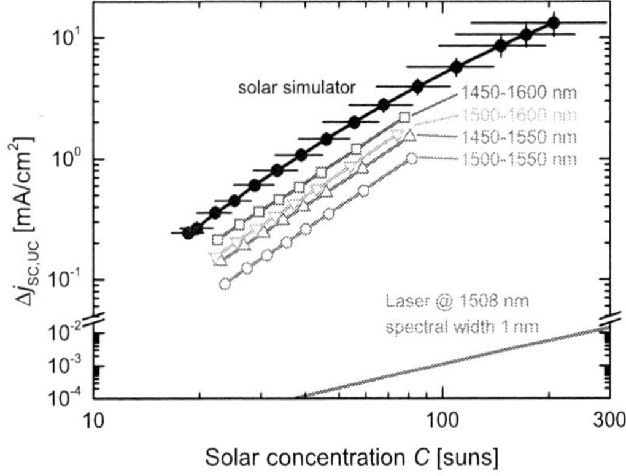

Fig. 7. Comparison of the estimated additional short-circuit current density due to upconversion of sub-band-gap photons $\Delta j_{SC,UC}$ for the various excitation sources in a double log scale. We found larger $\Delta j_{SC,UC}$ values for broader excitation spectra. Not shown are the errors of around 15% for the $\Delta j_{SC,UC}$ values under broad-band excitation.

D. Comparison of the Different Illumination Conditions

The estimated additional short-circuit current density due to UC of sub-band-gap photons $\Delta j_{SC,UC}$ obtained under the different illumination conditions are depicted in Fig. 7. The larger the spectral bandwidth, the larger is the expected $\Delta j_{SC,UC}$. We determined a $\Delta j_{SC,UC}$ of 2.2 $\pm$ 0.3 mA/cm^2 for a broad-band excitation band that ranges from 1450 to 1600 nm and a concentration of 78$\pm$6 suns.

Since the spectral width of the laser is very narrow even the large EQE_{UC} values do not compensate for the much lower photon flux density provided by a broader excitation spectrum.

Larger $\Delta j_{SC,UC}$ values are achieved for the solar simulator measurement than the broadest broad-band excitation spectrum. We calculated an additional short-circuit current density of 13.3 $\pm$ 3.0 mA/cm^2 due to UC of sub-band-gap photons under a solar concentration of 207 $\pm$ 86 suns. This value translates to a relative enhancement of the used silicon solar cell of 0.19 $\pm$ 0.04%. The intrinsic j_{SC} of the solar cell is 33.4 mA/cm^2 and a corresponding cell efficiency of 17.6% under 1 sun standard measurement conditions.

IV. Discussion

The key result of this study is that a relatively high increase in the short-circuit current density can be expected due to UC at low concentration levels of the broad solar radiation. However, since some estimations and approximations have been necessary to calculate the $\Delta j_{SC,UC}$, we would like to point out that the values for the solar simulator are only estimates yet. The main uncertainty stems from the estimation of the concentration and the area of the light spot A_{spot}. Another uncertainty comes from the incomplete coverage of the active solar cell area by the upconverter sample. For example, when A_{spot} is larger than the upconverter sample, some light transmitted by the solar cell does not hit the upconverter directly. Although this light is reflected by the PTFE rear reflector with high probability and can subsequently illuminate the upconverter. This process is less efficient than direct absorption by the upconverter. Hence, with increasing A_{spot} and decreasing concentration C, we can expect a stronger decrease of $\Delta j_{SC,UC}$ than we would observe when the full area of the solar cell was covered with an upconverter material.

Nevertheless, the values of $\Delta j_{SC,UC}$ fit into the series of the broad-band data, which show increasing enhancements of $\Delta j_{SC,UC}$ with increasing spectral width of the excitation. The fact that an increase is observed, even for excitation spectra that are considerably larger than the spectral region of efficient UC, which is shown by the excitation profile in Fig. 3(b), could be explained by excited state absorption, for example, pushing up the quantum yield of the upconverter, as it was suggested in [14]. This hypothesis could be tested by two-color UC quantum yield measurements.

V. Summary and Conclusion

We investigated upconverter solar cell devices, which are composed of a bifacial silicon solar cell with the upconverter powder β-NaYF$_4$ doped with 25% Er^{3+} embedded in perfluorocyclobutyl (PFCB). The upconverter samples are attached to the rear side of the solar cell. These devices are investigated under monochromatic laser excitation, broad-band excitation, and under the concentrated light from a solar simulator. The EQE_{UC} was determined under monochromatic laser excitation and under excitation with four different broad-band spectra. Due to the larger overlap with the absorption spectrum of the upconverter, we observed larger EQE_{UC} values for narrower excitation spectra. Under laser excitation, we determined an EQE_{UC} of 1.79% for an irradiance of 1000 Wm^{-2} and an incident wavelength of 1508 nm. This translates to a normalized efficiency of 0.179 cm^2/W, which constitutes a sixfold increase compared with previously published values. For the broad-band excitation ranging from 1500 to 1550 nm, we determined an EQE_{UC} of 0.77% for an irradiance of 1063 W/m^2 with a corresponding normalized efficiency of 0.072 cm^2/W.

We transformed the measured EQE_{UC} values to an expected additional short-circuit current density $\Delta j_{SC,UC}$ due to UC of sub-band-gap photons under a given solar concentration. A spectral mismatch correction method was used to account for the spectral differences between the excitation spectra and the solar spectrum, while considering the absorption spectrum of the upconverter. With broad-band excitations, we see larger $\Delta j_{SC,UC}$ values with broader excitation spectra. Accordingly, the measurements performed by concentrating the light of a solar concentrator with a Fresnel lens on the upconverter solar cell device, featuring the broadest excitation spectrum, yield the highest $\Delta j_{SC,UC}$ values. A $\Delta j_{SC,UC}$ of 13.3 $\pm$ 3.0 mA/cm^2 was achieved. This corresponds to a relative efficiency increase of 0.19 $\pm$ 0.04%.

References

[1] K. W. Krämer, D. Biner, G. Frei, H. U. Güdel, M. P. Hehlen, and S. R. Lüthi, "Hexagonal sodium yttrium fluoride based green and blue emitting upconversion phosphors," *Chem. Mater.*, vol. 16, pp. 1244–1251, 2004.

[2] F. Auzel, "Upconversion and anti-stokes processes with f and d ions in solids," *Chem. Rev.*, vol. 104, pp. 139–173, 2004.

[3] P. Gibart, F. Auzel, J. C. Guillaume, and K. Zahraman, "Below band-gap IR response of substrate-free GaAs solar cells using two- photon up-conversion," *Jpn. J. Appl. Phys.*, vol. 35, pp. 4401–4402, 1996.

[4] A. Shalav, B. S. Richards, and M. A. Green, "Luminescent layers for enhanced silicon solar cell performance: Up-conversion," *Solar Energy Mater. Solar Cells*, vol. 91, pp. 829–842, 2007.

[5] S. Fischer, J. C. Goldschmidt, P. Löper, G. H. Bauer, R. Brüggemann, K. Krämer, D. Biner, M. Hermle, and S. W. Glunz, "Enhancement of silicon solar cell efficiency by upconversion: Optical and electrical characterization," *J. Appl. Phys.*, vol. 108, pp. 044912, 2010.

[6] J. de Wild, J. K. Rath, A. Meijerink, W. G. J. H. M. van Sark, and R. E. I. Schropp, "Enhanced near-infrared response of a-Si: H solar cells with β-NaYF4:Yb3 +(18%), Er3+ (2%) upconversion phosphors," *Sol. Energy Mater. Sol. Cells*, vol. 94, pp. 2395–2398, 2010.

[7] T. F. Schulze, J. Czolk, Y.-Y. Cheng, B. Fückel, R. W. MacQueen, T. Khoury, M. J. Crossley, B. Stannowski, K. Lips, U. Lemmer, A. Colsmann, and T. W. Schmidt, "Efficiency enhancement of organic and thin-film silicon solar cells with photochemical upconversion," *J. Phys. Chem. C*, vol. 116, pp. 22794–22801, 2012.

[8] A. Nattestad, Y. Y. Cheng, R. W. MacQueen, T. F. Schulze, F. W. Thompson, A. J. Mozer, B. Fückel, T. Khoury, M. J. Crossley, K. Lips, G. G. Wallace, and T. W. Schmidt, "Dye-sensitized solar cell with integrated triplet–triplet annihilation upconversion system," *J. Phys. Chem. Lett.*, no. 4, pp. 2073–2078, 2013.

[9] J. de Wild, A. Meijerink, J. K. Rath, W. G. J. H. M. van Sark, and R. E. I. Schropp, "Upconverter solar cells: Materials and applications," *Energy Environ. Sci.*, vol. 4, pp. 4835–4848, 2011.

[10] X. Huang, S. Han, W. Huang, and X. Liu, "Enhancing solar cell efficiency: The search for luminescent materials as spectral converters," *Chem. Soc. Rev.*, vol. 42, pp. 173–201, 2013.

[11] S. Baluschev, T. Miteva, V. Yakutkin, G. Nelles, A. Yasuda, and G. Wegner, "Up-conversion fluorescence: Noncoherent excitation by sunlight," *Phys. Rev. Lett.*, vol. 97, pp. 143903, 2006.

[12] S. K. W. MacDougall, A. Ivaturi, J. Marques-Hueso, K. W. Krämer, and B. S. Richards, "Ultra-high photoluminescent quantum yield of b-NaYF4: 10% Er3+ via broadband excitation of upconversion for photovoltaic devices," *Opt. Exp.*, vol. 20, pp. A879–A887, 2012.

[13] S. Fischer, B. Fröhlich, H. Steinkemper, K. W. Krämer, and J. C. Goldschmidt, "Absolute upconversion quantum yield of b-NaYF4 doped with Er3+ and external quantum efficiency of upconverter solar cell devices under broad-band excitation considering spectral mismatch corrections," submitted for publication.

[14] J. C. Goldschmidt, S. Fischer, P. Löper, K. W. Krämer, D. Biner, M. Hermle, and S. W. Glunz, "Experimental analysis of upconversion with both coherent monochromatic irradiation and broad spectrum illumination," *Sol. Energy Mater. Sol. Cells*, vol. 95, pp. 1960–1963, 2011.

[15] J. De Wild, T. F. Duindam, J. K. Rath, A. Meijerink, W. G. J. H. M. Van Sark, and R. E. I. Schropp, "Increased upconversion response in a-Si: H solar cells with broad-band light," *IEEE J. Photovoltaics*, vol. 3, no. 1, pp. 17–21, Jan. 2013.

[16] M. Rüdiger, S. Fischer, J. Frank, A. Ivaturi, B. S. Richards, K. W. Krämer, M. Hermle, and J. C. Goldschmidt, "Bifacial n-type silicon solar cells for upconversion applications," submitted for publication.

[17] A. Ivaturi, S. K. W. MacDougall, R. Martin-Rodriguez, M. Quintanilla, J. Marques-Hueso, K. W. Kramer, A. Meijerink, and B. S. Richards, "Optimizing infrared to near infrared upconversion quantum yield of beta-NaYF$_4$: Er^{3+} in fluoropolymer matrix for photovoltaic devices," *J. Appl. Phys.*, vol. 114, pp. 013505–013509, 2013.

Armin Richter received the Diploma degree in physics from the University of Hamburg, Hamburg, Germany, in 2008. He is currently working toward the Ph.D. degree with the Fraunhofer Institute for Solar Energy Systems, Freiburg, Germany.

His research interests include the development and characterization of silicon surface passivation with ALD Al$_2$O$_3$ layers, Auger recombination in crystalline silicon, and the development of both sides contacted n-type silicon solar cells with front side boron-doped emitter by applying industrial feasible concepts.

Stefan Fischer studied physics at the University of Heidelberg, Germany, and the University of Freiburg, Germany. He received the Diploma degree from the University of Freiburg in 2009. He is currently working toward the Ph.D. degree with the Fraunhofer Institute for Solar Energy Systems, Freiburg.

In 2008, he joined the Fraunhofer Institute for Solar Energy Systems. His research interests include luminescent materials, light matter interactions, and photon management for solar applications, with a special focus on the characterization of upconverter materials and implementation of upconverters into solar cell devices.

Aruna Ivaturi received the Ph.D degree in 2006 in experimental solid-state physics from the Indian Institute of Technology Delhi, Delhi, India. Her thesis focused on the properties of rare-earth nanoparticle layers for "switchable mirrors."

She was with the University of Duisburg-Essen, Essen, Germany, working on the synthesis of metal and oxide nanoparticles for gas sensors (2006–07). During 2009–2010, her work at the University of Cambridge, Cambridge, U.K., dealt with the growth of metal oxide nanowires for solar cell technology. Since 2011, she has been working with the Renewable Energy Group, Heriot Watt University, Edinburgh, U.K.

Dr. Ivaturi received the Alexander von Humboldt Fellowship (2007–2009) to carry out self-proposed work on the synthesis of rare-earth oxide nanoparticles via gas phase.

Benjamin Fröhlich studied physics at the University of Freiburg, Germany. He received the Diploma degree on the "Characterization of upconverter materials for photovoltaics."

He is currently with the Fraunhofer Institute for Solar Energy Systems, Freiburg. His research interests include luminescent materials and photon management for photovoltaics, especially on the investigation of upconverters and their application to solar cell devices.

Marc Rüdiger received the diploma degree in physics from the University of Freiburg, Germany, in 2007. He completed his Ph.D. thesis, which was focused on the analysis and simulation of crystalline silicon solar cells, at the Fraunhofer Institute for Solar Energy Systems (ISE), and defended it at the University of Konstanz, Germany, in 2013. Since then, he has been with the group of strategic planning at the Fraunhofer ISE, Freiburg.

Karl W. Krämer studied chemistry at Justus-Liebig University, Giessen, Germany. He received the Diploma degree in 1988 and the Dr. rer. nat. in 1991 with Prof. G. Meyer from the Justus-Liebig University, Giessen, Germany.

He subsequently held a Postdoctoral position with Prof. H. Güdel in Bern, Switzerland. Since 2005, he has been the Head of the Solid-State Chemistry Group, Department of Chemistry and Biochemistry, University of Bern. His research interests include the synthesis of anhydrous metal halides, crystal growth, upconversion spectroscopy, Ce^{3+} doped rare- earth scintillators, and the investigation of magnetic interactions in low-dimensional systems by neutron scattering and magnetic measurements.

Bryce S. Richards received the B.Sc. degree in physics from Victoria University, Wellington, New Zealand, in 1994 and the Master's and the Ph.D. degrees from the University New South Wales, Kensington, N.S.W., Australia.

Subsequently, he was a Postdoctoral Fellow with the Australian National University before relocating to Scotland in 2006. He was promoted to a Full Professor in 2008 and also founded the Scottish Institute for Solar Energy Research. He is currently on sabbatical in Tanzania, undertaking capacity building in solar energy research. His primary research interest includes spectral conversion for photovoltaics.

Jan Christoph Goldschmidt received the Ph.D. (Dr. rer. nat.) degree from the University of Konstanz, Konstanz, Germany, for his work at the Fraunhofer Institute for Solar Energy Systems (ISE), Freiburg, Germany, on novel solar cell concepts in 2009.

He is currently the Head of the Novel Solar Cell Concepts Team with ISE and a Visiting Researcher with Imperial College, London, U.K. Among other things, he is the Coordinator of the EU FP7 project "Nanospec–Nanomaterials for harvesting sub-bandgap photons via upconversion to increase solar cell efficiencies." His research interests include photon management for photovoltaics, including luminescent solar concentrators, spectral splitting, upconversion, and advanced light trapping.

Real Time, In-line, and Mapping Spectroscopic Ellipsometry for Applications in $Cu(In_{1-x}Ga_x)Se_2$ Metrology

Puruswottam Aryal, Puja Pradhan, Dinesh Attygalle, Abdel-Rahman A. Ibdah,
Krishna Aryal, Vikash Ranjan, Sylvain Marsillac, Nikolas J. Podraza, and Robert W. Collins

Abstract — In the scale-up of $Cu(In_{1-x}Ga_x)Se_2$ (CIGS) solar cell processing for large area photovoltaics (PV) technology, the challenge is to achieve optimum values of layer thicknesses as well as CIGS Cu stoichiometry and alloy composition x within narrow ranges and simultaneously over large areas. As a result, contactless metrologies -- those that provide such information in real time or in-line process step by step, with the capabilities of large area mapping -- are of great interest in this technology. We have demonstrated high-speed multichannel spectroscopic ellipsometry (SE) in a number of modes for CIGS metrology including (i) single spot real time SE monitoring of $(In_{1-x}Ga_x)_2Se_3$ (IGS) as the first stage in multi-source evaporation of three-stage CIGS; (ii) control of Cu stoichiometry in the second and third stages of the process; (iii) single spot in situ SE analysis of alloy composition and grain size averaged through the thickness for the final CIGS film; (iv) off-line mapping of CIGS thickness and composition over large areas, as well as mapping after each device fabrication step for correlation with local small area cell performance; (v) ex situ single spot analysis of alloy composition profiles in CIGS and of completed solar cell stacks to extract thicknesses and properties of semiconductor and contact layers; and (vi) predictive capability for quantum efficiency based on the results of SE multilayer analysis. With the future development of new instrumentation, the off-line and ex-situ capabilities in multilayer analysis and mapping will be possible in-line for both rigid and roll-to-roll flexible substrates.

Index Terms — ellipsometry, gallium-based semiconductor materials, photovoltaic cells, thickness measurement.

Manuscript received June 18, 2013. This research was supported by the DOE/NSF F-PACE Program under contract No. DE-EE0005400, by NASA Glenn Research Center, and by Ohio's Wright Centers of Innovation Program.

Puruswottam Aryal is with the Department of Physics & Astronomy and the Center for Photovoltaics Innovation & Commercialization, University of Toledo, Toledo, OH 43606 USA (email: Puruswottam.Aryal@rockets. utoledo.edu).
Puja Pradhan is with the Department of Physics & Astronomy and the Center for Photovoltaics Innovation & Commercialization, University of Toledo, OH 43606 USA (email: Puja.Pradhan@rockets.utoledo.edu).
Dinesh Attygalle is with the Department of Physics & Astronomy and the Center for Photovoltaics Innovation & Commercialization, University of Toledo, OH 43606 USA (email: Dinesh.Attygalle2@rockets.utoledo.edu).
Abdel-Rahman A. Ibdah is with the Department of Physics & Astronomy and the Center for Photovoltaics Innovation & Commercialization, University of Toledo, OH 43606 USA (email: Abedl-Rahman.Ibdah@rockets.utoledo.edu).
Krishna Aryal is with the Department of Electrical and Computer Engineering, Old Dominion University, Norfolk, VA 23529 USA (email: karya001@odu.edu).
Vikash Ranjan was with the Department of Physics & Astronomy and the Center for Photovoltaics Innovation & Commercialization, University of Toledo, OH 43606 USA. He is currently with Pilkington, USA. (email: vikashphysics@gmail.com).
S. Marsillac is with the Department of Electrical and Computer Engineering, Old Dominion University, Norfolk, VA 23529 USA (email: smarsill@odu.edu).
N. J. Podraza is with the Department of Physics & Astronomy and the Center for Photovoltaics Innovation & Commercialization, University of Toledo, OH 43606 USA (email: Nikolas.Podraza@utoledo.edu).
R. W. Collins is with the Department of Physics & Astronomy and the Center for Photovoltaics Innovation & Commercialization, University of Toledo, OH 43606 USA (corresponding author; phone: 419-530-3843; fax: 419-530-3855; email: Robert.Collins@utoledo.edu).

I. INTRODUCTION

With the highest small-area efficiency among the low-cost polycrystalline thin film photovoltaic (PV) technologies, $Cu(In_{1-x}Ga_x)Se_2$ (CIGS) based solar cells have shown the greatest potential for success [1,2]. This technology also poses the greatest challenges in process scale up due to the need to achieve optimum values within narrow ranges of layer thicknesses, CIGS Cu stoichiometry [3], and alloy composition x [4-6] simultaneously over large areas. Thus in thin film PV, many key problems related to manufacturing scale-up may be addressed by advanced real-time, in-line, and mapping metrologies. Given the number of processing steps, it is critical to identify problems early -- even before a junction is formed or top contacts are deposited. Non-invasive probes, i.e., probes operating passively during the process, are superior but may ultimately limit the accessible information.

We have applied high-speed multichannel spectroscopic ellipsometry (SE) as a quantitive tool for real time, in situ, and mapping analysis of CIGS solar cell processing. Capabilities include the ability to extract the multilayer stack structure and the component layer dielectric functions. In the case of CIGS, the Cu stoichiometry, alloy composition, and grain size are accessible through the dielectric function. Recent progress is described in several applications of both real time spectroscopic ellipsometry (RTSE) and mapping SE to CIGS materials processing and scale-up issues.

The CIGS layers analyzed in this study range in thickness from 0.6 to 2.2 μm. Except where noted in subsections below, the depositions were performed on Mo-coated soda lime glass substrates by standard three-stage co-evaporation [7]. Substrate sizes range from 2.5 cm × 7.5 cm (single spot RTSE and ex-situ SE) to 10 cm x 10 cm (area mapping SE). RTSE was performed on the growing films using a rotating-compensator multichannel ellipsometer having a spectral range from 0.75 to 6.5 eV. Mapping SE was performed with a high speed instrument of similar design, but with a spatial scanning capability over a fixed substrate of maximum area ~ 1.1 m x 1.5 m (J.A. Woollam Co., M2000-DI, AccuMap-SE). The details of each experiment performed in this study are presented next.

A. RTSE monitoring and control of CIGS

Because ~65% of the final CIGS absorber layer thickness is generated in the first deposition stage that yields IGS, it is critical to study this stage and ensure the desired initial composition [x = Ga/(Ga+In)] and, thus, its ultimate profile throughout the absorber after all three stages are complete. In order to study this stage, IGS films were deposited having compositions x = 0 (In_2Se_3), 0.25, 0.31, 0.45, 0.56, 0.69, and 1 (Ga_2Se_3), as measured by energy-dispersive X-ray spectroscopy (EDS). The substrates were silicon wafers with ~25 nm thermally-grown SiO_2. Such substrates enabled deposition of optically opaque Mo with minimum surface roughness -- within the thickness range of 60-80 Å, as deduced by RTSE during Mo sputtering. In this case, the surface roughness is modeled as a discrete layer having a dielectric function determined using the Bruggeman effective medium approximation (EMA) assuming 50/50 vol.% Mo/void. The smoothest Mo leads to highest accuracy in IGS dielectric function analyses.

For the study of the second and the third stages of the three stage process, CIGS layers were deposited on Mo coated soda-lime glass substrates fabricated by the standard method that yields efficient solar cells. RTSE data were collected during all IGS and CIGS depositions.

B. In situ SE monitoring of alloy composition and grain size

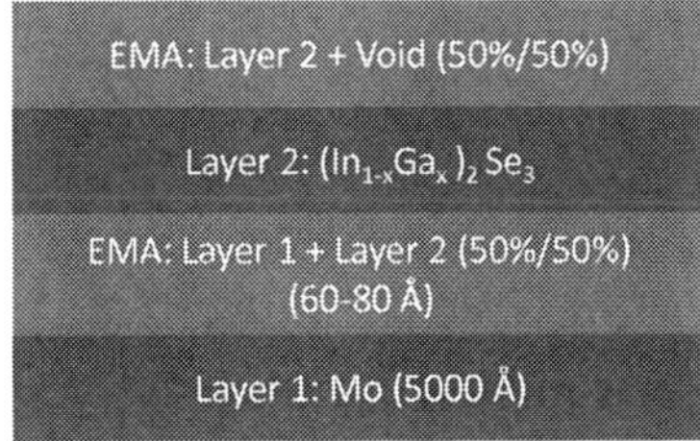

Fig. 1. Multilayer model used for analysis of RTSE data acquired on IGS thin films prepared in the first stage of CIGS co-evaporation. Interface and surface roughness layers were modeled assuming 50/50 vol.% mixtures of underlying/overlying materials with the EMA.

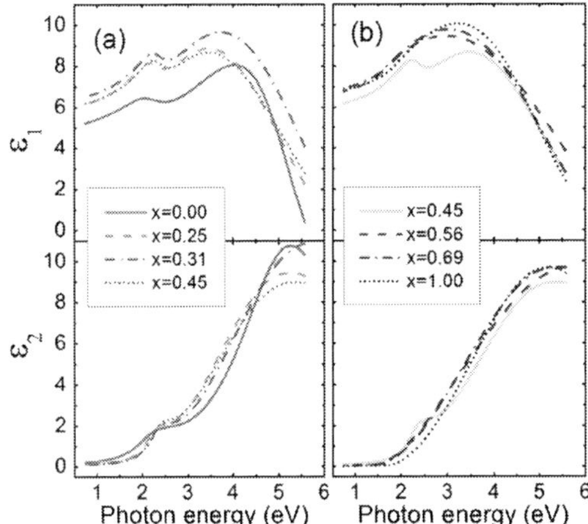

Fig. 2. Parameterized dielectric functions of IGS films measured at 400°C for (a) x ≤ 0.45 and (b) x ≥ 0.45. The dielectric function model includes a critical point oscillator near the fundamental band gap and a Tauc-Lorentz oscillator with a resonance at high-energy.

CIGS films and solar cells deposited by one stage, two stage, and three stage processes were also measured in-situ with SE. The measurements were performed at the end of the deposition process at both deposition and room temperatures. In this particular study, the same In:Ga flux ratio of 7:3 was used for all three processes and all IGS stages, implying the same thickness-averaged composition for all depositions.

C. Off-line mapping of CIGS solar cells

Thin film CIGS was deposited over a 10 cm × 10 cm area by co-evaporation using a three-stage process at a substrate temperature of 570°C. The average target thickness for CIGS was reduced from the standard 2.2 μm by > 3x to 0.65 μm.

Ex-situ mapping SE was performed after the following three deposition steps: (i) CIGS by multi-source evaporation, (ii) CdS by chemical bath deposition (CBD), and (iii) ZnO and ZnO:Al by magnetron sputtering. The thicknesses of all layers except CIGS were the same as those used for standard cells having 2.2 μm thick CIGS. SE data were collected on a 0.5 cm × 0.5 cm array from 361 locations. Ni-Al-Ni grids were deposited on top of the ZnO:Al, yielding an array of 162 cells 0.5 cm^2 in area via mechanical scribing. J-V curves were measured under AM1.5 illumination using commercial instrumentation (Model IVQE8-C, PV Measurements, Inc).

III. RESULTS AND DISCUSSION

A. Real time SE monitoring and control of CIGS

The RTSE data for the growing IGS samples were analyzed using the three layer model shown in Fig. 1. The layers consist of (i) a Mo/IGS interface roughness layer, having a fixed thickness assumed equal to the roughness layer thickness determined for the Mo surface, (ii) an IGS bulk layer of thickness d_b, and (iii) an IGS surface roughness layer of thickness d_s, the latter two determined individually at each time point in the analysis. For (i) and (iii), the Bruggeman effective medium approximation (EMA) was applied to extract the real and imaginary parts of the complex dielectric function for the roughness layers, denoted $\varepsilon = \varepsilon_1 + i\varepsilon_2$. A multi-time analysis approach was used to determine the structural evolution of the IGS with ε modeled with a B-spline function [8]. The structural results enabled exact inversion of the dielectric functions, which were parameterized using a critical point oscillator and a Tauc-Lorentz oscillator, representing the bandgap region and the higher energy region, respectively. The dielectric functions are shown in Fig. 2. The change in behavior of these dielectric functions at $x \sim 0.45$ is consistent with a well-defined hexagonal crystal structure for $x \leq 0.45$ and a disordered structure for $x > 0.5$.

Figure 3 shows the evolution of stage I $(In_{1-x}Ga_x)_2Se_3$ (IGS) with $x = 0.31$ obtained by RTSE. The ~ 50 vol.% voids of the ~ 76 Å thick roughness layer on the underlying Mo is filled in by IGS, leading to a rapid increase in the IGS vol.% in the layer from $t = 0$. Simultaneously, the surface roughness thickness d_s on the IGS increases from $d_s = 0$ as the Mo is covered. After the interface is filled, a bulk layer can be incorporated into the model. During initial bulk layer growth,

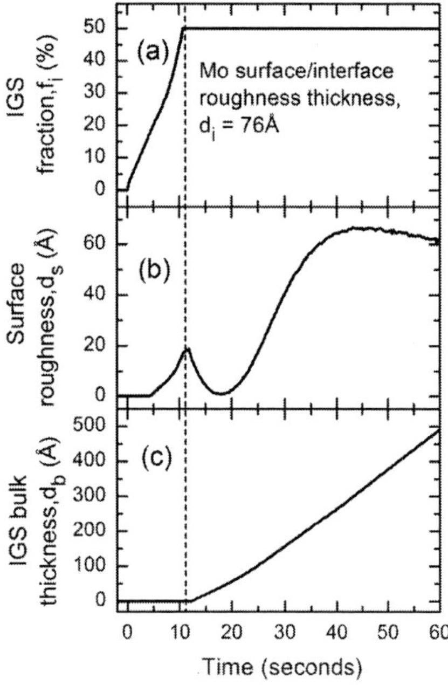

Fig. 3. Early stage structural evolution of $(In_{1-x}Ga_x)_2Se_3$ (IGS) on Mo coated soda lime glass; (a) IGS volume percentage filling the voids in the Mo surface roughness layer; (b) IGS surface roughness thickness, and (c) IGS bulk layer thickness. The interface and surface roughness regions are modeled as distinct layers having dielectric functions determined using the EMA assuming 50/50 vol.% Mo/IGS and 50/50 vol.% IGS/void, respectively.

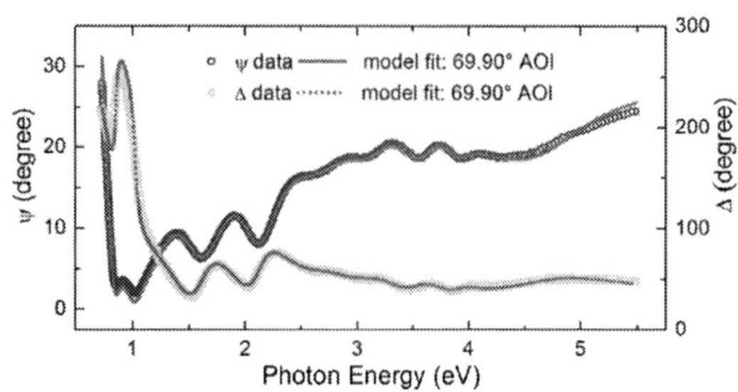

Fig. 4. RTSE measurement and analysis results depicted as the experimental ellipsometric (ψ, Δ) spectra and corresponding best fit for the CIGS stage III deposition at $t = 84.6$ min in Fig. 5, when the $Cu_{2-x}Se$ effective thickness is maximum. AOI refers to the angle of incidence.

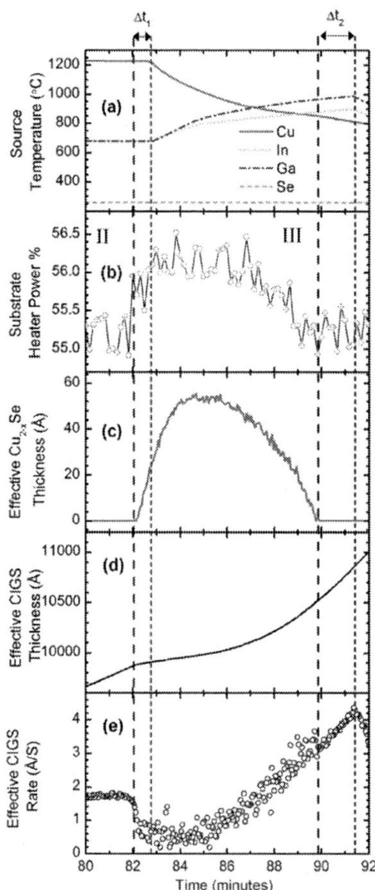

Fig. 5. Time evolution of (a) source temperatures; (b) heater power; (c) effective thickness of $Cu_{2-x}Se$; (d) effective thickness of CIGS, and (e) deposition rate in terms of effective thickness for CIGS. These results are shown near the Cu transitions (long dashed lines) and the times that end stages II and III (short dashed lines).

the roughness thickness on the IGS decreases, indicating suppression of substrate-induced roughness and apparent wetting of Mo. Later, the IGS roughness increases due to enlarging crystallites protruding above the surface. In addition to the film's structural evolution, its dielectric function can be obtained as a compositional fingerprint.

The Cu-rich CIGS film was analyzed by RTSE in stages II and III. In order to represent the phase segregation of $Cu_{2-x}Se$ in such films, an EMA model consisting of a mixture of stoichiometric CIGS, $Cu_{2-x}Se$, and void was used to describe the dielectric function of the CIGS surface layer. Several structural models were applied, and this one gave the best fitting quality versus time. Figure 4 shows the experimental data and best fit at 84.6 min during stage III that yields the structural parameters given in Fig. 5. Figure 5(c) shows the $Cu_{2-x}Se$ effective thickness versus time near the end of stage II and throughout stage III. The effective thickness in this case is the $Cu_{2-x}Se$ volume fraction multiplied by the surface layer thickness. From Figs. 5(b)-(c), it is clear that the Cu-poor $\rightarrow$ Cu-rich transition identified from a change in film surface emissivity corresponds to a rapid acceleration in the deposition of the $Cu_{2-x}Se$ phase as detected by RTSE. At the same time, the rate of CIGS growth in terms of effective thickness drops abruptly. This behavior indicates that at the end of stage II, much of the growth can be ascribed to $Cu_{2-x}Se$. By waiting a time Δt_1 as shown in Fig. 5, $Cu_{2-x}Se$ accumulation at the surface is ensured.

With the introduction of In and Ga in stage III, the rapid rise in the CIGS rate is due to the reaction of this $Cu_{2-x}Se$ with the In, Ga and Se fluxes, yielding CIGS. The Cu-rich $\rightarrow$ Cu-poor transition, identified by a more gradual drop in heater current corresponds to the reduction in $Cu_{2-x}Se$ effective thickness below 20 Å, as measured by RTSE. In, Ga, and Se fluxes are then maintained for a duration of Δt_2 as shown in Fig. 5, and the CIGS thickness continues to increase until the desired Cu-poor composition is achieved.

B. In situ SE monitoring of alloy composition and grain size

Values deduced by in situ SE for the energy position of the lowest energy $E_0(A,B)$ critical point (CP), corresponding to the bandgap, are presented in Fig. 6. These values were obtained at both deposition and room temperatures at the end of standard 1-, 2-, and 3-stage CIGS depositions by fitting

the dielectric functions using a critical point oscillator. All processes yield films having (room, deposition) temperature bandgaps of (1.17 eV, 1.05 eV), respectively. Due to the use of a two-layer bulk/roughness model in SE analysis, these gaps represent an average throughout the film thickness. Applying the known relationship between room temperature bandgap ($E_g = E_0$) and $x = [Ga]/\{[In]+[Ga]\}$, a composition of

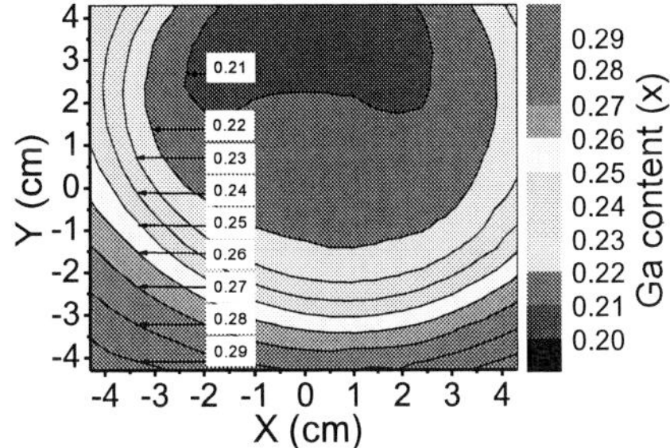

Fig. 7. Map of the Ga content x over the 10 cm x 10 cm area obtained from SE analysis of CIGS on Mo coated soda lime glass.

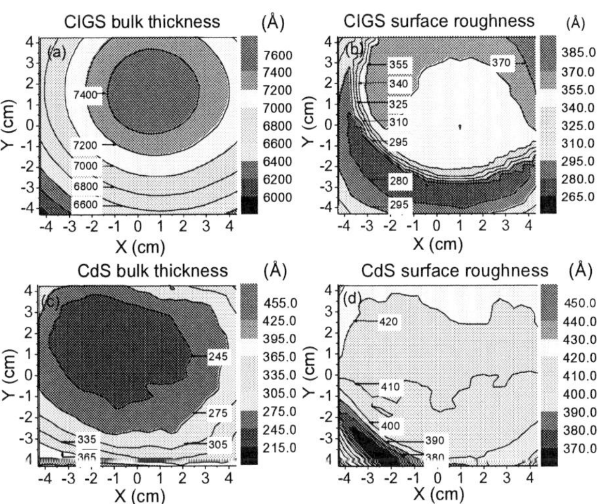

Fig. 8. Solar cell component layer thicknesses obtained using step-by-step mapping SE including: CIGS (a) bulk and (b) surface roughness, and CdS (c) bulk and (d) surface roughness

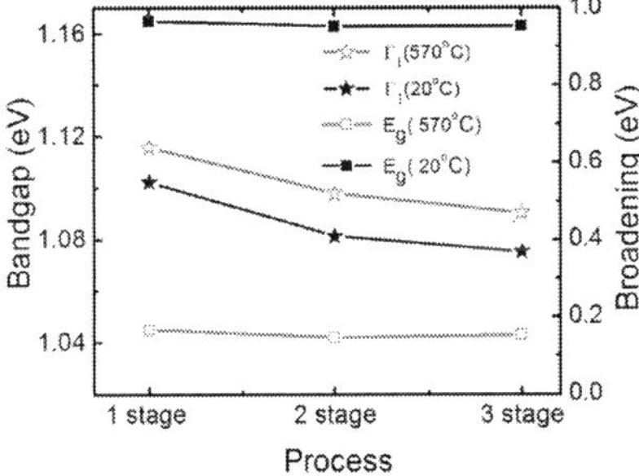

Fig. 6. Bandgap E_g and broadening parameter Γ values associated with the $E_0(A,B)$ critical point measured in situ at the end of the CIGS depositions, representing an average throughout the thickness, for CIGS films prepared in 1-, 2-, and 3-stage processes.

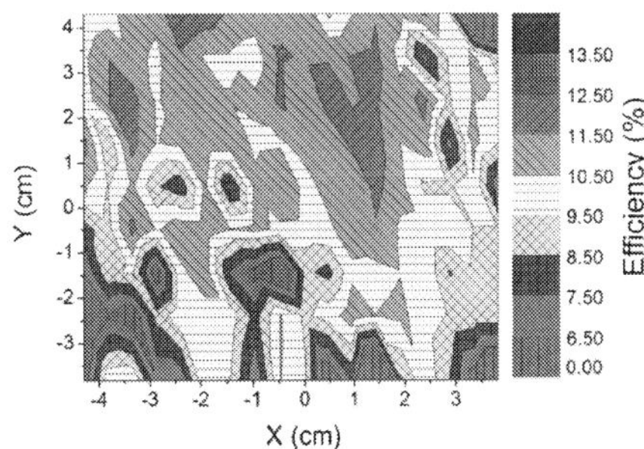

Fig. 9. A map of solar cell efficiency over a 10 cm × 10 cm area constructed from results obtained on 162 solar cells, each with an area of 0.5 cm^2.

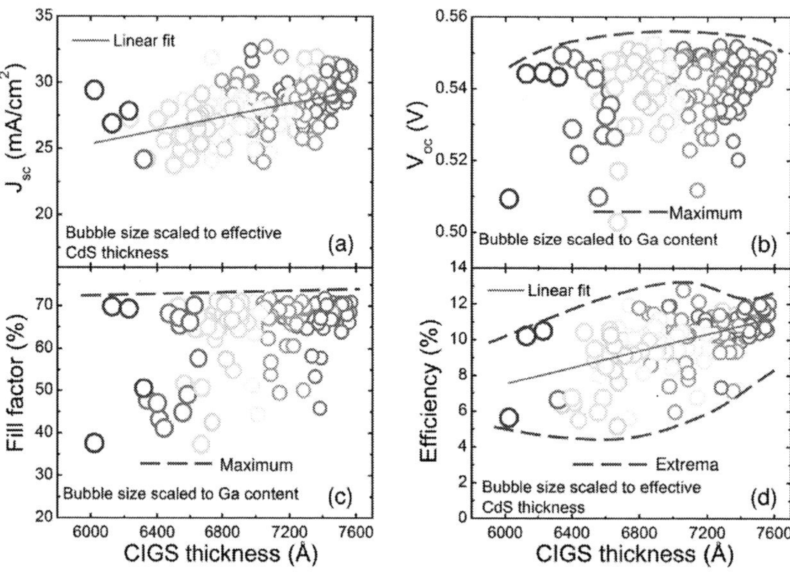

Fig. 10. Correlation plots of (a) J_{sc} vs. CIGS bulk thickness, (b) V_{oc} vs. CIGS bulk thickness, (c) FF vs. CIGS bulk thickness, and (d) efficiency vs. CIGS bulk thickness. The maximum confidence limits in the CIGS thickness is ± 35 Å in the above plots.

x = 0.31 was found and confirmed by EDS. The agreement among deduced 1, 2, and 3-stage CIGS compositions suggests that SE does indeed provide an average value throughout the CIGS thickness, irrespective of the compositional gradient. Since the linear temperature coefficients of the bandgap have been determined by us for the range between room and deposition temperature, the in situ bandgap measurement capability reported here also enables compositional monitoring via RTSE.

Single crystal materials exhibit sharp CP features compared to their polycrystalline counterparts. Broadening of the CP resonances results from a reduction in excited state lifetime due to the scattering of optically excited carriers by grain boundaries [9]. Applying this concept to the results for the bandgap broadening parameter from in situ SE shown in Fig.6, it becomes clear that the grain size increases successively with the number of stages in the deposition process. Because the broadening parameter values follow a similar trend at room and deposition temperatures, RTSE can be applied to monitor relative grain sizes for the various deposition processes.

C. Off-line mapping of CIGS solar cells

For SE analysis of the off-line mapping data, component layer dielectric functions were used along with the procedure reported previously for CIGS [10]. In this procedure, the dielectric functions deduced in situ for thin, 1-stage CIGS are parameterized versus x, as determined by EDS, enabling the use of x as a free parameter in least-squares regression of multilayer stacks that incorporate CIGS. A CIGS Ga content map spanning a 10 cm × 10 cm area is shown in Fig. 7. The map shows a circular compositional pattern with the Ga

content in the range from ~ 0.20 ± 0.01 to 0.30 ± 0.01. The lowest Ga content is found near the top of the map and the highest is found toward the bottom, which is consistent with the position of the sources in the deposition chamber.

Figures 8(a) and 8(b) show maps of the CIGS bulk and surface roughness layer thicknesses, the latter extracted using the EMA. These maps were obtained from the same SE analysis that yielded the Ga content map. The maps show well-defined circular patterns with bulk and surface roughness layer thicknesses in the ranges of 6000-7600 Å and 265-370 Å, respectively, yielding a CIGS effective thickness range from 6160 Å to 7820 Å. The effective thickness is the volume per unit substrate area and is the sum of contributions from the bulk, surface, and interface roughness layers. Figures 8(c) and 8(d) show maps for CdS deposited in the CBD process. In the SE analysis of the CdS layer, data above 2 eV were selected so that the CIGS layer is opaque. The effective thickness of the CdS layer is in the range of 420-660 Å and, in contrast to the CIGS layer, is thinner at the substrate center. The large CdS roughness (for such a thin layer), which smoothens with increasing CdS bulk thickness, is caused by the surface modulations of the underlying rough CIGS layer.

Figure 9 shows a map of solar cell efficiency η constructed on the basis of J-V measurements of 162 cells fabricated over the same 10 cm × 10 cm substrate area as the Ga composition and layer thickness maps. The low η values on the lower side of the map are due to low fill factor (FF) and short circuit current density (J_{sc}). Three materials characteristics associated with the lower side of the maps may account for this behavior: (i) smaller CIGS thickness, (ii) larger CdS thickness, and (iii) larger Ga content x. All three characteristics can reduce J_{sc}; however, it is likely that the reduction in FF is most directly related to CIGS thickness reduction due to an accompanying reduction in crystalline grain size. The outliers in η over the map are dominated by a poor FF due to the presence of shunts and series resistances, and do not depend on the SE-deduced layer properties. In fact, the localized microscopic pin-holes which give rise to shunting cannot be detected by SE.

Correlation plots can help to identify the optimum set of parameters in this study of thin CIGS, for which literature guidance is not readily available. The correlation plot of J_{sc} vs. CIGS bulk layer thickness d_b is shown in Fig. 10(a). The bubble size in the plot is scaled to the CdS effective thickness. This plot reveals the expected increase in J_{sc} with an increase in d_b and a decrease in CdS effective thickness. These correlation data were fit to a linear equation, $J_{sc} = a_1 + b_1 d_b$. The coefficients a_1 and b_1 were found to be 10.07 ± 3.72 mA/cm^2 and 0.002550 ± 0.000527 mA/cm^{2}Å, respectively.

Figure 10(b) shows the correlation of V_{oc} and CIGS bulk thickness d_b with the bubble size scaled to Ga content. The broken curve, which is a guide to the eye with an uncertainty controlled by the confidence limits on d_b ($< \pm 35$ Å), suggests that V_{oc} can be maximized at an intermediate d_b value. Since the increase in d_b causes an increase in grain size and consequently a decrease in junction defect density, V_{oc} first increases with d_b. The decrease in V_{oc} for $d_b > 0.7$ μm is likely due to a decrease in Ga content in that region, which can be inferred from the size of the bubbles.

Figure 10(c) shows the correlation of FF and CIGS bulk thickness. The bubbles in this case are scaled to Ga content. The FF increases with an increase in d_b also due to the increase in grain size with d_b which reduces bulk layer defects. The low values of FF in the plot are due to the presence of shunts and the series resistances, which are independent of the thicknesses and Ga content as described earlier. The broken line in Fig. 10(c) is a guide to the eye, which envelops the maximum FF, with an uncertainty controlled as noted above.

The efficiency exhibits the same trend vs. the CIGS and CdS thicknesses as does J_{sc}, as observed by comparing Figs. 10(a) and (d). A best fit line was obtained for Fig. 10(d) by fitting to a linear equation $\eta = a_2 + b_2 d_b$. The values of the coefficients a_2 and b_2 were found to be -6.50 ± 2.22 % and 0.002340 ± 0.000313 %/Å, respectively. The broken lines in the figure are guides to the eye that envelop the maximum and mimimum values of η. For thin CIGS, the change in J_{sc} dominates η relative to weaker trends in V_{oc} and FF.

IV. SUMMARY

We have applied high-speed multichannel spectroscopic ellipsometry (SE) in a number of modes for CIGS and its precursor films. Real time SE (RTSE) was employed to characterize the nucleation, interface filling, and roughness evolution during the growth of IGS, as well as to determine the optical properties of the films as a function of Ga content. We have reported for the first time the stage-I IGS dielectric functions versus composition, which are crucial for analysis of the full 3-stage CIGS process. We find that RTSE can identify the Cu-poor to Cu-rich and Cu-rich to Cu-poor transitions during the deposition of CIGS films by the 3-stage process. The procedure developed here provides monolayer-level thickness quantification for the $Cu_{2-x}Se$ layer that forms on the surface of the CIGS film during Cu-poor to Cu-rich transition. We have demonstrated the application of in situ SE for monitoring the alloy composition and grain size of CIGS films independent of the deposition method used. Finally, step by step ex situ SE mapping was employed to study nonuniformites that exist in large area solar cell depositions. A new methodology was demonstrated whereby correlations between basic properties from SE and device performance can used for insights into device optimization when intended deviations from standard conditions are employed, or for off-line monitoring to track unintended process deviations and drift. Future work will involve exploration of this latter capability in greater depth through more advanced statistical methods for correlating changes in a single material parameter with device performance and through an enlargement of the parameter set deduced in the SE measurement.

REFERENCES

[1] P. Jackson, D. Hariskos, E. Lotter, S. Paetel, R. Wuerz, R. Menner, W. Wischmann, and M. Powalla, "New world record efficiency for Cu(In,Ga)Se$_2$ thin-film solar cells beyond 20%," *Prog. Photovolt.: Res. Appl.*, vol. 19, pp. 894-897, 2011.

[2] I. Repins, M. A. Contreras, B. Egaas, C. DeHart, J. Scharf, C. L. Perkins, B. To, and R. Noufi, "19.9%-efficient ZnO/CdS/CuInGaSe$_2$ solar cell with 81.2% fill factor," *Prog. Photovolt.: Res. Appl.*, vol. 16, pp. 235-239, 2008.

[3] S. H. Han, F. S. Hasoon, H. A. Al-Thani, A. M. Hermann, and D. H. Levi, "Effect of Cu deficiency on the optical properties and electronic structure of CuIn$_{1-x}$Ga$_x$Se$_2$," *J. Phys. Chem. Solids*, vol. 66, pp. 1895-1898, 2005.

[4] K. Ramanathan, M. A. Contreras, C. L. Perkins, S. Asher, F. S. Hasoon, J. Keane, D. Young, M. Romero, W. Metzger, R. Noufi, J. Ward, and A. Duda, "Properties of 19.2% efficiency ZnO/CdS/CuInGaSe$_2$ thin-film solar cells," *Prog. Photovolt.: Res. Appl.*, vol. 11, pp. 225-230, 2003.

[5] W. Li, S. R. Cohen, K. Gartsman, and D. Cahen, "Ga composition dictates macroscopic photovoltaic and nanoscopic electrical characteristics of Cu(In$_{1-x}$Ga$_x$)Se$_2$ thin films via grain-boundary-type inversion," *IEEE J. Photovolt.*, vol. 2, pp. 191-195, 2012.

[6] W. N. Shafarman, R. Klenk, and B. E. McCandless, "Device and material characterization of Cu(In,Ga)Se$_2$ solar cells with increasing band gap," *J. Appl. Phys.*, vol. 79, pp. 7324-7328, 1996.

[7] Method of fabricating high-efficiency Cu(In,Ga)(SeS)$_2$ thin films for solar cells, by R. Noufi et al. (August 15, 1995), **Patent 5,441,897**.

[8] B. Johs and J. S. Hale, "Dielectric function representation by B-splines," *Phys. Stat. Sol. (a)*, vol. 205, pp. 715-719, 2008.

[9] R. W. Collins, H. Windischmann, J. M. Cavese, and J. Gonzalez-Hernandez, "Optical properties of dense thin-film Si and Ge prepared by ion-beam sputtering," *J. Appl. Phys.*, vol. 58, pp. 954-957, 1985.

[10] P. Aryal, D. Attygalle, P. Pradhan, N. J. Podraza, S. Marsillac, and R. W. Collins, "Large-area compositional mapping of Cu(In$_{1-x}$Ga$_x$)Se$_2$ materials and devices with spectroscopic ellipsometry," *IEEE J. Photovolt.*, vol. 3, no. 1, pp. 359–363, 2013.

Puruswottam Aryal is currently a doctoral student at the University of Toledo, Toledo OH. His thesis research involves applications of real time spectroscopic ellipsometry in studies of I-III-VI$_2$ thin-film PV materials and devices with a focus on accurate determination of the optical functions with applications in multilayer optical analysis.

Puja Pradhan is currently a doctoral student at the University of Toledo. Her thesis research includes the application of real time spectroscopic ellipsometry to the growth of materials used in I-III-VI$_2$ solar cells. Of particular interest is the observation of interface formation between Mo and the first stage of CIGS co-evaporation.

Dinesh Attygalle received the Ph.D. in Physics from the University of Toledo (UT) in 2010 and later served a Post-doctoral Research Scientist at UT. As a graduate student his research focus was thin film amorphous semiconductor photovoltaics; as a post-doctor, the focused on process development and optimization for CIGS solar cells.

Abdel-Rahman A. Ibdah is currently a doctoral student at the University of Toledo. His thesis research includes the optimization of multi-stack AR coatings for applications in thin CIGS technology.

Krishna Aryal is currently a doctoral student at Old Dominion University. His current research area includes fabrication and characterization of high-efficiency thin film CIGS solar cells, and spectroscopic ellipsometry for in-situ and real-time analysis.

Vikash Ranjan received the Ph.D. in Physics from the University of Toledo (UT) in 2010 and is currently a Research Scientist at Pilkington, USA. As a graduate student, his research focused on the enhancement of the deposition processes of Cu(In,Ga)Se$_2$ and CdS thin films via in-situ and ex-situ measurements including SE.

Sylvain Marsillac received the Ph.D. in Materials Science and Engineering from the University of Nantes (France) in 1996. He is currently Associate Professor of Electrical Engineering at Old Dominion University. His research interests include study of new inorganic materials for renewable energy applications.

Nikolas Podraza received the Ph.D. in Physics from University of Toledo in 2008 and is currently Assistant Professor at UT. His research interests include the physical mechanisms of film growth that control the electromagnetic, optical, and vibrational properties of thin film materials used in opto-electronic device applications.

Robert Collins is a Distinguished University Professor and the NEG Endowed Chair of Silicate and Materials Science in the Department of Physics & Astronomy at the University of Toledo, Toledo OH. He received the Ph.D. in Applied Physics from Harvard University in 1982. He co-directs the Center for Photovoltaics Innovation & Commercialization and has been involved in research and development of thin film PV since 1976.

Characterization of Cu(In,Ga)Se$_2$ Electrodeposited and Co-Evaporated Devices by Means of Concentrated Illumination

M. Paire, C. Jean, L. Lombez, T. Sidali, A. Duchatelet, E. Chassaing, G. Savidand, F. Donsanti, M. Jubault, S. Collin, J.-L. Pelouard, D. Lincot, and J.-F. Guillemoles

Abstract—We present a new Cu(In,Ga)Se$_2$ characterization tool: Cu(In,Ga)Se$_2$ microcells. By creating pixels on a Cu(In, Ga)Se$_2$ substrate, we are able to test electrically different locations. Moreover, because of the reduced size of the cells, (5-to 500-μm wide), heat and spreading resistance losses are made negligible, which make high flux characterizations available. We analyze current–voltage curves under high concentration to gain insight in the physical properties of Cu(In,Ga)Se$_2$ cells. From our analysis, Cu(In,Ga)Se$_2$ electrodeposited absorbers present resistivity fluctuations that are much more important than co-evaporated ones. These absorbers, as they present more electronic defects, are also more affected by the V$_{oc}$ increase under intense fluxes, and the efficiency gains can be very significant: up to 6% absolute efficiency points at less than 50 suns.

Index Terms—Current–voltage characteristics, photovoltaic cells.

I. Introduction

THE chalcopyrite compound Cu(In,Ga)Se$_2$ has proven to be very efficient as a solar cell absorber, with over 20% efficiency reached in 2011 [1]. Various techniques are available to synthesize Cu(In,Ga)Se$_2$, such as co-evaporation, sputtering, electrodeposition, and printing, to name a few. Each absorber deposition process leads to distinct opto-electronic properties of the corresponding solar cells. It is thus important to have characterization tools that can link final devices characteristic to features of the deposition process. In this paper, we propose to compare Cu(In,Ga)Se$_2$ solar cells with either co-evaporated or electrodeposited absorbers. In order to gain insight into the

Manuscript received June 10, 2013; revised November 27, 2013; accepted November 28, 2013.

M. Paire, T. Sidali, A. Duchatelet, G. Savidand, F. Donsanti, and M. Jubault, are with the EDF R&D, Institute of research and development on photovoltaic energy–IRDEP, F-78401 Chatou, France (e-mail: myriam. paire@gmail.com; tarik.sidali@edf.fr; aurelien.duchatelet@edf.fr; gregory. savidand@edf.fr; frederique.donsanti@edf.fr; marie.jubault@edf.fr).

C. Jean, L. Lombez, E. Chassaing, D. Lincot, and J.-F. Guillemoles are with the CNRS Institute of research and development on photovoltaic energy–IRDEP, F-78401 Chatou, France (e-mail: cyril-externe.jean@edf.fr; laurent-lombez@chimie-paristech.fr; elisabeth-chassaing@chimie-paristech. fr; daniel-lincot@chimie-paristech.fr; jf-guillemoles@chimie-paristech.fr).

S. Collin, and J-L. Pelouard are with the CNRS, Laboratoire de photonique et nanostructures–LPN, F-91460 Marcoussis, France (e-mail: stéphane.collin@lpn.cnrs.fr; jean-luc.pelouard@lpn.cnrs.fr).

Color versions of one or more of the figures in this paper are available online at http://ieeexplore.ieee.org.

Digital Object Identifier 10.1109/JPHOTOV.2013.2293889

differences between these two processes, we use a novel technique. We characterize a pixilated substrate under various illumination conditions (dark, AM1.5 G, or concentrated illumination). Conclusions on material quality, homogeneity, or sensitivity to temperature elevation are given.

II. Fabrication and Characterization Methods

A. Approach

Cu(In,Ga)Se$_2$ solar cells are studied by creating pixels on a large substrate. Thus, local characterization of opto-electronic properties is possible. The cells studied here are of the type sodalime glass/Mo/Cu(In,Ga)Se$_2$/CdS/ZnO/ZnO:Al, where Mo and ZnO layers are deposited by sputtering and CdS by chemical bath deposition. Two types of absorbers are used in this study.

B. Absorber Synthesis

Two different Cu(In,Ga)Se$_2$ absorber synthesis processes are compared in this paper.

The first absorber type is obtained by co-evaporation, in a three-stage process, as described in [2].

The second process is the electrodeposition of Cu(In,Ga)Se$_2$ precursors and subsequent annealing. The electrodeposition is carried out in a single step, in an aqueous solution of Cu(II), In(III), and Ga (III) nitrates [3]. The precursor layer is then transformed in a metallic layer by annealing in a reducing atmosphere (H_2 containing atmosphere). The Cu(In,Ga)Se$_2$ layer is formed after selenization by annealing in a selenium saturated atmosphere. This process can give on conventional laboratory cells (0.1 cm^2) around 10% efficiency [3].

C. Microcells Fabrication

The CdS and ZnO layer are subsequently deposited by chemical bath deposition and sputtering. In order to pixelate the substrate, microcells are created by using a patterned insulating layer. A SiO$_2$ layer is deposited on top of the ZnO layer prior to the deposition of ZnO:Al and patterned by UV-lithography. Thus, microdiodes are only created in the holes patterned in the insulating layer. More details on the patterning process can be found elsewhere [4].

The microcell size varies from 500-μm down to less than 10-μm in diameter. On each sample, 244 microcells are patterned. The pixels are distant from one another by 1 mm.

373

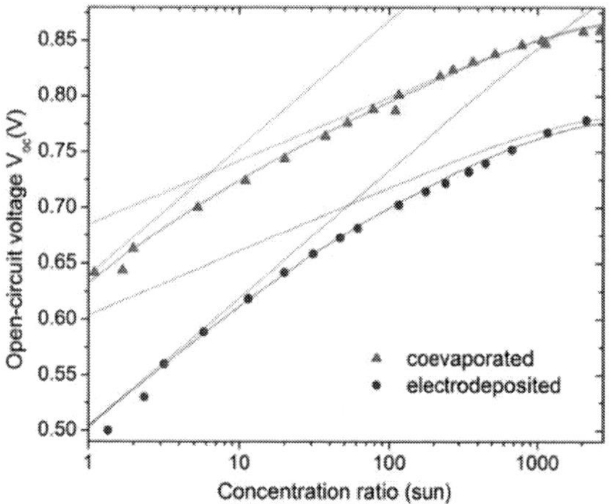

Fig. 1. V_{oc} versus concentration ratio for co-evaporated and electrodeposited Cu(In,Ga)Se$_2$ absorbers. The microcells have a diameter of 15 μm. The lines correspond to the component of open-circuit voltage of ideality factor 1 and 2. The lines deviates from linearity at high concentration because of a temperature increase [4].

D. Microcell Electrical Characterization

The microcells are tested individually by current–voltage measurements under dark and AM1.5 G illumination (class AAA Newport solar simulator). Tests under 532-nm laser illumination are also carried out, with varying incident light intensities, using neutral density filters.

The AM1.5 G tests enable us to determine the average short circuit current density. Then, in the range where short-circuit current density is proportional to the incident light power, the concentration ratio is calculated as $C = J_{sc}/J_{sc}\,(AM1.5G)$.

III. Results and Discussion

A. Comparison of Electrodeposited or Coevaporated Cu(In,Ga)Se$_2$ in Terms of V_{oc}–J_{sc}

Both Cu(In,Ga)Se$_2$ solar cells show logarithmically increasing open-circuit voltage under concentrated illumination (see Fig. 1). This behavior is in accordance with expected behavior, as the concentrated illumination increases the photogenerated carrier densities and, thus, the quasi-Fermi level splitting.

In Fig. 1, the experimental data are fitted with two lines, corresponding respectively to an ideality factor of 1 and 2, according to the equation

$$V_{oc} = \frac{2kT}{q} \ln\left(\frac{-J_{02} + \sqrt{J_{02}^2 + 4J_{01}C \times J_{sc}\,(AM1.5)}}{2J_{01}} \right) \tag{1}$$

where J_{01} and J_{02} are the saturation currents of ideality 1 and 2, respectively, and C is the concentration ratio, as defined earlier by $C = J_{sc}/J_{sc}(AM\,1.5\,G)$.

It is clear that the slope of the V_{oc} curve corresponding to the electrodeposited sample is steeper. This is because of the fact that on an electrodeposited sample, the saturation current corresponding to an ideality factor of 2, J_{02}, is more important than for the co-evaporated samples. Indeed, from dark measurements,

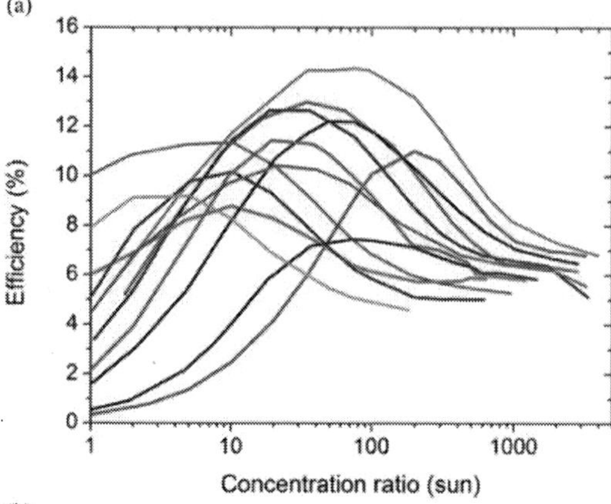

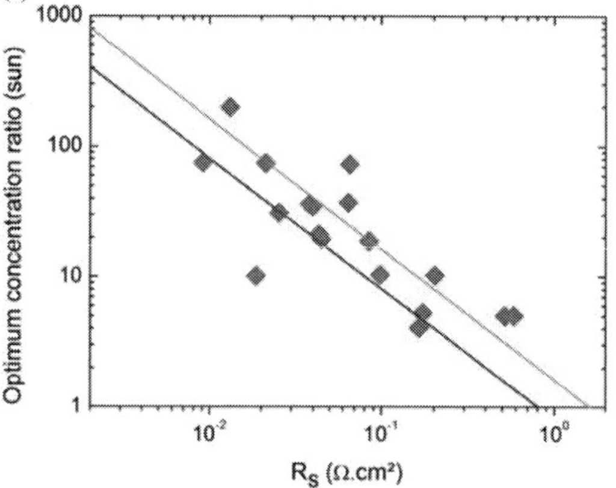

Fig. 2. (a) Efficiency versus concentration for the electrodeposited sample for different microcells of various sizes and (b) optimum concentration ratio as a function of the series resistance under AM1.5 G illumination. The orange line corresponds to the theoretical relation (2) with n = 2 and the brown one with n = 1.

we obtain J_{02} between 10^{-3}–10^{-2} mA/cm^2, compared with 10^{-4}–10^{-3} mA/cm^2 for co-evaporated samples, whereas J_{01} stays of the order of 10^{-10} mA/cm^2 for both samples. Thus, the points where the V_{oc}–J_{sc} curve change from a n = 2 slope to a n = 1 slope is pushed to higher concentration ratios on electrodeposited samples, which results in a higher V_{oc} gain under concentration. This behavior is in line with previously published results, which shows that defective solar cells are more sensitive to gains under concentration [5], [6].

B. Resistivity Analysis

To gain more insight in the differences between co-evaporated and electrodeposited samples, we analyze the efficiency as a function of the concentration level.

The efficiency increases with concentration at low concentration because of V_{oc} gains [see Fig. 2(a)]. Then, the efficiency decreases because of excessive resistive losses, according to the expected relationship [7]

$$R_s \times C \times J_{sc}\,(AM\,1.5) = nkT/q \tag{2}$$

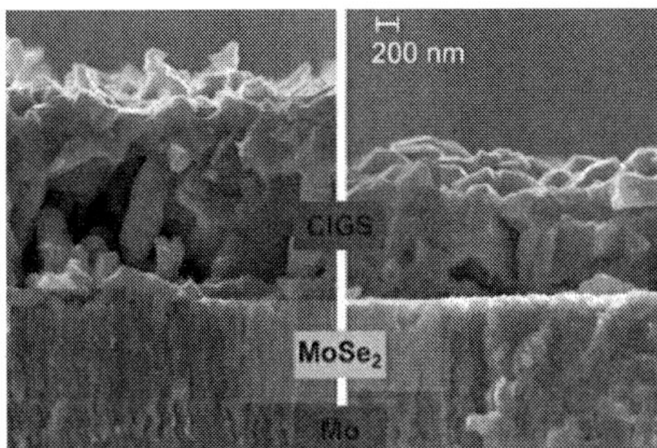

Fig. 3. SEM images of the cross section of the same electrodeposited Cu(In,Ga)Se$_2$ layer at two different locations. The colors highlight the Mo, MoSe$_2$, and Cu(In,Ga)Se$_2$ layers with various thicknesses.

where R_s is the series resistance, C is the concentration ratio, and $J_{sc}(AM\,1.5)$ is the short-circuit current at AM1.5 G illumination.

Contrary to what is usually seen on co-evaporated samples [4], the concentration ratio at which the efficiency is maximum, which is called optimum concentration ratio, is not constant over the sample. It varies from pixel to pixel, independently of the microcell size. Fig. 2(a) contains the characteristics of microcells of different sizes, but no correlation is found between the size and the form of the efficiency versus concentration curve. This indicates that the resistivity of the electrodeposited sample varies on the substrate at the mm scale, whereas that of the co-evaporated samples is highly homogeneous. We can directly correlate the optimum concentration ratio to the pixel series resistance under AM1.5 G illumination [see Fig. 2(b)].

A possible explanation for these local variations of resistivity is the inhomogeneity of Cu(In,Ga)Se$_2$ and MoSe$_2$ layer thickness on electrodeposited samples. A scanning electron microscopy analysis of an electrodeposited sample shows that the absorber thickness can vary up to a factor three on the sample. Moreover, during selenization, MoSe$_2$ is formed from the Mo layer, and its thickness varies on the sample from 750 to 1100 nm (see Fig. 3). On the contrary, on co-evaporated samples, the MoSe$_2$ layer is usually less than 20-nm thick. Another possible explanation for resistivity variations is the fact that the Cu(In,Ga)Se$_2$ electrodeposited layer can be denser or more porous, especially at the MoSe$_2$/Cu(In,Ga)Se$_2$ interface depending on the location. Thus, vertical current flow in the solar cell can encounter higher or lower resistance.

For the record microcell obtained on an electrodeposited substrate, we note a 15% efficiency at 33 suns equivalents, compared with 9% efficiency under AM1.5 G illumination.

It is interesting to note that the series resistance varies with the concentration level (see Fig. 4). This is primarily because of the photodoping of the Cu(In,Ga)Se$_2$ absorber. This behavior was observed on co-evaporated samples [8]. From the decay of series resistance, one can extract an effective diffusion length, as the series resistance can be expressed as [8]

$$R_{s_{\text{microcell}}} = R_c$$
$$+ \frac{R_{s0}}{\left(1 + \left(1 + \frac{\mu_p}{\mu_n}\right) \times \left(\frac{L_n}{t}\right)^2 \times \frac{q^2 \times EQE \times R_{s0} \times P_{\text{light}}}{kT \times h\nu}\right)} \quad (3)$$

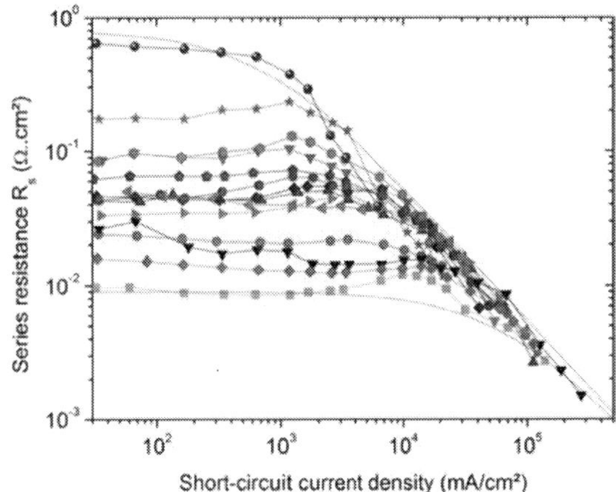

Fig. 4. Evolution of series resistance with concentration ratio of various electrodeposited microcells of different sizes.

where R_c is the light independent series resistance, R_{s0} the absorber resistance in dark condition, $R_{s0} = t/q\mu_p p_0$, with q the elementary charge, t the absorber thickness, μ_n (μ_p) the electron (hole) mobility, P_{light} the incident light power density, L_n the minority carrier diffusion length in the absorber, EQE the external quantum efficiency at 532 nm, kT/q the thermal voltage, and hν the energy of the incident photons. We can estimate that in electrodeposited samples the diffusion length is of the order of 0.4 μm, which is nearly one order of magnitude smaller than in co-evaporated samples. This is consistent with the lower crystallinity and higher defect concentration in electrodeposited absorbers. It can also stem from the fact that the Ga gradient in electrodeposited absorbers is not optimum, and thus, the effective diffusion length is not improved by grading, contrary to the co-evaporated samples with either V-shape or linear grading.

C. Temperature Effect

As we test the microcells under concentrated illumination, the temperature of the device can increase. This increase is linear with the incident light power, as thus the short-circuit current density: $T = T_0 + \kappa \times j_{\text{sc}}$, where T_0 is the temperature of the cell in the dark, or the ambient temperature, and κ is a proportionality factor. The consequence of this temperature elevation is the decrease of the open-circuit voltage at high concentration (see Fig. 1). Indeed, the V_{oc} can be expressed as a function of the short-circuit current density as [4]

$$V_{\text{oc}} = \frac{E_g}{q} - \frac{2kT_0}{q} \times \left(1 + \frac{\kappa}{T_0} J_{\text{sc}}\right)$$
$$\times \ln\left(\frac{2J_{001}}{-J_{002} + \sqrt{J_{002}^2 + 4J_{001}J_{\text{sc}}}}\right) \quad (4)$$

where q is the elementary charge, and T_0 the temperature of the cell in the dark, Eg the absorber bandgap energy, and J_{001} and J_{002} the dark saturation current prefactors. By fitting the $V_{\text{oc}} - J_{\text{sc}}$ curve in this high illumination regime, we can evaluate κ and, thus, conclude on the thermal conduction properties

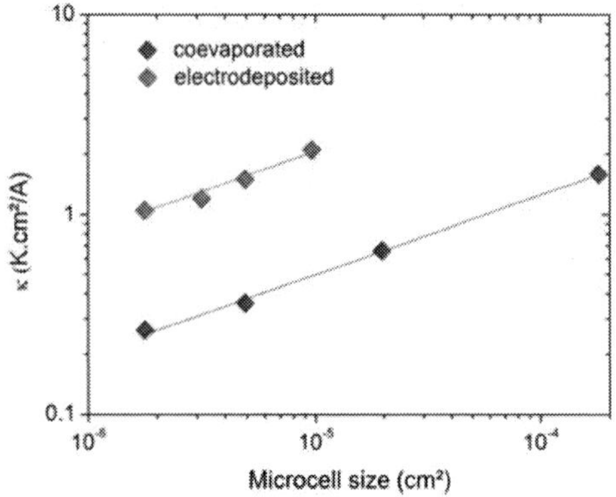

Fig. 5.   Factor κ as a function of the cell size.

of the different cells (see Fig. 5). One can see that the factor κ increases with increasing cell size. This scale effect is easily explained as with increasing laser spot size, the heat evacuation is less efficient [4], [9]–[11]. Indeed, the ratio of volume heated over the surface for heat exchange is increased. One can also see that the factor tends to be more important on electrodeposited samples. The Mo back contact layer plays the role of a heat spreading layer in the $Cu(In,Ga)Se_2$ stack, because of its large thermal conductivity (1.37 W/cm/K [12]). In electrodeposited cells, the Mo layer is partly consumed and transformed in $MoSe_2$ by selenization, whose thermal conductivity is lower (i.e., $\sim 10^{-2}$ W/cm/K [13]). This contributes to explain that these cells are more sensitive to temperature elevation than the co-evaporated ones. Other factors can also play a role in the temperature dependence of electrodeposited cells, such as the low density of $Cu(In,Ga)Se_2$ close to the molybdenum interface (see Fig. 3), that prevents an efficient thermal conduction between these two layers.

IV. Conclusion

By means of the pixelation of $Cu(In,Ga)Se_2$ solar cells, we were able to study co-evaporated and electrodeposited $Cu(In,Ga)Se_2$ solar cells. As expected, the electrodeposited cells are more inhomogeneous, in terms of resistivity, for example. Because of a higher concentration of defects, electrodeposited absorbers are also more sensitive to efficiency gains under concentration. The record electrodeposited microcell reaches 15% efficiency under 33 suns equivalent. It is very interesting in the perspective of using the $Cu(In,Ga)Se_2$ device under concentration. In the future, the pixelation could be used to couple

different characterization techniques, and complement classic cartographic measurements, by providing the local electrical properties of the device.

References

[1] P. Jackson, D. Hariskos, E. Lotter, S. Paetel, R. Wuerz, R. Menner, W. Wischmann, and M. Powalla, "New world record efficiency for $Cu(In,Ga)Se_2$ thin-film solar cells beyond 20%," *Prog. Photovolt: Res. Appl.*, vol. 19, pp. 894–897, 2011.

[2] M. Paire, L. Lombez, F. Donsanti, M. Jubault, S. Collin, J.-L. Pelouard, J.-F. Guillemoles, and D. Lincot, "Cu(In, Ga)Se$_2$ microcells: High efficiency and low material consumption," *J. Renewable Sustainable Energy*, vol. 5, p. 011202, 2013.

[3] A. Duchatelet, G. Savidand, R. N. Vannier, E. Chassaing, and D. Lincot, "A new deposition process for Cu(In,Ga)(S,Se)$_2$ solar cells by one-step electrodeposition of mixed oxide precursor films and thermochemical reduction," *J. Renewable Sustainable Energy*, vol. 5, no. 1, p. 011203, 2013.

[4] M. Paire, A. Shams, L. Lombez, N. Pere-Laperne, S. Collin, J.-L. Pelouard, J.-F. Guillemoles, and D. Lincot, "Resistive and thermal scale effects for $Cu(In,Ga)Se_2$ polycrystalline thin film microcells under concentration," *Energy Environ. Sci.*, vol. 4, no. 12, pp. 4972–4977, 2011.

[5] Y. Hirai, H. Nagashima, Y. Kurokawa, and A. Yamada, "Experimental and theoretical evaluation of Cu(In,Ga)Se$_2$ concentrator solar cells," *Jpn. J. Appl. Phys.*, vol. 51, no. 1, p. 014101, 2012.

[6] J. R. Tuttle, "The performance of Cu(In,Ga)Se$_2$-based solar cells in conventional and concentrator applications," in *Proc. Mater. Res. Soc.*, San Francisco, CA, USA, 1996, 426, pp. 143–151.

[7] E. Sanchez and G. L. Araujo, "Mathematical analysis of the efficiency-concentration characteristic of a solar cell," *Sol. Cells*, vol. 12, no. 3, pp. 263–276, 1984.

[8] M. Paire, L. Lombez, N. Pere-Laperne, S. Collin, J.-L. Pelouard, D. Lincot, and J.-F. Guillemoles, "Microscale solar cells for high concentration on polycrystalline Cu(In,Ga)Se$_2$ thin films," *Appl. Phys. Lett.*, vol. 98, no. 26, p. 264102, 2011.

[9] P. Thomas, "Some conduction problems in the heating of small areas on large solids," *Quart. J. Mech. Appl. Math.*, vol. 10, no. 4, p. 482, 1957.

[10] M. Paire, "Highly efficient solar cells in low dimensionality based on Cu(In,Ga)Se$_2$ chalcopyrite materials," Ph.D. dissertation, Inst. Res. Development Photovoltaic Energy (IRDEP), Univ. Pierre-and-Marie-Curie, Paris, France, 2012.

[11] M. Paire, L. Lombez, A. Delamarre, S. Collin, J.-L. Pelouard, J.-F. Guillemoles, and D. Lincot, "Physics of Cu(In, Ga)Se$_2$ solar cells in high injection regime," presented at the 39th IEEE Photovolt. Spec. Conf., Tampa, FL, USA, 2013.

[12] R. P. Tye, "Preliminary measurements on the thermal and electrical conductivities of molybdenum, niobium, tantalum and tungsten," *J. Less Common Metals*, vol. 3, no. 1, pp. 13–18, 1961.

[13] J.-Y. Kim, S.-M. Choi, W.-S. Seo, and W.-S. Cho, "Thermal and electronic properties of exfoliated metal chalcogenides," *Bull. Korean Chem. Soc.*, vol. 31, no. 11, pp. 3225–3227, 2010.

Authors' photographs and biographies not available at the time of publication.

High Efficiency Multi-busbar Solar Cells and Modules

Stefan Braun, Robin Nissler, Christian Ebert, Dirk Habermann, and Giso Hahn

Abstract—In this paper, a detailed overview of multi-busbar solar cells and modules with selective emitter, a fine line screen printed front side metallization, and full aluminum rear side are presented. The designs of three-busbar and multi-busbar solar cells and modules are compared and assessed by solar cell, module performance, and Ag metal consumption. Assembled multi-busbar solar cells and four-cell modules are compared with industrial type three-busbar solar cells and modules that demonstrate average fill factor gains of 0.6%$_{\mathrm{abs}}$ on the module level. A reduction in Ag paste consumption of about 50%$_{\mathrm{abs}}$ for the front grid is achieved using the multi-busbar front electrode design with a fine line screen printing process. An advanced front side metallization technique using an Ag seed and Ag LIP approach demonstrates the potential to further reduce Ag consumption to values as low as 32 mg/cell.

Index Terms—Photovoltaic cells, semiconductor device manufacture, silicon, solar energy.

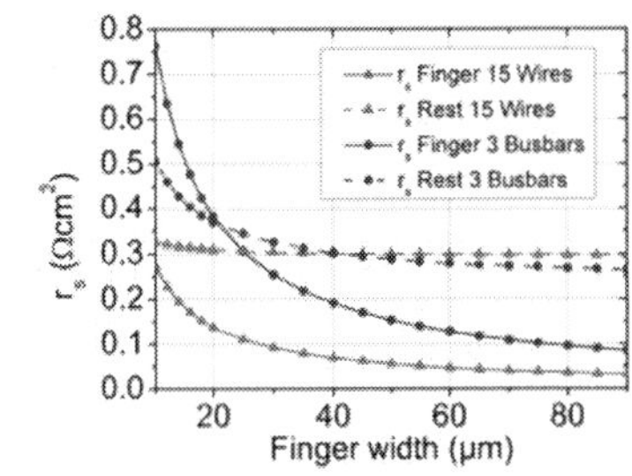

Fig. 1. Series resistance contribution plotted versus the width of a screen printed finger of a multi-busbar and a three-busbar solar cell. In the dashed lines, the remaining part of the series resistance is plotted. By adding the finger contribution to the rest, one obtains the total series resistance of the solar cells.

I. INTRODUCTION

HIGHER efficiencies with lower processing costs reached by lower metal consumption of the front side metallization are prerequisites for lower costs of Si photovoltaics. An optimized solar cell design using the same equipment as already available for state-of-the-art solar cells can easily be implemented into industrial solar cell production lines. In this paper, an approach for a front side design is discussed, using more busbars than the widely used three-busbar design. The idea for such a solar cell design based on multiple wires, which interconnect the cells in a module like ribbons, but substituting the busbar at the same time, was first introduced to the market by the Canadian company Day4 Energy [1].

The starting point is to optimize the solar cell series resistance under module conditions and not for a measurement on cell level [2]. For the optimization of the front grid, a simulation program based on the two-diode model is used to sum up the series resistances of each contributor in a module, optimizing the number and geometry as well as the shading of wires needed. The simulations reveal that the advantages of the multi-busbar design originate from a reduction of effective finger length,

opening up new possibilities for the front side design relating to metal consumption, and grid layout. It is demonstrated that the multi-busbar solar cell design with a screen printed front grid can increase the module efficiency by 0.2%$_{\mathrm{abs}}$ [3], and simulations predict that a reduction in the Ag consumption of 80% can be achieved using seed and plate techniques. Round wires offer the beneficial effect that reflected sunlight is partly guided to the solar cell surface. The effectively shaded area of the wires is therefore reduced [3]. This effect is also enhanced when incorporating the wire solar cell into a module because of internal back reflection on the glass/air interface.

II. SIMULATION

The two-diode model is used to simulate the *IV* characteristics [4]. An Excel spreadsheet determines the series resistance [5] for both solar cell types on cell and module level and solves the two-diode model equation for each given parameter using iteration algorithms. Additionally, the optimum number of wires is calculated for each wire diameter. In addition, the optimal amount of Ag needed for a sufficient front side metallization is calculated. The outcome of the simulations is presented in Section IV.

The simulations reveal the beneficial effects of the front grid design of multi-busbar solar cells. In Fig. 1, the series resistance contribution of a screen printed Ag finger is displayed for a three-busbar and a multi-busbar solar cell with 15 wires. The assumption is made for the *IV* setup that the current is collected with 15 pins on each busbar and that the rear side of the solar cell has full contact to the metal chuck. For the multi-busbar solar cell, the current is collected on both edges by the wires, which is more realistic to the situation in a module.

In addition, the remaining part of the series resistance (contribution of rear side, base, emitter, contact to the emitter, and

Manuscript received July 5, 2013; revised August 6, 2013 and September 17, 2013; accepted October 8, 2013. Date of publication November 1, 2013; date of current version December 16, 2013. This work was supported by the German BMU project FKZ 0325581.

S. Braun and G. Hahn are with the University of Konstanz, Konstanz D-78457, Germany (e-mail: stefan.braun-shirazi@uni-konstanz.de; giso.hahn@uni-konstanz.de).

R. Nissler, C. Ebert, and D. Habermann are with Gebr. Schmid GmbH&Co, Freudenstadt D-72250, Germany (e-mail: nissler.ro@schmid-group.com; ebert.ch@schmid-group.com; habermann.di@schmid-group.com).

Color versions of one or more of the figures in this paper are available online at http://ieeexplore.ieee.org.

Digital Object Identifier 10.1109/JPHOTOV.2013.2286525

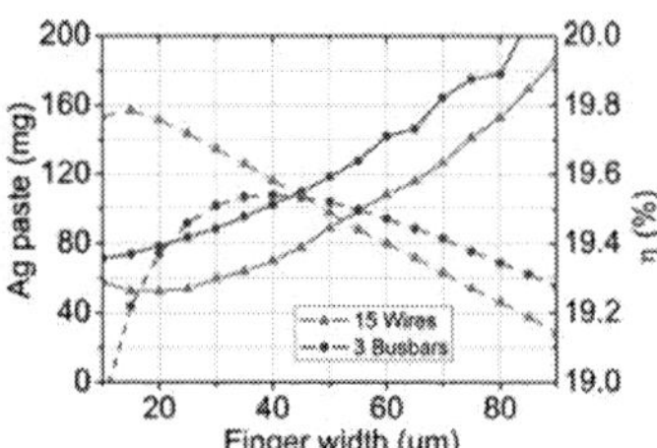

Fig. 2. Ag paste consumption (solid lines) and efficiency (dashed lines) plotted versus the finger width of screen printed solar cells.

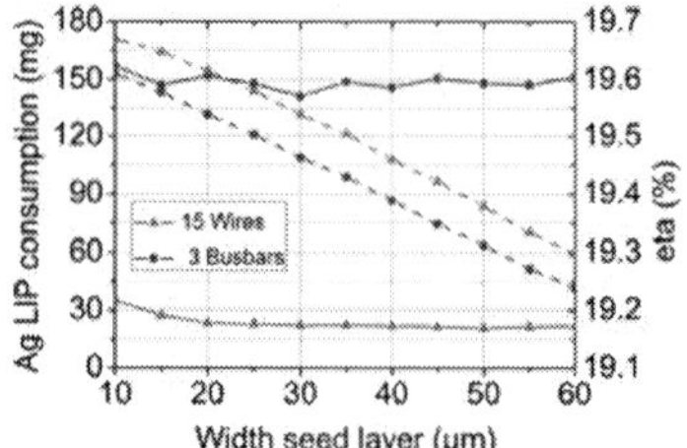

Fig. 3. Optimal amount of plated Ag needed plotted versus the seed layer width (solid lines). Efficiencies of both cell types (dashed lines).

busbars/pads) is displayed in dashed lines. By adding the remaining part to the series resistance contribution of the fingers, one obtains the total series resistance of the solar cell. A busbar width of 1.5 mm and a wire diameter of 250 μm are assumed. With decreasing finger width the series resistance contribution r_s of a Gaussian shaped finger with a height of 35 μm rises much faster for a three-busbar solar cell compared with a multi-busbar solar cell. This finger shape is more realistic compared with a rectangular finger form. Even more accurate would be to use a finger form, which also takes into account the nonuniformity of the screen printed finger [6]. In the simulation, the potential reflection of light on the grid structure was not taken into account, therefore the shading was set to 100% for the metallized area. For more accurate simulations material, roughness, and shape have to be taken into account.

The huge difference in series resistance is related to a reduced effective finger length for the multi-busbar solar cell. The shading for both solar cells is reduced with decreasing finger width. The results of the simulations indicate that the line resistance of the fingers for a multi-busbar solar cell is almost negligible. This offers possibilities not only for new metallization techniques but also for less conductive materials. Using screen printing techniques, the amount of Ag paste can be reduced significantly because the effective finger length is reduced from 25 mm for a three-busbar solar cell to only 5 mm for a solar cell with multi-busbar front grid with 15 wires and a wire diameter of 250 μm.

Taking a closer look at the Ag paste consumption and efficiency for both solar cell designs, one can observe the following. In Fig. 2, the Ag paste consumption and the efficiency are plotted versus the width of a screen printed finger with a Gaussian shaped form and an aspect ratio (finger width / finger height) of 0.5.

Both cell types benefit from a finger width reduction. The efficiency rises, however at a certain width, about 40 μm for the three-busbar and 15 μm for the multi-busbar solar cell, the efficiency drops because of the insufficient finger conductivity. This results in a higher efficiency for the multi-busbar design. The metal consumption was calculated as follows. For the three-busbar solar cell, a busbar width of 1.2 mm was assumed. For the multi-busbar solar cells, small front pads were also added in the simulation. These front pads increase the contact area to the wire and are needed to obtain a sufficient adhesion between the cell and the wire for the soldering process. These pads lead to higher Ag paste consumption and shading when going to smaller finger spacings. The size of such a pad is 500×500 μm^2. For each wire, one pad is needed for each finger. Depending on the finger spacing the number of pads varies.

The highest efficiency of the three-busbar solar cell is reached for an Ag paste consumption of 102 mg. The multi-busbar solar cell only needs 53 mg Ag paste to reach the highest efficiency.

For a seed and plate approach where a highly conductive metal is deposited onto a shallow seed layer, the multi-busbar design also demonstrates its advantages. The growth mode for a plated finger differs from a screen printed one. The screen printed fingers have a Gaussian shaped form and plated fingers grow during the metallization process. Its growth is two times faster in length than in height, which results in a hemicycle shape for long plating times. In Fig. 3, on the left y-axis, the optimal amount of plated Ag is plotted against the width of a seed layer indicated by solid lines. On the right y-axis, the efficiency is plotted and marked in dashed lines.

In the simulation, an Ag conductivity of 50×10^6 S/m is assumed for the plated base layer, which was also reported in [7]. The conductivity of the seed layer was set to zero. For the multi-busbar solar cell with 15 wires, a wire diameter of 250 μm (as the IV-setup) and small front pads of 500×500 μm^2 are assumed.

It is assumed that the growth rate of the plated Ag layer is the same on fingers, busbars, and pads. This assumption is not necessarily correct as reported in [8].

With decreasing seed layer width, the efficiency for both solar cell designs rises because the shading is reduced. At the same time, the finger spacing is reduced for decreasing width of the seed layer. The spikes in the blue line are related to a low resolution of the simulation in particularly the finger spacing which was varied in 100-μm steps. The results of the simulation indicate that the front side of a multi-busbar solar cell is sufficiently plated with 20–40 mg Ag, whereas the optimal Ag consumption for a three-busbar front grid lies in the range of 140–160 mg (optimized for efficiency, not for cost). Therefore, for a sufficient front side metallization of a multi-busbar solar cell, only a fifth of Ag is needed. In addition, a slight increase in efficiency is gained comparing the efficiencies of both cell types using the same seed layer width.

III. EXPERIMENT

In the experiment, common three-busbar solar cells are compared with multi-busbar solar cells on cell and module level. All six inch boron doped p-type semi-square Cz wafers, resistivity

2 Ω·cm, with an area of 239.12 mm^2 were alkaline textured and obtained a 55 Ω/sq. POCl$_3$ emitter diffusion. The wafers were masked by inkjet printing and etched back to about 110 Ω/sq. to form a selective emitter [9]. Edge isolation was performed by single side chemical etching. Afterwards, the wafers were cleaned and a PECVD SiN$_x$:H layer was deposited on the surface. The wafers were divided into three groups. Group 1 is the three-busbar front grid reference group. For the front side metallization process, 70-μm wide fingers and 1.2-mm wide busbars were printed. The width of the busbars should be reduced as much as possible to reduce the amount of Ag paste printed. On the other hand, the adhesion to the ribbon which will be soldered onto the busbar later on has also to be taken into account. The distance between the metal fingers was 2.07 mm. Around 150 mg Ag paste was used for the front side metallization with a single printing step. The rear side was screen printed with Al. Group 2 has a multi-busbar front grid design also with a full Al back surface field on the rear side. For the front side grid, a dual printing was used where only the fine line printed fingers of around 50-μm width contact the emitter structure. The amount of Ag paste used was around 40 mg, and the finger spacing for the solar cells was 1.8 mm. Group 2 obtained small Ag pads (700 × 500 μm^2) onto the conductive fingers which increase the contact area between the fingers and the wires attached later on. The amount of Ag paste used for the Ag front side pads was 30 mg. Finally, the solar cells were co-fired in a belt furnace. All solar cells were measured with a modified HALM IV flasher [10]. For contacting of the front side, a frame with 15 Cu wires with a diameter of 250 μm was used.

After this step, Group 1 and Group 2 solar cells obtained three 4-mm wide Sn stripes on the full area screen printed Al rear side, which are needed to solder the ribbons/wires on the Al rear side. The Sn was deposited via ultrasonic soldering using the TinPad technique [11]. For Group 1, the stripes were deposited in busbar direction. This leads to a continuous contact of the ribbons on the rear side. For the multi-busbar cells, the stripes were deposited perpendicular to the wire direction. In that way, each wire contacts three tin pads. In the following step, Group 1 solar cells were stringed with Cu ribbons (200 μm × 1.5 mm) on front and rear side, and the multi-busbar solar cells were interconnected with wires. For Group 2, 15 copper wires with Sn encapsulant and a diameter of 300 μm were used. Note that this wire diameter is larger than the one used for the *IV* measurement of the cells and the simulations. The increased wire diameter will decrease the series resistance further and lead to higher fill factors. Four solar cells of each group were integrated into a module. The module glass has a single sided antireflection coating. After that step, the modules were measured independently at the JRC–ESTI in Ispra (Italy). For the measurement, a square-shaped shadow mask with 318-mm edge length was used. The spacing between the solar cells was 3 mm and the space between the edges of the cells and the mask was 1.5 mm.

In a second experiment, a new front side metallization scheme was assessed. The optimal amount of Ag needed for the front side metallization was determined. These solar cells represent Group 3. A shallow Ag finger grid plus front pads, 15 pads for

TABLE I
OVERVIEW OF GROUPS

Group	Type	Rear side	Front side	Connector
G1	3-busbar	full Al BSF + TinPad	Screen Printed	200 µm x 1.5 mm
G2	multi-busbar	full Al BSF + TinPad	Screen Printed	300 µm wire
G3	multi-busbar	full Al BSF	Seed & Plate	

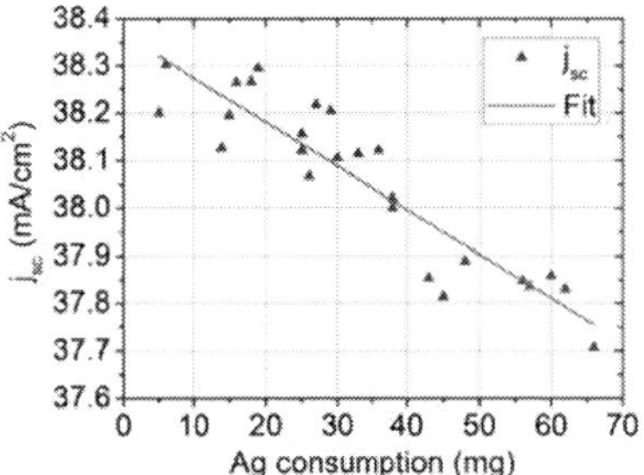

Fig. 4. Current density plotted versus the Ag consumption for solar cells with an Ag plated front grid. A reduction of Ag leads to higher current densities of the device because of reduced shading.

each finger with a dimension of 500 × 500 μm^2, was deposited. In a first step, a shallow Ag seed layer was deposited on the SiN$_x$:H layer over the highly doped region of the selective emitter structure using an inkjet device. After the firing process, the seed layer was strengthened using light induced Ag plating (Ag LIP). The amount of Ag deposited was varied between 5–70 mg. The solar cells were then measured with a HALM IV flasher to determine the cell parameters. The main attributes of all three groups are displayed in Table I.

IV. SOLAR CELL RESULTS

For *IV* measurement, the multi-busbar solar cells are contacted with 15 wires on the front side. The diameter of these wires was 250 μm. The current was collected at the edges of the solar cells from both sides. For the seed layer deposition, 12 mg of Ag nano-particle ink was applied. The resulting seed layer width was in the range of 30–35 μm.

In Fig. 4, one can observe the linear increase of current density (indicated by the red fit curve) by reducing the amount of Ag.

This effect can be easily explained. During the plating process, Ag is uniformly deposited on the seed layer. This broadens the finger structure with increasing plating duration leading to an increased shading of the front grid.

Taking a look at Fig. 5, where the fill factor of the solar cells is plotted versus the Ag consumption, a decrease in fill factor with decreasing amount of Ag is visible. This is indicated by the red fit curve. The reduction of Ag directly leads to higher line resistances of the front side metallization, and the higher series resistance contribution affects the fill factor. As a result, the fill factor drops. On the right side of the graph, the fill factor

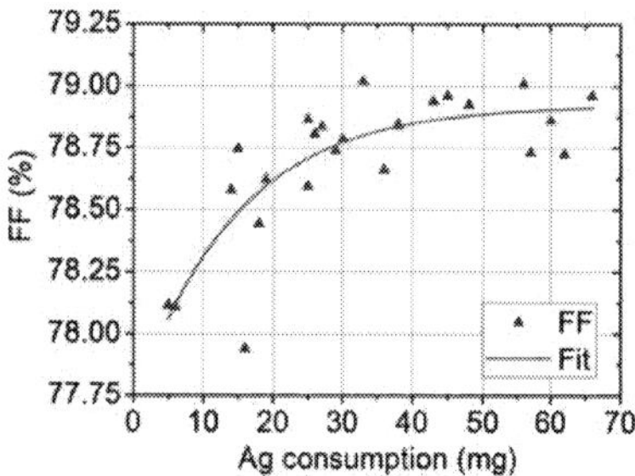

Fig. 5. Fill factor plotted versus the Ag consumption for solar cells with an Ag plated front grid. For a sufficient fill factor, the amount of Ag has to be adapted.

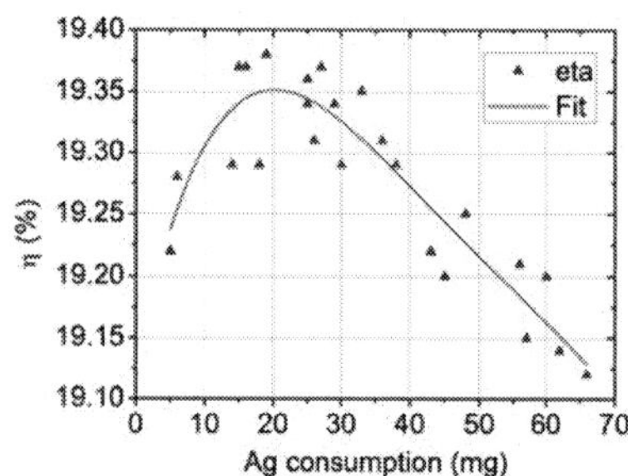

Fig. 6. The efficiency plotted versus the LIP Ag consumption for solar cells with an Ag plated front grid.

saturates because an adequate line resistance does not influence the fill factor anymore.

The efficiency plotted against the amount of plated Ag is displayed in Fig. 6. Going from 65 mg Ag to 20 mg, the efficiency rises. This effect is related to the fact that a reduced Ag consumption causes less shading of the front side, which was demonstrated in Fig. 4. The highest efficiencies can be reached in the range of 15–25 mg of plated Ag. When reducing the amount of Ag further, the efficiency drops. As a guide to the eye, a red fitting curve is also plotted in the graph.

The highest efficiencies are in the range of 19.3%–19.4% with fill factors of 78.5%–78.8%. This is a compromise between high current densities and adequate fill factors.

Even the solar cells with a sufficient Ag metallization could only reach fill factors in the range of 79%. Former experiments demonstrated higher fill factors in the range of 79.5%. This is why the authors believe that a further increase in efficiency could be reached by optimizing the processes sequence.

If we compare the results of plated Ag consumption for the experiment and the simulation, we obtain a Ag consumption of 22 mg for a seed layer with 30–35 μm in the simulation and a maximum efficiency of 20-mg Ag in the experiment. This demonstrates that the simulation is in good agreement with the experimental values.

The results of the *IV* measurement for Group 1, 2, and 3 are given in Table II. For Group 3 solar cells, the number indicates the amount of metal plated in mg. For Group 1 and 2, eight solar cells are taken to fabricate two four-cell modules.

TABLE II
IV MEASUREMENT ON CELL LEVEL

Group	V_{oc} (mV)	j_{sc} (mA/cm²)	FF (%)	eta (%)
G1-1A	641.7	38.0	79.9	19.5
G1-2A	643.1	38.0	79.8	19.5
G1-3A	642.6	38.1	79.5	19.5
G1-4A	643.1	38.0	79.8	19.5
G1-5B	642.6	38.0	79.8	19.5
G1-6B	642.7	38.0	79.8	19.5
G1-7B	642.6	38.0	79.8	19.5
G1-8B	642.9	38.1	79.7	19.5
G2-1A	644.5	37.9	79.1	19.3
G2-2A	644.5	37.9	79.5	19.5
G2-3A	644.5	38.0	79.5	19.5
G2-4A	644.9	37.9	79.7	19.5
G2-5B	643.6	37.9	79.3	19.4
G2-6B	644.4	38.0	79.6	19.4
G2-7B	643.1	38.0	79.4	19.4
G2-8B	644.7	37.9	79.6	19.5
G3-5	644.1	38.2	78.1	19.2
G3-6	644.5	38.3	78.1	19.3
G3-14	644.0	38.1	78.6	19.3
G3-15	643.9	38.2	78.7	19.4
G3-16	644.3	38.3	77.9	19.4
G3-18	642.7	38.3	78.4	19.3
G3-19	643.8	38.3	78.6	19.4
G3-25	644.9	38.2	78.6	19.3
G3-26	643.6	38.1	78.8	19.3
G3-27	642.8	38.2	78.8	19.4
G3-29	643.0	38.2	78.7	19.3
G3-30	642.4	38.1	78.8	19.3
G3-33	642.3	38.1	79.0	19.4
G3-36	643.9	38.1	78.7	19.3
G3-38	643.9	38.0	78.8	19.3
G3-43	643.3	37.9	78.9	19.2
G3-45	642.9	37.8	79.0	19.2
G3-48	643.6	37.9	78.9	19.3
G3-56	642.5	37.8	79.0	19.2
G3-57	642.6	37.8	78.7	19.2
G3-60	643.1	37.9	78.9	19.2
G3-62	643.1	37.8	78.7	19.1
G3-66	642.3	37.7	79.0	19.1

V. MODULE RESULTS

Four cells were stringed, laminated under module glass, and independently measured at the Joint Research Centre-European Solar Test Installation (JRC–ESTI). The results are presented in Table III. The edges of the modules were covered by a black polyethylene (PE) mask. The aperture area of the modules was 1011.24 cm² , whereas the total cell area was only 956.48 cm².

The modules were measured in outdoor conditions at a module temperature of 25 °C to make best use of the correct sun

TABLE III
RESULTS OF FOUR-CELL MODULES MEASURED AT JRC–ESTI

Group	V_{oc}	I_{sc}	j_{sc}	FF	eta	P_{max}
	(V)	(A)	(mA/cm²)	(%)	(%)	(W)
G1-A	2.556	9.151	36.2	76.08	17.58	17.77
G1-B	2.556	9.127	36.1	76.31	17.61	17.80
G2-A	2.570	9.104	36.0	76.98	17.79	17.98
G2-B	2.560	9.168	36.3	76.57	17.77	17.97

spectrum. All four modules show high efficiencies in the range of 17.6–17.8%. The short circuit current densities of the three-busbar modules also shown in Table III are the current densities for the four modules calculated with the total illuminated area, not the cell area only. It is hard to determine if the slight gain in j_{sc} can be related to the round shaped wires as reported in [12]. Please note that the *IV* measurement was performed with 250-μm thick wires, whereas the modules are stringed with 300-μm wide wires.

The increased fill factor (FF) can clearly be related to the amount and thickness of wires. The cross section of all wires is 1.06 mm^2, whereas the cross section of the three ribbons is only 0.9 mm^2. An average gain of 0.6%$_{abs}$ in FF can be observed. The increased fill factor can directly be related to the larger cross section of the wires. This also means that more Cu is used to increase the fill factor. A further broadening of the ribbons from 1.5 to 1.6 mm or more could also increase the amount of Cu and lower the fill factor, but would lead to higher shading. An increased ribbon height would cause more stress during the lamination process and could lead to cell breakage. In addition, the multi-busbar modules show higher open-circuit voltages. The difference of up to 14 mV can explained by the higher V_{oc} values on cell level originating from the dual printing of the front side metallization.

VI. DISCUSSION

The potential in Ag reduction for the front side metallization using a front grid with 15 wires instead of three busbars is presented in this paper. Using screen printing, an Ag reduction of more than 50% is achieved. At the same time, the solar cells demonstrate similar performance on cell level.

Changing the front side metallization to a seed and plate technique, a further Ag reduction can be seen. Twelve milligrams of Ag particle containing seed layer ink plus 20 mg Ag for LIP are sufficient for a cell performance of 19.4%. Compared with the three-busbar solar cells, the simulation predicts that an Ag reduction of 118 mg is possible.

Further process optimization offers the possibility to even increase the efficiency as the simulation reveals.

On module level efficiencies of 17.6% with a power of 17.8 W with three-busbar solar cells and an illuminated area of 1011.24 cm^2 are presented. The multi-busbar modules reach slightly higher efficiencies up to 17.8% and a module power of 18.0 W. Calculating the module power to a 60-cell module, the power of a three-busbar module would be 267 W and for a multi-busbar module a power of 270 W can be reached. A silver paste reduction of 4800 mg for such a module is possible.

VII. CONCLUSION

It was demonstrated that a multi-busbar module design shows benefits in fill factor, current density, and Ag paste consumption. Using a dual print approach, 80 mg of silver paste could be saved with the multi-busbar front design compared with the standard three-busbar front design, which is a reduction of >50%. With a seed and plate approach, the amount of Ag needed for the front side metallization could be further reduced to 12 mg for the seed layer and 20 mg for the plated base layer. Here, the multi-busbar cell design shows its benefits for Ag reduction.

The production of four-cell modules demonstrated the feasibility of the new design. Using only narrow fingers and small pads for the front side metallization, module efficiencies of 17.8% prove the high potential of this technology. The reference modules obtained efficiencies of 17.6%.

Because of further optimization of the cell, stringing, and lamination process, the authors believe a further increase of module efficiency is possible. A further cell optimization could be achieved using more elaborate metal deposition techniques, for example, optimized inkjet printers that can deposit narrower conduction lines or laser ablation of the SiN$_x$ layer and direct plating [13]. The automated stringing process could be further optimized using smaller pads, which would slightly increase the current and voltage of the solar cell. A further optimized lamination process could offer thicker wire diameters. This would lead to higher fill factors and slightly lower currents, but higher efficiencies.

ACKNOWLEDGMENT

The authors would like to thank L. Mahlstaedt for help and assistance during cell processing, the TCS team for their support, and E. Salis and H. Müllejans for the module measurements at the ESTI.

REFERENCES

[1] A. Schneider, L. Rubin, and G. Rubin, "Solar cell improvement by new metallization techniques—The DAY4TM electrode concept," in *Proc. 4th World Conf. Photovoltaic Energy Conversion*, 2006, pp. 1095–1098.

[2] S. Braun, G. Micard, and G. Hahn, "Solar cell improvement by using a multi-busbar design as front electrode," *Energy Procedia*, vol. 27, pp. 227–233, 2012.

[3] S. Braun, G. Hahn, R. Nissler, C. Pönisch, and D. Habermann, "Multi-busbar solar cells and modules: High efficiencies and low silver consumption," *Energy Procedia*, vol. 38, pp. 334–339, 2013.

[4] D. S. H. Chan and J. C. H. Phang, "Analytical methods for the extraction of solar-cell single- and double-diode model parameters from I–V characteristics," *IEEE Trans. Electron Devices*, vol. 34, pp. 286–293, Feb. 1987.

[5] A. Mette, New Concepts for Front Side Metallization of Industrial Silicon Solar Cells, Ph.D. Dissertation, Dept. Eng., Univ. Freiburg, Freiburg, Germany, 2007.

[6] L. Jiang, "An improved mathematical modeling to simulate metallization screen pattern trend for silicon solar cell," in *Proc. 39th IEEE Photovoltaic Spec. Conf.*, 2013, to be published.

[7] M. Hörteis, J. Bartsch, V. Radtke, A. Filipovic, and S.W. Glunz, "Different aspects of seed layer-printed and light-induced plated front side contacts," in *Proc. 24th Eur. Photovoltaic Solar Energy Conf. Exhib.*, 2009, pp. 985–988.

[8] J. Bartsch, Advanced Front Side Metallization for Crystalline Silicon Solar Cells with Electrochemical Techniques, Dept. Eng., Dissertation Univ. Freiburg, Freiburg, Germany, 2011.

[9] H. Haverkamp, A. Dastgheib-Shirazi, B. Raabe, F. Book, and G. Hahn, "Minimizing the electrical losses on the front side: Development of a

selective emitter process from a single diffusion," in *Proc. 33rd IEEE Photovoltaic Spec. Conf.*, 2008, pp. 430–433.

[10] A. Herguth, S. Braun, G. Hahn, C. Poenisch, R. Nissler, and D. Habermann, "Towards non-permanent contacting schemes for busbar-free solar cells," in *Proc. 28th Eur. Photovoltaic Solar Energy Conf. Exhib.*, 2013, to be published.

[11] H. van Campe, S. Huber, S. Meyer, S. Reif, and J. Vietor, "Direct tin-coating of aluminum rear contact by ultrasonic soldering," in *Proc. 27th Eur. Photovoltaic Solar Energy Conf. Exhib.*, 2012, pp. 1150–1153.

[12] A.W. Blakers, "Shading losses of solar-cell metal grids," *J. Appl. Phys.*, vol. 71, pp. 5237–5241, 1992.

[13] A. Grohe, A. Knorz, M. Alemán, C. Harmel, S.W. Glunz, R. Prei, and G.W. Willeke, "Novel low temperature front side metallization scheme using selective laser ablation of anti reflection coating and electroless nickel plating," in *Proc. 21st Eur. Photovoltaic Solar Energy Conf. Exhib.*, 2006, pp. 750–753.

Dirk Habermann was born in Herdecke, Germany, in 1962. He studied geoscience at Ruhr University, Bochum, Germany, where he received the Master's and Ph.D. degrees on the topic "Quantitative Cathodo-Luminescence Spectoscopy," in 1993 and 1997, respectively.

In 1998, he became an Assistant Professor of experimental physics with the Technical University Bergakademie Freiberg, Germany. In 2002 he joined the company RENA, where he became Senior Process Manager for semiconductor technology. In 2004, he left RENA and joined the Schmid Group, Freudenstadt, Germany, where he served as Director of Technology at the STN in Freudenstadt, where he was responsible for solar cell process and production technology, as well as automation technology. In 2008, he was promoted to Vice President for Research and Development at Schmid. He is the author/co-author of more than 50 publications in journals and conference proceedings and holds several patents.

Stefan Braun was born in Höxter, Germany, in 1981. He received a scholarship and received the Diploma degree in physics on the investigation of multicrystalline silicon solar cells with buried contact cell structures from the University of Konstanz, Konstanz, Germany, in 2009. He is currently working toward the Ph.D. degree with the Photovoltaics Division, University of Konstanz.

His research topics include novel silicon solar cell designs and metallization techniques for industrial solar cell applications. He is the author/co-author of more than ten publications in journals and conference proceedings and holds two patents, with several patents pending.

Giso Hahn was born in Frankfurt am Main, Germany, in 1969. He received the Diploma degree in physics from University of Stuttgart, Stuttgart, Germany, in 1995 and the Ph.D. degree in physics from University of Konstanz, Konstanz, Germany, in 1999. He received the Venia Legendi (Habilitation) degree in experimental physics from University of Konstanz in 2005.

Since 2009, he has been an Adjunct (Apl.) Professor with the Department of Physics, University of Konstanz. He is also the Head of the Photovoltaics Division, Department of Physics, University of Konstanz, which consists of more than 50 employees. His research interests include crystalline silicon materials and solar cell process development, characterization of promising low-cost materials for photovoltaic applications, and development of adapted solar cell processes for these and other materials. He is the author/co-author of more than 230 publications in journals, books, and conference proceedings and holds several patents.

Prof. Hahn is a member of the scientific committees of various conference series (e.g., IEEE, PVSC, EU PVSEC, and SiliconPV) and workshops. His other scientific and technological achievements include reaching record efficiencies for selected crystalline silicon materials and detailed characterization of efficiency limiting crystal defects. His group is interested in transferring technologies from the laboratory stage to industry.

Robin Nissler was born in Stuttgart, Germany, in 1977. He received the Diploma degree in physics from the Technical University of Munich, Munich, Germany, in 2003 and the Ph.D. degree in physics from University of Bonn, Bonn, Germany, in 2008.

He is currently with the R&D Department of the Schmid Group, Freudenstadt, Germany, where he is focusing on solar cell metallization and characterization.

Christian Ebert was born in Heidelberg, Germany, in 1981. He received the Diploma degree in physics from the University of Heidelberg in 2007.

He is currently an R&D Scientist with the Schmid Group, Freudenstadt, Germany. His work focuses on solar cell metallization for front and rear contacts, as well as solar cell contacting methods and solar module optimization.

Fully Ion-Implanted and Screen-Printed 20.2% Efficient Front Junction Silicon Cells on 239 cm² n-Type CZ Substrate

Yuguo Tao, Young-Woo Ok, Francesco Zimbardi, Ajay D. Upadhyaya, *Member, IEEE*, Jiun-Hong Lai, Steven Ning, Vijaykumar D. Upadhyaya, and Ajeet Rohatgi, *Fellow, IEEE*

Abstract—In this study, we present fully ion-implanted screen-printed high-efficiency 239 cm² n-type silicon solar cells that are fabricated on pseudosquare Czochralski wafers. Implanted boron emitter and phosphorous back-surface field (BSF) were optimized to produce n-type front junction cells with front and back SiO_2/SiN_x surface passivation and rear point contacts. Average efficiency of 19.8%, with the best efficiency of 20.2%, certified by Fraunhofer ISE, Freiburg, Germany, was achieved. In addition, the planarized rear side gave better surface passivation, in combination with optimized BSF profile, raised the average efficiency to ~20% for the fully implanted and screen-printed n-type passivated emitter, rear totally diffused cells.

Index Terms—Back-surface field (BSF), ion implantation, n-type wafer, planarization, screen printed.

I. Introduction

ION implantation has become an active area of investigation in photovoltaics (PV) because it can produce advanced high-efficiency cell structures with fewer processing steps [1]–[4]. It is also well known that n-type silicon (Si) provides several advantages over p-type, including better tolerance to common impurities (e.g., Fe), high bulk lifetime, and no light-induced degradation due to boron–oxygen complex [5], [6]. Benick *et al.*, demonstrated high quality of boron and phosphorus implantation by fabricating 22.3% efficient small-area (4 cm²) n-type passivated emitter, rear totally-diffused (PERT) cell with V_{oc} of 684 mV. It is worth mentioning that this fully implanted high-efficiency cell on float zone wafer had Al_2O_3/SiN_x passivated boron-doped emitter, thermally grown SiO_2 passivated phosphorous-doped back-surface field (BSF), and photolithographically defined front contacts (evaporated Ti/Pd/Ag) [7]. The Al_2O_3 films synthesized by plasma-assisted atomic layer

Manuscript received June 10, 2013; revised July 10, 2013 and August 13, 2013; accepted September 3, 2013. Date of publication September 23, 2013; date of current version December 16, 2013.

Y. Tao, Y.-W. Ok, F. Zimbardi, A. D. Upadhyaya, J.-H. Lai, S. Ning, and V. D. Upadhyaya are with the Georgia Institute of Technology, Atlanta, GA 30332 USA (e-mail: yuguo.tao@ece.gatech.edu; yok6@mail.gatech.edu; francesco@gatech.edu; ajayup@ece.gatech.edu; jhlai@gatech.edu; steven. ning@gatech.edu).

A. Rohatgi is with Suniva Inc., Norcross, GA 30092 USA and also with the Georgia Institute of Technology, Atlanta, GA 30332 USA (e-mail: ajeet.rohatgi@ece.gatech.edu).

Color versions of one or more of the figures in this paper are available online at http://ieeexplore.ieee.org.

Digital Object Identifier 10.1109/JPHOTOV.2013.2281106

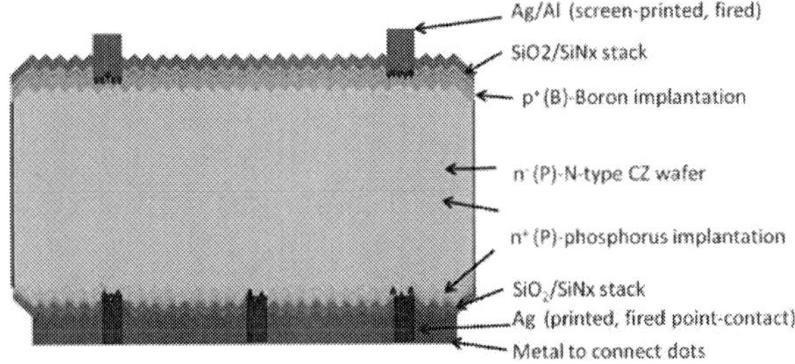

Fig. 1. Schematic of the front junction n-type Si solar cell structure.

deposition (ALD) have a high fixed negative charge density. Therefore, it provides excellent field-induced passivation on the boron-doped p^+-emitter with doping concentrations around 10^{19} cm^{-3} [8]–[11]. On the other hand, it has also been reported that the high quality oxide with low interface states density can be formed during implantation anneal at no additional cost [12]. Furthermore, an emitter saturation current density (J_{oe}) of ~80 fA/cm² was reported on highly boron-doped emitter passivated with SiO_2/SiN_x stack after firing of screen-printed contacts at high temperature [13]. Therefore, in this study, ion implantation and low-cost screen-printing technologies are combined with thermally grown SiO_2 passivation on both emitter and BSF. In a previous work, we reported 19.6% efficient n-type bifacial cells on large area (239 cm²) Czochralski (Cz) substrate using ion implantation and screen printing, and pointed out that ~8% metal coverage on the rear side was in part responsible for lower efficiency [13]. In this study, we present the development of higher efficiency n-type cells on 239 cm² Cz Si with less metal coverage (point contacts) on the back and the two different rear surface morphologies: textured and planar.

II. Experiments

Fig. 1 shows the structure of our front junction n-type cell that is fabricated on 1~6 Ωcm 200-μm thick wafers. The fabrication process involves saw damage removal in heated potassium hydroxide (KOH) solution followed by alkaline texturing of both sides of the starting wafers. The boron and phosphorus implantations were performed on a production-line implanter at Suniva Inc., Norcross, GA, USA. Hermle *et al.* [3] pointed out that the crystal defects created during implantation are different for different implanted ions, for example, amorphized

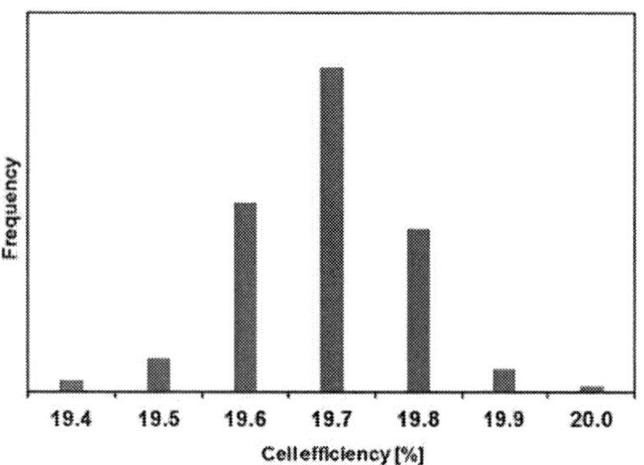

Fig. 2. Cell efficiency distribution of 75 cells (textured rear) in five different experiments with wafers supplied by three vendors.

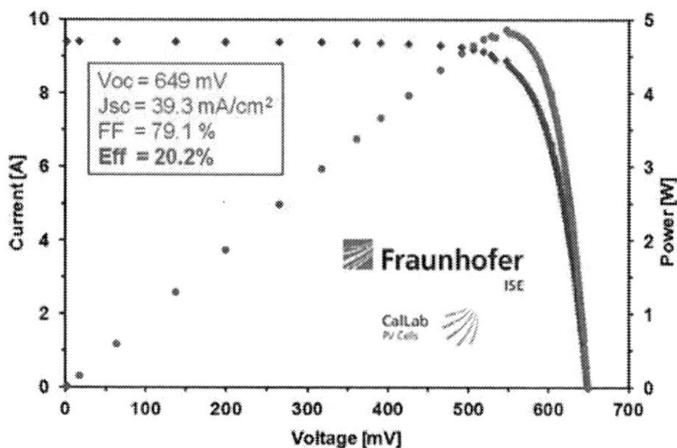

Fig. 3. Fraunhofer-certified full area (239.5 cm^2) 20.2% efficient n-type cell (textured rear surface).

surface is formed for heavy ion like phosphorus, and point defects (self-interstitials and vacancies) without amorphization are created for lighter element like boron. Therefore, two different anneals were performed in this study—the first right after the boron implantation and the second after the phosphorous implantation. To reduce surface recombination on boron-doped emitter and obtain low J_{oe}, a chemical etching treatment was performed after the first anneal [13], [14], while the SiO$_2$ passivation layer on both sides was grown as a byproduct of the second anneal [12], [13]. The appropriate implantation, annealing, and chemical etching treatment were applied to obtain sheet resistivity of $\sim$80 $\Omega/\square$ for the boron emitter and $\sim$60 $\Omega/\square$ for the phosphorus BSF. The resulting thickness of thermally grown oxide was $\sim$10 nm on the front and $\sim$20 nm on the rear side. Then, the SiN$_x$ films with appropriate thickness were deposited by the plasma-enhanced chemical vapor deposition (PECVD) tool on the front and rear surfaces. Prior to metallization, the implied open-circuited voltage (implied V_{oc}) of 660$\sim$665 mV were achieved after a simulated cofiring cycle. Implied V_{oc} was measured at a light intensity of one sun using the quasisteady-state photoconductance (QSSPC) method that is developed by Sinton Consulting [15].

In order to reduce the metal shading while maintaining good series resistance, the coverage of screen-printed front Ag/Al grid was limited to $\sim$8%. Ag dots were screen printed on the rear with diameter of 110$\sim$150 μm and pitch of $\sim$500 μm, which is equivalent to 4$\sim$5% metal coverage. Next, the cofiring was optimized in an industrial-style belt furnace to get good front and back ohmic contacts. Finally, a low temperature metal paste was screen printed and dried on the entire rear side to connect the Ag dots. Note that in term of the major material of this low temperature metal paste—Ag, it is more expensive than the Al paste for the standard Al-BSF cell.

III. RESULTS

A. Cells With Textured Back Surface

The resulting efficiency distribution of double side textured 75 cells is shown in Fig. 2. Note that these cells were fabricated in five different experiments using wafers from three different vendors. The average cell efficiency of 19.7% was obtained with a maximum of 20.0% (see Fig. 2). Reasonably narrow spread in the cell efficiency over a wide range of bulk resistivity (1$\sim$6 Ωcm) from different wafer suppliers suggests excellent stability of the established process and its capability of fabricating high-efficiency solar cells. However, further process refinement is necessary to achieve economic viability, such as replacing the two separated annealing steps by a single coannealing, and exploring an Al paste instead of the expensive metal paste for the entire rear side, etc.

Fig. 3 shows the I–V data of the best cell achieved on $\sim$3 Ωcm wafer, with V_{oc} of 649 mV, J_{sc} of 39.3 mA/cm^2, FF of 79.1%, and cell efficiency of 20.2% (certified by Fraunhofer ISE Cell Calibration Lab). These results demonstrate the high quality of boron and phosphorus impantation and *in situ* oxide passivation.

B. Cells With Planar Rear Surface

To obtain planar rear surface, the double side textured wafers with bulk resistivity of $\sim$2 Ωcm (after annealing) were coated with SiN$_x$ as a barrier layer on the front side, and then, etched in heated KOH solution to planarize the back. After planarization, the wafer thickness was reached to about 175 μm. To extract the saturation current density of phosphorus implanted BSF ($J_{ob'}$) on planar surface, four groups of wafers (five samples per group) with symmetric n^+nn^+ structure were implanted with four different doses ("D," "E," "F," and "G") but annealed under the same condition. Group "A" with textured rear surface was also included for comparison. Wafers for $J_{ob'}$ study had high base resistivity (5$\sim$6 Ωcm) and high bulk lifetime ($>$1 ms) to attain high level injection. The measured $J_{ob'}$ in Fig. 4 shows that all planar back samples have lower $J_{ob'}$ than the textured back samples, with the lowest $J_{ob'}$ value of 38 fA/cm^2 for group G. To account for the difference in surface morphology and area of the textured and planar surfaces, the implanted phosphorus dose in group A was increased by a factor of 1.8 compared with the counterpart group E.

Fig. 4 shows that group A has about 20 fA/cm^2 higher $J_{ob'}$ relative to group E. This suggests that oxide passivation quality is superior on a planar rear surface. In addition, model calculations

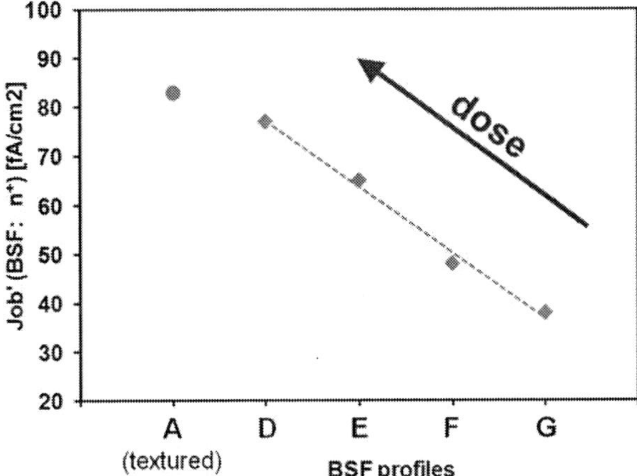

Fig. 4. Average saturation current density from the BSF ($J_{ob'}$) as a function of implanted BSF profiles.

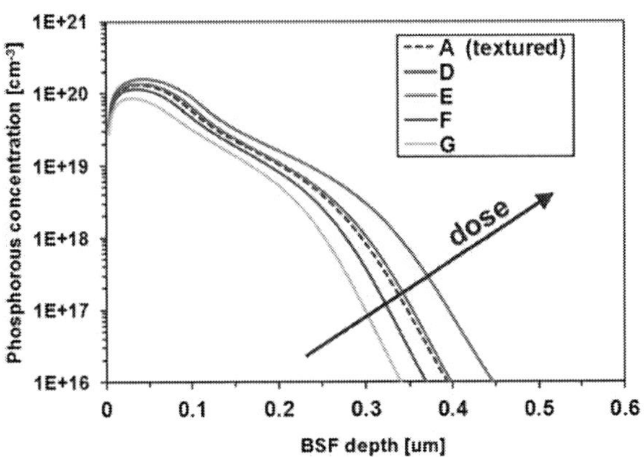

Fig. 5. Phosphorus concentration profiles obtained via Sentaurus simulation that is calibrated by the measurement results from the electrochemical capacitance–voltage (ECV) technique.

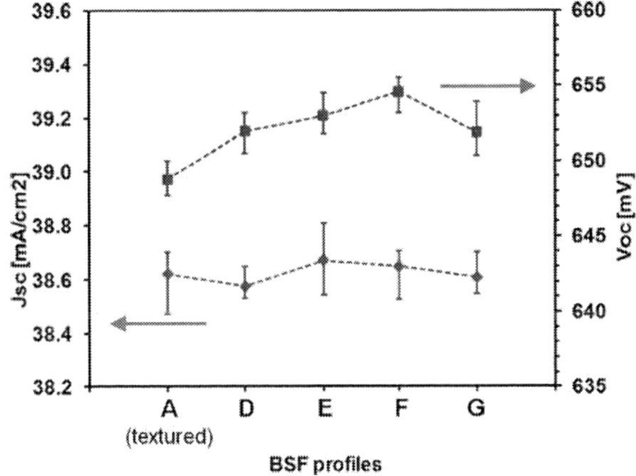

Fig. 6. Open-circuit voltage (V_{oc}) and short-circuit current density (J_{sc}) as a function of implanted BSF profiles.

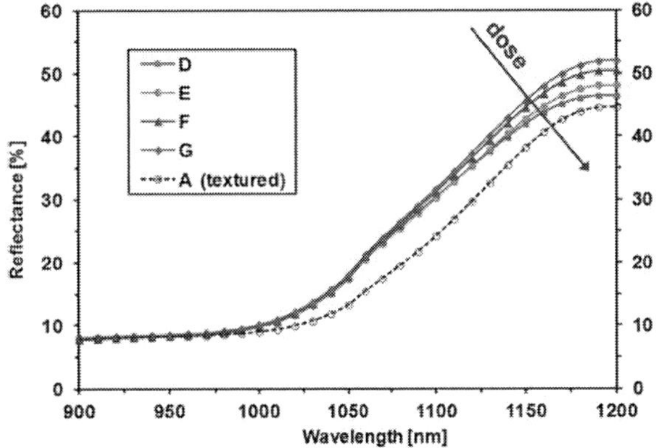

Fig. 7. Reflectance of front junction Si cells as a function of implanted BSF profiles.

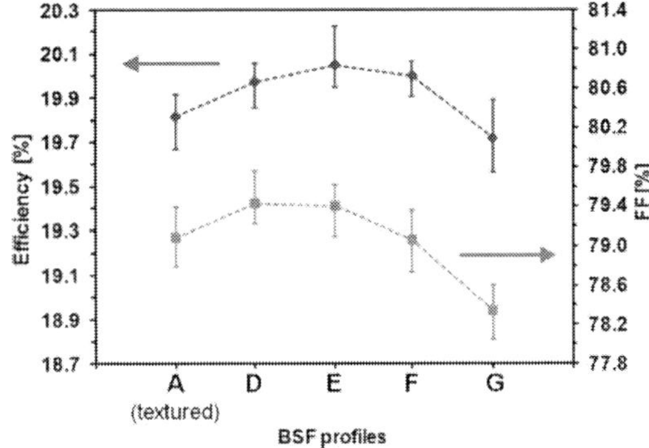

Fig. 8. Cell efficiency (η) and fill factor (FF) as a function of different BSF profiles.

in Fig. 5 shows that lower dose on planar surface produces shallower BSF for the same annealing conditions.

Fig. 6 shows the cell data for groups A–G (6~10 cells per group). Consistent with the decreasing $J_{ob'}$ trend shown in Fig. 4, open-circuit voltage (V_{oc}) gradually increases from group A to F. However, it drops for group G, in spite of lower $J_{ob'}$ prior to metallization. This is because group G has very shallow or transparent BSF. Therefore, it is more adversely affected by metal recombination, which negates the positive effect of reduced heavy doping in the BSF.

The measured reflectance in Fig. 7 shows that all the planar back cells (groups D, E, F, and G) have higher escape or back-surface reflectance than the textured back cells (group A) in the long wavelength range of 980~1200 nm. However, the average short circuit current density (J_{sc}) are similar for all the BSF conditions, about 38.6 mA/cm^2. Fig. 7 also indicates that the BSF with lower implanted phosphorus dose has slightly higher escape reflection possibly due to reduced free carrier absorption in the back.

Fig. 8 shows that the cells with lower phosphorus dose BSF gave lower fill factor (FF), which is attributed to higher series resistance (R_s) as well as higher n-factor (see Fig. 9). The measured sheet resistivity gradually increased from ~50 to ~90 $\Omega/\square$ as the phosphorus-doped BSF profile on the planar

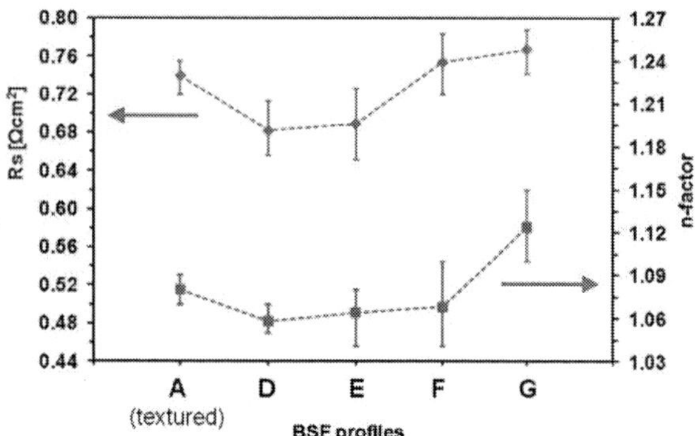

Fig. 9. Series resistance (R_s) and n-factor the rear side of cells as a function of different BSF profiles.

TABLE I
AVERAGE LIGHT I–V PARAMETERS OF THE $\sim$5 Ωcm n-TYPE CELLS WITH TEXTURED BACK (GROUP A) AND PLANAR BACK SURFACE (GROUP E) MEASURED AT AM1.5G, 100 mW/cm^2, 25 $^\circ$C (MEASURED IN-HOUSE)

Rear surface feature		V_{oc} [mV]	J_{sc} [mA/cm2]	FF [%]	η [%]
group A (10 cells: textured back)	average	648.8	38.6	79.1	19.8
	the best	650.4	38.6	79.3	20.0
group E (8 cells: planar back)	average	653.0	38.7	79.4	20.0
	the best	654.5	38.8	79.6	20.2

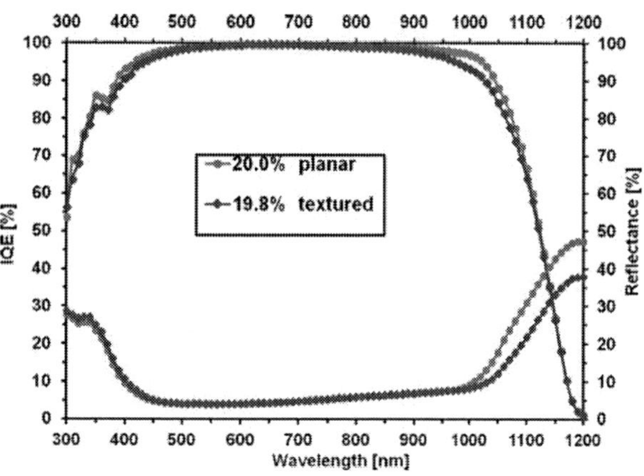

Fig. 10. Comparison of internal quantum efficiency (IQE) and reflectance of the cell with efficiency of 20.0% for planar rear surface from group E and 19.8% for textured rear surface from group A.

surface was changed from D to G. This is the result of increasing R_s. High n-factor (>1.1) for the group G is most likely due to shallow BSF and possibly metal spiking. Since the J_{sc} has a small variation for all the dose conditions, Fig. 8 reveals that the optimal phosphorus dose is mainly determined by the tradeoff between $J_{ob'}$ (hence, V_{oc}) and FF.

Table I and Fig. 10 summarize the cell parameters and internal quantum efficiency (IQE) of textured back group A and correspondent planar back group E cells. It is clear that planarization increases the long wavelength response and V_{oc} due to improved passivation and back-surface reflectance. This is supported by higher long wavelength response (passivation) and higher escape reflectance (BSR) in Fig. 10. Consequently, enhancement of $\sim$4 mV in V_{oc} and $\sim$0.1 mA/cm^2 in J_{sc} was achieved, in combination with $\sim$0.3% increase in absolute FF due to better ohmic contacts. As a result, rear planarization resulted in $\sim$0.2% increase in absolute average efficiency. Average efficiency for planar devices increased from 19.8% to 20% with a maximum of $\geq$20.2% in this experiment. Nevertheless, to the authors' knowledge, it is still not clear whether the 0.2% increase in the cell efficiency from rear planarization overcomes the cost of the additional processing required to obtain planar rear surface.

IV. SUMMARY

We have fabricated average 19.8% efficient fully ion-implanted and screen-printed front junction n-type cells on 239 cm^2 Cz substrate with textured surface and point contacts on the rear side. By applying planar rear surface and an optimal implanted phosphorus BSF profile, the average cell efficiency was increased to $\sim$20% with a maximum of $\geq$20.2% for the large area fully implanted and screen-printed n-type PERT cells.

ACKNOWLEDGMENT

The authors would like to thank Dr. A. Gupta and Dr. A. Payne of Suniva Inc. for support in ion implantation and all other group members at UCEP/GIT for their invaluable support and discussion.

REFERENCES

[1] R. Low, A. Gupta, N. Bateman, D. Ramappa, P. Sullivan, W. Skinner, J. Mullin, S. Peters, and H. Weiss-Wallrath, "High efficiency selective emitter enabled through patterned ion implantation," presented at the 35th IEEE Photovoltaic Specialist Conf., Honolulu, HI, USA, 2010.

[2] A. Rohagti, D. Meier, B. Mcperson, Y. Ok, A. D. Upadhyaya, J. Lai, and F. Zimbardi, "High-throughput ion-implantation for low-cost high-efficiency silicon solar cells," *Energy Procedia*, vol. 15, pp. 10–19, 2012.

[3] M. Hermle, J. Benick, M. Rüdiger, N. Bateman, and S. W. Glunz, "N-type silicon solar cells with implanted emitter," presented at the 26th Eur. Photovoltaic Solar Energy Conf., Hamburg, Germany, Sep. 2011.

[4] D. L. Meier, V. Chandrasekaran, H. P. Davis, A. M. Payne, X. Wang, V. Yelundur, J. E. O'Neill, Y. Ok, F. Zimbardi, and A. Rohatgi, "N-type, ion-implanted silicon solar cells and modules," *IEEE J. Photovoltaics*, vol. 1, no. 2, pp. 123–129, Oct. 2011.

[5] D. Macdonald and L. J. Geerligs, "Recombination activity of interstitial iron and other transition metal point defects in p-and n-type crystalline silicon," *Appl. Phys. Lett.*, vol. 85, pp. 4061–4063, 2004.

[6] S. W. Glunz, S. Rein, J. Y. Lee, and W. Warta, "Minority carrier lifetime degradation in boron-doped Czochralski silicon," *J. Appl. Phys.*, vol. 90, pp. 2397–404, 2001.

[7] J. Benick, R. Müller, N. Bateman, M. Hermle, and S. W. Glunz, "Fully implanted n-type PERT solar cells," presented at the 27th Eur. Photovoltaic Solar Energy Conf., Frankfurt, Germany, Sep. 2012.

[8] B. Hoex, J. Schmidt, R. Bock, P. P. Altermatt, M. C. M. van de Sanden, and W. M. M. Kessels, "Excellent passivation of highly doped p-type Si surfaces by the negative-charge-dielectric Al2 O3," *J. Appl. Phys.*, vol. 91, pp. 112107-1–112107-3, 2007.

[9] J. Benick, B. Hoex, M. C. M. van de Sanden, W. M. M. Kessels, O. Schultz, and S. W. Glunz, "High efficiency n-type Si solar cells on Al$_2$O$_3$-passivated boron emitters," *J. Appl. Phys.*, vol. 92, pp. 253504-1–253504-3, 2008.

[10] G. Dingemans, P. Engelhart, R. Seguin, F. Einsele, B. Hoex, M. C. M. van de Sanden, and W. M. M. Kessels, "Stability of Al2O3 and Al2O3/a-SiNx:H stacks for surface passivation of crystalline silicon," *J. Appl. Phys.*, vol. 106, pp. 114907-1–114907-4, 2009.

[11] P. Saint-Cast, A. Richter, E. Billot, M. Hofmann, J. Benick, J. Rentsch, R. Preu, and S. W. Glunz, "Very low surface recombination velocity of boron doped emitter passivated with plasma-enhanced chemical-vapor-deposited AlO_x layers," *Thin Solid Films*, vol. 522, pp. 336–339, 2012.

[12] J. Lai, A. Upadhyaya, S. Ramanathan, A. Das, K. Tate, V. Upadhyaya, A. Kapoor, C. Chen, and A. Rohatgi, "High-efficiency large-area rear passivated silicon solar cells with local Al-BSF and screen-printed contacts," *IEEE J. Photovoltaics*, vol. 1, no. 1, pp. 16–21, Jul. 2011.

[13] Y. W. Ok, A. D. Upadhyaya, Y. Tao, F. Zimbardi, S. Ning, and A. Rohatgi, "Ion-implanted and screen-printed large area 19.6% efficient *n*-type bifacial Si solar cells," presented at the 37th IEEE Photovoltaic Specialist Conf., Austin, TX, USA, 2012.

[14] K. Ryu, A. Upadhyaya, H. Song, C. Choi, A. Rohatgi, and Y. Ok, "Chemical etching of boron-rich layer and its impact on high efficiency n-type silicon solar cells," *Appl. Phys. Lett.*, vol. 101, pp. 073902-1–073902-4, 2012.

[15] R. A. Sinton, A. Cuevas, and M. Stuckings, "Quasi-steady-state photoconductance, a new method for solar cell material and device characterization," presented at the 25th IEEE Photovoltaic Specialist Conf., Washington, DC, USA, 1996.

Francesco Zimbardi received the Bachelor of Science degree in electrical engineering from the Georgia Institute of Technology, (Georgia Tech) Atlanta, GA, USA, in 2009.

While in college, he worked for two years with the National Electric Energy Testing Research and Application Center, Forest Park, GA, USA, testing new power transmission and distribution components qualifying them to industry standards. In 2008, he began working with the University Center of Excellence for Photovoltaics as a Student Researcher, becoming a Research Engineer upon graduating from Georgia Tech. He is involved in student projects and currently serves as a Faculty Advisor with the Solar Jackets Racing Team: a group which he helped found while in college.

Yuguo Tao received both the B.S. degree in mechanical engineering and the M.S. degree in power machinery engineering from Tianjin University, Tianjin, China, in 2002 and 2005, respectively, and the Ph.D. degree in photovoltaic engineering from the University of New South Wales (UNSW), Sydney, Australia, in 2012.

He was a Research Assistant from 2003 to 2005 with FAI Electronics Ltd., Hangzhou, China—founded by his supervisors. Upon graduating from the graduate school, he served as a Research Engineer with Robert Bosch GmbH, Wuxi, China. He joined SIEMENS, Shanghai, China, in 2006. Having strong interest in the renewable energy world, in 2008, he started to pursue new study in solar energy. Since graduating from UNSW, he has been a Research Engineer with the University Center of Excellence for Photovoltaics, Georgia Institute of Technology, Atlanta, GA, USA. His current research interests include the design and development of ion-implanted and screen-printed high-efficiency and cost-effective Si solar cells on commercially available large-area wafers.

Ajay D. Upadhyaya (M'06) was born on August 10, 1974, in India. He received the B.Sc. degree in electrical engineering from the Georgia Institute of Technology (Georgia Tech), Atlanta, GA, USA, in 2001 and the M.B.A. degree in marketing from Mercer University, Macon, GA, USA, in 2006.

He has been with Georgia Tech since 2001 in many capacities. He started as a Research Engineer I and was promoted to Research Engineer II during his career. He has been serving as the Operation Manager with research duties for the University Center of Excellence for Photovoltaics with Georgia Tech. He is the author or co-author of more than 40 publications in journals and conference proceedings. His current research interests include making monocrystalline silicon solar cells more efficient and cost effective through technology innovation. His past research interests were the enhancement of lower quality silicon materials such as multicrystalline, ribbon, and edge-defined film-fed growth silicon to improve the quality and performance of solar cells through existing processing steps.

Mr. Upadhyaya is on the Board of Directors of the Energy and Environment Expo. He received the Best Researcher Award in 2004 from Georgia Tech.

Young-Woo Ok received the B.S. degree from the School of Materials Science and Engineering, Korea University, Seoul, Korea, in 1999 and the M.S. and Ph.D. degrees from the Gwangju Institute of Science and Technology, Gwangju, Korea, in 2001 and 2005, respectively.

After receiving the Ph.D. degree, he worked with Solar Cell Laboratory, Korea University, as a Postdoctoral Fellow for two years and then with the Semiconductors and Solar Cells Laboratory, Australian National University, Canberra, Australia, as a Visiting Researcher for one year. He has been working with the University Center of Excellence, Georgia Institute of Technology, Atlanta, GA, USA, as a Research Engineer since 2009. He has published more than 50 papers in the research areas of semiconductor and photovoltaic Si devices. His research interests include the fabrication and characterization of Si-based photovoltaic devices. His current research interests include the development of new structure and passivation to realized low-cost and high-efficiency n-type Si solar cells.

Jiun-Hong Lai received the B.S. degree in electrical engineering from Chung-Hua University, Hsinchu, Taiwan, in 1996; the M.S. degree in electrical and control engineering from National Chiao-Tung University, Hsinchu, in 1997; and another M.S. degree from the Georgia Institute of Technology, Atlanta, GA, USA, in 2010, where he is currently working toward the Ph.D. degree under the guidance of Dr. A. Rohatgi with the University Center of Excellence for Photovoltaics.

Upon graduating early from graduate school, he was a Research Assistant with the Department of Bio-Industrial Mechatronics Engineering, National Taiwan University, Taipei, Taiwan. As a Principle Engineer with Taiwan Semiconductor Manufacturing Company from 2000 to 2007, he was responsible for developing control systems for gate formation of semiconductor devices. He has been awarded two patents in this field of advanced process control. His research focuses on design and fabrication of commercial grade low-cost high efficiency silicon solar cells.

Mr. Lai received the Best Student Paper Award at the 37th IEEE Photovoltaics Specialists Conference, Seattle, WA, USA, in 2011.

Steven Ning received the B.S. degree in physics from Harvey Mudd College, Claremont, CA, USA, and the M.S. degree in electrical and computer engineering from the Georgia Institute of Technology (Georgia Tech), Atlanta, GA, USA, where his research with the University Center of Excellence for Photovoltaic Research and Education focused on fabrication of novel n-type silicon solar cell structures, as well as Technology Computer-Aided Design simulation of fabrication processes and device physics.

He served as the Project Manager for the Georgia Tech Solar Jackets solar car racing team. He is currently working as a Design Engineer for Space Exploration Technologies, Hawthorne, CA, USA.

Vijaykumar D. Upadhyaya received the B.Sc. degree in electrical and computer engineering from the Georgia Institute of Technology (Georgia Tech), Atlanta, GA, USA, in 2003.

He is a currently a Research Engineer. He was also a Co-op student during his studies and worked for SoC Solutions, Tech Center, and the University of Excellence in Photovoltaics Research and Education (UCEP), Georgia Tech. After graduation, he became a Full-Time Research Engineer with UCEP, where he contributed to the development, fabrication, and characterization of low-cost, high-efficiency, Czochralski, and float-zone silicon solar cells. He has co-authored various technical papers, journals, and proceedings. He has also worked on emitter wrap-through/interdigitated back-contacts solar cell research that helped J. Gee of Advent Solar, Inc. He is also responsible for sponsored research with various paste-manufacturing companies like Ferro, Hereaus, Dupont, BASF, and Cermet, and he is currently working with companies like Suniva, Norcross, GA, USA, in advanced solar cell structures and advance processing using screen-printed technology.

Ajeet Rohatgi (F'08) received the B.S. degree in electrical engineering from the India Institute of Technology, Kanpur, India, in 1971, the M.S. degree in materials engineering from the Virginia Polytechnic Institute and State University, Blacksburg, VA, USA, in 1973, and the Ph.D. degree in metallurgy and material science from Lehigh University, Bethlehem, PA, USA, in 1977.

He is currently a Regent's Professor and a GRA Eminent Scholar with the School of Electrical Engineering, Georgia Institute of Technology (Georgia Tech), Atlanta, GA, USA. He is the Founding Director of the University Center of Excellence for Photovoltaic Research and Education, Georgia Tech, and the Founder and CTO of Suniva, Inc., Norcross, GA, USA. Before joining the Electrical Engineering Faculty with Georgia Tech, in 1985, he was a Westinghouse Fellow with the Research and Development Center, Pittsburgh, PA, USA. He has published more than 400 technical papers in this field and has received 16 patents. His current research interests include the design and development of low-cost and high-efficiency commercial ready Si solar cells and the economics of photovoltaic systems.

Dr. Rohatgi received the Westinghouse Engineering Achievement Award in 1985, the Georgia Tech Distinguished Professor Award in 1996, the IEEE PVSC William Cherry Award in 2003, the NREL/DOE Rappaport Award in 2003, and the EPA Climate Protection Award in 2009, and he was named a champion of PV in 2011 by *Renewable World Energy Magazine*.

High-Efficiency Full Back Contacted Cells Using Industrial Processes

Jingbing Dong, Longzhong Tao, Yanbin Zhu, Zhuojian Yang, Zhengyue Xia, Rubin Sidhu, and Guoqiang Xing

Abstract—Full-size (156 × 156 mm^2) interdigitated back contact (IBC) solar cells have been developed with conventional industry processes. With PC1D simulation and short-flow experiment verification, we found that the tunnel junction shunting of rear n^+/p^+ could be mitigated significantly by controlling the boron surface concentration; therefore, it is not necessary to form a gap between rear emitter and back surface field. Made by a novel yet relative simple process, the IBC cells preliminarily achieved 19.65% best efficiency with J_{sc} and V_{oc} as high as 40.5 mA/cm^2 and 655 mV, respectively, while FF was only 73.9% due to the low pseudo fill factor (Pff) and high series resistance. Through the optimization of the rear pattern process, Pff was improved up to 82.5% and FF up to 77%. With further optimization of emitter, front surface field, passivation, and rear pattern design, the cells potentially can achieve up to 22.0% efficiency in the near future.

Index Terms—Conventional process, high efficiency, interdigitated back contact (IBC) cells, tunnel junction shunting (TJS).

I. INTRODUCTION

INTERDIGITATED back contact (IBC) solar cells represent a promising approach toward high efficiencies for mass production [1]. The Zebra cell [2] developed by Halm has reached 21.3% using standard industrial processing equipment. Recently, a record efficiency of 24.2% has been announced by Sunpower [3].

High efficiency of IBC cells is mainly driven by nonmetallization of front side which can eliminate the optical shading loss and achieve extremely low front surface recombination velocity. Furthermore, light-doping of phosphorous of front side provides excellent front surface field (FSF) which can 1) repel the minority carriers at the physical semiconductor surface to improve the front surface passivation [4], [5], 2) enhance the lateral majority carrier current transport to reduce the series resistance losses, 3) improve the stability of the front surface passivation under UV-light exposure [5], [6], and 4) improve the cell performance at low-illumination conditions [7].

Manuscript received June 14, 2013; revised August 13, 2013 and September 22, 2013; accepted September 27, 2013. Date of publication October 23, 2013; date of current version December 16, 2013. This work was supported by Hareon Solar Technology Co., Ltd.

J. Dong, Y. Zhu, Z. Xia, and G. Xing are with Hareon Solar Technology, Jiangyin 214407, China (e-mail: dongjb@hareon.net; zhuyb@hareon.net; xiazy@hareon.net; xinggq@hareon.net).

L. Tao and Z. Yang were with Hareon Solar Technology Co., Ltd., Jiangyin 214407, China. They are now with Suzhou Runergy PV Technology Co., Ltd., Kunshan 215300, China (e-mail: taolz@hareon.net; yangzj@hareon.net).

R. Sidhu is with Hareon Solar USA, San Jose, CA 95110 USA (e-mail: rubin.sidhu@hareon.net).

Color versions of one or more of the figures in this paper are available online at http://ieeexplore.ieee.org.

Digital Object Identifier 10.1109/JPHOTOV.2013.2285623

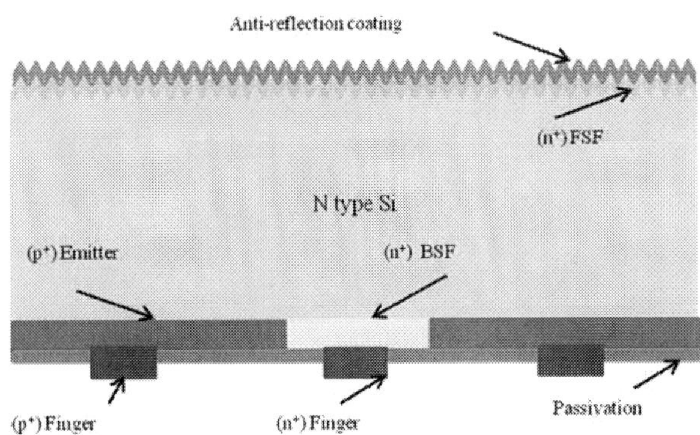

Fig. 1. Schematic structure of IBC cells.

Although the IBC cells obviously have high efficiency, however, very complicated process and high cost due to many steps involved in boron/phosphorous doping, masking, etching, passivation, alignments, and metallization limit the large-scale mass production of IBC cells.

In this paper, we tried to develop full-size IBC cells with conventional industry processes, such as alkaline texturing, POCl$_3$/BBr$_3$ diffusion, passivation, and screen-printing. Based on the PC1D simulations and short-flow experiment results, we verified that the tunnel junction shunting (TJS) between rear emitter and rear BSF can be mitigated significantly by controlling the boron-doping concentration at the rear n+/p+ interface. Therefore, without the gap between rear p^+ and n^+, the whole process flow of IBC can be simplified dramatically.

II. EXPERIMENTAL DETAILS

Full-size (156 × 156 mm^2) IBC solar cells were fabricated on 180-μm-thick n-type CZ Si wafers with resistivity of 3.8 Ω·cm. Fig. 1 shows the structure of IBC cells. The rear emitter is doped by BBr$_3$ diffusion, the rear-side POCl3 diffused zone width is about 200 μm, with pitch of 1.2 mm. The front side and rear open area are both doped by POCl$_3$ diffusion as FSF and back surface field (BSF). After front side passivated with SiN$_x$ and rear side passivated with SiO$_x$/SiN$_x$ stack layer, metal pastes are screen-printed and fired as positive and negative electrodes; at last, rear-side insulation layer and busbar are printed crossing the fingers. The detailed process flow is shown in Fig. 2.

III. RESULTS AND DISCUSSION

A. Tunnel Junction Shunting

As we know, TJS exists at the heavily doped n^+/p^+ interface [8]. Generally, in order to avoid the TJS problem for IBC

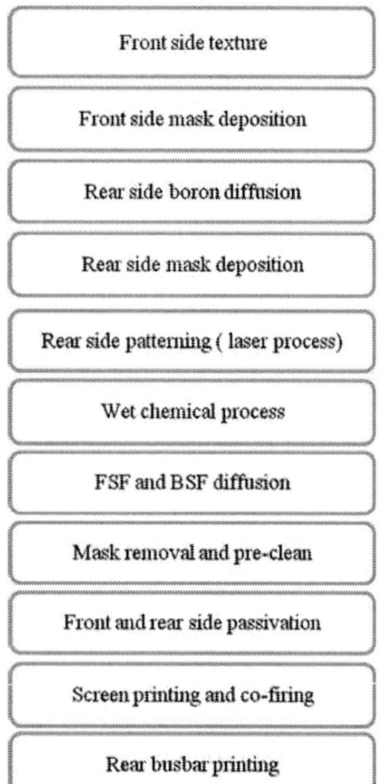

Fig. 2.   Process flow of IBC cells.

cells, an undoped gap is needed between rear n+ BSF and rear p+ emitter [9], but it would make the process much more complicated because it requires many steps of masking, opening, etching, and doping, with high-accuracy alignments. In order to mitigate the TJS problem, we simulate this issue by PC1D, which had been used for TJS study by Clugston and Basore [10]. An abrupt junction was formed by a 5-μm-thick n^+ emitter with a doping concentration of 3×10^{20} cm^{-3} and a 10-μm-thick p-type base with a varied doping concentration from 1×10^{16} to 1×10^{20} cm^{-3}. Dark current at 500 mV forward bias of such an abrupt junction is plotted in Fig. 3. By switching ON and OFF the trap-assisted tunneling model (Hurkx model, [11]) implemented in PC1D, influence of TJS is revealed by the difference between two dark current curves. The TJS problem is found when base doping concentration increases up to 3×10^{19} cm^{-3}. It gets worse if base doping concentration increases further. Fig. 3 also reveals that even without a gap between n+ emitter and p-type base, TJS can be mitigated by reducing the doping concentration of p-type base to less than 3×10^{19} cm^{-3}.

Fig. 4 shows the $I\text{–}V$ curves simulated by PC1D with n$^+$ doping at 3×10^{20} cm^{-3} and p$^+$ doping varied from 1.17×10^{19} to 3.0×10^{19} cm^{-3}. Typical characteristics of tunneling current can be clearly seen when p-type base doping concentration is higher than 2.0×10^{19} cm^{-3}.

In order to verify the simulated results, we made IBC devices with the process flow shown in Fig. 2. The doping profiles of rear n$^+$ BSF and rear p$^+$ emitter are shown in Fig. 5. In

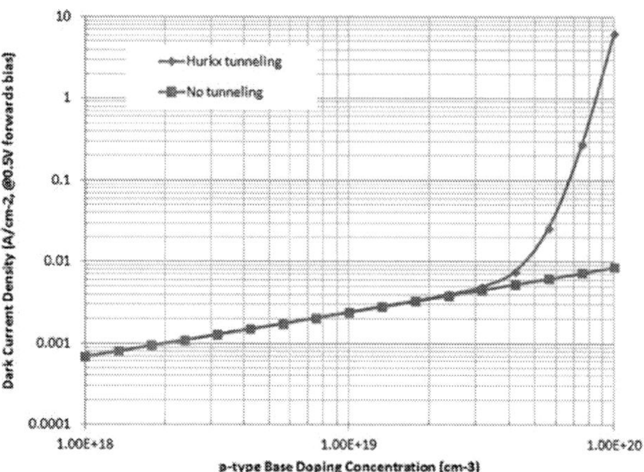

Fig. 3.   Comparison of dark current density at 500-mV forward bias with varied base doping concentration for the abrupt junction.

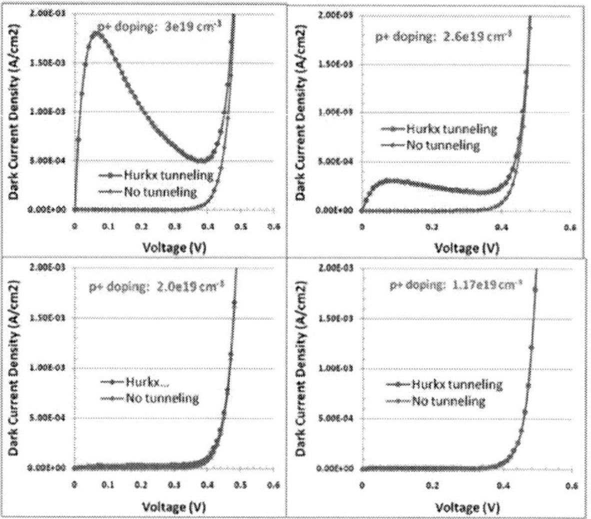

Fig. 4. $I\text{–}V$ curves simulated by PC1D with n$^+$ doping at 3×10^{20} cm^{-3} and p$^+$ doping varied from 1.17×10^{19} to 3×10^{19} cm^{-3}.

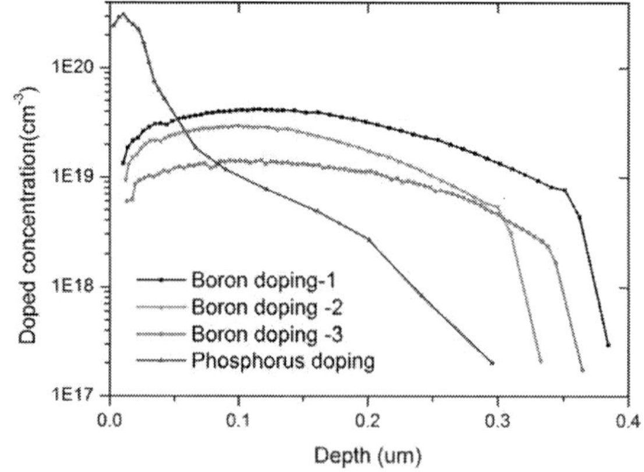

Fig. 5.   Doping profiles of rear n$^+$ BSF and p^+ emitter tested with the electrochemical capacitance voltage tool.

Surface doped concentration [cm^{-3}]	Shunt resistance [$\Omega \cdot$cm^{-2}]
Boron doping -1	215
Boron doping -2	520
Boron doping -3	7167

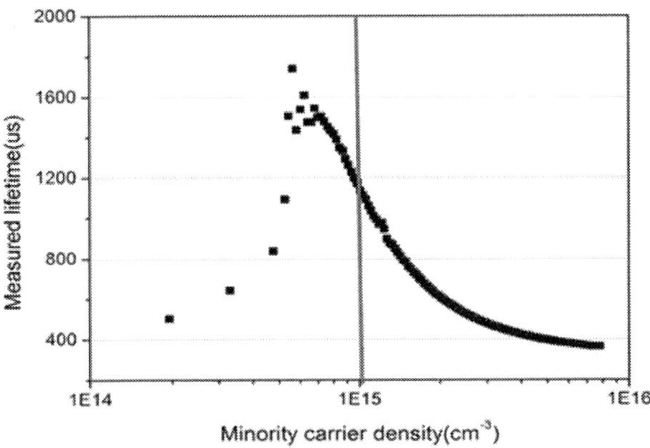

Fig. 6.   Typical effective lifetime of the IBC structure.

TABLE II
IBC CELL WITHOUT FSF OPTIMIZATION

Cell area [cm^2]	Jsc [mA/cm^2]	Voc [mV]	FF [%]	η [%]	Pff [%]	J02 [A/cm^2]
238.9	39.22	641.0	74.00	18.60	79.9	2.70E-8

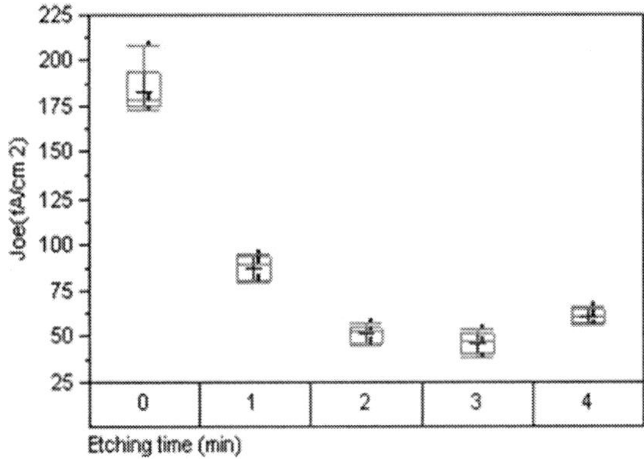

Fig. 7.   Changing of J_{oe} values as different etching time.

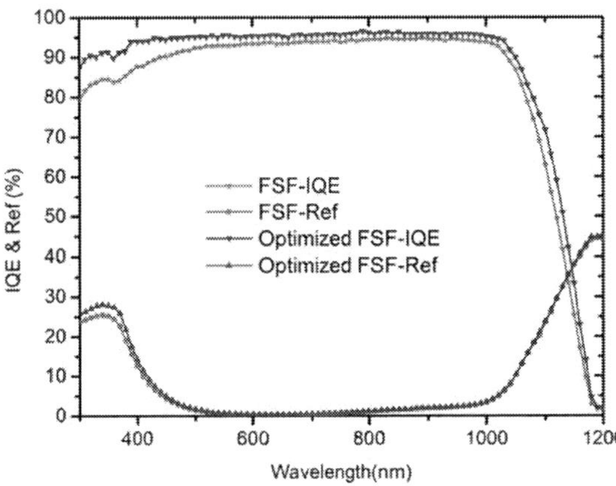

Fig. 8.   Measured IQE and reflectance of best IBC cells with and without FSF optimization.

this experiment, rear n$^+$ BSF were doped with the same profile, while rear p$^+$ emitters were doped with different concentrations. The shunt resistance of the cells calculated from dark I–V curve is shown in Table I.

The shunt resistance results coincide well with the simulation. When the boron doping concentration decreases down to $\sim 1.4 \times 10^{19}$ cm^{-3}, the shunt resistance increases up to 700 $\Omega \cdot$cm^2. Therefore, with the controlling of rear-side boron doping concentration, we decided to fabricate IBC cells with no gap between rear n$^+$ BSF and rear emitter by conventional industry process.

B. Performance of Interdigitated Back Contact Cells

The typical effective lifetime of bifacial-passivated IBC structure was tested by Sinton WCT-120 as shown in Fig. 6. However, for the rear p$^+$/n$^+$ structure used, the tested effective lifetime needs calculating. According to Dr. R. A. Sinton's calculating method (discussed with Dr. R. A. Sinton on e-mail), the effective lifetime of our IBC structure should be between 610 and 1200 μs @1E15 cm^{-3} and implied V_{oc} of 690 mV indicate that conventional processes for boron/phosphorus diffusion and passivation are feasible to make high-efficiency IBC cells. However, from the I–V data shown in Table II, we see that low V_{oc} of 641 mV and J_{sc} of 39.22 mA/cm^2 lead to only 18.6%

efficiency. Quantum efficiency (QE) measurements (see Fig. 8) show the heavy-doping front surface (same doping profile as rear BSF) leads to high front surface recombination and poor spectral response at short wavelengths.

C. Optimization of Front Surface Field

In order to reduce the front surface recombination, an accurate etch-back process was introduced in our IBC processes reported by Li [9]. The N$^+$/n/n$^+$ sandwich structure etched for different times was used to characterize the quality of FSF. Fig. 7 shows that 3-min etching-back can decrease emitter saturation current density (J_{oe}) obviously from 170 to 40 fA/cm^2, which means the "dead layer" at the front surface would be removed and Auger recombination decreased. The trend of J_{oe} with etching time is the same as reported by Li [9]. However, when the etch time increased to 4 min, J_{oe} increased a little on the contrary. The possible reason is that long etching time can lead to a very shallow junction so that the carriers can diffuse to the surface easily and result in higher surface recombination.

According to this result, we added FSF etching-back process into our IBC process flow before surface passivation. With FSF optimization, J_{sc} and V_{oc} of our cells improved significantly and

TABLE III
BEST IBC CELL WITH FSF OPTIMIZATION

Cell area [cm²]	Jsc [mA/cm²]	Voc [mV]	FF [%]	η [%]	Pff [%]	J02 [A/cm²]
238.9	40.54	655.0	73.90	19.65	79.8	3.10E-8

TABLE IV
IBC CELL WITH THE OPTIMIZATION OF LASER PATTERNING PROCESS

Cell area [cm²]	Jsc [mA/cm²]	Voc [mV]	FF [%]	η [%]	Pff [%]	J02 [A/cm²]
238.9	39.15	640.8	77.16	19.36	82.5	1.10E-8

cell efficiency increased up to 19.65%. Table III shows the data of best IBC cell with FSF optimization. The large discrepancy of J_{sc} between Tables II and III is caused by the lower front surface recombination of IBC cells.

Fig. 8 shows internal quantum efficiency (IQE) comparison (the spot size used for IQE test is about 10 mm × 10 mm) of two best IBC cells with and without FSF optimization (see Tables II and III cells). IQE at a short wavelength can be obviously improved by front surface etching-back. The large difference of QE results, especially at short wavelengths band, coincide well with our analysis.

D. Analysis on Pseudo Fill Factor

According to the Suns-V_{oc} results as shown in Tables II and III, our IBC cells show low pseudo fill factor (Pff), which might be affected by emitter quality. However, $p^+/n/p^+$ sandwich structures with bifacial passivation show only 100 fA/cm² low J_{oe}, which means that BBr3 diffusion can form high-quality emitters. We doubted that the laser-patterning step would form the serious damage on the device. In order to verify it, we optimized the patterning process and made the IBC cells, but without FSF etching-back. Table IV shows Pff improved up to 82.5%, indicating that the laser patterning process really form the damage on the device.

E. Potential of our Interdigitated Back Contact Cells

Although we have done some improvements, there is still a big room to optimize our process flow, including rear side passivation, pattern design, and metallization. With the improvement of FF, our IBC cells potentially can achieve >22% efficiency in the near future.

IV. CONCLUSION

We verified that TJS could be mitigated significantly by controlling boron-doping profile. Based on this result, we simplified IBC process flow without any gap between rear n^+ BSF and rear p^+ emitter. With FSF optimization, best IBC cell achieved 19.65% efficiency, but FF was only 73.9% due to low the Pff and high series resistance. Through the optimization of the rear pattern process, Pff can be improved up to 82.5% and FF up to 77%. With the further optimization of emitter, front surface field, passivation, and rear pattern design, the cells potentially can achieve >22.0% efficiency in the near future.

REFERENCES

[1] D. De Ceuster et al., "low cost, high volume production of > 22% efficiency silicon solar cells," presented at the 22nd Eur. Photovoltaic Sol. Energy Conf. Exhib., Milan, Italy, 2007.

[2] A. Halm et al., "The zebra cell concept: Large area N-type interdigitated back contact solar cells and one-cell modules fabricated using standard industrial processing equipment," presented at the 27th Eur. Photovoltaic Sol. Energy Conf. Exhib., Frankfurt, Germany, 2012.

[3] P. J. Cousins et al., "Gen III: Improved performance at lower cost," in Proc. 35th Photovoltaic Spec. Conf., 2010, pp. 000275–000278.

[4] M. Hermle et al., "Analyzing the effects of front-surface field on back-junction silicon solar cells using the charge-collection probability and the reciprocity theorem," J. Appl. Phys., vol. 103, 2008.

[5] F. Granek, M. Hermle et al., "Positive effective effects of front surface field in high-efficiency back-contact back-junction n-type silicon solar cells," presented at the 33rd IEEE Photovoltaic Spec. Conf., San Diego, CA, USA, 2008.

[6] P. E. Gruenbaum, R. A. Sinton, and R. M. Swanson, "Stability problems in point contact solar cells," in Proc. 20th IEEE Photovoltaic Spec. Conf., Las Vegas, NV, USA, 1988, pp. 423–428.

[7] F. Granek, M. Hermle, and S. W. Glunz, "Analysis of the current linearity at low illumination of high-efficiency back-junction back-contact silicon solar cells," Phys. Status Solidi (RRL), vol. 2, pp. 151–153, 2008.

[8] L. M. Fraas and L. D. Partain, Solar Cells and Their Applications, 2nd ed. New York, NY, USA: Wiley, 2010.

[9] X. Li et al., "Boron diffused emitter etch back and passivation," in Proc. 38th IEEE Photovoltaic Spec. Conf., 2012, pp. 001073–001076.

[10] D. A. Clugston and P. A. Basore, "PC1D version 5: 32-bit solar cell modeling on personal computers," in Proc. 26th IEEE Photovoltaic Spec. Conf., 1997, pp. 207–210.

[11] G. A. M. Hurkx et al., "A new recombination model for device simulation including tunneling," IEEE Trans. Electron Devices, vol. 39, no. 2, pp. 331–338, Feb. 1992.

Authors' photographs and biographies not available at the time of publication.

Evaluating Dynamic Maximum Power Point Tracking With Variable Solar Irradiance

Mohammad A. Huque, Member, IEEE, Steven J. Coley, and Thomas S. Key, Fellow, IEEE

Abstract—**Photovoltaic (PV) plant performance, among many factors, depends on inverter tracking of the maximum power point and its energy conversion efficiency. For a given PV array, under certain environmental conditions, the energy yield depends on the inverter's dynamic response for maximum power point tracking (MPPT) with highly variable array output. This paper describes the theoretical irradiance test profile proposed in a European Norm Standard (EN 50530:2010) for inverter Dynamic MPPT efficiency evaluation. Example test results from two inverters are included. This paper also reports some discrepancy in the standard test profile by comparing the required test environment with high resolution measured solar irradiance ramp rate data for a South-East and a Western part of USA.**

Index Terms—**Photovoltaic systems, inverter, efficiency, dynamic maximum power point tracking (MPPT), microinverter, string inverter, performance evaluation.**

I. INTRODUCTION

In any grid-tied photovoltaic (PV) system the inverter play an essential role in energy performance by converting the DC energy from the PV module into AC energy suitable for interconnect with the utility electric grid. Capturing maximum energy from a given PV array, in a certain geographic region, is one of the key factors that can minimize levelized-cost-of-energy (LCOE) for this renewable energy source. Hence energy performance is an important selection criterion for inverters for any PV project.

In USA the reference for energy performance comes from the California Energy Commission (CEC) defined PV inverter efficiency [1] database. In Europe, a similar "European Efficiency" approach has been defined to benchmark the energy performance of PV inverters. Both CEC and European efficiencies are a measure of only the static power conversion efficiencies, the ratio of the inverter AC output power to its DC input power. In real world, because of intermittency in solar irradiation, maximum DC energy that can be harvested also fluctuates. Hence PV plant's total energy yield over certain duration depends on inverter's ability to accurately and quickly tracking of solar irradiance changes.

Inverter's MPPT efficiency represents how well the inverter harvests the available PV array energy (DC) by adjusting the DC operating point under the changing solar irradiation conditions. Precise and faster maximum power point tracker (MPPT) provides quick and accurate tracking even in very fast changing environmental conditions [2 - 4]. A European Norm standard, EN 50530: 2010, proposed a laboratory test methodology along with irradiance test profiles to calculate PV inverter's dynamic MPPT efficiency [5, 6]. This paper briefly describes the theoretical irradiance profile proposed in this standard. Laboratory test results from two inverters are presented here to discuss potential concerns regarding the proposed test profiles. This paper also includes analysis of measured high speed irradiance data from two environmentally diverse locations across USA to evaluate the likelihood of experiencing the proposed ramp rates in the real world. Based on these analyses some planned modifications in the standard test profiles are also discussed.

II. EN 50530 DYNAMIC MPPT EFFICIENCY TEST PROFILES

EN 50530 includes two types of MPPT tests – static and dynamic. Static MPPT efficiency indicates how accurately an inverter can set its DC operating point to match with the actual peak power voltage and current values on a given static power curve of a PV array. Variations in the solar irradiation and temperature and the resulting transitions of the inverter operating points to the newer maximum power points (MPP) on the new characteristic curves are not captured by the static MPPT efficiency. Dynamic MPPT efficiency is the right metric to evaluate inverter performance to track fast changing solar irradiance, typically due to passing clouds. To evaluate PV inverter dynamic MPPT efficiency, EN50530 proposes several irradiance test profiles with varying ramp rates. It suggests loading these profiles into a PV simulator and subjecting the inverter under test to the variable DC operating conditions. AC energy generated by the inverter in response to these varying solar ramp events is an indication of its dynamic MPPT performance.

Fig. 1 shows the concept of the proposed solar irradiance test profile and parameters which defines the wave shape. All the ramp events are linearly carried out between two limits, which are defined as "Low" and "High" in Fig. 1. Slopes of the ramp up and ramp down events are equal. After every ramp events a dwell time is provided to allow the inverter to settle down before the start of the next ramp event. Ramp-up/down event with gradually increasing ramp rates are repeated increasing number of times to generate the overall test profile.

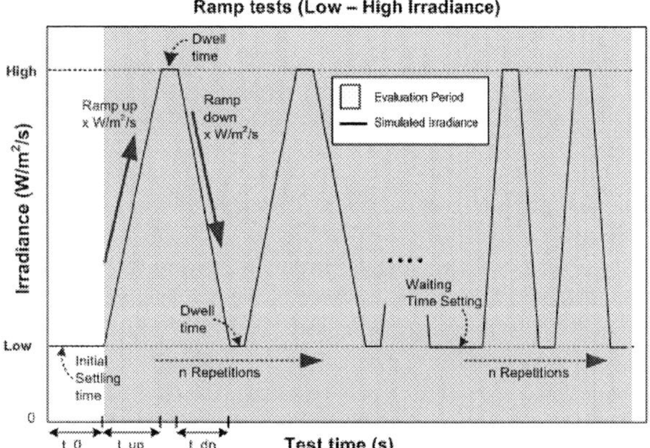

Fig. 1. EN50530 irradiance test profile for dynamic MPPT efficiency measurement.

Table I summarizes the parameter values proposed in EN 50530: 2010 that defines the test sequence for fluctuations between small (100 W/m^2) and medium (500 W/m^2) irradiation magnitudes. Ramp events with faster slopes are repeated larger number of times with shorter durations. Table II gives similar parameter values to generate test sequence for medium (300 W/m^2) to high (1000 W/m^2) irradiance fluctuations.

TABLE I
DYNAMIC MPPT TEST PROFILE: IRRADIANCE FROM 100 TO 500 W/M^2

# of repetitions	Ramp up/down slopes (W/m²/s)	Dwell time on high/low levels (s)
2	0.5	10
2	1	10
3	2	10
4	3	10
6	5	10
8	7	10
10	10	10
10	14	10
10	20	10
10	30	10
10	50	10

TABLE II
DYNAMIC MPPT TEST PROFILE: IRRADIANCE FROM 300 TO 1000 W/M^2

# of repetitions	Ramp up/down slopes (W/m²/s)	Dwell time on high/low levels (s)
10	10	10
10	14	10
10	20	10
10	30	10
10	50	10
10	100	10

III. SAMPLE DYNAMIC MPPT TEST RESULTS

A microinverter and a string inverter from two leading PV inverter manufacturing companies were tested in the laboratory to evaluate their dynamic MPPT performance. Objective of this initial test was to study the responses of these two power converter topologies to the irradiance test sequence defined in EN 50530. In this test a PV simulator was employed to generate the PV array DC output corresponding to the irradiance profile described in Table I and II. For both cases ratios of PV array's maximum DC power to inverter name plate AC power rating were maintained nearly identical. Fig. 2 and Fig. 3 show the microinverter and the string inverter AC power output respectively in response to EN 50530 small to medium irradiance test profile. Based on the observed results from these two particular units, the microinverter under test outperformed the string inverter especially at higher ramp rates. The string inverter's AC output frequently dropped to zero and even the inverter turned OFF quite often when the ramp rate was higher than 7 W/m^2/s. Whereas the microinverter's AC output closely followed the variations, even the one with fastest ramp, in the irradiance profile.

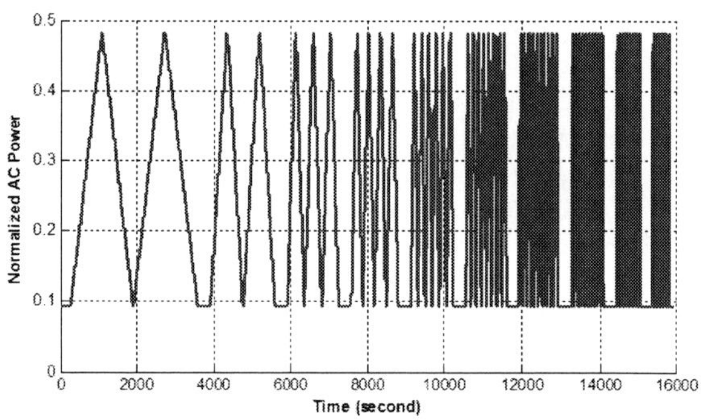

Fig. 2. Microinverter AC output power in response to EN50530 small to medium irradiance test profile defined in Table I.

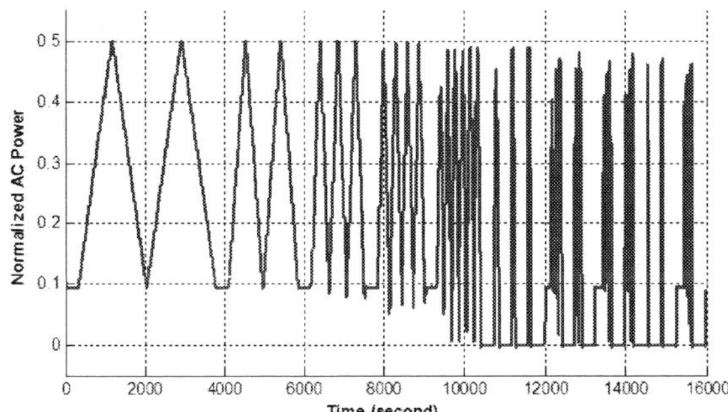

Fig. 3. String inverter AC output power in response to EN50530 small to medium irradiance test profile defined in Table I.

Similar tests were carried out for the medium to high irradiance test profile described in EN 50530. Responses of microinverter and string inverter under test to this test profile are shown in Fig. 4 and in Fig. 5 respectively. Unlike the previous test, this time string inverter output did not drop to zero. But often, especially at higher ramp rates, its output dropped below the lower limit. In many cases it also failed to reach the maximum achievable power level.

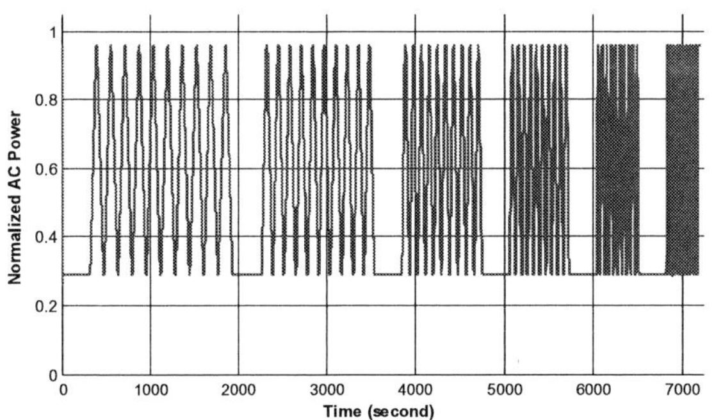

Fig. 4. Microinverter AC output power in response to EN50530 medium to high irradiance test profile shown in Table II.

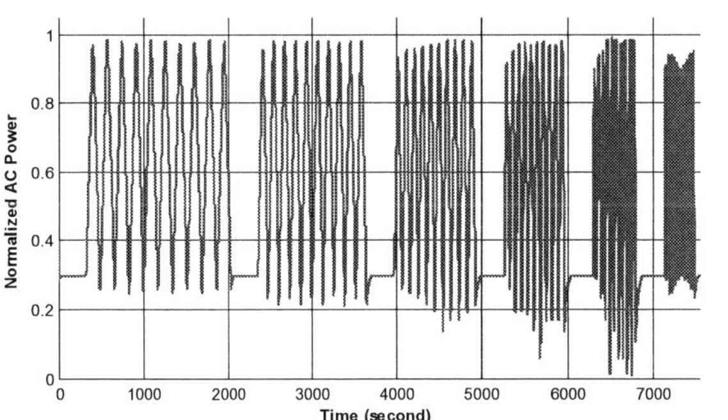

Fig. 5. String inverter AC output power in response to EN50530 medium to high irradiance test profile shown in Table II.

This discrepancy in microinverter and string inverter performance inspired the authors to investigate if such high irradiance variations are likely in real system. Field measured high resolution (1-sec) data from different parts of USA is analyzed and presented in the following sections.

IV. SOLAR IRRADIANCE MEASURED DATA IN TENNESSEE

High resolution (1-second) field measured data from a 1-MW PV plant in East Tennessee is analyzed to study the solar irradiance profile in the South East part of USA where high solar variable days are frequent [7]. Irradiance measurements were taken from a pyranometer in the plane of array (30° fixed tilt, south orientation) of the PV plant. Fig. 6 shows the irradiance profile for a typical clear sunny day in East Tennessee. From this 1-sec resolution data solar irradiance ramp rates are calculated for every second and distribution as a percentage of total day time seconds is shown in Fig. 7. In a clear day, like the one shown in this example, there are almost no ramp rate events with slopes faster than 10 W/m²/s.

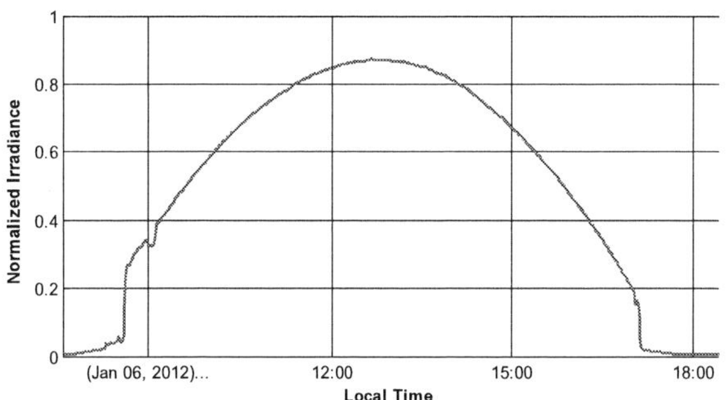

Fig. 6. Example clear day solar irradiance profile in East Tennessee.

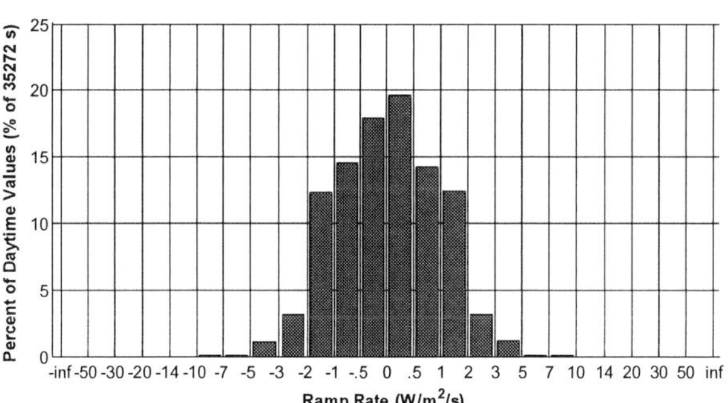

Fig. 7. Ramp rate distribution for the example clear day solar irradiance profile shown in Fig. 6.

An overcast day situation is quite different. Fig. 8 and Fig. 9 show solar irradiance profile and distribution of ramp rates for a highly variable solar day also in East Tennessee. On days like the one shown in this example, irradiance ramps higher than 10 W/m²/s and even higher than 50 W/m²/s may happen. However, it must be noted that, percent of daytime hours experiencing ramp rates higher than 10 W/m2/s are quite low compared to slower ramps.

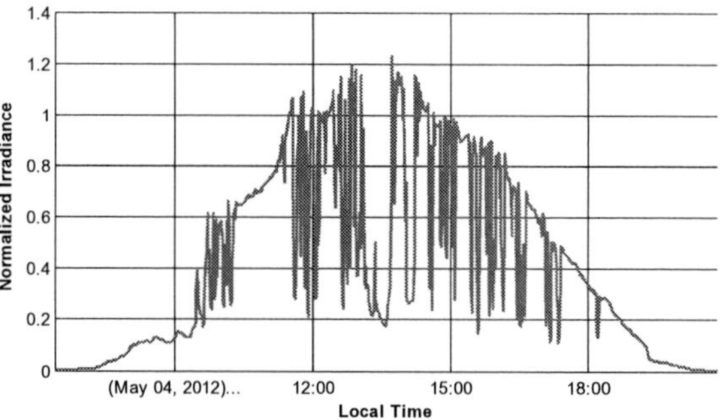

Fig. 8. Example solar irradiance profile for a highly variable day in East Tennessee.

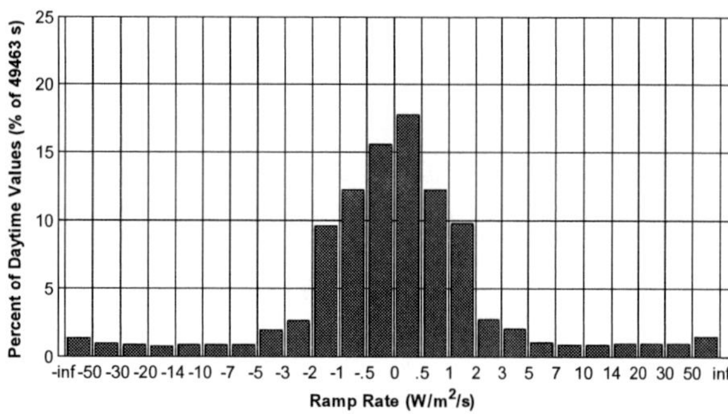

Fig. 9. Ramp rate distribution for the example highly variable day irradiance profile shown in Fig. 8.

Daytime irradiance data from the East Tennessee PV site is also analyzed for an entire year and distribution of irradiance ramp rates is presented in Fig. 10. The analysis for the whole year, which incorporates all the seasonal variations, reveals that irradiance ramping events higher than 10 W/m2 are quite rare.

If only the second-by-second variations in solar irradiance profile is taken into consideration then number of repetitions of ramping events, especially ones with faster rates, proposed in the EN 50530 test profiles do not represent the field experience presented in this section. However, this standard specifies testing profiles that consider magnitude of change in addition to rate of change as described in Table I and II. In the following section solar irradiance data from the same PV plant in Tennessee is also analyzed for ramp events between certain magnitudes.

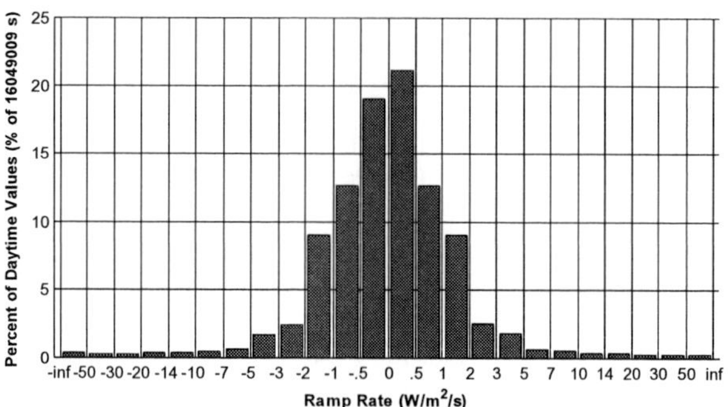

Fig. 10. Distribution of irradiance ramp rates over a year (2012) in East Tennessee.

V. Solar Irradiance Ramp – Magnitude Analysis

First analysis was performed to identify how frequently solar irradiance in Tennessee reaches 1000 W/m² or higher and drops at or below 100 W/m². The irradiance – duration curve in Fig. 11 shows the irradiance magnitude as a function of percentage of daytime hours experiencing that irradiance level or higher in year 2012. In this particular PV site in Tennessee in 2012, irradiance levels exceeded 1000 W/m² only 1.5% of the total daytime hours, or 65 hours out of the entire year. Irradiance levels were below 100 W/m² for 29.3% of the total daytime hours, or 1,267 hours in the entire year. Although the plant irradiance stayed below 100 W/m2 for a significant amount of time, however most of these low irradiance intervals are during sunrises and sunsets instead of mid-day when solar ramping up and down events typically occur.

In order to obtain a larger ramp rate dataset, which more closely aligns with real world ramping events, a modified range from 25% to 50% is used in this analysis instead of 10% to 50% as specified in the EN 50530: 2010 standard. Similarly for the medium-to-high irradiance range 30% to 80% is used instead of 30% to 100%. Fig. 11 shows that irradiance levels are below 250 W/m² for 47.5% of daytime hours (2,054 hours/yr) while irradiance levels are above 800 W/m² for 16.5% of daytime hours (714 hours/yr).

          396

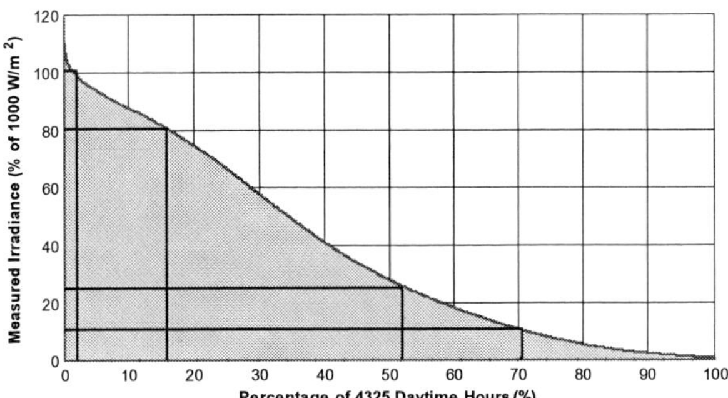

Fig. 11.   2012 Solar Irradiance – duration profile in East Tennessee.

To create the ramp rate dataset from the 1-second irradiance profile which considers magnitude of change, each ramping event, between a lower and upper bound was correlated to a linear ramp of the same magnitude and time frame. Ramping events which had a correlation coefficient below 0.9 were discarded in this analysis. Threshold 0.9 was chosen to maintain a fairly linear ramp without significantly sacrificing the size of the dataset. Fig. 12 shows examples of two irradiance ramping events with two different correlation coefficients. The ramp events with 0.88 correlation coefficient was discarded from the reminder of this study due to significant deviation from the linear ramp nature. Example ramp events with 0.95 coefficient depicts the closeness to linear ramp in Fig. 12 . All ramp events between the target magnitude level with correlation coefficient equal or higher than 0.90 were retained within the final ramp rate dataset for further analysis.

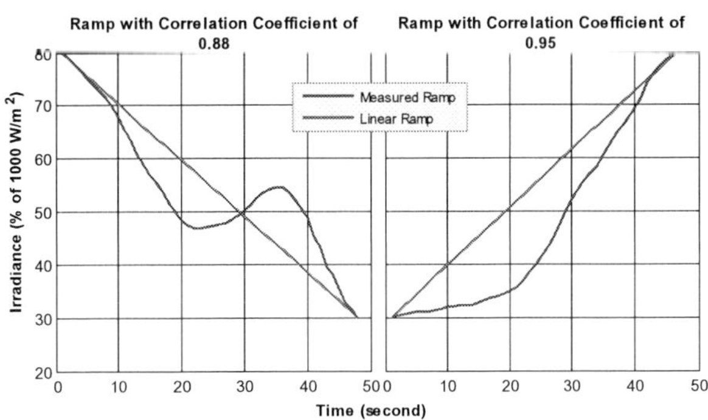

Fig. 12.   Example solar irradiance ramping events with two different correlation coefficients.

Distribution of number of ramp events between small (25%) to medium (50%) irradiance magnitudes are shown in Fig. 13. From this distribution it is clear that most ramping events in the filtered dataset occurred at rates faster than 50 W/m², for both ramping up and down slopes. Although the number of ramping events with higher ramp rates is larger, the total time duration during which these events occurred is a very small fraction of the total day time hours in a whole year. This observation is quite clear from the time-duration distribution shown in Fig. 14. This distribution also closely aligns with the 1-sec ramp rate distribution shown in Fig. 10 for the entire year.

Total duration of all the qualified ramp events between 250 W/m² and 500 W/m² is 305 hrs, which is only 7% of the total day time hours measured in East Tennessee in 2012. Percentage of this 305 hrs taken by different ramp rate ranges is shown in Table III. From this table it is quite obvious that percentage of time the irradiance profile changes faster than 2 W/m²/s is very low.

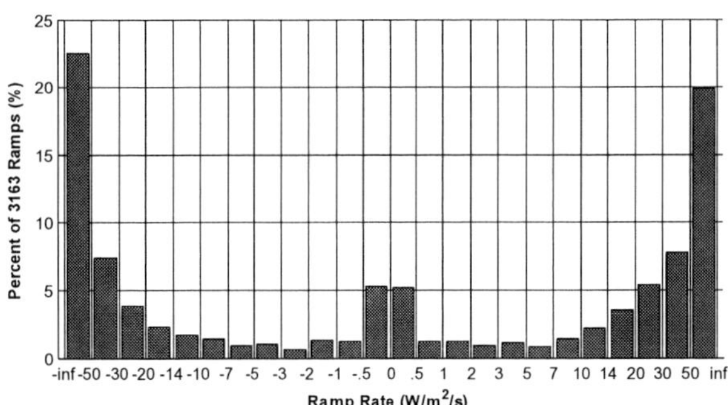

Fig. 13.   Distribution of ramp events between 250 W/m² and 500 W/m² calculated from year-long measured data in East Tennessee.

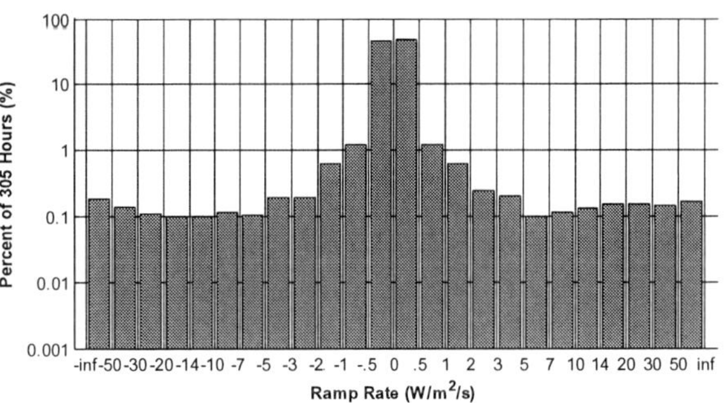

Fig. 14.   Distribution of time-duration of ramp events between 250 W/m² and 500 W/m² calculated from year-long measured data in East Tennessee.

Similar analysis of ramp events between medium (300 W/m²) and high (800 W/m²) irradiance magnitude levels were carried out and the distributions are presented in Fig. 15 and Fig. 16. This distribution is similar to those showed above for the lower range with slightly more ramping events occurring at faster rates.

Total duration of all the qualified ramp events between 330 W/m^2 and 800 W/m^2 is 548 hrs, which is less than 13% of the total day time hours measured in East Tennessee in 2012. During the 99% of this 548 hrs irradiance ramp rate was 10 W/m^2/s or lower. Percentage of this 548 hrs taken by different ranges of ramp rates is shown in Table IV.

TABLE III

WEIGHTING PERCENTAGES OF RAMP RATES IN TENNESSEE, LOWER RANGE

Ramp Rate (W/m^2/s)	Lower Range 250 W/m^2 to 500 W/m^2
0 to 0.5	93.67%
0.5 to 1	2.42%
1 to 2	1.26%
2 to 3	0.44%
3 to 5	0.40%
5 to 7	0.21%
7 to 10	0.23%
10 to 14	0.23%
14 to 20	0.25%
20 to 30	0.26%
30 to 50	0.28%
> 50	0.35%

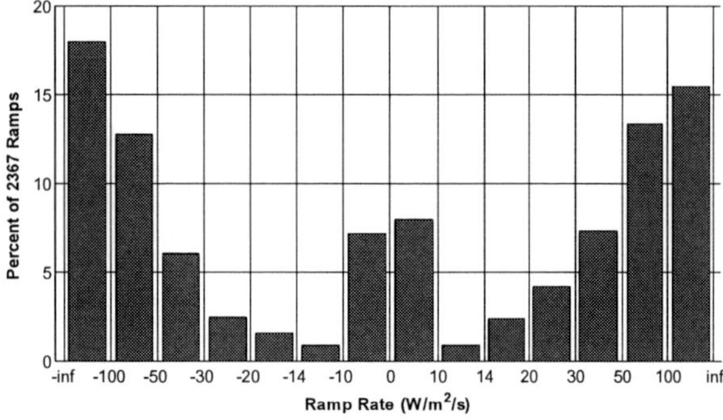

Fig. 15. Distribution of ramp events between 300 W/m^2 and 800 W/m^2 calculated from year-long measured data in East Tennessee.

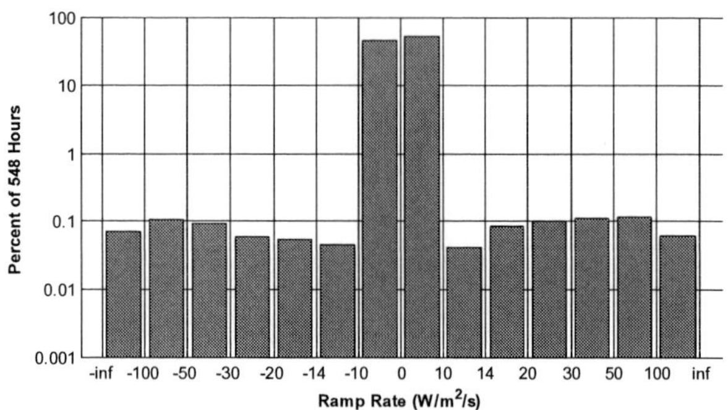

Fig. 16. Distribution of time-duration of ramp events between 300 W/m^2 and 800 W/m^2 calculated from year-long measured data in East Tennessee.

TABLE IV

WEIGHTING PERCENTAGES OF RAMP RATES IN TENNESSEE, UPPER RANGE

Ramp Rate (W/m^2/s)	UPPER Range 300 W/m^2 to 800 W/m^2
0 to 10	99.05%
10 to 14	0.09%
14 to 20	0.14%
20 to 30	0.16%
30 to 50	0.20%
50 to 100	0.22%
> 100	0.13%

VI. SOLAR IRRADIANCE MEASURED DATA IN CALIFORNIA

Weather patterns vary significantly form one geographic region to another. Solar variability conditions in two locations can be totally different depending on their weather regions [7]. The analysis presented in section III and IV were repeated for a PV plant in California, where high solar variable days are quite infrequent. Irradiance measurements were taken from a pyranometer in the plane of array (10° fixed tilt, south orientation) of a 200-kW PV plant. The ramp rate distribution for the entire 2012 is shown in Fig. 17. As expected this distribution has less frequent higher ramp rates than those shown in Fig. 10 for East Tennessee.

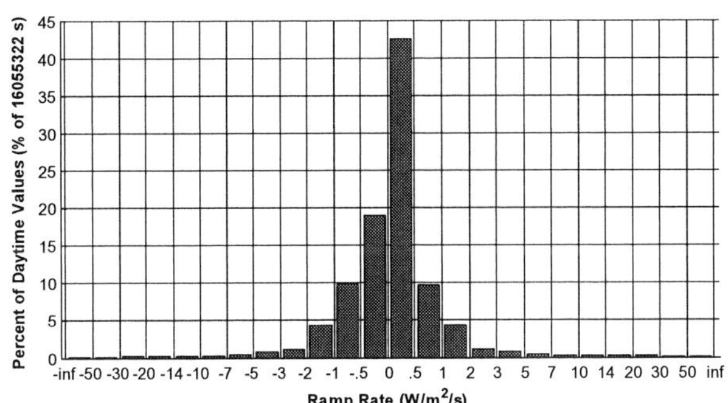

Fig. 17. Distribution of irradiance ramp rates over a year in California, 2012.

The distribution of ramp events follow the same general trend with more occurrences of higher ramp rates between the specified magnitude ranges yet a very small percentage of time is spent ramping at that high rates. Time-duration distributions for ramp events between small (250 W/m^2) and medium (500 W/m^2) and also for medium (300 W/m^2) and high (800 W/m^2) are shown in Fig. 18 and Fig. 19 respectively. Further, in California, the faster ramp events occur less often than in Tennessee which is expected. As shown in Table V, the slower ramp rates (less than 0.5 W/m^2/s) account for no less than 99% of the ramping time between the small and medium irradiance magnitude levels, compared with 93% in East Tennessee. Table VI shows the percentage of total time taken by different ranges of ramp rates for medium to high irradiance magnitude levels.

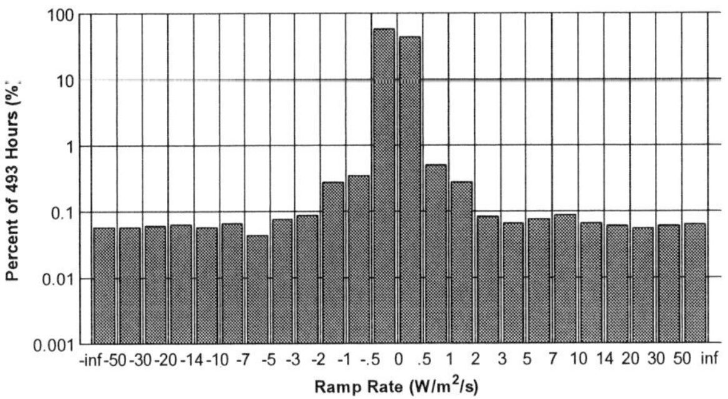

Fig. 18. Distribution of time-duration of ramp events between 250 W/m^2 and 500 W/m^2 calculated from year-long measured data in California.

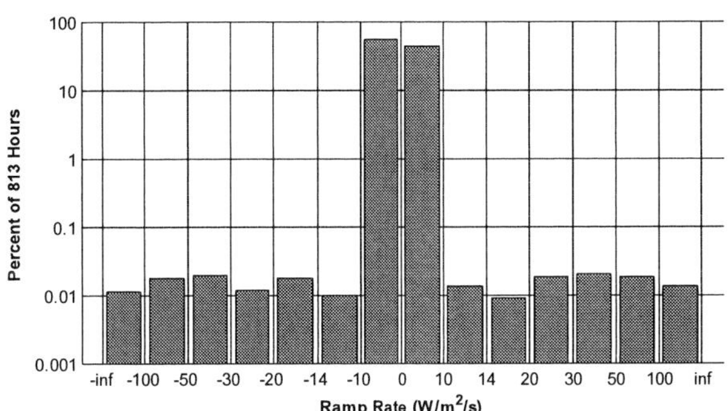

Fig. 19. Distribution of time-duration of ramp events between 300 W/m2 and 800 W/m2 calculated from year-long measured data in California.

TABLE V
WEIGHTING PERCENTAGES OF RAMP RATES IN CALIFORNIA, LOWER RANGE

Ramp Rate (W/m^2/s)	Lower Range 250 W/m^2 to 500 W/m^2
0 to 0.5	99.41%
0.5 to 1	0.12%
1 to 2	0.12%
2 to 3	0.08%
3 to 5	0.04%
5 to 7	0.02%
7 to 10	0.04%
10 to 14	0.02%
14 to 20	0.03%
20 to 30	0.03%
30 to 50	0.04%
> 50	0.06%

TABLE VI
WEIGHTING PERCENTAGES OF RAMP RATES IN CALIFORNIA, UPPER RANGE

Ramp Rate (W/m^2/s)	UPPER Range 300 W/m^2 to 800 W/m^2
0 to 10	99.82%
10 to 14	0.02%
14 to 20	0.03%
20 to 30	0.03%
30 to 50	0.04%
50 to 100	0.04%
> 100	0.02%

Dynamic MPPT efficiency can be critical for PV inverter performance in applications with frequent variable array output. This criterion is not normally specified in inverter selection even though it can enhance energy yield and lower the LCOE. EN 50530: 2010 did an excellent job defining the dynamic MPPT efficiency test protocol in addition to static conversion and MPPT efficiency tests. However, the irradiance test profiles proposed in the standard do not match field measurements reported in this paper. For example, in the small-to-medium irradiance variation test sequence summarized in Table I, events with ramp rate of 50 W/m²/s occupies 4.1% of the total test period. Whereas our analysis of field measured data from Tennessee shows that events with ramp rates 30 to 50 W/m²/s occurs for only 0.28% of the total time solar irradiance was varying between the magnitude limits specified for this test. For California this percentage was quite negligible, only 0.04%.

In the medium-to-high irradiance variation test sequence summarized in Table II, events with ramp rate of 10 W/m²/s occupies 27% of the total test period. Whereas our analysis of field measured data from Tennessee shows that events with ramp rates 10 W/m²/s or lower occurs for 99% of the total time solar irradiance was varying between the magnitude limits specified for this test. For California this percentage was even higher, 99.82%.

VII.   CONCLUSION

For both locations, more than 98% of the ramping events were experiencing 10 W/m²/s or lower ramp rates. Analysis of year long second-by-second ramp rate distributions for Tennessee and California presented in this paper shows that most solar irradiance variations are 5 W/m²/s or lower. Hence, in dynamic MPPT testing more emphasis need to be employed to ramp events with slopes up to 5 W/m2/s. Measured data presented in this work clearly showed that high ramp rates do occur in the field, but their duration, compared to total day time hours in an year, is quite insignificant.

In addition, string and central inverters run their MPPT algorithm over the aggregate current-voltage characteristics of the entire PV array. For PV plants, with larger footprint actual maximum power point does not vary as fast as the solar irradiance measured by a point source like pyranometer. On the other hand, microinverter converts the DC output of a single PV module whose DC output variations can be as fast as the variation in the irradiance. Hence, dynamic MPPT performance analysis is more important for microinverters, DC power optimizers, and small residential string inverters.

In order to evaluate accuracy of dynamic MPPT efficiency the number of repetitions of a ramp up and down events with certain slopes need to be representative of the percent of day time that particular ramp rates occurs in the field. Measured solar irradiance profiles from several geographic locations need to be analyzed to develop the proper test sequence. In future work measured irradiance data from other locations will be analyzed and revised irradiance test profiles, with necessary adjustments in the number of repetitions representing frequency of occurrence, will be developed.

REFERENCES

[1] State of California, California Energy Commission & California Public Utilities Commission. List of Eligible Inverters per SB1 Guidelines.
http://www.gosolarcalifornia.ca.gov/equipment/inverters.php

[2] D. Sera, R. Teodorescu, J. Hantschel, and M. Knoll, "Optimized maximum power point tracker for fast-changing environmental conditions," *IEEE Trans. Ind. Electron.*, vol. 55, no. 7, pp. 2629-2637, Jul. 2008.

[3] E. Koutroulis, and F. Blaabjerg, "A new technique for tracking the global maximum power point of PV arrays operating under partial-shading conditions," *IEEE J. Photovoltaics*, vol. 2, no. 2, pp. 184-190, Apr. 2012.

[4] U. Zimmermann, and M. Edoff, "A maximum power point tracker for long-term logging of PV module performance," *IEEE J. Photovoltaics*, vol. 2, no. 1, pp. 47-55, Jan. 2012.

[5] B. Yu, G. Yu, and Y. Kim, "Design and experimental results of improved dynamic MPPT performance by EN50530," in *Proc. Tel. Energy Conf. (INTELEC)*, 2011, pp. 1-4.

[6] Overall efficiency of grid connected photovoltaic inverters; European Committee for Electro-Technical Standardization (CENELEC) EN 50530: Apr. 2010, in close cooperation with, and providing input to, International Electro-technical Commission IES TC 82.

[7] C. Trueblood, S. Coley, T. Key, L. Rogers, A. Ellis, C. Hansen, and E. Philpot, "PV measures up for fleet duty," *IEEE Power & Energy*, vol. 11, no. 2, pp. 33-44, Apr. 2013.

Failure Analysis Techniques for Microsystems-Enabled Photovoltaics

Benjamin B. Yang, *Member, IEEE*, Jose L. Cruz-Campa, Gaddi S. Haase, Edward I. Cole Jr., *Senior Member, IEEE*, Paiboon Tangyunyong, Paul J. Resnick, Alice C. Kilgo, Murat Okandan, *Member, IEEE*, and Gregory N. Nielson

Abstract—Microsystems-enabled photovoltaics (MEPV) has great potential to meet the increasing demands for light-weight, photovoltaic solutions with high power density and efficiency. This paper describes effective failure analysis techniques to localize and characterize nonfunctional or underperforming MEPV cells. The defect localization methods such as electroluminescence under forward and reverse bias, as well as optical beam induced current using wavelengths above and below the device band gap, are presented. The current results also show that the MEPV has good resilience against degradation caused by reverse bias stresses.

Index Terms—Failure analysis, photovoltaic (PV) cells, silicon, solar energy.

I. Introduction

MANY applications of photovoltaics (PV), such as those for space and portable devices, have a strong need for light-weight, flexible, and efficient solutions with a high specific power. One approach to meet this demand is to utilize microfabrication techniques to produce thin miniature solar cells and take advantage of scaling effects, such as reduced material costs, lower bulk recombination, and improved heat dissipation [1]–[3].

Microsystems-enabled photovoltaics (MEPV) is an example of this approach. MEPV utilizes microfabrication techniques to create arrays of thin, interdigitated back contact (IBC), hexagonal solar cells that are 250 μm to 1 mm in diameter and 14 to 20 μm in thickness [4]. These cells are can be assembled onto flexible substrates and interconnected to produce arrays with high power density [5].

MEPVs have several features that require reexamination of new and existing failure analysis techniques commonly used in PV. These characteristics are also likely applicable to any researcher that is using new techniques to scale down certain PV device dimensions, such as the size of the electrical contacts. The evaluation of different failure analysis methods in this paper will be relevant to such situations.

Manuscript received June 16, 2013; revised August 6, 2013; accepted September 15, 2013. Date of publication October 24, 2013; date of current version December 16, 2013. Sandia National Laboratories is a multiprogram laboratory managed and operated by Sandia Corporation, a wholly owned subsidiary of Lockheed Martin Corporation, for the U.S. Department of Energy's National Nuclear Security Administration under contract DE-AC04-94AL85000.

The authors are with the Sandia National Laboratories, Albuquerque, NM 87185, USA (e-mail: bbyang@sandia.gov; jlcruzc@sandia.gov; gshaase@sandia.gov; coleei@sandia.gov; ptangyu@sandia.gov; resnicpj@sandia.gov; ackilgo@sandia.gov; mokanda@sandia.gov; gnniels@sandia.gov).

Color versions of one or more of the figures in this paper are available online at http://ieeexplore.ieee.org.

Digital Object Identifier 10.1109/JPHOTOV.2013.2284864

MEPV has characteristics and fabrication steps not found in conventional PV devices that could lead to new failure modes and require new evaluation techniques that include 1) the metal layer and doped regions are connected through small 3-μm diameter contacts; 2) the electrical connection between the MEPV cell and substrate are made through numerous 75-μm diameter metal pillars attached with solder; 3) the fabrication and release of the MEPV cells involve wet-etch steps where an over- or under-etch can significantly affect the device's electrical connectivity to the substrate; 4) the p-i-n nature of the MEPV means that failure analysis techniques for rectifiers, such as light-induced voltage alteration, are less effective than the optical beam induced current (OBIC) setup proposed in this paper; and 5) the active area of a single MEPV consists of multiple p-i-n regions, which may have nonuniform performance.

This paper describes the failure analysis techniques that were found to be effective for MEPV and summarizes the relative strengths and weaknesses of each method. In addition, the paper reports two experiments that demonstrate the robustness of MEPV to reverse bias stress and uses the resulting degraded samples as case studies for defect localization.

The results of this paper form the basic tools to build a reliability model for MEPV. The ability to nondestructively perform preliminary failure analysis on individual cells in an MEPV array allows simultaneous stress testing of multiple cells, as shown in the reverse bias tests in this paper. Stressing and analyzing larger arrays instead of individual cells results in a larger data set. In addition, the failure analysis techniques could uncover signatures that are precursors to early failure, which would allow them to also serve as a screening tool for infant mortality.

II. Microsystems-Enabled Photovoltaics Overview

MEPVs are single crystalline silicon solar cells that have IBCs and point contacts. The fabrication of MEPV cells is briefly covered here for the reader's convenience and described in greater detail in previous publications [6], [7]. The fabrication begins with a 6-in, 20–30 Ω-cm, p-type, (100)-oriented, silicon-on-insulator wafer with a 20-μm device layer and a 1-μm buried oxide layer. Circular islands of boron and phosphorous are implanted into the silicon and connected through an insulating nitride layer to two electrode pads in the metal layer. The positive electrode pad is connected to all p-type implantation regions and the negative electrode pad is connected to all n-type implantation regions.

A layout showing the p-type regions, n-type regions, and the point contacts to their respective electrode pads is illustrated at the top view of Fig. 1(a). The blue areas represent the p-type

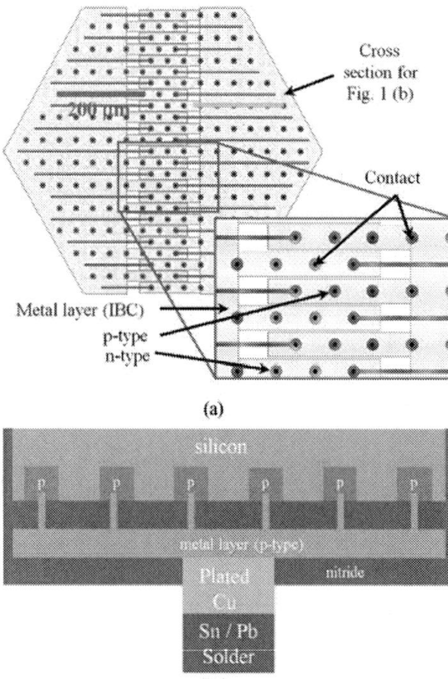

Fig. 1. Drawing illustrating the doping profile and metal layer is shown in Fig. 1(a). The blue regions represent the p-type areas, and the red regions represent the n-type areas. The black dots, which are visible in the close-up view, show the dimensions of the contacts that connect the p-type and n-type areas to their respective electrode in the metal layer. The IBC metal layer, which is shown in green, takes the form of two interdigitated halves: one connected to the p-type silicon and the other to the n-type silicon. Fig. 1(b) shows a cross-sectional sketch, not drawn to scale, along the orange line in Fig 1(a), where circular islands of p-doped silicon are connected to the metal layer by contacts. The electroplated pillars and solder, which are not visible in Fig. 1(a), connect the metal layer to the substrate. A nitride passivation layer surrounds the MEPV and functions as an antireflection layer.

TABLE I
SUMMARY OF CHARACTERIZATION METHODS

Technique	Description	Information Provided
Electrical Testing	Current vs. voltage measurement of the device in the dark	Leakage current
Electroluminescence (Forward Bias)	Collecting emitted photons with a thermally cooled camera while device is under *forward* biased.	Cell functionality and relative performance
Electroluminescence (Reverse Bias)	Collecting emitted photons with a thermally cooled camera while device is under *reverse* biased.	Localize high reverse-bias leakage current resulting from avalanche breakdown.
Optical Beam Induced Current (above band gap)	Monitoring amplified output current while raster-scanning unbiased device with a laser stimulus that has photon energy *above* the band gap.	Cell functionality and relative performance with better fidelity within a single cell than forward biased electroluminescence.
Optical Beam Induced Current (below band gap)	Monitoring amplified output current while raster-scanning unbiased device with a laser stimulus that has photon energy *below* the band gap.	Verification of electrical connectivity of nonfunctioning cell, evaluation of contacts between metal layer and doped regions.

regions and the brown areas correspond to the n-type regions. The black dots at the center of the p- and n-type areas are contacts connecting the implantation regions to the electrode pads in the IBC below, indicated in green. The left half is the n-type electrode pad and is connected to the n-type regions. The right half is the p-type electrode pad and is connected to the p-type region.

Fig. 1(b) shows a cross section of the p-type portion of the MEPV that is not drawn to scale. The sketch shows the contacts that connect the p-type regions to the metal layer. In the final configuration, the MEPV is back-contacted with the metal layer underneath so that no shading occurs. In addition, the picture shows one of four electroplated copper legs, which is not shown in Fig. 1(a), that connect the MEPV to the final substrate through a solder bond. These copper legs are shown in the mechanically-polished cross sectional image in Section III.

Once the fabrication of the functional features of the MEPV cells are complete, an etch step with hydrofluoric acid partially releases the cell such that it is held to the initial handle wafer with thin tethers. These tethers are broken when the cell is attached to the final substrate through a solder connection at the electroplated copper legs. The original handle wafer can be reused after the MEPV cells are fully released, thus saving on material costs.

III. FAILURE ANALYSIS TECHNIQUES AND RESULTS

The failure analysis techniques utilized in this paper include electrical characterization, electroluminescence (EL), and the OBIC. Table I provides a summary of the various techniques described in this section.

The EL image consists of light emission collected from the device under forward bias and is used to evaluate the relative performance of each cell [8]. In addition, the EL under reverse bias is used to localize the source of significant leakage currents. Because of the large depletion region which results from the p-i-n structure of MEPV, avalanche breakdown and associated heat damage is likely the dominant reverse bias breakdown mechanism. The high-field carrier populations in an avalanche breakdown generate sufficient photons for EL to localize the defect site [9].

Fig. 2 shows an example of a forward biased EL image. The hexagonal PV cells in the image are 720 μm in diameter.

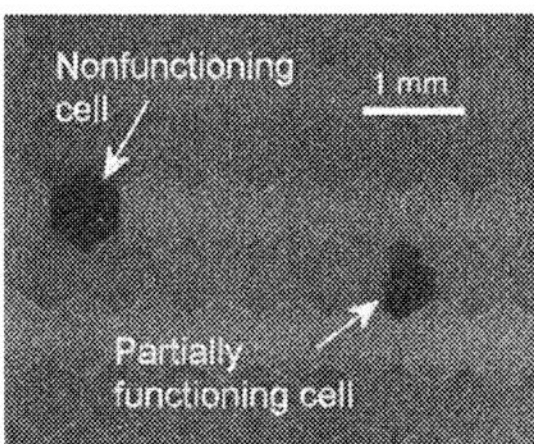

Fig. 2. EL is used to evaluate relative efficiency of MEPV arrays. This figure shows an example of a nonfunctioning cell and a partially functioning one. Certain cells have area defects that limit performance.

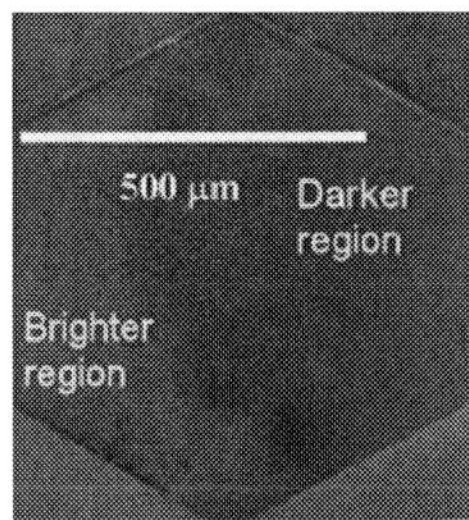

Fig. 3. OBIC image using an above-band-gap laser stimulus provides additional fidelity on the regional performance on a single MEPV cell. The darker half on the right indicates a possible carrier generation or collection issue.

Each horizontal row in the cell is connected in parallel, and the rows are connected in series. The relative brightness of each row is related to the number of functioning cells in that row. EL is able to identify nonfunctioning cells, as well as partially functioning ones. The examples of both situations are represented in Fig. 2. Under forward bias, all functioning cells emit light. The nonfunctioning cells do not appear in the image. If the cell has damaged regions, those areas can also be identified in the EL image.

The OBIC uses a raster-scanning laser stimulus to generate currents in the device [10]. Low-noise amplification is performed on the induced signal to form an image. When the laser stimulus has sufficient photon energy to generate electron-hole pairs, above-band-gap OBIC can be used to evaluate the cell performance and complements EL by providing additional information on localized efficiency in an individual cell. We use a laser wavelength of 543 nanometers (nm) for this mode of operation, with a laser power of approximately 50 to 100 mW (depending on the objective used) after attenuation and a spot size that is less than 1 μm at the highest magnification objective. The amplifier gain is approximately 10^9 to 10^{10} with a scan speed of approximately 16 s per frame. Both the laser power and the amplification are adjustable parameters so that the combination of stimulus and amplifier used that produces the best image is used.

Fig. 3 shows an example where the OBIC is used to determine localized efficiency within an individual MEPV cell. The right half of the cell is darker than the left half in the OBIC image. The contrast difference suggests a possible carrier collection issue with the right half of the cell. This nonuniform performance was not apparent under EL, which further demonstrates the complementary nature of the two techniques.

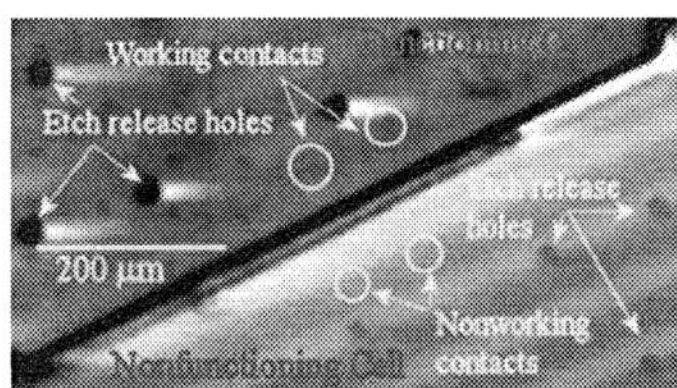

Fig. 4. A 1340-nm wavelength OBIC enables the evaluation of the contacts between the silicon and metal layer. Contacts in the functioning cell are shown as smaller dots that are not visible in the neighboring nonfunctioning cells.

Alternatively, below-band-gap OBIC can be used to provide additional device information. When the laser photon energy is below the device band gap, no electron-hole pairs are generated. Localized heating at interface regions between materials generates currents that are amplified to form the OBIC image. This configuration can be used to test the electrical contact and connectivity of the device separately from its ability to generate carriers. Two lasers are used in this mode of operation with wavelengths of 1064 nm and 1340 nm, respectively. The output power of both the lasers after attenuation varies between 50 to 120 mW, depending on the objective used. Both lasers are capable of having spot sizes that are less than 1 μm at the highest magnification objective. The amplifier gain is approximately 10^9 to 10^{10} with a scan speed of approximately 16 to 32 s per frame. As was the case with above-band-gap OBIC, both the laser power and the amplification are adjustable and the combination of stimulus and amplifier used are optimized to produce the best image.

Fig. 4 is an OBIC image of adjacent functioning and nonfunctioning MEPV cells. The contacts that connect the silicon to the metal interconnect layer are visible in the functioning cell and are not visible in the nonfunctioning cell. Note that the OBIC image has contrast changes at the etch-release holes and the edges of the MEPV cell. This contrast is because of the temperature gradient induced by the laser across material interfaces. Through this mechanism, we see that the etch release holes are still visible in the nonfunctioning cell, which suggests that it is still electrically connected with the array. The failure mechanism could be related to the contacts between the silicon and metal layer. Further defect localization is necessary before subsequent destructive analysis to determine the root cause.

In addition to the analysis through EL and OBIC, mechanically polished cross sections are analyzed to determine the quality of the electrical connection between the solar cell and the metal trace lines that connect them to each other. Fig. 5 illustrates two features of interest: voids in the solder connection and absorption of the metal trace lines into the solder. The voids could lead to increased series resistance or poor connection between the cell and the metal trace. Further analysis with scanning electron microscopy shows that the metal trace is thinner in regions under the solder where it is potentially consumed by alloying. Both the voids and the decreased thickness in metal traces are present in functioning cells. Additional cross sections of samples that have experienced temperature cycling will provide more insight into the long-term effects of these defects.

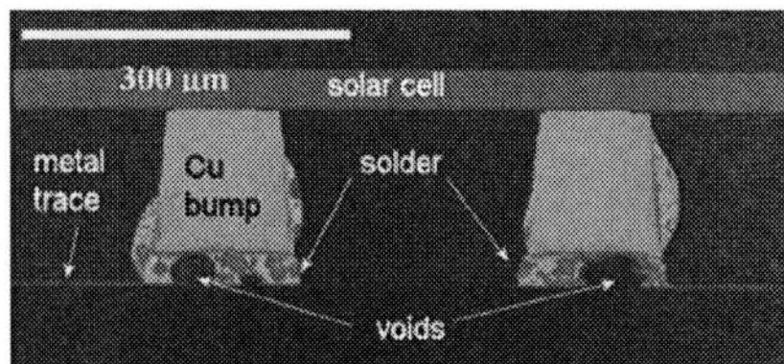

Fig. 5. Mechanical polishing and bright field optical microscopy has been used to evaluate the quality of the solder connection between the copper legs and the gold lines. Voids such as the one shown here could be a source for increased series resistance.

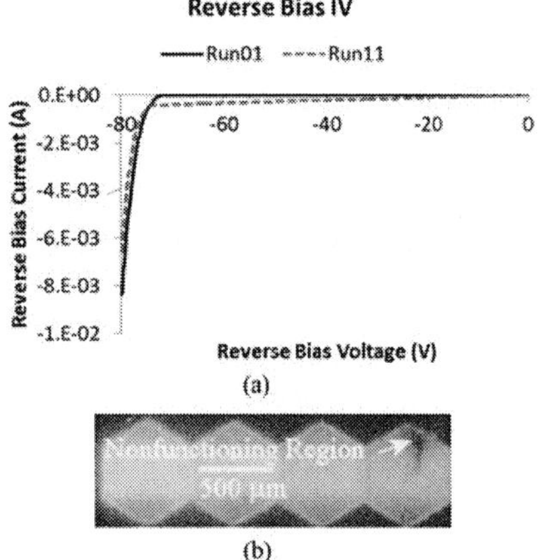

Fig. 6. *I–V* curves before and after reverse bias stress is shown in Fig. 6(a). Each voltage sweep takes approximately 10 s. Breakdown occurs at approximately –75 V. We can see that current leakage is aggravated after repeated voltage stress. A forward biased EL image of the damaged MEPV cell with a nonfunctioning region is shown in the far right of Fig. 6(b).

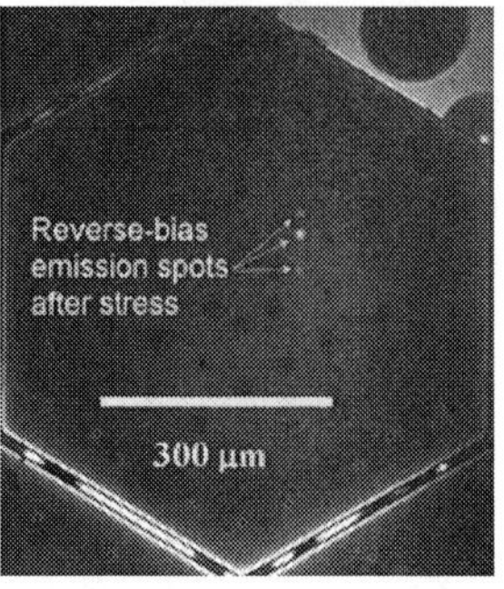

Fig. 7. EL imaging of the MEPV cell under reverse bias shows three local defects that are the source of the leakage current.

IV. Reverse Bias Breakdown Defect Localization

The reverse bias stress occurs in PV cells when a module experiences partial shading and is a source of degradation in PV modules [11]. We expect the MEPV to have good resistance towards reverse bias stress because the p-type and n-type regions are separated by a region of intrinsic silicon (a p-i-n device).

First, we present results of a MEPV device subjected to extreme reverse bias stress until there was a significant increase ($100\times$) in the leakage current. Breakdown onset did not occur until the reverse bias stress exceeded –75 V. Fig. 6(a) shows the reverse bias current–voltage (*I–V*) plot of 28 cells in parallel and illustrates the effect of extreme reverse bias stress. After 11 reverse bias voltage sweeps from 0 to –80 V lasting approximately 10 s each, the leakage current begins to increase dramatically, especially at the lower voltages. The two *I–V*-curves remain similar beyond –74 V, which suggests that the source of leakage currents at extremely high voltages is not significantly affected by the new failure.

Further analysis of the sample in Fig. 6(a) shows that the effects of reverse bias stress are localized. Fig. 6(b) shows a portion of the MEPV array forward biased EL image. The cell on the far right has a nonfunctioning region that is not emitting light.

This potential-induced defect was further localized by taking an EL image of the MEPV array under reverse (instead of forward) bias. Prior to the voltage stress, the MEPV array produced no detectable light emission under reverse bias. The poststress reverse bias EL image of the cell of interest is shown in Fig. 7. In order to display the location of the defect, the optical emission is converted to a green (false) color and overlaid on top of a bright-field image of the cell.

The EL signal suggests a current-induced dislocation path. The reverse bias light emission has higher intensity than the forward bias MEPV EL signal, which suggests a different photon generation mechanism. One possibility is that the photons are generated by microplasma that is characteristic of avalanche breakdown [12]. The small, discrete, and localized nature of the light emission also supports this suggested mechanism.

V. Reverse Bias Degradation Results

The subsequent study presented in this section focuses on lower reverse bias voltage stresses applied for longer periods of time for the purposes of building a reliability model for potential-induced degradation. Fig. 8 shows 300 reverse bias *I–V* measurements, taken every 2 hr over the course of 600 h of reverse bias stress at –50 V. The device under test had 34 MEPV cells connected in parallel. The color transition from blue to red identifies the relative order of each *I–V* sweep, with blue being the initial measurements and red being the last ones. The divisions on the left side of the plot provide estimations on the amount of stress applied prior to a given *I–V* measurement.

At the end of 600 h of reverse bias stress, the current leakage roughly doubled but still remained at an acceptable amount of approximately –15 μA per cell at –40 V. The transition to increased leakage current was gradual and continuous compared with the forward bias results, which are plotted separately in Fig. 9(a).

Unlike the reverse bias stress, the forward bias *I–V* curves exhibited very discrete increases in current for a given voltage. These changes occurred approximately after 100 and 210 h of stressing. These sharp changes suggest two breakdown events that increased the amount of current flow through the damaged device.

    404

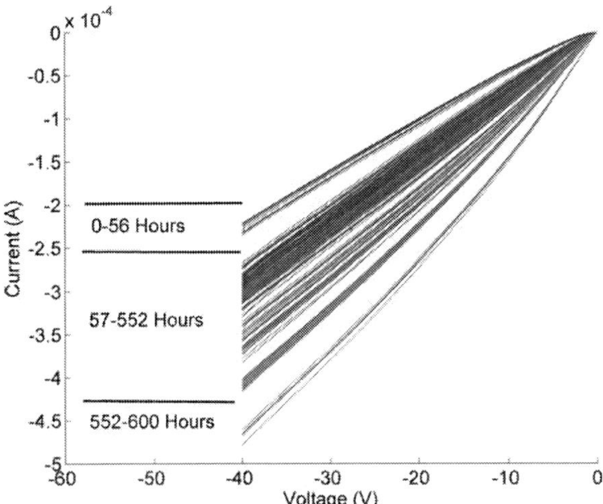

Fig. 8. Reverse bias *I–V* sweeps taken in 2-hr intervals during a 600-h reverse bias stress test at –50 V. The line color transition from blue to red indicates the relative order of the *I–V* sweeps, with red being the last measurement. The three regions in the plot show the duration of reverse bias stress that occurred prior to the *I–V* sweeps in the indicated area. We see that while the reverse bias current doubled during 600 h of stress, the overall leakage is still moderate.

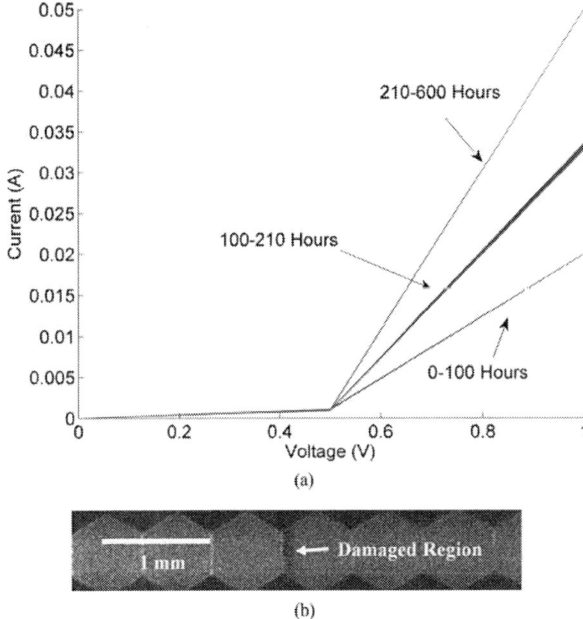

(b)

Fig. 9. The forward bias portion of the *I–V* sweeps of Fig. 8 are shown in Fig. 9(a). The measurements were taken in 2-hr intervals during a 600-h reverse bias stress test at –50 V. Unlike the continuous, steady increase of leakage current in the reverse bias *I–V* curves of Fig. 8, the forward bias current increase took place in two discrete transitions. This behavior suggests that two MEPV cells were damaged: one at approximately hour 100 and the other at approximately hour 210. When examining the EL image of the cells, we see two correspondingly damaged MEPV cells such as that shown in Fig. 9(b). The darker region labeled localizes the defect to the left edge of the cell shown.

A poststress, forward bias EL examination was able to identify two MEPV cells with damaged regions. Fig. 9(b) shows a forward bias EL image of one of these cells where the damaged area is apparent. Subsequent destructive failure analysis is needed to determine the exact nature of the breakdown.

Unlike the damaged sample in Section IV, there was insufficient leakage to generate a detectable reverse bias EL image. The lack of a strong, localized emission under reverse bias suggests that the avalanche breakdown failure mechanism observed in the previous section has not yet occurred on this sample. Therefore, when developing reliability data for an MEPV system, it is important not to overstress the device at voltages significantly beyond the partial shading reverse bias voltages expected for the specific application and operating conditions. Overstressing could lead to new failure modes such as the observed avalanche breakdown in Section IV that may not occur during actual operation of the system.

VI. Conclusion

The current research to explore the reliability of MEPV devices utilizes tools such as electrical characterization, EL, multiwavelength OBIC, and physical failure analysis to establish an effective set of failure analysis techniques for the technology. These methods are used to characterize MEPV devices and localized failure sites. EL and above-band-gap OBIC were demonstrated as methods to evaluate MEPV cell efficiency. The below-band-gap OBIC was shown to be an effective method to separately verify electrical connectivity of an MEPV cell.

We have also demonstrated good resilience to reverse bias voltage degradation. We found significant increases in leakage current, possibly because of avalanche breakdown, at voltage stresses exceeding –80 V. The minor increases in leakage current without the behavior of avalanche breakdown were observed after 600 h of voltage stress at –50 V. The evolution of the forward bias *I–V* curves correlated to the number of new defects, which was later verified using forward bias EL. Additional tests will enable development of a reliability model for reverse bias stress. The inclusion of additional stress testing such as temperature cycling and damp heat will lead to a comprehensive model to predict reliability. The failure analysis of accelerated testing samples will provide insight on how to further enhance the reliability of MEPV.

The failure analysis techniques described in this paper were found to be effective for MEPV and are likely good candidates to examine similar microfabricated PV devices, which include those with other materials systems such as III–Vs. The difference in band gap in the case of III–Vs, however, means that different detectors and optical stimulus may be required. These defect localization methods can be used to evaluate individual cells in large MEPV arrays which undergo stress tests. In addition, they can potentially serve as an early screening tool to identify future early failures in MEPV and other micro-PV arrays.

REFERENCES

[1] J. Yoon, A. J. Baca, S.-I. Park, P. Elvikis, J. B. Geddes, L. Li, R. H. Kim, J. Xiao, S. Wang, T.-H. Kim, M. J. Motala, B. Y. Ahn, E. B. Duoss, J. A. Lewis, R. G. Nuzzo, P. M. Ferreira, Y. Huang, A. Rockett, and J. A. Rogers, "Ultrathin silicon solar microcells for semitransparent, mechanically flexible and microconcentrator module designs," *Nature Mater.*, vol. 7, no. 11, pp. 907–915, Nov. 2008.

[2] K. J. Weber, A. W. Blackers, M. J. Stocks, J. H. Babaei, V. A. Everett, A. J. Neuendorf, and P. J. Verlinden, "A novel low-cost, high-efficiency micromachined silicon solar cell," *IEEE Electron Device Lett.*, vol. 25, no. 1, pp. 37–39, Jan. 2004.

[3] H. Arase1, A. Matsushita, A. Itou, T. Asano, N. Hayashi, D. Inoue, R. Futakuchi, K. Inoue, T. Nakagawa, M. Yamamoto, E. Fujii, Y. Anda, H. Ishida, T. Ueda, O. Fidaner, M. Wiemer, and D. Ueda, "A novel thin concentrator photovoltaic with micro solar cells directly attached to a lens array," in *Proc. 39th IEEE Photovolt. Spec. Conf.*, 2013.

[4] G. N. Nielson, M. Okandan, J. L. Cruz-Campa, A. L. Lentine, W. C. Sweatt, V. P. Gupta, and J. S. Nelson, "Leveraging scale effects to create next-generation photovoltaic systems through micro- and nanotechnologies," *Proc. SPIE*, vol. 8373, p. 837317, May 2012.

[5] J. L. Cruz-Campa, G. N. Nielson, P. J. Resnick, C. A. Sanchez, P. J. Clews, M. Okandan, T. Friedmann, and V. P. Gupta, "Ultrathin flexible crystalline silicon: Microsystems-enabled photovoltaics," *IEEE J. Photovolt.*, vol. 1, no. 1, pp. 3–8, Jul. 2011.

[6] G. N. Nielson, M. Okandan, J. L. Cruz-Campa, P. J. Resnick, M. W. Wanlass, P. J. Clews, T. C. Pluym, C. A. Sanchez, and V. P. Gupta, "Microfabrication of microsystem-enabled photovoltaic (MEPV) cells," in *Proc. SPIE 7927 Adv. Fabrication Technol. Micro/Nano Opt. Photon. IV*, Feb. 2011, vol. 7927.

[7] G. N. Nielson, M. Okandan, P. Resnick, J. L. Cruz-Campa, T. Pluym, P. J. Clews, E. Steenbergen, and V. P. Gupta, "Microscale c-Si (c)PV cells for low-cost power," in *Proc. 34th IEEE Photovolt. Spec. Conf.*, 2009, pp. 001816–001821.

[8] R. Ross, ed., *Microelectronic Failure Analysis Desk Reference*, 6th ed. Materials Park, OH, USA: ASM Int., 1999.

[9] N. Akil, S. E. Kerns, D. V. Kerns, Jr., A. Hoffman, and J.-P. Charles, "A multimechanism model for photon generation by silicon junctions in avalanche breakdown," *IEEE Trans. Electron Devices*, vol. 46, no. 5, pp. 1022–1028, May 1999.

[10] E. I. Cole, P. Tangyunyong, and D. L. Barton, "Backside localization of open and shorted IC interconnections," in *Proc. 36th Annu. IEEE Int. Rel. Phys. Symp.*, Reno, NV, USA, Mar./Apr. 1998, pp. 129–136.

[11] G. B. Alers, J. Zhou, C. Deline, P. Hacke, and S. R. Kurtz, "Degradation of individual cells in a module measured with differential IV analysis," *Prog. Photovolt. Res. Appl.*, vol. 19, no. 8, pp. 977–982, 2011.

[12] D. V. Kerns, K. Arora, S. Kurinec, and W. Power, "Si diode under avalanche breakdown as a light emitting source for VLSI optical interconnect," in *Proc. 21st Southeastern Symp. Syst. Theory*, Tallahassee, FL, USA, Mar. 1989, pp. 677–680.

Jose Luis Cruz-Campa received the B.S.M.E. degree from Universidad Autonoma Metropolitana, Mexico City, Mexico, in 2003, the M.S. degree in physics, and the Ph.D. degree in electrical engineering from The University of Texas at El Paso, El Paso, TX, USA, in 2007 and 2010, respectively.

He is currently at Sandia National Laboratories, Albuquerque, NM, USA. His research focuses on applying microtechnologies to attain new functionality and enhanced performance in photovoltaics. He has presented his research at 13 technical conferences, on scientific websites, in magazines, on local news, and on public television, and he has authored and co-authored 14 technical publications.

Dr. Cruz-Campa has received 17 awards and grants, including the R&D 100 in 2011.

Benjamin B. Yang (S'02–M'12) received the B.S. degree in mathematics in 2005 and the B.S. and M.S. degrees in electrical engineering in 2005 and 2006, respectively, from the University of Utah, Salt Lake City, UT, USA, and the Ph.D. degree in electrical engineering from the University of Wisconsin-Madison, Madison, WI, USA, in 2011.

In 2002, he was a lab technician with the University of Utahs HEDCO cleanroom facility. From 2003 to 2005, he was an NSF IGERT Fellow at the University of Utah. During his time at the University of Wisconsin-Madison, he held various teaching assistant and research assistant positions. He also completed a summer internship at L-3 Communications, Electron Devices in 2006. Since July 2011, he has been with the Validation and Failure Analysis Department at Sandia National Laboratories, Albuquerque, NM, USA. He has a broad range of past and current research interests including terahertz system engineering, nonlinear optics, photonics, microelectromechanical systems, and failure analysis and reliability techniques for next-generation integrated circuits, photovoltaic, and power electronics technologies.

Dr. Yang is a member of ASM International and the Electronic Device Failure Analysis Society. His recognitions include the 2011 IEEE International Conference on Plasma Science best student paper Award, the Gerald Holdridge Teaching Excellence Award from the University of Wisconsin-Madison, and the Engineering Service Scholar Award from the University of Utah.

Gaddi S. Haase received the Ph.D. degree in physical chemistry from the Hebrew University of Jerusalem, Israel, in 1989.

After post-doctoral research at Columbia University, New York, NY, USA, and at the University of Wisconsin, Madison, WI, USA, he became a professor at the Chemical Physics Department, the Weizmann Institute of Science, Israel. In 2001, He then moved to Texas Instruments, where he engaged in process development and novel materials reliability research. He then moved to Molecular Imprints (nano-imprint lithography) and later joined the Microsystems Science and Technology Center at Sandia National Laboratories, Albuquerque, NM, USA, in 2011. He has over 35 peer reviewed papers and one patent.

Edward I. Cole, Jr. (SM'13) received the Ph.D. degree in physics from the University of North Carolina, Chapel Hill, NC, USA, in 1987.

He joined the Failure Analysis Department of Sandia National Laboratories, Albuquerque, NM, USA, in 1987. His research interests are in the development and improvement of non-destructive IC failure analysis tools, with emphasis on electron and optical beam techniques.

Dr. Cole has led teams that have developed techniques, i.e., Charge-Induced Voltage Alteration (in 1995) and Light-Induced Voltage Alteration (in 1998), that have won R&D 100 awards. He has served on the executive and management committees of the ISTFA and IRPS conferences, chairing the ISTFA'96 and IRPS'07 events. He has served on the Electronic Device Failure Analysis Society (EDFAS) Board of Directors from 1998–2004 and was EDFAS President from 2000–2002. He is presently a past-editor of the EDFAS Societys magazine and serves on the IRPS Board of Directors and ASM Volunteerism committee. In 2013, he was appointed a Sandia Fellow and a Fellow of ASM International.

Paiboon Tangyunyong received the Ph.D. degree in engineering physics from Cornell University, Ithaca, NY, USA, in 1991.

In 1992, he joined Sandia National Labs, Albuquerque, NM, USA, where he worked in the area of surface science for two years. In 1994, he joined Sandias failure analysis department. He has worked extensively in developing and implementing SPM as a failure analysis tool, as well as the development of thermal and IR imaging for defect localization. His current research interest focuses on the development of several scanning laser-based techniques for defect localization. He has authored or co-authored over 55 technical papers (with eight invited papers and seven best or outstanding paper awards).

Paul J. Resnick received the B.S. and M.S. degrees in chemical engineering from the University of New Mexico, Albuquerque, NM, USA.

He is a MEMS process integration engineer at Sandia National Laboratories, Albuqueque, NM, USA, with 12 years of experience in silicon surface micromachining, bulk micromachining, and tungsten damascene microfabrication. He has related semiconductor processing experience in reactive ion etch, wet process, and supercritical fluid processes

Alice C. Kilgo photograph and biography not available at the time of publication.

Murat Okandan (M'98) received the Ph.D. degree in electrical engineering from Pennsylvania State University, University Park, PA, USA.

He is an electrical microsystems engineer at Sandia National Laboratories, Albuquerque, NM, USA. His work has focused on solid-state device physics, device design, microelectronics processing, and sensors. He has authored or co-authored over 30 technical publications, holds 12 patents, and has seven patents pending.

Gregory N. Nielson received the B.S. degree from Utah State University, Logan, UT, USA, and the M.S. and Ph.D. degrees from the Massachusetts Institute of Technology, Cambridge, MA, USA.

He is a Principal Member of Technical Staff at Sandia National Laboratories, Albuquerque, NM, USA. He has developed many unique optical MEMS technologies, including the first fully integrated wavelength selective optical MEMS switch and an ultrafast (225 ns) MEMS micromirror. He is an author on more than 40 publications and an inventor on over 30 patents or patent applications.

Dr. Nielson leads the "Microsystem-enabled Photovoltaic" project, which has received an SPIE Green Photonics Award, a Federal Laboratory Consortium Award, and an R&D 100 award.

Delta-Doping Effects on Quantum-Dot Solar Cells

Stephen J. Polly, *Student Member, IEEE*, David V. Forbes, *Member, IEEE*, Kristina Driscoll,
Staffan Hellström, *Member, IEEE*, and Seth M. Hubbard, *Member, IEEE*

Abstract—The effects of delta-doping InAs quantum-dot (QD)-enhanced GaAs solar cells were studied both through modeling and device experimentation. Delta doping of two, four, and eight electrons per QD, as well as nine holes per QD, was used in this study. It was observed that QD doping reduced Shockley–Read–Hall recombination in the QDs, which results in a reduced dark current and an improved open-circuit voltage over undoped QD devices. A voltage recovery of 121 mV was observed for the eight-electron sample compared with the undoped sample. QD doping had no positive effects on subbandgap photon collection but actually degraded bulk and QD response as doping levels were increased by limiting minority carrier collection through the QD region. Despite this, an absolute AM0 efficiency improvement of 1.41% was observed for the four-electron sample over the undoped QD device while maintaining a current enhancement.

Index Terms—InAs, delta doping, quantum dot (QD).

I. Introduction

THE use of InAs quantum dots (QDs) has become a proven method of increasing the photogenerated current density of GaAs solar cells through absorption and collection of subbandgap photons [1]–[3]. The ability to engineer the effective bandgap of a material has been of particular interest to the multijunction solar cell community, where an increase in current density of the middle (In)GaAs cell can significantly improve overall device efficiency [4]. Beyond bandgap engineering, QDs are a proposed method of achieving an intermediate band solar cell (IBSC), where a miniband of states exists in the normally forbidden region of the bandgap, allowing three distinct optical transitions [5], [6].

Further improvements in subgap collection efficiency may be possible by δ-doping the QDs, which provides carriers to partially fill the confined states so that they are more readily available for transitions into the conduction band continuum by photons with energies below the bandgap of the host. Through the introduction of delta doping, Sablon *et al.* have observed an increase in subgap current collection [7], while others have specifically observed carrier extraction via two-photon sequential absorption as opposed carrier escape through tunneling or

Manuscript received August 6, 2013; revised March 12, 2014; accepted March 29, 2014. This work was supported in part by the National Science Foundation (DMR-0955752), the Department of Energy (DE-FG36-08GO18012), the National Aeronautics and Space Administration (SAA3-844), and US Department of Education Graduate Assistance in Areas of National Need fellowship (P200A090225).

The authors are with the Rochester Institute of Technology, Rochester, NY 14623-5698 USA (e-mail: sjp5958@rit.edu; dvfsps@rit.edu; kmdsps@rit.edu; sdhnano@rit.edu; smhsps@rit.edu).

Color versions of one or more of the figures in this paper are available online at http://ieeexplore.ieee.org.

Digital Object Identifier 10.1109/JPHOTOV.2014.2316677

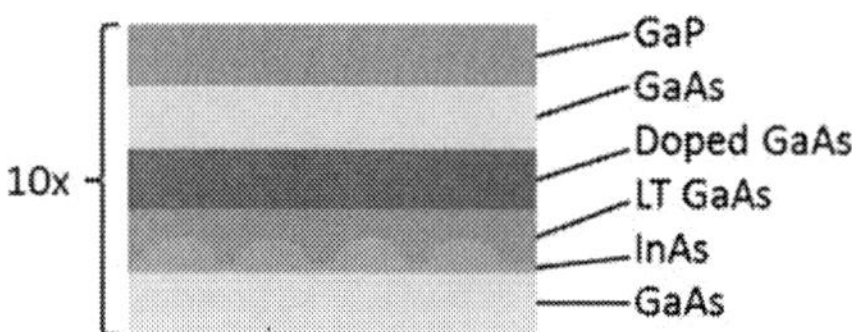

Fig. 1. Diagram (not to scale) of superlattice repeat unit incorporating UID GaAs, InAs QDs, intentionally doped GaAs, and GaP strain compensation.

interaction with a phonon—a requirement for the IBSC [8], [9]. Morioka *et al.* have also shown that flattening of the band structure caused by δ-doped QDs reduces Shockley–Read–Hall (SRH) recombination and dark current and should lead to an increase in photovoltage [10].

In this paper, GaAs *pin* solar cells incorporating ten-layer superlattice of GaP strain-compensated InAs QDs with and without various levels of silicon (n-type) and carbon (p-type) δ-doping were studied both through modeling and experimentation. It was shown that delta-doping reduced recombination in the QDs and resulted in more efficient devices by improving open-circuit voltage (V_{OC}) over undoped samples. No improvement was observed in subbandgap collection efficiency as a result of doping. At sufficiently high doping densities, collection efficiency in the QDs and the bulk was degraded due to reduced minority carrier collection efficiency through the QD region.

II. Sample Set and Experimental Setup

GaAs solar cells were grown by metal–organic vapor phase epitaxy (MOVPE) at the National Aeronautics and Space Administration (NASA) Glenn Research Center (GRC). The control device consisted of a *pin* design with a 100-nm *i*-region, incorporating InGaP$_2$ front and back surface fields. Further information on cell structure has been described in more detail elsewhere [11]. Devices incorporating QDs substituted a portion of the *i*-region with ten repeat units of a periodic structure shown in Fig. 1: first an unintentionally doped (UID) GaAs layer, followed by the InAs QDs grown by the Stranski–Krastanov method, then a low temperature (LT) UID GaAs capping layer, an intentionally doped GaAs layer, followed by a UID GaAs spacer layer, and finally, a GaP strain compensation layer [12]. In the undoped (0e$^-$/QD) sample, the doped GaAs layer was replaced with UID GaAs. The entirety of the QD region remained buffered on both sides between emitter and base by a region of intrinsic GaAs.

To determine how heavily to dope the QDs, the electronic band structure of the InAs QDs with and without doping was calculated using a conjugate gradients-based solver for the Poisson equation discretized by finite differences coupled to the eight-band k·p method, which is also discretized by finite differences [13]. The QDs were modeled as a hemisphere that is 16-nm wide and 2-nm high, within a 14-nm high simulation volume with periodic boundaries. All dimensions were taken from atomic force microscopy (AFM) measurements made on similar growth structures with a surface layer of uncapped QDs. The material parameters used in the model were obtained from well-established sources [14]. The model of the undoped QDs showed six bound electron states, one lower spin-pair, and two almost degenerate upper spin-paired states. Because of high hole effective mass, the calculated density of states for holes was large.

Doping was incorporated during growth in a layer approximately 0.5-nm thick with an areal density of Si or C equal to some multiple of the QD areal density measured previously by AFM as approximately $5 \times 10^{10}\,\mathrm{cm}^{-2}$. Here, the doping levels were chosen to equal two, four, and eight electrons per QD using silicon to partially fill and over fill the bound states, as well as a sample doped with carbon at nine holes per QD ($2e^-$/QD, $4e^-$/QD, $8e^-$/QD, $9h^+$/QD, respectively). This selection covered the range of what is possible given the limited number of confined states in the QDs. A precise determination of ideal partial filling fraction for a given system is discussed in [15]. Periodicity and strain of the samples were examined by symmetric high resolution x-ray diffraction about the (0 0 4) reflection, and were equivalent in all samples. Prior to final device growth, test structures were grown and analyzed using secondary ion mass spectroscopy (SIMS) to confirm periodic and controllable incorporation of dopant species.

Here, it should be noted that the diffusivity of silicon and the thermal budget necessary for the growth of the completed cell play an important role in the final dopant profile of the sample. The doping profile was calculated for a repeating period of delta doping, assuming a bulk GaAs medium using a solution for Fick's second law with a Gaussian distribution and fixed dopant population as shown in (1). Here, $N(x,t)$ is the doping profile as a function of position x and time t. The initial doping dose was Q, and a diffusivity value at the pertinent growth temperature D was taken from the literature [16]. This was a first-order approximation, ignoring any effects from the additional material systems (InAs, GaP) or strain that exists in the as-grown structure.

As calculated, the doping oscillated within an order of magnitude (about approximately 1×10^{17} cm^{-3}) throughout the superlattice, with peaks at the original doping locations and valleys near the QDs for what was originally ~4×10^{18} Si/cm^3 doping. Despite the simplistic nature of this model, the results agreed with the SIMS data, although the nature of diffusion may be exaggerated due to the granularity of the measurement technique. As the emitter and top InGaP$_2$ window layer of the devices were grown, the thermal energy was sufficient for the Si to diffuse out to some degree over the entire superlattice period, as can be seen in Fig. 2. The diffusion of carbon in the 9h+/QD sample was expected to be at least an order of magnitude less than silicon due to the decreased diffusivity of carbon in GaAs, but this was not measured via SIMS.

$$N(x,t) = \frac{Q}{\sqrt{\pi Dt}} \frac{e^{-\left(x/2\sqrt{Dt}\right)}}{2}. \tag{1}$$

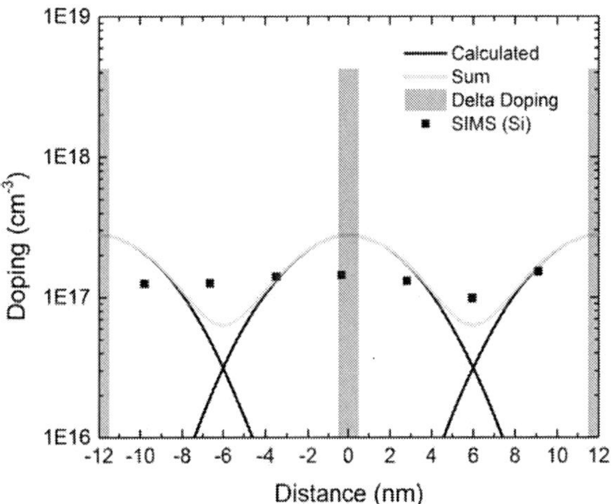

Fig. 2. Delta doping of silicon as-deposited (shaded region), compared with calculated (solid lines) and SIMS measured (squares) dopant profile after diffusion during growth of the remainder of the cell.

Cells were fabricated using standard photolithographic techniques, and a wet chemical mesa etch to isolate and define active areas of $1\,\mathrm{cm}^2$. Metallization for n-type contacts was Au/Ge/Ni/Au, and p-type was Au/Zn/Au, applied through a thermal evaporation and liftoff process. Antireflective coatings were not used in this study; contact grid shadowing was approximately 4%.

The 1-sun AM0 characterization was performed on a TS Space Systems dual-source close match solar simulator with a Keithley 2400 source meter, calibrated with cells provided by NASA GRC [17]. To determine dark diode behavior without the influence of series resistance, measurements of the short-circuit current (I_{SC}) and open-circuit voltage (V_{OC}) were taken at varying illumination levels using a Keithley 2400 under a quartz tungsten lamp array powered by a Sorensen DLM 80-7.5 power supply, all controlled using LabVIEW. External quantum efficiency (EQE) measurements were taken using a modified Gooch & Housego OL750 monochromator system.

III. Computational Modeling

Full devices were modeled using APSYS, a finite-element analysis software package developed by Crosslight. A previously created model with a good fit to experimental results was modified for the purposes of this study [18], [19]. Because of the diffusion of Si previously discussed, an average doping density was assumed for the silicon-doped samples rather than thin delta doped regions in the superlattice used for the carbon sample. The modeled band structure of the depletion region without illumination and at 0 V, applied bias is shown in Fig. 3 for the $0e^-$/QD and $4e^-$/QD devices. In this figure, as well as the remaining figures in this paper, the x-axis denoted as "Cell Depth" originates at the top of the contact layer above the front InGaP$_2$ window of the solar cell.

Typically, QDs are grown in a region of high electric field to quickly sweep carriers away from the nanostructures as soon

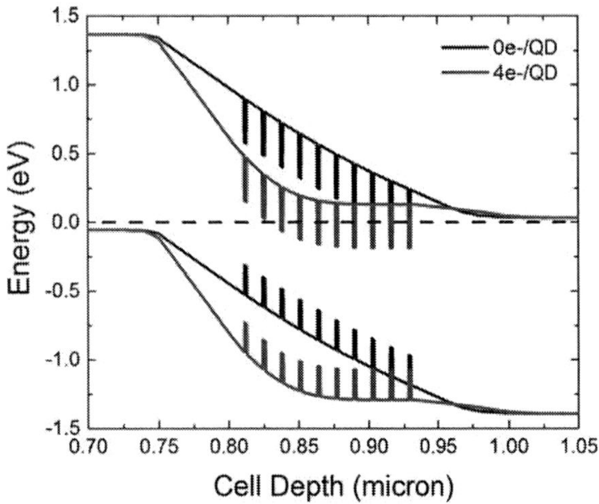

Fig. 3. APSYS modeled band diagram for 0e⁻/QD (black) and 4e⁻/QD (blue) structures in the dark at 0-V applied bias.

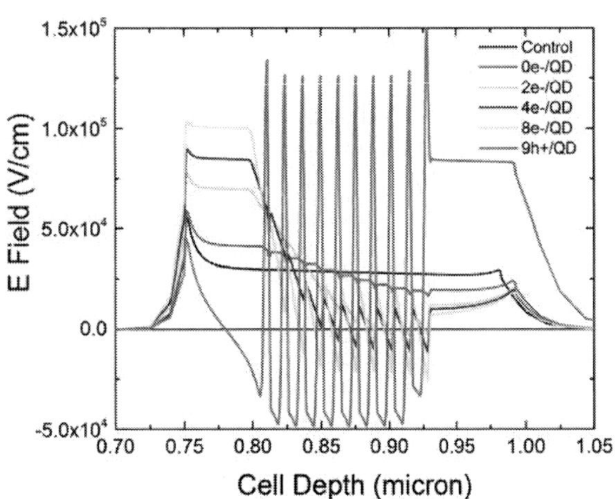

Fig. 4. APSYS modeled electric field for all samples in this study.

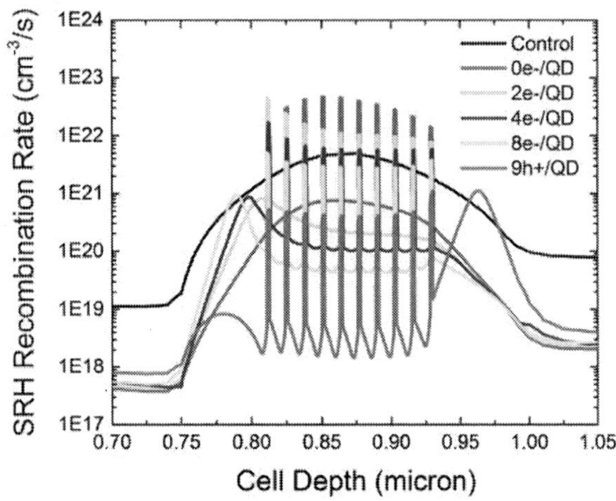

Fig. 5. APSYS modeled SRH recombination rates at 1.0-V applied bias across the i-region of varying delta-doping levels.

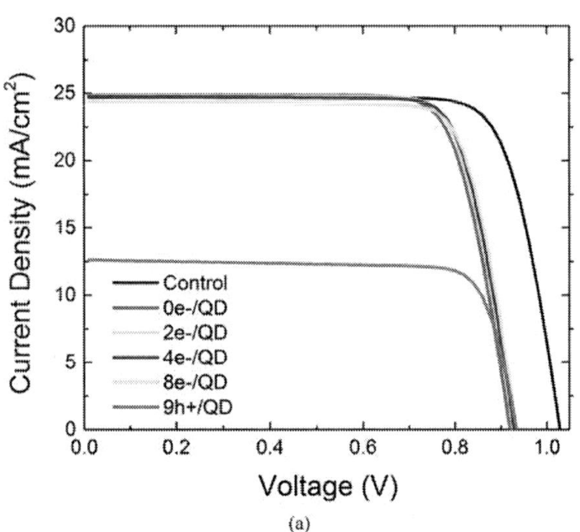

(a)

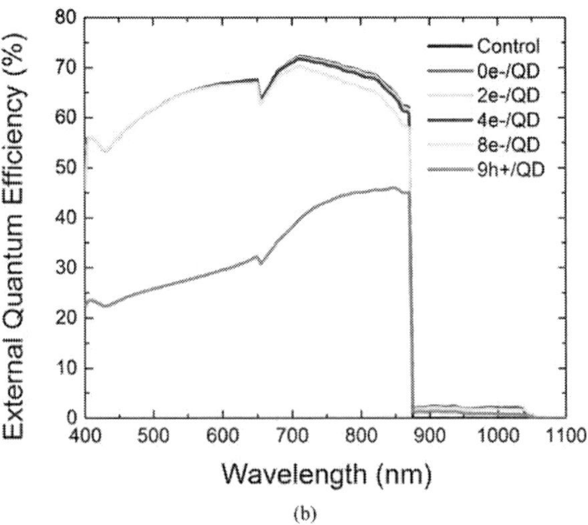

(b)

Fig. 6. (a) APSYS modeled 1-Sun AM0 J–V curves and (b) modeled EQE.

as they are excited into the bulk continuum. For purposes of bandgap engineering, this region has the additional benefit of increasing tunneling and thermal-assisted tunneling escape by the barrier narrowing due to the electric field, although this is not desirable for IBSC [20], [21]. The introduction of dopant flattened the band structure containing the QDs by shifting the peak of the electric field toward the p-type emitter or n-type base, for electron or hole delta doping, respectively. Calculated electric field strength is shown in Fig. 4, which is discussed further in Section IV.

A consequence of this shift in the electric field through the addition of doping can be seen in Fig. 5, showing the modeled SRH recombination rate at 1.0 V applied bias. The control (black), which contained no nanostructures, peaked in SRH recombination at the center of the i-region, at a depth of approximately 0.875 μm. As the InAs superlattice was incorporated into the model (red), recombination in the bulk was reduced as a consequence of strong recombination in the InAs itself, which is

	J_{SC} (mA/cm2)	V_{OC} (mV)	FF (%)	Eff (%)
Control	24.69	1027	81.45	15.12
0e-/QD	24.87	917	71.50	11.94
2e-/QD	24.85	923	73.01	12.26
4e-/QD	24.75	927	73.37	12.32
8e-/QD	24.38	932	73.77	12.27
9h+/QD	12.62	929	74.87	6.43

seen as ten distinct narrow regions of increased recombination. By introducing n-type dopant, the electric field shifted toward the p-type emitter, reducing the SRH recombination in the QD region while increasing it in the intrinsic buffer layer between the QDs and emitter (here, between approximately 0.75 and 0.8 μm). This trend continued as the doping level was increased. The introduction of p-type dopant had a similar effect, although the electric field was shifted in the opposite direction toward the base, and the effect of SRH reduction was increased due to the more delta-like doping density.

The reduction in SRH recombination led directly to an increase in V_{OC} for doped devices as compared with 0e$^-$/QD. This can be seen in the modeled J–V curves under 1-Sun AM0 in Fig. 6(a). Following the trend in SRH recombination, as InAs was introduced, V_{OC} decreased from the control value of 1027 to 917 mV. As n-type dopant is added at values of 2, 4, and 8e$^-$/QD, V_{OC} increased to 923, 927, and 932 mV, respectively. For 9h$^+$/QD doping, the V_{OC} improved to 929 mV as compared with the 0e$^-$/QD modeled result. Further consequences of dopant incorporation were seen in the short-circuit current density (J_{SC}) of these calculations. As shown in Table I, doping levels of 0, 2, and 4e$^-$/QD showed expected J_{SC} improvement over the control device due to subbandgap collection, but doped samples showed a reduction of J_{SC}, as compared with 0e$^-$/QD. At the highest electron doping level, J_{SC} began to degrade significantly. This effect was considerably larger in the 9h$^+$/QD device, which produced current densities half the magnitude of the control cell. The source of this reduction in J_{SC} can be seen in Fig. 6(b), showing EQE of the modeled devices. As n-type dopant was increased, the response of the cell between approximately 600 and 870 nm began to degrade, which can be seen most easily in the 8e$^-$/QD case. For p-type QD doping, short- and long-wavelength response was affected. This effect is discussed in the following section.

IV. RESULTS AND DISCUSSION

Representative experimental J–V curves of these devices are shown in Fig. 7, with specific characteristics shown in Table II. Under 1-sun AM0 characterization, trends were similar to the model predictions. At 2e$^-$/QD, the V_{OC} was improved 63 mV on average (across seven samples) over the 0e$^-$/QD sample, while the increased 4e$^-$/QD and 8e$^-$/QD doping furthered this average increase to 71 and 121 mV, respectively. These results show considerably larger voltage recovery as compared with

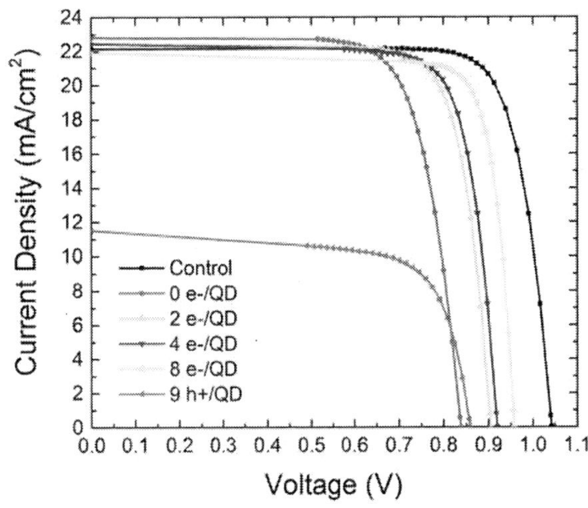

Fig. 7.   Measured 1-Sun AM0 J–V characteristics of devices.

the model predictions, although the largest difference is in the 0e$^-$/QD case. The model may be under-predicting the recombination effects caused by the insertion of InAs, which was later mitigated by the addition of localized doping. Samples with two and four electrons per QD showed absolute AM0 efficiency improvements of 1.25% and 1.41%, respectively, over the undoped QD cells. The 8e$^-$/QD sample continued to improve in efficiency but suffered a significant loss in J_{SC} below that of the 0e$^-$/QD sample, and the 9h$^+$/QD suffered efficiency losses compared with the 0e$^-$/QD sample due to severe loss of J_{SC}.

To further explore the voltage recovery, the $J_{SC} - V_{OC}$ technique was used, measuring J_{SC} and V_{OC} at increasing levels of illumination to create a dark-J–V-like curve without the influence of series resistance. The data were taken up to current densities of approximately 2 suns and were fit using a standard single-diode model about the 1-sun current density, over at least 30 data points with a delta of ~0.015 suns between points. The results of these fits, extracted as dark current densities and ideality factors, are shown in Table II. The range of measurement was not wide enough to observe transitions in recombination mechanisms, which would require testing under higher concentration.

Two-minority carrier recombination typical in the space charge region (SCR) region of the diode through capture and recombination via QD states is indicated by an ideality factor near 2. As n-type dopant was added, the band structure containing the QDs flattened and single-minority carrier recombination became dominant, as indicated by the reduction in both ideality factor and dark current.

The EQE measurements of the sample set are shown in Fig. 8(a). While bulk collection between the control 0e$^-$/QD and 2e$^-$/QD samples are nearly identical, as doping increases, the devices begin to degrade in performance, as predicted by the model. Specifically, increased n-type doping caused degradation of long-wavelength response, while the heavily doped p-type sample shows degradation throughout the spectrum.

TABLE II
EXPERIMENTALLY DETERMINED FIGURES OF MERIT FOR DOPED SAMPLES

Sample	J_{SC} (mA/cm2)	V_{OC} (mV)	FF (%)	Eff (%)	Dark Current (A/cm^2)	Ideality Factor	Integrated J_{SC} (350 nm – 1100 nm) (mA/cm^2)	Integrated J_{SC} (880 nm – 1100 nm) (mA/cm^2)
Control	22.15	1040	80.99	13.66	1.13×10^{-18}	1.08	22.97	0.079
0e-/QD	22.82	837	75.05	10.49	1.89×10^{-10}	1.77	23.62	0.291
2e-/QD	22.48	905	78.81	11.74	9.19×10^{-13}	1.45	23.76	0.298
4e-/QD	22.43	919	78.89	11.9	2.86×10^{-15}	1.2	23.45	0.289
8e-/QD	21.9	958	81.88	12.58	3.35×10^{-17}	1.09	22.91	0.265
9h+/QD	11.5	859	69.45	5.02	3.19×10^{-10}	1.9	10.33	0.136

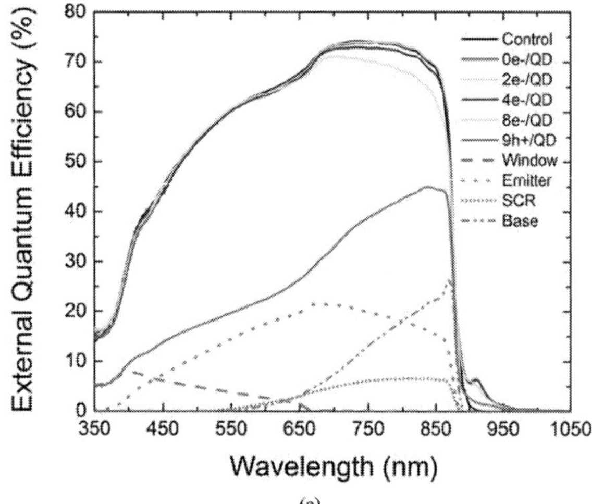

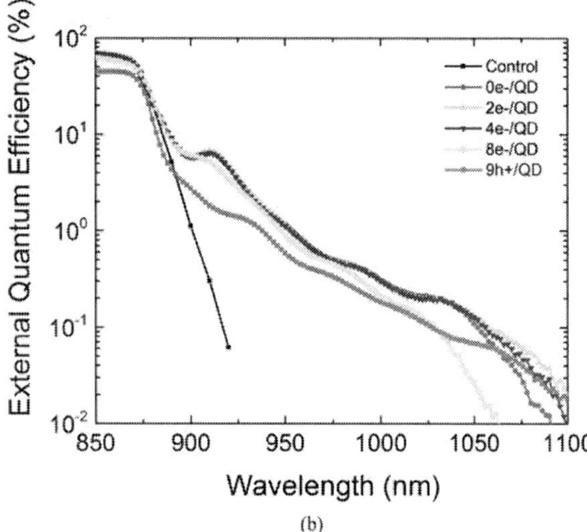

Fig. 8. External quantum efficiency measurements of devices in (a) bulk, also showing calculated regional collection through a fit from Hovel drift-diffusion model of 9h$^+$/QD sample, and (b) subbandgap regions.

Subbandgap collection experienced a similar trend to that of the bulk. Fig. 8(b) shows a semi-log plot of the subbandgap EQE of QD devices as compared with a GaAs control. To understand the current contribution of the QDs, these data were integrated against AM0, both in the full range of the measurement (350–1100 nm) and subgap, where only QDs collect (880–1100 nm). These results can be seen in Table II. The 0, 2, and 4e$^-$/QD devices showed improved total current density over the GaAs control and performed nearly identically for wavelengths below the bandgap. As doping was increased to 8e$^-$/QD, the subbandgap collection began to noticeably degrade.

The source of the degradation in bulk EQE can be explained in term of minority carrier collection. The n-type delta doping caused the overall doping in the QD portion of the i-region to approach, and in the case of 8e$^-$/QD sample, exceed the nominal doping of the n-type base. This changed the structure from pin to pin^+in, with an n^+-type region between two intrinsic buffers. This created two compounding impediments to minority holes generated in the n-type base region from collection at the junction. The first can be described without the inclusion of InAs nanostructures. Through the creation of a pin^+in structure, a potential barrier was established between the delta-doped region and the base, reflecting some minority holes back into the base and limiting their collection. Holes able to pass this barrier then encountered a region with little to no electric field to promote drift across the junction.

The second impediment was due to the charged QD, and was explained through the k·p model. To emulate the effect of a charged QD, the Fermi level inside the dot was set to a value higher than the two lower bound states, which led the coupled Schrödinger–Poisson solver to produce a local potential modification due to the electron wavefunction. This was equivalent to doping the dot with two electrons. The band bowing close to the dot due to this charging is shown in Fig. 9. As a QD was charged with electrons through doping, the local band structure at the QD shifted up to create a potential barriers at the borders of the QD to further electron capture in the conduction band but, as a consequence, created a potential well inviting hole capture in the valence band. This effect was also explored in [7]. As this individual effect was coupled in a ten-layer superlattice, it

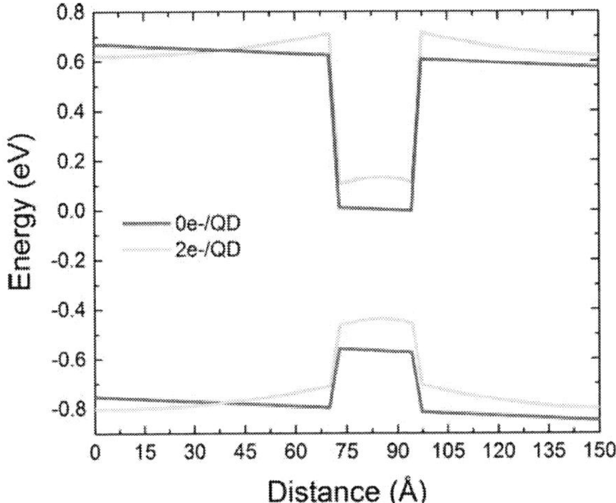

Fig. 9.   k•p modeled band structure of a single QD with and without captured charge.

formed a periodic oscillation in local electric field. Any minority holes passing the potential barrier first discussed must then cross a region of hole-depleted QDs fixed in an electric field oscillating positive and negative about 0 V/cm, where they may recombine and detract from the photocurrent. This oscillation can be seen on a more global scale in the APSYS simulated electric field shown in Fig. 4.

These results can be further quantified through the drift-diffusion model presented by Hovel and Woodall [22]. The reduction in long-wavelength collection through n-type QD doping can be explained in terms of a reduced effective minority carrier lifetime in the base. The base itself was not actually affected, but minority carriers generated there experienced reduced collection efficiency at the junction, as previously explained. A similar argument holds for hole doping. The device structure was then pip^+in, and the QDs were charged with holes, encouraging minority electrons to leave the emitter to be captured and recombine in the QD region, again subtracting from photocurrent.

An example fit using this model is shown in Fig. 8(a) for the $9h^+$/QD sample sectioning out the contribution to total EQE from the window layer, emitter, SCR, and base. Here, the minority electron lifetime in the emitter, fit as approximately 200 ps in both the control and $0e^-$/QD devices, was fit as approximately 15 ps for the $9h^+$/QD sample: more than an order of magnitude lower. For n-type doping, minority hole lifetime in the base remained approximately 15 ns for control, $0e^-$/QD and $2e^-$/QD samples but was reduced to fits of 5 and 1.3 ns for the 4 and $8e^-$/QD samples, respectively. As the effective minority carrier lifetime decreased, the number of carriers collected by the junction was reduced, and the photogenerated current density reduced with them.

Looking back to subbandgap collection, it can be seen in Fig. 8(b) that at doping levels of two and four electrons per QD, there was very little change in subgap collection compared with the undoped sample, despite the significant impacts on both the

overall electric field and local band structure shown previously. This suggests that the effective increase in barrier height caused by charging of QDs, and the reduction in local electric field, does not affect carrier extraction and collection at room temperature for QDs that are partially filled with electrons, where thermal escape is expected to be dominant for the confined states studied here [23].

At the highest electron doping level, the subbandgap current collection did begin to reduce, most significantly at the ground state transition. This may be due to an increased barrier height from further QD charging, or may speak to the carrier doping efficiency. If the ground state of the QD was saturated with electrons, a single photon corresponding to the ground state energy gap had nowhere to which to excite an electron, and the QD would be transparent to that photon energy. As this only occurred at the highest electron doping level, fewer electrons may have charged the QDs than was anticipated from the doping level incorporated during growth.

These results show promise both from the perspective of bandgap engineering and the IBSC. For either case, the introduction of dopant reduced SRH recombination in the QDs, allowing for larger V_{OC}, as compared with undoped cells. Additionally, by keeping the quanta of per-QD doping less than the total number of confined states, there was no negative impact on subbandgap collection. Because of the high thermal escape rate, additional experimentation at low temperature or high light concentration is necessary to explore conditions where evidence of a two-photon carrier extraction mechanism, as required for the IBSC, can be shown. Experimentation under concentration may allow for saturation of recombination pathways through higher injection of carriers, resulting in recovery of bulk-EQE loss for the heavily doped samples. This would also allow an extension of the $J_{SC} - V_{OC}$ analysis and further study of recombination mechanisms. Concentration may ultimately show improved efficiency for QD devices over the control, but that is beyond the scope of this paper.

V. Conclusion

The incorporation of delta doping in the barrier region of an InAs QD superlattice was investigated by both modeling and experimentation. The addition of doping flattened the band structure near the QDs, removing them from an area of highest electric field and, consequently, highest SRH recombination. This caused a decrease in the dark recombination current and ideality factor, which results in increased V_{OC} and ultimately increased efficiency, as compared with undoped QDs for samples doped with two or four electrons per QD. As doping levels approach and exceed the number of available confined states, minority carrier collection is affected, which causes a decrease in bulk EQE.

Acknowledgment

The authors would like to thank Z. Bittner and M. Slocum for their thoughtful insight on this work.

REFERENCES

[1] Y. Shoji, K. Akimoto, and Y. Okada, "Self-organized InGaAs/GaAs quantum dot arrays for use in high-efficiency intermediate-band solar cells," *J. Phys. D, Appl. Phys.*, vol. 46, no. 2, pp. 024002–024009, Jan. 2013.

[2] A. Luque, P. G. Linares, E. Antolín, I. Ramiro, C. D. Farmer, E. Hernández, I. Tobías, C. R. Stanley, and A. Martí, "Understanding the operation of quantum dot intermediate band solar cells," *J. Appl. Phys.*, vol. 111, no. 4, pp. 044502-1–044502-12, Feb. 2012.

[3] C. G. Bailey, D. V. Forbes, S. J. Polly, Z. S. Bittner, Y. Dai, C. Mackos, R. P. Raffaelle, and S. M. Hubbard, "Open-circuit voltage improvement of InAs/GaAs quantum-dot solar cells using reduced InAs coverage," *IEEE J. Photovoltaics*, vol. 2, no. 3, pp. 269–275, Jul. 2012.

[4] C. Kerestes, S. Polly, D. Forbes, C. Bailey, A. Podell, J. Spann, P. Patel, B. Richards, P. Sharps, and S. Hubbard, "Fabrication and analysis of multijunction solar cells with a quantum dot (In)GaAs junction," *Progress Photovoltaics, Res. Appl.*, 2013.

[5] A. Luque and A. Martí, "Increasing the efficiency of ideal solar cells by photon induced transitions at intermediate levels," *Phys. Rev. Lett.*, vol. 78, no. 26, pp. 5014–5017, Jun. 1997.

[6] A. Martí, L. Cuadra, and A. Luque, "Partial filling of a quantum dot intermediate band for solar cells," *IEEE Trans. Electron. Devices*, vol. 48, no. 10, pp. 2394–2399, Oct. 2001.

[7] K. A. Sablon, J. W. Little, V. Mitin, A. Sergeev, N. Vagidov, and K. Reinhardt, "Strong enhancement of solar cell efficiency due to quantum dots with built-in charge," *Nano Lett.*, vol. 11, no. 6, pp. 2311–2317, 2011.

[8] E. Antolin, A. Marti, P. G. Linares, I. Ramiro, E. Hernandez, C. D. Farmer, C. R. Stanley, and A. Luque, "Advances in quantum dot intermediate band solar cells," in *Proc. IEEE 35th Photovoltaic Spec. Conf.*, 2010, pp. 000065–000070.

[9] Y. Okada, T. Morioka, K. Yoshida, R. Oshima, Y. Shoji, T. Inoue, and T. Kita, "Increase in photocurrent by optical transitions via intermediate quantum states in direct-doped InAs/GaNAs strain-compensated quantum dot solar cell," *J. Appl. Phys.*, vol. 109, no. 2, pp. 024301–024305, Jan. 2011.

[10] T. Morioka and Y. Okada, "Dark current characteristics of InAs/GaNAs strain-compensated quantum dot solar cells," *Physica E: Low-Dimensional Syst. Nanostruct.*, vol. 44, no. 2, pp. 390–393, Nov. 2011.

[11] S. M. Hubbard, A. Podell, C. Mackos, S. Polly, C. G. Bailey, and D. V. Forbes, "Effect of vicinal substrates on the growth and device performance of quantum dot solar cells," *Sol. Energy Mater. Sol. Cells*, vol. 108, pp. 256–262, Jan. 2013.

[12] C. G. Bailey, S. M. Hubbard, D. V. Forbes, and R. P. Raffaelle, "Evaluation of strain balancing layer thickness for InAs/GaAs quantum dot arrays using high resolution x-ray diffraction and photoluminescence," *Appl. Phys. Lett.*, vol. 95, no. 20, pp. 203110-1–203110-3, Nov. 2009.

[13] O. Stier, M. Grundmann, and D. Bimberg, "Electronic and optical properties of strained quantum dots modeled by 8-band k·p theory," *Phys. Rev. B*, vol. 59, no. 8, pp. 5688–5701, Feb. 1999.

[14] I. Vurgaftman, J. R. Meyer, and L. R. Ram-Mohan, "Band parameters for III–V compound semiconductors and their alloys," *J. Appl. Phys.*, vol. 89, no. 11, pp. 5815–5875, Jun. 2001.

[15] A. Luque and A. Martí. "On the partial filling of the intermediate band in IB solar cells," *IEEE Trans. Electron. Devices*, vol. 57, no. 6, pp. 1201–1207, Jun. 2010.

[16] E. F. Schubert, J. B. Stark, T. H. Chiu, and B. Tell, "Diffusion of atomic silicon in gallium arsenide," *Appl. Phys. Lett.*, vol. 53, no. 4, pp. 293–295, Jul. 1988.

[17] S. J. Polly, Z. S. Bittner, M. F. Bennett, R. P. Raffaelle, and S. M. Hubbard, "Development of a multi-source solar simulator for spatial uniformity and close spectral matching to AM0 and AM1.5," in *Proc. IEEE 37th Photovoltaic Spec. Conf.*, 2011, pp. 001739–001743.

[18] K. Driscoll and S. Hubbard, "Modeling the optical and electrical response of nanostructured III–V solar cells," in *Proc. IEEE 38th Photovoltaic Spec. Conf.*, 2012, pp. 002985–002989.

[19] K. Driscoll, M. Bennett, S. Polly, D. V. Forbes, and S. M. Hubbard, "Investigation of the design parameters of quantum dot enhanced III–V solar cells," *Proc. SPIE*, vol. 8620, pp. 86200L-1–86200L-7, 2013.

[20] Y. Dai, C. G. Bailey, C. Kerestes, D. V. Forbes, and S. M. Hubbard, "Investigation of carrier escape mechanism in InAs/GaAs quantum dot solar cells," in *Proc. IEEE 38th Photovoltaic Spec. Conf.*, 2012, pp. 000039–000044.

[21] A. Alemu and A. Freundlich, "Resonant thermotunneling design for high-performance single-junction quantum-well solar cells," *IEEE J. Photovoltaics*, vol. 2, no. 3, pp. 256–260, Jul. 2012.

[22] H. J. Hovel and J. M. Woodall, "The effect of depletion region recombination currents on the efficiencies of Si and GaAs solar cells," presented at the 10th IEEE Photovolt. Specialist Conf., 1973, pp. 25–30.

[23] Y. Dai, S. Hellstroem, S. Polly, J. Hatakeyama, D. Forbes, and S. Hubbard, "Optical study of carrier transport in inas/gaas quantum dots solar cell," presented at the IEEE 39th Photovoltaic Spec. Conf., Tampa, FL, USA, 2013.

Stephen J. Polly (S'09) received the B.S. degree in microelectronic engineering from the Rochester Institute of Technology, Rochester, NY, USA, in 2009, where he is currently working toward the Ph.D. degree in microsystems engineering as a Department of Education GAANN Fellow.

He has performed research primarily on III-V nanostructured solar cells in the Photovoltaics team of the NanoPower Research Laboratory since 2007, and in that time, he has contributed to over 35 conference and journal publications.

David V. Forbes (M'12) received the Ph.D. degree in materials science and engineering from the University of Illinois-Urbana, Urbana, IL, USA, in 1995.

He has held positions as a Senior Member of Technical Staff with TRW, Director of Epitaxy with Alfalight, and Chief Scientist with Essential Research. Since 2008, he has been a Research Faculty member with the Rochester Institute of Technology, Rochester, NY, USA, developing nanostructured photovoltaic devices. His background includes epitaxial growth and characterization of IIIV materials for optoelectronics and photovoltaics. He has contributed to more than 50 technical publications and conference proceedings.

Kristina Driscoll studied electrical engineering at Boston University, Boston, MA, USA, and received the Ph.D. degree in 2009 from the Semiconductor Photonics Laboratory under the supervision of Prof. R. Paiella.

After receiving the Ph.D. degree, she was a Postdoctoral Researcher with the Cavendish Laboratory, University of Cambridge, Cambridge, U.K, during 2009–2011. She joined the Rochester Institute of Technology, Rochester, NY, USA, in 2012, where she is currently a Lecturer with the School of Physics and Astronomy.

Staffan Hellström (M'14) received the Ph.D. degree in theoretical chemistry from the Royal Institute of Technology, Stockholm, Sweden, in 2012.

He is currently a Postdoctoral Research Fellow with the Photovoltaics team of the NanoPower Research Laboratory, Rochester Institute of Technology, Rochester, NY, USA. His background includes numerical calculations of quantum dot optoelectronic devices.

Seth M. Hubbard (S'99–M'06) received the Ph.D. degree in electrical engineering from the University of Michigan, Ann Arbor, MI, USA, in 2005. His doctoral research consisted of studying the effects of materials properties and epitaxial device design on GaN heterojunction field effect transistors grown using vapor phase epitaxy.

He is currently an Associate Professor of physics and microsystems engineering with the Rochester Institute of Technology (RIT), Rochester, NY, USA. He currently leads the NanoPower Research Laboratory Photovoltaics team, working on the epitaxial growth, fabrication, and characterization of nanostructured solar photovoltaic devices. He has contributed to over 100 journal and conference publications on electronic and photovoltaic devices. Prior to RIT, he was a National Research Council (NRC) Postdoctoral Research Associate with NASA Glenn Research Center.

Dr. Hubbard serves as an Associate Editor of the IEEE JOURNAL OF PHOTOVOLTAICS and as part of the organizing committee of the IEEE Photovoltaics Specialist Conference. He received the National Science Foundation CAREER award in 2009.

414

CIGS Cells and Modules With High Efficiency on Glass and Flexible Substrates

Michael Powalla, Wolfram Witte, Philip Jackson, Stefan Paetel, Erwin Lotter, Roland Wuerz,
Friedrich Kessler, Carsten Tschamber, Wolfram Hempel, Dimitrios Hariskos, Richard Menner,
Andreas Bauer, Stefanie Spiering, Erik Ahlswede, Theresa Magorian Friedlmeier,
David Blázquez-Sánchez, Ines Klugius, and Wiltraud Wischmann

Abstract—Thin-film solar cells based on $Cu(In,Ga)(Se,S)_2$ (CIGS) have demonstrated both high efficiencies and a high cost-reduction potential in industrial production. This way, future CIGS module production lines can be profitable even for scales below the GW range. Among the different technologies, only the coevaporation method has demonstrated efficiencies above 20%, approaching the record values of polycrystalline Si cells. The main focus of this contribution is on the new results of the ZSW cell line with efficiencies above 20%, as well as on the mini-module line on glass substrates. Mini modules (10 cm $\times$ 10 cm) with efficiencies in the range of 17% give a proof of concept for industrial-sized modules. ZSW is also developing flexible cells and modules, transferring the processes from the glass-based technology. We achieved 18.6% cell efficiency on metal substrates and a 15.4% efficient mini module could be demonstrated with adapted methods of module patterning. In order to develop industrially relevant processes for foils, we are running a roll-to-roll deposition plant. Additionally, we have improved CIGS cell efficiencies with alternative buffers to certified 19.0% for solution-grown $Zn(O,S)$, to 16.4% for sputtered $Zn(O,S)$, and 17.1% for evaporated In_2S_3. Our cells deposited by vacuum-free methods exhibit an efficiency of 8.5% with a nanoparticle-based process.

Index Terms—Buffer layers, CIGS, coevaporation, modules, nonvacuum deposition, roll-to-roll, solar cells.

I. INTRODUCTION

OVER the past three years, a strong consolidation has been transforming the photovoltaic (PV) market. On the one hand, the world's cumulative solar PV capacity surpassed 100 GW_p in 2012, with a growth of ca. 31 GW_p in 2012 [1]. On the other hand, artificially low prices due to a worldwide overcapacity have driven many PV companies to reorganize or

Manuscript received June 21, 2013; revised August 9, 2013; accepted August 22, 2013. Date of publication October 21, 2013; date of current version December 16, 2013. This work was supported by the European Commission, the German Federal Ministries of Education and Research (BMBF), for the Environment, Nature Conservation and Nuclear Safety (BMU), and of Economics and Technology (BMWi) under various contracts.

The authors are with the Zentrum für Sonnenenergie- und Wasserstoff-Forschung Baden-Württemberg (ZSW), 70565 Stuttgart, Germany (e-mail: michael.powalla@zsw-bw.de; wolfram.witte@zsw-bw.de; philip.jackson@zsw-bw.de; stefan.paetel@zsw-bw.de; erwin.lotter@zsw-bw.de; roland.wuerz@zsw-bw.de; friedrich.kessler@zsw-bw.de; carsten.tschamber@zsw-bw.de; wolfram.hempel@zsw-bw.de; dimitrios.hariskos@zsw-bw.de; richard.menner@zsw-bw.de; andreas.bauer@zsw-bw.de; stefanie.spiering@zsw-bw.de; erik.ahlswede@zsw-bw.de; theresa.friedlmeier@zsw-bw.de; david.blazquez@zsw-bw.de; ines.klugius@zsw-bw.de; wiltraud.wischmann@zsw-bw.de).

Color versions of one or more of the figures in this paper are available online at http://ieeexplore.ieee.org.

Digital Object Identifier 10.1109/JPHOTOV.2013.2280468

TABLE I
SMALL-AREA CIGS CHAMPION CELLS WITH CDS AND ZN(O,S) BUFFER LAYERS. ALL EFFICIENCY VALUES η ARE WITH ANTIREFLECTIVE COATING (ARC)

Buffer	Method	η [%]	Institute	Year	Reference
CdS	CBD	20.4 cert.	EMPA	2013	[3]
CdS	CBD	20.3 cert.	ZSW	2011	[4]
CdS	CBD	20.0 cert.	NREL	2008	[5]
CdS	CBD	19.8 cert.	Solibro	2013	[6]
CdS	CBD	19.4 cert.	HZB	2011	[7]
CdS	CBD	19.4 a. a.	AIST	2013	[8]
Zn(O,S)	CBD	19.7 cert.	Solar Frontier	2013	[9]
Zn(O,S)	CBD	19.1	ZSW	2012	[10]
Zn(O,S)	CBD	18.6 cert.	NREL/ AGU	2003	[11]
Zn(O,S)	CBD	18.5	NREL	2012	[12]
Zn(O,S)	CBD	18.4	AGU	2013	[13]
Zn(O,S)	ALCVD	18.5 cert.	ÅSC	2006	[14]
Zn(O,S)	sputtering	18.3 cert.	HZB	2013	[15]

CBD: Chemical bath deposition.
ALCVD: Atomic layer chemical vapor deposition.
a. a.: active area.
EMPA: Swiss Federal Laboratories for Material Testing and Research, Dübendorf, Switzerland.
NREL: National Renewable Energy Laboratory, Golden, CO, USA.
HZB: Helmholtz-Zentrum Berlin für Materialien und Energie, Berlin, Germany.
AIST: National Institute of Advanced Industrial Science and Technology, Tsukuba, Ibaraki, Japan.
AGU: Aoyama Gakuin University, Sagamihara, Kanagawa, Japan.
ÅSC: Ångström Solar Center, Uppsala, Sweden.

even to file for bankruptcy. Because of low system prices on the market and the strong decrease of the module prices, only high-efficiency modules with low production costs will be competitive in the future. The $Cu(In,Ga)Se_2$ (CIGS) technology with its high efficiency potential comparable with polycrystalline wafer technology, has entered the GW market in this time frame. In the years 2010–2012, 1.5 GW_p CIGS modules were installed. Because of the excessive investment of the Chinese Si-based PV industry, the installation of CIGS modules decreased from 688 MW_p in 2011 to 516 MW_p in 2012 [2].

For the future development of CIGS, it is very important that the high efficiency potential from the lab can be quickly transferred to industrial production. It is very encouraging that efficiency values in the 19%–20% range are now reached by several groups around the world as listed in Table I. A remarkable progress has been made from 2011 to 2013 for CIGS cells with CdS as well as with $Zn(O,S)$ buffer layers. So far, the efficiency level above 20% is only reached for CIGS cells with CdS grown by chemical bath deposition (CBD).

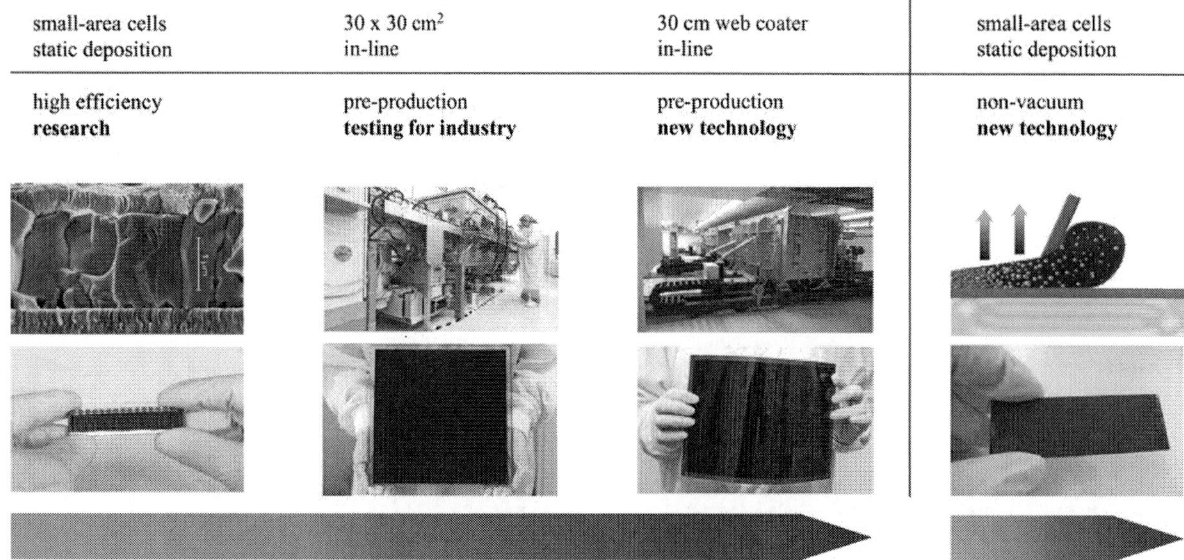

Fig. 1.   Development strategy at ZSW transferring results from laboratory processes to preproduction qualification.

Analyzing the operational expenditure (OPEX) of CIGS production, it can be demonstrated that it is possible to reach 0.55 $/W$_p$ by optimizing and harmonizing a production line even at capacities well below the GW region [16], [17]. The main impacts on OPEX are variable costs (65%) and depreciation (31%) and only 4% are due to personnel cost. Over 65% of the variable costs are driven by material costs like the glass, CIGS material, sputter targets, etc. Analyzing the depreciation, over 60% of capital expenditure (CAPEX) is related to the film deposition equipment.

To achieve these values and to further improve them, it is very important to have a long- and short-term research strategy as illustrated in Fig. 1. At ZSW, we run a development baseline for small cells with static deposition processes to exploit the whole efficiency potential of the CIGS technology. In parallel, we are transferring the consolidated findings to our preproduction line. After qualification in our in-line equipment for substrate sizes up to 30 cm × 30 cm, the knowledge and processes are finally tested at the Manz AG innovation line in Schwäbisch Hall, Germany. Furthermore, we are operating a preproduction web coater to qualify the developments on flexible substrates and roll-to-roll compatible processes. On the long-term time scale, nonvacuum coating processes like printing have the potential to further reduce costs in the future. ZSW is, therefore, running a nonvacuum CIGS cell line to initially qualify inks and develop high-efficiency processes. We are also testing alternative absorber materials like kesterites in combination with low-cost processing.

II. High-Efficiency CIGS Cells and Modules on Glass

A. Improvement of Small-Area Cells

The basis for the transfer of a new technology to industry is a thorough understanding of the core processes involved. For

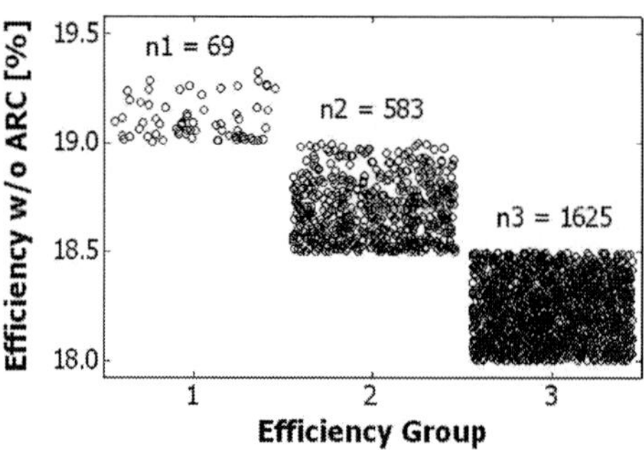

Fig. 2.   Process statistics of the ZSW high-efficiency production line with the number n of cells for each efficiency group. No ARC has been applied to the cells.

this reason, we run a small-area cell production line that has its focus precisely on the highest efficiency cells and a fundamental understanding of this technology. However, reliable parameter correlations in CIGS experimental research are hard to establish due to the variability of the material system. In addition, experimental phenomena observed on a medium-efficiency level often do not prove to be applicable on a high-efficiency level. This fact and the goal of further exploiting this promising technology make it necessary for us to employ a CIGS production line on the highest efficiency level possible.

We have established a procedure that will allow us to reproduce our top efficiency results not only once but on a regular basis. Fig. 2 shows the process statistics of the ZSW high-efficiency line segmented into three efficiency groups (60 cells with an area $A = 0.5$ cm^2 are produced with each CIGS run). Up to now, we have been able to produce a number of $n_3 = 1625$ CIGS cells with an efficiency between 18.0% and 18.5%, $n_2 = 583$ cells between 18.5% and 19.0%, and $n_1 = 69$ cells with an efficiency of 19.0% or more [all without

416

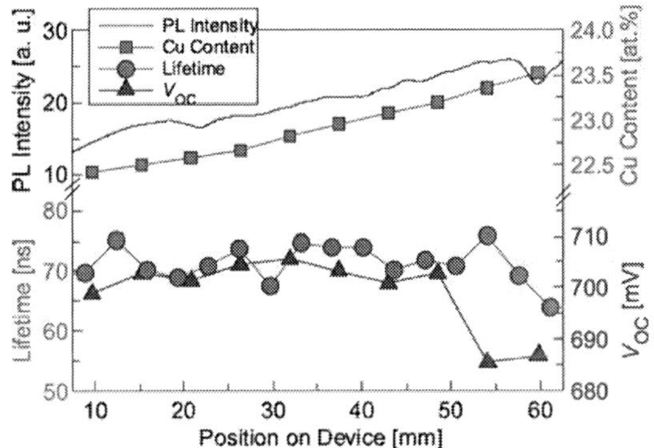

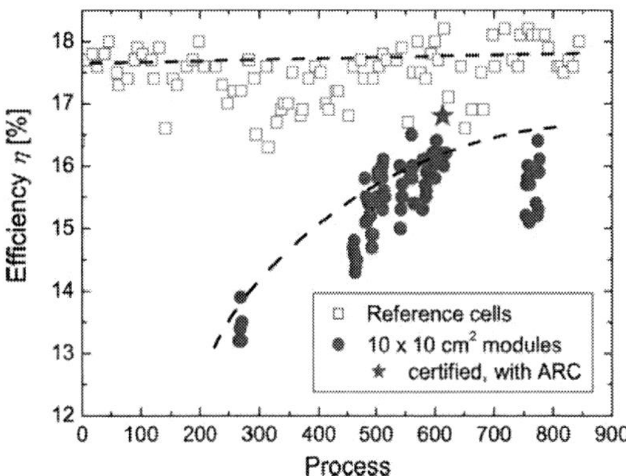

Fig. 3. PL intensity (black line) and carrier lifetimes (green circles) as extracted from TRPL of Mo/CIGS/CdS stacks of high-efficiency CIGS absorbers, Cu content of the CIGS absorber (red squares) from X-ray fluorescence, and the V_{OC} of the completed solar cell (blue triangles).

Fig. 4. Development of efficiency as a function of the process ID, covering a time span from late 2011 until early 2013. Values are given for 10 cm × 10 cm large submodules (full symbols) and for small-area reference cells (open symbols). The star symbol corresponds to the best 10 cm × 10 cm module prepared at ZSW with an aperture area efficiency of 16.8% (with ARC, certified by Fraunhofer ISE, Freiburg, Germany).

antireflective coating (ARC)]. Considering the fact that an MgF$_2$ ARC normally increases the absolute cell efficiency by approximately 1.0%–1.2%, we get 121 CIGS cells with an ARC-equivalent efficiency value of 20.0% or more (all cells counted that exhibit an efficiency equal to or above 18.9% without ARC). The ability to consistently produce CIGS cells on a high-efficiency level enables us to put the supposed positive influence of certain experimental parameters to the test. These tests have repeatedly shown that specific parameter settings that are capable of boosting cell efficiencies on a low- or medium-efficiency level do not yield any benefit for high-efficiency cells. Only true innovations prove to have a positive impact on these high-efficiency CIGS cells.

For the further development of high efficiencies in CIGS solar cells, however, it is essential to analyze the CIGS absorber layer on its own and not only through cell parameters of the device. One promising method is photoluminescence (PL) and time-resolved photoluminescence (TRPL). It is the goal of the latter method to extract carrier lifetimes from PL of the photoactive layers.

Our high-quality absorbers typically exhibit nearly single exponential decay with lifetimes of several tens of nanoseconds as depicted in Fig. 3 for a CIGS absorber with a Cu-content composition variation. The observed relationship between lifetimes and device performance is in general accordance with data reported by Repins *et al.* [18]. While the overall intensity of the PL signal is strongly influenced by the Cu concentration (see top part of Fig. 3), there is no apparent influence of the Cu content in the CIGS absorber on the carrier lifetime (see bottom part of Fig. 3).

B. Further Developments in the Module Line

ZSW runs a process line for modules up to 30 cm × 30 cm in size to facilitate and speed up the transfer of novel developments in CIGS PV to production maturity [19]. This line covers all steps from cutting and cleaning the glass substrates to the encapsulation of contacted modules. We use in-line deposition systems for the sputtered Mo back contact, the coevaporated CIGS absorber, and the sputtered transparent front contact involving i-ZnO and ZnO:Al. Compared with the small-area cells described earlier, modules employ a thicker ZnO:Al layer (approximately 900 nm) and no grid or ARC. The cells are monolithically integrated with P1 patterning by laser and mechanical P2 and P3 scribes. The timing for all processes is optimized so that the finished modules are electrically characterized within about 36 h after the CIGS deposition.

Over the past years, we have focused on the optimization of all layers of the heterostructure to improve the module efficiency in the module process line. It is equally important to have good process reproducibility and homogeneity over the full substrate size with only negligible effects of unintended variations in the deposition process. For the CIGS grown by the in-line multi-stage coevaporation process [19], the latter has been achieved by careful control of the substrate temperature and the evaporation rates of all elements. In-line process monitoring includes laser-light scattering to distinguish the important intermediate transition into the Cu-rich growth regime (Cu content of CIGS >24.8 at.%) by detecting the accompanying change in reflectivity [20], and X-ray fluorescence which is measured at the end of the multistage process to determine the final composition. Further steps include optimization of the CdS thickness and the ZnO in-line deposition. For the latter, a reduced peak temperature has been adopted following a monitoring of temperature as a function of process time. Via reduction of the distance between the patterning lines P1, P2, and P3, the dead area could be limited to 5% of the module aperture area.

The cumulated effects of the optimization are illustrated in Fig. 4, which shows the efficiency development of 10 cm × 10 cm modules and small-area reference cells starting from the end of 2011. The dashed lines are guides to the eye illustrating the reduction of the efficiency gap between cells and modules. Data spread is caused by intentional variations in the

TABLE II

DEVICE PARAMETERS OF OUR BEST SMALL-AREA CIGS CELLS WITH ALTERNATIVE BUFFER LAYERS (TOTAL AREA EFFICIENCIES, IN-HOUSE MEASUREMENTS) COMPARED WITH RECORD CELLS WITH STANDARD BUFFER/WINDOW LAYERS

Buffer	Method	Window	η [%]	V_{OC} [mV]	j_{SC} [mA/cm^2]	FF [%]	ARC	Treatment	Reference
CdS	CBD (TU)	i-ZnO/ZnO:Al	20.3* cert.	740	35.4	77.5	yes	-	[4]
CdS	CBD (TU)	i-ZnO/ZnO:Al	19.6 cert.	709	34.8	79.4	yes	-	[32]
Zn(O,S)	CBD (TU)	(Zn,Mg)O/ZnO:Al	19.0* cert.	684	36.7	75.6	yes	-	**this work**
Zn(O,S)	CBD (TAA)	(Zn,Mg)O/ZnO:Al	19.1	650	36.6	80.3	yes	PA + LS	[10]
Zn(O,S)	rf sputtering	ZnO:Al	16.4	662	34.3	72.4	no	-	**this work**
In$_x$S$_y$	evaporation	i-ZnO/ZnO:Al	17.1	655	34.8	74.9	yes	PA	**this work**

TU: Thiourea.
TAA: Thioacetamide.
*CIGS deposited in static small-area cell production line.
PA: Post-annealing of complete cell stack at 200 °C in air.
LS: Light soaking procedure under 1 sun AM 1.5G illumination at room temperature.
Cell area $A = 0.5$ cm^2.

processes and is not a measure for fluctuations in the module line using fixed conditions. An absolute increase of about 2.5% was realized for the 10 cm × 10 cm modules, with a best value of 16.8% for aperture area efficiency (certified, with ARC). Additionally, the efficiency of small reference cells with $A = 0.5$ cm^2 demonstrates the high quality of the multistage CIGS process. The continuous optimization of the multilayer system has considerably reduced the efficiency gap between small-area cells and modules.

III. BUFFER LAYERS

A source of photocurrent loss is the absorption in the commonly used CBD CdS buffer layer. Alternative materials with a higher transmission in the blue wavelength region have the potential to improve the conversion efficiency. Materials without cadmium are also attractive from an ecological point of view. The most promising alternative buffer materials for CIGS solar cells are Zn(O,S) with cell efficiencies in the range of 18%–20% [9], [11], [14] and In$_2$S$_3$ with cell efficiencies between 16% and 17% [21]–[23]. Additional candidates as a substitute for CdS are (Zn,Mg)O [24] and (Zn,Sn)O$_y$ [25], both on an 18% efficiency level. In some cases the alternative buffer materials work well with the standard i-ZnO/ZnO:Al window configuration as used for CdS. However, different cell architectures have often proven to be more advantageous. We refer to Naghavi *et al.* and references therein for an overview [26]. Besides high efficiencies for small-area cells, good results with values near 18% were also reported for Zn(O,S) buffer layers on 30 cm × 30 cm CIGS modules [27].

At ZSW, we focus on the two buffer materials Zn(O,S) and In$_2$S$_3$. Our CIGS contains no sulfur and no additional sulfurization of the CIGS surface was carried out before buffer deposition. For solution-grown Zn(O,S), we pursue two deposition routes.

1) A process very similar to the CBD CdS growth with the educts ZnSO$_4$, thiourea (TU) in an ammonia solution [28]. This process has typical deposition times between 15–20 min for a thickness of 20–30 nm which is slower than for CdS as a result of different growth kinetics.

2) A much faster, industrially relevant process that is based on the kinetically controlled reaction between ZnSO$_4$ and thioacetamide (TAA) by complexation of the zinc salt with an ammonia/nitrilotriacetate mixture [10].

For both CBD Zn(O,S) buffer layers, we use Zn$_{0.75}$Mg$_{0.25}$O instead of the standard i-ZnO layer in combination with ZnO:Al [29]. Our best cells with CBD Zn(O,S) are listed in Table II along with our record CdS-buffered cells. Note that the CIGS for the cell with the TU buffer, which exhibits a certified efficiency of 19.0% (with ARC), was deposited by the static small-area cell line and no postannealing was applied. The CIGS for the cell with 19.1% efficiency (with ARC) and the TAA-based Zn(O,S) buffer was grown in the 30 cm × 30 cm in-line machine. This cell was annealed at 200 °C for 30 min in air before the current–voltage measurement. During the postannealing step, which often has a beneficial effect for our cells with CBD Zn(O,S), primarily zinc diffuses into the CIGS absorber beside other processes [30]. Most of our cells with CBD Zn(O,S) buffers profit from a light soaking procedure with 1 sun AM1.5G at room temperature for several minutes which mainly improves the fill factor.

Concerning CIGS growth on flexible substrates by a roll-to-roll process as described in the following section, a buffer layer deposited by a dry process, e.g., sputtering or thermal evaporation would be more advantageous. Therefore, we are pursuing two approaches: sputtered Zn(O,S) and thermally evaporated In$_2$S$_3$. The Zn(O,S) buffer is grown at 150 °C substrate temperature by rf sputtering from a homogeneous mixed ZnO/ZnS target in Ar atmosphere. With the ZnO:Al window deposited directly on top of the sputtered Zn(O,S) buffer, we achieve an efficiency of 16.4% (without ARC; see Table II). These cells need no further treatment like postannealing or light soaking.

Our second approach for a dry buffer is the deposition of In$_x$S$_y$ by thermal evaporation of stoichiometric In$_2$S$_3$ from a linear source in a 30 cm × 30 cm in-line coater [23]. The current record cell we realized with an In$_x$S$_y$ buffer combined with an i-ZnO/ZnO:Al window bilayer has an efficiency of 17.1% (with ARC; see Table II). This value was achieved after a postannealing step, which is necessary for interdiffusion between the CIGS absorber and the In$_x$S$_y$ buffer layer [31], but without any light soaking.

418

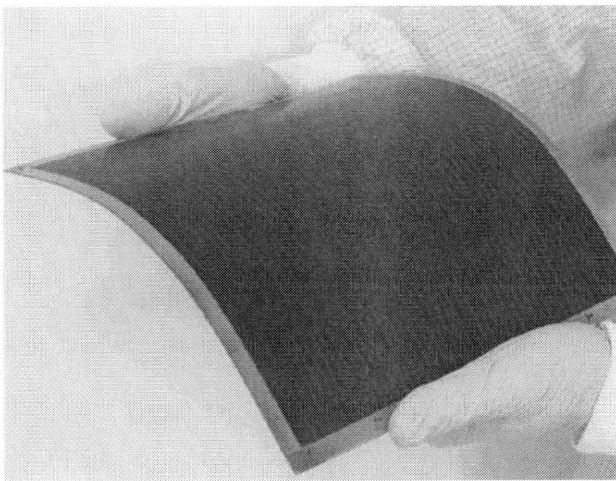

Fig. 5. CIGS module on an enameled steel substrate ($A = 23$ cm $\times$ 30 cm, $\eta_{aa} = 12.9\%$ without ARC).

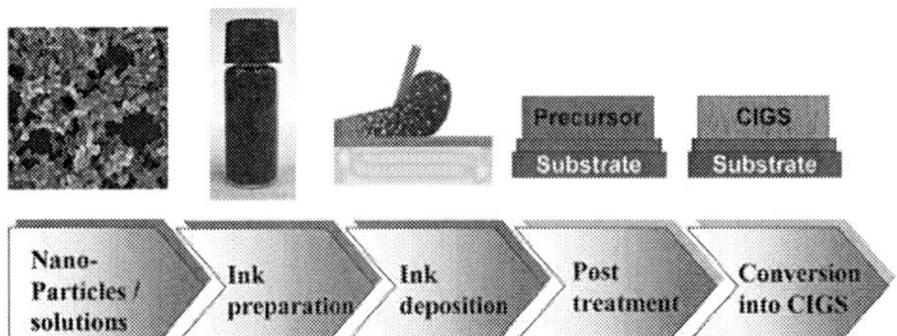

Fig. 6. Process sequence of printed CIGS absorbers.

IV. CIGS ON FLEXIBLE SUBSTRATES

The charm of flexible substrates is their low weight and their better suitability for building-integrated PV and consumer electronics. It has been shown that even on polyimide foil, an efficiency of 20.4% could be reached in a low-temperature CIGS process [3]. Flexible substrates enable CIGS deposition in a roll-to-roll process with promising cost reduction potential. The Na-free polyimide foil and alkali-containing enameled steel substrates were investigated as flexible substrates. The polyimide foil is attractive due to its: 1) low weight, 2) insulating property enabling monolithical cell interconnection, and 3) comparably low costs per square meter.

In the EUproject hipoCIGS (no. 241384), a special high-temperature enamel on the steel was jointly developed and supplied by PEMCO (Belgium) with well-matched alkali content to allow sufficient absorber doping without the need of any external Na supply. The flexibility of enameled substrates was rather restricted due to the comparatively high thicknesses of the low-carbon steel sheets (0.5 and 0.8 mm). The major advantages of enameled steel are its 1) insulating properties, hence, enabling monolithic interconnection on large-scale area, 2) high-temperature stability, thus, allowing high-temperature CIGS processing such as on soda-lime glass (SLG) substrates, 3) adjustable alkali content, which leads to even better cell performances compared with the SLG [33], and 4) a good barrier against diffusion of detrimental substrate elements like Fe from the steel substrate.

A. Roll-to-Roll

A special feature of the roll-to-roll setup at ZSW is that all active layers of the cell stack can be deposited in the same machine with only one winding and unwinding unit. So far, Mo sputtering as well as CIGS and In_2S_3 evaporation can be performed without breaking the vacuum. On 25-μm-thin polyimide films, a cell efficiency of $\eta = 13.1\%$ (with ARC, $A = 0.5$ cm^2) was achieved in a single-stage CIGS process with a CdS buffer and

a Mo:Na layer as Na source. In the meantime, growth of CIGS layers via a multistage process was implemented in the roll-to-roll setup. First and nonoptimized cells exhibit an efficiency of 10.8% (without ARC).

B. Enameled Steel as a Flexible Nonglass Substrate

CIGS layers were grown on enameled steel substrates in a high-temperature multistage in-line CIGS process [19], and, finally, processed to cells by using wet chemical deposition of a CdS buffer layer, sputtering of an i-ZnO/ZnO:Al window layer and evaporation of a metallic grid. The maximum cell efficiency (with ARC, $A = 0.5$ cm^2) achieved so far on an enameled steel is $\eta = 18.6\%$ ($V_{OC} = 726$ mV, $FF = 76.4\%$, $j_{SC} = 33.6$ mA/cm^2), which is even higher than on the SLG reference substrate ($\eta = 18.3\%$, $V_{OC} = 711$ mV, $FF = 78.5\%$, $j_{SC} = 32.8$ mA/cm^2). Generally the open-circuit voltage and the short-circuit current density are higher on the enameled steel compared with SLG, as potassium leads to a higher doping and a stronger Ga grading of the CIGS layer [33]. An advantage of an enameled steel is that standard structuring methods as used for SLG substrates can be applied, i.e., laser scribing for the P1 trench and mechanical scribing for the P2 and P3 trench. Hereby, a 10 cm $\times$ 10 cm module with an active-area efficiency of $\eta_{aa} = 15.4\%$ (with ARC) and a large-area module (23 cm $\times$ 30 cm) with an efficiency of $\eta_{aa} = 12.9\%$ (without ARC) could be processed (see Fig. 5). These results show the high potential of the enameled steel as alternative substrate.

V. VACUUM-FREE CIGS

The vacuum-free deposition of suitable precursor pastes and subsequent selenization has attracted increasing attention due to the possibility of low-cost high-throughput coating and production of CIGS thin-film solar cells [34], [35]. Nanoparticles are often used for paste formulation as they allow a direct microscopical control of the chemical composition and high reactivity due to their confined sizes. Quaternary chalcogenide $Cu(In,Ga)S_2$ nanoparticles that have been directly synthesized via coprecipitation reactions are especially interesting [36], [37]. The precursor films are heated after coating and exposed to selenium vapor where most of the sulfur is replaced by selenium. This replacement produces a volume expansion and leads to $Cu(In,Ga)(S,Se)_2$ absorber films with reduced inclusion of void space.

Fig. 6 describes our process sequence for the printed CIGS absorbers. The nanoparticle coprecipitation reaction and ink formulation is carried out as described by Klugius *et al.* [38] and has been performed and developed by R. Miller from EMD Millipore (USA) within the TEDD project (BMBF). The particles are suspended in toluene together with oleylamine and show a diameter of about 10 nm. The nanoparticle inks are washed and concentrated to obtain the desired stabilizing additive concentration suitable for the doctor blading technique. The final ink solution is deposited on Mo-coated SLG substrates.

Selenization is done in a rapid thermal annealing system in elemental selenium vapor, enabling a fast process that is suitable for high throughput with a short selenization duration of 3–5 min. With such an approach, we could demonstrate a cell efficiency of 8.5%, showing the promising potential of a vacuum-free CIGS route [38].

VI. Conclusion

This contribution summarizes the CIGS-related activities at ZSW including further developments and improvements for the static high-efficiency cell line, the 30 cm $\times$ 30 cm in-line modules and processes, alternative buffer layers Zn(O,S) and In$_2$S$_3$, alternative substrates like polyimide and enameled steel, as well as vacuum-free CIGS deposition processes.

We have demonstrated that our static CIGS process is very reliable and we could produce more than 100 small-area CIGS cells with efficiencies above 20% (with ARC and postannealing). Time-resolved photo-luminescence proved to be a very powerful tool to qualify these high-efficiency absorbers directly after the growth process. The gap between cell and module efficiencies (10 cm $\times$ 10 cm modules) could be significantly reduced and we achieved a certified 16.8% efficiency (with ARC) for our best monolithically integrated 10 cm $\times$ 10 cm module with the 30 cm $\times$ 30 cm in-line equipment.

Additionally, we are developing Zn(O,S) and In$_2$S$_3$ buffer materials as alternatives to CdS. Here, we could improve our efficiencies to 19.1% (with ARC and postannealing) for CIGS cells with a CBD (TAA) Zn(O,S) buffer, to 19.0% (certified, with ARC) with CBD (TU) Zn(O,S) without postannealing, to 16.4% (without ARC) for sputtered Zn(O,S), and to 17.1% (with ARC) for In$_2$S$_3$ deposited by thermal evaporation.

A CIGS cell with 13.1% efficiency (with ARC) could be realized in a roll-to-roll coater on a polyimide substrate. Furthermore, very promising results were achieved on enameled steel substrates like 18.6% (with ARC) for a cell, 15.4% (with ARC, active area) for a 10 cm $\times$ 10 cm, and 12.9% (without ARC, active area) for a 23 cm $\times$ 30 cm monolithically integrated module.

For our CIGS cells deposited by vacuum-free methods, we could achieve an efficiency of 8.5% with a process that is based on selenization of Cu(In,Ga)S$_2$ nanoparticles.

Acknowledgment

The authors would like to thank the CIGS team at ZSW for technical support and also B. Dimmler and K. Orgassa from Manz AG for their collaboration and support.

References

[1] Source: EPIA. (May 2013). Global Market Outlook for Photovoltaics 2013–2017. [Online]. Available: http://www.epia.org/home/ download at 20th May 2013.

[2] P. Mints, Solar PV Market Research in partnership with Strategies Unlimited, San Jose, CA, USA, private communication, May 2013.

[3] EMPA press release January 17 2013, Dübendorf, Switzerland. (Sep. 2013). [Online]. Available: http://www.empa.ch/plugin/template/empa/ 1/131438/- - -/l=2

[4] P. Jackson, D. Hariskos, E. Lotter, S. Paetel, R. Wuerz, R. Menner, W. Wischmann, and M. Powalla, "New world record efficiency for Cu(In,Ga)Se$_2$ thin-film solar cells beyond 20%," *Prog. Photovolt. Res. Appl.*, vol. 19, pp. 894–897, 2011.

[5] I. Repins, M. A. Contreras, B. Egaas, C. DeHart, J. Scharf, C. L. Perkins, B. To, and R. Noufi, "19.9%-efficient ZnO/CdS/CuInGaSe$_2$ solar cell with 81.2% fill factor," *Prog. Photovolt. Res. Appl.*, vol. 16, pp. 235–239, 2008.

[6] E. Wallin, U. Malm, R. Hunger, T. Jarmar, O. Lundberg, S. Weeke, P. Kratzert, M. Edoff, and L. Stolt, "Effects of Ga-grading in Cu(In,Ga)Se$_2$ absorber layers synthesized under industrial conditions," presented at the MRS Spring Meet. 2013, San Francisco, CA, USA, 2013.

[7] J. Haarstrich, H. Metzner, M. Oertel, C. Ronning, T. Rissom, C. A. Kaufmann, T. Unold, H. W. Schock, J. Windeln, W. Mannstadt, and E. Rudigier-Voigt, "Increased homogeneity and open-circuit voltage of Cu(In,Ga)Se$_2$ solar cells due to higher deposition temperature," *Sol. Energy Mater. Sol. Cells*, vol. 95, pp. 1028–1030, 2011.

[8] S. Ishizuka, A. Yamada, P. Fons, and S. Niki, "Texture and morphology variations in (In,Ga)$_2$Se$_3$ and Cu(In,Ga)Se$_2$ thin films grown with various Se source conditions," *Prog. Photovolt. Res. Appl.*, vol. 21, pp. 544–553, 2013.

[9] M. Nakamura, Y. Kouji, Y. Chiba, H. Hakuma, T. Kobayashi, and T. Nakada, "Achievement of 19.7% efficiency with a small-sized Cu(InGa)(SeS)$_2$ solar cell prepared by sulfurization after selenization process with Zn-based buffer," presented at the IEEE 39th Photovoltaic Specialists Conf., Tampa, FL, USA, 2013.

[10] D. Hariskos, R. Menner, P. Jackson, S. Paetel, W. Witte, W. Wischmann, M. Powalla, L. Bürkert, T. Kolb, M. Oertel, B. Dimmler, and B. Fuchs, "New reaction kinetics for a high-rate chemical bath deposition of the Zn(S,O) buffer layer for Cu(In,Ga)Se$_2$-based solar cells," *Prog. Photovolt. Res. Appl.*, vol. 20, pp. 534–542, 2012.

[11] M. A. Contreras, T. Nakada, M. Hongo, A. O. Pudov, and J. R. Sites, "ZnO/ZnS(O,OH)/Cu(In,Ga)Se$_2$/Mo solar cell with 18.6% efficiency," in *Proc. 3rd World Conf. Photovolt. Energy Convers.*, Osaka, Japan, 2003, pp. 570–573.

[12] K. Ramanathan, J. Mann, S. Glynn, S. Christensen, J. Pankow, J. Li, J. Scharf, L. Mansfield, M. Contreras, and R. Noufi, "A comparative study of Zn(O,S) buffer layers and CIGS solar cells fabricated by CBD, ALD, and sputtering," in *Proc. IEEE 38th Photovoltaic Spec. Conf.*, Austin, TX, USA, 2012, pp. 001677–001681.

[13] T. Kobayashi, H. Yamaguchi, and T. Nakada, "Effects of combined heat and light soaking on device performance of Cu(In,Ga)Se$_2$ solar cells with ZnS(O,OH) buffer layer," *Prog. Photovolt. Res. Appl.*, 2013, to be published. DOI: 10.1002/pip.2339.

[14] U. Zimmermann, M. Ruth, and M. Edoff, "Cadmium-free CIGS mini-modules with ALD-grown Zn(O,S)-based buffer layers," in *Proc. 21st Eur. Photovoltaic Sol. Energy Conf.*, Dresden, Germany, 2006, pp. 1831–1834.

[15] R. Klenk, "Design, preparation and performance of CIGS/Zn(O,S)/ ZnO:Al solar cells," presented at the 4th Int. Workshop on CIGS Solar Cell Technology, Berlin, Germany.

[16] K. Orgassa, Manz AG, Schwäbisch Hall, Germany, private communication, May 2013.

[17] B. Dimmler, "CIGS and CdTe based thin film PV modules, an industrial r/evolution," in *Proc. IEEE 38th Photovoltaic Spec. Conf.*, Austin, TX, USA, 2012, pp. 002494–002499.

[18] I. L. Repins, W. K. Metzger, C. L. Perkins, J. V. Li, and M. A. Contreras, "Correlation between measured minority-carrier lifetime and Cu(In,Ga)Se$_2$ device performance," *IEEE Trans. Electron Devices*, vol. 57, no. 11, pp. 2957–2963, Nov. 2010.

[19] G. Voorwinden, R. Kniese, P. Jackson, and M. Powalla, "In-Line Cu(In,Ga)Se$_2$ co-evaporation process on 30 cm $\times$ 30 cm substrates with multiple deposition stages," in *Proc. 22nd Eur. Photovolt. Sol. Energy Conf.*, Milan, Italy, 2007, pp. 2115–2118.

[20] M. Powalla, P. Jackson, W. Witte, D. Hariskos, S. Paetel, C. Tschamber, and W. Wischmann, "High-efficiency Cu(In,Ga)Se$_2$ cells and modules," *Sol. Energy Mater. Sol. Cells*, vol. 119, pp. 51–58, 2013.

[21] N. Naghavi, S. Spiering, M. Powalla, B. Canava, and D. Lincot, "High-efficiency copper indium gallium diselenide (CIGS) solar cells with indium sulfide buffer layers deposited by atomic layer chemical vapor deposition (ALCVD)," *Prog. Photovolt. Res. Appl.*, vol. 11, pp. 437–443, 2003.

[22] R. Sáez-Araoz, J. Krammer, S. Harndt, T. Koehler, M. Krueger, P. Pistor, A. Jasenek, F. Hergert, M. C. Lux-Steiner, and C.-H. Fischer, "ILGAR In$_2$S$_3$ buffer layers for Cd-free Cu(In,Ga)(S,Se)$_2$ solar cells with certified efficiencies above 16%," *Prog. Photovolt. Res. Appl.*, vol. 20, pp. 855–861, 2012.

[23] S. Spiering, F. Kessler, and W. Wischmann, "Indium sulphide buffer layers by in-line evaporation for CIGS thin film devices," in *Proc. 26th Eur. Photovolt. Sol. Energy Conf.*, Hamburg, Germany, 2011, pp. 2886–2889.

[24] A. Hultqvist, C. Platzer-Björkman, T. Törndahl, M. Ruth, and M. Edoff, "Optimization of i-ZnO window layers for Cu(In,Ga)Se$_2$ solar cells with ALD buffers," in *Proc. 22nd Eur. Photovoltaic Sol. Energy Conf.*, Milan, Italy, 2007, pp. 2381–2384.

[25] J. Lindahl, J. T. Wätjen, A. Hultqvist, T. Ericson, M. Edoff, and T. Törndahl, "The effect of Zn$_{1-x}$Sn$_x$O$_y$ buffer layer thickness in 18.0% efficient Cd-free Cu(In,Ga)Se$_2$ solar cells," *Prog. Photovolt. Res. Appl.*, 2012. DOI: 10.1002/pip.2239.

[26] N. Naghavi, D. Abou-Ras, N. Allsop, N. Barreau, S. Bücheler, A. Ennaoui, C.-H. Fischer, C. Guillen, D. Hariskos, J. Herrero, R. Klenk, K. Kushiya, D. Lincot, R. Menner, T. Nakada, C. Platzer-Björkman, S. Spiering, A. N. Tiwari, and T. Törndahl, "Buffer layers and transparent conducting oxides for chalcopyrite Cu(In,Ga)(S,Se)$_2$ based thin film photovoltaics: Present status and current developments," *Prog. Photovolt. Res. Appl.*, vol. 18, pp. 411–433, 2010.

[27] M. Nakamura, Y. Chiba, S. Kijima, K. Horiguchi, Y. Yanagisawa, Y. Sawai, K. Ishikawa, and H. Hakuma, "Achievement of 17.5% efficiency with 30 × 30 cm^2-sized Cu(In,Ga)(Se,S)$_2$ submodules," in *Proc. IEEE 38th Photovolt. Spec. Conf.*, Austin, TX, USA, 2012, pp. 001807–001810.

[28] C. Hubert, N. Naghavi, O. Roussel, A. Etcheberry, D. Hariskos, R. Menner, M. Powalla, O. Kerrec, and D. Lincot, "The Zn(S,O,OH)/ZnMgO buffer in thin film Cu(In,Ga)(S,Se)$_2$-based solar cells part I: Fast chemical bath deposition of Zn(S,O,OH) buffer layers for industrial application on co-evaporated Cu(In,Ga)Se$_2$ and electrodeposited CuIn(S,Se)$_2$ solar cells," *Prog. Photovolt. Res. Appl.*, vol. 17, pp. 470–478, 2009.

[29] D. Hariskos, B. Fuchs, R. Menner, N. Naghavi, C. Hubert, D. Lincot, and M. Powalla, "The Zn(S,O,OH)/ZnMgO buffer in thin-film Cu(In,Ga)(Se,S)$_2$-based solar cells part II: Magnetron sputtering of the ZnMgO buffer layer for in-line co-evaporated Cu(In,Ga)Se$_2$ solar cells," *Prog. Photovolt. Res. Appl.*, vol. 17, pp. 479–488, 2009.

[30] W. Witte, D. Hariskos, A. Eicke, R. Menner, O. Kiowski, and M. Powalla, "Impact of annealing on Cu(In,Ga)Se$_2$ solar cells with Zn(O,S)/(Zn,Mg)O buffers," *Thin Solid Films*, vol. 535, pp. 180–183, 2013.

[31] D. Abou-Ras, D. Rudmann, G. Kostorz, S. Spiering, M. Powalla, and A. N. Tiwari, "Microstructural and chemical studies of interfaces between Cu(In,Ga)Se$_2$ and In$_2$S$_3$ layers," *J. Appl. Phys.*, vol. 97, pp. 084908-1–084908-8, 2005.

[32] M. Powalla, D. Hariskos, P. Jackson, F. Kessler, S. Paetel, W. Wischmann, W. Witte, and R. Würz, "CIGS solar cells with efficiencies >20%: Current status and new developments," in *Proc. 26th Eur. Photovolt. Sol. Energy Conf.*, Hamburg, Germany, 2011, pp. 2416–2420.

[33] R. Wuerz, A. Eicke, F. Kessler, S. Paetel, S. Efimenko, and C. Schlegel, "CIGS thin-film solar cells and modules on enamelled steel substrates," *Sol. Energy Mater. Sol. Cells*, vol. 100, pp. 132–137, 2012.

[34] C. J. Hibberd, E. Chassaing, W. Liu, D. B. Mitzi, D. Lincot, and A. N. Tiwari, "Non-vacuum methods for formation of Cu(In,Ga)(Se,S)$_2$ thin film photovoltaic absorbers," *Prog. Photovolt. Res. Appl.*, vol. 18, pp. 434–452, 2010.

[35] T. Todorov and D. B. Mitzi, "Direct liquid coating of chalcopyrite light-absorbing layers for photovoltaic devices," *Eur. J. Inorg. Chem.*, pp. 17–28, 2010.

[36] Q. Guo, G. M. Ford, H. W. Hillhouse, and R. Agrawal, "Sulfide nanocrystal inks for dense Cu(In$_{1-x}$Ga$_x$)(S$_{1-y}$Se$_y$)$_2$ absorber films and their photovoltaic performance," *Nano Lett.*, vol. 9, pp. 3060–3065, 2009.

[37] Q. Guo, G. M. Ford, R. Agrawal, and H. W. Hillhouse, "Ink formulation and low-temperature incorporation of sodium to yield 12% efficient Cu(In,Ga)(S,Se)$_2$ solar cells from sulfide nanocrystal inks," *Prog. Photovolt. Res. Appl.*, vol. 21, pp. 64–71, 2013.

[38] I. Klugius, R. Miller, A. Quintilla, T. M. Friedlmeier, D. Blázquez-Sánchez, E. Ahlswede, and M. Powalla, "Growth mechanism of thermally processed Cu(In,Ga)S$_2$ precursors for printed Cu(In,Ga)(S,Se)$_2$ solar cells," *Phys. Status Solidi (RRL)*, vol. 6, pp. 297–299, 2012.

Authors' photographs and biographies not available at the time of publication.

CdTe Solar Cells at the Threshold to 20% Efficiency

M. Gloeckler, I. Sankin, and Z. Zhao

Abstract—After a long period of stagnancy for record cell efficiency and several years of growth of the industry, CdTe solar cell efficiency has been rapidly increasing recently. First Solar (FSLR) fabricated an 18.7% NREL certified cell at the end of 2012 and reports an increase to a certified 19.0% in this paper. Although the improvements were dominated by increases in short-circuit current and fill factor, there is now evidence that the open-circuit voltage of polycrystalline CdTe is not fundamentally limited to ~850 mV, and first devices exceeding 900 mV have been demonstrated. In-depth device characterization indicates that the responsible third-level metric is the increase of carrier lifetime, which can be characterized by transient photoluminescence. The progress at hand suggests that the near-term achievable target for CdTe solar cells should be raised from 19% to 22%. A detailed numerical model is used to translate cell results into predicted module efficiency. These simulations are in agreement with FSLR's recently certified 16.1% total-area module efficiency record. Forward-looking simulations show that with already demonstrated technology components, a module efficiency exceeding 17% is attainable. Disruptive changes and implementation of new device architectures can provide further room for improvement for cell efficiency beyond 22%.

Index Terms—Cadmium telluride, entitlement, open-circuit voltage, photovoltaic cells.

I. Introduction

IN their 2006 paper, Demtsu and Sites [1] reviewed CdTe state-of-the-art manufacturing and record cell performance, discussed the efficiency limitations, and proposed an achievable performance target for CdTe solar cells of 19%. The current–voltage (I–V) parameters were predicted to reach 900-mV open-circuit voltage (V_{oc}), 27-mA/cm^2 short-circuit current density (J_{sc}), and 77% fill factor (FF). At the time, this was compared against an established 16.5% world record, which happened to be the record from 2001 through 2011. Until 2011, no increase in champion cell efficiency was reported, although polycrystalline CdTe technology created a substantial market presence over this timeframe and received a high level of attention from numerous technology companies.

In addition, it is noteworthy that there has been no significant improvement in the open-circuit voltage for nearly 20 years, and numbers in the 840–860 mV range have been reported since the early 1990s. Many arguments have been made to justify the apparent V_{oc}-*limitation* [2], [3], most frequently 1) a poor heterointerface with CdS, 2) the difficulty to dope polycrystalline CdTe, 3) poor material quality of CdTe, 4) "grain-boundary" limitations, 5) poor back-contact, or 6) nonuniformities at the nano- or microscale. Voltage limitations are indeed very difficult to characterize, and hence, there is a reliance on measurable metrics that can be correlated to the open-circuit voltage. Such metrics have been previously termed "third-level metrics (3LM)" [1]. Unfortunately, due to the lack of detailed understanding of the complex physics of these polycrystalline devices, there is no direct measure. Finally, the matter is complicated by the fact that competing mechanisms limit the voltage. Low open-circuit voltage can be achieved in many ways, and hence, correlations established in a group of devices do not necessarily have predictive power beyond the already accomplished performance range.

Scaling from a laboratory cell to a module-sized process is different for each technology. While, for example, composition control over large areas can be very daunting, some technologies scale easily with little issues. First Solar's experience has been that nonuniformities played a small role in the difference between cell and module level efficiency. Correctly accounted for, area losses and resistive losses can explain the differences to the degree of accuracy that can be expected. Neglecting process-related nonuniformities, it is possible to compute the module-level entitlement of a technology based on its champion cell performance.

II. Recent Progress in Cell Efficiency

The history of photovoltaic technologies can be tracked by the well-known NREL champion cell efficiency chart [4]. Interestingly, many of the technologies shown in this chart show stagnation over long time periods, followed by rapid increase in cell efficiency that coincides with some technological breakthrough. Fig. 1 is a free reproduction of this chart for CdTe technology with slight additions; all references are provided in Table I. In 1993, Britt and Ferekides [5] reported on a 15.8% efficient cell; eight years later, the application of a cadmium stannate transparent conductive oxide (TCO) layer allowed Wu *et al.* [6] to increase this efficiency to 16.5% (16.7%). In the past 24 months, the CdTe record was broken four times and increased from 16.7% to 19.0%.

The I–V parameters for record cells of the last 20 years are listed in Table I. All results represent NREL-certified measurements with the exception of the 19.0% measurement certified at Newport. For reference, the previously mentioned Demtsu/Sites target is listed. The comparison leads to the conclusion that the efficiency and FF targets have been met, the J_{sc} exceeded the expectation, and the V_{oc} fell short of the expectation. Losses related to the short-circuit current are additive and can be optimized near independently of one another by improving the antireflective coating, the glass absorption, the absorption in the

Manuscript received June 10, 2013; revised August 7, 2013; accepted August 8, 2013. Date of publication September 5, 2013; date of current version September 18, 2013.

The authors are with First Solar, Inc., Perrysburg, OH 43551 USA (e-mail: mgloeckler@firstsolar.com; isankin@firstsolar.com; zzhao@firstsolar.com).

Color versions of one or more of the figures in this paper are available online at http://ieeexplore.ieee.org.

Digital Object Identifier 10.1109/JPHOTOV.2013.2278661

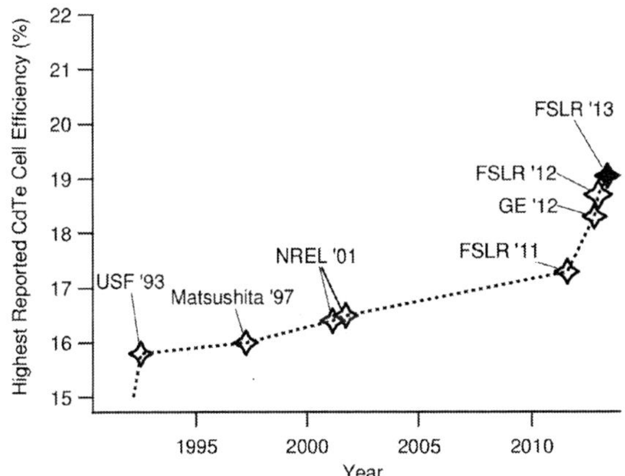

Fig. 1.   Reported CdTe record cell efficiencies.

TABLE I
CDTE RECORD CELL I–V PARAMETERS

Year	Team	Eff	Voc	Jsc	FF	Ref
1993	USF*	15.8%	843	25.1	74.5%	[5]
1997	Matsushita[t]	16.0%	840	26.1	73.1	[7]
2001	NREL*	16.4%	848	25.9	74.5	[8]
2001	NREL*	16.7%	845	26.1	75.5%	[6]
2011	FSLR*	17.3%	845	27.0	75.8%	[9]
2012	GE*	18.3%	857	27.0	79.0%	[10]
2012	FSLR*	18.7%	852	28.6	76.7%	
2013	**FSLR[S]**	**19.0%**	**872**	**28.0**	**78.0%**	
	Demtsu/Sites – Target	19.0%	900	27.0	78.5%	[1]

*NREL certified; [t]JQA certified; [S]Newport certified.

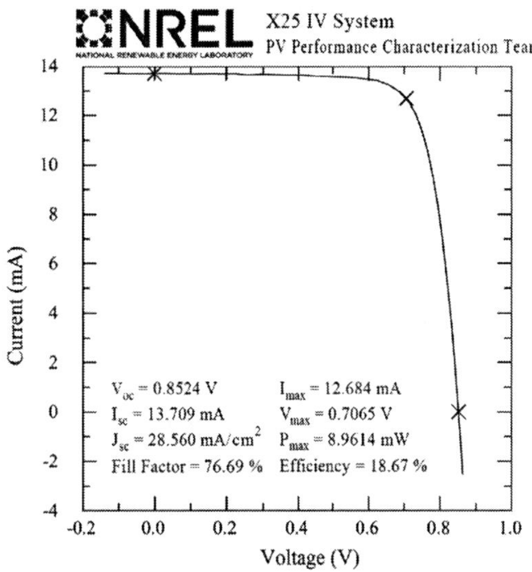

Fig. 2.   NREL certified I–V curve of the 18.7% cell.

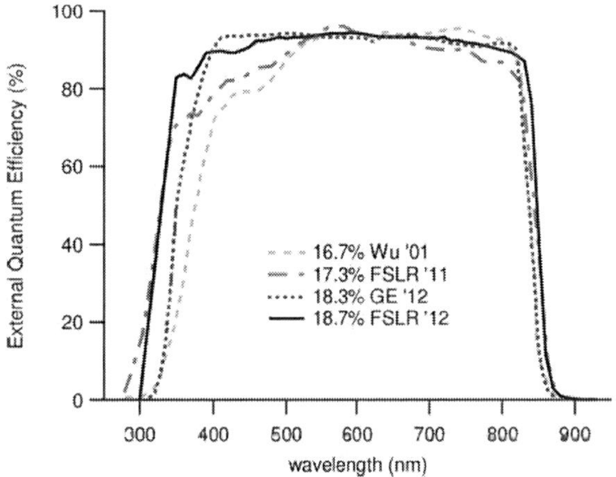

Fig. 3.   QE of recent CdTe champion cells.

TCO stack, the window layer, and the absorber collection. The layers are listed here in the order in which the light transmits through the device. Losses related to the open-circuit voltage are much more difficult to quantify and to reduce. In essence, the sum of all recombination currents competes with the light-generated current. Typically, it helps to separate recombination occurring at the heterointerface, inside the junction, in the quasi-neutral region, and at the back-surface.

The I–V curve of the NREL certified 18.7% cell is shown in Fig. 2. An overlay of the quantum efficiency (QE) curves of the last four cell records is shown in Fig. 3. The curves are reproductions from references listed in Table I and are all measured at NREL. Optical losses have been minimized to a great degree. Notably, losses in the CdS window layer have been nearly eliminated leading to relatively square QEs that are limited by the optical absorption of the substrate structure (glass/TCO) at the short wavelength and the bandgap of CdTe absorber at the long wavelength. The J_{sc} of the 18.7% cell is 28.6 mA/cm^2, which is the highest J_{sc} of any CdTe record cell ever reported. First Solar's best estimate for an achievable champion cell short-circuit current is 30 mA/cm^2, achieved through improvements in residual window layer transparency and substrate optimization. Further gains could be imagined by complex photon up/down conversion or by enhancing the near bandgap absorption through shrinking of the semiconductor bandgap; the latter, however, would likely be offset by losses in open-circuit voltage.

The 19.0% cell reported in Table I shows the first noticeable increase in V_{oc} of a record cell beyond the 860 mV in more

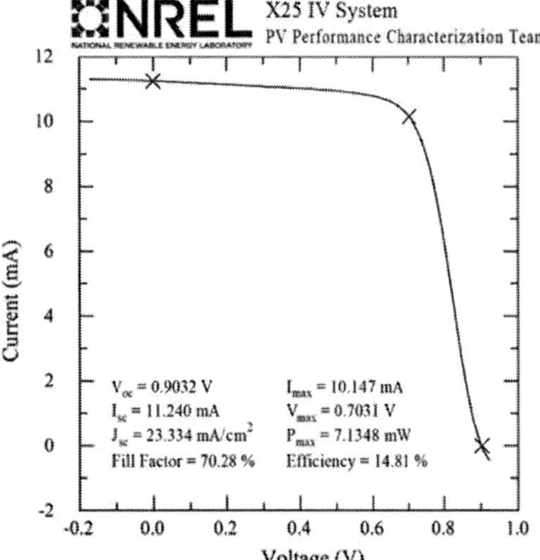

Fig. 4. NREL certified *I–V* curve of a 903 mV cell.

than 20 years. Albeit a modest gain, First Solar has been able to demonstrate a significant improvement in V_{oc} to 903 mV as shown in the NREL-certified *I–V* curve in Fig. 4. Given these positive signs of change, one can be optimistic that fundamentally polycrystalline CdTe material is not limited in the achievable voltage. In Section III, the device characteristics of high-voltage devices constructed at First Solar are discussed.

Concluding the discussion of record cell efficiencies, the newly identified boundaries to be discovered and next significant stepping stone for CdTe cell efficiency should be a V_{oc} of 925 mV, J_{sc} of 30 mA/cm2, and an FF near 80%, which equate to a cell efficiency of 22%.

III. PROGRESS IN OPEN-CIRCUIT VOLTAGE

Characterization of V_{oc}-limiting mechanisms is difficult, because multiple mechanisms are likely simultaneously at play and there is no direct measurement of any of them. Each mechanism can at best be derived from an indirect measurement of a 3LM and the interpretation utilizing a correct model. Both the good measurement of the metric and the use of appropriate models are very challenging. In the following, we compare properties of devices with V_{oc} in the range from 840 mV to 900 mV, based upon the following 3LMs:

DOPING: measured by room temperature junction capacitance versus voltage (*C–V*) profiling performed at 100 kHz. *C–V* is an inferior technique as the measurement gathers the net charge change at any given bias, which may include charge released or trapped from deeper levels in the junction and the heterointerface in addition to the dopant density [11]. However, an inherent expectation exists that higher doping derived from simple *C–V* should deliver higher V_{oc}. High doping would increase the built-in potential and reduce recombination in a narrower p-n junction.

LIFETIME: measured by transient photoluminescence (TRPL), performed at NREL. Carrier lifetimes are complex to interpret since drift and diffusion components can alter the net response of the measurement. Kanevce *et al.* [12] recently provided an in-depth analysis of the problem and concluded that the second decay time may be a better proxy for the actual bulk minority carrier lifetime. Further, lifetime in the CdTe bulk of the absorber can be limited by grain-boundary recombination or recombination in the grain bulk due to point defects. No attempt to separate these effects is made, and only the effective absorber lifetime response is reported. Decay constants for the second exponential fitted in the TRPL decay curve are used as a metric, and a representative range is reported due to the variability that can be seen even in repeat measurements on the same sample. In general, higher lifetimes are expected to be a sign of less recombination in the junction and quasi-neutral region and, hence, improved V_{oc} and improved carrier collection. With higher lifetime, it is expected that a greater fraction of the recombination may occur at the back-contact due to increased electron diffusion through the absorber.

INTERFACE: recombination parameter is extracted from the *I–V* curve measured at varying temperature. Typically, one of two approaches is followed, either characterization of the product of diode-quality factor and the log of the saturation current versus inverse temperature, or more simply, V_{oc} versus temperature [13]. Here, we only report numbers for the latter approach. The parameter represents the effective "activation energy" of recombination, and if this number is less than the bandgap energy, the recombination is interpreted to be dominated by the interface.

The results are summarized in Table II. The first row represents a typical experience value for nonexceptional CdTe device fabricated at First Solar. We derive the following conclusions regards the contribution to the enhancement of V_{oc} from 850 to 900 mV.

1) *C–V*-derived doping, characterized by the zero bias depletion width (W_0) or zero bias doping density (N_A), is uncorrelated with performance or open-circuit voltage.
2) TRPL lifetime, as measured by the second decay constant in a double-exponential fit of the response curve, is enhanced in high-Voc devices. A nearly tenfold increase up to 30 ns is observed.
3) All high-V_{oc} devices show an E_A approximately equal to the bandgap of the absorber layer. The interface is not a limiting mechanism in devices with high V_{oc} or record setting efficiencies.

The change in TRPL lifetime is the dominant shift in the discussed 3LMs and expresses an improvement in the overall CdTe absorber quality, may it be due to a reduction of grain boundary or bulk recombination.

IV. CELL TO MODULE

A fully self-consistent solver was developed that translates measured *I–V* characteristic at the cell level to the total area efficiency or power at the module level. Different module designs can be considered in this translation. This solver assumes that the virtual module is created uniform, incorporates all known loss mechanism, and can consider past and current module designs offered by First Solar. The algorithm: 1) corrects

3LM Parameters for Devices With V_{oc} in the Range of 840–900 mV (840, 852, 875, and 903 mV are NREL Certified Measurements, 872 mV is Certified by Newport); Shown are Efficiency (η), Zero-Bias Depletion Width (W_0), Zero-Bias Doping Density (N_A), TRPL Second Decay Time Constant (τ_2), and Zero Kelvin Intercept of V_{oc} Versus T Measurements

V_{oc}	η	W_0	N_A	τ_2*	$V_{oc}@0K^\$$
(mV)	(%)	(μm)	($\times 10^{15}$/cm^{-3})	(ns)	(V)
"typical" 840	15-16	0.9-1.5	0.5-1	2-5	1.4+/-0.05
840	17.3	0.9	1.2	(5-8)†	~1.4
852	18.7	1.2	0.6	10-15	1.6
872	19.0	1.3	0.6	10-15	1.6
875	18.3	0.9	1.0	10-15	1.5
903	14.9	1.3	0.4	20-30	1.5

*second exponential decay constant, characterized at NREL.

† estimate based on comparative analysis using a different TRPL system.

$^\$$ IV-T values are extracted from a variety of instruments utilizing overlapping but slightly varying temperature ranges.

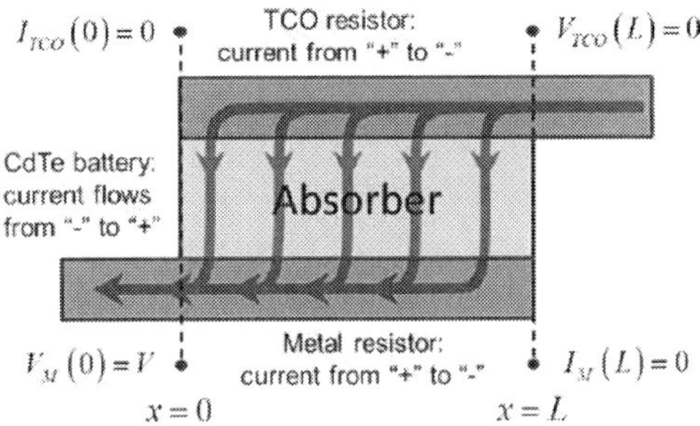

Fig. 5. "Unit cell" of the cell to module solver with boundary conditions.

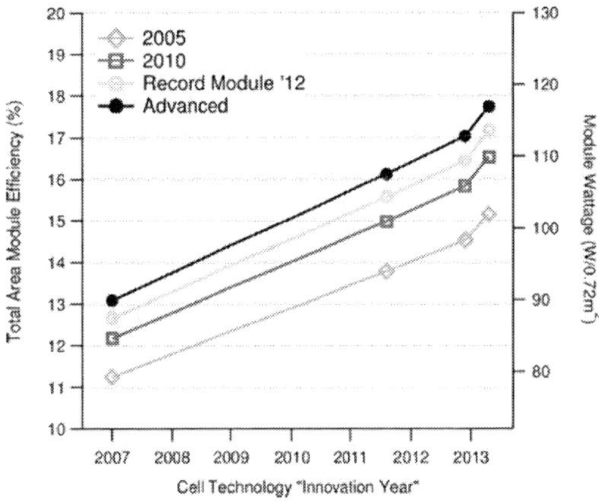

Fig. 6. Module efficiencies predicted from cell champion results assuming four different module integration schemes.

the measured cell *I–V* curve for known parasitic impacts; 2) calculates the net distributed resistance impact; and 3) accounts for dead areas in the module periphery as well as losses caused by the monolithic integration. Fig. 5 shows the unit cell and the boundary conditions considered for each unit cell.

Over the past decade, First Solar has made numerous changes to the device architecture, but also changes to the module integration aspects. The latter are typically more visible, e.g., the change from a wider edge delete pattern to a narrower edge, the reduction of the laser scribe pitch, or the switch from First Solar's Series 2 to Series 3 design. For the analysis, we considered four "module" technologies:

1) "2005" is representative of the First Solar Series 2 module with automatic edge delete and single-submodule circuit;
2) "2010" is representative of the First Solar Series 3 module with a narrower edge delete and two parallel submodule circuits;
3) "Record Module 12" is representative of the configuration used in the 16.1% total-area efficiency module reported by First Solar earlier [14];
4) An "Advanced" configuration considered attainable through continuous improvement of the current configuration without disruptive changes.

Utilizing *I–V* curves representing First Solar's certified record cell characteristics and the module designs described above, the results shown in Fig. 6 are obtained. Also included for this analysis is a 14.1% cell result that was certified by NREL in 2007. The horizontal axis describes the year; the cell performances

(>14% 2007, >17% 2011, >18% 2012, >19% 2013) were demonstrated and certified; the four curves show the results given the assumptions of the module design characteristics as described above. The recently reported total-area 16.1% record module [14] utilized module designs represented by the green circles and a cell technology that was advanced from the 2011 record cell. We find the prediction and module-level results in good agreement. Cell efficiencies exceeding 18% enable module efficiency exceeding 16%. Implementation of a 19% cell technology coupled with further optimization of the module design beyond the present allows efficiency to increase into the 17–18% territory without disruptive technology changes at the cell or module level.

V. Conclusions

Technological boundaries are shifting for CdTe thin-film solar cells. The previously believed target of 19% has been demonstrated and there is reason for optimism that CdTe will be able to significantly exceed 20% in the near future. We propose that a new attainable target should be formulated as 22% cell efficiency, and the improvements will be dominated by further increases in J_{sc} and V_{oc} beyond 900 mV. Cell efficiencies at today's record cell level will enable total-area module efficiencies exceeding 17% without disruptive design changes at the cell or module level.

REFERENCES

[1] S. H. Demtsu and J. R. Sites, "Quantification of losses in thin-film CdS/CdTe solar cells," presented at the Conf. Rec. 31st IEEE Photovoltaic Spec. Conf., Lake Buena Vista, FL, USA, 2006.

[2] J. Sites and J. Pan, "Strategies to increase CdTe solar-cell voltage," *Thin Solid Films*, vol. 515, no. 15, pp. 6099–6102, 2007.

[3] "Voc Workshop," in *Proc. 19th Nat. CdTe R&D Team Meeting*, Golden, CO, USA, 2006.

[4] NREL. (2013). [Online]. Available: http://www.nrel.gov/ncpv/images/efficiency_chart.jpg

[5] J. Britt and C. Ferekides, "Thin-film CdS/CdTe solar cell with 15.8% efficiency," *Appl. Phys. Lett.*, vol. 62, no. 22, pp. 2851–2852, 1993.

[6] X. Wu, J. C. Keane, R. G. Dhere, C. DeHart, D. S. Albin, A. Duda, T. A. Gessert, S. Asher, D. H. Levi, and P. Sheldon, "16.5%-efficient CdS/CdTe polycrystalline thin-film solar cell," in *Proc. 17th Eur. Photovoltaic Sol. Energy Conf.*, 2001, pp. 995–1000.

[7] H. Ohyama, T. Aramoto, S. Kumazawa, H. Higuchi, T. Arita, S. Shibutani, T. Nishio, J. Nakajima, M. Tsuji, A. Hanafusa, T. Hibino, K. Omura, and M. Murozono, "16.0% efficient thin-film CdS/CdTe solar cells," in *Proc. Conf. Rec. 26th IEEE Photovoltaic Spec. Conf.*, Anaheim, CA, USA, 1997.

[8] M. A. Green, K. Emery, D. L. King, S. Igari, and W. Warta, "Solar cell efficiency tables (version 18)," *Progr. Photovoltaics: Res. Appl.*, vol. 9, pp. 287–293, 2001.

[9] M. A. Green, K. Emery, Y. Hishikawa, W. Warta, and E. D. Dunlop, "Solar cell efficiency tables (version 40)," *Progr. Photovoltaics: Res. Appl.*, vol. 20, pp. 606–614, 2012.

[10] M. A. Green, K. Emery, Y. Hishikawa, W. Warta, and E. D. Dunlop, "Solar cell efficiency tables (version 41)," *Progr. Photovoltaics: Res. Appl.*, vol. 21, pp. 1–11, 2013.

[11] J. T. Heath, J. D. Cohen, and W. N. Shafarman, "Bulk and metastable defects in $CuIn_{1-x}Ga_x Se_2$ thin films using drive level capacitance profiling," *J. Appl. Phys.*, vol. 95, no. 3, pp. 1000–1010, 2004.

[12] A. Kanevce, D. H. Levi, and D. Kuciauskas, "The role of drift, diffusion, and recombination in time-resolved photoluminescence of CdTe solar cells determined through numerical simulation," *Progr. Photovoltaic*, 2013. DOI: 10.1002/pip.2369.

[13] S. Hegedus and W. N. Shafarman, "Thin-film solar cells: Device measurements and analysis," *Progr. Photovoltaics: Res. Appl.*, vol. 12, pp. 155–176, 2004.

[14] Press Release, First Solar Inc., Perrysburg, OH, USA, Apr. 22, 2013.

Authors' photographs and biographies not available at the time of publication.

Current Conduction Mechanism of Front-Side Contact of N-Type Crystalline Si Solar Cells With Ag/Al Pastes

Liang Liang, Zhigang Li, Lap Kin Cheng, Norihiko Takeda, R. J. S. Young, and Alan Carroll

Abstract—Recently, n-type crystalline Si (c-Si) cells with front-side (FS) metallization Ag/Al paste have attracted considerable attention. However, a clear understanding of current conduction mechanism is still lacking. We report here the results of our microstructural investigation of the interfacial contact region using electron microscopy techniques. In optimally fired cells, we did not find any Al–Si eutectic layer on the emitter surface that would support a regrowth mechanism as found during the back surface field formation process commonly practiced to create the full plane Al back contact of p-type industrial solar cells. The presence of SiN_x antireflection coating has possibly altered significantly the chemistry between Si and Al. The observed microstructures suggest that the current conduction is predominantly tunneling through ultrathin interfacial glass, assisted by the presence of nano-Ag colloids. We believe this mechanism is similar to the current conduction model we have proposed previously for FS Ag-contact of p-type c-Si solar cells with Ag paste.

Index Terms—Current conduction mechanism, front-side (FS) contact, microstructural investigation, n-type crystalline Si solar cells.

I. Introduction

RECENTLY, n-type crystalline Si (c-Si) cells have attracted considerable attention especially with respect to their potential as next-generation high-efficiency industrial devices. Modules made with n-type c-Si cells possess several important advantages over incumbent p-type c-Si ones. For instance, light-induced degradation, suffered by p-type Cz c-Si solar modules [1], [2], is absent in n-type panels. Attempts to reduce production costs of these next generation devices have led to the commercialization of n-type c-Si solar modules, such as Yingli's PANDA, and their large-scale installations [3]. In contrast with earlier state-of-the-art technology, such as interdigitated back-contact or heterojunction with intrinsic thin layer

solar cells, which emphasized highest performance, recent research and development efforts have been aimed at adapting low-cost conventional p-type manufacturing processes (dopant diffusion, plasma-enhanced chemical vapor deposition SiN_x, screen-printed contacts, etc.) to the production of higher efficiency n-type devices. These efforts have led to an average cell efficiency of $>19\%$ from production lines. The metallization is one of the most critical processing steps in n-type c-Si solar cell production. The commercially available Ag metallization paste for front-side (FS) metallization of p-type c-Si solar cells was initially tried on contact FS of n-type c-Si cells, but the measured contact resistivity was too high and cell efficiency was low [4]. On the other hand, Al paste has been successfully employed on the backside of p-type c-Si solar cells [5]. During rapid thermal processing of an industrial p-type c-Si solar cell, back surface field (BSF) Al-doped Si layer was regrown from a molten Al–Si alloy pool [5], [6]. During cool down, the molten Al–Si solidifies into a $\sim 12\%$ Si "eutectic layer," which can be best described as an Al matrix embedded with lots of small Si lamellae crystals. The microstructure of the backside of a p-type c-Si cell has been described in detail in the literature [7]–[9]. Later, Al powders (~ 1 micron in size) as additive were added in the Ag paste. When Ag/Al paste is used as the FS metallization paste of n-type c-Si cells, the cell efficiency improves significantly and the Ag/Al paste has been broadly adopted in commercial-scale production of n-type c-Si solar cells. Several papers have been published discussing the microstructure of screen-printed FS contact to n-type c-Si cells and the associated current conduction mechanism. Lago *et al.* [10] and Riegel *et al.* [11]–[13] reported their microstructural investigation of FS contacts printed with Ag/Al pastes on "model" n-type c-Si cells *without* SiN_x antireflective coating (ARC). However, it remains unclear whether their findings are applicable to an actual industrial cell where a $SiNx$ ARC is always present. Here, we report our microstructural investigation of $SiNx$ coated n-type c-Si solar cells contacts printed with commercially optimized Ag/Al pastes. To date, two main current conduction models of p-type FS contact of c-Si solar cells have been proposed: "nano-Ag colloids assisted tunneling" and "Ag crystallites" [14]–[17]. We will propose the current conduction mechanism of FS contact of n-type c-Si solar cells in this paper.

Manuscript received June 15, 2013; revised August 12, 2013 and September 18, 2013; accepted November 4, 2013.

L. Liang, Z. G. Li, and L. K. Cheng are with DuPont Central Research and Development, Wilmington, DE 19880-0500 USA (e-mail: liang.lliang@dupont.com; zhigang-rick.li@dupont.com; lapkin.K.cheng@dupont.com).

N. Takeda is with DuPont Microcircuit Materials, KSP, Kawasaki, Kanagawa 213-0012, Japan (e-mail: norihiko.taketa@dupont.com).

R. J. S. Young was with DuPont Microcircuit Materials, Bristol BS16 1QD, U.K.

A. F. Carroll is with DuPont Microcircuit Materials, Research Triangle Park, NC 27709 USA (e-mail: alan.F.carroll@dupont.com).

Color versions of one or more of the figures in this paper are available online at http://ieeexplore.ieee.org.

Digital Object Identifier 10.1109/JPHOTOV.2013.2292350

II. Experimental Setup

Our basic experimental procedures for paste and cell fabrication can be found in previous publications [18]. Small 30 mm $\times$

30 mm wafers were diced from textured 156 mm × 156 mm n-type wafers that are equipped with B-doped FS emitter (with sheet resistance of 60 Ω/square), P-doped back surface field, and front and back surface-passivated SiNx ARC optimized for light trapping. A 14-fingers FS contact grid was printed on these 9-cm^2 wafers with a commercially available Ag/Al paste, while a similar backside grid, with a commercially available Ag paste [19], [20]. After drying, these printed cells were fired at progressively higher peak set-point temperatures in an infrared belt furnace. Their J–V and Suns-V_{oc} curves were characterized using commercial testers. The Xe arc lamp in our J–V tester (ST-1000, Telecom-STV Co., Moscow, Russia) simulated sunlight at 1-Sun intensity and briefly irradiated the front surface of the cell to ensure 25 °C operation. The J–V tester used a four-point contact method to obtain J–V curves from which the fill factor, series resistance, and cell efficiency of n-type cells were calculated. Under-fired (with our belt furnace peak set point at 785 °C) and optimally fired (set points at 825 °C–905 °C) cells were identified based on measured efficiency (the paste has a wide optimal firing window). Contact resistance was obtained from 2-cm-wide sample strips cut directly from these solar cells. A custom-built tester, based on a technique similar to the transmission line method, was used to measure contact resistivity with accuracy down to ±0.1 mΩ·cm^2 [21]. Scanning electron microscope (SEM), JEM-7600 F, equipped with energy dispersive spectroscopy (EDS) was used to analyze the interfacial region of these cells.

III. RESULTS

Experimentally, we have found that the presence of Al influences contact resistance positively in our Al–Ag paste, although Al's oxidation does degrade bulk resistivity of the printed Ag–Al lines. Since aluminum forms low-melting eutectic with silicon at relatively low temperature (∼577 °C), we decided to focus our microstructure investigation on cells that perform with maximum efficiency (i.e., optimally fired, with belt furnace set points at 825 °C and 905 °C, "optimally-fired cells"), and cells that just fell short of forming an optimal contact (i.e., under-fired, with set point at 785 °C, "under fired cell"). The efficiency for the two optimally-fired cells studied here was ∼17.4%, and for under-fired cells, 13.8%. Most of the difference in cell efficiency can be attributed to a ∼5× lower contact resistivity of the optimally fired (905 °C) cell (i.e., 4.6 mΩ·cm^2 versus 23 mΩ·cm^2). For the optimally fired cells, no shunting problem is observed as judged from high V_{oc} value. A detailed SEM study of the interfacial region between the FS contact and p$^+$ Si emitter of these cells was then carried out to investigate if the difference in electrical performance can be qualitatively explained by microstructural features. SEM samples were taken from multiple locations of several of these cells to ensure that our images are representative.

We found that in general the microstructure of the front-side's interfacial contact region of screen-printed n-type c-Si solar cells is similar to the FS contact of p-type c-Si cells, which we have previously reported [14]–[16], [18]–[20]. Fig. 1 is a low magnification SEM image that gives a cross-sectional overview of an Ag finger line of an n-type optimal-fired cell. The image

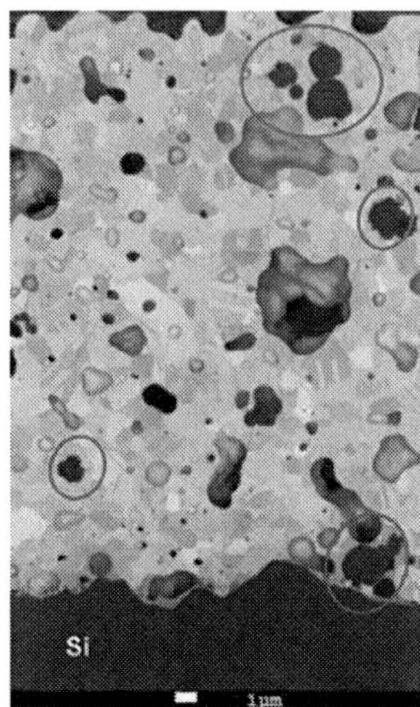

Fig. 1.   Low magnification cross-sectional SEM image of front-side contact of n-type c-Si optimally fired cell (Al particles, identified by EDS, are circled).

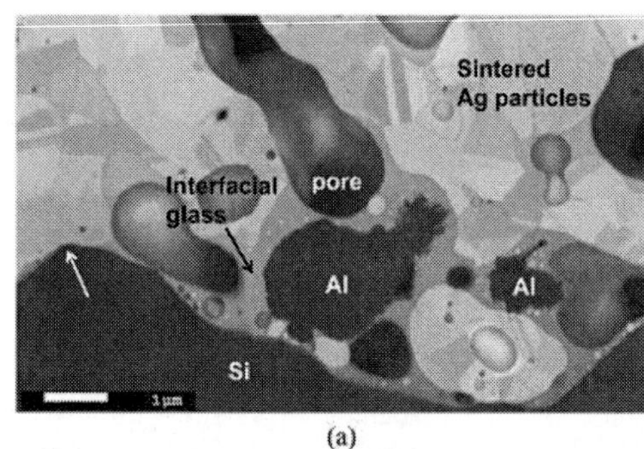

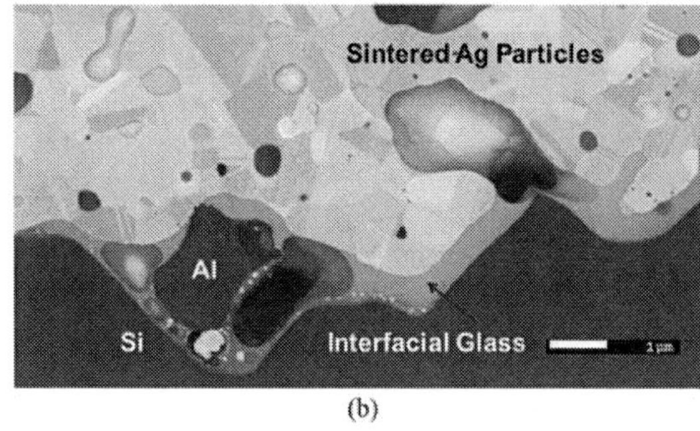

Fig. 2.   Cross-sectional SEM images of Al particles near the interface of cells fired at (a) 825 °C and (b) 905 °C. No Al–Si eutectic layer was found in either cells.

includes the interfacial region between sintered Ag line bulk and the p$^+$ Si emitter. A continuous interfacial glass layer with nano-Ag colloids was found between FS contact and the p$^+$ Si emitter. Relatively isolated Al particles were seen randomly distributed throughout the Ag conductor line. At a few locations, Al particles were found adjacent to but not embedded in the Si emitter surface.

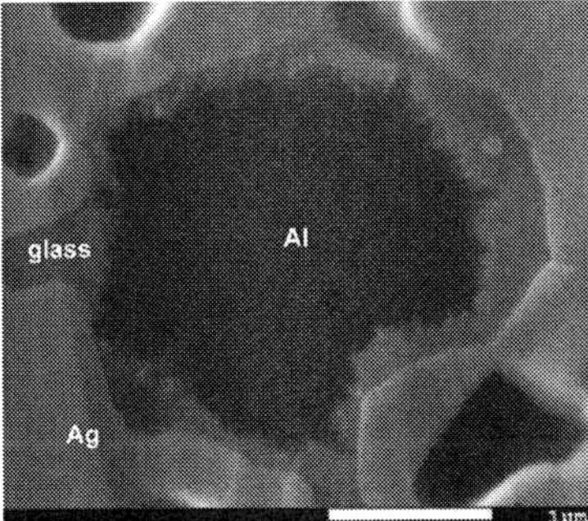

Fig. 3. Cross-sectional SEM image of an Al surrounded by melted glass in the FS conductor line.

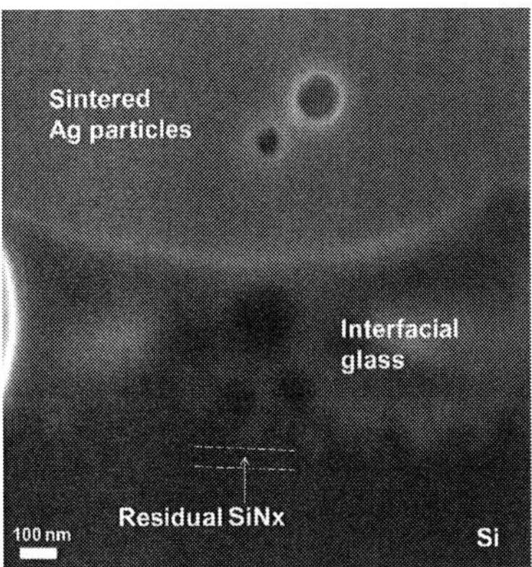

Fig. 4. Cross-sectional SEM image showing residual SiN_x at the interface between FS contact and p^+ emitter of the "under-fired" cell.

Fig. 2 presents the microstructure of Al particles found near the interface between FS contact and p^+ emitter of our optimally fired cells. Microstructural features can be readily identified such as Al particles surrounded by melted glass, pores, interfacial glass with different thicknesses containing nano-Ag colloids; these can all strongly affect current collection. Some of the content of the interfacial glass are the products of the reaction between the chemically active ingredients in the Ag/Al paste and the SiN_x ARC formed during the etching process. The white arrow in Fig. 2(a) identifies an area where Si and bulk Ag conductor line (sintered Ag particles) appears to be "touching." These ultrathin interfacial glass with nano-Ag colloids regions of FS contact of p-type Si cells were in detail investigated and previously reported [8]–[10], [12]–[14]. The microstructures revealed by our SEM images of these n-type Si cell contacts are consistent with our previously proposed conduction model using nano-Ag colloids-assisted tunneling [14]–[16]. It is worth noting that in all of the SEM investigation that we have done, we found practically no Ag crystallites on the emitter surface of optimally fired n-type c-Si solar cells. Since SEM can easily distinguish between Al and Si phases, high-quality images can be readily obtained to reveal them. For the devices investigated in this study, we did not observe Al–Si eutectic layer structure in the interfacial region between FS contact and p^+ Si emitter.

Within the bulk Ag conductor line, isolated Al particles were found randomly distributed throughout the sintered network of Ag particles and resolidified glass. Fig. 3 presents the microstructure of one Al particle, surrounded by resolidified glass, and sintered Ag particles. The melting temperatures of both Al and glass frit are usually low, and Al and glass frit readily reacted during firing (at 825 °C set point temperature). Nevertheless, some larger Al particles have survived the firing process resulting in the microstructure shown in Fig. 3. Consistent with the Al–Ag phase diagram [22], we also occasionally observed Al–Ag alloy embedded in the Ag line.

To investigate the relationship between microstructure and cell performance, we have included a detailed characterization of an under-fired cell. We found that a large portion of residual SiN_x still remains, as illustrated by Fig. 4. Residual SiN_x's high electrical resistance causes higher contact resistivity and lowers cell efficiency. Our SEM result reinforces the importance of a more complete removal of the insulating SiN_x ARC during the cell firing process to achieve the highest efficiency.

IV. DISCUSSION AND CONCLUSION

In previous studies of FS contact of boron-doped p^+ emitter of n-type c-Si solar cells, devices without SiN_x ARC were used, and Al–Si eutectic regrowth features were recognized as playing an important role in contacting such cells [10]–[13]. In this paper, we report, in detail, the microstructure of FS contact of n-type c-Si solar cells (B-doped p^+-Si emitter and our commercial Ag/Al paste) *with* SiN_x ARC. Features such as residual SiNx layer, Al particles surrounded with glass, Ag–Al alloy, and ultrathin glass with nano-Ag colloids, were observed in the FS contact of n-type Si solar cells. We found no evidence of Al–Si eutectic layer on top of the boron-doped Si emitter, which indicates its absence or much reduced presence. This finding is very different from the microstructure of both the backside of p-type c-Si cells and the FS of n-type c-Si cells without SiN_x ARC [10]–[13], where eutectic layers were formed after firing in both cases. We attributed this key difference to the presence of FS SiNx ARC, which interferes with Al's reaction with the silicon emitter.

Our investigation of FS contact of n-type c-Si cells reveals microstructural features that are consistent with electron tunneling being the dominant conduction mechanism. The presence of copious quantities of Ag colloids in the interfacial glass also supports the view that they could aid in carrier tunneling. We suggest, therefore, that the "nano-Ag colloids assisted tunneling" mechanism [14]–[16] we had proposed previously is also operative in n-type c-Si solar cells. In contrast, the absence of Al–Si eutectic layers would suggest that Al–Si contacts cannot be responsible for photocurrent extraction in our devices. In addition, we would like to point out that with SEM study of our under-fired and optimally fired devices, we practically found no Ag crystallites on the surface of these emitters. It is, therefore, highly unlikely that an alternative interpretation of conduction via Ag crystallites can be considered plausible. In a recent report, Jiang *et al.* observed that the presence of Ag crystallites on the emitter would damage the emitter/junction [23]. The study presented here shows that the key to high cell efficiency/low contact resistivity is the formation of well distributed high areal percentage of ultrathin interfacial glass with nano-Ag colloids at the interface. We describe in a recent publication that Ag crystallites and nano-Ag colloids were both observed if the distinction in the "thermal evolution" of these two microstructures was not sharp but more gradual as we swept across the optimal firing temperature [16]. It appears that for the n-type solar cells reported here, the microstructural features that delivered the best cell performance were formed at a temperature where the nucleation and growth of Ag crystallites were still disfavored.

In conclusion, we investigated by SEM the microstructure of the interfacial region between screen-printed FS Ag/Al contact and Si emitter of n-type c-Si solar cells with SiN_x ARC. No Al–Si eutectic layer was found at the interface between FS conductor lines and p^+ Si emitter. Our microstructure results suggest that FS contacts to p-type and n-type cells share a common dominant current conduction mechanism, namely, nano-Ag colloids-assisted tunneling. Our work also indicated the significant influence of the SiN_x in altering the Al–Si reaction chemistry.

ACKNOWLEDGMENT

The authors would like to thank their DuPont colleagues M. Lu, J. Casper, L. Zhang, M. Lewittes, J. Sternberg, S. Freilich, P. O'Callaghan, R. Leach, T. Suess, and M. Barker for the fruitful discussions and support of their experiments.

REFERENCES

[1] D. Macdonald and L. Geerligs, "Recombination activity of interstitial iron and other transition metal point defects in *p*- and *n*-type crystalline silicon," *Appl. Phys. Lett.*, vol. 85, pp. 4061–4063, 2004.

[2] S. Glunz, S. Rein, J. Lee, and W. Warta, "Minority carrier lifetime degradation in boron-doped Czochralski silicon," *J. Appl. Phys.*, vol. 90, pp. 2397–2404, 2001.

[3] D. Song, "Progress in *n*-type Si solar cell and module technology for high efficiency and low cost," presented at the 38th IEEE Photovoltaic Spec. Conf., Austin, TX, USA, 2012.

[4] H. Kerp, S. Kim, R. Lago, F. Recart, I. Freire, L. Perez, K. Albertsen, J. Carlos, and A. Shaikh, "Develop of screenprintable contacts for p+ emitter in bifacial solar cells," in *Proc. 21st Eur. Photovoltaic Sol. Energy Conf.*, Dresden, Germany, 2006, pp. 892–895.

[5] P. Loelgen, C. Leguijt, J. A. Eikelboom, R. A. Steeman, W. C. Sinke, L. A. Verhoef, P. F. A. Alkemade, and E. Algra, "Aluminum back-surface field doping profiles with surface recombination velocities below 200 cm/s," in *Proc. 23rd IEEE Photovoltaic Spec. Conf.*, Louisville, KY, USA, 1993, pp. 236–238.

[6] E. Peiner, A. Schlachetzi, and D. Kruger, "Doping profile analysis in Si by electrochemical capacitance-voltage measurements," *J. Electrochem. Soc.*, vol. 142, pp. 576–580, 1995.

[7] F. Huster, "Aluminum-back surface field: Bow investigation and elimination," in *Proc. 20th Eur. Photovoltaic Sol. Energy Conf.*, Barcelona, Spain, 2005, pp. 635–638.

[8] F. Huster and G. Schubert, "ECV doping profile measurements of aluminum alloyed back surface fields," in *Proc. 20th Eur. Photovoltaic Sol. Energy Conf.*, Barcelona, Spain, 2005, pp. 1462–1475.

[9] F. Huster, "Investigation of the alloying process of screen printed aluminum pastes for the BSF formation on silicon solar cells," in *Proc. 20th Eur. Photovoltaic Sol. Energy Conf.*, Barcelona, Spain, 2005, pp. 1071–1074.

[10] R. Lago, L. Perez, H. Kerp, I. Freire, I. Hoces, N. Azkona, F. Recart, and J. Jimeno, "Screen printing metallization of boron emitters," *Progress Photovotaics, Res. Appl.*, vol. 18, pp. 20–27, 2010.

[11] S. Riegel, F. Mutter, G. Hahn, and B. Terheiden, "Contact formation in the silver/aluminum thick film firing process – a phenomenological approach," in *Proc. 25th Eur. Photovoltaic Sol. Energy Conf.*, Valencia, Spain, Sep. 2010, pp. 2353–2356.

[12] S. Riegel, F. Mutter, G. Hahn, and B. Terheiden, "Influence of the dopant on the contact formation to p+-type Silicon," *Energy Procedia*, vol. 8, pp. 533–539, 2011.

[13] S. Riegel, F. Mutter, T. Lauermann, B. Terheiden, and G. Hahn, "Review on screen printed metallization on p-type silicon," *Energy Procedia*, vol. 21, pp. 14–23, 2012.

[14] Z. G. Li, L. Liang, and L. K. Cheng, "Electron microscopy study of front-side Ag contact in crystalline Si solar cells," *J. Appl. Phys.*, vol. 105, pp. 66102–66104, 2009.

[15] L. K. Cheng, L. Liang, and Z. G. Li, "Nano-Ag colloids assisted tunneling mechanism for current conduction in front contact of crystalline Si solar cells," in *Proc. 34th IEEE Photovoltaic Spec. Conf.*, Philadelphia, PA, USA, 2009, pp. 2344–2046.

[16] Z. G. Li, L. Liang, A. S. Ionkin, B. M. Fish, M. E. Lewittes, L. K. Cheng, and K. R. Mikeska, "Microstructural comparison of silicon solar cells' front-side Ag contact and the evolution of current conduction mechanisms," *J. Appl. Phys.*, vol. 110, pp. 074304–074311, 2011.

[17] C. Ballif, D. Huljic, G. Willeke, and A. Hessler-Wyser, "Silver thick-film contacts on highly doped *n*-type silicon emitter: Structure and electronic properties of the interface," *Appl. Phys. Lett.*, vol. 82, pp. 1878–1880, 2003.

[18] A. S. Ionkin, B. M. Fish, Z. G. Li, M. E. Lewittes, P. Soper, J. G. Pepin, and A. F. Carroll, "Screen-printable silver pastes with metallic nano-zinc and nano-zinc alloys for crystalline silicon photovoltaic cells," *ACS Appl. Mater. Interfaces*, vol. 3, pp. 606–610, 2011.

[19] Z. G. Li, K. R. Mikeska, P. D. VerNooy, and L. Liang, "Microstructural investigation of new thick-film paste flux for contacting silicon solar cells," in *Proc. 37th IEEE Photovoltaic Spec. Conf.*, Seattle, WA, USA, 2011, pp. 120–122.

[20] K. Mikeska, Z. G. Li, P. D. VerNooy, L. Liang, A. F. Carroll, J. Chou, and K. Shih, "New thick film paste flux for contacting silicon solar cells," in *Proc. 26th Eur. Photovoltaic Sol. Energy Conf.*, Hamburg, Germany, 2011, pp. 502–504.

[21] D. K. Schroder and D. L. Meier, "Solar cell contact resistance—A Review," *IEEE Trans. Electron Dev.*, vol. 31, pp. 637–647, 1984.

[22] Ag–Al phase diagram. [Online]. Available: http://www.crct.polymtl.ca/fact/documentation/TDNucl/Ag-Al.jpg

[23] C. Jiang, Z. G. Li, H. R. Moutinho, L. Liang, A. Ionkin, and M. M. Al-Jassim, "Real-space microscopic electrical imaging of n^+-p junction beneath front-side Ag contact of multicrystalline Si solar cells," *J. Appl. Phys.*, vol. 111, pp. 083704–083710, 2012.

Liang Liang received the B.E. degree from the Huazhong Institute of Technology, Huazhong, China, in 1982 and the Ph.D. degree in electronic engineering from the Institut Nationale Polytechnique de Toulouse, Toulouse, France in 1987.

She is currently a Research Associate with DuPont Central Research and Development, Wilmington, DE, USA. Her research interests include developing high-efficiency Ag paste for silicon solar cells. Her work has focused on the investigation of the microstructure of the front-side contact of p- and n-type crystalline Si solar cells and understanding current conduction mechanisms.

Zhigang Li received the Ph.D degree in applied physics from the University of Paul Sabatier, Toulouse, France.

He is currently a Research Associate with DuPont Central Research and Development, Wilmington, DE, USA. His research interests include current conduction mechanisms of front-side contact of p- and n-type crystalline Si solar cells, new paste development, and industrial applications of advanced electron microscopy techniques. He was the editor/co-editor of two books: *Industrial Applications of Electron Microscopy* (New York: Marcel Dekker, 2003) and *Organic Light-Emitting Materials and Devices* (New York: CRC, 2006).

Lap Kin Cheng received the Ph.D. degree in applied physics from Cornell University.

Upon graduation, he joined DuPont Central Research, Wilmington, DE, USA, as a crystal grower of nonlinear optical materials for data storage applications. During the past two decades, he has worked on a broad range of technologies, including catalysis, flexographic printing, Li-polymer batteries, and photovoltaics. His recent professional interests have focused on silicon solar cells, particularly relating to gaining a deeper understanding of the contact mechanism as it related to the design of better silver pastes.

Norihiko Takeda received the Ph.D. (Eng.) degree in materials chemistry from Osaka University, Osaka, Japan in 1998.

After working as a Researcher at several institutes, he joined DuPont Microcircuit Materials, Kanagawa, Japan, in 2006, where he has been working on thick-film paste for crystalline silicon solar cells ever since. He is currently a Senior Technical Specialist with DuPont Microcircuit Materials and leading the development of DuPont™ Solamet metallization for n-type cells.

R. J. S. Young, photograph and biography not available at the time of publication.

Alan Carroll received the Ph.D. degree in materials engineering science from Virginia Tech, Blacksburg, VA, USA, in 1980.

He is a Research Fellow with DuPont Microcircuit Materials, Research Triangle Park, NC, USA, where, for 28 years, he has developed numerous thick-film paste products, including DuPont™ Solamet metallization. His collaborative research on metal contact mechanisms has led to several product generations that have enabled advances in crystalline Si solar cell technology.

24.7% Record Efficiency HIT Solar Cell on Thin Silicon Wafer

Mikio Taguchi, Ayumu Yano, Satoshi Tohoda, Kenta Matsuyama, Yuya Nakamura, Takeshi Nishiwaki, Kazunori Fujita, and Eiji Maruyama

Abstract—A new record conversion efficiency of 24.7% was attained at the research level by using a heterojunction with intrinsic thin-layer structure of practical size (101.8 cm^2, total area) at a 98-μm thickness. This is a world height record for any crystalline silicon-based solar cell of practical size (100 cm^2 and above). Since we announced our former record of 23.7%, we have continued to reduce recombination losses at the hetero interface between a-Si and c-Si along with cutting down resistive losses by improving the silver paste with lower resistivity and optimization of the thicknesses in a-Si layers. Using a new technology that enables the formation of a-Si layer of even higher quality on the c-Si substrate, while limiting damage to the surface of the substrate, the V_{oc} has been improved from 0.745 to 0.750 V. We also succeeded in improving the fill factor from 0.809 to 0.832.

Index Terms—Amorphous materials, heterojunction, photovoltaic (PV) cells, silicon, surface passivation.

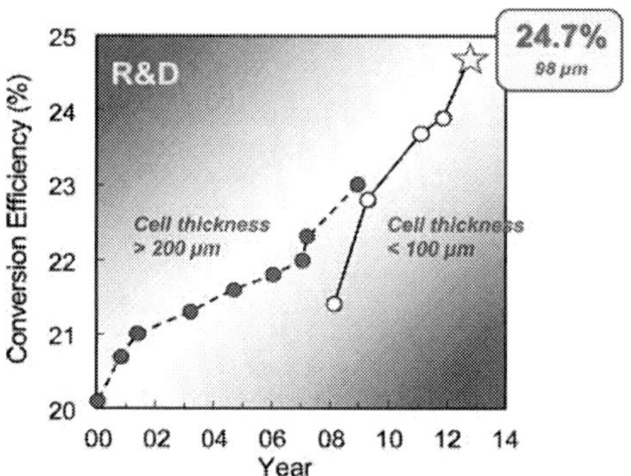

Fig. 1. Progress in conversion efficiency of HIT cells at R&D stage.

I. Introduction

SOLAR photovoltaic (PV) demand reached 29 GW in 2012 and can be expected to keep growing. Moreover, large-scale PV power stations have started appearing in many countries, and the globalization of the PV market is growing ever more noticeable year by year. It goes without saying that this rapid growth of global PV demand has thus far been caused in large part by the sharp reduction of solar module pricing.

Currently, the balance-of-systems cost has become the most important issue for the PV system cost. The ratio of the cost of the mounting materials, the power conditioners, and the land is now more significant than ever with lower module prices; therefore, it has become crucial to consider how the whole system cost can be reduced.

A more efficient solar module would be one solution. The area of a PV power station can be reduced without losing any output power, thus reducing the cost except for the PV module. A decrease in the area of a power station could also reduce maintenance costs such as weeding the PV fields, which is never negligible and is a continuous expense. Thus, many PV energy providers are working on the next technological advance of their products and are desperate for high-efficiency PV modules with reasonable production costs.

The heterojunction with intrinsic thin-layer (HIT) solar cell is one of the most promising solar cell structures that enable both high efficiency and low cost. Its symmetrical structure and low temperature process are well suited to using thin silicon wafers, which still account for the major cost of typical crystalline silicon (c-Si)-based solar modules.

Fig. 1 shows the progress in the conversion efficiency for HIT solar cells at the R&D stage. We started research on amorphous silicon (a-Si)/c-Si heterojunction solar cells in 1990 [1] and have been accumulating technologies to fabricate high-efficiency solar cells for long time. In our history of the development, we have shown some unique results that were beyond common knowledge in those days, namely, the usage of the n-type Si wafer, an unusually high open-circuit voltage (V_{oc}) of more than 0.700 V, a simple and low temperature process, and so on.

From about 2000, many researchers joined this field, which accelerated and deepened the fundamental knowledge about this structure [2]–[5].

Since we reported an excellent conversion efficiency of 22.8% with a thin (98 μm) wafer and 23.0% with a thick (>200 μm) wafer in 2009 [6], we have focused on developing technologies for higher conversion efficiency with the thin c-Si wafer with the aim of reducing material cost. Recently, we attained the superb conversion efficiency of 24.7% with a thin wafer of 98 μm. In this paper, we describe our approaches to achieving higher conversion efficiency in HIT solar cells. (Wafer thicknesses are calculated from the weight.)

Manuscript received June 16, 2013; revised August 26, 2013; accepted September 10, 2013. Date of publication October 4, 2013; date of current version December 16, 2013.

The authors are with the Solar Business Unit, Eco Solutions Division, Sanyo Electric Co., Ltd., Eco Solutions Company of Panasonic Group, Kobe 651–2242, Japan (e-mail: taguchi.mikio@jp.panasonic.com; yano.ayumu@jp.panasonic.com; tohoda.satoshi@jp.panasonic.com; matsuyama.kenta@jp.panasonic.com; nakamura.yuya@jp.panasonic.com; nishiwaki.takeshi@jp.panasonic.com; fujita.kazunori@jp.panasonic.com; maruyama.eiji@jp.panasonic.com).

Color versions of one or more of the figures in this paper are available online at http://ieeexplore.ieee.org.

Digital Object Identifier 10.1109/JPHOTOV.2013.2282737

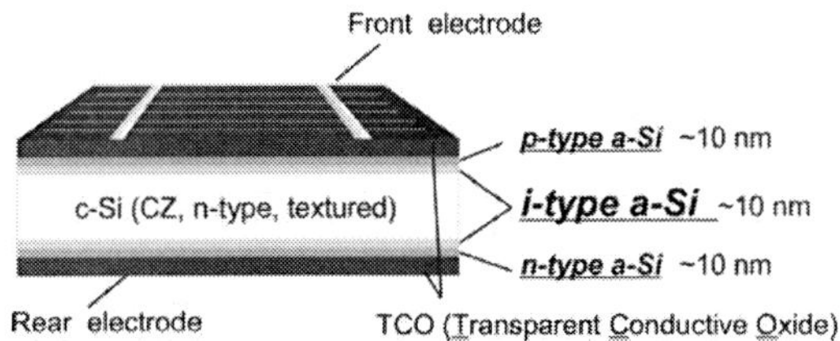

Fig. 2.   Structure of an HIT solar cell.

TABLE I

RECENT PROGRESS IN THE EFFICIENCY OF THE HIT SOLAR CELLS
WITH 98-μM THICKNESS AT THE R&D STAGE

Year	Voc [V]	Jsc [mA/cm2]	F.F. [%]	Effi. [%]
2013	0.750	39.5	83.2	24.7
2011	0.745	39.4	80.9	23.7
2009	0.743	38.8	79.1	22.8

II. STRUCTURE OF THE HETEROJUNCTION WITH INTRINSIC THIN-LAYER SOLAR CELL

Fig. 2 shows the structure of an HIT solar cell. The HIT solar cell, which is our original structure, is comprised of an intrinsic (i-type) a-Si layer and a p-type a-Si layer deposited on a randomly textured n-type Czochralski (CZ) crystalline silicon wafer to form a p/n heterojunction and i-type and n-type a-Si layers deposited on the opposite side of the wafer to obtain a back surface field structure. On both sides of the doped a-Si layers, transparent conductive oxide (TCO) layers and metal grid electrodes are fabricated. All of the processes described previously are done at low temperature ($<$200 °C) to avoid any thermal damage to the components of the cell.

By inserting the high-quality intrinsic a-Si layer between the c-Si wafer and the doped a-Si layer using a low-damage process, the surface dangling bonds of c-Si can be well passivated. This is based on our technologies to fabricate high-efficiency a-Si solar cells [7]. This effective passivation on both surfaces enables us to obtain an HIT solar cell with a high V_{oc} compared with conventional c-Si-based solar cells and leads to not only a high conversion efficiency but also an excellent temperature coefficient. The good temperature coefficient of HIT solar cells benefits consumers because the PV systems often work at temperatures of more than 25 °C (the standard condition to estimate the efficiency for the specification). In addition, as shown in Fig. 2, the HIT solar cell has a symmetrical structure that provides two advantages. One is the applicability of the cell to a so-called bifacial module, which can generate more electricity than an ordinary module, and the other is a less stressed structure, which is very important for thinner wafer processing.

III. APPROACHES TO IMPROVING THE EFFICIENCY OF THE HETEROJUNCTION WITH INTRINSIC THIN-LAYER SOLAR CELL

Table I shows the cell parameters of HIT solar cells with a 98-μm thick Si wafer and the record efficiency of 24.7%.

The V_{oc} of the HIT cell has been consistently increased step by step. We reported the very high value of 0.745 V in 2011 with a decrease in the surface recombination velocity to 2 cm/s accomplished by optimizing the wafer preparing before the a-Si deposition and modifying the deposition process of the a-Si layers [8]. We also reported that with an excellent passivation quality we could make the a-Si layers in the front surface thinner without sacrificing the V_{oc} and could increase the J_{sc} with the bandgap widening of the a-Si layers. It was reported that a certain thickness of i-layer would be necessary to complete the well-passivated surface for a specified V_{oc} [9], [10], but we found there is still a way to overcome the tradeoff between J_{sc} and V_{oc}. In the 2013 trial, utilizing the knowledge we had accrued in the past, we reviewed our material again and improved the film properties and the optimized thickness with great care. As a result, we were able to increase the V_{oc} to 0.750 V.

The optical losses in a-Si layers and TCO layers are problems peculiar to HIT solar cells and must be improved. The absorption loss in the short wavelength region is led by the layers on the front side of the HIT solar cell, which consists of a-Si and TCO layers. The absorption loss in the TCO layer on the back caused by free carrier absorption lowers the quantum efficiency at the near infrared region. The improvement of TCO will be described later.

The fill factor (FF) is affected by both the junction property and the resistive loss. We tried to increase the FF by improving the surface passivation quality of a-Si layers that increases the V_{oc} as well and by decreasing the resistive losses in electrodes, i.e., silver paste and TCO. The silver paste used for HIT solar cells is hardened at around or less than 200 °C and is more resistive compared with general fired-type silver pastes for conventional Si solar cells. Consequently, we have to develop an original silver paste for our cells. This material must be able to realize finer lines to reduce the shadow loss for a higher I_{sc} and simultaneously ensure lower resistance to increase the FF.

The bulk property of the CZ Si wafer is also important for high-efficiency solar cells because the HIT structure can derive the true potential of the silicon material with such low surface recombination velocity. To obtain the highest efficiency, none of three key items—wafer quality, wafer preparation, and high-quality a-Si—can be missed.

The fundamental strategy to achieve the high conversion efficiency in HIT solar cells described previously has not been changed for years, as shown in Fig. 3.

A. Improving the Characteristics of TCO Layers

A TCO layer, which is not used in other crystalline Si-based solar cells, plays the roles of electrodes and antireflection films for HIT solar cells. Improvement of this layer is quite important for the output performance of the HIT solar cell. In the backside of the TCO layer, the absorption loss in the near infrared region is caused by free carrier absorption. In order to suppress this absorption, the carrier concentration should be as low as possible, while maintaining sufficiently high conductivity. To this end, we investigated the best high-mobility material as well as the best deposition process. We succeeded in improving the electrical

        433

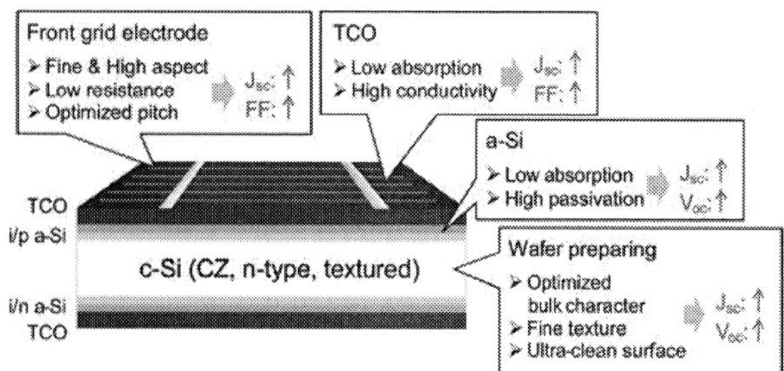

Fig. 3. Approaches for achieving higher conversion efficiency in HIT solar cells.

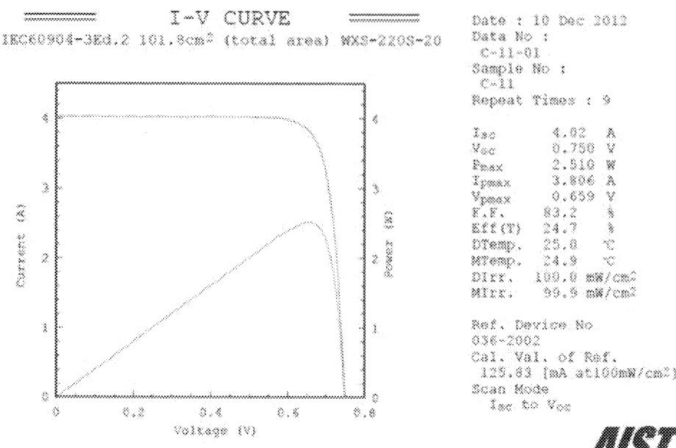

Fig. 4. I–V characteristics of the 24.7% efficiency an HIT solar cell with 98-μm thickness at the R&D stage (certified by Advanced Industrial Science and Technology). The cell is with a silver back reflector to avoid any fluctuation of the reflection with the measurement stage.

TABLE II
I–V CHARACTERISTICS OF THE HIT SOLAR CELLS FABRICATED WITH 98-μM-THICK AND 151-μM-THICK WAFERS (R&D STAGE)

Thickness [micron]	Voc [V]	Jsc [mA/cm2]	F.F. [%]	Effi. [%]
98	0.750	39.5	83.2	24.7
151	0.744	39.8	83.2	24.6

conductivity and the optical transmittance of TCO layers at the same time by designing the deposition process and optimizing the materials. We raised the Hall mobility in our TCO films step by step in 2009 and 2011 by reducing the carrier density and enhancing the spectral response at the near infrared region [11]. In this paper, we built on our recent results and obtained a spectrum response at the long wavelength region at a level similar to that in 2011.

B. Optimizing the Grid Electrode to Suppress the Shadow and Resistance Loss

For the HIT solar cell, we use screen-printed silver paste that can be hardened at a low temperature. This paste has a relatively high resistivity compared with that of conventional silicon solar cells. Therefore, we have had to continuously develop lower resistive materials by ourselves as well as the printing technology to minimize the resistive loss and the shadow loss at the grid electrode. Moreover, we have built up our knowledge about the silver paste materials that could balance long-term reliability with the electric characteristics.

With our efforts in developing the silver paste, we have succeeded in improving the uniformity of the contact resistance within the cell, while maintaining the high aspect ratio to minimize the shadow and resistance loss of the grid electrode that was present in the former 23.7% HIT cell in 2011.

C. Optimizing the Resistance Loss

The resistance loss in the HIT solar cell originates (except for the electrodes, as explained previously) from the characteristics of the a-Si layers. Because a certain thickness of the i-layer is required for surface passivation at the heterointerface, the resistive loss within the i-layer cannot be avoided. We have investigated thoroughly the improvement of our deposition process for the a-Si layers and their passivation quality by assuming that we could reduce the thickness of the i-layer if we had a better heterointerface with improved a-Si film. As a result, we again succeeded in improving the slight decrease in a-Si i-layer thickness with an even more enhanced V_{oc}.

IV. 24.7% EFFICIENCY WITH 98-μM-THICK SI SUBSTRATE AT THE RESEARCH & DEVELOPMENT STAGE

The approaches described in this paper led to our achievement of the world record efficiency of 24.7% with a 98-μm, 101.8 cm^2 wafer. This value was certified by AIST (see Fig. 4). The high V_{oc} of 0.750 V demonstrates the excellent passivation quality of the HIT structure.

We have made great efforts to not only raise the conversion efficiency of the HIT solar cells because the conversion efficiency has a great impact on the cost of a solar power system but also to apply a thinner wafer because the wafer cost is the main parameter of the production cost.

As we reported before, the V_{oc} of the HIT solar cell increases as cell thickness decreases because of the low surface recombination velocity of the HIT solar cells [6]. A decrease in the photocurrent, which is because of the shorter optical path length in the thinner Si, can be compensated for by an increase in the V_{oc} for the HIT structure. Therefore, the HIT solar cell can achieve a high conversion efficiency with a thin wafer.

To determine the impact of the wafer thickness on the efficiency of the HIT solar cell, we prepared a HIT solar cell with a c-Si wafer with a thickness of around 150 μm and compared it with a thin wafer. A high conversion efficiency of 24.6% was obtained in the 151-μm-thick HIT solar cell, certified by AIST. While a tradeoff between V_{oc} and I_{sc} was found by comparing the parameters of the output characteristics (shown in Table II), the conversion efficiency of both cells was almost equal. Since the growing lots of the c-Si ingot used for this experiment are different, it might be inadequate to compare both cells directly in terms of only wafer thickness, but it is found experimentally that, if the V_{oc} is at a high level of 0.750 V, we can maintain conversion efficiency at a high level with the HIT structure from 150 down to 100 μm because of the lower surface recombination velocity that the HIT structure provides.

V. Aiming for Higher Efficiency

As shown in Table I, the FF has been remarkably improved by the approaches explained in this paper. From our analysis, there are still some possibilities for raising the conversion efficiency even more by reducing the recombination losses with higher quality and more uniform deposition of the a-Si film. We have now upgraded our target of the conversion efficiency in the HIT cell in R&D to 25.5% and are aiming to achieve that in the near future.

The J_{sc}, however, has remained at the same level for these past two years. The shadow loss by the electrode on the front surface of the solar cell is the main reason and is hard to eliminate completely. To overcome this in practical PV modules, it is important to manage the optical path of the light incident on an electrode part in an entire PV module rather than a specific cell. This seems to be the key to raising the J_{sc} of an HIT PV module to the high level of the back contact type PV module.

VI. Conclusion

In this paper, we showed our recent activities to achieve high conversion efficiency HIT solar cells with thin silicon wafer at the R&D stage. We have continuously been improving the optical and electrical properties of each material, such as the a-Si and TCO layers and the metal grid electrode, to raise the conversion efficiency. As a result, we achieved the world's highest conversion efficiency of 24.7% with a 98-μm wafer for a total cell area of 101.8 cm^2.

References

[1] M. Taguchi, M. Tanaka, T. Matsuyama, T. Matsuoka, S. Tsuda, S. Nakano, Y. Kishi, and Y. Kuwano, "Improvement of the conversion efficiency of polycrystalline silicon thin film solar cell," in *Proc. Int. Photovoltaic Sci. Eng. Conf.-5 Tech. Dig.*, 1990, pp. 689–692.

[2] T. F. Schulze, L. Korte, F. Ruske, and B. Rech, "Band lineup in amorphous/crystalline silicon heterojunctions and the impact of hydrogen microstructure and topological disorder," *Phys. Rev. B*, vol. 83, pp. 165314-1–165314-11, 2011.

[3] A. Descoeudres, Z. Holman, L. Barraud, S. Morel, S. De Wolf, and C. Ballif, ">21% efficient silicon heterojunction solar cells on n- and p-type wafers compared," *IEEE J. Photovoltaics*, vol. 3, no. 1, pp. 83–89, Jan. 2013.

[4] S. De Wolf and M. Kondo, "Abruptness of a-Si:H/c-Si interface revealed by carrier lifetime measurements," *Appl. Phys. Lett.*, vol. 90, pp. 042111-1–042111-3, 2007.

[5] T. Koida, H. Fujiwara, and M. Kondo, "Reduction of optical loss in hydrogenated amorphous silicon/crystalline silicon heterojunction solar cells by high-mobility hydrogen-doped In2O3 transparent conductive oxide," *Appl. Phys. Exp.*, vol. 1, pp. 04501-1–04501-3, 2008.

[6] M. Taguchi, Y. Tsunomura, H. Inoue, S. Taira, T. Nakashima, T. Baba, H. Sakata, and E. Maruyama, "High-efficiency HIT solar cell on thin (<100 μm) silicon wafer," in *Proc. 24th Eur. Photovoltaic Sol. Energy Conf.*, 2009, pp. 1690–1693.

[7] T. Kinoshita, M. Shima, A. Terakawa, M. Isomura, H. Haku, K. Wakisaka, M. Tanaka, S. Kiyama, and S. Tsuda, "Effects of hydrogen dilution on a-Si/a-SiGe tandem solar cells," in *Proc. 14th Eur. Photovoltaic Sol. Energy Conf.*, 1997, pp. 566–569.

[8] A. Ogane, Y. Tsunomura, D. Fujishima, A. Yano, H. Kanno, T. Kinoshita, H. Sakata, M. Taguchi, H. Inoue, and E. Maruyama, "Recent progress of HIT solar cells heading for the higher conversion efficiencies," in *Proc. Int. Photovoltaic Sci. Eng. Conf.-21 Tech. Dig.*, 2011, 3A-1O-01.

[9] M. Tanaka, M. Taguchi, T. Matsuyama, T. Sawada, S. Tsuda, S. Nakano, H. Hanafusa, and Y. Kuwano, "Development of new a-Si/c-Si heterojunction solar cells: ACJ-HIT (artificially constructed junction-heterojunction with intrinsic thin-layer)," *Jpn. J. Appl. Phys., Part 1*, vol. 31, pp. 3518–3522, 1992.

[10] H. Fujiwara and M. Kondo, "Effects of a-Si:H layer thicknesses on the performance of a-Si:H/c-Si heterojunction solar cells," *J. Appl. Phys.*, vol. 101, pp. 054516-1–054516-9, 2007.

[11] T. Kinoshita, D. Fujishima, A. Yano, A. Ogane, S. Tohoda, K. Matsuyama, Y. Nakamura, N. Tokuoka, H. Kanno, H. Sakata, M. Taguchi, and E. Maruyama, "The approaches for high efficiency HIT solar cell with very thin (<100 μm) silicon wafer over 23%," in *Proc. 26th Eur. PV Solar Energy Conf.*, 2011, pp. 871–874.

Authors' photographs and biographies not available at the time of publication.

Quantum-Well Solar Cells for Space: The Impact of Carrier Removal on End-of-Life Device Performance

R. Hoheisel, M. Gonzalez, M. P. Lumb, D. A. Scheiman, S. R. Messenger, C. G. Bailey, J. Lorentzen, T. N. D. Tibbits, M. Imaizumi, T. Ohshima, S. Sato, P. P. Jenkins, and R. J. Walters

Abstract—In this paper, a detailed analysis on the radiation response of solar cells with multi quantum wells (MQW) included in the quasi-intrinsic region between the emitter and the base layer is presented. While the primary source of radiation damage of photovoltaic devices is minority carrier lifetime reduction, we found that in the case of MQW devices, carrier removal (CR) effects are also observed. Experimental measurements and numerical simulations reveal that with increasing radiation dose, CR can cause the initially quasi-intrinsic background doping of the MQW region to become specifically n- or p-type. This can result in a significant narrowing and even the collapse of the electric field between the emitter and the base where the MQWs are located. The implications of the CR-induced modification of the electric field on the current–voltage characteristics and on the collection efficiency of carriers generated within the emitter, the MQW region, and the base are discussed for different radiation dose conditions. This paper concludes with a discussion of improved radiation hard MQW device designs.

Index Terms—III–V semiconductor materials, photovoltaic cells, quantum-well devices, radiation effects.

I. Introduction

MULTIJUNCTION solar cells made of III–V semiconductor compounds yield the highest conversion efficiencies among today's photovoltaic technologies. Their high specific power and new fabrication processes, which allow them to be also mechanically flexible, make them the devices of choice for present and future space applications. To achieve highest conversion efficiencies, the photocurrents of all subcells within a multijunction (MJ) device have to be balanced. The inclusion of multiquantum-well (MQW) structures in one or more subcells of an MJ device has recently gained increased attention as a promising approach to attain or to further improve the current matching conditions in various MJ configurations such as GaInP/GaInAs/Ge, InAlAsSb/InGaAsP/InGaAs, or In-AlAsSb/InGaAlAs/InGaAs [1]–[4]. In these devices, by varying the composition and the thickness of the MQW structure, the bandgap of the subcells can be optimized for absorption, thereby maximizing the current through the MJ device and yielding increased MJ efficiencies. Successful operation of MQW cells has already been reported for GaAs-based single- and triple-junction solar cells [1]–[6]. For use in space, the radiation response of MQW solar cells has to be understood first. Indeed, the ultimate goal of the present research is to analyze the possible use of the MQWs to enhance the MJ performance at both beginning of life (BOL), i.e., prior to radiation, and end of life (EOL), i.e., after radiation.

Previous publications have shown that the radiation response of an MQW solar cell can vary significantly, depending on the specific solar cell design [3], [6]–[13]. The external quantum efficiency (EQE) at wavelengths associated with the MQW region, i.e., at wavelengths longer than the bandgap of the bulk material, has been reported to be relatively insensitive to radiation. However, and especially in comparison to their p-n junction counterparts, an increased degradation in the fill factor (FF), resembling a shunt-like behavior in the current versus voltage (J/V) characteristics, has been observed [3], [8], [12]–[14]. This has also been seen in this study; see Fig. 1.

Dark-J/V measurements showed that the shunt resistance remains virtually unaffected after radiation, meaning that the shape of the EOL J/V characteristics is not due to a low shunt. The high variation in the reported radiation response of different MQW designs, as well as the as-yet unaddressed cause for the untypical shape of the J/V characteristics, gives rise to a thorough analysis and a better understanding of the degradation behavior of MQW solar cells. In the following, we discuss the complex radiation response of MQW devices considering the radiation-induced effects of lifetime degradation, carrier removal, changes in carrier mobilities, as well as the importance of device geometries, in particular, the width of the quasi-intrinsic

Manuscript received June 16, 2013; revised August 16, 2013 and October 7, 2013; accepted October 17, 2013. Date of publication November 27, 2013; date of current version December 16, 2013. This work was supported by the Office of Naval Research.

R. Hoheisel and M. P. Lumb are with the The George Washington University, Washington DC 20052 USA (e-mail: hoheisel@gwu.edu; mlumb@gwu.edu).

M. Gonzalez is with the Sotera Defense Solutions, Crofton, MD 20701 USA (e-mail: maria.gonzalez@soteradefense.com).

D. A. Scheiman, S. R. Messenger, C. G. Bailey, J. Lorentzen, P. P. Jenkins, and R. J. Walters are with the U.S. Naval Research Laboratory, Washington, DC 20375 USA (e-mail: david.scheiman@nrl_pv_research@nrl.navy. mil; Scott.Messenger@nrl_pv_research@nrl.navy.mil; christopher.bailey.ctr@ nrl_pv_research@nrl.navy.mil; justin.lorentzen@nrl_pv_research@nrl.navy. mil; phillip.jenkins@nrl_pv_research@nrl.navy.mil; robert.walters@nrl_pv_ research@nrl.navy.mil).

T. N. D. Tibbits is with the formerly QuantaSol Ltd., Kingston-upon-Thames, Surrey KT1 3GZ, U.K. (e-mail: tom.tibbits@gmail.com).

M. Imaizumi is with the Japan Aerospace Exploration Agency, Ibaraki 305–8505, Japan (e-mail: imaizumi.mitsuru@jaxa.jp).

T. Ohshima and S. Sato are with the Japan Atomic Energy Agency, Gunma, 370–1292, Japan (e-mail: ohshima.takeshi20@jaea.go.jp; sato.shinichiro@ jaea.go.jp).

Digital Object Identifier 10.1109/JPHOTOV.2013.2289935

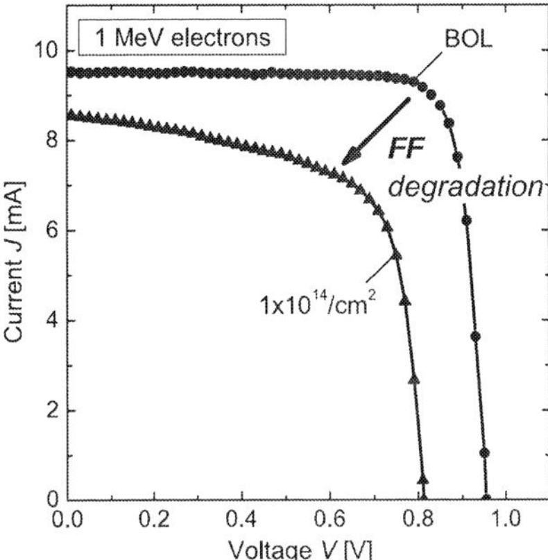

Fig. 1. MQW solar cell J/V characteristics before (BOL) and after radiation with 1 MeV 1×10^{14}/cm^2 electrons. Significant degradation in FF is observed. The MQW solar cell is composed of an n-type GaAs-emitter, a p-type GaAs-base and multiple strain balanced InGaAs/GaAsP quantum wells within a 1.2-μm-thick quasi-intrinsic region.

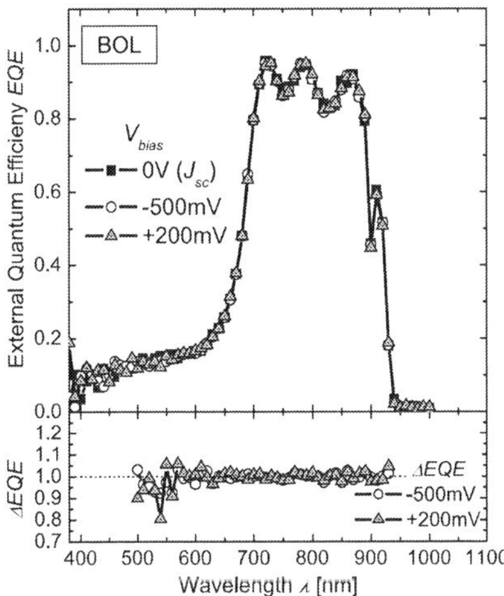

Fig. 2. EQE measurements as a function of the bias voltage V_{bias} (0 mV, -500 mV, $+200$ mV) before radiation (BOL). The ratios of the EQE under bias to that at zero bias (ΔEQE(V_{bias},λ) = EQE(V_{bias},λ) / EQE(V_{bias} = 0 V,λ)) are shown. For BOL conditions, no bias voltage dependence of the EQE is observed.

region, by both experimental characterization and numerical simulation.

II. EXPERIMENTAL DETAILS

To better understand the degradation in FF, EQE measurements at different bias voltages (V_{bias}) were performed, and the results are presented in Figs. 2 and 3.

Under BOL conditions, no V_{bias} dependence of the EQE is observed, see Fig. 2. This is consistent with the J/V curve in Fig. 1 showing only little voltage dependence of the photocurrent from short-circuit current (J_{sc}) conditions to the maximum power point, indicating that the carrier collection is independent of V_{bias}.

After 1-MeV electron radiation at a fluence of 1×10^{14}/cm^2, however, the EQE decreases over the entire wavelength range when V_{bias} is increased; see Fig. 3.

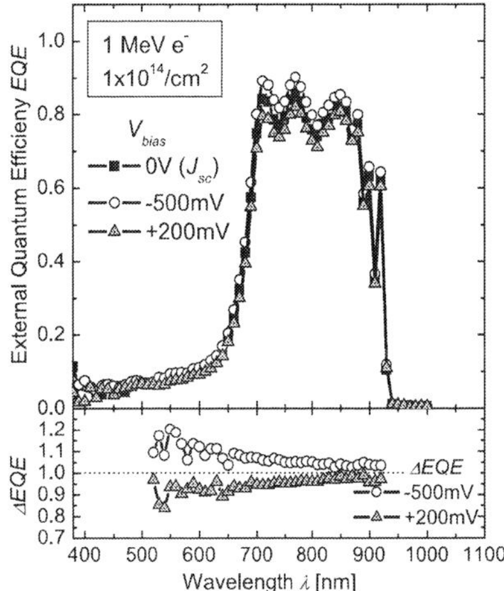

Fig. 3. EQE measurements as a function of V_{bias} (0 mV, -500 mV, $+200$ mV) after radiation with 1 MeV 1×10^{14}/cm^2 electrons. Relative ratios ΔEQE(V_{bias},λ) of the bias voltage dependent EQE measurements are shown. A V_{bias} dependence of the EQE is observed, which is pronounced at shorter wavelengths.

In the case of a negative V_{bias}, the EQE increases, while under positive V_{bias} the EQE decreases. It is noteworthy that a typical shunt resistance does not affect the EQE when different bias voltages are applied. This is further emphasized when considering the relative ratios of the EQE measurements

$$\Delta \mathrm{EQE}\,(V,\lambda) = {\mathrm{EQE}\,(V,\lambda)}/{\mathrm{EQE}\,(V = 0V,\lambda)}$$

as shown in the subsets of Figs. 2 and 3. After radiation, for both bias cases, the EQE at longer wavelengths shows much less V_{bias} dependence than at shorter wavelengths, i.e., for photons absorbed near the top of the cell (the emitter region). The decreased response under positive bias suggests that the collection of carriers generated by short-wavelength photons is reduced at higher voltages, e.g., at the maximum power point V_{mpp}. This then leads to a lower photocurrent at V_{mpp} and causes consequently a poorer FF. In the following, the mechanisms and dependences behind these radiation-, voltage- and wavelength-sensitive effects are investigated by numerical simulation.

III. NUMERICAL SIMULATION OF CARRIER REMOVAL IN THE "i"-REGION

To numerically simulate the complex radiation response of MQW solar cells, the device structure given in Table I, resembling the cells used in the experimental part, is considered.

Electric and optical parameters for the emitter and the base layer were taken from [15]. The optical properties of the MQWs were calculated using a combination of the effective medium approximation and an 8 band k·p simulation to calculate the bandstructure of the quantum-well confined states. The bulk dielectric function of the well and barrier materials was computed using the interpolation scheme described by Lumb [16]. The dielectric function of a planar, stratified medium in the regime where the thicknesses of the layers are significantly thinner than the wavelength of the light are computed from the effective

TABLE I
LAYER STRUCTURE AND PHYSICAL PARAMETERS OF THE MODELED
MULTIQUANTUM-WELL (MQW) SOLAR CELLS

Layer	Parameter	Value
n-GaAs emitter	carrier concentration	1×10^{18} cm^{-3}
	layer thickness	100 nm
	SRH lifetime	10 ns
	hole mobility	57 cm V^{-1} s^{-1}
quasi-intrinsic MQW region	carrier concentration	**1×10^{14} - 1×10^{16} cm^{-3}**
	layer thickness	1000 nm
	GaAs$_{1-x}$P$_x$ barrier	0.19 (x)
	In$_y$Ga$_{1-y}$ As well	0.12 (y)
	SRH lifetime	**1×10^{1} - 1×10^{-2} ns**
	hole mobility	**300 - 30 cm^2 V^{-1} s^{-1}**
	electron mobility	**6000 - 600 cm^2 V^{-1} s^{-1}**
p-GaAs base	carrier concentration	1×10^{17} cm^{-3}
	layer thickness	2000 nm
	SRH lifetime	10 ns
	electron mobility	4700 cm V^{-1} s^{-1}

Parameter variations used in the subsequent numerical simulation runs are highlighted. The series resistance is assumed to be zero, and the shunt resistance is set to infinity.

medium theory described by Aspnes [17]. For a material with two layers per period, having dielectric functions ε_1 and ε_2 and thicknesses d_1 and d_2, the dielectric function of the effective medium is given by

$$\varepsilon^{-1} = f_1 \varepsilon_1^{-1} + f_2 \varepsilon_2^{-1}.$$

Here, f_1 and f_2 are the fractional thickness of each layer given by $f_1 = d_1/(d_1+d_2)$ and $f_2 = d_2/(d_1+d_2)$, respectively. This averaging procedure was used to generate the optical constants of a bulk medium consisting of the well and barrier materials. However, the optical constants of the actual MQW system are modified by the effects of quantum confinement. The confinement of the electrons and holes modifies the density of states and of the material and the oscillator strength of interband transitions. Consequently, the dielectric function of the material is altered. To simulate the confined energy levels and dispersions of the MQW region, NRL MultiBands, a numerical bandsolver using the k·p method that was developed at the Naval Research Laboratory [18], was used. The resulting bandstructure was used to generate the absorption coefficient of the MQW stack, considering contributions from the lowest energy electron level and four lowest energy hole states. The calculated absorption coefficient was then used to generate the extinction coefficient of the MQW.

For energies greater than the barrier bandgap, the refractive index calculated from the averaging procedure was used. For energies lower than the barrier bandgap, the real part of the refractive index was calculated using the averaged dielectric function of the well and barrier, and the imaginary part of the refractive index was computed from the calculated MQW absorption coefficient. It should be noted that this approach neglects the impact of the Kramers–Kronig relations on the real part of the index and, therefore, is only a first-order approximation. The

calculation of the carrier generation and recombination profiles and the solving of the Poisson equation were carried out via the simulation environment PC1d [19].

The effects of lifetime degradation, carrier removal, changes in carrier mobilities, and the importance of different device geometries will now be discussed. Under steady-state conditions, the built-in voltage of a solar cell is related to the electric field across the semiconductor junction via the Poisson equation. Applying a negative external voltage across the terminals of the device increases the electric field, while a positive external voltage decreases the electric field [20]. In the case of an MQW solar cell, the presence of an electric field across the depletion region is critical for the collection of carriers generated in the wells [21]. From Fig. 2, it is observed that under BOL conditions, the electric field is sufficiently high such that the carrier collection, i.e., the EQE, is not affected by changes of the applied voltage. After radiation, however, a voltage dependent and, thus, a field dependent carrier collection at shorter wavelengths is observed; see Fig. 3. This suggests that the radiation causes a reduction of the strength of the electric field in the region close to the emitter, hindering carrier collection.

Local changes of the electrical field are also related via the Poisson equation to the ionized carrier density, i.e., the doping concentration. One radiation damage effect responsible for modifying the effective doping concentration is carrier removal (CR) [22], [23]. CR describes the effect of radiation-induced crystal defects that cause an energy state within the forbidden gap that can localize a free carrier thereby acquire a charge and act like a dopant. Depending on the semiconductor material as well as the irradiating particle type and energy, different crystal defects with different energy states are possible, and depending on the electrical properties of these states, CR can render the material further p- or n-type. Since n-type conversion has been typically reported for III–V materials, our discussion focuses on this kind of type conversion [24]–[28]. The change of the effective doping concentration Δn with particle fluence ϕ is described by the carrier removal rate $R_c = \Delta n / \phi$. In the case of low doped GaAs, values of $R_c \sim$ 1-5/cm have been measured [25]. For a total fluence of 1-MeV 1×10^{15}/cm^2 electrons, which is considered to be representative for a 15 year mission in a geostationary orbit (GEO), a change in the effective doping concentration of $\Delta n =$ 1-5 $\times 10^{15}$/cm^3 is expected. For other semiconductor materials, similar CR behavior has been reported [24], [26]–[28].

The field across the quasi-intrinsic region is particularly sensitive to CR for two main reasons: its comparatively large width with respect to both the emitter and the base layer and its initially low background doping concentration. As shown in Fig. 4(a), even small changes in the background doping concentration in the quasi-intrinsic MQW region can lead to a significant modulation of the location and strength of the electrical field within the overall device.

With the initially quasi-intrinsic MQW region becoming slightly n-type (as radiation impinges) the electric field becomes narrower and moves further towards the p-type base. Simulating CR effects as an increase in n-type background doping concentration, the electric field close to the n-type emitter is seen to

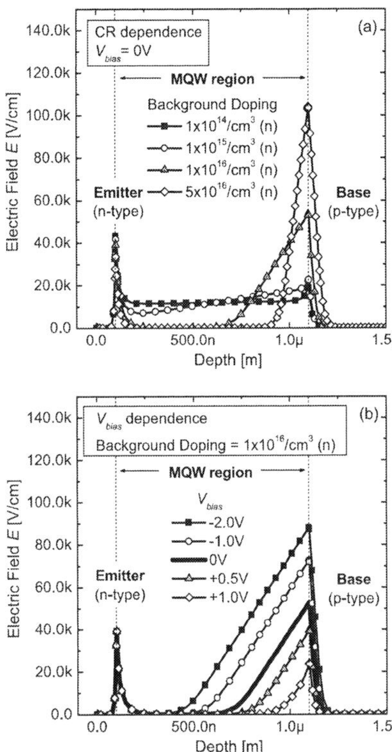

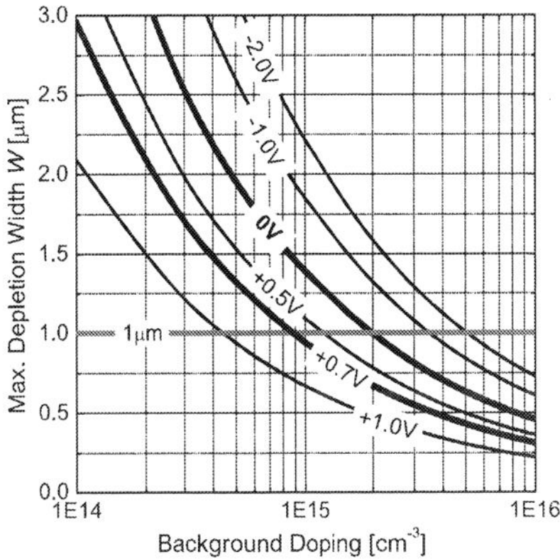

Fig. 5. Simulation of the maximum depletion width as a function of CR-induced n-type background doping concentration for a series of V_{bias} conditions. The curves $V_{\text{bias}} = 0$ V (J_{sc} condition) and $V_{\text{bias}} = 0.7$ V ($\sim$MPP condition) are highlighted.

Fig. 4. (a) Simulation of the impact of the background doping concentration in the MQW region on the electric field across the active regions of a MQW solar cell. Changes in the background doping concentration are used to simulate carrier removal (CR) effects. The simulation is based on the assumption that CR renders the initially quasi-intrinsic region slightly n-type ($n = 1 \times 10^{14} - 5 \times 10^{16}$/cm^3). The electric field is given at short-circuit conditions, i.e., $V_{\text{bias}} = 0$ V. (b) Simulation of the electric field as a function of the bias voltage V_{bias} at a constant n-type background doping concentration of 1×10^{16}/cm^3 in the MQW region.

eventually collapse due to CR; see Fig. 4(a). At increased positive bias voltages, the weakening of the electric field close to the emitter becomes even more pronounced; see Fig. 4(b). This is also in agreement with the V_{bias}-dependent EQE measurements after radiation where carrier collection at short wavelengths is reduced; see Fig. 3. In the next section, the implications of the radiation-induced modulation of the electric field on the device performance is discussed.

IV. NUMERICAL SIMULATION OF MULTIQUANTUM WELL SOLAR CELL PERFORMANCE

The electric field across the quasi-intrinsic region is necessary to achieve carrier collection from the MQW region at room temperature [20], [21]. Therefore, an important parameter in designing MQW solar cell devices is the width of the quasi-intrinsic region in which the quantum-well structures are included. In Fig. 5, the depletion widths for different background doping concentrations are depicted as a simulation of varied levels of CR. For background doping concentrations of less than 1×10^{15}/cm^3—which can be considered as a rough estimate for

a 15 year mission in GEO—maximum depletion region widths of around 1 μm under both J_{sc} and MPP conditions are possible.

The collection efficiency of carriers generated within the MQW region, however, is not only dependent on the strength and the width of the electric field but on the likelihood of recombination as well, i.e., the concentration and recombination rate of Shockley–Read–Hall (SRH) centers; see Figs. 6 and 7. The J/V characteristics for different background doping and SRH conditions are shown in Fig. 6. With SRH lifetimes of 10 ns in the MQW region [see Fig. 6(a)], the FF is only slightly affected by changes in background doping concentration, i.e., by CR, since even with a narrow depletion region under MPP conditions ($\sim$0.3 μm, $\Delta n = 1 \times 10^{16}$/cm^3), the diffusion lengths of carriers generated in the emitter and the MQW region are large enough to ensure that these carriers reach the base.

With reduced SRH lifetimes of 1 and 0.1 ns, as is the case with increasing radiation fluence, the impact of CR on the J/V characteristics becomes evident; see Figs. 6(b) and (c). Shorter SRH lifetimes indicate increased nonradiative recombination, meaning that carriers generated within the emitter and the MQW region are more likely to recombine on their way to the junction, leading to a lower photocurrent—an effect that is significantly intensified by CR since the decreased field lowers their drift velocity on their path. With applied forward bias, the junction field and drift velocities are further decreased, which leads to the pronounced voltage-dependent drop of the current and, hence, FF.

Simulations of the EQE of an MQW solar cell are shown in Fig. 7, where the impact of particle radiation has been included by considering different SRH lifetimes and CR conditions. Two main effects are observable. First, with increased CR-induced background doping concentration and reduced SRH lifetimes in the quasi-intrinsic region, the EQE at shorter wavelengths up to $\sim$700 nm, which are associated with carriers generated mostly in the emitter, degrades to a large extent. Second, the EQE at wavelengths of around 920 nm, which is associated with carriers generated in the MQW, is virtually unaffected until a heavy

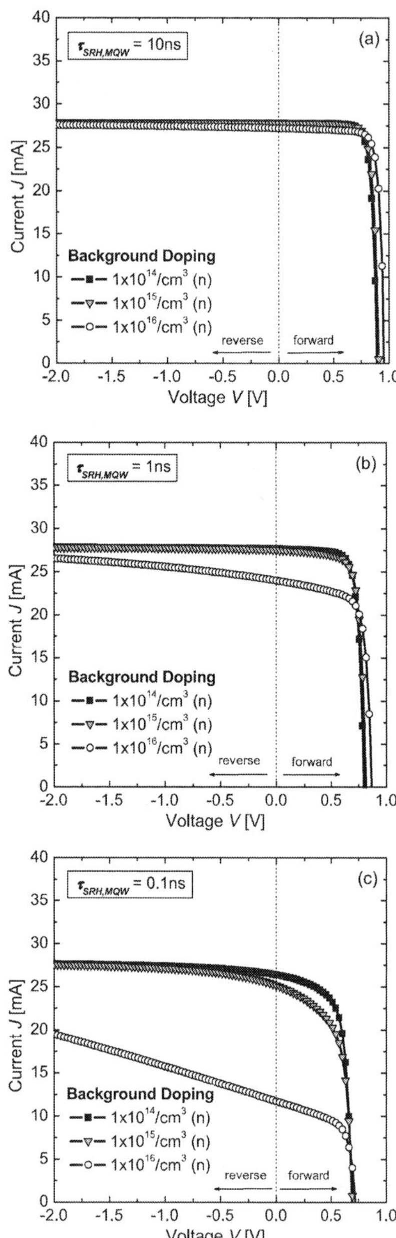

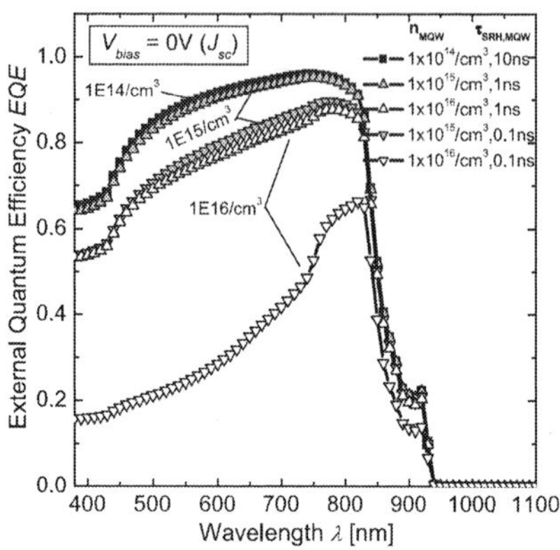

Fig. 7. Simulated quantum efficiency (EQE) as a function of CR-induced n-type background doping concentration and different SRH lifetimes in the MQW region. With increased CR-induced background doping concentration and reduced SRH lifetimes, a strong degradation of the EQE at shorter wavelengths is observed. SRH-lifetimes in the emitter and the base layer were kept constant; see Table I. The mobilities for electrons and holes within the MQW region were set to 6000 and 300 cm^2/V/s.

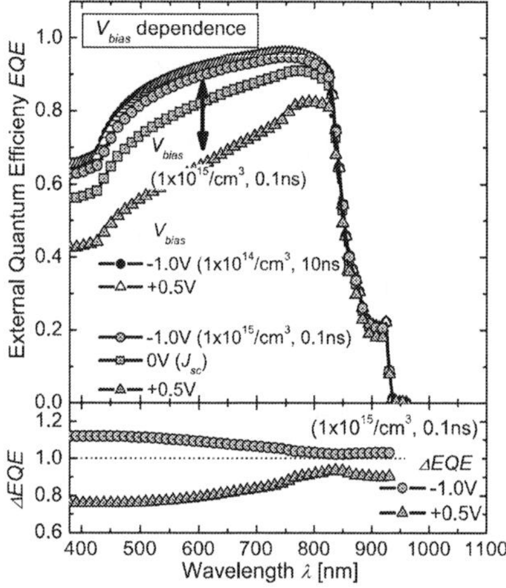

Fig. 8. Simulated EQE as a function of the bias voltage V_{bias}. Two radiation dose conditions are depicted. Before radiation (BOL) with a background doping concentration of 1×10^{14}/cm^3 and SRH lifetimes of 10 ns and after radiation such that a CR-induced n-type background doping concentration of 1×10^{15}/cm^3 and SRH lifetimes of 0.1 ns were induced. The combined effect of CR and reduced SRH lifetimes leads to a strong V_{bias}-dependence of the EQE at shorter wavelengths; see the relative ratios $\Delta\text{EQE}(V_{\text{bias}},\lambda)$ in the subset. SRH-lifetimes in the emitter and base layer were kept constant; see Table I. The mobilities for electrons and holes within the MQW region were set to 6000 and 300 cm^2/V/s.

Fig. 6. Simulation of the J/V characteristics of an MQW solar cell as a function of CR-induced background doping concentration and different SRH lifetimes within the quasi-intrinsic MQW region of (a) 10 ns, (b) 1 ns, and (c) 0.1 ns. With reduced SRH lifetimes, the impact of CR becomes more pronounced and leads to a reduction of the FF and a shunt-like shape of the J/V characteristics. SRH lifetimes in the emitter and base layer were kept constant; see Table I. The mobilities for electrons and holes within the MQW region were set to 6000 and 300 cm^2/V/s, respectively.

radiation fluence causes a very high CR-induced background doping concentration of 1×10^{16}/cm^3 and significantly reduced SRH lifetimes of 0.1 ns. These effects are caused by the CR-induced field effect, which leads to higher recombination rates in the absence of an electric field, especially close to the emitter where photons with shorter wavelengths are primarily absorbed.

It is noteworthy that in MQW cells, the dominant degradation mechanism for the EQE at shorter wavelengths differs from that of standard pn-junction solar cells, where the principal degradation mechanism is diffusion length degradation [29].

Simulation of the EQE as a function of different bias voltages is shown in Fig. 8. Before radiation (BOL), the change in the bias voltage has no impact on the carrier collection. After heavy radiation, however, a clear bias voltage dependence of the EQE is observed. In these simulations, a CR-induced background doping of 1×10^{15}/cm^3 and reduced SRH lifetimes of 0.1 ns in

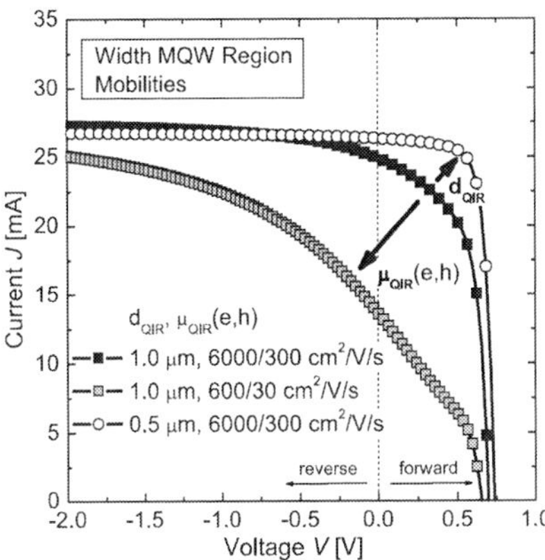

Fig. 9.   Simulated J/V characteristics showing the impact of CR in a MQW solar cell for reduced widths of the quasi-intrinsic region, d_{QIR}, which leads to an improved FF. In addition, the influence of changes in electron and hole mobilities μ_{QIR} in the quasi-intrinsic region are shown. A CR-induced background doping concentration in the MQW region of 1E15/cm^3 and SRH lifetimes of 0.1 ns were assumed, respectively.

the MQW region were assumed, which are representative of a high fluence irradiation.

The significant decrease in EQE at shorter wavelengths with increasing voltages explains the reduction in the FF after radiation as shown in Fig. 1. Carriers that were generated by short wavelength photons close to the emitter are less likely to reach the base due to decreased drift velocities caused by the reduced electric field close to the emitter region. This is in good agreement with the experimental data shown in Figs. 2 and 3.

The impact of CR and reduced SRH lifetimes on the radiation response of the J/V and EQE characteristics of an MQW solar cell described thus far can also be interpreted in terms of the width of the quasi-intrinsic region; see Fig. 9. Since the field attenuation by the CR-induced background doping concentration is mostly linear with the width of the quasi-intrinsic region, d_{QIR}, devices with reduced d_{QIR} are generally considered to be less affected by CR. In the case of a smaller MQW region of $d_{\mathrm{QIR}} = 0.5\ \mu$m, the impact of CR on the J/V characteristics is significantly reduced; see Fig. 9.

Another parameter of interest is the drift mobility, μ_{QIR}, of electrons and holes. With respect to the semiconductor bulk material, mobilities within the MQW region can be reduced as a cause of the replicating MQW heterostructures. Furthermore, the band offsets of barriers and wells can vary in the valence and conduction band. Consequently, the mobilities of electrons and holes can be affected differently. The effect of a reduction of the electron and hole mobilities in the MQW region by one order of magnitude is shown in Fig. 9. With lower drift mobilities, the impact of CR on the J/V characteristics becomes more distinct and leads to a greatly reduced FF.

V. Discussion of Multi Quantum Well Solar Cell Radiation Response

The presented results and analysis have demonstrated the significant impact of CR on the performance of MQW solar cells.

In addition, the interplay between CR and other physical parameters like the minority carrier lifetime, the carrier mobility, and the device dimensions were discussed. It is important to point out that the effect of CR can underlie specific irradiating particle, operation temperature, defect annealing, doping type, and initial doping concentration dependences, which can differ largely between semiconductor materials. Although CR renders most III–V solar cell materials n-type—as discussed in the paper—p-type conversion is also possible in principle. In this case, the electric field moves closer to the emitter with increasing fluence, and the collection of carriers generated in the field-less parts close to the base is primarily affected by CR. Remarkably, this leads to a significantly better radiation response compared with CR-induced n-type conversion. Because of the exponential photon absorption and carrier generation profile with device depth, considerably fewer carriers are affected by a higher recombination rate in the base region. For CR-induced n-type conversion, a similar improvement of the radiation response can be achieved by growing the structure upside-down, i.e., p on n. In this case, the electric field shifts to the upper part of the device, where the photon absorption and carrier generation is highest. For n on p structures with CR-induced n-type conversion, a slight initial p-type counter-doping can be used to ensure a high-enough electric field throughout the entire mission lifetime, resulting in a significantly more radiation hard device design. Apart from the discussed changes in the background doping concentration due to CR and the degradation of effective lifetimes and mobilities, strain-induced crystal and interface defects could potentially lead to additional device degradation. In addition, radiation-induced crystal defects might also affect the energy levels of the MQW states, causing a minor shift of the exciton energy peak comparable to the quantum confined Stark effect and detectable by high-resolution EQE and photoluminescence measurements. However, this effect is considered to be less critical than the collapse of the electric field within the depletion region of MQW device and, hence, negligible in terms of the device performance.

VI. Summary

The impact of CR on the radiation response of MQW solar cells was investigated. EQE and J/V measurements as well as numerical simulations under BOL and EOL conditions were presented. Significant degradation of the FF after radiation was observed which was explained by CR effects in the quasi-intrinsic MQW region. With increasing radiation dose, CR renders the background doping of the formerly quasi-intrinsic MQW region slightly n-type, which leads to a weakening and eventual collapse of the electric field close to the emitter region. The recombination rate of carriers that were generated by short-wavelength photons close to the emitter region is mostly affected and increases with a reduction of the electric field as a cause of lower drift velocities. This eventually causes a degradation of the quantum efficiency at shorter wavelengths. At increasing voltages, e.g., close to V_{mpp}, the electric field is even further narrowed, and the collection efficiency of carriers generated in the emitter and quasi-neutral parts of the MQW region is reduced. This leads to a decreased photocurrent at higher voltages, i.e., a lower FF and J/V characteristics with a shunt-like shape. With radiation, SRH lifetimes are also reduced so that the carrier collection and, consequently, the device performance become even more sensitive to the CR-induced electric field effect. Good agreement between numerical simulations and measured data was achieved for the radiation response of both J/V and EQE characteristics. The influence of other important physical parameters, like mobilities and the width of the MQW region on the device performance, has been discussed, and design considerations for radiation hard MQW solar cell structures were provided.

REFERENCES

[1] K. W. J. Barnham and G. Duggan, "A new approach to high-efficiency multi-band-gap solar cells," *J. Appl. Phys.*, vol. 67, no. 7, pp. 3490–3493, Apr. 1990.

[2] R. J. Walters, M. Gonzalez, J. G. Tischler, M. P. Lumb, J. R. Meyer, I. Vurgaftman, J. Abell, M. K. Yakes, N. Ekins-Daukes, J. G. J. Adams, N. Chan, P. Stavrinou, and P. P. Jenkins, "Design of an achievable, all lattice-matched multijunction solar cell using InGaAlAsSb," in *Proc. 37th IEEE Photovoltaic Spec. Conf.*, Jun. 19–24, 2011, pp. 000122–000126.

[3] R. Kellenbenz, R. Hoheisel, P. Kailuweit, W. Guter, F. Dimroth, and A. W. Bett, "Development of radiation hard Ga0.50In0.50P/Ga0.99In0.01 As/Ge space solar cells with multi quantum wells," in *Proc. 35th IEEE Photovoltaic Spec. Conf.*, Jun. 20–25, 2010, pp. 000117–000122.

[4] H. Fujii, Y. Wang, K. Watanabe, M. Sugiyama, and Y. Nakano, "High-Aspect ratio structures for efficient light absorption and carrier transport in InGaAs/GaAsP multiple quantum-well solar cells," *IEEE J. Photovoltaics*, vol. 3, no. 2, pp. 859–867, Apr. 2013.

[5] R. E. Welser, "Exploring the radiative limits of dark current operation in InGaAs quantum well solar cells," in *Proc. SPIE, Phys.*, vol. 8256, 2012. doi:10.1117/12.910609.

[6] M. Sugiyama, Y. Wang, S. Choi, Y. Wen, and Y. Nakano, "How shall we put multiple quantum wells in p-i-n structure for efficiency enhancement?" in *Proc. 35th IEEE Photovoltaic Spec. Conf.*, 2010, pp. 000376–000379.

[7] R. J. Walters, G. P. Summers, S. R. Messenger, A. Freundlich, C. Monier, and F. Newman, "Radiation hard multi-quantum well InP/InAsP Solar cells for space applications," *Prog. Photovolt, Res. App.*, vol. 8, no. 3, pp. 349–354, 2000.

[8] M. González, R. Hoheisel, M. P. Lumb, D. A. Scheiman, C. G. Bailey, J. Lorentzen, S. Maximenko, S. R. Messenger, P. P. Jenkins, T. N. D. Tibbits, M. Imaizumi, T. Ohshima, S. Sato, and R. J. Walters, "Radiation study in quantum Well III–V multi-junction solar cells," in *Proc. Photovoltaic Spec. Conf.*, 2013, to be published.

[9] A. Freundlich and A. Alemu, "Multi quantum well multijunction solar cell for space applications," *Phys. Stat. Sol.(c)*, vol. 2, no. 8, pp. 2978–2981, 2005.

[10] T. Ohshima, S. Sato, Imaizumi, Mitsuru, T. Sugaya, Niki, and Shigeru, "Radiation response of the electric characteristics of GaAs solar cells with quantum dot layers," in *Proc. 37th IEEE Photovoltaic Spec. Conf.*, Jun. 19–24, 2011, pp. 001605–001609. DOI: 10.1109/PVSC.2011.6186263.

[11] C. D. Cress, Bailey, G. Christopher, S. M. Hubbard, D. M. Wilt, Bailey, G. Sheila, and R. P. Raffaelle, "Radiation effects on strain compensated quantum dot solar cells," in *Proc. 33rd IEEE Photovoltaic Spec. Conf.*, 2008, pp. 1–6.

[12] C. Kerestes, D. Forbes, C. G. Bailey, J. Spann, B. Richards, P. Sharps, and S. Hubbard, "Radiation effects on quantum dot enhanced solar cells," *Proc. SPIE*, vol. 8256, Feb. 9, 2012. doi:10.1117/12.910835.

[13] C. Kerestes, D. V. Forbes, Z. Bittner, S. Polly, L. Yong, B. Richards, P. Sharps, and S. Hubbard, "Strain effects on radiation tolerance of quantum dot solar cells," in *Proc. 38th IEEE Photovoltaic Spec. Conf.*, Jun. 3–8, 2012, pp. 002792–002796.

[14] T. Ohshima, S. Sato, C. Morioka, M. Imaizumi, T. Sugaya, and S. Niki, "Change in the electric performance of InGaAs quantum dot solar cells due to irradiation," in *Proc. 35th IEEE Photovoltaic Spec. Conf.*, Jun. 20–25, 2010, pp. 002594–002598.

[15] M. Levinshtein, S. Rumyantsev, and M. Shur, *Handbook Series on Semiconductor Parameters: Volume 1: Si, Ge, C, GaAs, GaP, GaSb, InAs, InP, InSb*. Singapore: World Scientific, 1996.

[16] M. P. Lumb, M. Gonzalez, I. Vurgaftman, J. R. Meyer, J. Abell, M. Yakes, R. Hoheisel, J. G. Tischler, P. P. Jenkins, P. N. Stavrinou, M. Fuhrer, N. J. Ekins-Daukes, and R. J. Walters, "Simulation of novel InAlAsSb solar cells," *Proc. SPIE*, vol. 8256, p. 82560S, Feb. 9, 2012.

[17] D. E. Aspnes, "Optical properties of thin films," *Thin Solid Films*, vol. 89, no. 3, pp. 249–262, Mar. 19, 1982.

[18] M. P. Lumb, I. Vurgaftman, C. A. Affouda, J. R. Meyer, E. H. Aifer, and R. J. Walters, "Quantum wells and superlattices for III-V photovoltaics and photodetectors," *Proc. SPIE*, p. 84710A, Oct. 15, 2012.

[19] D. A. Clugston and P. A. Basore, "PC1D version 5: 32-bit solar cell modeling on personal computers," in *Proc. 26th IEEE Photovolt. Spec. Conf.*, 1997, pp. 207–210.

[20] S. M. Sze, *Physics of Semiconductor Devices*. New York, NY, USA: Wiley, 1981.

[21] I. Serdiukova, C. Monier, M. F. Vilela, and A. Freundlich, "Critical built-in electric field for an optimum carrier collection in multiquantum well p-i-n diodes," *Appl. Phys. Lett.*, vol. 74, no. 19, pp. 2812–2814, 1999.

[22] C. Claeys and E. Simoen, *Radiation Effects in Advanced Semiconductor Materials and Devices*. New York, NY, USA: Springer, 2002.

[23] D. V. Lang, "Review of radiation-induced defects in III–V compounds," in *Proc. Inst. Phys. Conf. Ser. No. 31*, 1997, ch. 1.

[24] N. J. Ekins-Daukes, H. S. Lee, T. Sasaki, M. Yamaguchi, A. Khan, T. Takamoto, T. Agui, K. Kamimura, M. Kaneiwa, M. Imaizumi, T. Ohshima, and T. Kamiya, "Carrier removal in lattice-mismatched InGaP solar cells under 1-MeV-electron irradiation," *Appl. Phys. Lett.*, vol. 85, no. 13, pp. 2511–2513, Sep. 2004. http://dx.doi.org/10.1063/1.1794371.

[25] M. Yamaguchi, Amano, and Chikara, "Numerical analysis for radiation-resistant GaAs heteroface solar cell structures," *J. Appl. Phys.*, vol. 57, no. 2, pp. 537–544, Jan 1985. http://dx.doi.org/10.1063/1.334788.

[26] S. I. Maximenko, S. R. Messenger, C. D. Cress, J. A. Freitas, and R. J. Walters, "Application of CL/EBIC-SEM techniques for characterization of radiation effects in multijunction solar cells," *IEEE Trans. Nucl. Sci.*, vol. 57, no. 6, pp. 3095–3100, Dec. 2010. DOI:10.1109/TNS.2010.2083691.

[27] S. R. Messenger, E. M. Jackson, E. A. Burke, R. J. Walters, M. A. Xapsos, and G. P. Summers, "Structural changes in InP/Si solar cells following irradiation with protons to very high fluences," *J. Appl. Phys.*, vol. 86, no. 3, pp. 1230–1235, 1 Aug. 1999.

[28] K. A. Bertness, B. T. Cavicchi, S. R. Kurtz, J. M. Olson, A. E. Kibbler, and C. Kramer, "Effect of base doping on radiation damage in GaAs single-junction solar cells," in *Proc. 22nd IEEE Photovoltaic Spec. Conf.*, Oct. 7-11, 1991, pp. 1582–1587.

[29] H. Y. Tada, J. R. Carter, B. E. Anspaugh, and R. G. Downing, *Solar Cell Radiation Handbook*: Nat. Aeronaut. Space Admin., Jet Propulsion Lab., Calif. Inst. Technol., 1982.

Authors' photograph and biographies not available at the time of publication.

Charged Particle Radiation Effects on Flexible a-Si/a-SiGe/a-SiGe Triple Junction Solar Cells for Space Use

Shin-ichiro Sato, Kevin Beernink, and Takeshi Ohshima

Abstract—Performance degradation of a-Si/a-SiGe/a-SiGe triple-junction solar cells due to irradiation of silicon ions, high-energy electrons, and protons are investigated using an *in-situ* current-voltage measurement system. The room temperature (RT) annealing effects immediately after irradiation are also investigated and the significant RT annealing is always observed independent of radiation species. By analyzing the energy loss process of incident particles (ionizing energy loss and non-ionizing energy loss), the radiation degradation mechanism is discussed. It is concluded that both the ionizing energy loss and the non-ionizing energy loss contribute the degradation.

Index Terms— amorphous semiconductors, photovoltaic cells, ion radiation effects, radiation hardening

I. Introduction

IN order to widely use amorphous silicon (a-Si) solar cells in space, it is required to clarify the radiation degradation mechanism. a-Si thin film solar cells are quite attractive for space application since it is known they have many advantages: good radiation tolerance, high specific power, high flexibility, ruggedness, and tight rollup feature for stowage [1]. Additionally, they also have the potential for reductions of both cost and stowage volume. The specific power of 1,200 W/kg has been currently attained by triple-junction (TJ) amorphous silicon alloy solar cells using roll-to-roll processing [2]. Unfortunately, however, the radiation degradation mechanism of a-Si solar cells is less well understood despite that the radiation degradation and their thermal recovery at post-irradiation have been investigated by several research groups [3]–[5].

Radiation degradation of crystalline silicon (c-Si) solar cells has been extensively studied for decades and their degradation mechanism has been substantially understood [6], [7]. In general, when exposed to radiations, radiation induced defects are created by the displacement damage effect, and they provides the decrease in minority carrier lifetime and majority carrier concentration. On the other hand, the degradation of a-Si solar cells is thought to be caused by the displacement damage effect as well as the electronic excitation effect (i.e. ionization), although it is not clarified yet which effect the radiation degradation dominates. This implies that the degradation mechanism is much more complicated than that of c-Si solar cells. In addition to this, it is known that the radiation degradation significantly recovers immediately after irradiation even at room temperature (RT) [4], [5]. This kind of instability strongly affects radiation experiments and makes it difficult to understand the obtained results.

We have recently investigated radiation degradation of a-Si solar cells and the followings have been clarified [8], [9]:

- Irradiation temperature strongly affects the performance degradation.
- Irradiation temperature, irradiation beam flux, and the elapsed time between irradiation and measurement should be carefully controlled in conducting radiation ground tests.

Therefore, *in-situ* measurement techniques are necessary to investigate the radiation degradation and the annealing effects after irradiation. The ion irradiation facility at JAEA has a unique feature that allows for both irradiation and illuminated current-voltage (*I-V*) measurement to be performed *in-situ* directly in the irradiation chamber where the temperatures can be carefully controlled. Using this system, we have investigated the degradation behavior of a-Si/a-SiGe/a-SiGe triple-junction (a-Si TJ) solar cells irradiated with various energy protons and

Manuscript received June 10, 2013; revised xxx xx, 2013. Current version published xx x, xxxx. This work was supported in part by Air Force Research Laboratory, Space Vehicles Directorate under contract FA9453-06-C-0339.

Shin-ichiro Sato and Takeshi Ohshima are with Japan Atomic Energy Agency, Takasaki, Gunma, 370-1292, Japan (corresponding author to provide phone: +81 27 346 9421; fax: +81 27 346 9687; e-mail: sato.shinichiro@jaea.go.jp, ohshima.takeshi20@jaea.go.jp).

Kevin Beernink is with United Solar Ovonic LLC, Troy, MI 48084-5352, USA (e-mail: kbeernink@uni-solar.com).

Digital Object Identifier xxxxxxx

TABLE I
TYPICAL CELL STRUCTURE

Layer	Thickness (nm)
ITO	~70
Top (a-Si)	~150
Middle (a-Si$_{0.8}$Ge$_{0.2}$)	~200
Bottom (a-Si$_{0.6}$Ge$_{0.4}$)	~200
ZnO, Ag + Stainless Steel	Substrate

TABLE II
REPRESENTATIVE INITIAL PERFORMANCES MEASURED AT 298 K UNDER AM0,
1 SUN CONDITIONS.

Isc (mA/cm^2)	8.84
Voc (V)	2.18
Pmax (mW/cm^2)	13.3
FF	0.689
Efficiency (%)	9.73
Active Area (cm²)	1.00

the performance recovery immediately after irradiation [10]. As a result, it has been shown that a single degradation curve could be drawn by the displacement damage dose scaling and thus, the proton-induced degradation was dominated by the displacement damage effect. It has been also shown that the RT annealing of the top subcell was more remarkable at RT than the other subcells.

In this paper, we investigate the heavy ion irradiation effects and the high energy electron irradiation effects on a-Si TJ solar cells and compare these results to the proton irradiation effects, which were reported previously. We aim to clarify the radiation degradation mechanism and to obtain a systematic interpretation of radiation degradation of a-Si TJ solar cells.

II. EXPERIMENTAL

Samples used in this study were a-Si/a-Si$_{0.8}$Ge$_{0.2}$/a-Si$_{0.6}$Ge$_{0.4}$ TJ solar cells. The cells were fabricated at United Solar Ovonic LLC. The cell structure and typical characteristics of the cells are listed in Tables I and II, respectively.

Silicon (Si) ion and electron irradiations were performed at the Takasaki Advanced Radiation Research Institute, Japan Atomic Energy Agency (JAEA Takasaki). *I-V* characteristics under AM0, 1 sun conditions were measured *in-situ* in an irradiation chamber (*in-situ* measurement). No light induced degradation due to the *in-situ I-V* measurement was observed in the irradiation experiments.

In this study, ion/electron beam flux, temperature during irradiation, and elapsed time between irradiation and measurement were carefully controlled in order to compare the degradation behavior accurately. The irradiation conditions are listed in Table III. Average values of Ionizing Energy Loss (IEL,

MeV·cm^2/g) and Non-Ionizing Energy Loss (NIEL, MeV·cm^2/g) in the whole region of the cells are also shown in Table III. All the *I-V* measurement was done 1 minute after irradiation was stopped. Also, the irradiation was performed until the short-circuit current (Isc) decreased to around 45 %, and the annealing effect of the cell performance after irradiation was investigated for 60 minutes at 298 K in vacuum or nitrogen atmosphere. The cells were kept under dark conditions except when the *I-V* measurement was performed. Finally, post-irradiation cells were annealed at 423 K for 4 hours in nitrogen atmosphere (thermal annealing).

III. RESULTS

A. Degradation Curves

Figure 1 shows degradation curves of the cells irradiated with 2 MeV and 0.5 MeV electrons (short-circuit current: Isc, open-circuit voltage: Voc, maximum output: Pmax, and fill factor: FF). All the parameters decreased monotonically with increasing fluence. The amount of degradation due to 0.5 MeV electrons was around twice compared to that due to 2 MeV electrons. The similar tendency has been reported elsewhere [12], even though the degradation is more intense as the electron energy is higher in the case of c-Si solar cells. The details are mentioned in the section IV.

Figure 2 shows degradation curves of the cells irradiated with 18 MeV, 5 MeV, 350 keV, and 110 keV Si ions. Si ions with energies of 110 keV stop in the interface between the top and the middle subcells, and provide the radiation damage non-uniformly. The radiation damage of 18 MeV and 5 MeV Si ions is provided almost uniformly in the cell. The shape of degradation curves was very similar to the results of electron and proton irradiations. The remaining factor of Voc was around 80 % when the Isc decreased to around 50 %. Unlike in the case of high energy electrons, the degradation was more intensive as the Si ion energy was higher, although the difference was small except the case of 110 keV Si ions.

B. Performance Recovery after Irradiation

Results of performance recovery of the cells after irradiation are listed in Table IV. Here, relative recovery amount described in Table IV is defined as the amount of increase 60 minutes after irradiation at 298 K. Figure 3 shows the performance recovery

TABLE III
IRRADIATION CONDITIONS AND DEPOSITED ENERGY OF INCIDENT PARTICLES (IEL AND NIEL)

Particle		Atmosphere	Temperature (K)	Beam Flux (cm^{-2}s^{-1})	Fluence (cm^{-2})	Average IEL (MeV·cm^2/g)	Average NIEL (MeV·cm^2/g)
Silicon	18 MeV	Vacuum	298±1	1.0×10^9	5.0×10^{10}	1.22×10^4	18.3
	5 MeV				1.0×10^{11}	8.84×10^3	60.0
	350 keV				8.0×10^{10}	1.58×10^3	696
	110 keV				3.0×10^{11}	216	302
Electron	2 MeV	N$_2$ Flow	300±4	1.0×10^{12}	3.0×10^{16}	1.41	5.07×10^{-5}
	0.5 MeV		298±2	1.1×10^{12}	1.6×10^{16}	1.63	1.81×10^{-5}

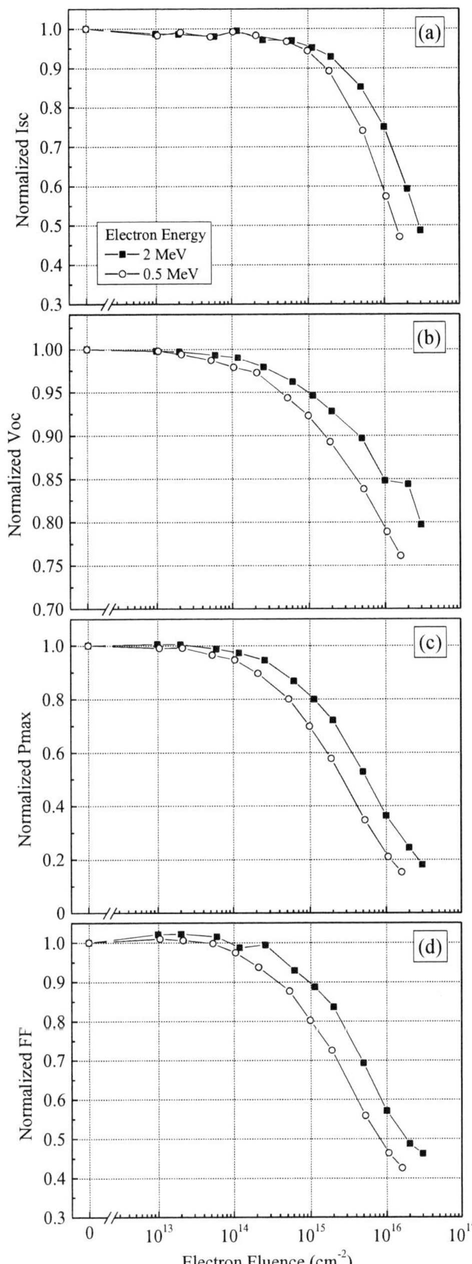

Fig. 1.   Degradation curves of the cells irradiated with 2 MeV and 0.5 MeV electrons: (a) Isc, (b) Voc, (c) Pmax, and (d) FF. All the values are normalized by the values before irradiation.

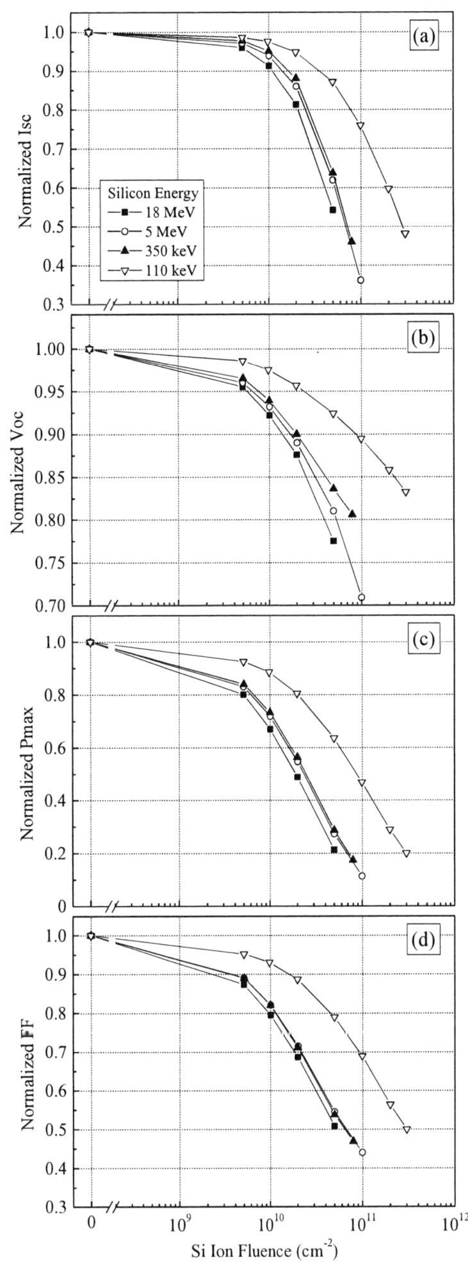

Fig. 2.   Degradation curves of the cells irradiated with 18 MeV, 5 MeV, 350 keV, and 110 keV Si ions: (a) Isc, (b) Voc, (c) Pmax, and (d) FF. All the values are normalized by the values before irradiation.

immediately after 18 MeV Si ion irradiation at the fluence of 1.0×10^{11} cm^{-2}. All the parameters (Isc, Voc, Pmax, and FF) significantly recovered and in particular, the Isc values prominently recovered in all cases. This indicates that radiation defects in the active layers were annealed and the minority carrier lifetime recovered (RT annealing). We conclude that the significant RT annealing occurs regardless of radiation species

and thus, the *in-situ* measurement technique is necessary to investigate the radiation degradation of a-Si solar cells.

The results of *I-V* measurements after the thermal annealing of 423 K for 4 hours are shown in the rightmost column in Table IV. It was shown that the Isc almost completely recovered while the values of Voc and FF did not, indicating that the shunt resistance did not completely recover. The similar results have also been obtained in the case of proton irradiation [10, 12].

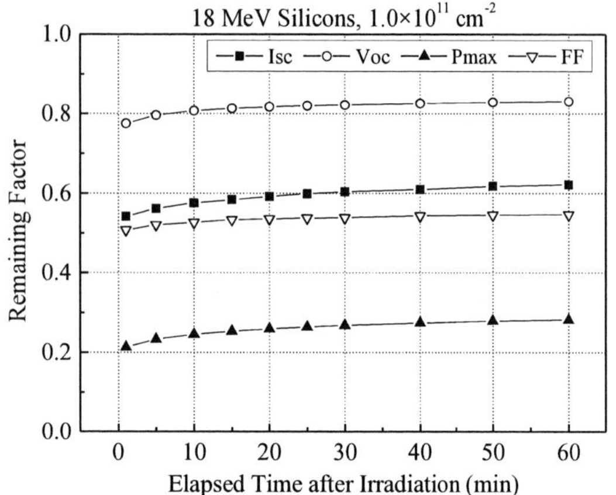

Fig. 3. Performance recovery after 18 MeV Si ion irradiation at the fluence of 1.0×10^{11} cm^{-2} at 298 K. Isc: closed squares, Voc: open circles, Pmax: closed triangles, and FF: open inverted triangles. All the values are normalized by the values before irradiation.

IV. DISCUSSION

In this section, we discuss the energy deposition process which dominates the radiation degradation of the cell performance. As explained in Introduction, the radiation degradation of a-Si solar cells is expected to be affected by both the electronic excitation effect (i.e. ionization) and the displacement damage effect, although it is unclear which effect is the main cause of the electrical degradation. However, by analyzing the degradation curves of Isc and Voc based on the energy deposition process of energetic particles, the degradation mechanism is revealed. The IEL value and the Ionizing Dose (ID), which is defined as the product of the IEL and the irradiation fluence, strongly correlate with the electronic excitation effect, whereas the NIEL value and the Displacement Damage Dose (DDD), which is defined as the produce of the NIEL and the irradiation fluence, strongly correlate with the displacement damage effect. Therefore, for example, if the degradation data collapse to a single curve using the ID as the abscissa, the radiation degradation is dominated by the electronic excitation effect, and vice versa. In this way, we have clarified that the proton induced degradation is dominated by the displacement damage effect, although the electronic excitation effect may partly contribute [10, 12].

Figure 4 shows the depth profiles of IEL and NIEL values for Si ions (110 keV, 350 keV, 5 MeV, and 18 MeV) and electrons (0.5 MeV and 2 MeV). The data of protons with energies of 40 keV, 200 keV, 2 MeV, and 10 MeV are also shown for comparison. Both the IEL and the NIEL per unit depth were calculated using TRIM-code [13] and refs. [14, 15]. Both the IEL and the NIEL values of all particles provide almost uniformly along the depth direction, except that of 110 keV Si ions. Both the IEL and the NIEL values of Si ions are much

TABLE IV

REMAINING FACTORS OF THE IRRADIATED CELLS, RELATIVE RECOVERY AMOUNT AFTER IRRADIATION, AND THERMAL ANNEALING RESULTS.

	Particle	Fluence (cm^{-2})	Remaining Factor (%)	Recovery Amount (60 min, +%)	After Annealing (423 K, 4h)
Isc	18 MeV Si	5.0×10^{10}	54.2	+8.0	100.1
	5 MeV Si	1.0×10^{11}	36.1	+8.8	98.9
	350 keV Si	8.0×10^{10}	46.0	+5.1	—
	110 keV Si	3.0×10^{11}	48.1	+7.4	—
	0.5 MeV Electrons	1.6×10^{16}	47.1	+4.9	—
Voc	18 MeV Si	5.0×10^{10}	77.5	+5.6	98.7
	5 MeV Si	1.0×10^{11}	70.9	+7.1	97.8
	350 keV Si	8.0×10^{10}	80.6	+1.3	—
	110 keV Si	3.0×10^{11}	83.3	+1.6	—
	0.5 MeV Electrons	1.6×10^{16}	76.1	+3.6	—
Pmax	18 MeV Si	5.0×10^{10}	21.3	+6.9	96.3
	5 MeV Si	1.0×10^{11}	11.3	+5.1	93.4
	350 keV Si	8.0×10^{10}	17.4	+2.5	—
	110 keV Si	3.0×10^{11}	20.0	+4.2	—
	0.5 MeV Electrons	1.6×10^{16}	15.3	+3.4	—
FF	18 MeV Si	5.0×10^{10}	50.8	+3.9	97.4
	5 MeV Si	1.0×10^{11}	44.0	+2.8	96.7
	350 keV Si	8.0×10^{10}	46.9	+0.6	—
	110 keV Si	3.0×10^{11}	50.0	+1.4	—

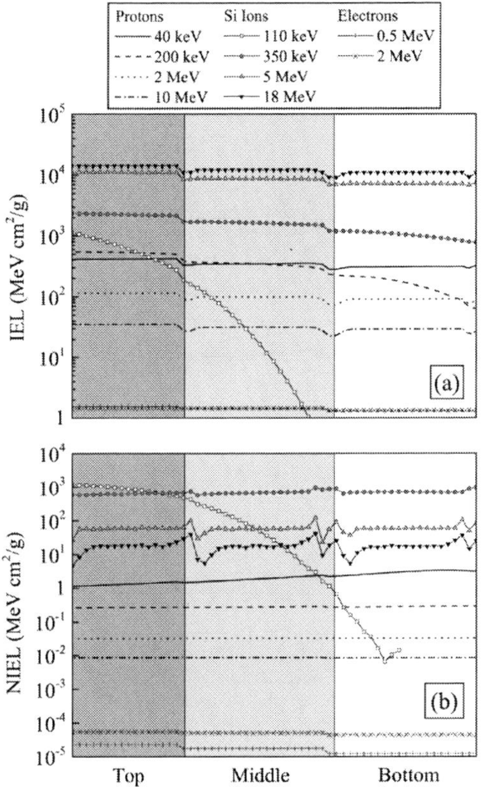

Fig. 4. Depth profiles of (a) ionizing energy loss (IEL) and (b) non-ionizing energy loss (NIEL) for protons, Si ions, and electrons. Top, middle, and bottom subcells are represented by dark-gray, light-gray, and white areas,

larger than that of protons. In particular, the very large IEL values are found in 5 MeV and 18 MeV Si ions and the very large NIEL values are found in 350 keV Si ions. On the other hand, both the IEL and the NIEL values of electrons are much smaller than that of protons and Si ions. Also, it is found that IEL > NIEL is true except for 110 keV Si ions and thus, most of particle energies are given through IEL.

Figure 5 (a, b, d, e) shows the degradation curves of Isc and Voc which are scaled using the ID and the DDD. The data in Figs. 1 and 2 as well as the proton degradation data [10, 12] are also shown in Fig. 5, although the data of 110 keV Si ions are not shown here in order not to consider the effects of extremely non-uniform energy deposition along the depth profile. However, average IEL and NIEL values in the whole region of the cells were used for ID and DDD calculations. Also, the ID was represented by a unit of MeV/g to be the same as the DDD, not by a unit of "rad" or "Gy" which was usually used.

The results in Fig. 5 (a, b, d, e) show that a universal degradation curve was not obtained by both the ID scaling and the DDD scaling. This fact indicates that both the electronic excitation effect (IEL) and the displacement damage effect (NIEL) contribute the degradation and neither of them is negligible. However, a single degradation curve was obtained by the DDD scaling only in the case of proton irradiation (open symbols in Fig. 5 (b, e)). Therefore, it may be concluded that the

proton degradation is significantly dominated by the displacement damage effect whereas the Si ion degradation and the electron degradation are not. This conclusion is seemingly controversial, but may be causally related to a difference of "radiation quality effect" among Si ions, electrons, and protons. In other words, since both the IEL and the NIEL values are an average energy deposition per unit area and do not consider the spatial distribution of deposited energy density, the density effect of deposited energy should be taken into account.

In the case of swift heavy ion irradiation on non-metallic materials, the high-density electronic excitation along the ion tracks often provides unique radiation effects [16]. In this study, 5 MeV and 18 MeV Si ions were regarded as swift heavy ions and they had much higher IEL values (around 10^4 MeV·cm²/g on average, see Table III) than the other particles. The high-density electronic excitation effect does not contribute the defect formation in c-Si and thus does not affect the performance degradation of c-Si solar cells. The creation ratio of radiation defects in amorphous materials is, however, likely to depend on the electronic excitation density of radiations and it may strongly affect the performance degradation of a-Si solar cells. In addition, heavy ions produce the cascade damage more seriously than protons and electrons, and it may also affect the performance degradation per unit DDD. As shown in Fig. 4 (b), the very high NIEL values were found in 350 keV Si ions (696 MeV·cm²/g on average, see Table III) and they were expected to induce a large amount of cascade damage.

Here, Effective Damage Dose (EDD) is defined by the following equation:

$$EDD = DDD + A \times ID \qquad (1)$$

where A is a relative damage factor. The relative damage factor is considered as the damage induction ratio of the IDD to the DDD which depends on radiation species, and the damage caused by the ID (the electronic excitation effect) is relatively higher as the value of A is larger. In other words, the factor A is mainly to consider the high-density electronic excitation effect. Note however that no physical meaning is included in the absolute value of EDD, and only the relative value of A is meaningful. The degradation curves of Isc and Voc scaled by the EDD are shown in Fig. 5 (c, f). In this figure, 4×10^{-4} was used for A value of protons and electrons, and 0.02 for Si ions. The results in Fig. 5 (c, f) clearly show that a single curve was drawn using the EDD scaling except the results of 0.5 MeV electrons and 350 keV Si ions, indicating that the ratio of the damage due to the IEL to the damage due to the NIEL in the cases of 5 MeV and 18 MeV Si ions is 50 times higher than that in the case of protons and electrons. This is thought to be due to the fact that the high-density electronic excitation effect enhances the damage induction ratio. On the other hand, protons and electrons have the same relative damage factor, indicating that the high density electronic excitation effect is not significant in the cases of proton and electrons. The important thing is that the ratios of the NIEL to the IEL in the case of protons are much higher than that in the case of electrons. For

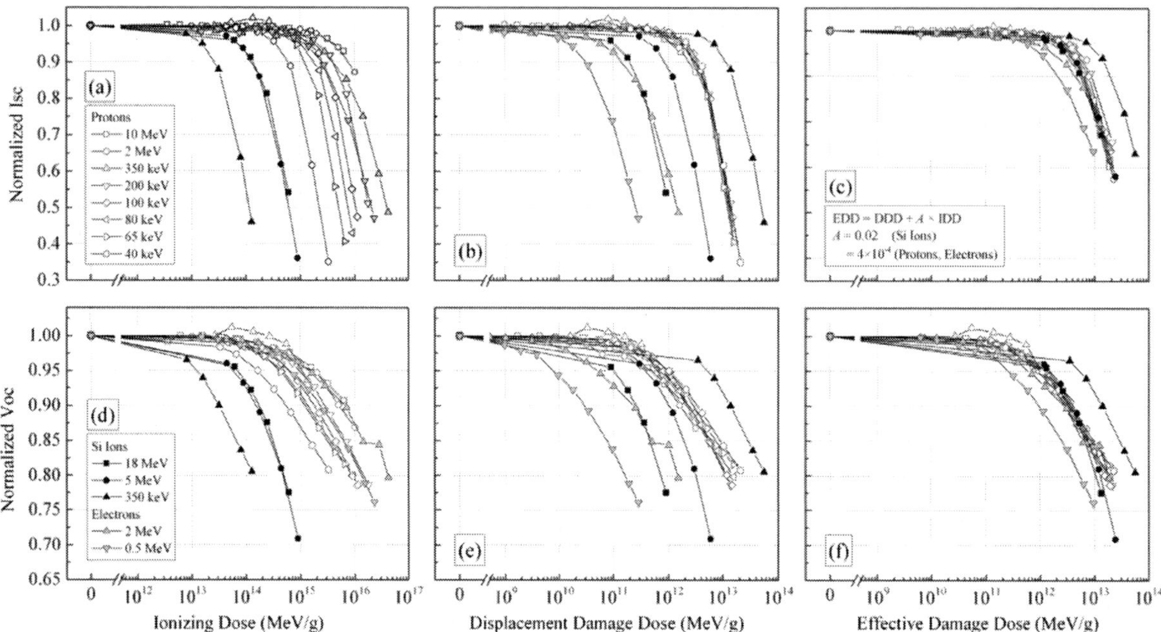

Fig. 5. Ionizing dose (ID) scaling, displacement damage dose (DDD) scaling, and effective damage dose (EDD) scaling for the degradation curves of Isc and Voc. The abscissa axes are converted from fluence (cm^{-2}) to ID in (a) and (d), DDD in (b) and (e), and EDD in (c) and (f). The ordinate axes are the remaining factors of Isc in (a), (b), and (c), Voc in (d), (e), and (f).

example, this ratio for 2 MeV protons is around 10 times higher than the ratio for 2 MeV electrons (3.20×10^{-4} for 2 MeV protons and 3.20×10^{-5} for 2 MeV electrons). Because of this, the proton degradation is mainly induced by the NIEL whereas the electron degradation is induced by both the NIEL and the IEL. The reason that the degradation curve of 350 keV Si ions did not follow the rest of the data could be interpreted as the effect of the cascade damage. It is possible that the cascade damage in amorphous materials rather reduce the degradation (defect creation) since the dense defects created by the cascade damage immediately annihilate through a structural relaxation even at RT. Unfortunately, speculations are still included in the discussion above at the present and further studies are needed to justify this. In particular, the very high energy Si ion irradiation effects should be investigated.

Finally, the results of 0.5 MeV electrons which did not follow the rest of the data in Fig. 4 (c, f) are mentioned. The degradation due to 0.5 MeV electrons was significantly larger than that due to 2 MeV electrons, as shown in Fig. 1. The NIEL value of 2 MeV electrons is around 3 times larger than that of 0.5 MeV whereas the IEL values are roughly the same (see Table III). Hence, this result cannot be explained in terms of the IEL and the NIEL. It is unlikely that the slight difference of IEL value resulted in the significant difference of degradation. Also, if the difference of NIEL value dominantly affected the degradation, the higher degradation should have been observed in 2 MeV electrons than 0.5 MeV electrons. Unfortunately, this result remains to be elucidated at the present stage, although at least thermal annealing effect based on the increase in irradiation temperature was excluded since the temperature during irradiation was carefully controlled in this study. Low energy electrons scattered backward from the sample stage may affect the cell degradation [17], since the degradation of a-Si solar cells can be induced by low energy electrons which do not produce the displacement damage. Actual energy spectrum of irradiated electrons should be investigated in order to estimate a more correct damage dose.

V. Summary

In this study, we investigated the degradation behavior of a-Si/a-SiGe/a-SiGe TJ solar cells due to Si ion irradiation and high energy electron irradiation. The results showed that the similar degradation curves are obtained regardless of radiation species. The degradation mechanism due to energetic particles (Si ions, electrons, and protons) was discussed on the basis of energy deposition process (IEL and NIEL) and it was found that the radiation quality effect such as the high-density electronic excitation effect and the cascade damage might affect the degradation. It was shown that the radiation degradation could be systematically explained by defining the effective damage dose. Performance recoveries immediately after irradiation were also investigated at RT and it was found that the RT annealing after irradiation always occurs. The cell performance did not completely recover by the thermal annealing of 423 K for 4 hours.

REFERENCES

[1] S. G. Bailey, J. McNatt, R. Raffaelle, S. Hubbard, D. Forbes, and L. Fritzenmeier, "The Future of Space Photovoltaics," in *Proc. 34th IEEE Photovoltaic Specialist Conf.*, Philadelphia, PA, 2009, pp. 001909–001913.

[2] A. Banerjee, X. Xu, K. Beernink, F. Liu, K. Lord, G. DeMaggio, B. Yan, T. Su, G. Pietka, C. Worrel, S. Ehlert, D. Beglau, J. Yang, and S. Guha, "Advances in Cell Efficiency of a-Si:H and nc-Si:H-Based Multi Junction Solar Cells for Space and Near-Space Applications," in *Proc. 34th IEEE Photovoltaic Specialist Conf.*, Philadelphia, PA, 2009, pp. 002651–002655.

[3] R. A. C. M. M. van Swaaij and A. Klaver, "Comparison of Amorphous Silicon Solar Cell Performance Following Light and High-Energy Electron-Beam Induced Degradation," *J. Non-Cryst. Solids*, vol. 354, pp. 2464–2467, Feb. 2008.

[4] J. R. Srour, G. J. Vendura, Jr., D. H. Lo, C. M. C. Toporow, M. Dooley, R. P. Nakano, and E. E. King, "Damage Mechanism in Radiation-Tolerant Amorphous Silicon Solar Cells," *IEEE Trans. Nucl. Sci.*, vol. 45, pp. 2624–2631, Dec. 1998.

[5] K. Shimazaki, M. Imaizumi, T. Ohshima, H. Itoh, and K. Kibe, "Analysis of Radiation Response and Recovery Characteristics of Amorphous Silicon Solar Cells," in *Proc. 4th World Conf. on Photovoltaic Energy Conversion*, Hawaii, HI, 2006, pp. 1797–1800.

[6] M. Yamaguchi, "Radiation-Resistant Solar Cells for Space Use," *Solar Energy Materials & Solar Cells*, vol. 68, pp. 31–53, 2001.

[7] M. Yamaguchi, S. J. Taylor, M. Yang, S. Matsuda, O. Kawasaki, and T. Hisamatsu, "High energy and high fluence proton irradiation effects in silicon solar cells," *J. Appl. Phys.*, vol. 80, pp. 4916–4920, 1996.

[8] S. Sato, H. Sai, T. Ohshima, M. Imaizumi, K. Shimazaki, and M. Kondo, "Electron and Proton Irradiation Effects on Substrate-Type Amorphous Silicon Solar Cells," in *Proc. 37th IEEE Photovoltaic Specialist Conf.*, Seattle, WA, 2011, pp. 001615–001619.

[9] S.-i. Sato, H. Sai, T. Ohshima, M. Imaizumi, K. Shimazaki, and K. Kondo, "Temperature Influence on Performance Degradation of Hydrogenated Amorphous Silicon Solar Cells Irradiated with Protons," *Prog. Photovolot: Res. Appl.*, in Press.

[10] S. Sato, K. Beernink, and T. Ohshima, "Degradation Behavior of Flexible a-Si/a-SiGe/a-SiGe Triple Junction Solar Cells Irradiated with 20-350 keV Protons," in *Proc. 38th IEEE Photovoltaic Specialist Conf.*, Austin, TX, 2012, in Press.

[11] R. J. Walters, J. H. Warner, G. P. Summers, S. R. Messenger, J. R. Lorentzen, P. Tlomak, J.E. Granata, and P. E. Hausgen, "Radiation Response and Annealing Characteristics of Thin Film Photovoltaics," in *19th European Photovoltaic Solar Energy Conference*, 2004, pp. 3606–3609.

[12] S. Sato, K. Beernink, and T. Ohshima, "Degradation Behavior of Flexible a-Si/a-SiGe/a-SiGe Triple Junction Solar Cells Irradiated with Protons," *IEEE J. Photovolt., Under Review*.

[13] Available online: http://www.srim.org/

[14] I. Jun, M. A. Xapsos, S. R Messenger, E. A. Burke, R. J. Walters, G. P. Summers, and T. Jordan, "Proton Nonionizing Energy Loss (NIEL) for Device Application," *IEEE Trans. Nucl. Sci.*, vol. 50, pp. 1924-1928, Sep. 2003.

[15] S. R. Messenger, E. A. Burke, G. P. Summers, M. A. Xapsos, R. J. Walters, E. M. Jackson, and B. D. Weaver, "Nonionizing Energy Loss (NIEL) for Heavy Ions," *IEEE Trans. Nucl. Sci.*, vol. 46, pp. 1595–1602, Dec. 1999.

[16] For example: N. Ishikawa, K. Ohhara, Y. Ohta, and O. Michikami, "Binominal Distribution Function for Intuitive Understanding of Fluence Dependence of Non-Amorphous Ion-Track Area," *Nucl. Instr. Meth. B*, vol. 268, pp. 3273–3276, Jun. 2010.

[17] S. R. Messenger, J. H. Warner, R. Uribe, and R. J. Walters, "Monte Carlo Analyses of the NEO Beam Electron Beam Facility for Space Solar Cell Radiation Qualification," *IEEE Trans. Nucl. Sci.*, vol. 57, pp. 3470–3476, Dec. 2010.

Mapping the Local Photoelectronic Properties of Polycrystalline Solar Cells Through High Resolution Laser-Beam-Induced Current Microscopy

Marina S. Leite, *Member, IEEE*, Maxim Abashin, Henri J. Lezec, Anthony G. Gianfrancesco, A. Alec Talin, and Nikolai B. Zhitenev

Abstract—To boost the efficiency of thin-film polycrystalline solar cells that are microscopically inhomogeneous, it is imperative to understand how the grain interiors (GIs) and grain boundaries (GBs) within these materials affect its overall electronic properties. By using an apertured near-field scanning optical microscope in an illumination mode, we determined the local photocurrent that is generated within the GIs and at the GBs with nanoscale resolution and correlate the results with surface morphology and composition.

Index Terms—Cadmium compounds, current measurement, grain boundaries (GBs), photovoltaic (PV) cells, scanning probe microscopy, thin-film devices, wavelength measurement.

I. INTRODUCTION

THE understanding of how the grain interiors (GIs) and grain boundaries (GBs) affect and favor the overall performance of polycrystalline thin-film solar cells is still an open question [1]–[3]. The presence of grains with different crystallographic orientations [see Fig. 1(a)] induces microscopic dislocations, vacancies, and distorted bonds at the interfaces, among other imperfections in the crystal lattice. In CdTe/CdS solar cells, these defects introduce extra electronic states and, consequently, significant band bending, as represented in Fig. 1(b) and (c). In the case of a p-type material, these gap states, also called "trap states," are spatially localized and trap holes, giving rise to an accumulation of positive charges p at the boundaries.

Manuscript received June 14, 2013; revised August 14, 2013; accepted September 9, 2013. Date of publication October 28, 2013; date of current version December 16, 2013. This work was supported by the Cooperative Research Agreement between the University of Maryland and the National Institute of Standards and Technology Center for Nanoscale Science and Technology, Award 70NANB10H193, through the University of Maryland.

M. S. Leite and M. Abashin are with the Center for Nanoscale Science and Technology, National Institutes of Standards and Technology, Gaithersburg, MD 20899 USA, and also with Maryland Nanocenter, University of Maryland, College Park, MD 20742 USA (e-mail: mleite@umd.edu; maxim.abashin@nist.gov).

H. J. Lezec, A. G. Gianfrancesco, and N. B. Zhitenev are with the Center for Nanoscale Science and Technology, National Institutes of Standards and Technology, Gaithersburg, MD 20899 USA (e-mail: henri.lezec@nist.gov; anthony.gianfrancesco@nist.gov; nikolai.zhitenev@nist.gov).

A. A. Talin is with the Center for Nanoscale Science and Technology, National Institutes of Standards and Technology, Gaithersburg, MD 2089 USA, and also with the Sandia National Laboratories, Livermore, CA 94550 USA. (e-mail: aatalin@sandia.gov).

Color versions of one or more of the figures in this paper are available online at http://ieeexplore.ieee.org.

Digital Object Identifier 10.1109/JPHOTOV.2013.2284860

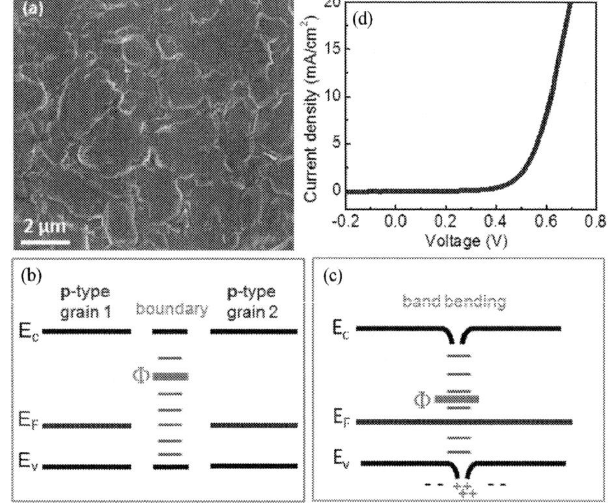

Fig. 1. (a) SEM image of thin-film CdTe layer showing micrometer-scale grains and interfaces with structural defects. (b) Band diagram for two grains and (c) band bending caused by the interface states. The extra states trap holes, resulting in electric field on both sides of the grain boundary. E_C, E_F, E_V, and Φ refer to the conduction, Fermi and valence energies, and the neutrality level, respectively. (d) Dark J–V curve showing diode behavior of CdTe/CdS solar cell device.

The presence of GBs affects, therefore, the transport properties of both majority and minority carriers, as well as the overall performance of the polycrystalline device, in particular, the open-circuit voltage (V_{oc}) [1]. Historically, the somewhat beneficial role of the GBs in CdTe/CdS devices has been mainly attributed to built-in electric fields [4], [5], while the composition variations within the polycrystalline grains [6], [7] were also discussed. In the latter case, S from the CdS layer was found to preferentially interdiffuse into the GBs as a result of grain-boundary-assisted diffusion mechanism, which lead to a $CdTe_{1-x}S_x$ ternary phase.

Presently, there is a great effort to engineer and increase the V_{oc} of polycrystalline CdTe/CdS devices. Although the bandgap of CdTe is 1.44 eV, the V_{oc} of world record cells is currently limited at 0.86 V, leading to an efficiency of 18.7% [8], [9]. For total area modules, the current V_{oc} record is 0.90 V, with efficiency record of 16.1% under global AM1.5 illumination [10]. The significant difference between the material bandgap and the best qV_{oc} achieved is limited by a consistently high forward dark current [see Fig. 1(d)] and indicates that proper

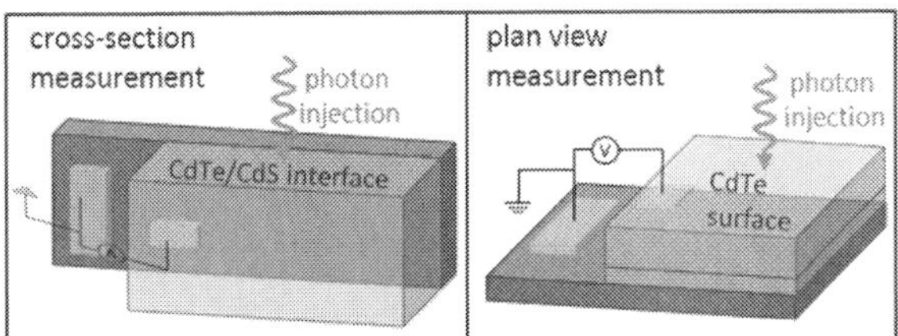

Fig. 2.   LBIC microscopy setup, which allows for both cross-sectional and plan-view measurements. In both cases, photons are injected through an apertured NSOM probe. The wavelength of the photons can be selected by using various laser sources, permitting the investigation of bandgap variations and/or subgap absorption within the polycrystalline material.

material engineering and device processing can lead to higher V_{oc} ($\approx$ 1.1 V), comparable with III–V compound semiconductor solar cells, such as GaAs. The open-circuit voltage in CdTe solar cells can be increased through the optimization of the device structure, including the microstructure of the absorber layer, and by a better control of the dopant distribution within the p-layer. Moreover, segregation and defect passivation can limit the recombination and leakage current within the polycrystals.

Here, we use laser-beam-induced current (LBIC) microscopy to measure the photoelectronic properties of the GIs and GBs. LBIC microscopy is used to spatially resolve and quantify the current distribution within the CdTe polycrystalline layer of the solar cell. This technique allows us to assess composition variations at the GBs, which can give us valuable information about the recombination sources at the grains' interfaces.

II. Laser-Beam-Induced Current Microscopy

Several scanning probe microscopy techniques, including conductive atomic force, Kelvin probe, and capacitance microscopies, have been employed to characterize the role of GBs on the performance of CdTe/CdS and CIGS solar cells [3], [11]–[18]. Nevertheless, scanning probe measurements often do not reproduce the operation conditions of the solar cells. Here, we use LBIC microscopy [6], [19]–[21] to locally probe the photoconductivity of the polycrystals constituting CdTe/CdS solar cells with nanoscale resolution. By using a subwavelength apertured near-field scanning optical microscope (NSOM) in an illumination mode, we determine the local photocurrent that is generated within the GIs and at the GBs through the electrical signal detection of the *in operando* device under different illumination conditions. Measurements are performed at multiple wavelengths that excite CdTe above, near, and below the bandgap with the aim to differentiate between the effects of the built-in electric fields and the local variations of optical absorption that are related to compositional inhomogeneity. While other techniques such as electron-beam-induced current microscopy [17], [22] can detect local variation of collection due to built-in electric fields, the additional advantage of LBIC lies on the fact that the photocurrent signal can be also be sensitive to local absorption and the compositional variation, depending on the wavelength of the excitation source.

Fig. 2 shows a schematic of the LBIC microscopy setup, which allows for both cross-sectional and plan-view measure-

ments on the device. Topography and photocurrent were acquired simultaneously using a *XYZ-piezo* feedback-controlled setup. Therefore, the surface topography and electrical signal can be directly correlated. Incident light wavelength was varied either using an optical parametric oscillator (OPO) laser or a supercontinuum laser with the appropriate combination of bandpass and neutral density filters. The photons are injected through an apertured NSOM probe. Nanoscale spatial resolution is achieved by placing the tapered fiber probes (with 50–500 nm in diameter) extremely close to the surface of the grains (10 nm), therefore providing a local source of excitation. Thus, the resolution is primarily affected by the probe diameter and the materials' absorption coefficient α. The transmittance of the optical fibers used varies from 10^{-5} to 10^{-1}, depending on the diameter of the fiber. For 300-nm probes, we measured transmittance of $\sim 10^{-4}$.

The samples used in this study are commercially available CdTe solar cells formed by the following layers (from top to bottom): 4.0 mm of glass substrate, 550 nm of In_2O_3/SnO_2 (bilayer transparent conductive oxide—TCO), 50 nm of n-type CdS, and 3.5 μm of p-type CdTe. The LBIC microscopy measurements were performed on the exposed p-doped CdTe grains of the backside of the cell injecting light in a region without back contact. The 100-nm thick platinum contact pads were evaporated through stencil masks, and the measurements were performed with the tip that is positioned off the contact edge. As a result, the tip can be placed in a close proximity to CdTe surface to analyze variations of photocurrent within the CdTe grain, as well as at the GIs and GBs' surface. In this particular geometry, holes (p) and electrons (n) are majority and minority carriers, respectively.

Most of the LBIC measurements were performed on "as-is grains" injecting light at different wavelengths through 200–400 nm NSOM probes. The plan-view LBIC microscopy measurements consistently showed higher photocurrent generation at the GBs than at the GIs, as shown by the representative image in Fig. 3(a). The overlay between the 3-D topography with the photocurrent measurement shows the spatial distribution of photocurrent and its correlation with the surface topography (valleys at GBs), as highlighted by the line profiles shown in Fig 3(b).

To evaluate the possible effects of rough topography on local light absorption, smooth surfaces were obtained by milling wedges at grazing angles using a Ga focused ion beam (FIB). A sequence of low-current milling steps at grazing incidence ($5°–7°$) was used during the wedge milling process in order to preserve the CdTe polycrystals. This unique geometry allowed us to deconvolute topography effects from the photocurrent variations at the material surface. The line profiles in Fig. 4(a) display the surface of the same CdTe sample before (as-is grains, in light gray) and after milling the wedge (dotted line, dark gray). As expected, the wedge fabrication dramatically modified the topography of the CdTe grains, making them significantly smoother. The presence of a randomly oriented texture (with root mean square of 0.1 μm in height) is a direct result of the original rough surface. This well-known "curtain effect" does not affect the structural properties of the grains, as confirmed by electron

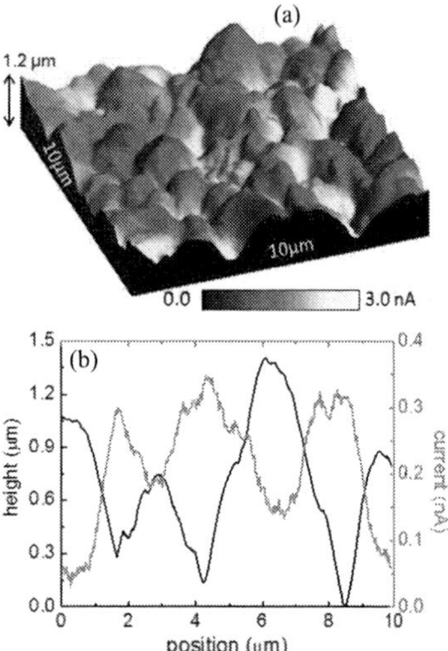

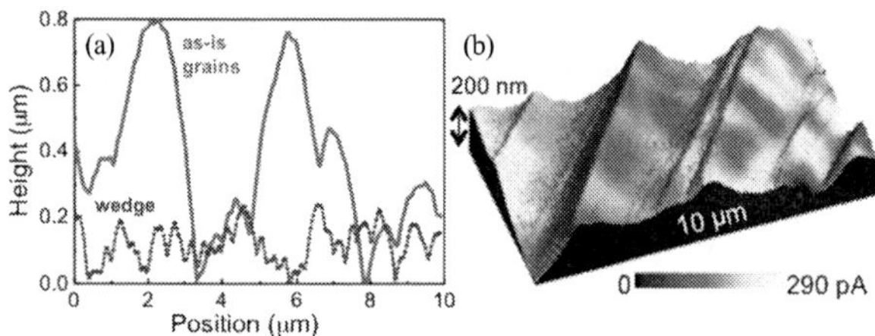

Fig. 3. (a) Three-dimensional topography overlaid with LBIC microscopy measurement of p-CdTe layer showing. The color scale refers to the photocurrent generated by the solar cell. (b) Line profile showing consistent better current transport at grain boundaries. Illumination source: 532 nm laser, power = 14 mW, NSOM probe = 300 nm.

Fig. 4. (a) Surface topography of CdTe grains before and after milling process. (b) 3-D topography overlaid with photocurrent measurement. Illumination source: 532 nm laser, power = 2 mW, NSOM probe = 200 nm.

back-scattering diffraction measurements. The overlay of a representative LBIC map with the corresponding wedge surface showed that the higher photocurrent was indeed generated in the vicinity of GBs. This result demonstrates that variations in photocurrent are in fact due to inhomogeneities within the GIs and GBs of the device that can be related to the band bending efficiently separating electrons and holes [see Fig. 4(b)].

III. PHOTOCURRENT DISTRIBUTION IN CDTE SOLAR CELLS

To assess the bandgap, and therefore, stoichiometry variations within the GBs, separating these from the effect of built-in electric field, we measured the same grains in plan view (see Fig. 2) exciting CdTe at different wavelengths (λ) from well above the bandgap to close and below the band edge (see Fig. 5). Optical filters were used to adjust the intensity of the focused laser illumination.

For $\lambda = 532$ nm, the absorption coefficient α is 10^7 m^{-1}, and the incoming light is absorbed at 100 nm from the material top surface, far away from the p-n junction. As a result, the generated photocurrent is very small. The contrast between the

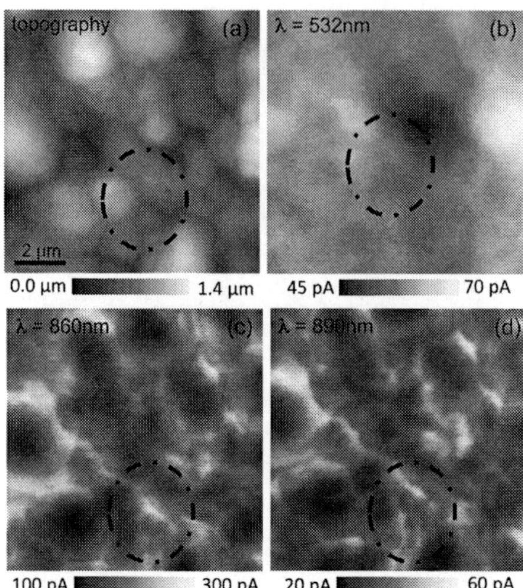

Fig. 5. (a) Topography and (b)–(d) LBIC microscopy measurements of p-CdTe layer under different illumination wavelengths (λ). The current scale was adjusted to clearly show the contrast between GIs and GBs in all images. The highlighted area shows variations in contrast due to composition variations within the grain boundaries. Illumination source: OPO laser, power $\approx$ 1 mW, probe diameter = 300 nm.

GIs and the GBs is rather poor [see Fig. 5(b)], and it can be additionally affected by a high recombination at the exposed top surface of CdTe.

Close to the bandgap ($E_g = 1.44$ eV, $\lambda = 860$ nm), the current generated at the GBs is consistently larger (3x) than the current generated by the GIs [see Fig. 5(c)], confirming that the GBs are efficient local collectors for the minority carriers (electrons). At this wavelength, $\alpha = 6 \times 10^3$ m^{-1} for CdTe, and the penetration depth is 200 μm. The exciting photons can fully penetrate the CdTe layer, assessing the p-n junction. The resulting photocurrent signal is, therefore, generated by the volume of the CdTe layer corresponding to the area that is being scanned. At energies below the bandgap, the absorption quickly vanishes, which results in a significant reduction of the generated photocurrent [see Fig. 5(d)]. At $\lambda = 890$ nm, additional current contrast that was not evident at $\lambda = 860$ nm could be resolved (for example, see highlighted region in Fig. 5). These sharp features could be caused by stoichiometry variations at the GBs or by additional absorption due to impurities.

The precise identification of the chemical composition of the alloy forming the GBs requires the use of high resolution destructive techniques, such as atom probe tomography [23]. Another possible origin of the spatially sharp contrast can still be related to the wavelength-dependent light out-coupling in the near-field affected by the topographic features. Currently, 3-D finite-difference time-domain simulations mimicking the measurement conditions are in progress.

IV. ASSESSING THE P-N JUNCTION

We performed cross-sectional LBIC microscopy measurements (as represented in Fig. 2) under constant illumination ($\lambda = 532$ nm, 14 mW) to access the device p-n junction. A

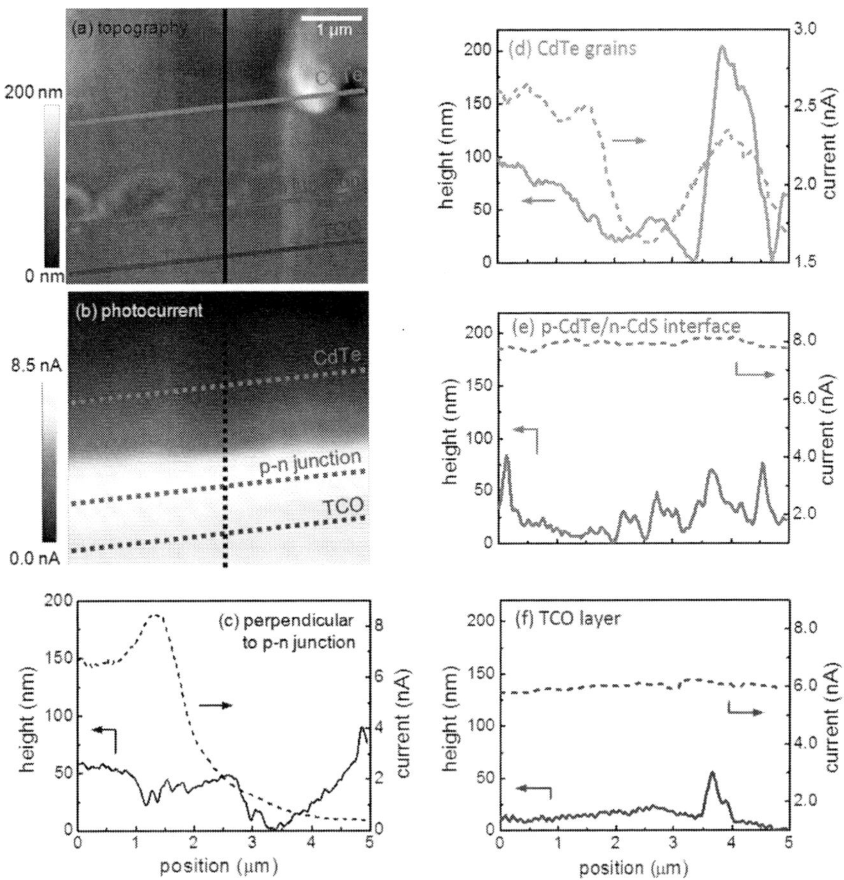

Fig. 6. Cross-sectional (a) topography and (b) LBIC measurements. (c) Line profiles perpendicular to the p-n junction; from the TCO layer ($x = 0$) to the CdTe layer ($x = 5~\mu$m). (d)–(f) Line profiles parallel to the p-n junction. In all cases, the solid and dashed lines refer to topography and current, respectively. Illumination source: 532 nm laser at 14 mW, probe = 500 nm in diameter.

cross section of the sample was milled using a Ga focused ion beam source to provide a fairly smooth surface, as shown by the topography measurement in Fig. 6(a). The white region in the image corresponds to a piece of CdTe that was not fully "polished away" during the final milling steps. Here, this topographic feature is used to corroborate the results of our plan-view measurements.

The CdTe grains' photocurrent [see Fig. 6(b)] varied as a function of distance to the p-n junction. Fig. 6(c) shows the line scans for the topography and photocurrent perpendicular to the p-n junction. As expected, the maximum current is generated at the p-n junction region. The line profiles parallel to the p-n junction for height and photocurrent taken at the same region of the CdTe grains are displayed in Fig. 6(d)–(f) and showed no correlation between topography and photocurrent, consistent with our plan-view and wedge measurements at $\lambda = 532$ nm. The CdTe/CdS interface, i.e., the p-n junction [see line profiles in Fig. 6(d)] was found to generate most of the photocurrent (≈ 8.0 nA), with very small variations, as displayed by the very bright region of Fig. 6(b). However, photocurrent was also generated when the probe was positioned on top of the TCO layer [see Fig. 6(e)]. This can be related to multiple scattering effects

at the contact and substrate interfaces that lead to light injection into the device, and the effect is likely nonlocal. A detailed analysis of the light-semiconductor interaction at the near field involving 3-D finite-difference time-domain simulations will be conducted in a future work.

V. Conclusion

In summary, we mapped and quantified the photocurrent that is generated at CdTe/CdS solar cells GBs under different illumination conditions. We found that the GBs are very efficient current collectors and that the enhanced collection at GBs can be reliably resolved by LBIC microscopy. Modified CdTe surfaces were investigated to exclude possible artifacts caused by surface topography on coupling of the near-field localized light source. Plan-view measurements were performed as a function of different illumination wavelengths to investigate material's bandgap variations or absorption by the states in the gap within the GBs. Cross-sectional LBIC measurements were used to access the p-n junction of the device, showing a clear dependence of the GBs transport properties with distance from the junction.

Furthermore, LBIC microscopy can be used to probe the photoelectronic properties of devices under forward bias (at V_{oc} operation) and can be expanded to other polycrystalline materials, such as CIGS and mc-Si. The local measurement of the photoelectronic properties of GBs and GIs in thin-film CdTe solar cells by LBIC microscopy represents an important step toward the understanding of how the GBs impacts the device performance and how it can be used to map the diffusion length and recombination rates of the GBs and GIs [24], which can be further used to engineer a device with enhanced V_{oc}.

ACKNOWLEDGMENT

The authors would like to thank A. Band, A. Centrone, M. Davanco, B. Hamadani, P. Haney, G. Holland, T. Landin, J. Munday, K. Srinivasan, J. Schumacher, H. Yoon, and all the CNST NanoFab staff. Sandia is a multi-program laboratory operated by Sandia Corporation, a Lockheed Martin Company, for the U.S. Department of Energy National Nuclear Security Administration under Contract DE-AC04-94AL85000.

REFERENCES

[1] A. L. a. S. Hegedus, *Handbook of Photovoltaic Science and Engineering*, vol. 1, 2nd ed. New York, NY, USA: Wiley, 2011.

[2] I. Visoly-Fisher, S. R. Cohen, K. Gartsman, A. Ruzin, and D. Cahen, "Understanding the beneficial role of grain boundaries in polycrystalline solar cells from single-grain-boundary scanning probe microscopy," *Adv. Functional Mater.*, vol. 16, pp. 649–660, Mar. 2006.

[3] I. Visoly-Fisher, S. R. Cohen, A. Ruzin, and D. Cahen, "How polycrystalline devices can outperform single-crystal ones: Thin film CdTe/CdS solar cells," *Adv. Mater.*, vol. 16, pp. 879–883, Jun. 2004.

[4] K. Durose, S. E. Asher, W. Jaegermann, D. Levi, B. E. McCandless, W. Metzger, H. Moutinho, P. D. Paulson, C. L. Perkins, J. R. Sites, G. Teeter, and M. Terheggen, "Physical characterization of thin-film solar cells," *Progr. Photovolt.*, vol. 12, pp. 177–217, Mar.–May 2004.

[5] K. L. Chopra, P. D. Paulson, and V. Dutta, "Thin-film solar cells: An overview," *Progr. Photovolt.*, vol. 12, pp. 69–92, Mar.-May 2004.

[6] M. K. Herndon, A. Gupta, V. Kaydanov, and R. T. Collins, "Evidence for grain-boundary-assisted diffusion of sulfur in polycrystalline CdS/CdTe heterojunctions," *Appl. Phys. Lett.*, vol. 75, pp. 3503–3505, Nov. 1999.

[7] A. A. McDaniel, J. W. P. Hsu, and A. M. Gabor, "Near-field scanning optical microscopy studies of Cu(In,Ga)Se-2 solar cells," *Appl. Phys. Lett.*, vol. 70, pp. 3555–3557, Jun. 1997.

[8] M. A. Green, K. Emery, Y. Hishikawa, W. Warta, and E. D. Dunlop, "Solar cell efficiency tables (ver. 41)," *Progr. Photovolt.*, vol. 21, pp. 1–11, Jan. 2013.

[9] P. K. Nayak, J. Bisquert, and D. Cahen, "Assessing possibilities and limits for solar cells," *Adv. Mater.*, vol. 23, pp. 2870–2876, Jul. 2011.

[10] (2012). [Online]. Available: http://www.pv-tech.org

[11] H. R. Moutinho, R. G. Dhere, C. S. Jiang, M. M. Al-Jassim, and L. L. Kazmerski, "Electrical properties of CdTe/CdS solar cells investigated with conductive atomic force microscopy," *Thin Solid Films*, vol. 514, pp. 150–155, Aug. 2006.

[12] H. R. Moutinho, R. G. Dhere, C. S. Jiang, Y. F. Yan, D. S. Albin, and M. M. Al-Jassim, "Investigation of potential and electric field profiles in cross sections of CdTe/CdS solar cells using scanning Kelvin probe microscopy," *J. Appl. Phys.*, vol. 108, pp. 074503-1-074503-7, Oct. 2010.

[13] C. Ballif, H. R. Moutinho, and M. M. Al-Jassim, "Cross-sectional electrostatic force microscopy of thin-film solar cells," *J. Appl. Phys.*, vol. 89, pp. 1418–1424, Jan. 2001.

[14] I. Visoly-Fisher, S. R. Cohen, and D. Cahen, "Direct evidence for grain-boundary depletion in polycrystalline CdTe from nanoscale-resolved measurements," *Appl. Phys. Lett.*, vol. 82, pp. 556–558, Jan. 2003.

[15] R. Baier, C. Leendertz, M. C. Lux-Steiner, and S. Sadewasser, "Toward quantitative Kelvin probe force microscopy of nanoscale potential distributions," *Phys. Rev. B*, vol. 85, pp. 165436-1–165436-6, Apr. 2012.

[16] M. Hafemeister, S. Siebentritt, J. Albert, M. C. Lux-Steiner, and S. Sadewasser, "Large neutral barrier at grain boundaries in chalcopyrite thin films," *Phys. Rev. Lett.*, vol. 104, pp. 196602-1–196602-4, May 2010.

[17] S. Sadewasser, D. Abou-Ras, D. Azulay, R. Baier, I. Balberg, D. Cahen, S. Cohen, K. Gartsman, K. Ganesan, J. Kavalakkatt, W. Li, O. Millo, T. Rissom, Y. Rosenwaks, H. W. Schock, A. Schwarzman, and T. Unold, "Nanometer-scale electronic and microstructural properties of grain boundaries in Cu(In,Ga)Se-2," *Thin Solid Films*, vol. 519, pp. 7341–7346, Aug. 2011.

[18] S. S. Schmidt, D. Abou-Ras, S. Sadewasser, W. J. Yin, C. B. Feng, and Y. F. Yan, "Electrostatic potentials at Cu(In,Ga)Se-2 grain boundaries: Experiment and simulations," *Phys. Rev. Lett.*, vol. 109, pp. 095506-1–095506-5, Aug. 2012.

[19] B. Rezek, C. E. Nebel, and M. Stutzmann, "Laser beam induced currents in polycrystalline silicon thin films prepared by interference laser crystallization," *J. Appl. Phys.*, vol. 91, pp. 4220–4228, Apr. 2002.

[20] S. A. Galloway, P. R. Edwards, and K. Durose, "Characterisation of thin film CdS/CdTe solar cells using electron and optical beam induced current," *Sol. Energy Mater. Sol. Cells*, vol. 57, pp. 61–74, Feb. 1999.

[21] C. R. McNeill, H. Frohne, J. L. Holdsworth, and P. C. Dastoor, "Near-field scanning photocurrent measurements of polyfluorene blend devices: Directly correlating morphology with current generation," *Nano Lett.*, vol. 4, pp. 2503–2507, Dec. 2004.

[22] H. P. Yoon, P. M. Haney, D. Ruzmetov, H. Xu, M. S. Leite, B. H. Hamadani, A. A. Talin, and N. B. Zhitenev, "Local electrical characterization of cadmium telluride solar cells using low-energy electron beam," *Solar Energy Mater. Solar Cells*, vol. 117, pp. 499–504, Aug. 2013.

[23] O. Cojocaru-Miredin, P. Choi, R. Wuerz, and D. Raabe, "Exploring the p-n junction region in Cu(In,Ga)Se-2 thin-film solar cells at the nanometer-scale," *Appl. Phys. Lett.*, vol. 101, pp. 181603-1–181603-5, Oct. 2012.

[24] C. Donolato, "Evaluation of diffusion lengths and surface recombination velocities from electron-beam induced current scans," *Appl. Phys. Lett.*, vol. 43, pp. 120–122, 1983.

Marina S. Leite (M'09) received the B.S. degree in chemistry in 2001 and the M.A. and Ph.D. degrees in physics in 2003 and 2007, respectively, from Campinas State University, Campinas, Brazil.

She is currently an Assistant Professor with the Department of Materials Science and Engineering and the Institute for Research in Electronics and Applied Physics, University of Maryland, College Park, MD, USA. Prior to her current appointment, she worked with the Center for Nanoscale Science and Technology, National Institute of Standards and Technology, Gaithersburg, MD, and she was a Postdoctoral Research Scholar with California Institute of Technology, Pasadena, CA, USA. Her research interests include multijunction and thin-film solar cells, metrology for photovoltaic materials characterization, solid-state batteries, alternative energy, and thermodynamics at the nanoscale.

Maxim Abashin received the M.S. degree in applied physics from the Moscow Institute of Physics and Technology, Dolgoprudny, Russia, in 2003 and the Ph.D. degree in photonics from the University of California, San Diego, CA, USA, in 2009.

He is an Expert in nanophotonics and near-field microscopy. He was with the National Institute of Standards and Technology, Gaithersburg, MD, USA, as a Postdoctoral Research Associate from 2009 to 2012.

Henri J. Lezec received the B.S., M.S., and Ph.D. degrees in electrical engineering from the Massachusetts Institute of Technology, Cambridge, MA, USA.

He is a Project Leader with the National Institute of Standards and Technology Center for Nanoscale Science and Technology, Gaithersburg, MD, USA, and has held research positions with NEC Fundamental Research Laboratories, Tsukuba, Japan; FEI Corporation, Munich, Germany; the Centre National de la Recherche Scientifique, Strasbourg, France; and the California Institute of Technology, Pasadena, CA, USA. His research interests include nanoplasmonics, nanophotonics, metamaterials, and nanofabrication with focused ion beams.

Dr. Lezec is a Fellow of the Optical Society of America and a corecipient of the 2012 Julius Springer Prize for Applied Physics.

A. Alec Talin received the B.A. degree in chemistry from the University of California, San Diego, CA, USA, in 1989 and the Ph.D. degree in materials science and engineering from the University of California, Los Angeles, CA, in 1995.

He is a Principal Member of technical staff with Sandia National Laboratories, Livermore, CA, an adjunct Fellow with the Center for Nanoscale Science and Technology, National Institute of Standards and Technology, Gaithersburg, MD, USA, and an adjunct Associate Professor of materials science and engineering with the University of Maryland, College Park, MD. Prior to joining Sandia in 2002, he spent six years as a Research Scientist with the Motorola Corporate Labs, Phoenix, AZ, USA. His research interests include charge transport in nanostructures, contacts, novel electronic materials, solid-state batteries, and photoelectrochemistry.

Anthony G. Gianfrancesco received the double B.S. degree in physics and mathematics and the M.S. degree in physics from Worcester Polytechnic Institute, Worcester, MA, USA, in 2012 and 2013, respectively. He is currently working toward the Ph.D. degree with the University of Tennessee, Knoxville, TN, USA, in energy science and engineering under a fellowship from the Bredesen Center for interdisciplinary research.

He was with the National Institute of Standards and Technology, Gaithersburg, MD, USA, as a Guest Student Researcher.

Nikolai B. Zhitenev received the M.S. (with Hons., eq. summa cum laude) degree in physics from the Moscow Institute of Physics and Technology, Dolgoprudny, Russia, and the Ph.D. degree in condensed matter physics from the Institute of Solid State Physics, Russia.

He is the Group Leader with the Center for Nanoscale Science and Technology (CNST) Energy Research Group, Gaithersburg, MD, USA. Prior to joining National Institute of Standards and Technology, he was an Alexander von Humboldt Fellow with the Max-Planck Institute for Solid State Physics, Stuttgart, Germany, then a Postdoctoral Fellow with the Massachusetts Institute of Technology, and then a Staff Member with Bell Laboratories, Lucent Technologies. As a Staff Member with CNST, he leads multiple projects related to the measurement of electronic properties of novel materials patterned into nanoscale devices and of photovoltaic materials.

Minority Carrier Lifetime Analysis in the Bulk of Thin-Film Absorbers Using Subbandgap (Two-Photon) Excitation

Darius Kuciauskas, Ana Kanevce, James M. Burst, Joel N. Duenow, Ramesh Dhere, David S. Albin, Dean H. Levi, and Richard K. Ahrenkiel

Abstract—**We describe a new time-resolved photoluminescence (TRPL) analysis method for the determination of minority carrier lifetime τ_B. This analysis is based on subbandgap excitation (two-photon excitation, or 2PE) and allows selective lifetime determination at the surface or in the bulk of semiconductor absorbers. We show that for single-crystal CdTe, τ_B could be determined even if surface recombination velocity is $> 10^5$ cm s^{-1}. Two-photon excitation TRPL measurements indicate that radiative lifetime in undoped CdTe is $\gg 66$ ns. We also compare one-photon excitation (1PE) and 2PE TRPL data for polycrystalline CdS/CdTe thin films.**

Index Terms—**Cadmium telluride, minority carrier lifetime, photovoltaic (PV) device, time-resolved photoluminescence (TRPL).**

I. Introduction

MINORITY carrier lifetime τ_B is an important characteristic of photovoltaic (PV) absorbers. For efficient PV devices, τ_B needs to be sufficiently large to enable collection of all photogenerated charge carriers. For example, if transport is due to diffusion, τ needs to be

$$\tau_B \geq \frac{qL^2}{kT\mu} \tag{1}$$

where L is the absorber thickness, μ is the mobility, q is the elementary charge, k is Boltzmann's constant, and T is the temperature. Several methods could be used to determine τ_B [1]. Time-resolved photoluminescence (TRPL) directly probes minority carrier dynamics [1] and provides the best time resolution (≥ 10 ps). One of the limitations of all analyses that employ excitation with laser pulses, such as TRPL, is absorption depth of the laser radiation. For example, when excitation is at 630 nm, $1/\alpha_{630\text{nm}} \approx 200$ nm for CdTe [2], ≈ 100 nm for CIGS [3], and ≈ 50 nm for CZTSe absorbers [4] (α is absorption coefficient). Therefore, immediately after laser excitation (at $t = 0$ ns) a photoluminescence (PL) signal will be emitted only

Manuscript received May 1, 2013; accepted June 11, 2013. Date of publication July 5, 2013; date of current version September 18, 2013. This work was supported by the U.S. Department of Energy under Contract DE-AC36-08-GO28308 with the National Renewable Energy Laboratory.

The authors are with the National Renewable Energy Laboratory, Golden, CO 80401-3305 USA (e-mail: darius.kuciauskas@nrel.gov; Ana.Kanevce@nrel.gov; james.burst@nrel.gov; joel.duenow@nrel.gov; ramesh.dhere@nrel.gov; David.albin@nrel.gov; dean.levi@nrel.gov; richard.ahrenkiel@nrel.gov).

Color versions of one or more of the figures in this paper are available online at http://ieeexplore.ieee.org.

Digital Object Identifier 10.1109/JPHOTOV.2013.2270354

from the surface/interface region of the absorber, and investigation of the bulk might not be possible. Further, in samples with large surface recombination velocity, TRPL decays will be dominated by surface/interface recombination and determination of minority carrier lifetime might not be possible [5].

In this paper, we describe a novel analysis method that enables minority carrier lifetime determination in the bulk of the semiconductor absorber. This analysis does not require any special sample preparation but is instead based on a different method to photogenerate electron–hole pairs by employing subbandgap excitation. When laser pulse intensity is sufficiently high, nonlinear two-photon absorption will occur in the laser beam focus region, which could be selectively moved to the sample surface or bulk. Therefore, the one-photon excitation (1PE) limitation that is imposed by Beer's law could be avoided. We demonstrate that two-photon excitation (2PE) TRPL allows minority carrier lifetime determination at least 0.5 mm from the single-crystal (sc) surface. By using 2PE, we describe initial TRPL measurements on sc-CdTe and on polycrystalline CdS/CdTe thin films.

II. Results and Discussion

A. Two-Photon Excitation Time-Resolved Photoluminescence

Nonlinear two-photon absorption in semiconductors is well known [6]. In the presence of both one- and two-photon absorption, the change in the intensity of the light I, as it passes through the sample in the direction z, is given by [6]

$$\frac{dI}{dz} = -\alpha I - \beta I^2 \tag{2}$$

where α is the absorption coefficient, and β is the two-photon absorption coefficient. (If ignoring the quadratic term, integration would yield the well-known Beer's law.) Two-photon absorption probability is smaller than that for one photon. For example, for n-CdTe using 30-ps pulses at 1064 nm, $\beta = 0.025$ cm/MW [6], and high excitation intensity is needed to achieve two-photon absorption. To avoid thermal effects and other possible complications, ultrafast laser pulses (< 1 ps) are typically employed for 2PE. As illustrated in Fig. 1, using 2PE light will be absorbed in the laser beam focus region, which could be either at the sample surface or in the bulk. Electron–hole pairs created due to 1PE or 2PE will undergo the same dynamics (recombination, drift, and diffusion), and by measuring time decays of PL signals, we are able to determine minority carrier lifetime using standard methods of such analysis [1].

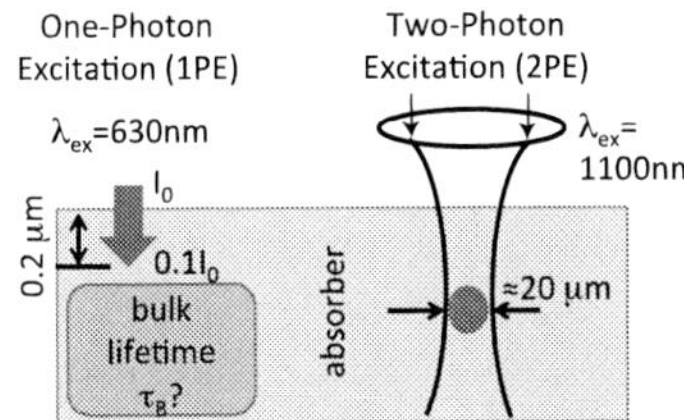

Fig. 1.   One- and two-photon excitation.

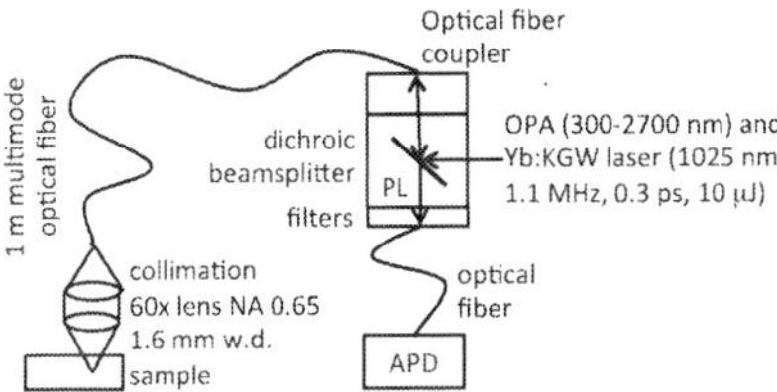

Fig. 2.   Experimental scheme for 2PE TRPL measurements. APD: avalanche: photodiode. NA: numerical aperture. w.d. working distance. OPA: optical parametric amplifier.

Our earlier paper described an optical-fiber-based TRPL spectrometer that affords measurements in room atmosphere or in a high-vacuum chamber using a 1–5 second integration time per measurement [7]. The same setup (Fig. 2) is used in 2PE measurements, except that optical parametric amplifier (OPA) is tuned to 1100 nm and a large numerical aperture aspheric lens (NA 0.65, working distance 1.6 mm) is used to focus laser excitation and to collect PL signals. A laser system (Yb:KGW Pharos laser and Orpheus OPA, Light Conversion Ltd.) provides ~0.3-ps pulses at a 1.1-MHz repetition rate. Because of the propagation in the optical fiber, laser pulse width increases to about 0.4–0.5 ps. No attempt was made to compensate for this temporal broadening. TRPL decays were determined using time-correlated single photon counting [7], and PL spectra were measured with an Ocean Optics USB2000+ spectrometer. Because we employ a multimode optical-fiber-based setup, the excitation spot is relatively large. By scanning samples with known thickness (1 μm or 5 μm), we estimated the laser beam diameter to be 20 μm. This means that for measurements on sc- samples, we can selectively excite the surface and bulk regions, while for thin-film samples excitation is approximately uniformly distributed over the film thickness. Finally, according to (2), βI product is equivalent to absorption coefficient α. When average laser power is 30 mW, $\beta I \approx 20$ cm^{-1}—much smaller than $\alpha = 10^4$–10^5 cm^{-1}, which is typical for direct-bandgap semiconductors. Estimate suggests that 2PE measurements using the optics described earlier correspond to low-injection conditions; data support this estimate.

B. One-Photon Excitation Photoluminescence and Time-Resolved Photoluminescence Analysis for sc-CdTe

Fig. 3 shows room temperature near-bandgap PL emission spectra for undoped sc-CdTe (JX Nippon Mining and Metals). The spectrum measured with 1PE (630 nm) has a maximum at 823 nm and is in good agreement with the data described in the

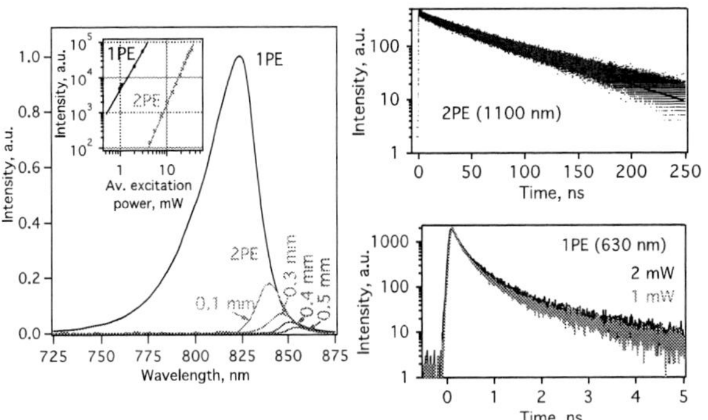

Fig. 3.   (Left) Near-bandgap 1PE and 2PE PL emission spectra for sc-CdTe. 2PE spectra measured ≈0.1 mm to ≈0.5 mm from the sample surface are normalized at 860–875 nm. Inset shows intensity dependence and fits to (3). (Right) TRPL decays measured with 1PE (630 nm) and 2PE (1100 nm).

TABLE I
ONE-PHOTON EXCITATION AND 2PE TRPL LIFETIMES FOR UNDOPEDsc-CdTe

	τ_1, ns (amplitude, %)	τ_2, ns
1PE (630 nm)	0.14 ± 0.02 (69%)	0.54 ± 0.05
2PE (1100 nm)	66 ± 2 (100%)	-

literature [8]. The inset of this figure shows PL signal amplitude intensity dependence. The dependence of PL intensity I_{PL} on excitation intensity I_{excit} is usually described as

$$I_{PL} \propto I_{excit}^a \qquad (3)$$

where the value of exponent a provides some information about recombination. For 1PE, $a = 2.3 \pm 0.3$, which is consistent with recombination through defect states [8].

One-photon excitation TRPL decays (see Fig. 3, measured at 830 nm) are essentially the same when average excitation power is between 1 and 2 mW. Two-exponential fitting of the 1PE data yields $\tau_1 = 0.14$ ns and $\tau_2 = 0.54$ ns (see Table I). As shown later, these decay components are not representative of the minority carrier lifetime. Ahrenkiel and Johnston have described analysis of time-dependent transients for samples with large surface recombination velocity S [9]. According to this model, the instantaneous lifetime after laser excitation (at $t = 0$ ns) is

$$\tau_1 = \frac{\tau_B}{1 + \alpha S \tau_B} \approx \frac{1}{\alpha S} \qquad (4)$$

where τ_B is bulk lifetime, and S is surface recombination velocity. Using $\tau_1 = 0.14$ ns, we estimate $S = 1.4 \times 10^5$ cm s^{-1}.

To further analyze surface recombination effects on 1PE TRPL decays, we used modeling with Sentaurus device software [10]. We have shown that computational analysis is very useful for interpreting TRPL data measured for polycrystalline CdS/CdTe thin-film PV devices (see below); thus, we applied the same approach to analyze TRPL dynamics for absorbers with large surface recombination velocity. Fig. 4 shows 1PE TRPL decay calculated for 2-mW excitation at 630 nm. We assumed $\tau_B = 66$ ns (see next section) and $S = 1.4 \times 10^5$ cm s^{-1}. Simulated 1PE TRPL decay is very similar to the experimental 1PE TRPL data in Fig. 3: In 5-ns, signal amplitude decreases to

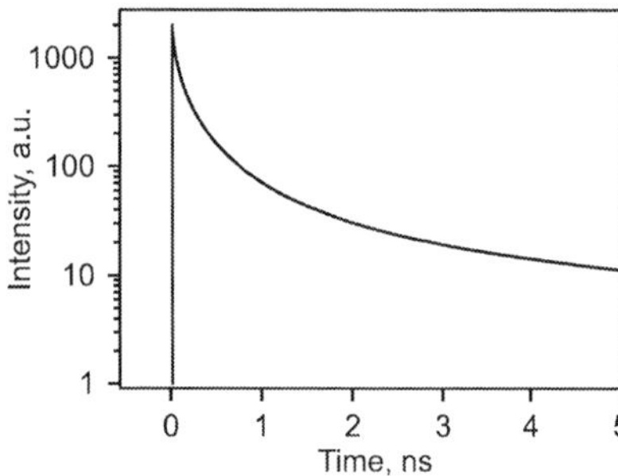

Fig. 4. TRPL decays calculated with Sentaurus device software for a crystalline CdTe absorber assuming electron/hole mobility μ_e /μ_h = 1000 / 125 Vcm^{-1}s^{-1}, τ_B = 66 ns, and $S = 1.4 \times 10^5$ cm s^{-1}.

about 0.5% from the initial maximum, and both decays could be approximated by two exponential functions. Based on good agreement of simulated 1PE TRPL decays and experimental data, it appears that estimation of the surface recombination velocity according to (4) is sufficiently accurate.

We conclude that for absorbers with a large absorption coefficient and large surface recombination velocity, 1PE TRPL analysis does not allow determination of the bulk minority carrier lifetime. Thus, surface passivation is necessary before minority carrier lifetime can be determined. Surface passivation using specially grown double heterostructures is common for III–V semiconductors [11] but not for II–VI semiconductors. Sometimes, a chemical treatment of the crystal surface affords a reduction of the surface recombination velocity and enables minority carrier lifetime determination with 1PE TRPL [12].

C. Two-Photon Excitation Photoluminescence and Time-Resolved Photoluminescence Analysis for sc-CdTe

Two-photon absorption in CdTe was reported in 1975 [13]. That study utilized nanosecond pulses, and it is not clear if thermal effects contributed to the results. Later, two-photon absorption in CdTe was investigated using picosecond pulses [6]. The value of the two-photon absorption coefficient, β, is in the same range as that for other semiconductors. For example, β = 0.025 cm/MW for CdTe, and β = 0.028 cm/MW for GaAs [6]. To our knowledge, the 2PE PL emission spectrum for CdTe was not reported in the literature. Therefore, we show this data in Fig. 3. When measurement is taken 0.1–0.5 mm from the crystal surface, 2PE PL emission spectra are red shifted to 840, 846, 851, and 855 nm (see Fig. 3). Because red shifts increase for measurements taken from the deeper regions of the sample, this shift is attributed to PL reabsorption [14]. This means that only the low-energy (longer-wavelength) photons propagate from the sample and are collected for analysis. Because of reabsorption, the full width at half maximum of the PL emission spectrum decreases from 32.7 nm (1PE) to 12.8 nm (2PE 0.5 mm from the sample surface).

The inset of Fig. 3 shows PL signal amplitude intensity dependence. When fitted to the model of (3), the value of exponent $a = 3.1 \pm 0.1$. These data further support our argument that 630

and 1100 nm excitation correspond to different electron–hole pair generation mechanisms and, in particular, that with 1100-nm excitation, electron–hole pairs are generated in a nonlinear absorption process.

Because of reabsorption in sc-CdTe, 2PE TRPL decays were collected at 850 nm. As shown in Fig. 3, 2PE TRPL decays are single exponential with τ_B = 66 ± 2 ns. (Uncertainty was determined from repeated measurements on different areas of the sample.) Importantly, within the uncertainty of the measurement, 2PE TRPL lifetimes are the same when data are collected from different depths of the CdTe crystal. Therefore, reabsorption does not appear to lead to photon recycling. In contrast, in epitaxial GaAs TRPL lifetime could be an order of magnitude larger than radiative lifetime due to photon recycling [14]. This result can be attributed to different recombination mechanisms in GaAs and CdTe. In CdTe, recombination is mostly nonradiative [5], and electron–hole pairs generated due to reabsorption have only negligible probability to recombine radiatively. Therefore, reabsorption only decreases PL signal intensity. In GaAs, recombination is largely radiative, electron–hole pairs generated by reabsorption are most likely to recombine radiatively, and photon recycling must be accounted for when determining minority carrier lifetime even in relatively thin (epitaxial) samples [14].

Two-photon excitation TRPL decays were essentially the same when average laser power was varied between 4 and 35 mW. Therefore, measurements correspond to low-injection conditions and τ_B = 66 ± 2 ns can be considered minority carrier lifetime. Recombination is largely nonradiative (Shockley–Reed–Hall, or SRH, recombination dominates in undoped CdTe [5]), and radiative lifetime could be estimated to be $\gg$66 ns. Unambiguously establishing radiative lifetime in undoped CdTe will require further analysis. For an initial estimate, we can use the value of the radiative rate constant reported by Cohen et al.: $B = 3 \times 10^{-9}$ cm^{3}s^{-1} [12]. Hall measurements on the undoped sc-CdTe samples from Nippon indicated that $p_0 = (3.5 \pm 0.3) \times 10^{14}$ cm^{-3}. Under low-injection conditions, the radiative bulk lifetime could be approximated as

$$\tau_R = \frac{1}{Bp_0} \approx 950 \text{ ns.} \tag{5}$$

This estimate suggests that radiative efficiency for undoped sc-CdTe is <10% and further increase in minority carrier lifetime should be possible by reducing the concentration of defects that act as SRH recombination centers.

The low-temperature PL emission spectrum for this sample (not shown) was similar to the data reported in the literature [15]. While spectral assignments are complex and in some cases uncertain, data indicate the presence of various point defects and defect complexes [15]. In contrast, in high-quality sc-CdTe, only the exciton PL emission peak is observed at low temperatures [16]. Single-crystal samples with reduced defect concentration that exhibit only excitonic low-temperature PL emission might have TRPL lifetimes that increase toward the radiative limit.

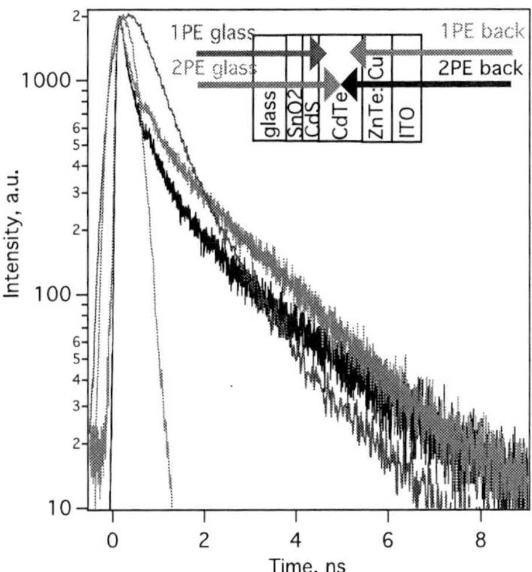

Fig. 5. One-photon excitation and 2PE TRPL decays for glass/SnO$_2$/CdS/CdTe/ZnTe:Cu/ITO. Inset illustrates directions from which excitation is applied and PL signals are collected. 1PE was at 630 nm (2 mW average power), and 2PE was at 1100 nm (20 mW). PL was measured at 840 nm. 1PE and 2PE decays are not identical at $t = 0$ ns due to different instrumental response functions (IRFs) of 1PE [7] and 2PE setups: 1PE data were measured with a R5509 PMT and 2PE data with an APD. Deconvolution of the IRF allows reliable lifetime determination up to 0.1 ns (PMT) and 0.05 ns (APD). Lifetimes determined with deconvolution of the IRF are given in Table II.

D. Comparison of One-Photon Excitation and Two-Photon Excitation Time-Resolved Photoluminescence Data for Superstrate Polycrystalline CdS/CdTe Photovoltaic Devices

We have reported experimental and computational 1PE TRPL studies for "superstrate" CdS/CdTe PV devices schematically illustrated in the inset of Fig. 5 [7], [17]–[19]. (This structure is used in most commercial thin-film PV devices.) Results could be summarized as follows.

1) When 1PE excitation is applied from the back of the PV device (through the transparent back contact [7]), TRPL decay is dominated by the surface recombination [20]. TRPL decay shown as a red solid line in Fig. 5 corresponds to this measurement geometry. When a single-exponential fit is used to analyze this data, lifetime $\tau_1 = 0.17$ ns. Applying the model of (4) yields $S = 1.2 \times 10^5$ cm s^{-1}—similar to the S value for a single crystal. Thus, 1PE TRPL measurement in this geometry does not allow determination of the bulk minority carrier lifetime.

2) When 1PE TRPL measurement is carried out through the glass, light is absorbed in the depletion region of the PV device. With excitation in the depleted region, the carrier dynamics are complex, and computational analysis is needed to understand this data [17], [18]. One-photon excitation TRPL decay in Fig. 5 (shown in blue) can be fit with $\tau_1 = 0.7$ ns and $\tau_2 = 2.0$ ns lifetime components. (Use of two exponential functions is an approximation typically sufficient to describe the data [7], [17]–[19], [21].) Computational analysis shows that the initial part of the 1PE TRPL decay (i.e., τ_1) is dominated by drift and diffusion [18], while the slower part of the TRPL decay could

459

TABLE II
1PE AND 2PE TRPL LIFETIMES FOR POLYCRYSTALLINE SUPERSTRATE CdS/CdTe DEVICE

		τ_1, ns (amplitude, %)	τ_2, ns
1PE	front	0.70 ± 0.02 (90%)	2.0 ± 0.1
(630 nm)	back	0.17 ± 0.02 (100%)	-
2PE	front	0.20 ± 0.02 (68%)	1.6 ± 0.1
(1100 nm)	back	0.16 ± 0.02 (85%)	1.7 ± 0.1

be related to the minority carrier lifetime (τ_2 is similar, but not equal, to τ_B). Detailed analysis of the relationship between 1PE TRPL lifetime components τ_1 and τ_2 to surface recombination velocity and minority carrier lifetime was presented in [17] and [18].

3) Experimentally, electron drift corresponding to the early part of the TRPL decay could be analyzed from time-dependent spectral shifts in the TRPL spectra [19]. Spectral shifts are attributed to time-dependent recombination changes in the CdSTe and CdTe layers [19].

With this background on 1PE TRPL analysis for polycrystalline thin-film CdS/CdTe PV devices, we discuss 2PE TRPL data measured as shown in the inset of Fig. 5. Note that 0.8-mm-thick glass was used as a substrate [7]; thus, 2PE TRPL measurements (with 1.6 mm working distance objective) were possible from both sides of the sample. As described earlier, in 2PE measurements with a multimode optical fiber, excitation volume is relatively large. Polycrystalline CdS/CdTe film is about 4–5 μm thick, and 2PE will be (almost) uniformly distributed over the whole film thickness. In contrast, 1PE is confined to <10% of the film thickness. Therefore, contrasting 1PE and 2PE data for the same sample enables us to compare recombination when excitation is uniformly distributed through the film (2PE) or confined to the surface/interface region (1PE).

Two-photon excitation TRPL decays measured from two sides of the sample (see the black and green solid lines in Fig. 5) are similar. This is perhaps expected; as explained earlier, excitation volume is distributed through the sample volume regardless of the excitation direction.

One-photon excitation and 2PE TRPL lifetimes are summarized in Table II. When 2PE TRPL is measured from both sides of the sample, $\tau_1 = 0.16$–0.20 ns—very similar to $\tau_1 = 0.17$ ns lifetime measured with 1PE from the back. This decay component is thus attributed to interface recombination with $S = (1.0$–$1.3) \times 10^5$ cm s^{-1} [based on (4)]. Limited spatial resolution does not allows us to determine whether such interface recombination occurs at the CdTe/ZnTe:Cu interface (as is the case with 1PE) or at other interfaces, including, for example, grain boundaries. The large amplitude of the first decay component (68%–85% of the total decay; see Table II) suggests that multiple interfaces might contribute to the fast recombination observed with 2PE.

The second (slower) 2PE TRPL decay component has a lifetime of $\tau_2 = 1.6$–1.7 ns. This lifetime is similar to that of the 1PE TRPL decay when excitation is through glass/junction ($\tau_2 = 2.0$ ns), which was shown to be related to the bulk lifetime τ_B [17]. We note that while the 2PE and PL collection span

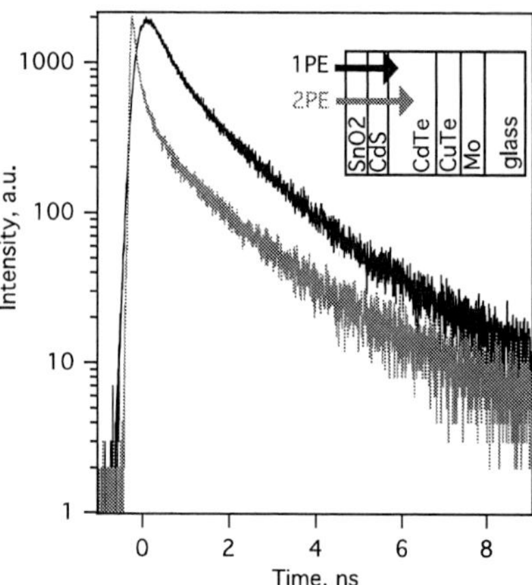

Fig. 6. One-photon excitation and 2PE TRPL decays for CdS/CdTe/Mo/glass sample. Inset illustrates directions from which excitation is applied and PL signals are collected. Measurement conditions were the same as for superstrate PV devices (see Fig. 5).

TABLE III
ONE-PHOTON EXCITATION AND 2PE TRPL LIFETIMES FOR POLYCRYSTALLINE SUBSTRATE CdS/CdTe DEVICE

	τ_1, ns (amplitude, %)	τ_2, ns
1PE (630 nm)	0.47 ± 0.02 (88%)	1.9 ± 0.1
2PE (1100 nm)	0.20 ± 0.02 (76%)	2.4 ± 0.1

all film thickness, 2PE TRPL data does not indicate additional longer lifetime components.

E. Comparison of One-Photon Excitation and Two-Photon Excitation Time-Resolved Photoluminescence Data for Substrate Polycrystalline CdS/CdTe Photovoltaic Devices

Fig. 6 shows 1PE and 2PE TRPL data for a SnO_2/CdS/CdTe/CuTe/Mo/glass "substrate" PV device [22], [23]. Because a metal (Mo) layer is part of the structure, this sample could only be measured with CdTe excitation through CdS. We have reported initial 1PE TRPL data for such devices [23], however, analysis of the minority carrier lifetime in this system is less developed. Among several key differences between superstrate and substrate samples are different alloying and crystalline grain size at the CdS/CdTe interface [22], [23]. Such changes appear to affect charge separation dynamics [24].

Two-photon excitation TRPL lifetimes are comparable for substrate (see Table III) and superstrate (see Table II) polycrystalline thin-film CdS/CdTe. Thus, the component with $\tau_1 = 0.2$ ns could be attributed to surface recombination ($S = 1 \times 10^5$ cm s^{-1}), and $\tau_2 = 2.4$ ns could be similar to the lifetime in the bulk.

We conclude that 1PE and 2PE TRPL data for polycrystalline CdS/CdTe PV devices are rather similar. This is an interesting result, because 1PE and 2PE create electron–hole pairs and collect PL from different parts of the sample: the surface region (1PE) and all film (2PE). The data suggest that minority carrier lifetime does not differ significantly within polycrystalline CdS/CdTe film, at least for samples with $\tau_B \approx 2$ ns. For a more definite analysis of lifetime distribution in polycrystalline absorbers, 2PE measurements with better spatial resolution are necessary. State-of-the-art 2PE microscopy affords spatial resolution of <0.5 μm [25]; thus, PL/TRPL analysis of some polycrystalline thin-film interfaces might be possible in the future.

III. CONCLUSION

We developed a new method for minority carrier lifetime determination in the bulk of semiconductor absorbers. Nonlinear 2PE enables characterization of bulk properties for samples with large surface recombination velocity S. Initial 2PE TRPL data for sc-CdTe and polycrystalline CdS/CdTe were analyzed. For sc-CdTe and polycrystalline CdTe, we consistently find $S = (1.0–1.4) \times 10^5$ cm s^{-1}. This large surface recombination velocity suggests that developing surface passivation for II–VI semiconductors/solar cell absorbers is important. Until then, 2PE TRPL analysis could be very valuable in evaluating recombination in the bulk. For undoped sc-CdTe, 2PE allowed determination of the bulk minority carrier lifetime $\tau_B = 66$ ns. Low radiative efficiency suggests that radiative lifetime for undoped CdTe could be much larger. The largest reported minority carrier lifetimes in polycrystalline CdS/CdTe thin-film PV devices are in the range of $\tau_B = 8–10$ ns [5], [21]. Significantly higher polycrystalline PV device efficiencies could be achieved if τ_B (and the net acceptor concentration) could be increased [26]. Our data show that achieving much longer minority carrier lifetimes should be possible before reaching the limit of radiative recombination.

ACKNOWLEDGMENT

The authors would like to thank Dr. R. Hirano, JX Nippon Mining and Metals, for providing sc-CdTe samples.

REFERENCES

[1] R. K. Ahrenkiel, N. Call, S. W. Johnston, and W. K. Metzger, "Comparison of techniques for measuring carrier lifetime in thin-film and multicrystalline photovoltaic materials," *Solar Energy Mat. Solar Cells*, vol. 94, pp. 2197–2204, 2010.

[2] D. E. Aspnes and H. Arwin, "Nondestructive analysis of $Hg_{1-x}Cd_x$Te (x = 0.00, 0.20, 0.29, and 1.00) by spectroscopic ellipsometry: I. Chemical oxidation and etching," *J. Vac. Sci. Technol. A2*, pp. 1309–1315, 1984.

[3] S. G. Choi, R. Chen, C. Persson, T. J. Kim, S. Y. Hwang, Y. D. Kim, and L. M. Mansfield, "Dielectric function spectra at 40 K and critical-point energies for $CuIn_{0.7}Ga_{0.3}Se_2$," *Appl. Phys. Lett.*, vol. 101, p. 261903, 2012.

[4] S. G. Choi, H. Y. Zhao, C. Persson, C. L. Perkins, A. L. Donohue, B. To, A. G. Norman, J. Li, and I. L. Repins, "Dielectric function spectra and critical-point energies of $Cu_2ZnSnSe_4$ from 0.5 to 9.0 eV," *J. Appl. Phys.*, vol. 111, p. 033506, 2012.

[5] J. Ma, D. Kuciauskas, D. Albin, R. Bhattacharya, M. Reese, T. Barnes, J. V. Li, T. Gessert, and S.-H. Wei, "Dependence of the minority-carrier lifetime on the stoichiometry of CdTe using time-resolved photoluminescence and first-principles calculations," *Phys. Rev. Lett.*, vol. 111, 2013, in press.

[6] V. Nathan, A. H. Guenther, and S. S. Mitra, "Review of multiphoton absorption in crystalline solids," *J. Opt. Soc. Amer. B*, vol. 2, pp. 294–316, 1985.

[7] D. Kuciauskas, J. N. Duenow, J. V. Li, M. R. Young, P. Dippo, and D. H. Levi, "Time resolved photoluminescence spectrometer for thin-film absorber characterization and analysis of TRPL Data for CdS/CdTe interface," in *Proc. IEEE 38th Photovoltaic Spec. Conf.*, 2012, pp. 1721–1726.

[8] J. Lee, N. C. Giles, D. Rajavel, and C. J. Summers, "Room-temperature band-edge photoluminescence from cadmium telluride," *Phys. Rev. B*, vol. 49, pp. 1668–1676, 1994.

[9] R. K. Ahrenkiel and S. W. Johnston, "An optical technique for measuring surface recombination velocity," *Solar Energy Mat. Solar Cells*, vol. 93, pp. 645–649, 2009.

[10] (2013). Sentaurus Device Manual, Ver. H-2013.03, Synopsys Inc., [Online]. Available: www.synopsys.com

[11] R. K. Ahrenkiel, "Minority carrier lifetime in III-V semiconductors," in *Semiconductors and Semimetals*. vol. 39, New York, NY, USA: Academic, 1993, pp. 39–150, 1993.

[12] R. Cohen, V. Lyahovitskaya, E. Poles, A. Liu, and Y. Rosenwaks, "Unusually low surface recombination and long bulk lifetime in n-CdTe single crystals," *Appl. Phys. Lett.*, vol. 73, pp. 1400–1402, 1998.

[13] S. J. Bepko, "Anisotropy of two-photon absorption in GaAs and CdTe," *Phys. Rev. B*, vol. 12, pp. 669–672, 1975.

[14] R. K. Ahrenkiel, B. M. Keyes, G. B. Lush, M. R. Melloch, M. S. Lundstrom, and H. F. MacMillan, "Minority-carrier lifetime and photon recycling in n-GaAs," *J. Vac. Sci. Tech. A*, vol. 10, pp. 990–995, 1992.

[15] D. P. Halliday, M. D. G. Potter, J. T. Mullins, and A. W. Brinkman, "Photoluminescence study of a bulk vapour grown CdTe crystal," *J. Cryst. Growth*, vol. 220, pp. 30–38, 2000.

[16] A. V. Kvit, Y. V. Klevkov, S. A. Medvedev, V. S. Bagaev, A. V. Perestoronin, and A. F. Plotnikov, "Evolution of photoluminescence spectra of stoichiometric CdTe: Dependence on the purity of starting components," *Semiconductors*, vol. 34, pp. 19–22, 2000.

[17] A. Kanevce, D. Kuciauskas, T. A. Gessert, D. H. Levi, and D. S. Albin, "Impact of interface recombination on time resolved photoluminescence (TRPL) decays in CdTe solar cells (numerical simulation analysis)," in *Proc. IEEE 38th Photovoltaic Spec. Conf.*, 2012, pp. 848–853.

[18] A. Kanevce, D. H. Levi, and D. Kuciauskas, "The role of drift, diffusion, and recombination in time-resolved photoluminescence of CdTe solar cells determined through numerical simulation," *Prog. Photovolt: Res. Appl.*, vol. 21, 2013, DOI: 10.1002/pip.2369.

[19] D. Kuciauskas, A. Kanevce, J. N. Duenow, P. Dippo, M. Young, J. V. Li, D. H. Levi, and T. A. Gessert, "Spectrally and time resolved photoluminescence analysis of the CdS/CdTe interface in thin-film photovoltaic solar cells," *Appl. Phys. Lett.*, p. 003319, 2013.

[20] W. K. Metzger, D. Albin, M. J. Romero, P. Dippo, and M. Young, "CdCl$_2$ treatment, S diffusion, and recombination in polycrystalline CdTe," *J. Appl. Phys.*, vol. 99, p. 103703, 2006.

[21] T. A. Gessert, W. K. Metzger, P. Dippo, S. E. Asher, R. G. Dhere, and M. R. Young, "Dependence of carrier lifetime on Cu-contacting temperature and ZnTe: Cu thickness in CdS/CdTe thin film solar cells," *Thin Solid Films*, vol. 517, pp. 2370–2373, 2009.

[22] R. G. Dhere, J. N. Duenow, C. M. DeHart, J. V. Li, D. Kuciauskas, and T. A. Gessert, "Development of substrate structure CdTe photovoltaic devices with performance exceeding 10%," in *Proc. IEEE 38th Photovoltaic Spec. Conf.*, 2012, pp. 3208–3211.

[23] J. N. Duenow, R. G. Dhere, D. Kuciauskas, J. V. Li, J. W. Pankow, P. C. Dippo, C. M. Dehart, and T. A. Gessert, "Oxygen incorporation during fabrication of substrate CdTe photovoltaic devices," in *Proc. IEEE 38th Photovoltaic Spec. Conf.*, 2012, pp. 3225–3229.

[24] T. A. Gessert, R. G. Dhere, J. N. Duenow, D. Kuciauskas, A. Kanevce, and J. D. Bergeson, "Comparison of minority carrier lifetime measurements in superstrate and substrate CdTe PV devices," in *Proc. IEEE 37th Photovoltaic Spec. Conf.*, 2011, pp. 1271–1274.

[25] E. E. Hoover and J. A. Squier, "Advances in multiphoton microscopy technology," *Nature Photonics*, vol. 7, pp. 93–101, 2013.

[26] J. Sites and J. Pan, "Strategies to increase CdTe solar-cell voltage," *Thin Solid Films*, vol. 515, pp. 6099–6102, 2007.

Authors' photographs and biographies not available at the time of publication.

The Dark Horse of Evaluating Long-Term Field Performance—Data Filtering

Dirk C. Jordan and Sarah R. Kurtz

Abstract—This paper addresses an issue of long-term performance that has seen relatively little attention in the industry, yet we will show that it can be of vital importance, not only for obvious financial reasons but, technically, because of its linkage to field failure as well. We will discuss how different data filtering on one particular system can lead to a variety of different degradation rates compared with indoor measurements and how it may change the field failure interpretation for a single module. A method based on the variation of the uncertainty in the determined degradation rates is proposed to aid the data filtering process when no baseline measurements exist. Finally, based on this experience, we propose a set of guidelines as a basis for a standardized approach to long-term performance assessment.

Index Terms—Data filtering, degradation rate, field failure, field performance, performance, photovoltaics (PVs).

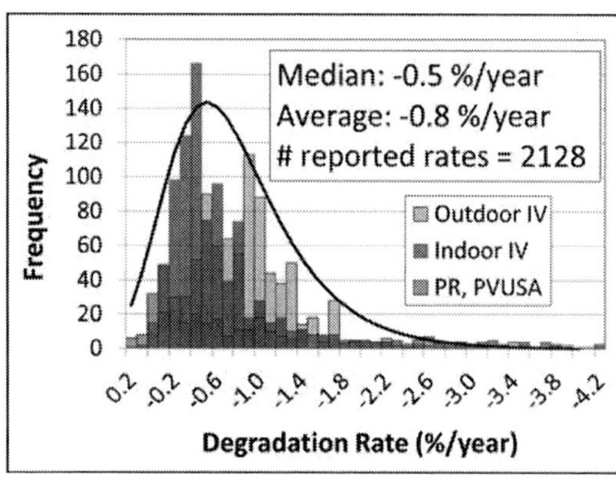

Fig. 1. Histogram of historical degradation rates, and itemized by method of measurement, with an extreme value distribution fit.

I. INTRODUCTION

WORLDWIDE photovoltaic (PV) installations represent investments that can be already measured as a percentage of gross domestic products of respective countries. At this magnitude, it is critical to all stakeholders to determine and predict long-term performance accurately. Fig. 1 shows a histogram of historical degradation rates (R_d) partitioned by method of measurement with an extreme value distribution [1]. A significant number of degradation rates—a negative degradation rate is defined in this paper as a performance loss—have been determined using continuous performance data. Contrary to current-voltage (IV) data that are typically taken under carefully controlled conditions, continuous data need to be reduced for performance evaluation. The process of preferentially choosing a subset (data filtering), such as data for sunny-only days, can increase the accuracy of the long-term analysis, as it has been shown using the photovoltaics for utility scale applications (PVUSA) methodology and is also incorporated in the standard ASTM E2848–11 [2], [3]. Furthermore, a combination of binning, data filtering, and data only from the same time period of the year has been shown to reduce degradation rate uncertainty [4], [5]. However, the filtering process may not only affect the uncertainty but the degradation rate itself as well. In some cases, differences in degradation rates reflect a true difference, as when a module decreases in low-light performance relatively faster than at full-sun conditions, but in most cases, the difference reflects the variability of the data. As there are different metrics and filtering methods in use, a standard approach would be useful such that two analysts derive the same result for the same dataset. To this end, we have determined degradation rates for a mono-crystalline Si (mono-Si) system for a variety of different performance metrics and filtering conditions on the same dataset, as we discuss in the first section. The second part examines the impact of data filtering on the salient IV parameters—maximum power $(P_{\max})$, short-circuit current (I_{sc}), open-circuit voltage (V_{oc}), and fill factor (FF)—on a mono-Si module collected automatically over the last 17 years and establishes the link with field failure. Finally, we introduce a filtering optimization based on uncertainty minimization and summarize our overall findings in a set of guidelines that may be utilized in the development of a standard approach to long-term performance assessment.

Manuscript received June 10, 2013; revised September 3, 2013; accepted September 8, 2013. Date of publication October 3, 2013; date of current version December 16, 2013. This work was supported by the U.S. Department of Energy under Contract DE-AC36–08-GO28308 with the National Renewable Energy Laboratory.

The authors are with the National Renewable Energy Laboratory, Golden, CO 80401 USA (e-mail: dirk.jordan@nrel.gov; Sarah.Kurtz@nrel.gov).

Color versions of one or more of the figures in this paper are available online at http://ieeexplore.ieee.org.

Digital Object Identifier 10.1109/JPHOTOV.2013.2282741

II. SYSTEM DATA

Fig. 2 shows the degradation rate for a 1.4-kW-mono-Si system fielded for almost ten years at NREL as a function of different metrics and filtering conditions. The system consists of five modules, installed in portrait orientation in one string. The array was mounted at a latitude tilt of $40°$ facing due south and was utility grid tied through an SMA Sunnyboy inverter with its own maximum-power-point-tracking algorithm [6]. The metrics used for the determination of the degradation rates are a temperature-corrected ratio of dc power over the plane-of-array irradiance (DC/G_{POA}) [7], the performance ratio (PR) utilizing

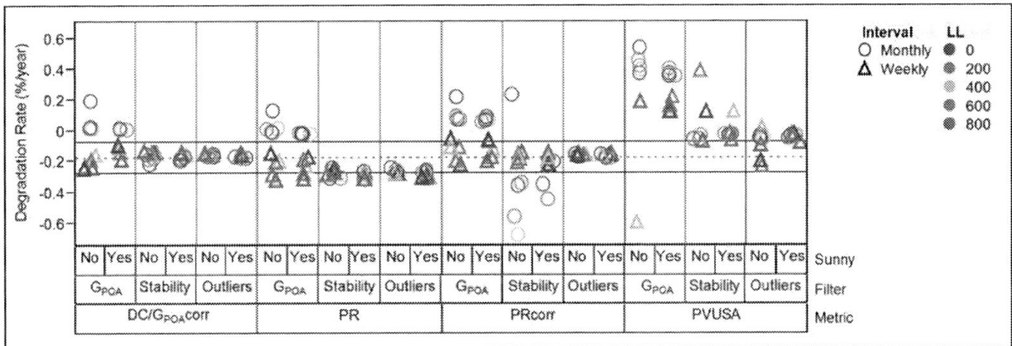

Fig. 2. Degradation rates for a mono-crystalline Si system as a function of different metrics and filtering conditions. Degradation rate determined by indoor IV measurements (red-dashed line) and a 0.1%/year interval (black lines) are given as guide to the eye.

nameplate rating with and without temperature correction [8], and lastly the regression PVUSA method. [9]

The analysis is based on dc power data to minimize inverter effects; however, a comparable analysis could be applied to ac power data. Manufacturer temperature coefficients were used for the temperature-corrected metrics to adjust to 45 °C module temperature. Two remaining effects, spectral and angle-of-incidence corrections have not been applied and may contribute to some residual variability. The time interval in which the performance metric is evaluated is given in monthly and weekly increments. The upper limit for G_{POA} was fixed at 1200 W/m^2, which, for the Colorado climate, is a good way to reduce the effect of cloud brightening. The lower limit (LL) was varied between 0 and 800 W/m^2. Two filters were applied in addition to the G_{POA} filtering and are denoted by "stability" and "outliers." The aptly named stability filter eliminates data points when the G_{POA} changes more than 20 W/m^2/min and the module temperature more than 1 °C/min. In addition to the stability screening, the outlier filter uses the difference between module and ambient temperature and the ratio DC/G_{POA} to eliminate snow days and partial-shading conditions, as illustrated more clearly in Section IV. Furthermore, the data for sunny days were selected by filtering for clearness index > 0.5. (Clearness index is the ratio of measured global irradiance over the extraterrestrial beam irradiance on a similarly tilted surface [10].)

The calculated degradation rates can be compared with rates obtained from indoor IV measurements taken before field deployment and after six years of exposure (dashed line). The temperature-corrected DC/G_{POA} ratio is in excellent agreement with the indoor IV data when all three data filters are applied. The PR shows good precision but indicates some deviation from the indoor IV for the same filtering. The accuracy, the deviation from the indoor measurements, and precision, i.e., the scatter of the data in each category, is improved if the PR is temperature corrected. The PVUSA methodology shows fairly large scatter, especially when using weekly increments. It is also the metric that benefits the most by using only sunny days, which has been previously shown [2].

Seasonal fluctuations can have significant impact on the determined degradation rates not only by increasing the uncertainties, but by leading to systematic deviations, particularly for non-

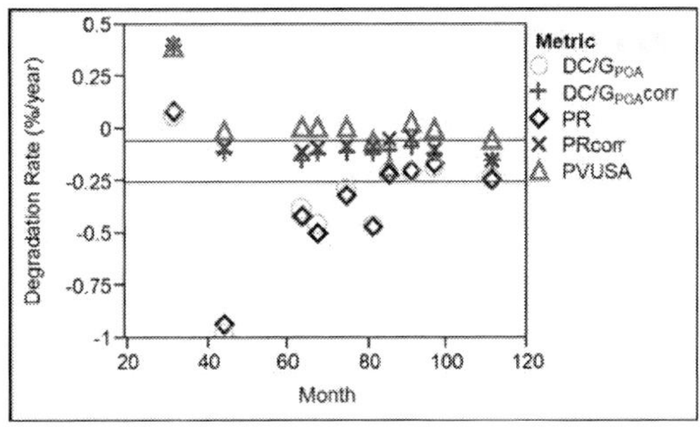

Fig. 3. Degradation rates as a function of field exposure for different metrics using weekly increments, as described in the text.

temperature metrics. Fig. 3 shows degradation rates determined when the "outlier" filter was used as a function of field exposure using weekly increments. In addition to the metrics used in Fig. 2, the uncorrected ratio DC/G_{POA} was used. A 0.1%/year interval around the rate determined from the indoor IV data is indicated by the solid blue lines. The temperature-corrected metrics show minimal fluctuations and are in excellent agreement even for three and half years of field data. The uncorrected metrics, both DC/G_{POA} and PR show significant fluctuations depending on the time of the year in addition to more systematic bias. The regression approach, i.e., PVUSA, also shows a dependence on seasonality and a systematic bias for almost the entire field exposure.

III. INDIVIDUAL MODULE

Fig. 4 illustrates the quandary of data filtering for an individual module. The 75-W mono-Si module, that is different from the ones comprising the system of Section II, was mounted on the performance and energy rating testbed which has been previously described in detail [11]. IV parameters collected automatically over the last 17 years in 15-min increments were investigated. The degradation rates for the salient IV parameters—maximum power (P_{max}), short-circuit current (I_{sc}), open-circuit voltage (V_{oc}), fill factor (FF)—are shown as a function of a stability filter. The upper G_{POA} limit was fixed at 1200 W/m^2, and two different lower G_{POA} limits were used.

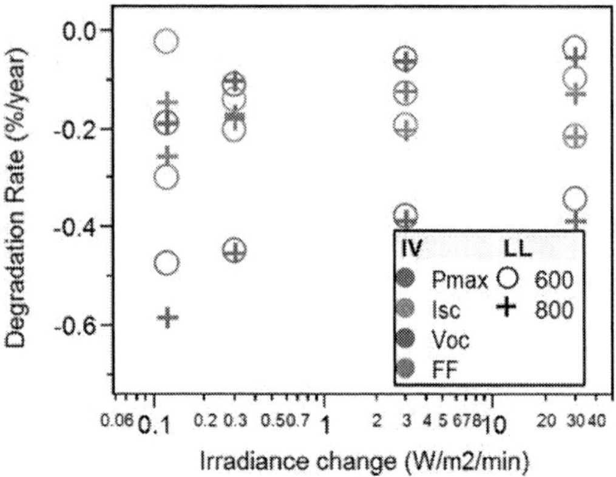

Fig. 4. Degradation rates of IV parameters for mono-Si module. The G_{POA} upper limit was fixed at 1200 W/m^2, and two different lower limits were used (LL).

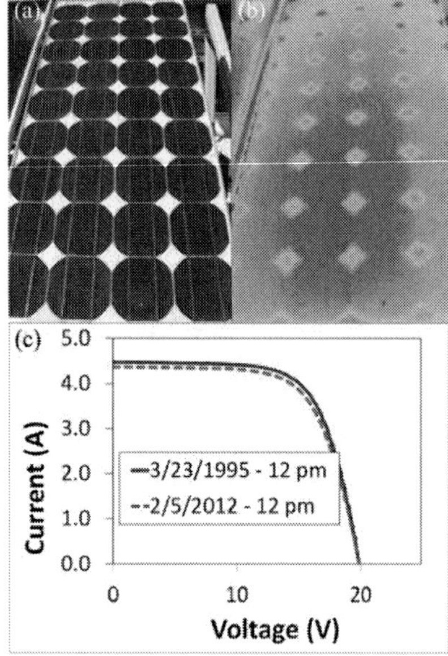

Fig. 5. (a) Optical image, (b) infrared image of the mono-Si module, and (c) irradiance- and temperature-corrected I–V curves, before and after 17 years of field exposure.

Significant changes can be discerned, as the irradiance stability is tightened. The lowest points in the figure show a degradation that is mostly dominated by FF loss, while a less-stringent filter on G_{POA} change shows a tendency toward I_{sc} loss. The difference is exacerbated for a lower G_{POA} limit. The following question arises: Is this module suffering more from I_{sc} or FF loss?

Fig. 5 shows (a) an optical and (b) infrared image of the individual module and (c) a pair of irradiance- and temperature-corrected IV curves according to IEC 60891 before and after 17 years of field exposure. No evidence of shunting or series resistance increase was observed (as is typically associated with FF loss). In addition, the IR image revealed no hot spots. The only visual degradation observed was some permanent soiling and encapsulant discoloration.

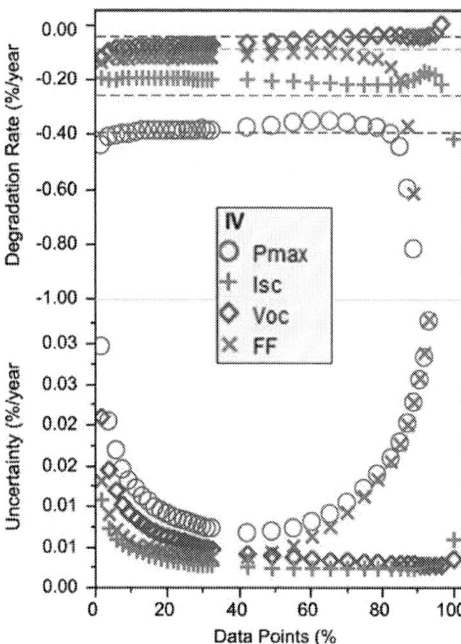

Fig. 6. Degradation rates and uncertainty as a function of percentage of data points left in the dataset. Rates determined from indoor IV measurements are indicated by dashed lines.

In Fig. 6, we provide additional indoor IV characterization results (dashed lines) that show a more I_{sc}-dominated loss historically attributed to delamination, discoloration, and cracked individual cells, while a smaller percentage can be attributed to light-induced degradation and soiling [12]–[14]. Additionally, Fig. 6 may also hold the key for assessing the situation more accurately when no indoor IV measurements are available.

Degradation rates (top panel) and calculated uncertainties, i.e., Type A, (bottom panel) are shown as a function of the percentage of data points left in the dataset for each IV parameter. The uncertainty utilized in this paper is obtained by statistical methods only and does not include measurement uncertainty [15]. When no data filtering is done, the uncertainty is fairly high. As the filtering increases around the median of the filtering parameter, so does the "cleanliness" of the dataset; meanwhile, the uncertainty decreases. If the filtering continues to tighten, a greater and greater number of data points are removed from the dataset, ultimately resulting in an increase of the uncertainty again. Between those two extremes is a region where the uncertainty is relatively constant. In that regime, the determined degradation rates are in good agreement with the rates determined from indoor characterization. Thus, the uncertainty curve can be used when filtering changes to determine the most likely regime for degradation rate determination.

IV. OUTLIER AND STABILITY FILTER

In the previous two sections, we showed the impact that outlier and stability filters of various strengths can have on system and module evaluation. The following section illustrates the importance of these filters in combination with the uncertainty

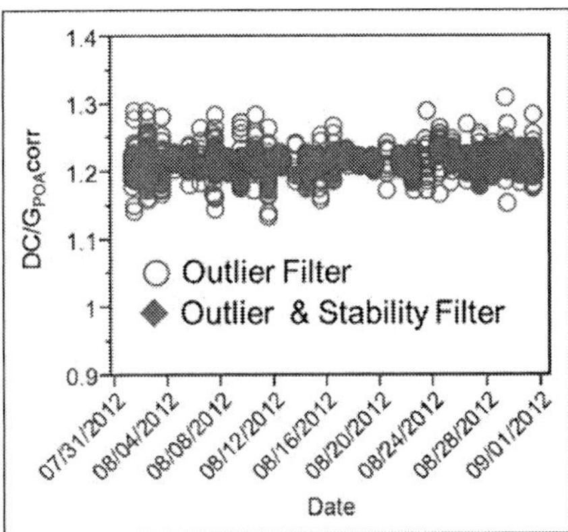

Fig. 7. Ratio dc power over POA irradiance using only an outlier filter (blue circles) and an additional stability filter (red triangles) for the month of August 2012.

minimization for common long-term field performance evaluation problems, extremely variable days, shading, and snow. Fig. 7 illustrates the impact of using only an outlier filter and an additional stability filter on the temperature-corrected DC/G_{POA} ratio for the month of August 2012. This month showed a particular large number of variable days. It can be seen that the outlier filter removes extreme outliers, however, the addition of the stability filter leads to a much improved signal-to-noise ratio.

Furthermore, the utility of these filters is demonstrated on two frequent problems in evaluating field data, losses due shading and snow coverage (in applicable climates). When field data are used to compare to a model it is imperative to identify those loss situations and incorporate them into the modeling. For long-term performance assessment, these situations can lead to an increase in the uncertainty and should be removed. The filtering method utilizing the degradation rate uncertainty developed in the previous section will be used for these two loss situations. Fig. 8 shows the DC/G_{POA} irradiance on the left axis and the change of the same ratio on the right axis as a function of time on January 8, 2012. (a) Data for the same mono-Si systems of Section II are shown unfiltered, (b) using only an outlier filter, and (c) using both an outlier and stability filter. The night before January 8, 2012, about 5 cm of snow fell and covered the modules of the system, while January 8 itself was a cloudless day. Fig. 8 is divided into three different sections; in section 1, the modules are still at least partially covered by snow. As the temperature increased, snow started sliding off the system, increasing the DC/I_{POA} ratio and eventually resulting in a clear system: section 2. However, the snow removal did not occur evenly, and especially just before the modules cleared completely, they showed rapid changes in the DC/G_{POA} ratio (blue crosses).

In Section III-A, decrease in the DC/G_{POA} ratio can again be discerned, but this time, it is because of shading, especially the area highlighted by the green oval. The system's azimuth is 180° south, but the slope on which the system is located does not face due south. Thus, multiple systems are offset by about 40 cm,

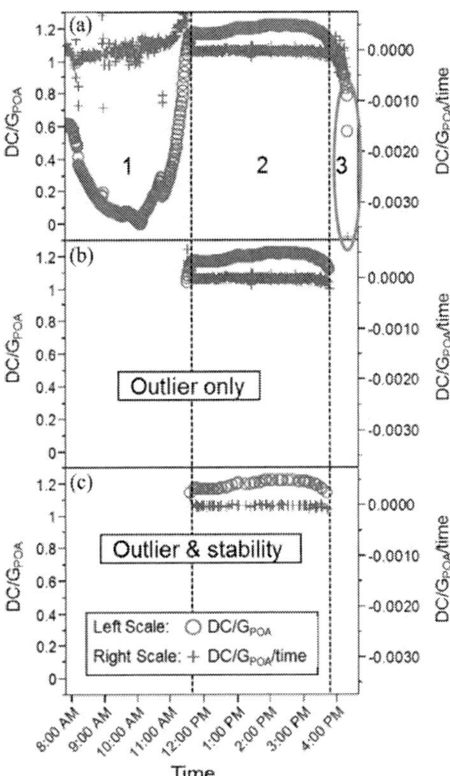

Fig. 8. Ratio dc power over POA irradiance (left axis) and change of that ratio in time (right axis) for a single day on January 8, 2012. (a) Data for the mono-Si systems are shown unfiltered, (b) using only an outlier filter, and (c) both outlier and stability filter.

resulting in the systems shading each other on afternoon winter days. Part (b) shows the same data using only the outlier filter of the DC/G_{POA} ratio where the optimum filter determined by the entire dataset of ten years, and the minimization of the uncertainty was used. The shading situation is completely removed, probably because the shading of the neighboring system is not severe. Most of the data points when snow still covered the system are also removed. However, not all data points just before the system is clear are removed. If a stability filter, using the change of the DC/G_{POA} ratio, is used in addition to the outlier filter (c), a clean dataset may be obtained.

V. Uncertainty Minimization for Systems

The results of the uncertainty minimization methodology, introduced in Section III and applied to three different systems, are shown in Fig. 9. The mono-Si system is the same system as in Section II. Outlier and stability filters were used, as previously discussed. As in Fig. 6, indoor IV measurements are indicated by dashed lines. The uncertainty minimum and the corresponding point on the degradation rate curve are highlighted to guide the eye. The uncertainty minimization method was used directly with the raw datasets. It can be seen that the uncertainty minimum occurs at different points for the different datasets.

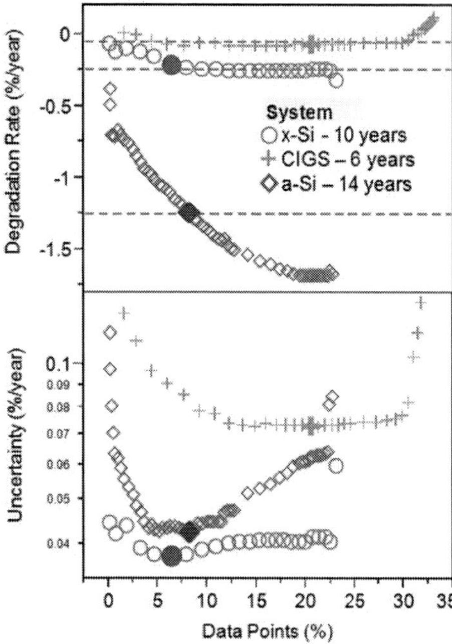

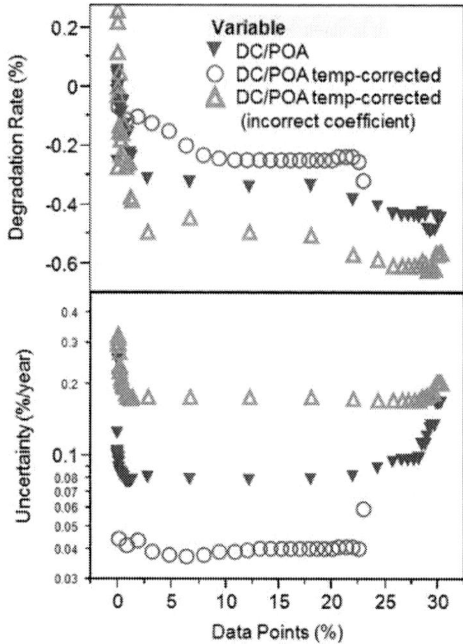

Fig. 9.   Degradation rates and uncertainty as a function of percentage of data points left in the dataset for three different systems. Rates determined from indoor IV measurements are indicated by dashed lines. The minimum of the uncertainty curve and the corresponding point on the degradation rate curve are highlighted by a solid symbol.

Fig. 10.   Degradation rates and uncertainty as a function of percentage of data points left in the dataset for mono-Si system using three different metrics.

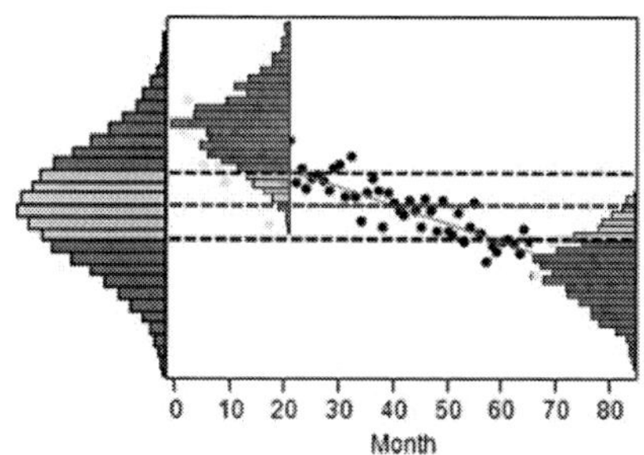

Fig. 11.   DC/G_{POA} ratio for a hypothetical dataset with a degradation of −1.3%/year is shown for more than six years. The overall distribution of the filtering parameter DC/G_{POA} is given outside the frame on the left. The inset histograms display the DC/G_{POA} distribution in the first and last month, respectively.

The highest absolute uncertainty corresponds to the dataset with the fewest number of years; however, the corresponding point on the degradation rate curve agrees with the indoor IV measurements. Furthermore, the asymmetry of the uncertainty curve is directly related to the distributions of the filter parameters. If the filter parameter such as the change in module temperature per time were normally distributed and the filtering proceeds in increasing steps around the median of the distribution a symmetric uncertainty curve would result. However, for most datasets most filter parameters are not only not-normally distributed but are most likely correlated. For instance, filtering out the tails of the G_{POA} change per time may not result in removing the tails of DC/G_{POA} distribution. Another interesting feature of Fig. 9 is that the degradation rate curve for the a-Si system displays a significant slope, while similar curves for the other two systems show a more level profile. Figs. 10 and 11 elucidate this particular feature.

Fig. 10 shows degradation rate and uncertainty curve as a function of the percentage of data points left in the dataset for the same mono-Si system of Section II. The temperature-corrected DC/G_{POA} ratio (red circles) is the same as in Fig. 9. The uncorrected DC/G_{POA} ratio (inverted purple triangles) displays not only a higher uncertainty curve than the corrected ratio but the degradation rate curve shows steeper tails than the corrected ratio as well. Finally, a temperature-corrected DC/G_{POA} ratio is shown, but with an incorrect temperature coefficient, resulting in an overcorrection. The overcorrection resulted in a significantly higher uncertainty curve and a substantially smaller plateau

on the degradation rate curve. Thus, possible explanations for the steep slope for the a-Si system in Fig. 9 may be with the temperature correction and/or connected with seasonal annealing of the a-Si system.

Fig. 11 illustrates schematically another explanation possibility on a hypothetical dataset. The DC/G_{POA} ratio is shown and assumed to have an overall normal distribution indicated by the histogram outside the frame on the left-hand side. For the sake of simplicity, changes in width and shape of the distribution, as was observed in field observation, has not been taken into account in this simulation [16]. A high degradation of −1.3%/year, similar to the a- Si system in Fig. 9, over more than six years is assumed. The two inset histograms are the DC/G_{POA} distributions in the first and last month, respectively. The overall median is indicated by the blue-dashed line. If a

466

tight data filtering interval around the median of the DC/G_{POA} ratio is implemented (black-dashed lines), the upper tail in the early months are disproportionally more removed (dark green) than the lower tail. Conversely, the same tight filtering interval leads to a disproportionally larger removal of the lower tail in the later months. Therefore, the remaining data will lead to a much smaller degradation rate. As the overall filtering interval is increased, the degradation quickly increases leading to a fairly high slope in the degradation curve. The situation is exaggerated for clarity purposes.

VI. Elements of a Standard Method

In calculating degradation rates, data filtering plays a very important role but is often neglected. Here, we bring this dark horse out into the light and propose a systematic approach to applying filters, with the goal of defining a consistent way to derive the most accurate degradation rate from a dataset. Such a standardized approach may encompass but is not limited to three distinct sections: 1) data integrity check, 2) data cleaning, and 3) performance analysis.

1) *Data integrity:*

a) Proceeding directly to the data cleaning or the analysis without proper data integrity check seems intuitive but occurs not infrequently. Simple time series graphs or histograms of the salient analytical parameters often can reveal serious integrity issues such as data shifts. More subtle discontinuities can often be detected through a 12-month moving average. If data shifts are present they can be statistically corrected, as detailed previously [17].

b) Missing data can be identified easily by a time series graph of the time difference between subsequent data rows: a step that is required in the calculation of the stability filter.

c) Several strategies exist to address missing data depending on the percentage of data such as replacement with average values or historical values [18], [19].

d) The same graph can be used to detect changes in data collection frequency. If there is a change in the frequency of data collection, it is useful to equalize the number of points over time.

e) Sensor redundancy, if present, can be used to detect sensor issues by graphing the mean sensor data versus production data.

f) Graphing meteorological versus production data in different time increments (weekly, monthly) can often be used in combination with the above checks to detect serious issues with either data.

2) *Data cleaning:*

a) An outlier filter such as the ratio of power production over irradiance is essential to reduce the effect of undocumented maintenance events: snow or shading.

b) A stability filter can reduce noise caused by variable days or partial snow covering. It is important that the filter is based on the width of the filter parameter distribution, for instance, the interquartile range.

c) The minimization of the degradation rate uncertainty may be used to find the best filtering conditions. As different filtering parameters are most likely correlated, simultaneous changing of the individual parameters in increments based on the width of their respective distributions is recommended. If the uncertainty is minimized for each individual parameter successively, stepping through a wider interval simultaneously in order to ascertain that the global minimum was found is recommended.

d) Finally, filtering for the irradiance of interest can further reduce uncertainty.

3) *Performance analysis:*

a) Seasonality caused by variables, such as temperature, spectrum, or angle-of-incidence, can have significant impact on long-term field performance. Therefore, corrected metrics such as the temperature-corrected PR are preferred over noncorrected metrics.

b) Evaluating data only from the same seasonal cycle or using data from the same time of the year may be used to minimize the effects of seasonality, especially for noncorrected metrics.

c) In addition, a 12-month or 52-week moving average may be used to minimize seasonality.

d) Varying the temperature coefficient to minimize uncertainty may assist in more accurate degradation rate determination.

e) The PVUSA regression method uses two regressions: the first to normalize and the second in the time series to assess performance. Most regressions use a standard least square approach based on minimization of the squared residuals making it susceptible to outliers. It may be possible to improve the regression methodology by using for example a robust regression approach based on the minimization of the absolute error.

Acknowledgment

The authors would like to thank the Reliability group at NREL, in addition to E. Maas, K. Luce, H. Groenendaal, and K. Jordan.

References

[1] D. C. Jordan and S. R. Kurtz, "Photovoltaic degradation rates—An analytical review," *Progress Photovoltaics Res. Appl.*, vol. 21, pp. 12–29, 2011.

[2] A. Kimber, T. Dierauf, L. Mitchell, C. Whitaker, T. Townsend, J. Newmiller, D. King, J. Granata, K. Emery, C. Osterwald, D. Myers, B. Marion, A. Pligavko, A. Panchula, T. Levitsky, J. Forbess, and F. Talmud, "Improved test method to verify the power rating of a photovoltaic (PV) project," in *Proc. 34th IEEE Photovoltaic Spec. Conf.*, Philadelphia, PA, USA, 2009, pp. 316–321.

[3] *Standard Test Method for Reporting Photovoltaic Non-Concentrator System Performance*, ASTM E2848–11, 2011.

     467

[4] K. Kiefer, D. Dirnberger, B. Müller, W. Heydenreich, and A. Kröger-Vodde, "A degradation analysis of PV power plants," in *Proc. 25th Eur. Photovoltaic Sol. Energy Conf.*, Valencia, Spain, 2010, pp. 5032–5037.

[5] N. H. Reich, A. Goebel, D. Dirnberger, and K. Kiefer, "System performance analysis and estimation of degradation rates based on 500 years of monitoring data," in *Proc. 38th IEEE Photovoltaics Spec. Conf.*, Austin, TX, USA, 2012, pp. 1551–1555.

[6] J. Adelstein and B. Sekulic, "Performance and reliability of a 1-kW amorphous silicon photovoltaic roofing system." in *Proc. 31st IEEE Photovoltaics Spec. Conf.*, Lake Buena Vista, FL, USA, 2005, pp. 1627–1630.

[7] D. C. Jordan and S. R. Kurtz, "PV degradation Risk," presented at the World Renewable Energy Forum, Denver, CO, USA, May 2012.

[8] H. Haeberlin and Ch. Beutler, "Normalized representation of energy and power for analysis of performance and on-line error detection in PV systems," presented at the 13th Eur. Photovoltaic Sol. Energy Conf., Nice, France, 1995.

[9] C. Jennings, "PV module performance at PG&E," in *Proc. 20th Photovoltaic Spec. Conf.*, Las Vegas, NV, USA, 1988, pp. 1225–1229.

[10] S. Ransome, "Array performance analysis using imperfect or incomplete input data," in *Proc. 23rd Eur. Photovoltaic Solar Energy Conf.*, Valencia, Spain, USA, 2008, pp. 3187–3191.

[11] J. A. del Cueto, "Closed-form solutions and parameterization of the problem of current-voltage performance of polycrystalline photovoltaic modules deployed at fixed latitude tilt," in *Proc. 31st IEEE Photovoltaic Spec. Conf.*, Orlando, FL, USA, 2005, pp. 331–335.

[12] M. A. Quintana, D. L. King, T. J. McMahon, and C. R. Osterwald, "Commonly observed degradation in field-aged PV modules," in *Proc. 29th IEEE Photovoltaic Spec. Conf.*, 2002, pp. 1436–1439.

[13] S. Sakamoto and T. Oshiro, "Field test results on the stability of crystalline silicon photovoltaic modules manufactured in the 1990 s." in *Proc. 3rd World Conf. Photovoltaic Energy Convers.*, Osaka, Japan, 2003, pp. 1888–1891.

[14] K. Morita, T. Inoue, H. Kato, I. Tsuda, and Y. Hishikawa, "Degradation factor analysis of crystalline-Si PV modules through long-term field exposure test," in *Proc. 3rd Conf. Photovoltaic Energy Convers.*, Osaka, Japan, 2003, pp. 1948–1951.

[15] *ISO Guide to the Expression of Uncertainty in Measurement or GUM, 1995. The U.S. edition of the GUM is entitled: American National Standard for Expressing Uncertainty–U.S. Guide to the Expression of Uncertainty in Measurement*, ANSI/NCSL Z540–2–1997.

[16] D. C. Jordan, J. H. Wohlgemuth, and S. R. Kurtz, "Technology and climate trends in PV module degradation," in *Proc. 27th Eur. Photovoltaic Solar Energy Conf.*, Frankfurt, Germany, 2012, pp. 3118–3124.

[17] D. C. Jordan and S. R. Kurtz, "Analytical improvements in PV degradation rate determination," in *Proc. 35th IEEE Photovoltaic Spec. Conf.*, Honolulu, HI, USA, 2010, pp. 2688–2693.

[18] D. C. Jordan, "Degradation rates," presented at the Nat. Renewable Energy Lab. PV Module Rel. Worksh., Golden, CO, USA, Feb. 2010.

[19] Nat. Renewable Energy Lab., Tech. Rep., in press.

Authors' photographs and biographies not available at the time of publication.

A 12% Efficient Silicon/PEDOT:PSS Heterojunction Solar Cell Fabricated at $< 100\ ^\circ$C

Ken A. Nagamatsu, *Student Member, IEEE*, Sushobhan Avasthi, Janam Jhaveri, *Student Member, IEEE*, and James C. Sturm, *Fellow, IEEE*

Abstract—Solar cells based on a heterojunction between crystalline silicon and the organic polymer PEDOT:PSS were fabricated at temperatures $<100\ ^\circ$C by spin coating. The Si/PEDOT interface blocks electrons in n-type silicon from moving to the anode and functions as a low-temperature alternative to diffused p-n junctions. The device takes advantage of the light absorption and transport properties of silicon and combines it with the simplicity of fabrication afforded by organics. Reverse recovery measurements were used to analyze the electron-blocking effectiveness of the heterojunction. The data show that current in the device is primarily due to holes injected from the anode into the silicon. At AM1.5, Si/PEDOT heterojunction solar cells achieve power conversion efficiency of 11.7%, which is among the highest reported values for this class of devices.

Index Terms—Heterojunction, hybrid photovoltaics, PEDOT: PSS, silicon organic.

I. INTRODUCTION

HYBRID photovoltaic devices incorporating inorganic and organic materials are receiving great interest as an approach to next generation photovoltaics. These technologies are aimed at combining the advantages of different material systems to provide better efficiency, more cost efficient manufacturing, or both. Silicon/organic heterojunctions (SOH) are attractive because they can be fabricated at temperatures $<100\ ^\circ$C, using simple methods such as spin coating [1], [2]. In comparison, conventional crystalline silicon solar cells require p-n junctions that are fabricated at temperatures higher than $800\ ^\circ$C [3]. SOH-based solar cells also do not require a plasma-enhanced chemical vapor deposition process to deposit amorphous silicon, as in the heterojunction with intrinsic thin-layer (HIT) technology. However, like HIT cells, SOH-based solar cells make use of crystalline silicon as the absorbing material, and therefore may reach the high efficiency ($>24\%$) reported by the best crystalline silicon solar cells [4], [5]. Due to the simplicity of fabrication and the potential for high efficiency, SOH solar cells may sub-

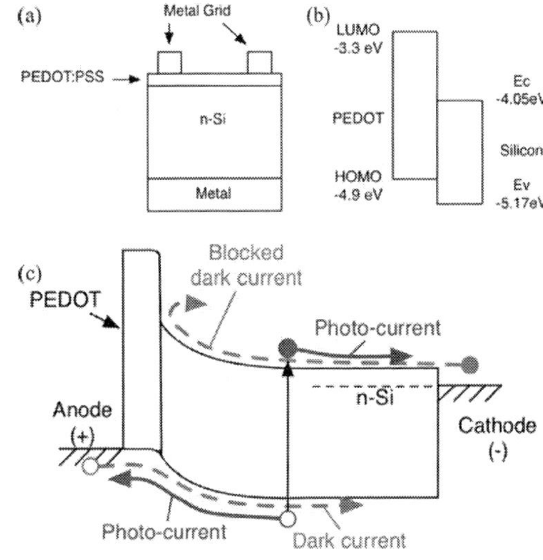

Fig. 1. (a) Physical structure and (b) electronic band alignment of SOH device. (c) Band diagram of device under illumination with positive bias. Dashed red lines represent dark current, solid blue lines represent photocurrent.

stantially reduce the cost of silicon photovoltaics. Previously, a Si/P3HT heterojunction solar cell with 10% power conversion efficiency was demonstrated [1]. In this paper, we report an investigation of the origin of dark current in SOH devices, and demonstrate a SOH solar cell with an AM1.5 power conversion efficiency of 11.7%.

Poly(3,4-ethylenedioxythiophene) poly(styrenesulfonate) (PEDOT:PSS) is an organic polymer that is commonly used as a transparent conductor. The PEDOT polymer and PSS together form a macromolecular salt, in which the PSS is reduced, forming the anion and the PEDOT is oxidized, forming the cation. PEDOT:PSS is readily dispersed in the aqueous solution [6]. The dispersion is readily spin cast and the resulting films are highly conductive and transparent. Several methods have been demonstrated to increase the conductivity further via solvent modification [7]–[9]. PEDOT thin films act as heavily doped p-type semiconductor with a large bandgap of $\sim$1.6 eV [10]–[12].

The structure of Si/PEDOT heterojunction solar cell is shown in Fig. 1(a), and the electronic band structure is shown in Fig. 1(b). The diagram reflects the highest occupied molecular orbital/lowest unoccupied molecular orbital (HOMO/LUMO) levels in low-conductivity (<10 S/cm) PEDOT:PSS [11]. Our work uses high-conductivity ($\sim$1000 S/cm) PEDOT:PSS, which

Manuscript received June 11, 2013; accepted October 5, 2013. Date of publication November 20, 2013; date of current version December 16, 2013. This work was supported by the National Science Foundation under MRSEC Grant #DMR-0819860 and the DOE Sunshot Grant #DE-EE0005315.

K. A. Nagamatsu, J. Jhaveri, and J. C. Sturm are with the Department of Electrical Engineering and Princeton Institute for the Science and Technology of Materials, Princeton University, Princeton, NJ 08544 USA (e-mail: knagamat@princeton.edu; jjhaveri@princeton.edu; sturm@princeton.edu).

S. Avasthi is with the Princeton Institute for the Science and Technology of Materials, Princeton, NJ, 08544, USA (e-mail: savasthi@princeton.edu).

Digital Object Identifier 10.1109/JPHOTOV.2013.2287758

has the same doping characteristics to first order. The conductivity enhancements result primarily through morphology changes of the insulating PSS surrounding conductive PEDOT grains [13]. Therefore, we model the high-conductivity PEDOT:PSS in our work with a HOMO/LUMO of 3.3 and 4.9 eV as measured in low-conductivity PEDOT:PSS. Light enters from the top of the cell, where the PEDOT:PSS is coated. The PEDOT:PSS layer is more than 90% transparent at such film thicknesses (<100 nm); therefore, under illumination, most of the light is absorbed in silicon. As shown in Fig. 1(b), the LUMO level of PEDOT is much higher than the conduction band of silicon; therefore, the electrons in silicon should be blocked from flowing into PEDOT. On the other hand, the HOMO level of PEDOT is closely aligned with the valence band of silicon, allowing holes in silicon to flow into PEDOT unimpeded. This is illustrated in the band diagram of the SOH device in Fig. 1(c). Due to the high work-function of the conductive, heavily-doped PEDOT layer ($\sim$4.9 eV), there exists a depletion region in n-type silicon at the Si/PEDOT interface (expected $\sim$1 um for $N_D = 10^{15}$ cm^{-3}). The depletion region separates the photogenerated carriers in silicon, causing a photocurrent. The negligible hole barrier at the Si/PEDOT interface allows the efficient collection of holes at the anode [solid blue line in valence band of Fig. 1(c)] and the large electron barrier at the Si/PEDOT interface reduces the electron dark current to the anode [dotted red lines in the conduction band of Fig. 1(c)] leading to low J_0 and high V_{OC}.

II. Experimental Details

PEDOT:PSS was purchased as 1.4% dispersion by weight in water (Clevios PH1000) and 10% w/w dimethyl sulfoxide was added to enhance the conductivity of the film [12], [13]. The silicon wafers were cleaned using the standard RCA cleaning procedure [14]. Si/PEDOT devices were fabricated by spin coating a 70-nm thick layer of PEDOT on 2–4 Ω·cm ($\sim$1.5 $\times$ 10^{15} cm^{-3}) phosphorus-doped n-type silicon wafers. To make electrical contacts, thermally evaporated silver and aluminum were deposited on the front and backside of the wafer to form anode and cathode, respectively. The anode (front side contact) was patterned by a shadow mask to allow light to be absorbed in silicon [Fig. 1(a)]. The top metal grid covers $\sim$10% of the surface. The device size was 4 mm $\times$ 4 mm. Lowering the PEDOT conductivity or increasing the metal grid spacing increases the parasitic lateral resistance. The maximum process temperature was 100 °C. The Si/ PEDOT solar cell does not require the fabrication of the p-n junction. The devices also did not have any back surface fields.

Electrical measurement of the devices was performed with an Agilent/Hewlett-Packard 4155 parameter analyzer. For characterization at AM1.5 illumination, a xenon lamp solar simulator was used. The illumination was calibrated to 1000 W/m^2 using a silicon reference cell. A 4 mm $\times$ 4 mm aperture was used to illuminate a fixed active area of a single device and prevent overestimation of photocurrent due to laterally diffusing carriers.

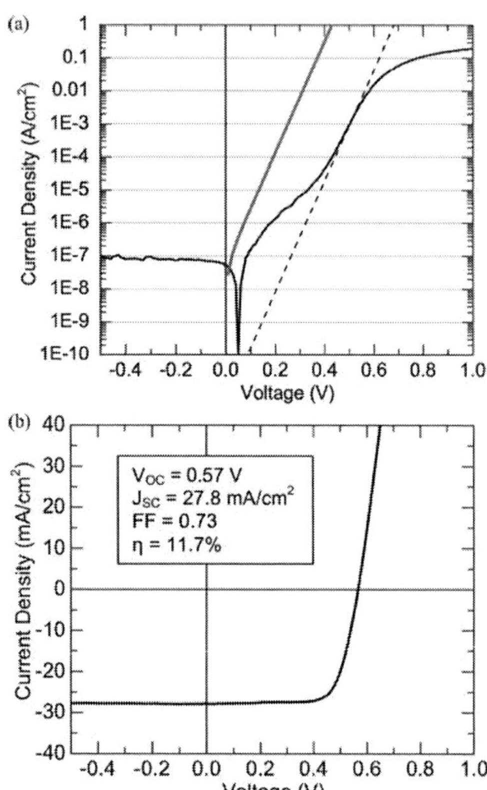

Fig. 2. (a) J–V characteristic of the SOH solar cell in the dark and calculated from a Schottky barrier (1). (b) J–V characteristic and parameters of SOH solar cell under AM1.5 illumination.

III. Results and Analysis

A. Current–Voltage Measurements

Fig. 2(a) presents the J–V characteristics for a Si/PEDOT heterojunction cell under dark conditions (continuous black line). The diode shows some nonideality ($n = 2$) at lower current levels ($\sim$10^{-6}–10^{-7} A/cm^2), which may be due to surface defect states at the Si/PEDOT interface. The diode regains an ideality factor of close to 1 at higher values of forward-bias (>0.4 V). At 1.3-mA/cm^2 forward current, and using an ideality factor of 1, we can extract a saturation current (J_0) to be 3.8 $\times$ 10^{-12} A/cm^2 [dashed line in Fig. 2(a)].

If the Si/PEDOT:PSS interface does not function as an electron-blocking barrier then one would expect the Si/PEDOT junction to behave just like a regular Schottky diode. The saturation current for such a Schottky diode is dominated by electrons, the majority carrier, and is given as

$$J_{0_{\text{electrons}}} = A^* T^2 e^{-\frac{\phi_B}{kT}} \qquad (1)$$

where A^* is the Richardson constant, T is temperature, ϕ_B is the Schottky barrier height, and k is the Boltzmann constant. Given the work function of PEDOT:PSS ($\sim$4.9 eV), the n-Si PEDOT Schottky junction would have a barrier height of $\phi_B = 0.8$ eV. Fig. 2(a) presents the current expected for such a metal/Si Schottky barrier (red line). Fig. 2(a) clearly shows the dark current in the SOH device is lowered by over four orders of magnitude than that expected from a simple Schottky device. This suggests that the PEDOT:PSS heterojunction does indeed act as a barrier to the electron current.

Fig. 2(b) shows that under AM1.5 illumination, an open-circuit voltage of 0.57 V was achieved along with a short-circuit current of 27.8 mA/cm^2 and fill factor of 73%. The overall power conversion efficiency of this device was 11.7%, which is among the best reported for this class of the photovoltaic device.

B. Reverse Recovery

The open-circuit voltage of a solar cell is limited by the amount of dark current in the device. To further increase the V_{OC} of the Si/PEDOT devices, the dark current should be reduced. The V_{OC} ideally depends on the saturation current (J_0), as

$$V_{OC} \equiv \frac{kT}{q} \ln \left(1 + \frac{J_{SC}}{J_0} \right) \tag{2}$$

where q is the elementary charge and J_{SC} is the short-circuit current. The first step toward reducing the J_0 is to determine which carrier contributes most to the dark current—electron or hole? It has been previously shown that in Si/P3HT devices, the electron-blocking is so good that the dark current is mostly caused by holes [minority carriers; the dashed red curve in the valence band Fig. 1(c)], not electrons (majority carriers) [1]. Si/PEDOT devices operate under the same principle in that the organic heterojunction blocks the electron current. To investigate this, we tested the device for stored minority carriers using the diode reverse recovery method [15]–[17].

In forward-bias, minority carriers will be injected from the anode into the quasi-neutral region of the diode, as shown in Fig. 1(c) (dashed red line in the valence band). In the steady state, a stored charge of holes will be built up in the n-type silicon. Another possible current mechanism is electrons overcoming the barrier presented by the heterojunction (thermionic emission). However, in this case, no stored charge would be observed because of the short electron lifetime in PEDOT:PSS [13]. The current may also be due to recombination at the heterojunction interface (silicon surface defects); however, this would not contribute to stored charge either. Therefore, the stored charges can be used to estimate the current due to minority carriers.

The extracted minority carrier charge can be measured by switching the diode from forward to reverse bias. Under reverse-bias the stored carriers (holes) get swept back out of the device to the PEDOT:PSS, momentarily causing a large reverse current (I_R). The circuit used to measure the transient along with the voltage and current waveforms is shown in Fig. 3(a) and (b). The area under the curve until the beginning of the decay point in reverse bias is defined as the charge extracted from the diode ($Q_{extracted}$). For a given forward-bias current (I_F), $Q_{extracted}$ depends on the transient current in reverse bias (I_R) by the following equation [15]:

$$Q_{extracted} = I_R \tau_{bulk} \left[\mathrm{erfc}^{-1} \left(\frac{1}{1 + \frac{I_R}{\alpha I_F}} \right) \right]^2 \tag{3}$$

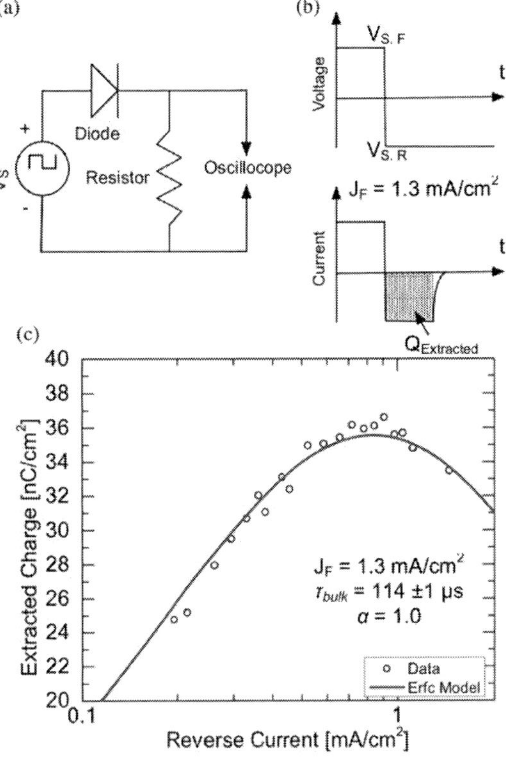

Fig. 3. (a) Circuit used for the reverse recovery experiment to measure effective injected hole lifetime τ_{bulk} and hole injection ratio α. (b) Typical waveforms for a device which has substantial minority carrier current, showing the $Q_{extracted}$. (c) $Q_{extracted}$ as a function of I_R. Black circles represent measured data and blue line shows best fit to the data for τ_{bulk} = 114 μs and α = 1.0.

where τ_{bulk} is the bulk recombination lifetime and α is the ratio of the minority-carrier current to the total current. If the dark current is composed only of holes injected into silicon, $\alpha = 1$.

Fig. 3(c) shows the measured value of $Q_{extracted}$ as a function of J_R, for an J_F = 1.3 mA/cm^2. At low J_R, the holes are not extracted fast enough; therefore, most of them recombine in silicon, leading to low value of $Q_{extracted}$. At higher J_R, the holes are removed quickly, before they can recombine, and hence, the $Q_{extracted}$ is large. The blue line in Fig. 3(c) is the best fit of the data to (3). From the best fit, the extracted value of α and τ_{bulk} are 1.0 and 114 μs, respectively.

The value of $\alpha = 1.0$ proves that most of the dark current is indeed caused by minority carriers and subsequently shows that the barrier is effective at blocking electrons. The τ_{bulk} can be further used to estimate the value of minority carrier current ($J_{0,hole}$), using the following equation:

$$J_{0,hole} = q \frac{n_i^2}{N_D} \sqrt{\frac{D_{hole}}{\tau_{bulk}}} \tag{4}$$

where N_D is the silicon doping level, D_{hole} is the hole diffusion coefficient, and n_i is the intrinsic carrier concentration of silicon. From the extracted value of τ_{bulk} = 114 μs, we estimate the $J_{0,hole}$ to be 6.64 × 10^{-12} A/cm^2.

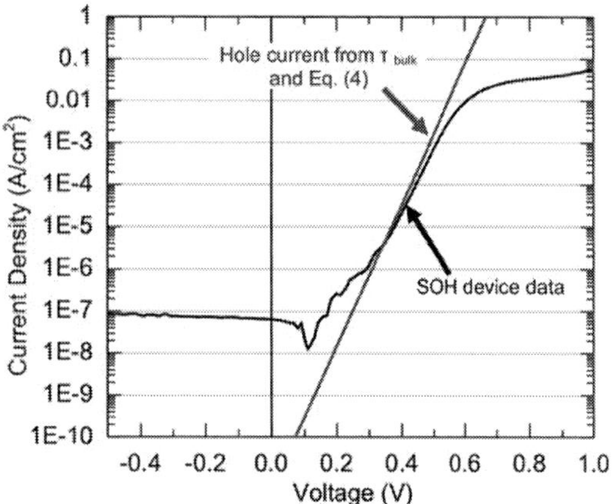

Fig. 4. $J-V$ characteristic of SOH device measured with reverse recovery and hole current calculated from the measured τ_{bulk} and (4).

Fig. 4 plots the $J-V$ characteristics of the SOH device measured with the reverse recovery experiment (black curve). In addition, shown is the hole current expected in the device, as calculated from (4) (blue line). Comparing the curves, we see excellent agreement in the ideal diode region of the device. This shows that in the $n\sim1$ region, the dark current is entirely accounted for by the hole current and that the contribution of electron current is negligible. Clearly, the PEDOT layer is an effective electron-blocker. The forward bias current used for the reverse recovery measurement was intentionally chosen to lie in this region, as this is the relevant operating region for the solar cell. This gives us confidence that our approach accurately extracts the minority carrier lifetime, and that $\alpha = 1$ for our devices.

Furthermore, by using measured values of J_{SC} (~25 mA/cm²) and the calculated $J_{0,\text{hole}}$ from (4), one can calculate an *expected* value of V_{OC} using (1): i.e., the V_{OC} one expects if the dark current is composed of only holes as measured via the reverse recovery experiment. The expected V_{OC} is 0.57 V, which agrees with the experimentally measured value of 0.57 V. These results suggest that in Si/PEDOT devices, dark current is predominantly composed of hole (minority) carriers and not electrons (majority) carriers.

IV. Conclusion

We have demonstrated an electron-blocking Si/PEDOT heterojunction that is fabricated by a room temperature spin coating process. Reverse recovery experiments provide a measurement of the stored charge provided by injection of minority carriers in forward bias. This provides a measurement of the current in the Si/PEDOT device that is carried by minority carrier hole injection from the anode. The data show that the Si/PEDOT interface is very effective at blocking electrons, to the extent that dark current in heterojunction devices on n-Si is not limited by electrons, but by the minority-carrier hole injection from anode into silicon. The best Si/PEDOT solar cells yield a high open-circuit voltage of 0.57 V and an efficiency of 11.7%, which is among the highest reported for this class of devices.

References

[1] S. Avasthi, S. Lee, Y. Loo, and J. C. Sturm, "Role of majority and minority carrier barriers silicon/organic hybrid heterojunction solar cells," *Adv. Mater.*, vol. 23, pp. 5762–5766, 2011.

[2] S. Avasthi and J. C. Sturm, "Charge separation and minority carrier injection in P3HT-silicon heterojunction solar cells," in *Proc. IEEE 37th Photovoltaics Spec. Conf.*, Jun. 19–24, 2009, pp. 002487–002489.

[3] A. Wang, J. Zhao, and M. A. Green, "24% efficient silicon solar cells," *Appl. Phys. Lett.*, vol. 57, pp. 602–604, 1990.

[4] J. Zhao, A. Wang, M. A. Green, and F. Ferrazza, "19.8% efficient 'honeycomb' textured multicrystalline and 24.4% monocrystalline silicon solar cells," *Appl. Phys. Lett.*, vol. 73, pp. 1991–1993, 1998.

[5] T. G. Chen, B. Y. Huang, E. C. Chen, P. Yu, and H. F. Meng, "Microtextured conductive polymer/silicon heterojunction photovoltaic devices with high efficiency," *Appl. Phys. Lett.*, vol. 101, pp. 033301-1–033301-5, 2012.

[6] L. Groenendaal, F. Jonas, D. Freitag, H. Pielartzik, and J. R. Reynolds, "Poly(3,4 = ethylenedioxythiophene) and its derivatives: Past, present, and future," *Adv. Mater.*, vol. 12, no. 7, pp. 481–494, 2000.

[7] Y. Xia, K. Sun, and J. Ouyang, "Solution-processed metallic conducting polymer films as transparent electrode of optoelectronic devices," *Adv. Mater.*, vol. 24, pp. 2436–2440, 2012.

[8] T. Stocker, A. Kohler, and R. Moos, "Why does the electrical conductivity in PEDOT:PSS decrease with PSS content? A study combining thermoelectric measurements with impedance spectroscopy," *J. Polym. Sci. Part B: Polym. Phys.*, vol. 50, pp. 967–983, 2012.

[9] A. M. Nardes, M. Kemerink, M. M. de Kok, E. Vinken, K. Maturova, and R. A. J. Janssen, "Conductivity, work function, and environmental stability of PEDOT:PSS thin films treated with sorbitol," *Org. Elec.*, vol. 9, pp. 727–734, 2008.

[10] J. Hwang, F. Amy, and A. Kahn, "Spectroscopic study on sputtered PEDOT:PSS: Role of surface PSS layer," *Org. Elec.*, vol. 7, pp. 387–396, 2006.

[11] E. L. Ratcliff, J. Meyer, K. X. Steirer, N. R. Armstrong, D. Olson, and A. Khan, "Energy level alignment in PCDTBT:PC70 BM solar cells: Solution processed NiOx for improved hole collection and efficiency," *Org. Elec.*, vol. 13, pp. 744–749, 2012.

[12] H. Do, M. Reinhard, H. Vogeler, A. Puetz, M. F. G. Klein, W. Schabel, A. Colsmann, and U. Lemmer, "Polymeric anodes from poly(3,4-ethylenedioxythiophene):poly(styrenesulfonate) for 3.5% efficient organic solar cells," *Thin Solid Films*, vol. 517, pp. 5900–5902, 2009.

[13] A. Elschner, S. Kirchmeyer, W. Lövenich, U. Merker, and K. Reuter, *PEDOT: Principles and Applications of an Intrinsically Conductive Polymer*. Boca Raton, FL, USA: CRC, Ch. 9.

[14] W. Kern, "The evolution of silicon-wafer cleaning technology," *J. Electrochem. Soc.*, vol. 137, no. 1887, 1990.

[15] D. K. Schroder, "Recombination lifetime—electrical measurement techniques," in *Semiconductor Material and Device Characterization*. Hoboken, NJ, USA: Wiley, 1990, ch. 8.5, p. 394.

[16] S. M. Sze, *Physics of Semiconductor Devices*. Hoboken, NJ, USA: Wiley, 1969, p. 128.

[17] B. Lax and S. F. Neustadter, "Transient Response of a pn Junction," *J. Appl. Phys.*, vol. 25, pp. 1148–1154, 1954.

Ken A. Nagamatsu (S'07) received the B.S. (Hons.) degree in microelectronic engineering from the Rochester Institute of Technology, Rochester, NY, USA, in 2010 and the M.A. degree in electrical engineering from Princeton University, Princeton, NJ, USA, in 2012, where he is currently working toward the Ph.D. degree in electrical engineering.

His research interests include hybrid silicon heterojunctions for photovoltaic applications and the device physics thereof.

Sushobhan Avasthi received the B.Tech degree in electrical engineering from the Indian Institute of Technology Kanpur, Kanpur, India, in 2005 and the M.A. and Ph.D. degrees in electrical engineering from Princeton University, Princeton, NJ, USA, in 2007 and 2013, respectively.

Since 2013, he has been a Postdoctoral Associate with the Princeton Institute of Science and Technology of Materials, Princeton University. His research focuses on photovoltaics, specifically silicon/organic and silicon/metal-oxide heterojunctions.

Dr. Avasthi received the Edith and Martin B. Stein Solar Energy Innovation Award from the Global Photonic Energy Corporation.

Janam Jhaveri (S'13) received the B.S. degree in electrical engineering from Purdue University, West Lafayette, IN, USA, in 2011 and the M.A degree in electrical engineering from Princeton University, Princeton, NJ, USA in 2013, where he is currently working toward the Ph.D. degree in electrical engineering.

His research interests include silicon/organic and silicon/metal oxide heterojunctions for photovoltaic applications.

James C. Sturm (S'81–M'85–SM'95–F'01) received the B.S.E. degree in electrical engineering and engineering physics from Princeton University, Princeton, NJ, USA, and the M.S.E.E and Ph.D. degrees in electrical engineering from Stanford University, Stanford, CA, USA, in 1981 and 1985, respectively.

He was a Microprocessor Design Engineer with Intel Corporation, as well as Siemens, Munich, Germany. He has been with the Faculty of Princeton University since 1986, where he is currently a Professor of electrical engineering and the PRISM Director. During 1994–1995, he was a von Humboldt Fellow with the Institüt Für Halbleitertechnik, University of Stuttgart, Germany. He has worked in the fields of silicon-based heterojunctions, 3-D integration, silicon-on-insulator, optical interconnects, TFT's, and organic light-emitting diodes. His current research interests include silicon–germanium–carbon and related heterojunctions on silicon, silicon-on-insulator, and 3-D integration; large-area electronics; flat-panel displays; organic semiconductors; and the nanotechnology–biology interface.

Prof. Sturm is a member of the American Physical Society and the Materials Research Society. He was a National Science Foundation Presidential Young Investigator. He received ten awards for teaching excellence from both Princeton University and the Keck Foundation and the President's Distinguished Teaching Award at Princeton in 2004. In 1996 and 1997, he was the Technical Program Chair and General Chair of the IEEE Device Research Conference, for which he is now a Charter Trustee. He served on the organizing committee of IEDM (1988–1992 and 1997–1999), having chaired both the Solid-State Device and Detectors/Sensors/Displays committees. In 2005, he was named the William and Edna Macaleer Professor of Engineering and Applied Science. He also has been a Symposium Organizer for the Materials Research Society and on the SOS/SOI, EMC, and several other conference committees. He was the organizing Chair for ISTDM in 2006.

473

A Novel Architecture for Photovoltaic Devices: Field-effect Solar Cells Using Screening-engineered Nanoelectrodes for Silicon and Earth Abundant Cuprous Oxide

Oscar Vazquez-Mena, William Regan, Steven Byrnes, Onur Ergen, Will Gannett, Feng Wang, Alex Zettl

Department of Physics, University of California, and Materials Sciences Division, Lawrence Berkeley National Laboratory, Berkeley, California 94720, U.S.A.

Abstract — **A field effect cuprous oxide solar cell device based on a gate that controls carrier concentration in semiconductors and using screening-engineered nanostructured electrodes is presented. The cell works in inversion mode, with a top gate that forms a depletion layer and a p-n junction, and with nanostructured electrodes that collect the photocurrent across the junction. This device does not require any doping process or a heterojunction, opening a novel route for materials that are difficult to dope. As a proof of principle, we present experimental results of a silicon field effect solar cell. To demonstrate the potential of this configuration for alternative materials, we present a field-effect solar cell made of earth abundant cuprous oxide, which has a favorable band gap but that is difficult to dope. We show the synthesis of the material, the effect of the gate on the carrier concentration and a photovoltaic power conversion efficiency of ~0.2%.**

Index Terms — **nanostructures, photovoltaic cells, solar energy, cuprous oxide, field effect**

I. Introduction

An important alternative for low cost solar energy is the use of cheap and earth abundant materials besides conventional silicon for solar cells. Actually, it has been claimed that materials such as copper oxides and sulfide, zinc phosphide and iron sulfide can potentially produce more photovoltaic energy and at lower cost than crystalline silicon [1]. However, so far the efficiencies achieved from these materials have significantly underperformed compared to Si or GaAs solar cells.

Solar cells are based on p-n junctions that can be either homojunctions or heterojunctions. The most common material for homojunctions is Si since doping is a well-controlled process for this material. In the case of heterojunctions, two materials with natural "p" and "n" doping are employed, such as "p" CdTe or CIGS and CdS as "n" material. The main limitation for homojunctions is that doping is well controlled only for few semiconductors such as Si or GaAs. However, for other materials the doping is still not well controlled. For heterojunctions, the main limitation is the quality of the interface between the two materials. Lattice mismatch and defects at the junction interface can produce recombination sites and reduce the cell performance.

In this paper, we present a novel configuration based on the field effect in semiconductors using a gate to control the carrier concentration in the semiconductor. This configuration avoids any doping implantation process or the formation of a heterojunction between two different materials. First, we describe the principle of the field effect solar cells based on the configuration proposed by Regan *et al* [2]. Then, we present experimental proof of this principle using conventional Si. Our main result is a field effect solar cell using cuprous oxide, opening a novel route for cells using earth abundant materials. We present the synthesis of Cu_2O by reactive sputtering. Then we show the control of carrier concentration in the Cu_2O by the gate voltage. Finally, we demonstrate the photovoltaic response of the solar cell as a function of the gate voltage and obtaining an efficiency of ~0.2%.

II. Field Effect Solar Cells: Principle and Proof

Field effect solar cells were developed based on the field effect transistors [3], however, the devices showed fast degradation at the insulator and screening of the gate field by the top contact [4-7]. In this work we use a novel configuration for field effect solar cells based on screening-engineered nanoelectrodes proposed and demonstrated by Regan *et al* [2]. The principle of the field effect solar cells is shown in Figure 1. In a conventional FET an inverted carrier layer is formed at the semiconductor-insulator interface when the gate voltage reaches the threshold value. This forms a conduction channel in the semiconductor with carriers of the opposite charge to the bulk doping (Figure 1.a). This principle can be applied to a solar cell by adding top and bottom electrodes to obtain a current across the junction (Figure 1.b). The main problem for this approach is that the top electrode screens the gate field. To avoid such screening, Regan *et al* proposed nanostructured electrodes narrower than the depletion width of the semiconductor that allow a continuous depletion layer in the semiconductor under the nanostructured electrodes (Figure 1.c). If the electrodes are wider than the depletion width, then no inversion layer and hence no p-n junction will be formed under the nanostructured electrodes to separate charges. Recently, another approach was reported using electrolyte liquids to induce inversion in the solar cells. [8, 9]

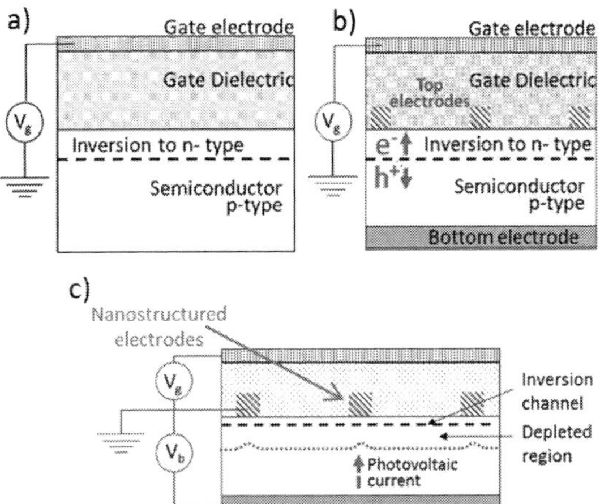

Fig. 1. Field effect solar cell principle (cross sections). a) Field effect in a semiconductor device in inversion mode, creating a junction under the gate dielectric. b) In a solar cell, top and bottom electrodes are added to extract the photocurrent across the p-n junction. To prevent the screening of the field, the nanostructured electrodes should not be wider than the depletion width in the semiconductor. c) Depleted region under the top nanostructured electrodes when $V_g \approx V_{th}$.

Figure 2 shows the experimental result for a Si solar cell reported by Regan *et al* [2]. It is based on a p-doped Si wafer with hole concentration of $N_A \sim 1 \times 10^{16}$ cm^{-3}. The nanostructured electrodes are 250 nm wide Al fingers. The gate dielectric is an evaporated 150 nm SiO$_2$ and the gate electrode is a thin Cr/Au layer. As shown in Figure 2, as V_g increases the photocurrent increases. When V_g increases, an inverted n- layer is formed under the gate dielectric forming a rectifying p-n junction. At V_g=3.2 V the efficiency is 1.4% with AM 1 5 illumination.

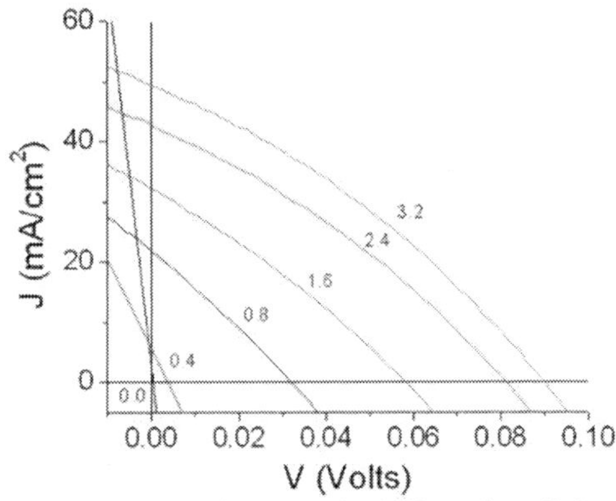

Figure. 2. I-V characteristics of a Si field effect solar cell showing the rectification due to induced p-n junction as gate voltage is increased forming an 'n' inversion layer in a 'p'-silicon chip. [2]

III. CUPROUS OXIDE CELLS

To demonstrate the potential of field effect solar cells for other earth abundament materials, a cuprous oxide (Cu$_2$O) cell was designed and fabricated. Cuprous oxide films 1 μm thick were prepared by reactive sputtering deposition using a copper metallic target and an oxygen flow in the deposition chamber to oxidize the copper.[10-12] Argon was used as sputtering gas. The process required the fine tuning of power, pressure and flows of Ar and O$_2$ gases to obtain the correct stoichiometry (Cu$_2$O), and avoid Cu or CuO deposition. The optimized parameters are 200 Watts RF power, working pressure of 5 mtorr and O$_2$ partial pressure of 0.62 mtorr. Optical absorption spectra show a band gap of ~2.0 eV for Cu$_2$O as expected. The X-Ray Diffraction (XRD) crystallographic data confirm the Cu$_2$O phase giving a peak corresponding to the (200) plane. These results are shown in Figure 3.

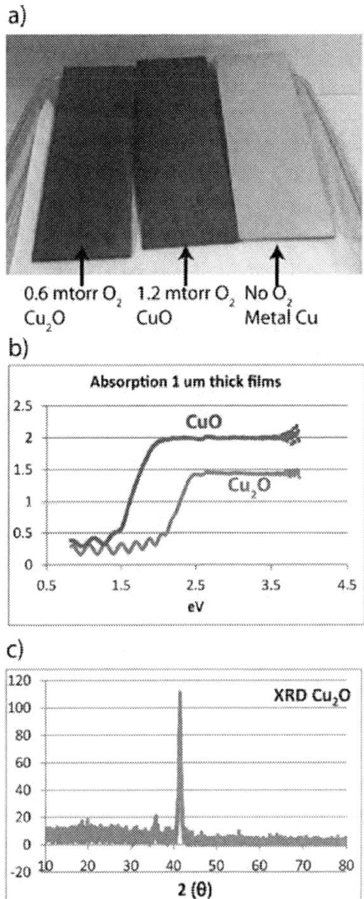

Fig. 3. a) One micron thick films of Cu$_2$O, CuO and Cu prepared by sputtering with varying O$_2$ flows. b) Light absorption showing the expected band gaps of Cu$_2$O (~2.0 eV) and CuO (~1.3 eV). c) XRD diffraction of a Cu$_2$O film showing the (200) peak.

In order to estimate the depletion width of the Cu_2O, a test structure next to the device was prepared. It consists of a gate contact pad of 500x500 μm^2 on top of a 100 nm thick SiO_2 evaporated film on the Cu_2O substrate. This structure allows realizing capacitance-voltage measurements and estimating the depletion width and carrier concentration of the Cu_2O. The measurements are shown in Figure 4. A depletion width of 260 nm and a hole concentration of $\sim N_A \sim 5x10^{15}$ cm^{-3} are estimated from such measurements.

The Cu_2O field effect solar cell build is shown in Figure 5.a. The fingers were made of 50 nm thick Au with a width of 150 nm defined by electron beam lithography and deposited by e-beam evaporation. The gate dielectric is a 100 nm thick evaporated SiO_2 film. The gate contact is a 50 nm sputtered ITO film. Figure 5.b shows the nanostructured electrodes (nanofingers). The rectifying behavior under AM1.5 illumination is shown in Figure 5.c. When $V_g=-0.2$, there is no photocurrent due to an ohmic contact between the semiconductor and the electrodes. When $V_g=2.3$, an inversion layer is formed under the gate dielectric. The n-p junction gives a diode behavior and a photocurrent is generated in the device under illumination achiving an efficiency of $\sim0.2\%$.

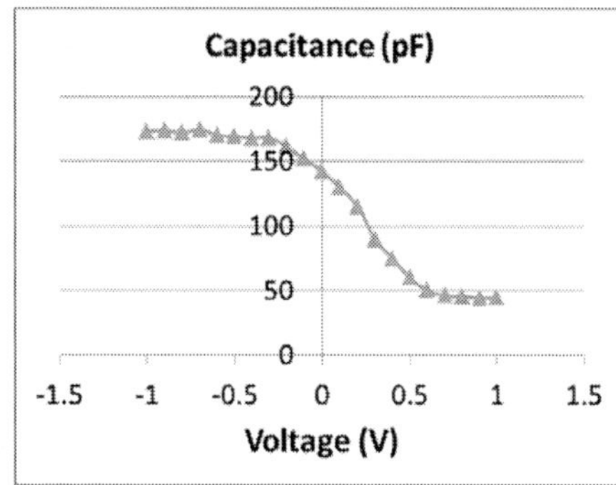

Fig. 4 a) Capacitance vs. Voltage measurements showing the depletion on Cu_2O as the gate voltage is increased to positive values. As the semiconductor is depleted the capacitance decreases. From this measurement a depletion width of 260 nm and a carrier concentration of $\sim N_A \sim 5x10^{15}$ cm^{-3} are estimated.

The efficiency achieved is small compared with higher values of $\sim4\%$ reported with Cu_2O, [13, 14] but it shows that the field effect principle can be used to explore the photovoltaic properties of novel materials that are more difficult to process. Higher purity Cu_2O and other materials such as ultrathin graphene as top electrodes are possible routes to improve the performance of this type of cells.

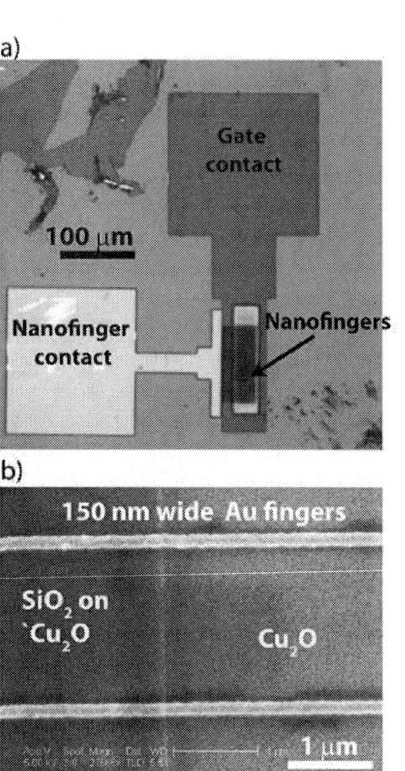

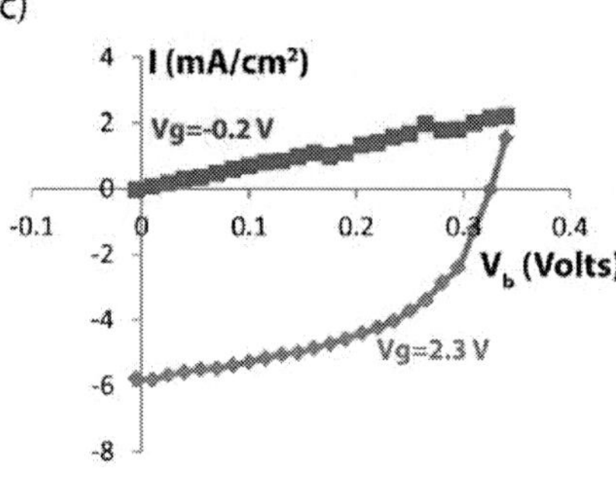

Fig. 5. a) Cu_2O field effect solar cell with Au nanostructured electrodes (nanofingers) and an ITO transparent gate. b) SEM image of the nanostructured electrodes on Cu_2O. c) I-V characteristics of the device under illumination (AM 1.5) showing the rectifying behavior when V_g is increased and the photocurrent generated. The estimated efficiency of the device is $\sim0.2\%$.

IV. CONCLUSION

We have demonstrated that the field effect solar cells using nanostructured electrodes allow the conversion of light into electricity without any implantation process and with a single material avoiding a heterojunction. This opens a new route for solar cells with materials like copper oxide that are hard to dope, or hard to synthesize on a different material to form heterojunctions. The use of these materials can lead to lower cost and larger scale production of photovoltaic energy. Currently we are working with similar architectures on other materials such as zinc phosphide and tin sulfide that are also earth abundant. New types of nanostructured materials and gating configurations are also being explored to simplify the realization of field effect solar cells.

ACKNOWLEDGMENTS

This authors acknowledge the support from the Office of Energy Research, Materials Sciences and Engineering Division, of the US Department of Energy under contract No. DEAC02- 05CH11231, from the National Science Foundation within the Center of Integrated Nanomechanical Systems, under Grant EEC-832819, and from the Office of Naval Research (MURI). O. V. acknowledges support by the Swiss National Science Foundation (PBELP2-135864) and W.R. acknowledges support through a National Science Foundation Graduate Research Fellowship.

REFERENCES

[1] C. Wadia, A. P. Alivisatos, and D. M. Kammen, "Materials Availability Expands the Opportunity for Large-Scale Photovoltaics Deployment," *Environmental Science & Technology,* vol. 43, pp. 2072-2077, Mar 2009.

[2] W. Regan, S. Byrnes, W. Gannett, O. Ergen, O. Vazquez-Mena, F. Wang, and A. Zettl, "Screening-Engineered Field-Effect Solar Cells," *Nano Letters,* vol. 12, pp. 4300-4304, Aug 2012.

[3] R. Godfrey and M. Green, "655 mV open circuit voltage, 17.6% efficient silicon MIS solar cells," *Applied Physics Letters,* vol. 34, p. 790, 1979.

[4] G. De Cesare, F. Chicarella, F. Palma, G. Nobile, and M. Tucci, "Experimental realization of field effect a-Si:H solar cells," *Thin Solid Films,* vol. 427, pp. 166-170, 2003.

[5] H. Fujioka, M. Oshima, C. Hu, M. Sumiya, N. Matsuki, K. Miyazaki, and H. Koinuma, "Characteristics of field effect a-Si:H solar cells," *Journal of Non-Crystalline Solids,* vol. 227–230, Part 2, pp. 1287-1290, 1998.

[6] D.-K. Yeh and T. A. DeMassa, "Computer analysis of induced-inversion layer MOS solar cells," *Solid-State Electronics,* vol. 27, pp. 283-292, 1984.

[7] V. Y. Yerokhov and I. I. Melnyk, "Influence of external bias on photoelectric properties of silicon MIS/IL structures," *Solid-State Electronics,* vol. 42, pp. 883-889, 1998.

[8] P. Wadhwa, B. Liu, M. A. McCarthy, Z. Wu, and A. G. Rinzler, "Electronic Junction Control in a Nanotube-Semiconductor Schottky Junction Solar Cell," *Nano Letters,* vol. 10, pp. 5001-5005, 2011/10/09 2010.

[9] P. Wadhwa, G. Seol, M. K. Petterson, J. Guo, and A. G. Rinzler, "Electrolyte-Induced Inversion Layer Schottky Junction Solar Cells," *Nano Letters,* vol. 11, pp. 2419-2423, 2011/10/09 2011.

[10] K. Akimoto, S. Ishizuka, M. Yanagita, Y. Nawa, G. K. Paul, and T. Sakurai, "Thin film deposition of Cu2O and application for solar cells," *Solar Energy,* vol. 80, pp. 715-722, 2006.

[11] R. Chandra, P. Taneja, and P. Ayyub, "Optical properties of transparent nanocrystalline Cu2O thin films synthesized by high pressure gas sputtering," *Nanostructured Materials,* vol. 11, pp. 505-512, 1999.

[12] S. O. Ishizuka, S. Kato, T. Maruyama, and K. Akimoto, "Nitrogen doping into Cu2O thin films deposited by reactive radio-frequency magnetron sputtering," *Japanese Journal of Applied Physics Part 1-Regular Papers Short Notes & Review Papers,* vol. 40, pp. 2765-2768, Apr 2001.

[13] T. Minami, Y. Nishi, T. Miyata, and J.-i. Nomoto, "High-Efficiency Oxide Solar Cells with ZnO/Cu2O Heterojunction Fabricated on Thermally Oxidized Cu2O Sheets," *Applied Physics Express,* vol. 4, Jun 2011.

[14] A. Mittiga, E. Salza, F. Sarto, M. Tucci, and R. Vasanthi, "Heterojunction solar cell with 2% efficiency based on a Cu2O substrate," *Applied Physics Letters,* vol. 88, Apr 17 2006.

Improved Rear Surface Passivation of Cu(In,Ga)Se$_2$ Solar Cells: A Combination of an Al$_2$O$_3$ Rear Surface Passivation Layer and Nanosized Local Rear Point Contacts

Bart Vermang, Viktor Fjällström, Xindong Gao, and Marika Edoff

Abstract—An innovative rear contacting structure for copper indium gallium (di) selenide (CIGS) thin-film solar cells is developed in an industrially viable way and demonstrated in tangible devices. The idea stems from the silicon (Si) industry, where rear surface passivation layers are combined with micron-sized local point contacts to boost the open-circuit voltage (V_{OC}) and, hence, cell efficiency. However, compared with Si solar cells, CIGS solar cell minority carrier diffusion lengths are several orders lower in magnitude. Therefore, the proposed CIGS cell design reduces rear surface recombination by combining a rear surface passivation layer and nanosized local point contacts. Atomic layer deposition of Al$_2$O$_3$ is used to passivate the CIGS surface and the formation of nanosphere-shaped precipitates in chemical bath deposition of CdS to generate nanosized point contact openings. The manufactured Al$_2$O$_3$ rear surface passivated CIGS solar cells with nanosized local rear point contacts show a significant improvement in V_{OC} compared with unpassivated reference cells.

Index Terms—Al$_2$O$_3$, atomic layer deposition, copper indium gallium selenide (CIGS), Cu(In,Ga)Se$_2$, Ga grading, nanosized, passivated emitter, passivated emitter and rear cell (PERC), photovoltaics, point contact openings rear locally diffused cell (PERL), rear surface passivation, Si, solar cells, thin film.

I. Introduction

AT present, rear surface recombination in highly efficient copper indium gallium (di)selenide (CIGS) solar cells is limited by using Ga grading to create a back surface field (BSF). World record conversion efficiencies (Eff.) of lab-scale CIGS solar cells are around 20%. Some recent outstanding examples are 1) the Japanese thin film manufacturer Solar Frontier, claiming a cadmium-free CIGS solar cell efficiency record of 19.7%, and 2) the Swiss Federal Laboratories for Materials Science and

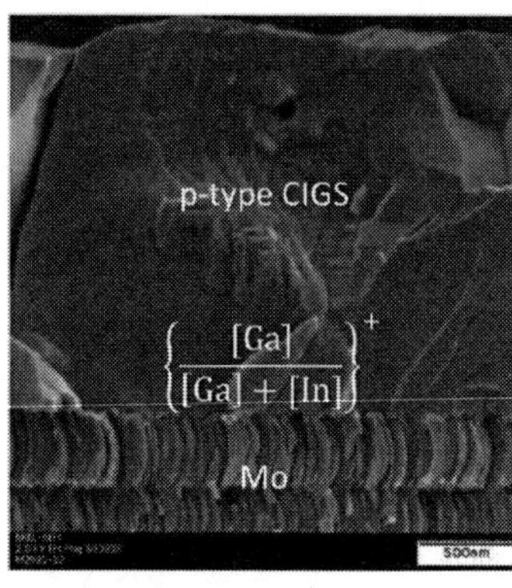

Fig. 1. SEM cross-section picture of a Mo/CIGS structure with a cell efficiency potential of 20.0% (taken from [4]).

Technology (EMPA), who have announced a thin-film CIGS solar cell record of 20.4% on a flexible polymer substrate [1]–[5]. These high efficiencies are achieved by varying the [Ga]/([Ga]+[In]) ratio to obtain different band gaps at different depths in the CIGS film. To reduce rear surface recombination, an increase of this ratio and, thus, bandgap toward the Mo back contact is a standard practice [6]. See, e.g., Fig. 1, which shows a scanning electron microscopy (SEM) cross section of a Mo/CIGS structure (produced adjacent to a 20.0% CIGS solar cell) fabricated by increasing the [Ga]/([Ga]+[In]) ratio toward the Mo/CIGS rear interface [4]. This gradient causes a quasi-electrical BSF that keeps the minority charge carriers away from the Mo/CIGS interface, and effectively reduces rear surface recombination [6].

In Si solar cell manufacturing, the present-day workhorse is the full aluminum (Al) BSF p-type silicon (Si) solar cell, whose rear structure is very comparable with those high-efficient CIGS cells. Fig. 2(a) represents a sketch of such a traditional full Al BSF cell. At the rear Al/Si interface, a BSF is formed thanks to a highly Al-doped p$^+$ region. In addition, in this case, the purpose of this BSF is to keep photo-electrons away from the metal/semiconductor (Al/Si) interface and, as a result, to reduce rear surface recombination [7].

Nevertheless, more advanced passivated emitter and rear cell (PERC) and analogous cell designs are on their way to substitute conventional aluminum Al BSF Si solar cells [8]–[10]. Fig. 2(b) represents a sketch of this alternative PERC [7]. As can be seen,

Manuscript received June 10, 2013; revised August 29, 2013; accepted October 15, 2013. Date of publication November 12, 2013; date of current version December 16, 2013. This work was supported by the Swedish Science Foundation (VR) and the Swedish Energy Agency. The work of B. Vermang was supported by the European Commission via FP7 Marie Curie IEF 2011 Action No. 300998.

B. Vermang, V. Fjällström, and M. Edoff are with the Ångström Solar Center, Division of Solid State Electronics, Department of Engineering Sciences, Uppsala University, 75121 Uppsala, Sweden (e-mail: Bart.Vermang@angstrom.uu.se; Viktor.Fjallstrom@angstrom.uu.se; Marika.Edoff@angstrom.uu.se).

X. Gao is with the Division of Solid State Electronics, Department of Engineering Sciences, Uppsala University, 75121 Uppsala, Sweden (e-mail: Gao.Xindong@angstrom.uu.se).

Color versions of one or more of the figures in this paper are available online at http://ieeexplore.ieee.org.

Digital Object Identifier 10.1109/JPHOTOV.2013.2287769

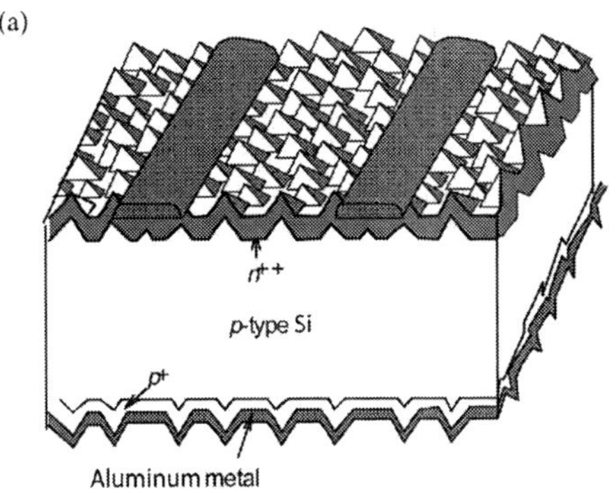

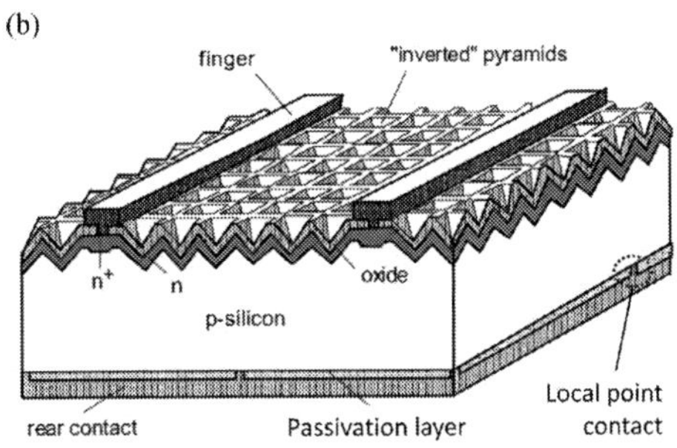

Fig. 2. Schematic drawing of (a) the conventional full Al back surface field p-type Si solar cell and (b) the passivated emitter and rear p-type Si solar cell (taken from [7]).

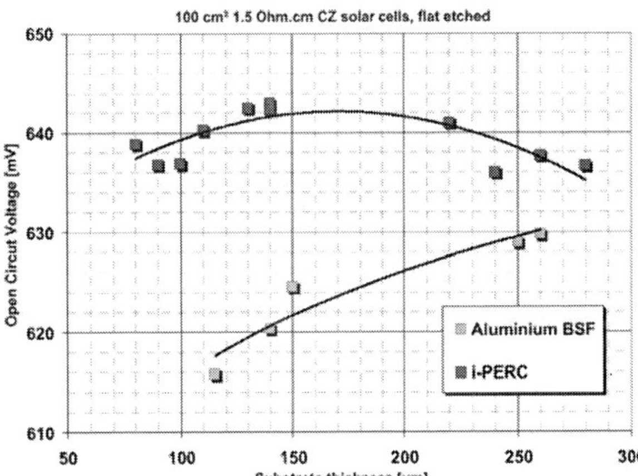

Fig. 3. Comparison of open-circuit voltages as a function of Si substrate thickness for (■) rear surface passivated industrial PERC (i-PERC) cells and (▨) standard full Al BSF reference cells (taken from [20]).

with respect to a conventional Al BSF solar cell production line, only a few extra steps are needed to introduce PERC processing: single-side texturing, local diffusion technologies, passivation layer deposition, and passivation layer opening. The potential of this more advanced cell processing is exposed by referring to the 25% world record cell conversion efficiency for single-junction Si solar cells as this record is achieved applying the passivated emitter, rear locally diffused cell (PERL) design, which is a PERC combined with locally diffused rear point contacts [1], [11].

Compared with conventional Al BSF processing, the rear of those advanced Si cell designs (PERC/PERL) is improved by a combination of an adequate rear surface passivation layer and micron-sized local point contacts—as shown in Fig. 2(b). Such a passivition layer combines two passivation mechanisms: 1) chemical passivation—a low density of interface defects D_{it} and 2) field-effect passivation—caused by a high density of fixed charges within the passivation layer. Roughly said, the point contact opening diameter has to be on the order of 50 to 200 μm, with a distance of 400 to 1600 μm between contact openings, as the minority carrier diffusion length L_n in industrial p-type Si wafers is in the order of 200 to 800 μm—depending on Si material quality and the doping level [8]–[10], [12]. Characteristic surface passivation layers for p-type Si are a combination of aluminum oxide (Al_2O_3), silicon oxide (SiO_2), and hydrogenated silicon nitride (SiN_x:H) [13], [14], while the local point contacts

are generated industrially by applying laser technology and represent 2 to 5% of the total rear surface area [8]–[10], [15]–[17].

Those rear surface passivation technologies are cost-effective for Si solar industry. They increase cell efficiency and allow the use of ever thinner wafers (resulting in a reduction in material cost), by improvements in rear surface passivation and rear internal reflection. In the case of standard full Al BSF solar cells, the rear surface recombination velocity S_b and rear internal reflection R_b generally are in the order of 1×10^4 to 1×10^6 cm/s and 60 to 70%, respectively. Unfortunately, this means that for full Al BSF cells a reduction in wafer thickness will decrease cell efficiency, because of 1) a raise in surface recombination—due to an increased surface-to-volume ratio combined with insufficient surface passivation and 2) a loss in absorption—due to thinner cells combined with low rear internal reflection. Rear surface passivated cell designs, on the other hand, lead to S_b as low as 1×10^2 cm/s and R_b above 85% and, hence, enhanced cell efficiencies for thinner Si wafers [8], [14], [18], [19]. Typically, short-circuit current J_{SC} is increased slightly due to higher R_b, while the fill factor FF is reduced somewhat due to more challenging contacting schemes. Nevertheless, due to an absolute improvement in rear surface passivation the open-circuit voltage V_{OC} is enhanced significantly. See, for example, Fig. 3, which compares V_{OC} of rear surface passivated i-PERC Si solar cells with standard full Al BSF cells as a function of Si wafer thickness [20]. Practically speaking, 300-μm-thick standard Al BSF Si solar cells can be substituted by more efficient rear surface passivated cells with a thickness between 100 and 200 μm.

Therefore, the purpose of this study is to assess the potential of these rear surface passivation technologies in CIGS solar cells. As for Al BSF Si cells, the Mo/CIGS rear surface of normal Ga-graded CIGS cells is known to show high S_b (also between 1×10^4 and 1×10^6 cm/s [21]–[23]) and low R_b (see the next section for R_b as a function of wavelength for the Mo/CIGS interface). Hence, analogous to Si PERC, the proposed cell design combines a rear surface passivation layer and local rear point contacts (LRPC), enabling reduced back contact

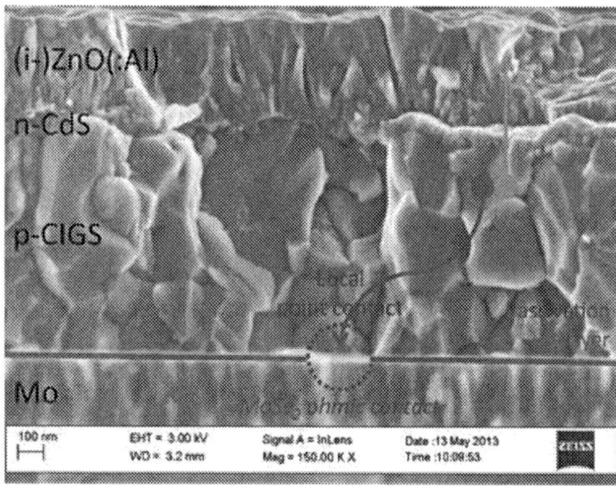

Fig. 4. Proposed CIGS solar cell design to reduce back contact recombination, by combining a rear surface passivation layer and local rear point contacts.

recombination and, thus, higher efficiencies—particularly for ever thinner CIGS absorber layers. However, thin film solar cells are known to have very short minority carrier lifetimes, which means that LRPC for rear passivated CIGS cells require to be nanosized and closely spaced. Assuming that L_n between 0.75 and 1.50 μm is feasible [24], [25], the contact openings targeted are between 200 and 400 nm in diameter with internal spacing between 1.5 and 3.0 μm, as scaled from the Si PERC design and keeping the contacting area between 2 and 5% of the total rear surface area. Fig. 4 shows a graphical representation of this proposed cell design.

This novel rear contacting structure for CIGS solar cells is developed in an industrially viable way and its improvement—compared with state-of-the-art reference cells—is demonstrated in tangible devices as a function of CIGS absorber layer thickness.

II. METHODOLOGY

The formation and subsequent removal of spherical particles (so-called colloids or precipitates) in chemical bath deposition (CBD) of CdS is applied to generate nanosized point contacts. In this study, standard CBD CdS is grown in a solution with 1.136 M ammonia, 0.100 M thiourea, and 0.003 M cadmium acetate, at 60 °C. However, to obtain particle-rich CdS deposition conditions, an alternative approach is required: 1) After preparing the CBD solution, soda lime glass (SLG)/Mo substrates are only immersed when the CBD solution reacted for X min—during which time CdS nanoparticles are formed within the solution [26]. 2) Thereafter, the substrates are dipped for Y min, and a thin particle-rich CdS film is grown. By varying time intervals X and Y the particle-density can be varied. Fig. 5 shows top-view SEM pictures of thin particle-rich CdS layers deposited on SLG/Mo substrates before and after removal of these particles [27]; in this case, both X and Y equal 4 min, and an extra layer of CdS is grown to intensify the contrast in Fig. 5(b). Particle removal is established in various ways: via 1) ultrasonic agitation, 2) dry ice (liquid CO_2) cleaning, or 3) mechanical wiping. Using numerous SEM measurements, an average particle diameter of 285 $\pm$ 30 nm and average point

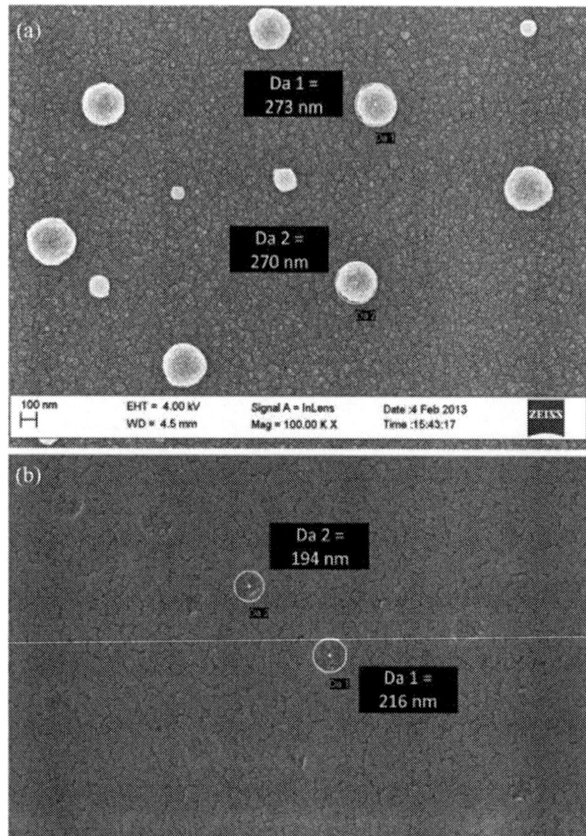

Fig. 5. SEM pictures of (a) a particle-rich CdS layer grown on a SLG/Mo substrate and (b) the same substrate after CdS particle removal (taken from [27]).

opening diameter of 220 $\pm$ 25 nm is calculated. In conclusion, to actually create nanosized point openings in rear surface passivation layers for CIGS, the passivation layer is 1) first grown on this particle-rich CdS layer, and 2) subsequently, the particles are removed. This way, a passivation layer with nanosized point openings having a diameter around 220 nm is obtained.

Atomic layer deposition (ALD) of Al_2O_3 is applied as CIGS surface passivation layer. In this study, ALD Al_2O_3 passivation layers are deposited in a temporal ALD reactor at 300 °C, using trimethylaluminum (TMA) and an oxygen source (both water (H_2O) and ozone (O_3) are used) as precursors [28]. Previously, Al_2O_3 is verified to be an adequate CIGS surface passivation layer, thanks to its 1) chemical passivation—first principles calculations indicate that the deposition of Al_2O_3 reduces about 35% of the interface defect density—and 2) field effect passivation—Al_2O_3 exhibits a large density of negative charges, causing a field effect that reduces the CIGS surface minority charge carrier concentration and, hence, passivates the interface effectively [23]. In the same work, an improvement of two orders in magnitude is reported for the integrated photoluminescence intensity of Al_2O_3 passivated CIGS compared

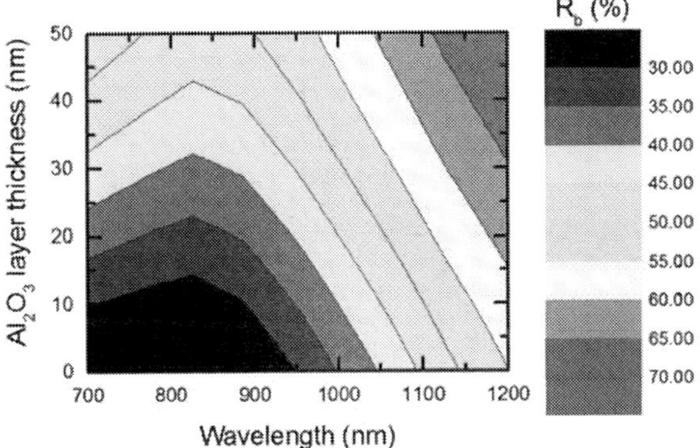

Fig. 6. Calculated rear internal reflection as a function of wavelength and Al_2O_3 layer thickness for a Mo/(CdS/)Al_2O_3/CIGS device [29].

with unpassivated CIGS. Hence, a significant reduction in S_b is expected for Al_2O_3 passivated CIGS surfaces compared with standard Mo/CIGS surfaces. To also have an idea about its optical confinement, R_b at the Mo/(CdS/)Al_2O_3/CIGS interface is calculated as in [29]; applying thickness, refractive index and extinction coefficient of the Al_2O_3 layer as measured on an Si substrate using spectrally resolved ellipsometry. In Fig. 6, R_b is depicted as a function of long wavelength and Al_2O_3 layer thickness in the case of a Mo/(CdS/)Al_2O_3/CIGS structure. This shows that—compared with the standard Mo/CIGS interface (equivalent to an Al_2O_3 layer thickness of 0 nm)—applying a thin layer (e.g., 5 nm) of Al_2O_3 as rear surface passivation increases R_b only slightly, while a thicker Al_2O_3 layer (e.g., 50 nm) leads to a larger R_b enhancement.

Ungraded CIGS absorber layers are used [30] 1) to allow evaluation of an obvious improvement in V_{OC} if rear surface passivation is enhanced and 2) to exclude any other surface passivation effects. CIGS layers are deposited in a high-vacuum chamber equipped with open-boat evaporation sources, while evaporation rates are monitored using a mass spectrometer. During CIGS growth, the maximum substrate temperature is 540 °C; Se is evaporated in excess; and constant rates of Cu, In, and Ga are applied until a desired CIGS thickness is reached. All studied samples have compositional values of $[Cu]/([Ga]+[In]) = 0.90 \pm 0.02$ and $[Ga]/([Ga]+[In]) = 0.30 \pm 0.01$, which are calculated from X-ray fluorescence (XRF) measurements. CIGS film thicknesses are measured with a profilometer and are varied between 0.48 ± 0.02 and 1.58 ± 0.04 μm. These "flat-evaporation-rate-CIGS" absorbers with uniform low Ga concentration are favored to assess rear surface passivation, because of their high reproducibility, their characteristic high L_n [24], and to exclude complementary rear surface passivation effects (e.g., a quasi-electrical field created by a Ga gradient causing a slope in the conduction band—as is the case in standard high-efficient CIGS cells). This approach leads to cell efficiencies below 16.5%, but allows an evident boost in solar cell characterization results if the advanced CIGS cell design functions.

Table I gives an overview of all steps required to fabricate rear surface passivated CIGS solar cells with nanosized LRPC. A detailed description of standard CIGS solar cell processing at the Ångström Solar Center can be found in [31], i.e., excluding

Step	Description
0	Start: low-iron soda lime glass
1	Glass cleaning
2	Mo rear contact sputtering
3	Particle-rich CBD CdS deposition
4	ALD Al_2O_3 passivation deposition
5	CdS particle removal
6	Ungraded CIGS absorber co-evaporation
7	CBD CdS buffer deposition
8	(i-)ZnO(:Al) window sputtering
9	Ni/Al/Ni front contact evaporation
10	Mechanical scribing of 0.5 cm^2 solar cells

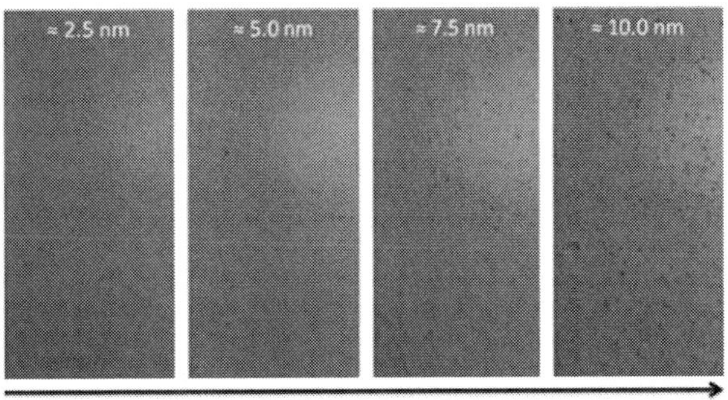

Fig. 7. Top-view optical microscopy pictures after particle removal of SLG/Mo/particle-rich-CdS/Al_2O_3 samples as a function Al_2O_3 layer thickness.

the ungraded absorber layer formation and the advanced back contact design. The starting substrate is low-iron SLG with a thickness of 1 mm, which first undergoes a cleaning process. As back contact, a Mo layer is deposited in an inline sputtering system. It has a sheet resistance of 0.6 $\Omega/\square$ and a typical thickness of 350 nm. The advanced back contact design combines an ALD Al_2O_3 rear surface passivation layer and CBD of CdS to generate nanosized LRPC, as described previously. On top of this rear contact structure, an ungraded CIGS absorber layer of desired thickness is evaporated, also described previously. The buffer layer is deposited using a standard CBD CdS process. Next, the shunt reducing intrinsic ZnO layer (i-ZnO) and, subsequently, the Al-doped ZnO (ZnO:Al) front contact of the cells are sputtered. As front contact grid, a Ni/Al/Ni stack is deposited by evaporation through a shadow mask. The (i-)ZnO(:Al) and Ni/Al/Ni stack have a total thickness around 400 and 3000 nm, respectively. Finally 0.5 cm^2 solar cells are defined by mechanical scribing with a stylus. No antireflective coating is used.

Light J–V measurements are performed at 25 °C under standard AM1.5 G conditions in a home-made system with a tungsten halogen lamp, which is calibrated using a certified silicon photo diode [31].

III. RESULTS AND DISCUSSION

The proposed technique to create nanosized point openings in Al_2O_3 passivation layers—by removing spherical particles deposited by CBD CdS—works fine for Al_2O_3 layers that are not too thick ($\leq$5 nm). Fig. 7 depicts for various Al_2O_3 thicknesses and top-view optical microscopy pictures of SLG/Mo/

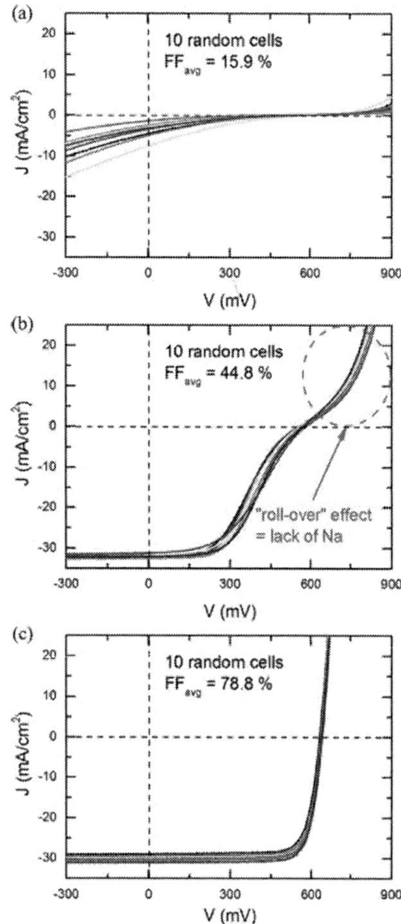

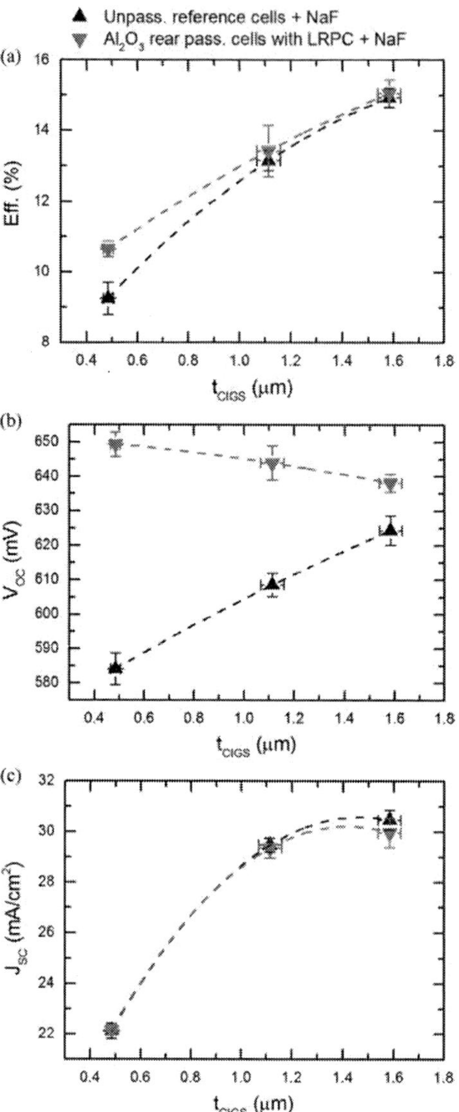

Fig. 8. Representative *J–V* curves for (a) Al$_2$O$_3$ rear surface passivated CIGS solar cells without nanosized LRPC, (b) Al$_2$O$_3$ rear surface passivated CIGS cells with nanosized LRPC, and (c) Al$_2$O$_3$ rear surface passivated CIGS cells having nanosized LRPC and an additional NaF layer evaporated on top of the Al$_2$O$_3$ layer (after particle removal). In all examples, the Al$_2$O$_3$ and CIGS layer thickness are around 5.0 nm and 1.58 μm, respectively. In each case, 10 random *J–V* curves are shown, and the average fill factor is given.

Fig. 9. Average (a) cell conversion efficiency, (b) open-circuit voltage, and (c) short-circuit current as a function of CIGS absorber layer thickness for Al$_2$O$_3$ rear surface passivated CIGS solar cells having nanosized LRPC compared with unpassivated reference CIGS cells. For each CIGS thickness, the same optimized NaF thickness is used for both the passivated and the unpassivated cells. Standard deviation is shown as error bars.

particle-rich-CdS/Al$_2$O$_3$ structures after particle removal. These pictures show that for too-thick ALD Al$_2$O$_3$ films ($\geq$7.5 nm), the particle removal becomes unsatisfactory. The self-limiting nature of ALD reactions leads to an ideal growth control and the ability to coat high-aspect-ratio structures, as desired for the suggested point opening approach. However, these ALD advantages also mean that CdS nanoparticles embedded in too-thick Al$_2$O$_3$ films become irremovable. Therefore, 5 nm of Al$_2$O$_3$ has been used for all passivated cells with LRPC, which are described next.

Al$_2$O$_3$ rear surface passivated CIGS solar cells require 1) LRPC for appropriate contacting and 2) extra supply of Na—since Al$_2$O$_3$ layers act as a barrier for Na diffusion from the SLG substrate. Fig. 8(a) shows representative *J–V* curves for ten random Al$_2$O$_3$ rear surface passivated CIGS solar cells without LRPC. These cells have an average FF of 16%, which 1) proves that there is no appropriate back contacting without point contacts and 2) indicates that the passivation layer

is intact after CIGS processing. Fig. 8(b), on the other hand, shows representative *J–V* curves for 10 random Al$_2$O$_3$ rear surface passivated CIGS cells with nanosized LRPC. The average FF increases to 45%, higher compared with the cells without LRPC but still rather low. In addition, these *J–V* curves show a "roll-over" effect, characteristic for devices lacking Na [32]. Note that 1) Al$_2$O$_3$ films are known to be excellent gas diffusion barriers [33] and that 2) this roll-over effect is not as pronounced as in Na-free cells [32]. Therefore, Fig. 8(c) shows representative *J–V* curves for 10 random Al$_2$O$_3$ rear surface passivated CIGS cells having LRPC and—after removal of the

CdS nanoparticles—an additional NaF layer evaporated on top of this Al_2O_3 layer. Fig. 8(c) proves that the low FF's in Fig. 8(b) are indeed caused by Al_2O_3 acting as an Na diffusion barrier. Even more, the combination of LRPC and extra Na supply leads to a high average FF of 79%.

The rear surface of Al_2O_3 rear surface passivated CIGS solar cells with nanosized LRPC are better passivated compared with unpassivated reference cells, which becomes more obvious in the case of thinner CIGS absorber layers. Fig. 9 shows the average 1) Eff., (b) V_{OC}, and (c) J_{SC} as a function of CIGS absorber layer thickness for Al_2O_3 rear surface passivated CIGS solar cells having nanosized LRPC and unpassivated reference CIGS cells. Note that for each CIGS thickness, the same optimized NaF thickness is used for both the Al_2O_3 passivated and the unpassivated reference cells. Fig. 9(a) shows that higher average efficiencies are measured for all the Al_2O_3 rear passivated cells. In addition, the difference becomes more apparent for the thinnest CIGS layers. Fig. 9(b) demonstrates that this increase in efficiency is obtained thanks to an improvement in V_{OC} for the Al_2O_3 rear passivated cells. The most logical explanation for this increase in V_{OC} is a significant enhancement in rear surface passivation (=lower S_b) for the Al_2O_3 rear-passivated cells [23], [27]. This boost in surface passivation becomes clearer for thinner CIGS absorber layers, as this well-passivated rear surface then gets closer to the space charge region of the cell. In addition, it is remarkable that this change in V_{OC} as a function of absorber layer thickness for rear passivated compared with unpassivated cells is very similar to Fig. 3. Unfortunately, the average J_{SC} of the passivated and unpassivated cells is similar for all CIGS thicknesses, as seen in Fig. 9(c). This comparable behavior in J_{SC} for passivated and unpassivated cells can be explained by a too-small improvement in R_b for only 5 nm of Al_2O_3 as rear surface passivation layer, as already shown in Fig. 6.

IV. Conclusion and Outlook

For the first time, the concept of rear surface passivation—as used in advanced Si cell technologies (PERC/PERL)—is developed for and shown in industrially viable CIGS solar cells: 5 nm of ALD Al_2O_3 is used to passivate the CIGS rear surface and the formation of nanosphere-shaped precipitates in CBD CdS to generate point contact openings. The same (V_{OC}) behavior is shown for rear surface passivated CIGS solar cells compared with unpassivated reference cells [see Fig. 9(b)] as for rear surface passivated Si solar cells compared unpassivated Si cells (see Fig. 3). Thanks to a significant improvement in rear surface passivation, an obvious increase in V_{OC} is measured, especially for ever thinner CIGS absorber layers, as this well-passivated rear surface gets closer to the most active region of the cells.

However, more reflective rear surface passivation layers need to be integrated to increase J_{SC} and, hence, efficiency, even further. As seen in Fig. 6, 5 nm of ALD Al_2O_3 increases R_b only slightly compared with the referential Mo/CIGS rear interface. Therefore, the focus is now on integrating thicker passivation layers to combine improved rear surface passivation with en-

hanced optical confinement. For that reason, research is ongoing to 1) combine Al_2O_3 rear surface passivation with other point contact opening approaches (lithography, laser ablation) or 2) combine the CBD CdS proposed technique to create nanosized point openings with other CIGS passivation layer candidates. The final target is—compared with unpassivated state-of-the-art CIGS solar cells of normal thickness—to develop CIGS cells having improved rear surface passivation and rear internal reflection, leading to a substantial increase in cell efficiency, even for thinner CIGS absorber layers.

References

[1] M. A. Green, "Solar cell efficiency tables (version 41)," *Prog. Photovoltaics, Res. Appl.*, vol. 21, pp. 1–11, 2013.

[2] P. Reinhard, A. Chirila, P. Blosch, F. Pianezzi, S. Nishiwaki, S. Buecheler, and A. N. Tiwari, "Review of progress toward 20% efficiency flexible CIGS solar cells and manufacturing issues of solar modules," *IEEE J. Photovoltaics*, vol. 3, no. 1, pp. 572–580, Jan. 2013.

[3] P. Jackson, D. Hariskos, E. Lotter, S. Paetel, R. Wuerz, R. Menner, W. Wischmann. and M. Powalla, "New world record efficiency for $Cu(In,Ga)Se_2$ thin-film solar cells beyond 20%," *Prog. Photovoltaics, Res. Appl.*, vol. 19, pp. 894–897, 2011.

[4] S. Niki, M. Contreras, I. Repins, M. Powalla, K. Kushiya, S. Ishizuka, and K. Matsubara, "CIGS absorbers and processes," *Prog. Photovolt, Res. Appl.*, vol. 18, pp. 453–466, 2010.

[5] I. Repins, S. Glynn, J. Duenow, T. J. Coutts, W. Metzger, and M.A. Contreras, "Required material properties for high-efficiency CIGS modules," *Proc. SPIE*, vol. 7409, pp. 1–14, 2009.

[6] O. Lundberg, M. Edoff, and L. Stolt, "The effect of Ga-grading in CIGS thin film solar cells," *Thin Solid Films*, vol. 480–481, pp. 520–525, 2005.

[7] M.A. Green, "Crystalline silicon solar cells," in *Clean Electricity from Photovoltaics*. London, U.K.: Imperial College Press, 2001.

[8] Z. Wang, P. Han, H. Lu, H. Qian, L. Chen, Q. Meng, N. Tang, F. Gao, Y. Jiang, J. Wu, W. Wu, H. Zhu, J. Ji, Z. Shi, A. Sugianto, L. Mai, B. Hallam, and S. Wenham, "Advanced PERC and PERL production cells with 20.3% record efficiency for standard commercial p-type silicon wafers," *Prog. Photovoltaics, Res. Appl*, vol. 20, pp. 260–268, 2012.

[9] M. Moors, K. Baert, T. Caremans, F. Duerinckx, A. Cacciato, and J. Szlufcik, "Industrial PERL-type solar cells exceeding 19% with screen-printed contacts and homogeneous emitter," *Solar Energy Mater. Solar Cells*, vol. 106, pp. 84–88, 2012.

[10] A. Cacciato, F. Duerinckx, K. Baert, M. Moors, T. Caremans, G. Leys, M. Mrearica, E. Picard, A. Ristow, and J. Szlufcik, "Industrial PERL-type Si solar cells with efficiencies exceeding 19.5%." *IEEE J. Photovoltaics*, vol. 3, no. 2, pp. 628–634, Apr. 2013.

[11] J. Zhao, A. Wang, and M.A. Green, "24% efficient PERL structure silicon solar cells," in *Proc. 21st IEEE Photovoltaic Spec. Conf.*, 1990, pp. 333–335.

[12] J. A. Giesecke, M. Kasemann, and W. Warta, "Determination of local minority carrier diffusion lengths in crystalline silicon from luminescence images," *J. Appl. Phys.*, vol. 106, pp. 014907-1–014907-8, 2009.

[13] B. Vermang, H. Goverde, L. Tous, A. Lorenz, P. Choulat, J. Horzel, J. John, J. Poortmans, and R. Mertens, "Approach for Al_2O_3 rear surface passivation of industrial p-type Si PERC above 19%," *Prog. Photovoltaics, Res. Appl.*, vol. 20, pp. 269–273, 2012.

[14] T. Dullweber, S. Gatz, H. Hannebauer, T. Falcon, R. Hesse, J. Schmidt, and R. Brendel, "Towards 20% efficient large-area screen-printed rear-passivated silicon solar cells," *Prog. Photovoltaics, Res. Appl.*, vol. 20, pp. 630–638, 2012.

[15] G. Agostinelli, J. Szlufcik, P. Choulat, and G. Beaucarne, "Local contact structures for industrial PERC-type solar cells," in *Proc. 20th Eur. Photovoltaic Sol. Energy Conf.*, 2005, pp. 942–945.

[16] E. Schneiderlöchner, R. Preu, R. Lüdemann, and S.W. Glunz, "Laser-fired rear contacts for crystalline silicon solar cells," *Prog. Photovoltaics, Res. Appl.*, vol. 10, pp. 29–34, 2002.

[17] T. Böscke, R. Hellriegel, T. Wütherich, L. Bornschein, A. Helbig, R. Carl, M. Dupke, D. Stichtenoth, T. Aichele, R. Jesswein, T. Roth, C. Schöllhorn, T. Geppert, A. Grohe, J. Lossen, and H.-J. Krokoszinski, "Fully screen-printed PERC cells with laser-fired contacts—An industrial cell concept with 19.5% efficiency," in *Proc. 37th Photovoltaic Spec. Conf.*, 2011, pp. 3663–3666.

[18] A. Lorenz, J. John, B. Vermang, E. Cornagliotti, and J. Poortmans, "Comparison of illumination level dependency and rear internal reflectance of PERC-type cells with different dielectric passivation stacks," in *Proc. 26th Eur. Photovoltaic Sol. Energy Conf.*, 2011, pp. 1486–1488.

[19] K.O. Davis, K. Jiang, C. Demberger, H. Zunft, H. Haverkamp, D. Habermann, and W. V. Schoenfeld, "Investigation of the internal back reflectance of rear-side dielectric stacks for c-Si solar cells," *IEEE J. Photovoltaics*, vol. 3, no. 2, pp. 641–648, Apr. 2013.

[20] G. Agostinelli, P. Choulat, H. F. W. Dekkers, E. Vermariën, and G. Beaucarne, "Rear surface passivation for industrial solar cells on thin substrates," in *Proc. 4th IEEE World Conf. Photovoltaic Energy Conv.*, 2006, pp. 1004–1007.

[21] K. Bothe, G.H. Bauer, and T. Unold, "Spatially resolved photoluminescence measurements on Cu(In,Ga)Se$_2$ thin films," *Thin Solid Films*, vol. 403–404, pp. 453–456, 2002.

[22] W. K. Metzger, I. L. Repins, M. Romero, P. Dippo, M. Contreras, R. Noufi, and D. Levi, "Recombination kinetics and stability in polycrystalline Cu(In,Ga)Se$_2$ solar cells," *Thin Solid Films*, vol. 517, pp. 2360–2364, 2009.

[23] W.-W. Hsu, J. Y. Chen, T.-H. Cheng, S. C. Lu, W.-S. Ho, Y.-Y. Chen, Y.-J. Chien, and C.W. Liu, "Surface passivation of Cu(In,Ga)Se$_2$ using atomic layer deposited Al$_2$O$_3$," *Appl. Phys. Lett.*, vol. 100, pp. 023508-1–023508-3, 2012.

[24] G. Brown, V. Faifer, A. Pudov, S. Anikeev, E. Bykov, M. Contreras, and J. Wu, "Determination of the minority carrier diffusion length in compositionally graded Cu(In,Ga)Se$_2$ solar cells using electron beam induced current," *Appl. Phys. Lett.*, vol. 96, pp. 022104-1–022104-3, 2010.

[25] R. Kniese, M. Powalla, and U. Rau, "Evaluation of electron beam induced current profiles of Cu(In,Ga)Se$_2$ solar cells with different Ga-contents," *Thin Solid Films*, vol. 517, pp. 2357–2359, 2009.

[26] R. Ortega-Borges and D. Lincot, "Mechanism of chemical bath deposition of cadmium sulfide thin films in the ammonia-thiourea system," *J. Electrochem. Soc.*, vol. 140, pp. 3464–3473, 1993.

[27] B. Vermang, V. Fjällström, J. Pettersson, P. Salomé, and M. Edoff, "Development of rear surface passivated Cu(In,Ga)Se$_2$ thin film solar cells with nano-sized local rear point contacts," *Solar Energy Mater. Solar Cells*, vol. 117, pp. 505–511, 2013.

[28] B. Vermang, *Aluminum Oxide as Negatively Charged Surface Passivation for Industrial Crystalline Silicon Solar Cells.* Leuven, Belgium: Univ. Leuven Press, 2012.

[29] F. Duerinckx, I. Kuzma-Filipek, K. Van Nieuwenhuysen, G. Beaucarne, and J. Poortmans, "Simulation and implementation of a porous silicon reflector for epitaxial silicon solar cells," *Prog. Photovoltaics, Res. Appl.*, vol. 16, pp. 399–407, 2008.

[30] W. N. Shafarman, R. S. Huang, and S.H. Stephens, "Characterization of Cu(InGa)Se$_2$ solar cells using etched absorber layers," in *Proc. 4th IEEE 4th World Conf. Photovoltaic Energy Conv.*, 2006, pp. 420–423.

[31] J. Lindahl, U. Zimmermann, P. Szaniawski, T. Törndahl, A. Hultqvist, P. Salomé, C. Platzer-Björkman, and M. Edoff, "Inline Cu(In,Ga)Se$_2$ coevaporation for high-efficiency solar cells and modules," *IEEE J. Photovoltaics*, vol. 3, no. 3, pp. 1100–1105, Jul. 2013. DOI: 10.1109/JPHOTOV.2013.2256232.

[32] P. Salomé, V. Fjällström, A. Hultqvist, and M. Edoff, "Na doping of CIGS solar cells using low sodium-doped Mo layer," *IEEE J. Photovoltaics*, vol. 3, no. 1, pp. 509–513, Jan. 2013.

[33] D. Bae, S. Kwon, J. Oh, W. K. Kim, and H. Park, "Investigation of Al$_2$O$_3$ diffusion barrier layer fabricated by atomic layer deposition for flexible Cu(In,Ga)Se$_2$ solar cells," *Renew. Energ.*, vol. 55, pp. 62–68, 2013.

Bart Vermang received the M.Sc. degree in experimental physics from the University of Ghent, Ghent, Belgium, in 2005, and the Ph.D. degree in electrical engineering from the University of Leuven, Leuven, Belgium, in 2012. During the M.Sc. final research project he studied surface reactions in model metallic catalyst systems at the Norwegian University of Science and Technology (NTNU) in Trondheim, Norway. His Ph.D. research he performed at Imec in Belgium, where he developed novel surface passivation structures for industrial silicon solar cells.

At present, he holds a Postdoctoral position at the University of Uppsala, Uppsala, Sweden, where his challenge is to integrate progressive Si solar cell concepts in CIGS thin-film cells.

Viktor Fjällström was born in Uddevalla, Sweden, in 1986. He received the Master's degree in energy systems engineering from Uppsala University, Uppsala, Sweden, in 2010. The main focus of his studies was renewable energy. His Master thesis was based on experiments in the field of concentrated solar power.

Since the end of 2010, he has been a Research Engineer with the Thin Film Solar Cell Group, Division of Solid State Electronics, Uppsala University.

Xindong Gao received the Ph.D. degree in physics from Fudan University, Shanghai, China, in 2010. His Ph.D. dissertation was based on the study on organic light-emitting device optimization and charge transport mechanisms.

From 2010 to 2011, he held a Postdoctoral. position within the Emerging Electronics group, Division of Solid State Electronics, University of Uppsala, Sweden. The main focus was developing the atomic layer deposition process and the Ni silicide process for advanced complementary metal–oxide semiconductor technology. Since the end of 2011, he has been a Researcher with the same group. His research interests include ion sensors based on both graphene and Si devices with a focus on ion sensitivity and selectivity.

Marika Edoff received the M.Sc. degree in electrical engineering and the Ph.D. degree in solid-state electronics from the Royal Institute of Technology, Stockholm, Sweden, in 1990 and 1997, respectively.

Since 2003, she has been leading research activities on solid-state thin-film solar cells with Uppsala University, Uppsala, Sweden. She was one of the four founders of Solibro, where since 2005, she has also been a part-time employee. Her research interests include CIGS-based thin-film solar cells, with a focus on material synthesis and device characterization.

Lattice-Mismatched 0.7-eV GaInAs Solar Cells Grown on GaAs Using GaInP Compositionally Graded Buffers

Ryan M. France, Iván García, William E. McMahon, Andrew G. Norman, John Simon, John F. Geisz, Daniel J. Friedman, and Manuel J. Romero

Abstract—The three-junction 1.8/1.4/1.0-eV inverted metamorphic multijunction solar cell can be extended to four junctions by adding another lattice-mismatched GaInAs junction with a bandgap of 0.7 eV. However, this requires a significant amount of mismatch to GaAs substrates, i.e., 3.8%, which is difficult to obtain while maintaining high-quality material. In this paper, we perform an in-depth investigation of a GaInP compositionally graded buffer varying in composition between $Ga_{0.5}In_{0.5}P$ and InP in order to identify limitations to dislocation glide and sources of excess dislocation formation. *In situ* wafer curvature, cathodoluminescence, and X-ray diffraction (XRD) are used to analyze dislocation glide; transmission electron microscopy, atomic force microscope, and XRD are used to analyze material structural properties. Composition nonuniformities and roughness are observed, and a region in the compositionally graded buffer where a significant number of excess dislocations are formed is identified. The formation of these dislocations is related to atomic ordering, which has a large influence on the dislocation behavior. Adding thickness to the region in the buffer where dislocations are formed reduces the threading dislocation density an order of magnitude. Metamorphic 0.74 eV solar cells grown on this template have internal quantum efficiency > 90% and V_{oc} > 0.3 V with J_{sc} set to 13 mA/cm^2, which is the expected current in a multijunction device. These results are compared with lattice-matched GaInAs/InP solar cells to evaluate the loss associated with the lattice-mismatch.

Index Terms—Concentrator, inverted metamorphic, lattice-mismatch, multijunction, solar cells, III–V.

I. Introduction

THREE-JUNCTION solar cells with over 40% efficiency have been demonstrated using a wide variety of device designs [1]–[6]. As these three-junction (3-J) designs approach their efficiency limit, four-junction (4-J) designs are desired to drive efficiency higher. The 1.8/1.4/1.0-eV 3-J inverted metamorphic multijunction (IMM) solar cell targets an optimal

Manuscript received June 13, 2013; revised August 7, 2013; accepted September 3, 2013. Date of publication September 30, 2013; date of current version December 16, 2013. This work was supported by the U.S. Department of Energy under Contract DE-AC36–08-GO28308 with the National Renewable Energy Laboratory. I. García holds an IOF grant from the People Programme (Marie Curie Actions) of the European Union's Seventh Framework Programme (FP7/2007–2013) under REA Grant 299878.

The authors are with the National Renewable Energy Laboratory, Golden, CO 80401 USA (e-mail: ryan.france@nrel.gov; ivan.garcia@nrel.gov; bill.mcmahon@nrel.gov; andrew.norman@nrel.gov; john.simon@nrel.gov; john.geisz@nrel.gov; daniel.friedman@nrel.gov; manuel.romero@nrel.gov).

Color versions of one or more of the figures in this paper are available online at http://ieeexplore.ieee.org.

Digital Object Identifier 10.1109/JPHOTOV.2013.2281724

bandgap combination by utilizing the lattice-mismatched material [7]. IMM designs with one and two independently lattice-mismatched junctions have achieved efficiencies over 40%, showing the performance capability of the lattice-mismatched junctions. The 3-J IMM can be extended to a 4-J IMM by adding another lattice-mismatched $Ga_x In_{1-x}As$ junction with a bandgap of 0.7 eV at a composition of x = 0.5 [8], [9]. However, this material has a substantial 3.8% misfit to the GaAs substrate, and therefore, research into lattice-mismatched growth is required.

Compositionally graded buffers (CGBs) allow strain-free growth of the lattice-mismatched material. During the growth of the buffer, the strain is relieved by the intentional formation and glide of dislocations. The portions of the dislocations parallel to the growth interfaces, termed misfit dislocations, are largely responsible for the strain relief. The portions of the dislocations inclined to the growth interfaces are termed threading dislocations, and are efficient recombination centers that lower the performance of lattice-mismatched solar cells if they propagate into the active region of the device. Research into CGBs is aimed at generating and confining dislocations within the CGB. The residual threading dislocation density (TDD) at the end of the buffer is a key metric of the CGB quality. Maximizing the average misfit dislocation glide length ensures the most in-plane lattice change per dislocation, which in turn reduces the residual TDD. Many factors influence dislocation glide throughout the buffer, including intrinsic material properties such as the elastic coefficients, as well as extrinsic factors such as surface roughness, composition variations, and other structural defects [10]. Recently, we have also shown that atomic ordering in III–V materials also has a strong influence on the dislocation behavior [11], [12], and therefore, the factors influencing atomic ordering also need to be considered in the CGB design. Researchers have shown that CGBs with very low residual TDD are possible by maintaining very high material quality and using appropriate growth conditions and CGB structures [13]–[15].

The IMM solar cell is grown on a GaAs substrate and targets specific GaInAs compositions and, therefore, specific amounts of compressive lattice-mismatch, to achieve the optimum bandgap combination. CGBs are placed between junctions with different lattice constants and, therefore, must be electrically conductive and optically transparent to wavelengths used by the lower junctions. These restrictions limit the selection of CGB materials. Previous research on GaInP CGBs for 1.0-eV GaInAs solar cells has resulted in low-TDD material and

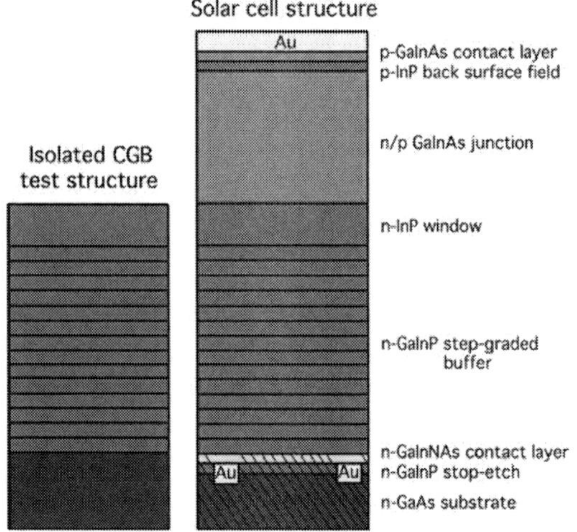

Fig. 1. Graded-buffer test structure and the solar cell structure. The CGB test structure is undoped and does not contain the cell layers.

high-quality metamorphic solar cells [15]. This paper extends research on GaInP CGBs to lattice constants that allow 0.7-eV GaInAs solar cells, which is required for the development of a 4-J IMM. Other research toward this goal has been performed [9], [16], [17]; here, we present detailed materials and device characterization. Several materials characterizations are performed on the required GaInP CGB in order to qualify the buffer and identify limitations to dislocation glide or sources of excess threading dislocations. The buffer is improved by focusing on a source of dislocations related to atomic ordering, and 0.7-eV GaInAs solar cells are demonstrated on improved buffers.

II. EXPERIMENTAL DETAILS

Both isolated CGB structures as well as lattice-mismatched GaInAs solar cells using CGB templates were grown by atmospheric pressure metalorganic vapor phase epitaxy on (0 0 1) GaAs:Si substrates miscut 2° toward $(\bar{1}\,1\,1)$B. These structures are illustrated in Fig. 1. The growth conditions of the CGB previously established for GaInP CGBs with 1.9% misfit [15] were extended to 3.8% misfit in this paper. The growth was performed at 675 °C using a fast growth rate (7 μm/h) and high phosphine partial pressure (10 Torr). Fourteen 0.25-μm-thick layers of undoped GaInP with varying composition were used to transition between nominally lattice-matched $Ga_{0.5}In_{0.5}P$ and InP, whose lattice constant equals that of the desired 0.7-eV $Ga_{0.5}In_{0.5}As$ active layer. The misfit change per step was 0.25%, equivalent to a misfit grade rate of 1%/μm of growth. The final layer of the CGB was 1 μm thick. Variations to this structure will be described in the text. The solar cell structure utilized a similar CGB structure but included Si doping throughout the CGB and a GaInNAs contact layer prior to the CGB. The GaInAs cell was grown directly on the final layer of the CGB and consists of a 0.1-μm emitter and a 4-μm base. After the cell growth, a 0.3-μm InP rear-passivation layer and a 0.1-μm GaInAs contact layer were grown. A gold back contact was electroplated to the

front surface of the growth, which was then bonded to a Si handle using epoxy. The GaAs substrate and GaInP stop-etch were then removed, and front contact grids were patterned using photolithography and gold electroplating. The devices were then mesa isolated and the exposed top contact layer was removed using selective etchants.

High-resolution X-ray diffraction (XRD) was performed using a Panalytical X-pert Pro with a Ge 4-bounce (0 0 4) hybrid monochromator and a PIXcel area detector. The tilt and strain of the InP layer were determined by analyzing reciprocal space maps (RSMs) of the symmetric (0 0 4) reflection with X-rays incident in the (1 1 0) plane. Transmission electron microscopy (TEM) was performed in a FEI ST30 microscope on cross-sectional [1 1 0] and $[\bar{1}\,1\,0]$ samples prepared by cleaving, dimpling, and ion milling. The TDD in the final layer was determined using cathodoluminescence (CL) imaging at 300 K in a JEOL JSM-7600 F scanning electron microscope equipped with Ge and GaInAs detectors. The root-mean-squared (RMS) roughness was evaluated from a 100 μm × 100 μm area using the tapping mode of a Veeco Dimension 3100 atomic force microscope (AFM). *In situ* wafer curvature measurements were performed using a 2-D k-space multibeam optical stress sensor (MOS) with the axes of measurement set along [1 1 0] and $[\bar{1}\,1\,0]$.

Light *J–V* curves were measured using an XT-10 1-sun continuous solar simulator. Quantum efficiency and specular reflectance measurements were performed in a custom-built instrument. The bandgap of the solar cells was determined from the external quantum efficiency.

III. MEASUREMENT AND ANALYSIS OF GaInP BUFFER

Composition nonuniformities, roughness, and other defects must be minimized in order to maximize dislocation glide and lower the residual TDD of CGBs [10]. Each material system has unique structural characteristics and growth issues that affect dislocation behavior. GaInP displays $CuPt_B$ atomic ordering [18] and phase separation [19], both of which can greatly influence dislocation glide [11], [13]. Here, we perform an in-depth measurement of a GaInP CGB varying in composition from $Ga_{0.5}In_{0.5}P$ to InP in order to identify any material characteristics which limit glide or produce excess dislocations. Dislocation properties are studied by measuring the TDD and the strain relaxation throughout growth, and material structural properties are measured using surface measurements and bulk microstructure analysis.

Fig. 2 shows a CL map of the GaInP CGB, used to analyze the TDD in the final 1.0-μm-thick InP layer. This CGB shows a TDD of 2.2×10^7 cm^{-2}, which is an order of magnitude higher than CGBs ending in $Ga_{0.2}In_{0.8}P$ [15] used to access 1.0-eV GaInAs. This magnitude of TDD is expected to significantly lower the performance of the solar cell devices [20].

In situ wafer curvature is used to monitor the stress–thickness throughout the growth (see Fig. 3) and calculate the residual strain of the final layer at growth temperature. The curvature throughout growth is related to the stress–thickness product using the Stoney formula [21], and the strain of the InP layer is

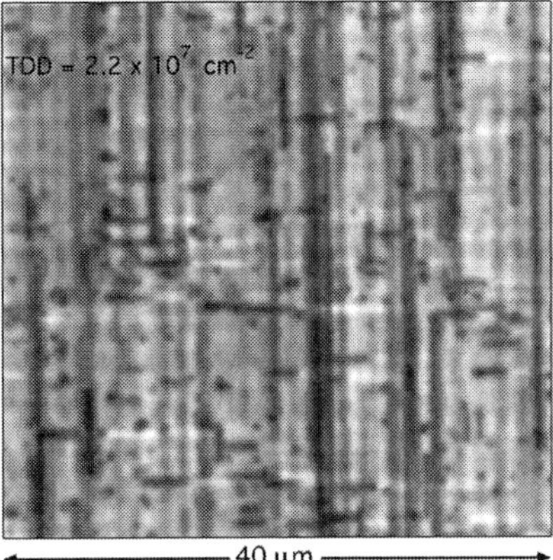

Fig. 2. CL map of the graded-buffer test structure: A GaInP CGB ending in InP (MK134). Both misfit dislocations (dark lines) and threading dislocations (dark spots) are visible.

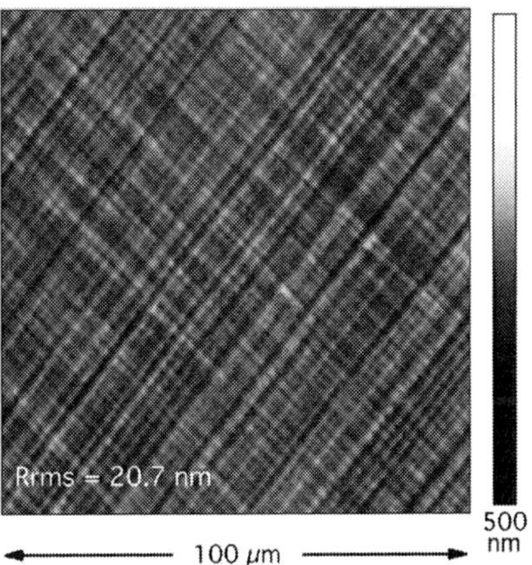

Fig. 4. Large area, i.e., $100\ \mu m \times 100\ \mu m$, AFM of the GaInP CGB test structure ending with InP, rotated 45° with respect to Fig. 2. The typical crosshatched surface of lattice-mismatch epitaxy results in an RMS roughness of 20.7 nm.

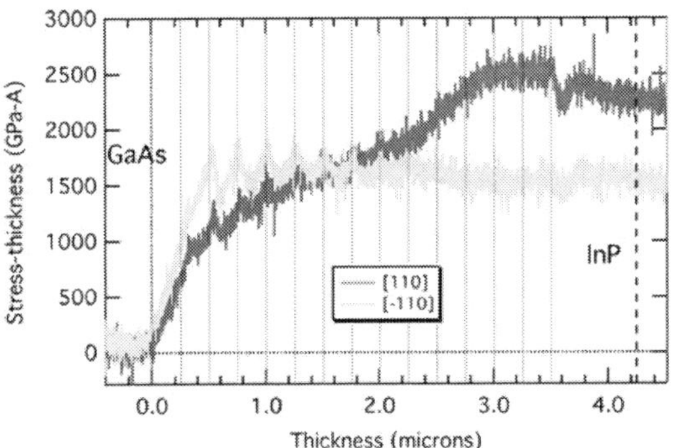

Fig. 3. Stress–thickness product throughout the growth of the GaInP CGB. Solid vertical lines delineate each layer of the buffer. The final 0.25 μm of the InP layer, demarcated by the dashed line, is analyzed for strain.

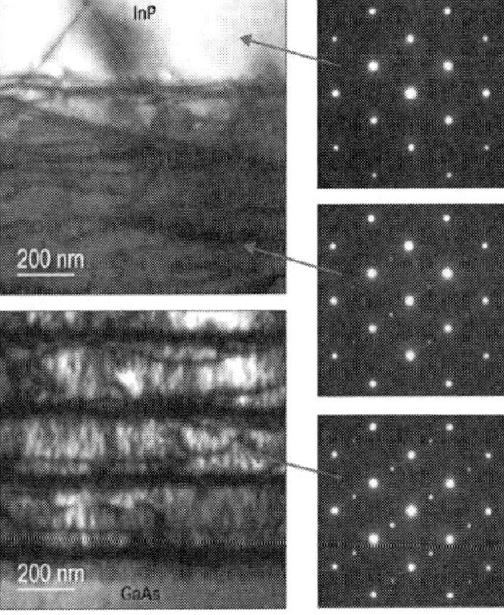

Fig. 5. (Left) Dark field 220 TEM images from the $[1\ 1\ 1]$ cross-section and (Right) TED images from the $[1\ 1\ 0]$ cross section. Beginning, $Ga_{0.5}In_{0.5}P$, (bottom), and end, InP, (top) of the CGB structure. Composition nonuniformities and atomic ordering are observed near the beginning of the CGB but not at the end.

calculated from the slope of the stress–thickness during the final 0.25 μm of growth [22]. The measured strain of the InP layer, averaged between $[1\ 1\ 0]$ and $[\bar{1}\ 1\ 0]$ directions, is 0.01% at growth temperature (675 °C), nominally completely relaxed. This is observed in Fig. 3 by noting the very low slope during the growth of the final 0.25 μm of growth. The XRD RSM analysis of the last layer determines a strain of –0.15% at the room temperature, which translates to –0.001% at growth temperature [23] due to the difference in thermal expansion coefficients between the substrate and epilayer. The agreement between XRD and MOS measurements indicates no large relaxation events occurred during cooldown from growth temperature. The lack of residual strain in the InP layer relieves the necessity of overshooting the target lattice constant for strain-free device growth [22].

The surface roughness is quantified *ex situ* using AFM (see Fig. 4). The large-area RMS roughness related to the typical crosshatch roughening of lattice-mismatched growth is 20.7 nm over a 0.01-mm² area, which is indeed much higher than the roughness of graded buffers ending with $Ga_{0.2}In_{0.8}P$ [15]. Surface roughness is undesirable in CGBs. The topology can both aid dislocation nucleation [24] and inhibit dislocation glide by reducing the glide channel [25]. Some lattice-mismatched devices also require low roughness for sharp material interfaces. Because limiting the roughness is beneficial for dislocation glide and lattice-mismatched devices, it must be characterized and considered when determining the quality of the CGB.

TEM is used to investigate material properties such as compositional nonuniformities, ordering, and other growth defects. Fig. 5 shows the 220 dark-field image near the start ($Ga_{0.5}In_{0.5}P$) and end (InP) of the GaInP graded buffer. Nanoscale strain contrast, due to composition nonuniformities from surface-driven phase separation [26], is observed near the beginning of the buffer but not at the end. Thus, for the same growth conditions, the composition affects the magnitude of the composition variation, similar to observations in GaInAsP [27]. Other work

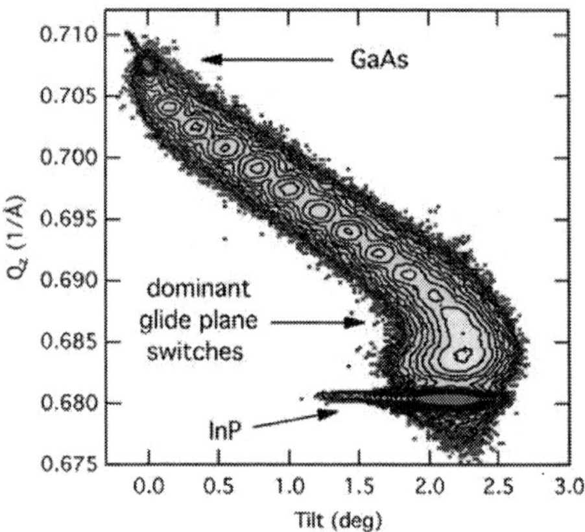

Fig. 6. XRD RSM of (0 0 4) from the CGB structure. The symmetric RSM shows the progression of tilt throughout the buffer.

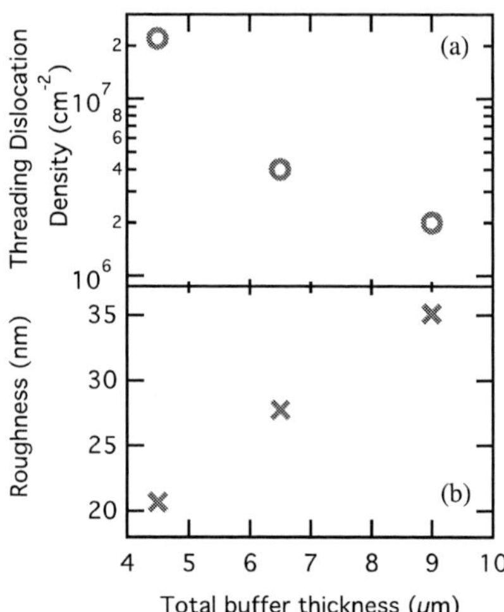

Fig. 7. (a) Residual TDD and (b) RMS roughness of CGBs with varying total thickness.

has observed phase separation in GaInP [28], [29] and shown a large impact on the residual TDD. In this case, the nanoscale composition variation is likely not the dominant reason for the increase in TDD between $Ga_{0.2}In_{0.8}P$ and InP. Its influence on dislocation glide is expected to decrease throughout the buffer, and similar buffers graded to $Ga_{0.2}In_{0.8}P$ have produced low-TDD material and high-quality solar cells [15]. Transmission electron diffraction (TED) patterns (see Fig. 5) from the [1 1 0] cross section show single-domain $CuPt_B$ ordering. The ordering parameter also decreases throughout the buffer toward InP, which can be observed by noting a decrease in intensity of the $1/2\,(\bar{1}\,1\,1)$ diffraction spots. The influence of ordering on dislocations is discussed below.

Fig. 6 shows the XRD RSM of the (0 0 4) reflection taken from (1 1 0) incidence, which shows a steady increase in tilt, or epilayer rotation around [1 1 0], throughout the graded buffer. The distribution of dislocation glide along either $(\bar{1}\,1\,1)$ or $(1\bar{1}1)$ (both of these glide planes have [1 1 0] dislocation lines and are called β dislocations in this compressive zincblende material) can be determined from the [1 1 0] rotation [11], [30], [31]. Nearly 100% of β dislocation glide is along $(1\bar{1}1)$ until the end of the buffer, where the β glide transitions to $(\bar{1}\,1\,1)$. Roughly 60% of β glide is along $(\bar{1}\,1\,1)$ near the end of the buffer. A change in the distribution of dislocation glide along either glide plane indicates a change in the energetics of dislocation glide. In this case, our earlier work showed that the change in the glide plane of β dislocations is related to the relationship between $CuPt_B$ ordering in III–V materials and the dislocation glide force. Near the beginning of the CGB, almost all β dislocations glide on $(1\bar{1}1)$ in GaInP with $(\bar{1}\,1\,1)$ ordering because the glide on this plane produces an antiphase boundary in the ordering pattern, which reduces the internal stress [11], [12]. Near the end of the CGB, the ordering parameter becomes smaller (shown in Fig. 5) because the GaInP becomes very In-rich, and relaxation on the $(\bar{1}\,1\,1)$ glide plane becomes more favorable due to the substrate miscut. Unfortunately, new dislocations form during this transition to accommodate glide on $(\bar{1}\,1\,1)$ [11].

However, knowledge of the formation mechanism allows targeted approaches to CGB improvement.

IV. Reduction of Dislocation Density

In-depth characterization of the GaInP CGB reveals several buffer imperfections: roughness, composition variations, and a glide plane transition that forms new dislocations. The formation of new dislocations occurs near the end of the buffer, around $Ga_{0.1}In_{0.9}P$, and has a large impact on the residual TDD in the InP layer [11]. The measured TDD, 2.2×10^7 cm^{-2}, is expected to have a large negative impact on the 0.7-eV GaInAs solar cell performance. For this reason, the formation of dislocations associated with the transition between glide planes merits particular attention and is the focus of this section.

Thickening the region of the buffer surrounding $Ga_{0.1}In_{0.9}P$ is investigated as a method of reducing the dislocation formation associated with the glide plane transition. Adding thickness is known to increase annihilation of existing dislocations [32] and reduce the required minimum TDD for strain relaxation of ideal CGBs [33], potentially reducing the nucleation of new dislocations on $(\bar{1}11)$. The thickness is added by reducing the misfit grade rate between $Ga_{0.2}In_{0.8}P$ and InP. Fig. 7 shows the residual TDD and RMS roughness of GaInP CGBs from GaInP to InP with varying total thickness. The initial misfit grade rate is 1%/μm and is changed to 0.5 and 0.25%/μm in the region surrounding the glide plane transition by adding additional low-misfit steps to the structure, resulting in total thicknesses of 4.5, 6.5, and 9 μm, respectively. The surface roughness from the crosshatch increases with buffer thickness. However, the additional material reduces the TDD by an order of magnitude to 2×10^6 cm^{-2}, which is an acceptable TDD for solar cell devices.

V. Solar Cell Results

Inverted metamorphic $Ga_{0.47}In_{0.53}As$ solar cells are grown on the GaInP CGB with 6.5-μm total thickness, described

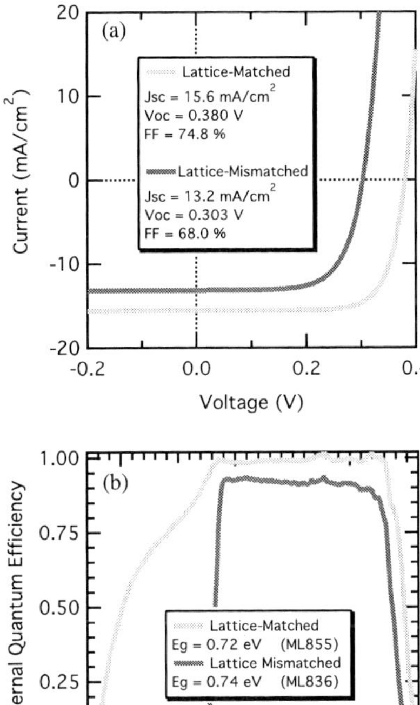

Fig. 8. (a) J–V and (b) IQE comparison between lattice-mismatched and lattice-matched GaInAs solar cells. J_{sc} for the J–V measurement is determined by integration of the product of the IQE and the G173 AM1.5 direct spectrum between the bandedge and 1.06 eV.

previously. This buffer was chosen as a compromise between the growth time, material usage, roughness, and TDD. The lattice-matching of the solar cell to the CGB was verified using *in situ* wafer curvature measurements. The active layers of the cell must be nearly strain free for best performance [22]. This ensures no additional dislocation formation or glide in the active region of the device. Inverted *lattice-matched* $Ga_{0.47}In_{0.53}As$ solar cells are also grown on InP substrates. Comparing lattice-mismatched and lattice-matched cells of the same bandgap provides a method to determine the loss associated with the lattice-mismatch, from differences in the TDD and other mismatch-related differences such as interface and bulk material quality. Fig. 8 shows the internal quantum efficiency (IQE) and J–V characteristics of both cells. The IQE of the lattice-mismatched cell is over 90% in the wavelength region of importance for the bottom junction of a 4-J IMM device. The expected J_{sc} of these devices in a multijunction cell is determined by integrating the product of the IQE and the G173 AM1.5 direct spectrum between the bandedge and 1.06 eV, which is the modeled optimal bandgap for the junction above this subcell in an IMM. We note that this technique overestimates J_{sc} by assuming no loss from the AR coating and because the IQE is overestimated at the bandedge from errors in the reflectivity measurement of inverted devices. Using this technique, the estimated J_{sc} of the lattice-mismatched device is 13.2 mA/cm^2, which is similar to the 1-sun J_{sc} of various 3-J

IMM designs [34]. The V_{oc} of the lattice-mismatched device is >0.3 V but is 80 mV less than the lattice-matched device. The bandgap of the lattice-mismatched cell is 20 meV higher, potentially due to small differences in composition and atomic ordering [35]. W_{oc} ($=E_g/q - V_{\text{oc}}$) of the lattice-mismatched solar cell, which takes into account the difference in the bandgap between the devices, is 0.44 V, 100 mV higher than the lattice-matched cell. The fill factor of the lattice-mismatched device is 68%, which is 7% lower than the lattice-matched cell.

These lattice-mismatched devices perform significantly better than previous results [8]. Compared with lattice-matched devices, the V_{oc} loss is significant. However, because the device has a high IQE and current, this structure has the potential to significantly increase the performance of IMM solar cells. A straightforward addition of 0.3 V to existing three-junction IMM devices would produce over 9% relative efficiency increase at under 1-sun conditions and a greater relative increase under concentrated light. Achieving this type of gain is only possible if the current and fill factor do not limit the other multijunction subcells, which depends on the bandgap combination and design of the 4-J IMM. Higher current, if needed, is possible by lowering the bandgap of this GaInAs subcell, either by increasing the atomic ordering of the GaInAs or extending the CGB to a larger lattice constant.

VI. Conclusion

GaInP CGBs with a total misfit of 3.8% are analyzed and improved, and lattice-mismatched 0.7-eV GaInAs solar cells are demonstrated. Roughness, bulk composition nonuniformities, and a residual TDD of 2.2×10^7 cm^{-2} are observed in standard buffers. Excess dislocations are generated near the end of the buffer due to a change in the distribution of dislocations that has been related to atomic ordering. The buffer structure is improved by adding thickness to the region of the buffer where these new dislocations are formed, which lowers the TDD by an order of magnitude. Lattice-mismatched solar cells are grown on GaInP CGB templates with low TDD, and show an IQE over 90% in the wavelength range of interest for the bottom junction of a 4-J IMM. The estimated current, 13.2 mA/cm^2 under a 1.06-eV filter, is sufficient for some potential IMM designs. The V_{oc} is 0.303 V and the fill factor is 68.0% when the J_{sc} is set to 13.2 mA/cm^2. While lattice-matched GaInP/InP solar cells perform significantly better, this lattice-mismatched device has the potential to appreciably increase the efficiency of metamorphic multijunction designs.

Acknowledgment

The authors would like to thank W. Olavarria, M. Young, B. To, and M. Steiner for growth, processing, and measurement contributions.

References

[1] R. M. France, J. F. Geisz, M. A. Steiner, D. J. Friedman, J. S. Ward, J. M. Olson, W. Olavarria, M. Young, and A. Duda, "Pushing inverted metamorphic multijunction solar cells towards higher efficiency at

realistic operating conditions," *IEEE J. Photovoltaic*, vol. 3, no. 2, pp. 893–898, Apr. 2013.

[2] J. F Geisz, D. J. Friedman, J. S. Ward, A. Duda, W. J. Olavarria, T. E. Moriarty, J. T. Kiehl, M. J. Romero, A. G. Norman, and K. M. Jones, "40.8% efficient inverted triple-junction solar cell with two independently metamorphic junctions," *Appl. Phys. Lett.*, vol. 93, pp. 123505-1–123505-3, 2008.

[3] W. Guter, J. Schöne, S. P. Philipps, M. Steiner, G. Siefer, A. Wekkeli, E. Welser, E. Oliva, A. W. Bett, and F. Dimroth, "Current-matched triple-junction solar cell reaching 41.1% conversion efficiency under concentrated sunlight," *Appl. Phys. Lett.*, vol. 94, pp. 223504-1–223504-3, 2009.

[4] R. R. King, D. Bhusari, A. Boca, D. Larrabee, X.-Q. Liu, W. Hong, C. M. Fetzer, D. C. Law, and N. H. Karam, "Band gap-voltage offset and energy production in next-generation multijunction solar cells," *Progress Photovoltaics*, vol. 19, pp. 797–812, 2011.

[5] V. Sabnis, H. Yuen, and M. Wiemer, "High-efficiency multijunction solar cells employing dilute nitrides," in *Proc. 8th Int. Conf. Concentrating Photovoltaic Syst.*, Toledo, Spain, 2012, pp. 14–19.

[6] C. Valdivia, S. Chow, S. Fafard, O. Theriault, M. Yandt, J. Wheeldon, A. J. Springthorpe, B. Rioux, D. McMeekin, D. Masson, B. Riel, V. Aimez, R. Ares, J. Cook, T. Hall, F. Shepherd, and K. Hinzer, "Measurement of high efficiency 1 cm^2 AlGaInP/InGaAs/Ge solar cells with embedded InAs quantum dots at up to 1000 suns concentration," in *Proc. Photovoltaic Spec. Conf.*, Honolulu, HI, USA, 2010, pp. 1253–1258.

[7] J. F. Geisz, S. R. Kurtz, M. W. Wanlass, J. S. Ward, A. Duda, D. J. Friedman, J. M. Olson, W. E. McMahon, T. Moriarty, and J. Kiehl, "High-efficiency GaInP/GaAs/InGaAs triple-junction solar cells grown inverted with a metamorphic bottom junction," *Appl. Phys. Lett.*, vol. 91, pp. 023502-1–023502-3, 2007.

[8] D. J. Friedman, J. F. Geisz, A. G. Norman, M. W. Wanlass, and S. R. Kurtz, "0.7-eV GaInAs Junction for a GaInP/GaAs/GaInAs (1 eV)/GaInAs(0.7 eV) four-junction solar cell," in *Proc. 4th World Conf. Photovoltaic Energy Convers.*, Waikoloa, HI, USA, 2006, pp. 598–602.

[9] M. Stan, D. Aiken, B. Cho, A. Cornfeld, V. Ley, P. Patel, P. Sharps, and T. Varghese, "High-efficiency quadruple junction solar cells using OMVPE with inverted metamorphic device structures," *J. Cryst. Growth*, vol. 312, pp. 1370–1374, 2010.

[10] E. A. Fitzgerald, S. B. Samavedam, Y. H. Xie, and L. M. Giovane, "Influence of strain on semiconductor thin film epitaxy," *J. Vac. Sci. Technol. A*, vol. 15, pp. 1048–1056, 1997.

[11] R. M. France, W. E. McMahon, A. G. Norman, J. F. Geisz, and M. J. Romero, "Control of misfit dislocation glide plane distribution during strain relaxation of CuPt-ordered GaInAs and GaInP," *J. Appl. Phys.*, vol. 112, pp. 023520-1–023520-6, 2012.

[12] W. E. McMahon, J. Kang, R. M. France, A. G. Norman, D. J. Friedman, and S. H. Wei, "Ordering-enhanced dislocation glide in III-V alloys," submitted for publication.

[13] N. J. Quitoriano and E. A. Fitzgerald, "Relaxed, high-quality InP on GaAs by using InGaAs and InGaP graded buffers to avoid phase separation," *J. Appl. Phys.*, vol. 102, pp. 033511-1–033511-17, 2007.

[14] K. E. Lee and E. A. Fitzgerald, "High-quality metamorphic compositionally graded InGaAs buffers," *J. Cryst. Growth*, vol. 312, pp. 250–257, 2010.

[15] R. M. France, J. F. Geisz, M. A. Steiner, B. To, M. J. Romero, W. J. Olavarria, and R. R. King, "Reduction of crosshatch roughness and threading dislocation density in metamorphic GaInP buffers and GaInAs solar cells," *J. Appl. Phys.*, vol. 111, pp. 103528-1–103528-7, 2012.

[16] P. Patel, D. Aiken, A. Boca, B. Cho, D. Chumney, M. B. Clevenger, A. Cornfeld, N. Fatemi, Y. Lin, J. McCarty, F. Newman, P. Sharps, J. Spann, M. Stan, J. Steinfeldt, C. Strautin, and T. Varghese, "Experimental results from performance improvement and radiation hardening of inverted metamorphic solar cells," *IEEE J. Photovoltaic*, vol. 2, no. 3, pp. 377–381, Jul. 2012.

[17] A. B. Cornfeld, D. Aiken, B. Cho, A. V. Ley, P. Sharps, M. Stan, and T. Varghese, "Development of a four sub-cell inverted metamorphic multijunction (IMM) highly efficient AM0 solar cell," in *Proc. Photovoltaic Spec. Conf.*, Honolulu, HI, USA, 2010, pp. 105–109.

[18] A. Gomyo, T. Suzuki, and S. Iijima, "Observation of strong ordering in Ga$_x$In$_{1-x}$P alloy semiconductors," *Phys. Rev. Lett.*, vol. 60, pp. 2645–2648, 1988.

[19] D. M. Follstaedt, R. P. Schneider, and E. D. Jones, "Microstructures of (In,Ga)P alloys grown on GaAs by metalorganic vapor-phase epitaxy," *J. Appl. Phys.*, vol. 77, pp. 3077–3087, 1995.

[20] C. L. Andre, D. M. Wilt, A. J. Pitera, M. L. Lee, E. A. Fitzgerald, and S. A. Ringel, "Impact of dislocation densities on n+/p and p+/n junction GaAs diodes and solar cells on SiGe virtual substrates," *J. Appl. Phys.*, vol. 98, pp. 014502-1–014502-5, 2005.

[21] G. G. Stoney, "The tension of metallic films deposited by electrolysis," in *Proc. R. Soc. Lond. Ser. A*, 1909, vol. 82, pp. 172–175.

[22] J. F. Geisz, A. X. Levandor, A. G. Norman, K. M. Jones, and M. J. Romero, "In-situ stress measurement for MOVPE growth of high efficiency lattice-mismatched solar cells," *J. Cryst. Growth*, vol. 310, pp. 2339–2344, 2008.

[23] T. Roesener, V. Klinger, C. Weuffen, D. Lackner, and F. Dimroth, "Determination of heteroepitaxial layer relaxation at growth temperature from room temperature X-ray reciprocal space maps," *J. Cryst. Growth*, vol. 368, pp. 21–28, 2013.

[24] A. G. Cullis, A. J. Pidduck, and M. T. Emeny, "Misfit dislocation sources at surface ripple troughs in continuous heteroepitaxial layers," *Phys. Rev. Lett.*, vol. 75, pp. 2368–2371, 1995.

[25] S. B. Samavedam and E. A. Fitzgerald, "Novel dislocation structure and surface morphology effects in relaxed Ge/Si-Ge(graded)/Si structures," *J. Appl. Phys.*, vol. 81, pp. 3108–3116, 1997.

[26] S. Mahajan, "Two-dimensional phase separation and surface-reconstruction driven atomic ordering in mixed III-V layers," *Mater. Sci. Eng. B*, vol. 30, pp. 187–196, 1995.

[27] A. G. Norman and G. R. Booker, "Transmission electron microscope and transmission electron diffraction observations of alloy clustering in liquid-phase epitaxial (001) GaInAsP layers," *J. Appl. Phys.*, vol. 57, pp. 4715–4720, 1985.

[28] A. Y. Kim, W. S. McCullough, and E. A. Fitzgerald, "Evolution of microstructure and dislocation dynamics in In$_x$Ga$_{1-x}$P graded buffers grown on GaP by metalorganic vapor phase epitaxy: Engineering device-quality substrate materials," *J. Vac. Sci. Technol. B*, vol. 17, pp. 1485–1501, 1999.

[29] L. M. McGill, E. A. Fitzgerald, A. Y. Kim, J. W. Huang, S. S. Yi, P. N. Grillot, and S. A. Stockman, "Microstructural defects in metalorganic vapor phase epitaxy of relaxed, graded InGaP: Branch defect origins and engineering," *J. Vac. Sci. Technol. B*, vol. 22, pp. 1899–2011, 2004.

[30] P. M. Mooney, F. K. LeGoues, J. Tersoff, and J. O. Chu, "Nucleation of dislocations in SiGe layers grown on (001)Si," *J. Appl. Phys.*, vol. 75, pp. 3968–3977, 1993.

[31] J. E. Ayers, S. K. Ghandhi, and L. J. Schowalter, "Crystallographic tilting of heteroepitaxial layers," *J. Cryst. Growth*, vol. 113, pp. 430–440, 1991.

[32] J. S. Speck, M. A. Brewer, G. Beltz, A. E. Romanov, and W. Pompe, "Scaling laws for the reduction of threading dislocation densities in homogeneous buffer layers," *J. Appl. Phys.*, vol. 80, pp. 3808–3816, 1996.

[33] E. A. Fitzgerald, A. Y. Kim, M. T. Currie, T. A. Langdo, G. Taraschi, and M. T. Bulsara, "Dislocation dynamics in relaxed graded composition semiconductors," *Mater. Sci. Eng. B*, vol. 67, pp. 53–61, 1999.

[34] J. F. Geisz, A. Duda, R. M. France, D. J. Friedman, I. Garcia, W. J. Olavarria, J. M. Olson, M. A. Steiner, J. S. Ward, and M. Young, "Optimization of 3-junction inverted metamorphic solar cells for high-temperature and high-concentration operation," in *Proc. 8th Int. Conf. Concentrating Photovoltaic Syst.*, Toledo, Spain, 2012, pp. 44–48.

[35] D. J. Arent, M. Bode, K. A. Bertness, S. R. Kurtz, and J. M. Olson, "Band-gap narrowing in ordered Ga$_{0.47}$In$_{0.53}$As," *Appl. Phys. Lett.*, vol. 62, pp. 1806–1808, 1993.

Authors' photographs and biographies not available at the time of publication.

Impact of Impurities From Crucible and Coating on mc-Silicon Quality—the Example of Iron and Cobalt

Martin C. Schubert, Jonas Schön, Florian Schindler, Wolfram Kwapil, Alireza Abdollahinia, Bernhard Michl, Stephan Riepe, Claudia Schmid, Mark Schumann, Sylke Meyer, and Wilhelm Warta

Abstract—The aim of this paper is to analyze the limiting role of crucible and coating impurities on material quality of multicrystalline silicon. Both solid body diffusion and diffusion into the silicon melt are considered in this study. Two ingots of size G1 have been analyzed. One of them was crystallized in a standard crucible, whereas the other was crystallized in a quartz crucible of very high purity. Focus is put on iron and cobalt as examples of typical impurity species. Iron was found in large concentrations in standard crucibles, and cobalt was proven to be a suitable marker impurity that is mainly found in the coating. Inductively coupled plasma mass spectroscopy data are exploited for the determination of impurity concentrations in crucible, coating, and within the crystal. With higher sensitivity for low concentration, PL imaging is applied for carrier lifetime and interstitial iron concentration measurements. The different findings are compared with modeling results of iron and cobalt in-diffusion by *Sentaurus Process*. The analysis of silicon wafers before and after gettering steps enable a quantification of impurity-limiting cell efficiency potential. Conclusions about the role of impurities from coated crucibles in large-scale crystallization are deduced.

Index Terms—Crucible, iron, silicon, simulation, vertical gradient freeze (VGF).

I. Introduction

THE electrical quality of directionally solidified block silicon has improved significantly in the recent past yielding an impressive increase of mc-Si cell efficiency potential (see, e.g., [1]). Novel crystallization processes have been developed that either reduce dislocation density significantly [2] or reduce or completely suppress the generation of grain boundaries [3].

Manuscript received June 14, 2013; revised July 31, 2013; accepted July 31, 2013. Date of publication September 5, 2013; date of current version September 18, 2013. This work has been supported by the German Ministry for the Environment, Nature Conservation and Nuclear Safety (BMU) under the frame of the project SolarWinS (0325270G).

M. C. Schubert, J. Schön, B. Michl, S. Riepe, C. Schmid, M. Schumann, and W. Warta are with the Fraunhofer Institute for Solar Energy Systems, Freiburg, Germany (e-mail: martin.schubert@ise.fraunhofer.de; jonas.schoen@ise.fraunhofer.de; bernhard.michl@ise.fraunhofer.de; stephan.riepe@ise.fraunhofer.de; claudia.schmid@ise.fraunhofer.de; mark.schumann@ise.fraunhofer.de; wilhelm.warta@ise.fraunhofer.de).

F. Schindler, A. Abdollahinia, and W. Kwapil are with the Fraunhofer Institute for Solar Energy Systems, Freiburg, Germany, and also with the Freiburg Materials Research Center FMF, Freiburg, Germany (e-mail: florian.schindler@ise.fraunhofer.de; alireza.abdollahinia@ise.fraunhofer.de; wolfram.kwapil@ise.fraunhofer.de).

S. Meyer is with the Fraunhofer Center for Silicon Photovoltaics, Halle, Germany (e-mail: sylke.meyer@csp.fraunhofer.de).

Color versions of one or more of the figures in this paper are available online at http://ieeexplore.ieee.org.

Digital Object Identifier 10.1109/JPHOTOV.2013.2279116

In addition to optimizing the crystal quality, the efficiency limitation due to impurities remains to be considered.

A dominant source of impurities was identified to be the coated crucible [4]–[6]. Both the silicon oxide crucible and the silicon nitride coating are sources of contamination. The use of cleaner crucible and coating materials are shown to improve carrier lifetime and, as a consequence, cell efficiency. Iron in-diffusion from the crucible wall that results in a contamination with iron point defects of the edge zone was identified as limiting the carrier lifetime [7]. It was suspected that the crystallization time besides the impurity concentration of crucible and coating influences the contamination of the silicon [4]. However, in these studies, the role of crucible and coating in the contamination of the silicon melt and crystal was not further quantified.

Based on these results, we aim for a quantitative analysis of impurity contamination in this paper by combining impurity analysis with inductively coupled remote plasma mass spectroscopy (ICP-MS) and PL-Imaging of carrier lifetime and iron point defects with modeling of impurity diffusion in the molten and solidified silicon.

For this purpose, we analyzed silicon crystals that were crystallized with the same recipe except for a variation of the crucible material where the standard fused silica type and very pure quartz type crucibles were used. The pure feedstock was used for the experiments ([Fe] approximately 10^{13} cm^{-3}). Similar processing conditions are a prerequisite for comparable crystal quality that is necessary to quantify the role of impurities on the electrical material quality of the produced vertical gradient freeze silicon for a given crystal structure.

In addition to a direct contamination of the feedstock or added dopants, impurities enter the silicon melt via solid–liquid diffusion and Si_3N_4 coating erosion or after solidification at high temperatures via solid state in-diffusion. Impurity contributions into the melt affect the whole ingot with increasing impact toward its top, whereas solid body in-diffusion is responsible for the edge zone of poor material quality in the vicinity of the crucible walls. Both effects are relevant for achievable cell efficiency potential and will be treated in the following.

The quantitative tracing of impurities is performed by ICP-MS [8] and iron imaging measurements [9], [10]. The latter is restricted to the analysis of silicon albeit with much higher sensitivity, whereas the first method was also applied to crucible and coating materials.

Iron and cobalt have been identified as ideal representative impurity species for five reasons: 1) Iron is known to be one of the most crucial impurities in p-type silicon; 2) iron was found in large quantities within the industrial standard ceramic

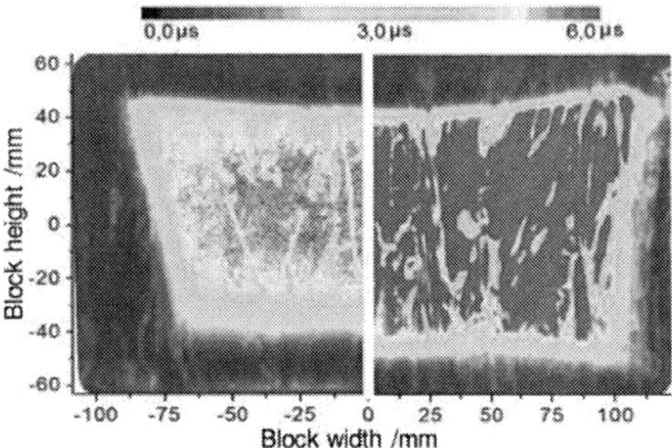

Fig. 1. μW-PCD effective carrier lifetime measurement of silicon ingots that were crystallized in a (left) standard and (right) high purity crucible.

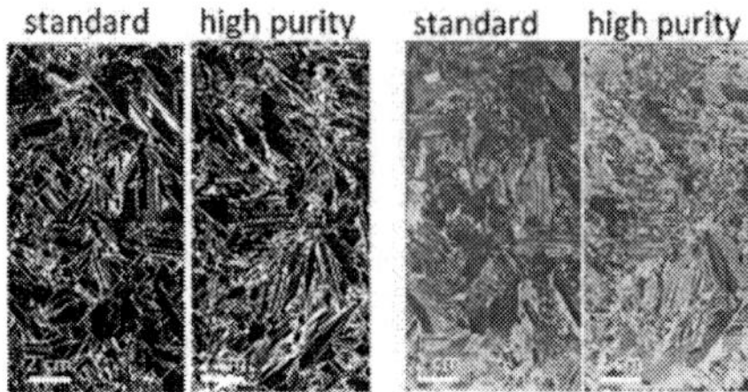

Fig. 2. (Left) Grain boundary image and (right) structural defect density image for midheight wafers from standard and high purity crystallization. Fifty percent of the wafer area (crucible wall was adjacent to left edge of images) under test is shown for both wafers.

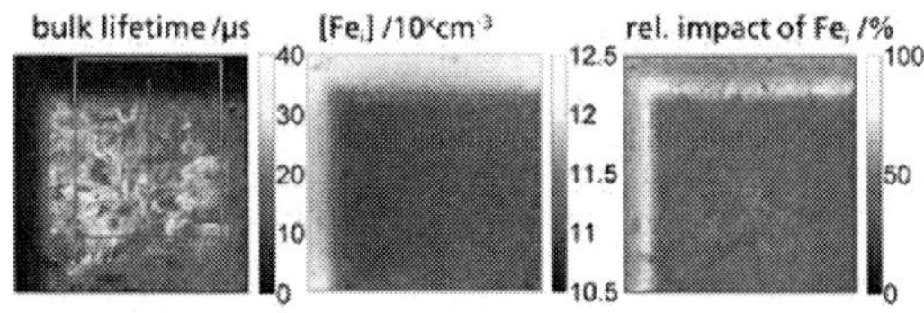

Fig. 3. Carrier lifetime, interstitial iron concentration, and relative limitation of carrier lifetime by iron point defects (see [10] for details), measured with photoluminescence imaging (from left to right, 156 mm $\times$ 156 mm). The top and left parts of the wafer are adjacent to the crucible walls. The rectangle in the left image represents the area where the linescans of Fig. 4 were taken (averaged over the horizontal axis).

crucible material; 3) iron in its interstitial form is quantitatively accessible with highest sensitivity by carrier lifetime images (down to concentrations of approximately 10^{10} cm^{-3}); 4) cobalt was mainly found in the coating as a suitable trace element; and 5) the sensitivity limit of ICP-MS for cobalt is much lower compared with iron. The impact of the coating on contamination can, therefore, be nicely exemplified and separated from the influence of the crucible.

The experimental findings are corroborated by numerical simulations quantifying the in-diffusion in both silicon melt and solidified crystal. These simulations take into account the heterogeneous interaction of metal impurities with crystal defects.

II. Experimental Results

A. Details on Crystallization Experiments

Two different G1 silicon ingots were prepared and investigated. The crystallization was performed with an initial silicon feedstock weight of approximately 14 kg and a net crystallization time of approximately 15 h. Two different crucible types were used: 1) a standard industrial type fused silica crucible and 2) a high purity quartz crucible. Both crucibles were coated with silicon nitride (Si_3N_4). Care was taken to use the same crystallization conditions including comparable temperature profiles. Because of the higher heat conductivity of the high purity crucible, the crystallization time was slightly shorter. The ingots were cut into a complex scheme in order to extract small samples for ICP-MS measurements, as well as asymmetrically cut wafers. Those wafers show the influence of the contaminated edge regions, as well as the quality of the center area. Sister wafers were prepared to assess the material quality after different cell processing steps, as well as after industrial cell processing. Our analysis in this paper is restricted to midheight of the ingot from where both the wafers and the ICP-MS samples had been taken.

In Fig. 1, measurements of the effective carrier lifetime on ingot level with Microwave Photoconductance Decay (μW-PCD) [11] are shown for both standard crucible and high-purity crucible. From these measurements, the different qualitative influence of the crucible is apparent. The zone of poor lifetime in the vicinity of the crucible bottom and walls is significantly

smaller, and the center part is of slightly higher lifetime when using the high purity crucible. In contrast with this observation, the upper area of poor material quality is governed by back-diffusion of segregated and precipitated metal impurities from the topmost part of the ingot and, in good approximation, independent of the crucible.

In order to test the crystal quality of both experiments, grain size distribution and dislocation density were measured for both materials as a function of block height. The grain boundary image was determined by visual inspection with an Intego Gemini tool [12] and the dislocation density by the structural defect density (SDD) method [13].

In Fig. 2, the results from midheight wafers of standard and high purity crystallization that were adjacent to the wafers under test in this paper are compared. Slightly higher grain sizes (area-weighted mean grain size approximately 170 mm^2) are found for the standard crystallization compared with the high purity crystallization (100 mm^2). The dislocation density can qualitatively be compared from the SDD image, where the red pixels represent areas of higher dislocation density.

The variation of grain sizes and dislocation density in both wafers is significantly larger than the difference between both wafers. We, therefore, do not expect a large effect of the different crystal structure on the diffusion properties of impurities.

B. Carrier Lifetime and Interstitial Iron Concentration

Wafers, asymmetrically cut from 50% block height, were analyzed for bulk carrier lifetime and interstitial iron concentration in the as-grown state as well as after standard phosphorus diffusion. Fig. 3 shows the carrier lifetime and iron imaging results of

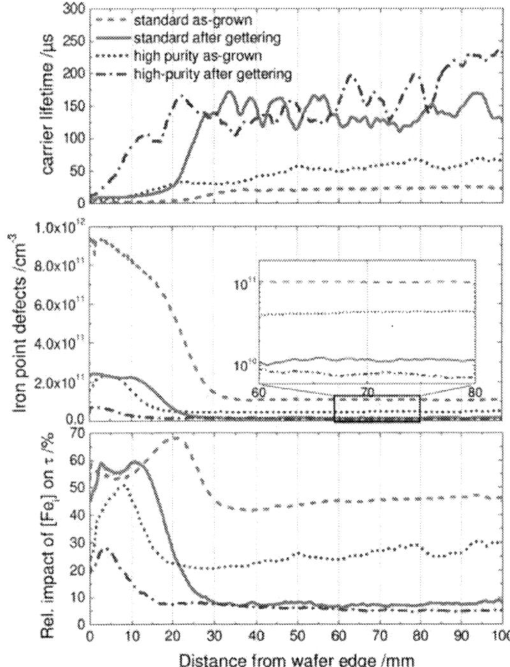

Fig. 4. Linescans for bulk carrier lifetime, iron point defect concentration, and relative impact of iron point defects on carrier lifetime (from top to bottom). As-grown and gettered wafers crystallized with the standard crucible are compared with those from the high purity crucible. The linescans were calculated from edge of the wafers toward the center (see Fig. 3). Note that the wafer edge's distance to the crucible wall is approximately 1–1.5 cm.

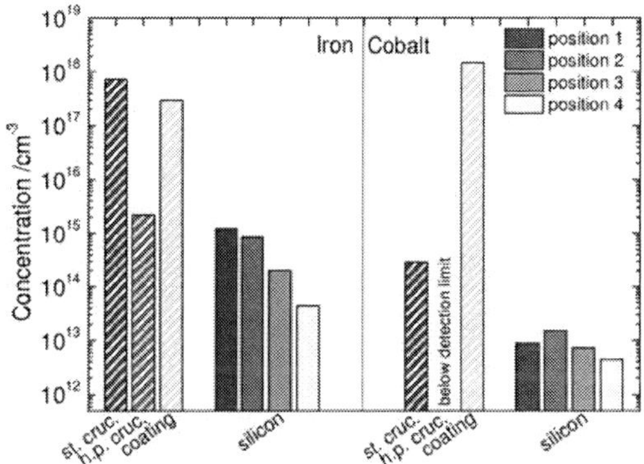

Fig. 5. Iron and cobalt impurity measurements with ICP-MS of standard crucible, high purity crucible, and crucible coating powder (shaded bars) and for different positions horizontally from the edge toward the inner part of the crystal (at 50% block height).

an as-grown wafer (standard crucible) that was passivated with $Al_2 O_3$ and analyzed with QSSPL calibrated photoluminescence imaging [14], [15]. The images show the material quality degrading effect of the crucible or coating on the left and upper parts of the wafer.

Fig. 4 depicts linescans of carrier lifetime, interstitial iron concentration, and relative limitation of carrier lifetime by iron point defects from the wafer edge close to the crucible wall to the central part of the ingot. The interstitial iron concentration is strongly increased near the crucible wall and decreases within a few centimeters in all cases.

As expected, gettering during phosphorus diffusion reduces the interstitial iron concentration. From the relative impact of interstitial iron on the total recombination rate it is apparent that the edge region of the ingot crystallized in the standard crucible is mainly limited by interstitial iron, whereas this type of defect has less influence on the center part. In the case of the high purity quartz crucible, the measured iron concentrations are lower compared with the case of the standard crucible and show the same relative trend.

The edge zone of poor material quality is significantly smaller in the case of the high purity crucible. The maximum carrier lifetime values in the core region of wafers from this crystallization attain higher values, as compared with wafers from the standard crucible, even after gettering.

C. Impurity Analyses of Crucible, Coating, and Silicon

The impurity concentrations of iron and cobalt for crucibles, coating, and the silicon crystals were analyzed with ICP-MS. It can be seen from Fig. 5 that the iron concentration is high in the standard crucible and the coating powder compared with the high purity crucible. Cobalt is prominent in the coating material but low concentrations were found in the crucible.

Iron and cobalt are ideal impurity species to compare: iron in the crucible is an infinite source in good approximation, whereas cobalt from the coating is a finite impurity source and behaves qualitatively differently. Furthermore, the interstitial iron concentration is accessible with very high sensitivity (down to concentrations of 10^{10} cm^{-3}) with iron imaging, which is a very valuable source of experimental verification of iron diffusion. The ICP-MS results of cobalt featured a low detection limit in the order of 2×10^{12} cm^{-3} (detection limit of iron is in the order of 2×10^{13} cm^{-3} with large uncertainties below 10^{14} cm^{-3}, deduced from multiple measurements at same distance from crucible wall; see Fig. 6) which enables the quantitative study of the in-diffusion profile of cobalt in the solid silicon.

In order to access the in-diffusion of iron and cobalt, ICP-MS measurements on samples from the midheight position with distances of approximately 0.2, 1.2, 2.2, 3.15, and 4.1 cm to the crucible walls were conducted.

III. Comparison of Experimental Data and Modeling

Since impurity in-diffusion into the silicon melt cannot be investigated directly via experiments, the comparison between measurement and modeling starts in Section III-A with the solid in-diffusion process. The resulting model parameters are then applied to the description of the solid-liquid in-diffusion into the melt in Section III-B.

A. Solid State In-Diffusion of Iron and Cobalt

While in the liquid phase metals from crucible and coating are distributed equally in the melt (see Section III-B), the

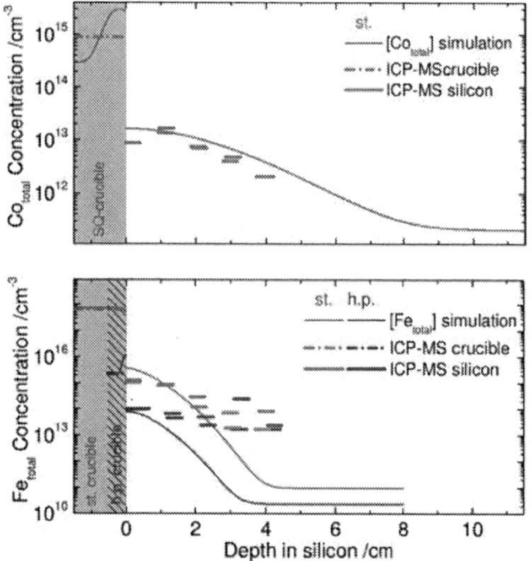

Fig. 6. Simulation of horizontal cobalt (upper image) and iron (lower image) diffusion profiles within crucible wall and solidified silicon at 50% block height. The simulation is compared with ICP-MS data of both, crucible and silicon. The three lowest measured iron concentrations are below the detection limit of the ICP-MS but higher iron concentrations also have large uncertainties. Note that the crucible coating is included in the simulation but too thin to be displayed.

impurity concentrations in the vicinity of the crucible walls are determined by solid state in-diffusion into the silicon crystal.

Inside the solid silicon, the physical mechanisms of Co and Fe diffusion described by the Fickian equations and the precipitation behavior of Fe at nucleation sites are well known. For the latter, a precipitation model based on the Fokker–Planck equation has been developed [16], [17], which successfully predicts iron precipitate densities [18] and interstitial iron concentrations after crystallization and solar cell processes [17], [19]. In the precipitation model, an effective local solubility [16] and radius [20], depending on the size of precipitates, is used for the calculation of the growth rates of iron-silicide precipitates. The Fe diffusivity coefficient was taken from Istratov *et al.* [21]. For Co, two diffusivity equations with different migration enthalpies are found in the literature [22]. We use $9 \times 10^{-4} \times \exp(-0.37\text{eV/kT})$ cm^2/s [22] for our simulations, which gives lower diffusivities at temperatures above 950 °C than in [23].

While the impurity modeling in solid silicon is thus well established, to the authors' knowledge several parameters needed for the description of the impurity diffusion in the crucible and coating and the impurity segregation between crucible, coating, and solid silicon have not been experimentally investigated so far. Only a few measurements of the diffusivity of metal impurities in silicon oxide and silicon nitride [24], [25] and possible segregation effects are published in [26]–[29]. As these experiments were conducted with materials of different stoichiometry, morphology and thickness, it is unclear as to what extent this data are useful for the description of the porous Si$_3$N$_4$ coating and the differently fabricated crucibles.

Thus, we estimate the diffusivity of iron and cobalt within the silicon nitride coating, as well as within the crucible by comparing simulated and measured diffusion profiles. Since our

TABLE I
DIFFUSIVITIES IN THE CRUCIBLE AND THE COATING AS WELL AS THE SEGREGATION COEFFICIENT BETWEEN SILICON AND COATING EXTRACTED FROM SIMULATION[1]

Impurity	D (in coating)	D (in crucible)	Segregation coeff. silicon/coating
Co	$90\times\exp^{-3.05\text{eV/kT}}$	$1000\times\exp^{-3.05\text{eV/kT}}$	0.01
Fe	$3\times\exp^{-3.05\text{eV/kT}}$	$50\times\exp^{-3.05\text{eV/kT}}$	1

[1]Note that the migration enthalpy is taken from [24] and only the prefactors are determined.

experimental data correspond to the effective diffusivities averaged over the whole temperature ramp of the crystallization process, the migration enthalpies could not be extracted. Hence, for the simulations, we use the migration enthalpy for iron in silicon oxide given in [26], using the prefactors as fitting parameters.

We would like to stress that the diffusivity in the crucible and coating and the segregation between coating and silicon ingot are our only fitting parameters in the simulations. All other parameters are measured or determined and experimentally verified in previous work.

We simulate the diffusion of impurities through the whole thickness of the crucible in the coating and in a crucible edge region with 5-cm (Fe) or 11-cm (Co) thickness [30]. The thickness of the crucibles (high purity: 0.6 cm / standard: 1.5 cm) and the coating (90 μm) are taken from measurements.

Inside the silicon, we use a 2-D model structure (8 cm $\times$ 100 μm) to take the inhomogeneous distribution of crystal defects in multicrystalline silicon into account. The mean distance of the detached dislocations within the model structure is 112 μm, which corresponds to a dislocation density of 8 $\times$ 10^3 cm^{-2}. The dislocations are all assumed to be perpendicular to the simulated 2-D plane. The density of nucleation sites is assumed to be proportional to the dislocations density, with a nucleation site line density along dislocations of 3.3 $\times$ 10^5 cm^{-1} [17]. Areas with higher nucleation site densities, i.e., highly dislocated areas and grain boundaries, have lower interstitial iron concentrations, especially in the edge region [17]. From the analyses of the Fe$_i$ imagings (see Fig. 2) and simulations with additional areas of high nucleation site density, we found that the influence of these areas on the averaged Fe$_i$ concentrations is rather weak for the simulated cases. The temperature profiles at 50% ingot height that we use for the simulation [31] of impurity in-diffusion are extracted from transient 2-D simulations of the temperature distribution and the crystallization processes in the crystallization furnace.

The ICP-MS measurements of the impurity concentrations in the crucible and the coating (see Fig. 5) are used as input parameters. The impurity concentration after solidification (i.e., before solid state in-diffusion) is taken from the simulations in Section III-B, which take the diffusion of iron into the silicon melt into account and agree well with our experimental values.

The best consistency with the measurements was found for the diffusivities and segregation coefficients listed in Table I. The simulated Co concentrations agree well with the ICP-MS data in silicon and in the crucible after the crystallization process (see Fig. 6). These material parameters have been successfully

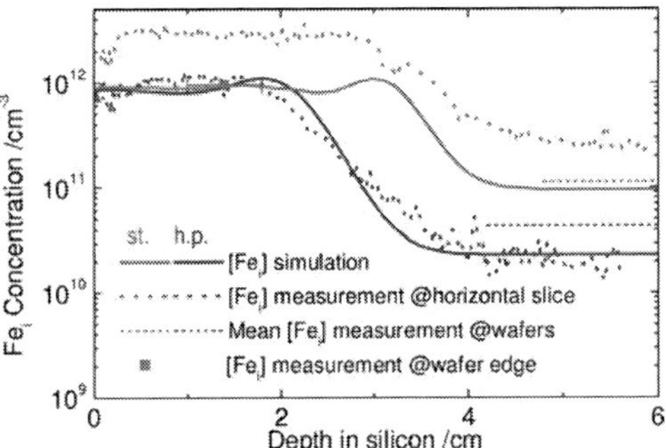

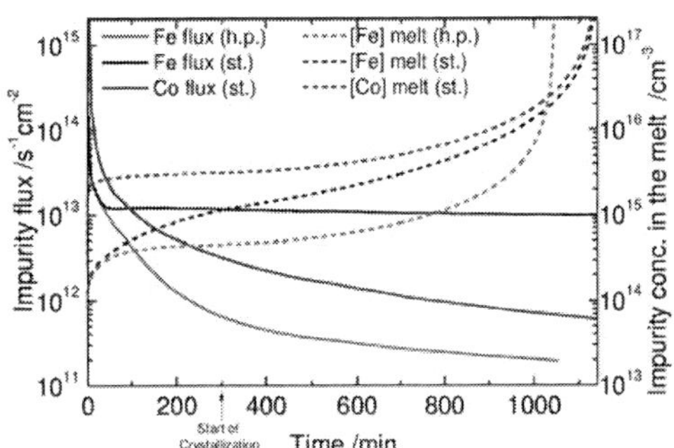

Fig. 7. Simulation of interstitial iron concentration profiles at 50% block height and comparison with experimental data from PL-based iron imaging.

Fig. 8. Simulation of impurity flux for iron (standard and high purity crucible) and cobalt (standard crucible) (left axis) and impurity concentration in the melt (right axis).

tested for consistency on a larger set of four different ingots (not shown).

For the comparison of the total iron concentration, the uncertainties of the ICP-MS measurements (see Section II) in combination with the relatively high detection limit in silicon have to be taken into account. For example, the relatively high Fe values measured via ICP-MS at 4-cm depth are close to the detection limit and appear to overestimate the iron concentration since they are inconsistent with the low Fe_i concentration at that depth (see Fig. 7) and the high lifetime in this area (see Fig. 4). The differences of ICP-MS data at same distance from the crucible wall indicate the uncertainty of the measurement. A relation to iron rich particles is improbable, because of the quite low and homogeneous Fe_i concentrations at these distances. Iron atoms from iron rich particles should diffuse out during high temperatures and increase the Fe_i concentration in the surroundings of the particles. Agglomeration of iron at lower temperature (<1000 °C) influences only a small region around the agglomeration center and, thus, should not have a large influence on ICP-MS measurements.

Since iron interstitials can be measured with high precision provided that the carrier lifetime is measurable, the diffusivities of iron in the crucible and coating are extracted from the comparison of the simulated and measured interstitial iron concentrations for the two different ingots (see Fig. 7). In this graph, interstitial iron profiles from 2-mm thick silicon slices that include the entire low lifetime edge region are compared with the simulations. The latter are averaged over the width of a 2-D model structure taking into account the heterogeneous crystal structure (see Figs. 6 and 7).

The high Fe_i concentration plateau close to the crucible wall is dominated by the cooling ramp at temperatures below 800 °C and corresponds to the low lifetime edge region. Next, the gradual decrease of the concentration toward the block center marks the tail of the Fe in-diffusion profile that is a sensitive function of the temperature ramp during cool-down, the initial concentrations in crucible and coating, and the diffusion and segregation parameters. The low Fe_i concentration plateau at the block center depends only on the Fe concentration in the silicon melt, as described earlier. All main features are well reproduced by our simulations. Slight deviations are observed for the standard

crucible that we explain by measurement uncertainties due to the lower carrier lifetime in combination with the thick sample from the standard crucible. A comparison with wafer data shows good agreement. Additional DLTS measurements confirmed the wafer results (see [32] for details).

It is interesting to note that the iron concentration within the high purity crucible increases during crystallization since iron diffuses from the coating in both directions; an effect that is well reproduced by the simulation (see Fig. 6). In contrast with this observation, the iron concentration within the standard crucible decreases during crystallization as shown by simulation and ICP-MS data.

Because of the porosity of the silicon nitride coating and the crucible, it is not surprising that we have to use diffusivities that are more than one order of magnitude larger than the published data for rather dense material [26]–[29]. The effect of a variation of the segregation coefficient between silicon and silicon nitride is very small, as long as we keep it between 0.1 and 10.

B. Contamination of Silicon Melt With Iron

Before solid state diffusion contaminates the edge region of a silicon block, impurities from crucible and coating can enter the silicon melt via diffusion or erosion of the coating. This effect causes a continuous increase of impurity concentration with time. With the assumption of perfect stirring and infinite impurity solubility, the amount of iron atoms that enter the melt can be quantitatively estimated. Basis of this calculation is the rate of iron atoms entering the melt per crucible area as a function of time $Fe_{Crucible}(t)$ (see Fig. 8). This rate is simulated with the diffusivity in the crucible and coating determined in the previous section. In addition, the aforementioned transient 2-D simulations of the temperature distribution and crystallization process in the furnace was taken as input, which yield, for example, the crystallization velocity $v(t)$ (see Fig. 9). Note that the high purity ingot is already fully solidified after 1080 min, due to differences in the thermal boundary conditions.

For the high purity crucible, we observe a strong decrease of the iron flux per crucible wall area with time. This decrease is typical for a finite impurity source provided by the coating. As to be expected, the shape of the simulated cobalt flux also

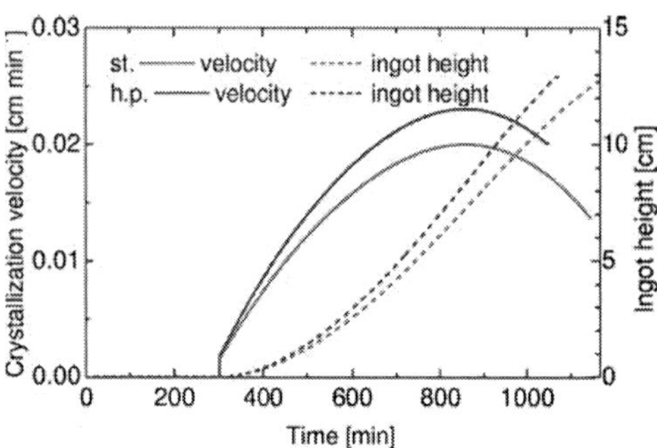 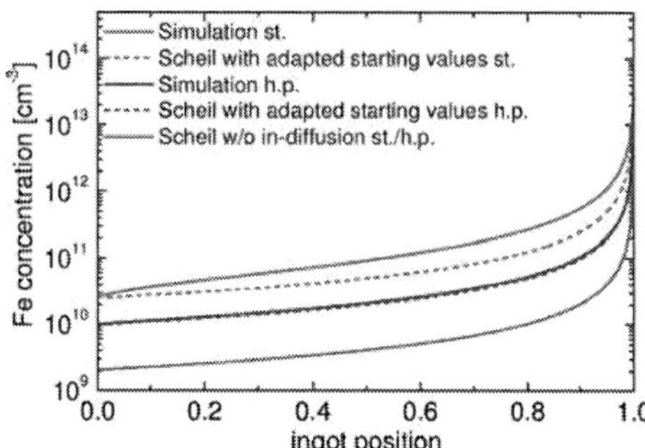

Fig. 9. Simulated crystallization velocity and ingot height as a function of time for crystallization with standard and with high purity crucible.

Fig. 10. Simulation of total iron concentration in crystallized silicon ingot as a function of block height accounting for continuous diffusion of iron into the melt for both standard crucible (black) and high purity crucible (red). For comparison, iron profiles are calculated from Scheil's equation (dotted line). The dashed lines represent calculations from Scheil's equation with a starting impurity concentration accounting for diffusion of iron into the melt before crystallization begins.

corresponds to a finite impurity source since it mainly comes from the thin coating.

In contrast, the iron flux from the standard crucible system decreases rapidly only in the first 30 min, then most of the iron from the coating is consumed, and the continuous iron flux from the crucible dominates.

With climbing crystallization front, the area of the crucible being in contact with the melt decreases. Before crystallization, the overall contact area is

$$A_{\text{contact}}\left(t \leq t_o\right) = a^2 + 4 \times a \times h \tag{1}$$

where a is the crucible width, and h is the filling height of liquid silicon. h is very weakly time dependent during crystallization that originates from the density of silicon being slightly higher for solid than for liquid silicon. This effect is, however, neglected in the following.

When crystallization starts at t_0, the contact area can be described by

$$A_{\text{contact}}\left(t\right)|_{t \geq t_0} = 4 \times a \left(h - h_{\text{interface}}\left(t\right)\right). \tag{2}$$

Two effects increase the iron concentration in the melt: the direct in-diffusion from or erosion of the coating and the segregation mechanism due the lower solubility of iron in solid silicon. In the widely used Scheil equation [33], only the segregation effect is taken into account. The in-diffusion from the crucible walls is given by the impurity flux per crucible area $\text{Fe}_{\text{Crucible}}(t)$ shown in Fig. 8 scaled with the area of the interface of liquid silicon and crucible. The iron concentration in the melt $C_{\text{liquid}}^{\text{Fe}}\left(t\right)$ as a function of time is then as follows:

$$C_{\text{liquid}}^{\text{Fe}}\left(t\right) = C_{\text{initial}}^{\text{Fe}} + \int_0^t \frac{1}{h - h_{\text{interface}}\left(t'\right)}$$

$$\times \left(\frac{A_{\text{contact}}\left(t'\right)}{a^2} \times \text{Fe}_{\text{Crucible}}\left(t'\right) + \left(1 - k_s\right)\right.$$

$$\left. \times v\left(t'\right) \times C_{\text{liquid}}^{\text{Fe}}\left(t'\right)\right) dt' \tag{3}$$

with the crystallization velocity $v(t)$ (see Fig. 9) and the effective segregation coefficient of iron between solid and liquid silicon $k = 2 \times 10^{-5}$ that is determined in [34]. In [34], the influence of iron in-diffusion from the crucible on the effective segregation

coefficient could be neglected, due to the high concentration of iron intentionally added to the melt.

We assume that around 10 μm of the initial coating (100-μm thickness) dissolves into the silicon melt. The initial iron concentration $C_{\text{initial}}^{\text{Fe}}$ is the sum of the iron concentration in the feedstock ($\sim 1.5 \times 10^{13}$ cm^{-3}) and the iron inside the dissolved fraction of the coating.

The resulting iron concentrations in the melt $C_{\text{liquid}}^{\text{Fe}}\left(t\right)$ for the two ingots and the cobalt concentration for the standard ingot, which is calculated in the same way, are shown in Fig. 8.

The Fe concentration in the central regions of the ingot directly after solidification can be calculated from the previous simulations with

$$C_{\text{solid}}^{\text{Fe}}\left(h\right) = k_s \times C_{\text{liquid}}^{\text{Fe}}\left(t'\right)|_{h = h_{\text{interface}}\left(t'\right)}. \tag{4}$$

In Fig. 10, we compare these iron concentrations for high purity and standard ingot as a function of the ingot position with results calculated with the Scheil equation, neglecting the in-diffusion from the crucible.

If iron in-diffusion is neglected (using Scheil's equation with the iron concentration of the feedstock only), the iron profile is significantly underestimated in all cases compared with the full simulation accounting for the continuous impurity flux during crystallization. This severe underestimation demonstrates that the iron concentration in the melt is dominated by the in-diffusion from the crucible system for both standard and high purity quality. If the iron in-diffusion into the melt before the beginning of the crystallization in addition to the feedstock contamination is taken into account (see the dashed lines Fig. 10), the iron concentrations calculated with the simple Scheil equation already give a good approximation for the high purity ingot. However, the large deviation between this calculation for the standard ingot and the simulations demonstrate that, in general, the Fe concentration in the ingot could not be described with a Scheil equation alone because the continuous Fe in-diffusion into the melt during crystallization has a significant impact.

As mentioned earlier, we use the simulated total iron concentrations for 50% ingot height shown in Fig. 10 as "background"

496

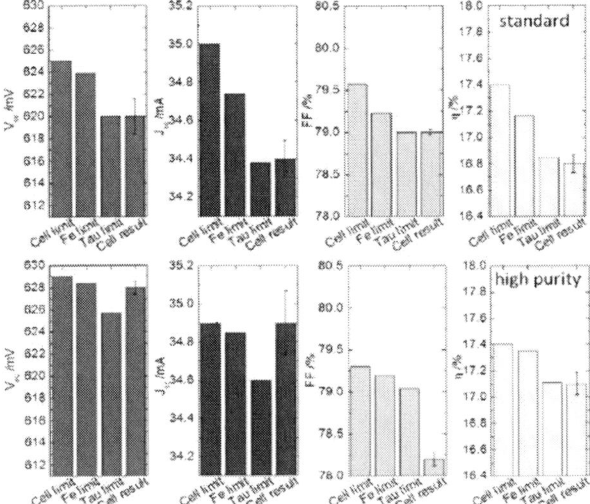

Fig. 11. ELBA cell parameter simulation results for both wafers from the standard (first row) and from the high purity crucible (second row) and comparison with cell results from an industrial cell process.

concentrations in the block center for the simulations shown in Section III-A. We obtain a very good agreement between the measured and simulated interstitial iron concentrations in the block center (see Fig. 7). Hence, by merely fitting the diffusivities in the crucible and coating and fitting the segregation coefficient, our modeling yields a consistent description of the interactions between crucible, coating, the silicon melt, and the crystal starting with the melting of the silicon in the crucible.

IV. Discussion

A. Impact of Iron on Cell Efficiency Potential

Fig. 11 shows cell simulations by the efficiency limiting bulk recombination analysis (ELBA) approach [35] and a comparison with cell results that were obtained on parallel wafers in an industrial line. The wafers contain both a part of the edge region as well as the core region of higher material quality (see Fig. 3). Fig. 11 compares the following cell parameters of a simulated Al-BSF cell: 1) simulated cell limit with neglected bulk recombination, incorporating only cell process-related losses; 2) simulated cell limit if recombination at (measured) interstitial iron is taken into account; 3) simulated cell limit considering all measured recombination (i.e., measured carrier lifetime, tau limit); and 4) experimental cell results of industrial cells on parallel wafers.

Since neither monocrystalline reference cells nor detailed information on the cell processing conditions have been available the cell model for the simulations was adapted to match the open-circuit voltage and short-circuit current of the cells from standard crystallization. Although this cell model might still differ from the real cell to some extent, it allows an insightful analysis of material related limiting effects on cell parameters.

The simulated cell limits for V_{oc} and J_{sc} of the standard and high purity material differ slightly because of slightly different doping concentrations ($N_{\mathrm{A,standard}} = 1.4 \times 10^{16}$ cm^{-3}, $N_{\mathrm{A,high\ purity}} = 1.7 \times 10^{16}$ cm^{-3}). Furthermore, slight differences in measured series resistances were considered for the simulation of fill factor values ($R_{\mathrm{S,standard}} = 0.73\ \Omega\mathrm{cm}^2$, $R_{\mathrm{S,high\ purity}} = 0.8\ \Omega\mathrm{cm}^2$).

The analysis of the results for cell efficiency (graphs on the right of Fig. 11) allow for the following statements. 1) The reduction of attainable cell efficiency due to interstitial iron (cell limit compared with Fe limit) is significant for standard wafers and smaller for the high purity wafers. 2) In addition to interstitial iron, other defects (iron related or due to other impurities/crystal defects) further reduce the attainable efficiency (Fe limit compared with tau limit). The reduction is slightly smaller for the high purity wafers. 3) These effects sum up to an overall higher simulated cell efficiency (tau limit) of the high purity wafers that is confirmed by the experimental values (cell results).

The analysis of the cell parameters of the standard material shows that the relative impact of interstitial iron is more pronounced for J_{sc} compared with V_{oc}. This effect reflects the strong injection dependence of carrier recombination at interstitial iron: At V_{oc}, the injection density is higher than at J_{sc}, and recombination is rather weak for the first case. At J_{sc}, the lower injection density causes higher recombination, and therefore, a stronger influence of interstitial iron on this parameter. This observation shows that the V_{oc} may not be well suited as a qualitative measure for the iron limited electrical material quality as J_{sc} provides a more sensitive measure to carrier recombination at iron interstitials.

The strong injection dependence of recombination at interstitial iron atoms is reflected by a reduced fill factor (PFF and FF, cell limit compared with Fe limit). The observed differences of V_{oc}, J_{sc}, and FF between simulated cell results (tau limit) and experimental cell results in the case of the high purity material are explained by uncertainties of the assumed cell model for the industrial process and possible differences of the phosphorus diffusion step that might be more efficient for the industrial cell processing, compared with the lifetime samples after gettering of this study.

B. Projection of Results to Large Ingots

The presented results have been obtained for crystallization experiments with G1 size. The experiments with this size are easier to handle and changes of the crucible material have been feasible. On the basis of the validated simulation approach, the results can be extrapolated to predict impurity in-diffusion for larger ingot sizes. The crystallization of those ingots differs in silicon-crucible contact area in volume, as well as in temperature ramps.

The geometric parameters and the crystallization time that are used as input parameters for the simulations are listed in Table II. The crystallization recipes used for the simulation of G1 and G2 are laboratory type, whereas the recipe for G4 is optimized for faster crystallization velocity. The crystallization recipes for G5 and G6 are estimations of industrial type crystallization processes. The comparison of iron in-diffusion profiles and center iron concentrations should, therefore, be done within

TABLE II

SIMULATION OF THE DEPTH OF IRON IN-DIFFUSION PROFILES AND IRON CONCENTRATION IN THE CENTER OF THE INGOT AS A FUNCTION OF INGOT SIZE[2]

	G1	G2	G4	G5	G6
Si weight /kg	14	77	230	450	800
Ingot width × height /cm	22 × 12.8	40 × 22.5	70 × 22.5	85 × 30	102 × 37
Contact area between crucible and silicon /m^2	0.16	0.52	1.12	1.45	2.55
Fraction of contact area per volume /cm^{-1}	0.26	0.14	0.1	0.08	0.066
Assumed crystallisation time /h (standard)	5+15 +14	5+29 +16	2+ 22.5 + 14	2+25 +15	2+31 +16
Depth of in-diffusion for iron (50% height) /cm (standard)	3.5	4.3	4.1	4.3	4.7
Iron concentration in the center /cm^{-3} (standard)	9.5× 10^{10}	7.4× 10^{10}	3.2× 10^{10}	2.8× 10^{10}	2.7× 10^{10}
Assumed crystallisation time (high purity)	5+15 +14	5+29 +16	2+ 22.5 +14	2+25 +15	2+31 +16
Depth of in-diffusion for iron (50% height) /cm (high purity)	2.8	3.7	3.5	3.7	4
Iron concentration in the center /cm^{-3} (high purity)	2.1× 10^{10}	1.3× 10^{10}	0.89 ×10^{10}	0.72 ×10^{10}	0.61 ×10^{10}

[2]The process time is divided in three sections: the time before crystallization with melted silicon, net crystallization time, and the time until the whole ingot is cooled below 1000 °C.

the groups G1 and G2 and G4 to G6, respectively. From the simulations, we extract the iron concentration in the ingot center at 50% height similar to Section III. In addition, the depth of the zone that is influenced by the solid state in-diffusion from the crucible system is listed in Table II. We define this zone as the area with more than five times higher iron concentration compared with the ingot center. The area with lower solar cell performance will be smaller, due to gettering during cell processing.

The two main following effects can be observed: 1) The depth of iron in-diffusion increases with size due to prolonged cooling times, and 2) the iron concentration in the center decreases with size. The latter effect is due to the fact that the fraction of melt-contaminating crucible surface to silicon volume is in favor for large ingots.

V. CONCLUSION

Iron and cobalt were studied as silicon-contaminating impurity species from crucible and coating. Iron in standard crucibles considerably affects the material quality as well as has a significant effect on cell efficiency potential. While a standard crucible can be considered as an infinite source of iron impurities, high purity quartz crucibles hardly contribute to the iron in-diffusion, while the coating that behaves like a finite iron source. Cobalt as a typical impurity species of the coating is a finite source that is independent of the crucible.

Experimental values of interstitial iron concentration, as well as ICP-MS values for total iron and cobalt concentrations, are (within the uncertainty limits of ICP-MS) in good agreement with the simulated results. We show that Scheil's equation simply using the initial contamination of the feedstock for the height-dependent iron concentration in a standard ingot is insufficient since iron continuously enters the melt during crystallization.

The effect of iron contamination on the solar cell performance has been demonstrated with cell simulations and industrial solar cells. Cells on wafers with influence from the edge region from the standard crucible show a significant impact of interstitial iron. This effect is strongly reduced for cells from high-purity crystallization.

Extrapolations to larger crucibles with the help of simulations show that the in-diffusion depth of iron increases with size, whereas the iron concentration in the center of an ingot decreases at the same time.

ACKNOWLEDGMENT

The authors would like to thank R. Krain for cell measurements, L. Mundt and J. Weiß for measurements of carrier lifetime and iron distribution, and R. Bakowskie from Hanwha Q-Cells and A. Seidl from Schott AG for providing measurements of structural defect density and grain boundary distribution.

REFERENCES

[1] P. Engelhart, D. Manger, B. Klöter, S. Hermann, A. A. Stekolnikov, S. Peters, H.-C. Ploigt, A. Eifler, C. Klenke, A. Mohr, G. Zimmermann, B. Barkenfelt, K. Suva, J. Wendt, T. Kaden, S. Rupp, D. Rychtarik, M. Fischer, and J. W. Müller, "Q.ANTUM: Q-Cells nect generation high-power silicon solar cell & module concept," in *Proc. 26th Eur. Photovoltaic Solar Energy Conf. Exhib.*, Hamburg, Germany, 2011.

[2] K. M. Yeh, C. K. Hseih, W. C. Hsu, and C. W. Lan, "High-quality multicrystalline silicon growth for solar cells by grain-controlled directional solidification," *Progr. Photovoltaics*, vol. 18, pp. 265–271, 2010.

[3] N. Stoddard, B. Wu, I. Witting, M. C. Wagener, Y. Park, G. Rozgonyi, and R. Clark, "Casting single crystal silicon: novel defect profiles from BP Solar's Mono2 TM Wafer," *Solid State Phenomena*, vol. 131, pp. 1–8, 2007.

[4] B. Geyer, G. Schwichtenberg, and A. Müller, "Increased wafer yield in silicon ingots by the applications of high purity silicon nitride-coating and high-purity crucibles," in *Proc. IEEE 31st Photovoltaic Spec. Conf.*, 2005.

[5] E. Olsen and E. J. Ovrelid, "Silicon nitride coating and crucible: Effects of using upgraded materials in the casting of multicrystalline silicon ingots," *Progr. Photovoltaics*, vol. 16, pp. 93–100, 2008.

[6] R. Kvande, L. Arnberg, and C. Martin, "Influence of crucible and coating quality on the properties of multicrystalline silicon for solar cells," *J. Crystal Growth*, vol. 311, pp. 765–768, 2009.

[7] T. Naerland, L. Arnberg, and A. Holt, "Origin of the low carrier lifetime edge zone in multicrystalline Pv silicon," *Progr. Photovoltaics: Res. Appl.*, vol. 17, pp. 289–296, 2009.

[8] A. Montaser,, *Inductively Coupled Plasma Mass Spectrometry*. New York, NY, USA: Wiley-vch, 1998.

[9] D. Macdonald, J. Tan, and T. Trupke, "Imaging interstitial iron concentrations in boron-doped crystalline silicon unsing photoluminescence," *J. Appl. Phys.*, vol. 103, p. 073710, 2008.

[10] M. C. Schubert, H. Habenicht, and W. Warta, "Imaging of metastable defects in silicon," *J. Photovoltaics*, vol. 1, pp. 168–173, 2011.

[11] M. Schöfthaler and R. Brendel, "Sensitivity and transient response of microwave reflection measurements," *J. Appl. Phys.*, vol. 77, pp. 3162–3173, 1995.

[12] Intego (2013). Gemini Kornstrukturanalyse. Available: www.intego.de.

[13] R. Bakowskie, G. Kesser, R. Richter, D. Lausch, A. Eidner, P. Clemens, and K. Petter, "Fast method to determine the structural defect density of 156 × 156 mm^2 Mc-Si Wafers," *Energy Procedia*, vol. 27, pp. 179–184, 2012.

[14] T. Trupke, R. A. Bardos, M. C. Schubert, and W. Warta, "Photoluminescence imaging of silicon wafers," *Appl. Phys. Lett.*, vol. 89, pp. 1–3, 2006.

[15] J. Giesecke, M. C. Schubert, D. Walter, and W. Warta, "Minority carrier lifetime in silicon wafers from quasi-steady-state photoluminescence," *Appl. Phys. Lett.*, vol. 97, p. 092109, 2010.

[16] A. Haarahiltunen, H. Väinölä, O. Anttila, M. Yli-Koski, and J. Sinkkonen, "Experimental and theoretical study of heterogeneous iron precipitation in silicon," *J. Appl. Phys.*, vol. 101, p. 043507, 2007.

[17] J. Schön, H. Habenicht, M. C. Schubert, and W. Warta, "Understanding the distribution of iron in multicrystalline silicon after emitter formation: theoretical model and experiments," *J. Appl. Phys.*, vol. 109, pp. 1–8, 2011.

[18] J. Schön, A. Haarahiltunen, H. Savin, D. P. Fenning, T. Buonassisi, W. Warta, and M. C. Schubert, "Analyses of the evolution of iron-silicide precipitates in multicrystalline silicon during solar cell processing," *J. Photovoltaics*, vol. 3, pp. 131–137, 2013.

[19] B. Michl, J. Schön, W. Warta, and M. C. Schubert, "The impact of different diffusion temperature profiles on iron concentrations and carrier lifetimes in multicrystalline silicon wafers," *J. Photovoltaics*, vol. 3, pp. 635–640, 2012.

[20] A. Haarahiltunen, H. Talvitie, H. Savin, M. Yli-Koski, M. I. Asghar, and J. Sinkkonen, "Modeling boron diffusion gettering of iron in silicon solar cells," *Appl. Phys. Lett.*, vol. 92, pp. 021902-1–021902-3, 2008.

[21] A. A. Istratov, H. Hieslmair, and E. R. Weber, "Iron and its complexes in silicon," *Appl. Phys. A*, vol. 69, pp. 13–44, 1999.

[22] D. Gilles, "Einfluss der elektronischen Struktur auf Diffusion, Löslichkeit und Paarbildung von 3d-Übergangselementen in Silizium," Ph.D. dissertation, Univ. Göttingen, Göttingen, Germany, 1987.

[23] J. Utzig and D. Gilles, *Mater. Sci. Forum*, vol. 38–41, p. 729, 1989.

[24] R. N. Ghoshtagore, "Diffusion of nickel in amorphous silicon dioxide and silicon nitride films," *J. Appl. Phys.*, vol. 40, p. 4374, 1969.

[25] J. D. McBrayer, R. M. Swanson, and T. W. Sigmon, "Diffusion of metals in silicon dioxide," *J. Electrochemical Soc.*, vol. 133, p. 1242, 1986.

[26] A. A. Istratov, H. Väinölä, W. Huber, and E. R. Weber, "Gettering in silicon-on-insulator wafers: experimental studies and modelling," *Semicond. Sci. Technol.*, vol. 20, pp. 568–575, 2005.

[27] J. Isenberg, S. Reber, S. Aschaber, and W. Warta, "Silicon dioxide and silicon nitride as diffusion barrier for transition metals in solar cell applications," in *Proc. 16th EU-PVSEC*, Glasgow, U.K., 2000.

[28] S. Reber, "Electrical confinement for the crystalline silicon thin-film solar cell on foreign substrate," in *Fachbereich Physik*, Vol. Dr. rer. nat., Univ. Mainz, Mainz, Germany, 2000, p. 158.

[29] D. A. Ramappa and W. B. Henley, "Diffusion of iron in silicon dioxide," *J. Electrochemical Soc.*, vol. 146, p. 3773, 1999.

[30] (2012). Synopsis, Synopsis TCAD, Rel. G-2012.06. [Online]. Available: http:/www.synopsis.com

[31] STR, I., Graphical User Interface Reference Guide, Ver. 12.2.2012, 2012.

[32] F. Schindler, B. Michl, J. Schön, W. Kwapil, W. Warta, and M. C. Schubert, "Solar cell efficiency losses due to impurities from the crucible in multicrystalline silicon," *J. Photovoltaics*, to be published.

[33] E. Scheil and Z. Metallk. vol. 34, 1942, p. 70.

[34] J. Schön, H. Habenicht, M. C. Schubert, and W. Warta, "Simulation of iron distribution after crystallization of mc silicon," *Solid State Phenomena*, vol. 156–158, pp. 223–228, 2010.

[35] B. Michl, M. Rüdiger, J. Giesecke, M. Hermle, W. Warta, and M. C. Schubert, "Efficiency limiting bulk recombination in multicrystalline silicon solar cells," *Solar Energy Mater. Solar Cells*, vol. 98, pp. 441–447, 2012.

Authors' photographs and biographies not available at the time of publication.

An Analytical Model for Interdigitated Back Contact Solar Cells

Pierre Saint-Cast, Milan Padilla, Achim Kimmerle, and Christian Reichel

Abstract—An analytical model for an interdigitated back contact solar cell structure is presented. This model is based on the concept of diffusion resistance and on the superposition principle. The analytical model is compared with finite-element simulations that are based on a conductive boundary model. For most practical cases, the model presented here is in very good agreement with the simulation, with less than 1% deviation on the V_{oc}, j_{sc}, fill factor (FF) and efficiency.

Index Terms—Analytical model, interdigitated back contact (IBC) solar cell, simulation.

I. INTRODUCTION

INTERDIGITATED back contact (IBC) solar cells are one of the most efficient device concepts for the conversion of sun light into electricity by Si. From the early modeling and realization of this concept [1]–[3] until today [4] with the industrial solar cell from SunPower, IBC cells are counting among the most efficient Si solar cells. The growing competition on the photovoltaic (PV) market is pushing for innovation, high efficiency, and low-cost per watt peak. Therefore, many solar cells manufacturer are currently developing IBC cells aiming for high efficiency.

The realization of such a structure remains a challenge, since many processes steps are necessary. For laboratory type solar cells, thermal oxides are used for the masking, the formation of diffusion barriers, and the passivation of the surfaces. The structure is created by photolithography and the contacts are made by evaporation through a shadow mask or by photolithographic structuring and lift-off techniques [5]–[8].

The development of this process in combination with the optimization of the structure design lead to solar cell efficiencies of 22.2% at 1 sun concentration and 27.5% under a concentration of 100 suns, obtained by Sinton *et al.* [5]. This result was obtained on a point contact structure whose design was optimized with an analytical model developed by Swanson and Sinton [6]–[10]. From the early works on IBC solar cells, the optimization of the fabrication processes and the solar cell design needed to be carried out together [11].

Manuscript received June 10, 2013; revised September 3, 2013; accepted September 21, 2013. Date of publication November 13, 2013; date of current version December 16, 2013.

The authors are with the Fraunhofer Institute for Solar Energy Systems, Freiburg, 79110 Germany (e-mail: pierre.saint-cast@ise.fraunhofer.de; milan.padilla@ise.fraunhofer.de; achim.kimmerle@ise.fraunhofer.de; christian.reichel@ise.fraunhofer.de).

Color versions of one or more of the figures in this paper are available online at http://ieeexplore.ieee.org.

Digital Object Identifier 10.1109/JPHOTOV.2013.2287771

TABLE I
SYMBOLS USED IN OUR MODEL

Symbol	Quantity	Unit
α_i, β_i, χ	Coefficient for the calculation of excess carrier density in region i [a]	a. u.
D_α	Ambipolar diffusivity	cm^2 s^{-1}
D_n	Diffusivity of electrons	cm^2 s^{-1}
D_p	Diffusivity of holes	cm^2 s^{-1}
f	Emitter fraction on the rear surface	
f_E^*, f_{BSF}^*	Fraction of the rear surface which is not contacted	
$F_{\Delta n}$	Injection factor	
FF	Fill factor	
η	Solar cell efficiency	
j_{0i}	Saturation current density for the region i [a]	fA cm^{-2}
j_{lum}	Generated current, due to illumination	mA cm^{-2}
j_{out}	Output current of the solar cell	mA cm^{-2}
j_{sc}	Output current in short circuit condition	mA cm^{-2}
$j_{i\to j}$	Diffusion current flowing from the region i [a] to the region j [a]	mA cm^{-2}
p_0	Hole carrier density at equilibrium	cm^{-3}
Δp_i	Excess carrier density for region i [a]	cm^{-3}
$R_{d\_i\text{-}j}$	Diffusion resistance between i [a] and j [a]	fA^{-1} cm^{-1}
R_{s_int}/R_{s_out}	Series resistance in the bulk / external	Ω cm^2
ρ_i	Sheet resistance of the region i [a]	Ω / sq.
σ	Specific conductivity	S cm^{-1}
U_i	Recombination rate at region i [a]	
V_d	Potential losses due to Dember effect	V
V_i	Potential difference at region i [a]	V
V_{Rs}	Potential losses due to series resistance	V
V_{out}	Output voltage of the solar cell	V
V_{oc}	Voltage of the solar cell in open circuit	V
W	Wafer thickness	cm

[a]Region of the solar cell; B = bulk, E = emitter, eq = equivalent value representing solar cell, F = front surface or front surface field, BSF = back surface field, R = rear of the solar cell including the emitter and back surface field.

IBC cells benefit from a low total light reflectance due to the lack of front finger contacts. Therefore, they show less optical losses in comparison with conventional solar cells. However, as most of the charge carriers are generated close to the front surface of the solar cell, they need to diffuse through the bulk in order to be collected on the rear. This particularity makes IBC cells very sensitive to the effective diffusion length of the carriers. If the diffusion length is low, an important part of the generated carriers will be lost due to recombination [12]. For this type of solar cells, a diffusion related recombination loss (often call by the name of "electrical shading") is observed when the design of the rear surface is not optimized. Finally, the resistance loss in the metal and the resistance in the wafer need to be taken into account [13]. All these losses are related to the design of the solar cell, which needs an accurate modeling of the carrier transport in order to be understood.

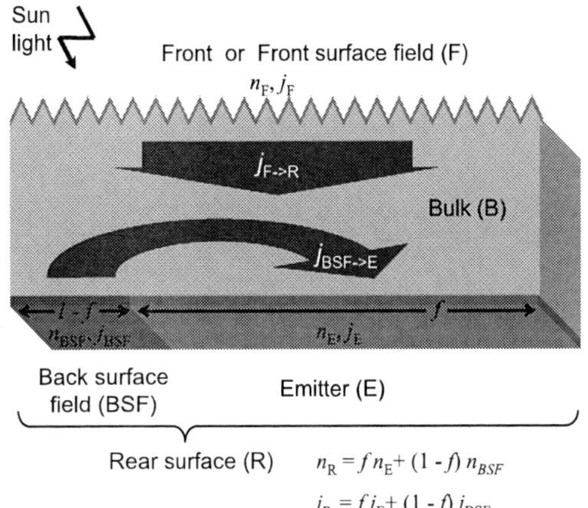

Fig. 1.   Schematic of the modeled IBC solar cell showing the different regions and diffusion currents.

II. Model Construction

A. Transport of Minority Carriers

A correct modeling of the minority carrier transport is essential for rear junction solar cells. For this solar cell structure, most of the charge carriers need to diffuse from the front surface, where they are generated, to the emitter partially covering the rear, where they are collected. The accuracy with which the recombination rates are calculated depends strongly on the accuracy of the transport model.

In this paper, we suppose that the diffusion of the carriers can be described by ambipolar diffusion

$$\vec{j}_p = -D_\alpha \vec{\nabla} p \tag{1}$$

where j_p is the minority carrier current density, D_α is the ambipolar diffusivity, and p the density of holes [22], [23]. In this paper, the wafer is supposed to be n-type, therefore the hole are the minority carriers. In a steady state, by integrating (1) between a region i and j, we obtain

$$p_i - p_j = R_{d\_i-j}\, j_{i\to j} \tag{2}$$

where $j_{i\to j}$ is the minority carrier current exchanged between regions i and j, p_i is the average hole density on the region i, and R_{d_i-j} is the diffusion resistance between regions i and j. For a homogenously doped bulk, p_i can be replaced by the average excess carrier density (Δp_i) in (2). Note that the diffusion resistance corresponds to an analogy between diffusion and electrical conduction. For diffusion (electrical conduction), there is a linear relation between the concentration difference (potential difference) and the particle flux (current), the proportionality factor is call diffusion resistance (resistance).

In this model, four regions are considered as shown in Fig. 1. The front or front surface field (F), the bulk (B), the back surface field (BSF), and the rear emitter (E). The BSF and the emitter are both located at the rear surface (R). The emitter covers the rear with the fraction f and the BSF with the fraction $(1-f)$. This model does not take into account a rear passivated area

or gap between the emitter and BSF [14]; however, this case is treated in [15].

An intuitive description of the current flow would be that the carriers are generated close to the front surface, a part recombines. The rest diffuse toward the rear splitting between emitter and BSF, this splitting ratio changes with the working point of the solar cell.

A nonintuitive description would be that the carriers are generated close to the front surface, a part recombines. The rest diffuse toward the rear. The emitter and the BSF receive the same current per unit of surface. At the same time, a purely lateral diffusion between the emitter and the BSF establish the equilibrium between the current collected and the recombinations.

However these descriptions seem different, they are equivalent. The non intuitive description is much easier to describe mathematically. Therefore, two main diffusion currents are considered.

1) $j_{F\to R}$ is the current diffusing vertically form the front to the rear.
2) $j_{BSF\to E}$ is the current diffusing laterally form the back surface field to the emitter.

Equation (2) implies the following relation between the front and the rear surface

$$\Delta p_F - \Delta p_R = R_{d\_F-R}\, j_{F\to R} \tag{3}$$

where R_{dF-R} is the diffusion resistance between the front and the rear. As the rear is the combination of the emitter and the BSF, we have $\Delta p_R = f\Delta p_E + (1-f)\Delta p_{BSF}$ for the carrier density and the same relation for current (see Fig. 1). For high carrier lifetime in the bulk,[1] the excess carrier density in the bulk (Δp_B) can be approximated by $\Delta p_B = (\Delta p_F + \Delta p_R)/2$. If this approximation is not valid, a proper diffusion resistance need to be considered for diffusion current from the front to the bulk.

For the lateral diffusion current in the solar cell, we can write

$$\Delta p_{BSF} - \Delta p_E = R_{d\_BSF-E}\, j_{BSF\to E} \tag{4}$$

where R_{d_BSF-E} is the diffusion resistance between the emitter and BSF.

Appendix A provides an example for the calculation of the diffusion resistances. Note that the diffusion resistance depends on the injection factor ($F_{\Delta n}$) and the ambipolar diffusion coefficient.

B. Generation and Recombination of Carriers

1) Generation: For the AM1.5G solar spectrum, the generation mainly occurs close to the front surface of the solar cell. Indeed, nearly the whole short wavelength part of the solar spectrum is absorbed in the first micrometers of the solar cell, whereas the long wavelength part of the spectrum can be described as homogeneous absorption in the bulk. A simple approximation is to consider that the light is absorbed at the

---

[1] High bulk carrier lifetime can be considered when $\tau_B \gg q\, W\, R_{d\_F-R}$, where τ_B is the bulk lifetime, W is the wafer thickness, and q is the elementary charge.

front surface of the solar cell. We followed this approach in this paper.

The model of this paper is only an electrical model of the solar cells, therefore the integrated carrier generation (j_{lum}) should be determined by a separated optical model. For the application in Section III, $j_{\text{lum}} = 43.23$ mA cm^{-2} was used [15].

2) Recombination: For this model, we describe the carrier recombination by diode saturation currents (j_{0i}). The recombination current at the region i (U_i) is then [16]

$$U_i = j_{0i} \frac{(N_D + \Delta p_i)\Delta p_i}{n_i^2} \tag{5}$$

where N_D is the ionized donor concentration, and n_i is the intrinsic carrier concentration (we assume $n_i \sim 10^{10}$ cm^{-3}).

In principle, j_{0i} does not depend on the carrier injection. In reality, many recombination mechanisms would lead to an injection dependence of j_{0i}. In order to take this effect into account, we define an injection factor ($F_{\Delta n} = 1 + \Delta p/N_D$) that is supposed to be almost constant in the solar cell[2][3] [17]. j_{0i} is therefore a function of the injection factor, and a different j_{0i} can be used for each working point of the solar cell. This approximation will be meaningful only if j_{0i} varies slowly relatively to the injection level and if the inhomogeneity in Δp is low enough.[3] These conditions lead to

$$U_i = j_{0i} F_{\Delta n} \frac{\Delta p_i}{p_0} \tag{6}$$

where p_0 is the hole density in the thermal equilibrium. It is more common to describe the bulk recombination using the carrier lifetime in the bulk (τ_B). j_{0B} can then be calculated from

$$j_{0B} = \frac{qW p_0}{F_{\Delta n}\tau_B} \tag{7}$$

where W is the wafer thickness. For the numerical examples Section III, the lifetime in the bulk is approximated by the Auger lifetime [18].

C. Solution for the Minority Carriers

For the carriers that are generated in the solar cell there are only two possibilities. They recombine or they are collected and contribute to the current of the solar cell (j_{out}). Therefore, we can write

$$j_{\text{lum}} = \sum_i U_i + j_{\text{out}}$$

$$j_{\text{lum}} = F_{\Delta n} \left[j_{0F} \frac{\Delta p_F}{p_0} + j_{0B} \frac{\Delta p_B}{p_0} \right.$$
$$\left. + (1-f) j_{0\text{BSF}} \frac{\Delta p_{\text{BSF}}}{p_0} + f j_{0E} \frac{\Delta p_E}{p_0} \right] + j_{\text{out}}. \tag{8}$$

As defined previously, $j_{F->R}$ correspond to the current of minority carriers from the front to the rear. This current includes the recombination current on the rear and j_{out}

$$j_{F->R} = F_{\Delta n} \left[(1-f) j_{0\text{BSF}} \frac{\Delta p_{\text{BSF}}}{p_0} + f j_{0E} \frac{\Delta p_E}{p_0} \right] + j_{\text{out}}. \tag{9}$$

The emitter receives the current from the front and from the BSF, this current is than split into the current that recombine and j_{out}. Therefore, we have

$$f j_{F->R} + j_{\text{BSF->E}} = F_{\Delta n} f j_{0E} \frac{\Delta p_E}{p_0} + j_{\text{out}}. \tag{10}$$

Now, we have enough independent equations in order to solve our problem. We consider a system of equations, with (3), (4), and (8)–(10). By solving it, we obtain the excess carrier concentration on each area (Δp_i) as a function of Δp_E and j_{out}. The result can be written as the general expression

$$\Delta p_i = (\alpha_i \Delta p_E + \beta_i j_{\text{out}}) / \chi \tag{11}$$

where the coefficient χ is the same for every region

$$\chi = 1 + R_{d\_BSF-E} F_{\Delta n} (1-f) f j_{0\text{BSF}} p_0^{-1}. \tag{12}$$

For the front, we have

$$\alpha_F = 1 + \left[R_{d\_F-R} + (1-f)^2 R_{d\_BSF-E} \right] F_{\Delta n} f j_{0E} p_0^{-1}$$
$$+ [R_{d\_F-R} + f (f + R_{d\_F-R} F_{\Delta n} j_{0E} p_0^{-1})$$
$$\times R_{d\_BSF-E}] F_{\Delta n} (1-f) j_{0\text{BSF}} p_0^{-1} \tag{13}$$

$$\beta_F = \left[1 + R_{d\_BSF-E} (1-f) F_{\Delta n} j_{0\text{BSF}} p_0^{-1} \right] R_{d\_F-R}$$
$$+ R_{d\_BSF-E} (1-f)^2. \tag{14}$$

For the BSF region, we have

$$\alpha_{\text{BSF}} = 1 + R_{d\_BSF-E} F_{\Delta n} (1-f) f j_{0E} p_0^{-1} \tag{15}$$

$$\beta_{\text{BSF}} = R_{d\_BSF-E} (1-f) p_0. \tag{16}$$

For the bulk region, we have

$$\alpha_B = [(1-f) \alpha_{\text{BSF}} + \alpha_F + f\chi]/2 \tag{17}$$

$$\beta_B = [(1-f) \beta_{\text{BSF}} + \beta_F]/2. \tag{18}$$

Finally, the general relation between the current of the solar cell and the excess carrier density at the emitter region can be calculated as

$$j_{\text{lum}} = [\{ j_{0F}\ \alpha_F + j_{0B}\alpha_B + (1-f) j_{0\text{BSF}}\ \alpha_{\text{BSF}} \} \chi^{-1}$$
$$+ f j_{0E}] F_{\Delta n} \Delta p_E p_0^{-1} + [\{ j_{0F}\ \beta_F + j_{0B}\beta_B$$
$$+ (1-f) j_{0\text{BSF}}\ \beta_{\text{BSF}} \} F_{\Delta n} j_{\text{out}} (p_0\chi)^{-1} + 1] j_{\text{out}}. \tag{19}$$

In order to simplify this equation, we introduce the equivalent saturation current density ($j_{0\text{eq}}$) and the equivalent diffusion resistance (R_{d_eq}). (19) can then be written as

$$j_{\text{lum}} = j_{0\text{eq}} F_{\Delta n} p_0^{-1} [\Delta p_E + R_{d\_\text{eq}} j_{\text{out}}] + j_{\text{out}}. \tag{20}$$

The expanded expressions of $j_{0\mathrm{eq}}$ and R_{d_eq} are the following:

$$j_{0\mathrm{eq}} = \Big\langle j_{0B} + j_{0F} + [(1-f)\,j_{0\mathrm{BSF}} + f j_{0E}] \times [1 + R_{d\_F-R}$$
$$\times \{ j_{0B}/2 + j_{0E}\} F_{\Delta n} p_0^{-1}] + R_{d\_\mathrm{BSF}-E}\,(1-f)\,f$$
$$\times [f\,(j_{0\mathrm{BSF}} - j_{0E})\,(j_{0B} + j_{0F})$$
$$+ j_{0E}\,(j_{0\mathrm{BSF}} + j_{0B} + j_{0F})$$
$$+ R_{d\_F-R} F_{\Delta n} j_{0F} p_0^{-1} j_{0\mathrm{BSF}}\,(j_{0B}/2 + j_{0F})]\,F_{\Delta n}\,p_0^{-1}\Big\rangle$$
$$\times \left[1 + R_{d\_\mathrm{BSF}-E} F_{\Delta n}\,(1-f)\,f j_{0\mathrm{BSF}} p_0^{-1} \right]^{-1}.$$

$$R_{d\_\mathrm{eq}} = \langle (j_{0B}/2 + j_{0F})\,R_{d\_F-R} + (1-f)\,[(1-f)$$
$$\times (j_{0\mathrm{BSF}} + j_{0B} + j_{0F}) + F_{\Delta n} j_{0\mathrm{BSF}} p_0^{-1}\,(j_{0B}/2 + j_{0F})$$
$$\times R_{d\_F-R}]\,R_{d\_\mathrm{BSF}-E} \rangle \times [1 + R_{d\_\mathrm{BSF}-E} F_{\Delta n}\,(1-f)$$
$$f j_{0\mathrm{BSF}} p_0^{-1}]^{-1}\,j_{0\mathrm{eq}}^{-1}.$$

D. Simplified Solution for the Minority Carriers

The complete expressions of $j_{0\mathrm{eq}}$ and R_{d_eq} are valid without conditions on the geometry and very weak conditions on the diode saturation current.[2] However, most of the IBC solar cells will meet certain conditions, leading to a much simpler approximation of $j_{0\mathrm{eq}}$ and R_{d_eq}.

The recombination at region i might be limited by one of the following:

1) the saturation current of the region, e.g., when the region i is well passivate;
2) the diffusion of the carriers to the region i, e.g., when the region i is very small and covers only a few percent of the surface. This was reported to be the case of laser fired contacts on rear passivated cells [19].

For IBC solar cells, it is important to obtain a low saturation current and a low diffusion resistance for each region. Therefore, it is very probable that the recombination is limited by the saturation current ($j_{0i}\,F_{\Delta n} p_0^{-1} \ll R_{di-j}^{-1}$). Concretely, this condition can be written under the form $j_{0F} \mathrm{F\_} \Delta n p_0^{-1} \ll R_{d\_F-R}^{-1}$ for the front, $j_{0B}\,F_{\Delta n} p_0^{-1} \ll R_{d\_F-R}^{-1}$ for the bulk, $j_{0\mathrm{BSF}}\,F_{\Delta n} p_0^{-1} \ll R_{d\_\mathrm{BSF}-E}^{-1}$ for the BSF, and $j_{0E}\,F_{\Delta n} p_0^{-1} \ll R_{d\_\mathrm{BSF}-E}^{-1}$ for the emitter. When these conditions are fulfilled, the following simplified expression of $j_{0\mathrm{eq}}$ and R_{d_eq} can be used:

$$j_{0\mathrm{eq}} = j_{0B} + j_{0F} + (1-f)\,j_{0\mathrm{BSF}} + f j_{0E} \qquad (21)$$

$$R_{d\_\mathrm{eq}} = [(j_{0B}/2 + j_{0F})\,R_{d\_F-R} + (1-f)^2$$
$$\times (j_{0\mathrm{BSF}} + j_{0B} + j_{0F})\,R_{d\_\mathrm{BSF}-E}]\,j_{0\mathrm{eq}}^{-1}. \qquad (22)$$

By implementing (21) and (22) in (20), we obtain

$$j_{\mathrm{lum}} = \{ j_{0B} + j_{0F} + (1-f)\,j_{0\mathrm{BSF}} + f j_{0E} \}\,F_{\Delta n}\frac{\Delta p_E}{p_0}$$
$$+ \Bigg\{ [(j_{0B}/2 + j_{0F})\,R_{d\_F-R} + (1-f)^2$$
$$\times (j_{0\mathrm{BSF}} + j_{0B} + j_{0F})\,R_{d\_\mathrm{BSF}-E}]\,\frac{F_{\Delta n}}{p_0} + 1 \Bigg\}\,j_{\mathrm{out}} \qquad (23)$$

which is a simple description of the recombination losses in an IBC solar cell.

In the next step, we focus on the majority carrier transport and, particularly, on the calculation of the solar cell voltage.

E. Voltage of the Solar Cell

The potential of the solar cell builds up toward the p-n junction and at the back surface field (V_{BSF}). The electrical potential difference (V_E) at the p-n junction is

$$V_E = V_{\mathrm{th}} \ln\left(\frac{\Delta p_E}{p_0}\right). \qquad (24)$$

The electrical potential difference (V_{BSF}) at the BSF region is

$$V_{\mathrm{BSF}} = V_{\mathrm{th}} \ln\left(\frac{N_D + \Delta p_{\mathrm{BSF}}}{N_D}\right)$$
$$= V_{\mathrm{th}} \ln\left(1 + \frac{\alpha_{\mathrm{BSF}}\Delta p_E + \beta_{\mathrm{BSF}} j_{\mathrm{out}}}{N_D \chi}\right). \qquad (25)$$

There are two electrical potential losses due to the majority carrier transport in the bulk. The net current (j_{net}) can be described as follows:

$$\vec{j}_{\mathrm{net}} = -\sigma \vec{\nabla} V + (D_n - D_p)\,q^{-1} \vec{\nabla} p$$
$$\vec{\nabla} V = \vec{j}_{\mathrm{net}}/\sigma - (D_n - D_p)\,\vec{\nabla} p / (q\sigma). \qquad (26)$$

The first part of (26) corresponds to the ohmic losses and the second to the Dember potential. The Dember potential losses (V_{dem}) can be expressed as the form [19]

$$V_{\mathrm{dem}} = \frac{D_n - D_p}{D_n + D_p} V_{\mathrm{th}} \ln\left[\frac{\Delta p_{\mathrm{BSF}}\,(\mu_n + \mu_p) + N_D \mu_n}{\Delta p_E\,(\mu_n + \mu_p) + N_D \mu_n} \right]$$
$$V_{\mathrm{dem}} = \frac{D_n - D_p}{D_n + D_p} V_{\mathrm{th}} \ln\left[\frac{\alpha_{\mathrm{BSF}}}{\chi} + \frac{\beta_{\mathrm{BSF}} j_{\mathrm{out}} \chi^{-1}\,(\mu_n + \mu_p)}{\Delta p_E\,(\mu_n + \mu_p) + N_D \mu_n} \right].$$
$$(27)$$

We still need to take into account the potential losses (V_{res}) due to series resistance

$$V_{\mathrm{res}} = (R_{s\_\mathrm{int}} + R_{s\_\mathrm{ext}})\,j_{\mathrm{out}} \qquad (28)$$

where R_{s_int} and R_{s_ext} are the internal and the external series resistance, respectively. R_{s_int} only includes the resistance losses in the bulk of the wafer. All the other resistances (contact resistance, resistance in the fingers, and bus-bars …) are included in R_{s_ext}. Note that R_{s_int} depends on the injection level ($F_{\Delta n}$), as the bulk resistivity decreases with the injection. The way R_{s_int} might be calculated is described in Appendix B.

Finally, the output voltage (V_{out}) of the solar cell can be obtained from

$$V_E + V_{\mathrm{BSF}} = V_{\mathrm{dem}} + V_{\mathrm{res}} + V_{\mathrm{out}}. \qquad (29)$$

F. Current Voltage Characteristic

Equation (20) gives a relation between the output current (j_{out}) and the carrier concentration at the emitter (p_E). In Section II-E, a relation (see (28)) between the output voltage (V_{out})

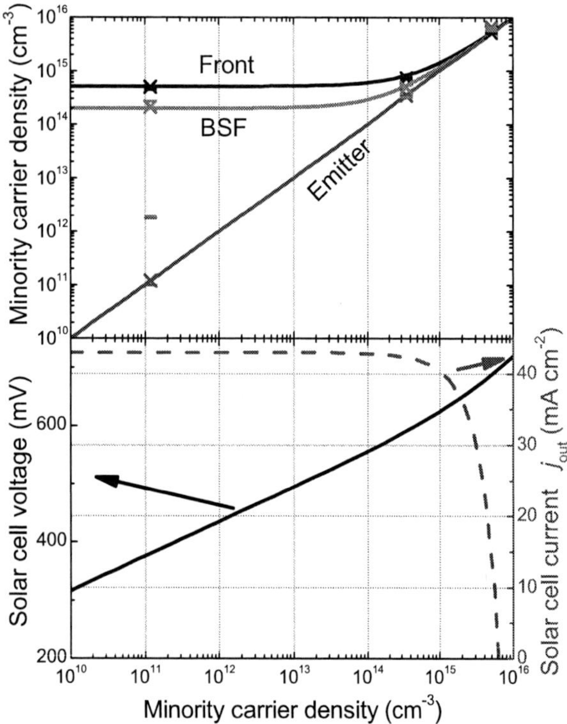

Fig. 2. Minority carrier density on the front, BSF and emitter, output voltage, and output current as a function of the minority carrier density on the emitter region (p_E). On the upper part of the graph, the crosses correspond to the average minority carrier density for the FEM simulation, and the — symbols correspond to the minmum and maximal values. The FEM simulation results are given around the short circuit, maximum power point, and open circuit conditions

and p_E is given. Therefore, the current–voltage (*I–V*) characteristic is obtained by varying p_E and by calculating the corresponding V_{out} and j_{out}. An example is given in the bottom part of Fig. 2.

III. Results and Discussion

A. Simulation Using a Conductive Boundary Model

In order to proove the validity of this model, we implemented a conductive boundary finite-element simulation in COMSOL Multiphysics based on the freely available CoBo model introduced by Brendel *et al.* [21]. The bulk lifetime and the Auger recombination models are the same as for the analytical model. For the generation, a fit from Fischer was used [15]. Each conductive boundary (Emitter, BSF, front) is represented by a dark saturation current density (j_{0i}) and a sheet resistance (ρ_i).

The presented analytical model does not explicitly include the sheet resistance. For this reason, all the sheet resistances (except for the front) were set to zero in the CoBo model. The authors expect that the sheet resistance would mainly impact the series resistance of the solar cell. This was verified comparing the model of this paper with CoBo for sheet resistance from 20–150 Ω^-2. An external series resistance obtained by solving the Poisson equation for a homogenous current ($R_{s\_\text{ext}} = L_p^2(f_E^* \rho_E$

$+ f_{\text{BSF}}^* \rho_{\text{BSF}})/12$) was used for the analytical model. Less than 0.2% deviation for the $V_{\text{oc}}, j_{\text{sc}}$, FF, and η was observed.

B. Comparison Between the Analytical Model and Numerical Simulations

For the comparison of both models the saturation current density (j_0) of the emitter, the BSF, and the front surface field were varied independently. j_{0E} and $j_{0\text{BSF}}$ were varied from 20 to 500 fA/cm^2, which cover most of the typical range of application. The emitter fraction was varied between three values 30%, 50%, and 70%. In addition, the period (l_p) of the rear pattern were varied from 200 μm to 4 mm. This model was tested for a very large range of parameters, including most of the practical cases.

In Fig. 3(a), j_{0E} is varied. A very good agreement was found between the simulation and the analytical model. The variation of j_{0E} leaves the j_{sc} almost unchanged.

In Fig. 3(b), $j_{0\text{BSF}}$ is varied. Here, a very good agreement is obtained for $j_{0\text{BSF}} < 500$ fA/cm^2. For high $j_{0\text{BSF}}$, the analytical model losses accuracy, however the deviation stays in an acceptable range ($<3\%$). It should be noticed that $j_{0\text{BSF}}$ has a higher impact on the efficiency than j_{0E}. Both parameters show a similar impact on V_{oc} and FF; however, $j_{0\text{BSF}}$ also impacts j_{sc}. This effect, known as "electrical shading," is due to an increased recombination on the BSF.

In Fig. 3(c), j_{0FSF} is varied. For this variation, the simulation and the analytical model agreed very well.

In Fig. 3(d), l_p is varied. For l_p lower than 4 mm, a very good agreement was found. For very large l_p, a significant deviation is observed. However, so large distances between the contacts are not relevant for the practical application, as almost all the relevant technologies allow optimal l_p of 2 mm or lower.

The range of parameters investigated allows finding the following limits of the analytical model:

1) For $j_{0\text{BSF}} > 500$ fA/cm^2, the inhomogeneity of the recombination current on the BSF becomes significant. Such inhomogenities are not taken into account in the calculation of $R_{d\_\text{BSF-E}}$ given in Appendix A. A refined calculation of $R_{d\_\text{BSF-E}}$ should lead to better results.

2) For $L_p > 4$ mm, a refined analytical calculation of $R_{d\_\text{BSF-E}}$ would have been needed for the same reason as above. In addition, one condition for validity of the model (see footnote three,[3]) is not verified for this case. This condition guaranties a low inhomogeneity of the excess carrier density in the solar cell.

For a large majority of cases investigated here, a very good agreement between both models is observed. In Fig. 4, the $V_{\text{oc}}, j_{\text{sc}}$, FF, and η are plotted for the analytical model and for CoBo model. For all the cases studied apart from $j_{0\text{BSF}} = 500$ fA/cm^2 and $l_p = 4$ mm, both models agree with less than 1% deviation. The analytical model shown here is therefore very accurate for most of the practical applications for the studied cell structure.

IV. Summary

An analytical model for IBC solar cells is developed. The results of this model are in very good agreement with the

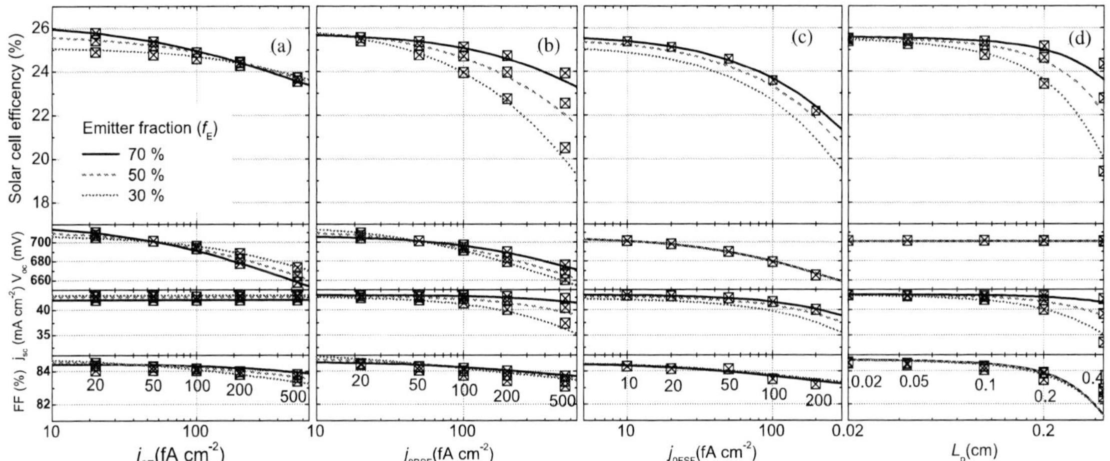

Fig. 3. Results of the analytical model of this work (lines) and the numerical simulations using a CoBo model (squares). The bulk is n-type 2 Ω cm, and the wafer thickness is 250 μm, when they are not varied $j_{0E} = j_{0BSF} = 50$ fA/cm^2, $j_{0FSF} = 20$ fA/cm^2, $l_p = 1$ mm. (a) Variation of the emitter saturation current $-j_{0E}$, (b) variation of the back surface field saturation current $-j_{0BSF}$, (c) variation of the front surface field saturation current $- j_{0FSF}$, (d) variation of the distance between to contacts $-L_p$.

conductive boundary model in the investigated range. The deviation obtained is less than 1% for most of the relevant solar cell structures. In extreme case of very high j_0 or very large structure ($l_p = 4$ mm), the deviations increase to more than 2%.

This model offers a very interesting compromise between invested resources and results accuracy. On one hand, it needs fewer resources (computing time, license expense, expert, accuracy of input data) than a computer simulation, for a minimal loss of accuracy. On the other hand, it is more complex than a 1-D model. However, the gain of accuracy is substantial, as it includes the "electrical shading."

Finally, a more refined calculation of the diffusion resistance would probably increase the accuracy of this model. In addition, a model including a passivated area between the emitter and the BSF would enlarge the range of application.

APPENDIX A
CALCULATION OF THE DIFFUSION RESISTANCE

A. Diffusion Resistance Between the Front and the Rear

All the generation is supposed to occur only at the front surface. Therefore, the continuity equation in the bulk is

$$\nabla^2 \Delta p \approx \frac{\Delta p}{L_{\text{diff}}^2} \qquad (A.1)$$

where L_{diff} is the diffusion length ($L_{\text{diff}}^2 = \tau_{\text{bulk}} D_\alpha$) [22], [23]. We define $\varepsilon = \Delta p - \Delta p_{\text{avr}}$, where Δp_{avr} is the average excess carrier density in the bulk. From the superposition principle, (A.1) is also valid for ε replacing Δp.

The next step is to calculate R_{d_F-R}. (A.1) is solved supposing a 1-D flow of minority carriers from front to rear $j_{F->R}$. We call ε_F and ε_R the average value of ε on the front and the rear, respectively, $\varepsilon_F - \varepsilon_R = R_{d\_F-R} \, j_{F->R}$. By solving (A.1)

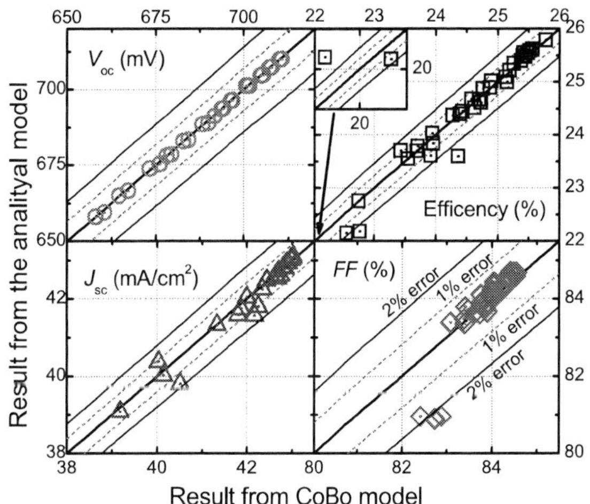

Fig. 4. Result of the analytical model as a function of the result of the CoBo model. V_{oc}, j_{sc}, FF, and η are given for all the simulation shown in Fig. 3.

for ε, we obtain

$$R_{d\_E-R} = \frac{2L_{\text{diff}} \tanh\left(W/\left(2L_{\text{diff}}\right)\right)}{qD_\alpha} \underset{L_{\text{diff}} \gg W}{\approx} \frac{W}{qD_\alpha}. \quad (A.2)$$

B. Diffusion Resistance Between the Emitter and BSF

In order to calculate the $R_{d\_BSF\_E}$, (A.1) needs to be solved for the following boundary conditions:
1) at the front $j_p = j_{0F} \Delta p / p_0$;
2) at the emitter j_p is supposed to be constant, with $f j_p = j_{BSF->E}$;
3) at the BSF j_p is supposed to be constant, with $(1 - f) j_p = j_{BSF->E}$.

Using the Fourier transform resolution method, for line contacts, we obtain

$$R_{d\_BSF-E} = \frac{1}{qD_\alpha} \frac{2}{(1-f)^2 f^2} \sum_{i \in \mathbb{N}^*} \left[\frac{\sin(i\pi f)}{i\pi} \right]^2 \kappa_i a_i$$

$$\kappa_i = \left(L_{\text{diff}}^{-2} + (i2\pi)^2 l_p^{-2} \right)^{-.5}$$

$$a_i = \frac{j_{0F} F_{\Delta n} \kappa_i \tanh(W/\kappa_i) + qp_0 D_\alpha}{j_{0F} F_{\Delta n} \kappa_i + qp_0 D_\alpha \tanh(W/\kappa_i)}. \qquad (A.3)$$

where L_p is the distance between the lines.

For square points BSF geometries with the emitter covering the rest of the surface, we have

$$R_{d\_BSF-E} = \frac{1}{qD_\alpha} \frac{2}{(1-f)^2 f^2}$$

$$\times \left\{ \sum_{i,j \in \mathbb{N}^*} \left[\frac{\sin(i\pi\sqrt{f})\sin(j\pi\sqrt{f})}{ij\pi^2} \right]^2 \kappa_{i,j} a_{i,j} \right.$$

$$\left. + f \sum_{i \in \mathbb{N}^*} \left[\frac{\sin(i\pi\sqrt{f})}{i\pi} \right]^2 \kappa_{i,0} a_{i,0} \right\}$$

$$\kappa_{i,j} = \left[L_{\text{diff}}^{-2} + (2\pi)^2 l_p^{-2} (i^2 + j^2) \right]^{-.5}$$

$$a_{i,j} = \frac{j_{0F} F_{\Delta n} \kappa_{i,j} \tanh(W/\kappa_{i,j}) + qp_0 D_\alpha}{j_{0F} F_{\Delta n} \kappa_{i,j} + qp_0 D_\alpha \tanh(W/\kappa_{i,j})}. \qquad (A.4)$$

Appendix B
Calculation of the Internal Series Resistance

For the calculation of the series resistance, the Poisson equation is solved for the electrical potential using the following boundary conditions.

1) At the front side, the net current is zero $j_{\text{net}} = 0$.
2) At the emitter, j_{net} is assumed constant, with $f j_{\text{net}} = j_{\text{out}}$.
3) At the BSF, j_{net} is assumed constant, with $(1-f)j_{\text{net}} = -j_{\text{out}}$.

Using the Fourier transform resolution method, for line contacts we obtain

$$R_{s\_\text{int}} = \frac{1}{F_{\Delta n}\sigma} \frac{2}{(1-f)^2 f^2} \sum_{i \in \mathbb{N}^*} \left[\frac{\sin(i\pi f)}{i\pi} \right]^2 \kappa_i a_i$$

$$\kappa_i = l_p (i2\pi)^{-1}, \quad a_i = \tanh(W/\kappa_i)^{-1}. \qquad (B.1)$$

For square points BSF geometries with the emitter covering the rest of the surface, we have

$$R_{s\_\text{int}} = \frac{1}{F_{\Delta n}\sigma} \frac{2}{(1-f)^2 f^2}$$

$$\times \left\{ \sum_{i,j \in \mathbb{N}^*} \left[\frac{\sin(i\pi\sqrt{f})\sin(j\pi\sqrt{f})}{ij\pi^2} \right]^2 \kappa_{i,j} a_{i,j} \right.$$

$$\left. + f \sum_{i \in \mathbb{N}^*} \left[\frac{\sin(i\pi\sqrt{f})}{i\pi} \right]^2 \kappa_{i,0} a_{i,0} \right\}$$

$$\kappa_{i,j} = l_p \left[(2\pi)^2 (i^2 + j^2) \right]^{-.5}, \quad a_{i,j} = \tanh(W/\kappa_{i,j})^{-1}. \qquad (B.2)$$

References

[1] M. D. Lammert and R. J. Schwartz, "The interdigitated back contact solar cell: A silicon solar cell for use in concentrated sunlight," *IEEE Trans. Electron. Devices*, vol. ED-24, no. 4, pp. 337–342, Apr. 1977.

[2] R. J. Schwartz and M. D. Lammert, "Silicon solar cells for high concentration applications," presented at the Int. Electron Devices Meeting, Washington, DC, USA, 1975.

[3] D. D. Smith, P. J. Cousins, A. Masad, A. Waldhauer, S. Westerberg, M. Johnson, T. Xiuwen, T. Dennis, G. Harley, G. Solomon, R. Seung, M. Shepherd, S. Harrington, M. Defensor, A. Leygo, P. Tomada, W. Junbo, T. Pass, L. Ann, L. Smith, N. Bergstrom, C. Nicdao, P. Tipones, and D. Vicente, "Generation III high efficiency lower cost technology: Transition to full scale manufacturing," presented at the 38th IEEE Photovoltaic Specialists Conf., Austin, TX, USA, 2012.

[4] P. J. Cousins, D. D. Smith, H.-C. Luan, J. Manning, T. D. Dennis, A. Waldhauer, K. E. Wilson, G. Harley, and W. P. Mulligan, "Generation 3: Improved performance at lower cost," presented at the 35th IEEE Photovoltaic Specialists Conf., Honolulu, HI, USA, 2010.

[5] R. A. Sinton, Y. Kwark, J. Y. Gan, and R. M. Swanson, "27.5-percent silicon concentrator solar cells," *IEEE Electron. Device Lett.*, vol. EDL-7, no. 10, pp. 567–569, Oct. 1986.

[6] R. A. Sinton, "Device physics and characterization of silicon point-contact solar cells," M.S. Thesis, Stanford Univ., Stanford, CA, USA, 1987.

[7] R. M. Swanson, "Point contact solar cells: Theory and modeling," presented at the 18th IEEE Photovoltaic Specialists Conf., Las Vegas, NV, USA, 1985.

[8] R. M. Swanson and R. A. Sinton, "High-efficiency silicon solar cells," in *Advances in solar energy, vol. 6*, K. W. Böer, Ed. New York, NY, USA: Plenum, 1990, pp. 427–84.

[9] R. M. Swanson, "Point-contact solar cells: Modeling and experiment," *Solar Cells*, vol. 17, pp. 85–118, 1986.

[10] R. M. Swanson and R. A. Sinton, "Point contact silicon solar cells," presented at the 7th Eur. Photovoltaic Solar Energy Conf., Sevilla, Spain, 1986.

[11] P. Verlinden, F. Van de Wiele, G. Stehelin, and J. P. David, "Optimized interdigitated back contact (IBC) solar cell for high concentrated sunlight," presented at the 18th IEEE Photovoltaic Specialists Conf., Las Vegas, NV, USA, 1985.

[12] M. Hermle, F. Granek, O. Schultz, and S. W. Glunz, "Analyzing the effects of front-surface fields on back-junction silicon solar cells using the charge-collection probability and the reciprocity theorem," *J. Appl. Phys.*, vol. 103, p. 054507, 2008.

[13] S. Kluska, F. Granek, M. Rüdiger, M. Hermle, and S. W. Glunz, "Modeling and optimization study of industrial n-type high-efficiency back-contact back-junction silicon solar cells," *Sol. Energ. Mat. Sol. Cells*, vol. 94, pp. 568–577, 2010.

[14] P. Saint-Cast, "Passivation of Si Surfaces by PECVD Aluminum Oxide," Ph.D. dissertation, Univ. Konstance, Konstanz, Germany, 2012, pp. 79–80.

[15] B. Fischer, "Loss analysis of crystalline silicon solar cells using photoconductance and quantum efficiency measurements," in *Physics*. Konstanz: Universität, Konstanz, Germany, 2003, p. 198.

[16] D. E. Kane and R. M. Swanson, "Measurement of the emitter saturation current by a contactless photoconductivity decay method (silicon solar cells)," presented at the 18th IEEE Photovoltaic Specialists Conf., Las Vegas, NV, USA, 1985.

[17] J. A. Giesecke, M. Kasemann, and W. Warta, "Separation of recombination properties of silicon solar cells and wafers via luminescence imaging," presented at the 24th European Photovoltaic Solar Energy Conf., Hamburg, Germany, 2009.

[18] A. Richter, S. W. Glunz, F. Werner, J. Schmidt, and A. Cuevas, "Improved quantitative description of Auger recombination in crystalline silicon," *Phys. Rev. B*, vol. 86, p. 165202, 2012.

[19] P. Saint-Cast, J. Nekarda, M. Hofmann, S. Kuehnhold, and R. Preu, "Recombination on locally processed wafer surfaces," *Energy Procedia*, vol. 27, pp. 259–266, 2012.

[20] P. Würfel, *Physics of Solar Cells*. Weinheim, Germany: Wiley, 2005.

[21] R. Brendel, "Modeling solar cells with the dopant-diffused layers treated as conductive boundaries," *Prog. Photov., Res. Appl.*, vol. 20, pp. 31–43, 2012.

[22] W. R. Thurber, R. L. Mattis, Y. M. Liu, and J. J. Filliben, "Resistivity-dopant density relationship for boron-doped silicon," *J. Electrochem. Soc.*, vol. 127, pp. 2291–4, 1980.

[23] W. R. Thurber, R. L. Mattis, Y. M. Liu, and J. J. Filliben, "Resistivity-dopant density relationship for phosphorus-doped silicon," *J. Electrochem. Soc.*, vol. 127, pp. 1807–12, 1980.

Pierre Saint-Cast was born in Lorient, France, in 1982. He received the M.Sc. degree in micro- and nanoelectronics from Joseph Fourier University, Grenoble, France, and the Engineering degree from the Polytechnic Institute of Grenoble, both in 2007, and the Ph.D. degree from the University of Konstanz, Konstanz, Germany.

Since 2008, he has been with Fraunhofer Institute for Solar Energy Systems, Freiburg, Germany. His research interests include the development of passivation layers for solar cell applications, especially plasma-enhanced chemical vapor deposition of Al_2O_3 layers and the analytical modeling of the electrical transport in Si solar cells devices.

Achim Kimmerle was born in 1983. He studied physics at the University of Freiburg, Germany, and the University of Sevilla, Spain. In 2011, he received the Diploma thesis from the Fraunhofer Institute for Solar Energy Systems, Freiburg, Germany, where he is currently working toward the Ph.D. degree, developing different concepts for back-contact back-junction silicon solar cells with industrially feasible technologies.

Christian Reichel, photograph and biography not available at the time of publication.

Milan Padilla was born in Berlin, Germany, in 1985. He received the Diploma degree in physics from Technische Universität München, Munich, Germany, in 2011, on the study of photo-current dynamics of single GaAs nanowires. He is currently working toward the Ph.D. degree with Fraunhofer ISE, Freiburg, Germany. His research interests include the development of new characterization methods for spatially resolved loss analysis of high-efficiency silicon solar cells, using luminescence-imaging and dark- and illuminated lock-in thermography. His dissertation is funded by the Reiner Lemoine Stiftung.

Correlating Multicrystalline Silicon Defect Types Using Photoluminescence, Defect-band Emission, and Lock-in Thermography Imaging Techniques

Steve Johnston, Harvey Guthrey, Fei Yan, Katherine Zaunbrecher, Mowafak Al-Jassim, Pati Rakotoniaina, and Martin Kaes

Abstract—A set of neighboring multicrystalline silicon wafers has been processed through different steps of solar cell manufacturing and then images were collected for characterization. The imaging techniques include band-to-band photoluminescence (PL), defect-band or subbandgap PL (subPL), and dark lock-in thermography (DLIT). Defect regions can be tracked from as-cut wafers throughout processing to the finished cells. The finished cell's defect regions detected by band-to-band PL imaging correlate well to diffusion length and quantum efficiency maps. The most detrimental defect regions, type A, also correlate well to reverse-bias breakdown areas as shown in DLIT images. These type A defect regions appear dark in band-to-band PL images, and have subPL emissions. The subPL of type A defects shows strong correlations to poor cell performance and high reverse breakdown at the starting wafer steps (as-cut and textured), but the subPL becomes relatively weak after antireflection coating (ARC) and on the finished cell. Type B defects are regions that have lower defect density but still show detrimental cell performance. After ARC, type B defects emit more intense subPL than type A regions; consequently, type B subPL also shows better correlation to cell performance at the starting wafer steps rather than at the ARC process step and in the finished cell.

Index Terms—Imaging, impurities, infrared imaging, photoluminescence, photovoltaic cells, silicon.

I. INTRODUCTION

WHILE multicrystalline silicon (mc-Si) has cost advantages over single-crystalline Si, mc-Si has slightly lower efficiency because of cast-in defect regions. Clusters of dis-

Manuscript received June 10, 2013; revised August 16, 2013; accepted September 16, 2013. Date of publication October 17, 2013; date of current version December 16, 2013. This work was supported in part by the U.S. Department of Energy under Contract DE-AC36-08GO28308 with the National Renewable Energy Laboratory and also in part by the American Recovery and Reinvestment Act.

S. Johnston, H. Guthrey, and M. Al-Jassim are with the National Renewable Energy Laboratory, Golden, CO 80401 USA (e-mail: steve_johnston@nrel.gov; harvey.guthrey@nrel.gov; mowafak.aljassim@nrel.gov).

F. Yan is with Applied Materials, Santa Clara, CA 95054 USA (e-mail: feiyan@gmail.com).

K. Zaunbrecher is with the National Renewable Energy Laboratory, Golden, CO 80401 USA and also with Colorado State University, Fort Collins, CO 80526 USA (e-mail: kzaunbrecher@gmail.com).

P. Rakotoniaina is with the Silicor Materials, San Jose, CA 95161, USA (e-mail: pati.rakotoniaina@silicormaterials.com).

M. Kaes is with the Calisolar GmbH, Berlin D-12489, Germany (e-mail: martin.kaes@silicormaterials.com).

Color versions of one or more of the figures in this paper are available online at http://ieeexplore.ieee.org.

Digital Object Identifier 10.1109/JPHOTOV.2013.2283575

locations and small-angle grain boundaries become decorated with oxygen and metal impurities and form the regions of high carrier recombination [1]–[6]. These defect areas have been detected and characterized using various imaging techniques, such as electroluminescence (EL) [7] and photoluminescence (PL) [8], [9], including both band-to-band and defect-band emissions [10]–[17], and lock-in thermography (LIT) [18]–[23]. EL imaging on finished cells has shown two types of defect regions with different characteristics [24]–[26]. Type A defect regions exhibit strong band-to-band recombination, but weak defect band or sub-bandgap EL (subEL) emissions. Type A defects show strong correlation to prebreakdown regions identified by reverse-bias EL [27] or dark LIT (DLIT). Type B defect regions show strong subEL emissions but less detrimental band-to-band recombination (lower contrast EL) and less breakdown at reverse bias [25], [26]. We have collected images not only of the finished cell, but also from neighbor wafers that were pulled from the processing line at each process step. Contrary to finished cell characterization, strong sub-bandgap PL (subPL) emissions exist in Type A defects for process steps prior to the silicon nitride anti-reflection coating (ARC) deposition. Relatively stronger subEL emissions in Type B defects occur because of the temperature processing associated with the ARC deposition [28], [29]. In this paper, we spatially compare defect areas with cell performance; we show differences in defect density when comparing Type A and Type B defect regions; and we observe that the relatively low temperatures used during ARC processing can induce changes in subPL even on the starting as-cut wafer.

II. EXPERIMENTAL SETUP

We have used a Princeton Instruments PIXIS 1024BR Si-charge-coupled-device camera with sensitivity into the near-infrared range ($\sim$1100 nm) for band-to-band PL imaging. Defect-band emission images are collected using a FLIR SC2500 N InGaAs camera with lock-in data acquisition and sensitivity out to $\sim$1700 nm. A long-pass filter ($>$1350 nm) is used to block band-to-band emissions. Excitation light is provided by fiber-coupled 810-nm laser diodes such that $\sim$100 mW/cm^2 is uniformly ($\pm$10%) illuminated upon the wafers. Image acquisition times range from 1 to 2 min for starting wafers to just a few seconds for diffused and passivated wafers. Images of both band-to-band PL and defect-band, or subPL, emissions have been collected on neighbor wafers that have been processed through to different steps of cell manufacturing. (See

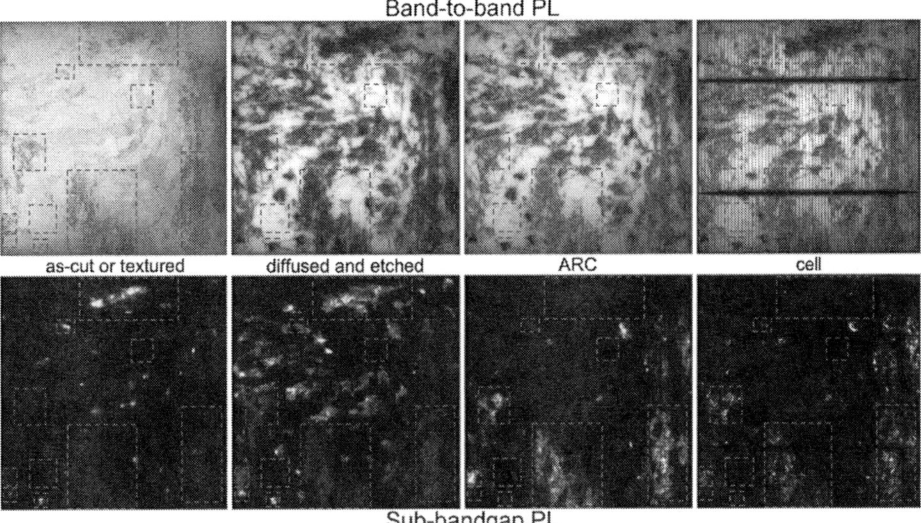

Fig. 1. Defect regions are identified on the images of neighbor wafers that were processed through different steps of cell manufacturing. The top row shows band-to-band PL imaging and the bottom row shows subPL imaging. Type A defects are highlighted in red, while Type B defects are highlighted in green. Defect-free regions are shown in blue.

Fig. 1). These wafers are from an interior brick of an ingot cast with electronic grade silicon. The wafers were selected from approximately half-way up within the brick (approximately wafer numbers 300 through 306 of about 600 total). The as-cut wafers are $\sim$200 μm thick. Various defect areas of this set provide examples of Type A and Type B regions. These regions vary in concentration from the bottom to the top of each brick. Other images not presented here also illustrated very similar examples of these defect regions in sets of wafers from ingot edge bricks, and ingots cast from upgraded metallurgical-grade (or solar grade) silicon. These other examples showed similar processing-related changes in band-to-band PL and subPL.

III. RESULTS AND DISCUSSION

A. Comparison of Band-to-band Photoluminescence and Sub Photoluminescence

There are six processing steps in which neighbor wafers were pulled from the processing line. In order, these steps are as-cut, textured, diffused, etched, ARC, and the finished cell. In Fig. 1, both band-to-band PL and subPL images for as-cut and textured wafers are very similar, therefore, only one of these is shown. Diffused wafers have stronger signals because of surface passivation and junction formation. After diffusion, the phosphosilicate glass (PSG) passivation leads to very high band-to-band PL image contrast between the high quality, defect-free silicon regions (bright) and the high-recombination regions (dark). When avoiding saturation of the bright areas, contrast scaling leads to poor visual clarity of the remaining image. Standard processing requires edge isolation and removal of the PSG for later contacting. This etching increases surface recombination and reduces the overall PL signal; thus, the lifetime distribution is smaller, and the image can be scaled so that more contrast is available to view the darker, recombination-active features. The second column of images in Fig. 1 shows the wafers after diffusion and etching. After diffusion, band-to-band PL and subPL images show more areas of recombination and defect band emission that were not as apparent in the starting wafer.

The ARC process step consists of depositing silicon nitride for 30 min at 450 °C. While rather small changes in band-to-band PL occur from the previous step, the subPL image changes dramatically. Many of the brightest subPL regions at the previous process step now have negligible subPL emissions compared with others. These defect regions that are characterized by a bright-to-dim transition of subPL during processing have been labeled Type A [25], [26] at the cell level, and a few such regions are outlined in red in Fig. 1. The brightest subPL regions after ARC had relatively dim emissions at the previous process step. These dim-to-bright defect regions have been labeled Type B [25], [26] at the cell level, and some select regions are outlined in green in Fig. 1.

Previously, we have shown that the temperatures of the ARC process promote large increases of subPL in the relatively less-dense, small-angle grain boundary regions, while higher-density grain boundary regions have less increase in subPL [28]. We also reported that higher temperatures ($>$500 °C) then caused the subPL to revert back to how it appeared before the ARC processing step [28].

B. Comparison of Photoluminescence to Internal Quantum Efficiency and Diffusion Length

The Type A defects, highlighted in red in Fig. 1, are the darkest features in the finished cell's band to band PL. These regions also represent the most detrimental defect areas, as shown in Fig. 2, where the internal quantum efficiency (IQE) is typically lowest at these Type A defect clusters. The IQE is collected using a Semilab mapping tool, which has a spot size of $\sim$100 μm.

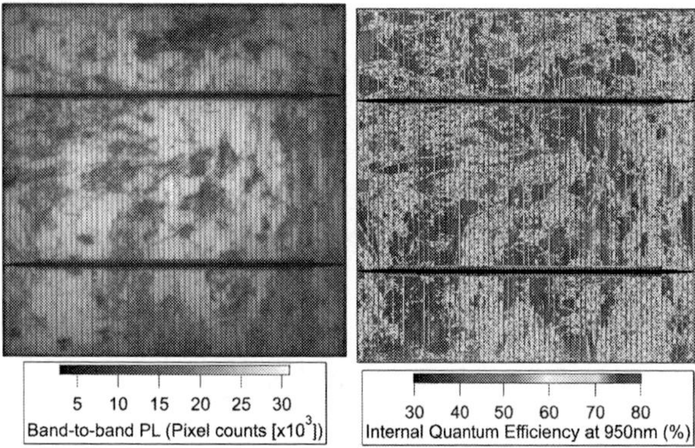

Fig. 2. Comparison of band-to-band PL and IQE (950 nm excitation) measured at the finished cell.

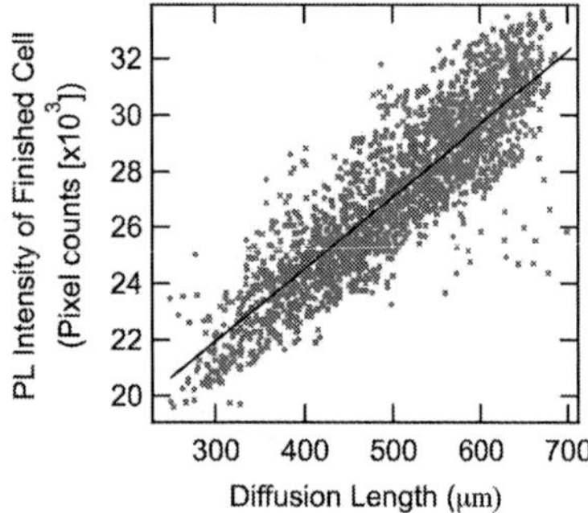

Fig. 3. Spatial comparison of PL intensity to mapped diffusion length on the finished cell.

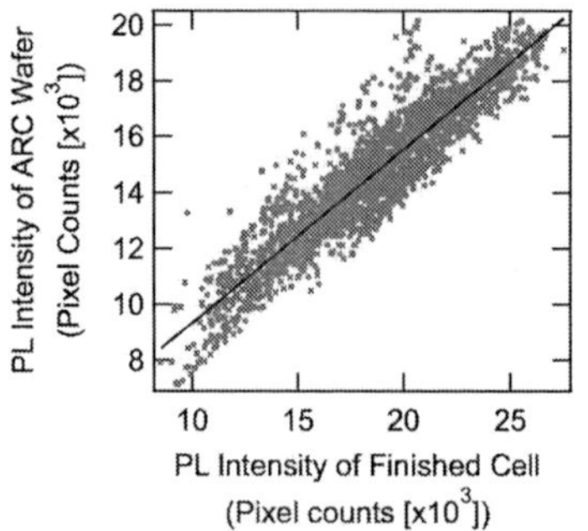

Fig. 4. Spatial PL intensity comparison of the finished cell to the neighbor wafer processed only through the ARC step. Bus bar areas were cropped from the images.

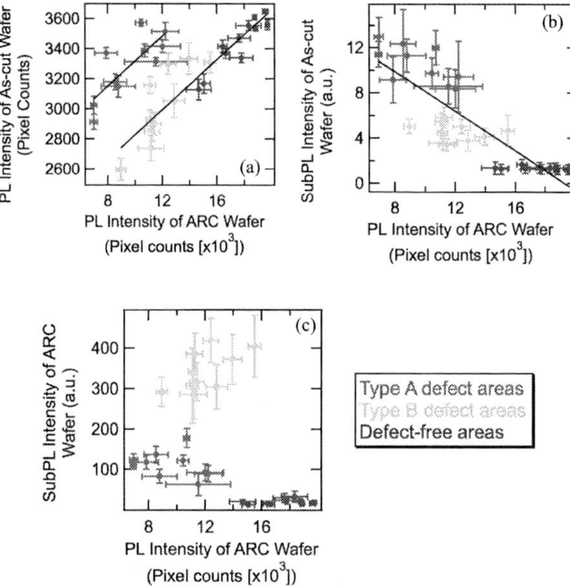

Fig. 5. Plots of image intensities compared with the band-to-band PL of the ARC wafer. Red points represent Type A defect areas, green points represent Type B defect areas, and blue points represent defect-free areas. The standard deviation of the selected area's averaging is shown by the error bars.

Fig. 2 shows a side-by-side comparison of the band-to-band PL image of the finished cell and the 950-nm excitation IQE map using a step size of 250 μm.

The plot of Fig. 3 shows a correlation of PL image intensity to diffusion length, calculated from IQE maps from a Semilab instrument at wavelengths of 1015, 950, and 850 nm. The PL image and diffusion length map are averaged down, or binned, to 50×50 pixels in size, and then the values of pixels in each spatial position are plotted against each other. This binning reduces the effect of misalignment of the grid lines and bus bars in the images. The good correlation shows that a PL image of the finished cell represents the defect-related spatial variation in cell performance.

Minimal changes in the PL image occur between the ARC and the cell screen-printing and firing steps. Fig. 4 shows strong correlation between the band-to-band PL images at the ARC and finished cell steps. The bus bar areas were cropped from each image for this comparison. This establishes that for this sample set, the ARC band-to-band PL image can be used to represent cell performance, and images from prior steps can be compared with the ARC PL to correlate to the finished cell's performance. The comparison of starting wafer images to ARC instead of the finished cell helps reduce analysis error and noise induced from the metallization pattern.

C. Correlation of Defect Areas to Cell Performance

Fig. 1 shows Type A defect regions highlighted in red, Type B defect regions highlighted in green, and defect-free regions in blue. These regions plus several other similar-type regions were more precisely outlined so that the selected areas were mostly dominated by that characteristic. Then, these defined areas were analyzed to give an average value and corresponding standard deviation. Fig. 5 shows plots of band-to-band PL and subPL from the as-cut wafer compared with band-to-band PL of the ARC wafer, which is the representative for cell performance.

In Fig. 5(a), the red points representing Type A defects, and green points representing Type B defects do not show significant differences in band-to-band PL intensity at the as-cut wafer phase. However, in Fig. 5(b), the subPL does show a trend that type A has the highest sub PL at the as-cut wafer stage,

     510

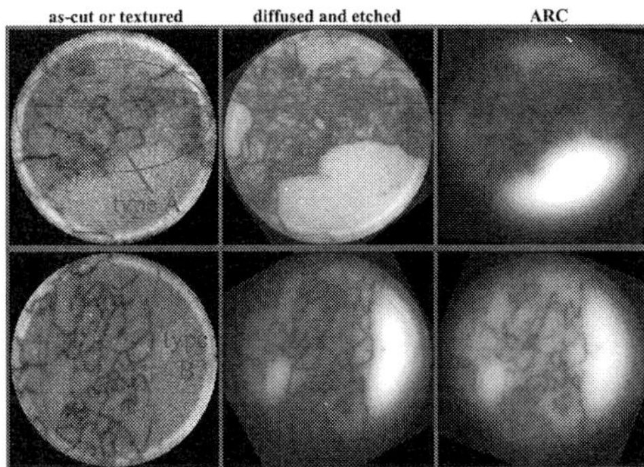

Fig. 6. Band-to-band PL zoomed-in images of defect areas at different process steps. The disks are ~1 cm in diameter.

which correlates to the lowest band-to-band PL intensity of the ARC wafer. The Type B regions represented by green points then follow the trend by showing correlation of the lower subPL intensity with higher band-to-band PL at the ARC wafer. Finally, the defect-free regions complete the trend by showing no subPL emissions and the highest band-to-band PL at the ARC wafer. In Fig. 5(c), the ARC-processing temperature-induced effect of the Type A and B defects is observed. The subPL of the Type B defect areas increases dramatically compared with that of the Type A defects, and the good correlation to ARC band-to-band PL, and cell performance, is no longer apparent.

D. Defect Density Comparison

For band-to-band PL, the Type A defects of the as-cut wafer show a correlation to the ARC band-to-band PL that is offset to larger values than the fit for Type B and relatively defect-free areas, as was shown in Fig. 5(a). Fig. 1 shows a trend—these Type A areas become relatively darker after the emitter diffusion process. A higher resolution example is shown in Fig. 6, in which grain boundaries within the high-defect density region of Type A become more apparent, likely because of gettering of impurities at the grain boundaries. The Type A grain boundaries become more recombination active after the diffusion process, and this results in the poor correlation between band-to-band PL of the as-cut and ARC wafers.

Grain boundaries of the Type B defect regions initially show recombination along the entire lengths of the grain boundaries and change relatively little throughout processing. The examples in Fig. 6 also reemphasize the higher density of grain boundaries prevalent in Type A defects, as mentioned previously [28].

E. Temperature Dependence of Defect Types

The Type A defects have been classified as having strong recombination but without showing strong subEL or subPL at the cell level. We have shown that a substantial change in subPL occurs at the ARC step; that Type A defects have relatively high subPL prior to ARC, and that the Type A/Type B switch of high subPL intensity occurs during the low temperature (~350° to 450 °C) processing of ARC. [28] As shown in Fig. 7, the low-temperature anneal of ~350 °C can even show such changes

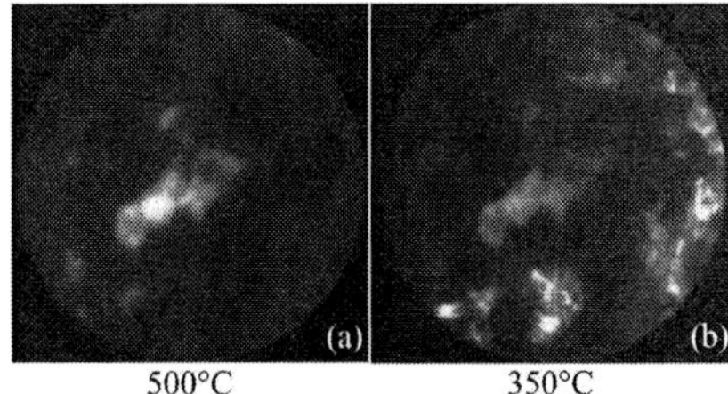

Fig. 7. SubPL of as-cut wafer section (~5 cm diameter) after heating at indicated temperature for 1 h.

in the as-cut wafer. Here, a sample of ~5-cm diameter in size shows a central Type A defect region surrounded by Type B defect regions near the edge. The subPL images of the starting condition (not shown) and after heating to a temperature of ~500 °C appear similar for both regions, as reported previously [28], but heating at ~350 °C causes a substantial increase of subPL in Type B regions.

Oxygen precipitates exist at the grain boundaries within the defect types, and such precipitates are thought to induce strain, which can trap secondary defects or impurities [1]–[3]. Enhanced diffusivity of oxygen to dislocations at temperatures as low as 350 °C has also been reported [30]–[32], suggesting that oxygen precipitates and perhaps other impurities such as iron [4]–[6] cause the dramatic changes in subPL at the ARC processing step, or equivalent heating. Because of the larger spacing between grain boundaries, Type B defects may getter more impurities from larger volumes of crystalline silicon between the grain boundaries. Thus, the Type B subPL intensity could increase to larger values than in Type A regions. While temperatures lower than 500 °C can allow impurities to getter and precipitates to possibly form and/or grow, temperatures greater than 500 °C may be dissolving precipitates and allowing impurities to diffuse throughout the silicon again.

F. Correlation of Defect Areas to Reverse Breakdown

DLIT imaging is used to characterize nonuniform heating of the cell induced from defect regions or other variations. A reverse-bias breakdown DLIT image of the cell of Fig. 1 is shown in Fig. 8. To collect the image, we used a Cedip Silver 660M (FLIR SC5600-M) InSb camera with 640 × 512 pixels. Reverse bias is applied to the cell by alternating from −12.9 to −13.1 V at a frequency of 25 Hz and 50% duty cycle. This is effectively a slope-DLIT measurement and emphasizes mostly the Type II impurity-related defects that induce breakdown currents [21]–[23].

The same defined areas used to create the plots of Fig. 5 are averaged to create the plots of Fig. 9. While a correlation of band-to-band PL on the as-cut wafer is not apparent in Fig. 9(a), Fig 9(b) shows that the subPL of the as-cut wafer correlates well to the breakdown regions for Type A and B defects.

Fig. 9(c) shows a correlation between band-to-band PL of the ARC wafer and the cell DLIT. This band-to-band PL correlation is now more evident because of the darkening of Type A defects after the diffusion process. However, because of the relative

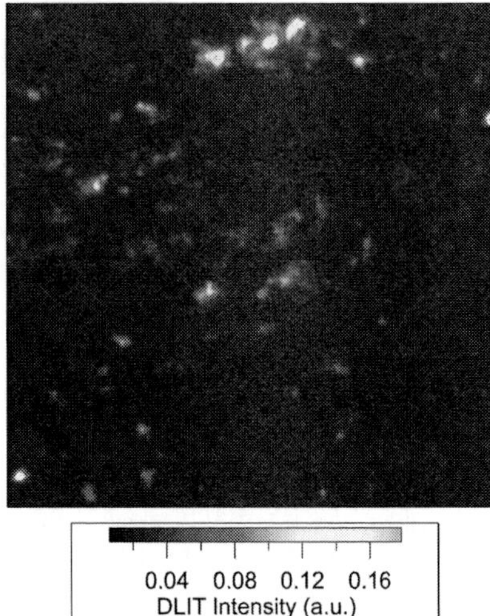

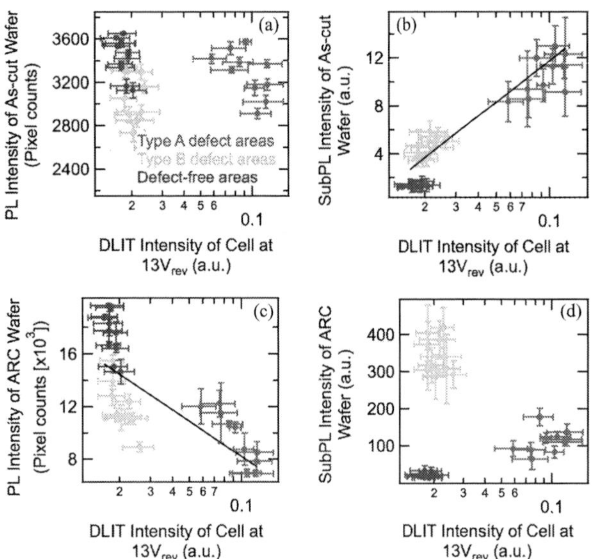

Fig. 8. DLIT image of the finished cell of Fig. 1 using slope-DLIT centered at a reverse bias of 13 V.

Fig. 9. Plots of image intensities compared to the cell's $13V_{rev}$ DLIT values. Red points represent Type A defect areas, green points represent Type B defect areas, and blue points represent defect-free areas. The standard deviation of the selected area's averaging is shown by the error bars.

switch of Type A and Type B subPL intensities at the ARC step, the subPL, in Fig. 9(d), no longer shows a good correlation to cell DLIT at the final two steps of processing.

G. Small Angle Grain Boundaries

The substantial differences between Type A and Type B defect areas are shown, by imaging, to be grain boundary density, activation of strong recombination for Type A defects at the diffusion step, and increasing subPL of Type B defects at ARC-processing temperatures. Fig. 10 shows images of a region that is predominantly Type A on the right side and Type B on the left

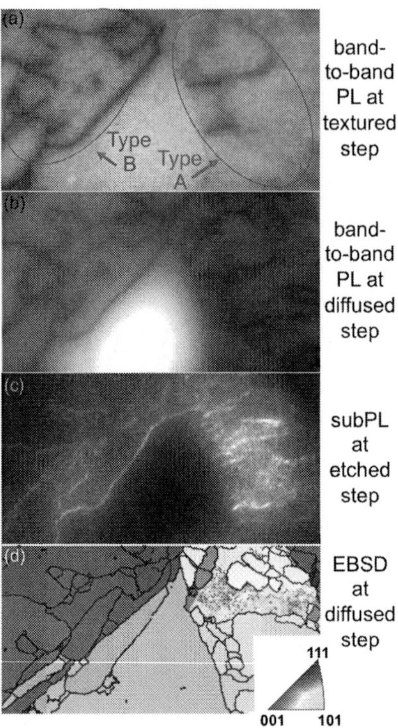

Fig. 10. Region ~5 mm wide composed of predominantly Type A defects on the right side and Type B defects on the left. (a) Band-to-band PL at textured step. (b) Band-to-band PL at diffused step. (c) SubPL at etched step. (d) EBSD map at diffused step.

side. Fig. 10(a) is a band-to-band PL image at the textured step, which shows low recombination activity in the Type A region. Fig. 10(b) shows a band-to-band PL image at the diffusion process step, and it shows increased recombination activity at the Type A grain boundaries. Fig. 10(c) shows subPL of this same region on a neighbor wafer at the etched step. Before ARC, the Type A region shows the dominant subPL intensity. Fig. 10(d) shows a map of electron backscatter diffraction (EBSD) that shows crystal orientation. The large map size and technique resolution can lead to some error or omission of grain boundaries when the angle of orientation between grains is very small, such as less than 1 to 2 degrees. The Type B defect region is predominantly blue in color, and the crystal orientation is mostly the same with small angle grain boundaries. Similarly, the Type A defect region is mostly yellow in color and contains many small angle grain boundaries, as well. Although the overall crystal orientations are different for the different defect types, the EBSD map shows that small angle grain boundaries dominate the Type A and B defect areas where subPL emission is detected [2].

IV. SUMMARY

PL imaging used throughout the production processing steps has shown striking changes in the appearance of Type A and Type B defect regions in multicrystalline silicon. Type A defects show strong subPL prior to ARC processing, which correlates very well to poor cell performance areas that are determined by

IQE mapping and DLIT imaging. Type A defects have higher grain boundary density than Type B defects, and show the most intense subPL on starting wafers and the highest recombination, or dark features, in band-to-band PL after the diffusion step. Type B defects show dramatic increase in subPL intensity after the ARC processing step or an equivalent temperature anneal step.

REFERENCES

[1] K. Bothe, K. Ramspeck, D. Hinken, C. Schinke, J. Schmidt, S. Herlufsen, R. Brendel, J. Bauer, J.-M. Wagner, N. Zakharov, and O. Breitenstein, "Luminescence emission from forward- and reverse-biased multicrystalline silicon solar cells," *J. Appl. Phys.*, vol. 106, pp. 104510-1–104510-8, 2009.

[2] M. Tajima, Y. Iwata, F. Okayama, H. Toyota, H. Onodera, and T. Sekiguchi, "Deep-level photoluminescence due to dislocations and oxygen precipitates in multicrystalline Si," *J. Appl. Phys.*, vol. 111, pp. 113523-1–113523-6, 2012.

[3] L. Xiang, D. Li, L. Jin, S. Wang, and D. Yang, "Enhancement of room temperature dislocation-related photoluminescence of electron irradiated silicon," *J. Appl. Phys.*, vol. 113, pp. 033518-1–033518-5, 2013.

[4] M. C. Schubert, J. Schon, P. Gundel, H. Habenicht, W. Kwapil, and W. Warta, "Imaging of metal impurities in silicon by luminescence spectroscopy and synchrotron techniques," *J. Electron. Mater.*, vol. 39, pp. 787–793, 2010.

[5] D. Lausch, K. Petter, R. Bakowskie, J. Bauer, O. Breitenstein, and C. Hagendorf, "Classification and investigation of recombination active defect structures in multicrystalline silicon solar-cells," in *Proc. 27th Eur. Photovoltaic Solar Energy Conf. Exhib.*, 2012, pp. 723–728.

[6] M. P. Peloso, N. Palina, K. Banas, A. Banas, H. Hidayat, B. Hoex, M. B. H. Breese, and A. Aberle, "Investigation of defect luminescence from multicrystalline Si wafer solar cells using X-ray fluorescence and luminescence imaging," *Phys. Status Solidi RRL*, vol. 6, pp. 460–462, 2012.

[7] T. Fuyuki, H. Kondo, T. Yamazaki, Y. Takahashi, and Y. Uraoka, "Photographic Surveying of Minority Carrier Diffusion Length in Polycrystalline Silicon Solar Cells by Electroluminescence," *Appl. Phys. Lett.*, vol. 86, pp. 262108-1–262108-3, 2005.

[8] T. Trupke, R. A. Bardos, M. C. Schubert, and W. Warta, "Photoluminescence imaging of silicon wafers," *Appl. Phys. Lett.*, vol. 89, pp. 044107-1–044107-3, 2006.

[9] T. Trupke, R. A. Bardos, M. D. Abbott, F. W. Chen, J. E. Cotter, and A. Lorenz, "Fast photoluminescence imaging of silicon wafers," in *Proc. 32nd IEEE Photovoltaic Spec.Conf., 4th World Conf. Photovoltaic Energy Convers.*, 2006, pp. 928–931.

[10] N. A. Drozdov, A. A. Patrin, and V. D. Tkachev, "Recombination radiation of dislocations in silicon," *JETP Lett.*, vol. 23, pp. 597–599, 1976.

[11] I. Tarasov, S. Ostapenko, C. Haessler, and E. U. Reisner, "Spatially resolved defect diagnostics in multicrystalline silicon for solar cells," *Mat. Sci. Engr. B*, vol. 71, no. 1–3, pp. 51–55, 2000.

[12] M. Kittler, W. Seifert, T. Arguirov, I. Tarasov, and S. Ostapenko, "Room-temperature luminescence and electron-beam-induced current (EBIC) recombination behaviour of crystal defects in multicrystalline silicon," *Sol. Ener. Mat. Sol. Cells*, vol. 72, pp. 465–472, 2002.

[13] M. Kasemann, W. Kwapil, M. C. Schubert, H. Habenicht, B. Walter, M. The, S. Kontermann, S. Rein, O. Breitenstein, J. Bauer, A. Lotnyk, B. Michl, H. Nagel, A. Schutt, J. Carstensen, H. Foll, T. Trupke, Y. Augarten, H. Kampwerth, R. A. Bardos, S. Pingel, J. Berghold, W. Warta, and S. W. Glunz, "Spatially resolved silicon solar cell characterization using infrared imaging methods," presented at the 33rd IEEE Photovoltaic Specialist Conf., San Diego, CA, USA, 2008.

[14] F. Dreckschmidt, H. Fiedler, D. Kreßner-Kiel, and H. J. Möller, "Sub-bandgap electroluminescence at room temperature of extended defects in multicrystalline silicon," in *Proc. 23rd Eur. Photovoltaic Solar Energy Conf. Exhib.*, Valencia, Spain, 2008, pp. 407–410.

[15] P. Gundel, M. C. Schubert, and W. Warta, "Simultaneous stress and defect luminescence study on silicon," *Phys. Status Solidi A*, vol. 207, pp. 436–441, 2010.

[16] M. C. Schubert, W. Kwapil, J. Schon, H. Habenicht, M. Kasemann, P. Gundel, M. Blazek, and W. Warta, "Analysis of performance limiting material properties of multicrystalline silicon," *Sol. Ener. Mat. Sol. Cells*, vol. 94, pp. 1451–1456, 2010.

[17] R. P. Schmid, D. Mankovics, T. Arguirov, M. Ratzke, T. Mchedlidze, and M. Kittler, "Rapid dislocation-related D1-photoluminescence imaging of multicrystalline Si wafers at room temperature," *Phys. Status Solidi A*, vol. 208, pp. 888–892, 2011.

[18] O. Breitenstein, M. Langenkamp, O. Lang, and A. Schirrmacher, "Shunts due to laser scribing of solar cells evaluated by highly sensitive lock-in thermography," *Sol. Ener. Mat. Sol. Cells*, vol. 65, pp. 55–62, 2001.

[19] O. Breitenstein, J. Bauer, J.-M. Wagner, and A. Lotnyk, "Imaging physical parameters of pre-breakdown sites by lock-in thermography techniques," *Prog. Photovolt, Res. Appl.*, vol. 16, pp. 679–685, 2008.

[20] O. Breitenstein, W. Warta, and M. Langenkamp, *Lock-in Thermography: Basics and Use for Evaluating Electronic Devices and Materials*, 2nd ed. Berlin, Germany, Springer-Verlag, 2010.

[21] O. Breitenstein, J. Bauer, J.-M. Wagner, H. Blumtritt, A. Lotnyk, M. Kasemann, W. Kwapil, and W. Warta, "Physical mechanisms of breakdown in multicrystalline silicon solar cells," presented at the 34th IEEE Photovoltaic Specialists Conf., Philadelphia, PA, USA, 2009.

[22] O. Breitenstein, J. Bauer, K. Bothe, W. Kwapil, D. Lausch, U. Rau, J. Schmidt, M. Schneemann, M. C. Schubert, J.-M. Wagner, and W. Warta, "Understanding junction breakdown in multicrystalline solar cells," *J. Appl. Phys.*, vol. 109, pp. 071101-1–071101-10, 2011.

[23] W. Kwapil, J. Nievendick, A. Zuschlag, P. Gundel, M. C. Schubert, and W. Warta, "Influence of surface texture on the defect-induced breakdown behavior of multicrystalline silicon solar cells," *Prog. Photovolt, Res. Appl.*, vol. 21, pp. 534–543, Jun. 2013.

[24] M. P. Peloso, P. Chaturvedi, P. Wurfel, B. Hoex, and A. G. Aberle, "Observations on the spectral characteristics of defect luminescence of silicon wafer solar cells," in *Proc. 35th IEEE Photovoltaic Spec. Conf.*, 2010, pp. 2714–2717.

[25] D. Lausch, R. Bakowskie, M. Lorenz, S. Schweizer, K. Petter, and C. Hagendorf, "Classification of recombination-active defects in multicrystalline solar cells made from upgraded metallurgical grade (UMG) silicon," *Sol. St. Phenom.*, vol. 178–179, pp. 88–93, 2011.

[26] R. Bakowskie, R. Lantzsch, T. Kaden, K. G. Eller, D. Lausch, Y. Ludwig, and K. Petter, "Comparison of recombination active defects in multicrystalline silicon by means of photoluminescence imaging and reverse biased electroluminescence," in *Proc. 26th Eur. Photovoltaic Solar Energy Conf. Exhib.*, 2011, pp. 1839–1842.

[27] D. Lausch, K. Petter, H. von Wenckstern, and M. Grundmann, "Correlation of pre-breakdown sites and bulk defects in multicrystalline silicon solar cells," *Phys. Status Solidi RRL*, vol. 3, pp. 70–72, 2009.

[28] S. Johnston, F. Yan, D. Dorn, K. Zaunbrecher, M. Al-Jassim, O. Sidelkheir, and K. Ounadjela, "Comparison of photoluminescence imaging on starting multi-crystalline silicon wafers to finished cell performance," in *Proc. 37th IEEE Photovoltaic Spec. Conf.*, Austin, TX, USA, 2012, pp. 2161–2166.

[29] F. Yan, S. Johnston, K. Zaunbrecher, M. Al-Jassim, O. Sidelkheir, and K. Ounadjela, "Defect-band photoluminescence imaging on multicrystalline silicon wafers," *Phys. Status Solidi RRL*, vol. 6, pp. 190–192, 2012.

[30] R. C. Newman, A. K. Tipping, and J. H. Tucker, "The effect of metallic contamination on enhanced oxygen diffusion in silicon at low temperatures," *J. Phys. C, Solid State Phys.*, vol. 18, pp. L861–L866, 1985.

[31] S.-T. Lee and P. Fellinger, "Enhanced oxygen diffusion in silicon at thermal donor formation temperature," *Appl. Phys. Lett.*, vol. 49, pp. 1793–1795, 1986.

[32] S. Senkader, P. R. Wilshaw, and R. J. Falster, "Oxygen-dislocation interactions in silicon at temperatures below 700 °C: Dislocation locking and oxygen diffusion," *J. Appl. Phys.*, vol. 89, pp. 4803–4808, 2001.

Steve Johnston received the B.S. degree in engineering from the Colorado School of Mines (CSM), Golden, CO, USA, in 1991, the M.S. degree in electrical engineering from the University of Illinois at Urbana-Champaign, Urbana, IL, USA, in 1995, and the Ph.D. degree in materials science from CSM in 1999.

From 1991 to 1993, he was with integrated-circuit manufacturer Texas Instruments. Since 1996, he has been with the National Renewable Energy Laboratory, Golden. His work and research interests have included minority-carrier lifetime by photoconductive decay and time-resolved photoluminescence, deep-level transient spectroscopy, and imaging techniques that include photoluminescence, electroluminescence, and lock-in thermography.

Harvey Guthrey received the B.S. degree from the University of North Texas, Denton, TX, USA, in 2008 and the Master's and Ph.D. degrees from the Colorado School of Mines, Golden, CO, USA, in 2010 and 2013, respectively.

He joined the National Renewable Energy Laboratory in May 2013, where his work focuses on determining how extended defects and impurities impact the performance of photovoltaic materials. His research interests include SEM-based electrical and optical characterization, laser pulsed atom probe tomography, and the development of novel characterization techniques.

Mowafak Al-Jassim received the B.S. degree in physics from the University of Baghdad, Baghdad, Iraq, the M.S. degree in materials science from Imperial College, London, U.K., in 1977, and the Ph.D. degree in materials science from Oxford University, Oxford, U.K., in 1983.

He joined the Solar Energy Research Institute (now the National Renewable Energy Laboratory) Golden, CO, USA, as a Postdoctoral Researcher in 1983, and then became a Staff Scientist in 1984. In 1985, he assumed the responsibility of Senior Scientist and Group Leader of the Materials Characterization Group. Since then, his work has involved the structural, electrical, luminescent, and chemical characterization of a wide variety of photovoltaic materials and devices by various electron and scanning probe microscopy techniques.

Fei Yan received the B.S. degree from Nanjing University, Nanjing, China, in 2002 and the Ph.D. degree from the University of Pittsburgh, Pittsburgh, PA, USA, in 2009, both in physics.

He was a Postdoctoral Researcher with the National Renewable Energy Laboratory, Golden CO, USA, from 2010 to 2011. He is currently a Senior Process Engineer at with Applied Materials, Santa Clara, CA, USA, working on the development of high-efficiency silicon wafer solar cells. His research interests include crystalline silicon and thin-film solar cells and growth and characterization of wide bandgap semiconductors.

Pati Rakotoniaina received the Diploma degree in physics from the University of Cologne, Cologne, Germany, in 1994, from which he received the Ph.D. degree in 1996.

He joined the Max Planck Institute of Microstructure Physics, Halle, Germany, in 2000 and worked in the field of silicon solar cells characterization. He joined Q-cells AG in 2005 as a Characterization Engineer. He has been with Silicor Materials, Inc., San Jose, CA, USA, since 2006, where his current position is Senior Manager of technical support.

Katherine Zaunbrecher received the B.S. degree from the University of Louisiana at Lafayette, Lafayette, LA, USA, in 2007 and the M.S. degree in physics from Colorado State University, Fort Collins, CO, USA, in 2010, where she is currently working toward the Ph.D. degree.

She is currently with the National Renewable Energy Laboratory, Golden, CO, as a Graduate Research Assistant. Her research interests include using imaging techniques such as electroluminescence and photoluminescence to characterize thin-film solar cells.

Martin Kaes received the Diploma degree in physics from the University of Konstanz, Konstanz, Germany in 2003.

Until 2007, he was a member of the scientific staff with the Photovoltaic Division, University of Konstanz. He has been with Calisolar GmbH, Berlin, Germany, since 2007, where he is currently a Managing Director.

Performance of Mismatched PV Systems With Submodule Integrated Converters

Carlos Olalla, *Member, IEEE*, Chris Deline, *Member, IEEE*, and Dragan Maksimovic, *Senior Member, IEEE*

Abstract—Mismatch power losses in photovoltaic (PV) systems can be reduced by the use of distributed power electronics at the module or submodule level. This paper presents an experimentally validated numerical model that can be used to predict power production with distributed maximum power point tracking (DMPPT) down to the cell level. The model allows the investigations of different DMPPT architectures, as well as the impact of conversion efficiencies and power constraints. Results are presented for annual simulations of three representative partial shading scenarios and two scenarios where mismatches are due to aging over a period of 25 years. It is shown that DMPPT solutions that are based on submodule integrated converters offer 6.9–11.1% improvements in annual energy yield relative to a baseline centralized MPPT scenario.

Index Terms—DC–DC converters, modeling and control of power electronics, photovoltaic modules, renewable energy systems, SubMICs, SubModule integrated converters.

I. INTRODUCTION

SOILING, partial shading, temperature gradients, manufacturing tolerances, and aging introduce mismatch-related losses in photovoltaic (PV) power systems due to dispersion in the maximum power point of the cells and modules in the system. By performing peak-power tracking at a finer granularity, distributed maximum power point tracking (DMPPT) using distributed power electronics has been shown to improve power production in photovoltaic (PV) systems under mismatched conditions [1] [4].

Module-level power electronics (MLPE) including microinverters (module-level dc–ac inverters) and dc optimizers (module-level dc–dc converters) have been explored [5]–[13] and are currently available. As an example, Fig. 1(a) shows a dc optimizer architecture. While MLPE approaches reduce mismatch-related losses, the converters typically process the

Manuscript received June 24, 2013; revised August 14, 2013; accepted September 5, 2013. Date of publication October 9, 2013; date of current version December 16, 2013. This work was supported in part by the Advanced Research Projects Agency-Energy, U.S. Department of Energy, under Award DE-AR0000216 and in part by the Generalitat de Catalunya, Beatriu de Pinós programme, under Award BP-B00047.

C. Olalla is with the Department of Electrical, Electronic, and Automatic Control Engineering, Rovira i Virgili University, Tarragona, 43007 Spain (e-mail: carlos.olalla@urv.cat).

C. Deline is with the National Renewable Energy Laboratory, Golden, CO 80401 USA (e-mail: chris.deline@nrel.gov).

D. Maksimovic is with the Department of Electrical, Computer, and Energy Engineering, University of Colorado, Boulder, CO 80309 USA (e-mail: maksimov@colorado.edu).

Color versions of one or more of the figures in this paper are available online at http://ieeexplore.ieee.org.

Digital Object Identifier 10.1109/JPHOTOV.2013.2281878

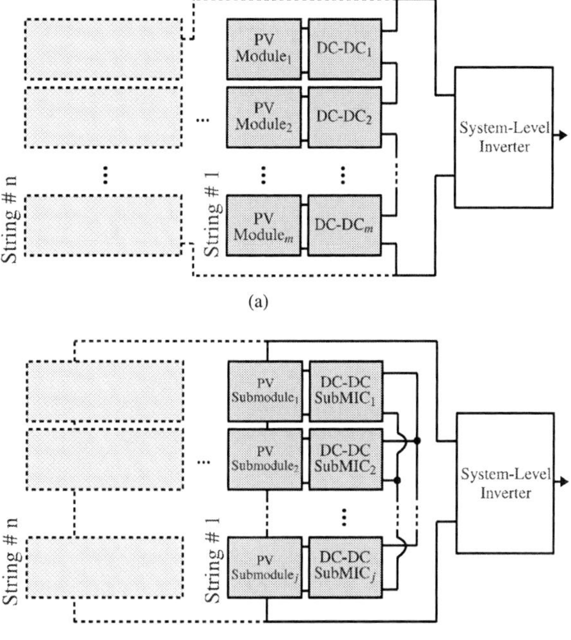

Fig. 1. PV systems with power electronics performing DMPPT. (a) Cascaded module-level DC-DC converters (MLPE) connected to conventional PV modules with bypass diodes in parallel. (b) Submodule bypass diodes are replaced by differential power processing submodule integrated converter (subMIC) circuitry. While total system power must be processed by dc-dc converters in (a), only the mismatch power is processed by subMICs in (b).

full power of the module and introduce insertion losses, even under no-mismatch conditions. Because the recoverable mismatch loss is generally small with respect to the total system power, the MLPE conversion efficiency must be very high in order to result in a net positive performance improvement [1]. In contrast with this approach, differential power processing (DPP) architectures, which are originally investigated in the context of battery balancing [14]–[17], only process the amount of power required to reduce the mismatch, presenting no insertion loss and allowing power converters rated at a fraction of the power [18]–[24]. Besides, these approaches can be applied at the submodule or bypass-diode level, increasing the granularity of DMPPT and recovering even more energy [4], [25]–[29].

To investigate the performance benefit of DMPPT that include submodule-integrated converters (subMICs), a cell-level simulation model has been developed with the ability to accurately reproduce partial-shading and other mismatch effects at high granularity [30]. The model is used here to predict the energy yield improvements of a specific DMPPT subMIC architecture that is illustrated in Fig. 1(b) [31], when compared with an MLPE architecture [see Fig. 1(a)] and a conventional system-level MPPT solution. While these results may not extend to other DMPPT architectures, a study of the differences between DMPPT approaches can be found in [24]. In addition, note that the specific values of power limit have been considered in the subMIC architecture, but the research on the effects of this limitation are left out for future investigations. Several representative scenarios have been examined, and two sources of mismatch have been considered: partial shading and aging, leading to an increased standard deviation in peak-power current I_{mpp}. The reported predictions consider long time spans of up to 25 years and, where possible, experimental measurements have been used to verify the simulations.

This paper is organized as follows. Section II briefly describes the cell-level simulation model and how partial shading and PV tolerances have been taken into account, together with simulation and experimental results verifying the model. Section III presents the predictions of the benefits of DMPPT architectures and compares the results with conventional PV systems. Finally, conclusions are provided in Section IV.

II. Cell-Level Simulation Model

This section briefly describes the cell-level simulation model that is presented in [30]. The model has the advantage that it can be solved very efficiently using standard numerical methods. As a consequence, it is well suited for evaluations of energy capture in large PV systems over long periods of time, including the effects of mismatches and the impact of DMPPT.

The PV cell model is described by the standard five-parameters cell equations, as in [32], with an additional term that accounts for the effects of breakdown voltage V_{br}:

$$I_{\mathrm{cell}} = f(V_{\mathrm{cell}_{jk}}, I_{\mathrm{cell}}) = I_{g_{jk}} - I_{drs}\left(e^{\frac{V_{d_{jk}}}{a \cdot V_T}} - 1\right) \ldots$$

$$- \frac{V_{d_{jk}}}{R_p} + I'_{drs}e^{\frac{V_{\mathrm{br}} - V_{d_{jk}}}{V_T}} \tag{1}$$

where $V_{d_{jk}} = V_{\mathrm{cell}_{jk}} + I_{\mathrm{cell}} \cdot R_s$, I_{drs} and I'_{drs} are the diode reverse saturation currents, R_p stands for the shunt resistance, R_s is the series resistance, V_T is the thermal voltage, and a is the diode quality factor. A standard V_{br} of -12 V is assumed. Note that $I_{g_{jk}}$ is the photocurrent at submodule j and cell k. As a consequence, each cell may have a unique maximum-power point, as explained below.

A. Shading Mismatch

Photocurrent $I_{g_{jk}}$ depends linearly on the incident irradiance and the fraction of shaded cell area α_{jk}, as depicted in Fig. 2.

$$I_{g_{jk}} = \left(G_{\mathrm{irr}}(1 - \alpha_{jk}) + D_{\mathrm{irr}} \cdot \alpha_{jk}\right)\frac{I_{\mathrm{sc}}}{G_{\mathrm{n}}} \tag{2}$$

where G_{irr} and D_{irr} are global and diffuse irradiance, respectively, and G_{n} is the global plane-of-array irradiance under standard test conditions. In experiments, irradiance data G_{irr} and

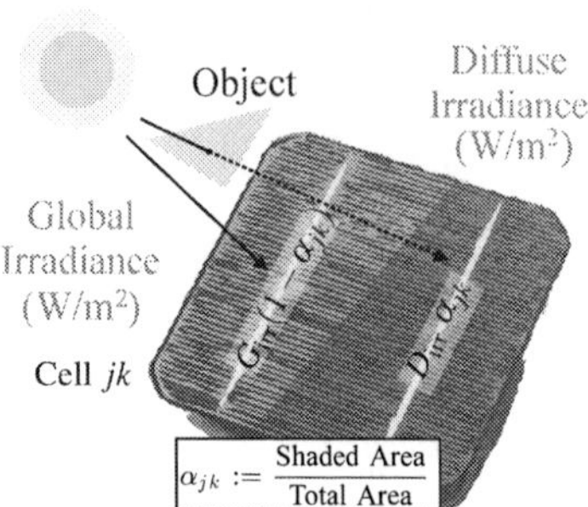

Fig. 2. Photocurrent of a cell $I_{g_{jk}}$ is determined by a linear combination of diffuse irradiance over the shaded fraction of the cell α_{jk} and global irradiance over the unshaded fraction of the cell $1 - \alpha_{jk}$.

D_{irr} were measured onsite, along with shading data α_{jk}. For simulations, G_{irr} and D_{irr} were obtained from an NREL historical database [33], and shading data was obtained by ray-tracing models, as in [4].

B. Aging Mismatch

PV system aging studies have indicated that PV module degradation is not uniform. In other words, some modules in a system will degrade more rapidly than other modules. This is represented by an increase in the standard deviation of device parameters over time, which also known as the coefficient of variation or standard deviation divided by the mean (σ/μ). Surveys of aging PV systems employing silicon modules have indicated that the coefficient of variation for a short-circuit current I_{sc} increases linearly from $\sigma/\mu = 1\%$ at beginning of life to $\sigma/\mu = 10\%$ after 25 years of deployment [34]. An increase in *skewness* is also observed, suggesting a tail-heavy distribution which further accentuates mismatch within the system. Compared with large changes in I_{sc} and fill factor over time, open-circuit voltage V_{oc} changes very little over module lifetime [34], [35]. Aside from the associated power loss, such a mismatch increases the incidence of hot spots, which may result in the permanent damage of the affected cells. It has been reported that this is the main cause of the increase in the standard deviation of peak-power voltage V_{mpp} in experimentally measured modules [35].

In order to model aging-related mismatch over time, several simplifications are considered, namely, that I_{sc} and I_{mpp} have similar σ/μ, and that its value increases linearly from 1% to 10% over the 25 year module lifetime. The distribution of I_{sc} and I_{mpp} is assumed to be normal, ignoring the observed increase in "skewness" over time. The open-circuit voltage is assumed constant. For any given year in the simulation, the mean values of I_{sc} and I_{mpp} are used to derive the remaining coefficients in the five-parameter model. Hence, each cell is considered identical and characterized by the same I_{drs}, R_p, R_s, V_{oc}, and V_{mpp} parameters. Since aging mismatch manifests primarily as a change in I_{sc} and I_{mpp}, its effects can be considered in a manner similar to the shading mismatch. The photocurrent $I_{g_{jk}}$ for a cell in the absence of shade is equal to

$$I_{g_{jk}} = G_{\mathrm{irr}} I_{\mathrm{sc}_{jk}}. \tag{3}$$

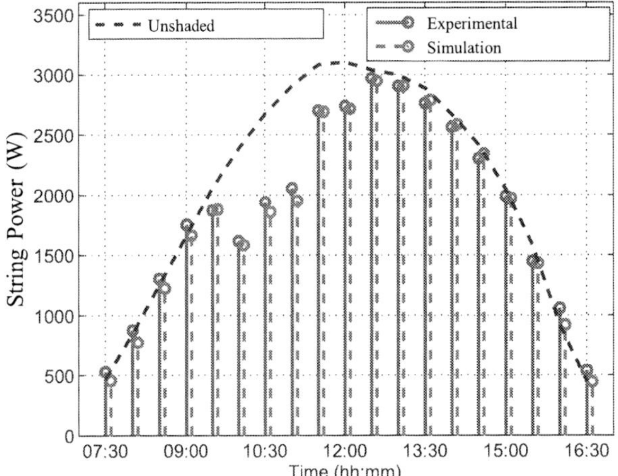

Fig. 3. Single day power production of a partially shaded string in a utility-scale installation, indicating agreement $<2\%$ between measured and modeled power.

Then, every short-circuit current $I_{\mathrm{sc}_{jk}}$ can be characterized with respect to the mean value $\overline{I_{\mathrm{sc}}}$ as

$$I_{\mathrm{sc}_{jk}} = \overline{I_{\mathrm{sc}}}(1 - \beta_{jk}). \tag{4}$$

Consequently, for a known set of $I_{\mathrm{sc}_{jk}}$ from a random normal distribution as defined previously, the set of shading values β_{jk} can be derived:

$$\beta_{jk} = 1 - \frac{I_{\mathrm{sc}_{jk}}}{\overline{I_{\mathrm{sc}}}}. \tag{5}$$

This approach could be applied equally to aging mismatch or mismatch due to manufacturing tolerances, if binning or distribution information for a given module type is known.

C. Model Verification and Experimental Results

The model has been verified with a short-term simulation of 1 day, using irradiance and shading data monitored onsite at a large utility-scale installation affected by partial shading (see Scenario I in Section III-A). Fig. 3 shows experimental measurements of string power collected every 30 min. System voltage was not monitored and is assumed to be constant for both the experimental and modeled results. The irradiance throughout the day was completely clear; therefore, the reduction in power in the morning hours, as shown in Fig. 3, was due to the shadow of a light pole passing across the array. At each 30-min interval, a photograph was taken of the shaded modules to determine which modules and cells received partial shading. These partial shading details along with measured values of G_{irr} and D_{irr} were used to conduct a simulation of predicted power output, which is also shown in Fig. 3. The power output that is obtained by simulation agrees with the measurements within 2%.

III. Energy Improvement Predictions for Representative Photovoltaic Systems

This section presents modeled results to illustrate the performance improvement from higher granularity power processing using module-level converters as in Fig. 1(a) or using subMICs, as shown in Fig. 1(b) [30]. Three partial shading and two aging mismatch scenarios are considered:

1) Scenario I: a large utility-scale system affected by partial shading;
2) Scenario II: a residential system shaded by nearby trees;
3) Scenario III: a residential system shaded by a chimney;
4) Scenario IV: an aging mismatch simulation applied to the utility-scale system in Scenario I;
5) Scenario V: an aging mismatch simulation applied to the residential system of Scenario II.

Scenarios IV and V consider only aging-related mismatches, neglecting any other mismatch effects.

System-level MPPT with a central inverter is considered *conventional* operation. Whenever module-level MPPT simulations are shown, dc optimizers are considered to be 97.5% efficient, corresponding to the measured weighted efficiency for a commercial dc–dc converter device [36]. For subMIC simulations, the devices are either assumed to have ideal $\eta = 100\%$ conversion efficiency or to be *nonideal* subMICs with a conversion efficiency of $\eta = 90\%$. The ideal case is shown here to identify the maximum recoverable power at this submodule granularity. Furthermore, nonideal 90% efficient subMICs can be rated at the full power (100% of the submodule power rating P_{mpp}) or at a fraction of the full power.

It is worth noting that subMIC-based balancing produces an almost constant MPP voltage at the string output, regardless of the mismatch conditions [30]. As a result, the downstream inverter could be designed to operate over a narrower voltage range, which could result in additional efficiency improvements. These considerations have not been included in the results reported in this paper assuming, instead, that characteristics of the downstream inverter are the same in all cases considered. Note that, while subMIC balancing also eases MPPT operation, it has been considered that the absolute MPP can be always found, even in case of multiple maxima. This can also result in conservative predictions of the improvement with subMIC architectures. One practical aspect of the inverter operation that is considered here is a minimum dc operating voltage. For Scenario III, nominal MPP voltage is about 110 V; hence, the inverter minimum dc input voltage is taken to be 50 V. For all other mismatch scenarios, the inverter minimum voltage is assumed to be 150 V.

A. Scenario I: Partial Shading in a Utility-Scale System

The first scenario, which is shown in Fig. 4, considers an existing utility-scale system (350 kW) that consists of multiple parallel strings of 16 modules. Modules are composed of three submodules of 20 cells apiece, each submodule being rated at 81 W. Nearby light poles cause partial shading on some strings throughout the day. Because of the large parallel configuration of strings, the MPP voltage at the central inverter remains

517

	Daily Production Pr_i (Wh)	$\frac{\mathrm{Pr}_i}{\mathrm{Pr}_0}$	Energy Improvement
No Shade	$\mathrm{Pr}_0 = 19715$	100 %	-
System-Level MPPT	$\mathrm{Pr}_1 = 17563$	89.08 %	-
Module-Level MPPT ($\eta = 97.5$ %)	$\mathrm{Pr}_2 = 18268$	92.67 %	4.01 %
SubMIC MPPT ($\eta = 100$ %)	$\mathrm{Pr}_3 = 19167$	97.2 %	9.13 %
SubMIC MPPT ($\eta = 90$ % , Rated at 100 % of P_{mpp})	$\mathrm{Pr}_4 = 19012$	96.43 %	8.25 %
SubMIC MPPT ($\eta = 90$ % , Rated at 33 % of P_{mpp})	$\mathrm{Pr}_5 = 18845$	95.56 %	7.30 %

Fig. 4. Scenario I: Picture of utility-scale system. (Top) Detail of partial shading from nearby light poles. Photo credit: C. Deline

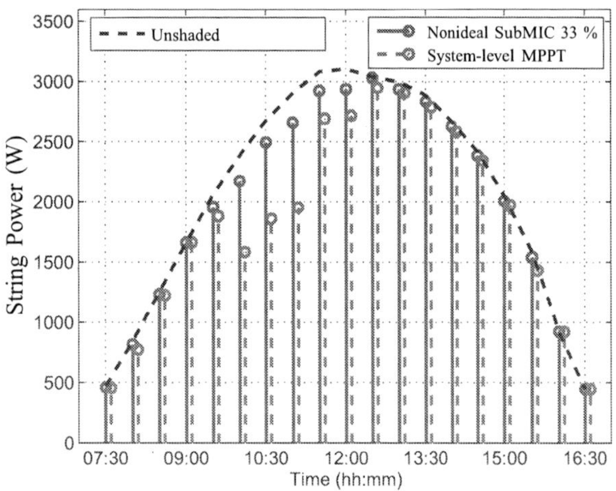

Fig. 5. Scenario I: Available Power simulation results for SubMICs rated at 33% versus system-level MPPT architecture.

unchanged, leading to relatively high mismatch loss. This particular circumstance provides the ability to gauge the benefit of distributed power processing architectures in large systems, where a relatively small portion of the system is affected by shading-induced mismatch.

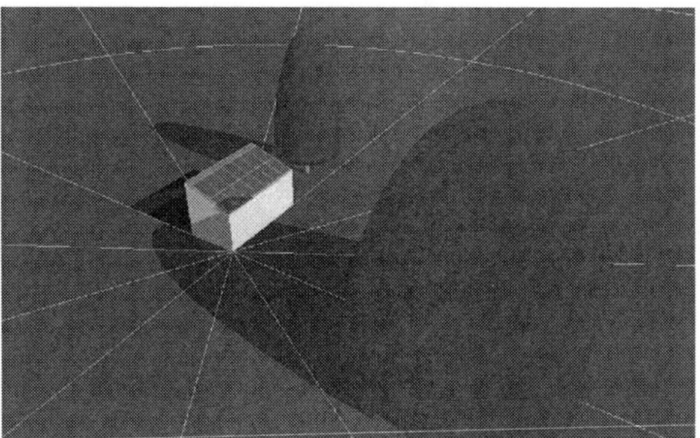

Fig. 6. Scenario II: Conditions in a residential PV system with shading that is caused by nearby trees. Annual shading calculated by ray-tracing simulation.

Fig. 5 shows a comparison of simulated daily production of a single-shaded string against an unshaded string. The simulated output with shade indicates a reduction in power throughout the morning as a shadow passes across the string. Approximately, 11% of the total energy of the string is lost due to shading, illustrating the disproportionate effects of this mismatch, given the small area being shaded each day by the light poles.

Part of the energy lost can be recovered with higher granularity MPPT. Table I shows simulation results that present the available power with module-level power electronics (MLPE) (a), ideal subMIC (b), and nonideal subMICs at 100% or 33% power rating. Those results illustrate that compared with the conventional approach, module-level DMPPT improves the day's performance by 4%, while subMICs improve performance by 7%–9%, depending on conversion efficiency. In particular, the subMIC approach shows performance advantages relative to module-level approach due to zero insertion loss during periods of no mismatch.

B. Scenario II: Residential System With Tree Shading

The second installation is a residential system for which experimental measurements have been collected since 2011. The system, rated at 2.9 kW, consists of two series strings of seven modules, each rated at 210 W. Hence, each submodule of 36 cells (three per module) is rated at 70 W. Fig. 6 gives an indication of the system configuration, along with nearby trees, which mostly provide shade in the morning and in winter. In contrast with Scenario I, shading affects a large fraction of the array, resulting in an estimated annual irradiance loss of about 20%.

	Annual Production Pr_i (kWh)	$\frac{\mathrm{Pr}_i}{\mathrm{Pr}_0}$	Energy Improvement
No Shade	$\mathrm{Pr}_0 = 5201$	100 %	-
System-Level MPPT	$\mathrm{Pr}_1 = 4041$	77.70 %	-
Module-Level MPPT ($\eta = 97.5$ %)	$\mathrm{Pr}_2 = 4193$	80.62 %	3.76 %
SubMIC MPPT ($\eta = 100$ %)	$\mathrm{Pr}_3 = 4305$	82.77 %	6.53 %
SubMIC MPPT ($\eta = 90$ % , Rated at 100 % of P_{mpp})	$\mathrm{Pr}_4 = 4264$	81.98 %	5.52%
SubMIC MPPT ($\eta = 90$ % , Rated at 40 % of P_{mpp})	$\mathrm{Pr}_5 = 4230$	81.33 %	4.68 %

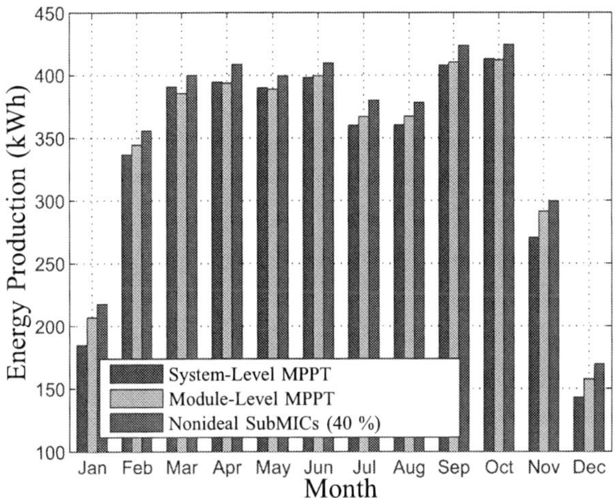

Fig. 7. Scenario II: Yearly simulation with system-level MPPT (first column of each month), module-level MPPT (second column), and nonideal subMICs rated at 40% of submodule rating (third column).

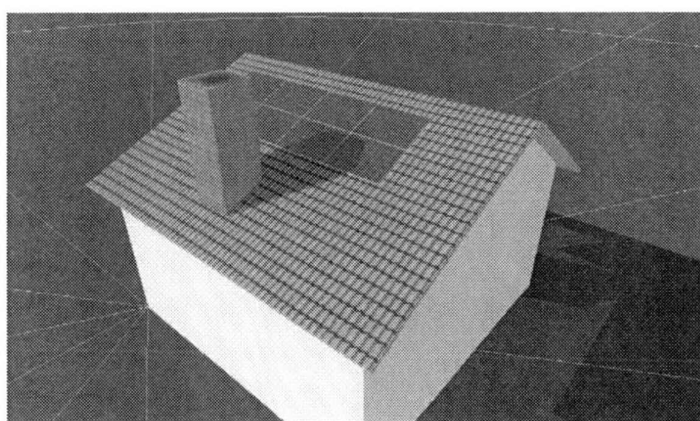

Fig. 8. Scenario III: Example shading conditions assumed for the residential chimney shading.

Yearly simulations were carried out using hourly measured irradiance data from NREL installations in Golden, CO, USA [33] and shading data from the ray-tracing irradiance model [4]. Annual partial shading performance is modeled for a conventional (system-level MPPT) configuration, as well as for MLPE and subMIC devices. Results in Table II and Fig. 7 indicate that of the 22.3% performance lost due to shade, a 3.6% performance improvement is achieved with 97.5% efficient MLPE, while a 5.5% performance improvement is achieved with 90% efficient subMICs. If the subMICs were assumed to be ideally efficient, the maximum performance improvement at this granularity would be 6.5%.

The performance advantage of subMICs relative to MLPE is partly due to the fact that the power processed by the subMICs is typically very small, being less than 20 W for 85% of the time in this simulation. Given the low overall power processed, the annual power conversion loss for the 90% efficient subMICs is only 1.1%.

It is also worth noting that subMIC balancing is more intense during the winter months and is less active during summer. This fact can also be seen in Fig. 7, where DMPPT power gain is lower during April and May. During these months, the module-level MPPT can in fact perform worse than the system-level MPPT due to insertion losses. This behavior has also been identified in Scenario III, where shade occurs only during winter months.

C. Scenario III: Residential System With Chimney Shading

A residential installation affected by rooftop chimney shade has been considered as the third partial shading scenario, which is shown in Fig. 8. This system is similar to the one considered in [28] and consists of two strings of four modules rated at 210 W, consisting of three submodules of 36 cells per module (70 W). Shading affects the array only during the winter months, with essentially no shading-induced mismatch during summer. Given the orientation of the array and the shading object, the top string is less shaded than the bottom string. This scenario can be considered to be a section of a rooftop PV array or a small standalone rooftop PV array with a low-voltage inverter.

Simulation results given in Table III indicate that annual shading loss for conventional MPPT is 13.3%. The performance improvement from MLPE is relatively small for this chimney shading case. This can be attributed to the insertion loss of the MLPE, even when conversion efficiency is as high as 97.5%. The monthly results of Fig. 9 show that the small performance gains in the winter months are outweighed by conversion losses in the summer. In contrast, the subMIC devices are shown to improve performance by 4.6% annually, due to the higher MPPT granularity and the lack of any insertion loss. The nonideal subMICs result in 35% of the shading loss being recovered and only waste 1.3% annually through conversion losses.

Scenario III may be considered ideal for the use of the subMIC architecture because shadows occur at high irradiance parts of the day, when mismatch is greater, and shadows cross only a few submodules, as opposed to a large uniform shadow over several modules. Additionally, large fractions of the year display

	Annual Production Pr_i (kWh)	$\frac{\mathrm{Pr}_i}{\mathrm{Pr}_0}$	Energy Improvement
No Shade	$\mathrm{Pr}_0 = 2968$	100 %	-
System-Level MPPT	$\mathrm{Pr}_1 = 2576$	86.79 %	-
Module-Level MPPT ($\eta_1 = 97.5$ %)	$\mathrm{Pr}_2 = 2629$	88.60 %	2.17 %
SubMIC MPPT ($\eta = 100$ %)	$\mathrm{Pr}_3 = 2719$	91.61 %	5.55 %
SubMIC MPPT ($\eta = 90$ % , Rated at 100 % of P_{mpp})	$\mathrm{Pr}_4 = 2694$	90.77 %	4.58 %
SubMIC MPPT ($\eta = 90$ % , Rated at 40 % of P_{mpp})	$\mathrm{Pr}_5 = 2665$	89.79 %	3.45 %

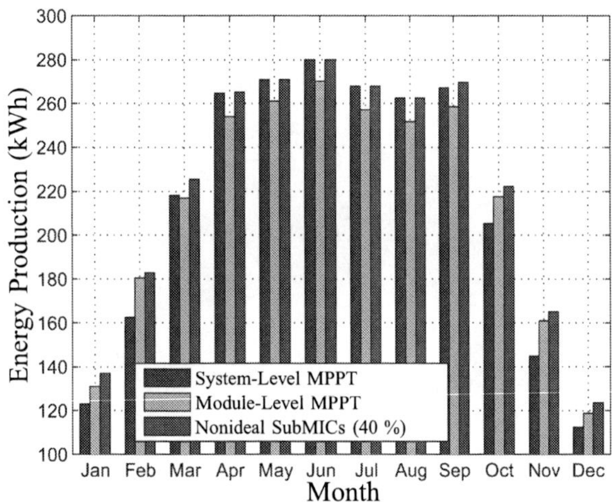

Fig. 9. Scenario III: Yearly simulation with system-level MPPT (first column of each month), module-level MPPT (second column), and nonideal subMICs rated at 40% of submodule rating (third column).

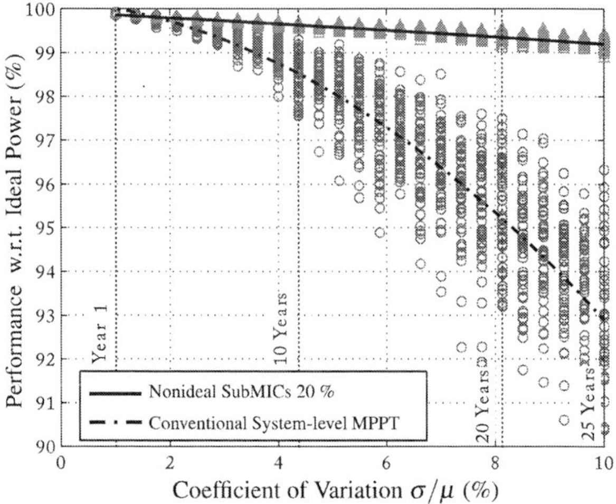

Fig. 10. Scenario IV: Performance (ratio between actual and ideal power) for a coefficient of variation between 1% and 10%. System-level MPPT (circles) and its best-fit curve (dash-dotted line). Nonideal 90% efficient SubMICs rated at 20% (triangles) and its best-fit curve (solid line).

little mismatch. At these times, insertion losses of module-level MPPT solutions outweigh their performance benefits.

D. Scenario IV: Aging Mismatch in a Utility-Scale System

In order to evaluate the energy loss due to aging effects and possible gains with the subMIC architecture, a Monte Carlo simulation was conducted using the method described in Section II. One string of the utility-scale system of Scenario I was chosen as the basis for the simulation, with random normally distributed values of I_{sc} and I_{mpp} for each submodule. The coefficient of variation is assumed to increase linearly from $\sigma/\mu = 1\%$ to $\sigma/\mu = 10\%$ after 25 years, as mentioned in Section II. These variations are carried out by increasing σ accordingly with the decrease of the average short-circuit current μ with time, also as reported in [35]. Note that I_{sc} and I_{mpp} are considered constant across each submodule, i.e., all cells in a particular submodule are equal. This approach is similar to that taken in [29].

The results of the Monte Carlo simulation are depicted in Fig. 10, and show a distribution of annual production over 25 years both with subMIC devices rated at only 20% of the submodule power (shown by blue triangles) and with conventional system-level MPPT (shown by red circles). A key point is that initial performance improvement is negligible. However, by the end of life of the PV system, mismatch power loss can be significant. By the time the coefficient of variation of the field

		20 Yrs. Production Pr_i (kWh)	Energy Improvement
System-Level MPPT		$\mathrm{Pr}_1 = 90650$	-
SubMIC MPPT ($\eta = 100$) %		$\mathrm{Pr}_2 = 93016$	2.61 %
SubMIC MPPT ($\eta = 90$ %)	Rated at 100 % of P_{mpp}	$\mathrm{Pr}_3 = 92780$	2.35 %
	Rated at 20 % of P_{mpp}	$\mathrm{Pr}_4 = 92780$	2.35 %

reaches $\sigma/\mu = 10\%$, the use of subMICs can net an average of 6% performance improvement over the system-level MPPT approach.

A more detailed lifetime simulation is conducted for the typical scenario uncovered by Monte Carlo simulation (indicated by the solid and dash-dotted lines in Fig. 11). For this specific case simulation, irradiance values remain unchanged, in order to examine the effect of aging mismatch over time. In this case, the element closest to the fitting line in the coefficient of variation of 20 years was chosen and simulated assuming linear increments of the short-circuit current of each submodule from an initial case that corresponds to the initial coefficient of variation of 1%. The results of this typical simulation are given in Table IV, indicating a lifetime energy improvement due to subMICs of 2.35%.

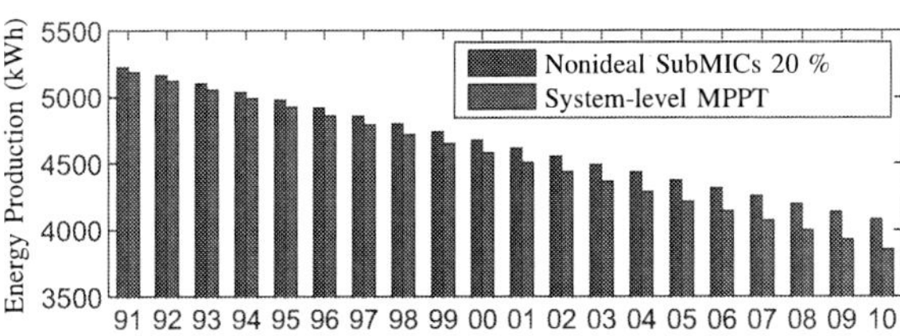

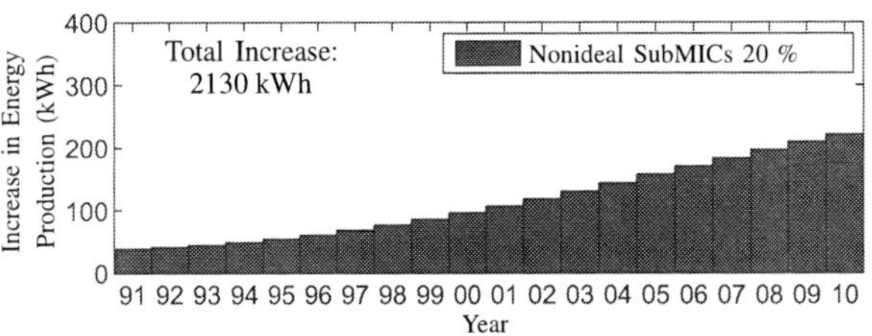

Fig. 11. Scenario IV: Comparison of the energy production over 20 years with system level MPPT and with subMICs if aging effects are taken into account. (Bottom) Perfomance increase by subMICs relative to system-level MPPT.

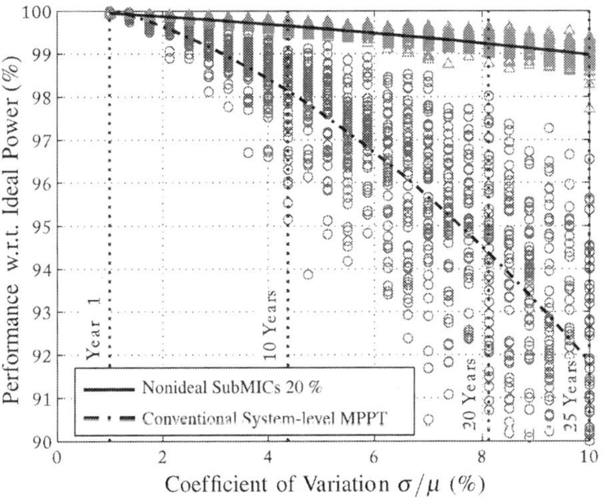

Fig. 12. Scenario V: Performance (the ratio between actual and ideal power) for a coefficient of variation between 1% and 10%. System-level MPPT (indicated by circles) and its best-fit curve (indicated by the dash-dotted line). Nonideal 90% efficient SubMICs rated at 20% (indicated by triangles) and its best-fit curve (indicated by solid line).

E. Scenario V: Aging Mismatch in a Residential System

The same simulations of the previous section have also been carried out for the residential system of Scenario II: a small PV array of 14 modules distributed in two strings.

The first simulation, depicted in Fig. 12, predicts an average mismatch loss of 5.5% after 20 years and of 8% after 25 years. Despite having fewer modules in series, this system presents more PV cells per submodule and two strings in parallel, such that mismatch can cause different MPPs of the strings and more adverse power loss. SubMICs rated at 20% of the submodule power allow to recover an average of 7% annually at the end of the PV lifetime.

TABLE V
SCENARIO V: ENERGY PRODUCTION SIMULATION RESULTS

TABLE V

SCENARIO V: ENERGY PRODUCTION SIMULATION RESULTS

		20 Yrs. Production Pr_i (kWh)	Energy Improvement
System-Level MPPT		$\mathrm{Pr}_1 = 90821$	-
SubMIC MPPT ($\eta = 100$) %		$\mathrm{Pr}_2 = 93707$	3.17 %
SubMIC MPPT ($\eta = 90$ %)	Rated at 100 % of P_{mpp}	$\mathrm{Pr}_3 = 93418$	2.86 %
	Rated at 20 % of P_{mpp}	$\mathrm{Pr}_4 = 93418$	2.86 %

TABLE VI

SUMMARY OF RESULTS

	Conventional System Power Loss	Energy Improvement with subMICs ($\eta = 90$ %)
Scenario I: Light Poles	10.92 %	8.25 %
Scenario II: Tree Shading	22.30 %	5.52 %
Scenario III: Chimney Shading	13.21 %	4.58 %
Scenario IV: Utility-Scale Aging	2.61 %	2.35 %
Scenario V: Residential-System Aging	3.17 %	2.86 %

The second simulation, with results shown in Table V, shows a 2.86% energy gain improvement achieved throughout the life span of the PV system, using the subMIC architecture with 90% efficient subMICs rated at 20% power.

IV. SUMMARY OF RESULTS AND CONCLUSION

The reported simulations predict significant losses due to partial shading and mismatches due to aging. The results, summarized in Table VI, attest that up to about 20% of the power can be lost in the presence of partial shading, while an additional 3% is lost due to aging effects. The results also demonstrate that a portion of the mismatch-induced energy loss can be recovered by distributed power electronics. Significant differences have been found between DMPPT approaches based on module-level power electronics [MLPE, as in Fig. 1(a)] and differential power processing architectures such as the subMIC architecture shown in Fig. 1(b).

The MLPE architecture is well suited for systems where mismatch is present at all times. Full power rating and very high efficiency (typically 97–98%) is required such that the DMPPT benefits outweigh insertion losses in the absence of mismatch. In contrast, the subMIC architecture not only eliminates the insertion loss but performs DMPPT at higher granularity, thus providing an opportunity to recover more power. Fig. 13 compares the annual performance increase of these DMPPT approaches with respect to the conventional case. It can be seen how the subMIC architecture performs about a 50–110% better than MLPE in the examples shown.

The advantages of subMIC balancing in the presence of partial shading are illustrated in Scenarios I–III. The first scenario shows how relatively small shadows can cause relatively large losses. In this case, most of the loss (up to about 70%) can be recovered using subMICs. The partial shading results in

978-1-4799-0511-9/13 $31.00 © 2013 IEEE

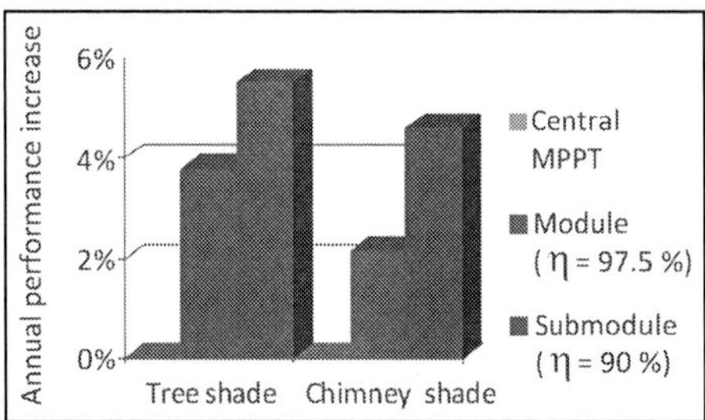

Fig. 13. Annual energy gain with central inverter (first column), module-level power electronics (second column), and submodule converters (third column) for Scenario II (Tree shade) and Scenario III (Chimney shade).

Scenarios II and III, with larger areas affected by shade, are more representative of residential systems, and the recoverable energy is approximately 20–35% of the loss. Table VI shows that the energy improvement with 90% efficient subMICs is within 4–8%, depending on the shade characteristics. In summary, small shades produce less power loss, but a larger part of the total loss can be recovered.

In systems where mismatches are due to the effects of ageing, the results show that approximately 90% of the loss can be recovered using practical 90% efficient subMICs rated at only 20% of the full power. This represents a lifetime improvement of the PV energy yield of approximately 3%, in addition to potentials for system reliability improvements, given the protection against the appearance of hot spots.

In summary, the submodule integrated converter (subMIC) architecture [31] is able to recover more of the lost power than module-level devices, even when considering practical subMIC implementations having moderate conversion efficiency (90%) and rated at partial power. If partial shading and aging are considered at the same time, the subMIC architecture allows an improvement of the energy yield within 6.9%–11.1%.

ACKNOWLEDGMENT

The authors would like to thank S. M. MacAlpine for providing shading data in Scenarios II and III. The information, data, or work presented herein was funded in part by an agency of the United States Government. Neither the United States Government nor any agency thereof, nor any of their employees, makes any warranty, express or implied, or assumes any legal liability or responsibility for the accuracy, completeness, or usefulness of any information, apparatus, product, or process disclosed, or represents that its use would not infringe privately owned rights. Reference herein to any specific commercial product, process, or service by trade name, trademark, manufacturer, or otherwise does not necessarily constitute or imply its endorsement, recommendation, or favoring by the United States Government or any agency thereof. The views and opinions of authors expressed herein do not necessarily state or reflect those of the United States Government or any agency thereof.

REFERENCES

[1] C. Deline, B. Marion, J. Granata, and S. Gonzales, "A performance and economic analysis of distributed power electronics in photovoltaic systems," Nat. Renewable Energy Lab., Tech. Rep. NREL/TP-5200-50003, 2010. Available: www.nrel.gov/docs/fy11osti/50003.pdf

[2] C. Deline, J. Meydbray, M. Donovan, and J. Forrest, "Photovoltaic shading testbed for module-level power electronics," Nat. Renewable Energy Lab., Tech. Rep. NREL/TP-5200-54876, 2012. Available: www.nrel.gov/docs/fy12osti/54876.pdf

[3] C. Podewils and M. Levitin, "Hidden powers," *Photon Int.*, pp. 136–147, Feb. 2011.

[4] S. M. MacAlpine, R. W. Erickson, and M. J. Brandemuehl, "Characterization of power optimizer potential to increase energy capture in photovoltaic systems operating under nonuniform conditions," *IEEE Trans. Power Electron.*, vol. 28, no. 6, pp. 2936–2945, Jun. 2013.

[5] R. Wills, S. Krauthamer, A. Bulawka, and J. Posbic, "The AC photovoltaic module concept," in *Proc. Intersoc. Energy Convers. Eng. Conf.*, Aug. 1997, vol. 3, pp. 1562–1563.

[6] Q. Li and P. Wolfs, "A review of the single phase photovoltaic module integrated converter topologies with three different DC link configurations," *IEEE Trans. Power Electron.*, vol. 23, no. 3, pp. 1320–1333, May 2008.

[7] R. W. Erickson and A. P. Rogers, "A microinverter for building-integrated photovoltaics," in *Proc. IEEE Appl. Power Electron. Conf. Expo.*, Feb. 15–19, 2009, pp. 911–917.

[8] D. Meneses, O. Garcia, P. Alou, J. Oliver, R. Prieto, and J. Cobos, "Single-stage grid-connected forward microinverter with constant off-time boundary mode control," in *Proc. IEEE Appl. Power Electron. Conf. Expo.*, Feb. 2012, pp. 568–574.

[9] G. Walker and P. Sernia, "Cascaded DC–DC converter connection of photovoltaic modules," *IEEE Trans. Power Electron.*, vol. 19, no. 4, pp. 1130–1139, Jul. 2004.

[10] N. Femia, G. Lisi, G. Petrone, G. Spagnuolo, and M. Vitelli, "Distributed maximum power point tracking of photovoltaic arrays: Novel approach and system analysis," *IEEE Trans. Ind. Electron.*, vol. 55, no. 7, pp. 2610–2621, Jul. 2008.

[11] L. Linares, R. W. Erickson, S. MacAlpine, and M. Brandemuehl, "Improved energy capture in series string photovoltaics via smart distributed power electronics," in *Proc. IEEE Appl. Power Electron. Conf. Expo.*, Feb. 15–19, 2009, pp. 904–910.

[12] P. Tsao, S. Sarhan, and I. Jorio, "Distributed max power point tracking for photovoltaic arrays," in *Proc. IEEE Photovolt. Spec. Conf.*, Jun. 7–12, 2009, pp. 2293–2298.

[13] P. Krein and R. Balog, "Minimm energy and capacitance requirements for single-phase inverters and rectifiers using a ripple port," *IEEE Trans. Power Electron.*, vol. 27, pp. 4690–4698, Nov. 2012.

[14] C. Pascual and P. Krein, "Switched capacitor system for automatic series battery equalization," in *Proc. IEEE Appl. Power Electron. Conf. Expo.*, 1997, pp. 848–854.

[15] J. Cao, N. Schofield, and A. Emadi, "Battery balancing methods: A comprehensive review," in *Proc. IEEE Veh. Power Propuls. Conf.*, Sep. 2008, pp. 1–6.

[16] V. Tikhonov, "Battery optimization system and method of use," U.S. Patent No. 17 489 106, 2009.

[17] M. Einhorn, W. Guertlschmid, T. Blochberger, R. Kumpusch, R. Permann, F. Conte, C. Kral, and J. Fleig, "A current equalization method for serially connected battery cells using a single power converter for each cell," *IEEE Trans. Veh. Technol.*, vol. 60, no. 9, pp. 4227–4237, Nov. 2011.

[18] G. Walker, J. Xue, and P. Sernia, "PV string per-module maximum power point enabling converters," in *Proc. Australas. Univ. Power Eng. Conf.*, Sep. 2003, pp. 112–117.

[19] Y. Nimni and D. Shmilovitz, "A returned energy architecture for improved photovoltaic systems efficiency," in *Proc. IEEE Int. Symp. Circuits Syst.*, May 30–Jun. 2, 2010, pp. 2191–2194.

[20] R. Giral, C. Ramos-Paja, D. Gonzalez, J. Calvente, A. Cid-Pastor, and L. Martinez-Salamero, "Minimizing the effects of shadowing in a PV module by means of active voltage sharing," in *Proc. IEEE Int. Conf. Ind. Technol.*, 2010, pp. 943–948.

[21] R. Giral, C. E. Carrejo, M. Vermeersh, A. J. S. Montes, and C. A. Ramos-Paja, "PV field distributed maximum power point tracking by means of an active bypass converter," in *Proc. Int. Conf. Clean Electr. Power*, 2011, pp. 94–98.

[22] S. Poshtkouhi, A. Biswas, and O. Trescases, "DC–DC converter for high granularity, sub-string MPPT in photovoltaic applications using a virtual-parallel connection," in *Proc. IEEE Appl. Power Electron. Conf. Expo.*, Orlando, FL, USA, 2012, pp. 86–92.

[23] D. Shmilovitz and Y. Levron, "Distributed maximum power point tracking in photovoltaic systems—Emerging architectures and control methods," *Automatika—J. Control, Meas., Electron., Comput. Commun.*, vol. 53, no. 2, 2012.

[24] P. S. Shenoy, K. A. Kim, B. B. Johnson, and P. T. Krein, "Differential power processing for increased energy production and reliability of photovoltaic systems," *IEEE Trans. Power Electron.*, vol. 28, no. 6, pp. 2968–2979, Jun. 2013.

[25] S. MacAlpine, M. Brandemuehl, and R. Erickson, "Analysis of potential for mitigation of building-integrated pv array shading losses through use of distributed power converters," in *Proc. ASME Int. Conf. Energy Sustainabil.*, Phoenix, AZ, USA, 2010, pp. 447–456.

[26] A. Sanz, I. Vidaurrazaga, A. Pereda, R. Alonso, E. Roman, and V. Martinez, "Centralized versus distributed (power optimizer) PV system architecture field test results under mismatched operating conditions," in *Proc. IEEE Photovolt. Spec. Conf.*, Jun. 19–24, 2011, pp. 2435–2440.

[27] C. Deline, J. Meydbray, M. Donovan, and J. Forrest, "Partial shade evaluation of distributed power electronics for photovoltaic systems," presented at the IEEE Photovoltaic Specialist Conf., Austin, TX, USA, 2012.

[28] S. Poshtkouhi, V. Palaniappan, M. Fard, and O. Trescases, "A general approach for quantifying the benefit of distributed power electronics for fine grained MPPT in photovoltaic applications using 3-D modeling," *IEEE Trans. Power Electron.*, vol. 27, no. 11, pp. 4656–4666, Nov. 2012.

[29] K. A. Kim, P. S. Shenoy, and P. T. Krein, "Photovoltaic differential power converter trade-offs as a consequence of panel variation," in *Proc. IEEE Worksh. Contr. Model. Power Electron.*, Jun. 10–13, 2012, pp. 1–7.

[30] C. Olalla, D. Clement, D. Maksimovic, and C. Deline, "A cell-level photovoltaic model for high-granularity simulations," presented at the IEEE Eur. Conf. Power Electron. Appl., Lille, France, 2013.

[31] C. Olalla, M. Rodriguez, D. Clement, and D. Maksimovic, "Architectures and control of submodule integrated DC-DC converters for photovoltaic applications," *IEEE Trans. Power Electron.*, vol. 28, no. 6, pp. 2980–2997, Jun. 2013.

[32] J. A. Duffie and W. A. Beckman, *Solar Engineering of Thermal Processes*, vol. 13, 3rd ed. New York, NY, USA: Wiley, 2006.

[33] (2012). *Measurement and Instrumentation Data Center* (Series Nat. Renewable Energy Lab.). [Online]. Available http://www.nrel.gov/midc/

[34] D. Jordan, J. Wohlgemuth, and S. Kurtz, "Technology and climate trends in PV module degradation," presented at the 27th Eur. Photovolt. Solar Energy Conf. Exhib., Frankfurt, Germany, Sep. 24–28, 2012.

[35] C. E. Chamberlin, M. A. Rocheleau, M. W. Marshall, A. M. Reis, N. T. Coleman, and P. A. Lehman, "Comparison of PV module performance before and after 11 and 20 years of field exposure," in *Proc. IEEE Photovolt. Spec. Conf.*, Jun. 19–24, 2011, pp. 101–105.

[36] C. Deline and S. MacAlpine, "Use conditions and efficiency measurements of DC power optimizers for photovoltaic systems," presented at the IEEE Energy Convers. Congress Expo., Denver, CO, USA, 2013.

Christopher Deline received the B.S., M.S., and Ph.D. degrees from the University of Michigan, Ann Arbor, USA, in 2003, 2005, and 2008, respectively, all in electrical engineering. His Ph.D. work involved experimental investigation of the magnetic nozzle region of electric propulsion thrusters at NASA MSFC, and JSC.

Since 2008, he has been a Research Engineer with the National Renewable Energy Laboratory, Golden, CO, USA, in the photovoltaic test and evaluation group. He has coauthored several reports on the performance impact of microinverters and DC-DC converters in photovoltaic (PV) systems under mismatched and shaded conditions. His research includes thin-film PV performance and stabilization, mismatch and partial shading in PV systems, and distributed power electronics for PV.

Dragan Maksimovic (M'89–SM'04) received the B.S. and M.S. degrees in electrical engineering from the University of Belgrade, Yugoslavia, in 1984 and 1986, respectively, and the Ph.D. degree from the California Institute of Technology, Pasadena, CA, USA, in 1989.

From 1989 to 1992, he was with the University of Belgrade, Serbia (Yugoslavia). Since 1992, he has been with the Department of Electrical, Computer, and Energy Engineering, University of Colorado, Boulder, CO, USA, where he is currently a Professor and Director of the Colorado Power Electronics Center (CoPEC). His current research interests include mixed-signal integrated circuit design for control of power electronics, digital control techniques, as well as energy efficiency and renewable energy applications of power electronics. He has co-authored over 200 publications and the textbook *Fundamentals of Power Electronics*.

Prof. Maksimovic received the 1997 NSF CAREER Award, the IEEE Power Electronics Society Transactions Prize Paper Award in 1997, the IEEE Power Electronics Society Prize Letter Awards in 2009 and 2010, the Holland Excellence in Teaching Awards in 2004 and 2011, the University of Colorado Inventor of the Year Award in 2006, the Bruce Holland Excellence in Teaching Awards in 2004 and 2011, the Charles Hutchinson Memorial Teaching Award for 2012, the 2013 Boulder Faculty Assembly Excellence in Teaching Award, and the IEEE PELS Modeling and Control Technical Achievement Award for 2012.

Carlos Olalla (S'06–M'09) received the M.S. degree in electronic engineering from the Universitat Rovira i Virgili, Tarragona, Spain, in 2004 and the Ph.D. degree in advanced automatic control from the Universitat Politécnica de Catalunya, Barcelona, Spain, in 2009, for his work on robust linear control of power converters, carried out in the GAEI research group of the Universitat Rovira i Virgili.

In 2007 and 2009, he was a Visiting Scholar with the Laboratoire d'Analyse et d'Architecture des Systémes (LAAS-CNRS), Toulouse, France, where he also held a postdoctoral position until March 2010. From 2010 to 2012, he was a Visiting Scholar and a Research Associate with the Colorado Power Electronics Center (CoPEC), University of Colorado, Boulder, CO, USA. Since 2013, he has been a Research Associate with the Department of Electrical, Electronics, and Automatic Control Engineering, Universitat Rovira i Virgili, where he works on modeling, optimization, and robust control synthesis methods for power converters and renewable energy systems.

Field Installation and Evaluation of a 20kW Rooftop PV System Using 3.5kW String Level MPPT DC/DC Converters and a Central Inverter

Ahmed Elasser[1], Mohammed Agamy[2], Maja Harfman Todorovic[1], Song Chi[1], Adam McCann[1], Li Zhang[1], Lei Wang[1], Fengfeng Tao[1], Bex Thomas[1], Juan Sabate[1], Raj Bahadur[1], Frank Mueller[1], Brian Baxter[3], Brian Smith[3], John Dodge[4], Sigifredo Gonzalez[5], Armando Fresquez[5]

1- GE Global Research Center, Niskayuna, NY, 2- University of British Columbia, Kelowna, BC, 3- GE Power &Water, Schenectady, NY, 4- GE Energy Management, Rotterdam, NY, 5- Sandia National Laboratories, Albuquerque, NM

Abstract — **High energy yield has been and continues to be a major driver in PV installations. With the continuous improvement in PV modules' performance, there is a need to extract as much power as possible from the modules under various weather conditions. Over the past three years, we proposed, analyzed, built, installed, and monitored a PV system with string level MPPT dc/dc converters and a central inverter to understand and quantify the benefits of distributed MPPT. Our team performed detailed simulation studies on multiple architectures (module level to multi-string level MPPT), quantified the benefits of each architecture, selected an approach (string level), and designed a novel high efficiency partial power dc/dc converter, built it and tested it in the lab (with a PV emulator) and in the field with actual PV strings and a grid tied inverter. A rooftop installation was built with two systems side by side (a distributed and a central inverter) and has been monitored over the past 9 months.**

Index Terms — **MPPT, Distributed, DC/DC Converter, Partial Power, High Energy Yield**

I. INTRODUCTION

The work described in this paper is the culmination of three years of work at GE Global research Center in Niskayuna, NY in collaboration with GE Power & Water in Schenectady, NY. It started as a proposal to DoE to look at the benefits of distributed MPPT architectures for commercial and utility scale installations. In 2008, when the work was proposed, there were few installations with distributed MPPT and it was not clear if distributed MPPT architectures are viable from a cost/performance point of view. Several small companies were exploring module level MPPT (Microinverters and Microconverters - later called optimizers), but no major analysis or field study was performed on the actual benefit and on the viability of the approach. At the time, Solar LCOE numbers were still high and there was a need to increase the energy output in order to reduce the LCOE. The big question was: which approach is best, which approach provides a better cost/performance ratio, what size of the converters is optimal, which type of installations can benefit from these architectures? To answer these questions and to provide quantitative data on the increase in energy yield with a

distributed MPPT architecture, our team started the work by performing a detailed trade-off of the various architectures as shown in Fig. 1

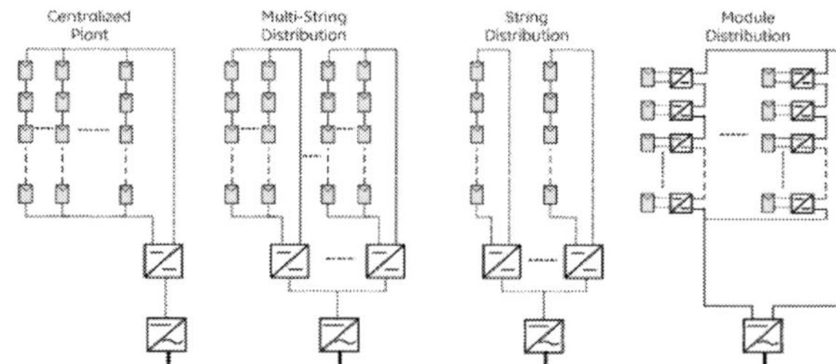

Figure 1: Distributed and central inverter MPPT architectures

The architectures of Fig. 1 were simulated for a 1MW plant with both Si and CdTe modules for different US locations. Detailed models of PV modules were developed in Pspice and were used to quantify the impact of shading [1]. Other tools such as Saber, Matlab Simulink, and Excel were used to compute the energy yield of the various architectures as well as determine the effect of various factors such as cabling, MPPT , shading, mismatch, soiling, etc.. on the energy yield [2-3]. Each factor was analyzed and its loss contribution was calculated for the central inverter architecture. We then quantified the percentage of losses that are recovered with MPPT distribution. The detailed results of this analysis were published in a conference paper [4]. In addition to computing the energy yield for these architectures, we also did a detailed cost, and reliability analysis. With the energy yield values, the cost and reliability data, we computed the net present value for each architecture and concluded that the best approach for large scale commercial plants is a string level MPPT solution with Si modules. The string level MPPT architecture provides an increase in energy yield of 6% to 8% over a central inverter solution. In addition, it allows for string monitoring, a constant dc link voltage, and an optimized inverter. With a string level solution chosen, we then looked at selecting a high efficiency dc/dc converter that will operate with a string of Si modules. Several converter concepts were considered and were simulated. A summary of this study findings were summarized in a conference paper [5].

II SELECTED DC/DC CONVERTER TOPOLOGY

A buck-boost partial power topology as shown in Fig. 2 operating in a boost mode with two channels is selected for its high composite efficiency, and its ability to operate in parallel mode with no need for voltage balance control on the dc link.

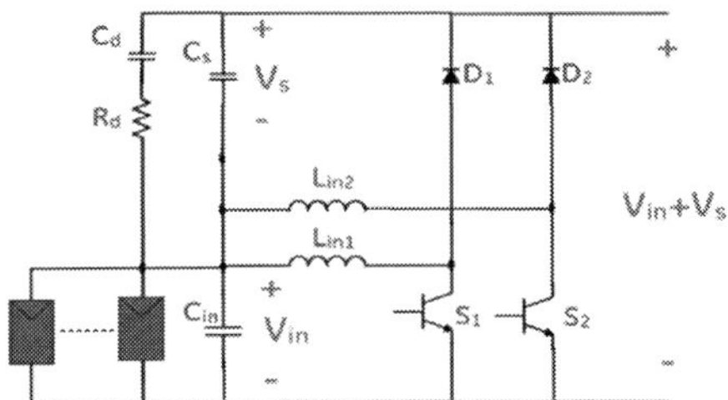

Figure 2: Partial power two channels string level MPPT DC/DC converter

Note that the converter is only processing a fraction of the total power given by:

$$\mathrm{Pr}\,ocessedPower = (V_s/V_{in})/(1 + V_s/V_{in}) \qquad (1)$$

The rest of the power is directly fed forward at 100% efficiency. Note also that with two paralleled channels, the converter can operate at higher efficiency at light load. We implemented a team-concept approach whereas only one channel operates when power is less than 1.75kW and two channels operate at higher power levels. Figure 3 shows the efficiency of the converter using the team operation.

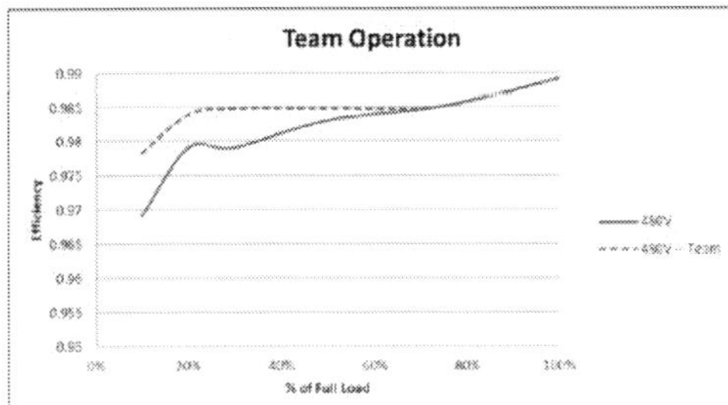

Figure 3: Converter composite efficiency with and without team operation

The converter was operated in a lab environment using a PV emulator and a grid tied constant voltage PV inverter. Control algorithms were tested under realistic conditions such as shading, wake-up, shutdown, and multiple maximum power points. With lab data, our next step was to field test the converter with actual PV modules and run multiple converters in parallel with a grid tied converter operating at a constant dc voltage.

In addition to our own testing at GRC, our converters were independently assessed by Sandia National Lab at their Distributed Energy Technology Lab. Figure 4 shows the measured efficiency results from Sandia National Lab.

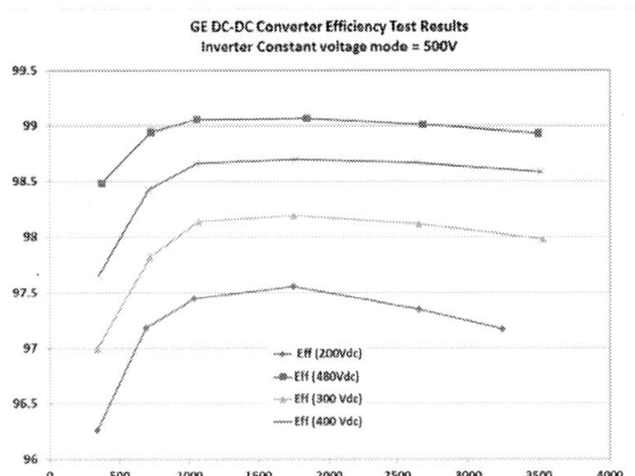

Figure 4: DC-DC converter efficiency as a function of load (X-axis in Watts) and input voltage (200V-400Vdc), output voltage is kept constant at 500Vdc. Y Axis- Efficiency (%)

A control platform and strategy was developed for the converter to perform local and global MPPT as well as all of the various protections such as overcurrent and overvoltage. A complete block diagram of the converter controls is shown in Figure 5 [6]. Note that in addition to the basic controls such as PWM signal generation, MPPT algorithm, there is also a communication block, a debugger block, and a protection block. The communication between the converter and the inverter is through RS485.

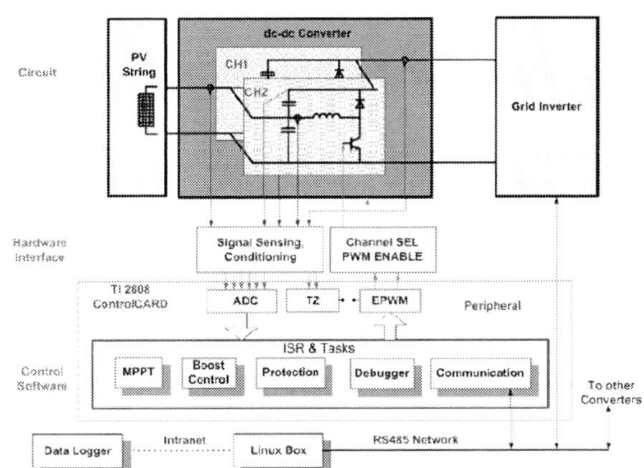

Figure 5: DC/DC converter control block diagram and interface with the grid tied inverter and other paralleled converters

The control platform includes software for enabling operation of the converter in a team operation mode as well as communicating with other converters to ensure robust paralleling and connection to the constant voltage dc bus. The latter is performed in conjunction with the communication

     525

platform to ensure seamless operation during startup in the mornings and during shutdowns.

III. SYSTEM DESIGN AND INSTALLATION

Prior to testing the converter in the field, a second version of the two channel converter was built which incorporates many of the changes and lessons learned from the lab tests. In addition, communication protocols were added to the converter to enable inter-converter and inverter communication as well as system supervisory control, data monitoring, and diagnostics of the converter and the system itself. The updated version of the converter is shown in Fig. 6. It uses Silicon IGBTs for the main switches and SiC Schottky diodes as freewheeling diodes. With SiC diodes, we basically eliminated all of the reverse recovery losses and reduced the turn-on losses of the IGBTs. An all SiC version of this converter was built and described in a recent IEEE Journal of Photovoltaics paper [7]

Figure 6: 3.5kW string level MPPT dc/dc converter board

Initially, single converters were tested with PV strings and a constant voltage dc electronic load. As the team gained experience with the setup, the converters were subsequently tested with PV strings and with the grid tied inverter operating at a constant dc voltage. Multiple converters (three) were then tested to verify the paralleling function and to synchronize the startup, shutdown, and grid connection. Communication protocols using RS485 were also tested, startup and shutdown procedures were developed and implemented. Global MPPT operation was calibrated. An example of the converters performing global MPPT is shown in Figure 7.

Prior to installing the three converters on the rooftop, the team had tested them on the ground. A NEMA 3R enclosure with a custom heatsink was designed and built to house the three converters, power supplies, and various protection equipment. Figure 8 shows a picture of the enclosure. Figure 9 shows the ground-level testing setup which shows the enclosure, the string combiners, and the grid tied inverter.

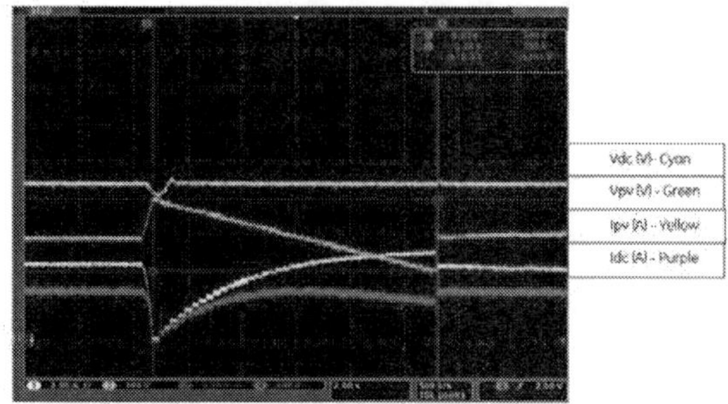

Figure 7: MPPT waveforms as a converter is going through a global MPPT sweeping event: Channel 1 (2A/div)- Yellow- I_{pv} (PV current), Channel 2 (100V/div)- Cyan- V_{dc} – DC bus voltage, Channel 3 (2A/div)- Purple- I_{dc} (dc output current), Channel 4 (100V/div)- Green- V_{pv}- PV Voltage

Figure 8 shows an example of all three converters going through a global MPPT sweeping event.

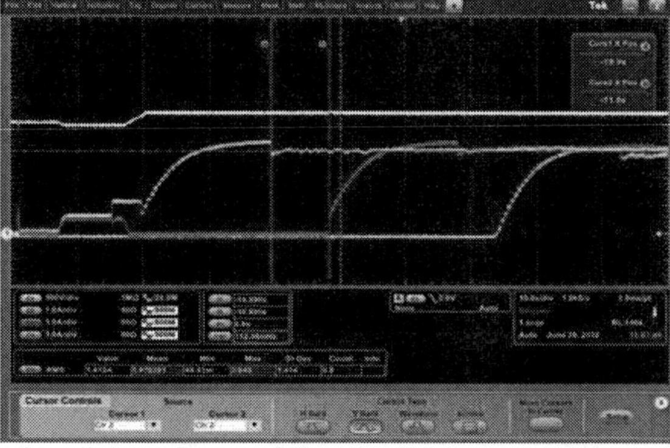

Figure 8: Input Current of Three Parallel Converters Connected to a PV Array and Feeding an Inverter During Shifted Global MPPT Sweeps. Ch1 (Yellow): Dc-Link Voltage (100V/div), Ch2 (Blue): Input Current of DC/DC Converter #1 (1A/div), Ch3 (Magenta): Input Current of DC/DC Converter #2 (1A/div), Ch4 (Green): Input Current of DC/DC Converter #3 (1A/div)

For the field installation, a webserver was designed and implemented to continuously monitor the three converters as well as the inverter. To ensure safety of the building, the system was tested temporarily for 3 months on the ground. After debugging most of the control and communication issues, the system was moved to a rooftop and installed permanently. Two systems were installed, a central inverter system and a distributed MPPT system with three dc/dc converters and a constant voltage PV inverter. Figure 11 shows the installed rooftop system. In addition to the power electronics and the modules, we also installed a weather station and numerous sensors to keep track of the modules and collect relevant information. Figure 12 shows another view of the rooftop installation with the communication box and the weather station on the background.

Figure 9: Prototype power enclosure with three 3.5kW dc/dc converters

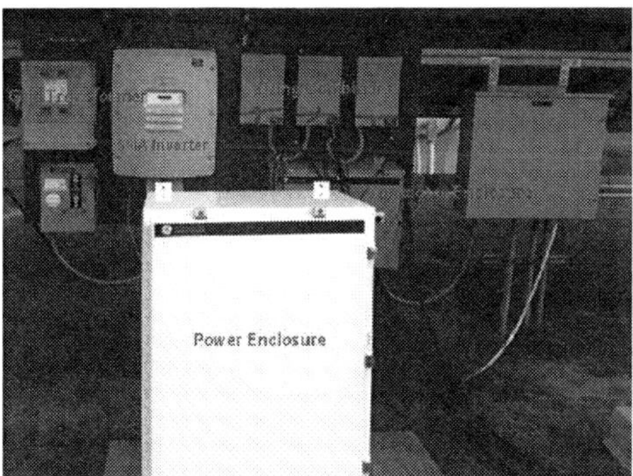

Figure 10: Ground-level testing installation

Figure 11: Rooftop installation - central and distributed systems

IV. SYSTEM OPERATION

We initially planned on using Si modules in our installation since we did all our modeling using Si modules and concluded that Si based plants can benefit from these string level architectures. Our business team was mostly interested in CIGS based plants for commercial roof back in 2012 and we ended up using the CIGS modules instead. By using CIGS modules, our string is now only 4 modules in series and we require few strings in parallel to meet the dc/dc converter requirements. 5 strings of 4 modules in series are used in our installation. With CIGS modules being rated at 120W each, which is about 2.4kW instead of the full 3.5kW converter rating. This choice was driven by the inverter availability. We used the SMA inverters in our installation in a constant voltage mode [8]. We need two inverters, one for the central inverter system (operating in MPPT mode) and one for the distributed system (operating in a constant voltage mode). With CIGS modules, a 10kW SMA inverter which would be needed for three converters has an MPPT window that is outside the CIGS modules MPPT window, hence is not suitable as a central inverter. We chose a 7.5kW inverter instead which works for both systems, hence the converters are limited to 2.4-2.5kW.

Since the distributed system requires the inverter to operate in a constant voltage mode, we characterized the inverter under constant voltage mode to select the optimal dc bus voltage. A dc bus voltage of 440V yielded the highest CEC efficiency for the inverter. Our converters were therefore operated in combination with the inverter to maintain a constant dc voltage of 440V. By operating the distributed inverter at 440V instead of its MPPT window, the ac efficiency is reduced by almost a percentage point as shown in Figure 13, hence impacting the ac energy yield output from the distributed architecture.

The rooftop installation has been operating since late August, 2012. In addition to all the debugging and fixes we performed while on the ground, several new challenges rose in our rooftop installation. Overvoltages, overcurrents as well as power curtailment issues were addressed and improvements to the control algorithm were implemented. In addition to electrical parameters such as voltages, currents, power, and energy yield, we also monitored weather data such as irradiance, humidity, rain level, wind speed, module temperature, and power enclosure temperature.

Figure 12: Rooftop installation: Two systems side by side -one central and one distributed. The weather station (wind, rain gauge, ambient temp, humidity sensors) is seen in the background. Irradiance sensors are placed by the modules, module temperature sensors are also used to monitor module temperature

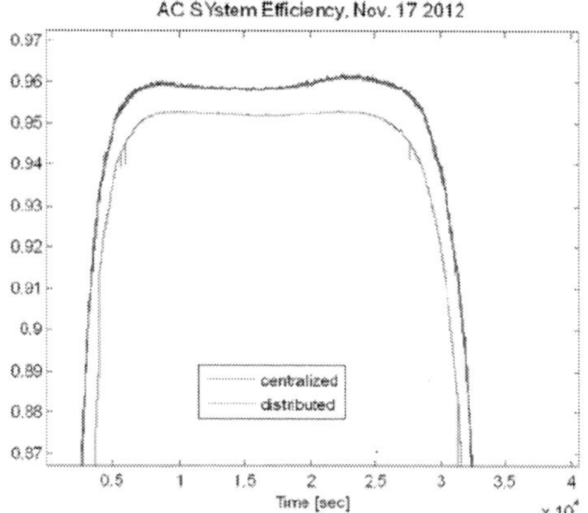

Figure 13: Inverter Efficiency - Central vs. Distributed. Note how almost a percentage point is lost in the distributed inverter as it operates at a higher and constant voltage

Our system has seen many conditions such as hot days, cloudy days, high irradiance days, rainy days, snowy days, and finally extremely cold days. The system has performed well under all these conditions and continues to run. In addition, we have a second system operating at the Sandia National Lab with Si modules. Figure 14 shows the inverter output for a cold sunny fall day and a semi-cloudy fall day.

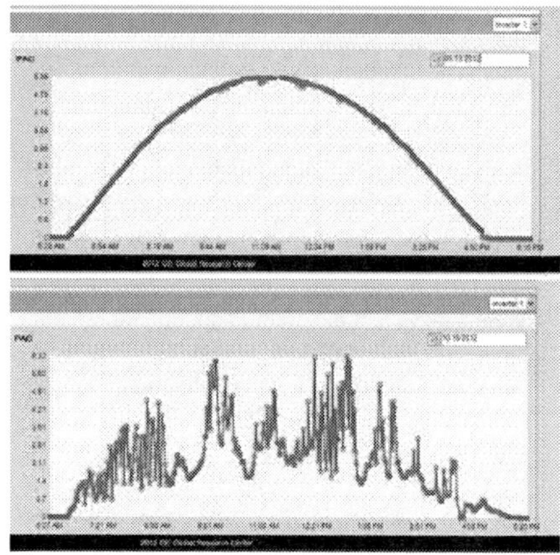

Figure 14: Inverter Output on a sunny & cloudy day

Figure 15 shows the Energy output from both the central and the distributed inverter on a hot sunny and cloudless day. Note that both systems go into power curtailment mode as early as 9:30 in the morning and operate at constant power for almost 5 hours. The inverter is limited to 7100W ac power. For the central inverter, power curtailment is performed by moving off the MPPT point. For the distributed architecture, the only way to do power curtailment is at the

dc/dc converter level, hence we limit the power of the dc/dc converter to 2.4kW.

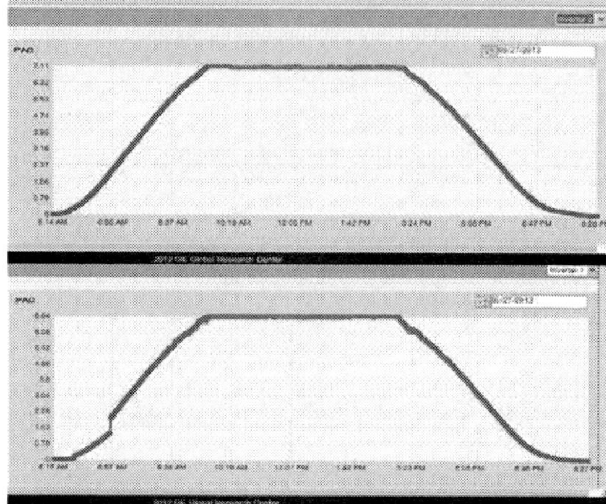

Figure 15: Central and distributed inverter ac power on a cloudless day in May 2013 (27th). Note how both curves are flat from 9:30am to 3:00pm. The central inverter power is curtailed to 7.11kW while the distributed inverter is only curtailed to 6.84kW. The difference is due to the lower efficiency of the distributed inverter as shown above and to the difference in the curtailment accuracy of both systems.

While we did our simulation using Si modules, we ended up installing CIGS modules [9]. With CIGS modules, the comparison between the distributed and the central inverter systems became difficult due to a number of reasons: CIGS modules have only 4 modules in series for a string, hence they are less sensitive to shading; dc/dc converters are now operating at only 68% of their rated power, hence their composite efficiency is reduced; the distributed inverter is not optimized to operate at a constant dc voltage, hence its efficiency is less than that of the central inverter; the installation is small, hence mismatch effect, cabling loss effect, and MPPT effects are all minimal. In the end the two installations are competing on the efficiency and the central inverter installation has a much higher efficiency than the distributed installation as shown in Figure 16.

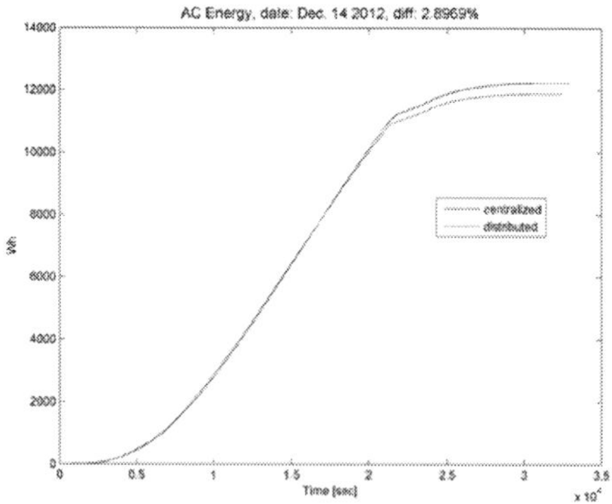

Figure 16: Distributed (Red) vs. central (Blue) AC energy (Wh)

When we measure the energy yield at the dc side, the difference between the two systems goes from 2.9% to 1.75% as shown in Figure 17.

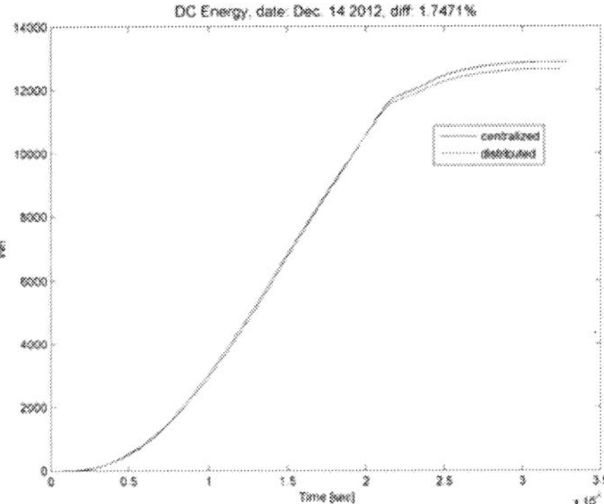

Figure 17: Distributed (Red) vs. central (Blue) DC energy (Wh)

While this data is not conclusive as to which architecture is better, it does show that under the right conditions and with an optimal inverter for the distributed inverter, the distributed architecture can outperform the central inverter architecture. A larger installation using Si modules is being considered and should answer the comparison question in a definitive way. While we used CIGS modules in our rooftop installation, we also tested the converters with Si modules at the Sandia National Lab. No comparison was made as we were nearing the end of the project. Figure 18 shows the test setup used at Sandia National Lab to test two converters in parallel with a single SMA grid tied inverter.

The evaluations involved connecting two dc-dc converters (mounted in an enclosure that was custom made by GE for the Sandia Lab Testing) to the SMA inverter and operating them using actual PV Modules (Two Sanyo HIP-200BA-19PV arrays, two parallel strings of six modules each). For these tests, the converters were not running at rated power, because the inverter is rated to 5kW only. Each PV array is made up of two six-module strings, for a standard test condition rating of 2.4kW per dc-dc converter.

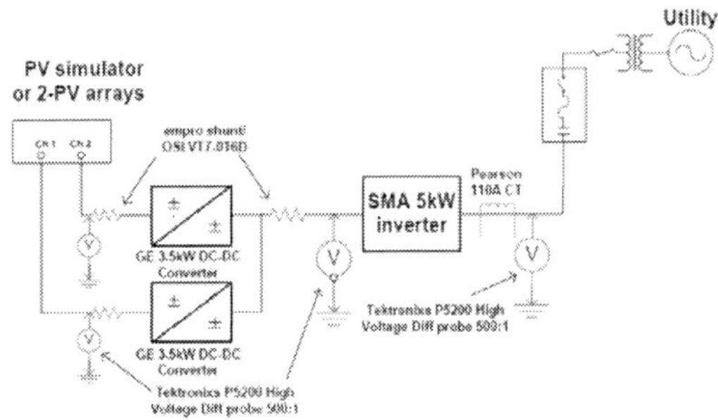

Figure 18: Two GE dc-to-dc converter configuration one-line diagram.

Figure 19 shows the converter power output as DC_Watts_2 and DC_Watts_3, the total power is denoted by DC_Watts_1. The lower power in the morning on this clear day is attributed to ice and to a slight snow accumulation on the modules.

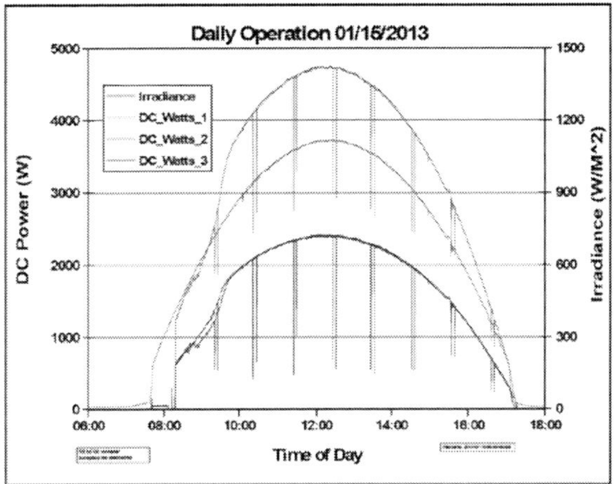

Figure 19: Enclosure unit converters' DC power output, Jan. 15th, 2013. Red curve is irradiance. The spikes seen in the power curves is due to the global MPPT sweep every hour.

V. Conclusion

A 20kW distributed & central inverter system installation and operation process from initial concept, to field testing, to rooftop installation has been described. The aim of this study was to compare these two architectures from an energy yield point of view. The simulation results were based on Si modules. The rooftop installation used CIGS modules, and as we explained above, the data obtained shows that all of the factors that are favorable to distributed architectures are not significant in our small installation. At the end the two systems were competing on efficiency and the central inverter system has a better efficiency since it is optimized for this operation.

The rooftop installation allowed us to prove the concept of our dc/dc converters, exercise our local and global MPPT algorithms, our power curtailment method. It also allowed us to field test the communication protocols, the monitoring, and the website. By installing the distributed architecture in the field, we debugged the system in a real installation and learned a lot about how these architectures operate and how to optimize them during startup, shutdown, to protect them from overvoltages, overcurrents, to curtail power, and most importantly how to operate them safely and in concert with a constant dc voltage inverter. The rooftop installation is still operating and has been generating many kWhs, the learning continues and a larger optimized installation using Si modules and with an optimized inverter is being considered to show that distributed (string level) architectures do indeed provide higher energy yields than central architectures for large commercial installations.

VII. REFERENCES

[1] H. Patel & V. Agarwal, "MATLAB-Based Modeling to Study the Effects of Partial Shading on PV Array Characteristics," IEEE Trans. on Energy Conversion, Vol. 23, No. 1, March 2008, pp. 302-310.

[2] A. Chouder & S. Silvestre, "Analysis Model of Mismatch Power Losses in PV Systems," Journal of Solar Engineering, May 2009, Vol. 131.

[3] N. Femia, G. Lisi, G. Petrone, G. Spagnuolo & M. Vitteli, " Distributed Maximum Power Point Tracking of Photovoltaic Arrays: Novel Approach and System Analysis," IEEE Trans. On Industrial Electronics, Vol. 55, No. 7, July 2008, pp. 2610-2621.

[4] A. Elasser et al., "A Comparative Study of Central and Distributed MPPT Architectures for Megawatt Utility and Large Scale Commercial Photovoltaic Plants," in IECON 2010, p. 2753

[5] M. Agamy et al.," DC/DC Converter Topology Assessment for Large Scale Distributed Photovoltaic Plant Architectures," in Proceedings of ECCE 2011, p. 764.

[6] TI DSP TMS320F2808 http://www.ti.com/product/tms320f2808

[7] M. Agamy et al., "A High Power Density Dc-Dc Converter for Distributed PV Architectures," in PVSC, June 2012 and now in IEEE Journal of Photovoltaics, Issue 99, 2013.

[8] SMA Sunny Boy Inverters http://www.sma-america.com/en_US/products/grid-tied-inverters/sunny-boy.html

[9] CIGS Solar Modules - http://www.solar-frontier.com/eng/products/index.html

VI. ACKNOWLEDGEMENTS

This work was supported in part by the U.S. Department of Energy under Grant DE-EE0000572.

VII. DISCLAIMER

This report was prepared as an account of work sponsored by an agency of the United States Government. Neither the United States Government nor any agency thereof, nor any of their employees, makes any warranty, express or implied, or assumes any legal liability or responsibility for the accuracy, completeness, or usefulness of any information, apparatus, product, or process disclosed, or represents that its use would not infringe privately owned rights. References herein to any specific commercial product, process, or service by trade name, trademark, manufacturer or otherwise does not necessarily constitute or imply its endorsement, recommendation, or favoring by the United States Government or any agency thereof. The views and opinions of the authors expressed herein do not necessarily state or reflect those of the United States government or any agency thereof.

Oscillator-Based Inverter Control for Islanded Three-Phase Microgrids

Brian B. Johnson, *Member, IEEE*, Sairaj V. Dhople, *Member, IEEE*, James L. Cale, *Member, IEEE*,
Abdullah O. Hamadeh, and Philip T. Krein, *Fellow, IEEE*

Abstract—A control scheme is proposed for an islanded low-inertia three-phase inverter-based microgrid with a high penetration of photovoltaic (PV) generation resources. The output of each inverter is programmed to emulate the dynamics of a nonlinear oscillator. The virtual oscillators within each controller are implicitly coupled through the physical electrical network. The asymptotic synchronization of the oscillators can be guaranteed by design, and as a result, a stable power system emerges innately with no communication between the inverters. Time-domain switching-level simulation results for a 45-kW microgrid with 33% PV penetration demonstrate the merits of the proposed technique; in particular they show that the load voltage can be maintained between prescribed bounds in spite of variations in incident irradiance and step changes in the load.

Index Terms—Microgrids, oscillators, photovoltaic inverter control, synchronization.

I. Introduction

MICROGRIDS offer the potential for increased renewable generation, improved reliability, and reduced transmission losses. This study is focused on low-inertia islanded microgrids, where sustainable generation resources, such as photovoltaic (PV) arrays and fuel cells (in contrast with diesel-engine or natural-gas-driven generators), are interfaced to the electric network through voltage-source inverters (VSIs), and intermittency in supply is managed by energy storage devices.

Key control challenges in such microgrids include 1) maximizing system availability in the face of uncertain renewable generation, 2) eliminating centralized controllers to ensure there are no single points of failure, and 3) minimizing communication between inverters to enhance resilience against cyber-level failures/attacks. Focused on these challenges, we propose an inverter control paradigm that is inspired by the *synchronization of coupled oscillators*. In particular, a stable islanded microgrid is realized by controlling the VSIs to emulate the dynamics of nonlinear oscillators. When coupled through the underlying electrical network, the virtual oscillators (we use the terminology *virtual* to emphasize that the oscillator dynamics are emulated on a digital controller) synchronize without any supervisory control effort or information exchanges over a communication network; in other words, a stable power system emerges innately by design.

Passivity- and $\mathcal{L}_2$ input-output stability-based methods [1] have recently been proposed in [2]–[4], respectively, to explore the synchronization of coupled nonlinear oscillators with the goal of formulating control strategies for inverters in islanded power systems. In this study, we extend our previous effort in [3] and [4], which was tailored to single-phase inverters, to the control of three-phase inverter-based microgrids with high PV penetration. Toward this end, we also formulate a maximum power point tracking (MPPT) method compatible with the virtual-oscillator-based controller for the subset of PV-interfaced inverters in the microgrid.

Relevant to this study is a wide body of literature on droop control of inverters in islanded microgrids [5]–[11]. Inspired by the control of synchronous generators, this approach is based on modulating the frequency and output voltage of inverters to be inversely proportional to the real and reactive power, respectively [5], [6], [12]–[14]. While the original formulation [5] did not necessitate communication, several drawbacks relating to load sharing accuracy and frequency/voltage deviations have prompted the supplementation of higher level controls, which require a communication network [15]–[19].

The proposed approach that is based on the dynamics of coupled oscillators offers a fundamentally different method for islanded inverter-based microgrids. The intrinsic electrical coupling between inverters is leveraged to synchronize virtual oscillators, hence realizing a control strategy that promotes dynamic load sharing with minimal frequency/voltage deviations. Since each controller is fundamentally identical, the system tolerates failures in any number of inverters so long as the load can be satisfied. The main contributions of this paper are as follows: 1) a method for the synthesis of oscillator-based controllers for three-phase inverters is outlined and 2) an MPPT method is integrated with the oscillator-based controller to maximize the power delivered by PV-interfaced inverters.

Manuscript received June 10, 2013; revised July 24, 2013 and August 22, 2013; accepted August 28, 2013. Date of publication October 4, 2013; date of current version December 16, 2013. The work of B. B. Johnson was supported in part by a National Science Foundation Graduate Research Fellowship and in part by the Grainger Center for Electric Machinery and Electromechanics at the University of Illinois. The work of P. T. Krein was supported in part by the Global Climate and Energy Project at Stanford University.

B. B. Johnson and J. L. Cale are with the Distributed Energy Systems Integration group, National Renewable Energy Laboratory, Golden, CO 80401 USA (e-mail: brian.johnson@nrel.gov; james.cale@nrel.gov).

S. V. Dhople is with the Department of Electrical and Computer Engineering, University of Minnesota, Minneapolis, MN 55455 USA (e-mail: sdhople@umn.edu).

A. O. Hamadeh is with the Department of Mechanical Engineering, Massachusetts Institute of Technology, Cambridge, MA 02139 USA (e-mail: ahamadeh@mit.edu).

P. T. Krein is with the Department of Electrical and Computer Engineering, University of Illinois, Urbana, IL 61820 USA (e-mail: krein@illinois.edu).

Color versions of one or more of the figures in this paper are available online at http://ieeexplore.ieee.org.

Digital Object Identifier 10.1109/JPHOTOV.2013.2280953

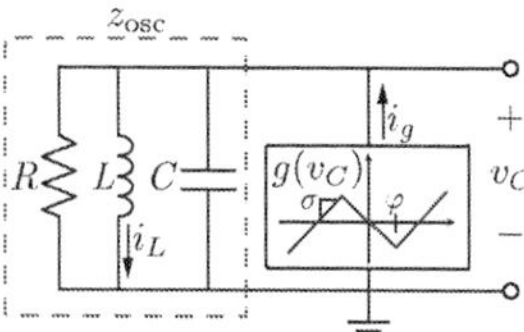

Fig. 1. Schematic of a single dead-zone oscillator.

The remainder of this paper is organized as follows. In Section II, the nonlinear oscillator is introduced, and a method for parameter selection and system design is outlined. Controller implementation details for a three-phase inverter and the MPPT method are described in Section III. Case-studies are presented in Section IV, and these are followed by concluding remarks in Section V.

II. Oscillator Model Fundamentals

In this section, we first present the oscillator model that constitutes the mainstay of the proposed three-phase inverter control method. Then, we provide a sufficient condition that ensures the synchronization of a system of three-phase inverters controlled with the proposed oscillator-based approach. Finally, we describe the parameter selection and system design process.

A. Oscillator Model

Fig. 1 illustrates the nonlinear *dead-zone oscillator* utilized in this study. Each oscillator consists of a resonant LC tank that sets the system frequency, a nonlinear voltage-dependent current source that sustains the oscillations $g\left(\cdot\right)$, and a damping element R. The terminal-voltage amplitude is proportional to $(\sigma - 1/R)$, where $\sigma = |dg/dv|$, and to ensure oscillations, we must have $\sigma > 1/R$ [3].[1] It can be shown that as $\epsilon := \sqrt{L/C}(\sigma - 1/R) \to 0$, the oscillator terminal voltage is approximately sinusoidal, with frequency $\omega \approx 1/\sqrt{LC}$. This is typically referred to as the quasi-harmonic regime [20].

B. Sufficient Condition for Synchronization

The basic microgrid topology under consideration is composed of parallel VSIs connected to an impedance load as shown in Fig. 2(a). Assume that a subset of the (N total) inverters in the microgrid are interfaced to PV arrays, while the others are interfaced to fuel cells/energy-storage devices (modeled as dc-voltage sources). Each inverter is controlled to emulate the dynamics of the dead-zone oscillator by using the digital controller depicted in Fig. 3 (controller details are outlined subsequently in Section III). With the implementation of the proposed controller, the dynamics of the three-phase microgrid in Fig. 2(a) can be described by the equivalent single-phase system in Fig. 2(b).

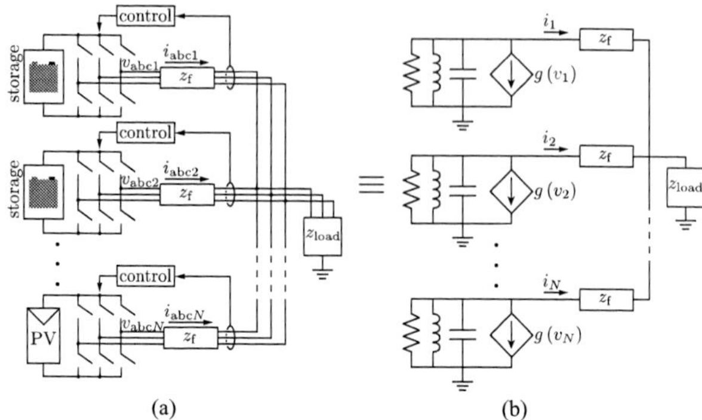

Fig. 2. Microgrid composed of parallel three-phase VSIs in (a) is controlled to emulate the corresponding single-phase system of coupled oscillators in (b).

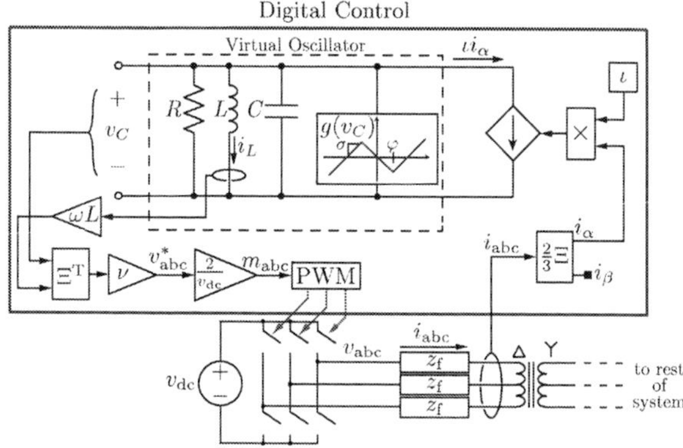

Fig. 3. Implementation of the proposed controller.

The synchronization of the terminal voltages in the system of coupled oscillators depicted in Fig. 2(b) can be guaranteed if

$$\max_{\omega} \left\| \frac{(\nu\iota)^{-1} z_{\mathrm{f}} z_{\mathrm{osc}}}{(\nu\iota)^{-1} z_{\mathrm{f}} + z_{\mathrm{osc}}} \right\|_2 \sigma < 1 \qquad (1)$$

where $\| \cdot \|_2$ denotes the Euclidean norm [1], $z_{\mathrm{f}} = R_{\mathrm{f}} + \mathrm{j}\omega L_{\mathrm{f}}$ is the inverter output-filter impedance, and $z_{\mathrm{osc}} = R \| \mathrm{j}\omega L \| (\mathrm{j}\omega C)^{-1}$ is the impedance of the passive RLC circuit in each oscillator (see Fig. 1). Furthermore, the condition in (1) depends on two design parameters, ν and ι (see Fig. 3), that are referred as the voltage and current gains, respectively. The values these parameters are tuned to depend on the voltage and power ratings. Note that for this particular network, the synchronization condition does not depend on the number of inverters N, or the load impedance z_{load}. Assuming a balanced three-phase system, synchronization in the single-phase equivalent system translates to a stable three-phase microgrid. An outline of the proof for the synchronization condition in (1) is provided in Appendix A. Details are in [3].

C. Parameter Selection and System Design

With reference to the controller that is depicted in Fig. 3, the design objective is to select the current gain ι, the voltage gain ν, and the oscillator parameters R, L, C, φ, and σ, for a

---

[1]The terminology *dead-zone oscillator* follows from the fact that we can write $g(v) = f(v) - \sigma v$, where $f(v)$ is a dead-zone function with slope 2σ and $f(v) = 0$ for $v \in (-\varphi, \varphi)$.

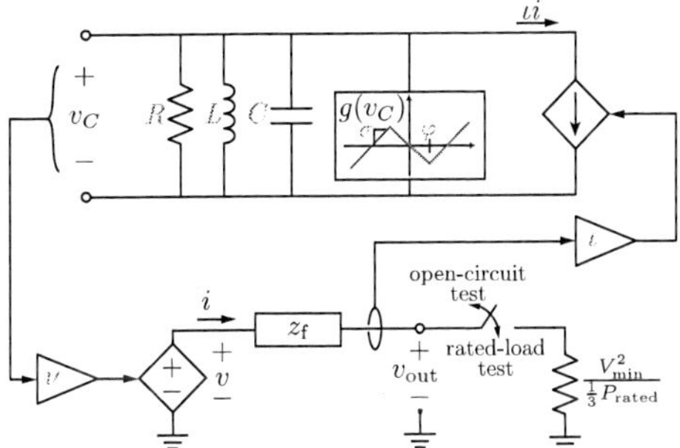

Fig. 4. Circuit model used to perform the open-circuit and rated-load tests for parameter selection. Design parameters that are tuned in Section II-C (R, L, C, σ, φ, ι, and ν) are highlighted in red.

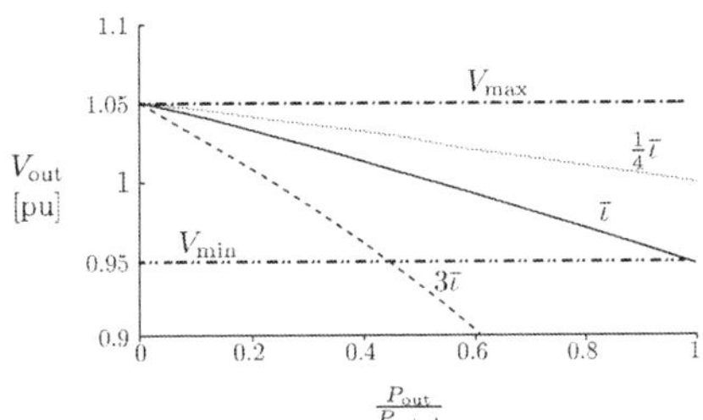

Fig. 5. Inverter output voltage as a function of real power for different values of the current gain. Note that when the current gain is equal to the nominal value, i.e., $\iota = \bar{\iota}$, the output voltage is between $V_{\min} = 0.95$ pu and $V_{\max} = 1.05$ pu for the whole load range.

given filter impedance z_f, such that the load voltage and system frequency meet performance specifications. Additionally, the choice of parameters must ensure that the condition in (1) is satisfied. Once all parameters are selected, it is straightforward to discretize the differential equations of the oscillator circuit in Fig. 3 for implementation on a microcontroller.

First, we set $\nu = \sqrt{2}V_{\mathrm{rated}}$, where V_{rated} is the rated RMS line-neutral voltage. This ensures that the virtual oscillator voltage corresponds to the per-unitized inverter voltage. To ensure oscillations at the rated system frequency ω_{rated}, the values of R, L, and C must be selected such that $R > 1/\sigma$, and $LC = 1/\omega_{\mathrm{rated}}^2$. Next, we perform two tests to tune φ and ι such that the RMS load voltage is between prescribed minimum and maximum values, denoted as $V_{\min}$ and $V_{\max}$, respectively. These tests are run for the equivalent single-phase test circuit shown in Fig. 4. In the open-circuit test, the value of φ is tuned so that the RMS voltage at the inverter output V_{out}, equals $V_{\max}$. In the rated-load test, the maximum rated load is connected to the inverter, and ι is adjusted such that $V_{\mathrm{out}} = V_{\min}$. The value of ι computed after the rated-load test is referred to as the nominal current gain, and denoted by $\bar{\iota}$. Finally, (1) is evaluated to validate that the synchronization condition is satisfied.

Fig. 5 illustrates the voltage versus power characteristic of a single inverter for three different choices of the current gain. The complete list of parameters for this particular inverter design is summarized in Appendix B. Note that for a fixed terminal voltage, the inverter output power is inversely proportional to

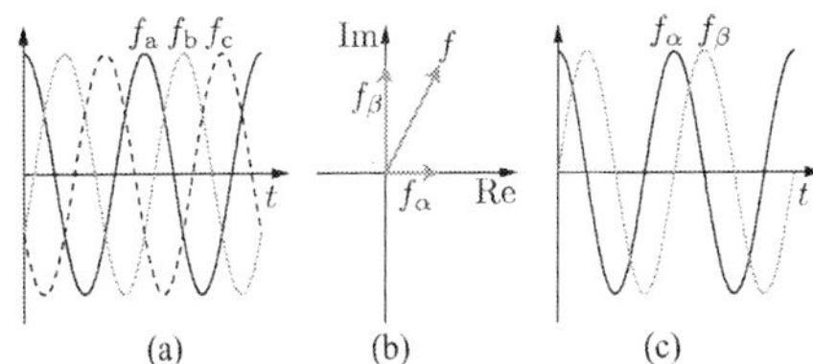

Fig. 6. (a) Illustrative three-phase balanced waveforms (b) Space-vector signal in the complex plane. (c) Corresponding waveforms in the $\alpha\beta$-frame.

ι. This characteristic forms the basis of the MPPT method (see Section IV-B) for the PV-interfaced inverters.

III. Oscillator-Based Inverter Control Method

In this section, we outline key controller implementation details that ensure the three-phase inverters emulate the behavior of the dead-zone oscillator described in Section II-A (the schematic of the controller is illustrated in Fig. 3). In the forthcoming discussions, we particularly focus on the coordinate transformations that interface the oscillator to the three-phase inverter, and describe the MPPT strategy that has been adopted for the PV-interfaced inverters in the microgrid.

A. Three-Phase Controller Design

Controller design in three-phase inverters can be simplified by formulating suitable coordinate transformations that refer three-phase voltages and currents to a different reference frame [21]. In this study, we focus on controller design in the $\alpha\beta$ frame [21]. Toward this end, for a set of balanced, sinusoidal, three-phase waveforms $f_\mathrm{a}(t)$, $f_\mathrm{b}(t)$, $f_\mathrm{c}(t)$, define the *space vector* signal

$$f(t) := \frac{2}{3}(f_\mathrm{a}(t) + f_\mathrm{b}(t)e^{-\frac{2\pi}{3}\mathrm{j}} + f_\mathrm{c}(t)e^{\frac{2\pi}{3}\mathrm{j}}). \tag{2}$$

The real and imaginary components of $f(t)$ are denoted by $f_\alpha(t)$ and $f_\beta(t)$, respectively. The relationship between the original three-phase signals and the transformed signals in the $\alpha\beta$ frame is captured by the following:

$$\begin{bmatrix} f_\alpha \\ f_\beta \end{bmatrix} = \frac{2}{3}\Xi \begin{bmatrix} f_\mathrm{a} \\ f_\mathrm{b} \\ f_\mathrm{c} \end{bmatrix}, \quad \begin{bmatrix} f_\mathrm{a} \\ f_\mathrm{b} \\ f_\mathrm{c} \end{bmatrix} = \Xi^\mathrm{T} \begin{bmatrix} f_\alpha \\ f_\beta \end{bmatrix} \tag{3}$$

where

$$\Xi := \begin{bmatrix} 1 & -\dfrac{1}{2} & -\dfrac{1}{2} \\ 0 & \dfrac{\sqrt{3}}{2} & -\dfrac{\sqrt{3}}{2} \end{bmatrix}. \tag{4}$$

Fig. 6 depicts the coordinate transformation described previously for an illustrative set of three-phase signals.

As shown in Fig. 3, the aforementioned coordinate transformation is used in the controller in two key ways. First, the inverter output currents, $i_{\mathrm{abc}}(t) = [i_\mathrm{a}(t), i_\mathrm{b}(t), i_\mathrm{c}(t)]^\mathrm{T}$, are sensed and transformed to obtain $i_\alpha(t)$ and $i_\beta(t)$ with (3). Since $i_\mathrm{a}(t) = i_\alpha(t)$ under balanced conditions, the current $\iota i_\alpha(t)$ is extracted from the virtual oscillator to establish the link with the single-phase equivalent of the three-phase inverter. Next,

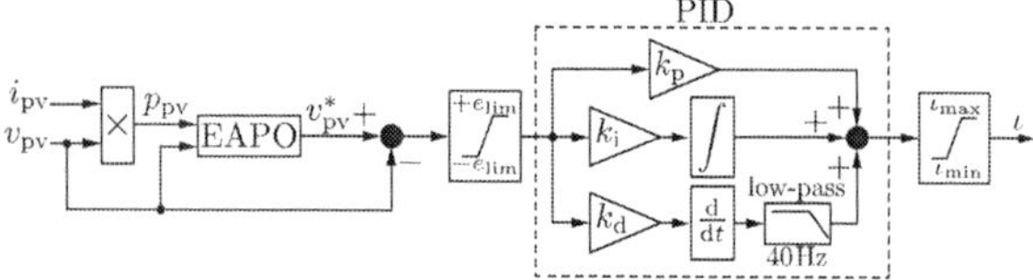

Fig. 7. Block diagram of MPPT controller for PV-interfaced inverters.

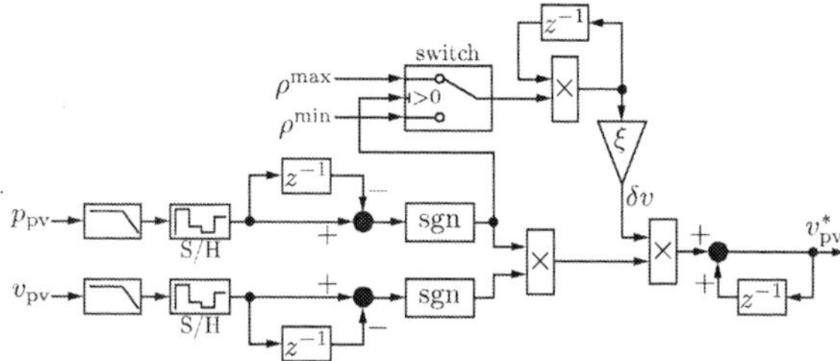

Fig. 8. Details of the exponential adaptive perturb and observe MPPT algorithm utilized in this study.

to control the switching action of the three-phase inverter, a set of three-phase modulation signals must be generated. In the quasi-harmonic regime, we can approximate the oscillator terminal voltage as $v_C(t) = V\cos(\omega t)$, where, as described in Section II, the amplitude V, is governed by the choice of σ and R, and the frequency $\omega \approx 1/\sqrt{LC}$. Since $di_L/dt = v_C$, it follows that the current through the inductor in the RLC subcircuit is given by $i_L(t) = V/(\omega L)\sin(\omega t)$. Since $v_C(t)$ and $i_L(t)$ are orthogonal, they can be used to derive a set of three-phase modulation signals. In particular, v_C and i_L are transformed from the $\alpha\beta$-frame to the abc-frame, multiplied by ν, and scaled by the dc-link voltage to yield a set of three-phase modulation signals $m_{abc}(t) = [m_a(t), m_b(t), m_c(t)]^T$. Finally, a conventional sine-triangle pulse width modulation scheme [22] is used to generate the switching signals. With the proposed approach, the inverter terminal voltages follow the commanded voltages, i.e., $v_{abc} \rightarrow v^*_{abc}$.

Remark 1: Note that with the proposed approach, the controller state variables corresponding to the nonlinear oscillator [i.e., $v_C(t)$ and $i_L(t)$] are directly utilized to generate the three-phase modulation signals. This eliminates the need for explicit orthogonal-signal generators [23], [24].

B. Maximum Power Point Tracking Method

We now describe the MPPT controller for the subset of PV-interfaced inverters in the microgrid. The exponential adaptive perturb and observe (EAPO) algorithm is utilized for MPPT [25]. This method is similar in construction to other adaptive perturb and observe (PO) algorithms (see, e.g., [26]–[28]) that modulate the perturbation step size with a goal of improving the dynamic and steady-state performance. In particular, these methods can potentially increase tracking speed and improve tracking efficiency by reducing oscillations around the maximum power point in a periodic steady state.

A block diagram of the MPPT controller is shown in Fig. 7, and the details of the EAPO algorithm are illustrated in Fig. 8.

We utilize the PV voltage as the MPPT perturbation control variable. As demonstrated in [29], this results in a fast response to irradiance changes and presents significant advantages compared with using the PV current as the control variable. Before discussing the details of the EAPO algorithm, it will be useful to briefly summarize the conventional PO algorithm. In a conventional PO algorithm, the dc-bus voltage reference in the $k+1$ iteration, $v^*_{pv}[k+1]$, is updated as follows:

$$v^*_{pv}[k+1] = v^*_{pv}[k] + \delta v \cdot \mathrm{sgn}(\Delta v_{pv}[k])\mathrm{sgn}(\Delta p_{pv}[k]) \quad (5)$$

where δv is the size of the perturbation step, $v^*_{pv}[k]$ is the dc-bus voltage reference, $\mathrm{sgn}(\Delta v_{pv}[k])$ is the sign of the difference in the dc-bus voltage, and $\mathrm{sgn}(\Delta p_{pv}[k])$ is the sign of the difference in the extracted PV power (all for the kth iteration). With a conventional PO algorithm, note that the perturbation step size δv, is fixed; the precise choice is based on a tradeoff in tracking speed and size of periodic steady-state oscillations around the maximum power point. To address these concerns, in the EAPO algorithm, the dc-bus voltage reference is updated as follows:

$$v^*_{pv}[k+1] = v^*_{pv}[k] + \delta v[k+1] \cdot \mathrm{sgn}(\Delta v_{pv}[k])\mathrm{sgn}(\Delta p_{pv}[k]) \quad (6)$$

where the perturbation step size is updated according to

$$\delta v[k+1] = \begin{cases} \rho^{\max}\delta v[k], & \text{if } \Delta p_{pv}[k] > 0 \\ \rho^{\min}\delta v[k], & \text{otherwise.} \end{cases} \quad (7)$$

Essentially, the perturbation step size is increased by a large factor $\rho^{\max}$ (small factor $\rho^{\min}$) if the extracted power increased (decreased) in the previous iteration. As shown in Fig. 8, a scaling factor ξ, can be included if required. In particular, the algorithm formulation ensures that the perturbation step size is reduced close to the maximum power point; this significantly increases the tracking efficiency in a periodic steady state [25].

A PID controller acts on the dc-bus voltage error $v^*_{pv} - v_{pv}$, and modulates the current gain ι. Since the power output of each inverter is inversely proportional to ι (see Fig. 5), this strategy ultimately controls the power output to ensure the dc-bus voltage is regulated to the reference that is generated by the MPPT algorithm. This general approach, where the dc-link voltage is regulated via the inverter power output, is widely adopted in VSIs with dc power-source inputs [21].

It is worth mentioning that while we apply the EAPO method for simplicity and ease of implementation, other approaches could be investigated to generate the dc-bus voltage reference (see [30]–[33] for comparisons and reviews of established MPPT methods, and [34]–[37] for some recent work in this area).

Remark 2: The controller depicted in Fig. 3 is utilized to regulate *all* inverters. The MPPT algorithm essentially constitutes a secondary outer control loop to modulate the current gain *only* in the PV-interfaced inverters. The current gains of the other inverters are fixed to the nominal value $\bar{\iota}$, determined following the design procedure outlined in Section II-C.

IV. Case Studies

In this section, we demonstrate the performance of the proposed oscillator-based controller with three case studies. The

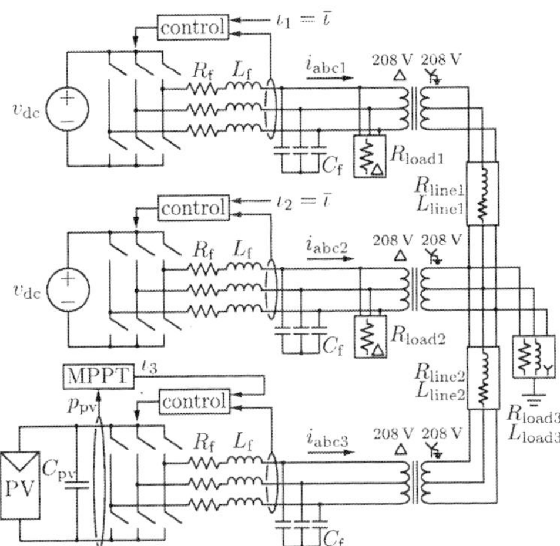

Fig. 9. Islanded microgrid composed of two inverters interfaced to energy-storage devices and one inverter interfaced to a PV array.

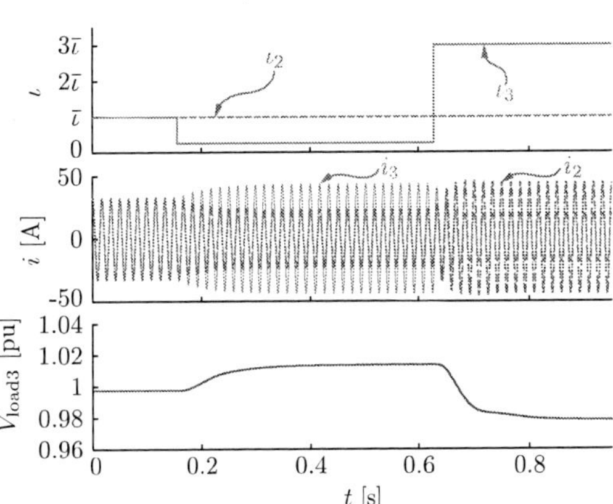

Fig. 10. Dynamics of a two inverter system when ι_2 is fixed and ι_3 undergoes step changes.

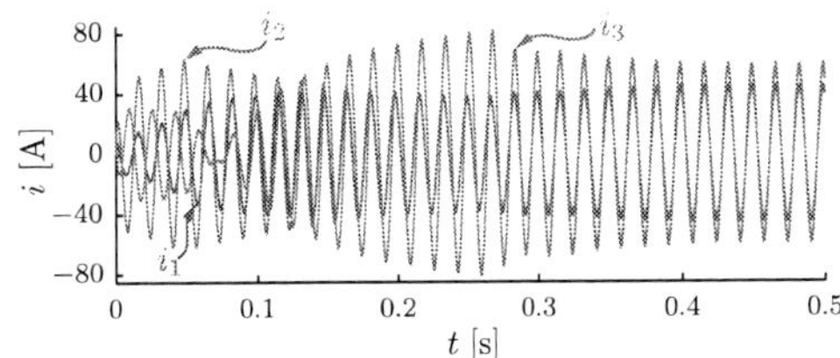

Fig. 11. Microgrid synchronization during startup.

simulations are performed for different abstractions (with increasing complexity) of the islanded microgrid system illustrated in Fig. 9. The three-phase inverters are each rated to deliver 15 kW. Two of the inverters (inverters 1 and 2) are connected to energy-storage devices (modeled as dc-voltage sources for the time scales investigated), and one inverter (inverter 3) is interfaced to a PV array, which is modeled using the single-diode model [38]. There are three loads in the system: loads 1 and 2 are resistive, and local to inverters 1 and 2 ($R_{\text{load}1}$ and $R_{\text{load}2}$ in Fig. 9), while load 3 is an inductive load ($R_{\text{load}3}$, $L_{\text{load}3}$ in Fig. 9). Delta-wye transformers facilitate lower dc-link voltages and are not a fundamental requirement of the proposed approach. The rated line-line voltage is 208 V and control parameters are selected to ensure that the common-load voltage is within $\pm 5\%$ of the rated value at 60 Hz under all operating conditions. The virtual-oscillator controller that has been depicted in Fig. 3 is employed in all three inverters. For the PV-interfaced inverter, MPPT is implemented following the approach described in Section IV-B. The parameters of the controller and the PV array are summarized in Appendix B. The perturbation frequency is set to 4 Hz, and this choice is based on the PV dc-link capacitance, which governs the PID voltage regulator settling time. For all cases, controller parameters are picked so that the synchronization condition in (1) is satisfied.

In the first case study, we demonstrate how dynamic load sharing between inverters is promoted by the terminal voltage-power characteristics in Fig. 5. The second and third case studies investigate system performance under variable irradiance and load conditions, respectively.

A. Dynamic Load Sharing

As described in Section II-C, the current gain of each inverter is selected such that the steady-state inverter output voltage is between prescribed lower and upper voltage limits (V_{min} and V_{max}, respectively) across the entire load range (open-circuit to full rated load). Additionally, for a given terminal voltage,

the power output is inversely proportional to the value of ι, as shown in Fig. 5. In this case study, we demonstrate that when a subset of inverters is allowed to vary the current gain (as would be the case with the MPPT controller in Fig. 7), the proportion of power delivered by each inverter also varies.

Consider the microgrid in Fig. 9, except, only with inverters 2 and 3. For simplicity, neglect the line impedances and the local loads, and assume a common resistive load. Since the primary aim of this case study is to illustrate the impact of variable current gains on load sharing, the inputs to the inverters are fixed to be dc-voltage sources. Furthermore, the current gain of inverter 2 ι_2, is fixed, while that of inverter 3 ι_3, is varied manually. Fig. 10 shows the system dynamics as ι_3 undergoes a series of step changes. The inverters share the load equally when $\iota_2 = \iota_3$. However, as ι_3 rises above and falls below ι_2, its fraction of load current (power) decreases and increases, respectively. In light of the terminal characteristics in Fig. 5, the load voltage is always constrained to lie between V_{min} and V_{max} as ι_3 varies. In subsequent simulation studies, we will find that consequently, the common-load voltage satisfies performance objectives in spite of variations in ambient conditions and load power.

B. Synchronization and MPPT Operation

At startup, the virtual-oscillator capacitor voltages were initialized to $v_C(0) = [0.25, 0.28, 0.22 \, \text{V}]^{\text{T}}$. Fig. 11 illustrates the phase-a currents of the three inverters during this startup. In spite of mismatched initial conditions, the inverters successfully reach the desired synchronized steady-state condition with

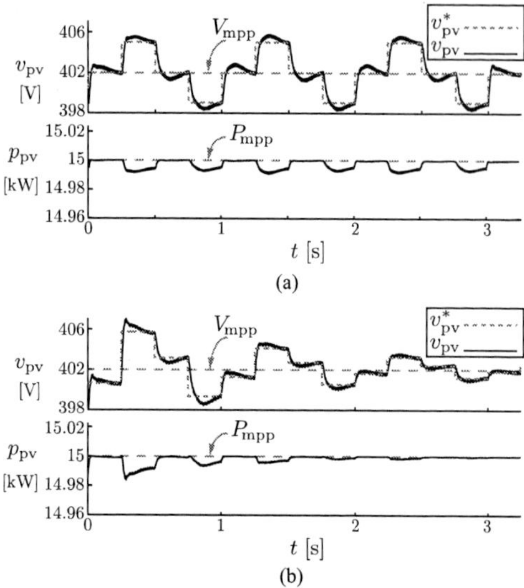

(a)

(b)

Fig. 12. Dynamics of the PV dc bus approaching the steady state as MPPT algorithms are initiated, comparing (a) the conventional PO algorithm of (5) to (b) the EAPO algorithm of (6). The maximum power point voltage and power are given by $V_{\mathrm{mpp}} = 402$ V and $P_{\mathrm{mpp}} = 15$ kW, respectively. The system control parameters support a perturbation frequency of 4Hz, and the PV dc bus recovers within about 0.2 s from each algorithm step. Note that the adaptive step size of the EAPO algorithm gets closer to the maximum power point and provides better tracking efficiency than conventional PO within 1 s after the MPPT algorithms begin to act.

all currents in phase. The start-up process limits current flows. Inverter 3 shows the highest overshoot, less than 35% of the final steady-state condition, and the overshoot lasts only about five cycles. Convergence is achieved for the three-inverter system from this blackstart condition in less than 20 cycles. Inverters 1 and 2 are in phase within about three cycles, and inverter 3 pulls into phase in the transition between cycles five and six— changing by more than 90° in one cycle but without imposing substantial current. Thus, the synchronization process takes only about 0.1 s and convergence to target power flows takes a bit longer, at about 0.3 s. The steady-state power injected by the PV inverter (unit 3) is 15 kW and corresponds to the maximum power point. Fig. 12 compares the dynamic recovery of the PV dc-bus voltage as the system approaches the steady state. The upper traces in Fig. 12(a) show a conventional PO process with about 1% voltage resolution. It oscillates around the maximum power point ($V_{\mathrm{mpp}} = 402$ V and $P_{\mathrm{mpp}} = 15$ kW), imposing a continuing small power error. The traces confirm that this system will support perturbation step rates of at least four steps per second, only a little more aggressive than the 0.3 s large-signal convergence time of the synchronizing control. When the PO algorithm imposes a voltage step, the system recovers within about 0.2 s (essentially a small perturbation effect related to Fig. 11) to allow the assessment of the new power level and provide information for a decision about the next step. In contrast, the EAPO algorithm results represented in the lower traces (see Fig. 12(b)) show that step size can reduce adaptively and quickly. The EAPO algorithm also allows at least four steps per second and recovers within 0.2 s for each step, but in this case,

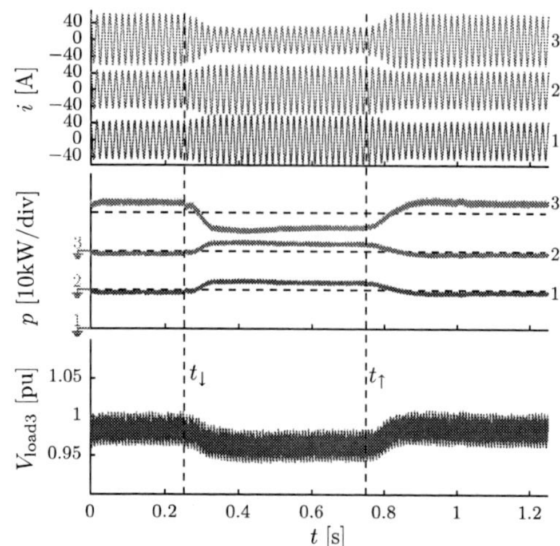

Fig. 13. Inverter (phase-a) currents, power outputs, and load voltage in the microgrid network with a resistive common load and no local loads. The PV irradiance decreases and increases abruptly at $t_\downarrow$ and $t_\uparrow$, respectively.

after four steps it is closer to the the maximum power point than the conventional PO controller, and continues to refine the accuracy to drive power error close to zero. With conventional PO, such a small step size would compromise dynamic response, but the EAPO large-signal dynamics can be designed to be just as fast as conventional PO.

C. Robustness to Irradiance and Load Variations

In this case study, we demonstrate that variations in incident irradiance and load power tend to be absorbed by the energy-storage-interfaced inverters, hence minimizing disruptions in the synchronized operation of the inverters. First, assume that the local loads at inverters 1 and 2 do not consume any power. In addition, the impedances of lines 1 and 2 are set to zero, such that all three inverters are directly connected across the common load. With these assumptions, we recover the network introduced in Section II-B (see Fig. 2), for which satisfying (1) ensures the inverter terminal voltages are synchronized in the steady state. Fig. 13 illustrates system dynamics when a 50% drop in incident illumination is effected at time $t = t_\downarrow$. As a result, power delivered by the PV inverter decreases quickly, and must be made up by the other inverters. As the center power traces in Fig. 13 show, the PV inverter tracks the step change within less than 0.1 s. The other inverters pick up quickly enough that the voltage trace at the bottom of Fig. 13 drops by less than 3% during the transient. The ac currents in the top traces mirror the power change, demonstrating that synchronization is maintained even in the face of this fast dynamic imbalance. Subsequently, at time $t = t_\uparrow$, the illumination is restored and the inverters recover to the prior condition within 0.1 s. The voltage also recovers. In general, the selected design parameters support extreme dynamic changes, while maintaining the output voltage magnitude inside a $\pm 5\%$ window with no communication between the three inverters.

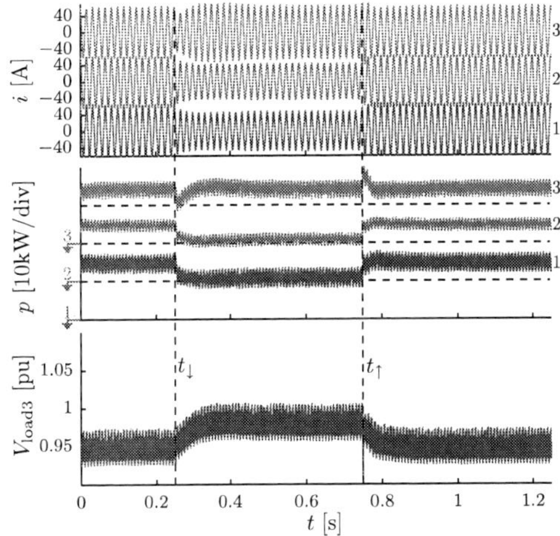

Fig. 14. Inverter (phase-a) currents, power outputs, and load voltage in the microgrid network with local loads and feeder impedances. The common-load power decreases and increases instantaneously at $t_\downarrow$ and $t_\uparrow$, respectively.

Now consider that the local loads at the terminals of inverters 1 and 2 are designed to consume 10 and 5 kW, respectively. As indicated in Appendix B, the common load is inductive, and therefore, the total load power factor is not unity. Additionally, nonzero and nonidentical line impedances connect each inverter to the central load. With this setup, while the inverters are still designed to satisfy (1), the inverter terminal voltages are no longer expected to be synchronized. Nonetheless, we will find that stable operation can be ensured irrespective of load variations. For simplicity, we hold the irradiance constant in this case study. Fig. 14 illustrates the load voltage, and the inverter current and power outputs as the common load undergoes a series of changes. In particular, at time $t = t_\downarrow$, the load is suddenly decreased. Despite the load change, the PV inverter continues to deliver maximum PV power while the other inverters decrease their power output. Next, the load is increased to its original value at time $t = t_\uparrow$ and the power extracted from the energy-storage devices is automatically increased. As before, in all cases the load voltage is maintained within $\pm 5\%$ of the rated value with no communication between the three inverters.

V. Conclusion

A technique for controlling a system of inverters in a microgrid has been presented. The proposed method is based on modulating the ac output of each inverter such that it emulates the dynamics of a nonlinear oscillator. Due to the inherent coupling between the oscillators introduced by the electrical network, the inverter ac outputs synchronize. The controllers only require local measurements available at the ac terminals; communication between inverters is not necessary. Oscillator-based control is applied toward the design of a three-phase microgrid with high PV penetration. Simulation results for a 45 kW system demonstrated that the system of inverters continually adjust their output to match load while maximizing PV energy delivery in the face

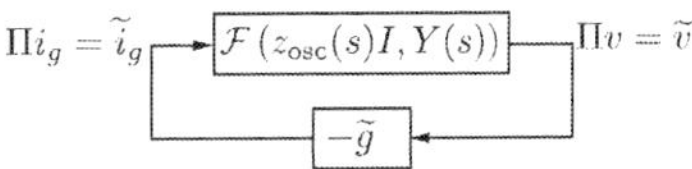

Fig. 15. Block-diagram representation of the differential system. The linear and nonlinear portions of the system are compartmentalized in $\mathcal{F}(\cdot,\cdot)$ and $\widetilde{g}$, respectively.

of uncertainty in ambient conditions and variations in the load power.

Appendix A

Sketch of the Proof for the Result in (1)

The forthcoming discussion is abstracted from [3, Th. 1]. Denote the vector of output currents and terminal voltages of the system of oscillators in Fig. 2(b) by $i = [i_1, \ldots, i_N]^{\mathrm{T}}$ and $v = [v_1, \ldots, v_N]^{\mathrm{T}}$, respectively. Additionally, denote the vector of currents sourced by the nonlinear voltage-dependent current sources in the oscillators by $i_{\mathrm{g}} = [i_{\mathrm{g}1}, \ldots, i_{\mathrm{g}N}]^{\mathrm{T}}$. Note that $i_{\mathrm{g}} = -g(v) := [-g(v_1), \ldots, -g(v_N)]^{\mathrm{T}}$.

We can express $i(s) = Yv(s)$, where Y is the admittance matrix of the microgrid electrical network given by $Y = \alpha I + \beta \Gamma$, where $\alpha = (z_{\mathrm{f}} + N z_{\mathrm{load}})^{-1}$, $\beta = z_{\mathrm{load}}(z_{\mathrm{f}}(z_{\mathrm{f}} + N z_{\mathrm{load}}))^{-1}$, I is the $N \times N$ identity matrix, and Γ denotes the Laplacian of the underlying graph.

To explore voltage synchronization, it is easier to consider the corresponding *differential system*, $\widetilde{i} = \Pi i$, $\widetilde{v} = \Pi v$, and $\widetilde{i}_{\mathrm{g}} = \Pi i_{\mathrm{g}}$, with $\Pi = (I - (1/N)\mathbf{1}\mathbf{1}^{\mathrm{T}})$, where $\mathbf{1} \in \mathbb{R}^N$ denotes the column vector of all ones. The entries of $\widetilde{v}(t)$ track the differences between corresponding entries of $v(t)$ and the average of all entries of $v(t)$ [39]. Consequently, to ensure synchronization, we need to ensure that $\widetilde{v}(t) \to 0$, i.e., the stability of the differential system implies synchronization of the original system.

For ease of analysis, we compartmentalize the differential system into linear and nonlinear subsystems as shown in Fig. 15. The nonlinear subsystem is defined by the map $\widetilde{g} : \widetilde{v} \to \widetilde{i}_{\mathrm{g}}$. The linear subsystem maps $\widetilde{i}_{\mathrm{g}}$ to $\widetilde{v}$ through the *linear fractional transformation*, $\mathcal{F} : \mathbb{R}^N \to \mathbb{R}^N$, which is defined as follows:

$$\widetilde{v} = \mathcal{F}(z_{\mathrm{osc}}I, Y)\widetilde{i}_{\mathrm{g}} := (I + z_{\mathrm{osc}}Y)^{-1} z_{\mathrm{osc}}\widetilde{i}_{\mathrm{g}}. \tag{8}$$

Using the small-gain theorem, we can show that the differential system illustrated in Fig. 15 is stable if

$$\widetilde{\gamma}(\mathcal{F}(z_{\mathrm{osc}}I, Y))\sigma < 1 \tag{9}$$

where $\widetilde{\gamma} := \sup_{\omega \in \mathbb{R}} \|\mathcal{F}(z_{\mathrm{osc}}I, Y)\widetilde{i}_{\mathrm{g}}\|_2 / \|\widetilde{i}_{\mathrm{g}}\|_2$ is the differential $\mathcal{L}_2$ gain of the linear fractional transformation [39], and $\sigma = |dg/dv|$. The $\mathcal{L}_2$ gain of a system provides a measure of the largest amplification imparted to a signal as it propagates through a system. Therefore, (9) implies that as long as the maximum possible amplification around the differential closed-loop system in Fig. 15 is less than unity, then $\widetilde{v}, \widetilde{i}_g \to 0$. Following the approach outlined in [39], and incorporating the current and voltage scaling parameters, ι and ν (see Fig. 3), it can be shown that $\widetilde{\gamma} = \left\| (\iota\nu)^{-1} z_{\mathrm{f}} z_{\mathrm{osc}} / ((\iota\nu)^{-1} z_{\mathrm{f}} + z_{\mathrm{osc}}) \right\|_2$, which establishes the synchronization condition in (1).

APPENDIX B

CASE-STUDY PARAMETERS

Electrical Network and Inverter-Design Parameters: Oscillator linear-subsystem parameters: $R = 10\,\Omega$, $L = 250\,\mu$H, $C = 28.14$ mF. Oscillator nonlinear-subsystem parameters: $\sigma = 1$ S, $\varphi = 0.47$ V. Inverter voltage gain and nominal current gain: $\nu = 208\sqrt{1/3}$ and $\bar{\iota} = 1.0568 \times 10^{-3}$, respectively. Inverter output filter parameters: $R_{\mathrm{f}} = 0.1\,\Omega$, $L_{\mathrm{f}} = 250\,\mu$H, $C_{\mathrm{f}} = 24\,\mu$F. Dc-bus filter capacitance for Inverter 3: $C_{\mathrm{pv}} = 20$ mF. Dc-voltage sources: $v_{\mathrm{dc}} = 400$ V. Inverter switching frequency $f_{\mathrm{sw}} = 12$ kHz. Line and load parameters (Case studies in Sections IV-A, IV-B, IV-C): $R_{\mathrm{load1}} = -, -, 25.94\,\Omega$, $R_{\mathrm{load2}} = -, -, 12.98\,\Omega$, $R_{\mathrm{load3}} = 2.60\,\Omega$, $1.16\,\Omega$, $(1.29 \to 1.92 \to 1.29)\,\Omega$, $L_{\mathrm{load3}} = -, -, 6.90$ mH, $L_{\mathrm{line1}} = -, -, 2\,\mu$H, $R_{\mathrm{line1}} = -, -, 2$ mΩ, $L_{\mathrm{line2}} = -, -, 1\,\mu$H, $R_{\mathrm{line2}} = -, -, 1$ mΩ.

PV Array and MPPT Controller Parameters: Open-circuit voltage: $V_{\mathrm{oc}} = 491$ V, Short-circuit current: $I_{\mathrm{sc}} = 41.74$ A, Maximum power point voltage and current: $V_{\mathrm{mpp}} = 402$ V, $I_{\mathrm{mpp}} = 37.3$ A, respectively. PID-controller parameters: $k_{\mathrm{p}} = 1.057 \times 10^{-4}$ V^{-1}, $k_{\mathrm{i}} = 1.7 \times 10^{-3}$ (V s)$^{-1}$, $k_{\mathrm{d}} = 4.227 \times 10^{-6}$ V^{-1} s, $e_{\mathrm{lim}} = 25$ V, $\iota_{\mathrm{min}} = -(1/10)\bar{\iota}$, $\iota_{\mathrm{max}} = \infty$. EAPO perturbation frequency $= 4$ Hz, $\rho^{\mathrm{max}} = 1.5$, $\rho^{\mathrm{min}} = 0.5$, $\xi = 0.0167$.

REFERENCES

[1] H. Khalil, *Nonlinear Systems*, 3rd ed. Upper Saddle River, NJ, USA: Prentice–Hall, 2002.

[2] L. A. B. Tôrres, J. P. Hespanha, and J. Moehlis, "Power supplies synchronization without communication," in *Proc. Power Energy Soc. General Meet.*, Jul. 2012, pp. 1–6.

[3] B. B. Johnson, S. V. Dhople, A. O. Hamadeh, and P. T. Krein, "Synchronization of nonlinear oscillators in an LTI power network," *IEEE Trans. Circuits Syst. I, Fundam. Theory Appl.*, to be published.

[4] B. Johnson, S. Dhople, A. Hamadeh, and P. Krein, "Synchronization of parallel single-phase inverters using virtual oscillator control," *IEEE Trans. Power Electron.*, submitted for publication.

[5] M. Chandorkar, D. Divan, and R. Adapa, "Control of parallel connected inverters in standalone AC supply systems," *IEEE Trans. Ind. Appl.*, vol. 29, no. 1, pp. 136–143, Jan. 1993.

[6] J. Lopes, C. Moreira, and A. Madureira, "Defining control strategies for microgrids islanded operation," *IEEE Trans. Power Syst.*, vol. 21, no. 2, pp. 916–924, May 2006.

[7] R. Lasseter, "Microgrids," in *Proc. IEEE Power Eng. Soc. Winter Meet.*, 2002, vol. 1, pp. 305–308.

[8] P. Piagi and R. Lasseter, "Autonomous control of microgrids," in *Proc. IEEE Power Eng. Soc. General Meet.*, Jun. 2006, vol. 6, pp. 1–8.

[9] J. M. Guerrero, J. Matas, L. G. de Vicuña, M. Castilla, and J. Miret, "Wireless-control strategy for parallel operation of distributed-generation inverters," *IEEE Trans. Ind. Electron.*, vol. 53, no. 5, pp. 1461–1470, Oct. 2006.

[10] J. M. Guerrero, J. C. Vasquez, J. Matas, M. Castilla, and L. G. de Vicuna, "Control strategy for flexible microgrid based on parallel line-interactive UPS systems," *IEEE Trans. Ind. Electron.*, vol. 56, no. 3, pp. 726–736, Mar. 2009.

[11] J. Vasquez, J. Guerrero, M. Savaghebi, J. Eloy-Garcia, and R. Teodorescu, "Modeling, analysis, and design of stationary-reference-frame droop-controlled parallel three-phase voltage source inverters," *IEEE Trans. Ind. Electron.*, vol. 60, no. 4, pp. 1271–1280, Apr. 2013.

[12] J. Guerrero, L. de Vicuna, J. Matas, M. Castilla, and J. Miret, "A wireless controller to enhance dynamic performance of parallel inverters in distributed generation systems," *IEEE Trans. Power Electron.*, vol. 19, no. 5, pp. 1205–1213, Sep. 2004.

[13] F. Katiraei and M. Iravani, "Power management strategies for a microgrid with multiple distributed generation units," *IEEE Trans. Power Syst.*, vol. 21, no. 4, pp. 1821–1831, Nov. 2006.

[14] A. Mohd, D. Ortjohann, and O. Omari, "Review of control techniques for inverters parallel operation," *Electr. Power Syst. Res.*, vol. 80, pp. 1477–1487, Dec. 2010.

[15] M. Marwali, J.-W. Jung, and A. Keyhani, "Control of distributed generation systems—Part II: Load sharing control," *IEEE Trans. Power Electron.*, vol. 19, no. 6, pp. 1551–1561, Nov. 2004.

[16] J. M. Guerrero, J. C. Vasquez, J. Matas, L. G. de Vicuña, and M. Castilla, "Hierarchical control of droop-controlled AC and DC microgrids—A general approach toward standardization," *IEEE Trans. Ind. Electron.*, vol. 58, no. 1, pp. 158–172, Jan. 2011.

[17] J. He and Y. W. Li, "An enhanced microgrid load demand sharing strategy," *IEEE Trans. Power Electron.*, vol. 27, no. 9, pp. 3984–3995, Sep. 2012.

[18] Q.-C. Zhong, "Robust droop controller for accurate proportional load sharing among inverters operated in parallel," *IEEE Trans. Ind. Electron.*, vol. 60, no. 4, pp. 1281–1290, Apr. 2013.

[19] J. M. Guerrero, M. Chandorkar, T. Lee, and P. C. Loh, "Advanced control architectures for intelligent microgrids—Part I: Decentralized and hierarchical control," *IEEE Trans. Ind. Electron.*, vol. 60, no. 4, pp. 1254–1262, Apr. 2013.

[20] A. Mauroy, P. Sacré, and R. J. Sepulchre, "Kick synchronization versus diffusive synchronization," in *Proc. IEEE Conf. Decis. Control*, 2012, pp. 7171–7183.

[21] A. Yazdani and R. Iravani, *Voltage-Sourced Converters in Power Systems*. Hoboken, NJ, USA: Wiley, 2010.

[22] D. Holmes and T. Lipo, *Pulse Width Modulation for Power Converters*. Piscataway, NJ, USA: IEEE Press, 2003.

[23] S. Golestan, M. Joorabian, H. Rastegar, A. Roshan, and J. Guerrero, "Droop based control of parallel-connected single-phase inverters in D-Q rotating frame," in *Proc. IEEE Int. Conf. Ind. Tech.*, 2009, pp. 1–6.

[24] U. A. Miranda, L. G. B. Rolim, and M. Aredes, "A DQ synchronous reference frame current control for single-phase converters," in *Proc. IEEE Power Electron. Spec. Conf.*, 2005, pp. 1377–1381.

[25] V. T. Buyukdegirmenci, A. M. Bazzi, and P. T. Krein, "A comparative study of an exponential adaptive perturb and observe algorithm and ripple correlation control for real-time optimization," in *Proc. IEEE Workshop Control Model. Power Electron.*, 2010, pp. 1–8.

[26] W. Xiao and W. G. Dunford, "A modified adaptive hill climbing MPPT method for photovoltaic power systems," in *Proc. IEEE Power Electron. Spec. Conf.*, 2004, vol. 3, pp. 1957–1963.

[27] N. Fermia, D. Granozio, G. Petrone, and M. Vitelli, "Predictive adaptive MPPT perturb and observe method," *IEEE Trans. Aerosp. Electron. Syst.*, vol. 43, no. 3, pp. 934–950, Jul. 2007.

[28] C. Zhang and D. Zhao, "A novel MPPT method with variable perturbation step for photovoltaic system," in *Proc. IEEE Conf. Ind. Electron. Appl.*, 2009, pp. 2184–2187.

[29] K. A. Kim, P. T. Krein, J. J. Lee, H. Bae, and B.-H. Cho, "Irradiance and temperature transient sensitivity analysis for photovoltaic control," in *Proc. IEEE Int. Conf. Power Electron. Energy Convers. Congr. Expo Asia*, 2011, pp. 393–400.

[30] T. Esram and P. L. Chapman, "Comparison of photovoltaic array maximum power point tracking techniques," *IEEE Trans. Energy Convers.*, vol. 22, no. 2, pp. 439–449, Jun. 2007.

[31] A. Bidram, A. Davoudi, and R. S. Balog, "Control and circuit techniques to mitigate partial shading effects in photovoltaic arrays," *IEEE J. Photovolt.*, vol. 2, no. 4, pp. 532–546, Oct. 2012.

[32] M. de Brito, L. Galotto, L. Sampaio, G. de Azevedo e Melo, and G. Canesin, "Evaluation of the main MPPT techniques for photovoltaic applications," *IEEE Trans. Ind. Electron.*, vol. 60, no. 3, pp. 1156–1167, Mar. 2013.

[33] D. Sera, L. Mathe, T. Kerekes, S. Spataru, and R. Teodorescu, "On the perturb-and-observe and incremental conductance MPPT methods for PV systems," *IEEE J. Photovolt.*, vol. 3, no. 3, pp. 1070–1078, Jul. 2013.

[34] P. E. Kakosimos, A. G. Kladas, and S. N. Manias, "Fast photovoltaic-system voltage- or current-oriented MPPT employing a predictive digital current-controlled converter," *IEEE Trans. Ind. Electron.*, vol. 60, no. 12, pp. 5673–5685, Dec. 2013.

[35] B. N. Alajmi, K. H. Ahmed, S. J. Finney, and B. W. Williams, "A maximum power point tracking technique for partially shaded photovoltaic systems in microgrids," *IEEE Trans. Ind. Electron.*, vol. 60, no. 4, pp. 1596–1606, Apr. 2013.

[36] G.-C. Hsieh, H.-I. Hsieh, C.-Y. Tsai, and C.-H. Wang, "Photovoltaic power-increment-aided incremental-conductance MPPT with two-phased

tracking," *IEEE Trans. Power Electron.*, vol. 28, no. 6, pp. 2895–2911, Jun. 2013.

[37] E. Dallago, D. G. Finarelli, U. P. Gianazza, A. L. Barnabei, and A. Liberale, "Theoretical and experimental analysis of an MPP detection algorithm employing a single-voltage sensor only and a noisy signal," *IEEE Trans. Power Electron.*, vol. 28, no. 11, pp. 5088–5097, Nov. 2013.

[38] G. M. Masters, *Renewable and Efficient Electric Power Systems.* Hoboken, NJ, USA: Wiley-Interscience, 2004.

[39] A. Hamadeh, "Constructive robust synchronization of networked control systems," Ph.D. dissertation, Dept. Eng., Univ. Cambridge, U.K., Jun. 2010.

Abdullah O. Hamadeh received the M.Eng., M.A., and Ph.D. degrees in electrical engineering from the University of Cambridge, Cambridge, U.K., in 2005, 2008, and 2010 respectively. His doctoral research concerned the control and synchronization of networked dynamical systems.

Between 2010 and 2013, he held Postdoctoral positions with the University of Waterloo, Waterloo, ON, Canada, and Rutgers University, New Brunswick, NJ, USA. He is currently a Post-Doctoral Associate with the Department of Mechanical Engineering, Massachusetts Institute of Technology, Cambridge, MA, USA. His current research interests are in the applications of control theoretic techniques to systems and synthetic biology and in the control of electrical power networks.

Brian B. Johnson (S'08–M'13) received the B.S. degree in physics from Texas State University, San Marcos, TX, USA, in 2008 and the M.S. and Ph.D. degrees in electrical and computer engineering from the University of Illinois at Urbana-Champaign, Urbana, IL, USA, in 2010 and 2013, respectively.

He is currently an Electrical Engineer with the National Renewable Energy Laboratory, Golden, CO, USA. His research interests include power electronics, distributed generation, renewable energy systems, and nonlinear controls.

Dr. Johnson received a National Science Foundation Graduate Research Fellowship in 2010.

Sairaj V. Dhople (S'09–M'13) received the B.S., M.S., and Ph.D. degrees in electrical engineering, in 2007, 2009, and 2012, respectively, from the University of Illinois, Urbana-Champaign, Urbana, IL, USA.

He is currently an Assistant Professor with the Department of Electrical and Computer Engineering, University of Minnesota, Minneapolis, MN, USA, where he is affiliated with the Power and Energy Systems research group. His research interests include modeling, analysis, and control of power electronics and power systems with a focus on renewable integration.

Philip T. Krein (S'76–M'82–SM'93–F'00) received the B.S. degree in electrical engineering and the A.B. degree in economics and business from Lafayette College, Easton, PA, USA, and the M.S. and Ph.D. degrees in electrical engineering from the University of Illinois (UI), Urbana, IL, USA.

He was an Engineer with Tektronix, Beaverton, OR, USA, and then returned to UI. He currently holds the Grainger Endowed Director's Chair with Electric Machinery and Electromechanics as a Professor and the Director of the Department of Electrical and Computer Engineering, Grainger Center for Electric Machinery and Electromechanics, UI. He has published an undergraduate textbook *Elements of Power Electronics* (Oxford, U.K.: Oxford Univ. Press, 1998). In 2001, he helped initiate the IEEE International Future Energy Challenge: a major student competition involving fuel cell power conversion and energy efficiency. He holds 26 U.S. patents with additional patents pending. His research interests include all the aspects of power electronics, machines, drives, and electrical energy, with emphasis on nonlinear control and distributed systems.

Dr. Krein is a Registered Professional Engineer in Illinois and Oregon. He was a senior Fulbright Scholar with the University of Surrey, Surrey, U.K., and was recognized as a University Scholar, which is the highest research award at UI. In 2003, he received the IEEE William E. Newell Award in Power Electronics. He is a past President of the IEEE Power Electronics Society and served as a member of the IEEE Board of Directors. During 2005–2007, he was a Distinguished Lecturer for the IEEE Power Electronics Society. In 2008, he received the Distinguished Service Award from the IEEE Power Electronics Society. He is an Associate Editor of the IEEE TRANSACTIONS ON POWER ELECTRONICS and serves as an Academic Advisor for the Department of Electronic and Information Engineering, Hong Kong Polytechnic University. He is a Founder and the Director of SolarBridge Technologies: a developer of long-life integrated solar energy systems.

James L. Cale (M'03) received the B.S. (summa cum laude) degree in electrical engineering from the University of Missouri-Rolla, Rolla, MO, USA, in 2001 and the M.S. and Ph.D. degrees in electrical engineering from Purdue University, West Lafayette, IN, USA, in 2003 and 2007, respectively.

His background and research interests include areas of high-penetration photovoltaic (PV) integration on the electric grid, power electronic controls, and microgrids. Prior to joining The National Renewable Energy Laboratory (NREL), Golden, CO, USA, he was a Member of Technical Staff with Advanced Energy, where he designed controls for advanced utility-scale PV inverters. He currently manages the Distributed Energy Systems Integration group, NREL.

Simulations, Practical Limitations, and Novel Growth Technology for InGaN-Based Solar Cells

Chloe A. M. Fabien, *Student Member, IEEE*, Michael Moseley, Brendan Gunning,
W. Alan Doolittle, *Senior Member, IEEE*, Alec M. Fischer, Yong O. Wei, and Fernando A. Ponce

Abstract—Indium gallium nitride (InGaN) alloys exhibit substantial potential for high-efficiency photovoltaics. However, theoretical promise still needs to be experimentally realized. This paper presents a detailed theoretical study to provide guidelines to achieve high-efficiency InGaN solar cells. While the efficiency of heterojunction devices is limited to ~11%, homojunction devices can achieve suitable efficiencies, provided that highly p-type-doped InGaN layers and thick, single-phase InGaN films can be grown. Thus, we have developed a novel growth technology that facilitates growth of p-type nitride films with greatly improved hole concentration and growth of InGaN without phase separation, offering promise for future high-efficiency InGaN solar cells.

Index Terms—Crystal microstructure, doping, indium gallium nitride (InGaN), semiconductor device modeling, semiconductor growth, solar cell.

I. INTRODUCTION

INDIUM gallium nitride (InGaN) alloys are promising candidates for full-solar-spectrum photovoltaic application because of tunable bandgaps ranging from 0.65 to 3.42 eV and, thus, covering the entire visible solar spectrum [1], [2]. Because of this wide range of bandgaps, InGaN alloys offer great potential for a multijunction solar cell. Several InGaN subcells can be theoretically stacked to form multijunction solar cells from a single material system by varying the indium and gallium compositions [3]. Furthermore, InGaN alloys exhibit high absorption coefficients (approximately $10^5 \, \text{cm}^{-1}$ at the band edge) [4]. Only a few hundred nanometers of InGaN material is required to absorb most of the incident light, thereby relieving the cost constraint due to moderately expensive indium. Other suitable photovoltaic properties include a direct bandgap over the alloy composition range, high carrier mobility [5], and superior radiation resistance for space-based photovoltaic applications [6].

Despite these advantages, InGaN alloys have several challenges that need to be overcome to achieve high-efficiency InGaN solar cells. Experimental studies on InGaN solar cells have demonstrated conversion efficiency of less than 2% for both InGaN/GaN heterostructures [7]–[9] and p-i-n homojunction devices [10], [11] at solar-relevant compositions. A critical issue is p-type doping in nitride alloys as typical hole concentrations for p-type GaN and low-indium-content InGaN are in the mid-10^{18}-cm^{-3} range [12], [13]. The growth of highly p-type layers remains difficult because of the limited solubility of magnesium (Mg) acceptors, large activation energy of Mg acceptors (160–170 meV), and compensation by native defects [14]. Because of these compensating native defects, undoped InGaN films usually display high background donor concentrations [15].

Another major challenge to the development of III-nitride solar cells is the growth of thick, high-quality InGaN layers with high indium composition needed to absorb lower-energy photons. Because of the miscibility gap between InN and GaN, indium-rich InGaN films commonly demonstrate phase separation, which results in the formation of a nonuniform alloy [16]. Furthermore, due to the lack of a native substrate and the large difference in lattice spacing between InN and GaN, InGaN films usually demonstrate a high density of threading dislocations that can act as shunt pathways [17] and nonradiative recombination centers (NRCs) [18]. This high density of NRCs in InGaN drastically reduces the carrier diffusion length. As a result, InGaN-based solar cells must rely on a drift process to efficiently separate minority carriers. The built-in field can be extended by introducing an intrinsic InGaN layer between the n- and p-type InGaN layers, forming a p-i-n device structure. While intrinsic InGaN layers are crucial for drift devices, the growth of such films is extremely challenging since undoped InGaN typically demonstrates n-type conductivity resulting from a high background donor concentration [15]. This high concentration of residual donors negatively affects the width of the depletion region. III-nitrides also display strong spontaneous and piezoelectric polarization effects [19]. At an abrupt heterojunction interface, the discontinuity in spontaneous and piezoelectric polarization generates interface charges that produce strong band bending and potential barriers. The polarization field in a III-polar structure induces an electric field that hinders separation of photogenerated carriers [20], [21].

This study investigates the performance of InGaN-based p-i-n solar cells to optimize device design given realistic material properties, and both present and future material limitations.

Manuscript received June 10, 2013; revised October 4, 2013; accepted November 17, 2013. This material is based upon work primarily supported by the National Science Foundation (NSF) and the Department of Energy (DOE) under NSF CA No. EEC-1041895. Any opinions, findings and conclusions or recommendations expressed in this material are those of the author(s) and do not necessarily reflect those of NSF or DOE.

C. A. M. Fabien, B. Gunning, and W. A. Doolittle are with the Georgia Institute of Technology, Atlanta, GA 30332 USA (e-mail: chloe.fabien@gatech.edu; bpgunning@gatech.edu; alan.doolittle@ece.gatech.edu).

M. Moseley was with the Georgia Institute of Technology, Atlanta, GA 30332 USA. He is now with Sandia National Laboratories, Albuquerque, NM 87123 USA (e-mail: mwmosel@sandia.gov).

A. M. Fischer, Y. O. Wei, and F. A. Ponce are with the Department of Physics, Arizona State University, Tempe, AZ 85287–1504 USA (e-mail: amfisch1@asu.edu; Yong.Wei@asu.edu; ponce@asu.edu).

Color versions of one or more of the figures in this paper are available online at http://ieeexplore.ieee.org.

Digital Object Identifier 10.1109/JPHOTOV.2013.2292748

The performance of both p-i-n InGaN/GaN heterojunction devices that are presently feasible and InGaN homojunction solar cells that are expected to be achievable in the future are studied and compared using a realistic approach. These numerical simulations aim to provide guidelines for experimental devices. Primary experimental results show substantial promise for the growth of future InGaN homojunction solar cells with high indium composition.

II. SIMULATION RESULTS

A. Simulation Parameters

In this study, the performance of p-i-n solar cells is investigated with the finite-element analysis software APSYS [22]. The electrical and optical properties of GaN and InN used in the simulations can be found elsewhere [23]. The unstrained bandgap of InGaN is expressed by

$$E_g\left(\text{In}_x\text{Ga}_{1-x}\text{N}\right) = E_{g,\text{InN}}\,x + E_{g,\text{GaN}}\left(1-x\right) - b\,x\left(1-x\right) \tag{1}$$

where $E_{g,\text{InN}} = 0.65$ eV and $E_{g,\text{GaN}} = 3.42$ eV are the bandgap energies of InN and GaN, respectively, and b = 1.43 eV is the bowing parameter for $\text{In}_x\text{Ga}_{1-x}\text{N}$ [24]. The electron and hole mobilities are calculated using the Caughey–Thomas approximation [25]. Minority carrier lifetimes as high as 5.4 and 6.5 ns have been observed in GaN and InN, respectively [26], [27]. However, $\text{In}_x\text{Ga}_{1-x}\text{N}$ alloys are expected to have lower lifetimes due to inferior crystal quality. Thus, a conservative 1-ns minority carrier lifetime is assumed and held constant over the entire composition range for fair comparisons of device designs. According to experimental measurements [28]–[30], a front surface recombination velocity of 10^4 cm/s is used. The interface charge density induced by spontaneous and piezoelectric polarizations is calculated with the method developed by Fiorentini et al. [31]. To account for screening effects, we scale the theoretical polarization surface charges by a factor of 0.4, which is in agreement with prior investigations [20], [32].

B. Indium Gallium Nitride/Gallium Nitride Heterojunction Structure

The InGaN/GaN p-i-n heterostructure consists of a 1-μm-thick n-GaN layer, a 500-nm-thick unintentionally doped (UID) $\text{In}_x\text{Ga}_{1-x}\text{N}$ layer, and a 50-nm-thick p-$\text{In}_{0.25}\text{Ga}_{0.75}\text{N}$ top layer. The residual donor concentration in the UID-$\text{In}_x\text{Ga}_{1-x}\text{N}$ is 10^{17} cm^{-3}. The electron and hole concentrations in the n-GaN and p-InGaN layers are 8×10^{18} and 4×10^{18} cm^{-3}, respectively. Similar hole concentrations in Mg-doped $\text{In}_{0.25}\text{Ga}_{0.75}\text{N}$ have already been demonstrated [33]. Thus, such devices are presently realizable using the state-of-the-art nitride technology [7], [8]. The conversion efficiency (η) as a function the composition of the UID-InGaN layer is shown in Fig. 1. As the bandgap decreases, η initially increases due to the increased photocurrent. However, for high indium compositions needed for longer wavelength absorption, η drops abruptly because of two polarization effects [20], [21]. First, the polarization-induced field strongly affects the depletion region near the UID-InGaN/p-InGaN interface. As the indium composition increases, the total electric

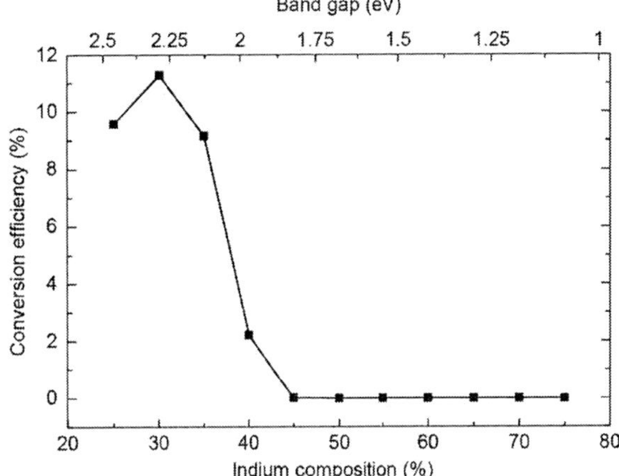

Fig. 1. Conversion efficiency of an n-GaN/UID-$\text{In}_x\text{Ga}_{1-x}$N/p-$\text{In}_{0.25}$ $\text{Ga}_{0.75}$N structure as a function of indium composition (i.e., bandgap) in the UID-InGaN layer. For high indium compositions needed for longer wavelength absorption, the efficiency drops abruptly due to polarization effects.

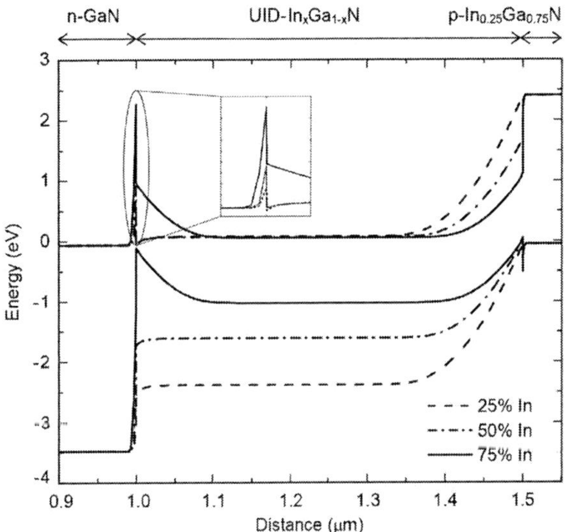

Fig. 2. Band diagrams at equilibrium for an n-GaN/UID-$\text{In}_x\text{Ga}_{1-x}$N/p-$\text{In}_{0.25}\text{Ga}_{0.75}$N structure with various indium compositions in the UID-layer. The inset shows a closeup view of the potential barriers at the GaN/InGaN interface.

field, required for carrier drift, decreases as illustrated in Fig. 2. Second, the polarization discontinuity creates a potential barrier at the GaN/InGaN heterointerface. As the indium composition increases, the polarization-induced potential barrier becomes more prominent (see Fig. 2 inset). Because of these combined polarization effects, the collection efficiency and, thus, η, decrease. Above an indium composition of 45%, the device stops operating as a solar cell.

Therefore, the conversion efficiency of the modeled InGaN/GaN heterojunction solar cell is limited to 11.3% for an UID-InGaN layer with an indium fraction of 30%. While such cells would be suitable as subcells in multijunction solar

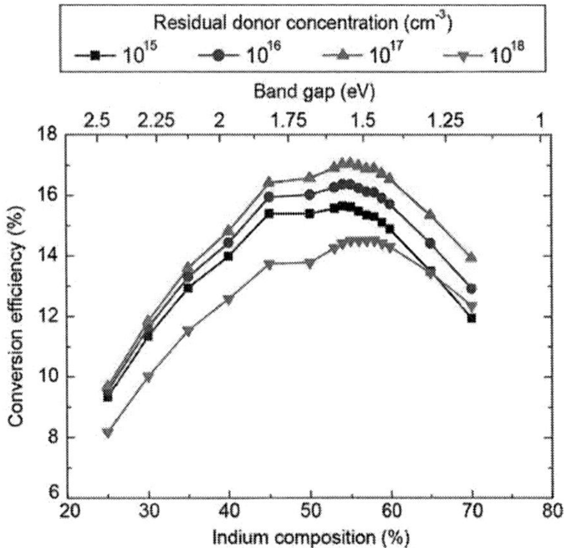

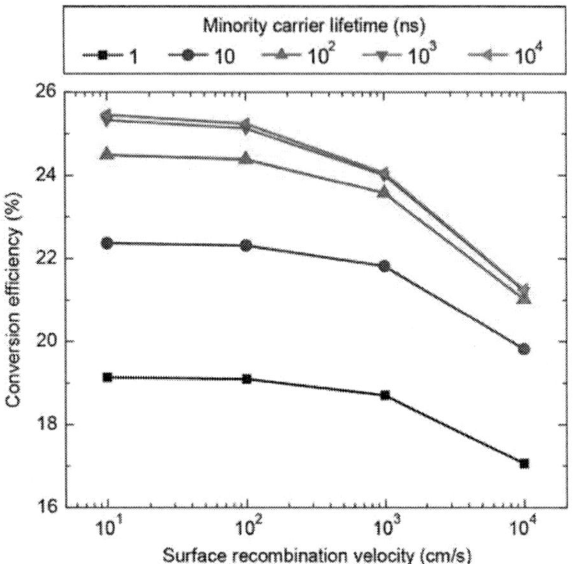

Fig. 3. Conversion efficiency as a function of indium composition (i.e., bandgap) for an InGaN p-i-n homojunction structure with various background concentrations. The optimal parameters for the modeled InGaN p-i-n homojunction solar cell are an indium composition of 55% (i.e., 1.54 eV) and a residual donor concentration of 10^{17} cm^{-3}.

Fig. 4. Conversion efficiency as a function of surface recombination velocity for a 55%-InGaN p-i-n homojunction structure with various minority carrier lifetimes.

cells, particularly for four- or more-junction devices [34], they are inadequate as single junction devices.

C. Indium Gallium Nitride p-i-n Homojunction Structure

To address this polarization issue, we investigate the photovoltaic characteristics of an InGaN p-i-n homojunction structure. In the n-In$_x$Ga$_{1-x}$N/UID-In$_x$Ga$_{1-x}$N/p-In$_x$Ga$_{1-x}$N design, the indium composition throughout the cell is constant so that the polarization-induced barriers that hinder carrier collection are eliminated. Unlike the previous design, such devices are presently very challenging to fabricate because of the need for p-doping at high indium composition and the difficulty in growing thick, In-rich InGaN layers. Simulation results show that band diagram, short-circuit current density (J_{sc}), open-circuit voltage (V_{oc}), and conversion efficiency strongly depend on indium content and the residual background doping of the UID-InGaN layer.

Fig. 3 shows the influence of composition and background doping on conversion efficiency. As the bandgap decreases, light absorption improves leading to higher photocurrents but the open-circuit voltages decrease. These opposite trends lead to an optimum bandgap for highest efficiency. For all background doping in the UID-layer, the peak efficiency occurs in the range 1.4 to 1.6 eV, which corresponds to 53–60% indium content. At the optimal composition, the maximum conversion efficiency for the InGaN p-i-n homojunction devices is within the range 14–18% for all UID-InGaN-layer background doping. Moreover, as the residual donor concentration increases, the depletion region narrows, leading to reduced J_{sc} but increased V_{oc}. The optimal background doping must account for a tradeoff between J_{sc} and V_{oc}. Simulation results show that the optimal parame-

ters for the modeled InGaN p-i-n homojunction solar cell are an indium composition of 55% (i.e., 1.54 eV) and a residual donor concentration of 10^{17} cm^{-3}. This optimized structure leads to a maximum conversion efficiency of 17.1%, which is substantially lower than the theoretical maximum energy-conversion efficiency for AM1.5 illumination [35], but comparable with the efficiency of the p-GaN/n-In$_x$Ga$_{1-x}$N/n-In$_{0.5}$Ga$_{0.5}$N structure with a 50 nm-thick and 10^{17} cm^{-3}-doped graded InGaN layer described in [23]. This efficiency is limited by presently achievable values of surface recombination velocity (10^4 cm/s) and minority carrier lifetime (1 ns). Fig. 4 shows the conversion efficiency for identical InGaN p-i-n homojunction devices with various surface recombination velocity and various minority carrier lifetimes. Using a minority carrier lifetime of 10 μs and a surface recombination lifetime of 10 cm/s, the conversion efficiency rises to 25.5%, which is closer to the predicted theoretical maximum efficiency.

III. EXPERIMENTAL RESULTS

As demonstrated by the simulation results, the only viable design for a high-efficiency single-junction InGaN solar cell is the homojunction structure. While InGaN p-i-n homojunction solar cells with indium composition up to 20% have been previously demonstrated [11], the fabrication of p-i-n solar cells with higher indium content requires further improvements in InGaN material. Major issues include suitable p-type doping and growth of thick, high-quality InGaN layers with high indium content and no phase separation.

These material-quality limitations can be partially overcome using a modified form of molecular beam epitaxy called metal-modulated epitaxy (MME) [36], [37]. MME is a growth technique in which the metal shutters are modulated with a fixed

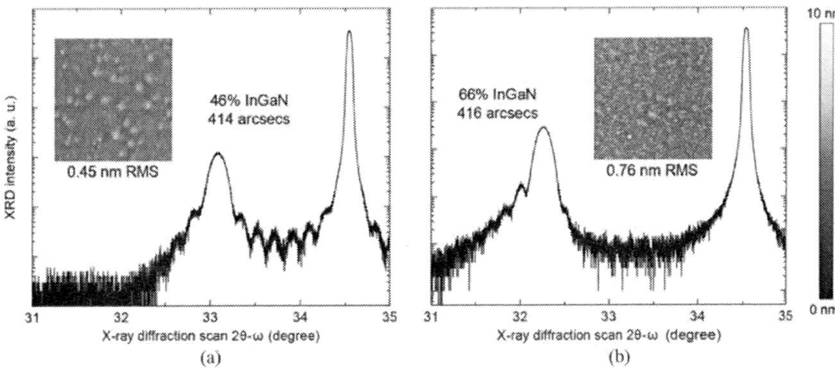

Fig. 5. X-ray diffraction scans, rocking curve FWHMs, AFM morphologies, and root-mean-square roughness values of InGaN layers at solar-relevant compositions. (a) 46% In. (b) 66% In. AFM images are $5 \times 5\ \mu\mathrm{m}^2$.

duty cycle, while a constant nitrogen flux is maintained. MME alternates between N-rich and metal-rich growth regimes by employing a metal-rich group-III flux, but periodically opening and closing the metal shutters. A metal adlayer builds up, while the metal shutters are opened and is consumed into the film, while the metal shutters are closed. This novel growth technique allows for control of the kinetics of Mg incorporation, while using low substrate temperatures, resulting in highly p-type nitride films with adequate crystal quality [38]–[40]. By periodically modulating the metal fluxes, MME takes advantage of both N-rich and metal-rich growth conditions. Under N-rich conditions, Mg dopants preferentially incorporate into Ga/In-substitutional sites [41]. Furthermore, under N-rich conditions, the formation energy of nitrogen vacancies that can act as compensating centers is higher than that under metal-rich condition [42]. However, N-rich growth usually results in lower material quality due to surface faceting that can create crystalline defects such as grain boundaries and dislocations [38]. In contrast, metal-rich growth results in smooth surfaces that prevent the formation of defects resulting from faceting. Under the metal-rich regime, however, the formation energy of nitrogen vacancies decreases, leading to a higher density of compensating centers. Experimental studies have resulted in highly p-type III-nitride films with hole concentrations exceeding $7 \times 10^{19}\ \mathrm{cm}^{-3}$ in GaN [40], offering promise for future subcells and tunnel junctions. The increased hole concentration can be attributed to optimal incorporation of surface-accumulated Mg dopants into Ga-substitutional sites with minimal formation of compensating defects.

In addition to p-type doping, MME has also been applied to the growth of high-indium-content InGaN throughout the miscibility gap [43], [44]. The InGaN films grown at solar-relevant compositions exhibit no phase separation or indium segregation, as shown in Fig. 5. Indium segregation is prevented by limiting the metal adlayer dose [44]. Lumilog MOCVD-grown GaN templates were used as substrates. The InGaN layers display GaN-template-limited crystal quality and very smooth surfaces with sub-nm RMS roughness. The microstructure of the 66% InGaN layer, analyzed by transmission electron microscopy (TEM), re-

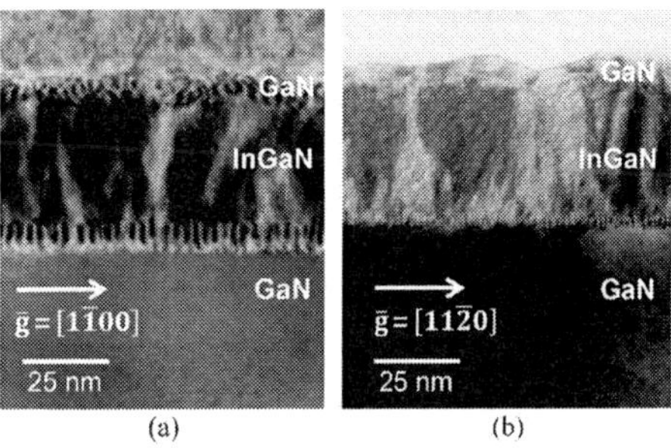

Fig. 6. TEM images of the 66% InGaN layer grown on GaN with a GaN cap layer under various diffraction conditions. (a) $g = [1\bar{1}00]$. (b) $g = [11\bar{2}0]$.

veals the presence of moiré fringes at the InGaN/GaN interface as shown in Fig. 6(a). These moiré patterns indicate that strain is mainly released at the interface through misfit dislocations, while the InGaN material remains relaxed [45]. Fig. 6(b) shows alternating bright and dark regions across the InGaN layer, indicating that the InGaN film grows in columns with a slight crystal rotation about the c-axis. Because of the large lattice mismatch between GaN and In-rich InGaN, plastic relaxation happens at a critical thickness of 1–2 monolayers [46], creating a uniform array of moiré fringes. The subsequent growth happens under relaxed conditions leading to a low density of threading dislocations. This reduced defect density is expected to increase the minority carrier lifetime and, thus, enhance future solar cell performance. This significant improvement in the crystalline structure is attributed to the large migration length and low growth temperature of MME, combined with this small critical thickness. As a result, MME offers great potential to overcome both p-doping and phase-separation limitations in In-rich InGaN.

While these advances in growth technology are very promising for the growth of high-efficiency InGaN solar cells, other material and device challenges still need to be solved. Further efforts must be made to achieve InGaN homojunction solar cells with suitable p-doping at all compositions and thick InGaN layers without phase separation.

IV. Conclusion

In conclusion, we numerically investigated the photovoltaic characteristics of InGaN p-i-n solar cells. For currently feasible InGaN/GaN heterostructures, the conversion efficiency is limited to ~11% as a result of polarization effects that impede carrier collection. These detrimental polarization effects can be eliminated by using InGaN p-i-n homojunction devices that are currently challenging to fabricate but are expected to be achievable in the future. Advances in growth technology have demonstrated the growth of highly p-type III-nitride films and the growth of high indium content InGaN throughout the miscibility gap without phase separation, offering great potential for high-efficiency InGaN photovoltaics.

References

[1] A. Bhuiyan, K. Sugita, A. Hashimoto, and A. Yamamoto, "InGaN solar cells: Present state of the art and important challenges," *IEEE J. Photovoltaics*, vol. 2, no. 3, pp. 276–293, Jul. 2012.

[2] E. Trybus, G. Namkoong, W. Henderson, S. Burnham, W. A. Doolittle, M. Cheung, and A. Cartwright, "InN: A material with photovoltaic promise and challenges," *J. Cryst. Growth*, vol. 288, pp. 218–224, Mar. 2006.

[3] A. S. Bouazzi, H. Hamzaoui, and B. Rezig, "Theoretical possibilities of In$_x$Ga$_{1-x}$N tandem PV structures," *Sol. Energy Mater. Sol. Cells*, vol. 87, pp. 595–603, May 2005.

[4] J. F. Muth, A. J. H. Lee, I. K. Shmagin, R. M. Kolbas, H. C. Casey, B. P. Keller, U. K. Mishra, and S. P. DenBaars, "Absorption coefficient, energy gap, exciton binding energy, and recombination lifetime of GaN obtained from transmission measurements," *Appl. Phys. Lett.*, vol. 71, pp. 2572–2574, Dec. 1997.

[5] Y. Nanishi, Y. Saito, and T. Yamaguchi, "RF-molecular beam epitaxy growth and properties of InN and related alloys," *Jpn. J. Appl. Phys.*, vol. 42, pp. 2549–2559, May 2003.

[6] J. Wu, W. Walukiewicz, K. M. Yu, W. Shan, J. W. Ager, E. E. Haller, L. Hai, W. J. Schaff, W. K. Metzger, and S. Kurtz, "Superior radiation resistance of In$_{1-x}$Ga$_x$N alloys: Full-solar-spectrum photovoltaic material system," *J. Appl. Phys.*, vol. 94, pp. 6477–6482, 2003.

[7] J. R. Lang, C. J. Neufeld, C. A. Hurni, S. C. Cruz, E. Matioli, U. K. Mishra, and J. S. Speck, "High external quantum efficiency and fill-factor InGaN/GaN heterojunction solar cells grown by NH$_3$-based molecular beam epitaxy," *Appl. Phys. Lett.*, vol. 98, pp. 131115-1–131115-3, Mar. 2011.

[8] E. Matioli, C. Neufeld, M. Iza, S. C. Cruz, A. A. Al-Heji, C. Xu, R. M. Farrell, S. Keller, S. DenBaars, U. Mishra, S. Nakamura, J. Speck, and C. Weisbuch, "High internal and external quantum efficiency InGaN/GaN solar cells," *Appl. Phys. Lett.*, vol. 98, pp. 021102-1–021102-3, Jan. 2011.

[9] J. P. Shim, M. Choe, S. R. Jeon, D. Seo, T. Lee, and D. S. Lee, "InGaN-based p-i-n solar cells with graphene electrodes," *Appl. Phys. Exp.*, vol. 4, pp. 052302-1-052302-3, May 2011.

[10] L. Sang, M. Liao, N. Ikeda, Y. Koide, and M. Sumiya, "Enhanced performance of InGaN solar cell by using a super-thin AlN interlayer," *Appl. Phys. Lett.*, vol. 99, pp. 161109-1–161109-3, Oct. 2011.

[11] X.-M. Cai, S.-W. Zeng, and B.-P. Zhang, "Fabrication and characterization of InGaN p-i-n homojunction solar cell," *Appl. Phys. Lett.*, vol. 95, pp. 173504-1–173504-3, Oct. 2009.

[12] S.-N. Lee, T. Sakong, W. Lee, H. Paek, J. Son, E. Yoon, O. Nam, and Y. Park, "Characterization of optical and electrical quality of Mg-doped In$_x$Ga$_{1-x}$N grown by MOCVD," *J. Cryst. Growth*, vol. 261, pp. 249–252, Jan. 2004.

[13] S. Brochen, J. Brault, S. Chenot, A. Dussaigne, M. Leroux, and B. Damilano, "Dependence of the Mg-related acceptor ionization energy with the acceptor concentration in p-type GaN layers grown by molecular beam epitaxy," *Appl. Phys. Lett.*, vol. 103, pp. 032102-1–032102-4, Jul. 2013.

[14] C. G. Van de Walle, C. Stampfl, and J. Neugebauer, "Theory of doping and defects in III-V nitrides," *J. Cryst. Growth*, vol. 189–190, pp. 505–510, Jun. 1998.

[15] B. N. Pantha, H. Wang, N. Khan, J. Y. Lin, and H. X. Jiang, "Origin of background electron concentration in In$_x$Ga$_{1-x}$N alloys," *Phys. Rev. B*, vol. 84, pp. 075327-1–075327-6, Aug. 2011.

[16] G. B. Stringfellow, "Microstructures produced during the epitaxial growth of InGaN alloys," *J. Cryst. Growth*, vol. 312, pp. 735–49, Mar. 2010.

[17] P. Kozodoy, J. P. Ibbetson, H. Marchand, P. T. Fini, S. Keller, J. S. Speck, S. P. DenBaars, and U. K. Mishra, "Electrical characterization of GaN p-n junctions with and without threading dislocations," *Appl. Phys. Lett.*, vol. 73, pp. 975–977, Aug. 1998.

[18] J. Abell and T. D. Moustakas, "The role of dislocations as nonradiative recombination centers in InGaN quantum wells," *Appl. Phys. Lett.*, vol. 92, pp. 091901-1–091901-3, Mar. 2008.

[19] E. T. Yu, X. Z. Dang, P. M. Asbeck, S. S. Lau, and G. J. Sullivan, "Spontaneous and piezoelectric polarization effects in III-V nitride heterostructures," *J. Vac. Sci. Technol. B*, vol. 17, pp. 1742–1749, Jul. 1999.

[20] Z. Q. Li, M. Lestradet, Y. G. Xiao, and S. Li, "Effects of polarization charge on the photovoltaic properties of InGaN solar cells," *Phys. Status Solidi A*, vol. 208, pp. 928–931, Apr. 2011.

[21] J.-Y. Chang and Y.-K. Kuo, "Numerical study on the influence of piezoelectric polarization on the performance of p-on-n (0001)-face GaN/InGaN p-i-n solar cells," *IEEE Electron Device Lett.*, vol. 32, no. 7, pp. 937–939, Jul. 2011.

[22] APSYS (Nov. 2013). [Online]. Available: http://www.crosslight.com

[23] G. F. Brown, J. W. Ager, III, W. Walukiewicz, and J. Wu, "Finite element simulations of compositionally graded InGaN solar cells," *Sol. Energy Mater. Sol. Cells*, vol. 94, pp. 478–483, Mar. 2010.

[24] J. Wu, W. Walukiewicz, K. M. Yu, J. W. Ager, E. E. Haller, L. Hai, and W. J. Schaff, "Small band gap bowing in In$_{1-x}$Ga$_x$N alloys," *Appl. Phys. Lett.*, vol. 80, pp. 4741–4743, Jun. 2002.

[25] D. M. Caughey and R. E. Thomas, "Carrier mobilities in silicon empirically related to doping and field," *Proc. IEEE*, vol. 55, no. 12, pp. 2192–2193, Dec. 1967.

[26] Z. Z. Bandic, P. M. Bridger, E. C. Piquette, and T. C. McGill, "Minority carrier diffusion length and lifetime in GaN," *Appl. Phys. Lett.*, vol. 72, pp. 3166–3168, Jun. 1998.

[27] F. Chen, A. N. Cartwright, H. Lu, and W. J. Schaff, "Temperature dependence of carrier lifetimes in InN," *Phys. Status Solidi A*, vol. 202, pp. 768–772, Apr. 2005.

[28] P. Scajev, K. Jarasiunas, S. Okur, U. Ozgur, and H. Morkoc, "Carrier dynamics in bulk GaN," *J. Appl. Phys.*, vol. 111, pp. 023702-1–023702-8, Jan. 2012.

[29] M. Boroditsky, I. Gontijo, M. Jackson, R. Vrijen, E. Yablonovitch, T. Krauss, C.-C. Cheng, A. Scherer, R. Bhat, and M. Krames, "Surface recombination measurements on III-V candidate materials for nanostructure light-emitting diodes," *J. Appl. Phys.*, vol. 87, pp. 3497–3504, Apr. 2000.

[30] H. Kitagawa, T. Suto, M. Fujita, Y. Tanaka, T. Asano, and S. Noda, "Green photoluminescence from GaInN photonic crystals," *Appl. Phys. Exp.*, vol. 1, pp. 032004-1–032004-3, Mar. 2008.

[31] V. Fiorentini, F. Bernardini, and O. Ambacher, "Evidence for nonlinear macroscopic polarization in III-V nitride alloy heterostructures," *Appl. Phys. Lett.*, vol. 80, pp. 1204–1206, Feb. 2002.

[32] H. Zhang, E. J. Miller, E. T. Yu, C. Poblenz, and J. S. Speck, "Measurement of polarization charge and conduction-band offset at In$_x$Ga$_{1-x}$N/GaN heterojunction interfaces," *Appl. Phys. Lett.*, vol. 84, pp. 4644–4646, Jun. 2004.

[33] B. N. Pantha, A. Sedhain, J. Li, J. Y. Lin, and H. X. Jiang, "Electrical and optical properties of p-type InGaN," *Appl. Phys. Lett.*, vol. 95, pp. 261904-1–261904-3, Dec. 2009.

[34] C. Honsberg, O. Jani, A. Doolittle, E. Trybus, G. Namkoong, I. Ferguson, D. Nicol, and A. Payne, "InGaN – A new solar cell material," presented at the 19th Eur. Photovoltaic Sol. Energy Conf. Exhib., Paris, France, 2004.

[35] M. A. Green, "Efficiency limits, losses and measurement," in *Solar Cells: Operating Principles, Technology, and System Applications.* Englewood Cliffs, NJ, USA: Prentice-Hall, 1982, pp. 85–91.

[36] S. D. Burnham, G. Namkoong, D. C. Look, B. Clafin, and W. A. Doolittle, "Reproducible increased Mg incorporation and large hole concentration in GaN using metal modulated epitaxy," *J. Appl. Phys.*, vol. 104, pp. 024902-1–024902-5, Jul. 2008.

[37] S. D. Burnham, G. Namkoong, K.-K. Lee, and W. A. Doolittle, "Reproducible reflection high energy electron diffraction signatures for improvement of AlN growth in situ growth regime characterization," *J. Vac. Sci. Technol. B*, vol. 25, pp. 1009–1013, May 2007.

[38] G. Namkoong, E. Trybus, K. K. Lee, M. Moseley, W. A. Doolittle, and D. C. Look, "Metal modulation epitaxy growth for extremely high hole concentrations above 10^{19} cm^{-3} in GaN," *Appl. Phys. Lett.*, vol. 93, pp. 172112-1–172112-3, Oct. 2008.

[39] E. Trybus, W. A. Doolittle, M. Moseley, W. Henderson, D. Billingsley, G. Namkoong, and D. C. Look, "Extremely high hole concentrations in c-plane GaN," *Phys. Status Solidi C*, vol. 6, pp. S788–S791, Jun. 2009.

[40] B. Gunning, J. Lowder, M. Moseley, and W. A. Doolittle, "Negligible carrier freeze-out facilitated by impurity band conduction in highly p-type GaN," *Appl. Phys. Lett.*, vol. 101, pp. 082106-1–082106-5, Aug. 2012.

[41] N. Sipe and R. Venkat, "Modeling GaN growth by plasma assisted MBE in the presence of low Mg flux," *Mater. Res. Soc. Internet J. Nitride Semicond. Res.*, vol. 7, pp. 11–1, 2002.

[42] C. G. Van de Walle and J. Neugebauer, "Defects, impurities and doping levels in wide-band-gap semiconductors," *Braz. J. Phys.*, vol. 26, pp. 163–166, Mar. 1996.

[43] M. Moseley, J. Lowder, D. Billingsley, and W. A. Doolittle, "Control of surface adatom kinetics for the growth of high-indium content InGaN throughout the miscibility gap," *Appl. Phys. Lett.*, vol. 97, pp. 191902-1–191902-3, Nov. 2010.

[44] M. Moseley, B. Gunning, J. Greenlee, J. Lowder, G. Namkoong, and W. A. Doolittle, "Observation and control of the surface kinetics of InGaN for the elimination of phase separation," *J. Appl. Phys.*, vol. 112, pp. 014909-1–014909-9, Jul. 2012.

[45] A. M. Fischer, Y. O. Wei, F. A. Ponce, M. Moseley, B. Gunning, and W. A. Doolittle, "Highly luminescent, high-indium-content InGaN film with uniform composition and full misfit-strain relaxation," *Appl. Phys. Lett.*, vol. 103, pp. 131101-1–131101-4, Sep. 2013.

[46] D. Holec, P. M. F. J. Costa, M. J. Kappers, and C. J. Humphreys, "Critical thickness calculations for InGaN/GaN," *J. Cryst. Growth*, vol. 303, pp. 314–317, May 2007.

Chloe A. M. Fabien (S'13) received the M.S. degrees in electrical engineering in 2011 from Supélec, Metz, France, and the Georgia Institute of Technology, Atlanta, USA, where she is currently working toward the Ph.D. degree.

Michael Moseley received the B.S., M.S., and Ph.D. degrees in electrical engineering from the Georgia Institute of Technology, Atlanta, GA, USA, in 2007, 2011, and 2013, respectively.

He is currently with Sandia National Laboratories, Albuquerque, NM, USA.

Brendan Gunning received the B.S. and M.S. degrees in electrical engineering from the Georgia Institute of Technology, Atlanta, GA, USA, in 2010 and 2012, respectively, where he is currently working toward the Ph.D. degree in electrical engineering.

W. Alan Doolittle (SM'89) received the Ph.D. degree in electrical engineering in 1996 from the Georgia Institute of Technology (Georgia Tech), Atlanta, GA, USA.

He is currently a Professor with the Department of Electrical and Computer Engineering at Georgia Tech. His principal interest is in the development of nitride-based and crystalline oxide-based devices, as well as applying new growth techniques to facilitate material and device improvements. His research interests include plasma-enhanced molecular beam epitaxy for III-Nitride and complex oxide growth for electronic, optoelectronic devices, and neuromorphic computational devices. He has authored/coauthored more than 118 research papers and 101 presentations (34 invited), as well as numerous technical reports and patents.

Dr. Doolittle received numerous awards, including a 2004 National Science Foundation CAREER Award, the 2003 Georgia Tech Faculty of the Year award, the 2005 ECE Outstanding Junior Faculty Member Award, the 2005 Lockheed Martin Aeronautics Company's Dean's Award for Teaching Excellence, and the 2008 Georgia Tech Outstanding Achievement in Research Program Development Award.

Alec M. Fischer received the B.S. degree in physics from the National University of Engineering, Lima, Peru, in 2004 and the Ph.D. degree in physics from Arizona State University, Tempe, AZ, USA, in 2009.

He is currently a Research Scientist with the Department of Physics, Arizona State University. His current research interests include optical and structural characterization of III-nitride semiconductors for optoelectronic and solar cell applications.

Yong O. Wei was born in Chongqing, China. He received the B.S. degree in condensed matter physics from the University of Science and Technology of China, Hefei, China, in 2007. He is currently working toward the Ph.D. degree with the Department of Physics, Arizona State University, Tempe, AZ, USA.

His current research focuses on the microstructural properties of III-nitride semiconductors.

Fernando A. Ponce received the B.S. degree in physics from the National University of Engineering, Lima, Peru, and the Ph.D. degree in materials science and engineering from Stanford University, Stanford, CA, USA.

He has been a Professor of Physics with the Department of Physics, Arizona State University, Tempe, AZ, USA, since 1999. His research focuses on the physics of semiconductor materials, in particular for light emitting and sensing applications. His current interest is in the understanding of the materials properties of III–V nitrides and their correlation to growth and to device performance for solid-state lighting. He was with Hewlett-Packard Laboratories Palo Alto, CA, USA (1980–1984) and with the Xerox Palo Alto Research Center (1977–1980 and 1984–1998). He has contributed to the growth and characterization of photovoltaic materials and to the development of materials for optoelectronic applications and of high-resolution transmission electron microscopy. He has coauthored more than 200 papers and eight patents and has coedited nine books.

Dr. Ponce was the Meeting Chair of the 1999 Fall MRS Meeting and Chair of the 27th International Conference on the Physics of Semiconductors held in Arizona in 2004. He is a fellow of the American Physical Society.

Development of High-performance Solar Cells Using Solar Spectrum Splitting Technique

M. Konagai[1,2*], S. Kim[1], Y. Takiguchi[1], P. Sichanugrist[1], T. Kobayashi[3], T. Nakada[3]

1.) Department of Physical Electronics, Tokyo Institute of Technology

2.) Photovoltaic Research Center (PVREC), Tokyo Institute of Technology

2-12-1-NE-15, O-okayama, Meguro-ku, Tokyo 152-8552, Japan

3.) Photovoltaic Science and Technology Research Division, Tokyo University of Science

5-4-30 Nishihashimoto, Sagamihara, Kanagawa 252-0131, Japan

*.) Corresponding author: konagai.m.aa@m.titech.ac.jp

Abstract —To increase the performance of solar cells, solar spectrum splitting technique has been considered and studied. It was found from the simulation that the total efficiency of nearly 25% can be obtained at the splitting wavelength of 600 nm for thin-film type solar cell using a-Si and CIGS as the top and bottom cells, respectively. The experiment has been carried out to verify the simulation results. By the optimization of device and splitter, up to now the total efficiency of about 22 % has been obtained at the splitting wavelength of 620 nm which is similar to the simulation results. Further work has been done using InGaP as the top cell instead of a-Si. Up to now an high efficiency of 26% has been measured for InGaP//CIGS configuration using the developed spectrum splitting technique. Higher performance can be expected with c-Si bottom cell or under concentration application. For higher cell efficiency, the configuration using InGaP//GaAs//CIGS using 2 optical splitters has been considered and its potential efficiency has been calculated. It was found that the maximum effiency of more than 30% can be expected with this configuration.

Index Terms — Photovoltaic, tandem, spectrum splitting

I. INTRODUCTION

Higher performance tandem cell needs to be developed and several ways to increase its efficiency are to use a mechanical stacked-type approach or to use a solar spectrum splitting technique. For the mechanical stacked-type structure, it is difficult to develop back semi-transparent electrode and optical coupler between the cells. On the other hand, these requirements are not necessary for splitting type one and it is easier to apply to the cells with other type of materials. However, it is required to develop an optical splitter at certain wavelength with low optical loss.

Various kind of splitting techniques have been proposed and discussed in the literature [1] and they included dichroic filter with dielectric multilayer, luminescent solar concentrator with fluorescent dye, prism refraction, and holographic filter. The first demonstration of this spectrum splitting system at PV module level was presented by Borden et al. [2,3]. However expensive crystalline AlGaAs and Si have been used.

Furthermore, a research with the same approach using low cost dichroic mirror has been carried out [4]. GaInP and pc-Si type cells have been used, but again all of them are crystalline type solar cells which are considered to use high manufacturing cost.

In this paper, we have carried out a study to apply the splitting techniques to thin-film type solar cells such as amorphous silicon (a-Si) and $Cu(In_{1-x}Ga_x)Se_2$ (CIGS) since their manufacturing costs are lower. Besides that low cost dichroic mirror has also been developed. A-Si has been chosen since its band gap is more than 1.7 eV and can be changed by varying the deposition temperature and hydrogen dilution ratio. On the other hand, CIGS has been used as the bottom cell since its band gap can be minimized as low as 1.0 eV.

Our spectrum splitting system was designed as shown in Fig.1. First, optical filter has been located at 45 degree and a-Si top and CIGS bottom cells are placed to absorb the light at short and long wavelength regions. In this study we first theoretically calculated its performance and then the cells have been fabricated and measured.

      546

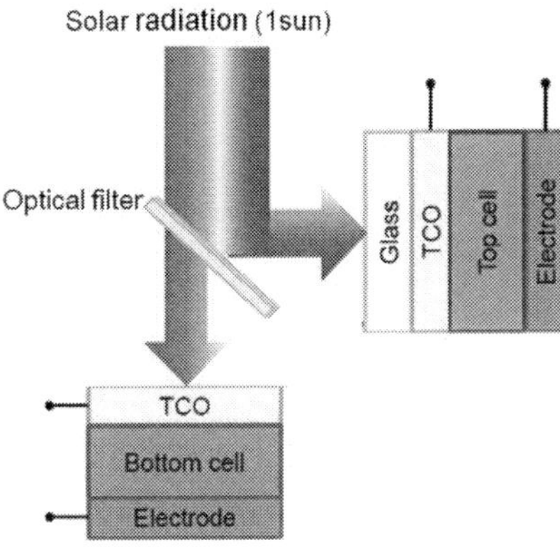

Fig. 1. Schematic diagram of full spectrum splitting

The new low-loss splitter has been developed and further work has been done using InGaP cell as the top cell instead of a-Si cell.

Furthermore, for high cell performance we have calculated the splitting cell using double optocal splitters based on the configuration of InGaP//GaAs//CIGS solar cells

II. SIMULATION MODEL

First the simulation has been carried out for a-Si//CIGS type structure. The band gap and the thickness of both top (a-Si) and bottom cells (CIGS) were changed to determine the ideal combination for each splitting or cut-on wavelength. In this study, A numerical analysis was carried out using a one-dimensional device simulation program AMPS-1D (Analysis of Microelectronic and Photonic Structures) [5].

Figure 2 shows the simulation results of top and bottom solar cell performance under various band gaps of active layers and splitting wavelength. As can be seen from this figure, the bottom cell has higher performance at short splitting wavelength while the top cell with higher performance at that wavelength should use wider bang gap.

Figure 3 shows the simulated total efficiency of overall solar cell performance which obtained from the efficiency sum of the top and bottom cells. The total efficiency which combines top cell with wider band gap achieved higher total

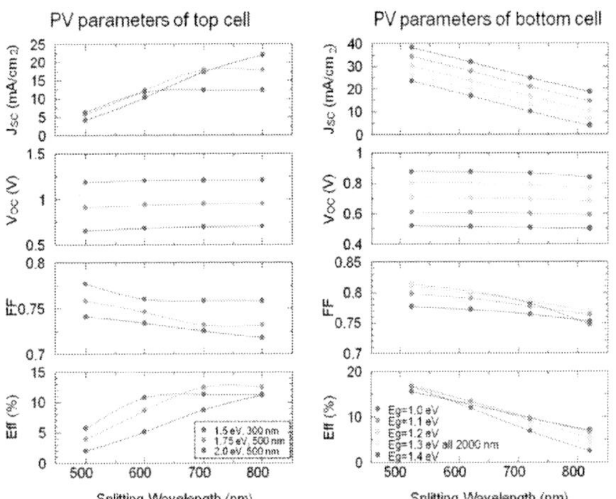

Fig. 2. Simulation results of top and bottom solar cells performances under various band gaps and splitting wavelengths

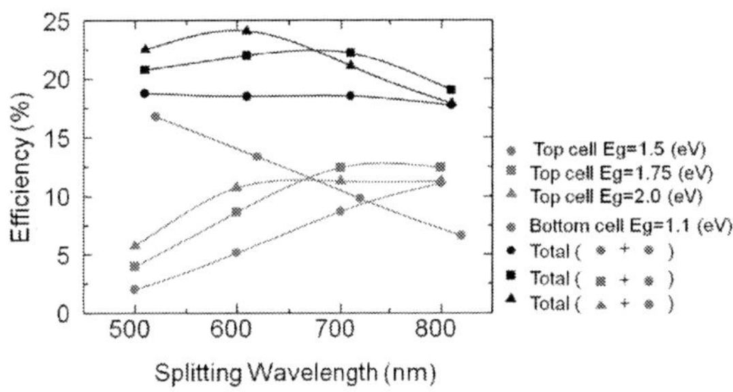

Fig. 3. Simulated total efficiency under various splitting wavelengths

efficiency. It should be noted here that it is possible to obtain the total efficiency of nearly 25% at the splitting wavelength of about 600 nm.

III. EXPERIMENTAL DETAIL

In order to make the best match to the spectral response of the top and bottom solar cell in each wavelength range, five filters (splitter) having the wavelength of 576, 614, 671, 728 and 741 nm are used to divide solar spectrum. These filters are manufactured by CVI Laser Optics LLC. Furthermore, to obtain higher performance, new splitters with very low optical loss has been developed by Kaneka Corp. Their splitting wavelength are 580, 600 and 620 nm.

To verify our simulation results, a-Si:H solar cell with a 1.75 eV band-gap i-layer has been fabricated. Solar cell with an area of 0.086cm^2 were fabricated on the SnO$_2$:F coated glass (Asahi U-type) and the cell structure is glass / SnO$_2$:F / p-a-SiC:H / buffer / i-a-Si:H (1.75eV, 300nm) / n-a-Si:H / ZnO:Al / Ag / Al. The CIGS solar cell with an area of 0.16 cm^2 was fabricated with a structure of Al grid / n-ZnO:B / i-ZnO / n-CdS / p-CIGS (1.15 eV, 2μm) / Mo / SLG glass. The CIGS solar cells have been developed by the group of T. Nakada [6,7]. Furthermore, high-performance InGaP and GaAs cells developed by Sharp Corp. has also been used as the top and middle cells with the combination of CIS bottom cell. The photo J-V characteristics for the fabricated cells were measured at 25 °C under AM 1.5, 100 mW/cm^2 illumination.

IV. RESULTS AND DISCUSSION

A. In case of a-Si//CIGS configuration

The a-Si:H and CIGS solar cells are measured under 5 different splitting wavelength filters as mentioned in experimental details. And the measured efficiencies are presented in Fig.4 with their total efficiency. The efficiency of top cell becomes much lower at shorter splitting wavelength. This low performance of top cell can be improved if high-voltage cell with large band gap a-Si:H has been used. Based on fundamental results, the conversion efficiency of 18.6% was obtained at the splitting wavelength of 614 nm.

B. In case of a-Si//CIGS configuration under optimized condition

To increase the conversion efficiency higher, we have tried to minimize the optical loss occurred at the optical splitter. Instead of using commercial filters, we have used developed the new filter developed by Kanaka Corp. which has relatively low absorption loss. Furthermore, we have also optimized the top a-Si cell by depositing it at lower deposition temperature. By using these two approach, we can obtain higher efficiency of 22% as shown in Table 1.

Figure 5 shows the spectral response of both cells shown in Table I. As can be seen the CIS cell has poor response at the wavelength below 500 nm while the a-Si one is higher. So it can be easily understood why splitting cell using both of them has higher efficiency than the stand-alone one.

TABLE I
EACH OF MAXIMUM SOLAR CELL PERFORMANCE AT SPLITTING
WAVELENGTH OF 620 NM

λsp = 620nm	Jsc (mA/cm^2)	Voc (V)	FF	Eff (%)
a-Si:H	12.9	0.99	0.72	9.15
CIGS	26.4	0.633	0.751	12.6
Total	—	—	—	21.75
Total	Input power corrected			22

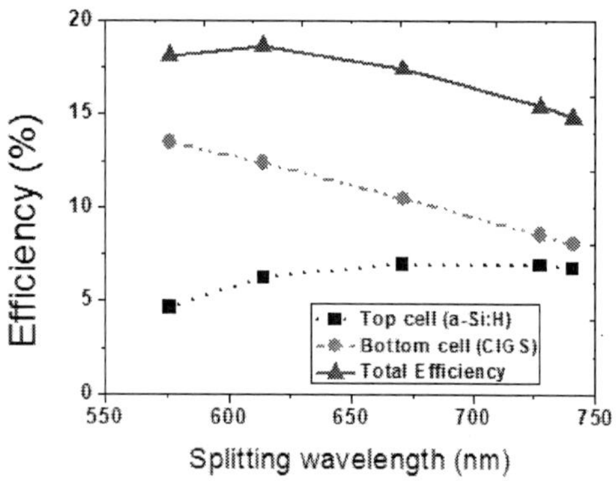

Fig. 4. Efficiency under various splitting wavelengths

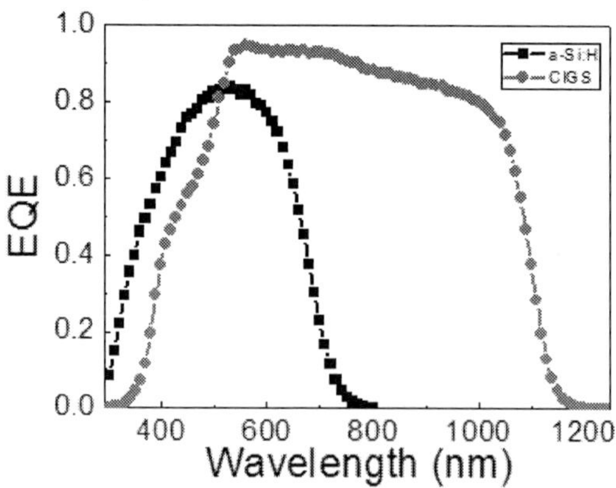

Fig. 5. Spectral response of fabricated a-Si:H and CIGS solar cells

C. *In case of InGaP//CIGS configuration*

Besides a-Si//CIGS cell structure InGaP//CIGS combination has been tried based on developed splitting technique. In this case high-performance InGaP solar cell has been used as the top cell instead of a-Si cell.

Table II shows the cell performance of InGaP measured under three develop splitters having splitting wavelength of 580, 600 and 620 nm and under 1 sun. Voc and FF are much higher than the one of a-Si cell.

TABLE II

CELL PERFORMANCE OF INGAP MEASURED UNDER THREE DEVELOPED SPLITTERS AND UNDER 1 SUN

λ sp (nm)	Jsc (mA/cm^2)	Voc (V)	FF	Eff (%)
580	10.0	1.41	0.842	12.0
600	10.4	1.42	0.838	12.4
620	11.3	1.42	0.837	13.4
w/o (1Sun)	13.0	1.42	0.833	15.4

Table III shows the details of maximum solar cell performance which was achieved at the splitting wavelength of 620 nm for InGaP top cell and CIGS bottom cell. Efficiency of nearly 26% has been achieved so far. The spectral responses of each cell were shown in Fig. 6. As can be seen in this figure, the InGaP cell has higher response at the short wavelength comparing to the one of CIGS. This efficiency of nearly 26% is higher than the one of standalone CIGS or InGaP showing that our developed splitting technique is a promising technique to obtain high performance solar cell.

TABLE III

EACH OF MAXIMUM SOLAR CELL PERFORMANCE AT SPLITTING WAVELENGTH OF 620 NM FOR INGAP//CIGS CONFIGURATION

λsp = 620nm	Jsc (mA/cm^2)	Voc (V)	FF	Eff (%)
InGaP	11.3	1.42	0.734	12.5
CIGS	26.4	0.633	0.751	13.4
Total	—	—	—	25.9

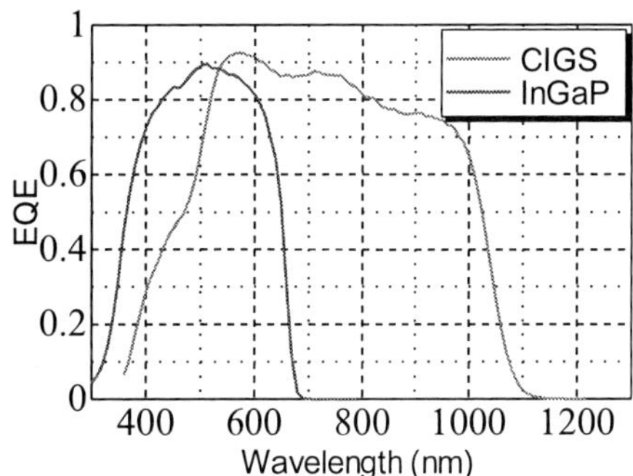

Fig. 6. Spectral response of fabricated InGaP and CIGS solar cells

D. *The higher efficiency expected in case of InGaP//GaAs//CIGS configuration*

There is a possibility that higher efficiency of this splitting solar cell can be expected with more optical splitters at different splitting wavelengths and more cells having different light absorption materials. Here as the first stage we consider the device configuration of InGaP//GaAs//CIGS which will have GaAs cell as the device to absorb the light in middle range and will use two optical splitters.

Figure 7 shows the QE of each fabricated cells. These real QE have been used in calculation while their Voc and FF are assumed to be constant under splitting condition.

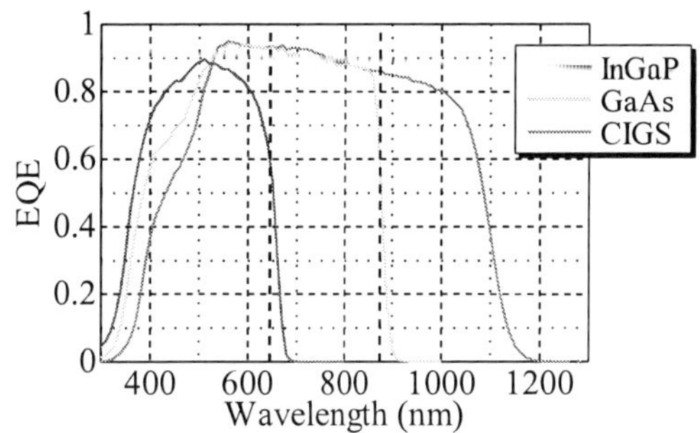

Fig. 7. Spectral response of fabricated InGaP, GaAs and CIGS solar cells

Table IV shows the cell performance of the splitting cell under the device configuration InGaP//GaAs//CIGS. The splitting wavelengths of 2 splitters have been varied in order to achieve the best performance. It was found from the calculation that when the splitting wavelengths are 645 and 875 nm, the cell efficiency as high as 30.6% under 1 Sun has been achieved. In this case, InGaP, GaAs and CIGS solar cells absorbed the lights between 300-640, 650-870 and 880-2000 nm, respectively and the total generated current density is around 36 mA/cm^2.

TABLE IV

EACH OF MAXIMUM SOLAR CELL PERFORMANCE AT SPLITTING WAVELENGTH OF 620 NM FOR INGAP//CIGS CONFIGURATION

	InGaP	GaAs	CIGS
λsp (nm)	645 nm for the 1st splitter		
	875 nm for the 2nd splitter		
Calculated wavelength (nm)	300-640	650-870	880-2000
Jsc (mA/cm^2)	13.0	14.0	8.90
Total Jsc (mA/cm^2)	35.9		
Voc (V)	1.42	1.01	0.641
FF	0.835	0.783	0.735
Eff (%)	15.4	11.0	4.19
Total Eff(%)	30.6		

V. CONCLUSION

To increase the performance of tandem type solar cells, solar spectrum splitting technique has been considered and studied. Simulation which has been carried out for cell and system design for a-Si//CIGS configuration shows that the total efficiency of nearly 25% can be obtained at the splitting wavelength of 600 nm with top cell using higher band gap material. By cell and splitter optimization, up to now the total efficiency of about 22 % and 26 % have been developed for a-Si//CIGS and InGaP//CIGS cell structure by using spectrum splitting technique.

Furthermore, it was found from the calculation based on the real spectral response that higher cell efficiency of more than 30% under 1 sun can also be obtained by using 2 optical splitters and the device configuration of InGaP//GaAs//CIGS. Higher performance can be expected with c-Si bottom cell or under concentration application.

ACKNOWLEDGEMENTS

This work was supported by the New Energy and Industrial Technology Development Organization (NEDO) under the Ministry of Economy, Trade and Industry (METI), Japan.

REFERENCES

[1] A. G. Imenes and D. R. Mills, "Spectral beam splitting technology for increased conversion in solar concentrating systems: a review" Sol. Energy Mater. Sol. Cells 84 (2004) 19.

[2] P.G. Borden, P.E. Gregory, O.E. Moore, L.W. James and H. Vander Plas, "A s10-unit dichroic filter spectral splitter module", in *Proc. 15th IEEE PVSC*, Florida, USA, 1981, pp. 311–316.

[3] P.G. Borden, P.E. Gregory, O.E. Moore, Design and demonstration spectrum splitting photovoltaic concentration module, Sandia Report SAND 82-7120, November 1982.J.Renewable Sustainable Energy 1, 013106 'A two junction, four terminal photovoltaic device for enhanced light to electric power conversion using a low-cost dichroic mirror (2009)

[4] A.G. Imenes and D.R. Mills, "Spectral beam splitting technology for increased conversion efficiency in solar concentrating systems: a review", Sol. Energy Mater. 84 (2004) 19–69.

[5] H. Zhu, A. K. Kalkan, J. Hou and S.J. Fonash, "Applications of AMPS-1D for solar cell simulation", in *AIP Conf. Proc. 462* , 1999, pp. 309.

[6] T. Nakada and S. Shirakata, "Impacts of Pulsed-Laser Assisted Deposition on CIGS Thin Films and Solar Cells", *Solar Energy Materials and Solar Cells 95(6)* , 2011, pp. 1463-1470.

[7] H. Nakakoba, Y. Yatsushiro, T. Mise, T. Kobayashi and T. Nakada, "Effects of Bi incorporation on Cu(In$_{1-x}$,Ga$_x$)Se$_2$ Thin Films and Solar Cells", *Jpn. J. Appl. Phys. 51(10)*, 2012.

A Novel Thin Concentrator Photovoltaic With Microsolar Cells Directly Attached to a Lens Array

Hidekazu Arase, Akio Matsushita, Akihiro Itou, Tetsuya Asano, Nobuhiko Hayashi, Daijiro Inoue,
Ryutaro Futakuchi, Kazuo Inoue, Tohru Nakagawa, Masaki Yamamoto, Eiji Fujii, Yoshiharu Anda,
Hidetoshi Ishida, Tetsuzo Ueda, Onur Fidaner, Michael Wiemer, and Daisuke Ueda

Abstract—We propose a novel concept of thin and compact CPV modules in which submillimeter solar cells are directly attached to lens arrays without secondary optics or an extra heat sink. With this small cell size, the optical path length of the module can be brought down to one-twentieth that of conventional CPV modules. To achieve precise alignment of the microsolar cells at the lens focal points, we have developed a fluidic self-assembly technique that utilizes surface tension. This novel CPV module with triple junction microsolar cells demonstrated an efficiency of 34.7% under sunlight in the particular measured condition.

Index Terms—III–V multijunction solar cells, photovoltaic cells, photovoltaic systems, self-assembly, surface tension.

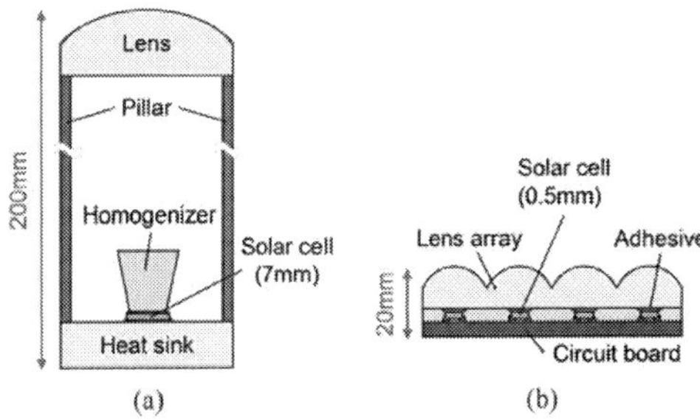

Fig. 1. Schematic images of (a) a conventional CPV module and (b) our compact CPV module.

I. Introduction

CONCENTRATOR photovoltaics (CPV) may help realize significantly higher solar energy conversion efficiency than flat panel modules [1]. In CPV, solar cells need to be placed only at the focused area of concentrators; therefore, high-performance tandem solar cell structures can be employed at an economically viable cost. Furthermore, cell efficiency can be improved by concentrating the incident light by concentrator [2]. Over the past decade, cell efficiency has been rapidly improved by about 10 absolute percent, and Solar Junction Corporation has achieved 44.0% under 947 Suns [3]. Nevertheless, application scenes of the CPV modules remain rather limited, partly because conventional CPV modules are extremely bulky.

Manuscript received June 10, 2013; revised August 30, 2013; accepted October 17, 2013.

H. Arase, A. Matsushita, A. Itou, T. Asano, N. Hayashi, D. Inoue, R. Futakuchi, K. Inoue, T. Nakagawa, M. Yamamoto, E. Fujii, and D. Ueda are with Advanced Technology Research Laboratories, Panasonic Corporation, Kyoto 619-0237, Japan. (e-mail: arase.hidekazu@jp.panasonic.com; matsushita.akio@jp.panasonic.com; itou.akihiro@jp.panasonic.com; asano.tetsuya001@jp.panasonic.com; hayashi.nobuhiko1@jp.panasonic.com; inoue.daijiro@jp.panasonic.com; futakuchi.ryutaro@jp.panasonic.com; inoue.kazuo@jp.panasonic.com; nakagawa.t@jp.panasonic.com; yamamoto.mas@jp.panasonic.com; fujii.e710@jp.panasonic.com; ueda.daisuke@jp.panasonic.com).

Y. Anda and H. Ishida are with the Corporate Business Development Division, Automotive and Industrial Systems Company, Panasonic Corporation, Kyoto 617-8520, Japan (e-mail: anda.yoshiharu@jp.panasonic.com; ishida.hi@jp.panasonic.com).

T. Ueda is with the Corporate Engineering Division, Automotive and Industrial Systems Company, Panasonic Corporation, Osaka 570-8501, Japan (e-mail: ueda.tetsuzo@jp.panasonic.com).

O. Fidaner and M. Wiemer are with Solar Junction Corporation, San Jose, CA 95131 USA (e-mail: ofidaner@sj-solar.com; mwiemer@sj-solar.com).

Color versions of one or more of the figures in this paper are available online at http://ieeexplore.ieee.org.

Digital Object Identifier 10.1109/JPHOTOV.2013.2292364

Large lenses are required for high concentration of sunlight, which, in turn, requires large heat sinks to prevent the cells from overheating. Furthermore, for CPV modules with Fresnel concentrators, homogenizers are needed to circumvent the adverse effects of the lens's chromatic aberration. This bulky and complex module structure has raised the installation cost of CPV modules and thus limited their potential application.

To alleviate the shortcomings of conventional CPV modules, in this paper, we propose a novel concept of thin and compact CPV modules in which high-efficiency GaAs-based multijunctions are directly attached to lens arrays with no secondary optics or extra heat sinks. This module design combines the advantages of good heat dissipation and high transmittance of the optical system. For automatic assembly of the microsolar cells with precise alignment at the focal point of the lenses, we have developed a unique fluidic self-assembly (FSA) technique that utilizes air/liquid or liquid/liquid interfacial forces [4]–[6]. The prototype module with this novel design shows 34.7% efficiency under on-Sun measurement.

II. Results and Discussion

A. Novel Concept of Our Compact CPV

Fig. 1 shows schematic images of the typical conventional CPV module [see Fig. 1(a)] and our novel CPV module [see Fig. 1(b)], in which the microsolar cells are directly attached to lens arrays. Unlike the typical conventional CPV modules, our CPV module is compact in thickness and is simple in design with no homogenizers or pillars. In our CPV modules, the microsolar cells [7] with 0.2–0.5 mm are assembled with a lens array and a circuit board, and connected to electrode pads on a circuit board using a reflow process. With this cell size, the lateral lens size can

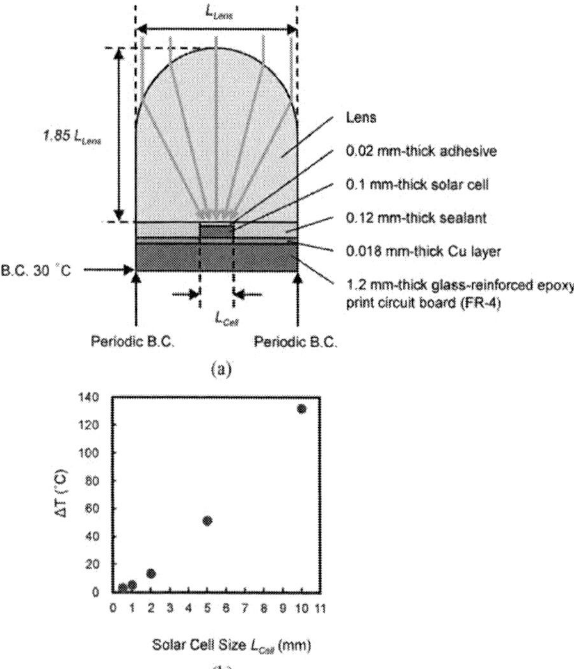

Fig. 2. (a) Model structure for 2-D heat simulation. L_{Cell} and L_{Lens} represent lateral solar cell size and lens size, respectively. The focal length of the lens is $1.85L_{Lens}$ based on our lens design. (b) Simulated result of the size-dependence of the cell temperature rise against the back surface of the module. The concentration ratio is fixed at 625 Suns, and the back sides of the cells are attached to 1.2-mm-thick glass-reinforced epoxy printed circuit board.

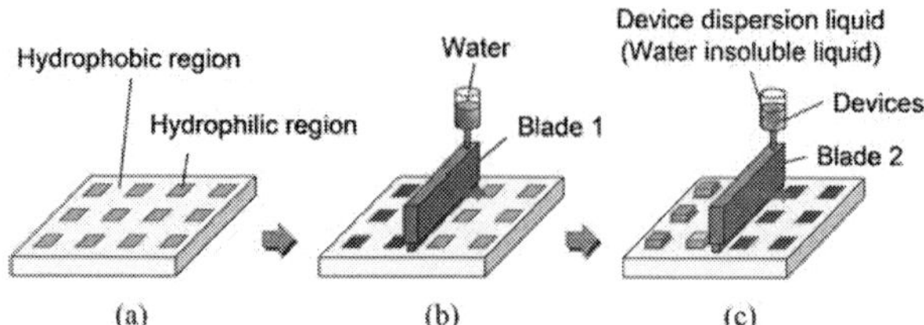

Fig. 3. Schematic images of our FSA technique. The description of the FSA process is in the text and in [4]–[6].

be reduced to ∼4–10 mm for the concentration of sunlight up to hundreds of Suns. The focal length of the lens is proportionally scaled down, taking into account the lateral lens size for a given lens material and curvature so that in our module, the distance from the lens apex to the cell can be reduced to ∼10–20 mm [see Fig. 1(b)] when using polymethyl methacrylate (PMMA) lens, making it one order of magnitude thinner than a conventional CPV module [see Fig. 1(a)].

In our compact CPV module, the cell temperature under sunlight is likely to be lower than for a conventional CPV module owing to fast lateral dissipation of the microsolar cells. To gain an approximate measure of the cell size-dependence of the cell temperature under concentrated sunlight, we performed a 2-D heat simulation of CPV modules with various cell sizes using the finite element method. The model structure we employed for the heat simulation is similar to our CPV module structure as shown in Fig. 2(a). A PMMA lens was placed in contact with the solar cell through 0.02-mm-thick adhesive. An 18 μm-thick Cu layer was placed beneath the solar cell, followed by a 1.2-mm-thick glass-reinforced epoxy printed circuit board (FR-4). The solar cell was surrounded by a sealant. The cell absorbed heat equivalent to 625× concentrated sunlight. We set the boundary conditions such that the back surfaces of FR-4 were at 30 °C and designated the periodic boundary condition in the horizontal direction, namely assigned the lateral temperature gradient at

both edges as zero. Fig. 2(b) shows the simulated result for cell size dependence of cell temperature rise against the temperature of the back surface of the CPV module under 625 Suns. As expected, the smaller the cell the lower its temperature, due to faster lateral heat dissipation characteristic of small cells. Under the particular conditions of this simulation, the temperature of submillimeter cells is only about 3 °C higher than the temperature of the back surface of the CPV module under 625 Suns. Although the actual temperature of CPV modules during operation will vary with the weather, this simulated result indicates that the CPV module with microsolar cells may not require an extra heat sink, thus reducing the size and weight of the module.

Because resistive and chromatic aberration losses are reduced with decreasing cell size [8], we employed a module design with no secondary optics. This allowed us to mount the solar cells directly on the lens arrays using transparent adhesive that has almost the same refractive index as the lens material. This module design eliminates the two reflective interfaces compared with the conventional CPV module (see Fig. 1), and can thus take advantage of more incoming sunlight for energy conversion.

B. FSA for Precise Cell Alignment

One possible drawback of our compact CPV with microsolar cells is that huge numbers of microsolar cells need to be precisely placed at the focal points of the lenses. The requirement for precision becomes even more stringent if there is no secondary optics.

To achieve the simultaneous and precise alignment of numerous microsolar cells at the focal point of the lenses, we have been developing an FSA technique that utilizes air/liquid or liquid/liquid interfacial forces [4]–[6]. Fig. 3 schematically shows the FSA technique that we have developed for the self-assembly of microelectronic chips [4]–[6]. First, a chemically patterned substrate with hydrophilic areas surrounded by a hydrophobic self-assembled monolayer is prepared, as shown in Fig. 3(a). Second, water is blade-coated onto the substrate. In this step, water droplets are selectively deposited on the hydrophilic areas as shown in Fig. 3(b). Third, before the water droplets evaporate, a water-insoluble dispersion liquid of chemically modified microsolar cells is applied to the substrate as shown in Fig. 3(c). This creates water/solvent interfaces on the water droplet surfaces. Because the microsolar cells have been chemically modified to be adsorbed onto the water surfaces by interfacial forces, the microsolar cells can be selectively assembled and aligned on

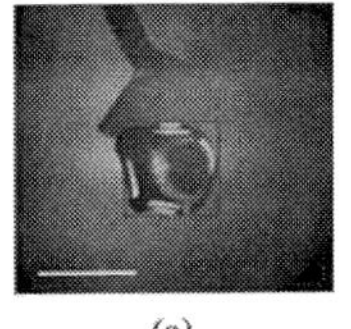 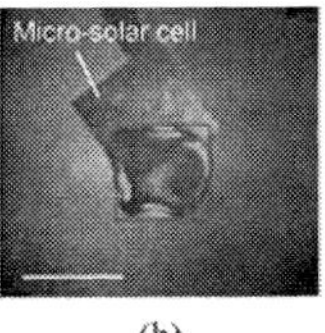 

(a)　　　(b)　　　(c)

Fig. 4. Photographs of self-alignment of a microsolar cell captured using a high-speed camera. (a) First, adhesive is selectively deposited. (b) Second, the microsolar cell comes into contact with the adhesive. (c) Third, the microsolar cell is automatically aligned at the focal position of the lens by interfacial force. The red lines in the figures outline the focal position (hydrophilic area). The scale bars represent 500 μm.

the hydrophilic areas. They are then anchored to the substrate after the water and solvent have evaporated.

In our CPV module assembly, the above FSA technique was implemented in a modified fashion. First, we patterned the back side of the lens array to create hydrophilic regions exactly at the focal points of the lenses, surrounded by a hydrophobic mono-layer [4]–[6]. We then placed adhesives, followed by microsolar cells, in the vicinity of the focal points of the lenses in such a way that a portion of the adhesive and microsolar cells over-lapped with the hydrophilic area but not necessarily at the exact focal points. Both the adhesives and microsolar cells were then automatically pulled into the focal points by the surface tension of the adhesive.

The motion of the microsolar cells during this self-alignment process was captured using a high-speed camera and is shown in Fig. 4. In Fig. 4(a), adhesive is selectively deposited at the focal points that have been applied with hydrophilic treatment. Next, the microsolar cell comes into contact with the adhesive, but at a rotated angle [see Fig. 4(b)]. The interfacial force then acts on the microsolar cell to automatically align it at the focal point of the lens [see Fig. 4(c)]. Using this self-assembly technique, we can accurately align large numbers of microsolar cells at the focal points of the lens array at a low manufacturing cost.

C. CPV Module Assembly Process

Fig. 5(a) is a photograph of the triple junction solar cell with a 500 μm $\times$ 500 μm aperture area as viewed from the light incident surface. The solar cell was designed with its electrodes on the back side to permit electrical connection to the circuit board. The 25 cells were positioned on the back side of the lens array using the abovementioned FSA technique. The microsolar cells were placed at the focal points of the lens array to an accuracy of ±25 μm. Fig. 5(b) shows a photograph of the lens array after having positioned the solar cells. Fig. 5(c) shows the electrical connection process between the cells and the electrode pads on the circuit board. All the microsolar cells were simultaneously connected to the circuit board using solder paste. The space between the lens array and the circuit board was filled with a sealant material that was then cured.

D. Performance Demonstration

To measure the solar characteristics of our compact CPV module, we created the module in which all 25 microsolar cells

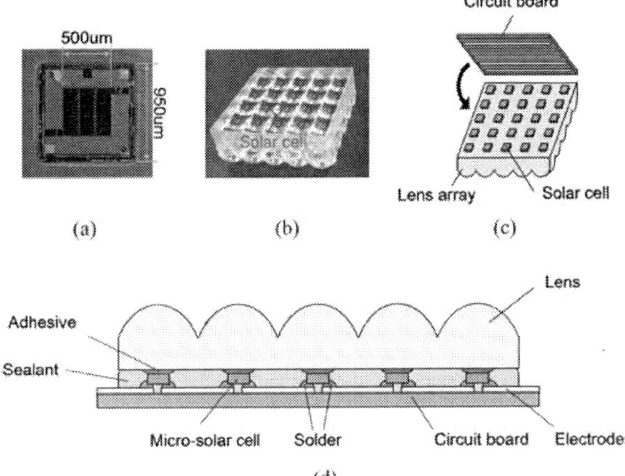

(a)　　　(b)　　　(c)

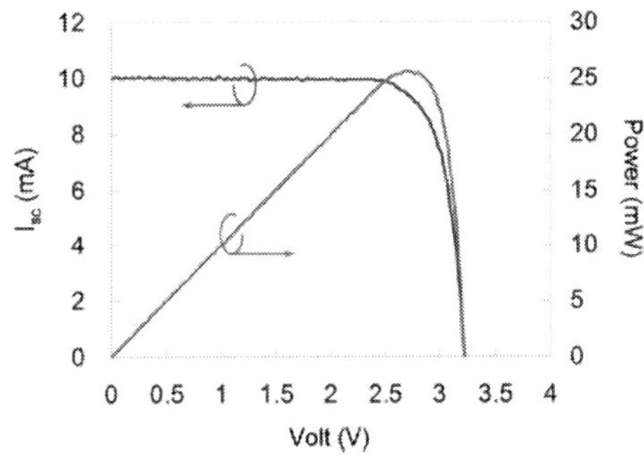

(d)

Fig. 5. (a) Photograph of the microsolar cell as viewed from the light-incident surface. (b) Photograph of the lens array with solar cells attached. (c) Schematic image of CPV module assembly process. (d) Cross-sectional view of the CPV module.

Fig. 6. P–I–V curves for one unit in our prototype module.

are electrically isolated with each other. A typical measured P–I–V curve of the isolated one-unit, which is equivalent to the CPV module with a single microsolar cell, is shown in Fig. 6. These measurements were taken on May 24, 2013 in Kyoto, Japan, under the following conditions: direct normal incidence = 735 W/m^2, ambient temperature = 30.5 °C, and wind speed = 1.2 m/s. These measurements showed the solar characteristics to be open circuit voltage V_{OC} = 3.23 V, short circuit current density I_{SC} = 10.0 mA (the size of the lens aperture is 10 mm $\times$ 10 mm), and the maximum power point P_{MAX} = 25.6 mW, efficiency = 34.7%, and fill factor FF = 0.789. Note that these measured values are raw data under the aforementioned particular condition, which is different from in-ternational standard operating conditions for CPV of 900 W/m^2, 20 °C ambient temperature, and 2 m/s wind speed. This high I_{SC} indicates the high optical transmittance of our module design as well as the precise alignment of the microsolar cells using our self alignment technique. The high FF shows that the resis-tive loss of the microsolar cell is not significant, in spite of the absence of the secondary optics.

We built the 50 mm $\times$ 50 mm CPV modules shown in Fig. 7(a). The thickness of the module is 20 mm, within which

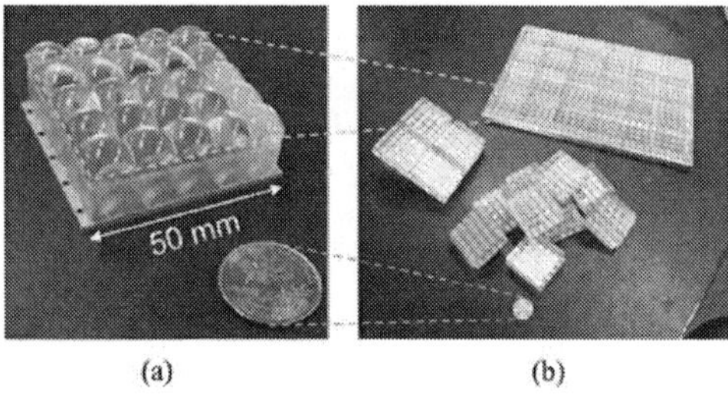

(a)   (b)

Fig. 7. Photographs of (a) our CPV module; a "CPV Block" and (b) a prototype A4-size CPV panel. The U.S. 25-cent coin gives a general impression of their size.

the heat sink is only a 1.5-mm-thick Al-based circuit board. The module is rigidly constructed with no gaps between individual module constituents (we call them "CPV blocks"). They can be scaled up by simply laying out the blocks on a frame, like the prototype A4-size (20 cm × 30 cm) CPV panel that consists of 24 CPV blocks shown in Fig. 7(b). These results indicate that our CPV module has the potential to achieve thin, compact, lightweight, and high-efficiency modules at low-manufacturing cost.

III. Conclusion

We propose a novel concept for a thin, compact, and high-performance CPV module in which microsolar cells are directly attached to lens arrays using our unique FSA techniques. The proposed CPV module design has the advantages of 1) effective heat dissipation; 2) high optical transmittance; and 3) minimal influence of chromatic aberration. The microsolar cells were precisely positioned, using our FSA technique, at the focal points of the lenses. The CPV module exhibited an efficiency of 34.7% under on-Sun measurement. These results indicate that our CPV module has the potential to achieve thin, compact, lightweight, and high-efficiency modules at low-manufacturing cost.

References

[1] M. Yamaguchi and A. Luque, "High efficiency and high concentration in photovoltaics," *IEEE Trans. Electron. Devices*, vol. 46, no. 10, pp. 2139–2144, Oct. 1999.

[2] A. Luqeue and V. Andreev, *Concentrator Photovoltaics*. Berlin, Heidelberg: Springer-Verlag, 2007.

[3] M. Green, K. Emery, Y. Hishikawa, W. Warta, and E. D. Dunlop, "Solar cell efficiency tables (version 41)," *Prog Photovoltaics: Res. Appl.*, vol. 21, pp. 1–11, 2013.

[4] T. Nakagawa, H. Torii, T. Kawashima, and T. Saitoh, "Controlled deposition of silicon nanowires on chemically patterned substrate by capillary force using a blade-coating method," *J. Phys. Chem. C*, vol. 112, pp. 5390–5396, 2008.

[5] H. Arase and T. Nakagawa, "Interfacial-energy-controlled deposition technique of microstructures using blade-coatings," *J. Phys. Chem. B*, vol. 113, pp. 15278–15283, 2009.

[6] H. Arase and T. Nakagawa, "Fluidic self-assembly of microstructures using a blade-coating technique: influence of volume of water droplets on probability of microstructure placement," *Jpn. J. Appl. Phys.*, vol. 51, pp. 036501-1–036501-6, 2012.

[7] J. Yoon, A. J. Baca, S. I. Park, P. Elvikis, J. B. Geddes, L. F. Li, R. H. Kim, J. L. Xiao, S. D. Wang, T. H. Kim, M. J. Motala, B. Y. Ahn, E. B. Duoss, J. A. Lewis, R. G. Nuzzo, P. M. Ferreira, Y. G. Huang, A. Rockett, and J. A. Rogers, "Ultrathin silicon solar microcells for semitransparent, mechanically flexible and microconcentrator module designs," *Nature Mater.*, vol. 7, pp. 907–915, 2008.

[8] S. R. Kurtz and M. J. O'Neill, "Estimating and controlling chromatic aberration losses for two-junction, two-terminal devices in refractive concentrator systems," in *Proc. 25th IEEE Photovoltaic Spec. Conf.*, 1996, pp. 361–364.

Authors' photographs and biographies not available at the time of publication.

Front-side metallization with high aspect ratio by stencil printing for crystal Si solar cell

Chien-Ming Chen, Yu-Chia Liao, Wei-Ming Su, Po-Sheng Huang, Li-Wei Cheng

TOPCELL SOLAR INTERNATIOMAL CO. LTD., Taoyuan, Taiwan

Abstract — **In order to reduce shading loss and keep low Rs under fine-line printing process, front-side metallization with high aspect ratio is necessary. In this paper, stencil screen with several opening widths are compared with mesh screen. While opening width in mesh screen is confined to about <40um, cells with high series resistance are generated because of the low cross section area of the finger. Nevertheless, stencil printing with 100% open areas could raise the aspect ratio in fine-line printing and effectively improve finger uniformity, leading to lower series resistance. In this work, fingers with aspect ratio over 0.5 have been achieved by stencil printing and kept low width. On the other hand, five pastes with different viscosity are applied to optimize stencil printing for 35μm and 45μm opening width respectively. The paste with higher viscosity has larger aspect ratio but poor printing quality. Finally, through line resistance measurement, larger aspect ratio performed by stencil printing actually exhibits lower resistance than that by mesh printing, making stencil suitable in fine-line printing production. With stencil printing for only fingers, followed by mesh printing of the busbars, +0.06% efficiency gain was achieved compared with single mesh printing as the result of the low resistance and high FF.**

Keywords — **fine-line printing, high aspect ratio, stencil printing, paste viscosity**

I. INTRODUCTION

It's the trend nowadays to print narrow fingers on crystal Si solar cell with high sheet resistance to reduce surface recombination and series resistance at the same time. Low phosphorus concentration accompanied by high lateral resistance makes better blue response and lower surface recombination so as to enhance the Isc and Voc. Once emitter resistance is higher does the front side grid design must be optimized to lower series resistance.

Single mesh printing will suffer the risks of line interruptions and poor line cross sectional uniformity if finger width is narrower than about 40um, which is due to the restriction of meshes and emulsion quality. On the contrary, stencil printing is used to print ultra fine line since the opening ratio is larger so as to enhance the ability of paste to penetrate through the screen and reduce line interruptions. Various types of stencil have been manufactured for solar cell printing like electroformed, laser cut, hybrid(metal with emulsion, metal with metal mesh) single and double layer. There are some researches concerning stencil have been proposed. In ECN, it's shown that full transfer of paste is ideal for opening with aspect ratio smaller than 1:1 [1]. DEK has tested two types of stencil and aspect ratio of finger has reached to 0.39 by using electroformed stencil with 30μm opening width [2]-[3]. The other ultra fine line stencil printing results are shown in TABLE I [1]-[4].

TABLE I

STENCIL PRINTING RESULTS FROM OTHER COMPANIES

Company	Stencil type	Stencil thickness (μm)	Opening (μm)	Width (μm)	Height (μm)	Aspect ratio
ECN	electroformed	30	30	42	15.0	0.36
DEK	Hybrid	20(EOM) +20(foil)	40	61	17.4	0.29
DEK	electroformed	30	30	45	17.6	0.39
DEK	electroformed	30	30	35	11.0	0.31
Applied	electroformed	x	40	55	19.0	0.35

In this work, various types of paste and stencil are applied. It's found that the highest aspect ratio of stencil approaches up to 0.5, which is far larger than that of other mesh printing result under the same opening width conditon. Therefore, for the following development of fine-line printing, stencil could provide an alternative way to improve the quality of fingers.

II. EXPERIMENTAL SETUP

Before printing, all p-type wafers with 200±20μm thick and 1~3 Ω.cm bulk resistivity undergo standard Si solar cell process: texturing, Phosphorous diffusion, wet-etching isolation, and anti-reflection coating. Then, the cells are printed with 3 busbars H pattern grid. Paste A~E with different viscosity are implemented on electroformed stencil printing in this work. Their viscosities have been measured respectively after spinning in the environment of 10rpm for 2 minutes. Single mesh printing is used as baseline while stencil printing is made by two step metallization process: first, the busbars are printed by mesh screen. Second, the fingers are printed by stencil screen. The details of mesh and stencil screens are displayed in TABLE II.

After printing, all of the groups are kept the same firing temperature in the Despatch belt furnace. Afterwards, IV measurement under standard testing condition is executed to quantify electrical properties. On the other hand, the finger geometry after co-firing is measured with a range of 3D & 2D microscopes.

TABLE II
MESH AND STENCIL SCREEN DIMENSIONS

Types	Mesh & Wire dia.	EOM (µm)	Opening (µm)
Mesh Screen	360.16	18	40
Busbars	325.23	8	NA
Fingers(stencil)	NA	NA	45
Fingers(stencil)	NA	NA	35

III. RESULTS AND DISCUSSION

In ultra fine line printing, fingers printed by mesh screen have very low aspect ratio because mesh confines paste transport. TABLE III shows respective finger width and height by the mesh and stencil screens with a typical paste called paste A. Aspect ratio of fingers printed via stencil screen with 100% open areas is almost three times higher than that through mesh screen. Due to the excellent paste penetration by stencil, the finger is wider than that via mesh screen under the same opening condition, also as shown in TABLE III.

TABLE III
PRINTING RESULT VIA MESH AND STENCIL SCREENS

Type	Opening (µm)	Width (µm)	Height (µm)	Aspect ratio
Mesh	27	41.36	6.28	0.15
	30	44.27	8.49	0.19
Stencil	25	36.60	18.39	0.50
	30	46.55	20.45	0.44
	35	59.47	31.89	0.54
	40	64.81	33.51	0.52

The aspect ratio of five pastes with different viscosity through stencil printing is shown in Fig. 1 and TABLE IV. Superior aspect ratio of 0.5 and < 55µm finger width have been achieved by using paste B and C for 35µm opening width. In addition, more viscous of the paste is, higher aspect ratio the finger will hold. The high aspect ratio performed by paste with large viscosity could be explained that the shape of finger made by high viscosity paste is simple to be maintained. In other words, through stencil printing with 100% open area, the paste with low viscosity easily diffuse over the neighbor region to make larger finger width.

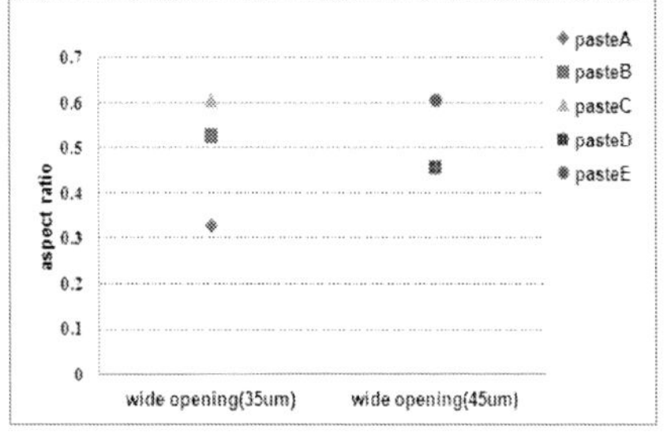

Fig. 1. The aspect ratio of five different pastes for stencil screen with 35µm and 45µm opening width.

TABLE IV
FINGER GEOMETRY AND VISCOSITY FOR EACH PASTE

Paste	Opening (µm)	Width (µm)	Height (µm)	Aspect ratio	Viscosity (Pa*s)
A	35	59.97	19.72	0.33	370
B	35	50.68	26.83	0.53	420
C	35	53.24	32.61	0.61	470
D	45	68.12	31.24	0.46	500
E	45	63.20	38.80	0.61	900

The highest aspect ratio of 0.61 can be reached by using paste C, but it will lead to worse finger quality in continuous printing due to its excessive viscosity. After printing the first wafer, paste with high viscosity sticks on the squeegee and the paste cannot be overlaid uniformly by blade before next printing, which will result in worse print quality.

Stencil printing using paste A and B are compared with mesh printing by means of the screen with same grid design. 2D and 3D visual images of mesh and stencil printing are shown in Fig. 2. High aspect ratio and uniform cross section of the fingers are observed by stencil printing, expectedly reducing the line resistance. The measured electrical properties are shown in TABLE V and the relation between the aspect ratio and efficiency with different printing parameters is displayed in Fig. 3. The efficiency over 0.06% gain has been achieved compared with mesh printing by using paste B on stencil printing. The higher Jsc and FF are due to narrower finger, more uniform finger quality, and the higher aspect ratio. Stencil printing with paste A has no higher efficiency in consequence of its wider finger which leads to increasing shading loss and surface recombination.

The line resistance of fingers by mesh and stencil printing are measured with the same grid design and paste, as shown in Fig. 4. Obviously, fingers by stencil printing have lower line resistance, which results from better printing quality and higher aspect ratio.

TABLE V
ELECTRICAL PROPERTIES BY MESH AND STENCIL PRINTING

Type	Paste	Voc (V)	Jsc (mA/cm2)	FF (%)	Eta (%)	Rs (mohm)
Mesh	A	0.6165	35.39	78.71	17.18	2.118
Stencil	A	0.6158	35.26	78.77	17.10	1.863
	B	0.6161	35.44	78.96	17.24	1.951

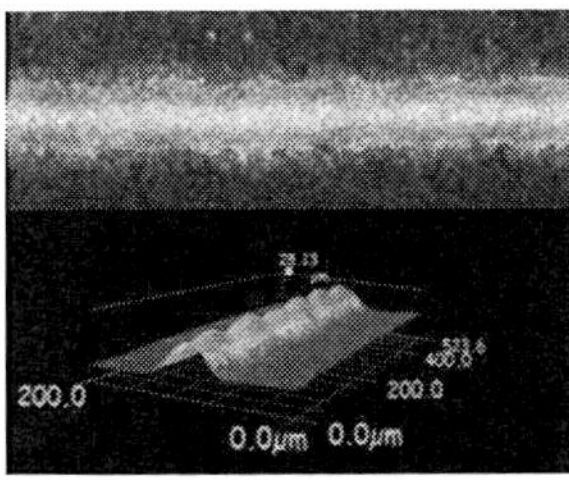

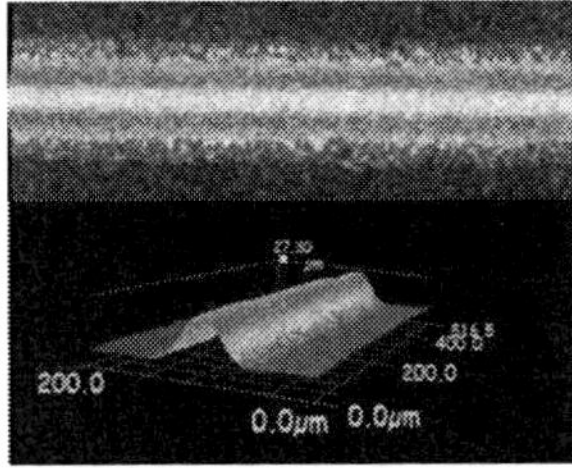

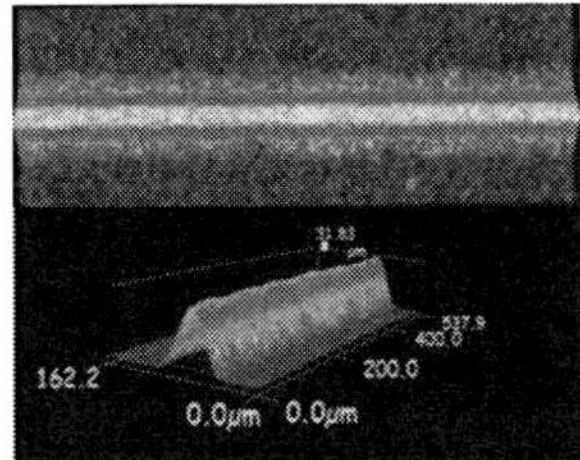

Fig. 2. 2D and 3D visual images of (a) mesh printing with paste A, (b) stencil printing with paste A, and (c) stencil printing with paste B.

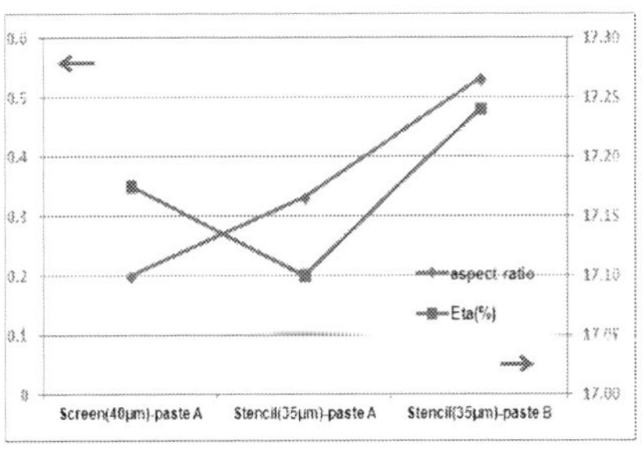

Fig. 3. The relation between aspect ratio and efficiency with different printing process

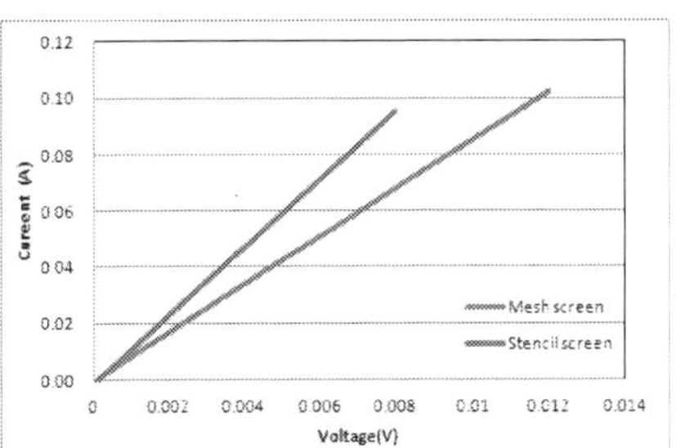

Fig. 4. The line resistance measurement of fingers by mesh and stencil printing respectively.

The specific contact resistivity of paste A and B are also measured individually by CTLM technique. Since paste A has lower contact resistance as shown in TABLE VI, the series resistance of stencil printing with paste A is still lower than that with paste B. Nevertheless, by stencil printing does the metal resistance actually lower down when using the same paste. In summary, reduced series resistance originates from high aspect ratio via stencil printing rather than paste properties.

TABLE VI

THE SPECIFIC CONTACT RESISTANCE OF PASTE A AND B

Paste	$\rho c(\text{ohm-cm}^2)$
A	1.02×10^{-4}
B	1.69×10^{-3}

IV. CONCLUSION

Two-step stencil printing process has been optimized and applied with narrow fingers. The aspect ratio over 0.5 has been achieved by choosing high viscosity paste on stencil printing. On the premise of no effect on the finger quality in continuous printing, paste A and B are better choices to be applied on production. +0.06% efficiency gain has been reached compared with mesh printing using the same grid design and paste. The highest efficiency by using paste B on stencil printing is due to both narrower finger and higher aspect ratio. At last, IV and CTLM results indicate that the reduced series resistance originates from high aspect ratio rather than paste properties. It's expected that more efficiency gain will be achieved while increasing viscosity of paste A which has lower contact resistance.

REFERENCES

[1] B. Heurtault and J. Hoornstra "Towards industrial application of stencil printing for crystalline Silicon solar cells," in 25th EPSEC, 2010, p. 1912.

[2] T. Falcon, "Ultra fine line frontside metallisation on crystalline silicon solar cells by screen & stencil printing," in 26th EPSEC, 2011, p. 1686.

[3] T. Falcon, R. D. Anderson, and D. V. Clark "Fine line printing of frontside metallisations using ultra fine mesh and stencil technologies" in 27th EPSEC, 2012, p. 1739.

[4] C. Bottosso, M. Martire, and M. Galiazzo "Fine line metallization through screen and stencil printing," in 27th EPSEC, 2012, p. 1645.

Photovoltaic Investment Risk and Uncertainty for Residential Customers

Easan Drury, Thomas Jenkin, Dirk Jordan, and Robert Margolis

Abstract—The revenues generated by rooftop photovoltaic (PV) systems have several sources of uncertainty. We use a Monte Carlo framework to explore the sensitivity of PV investment returns to three categories of PV investment uncertainty: 1) interannual solar variability, 2) PV technical performance and maintenance costs, and 3) market risks including future electricity rates and the possibility that retail electricity rates will be restructured for PV customers. We find that PV investment risk and uncertainty is driven by market factors in some U.S. regions (California and Massachusetts) and by the PV technical performance in other U.S. regions (Missouri and Florida). We explore the relative impacts of three methods for reducing PV investment uncertainty: research-and-development-driven performance improvements, system performance guarantees that are common for third-party owned systems, and long-term power purchase contracts. We find that the effectiveness of each risk reduction option varies by region, depending on which factors drive regional PV investment uncertainty.

Index Terms—Investment risk, rooftop photovoltaics, third-party ownership.

I. Introduction

RESIDENTIAL photovoltaic (PV) customers frequently think of PV investment costs and benefits in terms of a single point estimate, such as payback time, a fixed savings on electricity bills, or other similar values [1]–[3]. However, the costs and benefits of PV ownership are driven by several factors that are largely unknown to prospective customers when they make an investment decision.

Residential PV revenues are subject to three main categories of uncertainty in the U.S.: 1) interannual solar variability and weather trends, 2) PV technical performance and maintenance costs, and 3) market uncertainty including future electricity rate escalations and net-metering policies.[1]

We use several sources of data to develop probability distributions for these three categories of PV investment risk and uncertainty. Many input distributions are informed by historical data that are likely to be predictive of future trends (e.g., solar resource data, PV degradation rates, etc.), while other input distributions rely on historical data that may not be representative of future trends (electricity rate escalations) or cannot be inferred from historical data (likelihood of electricity rate restructuring for PV customers). While input distributions for several PV investment parameters are inherently unknowable, this analysis develops a framework to characterize the relative sensitivity of PV revenues to multiple input parameters.

We use a Monte Carlo framework to calculate distributions of possible future PV cash flows based on the uncertainty of PV input parameters. By sampling input distributions individually and collectively, we identify which variables drive the uncertainty in PV investment returns in four different regions of the U.S. (California, Missouri, Massachusetts, and Florida). These states were selected to sample a range of different solar resources, residential electricity prices, and historical price trends.

PV investment uncertainty is frequently reduced in the marketplace through various ownership structures and equipment warranties. We explore the potential impact of three methods for reducing PV investment uncertainty to residential customers: 1) research and development (R&D)-driven performance improvements, 2) performance guarantees that are common for third-party owned (TPO) PV systems, and 3) long-term power purchase contracts that set the value of future PV-generated electricity.[2]

II. Methodology

We use several sources of data to develop probability distributions for three categories of PV investment uncertainty.

A. Interannual Solar Variability

We simulate the interannual variability in PV generation for each study region using the National Renewable Energy Laboratory's System Advisor Model [5]. Fig. 1 shows 45 years of the simulated PV performance in units of kilowatt-hours (kWh) of electrical energy generated annually by one kilowatt of direct current PV capacity (kW_{DC}) for 19 U.S. locations. All PV systems are assumed to be oriented facing south with a 25° tilt.

Annual PV generation is impacted by several factors, including large volcanic eruptions and persistent weather events (e.g., La Ninas and El Ninos), which can lead to annual deviations of up to ±15% from mean performance trends. However, these annual deviations largely cancel over multiple years, and we find that deviations in PV generation over 20-year investment

Manuscript received June 14, 2013; revised August 19, 2013; accepted August 28, 2013. Date of publication September 24, 2013; date of current version December 16, 2013. This work was supported by the U.S. Department of Energy under Contract DE-AC36-08GO28308.

The authors are with the National Renewable Energy Laboratory, Golden, CO 80401 USA (e-mail: easan.drury@nrel.gov; thomas.jenkin@nrel.gov; dirk.jordan@nrel.gov; robert.margolis@nrel.gov).

Color versions of one or more of the figures in this paper are available online at http://ieeexplore.ieee.org.

Digital Object Identifier 10.1109/JPHOTOV.2013.2280469

[1]Net-metering policies set the value of rooftop PV electricity for grid-connected systems [4].

[2]The second and third methods shift investment uncertainty from residential customers to other parties, and these risk-reduction services might add additional costs to PV systems.

"

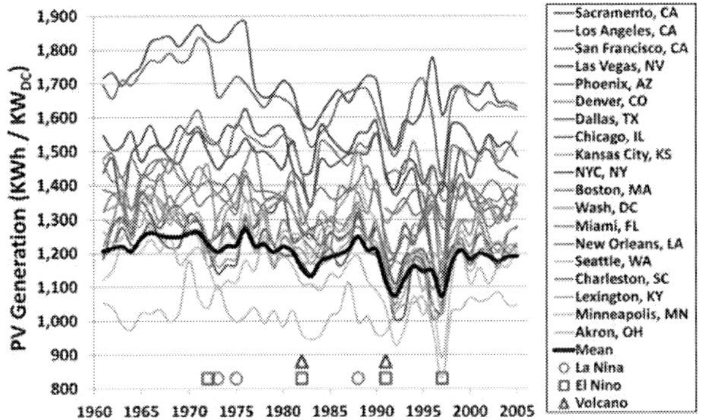

Fig. 1. Forty-five years of simulated annual PV generation (kWh/kW$_{DC}$) for 19 spatially dispersed U.S. cities.

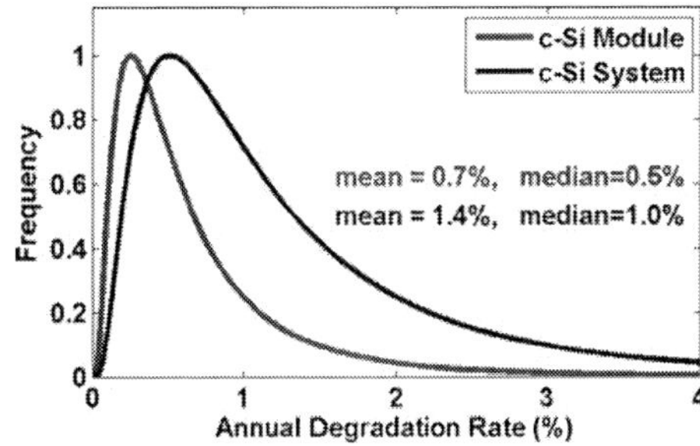

Fig. 2. Annual degradation rate distributions used for c-Si PV modules and residentially sized (<10 kW$_{DC}$) c-Si PV systems.

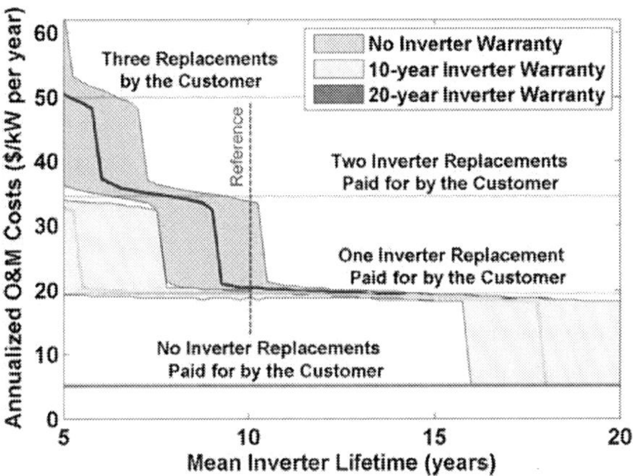

Fig. 3. Range in annualized PV operations and maintenance (O&M) costs as a function of mean inverter lifetimes for two inverter warranty options and a no-warranty option. Bold colored lines show median O&M costs, and shaded colored areas show the 25th–75th percentile O&M cost range.

lifetimes vary by only $\pm2\%$ from the mean based on 45 years of simulated PV performance.[3]

B. Photovoltaic Technical Performance Uncertainty

Both long-term PV technical performance and system maintenance costs are frequently uncertain when residential customers invest in PV. We characterize two sources of PV technical uncertainty: 1) a distribution of PV degradation rates that is based on historical PV performance [6], [7] and (2) a distribution of PV operations and maintenance (O&M) costs that is based on the uncertainty in inverter lifetimes.

PV degradation rate distributions are calculated using module-level PV performance data for crystalline silicon (c-Si) modules [6] that are used in most rooftop applications. We fit a log-normal distribution to historical module degradation rates, which results in a distribution with a mean of 0.7%/year and median of 0.5%/year [6]. System-level PV degradation rates are higher than module degradation rates because they are driven by the worst-performing PV modules [7]. We calculate system-level PV degradation rates by scaling the log-normal distribution of module-level degradation rates to fit the measured system-level PV performance for systems smaller than 10 kW$_{DC}$ [7] that are representative of residential systems. This results in a log-normal distribution of system-level PV degradation rates with a mean of 1.4%/year and a median of 1.0%/year (coefficient of variation of 3.2%, and skewness of 1.33), which is within the range of recent measurements [7].[4]

Fig. 2 shows annualized degradation rate distributions for PV modules and PV systems smaller than 10 kW$_{DC}$. Actual system degradation rates are characterized in the Monte Carlo simulations by drawing one degradation rate from the system-level distribution and applying it to all years in the PV cash flow calculation. This methodology is consistent with how the PV performance measurements are made.

Fig. 3 shows annualized O&M cost distributions for a range of mean PV inverter lifetimes and warranty options. Inverter lifetimes were assumed to be normally distributed with a 3-year standard deviation and means ranging from 5 to 20 years, corresponding to the x-axis in Fig. 3. Annualized O&M cost ranges are shown for two warranty options and a no warranty option. The widths of the cost ranges represent the 25th through 75th percentiles of O&M costs and the bold lines represent median O&M costs. The cost of inverter replacements and routine maintenance were calculated based on [8].[5] Routine maintenance costs—including cleaning, inspecting, and maintaining a PV system—are estimated to be $5/kW$_{DC}$ per year (real dollars). Routine maintenance costs likely vary both within regions and between regions, but we did not consider this source of uncertainty in the present analysis.

O&M costs are primarily driven by the expected number of inverter replacements that are not covered by a warranty, as seen by the cost "steps" in Fig. 3. If no inverter replacements are paid for by the residential customer, O&M costs are represented

---

[3]Lifetime generation statistics are calculated by randomly selecting 20 years out of the 45-year PV datasets.

[4]There is considerable spread in these measured variables between different systems. Interpreting PV performance data is an active area of research, in particular identifying location-specific and technology-specific degradation pathways.

[5]We assume that PV inverter hardware will cost $250/kW$_{DC}$ (real dollars), inverter replacement labor will cost $600/system (real dollars), and routine maintenance will cost $100/system (real dollars) every 4 years. We also assume that residential systems are 5 kW$_{DC}$.

by routine maintenance that we estimate as $5/kW_{DC}$ per year. Each additional inverter replacement increases annualized O&M costs by about $15/kW_{DC}$ per year.

Inverter warranties can significantly reduce PV O&M costs and cost uncertainty, however, the impact of warranties depends strongly on the combination of warranty length and the expected distribution of inverter lifetimes. For example, if mean inverter lifetimes range from 11 to 15 years, a 10-year warranty does not significantly reduce O&M costs because there is a strong likelihood that one inverter replacement will be required over the 20-year PV lifetime (and paid for by the PV owner) regardless of the 10-year warranty. However, longer warranties or performance guarantees (frequently included in TPO contracts) can significantly reduce annual O&M costs and cost uncertainty.

We estimate reference PV O&M cost distributions by assuming 1) normally distributed inverter lifetimes with a mean of 10 years and a standard deviation of 3 years, 2) 10-year inverter warranties based on [9], and 3) routine maintenance costs of about $5/kW_{DC}$ per year as discussed earlier. Using this methodology, annualized O&M costs are $19 \pm 7/kW_{DC}$ per year (15% require no inverter replacements that are not covered by a warranty, 75% require one replacement, and 10% require two replacements). Reference O&M cost ranges are roughly in line with recent estimates (e.g., see [8]).

C. Photovoltaic Market Risk and Uncertainty

All electricity customers face uncertain future energy costs. This uncertainty is driven by several factors like future natural gas and coal prices, fuel contracts, power purchase agreements that often include escalation provisions, environmental policies including the possibility of future carbon prices or accelerated generator retirement schedules, evolving utility business models, and others. Many residential PV customers decide to adopt PV because it can, under some circumstances, provide insurance against rising future energy prices. However, the ability of a PV investment to protect against escalating electricity rates is tied directly to current and future net metering policy.

We explore the impact of two sources of market uncertainty on PV net revenues: 1) uncertain future electricity rate escalations and 2) uncertain future rate structures that could significantly modify the value of PV-generated electricity.

Fig. 4 shows the distribution of annualized residential electricity rate escalations (2011 nominal U.S. dollars) for 50 states in the U.S. for periods ending in 2011 and starting at times ranging from 1990 to 2009, based on data from [10]. Median escalation rates are shown by the bold blue line, 25th/75th percentile escalations shown by dashed blue lines, and 10th/90th percentile escalations shown by dotted blue lines. The consumer price index (CPI) is also shown for the same time periods.

Residential electricity rates were relatively stable during the 1990s in nominal dollars, corresponding to periods of decreasing real electricity costs in several states where escalation rates were lower than the rate of inflation (as measured by the CPI). Electricity rates increased in real terms during the mid-2000s (as measured by a premium over the CPI) based on several factors, including the development of new natural gas generation resources, increasing natural gas prices, and others.

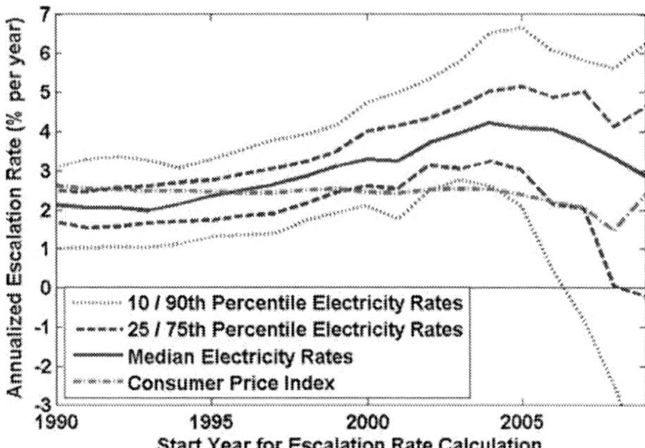

Fig. 4.   Distribution of annualized residential electricity rate escalations (nominal dollars) for 50 U.S. states, calculated for time periods ending in 2011 and starting at times ranging from 1990 through 2009 (x-axis) [10]. The annualized consumer price index is also shown for the same time periods.

We use historical electricity rates to develop electricity escalation rate distributions for each state. In reality, the key factors that will drive future electricity rates are inherently unknowable and cannot be inferred from historical trends. Historical rate escalations are used in this analysis to estimate the relative sensitivity of PV revenues to this uncertain parameter, and not as an estimate of future electricity rate trends.

Finally, retail electricity rates could be restructured during the lifetime of a PV investment by electric service providers in a way that significantly reduces PV revenues. The electricity generated by residential PV systems is frequently valued at retail electricity rates, based on local net metering policies [4]. However, electric service providers might be interested in restructuring electricity rates in the future so that PV-generated electricity is valued more closely to the variable cost of the marginal generating unit.

While there are no historical precedents to inform the likelihood of residential rate restructuring, we evaluate the sensitivity of PV investment revenues to uncertain future rate structures using the following steps. First, we assume that there is a 50% likelihood that electric service providers will modify rates for PV customers during the lifetime of a PV investment, as illustrated in Fig. 5. Then, we assume that the likelihood of restructuring increases linearly from 0% to 50% over the course of the PV investment and the actual timing of a rate restructuring event is simulated in the Monte Carlo model based on this increasing cumulative probability. If rates are restructured for a PV customer, we assume that PV-generated electricity will be valued at $0.07/kWh (real dollars) based roughly on the variable cost of natural gas generation.[6]

---

[6]This value is dependent on several factors including future natural gas prices, the local mix of combined cycle (CC) and combustion turbine (CT) generation, transmission congestion, avoided transmission and distribution line losses, emissions controls, and others. The value of $0.07/kWh is consistent with PV electricity offsetting the variable cost of a 50:50 split between natural gas CC and CT generation based on [11] (which assumes future natural gas price projections from the Annual Energy Outlook 2013 [12]) and assuming 7% line losses in the transmission and distribution system [13].

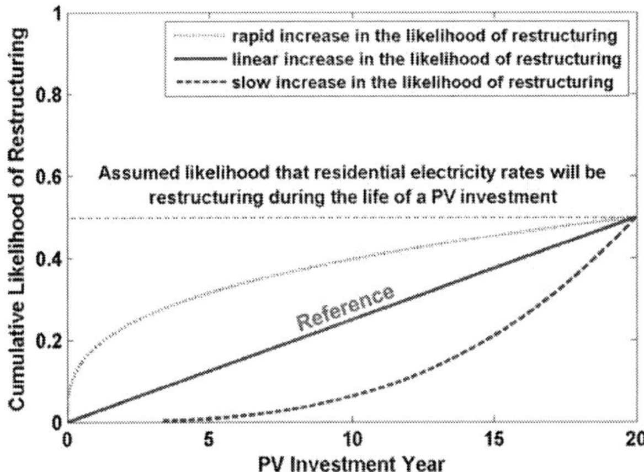

Fig. 5. Illustrative representation of the increasing likelihood of electricity rates being restructured for PV customers over the life of a PV investment. The linear increase in restructuring likelihood is assumed in all scenarios.

III. RESULTS

To characterize the relative impact of several sources of PV investment uncertainty, we developed a Monte Carlo simulation framework to generate probability distributions of PV net revenues. These are calculated by sampling each input distribution tens of thousands of times, both in isolation (to characterize the relative impact of each input parameter) and collectively (to characterize the combined impact of multiple uncertain parameters). For scenarios varying only one input distribution, the medians of all other distributions were used. For scenarios varying multiple parameters, we assume uncorrelated input distributions.[7]

We simulate PV net revenue distributions in four U.S. regions—Los Angeles, CA; Kansas City, MO; Boston, MA; and Miami, FL—to evaluate general trends and regional differences. We do not include state or local PV incentives [14] in this analysis, which particularly impacts PV revenue calculations for Boston where PV qualifies for solar renewable energy credit payments. In addition, we use mean residential electricity rates for all states [10], which can underestimate PV revenues for high energy-use customers on tiered rate structures that are common in California. This analysis is intended to identify broad market trends, and individual PV customers could use this framework to evaluate PV investment risk and uncertainty for specific projects.

Fig. 6 shows the simulated range of PV investment returns for a residential system in Los Angeles. The impacts of each of the five input distributions (see Section II) are characterized individually and collectively for the three categories of investment uncertainty and the total investment uncertainty. PV investment revenues are shown in units of the present value of PV net revenues generated by 1 kW of PV capacity ($/kW$_{DC}$) in 2013 U.S. dollars. In this analysis, we define PV net revenues as system

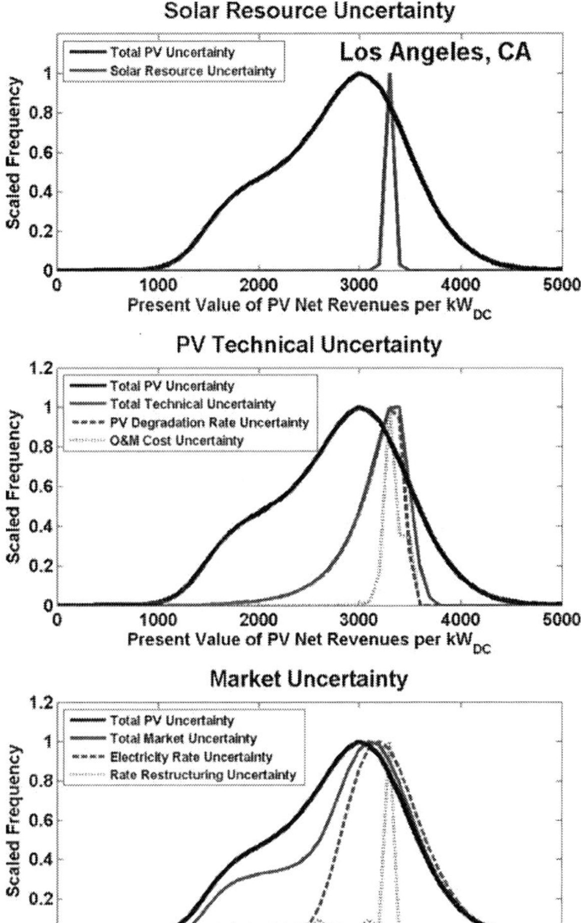

Fig. 6. Distribution of the present value of PV net revenues ($/kW$_{DC}$ in 2013 U.S. dollars) for residential systems in Los Angeles, CA, USA, plotted for several project variables individually and for the combination of all variables.

revenues minus O&M costs, and assume a 4% nominal discount rate[8] to calculate the present value of future net revenues.

For the PV system simulated in Los Angeles, market uncertainty primarily drives the range in PV investment returns.[9] The upper bound of PV net revenues is set by the range of retail escalation rates, and the lower bound of PV net revenues is set by the possibility that electricity rates will be restructured in the early years of a PV investment. The impact of rate restructuring is not symmetric because we assume that PV electricity will continue to be valued at retail rates in the reference scenario, whereas rate restructuring is assumed to decrease the value of PV-generated

---

[7]Characterizing correlations between input variables, like PV degradation rates and O&M costs, is an active area of research but was outside the scope of this analysis.

[8]The choice of discount rate is complicated and, in general, will vary with the investment risk. We use a low value of 4% nominal because residential customers might view PV cash flows similar to bond payments. However, the required rate of return (and associated discount rate) will likely vary significantly with the investment risk profile, ownership structure, and other factors.

[9]Although this finding is strongly dependent on the assumptions made about future market risk and uncertainty.

electricity to $0.07/kWh (real dollars). The present value of PV net revenues is very sensitive to the timing of rate restructuring, which leads to a continuous[10] downside tail in the aggregate distribution. This characterization of rate restructuring does not capture the possible benefits of restructuring to PV value—such as transitioning to time-of-use rates or demand-based rates—which could potentially lead to higher PV revenues for some customers.

Interannual solar variability adds a relatively small component to total PV investment uncertainty because annual solar deviations are typically small and these deviations largely cancel over multiple years. PV technical uncertainty (as simulated in this study) is primarily driven by system degradation rates with a smaller component of uncertainty from O&M costs. O&M uncertainty is relatively small because we assume 10-year inverter warranties that decrease both the number of inverter replacements paid for by a PV customer, and the discounted cost of inverter replacements that occur 10 years or more in the future.

Fig. 7 shows similar simulations of PV net revenues for Kansas City, Boston, and Miami. PV revenues in these regions show several similarities to those in Los Angeles and a few key differences. For example, PV net revenues are lower in Boston than Los Angeles primarily because solar insolation is lower, and PV net revenues are lower in Miami and Kansas City because both solar insolation and residential electricity rates are lower. The impact of rate restructuring is smaller in regions where retail rates are closer to the assumed variable cost of electricity generation (e.g., Kansas City and Miami). In these regions, other input parameters, like PV technical performance, can become more significant drivers of PV investment returns.

IV. METHODS FOR REDUCING PHOTOVOLTAIC INVESTMENT UNCERTAINTY

Residential PV investment risk and uncertainty can be reduced in several ways. Here, we explore the impact of 1) R&D-driven PV performance improvements, 2) PV performance guarantees that are common for TPO systems [15], and 3) long-term contracts that set a fixed price for PV-generated electricity over the lifetime of a PV investment. Both performance guarantees and long-term contracts shift investment risk from residential PV customers to other parties, and would likely increase the cost of PV systems.[11] However, since there is little data on how much performance guarantees or long-term contracts would cost PV customers, we do not add scenario-dependent costs in this analysis.

We simulate the R&D scenario[12] by assuming that the mean and median of the log-normal degradation rate distribution are halved (0.7%/year and 0.5%/year, respectively) and that inverter costs are halved, while leaving all other parameters unchanged.

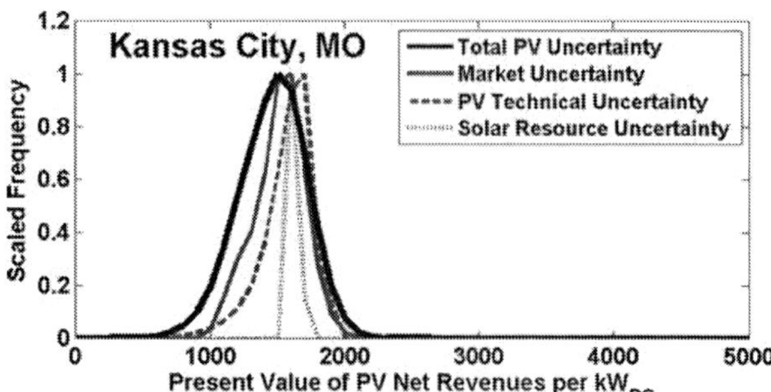

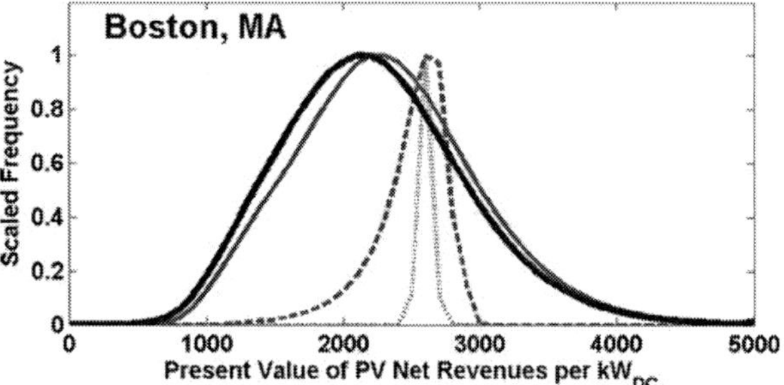

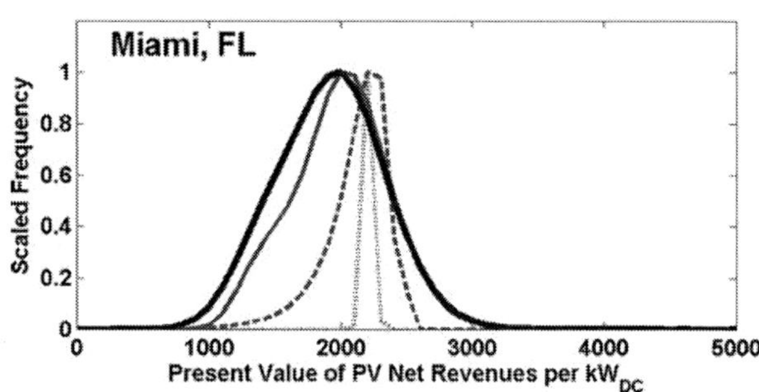

Fig. 7. Distribution of the present value of PV net revenues ($/kW$_{DC}$ in 2013 U.S. dollars) for residential systems modeled in three cities. Distributions are plotted for the three categories of investment uncertainty individually and for the total investment uncertainty.

We simulate PV performance guarantees by removing all PV O&M costs, and ensuring that annual PV generation is at least 90% of the mean first-year system performance. We simulate long-term contracts by setting the value of PV-generated electricity to retail electricity rates for each region and increase the value of PV-generated electricity in the future based on the median of historical escalation rates for each region [10].

Fig. 8 shows the cumulative likelihood that the present value of PV net revenues will reach or exceed amounts ranging from $0/kW$_{DC}$ to $5000/kW$_{DC}$ (2013 U.S. dollars) for a PV system located in Los Angeles The reference scenario shows a 50% likelihood of $2840/kW$_{DC}$ or higher PV net revenues. However, the width of the net revenue distribution is relatively large, with a 75% likelihood of earning at least $2310/kW$_{DC}$ to a 25% likelihood of earning at least $3240/kW$_{DC}$.

Each of the three methods for reducing PV investment uncertainty increases the 50% likelihood PV net revenue values since

---

[10]The downside tail of the restructuring distribution shows small oscillations which are likely caused by an incomplete sampling of the full distribution.

[11]These costs would likely include both the expected cost of providing performance guarantees and a reasonable rate of return for a company to assume additional project risk.

[12]Various R&D activities could drive PV price and performance improvements from fundamental advancements in materials science to developing new manufacturing techniques.

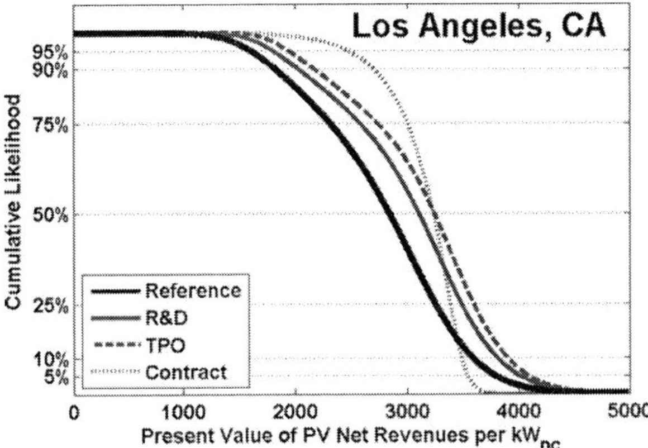
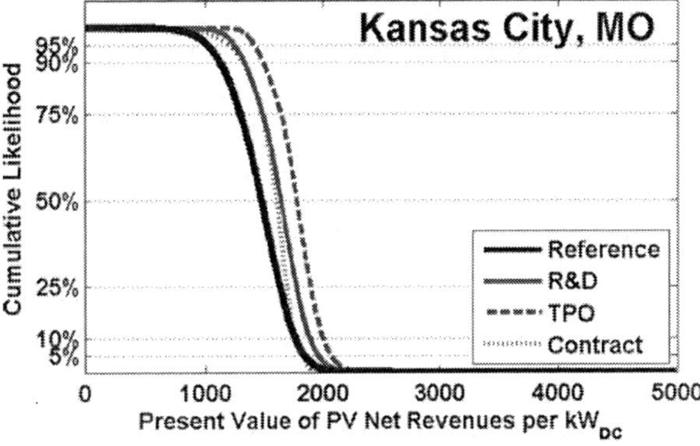

Fig. 8. Likelihood that the present value of PV net revenues ($/kW$_{DC}$ in 2013 U.S. dollars) will be at least high as the values on the x-axis, for the reference scenario and three sensitivity scenarios.

they either reduce system costs (R&D, TPO) or increase median revenues (all scenarios). Both the TPO and contract scenarios shift costs or uncertainty from the residential customer to another party that would likely increase system costs, and this is not captured in the analysis.

The main difference between scenarios is that the R&D and TPO scenarios shift the distributions to higher revenues without significantly modifying the width of the distribution, while the contract scenario significantly decreases PV net revenue uncertainty, seen by the steeper decline in the cumulative likelihood curve.

In Los Angeles, the contract scenario reduces the likelihood of very low PV net revenues by eliminating both the risk of rate restructuring and the possibility of realizing very low electricity rate escalations. However, the contracts scenario also reduces the likelihood of realizing very high PV net revenues by reducing the benefits of PV ownership in circumstances with very high retail rate escalations. While contracts can significantly reduce the uncertainty of PV investment returns, PV customers are still exposed to future electricity price risk because they sell PV electricity at a fixed price but still need to purchase electricity at an uncertain future price. In the R&D and TPO scenarios, customers have, to some extent, locked-in long-term electricity costs by reducing the amount of electricity they will need to purchase from their electric service provider at uncertain future prices.

Fig. 9 similarly shows the likelihood of PV generating a range of net revenues for the three additional regions. The R&D and TPO scenarios shift PV net revenues higher by a similar amount in all regions since we assume that they will reduce maintenance costs and increase PV generation similarly in all regions. However, the contract scenarios impact PV net revenue distributions differently in each region, based on differences in electricity prices (before restructuring) and historical price variability. For example, residential electricity prices were relatively low and stable in Kansas City (average electricity price was 10.1 cents/kWh in 2013 U.S. dollars from 1990–2011), and the contracts scenario performs similarly to the R&D sce-

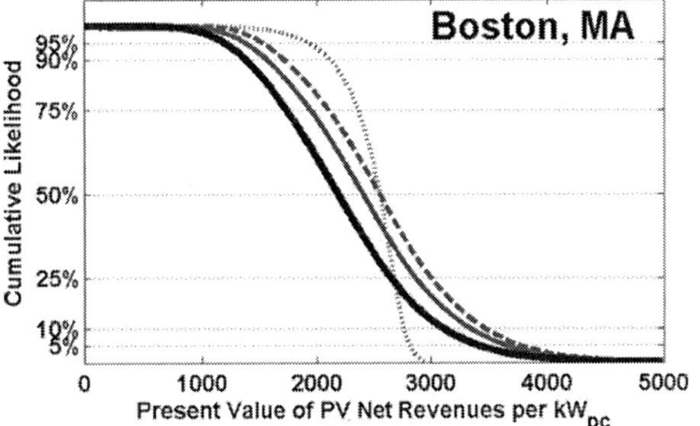
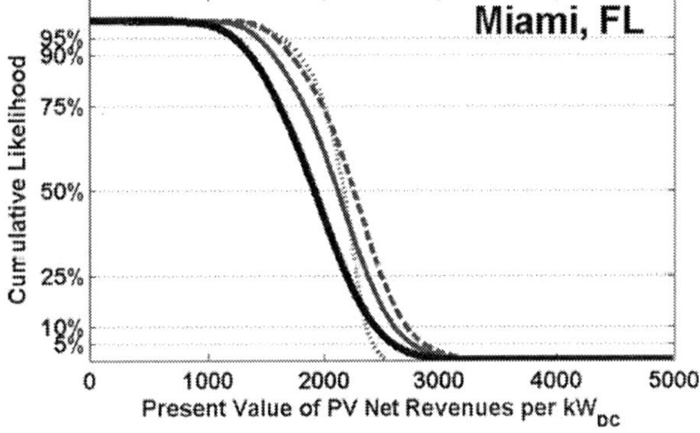

Fig. 9. Same as Fig. 8 but for three additional U.S. locations.

nario at the lower end of the PV net revenue distribution and performs similarly to the reference scenario at the upper end of the PV net revenue distribution. Conversely, residential electricity prices were relatively high and variable in Boston (average electricity price was 16.6 cents/kWh in 2013 U.S. dollars from 1990 to 2011) and the contracts scenario significantly reduces the likelihood of very low and very high PV net revenues.

By reducing the likelihood of very low and high PV net revenues, the contract scenario suggests a potential new business model where a company might be willing to issue contracts that reduce downside risk to customers, while having the potential to realize upside returns if future electricity rate escalations outpace historical trends. By offering contracts, a company would effectively be taking a long position on future electricity rates and could use this as a hedge against large future rate increases. In addition, if companies were to offer contracts in several electric service territories they may be able to manage market risk more effectively than individual customers who are inherently tied to one service territory.

While each of the three scenarios leads to an increase in PV net revenues on an expected basis, it is less clear how these would change a PV project's economic returns or the costs faced by a residential customer. To estimate this for each scenario, the incremental costs would need to be added (e.g., for warranties) and the net revenues discounted at a rate that properly reflects changes in overall project risk, risk allocation, and ownership structure. This lies outsides the scope of this paper but is the focus of current work.

V. Conclusion

The revenues generated by residential PV systems have several sources of uncertainty. We estimate three categories of PV investment risk and uncertainty: 1) interannual solar variability, 2) PV technical performance and maintenance costs, and 3) market risks including future retail rate escalations and the possibility of rate restructuring.

We use a Monte Carlo framework to characterize the relative impact of different sources of uncertainty. PV technical risk and uncertainty is significant in all regions, and is several times larger than the impact of interannual solar variability. However, market risk and uncertainty can overshadow PV technical risk in some regions where retail electricity prices are high and variable (California and Massachusetts).

Several market mechanisms have been developed to reduce PV investment risk to customers ranging from equipment warranties, to system performance guarantees, to long-term contracts with electric service providers. We find that the relative effectiveness of different methods for reducing investment risk varies by region. This research suggests that various market mechanisms could effectively reduce PV investment risk, in conjunction with R&D driven performance improvements. In particular, individual PV customers are in a poor position to manage investment risks because their investment is inherently tied to one region (electric service provider) and a specific PV technology and/or brand (PV module and inverter). By bundling PV projects across different regions and system types, commercial companies might be in a better position to manage and reduce PV customer risk exposure. However, the overall impact of these risk reducing mechanisms on PV economic returns and costs faced by PV customers is not clear and will depend on a number of factors. These include the economies of scale that arise from buying and maintaining a large number of systems, the benefits of diversifying across geographic regions and PV technologies, as well as the rates of return required by a companies to assume project risk and provide services. Incorporating these and other factors is the focus of our current research.

Acknowledgment

The authors would like to thank M. Bolinger, E. Kalendra, T. Mai, and B. Sigrin for comments and input.

References

[1] A. Audenaert, L. De Boeck, S. De Cleyn, S. Lizin, and J-F. Adam, "An economic evaluation of Photovoltaic Grid Connected Systems (PVGCS) in flanders for companies: A generic model," *Renew. Energ.*, vol. 35, pp. 2674–2682, 2010.

[2] E. Drury, P. Denholm, and R. Margolis, "The impact of different economic performance metrics on the perceived value of solar photovoltaics," Nat. Renewable Energy Lab., Golden, CO, USA, NREL/TP-6A20-52197, 2011.

[3] V. Rai and B. Sigrin, "Diffusion of environmentally-friendly energy technologies: Buy versus lease differences in residential PV markets," *Environ. Res. Lett.*, vol. 8, no. 1, 2013. doi:10.1088/1748-9326/8/1/014022.

[4] Interstate Renewable Energy Council. (2012). Freeing the Grid 2.0. [Online]. Available: http://freeingthegrid.org

[5] Nat. Renewable Energy Lab. System Advisor Model (SAM). (2013). [Online]. Available: https://sam.nrel.gov/

[6] D. C. Jordan and S. R. Kurtz, "Photovoltaic degradation rates—An analytical review," *Prog. Photovol. Res. Appl.*, vol. 1, pp. 12–29, 2013.

[7] D. C. Jordan, J. H. Wohlgemuth, and S. R. Kurtz, "Technology and climate trends in PV module degradation," presented at the 27th Eur. Photovoltaic Solar Energy Conf. Exhib., Frankfurt, Germany, Sep. 24–28. 2012.

[8] "SunShot Vision Study," U.S. Dept. Energy, Washington, DC, USA, DOE/GO-102012-3037, 2012.

[9] Photon Int., "2012 Inverter Survey," Apr. 2012, pp. 144–191.

[10] Energy Information Admin. (2012). Annual electric power industry report (EIA-861 data file). [Online]. Available: http://www.eia.gov/electricity/data/eia861/

[11] Energy Information Admin. (2013). Levelized cost of new generation resources in the annual energy outlook 2013. [Online]. http://www.eia.gov/forecasts/aeo/er/electricity_generation.cfm

[12] Energy Information Admin. (2013). Annual Energy Outlook 2013 with Projections to 2040. [Online]. Available: http://www.eia.gov/forecasts/aeo/pdf/0383(2013).pdf

[13] "A review of transmission losses in planning studies," Calif. Energy Commision Staff Paper, CEC-200-2011-009, 2011.

[14] Database of State Incentives for Renewable Energy. (2012). [Online]. Available: www.dsireusa.org. Accessed Nov. 2012.

[15] E. Drury, M. Miller, C. Macal, D. Graziano, D. Heimiller, J. Ozik, and T. Perry, "The transformation of Southern California's residential photovoltaics market through third-party ownership," *Energy Policy*, vol. 42, pp. 681–690, 2012.

Authors' photographs and biographies not available at the time of publication.

AUTHOR INDEX

AUTHOR INDEX

AUTHOR INDEX